016.8230872 H878C
1994 V2
35240000853615
25ar
Hubin, Allen J.
Crime fiction II : a
comprehensive bibliography,
1748-1980

016.8230872 H878C
1994 V2
35240000853615
25ar
Hubin, Allen J.
Crime fiction II : a
comprehensive bibliography,

CRIME FICTION II

GARLAND REFERENCE LIBRARY OF THE HUMANITIES (VOL. 1353)

CRIME FICTION II

A COMPREHENSIVE BIBLIOGRAPHY
1749–1990

A COMPLETELY REVISED
AND UPDATED EDITION

VOLUME 2

ALLEN J. HUBIN

GARLAND PUBLISHING, INC.
NEW YORK & LONDON / 1994

© 1994 Allen J. Hubin
All Rights Reserved

Library of Congress Cataloging-in-Publication Data

Hubin, Allen J.
    Crime fiction II : a comprehensive bibliography, 1749–1990 / Allen J. Hubin. — A completely rev. and updated ed.
       p.   cm. — (Garland reference library of the humanities ; vol. 1353)
    Includes bibliographical references (p.) and indexes.
    ISBN 0–8240–6891–2 (v. 2 : acid-free paper)
    1. Detective and mystery stories, English—Bibliography.   2. Detective and mystery stories, American—Bibliography.   3. Detective and mystery stories—Translations into English—Bibliography.   4. Crime in literature—Bibliography.   I. Title. II. Title: Crime fiction two.   III. Series.
Z2014.F4H83   1994
[PR830.D4]
016.823'087208—dc20
                                                                  93–41230
                                                                         CIP

Printed on acid-free, 250-year-life paper
Manufactured in the United States of America

CONTENTS

Preface / vii

Introduction / ix

Abbreviations / xix

Missing Contents of Story Collections / xxiii

Author Index / 1

Title Index / 889

Settings Index / 1215

Series Index / 1313

Series Character Chronology / 1337

Film Index / 1355

Screenwriters Index / 1491

Directors Index / 1539

TITLE INDEX

Title Index

ABC Affair. P. Winston
A.B.C. Investigates. Ephesian
ABC Murders. A. Christie
A.B.C. Solves Five. Ephesian
A.B.C.'s Test Case. Ephesian
ABCD. D. R. Slavitt
A4 Murder. P. A. Foxall
A-Haunting We Will Go. T. J. Kelly
"A" Is for Alibi. S. Grafton
A. J. Alan's Second Book. A. J. Alan
AK-47 Firefight. J. Lansing
A.K.A. D. Pedneau
A.O. Caper. D. Haring
A-100. Bruce Harrison
A.P.B. D. Pedneau
A.R.P. Murder. Sutherland Scott
A.R.P. Mystery. B. Perowne
A.R.P. Spy. A. O. Pollard
A.S.F. J. Rhode
ATS Mystery. G. Coverack
A-Team. C. Heath
A-Train. Roger Williams
Aardvark Affair. G. Brandner
Aaron Rod, Diviner. E. P. Oppenheim
Aaron's Serpent. E. Thorne
Abaft 'Midships. E. L. Long
Abandon Hope. I. Garland
Abandoned. J. Du Crane
Abandoned Car Crime. Gwyn Evans
Abandoned Doll. L. Meynell
Abandoned Power. J. Fores
Abandoned Prayers. Gregg Olsen
Abandoned Room. Wadsworth Camp
Abbess. W. H. Ireland
Abbey Court. M. Thum
Abbey Court Murder. A. Haynes
Abbey Murder. J. Hatton
Abbey Mystery. R. M. Gilchrist
Abbey of Clugny. M. Meeke
Abbey of St. Asaph. I. Kelly
Abbeygate. C. Crowe
Abbot of Monserrat. W. C. Green
Abbot's Cup. C. A. Alington
Abbot's House. L. Conway
Abbot's Moat. F. Warden
Abduction. D. Bischoff
Abduction. T. Burke
Abduction. S. Cohen
Abduction. Harrison James
Abduction. G. F. Newman
Abduction. G. C. Seeber
Abduction of a Royal. Ashland Price
Abduction of Princess Chriemhild. L. F. Griffin
Abduction of Virginia Lee. F. O'Rourke
Abductor. D. Hitchens
Abductors. R. Reid
Abe and Mawruss. M. Glass
Abel/Baker/Charley. J. Maxim
Abel Coincidence. J. N. Chance
Abel's War. N. Cain
Aberdeen Conundrum. Angus Ross
Abimelech Pott, the Don Quixote of the Bar. H. W. Jessup
Able Baker and others. J. Whitehill
Abner Crane's Vengeance. A. G. Hales
Abner Ferret, the Lawyer Detective. H. Rockwood
Abner Ferret, the Lawyer Detective. J. R. Taylor
Aboard the American Duchess. H. Hill
Aboard "The American Duchess". G. L. Meyers
Aboard the Aquitaine. G. Simenon
Abode of Love. J. Shearing
Abolition of Death. James Anderson
Abominable History of the Man with Copper Fingers. D. L. Sayers
Abominable Man. M. Sjowall
Abominable Snowman. M. Waugh
Abominable Twilight. Reginald Campbell
Abomination. H. Janson
Abort Project K! L. Wilhelm
About Doctor Ferrel. D. Kenne
About Face. F. Kane
About Levy. A. Calder-Marshall
About Life. Basil Watson
About Ourselves. H. Wood

About the Murder of a Man Afraid of Women. A. Abbot
About the Murder of a Startled Lady. A. Abbot
About the Murder of Geraldine Foster. A. Abbot
About the Murder of the Circus Queen. A. Abbot
About the Murder of the Clergyman's Mistress. A. Abbot
About the Murder of the Night Club Lady. A. Abbot
About Two A.M. C. F. Coe
Above All, Love. J. M. Greenleaf
Above and Below. J. Palmer
Above Reproach. J. Flores
Above Suspicion. R. O. Chipperfield
Above Suspicion. Helen MacInnes
Above the Dark Circus. H. Walpole
Above the Dark Tumult. H. Walpole
Above the Law. J. Goodwin
Above the Law. W. Pitt-Simmonds
Abra-Cadaver. C. Monig
Abra Cadaver. J. Mattera
Abracadabra. W. Mankowitz
Abracadaver. P. Lovesey
Abracadaver. R. McInerny
Abrams and Jones, Homicide. M. Dines
Abroad with Twitty. E. Mulliner
Abrus Necklace. E. G. Seibert
Absence. M. Eyre
Absent Friends. F. Busch
Absent Friends. C. J. C. Hyne
Absolute Proof. P. Kuttner
Absolutely Murder. G. Le Pelley
Absolutely True. I. Montagu
Absolution. A. Shaffer
Abu Wahab Caper. R. H. Spencer
Abundance of Rain. C. Drinkwater
Abuse of Justice. R. Parkes
Abyssinian Mystery. G. Chester
Academic Factor. C. A. Haddad
Academic Murder. D. Fiske
Academic Question. R. H. R. Smithies
Acapulco Rampage. D. Pendleton
Accent on Murder. R. Lockridge
Accent on Treason. C. W. Casewit
Acceptable Loses. F. Shaw
Accessory. M. Lockwood
Accessory After. E. C. Vivian
Accessory After the Fact. W. A. Hobday
Accessory After the Fact. Mrs. Leith-Adams
Accessory After the Fact. B. Reynolds
Accessory After the Fact. L. Thayer
Accessory for Murder. J. M. Rowe
Accessory to Murder. P. Barrington
Accident. A. A. Josey
Accident by Design. E. C. R. Lorac
Accident for Inspector West. J. Creasey
Accident in Piccadilly. H. Willett
Accident, Manslaughter or Murder? L. Thayer
Accident of Robert Luman. D. Fletcher
Accident or Murder? Nicholas Carter
Accident Prone. John Penn
Accident to Adeline. E. Burgess
Accident Ward Mystery. R. Truax
Accidental Accomplice. W. A. Johnston
Accidental Adventurer. S. M. Parkman
Accidental Clue. B. Graeme
Accidental Crimes. J. Hutton
Accidental Death of an Anarchist. D. Fo
Accidental Don Juan. E. Jepson
Accidental Murder. C. F. Gregg
Accidental Password. Nicholas Carter
Accidental Spy. James Watson
Accidental Woman. R. Neely
Accidents Do Happen. M. Burton
Accidents Will Happen. V. Bridges
Accomplice. J. Bland
Accomplice. M. Head
Accomplice. F. T. Hill
Accomplice. D. Mortola
Accomplice. J. Pudney
Accomplices. Leonard Cooper
Accomplices. David Fletcher
Accomplices. G. Simenon
According to Gibson. D. MacKail

According to Orders. F. B. Austin
According to Plan. L. Jackson
According to Plan. G. Seton
According to St. John. W. Babula
According to the Evidence. H. Cecil
According to the Evidence. F. Douglas
Accosting the Golden Spire. I. W. Collett
Account Closed. S. M. Parkman
Account of Capers. Bruce Marshall
Account of Martin Bron. F. Olrich
Account Paid. C. Brooks
Account Rendered. P. Barrington
Account Rendered. P. Cheyney
Account Rendered. F. Ryck
Account Rendered. P. Wentworth
Account to Render. S. Coulter
Account Unsettled. G. Simenon
Accounting. B. Marshall
Accounting for Murder. E. Lathen
Accurate Watch. D. W. Doyle
Accursed. C. Seignolle
Accuse the Toff. J. Creasey
Accused. D. Chiel
Accused. H. R. Daniels
Accused. H. Janson
Accused and Accuser. A. Sergeant
Accused Princess. A. Upward
Accusing Finger. M. Doran
Accusing Hand. E. MacArthur
Accusing Spirit. Mrs. Pilkington
Ace High. G. Goodchild
Ace High. Mark Ross
Ace High, the 'Frisco Detective. C. E. Tripp
Ace in the Hole. F. Martin
Ace Is Trumped. H. H. Stimson
Ace of Assassins. D. Haring
Ace of Clubs Murder. R. Trevor
Ace of Danger. L. Grex
Ace of Danger. Augustus Muir
Ace of Death. J. Callahan
Ace of Death. T. A. Plummer
Ace of Diamonds. A. Hurry
Ace of Diamonds. M. Schorr
Ace of Hearts. F. Du Boisgobey
Ace of Hearts. C. Thomas-Stanford
Ace of Jades. J. Cello
Ace of Jades. S. Palmer
Ace of Knaves. L. Charteris
Ace of Spades. R. Andre
Ace of Spades. J. C. Fraser
Ace of Spades. H. Holt
Ace of Spades. A. Nasielski
Ace of Spades. Dell Shannon
Ace of Spades Murder. H. S. Keeler
Ace of Spies. D. Von Elsner
Ace Squadron. Glen Allen
Ace Up My Sleeve. J. H. Chase
Aces & Eights. P. Garlington
Aces and Eights. T. Thackrey, Jr.
Aces, Eights, and Murder. M. V. Heberden
Aces of the White Death. R. J. Hogan
Aces Run Wild. J. A. Rennie
Achievements of John Carruthers. E. C. Cox
Achievements of Luther Trant. E. Balmer
Achilles Affair. B. Mather
Achilles' Isle. R. Batchelor
Achilles Mandate. M. Fogarty
Acid. H. Imbert-Terry
Acid Bath Murders. S. Brody
Acid Drop. S. George
Acid Rock. R. Sapir
Acid Test. C. Lewis
Ackroyd. J. Feiffer
Acolytes of Darkness. F. Dille
Aconite Murders. S. Williams
Acquainted with Murder. F. Hurt
Acquitaine Progression. R. Ludlum
Acquittal. G. Lorimer
Acquittal. H. Simpson
Acquittal. J. Wainwright
Acquitted! M. Frazer
Acrefield Mystery. F. Grierson
Across 110th. W. Ferris
Across That River. H. Whittington

Across the Border. J. G. Sarasin
Across the Common. E. Berridge
Across the Divide. A. Murray
Across the Equator. W. M. Graydon
Across the Footlights. F. Hume
Across the Frontiers. H. Edmonds
Across the Lawn. E. Verity
Across the Narrow Seas. J. Pattinson
Across the Pacific. C. E. Blaney
Across the Street. G. Simenon
Across the Water. S. Binnie
Across the World for a Wife. G. Boothby
Acrostic Mysteries. H. Slesar
Act of Anger. B. Spicer
Act of Betrayal. R. A. Sandys
Act of Darkness. P. Hastings
Act of Darkness. F. King
Act of Fear. Michael Collins
Act of Fear. W. D. Roberts
Act of God. J. M. Roberts
Act of God. C. Templeton
Act of Impulse. H. Bayliss
Act of Love. J. R. Lansdale
Act of Love. W. E. D. Ross
Act of Mercy. F. Clifford
Act of Murder. P. Reakes
Act of Passion. Wenzell Brown
Act of Passion. G. Simenon
Act of Providence. J. P. Brennan
Act of Providence. H. C. McNeile
Act of Rage. Joseph Hayes
Act of Silence. Anthony Graham
Act of Terror. P. A. Foxall
Act of Violence. E. Fadiman
Act of Violence. B. Heatter
Act of Violence. P. Saxon
Act of Violence. K. Wade
Act of War. B. Callison
Act of War. Leonard Sanders
Actes and Monuments. J. W. Corrington
Acting on Information Received. G. Hardwicke
Acting Second Mate. S. M. Parkman
Action at Arcanum. W. C. MacDonald
Action at World's End. W. Chambers
Action for the Picaroon. J. Cassells
Action in Diamonds. C. R. Cooper
Action Man. J. Flynn
Action of the Tiger. A. Kent
Action of the Tiger. G. Parker
Action of the Tiger. T. Walsh
Action of the Tiger. J. Wellard
Active Measures. J. Morris
Activities of Lavie Jutt. M. Barclay
Actor Manager. A. Askew
Actor's Blood. B. Hecht
Actor's Knife. Howel Evans
Actor's Secret. H. E. Hill
Actress. A. Applin
Actress Detective. Anonymous
Actress's Daughter. M. A. Fleming
Actress's Husband. G. Warden
Acts of Betrayal. J. Trenhaile
Acts of Black Night. K. M. Knight
Acts of Contrition. W. Heffernan
Acts of Faith. H. Koning
Acts of Homicide. Kenn Davis
Acts of Mercy. B. Pronzini
Acts of Theft. A. A. Cohen
Acupuncture Murders. D. Steward
Ad for Murder. J. Penn
Ad Statum Perspicuum. F. P. Wilson
Ada Vernham, Actress. R. Marsh
Adair and Son. P. Trent
Adam. P. Trent
Adam and Eve. L. Parr
Adam and Evelina. P. Allardyce
Adam and Evil. J. Carlova
Adam Grainger. H. Wood
Adam Grey. Jack Wilson
Adam Project. W. Woolfolk
Adam Sleep. W. Van Atta
Adam's Case. M. Underwood
Adam's Child. R. Breen
Adam's Fall. J. Ridgway

Adam's Rib. P. Allardyce
Adam's Tale. G. Honeycombe
Adapted to Stress. C. D. Peel
Add a Pinch of Cyanide. E. Page
Adders Abounding. J. Lukens
Adder's Brood. Nicholas Carter
Adders on the Heath. G. Mitchell
Addicted to Murder. T. S. Drachman
Additional Evidence. James Anderson
Addle. D. Durrant
Address Unknown. M. Hutton
Address Unknown. E. Phillpotts
Address Unknown. K. Taylor
Adela's Ordeal. F. Warden
Adele & Co. D. Yates
Adelgitha. Matthew Gregory Lewis
Adeline Saint Julian. A. Ker
Adirondack Tales. W. H. H. Murray
Adjuster. P. Malloch
Adjusters. Valentine
Adjustments. I. R. G. Hart
Adlon Link. Z. Hughes
Admirable Carfew. E. Wallace
Admirable Lady Biddy Fane. F. Barrett
Admiral Teach. C. J. C. Hyne
Admiral's a Spy. W. Taylor
Admiral's Light. H. M. Rideout
Admiral's Million. A. D. Divine
Admiral's Secret. A. Murray
Admiralty Murders. M. Adam
Admiralty Regrets—. Reginald Campbell
Admiralty's Secret. C. Dawe
Admit to Murder. Margaret Yorke
Adolescence of P-1. T. J. Ryan
Adopted. A. L. Halstead
Adopted Daughter. J. H. Robinson
Adopted Face. A. S. Carter
Adopters. W. Hegner
Adrenaline. J. Dillinger
Adria. R. Davis
Adrian and Jonathan. Richard Martin
Adriana. G. Dyer
Adriatic Formula. M. Lederer
Adrienne de Portalis. A. C. Gunter
Adrift with a Vengeance. K. Cornwallis
Advance Agent. J. August
Advance South. J. Robb
Advanced Calculus of Murder. E. Rosenthal
Advancement of Learning. R. Hill
Advancement of Mr. Simpkin. J. Last
Advantage Miss Seeton. H. Charles
Advent of Dying. C. O'Marie
Adventure. B. Deal
Adventure. C. Moberly
Adventure at Eighty. J. J. Farjeon
Adventure Calling! S. Horler
Adventure for Nine. J. J. Farjeon
Adventure for Two. A. Applin
Adventure for Wealth. C. T. Stoneham
Adventure in the Night. W. Dawson
Adventure in Venus. R. Michelmore
Adventure in Washington. L. Ross
Adventure Island. N. W. Firth
Adventure Isle. G. A. England
Adventure Mysterious. F. Marlowe
Adventure of Blue Peter. J. Ruyle
Adventure of Clay Fisk and Other Citizens. W. McEwan
Adventure of Lieut. Lawless, R. N. Rolf Bennett
Adventure of Red Head of the Red Sea. W. J. Makin
Adventure of State. P. Cosgrave
Adventure of the Albanian Avenger. W. W. Sayer
Adventure of the Annamese Prince. W. M. Graydon
Adventure of the Blue Room. S. Fowler
Adventure of the Bogus Sheik. G. H. Teed
Adventure of the Broad Arrow. Morley Roberts
Adventure of the Cardboard Lox. J. Ruyle
Adventure of the Cheesemonger's Bark. J. Ruyle
Adventure of the Christmas Pudding. A. Christie
Adventure of the Christmas Visitor. D. O. Smith
Adventure of the Clouded Crystal. T. J. Kelly
Adventure of the Copper Beeches. C. Fischer
Adventure of the Dancing Hen. J. Ruyle
Adventure of the Ectoplasmic Man. D. Stashower

Adventure of the Egyptian Student. R. C. Armour
Adventure of the Eleven Cuff-Buttons. J. F. Thierry
Adventure of the Fairfax Umpire. J. Ruyle
Adventure of the Five Buffalo Chips. J. Ruyle
Adventure of the Frail Codger. J. Ruyle
Adventure of the Freckled Hand. J. Ruyle
Adventure of the Frying Detective. J. Ruyle
Adventure of the Giant Bat of Sonoma. J. Ruyle
Adventure of the Jogging Man. J. Ruyle
Adventure of the Logophagous Client. J. Ruyle
Adventure of the Lost Manuscript. E. Pearson
Adventure of the Man "On Bail". W. J. Mayfield
Adventure of the Marked Man and One Other. S. Palmer
Adventure of the Missing Third Quarter. J. Ruyle
Adventure of the Mysterious Lodger. G. Gravatt
Adventure of the Oil Pirates. R. C. Armour
Adventure of the Orient Express. A. Derleth
Adventure of the Peerless Peer. P. J. Farmer
Adventure of the Purple Hand. D. O. Smith
Adventure of the Red-Headed Man. W. J. Bayfield
Adventure of the Retired Weatherman. J. Ruyle
Adventure of the Rogue's Apprentice. W. M. Graydon
Adventure of the Second Swag. Luke Sharp
Adventure of the Silk Smugglers. R. C. Armour
Adventure of the Smiling Judge. M. Fantina
Adventure of the Soledad Cyclist. J. Ruyle
Adventure of the Speckled Band. T. J. Kelly
Adventure of the Speed Mad Camden. E. J. Murray
Adventure of the Stalwart Companions. H. P. Jeffers
Adventure of the Unique Dickensians. A. Derleth
Adventure of the Unseen Traveler. D. O. Smith
Adventure of the Voodoo Queen. G. H. Teed
Adventure of the Zodiac Plate. D. O. Smith
Adventure Trail. D. B. Hobart
Adventure with a Goat. R. T. Campbell
Adventure with Crime. Josephine Bell
Adventurer. R. Miall
Adventurer from the West. M. J. Pemberton
Adventurer of the Bay. O. Binns
Adventurers. J. A. Hodge
Adventurers. H. B. M. Watson
Adventurers of the Night. G. A. Birmingham
Adventures at Greystones. G. E. Rochester
Adventures by Night. T. P. Prest
Adventure's End. J. Harris
Adventures in the Dark. J. Keating
Adventures of a Bashful Bachelor. C. Augusta
Adventures of a Chemist. F. A. Fawkes
Adventures of a Coquette. G. Leroux
Adventures of a Journalist. H. Cadett
Adventures of a Lady Detective. Mrs. G. Corbett
Adventures of a Lady Pearl Broker. B. Heron-Maxwell
Adventures of a Nice Young Man. Aix
Adventures of a Pretty Woman. F. Warden
Adventures of a Ship's Doctor. Morley Roberts
Adventures of a Skeleton. B. W. Waltermire
Adventures of a Social Detective. C. Bramley
Adventures of a Solicitor. W. Chesney
Adventures of a Stowaway. F. Whishaw
Adventures of a Turf Detective. F. D. A. C. De L'Isle
Adventures of a Wanderer. S. W. Powell
Adventures of Ah Foo, the Chinese Sherlock Holmes. C. Bishop
Adventures of Alonzo MacTavish. P. Cheyney
Adventures of an Attorney in Search of Practice. Anonymous
Adventures of an Engineer. W. Chesney
Adventures of an Equerry. M. Gerard
Adventures of an Ugly Girl. Mrs. G. Corbett
Adventures of Antoine. H. Collinson Owen
Adventures of Archer Dawe, Sleuth-Hound. J. S. Fletcher
Adventures of Bill Holmes. G. F. Hughes
Adventures of Blackshirt. B. Graeme
Adventures of Bobby Orde. S. E. White
Adventures of Burnaby Lee. E. Thomson
Adventures of Caleb Williams. W. Godwin
Adventures of Captain Ivan Koravitch. V. L. Whitchurch
Adventures of Captain Jack. M. Pemberton

Adventures of Captain Kettle. C. J. C. Kyne
Adventures of Captain Mounsell. W. W. Dixon
Adventures of Captain Spink. Morley Roberts
Adventures of Cardigan. F. Nebel
Adventures of Charles Edward. H. G. Rhodes
Adventures of Cigarette. J. Roland
Adventures of Creighton Holmes. N. Hubell
Adventures of D'Arcy Dewpond, Detective. W. Slater
Adventures of Detective Barney. H. J. O'Higgins
Adventures of Dick Boss. Maz
Adventures of Dr. Burton. A. C. Gunter
Adventures of Doctor Eszterhazy. A. Davidson
Adventures of Dr. Thorndyke. R. A. Freeman
Adventures of Doctor Whitty. G. A. Birmingham
Adventures of Ellery Queen. E. Queen
Adventures of Ephraim Tutt. A. Train
Adventures of Felix Boyd. S. Campbell
Adventures of Feluda. S. Ray
Adventures of Francois. S. W. Mitchell
Adventures of Gerard. A. C. Doyle
Adventures of Harrison Keith, Detective. Nicholas Carter
Adventures of Heine. E. Wallace
Adventures of Henry Turnbuckle. J. Ritchie
Adventures of Herlock Sholmes. Peter Todd
Adventures of Hiram Holliday. P. Gallico
Adventures of Husky Hillier. F. A. M. Webster
Adventures of Inspector Lestrade. M. J. Trow
Adventures of Jerry Parker, Mobile Investigator. J. Gunn
Adventures of Jimmie Dale. F. Packard
Adventures of Jimmy Strange. E. Dudley
Adventures of John Johns. F. Carrell
Adventures of Johnnie Pascoe. G. Norway
Adventures of Judith Lee. R. Marsh
Adventures of Jules de Grandin. Seabury Quinn
Adventures of Julia. P. Cheyney
Adventures of Julia and Two Other Spy Stories. P. Cheyney
Adventures of Kathlyn. H. MacGrath
Adventures of Kerlock Shomes and Dr. Warsaw. T. Gross
Adventures of Latimer Field, Curate. S. Hocking
Adventures of Louis Dural. Marguerite Bryant
Adventures of Lucius Leffing. J. P. Brennan
Adventures of Marmaduke Clegg. M. Gerard
Adventures of Martin Hewitt. Arthur Morrison
Adventures of Max Latin. Norbert Davis
Adventures of Mike Blair. H. Searls
Adventures of Miranda. L. T. Meade
Adventures of Miss Gregory. P. Gibbon
Adventures of Mr. Joseph P. Cray. E. P. Oppenheim
Adventures of Mr. Pitkin. B. Boothroyd
Adventures of Mr. Topham, Comedian. C. R. Gull
Adventures of Mr. Wellaby Johnson. O. Booth
Adventures of Mrs. Russell. S. B. Vandyopadhyaya
Adventures of M. D'Haricot. J. S. Clouston
Adventures of Mortimer Dixon. A. Ramsey
Adventures of Napoleon Prince. M. Edginton
Adventures of Paul Pry. E. S. Gardner
Adventures of Picklock Holes. R. C. Lehman
Adventures of Police Constable Vane, M. A. A. Askew
Adventures of Private Faust. H. H. Kirst
Adventures of Race Williams. C. J. Daly
Adventures of Raven Trail. Anonymous
Adventures of Richard O'Boy. B. Siegel
Adventures of Romney Pringle. C. Ashdown
Adventures of Russell Howard. A. E. Jobson
Adventures of Sam Spade and other stories. D. Hammett
Adventures of Sandy West, Private Eye. Stephen Wright
Adventures of Satan Hall. C. J. Daly
Adventures of Scout Grey. R. L. Bellamy
Adventures of Sheeluck Ohms. Dr. W. Ion
Adventures of Sherlaw Kombs. R. Barr
Adventures of Sherlock Holmes. A. C. Doyle
Adventures of Sherlock Holmes' Smarter Brother. G. Pearlman
Adventures of Shylar Homes. S. D. Williams
Adventures of Solar Pons. A. Derleth
Adventures of Susan Hopley. Mrs. C. Crowe

Adventures of Terra Tarkington. S. Webb
Adventures of the Black Pilgrim. G. Stanley
Adventures of the D.C.I. C. E. Russell
Adventures of the Five Puce Map Tacks. P. Nizza
Adventures of the Infallible Godahl. F. I. Anderson
Adventures of the Scarlet Pimpernel. Baroness Orczy
Adventures of the World's Greatest Detectives. G. Barton
Adventures of Turco Bullworthy. J. S. Fletcher
Adventures of Tyler Tatlock, Private Detective. D. Donovan
Adventures with Dangerous Women. P. Gurin
Adventuress. A. B. Reeve
Adventuress. C. Stanton
Adventuress. D. Winston
Adventuress of France. E. Gaboriau
Adventurous Annie. E. Everett-Green
Adventurous Exploits of the Younger Brothers. H. Dale
Adversaries. E. Linn
Adversary. G. Household
Adversary. A. M. Kabal
Adversary. D. Rhodes
Adversary. B. Spicer
Adverse Report. Gerald Hammond
Advertise for Treasure. D. Williams
Advice Limited. E. P. Oppenheim
Advisory Service. M. Russell
Advocate's Wig. L. M. Watt
Aegean Affair. W. Satterthwaite
Aelian Fragment. G. Bartram
Aerial Burglars. J. Blyth
Aerie. J. S. McClean
Aero Clubs Mystery. E. J. Millward
Aerodynamics of Pork. P. Gale
Aeroplane Mystery. D. T. Hughes
Affacombe Affair. E. Lemarchand
Affair at Abu Mina. P. William
Affair at Aliquid. G. D. H. Cole
Affair at Alkali. V. Coffman
Affair at Barwold. L. Meynell
Affair at Cralla Voe. J. Shelynn
Affair at Dead End. J. N. Chance
Affair at Falconers. M. Howe
Affair at Flower Acres. C. Wells
Affair at Helen's Court. C. Carnac
Affair at Islington. Matthew White
Affair at Little Todsham. G. Greenaway
Affair at Little Wokeham. F. W. Crofts
Affair at Lover's Leap. R. G. Dean
Affair at Palm Springs. C. Knight
Affair at Pine Court. N. R. Gilbert
Affair at Quala. T. Helmore
Affair at Ritos Bay. Muriel Bradley
Affair at Royalties. G. Baxt
Affair at Sidi Brahim. Brian Stuart
Affair at the Boat Landing. A. B. Cunningham
Affair at the Chateau. B. Reynolds
Affair at the Grotto. E H. Fonseca
Affair at the Semiramis Hotel. A. E. W. Mason
Affair at the "Vere Arms". A. R. Weekes
Affair at Tideways. E. A. Heath
Affair at Timber Lake. A. Anderson
Affair for the Baron. Anthony Morton
Affair in Araby. T. Mundy
Affair in Death Valley. C. Knight
Affair in Duplex 9B. W. A. Johnston
Affair in Hong Kong. D. Daniels
Affair in Marakesh. D. Daniels
Affair in Rome. J. Rejaunier
Affair in Tokyo. J. McPartland
Affair of Chief Strongheart. P. O'Malley
Affair of Danny the "Dip." W. Tyrer
Affair of Hearts. D. Noel
Affair of Honor. R. Wilder
Affair of John Donne. P. O'Malley
Affair of Jolie Madame. P. O'Malley
Affair of Nina B. J. M. Simmel
Affair of Sorcerers. G. Chesbro
Affair of State. P. Frank
Affair of Strangers. J. Crosby
Affair of Swan Lake. P. O'Malley
Affair of the Atlantic Mail Robbery. R. C. Armour
Affair of the Black Sombrero. C. Knight

Affair of the Blackfriars Financier. L. H. Brooks
Affair of the Bloodstained Egg-Cosy. James Anderson
Affair of the Blue Pig. P. O'Malley
Affair of the Bronzed Basilisk. A. Skene
Affair of the Bumbling Briton. P. O'Malley
Affair of the Circus Queen. C. Knight
Affair of the Corpse Escort. C. Knight
Affair of the Country Club. H. H. C. Gibbons
Affair of the Crimson Gull. C. Knight
Affair of the Crook Explorer. R. C. Armour
Affair of the Cross-Roads. H. H. C. Gibbons
Affair of the Dead Stranger. C. Knight
Affair of the Demobilized Soldier. W. J. Bayfield
Affair of the Diamond Star. H. H. C. Gibbons
Affair of the Envelope. E. Wigram
Affair of the Exotic Dancer. B. Benson
Affair of the Fainting Butler. C. Knight
Affair of the Family Diamonds. W. J. Bayfield
Affair of the Fatal Elm. John Hunter
Affair of the Fraternizing Soldier. P. Meriton
Affair of the Frigid Blonde. R. O. Saber
Affair of the Gallows Tree. S. Chalmers
Affair of the Ginger Lei. C. Knight
Affair of the Golden Buzzard. C. Knight
Affair of the Heart. J. Potts
Affair of the Heavenly Voice. C. Knight
Affair of the Hollywood Contract. W. Tyrer
Affair of the Jade Monkey. C. Knight
Affair of the Kidnapped Crook. H. H. C. Gibbons
Affair of the Limping Sailor. C. Knight
Affair of the Malacca Stick. C. Andrews
Affair of the Missing Parachutist. A. Parsons
Affair of the Missing Witness. W. M. Graydon
Affair of the Mutilated Mink Coat. James Anderson
Affair of the Oriental Doctor. Jack Lewis
Affair of the Phantom Car. E. J. Murray
Affair of the Red Mosaic. P. O'Malley
Affair of the Rival Cinema Kings. W. Shute
Affair of the Scarlet Crab. C. Knight
Affair of the Seven Mummy Cases. W. J. Bayfield
Affair of the Seven Warnings. G. N. Philips
Affair of the Sixth Button. C. Knight
Affair of the Skiing Clown. C. Knight
Affair of the Smuggled Millions. M. B. Dix
Affair of the Spiv's Secret. J. Hunter
Affair of the Splintered Heart. C. Knight
Affair of the Substitute Doctor. J. Rhode
Affair of the Syrian Dagger. C. Andrews
Affair of the Three Gunmen. W. M. Graydon
Affair of the Trade Rivals. R. C. Armour
Affair of the Unprincipled Publisher. L. Garland
Affair of the World's Champion. Jack Lewis
Affair on the Appian Way. M. Levey
Affair on the Bridge. J. M. DeGroot
Affair on the Painted Desert. C. Knight
Affair on Thor's Head. E. C. R. Lorac
Affair Ravel. J. Courage
Affair with a Rich Girl. J. N. Chance
Affaire Mysterieuse. G. Osmon
Affairs of Death. N. Fitzgerald
Affairs of Destiny. G. Simenon
Affairs of O'Malley. W. MacHarg
Affairs of Paludale. W. Slater
Affairs of Paula. H. Janson
Affairs of State. B. E. Stevenson
Affairs of the Generals. H. H. Kirst
Affairs of the Heart. M. Muggeridge
Affinities. M. R. Rinehart
Affliction. Russell Banks
Afghan Agent. J. Tabler
Afghan Assault. A. Caillou
Afghan Intercept. Nick Carter
Afghanistan Crashout. J. Rosenberger
Afghanistan Penetration. A. Kilgore
Afield and Afloat. F. R. Stockton
Afraid in the Dark. M. Derby
Afraid in the Dark. J. Reach
Afraid of the Dark. M. L. Roby
Africa Chess. F. Graves
African Assignment. P. McAdam
African Burn. Gar Wilson
African Contract. S. Jason
African Gold. W. M. Graydon

African Millionaire. G. Allen
African Millionaire. E. Wallace
African Mistress. L. Royer
African Nights. Rooiner
African Nights. I. M. Vinter
African Poison Murders. E. Huxley
African Terror. N. Sheraton
African Trio. G. Simenon
Afrit Affair. K. Laumer
After Alice Died. M. Bingley
After Baxtow's Death. M. Farrow
After Dark. D. Boucicault
After Dark. W. Collins
After-Dark. Ron Fraser
After Dark. William Katz
After Dark, My Sweet. J. Thompson
After Darvray Died. P. Meriton
After Delores. S. Schulman
After-Dinner Stories. M. Van Vorst
After-Dinner Story. W. Irish
After Doomsday. P. Anderson
After Eli. T. Kay
After Hours. E. Torres
After House. M. R. Rinehart
After Innocence. I. Gordon
After Magritte. T. Stoppard
After Many Days. C. Dawe
After Many Years. R. H. Savage
After Midnight. M. Albrand
After Midnight. E. Burfield
After Midnight. W. F. Fauley
After Midnight. E. Fletcher-Allen
After Midnight. H. Nielsen
After Office-Hours. E. Yates
After Rome, Africa. B. Glanville
After School Hours. R. Timperley
After-Shock. D. Howell
After Sundown. W. W. Penn
After the Act. Winston Graham
After the Ball. E. Dewhurst
After the Battle. D. Learmonth
After the Bribe Takers. Lieut. Carlton
After the Deacon Was Murdered. C. Penfield
After the Deed. J. S. Clouston
After the Execution. T. Hyde
After the Fact. A. Brock
After the Fault. R. H. Sherard
After the Fine Weather. M. Gilbert
After the First Death. Lawrence Block
After the First Death. R. Cormier
After the Funeral. A. Christie
After the Island. H. Bourne
After the Kill. S. Cunningham
After the Lady. P. Allardyce
After the Last Race. D. Koontz
After the Night Has Passed. A. L. Halstead
After the Race. M. Elkoff
After the Revolution. W. Wallace
After the Trial. E. Roman
After the Verdict. Nicholas Carter
After the Verdict. Anthony Gilbert
After the Verdict. R. Hichens
After the Verdict. P. Johnson
After the Verdict. E. Jordan
After the Wedding. K. Lindsay
After the Widow Changed Her Mind. C. Penfield
After Things Fell Apart. R. Goulart
After You with the Pistol. K. Bonfiglioli
Aftermath. O. T. Jackson
Aftermath. H. B. M. Watson
Aftermath of Murder. M. Fitt
Aftermath of Murder. R. Harrison
Aftermath of Murder. T. Newman
Afternoon at the Seaside. A. Christie
Afternoon for Lizards. D. Eden
Afternoon of a Counterspy. R. Tronson
Afternoon of a Gosling. M. Huffman
Afternoon of a Loser. T. Pace
Afternoon of Violence. C. Barling
Afternoon Walk. D. Eden
Aftershock. L. O'Donnell
Aftershock. C. Wilcox
Afterwards. M. B. Lowndes
Again Inspector Flagg. J. Cassells

Again McLean. G. Goodchild
Again, Mr. Sandyman. Neill Graham
Again Sanders. E. Wallace
Again the Dreamer. W. M. Duncan
Again the Remover. Roland Daniel
Again the Ringer. E. Wallace
Again the Three. E. Wallace
Again the Three Just Men. E. Wallace
Against All Odds. Arthur Smith
Against Desperate Odds. Nicholas Carter
Against My Fire. D. G. Waring
Against Odds. L. L. Lynch
Against the Evidence. L. Egan
Against the F.B.I. R. Carni
Against the Flame. Evelyn Harris
Against the Grain. J. O'Hagan
Against the Law. D. Durham
Against the Public Interest. R. Gaines
Against the Stream. J. Hatton
Against the Tides of Fate. J. A. Barry
Against Time. C. Hayter
Against Time. R. Jeffries
Agatha. K. Tynan
Agatha Christie Hour. A. Christie
Agatha Christie Made Me Do It. E. Cope
Agatha Christie's Poirot. A. Christie
Agatha Webb. A. K. Green
Agatha's Friends. T. Hauser
Agatha's Quest. R. H. Sherard
Agatite. C. Reynolds
Age of the Junkman. P. D. Ballard
Agency. P. Gottlieb
Agency House. S. Yorke
Agency House, Malaya. S. Yorke
Agent. T. Hinde
Agent. D. R. Slavitt
Agent B-7. Ared White
Agent Counter Agent. Nick Carter
Agent Extraordinary. S. Bayne
Agent from the West. D. Williams
Agent in Place. Helen MacInnes
Agent Intervenes. M. Annesley
Agent No. 5. J. Corbett
Agent of Byzantium. H. Turtledove
Agent of Change. Steve Miller
Agent of Death. N. De Mille
Agent of Influence. D. Aaron
Agent of Influence. Richard Cox
Agent of the Devil. H. Habe
Agent of the Falcon. L. McFarlane
Agent of the Id. B. Byers
Agent of Vega. J. H. Schmitz
Agent on the Other Side. G. O'Toole
Agent Orange Affair. James Watson
Agent Ordinaire. F. Jordison
Agent Out of Place. I. A. Greenfield
Agent Outside. P. Wynnton
Agent Provocateur. D. Young
Agents of Influence. P. Harcourt
Agents of Innocence. D. Ignatius
Agents of Sympathy. F. O'Neill
Agents of the League. C. Davy
Aggravating Joe, the Prince of Mischief. Old Sleuth
Agile Retrieval. J. Hild
Agnes of God. L. Fleischer
Agnes of God. J. Pielmeier
Agnes the Unknown. T. P. Prest
Agony Column. E. D. Biggers
Agony Column Murders. R. T. M. Scott
Agony Terrace. A. Griffiths
Agreement. S. L. McMurray
Agreement to Kill. P. Rabe
Aground. C. Williams
Ah King. W. S. Maugham
Ah, Sweet Mystery. J. Kirkpatrick
Ah, Sweet Mystery of Life. R. Dahl
Ahead of the Game. Nicholas Carter
Aila. K. Thomas
Aim for the Heart. W. McCall
Aim to Kill. R. Gatenby
Ainceworth Mystery. G. Baxter
Ainsley Case. B. Partridge
Air Apparent. J. Gardner
Air Bandits. D. T. Lindsay

Air Bandits. P. Trent
Air Bridge. H. Innes
Air Cavalier. T. Wallace
Air Devil. B. Beverley
Air Disaster. H. Innes
Air Feud. W. A. Hansbro
Air for Murder. F. L. Cary
Air Force One. E. Corley
Air Force One Is Haunted. R. J. Serling
Air Fugitives. P. J. Clancy
Air Glow Red. I. Slater
Air Gold. Colin Hope
Air Killer. J. Corbett
Air Ministry, Room 18. G. Frankau
Air Murders. R. H. Watkins
Air of Glory. S. Neilan
Air Peril. Colin Hope
Air Pilot. R. Parrish
Air Pirate. C. R. Gull
Air Raiders. S. Drew
Air Ranger. G. E. Rochester
Air Reprisal. A. O. Pollard
Air-Ship. J. S. Fletcher
Air Sleuth. J. Bolton
Air Smugglers. J. Bolton
Air That Kills. Francis King
Air That Kills. M. Millar
Air Tight Alibi. W. A. Hackett
Air Trail. G. E. Rochester
Airburst. S. L. Thompson
Airesboro Castle. E. M. Layman
Airing in a Closed Carriage. J. Shearing
Airline Pirates. J. Gardner
Airport Affair. D. Toma
Airport Cop. C. Miron
Airs Above the Ground. Mary Stewart
Airtight Alibi. C. F. Gregg
Akbar Contract. M. McCray
Akin to Murder. K. M. Knight
Al Capone. J. Roeburt
Al Jazzar. Christopher Matthews
Aladdin in London. F. Hume
Aladdin in London. M. Pemberton
Alain of Halfdene. A. Burr
Alamein. M. Urquhart
Alamut Ambush. A. Price
Alan! Alan! E. Wigram
Alan Fitz Osborne. Miss Muller
Alan Thorne. M. L. Moodey
Alaric Spenceley. J. H. Riddell
Alarm. E. R. Jones
Alarm. J. Rhode
Alarm at Black Brake. J. N. Chance
Alarm in the Night. S. Sterling
Alarm of the Black Cat. D. B. Olsen
Alarming Clock. M. Avallone
Alarum. G. Marton
Alarum and Excursion. V. Perdue
Alarums and Excursions. H. B. M. Watson
Alas for Her That Met Me! M. A. Ashe
Alas, Poor Father. Joan Fleming
Alaska Conspiracy. J. Rosenberger
Alaska Deception. W. M. Brinton
Alaska Deception. J. Hild
Alaska Project. J. Baddock
Alaskan. G. Goodchild
Alaskan Gold. Jim Mack
Alba. Delacorta
Albani. Anonymous
Albanian Connection. J. Rosenberger
Albanian Incident. S. Dodds
Albatross. E. Anthony
Albatross. C. Armstrong
Albatross Murders. I. Jones
Albert Gate Affair. L. Tracy
Albert Gate Mystery. L. Tracy
Albert Rides Again. J. T. Story
Albino's Double. G. N. Philips
Albion Case. D. Craig
Album. M. R. Rinehart
Album Leaf. J. Shearing
Alcatraz Break. S. Markham
Alcatraz Incident. R. O'Neil
Alchemist. K. Goddard

Title Index

Alchemy Deception. H. W. Holzer
Alchemy Murder. P. Oldfeld
Alcoholics. J. Thompson
Alda Abducted. A. R. Weekes
Aldeburg Cezanne. J. A. Graham
Alden Case. R. Bridges
Alderman's Children. J. B. Richards
Aldringham's Last Chance. A. J. Rees
Aleph. J. L. Borges
Aleph Solution. S. Frankel
Alert State Black. Frederick Nolan
Aleta's Terrible Secret. L. J. Libbey
Aletta. B. Mitford
Aleutian Blue Mink. J. M. Fox
Alexander Botts, Earthworm Tractors. W. H. Upson
Alexander the Greatest. W. H. Upson
Alexandra, the Ambivalent. K. Kimbrough
Alexandrovitch Is Missing! Anne Edwards
Alexena. Anonymous
Alfred Hitchcock Murder Case. G. Baxt
Alfred Hitchcock's Solve Them Yourself Mysteries. R. Arthur
Alfred Leslie. Anonymous
Algarve Affair. Nick Carter
Algarve Affair. R. Derwent
Algerian Incident. C. Sellers
Algonquin Project. F. Nolan
Algorithm. J. M. Gawron
Alias. F. Andreas
Alias a Lady. Carter Brown
Alias Basil Willing. H. McCloy
Alias Ben Alibi. T. S. Cobb
Alias Blackshirt. B. Graeme
Alias Blue Mask. Anthony Morton
Alias Dr. Ely. L. Thayer
Alias for Death. B. L. Reynolds
Alias His Wife. S. Ransome
Alias Jack the Ripper. G. Traylor
Alias John Doe. P. E. Triem
Alias John Smith. G. Wade
Alias Man. D. Craig
Alias Mr. Death. G. W. Jones
Alias Mr. Orson. A. Spiller
Alias Norman Conquest. B. Gray
Alias Red Ryan. C. N. Buck
Alias Richard Power. W. Allison
Alias Richard Power. C. N. Williamson
Alias the Baron. Anthony Morton
Alias the Bearded Lady. A. C. Headley
Alias—The Crimson Snake. T. A. Plummer
Alias the Dead. G. H. Coxe
Alias the Eagle. M. Harvey
Alias the Ghost. G. Verner
Alias the Hangman. V. Gunn
Alias the Lone Wolf. L. J. Vance
Alias the Maestro. L. Mantz
Alias the Night Wind. V. Vanardy
Alias the Saint. L. Charteris
Alias the Thunderbolt. J. McCulley
Alias the Victim. L. Gribble
Alias Uncle Hugo. M. Coles
Alibeg, the Tempter. W. C. Child
Alibi. H. Carmichael
Alibi. J. Creasey
Alibi. G. A. England
Alibi. R. Kroetsch
Alibi. M. Morton
Alibi. Mark Ross
Alibi. F. F. Van De Water
Alibi and Dr. Morelle. E. Dudley
Alibi Angel. D. Haring
Alibi at Dusk. B. Benson
Alibi Baby. S. Sterling
Alibi for a Corpse. E. Lemarchand
Alibi for a Judge. H. Cecil
Alibi for a Witch. E. Ferrars
Alibi for Arson. D. Haring
Alibi for Isabel. M. R. Rinehart
Alibi for Murder. C. Armstrong
Alibi in Black. Colin Robertson
Alibi in the Rough. S. Box
Alibi in Time. J. Thomson
Alibi Innings. B. Worsley-Gough
Alibi of Guilt. Philip Daniels
Alibi Off Broadway. H. Zore
Alibi Too Much. H. Kaner
Alibi Too Soon. R. Ormerod
Alice. E. Bulwer-Lytton
Alice. E. V. Cunningham
Alice. F. W. Pangborn
Alice and Me. W. Judson
Alice Devine. E. Jepson
Alice Dies Twice. B. Grant
Alice in La-La Land. Robert Campbell
Alice Leighton. T. Frost
Alice to Nowhere. Evan Green
Alice, Where Art Thou? E. Cadell
Alicia's Trump. J. Mathewson
Alien. Josephine Bell
Alien. L. P. Davies
Alien Archipelago. San Antonio
Alien Minds. E. E. Evans
Alien Nation. A. D. Foster
Alien Souls. A. Abdullah
Alien Trace. H. M. Major
Alien Virus. A. Caillou
Alington Inheritance. P. Wentworth
Alinsky's Diamond. T. McHale
Alise of Astra. H. B. M. Watson
Alive and Dead. E. Ferrars
Alive or Dead. G. B. Savi
Alixe Derring. E. Nisot
All About Women. A. M. Greeley
All Ages. J. J. Bell
All Along the River. M. E. Braddon
All at Sea. C. Wells
All Booked Up. T. Curran
All Brides Are Beautiful. M. Corrigan
All Cats Are Grey. C. G. Givens
All Change for Murder. V. Gunn
All Change, Humanity! C. Houghton
All Concerned Notified. H. Reilly
All Dames Are Dynamite. T. Trent
All Done by Kindness. Doris Langley Moore
All Dreams Denied. Adam Kennedy
All Dressed Up to Die. R. Nordan
All England at Home. John Gloag
All Evil Shed Away. A. Roy
All Exits Barred. C. Portway
All Exits Blocked. B. Perowne
All Fall Down. A. Kennington
All Fall Down. J. Saul
All Fall Down. L. A. G. Strong
All for a Woman. J. J. Dratler
All for Him. Anonymous
All for One and One for Death. S. Forbes
All for the Apple. J. MacKenzie
All for the Love of a Lady. L. Ford
All God's Children. A. Lyons
All Good Men. J. Daley
All Grass Isn't Green. A. A. Fair
All Hands. L. Luard
All Heads Turn When the Hunt Goes By. J. Farris
All Heaven in a Rage. M. Duffy
All Her Vices. S. Rand
All Honorable Men. D. Karp
All I Can Get. W. Ard
All in a Day. L. Barbee
All in a Day's Work. D. Ray
All in Good Crime. M. Hervey
All in One. H. Conway
All in the Dark. J. S. Le Fanu
All in the Night's Work. E. W. Mumford
All in the Racket. W. E. Weeks
All Is Discovered. J. Cannan
All Is Not Fair in Love. C. Garvice
All Is Not Gold. F. A. M. Webster
All Is Vanity. Josephine Bell
All Killers Aren't Ugly. T. K. Makagon
All Leads Negative. P. Aldine
All Men Are Liars. J. S. Strange
All Men Are Lonely Now. F. Clifford
All Men Are Murderers. C. Blackstock
All My Dead Men. B. Byers
All My Enemies. S. Baron
All My Enemies. Rosemary Harris
All My Sins Remembered. J. Haldemann
All Night at Mr. Stanyhurst's. H. Edwards

ALLIGATOR RING / 895

All Night Long. F. Metcalfe
All Night Service. B. Merivale
All of Our Aircraft Are Missing. J. P. Radford
All on a Summer's Day. J. Garden
All on a Summer's Day. J. Wainwright
All or Nothing. A. Bocca
All or Nothing. M. Catto
All or Nothing. R. Marlowe
All or Something. H. Brand
All Other Perils. Robert MacLeod
All Our Tomorrows. T. Allbeury
All Over But the Shooting. R. Powell
All Part of the Service. M. Russell
All Points Bulletin. M. Weiss
All Possible Avenues. Tom Howard
All-Purpose Bodies. P. McCutchan
All Risks Mortality. P. Cunningham
All Roads Lead to Friday. H. Innes
All Roads Lead to Sospel. G. Bellairs
All Set for Murder. B. Carter
All Shot Up. C. Himes
All Sorts. Vince Kelly
All Sorts. D. Wyllarde
All Souls' Night. H. Walpole
All Square with Fate. T. C. St. C. Morton
All Star Cast. N. Royde-Smith
All Stations to Malta. G. Hackforth-Jones
All Suspect. K. Methold
All Suspected. W. J. Bayfield
All That Glistens. M. Ashton
All That Glitters. M. Anthony
All That Glitters. M. Coles
All That Glitters. N. B. Gerson
All That Glitters. Magali
All That Glitters. E. Powers
All That Glitters. M. Richmond
All That Glitters. R. Spencer
All That Sparkles. S. Cameron
All the Better to Kill You. F. Carmichael
All the Colors of Darkness. L. Biggle
All the Dead Lay Down. James Fletcher
All the Grey Cats. Craig Thomas
All the King's Men. J. L. Johnson
All the Muscle You Need. D. McRae
All the Nice Girls. E. Kyle
All the Old Bargains. B. M. Schutz
All the Pretty People. J. S. Scott
All the Queen's Men. G. DeMontfort
All the Silent Voices. Roger Fuller
All the Skeletons in All the Closets. K. Fowler
All the Things You Ain't. N. Karta
All the Virtues of the Dead. I. Cecil
All the Way. C. Williams
All the Way Down. M. E. Chaber
All the Way Home and All the Night Through. T. Lewis
All the Winners. N. Gubbins
All the World to Nothing. W. Martyn
All the World Wondered. L. Merrick
All These Condemned. J. D. MacDonald
All This, and Heaven Too. R. Field
All This and That. D. Runyon
All This Is Ended. A. W. Wells
All This Shall Perish. M. Vinter
All Through the Night. W. Masterson
All Through the Night. E. Title
All Through the Night. J. Wainwright
All Thugs Are Dangerous. Roland Daniel
All Tramps Are Trouble. H. Janson
All Very Irregular. V. Bridges
All-White Elf. K. Robeson
All Your Lovely Words Are Spoken. M. L. Roby
Allah Conspiracy. C. Warren
Allah's Eye. A. Parsons
Allan Dare and Robert le Diable. A. Porter
Allan Keene, the War Detective. H. Rockwood
Alleged Great Aunt. H. K. Webster
Allegra's Child. J. Letton
Alley Girl. Jonathan Craig
Alley Kids. B. Appel
Allie Baird, the Settler's Son. Old Sleuth
Allies. M. Sellar
Alligator. I*n Fl*m*ng
Alligator Ring. Donald Ross

A

Allingham Case-Book. M. Allingham
Allingham Minibus. M. Allingham
Allison's Baby. Mike Stone
All's Fair on Lake Garda. A. J. Evans
Allworth Abbey. E. Southworth
Allyson. J. Jenkins
Almack, the Detective. E. H. Cragg
Almagro and Claude. Anonymous
Almeda. N. T. Oliver
Almighty. I. Wallace
Almira's Curse. T. P. Prest
Almon Mitchell's Double. Old Sleuth
Almost Dead. W. Herber
Almost Midnight. M. Caidin
Almost Murder. R. Jeffries
Almost Perfect Murder. H. Footner
Almost Without Murder. B. Graeme
Aloha. Robin Moore
Aloha Means Goodbye. N. A. Hintze
Alone at Night. V. Packer
Alone in the Grass. C. Phillips
Alone on a Wide, Wide Sea. W. C. Russell
Along a Dark Path. V. Johnston
Along Came a Spider. E. Davis
Along Came a Spider. Maude Parker
Along for the Ride. T. Newman
Along the Road. A. Hodges
Alonzo MacTavish Again. P. Cheyney
Alp Murder. A. M. Stein
Alperfol Affair. A. Kullar
Alpha and Omega. N. Bell
Alpha and Omega. B. Whittier
Alpha Bug. M. E. Morris
Alpha Deception. J. Land
Alpha-I Conspiracy. R. Jontas
Alpha List. T. Allbeury
Alpha List. James Anderson
Alpha-Omega. W. Glassford
Alpha Raid. A. Scholefield
Alpha Trip. G. Billing
Alphabet Hicks. R. Stout
Alphabet Murders. A. Christie
Alphonsine. A. Belot
Alpine Affair. J. F. Vignant
Alpine Coach. V. Coffman
Alpine Condo Cross Fire. M. G. Eberhart
Alpine Crack-Up. J. W. Hornby
Alpine Encounter. H. Rowan
Alpine Gambit. N. Cort
Alpine Treason. G. Wark
Alps Assignment. A. Sugar
Alraune. H. H. Ewers
Alscott Experiment. B. Stanley
Also Ran. B. Reynolds
Also Ran. N. Williams
Alster Case. R. Gillmore
Altar. P. Walker
Altar Boy. S. J. Cassidy
Altar of Evil. F. Stevenson
Altar-Piece. N. Royde-Smith
Altars of the Heart. R. Lebherz
Alter Ego. M. Arrighi
Alter Ego. E. Linington
Alter Ego. P. Watson
Altered Ego. J. Sohl
Altered Egos. K. Girard
Alternate Case. J. F. Dinneen
Alternate Casts. M. Cassady
Althea. M. McDonell
Althea's Flacon. D. M. Carlisle
Altheimer Inheritance. J. Herbrand
Alton Crucis. H. Shipton
Aluminum Turtle. B. Kendrick
Alumni Murders. P. Ruse
Alvarez Journal. R. Burns
Always a Body to Trade. K. C. Constantine
Always a Dame. B. Vane
Always a Spy. R. Footman
Always a Thief. J. W. Deaver
Always Aim High. D. Haring
Always Anonymous Beast. L. W. Douglas
Always Ask a Policeman. S. Truss
Always Expect the Unexpected. B. Graeme
Always Fight Back. A. MacKenzie

Always in August. A. Head
Always Kill a Stranger. R. L. Fish
Always Leave 'Em Dying. R. S. Prather
Always Lock Your Bedroom Door. R. Winsor
Always Murder a Friend. M. Scherf
Always Say Die. E. Ferrars
Always Say Goodbye. M. Heath-Miller
Always Take the Big Ones. Peter Chambers
Always Tell the Truth. Kevin O'Hara
Always the Wolf. N. Easton
Always Tip the Dealer. Gary Ross
Amadora. V. McConnor
Amanda in Berlin. G. Revelli
Amanda in Spain. G. Revelli
Amanda's Castle. G. Revelli
Amaranth Club. J. S. Fletcher
Amateur. R. Littell
Amateur Adventuress. C. Stanton
Amateur Agent. Christopher Adams
Amateur Agent. D. Vallance
Amateur Boxer. R. Worth
Amateur City. K. V. Forrest
Amateur Corpse. Simon Brett
Amateur Cracksman. E. W. Hornung
Amateur Crime. A. B. Cox
Amateur Criminal. G. S. Lavard
Amateur Crook. H. Clevely
Amateur Detective. S. Janney
Amateur Detectives. C. B. Booth
Amateur Emigrants. T. Cobb
Amateur Gentleman. J. Farnol
Amateur Governess. M. A. Gibbs
Amateur Hour. R. Hardin
Amateur in Crime. W. M. Graydon
Amateur in Violence. M. Gilbert
Amateur Inn. A. P. Terhune
Amateur Murderer. C. J. Daly
Amateurs. W. Cook
Amateur's Entertainment Book. A. L. Kaser
Amazing Adventures of Carolus Herbert. G. Leroux
Amazing Adventures of Dan Daredevil. Tim Kelly
Amazing Adventures of Lester Leith. E. S. Gardner
Amazing Adventures of Letitia Carberry. M. R. Rinehart
Amazing Adventures of Mr. Henry Button. L. Despard
Amazing Adventures of Sophie Lyons. S. Lyons
Amazing Affair of the Renegade Prince. G. N. Philips
Amazing Affair of the Shipyard Sabotage. S. Hope
Amazing Chance. P. Wentworth
Amazing Corpse. Colin Robertson
Amazing Count. W. LeQueux
Amazing Dr. Clitterhouse. B. Lyndon
Amazing Dr. Khan. H. Metcalfe
Amazing Duke. W. Magnay
Amazing Faith. L. Waller
Amazing Judgment. E. P. Oppenheim
Amazing Mr. Blackshirt. R. Graeme
Amazing Mr. Bunn. B. Atkey
Amazing Mr. Lutterworth. D. Leslie
Amazing Mr. Sandyman. Neill Graham
Amazing Mr. Smith. F. Dare
Amazing Mrs. Pollifax. D. Gilman
Amazing Partnership. E. P. Oppenheim
Amazing Quest of Doctor Syn. R. Thorndike
Amazing Quest of Mr. Ernest Bliss. E. P. Oppenheim
Amazing Scoundrel. Nicholas Carter
Amazing Test Match Crime. A. Alington
Amazing Verdict. M. Leighton
Amazing Web. H. S. Keeler
Amazing Witness. A. Shire
Amazing Wizard. Old Sleuth
Amazon. Nick Carter
Amazon Factor. W. Wise
Amazon Gold. P. Andrews
Amazon Slaughter. D. Stivers
Amazon Strike. Gar Wilson
Amazons. I. Ross
Ambart Trial. K. Ingram
Ambassador. S. Longstreet
Ambassador. M. L. West
Ambassador of Death. J. F. Fishter

Ambassador's Adventure. A. Upward
Ambassador's Glove. R. Machray
Ambassador's Kiss. W. J. Lomax
Ambassador's Plot. S. D. Frances
Ambassador's Trunk. G. Barton
Ambassador's Wife. P. Gibbs
Amber and Jade. A. Griffin
Amber Bead. J. Spiess
Amber Cat. Elizabeth Ford
Amber Effect. R. A. Prather
Amber Eyes. F. Crane
Amber Eyes. Roland Daniel
Amber Eyes of the Lion. S. Dembo
Amber for Anna. A. Watkyn
Amber Girl. C. Mayne
Amber Gods. S. C. Prescott
Amber Gods and Other Stories. H. Spofford
Amber Junk. M. E. Hanshew
Amber Nine. J. Gardner
Amber Palace. J. Freytag
Amber to Red. V. Hill
Amber Twilight. M. Lynch
Ambergris! A. Murray
Amberleigh. C. N. Douglas
Amberleigh. M. E. Edward
Amberley Affair. P. Parrish
Amberley Diamonds. A. W. Madden
Amberstone. P. Bennetts
Amberwood. A. Rundle
Ambient. J. Womack
Ambiguous Man. R. Tashkent
Ambition's Slave. F. M. White
Ambitious Lady. J. S. Fletcher
Ambler. F. Halliday
Amblers. B. L. Farjeon
Amboy Dukes. I. Shulman
Ambrose in London. P. Levene
Ambrose in Paris. P. Levene
Ambrose Lavendale, Diplomat. E. P. Oppenheim
Ambrosio. M. G. Lewis
Ambrotox and Limping Dick. O. Fleming
Ambulance. H. Miller
Ambush. M. Buckley
Ambush. W. Edwards
Ambush. B. G. High
Ambush! Steve Mackenzie
Ambush. J. G. Sarasin
Ambush at Derati Wells. P. McCurtin
Ambush at Osirak. H. Crowder
Ambush for Anatol. J. Sherwood
Ambush for the Hunter. F. L. Green
Ambush House. K. Steel
Ambush on Blood River. D. Pendleton
Ambushed. P. Rosemoor
Ambushers. D. Hamilton
Amendment. Sue Robinson
Amends for Murder. M. D. Lake
American. L. Waller
American Ambassador. W. Just
American Apetites. J. C. Oates
American Baron. J. De Mille
American Blood. J. Nichols
American Cavalier. W. C. Hudson
American Counterfeits. G. P. Burnham
American Crime Stories. J. Theydon
American Detective in Russia. Old Sleuth
American Dream. N. Mailer
American Gothic. R. Bloch
American Gun Mystery. E. Queen
American Legionnaire. J. Robb
American Marquis. Nicholas Carter
American Marquis. R. H. Sherard
American Monte Cristo. J. Hawthorne
American Monte Cristo. Old Sleuth
American Nightmare. C. Bainbridge
American Nightmare. D. Pendleton
American Penman. J. Hawthorne
American Pep. A. Stone
American Prisoner. E. Phillpotts
American Quartet. W. Adler
American Reich. D. Muir
American Satan. K. Farrell
American Sextet. W. Adler
American Spy Story. N. Quint

Title Index

American Surrender. Michael Brady
American Thug. Old Sleuth
American Tragedy. T. Dreiser
American Vengeance. J. Cutter
American Venus. E. Preston
American Widow. A. Kevill-Davies
America's Heroes. R. Coram
Amethyst Box. A. K. Green
Amethyst Button. B. Baskerville
Amethyst Cross. F. Hume
Amethyst Quest. L. A. Sunagel
Amethyst Spectacles. F. Crane
Amethyst Tears. Marilyn Ross
Amiable Charlatan. E. P. Oppenheim
Amiable Crimes of Dirk Memling. Rupert Hughes
Amigo, Amigo. F. Clifford
Aminda Gamble. J. Sherlock
Ammie, Come Home. B. Michaels
Amnesia Trap. R. Ormerod
Amok. G. Fox
Amok. H. Janson
Among Arabian Sands. J. Mitchell
Among the Brigands. J. De Mille
Among the Counterfeiters. Nicholas Carter
Among the Cranks. James Greenwood
Among the Freaks. W. L. Alden
Among the Nihilists. Nicholas Carter
Among the Ruins and Other Stories. M. C. Hay
Among the Water Lilies. C. M. Blake
Among Thieves. G. Cuomo
Among Those Absent. M. Coles
Among Those Hunted. M. Skinner
Among Those Present. P. Barrington
Among Those Present. A. Feist
Among Those Present. A. S. Roche
Amongst Those Missing. P. Capon
Amoret. C. Gibbon
Amorous Adventuress. R. Vane
Amorous Avenger. R. Kelsey
Amorous Leander. A. Hunter
Amorous Rogue. R. Foxall
Amos. S. G. West
Amos Petrie's Puzzle. J. V. Turner
Ampersand Papers. M. Innes
Amphetamines and Pearls. J. Harvey
Amphitheatre Plot. Nicholas Carter
Amphorae Pirates. L. Cameron
Ampuras Exchange. Angus Ross
Amsterdam. Nick Carter
Amsterdam Connection. L. Grimsey
Amsterdam Diversion. Angus Ross
Amsterdam Silver. R. Wilson
Amusement Only. R. Marsh
Amy. K. W. Eyre
Amy Girl. Bari Wood
Amyas Egerton, Cavalier. M. H. Hervey
Amzi, the Detective. Old Sleuth
Ana Mistral. S. Olson
Ana P. I. I. Magdalen
Anagram Detectives. N. Schier
Anagram of Murder. S. Matthews
Analog Bullet. Martin Smith
Anarchaos. Curt Clark
Anarchist. R. H. Savage
Anarchist's Moon. J. Griffin
Anarchist's Oath. B. Wayde
Anarchist's Pluck. B. Wayde
Anarchy Plot. P. B. Van Orsdol
Anastasia Syndrome and other stories. M. H. Clark
Anathema Stone. J. B. Hilton
Anatomy Lesson. M. Goldberg
Anatomy of a Crime. J. F. Dinneen
Anatomy of a Killer. P. Rabe
Anatomy of a Murder. R. Traver
Anatomy of a Murder. E. Winer
Anatomy of a Riot. J. Wainwright
Anatomy of an Arsonist. G. Mahoney
Anatomy of Violence. C. Runyon
Ancestor. R. Carol
Ancestral Precipice. J. Ekstrom
Anchor Island. P. Malloch
Anchor Watch Yarns. E. Downey
Anchor's Aweigh. E. L. Long
Ancient Evil. C. Arkham

Ancient Firm of Camouflage and Co. W. Beacon
Ancient Images. Ramsey Campbell
Ancient Mariners. Morley Roberts
Ancient Pond. Courtney Browne
Ancient Rage. J. La Tourrette
Ancient Records. T. C. H. Curties
Ancora Scipio. T. Gates
And a Bottle of Rum. B. Graeme
And Afterward, the Dark. B. Copper
And All That Beauty—. R. Bridges
And All the King's Men. Gordon Stevens
And Baby Will Fall. M. Z. Lewin
And Bay the Moon. P. Bourne
And Be a Villain. J. Cannan
And Be a Villain. L. Meynell
And Be a Villain. R. Stout
And Be My Love. Ledru Baker
And Being Dead. M. Erskine
And Berry Came Too. D. Yates
And Billy Disappeared. W. B. Hare
And Call It Accident. M. B. Lowndes
And Cauldron Bubble. B. Flynn
And Dangerous to Know. E. Daly
And Death Came Too. Anthony Gilbert
And Death Came Too. R. Hull
And Death Came Too. H. Mace
And Death Drove On. Robert Fleming
And Delilah. N. Paterson
And Die Remembering. M. L. Roby
And Die She Did. I. Oellrichs
And Died So? V. Gielgud
And Dream of Evil. T. Thomey
And Four to Go. R. Stout
And Hang Him. K. P. Arbuthnot
And He Did Eat. M. Zumsteg
And Here Is the Noose! Kevin O'Hara
And High Water. A. M. Stein
And Home Came Ted. W. B. Hare
And Hope to Die. L. Charbonneau
And Hope to Die. R. Powell
And If I Laugh. D. G. Waring
And Incidentally, Murder! B. E. Lovell
And Justice for All. R. Grossbach
And Kill Once More. A. Fray
And Leave Her Lay Dying. J. L. Reynolds
And Left for Dead. F. Lockridge
And Let the Coffin Pass. K. Abbey
And Love Survived. R. Chetwynd-Hayes
And Loving It! W. Johnston
And Murder Came Too. G. Compton
And Murder Won. H. C. Davis
And Next the King. Nick Carter
And No One Wept. A. Hocking
And Not for Love. P. Mechem
And Now the Screaming Starts. D. Case
And on the Eighth Day. E. Queen
And One Cried Murder. L. Thayer
And One for the Dead. P. Audemars
And One for the Pot. M. E. Simpson
And One Must Die. P. Henneker
And Only Man. A. Dick
And Presumed Dead. L. Fletcher
And Shall Trelawney Die? J. Hocking
And Shame the Devil. Sara Woods
And She Had a Little Knife. J. L. Linklater
And So He Died. M. Hunter
And So He Had to Die. D. C. Cameron
And So to Bed. W. Ard
And So to Death. W. Irish
And So to Death. G. Shayne
And So to Eternity. Whitney Brown
And So to Murder. Carter Dickson
And So We Die. J. Sandys
And Some Were Evil. E. Willie
And Sometimes Death. J. Valentine
And Still I Cheat the Gallows. E. P. Oppenheim
And Sudden Death. C. F. Adams
And Sudden Death. J. S. Fletcher
And the Body Came Too. L. Boden
And the Bullets Were Made of Lead. P. Wheeler
And the Deep Blue Sea. R. Knotts
And the Deep Blue Sea. C. Williams
And the Devil. C. Cannell
And the Girl Screamed. G. Brewer

And the Gods Laughed. Fredric Brown
And the Moon Was Full. H. McCutcheon
And the Shouting Dies. Robert Mason
And the Undead Sing. Carter Brown
And the Villain Still Pursued Her. A. L. Kaser
And the Winds Blew. H. J. Heinecke
And Then—? E. Mordaunt
And Then Came Fear. M. Cumberland
And Then Look Down. M. Garratt
And Then Murder. J. Fast
And Then...One Dark Night. E. Snell
And Then Put Out the Light. E. C. R. Lorac
And Then Silence. M. Propper
And Then the Screaming Started. O. Blakeston
And Then There Was Georgia. J. Blackmore
And Then There Was None. E. C. Vivian
And Then There Was Nun. M. Quill
And Then There Were Nine. W. H. L. Crauford
And Then There Were None. A. Christie
And Then They Die. R. McCollum
And Thereby Hangs. M. Merwin
And Thereby Hangs—. A. Spiller
And They Say You Can't Buy Happiness. M. Lovell
And to My Beloved Husband—. P. Loraine
And Turned to Clay. L. G. Offord
And Two Shall Meet. Raymond Mason
And When She Was Bad She Was Murdered. R. Starnes
And Where She Stops. T. B. Dewey
And Where's Mr. Bellamy? S. M. Wick
And, Which, the Knave? B. M. Scott
And Why Not? V. G. Malo
And Worms Have Eaten Them. M. Cumberland
And Worms Have Eaten Them. W. J. Elliott
Andean Murders. L. Hazard
Anderson Crow, Detective. G. B. McCutcheon
Anderson Tapes. L. Sanders
Andra Fiasco. W. Garner
Andre Cornelis. P. Bourget
Andrew and His Wife. T. Cobb
Andrew Reforms. P. Trent
Andrewlina. J. S. Fletcher
Andrew's Wife. K. Booton
Androcles and the Tiger. T. Gay
Andromache. H. Monteilhet
Andromeda Assignment. David Lewis
Andropov Deception. B. Crozier
Andropov Deception. J. Rossiter
Andropov File. Nick Carter
Anecdotes of Two Well-Known Families. Mrs. Parsons
Angel. G. Brewer
Angel! Carter Brown
Angel. C. Lucas
Angel. P. Traill
Angel. G. Verner
Angel Abroad. G. Montrose
Angel Among Witches. A. Gale
Angel and the Cuckoo. G. Kersh
Angel and the Nero. G. Montrose
Angel and the Red Admiral. G. Montrose
Angel, Angel, Down We Go. W. Johnston
Angel, Archangel. Nick Cook
Angel Astray. H. Janson
Angel at Arms. G. Montrose
Angel Came Down. M. Pereira
Angel Dance. M. F. Beal
Angel Death. P. Moyes
Angel Dust. Anthea Cohen
Angel Esquire. E. Wallace
Angel Eyes. R. Dietrich
Angel Eyes. L. Estleman
Angel Face. S. Cohen
Angel Face. F. Nichols
Angel Face Tatters the Kimono. A. St. Moore
Angel Falls. P. Guernsey
Angel Fire. A. M. Greeley
Angel Food. J. L. Martin
Angel for Paradise. J. Canon
Angel Hold Fire. K. T. McCall
Angel Hunt. Mike Ripley
Angel in Paradise. G. Montrose
Angel in the Case. E. Elder
Angel in the Pawnshop. A. B. Shiffrin

Angel in the Snow. P. Welles
Angel Loves Nobody. R. Miles
Angel Maker. H. Michelson
Angel of Comical Corner. F. Daniel
Angel of Death. D. Alexander
Angel of Death. James Anderson
Angel of Death. P. D. Ballard
Angel of Death. Nicholas Carter
Angel of Death. A. Cohen
Angel of Death. A. Dlovu
Angel of Death. P. C. Doherty
Angel of Death. P. Loraine
Angel of Death. G. Montrose
Angel of Death. R. Storey
Angel of Destruction. J. Hedges
Angel of Evil. G. Warden
Angel of Light. B. W. Battin
Angel of Light. H. McCutcheon
Angel of Light. J. C. Oates
Angel of Mercy. D. Haring
Angel of No Mercy. G. Montrose
Angel of Terror. E. Wallace
Angel of the Bells. F. Du Boisgobey
Angel of the Chimes. F. Du Boisgobey
Angel of the Revolution. G. Griffith
Angel of Torremolinos. D. Serafin
Angel of Vengeance. A. Cohen
Angel of Vengeance. G. De Villiers
Angel of Vengeance. G. Montrose
Angel of Zin. C. Irving
Angel Possessed. J. C. Conaway
Angel, Shoot to Kill. H. Janson
Angel Steps In. E. P. Thorne
Angel Street. P. Hamilton
Angel Take Care. R. Lakin
Angel Touch. Mike Ripley
Angel with a Gun. B. Raymond
Angel with Dirty Wings. J. E. Hasty
Angel Without Mercy. A. Cohen
Angela. S. Hanna
Angela. J. H. Hull
Angelic Avengers. P. Andrezel
Angelica. J. A. Bartlett
Angelica. F. Swann
Angelica. T. P. Prest
Angell, Pearl and Little God. Winston Graham
Angels Are Cowards. D. Garth
Angels Are Painted Fair. P. Whelton
Angels Are So Few. E. Ellison
Angels at the Ritz. W. Trevor
Angel's Blood. V. B. Miller
Angels Bruise Easy. Larry O'Brien
Angels Fell. B. Fischer
Angel's Flight. L. Cameron
Angels in Aldgate. W. J. Passingham
Angels in Chains. M. Franklin
Angels in the Gutter. J. Hilton
Angels in the Snow. Derek Lambert
Angels in Undress. M. Benney
Angels in Your Beer. Jeremy Scott
Angels of Darkness. C. Woolrich
Angels of Death. R. Peart
Angels of Doom. L. Charteris
Angels of Double Faces. R. O. Abio
Angels of Light. Jeff Long
Angels of September. A. M. Greeley
Angels on a String. M. Franklin
Angels on Ice. M. Franklin
Angel's Ransom. D. Dodge
Angels' Share. R. Irvine
Angels Sleep in Bed. N. Karta
Angel's Tear. J. Blackmore
Angels Weep! D. Leslie
Angeltread. K. Mendenhall
Anger at World's End. D. Reid
Anger of Fear. J. Ashford
Anger of Olivia. T. Cobb
Anger of the Bells. V. Rath
Angkor Massacre. L. Durand
Angle of Attack. R. Burns
Angry Amazons. Carter Brown
Angry Battalion. Herbert Harris
Angry Canary. K. Robeson
Angry Candy. H. Ellison

Angry Darkness. C. Leader
Angry Dead. M. A. Allen
Angry Dream. G. Brewer
Angry Dust. C. R. Hoopes
Angry Ghost. K. Robeson
Angry Heart. L. Edgley
Angry Hills. L. Uris
Angry Island. P. Haden
Angry Island. J. Pattinson
Angry Island. K. Royce
Angry Millionaire. S. Jepson
Angry Mountain. H. Innes
Angry Night. W. H. Baker
Angry Ocean. R. Johnston
Angry Silence. John Burke
Angry Wind. L. Ames
Angry Woman. J. Ronald
Angst-Ridden Executive. M. V. Montalban
Animal Episodes and Studies in Sensation. G. H. Powell
Animal Factory. E. Bunker
Animal Game. L. Derrick
Animal Letter. Rod Miller
Animal-Lover's Book of Beastly Murder. P. Highsmith
Animal Shop. Oriel Gray
Animated Skeleton. Anonymous
Anita, the Cuban Spy. G. Willets
Ann, the Gentle. K. Kimbrough
Ann Turns Detective. Roland Daniel
Anna (I) Anna. K. Rifbjerg
Anna of the Plains. J. Askew
Anna of the Underworld. G. R. Sims
Anna the Adventuress. E. P. Oppenheim
Anna, the Gentle. K. Kimbrough
Anna, Where Are You? P. Wentworth
Annalisa. F. Rydell
Annalise Experiment. W. D. Roberts
Annals of a Doss House. S. Hallifax
Annals of the Age. Anonymous
Annals of the Horse-Shoe Club. Finch Mason
Annam Jewel. P. Wentworth
Anna's. C. N. Boyle
Anne Belinda. P. Wentworth
Anne Hereford. H. Wood
Anne Hyde, Travling Companion. A. S. Swan
Anne of Destiny House. Wilma Forrest
Anne of the Flying Cap. H. H. Hill
Annette of the Argonne. W. LeQueux
Annexation Society. J. S. Fletcher
Annie Deane. R. H. Adelman
Annie Wallace. H. P. Halsey
Annihilation. I. Fischler
Annihilators. D. Hamilton
Annihilist. K. Robeson
Anniversary Murder. E. Phillpotts
Announcer. D. H. Landels
Ann's Crime. R. T. M. Scott
Annulet of Gilt. P. A. Taylor
Annulment. R. Rubin
Anodyne Necklace. M. Grimes
Anonymous Assassin. J. F. Drexler
Anonymous Client. J. P. Hailey
Anonymous Footsteps. J. M. O'Connor
Another Case for Inspector Jackson. D. T. Lindsay
Another Chorus. John Burke
Another Crime. C. Rushton
Another Day. J. Farnol
Another Day—Another Death. G. Bagby
Another Day, Another Stiff. Michael Brett
Another Day Toward Dying. M. Marlette
Another Death in Venice. R. Hill
Another 48 Hours. D. Chiel
Another Job for Biggles. W. E. Johns
Another Little Death. Bill Turner
Another Little Drink. P. Cheyney
Another Little Murder. L. N. Morgan
Another Man's Life. M. Head
Another Man's Murder. M. G. Eberhart
Another Man's Poison. H. Holman
Another Man's Poison. J. F. Straker
Another Man's Shadow. J. Bude
Another Man's Shoes. V. Bridges
Another Man's Wife. J. Chancellor

Another Man's Wife. M. B. Lowndes
Another Man's Wife. Lady A. Scott
Another Morgue Heard From. F. C. Davis
Another Mug for the Bier. R. Starnes
Another Mystery in Suva. F. Arthur
Another Night, Another Day. D. F. Gardiner
Another Part of the City. E. McBain
Another Path, Another Dragon. E. Mathis
Another Spring. H. S. Maxfield
Another Stretch of Porridge. Paul Victor
Another Time, Another Woman. W. Kaylin
Another Way of Dying. F. Clifford
Another Way to Die. J. Crowe
Another Weeping Woman. D. Zochert
Another Woman's House. M. G. Eberhart
Another Woman's Love. K. Lindsay
Another Woman's Man. Norma Lee
Another Woman's Poison. W. H. L. Crauford
Another Woman's Shoes. F. Durbridge
Another's Burden. J. Payn
Another's Crime. J. Hawthorne
Answer from a Dead Man. G. P. Cronin
Answer in the Negative. H. Hamilton
Answer in the Negative. E. Scholey
Answer That Bell! M. Baillie-Saunders
Answer to Heaven. P. Gallagher
Answered. F. Hume
Answers. T. Topor
Ant Heap. A. Mills
Antagonists. O. Cameron
Antagonists. W. Haggard
Antarctic Convergence. J. Griffin
Antenna Syndrome. A. Marks
Anthill. D. Gilles
Anthony Ravehill, Crime Merchant. R. Francis Foster
Anthony Trent: Avenger. W. Martyn
Anthropol. L. Trimble
Anti-Crime Ltd. E. Snell
Anti-Death League. K. Amis
Antidote. S. Murray
Antidote to Venom. F. W. Crofts
Antiphonary. H. Aquin
Antipodes. M.-A. Oliver
Antique and Deadly. L. H. Flynn
Antique Dust. R. Westall
Antoinette. G. Ohnet
Antonov Project. A. Trew
Antrobus Trust. R. Haig
Antwerp Appointment. J. Pattinson
Anubis Murders. G. Gygax
Anvil Agreement. K. Begg
Anvil Chorus. S. Stevens
Anvil of Hell. D. Pendleton
Anxious Conspirator. M. Underwood
Anxious Lady. J. Pendower
Any Body. G. Whitehead
Any Body for Tennis? J. Last
Any Four Women Could Rob the Bank of Italy. A. Cornelisen
Any God Will Do. R. Condon
Any Guy Can Die in Bed! D. Haring
Any Kind of Danger. E. G. Cousins
Any Man's Death. L. D. Estleman
Any Man's Girl. B. Heatter
Any Minute Now. A. Bocca
Any Number Can Die. F. Carmichael
Any Number Can Die! Morgan Ross
Any Number Can Play. D. Bloodworth
Any Number Can Play. E. H. Heth
Any Number Can Win. J. Trinian
Any Old Port in a Storm. Henry Clement
Any Price Blackmail! Bat Masters
Any Shape or Form. E. Daly
Any War Will Do. E. Pace
Anybody But Anne. C. Wells
Anybody for Murder? B. Clemens
Anybody's Pearls. H. Footner
Anyone's Grief. R. Drayton
Anyone's My Name. S. Shubin
Anything But Saintly. R. Deming
Anything But the Truth. M. Underwood
Anything But the Truth. C. Wells
Anything Can Happen. G. F. Gibbs

Title Index

Anything for a Quiet Life. A. A. Avery
Anything for a Quiet Life. M. Gilbert
Anything for Kicks. Morton Cooper
Anything Might Happen. H. Balfour
Anything Once. Douglas Grant
Anything to Declare? F. W. Crofts
Anytime, Anywhere. M. Caidin
Anywhere But Here. E. L. Adams
Anywhere Else. H. J. Kaplin
Apache. A. Askew
Apache Girl. A. Mills
Apaches of New York. Alfred H. Lewis
Apartment Hotel. M. Morell
Apartment Next Door. W. A. Johnston
Apartment on K Street. R. Travers
Apartment 13. J. C. McMullen
Ape, a Dog, and a Serpent. G. Kersh
Ape and the Diamond. Richard Marsh
Ape in Velvet. R. Foley
Ape Man. H. T. Johnson
Ape of London. F. Crisp
Ape, the Idiot and Other People. W. C. Morrow
Aphrodite. D. Chandler
Aphrodite Cargo. A. Fullerton.
Aphrodite Inheritance. M. J. Bird
Aphrodite Means Death. J. Appleby
Apocalypse. J. Rosenberger
Apocalypse. M. Stanton
Apocalypse U.S.A! J. Rosenberger
Apollo Fountain. D. Daniels
Apollo Legacy. A. Barker
Apollo Wore a Wig. R. T. Campbell
Apologetic Tiger. J. Workman
Apostles of Violence. M. G. Braun
Apostles of Violence. D. Perring
Appalachin. Jack Kelly
Apparition. G. Bishop
Apparition. T. P. Prest
Apparition. R. Stewart
Appearance of Evil. James Anderson
Appearances of Death. Dell Shannon
Apperson's Folly. A. Mallory
Apple a Day. H. Brinton
Apple Crunch. F. V. Huber
Apple of Discord. M. Blake
Apple of Discord. H. C. Rowland
Apple Spy in the Sky. M. Lovell
Apple to the Core. M. Lovell
Apple Tree. D. Du Maurier
Appleby and Honeybath. M. Innes
Appleby and the Ospreys. M. Innes
Appleby at Allington. M. Innes
Appleby File. M. Innes
Appleby on Ararat. M. Innes
Appleby Plays Chicken. M. Innes
Appleby Talking. M. Innes
Appleby Talks Again. M. Innes
Appleby's Answer. M. Innes
Appleby's End. M. Innes
Appleby's Other Story. M. Innes
Applegreen Cat. F. Crane
Apples by Night. H. A. Manhood
Apples of Sin. C. Kernahan
Appleshaw. C. Damien
Applewood Mystery. F. Burleigh
Appointed Date. J. J. Farjeon
Appointment at Eight. H. Desmond
Appointment at Midnight. Peter Williams
Appointment at Nine. D. M. Disney
Appointment in Andalusia. M. MacKintosh
Appointment in Cairo. G. Brewer
Appointment in Cairo. B. Kneale
Appointment in Calcutta. E. Tokson
Appointment in Haiphong. Nick Carter
Appointment in Hell. G. Brewer
Appointment in Hell. V. Warren
Appointment in Iran. S. Jason
Appointment in Kabul. D. Pendleton
Appointment in Manila. Elinor Chamberlain
Appointment in New Orleans. T. Claymore
Appointment in Peking. F. Drake
Appointment in Tangier. L. Wilkinson
Appointment in Tenerife. R. Harding
Appointment in Tibet. W. H. Murray

Appointment in Topeka. B. Harding
Appointment in Verona. M. A. Taylor
Appointment in Vienna. S. Gainham
Appointment in Zahrein. Michael Barrett
Appointment with Danger. W. H. Baker
Appointment with Danger. D. Garth
Appointment with Danger. A. Hughes
Appointment with Death. C. Barling
Appointment with Death. A. Christie
Appointment with Death. P. Frankau
Appointment with Death. M. Hervey
Appointment with Desire. H. Lugar
Appointment with Dishonor. W. H. Gage
Appointment with Fear. D. Stokes
Appointment with Murder. H. Seymour
Appointment with My Lady. F. Griffin
Appointment with Terror. J. Davidson
Appointment with the Hangman. T. C. H. Jacobs
Appointment with Venus. J. Tickell
Appointment with Yesterday. C. Fremlin
Apprehensive Dog. H. C. Bailey
Apprentice Fiction of F. Scott Fitzgerald. F. S. Fitzgerald
Apprentice in Terror. P. Warren
Apprentice to Fear. H. Brinton
April Evil. J. D. MacDonald
April Fool's Day. J. Rovin
April, May and June. H. Willett
April Rainers. Antheo Fraser
April Robin Murders. C. Rice
April Shroud. R. Hill
April Snow. N. O'Donohoe
April Thirteenth. B. St. James
April When They Woo. M. J. Adamson
April's Grave. S. Howatch
Apron-Strings. R. Marsh
Aquanauts. D. Bard
Aquarius Angel. L. Bullock
Aquarius Curse. Marilyn Ross
Aquarius Mission. M. Caidin
Aquarius, My Evil. J. De Pre
Aquarius Transfer. R. F. Joseph
Arab. G. L. Tippin
Arab Agent. Robert Mason
Arab Plague. Nick Carter
Arab Wife and A Strange Clue. Anonymous
Arabella. B. Vane
Arabesque. G. Household
Arabian Assault. P. McAdam
Arabian Nights Murder. J. D. Carr
Arabian Pearl. M. J. A. Jackson
Araby's Husband. A. Askew
Arafat is Here! Lionel Black
Araminta and the River. Alan Graham
Ararat. R. Houston
Araway Oath. H. Adams
Arcade. R. Maxxe
Arch-Criminal. Roland Daniel
Archangel. G. Seymour
Archangel 006. R. Hitchcock
Archdeacons Afloat. C. A. Alington
Archdeacons Ashore. C. A. Alington
Archdeacon's Daughters and other stories. G. A. Musgrove
Archer in the Arras, and other tales of mystery. L. Spence
Archer Plus Twenty. H. Clevely
Archers of the Long Bow. A. Moore
Archibald the Great. C. B. Kelland
Archie. C. Morley
Archie the Tumbler. Old Sleuth
Architect's Secret. W. J. Bayfield
Archon Conspiracy. Dave Hunt
Arctic Abduction. Nick Carter
Arctic Assignment. R. Charles
Arctic Convoy. Taffrail
Arctic Patrols. W. Campbell
Arctic Submarine. A. Mars
Arctic Trail. W. M. Graydon
Arden Mystery. M. Harvey
Ardreys. K. R. Vernon
Are You Mr. Butterworth? F. Metcalfe
Are You My Wife? M. Marcin
Area of Suspicion. J. D. MacDonald

Arena. W. Haggard
Arena of Fear. L. Erickson
Argentine Deadline. G. Wilson
Argon Furnace. R. L. Graves
Argosy Project. J. A. G. Kitchener
Argus Eye. F. M. White
Argus Gambit. D. D. Ross
Argus Pheasant. J. C. Beecham
Argyle Case. H. Ford
Argyle Case. A. Hornblow
Argyll Killings. Daniel Benson
Ariadne Clue. C. Clemeau
Ariel. J. Bickham
Ariel. Lawrence Block
Aries Rising. A. Herzog
Arigato. R. Condon
Arising from an Accident. P. Dewdney
Aristocratic Detective. R. Marsh
Aristocrats. Gwen Davis
Aristotle Detective. M. Doody
Aristotle System. R. Dzagoyan
Arizona. Augustus Thomas
Arizona Ambush. D. Pendleton
Arizona Drifters. W. C. Tuttle
Ark. J. Clive
Ark. D. Daniel
Arkansas Ranger. M. M. Murray
Arkham Asylum. Grant Morrison
Arkie, the Runaway. Old Sleuth
Arlette. N. Freeling
Arlett's Death. H. Falkner
Arlie Bright. Old Sleuth
Arm of Mrs. Egan and other strange stories. W. F. Harvey
Arm of the Law. Lieut. Carlton
Arm of the Law. M. Underwood
Arm of the Starfish. M. L'Engle
Arm of the Unwritten Law. A. Arp
Armada Gold. Edgar Turner
Armadale. W. Collins
Armageddon Conspiracy. J. Ahern
Armageddon Crazy. M. Farren
Armageddon Game. J. N. Frey
Armageddon Game. M. Washburn
Armageddon Rag. G. R. R. Martin
Armageddon, USA! J. Rosenberger
Armalite Maiden. J. Kebbe
Armchair in Hell. H. Kane
Armchair Stories. I. A. R. Wylie
Armed and Dangerous. J. Pence
Armed . . . Dangerous . . . B. Halliday
Armed with a New Terror. T. Du Bois
Armitage Case. Michael Kent
Armitage Secret. H. Howard
Armorer of Tyre. S. Cobb
Arms and the Spy. M. McKenna
Arms for Adonis. C. Jay
Arms for Oblivion. J. Hedges
Arms for the Love of Allah. Anthony Harding
Arms'-Length. J. Metcalfe
Arms of Death. M. Wainwright
Arms of Kali. W. B. Murphy
Arms of Phaedra. N. Worth
Arms of the Law. J. L. Latham
Arms of the Mantis. R. Charles
Arms of Vengeance. Nick Carter
Arms of Venus. J. Appleby
Armstrong. Alan White
Army Blue. L. K. Truscott, IV
Army Defaulter's Secret. L. C. Douthwaite
Army Doctor's Romance. G. Allen
Army of Devils. D. Stiver
Army of Shadows. E. Ambler
Army of Shadows. J. Kessel
Army of the Dead. C. Steele
Army of the Undead. Rafe Bernard
Army Post Murders. M. Wright
Arncliffe Puzzle. Gordon Holmes
Arnholt Makes His Bow. G. Latta
Arnold Robur. M. Combe
Around Dark Corners. H. Pentecost
Around the Fire. S. Hardman
Arrangement for Murder. R. Simons
Arranways Mystery. E. Wallace

A

Array of Eagles. R. Severn
Arrest. W. Proudfoot
Arrest 'Ace' Lannigan. L. Halward
Arrest and Trial. N. Daniels
Arrest of Arsene Lupin. M. Leblanc
Arrest the Bishop? W. Peck
Arrest the Saint. L. Charteris
Arrest These Men! B. Perowne
Arrested. Eame Stuart
Arrested. E. C. Vivian
Arrested for Murder. Roland Daniel
Arrested Moment and other stories. C. C. Dobie
Arresting Delia. S. Fowler
Arrival in Suspicion. S. Harvester
Arriverderci, Baby! James Peterson
Arrogant Alibi. C. D. King
Arrogant Duke. Rona Randall
Arrow in the Dark. S. Allan
Arrow of Death. Roland Daniel
Arrow of Death. F. Vivian
Arrow of God. R. Cassilis
Arrow of Terror. J. Marie
Arrow Pointing Nowhere. E. Daly
Arrow Points to Murder. F. De Laguna
Arrowheart. Ann Paris
Arrows of Chance. E. R. Plunshon
Arrows of Desire. G. Household
Arsenal Stadium Mystery. L. Gribble
Arsene Lepine—Herlock Soames Affair. S. B. Chester
Arsene Lupin. E. Jepson
Arsene Lupin, Gentleman Burglar. M. Leblanc
Arsene Lupin Intervenes. M. Leblanc
Arsene Lupin, Super Sleuth. M. Leblanc
Arsene Lupin Versus Herlock Sholmes. M. Leblanc
Arsene Lupin Versus Holmlock Shears. M. Leblanc
Arsenic. J. Remenham
Arsenic and Gold. B. Atkey
Arsenic and Old Lace. J. Kesselring
Arsenic for the Teacher. O. Keystone
Arsenic in Richmond. D. Frome
Arsenic on the Menu. B. H. Homersham
Arson. E. Fackler
Arson and Old Lace. S. Angus
Arson by Proxy. Ray Turner
Arson Job. J. Moss
Art Boggs, Private Investigator. M. Scheele
Art for Keeps. C. B. Block
Art of Death. A. Fliegel
Art of Disappearing. J. T. Smith
Art of Survival. A. E. Maxwell
Art School Murders. M. Dalton
Art Studio Murders. E. Ronns
Art Thou the Man? G. Berton
Art Treasure Murders. J. L. Benton
Artemis Flint: Detective. B. Goldsweig
Artemis Sanction. A. Aasheim
Arterial Road Murder. A. Blair
Artful Egg. J. McClure
Artful Schemer. Nicholas Carter
Arthur. J. A. Graham
Arthur Mervyn. C. B. Brown
Arthur's Night. J. F. Straker
Article 92: Murder-Rape. W. Beech
Artifact. G. Benford
Artifex Intervenes. R. Keverne
Artificial Fate. C. Boutelle
Artificial Girl. R. W. Cole
Artificial Jungle. C. Ludlam
Artificial Man. L. P. Davies
Artist and a Magician. H. Fleetwood
Artist and Model. R. de Pont-Jest
Artist Detective. Anonymous
Artist Dies. J. Rhode
Artist in Crime. R. Ottolengui
Artist in Crime. K. M. Sheahan
Artist in Crime. C. Somerville
Artist's Daughter. L. O'Grady
Artists in Crime. N. Marsh
Artist's Love. E. Southworth
Artist's Model. Mrs. C. Kernahan
Artists, Models and Murder. Tedd Steele
Artist's Murder. F. L. Cary
Artless Heiress. C. B. Kelland

Arundel Motto. M. C. Hay
Aryan Onslaught. L. Derrick
As a Bird to the Snare. G. Warden
As a Crook Sows. Nicholas Carter
As a Favor. S. Dunlap
As a Man Falls. H. Rigsby
As a Man Lives. E. P. Oppenheim
As a Man Sows. W. Westall
As a Thief in the Night. R. A. Freeman
As Bad As I Am. W. Ard
As Crime Goes By. D. K. Shah
As Darker Grows the Night. E. Giles
As Deadly Does. J. Corby
As Empty As Hate. M. Halliday
As Evil Does. J. Tigges
As for the Woman. F. Iles
As Good As a Mile. E. Albert
As Good As Dead. T. B. Dewey
As Good As Gold. E. Wymark
As Good As Murdered. J. D. O'Hanlon
As He Was Born. T. Gallon
As I Was Going to St. Ives. A. Hocking
As If She Were Mine. Alex Hamilton
As It Chanced. H. B. M. Watson
As It Was in the Beginning. G. R. Sims
As It Was Written. S. Luska
As It Was Written. T. W. Speight
As Lonely As the Damned. M. Halliday
As Long As I Live. I. S. Shriber
As Luck Would Have It. W. Westall
As Merry as Hell. M. Halliday
As October Dies. Kenn Davis
As Old As Cain. M. E. Chaber
As Peace Lay Dying. David Milton
As Strange a Maze. F. Leighton
As Tall As Pride. S. Kerr
As the Clock Strikes. E. Armstrong
As the Cock Crew and other stories. E. B. Rowlands
As the Devil Burned. H. Kemp
As the Sparks Fly. M. Eastvale
As the Stars Fade. B. Hector
As They Do Unto Me. G. C. Anderson
As They Rise. E. L. Long
As They Shall Sow. A. Spiller
As We Forgave Them. W. LeQueux
As We Sow. John O'Neill
Asbestos Mask. J. Nicholas
Ascendancy House. J. L. Rickard
Ascent of D-13. A. Garve
Ascot Mystery. Bat Masters
Aseptic Murders. Carter Brown
Asey Mayo Trio. P. A. Taylor
Asgard Solution. J. Marino
Ash. C. Cannel
Ash. James Murphy
Ash. D. Walker
Ashdown Summer. C. Gaines
Ashenden. W. S. Maugham
Ashes. C. F. Coe
Ashes. H. Nisbet
Ashes and Diamonds. J. Andrzyeyvski
Ashes for the Living. N. Cormarty
Ashes in an Urn. J. Roffman
Ashes in the Cellar. T. C. H. Jacobs
Ashes of Evidence. E. Levison
Ashes of Falconwyck. Angela Gray
Ashes of Loda. A. Garve
Ashes of Murder. G. Morton
Ashes of Windrow. J. T. Osborne
Ashes to Ashes. L. S. Carl
Ashes to Ashes. E. Lathen
Ashes to Ashes. I. Ostrander
Ashes to Ashes. D. Pendleton
Ashes to Ashes. M. M. Pulver
Ashes to Ashes. John Stuart
Ashiel Mystery. C. Bryce
Ashley, and other stories. H. Wood
Ashley Hall. S. Richard
Ashton-Kirk: Criminologist. J. T. MacIntyre
Ashton Kirk: Investigator. J. T. MacIntyre
Ashton-Kirk: Secret Agent. J. T. MacIntyre
Ashton-Kirk: Special Detective. J. T. MacIntyre
Ashton Priory. Anonymous
Asia Rip. G. Foy

Asian Affair. R. Holt
Asian Eyes. K. Crowder
Asian Mantrap. Nick Carter
Asimov's Mysteries. I. Asimov
Ask a Policeman. Detection Club
Ask a Policeman. E. C. R. Lorac
Ask a River. Charles Francis
Ask Agamemnon. Jenni Hall
Ask an Angel. G. Montrose
Ask 'Beccles. C. Campion
Ask for King Billy. H. Treece
Ask for Linda. F. Nichols
Ask for Lois. J. Barclay
Ask for Me Tomorrow. M. Millar
Ask for Ronald Standish. H. C. McNeile
Ask for Trouble. M. Cronin
Ask Me No Questions. L. Edwards
Ask Me Now. A. Young
Ask Miss Mott. E. P. Oppenheim
Ask No Mercy. B. Perowne
Ask No Question. M. Hocking
Ask No Questions. L. Dean
Ask No Questions. B. Duff
Ask Taffin Nicely. L. Mallet
Ask the Cards a Question. M. Muller
Ask the Rattlesnake. P. Loraine
Ask the Right Question. M. Z. Lewin
Asking for It. J. Mayo
Asking for Trouble. L. Meynell
Asking for Trouble. J. Rayter
Asking Price. H. Cecil
Asking Price. J. B. Hilton
Asp, and other stories. J. Knittel
Aspen Affair. B. Hirschfeld
Aspen Incident. T. Murphy
Aspern Papers. H. James
Aspern Papers. M. Redgrave
Asphalt Jungle. W. R. Burnett
Asphalt Jungle. B. Maddow
Asphodel. M. E. Braddon
Assassin. James Anderson
Assassin. Evelyn Anthony
Assassin! K. Blake
Assassin. R. Butler
Assassin. M. Edwards
Assassin. E. M. Harper
Assassin. S. Hutson
Assassin. S. Jepson
Assassin. U. Levi
Assassin. Liam O'Flaherty
Assassin. J. D. Revere
Assassin. L. W. Robinson
Assassin. Paul Ross
Assassin. Irwin Shaw
Assassin. Nick Stone
Assassin. W. Wager
Assassin. D. Wiltse
Assassin and the Peer. D. Weyer
Assassin Code. B. Mochan
Assassin—Code Name Vulture. Nick Carter
Assassin Convention. Nick Carter
Assassin for Hire. R. Rienits
Assassin of Saint Glenroy. A. F. Holstein
Assassin Prepares. N. J. McIver
Assassin Take All. D. Haring
Assassin Trail. Dan Morgan
Assassin Who Gave Up His Gun. E. V. Cunningham
Assassination. B. Abro
Assassination Affair. J. H. Hunter
Assassination Brigade. Nick Carter
Assassination Bureau, Ltd. J. London
Assassination Day. O. Jacks
Assassination Factor. L. Derrick
Assassination File. J. Gardner
Assassination Is Set for July 4. L. Parker
Assassination of Gorbachov. M. Khoury
Assassination of Mozart. D. Weiss
Assassination on Maya Bay. J. Cassidy
Assassination Run. J. Gerson
Assassinator. D. Vowell
Assassinators. P. Boast
Assassini. T. Gifford
Assassins. J. A. Brown

Title Index

Assassins. L. Falk
Assassins. E. Kazan
Assassins. N. Mosley
Assassins. F. Mullally
Assassins. F. M. Parker
Assassins. H. T. Teilhet
Assassins and Victims. C. Black
Assassin's Diary. A. Bremer
Assassins Don't Die in Bed. M. Avallone
Assassin's Express. A. Kilgore
Assassins for Peace. R. Charles
Assassins for Tomorrow. P. Heath
Assassins Have Starry Eyes. D. Hamilton
Assassin's Hideaway. H. D. Steward
Assassins in White. Robert Callahan
Assassins on Safari. D. Duchi
Assassin's Playoff. R. Sapir
Assassins Road. S. Harvester
Assassin's Shadow. R. Striker
Assault! S. Mackenzie
Assault. H. Mulisch
Assault. D. Pendleton
Assault and Matrimony. James Anderson
Assault and Pepper. J. T. Story
Assault Into Libya. Jim Case
Assault on a Queen. J. Finney
Assault on Agathon. A. Caillou
Assault on Aimata. A. Caillou
Assault on Alpha Base. D. Beason
Assault on England. Nick Carter
Assault on Fellawi. A. Caillou
Assault on Kolchak. A. Caillou
Assault on Loveless. A. Caillou
Assault on Mavis A. N. Stahl
Assault on Ming. A. Caillou
Assault on Rome. D. Pendleton
Assault on Soho. D. Pendleton
Assault on the Empress. J. Ahern
Assault with Intent. W. X. Kienzle
Assemblers. Speer Morgan
Assessor. H. Henn
Asset in Black. C. Prescott
Assignment. F. Duerrenmatt
Assignment. L. Leamer
Assignment. P. Wahloo
Assignment Abacus. L. P. Davies
Assignment—Amazon Queen. E. S. Aarons
Assignment Andalusia. R. C. Galway
Assignment—Angelina. E. S. Aarons
Assignment—Ankara. E. S. Aarons
Assignment Argentina. R. C. Galway
Assignment: Assassination. J. Milton
Assignment—Bangkok. E. S. Aarons
Assignment Basra. F. Pontheir
Assignment—Black Gold. E. S. Aarons
Assignment—Black Viking. E. S. Aarons
Assignment—Budapest. E. S. Aarons
Assignment—Burma Girl. E. S. Aarons
Assignment—Carlotta Cortez. E. S. Aarons
Assignment—Ceylon. E. S. Aarons
Assignment—Cong Hai Kill. E. S. Aarons
Assignment: Danger. Marilyn Ross
Assignment: Death Ship. W. B. Aarons
Assignment Death Squad. R. C. Galway
Assignment Doomsday. Martin Thomas
Assignment Fenland. R. C. Galway
Assignment: Find Cherry. J. Seward
Assignment for a Mercenary. Howard R. Simpson
Assignment for Rusty Brown. C. Regan
Assignment for Trouble. M. Carrel
Assignment Gaolbreak. R. C. Galway
Assignment—Golden Girl. E. S. Aarons
Assignment Greece. G. Sheen
Assignment Haiti. E. P. Thorne
Assignment—Helene. E. S. Aarons
Assignment Hong Kong. James Dark
Assignment in Algeria. John Lee
Assignment in Andorra. A. MacKintosh
Assignment in Beirut. J. Stagg
Assignment in Brittany. Helen MacInnes
Assignment in Guiana. G. H. Coxe
Assignment in Iraq. A. MacKinnon
Assignment in the Islands. J. Blair
Assignment in Tokyo. J. T. Elton

Assignment in Venice. G. Ferrand
Assignment: Intercept. Nick Carter
Assignment: Israel. Nick Carter
Assignment K. H. Howard
Assignment—Karachi. E. S. Aarons
Assignment—Lili Lemaris. E. S. Aarons
Assignment London. R. C. Galway
Assignment—Lowlands. E. S. Aarons
Assignment—Madeleine. E. S. Aarons
Assignment Malta. R. C. Galway
Assignment—Maltese Maiden. E. S. Aarons
Assignment—Manchurian Doll. E. S. Aarons
Assignment—Mara Tirana. E. S. Aarons
Assignment Mermaid. W. B. Aarons
Assignment—Moon Girl. E. S. Aarons
Assignment, Murder. Neill Graham
Assignment: Murder. D. Hamilton
Assignment New York. R. C. Galway
Assignment New York. M. Lantry
Assignment—Nuclear Nude. E. S. Aarons
Assignment—Palermo. E. S. Aarons
Assignment—Peking. E. S. Aarons
Assignment—Quayle Question. E. S. Aarons
Assignment: Rio. Nick Carter
Assignment—School for Spies. E. S. Aarons
Assignment Sea Bed. R. C. Galway
Assignment Sheba. W. B. Aarons
Assignment—Silver Scorpion. E. S. Aarons
Assignment—Sorrento Siren. E. S. Aarons
Assignment—Star Stealers. E. S. Aarons
Assignment—Stella Marni. E. S. Aarons
Assignment—Suicide. E. S. Aarons
Assignment—Sulu Sea. E. S. Aarons
Assignment Sydney. R. C. Galway
Assignment Tahiti. A. Gardner
Assignment—The Cairo Dancers. E. S. Aarons
Assignment—The Girl in the Gondola. E. S. Aarons
Assignment 13th Princess. W. B. Aarons
Assignment Tiger Devil. W. B. Aarons
Assignment to Bahrein. P. Winston
Assignment to Death. C. L. Leonard
Assignment to Disaster. E. S. Aarons
Assignment to Sante Fe. Dan Morgan
Assignment to Vengeance. B. Cleeve
Assignment—Tokyo. E. S. Aarons
Assignment Tokyo. James Dark
Assignment—Treason. E. S. Aarons
Assignment Tyrant's Bride. W. B. Aarons
Assignment Unicorn. E. S. Aarons
Assignment—White Rajah. E. S. Aarons
Assignment Without Glory. M. Spinelli
Assignment X. E. C. Shurmacher
Assignment—Zoraya. E. S. Aarons
Assisi Murders. T. Holme
Assisted by Lessinger. R. Essex
Assisted by Sadie. W. B. Hare
Assize of the Dying. E. Pargeter
Assorted Chocolates. O. R. Cohen
Assurance Double Sure. J. Esteven
Asterisk. Campbell Black
Asterisk Destiny. Campbell Black
Astonished Guardsman. Surrey Smith
Astonishing Adventure of Jane Smith. P. Wentworth
Astonishment! F. Lathom
Astounding Crime. P. Yorke
Astounding Crime on Torrington Road. W. Gillette
Astounding Dr. Yell. L. A. Knight
Astrea. E. Southworth
Astrakhan Coat. P. Macaulay
Astrid Factor. D. Orgill
Astronaut. J. Baumgarten
Aswan Assignment. A. Sugar
Aswan Hellbox. G. Wilson
Aswan High. R. E. Harrington
Aswan Solution. J. Rowe
Asylum. W. Johnston
Asylum. O. Knox
Asylum. Isaac Mitchell
At a Farthing's Rate. H. Gibbs
At a Venture. H. B. M. Watson
At Bay. Mrs. Alexander
At Bay. G. Greenfield
At Bay. P. Philips
At Bertram's Hotel. A. Christie

At Break of Dawn. G. James
At Button's. G. Wills
At Close Quarters. G. Seymour
At Dark of the Moon. A. C. Ley
At Dawn I Die. J. Corbett
At Dead of Night. N. Perrelli
At Death's Call. I. Stark
At Death's Door. R. Barnard
At Death's Door. L. Bruce
At Devil's Bridge. H. Marval
At Dusk All Cats Are Grey. J. Tickell
At Ease with Death. W. Satterthwait
At Face Value. Nicholas Carter
At Fault. H. Smart
At Friendly Point. G. F. Scott
At Government House. A. Beaman
At Her Mercy. J. Payn
At High Risk. P. Harcourt
At Large. E. W. Hornung
At Last, Mr. Tolliver. W. Wiegand
At Last We Are Alone. F. Sladen-Smith
At Market Value. G. Allen
At Midnight and other stories. A. Cambridge
At Midnight's Chime. W. J. Newton
At Mystery's Threshold. Nicholas Carter
At Night All Wolves Are Grey. G. Staalesen
At Night I Live. H. Vogel
At Night to Die. H. Hamilton
At Nine Bells. S. Emery
At 9:45. Owen Davis
At Odds with Scotland Yard. Nicholas Carter
At One Fell Swoop. O. Mills
At One Fell Swoop. S. Palmer
At One-Thirty. I. Ostrander
At Sixty Miles Per Hour. J. Drummond
At Some Forgotten Door. D. M. Disney
At Sword's Point. A. Norton
At Ten Paces. C. G. Booth
At the Back o' Beyond. R. Remnant
At the Back of the World. L. T. Meade
At the Bar. C. A. Collins
At the Blue Bell Inn. J. S. Fletcher
At the Blue Gates. R. Keverne
At the Call of Honour. A. W. Marchmont
At "The Cedars." A. Hocking
At the Change of the Moon. B. C. Blake
At the Court of the Maharaja. L. Tracy
At the Edge of the Sun. Anne Stuart
At the End of a Road. C. Houghton
At the Foot of the Rainbow. J. B. Hendryx
At the Foot of the Stairs. E. S. Porter
At the Gai-Moulin. G. Simenon
At the Green Dragon. J. J. Farjeon
At the Hands of Another. Arthur Lyons
At the House of Dree. G. Gardiner
At the House of the Priest. J. Adye
At the Knife's Point. Nicholas Carter
At the Lake of Sudden Death. T. Holme
At the Mercy of Tiberius. A. J. Wilson
At the Point of a .38. B. Halliday
At the Seaside, and other stories. M. C. Hay
At the Shrine of the Buddha. W. M. Graydon
At the Sign of the Clove and Hoof. Z. Johnson
At the Sign of the Eel. R. B. Whorf
At the Sign of the Golden Horn. J. K. Leys
At the Sign of the Grid. H. A. Vachell
At the Sign of the Sword. W. LeQueux
At the Silver Butterfly. Roland Daniel
At the Tenth Clue. H. H. Stanners
At the Time Appointed. A. M. Barbour
At the Top. M. Donovan
At the Villa Rose. A. E. W. Mason
At the World's Mercy. P. Trent
At the World's Mercy. F. Warden
At Thompson's Ranch. Nicholas Carter
At War with Society. J. M'Levy
At War with the Unknown. C. Frisbie
At What Cost, and Other Stories. H. Conway
Atascadero Island. G. Larsen
Atavar, the Dream Dancer. A. B. Reeve
Athabasca. Alistair MacLean
Athelstane Ford. A. Upward
Athena. F. Bandy
Athens Affair. H. Greene

Atherwood Terminal. H. Henn
Atlanta Burn. B. Ham
Atlanta Deathwatch. R. Dennis
Atlanta Extreme. C. Ramm
Atlantean Horror. J. Rosenberger
Atlantic City. W. B. Murphy
Atlantic City Murder Mystery. N. Goldsmith
Atlantic City Proof. C. C. Gilmore
Atlantic Fury. H. Innes
Atlantic Incident. Jack Davies
Atlantic Murder. F. H. Shaw
Atlantic Murders! E. T. Woodhall
Atlantic Nights and other tales. F. H. Shaw
Atlantic Scramble. G. Wilson
Atlantic Tragedy and other stories. W. C. Russell
Atlantis Fire. G. Goshgarian
Atom at Spithead. D. Divine
Atom Bomb Angel. P. James
Atom-Busters. P. Graham
Atom of Doubt. B. George
Atomic Death. H. Kasirov
Atomic Murder. L. Gribble
Atomic Submarine. A. Mars
Atoms and Evil. R. Bloch
Atoms of Empire. C. J. C. Hyne
Atomsk. Carmichael Smith
Atone with Evil. J. Fiedler
Atrocity. J. Ahern
Atropos. W. L. DeAndrea
Attack. C. Ehrlich
Attack. S. Mackenzie
Attack Alarm. H. Innes
Attack in the Desert. M. Home
Attack on the Farm, and other stories. A. W. Arnold
Attack on Vienna. Alan Nixon
Attack the Baron. Anthony Morton
Attack the Lusitania. R. Hitchcock
Attar's Revenge. Robert Graham
Attempt. J. Dennison
Attempted Murder of Peggy Sweetwater. J. Rustan
Attending Physician. R. B. Dominic
Attending Truth. E. R. Punshon
Attention! Saturnin Dax. M. Cumberland
Attic Child. G. Corren
Attic Murder. S. Fowler
Attic Room. K. Wolffe
Attic Rope. D. Daniels
Attorney. Anonymous
Attorney. H. Q. Masur
Attorney Conspiracy. C. T. Cline
Attraction. B. W. Battin
Auber File. M. Home
Auction. Alexander Cole
Auction. R. Cox
Auction. T. Murphy
Auction. Justin Scott
Auction Mart. S. Tremayne
Auctioned. H. Janson
Auctioneer. J. Samson
Audacious Adventures of Miles McConaughy. A. D. H. Smith
Audacious Picaroon. J. Cassells
Audacity. A. Evans
Audacity. B. A. Williams
Audit in Death. E. Norwood
Audition for Murder. P. M. Carlson
Auditorium Affair. Hugh C. McDonald
Audrey Rose. F. De Felitta
August Heat. S. Richards
August Ice. Deforest Day
August Incident. A. Dean
Augusta, the First. K. Kimbrough
Augusta, the Second. K. Kimbrough
Auld Acquaintance. Richard Harris
Auldearn House. B. Riefe
Aunt Beardie. J. Shearing
Aunt Cathie's Cat. F. Metcalfe
Aunt Isabel's Lover. M. Fox
Aunt Ivy Diddit. E. G. Gless
Aunt Jeanne. G. Simenon
Aunt Miranda's Murder. J. N. Chase
Aunt Phipps. T. Gallon
Aunt Sally and the Crime Wave. M. Short
Aunt Sophie Takes Charge. L. P. Martin

Aunt Sunday Sees It Through. J. J. Farjeon
Aunt Sunday Takes Command. J. J. Farjeon
Aunt Susie Shoots the Works! F. Caldwell
Aunt What's-Her-Name! W. B. Hare
Aupres de ma Blonde. N. Freeling
Aurelius Smith—Detective. R. T. M. Scott
Aurora. S. Lowe
Aurora Floyd. M. E. Braddon
Aurora's Motive. E. Hackl
Aussie Lawman. Glenn Holt
Austenburn Castle. Anonymous
Austin Melville, Turf Investigator. H. Graham
Australian Bush Track. D. Hennessey
Australian Eyes Only. M. Sexton
Australian Life. F. Adams
Aut Diabolus, Aut Nihil. X. L.
Authentic Death of Hendry Jones. C. Neider
Author Bites the Dust. A. W. Upfield
Author in Distress. C. M. Wills
Author Unknown. C. Dane
Authorized Murder. I. Asimov
Author's Choice. M. Kantor
Autobiography of a Blackguard. R. Paton
Autobiography of a Bottle of Bourbon. Old Sleuth
Autobiography of a French Detective. M. Canler
Autobiography of a London Detective. Waters
Autobiography of a Quack, and The Case of George Dedlow. S. W. Mitchell
Autobiography of a Thief. H. Hapgood
Autobiography of an English Detective. Waters
Autobiography of an Italian Police-Officer. Anonymous
Autopsy. J. R. Feegel
Autopsy. H. A. Olgin
Autumn Accelerator. P. Leslie
Autumn Dead. E. Gorman
Autumn Heroes. O. Jacks
Autumn in Araby. C. Salisbury
Autumn Lace. Eileen Jackson
Autumn of a Hunter. P. Stadley
Autumn Rose. Margery Lawrence
Autumn Tiger. B. Langley
Ava Mining Syndicate. C. C. Lowis
Avalanche. G. Atherton
Avalanche. K. Boyle
Avalanche. J. Wingate
Avalanche Express. C. Forbes
Avalanche Run. W. Grant
Avenged on Society. H. F. Wood
Avenger. Anonymous
Avenger. M. Blood
Avenger. C. Cunningham
Avenger. W. Forder
Avenger. R. Gar
Avenger. J. Goodwin
Avenger. Samuel Gordon
Avenger. H. Kane
Avenger. E. P. Oppenheim
Avenger. H. Rigsby
Avenger. D. Steele
Avenger. E. Wallace
Avenger at Bay. J. Salt
Avenger of Blood. J. M. Cobban
Avenger Strikes. W. S. Masterman
Avenger Tapes. R. G. Stimson
Avengers. D. Enefer
Avengers. H. Hill
Avengers: Too Many Targets. J. Peel
Avenging Angel. A. Appiah
Avenging Angel. Rex Burns
Avenging Brotherhood. I. Tattersall
Avenging Eagle. T. P. Hurley
Avenging Ikon. C. Barry
Avenging Kiss. C. Rae-Brown
Avenging Maid. J. S. May
Avenging Note. A. Sprissler
Avenging Nymph. H. Janson
Avenging of Ruthanna. Mrs. C. Kernahan
Avenging Parrot. Anne Austin
Avenging Picaroon. J. Cassells
Avenging Ray. Seamark
Avenging Saint. L. Charteris
Avenging Seven. L. H. Brooks
Avenging the Belgrano. B. Langley

Avenging Twins. J. McCulley
Avenging Twins Collect. J. McCulley
Avenue of the Dead. E. Anthony
Avenue of the Stars. J. Bacar
Average Jones. S. H. Adams
Average Man. A. C. Fox-Davies
Averno. B. Mitford
Avery's Fortune. W. M. Green
Avery's Knot. M. Cable
Avila Gold. D. Westheimer
Avima Affair. N. Calmer
Awake and Die. R. Ames
Awake Deborah! E. Phillpotts
Awake to Die. J. V. Nolan
Awake to Terror. Marilyn Ross
Awakening. R. C. Meredith
Awakening Dream. K. Cameron
Awakening of Theodore Wrenn. M. Crombie
Award of Justice. A. M. Barbour
Away Went the Little Fish. M. Bennett
Away with Murder. J. Pattinson
Away with Them to Prison. Sara Woods
Awful Destiny. K. Robeson
Awful Egg. K. Robeson
Awful Legacy. W. P. Naish
Awkward Lie. M. Innes
Awkward Marine. J. Spenser
Ax. E. McBain
Ax of Atlantis. L. Grimes
Axe for the Rani. R. Bond
Axe Is Laid. J. Mackworth
Axe to Grind. A. A. Fair
Axe to Grind. Robert Wallace
Axes of Hate. James Preston
Axis. Clive Irving
Axman Cometh. J. Farris
Axmann Agenda. M. Pettit
Axwater. Jennie Melville
Axx Goes South. F. Huber
Aynsley's Case. G. M. Fenn
Ayrshire Idylls. N. Munro
Azanian Assignment. I. Finlay
Azor! J. Henaghan
Azrael. W. L. DeAndrea
Aztec Avenger. Nick Carter
Azure Rose. R. W. Kauffman

B As in Banshee. L. Treat
BB of Ardlegay. W. H. Rainsford
B14. R. K. Weekes
B-Girl Decoy. E. Linkletter
"B" Is for Burglar. S. Grafton
B-Movie. S. Barstow
B.O.L.O. D. Pedneau
Babbington Case. Nicholas Carter
Babcock Boys. D. Reid
Babe Bound to Kill. M. Brody
Babe Gordon. Mae West
Babe in the Woods. W. Ard
Babe Jardine. Stuart Martin
Babe Up in Arms. K. T. McCall
Babe with the Twistable Arm. Hampton Stone
Babes in the Woods. L. O'Donnell
Babiole, the Pretty Milliner. F. Du Boisgobey
Baboon's Paw. R. C. Armour
Babs. B. Vane
Baby Blue Rip-Off. M. A. Collins
Baby Doll! D. Haring
Baby Doll Blues. D. Haring
Baby Doll Games. M. Maron
Baby Doll Murders. J. O. Causey
Baby, Don't Dare Squeal. H. Janson
Baby, Don't Get Rough. C. Wheatley
Baby Don't Love Hoodlums. M. Storme
Baby Don't Say Goodbye. M. Storme
Baby Face. M. Corrigan
Baby Face. Dulcie Gray
Baby Face Gangster. R. Steel
Baby Factory. C. Rayner
Baby Farm. M. Lundy
Baby Grand and other stories. S. Aumonier
Baby in the Ash Can. S. Shane
Baby in the Icebox. J. M. Cain
Baby Merchants. L. O'Donnell

Baby Mind Your Step. Rex Richards
Baby Moll. S. Brackeen
Baby Moll. B. Sarto
Baby of Baker Street. W. Butts
Baby Sitter. R. Boyle
Baby Sitters. J. Salisbury
Baby-Snatcher. C. Kendall
Baby, the Rain Must Fall. H. Foote
Baby Wilkinson's V.C. and other stories. N. Newham-Davis
Baby, You Slay Me. C. Defoe
Baby, Your Type's Murder. M. Brody
Baby, Your Racket's Busted. M. Brody
Baby, You're Better Dead. A. Cappeli
Baby, You're Grief. C. Macey
Baby, You're Guilt-Edged. Carter Brown
Babykiller. Joy Carroll
Babylon. G. Allen
Babylon South. J. Cleary
Babylonian Night's Entertainment. J. D. Kerruish
Babysitter. A. Coburn
Babysitter. John Fraser
Baccarat. H. Malot
Baccarat Club. J. L. Rickard
Bach Festival Murders. B. Bloch
Bachelor Flat Mystery. R. A. J. Walling
Bachelor Party. H. Hickman
Bachelor to the Rescue. A. Bethune
Bachelor's Christmas. Robert Grant
Bachelors Get Lonely. A. A. Fair
Bachelors of Broken Hill. A. W. Upfield
Bachelor's Widow. M. Dekobra
Back-Alley Blond. Griff
Back Bay. W. Martin
Back Bay Murders. R. Scarlett
Back Country. W. Fuller
Back County Crimes. L. Robertson
Back Door Man. R. Kantner
Back Door to Death. R. Foley
Back from the Dead. E. Snell
Back from the Dead. A. Soutar
Back from the Dead. M. Waugh
Back from the Grave. W. S. Masterman
Back from the Grave. J. K. Stafford
Back Home. I. S. Cobb
Back in Daylight. E. H. Clements
Back in the Real World. M. H. Albert
Back Number. E. Everett-Green
Back of Beyond. E. Snell
Back of the North Wind. N. Freeling
Back of the Tiger. J. Gerson
Back Room Girl. F. Durbridge
Back Room in Somers Town. J. Malcolm
Back-Seat Murder. Herman Landon
Back to Africa. W. Westall
Back to Bandola. R. Castle
Back to Eden. A. Soutar
Back to Fire Mountain. R. Scowcroft
Back to God's Country. J. O. Curwood
Back to Life. T. W. Speight
Back to Life. Jonathan Wade
Back to Lilac Land. G. Thorne
Back to 'Nam. J. Buchanan
Back to the Old Country. M. C. Hay
Back to the Wall. R. P. Hansen
Back to Victoria. J. J. Farjeon
Back to Your Knitting. J. E. Goodman
Back Toward Lisbon. Allison Cole
Backfire. C. L. Burgess
Backfire. C. Egleton
Backfire. D. J. Marlowe
Backfire. Christopher Newman
Backfire. E. Sherry
Backfire Is Hostile. J. Barnett
Background for Murder. Shelley Smith
Background to Danger. E. Ambler
Background to Death. J. W. Lee
Background to Murder, and other stories. T. S. Denham
Backhoe Gothic. J. DeWeese
Backing Winds. Josephine Bell
Backlash. P. Durst
Backlash. P. Gosling
Backlash. A. Melville-Ross

Backlash. J. B. O'Sullivan
Backlash. D. Pendleton
Backlash. J. Philips
Backlash. M. Russell
Backlash. V. Warren
Backlash. M. L. West
Backlash of Infamy. H. Janson
Backslider. G. Allen
Backstage Mystery. O. R. Cohen
Backstreets of Soho. J. Wingrave
Backtrack. Joseph Hansen
Backtrack. M. Nunes
Backup Men. Ross Thomas
Backwash. P. Malloch
Backwaters. M. S. Boyd
Backwoods Menace. R. Renauld
Backwoods Princess. H. Footner
Backwoods Teaser. G. Brewer
Backwoods Tramp. H. Whittington
Backyard. J. Femling
Bad Angel. E. K. Gann
Bad April. A. Ross
Bad As Could Be. Griff
Bad August. D. Hearn
Bad Blonde. J. Webb
Bad Blood. A. Bruno
Bad Blood. B. Petty
Bad Boy. S. D. Frances
Bad Boy. E. Schiddel
Bad Boy. J. Thompson
Bad Circle. J. N. Chance
Bad Communist. M. Crawford
Bad Company. L. Cody
Bad Conscience. J. Roffman
Bad Day at Black Rock. M. Niall
Bad Day for a Black Brother. B. B. Johnson
Bad Day in the Bahamas. A. Cullimore
Bad Debt. Stuart Kay
Bad Desire. G. Devon
Bad Die Young. Peter Chambers
Bad Die Young. R. Norman
Bad Dream. M. Gair
Bad Dream of Death. J. N. Chance
Bad Dreams. Kim Newman
Bad Dreams. Robert Robinson
Bad End Valley. W. B. Bannerman
Bad for Business. R. Stout
Bad for the Baron. Anthony Morton
Bad Fortune. D. Lynch
Bad Girl. H. Janson
Bad Girls. B. Clifton
Bad Guy. N. Brady
Bad Guys. Elizabeth Arthur
Bad Guys. A. Bruno
Bad Guys. E. Izzi
Bad Investment. L. Cassels
Bad Lord Lockington. F. Warden
Bad Luck. A. Bruno
Bad-Luck Cutie. H. Spencer
Bad Man of Cairo. A. Parsons
Bad Medicine. M. Borgenicht
Bad Medicine. C. Q. Yarbro
Bad Men Make Good Wives. M. Hayes
Bad Money. A. M. Kabal
Bad Money Baby. Harding Cole
Bad Moon Rising. J. Kirsch
Bad Name. J. J. Ellis
Bad Neighbor Murder. C. M. Russell
Bad Neighbors. I. Haiblum
Bad-News Man. M. McMullen
Bad Night's Work. O. J. Currington
Bad One. L. Barrington
Bad Penny. J. Blackburn
Bad Place. D. R. Koontz
Bad Ronald. J. H. Vance
Bad Room. C. C. Gilmore
Bad Samaritan. W. C. Gault
Bad Samaritan. A. Rider
Bad Scene. B. Copper
Bad Scene at Bong Son. J. Lansing
Bad Seed. Maxwell Anderson
Bad Seed. W. March
Bad Sister. E. Tennant
Bad Step. M. Derby

Bad Summer. J. Appleby
Bad Timing. O. De St. Jeor
Bad to Beat. H. Smart
Bad Track. M. Booth
Bad Trip. K. Roos
Bad Woman. H. Vogel
Baddington Horror. W. S. Masterman
Baddington Peerage. G. A. Sala
Badge. B. Bolt
Badge for a Gunfighter. R. Wilkes-Hunter
Badge of Madness. J. Willwerth
Badge of Evil. W. Masterson
Badge of Honor. D. Barnes
Badge of Honor. D. Brennan
Badge of Honor. J. K. Dugan
Badge of Infamy. P. Durst
Badge of Shame. A. Abram
Badge 373. M. Roote
Badger Game. Michael Bowen
Badger in the Dusk. N. Brent
Badger on the Barge. J. Howker
Badger's Daughter. R. Crawford
Badlands. J. Frost
Badmen on Halfaday Creek. J. B. Hendryx
Baffle Book. L. Wren
Baffled, But Not Beaten. Nicholas Carter
Baffled Conspirators. W. E. Norris
Baffled Imposter. S. W. Hopkins
Baffled Oath. Nicholas Carter
Baffling Quest. R. Dowling
Bag and Baggage. B. Capes
Bag Man. F. McAuliffe
Bag of Diamonds. G. M. Fenn
Bag o' Gold. N. Giltspar
Bagatelle and some other diversions. G. R. Preedy
Bagful of Bones. A. Kennington
Baghdad Blues. S. Greenlee
Baghdad Defections. B. Keller
Bagman. R. Dick
Bagman. P. Lacey
Bagman in Jewels. M. Pemberton
Bags of Blackmail. C. Litchfield
Bagshot Mystery. O. Gray
Bahama Crisis. D. Bagley
Bahamas Murder Case. L. Ford
Bail Jumper. R. J. C. Stead
Bail Up! H. Nisbet
Bailiff's Secret. G. H. Teed
Bainbridge Holme. Charles Henry
Bainbridge Murder. C. Fitzsimmons
Bainbridge Mystery. G. T. Pratt
Bait. Lionel Black
Bait. M. Carroll
Bait. L. Martin
Bait. D. Uhnak
Bait for a Killer. G. Bagby
Bait for a Tiger. B. Veiller
Bait for Murder. K. M. Knight
Bait Money. Max Collins
Bait of Lies. Hardiman Scott
Bait of Perjury. W. Savage
Bait on the Hook. F. Parrish
Baited Blonde. R. MacLean
Baited Hook. D. Keene
Baiting the Trap. J. Middlemass
Baja. Jack Jones
Baja Bandidos. L. Derrick
Baja Run. L. Chance
Baked Bean Supper Murders. V. Rich
Baker Street. J. Coopersmith
Baker Street Boys. B. N. Ball
Baker's Dozen. Mrs. H. Dudeney
Bakke's Night of Fame. J. McGrath
Baksheesh and Roses. C. Beardsley
Balance. W. D. Orcott
Balance of Dangers. A. Forrest
Balance of Fear. H. Matheson
Balance of Fear. G. Osborne
Balance of Power. W. B. Murphy
Balance of Power. Jack Peterson
Balance of Terror. C. Van Hazinga
Balaoo. G. Leroux
Balcony. F. Cowen
Balcony. D. C. Disney

Balcony. J. Genet
Beldragon. J. B. Harris-Burland
Balefire. K. Goddard
Balefire. N. Tranter
Bales of Trouble. G. W. Wicking
Balfour Conspiracy. I. St. James
Bali Ballet Murder. C. Conyn
Balinese Pearls. L. Lambert
Balkan Assignment. J. Poyer
Balkan Express. L. Ross
Balkan Saga. D. Weir
Balkan Spy. D. Betteridge
Ball Bearing Run. W. Winward
Ball of Fortune. C. E. Pearce
Ballad of Dogs' Beach. J. C. Pires
Ballad of Loving Jenny. Carter Brown
Ballad of the Fat Bushranger and other stories. D. Niland
Ballad of the Flim Flam Man. G. Owen
Ballad of the Running Man. Shelley Smith
Ballarat. Eric Lambert
Ballet! T. Murphy
Ballet of Death. Elizabeth Anthony
Ballet of Fear. Elizabeth Anthony
Ballet of Moments Unborn. A. Viney
Balloon Affair. M. M. Layne
Balloon Girl. M. MacKintosh
Balloon Man. C. Armstrong
Ballot. R. Summerscales
Ballot Box Murders. J. S. Strange
Ballot Box Mystery. H. H. C. Gibbons
Ballots for Violence. S. Dave
Ballycronin Mystery. H. M. Webster
Ballyho Bey. A. C. Gunter
Balmoral Nude. C. Coker
Baltic Business. P. Corris
Baltic Emerald. E. Ward
Baltic Mystery. F. S. Webber
Baltic Wolf. P. Allenby
Baltimore Madame. H. Knowland
Baltimore Trackdown. D. Pendleton
Bamboo. K. West
Bamboo Bay. G. Volk
Bamboo Blonde. D. B. Hughes
Bamboo Bloodbath. P. Anthony
Bamboo Bomb. James Dark
Bamboo Demons. J. Sherman
Bamboo Elephants. N. Thurley
Bamboo Girl. F. Lester
Bamboo Grove. Alixe Carter
Bamboo Prison. H. Gibbs
Bamboo Screen. S. Harvester
Bamboo Terror. W. Ross
Bamboo Whistle. C. V. Frost
Banacek. Deane Romano
Banana Men. M. Catto
Banana Murders. Y. Smith
Banana Tourist. G. Simenon
Banbury Bog. P. A. Taylor
Bancaster Mystery. A. N. Hodges
Bancock Murder Case. A. B. Cunningham
Band of Mystery. M. O. Rolfe
Band Played Murder. E. Howie
Bandaberry. L. Meynell
Bandaged Face. Z. I. Ponder
Bandaged Nude. R. Finnegan
Bandar-Log Mruder. C. Comstock
Bandbox. L. J. Vance
Bandersnatch. Mollie Hardwick
Bandersnatch. D. Lowden
Bandicoot. R. Condon
Bandini Affair. M. Bass
Bandit. L. Charteris
Bandit Love. J. Savage
Bandit of Syracuse. S. Cobb
Bandit Trust. M. Warrick
Bandits. E. Leonard
Bandits. P. Whalley
Bandits Aloft. T. Wallace
Bandit's Moon. N. MacKenzie
Bandits of the Air. Nicholas Carter
Bandits of the Night. J. M. Walsh
Bandits of the Sea. Anonymous
Bane. J. Donnelly

Bang! Bang! G. Ade
Bang Bang Beirut. R. Cooney
Bang Bang Birds. A. Diment
Bang! Bang! You're Dead! June Drummond
Bang, You're Dead! H. Treece
Bang, You're Death. P. Reakes
Bangkok Collection. J. Schoonover
Bangkok Murders. Reginald Campbell
Bangkok Secret. Anthony Grey
Banishment of Jessop Blythe. J. Hatton
Banjo. J. Curtis
Bank Draft Puzzle. Nicholas Carter
Bank Job. R. L. Pike
Bank Job. T. B. Reagan
Bank Manager. E. P. Oppenheim
Bank Note Plates. Lieut. Carlton
Bank Robber. G. Tippette
Bank Robbers. A. Griffith
Bank Robbers. Old Sleuth
Bank-Robbers and the Detectives. A. Pinkerton
Bank Robbery. M. Ulrich
Bank Robbery Hostage. R. Wilkes-Hunter
Bank Shot. D. E. Westlake
Bank Tragedy. M. R. Hatch
Bank Vault Mystery. L. F. Booth
Bank with the Bamboo Door. D. Hitchens
Banker. D. Francis
Banker and Broker. N. Gould
Banker's Bones. M. Scherf
Banker's Millions. Warren Miller
Banker's Trust. J. W. Bobin
Banker's Victim. O. Bradbury
Banking on Death. E. Lathen
Bankroll. B. Ducker
Banksters. Robin Moore
Bannantyne Sapphires. F. Hird
Banner for Pegasus. J. Bonett
Banner of the Bull. R. Sabatini
Banner of the Prophet. Robert Harding
Bannerman. F. Flynn
Bannerman Case. J. Lord
Bannerman Effect. J. R. Maxim
Bannerman Solution. J. R. Maxim
Banners of Blood. J. H. Hunter
Banners Yellow. J. E. Gordon
Bannon. A. Evans
Banquet Ceases. M. Fitt
Banquets of the Black Widowers. I. Asimov
Banshee. D. Barton
Banshee. M. Millar
Banyon. W. Johnston
Baptism. D. E. Zlotnick
Baptism for the Dead. R. Irvine
Bar Sinister. K. G. Ballard
Bar Sinister. C. A. Collins
Bar Sinister. J. M. DeGroot
Bar Sinister. P. MacTyre
Bar Sinister. S. Rathbone
Baraka. J. Saul
Barbara. M. E. Braddon
Barbara Heathcote's Trial. R. N. Carey
Barbara on Her Own. E. Wallace
Barbara, the Valiant. K. Kimbrough
Barbara's Rival. E. A. Young
Barbarossa Red. Dennis Jones
Barbarous Coast. R. Macdonald
Barbary Freight. R. Burke
Barbary Hoard. J. Appleby
Barbary Kate. F. Hay
Barbed Wire. E. Everett-Green
Barbed Wire. E. Fackler
Barbed Wire. M. Richmond
Barbed-Wire Hurdlers. P. Quinn
Barbed Wire Noose. Harold Adams
Barber of Littlewick. M. Drewe
Barber's Shop Crime. W. Edwards
Barber's Wife. C. Phillips
Barberton Intrigue. S. Truss
Barbie Murders. J. Varley
Barbouse. Alan Williams
Barboza Credentials. P. Driscoll
Barbs. Bill Walsh
Barca. L. Cameron
Barclay Place. R. Foley

Bardelow's Heir. Roy Vickers
Bardel's Murder. E. McGirr
Bardot M.P.? A. P. Herbert
Bare Acquaintances. K. Berne
Bare Bodkin. F. Gerard
Bare Facts. D. Haring
Bare-Top Babe. D. Haring
Bare Trap. F. Kane
Barefoot Mailman. T. Pratt
Barefoot Witch. M. Clare
Barely Seen. F. Kane
Bargain. M. Gilbert
Bargain for Death. Robert Martin
Bargain in Blood. Arthur MacLean
Bargain in Blood. D. Stanford
Bargain in Crime. Nicholas Carter
Bargain in Souls. E. D. Pierson
Bargain with Death. H. Pentecost
Barge Girl. C. Clements
Barge of Haunted Lives. J. A. Tyson
Baring Fault. J. Stonehouse
Barker Case. G. Barrett
Barker's Drift. C. Cannell
Barking Clock. H. S. Keeler
Barking Dog Murder Case. E. C. Vivian
Barking Dogs. T. M. Green
Barlow Casebook. Elwyn Jones
Barlow Comes to Judgment. Elwyn Jones
Barlow Dale's Casebook. R. Siverns
Barlow Down Under. Elwyn Jones
Barlow Exposed. Elwyn Jones
Barlow in Charge. Elwyn Jones
Barn Stormers. A. M. Williamson
Barnabas Collins. Marilyn Ross
Barnabas Collins and Quentin's Doom. Marilyn Ross
Barnabas Collins and the Gypsy Witch. Marilyn Ross
Barnabas Collins and the Mysterious Ghost. Marilyn Ross
Barnabas Collins vs. the Warlock. Marilyn Ross
Barnabas, Quentin and Dr. Jekyll's Son. Marilyn Ross
Barnabas, Quentin and the Body Snatchers. Marilyn Ross
Barnabas, Quentin and the Crystal Coffin. Marilyn Ross
Barnabas, Quentin and the Frightened Bride. Marilyn Ross
Barnabas, Quentin and the Grave Robbers. Marilyn Ross
Barnabas, Quentin and the Haunted Cave. Marilyn Ross
Barnabas, Quentin and the Hidden Tomb. Marilyn Ross
Barnabas, Quentin and the Mad Magician. Marilyn Ross
Barnabas, Quentin and the Magic Potion. Marilyn Ross
Barnabas, Quentin and the Mummy's Curse. Marilyn Ross
Barnabas, Quentin and the Nightmare Assassin. Marilyn Ross
Barnabas, Quentin and the Scorpio Curse. Marilyn Ross
Barnabas, Quentin and the Sea Ghost. Marilyn Ross
Barnabas, Quentin and the Serpent. Marilyn Ross
Barnabas, Quentin and the Vampire Beauty. Marilyn Ross
Barnabas, Quentin and the Witch's Curse. Marilyn Ross
Barney. W. Johnston
Baron Again. Anthony Morton
Baron and the Arrogant Alibi. Anthony Morton
Baron and the Beggar. Anthony Morton
Baron and the Chinese Puzzle. Anthony Morton
Baron and the Missing Old Masters. Anthony Morton
Baron and the Mogul Swords. Anthony Morton
Baron and the Stolen Legacy. Anthony Morton
Baron and the Unfinished Portrait. Anthony Morton
Baron at Bay. Anthony Morton
Baron at Large. Anthony Morton
Baron Branches Out. Anthony Morton

Title Index

Baron Comes Back. Anthony Morton
Baron Goes A-Buying. Anthony Morton
Baron Goes East. Anthony Morton
Baron Goes Fast. Anthony Morton
Baron in France. Anthony Morton
Baron Ixell, Crime Breaker. O. Schisgall
Baron—King Maker. Anthony Morton
Baron Montez of Panama and Paris. A. C. Gunter
Baron of Hong Kong. N. Daniels
Baron on Board. Anthony Morton
Baron Orgaz. F. Lauria
Baron Returns. Anthony Morton
Baron Sam. St. George Rathborne
Baron Sinister. J. Milton
Baron Trigault's Vengeance. E. Gaboriau
Baroness of Bow Street. G. Clark
Baronet Rag-Picker. C. S. Coom
Baronet's Bride. M. A. Fleming
Baronet's Crime. J. B. Williams
Baronet's Wife. F. Warden
Baroni. Alfred Harris
Baron's Daughter. I. Kelly
Baron's Mission to Peking. N. Daniels
Baroque. L. J. Vance
Barossa. J. Clive
Barotique Mystery. G. H. Coxe
Barozzi. Catharine Smith
Barrabas Blitz. J. Hild
Barrabas Creed. J. Hild
Barrabas Edge. J. Hild
Barrabas Fallout. J. Hild
Barrabas Fix. J. Hild
Barrabas Heist. J. Hild
Barrabas Hit. J. Hild
Barrabas Kill. J. Hild
Barrabas Raid. J. Hild
Barrabas Run. S. Otfinoski
Barrabas Sting. J. Hild
Barrabas Strike. J. Hild
Barrabas Sweep. J. Hild
Barrabas Thrust. J. Hild
Barrabas War. J. Hild
Barracks, Bivouacs and Battles. Archibald Forbes
Barracuda. I. A. Greenfield
Barracuda. R. Magowan
Barracuda Run. Gar Wilson
Barradine Detects. E. Jepson
Barrakee Mystery. A. W. Upfield
Barrancourt Destiny. A. Worboys
Barred from the West End. J. Hunter
Barrel Mystery. Nicholas Carter
Barrel Mystery. W. J. Flynn
Barren Harvest. C. M. Nelson
Barren Heritage. L. R. Davis
Barren Honor. H. Wood
Barren Land Murders. L. Short
Barren Land Showdown. L. Short
Barren Revenge. John Penn
Barren Title. T. W. Speight
Barrier. S. L. Bell
Barrier. R. Maugham
Barrier Island. J. D. MacDonald
Barrier Reef. M. Grant
Barrier Reef Mystery. A. Murray
Barringher House. B. Riefe
Barrington Mystery. L. Brock
Barronwell Mystery. H. Leyford
Barrow Sinister. Elsie Lee
Barry Bayne. A. Graves
Bars of Gold. G. Ellinger
Bars of Steel. L. Noel
Barsroom Project. L. Niven
Bartenstein Case. J. S. Fletcher
Bartenstein Mystery. J. S. Fletcher
Bartered Honour. R. H. Sherard
Bartholomew Fair Murders. L. Tourney
Bartlett Mystery. L. Tracy
Barton Manor Mystery. Gwyn Evans
Barton Mystery. G. Goodchild
Barton Mystery. W. Hackett
Barush Mystery. T. A. Plummer
Base Case. J. Rathbone
Basement Room and other stories. G. Greene
Basikasingo. J. Matthews

Basil. W. Collins
Basil and Annette. B. L. Farjeon
Basilisk. H. P. Stephens
Baskerville Caper. F. Norman
Basket Case. R. McInerny
Basket of Summer Fruit. R. McCullough
Basle Express. M. Coles
Bass Derby Murder. K. M. Knight
Bassington Murder. C. Hough
Bastard. J. Wainwright
Bastard Brigade. P. Leslie
Bastard Verdict. Winifred Duke
Bastard's Name was Bristow. J. S. Scott
Bastion of the Damned. J. Cassells
Bat. M. R. Rinehart
Bat Flies Low. S. Rohmer
Bat of the Belfrey. Anonymous
Bat Out of Hell. F. Durbridge
Bat Staffel. R. J. Hogan
Bat That Flits. N. Collins
Bat-Wing. S. Rohmer
Bat Woman. C. Gibbons
Bateman Household. J. Payn
Bates and His Bicycle. F. Whishaw
Bath Belles. Joan Smith
Bath Mysteries. E. R. Punshon
Bath of Acid. C. Franklin
Bathchair Mystery. A. Murray
Bathing Pool Mystery. A. Blair
Bathtub Murder. D. Lyon
Bathtub Murder Case. E. R. Punshon
Bathurst Complex. W. Martyn
Batman. Anonymous
Batman. C. S. Gardner
Batman. B. Kane
Batman: Head of the Demon. D. O'Neil
Batman Murders. C. S. Gardner
Batman: The Dark Night Returns. Frank Miller
Batman: The Killing Joke. Alan Moore
Batman: The Track of the Hook. Neal Adams
Batman vs. the Fearsome Foursome. W. Lyon
Batman vs. the Joker. B. Kane
Batman vs. the Penguin. B. Kane
Batman vs. Three Villains of Doom. W. Lyon
Batman: Year One. Frank Miller
Batman: Year Two. Frank Miller
Baton for the Conductor. T. L. Hubbard
Bats Fly at Dusk. A. A. Fair
Bats Fly Up for Inspector Ghote. H. R. F. Keating
Bats in the Belfrey. E. C. R. Lorac
Bats with Baby Faces. W. S. Moss
Battered Caravanserai. P. Capon
Battle. Douglas Newton
Battle Begins. J. Ahern
Battle for Inspector West. J. Creasey
Battle for the Cup. P. Gill
Battle for the Right. Nicholas Carter
Battle Group Peiper. J. Lucas
Battle in Botswana. Steve White
Battle in the Air. Anonymous
Battle Lines. D. Pendleton
Battle Mask. D. Pendleton
Battle of Basinghall Street. E. P. Oppenheim
Battle of Brains. F. Tuohy
Battle of Giants. P. Trent
Battle of Hate. N. Buntline
Battle of Jericho Street. F. Everton
Battle of Nerves. G. Simenon
Battle of the April Storm. H. Forrester
Battle of the Singing Men. G. Kersh
Battle of Wits. S. Campbell
Battle Pay. P. McCurtin
Battle Road. S. Harvester
Battle Song. W. H. Baker
Battle Without Glory. R. C. Trown
Battle Zone. M. Dixon
Battle Zone. Greg Walker
Battles of Life. Austin Philips
Battlewrack. F. B. Austin
Battling Barker. A. Soutar
Battling Prophet. A. W. Upfield
Battling Skyman. T. Wallace
Bavarian Connection. Don Smith
Bawlerout. F. Halsey

Baxter Family. A. Askew
Baxter Letters. D. Hitchens
Baxter Trust. J. P. Hailey
Baxter's Choice. H. Arnston
Baxter's Second Death. I. Greig
Baxter's Son. P. Trent
Bay City Blast. W. B. Murphy
Bay City Burnout. R. Harding
Bay of Deception. S. Shelley
Bay of Seals. J. Wood
Bay of the Damned. W. Carrier
Bay Prowler. M. Barry
Bay Psalm Book Murder. W. Harriss
Baying Hound. A. West
Bayou Brigade. B. Sanders
Bayou Road. M. G. Eberhart
Bazi Bazoum. C. Matthew
Be a Good Boy. Joan Fleming
Be Absolute for Death. R. Chance
Be All and End All. E. Berckman
Be Buried in the Rain. B. Michaels
Be Careful How You Live. E. Lacy
Be Home by Eleven. A. Dean
Be Kind to the Killer. Henry Wade
Be My Ghost. R. Chapman
Be My Love. M. Richmond
Be My Victim. R. Dietrich
Be Our Guest. C. Sodaro
Be Shot for Sixpence. M. Gilbert
Be Silent, Love. F. Nichols
Be Still, My Love. J. Truesdell
Be Thou My Judge. J. Wood
Beach Combings. R. Stock
Beach-Front Murders. Tom Howard
Beach Girls. J. D. MacDonald
Beach House. V. Coffman
Beach House 7. P. Roadarmel
Beach of Atonement. A. W. Upfield
Beach of Skulls. A. West
Beach of Terror, and other stories. B. Grimshaw
Beach Patrol. K. Rogers
Beach Queen Blowout. P. Morgan
Beachcomber. A. Murray
Beachy Head Murder. A. Gask
Beacon Fires. M. Gerard
Beacon Fires. Headon Hill
Beacon Hill Murders. R. Scarlett
Beacon in the Night. B. S. Ballinger
Beacons of Death. M. B. Dix
Beaded Banana. M. Scherf
Beads of Silence. L. Bamburg
Beagle Scented Murder. F. Gruber
Beak of Death. L. Bennet-Thompson
Beam of Black Light. O. John
Beam of Malice. Alex Hamilton
Beanball. T. Seaver
Bear Island. Alistair MacLean
Bear Raid. K. Follett
Bear Squeeze. M. M. Bodkin
Bear Witness. J. Reach
Beard the Lion. W. Manchester
Bearded Slayer. T. Roscoe
Bearer Plot. O. Sela
Bearers of the Burden. W. P. Drury
Bearpit. B. Freemantle
Bear's Requiem. P. Cunningham
Bear's Tears. C. Thomas
Beast. L. Allan
Beast. H. Fleetwood
Beast. E. C. Litsey
Beast. A. Masters
Beast in View. M. Millar
Beast-King Murders. R. Wallace
Beast Must Die. N. Blake
Beast of the Baskervilles. T. J. Kelly
Beast of the City. J. Lait
Beast on Broadway. M. Wolk
Beast with Five Fingers. W. F. Harvey
Beast with the Red Hands. S. Stuart
Beast with Two Backs. N. Sligh
Beastly Business. J. Blackburn
Beastmaker. J. V. Smith, Jr.
Beastmark the Spy. J. B. Clouston
Beastnights. C. Q. Yarbro

B

Beasts and Escapades. J. Delmont
Beasts and Superbeasts. H. H. Munro
Beasts of Brahm. M. Hansom
Beasts of Valhalla. G. Chesbro
Beaststalker. J. V. Smith, Jr.
Beat a Distant Drum. R. Emmett
Beat Back the Tide. D. Hitchens
Beat Not the Bones. C. Jay
Beat on an Orange Drum. D. Reid
Beat the Devil. J. Helvick
Beaten at the Post. B. Delannoy
Beating the Nobblers. J. Fairfax-Blakeborough
Beatnik Babe. D. Haring
Beatrice. E. Southworth
Beatrice and Fenedick. H. Smart
Beatrice Foyle's Crime. F. Warden
Beatrice Mystery. D. Johns
Beatrix Randolph. J. Hawthorne
Beau Blackstone. R. Falkirk
Beau Revel. L. J. Vance
Beaufort Dossier. D. Mariner
Beaufoy Romances. H. Drummond
Beaumaroy Home from the Wars. Anthony Hope
Beamont Tradition. D. Daniels
Beaurand Mystery. H. Greville
Beautiful Alien. S. Hocking
Beautiful and Dead. R. MacRoss
Beautiful and Dead. F. Winter
Beautiful Bait. R. Dudgeon
Beautiful Bait. D. Haring
Beautiful Birthday Cake. M. Scherf
Beautiful Blackmailer. Old Sleuth
Beautiful But Bad. R. Colby
Beautiful But Damned. F. Lorenz
Beautiful But Dangerous. T. W. Hanshew
Beautiful Crook. M. O'Nair
Beautiful Dead. H. Pentecost
Beautiful Derelict. C. Wells
Beautiful Devil. Detective Dunn
Beautiful Frame. W. Pearson
Beautiful Friend. R. Collier
Beautiful Fugitive. Old Sleuth
Beautiful Golden Frame. Peter Chambers
Beautiful Gunner. Norma Lee
Beautiful Jack, the Double-Edged Detective. Anonymous
Beautiful Jim of the Blankshire Regiment. J. S. Winter
Beautiful Mrs. Davenant. V. Tweedale
Beautiful Mrs. Leach. W. Graham
Beautiful Murder. J. Ingersol
Beautiful Place to Die. P. R. Craig
Beautiful Savage. Mrs. C. Kernahan
Beautiful Schemer. D. T. Hughes
Beautiful Scourge. E. Gaboriau
Beautiful Stranger. Bernice Carey
Beautiful Suspect. H. Richards
Beautiful Trap. B. S. Ballinger
Beautiful White Devil. G. Boothby
Beautiful Woman's Sin. Hero Strong
Beauty—A Snare. Glint Green
Beauty and the Bank Manager. M. Velis
Beauty and the Beast. E. McBain
Beauty and the Beat. H. Janson
Beauty and the Policeman and other stories. S. Horler
Beauty Can Kill. M. McCretton
Beauty Doctor. F. Warden
Beauty for Inspector West. J. Creasey
Beauty Found a Grave. Dave Steel
Beauty in Distress. G. Warden
Beauty Is a Beast. K. M. Knight
Beauty Is Found in a Grave. D. Steel
Beauty Kill. R. Hawkes
Beauty-Killer. B. Fleming
Beauty Marks the Spot. K. Roos
Beauty-Mask Murder. V. B. Shore
Beauty-Mask Mystery. V. B. Shore
Beauty of the Family. F. Warden
Beauty Parlor Murder. G. Chester
Beauty Queen Killer. J. Creasey
Beauty Sleep. R. Darby
Beauty Sleep. H. Dolson
Beauty Sleep. D. M. Klein

Beauty Spot. H. Mee
Beauty That Must Die. Barbara James
Beauty Vanishes. D. Brande
Beauty Wins. Aintree
Beauty's Queen. M. Leighton
Beaver to Fox. D. Kartun
Because It Is Bitter, and Because It Is My Heart. J. C. Oates
Because of Misella. A. W. Marchmont
Because of the Cats. N. Freeling
Because of the Night. J. Ellroy
Because of the Woman. C. H. Bullivant
Because Their Hearts Were Pure. M. Cary
Becca's Child. W. D. Roberts
Becket Factor. M. D. Anthony
Beckford Don. R. Haley
Beckoning. V. Coffman
Beckoning Door. M. Seeley
Beckoning Dream. E. Berckman
Beckoning Finger. H. Harding
Beckoning Hand and other stories. G. Allen
Beckoning Hands. M. M. Dreyer
Beckoning Idol. C. Dekker
Beckoning Lady. M. Allingham
Beckoning Shadow. Denis Scott
Becky. H. Janson
Becoming Tania. I. Adams
Bed Bugs. C. Sinclair
Bed by the Window. M. S. Peck
Bed Distrubed. Elbur Ford
Bed of Ashes. D. Daniels
Bed of Nails. Andrew Puckett
Bed Tramps. K. North
Bedchamber Mystery. C. S. Forester
Bedelia. V. Caspary
Bedeviled. Libbie Block
Bedford Row Mystery. J. S. Fletcher
Bedroom Agent. F. Branch
Bedroom Alibi. P. Kruger
Bedroom Bang Bang. D. Davis
Bedroom Bolero. M. Avallone
Bedroom in Hell. N. Daniels
Bedroom Window. A. Holden
Bedroom with a View. D. Wade
Bedrooms Have Windows. A. A. Fair
Bedside Corpse. S. Friedman
Bedtime at Eleven. Max Mills
Bee Sting Deal. G. Beare
Beech of the Boulevard. B. Sarto
Beechcourt Mystery. C. Strange
Beecher. V. O'Neal
Beef Wellington Blue. M. Davidson
Beehive. M. O'Donnell
Beekeeper. V. Andrews
Beelfontaine. S. O'Brien
Beelzebub Business. G. Brandner
Beer and Oysters. David Lynn
Beer and Skittles. B. J. Morison
Beer for Psyche. D. Gardiner
Beersheba Triangle. M. A. Yamani
Beethoven Conspiracy. T. Hauser
Beetle. R. Marsh
Before and After Edith. P. Popescu
Before I Die. G. Joseph
Before I Die. H. McCloy
Before I Die. M. L. Roby
Before I Die. L. White
Before I Wake. H. Debrett
Before I Wake. M. Echard
Before I Wake. B. Halliday
Before It's Too Late. L. Cameron
Before It's Too Late. Jay Stewart
Before Midnight. R. Stout
Before Morning. Edna Riley
Before She Kills. Fredric Brown
Before the Ball Was Over. A. Roudybush
Before the Beginning. M. Reison
Before the British Raj. A. Griffiths
Before the Cock Crowed. W. E. Hayes
Before the Crossing. S. Jameson
Before the Fact. F. Iles
Before the Fourteenth. S. D. Stevens
Before the Party. R. Ackland
Before the Storm. M. B. Lowndes

Before the Wind. E. F. Charles
Before the Wind. J. Laing
Beg Pardon, Sir! R. W. Kauffman
Beggar, and other stories. D. Newton
Beggar in Purple. A. Soutar
Beggar on Horseback. J. Payn
Beggars All. K. N. Burt
Beggars All. L. Dougall
Beggar's Choice. H. C. Branson
Beggar's Choice. P. Wentworth
Beggar's Manor. R. M. Gilchrist
Beggars of Kashapore. J. Andrews
Beggars of Life. J. Tully
Begin, Murderer! D. Cory
Begin with a Gun. M. Cronin
Beginner's Luck. P. Somers
Beginning of a Crime. Dorris Roberts
Beginning the Adventure. Augustus Muir
Beginning with a Bash. A. Tilton
Beginnings of Mr. P. J. Davenant. F. S. Hamilton
Begins with Murder. W. Collison
Begonia Walk. Gavin Holt
Begotten Murder. M. Carroll
Beguiling Shore. D. F. Gardiner
Begumbagh. Anonymous
Behind a Brass Knocker. F. Barnard
Behind a Bus. James Greenwood
Behind a Mask. L. M. Alcott
Behind a Mask. Nicholas Carter
Behind a Mask. T. Douglas
Behind a Mask. J. Hatton
Behind a Throne. Nicholas Carter
Behind Closed Doors. Nicholas Carter
Behind Closed Doors. A. K. Green
Behind Dark Shutters. J. Drummond
Behind Locked Doors. E. M. Poate
Behind Locked Shutters. W. E. D. Ross
Behind Prison Bars. Gordon Carr
Behind Red Curtains. Mansfield Scott
Behind Shuttered Windows. A. Askew
Behind That Curtain. E. D. Biggers
Behind That Door. G. Goodchild
Behind That Mask. H. S. Keeler
Behind the Arras. Anthony Graham
Behind the Badge. B. Chandler
Behind the Black Mask. Nicholas Carter
Behind the Blank. Creighton Dale
Behind the Bolted Door? A. E. McFarlane
Behind the Bronze Door. W. LeQueux
Behind the Crimson Blind. Carter Dickson
Behind the Curtain. H. R. Addison
Behind the Curtain. D. Haring
Behind the Curtain. M. Pemberton
Behind the Devil Screen. M. Keck
Behind the Door. E. J. Anders
Behind the Door. F. Lambirth
Behind the Enemy. G. Marlowe
Behind the Evidence. L. Blackledge
Behind the Evidence. P. Reynolds
Behind the Evil Eye! Anonymous
Behind the Fact. R. Hilary
Behind the First Wall. P. Graham
Behind the Fog. H. H. Bashford
Behind the German Lines. W. LeQueux
Behind the Granite Gateway. W. S. King
Behind the Green Mask. R. Trevor
Behind the Head-Lines. W. Sutherland
Behind the Headlines. R. Chapman
Behind the Monocle. J. S. Fletcher
Behind the Panel. J. S. Fletcher
Behind the Paragraph. H. M. E. Clamp
Behind the Picture. M. M. Bodkin
Behind the Purple Mask. J. H. Chase
Behind the Purple Veil. Marilyn Ross
Behind the Ranges. O. Binns
Behind the Scarlet Door. L. Cameron
Behind the Screen. D. Doubtfire
Behind the Throne. W. LeQueux
Behind the Veil. D. E. L. Patch
Behind the Veil. George R. Sims
Behind the Veils. W. M. Graydon
Behind the Wire Fence. L. Allan
Behind the Yellow Blind. R. A. J. Walling
Behind You. T. Millstead

Title Index

Behold a Fair Woman. F. Duncan
Behold, Here's Poison! G. Heyer
Behold the Body! O. Cecil
Behold the City. R. W. Howe
Behold, the Druid Weeps. M. Rippon
Behold! The Executioner! E. Harding
Behold the Fire. M. Blankfort
Behold the Judge. J. Brophy
Behold This Woman. D. Goodis
Beholder. P. Freund
Beiderbecke Affair. A. Plater
Beirut Contract. C. Bainbridge
Beirut Contract. P. Mann
Beirut Incident. Nick Carter
Beirut Payback. D. Pendleton
Beirut Pipeline. R. Alan
Beirut Playback. D. Pendleton
Beirut Retaliation. J. Cutter
Bejeweled Death. M. Babson
Belchamber Scandal. F. Murray
Belfast Blitz. Jim Case
Belfast Connection. M. Bass
Belfast Connection. G. DeVilliers
Belfriere. K. Gooding
Belfry Murder. M. Dalton
Belgrade Battleground. J. Rosenberger
Belgrade Case. C. Bradley
Belgrade Deception. Gar Wilson
Belgrade Drop. G. Vaughan
Belgrave Manor Crime. M. Dalton
Belgravia. D. Linzee
Belgrove Castle. T. H. White
Believe Me, Xantippe. F. Ballard
Believe This . . . You'll Believe Anything. J. H. Chase
Believed Violent. J. H. Chase
Believers. N. Conde
Belinda's Beaux. A. Kenealy
Bell. D. Daniels
Bell, Book and Candleflame. I. S. Way
Bell in the Fog. J. S. Strange
Bell Is Answered. R. East
Bell of Death. Anthony Gilbert
Bell on Lonely. M. P. Hood
Bell Ringer of Angel's. B. Harte
Bell Street Murders. S. Fowler
Bell Tower of Wyndspelle. A. Vandergriff
Bella. D. Eden
Bella Donna. R. Hichens
Bella Donna Was Poisoned. Carter Brown
Bella Mafia. L. LaPlante
Bella on the Roof. H. Ford
Belladonna. E. Lindley
Belladonna. D. Thomas
Bellamy Case. J. Hay
Bellamy Trial. F. N. Hart
Bellarmine Jug. N. Hasluck
Bellcroft Priory. W. B. Cooke
Belle. E. George
Belle. G. Simenon
Belle. Michael Stewart
Belle Claudine. P. Muse
Belle Haven. J. Fitzgerald
Belle of Australia. W. H. Thomas
Belle of the Ballet. A. Applin
Belle of the Bush. G. Darrell
Belle of Toorak. E. W. Hornung
Belle Starr, the Bandit Queen. Anonymous
Belles and Ringers. H. Smart
Bellini Look. C. Brink
Bellman and True. D. Lowden
Bellmer Mystery. B. A. Williams
Bellringer. L. Kamarck
Bellringer Street. Robert Richardson
Bells at Old Bailey. D. Bowers
Bells for the Dead. K. M. Knight
Bells of Agony. A. Dourado
Bells of Bicetre. G. Simenon
Bells of Doom. A. S. Falkner
Bells of Doom. Donald Stuart
Bells of Hallowdene. C. H. Bullivant
Bells of Old Bailey. D. Bowers
Bells of Palmdale, and other stories. W. Slater
Bells of Penraven. B. L. Farjeon

Bells of St. Martin. Karen Campbell
Bells of Widows Bay. M. Lynch
Belltower. K. A. Shoesmith
Bellwood. E. Ogilvie
Belonging. O. Wadsley
Beloved Diana. A. C. Ley
Beloved Enemy. P. Allardyce
Beloved Enemy. M. K. Douglas
Beloved Enemy. A. Maybury
Beloved Enemy. M. Richmond
Beloved Lady. B. Jefferis
Beloved of Ishmael. V. M. Steele
Beloved Sinner. M. Tomlinson
Beloved Stranger. J. Blackmore
Beloved Thief. O. Wadsley
Beloved Traitor. E. Bond
Beloved Traitor. H. Janson
Beloved Victim. J. Arliss
Below Bridge. R. Dowling
Below Bridges. P. Belloc
Below Suspicion. J. D. Carr
Below the Belt. David Hume
Below the Clock. J. V. Turner
Below the Dead-Line. S. Campbell
Below the Surface. E. K. Chatterton
Below Third Street. S. J. Simonsen
Belrox Mystery. Dick Stewart
Belshazzar's Feast. P. Way
Belshazzer Affair. M. Stall
Belt of Diamonds. B. Wayde
Belt of Suspicion. H. R. Wakefield
Beltane the Smith. J. Farnol
Belting Inheritance. J. Symons
Belvedere. Elizabeth Ford
Belvedere. R. Pearsall
Ben. G. A. Ralston
Ben Bradley's Puzzle. W. G. Forbes
Ben Bradley's Weirdest Case. W. G. Forbes
Ben Clough and other stories. W. Westall
Ben Gates Is Hot. R. Kyle
Ben Hassan's Secret. W. V. Cook
Ben on the Job. J. J. Farjeon
Ben Sees It Through. J. J. Farjeon
Benchley's Chip. C. A. Posey
Bend in the River. D. G. Deutsch
Beneath the Low Light. D. Hacker
Beneath the Mask. F. A. M. Webster
Beneath the Night Sky. A. M. Mountford
Beneath the Passion Flower. G. R. Preedy
Beneath the Precipice. J. Ritson
Beneath the Sea. G. M. Fenn
Beneath the Silent Sea. R. P. Henrick
Beneath the Veil. A. Sergeant
Beneath the Wheels. F. E. M. Notley
Beneath Your Very Boots. C. J. C. Hyne
Benedict Arnold Connection. J. DiMona
Benefactors' Club. A. Abdullah
Benefit. N. Mayo
Benefit Performance. R. Sale
Benefits of Death. R. Jeffries
Benevent Treasure. P. Wentworth
Benevolent Blackmail. W. R. M. Churcher
Benevolent Blackmailer. T. Harknett
Benevolent Monk. T. Melville
Benevolent Picaroon. J. Cassells
Bengal Fire. L. G. Blochman
Bengal Spider Plan. E. P. Thorne
Bengali Inheritance. O. Sela
Benighted. J. B. Priestley
Benjamin & Co. C. S. Abraham
Benjamin Butts Junr. Anonymous
Benjamin Franklin Takes the Case. R. L. Hall
Benjamin Seven. M. Kerr
Bennett. D. Cory
Bennett's World. E. Lewis
Benny Muscles In. P. Rabe
Benny Went First. V. Kathrens
Benson Murder Case. S. S. Van Dine
Bent Copper. J. Ashford
Bent for Blackmail. G. Monro
Bent Man. A. Maling
Bent, Not Broken. G. M. Fenn
Bentfinger. T. Roscoe
Bentinck's Tutor. J. Payn

Bentley's Conscience. P. Trent
Benton of the Royal Mounted. R. S. Kendall
Benwell Mystery. Hawkshaw
Bequeath Them No Tumbled House. Y. MacManus
Bequest of Evil. K. Robeson
Berenice. E. P. Oppenheim
Berg. A. Quin
Berg Case. John Bentley
Bergen Worth. W. Lloyd
Bergerac. M. Hardwick
Bergerac and the Fatal Weakness. A. Saville
Bergerac and the Jersey Rose. A. Saville
Bergerac and the Moving Fever. A. Saville
Bergerac and the Traitor's Child. A. Saville
Bergerac Is Back. A. Saville
Bergman's Blitz. T. Barling
Beria Papers. Alan Williams
Berkeley Street Mystery. M. R. Hatch
Berkshire Mystery. G. D. H. Cole
Berkut. J. Heywood
Berlin. Nick Carter
Berlin at Midnight. R. Joseph
Berlin Bait. D. Haring
Berlin Blind. A. Scholefield
Berlin Breakout. J. Romanes
Berlin Briefing. H. Janson
Berlin Couriers. J. McGovern
Berlin Ending. Howard Hunt
Berlin Epitaph. A. Winnington
Berlin Fugue. J. C. Winters
Berlin Game. L. Deighton
Berlin Halt. A. Winnington
Berlin Hotel. V. Baum
Berlin Indictment. E. Fischer
Berlin Memorandum. Adam Hall
Berlin Message. Ken Lawrence
Berlin Spy Trap. Geoffrey Davison
Berlin Target. Nick Carter
Berlin Tunnel 21. D. Lindquist
Berlin Warning. N. Guild
Bermuda Burial. C. D. King
Bermuda Calling. D. Garth
Bermuda Triangle Action. J. Rosenberger
Bernan Affair. J. Kessel
Bernard Treve's Boots. L. Clarke
Bernhardt's Edge. Collin Wilcox
Berrigan. V. McConnell
Berry and Co. D. Yates
Berry Green. E. H. Clements
Berry Goes to Monte Carlo. C. N. Williamson
Berry Scene. Dornford Yates
Berryhill. B. C. Bennett
Berserker. D. Schmidt
Berserker. F. Spiering
Bertha, the Bartender's Beautiful Baby. C. George
Bertha, the Beautiful Typewriter Girl. C. George
Bertha's Secret. F. Du Boisgobey
Bertie and the Seven Bodies. P. Lovesey
Bertie and the Tinman. P. Lovesey
Bertie Bland, the Detective. Old Sleuth
Bertram. C. R. Maturin
Bertram's Right. L. G. C.
Beryl of the Biplane. W. LeQueux
Beryl of the Movies. C. H. Bullivant
Beset by Spies. J. Blyth
Beside the Seaside. R. Kerridge
Besides the Wench Is Dead. M. Erskine
Besieged. L. Cullinan
Bess of Bentley's. A. Askew
Bessie Kitson. G. Norway
Bessie, the Bandit's Beautiful Baby. L. Price
Bessy Rane. H. Wood
Bessy Wells. H. Wood
Best Cellar. C. Goodrum
Best Detective Stories of Cyril Hare. Cyril Hare
Best Detective Stories of Roy Vickers. Roy Vickers
Best Dr. Poggioli Detective Stories. T. S. Stribling
Best Dr. Thorndyke Detective Stories. R. A. Freeman
Best Go First. F. O'Malley
Best Horror Stories of Arthur Conan Doyle. A. C. Doyle
Best Indian Chutney (Sweetened). Afghan
Best Kept Secrets. Sandra Brown

B

Best Laid Plans. F. Carmichael
Best Laid Plans. A. Hocking
Best-Laid Schemes. Mark Cross
Best Laid Schemes. Meredith Nicholson
Best Man. G. L. Hill
Best Man. H. MacGrath
Best Man to Die. R. Rendell
Best Max Carrados Detective Stories. E. Bramah
Best Mysteries of Isaac Asimov. I. Asimov
Best Mystery Stories. M. G. Eberhart
Best of Berry. Dornford Yates
Best of Damon Runyon. D. Runyon
Best of Ellery Queen. E. Queen
Best of Her Sex. F. Hume
Best of Husbands. J. Payn
Best of John Collier. J. Collier
Best of John Sladek. J. Sladek
Best of Mr. Fortune. H. C. Bailey
Best of Randall Garrett. R. Garrett
Best of Robert Bloch. R. Bloch
Best of Three. P. Trent
Best Short Stories of M. P. Shiel. M. P. Shiel
Best Stories of Peter Cheyney. P. Cheyney
Best Stories of Wilbur Daniel Steele. W. D. Steele
Best Story Ever. J. S. Clouston
Best That Ever Did It. E. Lacy
Best Thinking Machine Detective Stories. J. Futrelle
Best Western Stories of Bill Pronzini. B. Pronzini
Best Western Stories of Loren D. Estleman. L. D. Estleman
Best Will Always Do. E. Clarke
Bestseller. L. Ramsey
Betencourt Five. S. F. Griffin
Beth Takes Charge. Brian Stuart
Bethleham Road. Anne Perry
Bethnel Green. M. Fisher
Bethnel Inheritance. M. Whitfield
Betray Me—If You Dare. P. Carlon
Betrayal. E. P. Oppenheim
Betrayal. A. E. Walter
Betrayal and other stories. H. Acton
Betrayal at Blackcrest. Beatrice Parker
Betrayal in Eden. P. Chase
Betrayal into Darkness. R. S. S. Hall
Betrayal of John Fordham. B. L. Farjeon
Betrayals. B. Freemantle
Betrayals. A. Harrell
Betrayed. D. Essex
Betrayed. L. Fleischer
Betrayed!! C. M. Lindsay
Betrayed. J. Pendower
Betrayed. Dora Russell
Betrayed. D. B. Wilson
Betrayed by Death. P. Alding
Betrayer. D. Wiles
Betrayers. D. Hamilton
Betrayers. P. Leslie
Bettaley Jewels. E. M. C. Balfour-Browne
Better Angels. C. McCarry
Better Class of Business. J. S. Scott
Better Corpses. C. J. Daly
Better Dead. G. Bagby
Better Dead. J. M. Barrie
Better Dead. J. Bonett
Better Forgotten. D. Footman
Better Luck Next Crime. M. Hervey
Better Mousetraps. J. Lutz
Better Off Dead. J. Bonett
Better Off Dead. R. M. Laurenson
Better Off Dead. H. McCloy
Better Off Dead. M. McMullen
Better Part of Valour. B. Heatter
Better Than a Kick in the Pants. J. MacLaren-Ross
Better Than Dying. R. Faherty
Better Than Weapons. L. Christie
Better to Eat You. C. Armstrong
Better Wed Than Dead. H. Kane
Betty. G. Simenon
Betty Philpott's Release and other stories. W. J. Sharkey
Between Darkness and Day. G. Merrick
Between Life and Death. F. Barrett
Between Midnight and Dawn. I. L. Cassilis
Between Murders. Sherwood King
Between the Dark and the Daylight. R. Marsh
Between the Lines. B. Delannoy
Between the Tides. J. Templeton
Between Twelve and One. V. Loder
Between Two Evils. R. Thurston
Between Us and Evil. C. M. Russell
Beverly. M. T. Walworth
Beverly Hills Browning. P. Corris
Beverly Hills Cop II. R. Tine
Beverly Malibu. K. V. Forrest
Beware My Love. Lee Karr
Beware, My Love. Marilyn Ross
Beware of Johnny Washington. F. Durbridge
Beware of Midnight. J. Welcome
Beware of the Bouquet. Joan Aiken
Beware of the Cat. Roger Sherman
Beware of the Dawn. K. Lindsay
Beware of the Dog! Charles North
Beware of the Dog. B. Reynolds
Beware of the Dog. J. Varnam
Beware of the Trains. E. Crispin
Beware of Wantons. H. Vogel
Beware, Sweet Maggie. D. Olson
Beware the Bog. M. Kingsbury
Beware the Child. R. Foster
Beware the Crimson Cord. B. Edmunds
Beware the Curves. A. A. Fair
Beware the Hoot Owl. N. Rutledge
Beware the Hunter. H. Jones
Beware the Kindly Stranger. Clarissa Ross
Beware the Lady. C. Woolrich
Beware the Lurking Scorpion. S. Milne
Beware the Night. J. Blackmore
Beware the Pale Horse. B. Benson
Beware! The Picaroon. J. Cassells
Beware the Shadows. J. Carrick
Beware the Yellow Packard. L. Malloy
Beware the Young Stranger. E. Queen
Beware Young Lovers. H. Pentecost
Beware Your Neighbor. M. Burton
Bewitched. R. Gilmour
Bewitched. H. Janson
Bewitched. A. M. Williamson
Bewitching Grace. Patricia Maxwell
Beyond a Reasonable Doubt. C. W. Grafton
Beyond All Fear. F. A. M. Webster
Beyond Baker Street. M. Jaffee
Beyond Belief. Emlyn Williams
Beyond Blame. S. Greenleaf
Beyond Capricorn. B. Roland
Beyond Compare. C. Gibbon
Beyond Control. G. Leonard
Beyond Desire. C. Fayet
Beyond Desire. R. Himmel
Beyond Dover. V. Gielgud
Beyond Hope. E. Zaremba
Beyond Mombassa. J. Hilton
Beyond Murder. J. Buckley
Beyond Pursuit. Nicholas Carter
Beyond Reason. A. Goetz
Beyond Reasonable Doubt. R. Hull
Beyond Recall. Dorothy Fletcher
Beyond the Atlas. J. Trench
Beyond the DMZ. J. Lansing
Beyond the Danube. R. Meade
Beyond the Dark. K. Abbey
Beyond the Dark. Jennifer Hale
Beyond the End. C. Boutelle
Beyond the Eternal Ice. S. Drew
Beyond the Forest. S. Engstrand
Beyond the Fourth Door. J. J. Deegan
Beyond the Frontier. F. A. M. Webster
Beyond the Frontiers. L. Cargill
Beyond the Grave. M. Muller
Beyond the Law. E. Dalton
Beyond the Law. A. Murray
Beyond the Law. A. Patrick
Beyond the Law. A. H. Vincent
Beyond the Law. G. Warden
Beyond the Locked Door. L. Allan
Beyond the Mountain. W. Dieter
Beyond the Night. C. Woolrich
Beyond the Outposts. J. B. Hendryx
Beyond the Prize. M. Denning
Beyond the Rainbow. M. Chittenden
Beyond the Rim. G. K. Lovelady
Beyond the Skyline. R. Aitken
Beyond the Skyline. R. Hardinge
Beyond the Stone Heaps. Ian Anderson
Beyond the Wicked. W. H. Bagbey
Beyond the Windswept Sea. C. G. Page
Beyond These Voices. M. E. Braddon
Beyond This Place. A. J. Cronin
Beyond This Point Are Monsters. M. Millar
Beyond Tolerance. Hank Hobson
Bhunda Jewels. A. Worboys
Bianca. F. Stevenson
Bianca in Black. E. S. Rohmer
Bicycle Detective. Old Sleuth
Bicycle Highwayman. F. M. Bicknell
Bicycle Jim. Old Sleuth
Bicycle Ride. G. F. Turner
Bid. P. Palliser
Bid for a Coronet. A. M. Williamson
Bid for Beauty. H. Janson
Bid for Empire. A. Griffiths
Bid for Fortune. G. Boothby
Bid for Freedom. G. Boothby
Bid for Life. S. Campbell
Bid Me Discourse. M. C. Hay
Bid the Babe Bye-Bye. Carter Brown
Bidders. John Baxter
Bidding. John Baxter
Bier for a Chaser. R. Foster
Bier for a Hussy. A. Holt
Big Apple. S. Myles
Big Apple Money Is Rotten to the Core. J. M. Glazner
Big Bang. R. Goulart
Big Bear, Little Bear. D. Brierley
Big Bedroom. E. Ronns
Big Ben Alibi. Neil Gordon
Big Ben Looks On! J. Guildford
Big Ben Strikes Eleven. D. Magarshack
Big Ben Struck Twelve. A. Wood
Big Bet. E. H. Heth
Big Bite. Gerry Travis
Big Bite. C. Williams
Big Black. S. Myles
Big Blackmail. Frank King
Big Blackout. D. Tracy
Big Blonde. D. Haring
Big Blue Death. J. Milton
Big Bob. G. Simenon
Big Boodle. R. Sylvester
Big Boss. R. Gar
Big Bounce. E. Leonard
Big Bow Mystery. I. Zangwill
Big Boys. M. Ehrlich
Big Boys. D. Leach
Big Boys Don't Cry. M. Corrigan
Big Brain. B. Gray
Big Brass Ring. D. Tracy
Big Breakout. C. Whiting
Big Bridge. R. M. Stern
Big Brokers. I. Shulman
Big Brother, and other stories. R. Beach
Big Bruiser. A. Eichler
Big Business Murder. G. D. H. Cole
Big Bust. E. Lacy
Big Byte. P. J. Ognibene
Big C. M. Cronin
Big Call. G. Ashe
Big Caper. D. Haring
Big Caper. L. White
Big Cat. C. Short
Big Chance. V. Scannell
Big Chill. B. Copper
Big Chip. E. Cannon
Big Chip. W. R. Philbrick
Big Circus Mystery. H. King
Big City. J. G. Brandon
Big City Girl. C. Williams
Big Clock. K. Fearing
Big Come-On. D. Haring
Big Contract. D. Haring
Big Cough. A. Saunders
Big Dano. R. Arana

Title Index

Big Dark. S. Hanlon
Big Day. B. Unsworth
Big Deal. E. Ellison
Big Deal. A. Evans
Big Deal. P. Malloch
Big Deal in Veraqua. P. Morales
Big Dig. S. McGurk
Big Dive. K. F. Crossen
Big Dream. S. Fisher
Big Drop and other Cliff Hardy stories. P. Corris
Big Ear. S. Sterling
Big Easy. J. Conaway
Big Enchilada. L. A. Morse
Big Enough Wreath. W. Garner
Big Fake. M. Forbes
Big Fall. Ralph Hayes
Big Fall. T. B. Reagan
Big Fear. T. Durrant
Big Feeling. D. Karp
Big Fish. F. Beeding
Big Fish. R. Charles
Big Fish. T. Perry
Big Fish. R. Wills
Big Fix. A. Barker
Big Fix. M. Colton
Big Fix. R. Drayton
Big Fix. Spike Gordon
Big Fix. E. Jarvis
Big Fix. E. Lacy
Big Fix. R. L. Simon
Big Foot. E. Wallace
Big Four. A. Christie
Big Four. E. Wallace
Big Frame. J. K. Baxter
Big Frame. The Gordons
Big Frame. Sam Merwin
Big Frogs and Little Frogs. S. Ertz
Big Gamble. G. H. Coxe
Big Game. M. Brand
Big Game. P. Quinn
Big Game. L. L. Stevenson
Big Game. F. Wallace
Big Gold Dream. C. Himes
Big Goodbye. Peter Chambers
Big Goodnight. J. Gardiner
Big Grab. D. Haring
Big Grab. J. Trinian
Big Greed. K. Giles
Big Grouse. Douglas Clark
Big Guy. Wade Miller
Big H. H. Janson
Big H. Bryan Peters
Big Hamburger. H. Helfer
Big Hand for the Corpse. G. Bagby
Big Haul. A. S. Sherring
Big Heart. J. G. Brandon
Big Heat. W. P. McGivern
Big Heist. H. C. Davis
Big Hit. J. Readus
Big House. J. Lait
Big Island. J. Raines
Big Ivy. J. McCague
Big Job. J. Boland
Big Kidnap. A. Tack
Big Kill. R. Hausfeld
Big Kill. D. Pendleton
Big Kill. M. Spillane
Big Killing. P. Malloch
Big Killing. Annette Meyers
Big Killing. N. Morland
Big Kiss. O. Denoux
Big Kiss-Off. D. Haring
Big Kiss-Off. D. Keene
Big Kiss-Off of 1944. A. Bergman
Big Knife. C. Odets
Big Knockover. D. Hammett
Big League Lady! D. Haring
Big Lie. H. Janson
Big Loser. E. Kennedy
Big Lure. W. Manners
Big M. L. Powell
Big Make. G. Paul
Big Man. Edward Brown
Big Man. W. McIlvanney

Big Man. R. Marsten
Big Man, a Fast Man. B. Appel
Big Man in Saludas. F. Rosenwald
Big Midget Murders. C. Rice
Big Mike. C. G. Givens
Big Money. H. Atkinson
Big Money. H. Q. Masur
Big Money-Box. A. La Bern
Big Morning Blues. Gordon M. Williams
Big Needle. S. Myles
Big Nick. P. Buranelli
Big Night. I. Andersen
Big Night. S. Ellin
Big Night at Mrs. Maria's. B. Parrish
Big Noise. G. Courtis
Big Nowhere. J. Ellroy
Big One. H. Arnston
Big One. J. Cutter
Big Paddle. Robin Moore
Big Panic. B. Banarto
Big Payoff. J. Law
Big Payoff. R. Novak
Big Phil's Kid. M. M. Parker
Big Picture. D. Whitelaw
Big Picture. M. Wolk
Big Racket. Roland Daniel
Big Radium Mystery. M. E. Cooke
Big Red Sun. D. Larany
Big Red's Daughter. J. McPartland
Big Rip-Off. B. Copper
Big Rip-Off. S. Stewart
Big Round Bed. H. Janson
Big Rumble. Wenzell Brown
Big Runaround. D. L. Teilhet
Big Scam. D. Haring
Big Score. H. Barron
Big Score. Clayton Matthews
Big Scratch. Christopher Reed
Big Secret, Suzuki. J. P. Conty
Big Shot. Roland Daniel
Big Shot. D. Haring
Big Shot. F. Packard
Big Shot. D. Scanlon
Big Shot. L. Treat
Big Shot Racketeer. A. Capelli
Big Shot's Final Edition. M. Brody
Big Silence. B. Schopen
Big Sin. J. Webb
Big Sin. J. Wingrave
Big Sky Blues. R. S. Reid
Big Slam. John Powers
Big Slay. D. Haring
Big Sleep. R. Chandler
Big Smear. W. H. Baker
Big Snatch. Anthony Ferguson
Big Snatch. H. Howard
Big Snatch. B. Shannon
Big Sol. H. Von Rhau
Big Splash for Belinda. M. Brody
Big Spy Plot. D. Hill
Big Squeal. Roland Daniel
Big Squeeze. B. Arthur
Big Squeeze. M. Corrigan
Big Stake. R. Jocelyn
Big Stan. J. Monahan
Big Stash. R. Peters
Big Steal. W. H. Baker
Big Steal. E. Basinsky
Big Steal. E. A. Beilke
Big Steal. P. Malloch
Big Steal. H. Seymour
Big Steal! J. T. Story
Big Stick. L. Alexander
Big Stick-Up at Brink's! N. Behn
Big Stiffs. M. Avallone
Big Still. Roderic Wilkinson
Big Stopper. H. Kantor
Big Story. M. L. West
Big Straw Hat. Carlton Grey
Big, Strong Man! C. Edwards
Big Success. I. Gordon
Big Take. W. B. M. Ferguson
Big Tickle. M. Cronin
Big Tickle. J. Wainwright

Big Time. A. Capelli
Big Time. M. Montecino
Big Time. V. Scannell
Big Time Baby! D. Haring
Big Time Baby. R. Sterling
Big Time Girl. N. Baroni
Big Time Girl. R. Marlowe
Big-Time Racketeer. D. Linton
Big Time Tommy Sloane. J. Reardon
Big Timer. W. M. Duncan
Big Timer. P. A. Foxall
Big Tomorrow. D. Bateson
Big Top Dame. N. Karta
Big Town Round-Up. W. M. Raine
Big Trail. C. Houghton
Big Twist. Hank Hobson
Big Water. M. Derby
Big Wind for Summer. G. Black
Big Woman. M. Colton
Big X. D. Tracy
Bigamist. J. J. Chichester
Bigamy Kiss. S. Harragan
Bigger They Are. J. Ditton
Bigger They Are. H. Lugar
Bigger They Come. A. A. Fair
Biggest Holdup. J. F. Dinneen
Biggles—Air Commodore. W. E. Johns
Biggles—Air Detective. W. E. Johns
Biggles & Co. W. E. Johns
Biggles and the Black Mask. W. E. Johns
Biggles and the Black Pearl. W. E. Johns
Biggles and the Black-Raider. W. E. Johns
Biggles and the Blue Moon. W. E. Johns
Biggles and the Dark Intruder. W. E. Johns
Biggles and the Deep Blue Sea. W. E. Johns
Biggles and the Gun-Runners. W. E. Johns
Biggles and the Leopards of Zinn. W. E. Johns
Biggles and the Little Green God. W. E. Johns
Biggles and the Lost Sovereigns. W. E. Johns
Biggles and the Missing Millionaire. W. E. Johns
Biggles and the Noble Lord. W. E. Johns
Biggles and the Penitent Thief. W. E. Johns
Biggles and the Pirate Treasure. W. E. Johns
Biggles and the Plane That Disappeared. W. E. Johns
Biggles and the Plot That Failed. W. E. Johns
Biggles and the Poor Rich Boy. W. E. Johns
Biggles at World's End. W. E. Johns
Biggles Breaks the Silence. W. E. Johns
Biggles Buries a Hatchet. W. E. Johns
Biggles—Charter Pilot. W. E. Johns
Biggles' Chinese Puzzle. W. E. Johns
Biggles' Combined Operation. W. E. Johns
Biggles Cuts It Fine. W. E. Johns
Biggles Defies the Swastika. W. E. Johns
Biggles Delivers the Goods. W. E. Johns
Biggles Fails to Return. W. E. Johns
Biggles Flies Again. W. E. Johns
Biggles Flies East. W. E. Johns
Biggles Flies North. W. E. Johns
Biggles Flies South. W. E. Johns
Biggles Flies to Work. W. E. Johns
Biggles Flies West. W. E. Johns
Biggles Follows On. W. E. Johns
Biggles, Foreign Legionnaire. W. E. Johns
Biggles Forms a Syndicate. W. E. Johns
Biggles Gets His Man. W. E. Johns
Biggles Goes Alone. W. E. Johns
Biggles Goes Home. W. E. Johns
Biggles Goes to School. W. E. Johns
Biggles Goes to War. W. E. Johns
Biggles Hunts Big Game. W. E. Johns
Biggles in Africa. W. E. Johns
Biggles in Australia. W. E. Johns
Biggles in Borneo. W. E. Johns
Biggles in Mexico. W. E. Johns
Biggles in Spain. W. E. Johns
Biggles in the Baltic. W. E. Johns
Biggles in the Blue. W. E. Johns
Biggles in the Cruise of the Condor. W. E. Johns
Biggles in the Gobi. W. E. Johns
Biggles in the Orient. W. E. Johns
Biggles in the South Seas. W. E. Johns
Biggles in the Terai. W. E. Johns

B

B

Biggles in the Underworld. W. E. Johns
Biggles Investigates. W. E. Johns
Biggles Learns to Fly. W. E. Johns
Biggles Looks Back. W. E. Johns
Biggles Makes Ends Meet. W. E. Johns
Biggles of the Camel Squadron. W. E. Johns
Biggles of the Interpol. W. E. Johns
Biggles of the Special Air Police. W. E. Johns
Biggles of 266. W. E. Johns
Biggles on Mystery Island. W. E. Johns
Biggles on the Home Front. W. E. Johns
Biggles, Pioneer Air Fighter. W. E. Johns
Biggles Presses On. W. E. Johns
Biggles Scores a Bull. W. E. Johns
Biggles' Second Case. W. E. Johns
Biggles—Secret Agent. W. E. Johns
Biggles Sees It Through. W. E. Johns
Biggles Sees Too Much. W. E. Johns
Biggles Sets a Trap. W. E. Johns
Biggles Sorts It Out. W. E. Johns
Biggles' Special Case. W. E. Johns
Biggles Sweeps the Desert. W. E. Johns
Biggles Takes a Hand. W. E. Johns
Biggles Takes a Holiday. W. E. Johns
Biggles Takes Charge. W. E. Johns
Biggles Takes It Rough. W. E. Johns
Biggles Takes the Case. W. E. Johns
Biggle's Wharf. Brothers Owen
Biggles Works It Out. W. E. Johns
Bigtime Payoff. R. Banarto
Bijoux. F. Des Ligneris
Bike Bastards. G. Warren
Bikie Birds. Stuart Hall
Bikie Hell. Stuart Hall
Bikie Hellcats. Stuart Hall
Bikie Rumble. Stuart Hall
Bikini Bombshell. B. McKnight
Bikini Red North. T. Barling
Bilbao Looking Glass. C. MacLeod
Bill. John Burke
Bill 2. John Burke
Bill 3. John Burke
Bill 4. John Burke
Bill Blunders Through. A. Webb
Bill for Damages. N. Easton
Bill for the Use of a Body. D. Wheatley
Bill Marshall, Turf Sleuth. E. Woodward
Bill of Intictment. G. Sava
Bill Speed on Hot Ice. J. B. Donovan
Bill Speed—Special Squad. J. B. Donovan
Billboard Madonna. J. Trevor
Billiard Marker. W. V. Burgess
Billiard-Room Mystery. B. Flynn
Billiard Table Murders. G. Baxter
Billiards in Mufti. F. L. B. Greig
Billie Finds the Answer. H. C. McNeile
Billikin Courier. T. C. Lewellen
Billingsgate Shoal. R. Boyer
Billion Dollar Body. J. Shallit
Billion Dollar Brain. L. Deighton
Billion Dollar Catch. J. J. McNamara, Jr.
Billion Dollar Death. J. Nazel
Billion-Dollar Hold-Up. M. Calland
Billion Dollar Killing. P. E. Erdman
Billion Dollar Sure Thing. P. E. Erdman
Billionaire. P. James
Billionaire Mission. J. Rosenberger
Billions. I. K. Martin
Billy. W. Strieber
Billy Bathgate. E. L. Doctorow
Billy Binks, Hero, and other stories. G. Boothby
Billy Cantrell Case. H. Waugh
Billy Hamilton. A. C. Gunter
Billy Irish. T. Babe
Billy Mischief, a Regular Trained Detective. Old Sleuth
Billy Pagan, Mining Engineer. Randolph Bedford
Billy Preston. Old Sleuth
Billy Rags. T. Lewis
Billy, the Tramp. Old Sleuth
Billy's Army. N. Babcock
Billy's Bargain. E. Everett-Green
Billy's Brother. Kenneth Martin
Biltmore Call. V. Siller

Bimbashi Baruk of Egypt. S. Rohmer
Bimbo Heaven. M. H. Albert
Bimbos of the Death Sun. S. McCrumb
Bimini Run. Howard Hunt
Binary. J. Lange
Bind. S. Ellin
Binding Spell. Elizabeth Arthur
Bindlestiff. B. Pronzini
Binnacle Jack. Anonymous
Binnacle Jack. M. Mizzen
Bino. A. W. Gray
Bio-Assassins. G. Posner
Bio Blitz. A. Sugar
Biographs of Babylon. G. R. Sims
Birch Dene. W. Westall
Birchwood. J. Banville
Bird. T. Hinde
Bird Cage. E. O'Duffy
Bird-Cage. Kenneth O'Hara
Bird in a Guilt-Edged Cage. Carter Brown
Bird in Last Year's Nest. S. Herron
Bird in the Chimney. D. Eden
Bird in the Hand. A. Cleeves
Bird in the Hand. G. T. Root
Bird in the Hand. Lee Trench
Bird in the Net. F. Parrish
Bird Isle. A. Wade
Bird of Paradise. C. T. C. James
Bird of Paradise. E. P. Oppenheim
Bird of Prey. V. Canning
Bird of Prey. M. Cumberland
Bird of Prey. C. Toomey
Bird of Strange Plumage. J. L. Rickard
Bird Walking Weather. G. Bagby
Bird Watcher. J. A. Morris
Bird Watchers. M. Taylor
Birdcage. J. Cannan
Birdcage. V. Canning
Birdcage Murders. G. L. Westbie
Birds and other stories. D. Du Maurier
Birds in the Belfry. L. Payne
Bird's Nest. S. Jackson
Birds of a Bloodied Feather. R. Tate
Birds of a Feather. A. Spiller
Birds of a Feather Affair. M. Avallone
Birds of Death. K. Robeson
Birds of Destruction. Stuart Hall
Birds of Ill Omen. K. M. Knight
Birds of Prey. M. E. Braddon
Birds of Prey. G. Bronson-Howard
Birds of Prey. A. C. Brown
Birds of Prey. Nicholas Carter
Birds of Prey. G. Fairlie
Birds of Prey. J. R. Saul
Birds of Prey. Maxwell Scott
Birds of the Night. Austin Moore
Birdwatcher. E. Gordon
Birdwatcher's Quarry. M. Coles
Birkinshaw. A. Du Maurier
Birth of a Dark Soul. B. Cleeve
Birthday. E. L. Withers
Birthday, Deathday. H. Pentecost
Birthday Gift. U. Curtiss
Birthday Gifts and other stories. G. D. H. Cole
Birthday Girl. R. Rush
Birthday Murder. Lange Lewis
Birthday Murder. W. Sproul
Birthday Party. H. Pinter
Birthday Party and other stories. A. A. Milne
Birthday Treat. R. Rush
Birthmark. C. Houghton
Birthmark of Fear. Marsha Alexander
Bishop As Pawn. R. McInerny
Bishop in Check. S. Rattray
Bishop in the Back Seat. Clarissa Watson
Bishop Misbehaves. Frederick Jackson
Bishop Murder Case. S. S. Van Dine
Bishop Must Move. K. Bird
Bishop of Hell. M. Bowen
Bishop Pendle. F. Hume
Bishop's Amazement. D. C. Murray
Bishop's Bible. D. C. Murray
Bishop's Cap. J. L. Linklater
Bishop's Cap Murder. J. L. Linklater

Bishop's Crime. H. C. Bailey
Bishop's Emeralds. H. Townley
Bishop's Gambit. T. Cobb
Bishop's Gambit. C. Haynes
Bishop's Move. L. Hiscott
Bishop's Palace. Jan Alexander
Bishop's Park Mystery. D. Dike
Bishop's Pawn. Ritchie Perry
Bishop's Purse. C. Moffett
Bishop's Room. K. Meyer
Bishop's Scapegoat. T. B. Clegg
Bishop's Secret. F. Hume
Bishop's Sword. N. Berrow
Bismarck Cross. S. L. Thompson
Bismarck Herrings. M. Torrie
Bit and Bridal. H. Smart
Bit of a Shunt Up the River. D. Cory
Bit of Human Nature. D. C. Murray
Bit of Red May. O. Dale
Bitch. G. Brewer
Bitch. Jackie Collins
Bite. E. Corder
Bite. C. E. Dibb
Bite of an Apple, and other stories. Nicholas Carter
Bite of the Leech. W. A. MacKenzie
Bite of the Tigress. C. J. Wohlfrom
Bite the Hand. R. Fenisong
Biter. Jack Lang
Biting Fortune. W. Mills
Bits and Pieces. J. C. Masterman
Bits and Pieces. G. Robey
Bits of Broken China. W. E. S. Fales
Bits of Paradise. F. S. Fitzgerald
Bitten by the Tarantula. J. MacLaren-Ross
Bitter Autumn. C. D. Peel
Bitter Beauty. R. Dudgeon
Bitter Conquest. C. Blackstock
Bitter Enders. P. Leslie
Bitter Ending. A. Irving
Bitter Ends. R. Bloch
Bitter Finish. L. J. Barnes
Bitter Fortune. J. Boland
Bitter Gold Hearts. Glen Cook
Bitter Harvest. W. Haggard
Bitter Heritage. D. Noel
Bitter Homicide. M. Warden
Bitter Honey. J. Blackmore
Bitter Honey. D. Noel
Bitter Honeycomb. June Scott
Bitter Is the Fruit. C. J. Collins
Bitter Is the Harvest. T. Craig
Bitter Is the Rind. H. Smart
Bitter Justice. S. Cowan
Bitter Lake. L. P. Bachmann
Bitter Lemon Mob. M. Urquhart
Bitter Love. J. Blackmore
Bitter Love. E. Woodward
Bitter Medicine. S. Paretsky
Bitter Orange. Desmond Hamill
Bitter Path of Death. P. Audemars
Bitter Reason. F. Cowen
Bitter Reckoning. J. Payn
Bitter Rubies. J. Storm
Bitter Springs. Clifford King
Bitter Sweet Summer. O. Sinclair
Bitter Tea. G. Black
Bitter Test. J. Templeton
Bitter Water. Douglas Clark
Bittermeads Mystery. E. R. Punshon
Bittern Point. V. MacFadyen
Bitters Wood. U. Nightingale
Bittersweet. S. Clausse
Bizzy-Quizzy the Great. W. R. Bowker
Black. E. Wallace
Black Abbot. E. Wallace
Black Abolitionist. J. F. Bradley
Black Account. D. Jordan
Black Ace. G. Dilnot
Black Ace. K. Gordon
Black Against the Mob. O. Fletcher
Black Agent. B. Flynn
Black Alchemists. G. Wilson
Black Alert. A. White
Black Alibi. F. Vivian

Black Alibi. C. Woolrich
Black Alice. T. Demijohn
Black Amber. P. A. Whitney
Black Ambrosia. E. Engstrom
Black and Deadly. C. A. Harris
Black and the Red. Elliot Paul
Black and the White. H. Towson
Black Angel. Anonymous
Black Angel. D. Brandt
Black Angel. B. Kingsley
Black Angel. Snip Taylor
Black Angel. C. Woolrich
Black Angels. S. Hobbs
Black Angus. N. Thornburg
Black Arab. J. Halstead
Black Arab. Operator 1384
Black Arrows. F. Beeding
Black As He's Painted. N. Marsh
Black Asp. J. L. Hamilton
Black Assassin. J. Readus
Black Attendant. H. McCutcheon
Black August. D. Wheatley
Black Aura. J. Sladek
Black Automatic. W. B. Mowery
Black Autumn. E. Evans
Black Bag. E. Jones-Evans
Black Bag. L. J. Vance
Black Ball. E. D. Pierson
Black Band. Anonymous
Black Band. M. E. Braddon
Black Bar. G. M. Fenn
Black Baroness. D. Wheatley
Black Bartlemy's Treasure. J. Farnol
Black Bat. A. Murray
Black Bat Rides the Sky. G. E. Rochester
Black Bat's Invisible Enemy. G. W. Jones
Black Beadle. E. C. R. Lorac
Black Bean. Thormanby
Black Beret. P. Fry
Black Berets. M. McCray
Black Bess. N. Gould
Black Bird. Alexander Edwards
Black Bird. Steve Mackenzie
Black, Black Hearse. F. Freyer
Black, Black Witch. K. Robeson
Black Blood. G. M. Fenn
Black Blood. Jon Hart
Black Blood. A. L. Martin
Black Book. G. Bronson-Howard
Black Bottle. R. S. L. Harding
Black Box. T. C. H. Jacobs
Black Box. C. Kearey
Black Box. E. P. Oppenheim
Black Box. M. P. Shiel
Black Box Murder. Anonymous
Black Bread. W. B. M. Ferguson
Black Bridge to China. Nancy Martin
Black Buck. L. C. Hopkins
Black Bullets. Gavin Holt
Black Burying. H. Carstairs
Black Business. H. Smart
Black Butterfly. W. A. MacKenzie
Black Cabinet. A. Feist
Black Cabinet. P. Wentworth
Black Caesar. T. Strauss
Black Caesar's Clan. A. P. Terhune
Black Camel. E. D. Biggers
Black Camelot. D. Kyle
Black Camels. R. Johnston
Black Camels of Qashran. R. Johnston
Black Candle. E. Harris
Black Candle. C. Randell
Black Cap. Gwyn Evans
Black Cap for Murder. A. Spiller
Black Cap Murder. V. Gunn
Black Card. P. Brebner
Black Card. C. Lys
Black Cargo. W. M. Graydon
Black Carnation. F. Hume
Black Casket. L. Powell
Black Castle. Anonymous
Black Castle. J. J. Farjeon
Black Cat. R. Brome
Black Cat. R. St. Clair

Black Cat. L. Tracy
Black Cat Murder. R. McRae
Black Cat Murders. B. E. M. Ward
Black Cats Are Lucky. A. Fielding
Black Chalice. C. Goodall
Black Chamber. D. Chacko
Black Champagne. G. B. Mair
Black Charade. John Burke
Black Chariots. K. Robeson
Black Chateau. G. E. Rochester
Black Cherry Blues. J. L. Burke
Black Christmas. T. Altman
Black Christmas. L. Hays
Black Chronicle. W. E. Hayes
Black Chrysanethemum. A. Murray
Black Circle. C. Baines
Black Circle. Mansfield Scott
Black Cloak Murders. C. Buchanan
Black Coat. Constance Little
Black Coffee. A. Christie
Black Company. W. B. M. Ferguson
Black Connection. Randolph Harris
Black Cop. D. Gober
Black Coral. N. Ferguson
Black Corridors. Constance Little
Black Cotton Gloves. P. Fry
Black Country Sketches. Amy Lyons
Black Cripple. R. Keverne
Black Cross. J. M. Walsh
Black Cross Mystery. H. Corkran
Black Curl. Constance Little
Black Curtain. C. Woolrich
Black Cypress. F. Crane
Black Dagger. E. S. Brooks
Black Dahlia. J. Ellroy
Black Dark Murders. R. O. Saber
Black Death. H. Adams
Black Death. Nick Carter
Black Death. M. Dalton
Black Death. Anthony Gilbert
Black Death. R. K. Largent
Black Death. M. McCracken
Black Death. K. Robeson
Black Death. T. H. Stone
Black Deeds in Whitehorse. A. McDonald
Black Destiny. C. Rushton
Black Devil. T. C. H. Jacobs
Black Dice. D. Pendleton
Black Doctor and other tales of terror and mystery. A. C. Doyle
Black Dog. G. Goff
Black Doll. W. E. Hayes
Black Door. C. F. Adams
Black Door. V. Markham
Black Door. C. Wilcox
Black Dougal. D. Walker
Black Douglas. John Brown
Black Dragon. Kirk Mitchell
Black Dragon. J. M. Walsh
Black Dream. Constance Little
Black Drop. Alice Brown
Black Drop. H. Nisbet
Black Dudley Murder. M. Allingham
Black Dwarf. M. Molloy
Black Eagle. Roland Daniel
Black Eagle. G. H. Teed
Black Eagle Mystery. G. Bonner
Black Eagle Mystery. Anthony Thomas
Black Eagles Are Flying. F. V. Morse
Black Eagle's Last Round. Anonymous
Black Eagle's Millions. Anthony Thomas
Black Eagle's Return. Anthony Thomas
Black Eagle's Treasure Trail. Anthony Thomas
Black Edged. B. Flynn
Black Emperor. F. Gerard
Black Emperor. G. H. Teed
Black Envelope. D. Frome
Black Exorcist. J. Nazel
Black Express. Constance Little
Black Eye. Constance Little
Black Eye. N. Steed
Black Eye Snapshot. B. Lebhar
Black-Eyed Stranger. C. Armstrong
Black Fame. J. C. Ellis

Black Fan. M. B. O'Reilly
Black Fear. J. Halstead
Black Feather. B. Atlee
Black Feather. E. Cutcheon
Black Fedora. H. Lugar
Black Fetish. D. T. Lindsey
Black Finger. D. Newton
Black Fire. L. Goldman
Black Flame. J. Halstead
Black Flamingo. V. Canning
Black Flamingo. K. Norris
Black Fog. C. J. Dutton
Black Folder. D. Brett
Black for a Bride. J. Marie
Black for the Baron. Anthony Morton
Black Fox. H. F. Heard
Black Friday. D. Goodis
Black Fugitive. Eddie Stone
Black Fury. J. Nazel
Black Gambit. Eric Clark
Black Gang. H. C. McNeile
Black Gangster. D. Goines
Black Gangster. D. Steele
Black Garden. C. Arnothy
Black Gardenia. Elliot Paul
Black General. A. Southcott
Black Gestapo. J. Nazel
Black Ghost. R. Carlisle
Black Ghost. A. C. Martens
Black Ghost. J. M. Walsh
Black Ghost of the Highway. G. Linnell
Black Girl Lost. D. Goines
Black Girl, White Girl. P. Moyes
Black-Girl, White-Lady. A. Hyder
Black Glass City. J. Philips
Black Glove. G. Miller
Black Glove. J. G. Sarasin
Black Gloves. Constance Little
Black Goatee. Constance Little
Black Godfather. O. Fletcher
Black Gold. G. Morton
Black Gold. A. P. Terhune
Black Gold Briefing. P. Buck
Black Gold Murders. J. B. Ethan
Black Gold of Malverde. R. L. Graves
Black Gold, Red Death. D. L. Lindsay
Black Grandee. J. McCulley
Black Gravity. C. Ryan
Black Gull Rock. M. Gerard
Black Gunn. L. Pryce
Black Hammer. M. McCracken
Black Hand. Anonymous
Black Hand. W. C. Blakeman
Black Hand. A. B. Reeve
Black Hate. J. Halstead
Black Hawk. J. Reach
Black Hawk. G. E. Rochester
Black Hawthorn. J. S. Strange
Black Hazard. M. Reisner
Black-Headed Pins. Constance Little
Black Heart. M. E. Cooke
Black Heart. S. Horler
Black Heart. E. V. Lustbader
Black Hearts and Slow Dancing. E. W. Emerson
Black Hearts Murder. E. Queen
Black Heather. V. Coffman
Black Highway. J. N. Chance
Black-Hill Murder Case. R. Hardinge
Black Hogan Strikes Again. P. Renwick
Black Hole of Carcos. J. Shirley
Black Honey. C. R. Gull
Black Honey. P. Saxon
Black Honeymoon. Constance Little
Black Horse Running. J. Wood
Black Horse Tavern. R. Danton
Black Hotel. A. Laurance
Black Hour. R. Dudgeon
Black House. R. Bridges
Black House. P. Highsmith
Black House. Constance Little
Black House. Maxwell Scott
Black House in Harley Street. J. S. Fletcher
Black Hunchback. G. Verner
Black Hunter. Eddie Stone

Black Ice. C. Dunne
Black Ice Score. R. Stark
Black Image. F. Hume
Black Incense. A. M. Williamson
Black Inheritance. J. MacEnery
Black Ink Mystery. Gareth H. Browning
Black Inquisitor. Rex Madison
Black Iris. Constance Little
Black Is Beautiful. B. B. Johnson
Black Is Black. J. Nazel
Black Is the Color. J. Brunner
Black Is the Colour of My True Love's Heart. Ellis Peters
Black Is the Colour of My True Love's Heart. C. Reynolds
Black Is the Fashion for Dying. Jonathan Latimer
Black Italian. S. Jepson
Black Jack. G. Watson
Black Jack Rides Again. L. Wibberley
Black Jess, the Outlaw. Old Sleuth
Black John of Halfaday Creek. J. B. Hendryx
Black Joker. I. Ostrander
Black Joss. J. G. Brandon
Black Judas. B. Wilkinson
Black Justice. Stella Shepherd
Black Key. M. S. Michel
Black Knight in Red Square. S. M. Kaminsky
Black Knights. G. N. Smith
Black Lace Blackmail. K. T. McCall
Black Lace Hangover. Carter Brown
Black Lady. Constance Little
Black Lake. W. Magnay
Black Land, White Land. H. C. Bailey
Black Leather Barbarians. P. Stadley
Black Leather Case. M. Cronin
Black Leather Murders. D. Rutherford
Black Legend. J. Horton
Black Light. T. Howard
Black Light. G. Kinnell
Black Light. T. Mundy
Black Light. B. Reynolds
Black Limelight. G. Sherry
Black Limousine. W. W. Sayer
Black Lobster. D. Weir
Black Look. M. Butterworth
Black Madonna. D. Haring
Black Mafia. P. Rabe
Black Magic. Chris Allen
Black Magic. "Capstan"
Black Magic. A. Goetz
Black Magic. T. S. King
Black Magic. W. Strieber
Black Magician. R. T. M. Scott
Black Mail. D. M. Disney
Black Mail. N. Steed
Black Mamba. A. Broome
Black Man—White Maiden. G. R. Preedy
Black Man, White Man, Dead Man. M. J. Kingsley
Black Mantle. T. P. Prest
Black Marble. J. Wambaugh
Black Marble Pool. S. Leventhal
Black Maria. L. O. Johnson
Black Maria, M.A. J. Slate
Black Maria Mystery. W. J. Bayfield
Black Market. Roland Daniel
Black Market. B. Newman
Black Market. J. Patterson
Black Market. D. E. Zlotnik
Black Market Murders. Anonymous
Black Market Murders. H. Keyworth
Black Market Murders. J. Van Dyke
Black Market Soldiers. A. J. Levatino
Black Mask. J. Cournos
Black Mask. D. Goodwin
Black Mask. E. W. Hornung
Black Mask. A. L. Smith
Black Mass. F. Breton
Black Mass. G. C. Lethbridge
Black Massacre. L. Derrick
Black Master. M. Grant
Black Mastery. J. Turtle
Black Matador. A. West
Black Mesa. A. Thurlo
Black Midnight. G. Diamond

Black Midnight. A. Lowing
Black Mirror. B. Benson
Black Mirror. Winifred Duke
Black Mitre. W. M. Duncan
Black Mole. G. E. Rochester
Black Money. R. Macdonald
Black Money. G. H. Rosen
Black Monk. Anonymous
Black Monk. T. P. Prest
Black Monk. P. Urquhart
Black Moon. Alison Drake
Black Moon. L. D. Estleman
Black Moon. R. Potts
Black Morning. A. Bocca
Black Moth. G. Heyer
Black Moth. C. Runyon
Black Motor-Car. J. B. Harris-Burland
Black Mountain. R. Stout
Black Nail. A. Applin
Black Napoleon. J. Dark
Black Narc. J. Feinman
Black Nat. J. Halstead
Black Night in Red Square. S. M. Kaminsky
Black Night Murders. C. Well
Black Octopus. G. E. Rochester
Black Office. A. Castle
Black Onyx Ring. Colin Robertson
Black Opal. L. Allan
Black Opal. A. De Bremont
Black Opal. Maxwell Gray
Black Opal. J. L. Linklater
Black Opal Mine. A. Murray
Black Orchestra. R. Vacha
Black Orchid. G. Goodchild
Black Orchid. N. Meyer
Black Orchid. E. Ronns
Black Orchid. B. Vane
Black Orchid. H. Zore
Black Orchids. R. Stout
Black Out. E. Dane
Black Out. A. O. Pollard
Black Out. D. Whitelaw
Black-Out Crime. G. Chester
Black-Out in Gretley. J. B. Priestley
Black-Out Murder. D. Whitelaw
Black-Out Murders. L. Grex
Black Owl. W. LeQueux
Black Palm. M. McCray
Black Panther. Anonymous
Black Parrot. H. Hervey
Black Parrot. O. Lethbridge
Black Patch. F. Hume
Black Patch. G. C. K. Seymer
Black Path of Fear. C. Woolrich
Black Pavilion. Augustus Muir
Black Paw. Constance Little
Black Pawn. Bruce Norman
Black Pearl. J. Kaiser
Black Pearl. V. Sardou
Black Pearl. Mrs. W. Woodrow
Black Pearl and The Vikings. P. O'Donnell
Black Pearl Murders. M. S. Buchanan
Black Pearl of Passion. D. Day
Black Pearls. J. L. Roberts
Black Peril. W. E. Johns
Black Phantoms. P. Cruger
Black Piano. Constance Little
Black Pigeon. Anne Austin
Black Plume. D. Madsen
Black Plumes. M. Allingham
Black Police. A. J. Vogan
Black Poppy. D. Haring
Black Prince. Anonymous
Black Prophet. J. Nazel
Black Rage. Butch Holmes
Black Raiders. G. E. Rochester
Black Rain. M. Cogan
Black Rain. G. Simenon
Black Rainbow. B. Michaels
Black Rat. T. A. Plummer
Black Raven. Roland Daniel
Black Renegades. J. Readus
Black Reprieve. D. Sanderson
Black Ribbon Murders. T. A. Plummer

Black River Emerald. Peter Ryan
Black Robber. E. Ball
Black Robe. W. Collins
Black Robe. G. Morton
Black Rook. Mary Douglas
Black Room. C. Short
Black Room. Colin Wilson
Black Rose. G. Croudace
Black Rose. F. Huebner
Black Rose Murder. P. McGuire
Black Royalty. A. Mills
Black Rustle. Constance Little
Black Sabbat. J. B. Herman
Black Sadhu. E. P. Thorne
Black Sambo Affair. V. Gielgud
Black Samurai. M. Olden
Black Sand. W. J. Caunitz
Black Satchel. H. S. Keeler
Black Scorpion. A. Shannon
Black Sea Bloodbath. Nick Carter
Black Sea Caper. Robin Moore
Black Sea Connection. Robin Moore
Black Seraphim. M. Gilbert
Black Seven. C. Kendall
Black Shadow. J. W. Kneeshaw
Black Shadow. P. Sebastian
Black Shadow. F. A. M. Webster
Black Shadows. G. M. Fenn
Black Sheep. S. P. Hyatt
Black Sheep. B. Spicer
Black Sheep. E. Woodward
Black Sheep. E. Yates
Black Sheep, White Lamb. D. S. Davis
Black Ship. P. Mandel
Black Shrike. I. Stuart
Black Shrouds. Constance Little
Black Shrouds the Bride. P. G. Larbalester
Black Silence. M. Leighton
Black Sister. D. Edqvist
Black Skull. D. W. Steward
Black Skull. G. Verner
Black Skull Murders. Carlton Ross
Black Sky. W. H. Lovejoy
Black Slaver. S. Hope
Black Sleeves. A. M. Williamson
Black Smith. Constance Little
Black Sombrero Mystery. H. Pink
Black Spear. J. DeVries
Black Spectacles. J. D. Carr
Black Spider. Mark Cross
Black Spider. C. Dawe
Black Spider. S. P. B. Mais
Black Spiders. J. Creasey
Black Spot. K. Robeson
Black Spot. John Ross
Black Spot Mystery. A. Soutar
Black Squadron. J. Carol
Black Stage. Anthony Gilbert
Black Stamp. Will Scott
Black Star. J. McCulley
Black Star Again. J. McCulley
Black Star Murders. D. L. Gilbert
Black Star's Campaign. J. McCulley
Black Star's Return. J. McCulley
Black Star's Revenge. J. McCulley
Black Stocking. Constance Little
Black Stockings for Chelsea. P. Denver
Black Stone. G. F. Gibbs
Black Streak. W. M. Graydon
Black Summer Day. Hilary Brand
Black Sunday. Thomas Harris
Black Sunday. A. Kent
Black Sunset. E. P. Thorne
Black Swan. Nancy Graham
Black Swan. R. C. Payes
Black Swan. W. Penmare
Black Swan. R. Sabatini
Black Swastika. J. G. Brandon
Black Tarn. P. W. Wilson
Black Templar. J. Halstead
Black Temple. M. T. Garba
Black Terrace. K. Kendall
Black Terror. C. Bishop
Black Terror. F. W. Irwin

Black Terror. J. K. Leys
Black Thumb. Constance Little
Black Tide. H. Innes
Black Tide Rising. L. P. Greene
Black Tie Only. J. Fenton
Black Tortoise. F. Viller
Black Tower. P. D. James
Black Trail. E. M. Hall
Black Triangle. H. Somerville
Black Trinity. T. C. H. Jacobs
Black Troopers. J. N. Smith
Black Troopers and other stories. Anonymous
Black Tulip. S. Bate
Black Turret. P. Wynnton
Black Unicorn. June Drummond
Black Unicorns. C. Leach
Black Uprising. J. Nazel
Black Valentine. P. Sargent
Black Valise. A. Baxter
Black Valley. Anonymous
Black Valley Murders. A. Mallory
Black Vanguard. E. Atiyah
Black Velvet. C. B. Dignan
Black Velvet. Stuart Hall
Black Velvet. G. McMunn
Black Vendetta. D. Chesley
Black Vendetta. M. Gattzden
Black Venus Contract. P. Atlee
Black Vintage. M. Gerard
Black Vulture. G. Ashcroft
Black Watcher. A. Partridge
Black Weather. B. Roueche
Black Wedding. P. Jenkins
Black Wednesday. B. Crowther
Black Weever. R. Wills
Black Welcome. N. Fitzgerald
Black Whip—Gang Buster. J. Brearley
Black Whip of Arabia. J. Brearley
Black, White, and Brindled. E. Phillpotts
Black Widow. J. N. Chance
Black Widow. Bart Davis
Black Widow. Stuart Hall
Black Widow. R. Harrison
Black Widow. P. Quentin
Black Widow. J. Tobias
Black Widow. B. Tutton
Black Widow Weeps. Carter Brown
Black Widower. P. Moyes
Black Widower. A. Riefe
Black Wind. M. Asher
Black Wind. F. P. Wilson
Black Wind Blowing. P. Essex
Black Wind of Primrose Island. K. Frederick
Black Windmill. C. Egleton
Black Wings. M. Dalton
Black Wings Has My Angel. E. Chaze
Black Wolf Mystery. R. J. Diven
Black Work. M. Frederics
Black Wraith. R. Buxton
Black Yacht. J. Baxter
Blackadder. G. Croudace
Blackball. J. Sangster
Blackbird. T. Cartano
Blackbird. D. McMillan
Blackbird. J. Merek
Blackbird. R. Stark
Blackbird Sings of Murder. W. M. Duncan
Blackbirder. D. B. Hughes
Blackboard Jungle. E. Hunter
Blackbourne Hall. E. Grandower
Blackdrop Hall. H. Carstairs
Blacker Than Murder. W. Woolfolk
Blackeyes. D. Potter
Blackfingers. J. Cassells
Blackgable Inn. M. Eyre
Blackground. Joan Aiken
Blackguard. P. Trent
Blackhall Ghosts. S. Tytler
Blackheath Poisonings. J. Symons
Blackhope Legend. G. Fraser
Blackjack Blonde. P. Haring
Blackjack Hijack. C. Einstein
Blackladies. E. Everett-Green
Blacklash. J. Brunner

Blacklash. R. Vincent
Blacklight. B. Knox
Blacklist. Andrew Taylor
Blackmail. Ruth Alexander
Blackmail. C. Bennett
Blackmail. W. T. Call
Blackmail. V. Chute
Blackmail. J. Goodwin
Blackmail. H. I. Hancock
Blackmail. J. Ironsides
Blackmail. R. Mouteney-Jephson
Blackmail. Mark Ross
Blackmail! F. M. White
Blackmail and Old Lace. T. Vail
Blackmail Beauty. Carter Brown
Blackmail de Luxe. D. Whitelaw
Blackmail for a Brunette. Carter Brown
Blackmail Gang. C. Bishop
Blackmail in Blankshire. C. A. Alington
Blackmail in Red. F. Grierson
Blackmail in Red Headlines. M. Brody
Blackmail, Inc. R. Kyle
Blackmail Incorporated. N. Harman
Blackmail Is Murder. Craig Cooper
Blackmail North. P. McCutchan
Blackmail Was a Brunette. M. Brody
Blackmailed. A. Applin
Blackmailed. W. LeQueux
Blackmailed Baronet. H. E. Hill
Blackmailed Beauty. B. Raymond
Blackmailed Redhead. B. Raymond
Blackmailed Refugee. A. Parsons
Blackmailer. G. Axelrod
Blackmailer. Roland Daniel
Blackmailer. R. C. Elliott
Blackmailer. R. Fenisong
Blackmailer. E. Klein
Blackmailer. J. Miles
Blackmailer. J. Oakley
Blackmailer. P. Trent
Blackmailer and the Blonde. Leslie Carroll
Blackmailers. H. Cecil
Blackmailers. E. Gaboriau
Blackmailers. J. Mangut
Blackmailers & Co. J. C. Ellis
Blackmailer's Bluff. Nicholas Carter
Blackmailer's Summer. P. Whalley
Blackman's Wood. E. P. Oppenheim
Blackmarket Brains. K. Hoffman
Blackmoor. J. Trevelyan
Blackout. Mark Andrews
Blackout. H. Aquin
Blackout. Constance Little
Blackout at Rehearsal. M. P. Rea
Blackout Murders. G. W. Jones
Blackout Mystery. J. Reach
Blackpool Mystery. L. Bidston
Blackpool Vanishes. R. H. Francis
Blackshirt. B. Graeme
Blackshirt Again. B. Graeme
Blackshirt at Large. B. Graeme
Blackshirt, Counter-Spy. B. Graeme
Blackshirt Finds Trouble. R. Graeme
Blackshirt Helps Himself. R. Graeme
Blackshirt in Peril. R. Graeme
Blackshirt Interferes. B. Graeme
Blackshirt Meets the Lady. R. Gareme
Blackshirt Mystery. W. M. Graydon
Blackshirt on the Spot. B. Graeme
Blackshirt Passes By. R. Graeme
Blackshirt Saves the Day. R. Graeme
Blackshirt Sees It Through. R. Graeme
Blackshirt Sets the Pace. R. Graeme
Blackshirt Stirs Things Up. R. Graeme
Blackshirt Strikes Back. B. Graeme
Blackshirt Takes a Hand. B. Graeme
Blackshirt Takes the Trail. R. Graeme
Blackshirt the Adventurer. B. Graeme
Blackshirt the Audacious. B. Graeme
Blackshirt Wins the Trick. R. Graeme
Blacksmith of Voe. P. Cushing
Blackstock Affair. F. Bandy
Blackstone. R. Falkirk
Blackstone and the Scourge of Europe. R. Falkirk

Blackstone on Broadway. R. Falkirk
Blackstone Underground. R. Falkirk
Blackstone's Fancy. R. Falkirk
Blackthorn. D. Daniels
Blackthorn. A. J. Fitzgerald
Blackthorn House. J. Rhode
Blackthorn Winter and other stories. J. D. Beresford
Blacktower. M. Lynch
Blackwater Bayou. Marilyn Austin
Blackwell's Ghost. Angela Gray
Blackwood. J. Radcliffe
Blackwood Cult. T. A. Waters
Blackwood's Daughter. H. La Barre
Blade Is Bright. S. Horler
Blade of Castlemayne. A. Esler
Blade-o'-Grass. B. L. Farjeon
Blade of Light. D. Carpenter
Blag. J. Balham
Blairmount? Blinkhoolie
Blair's Attic. J. C. Lincoln
Blake House. A. Savage
Blame the Baron. Anthony Morton
Blame the Dead. G. Lyall
Blanche. T. P. Prest
Blanche Coningham's Surrender. J. Middlemass
Blanche de Maletroit. A. E. W. Mason
Blanche Fury. E. Britton
Blanche Fury. J. Shearing
Blanche Heriot. T. P. Prest
Blanco Case. S. Horler
Bland Beginning. J. Symons
Blane Document. N. Rich
Blank Cheque. Richard Brown
Blank Cheque for Murder. O. Beeby
Blank Page. K. C. Constantine
Blank Wall. E. S. Holding
Blanket. A. A. Murray
Blanket. H. Stratton
Blanket of the Dark. B. Healey
Blast. T. Kenrick
Blast of Trumpets. G. Ashe
Blast Out in Lebanon. D. Kramer
Blasted Acre. G. Ellinger
Blatchington Tangle. G. D. H. Cole
Blayde R.I.P. J. Wainwright
Blaze at Noon. M. Clare
Blaze of Riot. J. Tucker
Blaze of Roses. E. Trevor
Blaze of Vengeance. Stuart Hall
Blazed Trail Stories. S. E. White
Blazing Affair. M. Avallone
Blazing Garage Crime. A. Blair
Blazing Launch Murder. R. Hardinge
Blazing Star. Constance Rutherford
Bleak House. C. Dickens
Bleak November. R. O'Grady
Bleak Strand. G. K. Hohn
Bled White. I. St. Clair
Bledding Sorrow. Marilyn Harris
Bleeding Heart. L. Shriver
Bleeding Hearts. T. White
Bleeding Hooks. H. Rutland
Bleeding House. Hilda Lawrence
Bleeding Sapphire. J. W. Phelps
Bleeding Scissors. B. Fischer
Bleke, the Butler. W. LeQueux
Bless the Wasp. John Ross
Blessed Among Women. A. MacLeod
Blessed Plot. E. Berckman
Blessing Way. T. Hillerman
Blessington Method, and other strange tales. S. Ellin
Bleston Mystery. R. M. Kennedy
Blight. J. Creasey
Blighted Heart. T. P. Prest
Blind. J. Harvey
Blind Alley. J. Popplewell
Blind Alley. G. Simenon
Blind Alley. B. Singer
Blind Alley. James Warwick
Blind Barber. J. D. Carr
Blind Bargain. T. B. Morris
Blind Beak. E. Dudley
Blind Beggar Murder. C. Ryland

Blind Beggar of Bethnal Green and Bessy. Anonymous
Blind Brag. J. Wainwright
Blind Cartridges. W. C. MacDonald
Blind Cave. L. Katcher
Blind Chance. J. James
Blind Chance. B. Kinglsey
Blind Chance. Mary Napier
Blind Circle. M. Renard
Blind Conspiracy. A. Hernandez
Blind Corner. D. Yates
Blind Date. D. Haring
Blind Date. Leigh Howard
Blind Date. J. Pattinson
Blind Date for a Private Eye. B. Graeme
Blind Date for a Spy. Carl Johnson
Blind Date with Death. C. Woolrich
Blind Drifts. C. B. Clason
Blind Drop. J. Nicholas
Blind Eye. J. Raymond
Blind Fear, and other stories. S. Gardiner
Blind Frog. F. Grierson
Blind Fury. S. Gluck
Blind Gambit. J. Reach
Blind Geese. Winifred Duke
Blind Girl's Buff. E. Berckman
Blind Goddess. P. Hastings
Blind Goddess. E. Troller
Blind Goddess. A. Train
Blind Hypnotist. M. Lovell
Blind Justice. I. L. Cassilis
Blind Justice. H. B. Mathers
Blind Justice. B. Symons
Blind Lead. L. L. Lynch
Blind Love. W. Collins
Blind Man. R. W. Kauffman
Blind Man with a Pistol. C. Himes
Blind Man's Bluff. E. R. Johnson
Blind Man's Bluff. B. Kendrick
Blind Man's Bluff. R. Rodd
Blind Man's Bluff. E. Toller
Blind Man's Buff. J. Futrelle
Blind Man's Buff. F. Lynde
Blind Man's Buff. A. M. Meadows
Blind Man's Buff. F. Ryerson
Blind Man's Buff. A. Wood
Blind Man's Daughter. Nicholas Carter
Blind Man's Eyes. W. MacHarg
Blind Man's Garden. S. Troy
Blind Man's Mark. B. Palmer
Blind Man's Night. J. Esteven
Blind Man's Secret. C. Brisbane
Blind Marriage, and other stories. G. R. Sims
Blind Miller. C. A. Cookson
Blind Murder. N. Perrelli
Blind Obsession. D. Noel
Blind Path. G. Simenon
Blind Pig. J. A. Jackson
Blind Pilot. A. Clancy
Blind Policy. G. M. Fenn
Blind Prophet. B. Davis
Blind Quest. W. Dainton
Blind Rage. P. Rawls
Blind Reckoning. W. Mills
Blind Run. Ken Blake
Blind Run. B. Freemantle
Blind Saw Murder. H. C. Huston
Blind Search. L. Egan
Blind Side. W. Bayer
Blind Side. F. Clifford
Blind Side. N. Cromarty
Blind Side. D. Klein
Blind Side. P. Wentworth
Blind Sight. B. Y. Benediall
Blind Spot. J. Creasey
Blind Spot. Joseph Harrington
Blind Spot. Randy Russell
Blind Spring Rambler. John Douglas
Blind Terror. W. Hughes
Blind Trust. Linda Grant
Blind Trust Kills. J. P. Wohl
Blind Villain. E. Berckman
Blindfold. L. Fletcher
Blindfold. F. Marryat
Blindfold. A. Melville-Ross
Blindfold. J. L. Rickard
Blindfold. P. Wentworth
Blindfold Game. D. Thomas
Blindfold Mystery. Nicholas Carter
Blindfolded. E. A. Walcott
Blinding Light. C. Collins
Blindman. E. C. Mayne
Blindman's Bluff. M. Carr
Blindman's Marriage. F. Warden
Blindness of Flynn. E. L. Long
Blindpits. Anonymous
Blindside. M. Schorr
Blindsight. Michael Stewart
Blinkey Morgan, the Detective's Foe. Hawkshaw
Blithe Sheriff. F. R. Buckley
Blitzlicht Passage. D. Mason
Blizzard. G. Stone
Blizzard. W. Woodward
Block Busters. L. Cameron
Blockbuster. S. Barlay
Blockade Runners. W. M. Graydon
Blocked Trail. J. McCulley
Blond Baboon. J. Van de Wetering
Blond Spider. V. Brun
Blonde. Carter Brown
Blonde and Beautiful. R. Foster
Blonde and Johnny Malloy. B. Kerr
Blonde and the Boodle. J. T. Story
Blonde Angel. D. Haring
Blonde at Bay. M. Brody
Blonde Avalanche. Carter Brown
Blonde Baby. N. Baroni
Blonde, Bad and Beautiful. Carter Brown
Blonde Baggage. M. Holland
Blonde Bait. E. Lacy
Blonde Bait. S. Marlowe
Blonde, Beautiful—and BLAM! Carter Brown
Blonde Betrayer. J. Godey
Blonde Blackmail. B. Sanders
Blonde Body. Michael Morgan
Blonde Bombshell. D. Foster
Blonde Countess. H. O. Yardley
Blonde Cried Murder. J. Creighton
Blonde Cried Murder. B. Halliday
Blonde Cries Blackmail. M. Brody
Blonde, Cute and Wicked. D. Glinto
Blonde Died Dancing. K. Roos
Blonde Died First. D. Chambers
Blonde Dies First. J. Evans
Blonde Dynamite. A. Bocca
Blonde for a Punchline. M. Brody
Blonde for Ambush. T. Conrad
Blonde for Burial. N. Perrelli
Blonde for Danger. B. Gray
Blonde for Danger. L. Lambert
Blonde for Danger. N. Perrelli
Blonde for Murder. W. B. Gibson
Blonde Gangster. R. Sharp
Blonde Genius. J. T. Edson
Blonde Horror. B. Sarto
Blonde in Black. B. Benson
Blonde in Lower Six. E. S. Gardner
Blonde in Suite 14. S. Sterling
Blonde Indemnity. D. Haring
Blonde Is a Hurricane. C. Dekker
Blonde Is Dead. J. Dow
Blonde Lady. M. Leblanc
Blonde Madonna. H. D. Dearden
Blonde Menace. Don Martin
Blonde Murder Case. Roland Daniel
Blonde on a Broomstick. Carter Brown
Blonde on Borrowed Time. B. X. Sanborn
Blonde on Ice. A. Bocca
Blonde on Ice. Derek Cole
Blonde on the Rocks. Carter Brown
Blonde on the Spot. H. Janson
Blonde on the Street Corner. D. Goodis
Blonde Target. R. Reinsmith
Blonde Target. W. Wright
Blonde, the Gangster and the Private Eye. Dale Clark
Blonde to Burn. D. Reece
Blonde Trouble. Pete Costello
Blonde Vampire. D. Mooers
Blonde Verdict. Carter Brown
Blonde with the Deadly Past. M. Seeley
Blonde Without Escort. B. Perowne
Blonde Wore Black. Peter Chambers
Blondel Parva. J. Payn
Blondes Are My Trouble. Martin Brett
Blondes Are Skin Deep. L. Trimble
Blondes Aren't So Dumb. E. Ellison
Blondes Can Be Bitter! D. Haring
Blondes Die Young. Bill Peters
Blondes Don't Bruise. D. Haring
Blondes Don't Cry. M. Mace
Blondes End Up Dead. B. Winter
Blondes Prefer Bullets. Carter Brown
Blondes' Requiem. Raymond Marshall
Blonde's Stickpin. D. Haring
Blondie Beg Your Bullet. R. Razio
Blondie Iscariot. E. Lustgarten
Blondie Kiss Your Doom. R. Razio
Blondy's Boy Friend. L. Homesley
Blood. Allan Morgan
Blood All Over. Paul Todd
Blood-Amber. J. Mackworth
Blood and Blondes. B. Sarto
Blood and Caviare. M. Dekobra
Blood and Gold. R. Severn
Blood and Honey. G. G. Fickling
Blood and Judgment. M. Gilbert
Blood and Orchids. N. Katkov
Blood and Sable. C. J. Kane
Blood and Sun-Tan. T. C. H. Jacobs
Blood and Thirsty. F. Bonnamy
Blood and Thunder. H. Clevely
Blood and Thunder. D. Pendleton
Blood and Water. P. De Polnay
Blood Bargain. Michael Bradley
Blood Bath. L. S. Borlik
Blood Bath. H. Janson
Blood Bath. C. C. Risenhoover
Blood Bath. J. Rosenberger
Blood Bath. B. Rossi
Blood Beach. F. Garrett
Blood Beast. D. Ballenger
Blood Bond. E. Cave
Blood Bond. H. Curties
Blood Brother. Brian Morrison
Blood Brother, Blood Brother. N. N. Peebles
Blood Brotherhood. R. Barnard
Blood-Brotherhood. A. Murray
Blood Brotherhood. J. Van Der Zee
Blood Brothers. D. Sinclair
Blood Carnelian. J. Raynes
Blood Count. Dell Shannon
Blood Countess. K. Robeson
Blood Country. I. Ruff
Blood Cries. J. Weisman
Blood Cries for Vengeance. H. Desmond
Blood Cult. M. Dixon
Blood Dance. D. Monroe
Blood Debt. S. Jason
Blood Deep. C. Stubbington
Blood Doesn't Tell. R. Barth
Blood Dreams. J. MacLane
Blood Dues. D. Pendleton
Blood Eagle, and other mystery tales. P. H. Emerson
Blood Emerald. V. Blake
Blood Enemies. Glover Wright
Blood Feast. L. E. Murphy
Blood Feud. B. Harding
Blood Fever. B. Forester
Blood Fever. D. Pendleton
Blood Fix. D. Ballenger
Blood Flies Upwards. E. Ferrars
Blood for a Reckless Lady. W. Standish
Blood for Blood. J. Gloag
Blood for Breakfast. D. Ballenger
Blood from a Stone. R. S. Wallis
Blood Fugue. S. Eskapa
Blood Gambit. D. Stivers
Blood Game. E. Gorman
Blood Games. C. Leach
Blood Group O. D. Brierley
Blood Harvest. G. Gottesfeld

Title Index

Blood Heat. S. Pieczenik
Blood Heat Zero. D. Pendleton
Blood Highway. R. Harding
Blood Hunt. N. M. Gunn
Blood Hunt. L. Killough
Blood Hunt. A. O. Pollard
Blood in the Ashes. W. W. Johnstone
Blood in the Ashes. W. Wright
Blood in Your Eye. R. P. Wilmot
Blood Innocents. T. H. Cook
Blood Is a Beggar. T. Kyd
Blood Is a Personal Thing. J. Moffat
Blood Is a Stranger. Roland Perry
Blood Is Thicker. A. C. Fallon
Blood Island. P. McCurtin
Blood Ivory. A. McCoy
Blood Kin. M. McGann
Blood Kin. B. A. Pauley
Blood Lake. F. McConnell
Blood Libel. P. Kerrigan
Blood Lies. Virginia Anderson
Blood Lilies. W. A. Fraser
Blood Links. D. C. Miller
Blood Mark. D. Stivers
Blood, M'Lud. H. Carstairs
Blood Money. C. H. Bullivant
Blood Money. Max Collins
Blood Money. J. Goodwin
Blood Money. D. Hammett
Blood Money. Jack Lewis
Blood Money. Roy Lewis
Blood Money. F. J. Lowe
Blood Money. P. Malloch
Blood Money. W. C. Morrow
Blood Money. T. B. Reagan
Blood Money. G. Seton
Blood Money, and other stories. C. Gibbon
Blood Moon. Jan Alexander
Blood Moon. K. P. Connor
Blood Moon. L. Horvitz
Blood Moon. N. Kazan
Blood-Moon. I. Osgood
Blood Oath. B. Rossi
Blood of an Englishman. J. McClure
Blood of Angels. A. Barker
Blood of Buddha. Harold Ward
Blood of Eagles. D. Ing
Blood of My Blood. E. Lecale
Blood of My Brother. C. H. Thames
Blood of October. D. Lippincott
Blood of Poets. Kenn Davis
Blood of Strawberries. H. Van Dyke
Blood of the Albatross. Ridley Pearson
Blood of the Dragon. E. Ellison
Blood of the Falcon. Nick Carter
Blood of the Lamb. D. Pendleton
Blood of the North. J. B. Hendryx
Blood of the Vampire. F. Marryat
Blood of Vintage. T. Kyd
Blood on a Harvest Moon. D. Anthony
Blood on a Window's Cross. James Fraser
Blood on Baker Street. A. Boucher
Blood on Biscayne Bay. B. Halliday
Blood on Blue Denim. R. Cooper
Blood on Frisco Bay. J. Flynn
Blood on Her Shoe. Medora Field
Blood on His Hands! M. Afford
Blood on Lake Louisa. B. Kendrick
Blood on My Pillow. D. Haring
Blood on My Rug. E. L. Cushing
Blood on My Shadow. A. J. Merak
Blood on My Shoes. Jean Leslie
Blood on My Sleeve. I. Baker
Blood on Nassau's Moon. W. McCully
Blood on Pale Fingers. P. Malloch
Blood on the Beach. H. Holley
Blood on the Bearskin. R. Woodford
Blood on the Black Market. B. Halliday
Blood on the Blonde. G. Jackson
Blood on the Blotter. L. Marshall
Blood on the Boards. W. C. Gault
Blood on the Bosom Divine. T. Kyd
Blood on the Braches. O. Crawford
Blood on the Cat. N. Rutledge
Blood on the Common. A. Fuller
Blood on the Curb. J. T. Shaw
Blood on the Desert. P. Rabe
Blood on the Dining Room Floor. G. Stein
Blood on the Floor. W. S. Masterman
Blood on the Happy Highway. S. Radley
Blood on the Heather. S. Chalmers
Blood on the Ivy. H. Ellson
Blood on the Keys. John Leslie
Blood on the Knight. L. Thayer
Blood on the Lake. R. Hobart
Blood on the Moon. Barney Cohen
Blood on the Moon. B. Copper
Blood on the Moon. J. Ellroy
Blood on the Pavement. Neill Graham
Blood on the River. W. L. Heath
Blood on the Rocks. A. Venters
Blood on the Sand. C. Dekker
Blood on the Sand. F. Martin
Blood on the Shrine. J. G. Brenter
Blood on the Snow. E. Litvinoff
Blood on the Snow. N. MacKenzie
Blood on the Stars. B. Halliday
Blood on the Stars. N. Morland
Blood on the Stars. A. M. Stein
Blood on the Strip. L. Derrick
Blood on the Tracks. C. Brooks
Blood on the Turf. Glenis Wilson
Blood on the Yukon Trail. J. B. Hendryx
Blood Orange. Sam Llewellyn
Blood Pearls of Sulu. D. Del Mar
Blood Pit. M. Carrel
Blood Race. M. Olshaker
Blood Raid. Nick Carter
Blood Red. Anthony Morton
Blood-Red Badge. Nicholas Carter
Blood Red Death. M. Bardon
Blood-Red Dream. Michael Collins
Blood-Red Earth. R. Kershaw
Blood Red Gold. G. Blumberg
Blood Red Leaf. W. M. Duncan
Blood Red Oscar. Elsie Lee
Blood-Red Rose. A. Wise
Blood Red Sky. A. Emmerton
Blood Reign of the Dictator. C. Steele
Blood Relation. Andrew Taylor
Blood Relations. B. Feld
Blood Relations. F. Stewart
Blood Relatives. E. McBain
Blood Ride. P. Hofrichter
Blood Rights. Mike Phillips
Blood Ring. K. Robeson
Blood Risk. B. Coffey
Blood River. Bob Langley
Blood Royal. G. Allen
Blood Royal. A. Winch
Blood Royal. D. Yates
Blood Rubies. A. Young
Blood Ruby. Jan Alexander
Blood Run. Al Conroy
Blood Run. D. Kellerman
Blood Run. D. Pendleton
Blood Run. L. R. Robinson
Blood Run. A. Webb
Blood Run East. P. McCutchan
Blood Running Cold. Jonathan Ross
Blood Runs Cold. R. Bloch
Blood Runs Cold. A. B. Cunningham
Blood Runs Cold. L. Eby
Blood Runs Hot. R. Dacre
Blood Russian. R. D. Zimmerman
Blood Scenario. P. Spain
Blood Secrets. C. Jones
Blood Ship. N. Springer
Blood Shot. S. Paretsky
Blood Simple. J. Coen
Blood Solstice. J. H. Kunstler
Blood Sport. D. K. Cohler
Blood Sport. V. Cross
Blood Sport. D. Francis
Blood Sport. Michael Newton
Blood Sports. P. R. Rothweiler
Blood Stays Red. Austin Stone
Blood Stock. J. Francome
Blood Stone. M. Allegretto
Blood Storm. J. Buchanan
Blood Stripe. W. D. Blankenship
Blood Tango. R. Houston
Blood Tapes. L. Starr
Blood Tells. T. Armour
Blood Tells. Stephen Robertson
Blood Test. J. Kellerman
Blood Tide. R. F. Jones
Blood Tide. S. Wernick
Blood-Tie. S. Coulter
Blood Tie. M. L. Settle
Blood Ties. K. D. Frost
Blood Ties. I. Lambot
Blood Ties. W. B. Murphy
Blood Ties. A. J. Quinnell
Blood Ties. Stephen Robertson
Blood Ties. A. Roudybush
Blood Tracks of the Bush. S. Newland
Blood Trail. W. H. Baker
Blood Transfusion Murders. M. Propper
Blood Ultimatum. Nick Carter
Blood Under the Bridge. B. Zimmerman
Blood Upon the Snow. Hilda Lawrence
Blood Velvet. A. Kennington
Blood Vengeance. M. Carroll
Blood Vengeance. S. Jason
Blood Warning. J. Dillman
Blood White Rose. B. L. Farjeon
Blood Will Have Blood. L. J. Barnes
Blood Will Out. M. Carr
Blood Will Tell. G. Bagby
Blood Will Tell. Nicholas Carter
Blood Will Tell. A. Christie
Blood Will Tell. Maude Parker
Blood Will Tell. J. Potts
Blood Winter. William Patrick
Blood Wrath. C. Krone
Bloodbath. P. McCurtin
Bloodbath. W. Wingate
Bloodbrothers. R. Price
Bloodcircle. P. N. Elrod
Bloodcount. B. Brampton
Bloodhound of the Law. G. S. Trevor
Bloodhounds Bay. W. S. Masterman
Bloodhounds of Broadway. D. Runyon
Bloodhound's Revenge. W. M. Graydon
Bloodhouse. K. Cook
Bloodhunt. N. M. Gunn
Bloodied Ivy. R. Goldsborough
Blooding. F. Geron
Blooding. J. Wambaugh
Blooding Mr. Naylor. C. Boyce
Bloodland. W. W. Johnstone
Bloodland. B. S. Mosiman
Bloodletting. R. Skimin
Bloodline. Alanna Knight
Bloodline. S. Sheldon
Bloodline and Feathers. H. P. Fleming
Bloodline to Murder. E. McDowell
Bloodlust. P. N. Elrod
Bloodmoon. R. Kalish
Bloodroots Manor. Claudette Nicole
Bloodrose House. C. Crowe
Bloodrun. R. Kalish
Bloodrush. H. Zachary
Bloodshed in Bayswater. J. Rowland
Bloodsnarl. I. Watkins
Bloodspoor. J. McVean
Bloodsport. D. Pendleton
Bloodstain. David Alexander
Bloodstained Bokhara. W. C. Gault
Bloodstained Toy. Alice Campbell
Bloodstains. Andrew Puckett
Bloodstar. T. Topar
Bloodstone. L. Benedict
Bloodstone. K. J. Bjorgum
Bloodstone. M. J. Rodgers
Bloodstone. K. E. Wagner
Bloodstone Inheritance. S. D. Stevens
Bloodstorm. K. Maning
Bloodthirst. M. Ronson
Bloodtide. R. Kalish
Bloodtide. B. Knox

Bloodties. Gloria Murphy
Bloodtrail to Mecca. Nick Carter
Bloodwater. J. Crowe
Bloodwealth. Blair Stuart
Bloody Benders. R. H. Adleman
Bloody Bokhara. W. C. Gault
Bloody Book of Law. Sara Woods
Bloody Boston. L. Derrick
Bloody Chamber. Angela Carter
Bloody Chasm. J. W. De Forrest
Bloody Hand. Anonymous
Bloody Hand. M. Braun
Bloody Instructions. Sara Woods
Bloody Ivory. Robin Brown
Bloody Jack. T. J. Kelly
Bloody Jungle. C. Runyon
Bloody Kin. M. Maron
Bloody Mama. R. Thom
Bloody Marvelous. J. Rathbone
Bloody Mary. G. Kraft
Bloody Medallion. R. Telfair
Bloody Monday Conspiracy. Ralph Hayes
Bloody Moonlight. F. Brown
Bloody Murder. S. C. Mason
Bloody Murdock. R. Ray
Bloody Passage. J. Graham
Bloody Precinct. B. Douglas
Bloody Rose. D. Streib
Bloody Scandal. G. Milner
Bloody September. C. A. Haddad
Bloody Silks. M. Horwitz
Bloody Soaps. J. Babbin
Bloody Special. J. Babbin
Bloody Spur. C. Einstein
Bloody Success. M. Culpan
Bloody Sun at Noon. G. Beare
Bloody Sunday. F. Scarpetta
Bloody Sunrise. M. Spillane
Bloody Tower. J. Rhode
Bloody Vengeance. J. Ehrlich
Bloody Wednesday. Joel Harrison
Bloody Wig Murders. G. Bagby
Bloody with Spurring. C. Rushton
Bloody Wood. M. Innes
Bloom o' the Heather. S. R. Crockett
Bloomsbury Mystery. C. Woolf
Bloomsbury Treasure. S. Kyle
Bloomsbury Wonder. T. Burke
Blossom. A. Vachss
Blot. S. Torre
Blotting Book. E. F. Benson
Blow-Down. L. G. Blochman
Blow for Vengeance. Nicholas Carter
Blow Hot, Blow Cold. Gerald Butler
Blow Hot, Blow Cold. E. Queen
Blow of a Hammer and other stories. Nicholas Carter
Blow Out. N. Williams
Blow Out My Torch. J. A. Howard
Blow Over the Heart. R. Machray
Blow the Four Winds. H. Arvay
Blow the House Down. J. Blackburn
Blow Your House Down. P. Barker
Blowback. D. Kilcommons
Blowback. B. Pronzini
Blowdown. C. MacHardy
Blown Away. Hal Kantor
Blown Dead. B. Sloane
Blowout. D. Pendleton
Blowout! T. N. Scortia
Blowtop. A. Schwartz
Blowtorch: O'Reilly. E. Agry
Bludgeon. Jim Ryan
Blue Angels. I. Moffitt
Blue Bed. Glyn Jones
Blue Bell. A. Vachss
Blue Blood. A. Thynne
Blue Blood Flows East. D. Glinto
Blue Blood Runs Red. W. E. Johns
Blue Blood Will Out. T. Heald
Blue Bone. M. Woodhouse
Blue Bonnet. Augustus Muir
Blue Brotherhood. E. O. Zimmerman
Blue Bucket Mystery. F. Grierson

Blue Buckle. W. H. Osborne
Blue Bungalow. W. LeQueux
Blue Car Mystery. N. S. Lincoln
Blue Circle. E. Jones
Blue City. K. Millar
Blue Crochet Coathanger Cover. D. Foster
Blue Dahlia. R. Chandler
Blue Days and Fair. H. Gibbs
Blue Death. Michael Collins
Blue Devil Suite. D. Daniels
Blue Diamond. A. Askew
Blue Diamond. Paul Costello
Blue Diamond. A. Haynes
Blue Diamond. R. W. Keene
Blue Diamond. Mrs. C. Kernahan
Blue Diamond. L. T. Meade
Blue Door. V. Starrett
Blue Dryad. G. H. Powell
Blue Dwarf. P. B. St. John
Blue Envelope. S. Kerr
Blue-Eyed Boy. C. Curzon
Blue-Eyed Boy. C. Short
Blue-Eyed Gypsy. Janette Radcliff
Blue-Eyed Manchu. A. Abdullah
Blue-Eyed Shan. S. Becker
Blue Eyes. J. Charyn
Blue Fire. P. A. Whitney
Blue Flame. J. Gilmore
Blue Flames. H. Wales
Blue Flower Mystery. N. Cassera
Blue Fox. W. H. Helm
Blue Freckle. R. Mooney
Blue Frogs. J. Helterman
Blue Geranium. D. Birkley
Blue Geranium and Tuesday Club murders. A. Christie
Blue Germ. M. Swayne
Blue Ghost. B. J. McOwen
Blue Guitar. N. Hasluck
Blue Hammer. R. Macdonald
Blue Hand. M. E. Braddon
Blue Hand. E. Wallace
Blue Harpsichord. D. Keith
Blue Haze. F. Nunn
Blue Heron. P. Ross
Blue Horse of Taxco. K. M. Knight
Blue Hour. J. Godey
Blue Hour. J. P. Smith
Blue House. Dolores Holliday
Blue Hurricane. J. Dyson
Blue Ice. H. Innes
Blue Ice Affair. Nick Carter
Blue Invective. J. C. Manning
Blue Jean Billy. C. W. Tyler
Blue John Diamond. E. R. Punshon
Blue Key. K. Krause
Blue Kimono Kill. W. J. Sheldon
Blue Knight. J. Wambaugh
Blue Lacquer Box. G. F. Worts
Blue Lamp. W. D. Pelley
Blue Lamp. T. Willis
Blue Leader. W. Wager
Blue Lenses and other stories. D. Du Maurier
Blue Light. G. Stanley
Blue Lightning. G. Baxter
Blue Lightning. C. Stella
Blue Lights. A. Fredericks
Blue Line Murder. J. Moffatt
Blue List. Nigel West
Blue Lupines. L. A. Cuddy
Blue Macaw. C. Edwards
Blue Man. T. Atkins
Blue Mandarin. D. Lenton
Blue Marsh. T. R. Bernard
Blue Mascara Tears. J. McKimmey
Blue Mask. J. Cassells
Blue Mask at Bay. Anthony Morton
Blue Mask Strikes Again. Anthony Morton
Blue Mask Victorious. Anthony Morton
Blue Mauritius. V. Warren
Blue Messiah. J. D. Horan
Blue Mirage. J. D. McNamara
Blue Mirror. J. Turner
Blue Mist and Mystery. E. Everett-Green

Blue Moon. W. Wager
Blue Mountains Murderer. F. P. Clune
Blue Movie. D. Elliott
Blue Movie Murders. E. Queen
Blue Murder. R. L. Bellem
Blue Murder. E. Hale
Blue Murder. B. Halliday
Blue Murder. H. Rutland
Blue Murder. E. Snell
Blue Murder. W. Wager
Blue Murder. Colin Watson
Blue Numbers. B. Goldsmith
Blue Octavo. J. Blackburn
Blue Orchid. S. Drew
Blue Orchid. H. Zore
Blue Parakeet Murders. R. P. Koehler
Blue Paroquet. E. Y. Miller
Blue Parrot. M. Dekobra
Blue Pavilion. W. Buchan
Blue Pete. L. Allan
Blue Pete and the Kid. L. Allan
Blue Pete and the Pinto. L. Allan
Blue Pete at Bay. L. Allan
Blue Pete Breaks the Rules. L. Allan
Blue Pete: Detective. L. Allan
Blue Pete: Half-Breed. L. Allan
Blue Pete in the Badlands. L. Allan
Blue Pete: Indian Scout. L. Allan
Blue Pete: Outlaw. L. Allan
Blue Pete Pays a Debt. L. Allan
Blue Pete: Rebel. L. Allan
Blue Pete Rides the Foothills. L. Allan
Blue Pete to the Rescue. L. Allan
Blue Pete, Unofficially. L. Allan
Blue Pete Works Alone. L. Allan
Blue Peter. Morley Roberts
Blue Pete's Dilemma. L. Allan
Blue Pete's Vendetta. L. Allan
Blue Peter. P. Trent
Blue Pheasant. J. Boswell
Blue Plate Special. D. Runyon
Blue Poppy. C. Baines
Blue Print for Execution. L. Parker
Blue Print Murders. J. G. Brandon
Blue Rajah Murder. H. MacGrath
Blue Ribbon. W. Irish
Blue Ridge Crime. W. Martyn
Blue Ridge Patrol. Rowland Walker
Blue Ridge Mystery. Caroline Martin
Blue Room. G. Simenon
Blue Room. Monroe Thompson
Blue Rum. E. Souza
Blue Russell. W. Bryant
Blue Santo Murder Mystery. M. Armstrong
Blue Sash. O. Binns
Blue Scarab. D. G. Adee
Blue Scarab. R. A. Freeman
Blue Sea & Yellow Sun. R. Batchelor
Blue Shadow Mystery. J. H. Chase
Blue Shroud. D. Haring
Blue Silver. V. Bridges
Blue Skies Dame. J. Olsen
Blue Smoke and Mirrors. W. B. Murphy
Blue Smoke for My Lovely. B. Cabot
Blue Spectacles. H. S. Keeler
Blue Spider. A. Mills
Blue Sunshine. K. Johnson
Blue Talisman. F. Hume
Blue Taper. Gimone Hall
Blue Taxi. A. W. Barrett
Blue Vase. Lady A. Scott
Blue Veil. F. Du Boisgobey
Blue Vesuvius. A. Wynne
Blue Waistcoat. L. A. Ryan
Blue Wall. R. W. Child
Blue Water. C. H. Barker
Blue Water Contract. M. McCray
Blue Water Murder. P. Atkey
Blue Wolf. W. L. Amy
Blue World. R. R. McCammon
Blueback. B. Knox
Bluebeard. M. Frisch
Bluebeard. C. Ludlam
Bluebeard's Daughter. M. Z. Bradley

Bluebeard's Keys. Gwyn Evans
Bluebeard's Seventh Wife. W. Irish
Bluebeard's Wife. H. Desmond
Bluebird Canyon. D. McCall
Bluebolt One. P. McCutchan
Bluebottle. M. Urquhart
Bluefeather. L. Meynell
Bluegate Fields. A. Perry
Blueprint. P. Van Rjndt
Blueprint for a Terrorist. H. Scott
Blueprint for Larceny. P. Chester
Blueprint for Murder. R. Bax
Blueprint for Murder. M. K. Robertson
Blueprint for Terror. B. Temmey
Blueprint to Kill. K. Evans
Blueprints for a Blonde. M. Brody
Blueprints for Murder. M. Brody
Blues for a Black Sister. B. B. Johnson
Blues for a Dead Lover. J. Davidson
Blues for Charlie Darwin. N. Hentoff
Blues for My Baby. B. Shannon
Blues for the Prince. B. Spicer
Bluethorne. F. Y. McHugh
Bluff. H. Adams
Bluff! H. M. Paull
Bluffer's Luck. W. C. Tuttle
Bluffing of Gaston Leroux. W. Dinner
Blundell's Last Guest. A. P. Terhune
Blunderer. P. Highsmith
Blunt Darts. J. F. Healy
Blunt Instrument. G. Heyer
Blunted Sword. D. Divine
Blurred Reality. R. Lewis
Blushing Monkey. R. McDougald
Blye, Private Eye. N. Pileggi
Bo-Binh Commandos. J. Lansing
Board Stiff. Robert James
Boarder Runners. J. Irungu
Boarding-House Mystery. E. S. Brooks
Boarding House Mystery. M. Osborne
Boarding-House Reminiscences. Juloc
Boarding Party. J. Leasor
Boast. M. Donald
Boat-House Riddle. J. J. Connington
Boat Off the Coast. S. Dobyns
Boat Race Murder. R. E. Swartout
Boat Train Mystery. C. Barry
Bob Bridger, Detective. Anonymous
Bob Covington. A. C. Gunter
Bob Ford, the Slayer of Jesse James. W. B. Lawson
Bob Hits the Headlines. J. J. Farjeon
Bob Martin's Little Girl. D. C. Murray
Bob Younger's Fate. Anonymous
Bob Younger's Fate. E. S. Deane
Bobbed Hair Detective. R. Goyne
Bobbie and Certain Other Pickletillie Folk. I. Farquhar
Bobby Trap. William Stevenson
Boca Grande. L. Singer
Boden's Boy. T. Gallon
Bodies. Robert Barnard
Bodies Are Dust. P. J. Wolfson
Bodies Are Where You Find Them. B. Halliday
Bodies Fetch Good Prices. B. Sarton
Bodies in a Bookshop. R. T. Campbell
Bodies in a Cupboard. H. Desmond
Bodies in Bedlam. R. S. Prather
Bodies of Water. J. S. Borthwick
Bodily Harm. M. Atwood
Body. Carter Brown
Body. R. B. Sapir
Body and Passon. Whit Harrison
Body and Soil. R. McInerny
Body and Soul. A. Dare
Body and Soul. J. Dark
Body and Soul. J. R. Dimmock
Body and Soul. J. P. Smith
Body and Soul. Sherryl Woods
Body and Soul. J. Wingrave
Body at Busman's Hollow. F. Hurt
Body at Dead Dog Corner. A. P. Ward
Body at Madman's Bend. A. W. Upfield
Body Beautiful. B. S. Ballinger
Body Beautiful Murder. K. Platt

Body Behind the Bar. C. F. Gregg
Body Behind the Curtain. E. G. Cousins
Body Below. Howard Mason
Body Beneath a Mandarin Tree. F. Crane
Body Blow. K. Hopkins
Body Blows. S. Simmons
Body Came Back. B. Halliday
Body Count. M. Dixon
Body Count. F. Garrett
Body Count. E. Helm
Body Count. P. McCurtin
Body Count. F. Scarpetta
Body Drank Coffee. N. Hill
Body Dutiful. J. Cairo
Body Fell on Berlin. R. Lakin
Body for a Blonde. K. McLeod
Body for a Buddy. A. M. Stein
Body for Bill. I. S. Shriber
Body for Christmas. R. Reinsmith
Body for McHugh. J. Flynn
Body for Sale. R. Deming
Body for the Bride. G. Bagby
Body for the Widow. G. Warren
Body Found Stabbed. J. Cameron
Body Glow. D. V. Carleson
Body Goes Round and Round. T. Du Bois
Body Hunters. D. Streib
Body in Bedford Square. D. Frome
Body in Cadiz Bay. D. Serafin
Body in My Arms. R. Stephenson
Body in Paradise. R. Reinsmith
Body in Sokolniki Park. F. Neznansky
Body in the Barrage Balloon. Colin Curzon
Body in the Basket. G. Bagby
Body in the Beck. J. Cannan
Body in the Bed. B. S. Ballinger
Body in the Bed. S. Sterling
Body in the Belfry. K. H. Page
Body in the Billiard Room. H. R. F. Keating
Body in the Blue Room. S. Williams
Body in the Boathouse. Johnny Mack
Body in the Bonfire. C. Bush
Body in the Boot. V. Gunn
Body in the Boudoir. C. E. Vulliamy
Body in the Bridal Bed. R. Shattuck
Body in the Bungalow. J. Corbett
Body in the Bunker. H. Adams
Body in the Car. A. Hodges
Body in the Dawn. C. M. Wills
Body in the Drum Mystery. M. Harvey
Body in the Dumb River. G. Bellairs
Body in the Kiosk. R. Baxter
Body in the Library. A. Christie
Body in the Pound. O. Martyn
Body in the Road. M. Dalton
Body in the Safe. C. F. Gregg
Body in the Safe. S. Kyle
Body in the Shaft. R. Francis Foster
Body in the Silo. R. A. Knox
Body in the Trawl. A. Glanville
Body in the Turl. D. Frome
Body in the Volvo. K. K. Beck
Body in Velvet. F. Usher
Body Lies. E. J. Millward
Body Looks Familiar. R. Wormser
Body Lovers. M. Spillane
Body Made Alive. John Marsh
Body Missed the Boat. J. Iams
Body Mortgage. R. Engling
Body Next Door. E. K. Goldthwaite
Body of a Girl. M. Gilbert
Body of Evidence. D. A. Van Meter
Body of Opinion. J. Staynes
Body of the Crime. L. Heller
Body on Mount Royal. D. Montrose
Body on Page One. D. Ames
Body on the Beach. S. Brackeen
Body on the Beach. J. Decrest
Body on the Beach. R. Hardinge
Body on the Beach. R. Wallace
Body on the Beam. Anthony Gilbert
Body on the Bench. D. B. Hughes
Body on the Bus. L. Hollingsworth
Body on the Floor. N. B. Mavity

Body on the Line. Mary Archer
Body on the Pavement. G. Meyrick
Body on the Sidewalk. Bernice Carey
Body Politic. C. Aird
Body Ran Home. N. Perrelli
Body Rolled Downstairs. I. H. Irwin
Body Rub. Mark Andrews
Body Scissors. J. Doolittle
Body Search. A. M. Stein
Body Smasher. J. Stacy
Body Snatcher. R. L. Stevenson
Body Snatchers. C. Brooks
Body Surrounded by Water. Eric Wright
Body That Came by Post. G. W. Yates
Body That Wasn't Uncle. G. W. Yates
Body to Dye For. Grant Michaels
Body to Spare. M. Procter
Body Trade. Theodore Taylor
Body Unidentified. J. Rhode
Body Unknown. B. Graeme
Body Vanishes. V. Gunn
Body Vanishes. Jacquemard-Senecal
Body Was Lonely. B. Shannon
Body Was Missing. H. Brewis
Body Was of No Account. J. C. Cooper
Body Was Quite Cold. R. G. Dean
Bodyguard. A. Mitchell
Bodyguard. R. Reinsmith
Bodyguard Man. Philip Evans
Body's Mine. N. Karta
Body's Name Was Jones. P. Jaye
Bodysnatch. J. Hallums
Boffin's Find. R. Thynne
Bog Blossom Stories. J. Phelan
Bog-Myrtle and Peat. S. R. Crockett
Bogart 48. John Stanley
Bogey Men. R. Bloch
Bogeyman. John Raymond
Bogmail. P. McGinley
Bogue's Fortune. J. Symons
Bogus Buddha. James Melville
Bogus Clew. Nicholas Carter
Bogus Lover. H. Silver
Bogus Policeman. Anonymous
Bogus Tourist-Agency. W. M. Graydon
Bohannon's Book. Joseph Hanson
Boheme Combination. R. Close
Bohemian Connection. S. Dunlap
Bohemian Girls. F. Warden
Boiled Alive. B. Buckingham
Boka Lives! H. Calvin
Bold Buccaneer. Seafarer
Bold Desires. Stuart Hall
Bold Forager. T. Willard
Bold House Murders. Eugene Franklin
Bold Thing. M. Daniel
Boldt. T. Lewis
Bolero. M. Pflaum
Bolero Murders. M. Avallone
Bolivian Heat. Nick Carter
Bolo the Super-Spy. W. LeQueux
Bolt. D. Francis
Bolt. J. F. Howard
Bolt. P. R. Shore
Bolt from the Blue. Scott Graham
Bolthole. D. Craig
Bolts and Bars. F. C. V. Harcourt
Bolts from Blue Skies. Nicholas Carter
Bomb. A. Badger
Bomb for Atuna. B. Reade
Bomb Job. H. Kane
Bomb-Makers. W. LeQueux
Bomb Makers. V. Mayhew
Bomb Scare. P. Chambers
Bomb-Shell. M. Leblanc
Bomb Squad. Mark Andrews
Bomb That Could Lip Read. D. Seaman
Bomb Two. D. Henderson
Bomba, Bomba! S. Putnam
Bombay Mail. L. G. Blochman
Bombay Murder. S. K. Chettur
Bombe Surprise. Robin Cook
Bombers. P. Leslie
Bombing Run. A. M. Stein

Bombs Burst Once. G. Church
Bombs from the Murder Wolves. R. J. Hogan
Bombshell. Carter Brown
Bombshell. G. G. Fickling
Bombshell. Jennifer Phillips
Bombshell. R. Raine
Bombship. B. Knox
Bonanza Murder Case. C. H. Snow
Bonaparte Kiss. S. Cardiff
Bonaventure. C. Hastings
Boncoeur Affair. H. Wickman
Bond. M. Ehrlich
Bond Grayson Murdered! N. S. Bortner
Bond of Black. W. LeQueux
Bond of Evil. M. Cordell
Bond of Hate. J. Carrick
Bond Street Burlesque. Raymond Paul
Bond Street Murder. J. G. Brandon
Bond Street Mystery. Anonymous
Bond Street Raiders. J. G. Brandon
Bondage of Brandon. B. Hemyng
Bonded Dead. M. E. Chaber
Bonded Villain. Nicholas Carter
Bone. I. Blair
Bone. G. C. Chesbro
Bone and a Hank of Hair. L. Bruce
Bone House. W. Butler
Bone Is Pointed. A. W. Upfield
Bone of the Dinosaur. G. D. H. Cole
Bone Orchard. J. Trigoboff
Bone Pile. G. Dold
Bone Yard. D. Pendleton
Bonecrack. D. Francis
Bonegrinder. J. Lutz
Bones. B. Pronzini
Bones. E. Wallace
Bones and Silence. Reginald Hill
Bones Don't Lie. C. T. Gardner
Bones in London. E. Wallace
Bones in the Barrow. Josephine Bell
Bones in the Brickfield. M. Burton
Bones in the Sand. K. Royce
Bones in the Wilderness. G. Bellairs
Bones of Contention. E. Candy
Bones of Contention. R. Foley
Bones of Contention. N. Gage
Bones of Frankenstein. D. F. Glut
Bones of Napoleon. J. W. Bellah
Bones of the River. E. Wallace
Bonesetter's Brawl. C. Calderwood
Boney and the White Savage. A. W. Upfield
Bonfire Murder. T. A. Plummer
Bonn Blitz. Gar Wilson
Bonner Deception. D. Estey
Bonnet Man. G. Weill
Bonnie. H. Barron
Bonnie and Clyde. B. Hirschfeld
Bonus for Murder. J. G. Brandon
Bony and the Black Virgin. A. W. Upfield
Bony and the Kelly Gang. A. W. Upfield
Bony and the Mouse. A. W. Upfield
Bony and the White Savage. A. W. Upfield
Bony Buys a Woman. A. W. Upfield
Boocoo Death. J. Lansing
Boodle. L. Charteris
Boogey Man. B. W. Battin
Boogie Was a Gent. P. Lauben
Book a Hearse Now. J. Bogar
Book Early for Murder. Jennifer Jordan
Book for Banning. N. Easton
Book Her for Murder. M. Brody
Book Here. W. P. Ridge
Book of All Power. E. Wallace
Book of Bargains. V. O'Sullivan
Book of Changes. R. H. W. Dillard
Book of Clues. J. Sladek
Book of Dreams. J. Vance
Book of Evidence. J. Banville
Book of Master Crimes. M. Hervey
Book of Murder. F. I. Anderson
Book of Murder. R. Cowen
Book of Numbers. R. D. Pharr
Book of Numbers. David Thoreau

Book of Original Plays and How to Give Them. H. J. Gardner
Book of Robert E. Howard. R. E. Howard
Book of Stories. G. S. Street
Book of Strange Sins. C. Kernahan
Book of the Beast. Tanith Lee
Book of the Crime. E. Daly
Book of the Damned. Tanith Lee
Book of the Dead. J. Blackburn
Book of the Dead. E. Daly
Book of the Dead. Robert Richardson
Book of the Dead. J. Tigges
Book of the Lion. E. Daly
Book of Tish. M. R. Rinehart
Book with Orange Leaves. H. S. Keeler
Booked for Death. M. Borgenicht
Booked for Death. M. Cumberland
Bookmaker's Body. S. Stone
Bookmaker's Crime. A. Steffens Hardy
Books and Crooks. N. Mitzman
Books for the Baron. Anthony Morton
Bookshop Mystery. J. S. Childers
Boom-Time Gold. G. W. Wicking
Boomer. C. D. Taylor
Boomerang. A. Garve
Boomerang. B. Graeme
Boomerang. W. H. Osborne
Boomerang Clue. A. Christie
Boomerang Conspiracy. M. Stanley
Boomerang Murder. F. Grierson
Boon Companions. June Drummond
Boondocks. D. Lowden
Boonie-Rat Body Burning. J. Cain
Booster. E. Izzi
Boothroyd's Mill. E. C. Reed
Bootlaces for Bastion. R. Harrison
Bootleg Angel. E. Mazzaro
Bootlegger. V. Torrio
Bootlegger's Victim. R. C. Armour
Bootless Crime. T. W. Speight
Booty. Douglas Grant
Booty for a Babe. Carter Brown
Border Crossing. G. Blagowidow
Border Incident. Jay Flynn
Border Line. W. S. Masterman
Border Massacre. Greg Walker
Border of Darkness. John Latimer
Border Scourge. B. Mitford
Border Sweep. D. Pendleton
Border Town. Carroll Graham
Border Town Girl. J. D. MacDonald
Border Trail. H. Bindloss
Borderland of Hell. W. Barker
Borderland Studies. H. Pease
Borderlanders. J. Laing
Borderline. E. Crawshay-Williams
Borderline. J. T. Hospital
Borderline. J. Keener
Borderline. Vercors
Borderline Case. H. McLeave
Borderline Case. B. Williams
Borderline Cases. C. F. Adams
Borderline Murder. A. Amos
Borderlines. A. Madsen
Borderlines. A. Mayor
Borders of Barbarism. Eric Williams
Bored Stiff. J. Matera
Bored to Death. M. Delving
Borgia Blade. F. Ryerson
Borgia Cabinet. J. S. Fletcher
Borgia Head Mystery. V. Gunn
Borgia Testament. N. Balchin
Boris Story. V. Leigh
Bormann Brief. C. Egleton
Bormann Judgement. R. M. Stall
Bormann Receipt. M. Duke
Born Bad. Anonymous
Born Beautiful. Keith Campbell
Born Innocent. B. J. Hurwood
Born Loser. Carter Brown
Born Loser. M. Cronin
Born of Man and Woman. R. Matheson
Born of the Son. G. Wagner
Born Reckless. M. Rogers

Born Rotten. Joe Cannon
Born Soldier. J. S. Winter
Born Survivor. J. K. Lucas
Born to Be Hanged. M. E. Chaber
Born to Be Hanged. P. McGuire
Born to Be Murdered. Dennis Allan
Born to Betray. M. V. Victor
Born to Command. Hero Strong
Born to Die. K. David
Born to Die. D. Glinto
Born to Evil. B. Lippincott
Born to Kill. J. D. Revere
Born to Sin. H. L. Gates
Born to Win. M. Roote
Born Victim. H. Waugh
Borneo Patrol. R. Wilkes-Hunter
Bornless Keeper. P. B. Yuill
Borodino Mystery. M. L. Storer
Borough Council Murders. J. Austwick
Borough Council Ramp. P. Urquhart
Borough Treasurer. J. S. Fletcher
Borrow the Night. H. Nielsen
Borrowdale Tragedy. W. J. Dawson
Borrowed Alibi. L. Egan
Borrowed Alibi. M. Murphy
Borrowed Cottage. Alice Campbell
Borrowed Crime. W. Irish
Borrowed Liner. L. Clarke
Borrowed Rites. Judith Stephens
Borrowed Shield. R. E. Enright
Borrowed Time. A. Jackont
Borrowed Time. M. Shane
Borrower of the Night. Elizabeth Peters
Borzoi Control. S. Ellis
Bosambo of the River. E. Wallace
Boss. J. Greaves
Boss. J. W. McConaughy
Boss, and How He Came to Rule New York. Alfred Henry Lewis
Boss Man. R. B. Sparkia
Boss of Taroomba. E. W. Hornung
Boss of Terror. K. Robeson
Boss of the Skeletons. W. B. M. Ferguson
Bossa Nova Bed. E. Colby
Boston Avenger. M. Barry
Boston Belle Meets Murder. J. C. Lenehan
Boston Blackie. J. Boyle
Boston Blitz. D. Pendleton
Boston Bust-Out. P. McCurtin
Boston Conspiracy. J. H. Robinson
Boston Crab. F. Usher
Botanist at Bay. J. Sherwood
Botany Bay. John Lang
Both Sides of the Case. J. Prescot
Both Sides of the Road. B. A. Clarke
Both Sides of the Veil. R. Marsh
Botticelli Madonna. R. Cox
Bottle. Anonymous
Bottle Blonde. D. Haring
Bottle of Dust. A. Rutherford
Bottle Organ. R. Masson
Bottle with the Black Label. Nicholas Carter
Bottle with the Green Wax Seal. H. S. Keeler
Bottles of Scented Sweets. M. J. Pemberton
Bottletop Affair. G. Cotler
Bottom Deal. J. Philips
Bottom Line. J. Chaloner
Bottom Line. F. Knebel
Bottom Line. R. Sapir
Bottom Line Is Murder. R. Eversz
Bottom of Suez. G. H. Teed
Bottom of the Bottle. G. Simenon
Bottom of the Matter. A. Burr
Bottom of the Well. F. U. Adams
Boudapesti 3. D. Lowden
Boudoin's Moustache. J. W. Rhoads
Boudoir Murder. M. Propper
Boudoirs Are My Beat. J. Stewart
Boulevard. L. H. Brennan
Boulevard Mutes. Nicholas Carter
Boulevard Nights. D. Gram
Bound by a Spell. H. Conway
Bound by Honor. C. Virmonne
Bound by Love. C. Lanigan

Bound to Die. Bill Turner
Bound to John Company. M. E. Braddon
Bound to Kill. J. Blackburn
Bound to Murder. D. Fiske
Bound to Please. H. Spicer
Bound to Win. H. Smart
Bound Together. H. Conway
Boundaries. T. M. Wright
Bounty Hunter. A. Fletcher
Bounty Hunter. M. Franklin
Bounty Hunter Blues. John Leslie
Bouquet Garni. D. Clark
Bouquet of Clean Crimes and Neat Murders. H. Slesar
Bouquet of Thorns. John Sherwood
Bourbon Street. G. H. Otis
Bourne Identity. R. Ludlum
Bourne Supremacy. R. Ludlum
Bourne Ultimatum. R. Lundlum
Bournewick Murders. L. Blow
Bout with the Mildew Gang. S. Fowler
Bow Street Brangle. M. Sebastian
Bow Street Gentleman. M. Sebastian
Bow Street Terror. T. A. Waters
Bowerings' Breakwater. P. McCutchan
Bowery Birdie. B. Sarto
Bowery Blonde. Pete Costello
Bowery Blonde. B. Diamond
Bowery Murder. W. K. Smith
Bowie. G. Mac
Bowie. Greg Walker
Bowler, Batsman, Spy. A. Synge
Bowling Green Murder. M. Taylor
Bowling Green Murders. H. Woodward
Bowman at a Venture. H. Howard
Bowman on Broadway. H. Howard
Bowman Strikes Again. H. Howard
Bowman Test. A. J. Ellis
Bowman Touch. H. Howard
Bowmanville Break. S. Shelley
Bowsham Puzzle. J. Habberton
Bowstring Murders. Carr Dickson
Box. P. Rabe
Box for a Long Journey. E. E. Cameron
Box for One. P. Brook
Bow from Japan. H. S. Keeler
Box Hill Murder. J. S. Fletcher
Box of Doom. D. W. Steward
Box of Secrets. M. Crossley
Box of Tricks. S. Brett
Box Office Browning. P. Corris
Box Office Murders. F. W. Crofts
Box 100. F. Leonard
Box with Broken Seals. E. P. Oppenheim
Boxing Mystery. Gregory Wilson
Boxing Spy. P. Weldon
Boxing Tales. L. Golding
Boxwood Maze. B. Plagemann
Boy at the Bank. A. Philips
Boy Behind the Gun. C. E. Blaney
Boy Blue. S. Davies
Boy Crazy. A. L. Quandt
Boy Detective. Anonymous
Boy Detective. C. E. Blaney
Boy Detective. Old Sleuth
Boy Detectives. M. Everard
Boy from Nowhere. M. Hinxman
Boy Fugitive. Old Sleuth
Boy in the Pool. C. R. Bittle
Boy Next Door. C. Loken
Boy on a Chain. R. Parker
Boy on a Dolphin. D. Divine
Boy on Platform One. V. Canning
Boy Scout's Craig Kennedy. A. B. Reeve
Boy Who Followed Ripley. P. Highsmith
Boy Who Invented Bubble Gum. P. Gallico
Boy Who Liked Monsters. P. McCutchan
Boy Who Was Buried This Morning. Joseph Hansen
Boy with a Sling. Jonathan Wade
Boy Without a Memory. J. W. Bobin
Boys from Binjiwunyawunya. R. G. Barrett
Boys from Brazil. I. Levin
Boys in Brown. R. Beckwith
Boys in the Island. C. J. Koch

Boys of Red House. E. Everett-Green
Brace for the Law. Marsden Richards
Brace of Rogues. N. Islay
Brace of Sixes. J. A. Davitt
Brace of Skeet. Gerald Hammond
Brace of Yarns. W. B. Jones
Bracelet of Doom. V. Mayo
Brackenridge Enigma. L. Geoghegan
Brackenroyd Inheritance. E. Lindley
Brackenthorpe. K. A. Shoesmith
Bracknell's Law. W. Hildick
Brad Dolan's Blonde Cargo. W. Fuller
Brad Dolan's Miami Manhunt. W. Fuller
Braddigan Murder. I. Ostrander
Bradfield Case. J. Graystone
Bradford's Trials. J. R. Beek
Brading Collection. P. Wentworth
Bradmoor Murder. M. D. Post
Bradovich. W. Herrick
Braes of Yarrow. C. Gibbon
Braganza Pursuit. S. Neilan
Bragg's Hunch. J. Lynch
Brahmin Arrangement. A. Tully
Brain. R. Cook
Brain and Ten Fingers. G. Kersh
Brain Child. B. Dibble
Brain Dead. L. Brieno
Brain Death. Sandra Wilkinson
Brain Drain. R. Sapir
Brain Drain Docket. S. Dave
Brain Fever. R. Dee
Brain Guy. B. Appel
Brain Master. V. Van Der Elst
Brain of Agent Blue. T. Richards
Brain of Paul Menoloff. John Marsh
Brain Robbers. H. Munro
Brain Scavengers. P. Edwards
Brain Trust Murder. Diplomat
Brain Twister. Mark Phillips
Brain Watch. R. N. Walker
Brain Wave. R. Obstfeld
Brain-Waves and Death. W. Rich
Brainchild. J. M. Johnston
Brainchild. A. Neiderman
Brainchild. J. Saul
Brainfade. P. Barthelme
Brainfire. C. Black
Brainpicker. P. J. Helm
Brains Trust for Murder. A. Spiller
Brainstorm. Reginald Campbell
Brainwash. J. Wainwright
Brainwashed. Martin Thomas
Brainwrack. K. Pedler
Brainz. R. Goulart
Braking Point. A. Neilson
Bramble Bush. D. Duncan
Bran Mak Morn. R. E. Howard
Branch Bearers. G. Petrie
Branch for the Baron. Anthony Morton
Branches of Evil. M. J. Kingsley
Brand for the Burning. H. McCutcheon
Brand Image. H. Janson
Brand Inheritance. Dorothy Fletcher
Brand of Cain. G. Norway
Brand of Fear. B. Lang
Brand of Silence. Harrington Strong
Brand of Silence. F. M. White
Brand of the Beast. Michael Lewis
Brand of the Broad Arrow. A. Griffiths
Brand of the Crook. F. Ramsdale
Brand of the Metal Maiden. B. House
Brand of the Werewolf. K. Robeson
Brand T. H. Brand
Brand X. C. Brand
Branded. G. Biss
Branded Hand. M. O. Rolfe
Branded Prince. W. Chesney
Branded Spy. O. Merland
Branded Spy Murders. V. W. Mason
Branded Woman. Wade Miller
Brandenburg Affair. J. D. White
Brandenburg Concerto. D. Williams
Brandenburg Hotel. P. G. Winslow
Brandon Affair. C. Whited

Brandon Case. J. J. Connington
Brandon Coyle's Wife. E. Southworth
Brandon in New York. V. Warren
Brandon Is Missing. Dennis Allan
Brandon Papers. Q. Bell
Brandon Returns. V. Warren
Brandon Takes Over. V. Warren
Brandon the Bushranger. C. Rowcroft
Brandstetter and Others. Joseph Hansen
Brandy for a Hero. W. O'Farrell
Brandy for the Parson. R. Foxall
Brandy on the Rocks. Maryl James
Brandy Pole. J. N. Chance
Brandywine Exchange. R. A. Liston
Brangwyn Mystery. D. C. Murray
Brannigan's Lot. Barney Douglas
Brannington's Leopard. F. Webb
Brant Adams, the Emperor of Detectives. Anonymous
Brant Adams, the Emperor of Detectives. Old Sleuth
Brass Bandit. P. Dickey
Brass Bed. F. Flora
Brass Bound Book. J. Letton
Brass Bowl. L. J. Vance
Brass Chills. H. Pentecost
Brass Cupcake. J. D. MacDonald
Brass Diamonds. B. Sandberg
Brass Eagle. M Duffy
Brass Faces. C. McEvoy
Brass for a Nude. Kane
Brass Go-Between. O. Bleeck
Brass Gong Tree. J. W. Bellah
Brass Halo. J. Nugent
Brass Halo. J. Webb
Brass Key. F. Swann
Brass Knocker. E. Rathbone
Brass Knuckle. L. Grex
Brass Knuckles. F. Gruber
Brass Knuckles. B. Mochan
Brass Monkey. H. Whittington
Brass Rainbow. Michael Collins
Brass Ring. L. Padgett
Brass Shroud. B. Cassiday
Brass Target. F. Nolan
Brassbound. M. D. Bickel
Brat. G. Brewer
Brat Farrar. J. Tey
Brave, Bad Girls. T. B. Dewey
Brave Cannot Yield. I. MacKintosh
Brave Heart of Youth. K. Lindsay
Brave Interlude. G. Goodchild
Brave Little Woman. M. A. Denison
Brave Shall Serve. C. Stevens
Bravely to Bed. N. Karta
Bravo. Stuart Hall
Bravo Charlie. C. M. Filgate
Bravo 9. W. B. Day
Bravo of London. E. Bramah
Bravo Romeo. R. Peters
Braydon Mystery. E. Healey
Brazen. Carter Brown
Brazen Bull. G. Kersh
Brazen Confession. C. F. Gregg
Brazen Head. L. A. Knight
Brazen Seductress. H. Janson
Brazen Tongue. G. Mitchell
Brazen Virtue. Nora Roberts
Brazilian Sleigh Ride. R. L. Fish
Brazilian Stardust. M. McEvoy
Brea File. L. Charbonneau
Breach of Fate. J. P. Evans
Breach of Promise. Roy Hart
Breach of Reason. E. H. John
Breach of Security. M. Penoyre
Breach of Trust. W. M. Graydon
Bread. E. McBain
Bread and a Stone. A. Bessie
Bread and Olives. P. Arundale
Bread for the Dead. B. Carson
Bread of Deceit. M. B. Lowndes
Breadfruit Lotteries. R. Elman
Break. J. Giovanni
Break. B. Mather
Break a Leg. L. DuBreuil

Break and Enter. Colin Harrison
Break for a Lovely. H. Janson
Break for Summer. L. Meynell
Break In. D. Francis
Break in the Circle. P. Loraine
Break in the Line. B. Mather
Break of Day. B. King
Break-Out. O. J. Currington
Break Out. W. McNeilly
Break Point. I. Nastase
Break the Toff. J. Creasey
Break-Through. P. Malloch
Breakaway. Lionel Black
Breakaway. E. Cannon
Breakaway. F. Durbridge
Breakaway House. A. W. Upfield
Breakdown. J. Boland
Breakdown. P. Marsh
Breakdown. James Preston
Breaker of Laws. W. P. Ridge
Breaker of Ships. F. Sleath
Breakers Ahead. A. M. Barbour
Breakers of the Law. A. S. Walker
Breakfast for Three. Marguerite Bryant
Breakfast with a Corpse. Max Murray
Breakheart Pass. Alistair MacLean
Breaking Point. B. Copper
Breaking Point. D. Du Maurier
Breaking Point. A. A. Flint
Breaking Point. W. Hewlett
Breaking Point. L. Meynell
Breaking Point. M. R. Rinehart
Breaking Point. K. Spore
Breaking Strain. J. Masters
Breaking the Shackles. F. Barrett
Breaking the Shell. Joseph Norwood
Breakout. Leo Kessler
Breakout! Steve Mackenzie
Breakthrough. M. Urquhart
Breastplate for Aaron. S. Harvester
Breath of Brimstone. Anthea Fraser
Breath of Genius. M. Channing
Breath of Murder. W. M. Duncan
Breath of Scandal. E. Balmer
Breath of Spring. P. Coke
Breath of Suspicion. H. Desmond
Breath of Suspicion. E. Ferrars
Breath of Suspicion. W. LeQueux
Breathe No More. C. Franklin
Breathe No More. M. Randolph
Breathe No More, My Lady. H. Bailey
Breathe No More, My Lady. E. Lacy
Brecon Castle. C. Farr
Bred in the Bone. J. Payn
Bred in the Bone. E. Phillpotts
Bred to Kill. Martin Thomas
Breed of the Beverleys. S. Horler
Breeder. Jim Morris
Breeze from the Backveldt. F. H. Sibson
Breezy Frank. Old Sleuth
Bren Hardy Again. W. J. Elliott
Bren Hardy, Tough Dame. W. J. Elliott
Brenda. L. Zane
Brenda Gets Married. Roy Vickers
Brenda Maneuver. S. N. Rosenberg
Brenda Yorke, and other tales. M. C. Hay
Brenda's Murder. T. Wells
Brent—of Bleak House. T. A. Plummer
Bressant. J. Hawthorne
Bressio. R. Sapir
Bret Harte's Choice Bits. B. Harte
Bretherton. W. F. Morris
Brethren of the Axe. J. Somers
Brethren of the Compass. J. M. Walsh
Breton Sisters. G. Simenon
Brezhnev Memo. M. Marcus
Briar Patch. C. Blackstock
Briar Rose. C. N. Williamson
Briarcliff Manor. S. A. Salvato
Briarlea. E. Zumwalt
Briarpatch. R. Thomas
Briarwood. K. Ashby
Bribe Was Beautiful. Carter Brown
Bric-a-Brac Man. R. H. Greenan

Brick Alley. D. Chacko
Brick Foxhole. R. Brooks
Brickbats for Bastian. R. Harrison
Bricklayer's Arms. J. Rhode
Bricks Upon Dust. P. Tabori
Bridal Bed Murders. A. E. Martin
Bridal Eve. E. Southworth
Bride. J. Garwood
Bride. G. Middleton
Bride and the Burglar. F. L. Speare
Bride Brings Death. Darby St. John
Bride by Candlelight. D. Eden
Bride Dined Alone. V. Kelsey
Bride Elect. T. Douglas
Bride for a Night. R. Vane
Bride for Arundel. Jan Daniels
Bride for Bedivere. Hilary Ford
Bride for Bombay. J. R. Warren
Bride for Hampton House. H. Waugh
Bride from the Desert. G. Allen
Bride from the Sea. G. Boothby
Bride in Black. A. Askew
Bride in Blue. J. Rees
Bride Laughed Once. M. K. Sanders
Bride of a Day. F. Du Boisgobey
Bride of a Moment. C. Wells
Bride of a Stranger. Patricia Maxwell
Bride of Alderburn. M. Neilson
Bride of an Evening. E. Southworth
Bride of Brackenloch! R. Abbot
Bride of Cairngorn. J. F. Webb
Bride of Chance. V. Blake
Bride of Darkness. Margery Lawrence
Bride of Death. N. Marsh
Bride of Death. M. Reisner
Bride of Death. K. Wolffe
Bride of Devil's Leap. S. Shulman
Bride of Donnybrook. L. Ames
Bride of Doom. Harriet Gray
Bride of Dutton Market. M. Leighton
Bride of Emersham. L. Lance
Bride of Frankenstein. M. Egremont
Bride of Frankenstein. G. Preston
Bride of Fu Manchu. S. Rohmer
Bride of Fury. R. C. Payes
Bride of Gaylord Hall. S. O'Brien
Bride of Hatfield Castle. B. C. Warren
Bride of Infelice. A. L. Halstead
Bride of Invercoe. C. Massey
Bride of Kilkerran. K. Westcott
Bride of Lenore. C. Kavanaugh
Bride of Llewellyn. E. Southworth
Bride of Lowther Fell. M. Forster
Bride of Menace. A. Barron
Bride of Misfortune. V. Blake
Bride of Moat House. P. Curtis
Bride of Newgate. J. D. Carr
Bride of Pendorric. V. Holt
Bride of Raven Island. E. Orford
Bride of Tancred. D. Pearson
Bride of Terror. E. Bond
Bride of the Dark Island. Dorine Moore
Bride of the Dullahan. S. Wagner
Bride of the Kalahari. F. H. Rose
Bride of the Shadows. L. M. Jansen
Bride of the Sun. G. Leroux
Bride of the Tomb. A. M. Miller
Bride of the Unliving. L. Churchill
Bride of the Wilderness. C. McCarry
Bride of the Wolf. W. E. Groves
Bride Regrets. M. Carleton
Bride That Got Away. S. Truss
Bride Wears Black. W. H. L. Crauford
Bride Wore Black. M. Brody
Bride Wore Black. C. Woolrich
Bride Wore Weeds. H. Janson
Bridegroom. C. V. McFadden
Brideprice. J. N. Catanach
Bride's Bouquet. K. Gordon
Bride's Castle. P. W. Wilson
Bride's Fate. E. Southworth
Bride's Madness. A. Upward
Bride's Mirror. M. Turnbull
Brides of Aberdar. C. Brand

Brides of Bellenmore. A. Maybury
Brides of Doom. A. Marsh
Brides of Doom. M. Richmond
Brides of Friedberg. Gwendoline Butler
Brides of Lucifer. M. Lynch
Brides of Mertonbridge Hall. H. C. McNeile
Brides of Saturn. Marilyn Ross
Brides of Solomon and other stories. G. Household
Bride's Ransom. L. Clausse
Bridesmaid. R. Rendell
Bridge at Branfield. J. E. Greene
Bridge Fall Down. N. Rinaldi
Bridge House. L. Crosby
Bridge of Asses. J. Gautier
Bridge of Birds. B. Hughart
Bridge of Fear. D. Eden
Bridge of Lions. H. Slesar
Bridge of Magpies. G. Jenkins
Bridge of Sand. F. Gruber
Bridge of Strange Music. J. Blackmore
Bridge of Wonder. Margery Lawrence
Bridge Players. C. R. Gull
Bridge That Went Nowhere. R. L. Fish
Bridge to Nowhere. L. R. Humes
Bridge to the Moon. A. Maybury
Bridge to Vengeance. Winston Graham
Bridgeport Dagger. J. Milbrook
Bridie and the Silver Lady. M. S. Power
Brief Candle. A. Spiller
Brief Candles. F. Gaite
Brief Case of Murder. P. Laing
Brief for O'Leary, and two other episodes in his career. B. Graeme
Brief Return. M. G. Eberhart
Brief Suspicion. Patricia Gordon
Brief Tales from the Bench. H. Cecil
Briefly . . . a Dame! D. Haring
Brierfield Tragedy. R. F. Redd
Briers Way. Lee Michaels
Brig Jane May. F. Marlowe
Brigade. J. Shirley
Brigade. M. J. Trow
Brigade of Terror. Hugh MacDonald
Brigand. T. P. Prest
Brigand. E. Wallace
Brigand's Secret. W. M. Graydon
Briggs Investigates. D. MacDonald
Bright Adventure. G. Rose
Bright Angel. A. Wood
Bright As a Diamond. A. Allyson
Bright Blue Death. Nick Carter
Bright Cantonese. A. Cordell
Bright Corner. J. B. Priestley
Bright Danger. H. M. Kahler
Bright Day. M. Hocking
Bright Deadly Summer. Barbara James
Bright Dummy. K. Sundelof-Asbrand
Bright Eyes of Danger. J. M. Scott
Bright Face of Danger. J. Fast
Bright Face of Danger. L. Meynell
Bright Face of Danger. R. Ormerod
Bright Green Waistcoat. P. Fry
Bright Lights. T. Benoit
Bright Lights. R. O. Chipperfield
Bright Lights, Dark Rooms. D. Nemec
Bright Like Blood. D. Rowden
Bright Morning. Rona Randall
Bright Nemesis. J. Gunther
Bright Orange for the Shroud. J. D. MacDonald
Bright Promise. J. Lukens
Bright Red Business Men. P. McCutchan
Bright Road to Fear. R. M. Stern
Bright Serpent. J. M. Fox
Bright Star. H. Coyle
Bright Star of Danger. W. Chambers
Bright Sun, Dark Shadow. M. Blake
Bright To-Morrow. W. J. Harding
Brightener. C. N. Williamson
Brighter Buccaneer. L. Charteris
Brightlight. T. Bernard
Brighton Alibi. A. Mills
Brighton Beach Mystery. C. Kingston
Brighton Belle. A. La Bern
Brighton Belle and other stories. Francis King

Title Index

Brighton Monster and others. G. Kersh
Brighton Murder Trial. B. Hamilton
Brighton Mystery. B. Hemyng
Brighton Rock. G. Greene
Brighton Tragedy. G. Boothby
Brilliant Kids. H. Lieberman
Brimstone. R. L. Duncan
Brimstone. R. Masefield
Brimstone Red. D. Keene
Bring Another Glass. Georgina Seton
Bring Back Her Body. S. Brock
Bring 'Em Back Dead! David Hume
Bring Him Back Dead. D. Keene
Bring Me Another Corpse. P. Rabe
Bring Me Another Murder. W. Chambers
Bring Me My Bow. M. Moiseiwitsch
Bring Me Sorrow. H. Janson
Bring the Bride a Shroud. D. B. Olsen
Bring the Monkey. Miles Franklin
Brink. N. J. Crisp
Brink. A. J. Rees
Brink of Disaster. G. Cullingford
Brink of Murder. H. Nielsen
Brink of Silence. G. M. Jay
Brinkman. D. Meiring
Brink's. N. Behm
Bristol Affair. H. Seymour
Bristol Express Mystery. C. H. Ogilvie
Bristow's Wreck. A. Howlett
Britain at Bay. J. Tregellis
Britain Invaded. J. Tregellis
Britain's Revenge. J. Tregellis
Britannia Obsession. Brett Woods
British Agent. H. B. Lockhart
British Cross. B. Granger
British Museum Mystery. W. Jardine
Brittany Stones. Lynna Cooper
Brittle Thread. D. Hall
Britz of Headquarters. M. Barber
Brixham Manor Mystery. E. S. Brooks
Broad Highway. J. Farnol
Broad Players. C. A. Harris
Broad Road. A. S. Swan
Broadcast. J. Mackworth
Broadcast Murder. "Capstan"
Broadcast Murders. F. Smith
Broadcast Mystery. W. LeQueux
Broads Don't Scare Easy. H. Janson
Broadway. P. Dunning
Broadway Bab. J. McCulley
Broadway Babylon. P. De Pietro
Broadway Bob, the Bounder Detective. Anonymous
Broadway Bounty. Josh Randall
Broadway Butterfly Murders. T. Bliss
Broadway Contraband. P. Granados
Broadway Cross. Nicholas Carter
Broadway Doll. N. W. Firth
Broadway Glamour Girl. J. Dekker
Broadway Jungle. Norma Lee
Broadway Lady. K. Slattery
Broadway Murders. E. J. Doherty
Broadway Murders. R. Wallace
Broadway Racket. W. R. Hutton
Broadway Racketeers. J. O'Connor
Broadway Siren. B. Banarto
Broadway Virgin. L. Bull
Brock. J. Bingham
Brock. G. Kersh
Brock and the Defector. J. Bingham
Brocken Spectre. Karen Campbell
Brocklebank Riddle. H. Wales
Broderick. W. Heffernan
Broke of Covenden. J. C. Snaith
Broken Alibi. T. C. H. Jacobs
Broken Angel. F. Mahannah
Broken Bars. Nicholas Carter
Broken Blossoms. T. Burke
Broken Body. F. Mahannah
Broken Bond. Nicholas Carter
Broken Bonds. H. Smart
Broken Boy. J. Blackburn
Broken Branch. Keith Campbell
Broken Butterfly. Ladbroke Black
Broken Cigarettes. H. Gaunt
Broken Circle. R. Goyne
Broken Circle. M. Saxton
Broken Codes. John Shannon
Broken Consort. J. Gollin
Broken Doll. A. Kent
Broken Doll. J. Webb
Broken Eagle. R. Tine
Broken Engagement. E. Southworth
Broken English. David Thompson
Broken Face Murders. D. L. Teilhet
Broken Faith. I. D. Hardy
Broken Fang. U. Key
Broken Fetter. J. K. Leys
Broken Glass. E. Kyle
Broken Gun. L. L'Amour
Broken Heart. Mary Bennett
Broken Heart. T. Thurston
Broken Honeymoon. C. H. Bullivant
Broken Idol. A. Sergeant
Broken Idols. S. Flannery
Broken Image. V. Ebert
Broken Jigsaw. P. Somers
Broken Key. M. L. Roby
Broken Knife. T. C. H. Jacobs
Broken Ladders. A. Soutar
Broken Law. J. B. Harris-Burland
Broken Link. C. Virmonne
Broken Marriage. S. Murray
Broken Memory. F. M. White
Broken Men. V. Gielgud
Broken Necks and other stories. B. Hecht
Broken Net. H. Bindloss
Broken O. C. Wells
Broken on Crime's Wheel. Nicholas Carter
Broken Pen. J. K. Stafford
Broken Penny. J. Symons
Broken Pledges. E. Southworth
Broken Promise. E. A. Rife
Broken Ramparts. J. Robb
Broken Reed. C. Braeme
Broken River. J. Hawkins
Broken Rosary. G. Johnson
Broken Seal. H. Hill
Broken Seal. Dora Russell
Broken Shield. B. Benson
Broken Sphinx. K. Kimbrough
Broken Stirrup-Leather. C. Granville
Broken Sword. M. Gerard
Broken Sword. A. Mills
Broken Symmetries. P. Preuss
Broken Tapestry. Rona Randall
Broken Thread. W. LeQueux
Broken Three. K. Detzer
Broken to Harness. E. Yates
Broken Toy. Arthur MacLean
Broken Trail. H. Bindloss
Broken Trail. Nicholas Carter
Broken Trail. A. Murray
Broken Vase. R. Stout
Broken Vase Mystery. M. Plum
Broken Waters. F. Packard
Broken Way. P. Trent
Broken Window. E. Booth
Brokenclaw. J. Gardner
Broker. Max Collins
Broker. H. Q. Masur
Broker's End. L. F. Booth
Brokers of Doom. A. Aikman
Broker's Wife. Max Collins
Brond. F. Lindsay
Bronkhurst Case. T. C. H. Jacobs
Bronsville Massacre. B. Toler
Bronx Number. Anonymous
Bronze Bell. S. Silliphant
Bronze Bell. L. J. Vance
Bronze Buddha. C. L. Daniels
Bronze Claws. P. Kruger
Bronze Door. Augustus Muir
Bronze Face. W. LeQueux
Bronze Hand. C. Wells
Bronze Heist. M. F. Callan
Bronze Mermaid. P. Ernst
Bronze Perseus. S. B. Hough
Brood of Folly. M. Erskine
Brood of the Witch-Queen. S. Rohmer
Brooding House. Alice Brennan
Brooding Lake. D. Eden
Brooding Mansion. P. Warren
Brooding Mist. Rose Dana
Brooding Wild. R. Cullum
Brookham Mystery. E. De Wil
Brooklands Mystery. W. B. Baldry
Brooklands Mystery. P. Urquhart
Brooklyn Angel. M. Hervey
Brooklyn Daughter. B. Vane
Brooklyn Moll Shoots Bedmate. Griff
Brooklyn Murders. G. D. H. Cole
Broomstick. I. Karlova
Broomstick in the Hall. J. Blackmore
Broomsticks over Flaxborough. Colin Watson
Brother and Sister. M. Nickolay
Brother Berserk. J. W. Hanson
Brother Cain. P. Capon
Brother Cain. S. Raven
Brother Death. J. Lodwick
Brother Esau. D. Orgill
Brother for Hugh. M. Coles
Brother Lowdown. S. K. Epperson
Brother Monster. F. Brown
Brother Orchid. L. Brady
Brother Rat. N. Karta
Brother Rogue and Brother Saint. T. Gallon
Brother Sinister. C. Bramwell
Brother Spy. T. C. H. Jacobs
Brother Strangler. J. Kelso
Brother Wolf. B. Reynolds
Brotherhood. L. J. Carlino
Brotherhood. P. Trent
Brotherhood. Alan Williams
Brotherhood of Blood. L. Derrick
Brotherhood of Death. Nicholas Carter
Brotherhood of Death. G. Stanley
Brotherhood of Evil. I. Zacharia
Brotherhood of Freedom. Dick Stewart
Brotherhood of Satan. L. Q. Jones
Brotherhood of the Rose. D. Morrell
Brotherhood of the Seven Kings. L. T. Meade
Brotherhood of the Stars. Stockton Heath
Brotherhood of the Tomb. D. Easterman
Brotherhood of the White Feather. X
Brotherhood of Velvet. D. Karp
Brotherly Love. W. Blankenship
Brotherly Love. P. Trent
Brothers. W. Goldman
Brothers. R. Huish
Brothers and Sisters Have I None. J. Usher
Brothers Brannigan. H. E. Helseth
Brothers in Arms. H. H. Kirst
Brothers in Blood. P. D. Ballard
Brothers in Blood. D. Pendleton
Brothers in Law. H. Cecil
Brothers Karamazov. J. Copeau
Brothers Karamazov. F. Dostoevskii
Brothers Keepers. A. Storey
Brothers Keepers. D. E. Westlake
Brothers Kresky. H. Bloomstein
Brothers of Benevolence. J. Cassells
Brothers of Judgment. W. M. Duncan
Brothers of Silence. F. Gruber
Brothers of the Chain. George Griffith
Brothers of the People. F. Whishaw
Brothers of the Thin Wire. F. Pitt
Brothers Rico. G. Simenon
Brothers Sackville. G. D. H. Cole
Brought in Dead. Harry Patterson
Brought to Bay. Nicholas Carter
Brought to Bay. J. M'Govan
Brought to Bay. M. Pereira
Brought to Bay. R. H. Savage
Brought to Book. T. Heald
Brought to Book. H. Spicer
Brought to Light. E. R. Punshon
Brought to Light. T. W. Speight
Brought to the Mark. Nicholas Carter
Brown Book. J. B. Harris-Burland
Brown Mask. P. Brebner
Brown Murder Case. Roland Daniel
Brown Paper Twice. C. Davy

Brown Portmanteau and other stories. Curtis Yorke
Brown Princess. M. V. Victor
Brown Satin Bomb. Anthea Goddard
Brown Suede Jacket. P. Fry
Browne Fights the Fifth Column. M. Poole
Browne Follows the Clue. M. Poole
Browne of the Secret Service. M. Poole
Browne's 50,000 Pound Mystery. M. Poole
Browne's First Case. M. Poole
Brownie's Plot. T. Cobb
Browning Takes Off. P. Corris
Browning Touch. D. Rohan
Browns of the Yard. A. Brock
Brown's Requiem. J. Ellroy
Brownstone Gothic. E. Shenkin
Brownstone House. R. Foley
Brownsville Murders. B. S. Keirstead
Bruce Angelo. Anonymous
Bruce Angelo, the City Detective. Old Sleuth
Bruce Douglas, A Man of the People. R. A. Gunn
Bruce Lee Lives? M. Caulfield
Bruised Fruit. A. Ephron
Brumblingham Hall. J. Blyth
Brunette on the Beam. M. Brody
Brunettes Are Dangerous. Roland Daniel
Brunettes Are No Better. S. Coburn
Bruno. W. H. Ireland
Brush Creek Murders. C. H. Snow
Brush of Death. James Warren
Brush with a Baby. M. McLoughlin
Brush with Death. S. Pim
Brush with Death. Joan Smith
Brush with Fate. C. Dawe
Brussels Dossier. W. H. Baker
Brutal Kook. M. Avallone
Brutal Question. O. W. Bayer
Brutal Years. G. Ledig
Brute. G. Des Cars
Brute. F. A. Kummer
Brute. D. Newton
Brute in Brass. H. Whittington
Bubble Moon. R. Bridges
Bubble Reputation. P. C. Wren
Bubbles. M. Foster
Bubbles We Buy. A. Jones
Buccaneer in Spats. A. Abdullah
Buccaneer's Parrot. J. Courage
Buccaneer's Pride. B. Bolt
Buccaneers' Tangle. Curt Lawrence
Buchanan of "The Press." S. Bent
Bucharest Ballerina Murders. V. M. Mason
Buchman's Law. R. Thorman
Bucholz and the Detectives. A. Pinkerton
Buck Passes Flynn. G. McDonald
Bucket in a Well. H. Willett
Buckhorn Murder Case. C. H. Snow
Bucking the Tiger. A. Abdullah
Buckingham Blowout. A. Kilgore
Buckingham Palace Connection. T. Willis
Buckled Bag. M. R. Rinehart
Bucks. P. Chandler
Bucks County Idyll. R. J. Seidman
Buckshot Range. W. C. Tuttle
Budapest Action. J. Rosenberger
Budapest Parade Murders. V. M. Mason
Budapest Risk. Patricia Wright
Budapest Run. Nick Carter
Budapest Tradeoff. R. Carroll
Buddha of Fleet Street. F. Grierson
Buddha's Secret. Roland Daniel
Buddy Boys. M. McAlary
Budget of Tares. Austin Philips
Budspy. D. Dvorkin
Buenos Aires Affair. M. Puig
Buffalo Box. F. Gruber
Buffalo Hook. Richard Butler
Buffaloes. C. Warburton
Buffet for Unwelcome Guests. C. Brand
Bufo & Spallanzini. R. Fonseca
Bugged for Murder. E. Lacy
Bugles Blowing. N. Freeling
Build Me a Blonde. A. Rocco
Build My Gallows High. G. Homes
Build My Gallows High. R. B. Sparkia

Builder. J. B. Harris-Burland
Builders of Ships. M. Leighton
Builders of the Black Empire. G. Stockbridge
Building Estate Murder. P. Urquhart
Built for Trouble. A. Fray
Built to Kill. R. Tine
Bulgarian Exchange. A. Grey
Bulgarian Termination. J. Rosenberger
Bull Moose. R. Cullum
Bulldog and Rats. M. Allain
Bulldog Breed. G. E. Rochester
Bulldog Carney. W. A. Fraser
Bulldog Drummond. H. C. McNeile
Bulldog Drummond and the Female of the Species. H. C. McNeile
Bulldog Drummond at Bay. H. C. McNeile
Bulldog Drummond Attacks. G. Fairlie
Bulldog Drummond Meets a Murderess. H. C. McNeile
Bulldog Drummond on Dartmoor. G. Fairlie
Bulldog Drummond Returns. H. C. McNeile
Bulldog Drummond Stands Fast. G. Fairlie
Bulldog Drummond Strikes Back. H. C. McNeile
Bulldog Drummond's Third Round. H. C. McNeile
Bulldog Has the Key. F. W. Bronson
Bulldog Murder. J. K. Tarpey
Bullet Creek. L. S. Carroll
Bullet for a Beast. R. Simons
Bullet for a Bedroom. M. Brody
Bullet for a Blonde. P. Kruger
Bullet for Bradford. M. Warden
Bullet for a Brunette. D. Haring
Bullet for a Star. S. Kaminsky
Bullet for Betty. C. Joyce
Bullet for Blondie. D. Haring
Bullet for Charles. H. Walter
Bullet for Cinderella. J. D. MacDonald
Bullet for Fidel. Nick Carter
Bullet for Georgie. E. M. Skehan
Bullet for Midas. N. Morland
Bullet for My Baby. Carter Brown
Bullet for My Lady. B. Mara
Bullet for My Love. O. R. Cohen
Bullet for Pretty Boy. M. Avallone
Bullet for Rhino. C. Witting
Bullet for Stonewall. Benjamin King
Bullet for the Bride. J. Messmann
Bullet for the Countess. S. Horler
Bullet for the Shah. Alan Williams
Bullet for Your Dreams. D. Von Elsner
Bullet Hole. Keith Miles
Bullet in His Cap. Robert Fleming
Bullet in the Ballet. C. Brahms
Bullet in the Cornice. M. Beckett
Bullet Proof. R. Angel
Bullet Proof. M. A. Collins
Bullet Proof. A. Dean
Bullet Proof. F. Kane
Bullet-Proof Man. A. Riefe
Bullet-Proof Martyr. J. A. Howard
Bullet-Proof Toga. L. Malloy
Bullet Train. J. Rance
Bulletin Blonde. M. Brody
Bullets and Brown Eyes. M. Corrigan
Bullets Are Final. E. Kennedy
Bullets Are My Business. J. B. West
Bullets Are Trumps. D. Reid
Bullets, Bikinis and Bells. R. Renauld
Bullets Bite Deep. J. Carlshon
Bullets Bite Deep. David Hume
Bullets for a Banker. Lee Thomas
Bullets for a Blonde. W. Oursler
Bullets for a Bride. B. Banarto
Bullets for Blondes. R. Hausfeld
Bullets for Brandon. V. Warren
Bullets for Breakfast. J. M. Walsh
Bullets for Macbeth. Marvin Kaye
Bullets for My Blonde. J. Bogar
Bullets for Snoopers. Griff
Bullets for the Bridegroom. D. Dodge
Bullets in the Bush. E. Norwood
Bullets Make Holes. John Bentley
Bullets of Palestine. H. Kaplan
Bullets Speak Louder. R. Marlowe

Bullets to Baghdad. Philip Chambers
Bullion. J. Goldsmith
Bullion. M. Woodman
Bullion Mystery. Nicholas Carter
Bullion Run 101. B. McAllister
Bullitt. R. L. Pike
Bullitzer Baby Case. J. Sword
Bull's Eye. M. Kennedy
Bulls Like Death. M. Fitt
Bulls of Ronda. E. P. Benson
Bullshot. G. Kraft
Bullshot Crummond. R. House
Bully! M. Schorr
Bully Hayes: Buccaneer, and other stories. L. Becke
Bulton's Revenge. H. C. McNeile
Bum Steer. N. Picard
Bumbledinky. A. A. Thomson
Bump and Grind Murders. Carter Brown
Bump in the Night. I. Holland
Bump in the Night. Colin Watson
Bunce. M. Delarrabeiti
Bunch Grass. H. A. Vachell
Bunch of Crooks. Roland Daniel
Bunch of Errors. S. De Madariaga
Bundle for the Toff. J. Creasey
Bundle of Clews. Nicholas Carter
Bundle of Lies. L. Castletown
Bundle of Nerves. Joan Aiken
Bungalow Crime. P. Urquhart
Bungalow Mystery. A. Haynes
Bungalow of Dead Birds. G. Varney
Bungalow on the Roof. A. Abdullah
Bungalow Tragedy. W. J. Bayfield
Bungalow Under the Lake. C. E. Pearce
Bungay Castle. E. Bonhote
Bunker at the 5th. M. Dods
Bunkum. F. Richardson
Bunkumelli. W. C. Platts
Bunnies. J. Quirk
Bunny Lake Is Missing. E. Piper
Buns from the Gutter. N. Melides
Bunyip of Barney's Elbow. Brian James
Buoyed Cables. E. L. Long
Burden of Guilt. Carter Brown
Burden of Guilt. I. Gordon
Burden of Isabel. J. M. Cobban
Burden of Proof. J. Ashford
Burden of Proof. J. Barlow
Burden of Proof. V. Canning
Burden of Proof. Nicholas Carter
Burden of Proof. M. Challis
Burden of Proof. J. Truesdell
Burden of Proof. S. Turow
Burden's End. B. Lowry
Burden's Mission. H. Whittington
Burdens of Proof. C. M. Oksner
Burdock. A. L. Elsworthy
Burglar. D. Goodis
Burglar Alarm. H. S. Griffith
Burglar and the Girl. M. Boulton
Burglar and the Lady. O. Harper
Burglar for a Night. R. H. Wilkinson
Burglar in Baulk. F. Martyn
Burglar in the Closet. Lawrence Block
Burglar of White Birches. W. M. Graydon
Burglar-Proof. M. Wilson
Burglar Who Liked to Quote Kipling. Lawrence Block
Burglar Who Moved Paradise. H. D. Ward
Burglar Who Painted Like Mondrian. Lawrence Block
Burglar Who Studied Spinoza. Lawrence Block
Burglars. J. Julian
Burglar's Accomplice. Beechwood
Burglar's Can't Be Choosers. Lawrence Block
Burglars' Club. H. A. Hering
Burglar's Fate and the Detectives. A. Pinkerton
Burglars in Bucks. G. D. H. Cole
Burglars Must Dine. E. P. Oppenheim
Burglary. E. A. Dillwyn
Burgle the Baron. Anthony Morton
Burgled Heart. G. Leroux
Burglings of Tutt. R. Andom
Burgomaster of Furnes. G. Simenon

Burgos Contract. Angus Ross
Burgo's Romance. T. W. Speight
Burial Deferred. J. Ross
Burial in Moscow. F. Dickey
Burial in Portugal. Robert MacLeod
Burial of M. Bouvet. G. Simenon
Burial of the Fruit. D. Dortort
Burial Service. P. McGuire
Buried. D. Helfgott
Buried Caesars. S. M. Kaminsky
Buried Crime. C. Elmore
Buried for Pleasure. E. Crispin
Buried in So Sweet a Place. S. Forbes
Buried in the Deep. Mrs. C. Hoey
Buried in the Past. E. Lemarchand
Buried Millions. J. Andrews
Buried Motive. B. Cassiday
Buried on Sunday. E. O. Phillips
Buried Once. M. Dalman
Buried Remembrance. N. G. Smith
Buried Rubies. E. Jepson
Buried Secret. Nicholas Carter
Buried Shadows. Leslie Lynn
Buried Sin. I. D. Hardy
Burke Foundation. A. McCandless
Burke's Law. Roger Fuller
Burleigh Murders. G. Morton
Burlesque of Frankenstein. G. Isaacs
Burma Probe. J. Rosenberger
Burma Ruby. J. S. Fletcher
Burma Strike. J. N. Pruitt
Burmese Dagger. Donald Stuart
Burn. N. Gant
Burn Down. Stuart Collins
Burn Forever. L. Ford
Burn, Killer, Burn. P. Crump
Burn Marks. S. Paretsky
Burn Season. J. Lantigua
Burn Sugar Burn. G. Clifton
Burn This. H. McCloy
Burn, Witch, Burn! A. Merritt
Burned Evidence. W. Woodrow
Burned Man. C. Monig
Burned Man. B. Spicer
Burned Man. N. Stahl
Burned Woman. E. Mathis
Burning. R. Charles
Burning Beacon. T. Charles
Burning Blue Death. J. Rosenberger
Burning Bush. H. Herald
Burning Conscience. C. Kingston
Burning Court. J. D. Carr
Burning Eye. V. Canning
Burning Fuse. B. Benson
Burning Fuse. Jay Bernard
Burning Gold. F. L. Cary
Burning Hill. E. Kyle
Burning Is a Substitute for Loving. Jennie Melville
Burning Man. T. J. Kelly
Burning Moon. A. Spilken
Burning Obsession. R. W. Walker
Burning of Billy Toober. Jonathan Ross
Burning of Troy. M. Gair
Burning Question. C. Carnac
Burning Sappho. G. Baxt
Burning Season. W. D. Dundee
Burning Secret. G. McDonell
Burning Shore. E. Trevor
Burning Sky. R. Faust
Burning Sky. J. H. Roberts
Burning Water. M. Lackey
Burning Woman. M. Ritter
Burnout. J. W. Thomas
Burnt Bones Mystery. M. Dalman
Burnt Caravan. B. Bolt
Burnt Earth. W. F. Fauley
Burnt Million. J. Payn
Burnt Offering. R. Lockridge
Burnt Offerings. R. Marasco
Burnt Orange Heresy. C. Willeford
Burnt-Out Case. G. Greene
Burnt Powder. A. P. Morris
Burnton Widows. V. McConnell
Burqa. H. Campbell

Burwyck's Wander. S. J. Treibich
Bury by Night. L. Foley
Bury Her Deep. D. Macomber
Bury Him Among Kings. E. Trevor
Bury Him Darkly. J. Blackburn
Bury Him Darkly. Henry Wade
Bury Him Deeper. R. A. J. Walling
Bury Him Gently. C. Rank
Bury in Haste. A. Eichler
Bury Me Deep. H. L. Ingham
Bury Me Deep. D. Linton
Bury Me Deep. H. Q. Masur
Bury Me in Gold Lame. S. Forbes
Bury Me in Lead. I. Goodwin
Bury Me Not. W. Francis
Bury Me Not at Sea. M. Eyre
Bury That Poker. G. M. Wilson
Bury the Guy! B. Shannon
Bury the Hatchet. Manning Long
Bury the Past. R. Reinsmith
Bury Their Dead. Alex Fraser
Bus Ran Late. G. M. Wilson
Bus Station Murders. L. Revell
Bus That Vanished. L. Groc
Bush Baby. M. Woodhouse
Bush Gypsies. A. Parsons
Bush King. P. Trent
Bush Mystery. J. Mackie
Bush Studies. B. Baynton
Bush Track. D. Hennessey
Bush Tracking. T. Collard
Bush Warfare. J. Kilgore
Bushfire. James Preston
Bushido. B. Osborne
Bushido Code. R. St. Louis
Bushigrams. G. Boothby
Bushman. A. Crane
Bushman Who Came Back. A. W. Upfield
Bushmaster. B. Bolt
Bushranger. C. Rowcroft
Bushranger of the Skies. A. W. Upfield
Bushranger of Van Diemen's Land. C. Rowcroft
Bushrangers. W. H. Thames
Bushtrackers. M. Mwangi
Business at Blanche Capel. B. Morgan
Business of Bodies. S. Forbes
Business of Loving. Godfrey Smith
Business of Murder. R. Harris
Business Unusual. T. Heald
Businessman. T. M. Disch
Busker. B. McNeill
Busman's Holiday. J. Pattinson
Busman's Honeymoon. D. L. Sayers
Bust! S. McPhilemy
Busted Wheeler. Carter Brown
Bustillo. K. Royce
Busy Bodies. Patrick Anderson
Busy Body. E. Ferrars
Busy Body. D. E. Westlake
Busy Whisper. T. Cobb
Busybody. J. Popplewell
But a Short Time to Live. Raymond Marshall
But Death Runs Faster. W. P. McGivern
But Don't Go Alone. K. Court
But He Was Already Dead When I Got There. Barbara Paul
But I Wouldn't Want to Die There. S. Forbes
But Ill He Lived. Bradshaw Jones
But Nellie Was So Nice. M. McMullen
But Not for Love. I. Wilson
But Not for Me. E. Ronns
But Not Forgotten. R. Fenisong
But Not Yet Slain. B. Appel
But Once a Year. A. A. Thomson
But She Won't Lie Down. P. Yeldham
But Soft—We Are Observed. H. Belloc
But the Doctor Died. C. Rice
But the Patient Died. J. G. Edwards
But the Patient Died. Fiona Sinclair
But We Are Exiles. E. Kyle
But We Didn't Get the Fox. R. Llewellyn
But Why Bump Off Barnaby? R. Abbot
Butcher, Baker, Nightmare Maker. R. Natale
Butcher Block. M. Mandell

Butcher of Belgrade. Nick Carter
Butcher of Bruton Street. A. Applin
Butcherknife Killings. S. Harkins
Butchers and other stories of crime. P. Lovesey
Butcher's Boy. T. Perry
Butcher's Dozen. M. A. Collins
Butcher's Moon. R. Stark
Butchers of Men. J. Hild
Butcher's Theatre. J. Kellerman
Butcher's Wife. Li Ang
Butcher's Wife. O. Cameron
Butler Did It. T. J. Kelly
Butler Did It. W. Marks
Butler Did It. R. Pendark
Butler Died in Brooklyn. R. Fenisong
Butler in a Box. C. H. Abrahall
Butler's Revenge. M. Powell
Butler What? Gary Campbell
Butter Market House. Elizabeth Ford
Buttercup. B. Vane
Buttercup Case. F. Crane
Buttercup Spell. H. Cecil
Butterfly. J. M. Cain
Butterfly. H. K. Webster
Butterfly Avengers. B. Atlee
Butterfly Flood. J. Wyllie
Butterfly Hunter. J. Van De Wetering
Butterfly Murder. C. Andrews
Butterfly Nett. Carter Brown
Butterfly of Paris. L. H. Brennan
Butterfly on the Wheel. G. Thorne
Butterfly Picnic. Joan Aiken
Butterfly Plague. T. Findley
Butterfly Revolution. W. Butler
Butterscotch Prince. Richard Hall
Button. B. Starr
Button, Button. M. Bramhall
Button, Button. W. L. Doty
Button, Button. Robin Francis
Button, Button. H. Roth
Button in the Plate. V. Loder
Button Zone. W. Greatorex
Buy Back Blues. R. Dennis
Buy Back the Dawn. H. Garland
Buy My Silence! Herman Landon
Buyer Beware. J. Lutz
Buying Time. J. Haldemann
Buzzards Pick the Bones. Murray Thomas
Buzzard's Roost. G. E. Rochester
By a Hair's Breadth. H. Hill
By a Hair's Breadth. E. S. Tupper
By a Vanished Hand. A. Feeny
By Advice of Counsel. A. Train
By an Unseen Hand. Nicholas Carter
By an Unseen Hand. E. Hughes
By Any Illegal Means. Donald Mackenzie
By Appointment Only. D. S. Mayleas
By Birth a Lady. G. M. Fenn
By Bitter Experience. Scott Graham
By Bizarre Hands. J. R. Lansdale
By Blood Alone. F. Corey
By Breathless Ways. B. Bolt
By Candle-Light. G. Knevels
By Dawn's Early Light. Henry Clement
By Death Possessed. R. Ormerod
By Demons Possessed. E. Grayson
By Executive Arrangement. T. McMordie
By Fair Means. J. Middlemass
By Fair Means or Foul. T. W. Speight
By Fate's Caprice. T. W. Speight
By Favour of Allah. G. E. Holt
By Flower and Dean Street, and The Love Apple. P. Chaplin
By Force of Circumstances. Gordon Holmes
By Fortune's Whim. T. W. Speight
By Foul Means. H. Leyford
By Frequent Anguish. S. F. X. Dean
By Hand Unseen. A. W. Marchmont
By Hate Possessed. M. Gagnon
By Her Own Hand. F. Bonham
By His Own Hand. M. Cronin
By Hook or by Crook. Anthony Gilbert
By Hook or by Crook. E. Lathen
By Hook or by Crook. R. A. J. Walling

By Hook or Crook. R. A. J. Walling
By Horror Haunted. C. Fremlin
By-Line for Murder. A. Garve
By Love Betrayed. M. Andrau
By Love Forgotten. C. Gayet
By Mead and Stream. C. Gibbon
By Means Unknown. E. Wooton
By Misadventure. F. Barrett
By Misadventure. A. Brock
By Misadventure. R. J. Fletcher
By Night. R. Clay
By Night at Dinsmore. J. Esteven
By Order of the Brotherhood. Le Voleur
By Order of the Czar. J. Hatton
By Order of the Dead. W. V. Cook
By Order of the Five. H. Adams
By Order of the King. A. Askew
By Order of the King! W. M. Graydon
By Order of the Magistrate. W. P. Ridge
By Order of the President. M. Kilian
By Order of the Soviet. F. A. Symonds
By Order of the Tong. J. G. Brandon
By Papuan Waters. O. Binns
By-Pass Control. M. Spillane
By-Pass Murder. D. Frome
By Peak and Pass. F. A. M. Webster
By Persons Unknown. J. York
By Proxy. J. Payn
By Reason Of. M. R. Henderson
By Reason of Doubt. E. Godfrey
By Reason of Insanity. J. N. Harvey
By Reason of Insanity. S. Stevens
By Reef and Palm. L. Becke
By Registered Post. J. Rhode
By Right Not Law. R. H. Sherard
By Right of Sword. A. W. Marchmont
By Rock and Pool on an Astral Shore. L. Becke
By Royal Command. D. Yates
By Saturday. S. Fowler
By Snare of Love. A. W. Marchmont
By Some Person Unknown. P. Barrington
By Telegraph. J. M. Cobban
By That Sin. B. Malim
By the Brown Bog. O. Roe
By the Fore Barbette. Anonymou
By the Gate of the Sea. D. C. Murray
By the Night Express. K. Fleming
By the North Door. M. E. Atkins
By the Pricking of My Thumbs. A. Christie
By the Skin of His Teeth. R. C. Armour
By the Sounding Sea. J. Barden
By the Terms of the Will. W. M. Graydon
By the Watchman's Clock. L. Ford
By the Waters of Babylon. N. DeMille
By the World Condemned. John Marsh
By Their Deeds. A. Peters
By Third Degree. H. S. Keeler
By Unseen Hands. E. Lisle
By Victories Undone. M. Olympitis
By Way of Confession. R. Gore-Brown
By-Ways of Braithe. F. Powell
By Whose Hand? B. Baskerville
By Whose Hand. F. Crisp
By Whose Hand? R. Hardinge
By Whose Hand? H. H. Lewis
By Whose Hand? Louise Rice
By Whose Hand? B. Symons
By Whose Hand? E. S. Tupper
By Wit of Woman. A. W. Marchmont
Bye, Baby Bunting. D. Keene
Bye, Bye, Baby! J. H. Bond
Bye, Bye, Benny. D. Haring
Bye-Bye, Blackbeard! N. Mapple
Bye-Bye Blackbird. R. Rowe
Byzantine Encounter. Andrea Harris

CAB-Intersec. D. Walker
C.A.T. Caper. Margaret Logan
CB Baby. C. Whelton
CB Logbook of the White Knight. M. Avallone
CC and Comapny. M. Roote
C.I.D. T. Mundy
C.I.D. Banner. M. Zleno
C.I.D. of Dexter Drake. E. Barker

C.I.D. Room. P. Alding
C.I.G. J. H. Jones
C Is for Corpse. S. Grafton
C.L.A.W. R. Graves
C.O.D. N. S. Lincoln
"C.Q." A. Train
C.V.C. Murders. K. Williams
CW2. L. C. Heath
Cab Driver's Secret. Nicholas Carter
Cab No. 44. Richard F. Foster
Cab of the Sleeping Horse. J. R. Scott
Cabal. N. Garbo
Cabana Murders. J. Y. Dane
Cabaret. L. H. Brennan
Cabaret Crime. F. Grierson
Cabaret Crime. G. H. Teed
Cabbages and Crime. A. Nash
Cabbages and Kings. O. Henry
Cabin Fever. J. Schenkar
Cabin Nineteen. M. Richmond
Cabin of Fear. D. Hitchens
Cabin 13. Anonymous
Cabin 3033. Anna Clarke
Cabinda Affair. M. Head
Cabine de Luxe. E. L. Long
Cabinet Minister Resigns. A. Duncan
Cabinet Minister's Wife and other stories. G. R. Sims
Cabinet Secret. G. Boothby
Cable-Car. June Drummond
Cable Car Murder. E. A. Taylor
Cable from Kabul. N. Tranter
Cable-Man. W. Chesney
Cabot Station. W. S. Schaill
Cabot Wright Begins. J. Purdy
Cache. L. Damore
Cache-Cache. A. Marsland
Cache on the Rocks. M. Sellers
Cachet. J. Ashford
Cactus. C. Chadwick
Cactus. H. Janson
Cactus Shroud. Carolyn Thomas
Cad Metti, the Female Detective. Old Sleuth
Cadaver of Gideon Wyck. A. Laing
Cadbury's Coffin. G. Swarthout
Cade. J. H. Chase
Cade Curse. W. E. D. Ross
Cadenza for Caruso. B. Paul
Cade's County. A. Lawrence
Cadre One. R. O'Riordan
Caemon's Song. Peter Rominson
Caesar Code. J. M. Simmel
Caesar Code. M. K. Shuman
Caesar Dies. T. Mundy
Cafe in Montparnasse. A. Mills
Cage. R. Gadney
Cage. S. Horler
Cage. E. R. Jones
Cage Five Is Going to Break. E. R. Johnson
Cage for the Nightingale. P. Paul
Cage of Corruption. Griff
Cage of Darkness. R. Masson
Cage of Eagles. J. Follett
Cage of Fear. S. Seaton
Cage of Ice. D. Kyle
Cage of Mirrors. R. Ray
Cage of Passion. I. Mari
Cage of Shadows. Archie Hill
Cage of Violence. R. Magowan
Cage Until Tame. L. Henderson
Cage Without Bars. P. Barrington
Caged. T. Brykcznski
Caged. C. R. Cooper
Caged! H. Hill
Caged. F. Nichols
Caging the Raven. W. Heffernan
Cahusac Mystery. K. Prichard
Cain '67. J. M. Simmel
Cain's Chinese Puzzle. S. A. Key
Cain's Girl Friend. W. Grote
Cain's Hundred. E. L. Heyman
Cain's Wife. O. G. Benson
Cain's Woman. O. G. Benson
Cairo. Percy White

Cairo Alternative. Terry Palmer
Cairo Cabal. A. Caillou
Cairo Communique. Robert Mason
Cairo Countdown Crisis. D. Stivers
Cairo Counterplot. L. J. Burke
Cairo Crisis. W. Martyn
Cairo Garter Murders. V. W. Mason
Cairo Intrigue. W. Manchester
Cairo Mafia. Nick Carter
Cairo Ring. N. Sheraton
Cairo Sleeper. W. Tute
Cajun Nights. D. Stivers
Cajun Nights. D. J. Donaldson
Cake for Caroline. G. M. Wilson
Cakes for Your Birthday. C. E. Vulliamy
Cakes to Kill. H. C. Beck
Calabrian Summer. M. McEvoy
Calamity at Harwood. G. Bellairs
Calamity Comes of Age. G. Baxter
Calamity Comes to Flenton. C. Ashton
Calamity Conquest. B. Gray
Calamity Fair. Wade Miller
Calamity House. M. Billett
Calamity in Kent. J. Rowland
Calamity Town. E. Queen
Calamityville Terror. W. Gleason
Calcroft Case. E. J. Murray
Calculated Risk. R. Foley
Calculated Risk. J. Hayes
Calculated Risk. C. Joyce
Calculus of Murder. E. Rosenthal
Calcutta. Alex Morrison
Calcutta Sweep Mystery. Bat Masters
Calderwood. M. Heath
Caldwell Shadow. D. Daniels
Caleb Clickett. A. Graves
Caleb, Who Is Hotter Than a $2 Pistol. S. Ashley
Caleb Williams. W. Godwin
Calendar. E. Wallace
Calendar of Crime. E. Queen
Calgary Challengers. T. M. Longstreth
Caliban's Castle. P. Warren
Calibre. I. Shulman
Calibre .50. R. Sheckley
Calico Cat. C. M. Thompson
California Conspiracy. R. Lamm
California Detective. Anonymous
California Factor. P. Vernier
California Hit. D. Pendleton
California in the Morning. B. Harding
California Roll. R. L. Simon
California Shakedown. D. Streib
California Street. D. Levin
California Thriller. M. Byrd
Caligari Complex. B. Copper
Calina. L. Gardner
Caliph Intrigue. L. James
Call a Hearse. J. Stagge
Call After Midnight. M. G. Eberhart
Call After Midnight. T. Gerritsen
Call Back to Crime. P. Alding
Call Back Yesterday. G. Ferrand
Call Back Yesterday. Sara Woods
Call-Box Murder. G. Barnett
Call-Box Mystery. J. Ironsides
Call Conquest for Danger. B. Gray
Call Down the Sky. H. Lillie
Call for Blackshirt. R. Graeme
Call for Michael Shayne. B. Halliday
Call for Murder. A. Robbins
Call for Simon Shard. P. McCutchan
Call for Superintendent Flagg. J. Cassells
Call for the Baron. Anthony Morton
Call for the Dead. J. Le Carre
Call for the Saint. L. Charteris
Call from Austria. M. Albrand
Call from L.A. A. Hansl
Call from the Past, and other stories. L. Merrick
Call Girl. Pete Costello
Call Girl Murders. J. G. Brandon
Call Girls for Murder. J. B. Ethan
Call Girls of New York. R. Vane
Call Her Savage. J. Grecco
Call Him Early for the Murder. N. Morland

Title Index

Call in Miss Hogg. A. Lee
Call in the Feds. "G-Man"
Call in the Feds. G. Greer
Call in the Night. Nicholas Carter
Call in the Night. S. Howatch
Call in the Yard. M. A. Clune
Call in the Yard. David Hume
Call It Accident. R. Foley
Call It Coincidence. F. Lockridge
Call It Murder. G. Tracey
Call It Treason. G. Howe
Call McLean. G. Goodchild
Call Me Al. D. Linton
Call Me Captain. P. Stanton
Call Me Deadly. H. Braham
Call Me Duke. H. Grey
Call Me Evil. Desmond Moore
Call Me Killer. H. Whittington
Call Me Miranda. B. Vane
Call Me Pandora. A. Dean
Call Me Shameless. B. Sarto
Call Me Sometime. R. Angel
Call Me Sugar. M. Lavelle
Call Mr. Fortune. H. C. Bailey
Call of Death. Anonymous
Call of Death. T. S. King
Call of Glengarron. N. Buckingham
Call of Honor. D. Bannerman
Call of the Banshee. W. D. Hepenstall
Call of the Blood. K. Kellow
Call of the Deep. I. Stark
Call of the East. M. Nyberg
Call of the Flesh. V. Coffman
Call of the Hand. L. Golding
Call of the North. J. Templeton
Call of the People. L. Clarke
Call of the South. L. Becke
Call of the World. C. H. Bullivant
Call Off the Corpse. John Bentley
Call on Kuprin. M. Edelman
Call on Kuprin. Jerome Lawrence
Call on the Phone. Nicholas Carter
Call Out the Flying Squad! H. Holt
Call or Fold. W. Hughes
Call Sign—Death. V. Wallace
Call the Lady Indiscreet. P. Whelton
Call the Next Witness. P. Woodruff
Call the Toff. J. Creasey
Call the Witness. E. Sherry
Call the Yard! H. Clevely
Call the Yard. J. Mowbray
Call to Danger. C. Coram
Call to Die. C. Coram
Callaghan. P. Cheyney
Callaghan Meets His Fate. M. Chesney
Callaghan of Intelligence. M. Chesney
Callan. J. Mitchell
Callander Square. A. Perry
Callao Clue. R. Howes
Called Back. H. Conway
Called Northwest. S. A. White
Called to Account. Nicholas Carter
Called to Judgment. C. Stanton
Called to the Bar. B. Hemyng
Caller. M. R. Hayes
Callers for Dr. Morelle. E. Dudley
Calling. J. Jenkins
Calling. R. Randall
Calling Alan Fraser. H. Desmond
Calling All Cars. A. W. Cook
Calling All Cars. H. Holt
Calling All Cars. E. Snell
Calling All Ghosts. J. F. Stone
Calling All Suspects. C. Wells
Calling All Z-Cars. W. Prendergast
Calling Bulldog Drummond. G. Fairlie
Calling Dr. Kill. A. Sugar
Calling Dr. Patchwork. R. Goulart
Calling Juliet Bravo. Mollie Hardwick
Calling Larry Kent. D. Haring
Calling Lord Blackshirt. B. Graeme
Calling Mr. Callaghan. P. Cheyney
Calling Mr. Spade. D. Spade
Calling Peter Grayleigh. Colin Robertson

Calling Scotland Yard. H. Holt
Calling Whitehall 1212. H. Clevely
Calling Whitehall 1212. A. Parsons
Callingham's Girl. A. S. Roche
Calliope Reef. H. Rigsby
Calloused Eye. E. H. Loban
Calverston Story. Alan Thomas
Caly. S. M. Combes
Calypso. E. McBain
Calypso. H. Slater
Calypso Magic. C. Coulter
Calypso Murders. P. H. Mulholland
Cambodia. Nick Carter
Cambodia Clash. D. Pendleton
Cambodia Kill-Zone. J. Lansing
Cambodian Quest. R. J. Casey
Cambri Plot. J. Moffatt
Cambridge Murders. A. Broome
Cambridge Murders. D. Rees
Cambridge Theorem. T. Cape
Camden Town Murder. D. Napley
Came a Spider. M. Hammonds
Came the Dawn. R. Bax
Camel. L. Berniers
Camelia Caper. J. K. Polk
Camelion's Dish. R. Pertwee
Camelot Caper. Elizabeth Peters
Camelot Club. B. Killick
Camelot Conundrum. J. Griffin
Cameo. Winston Graham
Cameo. W. Leeds
Cameos. O. R. Cohen
Camera Clue. G. H. Coxe
Camera Fiend. E. W. Hornung
Cameron Castle. Marilyn Ross
Cameron Hill. M. Flavin
Cameron Hill. M. K. Simmons
Cameron Mystery. C. Talbot
Cameron's Landing. Anne Scott
Camerton Slope. R. F. Bishop
Camilla. P. Paul
Camouflage! E. W. Alais
Camouflage. L. Meynell
Camouflage Revolution. H. McKay
Camp. A. Saperstein
Camp. Gordon M. Williams
Camp-Meeting Murders. V. Randolph
Camp of Fear. L. H. Gordon
Camp 7 Last Stop. H. H. Kirst
Camp, the Battlefield, and the Hospital. L. P. Brockett
Campaign Train. The Gordons
Campanile Murders. W. Chambers
Campbell of the Mounties. Robin Marshall
Campbell's Kingdom. H. Innes
Campden Hill Mystery. Elliot Bailey
Campden Ruby Murder. A. Bliss
Campion Diamonds. S. May
Campus Corpse. K. Hopkins
Campus Killings. E. B. Ruark
Campus Murders. E. Queen
Can a Mermaid Kill? T. B. Dewey
Can Death Be Sleep? H. Brinton
Can Ellen Be Saved? M. Z. Bradley
Can It Be True? A. Eedy
Can Ladies Kill? P. Cheyney
Can of Worms. J. H. Chase
Can of Worms. R. H. Greenan
Can Such Things Be? A. Bierce
Can Such Things Be? K. Fleming
Cana Diversion. W. C. Gault
Canaan Legacy. M. A. Kahn
Canadian Bomber Contract. P. Atlee
Canadian Crisis. D. Pendleton
Canadian Farm Mystery. B. Marchant
Canadian Kill. J. Nazel
Canadian Killing Ground. A. Kilgore
Canal Dreams. I. M. Banks
Canal Mystery. J. Remenham
Canal Street. J.-P. Conty
Canal Zone Conquest. Mark Roberts
Canaries Also Sing. E. Allen
Canaries Sometimes Croak. J. Cooper
Canaris File. W. Winward

CANTERBURY KILGRIMS / 925

Canaris Fragments. W. Winward
Canaris Legacy. R. Hitchcock
Canaris Papers. G. Richards
Canary. N. Aldyne
Canary. T. Cohan
Canary Murder Case. W. Butterfield
Canary Murder Case. S. S. Van Dine
Canary That Died. James Lewis
Canary Yellow. E. Cadell
Canceled Czech. Lawrence Block
Cancelled Accounts. H. Greene
Cancelled in Red. H. Pentecost
Cancelled Out. A. E. Redmond
Cancelled Score Mystery. Gret Lane
Cancelled Will. E. A. Dupuy
Candace. Alice Brennan
Candice Is Dead. A. S. Well
Candid Escort. T. B. Marle
Candid Impostor. G. H. Coxe
Candid Killer. J. Giltene
Candidate. R. Alonso
Candidate for a Coffin. J. G. Brandon
Candidate for a Coffin. Neill Graham
Candidate for Danger. E. Sherwood
Candidate for Hell. D. P. Neeley
Candidate for Lilies. R. East
Candidate for Murder. F. Earley
Candidate for Murder. F. Orenstein
Candidate for Murder. M. Post
Candidate's Blood. L. Derrick
Candidates for Glory. J. Fores
Candidates for Murder. A. Hocking
Candidates for Murder. Frank King
Candidate's Wife. V. Coffman
Candido. L. Sciascia
Candied Peel. F. L. Cary
Candle. L. C. Hopkins
Candle and the Tower. R. D. Spector
Candle at Midnight. F. Lynch
Candle for a Corpse. S. Sterling
Candle for Judas. David Fraser
Candle for the Dead. H. Marlowe
Candle for the Dragon. M. Craig
Candle-Holders. V. Gielgud
Candle in the Sun. D. Daniels
Candle in the Wind. G. Bernau
Candle in the Wind. P. Essex
Candle in the Wind. M. Richardson
Candle of the Night. M. Clare
Candle of the Wicked. E. Balmer
Candle of the Wicked. Elizabeth Brown
Candlelight in Avalon. Augustus Muir
Candles Are All Out. N. Fitzgerald
Candles for the Dead. H. Carmichael
Candles in the Night. A. Carr
Candles in the Wood. A. Manners
Candles of Katara. B. Grimshaw
Candleshoe. M. Innes
Candlestick with Seven Branches. M. Leblanc
Candy Kid. D. B. Hughes
Candy Killings. G. Stockwell
Candy Man. R. Cullum
Candyleg. O. Demaris
Candywine Development. John Morris
Cane-Patch Mystery. A. B. Cunningham
Canfield Decision. S. T. Agnew
Canisbay Conspiracy. A. MacVicar
Cankerworm. G. M. Fenn
Cannes. I. Johnstone
Cannibal. N. De Mille
Cannibal Heart. M. Millar
Cannibal Who Overate. H. Pentecost
Cannibals. D. Rome
Cannibals and Missionaries. M. McCarthy
Cannon Law. T. C. Paynter
Cannon, the Falling Blonde. P. Denver
Cannonball. J. Chamier
Cannon's Mouth. W. G. Duncan
Canon Bang-Bang. J. M. O'Neill
Canon in Residence. V. L. Whitechurch
Canon Lucifer. J. D. Delille
Canon's Dilemma. V. Whitechurch
Canon's Ward. J. Payn
Canterbury Kilgrims. J. N. Chance

C

C

Canterbury Mystery. J. S. Fletcher
Canter's Chase. Margaret Archer
Canto for a Gypsy. Martin Smith
Cantrell. R. Prickett
Canvas Coffin. W. C. Gault
Canvas Dagger. H. Reilly
Canvas Jungle. Arthur MacLean
Canvas Prison. G. De Marco
Canyon of Death. K. Edgar
Cap Across the River. J. M. Scott
Cap and Gown for a Shroud. E. N. Gilla
Cap Colt, the Quaker Detective. C. Morris
Capablanca Opening. D. T. Chandler
Capac Legacy. S. Gianetta
Cape. M. Caidin
Cape Cod Caper. M. Arnold
Cape Cod Caper. Carey Phillips
Cape Cod Mystery. P. A. Taylor
Cape Fear. J. D. MacDonald
Cape House. L. P. Shepherd
Cape Jasmine Murder. M. M. Mott
Cape Murders. D. Weeks
Cape of Black Sands. W. D. Roberts
Cape of Shadows. H. Gibbs
Cape Town Affair. A. Scobie
Caper. L. Andress
Caper. T. B. Reagan
Caper at Canaveral! Roger Blake
Caper of the Golden Bulls. W. P. McGivern
Caper Sauce. S. P. B. Mais
Capful o' Nails. D. C. Murray
Capillary Crime and other stories. F. D. Millet
Capital City Mystery. J. H. Wallis
Capital Crime. L. Ford
Capital Crime. A. Roudybush
Capital Killing. D. Everson
Capital Murder. J. Z. Alner
Capital Punishment. Stuart Martin
Capital Punishment. Sutherland Scott
Capitol Crime. Lawrence Meyer
Capitol Crimes. Lawrence Sanders
Capitol Hell. L. Derrick
Capitol Hill Affair. L. James
Capitol Offense. J. Davey
Capri Affair. D. Hanna
Capriccio. Joan Smith
Caprice. S. Hylton
Caprice. J. Withers
Capricorn and Cancer. G. Household
Capricorn One. R. Goulart
Capricorn Quadrant. Charles Ryan
Capricorn Run. D. J. Cleary
Capricorn Stone. M. Brent
Caprifoil. W. P. McGivern
Caprimulgus. W. F. Harvey
Capsule. D. Hagberg
Capsule Mystery. E. C. Vivian
Captain. S. Shubin
Captain and the Enemy. G. Greene
Captain Applejack. W. Hackett
Captain Balaam of the "Cormorant". Morley Roberts
Captain Black. M. Pemberton
Captain Blood. M. Blodgett
Captain Blood: His Odyssey. R. Sabatini
Captain Blood Returns. R. Sabatini
Captain Bolton's Corpse. J. Sturrock
Captain Bowker. S. M. Parkman
Captain Bulldog Drummond. G. Fairlie
Captain Butterfly. B. Leuci
Captain Castle. C. Dawe
Captain Christine. Basil Carey
Captain Clew, the Flying Detective. Anonymous
Captain Confetti. F. J. Dee
Captain Crash. G. Goodchild
Captain Cut-Throat. J. D. Carr
Captain Dack. P. Meriton
Captain Firebrace. Seafarer
Captain Firebrace and the Java Queen. Seafarer
Captain Flynn. E. L. Long
Captain Flynn Ret'd. E. L. Long
Captain Flynn, Sheriff. E. L. Long
Captain Fraser's Profession. J. S. Winter
Captain Gardiner of the International Police. R. Allen
Captain Gault. W. H. Hodgson
Captain Incognito. G. Gibson
Captain Jack. H. Outerbridge
Captain Jackman. W. C. Russell
Captain Justice. A. Forrest
Captain Kettle, Ambassador. C. J. C. Hyne
Captain Kettle, K.C.B. C. J. C. Hyne
Captain Kettle on the War-Path. C. J. C. Hyne
Captain Kettle's Bit. C. J. C. Hyne
Captain King Investigates. K. Trask
Captain Kirke Webb. F. W. Hayes
Captain Landon. R. H. Savage
Captain Lost His Bathroom. C. Winchester
Captain Lucifer. B. Bolt
Cap'n Luke, Filibuster. "Capstan"
Captain McBlaid of the Air Police. R. Walker
Captain Marraday's Marriage. T. Cobb
Captain Millett's Island. K. N. Burt
Captain Moonlight. Francis Warwick
Captain Must Die. R. Colby
Captain Nash and the Honour of England. Ragan Butler
Captain Nash and the Wroth Inheritance. Ragan Butler
Captain Nice. W. Johnston
Captain of the Guard. C. Houghton
Captain of the Kansas. L. Tracy
Captain of the Polestar, and other stories. A. C. Doyle
Captain of the Vulture. M. E. Braddon
Captain Overboard. F. Andreas
Captain Rock's Pet. E. Southworth
Captain Samson, A.B. Gavin Douglas
Captain Satan. J. Brearley
Captain Sentimental and other stories. E. Jepson
Captain Shannon. C. Kernahan
Captain Sinister. G. Goodchild
Captain Sparkle, Pirate. Nicholas Carter
Cap'n Sue. H. Footner
Captain Tatham of Tatham Island. Edgar Wallace
Captain Wardlaw's Kitbags. H. MacGrath
Captain Wunder. D. Thomas
Captains All. W. W. Jacobs
Captain's Cabin. Edward Jenkins
Captain's Curio. E. Phillpotts
Captain's House. M. K. Simmons
Captain's Lady. Rachelle Edwards
Captains of Death. G. W. Jones
Captains of Souls. E. Wallace
Captains of the "Calabar". F. Knight
Captain's Pawn. A. Lowing
Captain's Room. W. Besant
Captain's Walk. E. Welles
Captain's Woman, and other stories. Neil Bell
Captivator. A. York
Captive. N. Daniels
Captive. The Gordons
Captive. Victoria Holt
Captive. B. Kingsley
Captive Audience. Jessica Mann
Captive City. J. Appleby
Captive City. D. DaCruz
Captive Heart. C. Jauniere
Captive in Paradise. Magali
Captive in the Land. J. Aldridge
Captive in the Night. D. Stokes
Captive in Time. S. Dreher
Captive Princess. R. H. Savage
Captive Years. D. Lee
Captives of Mora Island. V. Canning
Captivity Captive. Rodney Hall
Captors. J. Farris
Capture. W. Martyn
Capture of Paul Beck. M. M. Bodkin
Capture of the Paddy Ryan Gang of Burglars. L. A. Newcome
Captured. M. Serrian
Captured by Cannibals. J. Hatton
Captured Cruiser. C. J. C. Hyne
Captures. J. Galsworthy
Car for Mr. Bradley. J. Pattinson
Car Park Mystery. A. Parsons
Cara Massimina. J. McDowell
Caracol Reef. Michael Andrews
Carambola. D. Dodge
Caravaggio Obsession. O. Banks
Caravaggio Shawl. S. M. Steward
Caravan Adventure. J. J. Farjeon
Caravan Crime. G. Chester
Caravan Days. G. Goodchild
Caravan Detective. S. C. Hook
Caravan Mystery. F. Hume
Caravan of Crime. E. O'Donnell
Caravan of Night. M. Erskine
Caravan to Vaccares. Alistair MacLean
Caravanners. J. Dering
Caravans by Night. H. Hervey
Carbon Copies. O. R. Cohen
Carbon Copy. Anthony Brennan
Carbon Copy Killer. M. Brody
Carbon Monoxide. J. Street
Carbuncle Clue. F. Hume
Carcase for Hounds. M. Mwangi
Carcellini Emerald, with other tales. Mrs. B. Harrison
Card Games. A. Fletcher
Card 13. M. L. Luther
Cardboard Castle. Margery Lawrence
Cardboard Castle. P. C. Wren
Cardboard City. Joe Cannon
Cardboard Hero. L. Noel
Cardiac Arrest. J. H. Way
Cardinal and the Corpse. S. Blakesley
Cardinal Error. M. Walton
Cardinal Moth. F. M. White
Cardinal of the Kremlin. T. Clancy
Cardinal Sin. H. Conway
Cardinal Virtues. A. M. Greeley
Cardinalli Contract. E. R. Johnson
Cardinal's Rose. V. Sutphen
Cardington Crescent. Anne Perry
Cardross Luck. J. L. Roberts
Cards of the Gambler. B. Kiely
Cards on the Table. A. Christie
Cards on the Table. L. Darbon
Cardyce for the Defence. B. Graeme
Care of Devils. S. Press
Care of Souls. J. M. Cobban
Care of the Commander. R. L. Dearden
Care of Time. E. Ambler
Careen. V. Coffman
Career for the Baron. Anthony Morton
Career in C Major and other stories. J. M. Cain
Career of a Nihilist. Stepniak
Career with Death. H. Tracy
Careful, He Might Hear You. S. L. Elliott
Careful Man. R. Deming
Careful with the Sharks. C. Phipps
Careless Corpse. B. Halliday
Careless Corpse. C. D. King
Careless Feast. M. Rostov
Careless Hangman. N. Morland
Careless Lives. D. Leslie
Careless Mrs. Christian. C. M. Russell
Careless Whispers. C. Stowers
Caress Before Killing. Carter Brown
Caress of Conquest. S. D. Frances
Caretaker. F. Hume
Caretakers. T. King
Carfax Abbey. B. Thomson
Carfax Baines. W. M. Graydon
Cargo Club. P. Corris
Cargo for Crooks. Sea Lion
Cargo for Death. T. Wallace
Cargo for the Styx. L. Trimble
Cargo Gods. D. Streib
Cargo of Death. H. McCutcheon
Cargo of Eagles. M. Allingham
Cargo of Fear. J. L. Currier
Cargo of Gold. J. G. Sarasin
Cargo of Spent Evil. J. M. Brett
Cargo of Tin. T. Henege
Cargo Risk. Robert MacLeod
Cargo to Saigon. C. Leader
Cargo—Trouble. P. Thomas
Cargo Unknown. K. Robeson

Title Index

Caribbean Account. A. Furst
Caribbean Adventure and other stories. M. Gann
Caribbean Affair. E. P. Thorne
Caribbean Blood Moon. J. Rosenberger
Caribbean Blues. M. H. Clark
Caribbean Caper. H. Janson
Caribbean Caper. Robin Moore
Caribbean Caper. J. Rosenberger
Caribbean Conspiracy. B. Conrad
Caribbean Conspiracy. L. Holden
Caribbean Coup. Nick Carter
Caribbean Crisis. D. E. Bingley
Caribbean Crisis. D. Reid
Caribbean Cutie. Griff
Caribbean Dreams. R. Friedman
Caribbean Kidnap. M. Cronin
Caribbean Kill. D. Pendleton
Caribbean Kill. A. Sugar
Caribbean Mystery. A. Christie
Caribbean Phantom and other stories. M. Gann
Caribbean Striker. J. E. MacDonnell
Caribbean Strip. I. S. Black
Caribe. L. Maracotta
Caribe. J. R. Sprechman
Caribou Patrol. C. Stoddard
Carioca Fletch. G. McDonald
Carla. J. R. Marshall
Carla Packs a Rod. R. Marlowe
Carlent Manor Crime. L. Grex
Carleton Case. E. H. Clark
Carlito's Way. E. Torres
Carlos Chadwick Mystery. G. Bell-Villada
Carlos Contract. D. A. Phillips
Carlos Is Dead. N. Harman
Carlos Must Die. U. Dan
Carlton Plot. P. N. Walker
Carlyon's Year. J. Payn
Carmen Was a Virgin. M. Storme
Carmen's Messenger. H. Bindloss
Carn. P. McCabe
Carnaby and the Assassins. P. N. Walker
Carnaby and the Campaigners. P. N. Walker
Carnaby and the Conspirators. P. N. Walker
Carnaby and the Counterfeiters. P. N. Walker
Carnaby and the Demonstrators. P. N. Walker
Carnaby and the Eliminators. P. N. Walker
Carnaby and the Gaolbreakers. P. N. Walker
Carnaby and the Hijackers. P. N. Walker
Carnaby and the Infiltrators. P. N. Walker
Carnaby and the Kidnappers. P. N. Walker
Carnaby and the Saboteurs. P. N. Walker
Carnaby Curse. D. Winston
Carnaby Rex. R. MacLeish
Carnacki, the Ghost Finder. W. H. Hodgson
Carnacki, the Ghost Finder, and a Poem. W. H. Hodgson
Carnage at Christhaven. Chrysostom Society
Carnage of the Realm. C. A. Goodrum
Carnal Days of Helen Seferis. A. Trocchi
Carnal Greed. P. C. Smith
Carnavaron's Castle. J. F. Webb
Carnecrane. Mary Williams
Carnelian Cat. J. Deweese
Carnellian Circle. H. John
Carney's Burlesque. S. Harragan
Carnival. W. W. Johnstone
Carnival! J. Rathbone
Carnival. Jenna Ryan
Carnival Confession. C. Zuckmayer
Carnival for Killing. Nick Carter
Carnival Girl. R. Glendinning
Carnival Murder. N. Brady
Carnival of Crime. Fredric Brown
Carnival of Crime. Nicholas Carter
Carnival of Death. A. Eadie
Carnival of Death. D. Keene
Carnival of Death. D. Kirby
Carnival of Death. J. C. Lenehan
Carnival of Death. H. Zore
Carnival of Spies. R. Moss
Carnivores. J. R. Levitt
Carny Kill. R. E. Alter
Caro. B. J. Packer
Carol in the Dark. C. Jordan

Carol, the Pursued. K. Kimbrough
Carolina House. E. Kyle
Carolina Skeletons. D. Stout
Caroline Affair. C. H. Gibbs-Smith
Caroline, Caroline. M. Ritter
Caroline Miniscule. Andrew Taylor
Caroline Ormesby's Crime. H. Adams
Carolinian. R. Sabatini
Carp Country. E. Kyle
Carpaccio Caper. B. Strutton
Carpathian Caper. J. Sandulescu
Carpe Diem. Steve Miller
Carpenter, Detective. H. T. Caine
Carpenter Investigates and other stories. H. L. Peacock
Carpet Courtship. T. Cobb
Carpet from Bagdad. H. MacGrath
Carpet of Death. R. McNear
Carpet-Slipper Murder. A. C. MacLean
Carquake. M. Avallone
Carr of Dimscaur. T. Douglas
Carradice Chain. S. Hylton
Carriage Clock. V. Andrews
Carriage 7 Seat 15. C. Aveline
Carried Away. E. L. Long
Carriers of Death. J. Creasey
Carrington Assignment. R. Child
Carrington V.C. D. Christie
Carrington's Cases. J. S. Clouston
Carrion Comfort. Dan Simmons
Carrion Crows. Dorothy Bennett
Carrion Eaters. W. A. Ballinger
Carrion Eaters. E. H. Rhodes
Carrion Experience. I. G. Slabber
Carrismore Ruby. J. S. Fletcher
Carriston's Gift and other stories. F. J. Fargus
Carroll Moore. Old Sleuth
Carrolls and other tales. Anonymous
Carrot for the Donkey. Les Roberts
Carry-Cot. A. Thynne
Carry Me Home. P. Traill
Carry My Coffin Slowly. L. Herrington
Carson Inheritance. D. Daniels
Carson Loan Mystery. A. De Brune
Carson's Conspiracy. M. Innes
Cart Before the Crime. J. Porter
Cart Before the Hearse. R. Ormerod
Cartel. E. J. Epstein
Carter Kidnapping Case. A. R. Long
Carteret Affair. S. Rathbone
Carteret Hotel Mystery. J. Corbett
Carteret's Cure. R. Keverne
Carter's Castle. Wilbur Wright
Carter's Triumph. H. Bindloss
Carthusian Friar. Sarah Green
Cartoon Crimes. K. Robeson
Cartoon for Crime. M. Catton
Cartoonist. Sean Costello
Cartsley Mystery. J. G. Rowe
Cartwright Gardens Murder. J. S. Fletcher
Cartwright Is Dead, Sir! H. Baker
Caruthers Affair. W. N. Harben
Carved Emerald. V. France
Carven Ball. J. Haslette
Carver. P. Barker
Carver of the Swamp. "Capstan"
Casa Madrone. M. G. Eberhart
Casablack. C. Leopold
Casablanca. J. J. Epstein
Casablanca Conspiracy. G. Wagner
Casablanca Intrigue. Clarissa Ross
Casanova Embrace. W. Adler
Casanova, Prince of Lovers. R. Vane
Casbah Killers. Nick Carter
Casco Deception. B. Reiss
Case. V. White
Case Against Aldor. C. Ryland
Case Against Andrew Fane. Anthony Gilbert
Case Against Butterfly. G. Tree
Case Against Dr. Ripon. W. Tyrer
Case Against Love. D. Decoin
Case Against Mrs. Ames. A. S. Roche
Case Against Mrs. Dane. D. Trevern
Case Against Myself. G. Tree

Case Against Paul Raeburn. J. Creasey
Case Against Philip Quest. M. Underwood
Case Against Satan. Ray Russell
Case and Exceptions. F. T. Hill
Case and the Girl. R. Parrish
Case Bird and other stories. F. B. Young
Case-Book of Anthony Slade. L. Gribble
Case Book of Ellery Queen. E. Queen
Case Book of Jimmie Lavender. V. Starrett
Case Book of Mr. Campion. M. Allingham
Case-Book of Sherlock Holmes. A. C. Doyle
Case Books of X 37. A. J. Dawson
Case Closed. J. Thomson
Case Continued. J. Prescot
Case Dead and Buried. C. Barry
Case File: FBI. The Gordons
Case for Appeal. L. Egan
Case for Charley. J. Spenser
Case for Compensation. Cameron Ross
Case for Court. J. Prescot
Case for Equity. K. Hill
Case for Hearing. J. Prescot
Case for Inspector Flagg. J. Cassells
Case for Inspector West. J. Creasey
Case for Mason. W. McCleery
Case for M.I.5. W. Jardine
Case for Mr. Crook. Anthony Gilbert
Case for Mr. Fortune. H. C. Bailey
Case for Mr. Paul Savoy. Jackson Gregory
Case for Mrs. Heydon. R. Bridges
Case for Punishment. H. Hunter
Case for Sergeant Beef. L. Bruce
Case for Solomon. B. Graeme
Case for the Accused. J. Prescot
Case for the Baron. Anthony Morton
Case for the C.I.D. P. C. De Crespigny
Case for the Cardinal. S. Blakesley
Case for the Courts. Mrs. C. Kernahan
Case for the Crown. F. M. White
Case for the Defence. M. Fitt
Case for the Defendent. H. Aufricht-Ruda
Case for the Dreamer. W. M. Duncan
Case for the Lady. F. Warden
Case for the Prosecution. W. M. Graydon
Case for Three Detectives. L. Bruce
Case for Treachery. V. White
Case for Tressider. C. Barry
Case for Trial. J. Prescot
Case in Camera. O. Onions
Case in Hand. N. A. Temple-Ellis
Case in Madrid. E. Naughton
Case in Nullity. E. Berckman
Case in the Clinic. E. C. R. Lorac
Case Is Altered. H. L. Jones
Case Is Altered. W. Plomer
Case Is Altered. Brian Stuart
Case Is Altered. Sara Woods
Case Is Closed. P. Wentworth
Case Load—Maximum. E. R. Johnson
Case No. 561. D. Knight
Case of Alisa Gray. G. M. Fenn
Case of Alan Copeland. M. Dalton
Case of Anne Bickerton. S. Fowler
Case of Art Failure. F. Bream
Case of Blackmail. E. W. Alais
Case of Blackmail. C. K. Moore
Case of Blind Fear. Martin Powell
Case of Books. B. Graeme
Case of Bottled Murder. E. Wagner
Case of Caroline Animus. D. Chambers
Case of Caspar Gault. W. Morton
Case of Colonel Marchand. E. C. R. Lorac
Case of Comrade Tulayev. V. Serge
Case of Constable Shields. R. Greaves
Case of Dan Morris. C. Jude
Case of Doctor Horace. J. H. Prentis
Case of Dr. Morel. K. Bramson
Case of Doctor Plemen. R. De Pont-Jest
Case of Doctor Tracey. R. A. Here
Case of Elinor Norton. M. R. Rinehart
Case of Elymas the Sorcerer. B. Flynn
Case of George Candlemas. G. R. Sims
Case of Give a Dog. Julian Roberts
Case of Identity. L. Brain

Case of Identity. R. Marsh
Case of Indelicate Champagne. F. Halliday
Case of Innocence. D. J. Keeling
Case of Jennie Brice. M. R. Rinehart
Case of John Muir of Merchant Navy. L. Jackson
Case of Joshua Locke. R. G. Dean
Case of Kitty Ogilvie. J. Stubbs
Case of L. A. C. Dickson. J. Drummond
Case of Lady Broadstone. A. W. Marchmont
Case of Lady Camber. H. A. Vachell
Case of Larachi the Lascar. O. Merland
Case of Libel. J. Bingham
Case of Lone Star. K. Friedman
Case of Lord Greyburn's Son. D. Long
Case of Loyalties. Marilyn Wallace
Case of Lucy Bending. Lawrence Sanders
Case of Many Clues. Nicholas Carter
Case of Marie Corwin. G. Dean
Case of Mary Fielding. M. Erskine
Case of Mary Sherman. J. E. Brady
Case of Matthew Crake. A. G. MacLeod
Case of Miss Dunstable. J. Hocking
Case of Miss Elliott. B. Orczy
Case of Mr. Budd. G. Verner
Case of Mr. Cassidy. W. Targ
Case of Mr. Crump. L. Lewisohn
Case of Mr. Lucraft and other tales. W. Besant
Case of Mrs. Wingate. O. Micheaux
Case of Mortimer Fenley. L. Tracy
Case of Naomi Clynes. B. Thomson
Case of Need. J. Hudson
Case of Oscar Brodsky. R. A. Freeman
Case of Paul Breen. A. Tudor
Case of Rape. D. Warren
Case of Red Diamonds. R. Pendark
Case of Reuben Malachi. H. Sutherland Edwards
Case of Richard Eden. Mark Allerton
Case of Richard Meynell. Mrs. H. Ward
Case of Robert Quarry. A. Garve
Case of Robert Robertson. S. Elvestad
Case of Sergeant Bill Mordon. Richard Standish
Case of Sir Adam Braid. M. Thynne
Case of Sir Edward Talbot. V. F. Taubman-Goldie
Case of Sir Geoffrey. F. Warden
Case of Sonia Wayward. M. Innes
Case of Spirits. P. Lovesey
Case of the Abominable Snowman. N. Blake
Case of the Absent Corpse. K. Hill
Case of the Absent-Minded Professor. A. M. Stein
Case of the Ace Accomplice. W. J. Passingham
Case of the Acid Throwers. J. Creasey
Case of the Adopted Daughter. W. M. Graydon
Case of the Advertised Murder. M. Bardon
Case of the African Emigrant. R. Hardinge
Case of the African Hoodoo. R. Hardinge
Case of the African Trader. R. Hardinge
Case of the Alpha Murders. S. Blakesley
Case of the Amateur Actor. C. Bush
Case of the Amber Crown. A. Murray
Case of the American Tourists. J. Hunter
Case of the Amorous Aunt. E. S. Gardner
Case of the Angels' Trumpets. Michael Burt
Case of the Angry Actress. E. V. Cunningham
Case of the Angry Mourner. E. S. Gardner
Case of the April Fools. C. Bush
Case of the Ashanti Gold. C. Mason
Case of the Back Seat Girl. C. Ryland
Case of the Backward Mule. E. S. Gardner
Case of the Baffled Policeman. Allen Sharp
Case of the Baited Hook. E. S. Gardner
Case of the Baker Street Irregulars. A. Boucher
Case of the Banned Film. A. Parsons
Case of the Barking Clock. E. S. Gardner
Case of the Baronet's Memoirs. Richard Grant
Case of the Beautiful Beggar. E. S. Gardner
Case of the Beautiful Body. Jonathan Craig
Case of the Beckoning Dead. J. Donavan
Case of the Bendigo Heirlooms. Jack Lewis
Case of the Benevolent Bookie. C. Bush
Case of the Berlin Spy. D. Betteridge
Case of the Bigamous Spouse. E. S. Gardner
Case of the Billion Dollar Body. J. Shallit
Case of the Biscay Pirate. L. Jackson
Case of the Bismarck Memoirs. P. Quiroule

Case of the Black-Eyed Blonde. E. S. Gardner
Case of the Black Magician. R. Hardinge
Case of the Black Orchids. R. Stout
Case of the Black Sheep. S. Finley
Case of the Black Twenty-Two. B. Flynn
Case of the Blackmailed Banker. A. Blair
Case of the Blackmailed King. Roland Daniel
Case of the Blackmailed Prince. A. Parsons
Case of the Blank Cartridge. L. Trimble
Case of the Blind Mouse. M. J. Freeman
Case of the Blonde Bonanza. E. S. Gardner
Case of the Blood-Stained Dime. M. Bardon
Case of the Bludgeoned Teacher. J. Hollis
Case of the Blue Lacquered Box. G. F. Worts
Case of the Blue Orchid. H. Desmond
Case of the Bogus Baron. W. Tyrer
Case of the Bogus Bride! H. H. C. Gibbons
Case of the Bogus Laird. J. W. Bobin
Case of the Bogus Monk. G. H. Teed
Case of the Bogus Prince. G. Chester
Case of the Bogus Treasure Hunt. W. M. Graydon
Case of the Bonfire Body. C. Bush
Case of the Bookmaker Baronet. J. W. Bobin
Case of the Borrowed Brunette. E. S. Gardner
Case of the Bouncing Better. M. Avallone
Case of the Brass-Bound Chest. G. Chester
Case of the Brazen Beauty. Jonathan Craig
Case of the Bronze Statue. J. Hunter
Case of the Brooklyn Mobster. L. Dexter
Case of the Brown-Eyed Housemaid. C. Ryland
Case of the Brunette Bombshell. H. Waugh
Case of the Buchanan Curse. Allen Sharp
Case of the Buried Clock. E. S. Gardner
Case of the Burmese Dagger. A. Murray
Case of the Burning Bequest. T. Chastain
Case of the Burnt Bohemian. C. Bush
Case of the Busy Bees. C. Witting
Case of the Cabaret Girl. W. W. Sayer
Case of the Calabar Bean. C. M. Wills
Case of the Calendar Girl. E. S. Gardner
Case of the Cancelled Redhead. H. Daly
Case of the Canny Killer. H. S. Keeler
Case of the Careless Cupid. E. S. Gardner
Case of the Careless Kitten. E. S. Gardner
Case of the Careless Thief. C. Bush
Case of the Caretaker's Cat. E. S. Gardner
Case of the Cashiered Officer. W. M. Graydon
Case of the Cautious Coquette. E. S. Gardner
Case of the Chased and the Unchaste. T. B. Dewey
Case of the Cheating Bride. M. Propper
Case of the Chief Rabbi's Problem. V. Andrews
Case of the Chinese Boxes. Marele Day
Case of the Chinese Courier. R. Hardinge
Case of the Chinese Gong. C. Bush
Case of the Chinese Pearls. G. H. Teed
Case of the Cinema Star. A. Murray
Case of the Clairvoyant's Ruse. G. H. Teed
Case of the Climbing Corpse. Gwyn Evans
Case of the Climbing Rat. C. Bush
Case of the Cold Coquette. Jonathan Craig
Case of the Cold Murderer. E. Godfrey
Case of the Coloured Wind. J. Donavan
Case of the Conscript Miner. W. Tyrer
Case of the Constant God. R. King
Case of the Constant Suicides. J. D. Carr
Case of the Copper Cat. L. W. Douglas
Case of the Cop's Wife. M. K. Ozaki
Case of the Copy-Hook Killing. R. Howes
Case of the Corner Cottage. C. Bush
Case of the Corporal's Leave. C. Bush
Case of the Cottage Crime. W. Tyrer
Case of the Cotton Beetle. A. Murray
Case of the Council Swindle. W. Tyrer
Case of the Counterfeit Colonel. C. Bush
Case of the Counterfeit Eye. E. S. Gardner
Case of the Courtland Jewels. G. H. Teed
Case of the Crawling Cockroach. Harlan Reed
Case of the Crazy Atom. H. Hawton
Case of the Crazy Pilot. P. Conde
Case of the Crime Reporter. R. Hardinge
Case of the Criminal's Daughter. H. Clevely
Case of the Crimson Conjurer. Gwyn Evans
Case of the Crimson Kiss. E. S. Gardner
Case of the Crimson Wizard. E. J. Murray

Case of the Crook Banker. Ladbroke Black
Case of the Crook Councilor. A. Blair
Case of the Crook Iron Master. M. Osborne
Case of the Crook M.P. G. N. Philips
Case of the Crook Rajah. A. Parsons
Case of the Crooked Candle. E. S. Gardner
Case of the Crooked Skipper. J. Hunter
Case of the Crumpled Knave. A. Boucher
Case of the Crying Swallow. E. S. Gardner
Case of the Cultured Pearls. J. W. Bobin
Case of the Curious Bride. E. S. Gardner
Case of the Curious Chair. R. Powell
Case of the Curious Client. C. Bush
Case of the Curious Heel. K. F. Crossen
Case of the Curious Moonstone. T. K. Kelly
Case of the Dancing Bees. Allen Sharp
Case of the Dancing Sandwiches. F. Brown
Case of the Dangerous Dowager. E. S. Gardner
Case of the Dangra Millions. A. Parsons
Case of the Daring Decoy. E. S. Gardner
Case of the Daring Divorcee. E. S. Gardner
Case of the Dark Hero. P. Cheyney
Case of the Dark Stranger. M. Dalton
Case of the Dark Wanton. P. Cheyney
Case of the Dead Cadet. R. P. Koehler
Case of the Dead Diplomat. B. Thomson
Case of the Dead Divorcee. W. Holder
Case of the Dead Doctor. V. Loder
Case of the Dead Grandmother. M. Bardon
Case of the Dead Man Gone. C. Bush
Case of the Dead Producer. V. MacClure
Case of the Dead Shepherd. C. Bush
Case of the "Dead" Spy. J. Drummond
Case of the Deadly Diamonds. C. Bush
Case of the Deadly Diary. William Du Bois
Case of the Deadly Kiss. M. K. Ozaki
Case of the Deadly Toy. E. S. Gardner
Case of the Deadly Triangle. R. Ayers
Case of the Death Computer. J. N. Chance
Case of the Defaulting Sailor. J. Hunter
Case of the Demented Spiv. G. Bellairs
Case of the Demure Defendant. E. S. Gardner
Case of the Deported Aliens. W. J. Bayfield
Case of the Deportee. G. Chester
Case of the Deserted War Bride. J. Hunter
Case of the Deserted Wife. W. J. Bayfield
Case of the Devil's Hoofmarks. Allen Sharp
Case of the Dictator's Double. A. Blair
Case of the Discharged P.C. W. Shute
Case of the Discharged Policeman. L. Jackson
Case of the Disguised Apache. G. H. Teed
Case of the Dope Dealers. M. Frazer
Case of the Doped Favourite. J. Hunter
Case of the Doped Heavyweight. L. Jackson
Case of the Double Event. J. Hunter
Case of the Double Tangle. W. J. Bayfield
Case of the Dowager's Etchings. R. King
Case of the Drowning Duck. E. S. Gardner
Case of the Drowsy Mosquito. E. S. Gardner
Case of the Dubious Bridegroom. E. S. Gardner
Case of the Duplicate Daughter. E. S. Gardner
Case of the Ebony Queen. C. Adkins
Case of the Eccentric Will. R. C. Armour
Case of the Eight Brothers. M. V. Heberden
Case of the Eighteenth Ostrich. Colin Curzon
Case of the Empty Beehive. C. M. Wills
Case of the Empty Tin. E. S. Gardner
Case of the Extra Grave. C. Bush
Case of the Extra Man. C. Bush
Case of the Fabulous Fake. E. S. Gardner
Case of the Face at the Window. W. Ecke
Case of the Faithful Heart. B. Flynn
Case of the Famished Parson. G. Bellairs
Case of the Fan-Dancer's Horse. E. S. Gardner
Case of the Fast Young Lady. Michael Burt
Case of the Fatal Film. J. Hunter
Case of the Fatal Souvenir. L. Jackson
Case of the Fatal Taxi Cab. W. M. Graydon
Case of the Fear Makers. J. N. Chance
Case of the Fenced-In Woman. E. S. Gardner
Case of the Fiery Fingers. E. S. Gardner
Case of the Fifth Key. G. Dean
Case of the Fighting Padre. L. Jackson
Case of the Fighting Soldier. C. Bush

Case of the First-Class Carriage. C. Carnac
Case of the Five Dummy Books. W. W. Sayer
Case of the Five Fugitives. L. Jackson
Case of the Five Merchants. W. M. Graydon
Case of the Five Red Herrings. L. Jackson
Case of the Flowery Corpse. C. Bush
Case of the Flying Ass. C. Bush
Case of the Flying Fifteen. O. Mills
Case of the Foot-Loose Doll. E. S. Gardner
Case of the Forbidden Island. W. Tyrer
Case of the Forty Thieves. J. Rhode
Case of the Foster Father. V. Perdue
Case of the Fotheringham Diamond. T. Bullimore
Case of the Four Barons. W. M. Graydon
Case of the Four Friends. J. C. Masterman
Case of the Four Pages. John Norman
Case of the Fourth Detective. C. Bush
Case of the Fragmented Woman. Cleo Jones
Case of the Frantic Ladies. L. Floyd
Case of the French Raiders. J. Hunter
Case of the Frightened Brother. Frank King
Case of the Frightened Fish. William Du Bois
Case of the Frightened Girl. R. Hardinge
Case of the Frightened Heiress. Allen Sharp
Case of the Frightened Lady. E. Wallace
Case of the Frightened Man. A. Parsons
Case of the Frightened Mannequin. C. Bush
Case of the Frozen Scream. T. B. Haughey
Case of the Fugitive Nurse. E. S. Gardner
Case of the Gambler's Corpse. R. Clarke
Case of the Gangster's Moll. J. G. Brandon
Case of the Gentle Conspirators. Allen Sharp
Case of the Giant Killer. H. C. Branson
Case of the Gilded Fly. E. Crispin
Case of the Gilded Lily. E. S. Gardner
Case of the Girl on Remand. J. Hunter
Case of the Girl Reporter. J. W. Bobin
Case of the Glamorous Ghost. E. S. Gardner
Case of the Glass Slipper. N. MacKenzie
Caes of the Gloating Landlord. R. Fenisong
Case of the Gold Coins. A. Wynne
Case of the Gold-Digger's Purse. E. S. Gardner
Case of the Golden Coins. D. A. Davey
Case of the Golden Stool. F. A. Symonds
Case of the Good Employer. C. Bush
Case of the Grand Alliance. C. Bush
Case of the Greedy Rainmaker. George Douglas
Case of the Green Caravan. R. Hardinge
Case of the Green-Eyed Sister. E. S. Gardner
Case of the Green Felt Hat. C. Bush
Case of the Green Knife. A. Wynne
Case of the Grieving Monkey. V. Perdue
Case of the Grinning Gorilla. E. S. Gardner
Case of the Half-Wakened Wife. E. S. Gardner
Case of the Handsome Stranger. R. Horton
Case of the Hanging Lady. N. Jones
Case of the Hanging Rope. C. Bush
Case of the Happy Medium. C. Bush
Case of the Happy Warrior. C. Bush
Case of the Hardboiled Dicks. J. Blumenthal
Case of the Hated Senator. M. Scherf
Case of the Haunted Brides. William Du Bois
Case of the Haunted Grange. E. H. Robinson
Case of the Haunted Husband. E. S. Gardner
Case of the Haven Hotel. C. Bush
Case of the Head Dispenser. J. W. Bobin
Case of the Headless Jesuit. G. Bellairs
Case of the Heavenly Twin. C. Bush
Case of the Hesitant Hostess. E. S. Gardner
Case of the Hijacked Moon. T. B. Haughey
Case of the Hold-Up King. F. A. Symonds
Case of the Hollow Man. M. Carrel
Case of the Hookbilled Kites. J. S. Borthwick
Case of the Horrified Heirs. E. S. Gardner
Case of the Housekeeper's Hair. C. Bush
Case of the Howling Dog. E. S. Gardner
Case of the Howling Dog. Allen Sharp
Case of the Hula Clock. D. Gardiner
Case of the Human Ape. W. M. Graydon
Case of the Human Mole. H. Townley
Case of the Hundred Clues. Anonymous
Case of the Hypnotized Virgin. J. Roeburt
Case of the Ice-Cold Hands. E. S. Gardner
Case of the Income-Tax Frauds. W. J. Bayfield

Case of the Indian Dancer. A. Parsons
Case of the Indian Millionaire. A. Parsons
Case of the Indian Watcher. A. Parsons
Case of the Indiana Torturer. E. E. Saks
Case of the Innocent Victims. J. Creasey
Case of the Innocent Wife. N. Morland
Case of the Innocent Witness. M. Carrel
Case of the International Adventurer. J. W. Bobin
Case of the Invisible Thief. T. B. Haughey
Case of the Irate Witness. E. S. Gardner
Case of the Island Princess. R. C. Armour
Case of the Island Trader. J. W. Bobin
Case of the Ivory Arrow. H. S. Keeler
Case of the Jack of Clubs. Gwyn Evans
Case of the Jade-Handled Knife. G. H. Teed
Case of the Japanese Contract. A. Parsons
Case of the Japanese Detective. T. C. Wignall
Case of the Jewelled Ragpicker. H. S. Keeler
Case of the Johannisberg Riesling. G. Maddren
Case of the Journeying Boy. M. Innes
Case of the Judas Spoon. M. L. Stokes
Case of the Jumbo Sandwich. C. Bush
Case of the Kidnapped Angel. E. V. Cunningham
Case of the Kidnapped Colonel. C. Bush
Case of the Kidnapped Legatee. R. C. Armour
Case of the Kidnapped Prisoner. A. Blair
Case of the Kidnapped Shadow. T. B. Haughey
Case of the Kidnapped Specialist. R. Hardinge
Case of the King of Montavia. Roland Daniel
Case of the King's Spy. W. W. Sayer
Case of the Kippered Corpse. M. Scherf
Case of the Lame Canary. E. S. Gardner
Case of the Langsdale Wanderers. Hedley Scott
Case of the Late Pig. M. Allingham
Case of the Laughing Cat. B. Marchant
Case of the Laughing Dwarf. J. Reach
Case of the Laughing Jesuit. Michael Burt
Case of the Laughing Virgin. Jonathan Craig
Case of the Lavender Gripsack. H. S. Keeler
Case of the Lazy Lover. E. S. Gardner
Case of the Leaning Man. C. Bush
Case of the Legion Deserter. H. Clevely
Case of the Little Doctor. Hilda Lewis
Case of the Little Green Man. M. Reynolds
Case of the Loaded Garter Holster. E. Willie
Case of the Lone Plantation. E. J. Murray
Case of the Lonely Heiress. E. S. Gardner
Case of the Lonely Lovers. W. Daemer
Case of the Long-Firm Frauds. J. W. Bobin
Case of the Long-Legged Models. E. S. Gardner
Case of the Lucky Legs. E. S. Gardner
Case of the Lucky Loser. E. S. Gardner
Case of the Mad Inventor. J. Creasey
Case of the Magic Mirror. C. Bush
Case of the Malevolent Twin. L. Eby
Case of the Maltese Treasure. T. B. Haughey
Case of the Malverne Diamonds. L. Gribble
Case of the Man in Black. O. Merland
Case of the Man on Leave. G. Chester
Case of the Man Who Followed Himself. Allen Sharp
Case of the Man Who Never Slept. Gwyn Evans
Case of the Man with No Name. J. Drummond
Case of the Mandarin's Mask. J. Wylde
Case of the Marsden Rubies. L. Gribble
Case of the Master Organizer. A. Murray
Case of the Mexican Knife. G. Homes
Case of the Michaelmas Goose. C. Witting
Case of the Mill Owner's Son. W. M. Graydon
Case of the Millionaire Newspaper Owner. R. C. Armour
Case of the Millionaire's Blackmail. W. J. Bayfield
Case of the Mischievous Doll. E. S. Gardner
Case of the Missing Airmen. G. Elliott
Case of the Missing Bridegroom. G. Dilnot
Case of the Missing Bronte. R. Barnard
Case of the Missing Bullion. Peter Gordon
Case of the Missing Co-Ed. W. Hardy
Case of the Missing Corpse. E. Lanham
Case of the Missing Corpse. J. Sanger
Case of the Missing D.F.C. A. Parsons
Case of the Missing Diary. A. Fielding
Case of the Missing Estate Agent. Donald Stuart
Case of the Missing G.I. Bride. A. Parsons

Case of the Missing Gardener. H. Walker
Case of the Missing Hand. M. Hervey
Case of the Missing Lady. R. T. Hopkins
Case of the Missing Lovers. Lee Roberts
Case of the Missing Major. A. Parsons
Case of the Missing Men. C. Bush
Case of the Missing Minutes. C. Bush
Case of the Missing Musician. R. Hardinge
Case of the Missing Nazi. W. Tyrer
Case of the Missing Sandals. N. B. Mavity
Case of the Missing Scientist. A. Parsons
Case of the Missing Ships. S. Hope
Case of the Missing Stoker. L. Jackson
Case of the Missing Surgeon. A. Parsons
Case of the Monday Murders. C. Bush
Case of the Monta Grandee Diamonds. S. Hope
Case of the Moth-Eaten Mink. E. S. Gardner
Case of the Moving Finger. A. Christie
Case of the Muckrakers. W. McNeilly
Case of the Mummified Hand. G. H. Teed
Case of the Murdered Caretaker. C. Gates
Case of the Murdered Commissionaire. J. G. Brandon
Case of the Murdered Financier. J. Creasey
Case of the Murdered Mackenzie. E. V. Cunningham
Case of the Murdered Madame. H. Kane
Case of the Murderd Mahout. W. M. Graydon
Case of the Murdered Major. C. Bush
Case of the Murdered Model. T. B. Dewey
Case of the Murdered Pawn Broker. W. Edwards
Case of the Murdered Postman. R. Hardinge
Case of the Murdered Redhead. F. Lockridge
Case of the Murdered Taxi Driver. A. Blair
Case of the Murdered Wedding Guest. W. Jardine
Case of the Murderer's Bride. E. S. Gardner
Case of the Musical Cow. E. S. Gardner
Case of the Mysterious Germs. R. C. Armour
Case of the Mysterious Jockey. W. M. Graydon
Case of the Mysterious Moll. H. S. Keeler
Case of the Mystery Champion. A. Steffens Hardy
Case of the Mystery Millionaire. A. Murray
Case of the Mythical Monkeys. E. S. Gardner
Case of the Nabob's Son. W. M. Graydon
Case of the Nameless Corpse. E. K. Goldthwaite
Case of the Nameless Corpse. C. B. Kelland
Case of the Nameless Man. O. Merland
Case of the Nameless Millionaire. A. Parsons
Case of the Naval Defaulter. W. Tyrer
Case of the Naval Stores Bucket. W. Tyrer
Case of the Negligent Nymph. E. S. Gardner
Case of the Nervous Accomplice. E. S. Gardner
Case of the Nervous Nude. Jonathan Craig
Case of the Night Club Queen. J. G. Brandon
Case of the Night Lorry Driver. L. Jackson
Case of the Old Oak Chest. H. H. C. Gibbons
Case of the One-Eyed Witness. E. S. Gardner
Case of the 100% Alibis. C. Bush
Case of the One-Penny Orange. E. V. Cunningham
Case of the Open Drawer. L. Allan
Case of the Painted Girl. Frank King
Case of the Painted Ladies. B. Flynn
Case of the Paralzyed Man. A. Murray
Case of the Perfect Alibi. M. Carrel
Case of the Perfumed Mouse. T. Du Bois
Case of the Perjured Parrot. E. S. Gardner
Case of the Petticoat Murder. Jonathan Craig
Case of the Phantom Baseball. J. E. Lawrence
Case of the Phantom Fingerprints. K. F. Crossen
Case of the Phantom Fortune. E. S. Gardner
Case of the Philosopher's Ring. R. Collins
Case of the Pink Macaw. G. H. Teed
Case of the Plastic Man. J. Donavan
Case of the Plastic Mask. J. Donavan
Case of the Platinum Blonde. C. Bush
Case of the Poisoned Cat. K. P. Bahadur
Case of the Poisoned Cocktails. O. Boyd
Case of the Poisoned Eclairs. E. V. Cunningham
Case of the Poisoned Pen. Gwyn Evans
Case of the Poisoned Pup. S. S. Pridham
Case of the Pornographic Photos. Lawrence Block
Case of the Portuguese Giantess. G. H. Teed
Case of the Postponed Murder. E. S. Gardner
Case of the Preying Evangelist. D. W. F. Hardie

Case of the President's Heads. M. L. Stokes
Case of the Press Photographer. W. J. Bayfield
Case of the Prince's Diary. A. Parsons
Case of the Prince's Prisoners. A. Parsons
Case of the Prodigal Daughter. C. Bush
Case of the Purloined Picture. C. Bush
Case of the Purple Calf. B. Flynn
Case of the Queenly Contestant. E. S. Gardner
Case of the Queer K.O. Anonymous
Case of the R. E. Pipe. C. M. Wills
Case of the Radioactive Redhead. G. G. Fickling
Case of the Rajah's Son. H. E. Hill
Case of the Red Box. R. Stout
Case of the Red Brunette. C. Bush
Case of the Red Crimona's. H. H. C. Gibbons
Case of the Red-Haired Girl. A. Wynne
Case of the Redoubled Cross. R. King
Case of the Rejuvenated Millionaire. G. N. Philips
Case of the Reluctant Redhead. E. S. Gardner
Case of the Renegade Agent. D. Reid
Case of the Renegade Naval Officer. A. Parsons
Case of the Rented Coffin. L. D. Smith
Case of the Repatriated Prisoner. G. Chester
Case of the Restless Redhead. E. S. Gardner
Case of the Returning Soldier. W. Tyrer
Case of the Revolutionist's Daughter. L. Feuer
Case of the Rival Race Gangs. H. C. Miln
Case of the River Smugglers. D. T. Hughes
Case of the Rolling Bones. E. S. Gardner
Case of the Runaway Corpse. E. S. Gardner
Case of the Running Man. C. Bush
Case of the Running Mouse. C. Bush
Case of the Russian Cross. C. Bush
Case of the Russian Crown Jewels. R. H. Poole
Case of the Rusted Room. J. Donavan
Case of the Sapphire Brooch. C. Bush
Case of the Scared Rabbits. G. Bellairs
Case of the Screaming Woman. E. S. Gardner
Case of the Seaside Crooks. A. Murray
Case of the Second Chance. C. Bush
Case of the Second Crime. A. Parsons
Case of the Secret Agent. R. Hardinge
Case of the Secret Plans. C. H. Barker
Case of the Secret Road. A. Parsons
Case of the Seven Bells. C. Bush
Case of the Seven Keys. G. Stanley
Case of the Seven Murders. E. Queen
Case of the Seven of Calvary. A. Boucher
Case of the Seven Sneezes. A. Boucher
Case of the Seven Whistlers. G. Bellairs
Case of the Severed Fingers. Anonymous
Case of the Severed Skull. H. Weiner
Case of the Shapely Shadow. E. S. Gardner
Case of the Shaven Blonde. R. Hobart
Case of the Shivering Chorus Girls. J. A. Phillips
Case of the Shoplifter's Shoe. E. S. Gardner
Case of the Shot Looter. M. Frazer
Case of the Silent Canary. Allen Sharp
Case of the Silent Partner. E. S. Gardner
Case of the Silent Safe-Cutters. H. H. C. Gibbons
Case of the Silent Stranger. Jonathan Craig
Case of the Silken Petticoat. C. Bush
Case of the Singing Skirt. E. S. Gardner
Case of the Sinister Farm. A. Parsons
Case of the Six Bullets. R. M. Laurenson
Case of the Six Coffins. R. J. Hogan
Case of the Six Mistresses. B. Maxwell
Case of the Six O'Clock Scream. A. Parsons
Case of the 16 Beans. H. S. Keeler
Case of the Sleeping Partner. E. S. Brooks
Case of the Sleepwalker's Niece. E. S. Gardner
Case of the Sliding Pool. E. V. Cunningham
Case of the Smoking Chimney. E. S. Gardner
Case of the Smuggled Currency. H. Clevely
Case of the Society Blackmailer. W. M. Graydon
Case of the Solid Key. A. Boucher
Case of the Spanish Legatee. A. Parsons
Case of the Spiv's Secret. A. Parsons
Case of the Spurious Spinster. E. S. Gardner
Case of the Squealing Cat. J. Reach
Case of the Stag at Bay. W. McNeilly
Case of the Stepdaughter's Secret. E. S. Gardner
Case of the Stolen Bridegroom. H. Adams
Case of the Stolen Evidence. A. Parsons

Case of the Stolen Mine. R. Hardinge
Case of the Stolen Paintings. W. Ecke
Case of the Stolen Police Dossier. A. Blair
Case of the Stolen Ransom. J. Hunter
Case of the Stranded Touring Company. L. Carlton
Case of the Strange Beauties. Frank King
Case of the Strange Wireless Message. W. W. Sayer
Case of the Strangled Seven. P. Yorke
Case of the Strangled Starlet. J. H. Chase
Case of the Straw Man. D. M. Disney
Case of the Stuttering Bishop. E. S. Gardner
Case of the Substitute Face. E. S. Gardner
Case of the Sulky Girl. R. F. Fernand
Case of the Sulky Girl. E. S. Gardner
Case of the Sun Bather's Diary. E. S. Gardner
Case of the Suppressed Will. W. M. Graydon
Case of the "Suspect" Watchmaker. L. Jackson
Case of the Swindled Guarantor. W. Tyrer
Case of the Swindler's "Stooge". A. Parsons
Case of the Swinging Spider. P. Yorke
Case of the Tainted Token. K. M. Knight
Case of the Talking Bug. The Gordons
Case of the Talking Dust. J. Donavan
Case of the Tattooed Man. Anonymous
Case of the Tattooed Torso. J. St. George
Case of the Tea-Cosy's Aunt. Anthony Gilbert
Case of the Tearless Widow. J. Roeburt
Case of the 10 Clues. Donald Dane
Case of the Ten Diamonds. G. H. Teed
Case of the Terrified Typist. E. S. Gardner
Case of the Theatrical Profiteer. W. M. Graydon
Case of the 13th Coach. E. G. Bartlett
Case of the Three Absconding Swindlers. C. Brisbane
Case of the Three Broken Necks. A. McClintock
Case of the Three Lost Letters. C. Bush
Case of the Three-Ring Puzzle. C. Bush
Case of the Three Strange Faces. C. Bush
Case of the Three Survivors. H. Clevely
Case of the Too Many Murders. T. Chastain
Case of the Topaz Flower. C. M. Russell
Case of the Trade Secret. J. W. Bobin
Case of the Transatlantic Flyers. Jack Lewis
Case of the Transposed Legs. H. S. Keeler
Case of the Treble Twist. C. Bush
Case of the Triple Twist. C. Bush
Case of the Troubled Trustee. E. S. Gardner
Case of the Tudor Queen. C. Bush
Case of the Turning Tide. E. S. Gardner
Case of the Twin Detectives. E. S. Brooks
Case of the Twisted Scarf. F. Durbridge
Case of the Twisted Trail. F. A. Symonds
Case of the Two Bankers. J. W. Bobin
Case of the Two Brothers. A. Murray
Case of the Two Crooked Baronets. W. Tyrer
Case of the Two Doctors. Nicholas Carter
Case of the Two-Faced Swindler. J. Drummond
Case of the Two Guardians. W. M. Graydon
Case of the Two Pearl Necklaces. A. Fielding
Case of the Two Scapegraces. W. M. Graydon
Case of the Two Strange Ladies. H. S. Keeler
Case of the Unbolted Lightning. T. B. Haughey
Case of the Unconquered Sisters. T. Downing
Case of the Uncut Gems. A. Murray
Case of the Undischarged Bankrupt. A. Murray
Case of the Unfortunate Village. C. Bush
Case of the Unhappy Angels. G. Homes
Case of the Unknown Heir. A. Parsons
Case of the Un-Named Film. A. Murray
Case of the Vagabond Virgin. E. S. Gardner
Case of the Vanished Husband. W. J. Bayfield
Case of the Vanishing Artist. Frank King
Case of the Vanishing Beauty. R. S. Prather
Case of the Vanishing Corpse. K. Richards
Case of the Vanishing Woman. R. Archer
Case of the Velvet Claws. E. S. Gardner
Case of the Village Tramp. Jonathan Craig
Case of the Violent Virgin. M. Avallone
Case of the Violet Smoke. J. Donavan
Case of the Walking Corpse. A. Livingston
Case of the Walking Corpse. B. Halliday
Case of the Waylaid Wolf. E. S. Gardner
Case of the Weird Sisters. C. Armstrong
Case of the Weird Sisters. W. Spence

Case of the Wicked Three. A. Parsons
Case of the Wicked Twin. L. Eby
Case of the Winking Buddha. M. L. Stokes
Case of the Withered Hand. J. G. Brandon
Case of the "Wizard" Jockey. W. J. Bayfield
Case of the Woman in Black. A. Murray
Case of the Worried Waitress. E. S. Gardner
Case of the Would-Be Widow. J. G. Brandon
Case of the Wounded Mastiff. N. Harman
Case of Thomas N. J. D. Morley
Case of Torches. Clark Smith
Case of William Smith. P. Wentworth
Case of Young Lord Folliot. N. H. Romanes
Case on Cloud Nine. L. Freeman
Case Pending. Dell Shannon
Case Proceeding. J. Prescot
Case to Answer. E. Lustgarten
Case 29. J. Cassells
Case with Four Clowns. L. Bruce
Case with Nine Solutions. J. J. Connington
Case with No Conclusion. L. Bruce
Case with Ropes and Rings. L. Bruce
Case with Three Husbands. M. Erskine
Case with Three Threads. Anthony Lang
Case Without a Clue. Nicholas Carter
Case Without a Clue. N. Morland
Case Without a Corpse. L. Bruce
Casebook of a Victorian Detective. J. M'Levy
Casebook of Crime. A. Brock
Casebook of Jules de Grandin. Seabury Quinn
Casebook of Lucius Leffing. J. P. Brennan
Casebook of Solar Pons. A. Derleth
Casebook of the Black Widowers. I. Asimov
Casefile. B. Pronzini
Cases of Martin Trackman. Anonymous
Cases of Susan Dare. M. G. Eberhart
Cash and Carry. C. Megahy
Cash on Delivery. F. Du Boisgobey
Cash on Destruction. S. Howatch
Cashelmara. S. Howatch
Cashier's Secret. Nicholas Carter
Casino. G. Norsworthy
Casino for Sale. C. Brahms
Casino Greystone. L. Bronte
Casino Murder Case. S. S. Van Dine
Casino Mystery. M. E. Cooke
Casino Mystery. Elaine Hamilton
Casino Royale. I. Fleming
Casino Strip. H. Janson
Casinopoly. H. Janson
Cask. F. W. Crofts
Cask of Amontillado. D. R. Gribble
Casket for a Lying Lady. R. R. Werry
Casket of Death. J. B. O'Sullivan
Caspian Song. J. G. Sarasin
Cass and the Stone Butch. A. Azolakov
Cassady. J. Sutton
"Cassandra" Bell. P. Van Greenaway
Cassandra Crossing. R. Katz
Cassandra, Goodbye. A. W. Berg
Cassia. M. Conte
Cassidy. Morris West
Cassidy the Con Man. G. H. Teed
Cassidy's Girl. D. Goodis
Cassidy's Yard. Alan White
Cassiodore Case. A. R. Martin
Cassis..Resort to Vengeance. Mark Walker
Cast a Cold Eye. M. Eccles
Cast a Green Shadow. M. V. Hunt
Cast a Long Shadow. H. Elsna
Cast a Yellow Shadow. Ross Thomas
Cast Away. E. Yates
Cast for Death. M. Yorke
Cast, in Order of Disappearance. Simon Brett
Cast in Wax. Jenna Ryan
Cast Iron Alibi. D. Betteridge
Cast Out. M. Gerard
Cast to Death. N. Orde-Powlette
Castang's City. N. Freeling
Castilian Caper. V. A. Paradis
Casting of the Shadows. J. Dory
Casting the Net. Dick Stewart
Castle and the Key. C. Knye
Castle at Glencarris. J. Vicary

Castle at Jade Cove. H. B. Hicks
Castle at Witch's Coven. V. Coffman
Castle Avalon. Alan Jenkins
Castle Barebane. Joan Aiken
Castle Barra. V. Coffman
Castle Black. J. Schubert
Castle by the Sea. H. B. M. Watson
Castle Captive. S. Ratcliffe
Castle Chapel. R. M. Roche
Castle Clodha. Alanna Knight
Castle Cloud. Joan Grant
Castle Cloud. Elizabeth Norman
Castle Conquest. B. Gray
Castle Craggs. V. Maas
Castle Craneycross. G. B. McCutcheon
Castle Danger. W. O'Meara
Castle Dangerous. V. Gunn
Castle Dangerous. A. Wood
Castle-Dinas. R. A. J. Walling
Castle Doom. M. McEvoy
Castle Dor. A. T. Quiller-Couch
Castle Enigma. J. R. Warren
Castle Fell. D. Duff
Castle Fenham Case. Charles Ross
Castle Foam. H. W. French
Castle for Sale. M. Messer
Castle for Tess. R. Simon
Castle for the Left Hand. Annjeanette Scott
Castle Garac. N. Monsarrat
Castle Gay. J. Buchan
Castle Heritage. E. Barr
Castle Hohenfels. Dorinne Moore
Castle in Bohemia. D. Whitelaw
Castle in Canada. C. Farr
Castle in Spain. J. De Mille
Castle in Spain. C. Farr
Castle in the Air. D. E. Westlake
Castle Island Case. V. W. Mason
Castle Malice. Marilyn Ross
Castle Malindone. H. Ford
Castle Mandragora. M. Durham
Castle Midnight. E. McKenna
Castle Minerva. V. Canning
Castle Mirage. Alice Brennan
Castle Morvant. D. Daniels
Castle of Berry Pomeroy. E. Montague
Castle of Caithness. F. H. P.
Castle of Closing Doors. D. Winston
Castle of Crushed Shamrocks. Lee Karr
Castle of Dark Evil. Melissa Napier
Castle of Doubt. J. H. Whitson
Castle of Dreams. P. Warren
Castle of Eagles. C. Heaven
Castle of Ehrenstein. G. P. R. James
Castle of Evil. S. Abbott
Castle of Fear. S. Abbott
Castle of Fear. J. J. Farjeon
Castle of Fear. R. S. L. Harding
Castle of Lies. A. H. Vesey
Castle of Lindenburg. M. G. Lewis
Castle of Lugas. A. Fernandez
Castle of Montalbano. Sarah Wilkinson
Castle of Mowbray. N. Harley
Castle of Ollada. F. Lathom
Castle of Otranto. H. Walpole
Castle of St. Vallery. Anonymous
Castle of Shadows. B. C. Warren
Castle of Shadows. A. M. Williamson
Castle of Sin. J. Cassells
Castle of Strathmay. Honoria Scott
Castle of Terror. C. Farr
Castle of the Demon. P. Ruell
Castle of the Sea. B. Dean
Castle of the Winds. Jeanne Montague
Castle of Tynemouth. Jane Harvey
Castle of Vengeance. M. Hastings
Castle of Villeroy. F. M. Mills
Castle of Vivaldi. C. Harwood
Castle of Wolfenbach. Mrs. Parsons
Castle on the Cliff. Dan Ross
Castle on the Hill. E. Randolph
Castle on the Hill. W. E. D. Ross
Castle on the Island. L. Ames
Castle on the Loch. C. Farr

Castle on the Mountain. J. Wellsley
Castle on the Rhine. C. Farr
Castle Perilous. V. Johnston
Castle Raven. Laura Black
Castle Rock. C. G. Hart
Castle Rock Mystery. G. F. Gibbs
Castle Sinister. Gwyn Evans
Castle Skull. J. D. Carr
Castle Spectre. M. G. Lewis
Castle Spectre. Sarah Wilkinson
Castle Terror. M. Z. Bradley
Castle That Whispered. M. Farnsworth
Castle to Let. B. Reynolds
Castle Ugly. Marianne Barrett
Castle Wafer. H. Wood
Castle Walk. M. Le Bas
Castlecliff. S. Shulman
Castlecourt Diamond Case. G. Bonner
Castledoom. E. Lecale
Castleford Conundrum. J. J. Connington
Castlereagh. M. Heath
Castlereagh. J. L. Roberts
Castles Burning. A. Lyons
Castle's Heir. H. Wood
Castles in the Air. Augustus Muir
Castles in the Air. B. Orczy
Castles of Athlin and Dunbayne. A. Radcliffe
Castleview. G. Wolfe
Castrato. Michael Collins
Castro File. J. Rosenberger
Casual Affairs. L. O'Donnell
Casual Murderer. H. Footner
Casual Slaughters. V. Hanson
Casual Slaughters. J. Quince
Casuarina Tree. W. S. Maugham
Cat. V. Gielgud
Cat. G. Simenon
Cat. A. Sinclair
Cat Among the Pigeons. A. Christie
Cat and Capricorn. D. B. Olson
Cat and Feather. D. Basil
Cat and Fiddle Murders. E. B. Ronald
Cat and Mouse. C. Brand
Cat and Mouse. W. C. Gault
Cat and Mouse. E. K. Goldthwaite
Cat and Mouse. M. Halliday
Cat and Mouse. H. Pentecost
Cat and Mouse. M. L. Roby
Cat and Mouse Murder. E. K. Goldthwaite
Cat and the Canary. G. Kingsley
Cat and the Canary. John Willard
Cat and the Cherub. C. B. Fernald
Cat and the Clock. C. G. Booth
Cat and the Corpse. R. A. J. Walling
Cat and the Fiddle. Paul Costello
Cat and the Mice. L. O. Mosley
Cat Burglar. E. Wallace
Cat Cay Warrant. Allen Morgan
Cat Chaser. E. Leonard
Cat Climbs. C. A. Tarrant
Cat Creeps. John Willard
Cat Dies First. W. H. L. Crauford
Cat-Eye. Lucille Palmer
Cat Got Your Tongue? C. Carpenter
Cat Got Your Tongue? A. Pearson
Cat in Gloves. D. Delaney
Cat in the Convoy. W. G. Schofield
Cat in the Hat Box. A. W. Upfield
Cat in the Manger. L. Adamson
Cat Jumps. M. Burton
Cat Jumps and other stories. E. Bowen
Cat of Bast and other stories of mystery. W. E. Thorner
Cat of Many Tails. E. Queen
Cat o' Nine Tails. P. J. Gillette
Cat of Nine Tails. V. Leigh
Cat Saw Murder. D. B. Olsen
Cat Screams. T. Downing
Cat Tails. W. L. Alden
Cat Trap. G. A. Ralston
Cat Trapper. P. Bryers
Cat Walk. D. B. Olsen
Cat Watchers. J. N. Chance
Cat Wears a Mask. D. B. Olsen

Cat Wears a Noose. D. B. Olsen
Cat Who Ate Danish Modern. L. J. Braun
Cat Who Could Read Backwards. L. J. Braun
Cat Who Had 14 Tales. L. J. Braun
Cat Who Knew Shakespeare. L. J. Braun
Cat Who Lived High. L. J. Braun
Cat Who Played Brahms. L. J. Braun
Cat Who Played Post Office. L. J. Braun
Cat Who Saw Red. L. J. Braun
Cat Who Sniffed Glue. L. J. Braun
Cat Who Talked to Ghosts. L. J. Braun
Cat Who Turned On and Off. L. J. Braun
Cat Who Went Underground. L. J. Braun
Cat Will Mew. Frederick Jackson
Cat with the Mustache. Simon
Catacomb. B. Glanville
Catacombs. Jay Bennett
Catacombs. J. Farris
Catacombs of Death. Operator 1384
Catafalgque. R. C. Goldston
Catalyst. Josephine Bell
Catalyst. K. Lowe
Catalyst Blue. R. F. Baylus
Catalyst Club. G. Dyer
Catamount Kid. Jim Mack
Catapult Ultimatum. Peter Leslie
Catastrophe. E. Gaboriau
Catastrophe at Cliff Haven. T. K. Cook
Catastrophe Club. Frank King
Catastrophe in Bohemia and other stories. H. S. Brooks
Catch. J. Boland
Catch a Fallen Starlet. D. Sanderson
Catch a Falling Angel. P. Engleman
Catch a Falling Clown. S. M. Kaminsky
Catch a Falling Spy. N. Benchley
Catch a Falling Spy. L. Deighton
Catch a Killer. U. Curtiss
Catch a Killer. Robert Martin
Catch a Tiger. O. Cameron
Catch a Tiger. Martin Thomas
Catch and Kill. N. Blake
Catch and Squeeze. Craig Cooper
Catch-as-Catch-Can. C. Armstrong
Catch as Catch Can. F. Lockridge
Catch-'Em-Alice-O! Michael Burt
Catch Her, Kill Her. M. Boone
Catch Me a Phoenix. Carter Brown
Catch Me a Renegade. H. Janson
Catch Me a Spy. G. Marton
Catch Me a Traitor. Henry Talbot
Catch Me—If You Can. B. Cobb
Catch Me If You Can. P. McGerr
Catch Me If You Can. Judi Miller
Catch Me If You Can. J. Weinstock
Catch Me, Kill Me. W. H. Hallahan
Catch That Thief! W. Spence
Catch the Brass Ring. S. Marlowe
Catch the Gold Ring. J. S. Strange
Catch the Saint. L. Charteris
Catch the Wind. H. Segal
Catchee Chinaman. May Phillips
Catching a Tartar. G. W. Appleton
Catching Fire. K. N. Smith
Catenary Exchange. J. Winters
Cater Street Hangman. A. Perry
Catering to Nobody. D. M. Davidson
Caterpillar Cop. J. McClure
Catfish Tangle. C. Williams
Cathedral. N. De Mille
Cathedral Option. R. Montana
Catherine. I. Solomons
Catherine Horeton. W. M. Sabelberg
Catherine Murders. E. Chaze
Catherine Wheel. P. Wentworth
Catherine's Twins. L. Raygor
Catherwood Mystery. A. P. Southwick
Cathkin Mystery. G. Woden
Catholic. W. H. Ireland
Catholina. J. H. Robinson
Cathra Mystery. A. G. MacLeod
Cathy Rossiter. J. L. Rickard
Catmur's Caves. R. Dowling
Catnapped. The Gordons

C

Cats. B. Roueche
Cats. N. Sharman
Cat's Claw. D. B. Olsen
Cat's Cradle. P. Flower
Cat's Cradle. S. Harvester
Cat's Cradle Murder. Jerome Barry
Cats Don't Need Coffins. D. B. Olsen
Cats Don't Smile. D. B. Olsen
Cat's Eye. C. Aveline
Cat's Eye. R. A. Freeman
Cat's-Eye Ring. F. Du Boisgobey
Cat's Eyes. Lee Jordan
Cat's Eyes. S. Warwick
Cats Have Tall Shadows. D. B. Olsen
Cats in Crime . . . and others. A. L. Germeshausen
Cat's Meow. Robert Campbell
Cat's Paw. J. Heron
Cat's Paw. A. Hocking
Cat's Paw. H. Janson
Cat's Paw. C. B. Kelland
Cat's Paw. N. S. Lincoln
Cat's-Paw. W. Mastrosimone
Cat's Paw. B. Pronzini
Cat's-Paw. M. Salter
Cat's Paw. R. Scarlett
Cat's Prey. D. Eden
Cats Prowl at Night. A. A. Fair
Cat's Whisker. H. C. Bailey
Catseyes. A. Winnington
Catskill Eagle. R. B. Parker
Catspaw. John Carroll
Catspaw. W. LeQueux
Catspaw. A. Murray
Catspaw. W. H. Osborne
Catspaw. P. Reakes
Catspaw. M. Russell
Catspaw. Anne Stuart
Catspaw. J. D. Vinge
Catspaw II. Anne Stuart
Catspaw for Murder. D. B. Olsen
Catspaw Ordeal. E. Ronns
Catspaws. C. Brooks
Catt Among the Pigeons. C. Connell
Catt Out of the Bag. C. Witting
Catwalk Kill. J. Munro
Caught and Bowled. Anonymous
Caught at Last! D. Donovan
Caught by Fate. Mageli
Caught Dead. B. Halliday
Caught Dead in Philadelphia. Gillian Roberts
Caught in a Corner. G. W. Waters
Caught in a Trap. J. C. Hutcheson
Caught in a Villain's Web. H. E. Swayne
Caught in a Web. R. St. Clair
Caught in a Whirlpool. Nicholas Carter
Caught in His Own Trap. Beatrice Walsh
Caught in Mid-Ocean. O. Harper
Caught in Terror. M. Bardsley
Caught in the Act. John Lee
Caught in the Machine. C. Campbell
Caught in the Middle. S. Waldron
Caught in the Net. E. Gaboriau
Caught in the Toils. Nicholas Carter
Caught Wet. R. Crothers
Cauldron Bubble. G. Goodchild
Cauldron Bubbles. N. A. Temple-Ellis
Cauldron of Evil. Marilyn Ross
Cauldron of Hell. Nick Carter
Cause and Effect. R. McInerny
Cause for a Killing. J. Wainwright
Cause for Alarm. E. Ambler
Cause for Alarm. J. Pendower
Cause for Malice. F. Hurt
Cause for Suspicion. T. C. H. Jacobs
Cause of Death. M. Underwood
Cause of the Crime. L. Frank
Cause of the Screaming. D. Elias
Cause Unknown. J. J. Farjeon
Causes Unknown. L. Horvitz
Causeway. P. M. Hubbard
Causeway to the Past. W. O'Farrell
Cautious Assassin. D. Orgill
Cautious Maiden. C. Saint-Laurent
Cautious Overshoes. M. Scherf

Cautley Conundrum. A. Fielding
Cautley Mystery. A. Fielding
Cavalier Case. Antonia Fraser
Cavalier Conquest. B. Gray
Cavalier of Chance. S. Horler
Cavalier of Crime. F. Hedley
Cavalier of the Night. R. Armstrong
Cavalier's Corpse. T. Du Bois
Cavalier's Cup. Carter Dickson
Cavaliers of Death. R. Forbes
Cavanaugh Keep. M. Leslie
Cavanaugh Quest. T. Gifford
Cave and the Beast. I. Garrick
Cave Man. L. Lane
Cave of Bats. Robert MacLeod
Cave of the Chinese Skeletons. J. Seward
Cave of the Moaning Wind. J. Deweese
Cave of the Moon. N. McGill
Cave of Toledo. A. A. Stuart
Cavender's Balkan Quest. E. Tokson
Cavern. A. MacVicar
Cavern of Death. A. Graves
Cavern of Horrors. Anonymous
Cavern of the Damned. C. Steele
Caverns of Falkenhorst. Dorinne Moore
Caves of Alienation. Stuart Evans
Caves of Blackscar. Haydon Dean
Caves of Claro. J. Palmer
Caves of Danger. J. Schenk
Caves of Darkness. J. Schenk
Caves of Death. V. Norwood
Caves of Fear. P. Morton
Caves of Guernica. Samuel Edwards
Caves of Night. J. Christopher
Caves of Segada. A. Aikman
Caves of Shend. D. Hennessey
Caves of Steel. I. Asimov
Caves of Terror. T. Mundy
Caviar Cruise. F. Webb
Caviar to Kill. K. T. McCall
Caviare. Godfrey Smith
Cawthorn Journals. S. Marlowe
Caxborough Scandal. F. Whishaw
Cease Upon the Midnight. S. Troy
Cecil Castlemaine's Gage. Ouida
Cecile. H. Smart
Cecile's Fortune. F. Du Boisgobey
Cecile's Tryst. J. Payn
Cecily. I. Holland
Cecily Disappears. A. M. Platts
Cedar. James Murphy
Cedar Haven. P. Campbell
Cedar Tree. Rona Randall
Ceiling of Hell. W. B. Murphy
Celebate's Wife. H. Flowerdew
Celebrated Cases of Dick Tracy, 1931-1951. C. Gould
Celebrated Cases of Judge Dee. R. Van Gulik
Celebrated Crimes and Their Solution. G. Barton
Celebrated Detective. Anonymous
Celebration for Murder. R. Wissman
Celebrity. T. Thompson
Celestial City. B. Orczy
Celestial Hit List. C. Ingrid
Celestial Navigation. A. Tyler
Celestial Ruby. T. W. Speight
Celia. P. Trent
Celia's Career. P. Trent
Cell. D. Case
Cell Car 54. J. M. Fox
Cell Cutie. D. Haring
Cell Murder Mystery. D. B. Hobart
Cell or a Throne? H. Hosken
Cell 13. E. H. Trafton
Cellar at No. 5. Shelley Smith
Cellar Boys. W. H. Baker
Cellars' Market. Douglas Stewart
Cellars of the Dead. Marilyn Ross
Cellini Plaque. H. MacGrath
Cellini Smith, Detective. Robert Reeves
Celluloid Caper. C. Miron
Celluloid Gangs. T. Tolnay
Celluloid Suicide. P. Valdez
Cemeteries Are for Dying. W. L. Story

Cemetery First Stop! D. Hume
Cemetery in Munich. C. Hilton
Censor. J. Gardner
Censor. M. Russell
Censored Tales. T. Rothman
Centaur Conspiracy. Carl Stevens
Centeola; and other tales. D. P. Thompson
Center Game. Robert Andrews
Center of the Web. K. Roberts
Centerfold Be Damned. D. Haring
Centerforce. T. A. Waters
Centipede. B. Boothby
Central Park Murder. B. Duff
Central Park Mystery. Old Sleuth
Centre Court Murder. B. Newman
Centre Holds. A. Storey
Centrifuge. J. C. Pollock
Centurion's Story. P. C. MacFarlane
Cepherine. J. H. Robinson
Cerberus Gambit. D. Houghton
Cerebus Murders. R. Quest
Ceremony. R. B. Parker
Ceremony in the Lincoln Tunnel. R. Cunningham
Ceremony of Innocence. A. J. Cassidy
Ceremony of Innocence. R. Kilroy-Silk
Ceremony of Innocence. S. F. X. Dean
Certain Blindness. Roy Lewis
Certain Blood. J. Ahern
Certain Dr. Mellor. P. P. Maguire
Certain Dr. Thorndyke. R. A. Freeman
Certain Evil. D. Kraslow
Certain Liveliness. H. F. Moulton
Certain Sleep. H. Reilly
Certified Check. Nicholas Carter
Certified Insane. R. C. Armour
Cesario Rosalba. J. A. K. Curtis
Cesspool. D. Haring
Chaff Before the Wind. S. Christiansen
Chain. D. Lowden
Chain. J. J. Maloney
Chain-Gang Queenie. B. Sarto
Chain Invisible. C. R. Gull
Chain Letter. E. K. Stirling
Chain Murder. A. Soutar
Chain Murders. P. Richmond
Chain of Chance. S. Lem
Chain of Circumstances. C. S. Smith
Chain of Clues. Nicholas Carter
Chain of Command. I. R. Blacker
Chain of Command. D. Buttenshaw
Chain of Darkness. K. Cook
Chain of Death. N. McLarty
Chain of Death. S. Noel
Chain of Evidence. Nicholas Carter
Chain of Evidence. C. Wells
Chain of Infamy. G. Beare
Chain of Vengeance. W. Beechcroft
Chain of Violence. A. Capelli
Chain of Violence. L. Egan
Chain Reaction. N. Guild
Chain Reaction. C. Hodder-Williams
Chain Reaction. Lee Jordan
Chain Reaction. G. Pape
Chain Reaction. G. A. Ralston
Chain Saw. J. Gillis
Chained. F. Hird
Chained Reaction. R. Sapir
Chained Crocodile. B. Whitaker
Chains. B. Moss
Chains. Douglas Scott
Chains of Circumstance. T. W. Speight
Chains of Gold. Margaret Lamb
Chainsaw Terror. Nick Blake
Chair for Death. J. Reddoch
Chair for Martin Rome. H. E. Helseth
Chair-Lift. E. H. Clements
Chair on the Boulevard. L. Merrick
Chairman. J. R. Kennedy
Chairman. G. Vaizey
Chairman of the Board. J. Evans
Chalet Bougy-Villars. S. Marvin
Chalet Diabolique. V. Coffman
Chalet of the Devil. V. Coffman
Chaleur Network. R. G. Stern

Chalice Caper. D. MacKenzie
Chalk Circle. A. Trew
Chalk Face. W. Frank
Chalk-Face. J. M. Walsh
Chalk Garden. E. Bagnold
Chalk Stream Killing. R. Pertwee
Challenge. J. Ahern
Challenge. G. Foy
Challenge. H. C. McNeile
Challenge at Castle Gap. Ben Douglas
Challenge at Le Mans. L. Kenyon
Challenge Blue Mask! Anthony Morton
Challenge for the Dreamer. W. M. Duncan
Challenge for the Picaroon. J. Cassells
Challenge for Three. D. Garth
Challenge of Evil. S. Metcalfe
Challenge of the Bush. C. R. Cooper
Challenge of the North. W. B. Mowery
Challenge to Murder. F. J. Whaley
Challenge to the Four. Mark Cross
Challoners of Bristol. L. Hayes
Chamber Music. A. Kopit
Chamber of Death. Orlando
Chamber of Horrors. R. Bloch
Chambered Tomb. Charlotte Hunt
Chameleon. W. Diehl
Chameleon. H. S. Keeler
Chameleon. W. LeQueux
Chameleon Corps. R. Goulart
Chameleon Course. D. Seaman
Chameleon File. L. James
Chameleon Kill. J. Quinn
Chameleon Variant. C. K. Mack
Chamois Murder. C. M. Wills
Champagne and a Gardener. B. J. Morison
Champagne and Choppers. B. Carson
Champagne Bandits. P. A. Foxall
Champagne Blues. N. Lyons
Champagne for One. R. Stout
Champagne Killer. H. Pentecost
Champagne Marxist. R. Gadney
Champagne Mystery. G. Garston
Champdoce Mystery. E. Gaboriau
Champington Mystery. Le Voleur
Champion. C. N. Williamson
Champion and Crook. T. Lloyd
Champion Clue-Finder. Anonymous
Champion from Far Away. B. Hecht
Champion of Virtue. Clara Reeve
Championship Crime. J. G. Brandon
Chance. S. McAulay
Chance Awakening. G. Markstein
Chance Child. Mrs. C. Kernahan
Chance Discovery. Nicholas Carter
Chance Elson. W. T. Ballard
Chance Encounter. J. Audrenn
Chance Encounter. E. E. Sumner
Chance in Chains. G. Thorne
Chance Marriage. E. Gaboriau
Chance Meeting. Leigh Howard
Chance Miracle. P. S. McCoy
Chance on Murder. S. S. Baker
Chance the Changeling. M. C. Knight
Chance the Piper. A. Castle
Chance to Die. Lionel Black
Chance to Die. F. Drake
Chance to Kill. R. Lait
Chance to Kill. Dell Shannon
Chance to Poison. G. Bromley
Chancellor Manuscript. R. Ludlum
Chancer. J. Brown
Chancery Lane Tragedy. R. F. Jupp
Chandler. W. Denbow
Chandler Policy. D. M. Disney
Chandu Men. F. Crisp
Change for Heaven. A. Hillgarth
Change for the Worse. E. Lemarchand
Change Here for Babylon. N. Bawden
Change in the Wind. L. Waller
Change of Heart. H. McCloy
Change of Heir. M. Innes
Change of Mind. C. Stratton
Change of Pace. T. Cobb
Change of Sky. F. Singleton

Changed Brides. E. Southworth
Changed Face. T. Craig
Changeling. C. Arnold
Changeling. M. Higgins
Changeling. A. Murray
Changeling. E. Phillpotts
Changeling. M. Wilson
Changing Heart. P. Barrington
Changing Pulse of Madame Touraine. A. C. Gunter
Changing Road. H. MacGrath
Channay Syndicate. E. P. Oppenheim
Channel Assault. K. Royce
Channel Million. G. Collins
Channel Mystery. L. H. Brennan
Channel Mystery. W. F. Morris
Channel Tunnel Mystery. S. G. Hedges
Channing Affair. R. Dark
Channings. Mrs. H. Wood
Chant. D. Cross
Chant of Jimmie Blacksmith. T. Keneally
Chantal. G. Des Cars
Chanter's Chase. J. Tattersall
Chantic Bird. D. Ireland
Chanticleer's Muffled Crow. A. Dean
Chanting of Children. M. Sand
Chaos. W. K. Wells
Chaos Contract. D. Weldon
Chaos in Lagrangia. M. Reynolds
Chaos of Crime. Dell Shannon
Chaperone. E. Gordon
Chaplain's Craze. G. M. Fenn
Chapman's Wares. W. B. M. Watson
Charabanc Mystery. M. Burton
Charade. J. Mortimer
Charade. P. Stone
Charades. J. Cresswell
Charaka Puja and other stories. Chola
Charg, Monster. M. Grant
Charge from the Grave. S. Gibney
Charge Is Murder. C. Cumberland
Charge Is Murder. L. B. McMahon
Charge Is Murder! J. M. Spender
Charge Is Rape. J. MacGowan
Charge Is Treason. W. H. Baker
Charing Cross Mystery. J. S. Fletcher
Chariot of Desire. D. Nabarro
Chariot of the Sun. M. Clare
Charioteer. G. Thorne
Charisma. M. G. Coney
Charitable End. Jessica Mann
Charity. S. Nichols
Charity Ends at Home. Colin Watson
Charity Fund Mystery. G. Chester
Charity Ghost. T. Gallon
Charity Murders. P. Manton
Charka Memorial. W. Ware
Charlatan. R. W. Buchanan
Charlatan. W. Hamilton
Charlatan. S. Horler
Charlatan. P. J. Stead
Charles and Elizabeth. W. J. Burley
Charles Beaumont: Selected Stories. C. Beaumont
Charles Edward. H. G. Rhodes
Charles Fort Never Mentioned Wombats. G. DeWeese
Charleston Knife's in Town. Ralph Dennis
Charley Gets the Picture. J. Spenser
Charley Hunter. Anonymous
Charlie and the Iceman. J. Eller
Charlie Boy. P. Feibleman
Charlie Chan and the Curse of the Dragon Queen. M. Avallone
Charlie Chan Carries On. E. D. Biggers
Charlie Chan Returns. D. Lynds
Charlie Dell. A. Wayne
Charlie Finds a Corpse. R. Denton
Charlie M. B. Freemantle
Charlie Muffin. B. Freemantle
Charlie Muffin and the Russian Rose. B. Freemantle
Charlie Muffin San. B. Freemantle
Charlie Muffin U.S.A. B. Freemantle
Charlie Muffin's Uncle Sam. B. Freemantle
Charlie Sent Me! Carter Brown
Charlie's Angels. M. Franklin

Charlie's Back in Town. Jacqueline Park
Charlotte. N. Lofts
Charlotte Wade. A. McElfresh
Charlotte's Inheritance. M. E. Braddon
Charm of Finches. B. Thielen
Charm School. N. De Mille
Charmed Circle. C. Gaskin
Charmed Death. M. Tripp
Charmed Lives. Stanley Rogers
Charmer. Patrick Hamilton
Charmer Chased. Carter Brown
Charmian, Lady Vibard. J. Farnol
Charming Couple. Elizabeth Ford
Charming Murder. F. Shay
Charms. W. S. N. Iddesleigh
Charred Witness. G. H. Coxe
Charter Lane Mystery. G. C. Keech
Charter to Danger. E. Reed
Charteris Mystery. A. Fielding
Charters and Caldicott. S. Bingham
Chartreuse Clue. W. F. Love
Chase. A. Carpentier
Chase. N. Daniels
Chase. K. R. Dwyer
Chase. H. Foote
Chase. R. M. Gilchrist
Chase. R. G. Hubler
Chase. D. Lambert
Chase. J. Lermina
Chase. R. Unekis
Chase a Dark Shadow. I. Valdes
Chase Around the World. Anonymous
Chase for Millions. Nicholas Carter
Chase in the Dark. Nicholas Carter
Chase Me Round the Houses. B. Winter
Chase of the Golden Plate. J. Futrelle
Chase of the Linda Belle. H. Footner
Chase of the Ruby. R. Marsh
Chase Round the World. R. Overton
Chase Round the World. M. Weir
Chase Royal. D. Seaman
Chase the Snowman. M. C. McDougall
Chase the Storm. Alison Tyler
Chase the Sun. Alison Tyler
Chase the Wind. Alison Tyler
Chased by Fire. N. Gould
Chaser's Luck. G. G.
Chasing Eights. Michael Collins
Chasing the Dragon. S. Gall
Chasm. V. Canning
Chasm. R. W. Kauffman
Chasm of Fear. L. Robin
Chastity House. John Burke
Chateau Chaumond. A. Delmonico
Chateau d'Or. M. J. Holmes
Chateau in Brittany. M. Young
Chateau in the Shadows. S. Marvin
Chateau of Mystery. L. T. Meade
Chateau of Secrets. J. Wellsley
Chateau of Shadows. M. Heath
Chateau of Wolves. C. Farr
Chateau Rocca. E. H. England
Chateau Saxony. S. Richard
Chateau Sinister. I. Moore
Chatham Rats. D. Mariner
Chattering Gods. R. Crawley
Chatterton. P. Ackroyd
Chatterton Mystery. E. Everett-Green
Chauffeur-Driven Pyre. J. Hedges
Chautauqua. D. Keene
Cheap Detective. R. Grossbach
Cheap Dream. R. Leigh
Cheap Shot. J. Cronley
Cheat. R. Dietrich
Cheat. D. Tracy
Cheat. Bill Walsh
Cheat the Hangman. E. Ferrars
Cheaters. Ledru Baker
Cheating Butcher. A. M. Stein
Cheating Cheaters. M. Marcin
Cheating Justice. J. K. Stafford
Cheating the Kidnappers. G. S. Kaufman
Check No. 77. Nicholas Carter
Check to the King. M. Gerard

C

Check 2134. E. S. Ellis
Checked Through, Missing Trunk No. 17580. R. H. Savage
Checkerboard Caper. John Morris
Checkmate. S. Horler
Checkmate. J. S. Le Fanu
Checkmate. N. Lofts
Checkmate. P. Meredith
Checkmate. A. M. Stokes
Checkmate and Deathmate. M. Ashley
Checkmate and Stalemate. D. Learmonth
Checkmate Budapest. R. Hitchcock
Checkmate by the Colonel. G. Griswold
Checkmate for China. G. Osborne
Checkmate in Rio. Nick Carter
Checkmate Mr. President. J. Gouriet
Checkmate to Murder. E. C. R. Lorac
Checkmated. A. Macey
Checkmated Scoundrel. Nicholas Carter
Checkmating a Countess. Dick Stewart
Checkpoint. C. W. Thayer
Checkpoint Charlie. G. De Villiers
Checkpoint Charlie. B. Garfield
Checkpoint Orinoco. A. Ekert-Rotholz
Cheer for the Dead. E. Colter
Cheerful Blackguard. R. Pocock
Cheerful Knave. Keble Howard
Cheerio Killings. D. Allyn
Cheerio! Some Soldier Yarns. J. F. Tilsley
Cheese from a Mousetrap. J. M. Fox
Cheim Manuscript. R. S. Prather
Chekhov Proposal. Constance Carey
Chelsea Ghost. A. Hunter
Chelsea Murders. L. Davidson
Chelsea Mystery. Elaine Hamilton
Cheltenham Square Murder. J. Bude
Chemes. Taffrail
Cheng Ling Mystery. Elliot Bailey
Chengtu Strain. M. Goldberg
Cheque for Three Thousand. A. H. Veysey
Chequers. J. Runciman
Cherbourg Mystery. J. Maske
Cherchez la Femme. B. Graeme
Cherchez la Femme. L. Hamilton
Cheri-Bibi. G. Leroux
Cheri-Bibi and Cecily. G. Leroux
Cheri-Bibi, Mystery Man. G. Leroux
Cherie—You Slay Me. C. Dekker
Cherished Ones. H. Elsna
Cherokee. J. Echenoz
Cherokee Diamondback. John Reese
Cherry Blossom Corpse. Robert Barnard
Cherry-Boy Body Bag. J. Cain
Cherry Brandy. S. Ready
Cherry-Fair. Winifred Duke
Cherry Gambol and other stories. E. Phillpotts
Cherry Harvest. E. H. Clements
Cherry in the Wine Glass. J. B. O'Sullivan
Cherrycake Death. I. Tain
Cherry's Choice. L. Cargill
Chesapeake Project. P. Horn
Cheshire Cat's Eye. M. Muller
Chess Murders. Means Davis
Chess Mysteries of Sherlock Holmes. R. Smullyan
Chessboard Spies. Geoffrey Davison
Chessmaster. Nick Carter
Chessplayer. W. Pearson
Chest of Opium. Mr. M—
Chestermarke Instinct. J. S. Fletcher
Cheung, Detective. H. S. Keeler
Chevalier Casse-Cou. F. Du Boisgobey
Cheviot Chase. N. Tranter
Chewton Abbot and other tales. Anonymous
Cheyne Mystery. F. W. Crofts
Cheyney's Law. P. Cosgrove
Chez Krull. G. Simenon
Chez Torpe. F. Billetdoux
Chiangmai Suitcase. S. Richards
Chianti Flask. M. B. Lowndes
Chiaroscuro. P. Clothier
Chic Chick Spy. R. Tralins
Chicago. C. Carroll
Chicago. M. Watkins
Chicago Assault. C. Ramm
Chicago Chick. H. Janson
Chicago Dames. B. Sarto
Chicago Deadline. E. Mazzaro
Chicago Deathwinds. N. Winski
Chicago 11. D. Keene
Chicago Girl. T. Kenrick
Chicago Hustle. O. Hawkins
Chicago Joe and the Showgirl. M. Gaynor
Chicago Jungle. M. Baroni
Chicago Loop. P. Theroux
Chicago Payoff. A. Capelli
Chicago Princess. R. Barr
Chicago Rod. L. Martin
Chicago-7. W. P. McGivern
Chicago Slaughter. M. Barry
Chicago Striptease. B. Sarto
Chicago Terror. M. Storme
Chicago Winter's Tale. A. B. Crunden
Chicago Wipeout. D. Pendleton
Chicago Woman. R. O. Saber
Chicane. O. Sandys
Chicano War. W. C. Gault
Chichester Intrigue. T. Cobb
Chick. E. Wallace
Chicken. M. Tripp
Chicken and Zella. J. Tripp
Chickens in the Airshaft. S. Franklin
Chidori's Room. R. Timperley
Chief. C. Dawe
Chief Constable. Vincent Brown
Chief Constable. C. F. Gregg
Chief Counsel. A. L. Furman
Chief in Embryo. E. L. Long
Chief Inspector McLean. G. Goodchild
Chief Inspector's Daughter. S. Radley
Chief Inspector's Statement. M. Procter
Chief Justice. E. Franzos
Chief K. F. G. Wood
Chief Legatee. A. K. Green
Chief of the Counterfeiters. Old Sleuth
Chief Tallon and the S.O.R. J. Ball
Chief Witness. H. Adams
Chiefs. Stuart Woods
Chiffon Scarf. M. G. Eberhart
Child and the Serpent. S. Cook
Child at the Window. W. Hewlett
Child Divided. H. Cecil
Child Is Missing. C. Paul
Child Killer. E. T. Hamill
Child of Blood. Michael Newton
Child of Darkness. D. Daniels
Child of Evil. O. R. Cohen
Child of Mystery. H. M. Jones
Child of Night. Anne Edwards
Child of Rage. J. Thompson
Child of Satan. Melissa Napier
Child of Shadows. J. Coyne
Child of the Menhir. A. Clare
Child of the North. R. Cullum
Child of the Regiment. C. E. Blaney
Child of Two Fathers. T. P. Prest
Child of Value. P. Morton
Child Player. W. Dobson
Child Sellers. W. Leeds
Child Slaves of New York. C. E. Blaney
Child Stalker. C. C. Risenhoover
Child Witness. H. C. Davis
Child Witness. H. N. Halsey
Childerbridge Mystery. G. Boothby
Childproof. M. Z. Lewin
Children. C. Robertson
Children Are Gone. A. Cavanaugh
Children Are Watching. P. L. Dixon
Children! Children! J. Horrigan
Children in a Burning House. D. Soesby
Children of Chance. A. Carlyle
Children of Chance. H. Lloyd
Children of Despair. J. Creasey
Children of Earth. S. Paternoster
Children of Fear. D. Morley
Children of Hate. J. Creasey
Children of Hermes. H. Nisbet
Children of Houndstooth. K. Kimbrough
Children of Light. Robert (G.) Curtis
Children of Light. H. L. Lawrence
Children of Mammon. J. K. Leys
Children of Men. W. R. Trowbridge
Children of Power. S. R. Shreve
Children of Tender Years. T. Allbeury
Children of the Abbey. R. M. Roche
Children of the Cloven Hoof. A. Dorrington
Children of the Dark. I. Shulman
Children of the Dark. C. Veley
Children of the Griffin. E. Giles
Children of the Gutter. A. Applin
Children of the Knife. B. Strickland
Children of the Mist. B. Knox
Children of the Mists. H. McEwen
Children of the Night. M. Bingley
Children of the Night. J. Blackburn
Children of the Night. M. Lackey
Children of the Night. W. B. Maxwell
Children of the Reich. James Gregory
Children of the Ruins. T. Wiseman
Children of the Storm. D. Dwyer
Children of the Whirlwind. L. Scott
Children of the Wind. K. Wilhelm
Children of the Zodiac. A. M. Williamson
Children, Racehorses and Ghosts. E. H. Cooper
Children's Game. D. Wise
Children's Games. J. LaPierre
Children's Overture. H. Gibbs
Children's Party. Arthur H. Lewis
Children's Ward. P. Wallace
Children's Zoo. L. O'Donnell
Child's Garden of Death. R. Forrest
Child's Play. Alice Campbell
Child's Play. K. Christie
Child's Play. U. Curtiss
Child's Play. Reginald Hill
Child's Play. D. Malouf
Child's Play. R. Marasco
Child's Play. R. Sapir
Chilean Club. G. Shipway
Chill. E. C. Bentley
Chill. R. Macdonald
Chill. J. Sherman
Chill and the Kill. Joan Fleming
Chill Factor. R. Falkirk
Chill Factor. A. M. Stein
Chill of a Corpse. G. Peters
Chill on Chili. Carter Brown
Chill Rain in January. L. R. Wright
Chill Wind of Freedom. J. Midgley
Chill Winds of Ravenhall. M. Bishop
Chiller. D. Sale
Chillers. P. Highsmith
Chillers and Thrillers. Anonymous
Chillery Court Mystery. R. Francis Foster
Chilling Deception. J. Castle
Chimera. S. Gallagher
Chimney Murder. E. M. Channon
Chin-Chin-Chinaman. P. Walsh
Chin Chin, the Chinese Detective. A. W. Aiken
China Alley. H. Henn
China Bloodhunt. A. Kilgore
China Blue. G. Tippette
China Bomb. R. Tregaskis
China Cane. M. Storm
China Card. J. Ehrlichman
China Card. D. Freed
China Coaster. Don Smith
China Command. Gar Wilson
China Doll. Nick Carter
China Doll. M. Yorke
China Expert. M. Delving
China Gate. W. Arnold
China Gold. J. Tarrant
China Governess. M. Allingham
China Hand. B. Skoggard
China Kill. S. Hamill
China Lovers. D. Bonavia
China Option. N. D. Milton
China Rose. L. Chrichton
China Roundabout. Josephine Bell
China Run. Eric Clark
China Sea Murders. V. W. Mason
China Servant. C. S. Archer

China Shadow. Clarissa Ross
China Shepherdess. F. Y. McHugh
China Silk. F. Hurd
China Spy. R. Footman
China Syndrome. B. Wohl
China Tape. P. L. Lyons
China Town Mystery. G. H. Teed
China White. S. Grave
China White. T. Kenrick
Chinaman's Chance. Ross Thomas
Chinatown Charlie, the Opien Fiend. J. P. Ritter
Chinatown Connection. D. Park
Chinatown Justice. W. B. Longley
Chinatown Stories. C. B. Fernald
Chinatown, The Last Detail, Shampoo. R. Towne
Chinatown Trunk Mystery. O. Harper
Chinese Agenda. J. Poyer
Chinese Agent. M. Moorcock
Chinese Assassin. A. Grey
Chinese Bandit. S. Becker
Chinese Bed Mysteries. A. E. Martin
Chinese Bell Murders. R. Van Gulik
Chinese Blake. James Bennett
Chinese Bottle. P. Street
Chinese Box. K. W. Eyre
Chinese Box. M. McEvoy
Chinese Brown of Scotland Yard. C. Bishop
Chinese Bungalow. M. Osmond
Chinese Burn. Eric Clark
Chinese Cabinet. A. Applin
Chinese Cabinet. "Capstan"
Chinese Chanty. V. Clemov
Chinese Chop. J. Sheridan
Chinese Clippers. O. D. Adams
Chinese Coats. F. Heller
Chinese Coffin. J. Hedges
Chinese Connection. William Crawford
Chinese Connection. D. Haring
Chinese Consortium. W. Rilla
Chinese Conspiracy. J. Rosenberger
Chinese Conundrum. W. Manson
Chinese Crimson. A. S. Fleischman
Chinese Detective. M. Hardwick
Chinese Doll. W. Tucker
Chinese Doll Affair. A. Nuttall
Chinese Donovan. Carter Brown
Chinese Door. V. Coffman
Chinese Executioner. P. Boulle
Chinese Fairy Tales. A. M. Fielde
Chinese Fire Drill. M. Wolfe
Chinese Fish. J. Bommart
Chinese Girl. M. Hutton
Chinese Godfather. P. Gillette
Chinese Gold Murders. R. Van Gulik
Chinese Goose. H. Robertson
Chinese Hammer. S. Harvester
Chinese Jade Affair. D. Miller
Chinese Jar. F. Hume
Chinese Jar Mystery. J. S. Strange
Chinese Justice. S. Murray
Chinese Keyhole. R. Himmel
Chinese Kiss. J. J. Montague
Chinese Label. J. F. Davis
Chinese Lake Murders. R. Van Gulik
Chinese Letter. Claudette Nicole
Chinese Lover. E. Lay
Chinese Mask. B. S. Ballinger
Chinese Maze Murders. R. Van Gulik
Chinese Nail Murders. R. Van Gulik
Chinese Nightmare. H. Pentecost
Chinese Nights' Entertainment. A. M. Fielde
Chinese Orange Mystery. E. Queen
Chinese Oxymoron. V. S. Pierce
Chinese Parrot. E. D. Biggers
Chinese Paymaster. Nick Carter
Chinese Pleasure Girl. J. Seward
Chinese Poison. G. Hackforth-Jones
Chinese Poker. E. P. Thorne
Chinese Puzzle. M. Bower
Chinese Puzzle. M. Burton
Chinese Puzzle. O. Dekobra
Chinese Puzzle. R. Sapir
Chinese Red. R. Burke
Chinese Red. G. Collins
Chinese Restaurants Never Serve Breakfast. R. Gilligan
Chinese Roulette. P. Kirk
Chinese Shawl. P. Wentworth
Chinese Spur. B. Sandberg
Chinese Stories. R. K. Douglas
Chinese Straight. J. J. Lamb
Chinese Ultimatum. Robin Moore
Chinese Vengeance. R. A. Kent
Chinese Visitor. J. Eastwood
Chinese White. H. B. Drake
Chinese Widow. J. Leasor
Ching Ching on the Trail. E. H. Burrage
Ching Lung's Wager. S. Drew
Chink in the Armour. Jack Lewis
Chink in the Armour. M. B. Lowndes
Chinkie's Flat and other stories. L. Becke
Chinks in the Curtain. J. Porter
Chink's Victim. J. G. Brandon
Chip on My Shoulder. Eric North
Chipped. N. Steed
Chipstead of the Lone Hand. S. Horler
Chiselers. Albert Conroy
Chiseller. Duff Johnson
Chislehurst Mystery. E. L. Mann
Chit of a Girl. G. Simenon
Chivalry. R. Sabatini
Chivalry and the Gibbet. G. Curtis
Chocolate Charlie. T. Fitzgerald
Chocolate Cobweb. C. Armstrong
Chocolate Mousse. H. L. Herbst
Chocolate Mousse Murders. F. Halliday
Chocolate Spy. D. M. Alexander
Chog. Q. Crisp
Choice. T. Allbeury
Choice. M. Brandel
Choice. P. MacDonald
Choice. E. R. Punshon
Choice Cuts. P. Boileau
Choice of Angels. H. Arvonen
Choice of Assassins. W. P. McGivern
Choice of Crimes. L. Egan
Choice of Eddie Franks. J. Winchester
Choice of Emilia. A. Sergeant
Choice of Enemies. T. Allbeury
Choice of Enemies. G. V. Higgins
Choice of Evils. Mrs. Alexander
Choice of Evils. Philip Ross
Choice of Nightmares. M. Dorner
Choice of Theodora. T. Cobb
Choice of Two Women. Gerald Butler
Choice of Victims. J. F. Straker
Choice of Violence. H. Pentecost
Choirboys. J. Wambaugh
Choke Chain. J. B. O'Sullivan
Choke Hold. L. Dykes
Choke Point. C. D. Taylor
Cholo. R. Houston
Choose Your Own Verdict. Hilary Landon
Choose Your Weapon. V. Loder
Chopin Express. H. Kaplan
Chopper Command. E. Helm
Chord in Crimson. G. Gallagher
Chorine Makes a Killing. Carter Brown
Chorus Ending. E. Raymond
Chorus of Detectives. Barbara Paul
Chorus of Echoes. E. Trevor
Chosen Child. V. Maxwell
Chosen Course. N. Tranter
Chosen Girl. J. Buell
Chosen Instrument. H. Calvin
Chosen Man. Anonymous
Chosen Man. H. P. Halsey
Chosen of the Gods. A. Soutar
Chosen Parents. M. Arrighi
Chosen People. B. Michelson
Chosen Prey. W. Brashler
Chosen Sparrow. V. Caspary
Chowra's Revenge. F. E. Penny
Chris: A Love Story. J. Ironside
Christ Commission. O. Mandino
Christabel's Room. A. Clement
Christie Case. Ronald Maxwell
Christie in Love. H. Brenton
Christina. R. Cameron
Christina. D. Rome
Christina. Dee Stuart
Christine Diamond. M. B. Lowndes
Christine in Murderland. F. Wells
Christmas Adventure and other tales. Anonymous
Christmas at Candleshoe. M. Innes
Christmas at Poverty Castle. T. Gallon
Christmas Bomber. T. Chastain
Christmas Card Murders. D. W. Meredith
Christmas Day and How It Was Spent. C. Le Ros
Christmas Egg. M. Kelly
Christmas Eve. S. C. Roberts
Christmas Fireside Tales. J. B. Sabin
Christmas Guest. E. Southworth
Christmas Hamper. M. Lemon
Christmas Hirelings. M. E. Braddon
Christmas Holiday. W. S. Maugham
Christmas Kill. Nick Carter
Christmas Murder. C. Hare
Christmas Pudding That Shook the World. Alex Hamilton
Christmas Rising. D. Serafin
Christmas Spy. J. Howlett
Christmas Tree Murders. J. Y. Dane
Christmas Without Roddy. W. Fennerton
Christobel. M. L. Roby
Christopher Bond, Adventurer. W. Martyn
Christopher Henrick. J. Hatton
Christopher Parkins, R.N. R. L. Dearden
Christopher Quarles, College Professor and Master Detective. P. Brebner
Christopher's Mansion. W. E. D. Ross
Christy King Is Kidnapped. Polan Banks
Chrome Connection. M. Simpson
Chronicle of the Fleet Street Prison. C. Rowcroft
Chronicles of a Cavalier. J. G. Sarasin
Chronicles of a Country Cricket Club. A. E. Bayly
Chronicles of a Death Foretold. G. G. Marquez
Chronicles of Addington Peace. B. F. Robinson
Chronicles of Bustos Domecq. J. L. Borges
Chronicles of Captain Blood. R. Sabatini
Chronicles of Cardewe Manor. L. Farmer
Chronicles of Choisy. J. Le Breton
Chronicles of Clovis. H. H. Munro
Chronicles of Dennis Chetwynd. H. J. Fidler
Chronicles of Don Q. K. Prichard
Chronicles of Golden Friars. J. S. Le Fanu
Chronicles of Humphrey Judd. V. L. Whitechurch
Chronicles of Lucius Leffing. J. P. Brennan
Chronicles of Martin Hewitt. Arthur Morrison
Chronicles of Melhampton. E. P. Oppenheim
Chronicles of Michael Danevitch of the Russian Secret Service. D. Donovan
Chronicles of No Man's Land. F. Boyle
Chronicles of Quincy Adams Sawyer, Detective. C. F. Pidgin
Chronicles of St. Tid. E. Phillpotts
Chronicles of Service Life in Malta. Mrs. A. T. Stuart
Chronicles of Shark Gotch. A. R. Wetjen
Chronicles of Slyme Court. H. M. Raleigh
Chronicles of Solar Pons. A. Derleth
Chronicles of the Bow Street Police-Office. Percy Fitzgerald
Chronicles of the "Crooked" Club. J. Greenwood
Chronicles of the Fleet Prison. C. Rowcroft
Chronicles of the Imp. J. Farnol
Chronicles of the Secret Service. A. Wilson
Chronicles of Tirlie Town. J. Porsnocke
Chronological History of the Boston Watch and Police. Edward Savage
Chrysalis. William Taylor
Chrysanthanum Chain. James Melville
Chuckling Fingers. M. Seeley
Church of Humanity. D. C. Murray
Churchill Commando. T. Willis
Churchill Diamonds. B. Langley
Churchill Mission. K. Netzen
Churchill's Gold. J. Follett
Churchyard Salad. M. Torrie
Churstons. P. Trent
Cider Row. W. K. McIntire
Cigar for Inspector Head. E. C. Vivian

Cigarette. P. T. Reynolds
Cigarette Clew. Nicholas Carter
Cinch. R. Martins
Cinder-Path Tales. W. Lindsey
Cinderella. E. McBain
Cinderella After Midnight. F. Zackel
Cinderella All Alone. A. Wood
Cinderella Goes to the Morgue. N. Spain
Cinderella Spy. P. Daniels
Cinderella's Dead. M. F. Callan
Cinders of Harley Street. W. LeQueux
Cinema City. C. R. Gull
Cinema Crime. R. Goyne
Cinema Crimes. J. Creasey
Cinema Crook. Anonymous
Cinema Murder. E. P. Oppenheim
Cinnabar Shroud. K. Ashley
Cinnamon Murder. F. Crane
Cinnamon Skin. J. D. MacDonald
Cinnebar. R. B. Oxnam
Cintra Story. M. Clare
Cipher. Alex Gordon
Cipher Detective. A. P. Morris
Cipher Five. A. O. Pollard
Cipher of Death. F. L. Gregory
Cipher Six. W. LeQueux
Cipher Stories Puzzle Book. K. S. Cooper
Ciphergrams. H. O. Yardley
Ciphered. S. Keech
Circe & Bravo. D. Freed
Circe Complex. D. Cory
Circle. L. E. McCormick
Circle. S. Shagan
Circle in the Water. J. McKimmey
Circle of Confusion. Palmer White
Circle of Danger. P. Alding
Circle of Darkness. J. Griffin
Circle of Death. H. Arvonen
Circle of Death. C. J. Dutton
Circle of Death. W. J. Elliott
Circle of Death. P. A. Foxall
Circle of Death. J. N. Frey
Circle of Death. Richard Grant
Circle of Death. P. Quiroule
Circle of Death. M. Rennert
Circle of Deceit. W. Winward
Circle of Deception. E. Title
Circle of Deception. C. Virmonne
Circle of Dust. J. Cassells
Circle of Evil. V. Johnston
Circle of Evil. S. Wagner
Circle of Fear. A. Brennan
Circle of Fear. P. Carlon
Circle of Fire. M. Sadler
Circle of Freedom. Mark Cross
Circle of Guilt. D. Daniels
Circle of Guilt. C. Kingston
Circle of Justice. P. Manton
Circle of Secrets. Claudette Nicole
Circle of Shadows. D. Holt
Circle of Squares. Bill Turner
Circle of Steel. D. Pendleton
Circle of the Earth. George Knight
Circle of the Snake. Anonymous
Circle of Thirteen. W. H. Graydon
Circle of Vengeance. N. Jorgenson
Circle of Von Boden. R. Harrison
Circle of Women. D. L. Pifer
Circle Round a Corpse. Hilary Landon
Circles of Deceit. N. Bawden
Circlet of Night. Stockton Heath
Circular Staircase. M. R. Rinehart
Circular Study. A. K. Green
Circumstances Beyond Control. A. Yudkoff
Circumstantial Case. E. H. Creeth
Circumstantial Evidence. A. I. Abbott
Circumstantial Evidence. Nicholas Carter
Circumstantial Evidence. F. W. Crofts
Circumstantial Evidence. F. J. Fargus
Circumstantial Evidence. E. Fitzmaurice
Circumstantial Evidence. Andrew Stewart
Circumstantial Evidence. J. H. Swingler
Circumstantial Evidence. Bessie Turner
Circumstantial Evidence. E. Wallace

Circus. Alistair MacLean
Circus Crime. A. Skene
Circus Couronne. R. W. Campbell
Circus Day. Caroline Crane
Circus Detective. Anonymous
Circus Master's Mission. J. Brinkley
Circus Mystery. D. T. Hughes
Circus Parade. J. Tully
Cire Perdue. W. Butler
Citadel of the Bats. M. Hastings
Citadel Run. P. Bishop
Cities of the Dead. Linda Barnes
Cities of the Red Night. W. Burroughs
Citizen of Brains. R. H. Williams
Citizens-to Arms! Garnett Weston
City and Suburban. F. Warden
City at Bay. D. Thoreau
City Beneath the Skin. J. Gathorne-Hardy
City Beyond. L. Emerick
City Called Holy. M. Callard
City Called July. H. Engel
City Destroyer. G. Stockbridge
City for Sale. J. Messmann
City in Heat. W. B. Murphy
City in the Clouds. C. R. Gull
City Limit Blonde. A. Bocca
City Limits. N. Marino
City of a Thousand Drums. H. Vernes
City of Angels. S. Shagan
City of Anger. W. Manchester
City of Apes. A. Murray
City of Blood. D. Hartman
City of Brass, and other Simon Ark stories. E. D. Hoch
City of Cain. K. Wilhelm
City of Crooks. S. Blake
City of Endless Night. M. M. Hastings
City of Evil. D. Haring
City of Fading Light. J. Cleary
City of Fear. F. Lady
City of Fear. John Marsh
City of Flaming Shadows. G. Stockbridge
City of Forever. B. Blackburn
City of Glass. P. Auster
City of Gold and Shadows. Ellis Peters
City of Horrors. W. J. Bayfield
City of Kites. T. Callas
City of Lies. C. Winchester
City of Light. T. Benoit
City of Lost Women. Griff
City of Masks. M. Browne
City of Masks. E. J. Murray
City of Mystery. A. C. Gunter
City of Passion. D. Barnes
City of Peril. A. Stringer
City of Purple Dreams. Anonymous
City of Refuge. J. G. Sarasin
City of Shadows. P. Meredith
City of Shadows, and other stories. J. Barnard-James
City of Silent Men. L. Lane
City of Silent Men. J. A. Moroso
City of Sin. R. O. Saber
City of Sin. B. Sarto
City of Strangers. Robert Barnard
City of Strife. Gwyn Evans
City of the Dead. L. Derrick
City of the Dead. H. Lieberman
City of the Golden Gate. E. Everett-Green
City of the Just. T. Terrell
City of the Living Dead. B. House
City of the Soul. M. Home
City of Whispering Stone. G. Chesbro
City of Wonders. E. Mendoza
City Office Mystery. M. B. Giles
City Primeval. E. Leonard
City Slicker and Our Nell. L. Price
City Solitary. N. Freeling
Civil Death. J. W. Corrington
Claim of Anthony Lockhart. A. Sergeant
Claim of the Fleshless Corpse. G. Bruce
Claim the Crown. C. Neggers
Claimant. W. Chesney
Claire. D. Malm
Clairvoyant. H. Clement

Clairvoyant Countess. D. Gilman
Clairvoyante. B. L. Farjeon
Clampdown. W. V. Butler
Clan of Golgotha Scalp. M. F. Anderson
Clancumara's Keep. M. Heath
Clancy. F. Mullally
Clancy of the Mounted Police. O. Binns
Clancy's Secret Mission. L. Thayer
Clandestine. J. Ellroy
Clang on the Anvil. H. C. Danby
Clangor in the Bell Tower. M. Graff
Clanmire Tor. M. Blair
Clans of the Alphane Moon. P. K. Dick
Clap Hands, Here Comes Charlie. B. Freemantle
Clap Hands If You Believe in Fairies. John Fraser
Clara Hopkins. O. Bradbury
Clara Lake's Dream. H. Wood
Clara Reeve. L. Hargrave
Clara Vaughan. R. D. Blackmore
Clare of Claresmede. C. Gibbon
Claret, Sandwiches and Sin. M. Donne
Clarice Dyke, the Female Detective. H. Rockwood
Clarinda Conspiracy. A. Campsie
Clash. E. Wilkinson
Clash by Night. C. Clarke
Clash by Night. R. Croft-Cooke
Clash of Distant Thunder. A. C. Marin
Clash of Eagles. L. Rutman
Clash of Hawks. R. Charles
Clash of Loyalties. P. Harcourt
Clash of Shadows. H. Rigsby
Clash of Steel. Colin Robertson
Class Distinctions. T. Heald
Classical Death. A. Marsland
Classics of the Macabre. D. Du Maurier
Classified Death. C. Taschjian
Clauberg Trigger. J. Tarrant
Claud the Charmer. E. Everett-Green
Claude Beauclerc. Ambofilius
Claude Du Val. H. D. Miles
Claude Duval of Ninety-Five. F. Hume
Claude Melnotte as a Detective, and other stories. A. Pinkerton
Clause in the Will. W. M. Graydon
Claustrophobia. R. Child
Claverleigh Curse. S. Dubay
Claverse Affair. J. G. Vermandel
Claverton Affair. J. Rhode
Claverton Case. R. Rodd
Claverton Mystery. J. Rhode
Claw. N. Lofts
Claw. M. Raynor
Claw. J. Younger
Claw of a Cat. G. Peters
Claws for a Cutie. B. Sarto
Claws in the Night. V. Hansen
Claws of Fate. D. Dayle
Claws of God. M. Tripp
Claws of Mercy. J. Harris
Claws of the Cougar. N. Berrow
Claws of the Crow. P. Wissmann
Claws of the Gryphon. Peter Turnbull
Claws of the Red Dragon. C. Bishop
Claws of the Scorpion. G. Johnston
Claws of the Tiger. Nicholas Carter
Claxton's Mill. F. M. White
Clay. H. Imbert-Terry
Clay Assassin. J. Godey
Clay-Face. J. Templeton
Clay Hand. D. S. Davis
Clean Break. L. White
Clean, Bright, and Slightly Oiled. G. Kersh
Clean Crimes and Neat Murders. H. Slesar
Clean Hand. M. B. Vandeburg
Clean Kill. M. Gilbert
Clean Sweep. J. M. Wallmann
Clean Up. Joe Barry
Clean-Up. L. C. Douthwaite
Clean-Up. D. Williamson
Clear and Present Danger. T. Clancy
Clear and Present Danger. B. Kendrick
Clear and Present Danger. B. Sanders
Clear Case of Murder. H. Desmond
Clear Case of Murder. W. Downing

Title Index

Clear Case of Suicide. M. Underwood
Clear Road to Archangel. G. Rose
Clear Round. E. L. Long
Clear Shot. D. Stivers
Clear Sky above. N. Sheraton
Clear the Fast Lane. D. Rutherford
Clearing in the Fog. D. Macomber
Cleaver. D. Rome
Cleek of Scotland Yard. T. W. Hanshew
Cleek, the Man of Forty Faces. T. W. Hanshew
Cleek, the Master Detective. T. W. Hanshew
Cleek's Government Cases. T. W. Hanshew
Cleek's Greatest Riddles. T. W. Hanshew
Cleft Chin Murder. R. A. Raymond
Cleft of Stars. G. Jenkins
Clement Lorimer. A. B. Reach
Clenched Antagonisms. L. Iram
Cleopatra Jones. R. Goulart
Cleopatra Jones and the Casino of Gold. R. Goulart
Cleopatra Needle Mystery. J. N. Pentelow
Cleopatra's Nose. T. B. Marle
Cleopatra's Tears. H. S. Keeler
Clerical Cracksman. A. F. King
Clerical Error. A. Rolls
Clerk Barton's Crime. Steele Penn
Clerk of Portwick. G. M. Fenn
Clermont. R. M. Roche
Clerycastle. M. Heath
Clevedon Case. N. Oakley
Cleveland Pipeline. D. Pendleton
Clevelands of the Peak. A. H. Fletcher
Clever Celestial. Nicholas Carter
Clever Criminals. John Lang
Clever Detective. Old Sleuth
Clever One. E. Wallace
Clever Ones. R. R. King
Clever Ones. J. E. Middleton
Cleverdale Mystery. W. A. Wilkins
Cleverest Woman in England. L. T. Meade
Cleverly Won. H. Smart
Cleverness of Mr. Budd. G. Verner
Clew Against Clew. Nicholas Carter
Clew by Clew. Nicholas Carter
Clew in the Glass. W. B. M. Ferguson
Clew of the Forgotten Murder. C. Kendrake
Click of the Gate. Alice Campbell
Client. Parnell Hall
Client. M. Russell
Client Is Cancelled. R. Lockridge
Client: Mafia. D. Haring
Client Privilege. W. G. Tapply
Clients of Doctor Bernagius. L. Biart
Clients of Omega. D. Bloodworth
Cliff Face. D. Buckingham
Cliff Mill Mystery. G. Volk
Cliff Mystery. H. Aide
Cliff-Path Mystery. H. Hill
Cliff Walk. M. Dickson
Cliffhanger. J. Yaffe
Cliffhaven. Dan Ross
Clifford Affair. A. Fielding
Clifford Mystery. A. Fielding
Cliff's End Farm and other stories. F. Warden
Cliff's Head. D. Kamm
Cliffs of Death. Claude Nicole
Cliffs of Dread. V. Coffman
Cliffs of Night. Beatrice Brandon
Cliffs of Sark. G. Volk
Cliffside Castle. D. Daniels
Clik! Julian Spencer
Climate for Conspiracy. P. Harcourt
Climate of Courage. J. Cleary
Climate of Hell. H. Lieberman
Climate of Hell. J. Roeburt
Climate of Revolt. Alan White
Climax. G. C. Jenks
Climax. N. Karta
Climax. F. J. Lewis
Climax. E. Locke
Climax at the Falls. G. Baxter
Climb a Broken Ladder. R. Novak
Climb a Dark Cliff. K. Ashby
Climb the Dark Mountain. J. Wellsley
Climb the Wall. M. Cronin

Climbing Corpse. A. Brede
Climbing Tree. C. McAfee
Cling of the Clay. M. Hayes
Clinging Shadows. M. Waring
Clinic. C. Johnson
Clinic of Dr. Aicadre. Muriel Harris
Clinton Is Assigned. M. McConnell
Clio Browne: Private Investigator. D. Komo
Clip-Joint. E. Olmstead
Clip Joint Girl. R. Vane
Clipped Hedges. F. Hird
Clique of Gold. E. Gaboriau
Clique of Knaves. Dick Stewart
Clive Lorimer's Marriage. E. Everett-Green
Cloak and Dagger. Jenna Ryan
Cloak and Dagger Lover. M. Greig
Cloak-and-Doctor. F. E. Gibson
Cloak for Malice. K. Wade
Cloak of Darkness. H. MacInnes
Cloak of Darkness. W. Magnay
Cloak of Guilt. Nicholas Carter
Cloak of St. Martin. Armine Grace
Cloakroom Murder. W. Jardine
Clock. R. Goyne
Clock. A. E. W. Mason
Clock and Bell. S. Claudia
Clock and the Key. A. H. Vesey
Clock at Ravenswood. J. Teta
Clock Face. M. K. Simmons
Clock in the Hatbox. Anthony Gilbert
Clock Strikes. P. Troubetzkoy
Clock Strikes Ten. M. Richmond
Clock Strikes Thirteen. H. Brean
Clock Strikes Twelve. P. Wentworth
Clock Strikes Two. H. K. Webster
Clock Struck One. F. Hume
Clock Struck Seven. G. Goodchild
Clock Struck Twelve. J. Reach
Clock That Wouldn't Stop. E. Ferrars
Clock Ticks. C. Houghton
Clock Ticks On. V. Williams
Clock Tower. J. Montague
Clock Without Hands. G. Kersh
Clockmaker. G. Simenon
Clockmaker of Heidelberg. H. Edmond
Clocks. A. Christie
Clocktower. G. McDonell
Clockwork. N. Steed
Clockwork Orange. A. Burgess
Cloggy Dick. Arthur Smith
Cloisonne Vase. E. Noone
Cloister Cat. A. Wight
Clone People. M. Johnson
Close All Roads to Sospel. G. Bellairs
Close Call. J. L. Berry
Close Call. E. Phillpotts
Close Doesn't Count. John Craig
Close Her Eyes. D. Simpson
Close Her Pale Blue Eyes. H. Hull
Close His Eyes. O. Dwight
Close of Play. S. Raven
Close Pursuit. C. Stroud
Close Quarters. M. Gilbert
Close Shave. S. Maddock
Close the Door on Murder. J. York
Close the Frontier. L. A. Knight
Close to Death. J. Crowe
Close to Home. C. Blair
Close to the Wind. J. Harris
Close-Up. M. Turnbull
Close-Up. D. Walshe
Close-Up of a Killing. R. M. Douglas
Close-Up of a Killing. Richard Hubbard
Close-Up on Death. Marueen O'Brien
Close Your Eyes and Sleep, My Beauty. A. Sewart
Closed Book. W. LeQueux
Closed Circle. W. Ebersohn
Closed Circuit. W. Haggard
Closed Door. R. M. Douglas
Closed Door. F. Du Boisgobey
Closed Door. S. Horler
Closely Confined. E. Burgess
Closeout. D. Conger
Closet Bones. T. Bunn

Closet Hanging. T. Fennelly
Closing Ceremonies. Harold King
Closing Circle. L. Cameron
Closing Costs. T. Bunn
Closing Door. J. Blackmore
Closing Net. H. C. Rowland
Closing the Circle. Dick Stewart
Cloud. R. Bridges
Cloud Nine. J. M. Cain
Cloud Nineteen. W. Stanley
Cloud Over Calderwood. K. A. Shoesmith
Cloud Over Malverton. N. Buckingham
Cloud the Smiter. A. Gask
Cloudburst. F. Keast
Clouded in Mystery. M. A. A. B.
Clouded Mirror. E. Bond
Clouded Moon. M. Saltmarsh
Clouds in the Wind. F. L. Green
Clouds of Fear. R. Bryant
Clouds of Guilt. J. Wainwright
Clouds of War. Ralph Hayes
Clouds of Witness. D. L. Sayers
Clouds Over Vellanti. Elsie Lee
Cloudy in the West. W. P. White
Cloudy Ladder. V. Barlow
Clough Plays Murder. L. Parsons
Clove Crest. I. A. Greenfield
Cloven Foot. M. E. Braddon
Cloven Foot. O. C. Kerr
Cloven-Footed Angel. M. Dekobra
Cloverdale Skeleton. C. L. Hooper
Clown. Carter Brown
Clowning Through. E. C. Reed
Clowns Wear Guns. V. Phillips
Cloze Papers. K. Livingston
Club. A. D. Wintle
Club Car Mystery. G. I. Colbron
Club Dead. J. Oster
Club Hostess. W. Standish
Club—Mink Lined Murder. M. Webb
Club of Masks. A. Upward
Club of Queer Trades. G. K. Chesterton
Club of Skulls. Anonymous
Club of Skulls. Wilfred Barclay
Club Paradis Murders. C. McCormick
Club 17. B. Kerr
Club Twelve. A. K. Williams
Clubbable Woman. R. Hill
Clubfoot the Avenger. V. Williams
Clubs and Hearts. P. Trent
Clue. A. V. Arnold
Clue. M. McDowell
Clue. O. Wadsley
Clue. C. Wells
Clue Armchair Detective. L. Treat
Clue for Clancy. L. Thayer
Clue for Clutha. H. Munro
Clue for Mr. Fortune. H. C. Bailey
Clue for Murder. R. Barker
Clue from the Clouds. Anonymous
Clue from the Past. G. Langdon
Clue from the Stars. E. Phillpotts
Clue from the Unknown. Nicholas Carter
Clue in the Air. I. Ostrander
Clue in the Clay. D. B. Olsen
Clue in the Glass. W. B. M. Ferguson
Clue in the Mirror. N. Morland
Clue in Two Flats. R. L. F. McCombs
Clue in Wax. F. M. White
Clue of Death. S. C. Hook
Clue of the Artificial Eye. J. S. Fletcher
Clue of the Bricklayer's Aunt. N. Morland
Clue of the Careless Hangman. N. Morland
Clue of the Charred Diary. W. J. Bayfield
Clue of the Cloak. R. DeMalahide
Clue of the Cloakroom Ticket. R. C. Armour
Clue of the Clock. M. Harvey
Clue of the Clot. C. Barry
Clue of the Cone. J. Arthur Williams
Clue of the Cross-Eyed Girl. N. Burnaby
Clue of the Curious Cat. R. Brode
Clue of the Dead Goldfish. V. MacClure
Clue of the Eyelash. C. Wells
Clue of the Forgotten Murder. C. Kendrake

C

C

Clue of the Four Wigs. G. H. Teed
Clue of the Fourteen Keys. M. Burton
Clue of the Frightening Coin. Jessica Ryan
Clue of the Golden Ear-Ring. C. M. Wills
Clue of the Golden Tooth. J. Brooks
Clue of the Green Candle. G. Verner
Clue of the Green Parrot. B. Moorhouse
Clue of the Hungry Corpse. I. Jones
Clue of the Ivory Claw. F. H. Dimmock
Clue of the Judas Tree. L. Ford
Clue of the Leather Noose. D. B. Hobart
Clue of the Lost Hour. C. M. Wills
Clue of the Missing Link. Gwyn Evans
Clue of the Naked Eye. C. M. Russell
Clue of the New Pin. E. Wallace
Clue of the New Shoe. A. W. Upfield
Clue of the Pin-Up Girl. W. Tyrer
Clue of the Poor Man's Shilling. K. M. Knight
Clue of the Postage Stamp. A. Bray
Clue of the Primrose Petal. H. Wickham
Clue of the Purple Asters. J. Cassells
Clue of the Rising Moon. V. Williams
Clue of the Scarlet Singers. Anonymous
Clue of the Second Murder. J. S. Strange
Clue of the Second Tooth. D. W. Steward
Clue of the Seventh Stain. J. Wylde
Clue of the Silver Brush. M. Burton
Clue of the Silver Cellar. M. Burton
Clue of the Silver Crescent. A. G. Pearson
Clue of the Silver Key. E. Wallace
Clue of the Six Kissing Girls. C. Herbert
Clue of the Stolen Rupees. A. Parsons
Clue of the Stone. H. A. Wrenn
Clue of the Tattooed Man. J. G. Brandon
Clue of the Twisted Candle. E. Wallace
Clue of the Twisted Face. F. A. Kummer
Clue Sinister. C. Carnac
Clue to Danger. A. Furness
Clue to the Labyrinth. C. B. Clason
Clueless Trail. P. Walsh
Clues. W. Henderson
Clues for Dr. Coffee. L. G. Blochman
Clues from a Detective's Camera. H. Hill
Clues of the Caribbees. T. S. Stribling
Clues to Burn. L. G. Offord
Clues to Christabel. M. Fitt
Clunk's Claiment. H. C. Bailey
Cluny Problem. A. Fielding
Cluster of Gems. R. Carr
Cluster of Separate Sparks. Joan Aiken
Clutch of Circumstance. J. Barnes
Clutch of Circumstance. M. B. Cooke
Clutch of Constables. N. Marsh
Clutch of Coppers. G. Ashe
Clutch of Diamonds. W. Christopher
Clutch of Dread. Nicholas Carter
Clutch of Vipers. J. S. Scott
Clutching Claw. R. Kettering
Clutching Hand. C. J. Dutton
Clutching Hand. A. B. Reeve
Clutha and the Lady. H. Munro
Clutha Plays a Hunch. H. Munro
Clutterbuck's Treasure. F. Whishaw
Clutterkill. G. Paulsen
Clyde, the Resolute Detective. Old Sleuth
Clyde, the Trailer. M. O. Rolfe
Clyffards of Clyffe. J. Payn
Clytie. J. Hatton
Co-Heiresses. E. Everett-Green
Coach Draws Near. M. Savage
Coach North. P. McCutchan
Coachman's Club. George R. Sims
Coachman's Daughter. D. Creekmore
Coal Tom. Old Sleuth
Coals of Fear and other stories. D. C. Murray
Coast Highway 1. E. C. Ward
Coast of Adventure. H. Bindloss
Coast of Bohemia. Z. Tomin
Coast of Chance. Esther Chamberlain
Coast of Echoes. J. C. Strange
Coast of Fear. K. G. Ballard
Coast of Fear. C. Crane
Coast of Fear. J. D'Astor
Coast of Fear. L. Waller

Coast of Intrigue. W. Chambers
Coast of No Return. M. Hastings
Coast Road Murder. M. Turnbull
Coaster. G. Foy
Coat of Arms. G. Sims
Coat of Arms. E. Wallace
Coat of Blackmail. J. T. McIntosh
Coat of Varnish. C. P. Snow
Coatine Case. A. J. Colton
Cobalt. N. Aldyne
Cobalt 60. R. L. Graves
Cobra Candlestick. E. Barker
Cobra Chase. J. Rosenberg
Cobra Diamond. A. Lillie
Cobra Kill. Nick Carter
Cobra Strike. R. Charles
Cobra Strike. J. B. Hadley
Cobra Team. E. E. Mayer
Cobra Venom. A. Rowe
Cobra Venom. J. B. West
Cobweb. P. Flower
Cobweb Across the Moon. C. Darby
Cobweb Castle. J. S. Fletcher
Cobweb House. E. H. Holloway
Cobwebs. Mabel Collins
Cobwebs and Clues. E. Malan
Cocaine. D. Forde
Cocaine. M. Olden
Cocaine and Blue Eyes. F. Zackel
Cocaine Blues. K. Greenwood
Cocaine Blues. W. Satterthwait
Cocaine Caper. V. A. Paradis
Cocaine Connection. R. L. Brent
Cocaine for Breakfast. G. Sava
Cocaine Kill. A. Destefano
Cocaine Run. J. Ahern
Cock Crow. A. Carlyle
Cock o' the North. T. Mundy
Cock-Pit of Roses. James Fraser
Cock Robin. E. L. Rice
Cockatoo Crime. B. Knox
Cockeyed Corpse. R. S. Prather
Cockleburr. R. Crawford
Cocklepfeiffer Case. B. Hewitt
Cockney Cavalcade. G. Ingram
Cockney of the Legion. J. D. Newsom
Cockpit. J. Kosinski
Cockpit. Warwick Scott
Cockroach Dance. M. Mwangi
Cockroach Sings. Alice Campbell
Cock's Tail Murder. H. Austin
Cocksure Dame. J. Cairo
Cocktail for Cupid and other stories. P. Cheyney
Cocktail Party and other stories. P. Cheyney
Cocktails and the Killer. P. Cheyney
Cocktails with a Stranger. C. Franklin
Cocoanut Inn. S. W. Powell
Coconut Killings. P. Moyes
Coconut Wireless. F. Kauffman
Coda. T. Topor
Coda Alliance. M. Brady
Code. Nick Carter
Code Conquistador. W. P. Kennedy
Code Ezra. G. Courter
Code-Letter Mystery. D. Sharp
Code Mobius. J. R. Zapor
Code-Name Caruso. George Sims
Code Name Cobra. Nick Carter
Code Name Emerald. R. Bass
Code Name Gadget. P. Rabe
Code Name: Grand Guignol. I. Melchior
Code Name Hangman. P. Geddes
Code Name Harlequin. B. Mitchell
Code Name "Icy." L. Agniel
Code Name: Judas. M. Walker
Code Name: Little Ivan. J. Tiger
Code Name: Love. M. Nicole
Code Name: Mamba. M. Marler
Code Name Nimrod. J. Leasor
Code Name: Rapier. M. Walker
Code Name: Rubble. P. Thomas
Code Name Sebastian. J. L. Johnson
Code Name: Werewolf. Nick Carter
Code of Arms. L. Block

Code of Blood. D. Cross
Code of Conduct. Elliott Arnold
Code of Dishonor. D. Pendleton
Code of Dishonour. B. Sanders
Code of the Northwest. S. A. White
Code 1013: Assassin. L. Trevor
Code Sakura. D. Unkefer
Code Seven. L. Cameron
Code Talkers. C. Bianchi
Code Three. J. M. Fox
Code Word Christmas Tree. J. J. Parnell
Code Word—Golden Fleece. D. Wheatley
Code Word "Proton". E. P. Thorne
Code Z. J. Swerdlow
Code Zero: Shots Fired. J. Cain
Codename—Bastille. B. Musto
Codename: Needlepoint. R. W. Marsh
Codename, Starlight. Hartshorne
Codeword Cromwell. P. Kelly
Codfish Watch. E. R. Knowlton
Cody's Army. Jim Case
Coffee for None. A. B. Caldwell
Coffee for One. E. Hale
Coffee for One. J. Last
Coffee in the Morning. G. Greenaway
Coffee on the Roof. J. Victor
Coffin & Co. N. Simon
Coffin and the Paper Man. Gwendoline Butler
Coffin Bird. Carter Brown
Coffin Corner. G. Bagby
Coffin Corner. Dell Shannon
Coffin Corner U.S.A. S. Jason
Coffin Country. A. M. Stein
Coffin Fits. A. Bocca
Coffin Following. Gwendoline Butler
Coffin for a Cutie. S. Morelli
Coffin for a Hood. L. White
Coffin for a Murderer. Reginald Campbell
Coffin for Baby. Gwendoline Butler
Coffin for Christopher. D. Ames
Coffin for Clara. B. Diamond
Coffin for Dimitrios. E. Ambler
Coffin for Lefty. B. Shannon
Coffin for One. F. Beeding
Coffin for Pandora. Gwendoline Butler
Coffin for the Body. N. Morland
Coffin for Two. Robert Martin
Coffin from Hong Kong. J. H. Chase
Coffin from the Past. Gwendoline Butler
Coffin in Fashion. Gwendoline Butler
Coffin in Malta. Gwendoline Butler
Coffin in Oxford. Gwendoline Butler
Coffin in the Black Museum. Gwendoline Butler
Coffin in the Museum of Crime. Gwendoline Butler
Coffin in the Sky. J. L. Morrissey
Coffin Island. M. Leblanc
Coffin on the Water. Gwendoline Butler
Coffin, Scarcely Used. Colin Watson
Coffin Ship. P. Tonkin
Coffin Things. M. Avallone
Coffin Underground. Gwendoline Butler
Coffin Waiting. Gwendoline Butler
Coffins Are Cheap. G. Surgman
Coffins Come in All Sizes. D. Benton
Coffin's Dark Number. Gwendoline Butler
Coffins for Three. F. C. Davis
Coffins for Two. Gwyn Evans
Coffins for Two. V. Starrett
Coffins in Her Eyes. Duff Johnson
Coffy. P. W. Fairman
Cogan's Trade. G. V. Higgins
Cohort of Dishonour. B. Schwarz
Coign of Vantage. J. McAleer
Coil of Mystery. B. Bolt
Coil of Rope. J. F. Straker
Coil of Serpents. A. Stevenson
Coin of Edward VII. F. Hume
Coin of the Realm. W. B. Murphy
Coiner's Cave. J. Herbrand
Coiner's League. B. Wayde
Colchicine Factor. R. Bryce
Colcorton. E. Pope
Cold and Unhonoured. F. Hurt
Cold Beauty. D. Haring

Title Index

Cold Bed in the Clay. R. S. Wallis
Cold Blood. L. Bruce
Cold Blood. Robin Richards
Cold-Blooded Murder. F. W. Crofts
Cold Blue Death. K. Stanton
Cold Cash. G. Dold
Cold Chill of Coptos. K. Ashley
Cold Chills. R. Bloch
Cold Chisel. J. B. O'Sullivan
Cold Coffin. E. Quest
Cold Comfort. M. D. Lake
Cold Comfort. D. R. Slavitt
Cold Coming. M. Kelly
Cold Companion. J. Sher
Cold Copper Tears. Glen Cook
Cold Cream. A. Applin
Cold Dark Hours. A. G. Yates
Cold Dark Night. S. Gainham
Cold Dawn. C. Virmonne
Cold Dead. Gar Wilson
Cold Dead Coed. H. Janson
Cold Death. K. Robeson
Cold Dish. M. A. Collins
Cold Evil. B. Flynn
Cold Eye. G. Blunt
Cold Eyes. J. F. Dwyer
Cold Finger Curse. E. D. Torgerson
Cold Front. B. Everitt
Cold Front. S. Hanlon
Cold Front. W. H. Lovejoy
Cold Hand in Mine. R. Aickman
Cold Harbour. Jack Higgins
Cold in July. J. R. Lansdale
Cold Iron. N. Freeling
Cold Is the Sea. E. L. Beach
Cold Judgment. J. Fluke
Cold Judgment. D. Pendleton
Cold Jungle. G. Black
Cold Killing. Deforest Day
Cold Light of Dawn. G. Ison
Cold Light of Day. E. Page
Cold Line to Moscow. Henry Talbot
Cold, Lone and Still. G. Mitchell
Cold Moon Over Babylon. M. McDowell
Cold New Dawn. I. St. James
Cold Night. A. Sarrantonio
Cold Night for Murder. Martin Thomas
Cold Night's Death. Barbara Harrison
Cold Ones. P. Kruger
Cold Poison. S. Palmer
Cold Rain. V. Tapner
Cold Red Sunrise. S. M. Kaminsky
Cold River. W. Judson
Cold Room. J. Caine
Cold Route to Freedom. C. D. Peel
Cold Smell of Sacred Stone. G. C. Chesbro
Cold Snap. Peter Leslie
Cold Spell. J. Bruce
Cold Spring Harbor. Richard Yates
Cold Steal. A. Tilton
Cold Steel. D. Stivers
Cold Steel. James Warren
Cold Steele. J. D. Masters
Cold Stove League. T. Boyle
Cold Terror. R. Chetwynd-Hayes
Cold Trail. Dell Shannon
Cold Turkey. T. Childs
Cold Vengeance. M. McCray
Cold War. D. Brierley
Cold War in a Country Garden. L. Gutteridge
Cold War Swap. Ross Thomas
Cold Waters. P. M. Hubbard
Cold Waters. L. Moore
Cold Wind in August. B. Wohl
Cold Wind of Death. H. Seymour
Colder Than the Grave. R. Haigh
Coldharbour. M. Cobb
Coldstone. P. Wentworth
Cole of Spyglass Mountain. A. P. Hankins
Coleraine Tragedy. E. T. Sawyer
Coleville Skeleton. R. C. Finney
Colfax Book-Plate. Agnes Miller
Coliseum. B. Cohen
Collaborators. Reginald Hill

Collapse of Stout Party. J. T. Story
Collar for the Killer. H. Brean
Collected Novellas. G. G. Marquez
Collected Short Fiction of Ngaio Marsh. Ngaio Marsh
Collected Short Stories. K. Amis
Collected Stories. R. L. Finn
Collected Stories. G. G. Marquez
Collected Stories of Ben Hecht. B. Hecht
Collected Stories of Chester Himes. C. Himes
Collected Stories of John William Corrington. J. W. Corrington
Collection. P. Montana
Collection of Strangers. D. Hitchens
Collector. J. Fowles
Collector of Photographs. D. Valentine
Collectors. E. Christie
Collectors. F. J. Mather
Collector's Choice. Peter Marks
Collector's Item. A. Dean
Colleen Bawn. D. Boucicault
College for Crooks. Anonymous
Collegians. G. Griffin
Collision. J. Gordon
Collision. J. Pulman
Collision Ahead. R. Johnston
Collision Course. William Grant
Collision Course. D. Rutherford
Collusion. T. Cobb
Collusion. T. D. Irwin
Colombia Crackdown. C. Cunningham
Colombian Connection. R. S. Silverman
Colombian Gold. J. Manrique
Colombo Night. A. Philips
Colonel and the Corpse. Tod Conrad
Colonel Blessington. P. Frankau
Colonel Bogus. J. Blackburn
Colonel Butler's Wolf. A. Price
Colonel Dam. J. S. Clouston
Colonel Gore's Second Case. L. Brock
Colonel Gore's Third Case. L. Brock
Colonel Grant's Tomorrow. G. Seton
Colonel Jack. D. Defoe
Colonel Paternoster. R. Inchbald
Col. Ross of Piedmont. J. E. Cooke
Colonel Sun. R. Markham
Colonel Thorndyke's Secret. G. A. Henty
Colonel's Foxhound. C. M. Wills
Colonel's Past. F. Warden
Colonial King. H. Nisbet
Color Him Dead. C. Runyon
Color Him Guilty. J. L. Hensley
Color Me Blood Red. H. G. Lewis
Color of Blood. Brian Moore
Color of Greed. G. F. Valcour
Color of Green. L. Kaufman
Color of Hate. J. L. Hensley
Colorado Jim. G. Goodchild
Colorado Kill-Zone. D. Pendleton
Colorado Special. William Grant
Colors. J. Norst
Colors. M. Schiffer
Colors for Murder. K. Robeson
Colors of Death. S. Wagner
Colossus. E. Wallace
Colossus of Arcadia. E. P. Oppenheim
Colour Blind. C. A. Cookson
Colour Blind. S. P. B. Mais
Colour Man. I. Moffitt
Colour of Darkness. A. Dipper
Colour of Dried Blood. M. Vinter
Colour of Fear. R. Ormerod
Colour of Murder. J. Symons
Colour of Murder. P. Winn
Colour of Violence. J. Ashford
Colour Scheme. N. Marsh
Coloured Glass. I. R. G. Hart
Colours Flying. N. Tranter
Colt & Co. in the Valley of Gold. J. E. MacDonnell
Colt from the Country. A. Wright
Coltray. D. Alexander
Columbella. P. A. Whitney
Columbia. Anonymous
Columbine Cabin Murders. P. Mechem

Columbo. A. Lawrence
Columbo and the Samurai Sword. B. Magee
Columbus Option. Richard Cox
Columnist Murder. L. Saunders
Colwyn Dane—the Outlawed Detective. M. Grimshaw
Coma. R. Cook
Comanche Scalp. W. C. MacDonald
Combat Pay. Robin Moore
Combat Zone—Miami. T. Conners
Combination. A. York
Combination-Lock Mystery. Anonymous
Combination Sweetheart. D. Haring
Combined Forces. J. Smithers
Come Again Pecker. M. Clinton
Come Along. W. Woodrow
Come Along with Me. S. Jackson
Come and Be Killed. Dorothy Bennett
Come and Be Killed. E. Ferrars
Come and Be Killed! Shelley Smith
Come and Get Me. Griff
Come and Get Me. D. Haring
Come and Go. F. Gaite
Come and Kill Me. S. Gluck
Come and Kill Me. J. Tey
Come Away, Death. J. Kirkpatrick
Come Away, Death. G. Mitchell
Come Away Death. A. G. Wilson
Come Away from Life. Cosmo Hamilton
Come Back. Duff Johnson
Come Back. Jonathan Smith
Come-Back. C. Wells
Come Back, Alice Smythereene! N. J. McIver
Come Back and Die. I. Lambot
Come Back, Charleston Blue. C. Himes
Come Back for More. A. Fray
Come Back for the Body. David Hume
Come Back, My Love. E. S. Aarons
Come Back to Murder. S. H. Courtier
Come Back When I'm Sober. M. Waddell
Come Blonde, Came Murder. P. George
Come Clean. Bill James
Come Clean, Baby. B. Cagson
Come Dark, Come Evil. W. McNeilly
Come Death and High Water. A. Cleeves
Come Destroy Me. V. Packer
Come Die for Me. D. P. Lyday
Come Die with Me. James Dark
Come Die with Me. J. Eastwood
Come Die with Me. W. C. Gault
Come Die with Me. D. Haring
Come Dwell with Death. M. W. Glidden
Come Easy—Go Easy. J. H. Chase
Come Feed on Me. Morton Cooper
Come, Follow Me. P. Michaels
Come Hell and High Water. R. Petrie
Come Here and Die. M. Halliday
Come Home and Be Killed. Jennie Melville
Come Home to Crime. N. Deane
Come Home to Death. G. Ashe
Come Home, Toby Brown. J. Pattinson
Come In. E. C. Mayne
Come In Number One, Your Time Is Up. D. Jewell
Come In Sinner. D. Haring
Come Into My Parlour. D. Wheatley
Come Kill with Me. H. Kane
Come Kill with Me. F. Kassak
Come Like a Storm. E. G. Cousins
Come Love, Come Death. S. P. B. Mais
Come Morning. J. Gores
Come Murder Me. J. Kieran
Come Night, Come Desire. D. Wade
Come Night, Come Evil. Jonathan Craig
Come Nightfall. G. Amo
Come-On. W. Chambers
Come On. J. Cirni
Come-On! D. Haring
Come-On. M. Yorke
Come On Fortune! E. Loring
Come Out, Come Out. G. Malcolm-Smith
Come Out, Come Out, Whoever You Are. T. McCann
Come Out Fighting. Duff Johnson
Come Out Killing. Robert Reeves

Come Out with Your Hands Up. H. Lugar
Come Over, Red Rover. S. Marlowe
Come Quickly, Honey. H. Janson
Come See Me Die. M. Neville
Come See Them Die. H. Hadley
Come Sweet Death. M. S. Curry
Come, Sweet Death. S. Mitchell
Come the Night. Nick Blake
Come, Thick Night. M. Neville
Come Thirteen. D. Silva
Come to Castlemoor. Beatrice Parker
Come to Dust. F. Drake
Come to Dust. E. Lathen
Come to Grief. H. Foley
Come to Judgment. J. S. Strange
Come to My Funeral. I. Wempe
Come to My House. A. S. Roche
Come Trouble. J. P. Heggy
Come-Uppance of Arthur Hearne. Angus Hall
Come Watch Him Die. S. Jason
Comeback. L. L. Enger
Comeback. J. Tomerlin
Comeback for Stark. H. Reade
Comeback to Crime. R. Dudgeon
Comedian. K. Hewitt
Comedian Dies. Simon Brett
Comedians. G. Greene
Comedy of Terrors. A. Carr
Comedy of Terrors. J. De Mille
Comedy of Terrors. M. Innes
Comedy of Terrors. Elsie Lee
Comedy of the Unexpected. G. W. Appleton
Comes a Stranger. E. R. Punshon
Comes the Blind Fury. H. McCutcheon
Comes the Blind Fury. D. Rutherford
Comes the Blind Fury. J. Saul
Comes the Dark Stranger. Harry Patterson
Comethup. T. Gallon
Comets Have Long Tails. M. Johnston
Comfort Me with Spies. M. Lovell
Comforters. M. Spark
Comic Book Killer. R. A. Lupoff
Comic Miscellany for 1845. J. Poole
Comic Strip. G. Panetta
Comic Tragedy. G. R. Kuhn
Coming Attractions. T. Tally
Coming Back of Laurence Averil. M. Drake
Coming Down Again. J. Balaban
Coming Home to Roost. G. M. Fenn
Coming of Age. R. Marsh
Coming of Age. T. Zahn
Coming of Aurora. P. C. De Crespigny
Coming of Carew. B. Graeme
Coming of Cosgrove. L. Y. Erskine
Coming of Jonathan Smith. H. Ludlam
Coming of Rain. R. Marius
Coming of the Monster. O. F. Dudley
Coming-Out Party. R. Frede
Coming Out Party. G. Petrie
Comlyn Alibi. H. Hill
Command. A. Melville-Ross
Command Strike. D. Pendleton
Commander Amanda Nightingale. G. Revelli
Commander Lawless, V.C. Rolf Bennett
Commander Leigh. R. H. Savage
Commander-1. P. George
Commandments Six and Eight. A. Griffin
Commando. R. Wilkes-Hunter
Commando Escape. Stagg Green
Commando Squad. M. K. Roberts
Commando X. P. Runyon
Commandos. E. Arnold
Commandos Are Expendable. R. Wilkes-Hunter
Commemorations. H. Herlin
Commencement Day Murders. L. M. Floyd
Commentary. J. Galsworthy
Commerce Patrol. I. F. Anderson
Commissar's Report. Martyn Burke
Commission for Disaster. J. N. Chance
Commission in London. S. Dabkowski
Commissioner. R. Dougherty
Commissioner's Cowboys. Rod Miller
Commitment. C. Illing
Committal Chamber. R. Bradden

Committed Agent. T. Gilchrist
Committee. H. Braxon
Committee. D. Seaman
Commodore Junk. G. M. Fenn
Common Death. Natasha Cooper
Common Enemy. Gayle Stone
Common Love. J. B. Watney
Common Murder. V. McDermid
Common or Garden Crime. S. Pim
Common People. A. E. Martin
Common Sense Is All You Need. J. J. Connington
Commons Killing. J. Fairfax
Commune's Child. S. Ascani
Communicating Door. S. Allan
Communicating Door. Wadsworth Camp
Communist's Corpse. R. Wormser
Commutation of Sentence. C. M. Hincks
Compact. R. Cullum
Compact of Crime. B. Wayde
Companion. K. Greenhall
Companion of Dishonour. J. Wellsley
Companion to Danger. J. Aeby
Companion to Evil. M. Farnsworth
Companion to Sirius. G. Goodchild
Company. J. Ehrlichman
Company Man. J. C. Faust
Company Man. J. Maggio
Company of Bandits. J. T. Story
Company of Friends. J. Crosby
Company of St. George. Kenneth O'Hara
Company of Saints. E. Anthony
Company of Shadows. J. M. Walsh
Company of Sinners. W. M. Duncan
Company of Strangers. J. Rosenberg
Company Secrets. A. Coburn
Company Spook. R. Weber
Compare These Dead! M. P. Rea
Compartment East. P. Remy
Compartment K. H. Reilly
Compass Points to Fear. J. Ward
Compass Stone. F. Arrabel
Compassionate Crook. P. Goulden
Compassionate Rogue. G. Goodchild
Compelling Case. Michael Underwood
Compkill. G. Paulson
Compleat Agent. W. Crisp
Compleat Werewolf and other tales of fantasy and science fiction. A. Boucher
Complete Casebook of Herlock Sholmes. Charles Hamilton
Complete Change. A. J. Philip
Complete Crow. B. Lumley
Complete Home Entertainer. Anonymous
Complete Magnus Ridolph. J. Vance
Complete State of Death. J. Gardner
Complete Steel. C. Aird
Complete Stranger. V. Siller
Compliments of a Fiend. F. Brown
Composite Lady. T. Cobb
Composition for Four Hands. Hilda Lawrence
Compost Heap Corpses. S. C. Williamson
Compound for Death. D. M. Disney
Comprador. D. R. Cudlip
Compromising Positions. S. Isaacs
Compton Connection. L. Holden
Compton Effect. L. Horvitz
Compulsion. M. Levin
Compulsively Murdering Mao. Bill Green
Compulsory Gangster. W. Darrell
Computer Connection. A. Bester
Computer Criminals . . . It Began at the World's Fair. S. Fawcette
Computer Kill. R. E. Banks
Computer Kill. L. Derrick
Comrade Charlie. B. Freemantle
Comrade Jill. H. Adams
Comrade Souvarin. M. Moiseiwitsch
Comrade Spy. L. S. Ovalov
Comrades. Matthew Hunter
Comrades in Arms. W. E. Johns
Comrades in Death. P. Turner
Comrades of Peril. R. Parrish
Comrades of the Black Cross. H. Nisbet
Comrades of the Right Hand. Nicholas Carter

Comrades Three! A. Saxby
Con Game. M. Cronin
Con Game. E. Naha
Con Game. H. Waugh
Con-Man. A. Draper
Con Man. C. A. Harris
Con Man. E. McBain
Con Man. G. Verner
Conant. W. R. Burnett
Concannon. F. O'Rourke
Conceal and Disguise. H. Kane
Concealed Identity. M. Richmond
Concept for Murder. Margo Lewis
Concerning a Woman of Sin and other stories. B. Hecht
Concerning Blackshirt. R. Graeme
Concerning Miss Duncan. Mary Archer
Concerning Peter Jackson and others. G. Frankau
Concerning the Saint. L. Charteris
Concerning This Woman. W. LeQueux
Concert Masters. J. Sligo
Concert Party Murders. John Norman
Concerto. P. Austin
Concerto. R. Burlinson
Concerto. Dennis Jones
Concerto for Fear. D. Richmond
Concerto for Murder. W. H. Rowley
Concerto in the Key of Death. B. Fried
Concerto of Death. G. J. Barrett
Conclave. L. D. Klausner
Concorde—Airport 1979. K. Stewart
Concrete Boot. K. Royce
Concrete Cage. R. Novak
Concrete Castle. F. Gerard
Concrete Castle Murders. F. Gerard
Concrete Crime. M. Coles
Concrete Curtain. J. Bogar
Concrete Evidence. M. Russell
Concrete Flamingo. C. Williams
Concrete Kimono. J. P. Carstairs
Concrete Maze. N. Morland
Concrete Nymph. N. Karta
Concubine. M. East
Condamine Case. M. Dalton
Condell. J. Turner
Condemned. H. Carmichael
Condemned. H. Desmond
Condemned. P. Kuttner
Condemned. J. Pagano
Condemned As a Nihilist. G. A. Henty
Condemned Door. F. Du Boisgobey
Condemned to Death. J. R. Eyre
Condemned to Live. T. A. Plummer
Condensed Novels. B. Harte
Condition Green. N. Goble
Condition Purple. Peter Turnbull
Conditional Sentence. H. Fleetwood
Condo Kill. R. Barth
Condor. T. Luke
Condor. G. Masterton
Condor Conspiracy. C. Yarborough
Condorman. H. Simon
Conduct of a Member. V. Gielgud
Conduct of Major Maxim. G. Lyall
Conduct Unbecoming. B. England
Cone of Silence. D. Beaty
Coney Island Quickstep. G. Gipe
Confederate. H. Fielding
Confederate Rogues. Dick Stewart
Confederate Spy. T. N. Conrad
Confess Fletch. G. Mcdonald
Confess to Dr. Morelle. E. Dudley
Confession. H. Carmichael
Confession. R. Francis Foster
Confession. P. McAlan
Confession Corner, and other stories. B. Reynolds
Confession of a Thug. Warren Miller
Confession of Andrew Clare. David Robinson
Confession of Brother Haluin. Ellis Peters
Confession of Hercule. P. Audemars
Confession of Joe Cullen. H. Fast
Confession of Lorraine Herschel. N. T. Oliver
Confession of Murder. C. Barling
Confession of Murder. M. Neville

Title Index

Confession to Murder. F. Arthur
Confession/Sight Unseen. M. R. Rinehart
Confessional. J. Higgins
Confessional. G. Simenon
Confessional of the Black Penitents. A. Radcliffe
Confessional of Valombre. L. S. Stanhope
Confessions. D. Silber
Confessions of a Chinatown Moll. J. Bogar
Confessions of a Climber. L. Cleeve
Confessions of a Coiner. E. Douglass
Confessions of a Con Man. Will Irwin
Confessions of a Court Milner. L. T. Meade
Confessions of a Crap Artist. P. K. Dick
Confessions of a Currency Girl. C. Dawe
Confessions of a Dangerous Mind. C. Barris
Confessions of a Detective. Alfred H. Lewis
Confessions of a Detective Policeman. Anonymous
Confessions of a Fanatic. Anonymous
Confessions of a Horse Coper. Ballinsloe
Confessions of a Ladies' Man. W. LeQueux
Confessions of a Lady Killer. G. Stade
Confessions of a Private Dick. T. Lea
Confessions of a Scoundrel. G. Spencer
Confessions of a Thug. Warren Miller
Confessions of a Thug. Meadows Taylor
Confessions of a Ticket-of-Leave Man. Anonymous
Confessions of a Wife. Grace M. White
Confessions of a Young Lady. Richard Marsh
Confessions of Alma Quartier. David Robinson
Confessions of Alphonse. B. Pain
Confessions of an Attorney. G. Sharp
Confessions of an Attorney. W. Warner
Confessions of an Imp. Old Sleuth
Confessions of an Old Burglar. Charles Morley
Confessions of Arsene Lupin. M. Leblanc
Confessions of Artemas Quibble. A. Train
Confessions of Claud. E. Fawcett
Confessions of Cleodora. C. Dawe
Confessions of Stephen Whopshare. E. Brooke
Confessor. J. Donohue
Confetti Can Be Red. M. Cumberland
Confetti for a Killing. C. Edwards
Confetti Man. B. J. Reynolds
Confidence King. Nicholas Carter
Confidence Man. L. V. Erskine
Confident Morning. V. Gielgud
Confidential. D. H. Clarke
Confidential Agent. G. Greene
Confidential Agent. J. Payn
Confidential Mission. W. L. Whitehouse
Confidentially Yours. C. Williams
Confirm or Deny. G. Ison
Conflict. M. E. Braddon
Conflict. H. Janson
Conflict. C. B. Kelland
Conflict. Alex Morrison
Conflict of Evidence. R. Ottolengui
Conflict of Interest. B. Williams
Conflict of Interests. J. Ashford
Conflict of Interests. C. Egleton
Conflict of Lions. T. Strong
Conflict of Shadows. Colin Robertson
Conflict of Women. E. Darby
Conflict Within. D. Reid
Conformist. A. Moravia
Confounding of Sergeant Cluff. G. North
Confrontation. N. Garbo
Confrontation. Ralph Vickers
Confucius Enigma. Margaret Jones
Confucius in a Tail-Coat. M. Dekobra
Confusion at Campden Trig. V. Beynon-Harris
Confusion of Eyes. J. N. Chance
Cong Kiss. J. J. Montague
Congleton Lark. Angus Ross
Congo. W. A. Ballinger
Congo Diamonds. R. W. Hunter
Congo Mercenary Major. R. W. Hunter
Congo Venus. M. Head
Congo War Cry. A. Caillou
Coniackers. R. Rivers
Conies in the Hay. Jane Lane
Conjugal Rights. Rita
Conjure Man Dies. Rudolph Fisher
Conjure Wife. F. Leiber

Conjurer of Phantoms. J. W. Harding
Conjurers. Marilyn Harris
Conjurer's Coffin. G. Cullingford
Conjurer's Tales. George Johnson
Connecting Link. Nicholas Carter
Connector. T. Williamson
Connie Burt. G. Boothby
Connie Morgan Hits the Trail. J. B. Hendryx
Connie Morgan in Alaska. J. B. Hendryx
Connie Morgan in Barren Lands. J. B. Hendryx
Connie Morgan in the Arctic. J. B. Hendryx
Connie Morgan in the Cattle Country. J. B. Hendryx
Connie Morgan in the Fur Country. J. B. Hendryx
Connie Morgan in the Lumber Camps. J. B. Hendryx
Connie Morgan, Prospector. J. B. Hendryx
Connie Morgan with the Forest Rangers. J. B. Hendryx
Connie Morgan with the Mounted. J. B. Hendryx
Connoisseur's Case. M. Innes
Connolly's Woman. H. Whittington
Conor Sands. E. Kyle
Conover's Folly. D. Daniels
Conquered Place. R. Shafer
Conqueror Down! B. Langley
Conqueror Inn. E. R. Punshon
Conqueror's Road. L. A. Knight
Conquest. H. Hatten
Conquest. R. Vane
Conquest After Midnight. B. Gray
Conquest Before Autumn. M. Eden
Conquest Calls the Tune. B. Gray
Conquest Goes Home. B. Gray
Conquest Goes West. B. Gray
Conquest in California. B. Gray
Conquest in Command. B. Gray
Conquest in Ireland. B. Gray
Conquest in Scotland. B. Gray
Conquest in the Underworld. B. Gray
Conquest Likes it Hot. B. Gray
Conquest Marches On. B. Gray
Conquest of Charlotte. D. S. Meldrum
Conquest of Fortune. George Griffith
Conquest of London. J. Tregellis
Conquest on the Run. B. Gray
Conquest Overboard. B. Gray
Conquest Takes All. B. Gray
Conquest Touch. B. Gray
Conquistadores. B. Langley
Cons at Large. Jack Roberts
Cons on the Run. B. Shannon
Conscience. A. Griffin
Conscience Makes Heroes. G. Abrahams
Conscience Money. S. Warwick
Conscience of a Killer. M. Arrighi
Conscience of a King. A. C. Gunter
Conscience of Dr. Holt. A. Clare
Conscience of the King. Jane Barry
Conscripts. W. Winward
Consequence of Crime. E. Linington
Consequence of Fear. T. Allbeury
Consequences of a Duel. F. Du Boisgobey
Conservatory. P. Hastings
Consider the Evidence. J. Ashford
Consider the Lilies. H. Ainsworth
Consider the Verdict. A. Bodelsen
Consider Your Verdict. R. Hardinge
Consider Your Verdict. N. MacKenzie
Consider Your Verdict. T. Mason
Consider Your Verdict. A. Soutar
Consider Yourself Dead. J. H. Chase
Consider Yourself Dead. G. Fredrics
Consignment of Ore. P. Warden
Consolation Bureau. D. Lyall
Conspiracy. R. Baker
Conspiracy. P. J. Cooper
Conspiracy. P. Meriton
Conspiracy. W. Proudfoot
Conspiracy. Robert Robinson
Conspiracy. A. S. Roche
Conspiracy at Angel. B. Flynn
Conspiracy Island. Peter Craig
Conspiracy of Angels. Frank Ross

Conspiracy of Assassins. G. Garofalo
Conspiracy of Eagles. B. Davis
Conspiracy of Love. L. Hoffman
Conspiracy of Mirrors. Richard Hugo
Conspiracy of Poisons. J. Sturrock
Conspiracy of Rumors. Nicholas Carter
Conspiracy of Silence. M. Blizard
Conspiracy of Silence. E. Butler
Conspiracy of Strangers. Lee Martin
Conspiracy of Vipers. P. Ordway
Conspiracy to Kill. C. Jauniere
Conspirator. H. Slater
Conspirator of Cordova. S. Cobb
Conspirators. W. Haggard
Conspirators. F. Kane
Conspirators. E. P. Oppenheim
Conspirators. F. Prokosch
Conspirators. A. Reife
Conspirators at Large. S. Maddock
Conspirators in Capri. S. Maddock
Conspirators Three. S. Maddock
Conspire to Kill. Jack Watson
Constable Across the Moors. N. Rhea
Constable Along the Lane. N. Rhea
Constable Among the Heather. N. Rhea
Constable and the Lady. J. Bude
Constable Around the Village. N. Rhea
Constable at the Double. N. Rhea
Constable by the Sea. N. Rhea
Constable 42Z. E. A. D. B.
Constable, Guard Thyself! Henry Wade
Constable in Disguise. N. Rhea
Constable in the Dale. N. Rhea
Constable on the Hill. N. Rhea
Constable Simple Simon. W. Edwards
Constable Through the Meadow. N. Rhea
Constables Don't Count. Alex Fraser
Constable's Stories. F. Schmalz
Constance, and Calbot's Rival. J. Hawthorne
Constance Dunlap, Woman Detective. A. B. Reeve
Constant Sinner. Mae West
Constant Sinner—Babe Gordon. Mae West
Constantine Cay. C. Dillon
Consul's File. P. Theroux
Consultant. J. McNeil
Consulting Room Crime. M. Osborne
Consulting Room Mystery. M. Osborne
Consummate Rose. L. Meynell
Consummate Scoundrel. G. Boothby
Contact and other stories. F. N. Hart
Contact Lens. M. Urquhart
Contact Lost. D. Craig
Contact Man. D. Betteridge
Contact Man. F. Struan
Contact Mercury. L. H. Nason
Contact Mr. Delgado. J. Pattinson
Container. M. Kaufman
Contaminant. L. Reiffel
Contamination. C. Pincher
Contango Day. B. Jefferis
Content Assignment. H. Roth
Contents of the Coffin. J. S. Fletcher
Contents Unknown. L. Barbee
Conte's Run. A. Lassiter
Contessa Came Too. J. Bryan
Contesting the County, and other tales. B. Hemyng
Continental Conspiracy. F. W. Irwin
Continental Contract. D. Pendleton
Continental Drift. J. D. Houston
Continental Op. D. Hammett
Contraband. C. F. Adams
Contraband. H. Janson
Contraband. C. B. Kelland
Contraband. L. A. Knight
Contraband. K. Michel
Contraband. R. Parrish
Contraband. D. Wheatley
Contraband Coast. W. Chambers
Contraband Cruises. Will Allen
Contrabandits. J. Workman
Contrabando. K. Detzer
Contract. H. Carlisle
Contract. O. Demaris
Contract! C. Dempster

C

C

Contract. J. Poyer
Contract. A. Prior
Contract. J. W. Rhoads
Contract. G. Seymour
Contract for a Killer. D. Reid
Contract for a Killing. R. L. Brent
Contract for Death. D. Ingham
Contract for Homicide. Dan Morgan
Contract for Slaughter. Dan Schmidt
Contract on Cherry Tree. P. Rosenberg
Contract on Stone. D. R. Addleman
Contract on the President. J. Crosby
Contract: Terror Summit. M. McCray
Contract with a Killer. H. Jobson
Contract: White Lady. M. McCray
Contractees Die Young. A. Azolakov
Control. Jack Anderson
Control. W. Goldman
Control. K. Jackson
Controller. O. John
Controlling Interest. B. Bannerman
Convenient Death. R. Galbraith
Convent Mystery. J. K. Stafford
Convent of the Grey Penitents. Sarah Wilkinson
Convent on Styx. G. Mitchell
Convent Spectre. Anonymous
Convention. F. Knebel
Convention for Killers. J. Whiffen
Convergence. J. Fuller
Converging Parallels. T. Williams
Conversation with a Corpse. R. C. Dennis
Conversion of Con Cregan, and other stories. D. Conyers
Convertible Hearse. W. C. Gault
Convict. N. Buntline
Convict. T. P. Prest
Convict and other stories. J. L. Burke
Convict B 14. R. K. Weekes
Convict by Proxy. A. Murray
Convict Captain. D. W. MacArthur
Convict Colonel. F. Du Boisgobey
Convict 88. T. C. Bridges
Convict 413L. M. Leighton
Convict Has Escaped. J. Budd
Convict International. W. D. Maydwell
Convict 999. Grace M. White
Convict 99. M. Leighton
Convict 100. M. Leighton
Convict 1066. B. Gray
Convict 72. N. Ned
Convict 66. A. S. Hardy
Convict Ship. W. C. Russell
Convicted. D. Goodis
Convict's Hoard. M. G. Hugi
Convict's Marriage. A. Bouvier
Convict's Sweetheart. Anonymous
Convict's Sweetheart. O. Harper
Convivial Codfish. C. MacLeod
Convoy. D. Pope
Convoy Strike. M. McGann
Conway, K. C. S. Stone
Cook General. J. Cashman
Cook Up a Crime. C. M. Russell
Cookie. J. Adkins
Cooking School Murders. V. Rich
Cool Clear Death. T. Hallernan
Cool Cottontail. J. Ball
Cool Day for Killing. W. Haggard
Cool Encounter. Liz Allen
Cool Hand Luke. Donn Pearce
Cool Jade. B. Girard
Cool-Kill Cutie! D. Haring
Cool Killing. Stephen Murray
Cool Man. W. R. Burnett
Cool Murder. P. George
Cool Ones. D. Haring
Cool Repentance. Antonia Fraser
Cool Runnings. R. Hoyt
Cool Sleeps Balaban. D. MacKenzie
Cool Sugar. H. Janson
Cool Tom, the Sailor Boy Detective. Old Sleuth
Cool War. F. Pohl
Cooler. G. Markstein
Coolie Tramp. E. L. Long

Coomsberrow Mystery. J. Colwall
Co-Op Kill. R. Barth
Co-Ordinator. A. York
Cop. J. Karney
Cop. E. J. Morris
Cop and the Corpse. R. Lynford
Cop Hater. E. McBain
Cop in a Tight Frame. Neill Graham
Cop in the Closet. J. Foscom
Cop-Kill. William Crawford
Cop Killer. G. Bagby
Cop Killer. D. Haring
Cop Killer. T. Philbin
Cop Killer. M. Sjowall
Cop Killers. M. Raboinowitz
Cop Killers. Steve Scott
Cop-Lover. P. Malloch
Cop on the Corner. J. Kirkpatrick
Cop Out. R. W. Jones
Cop Out. E. Queen
Cop Story. P. Andrews
Cop Without a Shield. L. O'Donnell
Copacabana Stud. John Allen
Copenhagen Affair. S. McGurk
Copenhagen Affair. J. Oram
Copenhagen Connection. Elizabeth Peters
Copley's Hunch. J. Ditton
Copp for Hire. D. Pendleton
Copp in Deep. D. Pendleton
Copp in the Dark. D. Pendleton
Copp on Fire. D. Pendleton
Copper. T. McGrath
Copper at Sea. G. Fairlie
Copper Beeches. Arthur H. Lewis
Copper Bottle. E. J. Millward
Copper Box. J. S. Fletcher
Copper Butterfly. S. Harvester
Copper Crash. F. Danby
Copper Disc. R. J. C. Stead
Copper Frame. E. Queen
Copper, Gold and Treasure. D. Williams
Copper House. J. Regis
Copper Lady. H. L. Nelson
Copper Mask, and other stories. H. Wiley
Copper Smoke. K. O'Malley
Copper Snare. Lawrence Williams
Coppergold. P. G. Winslow
Copperhead. J. Henderson
Copperhead. W. Katz
Copperhead Creek. Colin Mason
Coppers and Gold. H. Brinton
Coppers Don't Cry. J. Wainwright
Coppersmith. R. J. Griffin
Coppersmith's Dolls. R. J. Griffin
Cops. T. C. Fox
Cops. J. Pearl
Cops and Robbers. O. Henry
Cops 'n Robbers. J. Russell
Cops and Robbers. D. E. Westlake
Cop's Blood. L. Cassina
Copsford Mystery. W. C. Russell
Copy-Cat Killings. Martin Thomas
Copy for Crime. C. Carnac
Copycat. N. Jillett
Copycat Killers. H. Pentecost
Coral Kill. B. Chandler
Coral Lady. E. Southworth
Coral Palace. B. Grimshaw
Coral Pin. F. Du Boisgobey
Coral Princess Murders. F. Crane
Corbin Necklace. H. K. Webster
Cord and Cheese. J. De Mille
Cord for a Killer. W. M. Duncan
Cordelia the Magnificent. L. Scott
Corder Index. R. Raine
Cordially Invited to Meet Death. R. Stout
Cordley's Castle. J. Pattinson
Cords of Vanity. D. Hennessey
Cords of Vanity. M. Tripp
Co-Respondent. G. W. Appleton
Corfu Affair. J. T. Phillifent
Corinthian Days. A. Soutar
Corinthian Jack. C. E. Pearce
Corioli Affair. M. Deasy

Cork and the Serpent. Macdonald Hastings
Cork in Bottle. Macdonald Hastings
Cork in the Doghouse. Macdonald Hastings
Cork of the Colonies. S. S. Rafferty
Cork on Location. Macdonald Hastings
Cork on the Telly. Macdonald Hastings
Cork on the Water. Macdonald Hastings
Cork Street Crime. J. G. Brandon
Corkscrew. Ted Wood
Corkscrew Man. B. Gee
Cormac Legend. D. Daniels
Cormorant Crag. G. M. Fenn
Cormorant's Isle. A. MacKinnon
Corner House. F. M. White
Corner in Coffee. C. T. Brady
Corner in Corpses. A. Bocca
Corner in Crime. Norman Lucas
Corner in Diamonds. M. Gerard
Corner Men. J. Gardner
Corner of Paradise. L. Holton
Corner of the Playground. S. Harvester
Corner Shop. E. Cadell
Cornered. A. W. Cook
Cornered. L. King
Cornered! J. McKimmey
Cornered. S. Markham
Cornered. T. A. Plummer
Cornered at Last. Nicholas Carter
Cornered at Last. A. F. Pinkerton
Cornered at Six. T. P. McMahon
Cornish Coast Conspiracy. D. Ames
Cornish Coast Murder. J. Bude
Cornish Crime. A. Weymouth
Cornish Crusoe. G. Volk
Cornish Fox. C. H. B. Kitchin
Cornish Interlude. S. Murray
Cornish Mystery. M. Durham
Cornish Penny. C. T. Cade
Cornish Pixie Affair. P. Leslie
Cornish Riviera Mystery. J. Rowland
Corollary to Murder. R. White
Corona Affair. E. Simson
Coronation. W. J. Weatherby
Coronation Mysteries and other stories. H. Hill
Coronation Mystery. G. Chester
Coroner Doubts. R. A. J. Walling
Coroner Presides. S. Truss
Coroner's Jury. E. Marsh
Coroner's Pidgin. M. Allingham
Coroner's Understudy. Captain Coe
Coroner's Verdict. R. Keverne
Corporal Cameron. R. Connor
Corporal Cameron of the North West Mounted Police. R. Connor
Corporal Cavannagh. Ian Anderson
Corporal Died in Bed. B. Graeme
Corporal Downey Takes the Trail. J. B. Hendryx
Corporal Jacques of the Foreign Legion. H. D. Stacpoole
Corporal of the Mounted. L. C. Douthwaite
Corporal Sam and other stories. Q
Corporal Smithers, Deceased. J. S. Scott
Corporal Wanzi. F. Brownlee
Corporate Caper. S. Jason
Corpse. Carter Brown
Corpse. P. McCutchan
Corpse! Gerald Moon
Corpse and Robbers. D. Stapleton
Corpse and the Lady. J. S. Strange
Corpse and the Three Ex-Husbands. P. MacTyre
Corpse at Camp Two. G. Carr
Corpse at Casablanca. B. Cobb
Corpse at College. M. Risco
Corpse at Least. S. H. Courtier
Corpse at the Carnival. G. Bellairs
Corpse at the Quill Club. A. R. Long
Corpse Awaits. O. F. Jerome
Corpse-Bird Cries. O. Norton
Corpse by Any Other Name. R. A. J. Walling
Corpse by the River. H. Arre
Corpse Came Back. A. R. Long
Corpse Came C.O.D. Jimmy Starr
Corpse Came Calling. G. C. Bestor
Corpse Came Calling. B. Halliday

Corpse Came Too. D. Reid
Corpse Can Sure Louse Up a Weekend! D. Tracy
Corpse Candle. G. Bagby
Corpse Can't Walk. H. Long
Corpse Cargo. G. Stockbridge
Corpse Clocks In. M. LeBrun
Corpse Comes Ashore. J. Mersereau
Corpse de Ballet. L. Cores
Corpse Died Twice. B. Frost
Corpse Diplomatique. D. Ames
Corpse Errant. M. Durham
Corpse for a Candidate. M. Geller
Corpse for a Client. H. W. Gabriel
Corpse for Breakfast. Max Murray
Corpse for Charlie. J. Courage
Corpse for Charybdis. S. Gilruth
Corpse for Christmas. W. A. Ballinger
Corpse for Christmas. Carter Brown
Corpse for Christmas. D. Essex
Corpse for Christmas. H. Kane
Corpse for Kofi Katt. G. North
Corpse from "The City". J. G. Brandon
Corpse from the Sky. J. M. Crouch
Corpse Grows a Beard. M. Scherf
Corpse Guards Himself. M. Kennedy
Corpse Had Red Hair. Alice Campbell
Corpse, Hands Off! W. Dale
Corpse Hangs High. E. Ronns
Corpse in a Gilded Cage. R. Barnard
Corpse in Camera. D. Launay
Corpse in Canonicals. G. D. H. Cole
Corpse in Cold Storage. M. Kennedy
Corpse in Community. D. Fisher
Corpse in Company K. R. Avery
Corpse in Diplomacy. M. Borgenicht
Corpse in Handcuffs. F. A. Smith
Corpse in My Bed. David Alexander
Corpse in Oozak's Pond. C. MacLeod
Corpse in the Boudoir. Gene Ross
Corpse in the Cab. Aldin Vinton
Corpse in the Cabin. B. Sarto
Corpse in the Car. J. Rhode
Corpse in the Caravan. R. Trevor
Corpse in the Cargo. B. Cobb
Corpse in the Castle. E. Friend
Corpse in the Church. T. F. W. Hickey
Corpse in the Circus. N. Morland
Corpse in the Circus and other stories. N. Morland
Corpse in the Clouds. P. Conde
Corpse in the Constable's Garden. G. D. H. Cole
Corpse in the Coppice. R. A. J. Walling
Corpse in the Corner Saloon. Hampton Stone
Corpse in the Coupe. W. Paddon
Corpse in the Cove. E. Mack
Corpse in the Crevasse. G. Carr
Corpse in the Crimson Slippers. R. A. J. Walling
Corpse in the Derby Hat. H. Swiggett
Corpse in the Elevator. M. Mannon
Corpse in the Flannel Nightgown. M. Scherf
Corpse in the Green Pajamas. R. A. J. Walling
Corpse in the Guest Room. Clement Wood
Corpse in the Picture Window. B. Cassiday
Corpse in the Snowman. N. Blake
Corpse in the Waxworks. J. D. Carr
Corpse in the Wind. R. P. Koehler
Corpse Incognito. B. Cobb
Corpse Is Indignant. Douglas Stapleton
Corpse Maker. H. B. Cave
Corpse Maker. David Wilson
Corpse Moved Upstairs. F. Gruber
Corpse Named Ingrid. D. Haring
Corpse Next Door. J. Farris
Corpse Now Arriving. M. Hinxman
Corpse of the Old School. J. Iams
Corpse on Ice. J. Hedges
Corpse on London Bridge. L. Southworth
Corpse on the Bridge. C. Barry
Corpse on the Cruise. F. Bream
Corpse on the Dike. J. Van de Wetering
Corpse on the Flying Trapeze. N. Morland
Corpse on the Hearth. Harry Lang
Corpse on the Mat. M. Kennedy
Corpse on the Town. J. Roeburt
Corpse on the White House Lawn. Diplomat

Corpse Parade. M. Hervey
Corpse Parade. R. Wallace
Corpse Road. G. Moffat
Corpse Rode On. J. G. Brandon
Corpse Said No. B. Frost
Corpse Sat Up. R. Glenning
Corpse Spells Danger. M. Storme
Corpse Steps Out. C. Rice
Corpse That Came Back. P. Piper
Corpse That Got Away. S. Truss
Corpse That Knew Everybody. C. Worth
Corpse That Never Was. B. Halliday
Corpse That Refused to Stay Dead. Hampton Stone
Corpse That Spoke. R. H. Leitfred
Corpse That Talked. R. Telfair
Corpse That Traveled. A. J. Rees
Corpse That Walked. O. R. Cohen
Corpse That Walked. R. Winsor
Corpse to Bury. J. B. Fearnley
Corpse to Cairo. M. O'Brine
Corpse to California. B. Harding
Corpse to Copenhagen. Jonathan Burke
Corpse to Cuba. A. Kent
Corpse Too Many. J. Callendar
Corpse Was No Bargain at All. Hampton Stone
Corpse Was No Lady. N. Morland
Corpse Who Had Too Many Friends. Hampton Stone
Corpse Who Wouldn't Die. E. J. Doherty
Corpse with Camera. Jean Fraser
Corpse with Knee Action. B. J. Maylon
Corpse with One Shoe. M. Scherf
Corpse with the Blistered Hand. R. A. J. Walling
Corpse with the Blue Cravat. R. A. J. Walling
Corpse with the Dirty Face. R. A. J. Walling
Corpse with the Eerie Eye. R. A. J. Walling
Corpse with the Floating Foot. R. A. J. Walling
Corpse with the Grimy Glove. R. A. J. Walling
Corpse with the Listening Ear. L. D. Smith
Corpse with the Missing Watch. R. A. J. Walling
Corpse with the Purple Thighs. G. Bagby
Corpse with the Red-Headed Friend. R. A. J. Walling
Corpse with the Sticky Fingers. G. Bagby
Corpse with the Sunburnt Face. C. S. Sprigg
Corpse Without a Clue. R. A. J. Walling
Corpse Without a Country. L. Trimble
Corpse Without a Jacket. L. West
Corpse Without Boots. L. Hill
Corpse Without Flesh. G. Bruce
Corpse Won't Sing. S. H. Courtier
Corpse Wore a Wig. G. Bagby
Corpse Wore Nylon. L. Paradise
Corpse Wore No Shoes. D. Thompson
Corpse Wore Rubies. F. Lester
Corpses Ain't Smart. R. Callahan
Corpses at Indian Stones. P. Wylie
Corpses Can Walk. R. T. Hopkins
Corpses Can't Walk. Robert (G.) Curtis
Corpses Cause Trouble. J. T. Damony
Corpses Don't Care. E. Ellison
Corpses Don't Kill. C. Benson
Corpses Galore. J. Bruce
Corpses in Enderby. G. Bellairs
Corpses in the Cellar. B. Latham
Corpses Never Argue. David Hume
Corpus Christmas. M. Maron
Corpus Delectable. T. Powell
Corrector of Destinies. M. D. Post
Correspondent. R. H. Shimer
Corridor of Death. Lieut. Carlton
Corridor of Mirrors. Archie Hill
Corridor of Mirrors. C. Massie
Corridor of Venus. N. Bell
Corridor of Whispers. E. Noone
Corridors of Death. R. D. Edwards
Corridors of Fear. S. Horler
Corridors of Fear. J. D. Perry
Corridors of Fear. Clarissa Ross
Corridors of Guilt. J. B. Hilton
Corrie Who? M. Foster
Corrigan. C. Blackwood
Corrigan's Way. E. Snell
Corrupt and Ensure. F. M. Nevins

Corrupt City. E. Ellison
Corrupt Ones. J. C. Barton
Corrupted Women. B. Sarto
Corrupter. H. Barron
Corrupters. Clayton Moore
Corrupters. D. Telfer
Corruption. R. Curle
Corruption. H. Janson
Corruption. P. Saxon
Corruption. Percy White
Corruption City. J. Bogar
Corruption City. H. McCoy
Corruption in Cantock. J. Notley
Corruption's Tutor. J. Cello
Corruptors. W. Francis
Corruptors. G. G. Griffin
Corsage. R. Stout
Corsair. W. Green
Corsair. J. G. Sarasin
Corsican. B. S. Ballinger
Corsican. W. Heffernan
Corsican Contract. E. Clark
Corsican Cross. Michael Bradley
Corsican Death. R. Hawkes
Corsican Takeover. Don Smith
Corsican Woman. M. Swindells
Cortenay Treasure. P. C. Wren
Cortes Letter. M. Gillette
Cory's Losers. J. Whitlach
Cosa Nostra. P. McCurtin
Cosa Nostra Circus. G. Corbin
Cosgrove: Detective. M. M. Innes
Cosgrove Report. G. O'Toole
Cosmetic Effects. Clive Sinclair
Cosmic Calamity. B. Luigi
Cosmic Reality Kill. J. Rosenberger
Cosmopolitans. W. S. Maugham
Cossack Cowboy. L. S. Taube
Cossack Hideout. E. Webster
Cossack Mystery. H. Pink
Cossack's Bride. Justin Scott
Cost of a Clue. I. Stark
Cost of Living. R. D. MacDougall
Cost of Love. Alexis Rogers
Cost of Silence. M. Yorke
Cost Price. D. Yates
Costa del Sol. Des Wilson
Consa Rican Chaos. Mark Roberts
Costello. Richard Hall
Costello—Psychic Investigator. J. Nicholson
Coster King. E. W. Alais
Cosway Miniature. R. Ruben
Cosy Little Murder. E. Radford
Cotfold Conundrums. D. G. Browne
Cotswold Case. A. Wynne
Cotswold Connection. C. Vivian
Cotswold Manners. Michael Spicer
Cotswold Murders. Michael Spicer
Cottage. Gretchen Travis
Cottage at Avalanche. J. Wetherell
Cottage at Barron Ridge. J. T. Osborne
Cottage at Chapelyard. F. Keinzley
Cottage at Drimble. Elizabeth Ford
Cottage in the Chine. H. Hill
Cottage in the Woods. D. Quentin
Cottage Murder. E. R. Punshon
Cottage of Terror. Donald Stuart
Cottage on Catherine Cay. J. Aeby
Cottage on the Fells. H. D. Stacpoole
Cottage Sinister. Q. Patrick
Cottages to Let. G. Kerr
Cotton Comes to Harlem. C. Himes
Couch. R. Bloch
Couch of Earth. P. Somerville-Large
Couch Trip. K. Kolb
Cougar. W. Winward
Could It Be Murder? N. MacKenzie
Coulson Alone. Jack Mann
Coulson Goes South. Jack Mann
Coulter Conspiracy. K. Crowder
Council of Comforters. W. M. Duncan
Council of Crooks. W. J. Bayfield
Council of Death. Nicholas Carter
Council of Justice. E. Wallace

C

Council of Kings. D. Pendleton
Council of Seven. J. C. Snaith
Council of Six. Anonymous
Council of Ten. S. Cobb
Council of Ten. J. Land
Council of the Rat. J. Cassells
Councillors of Falconhoe. F. M. White
Counsel for the Defense. J. Ashford
Counsel for the Defense. J. Ronald
Counsel for the Defense. L. Scott
Counsel for the Killer. M. Carrel
Counsellor. J. J. Connington
Counsellor. G. Ziran
Counsellor Heart. P. G. Winslow
Counsels of the Night. L. Cleeve
Count Azar. V. Krymov
Count Backwards to Zero. B. Halliday
Count Bruga. B. Hecht
Count Bunker. J. S. Clouston
Count de Mornay. S. W. Wheeler
Count-Down. H. Howard
Count-Down. C. E. Maine
Count Down for Conquest. B. Gray
Count Dracula. T. Tiller
Count in Kensington. C. A. Alington
Count Me In. F. Nichols
Count Me Out! D. Spade
Count Netherleigh. H. Wood
Count Not the Cost. I. MacKintosh
Count of Nine. A. A. Fair
Count of Six. L. Powell
Count of Van Rheeden Castle. Annjeanette Scott
Count on the Saint. L. Charteris
Count Philip. P. Benoit
Count Remeny. J. Middlemass
Count Roderic's Castle. Anonymous
Count St. Blanchard. M. Meeke
Count the Cost. E. Ferrars
Count the Days. L. Summerfield
Count the Hours. C. Fraser-Simson
Count the Ways. D. M. Disney
Count Zarka. W. Magnay
Count Zero. W. Gibson
Countdown. W. Doxey
Countdown. D. J. Hagberg
Countdown at Monaco. L. Kenyon
Countdown for a Spy. D. Von Elsner
Countdown for Lisa. Vince Howard
Countdown for Murder. G. Sydney
Countdown 1000. D. Mariner
Countdown to Armageddon. Nick Carter
Countdown to Chaos. D. Pendleton
Countdown to China. S. L. Thompson
Countdown to Crisis. M. Eden
Countdown to Doomsday. R. Quest
Countdown to Murder. D. Haring
Countdown to Murder. H. D. Kastle
Countdown to Terror. L. Derrick
Counter Attack. F. Garrett
Counter-Clock World. P. K. Dick
Counter-Coup. M. Bradford
Counter Currents. E. Janis
Counter-Feat. H. Janson
Counter Force. D. Streib
Counter Paradise. N. Fleming
Counter Plot. E. Z. Frank
Counter-Spy. G. Dilnot
Counterattack. F. Scarpetta
Counterattack. J. Stevenson
Counterbalance. P. Trent
Counterblow. D. Stivers
Countercrime. O. Chase
Counterfeit. H. Howard
Counterfeit. L. Thayer
Counterfeit Agent. Nick Carter
Counterfeit Bill. L. Thayer
Counterfeit Bridegroom. L. M. Borden
Counterfeit Corpse. F. Findley
Counterfeit Corpse. N. A. Vanderpuije
Counterfeit Courier. J. C. Sheers
Counterfeit Death. W. Bannister
Counterfeit Gentleman. C. B. Kelland
Counterfeit Heiress. Andrea Hill
Counterfeit Hostage. C. H. Yaeger

Counterfeit Kill. Gordon Davis
Counterfeit Lady. B. Raymond
Counterfeit Murders. V. MacClure
Counterfeit of Murder. Ray Harrison
Counterfeit Spy. A. O. Pollard
Counterfeit Traitor. A. Klein
Counterfeit Wife. B. Halliday
Counterfeiter's Roguery. E. C. Derby
Coutnerfeiter's Wake. Lieut. Carlton
Counterflood. K. Thackeray
Counterforce. R. P. Henrick
Countermine. A. Welock
Counterpoint. I. Holland
Counterpoint Murder. G. D. H. Cole
Counterpoise of Death. H. Taylor
Counterpol. J. Boland
Counterpol in Paris. J. Boland
Counterprobe. C. N. Douglas
Countersnatch. J. F. Straker
Counterspy. B. Cleeve
Counterspy Express. A. S. Fleischman
Counterspy Murders. P. Cheyney
Counterstrike. S. Flannery
Counterstrike. P. A. Foxall
Counterstrike. C. D. Taylor
Counterstroke. A. Garve
Counterstroke. A. Pratt
Counterstroke. P. Wayland
Countertrap. J. Tiger
Counterweight. D. Brown
Countess and the Spy. G. De Villiers
Countess Dracula. N. Du Brock
Countess Ida. F. Whishaw
Countess Londa. G. Boothby
Countess Muta. C. H. Montague
Countess of Lowndes Square. E. F. Benson
Countess of Zelle. M. Gerard
Countess Vera. A. M. Miller
Countess, You Kill Me! D. Haring
Countless Steps. B. Shannon
Country and Fatal. G. Bagby
Country Beyond. J. O. Curwood
Country Club Murder. R. Verron
Country Code. R. P. Jones
Country Coffins. Dale Clark
Country Family. J. S. Clouston
Country Gothic. T. J. Kelly
Country Holiday. Elizabeth Ford
Country-House Burglar. M. Gilbert
Country Killing. M. F. Harris
Country Kind of Death. M. McMullen
Country Love and Poison Rain. P. Tate
Country of Again. P. M. Hubbard
Country of the Heart. K. N. Smith
Country of the Kind. S. Jennifer
Country of the Strangers. F. S. Wees
Country of the Wolf. S. Wagner
Country Squire. G. M. Fenn
Country Tragedy. F. C. Hall
Count's Chauffeur. W. LeQueux
Count's Millions. F. Du Boisgobey
Count's Millions. E. Gaboriau
Count's Secret. E. Gaboriau
County Affairs. R. Armfelt
County Court. R. Flanagan
County Family. J. Payn
County Kill. W. C. Gault
County Library Murders. J. Austwick
Coup! K. Okpi
Coup de Grass. P. Nash
Coup D'Etat. J. Harvey
Coup That Failed. R. Worth
Couple from Poitiers. G. Simenon
Couple of Cups Ago. N. W. Swan
Coupon Crimes. G. Verner
Coupons for Death. N. Brady
Courage for Sale. Robert Mason
Courage of the North. J. B. Hendryx
Couragous Exploits of Doctor Syn. R. Thorndike
Courier. G. Cole
Courier. D. Kartun
Courier for Crime. J. T. Story
Courier Job. J. Pattinson
Courier of Fortune. A. W. Marchmont

Courier of Lyons. E. Moreau
Courier to Danger. M. Blake
Courier to Marrakesh. V. Williams
Courier to Peking. J. Goodfield
Courier's Fist. H. A. Eysman
Course in Murder. L. Chaytor
Course of Villainy. J. Moffatt
Court Adjourns. W. F. Alexander
Court by Proceedings. W. R. Smith
Court Favorite. B. Reynolds
Court Intrigue. B. Thomson
Court-Martial. W. E. Butterworth
Court Martial. J. Ehrlich
Court-Martial. Robin Moore
Court Martial. D. E. Zlotnik
Court of Crows. R. A. Knowlton
Court of Dusty Feet. J. G. Sarasin
Court of Honor. W. LeQueux
Court of Last Resort. L. H. Hart
Court of Owls. R. Adicks
Court of St. Simon. E. P. Oppenheim
Court of Shadows. G. Jackson
Court of Silver Shadows. Beatrice Brandon
Court of the Stone Children. M. Bucci
Court of the Thorn Tree. Patricia Maxwell
Court Short. J. Balfour
Court Tragedy. A. D. Vandam
Courtesy Dame. R. M. Gilchrist
Courtesy of Death. G. Household
Courthouse. J. N. Iannuzzi
Courtier to Death. Anthony Gilbert
Courting of Nicholas. E. Phillpotts
Courtland's Crime. A. M. Burrage
Courtney. J. Jenkins
Courtney Entry. J. Harris
Courts of Idleness. Dornford Yates
Courts of Morning. J. Buchan
Courtway Case. R. Goyne
Courtyard. J. Moffatt
Cousin Henrietta. E. Cave
Cousin Hugh. Theo Douglas
Cousin Jess. M. Turni
Cousin Once Removed. G. Hammond
Cousin Phillis. E. Gaskell
Cousin to Terror. C. Bramwell
Cove in Darkness. S. Wagner
Cove of Fear. V. Smiley
Coven. Carter Brown
Coven. J. M. Fox
Coven. J. Hampton
Coven. David St. John
Coven Gibbet. J. N. Chance
Covenant with Death. S. Becker
Covenant with Death. F. Grierson
Covenant with Death. J. Harris
Covenant with Death. C. Victor
Covenant with Death. R. Walker
Covent Garden Murder. W. J. Makin
Covent Garden Mystery. W. J. Bayfield
Coventry Option. Anthony Burton
Cover. J. Ketchum
Cover for a Traitor. P. Harcourt
Cover Girl Cries Murder. M. Brody
Cover Girls. P. W. Fairman
Cover Her Face. P. D. James
Cover Her Face. H. McCutcheon
Cover Her with Roses. R. Anderson
Cover His Face. T. Kyd
Cover of Darkness. L. A. Olmsted
Cover Stories. R. Rosenblum
Cover Story. C. Forbes
Cover Story. R. Rosenblum
Cover That Corpse. H. Zore
Cover Up. H. A. Olgin
Cover-Up. Anthony Oliver
Cover-Up Story. M. Bagson
Cover Zero. W. Hughes
Covering Fire. H. Janson
Cove's End. S. Hufford
Coward. T. Ewen
Coward. A. Meredith
Coward Behind the Curtain. R. Marsh
Cowardly Custard. B. Von Hutten
Cowards' Castle. A. Soutar

Coward's Club. F. Grierson
Coward's Kiss. L. Block
Cowboy Blues. S. Lewis
Cowboy Conspiracy. L. D. Names
Cowboy Countess. C. N. Williamson
Cowboy Detective. Old Sleuth
Cowboy Detective. C. A. Sirengo
Cowboy's Revenge. D. Stivers
Cowl of Doom. E. Ronns
Cowled Menace. W. E. Hawkins
Coyote. Linda Barnes
Coyote Connection. Nick Carter
Coyote Cried Twice. A. Bay
Coyote Crossing. F. Roderus
Coyote Waits. T. Hillerman
Cozumel. H. Hunt
Crabtree Affair. M. Innes
Crabtree House. Howel Evans
Crack. L. Clancy
Crack in the Bell. P. C. MacFarlane
Crack in the House of God. G. Shannon
Crack in the Mirror. M. Haedrich
Crack in the Sidewalk. B. Copper
Crack in the Teacup. M. Gilbert
Crack of Dawn. L. Ford
Crack of Doom. L. Bruce
Crack of Doom. R. Cromie
Crack of Doom. G. Hackforth-Jones
Crack-Up. H. Atkinson
Crackdown. B. Cornwell
Crackdown. Nick Stone
Crackerjack. W. B. M. Ferguson
Crackerjack. B. J. Rockliff
Cracking of Spines. R. H. Lewis
Crackshot. R. Busby
Crackshot Detective. Anonymous
Cracksman on Velvet. F. Selwyn
Cracksmen All. G. C. Foster
Crackswoman. Roland Daniel
Crackswoman. C. Dawe
Cradle and All. F. N. Zachary
Cradle and the Grave. A. M. Stein
Cradle Kill. S. A. Hillman
Cradle of Crime. J. B. Hilton
Cradle Snatch. P. Conway
Cradle Will Fall. M. H. Clark
Cradled in Fear. A. Boutell
Cradled in Murder. Rudd Fleming
Cradle's Revenge. Eric Bailey
Craft and Cunning. W. M. Graydon
Craftsmen in Crime. Tom Fallon
Crafty Foe. H. Nisbet
Crag Island. W. M. Graydon
Craghold Creatures. E. Noone
Craghold Curse. E. Noone
Craghold Legacy. E. Noone
Cragsmoor. J. Letton
Craig and the Jaguar. K. Benton
Craig and the Midas Touch. K. Benton
Craig and the Tunisian Tangle. K. Benton
Craig Kennedy, Detective. A. B. Reeve
Craig Kennedy Listens In. A. B. Reeve
Craig Kennedy on the Farm. A. B. Reeve
Craig Poisoning Mystery. A. Fielding
Craigallen Castle. Mrs. Gore
Craig's Spur. E. S. Madden
Craigshaw Curse. J. F. Webb
Craine's First Case. E. P. Healey
Crambo. M. O'Brine
Cranes of Ibycus. M. Craig
Crang Plays the Ace. J. Batten
Crank in the Corner. C. Bush
Cranmer. S. Knickmeyer
Cranshaw Inheritance. C. Etheridge
Crash! A. Applin
Crash. H. Franklin
Crash and Carry. S. Christie
Crash Course. S. Barlay
Crash Into Murder. T. B. Morris
Crash Landing. M. Regan
Crash Out. H. Spencer
Crash Programme. J. R. Daniels
Crashlanding in the Congo. C. H. Wallace
Crashout. James Preston

Crater. R. Gore-Brown
Crater's Gold. P. E. Curtiss
Crave Pity from the Wind. B. Freestone
Craven Castle. L. Churchill
Craven Fortune. F. M. White
Craven Legacy. C. Heaven
Craven Mystery. P. Trent
Crawlspace. H. Lieberman
Crawshay Jewel Mystery. Roland Daniel
Crayfish Club. Roy Roberts
Crayfish Dinner. C. Keith
Crayon Clue. M. J. Reynolds
Craze of Christian Englehart. H. F. Darnell
Crazy Joe. M. Barone
Crazy Dame. W. Standish
Crazy for Kicks. D. Haring
Crazy Kill. C. Hamblett
Crazy Kill. C. Himes
Crazy Mixed-Up Corpse. M. Avallone
Crazy Mixed-Up Nude. G. G. Fickling
Crazy Murder Show. Sutherland Scott
Crazy-Quilt. F. Hume
Crazy Quilt Murders. H. W. Sandberg
Crazy to Kill. A. Cardwell
Crazy to Kill. D. Linton
Crazy Woman Blues. J. F. Burke
Crazyhead. J. Klawitter
Creaking Chair. L. Meynell
Creaking Chair. A. T. Wilkes
Creaking Door. H. Bridges
Creaking Floors. R. B. Whorf
Creaking Gallows. T. A. Plummer
Creaking Gate. V. Bridges
Creaking Tree Mystery. L. A. Knight
Cream and Cider. H. Gibbs
Created: The Destroyer. R. Sapir
Creative Kind of Killer. J. Early
Creative Murders. Carter Brown
Creator. M. T. Hinkemeyer
Creature. John Saul
Creature Creeps. J. Sharkey
Creature of the Night. F. Hume
Creature Was Stirring. T. Wells
Creatures. R. Masson
Creatures in a Dream. I. S. Black
Creatures of Satan. John Muir
Creatures of the Mist. V. Hanson
Creco the Swordsman. Old Sleuth
Credit for a Murder. S. Dean
Creedy Case. E. Crankshaw
Creep. B. W. Battin
Creep Into Thy Narrow Bed. Leonard Bishop
Creep, Shadow! A. Merritt
Creep, Shadow, Creep! A. Merritt
Creeper. P. Macaulay
Creepers. J. Creasey
Creeping Death. M. Grant
Creeping Death. L. A. Knight
Creeping Flesh. D. Rutherford
Creeping Hours. H. Pentecost
Creeping Jenny Mystery. B. Flynn
Creeping Shadow. Sam Merwin
Creeping Shadows. W. Usher
Creeping Siamese. D. Hammett
Creeping Tides. Kate Jordan
Creeping Venom. S. Pim
Creeping Vicar. I. Hamilton
Creeps. A. Abbot
Creeps by Night. T. J. Kelly
Creeps Medley. M. Hervey
Creepy Crest. W. E. Wright
Creggan Peerage. C. R. Gull
Creighton's Castle. M. Lynch
Crenland Castle. M. Gerard
Creole. S. J. Arnold
Creole Slave's Revenge. O. Harper
Creole's Crime. M. Pinkerton
Crepe Myrtle Tree. L. V. Stevens
Crescent Brotherhood. Nicholas Carter
Crescent Moon. L. Noel
Crescents of the Moon. J. Matthews
Cresselly Inheritance. J. Blackmore
Cressida. M. B. Lowndes
Crested Key. K. Orbison

Creston, the Detective. Old Sleuth
Crestwood Heights. C. Hyde
Crestwood Traps. G. M. Snodgress
Cretan. E. Ayrton
Cretan Cipher. J. Palmer
Cretan Counterfeit. K. Farrer
Crevasse. J. E. Brown
Crevice. W. J. Burns
Crew of L.C. 454. E. L. Long
Crew of the Anaconda. A. G. McDonell
Crib. H. Friedman
Cricket Cage. R. H. Shimer
Cricketeer Cracksman. Anonymous
Cricketeer Crook. Anonymous
Cried the Piper. J. Simmons
Cries from the Darkness. M. Fisher
Cries in the Night. J. H. Wallis
Crilly Court Mystery. H. S. Keeler
Crime. G. Bernanos
Crime. Anthony Lang
Crime. S. Longstreet
Crime. T. P. Prest
Crime a la Carte. M. Hervey
Crime Across the Way. F. Millington
Crime Against Judy Bishop. C. Barling
Crime Against Marcella. G. Milner
Crime Against Society. J. Spenser
Crime and a Clock. Whyte Hall
Crime and Again. R. Stout
Crime and Co. S. Fowler
Crime and Judy. R. L. Radford
Crime and Punishment. R. Ackland
Crime and Punishment. F. M. Dostoevski
Crime and Punishment. M. Dubois
Crime and Punishment Show. A. Hausvater
Crime and Puzzlement. L. Treat
Crime and Puzzlement II. L. Treat
Crime and Puzzlement #3. L. Treat
Crime and the Casket. J. Ironside
Crime and the Confessor. H. G. Hutchinson
Crime and the Criminal. R. Marsh
Crime and the Crystal. E. Ferrars
Crime and the Curator. J. Veitch
Crime and the Motive. Nicholas Carter
Crime and the Underworld. C. Bishop
Crime Apart. M. Underwood
Crime at Black Dudley. M. Allingham
Crime at Blossoms. M. Shairp
Crime at Cape Folly. S. Browning
Crime at Christmas. G. Evans
Crime at Christmas. C. H. B. Kitchin
Crime at Cloysters. R. Bayne-Powell
Crime at Cobb's House. H. Corey
Crime at Crooked Gables. T. A. Plummer
Crime at Crown Inn. M. Frazer
Crime at Diana's Pool. V. L. Whitechurch
Crime at Gargoyles. K. Wade
Crime at Grandison Hall. H. Leyford
Crime at Guildford. F. W. Crofts
Crime at Halfpenny Bridge. G. Bellairs
Crime at Honotassa. M. G. Eberhart
Crime at Keeper's. T. Cobb
Crime at Lock 14. G. Simenon
Crime at Nornes. F. W. Crofts
Crime at Orcival. E. Gaboriau
Crime at Porches Hill. R. Bayne-Powell
Crime at Red Towers. C. K. Steele
Crime at Tattenham Corner. A. Haynes
Crime at the Cedars. A. Feist
Crime at the Club. W. Massey
Crime at the Conquistador. S. Callaway
Crime at the Crossroads. P. Urquhart
Crime at the Crossways. B. Flynn
Crime at the Fair. H. King
Crime at the "Noah's Ark." M. Thynne
Crime at the Quay. A. Blair
Crime at the Quay Inn. E. Aldhouse
Crime at the Seaside Hotel. A. Blair
Crime at the Villa Gloria. G. Norsworthy
Crime at 3 A.M. H. Clevely
Crime Beat Crisis. H. Janson
Crime Boss. A. L. Quandt
Crime-Buster. S. Power
Crime Buster. J. Ratton

Crime by Chance. E. Linington
Crime by Persuasion. C. J. Burton
Crime Cargo. M. Knight
Crime City. H. Banarto
Crime Club. F. Froest
Crime Club. W. Holt-White
Crime Club. R. R.
Crime Coast. E. Gill
Crime Code. W. LeQueux
Crime Combine. David Hume
Crime Comes to Chimney's. Anonymous
Crime Commandoes. P. Cave
Crime Conductor. P. MacDonald
Crime Confessions. J. W. Firth
Crime Conscious. S. O. Giffen
Crime Cop. L. Holden
Crime Counter Crime. E. C. R. Lorac
Crime Cruise. E. L. Long
Crime Cult. M. Grant
Crime Cutie. D. Haring
Crime de Luxe. E. Gill
Crime Doctor. E. W. Hornung
Crime Does Pay. D. Bardens
Crime File. Dell Shannon
Crime Flies. B. Luigi
Crime for Christmas. L. Egan
Crime for Christmas. M. Lynch
Crime for Mothers and others. H. Slesar
Crime for Tea. W. Massey
Crime Gang. M. E. Cooke
Crime, Gentlemen, Please. D. Ames
Crime Harvest. P. Richmond
Crime Has No Friends. L. Rogers
Crime Haters. G. Ashe
Crime Hound. M. S. Scott
Crime in Cabin 66. A. Christie
Crime in Car 13. S. Chalmers
Crime in Carson's Shack. R. Hardinge
Crime in Concrete. M. Coles
Crime in Corn-Weather. M. M. Atwater
Crime in Crystal. H. R. Campbell
Crime in Cumberland Court. R. A. J. Walling
Crime in Holland. G. Simenon
Crime in Ink. C. Carvalho
Crime in Kensington. C. S. Sprigg
Crime in Lepers' Hollow. G. Bellairs
Crime in Paradise. Nicholas Carter
Crime in Park Lane. W. Jardine
Crime in Quarantine. Rosa Lambert
Crime in Question. Margaret Yorke
Crime in Reverse. J. D. Kennedy
Crime in Room 27. W. Tyrer
Crime in the Alps. G. Warden
Crime in the Arcade. B. Proudfoot
Crime in the Boulevard Raspail. R. Massey
Crime in the Close. A. Dick
Crime in the Crypt. F. W. Gumley
Crime in the Crypt. C. Wells
Crime in the Crystal. R. Hare
Crime in the Dutch Garden. H. Adams
Crime in the Kiosk. J. G. Brandon
Crime in the Wood. W. M. Graydon
Crime in the Wood. T. W. Speight
Crime in Threadneedle Street. George David
Crime in Time. M. Burton
Crime in Washington Mews. H. Crooken
Crime in Whispers. C. Witting
Crime Inc. J. S. Endicott
Crime Incarnate. C. Wells
Crime Insoluble. M. Durham
Crime Is Murder. H. Nielsen
Crime Is My Business. W. H. Baker
Crime Is of the Essence. J. Csida
Crime King's Challenge. Anonymous
Crime Lady. D. Haring
Crime Legitimate. P. Luck
Crime Limited. L. C. Douthwaite
Crime Looks Up. C. Rushton
Crime Maker. B. Fleming
Crime Master. W. M. Duncan
Crime Medley. M. Hervey
Crime Minister. I. Barclay
Crime Most Foul. George Douglas
Crime of a Century. Nicholas Carter

Crime of a Christmas Toy. H. Herman
Crime of a Countess. Nicholas Carter
Crime of Bohemia. J. K. Stafford
Crime of Colin Wise. M. Underwood
Crime of Constable Kelly. J. C. Snaith
Crime of Convict 13. W. M. Graydon
Crime of Corporal Sherwood. G. Chester
Crime of Count Dureen. P. Urquhart
Crime of Four. D. W. Steward
Crime of Golden Gully. G. Rock
Crime of Gunga Dass. C. Brisbane
Crime of Hallowe'en. L. J. Libbey
Crime of Henry Vane. Anonymous
Crime of Herbert Wratislaus. Michael Lewis
Crime of His Life. C. Conrad
Crime of Honor. G. Arpino
Crime of Innocence. N. Garland
Crime of Inspector Maigret. G. Simenon
Crime of Jane Dacre. S. C. Lethbridge
Crime of Julian Masters. E. Atiyah
Crime of Keziah Keene. V. Campbell
Crime of Laura Sarelle. J. Shearing
Crime of Margaret Foley. P. Robinson
Crime of Maunsell Grange. F. Breton
Crime of Mildred Bentham. T. B. Morris
Crime of Monte Carlo. Anonymous
Crime of One's Own. E. Grierson
Crime of Peter Ropner. H. Heslop
Crime of Philip Garrison. F. Marlowe
Crime of Philip Guthrie. L. Ragsdale
Crime of Silence. P. Carlon
Crime of Sybil Cresswell. E. F. Spence
Crime of the Boulevard. J. Claretie
Crime of the Camera. Nicholas Carter
Crime of the Cashiered Major. A. Parsons
Crime of the Catacombs. G. H. Teed
Crime of the Century. A. Abbot
Crime of the Century. K. Amis
Crime of the Century. D. Donovan
Crime of the Century. R. Ottolengui
Crime of the Chromium Bowl. E. B. Black
Crime of the Crimson Widow. J. Wylde
Crime of the Crossword. J. Garland
Crime of the Crystal. F. Hume
Crime of the Electric Torch. H. J. Peel
Crime of the French Cafe and other stories. Nicholas Carter
Crime of the 'Liza Jane. F. Hume
Crime of the Midnight Express. A. F. Pinkerton
Crime of the Opera House. F. Du Boisgobey
Crime of the Reckaviles. W. S. Masterman
Crime of the Under-Seas. G. Boothby
Crime of Their Life. F. Kane
Crime of Vera Seymour. B. Heygate
Crime of Violence. R. King
Crime of Violence. J. Stagg
Crime of Wilfred Hanson. Alfred James Alderson
Crime on a Convoy Cruiser. A. Whitehouse
Crime on a Cruise. K. Rhodes
Crime on Canvas. F. M. White
Crime on Cote des Neiges. D. Montrose
Crime on Gallows Hill. G. H. Teed
Crime on Her Hands. L. Gribble
Crime on Her Hands. R. Stout
Crime on My Hands. R. Chapman
Crime on My Hands. R. Drayton
Crime on My Hands. C. G. Hodges
Crime on My Hands. H. Janson
Crime on My Hands. J. Laffin
Crime on My Hands. G. Sanders
Crime on My Mind. W.H. Baker
Crime on the Cliff. L. Jackson
Crime on the Clyde. G. Chester
Crime on the Coast. Detection Club
Crime on the Cuff. H. Weiner
Crime on the French Frontier. J. Hunter
Crime on the Heath. C. V. Frost
Crime on the Kennet. C. A. Alington
Crime on the Limited. N. Ridley
Crime on the Moor. T. C. Bridges
Crime on the Moors. W. Tyrer
Crime on the Promenade. J. Hunter
Crime on the Solent. F. W. Crofts
Crime on Their Hands. Dell Shannon

Crime or Folly? B. M. Clay
Crime Oracle. M. Grant
Crime Out of Mind. D. Ames
Crime Over Casco. W. B. Gibson
Crime Partners. A. C. Clark
Crime Passionel. E. La Forge
Crime Pays No Dividends. E. Radford
Crime Philosopher. R. Goyne
Crime Photographers. S. Bristol
Crime Remembered. J. Ashford
Crime Reporter. J. L. T. E. Jones
Crime Reporter's Secret. G. Dilnot
Crime Scene at "O" Street. P. W. Valentine
Crime School. M. Cumberland
Crime Scientist. F. A. M. Webster
Crime Specialist. D. Newton
Crime Squadron. B. Waller
Crime Story. J. R. Nash
Crime Syndicate. A. Macey
Crime Syndicate. P. Manton
Crime Takes the Count. Elliott Dane
Crime Takes Wings. J. S. Dawe
Crime Tears On. C. Wells
Crime, the Place, and the Girl. D. Stapleton
Crime to Come. G. W. Jones
Crime to Fit the Punishment. C. Joyce
Crime to Music. P. Drax
Crime Unlimited. David Hume
Crime Upon Crime. A. Gask
Crime Upon Crime. M. Underwood
Crime Wave. M. Dixon
Crime Wave. M. Russell
Crime Wave. J. Wynne
Crime Wave at Little Cornford. H. Adams
Crime Wind. M. Holbrook
Crime with Karen. D. Whittaker
Crime with Many Voices. M. Halliday
Crime with Ten Solutions. H. Leyford
Crime Within Crime. F. Drax
Crime Without a Clue. T. Cobb
Crime Without a Flaw. L. Despard
Crime Without a Name. Dick Stewart
Crime Without Passion. R. Grayson
Crime Without Reason. George Douglas
Crimean and other stories. W. Addison
Crimebeat Crisis. H. Janson
Crimes at Fenton Towers. W. Tyrer
Crimes Club. W. LeQueux
Crime's Masquerader. A. MacVicar
Crimes of Cleopatra's Needle. J. M. Walsh
Crimes of Dr. K. Jack Savage
Crimes of Passion. J. Orton
Crimes of the Season. A. Saville
Crimes Past. M. Challis
Crimes Stalk the Fan World. F. L. Baldwin
Crimes Unpunished. G. Sava
Criminal. J. Thompson
Criminal Act. T. Wilson
Criminal Airman. A. O. Pollard
Criminal at Large. E. Wallace
Criminal C.O.D. P. A. Taylor
Criminal Code. M. Flavin
Criminal Comedy. J. Symons
Criminal Comedy of the Contented Couple. J. Symons
Criminal Conversation. N. Freeling
Criminal Court. W. Lyon
Criminal Croesus. George Griffith
Criminal Link. Nicholas Carter
Criminal Minds. R. Swicord
Criminal Mischief. P. Chevigny
Criminal of the Clouds. Anonymous
Criminal Queen. E. A. Young
Criminal Reminiscences and Detective Sketches. A. Pinkerton
Criminal Square. H. Hastings
Criminal Tendencies. J. Goodman
Criminal Tendencies. W. O'Rourke
Criminal Yarns. T. C. Bridges
Criminals. D. Kranes
Criminals All. W. Martyn
Criminals Caught. J. M'Govan
Criminals I Have Known. A. Griffiths
Criminals in Love. G. F. Walker

Criminals Run Down. Old Sleuth
Crimshaw Memorandum. L. White
Crimson Alibi. O. R. Cohen
Crimson Beetle. J. Andrews
Crimson Belt. G. H. Teed
Crimson Blade. M. S. Buchanan
Crimson Blind. F. M. White
Crimson Blotter. I. Ostrander
Crimson Box. H. S. Keeler
Crimson Butterfly. E. Snell
Crimson Candle. E. Bond
Crimson Car. F. Grierson
Crimson Cat Murders. S. E. Porcelain
Crimson Chair, and other stories. R. Dowling
Crimson Circle. E. Wallace
Crimson City. A. Coldeway
Crimson Claw. L. Bidston
Crimson Claw. W. Hewlett
Crimson Clay. B. Schwarz
Crimson Clown. J. McCulley
Crimson Clown Again. J. McCulley
Crimson Clue. G. H. Coxe
Crimson Clue. I. Stark
Crimson Corridor. E. Eagle
Crimson Crescent. Augustus Muir
Crimson Crime. G. M. Fenn
Crimson Cross. C. E. Walk
Crimson Cryptogram. F. Hume
Crimson Dacoit. A. Wilson
Crimson Death. J. Kelso
Crimson Dice. G. N. McCain
Crimson Domino. G. Goodchild
Crimson Domino. W. W. Sayer
Crimson Falcon. S. Hylton
Crimson Feather. M. Crossley
Crimson Feather. S. E. Mason
Crimson Flash. Nicholas Carter
Crimson Frame. A. L. Martin
Crimson Friday. D. C. Disney
Crimson Gardenia. R. Beach
Crimson Gargoyle. Anonymous
Crimson Glove. Warren Miller
Crimson Goddess. E. S. Carrington
Crimson Hair Murders. D. L. Teilhet
Crimson Hairs. Anonymous
Crimson Hairs. Whidden Graham
Crimson Hand. R. C. Finney
Crimson Holiday. P. Rosemoor
Crimson Honeymoon. H. Hill
Crimson Ice. C. Fitzsimmons
Crimson in the Purple. H. Roth
Crimson Jade. G. B. Mair
Crimson Joy. R. B. Parker
Crimson Kisses. A. Belot
Crimson Lady. D. Haring
Crimson Madness of Little Doom. M. McShane
Crimson Mascot. C. E. Pearse
Crimson Mask. W. H. L. Crauford
Crimson Mask. A. Steffens Hardy
Crimson Moon. I. Foster
Crimson Pall. W. Dawson
Crimson Patch. P. A. Taylor
Crimson Paw. M. G. Eberhart
Crimson Poppies. M. Benson
Crimson Query. A. Eadie
Crimson Quest. D. Barr
Crimson Ramblers. G. Verner
Crimson Rope. H. Ashbury
Crimson Secret. S. Warwick
Crimson Serpent. K. Robeson
Crimson Shadow. Roland Daniel
Crimson Stain. A. Bradshaw
Crimson Swastika. E. Snell
Crimson Thread. L. Lauferty
Crimson Threat. G. E. Rochester
Crimson Trail. J. Walker
Crimsoned Millions. J. Willoughby
Crinkled Crown. W. LeQueux
Crippled Canary. V. Gunn
Crippled Hand. F. S. Stewart
Crippler Gang. E. Woodward
Crises. M. Level
Crisis. J. Cello
Crisis. D. Fisher

Crisis. Steve Mackenzie
Crisis Comes to Mister Smith. Richard Fisher
Crisis for Two. Mark Ross
Crisis U.K. D. Tibbenham
Criss-Cross. Lee Jordan
Criss-Cross. T. Kakonis
Criss-Cross. D. Tracy
Criss-Crossing. P. Magdalany
Crisscross. P. Flower
Crisscross. H. Henkin
Criton Hunt Mystery. R. Jocelyn
Croaked the Raven. B. Fischer
Croaker. G. Ashe
Croaker. R. Garnett
Croaker. Arthur Russell
Croaking of the Raven. F. Lyall
Croaking Raven. G. Mitchell
Croation. T. B. Marle
Crock of Gold. M. F. Tupper
Crocker. M. Gaskey
Crockett on the Loose. B. Lang
Crockett's Woman. E. Hatch
Crocodile Club. A. Broome
Crocodile Down the River. G. C. Foster
Crocodile Man. P. Meredith
Crocodile on the Sandbank. Elizabeth Peters
Crocus List. G. Lyall
Croesus Affair. A. Segal
Croesus Conspiracy. B. Stein
Cromwell File. W. Harrington
Cromwell's Cavalier. John Sanders
Cromwell's Spy. Eva McDonald
Crone. B. Garnett
Cronin Mystery. John Arthur Fraser
Cronus. W. L. DeAndrea
Crook. Jonathan Starr
Crook Bait. L. C. Douthwaite
Crook Cargo. J. Hunter
Crook from Chicago. S. Hood
Crook in Paradise. D. Lynn
Crook in the Furrow. A. G. Street
Crook of Canada. G. H. Teed
Crook of Chinatown. W. M. Graydon
Crook of Costa Blanca. G. H. Teed
Crook of Crauford Court. L. Essex
Crook of Fleet Street. Gwyn Evans
Crook o' Lune. E. C. R. Lorac
Crook of Marsden Manor. G. H. Teed
Crook of Mayfair. H. H. C. Gibbons
Crook of Monte Carlo. G. H. Teed
Crook of Mosquito Creek. E. S. Brooks
Crook of Newmarket. A. Steffens Hardy
Crook of Paris. G. H. Teed
Crook of Shanghai. G. H. Teed
Crook Ship. M. Frazer
Crook Stuff. R. Keverne
Crook Town. A. Skene
Crook Who Came Back. Anonymous
Crook Who Wasn't There! P. Valdez
Crooked. M. Foster
Crooked Adam. D. E. Stevenson
Crooked Alley. Irene Alexander
Crooked Billet. V. Shaw
Crooked Billet. D. Titherage
Crooked Bough. J. Remenham
Crooked Business. F. Marlowe
Crooked Circle. M. L. Stokes
Crooked Circle. G. Verner
Crooked City. R. Kyle
Crooked Coffins. Griff
Crooked Company. F. Marlowe
Crooked Computer. W. G. Shingler
Crooked Cop. Bob Parker
Crooked Coronet. M. Arlen
Crooked Courtship. G. E. Bollans
Crooked Cross. C. J. Dutton
Crooked Cross. B. J. Sussman
Crooked Dwarf. A. W. Bradley
Crooked Eye. K. Virden
Crooked Finger. A. MacVicar
Crooked Finger. E. A. Treeton
Crooked Five! J. G. Brandon
Crooked Flight. B. Jackson
Crooked Frame. W. P. McGivern

Crooked Furrow. J. Farnol
Crooked Gambler. R. Hardinge
Crooked Game. A. Wright
Crooked Gold. L. Charteris
Crooked Highway. A. Spiller
Crooked Hinge. J. D. Carr
Crooked House. A. Christie
Crooked House. B. Fleming
Crooked House. J. Rowland
Crooked Inn. E. Dudley
Crooked Inspector. B. Wayde
Crooked Jacket. D. Dayle
Crooked Killer. P. Manton
Crooked Lady. B. Sarto
Crooked Lane. F. N. Hart
Crooked Lanes. R. S. Holland
Crooked Letter. L. DuBreuil
Crooked Lip. H. Adams
Crooked Man. Shelley Smith
Crooked Men Came. R. F. Lambert
Crooked Mile. N. Fagan
Crooked Money. J. E. Day
Crooked Paths. F. Allingham
Crooked Phoenix. Bradshaw Jones
Crooked Road. M. L. West
Crooked Samaritan. P. Trent
Crooked Shadow. K. Steel
Crooked Shadows. J. Crowe
Crooked Shadows. Gordon Young
Crooked Shamrock. C. B. Gilford
Crooked Sign. B. Bolt
Crooked Sixpence. L. Grex
Crooked Spur. R. Dawson
Crooked Staircase. V. Gunn
Crooked Straight. E. Dudley
Crooked Tree. T. B. Morris
Crooked Way. W. LeQueux
Crooked Wood. M. Underwood
Crooked Wreath. C. Brand
Crookedshaws. Winifred Duke
Crookery Inn. M. Crossley
Crooking Finger. C. F. Adams
Crooks. P. Whalley
Crook's Accomplice. A. Skene
Crooks and the Cup. J. Durston
Crooks and Vagabonds. R. Keverne
Crook's Bauble. Nicholas Carter
Crook's Blind. Nicholas Carter
Crooks' Caravan. Frank King
Crook's Cargo. J. G. Brandon
Crooks' Castle. B. Atkey
Crook's Castle. G. Dilnot
Crook's Contract. T. F. Moynihan
Crooks Convoy. A. Blair
Crooks' Cross. Frank King
Crook's Crossing. V. Lester
Crook's Cruise. Seafarer
Crook's Decoy. G. H. Teed
Crook's Deputy. A. Parsons
Crook's Double. W. J. Bayfield
Crook's Double. Nicholas Carter
Crook's Double. A. Murray
Crooks for a Month. G. F. Mountford
Crooks' Game. G. Dilnot
Crooks' Hill. San Antonio
Crook's Honeymoon. P. Swift
Crooks in Cabaret. S. Simpson
Crooks in Clover. G. H. Teed
Crooks in the Sunshine. E. P. Oppenheim
Crooks Ltd. L. Bidston
Crooks Limited. E. Snell
Crook's Loot. W. Jardine
Crooks of Paris. D. Lenton
Crooks of the Waldorf. Horace Smith
Crooks of Tunis. A. Parsons
Crook's Shadow. J. J. Farjeon
Crooks' Shepherd. S. Truss
Crook's Turning. John Muir
Crooks' Vendetta. G. H. Teed
Crookshaven Murder. Alexander Morrison
Crooner's Swan Song. L. Grex
Crop-Eared Jacquot. A. Dumas
Cropper's Cabin. J. Thompson
Cross and the Sickle. R. D. Zimmerman

Cross-Channel Crime. G. H. Teed
Cross-Country. H. D. Kastle
Cross Current. C. T. Cline
Cross Currents. R. Rostand
Cross Cut. C. R. Cooper
Cross-Eyed Bear. D. B. Hughes
Cross-Eyed Bear Murders. D. B. Hughes
Cross-Fire. K. Okpi
Cross Fire. Ralph Young
Cross-Fires. F. Warden
Cross for Tomorrow. M. Farnsworth
Cross in the Dust. M. O. Rolfe
Cross Marks the Spot. J. Ronald
Cross of Gold Affair. F. Davies
Cross of Lazzaro. J. Harris
Cross of Murder. Carter Dickson
Cross Over Nine. W. C. Butler
Cross Purposes. A. Dick
Cross Purposes. Jim Thomas
Cross Roads to Crime. F. Walton
Cross Section. Julian Spencer
Cross That Palm When I Come to It. A. Southcott
Cross the Red Creek. H. Whittington
Crossbow Murder. Carter Dickson
Crossed Needles. Nicholas Carter
Crossed Path. W. Collins
Crossed Skis. C. Carnac
Crossed Swords. S. Flannery
Crossed Wires. Nicholas Carter
Crossfire. D. Lynds
Crossfire. J. C. Pollock
Crossfire Kill. J. Buchanan
Crossfire Killings. Bill Knox
Crossfire Red. Nick Carter
Crossing. T. Allbeury
Crossing. J. Clive
Crossing. J. Flanagan
Crossing. C. Keane
Crossing at Ivalo. R. MacLeish
Crossing in Berlin. F. Knebel
Crossing of Clues. E. C. Derby
Crosskiller. M. Montecino
Crossover. W. Greatorex
Crossover. W. Karlin
Crossroad Murders. G. Simenon
Crossroads. J. D. MacDonald
Crosstalk. D. Bloodworth
Crossword Code. H. Resnicow
Crossword Hunt. H. Resnicow
Crossword Legacy. H. Resnicow
Crossword Murder. E. R. Punshon
Crossword Mystery. R. Gillespie
Crossword Mystery. E. R. Punshon
Crotchet Castle. T. L. Peacock
Crotchets and Foibles. A. Bligh
Crouching Beast. V. Williams
Crouching Hill. W. Blazey
Crouching Men. A. West
Crouching Spy. A. MacVicar
Crow and the Cat. P. De Polnay
Crow Eaters. B. Sidhwa
Crow Hollow. D. Eden
Crowborough Beacon. H. G. Hutchinson
Crowded and Dangerous. A. Lejeune
Crowded Cemetery. L. Williamson
Crowing Hen. R. Davis
Crown: Bamboo Shoot-Out. T. Harknett
Crown Colony. N. Harman
Crown Court. J. Follett
Crown Diamond. Nicholas Carter
Crown Estate. E. Berckman
Crown in Darkness. P. C. Doherty
Crown Kidnap. A. Crofts
Crown: Macao Mayhem. T. Harknett
Crown of India. S. Fuller
Crown of Night. P. Audemars
Crown of Stars. M. K. Simmons
Crown of Straw. A. Upward
Crown Swindle. M. L. Eadles
Crown: The Sweet and Sour Kill. T. Harknett
Crown Valley. K. Ashby
Crown vs. Dr. Watson. G. Lientz
Crowned Skull. F. Hume
Crowner's Quest. A. Broome

Crowning Design. L. Meacham
Crowning Murder. H. H. Stanners
Crowning of Esther. M. Gerard
Crowns Can Kill. H. Janson
Crows Are Black Everywhere. H. O. Yardley
Crows Can't Count. A. A. Fair
Crow's Inn Tragedy. A. Haynes
Crow's Parliament. Jack Curtis
Croyd. Ian Wallace
Crozart Stroy. K. Fearing
Crozier Pharoahs. G. Mitchell
Crucible. S. Murray
Crucible. B. A. Williams
Crucible of Circumstance. P. Brebner
Crucible of Courage. H. Neban
Crucible of Evil. Lydia Belknap Long
Crucifer of Blood. P. Giovanni
Crucifixion Squad. P. Beere
Cruciform Mark. Riccardo Stephens
Crude Kill. D. Pendleton
Cruel As a Cat. M. Halliday
Cruel As the Grave. I. Bayne
Cruel As the Grave. H. McCloy
Cruel As the Grave. E. Southworth
Cruel Betrayal. Coriola
Cruel Calumny. Mrs. Leith-Adams
Cruel Case. S. Rathbone
Cruel Dart. H. Carstairs
Cruel Deadline. R. Gaines
Cruel Designs. C. Wilder
Cruel Dilemma. M. H. Tennyson
Cruel Fire. E. Atiyah
Cruel Heart. J. La Tourrette
Cruel Is the Night. Howard Hunt
Cruel Lady. M. Corrigan
Cruel Legacy. L. H. Hudson
Cruel London. J. Hatton
Cruel Masquerade. H. Simart
Cruel Mother. J. LaPierre
Cruel Secret. Anonymous
Cruel Suspicion. F. P. Rathburne
Cruel Trade. F. Finlay
Cruel Triumph. N. Pierlain
Cruel Victim. M. Tripp
Cruise Breaker. A. Corbett
Cruise Into Chaos. L. Derrick
Cruise of a Deathtime. M. Babson
Cruise of Death. J. Rand
Cruise of Terror. S. Hope
Cruise of the Albatross. G. Allen
Cruise of the Carefree. John Marsh
Cruise of the Condor. W. E. Johns
Cruise of the Jasper B. Appleton. D. Marquis
Cruise of the Motor-Boat Conqueror. S. Paternoster
Cruice of the "Scandal", and other stories. V. Bridges
Cruise of the Sphinx. L. Robin
Cruise with Death. F. Draco
Cruiser in Action. Reginald Campbell
Cruiser on Wheels. G. Thorne
Cruising. Gerald Walker
Crumblerock Crime! W. J. Bayfield
Crumpled Cup. H. Kane
Crumpled Leaf. Mrs. Alexander
Crumpled Lilies. C. Dawe
Crumplin! M. S. Gretton
Crunch. J. M. Fox
Crunch. H. Janson
Crux. G. Rugarli
Crusade. Peter Watson
Crusade Into Crime. R. Wilkes-Hunter
Crusader's Cross. J. Pattinson
Crusader's Secret. J. Barre
Crusie Sketches. Fergus MacKenzie
Crusoe Harry. Old Sleuth
Crusoe Test. Mark Nelson
Crust on the Uppers. Robin Cook
Crux. R. Aellen
Cry Aloud for Murder. P. McGuire
Cry at Dusk. M. F. Ballard
Cry at Dusk. L. Dent
Cry, Baby, Cry! J. Ehrlich
Cry Baby Killer. J. Hilton
Cry Blood. H. V. Dixon
Cry, Brother, Cry. J. Karney

Cry Flesh. D. Karp
Cry Flood! E. J. Fredericks
Cry for Help. Nicholas Carter
Cry for Help. D. M. Disney
Cry for Kit. V. Heley
Cry for Love. A. L. Thompson
Cry for My Lovely. S. D. Frances
Cry for the Baron. Anthony Morton
Cry for the Lost. G. Dessart
Cry for the Strangers. J. R. Saul
Cry from the Dark. W. H. Baker
Cry from the Ether. R. Sharp
Cry Hallelujah! K. Orvis
Cry Hard, Cry Fast. J. D. MacDonald
Cry Havoc. D. Lowden
Cry Havoc. J. K. Mayo
Cry Havoc. B. Sadler
Cry Havoc. R. M. Stern
Cry Hold! P. Harris
Cry in Absence. Madison Jones
Cry in the City. P. G. Winslow
Cry in the Jungle. K. M. Knight
Cry in the Night. K. Brosnan
Cry in the Night. M. H. Clark
Cry in the Night. A. Golsworthy
Cry in the Night. W. Masterson
Cry in the Night. Judi Miller
Cry in the Night. D. Quick
Cry in the Night. K. Roos
Cry in the Night. P. Saxon
Cry in the Valley. G. K. Cowan
Cry Kill. Wenzell Brown
Cry Kill. D. Haring
Cry Killer! K. Fearing
Cry Lebanon. J. Morell
Cry Me a Killer. Garrity
Cry Me a Murder. D. Haring
Cry Murder. E. Howie
Cry Murder. W. M. Raine
Cry Murder. N. Rutledge
Cry Murder in the Market Place. W. M. Raine
Cry of Blood. F. Du Boisgobey
Cry of Neptune. A. Bretonne
Cry of Shadows. E. Gorman
Cry of the Banshee. T. J. Kelly
Cry of the Beast. V. Norwood
Cry of the Cat. M. Sellers
Cry of the Cat. S. Wagner
Cry of the Deep. R. P. Henrick
Cry of the Dingo. C. Phillips
Cry of the Flesh. B. Himmel
Cry of the Halidon. J. Ryder
Cry of the Hawk. H. Steirman
Cry of the Hunter. Harry Patterson
Cry of the Kestrel. J. Wood
Cry of the Nighthawk. N. Dorer
Cry of the Owl. P. Highsmith
Cry of the Owl. M. Mayhew
Cry of the Peacock. M. L. Roby
Cry of the Whippoorwill. J. T. Osborne
Cry of the Wind. S. MacIvers
Cry of Whiteness. T. J. Fleming
Cry on My Shoulder. H. Howard
Cry on the Wind. W. H. Boore
Cry Passion. R. Jessup
Cry Plague! T. S. Drachman
Cry Rape. R. Boyle
Cry Rape. Ruth Williams
Cry Revenge! A. C. Clark
Cry Scandal. W. Ard
Cry Shadow. M. Grant
Cry Spy. William Hood
Cry Terror. A. L. Stone
Cry the Soft Rain. A. Dwyer-Joyce
Cry, Tiger! M. Storm
Cry Torment. V. H. Johnson
Cry Tough. I. Shulman
Cry Treason Thrice. Eva McDonald
Cry Twice, Kitten! D. Haring
Cry Uncle! Michael Brett
Cry Vengeance. L. Peters
Cry Vengeance. B. Schwarz
Cry Witch. N. A. Hintze
Cry Wolf. K. Blake

Title Index

Cry Wolf. M. Carleton
Cry Wolf, Sister. N. Karta
Cry Wolfram. D. Sanderson
Crying Child. B. Michaels
Crying Makes Your Nose Run. J. T. Story
Crying Pig Murder. V. MacClure
Crying Sisters. M. Seeley
Cryogenic Nightmare. L. Derrick
Cryptic Clue. P. Conway
Crypto Man. K. Royce
Cryptogram. J. De Mille
Cryptogram. W. M. Graydon
Crystal. W. Wingate
Crystal Ball. D. Spicer
Crystal Beads Murder. A. Haynes
Crystal Blue Persuasion. W. R. Philbrick
Crystal Cat. V. Johnston
Crystal Cell. Gwyn Evans
Crystal Claw. W. LeQueux
Crystal Clear. E. Cadell
Crystal Clear. R. F. West
Crystal Clear Case. L. Head
Crystal Contract. J. Rathbone
Crystal Crow. Joan Aiken
Crystal Curtain. S. Bayer
Crystal Days. C. N. Douglas
Crystal Destiny. C. Blair
Crystal Eye. W. R. Randall
Crystal-Gazers. H. Robertson
Crystal Kill. J. Quinn
Crystal Mouse. B. H. Deal
Crystal Mystery. Nicholas Carter
Crystal Nights. C. N. Douglas
Crystal Palace. Max Barrett
Crystal Pawns. B. T. Haaf
Crystal Shadows. M. Y. Thomas
Crystal Skull. Warren Hill
Crystal Skull. J. McLaren
Crystal Stopper. M. Leblanc
Crystal Tower. X. Putnam
Crystal Wave. J. Turner
Crystal Window. P. Brisco
Crystallized Carbon Pig. J. Wainwright
Crystal's Secret. J. H. Connelly
Cub. C. L. Pancoast
Cuban Confetti. S. Barlay
Cuban Connection. P. Pembroke
Cuban Deathlift. R. Striker
Cuban Expedition. G. Null
Cuban Heel. B. Carson
Cuban Heel. S. Harragan
Cuban Heel. P. Jefferson
Cuban Inferno. S. Victor
Cuban Killer. R. Kleiner
Cuban Legacy. S. M. Parkman
Cuban Passage. N. Lewis
Cuban Treasure Island. W. P. Kelly
Cubano Caper. S. Jason
Cubwood. W. R. S. Lewis
Cuckoo Clock. M. K. Ozaki
Cuckoo Fair. Robin Temple
Cuckoo in Harley Street. S. Fairway
Cuckoo in the Nest. Laura Smith
Cuckoo Line Affair. A. Garve
Cuckoo Run. I. Pitt
Cuckoo Woman. H. Parker
Cuckoo's Egg. C. Stoll
Cuckoos on the Hearth. P. Fennelly
Cudgel. T. Polsky
Cue for a Killer. M. McFadden
Cue for Murder. Matt Bryant
Cue for Murder. H. McCloy
Cue for Passion. E. Chodorov
Cuernavaca Question. Lydia Kirk
Cuirass of Diamonds. E. Jepson
Cul-de-Sac. S. Dewes
Cul-de-Sac. J. Wainwright
Cult. E. J. Frail
Cult Breaker. A. Sugar
Cult Counter Cult. L. Davies
Cult Creatures. D. Haring
Cult .45. R. Rainey
Cult of Darkness. D. Reid
Cult of Killers. D. MacIvers

Cult of Terror. S. Cunningham
Cult of the Damned. S. Andrews
Cult of the Queer People. W. M. Duncan
Cult War. D. Stivers
Cumberland Decision. R. S. Silverman
Cummings Report. J. Brogan
Cumner's Son and other south sea tales. Gilbert Parker
Cumsha Cruise. E. L. Long
Cunning. R. Bloch
Cunning Against Force. Tom Steele
Cunning and the Haunted. R. Jessup
Cunning As a Fox. M. Halliday
Cunning Enemy. V. Hill
Cunning Mulatto and Other Cases of Ellis Parker, American Detective. F. Pratt
Cunningham Equations. G. C. Edmondson
Cuoto Snatch. J. Shelynn
Cup and the Lip. E. Ferrars
Cup Final Crime. L. Bidston
Cup Final Murder. B. Newman
Cup Final Mystery. A. Edgar
Cup of Cold Poison. Joan Fleming
Cup of Death. Gene Thompson
Cup of Silence. A. J. Rees
Cup of Thanatos. Charlotte Hunt
Cup That Kills. G. J. Barrett
Cup, the Blade or the Gun. M. Eberhart
Cup-Tie Murder. C. Dixon
Cup-Tie Mystery. F. W. Irwin
Cupboard. O. Ashdown
Cupid Among the Clues. F. G. Puzey
Cupid and the Creeds. W. J. Newton
Cupid on the Trapese. J. E. White
Cupid Turns Killer. H. Janson
Cupid's Executioners. H. Monteilhet
CUPPI. Sandi Johnson
Curate Finds the Corpse. A. T. Rich
Curate's Crime. A. Dick
Cure. K. Froth
Cure for Cancer. M. Moorcock
Cure for Death. V. Valentine
Cure for Dying. Jennie Melville
Cure It with Honey. Thurston Scott
Curio Murders. R. Wallace
Curio Shop. E. M. Penn
Curios. R. Marsh
Curiosities. B. Pain
Curiosities of Crime in Edinburgh. J. M'Levy
Curiosities of Detection. Robert Curtis
Curiosity Didn't Kill the Cat. M. K. Wren
Curiosity Killed a Cat. A. Rowe
Curiosity Killed Kitty. R. C. Payes
Curiosity Killed the Cat. J. Cockin
Curiosity of Etienne MacGregor. P. Cheyney
Curiosity of Mr. Treadgold. V. Williams
Curious Affair of the Third Dog. P. Moyes
Curious Case of Gen. Delaney Smythe. W. H. Gardner
Curious Case of Marie Dupont. A. Luehrmann
Curious Case of the Crook's Memoirs. W. M. Graydon
Curious Crime. A. E. Martin
Curious Crime of Miss Julia Blossom. L. Meynell
Curious Crimes. B. Hemyng
Curious Custard Pie. M. Scherf
Curious Facts Preceding My Execution. D. E. Westlake
Curious Happenings. Marjorie Bowen
Curious Happenings to the Rooke Legatees. E. P. Oppenheim
Curious Locket. L. Traugot
Curious Mr. Tarrant. C. D. King
Curious Quest. E. P. Oppenheim
Curious Were Killed. Dorothy Bennett
Curiouser and Curiouser. J. C. Snaith
Curiously Planned. Camilla Hope
Curl Up and Die Day. F. Dicken
Curlew Coombe Mystery. Gret Lane
Curls and the Penalty. L. McIver
Currie, Curtis & Co., Crammers. C. J. C. Hyne
Curry Experiment. A. A. Rayner
Curs in Clover. I. Mercer
Curse! N. Buntline

Curse. F. Hume
Curse at Wayfield. J. T. Osborne
Curse in the Colophon. E. Goodspeed
Curse of Amen-Tah. O. Sackville
Curse of an Aching Heart. H. E. Swayne
Curse of Anubis. J. Younger
Curse of Beauty. Geraldine Fleming
Curse of Black Charlie. Marilyn Ross
Curse of Blood. W. Herscholt
Curse of Cain. D. W. Rimel
Curse of Cantire. W. S. Masterman
Curse of Carlyon. E. Everett-Green
Curse of Carne's Hold. G. A. Henty
Curse of Carranca. Elsie Lee
Curse of Clement Waynflete. B. Mitford
Curse of Clifton. E. Southworth
Curse of Cloud. J. B. Harris-Burland
Curse of Collinwood. Marilyn Ross
Curse of Cowden. A. S. Swan
Curse of Craig's End. R. Verron
Curse of Deepwater. C. Randell
Curse of Doone. S. Horler
Curse of Drink. C. E. Blaney
Curse of Frankenstein. R. S. Mulligan
Curse of Halewood. B. Paul
Curse of Kali. A. Greening
Curse of Kali. H. E. Hill
Curse of Kalispoint. M. Richardson
Curse of Kama. W. F. Lovatt
Curse of Kenton. J. L. Roberts
Curse of Khatra. T. C. H. Jacobs
Curse of Kor. Anonymous
Curse of Leo. R. Lory
Curse of Magira. D. Bee
Curse of Mallory Hall. D. Daniels
Curse of Nightwind. Regina Hubbard
Curse of Pengrail Park. S. Farrant
Curse of Pocahontas. Wenona Gilman
Curse of Rathlaw. P. Saxon
Curse of Ravenswood. S. MacIvers
Curse of Red Shiva. V. Meik
Curse of Scotland. Gordon Bligh
Curse of Seabrea. Dewey Ward
Curse of Siva. R. St. Clair
Curse of Still Valley. S. Wagner
Curse of the Bronze Lamp. Carter Dickson
Curse of the Burdens. J. B. Harris
Curse of the Carrington's. W. Tyrer
Curse of the Casa Del Monte. E. E. Cameron
Curse of the Clodaghs. F. Cowen
Curse of the Concullens. F. Stevenson
Curse of the Crystal Ball. R. St. Clair
Curse of the Fevrills. Sylvia Penn
Curse of the Fleers. B. Copper
Curse of the Fultons. W. E. Grogan
Curse of the Giant Hogweed. C. MacLeod
Curse of the Golden Skull. J. Kains
Curse of the Hand. W. J. Elliott
Curse of the Island Pool. V. Coffman
Curse of the Kings. V. Holt
Curse of the Lhasa. G. E. Rochester
Curse of the Lion. F. A. M. Webster
Curse of the Mandarin's Fan. B. House
Curse of the Montrolfes. R. O'Grady
Curse of the Moors. F. Hurd
Curse of the Mummy. B. Luigi
Curse of the Nibelung. M. D'Agneau
Curse of the Obelisk. R. Goulart
Curse of the Pharaohs. Elizabeth Peters
Curse of the Pharaohs. J. Younger
Curse of the Reckaviles. W. S. Masterman
Curse of the Santyres. Gwyn Evans
Curse of the Sightless Fish. M. South
Curse of the Silver Wings. T. Wallace
Curse of the Snake. G. Boothby
Curse of the Track. J. Hunter
Curse of the Two-Headed Bull. L. Falk
Curse of the Wise Woman. Lord Dunsany
Curse of the Wolfskin. J. Crecy
Curse of Whispering Hills. K. Cameron
Curse the Darkness. L. Grant-Adamson
Curse This House. Barbara Wood
Curse You, Jack Dalton! W. Braun
Cursed Be the Treasure. H. B. Drake

C

Cursed by a Fortune. G. M. Fenn
Cursed Inheritance. L. Loghry
Cursed to Death. B. Crider
Curses! A. J. Elkins
Curses Come Home. E. C. Vivian
Cursing Stones Murder. G. Bellairs
Curtailed Voyage. E. L. Long
Curtain. A. Christie
Curtain at Eight. O. R. Cohen
Curtain Between. V. Siller
Curtain Call. M. Cronin
Curtain Call. R. Foley
Curtain Call for a Corpse. Josephine Bell
Curtain Call for Murder. A. Spiller
Curtain Call for Murder. P. Yates
Curtain Fall. E. Dewhurst
Curtain for a Jester. F. Lockridge
Curtain for Crime. M. P. Rea
Curtain Has Lace Fringes. G. Joseph
Curtain Killers. D. Haring
Curtain of Fear. D. Wheatley
Curtain of Glass. D. Ambler
Curtain of Hate. J. Moffatt
Curtain of Night. D. Petri
Curtain of Storm. J. Gollomb
Curtain of the Dark. H. McElroy
Curtained Sleep. A. Roy
Curtains. G. Gonzales
Curtains for a Chorine. Carter Brown
Curtains for a Lover. R. Dietrich
Curtains for Carla. M. Storme
Curtains for Carrie. D. Glinto
Curtains for Conquest? B. Gray
Curtains for Dulcie. B. Diamond
Curtains for Komespi. Ernest Paul
Curtains for the Cobra. P. Tabori
Curtains for the Copper. T. Polsky
Curtains for the Editor. T. Polsky
Curtains for the Judge. T. Polsky
Curtains for Three. R. Stout
Curtains of Solomon. M. Osmond
Curtis Wives. Marsha Alexander
Curve of the Catenary. M. R. Rinehart
Curved Blades. C. Wells
Curves and Angles. J. Farrell
Curves Can Cast Shadows. Griff
Curves Cause Trouble. Gene Ross
Curves for a Coroner. Carter Brown
Curves for Danger. A. Bocca
Curves Pay Off. N. Baroni
Curves Spell Death. M. Lavelle
Curzon. F. Durbridge
Custom House. Francis King
Custom House Fraud. B. Wayde
Custom of the Country. P. M. Hubbard
Customer's Always Wrong. Kevin O'Hara
Cut and Run. B. McGhee
Cut and Run. M. Tanner
Cut by Society. A. M. Meadows
Cut by the County. M. E. Braddon
Cut Direct. A. Tilton
Cut for Partners. E. K. Goldthwaite
Cut in Diamonds. R. MacLeod
Cut Me In. H. Collins
Cut Me In. J. Karney
Cut Numbers. N. Tosches
Cut of the Ax. D. Jackson
Cut of the Whip. P. Rabe
Cut-Out. Colin Smith
Cut Price Murder. M. Hervey
Cut the Cards, Lady. D. Lee
Cut Thin to Win. A. A. Fair
Cut Throat. C. Bush
Cut Throat. Simon Michael
Cute and Deadly Surf Twins. P. Morgan
Cute Boy Detective. Old Sleuth
Cute Courier. D. Haring
Cute Heat! D. Haring
Cuthbert Grahame's Will. R. Marsh
Cutie Cargo. C. Dekker
Cutie Cashed His Chips. Carter Brown
Cutie Cursed. C. Dekker
Cutie on Call. H. Janson
Cutie, Quit Calling. D. Haring

Cutie Takes the Count. Carter Brown
Cutie Wins a Corpse. Carter Brown
Cutter and Bone. N. Thornberg
Cutthroat. J. Frost
Cutthroat Cannibals. C. Sargent
Cutting Edge. L. Chance
Cutting Edge. K. Jackson
Cutting Edge. D. Pendleton
Cyanide! S. Toye
Cyanide for the Chorister. C. Wogan
Cyanide Girl. D. Haring
Cyanide Sweetheart. Carter Brown
Cyanide with Compliments. E. Lemarchand
Cyber Way. A. D. Foster
Cyberbooks. B. Bova
Cyborg. M. Caidin
Cybork King. R. Goulart
Cyborg IV. M. Caidin
Cyclops. C. Cussler
Cyclops Conspiracy. Nick Carter
Cyclops Goblet. J. Blackburn
Cynara. R. Gore-Brown
Cynara. H. M. Harwood
Cynic Fortune. D. C. Murray
Cynic's Desperate Mission. H. Kaner
Cynthia. M. Brenner
Cynthia. E. V. Cunningham
Cynthia-of-the-Minute. L. J. Vance
Cynthia Wakeham's Money. A. K. Green
Cynthia's Chauffeur. L. Tracy
Cypher 8. I. F. Anderson
Cypher K. Taffrail
Cypress Chest. G. Cumberland
Cypress Man. Jane Beynon
Cypress Road. M. Home
Cyrilla Maude's First Love. H. Wood
Czar of Fear. K. Robeson
Czar of Halfaday Creek. J. B. Hendryx
Czar's Spy. W. LeQueux
Czech Mate. W. Fennerton
Czech Point. N. Fleming
Czechmate. D. Brierley
Czechmate. L. Johns

D.A. Breaks a Seal. E. S. Gardner
D.A. Breaks an Egg. E. S. Gardner
D.A. Calls a Turn. E. S. Gardner
D.A. Calls It Murder. E. S. Gardner
D.A. Cooks a Goose. E. S. Gardner
D.A. Draws a Circle. E. S. Gardner
D.A. Goes to Trial. E. S. Gardner
D.A. Holds a Candle. E. S. Gardner
D.A. Takes a Chance. E. S. Gardner
D.A.'s Daughter. H. Peterson
D As in Dead. L. Treat
D.C. Death March. M. McCray
D.E.A.D. E. Whitmore
D.E.A.T.H. Hunters. J. Ahern
D.E.Q. L. Gorell
D for Delinquent. B. Clifton
D.I. J. Ashford
D Is for Danger. C. Emery
D Is for Deadbeat. S. Grafton
D.N.A. Business. H. Calvin
"D" Notice. B. Graeme
D.O.A. D. Pedneau
Da Vinci. L. Perdue
Da Vinci Deception. T. Swan
Da Vinci Rose. A. O'Neill
Dachau Treasure. M. Hervey
Dacobra. J. B. Harris-Burland
DADA Caper. R. H. Spencer
Dadda Jumped Over Two Elephants. D. Niland
Daddy. L. Durand
Daddy Cool. D. Goines
Daddy Goriot. H. Balzac
Daddy-O. P. Stadley
Daddy's Girl. John Milne
Daddy's Gone a'Hunting. M. St. Clair
Daddy's Gone A Hunting. J. Toral
Daddy's Home. P. D. Anderson
Daddy's Little Girl. D. Ransom
Daffodil Affair. M. Innes
Daffodil Blonde. F. Crane

Daffodil Murder. E. Wallace
Daffodil Mystery. E. Wallace
Dagger. Jeff Brown
Dagger. K. Grosse
Dagger. W. Mason
Dagger. J. Rovin
Dagger. A. Wynne
Dagger Affair. D. McDaniel
Dagger and Cord. A. De Brune
Dagger and the Cross. J. Hatton
Dagger Before Me. M. O'Brine
Dagger Drawn. L. Hill
Dagger in Fleet Street. R. C. Woodthorpe
Dagger in the Dark. W. F. Eberhardt
Dagger in the Sky. K. Robeson
Dagger in the Sleeve. K. Maclaren
Dagger of Fate. R. Marsh
Dagger of Flesh. R. S. Prather
Dagger of the Mind. K. Fearing
Daggerman. R. H. Francis
Daggers Drawn. M. Carr
Daggers Drawn. Alan Thomas
Daggers of Kali. R. Wallace
Dago. J. March
Dagwort Coombe Murder. L. Brock
Dahlia. B. Goldie
Dai-Sho. M. Olden
Dain Curse. D. Hammett
Dainty Was a Jane. D. Glinto
Dais. E. F. Ibbetson
Daisy Canfield. B. Haas
Daisy-Chain for Satan. Joan Fleming
Daisy Dilemma. D. Rico
Daisy Ducks. R. Boyer
Dakota Project. J. Beeching
Dakota Warpath. G. A. Ralston
Dale of the Secret Service. N. Wray
Dalehouse Murder. F. Everton
Daleth Effect. H. Harrison
Dallas Down. R. Moran
Dallas Drop. R. Abshire
Dallenger of the Police. Robert Harding
Dally with a Deadly Doll. J. Miles
Dalmation Tapes. Don Smith
Dalmayne Mystery. H. Leyford
Dalton Boys and the M. K. and T. Robbery. W. B. Lawson
Dalton Boys in California. W. B. Lawson
Dalton Brothers and Their Astounding Career of Crime. Anonymous
Dam. R. Byrne
Damascus Countdown. H. Avray
Dame. Carter Brown
Dame. R. Stark
Dame Ain't Safe. A. Bocca
Dame Between Two. D. Glinto
Dame Called Desire. N. Karta
Dame Called Murder. R, O. Saber
Dame Came Late. R. Angel
Dame Can't Cry Forever. D. Haring
Dame Dies Greedy. N. Perrelli
Dame Doles Death. N. Perrelli
Dame Gets Hers. D. Nolan
Dame in Danger. T. B. Dewey
Dame in Distress. Craig Cooper
Dame in My Bed. M. Storme
Dame Is Snatched. R. Commorde
Dame Laughed. Cliff Rogers
Dame Made for Love. Rex Richards
Dame Must Live. Tony Mann
Dame on a Deadline. M. Brody
Dame on a Death Round. M. Brody
Dame on a Drumbeat. D. Haring
Dame on the Lam. Johnny Dark
Dame on the Make. K. T. McCall
Dame Plays Rough. D. Spade
Dame to Discover. G. Usher
Dame Too Many. P. Garroway
Dame Trouble There. R. Angel
Dame Without Shame. M. Lavelle
Dames and Diamonds. D. Haring
Dames Are Deadly. D. Glinto
Dames Are Dynamite. A. Capelli
Dames Are Dynamite. D. Haring

Dames Are Dynamite. B. Schwarz
Dames Are No Dice. S. Vincent
Dames Are Out. D. Glinto
Dames Are So Dangerous. Rex Richards
Dames Are Welcome. W. Standish
Dames Can Be Deadly. Peter Chambers
Dames Can Be Poison. B. Sarto
Dames Can't Wait. S. Markham
Dames Come Deep-Freeze. D. Haring
Dames, Diamonds and Death! C. Wheatley
Dames Die Hard. Pete Costello
Dames Die Hard. D. Haring
Dames Die Too. D. Linton
Dames Don't Care. P. Cheyney
Dames Don't Dictate. R. Angel
Dames Don't Forget. Griff
Dames Don't Scorch. D. Haring
Dames-Errant. G. Norsworthy
Dames for Danger. J. Cairo
Dames for Hire. B. Sarto
Dames Fry Too. D. Hudson
Dames in Distress. L. Halward
Dames in His Death. M. Brody
Dames Is My Undoing. M. Horgan
Dames Never Tell. P. Pethick
Dames Out of the Ring. H. Enterkin
Dames Pay Off. P. Bruce
Dames Play Dumb. B. Banarto
Dames Play Rough. N. W. Firth
Dames Play Rough. J. Grecco
Dames Scare Easy. B. Carson
Dames Spell Homicide. H. R. Oldham
Dames Spell Trouble. P. Gallico
Dames Spell Trouble. M. Hervey
Dames Spell Trouble. S. Markham
Dames Take to Crime. D. Rogan
Dame's the Game. A. Fray
Damian. Melissa Mather
Damn Desmond Drake. Sea Lion
Damnation of Adam Blessing. V. Packer
Damnation Reef. J. Tattersall
Damned. R. Cordell
Damned. J. D. MacDonald
Damned and Destroyed. K. Orvis
Damned and the Destroyed. K. Orvis
Damned Disciples. C. Sargent
Damned Don't Die. J. Nisbet
Damned If He Does. B. Kerr
Damned Innocents. R. Neely
Damned Lovely. J. Webb
Damned One. G. Des Cars
Damned Serious Business. G. Ison
Damned Spot. H. Adams
Damned to Success. H. H. Kirst
Damning Trifles. M. C. Johnson
Damocles Factor. R. Chester
Damocles Sword. E. Trevor
Damosel Croft. R. M. Gilchrist
Damsel. R. Stark
Damsel for Discount. Jason
Damsel Not for Drowning. Kane
Dan Gunn, the Man from Mauston. L. Armstrong
Dan Sanda. F. Abbot
Dan, the Detective. H. Alger
Dan Turner, Hollywood Detective. R. L. Bellem
Dance Baby. J. Olsen
Dance Band Mystery. R. Sonin
Dance Card. J. R. Feegel
Dance for a Dead Uncle. C. Ashton
Dance for a Diamond. C. Murphy
Dance for Diplomats. P. Harcourt
Dance Hall of the Dead. T. Hillerman
Dance in Darkness. D. Daniels
Dance in the Sun. D. Jacobson
Dance Into Danger. S. Kuban
Dance of Death. Carter Brown
Dance of Death. H. McCloy
Dance of Death. J. Potter
Dance of Death. F. C. Ticknor
Dance of Death and other stories. O. Williams
Dance of Love. D. B. Dodson
Dance of Shiva. W. Deverell
Dance of the Dwarfs. G. Household
Dance on a Hornet's Nest. J. Blackmore

Dance on a Sinking Ship. M. Kilian
Dance to Your Daddy. G. Mitchell
Dance with a Ghost. K. Ostrander
Dance with Death. T. Barling
Dance with Me Deadly. K. T. McCall
Dance with the Dead. R. S. Prather
Dance with the Devil. T. Barling
Dance with the Devil. D. Dwyer
Dance Without Music. P. Cheyney
Dancehall. B. F. Conners
Dancer and the King. C. E. Blaney
Dancer Disappears. A. Sax
Dancer in Darkness. D. Stacton
Dancer in Yellow. E. Ogilvie
Dancer of San Jose. J. Laffin
Dancer with One Leg. S. Dobyns
Dancer's Daughter. J. Edgar
Dancer's Death. P. Davis
Dancer's Debt. J. Lutz
Dancer's End. D. Vane
Dancers in Mourning. M. Allingham
Dancers in the Reeds. L. Meynell
Dancing Aztecs. D. E. Westlake
Dancing Bear. P. Conway
Dancing Bear. J. Crumley
Dancing Beggars. E. B. Young
Dancing Cheat. D. Walshe
Dancing Cinderella. Rona Randall
Dancing Dead. R. Syvertsen
Dancing Dead. E. Thomas
Dancing Death. C. Bush
Dancing Detective. W. Irish
Dancing Dodo. J. Gardner
Dancing Doll. F. Condon
Dancing Doll. J. L. Roberts
Dancing Doll Murders. R. Wallace
Dancing Druids. G. Mitchell
Dancing Faun. Florence Farr
Dancing Floor. J. Buchan
Dancing Floor. M. M. McNamara
Dancing Ghost. L. Greth
Dancing Girl. G. Leroux
Dancing Horse. A. MacVicar
Dancing Leaves. G. Warden
Dancing Men. P. M. Hubbard
Dancing Men. D. Kyle
Dancing of the Fox. Winifred Duke
Dancing on the Wind. S. Chester
Dancing Silhouette. N. S. Lincoln
Dancing Spy. C. H. Bullivant
Dancing Star. Captain Ingram
Dancing Stones. L. A. Knight
Dancing Water. Y. Pickering
Dancing with a Tiger. S. Morrow
Dancing with Danger. P. Webb
Dancing with Death. J. Coggin
Dancing with Death. J. Corbett
Dancing Years. Clarissa Ross
Dandy. L. Meynell
Dandy. J. Middlemass
Dandy Against the Gangsters. G. Goodrich
Dandy Hangs Behind. G. Goodrich
Dandy in Aspic. D. Marlowe
Dandy Nabs "The Falcon". G. Goodchild
Danes Abbey. M. Gerard
Dane's Testament. D. Gethin
Danesbury House. H. Wood
Danger. D. Francis
Danger Adrift. F. Quilici
Danger Aft. N. Ashe
Danger After Dark. S. Maddock
Danger Ahead. M. Richmond
Danger Ahead. P. Saxon
Danger Ahead. J. T. Shaw
Danger Ahead. G. Simenon
Danger! and other stories. A. C. Doyle
Danger Ashore. G. Simenon
Danger at Bravo Key. Ronald Johnston
Danger at Cliff House. C. F. Gregg
Danger at Dahlkari. E. Marlow
Danger at Hand. Anne-Marie Cox
Danger at Midnight. F. Griffin
Danger at My Heels. G. Meyrich
Danger at Olduvai. J. Blair

Danger at Ringside. H. R. Cleaver
Danger at Sea. G. Simenon
Danger at Westway's. Donald Stuart
Danger Below. G. Goodchild
Danger Below. G. Hackforth-Jones
Danger by My Side. A. MacKinnon
Danger Calling. P. Wentworth
Danger Circuit. D. Bower
Danger—Dame at Work. P. Muller
Danger—Death at Work. R. Garnett
Danger Doll. C. Dekker
Danger Draws a Wild Card. T. Lennox
Danger Feeds My Fear. M. Strong
Danger Follows. C. Fraser-Simson
Danger for Blackshirt. R. Graeme
Danger for Breakfast. J. McPartland
Danger for Love. R. Lacroix
Danger for the Baron. Anthony Morton
Danger from Grassen. James Stewart
Danger Game. E. Hunt
Danger Game. A. Mills
Danger—Girls Working! J. Reach
Danger: Hospital Zone. U. Curtiss
Danger in Diamonds. G. J. Barrett
Danger in Eden. J. Ames
Danger in My Blood. S. Brackeen
Danger in Numbers. Noel Lee
Danger in Paradise. O. R. Cohen
Danger in Paradise. A. S. Fleischman
Danger in Suburbia. R. Goyne
Danger in the Cards. M. MacDougall
Danger in the Dark. P. Carlon
Danger in the Dark. A. M. Chase
Danger in the Dark. M. G. Eberhart
Danger in the Dark. C. F. Gregg
Danger in the Dark. C. Rushton
Danger Inside. F. L. Cary
Danger Is My Line. S. Marlowe
Danger Key. Nick Carter
Danger Lies East. K. Robeson
Danger Line. G. Goodchild
Danger Line. L. L. Lynch
Danger Line. S. Ready
Danger Mansion. D. Daniels
Danger Mansion. P. Wylie
Danger Maze. W. Rotsler
Danger Merchant. I. Lambot
Danger Money. A. Dean
Danger Money. M. G. Eberhart
Danger Money. T. C. H. Jacobs
Danger Money. M. Russell
Danger Next Door. Q. Patrick
Danger of Folly. Nicholas Carter
Danger on Cue. Rebecca Holland
Danger on Target. D. G. Deutsch
Danger on the Flip Side. J. T. Story
Danger on the Map. A. Aldous
Danger on the Mountain Express. Anonymous
Danger on the Right. L. Du G. Peach
Danger Point. P. Wentworth
Danger Preferred. S. Horler
Danger Road. M. Saxton
Danger Round the Corner. L. Meynell
Danger Signal. P. Bottome
Danger Signal. R. Peart
Danger Signal and other tales. B. Hemyng
Danger Trail. Hedley Scott
Danger Trail. W. C. Tuttle
Danger Under the Moon. M. Walsh
Danger Wakes My Heart. J. Ames
Danger Within. M. Gilbert
Danger Woman. Abel Mann
Danger: Woman at Work! Kevin O'Hara
Danger Zone. J. M. Flynn
Danger Zone. K. Lindsay
Danger Zone. J. M. Walsh
Dangerfield Talisman. J. J. Connington
Dangerous Affair. A. Andre
Dangerous Affair. D. Quentin
Dangerous Afternoon. G. Anstruther
Dangerous Age. A. J. Baker
Dangerous Age. M. Sylvester
Dangerous American. A. E. Hotchner
Dangerous Angel. C. B. Kelland

D

Dangerous Assignment. J. Blair
Dangerous Bargain. W. T. Ballard
Dangerous Bargain. J. Barry
Dangerous Beauty. J. J. Farjeon
Dangerous Blonde. B. Sarto
Dangerous Blondes. K. Roos
Dangerous Bridegroom. C. Kemp
Dangerous Brute. R. Jocelyn
Dangerous Business. E. Balmer
Dangerous Business. M. Underwood
Dangerous by Nature. M. Coles
Dangerous Cargo. H. Footner
Dangerous Cargoes. R. Hobart
Dangerous Catspaw. D. C. Murray
Dangerous Child. F. Cowen
Dangerous Company. W. Massey
Dangerous Company. Laura Parker
Dangerous Company. J. Rowland
Dangerous Conceits. Margaret Moore
Dangerous Connection. C. Gibbon
Dangerous Conspirator. G. Norway
Dangerous Corner. Ruth Holland
Dangerous Corner. J. B. Priestley
Dangerous Corpse. G. W. Jones
Dangerous Course. M. K. Douglas
Dangerous Cross-Roads. Laurence Kirk
Dangerous Curves. B. Banarto
Dangerous Curves. P. Cheyney
Dangerous Dames. R. Marlowe
Dangerous Davies: The Last Detective. Leslie Thomas
Dangerous Days. R. Overton
Dangerous Days. M. R. Rinehart
Dangerous Dead. W. Brandon
Dangerous Deadline. F. S. Wees
Dangerous Deceptions. A. Seymour
Dangerous Decor. D. Haring
Dangerous Design. L. Goldman
Dangerous Dilemmas. J. Peddie
Dangerous Diversion! E. Nepean
Dangerous Domicile. E. C. R. Lorac
Dangerous Dream. V. Nielsen
Dangerous Edge. R. Daley
Dangerous Edge. E. L. Hewitt
Dangerous Edge. W. F. Temple
Dangerous Enchantment. M. Garratt
Dangerous Enchantment. J. Pattinson
Dangerous Encounter. D. L. Teilhet
Dangerous Escapade. J. A. Park
Dangerous Exchange. M. Eden
Dangerous Experiment. Lady Duffus Hardy
Dangerous Fascination. L. Robin
Dangerous Fortune. T. C. H. Jacobs
Dangerous Fragrance. L. Graham
Dangerous Funeral. M. McMullen
Dangerous Game. A. Applin
Dangerous Game. F. Duerrenmatt
Dangerous Game. W. LeQueux
Dangerous Game. E. Yates
Dangerous Games. N. W. Firth
Dangerous Games. W. B. Murphy
Dangerous Games. L. Schreiber
Dangerous Games. B. Sowanda
Dangerous Glamour. M. Olden
Dangerous Ground. L. L. Lynch
Dangerous Ground. F. S. Wickware
Dangerous Guest. L. Leete-Hodge
Dangerous Guide. E. C. Vivian
Dangerous Harbour. W. E. Huntsberry
Dangerous Harem. J. B. Thompson
Dangerous Haven. G. Bettany
Dangerous Hideout. K. Lorraine
Dangerous Holiday. Elizabeth Ford
Dangerous Homecoming. V. F. Freethy
Dangerous Honeymoon. A. Kielland
Dangerous House. J. Herbrand
Dangerous Illusions. P. Rosemoor
Dangerous Impersonation. J. St. George
Dangerous in Love. Leslie Thomas
Dangerous Inheritance. V. Black
Dangerous Inheritance. G. Ferrand
Dangerous Inheritance. I. L. Forrester
Dangerous Inheritance. D. Wheatley
Dangerous Islands. A. Bridge
Dangerous Isles. Basil Carey
Dangerous Journey. N. Deane
Dangerous Knowledge. K. Bennett
Dangerous Knowledge. L. A. Knight
Dangerous Ladies. H. Manning
Dangerous Lady. O. R. Cohen
Dangerous Lady. M. Cronin
Dangerous Lady. M. O'Nair
Dangerous Landing. P. McGerr
Dangerous Landing. P. T. Owen
Dangerous Legacy. G. H. Coxe
Dangerous Legacy. J. Holden
Dangerous Legacy. M. Murphy
Dangerous Legacy. W. D. Roberts
Dangerous Liaison. J. Davey
Dangerous Limelight. R. Armstrong
Dangerous Love. J. Blackmore
Dangerous Love. D. Dayle
Dangerous Love. W. C. Stone
Dangerous Lovers. A. Applin
Dangerous Madonna. K. Lindsay
Dangerous Magic. F. Lynch
Dangerous Man. P. Haraday
Dangerous Maze. Brian Jones
Dangerous Memory. L. A. Olmsted
Dangerous Men. K. M. Sheahan
Dangerous Men. P. Steward
Dangerous Mission. Roland Daniel
Dangerous Mission. B. Marchant
Dangerous Mr. Dell. David Hume
Dangerous Mr. X. F. Duncan
Dangerous Mrs. Marsden. Monica Blake
Dangerous Moment. Roland Daniel
Dangerous Money. N. Hardinge
Dangerous Nan McGrew. G. Batson
Dangerous Oasis. M. Hastings
Dangerous Odyssey. Jane Edwards
Dangerous One. R. Ames
Dangerous Ones. C. Franklin
Dangerous Passenger. T. Walsh
Dangerous Paths. H. S. Cooper
Dangerous Pawn. Winston Graham
Dangerous Place to Die. David Wilson
Dangerous Place to Dwell. M. Russell
Dangerous Places. E. R. Chase
Dangerous Playmate. Philip Chambers
Dangerous Pretense. H. Simart
Dangerous Promise. R. Bell
Dangerous Quest. J. Creasey
Dangerous Quest. E. D. Pierson
Dangerous Rackets. N. Baroni
Dangerous Refuge. Joyce Bentley
Dangerous Refuge. I. Lambot
Dangerous Sanctuary. Andrea Hill
Dangerous Search. E. Wilmot
Dangerous Secret. Annie Thomas
Dangerous Shadow. J. B. Priestley
Dangerous Silence. D. MacKenzie
Dangerous Situation. L. Tracy
Dangerous Stable. N. Gould
Dangerous Stranger. M. Martin
Dangerous Sunlight. J. Bude
Dangerous Temptation. C. Virmonne
Dangerous to Know. M. Babson
Dangerous to Know. J. P. Duff
Dangerous to Know. K. Lindsay
Dangerous to Lean Out. K. Fitzgerald
Dangerous to Me. R. Foley
Dangerous Trade. G. Hackforth-Jones
Dangerous Twilight, and other stories. Arthur Gordon
Dangerous Twin. H. C. Davis
Dangerous Twins. E. Jepson
Dangerous Visit. F. Hurt
Dangerous Wanton. B. Banarto
Dangerous Water. W. Chambers
Dangerous Waters. John Bentley
Dangerous Waters. M. Frazer
Dangerous Waters. M. Sotabinda
Dangerous Woman. M. Blount
Dangerous Woman. G. A. Pierce
Dangerous Young Man. G. F. Worts
Dangerously Blonde. A. F. Witley
Danger's Bright Eyes. S. Horler
Danger's Child. J. T. Story
Danger's Green Eyes. M. Corrigan
Dangers of Working Girls. Grace M. White
Dangerville Inheritance. A. C. Fox-Davies
Dangling Carrot. D. Keene
Dangling Man. H. Kane
Daniel P. Wack, "Dumb-Bell". H. M. Kohler
Danish Gambit. W. Butler
Danju Gig. C. Weston
Danny Spade Sees Red. D. Ambler
Danny Spade Spells Danger. D. Ambler
Danovitch. W. B. Harris
Danse Macabre. K. Kellow
Danton, the "Shadow-Sharp." Anonymous
Danube Covenant. J. M. Elliot
Danube Flows Red. A. Melville
Danube Runs Red. R. Meade
Danvers Jewels. M. Cholmondeley
Danziger Transcript. C. Fick
Danziger's Cut. W. Warnock
Daphne Dead and Done For. Jonathan Ross
Daphne Decisions. Meg O'Brien
Darab's Wine-Cup and other stories. Bart Kennedy
D'Arblay Mystery. R. A. Freeman
Darby Trial. D. Pearce
Darcourt. I. Holland
Dardanelles Derelict. V. W. Mason
Dare-Devil Conquest. B. Gray
Dare Lorimer's Heritage. E. Everett-Green
Dare the Devil. M. Carr
Dared by a Dame. Griff
Daredevil. L. Charteris
Daredevils, Ltd. R. Goulart
Daring Abduction. N. Ridley
Daring Anna Alcott. A. Applin
Daring Conspiracy. Old Sleuth
Daring Diana. Anthony Lang
Daring Experiment and other stories. L. D. Blake
Daring Express Messenger. J. K. Stafford
Daring Horse Thief. P. Ryan
Daring Maddie. Old Sleuth
Daringfords. Mrs. Lodge
Dark. M. Derby
Dark. M. Franklin
Dark. J. Herbert
Dark Abyss. C. Knight
Dark Abyss. F. J. Thwaites
Dark-Adapted Eye. B. Vine
Dark Adventure. Augustus Muir
Dark Adventure. J. Tickell
Dark Amid the Blaze. C. Rushton
Dark and Brilliant Places. S. T. Robinson
Dark and Deadly. B. Winter
Dark and Deadly Love. E. Evans
Dark and Light Stories. M. Hope
Dark and Secret Place. M. Summerton
Dark Angel. S. Beauman
Dark Angel. L. Della
Dark Angel. S. Forestal
Dark Angel. J. Ronald
Dark Angel of Fear. C. Dekker
Dark Ann, and other stories. Marjorie Bowen
Dark Apostle. D. Kilcommons
Dark Arbor. I. S. Shriber
Dark Arches. G. Warden
Dark at Noon. J. Tattersall
Dark Avenue. F. Hume
Dark Avenue. J. Pendower
Dark Bahama. P. Cheyney
Dark Banner. R. Bentinck
Dark Bayou. J. T. Osborne
Dark Before Dawn. T. Dick
Dark Beginnings. K. Blickle
Dark Below. M. T. Hinkemeyer
Dark Beneath the Pines. A. Eliot
Dark Beneath the Stars. J. Blackmore
Dark Beyond Moura. V. Coffman
Dark Blood, Dark Terror. B. Cleeve
Dark Blue and Dangerous. J. Ross
Dark Boundary. A. Purdy
Dark Brings Death. D. Linton
Dark Brown. P. Johnson
Dark Bureau. E. Dudley
Dark Calypso. Dulcie Gray

Title Index

Dark Carnival. J. Ames
Dark Castle. D. Quentin
Dark Cavalier. V. Rath
Dark Chamber. L. Cline
Dark Chase. D. Goodis
Dark Circle. G. Ashe
Dark Citadel. C. Farr
Dark City. M. A. Collins
Dark Cliffs. D. Farrell
Dark Corner. M. Blizard
Dark Corner. C. Dale
Dark Corner. L. Q. Ross
Dark Corners. E. R. Chase
Dark Corners. F. E. Penny
Dark Corners of the Night. L. Olay
Dark Corsican. J. Appleby
Dark Countess. M. Richmond
Dark Cries of Gray Oaks. Lee Karr
Dark Crusade. J. M. Fox
Dark Crusader. I. Stuart
Dark Curtain. L. Dale
Dark Curtain. J. Packer
Dark Cypress. E. Noone
Dark Dame. W. Collison
Dark Danger. S. Horler
Dark Danger. M. Saville
Dark Days. F. J. Fargus
Dark Days Ahead. H. Desmond
Dark Dealing. A. C. Brown
Dark Death. Anthony Gilbert
Dark Death. C. Schurr
Dark Deception. Jane McCarthy
Dark Deeds. H. Desmond
Dark Deeds. D. Donovan
Dark Deeds. K. Welsh
Dark Deeds at Swan's Place. T. J. Kelly
Dark Descends. D. Ramsay
Dark Design. F. Hurt
Dark Desire. V. Coffman
Dark Desires. P. J. Cooper
Dark Destination. J. Potts
Dark Destiny. K. Lindsay
Dark Destiny. E. Ronns
Dark Device. H. Lees
Dark Diamond. D. Tower
Dark Disguise. John Bentley
Dark Doings. J. Reach
Dark Don't Catch Me. V. Packer
Dark Door. M. Collis
Dark Door. K. Wilhelm
Dark Dowry. W. D. Roberts
Dark Dream. H. Elsna
Dark Dream. Robert Martin
Dark Duet. P. Cheyney
Dark Echo. H. L. Nelson
Dark Eden. B. Kevern
Dark Edge of Violence. M. Carrel
Dark Emerald. J. Storm
Dark Enchantment. D. Macardle
Dark Encounter. Howard Hunt
Dark Encounter. W. Mills
Dark Encounter. C. Schurr
Dark Encounter. F. Stevenson
Dark Entry. B. Copper
Dark Eyes and Danger. H. Clevely
Dark Eyes of London. E. Wallace
Dark Fantastic. M. Echard
Dark Fantastic. S. Ellin
Dark Fantastic. W. Masterson
Dark Fields. T. J. MacGregor
Dark Flight. J. Rossiter
Dark Forest. R. Foxall
Dark Fountain. J. R. Nash
Dark Frontier. E. Ambler
Dark Frontier. Arthur MacLean
Dark Garden. M. G. Eberhart
Dark Garden. E. R. Punshon
Dark Gateway. Martin Long
Dark Geraldine. J. Ferguson
Dark Gethryn. H. H. Ross
Dark God. J. Chancellor
Dark Goddess. M. H. Albert
Dark Goddess. D. Haring
Dark Gondola. V. Coffman

Dark Green Circle. E. Shanks
Dark Guardian. V. Blake
Dark Half. Stephen King
Dark Hammock. M. Orr
Dark Harbor Haunting. Clarissa Ross
Dark Harbour. M. Browne
Dark Harvest. J. Creasey
Dark Harvest. C. Kenyon
Dark Hazard. W. R. Burnett
Dark Hazard. S. Styles
Dark Heritage. D. Daniels
Dark Heritage. John Foster
Dark Heritage. M. McEvoy
Dark Hero. P. Cheyney
Dark Highway. A. Gask
Dark Hill. R. Foley
Dark Holiday. M. K. Stevens
Dark Hollow. A. K. Green
Dark Horizon. M. Richmond
Dark Horse. N. Gould
Dark Horse. M. H. Herbert
Dark Horse. F. Knebel
Dark Horseman. J. Budd
Dark Host. A. Roy
Dark Hostess. S. Horler
Dark House. M. Cartwright
Dark House. M. Cumberland
Dark House. M. K. Douglas
Dark House. G. M. Fenn
Dark House. W. Spence
Dark House. A. S. Swan
Dark House, Dark Road. C. Wick
Dark House in Florissant. R. W. Kauffman
Dark Hunger. Don James
Dark Hunger. T. Strauss
Dark Index. J. Turner
Dark Inheritance. M. C. Hay
Dark Inheritance. C. Salisbury
Dark Intent. R. Foley
Dark Interlude. P. Cheyney
Dark Interval. John Aiken
Dark Intruder. R. Dowling
Dark Intruder. V. Packer
Dark Is Mine. C. Bartholomew
Dark Is My Destiny. H. S. Hurst
Dark Is My Shadow. W. E. D. Ross
Dark Is the Clue. E. R. Punshon
Dark Is the Tunnel. M. Burton
Dark Island. R. Barr
Dark Island. D. Daniels
Dark Journey. F. W. Crofts
Dark Journey. Julien Green
Dark Journey. S. Horler
Dark Journey Home. P. Hagan
Dark Kiss. D. Enefer
Dark Knight. Colin Robertson
Dark Labyrinth. L. Barth
Dark Labyrinth. S. Leigh
Dark Lady. D. M. Disney
Dark Lady. J. J. Farjeon
Dark Lady. Gavin Holt
Dark Lady. G. Robison
Dark Lady Murders. C. Ryland
Dark Lamp. L. Heilgers
Dark Lane. W. E. D. Ross
Dark Lantern. C. Short
Dark Legacy. M. Alan
Dark Legacy. T. Charles
Dark Legend. L. Hayes
Dark Legend. Marilyn Ross
Dark Light. B. Spicer
Dark Love, Dark Magic. O. T. Jackson
Dark Lucy. P. King
Dark Lullaby. J. Dalton
Dark Mambo. W. H. Baker
Dark Man. R. Chetwynd-Hayes
Dark Man. Robin Temple
Dark Man and others. R. E. Howard
Dark Mansion. C. Farr
Dark Mansion. H. R. Kaye
Dark Mansion. W. E. D. Ross
Dark Masquerade. Anonymous
Dark Masquerade. Patricia Maxwell
Dark Masquerade. Elna Stone

Dark Matter. G. Reeves-Stevens
Dark Memories. J. Morella
Dark Memory. E. Ronns
Dark Menace. C. Birkin
Dark Messenger. C. L. Cooper
Dark Mill. Claudette Nicole
Dark Mill Stream. A. Gask
Dark Mind. R. Goyne
Dark Mirror. B. Copper
Dark Mirror. P. Mason
Dark Mirror. L. J. Vance
Dark Moment. K. Wade
Dark Money. Colin Robertson
Dark Moon. A. D. Divine
Dark Moon. F. Vivian
Dark Moon, Lost Lady. Elsie Lee
Dark Moonshine. J. M. English
Dark Mosaic. C. Brooker
Dark Mountain. R. Laymon
Dark Mountain, and other stories. D. Hogan
Dark Music. C. Russell
Dark Mystery. G. Ashe
Dark Nantucket Moon. J. Langton
Dark Night. R. Francis Foster
Dark Night. S. Horler
Dark Night. N. MacKenzie
Dark Night of Love. C. Clements
Dark Night Offshore. M. Gagnon
Dark Nights. T. Burke
Dark Night's Work. Mrs. Gaskell
Dark Night's Work. P. Ingelow
Dark Number. E. Boyd
Dark Odyssey. F. Stevenson
Dark of Memory. P. Minton
Dark of Summer. D. Dwyer
Dark of the Moon. J. D. Carr
Dark of the Moon. W. E. D. Ross
Dark of the Moon. L. Thayer
Dark of the Sun. Wilbur Smith
Dark on Monday. M. Avallone
Dark on the Other Side. B. Michaels
Dark Over Arcadia. A. Talmage
Dark Page. N. Bell
Dark Page. S. Fuller
Dark Pages. Mrs. H. Dobell
Dark Palazzo. V. Coffman
Dark Paradise. M. MacKintosh
Dark Paradise. Dennis Schmidt
Dark Passage. D. Goodis
Dark Passage. A. York
Dark Passions Subdue. D. Sanderson
Dark Path. M. Neilson
Dark Pathway. D. Newton
Dark Peril. J. Creasey
Dark Peril. M. Leighton
Dark Persuasion. M. Andrau
Dark Place. Mildred Davis
Dark Place. A. J. Elkins
Dark Places. C. Allen
Dark Places. T. Altman
Dark Places. Alex Fraser
Dark Places. P. Gibbon
Dark Plot. S. Cobb
Dark Plunder. V. Rosen
Dark Power. W. Arden
Dark Power. E. S. Holding
Dark Power. L. J. Vance
Dark Prophecy. M. Alan
Dark Purpose. Doris Hume
Dark Rackets. B. Banarto
Dark Rainbow. Gerald Butler
Dark Red Star. I. Ruff
Dark Refuge. N. McFather
Dark Rendezvous at Dungariff. Lois Stewart
Dark Returners. J. P. Brennan
Dark Rider. G. Thayer
Dark River. P. Clark
Dark River Legacy. B. J. Hoff
Dark Road. J. Cross
Dark Road. D. M. Disney
Dark Road. C. Knight
Dark Road. G. Leroux
Dark Road. N. MacKenzie
Dark Road of Danger. C. H. Barker

D

954 / DARK ROOM

Dark Room. D. F. Mills
Dark Roots of Fear. B. Gaston
Dark Rose. J. L. Roberts
Dark Rose. Kenneth Thomas
Dark Rose the Phoenix. W. H. Murray
Dark Runner. R. Ashe
Dark Satanic. M. Z. Bradley
Dark Saviour. R. Harling
Dark Sea. P. C. De Crespigny
Dark Seas of Maltern Mansion. K. Vernon
Dark Season at Aerie. J. T. Osborne
Dark Secret. E. C. Clapp
Dark Secret. M. A. Fleming
Dark Secret of Josephine. D. Wheatley
Dark Secrets. W. M. Graydon
Dark Secrets of the Manor. G. A. Bruce
Dark Seed, Dark Flower. V. Leigh
Dark Shades of City Life. Anonymous
Dark Shadow. H. Desmond
Dark Shadow. R. Mattheson
Dark Shadow. P. Standish
Dark Shadow. R. S. Thorn
Dark Shadow at Bitterhill. P. Warren
Dark Shadow of Love. H. Simart
Dark Shadows. K. Lynn
Dark Shadows. Marilyn Ross
Dark Ships. H. Footner
Dark Shore. S. Howatch
Dark Side. D. Hornig
Dark Side. John Stanley
Dark Side Also. P. Conway
Dark Side of Destiny. S. Morgan
Dark Side of Love. O. Saul
Dark Side of Love. C. Virmonne
Dark Side of Love. C. Woolrich
Dark Side of Magic. R. Aspinall
Dark Side of Paradise. Alma Blair
Dark Side of Paradise. J. A. Creighton
Dark Side of Paradise. S. Wagner
Dark Side of the Island. M. Hebden
Dark Side of the Island. Harry Patterson
Dark Side of the Moon. W. Corlett
Dark Side of the Street. M. Fallon
Dark Sonata. E. Bond
Dark Sonata. B. Murray
Dark Spot. L. Allan
Dark Square. L. Meynell
Dark Stage. D. Daniels
Dark Stain. B. Appel
Dark Stain. Shubael
Dark Star. R. W. Chambers
Dark Star. A. Maybury
Dark Star. M. Muller
Dark Star Rising. D. Lee
Dark Stars Over Seacrest. Marilyn Ross
Dark Stone. Mildred Nelson
Dark Stranger. L. Lance
Dark Streaks and Empty Places. E. Mathis
Dark Stream. June Thomson
Dark Street. P. Cheyney
Dark Street. Gavin Holt
Dark Street Murders. P. Cheyney
Dark Summer. N. Buckingham
Dark Summer. M. Upton
Dark Sun, Pale Shadows. N. Grey
Dark Sunlight. J. Ames
Dark Surrender. Laurel Collins
Dark Suspicion. C. Gayet
Dark Symmetry. L. Conway
Dark Talisman. A. Bretonne
Dark the Summer Dies. W. Untermeyer
Dark Thirty. T. Kay
Dark Threat. P. Wentworth
Dark Threshold. G. Corren
Dark Tide. G. Croudace
Dark Tower. J. Edgar
Dark Tower. A. Woollcott
Dark Towers of Fog Island. Marilyn Ross
Dark Trade. A. Lejeune
Dark Trails Go East. F. A. M. Webster
Dark Tunnel. K. Millar
Dark Turnpike. J. G. Sarasin
Dark Understudy. E. Greenwood
Dark Valley. M. Stall

Dark Veil. N. Gerstner
Dark Vendetta. R. Charles
Dark Vengeance. A. Barron
Dark Villa. D. Daniels
Dark Villa of Capri. W. E. D. Ross
Dark Visions. M. O'Callaghan
Dark Voyage. H. Addis
Dark Wanton. P. Cheyney
Dark Watch. Genevieve St. John
Dark Waterfront. M. Hervey
Dark Waters. F. Cockrell
Dark Waters. W. Corcoran
Dark Waters. Ardath Wise
Dark Waters of Death. S. Wagner
Dark Ways of Death. P. Saxon
Dark Wheel. P. MacDonald
Dark Whispers. Claudette Nicole
Dark Wind. T. Hillerman
Dark Window. T. Walsh
Dark Winds. V. Coffman
Dark Wing. J. Wetherell
Dark Woman. Anonymous
Dark Wood. M. Farnsworth
Darke Darrell, the Boy Detective. F. H. Stauffer
Darken the Moon. F. B. Clark
Darkened Room. A. Clarke
Darkened Room. R. Goyne
Darkened Room. M. Harrison
Darkened Windows. C. K. Rathbone
Darkening Door. B. S. Ballinger
Darkening Glass. J. Wainwright
Darkening Night. Jane Elliott
Darkening Willows. P. Dalton
Darker Grows the Street. B. Winter
Darker Grows the Valley. Q. Patrick
Darker Heritage. G. A. Cerra
Darker Side of Death. M. Russell
Darker Than Amber. J. D. MacDonald
Darker the Night. H. Brean
Darker Traffic. Martin Brett
Darkest Death. R. Stephenson
Darkest Hour. Louna Ford
Darkest Hour. C. George
Darkest Hour. W. P. McGivern
Darkest Hour. H. Nielsen
Darkest Hour. L. Tracy
Darkest Night. P. Saxon
Darkest Room. G. Corren
Darkest Spot. L. Thayer
Darkest Under the Lamp. J. Sandys
Darkhaven. D. Daniels
Darkling Death. F. Vivian
Darkman. R. Boyle
Darkness As a Bride. M. Cumberland
Darkness at Bromley Hall. Maybeth Morgan
Darkness at Indian Key. K. Hess
Darkness at Mantia. I. Barry
Darkness at Middlebrook. J. T. Osborne
Darkness at Noon. S. Kinglsey
Darkness at Noon. A. Koestler
Darkness at Pemberley. T. H. White
Darkness at Sunrise. Rae Brown
Darkness Before the Dawn. Anne Stuart
Darkness Falling. B. Kevern
Darkness Falls. J. A. Schneider
Darkness Falls from the Air. N. Balchin
Darkness I Leave You. N. W. Hooke
Darkness in the Eye. M. S. Power
Darkness of Love. V. Stuart
Darkness of Slumber. R. Kutak
Darkness on the Stairs. F. Stevenson
Darkness Outside. G. H. Johnston
Darkness Over Hycroft. F. A. Chittenden
Darkness Visible. N. Lewis
Darkroom. C. Banks
Darkwater. Jan Alexander
Darkwater. D. Eden
Darkwater Hall Mystery. K. Amis
Darkworld Detective. J. M. Reaves
Darling Carey's Dead. M. G. Webb
Darling Clementine. D. Eden
Darling Daughter. R. Rayner
Darling Decoy. D. Haring
Darling Delinquent. H. Janson

Darling, Don't. Keith Campbell
Darling, Don't Be Dumb. P. G. Larbalestier
Darling, I Hate You. T. S. Matthews
Darling, It's Death. R. S. Prather
Darling Lili. H. Clement
Darling Murderess. C. Franklin
Darling Sin. Jean Leslie
Darling, This Is Death. D. Chambers
Darling You're Doomed. Carter Brown
Darlington Jaunt. A. Ross
Darnley's Bride. V. Stuart
Darrell Markham. M. E. Braddon
Darrell's Dream. C. Horner
Darrow Enigma. M. Severy
Darsham's Folly. H. Esmond
Darsham's Tower. H. Esmond
Dart Board Mystery. W. D. Maydwell
D'Artagnan Signature. R. Rostand
Dartmoor. M. H. Hervey
Dartmoor Enigma. B. Thomson
Dartmoor Mystery. M. B. Dix
Dartmouth Drop. P. Browne
Dartmouth Murders. C. Orr
Darwich Castle. B. Kingsley
Dash for a Throne. A. W. Marchmont
Dashiell Hammett Omnibus. D. Hammett
Dashiell Hammett Story Omnibus. D. Hammett
Dashing Dick's Daughter. E. Everett-Green
Dashing Female Detective. Anonymous
Dashing Fugitive. Old Sleuth
Dashmarton's Legacy and A Cast of the Net. Anonymous
Dastard "Dr." Anonymous
Datchet Diamonds. R. Marsh
Datchley Inheritance. S. McKenna
Date After Dark and other stories. P. Cheyney
Date for a Dame. C. Wheatley
Date for Homicide. R. Carni
Date for Murder. L. Trimble
Date in Detroit. S. Markham
Date with...? J. Grecco
Date with a Dead Man. B. Halliday
Date with a Spy. S. Maddock
Date with Danger. J. Ames
Date with Danger. G. Chester
Date with Danger! Martin Thomas
Date with Danger. Roy Vickers
Date with Darkness. D. Hamilton
Date with Death. W. H. L. Crauford
Date with Death. L. Ford
Date with Death. E. K. Goldthwaite
Date with Death. E. Linington
Date with Death. W. B. Murphy
Date with Despair. H. Vogel
Date with Destiny. J. Walker
Date with Doom. Ray Owen
Date with Fear. J. Pendower
Date with Murder. L. Marshall
Date with the Departed. E. P. Thorne
Dateless Bargain. C. L. Pirkis
Dateline Darlene. H. Janson
Dateline Debbie. H. Janson
Dateline Diane. H. Janson
Dateline: Europe. L. Ross
Dateline—Paris. F. Struan
Dating Service. B. Knister
Daughter Fair. P. Graaf
Daughter of Allah. C. H. Bullivant
Daughter of Belial. B. Tozer
Daughter of Bonnie & Clyde. L. W. Brent
Daughter of Darkness. H. P. Dunne
Daughter of Darkness. R. Goyne
Daughter of Darkness. E. Gresham
Daughter of Darkness. J. R. Lowell
Daughter of Darkness. P. McGerr
Daughter of Darkness. E. Noone
Daughter of Despair. Richard Hubbard
Daughter of Evil. P. Morton
Daughter of Evil. Genevieve St. John
Daughter of Evil. J. Weil
Daughter of France. J. Hatton
Daughter of Fu Manchu. S. Rohmer
Daughter of Illusion. J. Budd
Daughter of Judas. R. H. Savage

Title Index

Daughter of Kings. G. W. Gough
Daughter of Mars. B. Kingsley
Daughter of Mystery. R. N. Silver
Daughter of Satan. Harry Mills
Daughter of Silence. M. L. West
Daughter of Strife. J. H. Findlater
Daughter of the House. C. Wells
Daughter of the Marionis. E. P. Oppenheim
Daughter of the Pangaran. D. Divine
Daughter of the Sacred Mountain. M. Richardson
Daughter of the Scaffold. W. Tyrer
Daughter of the Sidewalk. D. Linton
Daughter of the Stars and other tales. H. Conway
Daughter of the States. M. Pemberton
Daughter of the Veldt. B. Marnan
Daughter of Time. J. Tey
Daughter of Two Worlds. L. Scott
Daughters in Law. H. Cecil
Daughters of Ardmore Hall. D. Eden
Daughters of Astaroth. S. Shulman
Daughters of Belial. S. Truss
Daughters of Cain. M. Lynch
Daughters of Jezebel. Henry Holt
Daughters of Lizzie. S. Lawrence
Daughters of Satan. S. Shulman
Daughters of the Night. E. Wallace
Daughter's Promise. J. Ellis
Dauntless Three. Andrew Gray
Dave Sulkin Cares. F. Knebel
Davenham Heritage. R. H. Poole
Davenport Dunn. C. Lever
Dave's Sweetheart. M. Gaunt
David Betterton. J. Ruegg
David Dimsdale, M.D. M. H. Hervey
David Goodis Omnibus. D. Goodis
David Lindsay. E. Southworth
David Poindexter's Disappearance, and other tales. J. Hawthorne
David the Avenger. W. J. Carroll
David Wilshaw Investigates. A. O. Pollard
Davidian Report. D. B. Hughes
David's War. H. D. Kastle
Davidson Case. J. Rhode
Davis Doesn't Live Here Any More. J. Ripley
Davy Chadwick. J. Buchan
Davy Jones. A. Hillgarth
Dawn. V. C. Andrews
Dawn. H. R. Haggard
Dawn and Vengeance. J. Keitgas
Dawn at Kahlenberg. J. Siegel
Dawn Comes Soon. U. Nightingale
Dawn for Danger. Edmund Stone
Dawn Must Come. O. Williams
Dawn of Darkness. J. Creasey
Dawn Patrol. K. Ford
Dawn's Early Light. Steve Johnson
Dawson Pedigree. D. L. Sayers
Day and Night Stories. A. Blackwood
Day Before Midnight. Stephen Hunter
Day Before Sunrise. T. Wiseman
Day Before Tomorrow. D. Helwig
Day Care. J. Russo
Day-Dreams and Night-Mares. F. G. Young
Day for Angels. E. Lindall
Day for Murder. K. McComb
Day Gibraltar Fell. B. Wynne
Day He Died. L. Padgett
Day I Died. L. Lariar
Day I Stopped Running. R. Wilkes-Hunter
Day in Monte Carlo. M. Albrand
Day in Summer. J. L. Carr
Day It Rained Diamonds. M. E. Chaber
Day Krushcev Panicked. G. B. Mair
Day Miss Bessie Lewis Disappeared. D. M. Disney
Day New York Trembled. I. Lewis
Day of Dark Memory. J. Phillips
Day of Days. L. J. Vance
Day of Disaster. J. Creasey
Day of Dwarfs. P. Everett
Day of Fate. T. A. R. Cheney
Day of Fear. G. Ashe
Day of Judgement. J. Higgins
Day of Judgment. E. Lipsky
Day of Judgment. N. MacKenzie

Day of Mourning. D. Pendleton
Day of Murder. B. Bearshaw
Day of Reckoning. Nicholas Carter
Day of Reckoning. F. Du Boisgobey
Day of Reckoning. J. Garden
Day of Reckoning. J. Katzenbach
Day of Temptation. W. LeQueux
Day of Terror. M. E. Cooke
Day of Terror. S. Frances
Day of the Adder. N. Fitzgerald
Day of the Arrow. P. Loraine
Day of the Assassin. Nick Carter
Day of the Big Dollar. Peter Chambers
Day of the Cheetah. Dale Brown
Day of the Coastwatch. P. McCutchan
Day of the Dead. C. Murray
Day of the Dead. B. Spicer
Day of the Dingo. Nick Carter
Day of the Dolphin. R. Merle
Day of the Donkey Derby. Joan Fleming
Day of the Dust. R. Verron
Day of the Fox. N. Lewis
Day of the Grocer. W. Rushton
Day of the Guns. M. Spillane
Day of the Jackal. F. Forsyth
Day of the Mahdi. Nick Carter
Day of the Moon. W. Jeffrey
Day of the Owl. L. Sciascia
Day of the Peppercorn Kill. J. Wainwright
Day of the Ram. W. C. Gault
Day of the Storm. Elizabeth Ford
Day of Uniting. E. Wallace
Day of Vengeance. J. Dayle
Day of Wrath. W. Coughlin
Day of Wrath. L. Tracy
Day of Wrath. J. Valin
Day One. J. Maccabee
Day Seven. J. Bickham
Day She Died. H. Reilly
Day That I Die. P. F. Kluge
Day the Bookies Took a Bath. A. P. Hagan
Day the Call Came. T. Hinde
Day the Children Vanished. H. Pentecost
Day the Fish Came Out. K. Cicellis
Day the Island Almost Sank. S. D. Frances
Day the Sun Fell. R. L. Duncan
Day the Sun Rose Twice. D. Thomas
Day the Thames Caught Fire. P. Chambers
Day the Whores Came Out to Play Tennis. A. Kopit
Day the Wind Dropped. K. Royce
Day the World Ended. S. Rohmer
Day They Hijacked Death. James Lake
Day They Invaded New York. I. Lewis
Day They Kidnapped Queen Victoria. H. K. Fleming
Day They Robbed the Bank of England. J. Brophy
Day They Stole the Queen Mary. T. Hughes
Day Will Come. M. E. Braddon
Day Without Sunshine. L. H. Whitten
Daybreak. Arnold Meredith
Daybreak at Deest. R. Gaines
Daydreams. Mitchell Smith
Daylight. Russell James
Daylight and Nightmare. G. K. Chesterton
Daylight Fear. F. Cowen
Daylight Intruder. J. Jenkins
Daylight Murder. P. McGuire
Daylight Robbery. J. W. Bobin
Daylight Robbery. M. Russell
Daylight Robbery. R. W. Tullipan
Days Among the Dead. I. Baker
Days and Nights of Peril. Old Sleuth
Days Are Long. R. Barker
Days Like These. N. Fountain
Day's Mischief. L. Storm
Days of Danger. J. Creasey
Days of Darkness. D. Orgill
Days of Disaster. A. M. Stein
Days of Doubt. A. M. Meadows
Days of Misfortune. A. M. Stein
Days of Power, Nights of Far. B. Shaw
Days of Starlight. Craig Harrison
Days of Thunder. M. Hartmann
Days of Vengeance. D. Enefer

Days of Vengeance. C. H. Guenter
Days of Wine and Murder. M. Glade
Days of Yellow. D. Culverwell
Days of Your Fathers. G. Household
Day's Tragedy. A. Upward
Daze of Fears. J. Roffman
Daze, the Magician. A. Baerlein
Dazzle the Natives. E. Howis
Dazzled. H. Townley
Dazzling Miss Davison. F. Warden
De Bercy Affair. Gordon Holmes
De Grey. Anonymous
De Marigny Affair. M. C. Pain
De Profundis. W. Gilbert
De Witt's War. H. Koning
Deacon and Actress. A. C. Gunter
Deacon Brodie. D. Donovan
Deacon's Daughter. R. Marsh
Deacon's Second Wind. A. C. Gunter
Dead Accomplice. Nicholas Carter
Dead Account. G. Burnett
Dead Against My Principles. K. Hopkins
Dead Against the Lawyers. R. Jeffries
Dead Ahead. R. Horansky
Dead Ahead. W. L. Stuart
Dead Aim. W. McCall
Dead Aim. C. Wilcox
Dead Air. M. Lupica
Dead and Alive. H. Innes
Dead and Buried. H. Engel
Dead and Doggone. S. Conant
Dead and Done For. Robert Reeves
Dead, and Done With. M. Cronin
Dead and Dumb. E. Crispin
Dead and Gone. B. Bird
Dead and Gone. M. Kittredge
Dead—and Kicking. F. Castle
Dead and Not Buried. H. F. M. Prescott
Dead and Paid For. N. Hollander
Dead and Paid For. M. Olden
Dead and the Damned. W. H. Baker
Dead and the Damned. B. Schwarz
Dead and the Deadly. L. Trimble
Dead Angel. J. Dolph
Dead Are Blind. M. Afford
Dead Are Dangerous. L. Marshall
Dead Are Discreet. A. Lyons
Dead Are Prowling. V. Markham
Dead Are Silent. L. Marshall
Dead Are So Dumb. L. Cargill
Dead As a Dinosaur. F. Lockridge
Dead As a Dodo. M. O'Brine
Dead As a Dummy. G. Homes
Dead As Diamonds. G. Trotta
Dead As They Come. K. Platt
Dead at 8 P.M. C. H. Ogilvie
Dead at First Hand. Jonathan Ross
Dead at the Take-Off. L. Dent
Dead Awkward. John Milne
Dead Babes in the Wood. D. B. Olsen
Dead Ball. B. Cork
Dead Bang. E. Naha
Dead-Bang. R. S. Prather
Dead Beat. R. Bloch
Dead Before Midnight. R. Charles
Dead Birds. John Milne
Dead Bolt. R. Obstfeld
Dead Bones Tell Tales. Griff
Dead Branch. G. Norham
Dead Bridal. J. F. Slingsby
Dead Bullfighter. D. Sanderson
Dead Butler Caper. F. Norman
Dead by Morning. D. Simpson
Dead by Now. M. Erskine
Dead by the Light of the Moon. T. Wells
Dead Calm. C. Williams
Dead Can Tell. H. Reilly
Dead Canary. J. M. Fox
Dead Can't Love. J. Philips
Dead Center. Mary Collins
Dead Center. L. Langley
Dead Center. Christopher Wood
Dead Centre. T. Wood
Dead Cert. D. Francis

D

Dead Certain. S. Sterling
Dead Certainties. N. Gubbins
Dead Certainty. N. Gould
Dead Certainty. H. Janson
Dead Circuit. S. Rattray
Dead City. J. Delmont
Dead City. S. Stevens
Dead Clever. R. Jeffries
Dead Collection. P. R. G. Birch
Dead Copy. H. Monteilhet
Dead Corse. M. Kelly
Dead Crazy. N. Picard
Dead Dames Can't Cheat. C. Wheatley
Dead Darling. Jonathan Craig
Dead Do Talk. John Bentley
Dead Dog. C. Harris
Dead Dogs Bite. E. M. Curtiss
Dead Dolls Don't Cry. Carter Brown
Dead Dolls Don't Talk. D. Keene
Dead Don't Bite. D. G. Browne
Dead Don't Care. Jonathan Latimer
Dead Don't Cry. C. Dekker
Dead Don't Cry. B. Sarto
Dead Don't Cry. B. Shannon
Dead Don't Matter. Spencer Smith
Dead Don't Rise. Duff Johnson
Dead Don't Scare. P. Marlowe
Dead Don't Scream. L. Gribble
Dead Don't Speak. M. Erskine
Dead Drop in Havana. C. H. Guenter
Dead Drunk. G. Bagby
Dead Drunk. P. Conway
Dead Drunk. H. Howard
Dead Duck. P. MacNee
Dead Easy. R. Angel
Dead Easy. D. Pendleton
Dead Easy. J. Popplewell
Dead Easy for Dover. J. Porter
Dead End. M. Cruz
Dead End. C. Hilton
Dead End. S. Kingsley
Dead End. E. Lacy
Dead End. Ritchie Perry
Dead End. J. S. Strange
Dead End Dame. Pete Costello
Dead End Delivery. T. J. Santiago
Dead End in Mayfair. L. Gribble
Dead-End Option. R. Obstfeld
Dead End Street. W. B. Murphy
Dead End Street. L. Thayer
Dead Ending. J. Philips
Dead-Ends? P. Fanchette
Dead Ernest. James Mitchell
Dead Ernest. A. Tilton
Dead Even. C. C. Risenhoover
Dead Eye. John Reese
Dead Eye. J. Ross
Dead Faces Laughing. D. Delman
Dead Fall. P. Kirk
Dead Fall. D. Wilmer
Dead Fellah. M. Palmer
Dead File. B. Copper
Dead Fingers. E. Sutton
Dead Fires. Joan Gardiner
Dead Fix. M. Geller
Dead Flowers. Joan Gardiner
Dead Flowers. E. R. Johnson
Dead for a Ducat. L. Bruce
Dead for a Ducat. L. Payne
Dead for a Ducat. H. Reilly
Dead for a Dead Thing. P. Turnbull
Dead for a Penny. C. A. Goodrum
Dead for Danger. L. Foley
Dead for Pleasure. Kent Howard
Dead Game. M. Avallone
Dead Game. G. Hammond
Dead Girl. M. Thernstrom
Dead Girls. J. Ibarguengoitia
Dead Girl's Shoes. B. Cobb
Dead Give Away. Dulcie Gray
Dead Giveaway. S. Allan
Dead Giveaway. D. Blunt
Dead Giveaway. S. Brett
Dead Giveaway. J. Fluke

Dead Giveaway. H. L. Nelson
Dead Giveaway. M. Orr
Dead Giveaway. D. Wheelock
Dead Ground. P. Kerrigan
Dead Hand. I. R. G. Hart
Dead Hands Reaching. Marion Scott
Dead Harm No One. E. B. Quinn
Dead Have No Friends. J. Donavan
Dead Have No Mouths. C. Barry
Dead Head. H. Brenton
Dead Head. M. Horwitz
Dead Heart. C. Gibbon
Dead Heat. P. Ayres
Dead Heat. L. J. Barnes
Dead Heat. B. Hemyng
Dead Heat. W. Kim
Dead Heat. R. Obstfeld
Dead Heat. R. S. Prather
Dead Heat. F. Roderus
Dead Heat. Martin Russell
Dead Heat. P. Saxon
Dead Heat. Nick Stone
Dead Heat on a Merry-Go-Round. E. L. Heyman
Dead Hero. W. C. Gault
Dead If I Remember. S. H. Courtier
Dead in a Ditch. V. Gunn
Dead in a Row. Gwendoline Butler
Dead in Aqaba. C. H. Guenter
Dead in Bed. H. Kane
Dead in Bed. D. Keene
Dead in Center Field. P. Engleman
Dead in Guanajuato. P. Rock
Dead in No Time. N. A. Temple-Ellis
Dead in the Eye of the Law. G. Parker
Dead in the Morning. M. Yorke
Dead in the Scrub. B. J. Oliphant
Dead in the Water. T. Wood
Dead in the Water. B. Yates
Dead in Transit. M. Cronin
Dead Indeed. M. R. Hodgkin
Dead Ingleby. T. Gallon
Dead Innocent. P. Winn
Dead Irish. J. T. Lescroart
Dead Is Forever. A. E. Redmond
Dead Is the Door-Nail. P. Haggard
Dead Issue. C. A. Posey
Dead Kachina Man. T. Van Etten
Dead Knock. P. Turnbull
Dead Last. M. Geller
Dead Letter. D. Clark
Dead Letter. M. Ehrlich
Dead Letter. W. B. Murphy
Dead Letter. S. Regester
Dead Letter. J. Valin
Dead Letter Drop. P. James
Dead Letters. J. George
Dead Level. Russell Gordon
Dead Liberty. C. Aird
Dead Liberty. D. Craig
Dead Lie Still. W. L. Stuart
Dead Line. P. McCutchan
Dead Line. D. Pendleton
Dead-Line. W. C. Tuttle
Dead Lion. J. Bonett
Dead Little Rich Girl. N. Davis
Dead Little Rich Girl. T. Harknett
Dead Look Down. S. Esmond
Dead Loss. M. Cronin
Dead Loss. W. Massey
Dead Loss. R. Petrie
Dead Love Has Chains. M. E. Braddon
Dead Low Tide. J. D. MacDonald
Dead Lucky. Tom Howard
Dead Magician. E. E. Sullivan
Dead Man at the Window. J. Toussaint-Samat
Dead Man Blues. W. Irish
Dead Man Calling. G. Black
Dead Man Control. H. Reilly
Dead, Man, Dead. David Alexander
Dead Man Drifting. A. Sewart
Dead Man Falling. D. Cory
Dead Man Friday. J. F. Hutton
Dead Man Inside. V. Starrett
Dead Man Laughs. V. Gunn

Dead Man Manor. V. Williams
Dead Man Murder. B. Newman
Dead Man Out. C. B. Gilford
Dead Man Over All. Walter Allen
Dead Man Running. J. Blackburn
Dead Man Running. C. R. Lajeunesse
Dead Man Running. D. Pendleton
Dead Man Running. S. Picard
Dead Man Running. J. Warmbold
Dead Man Sings. Roland Daniel
Dead Man Smiling. L. F. Meares
Dead Man Talks Too Much. W. Dickinson
Dead Man Twice. C. Bush
Dead Man Walkin'. Seth Morgan
Dead Man's Alibi. L. Hollingsworth
Dead Man's Bay. C. Arley
Dead Man's Bay. M. Osborne
Dead Man's Bluff. B. Dunne
Dead Man's Bluff. R. Jeffries
Dead Man's Booty. O. Bradshaw
Dead Man's Chest. P. Capon
Dead Man's Chest. Jack Mann
Dead Man's Cocktail. B. Crowther
Dead Man's Corner. Roland Daniel
Dead Man's Court. M. H. Hervey
Dead Man's Cross. H. C. Davis
Dead Man's Derby. Bat Masters
Dead Man's Destiny. Martin Thomas
Dead Man's Diary. B. Halliday
Dead Man's Diary. Robert Hunter
Dead Man's Diary. C. Kernahan
Dead Man's Dower. S. Kyle
Dead Man's Effects. H. C. Bailey
Dead Man's Evidence. J. G. Brandon
Dead Man's Face. F. J. Fargus
Dead Man's Float. Roger Carr
Dead Man's Float. A. Dean
Dead Man's Float. R. W. Walker
Dead Man's Flower. C. Christopher
Dead Man's Folly. A. Christie
Dead Man's Gang. F. Delmere
Dead Man's Gate. J. Hunter
Dead Man's Gift. Z. Popkin
Dead Man's Gold. R. Bridges
Dead Man's Gold. J. A. Dunn
Dead Man's Gold. G. E. Rochester
Dead Man's Grip. Nicholas Carter
Dead Man's Hand. G. R. R. Martin
Dead Man's Hand. S. Matthews
Dead Man's Handle. J. Blackburn
Dead Man's Handle. P. O'Donnell
Dead Man's Hat. H. Footner
Dead Man's Heath. J. J. Farjeon
Dead Man's Hoard. T. J. O'Connell
Dead Man's Island. J. Hunter
Dead Man's Isle. Hedley Scott
Dead Man's Knock. J. D. Carr
Dead Man's Knock. J. N. Chance
Dead Man's Letters and other stories. E. S. Gardner
Dead Man's Love. T. Gallon
Dead Man's Mirror. A. Christie
Dead Man's Mooring. Bill Knox
Dead Man's Music. C. Bush
Dead Man's Path. J. B. Hilton
Dead Man's Peak. C. Brisbane
Dead Man's Plaything. E. Woodward
Dead Man's Plunder. G. W. Jones
Dead Man's Profits. D. Astlin
Dead Man's Quarry. I. Jerrold
Dead Man's Ransom. Ellis Peters
Dead Man's Riddle. M. Kelly
Dead Man's Rock. Q
Dead Man's Rooms. B. Delannoy
Dead Man's Sands. Stanton Hope
Dead Man's Secret. H. Clevely
Dead Man's Secret. J. Paeon
Dead Man's Secret. M. Plum
Dead Man's Secret. A. O. Pollard
Dead Man's Secret. Maxwell Scott
Dead Man's Secret. Donald Stuart
Dead Man's Shadow. Basil Carey
Dead Man's Shoes. R. C. Armour
Dead Man's Shoes. H. C. Bailey
Dead Man's Shoes. L. Bruce

Dead Man's Shoes. E. Cameron
Dead Man's Shoes. J. N. Chance
Dead Man's Shoes. M. Innes
Dead Man's Shoes. M. Trevor
Dead Man's Shoes. H. Windsor
Dead Man's Slippers. J. W. Heming
Dead Man's Step. L. L. Lynch
Dead Man's Story, and other tales. H. Herman
Dead Man's Tale. D. Pendleton
Dead Man's Tale. H. Pentecost
Dead Man's Tale. E. Queen
Dead Man's Tears. J. Newman
Dead Man's Thoughts. C. Wheat
Dead Man's Tide. W. Richards
Dead Man's Treasure. M. Brand
Dead Man's Treasure. J. Goodwin
Dead Man's Vengeance. Roland Daniel
Dead Man's Walk. R. S. Prather
Dead Man's Warning. V. Gunn
Dead Man's Watch. G. D. H. Cole
Dead March for Penelope. G. Bellairs
Dead March for Penelope Blow. G. Bellairs
Dead March in Three Keys. P. Curtis
Dead Matter. S. Frimmer
Dead Meat. W. G. Tapply
Dead Men. C. Rushton
Dead Men Alive. D. Cory
Dead Men Are Dangerous. Garnett Weston
Dead Men at the Folly. J. Rhode
Dead Men Do Tell. K. Trask
Dead Men Do Tell Tales. Donald Ross
Dead Men Don't Answer. T. Claymore
Dead Men Don't Give Seminars. D. Sucher
Dead Men Don't Marry. D. Sucher
Dead Men Don't Love. L. Shelton
Dead Men Don't Ski. P. Moyes
Dead Men Grin. B. Fischer
Dead Men Leave No Fingerprints. W. Chambers
Dead Men of Eden. V. M. Grayland
Dead Men of Sestos. P. Loraine
Dead Men Rise Up Never. C. Landon
Dead Men Rise Up Never. J. Pattinson
Dead Men Running. D. Niland
Dead Men Sing No Songs. M. Stuart
Dead Men Tell . . . R. Dark
Dead Men Tell. Johnny James
Dead Men Tell No Tales. E. W. Hornung
Dead Men Tell No Tales. G. A. Sale
Dead Men Turn Green. H. E. Wheeler
Dead Men's Bells. V. Gunn
Dead Men's Dollars. M. Crommelin
Dead Men's Fingers. P. Helm
Dead Men's Money. J. S. Fletcher
Dead Men's Morris. G. Mitchell
Dead Men's Plans. M. G. Eberhart
Dead Men's Shoes. M. E. Braddon
Dead Men's Shoes. L. Thayer
Dead Men's Tales. C. Junor
Dead Men's Tales. F. H. Kitchin
Dead Mr. Nixon. T. H. White
Dead Mrs. Stratton. A. Berkeley
Dead Mouse. Austen Allen
Dead Needle. Alex Hamilton
Dead-Nettle. J. B. Hilton
Dead Nigger. Anthony Gray
Dead of a Counterplot. S. Nash
Dead of a Physician. Fiona Sinclair
Dead of Jericho. C. Dexter
Dead of Night. J. C. McMullen
Dead of Night. P. Phil-Ebosie
Dead of Night. K. Steel
Dead of Night. S. Sterling
Dead of Night. P. Whalley
Dead of Summer. Josephine Gill
Dead of Summer. M. Kelly
Dead of Summer. D. Moseley
Dead of the Night. H. Carmichael
Dead of the Night. J. Reach
Dead of the Night. J. Rhode
Dead of Winter. M. Allegretto
Dead of Winter. F. Bramble
Dead of Winter. D. Cooper
Dead of Winter. C. Cornish
Dead of Winter. C. Hale

Dead of Winter. W. H. Hallahan
Dead of Winter. J. Pattinson
Dead of Winter. David Poyer
Dead of Winter. Marilyn Ross
Dead on Account. Gary Evans
Dead on Arrival. G. Bagby
Dead on Arrival. H. Gordon
Dead on Arrival. S. Marlowe
Dead on Arrival. S. Mitchell
Dead on Arrival. D. Simpson
Dead on Arrival. C. Stratton
Dead on Arrival. L. Thayer
Dead on Course. M. Black
Dead on Cue. G. Compton
Dead on Cue. A. Morice
Dead on Cue. D. Reid
Dead on Delivery. A. Bocca
Dead on Delivery. George Douglas
Dead on Departure. A. MacKinnon
Dead on Nine. J. Popplewell
Dead on Noon. N. Tarrant
Dead on Prediction. O. Norton
Dead on Target. D. Haring
Dead on the Dot. George Douglas
Dead on the Level. H. Nielsen
Dead on the Stick. R. Upton
Dead on the Stone. R. Amberley
Dead on the Track. J. Rhode
Dead on Time. A. Bocca
Dead on Time. A. Capelli
Dead on Time. P. Denver
Dead on Time. C. F. Gregg
Dead on Time. Stephen Grey
Dead on Time. O. John
Dead on Time. H. R. F. Keating
Dead on Time. N. Perrelli
Dead on Time. Colin Robertson
Dead on Time. C. Witting
Dead One in Berlin. U. Miehe
Dead Ones Don't Talk. R. Gar
Dead Opposite the Church. F. Vivian
Dead Opposites. B. Campbell
Dead or Alive. Ian Anderson
Dead or Alive. Anonymous
Dead or Alive. Stanley Bruce
Dead or Alive. J. Creasey
Dead or Alive. J. Templeton
Dead or Alive! C. H. Webstead
Dead or Alive. P. Wentworth
Dead Orchid. D. Lawrence
Dead Parrot. M. Keyes
Dead Past. J. Scholey
Dead Piano. H. Van Dyke
Dead Pigeon. J. M. Fox
Dead Pigeon. R. P. Hansen
Dead Pigeon. D. Haring
Dead Pigeon on Beethoven Street. S. Fuller
Dead Pigs at Hungry Farm. B. Graeme
Dead Prior. C. D. Lampen
Dead Pull Hitter. Alison Gordon
Dead Reckoning. Ken Blake
Dead Reckoning. J. E. Bloundelle-Burton
Dead Reckoning. F. Bonnamy
Dead Reckoning. E. Cannon
Dead Reckoning. P. Conde
Dead Reckoning. George Douglas
Dead Reckoning. B. Hamilton
Dead Reckoning. Sam Llewelyn
Dead Reckoning. G. Mitcham
Dead Reckoning. Alex Morrison
Dead Reckoning. I. Ruff
Dead Reckoning. K. Sandford
Dead Reckoning. B. Sarto
Dead Reckoning. R. Simons
Dead Reckoning. L. Thayer
Dead Reckoning. Linda Walters
Dead Regimental. B. Bavin
Dead Respectable. D. Reid
Dead Return. W. Carter
Dead Ride Hard. L. J. Vance
Dead Riders. E. O'Donnell
Dead Right. Jennette Lee
Dead Right. S. Sterling
Dead Ringer. F. Brown

Dead-Ringer. E. Cannon
Dead Ringer. J. H. Chase
Dead Ringer. F. Findley
Dead Ringer. A. Lyons
Dead Ringer. G. Mandel
Dead Ringer. R. Ormerod
Dead Ringer. Charles Ross
Dead Ringer. Bob Thomas
Dead Ringer. M. Warden
Dead Rite. F. Kane
Dead Romantic. S. Brett
Dead Room. H. Resnicow
Dead Run. J. Black
Dead Run. J. Foxx
Dead Run. T. Gibbs
Dead Run. H. Holley
Dead Run. R. Lockridge
Dead Run. R. Sheckley
Dead Runner. F. Ross
Dead Sailor and other stories. J. C. Robinson
Dead Say No. Max Gordon
Dead Sea Cipher. Elizabeth Peters
Dead Sea Fruit. M. E. Braddon
Dead Sea Submarine. A. Caillou
Dead Season. J. B. Owen
Dead Secret. R. Ackland
Dead Secret. W. Collins
Dead Secret. K. Sandford
Dead Secret. G. Verner
Dead Secret. Alan Williams
Dead Seed. W. C. Gault
Dead: Senate Office Building. M. Scherf
Dead Sequence. S. Rattray
Dead Set. T. H. Stone
Dead Shall Be Raised. G. Bellairs
Dead, She Was Beautiful. W. Masterson
Dead Shot. J. M. Fox
Dead Side. K. Davis
Dead Side of the Mike. Simon Brett
Dead Silence. J. Bruce
Dead Silence. S. Rattray
Dead Sinners. N. Lazenby
Dead Skip. J. Gores
Dead Sleep for Keeps. B. Winter
Dead Sleep Late. E. Kennedy
Dead Sleep Lightly. J. D. Carr
Dead Snakes' Venom. H. Kemp
Dead So Soon. Richard Grayson
Dead Spit. J. Edmonds
Dead Spy, Dead Secret. W. E. Corfield
Dead Stay Dumb. J. H. Chase
Dead Stick. L. J. Washburn
Dead Stop. M. Burton
Dead Stop. D. M. Disney
Dead Storage. G. Bagby
Dead Storage. L. Thayer
Dead Straight. D. Mackenzie
Dead Straight. A. Neilson
Dead Straight. Old Sleuth
Dead Stranger. Nicholas Carter
Dead Sure. H. Brean
Dead Sure. S. Sterling
Dead Take No Bows. R. Burke
Dead Tale-Tellers. J. N. Chance
Dead Thing in the Pool. A. M. Stein
Dead to Rights. Dennis Allan
Dead to Rights. K. Davis
Dead to Rites. S. Angus
Dead to the World. N. Baker
Dead to the World. F. Durbridge
Dead to the World. D. X. Manners
Dead to the World. S. Sterling
Dead to the World and No Diamonds for Eve. K. Slattery
Dead Travel Fast. R. Tate
Dead Tree Gives No Shelter. V. Scott
Dead Trouble. M. Carroll
Dead Trouble. D. Devine
Dead 'Un Wins. Aintree
Dead, Upstairs in the Tub. Michael Brett
Dead Voice. C. M. Wills
Dead Walk. G. Collins
Dead Water. N. Marsh
Dead Water. E. Radford

Dead Weight. R. Fenisong
Dead Weight. F. Kane
Dead Weight. B. Lecomber
Dead Weight. T. Magnuson
Dead Weight. A. Simmons
Dead Were Strangers. M. Clinten
Dead White. A. Ryan
Dead Winter. W. G. Tapply
Dead with Sorrow. P. Audemars
Dead Witness. Old Spicer
Dead Witness. D. Pedneau
Dead Woman. E. Walter
Dead Woman of the Year. H. Penteocst
Dead Woman's Ditch. S. Nash
Dead Women's Handbags. S. MacKay
Dead Wood. B. Parvin
Dead Wrong. G. Bagby
Dead Wrong. A. D. Burke
Dead Wrong. M. Cruz
Dead Wrong. W. S. Doxey
Dead Wrong. Nick Hall
Dead Wrong. R. S. Hastings
Dead Wrong. L. Holden
Dead Wrong. S. Sterling
Dead Yellow Women. D. Hammett
Dead Yesterday. R. Fenisong
Dead Yet Living. J. B. Williams
Dead Zone. Stephen King
Dead Zone. D. Stivers
Deadbolt. Jay Brandon
Deader They Fall. Peter Chambers
Deadest Thing You Ever Saw. Jonathan Ross
Deadeye. Sam Llewellyn
Deadfall. D. Cory
Deadfall. Patti Davis
Deadfall. K. Laumer
Deadfall. J. MacLean
Deadfall. L. Orde
Deadfall. B. Pronzini
Deadfall. T. A. Schock
Deadfall Trap. Barry Taylor
Deadhand. G. Sims
Deadhead. C. Carpenter
Deadhead. C. M. Warren
Deadheads. Reginald Hill
Deadlier of the Species. D. Reid
Deadlier Sex. B. S. Ballinger
Deadlier Sex. G. Manceron
Deadlier Sex. R. Striker
Deadlier Than the Male. J. C. Conaway
Deadlier Than the Male. James Gunn
Deadlier Than the Male. G. Holden
Deadlier Than the Male. H. Reymond
Deadliest Game. M. Jahn
Deadliest Game. P. McCurtin
Deadliest Profession. W. Boyles
Deadliest Show in Town. M. McQuay
Deadlight. A. Roy
Deadline. P. Brickhill
Deadline. T. B. Dewey
Deadline. J. Dunning
Deadline. J. Eastwood
Deadline. H. Howard
Deadline. T. Heald
Deadline. A. Irving
Deadline. D. Linton
Deadline. P. MacNee
Deadline. M. Russell
Deadline. T. Stacey
Deadline. H. Stahl
Deadline at Dawn. W. Irish
Deadline Death. D. Corbett
Deadline Dolly. D. Enefer
Deadline Down Under. D. Haring
Deadline for a Critic. W. X. Kienzle
Deadline for a Dame. M. Brody
Deadline for a Diplomat. S. Truss
Deadline for a Doll. C. Macey
Deadline for a Dream. B. Knox
Deadline for Danger. Arthur MacLean
Deadline for Destruction. C. L. Leonard
Deadline for Final Art. J. Adkins
Deadline for Loren. M. Clare
Deadline for Lovers. F. Nichols

Deadline for Macall. G. Fairlie
Deadline for Murder. H. Gould
Deadline in Jakarta. I. Stewart
Deadline Moscow. A. Redwood
Deadline Story. M. Bingley
Deadline 2 A.M. R. L. Pike
Deadlines. C. Dunn
Deadlines. I. Moffitt
Deadlines. E. Travis
Deadlock. R. Busby
Deadlock. R. Fenisong
Deadlock. C. Forbes
Deadlock. S. Paretsky
Deadlocked! L. P. Kelley
Deadly Ackee. J. Hadley
Deadly Advice. L. Ericson
Deadly Affair. E. Lacy
Deadly Affair. J. Le Carre
Deadly Affections. B. S. Mosiman
Deadly Aims. R. L. Gerard
Deadly Alliance. William Crawford
Deadly Appearances. G. Bowen
Deadly Aria. Paul Myers
Deadly Bedfellows. F. C. Davis
Deadly Beloved. W. Ard
Deadly Beloved. D. Haring
Deadly Beloved. Alanna Knight
Deadly Beloved. J. S. Strange
Deadly Birdman. P. Buck
Deadly Blonde. R. O. Saber
Deadly Blunder. J. Ritson
Deadly Bonds. E. Ryp
Deadly Boodle. J. M. Flynn
Deadly Breed. C. Burnes
Deadly But Delectable. K. T. McCall
Deadly Cadence. Paul Myers
Deadly Chance. P. Denver
Deadly Charade. M. Stall
Deadly Chase. Carter Cullen
Deadly Chase. J. M. Eshleman
Deadly Circle. J. T. Osborne
Deadly Climate. R. Barth
Deadly Climate. U. Curtiss
Deadly Combo. J. Farr
Deadly Communion. O. Brookes
Deadly Companion. N. B. Jacobs
Deadly Companions. B. Sang
Deadly Company. G. Kent
Deadly Connection. C. Cunningham
Deadly Contact. A. Dean
Deadly Convictions. P. Luber
Deadly Cotton Heart. R. Dennis
Deadly Crescendo. Paul Myers
Deadly Crusade. P. Chase
Deadly Crusader. D. Streib
Deadly Curve. D. Haring
Deadly Curves. E. Ronns
Deadly Cyborgs. P. Edwards
Deadly Daffodils. R. Silverwood
Deadly Dames. Malcolm Douglas
Deadly Darling. R. S. Prather
Deadly Date. A. F. Daniels
Deadly, Deadly Art. G. A. Ralston
Deadly Deal. S. Jason
Deadly Deceit. E. Burgess
Deadly Decoy. D. Haring
Deadly Decoy. J. Tabler
Deadly Decree. J. C. Lenehan
Deadly Deep. J. Messmann
Deadly Delight. A. M. Stein
Deadly Desire. R. Colby
Deadly Diamond. J. Storm
Deadly Diary. William Du Bois
Deadly Discretion. D. Ramsay
Deadly Ditto. C. Hale
Deadly Diva. Nick Carter
Deadly Doctor. S. Jason
Deadly Document. M. Bar-Zohar
Deadly Doll. J. Barbette
Deadly Doll. H. Kane
Deadly Dolly. L. Lessing
Deadly Doubles. Nick Carter
Deadly Dove. R. King
Deadly Dowager. E. Greenwood

Deadly Downbeat. Jonathan Burke
Deadly Dream. T. S. Drachman
Deadly Duo. M. Allingham
Deadly Duo. R. Jessup
Deadly Dwarf. K. Robeson
Deadly Dyke. B. Parvin
Deadly Edge. R. Stark
Deadly Election. M. Castle
Deadly Encounter. R. Woodley
Deadly Ernest. A. Bocca
Deadly Ernest. J. Cockin
Deadly Ernest. D. Lynch
Deadly Errand. M. Hillary
Deadly Eurasian. A. Cordell
Deadly Feast. Jane Collier
Deadly Finger. H. Kane
Deadly Foe. A. Sergeant
Deadly Force. M. Dixon
Deadly Fresco. L. Southney
Deadly Friend. D. Henstell
Deadly Friend. H. Pentecost
Deadly Friendship. C. Arkham
Deadly Frost. T. Moan
Deadly Game. N. Daniels
Deadly Game. Graham Hastings
Deadly Game. J. MacKenzie
Deadly Game. W. Manson
Deadly Game. Vince Robinson
Deadly Game. J. Yaffe
Deadly Games. F. Neznansky
Deadly Gold. J. Rossiter
Deadly Green. E. Harris
Deadly Green. J. Rossiter
Deadly Grounds. Patricia Wallace
Deadly Group Down Under. P. Morgan
Deadly Hall. J. D. Carr
Deadly Harvest. P. Mallory
Deadly Homecoming. T. George
Deadly Honeymoon. Lawrence Block
Deadly Honeymoon. A. C. MacLean
Deadly Horse-Race. H. Janson
Deadly Illusion. G. P. Williams
Deadly Image. G. H. Coxe
Deadly Impulse. C. B. Mason
Deadly in New York. C. Ramm
Deadly Inheritance. A. Andre
Deadly Inheritance. F. Reeves
Deadly Inheritance. Janice Robinson
Deadly Innocents. M. Sadler
Deadly Intent. G. Rosellini
Deadly Intent. A. Rowe
Deadly Interlude. M. O'Brine
Deadly Intrusion. W. Dillon
Deadly Is the Diamond. M. G. Eberhart
Deadly Is the Evil Tongue. A. Hocking
Deadly Isles. J. H. Vance
Deadly Jade. B. Sanders
Deadly Jest. V. Markham
Deadly Jigsaw. R. Bay
Deadly Joke. H. Pentecost
Deadly Joker. N. Blake
Deadly Justice. D. Barnes
Deadly Kind of Lonely. S. Forbes
Deadly Kisses. P. Berger
Deadly Kitten. Carter Brown
Deadly Knighthood. J. O. Mayo
Deadly Lady. J. Dial
Deadly Lampshade. Dulcie Gray
Deadly Legacy. W. Arden
Deadly Legacy. Christina Blake
Deadly Legacy. F. Usher
Deadly Lover. R. O. Saber
Deadly Lovers. Anthony Graham
Deadly Lure. W. Chambers
Deadly Manhunt. J. Rosenberger
Deadly Marriage. R. Jeffries
Deadly Matrimony. Jon Stevens
Deadly Medicine. H. L. Klawans
Deadly Meeting. R. Bernard
Deadly Memorial. P. Perry
Deadly Mermaid. J. A. Phillips
Deadly Messiah. Andrea Hill
Deadly Miss. Carter Brown
Deadly Miss Ashley. F. C. Davis

Deadly Mission. Roland Daniel
Deadly Mission. H. Janson
Deadly Misunderstanding. C. Biddle
Deadly Nature. H. Scott
Deadly Night-Blade. Austin Stone
Deadly Night Call. W. Irish
Deadly Night-Cap. H. Carmichael
Deadly Nightcap. F. Durbridge
Deadly Nightcap. H. Hawton
Deadly Nightcap. F. Stewart
Deadly Nightshade. K. Cameron
Deadly Nightshade. E. Daly
Deadly Nightshade. James Fraser
Deadly Nightshade. Jean Fraser
Deadly Nightshed. W. Maner
Deadly Noose. R. Foley
Deadly Objectives. L. A. Taylor
Deadly Obsession. D. Keys
Deadly One. H. McCutcheon
Deadly Orbit Mission. V. W. Mason
Deadly Party. L. DuBreuil
Deadly Pattern. Douglas Clark
Deadly Pavilion. Hilda Lawrence
Deadly Pawn. Magali
Deadly Pay-Off. W. H. Duhart
Deadly Payoff. M. Clerc
Deadly Payoff. F. Mullally
Deadly Pearl. M. Olden
Deadly Percheron. J. F. Bardin
Deadly Persuasion. S. Mitchell
Deadly Persuasion. D. Reid
Deadly Petard. R. Jeffries
Deadly Pickup. M. K. Ozaki
Deadly Picnic. J. Bingham
Deadly Piece. P. Hamill
Deadly Place to Stay. Josephine Bell
Deadly Poison. M. Pertwee
Deadly Prey. Ralph Hayes
Deadly Promise. M. F. Ballard
Deadly Purpose. R. P. Hanson
Deadly Putter. T. Dexter
Deadly Quiet. D. Enefer
Deadly Race. T. C. H. Jacobs
Deadly Reaper. Clark Smith
Deadly Record. N. W. Hooke
Deadly Reflections. M. Friedman
Deadly Rehearsal. Audrey Peterson
Deadly Relations. R. Gatenby
Deadly Relations. J. Thomson
Deadly Resolutions. A. Ashwood-Collins
Deadly Resurrection. J. T. Doyle
Deadly Resurrection. J. McCarty
Deadly Return. I. Lambot
Deadly Reunion. J. Ekstrom
Deadly Reunion. W. L. Harter
Deadly Reunion. R. Hayes
Deadly Reunion. M. McCray
Deadly Revenge. A. Askew
Deadly Rose. M. Lynch
Deadly Rose. K. Rich
Deadly Safari. K. McQuillan
Deadly Scarab. Nicholas Carter
Deadly Score. Paul Myers
Deadly Sea, Deadly Sand. I. Foster
Deadly Secret. A. Abbot
Deadly Secrets. S. R. Hawley
Deadly Seeds. R. Sapir
Deadly September. K. Kramer
Deadly Sex. Stuart Hall
Deadly Sex. J. Webb
Deadly Shade of Gold. J. D. MacDonald
Deadly Shore. J. Pattinson
Deadly Sickness. J. Penn
Deadly Side of the Square. Lee Jordan
Deadly Sights. R. L. Gerard
Deadly Silence. L. Derrick
Deadly Silents. L. Killough
Deadly Snow. J. Decker
Deadly Sonata. P. Myers
Deadly Stakes. H. F. Wiser
Deadly State of Mind. L. Hays
Deadly Streak. D. Enefer
Deadly Streets. H. Ellison
Deadly Summer. G. M. Barnes

Deadly Sunshade. P. A. Taylor
Deadly the Daring. W. Randall
Deadly to Bed. D. Tracy
Deadly Trade. Bradshaw Jones
Deadly Transaction. A. Livingstone
Deadly Trap. H. Pentecost
Deadly Travelers. D. Eden
Deadly Treatment. C. Denman
Deadly Triangle. R. Roleine
Deadly Triplets. Adrienne Kennedy
Deadly Truth. H. McCloy
Deadly Valentine. C. G. Hart
Deadly Variations. P. Myers
Deadly Weapon. Wade Miller
Deadly Web. J. Gearon
Deadly Welcome. J. D. MacDonald
Deadly Welcome. K. Rothrock
Deadman's Bay. L. A. Knight
Deadman's Game. R. Dennis
Deadman's Rest. N. Dorer
Deadspeak. B. Lumley
Deadwood Dick. T. Taggart
Deadwood Dick's Last Shot. E. L. Wheeler
Deaf, Dumb and Blonde. Anthony Morton
Deaf-Mute Murders. V. Loder
Deafman No Hear. D. Fulani
Deaken's War. B. Freemantle
Deal in Death. A. O. Pollard
Deal in Diamonds. Anonymous
Deal in Diamonds. Nicholas Carter
Deal in Diamonds, and other stories. J. Burtt
Deal in Letters. F. M. White
Deal in Violence. W. Arden
Deal Me Out. J. S. Blazer
Deal Me Out. P. Corris
Deal Me Out. D. Haring
Deal Me Out. S. Morelli
Deal of Death Caps. G. M. Wilson
Deal of the Century. I. K. Martin
Dealer. Max Collins
Dealer. V. Torrio
Dealer in Antiques. B. Tozer
Dealer in Death and other stories. Arthur Morris
Dealer of Death. D. Hartman
Dealer of Death. F. MacIsaac
Dealer's Move. Steve Wilson
Dealer's War. Steve Wilson
Dealer's Wheels. Steve Wilson
Dealing Out Death. W. T. Ballard
Deals. B. Pain
Dean and Jecinora. V. L. Whitechurch
Dean Dunham. H. Alger
Dean of Clonbury. P. Roche
Dean's Daughters. H. Adams
Dean's Death. A. Lawrence
Dear Brother, Here Departed. Stella Phillips
Dear Conspirator. G. Goodchild
Dear Daughter Dead. S. B. Hough
Dear, Dead Days. J. Barbette
Dear, Dead Girls. N. Morland
Dear, Dead Harry. Milton Scott
Dear Dead Mother-in-Law. K. Hill
Dear Dead Professor. K. A. LaRoche
Dear Dead Woman. Anthony Gilbert
Dear, Dead Women. D. Chambers
Dear, Deadly Beloved. J. Flagg
Dear Dear Cara. G. Z. Stone
Dear Deadly Past. Whit Harrison
Dear Delinquent. J. Popplewell
Dear Delusion. E. Woodward
Dear Departed. Anne Burton
Dear Fatherland. J. M. Simmel
Dear Fools. A. Soutar
Dear Hannah. T. Hauser
Dear Hungarian Friend. G. Napier
Dear John. Susan Lee
Dear Judgment. J. Crosby
Dear Laura. J. Stubbs
Dear Liar. D. M. Low
Dear Life. H. E. Bates
Dear Lost Love. A. Maybury
Dear Miss Demeanor. Joan Hess
Dear Mr. Capote. G. Lish
Dear Mr. Right. E. Dewhurst

Dear Murderer. S. L. Clowes
Dear Murderer. R. Parry-Ellis
Dear Old Gentleman. G. Goodchild
Dear Phoebe. T. Taggart
Dear Pretender. A. R. Colver
Dear Traitor. J. March
Dearest Enemy. Sara Woods
Dearly Beloved Wives. W. H. L. Crauford
Death. Woody Allen
Death a la King. I. Waitt
Death About Face. F. Kane
Death Across the Tamagash. M. Hastings
Death Adder Dreaming. I. Moffitt
Death After Breakfast. H. Pentecost
Death After Dark. F. Griffin
Death After Evensong. Douglas Clark
Death After Lunch. R. D. Abrahams
Death After School. A. Holden
Death Against the Clock. Anthony Gilbert
Death Against Venus. D. Chambers
Death Ain't Commercial. G. Bagby
Death Amidst Satin. E. Woodward
Death Among Doctors. J. G. Edwards
Death Among Friends. H. Ainsworth
Death Among Friends. C. Hare
Death Among Friends. Lange Lewis
Death Among Strangers. D. Laiken
Death Among the Dunes. A. Infante
Death Among the Lilacs. A. Palen
Death Among the Orchids. T. B. Morris
Death Among the Professors. K. Sproul
Death Among the Sands. E. Mack
Death Among the Stars. K. Giles
Death Among the Stars. Jean Marsh
Death Among the Sunbathers. E. R. Punshon
Death Among the Tulips. A. Hocking
Death Among the Writers. E. De Caire
Death and a Dark Horse. Martin Thomas
Death and a Madonna. J. O'Hagen
Death and Benedict. I. Bayne
Death and Bitters. K. Christian
Death and Blintzes. S. Rosen
Death and Bright Water. J. Mitchell
Death and Chicanery. P. MacDonald
Death and Circumstance. H. Waugh
Death and Daisy Bland. N. Blake
Death and Festivals. Richard Blum
Death and His Brother. M. Bidwell
Death and His Sweetheart. Winifred Duke
Death and Letters. E. Daly
Death and Lila Fell. M. J. Johnson
Death and Lilacs. F. Bayard
Death and Little Brother. C. Knight
Death and Little Girl Blue. V. J. Hanson
Death and Mary Dazill. M. Fitt
Death and Mr. Gilly. W. M. Duncan
Death and Mr. Potter. R. Foley
Death and Mr. Prettyman. K. Giles
Death and Mrs. Lovely. E. Wake
Death and Still Life. D. Launay
Death and Taxes. T. B. Dewey
Death and Taxes. D. Dodge
Death and the Archdeacon. N. Harman
Death and the Bridegroom. F. Hurt
Death and the Bright Day. M. Fitt
Death and the Chaste Apprentice. Robert Barnard
Death and the Dancing Footman. N. Marsh
Death and the Dark Daughter. F. Hurt
Death and the Dear Girls. J. Stagge
Death and the Devil. P. Whelton
Death and the Diplomat. M. Scherf
Death and the Dogwalker. A. J. Orde
Death and the Durlings. V. Fletcher
Death and the Dutch Uncle. P. Moyes
Death and the Dutiful Daughter. A. Morice
Death and the Gentle Bull. R. Lockridge
Death and the Gilded Man. Carter Dickson
Death and the Golden Boy. N. Morland
Death and the Golden Image. Whyte Hall
Death and the Good Life. R. Hugo
Death and the I Ching. E. Michaels
Death and the I Ching. L. Rosenfeld
Death and the Jack Shade. W. S. Brady
Death and the Joyful Woman. Ellis Peters

Death and the Leaping Ladies. C. Drummond
Death and the Mad Heroine. S. F. X. Dean
Death and the Maiden. E. Lindall
Death and the Maiden. J. K. MacDougall
Death and the Maiden. G. Mitchell
Death and the Maiden. Q. Patrick
Death and the Maiden. S. Radley
Death and the Naked Lady. J. Flagg
Death and the Night Watches. V. Bell
Death and the Pleasant Voices. M. Fitt
Death and the Pregnant Virgin. S. T. Haymon
Death and the Princess. R. Barnard
Death and the Professor. E. Radford
Death and the Professors. K. Sproul
Death and the Remembrancer. F. Lyall
Death and the Shortest Day. M. Fitt
Death and the Single Girl. E. Lewis
Death and the Sky Above. A. Garve
Death and the South Wind. F. Lester
Death and the Spider. G. Stockbridge
Death and the Trumpets of Tuscany. H. W. Jones
Death and the Visiting Fireman. H. R. F. Keating
Death and the Women. A. Golsworthy
Death and Variations. I. Baker
Death Angel. Robert Black
Death Angel. C. B. Clason
Death Angel's Shadow. K. E. Wagner
Death Answers the Bell. V. Williams
Death Arms. K. W. Jeter
Death—As in Matador. L. V. Roper
Death at a Masquerade. M. E. Corne
Death at Abu Mina. P. William
Death at Appledore Towers. G. Lientz
Death at Aranshore. K. Wade
Death at Ash House. M. Burton
Death at Breakfast. J. Rhode
Death at Broadcasting House. V. Gielgud
Death at Charity's Point. W. G. Tapply
Death at Chestnut Hill. C. Nicolai
Death at Court Lady. S. Horler
Death at Crane's Court. E. Dillon
Death at Dakar. K. O'Neil
Death at Dale's End. J. Brooke
Death at Dancing Stones. M. Fitt
Death at Datchets. F. J. Whaley
Death at Dawn. D. Keene
Death at Dayton's Folly. V. Rath
Death at Deep End. P. Wentworth
Death at Deepwood Grange. Michael Underwood
Death at Devil-Fish Point. D. Boyle
Death at Duncan House. P. Garfield
Death at Dusk. P. Ketchum
Death at Dyke's Corner. E. C. R. Lorac
Death at Eight Bells. F. A. Kummer
Death at Every Door. A. Capelli
Death at Flight. C. Willock
Death at Flood Tide. L. A. Brennan
Death at Four Corners. Anthony Gilbert
Death at Half-Term. Josephine Bell
Death at Hallows End. L. Bruce
Death at Heel. F. Andreas
Death at Her Elbow. J. M. Walsh
Death at Her Fingertips. J. M. Fox
Death at Lord's. B. Newman
Death at Lover's Leap. R. G. Dean
Death at Low Tide. M. Burton
Death at My Elbow. H. Desmond
Death at My Heels. D. Kirby
Death at My Heels, and other stories. M. Hervey
Death at Newport. D. Hinch
Death at No. 47. C. Wallace
Death at Nostalgia Street. Wade Wright
Death at One Below. H. Hamilton
Death at Peak Hour. Jean Marsh
Death at Pyford Hall. D. Fisher
Death at Roman Farm. John Lloyd
Death at St. Anslem's. I. Holland
Death at St. Asprey's School. L. Bruce
Death at Salterton Court. R. Marr
Death at Screaming Pool. C. Ryland
Death at Sea. V. Robinson
Death at Sea. R. Sale
Death at Sea. L. White
Death at 7:10. H. F. S. Moore

Death at Shinglestrand. P. Capon
Death at Slack Water. D. W. MacArthur
Death at Springtime. D. C. Andrews
Death at Swaythling Court. J. J. Connington
Death at the BBC. J. Sherwood
Death at the Bank. B. Francis
Death at the Bar. C. Drummond
Death at the Bar. N. Marsh
Death at "The Bottoms." A. B. Cunningham
Death at the Cascades. B. J. Farmer
Death at the Chase. M. Innes
Death at the Chateau. M. Tinayre
Death at the Chateau Noir. E. Radford
Death at the Club. M. Burton
Death at the Crossings. J. Nowak
Death at the Crossroads. M. Burton
Death at the Cut. D. Kiker
Death at the Dam. C. F. Adams
Death at the Dance. J. Rhode
Death at the Depot. D. G. Hastings
Death at the Dog. J. Cannan
Death at the Dolphin. N. Marsh
Death at the Door. Anthony Gilbert
Death at the Dowager. B. Huber
Death at the Drome. W. R. Hutton
Death at the Drome. W. K. Watts
Death at the Easel. M. Baker
Death at the Feast. Nicholas Carter
Death at the Furlong Post. C. Drummond
Death at the Games. J. MacGowan
Death at the Golden Cockerel. W. R. Hutton
Death at the Golden Crown. A. Dick
Death at the Helm. J. Rhode
Death at the Horse Show. V. Loder
Death at the Inn. R. A. Freeman
Death at the Inn. L. Gribble
Death at the Inn. J. Rhode
Death at the Isthmus. G. H. Coxe
Death at the Manor. M. E. Corne
Death at the Medical Board. Josephine Bell
Death at the Mike. A. Eichler
Death at the Opera. G. Mitchell
Death at the Pelican. C. M. Wills
Death at the President's Lodging. M. Innes
Death at the Rodeo. E. Queen
Death at the Salutation. F. Vivian
Death at the Strike. C. Willock
Death at the Theatre. R. McRae
Death at the Towers. F. C. Tickner
Death at the Villa. M. Dalton
Death at the Wedding. M. Duke
Death at the Wedding. A. Hocking
Death at the Wheel. V. Loder
Death at Three. C. Rice
Death at Traitor's Gate. V. Gunn
Death at Windward Hill. H. J. Hultman
Death at Yew Corner. R. Forrest
Death Audit. J. A. Howard
Death Awaits Thee. M. Lang
Death Ball. E. Rees
Death Be My Destiny. N. H. Perrin
Death Be Nimble. R. N. Smith
Death Beads. B. Hagman
Death Beam. R. Moss
Death Beat. Mike Warden
Death Beats the Band. I. Shurman
Death Beats the Deadline. F. Struan
Death Beckons Quietly. W. M. Duncan
Death Bed. S. Greenleaf
Death Before Bedtime. E. Box
Death Before Breakfast. C. F. Adams
Death Before Breakfast. G. Bellairs
Death Before Breakfast. D. Fearon
Death Before Day. M. Dalman
Death Before Dinner. E. C. R. Lorac
Death Before Dying. Collin Wilcox
Death Before Honour. David Hume
Death Before Launching. H. J. Quartermain
Death Before Mirth. N. Spain
Death Begs the Question. L. Eby
Death Behind the Door. F. W. Gumley
Death Behind the Door. V. MacClure
Death Bell. Edison Marshall
Death Below the Dam. E. H. Fonseca

Death Below Zero. H. S. Head
Death Below Zero. T. Muir
Death Below Zero. A. Venters
Death Beneath Jerusalem. R. Bax
Death Beneath the River. J. Rowland
Death Beside the Sea. M. Babson
Death Beside the Seaside. M. Babson
Death Beyond the Go-Thru. B. Kendrick
Death Beyond the Nile. Jessica Mann
Death Bids for Corners. A. Dickson
Death Bird. R. St. Clair
Death Bird Contract. P. Atlee
Death Blade. P. Case
Death Blanks the Screen. L. O'Donnell
Death Blew Out the Match. K. M. Knight
Death Boards the Lazy Lady. R. Darby
Death Box. E. Lacale
Death Box. L. N. Morgan
Death Box. B. G. Quin
Death Brand. I. Gregory
Death Breaks the Ring. V. Rath
Death Bringers. D. Orgill
Death-Bringers. Dell Shannon
Death Brings a Storke. A. Boutell
Death Brings in the New Year. G. Bellairs
Death Brokers. P. D. Ballard
Death Burns the Candle. R. Trevor
Death Business. Anthony Graham
Death by Analysis. G. Slovo
Death by Apparition. Reginald Campbell
Death by Appointment. F. Bonnamy
Death—by Appointment. J. Corbett
Death by Appointment. C. Goodall
Death by Appointment. H. Lugar
Death by Arrangement. D. Alberts
Death by Arrangement. J. Kershaw
Death by Arrangement. L. Meynell
Death by Association. R. Lockridge
Death by Ballot. John Laffin
Death by Bequest. F. Hurt
Death by Bequest. M. McMullen
Death by Chalk Face. J. Gale
Death by Chocolates. P. Freed
Death by Clue. H. C. Beck
Death by Computer. D. M. Disney
Death by Deception. A. Wingate
Death by Demonstration. P. Carlon
Death by Design. A. Derleth
Death by Design. A. Nash
Death by Desire. R. Goyne
Death by Dreaming. J. M. White
Death by Drowning. Robin Daniel
Death by Dynamite. J. L. Bonney
Death by Fire. H. Pentecost
Death by Fire. C. F. Roe
Death by Gaslight. M. Kurland
Death by Hoax. Lionel Black
Death by Inches. Dell Shannon
Death by Invitation. G. Stockwell
Death by Marriage. E. G. Cousins
Death by Misadventure. K. Greenwood
Death by Misadventure. B. Malim
Death by Misadventure. M. Underwood
Death by Moonlight. M. Innes
Death by My Destiny. N. H. Perrin
Death by Night. J. Creasey
Death by Order. W. Byford-Jones
Death by Proxy. J. Crosby
Death by Proxy. E. B. Ronald
Death by Remote Control. E. Hogarth
Death by Request. R. John
Death by Sheer Torture. R. Barnard
Death by Surprise. C. G. Hart
Death by the Day. Lawrence Fisher
Death by the Gaff. J. H. Vahey
Death by the Lake. L. Bruce
Death by the Lake. Roland Daniel
Death by the Lake. W. Martyn
Death by the Mistletoe. A. MacVicar
Death by the Nile. A. Parsons
Death by the Radio. J. W. Lee
Death by the Riverside. J. M. Reddmann
Death by the Sea. J. Turner
Death by the Seine. B. Sarto

Death by the Zodiac. M. Farnsworth
Death by Treble Chance. E. G. Cousins
Death by Two Hands. P. Drax
Death by Water. M. Innes
Death Call. D. Haring
Death Called at Night. R. A. Bennett
Death Called China 2244. R. Carni
Death Called Twice. C. B. Molyneaux
Death Calling—Collect. D. Tracy
Death Calls at Scotland Yard. J. E. Nyson
Death Calls on the Witches. J. Martenson
Death Calls the Jester. H. E. Wheeler
Death Calls the Shots. B. Knox
Death Calls the Tune. F. W. Gumley
Death Calls Three Times. G. Barnett
Death Came Back. E. Hale
Death Came Back. C. Kingston
Death Came by Night. G. Bligh
Death Came Dancing. K. M. Knight
Death Came in Lucerne. M. Stand
Death Came in Straw. P. Piper
Death Came in the Studio. M. Stand
Death Came Late. J. B. O'Sullivan
Death Came Smiling. E. Dewhurst
Death Came Softly. E. C. R. Lorac
Death Came to Lighthouse Steps. M. Stand
Death Came Too Soon. M. Stand
Death Came Too Soon. I. E. Ward
Death Came Uninvited. E. Backhouse
Death Came with Darkness. M. Stand
Death Came with Diamonds. M. Stand
Death Came with Flowers. M. Stand
Death Camp Colombia. Dan Schmidt
Death Can Wait. G. W. Cooke
Death Cancels the Evidence. R. H. Leitfred
Death Cap. S. Brydon
Death Cap. R. T. Campbell
Death Cap. J. Thomson
Death-Cap Dancers. G. Mitchell
Death Car Surfside. P. Morgan
Death Card. J. B. O'Sullivan
Death Care. R. Haigh
Death Carries a Cane. Sherwood King
Death Casts a Long Shadow. Anthony Gilbert
Death Casts a Lure. M. Johnston
Death Casts a Shadow. L. Marshall
Death Casts a Vote. M. Yates
Death Casts No Shadow. P. G. Larbalestier
Death Catches Up with Mr. Kluck. Xantippe
Death Cell. R. Goulart
Death Ceremony. James Melville
Death Certificate. J. Wainwright
Death Changes His Mind. Frank King
Death Charge. A. Caillou
Death Charter. E. L. Adams
Death Check. R. Sapir
Death Checks In. S. Ransome
Death Chemist. J. N. Chance
Death Chime. L. Gribble
Death Circle. Nicholas Carter
Death Claims. Joan Banks
Death Claims. J. Hansen
Death Climbs a Hill. E. Backhouse
Death Code. D. Stivers
Death Coins. W. S. Masterman
Death Collection. M. Arrighi
Death Comes As the End. A. Christie
Death Comes Ashore. E. F. Charles
Death Comes at Night. K. Ingram
Death Comes by Air. N. Leslie
Death Comes by Post. J. Carr
Death Comes Courting. I. Garland
Death Comes Early. W. R. Cox
Death Comes Easy. B. Feltner
Death Comes Grinning. W. Creed
Death Comes Home. J. Dekker
Death Comes in the Night. J. M. Spender
Death Comes Incognito. R. Edwards
Death Comes Laughing. V. Gunn
Death Comes Like a Thief. V. Ellis
Death Comes on Derby Day. Alan Muir
Death Comes on Friday. L. Day
Death Comes Staccato. G. Slovo
Death Comes Swiftly. J. G. Brandon

Death Comes to a Party. A. McAllister
Death Comes to Cambers. E. R. Punshon
Death Comes to Casanova. H. G. Coulter
Death Comes to Dinner. A. Colin
Death Comes to Dinner. S. Gluck
Death Comes to Dinner. P. Yates
Death Comes to Fanshawe. J. Corbett
Death Comes to Kenya. N. Leslie
Death Comes to Lady's Steps. W. M. Duncan
Death Comes to Perigord. J. Ferguson
Death Comes to Rehearsal. R. Sharp
Death Comes to Tea. T. Du Bois
Death Comes to the Hermit. J. Harrell
Death Comes Too Late. R. Trevor
Death Comes Wholesale. R. Drayton
Death Commits Bigamy. J. M. Fox
Death Conducts a Tour. R. Darby
Death Connection. R. Brandt
Death Convention. D. Winsor
Death Counts Five. H. L. Gates
Death Counts Three. H. Carmichael
Death Cracks a Bottle. K. Giles
Death Crag. B. Gaston
Death Cries in the Street. S. A. Krasney
Death Cries Ole. M. Mundy
Death Croons the Blues. J. Ronald
Death Crosses the Line. E. F. Charles
Death Cruise. J. Cannon
Death Cruises South. R. Denbie
Death Cry. D. Hauck
Death Crystal. J. E. Ames
Death Cues the Pageant. E. Ainsworth
Death Curse. A. O. Pollard
Death Cuts a Caper. D. Magarshack
Death Cuts a Silhouette. D. B. Olsen
Death Cuts the Deck. R. L. Fish
Death Cuts the Film. C. Saxby
Death Cycle. C. Runyon
Death Dams the Tide. J. Guildford
Death Dances Thrice. J. C. Lenehan
Death Darkens Council. V. Bell
Death Date. R. Wilkes-Hunter
Death Date for Dolores. Carter Brown
Death Dates a Dame. J. Death
Death Deal. Anonymous
Death Deal. J. Hild
Death Deal. B. E. Miller
Death Dealer. Nick Carter
Death Dealer. James Scott
Death Dealers. I. Asimov
Death Dealers. B. Gaston
Death Dealers. F. Meadows
Death Dealers. M. Spillane
Death Deals a Diamond. N. Wray
Death Deals a Double. J. Bude
Death Deals in Diamonds. Bradshaw Jones
Death Deals in Diamonds. Hal Murray
Death Dealt the Cards. E. Hale
Death Deep Down. D. J. Marlowe
Death Defies the Doctor. B. Cobb
Death Defies the Doctor. Denis Muir
Death Delivers a Postcard. J. Philips
Death Demands an Audience. H. Reilly
Death Demon. J. K. Stafford
Death Department. B. Knox
Death Descending. Karen Campbell
Death Designs a Dress. E. M. Robinson
Death Devils. P. Edwards
Death Diamonds. Anonymous
Death Diamonds. L. Cotten
Death Dines Out. T. Du Bois
Death Disciple. Robin Moore
Death Disposes. M. Dalman
Death Disturbs Mr. Jefferson. A. Hocking
Death Dives Deep. M. Avallone
Death Do Not Praise. Pauline Bell
Death Do Us Part. S. Noel
Death Do Us Part. Maude Parker
Death-Doctor. W. LeQueux
Death Doll. A. Goddard
Death Doubles Death. G. Braddon
Death Down East. E. Blake
Death Down East. H. Norwood
Death Down Home. E. K. Sandstrom

Death Down Under. C. McNab
Death Draws the Curtain. R. Watkins
Death Draws the Line. J. Iams
Death Dream. G. Masterton
Death Dreams. W. Katz
Death Drive. M. E. Cooke
Death Drives the Lead Car. P. Moore
Death Drop. B. M. Gill
Death Drops Delilah. Q. Mario
Death Drops the Pilot. G. Bellairs
Death Drum. M. Peterson
Death Duel. A. Hocking
Death Dupes a Lady. R. Howes
Death Duty Swindle. W. J. Bayfield
Death Echo. J. Sandys
Death Elects a Mayor. J. G. Edwards
Death Elsewhere. Barbara Paul
Death en Voyage. R. Grayson
Death Enters the Lists. O. Mills
Death Enters the Ward. I. Bayne-Powell
Death Express. A. Eadie
Death-Face, the Detective. Anonymous
Death Fear. W. Martyn
Death Files for Congress. T. O. Henle
Death Filled the Glass. C. Armstrong
Death Film. P. R. Shore
Death Finds a Foothold. G. Carr
Death Finds a Target. M. Fitt
Death Finds the Day. Alan White
Death Finds the Gloves. J. Sandys
Death Fire. L. Bennet-Thompson
Death Fires. R. Faust
Death Flash. J. G. Rowe
Death Flies High. J. R. Holden
Death Flies High. D. L. Teilhet
Death Flies Low. H. Park
Death Flies Low. H. Shepherd
Death Flies West. J. F. Bonnell
Death Flight. C. Miron
Death Flight. A. O. Pollard
Death Flight. D. Wiles
Death Follows a Formula. N. Gayle
Death Follows the Flower Show. E. G. Seibert
Death for a Dancer. E. X. Giroux
Death for a Darling. E. X. Giroux
Death for a Dietician. E. X. Giroux
Death for a Dilettante. E. X. Giroux
Death for a Doctor. E. X. Giroux
Death for a Doll. S. Morelli
Death for a Double. E. X. Giroux
Death for a Dreamer. E. X. Giroux
Death for a Dropout. P. Bloxham
Death for a Dumb-Bell. B. Sarto
Death for a Holiday. D. P. Le Huray
Death for a Hussy. A. Holt
Death for a Hussy. A. L. Martin
Death for a Playmate. J. Ball
Death for a Theatre Filly. A. Williamson
Death for a Traitor. N. MacKenzie
Death for Adonis. E. X. Giroux
Death for an Emerald. R. H. Lees
Death for Auld Lang Syne. J. Sharkey
Death for Charity. G. W. Jones
Death for Dear Clara. Q. Patrick
Death for Deborah. V. Heley
Death for Dollars. N. Thurley
Death for Hire. J. Nazel
Death for Love. A. F. Garner
Death for Madame. R. T. Campbell
Death for Mr. Big. J. Gonzales
Death for My Beloved. D. M. Disney
Death for My Neighbor. Muriel Bradley
Death for Safe Custody. B. Francis
Death for Safety. E. Dennis
Death for Sale. N. Cain
Death for Sale. H. Kane
Death for Sale. N. Morland
Death for Short. J. Gale
Death for the Lady. S. Vanderveer
Death for the Surgeon. G. Eldredge
Death for Two. C. Ashton
Death Force. J. Arnett
Death Forms Threes. C. Robbins
Death Framed in Silver. Alice Campbell

Death Freak. J. Luckless
Death from a Top Hat. C. Rawson
Death from Below. G. Ashe
Death from Disclosure. Ian Stuart
Death from Nowhere. S. Towne
Death from the Air. P. Conde
Death Fugue. P. McGuire
Death Fungus. W. Allen
Death Fuse. M. Russell
Death Gamble. J. A. Dunn
Death Gamble. G. R. Sims
Death Gambit. J. Dekker
Death Game. A. O. Pollard
Death Game. Stuart White
Death Game—Five Players. A. Sewart
Death Games. M. Jahn
Death Games. D. Pendleton
Death Gang. D. Dell
Death Gang. A. Skene
Death Gets a Head. A. R. McKenzie
Death Gets a Place. J. Brown
Death Gets an A. R. H. R. Smithies
Death Giver. M. Grant
Death Glides In. A. L. Elsworthy
Death Glow. R. Wallace
Death Goes Ashore. A. Glanville
Death Goes by Bus. L. Cargill
Death Goes Caving. G. Usher
Death Goes Fishing. Edward Lee
Death Goes Hunting. C. Massie
Death Goes Native. Max Long
Death Goes on Skis. N. Spain
Death Goes Skiing. N. Schier
Death Goes to a Party. M. Jaffe
Death Goes to a Reunion. K. M. Knight
Death Goes to Brussels. Rosa Lamber
Death Goes to School. Q. Patrick
Death Goes to Sea. J. Robertson
Death Goes to the Bahamas. K. Hess
Death Goes to the Fair. J. Courage
Death Goes Touring. F. W. Gumley
Death Goes Window Shopping. F. A. Symonds
Death Gong. S. Jepson
Death Grasp. T. P. Prest
Death Greets a Guest. C. Ashton
Death Grip. J. Ahern
Death Grip. Al Conroy
Death Ground. E. Gorman
Death Grows on You. Niki Hill
Death Hall. M. Reisner
Death Hand Play. Nick Carter
Death Has a Double. Frank King
Death Has a Name. D. Pendleton
Death Has a Past. A. Boutell
Death Has a Shadow. M. Procter
Death Has a Small Voice. F. Lockridge
Death Has a Thousand Doors. W. Cooper
Death Has a Thousand Doors. M. Marlette
Death Has a Thousand Entrances. P. Helm
Death Has a Will. A. R. Long
Death Has Deep Roots. M. Gilbert
Death Has Four Hands. Hilda Lawrence
Death Has Green Eyes! Nicholas Carter
Death Has Green Fingers. Lionel Black
Death Has Many Doors. F. Brown
Death Has Many Doors. S. MacKenzie
Death Has My Number. J. Laffin
Death Has No Tongue. J. Cowdroy
Death Has No Weight. B. Luigi
Death Has Scarlet Candles. D. Lockwood
Death Has Seven Faces. H. Austin
Death Has Ten Thousand Doors. B. Chetwynd
Death Has Three Lives. B. Halliday
Death Has Two Doors. V. Bell
Death Has Two Faces. N. Herries
Death Has Two Faces. E. Radford
Death Has Two Hands. D. Lawrence
Death Haunts the Charnel Estate. Jackson Evans
Death Haunts the Dark Lane. A. B. Cunningham
Death Haunts the Lounge. A. C. Trevor
Death Haunts the Repertory. T. A. Plummer
Death Heads North. J. B. Hendryx
Death Her Destination. W. Jardine
Death Hides a Mask. M. E. Corne

Death Hitches a Ride. M. L. Weiss
Death Hits the Jackpot. J. Tiger
Death Holds His Court. N. MacKenzie
Death House. C. Brisbane
Death House. Roland Daniel
Death House Doll. D. Kenne
Death Hunch. R. Humphreys
Death Hunt. P. McCurtin
Death Importer. J. N. Chance
Death in a Bowl. R. Whitfield
Death in a Chilly Corner. I. Oellrichs
Death in a Cold Climate. R. Barnard
Death in a Dark Pool. H. Van Rensburg
Death in a Deck Chair. K. K. Beck
Death in a Deck-Chair. M. Kennedy
Death in a Distant Land. Nancy Livingston
Death in a Domino. R. Pertwee
Death in a Downpour. K. McComb
Death in a Duffle Coat. M. Burton
Death in a High Latitude. J. R. L. Anderson
Death in a Hurry. G. Ashe
Death in a Lighthouse. E. Ronns
Death in a Little Town. R. C. Woodthorpe
Death in a Million Living Rooms. P. McGerr
Death in a Mist. E. Salter
Death in a Pheasant's Eye. James Fraser
Death in a Quiet Place. E. G. Cousins
Death in a Salubrious Place. W. J. Burley
Death in a Serene City. E. Sklepowich
Death in a Sleeping City. J. Wainwright
Death in a Small Southern Town. R. L. McKinney
Death in a Small World. L. Colburn
Death in a Sunny Place. R. Lockridge
Death in a Tenured Position. A. Cross
Death in a Tokyo Family. D. Kenrick
Death in a Town. H. Waugh
Death in a Tranquil Place. Clare Dawson
Death in a White Tie. N. Marsh
Death in Aberration. J. C. Cooper
Death in Act IV. B. Francis
Death in Albert Park. L. Bruce
Death in Ambush. J. Bude
Death in Ambush. S. Gilruth
Death in Amsterdam. N. Freeling
Death in an Armchair. J. Street
Death in Ankara. Clement Wood
Death in April. A. M. Greeley
Death in Arcady. Stella Phillips
Death in Arms. R. Philmore
Death in Autumn. M. Nabb
Death in B-Minor. J. Lilly
Death in Berlin. M. M. Kaye
Death in Bermuda. Q. Patrick
Death in Blue Folders. M. Maron
Death in Botanist's Bay. E. Ferrars
Death in Brunswick. B. Oxlade
Death in Budapest. V. Gielgud
Death in Camera. M. Underwood
Death in Captivity. M. Gilbert
Death in China. W. D. Montalbano
Death in Claivoyance. Josephine Bell
Death in Close-Up. Nancy Livingston
Death in Cold Print. J. Creasey
Death in Cold Storage. E. Healey
Death in Connecticut. J. Linzee
Death in Costume. A. McRoyd
Death in Covert. C. Willock
Death in Cranford. C. Stone
Death in Cyprus. M. M. Kaye
Death in "D" Division. J. G. Brandon
Death in Dark Glasses. G. Bellairs
Death in Darkness. C. Barry
Death in Darkness. George Douglas
Death in Darkness. F. Struan
Death in Darkness. Alan White
Death in Dawson. J. Lotz
Death in Deakins Wood. R. Petrie
Death in Deep Green. M. Hastings
Death in Deep Shadows. W. Toole
Death in Desolation. G. Bellairs
Death in Despair. G. Bellairs
Death in Diamonds. G. Ashe
Death in Diamonds. K. Giles
Death in Diamonds. H. R. Taunton

Death in Disguise. H. Tracy
Death in Dockland. D. Reid
Death in Don Mills. H. Gardner
Death in Donegal Bay. W. C. Gault
Death in Downing Street. J. G. Brandon
Death in Dream Time. S. H. Courtier
Death in Duplicate. J. G. Brandon
Death in Duplicate. George Douglas
Death in Duplicate. Alan White
Death in Dwelly Lane. F. V. Morley
Death in Ecstasy. N. Marsh
Death in Error. F. Usher
Death in Fancy Dress. J. J. Farjeon
Death in Fancy Dress. Anthony Gilbert
Death in Fashion. M. Babson
Death in Five Boxes. Carter Dickson
Death in Flames. G. Ashe
Death in Four Colors. B. Bird
Death in Four Letters. F. Beeding
Death in Gelly Wood. H. Keyworth
Death in Geneva. A. D. Clift
Death in Gentle Grove. F. K. Allan
Death in Goblin Waters. M. Petrson
Death in Grease Paint. S. Palmer
Death in Harbour. R. Goyne
Death in Harley Street. J. Rhode
Death in Her Eyes. B. Vane
Death in High Heels. C. Brand
Death in High Places. G. Ashe
Death in High Provence. G. Bellairs
Death in Hollywood. P. Richmond
Death in Ireland. P. Everett
Death in Irish Town. J. S. Scott
Death in Jermyn Street. J. G. Brandon
Death in Kenya. M. M. Kaye
Death in Lebanon. J. Tyndall
Death in Leningrad. J. Lear
Death in Life. Nicholas Carter
Death in Lilac Time. F. Crane
Death in Little Houses. K. Robeson
Death in Lord Byron's Room. S. Wood
Death in Melting. Richard Grayson
Death in Mermaid Lane. Gret Lane
Death in Midwinter. J. B. Hilton
Death in Office. N. Longmate
Death in Office. J. Potter
Death in 1-2-3. R. D. Abrahams
Death in Our Wake. A. Glanville
Death in Paradise. D. Hinch
Death in Passing. E. Lacy
Death in Perpetuity. D. G. Browne
Death in Piccadilly. Elliot Bailey
Death in Piccadilly. R. Garnett
Death in Practice. C. A. Moreton
Death in Ptarmigan Forest. C. Coram
Death in Purple Prose. Robert Barnard
Death in Pursuit. G. Leaderman
Death in Quiet Places. Elliot Bailey
Death in Real Life. R. Latimer
Death in Regatta Week. Charles Mason
Death in Reserve. T. Muir
Death in Reserve. H. Tracy
Death in Retirement. Josephine Bell
Death in Retreat. George Douglas
Death in Room Five. G. Bellairs
Death in Russian Habit. Sea Lion
Death in Sanctuary. I. Baker
Death in Santiago. G. DeVilliers
Death in Seven Hours. Stratford Davis
Death in Seven Volumes. D. G. Browne
Death in Shallow Water. M. Burton
Death in Sheep's Clothing. Stella Phillips
Death in Silhouette. J. Slate
Death in Silver. K. Robeson
Death in Slow Motion. K. Robeson
Death in Small Corners. H. T. Smith
Death in Small Doses. Martin Thomas
Death in Soho. John Powers
Death in Sorrento. W. Charles
Death in Soundings. T. Muir
Death in Springtime. M. Nabb
Death in Stanley Street. W. J. Burley
Death in Still Water. A. Handley
Death in Sunlight. F. Lester

Title Index

Death in Ten Point Bold. E. Bruton
Death in the A.R.P. G. Davison
Death in the Air. A. Christie
Death in the Air. D. Hartman
Death in the Andamans. M. M. Kaye
Death in the Back Seat. D. C. Disney
Death in the Bag. G. Usher
Death in the Bathroom. B. Thomson
Death in the Blackout. Anthony Gilbert
Death in the Blue Hour. F. Crane
Death in the Blue Lake. B. Borge
Death-in-the-Box. M. Magill
Death in the Canongate. P. Piper
Death in the Cards. A. T. Smith
Death in the Caribbean. J. R. L. Anderson
Death in the Castle. P. S. Buck
Death in the Cemetery. A. L. Matthison
Death in the Chalkpit. E. R. Punshon
Death in the Channel. J. R. L. Anderson
Death in the Church. K. Giles
Death in the City. J. R. L. Anderson
Death in the Clouds. A. Christie
Death in the Colony. A. Sax
Death in the Copse. A. G. E. Cromwell
Death in the Coverts. R. Jeffries
Death in the Crease. Richard Curtis
Death in the Cup. M. Dalton
Death in the Cup. A. Hocking
Death in the Dark. Stacey Bishop
Death in the Dark. Michael Blake
Death in the Dark. M. Dalton
Death in the Dark. C. M. Wills
Death in the Deep South. Ward Greene
Death in the Desert. J. R. L. Anderson
Death in the Desert. Genevieve St. John
Death in the Devil's Acre. A. Perry
Death in the Dimness. I. B. Colley
Death in the Ditch. J. G. Brandon
Death in the Diving Pool. C. Carnac
Death in the Dog Watches. Sea Lion
Death in the Doll's House. H. Lees
Death in the Dormitory. M. Brucker
Death in the Dovecote. Q. Patrick
Death in the Drawing Room. R. A. Rathbone
Death in the Dunes. P. H. Dobbins
Death in the Dusk. V. Markham
Death in the East. C. Franklin
Death in the Faculty. A. Cross
Death in the Fearful Night. G. Bellairs
Death in the Fens. Colin Hope
Death in the Fifth Position. E. Box
Death in the Fog. M. G. Eberhart
Death in the Forest. N. Brand
Death in the Forest. M. Dalton
Death in the Forest. J. Potter
Death in the Garden. Jennie Melville
Death in the Glass. N. Gayle
Death in the Gorge. L. Thayer
Death in the Green Manor. A. Morice
Death in the Greenhouse. J. R. L. Anderson
Death in the Hands of Talent. P. Yates
Death in the Headlines. R. Sharp
Death in the Hop Fields. J. Rhode
Death in the House. A. Berkeley
Death in the House. S. Cameron
Death in the Inkwell. J. J. Farjeon
Death in the Inner Office. N. Wight
Death in the Jordan. J. Tyndall
Death in the Jungle. Gwyn Evans
Death in the Jungle. S. Nicholls
Death in the Kettle. C. Wallace
Death in the Library. J. Greenfield
Death in the Library. P. Ketchum
Death in the Life. D. S. Davis
Death in the Life Department. C. P. Cleary
Death in the Limelight. A. Applin
Death in the Limelight. A. E. Martin
Death in the Loch. T. Muir
Death in the Loving Cup. T. Girtin
Death in the Manger. A. M. Stewart
Death in the Mews. T. C. H. Jacobs
Death in the Mews. Eric Wood
Death in the Middle Watch. L. Bruce
Death in the Mind. R. Lockridge

Death in the Mist. R. C. Finney
Death in the Mist. F. Hurt
Death in the Morning. H. Hodge
Death in the Morning. S. Radley
Death in the Night. P. Ketchum
Death in the Night Watches. G. Bellairs
Death in the North Sea. J. R. L. Anderson
Death in the Old Country. E. Wright
Death in the Past. R. A. Moore
Death in the Past. B. Parvin
Death in the Picture. G. Braddon
Death in the Picture. M. Williamson
Death in the Pot. M. Van Loggem
Death in the Quadrangle. E. Dillon
Death in the Quarry. J. G. Brandon
Death in the Quarry. G. D. H. Cole
Death in the Rain. F. Parrish
Death in the Ring. R. Gilmour
Death in the Rising Sun. J. Creasey
Death in the Round. A. Morice
Death in the Saddle. N. Jackson
Death in the Scillies. H. C. Davis
Death in the Senate. Diplomat
Death in the Shingle. H. Desmond
Death in the Signal Box. H. Keyworth
Death in the Silver Ring. J. Brown
Death in the Smog. H. MacKenzie
Death in the Snow. R. M. Stern
Death in the Spanish Sun. N. Deane
Death in the Spring. M. J. Law
Death in the Stalls. J. R. Wilmot
Death in the Stars. N. Lazenby
Death in the State House. T. Knox
Death in the Stocks. G. Heyer
Death in the Straw. G. Usher
Death in the Sun. G. D. H. Cole
Death in the Sun. S. Coulter
Death in the Sun. C. Saxby
Death in the Sunday Supplement. Sam Merwin
Death in the Surgery. R. Trevor
Death in the Tankard. G. D. H. Cole
Death in the Thames. J. R. L. Anderson
Death in the Theatre. D. Dayle
Death in the Theatre. J. R. Wilmot
Death in the Thicket. V. Loder
Death in the 13th Dose. V. Loder
Death in the Top Twenty. W. McNeilly
Death in the Tote Box. W. D. Maydwell
Death in the Trees. G. Ashe
Death in the Tunnel. M. Burton
Death in the Village. J. Garden
Death in the Virgins. R. H. Barbour
Death in the Wasteland. G. Bellairs
Death in the Wet. G. Mitchell
Death in the Wheelbarrow. W. Gore
Death in the Willows. R. Forrest
Death in the Wind. J. A. Jordan
Death in the Wind. E. Lanham
Death in the Wind. R. Massey
Death in the Wood. C. Rushton
Death in the Wrong Bed. S. Farrar
Death in the Wrong Room. Anthony Gilbert
Death in the Yew Alley. M. Ervin
Death in Three Masks. B. Healey
Death in Tiger Valley. Reginald Campbell
Death in Time. F. Lyall
Death in Time. M. Warner
Death in Tokyo. G. Stanley
Death in Triplicate. E. C. R. Lorac
Death in Verona. R. H. Lewis
Death in View. T. Macrae
Death in Waiting. J. Bland
Death in Wellington Road. J. Rhode
Death in Wessex. Audrey Peterson
Death in White Bear Lake. B. Siegel
Death in White Pajamas. J. Bude
Death in Willow Pattern. W. J. Burley
Death in Yellow. S. Jason
Death in Zanzibar. M. M. Kaye
Death Inheritance. P. Swan
Death Intervened. A. O. Pollard
Death Invades the Meeting. J. Rhode
Death Is a Black Camel. H. B. Kaye
Death Is a Circus. Jason

Death Is a Cold, Keen Edge. E. Basinsky
Death Is a Dame. D. Steel
Death Is a Dark Man. D. Highland
Death Is a Dirty Trick. J. Philips
Death Is a Drag. D. Hoyt
Death Is a Drum . . . Beating Forever. J. Wyllie
Death Is a Family Affair. L. V. Sims
Death Is a Friend. D. MacKenzie
Death Is a Gold Coin. R. Fenisong
Death Is a Habit. O. Kensch
Death Is a Liar. Marc Miller
Death Is a Lizard. John Williams
Death Is a Lonely Business. R. Bradbury
Death Is a Lovely Dame. M. Blood
Death Is a Lovely Lady. R. Fenisong
Death Is a Lover. N. Tyre
Death Is a Red Rose. D. Eden
Death Is a Restless Sleeper. E. B. Quinn
Death Is a Round Black Ball. M. Roscoe
Death Is a Round Black Spot. K. Robeson
Death Is a Silent Room. Jay Bennett
Death Is a Stowaway. W. Price
Death Is a Swinger. Jason Morgan
Death Is a Tiger. M. Mundy
Death Is a Tory. K. Patrick
Death Is a Z. A. Yarrow
Death Is Academic. A. MacKay
Death Is an Artist. S. Gardiner
Death Is an Early Riser. J. M. Bigelow
Death Is Buttercups. G. M. Wilson
Death Is Confidential. L. Lariar
Death Is for Ever. L. Marshall
Death Is for Losers. W. Newton
Death Is for Losers. W. F. Nolan
Death Is Forever. M. O'Callaghan
Daeth Is in the Garden. M. Marlette
Death Is Late to Lunch. T. Du Bois
Death Is Like That. J. Spain
Death Is Merciful. J. Sandys
Death Is My Bridegroom. D. M. Devine
Death Is My Comrade. S. Marlowe
Death is My Dancing Partner. C. Woolrich
Death Is My Lover. S. Brock
Death is My Mistress. D. Haring
Death Is My Name. S. Wells
Death Is My Neighbor. A. Templeton
Death Is My Shadow. J. Corbett
Death Is My Shadow. E. Ronns
Death Is No Lady. M. E. Corne
Death Is No Sportsman. C. Hare
Death Is Not a Passing Grade. V. B. Miller
Death Is Our Playmate. P. Turnbull
Death Is Relative. E. Phillips
Death Is Skin Deep. C. Percy
Death Is So Final. Alex Fraser
Death Is So Kind. L. Redmond
Death Is So Lonely. L. Amino
Death Is the End. G. W. Cooke
Death Is the Host. L. Lariar
Death Is the Last Lover. H. Kane
Death Is the Pay-Off. Simon Burke
Death Is Thy Neighbor. L. D. Smith
Death Is Too Good for You. M. Alexander
Death Is Waiting. F. Usher
Death Is Where You Meet It. Max James
Death Island. Nick Carter
Death It Is. E. Mordaunt
Death Joins the Party. R. Boyd
Death Joins the Party. J. V. Turner
Death Joins the Women's Club. C. Saxby
Death Keeps a Secret. C. B. Kelland
Death Kicks a Pebble. A. Tack
Death Kiss. Gerald Moore
Death Kiss. M. St. Dennis
Death Kit. S. Sontag
Death Knell. C. T. Cline
Death Knell. B. Kendrick
Death Knock. D. Haring
Death Knocks Three Times. Anthony Gilbert
Death Knows No Calendar. J. Bude
Death Lady. K. Robeson
Death Laughs Aloft. P. Conde
Death Leaves a Diary. H. Carmichael
Death Leaves No Card. M. Burton

D

D

Death Leaves Us Naked. L. Hollingsworth
Death Let Loose. H. Desmond
Death Letter. T. A. Plummer
Death Lies Deep. W. Guinn
Death Lies in Waiting. B. Williams
Death Lifts the Latch. Anthony Gilbert
Death Light. Richard Grant
Death Lights a Candle. P. A. Taylor
Death Like Thunder. H. Holman
Death Likes It Hot. E. Box
Death-Line. J. Mercer
Death List. R. Casler
Death List. A. C. Clark
Death List. R. Hawkes
Death List. R. McKew
Death Listened In. K. Sproul
Death Lives in the Mansion. D. Locke
Death Lives Next Door. Gwendoline Butler
Death Looks Down. A. R. Long
Death Looks In. R. Sale
Death Looks On. P. Manton
Death Loop. P. Conde
Death Lottery. E. Hyams
Death Loves a Shining Mark. A. Hocking
Death Lust. A. Kilgore
Death Machine. K. Robeson
Death Machine Contract. M. McCray
Death Mail. Peter Leslie
Death Maker. A. J. Small
Death Makers. J. Milton
Death Makers Conspiracy. Ralph Hayes
Death Makes a Claim. Hank Hobson
Death Makes a Date. J. Corbett
Death Makes a Date. F. W. Irwin
Death Makes a Deal. Maude Parker
Death Makes a Prophet. J. Bude
Death Makes the Scene. Stella Phillips
Death Man. D. Kirby
Death Man. B. Swift
Death Mask. A. Applin
Death Mask. J. Dentinger
Death-Mask. R. Parkes
Death Mask. H. Pentecost
Death Mask. Ellis Peters
Death Mask of War. G. Marlowe
Death Masque. K. Hayles
Death Masque. H. McLeave
Death Master. B. Appel
Death Master. W. W. Johnston
Death Match. R. Glendinning
Death Match. J. Stacy
Death May Surprise Us. T. Willis
Death Mechanic. A. D. Hutter
Death Meets 400 Rabbits. A. M. Stein
Death Meets the Coroner. J. K. Ryland
Death Meets the Deadline. D. R. George
Death Meets the King's Messenger. G. Collins
Death Men from Mexico. Anonymous
Death Merchant. J. Rosenberger
Death Merchants. S. Murray
Death Merchants. J. Readus
Death Message: Oil 74-2. Nick Carter
Death Miser. J. Creasey
Death Mission: Havana. Nick Carter
Death Must Have Laughed. J. V. Turner
Death Must Wait. D. Kingery
Death, My Darling Daughters. J. Stagge
Death, My Lover. P. Allardyce
Death Mystery. Anonymous
Death-Mystery. N. Buntline
Death Near the River. Monte Cooper
Death Needs No Alibi. L. Gribble
Death Never Forgets. Robin Moore
Death Never Forgets. Garnett Weston
Death Never Weeps. S. Ryan
Death Notes. R. Rendell
Death Notice. M. S. Karl
Death Occurred. N. Hoult
Death of a Banker. A. Wynne
Death of a Barrow Boy. Charles Harris
Death of a Beauty Queen. E. R. Punshon
Death of a Best Seller. C. M. Wills
Death of a Big Man. J. Wainwright
Death of a Big Shot. George Douglas

Death of a Big Shot. C. Knight
Death of a Blue-Eyed Soul Brother. B. B. Johnson
Death of a Blue Movie Star. J. W. Deaver
Death of a Bogey. D. Warner
Death of a Bookseller. B. J. Farmer
Death of a Borgia. C. J. Stevermer
Death of a Bovver Boy. L. Bruce
Death of a Bride. G. D. H. Cole
Death of a Bridegroom. J. Rhode
Death of a Bridge Expert. C. C. Nicolet
Death of a Bullionaire. A. B. Cunningham
Death of a Burrowing Mole. G. Mitchell
Death of a Busybody. G. Bellairs
Death of a Busybody. Dell Shannon
Death of a Butterfly. M. Maron
Death of a Cad. M. C. Beaton
Death of a Cad. J. Bude
Death of a Call Girl. L. Trevor
Death of a Canary. Neill Graham
Death of a Celebrity. H. Footner
Death of a Chancellor. W. Carrier
Death of a Cheat. J. M. Eshleman
Death of a Citizen. D. Hamilton
Death of a City. L. White
Death of a Cloven Hoof. Frank King
Death of a Clown. E. Backhouse
Death of a Commuter. L. Bruce
Death of a Con Man. Josephine Bell
Death of a Convict. T. Herd
Death of a Corinthian. E. Lanham
Death of a Courier. R. Hawkes
Death of a Critic. W. Norman
Death of a Crow. U. Curtiss
Death of a Curate. K. H. Ashley
Death of a Daimyo. James Melville
Death of a Dancer. J. McGown
Death of a Dancing Lady. R. Harrison
Death of a Dandie Dinmont. M. Duke
Death of a Dastard. H. Kane
Death of a Dear Friend. A. Quinton
Death of a Decent Fellow. N. A. Temple-Ellis
Death of a Delegate. G. P. Cronin
Death of a Delft Blue. G. Mitchell
Death of a Designer. N. Brand
Death of a Detective. L. W. Brent
Death of a Diplomat. P. Oldfeld
Death of a Dissenter. L. Lamb
Death of a Dissident. S. M. Kaminsky
Death of a Doctor. J. Armour
Death of a Dog. L. Eyles
Death of a Doll. Carter Brown
Death of a Doll. Hilda Lawrence
Death of a Don. H. Shaw
Death of a Dormouse. P. Ruell
Death of a Doxy. R. Stout
Death of a Dreamer. R. A. Bennett
Death of a Dreamer. D. Warner
Death of a Dude. R. Stout
Death of a Dutchman. M. Nabb
Death of a Dwarf. H. Kemp
Death of a Fan Dancer. J. Carlshon
Death of a Fantasy Life. T. G. Gilpin
Death of a Fashion Writer. M. Charlton
Death of a Fat God. H. R. F. Keating
Death of a Favorite Girl. M. Gilbert
Death of a Fellow Traveller. D. Ames
Death of a Fire-Raiser. George Davis
Death of a First Mate. C. Barry
Death of a Flack. H. Kane
Death of a Flower Child. R. Clarke
Death of a Fool. N. Marsh
Death of a Fox. J. Roffman
Death of a Friend. R. Harris
Death of a Friend. N. Masterman
Death of a Frightened Editor. E. Radford
Death of a Frightened Traveller. F. Lester
Death of a Gay Dog. A. Morice
Death of a Gentleman. J. Courage
Death of a "Gentleman." E. Radford
Death of a Ghost. M. Allingham
Death of a Goblin. G. Hythe
Death of a God. S. T. Haymon
Death of a Godmother. J. Rhode
Death of a Golden Girl. E. Fulton

Death of a Golden Goose. H. Mace
Death of a Golfer. A. Wynne
Death of a Good Woman. M. Eccles
Death of a Good Woman. J. F. Straker
Death of a Gossip. M. C. Beaton
Death of a Governor. A. Parsons
Death of a Greek. J. G. Brandon
Death of a Halo. Frank King
Death of a Harbourmaster. G. Simenon
Death of a Harlot. B. Newman
Death of a Harvard Freshman. V. Silver
Death of a Hawker. J. Van De Wetering
Death of a Heavenly Twin. A. Morice
Death of a Hippie. Michael Brett
Death of a Hit-Man. Frederick Davies
Death of a Hittite. S. Angus
Death of a Hollow Man. Caroline Graham
Death of a Holy Murderer. M. Duke
Death of a Hooker. H. Kane
Death of a Hussy. M. C. Beaton
Death of a Jazz King. C. M. Walker
Death of a Jester. P. O'Donnell
Death of a Joyce Scholar. B. Gill
Death of a King. P. C. Doherty
Death of a King. A. Wynne
Death of a Ladies' Man. Lee Roberts
Death of a Lady Killer. C. Carnac
Death of a Lake. A. W. Upfield
Death of a Lawyer. E. Jones-Evans
Death of a Libertine. C. Wallace
Death of a Literary Widow. R. Barnard
Death of a Love. R. Hobart
Death of a Low-Handicap Man. B. Ball
Death of a Lucky Man. V. Rath
Death of a Man-Tamer. M. Tripp
Death of a Marine. C. Leader
Death of a Merchant of Death. N. S. Bortner
Death of a Mermaid. G. Brandon
Death of a Millionaire. G. D. H. Cole
Death of a Millionaire. R. Dana
Death of a Mind. J. Ritson
Death of a Minor Poet. W. Krasner
Death of a Moffy. K. O'Hara
Death of a Moral Person. A. Roudybush
Death of a Mystery Writer. R. Barnard
Death of a Next-Door Neighbor. D. Goodnough
Death of a Nude. D. Warner
Death of a Nurse. R. Marsten
Death of a Nurse. L. H. Whitten
Death of a Nymph. D. Delman
Death of a Nymph. E. Piper
Death of a Painted Lady. B. Cleeve
Death of a Pale Man. F. Lester
Death of a Patriot. R. E. Harrington
Death of a Peculiar Rabbit. E. Radford
Death of a Peeping Tom. B. Cobb
Death of a Peer. N. Marsh
Death of a Perfect Mother. R. Barnard
Death of a Perfect Wife. M. C. Beaton
Death of a Philanderer. L. Meynell
Death of a Player. L. O'Donnell
Death of a Poison-Tongue. Josephine Bell
Death of a Politician. R. Condon
Death of a Pornographer. A. Lejeune
Death of a Portrait. E. Mack
Death of a Portrait. L. Williamson
Death of a Postman. J. Creasey
Death of a Pregnant Virgin. S. T. Haymon
Death of a Prima Donna. L. Colburn
Death of a Prom Queen. Marie Oliver
Death of a Punk. J. Browner
Death of a Puppet. G. Hythe
Death of a Puppeteer. W. G. Beyer
Death of a Pusher. R. Deming
Death of a Queen. C. S. Sprigg
Death of a Racehorse. J. Creasey
Death of a Radcliffe Roommate. V. Silver
Death of a Raven. M. Duffy
Death of a Renaissance Man. L. Uccello
Death of a Revolutionist. J. Dall
Death of a Saboteur. H. Footner
Death of a Sadist. R. R. Ryan
Death of a Sahib. C. Egleton
Death of a Salesperson. Robert Barnard

Title Index

Death of a Sardine. Joan Fleming
Death of a Scandal Sister. M. Brody
Death of a Scapegoat. G. Hythe
Death of a Scavenger. K. Spore
Death of a Schoolboy. H. Koning
Death of a Scoundrel. T. C. H. Jacobs
Death of a Shadow. G. Bellairs
Death of a Shadow. A. Wynne
Death of a Shipowner. T. Henege
Death of a Shrew. C. Barling
Death of a Shrew. A. Kennington
Death of a Sinner. R. Arnold
Death of a Sinner. R. Quest
Death of a Sinner. P. Warwick
Death of a Skin-Diver. S. Jay
Death of a Snout. D. Warner
Death of a Socialite. J. G. Brandon
Death of a Source. R. A. Moore
Death of a Spinster. M. Dalton
Death of a Spinster. F. Duncombe
Death of a Spinster. Dorothy Johnson
Death of a Spy. S. Horler
Death of a Star. G. D. H. Cole
Death of a Stranger. W. Barrett
Death of a Stranger. M. Halliday
Death of a Stranger. D. Noel
Death of a Stray Cat. J. Potts
Death of a Supertanker. A. Trew
Death of a Swagman. A. W. Upfield
Death of a Tall Man. F. Lockridge
Death of a Tax Inspector. S. Chance
Death of a Terrorist. J. Beeching
Death of a Thin-Skinned Animal. P. Alexander
Death of a Tin God. G. Bellairs
Death of a Tom. D. Warner
Death of a Tough Guy. T. Trenton
Death of a Train. F. W. Crofts
Death of a Tyrant. E. R. Punshon
Death of a Unicorn. P. Dickinson
Death of a Viewer. H. Adams
Death of a Village. J. Courage
Death of a Voodoo Doll. M. Arnold
Death of a Wanton. B. Cabot
Death of a Wedding Guest. A. Morice
Death of a Weirdy. G. Carr
Death of a White Witch. I. Oellrichs
Death of a Wicked Servant. B. Cleeve
Death of a Wide-Boy. W. R. Hutton
Death of a Wife. C. Wallace
Death of a Wild Bird. J. N. Chance
Death of a Witch. H. Hawton
Death of a World. J. J. Farjeon
Death of a Worldly Woman. A. B. Cunningham
Death of an Ad Man. A. Eichler
Death of an Admiral. A. Gilchrist
Death of an Admiral. G. Hackforth-Jones
Death of an Airman. C. S. Sprigg
Death of an Alaskan Princess. B. A. Smith
Death of an Alderman. J. B. Hilton
Death of an Ambassador. M. Coles
Death of an Ancient Saxon. E. Radford
Death of an Angel. F. Lockridge
Death of an Angel. M. P. Rea
Death of an Angel. C. Richards
Death of an Angel. P. G. Winslow
Death of an Artist. A. Eichler
Death of an Artist. J. Rhode
Death of an Aryan. E. Huxley
Death of an Assassin. J. Creasey
Death of an Aunt. T. Harknett
Death of an Author. E. C. R. Lorac
Death of an Author. J. Rhode
Death of an Editor. V. Loder
Death of an Eloquent Man. C. M. Russell
Death of an Englishman. M. Nabb
Death of an Expert Witness. P. D. James
Death of an Expert Witness. P. H. Powell
Death of an Extra. V. Gielgud
Death of an Honourable Member. R. Barnard
Death of an Idol. W. A. Harbinson
Death of an Informer. W. Perry
Death of an Innocent. J. N. Chance
Death of an Innocent. R. Ormerod
Death of an Inquisitor and other stories. L. Sciascia

Death of an Intruder. N. Tyre
Death of an Oddfellow. Eric Wood
Death of an Old Flame. M. McClintick
Death of an Old Girl. E. Lemarchand
Death of an Old Goat. R. Barnard
Death of an Old Sinner. D. S. Davis
Death of an Outsider. M. C. Beaton
Death of an Uncle. P. Hambledon
Death of an Undertaker. D. Lynn
Death of an Unknown Man. M. Bringle
Death of Anton. A. Melville
Death of Captain Shand. E. Spencer
Death of Cecilia. H. Hartley
Death of Cold. L. Bruce
Death of Cosmo Revere. C. Bush
Death of Daddy-O. David Alexander
Death of Descartes. D. Bosworth
Death of Dr. Whitelaw. A. Wilson
Death of Duboyne. W. J. Bayfield
Death of Four. A. Skene
Death of Gold. Mervyn Lewis
Death of Henrietta. L. M. Armistead
Death of His Uncle. C. H. B. Kitchin
Death of Honor. J. C. Faust
Death of Humpty Dumpty. David Alexander
Death of Innocence. Z. Popkin
Death of Jason Darby. G. E. Taylor
Death of Jezebel. C. Brand
Death of John Tait. A. Fielding
Death of Kings. J. L. Johnson
Death of Kyralessa. C. V. Gheorgiu
Death of Laura. H. C. Davis
Death of Laurence Vining. Alan Thomas
Death of Lord Haw Haw. B. Rutledge
Death of Lorenzo Jones. B. Latham
Death of Maurice. B. Pain
Death of Me Yet. W. Masterson
Death of Men. A. Massie
Death of Minor Character. E. Ferrars
Death of Miss Cunningham. J. Cousseau
Death of Miss X. M. McMullen
Death of Mr. Balishberger. H. Hrabel
Death of Mr. Dodsley. J. Ferguson
Death of Mr. Gantley. M. Burton
Death of Mr. Lomas. F. Vivian
Death of Mrs. Preedy. L. Jackson
Death of Moishe Ganef. S. Louvish
Death of Monsieur Gallet. G. Simenon
Death of My Aunt. C. H. B. Kitchin
Death of Nevill Norway. J. Rowland
Death of Our Dear One. M. Erskine
Death of Ruth. E. Kata
Death of the Abbe Didier. R. Grayson
Death of the Claimant. A. R. Martin
Death of the Deputy. F. Didelot
Death of the Detective. Mark Smith
Death of the Doctor's Wife. Whyte Hall
Death of the Dragon. F. Drake
Death of the Falcon. Nick Carter
Death of the Family. S. George
Death of the Fuhrer. R. Puccetti
Death of the Good Samaritan. O. D. Johnston
Death of the Home Secretary. Alan Thomas
Death of the King's Canary. Dylan Thomas
Death of the Party. L. Cutter
Death of the Party. R. Fenisong
Death of the Red King. P. Bennetts
Death of the Vampire Baroness. V. Van Der Elst
Death of Two Brothers. M. Burton
Death of Virginia. O. Rees
Death Off the Fairway. H. Adams
Death on a Back Bench. F. Hobson
Death on a Broomstick. G. M. Wilson
Death on a Downbeat. Carter Brown
Death on a Dude Ranch. F. Bonnamy
Death on a Ferris Wheel. A. L. Martin
Death on a High Note. D. Reid
Death on a Hot Summer Night. A. Infante
Death on a No. 8 Hook. L. Gough
Death on a Pale Horse. Bradshaw Jones
Death on a Quiet Beach. S. Challis
Death on a Quiet Day. M. Innes
Death on a Smokeboat. Ross Graham
Death on a Summer Day. E. Booth

Death on a Sunday Morning. J. F. Straker
Death on a Warm Wind. D. Warner
Death on a Wet Sunday. P. Capon
Death on Account. M. Yorke
Death on All Hallows. A. C. MacLean
Death on Allhallowe'en. L. Bruce
Death on an Island. G. G. Roper
Death on Bodmin Moor. V. Gunn
Death on "Calamity." K. Wade
Death on Call. S. D. Wilkinson
Death on Capitol Hill. B. Whitehurst
Death on Danger Hill. T. A. Plummer
Death on Dartmoor. J. Rowland
Death on Deadline. R. Goldsborough
Death on Delivery. E. Allen
Death on Delivery. J. G. Brandon
Death on Delivery. R. Gore-Browne
Death on Delivery. F. W. Gumley
Death on Delivery. E. L. Sloane
Death on Demand. G. Ashe
Death on Demand. C. G. Hart
Death on Demand. Kim Hill
Death on Deposit. F. Grierson
Death on Display. R. Simons
Death on Doomsday. E. Lemarchand
Death on Herons' Mere. M. Fitt
Death on Ice. J. B. O'Sullivan
Death on Jerusalem Road. D. Angus
Death on Location. W. R. Cox
Death on May Morning. M. Dalman
Death on Milestone Buttress. G. Carr
Death on My Left. P. MacDonald
Death on My Shoulder. C. Franklin
Death on Paper. J. Bude
Death on Priority 1. P. Yorke
Death on Raven's Scar. Albert Harding
Death on Remand. M. Underwood
Death on Romney Marsh. L. Bruce
Death on Scurvy Street. B. A. Williams
Death on Shivering Sand. V. Gunn
Death on Site. Janet Neel
Death on Sunday. J. Rhode
Death on Television. H. Slesar
Death on the Agenda. M. Bidwell
Death on the Agenda. P. Moyes
Death on the Agenda. T. Muir
Death on the Air. Herman Landon
Death on the Aisle. F. Lockridge
Death on the Atoll. B. Francis
Death on the Barrier Reef. E. Antill
Death on the Beat. D. Logan
Death on the Black Sands. L. Bruce
Death on the Board. J. Rhode
Death on the Boardwalk. J. Cafferty
Death on the Boat Train. J. Rhode
Death on the Border. R. Chavis
Death on the Border. R. P. Holden
Death on the Borough Council. Josephine Bell
Death on the Bridge. R. Howes
Death on the Broadlands. A. Hunter
Death on the Broads. E. Radford
Death on the Campus. A. Simmons
Death on the Cards. R. Grayson
Death on the Centre Court. G. Goodchild
Death on the Champs-Elysees. F. Didelot
Death on the Cherwell. M. D. Hay
Death on the Circuit. J. Ellery
Death on the Cliff. T. Cobb
Death on the Clock. G. Knevels
Death on the Cuff. M. G. MacKnutt
Death on the Deep. H. M. Stephenson
Death on the Diamond. C. Fitzsimmons
Death on the Docks. D. Hartman
Death on the Door Mat. M. V. Heberden
Death on the Doorstep. George Douglas
Death on the Dordogne. Jean Fraser
Death on the Double. H. Kane
Death on the Down Beat. S. Farr
Death on the Downbeat. Carter Brown
Death on the Downs. A. Marsden
Death on the Dragon's Tongue. M. Arnold
Death on the Eno. A. MacKay
Death on the Files. M. Penrose
Death on the First Tee. H. Adams

Death on the Glass. L. O'Donnell
Death on the Heath. A. Hunter
Death on the High C's. R. Barnard
Death on the Highway. C. Robbins
Death on the Hit Parade. B. Gray
Death on the Hour. R. Lockridge
Death on the Last Train. G. Bellairs
Death on the Late Show. J. Michaels
Death on the Lawn. J. Rhode
Death on the Limited. R. Denbie
Death on the Line. C. M. Wills
Death on the Machar. A. MacVicar
Death on the Mall. A. Parsons
Death on the Mississippi. R. Forrest
Death on the Moor. J. Pendower
Death on the Motorway. C. Coram
Death on the Mountain. D. Ogburn
Death on the Move. G. Ashe
Death on the Move. B. Crider
Death on the Nile. A. Christie
Death on the Nose. H. D. Spatz
Death on the Outer Shoal. A. Fuller
Death on the Oxford Road. E. C. R. Lorac
Death on the Pack Road. H. Andover
Death on the Pampas. Clement Wood
Death on the Piazza. Jean Fraser
Death on the Reserve. Josephine Bell
Death on the River. A. MacKay
Death on the River Kwai. G. De Villiers
Death on the Riviera. J. Bude
Death on the Roads. G. W. Wray
Death on the Rocks. M. Allegretto
Death on the Rocks. J. R. L. Anderson
Death on the Rocks. J. B. West
Death on the Roof. B. Francis
Death on the Run. J. M. Hickman
Death on the Run. U. Rothwell
Death on the Set. V. MacClure
Death on the Sixth Day. H. Farrell
Death on the Slopes. N. Schier
Death on the Spike. D. Reid
Death on the Swim. Simon
Death on the Table. C. Rayner
Death on the Trooper. T. Muir
Death on the Viaduct. J. R. Traynor
Death on the Waterfront. R. Archer
Death on the Way. F. W. Crofts
Death on Their Doorsteps. M. Pender
Death on 30 Beat. Maynard Collins
Death on Tiptoe. R. C. Ashby
Death on Tour. J. Courage
Death on Wheels. M. Strongman
Death on Widow's Walk. L. Grant-Adamson
Death Opens the Ball. J. R. Benson
Death Orbit. Nick Carter
Death Out of Darkness. M. Halliday
Death Out of Focus. W. C. Gault
Death Out of Focus. C. Whitman
Death Out of Season. E. Litvinoff
Death Out of the Night. A. Wynne
Death Out of Thin Air. S. Towne
Death Over Deep Water. S. Nash
Death Over Her Shoulder. D. C. Meade
Death Over Hollywood. C. Saxby
Death Over London. M. Wheeler-Nicholson
Death Over Newark. Alexander Williams
Death Over San Silvestro. M. Teagle
Death Over Sunday. J. F. Bonnell
Death Overseas. C. Barry
Death Pack. R. Sonin
Death Packs a Suitcase. B. E. Wallace
Death Paints a Picture. M. Burton
Death Paints a Portrait. W. Herber
Death Paints the Picture. L. Lariar
Death Parade. H. Desmond
Death Parade. A. O. Pollard
Death Patrol. J. Ascott
Death Pays a Dividend. J. Rhode
Death Pays All Debts. M. Sharman
Death Pays Dividends. J. W. Hornby
Death Pays the Piper. L. Gribble
Death Pays the Wages. E. McGirr
Death Penalty. A. Draper
Death Penalty. C. Mellor

Death Play. G. Verner
Death Plays a Duet. A. L. Davies
Death Plays Solitaire. R. L. Goldman
Death Plays the Gramophone. Marjorie Stafford
Death Plays the Last Card. H. H. Kirst
Death Plot. L. H. Brenning
Death Points a Finger. W. Levinrew
Death Pool. J. Corbett
Death Pool. V. Loder
Death Prowls the Cove. Gret Lane
Death Pulls a Doublecross. Lawrence Block
Death Pulls No Punches. B. Shannon
Death Puppet. J. Nisbet
Death Race. S. Jason
Death Raid. Richard Harper
Death Raid. Jon Hart
Death Rattle. A. B. Caldwell
Death Ray Dictator. W. R. Titterton
Death Ray Mystery. L. Rutland
Death Ray Terror. L. Derrick
Death Reel. Hamish MacInnes
Death Registers at the Eagle Arms. K. Frost
Death Rehearses. J. Varnam
Death Reign of the Vampire King. G. Stockbridge
Death Renders Account. J. M. Spender
Death Ride. M. Franklin
Death Ride. P. Hofrichter
Death Ride. N. MacNeil
Death Ride. D. Stivers
Death-Riders. C. Cofyn
Death Riders. D. Streib
Death Rides a Black Steed. L. Churchill
Death Rides a Camel. J. Wolf
Death Rides a Hobby. R. Howes
Death Rides a Painted Horse. R. P. Wilmot
Death Rides a Sorrel Horse. A. B. Cunningham
Death Rides Swiftly. N. Shepherd
Death Rides Tandem. W. McCully
Death Rides the Air Line. W. Sutherland
Death Rides the Deep. F. MacIsaac
Death Rides the Desert. D. Adair
Death Rides the Dragon. E. Thomas
Death Rides the Forest. Rupert Grayson
Death Rides the Rail. R. Sharp
Death Rides the Rails. J. Hopwood
Death Rides the Rails. C. Stoddard
Death Rides the Range. B. Netton
Death Rides the Speedway. D. Forde
Death Rides the Storm. K. Kendall
Death Rides the Train. B. Sarto
Death Ring. E. S. Drewry
Death Rings a Bell. C. Fitzsimmons
Death Rings No Bell. G. Braddon
Death Road. Donald Stuart
Death Rocks the Cradle. P. Martens
Death Roll. Sam Llewellyn
Death Room. Edgar Wallace
Death Rope Island. P. Goulden
Death Round the Corner. J. Creasey
Death Run. Stuart Hall
Death Runs on Skis. H. Ritchie
Death Rust. E. P. Thorne
Death Sails in a High Wind. T. Du Bois
Death Sails the Bay. J. Feegel
Death Sails the Nile. F. B. McKinley
Death Says Good-Morning. J. O. Mayo
Death Scene. J. Beadle
Death Scene. B. Suyker
Death-Scented Flower. P. Hastings
Death Schuss. L. O'Donnell
Death Seance. F. W. Gumley
Death Seat. J. B. O'Sullivan
Death Seekers. Ross Richards
Death Sends a Cable. M. T. Yates
Death Sends for the Doctor. G. Bellairs
Death Sends for the Doctor. E. Heltai
Death Sentence. B. Garfield
Death Sentence. A. D. Miller
Death Sentence. W. B. Murphy
Death Sentence. T. Philbin
Death Serves a Fault. C. Ryland
Death Serves an Ace. H. Wills
Death Set in Diamonds. G. Verner
Death Set to Music. M. Hebden

Death Sets the Pace. L. Cargill
Death Shall Overcome. E. Lathen
Death Ship. A. Blair
Death Ship. H. Edmonds
Death Ship. S. Hope
Death Ship. T. P. Prest
Death Shock. H. Arnston
Death Shuttle. D. Streib
Death Sign. Gwyn Evans
Death Signs. H. E. Hunsburger
Death Singer. J. A. Jordan
Death Sits In. C. Glick
Death Sits In. H. A. Keller
Death Sits on the Board. J. Rhode
Death Slams the Door. P. Cade
Death Sleep. J. Sohl
Death Sleeps in Kensington. J. Ward
Death Sleeps Lightly. P. C. Payes
Death Smells of Cordite. M. McCracken
Death Smiles. R. R. Phillips
Death Song. R. Hawkes
Death Speaking. Gwyn Evans
Death Speaks Softly. Anthea Fraser
Death Specialists. G. Paulsen
Death Sped the Plough. G. Usher
Death Spins the Platter. E. Queen
Death Spins the Wheel. G. Bellairs
Death Spiral. Bill Kelly
Death Spiral. Meredith Phillips
Death Spiral. P. Rosemoor
Death Spoke Sweetly. R. Garnett
Death Springs the Trap. E. K. Goldthwaite
Death Squad. Nick Carter
Death Squad. B. Copper
Death Squad. H. Kastle
Death Squad. P. McCurtin
Death Squad. D. Pendleton
Death Squad London. J. Gerson
Death Squadron. A. O. Pollard
Death Stalk. T. Chastain
Death Stalk. R. Grayson
Death Stalk. B. Langley
Death Stalk in Spain. Don Smith
Death Stalked the Fells. A. G. MacLeod
Death Stalks a Lady. Shelley Smith
Death Stalks a Marriage. R. W. Larson
Death Stalks in Kenya. A. Peverett
Death Stalks in Soho. J. G. Brandon
Death Stalks My Lovely. N. Rosso
Death Stalks the Bride. Jean Marsh
Death Stalks the Cobbled Square. J. N. Chance
Death Stalks the Dykes. A. Lloyd
Death Stalks the Fleet. H. Cope
Death Stalks the Punjab. M. A. Casberg
Death Stalks the River. O. Williams
Death Stalks the Stadium. J. B. O'Sullivan
Death Stalks the Wakely Family. A. Derleth
Death Stalks the Ward. B. G. Williamson
Death Stalks the Waterway. S. Dewes
Death Stalks "The Wild Goose." R. Stahl
Death Stands By. J. Creasey
Death Stands Near. L. A. Knight
Death Stands Round the Corner. W. M. Duncan
Death Star Affair. Nick Carter
Death Starts a Rumour. M. Fitt
Death Steals the Show. J. Bude
Death Stills the Brush. F. W. Gumley
Death Stone. D. Weir
Death Stops at the Old Stone Inn. S. Seifert
Death Stops the Bells. R. M. Baker
Death Stops the Frolic. G. Bellairs
Death Stops the Manuscript. R. M. Baker
Death Stops the Rehearsal. R. M. Baker
Death Stops the Show. L. S. Thompson
Death Strain. Nick Carter
Death Strike. D. Stivers
Death Strikes at Dawn. H. Desmond
Death Strikes at Heron House. K. O'Neil
Death Strikes at Six Bells. G. Baxter
Death Strikes from the Rear. A. Marsden
Death Strikes Home. M. W. Glidden
Death Strikes in Darkness. L. Marshall
Death Strikes Out. G. Finley
Death Suite. P. De Pietro

Death Suspended. C. Whitman
Death Swap. M. Babson
Death Sweet. T. J. MacGregor
Death Switch. H. Henn
Death Symbol. T. A. Plummer
Death Syndicate. J. Philips
Death Takes a Bow. F. Lockridge
Death Takes a Detour. M. Burton
Death Takes a Dive. G. W. Cooke
Death Takes a Dive. E. Heath
Death Takes a Dive. A. Tack
Death Takes a Flat. M. Burton
Death Takes a Gamble. R. H. R. Smithies
Death Takes a Hand. F. Griffin
Death Takes a Hand. T. A. Plummer
Death Takes a Holiday. Walter Ferris
Death Takes a Holiday. N. MacKenzie
Death Takes a Partner. J. Rhode
Death Takes a Paying Guest. A. M. Stein
Death Takes a Redhead. Anthony Gilbert
Death Takes a Ride. R. C. Finney
Death Takes a Ride. H. E. Wheeler
Death Takes a Sabbatical. R. Bernard
Death Takes a Star. N. Morland
Death Takes a Teacher. G. Usher
Death Takes a Wife. Anthony Gilbert
Death Takes an Editor. N. Morland
Death Takes an Option. N. MacNeil
Death Takes Over. J. McFerran
Death Takes Revenge. James Preston
Death Takes Small Bites. G. H. Johnston
Death Takes the Bus. L. White
Death Takes the Joystick. P. Conde
Death Takes the Last Train. R. Bernard
Death Takes the Living. M. Burton
Death Takes the Low Road. P. Ruell
Death Takes the Stage. Gavin Holt
Death Takes the Stage. Donald Ward
Death Takes the Stump. E. H. Duthoit
Death Takes the Wheel. E. Radford
Death Talks Out of Turn. R. Powell
Death Talks Shop. P. Haggard
Death Tape. K. Gallison
Death Tears a Comic Strip. T. Du Bois
Death That Lurks Unseen. J. S. Fletcher
Death the Red Flower. O. Wynd
Death the Showman. John Fraser
Death the Sure Physician. J. Wakefield
Death Therapy. R. Sapir
Death Through the Looking Glass. R. Forrest
Death Through the Mill. L. Colburn
Death Throws a Party. Austin Stone
Death Throws No Shadow. L. Grex
Death Thumbs a Ride. J. Lilly
Death Tide. W. Norville
Death Times Three. R. Stout
Death to a Left-Handed Woman. C. Joyce
Death to Comrade X. John Morgan
Death to Drumbeat. J. Lane
Death to My Beloved. R. Neely
Death to My Killer. J. York
Death to Remember. R. Ormerod
Death to Slow Music. B. Nichols
Death to the Dancing Masters. R. Harper
Death to the Fifth Column. B. Newman
Death to the Killer. C. F. Caunter
Death to the Ladies. N. Morland
Death to the Landlords! Ellis Peters
Death to the Mafia. F. Scarpetta
Death to the Rescue. M. Kennedy
Death to the Spy. D. Dayle
Death to the Spy. B. Newman
Death to Windward. H. Brinton
Death Toll. W. E. Chambers
Death Tolls. J. E. Stith
Death Tolls the Bell. M. Hervey
Death Tolls the Bell. P. McGuire
Death Tolls the Gong. J. G. Brandon
Death Took a Greek God. N. Forrest
Death Took a Publisher. N. Forrest
Death-Torch Terror. B. House
Death Tour. D. J. Michael
Death Tower. M. Grant
Death Train. R. Byrne

Death Train. A. MacNeill
Death Trance. G. Masterton
Death Trap. H. Carmichael
Death Trap. R. W. Cole
Death Trap. P. H. Dobbins
Death Trap. E. P. Green
Death Trap. J. D. MacDonald
Death Trap. J. Rosenberger
Death Trap. A. Skene
Death Traps. K. C. Strahan
Death Traps the Killer. Mary Dane
Death Treads—. C. M. Wills
Death Treads Softly. G. Bellairs
Death Trick. J. F. Burke
Death Trick. R. Jeffries
Death Trick. R. Stevenson
Death Trust. Anonymous
Death Trust. A. L. Halstead
Death Turns a Trick. Julie Smith
Death Turns Right. T. B. Dewey
Death Turns Right. J. Mathewson
Death Turns the Tables. J. D. Carr
Death Turns Traitor. W. S. Masterman
Death-Twist. J. Tiger
Death Under Contract. R. Wallace
Death Under Desolate. J. N. Chance
Death Under Gibraltar. B. Newman
Death Under Par. J. Law
Death Under Sail. C. P. Snow
Death Under Snowdon. G. Carr
Death Under the Lilacs. R. Forrest
Death Under the Moonflower. T. Downing
Death Under the Stars. V. Bell
Death Under the Table. P. Godfrey
Death Under Virago. T. Muir
Death Unheralded. George Douglas
Death Upon a Spear. Hosanna Brown
Death Village. K. Netzen
Death Visits Downspring. M. Burton
Death Visits the Apple Hole. A. B. Cunningham
Death Visits the Cinema. F. W. Irwin
Death Visits the Circus. Jean Marsh
Death Visits the Parish. F. W. Gumley
Death Visits the Summer-House. Gret Lane
Death Vows. Max Hart
Death Waits in Tucson. D. Reid
Death Waits Outside. R. Verron
Death Walk. E. Quest
Death Walked In. B. Manktelow
Death Walked In. L. A. Olmsted
Death Walked in Berlin. M. M. Kaye
Death Walked in Cyprus. M. M. Kaye
Death Walked in Kashmir. M. M. Kaye
Death Walkers. G. Brandner
Death Walks. D. Haring
Death Walks by the River. V. Bell
Death Walks In. G. Chester
Death Walks In. D. Haring
Death Walks in Eastrepps. F. Beeding
Death Walks in Marble Halls. L. G. Blochman
Death Walks in Scarlet. L. Cargill
Death Walks in Shadow. L. Thayer
Death Walks on Cat Feet. P. Haggard
Death Walks on Cat Feet. D. B. Olsen
Death Walks Softly. Hazel C. MacDonald
Death Walks Softly. B. Shannon
Death Walks Softly. N. Shepherd
Death Walks the Dry Tortugas. M. P. Rea
Death Walks the Post. V. Hanson
Death Walks the Woods. C. Hare
Death Warmed Over. Mary Collins
Death Warmed Over. J. D. Forbes
Death Warmed Over. Lee Martin
Death Warmed Up. M. Babson
Death Warrant. S. Coburn
Death Warrant. Gary Hunter
Death Was a Wedding Guest. A. S. Roche
Death Was Her Desire. R. Himmel
Death Was Her Escort. E. Pawley
Death Was No Lady. S. Truss
Death Was the Echo. R. Dana
Death-Watch. J. D. Carr
Death Watch. D. Creed
Death Watch. J. Hawkins

Death Watch. R. Wilson
Death Watch. D. Winston
Death Watch Ladies. J. N. Chance
Death Waves. Nick Stone
Death Wears a Bridal Veil. K. M. Knight
Death Wears a Carnation. B. E. Stevenson
Death Wears a Copper Necktie and other stories. H. Pentecost
Death Wears a Green Hat. W. Creed
Death Wears a Lady's Smile. D. Haring
Death Wears a Mask. Therese Benson
Death Wears a Mask. D. G. Browne
Death Wears a Mask. Anthony Gilbert
Death Wears a Petticoat. H. Janson
Death Wears a Purple Shirt. R. C. Woodthorpe
Death Wears a Red Hat. W. X. Kienzle
Death Wears a Scarab. A. R. Long
Death Wears a Silk Stocking. W. M. Duncan
Death Wears a Veil. K. M. Knight
Death Wears a White Shirt. T. Du Bois
Death Wears a White Gardenia. Z. Popkin
Death Wears Cat's Eyes. D. B. Olsen
Death Wears Nylons. M. T. Dallas
Death Wears Pink Shoes. Robert James
Death Wears Red Shoes. Colin Robertson
Death Weed. L. Thayer
Death Went Hunting. George Douglas
Death When She Wakes. N. Morland
Death When You Want It. Desmond Martin
Death Whispers. J. B. Carr
Death Whispers Softly. P. Malloch
Death Whistle. R. Marsh
Death Will Find Me. H. Steers
Death Wind. D. Pendleton
Death Wish. R. Beck
Death Wish. V. Caspary
Death Wish. B. Garfield
Death Wish. E. S. Holding
Death-Wish Green. F. Crane
Death Wishes. P. Loraine
Death with a Difference. B. Cobb
Death with Blue Ribbon. L. Bruce
Death Within the Vault. L. Thayer
Death Without a Funeral. J. Ward
Death Without Honor. D. Moreau
Death Without Question. T. Muir
Death Woman. J. N. Chance
Death Won a Prize. I. Montgomery
Death Won't Wait. Anthony Gilbert
Death Won't Wait. Peter Williams
Death Won't Wash. N. Longmate
Death Wore a Diadem. I. McGregor
Death Wore a Petticoat. H. Janson
Death Wore Fins. Dale Clark
Death Wore Gloves. R. H. Spencer
Death Wore Gold Shoes. L. V. Stevens
Death Wore Roses. C. Saxby
Death Works to Rule. J. Bowyer
Death Writes a Message. T. Westgate
Death Writes an Ad. M. Holbrook
Deathampton Summer. M. Logan
Deathbed. W. X. Kienzle
Deathbed of Roses. Deborah Scott
Deathbird Stories. H. Ellison
Deathbites. D. Stivers
Deathblow Hill. P. A. Taylor
Deathbringer. M. Von Conta
Deathcalls. R. Montana
Deathday Song. E. Zumwalt
Deathgame. J. Ramsay
Deathhunter. I. Watson
Deathless and the Dead. A. Clarke
Deathly Pale. D. Lynch
Deathmaster. W. M. Duncan
Deathmate. M. Caidin
Death's Angel. W. B. Longley
Death's Bright Angel. H. Davie-Martin
Death's Bright Angel. Janet Neel
Death's Bright Angel. T. Warriner
Death's Bright Arrow. J. Sherburne
Death's Bright Dart. V. C. Clinton-Baddeley
Death's Busy Crossroads. S. Mitchell
Death's Clenched Fist. J. Sherburne
Death's Counterfeit. H. Clevely

D

Death's Dark Deceit. S. Clausse
Death's Dark Music. Marilyn Ross
Death's Darkest Face. J. Symons
Death's Dateless Night. T. Warriner
Death's Door. W. Barker
Death's Doorway. V. Gunn
Death's Duet. H. Carstairs
Death's Eye. L. Meynell
Death's Foot Forward. G. B. Mair
Death's Gray Angel. J. Sherburne
Death's Head. C. Black
Death's Head. J. Ross
Death's Head. Arthur Wise
Death's Head Berlin. J. Gerson
Death's Head Conspiracy. Nick Carter
Death's Inheritance. E. Radford
Death's Juggler. C. J. Daly
Death's Little Sister. J. Dekker
Death's Long Shadow. J. Barbette
Death's Long Shadow. K. Wolffe
Death's Lovely Mask. J. Flagg
Death's Mannikens. M. Afford
Death's No Antidote. G. Osborne
Deaths of Lora Karen. R. McDougald
Death's Old Sweet Song. J. Stagge
Death's Pale Face. E. Wiley
Death's Pale Horse. J. Sherburne
Death's Running Mate. J. D. Revere
Death's Savage Passion. O. Papazoglu
Death's Second Self. J. F. Drabble
Death's Sweet Music. N. Morland
Death's Sweet Song. Clifton Adams
Death's Treasure Hunt. W. C. Harvey
Death's Visiting Card. J. C. Woodiwiss
Deathsport. William Hughes
Deathstalk. B. Clark
Deathstar Voyage. Ian Wallace
Deathstone. E. L. Arch
Deathstorm. R. B. Gillespie
Deathstrike. Nick Carter
Deathtrap. I. Levin
Deathward. R. Byers
Deathwatch. J. Genet
Deathwatch. J. Gerson
Deathwatch. R. Harrison
Deathwatch. E. Trevor
Deathwatch '39. J. Gerson
Deathwishers. T. Journet
Deathwork. J. McLendon
Deaves Affair. H. Footner
Deborah's Legacy. S. Marlowe
Debriefing. R. Littell
Debt. O. Hogstrand
Debt Discharged. E. Wallace
Debt of Hatred. G. Ohnet
Debt of Honor. A. Kennedy
Debt of Vengeance. Mrs. E. B. Collins
Debt to Dishonour. A. Furness
Decameron of a Hypnotist. E. R. Suffling
Decayed Gentlewoman. E. Ferrars
Deceit. N. W. Firth
Deceit and Deadly Lies. F. Bandy
Deceitful Death. J. Penn
Deceivers. R. Goldhurst
Deceiver's Door. C. B. Booth
Deceiving Mirror. P. Traill
December Conspiracy. J. Crown
December Ultimatum. Michael Nicholson
Deception. J. Aiken
Deception. C. Dale
Deception. C. Kavanaugh
Deception by Design. L. Pace
Deception Island. M. K. Lorens
Deception of Death. V. Siller
Deception of Ursula. T. Cobb
Deception on Peregrine Island. L. A. Sunagel
Deceptions. H. L. Victor
Deceptive Clarity. A. J. Elkins
Decimate Decision. A. Heal
Decision. E. Chodorov
Decision. A. Drury
Decision. W. A. Hackett
Decision. H. Kane
Decision at Dawn. A. Calin

Decision at Delphi. Helen MacInnes
Decision Before Dawn. G. Howe
Decision in Berlin. R. D. Dege
Decision in the Dark. Philip Turner
Decision Time. J. Ahern
Deck with Flowers. E. Cadell
Decker. W. Graeme-Holder
Decks Ran Red. L. A. Stone
Declared Dead. J. Francome
Declined with Thanks. E. Mulliner
Declined with Thanks. U. L. Silberrad
Decoding of Edwin Drood. C. Forsyte
Decorated Corpse. R. Stratton
Decoration. K. Hewitt
Decoy. C. F. Adams
Decoy. J. D. Beresford
Decoy. Francis Dana
Decoy. A. Maling
Decoy. Michael Morgan
Decoy. D. Pope
Decoy. Stephen Robertson
Decoy. E. Ronns
Decoy Babes. B. Sarto
Decoy Detective. Anonymous
Decoy Doll. C. F. Adams
Decoy for Murder. P. Saxon
Decoy Hit. Nick Carter
Decoy in Diamonds. N. Gates
Decoy Murders. A. Douglas
Decoyed Across the Seas. R. Overton
Decoys. R. Hoyt
Dedicated Man. Peter Robinson
Dedicated to the End. P. De Pietro
Deductions of Colonel Gore. L. Brock
Dee Dee. E. H. Robinson
Dee Goong An. R. Van Gulik
Deed Is Drawn. W. A. Barber
Deed of a Night. Warren Miller
Deed of Darkness. I. Stark
Deed of Innocence. J. Blackmore
Deed Without a Name. D. Bowers
Deed Without a Name. E. Phillpotts
Deeds Ill Done. A. Seifert
Deeds of Darkness. G. T. Morley
Deeds of Dr. Deadcert. Joan Fleming
Deeds of the Disturber. Elizabeth Peters
Deep. P. Benchley
Deep. M. Spillane
Deep Among the Dead Men. J. Blackburn
Deep and Crisp and Even. L. Payne
Deep and Crisp and Even. P. Turnbull
Deep As the Grave. O. Keystone
Deep Blue Cradle. Peter Chambers
Deep Blue Good-By. J. D. MacDonald
Deep Blue Seize. D. McLarty
Deep Channels. E. L. Long
Deep Chill. I. Slater
Deep Coffyn. J. Laurence
Deep Cold Green. Carter Brown
Deep Cover. B. Garfield
Deep Cover Blastoff. L. Derrick
Deep Currents. A. Fielding
Deep, Dark and Dead. D. MacKenzie
Deep, Deep Freeze. W. Garner
Deep Disturbance. C. Rauch
Deep Dive. D. Hornig
Deep End. F. Brown
Deep End. O. Dudley
Deep End. J. Fielding
Deep End. J. Hayes
Deep Fall. B. Knox
Deep Flows the River. A. Wood
Deep Freeze. J. Bruce
Deep Furrows. R. W. Ritchie
Deep Gold. A. Mather
Deep Green Death. B. Gaston
Deep in Dark Country. P. Drew
Deep Is My Desire. I. Gordon
Deep Is My Grave. J. Death
Deep Is the Blue. M. Ehrlich
Deep Is the Lake. M. Clare
Deep Is the Pit. H. V. Dixon
Deep Kill. D. Da Cruz
Deep Kill. J. Dugan

Deep Knife. R. Dudgeon
Deep-Lake Mystery. C. Wells
Deep Lay the Dead. F. C. Davis
Deep Lie. Stuart Woods
Deep Malice. D. G. Waring
Deep Moat Grange. S. R. Crockett
Deep Pocket. M. Kenyon
Deep Pool. J. Blackmore
Deep Purple. T. Allbeury
Deep Quarry. J. E. Stith
Deep Sand. B. Munslow
Deep Sea Death. Nick Carter
Deep Sea Gold. Anonymous
Deep-Sea Tow. C. McManus
Deep Secret. R. Chapman
Deep Six. J. Cartwright
Deep Six. C. Cussler
Deep Six. J. M. Flynn
Deep Six. R. Striker
Deep South Slave. D. Glinto
Deep Valley. W. Anthony
Deep Water. P. Highsmith
Deep Water. S. Whalen
Deep Waters. W. W. Jacobs
Deep Waters. M. Leighton
Deepening Blue. S. M. Schley
Deeper Danger. J. Springer
Deeper Game. Nicholas Carter
Deeper Scar. S. Gluck
Deeper Stain. F. Hird
Deepsea Shootout. L. Derrick
Deepwater. A. Finer
Deer in Water. J. Reid
Deer Killers. G. Landers
Deer Leap. M. Grimes
Deerlover. E. H. Creeth
Deerstalker. T. Mustoo
Defame and Destroy. P. Chase
Defcon One. J. Weber
Defeat of a Detective. C. M. Wills
Defection! Steve Mackenzie
Defection of A. J. Lewinter. R. Littell
Defector. Evelyn Anthony
Defector. Nick Carter
Defector. C. Collingwood
Defector. R. Raphael
Defector. H. Reynolds
Defector. D. Seaman
Defector. P. Thomas
Defectors. R. Lehrman
Defectors Are Dead Men. F. A. Smith
Defence Against Terror. W. Rotsler
Defence of the Realm. J. O. Easton
"Defend the Rock." P. Groom
Defenders. E. S. Aarons
Defenders and Believers. D. Pendleton
Defenders of the Law. H. Del Ruth
Defending a Home. E. A. Young
Defense Does Not Rest. E. Sherry
Defense Rests. E. Pierson
Deferred Payment. J. Owen
Deficit Ending. Lee Martin
Definite Object. J. Farnol
Defrauded Yeggman. H. S. Keeler
Defrauding the Government. W. H. Theobald
Defy the Devil. Sara Woods
Defy the Tempest. S. Dannett
Degenerate. F. Whishaw
Degradation of Geoffrey Alwith. Morley Roberts
Degraded. Stuart Hall
Deirdre. J. Nicholas
Deja Vu. L. Pender
Deja-Vu. D. Saint-Alban
Dekker. L. Cameron
Dekker's Demons. A. Webb
Delacott Mystery. C. Kingston
Delafield Affair. F. F. Kelly
Delaney. Gilbert Morris
Delaplaine. M. T. Walworth
Delaware Dick. M. Mizzen
Delay in Danger. S. Harvester
Delay of Doom. P. Capon
Delay on Turtle. V. Canning
Delayed Action. R. W. Hatch

Delayed Action. N. Tranter
Delayed Harvest. Rona Randall
Delayed Payment. J. Rhode
Deldee. F. Warden
Deldee, the Ward of Warington. F. Warden
Delfina. S. Brackeen
Delgado Killings. R. Hawkes
Delia's Dilemma. A. Griffin
Delicate Ape. D. B. Hughes
Delicate Case of Murder. S. Gluck
Delicate Darling. J. Webb
Delicate Deceit. S. Hufford
Delicate Dilemmas. M. P. Willocks
Delicate Dust of Death. P. Audemars
Delicate Fiend. E. C. Vivian
Delicately Personal Matter. R. Werry
Delicious Danger. H. Janson
Delilah. P. Trent
Delilah of Harlem. R. H. Savage
Delilah of Mayfair. A. Soutar
Delilah Was Deadly. Carter Brown
Delinquent! Morton Cooper
Delinquents. A. Bloomfield
Delinquents. P. Malloch
Deliver the Baby. A. Bocca
Deliver Us from Evil. H. Desmond
Deliver Us from Evil. A. L. Harris
Deliver Us from Evil. S. Smoke
Deliver Us from Wolves. L. Holton
Deliver Us to Evil. J. L. Hensley
Deliverance. J. Dickey
Deliverers. B. M. Aitken
Delivery. G. Simenon
Delivery of Furies. V. Canning
Delorme in Deep Water. S. Lister
Delphi Betrayal. L. Perdue
Delphi Calculus. M. Green
Delphine. R. Henrey
Delta Crossing. J. Nazel
Delta Decision. Wilbur Smith
Delta Deputies. Carl Martin
Delta Factor. M. Spillane
Delta Flame. Marilyn Ross
Delta Force. J. Norst
Delta Knife. Kenneth O'Hara
Delta November. C. M. Filgate
Delta Star. J. Wambaugh
Demagogue. C. Dawe
Demand for Justice. I. Stark
Demarest Inheritance. M. Carleton
DeMaury Papers. I. Holland
Demented. B. W. Battin
Demented. D. J. Young
Demented Empire. L. Derrick
Demi-Paradise Regained. S. Stone
Demise of a Louse. W. T. Ballard
Democrat Dies. P. Frankau
Demolished Man. A. Bester
Demolishers. Donald Hamilton
Demon. J. McCulley
Demon. I. Watkins
Demon. C. N. Williamson
Demon Again. E. M. Keate
Demon Barber of Broadway. Griff
Demon Cat. L. B. Clark
Demon Child. D. Dwyer
Demon Count. Anne Stuart
Demon Count's Daughter. Ann Stuart
Demon Detective. Anonymous
Demon Device. R. Saffron
Demon-4. David Mace
Demon in My View. R. Rendell
Demon in the Blood. P. Marlowe
Demon in the Skull. F. Pohl
Demon Island. K. Robeson
Demon Jockey. B. Hemyng
Demon Lover. V. Holt
Demon of Barnabas Collins. Marilyn Ross
Demon of Desire. W. J. Elliott
Demon of Hong Kong. R. S. L. Harding
Demon of Raven's Cliff. P. Zawadsky
Demon of Sicily. E. Montague
Demon of the Air. E. M. Keate
Demon of the Darkness. Dana Ross

Demon of the Opera. N. Schier
Demon Stirs. O. Cameron
Demon Tower. V. Coffman
Demon Within. Brook Hastings
Demoniacs. J. D. Carr
Demonic Color. P. Dunn
Demon's Eye. Nicholas Carter
Demon's Moon. Colin Robertson
Demons of Highpoint House. C. Cunningham
Demons of the Night. Nicholas Carter
Demonwood. Anne Stewart
Dempsey Diamonds. A. Arnot
Den of Savage Men. Bradshaw Jones
Den of Thieves. K. Stall
Denbigh Affair. A. Lowing
Dene Hollow. H. Wood
Dene of the Secret Service. J. S. Barlow
Dene of the Secret Service. G. Verner
Deniable Man. S. Stein
Denis Delivers the Goods. C. Hand
Denis Dent. E. W. Hornung
Denmark Bus. S. McGurk
Denmede Mystery. W. Martyn
Dennecker Code. J. C. Pollock
Dennis, the Girl and the Case. Hugh
Dennisdale Tragedy. H. Andover
Dennison Hill. D. Winston
Dennison's War. A. Lassiter
Denton's Army. R. D. Cross
Denver Collection. D. Wright
Denver Lil. F. Foden
Denver Strike. C. Ramm
Denver's Double. George Griffith
Denzil Emeralds. P. Meredith
Denzil's Device. B. Delannoy
Depart This Life. E. Ferrars
Department K. H. Howard
Department of Dead Ends. Roy Vickers
Department of Death. J. Creasey
Department of Queer Complaints. Carter Dickson
Departmental. M. Rutherford
Departure Deferred. W. H. Baker
Departure Delayed. W. Oursler
Departure of Mr. Gaudette. D. M. Disney
Deposit Vault Puzzle. Nicholas Carter
Depository Mystery. G. Chester
Depraved Indifference. R. K. Tanenbaum
Depravity. H. Janson
Depth Charge. Nick Stone
Depths. J. Creasey
Depths of Death. B. Luigi
Depths of Yesterday. D. Lyons
Deputy. W. C. Tuttle
Deputy Avenger. H. Richards
Deputy Avenger. R. Trevor
Deputy for Cain. Roy Vickers
Deputy Wife. Norman Lee
Derelict. C. J. C. Hyne
Derelict. J. T. Shaw
Derelict House. A. Skene
Derelict of Skull Shoal. K. Robeson
Derelicts. W. M. Graydon
Derfflinger. B. Garland
Derision. C. Edwards
Derrick Devil. K. Robeson
Derring-Do. H. Craigie
Derry Down Death. A. Curry
Deruga Trial. R. Huch
Desborough Mystery. A. M. Diehl
Descent into the Dark. D. Ramsay
Desert Adventure. D. Spicer
Desert Bride. H. Nisbet
Desert Cain. Kathlyn Rhodes
Desert Captive. E. Tokson
Desert Castle Mystery. C. H. Snow
Desert Convoy. M. Hastings
Desert Crime. Roland Daniel
Desert Death Raid. J. Buchanan
Desert Demons. Anonymous
Desert Desire. J. Chancellor
Desert Episode. G. Greenfield
Desert Flower. Rona Randall
Desert Flyer. J. Bolton
Desert Fury. H. Janson

Desert Intrigue. E. Ellison
Desert Intrigue. J. Stagg
Desert Lake Mystery. K. C. Strahan
Desert Light. Chilton Williamson
Desert Look. B. Schopen
Desert Lovers. C. H. Bullivant
Desert Moon Mystery. K. C. Strahan
Desert Night. W. E. Johns
Desert of Darkness. P. Wissmann
Desert of Doom. W. M. Graydon
Desert of Salt. K. R. Butler
Desert of the Damned. B. McAllister
Desert Raid. Steve Mackenzie
Desert Shadows. B. Netton
Desert Squadron. J. R. Holden
Desert Stalker. M. Barry
Desert Strike. D. Pendleton
Desert Town. R. Stewart
Desert Trail. R. C. Armour
Desert Trail. D. Lenton
Desert Wooing. C. H. Bullivant
Deserted by the Devil. T. Irving-Jones
Deserted Date. D. Haring
Deserted Night. T. B. Morris
Deserted Wife. E. Southworth
Deserter of the Foreign Legion. W. M. Graydon
Deserters. D. Hann
Deserters. G. C. Jenks
Deserters Don't Come Back. R. Wilkes-Hunter
Design for an Accident. D. Egerton
Design for Blackmail. J. L. Morrissey
Design for Danger. E. Ellison
Design for Death. J. Day
Design for Death. E. Ronns
Design for Death. K. Summers
Design for Destruction. Deryck Phillips
Design for Dupes. H. Janson
Design for Dying. A. Jeffers
Design for Dying. S. A. Krasney
Design for Dying. H. McCloy
Design for Dying. A. Morice
Design for Dying. L. Trimble
Design for Murder. G. Batson
Design for Murder. F. Durbridge
Design for Murder. C. G. Hart
Design for Murder. F. A. Kummer
Design for Murder. E. Quest
Design for Murder. P. Wilde
Design for Murder, and five other stories. L. H. Fox
Design for November. R. E. Mitchell
Design for Treachery. C. C. Saunders
Design for Treason. G. Dickson
Design for Vengeance. Martin Thomas
Design in Diamonds. K. M. Knight
Design in Evil. R. King
Designated Assassin. Frederick Nolan
Designated Hitter. W. Wager
Designed to Deceive. Carter Brown
Designs on Life. E. Ferrars
Desirable Alien. A. Kennington
Desirable Dictator. J. Fores
Desirable Woman. C. Dawe
Desire After Dark. A. Bocca
Desire at Midnight. N. W. Firth
Desire in the Dust. H. Whittington
Desire of the Eyes and other stories. G. Allen
Desire to Kill. Alice Campbell
Desire to Kill. A. Clarke
Desired. Carter Brown
Desireless. Thomas York
Desmond Dare. Old Sleuth
Desmond Drake Goes West. Sea Lion
Desmond Rourke, Irishman. J. Haslette
Desouza in Stardust. F. Olbrich
Desouza Pays the Price. F. Olbrich
Despair. R. Kleiner
Despair. V. Nabokoff-Sirin
Despair and Delight. R. Arnold
Despair and Die. J. Midgley
Despair's Last Journey. D. C. Murray
Despatch of a Dove. R. Petrie
Desperado. J. Hunter
Desperate Adversaries. J. Hoffenberg
Desperate Art. J. Rosenberg

D

Desperate Chance. Nicholas Carter
Desperate Chance. O. Harper
Desperate Chance. J. D. J. Kelley
Desperate Chance. Old Sleuth
Desperate Conspiracy. G. Boothby
Desperate Criminals. R. Longrigg
Desperate Cure. R. Fenisong
Desperate Deed. N. T. Oliver
Desperate Desmond's Dastardly Deed. L. Price
Desperate Dilemma. M. Danvers
Desperate Encounter. Cecile Rutherford
Desperate Expedient. C. N. Boyle
Desperate Gamble. H. Desmond
Desperate Game. J. K. Leys
Desperate Game. Old Spicer
Desperate Game. F. Warden
Desperate Games. P. Boulle
Desperate Games. J. Castle
Desperate Heiress. Marilyn Ross
Desperate Holiday. F. Cowen
Desperate Hours. J. Hayes
Desperate Journey. H. Treece
Desperate Justice. Dan Morgan
Desperate Justice. R. Speight
Desperate Love. A. Andre
Desperate Love. C. Dawe
Desperate Measures. M. Arnold
Desperate Measures. D. Wheatley
Desperate Moment. M. Albrand
Desperate People. H. C. Davis
Desperate People. F. Durbridge
Desperate Remedies. Thomas Hardy
Desperate Remedy. B. Bolt
Desperate Rendezvous. R. Severn
Desperate Search. C. Eland
Desperate Search. A. Mayse
Desperate Steps. Mark Cross
Desperate Venture. J. Ritson
Desperate Voyage. E. F. Knight
Desperate Witch. Anthony Graham
Desperation. R. Rand
Despite the Evidence. P. Alding
Despoilers. E. Mitchell
Despotic Lady. W. E. Norris
Destination: Algiers. J. Rovin
Destination Dames. H. Janson
Destination Danger. W. C. MacDonald
Destination: Death. G. Bishop
Destination—Death. H. Desmond
Destination Dieppe. W. H. Baker
Destination: Norway. J. Rovin
Destination: Stalingrad. J. Rovin
Destination TNT. D. Haring
Destination: Terror. J. Paull
Destination Unknown. A. Christie
Destination Unknown. R. Goyne
Destination Unknown. J. Hunter
Destination Unknown. R. Sale
Destinations. G. Simenon
Destinies. H. Normanby
Destiny. A. Askew
Destiny Is My Name. David Hume
Destiny Man. P. Van Greenaway
Destiny of Death. Dell Shannon
Destiny on Demand. M. Butcher
Destiny's Child. P. Morton
Destiny's Daughter. C. H. Bullivant
Destroy the U.S.A. W. F. Jenkins
Destroyer. C. Goodall
Destroyer. J. Lodwick
Destroyer. B. E. Stevenson
Destroyer. B. Swift
Destroyer. R. W. West
Destroyer and the Red-Haired Death. S. Horler
Destroyers. A. W. Miller
Destroyers. H. E. South
Destroying Angel. Anthea Cohen
Destroying Angel. J. Creighton
Destroying Angel. Bernard King
Destroying Angel. N. Klein
Destroying Angel. L. J. Vance
Destroying Angel. E. Wallace
Destruction Committee. W. J. Coughlin
Destruction Man. Charles West

Destruction of Eva. K. Hurst
Destructive Vice. B. Bavin
Destructors. M. Franklin
Destur Mobed, and other stories. E. M. Birnstingl
Detail. W. McCarthy
Detail for the Dreamer. W. M. Duncan
Details of Jeremy Stratton. A. E. Lindop
Detection in a Topper. J. Oliver
Detection Unlimited. G. Heyer
Detections of Dr. Sam: Johnson. L. De La Torre
Detective. P. Ferris
Detective. Parnell Hall
Detective. R. Thorp
Detective. L. J. Vance
Detective Against Detective. D. J. MacKenzie
Detective Against Detective. M. Redwing
Detective and Mr. Dickens. W. J. Palmer
Detective and the Poisoner. S. Rathbone
Detective and the Somnambulist. A. Pinkerton
Detective Archie. Old Sleuth
Detective Ben. J. J. Farjeon
Detective Bob Bridger. R. M. Taylor
Detective Burr's Seven Clues. Anonymous
Detective Coulson. Jack Mann
Detective Crime Cases. A. L. Rankin
Detective Dale. Old Sleuth
Detective Duff Unravels It. H. J. O'Higgins
Detective Fleet of London. Anonymous
Detective for Vengeance. Anonymous
Detective Gay. Old Sleuth
Detective Gordon's Grip. Anonymous
Detective Grime's Triumph. A. Robertson
Detective Hanley. Old Sleuth
Detective in Distress. B. Cobb
Detective in Italy. H. Forbes
Detective in Spite of Himself. H. Manning
Detective Inspector Chance. G. R. Sims
Detective Janaki. K. Sathianadhan
Detective Johnson of New Orleans. H. I. Hancock
Detective Kennedy. Old Sleuth
Detective Murdock, the Silent. Old Sleuth
Detective Nipper. Maxwell Scott
Detective No. 1. F. Pratt
Detective Officer. Waters
Detective on the Prowl. L. W. Brent
Detective Payne. Old Sleuth
Detective Payne's Shadow. Old Sleuth
Detective Play. Paul Groves
Detective Reynold's Hardest Case. G. Macias
Detective Stories. Anonymous
Detective Stories. Nicholas Carter
Detective Stories. W. Henderson
Detective Story. S. Kingsley
Detective Sylvia Shale. S. Groom
Detective Thrash, the Trapper of Criminals. Old Sleuth
Detective Trio. Old Sleuth
Detective Unawares. G. F. P. Lea
Detective Warder Nelson Lee. Maxwell Scott
Detective Wore Silk Drawers. P. Lovesey
Detectives. N. Daniels
Detective's Album. W. W.
Detective's Clew. Old Hutch
Detective's Crime. F. Du Boisgobey
Detective's Crime. C. Morris
Detective's Daughter. L. L. Lynch
Detective's Daughter. Old Sleuth
Detective's Dilemma. F. Du Boisgobey
Detective's Dilemma. H. L. Phillips
Detective's Due. L. Egan
Detective's Enigma. Old Sleuth
Detective's Eye. F. Du Boisgobey
Detective's Holiday. C. Barry
Detective's Honeymoon. M. Danvers
Detectives in Gum Boots. R. East
Detectives, Limited. N. Goddard
Detectives, Ltd. F. S. Wees
Detective's Memoirs and other stories. E. M. L. Sturt
Detective's Note-Book. C. Martel
Detective's Notebook. Anonymous
Detectives of Europe and America. G. S. McWatters
Detective's Pretty Neighbor and other stories. Nicholas Carter

Detective's Secret. N. D. Urner
Detective's Tale. G. F. Newman
Detective's Theory. Nicholas Carter
Detective's Triumph. F. Du Boisgobey
Detective's Triumphs. D. Donovan
Detective's Victory. Anonymous
Detectograms and other puzzles. H. A. Ripley
Dethroned Heiress. E. A. Dupuy
Detling Murders. J. Symons
Detling Secret. J. Symons
Detonator. W. Garys
Detonators. D. Hamilton
Detour. M. M. Goldsmith
Detour. H. Nielsen
Detour. W. Wilson
Detour at Night. G. Endore
Detour Through Devon. G. Endor
Detour to a Funeral. V. J. Santiago
Detour to Death. H. Nielsen
Detour to Denmark. J. Ware
Detour to Oblivion. F. C. Davis
Detours. O. R. Cohen
Detroit Combat. C. Ramm
Detroit Deathwatch. D. Pendleton
Detroit Massacre. M. Barry
Deuce and All. G. Raffalovich
Deuces Wild. H. MacGrath
Deuces Wild. Dell Shannon
Deus Irae. P. K. Dick
Devalino Caper. A. J. Russell
Devastation. Mrs. C. Kernahan
Devastators. D. Hamilton
Devereaux File. R. H. Spencer
Devereaux Legacy. C. G. Hart
Devereux Court Mystery. M. Burton
Deveril's Diamond. A. Sergeant
Deveron Hall. V. Johnston
Deviant Behavior. E. W. Emerson
Deviant Death. G. Moffat
Deviations of Diana. H. Mitchell
Deviator. A. York
Device. E. Wallace
Device for Murder. G. M. Snodgress
Devices and Desires. P. D. James
Devices of Darkness. J. M. English
Devil and All. J. Collier
Devil and Ben Camden. H. Graat
Devil and Ben Franklin. T. Mathieson
Devil and Destiny. T. Du Bois
Devil and Mary Ann. C. Cookson
Devil and Miss Thrace, and other stories. M. Hervey
Devil and Mrs. Devine. Josphine Leslie
Devil and the C.I.D. E. C. R. Lorac
Devil and the Crusader. A. Askew
Devil and the Deep. S. Horler
Devil and the Deep. H. Janson
Devil and the Deep Blue Sea. E. Jordan
Devil and the Dolce Vita. T. Holme
Devil and Webster Daniels. T. L. Smith
Devil and X.Y.Z. B. Browne
Devil at Castelnero. J. Schubert
Devil at Home. O. Lange
Devil at Saxon Wall. G. Mitchell
Devil at the Crossroads. J. Barwick
Devil at the Door. D. Gilfillan
Devil at the Door. M. Seuffert
Devil at Westease. V. Sackville-West
Devil at Your Elbow. D. M. Devine
Devil Behind Me. F. E. Smith
Devil Boy. W. D. Roberts
Devil Breathes But Once. C. Wallace
Devil Builds a Chapel. M. Marlette
Devil by the Sea. N. Bawden
Devil Child. P. J. Cooper
Devil Comes to Bolobyn. S. Horler
Devil Comes to Devon. J. Rowland
Devil Daddy. J. Blackburn
Devil Dances for Gold. Regina Ross
Devil, Devil. M. Avallone
Devil Doctor. S. Rohmer
Devil Dolls. J. Nazel
Devil Drives. R. Ames
Devil Drives. J. N. Chance

Title Index

Devil Drives. V. Markham
Devil Dunes. M. Sheppard
Devil Finds Work. M. Delving
Devil Fish. P. Groom
Devil for the Witch. E. Lacy
Devil Force. D. Pendleton
Devil Genghis. K. Robeson
Devil Has a Racket. M. Storme
Devil Has Four Faces. J. Jakes
Devil Has the Best Tunes. H. L. V. Fletcher
Devil Has Wings. P. Conde
Devil Held the Aces. P. Doncaster
Devil His Due. W. O'Farrell
Devil in a Blue Dress. W. Mosley
Devil in a Domino. C. L'Epine
Devil in Broad Daylight. J. Bramlett
Devil in Crystal. E. Lindley
Devil in Davos. G. Brewer
Devil in Downing Street. R. Ladline
Devil in Dungarees. Albert Conroy
Devil in Greenlands. J. N. Chance
Devil in Harbour. C. Gavin
Devil in Her. H. Duval
Devil in Her. P. Trent
Devil in Kansas. Simon Quinn
Devil in London. G. R. Sims
Devil in Moonlight. M. Proctor
Devil in Tartan. E. Ogilvie
Devil in the Belfry. R. Thorndike
Devil in the Bush. M. Head
Devil-in-the-Dark. P. Wentworth
Devil in the Darkness. A. Roy
Devil in the Maze. V. Gunn
Devil in the Pines. L. Cameron
Devil in the Pulpit. E. O'Donnell
Devil in the Sky. Muriel Bradley
Devil in the Wind. G. Greenaway
Devil in Velvet. J. D. Carr
Devil Is a Skirt. W. Standish
Devil Is Dead. Roy Lewis
Devil Is Jones. K. Robeson
Devil Kinsmere. R. Fairbairn
Devil Laughed. M. Richmond
Devil Loves Me. M. Millar
Devil Man. E. Wallace
Devil Mask Mystery. J. Rains
Devil May Care. Wade Miller
Devil-May-Care. Elizabeth Peters
Devil-May-Care. A. S. Roche
Devil Must. T. Wicker
Devil of Aske. Pamela Hill
Devil of Danehurst. J. Hunter
Devil of Dragon House. J. S. May
Devil of Pei-Ling. H. Asbury
Devil of the Depths. J. McLaren
Devil on Board. G. T. Ockley
Devil on His Trail. J. Hawkins
Devil on Horseback. V. Holt
Devil on Lammas Night. S. Howatch
Devil on the Moon. K. Robeson
Devil on the Stairs. P. Root
Devil on Two Sticks. Wade Miller
Devil or Saint? Colin Robertson
Devil Rides Out. D. Wheatley
Devil Snar'd. G. R. Preedy
Devil Spider. Glint Green
Devil-Stick. F. Hume
Devil Take All. Alice Brennan
Devil Take All. M. Caidin
Devil Take Her. F. Nichols
Devil Take Him. R. DeToledano
Devil Take the Blue-Tail Fly. J. F. Bardin
Devil Take the Foremost. T. Kinney
Devil Take the Hindmost. H. F. Shefler
Devil Takes a Hill Town. C. G. Givens
Devil That Slumbers. W. Allen
Devil Threw Dice. A. Dean
Devil Thumbs a Ride. R. C. Du Soe
Devil to Pay. P. Conway
Devil to Pay. R. Dolphin
Devil to Pay. George Douglas
Devil to Pay. F. N. Greene
Devil to Pay. H. Kane
Devil to Pay. E. Queen

Devil to Play. L. Holton
Devil Was a Woman. B. Graeme
Devil Was Handsome. M. Procter
Devil Was Kind. Donald Ross
Devil Was Sick. M. Durham
Devil Wears No Halo. D. Haring
Devil Wears Wings. H. Whittington
Devil Within. B. M. Scott
Devil Within Us. D. Basinger
Devil Wolf. N. S. Schinke
Devil Woman. Roland Daniel
Devil Wore Scarlet. Dulcie Gray
Devil You Don't. Ron Moody
Devil You Don't. J. Wainwright
Devil You Know. W. J. White
Devilday. Angus Hall
Deville McKeene, the British Ace. R. Walker
Devil's Ace. F. Hume
Devil's Admiral. F. F. More
Devil's Advocate. H. T. Johnson
Devil's Advocate. A. Neiderman
Devil's Advocate. F. M. White
Devil's Agent. H. Habe
Devil's Alternative. F. Forsyth
Devil's Apprentice. G. Davison
Devil's Bargain. F. Warden
Devil's Beacon. C. Robbins
Devil's Behind You. H. E. Helseth
Devil's Bell. E. M. McMillan
Devil's Birthday. J. Lie
Devil's Black Rock. K. Robeson
Devil's Box. W. J. Sheldon
Devil's Bread. D. Mariner
Devil's Brew. M. W. Kaye
Devil's Bride. Rachelle Edwards
Devil's Bride. Seabury Quinn
Devil's Bridge. M. Deasy
Devil's Brood. C. H. Barker
Devils Burn Too. Clay Henry
Devil's Cameo. W. H. Dye
Devil's Can-Can. W. H. Baker
Devil's Caress. D. Wand
Devil's Caress. J. Wright
Devil's Carnival. W. LeQueux
Devil's Cavern. C. Morgan
Devil's Chapel. E. P. Thorne
Devil's Chaplain. G. Bronson-Howard
Devil's Child. M. Bingley
Devil's Church. F. Draco
Devil's Churchyard. T. Willis
Devil's Circus. B. Christiansen
Devil's Claw. D. Masters
Devil's Cloak. Colin Robertson
Devil's Cockpit. Nick Carter
Devil's Cocktail. A. Wilson
Devil's Coffin. H. Gordon
Devil's Cook. E. Queen
Devil's Court. R. C. Payes
Devil's Current. K. Bennett
Devil's Dagger. M. G. Kiddy
Devil's Dance. Jan Alexander
Devil's Daughter. Griff
Devil's Daughter. E. Lipsky
Devil's Daughter. P. Marsh
Devil's Daughter. Marilyn Ross
Devil's Daughter. O. Schisgall
Devil's Daughter. D. Shaw
Devil's Daughter. D. Winston
Devil's Den. L. Saunders
Devil's Derelicts. F. C. V. Harcourt
Devil's Destiny. D. Haring
Devil's Diamond. R. Marsh
Devil's Diamonds. G. Davison
Devil's Diary. P. McGinley
Devil's Dice. W. LeQueux
Devil's Die. G. Allen
Devil's Diplomats. Operator 1384
Devil's Dominion. K. Lindsay
Devil's Door. L. Halliday
Devil's Door. R. Neill
Devil's Doorstep. D. Kamm
Devil's Double. C. H. Bullivant
Devil's Double. W. D. Roberts
Devil's Doubloons. J. McCulley

Devil's Dozen. Nick Carter
Devil's Dozen. N. Vane
Devil's Dreamer. Alice Brennan
Devil's Dress. M. M. Fletcher
Devil's Drive. A. W. Allan
Devil's Drum. L. Gorell
Devil's Drum. W. C. MacDonald
Devil's Drum. V. Meik
Devil's Due. Lanora Miller
Devil's Due. M. Procter
Devil's Edge. J. N. Chance
Devil's Elbow. G. Mitchell
Devil's Emissary. J. Laffin
Devil's End. P. Dalton
Devil's Eye. J. A. Jordan
Devil's Finger. R. Emmett
Devil's Fire, Love's Revenge. B. Paul
Devil's Footprints. E. Bond
Devil's Footsteps. John Burke
Devil's Gate. A. J. Fitzgerald
Devil's Gate Road. John Ross
Devil's Gateway. T. Worthing
Devil's Goad. J. Laffin
Devil's Gold. J. B. Hendryx
Devil's Guard. T. Mundy
Devil's Half Acre. Alien
Devil's Heirloom. A. M. Rud
Devil's Henchman. J. Oldrey
Devil's Highway. H. Janson
Devil's Hole. P. Ainsworth
Devil's Home on Leave. D. Raymond
Devil's Horn. D. Pendleton
Devil's Horns. K. Robeson
Devil's Horseman. J. Davison
Devil's Host. C. Glick
Devil's House. J. Tremonte
Devils in Candy Houses. W. Wall
Devil's Innocents. J. Edgar
Devil's Instrument. M. M. Fletcher
Devil's Island. F. Garrett
Devil's Keg. R. Cullum
Devil's Kloof. L. P. Greene
Devil's Knell. M. Warner
Devil's Lady. H. L. Gates
Devil's Lady. Linden Howard
Devil's Lady. Colin Robertson
Devil's Laughter. L. H. Brenning
Devil's Lieutenant. M. Fagyas
Devil's Lighter. J. Ballem
Devil's Luck. O. Williams
Devil's Mansion. R. Jardin
Devil's Mantle. F. Packard
Devil's Mirror. M. Lynch
Devil's Mirror. R. Spencer
Devil's Mistress. J. W. Brodie-Innes
Devil's Mistress. V. Coffman
Devil's Mistress. Kenneth Thomas
Devil's Mountain. E. Harwood
Devil's Nest. H. H. Harper
Devil's Novice. Ellis Peters
Devils of the Deep. K. Robeson
Devil's Own. G. Bowman
Devil's Own. P. Curtis
Devil's Own. J. L. Roberts
Devil's Own. R. A. Scotti
Devil's Own Luck and other stories. H. A. Vachell
Devil's Paintbrush. M. Dibner
Devil's Paradise. E. Cannon
Devil's Paradise. R. Timperley
Devil's Passkey. J. Shannon
Devil's Passport. Gordon Young
Devil's Paw. E. P. Oppenheim
Devil's Pawn. E. Bruton
Devil's Payday. W. C. Tuttle
Devil's Payment. T. Roscoe
Devil's Playground. K. Robeson
Devil's Playground. R. Vane
Devil's Plunder. C. Bainbridge
Devil's Plunge. D. Walker
Devil's Portage. C. Stoddard
Devil's Post Office. John Muir
Devil's Power. C. Rushton
Devil's Princess. D. Winston
Devil's Prison. M. O'Donnell

D

D

Devil's Profession. G. d. S. W. James
Devil's Punchbowl. D. Decker
Devil's Quill. D. Horner
Devil's Rain. M. Willis
Devil's Reckoning. M. Burton
Devil's Ring. L. Kenyon
Devil's Shilling. C. Rae-Brown
Devil's Signpost. A. Drummond
Devil's Skull. G. M. Wilson
Devil's Smile. R. Foxall
Devil's Snare. M. Cumberland
Devil's Son. Nicholas Carter
Devil's Sonata. S. Hufford
Devil's Spawn. C. Birkin
Devil's Spawn. R. Foxall
Devil's Spy. M. Hastings
Devil's Staircase. B. Wilson
Devil's Steps. N. Thurley
Devil's Steps. A. W. Upfield
Devil's Stronghold. L. Ford
Devil's Tea-Party. T. A. Plummer
Devil's Tears. E. Hale
Devil's Torch. G. Dickson
Devil's Toy. Anita Stewart
Devil's Trashcan. J. Rosenberger
Devil's Triangle. M. Macao
Devil's Triangle. A. Soutar
Devil's Vicar. V. Coffman
Devil's Vicar. Rod Miller
Devil's Vineyard. B. Kevern
Devil's Virgin. V. Coffman
Devil's Walk. G. Hall
Devil's Whirlpool. G. Volk
Devil's Whisper. R. Barnett
Devil's Whisper. L. Borden
Devil's Work. J. Brunner
Devil's Work. A. Burgess
Devil's Work. C. Wells
Devil's Work. M. Yorke
Deviltower. U. Nightingale
Devilweed. B. Knox
Devine Court Mystery. B. Symons
Devious Defector. W. J. Saber
Devious Design. D. B. Olsen
Devious Duchess. Jean Smith
Devious Murder. G. Bellairs
Devious Ones. F. Lockridge
Devious Ways. P. Freund
Devlin. J. Younger
Devlin the Barber. B. J. Farjeon
Devlin's Triangle. B. Heatter
Devon Maze. J. D. Fitz
Devouring. F. M. Armstrong
Devouring Fire. L. Gorell
Dew and Mildew. P. C. Wren
Dew in the Morning. Marjorie Curtis
Dew of Slumber. W. D. Browne
Dew of the Sea and other stories. H. A. Vachell
Dewey Death. C. Blackstock
Dewey Decimated. C. A. Goodrum
DeWitt Manor. E. St. Clair
DeWitt's War. H. Koning
Dexter Bank Robbery. E. A. Young
Dhow Patrol. M. Gregg
Di Di Mau or Die. J. Cain
Di Montranzo. L. S. Stanhope
Diabella. H. Forbes
Diablo Manor. D. Daniels
Diabolic Candelabra. E. R. Punshon
Diabolist. M. A. Drew
Diabolist. P. W. Fairman
Diabolus. David St. John
Diagnosis: Homicide. L. G. Blochman
Diagnosis: Murder. J. Kahn
Diagnosis: Murder. R. King
Diagnosis—Murder. Sutherland Scott
Dial Death. M. Russell
Dial Death. D. Spade
Dial 577 R-A-P-E. L. O'Donnell
Dial M for Money. D. Taggart
Dial "M" for Murder. F. Knott
Dial "M" for Murdock. R. Ray
Dial 999. J. M. Walsh
Diamante. E. Siciliano

Diamond. E. Byrd
Diamond and the Lady. J. Blyth
Diamond Beach. L. Forrester
Diamond Before You Die. C. Wiltz
Diamond Bikini. C. Williams
Diamond Boomerang. L. S. Taube
Diamond Bracelet. H. Wood
Diamond Bubble. R. L. Fish
Diamond-Buckled Shoe. B. Bolt
Diamond Button. B. North
Diamond Coterie. L. L. Lynch
Diamond Crime Detective. Benett Hill
Diamond Cross Mystery. C. K. Steele
Diamond Cut Diamond. J. Bunker
Diamond Cut Diamond. Nicholas Carter
Diamond Cut Diamond. J. K. Prothero
Diamond Cut Diamond. Brian Stuart
Diamond Dragon. G. H. Teed
Diamond Dress. O. John
Diamond Duel. S. G. Hedges
Diamond Exchange. T. Chastain
Diamond Eyes. J. Lutz
Diamond Feather. H. Reilly
Diamond Fingers. J. Ingersol
Diamond Flood. R. C. Armour
Diamond from the Sky. N. L. McCardell
Diamond Hair Slide. H. C. McNeile
Diamond Hitch. A. Barker
Diamond Hitch. W. C. Tuttle
Diamond Hook. J. Quartermain
Diamond Hostage. J. Quartermain
Diamond Hunters. Wilbur Smith
Diamond in the Buff. Susan Dunlap
Diamond in the Hoof. T. Stevenson
Diamond Kill. Michael Brett
Diamond Lens and other stories. Fitz-James O'Brien
Diamond Master. J. Futrelle
Diamond Mercenaries. J. Carter
Diamond Merchant. John Shaw
Diamond Mine Case. Nicholas Carter
Diamond Mountain. T. Keeping
Diamond Murders. J. S. Fletcher
Diamond Necklace. Frederick Jackson
Diamond of Death. M. L. Gamble
Diamond of Evil. F. Whishaw
Diamond of Ti Lingo. J. G. Brandon
Diamond Pendant. Maxwell Gray
Diamond Pendant. T. Thurston
Diamond Pin. C. Wells
Diamond Plane. P. T. Owen
Diamond Queen. M. Dekobra
Diamond Queen. A. B. Reeve
Diamond Racket. N. Anthony
Diamond Ransom Murders. N. Child
Diamond Rock. M. Schorr
Diamond Rock. Sea Lion
Diamond Rose Mystery. G. Knevels
Diamond Seeker of Brazil. Leon Lewis
Diamond Ship. M. Pemberton
Diamond Spitfire. Robin Moore
Diamond Stud. N. Singer
Diamond-Studded Typewriter. C. Keith
Diamond Sunburst. G. H. Teed
Diamond Thieves. A. Stringer
Diamond Tolls. R. S. Spears
Diamond Trail. O. Binns
Diamond Trail. Nicholas Carter
Diamond Trail. T. Gallon
Diamond Trip. Jenni Hall
Diamond Web. L. Gribble
Diamonds. T. Beattie
Diamonds. J. S. Fletcher
Diamonds. A. Michaels
Diamonds and Blood. Robin Moore
Diamonds and Detectives. A. L. Kaser
Diamonds and Hearts. J. C. Goodwin
Diamonds Are Deadly. J. Eastwood
Diamonds Are Forever. I. Fleming
Diamonds Are Trumps. H. Adams
Diamonds Bid. J. Rathbone
Diamonds Can Be Dangerous. B. O'Keefe
Diamonds Can Be Trouble. E. Harrison
Diamonds Don't Burn. Gertrude Walker
Diamonds for a Blonde. B. Sarto

Diamonds for Danger. J. Pendower
Diamonds for Danger. D. Walker
Diamonds for Moscow. D. Walker
Diamonds Going and Coming. H. G. Dyar
Diamonds in the Dumplings. S. Shane
Diamonds of Alcazar. M. K. Simmons
Diamonds of Death. B. Chase
Diamonds of Death. W. Jackson
Diamonds of Death. B. Raymond
Diamonds of Death. J. Ronald
Diamonds of Death. H. Willett
Diamonds of Despair. R. Chester
Diamonds of Loreta. I. Drummond
Diamonds See in the Dark. T. Mundy
Diamonds Spell Death. L. Edgley
Diamonds Spell Death. J. Kelso
Diamonds to Amsterdam. M. Coles
Diamonds Wild. A. Caillou
Diamonds Worth a Death or Two. P. Campion
Diana and Destiny. C. Garvice
Diana Defiant. A. Applin
Diana Is Dead. M. Stand
Diana K.C. R. Lichfield
Diana Meets Murder. P. Tabori
Diana of Dartmoor. G. Warden
Diana of Kara Kara. E. Wallace
Diana of the Islands. B. Bolt
Diana of the Moorland. L. Tracy
Diana of the Moors. L. Tracy
Diana of the Woods. L. C. Douthwaite
Diana Tempest. M. Cholmondeley
Diana's Destiny. C. Garvice
Diana's Luck. A. Applin
Diane and Her Friends. A. Sherburne Hardy
Diane Game. S. Cohen
Diary. W. Ard
Diary of a Detective Police Officer. Waters
Diary of a Drop-Out. S. Box
Diary of a Judge. H. R. Addison
Diary of a Police Surgeon. G. Grant
Diary of a Red-Haired Girl. E. Price
Diary of a Scoundrel. M. Pemberton
Diary of an Ex-Detective. C. Martel
Diary of Death. W. Collison
Diary of Death. F. W. Gumley
Diary of Evil. V. Hawthorne
Diavola. M. E. Braddon
Dibchick. Richard Dark
Dice Are Dark. B. Flynn
Dice Spelled Murder. A. Fray
Dice Were Loaded. M. Cumberland
Dick. B. J. Friedman
Dick and Jane. A. Robinson
Dick Barton, Special Agent. Elwyn Jones
Dick Barton, Special Agent. Geoffrey Webb
Dick Diminy. Priam
Dick Merriwell's Detective Work. B. L. Standish
Dick Merriwell's Mystery. B. L. Standish
Dick o' the Highway. D. Goodwin
Dick of the Secret Service. Robert Harding
Dick, the Boy Detective. Old Sleuth
Dick Tracy. M. A. Collins
Dick Tracy. W. Johnston
Dick Tracy, Ace Detective. C. Gould
Dick Tracy and the Woo Woo Sisters. C. Gould
Dick Tracy Meets Angeltop. M. A. Collins
Dick Tracy Meets the Punks. M. A. Collins
Dick Tracy: The Secret Files. Anonymous
Dick Tracy: The Thirties. C. Gould
Dick Turpin. H. D. Miles
Dicker in Souls, and other stories. W. S. Gidley
Dictator. Justin McCarthy
Dictator of Death. Frank King
Dictator's Daughter. E. Jepson
Dictator's Destiny. D. Betteridge
Dictators Die Hard. R. A. Levey
Dictator's Secret. G. H. Teed
Dictator's Way. E. R. Punshon
Dictatorship of the Dove. F. Gerard
Dictionary of the Khazars. M. Pavic
Did She Fall? T. Smith
Did She Fall or Was She Pushed? D. M. Disney
Did You Kill Mona Leeds? J. Roebuck
Didn't Anybody Know My Wife? W. D. Roberts

Die a Little. T. Kennedy
Die a Little Every Day. Lawrence Fisher
Die After Dark. H. Pentecost
Die Again, Macready. J. Livingston
Die All, Die Merrily. L. Bruce
Die Anytime, After Tuesday! Carter Brown
Die—As in Murder. L. Grex
Die, Baby, Die. R. Wilde
Die by Night. M. S. Marble
Die by the Book. L. Meynell
Die-Cast. N. Stead
Die, Damn You! P. Durst
Die, Darling, Die. E. Bruton
Die, Darling, Die. D. Haring
Die Fast, Die Happy. M. Denning
Die for a Diamond. D. Haring
Die for Big Betsy. B. Knox
Die for Love. J. Oxford
Die for Love. Elizabeth Peters
Die for the Queen. Douglas Scott
Die Hard. R. Thorp
Die Harder. W. Wager
Die Here a Stranger. M. Vinter
Die in the Country. T. Wells
Die in the Dark. Anthony Gilbert
Die, Jessica, Die. J. De Pre
Die, Killer, Die. F. Scarpetta
Die Kinder. G. Richards
Die Laughing. R. Lockridge
Die Laughing. P. McGerr
Die Laughing. S. S. Rafferty
Die Like a Dog. F. Gruber
Die Like a Dog. B. Halliday
Die Like a Dog. G. Moffat
Die Like a Man. M. Delving
Die, Little Goose. David Alexander
Die, Lover. H. Whittington
Die, My Beloved. P. Malloch
Die, My Darling. F. Usher
Die, My Lovely. J. Brenner
Die Now, Live Later. B. Copper
Die of a Rose. W. Maner
Die on Easy Street. J. A. Howard
Die Quickly, Brother. J. W. Hornby
Die Quickly, Dear Mother. T. Wells
Die Rich Die Happy. J. Munro
Die Screaming. J. Pagano
Die She Must. B. Von Hutten
Die to a Distant Drum. W. Arden
Die Wearing a Rose. E. P. Thorne
Die with Me, Lady. R. Cocking
Diecast. Michael Brett
Died in the Grass. C. Franklin
Died in the Red. Dulcie Gray
Died in the Wool. N. Marsh
Died o'Wednesday. S. Carver
Died o'Wednesday. Paul Townend
Died on a Rainy Sunday. Joan Aiken
Diehard. J. A. Jackson
Diehard. J. Potts
Dies Irae. R. Spinell
Diet to Die For. Joan Hess
Difference in Death. Donn Russell
Difference to Me. J. Bryan
Different Drummer. C. Egleton
Different Kind of Rain. D. S. Copp
Different Kind of Summer. Jennie Melville
Different Night. O. Hesky
Different Problem and other stories. A. K. Green
Different Seasons. Stephen King
Dig a Dead Doll. G. G. Fickling
Dig a Little Deeper. U. Curtiss
Dig a Narrow Grave. M. L. Roby
Dig Another Grave. D. C. Cameron
Dig Deep for Julie. R. Rayner
Dig for a Corpse. M. Mundy
Dig Her a Grave. P. Kruger
Dig Me a Dame. D. Haring
Dig Me a Grave. J. Spain
Dig Me Later. M. Hagen
Dig Mine Deep. E. Ellison
Dig My Grave Deep. P. Rabe
Dig That Crazy Grave. R. S. Prather
Dig the Grave and Let Him Die. J. Wainwright

Dig the Grave Deep. N. Brent
Dig the Missing. M. Urquhart
Dig Those Heels. H. Janson
Dig: Two Heads Wanted. H. H. Woodbridge
Digby's Miracle. F. E. Wynne
Digger of the Pit. M. Hastings
Digger 'Tec. G. H. Teed
Diggers Die Hard. Eric Lambert
Digger's Game. G. V. Higgins
Digital Justice. P. Moreno
Dignity and Purity. I. Jefferies
Dil Dies Hard. K. P. Gast
Dilemma. J. Brampton
Dilemma. N. Edwards
Dilemma. H. C. McNeile
Dilemma. E. Phillpotts
Dilemma for Dax. M. Cumberland
Dilemma of Commander Brett. W. Chesney
Dilemma of Death. L. G. Redmond-Howard
Dilemma of Dr. Riley. W. Tyrer
Dilemma of the Dead Lady. W. Irish
Dilemmas. A. E. W. Mason
Dillinger. Henry Clement
Dillinger. H. Patterson
Dimbleby's. L. C. Douthwaite
Dime to Dance By. W. Walker
Diminished by Death. Jonathan Ross
Diminished Responsibility. J. Barnett
Diminished Responsibility. G. Toye
Diminishing Returns. E. L. Withers
Dimpled Racketeer. A. S. Scarberry
Dimples Died De-Luxe. Carter Brown
Din of Inequity. M. Denning
Dinah Faire. V. Coffman
Dinah for Danger. J. Bogar
Dinard Mystery. J. Maske
Dine and Be Dead. Gwendoline Butler
Dine with Murder. M. Halliday
Dine with the Devil. J. G. Vermandel
Diner on the Other Track. W. I. Frank
Diners a Deux. S. B. Chester
Ding Dong Bell. H. Reilly
Ding Dong Dead. Mawby Green
Dingane's War. W. Charles
Dingdong. A. Maling
Dining with Duke Humphrey. James Greenwood
Dinky-Dau Death. J. Cain
Dinky Died. T. Wells
Dinner After Death. T. Irving-James
Dinner and Death. W. R. Burnett
Dinner at Antoine's. F. P. Keyes
Dinner at Dupre's. B. Halliday
Dinner Club. H. C. McNeile
Dinner for None. M. Sarsfield
Dinner in New York. S. Fowler
Dinner-Party at Bardolph's. R. A. J. Walling
Dinner to Die For. Susan Dunlap
Dinner with the Dead. M. McLaren
Dinosaur. L. Kamarck
Dinosaur Hunters. H. Vernes
Diogenes of London and other fantasies and sketches. H. B. M. Watson
Dion O'Dare. C. E. Blaney
Dip Into Murder. R. Ormerod
Diplomacy. M. Donald
Diplomat. J. Aldridge
Diplomat and the Gold Piano. M. Scherf
Diplomat Dies. L. Gribble
Diplomates. V. Sardou
Diplomatic Adventures. S. W. Mitchell
Diplomatic Corpse. P. A. Taylor
Diplomatic Cover. D. Torr
Diplomatic Death. C. Forsyte
Diplomatic Immunity. E. Sydell
Diplomatic Immunity. T. Szulc
Diplomatic Incident. Judith Kelly
Diplomatic Lover. Elsie Lee
Diplomatic Mysteries. V. Thompson
Diplomatic Pleasures. A. Lelouche
Diplomatic Traffic. D. Miller
Diplomatic Woman. H. Mee
Diplomatist. W. Haggard
Diplomat's Diary. Julien Gorden
Diplomat's Folly. Henry Wade

Dipo Flight. L. Robert
Dire Departed. J. Matheson
Direct Hit. D. Pendleton
Directed by the Devil. Bruce Kent
Directive 16. Charles Robertson
Director. O. Fraley
Director. Alan Thomas
Directors' Corridor. Caroline Francis
Dirge for a Dead Witch. Winifred Duke
Dirge for a Dog. Jennifer Jones
Dirge for a Doll. T. Trenton
Dirge for a Lady. Alicen White
Dirge for Her. V. Rath
Dirk Gently's Holistic Detective Agency. Douglas Adams
Dirt Rich. Clark Howard
Dirty Area. N. Luard
Dirty Business. L. Edgley
Dirty Butter for Servants. Joan Fleming
Dirty-Down. P. Clothier
Dirty Duck. M. Grimes
Dirty Game. W. H. Baker
Dirty Gertie. H. Kane
Dirty Hands. R. Neely
Dirty Harry. P. Rock
Dirty Laundry. P. Hamill
Dirty Linen. Elliott Lewis
Dirty Money. M. Bass
Dirty Money. Ray Russell
Dirty Money Can't Wash Both Hands at Once. J. M. Glanzer
Dirty Pool. G. Bagby
Dirty Proof. B. Gregorich
Dirty Scenario. J. Ballem
Dirty Secrets. N. Garbo
Dirty Story. E. Ambler
Dirty Tricks. C. Pincher
Dirty Tricks. P. Way
Dirty War. D. Pendleton
Dirty Way to Die. G. Bagby
Dirty Way to Die. B. Rossi
Dirty Weekend. A. T. Scholefield
Dirty White. J. Evans
Dirty Work. R. Kantner
Dirty Work. R. Pertwee
Dirty Work at the Crossroads. B. Johnson
Disagreeable Woman. Julian Starr
Disappearance. R. Carroll
Disappearance. James Cohen
Disappearance. J. Cowdroy
Disappearance. Derek Marlowe
Disappearance. C. Wilcox
Disappearance of a Niece. K. Field
Disappearance of Archibald Forsyth. Ian Alexander
Disappearance of Cropton. J. Fairfax-Blakeborough
Disappearance of Dr. Bruderstein. J. Sherwood
Disappearance of George Driffell. J. Payn
Disappearance of Julie Hintz. S. Truss
Disappearance of Kimball Webb. R. Wright
Disappearance of Lady Diana. R. Machray
Disappearance of Martha Penny. H. A. Vachell
Disappearance of Mary Amber. B. Poynter
Disappearance of Mr. Derwent. T. Cobb
Disappearance of Nicholson. C. Ainsworth
Disappearance of Nigel Blair. F. Warden
Disappearance of Norman Langdale. P. Lancaster
Disappearance of Odile. G. Simenon
Disappearance of Penny. R. J. Randisi
Disappearance of Roger Tremayne. B. Graeme
Disappearance of "Straight Left" Smith. Ernest H. Robinson
Disappearance of the Duke. Mrs. C. Kernahan
Disappearance of Uncle David. J. J. Farjeon
Disappearances. W. Wiser
Disappearing Bridegroom. M. Erskine
Disappearing Bullets. G. J. Brenn
Disappearing Corpse. James Warren
Disappearing Eye. F. Hume
Disappearing Island. G. Jenkins
Disappearing Lady. K. Robeson
Disappearing Parson. M. Burton
Disappearing Princess. Nicholas Carter
Disaster at Dungeness. R. Johnston
Disaster Pit. A. C. Murray

D

Disc. J. B. Harris-Burland
Discarded Daughter. E. Southworth
Discarded Son. R. M. Roche
Discharge to Danger. W. Spann
Disciple of Satan. Nicholas Carter
Disciples of Dread. H. B. Cave
Disciples of Nemesis. B. Osborne
Disciples of Satan. M. Richmond
Discipline of Christine. B. Goldie
Disclosures of a Press Agent. D. Miall
Disco Deadly. D. Haring
Disco Deathbeat. M. Geller
Discord in Harmony. P. K. McAfee
Discord in the Air. E. H. Clements
Discords of the Deep. L. A. Cunningham
Discourse with Shadows. J. Malcolm
Discovery. J. Parry
Discovery. S. Shagan
Discretion. D. Linzee
Discretion of Dominick Ayres. M. Vaughan
Disenchanted Diva. R. Santini
Disentanglers. Andrew Lang
Disgrace and Favour. J. Potter
Disgrace to the College. G. D. H. Cole
Disguise for a Dead Gentleman. G. Compton
Dish Ran Away. H. Janson
Disher-Detective. Will Scott
Disheveled City. G. Dold
Dishonest Murderer. F. Lockridge
Dishonest Way to Die. P. A. Foxall
Dishonor Among Thieves. S. Dean
Dishonored. F. Vreeland
Dishonour Among Thieves. David Hume
Dishonour Among Thieves. E. C. R. Lorac
Dishonour Among Thieves. J. Pattinson
Dis-Honourable. D. Hennessey
Dishonourable Member. J. T. Story
Dishonoured Bones. J. Trench
Disillusioned. B. Sarto
Disinformer. O. John
Disinformer. P. Ustinov
Disinherited. K. Orvis
Disintegration of J.P.G. G. Simenon
Disintegrator. Arthur Morgan
Dismal Ravens Crying. D. Fletcher
Dismal Thing to Do. Alisa Craig
Dismissed with Prejudice. J. A. Jance
Disordered Death. J. B. O'Sullivan
Disoriented Man. P. Saxon
Dispatch and Secrecy. G. Grison
Dispensable Man. W. Rilla
Displaced Person. J. B. Hilton
Disposal Job. E. Harris
Disposal Unit. J. Roland
Disposing Mind. R. H. R. Smithies
Disposing of Henry. R. Bax
Dispossessed. D. Carpenter
Dispossessed. G. Wagner
Disputed Barricade. H. Gibbs
Disputed Quarry. D. Sharp
Disqualified. F. Johnston
Dissector. H. Miller
Dissemblers. T. Cobb
Dissemblers. J. Creasey
Dissertation Upon Second Fiddles. V. O'Sullivan
Dissident. P. Van Greenaway
Distaff Factor. J. Wainwright
Distant Banner. Roy Lewis
Distant Clue. R. Lockridge
Distant Landscape. H. Elsna
Distant Stranger. P. Harcourt
Distant View of Death. J. S. Scott
Distinguished Gathering. James Parish
Distracting Guest. R. Jocelyn
Distributors. A. Partridge
District Bungalow. C. C. Lowis
Disturbance on Berry Hill. Elizabeth Fenwick
Disturbing Affair of Noel Blake. N. Bell
Ditto, Brother Rat! W. Garner
Ditto List. S. Greenleaf
Diva's Emeralds. V. MacClure
Dive and Die. D. Haring
Dive Deep for Danger. H. T. Rothwell
Dive Deep for Death. E. Messenger

Dive Deep Into Danger. C. Forsyte
Dive Deep Into Darkness. L. O'Donnell
Dive Into Death. Clayton Matthews
Diver Went Down. J. McLaren
Divers. H. Nisbet
Divers Diamonds. A. Dekker
Divers Vanities. Arthur Morrison
Diversions of Dawnson. B. Copplestone
Dives and Son. E. Davies
Divide. W. Overgard
Divide by Seven. R. Chambers
Divide the Night. D. Honig
Divided Trail. J. K. Stafford
Divided Treasure. David Williams
Divided We Fall. E. Burgess
Dividend of Death. G. Malcolm-Smith
Dividend on Death. B. Halliday
Divident Was Death. W. J. Coughlin
Dividing Line. K.-O. Bornemark
Dividing Line. R. Maugham
Dividing Night. V. Scannell
Divinations of Kala Persad and other stories. H. Hill
Divine and Deadly. M. Scherf
Divine Assassin. B. Reiss
Divine Death. L. Derrick
Divine Gift. C. McLaren
Divine Spark. P. Traill
Diving Dames affair. P. Leslie
Diving Death. C. Forsyte
Diving for Pearls. H. Brenton
Divining Rod for Murder. M. Neville
Divinitas. J. Knowler
Division Bell Mystery. E. Wilkinson
Divorce. T. P. Prest
Divorce. G. Thorne
Divorce Court Murder. M. Propper
Divorced Princess. R. de Pont-Jest
Dixie Convoy. D. Pendleton
Dixie Death Squad. L. Derrick
Dixon Brett and the "Baker's Dozen". Anonymous
Dixon Brett and the Mystery Yacht. Anonymous
Dixon Hawke, Secret Agent. J. Creasey
Dixon Hawke's Case Book. Anonymous
Dixon of Dock Green. Rex Edwards
Dizzy Dames Die Fast. C. Wheatley
Do Butlers Burgle Banks? P. G. Wodehouse
Do Evil in Return. M. Millar
Do It Yourself Doom. S. Prickett
Do Me a Favor, Drop Dead. J. H. Chase
Do No Evil. F. Noro
Do Not Disturb. H. McCloy
Do Not Disturb. L. Thayer
Do Not Fold, Spindle or Mutilate. D. M. Disney
Do Not Go Gentle. Gordon Stevens
Do Not Murder Before Christmas. J. Iams
Do Not Sleep. G. M. Wilson
Do Nothing' Till You Hear from Me. J. Wainwright
Do—or Die! T. Taggart
Do the Dead Know? A. Kenealy
Do Unto Others. D. M. Disney
Do Unto Others. P. Rosemoor
Do You Deal in Murder? A. Allyson
Do You Know This Voice? E. Berckman
Do You Like Tahiti? E. Clerk
Do You Remember England? Derek Marlowe
Doberman Wore Black. Barbara Moore
Doc Churston. D. Binns
Doc Grip, the Sporting Detective. Anonymous
Doc Savage Omnibus #1. K. Robeson
Doc Savage Omnibus #2. K. Robeson
Doc Savage Omnibus #3. K. Robeson
Doc Savage Omnibus #4. K. Robeson
Doc Savage Omnibus #5. K. Robeson
Doc Savage Omnibus #6. K. Robeson
Doc Savage Omnibus #7. K. Robeson
Doc Savage Omnibus #8. K. Robeson
Doc Savage Omnibus #9. K. Robeson
Doc Savage Omnibus #10. K. Robeson
Doc Savage Omnibus #11. K. Robeson
Doc Savage Omnibus #12. K. Robeson
Doc Savage Omnibus #13. K. Robeson
Dock Brief. D. Barr
"Dock Rats" of New York. Old Sleuth
Dock Walloper. B. Appel

Docken Dead. J. Trench
Dockyard Mystery. S. Hope
Doctor and the Corpse. Max Murray
Doctor and the Devil. C. W. Gardner
Doctor and the Devils. D. Thomas
Doctor Artz. R. Hichens
Doctor Austin's Guests. W. Gilbert
Doctor Baxter's Invention. W. P. Kelly
Doctor Bentiron: Detective. E. M. Poate
Dr. Berkeley's Discovery. R. Slee
Doctor Bernard St. Vincent. H. Nisbet
Dr. Bruderstein Vanishes. J. Sherwood
Doctor Burton. A. C. Gunter
Doctor Burton's Success. A. C. Gunter
Dr. Campion's Patients. W. G. Waters
Doctor Caro. B. J. Packer
Doctor Chaos and the Devil Snar'd. G. R. Preedy
Doctor Claude. H. Malot
Doctor Cobb's Game. R. V. Cassill
Doctor Cockaigne. N. E. Davies
Dr. Cook's Garden. I. Levin
Dr. Crippen's Diary. Emlyn Williams
Dr. Cunliffe—Investigator. H. Frankish
Doctor Dale's Dilemma. G. W. Appleton
Doctor Darch's Wife. F. Warden
Doctor Deals with Murder. W. M. Duncan
Dr. Death. Nick Carter
Doctor Death. H. Fisher
Doctor Death. J. Hartenfels
Doctor Death. C. Whitman
Doctor Death. T. Worthing
Doctor Death and other terror tales. Zorro
Doctor Detective. P. Graham
Doctor Didn't Prescribe Murder. H. B. May
Doctor Died at Dusk. G. Homes
Doctor Disappears. M. Dalman
Doctor Dodds' Experiment. Sutherland Scott
Dr. Duvene's Crime. G. Chester
Dr. Endicott's Experiment. A. Sergeant
Dr. Falke of Harley Street. S. Fairway
Doctor Falls in Love. Rona Randall
Dr. Feel Good. J. Nazel
Dr. Fell, Detective, and other stories. J. D. Carr
Dr. Ferraro's Frame-Up. C. Brisbane
Doctor Fischer of Geneva. G. Greene
Doctor Fix. H. Janson
Doctor for the Dead. M. Higgins
Doctor Fram. S. Mackenzie
Doctor Frigo. E. Ambler
Doctor from Devil's Island. C. Rushton
Doctor Garrett's Girl. M. Lynch
Dr. Gatzkill's Blue Shoes. P. Conant
Doctor Glas. H. Soderberg
Dr. Glazebrook's Revenge. A. C. Brown
Doctor Glennie's Daughter. B. L. Farjeon
Dr. Goodwood's Locum. J. Rhode
Dr. Greenfingers. E. Woodward
Dr. Grimshawe's Secret. N. Hawthorne
Dr. Gully. Elizabeth Jenkins
Dr. Gully's Story. Elizabeth Jenkins
Dr. Hades. Arthur Russell
Doctor Havelock's Wife. Rona Randall
Doctor, His Wife, and the Clock. A. K. Green
Doctor Is Sick. A. Burgess
Doctor Izard. A. K. Green
Dr. Janet of Harley Street. A. Kenealy
Dr. Jekyll and Mr. Holmes. L. D. Estleman
Dr. Jekyll and Mr. Hyde. D. Barber
Dr. Jekyll and Mr. Hyde. G. Osterman
Dr. Krasinski's Secret. M. P. Shiel
Doctor Krook. A. Mallory
Doctor, Lawyer . . . C. Wilcox
Doctor Looks at Murder. D. Quick
Dr. Mabuse, Master of Mystery. N. Jacques
Dr. Manton. M. Gerard
Doctor Mephisto. J. Joseph-Renaud
Dr. Monte Cristo. I. P. Sobel
Doctor Moon. C. Meadows
Dr. Morel. K. Bramson
Dr. Morelle. E. Dudley
Dr. Morelle and Destiny. E. Dudley
Dr. Morelle and the Doll. E. Dudley
Dr. Morelle and the Drummer Girl. E. Dudley
Dr. Morelle at Midnight. E. Dudley

Dr. Morelle Meets Murder and other new adventures. E. Dudley
Dr. Morelle Takes a Box. E. Dudley
Dr. Nicholas Stone. E. S. De Puy
Doctor Nikola. G. Boothby
Dr. Nikola's Experiment. G. Boothby
Doctor No. I. Fleming
Doctor of Pimlico. W. LeQueux
Doctor of Souls. W. K. Knight
Dr. Orient. F. Lauria
Dr. Palliser's Patient. G. Allen
Doctor Paradise. J. J. Dratler
Dr. Phibes. W. Goldstein
Dr. Phibes Rises Again. W. Goldstein
Dr. Priestley Investigates. J. Rhode
Dr. Priestley Lays a Trap. J. Rhode
Dr. Priestley's Quest. J. Rhode
Dr. Quake. R. Sapir
Doctor Quartz, Magician. Nicholas Carter
Doctor Quartz's Quick Move. Nicholas Carter
Dr. Quick, the Masked Detective. Ernest H. Robinson
Doctor Rameau. G. Ohnet
Dr. Ricardo. W. Garrett
Dr. Rumsey's Patient. L. T. Meade
Doctor S.O.S. L. Thayer
Dr. Sam: Johnson, Detector. L. De La Torre
Doctor Samovar, Crook. Spike Gordon
Doctor Sax. J. Kerouac
Dr. Scarlett. A. Laing
Doctor Severin's Secret. S. Fairway
Dr. Silex. J. B. Harris-Burland
Doctor Sinister. G. Chester
Dr. Sinister. Gwyn Evans
Dr. Smith of Queen Anne Street. A. Kenealy
Dr. Somerville's Crime. M. H. Hervey
Dr. Strangelove. P. George
Doctor Syn. R. Thorndike
Doctor Syn on the High Seas. R. Thorndike
Doctor Syn Returns. R. Thorndike
Dr. Tancred Begins. G. D. H. Cole
Doctor—There's Danger. F. L. Cary
Dr. Thorndyke Intervenes. R. A. Freeman
Dr. Thorndyke Investigates. R. A. Freeman
Dr. Thorndyke Omnibus. R. A. Freeman
Dr. Thorndyke's Case-Book. R. A. Freeman
Dr. Thorndyke's Cases. R. A. Freeman
Dr. Thorndyke's Dilemma. J. H. Dirckx
Dr. Thorndyke's Discovery. R. A. Freeman
Dr. Time. K. Robeson
Doctor to the Stars. M. Leinster
Dr. Toby Finds Murder. S. M. Schley
Doctor Transit. I. S.
Doctor Vandyke. J. E. Cooke
Dr. Vane Answers the Call. W. E. Johns
Doctor vs. Murder. M. Ryerson
Doctor Villagos. F. Du Boisgobey
Dr. Wainwright's Patient. E. Yates
Doctor Was a Dame. S. Truss
Doctor Was a Lady. M. V. Heberden
Doctor Who Held Hands. H. Footner
Doctor Who Wouldn't Tell. W. M. Graydon
Dr. Wilbur's Note Book. N. T. Oliver
Dr. Willoughby Smith. M. A. M. Marks
Dr. Wynne's Revenge. W. Westall
Dr. Yen Sin. D. E. Keyhoe
Doctor Xavier. M. Pemberton
Dr. Zollinoff's Revenge. E. R. Owen
Doctors Also Die. D. M. Devine
Doctors Are Doubtful. A. Weymouth
Doctor's Beautiful Ward. J. H. Robinson
Doctors Beware! W. McCully
Doctor's Challenge. J. E. MacDonnell
Doctor's Crime. M. Danvers
Doctor's Daughter. P. Allardyce
Doctor's Daughter. H. Wood
Doctors, Death and Doomsday. H. Cabot
Doctor's Defence. S. Fairway
Doctor's Double. E. W. Alais
Doctor's Double. N. Gould
Doctor's First Murder. R. Hare
Doctor's Idol. C. Lys
Doctor's Mistake. C. H. Montague
Doctor's Murder Case. R. P. Koehler
Doctor's Note-Book. S. Guy
Doctor's Office. Elsie Lee
Doctor's Secret. W. J. Bayfield
Doctor's Secret. Rita
Doctor's Strategem. Nicholas Carter
Doctors' Tales. W. Hywel
Doctors Wear Scarlet. S. Raven
Doctor's Wife. M. E. Bradden
Document of the Last Nazi. M. Eden
Documentary Evidence. R. Halket
Documents in the Case. D. L. Sayers
Documents Marked "Secret". John Gloag
Documents of Death. J. Creasey
Documents of Murder. T. C. H. Jacobs
Dodd Cases. K. Livingston
Dodge Boys. G. Sibbald
Dodge City Bombers. L. Derrick
Dodging the Law. Nicholas Carter
Dodos Don't Duck. M. O'Brine
Does Mr. Jones Live Here? H. S. Snell
Doesn't Everyone. I. A. Greenfield
Dog and Duck Mystery. H. Bogue
Dog Collar Murders. Barbara Wilson
Dog Day Afternoon. P. Mann
Dog Detective. Anonymous
Dog Detective and His Young Master. M. M. Murray
Dog Eat Dog. W. Chambers
Dog Eat Dog. Mary Collins
Dog Eats Dog. M. H. Cooper
Dog-Face. J. Easton
Dog Fight with Death. G. Davison
Dog Fox. W. B. M. Ferguson
Dog Heavies. L. J. Washburn
Dog Horse Rat. Christopher Davis
Dog in the Dark. Gerald Hammond
Dog in the Manger. U. Curtiss
Dog It Was. R. Harrison
Dog It Was That Died. G. Braddon
Dog It Was That Died. H. R. F. Keating
Dog It Was That Died. C. E. R. Lorac
Dog Man. M. Procter
Dog Rock. D. Foster
Dog Soldiers. R. Stone
Dog Star. C. Stanton
Dog with a Bad Name. F. Warden
Dogcatcher. P. Prince
Dogheaded Death. R. F. Nelson
Doghouse. G. Hammond
Dogs. R. Calder
Dog's Body. J. Edmonds
Dog's Death. P. Motte
Dogs Do Bark. J. Stagge
Dogs of War. W. H. Baker
Dogs of War. F. Forsyth
Dog's Ransom. P. Highsmith
Dogwatch. C. Coffin
Doing Business. J. Beadle
Doing It. J. W. Thomas
Doings of Raffles Haw. A. C. Doyle
Doll. F. Durbridge
Doll. E. McBain
Doll Baby. H. Barron
Doll Baby. H. Janson
Doll Castle. M. Monigle
Doll for the Big House. Carter Brown
Doll for the Toff. J. Creasey
Doll Who Ate His Mother. Ramsey Campbell
Doll with Opal Eyes. J. DeWeese
Dollar Covenant. Michael Sinclair
Dollar Instinct. E. Seeley
Dollar Man. John Turner
$ Marked Her Sin. J. Brenner
Dollar Rackets. B. Vane
Dollars Are Trumps. A. Kevill-Davies
Dolls and Dollars. J. Dekker
Dolls Are Deadly. Don Boyd
Dolls Are Deadly. B. Halliday
Dolls Are Dynamite. F. Foden
Dolls Are Murder. H. Q. Masur
Doll's Bad News. J. H. Chase
Doll's Done Dancing. B. Flynn
Doll's Trunk Murder. H. Reilly
Dolls with Sad Faces. C. Phillips
Dolly and the Bird of Paradise. D. Dunnett
Dolly and the Cookie Bird. D. Halliday
Dolly and the Doctor Bird. D. Halliday
Dolly and the Nanny Bird. D. Halliday
Dolly and the Singing Bird. D. Halliday
Dolly and the Starry Bird. D. Halliday
Dolly Dolly Spy. A. Diment
Dolly the Romp. F. Warden
Dolly's Walk. C. Edwards
Dolomite Cavern. W. P. Kelly
Dolomite Memorandum. T. Willard
Dolores. G. Kelton
Dolores and Some Others. M. Pemberton
Dolores Divine, Guilty or Innocent? K. M. Ellis
Dolorosa Deal. B. Littell
Dolphin Mystery. J. P. Hutton
Dolphin Shore. P. Barstow
Dolphin Summer. C. Salisbury
Dombey and Daughter. R. Nicholson
Domes of Silence. O. J. Friend
Domesday Story. Warwick Scott
Domestic Affair. M. Russell
Domestic Agency. J. Rhode
Domestic Animal. Francis King
Dominant Third. E. Hely
Dominator. J. Follett
Dominator. A. York
Dominici Affair. J. Laborde
Domino. M. K. Simmons
Domino. P. A. Whitney
Domino Club. A. Upward
Domino Image. B. J. Hoff
Domino Plan. E. Granville
Domino Principle. A. Kennedy
Domino Spell. W. L. Story
Domino Vendetta. A. Kennedy
Dominoes. J. Wainwright
Don. F. V. Perrin
Don. G. Ziran
Don Algonah. Anonymous
Don Among the Dead Men. C. E. Vulliamy
Don Belasco of Key West. A. C. Gunter
Don Bueno. Z. Ghose
Don Caesar de Bazan. T. P. Prest
Don Chicago. C. E. B. Roberts
Don Is Dead. N. Quarry
Don or Devil? W. Westall
Don Q in the Sierra. K. Prichard
Don Q's Love Story. K. Prichard
Don Raphael. George Walker
Donald Dyke, the Down-East Detective. H. Rockwood
Donald Dyke, the Yankee Detective. H. Rockwood
Donalda. M. J. Young
Donato & Daughter. J. Early
Donavan. Carter Brown
Donavan's Day. Carter Brown
Donavan's Delight. Carter Brown
Done in the Dark. Nicholas Carter
Done to Death. F. Carmichael
Done to Death. Sara Woods
Dongola Script. L. Johns
Donkey from the Mountains. E. Atiyah
Donna. R. T. Larkin
Donna Died Laughing. Carter Brown
Donna with Green Eyes. B. Sarto
Donnolly Murders. W. Crichton
Donor. R. Tate
Donors. L. A. Horvitz
Donovan. J. Midgley
Donovan Affair. Owen Davis
Donovan Case. J. Monmouth
Donovan of Whitehall. W. LeQueux
Donovan's Brain. C. Siodmak
Donovan's Last Case. J. K. Lyons
Don't Argue with Death. L. Gribble
Don't Ask Questions. J. P. Marquand
Don't Be Afraid of the Dark. P. Henneker
Don't Be No Hero. Leonard Harris
Don't Bet on Living, Alice. K. Carr
Don't Betray Me. J. Berry
Don't Betray Me. J. Van Hearn
Don't Bleed on Me. B. Copper
Don't Bother to Knock. Peter Chambers

Don't Bother to Knock. C. Dekker
Don't Break the Seal. A. M. Burrage
Don't Call Back. R. O'Neil
Don't Call Me Madame. H. Kane
Don't Call Tonight. W. C. Gault
Don't Catch Me. R. Powell
Don't Come Back! W. Wright
Don't Come Crying to Me. W. Ard
Don't Count the Corpses. C. Monig
Don't Cross Me, Honey. R. Callahan
Don't Cross Me, Honey. J. Grecco
Don't Crowd Me. E. Hunter
Don't Crowd Me. G. Usher
Don't Cry, Beloved. E. Ronns
Don't Cry for Long. T. B. Dewey
Don't Cry for Me. W. C. Gault
Don't Cry, Little Girl. B. Hastings
Don't Cry, Little Girl. N. Parker
Don't Cry Little Sister. J. Letton
Don't Cry Now. H. Janson
Don't Dare Me, Sugar. H. Janson
Don't Die on Me. D. Spade
Don't Die on Me, Billie Jean. Stanton Forbes
Don't Die on Me, Diana. D. Haring
Don't Die Too Soon. A. Capelli
Don't Dig Deeper. W. Francis
Don't Drop Dead Tomorrow. H. Pentecost
Don't Embarrass the Bureau. B. F. Conners
Don't Ever Love Me. O. R. Cohen
Don't Expect Any Mercy. H. Treece
Don't Fall, Sucker! Rex Richards
Don't Feed the Animals. J. Farr
Don't Get Caught. M. E. Chaber
Don't Get Caught. Carter Cullen
Don't Get Me Wrong. P. Cheyney
Don't Give Me That. R. Norman
Don't Go Away Dead. H. Kane
Don't Go Away Mad. J. Hayes
Don't Go in Alone. G. Holden
Don't Go Into the Woods Today. D. M. Disney
Don't Go Out After Dark. N. Berrow
Don't Go to Ceuta. H. Franklin
Don't Go to Sleep in the Dark. C. Fremlin
Don't Hang Me Too High. J. B. O'Sullivan
Don't Hold Your Breath. W. Newton
Don't Jump, Mr. Boland! N. Berrow
Don't Just Die There. H. Kane
Don't Just Stand There. C. Williams
Don't Just Stand There, Do Someone. D. Von Elsner
Don't Kill Me Twice. D. Bogard
Don't Kill, My Love. R. Foley
Don't Leave Me This Way. Joan Smith
Don't Let Her Die. Tarn Scott
Don't Let Him Burn! F. MacIsaac
Don't Let Him Kill. G. Ashe
Don't Let Me Die, Darling. L. Berg
Don't Lie to Me. T. Coe
Don't Lie to the Police. B. Cobb
Don't Look Back. M. Borgenicht
Don't Look Behind You. M. Erskine
Don't Look Behind You! S. Rogers
Don't Look Behind You. Marilyn Ross
Don't Look Down. V. Katcha
Don't Look for Me, I'm Dead. W. Strathern
Don't Look Now. D. Du Maurier
Don't Look Now. M. Hayne
Don't Make Me Kill. M. Clinten
Don't Mention It. B. Shannon
Don't Mention My Name. E. K. Goldthwaite
Don't Mess with Murder. A. Allyson
Don't Mind Stella. B. Vane
Don't Monkey with Murder. E. Ferrars
Don't Mourn for Me. E. Ellison
Don't Mourn Me, Toots. H. Janson
Don't Neglect the Body. Kevin O'Hara
Don't Open the Door. U. Curtiss
Don't Open the Door! Anthony Gilbert
Don't Play with the Rough Boys. S. Troy
Don't Point That Thing at Me. K. Bonfiglioli
Don't Push Me Around. E. Gilbert
Don't Push Your Luck. P. Muller
Don't Rely on Gemini. V. Packer
Don't Say No. O. L. Rosmanith

Don't Scare Easy. H. Janson
Don't Scare Me, Sister. D. Foster
Don't Sell Me Cheap. W. Standish
Don't Shoot, Darling. H. Holt
Don't Shoot the Pianist. James Grant
Don't Shut Me Out. H. Elsna
Don't Slip, Delaney. B. Singer
Don't Speak to Strange Girls. H. Whittington
Don't Stop for Hooky Heffernan. L. Meynell
Don't Take It to Heart. S. Seaton
Don't Talk to Strangers. Beverly Hastings
Don't Tell Daddy. B. Petty
Don't Tell Mother! M. Ferris
Don't Tell the Police. Kevin O'Hara
Don't Tell the Press. H. Jobson
Don't Tempt Me. S. Coburn
Don't Tempt the Hangman. Spike Gordon
Don't Tie Me Down. V. Lloyd
Don't Touch Me. Spike Gordon
Don't Touch the Body. A. Mills
Don't Try Anything Funny. J. M. Fox
Don't Walk Home. B. Hastings
Don't Wear Your Wedding Ring. L. O'Donnell
Don't Whistle "MacBeth." David Fletcher
Doodled Asterisk. R. A. J. Walling
Doom. H. Imbert-Terry
Doom! Justin Huntly McCarthy
Doom Campaign. M. McMullen
Doom Candle. Richard Grant
Doom Dealer. D. Fox
Doom in the Midnight Sun. E. M. Boyd
Doom Indigo. Angus Ross
Doom-Maker. B. X. Sanborn
Doom of Glendour. K. Ostrander
Doom of Siva. T. W. Speight
Doom of the Demon Band. Old Sleuth
Doom of the Reds. Nicholas Carter
Doom Service. D. J. Marlowe
Doom Stone. C. Woolrich
Doom Trail of the Squeaker. Anonymous
Doom Window. M. Drake
Doomdate. J. Tiger
Doomed Five. C. Wells
Doomed Flight. J. R. Holden
Doomed Men. W. Jardine
Doomed Oasis. H. Innes
Doomed Sinner. D. Brennan
Doomed to Failure. Nicholas Carter
Doomed to Hate. J. Bowman
Dooming Eye. P. Edler
Doomington Wanderer. L. Golding
Doom's Caravan. G. Household
Doomsday. Warwick Scott
Doomsday Affair. H. Whittington
Doomsday Bag. M. Avallone
Doomsday Bells. M. Lynch
Doomsday Book. J. MacLaren-Ross
Doomsday Brain. P. Tabori
Doomsday Carrier. V. Canning
Doomsday Committee. R. Gallagher
Doomsday Conspiracy. Ralph Hayes
Doomsday Contract. T. Williamson
Doomsday Decree. P. MacAlan
Doomsday Deposit. Stanley Johnson
Doomsday Device. P. Fox
Doomsday Disciples. D. Pendleton
Doomsday England. M. Cooney
Doomsday Exercise. Bart Davis
Doomsday Formula. Nick Carter
Doomsday Game. R. E. Harrington
Doomsday List. K. Orvis
Doomsday Men. J. B. Priestley
Doomsday Mission. H. Whittington
Doomsday Morning. C. L. Moore
Doomsday Prophecy. R. Wenk
Doomsday Scroll. Barbara Rogers
Doomsday Ship. J. A. Price
Doomsday Spiral. J. Land
Doomsday Spore. Nick Carter
Doomsday Squad. D. Gober
Doomsday Squad. Clark Howard
Doomsday Square. R. W. Taylor
Doomsday Syndrome. Gar Wilson
Doomsday Ultimatum. J. Follett

Doomsday Vendetta. P. Winston
Doomsters. R. Macdonald
Doomway. E. Bond
Doone Walk. D. Clark
Door. M. R. Rinehart
Door. J. F. Rossmann
Door. G. Simenon
Door Between. E. Queen
Door Closed Softly. Alice Campbell
Door Fell Shut. M. Albrand
Door in the Wall. L. Meynell
Door Into Terror. J. Coulson
Door Nails Never Die. A. Wynne
Door of Death. J. Esteven
Door of Doubt. Nicholas Carter
Door of Dread. A. Stringer
Door of the Unreal. G. Biss
Door to Death. R. Stout
Door to December. R. Paige
Door to Doom. J. D. Carr
Door to Enigma. Ian Wallace
Door to the Moor. M. B. Vandeburg
Door to the Tower. S. Dannett
Door Was Violence. G. Leaderman
Door with Seven Locks. E. Wallace
Door Without a Key. Constance Rutherford
Doorbell Rang. R. Stout
Doors. E. Hannon
Doors of Sleep. T. Warriner
Doors of the Night. F. Packard
Doors Open. M. Gilbert
Doors to Death. L. Crosby
Doorstep Murders. C. Wells
Doorway to Danger. S. Maddock
Doorway to Death. H. Arvonen
Doorway to Death. J. Creasey
Doorway to Death. H. Desmond
Doorway to Death. D. J. Marlowe
Doorways to Death. Mark Napier
Doowinkle, D.A. H. Klingsberg
Dope. S. Rohmer
Dope-Darling. Leda Burke
Dope Dealer. E. Snell
Dope Dealers. L. Cross
Dope Devils. W. J. Elliott
Dope Doll. S. Harragan
Dope for Dolores. N. Perrelli
Dope Is for Dopes. Griff
Dope King. H. J. S. Anderton
Dope Opera. P. McDowell
Dope Racketeer. Rex Richards
Dope Ring. J. Hill
Dope Runners. G. Grantham
Dope Ship. E. L. Long
Dope Specialist. F. Johnston
Doped and the Damned. Griff
Dopefiend. D. Goines
Doppelganger. H. Innes
Doppelganger. P. Van Greenaway
Doppelganger Gambit. L. Killough
Doppelgangers. H. F. Heard
Dora Elmyr's Worst Enemy. M. V. Victor
Dora Livingstone, the Adulteress of Quaker City. Anonymous
Dora Myrl, the Lady Detective. M. M. Bodkin
Dora, the Beautiful Dishwasher. N. Albert
Dora's Device. G. P. Cather
Dorcas Dene, Detective. G. R. Sims
Doria Rafe Case. H. Waugh
Doris. Dorothy Johnson
Doris Moore. G. Thorne
Doris's Fortune. F. Warden
Dorit in Lesbos. T. Olson
Dorking Gap Affair. G. Petrie
Dormant. E. Nesbit
Dormitory Women. R. V. Cassill
Dormouse Has Nine Lives. Frank King
Dormouse—Peacemaker. Frank King
Dormouse—Undertaker. Frank King
Dornstein Ikon. J. L. Roberts
Dorothy and Agatha. G. Larsen
Dorothy Jordan, the Siren of Old Drury. P. Renin
Dorothy Marlow. A. W. Marchmont
Dorothy Parker Murder Case. G. Baxt

Dorothy the Rope Dancer. M. Leblanc
Dorothy, the Terrified. K. Kimbrough
Dorothy's Double. G. A. Henty
Dorothy's Venture. M. C. Hay
Dorrien of Cranston. B. Mitford
Dorrington Deed-Box. Arthur Morrison
Dorsey Disappears. L. Barbee
Dossier. P. Salinger
Dossier Closed. C. Eland
Dossier 51. G. Perrault
Dossier IX. B. Weil
Dossier No. 113. E. Gaboriau
Dossier of Solar Pons. B. Copper
Dossier on a Mantis. W. R. Bennett
Dotmakers. J. F. Beaman
Double. B. Pronzini
Double. E. Wallace
Double Acrostic. G. Goodchild
Double Agent. J. Bingham
Double Agent. G. Stackelberg
Double Agent. H. T. Teilhet
Double Alibi. M. R. Rinehart
Double Bang. H. Gould
Double Banked. E. L. Long
Double Barrel. N. Freeling
Double-Barrelled Detective Story. M. Twain
Double Blackmail. G. D. H. Cole
Double Blinded. L. A. Horvitz
Double Bluff. S. Mitchell
Double Bluff. Dell Shannon
Double Chance. J. S. Fletcher
Double Crime. J. J. Farjeon
Double Crime. Old Sleuth
Double Cross. M. Barak
Double Cross. A. Capelli
Double Cross. George Douglas
Double-Cross. M. Gicheru
Double Cross. C. H. Merrett
Double Cross. M. Moran
Double-Cross. A. O. Pollard
Double Cross. A. E. Thomas
Double Cross. P. Urquhart
Double Cross. G. Willets
Double-Cross Circuit. M. Dorland
Double Cross Inn. J. Laurence
Double-Cross Murder. R. Gilmour
Double Cross Purposes. R. A. Knox
Double Cross Purposes. Kenneth O'Hara
Double Cross Squadron. W. P. Evans
Double Crossed. D. Newton
Double-Crosser. J. Cassells
Double-Crossers of Ghost Tree. W. C. Tuttle
Double Crossfire. D. Pendleton
Double Crossing. E. Holzer
Double-Crossing Traitor. Roland Daniel
Double Cunning. G. M. Fenn
Double Cut. A. Shaughnessy
Double Dagger. N. Ridley
Double Dan. E. Wallace
Double Dare. E. Keyes
Double Darkness. E. Fenton
Double Daughter. V. McConnell
Double Deal. H. Miller
Double Deal. M. Russell
Double Dealer. F. Gruber
Double Dealers. M. MacKintosh
Double Dealing. F. P. Jordan
Double Dealing. Harold Trembath
Double Death. J. N. Chance
Double Death. F. W. Crofts
Double Death. Detection Club
Double Death. S. Elgar
Double Death. C. Forsyte
Double Death Mystery. L. Geoghegan
Double Death of Frederic Belot. C. Aveline
Double Deceit. P. Harcourt
Double Deception. Jan Allen
Double Decoy. D. Newton
Double Defector. P. Wayland
Double Delegate. G. Wark
Double Detection. B. Cobb
Double Diamond. J. Pendower
Double Disappearance. L. Winstanley
Double Doom. Josephine Bell

Double Door. E. McFadden
Double Double. E. Elice
Double Double. F. M. Kelsall
Double, Double. E. Queen
Double Double-Cross. D. Thurlow
Double, Double, Oil and Trouble. E. Lathen
Double Duel. S. Cobb
Double Eagle. Keith Miles
Double Entry. Constance Rutherford
Double Events. A. Wilson
Double Exposure. M. S. Bell
Double Exposure. F. W. Culver
Double Exposure. D. MacKenzie
Double Exposure. H. McLeave
Double Exposure. A. W. Sherring
Double Exposure. J. Stimson
Double Fault. L. Meynell
Double Feature. A. Fowles
Double Finesse. H. Howard
Double Fix. C. Lawton
Double Florin. J. Rhode
Double for Blackshirt. R. Graeme
Double for Danger. S. J. Maybridge
Double for Death. G. Ashe
Double for Death. R. Stout
Double for Murder. N. Deane
Double for the Toff. J. Creasey
Double Fortune. B. L. Hoskins
Double Four. E. P. Oppenheim
Double Frame. Anthony Morton
Double Frame. C. Rice
Double Game. D. Richards
Double Griffin. P. Blake
Double-Handed Game. Nicholas Carter
Double Hit. M. Russell
Double House. E. Dejeans
Double Identities. J. Rhode
Double Identity. Nick Carter
Double Identity. G. H. Coxe
Double Identity. F. Drake
Double Image. I. R. G. Hart
Double Image. R. MacDougall
Double Image. Helen MacInnes
Double Image and other stories. Roy Vickers
Double Images. P. Rosemoor
Double in Diamonds. F. Carmichael
Double in Trouble. R. S. Prather
Double Indemnity. J. M. Cain
Double Jeopardy. C. Forbes
Double Jeopardy. M. M. Goldsmith
Double Jeopardy. E. Lanham
Double Jeopardy. E. Levine
Double Jeopardy. F. Pratt
Double Jeopardy. W. C. Stiles
Double Jeopardy. M. Underwood
Double Jeopardy. Clement Wood
Double Kill. D. Bogard
Double Kill. D. Da Cruz
Double Knot. G. M. Fenn
Double Life. L. M. Alcott
Double Life. O. F. Jerome
Double Life. G. Leroux
Double Life. M. W. Wellman
Double Life and the Detectives. A. Pinkerton
Double Life of Mr. Alfred Burton. E. P. Oppenheim
Double Lives. S. Murray
Double M Man. C. Leader
Double Man. W. S. Cohen
Double Man. H. Reilly
Double Mask. R. N. Silver
Double Masquerade. A. Wilson
Double Menace. B. Newman
Double Motive. J. Creasey
Double Muscadine. F. O. Gaither
Double Mystery. Nicholas Carter
Double Mystery. L. Raphael
Double Mystery. A. Wynne
Double Negative. D. Carkeet
Double Negative. J. B. O'Sullivan
Double Nought. W. LeQueux
Double or Nothing. C. Dekker
Double or Nothing. C. Egerton-Thomas
Double or Quit. E. C. Vivian
Double or Quits. M. Dekobra

Double or Quits. A. A. Fair
Double or Quits. H. Lugar
Double Play. G. Leeds
Double Plot. Nicholas Carter
Double Problem. J. L. Morrissey
Double Quest. D. Timins
Double Red. D. Jordan
Double Revenge. L. T. Meade
Double Run. J. Ashford
Double Scoop. B. Cable
Double Shadow. W. LeQueux
Double Shadow Murders. A. McRoyd
Double Shuffle. J. H. Chase
Double Shuffle. D. B. Hobart
Double Shuffle Club. Nicholas Carter
Double Sin and other stories. A. Christie
Double Six. Maxwell Scott
Double Smile. M. Leblanc
Double Snare. Rosemary Harris
Double Snatch. G. Usher
Double Solution. C. F. Gregg
Double Spy. M. McKenna
Double Standard. L. DuBreuil
Double Take. D. Bloch
Double Take. J. Bruce
Double Take. M. Colton
Double Take. D. Craig
Double Take. G. Dowling
Double Take. R. Huggins
Double Take. H. Janson
Double Take. Roy Lewis
Double Take. R. Ormerod
Double Take. L. Peters
Double Take. Colin Robertson
Double Take. J. Stinson
Double Take. E. Violett
Double the Bluff. G. Fairlie
Double Thirteen. P. Marlowe
Double-Thirteen Mystery. A. Wynne
Double Thumb. F. Grierson
Double Tragedy. Anonymous
Double Tragedy. F. W. Crofts
Double Traitor. E. P. Oppenheim
Double Treasure. C. B. Kelland
Double Trouble. A. Bocca
Double Trouble. B. Graeme
Double Trouble. E. Lacy
Double Trouble. E. Lewis
Double Trouble. R. Mallory
Double Trouble. J. Stratton
Double Trouble. W. C. Tuttle
Double Trouble for a South American President. T. Barr
Double Turn. C. Carnac
Double Wedding. William Katz
Double Whammy. C. Hiassen
Double Who Double Crossed. T. D. Smith
Double Z. M. Grant
Doublecross. A. Livingston
Doublecross Dame. B. Banarto
Doublecross of Death. J. Creasey
Doublecrosser. Roland Daniel
Doublecrossers. M. Wells
Doubled in Diamonds. V. Canning
Doubled Up. T. J. Lustig
Doubles. V. Mikhanovsky
Doubles in Death. W. Grew
Doubling in Brass. C. C. Dobie
Doubling of Joseph Brereton. R. Hodder
Doubloons. E. Phillpotts
Doubly Dead. R. Cobb
Doubly Dead. E. Ferrars
Doubly Dead. J. M. Patterson
Doubtful Disciple. W. Haggard
Doubtful Motives. M. Gagon
Doubting Castle. R. Kavalier
Doubting Thomas. R. Reeves
Douce. E. Kyle
Dough for the Dormouse. Frank King
Douglas Affair. A. Mair
Douglas Castle. C. F. Barrett
Dove. R. O. Saber
Dove. W. Tucker
Dove in the Mulberry Tree. G. R. Preedy

Dove of War. Ian Mitchell
Dovebury Murders. J. Rhode
Dover and the Claret Tappers. J. Porter
Dover and the Unkindest Cut of All. J. Porter
Dover Beach. R. Bowker
Dover Beats the Band. J. Porter
Dover Goes to Pott. J. Porter
Dover One. J. Porter
Dover-Ostend. Taffrail
Dover Strikes Again. J. Porter
Dover Three. J. Porter
Dover Train Mystery. Anthony Gilbert
Dover Two. J. Porter
Doverfields' Diamonds. L. L. Lynch
Dovingsby Death. P. N. Walker
Dower Chest. A. Dean
Dower Court Manor. E. D. Bennett
Dower House Mystery. M. Beckett
Dower House Mystery. P. Wentworth
Dowker-Detective. F. Hume
Down. W. Grove
Down a Dark Alley. G. Holden
Down Among the Ad Men. W. A. Ballinger
Down Among the Dead Men. Evelyn Harris
Down Among the Dead Men. M. Hartland
Down Among the Dead Men. James Lake
Down Among the Dead Men. P. Moyes
Down Among the Dead Men. Sea Lion
Down Among the Dead Men. R. Stephenson
Down Among the Dead Men. S. Sterling
Down Among the Jocks. R. Dennis
Down an Alley Filled with Cats. W. Moss
Down and Dirty. Frank King
Down and Dirty. W. B. Murphy
Down and Dirty. D. Pendleton
Down and Out. W. J. Bayfield
Down and Out. Nicholas Carter
Down-Beat Kill. Peter Chambers
Down Dartmoor Way. E. Phillpotts
Down East. W. M. Graydon
Down East! L. Jackson
Down East Murders. J. S. Borthwick
Down Express. G. W. Appleton
Down for the Count. S. M. Kaminsky
Down Home. G. Mettler
Down I Go. B. Kerr
Down in the Valley. D. M. Pierce
Down Payment on Death. J. Eldridge
Down "Plug Street" Way, and other stories. G. Goodchild
Down River. S. Gallagher
Down River. Seamark
Down River. J. H. Vahey
Down-River Dolls. B. Sarto
Down the Dark Street. J. Fenton
Down the Garden Path. D. Cannell
Down the Green Stairs and other stories. J. J. Farjeon
Down the Long Slide. T. Hopkinson
Down the Water. E. Kyle
Down There. D. Goodis
Down Through the Night. J. Fast
Down to Death. Stella Phillips
Down Under. P. Wentworth
Down Under and Dirty. D. Streib
Down Under Donovan. E. Wallace
Down Under Thunder. Gar Wilson
Down Yonder with Judge Priest. I. S. Cobb
Downbeat for a Dirge. B. Bird
Downbeat on a Debutante. J. J. McCall
Downe Reserve. M. Blount
Downey of the Mounted. J. B. Hendryx
Downfall of a Lady. Rex Richards
Downfall of Gerdt Bladh. C. Kihlman
Downhill Ride of Leeman Popple. G. Bellairs
Downing of Flight Six Heavy. P. Lafferty
Downing Street Discovery. J. G. Brandon
Downriver. P. Collier
Downriver. P. Fox
Downtown. C. Borelli
Downtown. E. McBain
Downtown and Dead. M. Brody
Downtown Doll. H. Janson
Downward Path. R. Chapman

Downward Path. E. Gaboriau
Downward Path. Dick Stewart
Downwind. B. McKnight
Downwind of Death. B. McKnight
Dowry. M. Gould
Dowry of Danger. R. L. Smithson
Dowry of Death. M. A. Casberg
Dowry of Diamonds. L. V. Stevens
Doyle's Disciples. B. Leuci
Doyle's Rock and other stories. L. A. G. Strong
Dozen Ways of Love. L. Dougall
Dracula. H. Deane
Dracula. C. Johnson
Dracula. T. J. Kelly
Dracula. J. Mattera
Dracula. Anne Pearson
Dracula. B. Stoker
Dracula Archives. R. Rudorff
Dracula Murders. P. Daniels
Dracula's Guest. B. Stoker
Draftsman. F. Cockain
Drag Me Down. J. Brenner
Drag Me Down. E. B. Stuart
Drag the Dark. F. C. Davis
Dragnet. E. S. Barnett
Dragnet. J. G. Brandon
Dragnet. R. Deming
Dragnet. J. Reach
Dragnet. D. Spade
Dragnet: Case No. 561. D. Knight
Dragnet Drive. A. Capelli
Dragnet 1968. D. Vowell
Dragnet: The Case of the Courteous Killer. R. Deming
Dragnet: The Case of the Crime King. R. Deming
Dragoman Pass. Eric Williams
Dragon. Jack Bennett
Dragon. Alfred Coppel
Dragon. C. Cussler
Dragon Bowl. Anonymous
Dragon Fire. A. Kaplan
Dragon Flame. Nick Carter
Dragon for Christmas. G. Black
Dragon Harvest. U. Sinclair
Dragon Hunt. Garrity
Dragon in Harness. S. Gluck
Dragon in Spring. A. Barker
Dragon Island. M. Hastings
Dragon Keepers. Rodney Hughes
Dragon Lover. D. Randall
Dragon Murder Case. S. S. Van Dine
Dragon of Lung Wang. M. Harvey
Dragon Portfolio. R. Hoyt
Dragon Rising. W. Barker
Dragon Road. S. Harvester
Dragon Roars. C. Leader
Dragon Robe. C. C. Vance
Dragon Shadows. James Bennett
Dragon Slay. Nick Carter
Dragon Slayer. R. Pocock
Dragon Slayings. R. Rainey
Dragon Spoor. J. H. Crisp
Dragon Strike. P. Browne
Dragon Strikes Back. T. Roan
Dragon Tree. V. Canning
Dragon Tree Island. N. Lewis
Dragon Under Ground. R. Bell
Dragon Under the Hill. G. Honeycombe
Dragonfire. Nick Carter
Dragonfire. B. Pronzini
Dragonfire. P. G. Scott
Dragonfly. K. R. Dwyer
Dragonhead Deal. R. J. Harper
Dragonmede. Rona Randall
Dragonplague. Terence Strong
Dragons at the Gate. R. L. Duncan
Dragons at the Party. J. Cleary
Dragon's Blood. H. M. Rideout
Dragon's Breath. F. A. Smith
Dragons Can Be Dangerous. P. Chambers
Dragon's Cave. C. B. Clason
Dragon's Claw. Roland Daniel
Dragon's Claw. J. A. Dunn
Dragon's Claw. P. O'Donnell

Dragon's Claws. A. C. Hampshire
Dragons Come Expensive. M. Storme
Dragon's Daughter. C. C. Westover
Dragons Drive You. E. Balmer
Dragon's Eye. Jennie Melville
Dragon's Eye. S. C. S. Stone
Dragon's Eye. Linda Walters
Dragon's Gap. G. Harding
Dragon's Jaws. F. Packard
Dragon's Kill. G. Wilson
Dragon's Lair. I. D. Wenzell
Dragon's Mount. D. Rowan
Dragon's Play. John Pearson
Dragon's Silk. P. Herring
Dragon's Spine. L. Cameron
Dragon's Teeth. David Fraser
Dragon's Teeth. L. Killough
Dragon's Teeth. E. Queen
Dragons to Slay. Bok
Dragon's Tongue. Alick Harvey
Dragonseeds. B. Banks
Dragonship. Robert MacLeod
Dragonwyck. A. Seton
Drakmere Must Die. W. H. L. Crauford
Drakov Memorandum. J. Winters
Dram of Evil. D. J. Olson
Dram of Poison. C. Armstrong
Dram of Poison. M. Jackson
Drama in Mid Air. H. P. Bowden
Drama of Mr. Dilly. C. Edwards
Drama of Mount Street. H. Flatau
Drama of the Rue de la Paix. A. Belot
Drama of the Telephone and other tales. R. Marsh
Dramas of Life. G. R. Sims
Dramatic Murder. Elizabeth Anthony
Draper Solution. G. C. Dukes
Draught of Life. G. R. Sims
Draughts in the Sun. R. Parker
Draw Batons! B. Knox
Draw in Your Stool. O. Onions
Draw the Blinds. S. Truss
Draw the Curtain Close. T. B. Dewey
Draw the Dragon's Teeth. B. Newman
Draw the Teeth of a Dragon. M. Ashton
Drawback to Murder. W. A. Barber
Drawn Blanc. R. Gadney
Drawn Blank. R. Jocelyn
Drawn Conclusion. W. A. Barber
Drawn to Evil. H. Whittington
Drawstring. D. Locke
Draycott Murder Mystery. M. Thynne
Dread. B. Sarto
Dread and Water. Douglas Clark
Dread Brass Shadows. Glen Cook
Dread Cave. J. Courage
Dread Journey. D. B. Hughes
Dread of Night. E. O'Donnell
Dread of Night. A. Shivelley
Dread the Sunset. M. Carleton
Dreadful Hollow. N. Blake
Dreadful Hollow. I. Karlova
Dreadful Lemon Sky. J. D. MacDonald
Dreadful Night. B. A. Williams
Dreadful Reckoning. C. M. Russell
Dreadful Sanctuary. E. F. Russell
Dreadful Summit. S. Ellin
Dream. L. Freeman
Dream and a Forgetting. J. Hawthorne
Dream and the Dead. P. Audemars
Dream—and the Woman. T. Gallon
Dream Apart. L. Egan
Dream Baby. B. McAllister
Dream Before Dying. M. Alexander
Dream-Boaters. L. Frisch
Dream Buyers. M. Land
Dream Daughter. A. Askew
Dream-Detective. S. Rohmer
Dream Doctor. A. B. Reeve
Dream Girl Caper. J. D. Lawrence
Dream Horse. J. Griffiths
Dream Hunter. M. Fredericks
Dream Is Deadly. Carter Brown
Dream Killers. D. Winston
Dream Lover. M. Upton

Title Index

Dream Merchant. Carter Brown
Dream Murder. A. Broome
Dream Murder. E. C. Reed
Dream of a Woman. J. J. Dratler
Dream of Danger. A. Nolder
Dream of Darkness. P. Ruell
Dream of Death. M. O. Rank
Dream of Death. E. Trevor
Dream of Fair Serpents. C. Darby
Dream of Fair Women. C. Armstrong
Dream of Falling. M. O. Rank
Dream of Freedom. H. Nisbet
Dream of Madness. J. Pattinson
Dream of Orchids. P. A. Whitney
Dream of Raven. Anonymous
Dream of Romy Jackson. A. J. Benchley
Dream of Terror. R. Abbey
Dream of Treason. M. Edelman
Dream of Treason. M. Pugh
Dream of Unicorns. M. Naismith
Dream Park. L. Niven
Dream Sinister. S. M. Schley
Dream Spinners. C. G. Thacker
Dream Street. Bill Kelly
Dream Walker. C. Armstrong
Dream Watch. J. H. Way
Dreamer. Peter James
Dreamer at Large. W. M. Duncan
Dreamer Beware. R. Wissman
Dreamer Deals with Murder. W. M. Duncan
Dreamer Intervenes. W. M. Duncan
Dreamer, Lost in Terror. Alison King
Dreamers. R. Manvell
Dreamers: A Club. J. K. Bangs
Dreamers and Dealers. B. Hirschfeld
Dreamers in a Haunted House. M. Lovell
Dreaming Damozel. Mollie Hardwick
Dreaming God. Basil Carey
Dreaming of Babylon. R. Brautigan
Dreaming Summer. E. Ogilvie
Dreaming Witness. J. Davison
Dreamland. G. V. Higgins
Dreamland. N. Thornburg
Dreamland Mystery. M. Gilmore
Dreams Die Hard. M. Hayman
Dream's Fulfillment. H. C. Bentley
Dreams of Glory. T. J. Fleming
Dreams of Leaving. Rupert Thomson
Dreams to Sell. S. Warwick
Dreamspinner. J. Hinchman
Dreamspinner. B. D. Smith
Dreamwalker. J. Fitzpatrick
Dreamwatcher. T. Roszak
Drearloch. D. Kamm
Dreemz of the Night. J. Harrington
Dresden Green. N. Freeling
Dress Circle Murders. P. Yates
Dress Gray. L. Truscott
Dress Her in Indigo. J. D. MacDonald
Dress to Die In. Marion Cooper
Dress Up and Die. D. Elias
Dressed to Kill. C. Black
Dressed to Kill. A. Bocca
Dressed to Kill. B. Channing
Dressed to Kill. P. Cheyney
Dressed to Kill. E. L. Fetta
Dressed to Kill. K. Gordon
Dressed to Kill. D. H. Hyde
Dressed to Kill. M. Logan
Dressed to Kill. N. Morland
Dressed to Kill. M. K. Ozaki
Dressed Up to Kill. E. G. Cousins
Dressing of Diamond. N. Freeling
Dressing-Room Murder. J. S. Fletcher
Drexel Dream. W. A. MacKenzie
Drift of Fate. Dora Russell
Drifthaven. Clarissa Ross
Drifting Death. H. Carstairs
Drifting Death. B. Gaston
Drifting Diamond. L. Colcord
Drifting Mist. M. McGregor
Drifting Sands. Elsie Lee
Driftwood and Other Tales. J. C. Haywood
Drill Is Death. F. Lockridge

Drilling for Death. John Wolfe
Drink Alone and Die. B. Cobb
Drink for Mr. Cherry. D. Gardiner
Drink! For Once Dead. A. Sewart
Drink No Deeper. C. Edwards
Drink the Green Water. H. Austin
Drink This. E. Dewhurst
Drink to Yesterday. M. Coles
Drink with the Dead. J. M. Flynn
Drinks on the Victim. M. V. Heberden
Drip Dry Man. Eric Lambert
Dripping Tamarinds. C. C. Lewis
Driscoll's Diamonds. I. MacAlister
Drive East on 66. R. Wormser
Driven. R. Gehman
Driven Death. N. Orde-Powlett
Driven Flesh. L. Easton
Driven from Cover. Nicholas Carter
Driven from Home. Anonymous
Driven to Bay. F. Marryat
Driven to Death. J. C. Lenehan
Driven to Desperation. Nicholas Carter
Driven to Kill. D. M. Disney
Driven to Kill. B. Dolphin
Driven to Kill. C. Witting
Driven to Murder. A. D. Burke
Driven to Murder. A. W. Davison
Driven to Murder. O. Chase
Driven to the Wall. S. Campbell
Driver. C. B. Phillips
Driver's Seat. M. Spark
Drone-Man. John Ross
Droonin' Watter. J. S. Fletcher
Drop Dead. G. Ashe
Drop Dead. G. Bagby
Drop Dead. W. Braun
Drop Dead. R. Drayton
Drop Dead. June Drummond
Drop Dead. B. McKnight
Drop Dead. M. Neville
Drop Dead, Darling. D. Haring
Drop Dead in Desden. R. Vacha
Drop Dead, Sucker! H. Janson
Drop Dead, Sucker. B. Rigan
Drop Detective. Anonymous
Drop in the Ocean. Steve Wright
Drop of a Hat. R. Fenisong
Drop of Hot Gold. J. N. Chance
Drop of Murder. B. Joshua
Drof-Off. K. Grissom
Drop One, Carry Four. Frederic Sinclair
Drop Out. H. Miller
Drop That Gun. R. Angel
Drop to His Death. J. Rhode
Dropped Dead. J. Ross
Dropped from the Fast Express. F. M. White
Dropped Living Room. F. Y. McHugh
Dropshot. J. Bickham
Dross. M. E. Braddon
Drought. J. Creasey
Drove Road. Winifred Duke
Drown Her Remembrance. S. Gilruth
Drown Him Deep. Barbara Cooper
Drown the Wind. M. P. Hood
Drowned Hopes. D. E. Westlake
Drowned Queen. E. L. Laumer
Drowned Rat. E. Ferrars
Drowner. J. D. MacDonald
Drowning. J. Ehrlich
Drowning Day. A. Dipper
Drowning Pool. J. R. Macdonald
Drowning Stone. H. Fosburgh
Drowning Wire. M. Claire
Drug Called Power. I. MacKintosh
Drug Farm. P. A. Foxall
Drug in the Market. C. Baines
Drug of Choice. J. Lange
Drug on the Market. H. Brinton
Drug on the Market. D. Dodge
Drug on the Market. G. Sampson
Drug on the Market. N. Tranter
Drug Run. William Crawford
Drug-Run. P. Pettit
Drug Runner. P. Andrews

Drug Trial. Rosemary Richards
Drug Warriors. R. Coran
Drugstore Cowboy. J. Fogle
Druid's Blood. E. M. Friesner
Druid's Retreat. K. Kent
Drum Beat—Berlin. S. Marlowe
Drum Beat—Dominique. S. Marlowe
Drum Beat—Erica. S. Marlowe
Drum Beat—Madrid. S. Marlowe
Drum Beat—Marianne. S. Marlowe
Drum Madness. The Edingtons
Drum of Power. Robert MacLeod
Drum of Ungara. Robert MacLeod
Drumbuie House. M. D. Scott
Drummer in the Dark. F. Clifford
Drums Along the Amazon. V. Norwood
Drums Beat at Dusk. S. Maddock
Drums Beat at Night. Gavin Holt
Drums Beat Red. D. Graeme
Drums Call the Major. L. P. Greene
Drums in the Night. P. S. McCoy
Drums Never Beat. M. McKenna
Drums of Darkness. M. Z. Bradley
Drums of Death. J. Addiscombe
Drums of Death. H. Reed
Drums of Dombali. E. Phillpotts
Drums of Doom. O. Binns
Drums of Fu Manchu. S. Rohmer
Drums of Jeopardy. H. MacGrath
Drums of Kufu. J. Delft
Drums of Sacrifice. W. R. Foran
Drums of the Dark Gods. W. A. Ballinger
Drums of War. G. E. Rochester
Drums of War. J. G. Sarasin
Drums of Youth. Margery Lawrence
Drunkard. G. Thorne
Drunkard's End. S. Troy
Drury Affair. I. Valdes
Drury Club Case. S. Williams
Drury Lane's Last Case. B. Ross
Druze Document. G. Fitzgerald
Dry Spell. J. Creasey
Dry Taste of Fear. Dorothea Bennett
Dry Tortugas. W. Chambers
Dry White Season. A. Brink
Dry White Tear. S. F. Wilcox
Dual Enigma. M. Underwood
Dual Identity. C. G. Mitford
Duane and the Art Murders. J. L. Benton
Duane of the FBI. J. L. Benton
Duane of the G-Men. J. L. Benton
Dubai. Robin Moore
Dublin Affair. P. S. Donoghue
Dublin Nightmare. P. Loraine
Dublin Pawn. J. Keckhut
Dubrovnik Massacre. Nick Carter
Duca and the Milan Murders. G. Scerbanenco
Ducats in Her Coffin. T. Warriner
Ducetti Lair. L. Hitchcock
Duchess. J. Edgar
Duchess. L. L. Rogger
Duchess de Langeais. H. Balzac
Duchess Double D. Carter Brown
Duchess Grace. M. Leighton
Duchess in Difficulties. A. Griffiths
Duchess in Pursuit. I. A. R. Wylie
Duchess Intervenes. M. B. Lowndes
Duchess Laura: Some Days of Her Life. M. B. Lowndes
Duchess of Dope. B. Sarto
Duchess of Pontifex Square. G. W. Appleton
Duchess of Powysland. G. Allen
Duchess of Skid Row. L. Trimble
Duchess of Videl. D. Lindsey
Duckett's Condor. Roy Burns
Ducking of Herbert Polton, and Coincidence. H. C. McNeile
Ducks and Drakes. P. G. Labalestier
Ducks and Drakes. M. Leighton
Ducks and Drakes. N. Tranter
Ducks in Thunder. J. J. Dratler
Duckworth's Diamonds. E. Everett-Green
Ducrow Follow. J. N. Chance
Dude Ranch Murders. M. F. Ford

Dudie Dunne. Old Sleuth
Dudley Carleon. M. E. Braddon
Duds. H. C. Rowland
Due or Die. F. Kane
Due to a Death. M. Kelly
Due to Expire. H. A. Wrenn
Due to the Lion Tamer. L. M. Robertson
Duel. R. Marsh
Duel. D. Seaman
Duel Across the Water. D. Quentin
Duel for a Dark Lady. M. Marais
Duel for Cannons. D. Hartman
Duel in Glenfinnan. A. MacVicar
Duel in the Dark. Anonymous
Duel in the Shadows. A. Lejeune
Duel in the Snow. H. Meissner
Duel Murder. G. Bray
Duel of Brains. Nicholas Carter
Duel of Happiness. H. Simart
Duel of Shadows. L. R. Brown
Duel on the Song Cai. J. Lansing
Duel Resurrection. B. Mitford
Duel with Diamonds. H. L. Ruff
Dueling Missiles. D. Stivers
Dueling Oaks. D. Dorsett
Duenna to a Murder. R. King
Duet. D. Daniels
Duet for a Corpse. J. Bogar
Duet for Death. M. Cronin
Duet for Three Spies. H. T. Rothwell
Duet for Two Guns. D. Ambler
Duet for Two Hands. M. H. Bell
Duet in Death. Hilda Lawrence
Duet of Death. Hilda Lawrence
Duet to Corruption. J. Cello
Duff. I. Blair
Duffy. H. J. Brown, Jr.
Duffy. D. Kavanagh
Duffy Is Dead. J. M. O'Neill
Dugdale Millions. W. C. Hudson
Duke. J. S. Clouston
Duke. H. Ellson
Duke. W. Manson
Duke and the Dices. Holworthy Hall
Duke and the Veil. C. J. Stevermer
Duke Decides. H. Hill
Duke in the Suburbs. E. Wallace
Duke of Arcanum. F. C. Long
Duke of Cameron Avenue. A. R. Weekes
Duke of Clarence. E. M. F.
Duke of Omaha. Old Sleuth
Duke of York's Steps. Henry Wade
Dukedom of Portsea. A. M. Meadows
Duke's Daughters, and The Fugitives. M. Oliphant
Duke's Day. A. Travis
Duke's Dilemma. W. Magnay
Duke's Last Trick. C. F. Gregg
Duke's Sweetheart. R. Dowling
Dulcarnon. H. M. Rideout
Dulcie Bligh. G. Clark
Dull Dead. Gwendoline Butler
Dull Thud. Manning Long
Dull Tree. H. Canelstein
Dum-Dum for the President. Martin Brett
Dumaresq's Daughter. G. Allen
Dumb Alibi. N. Morland
Dumb As They Come. M. Corrigan
Dumb Babes Don't Die. H. Spencer
Dumb Detective. Anonymous
Dumb Gods Speak. E. P. Oppenheim
Dumb Man of Manchester. B. F. Rayner
Dumb Vengeance. S. Tower
Dumb Waiter. H. Pinter
Dumb Witness. A. Christie
Dumb Witness. M. Hervey
Dumb Witness. T. A. Plummer
Dumb Witness. N. Wylie
Dumb Witness and other stories. Nicholas Carter
Dumbo Dossier. E. Cannon
Dumdum Murder. Carter Brown
Dummy. A. L. Kaser
Dummy. H. J. O'Higgins
Dummy Murder Case. M. K. Ozaki
Dummy Robberies. M. E. Cooke

Dummy Run. Martin Russell
Dump. J. Remenham
Dumphry. B. Pain
Dumpling. C. Kernahan
Duncan Dynasty. D. Daniels
Duncan Is in His Grave. R. Wiseman
Duncan Ross—Detective-Sergeant. R. Stuart
Duncraig. M. Heath
Dunes. S. Walters
Dunfermline Affair. Angus Ross
Dungeon. M. L. Falcon
Dungeons of Crowley Hall. C. Alcott
Dunkirk Directive. D. Richmond
Dunleary. M. Heath
Dunleath Abbey. H. P. Diltz
Dunn's Conundrum. Stan Lee
Dunsan House. Gail St. John
Dunslow. E. R. Punshon
Dunthorpes of Westleigh. C. Lys
Duo. C. Armstrong
Dupe. G. Biss
Dupe. L. Cody
Dupe. C. Mansfield
Dupe Negative. A. Fowles
Dupes. E. W. Mumford
Duplicate. A. Mather
Duplicate. H. B. Taylor
Duplicate Death. A. C. Fox-Davies
Duplicate Death. G. Heyer
Duplicate Duke. H. Hill
Duplicate Keys. J. Smiley
Duplicate Stiff. A. O'Neill
Dupre Blues. D. Curran
Durable Fire. Sheila Bishop
Durand Case. S. Kyle
Durian Tree. M. Keon
During Her Majesty's Pleasure. M. E. Braddon
During His Majesty's Pleasure. S. Kyle
Durong Warriors. J. Lansing
Durrell Towers. Clarissa Ross
Dusk at Penarder. Gavin Holt
Dusk to Dawn. C. Grave
Dusky Cactus. M. McEvoy
Dusky Death. R. Garnett
Dusky Hour. E. R. Punshon
Dusky Innocent. Stuart Hall
Dusky Limelight. Colin Robertson
Dusky Night. V. Bridges
Dusseldorf. A. M. Mackenzie
Dust. J. Hawthorne
Dust and the Curious Boy. P. Graaf
Dust and the Heat. M. Gilbert
Dust in My Throat. J. Farrimond
Dust in the Balance. G. Knight
Dust in the Sun. J. Cleary
Dust in the Vault. R. A. J. Walling
Dust in Your Eyes. S. Seaton
Dust of Death. I. Ostrander
Dust to Dust. I. Ostrander
Dustman. F. D. Singer
Dustman to Ashes. R. S. Peltz
Dusty Coinage. W. Mills
Dusty Death. M. Burning
Dusty Death. O. Mills
Dusty Death. C. Robbins
Dusty Death. L. Thayer
Dusty Ermine. N. Grant
Dusty Sunset. P. Winn
Dutch Blue Error. W. G. Tapply
Dutch Caper. J. Baddock
Dutch Courage. Ritchie Perry
Dutch Detective. W. B. Hare
Dutch Justice. Richard Sanders
Dutch Shea, Jr. J. G. Dunne
Dutch Shoe Mystery. E. Queen
Dutch the Diver. G. M. Fenn
Dutch Treat. T. Jones
Dutch Uncle. S. Gray
Duty Be Damned! D. Walshe
Duty Elsewhere. J. Wainwright
Duty Free. F. Gaite
Duveen Letter. E. Leather
Dwarf of Westerbourg. C. H. Spiess
Dwarf's Chamber and other stories. F. Hume

Dwarves of Death. J. Coe
Dwell in Danger. R. Lewis
Dwellers in Darkness. A. Derleth
Dwellers of Riven Oak. J. T. Osborne
Dwelling. T. Elliott
Dwelly Lane. F. V. Morley
Dydeetown World. F. P. Wilson
Dyed for Death. W. W. Rider
Dying. L. A. Horvitz
Dying Alderman. Henry Wade
Dying Breath. J. Honeywood
Dying Breath. R. W. Walker
Dying Business. E. Dewar
Dying Day. James Mitchell
Dying Echo. K. N. Knight
Dying Fall. H. Dolson
Dying Fall. G. Milner
Dying Fall. J. Thomson
Dying Fall. Henry Wade
Dying for a Drink. R. Silverwood
Dying for Stardom. E. Fulton
Dying High. A. Curry
Dying, in Other Words. M. Gee
Dying in the Night. J. Roffman
Dying of the Light. Robert Richardson
Dying Place. D. A. Maurer
Dying Room. M. L. Stokes
Dying Room Only. S. Sterling
Dying Space. W. B. Murphy
Dying to Come Home. J. Jenkins
Dying to Live and other stories. S. Horler
Dying to Meet You. B. M. Gill
Dying Trade. P. Corris
Dying Ukrainian. P. Howarth
Dying Voices. B. Crider
Dying Witnesses. M. Halliday
Dyke and Burr, the Rival Detectives. H. Rockwood
Dyke Darrel, the Railroad Detective. A. F. Pinkerton
Dynamite! Rip Connolly
Dynamite. B. Sarto
Dynamite Days. W. C. Tuttle
Dynamite Doll. B. Sarto
Dynamite Drury. L. P. Greene
Dynamite Drury Again. L. P. Greene
Dynamite Drury Patrols. L. P. Greene
Dynamite Freaks. D. Ryan
Dynamite Monster Boogie Concert. Paul Ross
Dynamite on Wheels. Duff Johnson
Dynamite Trap. Nicholas Carter
Dynamiter. R. L. Stevenson
Dynamiters. M. Creighton
Dynasty of Desire. V. Coffman
Dynasty of Doom. P. A. Foxall
Dynasty of Dreams. V. Coffman
Dynasty of Fear. J. C. Sprague
Dynasty of Power. D. Thoreau
Dynasty of Spies. D. Sherman
Dzerzhinsky Square. J. O. Jackson

E Is for Evidence. S. Grafton
E Pluribus Bang! D. Lippincott
E.T.A. for Death. C. H. Wallace
Each Dawn I Die. J. Odlum
Each Life to Life. R. Gehman
Each Man's Destiny. M. Procter
Each Night We Die. E. Woodward
Eagle and the Wren. R. Pertwee
Eagle and Unicorn. G. Brook-Shepherd
Eagle at the Gate. R. Randall
Eagle Down. W. Mason
Eagle Flies from England. E. Atiyah
Eagle Has Landed. J. Higgins
Eagle Six. P. Long
Eagles. L. Orde
Eagle's Blood. Douglas Scott
Eagle's Eye. W. J. Flynn
Eagle's Feathers. N. Tranter
Eagles Fly. S. Flannery
Eagles Near His Carcase. P. Somerville-Large
Eagle's Nest. J. Carter
Eagle's Nest. D. Daniels
Eagle's Nest. J. Di Mona
Eaglescliffe. M. McEvoy
Eagrave Square Mystery. A. W. Marchmont

Eames-Erskine Case. A. Fielding
Ear for Murder. Michael Brett
Ear in the Wall. A. B. Reeve
Ear to the Ground. J. H. Chase
Earhart Betrayal. J. S. Thayer
Earhart Mission. P. Tanous
Earl Derr Biggers Tells Ten Stories. E. D. Biggers
Earl of Chicago. Brock Williams
Earl Without an Earldom. Scott Graham
Earl's End. L. Gorell
Earl's Heirs. H. Wood
Earl's Return. W. M. Graydon
Earl's Ward. S. Cobb
Early Autumn. R. B. Parker
Early Boyd. Carter Brown
Early Days of August. J. B. Kovalsky
Early Doors. Hugh Mills
Early Frost. D. F. Parkhirst
Early Graves. Joseph Hanson
Early Morning Murder. M. Burton
Early Morning Poison. B. Cobb
Early Stories. D. Du Maurier
Early Warning. C. Fitzsimons
Earmarked for Murder. G. Rayne
Earnshaw's Evidence. P. Bowland
Ears of the Jungle. P. Boulle
Earth. D. Brin
Earth Angels. G. Petievich
Earth-Bound. M. Macardle
Earth Descended. F. Saberhagen
Earth to Ashes. A. Brock
Earthfire North. Nick Carter
Earthly Pergatory. L. Dougall
Earthman's Burden. P. Anderson
Earthquake Machine. A. Mitchelson
Earthrace. T. Keene
Earth's Great Lord. E. R. Punshon
East All the Way. J. G. Lockhart
East and West. T. Mundy
East Coast Crisis. H. Weinstein
East Coast Mystery. H. Edmonds
East Coast Yarns. P. H. Emerson
East Hampton. Richard Hubbard
East India and Company. P. Morand
East Indian. M. J. Young
East London Mystery. A. Sergeant
East Lynn. N. Albert
East Lynne. B. J. Burton
East Lynne. H. Wood
East of Algiers. P. Temple
East of Broadway. O. R. Cohen
East of Desolation. J. Higgins
East of Elsa. R. Dudgeon
East of Everest. B. Langley
East of Hell. Nick Carter
East of Kashgar. F. A. M. Webster
East of Mansion House. T. Burke
East of Piccadilly. S. Maddock
East of Samarinda. C. Jacobi
East of Singapore. G. Goodchild
East of Singapore. M. McGrath
East of Singapore. S. M. Parkman
East of Suez. A. Perrin
East Side Assignment. R. Kirby
East Side Blonde. N. Rosso
East Side Detective. Anonymous
East Wind Coming. A. B. Cover
East Wind, Rain. N. R. Nash
East Zone Snatch. G. Vaughan
Easter Dinner. D. Downes
Easter Egg Hunt. G. Freeman
Easter Guests Mystery. J. K. Ryland
Easter Man. Evan Hunter
Easter Weekend. J. Bottoms
Eastern Men—Chicago Women. Griff
Eastern Question. M. Walker
Eastern Vendetta. Old Sleuth
Eastlake Affair. Colin Robertson
Eastside Exposure. B. Sarto
Eastward in Eden. D. Garth
Eastwind/Westwind. J. Nordhoff
Easy Access. R. Flanders
Easy Come. G. Wheeler
Easy Come, Easy Go. A. Bocca

Easy Come, Easy Go. O. Davis
Easy Curves. N. Baroni
Easy Dough. B. Logan
Easy for the Crook. R. Trevor
Easy Go. J. Lange
Easy Living. B. Vane
Easy Money. B. Atkey
Easy Money. F. Johnston
Easy Money. S. Koperwas
Easy Money. A. Mather
Easy Money. L. Osborn
Easy Money. J. Reid
Easy Nat. A. L. Stimson
Easy Pickings. P. A. Cruzer
Easy Prey. Josephine Bell
Easy Television Plays. L. J. Huber
Easy Thing. P. I. Taibo
Easy to Kill. A. Christie
Easy to Kill. H. Footner
Easy to Murder. N. Rutledge
Easy to Take. Duff Johnson
Easy Victim. L. Farago
Easy Way to Go. G. H. Coxe
Eat Me If You Must. N. Karta
Eater of Darkness. R. M. Coates
Eating the Big Fish. W. Rayner
Eavesdropper. J. Francome
Eavesdropper. J. Payn
Eavesdropping on Death. C. C. Estes
Ebbing of the Tide. L. Becke
Ebenezer Investigates. N. Brady
Eblis. S. Shaw
Ebony Bed Murder. J. R. Gillies
Ebony Box. J. S. Fletcher
Ebony Cross. Nick Carter
Ebony Diamond. Stuart Hall
Ebony Mirror. F. A. Gallimore
Ebony Stag. B. Flynn
Ebony Torso. J. C. Woodiwiss
Eccentricities of Capt. Tinker, R.N. C. Fitz-Graeme
Echo. K. Jupp
Echo. M. L. Vennum
Echo Answers Murder. N. Fitzgerald
Echo Chamber. R. Himmel
Echo from Silence. M. Pereira
Echo in a Dark Wind. J. Withers
Echo in the Cave. L. Meynell
Echo My Tears. Jan Foster
Echo of a Bomb. M. Derby
Echo of a Bomb. V. Siller
Echo of a Curse. R. R. Ryan
Echo of Barbara. Jonathan Burke
Echo of Guilt. P. Paul
Echo of Justice. Hugh Miller
Echo of Margaret. V. Black
Echo of Treason. Jonathan Burke
Echo of Weeping. M. Lynch
Echo on the Stairs. M. Jenson
Echo Vector. J. Kahn
Echoes. J. Hyman
Echoes and Shadows. L. Bobker
Echoes from Castor Hills. D. A. Stephens
Echoes from the Cornish Cliffs. D. V. Baker
Echoes from the Macabre. D. Du Maurier
Echoes from the Past. J. M. Backer
Echoes of an Ancient Love. S. Wagner
Echoes of Celandine. D. Marlowe
Echoes of Evil. K. Cameron
Echoes of Evil. I. Comfort
Echoes of Innocence. Coriola
Echoes of Landre House. A. Ainsley
Echoes of the Past. M. McEvoy
Echoes of War. J. Dial
Echoes of Zero. R. H. Spencer
Echoing Footsteps. F. A. M. Webster
Echoing Shore. Robert Martin
Echoing Strangers. G. Mitchell
Echoing Wave. D. Giberson
Eclipse. R. Belletto
Eclipse. William Stevenson
Eclipse. N. Wollaston
Eclipse of James Trent, D.I. L. Yates
Ecstasy. H. Janson
Ecstasy Business. R. Condon

Ecstasy's Captive. N. McFather
Ecstatic Thief. G. K. Chesterton
Ed Noon in London. M. Avallone
Ed. Somers, the Pinkerton Detective. E. Stark
Eddie and the Cruisers. P. F. Kluge
Eddie Black. W. F. Shapiro
Eddie Gorgon Calls the Tune. R. Hausfeld
Eddie Gorgon Takes the Rap. R. Hausfeld
Eddie Macon's Run. J. McLendon
Eddy. Riccardo Stephens
Eddy Deco's Last Caper. Gahan Wilson
Eden. J. Ellis
Eden Close. A. Shreve
Eden Eden. H. K. Fleming
Edenvile. I. Ruff
Edgar. R. Sickelmore
Edgar Allan Who—? P. Van Greenaway
Edgar Huntley. C. B. Brown
Edgar Wallace Reader. E. Wallace
Edge. Dick Francis
Edge of Beauty. B. Ferm
Edge of Beyond. J. B. Hendryx
Edge of Danger. M. Storm
Edge of Darkness. Joan Banks
Edge of Darkness. B. Clemens
Edge of Despair. M. L. Hinkel
Edge of Doom. L. Brady
Edge of Doom. M. Dalton
Edge of Eden. N. Proffitt
Edge of Extinction. J. Wainwright
Edge of Glass. C. Gaskin
Edge of Hate. E. Cannon
Edge of Hazard. G. Horton
Edge of Honesty. C. Gleig
Edge of Horror. H. Desmond
Edge of Nowhere. E. Thompson
Edge of Panic. H. Kane
Edge of Running Water. W. Sloan
Edge of Terror. F. Cowen
Edge of Terror. B. Flynn
Edge of Terror. Sean Gregory
Edge of Terror. M. Halliday
Edge of the Blade. Dan Schmidt
Edge of the City. F. Pohl
Edge of the Deep. A. Hutton
Edge of the Forest. R. Barr
Edge of the Forest. J. D. White
Edge of the Horizon. A. Tabucchi
Edge of the Law. R. Deming
Edge of the Pond. Robin Moore
Edge of the Sword. F. M. White
Edge of the Tightrope. J. H. Drew
Edge of Violence. S. Clausse
Edge of Violence. A. English
Edged Weapons. W. Goldman
Edgerston Audit. D. Akenson
Edina. H. Wood
Edinburgh Caper. S. McKelway
Edinburgh Exercise. Angus Ross
Edisto Sanctuary. J. R. Singleton
Edith Heron. Anonymous
Editha's Burglar. A. Thomas
Edith's Diary. P. Highsmith
Editor. D. Tracy
Edric the Forester. A. Ker
Educated Death. G. Larsen
Educated Evans. E. Wallace
Educated Man. E. Wallace
Educated Murder. J. R. Hulland
Educating of Quinton Quinn. A. Sewart
Education of Don Juan. Robin Hardy
Education of Mr. P. J. Davenant. F. S. Hamilton
Education of Oversoul Seven. Jane Roberts
Education of Patrick Silver. J. Charyn
Edward Barry, South Sea Pearler. L. Becke
Edwin of the Iron Shoes. M. Muller
Edwina Black. W. Dinner
Eel Pie Murders. D. Frome
Eel Pie Mystery. D. Frome
Eenie, Meenie, Minie—Murder! W. G. Beyer
Eeny Meeny Miny Mole. M. D'Agneau
Eferding Diaries. G. Brook-Shepherd
Efficiency Expert. E. R. Burroughs
Effigy of a Spy. C. Richardson

E

Efford Tangle. G. Goodchild
Egad, the Woman in White. T. J. Kelly
Egg-Shaped Thing. C. Hodder-Williams
Egremont Mystery. L. Elmont
Egypt Green. C. Hyde
Egyptian Cross Mystery. E. Queen
Egyptian Nights. Jack Mann
Egyptian Nights. S. Rohmer
Egyptian Tragedy and other stories. R. H. Savage
Egypt's Choice. D. Broun
Eichmann Syndrome. U. Dan
Eiger Sanction. Trevanian
Eight. K. Neville
Eight Black Horses. E. McBain
Eight Candles Glowing. P. Muse
Eight Card Stud. Nick Carter
Eight Crooked Tenches. F. Beeding
Eight Days. G. Fielding
Eight Days in Washington. A. Jute
8 Faces at 3. C. Rice
Eight Hours from England. A. Quayle
Eight Million Ways to Die. L. Block
Eight Murders in the Suburbs. Roy Vickers
Eight O'Clock Alibi. C. Bush
Eight O'Clock Tuesday. R. Wallsten
Eight of Diamonds. H. G. Hutchinson
Eight of Swords. J. D. Carr
Eight Penny Spy. A. Mallary
Eight-Pointed Star. G. H. Teed
Eight Short Stories. Lennox Robinson
Eight Short Stories. A. Waugh
Eight Strokes of the Clock. M. Leblanc
813. M. Leblanc
Eight Three Five. A. Soutar
VIII to IX. R. A. J. Walling
Eight Went Cruising. C. H. Barker
Eight Women—and a Ghost. J. Kirkpatrick
18 Nervous Gumshoes. Tim Kelly
Eighteen of Them—Singular Stories. W. Simpson
Eighteen Tales. L. Couperus
Eighteen-Wheel Avenger. W. W. Johnstone
Eighteenth Summer. L. Holland
Eighth Circle. S. Ellin
Eighth Commandment. Lawrence Sanders
Eighth Day. T. Wilder
Eighth Deadly Sin. Jessica Mann
Eighth Dwarf. Ross Thomas
Eighth Millionaire. G. H. Teed
Eighth Mrs. Bluebeard. H. Waugh
Eighth Sacrament. T. Cullinan
Eighth Seal. A. MacLeod
Eighth Square. H. Lieberman
Eighth Trumpet. J. Land
Eighth Veil. J. Moffatt
Eighth Victim. E. Izzi
Eighth Wonder. J. G. Sarasin
Eighty Dollars to Stamford. L. Fletcher
81st Site. T. Kenrick
Eighty Million Eyes. E. McBain
Eileen the Spy. Anonymous
Einstein Legacy. R. Elliott
Einstein Plot. B. Heatter
Einstein's Brain. M. Olshaker
Eisenhower Deception. C. Egleton
El Dorado. R. Cromie
El Greco Puzzle. J. Murphy
El Murders. B. Granger
El Rancho Rio. M. G. Eberhart
Ela the Outcast. T. P. Prest
Elberg Collection. A. Oliver
Elder Brother. A. Gibbs
Elderly Gentleman Shot. D. Sharp
Eldorado. Baroness Orczy
Eldorado Jane. P. Bottome
Eldorado Network. Derek Robinson
Eldorado Red. D. Goines
Eldrida, the Red Rover's Daughter. N. Buntline
Eleanor. Mrs. C. D. Haynes
Eleanor's Victory. M. E. Braddon
Election Booth Murder. M. Propper
Election by Murder. A. Eichler
Electric Beach. L. Rees
Electric Shock and other stories. E. Gerard
Electric Theft. N. W. Williams

Electric Train. D. Beaty
Electro Pete, the Man of Fire. A. P. Morris
Elegant Edward. E. Wallace
Elegy for a Revolutionary. C. J. Driver
Elegy for a Soprano. K. N. Smith
Elegy in a Country Churchyard. Audrey Peterson
Element of Chance. Emma Page
Element of Doubt. A. Booth
Element of Doubt. D. Simpson
Element of Risk. E. Cannon
Element of Risk. M. Derby
Elemental. R. Chetwynd-Hayes
Elementary, My Dear. P. King
Elementary, My Dear Freddie. W. H. L. Crauford
Elementary, My Dear Holmes. R. Mauro
Elementary, My Dear Watson. G. Nown
Elements of Chance. B. Wilkins
Elena. E. Francis
Eleni. N. Gage
Elephant. G. Goodchild
Elephant God. G. Casserly
Elephant Murders. E. S. Brown
Elephant Never Forgets. Ethel L. White
Elephant Valley. Finis Farr
Elephants Can Remember. A. Christie
Elephants in the Distance. D. Stashower
Elephant's Work. E. C. Bentley
Elevated Railroad Mystery and other stories. Nicholas Carter
Eleven. P. Highsmith
Eleven Bullets for Mohammed. H. Arvay
Eleven Came Back. M. Seeley
11 for Danger. A. MacVicar
11 Harrowhouse. G. A. Browne
Eleven Men Died. E. T. Woodhall
Eleven of Diamonds. B. Kendrick
Eleven Short Stories. G. Olya
Eleven-Thirty Till Twelve. R. Greene
Eleven Thrilling Mysteries. V. McCall
11.20 Glasgow Central. P. Malloch
Eleven Twenty-Seven. N. Carruthers
Eleven Were Brave. F. Beeding
Eleventh Commandment. M. Shavelson
Eleventh Hour. A. Armstrong
Eleventh Hour. G. Base
Eleventh Hour. J. S. Fletcher
Eleventh Hour. Donald Forbes
Eleventh Hour. C. N. Gattey
Eleventh Hour. H. C. McNeile
Eleventh Hour. W. B. Murphy
Eleventh Hour. R. B. Sinclair
Eleventh Little Indian. Jacquemard-Senecal
Eleventh Little Nigger. Jacquemard-Senecal
Eleventh Plague. N. Berrow
Eleventh Plague. L. T. Peters
Elfa. A. W. Marchmont
Elfrida, the Red Rover's Daughter. N. Buntline
Elgar Variation. M. Kenyon
Elgin Marble. B. Von Hutten
Eligible Connection. Elsie Lee
Elijah Conspiracy. Charles Robertson
Eliminate the Middle Man. M. Wilk
Elimination Process. C. Joyce
Elimination Syndicate. J. A. Dunn
Eliminator. A. York
Elixir. J. N. Frey
Eliza. J. A. Barlett
Eliza Gets Kissed. Dana Stevens
Eliza Grimwood. Anonymous
Elizabeth. J. Hamilton
Elizabeth Finds the Body. F. Kilpatrick
Elizabeth Glen, M.D.: The Experiences of a Lady Doctor. A. S. Swan
Elizabeth Is Missing. L. De La Torre
Elizabeth R.I.P. D. Lee
Elizabeth the Sleuth. F. Kilpatrick
Elizabeth X. V. Caspary
Eliza's Galiardo. J. Gollin
Elk and the Evidence. M. Scherf
Ellen Morgan. W. Tyrer
Ellena. C. Connell
Ellerby Case. J. Rhode
Ellery Queen, Master Detective. E. Queen
Ellery Queen Omnibus. E. Queen

Ellery Queen's The Four of Hearts Mystery. W. Rand
Ellice Quentin. J. Hawthorne
Elm Tree Murder. J. Rhode
Elmer. G. Menuhin
Elope to Death. G. Ashe
Elsa the Terrible. B. Sarto
Elsie and the Child. Arnold Bennett
Elspeth. S. Nichols
Elster's Folly. H. Wood
Elusive Bachelor. F. E. Penny
Elusive Bowman. F. Vivian
Elusive Clue. D. Stephens
Elusive Corpse. N. Karta
Elusive Criminal. R. Broemel
Elusive Epicure. C. Keith
Elusive Exile. M. Blake
Elusive Four. W. LeQueux
Elusive Isabel. J. Futrelle
Elusive Killer. T. A. Plummer
Elusive Knave. Nicholas Carter
Elusive Lady. M. Cronin
Elusive Legacy. K. A. Shoesmith
Elusive Lord Bagtor. B. Tozer
Elusive Lover. V. Woods
Elusive Mr. Drago. T. C. H. Jacobs
Elusive Mrs. Pollifax. D. Gilman
Elusive Nephew. M. Dalman
Elusive Picaroon. J. Cassells
Elusive Picaroon. H. Landon
Elusive Pimpernel. Baroness Orczy
Elusive Quest. F. Cowen
Elusive Vicky Van. C. Wells
Elusive Witness. D. E. Bingley
Elvin Court Mystery. A. I. Etheridge
Elvira Digs a Grave. M. Storme
Elvis Murders. A. Bourgeau
Em. E. Southworth
Emancipation of Ambrose. M. Cobb
Embankment Crime. Donald Stuart
Embankment Murder. G. Verner
Embarrassed Ladies Affair. H. Catalan
Embarrassed Murderer. G. Stockwell
Embarrassing Death. R. Jeffries
Embarrassment of Riches. M. Fischer
Embassy. V. Brome
Embassy. S. Coulter
Embassy. L. Waller
Embassy Ball. V. R. Coxe
Embassy Case. H. Hill
Embassy Detective. W. M. Graydon
Embassy House. N. Proffitt
Embassy Madonna. Lydia Kirk
Embassy Murder. A. Hodges
Embers of Hate. Bradshaw Jones
Embezzler. J. M. Cain
Embrace of Death. C. C. Estes
Embrace the Butcher. Anthony Burton
Embrace the Wolf. B. M. Schutz
Embraces. S. Wagner
Embroidered Sunset. Joan Aiken
Emerald. J. Baddock
Emerald. P. A. Whitney
Emerald Angel. S. Sackett
Emerald Buddha. J. B. Ames
Emerald Buddha. E. Morse
Emerald Chicks Caper. L. V. Roper
Emerald Clasp. F. Beeding
Emerald Decision. David Grant
Emerald Elephant Gambit. L. Maddock
Emerald Embassy. F. Gerard
Emerald Heart. M. Carrel
Emerald Hill. D. Daniels
Emerald Illusion. R. Bass
Emerald Kiss. C. Reeve
Emerald Mountain. F. Y. McHugh
Emerald Murder Case. Dennis Dean
Emerald Murder Trap. Jackson Gregory
Emerald Necklace. E. Fraser
Emerald Necklace. A. R. Weekes
Emerald of Catherine the Great. H. Belloc
Emerald of Death. E. Snell
Emerald Oil Caper. J. D. Lawrence
Emerald Pool. M. Andrau

Emerald Spider. Gavin Holt
Emerald Station. D. Winston
Emerald Tears of Foxfire Manor. C. Wimberly
Emerald Tiger. E. Jepson
Emerald Trap. L. St. Clair
Emergency Exit. H. Carmichael
Emergency Exit. M. Cronin
Emergency Exit. A. Wynne
Emergency in the Pyrenees. A. Bridge
Emergency Operator. D. Haring
Emergency Procedure. M. Frederics
Emergency Room. J. Kerr
Emigrants de Luxe. M. Dekobra
Emily. C. F. Barrington
Emily Coulton Dies. M. B. Dix
Emily Dickinson Is Dead. J. Langton
Emily Fitzormond. T. P. Prest
Emily Moreland. H. M. Jones
Emily Percy. T. P. Prest
Emily Will Know. N. Rutledge
Eminence. W. X. Kienzle
Eminent Persons. W. Greatorex
Emissary. Michael Mainwaring
Emma Chizzit and the Queen Anne Killer. M. B. Hall
Emma of Alkistan. Margery Lawrence
Emma Slasky. J. Grecco
Emperor Fu Manchu. S. Rohmer
Emperor of America. S. Rohmer
Emperor of Detectives. Anonymous
Emperor of Evil. C. J. Daly
Emperor of Hallelujah Island. G. Goodchild
Emperor of Ice. R. Tate
Emperor of the Air. J. Tregellis
Emperor's Candlesticks. B. Orczy
Emperor's Old Clothes. F. Heller
Emperor's Pearl. R. Van Gulik
Emperor's Secret. D. Pilgrim
Emperor's Servant. D. Pilgrim
Emperor's Snuff-Box. J. D. Carr
Empire 99. R. Goulart
Empire of Crime. Nicholas Carter
Empire of Evil. S. Noel
Empire of the World. C. J. C. Hyne
Empire on Arumac. M. Hale
Empire State. E. A. Pollitz, Jr.
Empress Eugenie. M. B. Lowndes
Empress of Coney Island. R. B. Gillespie
Empress of the Andes. F. Warden
Empty Beach. P. Corris
Empty Bed. H. Adams
Empty Copper Sea. J. D. MacDonald
Empty Cot. C. Phillips
Empty Flat. Frank King
Empty Glass. D. Learmonth
Empty Hands. A. Stringer
Empty Heart. Elizabeth Ford
Empty Hills. A. Holden
Empty Hotel. A. C. Gunter
Empty Hours. E. McBain
Empty House. A. Blackwood
Empty House. M. Gilbert
Empty House. F. Grierson
Empty House. I. Karlova
Empty House Murder. Donald Stuart
Empty House Mystery. B. Bolt
Empty Mail Bags. E. C. Derby
Empty Man. M. Heimer
Empty Nest. E. Cadell
Empty Palace. Ben Barclay
Empty Quarter. L. Cameron
Empty Saddle. L. Meynell
Empty Silence. B. Copper
Empty Tiger. M. Catto
Empty Tigers. I. Wilson
Empty Trap. J. D. MacDonald
Empty Villa. J. L. Rickard
Empty Years. James Preston
Em's Husband. E. Southworth
Emu's Head. C. Dawe
Enchanted. Roberta Murphy
Enchanted Casements. A. Castle
Enchanted Circle. A. Grace
Enchanted Desert. C. H. Bullivant

Enchanted Eden. Rona Randall
Enchanted Garden and other stories. H. A. Vachell
Enchanted Grotto. V. Black
Enchanted Hat. H. MacGrath
Enchanted Hill. P. B. Kyne
Enchanted Isle. J. M. Cain
Enchanted Isle. M. McEvoy
Enchanted Stone. C. L. Hind
Enchanted Type-Writer. J. K. Bangs
Enchanted Voyage. W. E. D. Ross
Enchanted Wooing. M. Richmond
Enchanter. R. Newman
Enchanter's Castle. J. Tattersall
Enchanter's Nightshade. K. Troy
Enchantment. H. MacGrath
Enchantress. G. Bolton
Enchantress. C. H. Bullivant
Enchantress of the Nile. K. Lindsay
Encore. O. Henry
Encore Allain! B. Graeme
Encore at Dien Bien Phu. J. Lansing
Encore Murder. M. Babson
Encore the Lone Wolf. L. J. Vance
Encore to Murder. H. P. Martin
Encounter. C. Blackstock
Encounter at Kharmel. R. Dentry
Encounter Darkness. S. Forbes
Encounter Group. W. B. Murphy
Encounter in Athens. G. Ferrand
Encounter Three. M. Caidin
Encounter with Evil. A. Dean
End from the Beginning. K. Slattery
End Game. M. Gilbert
End Game. James Underwood
End Game in Paris. I. Adams
End in Sight. Clifford King
End Is Known. G. H. Hall
End of a Big Wheel. C. Fox
End of a Call Girl. W. C. Gault
End of a Cigarette. E. Gillibrand
End of a Diplomat. Ronald Simpson
End of a Good Woman. M. Hinxman
End of a JD. J. Gonzales
End of a Life. E. Phillpotts
End of a Millionaire. P. D. Ballard
End of a Party. H. Waugh
End of a Shadow. A. Clarke
End of a Stripper. R. Dietrich
End of an Ancient Mariner. G. D. H. Cole
End of an Author. J. J. Farjeon
End of an Iron Man. J. N. Chance
End of Andrew Harrison. F. W. Crofts
End of Chapter. N. Blake
End of Count Rollo. E. Phillpotts
End of Count Rollo and other stories. E. Phillpotts
End of Her Honeymoon. M. B. Lowndes
End of Lieutenant Boruvka. J. Skvorccky
End of Mr. Garment. V. Starrett
End of Reckoning. Clayton Moore
End of Solomon Grundy. J. Symons
End of Someone Else's Rainbow. R. Rossner
End of Steel. C. R. Cooper
End of Term. A. Dunnett
End of the Affair. G. Greene
End of the Chase. C. Waye
End of the Family. A. Seymour
End of the Game. J. Cortazar
End of the Game. F. Duerrenmatt
End of the Game. W. B. Murphy
End of the Kill. V. J. Hanson
End of the Line. S. Baron
End of the Line. George Douglas
End of the Line. Graham Fisher
End of the Line. B. Hitchens
End of the Line. S. OCork
End of the Long Hot Summer. L. Meynell
End of the Mildew Gang. S. Fowler
End of the Night. J. D. MacDonald
End of the River. B. L. Van Vors
End of the Road. A. Armstrong
End of the Road. Ray Owen
End of the Rug. R. Llewellyn
End of the Running. A. Evans
End of the Street. M. Procter

End of the Tiger and other stories. J. D. MacDonald
End of the Track. A. Garve
End of the Trail. L. Allan
End of the Web. G. Sims
End of Tragedy. R. Ingalls
End of Violence. B. Benson
End on the Rocks. I. Stuart
End Play. R. Braddon
End to Mirth. B. A. Williams
End to Violence. Ed Lacy
Endangered. Barnaby Conrad
Endgame. H. Ardman
Endgame. James Mann
Endgame Enigma. J. P. Hogan
Endless Chain. N. Bell
Endless Colonnade. R. Harling
Endless Game. B. Forbes
Endless Night. A. Christie
Endless Tunnel. H. K. Hilton
Endplay. R. G. Toepfer
Ends of Justice. F. M. White
Ends of the Earth. M. Gaunt
Ends of the Earth. D. Haring
Endure No Longer. M. Albrand
Enduring Flame. N. Tranter
Enduring Old Charms. D. M. Disney
Enemies. Richard Harris
Enemies of England. C. R. Gull
Enemies of the Bride. O. Mills
Enemies Within. M. Z. Lewin
Enemy. D. Bagley
Enemy Agent. S. MacKinlay
Enemy and Brother. D. S. Davis
Enemy in My Arms. Ashland Price
Enemy in the House. M. G. Eberhart
Enemy of Love. V. Coffman
Enemy of Man. H. Janson
Enemy of Women. B. Perowne
Enemy Outpost. J. S. Childers
Enemy Territory. D. Terman
Enemy to Society. G. Bronson-Howard
Enemy Unseen. F. W. Crofts
Enemy Unseen. V. E. Mitchell
Enemy Within. J. Creasey
Enemy Within. N. Herbert
Enemy Within. D. Streib
Enemy Within. Roy Vickers
Enemy Within the Gates. S. Horler
Enforcer. W. Morgan
Enforcer. B. Appel
Enforcer. J. Cassells
Enforcer. O. Demaris
Enforcer. W. Morgan
Enforcer. A. Sugar
Engaged in Murder. N. Forde
Engaged to Murder. M. V. Heberden
Engagement with Death. G. Ashe
Engaging Picaroon. J. Cassells
England Commune. D. Pryce-Jones
England Made Me. G. Greene
England's Peril. W. LeQueux
England's Toughest Villain. Joe Cannon
English Assassin. M. Moorcock
English Captain and other stories. L. A. G. Strong
English Lady. W. Harrington
English Murder. C. Hare
English Nun. C. Selden
English Paragon. Marjorie Bowen
English Rose. Elizabeth Ford
English School of Murder. R. D. Edwards
English Wife. C. Blackstock
Englishman of the Rue Cain. H. F. Wood
Englishman's Daughter. P. Evans
Englishman's Home. G. Du Maurier
Englishwoman. A. Askew
Engraved in Evil. P. Minton
Enigma. M. Barak
Enigma. E. Gladstone
Enigma Files. C. Sparkes
Enigma of Conrad Stone. C. Houghton
Enigma Project. J. Rosenberger
Enigma Sacrifice. M. Barak
Enigma Variations. B. Murphy
Enigma Variations. J. Thurley

Enjoy Such Liberty. M. Latham
Enoch Strone. E. P. Oppenheim
Enormous Dwarf. R. Francis
Enormous Hour Glass. R. Goulart
Enormous Shadow. R. Harling
Enough. D. E. Westlake
Enough Blue Sky. Elizabeth North
Enough Rope. D. Linton
Enough to Kill a Horse. E. Ferrars
Enquiries Are Continuing. J. Ashford
Enquiries Are Proceeding. P. Daniels
Enquiries of Dr. Eszterhazy. A. Davidson
Enquiry. D. Francis
Enquiry Into the Existence of Vampires. M. Lovell
Enrollment Cancelled. D. B. Olsen
Ensign Knightley and other stories. A. E. W. Mason
Enslaved Ones. D. Haring
Entangled. P. Jason
Enter a Gentlewoman. Sara Woods
Enter a Murderer. N. Marsh
Enter a Spy. F. J. Whaley
Enter Bridget. T. Cobb
Enter Certain Murderers. Sara Woods
Enter Craig Kennedy. A. B. Reeve
Enter Dr. Nikola. G. Boothby
Enter Murderers. H. Slesar
Enter Pharoah Nussbaum. T. J. Kelly
Enter Second Murderer. Alanna Knight
Enter Sir John. C. Dane
Enter Sleeping. D. Karp
Enter Superintendent Flagg. J. Cassells
Enter the Ace. S. Horler
Enter the Corpse. Sara Woods
Enter the Dormouse. Frank King
Enter the Dragon. M. Roote
Enter the G-Men. W. Engle
Enter the Lion. M. P. Hodel
Enter the Picaroon. J. Cassells
Enter the Saint. L. Charteris
Enter Three Witches. P. McGuire
Enter Two Murderers. Hurst Marshall
Enter Without Desire. E. Lacy
Enterprising Burglar. H. Balfour
Enterprising Picaroon. J. Cassells
Entertaining Mrs. Sloane. J. Orton
Entertaining Murder. F. Grierson
Enthusiast. Peter Hill
Enticement. B. Johns
Enticement to Danger. Ralph Vickers
Entirely My Own Invention. C. Martin
Entombed Convict. E. A. Treeton
Entranced with a Dream. R. Rowlatt
Entrapment. J. Ahern
Entrapped. F. G. Bissager
Entrapped. A. M. Diehl
Entry from San Sebastian. B. Adkins
Entry of Death. E. McGirr
Entwining. R. Condon
Envious Casca. G. Heyer
Envoy Extraordinary. E. P. Oppenheim
Envoy of the Emperor. F. Gerard
Envoy on Excursion. C. Brahms
Envy of the Stranger. C. Graham
Epidemic 9. M. Gunther
Epilogue. B. Graeme
Epilogue for Selena. J. Shelynn
Episode. R. Pollack
Episode. William Taylor
Episode at Toledo. A. Bridge
Episode in Rome. T. Lester
Episode of the Stolen Voice. R. C. Armour
Episode of the Wandering Knife. M. R. Rinehart
Episode on an Autumn Evening. F. Duerrenmatt
Episodes. E. J. Gilbert
Episodes. G. S. Street
Episodes in the Lives of a Shropshire Lass and Lad. Lady C. M. Gaskell
Episodes of Marge. H. R. Cromarsh
Epitaph for a Blonde. I. Mercer
Epitaph for a Dead Actor. Dulcie Gray
Epitaph for a Dead Beat. D. Markson
Epitaph for a Lady. M. Cronin
Epitaph for a Lobbyist. R. B. Dominic
Epitaph for a Loser. J. T. Doyle

Epitaph for a Nurse. A. Hocking
Epitaph for a Spy. E. Ambler
Epitaph for a Teddy Bear. L. Barth
Epitaph for a Tramp. D. Markson
Epitaph for Emily. D. W. Christner
Epitaph for Joanna. H. Howard
Epitaph for Lemmings. S. Harvester
Epitaph for Love. D. Clewes
Epitaph for Lydia. V. Rath
Epitaph for Meredith. N. Cromarty
Epitaph for Mister Wynn. K. Wheeler
Epitaph for Poor Richard. A. S. Well
Epitaph to a Bad Cop. J. Fredman
Epitaph to Treason. W. A. Ballinger
Epworth Case. I. Patterson
Epsom Mystery. H. Hill
Equal Antagonism. M. Pereira
Equal Danger. L. Sciascia
Equal Opportunity. S. Dunlap
Equal Partners. H. Fielding
Equality Island. A. Soutar
Equalizer (Book 1). D. G. Deutsch
Equalizer (Book 2). D. G. Deutsch
Equalizer (Book 3). D. E. Deutsch
Equinox. Kurt Maxwell
Erase My Name. J. Donahue
Erasers. A. Robbe-Grillet
Erasmus Magister. C. Sheffield
Erection Set. M. Spillane
Eric Allen's Broadcast Stories. Eric Allen
Eric Hearle, Detective. A. Joscelyn
Eric Peters, Pullman Porter. O. R. Cohen
Eric Sykes of Sebastopol Terrace. E. Sykes
Eric the Archer. M. H. Hervey
Erika. J. McGovern
Erin. J. Jenkins
Erminie. M. A. Fleming
Ernest Grey. M. Maxwell
Ernest Maltravers. E. Bulwer-Lytton
Ernestine de Lacy. T. P. Prest
Eroica. M. Rostov
Eros Affair. P. McCutchan
Eros at Zenith. M. Resnik
Eros Is No Hangman. A. Wood
Erotica Caper. Jay Martin
Errant Knights. M. Hebden
Errant Sleuth. C. Joyce
Errant Target. C. Joyce
Errant Witness. C. Joyce
Erring Under-Secretary. F. Beeding
Erring Way. C. N. Whaley
Error in Judgment. D. C. Brod
Error in Judgment. A. Corliss
Error of Her Ways. F. Barrett
Error of Judgment. G. H. Coxe
Error of Judgment. H. Denker
Error of Judgment. Roy Lewis
Error of Judgment. Sara Woods
Error of the Moon. Sara Woods
Escalation. H. Janson
Escalator. A. Gardner
Escapade. A. Mills
Escapades of Mr. Alfred Dimmock. F. Russell
Escape. J. Ahern
Escape. M. Aldanov
Escape. Royal Brown
Escape. H. Desmond
Escape. C. Franklin
Escape. J. Galsworthy
Escape. H. Janson
Escape. M. Porlock
Escape. Jeremy Scott
Escape. E. Vance
Escape. K. Walker
Escape a Killer. J. Philips
Escape Agents. C. J. C. Hyne
Escape and Be Secret. C. H. Gibbs-Smith
Escape and Return. M. McLaren
Escape at Dawn. G. P. Willis
Escape at Sunrise. M. Cronin
Escape from Dartmoor. M. Beckett
Escape from Devil's Island. P. McCurtin
Escape from Five Shadows. E. Leonard
Escape from Gulag Taria. J. Rosenberger
Escape from Julia. C. Massie

Escape from Liberty. L. P. Greene
Escape from Murder. M. Stand
Escape from New York. M. McQuay
Escape from Nicaragua. J. Buchanan
Escape from Paris. C. G. Hart
Escape from Poland. J. Tabler
Escape from Prague. B. Cleeve
Escape from Spain. A. D. Divine
Escape from Zahrein. Michael Barrett
Escape If You Can. Robin Temple
Escape in Vain. G. Simenon
Escape Into Danger. M. S. Gaffney
Escape Into Danger. N. Rutledge
Escape Into Murder. M. Jackson
Escape of Andrew Cole. U. L. Silberrad
Escape of General Gerard. D. Betteridge
Escape of Mr. Trimm. I. S. Cobb
Escape of the Notorious Sir William Heans, and the Mystery of Mr. Daunt. W. Hay
Escape Out of Darkness. Anne Stuart
Escape Plus. B. Bova
Escape Route. S. Ready
Escape Route W6. J. H. Date
Escape the Night. M. G. Eberhart
Escape the Night. R. N. Patterson
Escape the Past. P. Parrish
Escape to Athena. P. Blake
Escape to Crime. James Stewart
Escape to Danger. P. Conway
Escape to Death. C. Franklin
Escape to Death. E. M. Williams
Escape to Eternity. W. B. M. Ferguson
Escape to Fear. S. Bate
Escape to Fear. R. Foley
Escape to Fear. T. D. Smith
Escape to Love. E. S. Aarons
Escape to Murder. Sutherland Scott
Escape to Nowhere. M. Boone
Escape to Nowhere. P. Covert
Escape to Nowhere. D. Karp
Escape to Quebec. M. Kennedy
Escape While I Can. M. Marlette
Escape with Gun Cotton. Rupert Grayson
Escaped from Sing Sing. Hawkshaw
Escapemanship. J. Ditton
Escapement. C. E. Maine
Escaping Club. A. J. Evans
Escort Job. H. Kane
Escort to Adventure. A. MacVicar
Escort to Danger. S. Truss
Espionage. W. S. Doxey
Espionage. H. Hayford
Espionage! G. Marlowe
Espionage. B. Sarto
Espionage. P. Sebastian
Espionage Agent. D. Clift
Espionage for a Lady. T. Ferris
Espionage Infection. D. Haysom
Espionage Killings. J. G. Brandon
ESPolksa Ploy. G. V. D'Amore
Esprit de Corpse. F. Kane
Ess Club. Dinsdale Walker
Essence of Murder. H. Klinger
Essential Man. Al Morgan
Essex Murders. V. Loder
Essex Road Crime. J. Drummond
Establishment. Robin Moore
Establishment of Innocence. H. Aronson
Estate of Grace. J. Powers
Estate of the Beckoning Lady. M. Allingham
Esther Lawes. E. Jepson
Esther, Ruth and Jennifer. Jack Davies
Estuary Pilgrim. D. Skeggs
Etched in Murder. K. Jones
Etched in Violence. M. Cumberland
Eternal Conflict. J. Templeton
Eternal Instinct. A. Applin
Eternal Moment. G. B. H. Logan
Eternal Reich. J. M. Knopp
Eternal Triangle. D. Pendleton
Eternity, Here I Come! David Hume
Eternity Ring. P. Wentworth
Ethel and the Naked Spy. M. Lovell
Ethel and the Terrorist. C. Jasmin

Title Index

Ethel Norman's Secret. P. Trent
Ethel Opens the Door. D. Fox
Ethelinde. T. P. Prest
Ethelwina. H. J. D. Curties
Ethical Man. Alane Mark
Ethical Solution. J. V. Gordon
Ethiopian's Secret. W. W. Sayer
Etonian. A. Askew
Etruscan Bull. F. Gruber
Etruscan Net. M. Gilbert
Etruscan Smile. V. Johnston
Eugene Aram. E. Bulwer-Lytton
Eugene Vidocq: Soldier, Thief, Spy, Detective. D. Donovan
Eugenia. Anonymous
Engenia. A. Hurlba
Eulalie. M. A. Earl
Eulalie. W. S. Hayward
Eunuch of Stamboul. D. Wheatley
Eurasian Virgins. J. Seward
Euridice. Taffrail
Euro-Killers. J. Rathbone
Europe That Was. G. Household
Europian Job. W. D. Russell
Euryale in London. C. Dane
Eustace Diamonds. A. Trollope
Euston Road Mystery. A. Parsons
Euthanasia. Anonymous
Eva. I. Melchior
Evan Less Legal! I. S. Black
Eve. J. H. Chase
Eve. P. Trent
Eve—and the Law. A. Askew
Eve As in Evil. C. Dekker
Eve Finds the Killer. R. Garnett
Eve—It's Extortion. Carter Brown
Eve of April Twenty. P. Upton
Eve of His Dying. Carter Brown
Eve of Judgment. Roger Fuller
Eve of the Wedding. Lionel Black
Evelina, the Pauper's Child. T. P. Prest
Evelyn. A. Askew
Evelyn Prentice. W. E. Woodward
Evelyn, the Ambitious. K. Kimbrough
Even Bishops Die. C. Saxby
Even Cop's Daughters. Martha Webb
Even Doctors Die. L. Anson
Even from the Law. M. Latham
Even If You Run. D. Cory
Even in Death. S. Devine
Even in the Best Families. R. Stout
Even Jericho. Warner Hall
Even My Foot's Asleep. L. Payne
Even the Butler Was Poor. R. Goulart
Even the Rainbow's Bent. C. Noone
Even the Rich Girl. H. L. Gates
Even the Wicked. R. Marsten
Evening at the Larches. H. Hearson
Evening in Paris. M. Richmond
Evening News. A. Hailey
Evening Walk. D. Collenette
Evens, Buster. D. Haring
Event Called Murder. Martin Thomas
Eventide. B. Ferm
Events at Midridge. C. R. Sumner
Events of That Week. N. Bentley
Ever-Loving Blues. Carter Brown
Ever Mohun. F. T. Jane
Ever Singing Die Oh! Die. O. Blakeston
Ever This Night. V. De Coursey
Evered. B. A. Williams
Everglades Assault. R. Striker
Evergreen Death. James Fraser
Everlasting. L. Bishop
Evermore. B. Steward
Every Bet's a Sure Thing. T. B. Dewey
Every Brillian Eye. L. D. Estleman
Every Creature of God Is Good. A. Gould
Every Inch a Lady. Joan Fleming
Every Inch a Soldier. J. S. Winter
Every Little Crook and Nanny. E. Hunter
Every Man a King. A. Worboys
Every Man a Murderer. H. Von Doderer
Every Man an Enemy. W. H. Baker

Every Man for Himself. H. Moorhouse
Every Man Has His Price. M. Leighton
Every Man Has His Price. A. Whitney
Every Man His Price. M. Rittenberg
Every Man's Brother. N. Lewis
Every Man's Hand. Charles Ross
Every Mother's Son. A. D. LeClaire
Every Night About Half Past Eight, and other stories. L. J. Beeston
Every Second Thursday. E. Page
Every Third Thought. D. Malm
Everybody Adored Cara. A. Head
Everybody Always Tells. E. R. Punshon
Everybody Comes to Cosmo's. R. Goulart
Everybody Does It. J. M. Cain
Everybody Had a Gun. R. S. Fletcher
Everybody Loves Opal. J. Patrick
Everybody Makes Mistakes. M. S. Marble
Everybody Suspect. D. Sharp
Everybody's Favorite Duck. Gahan Wilson
Everybody's Girl. D. Haring
Everybody's Metamorphosis. C. Willeford
Everybody's Ready to Die. J. Frederics
Everyone Suspect. N. Tyre
Everything But the Squeal. T. Hallinan
Everything Happens to Joe. D. O'Flanagan
Everything Has Its Price. H. H. Kirst
Everything He Touched. M. Cumberland
Everything Is Thunder. J. L. Hardy
Everything That Moves. B. Schulberg
Eve's Island. E. Wallace
Evidence. Anthony Lang
Evidence. N. Ravin
Evidence. J. Weisman
Evidence Before Gabriel. Conrad Forst
Evidence by Telephone. Nicholas Carter
Evidence Circumstantial. A. Sohland
Evidence I Shall Give. J. Wainwright
Evidence in Blue. E. C. Vivian
Evidence Most Blind. D. Keene
Evidence of the Accused. R. Jeffries
Evidence of Things Seen. E. Daly
Evidence to Destroy. Margaret Yorke
Evidence Unseen. L. R. Davis
Evidence You Will Hear. H. Jobson
Evidently Murdered. Jay Hall
Evie Was No Lady. R. Drayton
Evil. Richard O'Brien
Evil Always Ends. J. P. Brennan
Evil Among Us. J. Crecy
Evil Angel. J. Middlemass
Evil at Bayou Laforche. E. Hayworth
Evil at Hillcrest. J. Ellis
Evil at Nunnery Manor. R. Abbey
Evil at Queen's Priory. V. Coffman
Evil at Roger's Cross. C. Cookson
Evil at the Root. B. Crider
Evil at Whispering Hills. K. Cameron
Evil Became Them. P. Root
Evil Cargo. K. Stanton
Evil Chateau. S. Horler
Evil Children. W. D. Roberts
Evil Come, Evil Go. W. Masterson
Evil Cross. S. Esmond
Evil Damp. K. R. Butler
Evil Days. B. Fischer
Evil Ever After. B. Myers
Evil, Evil. L. DuBreuil
Evil Eye. P. Boileau
Evil Eye. Martin Thomas
Evil Eyes. Roland Daniel
Evil Formula. Nicholas Carter
Evil Friendship. V. Packer
Evil Genius. G. Bagby
Evil Genius. W. Collins
Evil Genius. E. Turland
Evil Gnome. K. Robeson
Evil Guest. J. S. Le Fanu
Evil Harvest. Margery Lawrence
Evil Hour. J. McGown
Evil Hour. L. Meynell
Evil in a Mask. D. Wheatley
Evil in High Places. P. Lunn
Evil in the Cup. E. P. Thorne

Evil in the Family. G. Corren
Evil in the House. E. Bond
Evil in the House. Elbur Ford
Evil in Waiting. Renate Chapman
Evil Innocence. H. Munro
Evil Intent. J. Wainwright
Evil Is a Quiet Word. Theodus Carroll
Evil Is As Evil Does. R. Gatenby
Evil Is the Night. J. Chadwick
Evil Is the Night. J. Creighton
Evil Island. J. Blair
Evil Lives Here. H. S. Nuelle
Evil Mark. G. Miles
Evil Men Do. C. Fitzsimmons
Evil Men Do. B. Kiely
Evil Men Do. D. Nile
Evil Messenger. S. Horler
Evil Money. T. Harknett
Evil of Dark Harbor. Clarissa Ross
Evil of the Day. T. Sterling
Evil of Time. E. Berckman
Evil Ones. G. J. Barrett
Evil Ones. J. Mitchell
Evil Phoenix. B. Newman
Evil Reputation. Dora Russell
Evil Root. L. Thayer
Evil Roots. W. Untermeyer
Evil Shadows. Roland Daniel
Evil Shepherd. E. P. Oppenheim
Evil Side of Eden. Sara North
Evil Sleep. E. Hunter
Evil Spell. W. Tyrer
Evil Star. J. Spain
Evil That Men Do. S. A. Curtis
Evil That Men Do. E. Fawcett
Evil That Men Do. R. L. Hill
Evil That Men Do. A. Hocking
Evil That Men Do. H. Pentecost
Evil That Men Do. M. P. Shiel
Evil That Men Do. A. Spiller
Evil That Men Do. G. Steuart
Evil That Waited. M. Farnsworth
Evil That Walks Invisible. Alicen White
Evil Under the Sun. A. Christie
Evil Vanguard. M. Hay
Evil Wish. J. Potts
Evvie. V. Caspary
Ewe Lamb. M. Erskine
Ex-Con. S. Friedman
Ex-Detective. E. P. Oppenheim
Ex-Duke. E. P. Oppenheim
Ex-Gangster. C. F. Caunter
Ex Officio. T. J. Culver
Ex-Pugilist Detective. Old Sleuth
Ex-Serviceman's Secret. R. Hardinge
Ex-Soldier Employment Swindle. A. Murray
Excalibur Disaster. J. Bickham
Excavator's Secret. H. H. C. Gibbons
Excellency. D. Beaty
Excellent Intentions. R. Hull
Excellent Knave. J. F. Molloy
Excellent Mystery. C. D. Jones
Excellent Mystery. Ellis Peters
Excellent Night for Murder. V. Rath
Excelsior. H. B. M. Watson
Except for One Thing. H. Blayn
Exception. S. Trott
Excess Baggage. H. M. Raleigh
Exchange. R. L. Brent
Exchange. T. Wilden
Exchange of Clowns. T. Wilden
Exchange of Doves. K. Royce
Exchange of Eagles. O. Sela
Exchanged Identity. F. Du Boisgobey
Exclusive. H. Janson
Exclusive Clue. J. Aeby
Excuse My Gun. R. Angel
Execution. M. Blais
Execution. O. Crawford
Execution. R. Mayer
Execution by Choice. D. Warbash
Execution Exchange. Nick Carter
Execution Exchange. J. Gluckman

Execution Night. R. Dade
Execution of Diamond Deutsch. C. F. Gregg
Execution of Justice. F. Duerrenmatt
Execution of Newcome Bowles. A. Mickle
Executioner. P. Boulle
Executioner. V. Torrio
Executioners. Nick Carter
Executioners. J. Creasey
Executioners. P. McCutchan
Executioners. J. D. MacDonald
Executioners. B. Moore
Executioner's Axe. P. Lancaster
Executioner's Rest. A. M. Stein
Executioner's Song. N. Mailer
Executive Privilege. G. Perrett
Executive Wife. R. Colby
Executor. Gerald Hammond
Exercise for Madmen. B. Paul
Exercise Hoodwink. M. Procter
Exercise in Terror. S. M. Kaminsky
Exes. D. Greenburg
Exeunt Murderers. A. Boucher
Exhibit. L. Hollander
Exhibit No. Thirteen. R. Jeffries
Exhumed! A. Blair
Exile. P. Essex
Exile. Madison Jones
Exile. W. Kotzwinkle
Exile from London. R. H. Savage
Exile Kiss. G. A. Effinger
Exiled. S. Greene
Exiled to Siberia. W. M. Graydon
Exiles. R. H. Carson
Exile's Bride. E. Southworth
Exit a Dictator. E. P. Oppenheim
Exit a Spy. H. T. Rothwell
Exit a Star. K. M. Knight
Exit Actors, Dying. M. Arnold
Exit an Admiral. A. W. Allen
Exit and Curtain. Kevin O'Hara
Exit Arnholt. G. Latta
Exit Charlie. A. Atkinson
Exit Dying. H. Olesker
Exit for a Dame. R. Ellington
Exit from Prague. B. Cleeve
Exit Funtopia. M. Farren
Exit Harlequin. C. F. Gregg
Exit Harlequin. Jessica Ryan
Exit in Green. Martin Brett
Exit John Horton. J. J. Farjeon
Exit Laughing. S. Palmer
Exit Lines. Reginald Hill
Exit Mr. Brent. G. Davison
Exit Mr. Marlowe. V. Bridges
Exit Mr. Shane. J. Cassells
Exit Murderer. Sara Woods
Exit Only. S. Maddock
Exit Pretty Poll. E. Burgess
Exit, Running. B. Spicer
Exit Screaming. H. Dalmas
Exit Screaming. C. Hale
Exit Second Murderer. D. Sharp
Exit Sherlock Holmes. R. L. Hall
Exit Silas Danvers. H. Leyford
Exit Simeon Hex. J. M. Walsh
Exit Sir John. B. Flynn
Exit Sir Toby Belch. Hilary Landon
Exit the Body. F. Carmichael
Exit the Disguiser. S. Horler
Exit the Grand Duchess. C. M. O'Hara
Exit—the Killer. J. Dyan
Exit the Skeleton. H. Adams
Exit This Way. M. V. Heberden
Exit to Music. N. Shepherd
Exit to Music and other stories. N. Morland
Exit to Violence. H. Jobson
Exit Who? F. Carmichael
Exit with Emeralds. I. Andrews
Exit with Intent. P. Loraine
Exit Without Permit. C. Franklin
Exit Wounds. Michael Baldwin
Exit Wounds. J. Westermann
Exits and Farewells. Marjorie Bowen
Exocet. J. Higgins

Exodus from Hell. J. Buchanan
Exodus of the Damned. S. Slappey
Exodus: 20. O. B. Davis
Exorcism. C. Blackstock
Exorcism of Angela Gray. N. T. Vane
Exorcism of Jenny Slade. D. Daniels
Exorcist. W. P. Blatty
Exotic. Carter Brown
Exotic Ecstasy. D. Haring
Exotic Island. Stuart Hall
Exotic Seductress. H. Janson
Expanded Universe. R. Heinlein
Expatriots. W. Haggard
Expect No Mercy. E. P. Thorne
Expectant Nymph. H. Janson
Expected Death. M. Fitt
Expecting Someone Taller. Tom Holt
Expendable. W. D. Roberts
Expendable Man. D. B. Hughes
Expendable Spy. J. D. Hunter
Expensive Place to Die. L. Deighton
Experience with Evil. J. R. MacDonald
Experiences of a Barrister. W. Warner
Experiences of a Bond Street Jeweller. H. A. Vachell
Experiences of a French Detective Officer. Waters
Experiences of a Lady Detective. Anonymous
Experiences of a Real Detective. Inspector F
Experiences of an American Detective. Anonymous
Experiences of Loveday Brooke, Lady Detective. C. L. Pirkis
Experiences of Mack. Himself
Experiment. W. Butler
Experiment. M. Carson
Experiment at Proto. P. Oakes
Experiment in Crime. J. Rhode
Experiment in Crime. P. Wyllie
Experiment in Springtime. M. Millar
Experiment in Terror. The Gordons
Experiment of Doctor Nevill. E. Hulme-Beaman
Experiment Perilous. M. Carpenter
Experiment with Death. E. Ferrars
Experiment with Eros. R. S. Thorn
Experiments in Crime. G. Frankau
Expert. B. Picton
Expert Evidence. C. F. Gregg
Expert Evidence. R. Pertwee
Expert in Craft. Dick Stewart
Expert in Murder. C. L. Leonard
Expert Witness. P. Conway
Expiation. E. P. Oppenheim
Expiation of Lady Anne. L. S. Oliver
Expiation of Wynne Palliser. B. Mitford
Expiration Date. A. Thurlo
Exploding Lake. K. Robeson
Exploited Woman. J. Keating
Exploiters. Samuel Edwards
Exploits of a Dead Man. P. Urquhart
Exploits of a Physician Detective. George Butler
Exploits of a Private Detective. S. Campbell
Exploits of a Race-Course Detective. N. Gould
Exploits of Arsene Lupin. M. Leblanc
Exploits of Asaf Khan. Afghan
Exploits of Billy the Page. Willoughby Lane
Exploits of Black Tumb. W. Bouchier
Exploits of Brigadier Gerard. A. C. Doyle
Exploits of Capt. McKeene. R. Walker
Exploits of Captain O'Hagan. S. Rohmer
Exploits of Danby Croker. R. A. Freeman
Exploits of Death. Dell Shannon
Exploits of Dick Tracy, Detective. C. Gould
Exploits of Dr. Sam: Johnson. L. De La Torre
Exploits of Elaine. A. B. Reeve
Exploits of Fidelity Dove. D. Durham
Exploits of Jo Salis, a British Spy. W. O. Greener
Exploits of Jonathan Jow. W. J. Makin
Exploits of Juve. P. Souvestre
Exploits of Kesho Naik, Dacoit. E. C. Cox
Exploits of Piccolo. A. A. Thomson
Exploits of Pudgy Pete & Co. E. P. Oppenheim
Exploits of Sherlock Holmes. Adrian C. Doyle
Exploits of the Chevalier Dupin. M. Harrison
Explosion. D. C. Disney
Explosion! Colin Robertson
Explosion. E. Wuorio

Explosion. H. H. Ziemann
Explosive Situation. G. Hackforth-Jones
Expo 80. John Burke
Expo '98: Sherlock Holmes in Omaha. B. Forsythe
Expo '77. C. Ike
Exporters. G. Norham
Exposure. J. D. Reed
Exposure of the Land Swindlers. E. C. Hall
Express Delivery. J. M. Walsh
Express Messenger and other tales of the rail. C. Warman
Express Train Murder. John Norman
Expressman and the Detective. A. Pinkerton
Expresso Jungle. W. H. Baker
Expressway. H. North
Expropriators. J. Blythe
Expurgator. A. York
Exquisite Corpse. Alfred Chester
Exquisite Lady. G. Fairlie
Extenuating Circumstances. E. Nisot
Extenuating Circumstances. J. Valin
Exterior to the Evidence. J. S. Fletcher
Exterminating Angels. P. Dunant
Extermination Camp. G. Sheen
Exterminator. P. McCurtin
Exterminators. V. Thorpe
Extinction Bomber. S. B. Hough
Extinction Cruise. J.-A. Price
Extortion. H. Howard
Extortion Incorporated. J. Cooper
Extortioners. J. Creasey
Extortioners. O. Demaris
Extortionist. C. Nwokolo
Extortionists. B. Bavin
Extra Body. R. Reinsmith
Extra Cover. A. C. Smith
Extra Credits. M. Lupica
Extra Kill. D. Shannon
Extra Passenger. D. Timins
Extraordinary Adventures of Arsene Lupin, Gentleman Burglar. M. Leblanc
Extraordinary Case of Mr. Bell. W. Jackson
Extraordinary Experience. L. Bryce
Extraordinary Seaman. P. Rock
Extracurricular Activities. E. Lottman
Extras. W. Karlin
Extreme Close-Up. L. Crews
Extreme License. Jerome Barry
Extreme Penalty. A. M. Meadows
Extreme Prejudice. R. Cobbins
Extreme Remedies. M. Borgenicht
Extremes Meet. C. MacKenzie
Extremists. P. Leslie
Extremities. W. Mastrosimone
Extricating Obadiah. J. C. Lincoln
Extro. A. Bester
Eye. B. Pronzini
Eye at the Keyhole. S. Maddock
Eye for a Tooth. D. Yates
Eye for an Eye. O. W. Bayer
Eye for an Eye. L. Brackett
Eye for an Eye. F. Hickok
Eye for an Eye. M. Leighton
Eye for an Eye. W. LeQueux
Eye for an Eye. M. O. Rolfe
Eye for an Eye. V. J. Santiago
Eye for an Eye. M. Schorr
Eye for an Eye. G. Seton
Eye for an Eye. G. Seymour
Eye for an Eye. J. Telushkin
Eye for an Eye. J. B. West
Eye for Eye. A. Kilgore
Eye Hath Not Seen... D. G. Rowlands
Eye in Attendance. V. Williams
Eye in Darkness. J. N. Chance
Eye in the Museum. J. J. Connington
Eye in the Pyramid. R. Shea
Eye in the Ring. R. J. Randisi
Eye in the Sky. P. K. Dick
Eye of a God. W. A. Fraser
Eye of a Serpent. G. Peters
Eye of Anna. A. Wingate
Eye of Fate. A. M. Meadows
Eye of Gold. I. Stark

Eye of Isis. M. Peterson
Eye of Itza. A. Aikman
Eye of Jinas and other stories. T. A. Fraser
Eye of Kali. E. R. Brayshaw
Eye of Lucifer. F. F. Van De Water
Eye of Nemesis. P. C. De Crespigny
Eye of One. G. Merrick
Eye of Osiris. R. A. Freeman
Eye of Shiva. L. Grimes
Eye of the Beholder. M. Behm
Eye of the Beholder. M. Marrin
Eye of the Beholder. A. R. Rooth
Eye of the Beholder. J. Wainwright
Eye of the Cat. D. Spicer
Eye of the Devil. P. Loraine
Eye of the Dragon. G. H. Teed
Eye of the Eagle. G. V. Basile
Eye of the Eagle. D. O'Connor
Eye of the Fire. J. Hild
Eye of the Gods. J. Neil
Eye of the Gods. Richard Owen
Eye of the Hurricane. H. Howard
Eye of the Mind. L. Biederstadt
Eye of the Needle. K. Follett
Eye of the Needle. Ronald Johnston
Eye of the Needle. T. Walsh
Eye of the Peacock. A. M. Dodge
Eye of the Peacock. O. Goff
Eye of the Sniper. Hal Kantor
Eye of the Storm. W. H. Baker
Eye of the Storm. M. Muller
Eye of the Sun. E. S. Ellis
Eye of the Tiger. Wilbur Smith
Eye of the Tornado. C. Pincher
Eye of Zeitoon. T. Mundy
Eye Spy. M. Finch
Eye Stones. H. Esmond
Eye to Eye. D. Pendleton
Eye with Mascara. M. Finch
Eye-Witness. G. H. Coxe
Eye-Witness. L. De Francquen
Eye-Witness! J. Doe
Eye Witness. E. Levison
Eye Witness. J. S. Strange
Eyecatcher. M. Kreciala
Eyes and Dolls. B. Vane
Eyes Around Me. G. Black
Eyes at the Window. O. S. Cornelius
Eyes at the Window. S. Truss
Eyes in the Corner. B. Grimshaw
Eyes in the Fire. D. Grabien
Eyes in the Night. Gavin Holt
Eyes in the Night. C. M. Howarth
Eyes in the Night. B. Kendrick
Eyes in the Wall. C. Wells
Eyes of a Stranger. J. Hyman
Eyes of Alicia. C. E. Pearce
Eyes of Buddha. J. Ball
Eyes of Darkness. L. Nichols
Eyes of Death. John Bentley
Eyes of Desire. C. H. Bullivant
Eyes of Green. N. Bawden
Eyes of Laura Mars. H. B. Gilmour
Eyes of Light. A. Moore
Eyes of Max Carrados. E. Bramah
Eyes of Men. D. Newton
Eyes of Omar. L. C. Douthwaite
Eyes of Pharaoh. G. Thorne
Eyes of St. Emlyn. A. Feist
Eyes of the Blind. G. W. Jones
Eyes of the Blind. A. S. Roche
Eyes of the Shadow. M. Grant
Eyes of the Tiger. Nick Carter
Eyes of Tlalac. A. E. Peterson
Eyes on Utopia Murders. B. D'Amato
Eyes That Watch You. W. Irish
Eyes Through the Mask. R. Trevor
Eyes Through the Tree. M. C. Keator
Eyes Upon a Wet Grave. V. Wallace
Eyewitness. M. Hebden
Eyewitness. J. Minahan
Eyewitness. J. P. Seabrooke
Eyre's Acquittal. H. B. Mathers
Eyrie of an Eagle. A. Delmonico

Eyrie of the Fox. M. Eyre
F As in Flight. L. Treat
FBI Girl. M. Marlowe
F.B.I. Showdown. "G-Man"
F.B.I. Special Agent. "G-Man"
FBI Story. The Gordons
FBN. M. Leonard
"F" Cipher. J. G. Bethune
F Corridor. J. G. Edwards
F-Cubed. D. Da Cruz
F.E.U.D. H. Janson
F Is for Fugitive. S. Grafton
F.O.B. Murder. B. Hitchens
FSO-1. H. Greene
Fablesinger. J. W. Colombo
Fabulists. B. Capes
Fabulous. Carter Brown
Fabulous Clipjoint. F. Brown
Fabulous Finn. D. Cushman
Fabulous Valley. D. Wheatley
Fabulous Wink. K. Bennett
Face. J. Vance
Face. Marvin Werlin
Face. D. Whitelaw
Face. D. Zec
Face and the Mask. R. Barr
Face at the Window. P. Parrish
Face at the Window. W. D. Roberts
Face Behind the Mask. J. Minahan
Face Cards. C. Wells
Face for a Clue. G. Simenon
Face in the Film. O. Merland
Face in the Flashlight. F. Warden
Face in the Fog. Marilyn Ross
Face in the Leaves. R. Timperley
Face in the Mirror. D. V. Baker
Face in the Mirror. G. F. Bradby
Face in the Mirror. M. Chittenden
Face in the Mirror. A. Furness
Face in the Mirror. E. Title
Face in the Night. E. Wallace
Face in the Pond. Clarissa Ross
Face in the Shadow. Nicholas Carter
Face in the Shadows. V. Johnston
Face in the Shadows. P. Ordway
Face in the Shadows. Marilyn Ross
Face in the Stone. C. Curzon
Face Me When You Walk Away. B. Freemantle
Face of a Hero. P. Boulle
Face of a Stranger. Anne Perry
Face of Air. G. L. Knapp
Face of an Angel. M. Paradise
Face of Chalk. Melissa Davies
Face of Danger. Graham Fisher
Face of Danger. W. D. Roberts
Face of Danger. Regina Ross
Face of Danger. M. Sharman
Face of Death. M. Gault
Face of Death. L. Grant-Adamson
Face of Evil. J. McPartland
Face of Fear. B. Coffey
Face of Fear. L. Crump
Face of Fortune. J. Workman
Face of Fury. P. A. Foxall
Face of Hate. T. Du Bois
Face of Him. I. A. Greenfield
Face of Innocence. E. Ogilvie
Face of Inspector Britt. E. P. Thorne
Face of Jalanath. Ronald Hardy
Face of Night. B. Brunner
Face of Rosenfel. C. H. Montagne
Face of Stone. S. Horler
Face of Terror. U. Dan
Face of Terror. E. Litvinoff
Face of the Crime. L. O'Donnell
Face of the Enemy. V. Scannell
Face of the Enemy. T. Walsh
Face of the Foe. J. Millson
Face of the Foe. P. Power
Face of the Lion. J. Blackburn
Face of the Man from Saturn. H. S. Keeler
Face of the Tiger. U. Curtiss
Face of Trespass. R. Rendell

Face on the Cutting Room Floor. C. McCabe
Face on the Stair. L. Winstanley
Face Out Front. R. R. Irvine
Face That Must Die. Ramsey Campbell
Face the Music. C. Franklin
Face to Face. J. Lynch
Face to Face. D. J. MacKenzie
Face to Face. E. Queen
Face to Face with Death. A. W. Marchmont
Face to the Sun. G. Household
Face Value. L. P. Greene
Face Value. R. Ormerod
Face Value. R. Powers
Face Value. J. M. Walsh
Faceless Adversary. F. Lockridge
Faceless Corpse Murders. L. L. Rogger
Faceless Enemy. F. S. Wees
Faceless Fugitive. R. Charles
Faceless Man. C. Wick
Faceless Men. O. Beeby
Faceless Mortals. Bob Cook
Faceless Ones. L. Hardy
Faceless Ones. G. Verner
Faceless Satan. G. W. Jones
Faceless Stranger. F. Usher
Facemaker. William Katz
Faces. S. Lord
Faces in the Dark. P. Boileau
Faces in the Rain. Roland Perry
Faces of a Bad Girl. J. N. Chance
Faces of Danger. R. King
Faces of Death. A. M. Stein
Faces of Murder. J. T. MacCargo
Facets. I. R. G. Hart
Facing Death. J. J. Farjeon
Facing East. A. Soutar
Fact X. P. Winn
Factor's Wife. C. Blackstock
Factory. B. Freemantle
Factory. J. Lynn
Factory Girl. C. E. Blaney
Factory Girl. M. E. Braddon
Factory Mystery. Gregory Wilson
Factory on the Cliff. Neil Gordon
Factotum and other stories. W. LeQueux
Facts About Floyd. S. M. Parkman
Facts and Phantasies. H. Compton
Facts in the Case of E. A. Poe. A. Sinclair
Faculty of Murder. J. Wright
Fade Into Murder. S. Holmes
Fade Out. R. Upton
Fade Out the Stars. M. Cumberland
Fade the Heat. J. Brandon
Fade to Black. J. Goldsborough
Fade to Black. P. Rawlings
Fade to Black. R. Renauld
Fadeaway. Richard Rosen
Faded Tattooes. J. S. Brandford
Fadeout. J. Hansen
Fading Blue. R. Busby
Fading Shrine. M. McCrory
Fagan. P. Gravesen
Fago. B. Roueche
Fahnsworth Manor. E. Welles
Fail-Safe. E. Burdick
Failure. G. Vaizey
Failure at the Mission Trust. B. Ducker
Faint Cold Fear. R. Daley
Fainting Lady. M. Frazer
Faintley Speaking. G. Mitchell
Fair. V. Andrews
Fair Affair. P. Champagne
Fair and the Dead. J. S. Strange
Fair at Sokolniki. F. Neznansky
Fair Brigand. G. Horton
Fair Colonist. E. Glanville
Fair Cops. C. N. Gattey
Fair Criminal. Nicholas Carter
Fair Crusader. W. Westall
Fair Devil. E. Greenwood
Fair Exchange. E. Colles
Fair Exchange. Anne-Marie Cox
Fair Exchange. K. Gordon
Fair Exchange. P. Harcourt

Fair Freebooter. B. Marnan
Fair Freelance. G. Campbell
Fair Friday. P. Turnbull
Fair Game. G. Bartram
Fair Game. G. Hammond
Fair Game. P. Harcourt
Fair Game. K. Kramer
Fair Game. D. O. Malek
Fair Game. N. Tranter
Fair Game. Gar Wilson
Fair-Haired lady. M. Leblanc
Fair Imposter. A. St. Aubyn
Fair in the Fearless Old Fashion. C. Farmlet
Fair Insurgent. E. Horton
Fair Intruder. K. Lindsay
Fair-Isle Jumper Mystery. Hallam James
Fair Kilmeny. V. Black
Fair Maids Missing. P. Audemars
Fair Murder. N. Brady
Fair Mystery. Anonymous
Fair Mystery. B. M. Clay
Fair Play. E. Southworth
Fair Prey. Will Duke
Fair Prisoner. M. Gerard
Fair Quakeress. O. Bradbury
Fair Refuge. M. Gerard
Fair Schemer. J. H. Robinson
Fair Sinner. Mrs. C. Kernahan
Fair Trial. J. Laborde
Fair Warning. M. G. Eberhart
Fair Warning. G. E. Simpson
Fair Weather Foul. S. Freeman
Fair Wind to Malabar. J. D. White
Fair Winds of Love. R. Baker
Fair Young Widow. G. R. Preedy
Fairbairn Case. John Bentley
Fairer Than She. T. Charles
Fairfax Millions. A. Winnington
Fairfax Mystery. J. Keating
Fairly Caught. D. Walshe
Fairly Dangerous Thing. R. Hill
Fairly Innocent Little Man. L. Meynell
Fairway Island. H. G. Hutchinson
Fairways and Foul. J. Carrick
Fairy of the Film. H. T. Johnson
Faith. C. Barnard
Faith Has No Country. R. V. Beste
Faith-Healer. A. W. Marchmont
Faith, Hope and Charity. I. S. Cobb
Faith, Hope and Charity. Rona Randall
Faith, Hope and Cyanide. D. Roome
Faith, Hope and Death. D. Craig
Faith That Kills. E. Hulme-Beaman
Faith Unfaithful. F. E. Wynne
Faithful Achates. A. Gould
Faithful Knave. E. Fitzgerald
Faithful Stranger. S. Kaye-Smith
Faithless. Clayton Matthews
Fake. P. Lunn-Rockliffe
Fake. Colin Robertson
Fake. H. Sprott
Faked Passports. D. Wheatley
Fakers. P. Leslie
Faking It. Gerald Green
Fakir's Curse. K. Bruce
Fakir's Secret. A. Cartwright
Fala Factor. S. M. Kaminsky
Falcon. N. Slater
Falcon and the Dove. J. Laborde
Falcon and the Moon. C. Darby
Falcon Cuts In. D. Drake
Falcon for a Witch. C. Darby
Falcon for the Hawks. C. Egleton
Falcon Meets a Lady. D. Drake
Falcon Memorandum. M. Judge
Falcon Mystery. S. Guise
Falcon of the Foreign Office. D. Newton
Falcon Ring. M. F. Callan
Falcon Rising. C. Darby
Falcon Road. C. Massie
Falcon Royal. C. Darby
Falcon Sunset. C. Darby
Falcon to the Lure. C. Darby
Falconhurst Mystery. E. T. Pickering

Falconer's Hall. J. Aeby
Falconlough. M. Heath
Falconridge. E. Marlow
Falcon's Claw. C. Darby
Falcon's Cry. Leona Karr
Falcon's Heir. C. Virmonne
Falcon's Island. Antonia Scott
Falcon's Malteser. A. Horowitz
Falcon's Nest. A. Lloyd
Falcon's Prey. D. Drake
Falcon's Shadow. K. Troy
Falkland's Choice. P. Trent
Falklands Factor. H. G. Ward
Falkland's Gambit. B. Langley
Falkner's of Greenhurst. J. Middlemass
Fall. C. Dekker
Fall Back and Kill. D. Stivers
Fall, Darkness, Fall. J. Corby
Fall from Grace. M. Borgenicht
Fall from Grace. V. Canning
Fall from Grace. L. Collins
Fall Girl. Ken Blake
Fall Girl. R. Deming
Fall Guy. G. Abbott
Fall Guy. Jerome Barry
Fall Guy. Joe Barry
Fall Guy. D. Haring
Fall Guy. N. Harman
Fall Guy. H. Howard
Fall Guy. Johnny Mack
Fall Guy. Ray Owen
Fall Guy. Ritchie Perry
Fall Guy. B. Shannon
Fall Guy. F. Struan
Fall Guy. T. Trent
Fall Guy for a Killer. S. Acre
Fall Guy for Murder. L. Goldman
Fall Into My Grave. F. Usher
Fall of a Dictator. A. Gask
Fall of a Saint. E. C. Scott
Fall of a Sparrow. V. Gielgud
Fall of a Star. W. Magnay
Fall of an Eagle. J. Cleary
Fall of Marty Moon. A. Frazer
Fall of Midas. J. Astley
Fall of Rock. K. R. Butler
Fall of Snow. J. Shelynn
Fall of Terror. L. Peters
Fall of the Curtain. P. Motte
Fall of the Eagle. P. Bourne
Fall of the House of Heron. E. Phillpotts
Fall of the House of Usher. R. Brome
Fall of the House of Usher. T. J. Kelly
Fall of the Mighty. A. Seymour
Fall of the Russian Empire. D. James
Fall of the Sparrow. N. Balchin
Fall of the Staincliffes. A. Colbeck
Fall Out. K. Royce
Fall-Out of Thieves. J. N. Chance
Fall Over Cliff. Josephine Bell
Fall Zion. Dennis Jones
Fallback. P. Niesewand
Fallen Among Thieves. A. W. A'Beckett
Fallen Among Thieves. O. Allan
Fallen Among Thieves. A. Applin
Fallen Among Thieves. S. P. Hyatt
Fallen Angel. M. Avallone
Fallen Angel. D. Camp
Fallen Angel. A. Cohen
Fallen Angel. P. Conway
Fallen Angel. W. Ericson
Fallen Angel. M. Holland
Fallen Curtain. R. Rendell
Fallen Eagles. Geoffrey Davison
Fallen Fortunes. J. Payn
Fallen from Favour. J. Middlemass
Fallen Hearts. V. C. Andrews
Fallen Into the Pit. E. Pargeter
Fallen Leaves. W. Collins
Fallen Nun. D. A. Hillman
Fallen Pride. E. Southworth
Fallen Sparrow. D. B. Hughes
Fallen Staircase. K. Hess
Fallen Star. Jack Lewis

Falling Angel. W. Hjortsberg
Falling Blonde. P. Denver
Falling Man. W. Forma
Falling Man. M. Sadler
Falling Star. P. Moyes
Falling Star. L. O'Donnell
Falling Star. E. P. Oppenheim
Fallout for a Spy. R. L. Hershatter
Falls the Shadow. E. Litvinoff
Falls the Shadow. Regina Ross
Falmont Claiments. A. Bercovici
False. G. Fleming
False Alarm. Manning Long
False Alibi. J. G. Brandon
False Alibi. Jack Lewis
False Alibi. C. Thornton
False Beards. Alan Williams
False Bounty. S. Ransome
False Cards. H. Smart
False Claim. B. Wayde
False Claimant. Nicholas Carter
False Colors. M. Borgenicht
False Colors. R. Powell
False Colours. Annie Thomas
False Colours. E. Woodward
False Combination. Nicholas Carter
False Cross. Stephen Forbes
False Evidence. H. Carmichael
False Evidence. E. P. Oppenheim
False Face. V. Caspary
False Face. L. Edgley
False-Face. S. Horler
False Face. J. Lilly
False-Face. F. MacIsaac
False Face. S. Truss
False Face of Death. Anita Allen
False Faces. L. J. Vance
False Finger Tip. S. Kearney
False Flags. N. Hynd
False Freedom. L. Emsley
False Front. Lawrence Meyer
False God. B. Vane
False Gods. G. H. Lorimer
False Gods. G. Thorne
False Gold. L. C. Davidson
False Idols. B. Ferm
False Impressions. K. Berne
False Inspector Dew. P. Lovesey
False Intruder. G. Goodchild
False Joanna. J. Fredman
False Notes. C. Q. Yarbro
False Pretences. T. Cobb
False Pretences. C. Coulter
False Pretences. W. J. Elliott
False Pretences. Annie Thomas
False Profit. R. Eversz
False Prophets. S. Flannery
False Purple. S. Horler
False Scent. Mrs. Alexander
False Scent. J. S. Fletcher
False Scent. I. Greig
False Scent. N. Marsh
False Scents. W. J. Bayfield
False to Any Man. L. Ford
False Truth. E. C. Vivian
False Witness. Mark Allerton
False Witness. Mary Cross
False Witness. S. Milne
False Witness. H. Nielsen
False Witness. E. Nisot
False Witness. D. Uhnak
False Witness. M. Underwood
Falseface. M. Sharp
Falsely Accused. G. Norway
Falstaff Cross. J. Kern
Familiar Faces. M. R. Rinehart
Familiar Spirits. L. Tourney
Familiar Stranger. F. E. Penny
Familiar Strangers. B. Forbes
Families Repaired. J. S. Fletcher
Family Affair. L. Benedict
Family Affair. H. Conway
Family Affair. M. G. Eberhart
Family Affair. M. Innes

Family Affair. I. S. Shriber
Family Affair. R. Stout
Family Affairs. J. Ellery
Family Affairs. J. Rhode
Family Affairs. G. Robey
Family and Friends. Emma Page
Family Arsenal. P. Theroux
Family at Tammerton. M. Erskine
Family Burial Murders. M. Propper
Family Business. V. Patrick
Family Closets. M. Dorner
Family Doom. E. Southworth
Family Failing. H. Smart
Family Fortune. M. G. Eberhart
Family Fortune. J. Weidman
Family Fortunes. J. Neufeld
Family Jewels. A. Gregg
Family Lie. G. Simenon
Family Likeness. Anna Gilbert
Family Linen. L. Smith
Family Man. Robin Moore
Family Matter. F. Gaite
Family Matter. J. Roosevelt
Family Matters. A. Rolls
Family Money. Doris Shannon
Family of Santraile. Harriet Jones
Family of Strangers. J. S. May
Family of Strangers. D. Winston
Family on Vendetta Street. L. Longo
Family Passions. B. Aswad
Family Plot. V. Canning
Family Property. P. Trent
Family Reunion. Joyce Harrington
Family Reunion. N. Sarazen
Family Secrets. M. Chevalier
Family Scapegrace. J. Payne
Family Sins and other stories. W. Trevor
Family Skeleton. D. M. Disney
Family Skeleton. J. Hawk
Family Skeleton. E. Tyler
Family Skeletons. H. Garnett
Family Skeletons. D. Hartman
Family Skeletons. P. Quentin
Family Tomb. M. Gilbert
Family Trade. James Carroll
Family Trouble. J. Masiello
Family Vault. C. MacLeod
Family Worth. J. Crosby
Famine. J. Creasey
Famine. G. Masterton
Famine Plot. J. Freivalds
Famous Boy. Old Sleuth
Famous Burdick Case. Anonymous
Famous Cases of Dr. Thorndyke. R. A. Freeman
Famous Detective Mysteries. G. Barton
Famous Detective Stories. Alexander Morton
Famous Last Words. T. Findley
Famous McGarry Stories. Matt Taylor
Famous Match. N. Gould
Fan. B. Randall
Fan. W. Caine
Fan Fare. H. Janson
Fan of Dirty Green. R. Rattray
Fan Tan of the Front Page. D. Dell
Fanatic of Fez. C. L. Leonard
Fanatics. Peter Hill
Fanatics of Al Asad. Nick Carter
Fancies and Goodnights. John Collier
Fancy Dress Ball. J. J. Farjeon
Fancy Free. E. Phillpotts
Fancy Free and other stories. C. Gibbon
Fancy Now! Evoe
Fancy's Knell. B. H. Deal
Fandango Involvement. T. Mahon
Fandom Is a Way of Death. B. Warren
Fanfare for a Murderer. J. Rosenberg
Fanfare for Angel. G. Montrose
Fanfare for Murder. H. Desmond
Fangs of Murder. R. Wallace
Fangs of the Hooded Demon. G. Marsh
Fangs of the Serpent. G. R. Fox
Fangs of the Sky Leopard. R. J. Hogan
Fannin. D. Markson
Fanny. H. Janson

Fanny McBride. C. Cookson
Fanny White and Her Friend Jack Rawlings. Anonymous
Fanshaw Case. G. K. Cowan
Fanshawe Court Mystery. J. Laurence
Fanshawe Murder. G. Thorne
Fantasist. P. McGinley
Fantastic Island. K. Robeson
Fantastic Saint. L. Charteris
Fantastic Stories of Cornell Woolrich. C. Woolrich
Fantastic Summer. D. Macardle
Fantasy and Fugue. Roy Fuller
Fantine Avenel. L. Maddock
Fantoccini. Countess Barcynska
Fantoccini. F. Barrett
Fantoccini. W. L. Gibson-Cowan
Fantomas. P. Souvestre
Fantomas Captured. M. Allain
Far and Away. A. Boucher
Far Away Man. W. Marshall
Far Better Dead! M. Cumberland
Far Cry. F. Brown
Far Cry. M. Stewart
Far Fly the Eagles. Evelyn Anthony
Far Forests. Joan Aiken
Far Horizon. B. Copper
Far Lands Other Days. E. H. Price
Far-Off Strands. Dale Collins
Far Place. B. Fuller
Far Pursuit. O. Binns
Far Sands. A. Garve
Far Side of Fear. B. Copper
Far Side of the Dollar. R. Macdonald
Far to Go. M. Aswell
Far Traveller. F. Gaite
Far Wandering Men. J. Russell
Far West Detective. Anonymous
Faraday's Flowers. T. Kenrick
Faraway Drums. J. Cleary
Farberge Egg. R. Upton
Fare Prey. Laine Fisher
Farewell by Death. V. Warren
Farewell Crown and Goodbye King. M. Bennett
Farewell, Lo Jolla. Demouzon
Farewell, Little Sister. D. Enefer
Farewell, My Dear Colonel. L. Koslov
Farewell, My Lovely. R. Chandler
'Farewell, Nikola.' G. Boothby
Farewell Party. F. Bandy
Farewell Party. June Drummond
Farewell Performance. E. P. Lehman
Farewell, Pretty Ladies. C. Massie
Farewell to Passion. D. Keene
Farewell to Peril. D. R. Dunn
Farewell to Russia. Richard Hugo
Farewell to the Admiral. P. Cheyney
Farewell to the Castle. J. Corby
Farewell to Vienna. Dorothy Fletcher
Farm at Paranao. Laurence Kirk
Farm at Sante Fe. Laurence Kirk
Farm Boy. M. Skedgell
Farm in the Hills. F. Warden
Farm Villains. J. N. Chance
Farmhouse. H. Reilly
Farmhouse by the Sea. Joyce Bell
Farndale Avenue Housing Estate Townswomen's Guild Dramatic Society Murder Mystery. D. McGillivray
Farnsworth Score. R. Burns
Farrowshot Park Affair. W. J. Bayfield
Farther Off from England. L. Chancellor
Fascinating Traitor. R. H. Savage
Fascinator. A. York
Fashion and Passion. Anonymous
Fashion in Shrouds. M. Allingham
Fashioned for Murder. C. Canyon
Fashioned for Murder. G. H. Coxe
Fast and Loose. L. Della
Fast and Loose. A. Griffiths
Fast and Loose. N. Tranter
Fast As the Wind. N. Gould
Fast Buck. J. H. Chase
Fast Buck. B. Fischer
Fast Buck. H. Janson

Fast Buck. R. Laurence
Fast Colors. M. Doran
Fast Company. Marco Page
Fast Copy. Dan Jenkins
Fast-Death Factor. V. Crosby
Fast Exit. M. Cronin
Fast Fade. Arthur Lyons
Fast Farewell. R. Dudgeon
Fast Fix. D. Haring
Fast Life in New York. Grace M. White
Fast Mail. C. Thornton
Fast Man with a Dollar. R. Avery
Fast Money. E. A. Clancy
Fast Money Shoots from the Hip. J. M. Glazner
Fast One. P. Cain
Fast Play! D. Haring
Fast Shuffle. T. Herd
Fast Shuffle. Robin Moore
Fast Track. C. A. Harris
Fast Train to Terror. D. Boyce
Fast with a Gun. R. Wilkes-Hunter
Fast Work. P. Cheyney
Fast Work and other stories. P. Cheyney
Fastburn. D. Pendleton
Faster She Runs. R. Colby
Faster We Live. B. Brennan
Fastest Boy in New York. Old Sleuth
Fat Boy Must Die. R. E. Pearson
Fat Cat Affair. K. Hagenbach
Fat Chance. K. Laumer
Fat Death. M. Avallone
Fat Guys Don't Wear Stripes. D. Dunham
Fat Lady's Song. R. W. Nolan
Fat Man's Agony. G. Carr
Fat Man's Shadow. R. Blake
Fat Men Laugh at Murder. M. Stephens
Fat Tuesday. E. W. Emerson
Fata Morgana. W. Kotzwinkle
Fatal Accident. P. N. Walker
Fatal Accident. C. M. Wills
Fatal Ace. A. Applin
Fatal Advent. I. Holland
Fatal Affair. V. Johnston
Fatal Affinity. S. L. Cumberland
Fatal Alibi. G. Bellairs
Fatal Alibi. L. Bidston
Fatal Alibi. L. Thayer
Fatal Amateur. D. L. Mathews
Fatal Amulet. G. H. Teed
Fatal Amusement. C. G. Thacker
Fatal Analysis. C. Patton
Fatal Assignation. A. C. Ley
Fatal Attraction. Craig Jones
Fatal Attraction. B. Slade
Fatal Bargain. Nicholas Carter
Fatal Beauty. G. D. H. Cole
Fatal Beauty. J. Godey
Fatal Beauty. W. Schoell
Fatal Bonds. R. Dowling
Fatal Bride. V. Siller
Fatal Call. A. Dorrington
Fatal Car. R. Hardinge
Fatal Cast. C. T. Gardner
Fatal Chair. Hawkshaw
Fatal Charm. A. Morice
Fatal Charms. E. Wiley
Fatal Choice. J. D'Astor
Fatal Choice. D. M. Disney
Fatal Choices. James Burke
Fatal Combination. P. De Pietro
Fatal Command. J. D. McNamara
Fatal Complaint. P. Quinn
Fatal Curtain. Arthur MacLean
Fatal Curiosity. G. Lillo
Fatal Curtain. J. B. Hilton
Fatal Descent. J. Rhode
Fatal Diagnosis. M. Kittredge
Fatal Diamonds. E. C. Donnelly
Fatal Dose. B. Cobb
Fatal Dose. F. M. White
Fatal Element. E. C. Clark
Fatal Entrance. R. Barratt
Fatal Entrance. N. Wishart
Fatal Equilibrium. M. Jevons

Fatal Errand. J. Pattinson
Fatal Error. J. Boland
Fatal Error. C. F. Gregg
Fatal Error. D. Pendleton
Fatal Face. W. LeQueux
Fatal Falsehood. Nicholas Carter
Fatal Fascination. J. N. Chance
Fatal Fetish. P. Hochstein
Fatal Fifth. M. Penrose
Fatal Finale. P. H. Dobbins
Fatal Finger Mark, Rose Courtenay's First Case. M. Danvers
Fatal Fingers. W. LeQueux
Fatal Finish. M. D'Alton
Fatal Five Minutes. R. A. J. Walling
Fatal Flashback. E. Fulton
Fatal Flaw. L. Meynell
Fatal Flaw. B. Musto
Fatal Flirt. D. Hitchens
Fatal Flourishes. S. S. Rafferty
Fatal Flower. L. Benedict
Fatal Focus. P. Valdez
Fatal Footsteps. C. Shannon
Fatal Forgery. J. G. Brandon
Fatal Formula. J. Rosenberger
Fatal Fortune. M. Babson
Fatal Fortune. J. Castle
Fatal Fortune. F. Hurt
Fatal Fortune. A. Murray
Fatal .45. J. Ronald
Fatal Foursome. F. Kane
Fatal Fragrance. D. M. Locke
Fatal Frails. D. J. Marlowe
Fatal Frame. Kane
Fatal Friday. F. Gerard
Fatal Friend. B. Falkson
Fatal Friends. K. Netzen
Fatal Friendship. Gwyn Evans
Fatal Games. B. McElwain
Fatal Garden. J. Rhode
Fatal Glove. C. Augusta
Fatal Grace. G. M. Edwards
Fatal Harvest. A. Amos
Fatal Holiday. B. Cobb
Fatal Hour. Nicholas Carter
Fatal Hour. E. Harrison
Fatal Image. T. S. King
Fatal Impressions. W. Warga
Fatal in Furs. J. M. Fox
Fatal in My Fashion. P. McGerr
Fatal Inversion. B. Vine
Fatal Kiss Mystery. R. King
Fatal Lady. R. Foley
Fatal Lady. J. West
Fatal Law. B. Kent
Fatal Legacy. L. Linares
Fatal Legacy. L. Tracy
Fatal Lover. V. Siller
Fatal Manuscript. D. W. Steward
Fatal Marriage. M. E. Braddon
Fatal Marriage. E. Southworth
Fatal Mascot. A. Skene
Fatal Memoirs. W. Edwards
Fatal Memory. B. Forester
Fatal Mistake. P. H. Powell
Fatal Move, and other stories. C. Conall
Fatal Nugget. E. H. Burrage
Fatal Number. W. Shute
Fatal Obsession. D. B. Baylor
Fatal Obsession. S. Greenleaf
Fatal Odds. J. Halkin
Fatal Past. Dora Russell
Fatal Picnic. Bernice Carey
Fatal Pit. J. W. Bobin
Fatal Pool. J. Rhode
Fatal Power. C. H. Bullivant
Fatal Prescription. Nicholas Carter
Fatal Purchase. A. Rose
Fatal Record. C. B. Booth
Fatal Relations. M. Erskine
Fatal Request. A. L. Harris
Fatal Resemblance. E. Ellerton
Fatal Resemblance. C. Faber
Fatal Resemblance. Old Sleuth

Fatal Reunion. C. McNab
Fatal Reunion. D. Saperstein
Fatal Revenge. Dennis J. Murphy
Fatal Ring. D. Donovan
Fatal Ring of Light. H. Eastwood
Fatal Rose. Ernest Clark
Fatal Ruby. C. Garvice
Fatal Run. Ernest Clark
Fatal Second. H. C. McNeile
Fatal Secret. Anonymous
Fatal Secret. E. Southworth
Fatal Shadow. G. Black
Fatal Shadows. S. George
Fatal Shadows. E. S. Lockwood
Fatal Shadows. D. C. Meade
Fatal Shadows. M. Peterson
Fatal Silence. F. Marryat
Fatal Sisters. W. G. Duncan
Fatal Song. F. Hume
Fatal Step. C. F. Cushman
Fatal Step. Wade Miller
Fatal Stranger. A. R. Rooth
Fatal Switch. Ian Stuart
Fatal Talisman. C. Brisbane
Fatal Thirteen. W. LeQueux
Fatal Three. M. E. Braddon
Fatal Tin Whistle. Anonymous
Fatal Trip. M. Underwood
Fatal Undertaking. F. Kane
Fatal V Sign. M. Frazer
Fatal Venture. F. W. Crofts
Fatal Vow. F. Lathom
Fatal Vows. Anonymous
Fatal Wager. A. Blair
Fatal Woman. D. Donovan
Fatal Woman. P. Quentin
Fatality at Bath & Wells. Nancy Livingston
Fatality in Fleet Street. C. S. Sprigg
Fatally Female. K. T. McCall
Fate Accompli. H. P. Raimes
Fate Accomplished. Jonathan Ross
Fate—and Drusilla. A. Askew
Fate and Fernand. P. Audemars
Fate and Four Sinners. H. L. Victor
Fate and the Man. T. W. Hanshew
Fate at the Fair. M. Burton
Fate Chose the Number. C. Dekker
Fate Cries Out. C. Dane
Fate Laughs. H. Adams
Fate of Austin Craige. S. Campbell
Fate of Fay Delray. J. Wilstach
Fate of Felix. Mrs. C. Kernahan
Fate of Felix Brand. F. F. Kelly
Fate of Herbert Wayne. E. J. Goodman
Fate of Jane McKenzie. N. B. Mavity
Fate of Luke Ormerod. R. Dowling
Fate of Mary Rose. C. Blackwood
Fate of O'Loughlin. D. McCarthy
Fate of Osmund Brett. H. G. Hutchinson
Fate of Princes. P. C. Doherty
Fate of Ralph Erard. C. Fleming
Fate of Sister Jessica. F. W. Robinson
Fate of the Hara Diamond. T. W. Speight
Fate of the Immodest Blonde. P. Quentin
Fate of the Lying Jade. J. N. Chance
Fate of the Malous. G. Simenon
Fate of the Plotter. L. Tracy
Fate Strikes Twice. C. Ashton
Fate Worse Than Death. S. Radley
Fate Worse Than Death. D. Weed
Fated Five. G. Biss
Fated to Love. R. Roleine
Fateful Abduction. M. A. Fleming
Fateful Departure. D. M. Disney
Fateful Hand. N. T. Oliver
Fateful Star Murder. H. Kerkow
Fateful Summer. V. Johnston
Fateful Tide. J. Wellsley
Fate's Pendulum. G. Comley
Father and Son. P. Maas
Father Anthony. R. W. Buchanan
Father Brown Omnibus. G. K. Chesterton
Father Goriot. H. Balzac
Father Hayes. P. Leslie

Father Hunt. R. Stout
Father Pig. B. Hirschfeld
Father Pink. A. W. Barrett
Fatherless Fanny. T. P. Prest
Fathers in Law. H. Cecil
Father's Law. D. W. Smith
Fathom. M. Hammond
Fauconberg. W. Magnay
Faulkner's Folly. C. Wells
Fault. C. T. Podmore
Fault in Our Stars. S. D. Frances
Fault in the Structure. G. Mitchell
Fault Lines. Teri White
Fault Tree. M. Friedman
Faultline. S. Leventhal
Faust Conspiracy. J. Baddock
Faust of the F.B.I. Jim Mack
Fausta. P. J. Stead
Faustian Pact. A. Beevor
Favilla. T. J. Corr
Favor. N. Guild
Favor. Parnell Hall
Favorite Son. S. Sohmer
Favourite Scratched. B. Hemyng
Faxon Secret. J. Ware
Fayolle Formula. T. G. Courtenay
Fazackerley's Millions. F. Crisp
Fear! L. C. Douthwaite
Fear. P. Hines
Fear. T. Keneally
Fear. E. Nesbit
Fear. B. Sarto
Fear Among the Shadows. L. Hoffman
Fear and Miss Betony. D. Bowers
Fear and the Dead Man. L. Smith
Fear and the Guilt. W. Shaw
Fear and Trembling. R. Bloch
Fear and Trembling. B. Flynn
Fear Business. H. Hossent
Fear by Installments. Jonathan Burke
Fear by Night. P. Wentworth
Fear Came First. V. Kelsey
Fear Cay. K. Robeson
Fear Comes Calling. A. L. Martin
Fear Comes to Chalfont. F. W. Crofts
Fear Dealers. R. Cade
Fear Dealers. Jack Thomas
Fear Familiar. C. Burnes
Fear Followed On. C. Kingston
Fear for Francis. V. Heley
Fear for Miss Betony. D. Bowers
Fear for the Hero. K. Welsh
Fear Fortune, Father. S. B. Hough
Fear Haunts the Fells. R. Goyne
Fear Haunts the Roses. C. Edwards
Fear Holds the Key. F. Duncan
Fear in a Desert Town. Roger Fuller
Fear in a Handful of Dust. J. Ives
Fear in Borzano. W. Jay
Fear in the Dark. Sinclair Russell
Fear in the Forest. Reginald Campbell
Fear in the Wind. S. Jepson
Fear Is a Weapon. F. Ford
Fear Is My Shadow. Martin Thomas
Fear Is the Key. Alistair MacLean
Fear Is the Same. Carter Dickson
Fear Itself. S. Kanfer
Fear Kissed My Lips. J. Ames
Fear Makers. D. L. Teilhet
Fear No Evil. L. Brackett
Fear No Evil. Alice Brennan
Fear No Evil. J. G. Davis
Fear No More. L. Edgley
Fear of a Stranger. R. Foley
Fear of Death. C. Conte
Fear of Death. A. M. Wells
Fear of Fear. F. Ryerson
Fear of Felix Corder. J. Creasey
Fear of God. D. Quinn
Fear of Heights. V. Coffman
Fear of Life. G. Maxwell
Fear of Mr. Taltry. E. G. Cousins
Fear of the Dark. G. A. Haywood
Fear of the Night. J. S. Fletcher

Title Index　　FIFTH ESTATE / 991

Fear Place. J. Ware
Fear Rides the Fog. E. C. Stone
Fear Round About. G. Bellairs
Fear Runs Softly. C. Franklin
Fear Shadowed. M. Peterson
Fear Sign. M. Allingham
Fear Stalks the Bayou. J. Coulson
Fear Stalks the City. N. MacKenzie
Fear Stalks the Footlights. Don Boyd
Fear Stalks the Village. Ethel L. White
Fear the Light. E. Ferrars
Fear to Tread. M. Gilbert
Fear Today—Gone Tomorrow. R. Bloch
Fear Treads Soft Shod. M. Clare
Fear Waits on Cypress Road. P. Wissmann
Fear Walked Behind. S. Horler
Fear Walks the Island. H. Desmond
Fear Without End. Noel Lee
Feared and the Fearless. Guthrie Wilson
Fearful Paradise. J. Ames
Fearful Passage. H. C. Branson
Fearful Symmetry. L. M. Waltch
Fearful Thing. V. Gielgud
Fearful Way to Die. J. C. Nolan
Fearless Investigator. F. U. Eaton
Fearless Lovers. A. Applin
Fearsome Riddle. M. Ehrmann
Feast for Spiders. K. Evans
Feast of Death. John Penn
Feast of Eggshells. F. Stevenson
Feast of Lanterns. M. Richmond
Feast of the Dead. G. M. Jay
Feast of the Scorpions. J. Pattinson
Feast of Vultures. P. G. Scott
Feast of Vultures. C. Weissner
Feather Cloak Murders. D. L. Teilhet
Feather on the Moon. P. A. Whitney
Feather Your Nest. G. Greenaway
Feathered Octopus. K. Robeson
Feathered Serpent. E. Wallace
Feathers for the Toff. J. Creasey
Feathers in the Fire. C. Cookson
Feathers Left Around. C. Wells
Feather's Weight. Amarala Martin
Featherstone's Story. H. Wood
Featuring the Saint. L. Charteris
February Doll Murders. M. Avallone
February Face. M. J. Adamson
February Morning. H. Wakefield
February Plan. J. H. Roberts
Fed Up. G. A. Birmingham
Federal Agent. "G-Man"
Federal Agent. John Ross
Federal Bullets. G. F. Eliot
Fedora. A. Belot
Fedora of the Halls. A. Applin
Feed Store Mystery. H. Reed
Feedback. B. Copper
Feedback. H. Miller
Feeding the Wind. J. E. Gurdon
Feet of a Snake. B. Chubin
Feet of Clay. B. Schwarz
Feet of Death. B. Flynn
Feet of Death. M. Peterson
Feldisham Mystery. Gordon Holmes
Felicia. Mark Dane
Felicia. G. A. Effinger
Felicity. C. Lansbury
Feline Frame-Up. P. Valdez
Felix Boyd's Final Problems. S. Campbell
Felix Boyd's Revelations. S. Campbell
Felix Running. H. Ford
Felix Stone. A. Askew
Felix Walking. H. Ford
Fell Clutch. P. Motte
Fell Murder. E. C. R. Lorac
Fell of Dark. R. Hill
Fell of Dark. J. Judson
Fell Purpose. A. Derleth
Fella's Choice. K. Omotoso
Fellow of Trinity. A. St. Aubyn
Fellow Passenger. G. Household
Fellow Passengers. R. Pyke
Fellow-Traveler. D. Montross

Fellowship of Fear. A. J. Elkins
Fellowship of Five. F. Johnston
Fellowship of the Feather. H. Pink
Fellowship of the Frog. E. Wallace
Fellowship of the Hand. E. D. Hoch
Felo De Se? R. A. Freeman
Felon Angel. Carter Brown
Felon in Disguise. L. Southworth
Feloniously and Wilfully. Ernest Wood
Felonry of New South Wales. T. Walker
Felon's Bequest. F. Du Boisgobey
Felon's Daughter. J. Middlemass
Felony at Random. Dell Shannon
Felony File. Dell Shannon
Felony Report. E. Linington
Felony Squad. M. Avallone
Felony Tank. M. Braly
Felthams. Franz
Female Bluebeard. E. Sue
Female Depravity. Anonymous
Female Depravity. O. Bradbury
Female Detective. A. Forrester
Female Detective. C. H. Hazlewood
Female Detective. Old Sleuth
Female Fatales. Stuart Hall
Female—Handle with Care. P. Chambers
Female Nihilist. E. Lavigne
Female of the Species. H. C. McNeile
Female of the Species. A. Roudybush
Female Spy. Emerson Bennett
Female Spy. Roland Daniel
Female Target. D. Onyeama
Female—The Huntress. Stuart Hall
Female Ventriloquist. Old Sleuth
Feminine for Spy. B. Sanders
Femme Fatale. C. Dekker
Femme Fatale. D. Haring
Fen Country. E. Crispin
Fen Tiger. C. Marchant
Fence. H. L. Nelson
Fence's Victim. Donald Stuart
Fengriffin. D. Case
Fenland Mystery. C. A. Brandreth
Fennell's Tower. L. Tracy
Fenner. G. H. Coxe
Fennister Affair. Josephine Bell
Fenokee Project. Roy Lewis
Fenris Option. R. D. Jones
Fenton Affair. R. Quest
Fenton of the Foreign Office. M. Annesley
Fentons. R. Goyne
Fenton's Quest. M. E. Braddon
Fenwick Houses. C. A. Cookson
Fenwood Murders. G. E. Locke
Feo. M. Pemberton
Fer-de-Lance. R. Stout
Fer-de-Lance Contract. P. Atlee
Feral. B. Roueche
Feramontov. D. Cory
Ferguson. R. Kruger
Ferguson Affair. Ross Macdonald
Fern Dead. R. H. R. Smithies
Fern Seed. H. M. Rideout
Fernanda. V. Miller
Fernande's Choice. F. Du Boisgobey
Fernwood. M. Thum
Ferocious Fern and other stories. C. B. Pulman
Ferret. G. Markstein
Ferret Detective. Anonymous
Ferrol Bond. J. Easton
Ferry Boat. F. Du Boisgobey
Ferrybridge Mystery. D. Vane
Ferryman, Take Him Across! V. Rath
Festered Lilies. K. D. Taylor
Fertig. S. Yurick
Fertility Rights. F. N. Zachary
Festering Lilies. Natasha Cooper
Festival. J. R. L. Anderson
Festival! M. Butterworth
Festival. N. J. Crisp
Festival. A. Jute
Festival Death. R. Stephenson
Festival for Spies. David St. John
Festival of Darkness. M. Garratt

Festival of St. Jago. Sarah Green
Fetch. P. Everett
Fetch. J. Shearing
Fetch Me a Rope. R. Boyd
Fetch Out No Shroud. Stephen Murray
Fete Fatale. R. Barnard
Fete Worse Than Death. J. Christmas
Fetish. Jeanne Hart
Fetish. K. Hewitt
Fetish Murders. A. Curry
Fettered. P. Trent
Fettered by Fate. G. W. Miller
Fettered by Fate. A. Wright
Fettered for Life. F. Barrett
Fettered Love. M. Richmond
Feud. "Capstan"
Feud. J. Templeton
Feud. D. Whitelaw
Feud Beyond the Law. A. Murray
Feud of Fear. W. M. Graydon
Feudal Tyrants. M. G. Lewis
Fever. R. Cook
Fever Grass. John Morris
Fever in the Blood. William Pearson
Fever of Life. F. Hume
Fever Tree. R. Mason
Fever Tree. R. Rendell
Fevered. Alison Drake
Feversham. Diane Davidson
Few Days in Endel. Diana Gordon
Few Days in Madrid. A. Roos
Few Die Well. S. Noel
Few Drops of Murder. I. Capeto
Few Fiends to Tea. V. Coffman
Few Good Men. W. Overgard
Few Small Bones. H. C. Rae
Fiasco in Fulham. Josephine Bell
Ficciones. J. L. Borges
Fickle Heart. F. Du Boisgobey
Fiction As She Is Wrote. Evoe
Fictional Lives. H. Fleetwood
Fiddle City. D. Kavanagh
Fiddle o' Dreams. A. Morrison
Fiddler's Bridge. K. Denton
Fiddler's Green. E. K. Gann
Fiddler's Place. R. Parker
Fiddlestrings. J. H. Vahey
Fiddling Cracksman. H. S. Keeler
Fidel Castro Assassinated. Lee Duncan
Fidelio Affair. H. Green
Fidelio Score. G. Sinstadt
Fidgets. G. A. Birmingham
Field of Blood. G. Seymour
Field of Fire. P. Alding
Field of Night. R. W. Krepps
Field of the Forty Footsteps. P. Hastings
Field Work. Maureen Moore
Fields of Eden. M. T. Hinkemeyer
Fields of Heather. A. Hunter
Fieldwork. M. Danielle
Fiend. M. Millar
Fiend in Need. M. K. Ozaki
Fiend Incarnate. D. Malcolm
Fiends. P. Boileau
Fiends of the Family. P. Flower
Fiery Chariot. E. Everett-Green
Fiery Cross. D. Pendleton
Fiery Furnace. Lawrence Williams
Fiery Menace. K. Robeson
Fiery Serpent. A. Mallory
Fiesta for Murder. P. O. McGuire
Fifteen Cells. Stuart Martin
Fifteen Keys. C. Dawe
Fifteen Odd Stories. Shane Leslie
Fifteen Streets. C. Cookson
Fifth Ace. Douglas Grant
Fifth Angel. D. Wiltse
Fifth Answer. M. Pereira
Fifth Avenue Number. Anonymous
Fifth Caller. H. Nielsen
Fifth Cord. D. M. Devine
Fifth Dagger. D. Quick
Fifth Defector. P. Jones
Fifth Estate. Robin Moore

Fifth Finger. W. LeQueux
Fifth Form Detective. R. Walker
Fifth Freedom. A. O. Pollard
Fifth Freedom. John Smith
Fifth Grave. Jonathan Latimer
Fifth Horseman. N. M. Adams
Fifth Horseman. L. Collins
Fifth Hostage. T. Strong
Fifth House. J. Godey
Fifth Key. G. H. Coxe
Fifth Latchkey. N. S. Lincoln
Fifth Law of Hawkins. C. Durden
Fifth Man. P. Beere
Fifth Man. M. Coles
Fifth Must Die! R. Verron
5th of November. M. Franklin
Fifth Passenger. E. Young
Fifth Point of the Compass. M. Tripp
Fifth Profession. D. Morrell
Fifth Sally. D. Keyes
Fifth Script. R. H. Spencer
Fifth Seal. M. Aldanov
Fifth Tumbler. C. B. Clason
Fifth Vase. Anonymous
Fifth Victim. D. Collins
Fifth Wheel. B. Heron-Maxwell
Fifth Woman. M. Fagyas
Fifty Bucks. B. Vane
Fifty Candles. E. D. Biggers
58 Minutes. W. Wager
Fifty-Fifty and other stories. P. Frankau
Fifty-First. M. Stewart
Fifty-Five. G. Volk
55 Guineas Reward. F. C. Milford
Fifty Million Hijack. A. Cecil
50 Pound Marriage Case. J. G. Brandon
Fifty Pounds for a Wife. A. L. Glyn
Fifty Roads to Town. F. Nebel
Fifty Thousand Dollars Ransom. D. Malcolm
Fifty-Two Pickup. E. Leonard
52 Suspects. M. Grove
Fig Connection. J. Franzen
Fig Leaves for a Lady. Johnny Dark
Fight. V. Scannell
Fight for a Fortune. F. Du Boisgobey
Fight for a Soul. F. Warden
Fight for a Throne. Nicholas Carter
Fight for Millions. Chris Allen
Fight for Right. Nicholas Carter
Fight for the Child. F. M. White
Fight for the Luck. J. Blyth
Fight Racket. L. Bell
Fight to a Finish. W. G. Forbes
Fight to a Finish. G. Hackforth-Jones
Fight to a Finish. E. Phillpotts
Fight to a Finish. F. Warden
Fight with a Fiend. Nicholas Carter
Fighter Pilot. R. Wilkes-Hunter
Fighting Against Millions. Nicholas Carter
Fighting Agents. A. Baldwin
Fighting an Unknown Power. W. G. Forbes
Fighting Back. C. Alverson
Fighting Back. J. Bowen
Fighting Back. R. Sandroff
Fighting Blood. J. Addiscombe
Fighting Byng. A. Stone
Fighting Cartoonist Detective. Hedley Trembath
Fighting Chance. M. G. Eberhart
Fighting Edge. W. M. Raine
Fighting Fool. G. Dilnot
Fighting Footballers. P. Gill
Fighting for a Fortune. Old Sleuth
Fighting Hearts. J. Dorrance
Fighting His Way. Old Sleuth
Fighting Irish. Steve White
Fighting Lieutenant. J. G. Rowe
Fighting Men. J. Cartwright
Fighting Snub Reilly. E. Wallace
Fighting the Red Shadow. Vigilant
Fighting Through. A. Abdullah
Fighting 'Tec. P. A. Clarke
Fighting Tramp. P. Gill
Fighting Troubadour. A. C. Gunter
"Fightingcocks." W. P. Drury

Figure Away. P. A. Taylor
Figure Eight. S. Regester
Figure in the Corner and other stories. M. E. Braddon
Figure in the Dusk. J. Creasey
Figure in the Shadows. Dana Ross
Figure It Out for Yourself. J. H. Chase
Figure of Eight. C. Waye
Figure on the Terrace. A. R. Weekes
Figurehead. B. Knox
File for Death. Janet Hart
File for Record. A. Tilton
File No. 115. H. Harper
File No. 114. E. A. Young
File No. 113. E. Gaboriau
File of the Golden Goose. John Watson
File of Ms. Tree. M. A. Collins
File on a Missing Redhead. L. Cameron
File on Bolitho Blane. D. Wheatley
File on Charlie. B. Copeland
File on Claudia Cragge. Q. Patrick
File on Death. K. Giles
File on Devlin. C. Gaskin
File on Fenton and Farr. Q. Patrick
File on Lester. A. Garve
File on Robert Prentice. D. Wheatley
File on Rufus Ray. H. Reilly
Filibusters. C. J. C. Hyne
Filibuster's Warning. G. Jerome
Filigree Ball. A. K. Green
Fillets on the Menu. J. Hague
Filly. I. Herbert
Filly Wore a Rod. H. Janson
Film Detective. Maxwell Scott
Film Faker. Anonymous
Film Mystery. A. B. Reeve
Film of Fear. A. Fredericks
Film Star Vanishes. D. Richmond
Film Studio Murder. C. Kenwood
Filmi, Filmi, Inspector Ghote. H. R. F. Keating
Filthy English. J. Meades
Filthy Five. Nick Carter
Filthy Ones. D. Haring
Filthy Rich. K. Colquhoun
Final. J. Greaves
Final Act. J. H. Crisp
Final Act. C. Hudson
Final Act. M. Spicer
Final Agenda. E. Hyams
Final Analysis of Dr. Stark. J. Telushkin
Final Appeal. J. Fluke
Final Appearance. J. C. Nolan
Final Appointment. M. Blair
Final Approach. P. Griffiths
Final Approach. C. Hodder-Williams
Final Approach. J. L. Nance
Final Bug. J. Blashfield
Final Caliph. F. Keast
Final Chance. P. Trent
Final Class: Murder and Mystery. J. Markham
Final Copy. J. Barbette
Final Count. H. C. McNeile
Final Covenant. A. Hernandez
Final Crossing. H. Ardman
Final Crossroads. Maude Parker
Final Crusade. W. B. Murphy
Final Curtain. W. H. L. Crauford
Final Curtain. F. Kane
Final Curtain. N. Marsh
Final Cut. P. Chais
Final Cut. Max Perry
Final Death. R. Sapir
Final Deception. R. Neidhardt
Final Deduction. R. Stout
Final Destiny. R. D. Ridyard
Final Dictation. L. M. Vincent
Final Doors. J. L. Hensley
Final Encore. M. Albrand
Final Encore. D. Haring
Final Ending of It. H. Wood
Final Exam. G. Meyer
Final Exploits of Nick Carter. Nicholas Carter
Final Exposure. P. H. Mansfield
Final Fair. M. Blair

Final Fear. L. M. Janifer
Final Flight. S. Coonts
Final Four. R. H. Parker
Final Glass. L. Henderson
Final Guest. M. Blair
Final Installment. M. Cronin
Final Judgement. P. Barrington
Final Judgment. M. Benjoya
Final Landscapes. K. Keller
Final Lie. M. Blair
Final Moments. E. Page
Final Night. R. Gaines
Final Notice. J. Gores
Final Notice. J. Valin
Final Option. G. Kriss
Final Option. S. Robinett
Final Payment. A. Applin
Final Payment. T. C. H. Jacobs
Final Payment. V. Shore
Final Portrait. V. Caspary
Final Pose. M. Blair
Final Proof. A. MacVicar
Final Proof. R. Ottolengui
Final Proof. M. Reno
Final Reckoning. L. Edgley
Final Reckonings. R. Bloch
Final Ring. M. Blair
Final Run. J. Pattinson
Final Run. D. Sanderson
Final Run. D. Stivers
Final Safari. P. Ordway
Final Score. George Douglas
Final Score. G. Goodchild
Final Score. E. Grogan
Final Sentence. M. Maurice
Final Set. P. Harris
Final Steal. P. George
Final Target. M. Blair
Final Thesis. W. L. Story
Final Things. R. B. Wright
Final Throw. M. Gilbert
Final Trace. B. R. Boylan
Final Triumph. Old Sleuth
Final Witness. J. F. Straker
Final Witness. R. W. Swaybill
Finale. M. Blair
Finalists. R. Braddon
Finally, a Kill. D. Haring
Finally, Sunday! C. Williams
Finances of Sir John Kynnersley. A. C. Fox-Davies
Financier. J. B. Harris-Burland
Financier's Wife. F. Warden
Finch Takes to Crime. F. Lester
Find a Crooked Sixpence. E. Thompson
Find a Victim. J. R. Macdonald
Find Actor Hart. H. S. Keeler
Find Eileen Hardin—Alive! A. Frazer
Find Inspector West. J. Creasey
Find Me a Killer! Arthur MacLean
Find Me a Villain. M. Yorke
Find My Killer. M. W. Wellman
Find Sherri! P. Swan
Find the Body. J. York
Find the Clock. H. S. Keeler
Find the Diamonds. J. Pattinson
Find the Don's Daughter. J. Jacks
Find the Girl. S. Ready
Find the Innocent. Roy Vickers
Find the Lady! Anonymous
Find the Lady. G. Barnett
Find the Lady. R. C. Finney
Find the Lady! G. Goodchild
Find the Lady! D. Walshe
Find the Motive. J. Woodford
Find the Professor. Mark Cross
Find the Tiger. P. Brooks
Find the Woman! W. Braun
Find the Woman. G. Burgess
Find the Woman. D. M. Disney
Find the Woman. J. S. Fletcher
Find the Woman. A. Hornblow
Find the Woman. H. J. Hultman
Find the Woman. A. S. Roche
Find This Woman. R. S. Prather

Find Tracy George. Ray Owen
Finder. Marilyn Greene
Findernes' Flowers. G. R. Preedy
Finders Keepers. G. Homes
Finders Keepers. B. Nickolae
Finders, Keepers. E. Travers
Finders, Losers—. P. Muller
Finders Weepers. M. Byrd
Finding Hoseyn. C. MacKinnon
Finding Maubee. A. H. Z. Carr
Finding of the Gentian. A. W. Rollins
Findings Is Keepings. J. B. Clarke
Findlay's Landing. M. Chittenden
Fine. S. Shem
Fine and Handsome Captain. F. Lynch
Fine and Private Place. M. Fitt
Fine and Private Place. E. Queen
Fine and Private Place. J. Simpson
Fine Art of Murder. A. Quogan
Fine Day for Dying. J. T. MacCargo
Find Day for Murder. J. Ingersol
Fine Feathers. Margery Lawrence
Fine Feathers. W. LeQueux
Fine Line. K. Gross
Fine Night for Dying. M. Fallon
Fine Pair. C. Stratton
Fine Red Rain. S. M. Kaminsky
Finger. H. Kane
Finger. A. M. Stein
Finger! Finger! H. S. Keeler
Finger in the Sky Affair. P. Leslie
Finger Man and other stories. R. Chandler
Finger of Death. H. Connolly
Finger of Destiny and other stories. E. Snell
Finger of Fate. H. C. McNeile
Finger of Fire. J. Braine
Finger of God. P. Wilde
Finger of Saturn. V. Canning
Finger of Smoke. R. M. Wells
Finger of Suspicion. Nicholas Carter
Finger of Suspicion. R. Umelo
Finger-Prints Never Lie! J. G. Brandon
Finger to Her Lips. E. Berckman
Fingered City. D. Hatch
Fingered Man. B. Fischer
Fingernail Beach. Richard Butler
Fingerprint. Anthony Gilbert
Fingerprint. P. Wentworth
Fingerprints. H. Stinson
Fingerprints of Fate! L. H. Brooks
Fingers Before Forks. E. Woodward
Fingers for Ransom. N. Berrow
Fingers of Death. M. Grant
Fingers of Fate. L. G. Moberly
Fingers of Fear. P. MacDonald
Fingers of Fear. J. U. Nicolson
Finger's on Me. J. Bodini
Finish Line. P. Kruger
Finish Me Off. H. Waugh
Finish of Three Rascals. Nicholas Carter
Finishing Stroke. E. Queen
Finishing Touch. A. Hocking
Finishing Touches. T. Essier
Finlay of the Sentinel. C. F. Gregg
Finnegan's Dilemma. C. Belmar
Finsbury Lot. G. Burnett
Finsbury Mob. E. Bruton
Fiona. C. Gaskin
Fire. A. Davenport
Fire and Forget. Bob Cook
Fire and Ice. R. Harding
Fire and Ice. K. Robeson
Fire and Maneuver. D. Stivers
Fire and the Clay. P. Audemars
Fire Ant. J. F. Drexler
Fire Arrow. F. A. Leib
Fire at Greycombe Farm. J. Rhode
Fire at Will. D. M. Disney
Fire Below. D. Yates
Fire Bomb. S. Jason
Fire-Bomb Jack. Old Sleuth
Fire Bug. E. Bruton
Fire-Bug. R. St. Clair
Fire, Burn! J. D. Carr

Fire Cloud. K. McKenney
Fire Down Below. N. Mastorakis
Fire Eaters. D. Pendleton
Fire Engine That Disappeared. M. Sjowall
Fire Escape. T. S. Strachan
Fire Eyes. D. F. Bailey
Fire Falcon. D. Hart-Davis
Fire Flingers. W. J. Neidig
Fire Fly. D. Haring
Fire Goddess. S. Rohmer
Fire Horse. D. M. Way
Fire in Anger. A. Mars
Fire in His Hand. M. Grieg
Fire in His Hand. L. Phillips
Fire in the Barley. F. Parrish
Fire in the Blood. M. K. Simmons
Fire in the Flesh. D. Goodis
Fire in the Ice. A. D. Divine
Fire in the Sky. D. Pendleton
Fire in the Snow. H. Innes
Fire in the Streets. J. Messmann
Fire in the Sun. G. A. Effinger
Fire in the Thatch. E. C. R. Lorac
Fire Island. G. M. Fenn
Fire Lake. J. Valin
Fire Lance. David Mace
Fire Like the Sun. M. Bond
Fire Mountain. H. Hastings
Fire of Death. M. E. Cooke
Fire of the Witches. Lydia Belknap Long
Fire on Fear Street. S. Sterling
Fire on the Cliffs. C. Waynar
Fire on the Seven Peaks. R. Arnold
Fire on the Wind. D. Garth
Fire Opal. Robert Fraser
Fire Opal. P. Monnow
Fire Opals. R. Danton
Fire Over Baghdad. G. Griffith
Fire Over India. W. H. Baker
Fire Past the Future. C. E. Maine
Fire-Raiser. E. Trevor
Fire Rock. J. Wood
Fire Ship. P. Tonkin
Fire Storm. R. L. Duncan
Fire Storm. R. Mackin
Fire Storm. Gar Wilson
Fire-Tongue. S. Rohmer
Fire Trap. O. Cameron
Fire Trumpet. B. Mitford
Fire-Watcher's Night. H. Kaner
Fire Will Freeze. M. Millar
Fire Within. G. F. Gibbs
Fire Within. P. Wentworth
Fire Zone. J. Bogar
Fireball. P. C. W. Davies
Fireball. H. Janson
Fireball. P. MacAlan
Fireball Assignment. A. Sugar
Firebase. J. Crowther
Firebase Seattle. D. Pendleton
Firebird. James Carroll
Firebird. W. Marchant
Firebrace and Father Kelly. Seafarer
Firebrand. S. R. Crockett
Firebrand Fakir. Robert Harding
Firebug. R. Bloch
Firecrest. V. Canning
Firecross. D. Stivers
Firefight. R. Parque
Fireflash 5. G. Masterton
Fireflood. P. Cave
Firefly Gadroon. Jonathan Gash
Firefox. Craig Thomas
Firegold. J. R. Daniels
Fireman. S. Leather
Fireman Hot. C. J. C. Hyne
Fireman, Save My Child! N. Albert
Fireplay. W. Wingate
Fireprint. G. Jenkins
Fires at Fairlawn. Josephine Bell
Fires at Fitch's Folly. K. Whipple
Fires of Ballymorris. V. Connolly
Fires of Brimstone. P. Gallagher
Fires of Fate. W. F. Fauley

Fires of Fu Manchu. C. Van Ash
Fires of Ghat. Anonymous
Fires of Glenlochy. C. Heaven
Fires of Hate. R. Bridges
Fires of Heaven. B. M. Miller
Fires of Kiwai. E. Lindall
Fires of Love. M. Leighton
Fires of Paris. Zachary Hughes
Fires That Destroy. H. Whittington
Fireside Omnibus. Anonymous
Firespill. I. Slater
Firestarter. Stephen King
Firestone. B. J. Rockliff
Firestorm. C. D. Peel
Firestorm at Dong Nam. J. Lansing
Firestorm U.S.A. J. Hild
Firestrike. Jim Case
Firewind. B. Pronzini
Firewind. H. Searls
Firework for Oliver. John Sanders
Fireworks. Jim Thompson
Firing Line. W. B. Murphy
Firing Line. E. Storm
Firing Squad. J. Barnett
Firm Hand. H. Bindloss
Firm of Girdlestone. A. C. Doyle
Firmly by the Tail. P. N. Gwynne
First a Murder. M. Halliday
First and Last Murder. R. Leigh
First Angel. E. Amrin
First Blood. P. McCurtin
First Blood. D. Morrell
First Body. L. Payne
First Born. R. M. Gilchrist
First-Born. G. Simenon
First Born. C. Thompson
First-Born. P. Trent
First Born of Egypt. Demouzon
First-Born Son. A. Murray
First Came a Murder. J. Creasey
First Case of Mr. Paul Savoy. Jackson Gregory
First Come, First Kill. F. Allan
First Come, First Kill. R. Lockridge
First Deadly Sin. Lawrence Sanders
First Directive. J. McNamara
First Englishman. R. Thorndike
First False Step. T. P. Prest
First Favourites. N. Gubbins
First Flight. J. R. Daniels
First Gravedigger. B. Paul
First Hit of the Season. J. Dentinger
First Immortals. E. L. Arch
First It Was Ordained. B. Thorne
First Just Men. P. Coussee
First Kill All the Lawyers. A. Storey
First Lady. R. Nessen
First Law. G. Willets
First Light. P. Ackroyd
First Light Fraser. Maurice Francis
First Loyalty. G. Kriss
First Loyalty. R. Lourie
First Mrs. Winston. R. Foley
First Night Murder. F. G. Parke
First Obsession. Judith Reese
First of the English. A. C. Gunter
First Ophelia. L. P. Kirby
First Person Paramount. A. Pratt
First Person Plural. R. Wiseman
First Person Singular. W. R. Benet
First Person Singular. D. C. Murray
First Prize. E. Cline
First Round Murder. J. V. Turner
First Saint Omnibus. L. Charteris
First Salvo. C. D. Taylor
First Sir Percy. Baroness Orczy
First Steps Inside the Zoo. J. Lodwick
First Stone. M. Peterson
First Stop to Hell. M. Urquhart
First Strike. D. Terman
First Team. J. Ball
First Television Murder. V. Gielgud
First Time for a Lady. D. Haring
First Time He Died. Ethel L. White
First to Kill. F. Usher

First Train to Babylon. M. Ehrlich
First Waltz. J. L. Roberts
First Wicket Down. John Parker
First You Have to Find Him. E. K. Goldthwaite
Fish and Company. R. Arnold
Fish and Kill. Macdonald Hastings
Fish Are So Trusting. N. Morland
Fish Are Such Liars! R. Pertwee
Fish for Murder. Edward Lee
Fish Lane. L. Corkill
Fish on a Hook. P. MacTyre
Fish or Cut Bail. A. A. Fair
Fish Out of Water. G. Hackforth-Jones
Fish Story. R. Hoyt
Fisherman Dies. P. T. Owen
Fisherman's End. K. D. Guinness
Fisherman's Gat. E. Noble
Fisherman's Luck. T. Pace
Fishers of Men. C. Dawe
Fisheye. Peter Townend
Fishing Is Dangerous. F. N. Millar
Fishport. G. Thorne
Fist in the Sky. M. Jopson
Fist of Fatima. P. Edwards
Fistful of Death. H. Kane
Fit As a Filly. Howard Mason
Fit of Shivers. Joan Aiken
Fit to Kill. B. Halliday
Fit to Kill. M. Cronin
Fit to Kill. M. Kane
Fit to Kill. H. C. Owen
Fit to Kill. L. Trimble
Fitch and His Fortunes. G. Dick
Fits and Starts. T. A. Fitzgerald
Fits and Starts. Maurice Richardson
Fitz. T. McNally
Fitzallan. R. Huish
Five. T. Field
Five Aces. David Hume
Five Against the House. J. Finney
Five Alarm Funeral. S. Sterling
Five and Dime Murders. R. Reinsmith
Five and Ten. T. Taggart
Five-and-Twenty Turkeys. J. J. Bell
Five Arrows. Allan Chase
Five Assassins. O. F. Jerome
Five Bells and Bladebone. M. Grimes
Five Brains. W. Sheridan
Five Bright Stars. E. Lambert
Five Bullets. L. Thayer
Five Came to Kill. R. Wilkes-Hunter
Five Crooked Chairs. F. Wells
Five-Day Nightmare. F. Brown
Five Days. D. Raymond
Five Days Till Noon. Sheila Ross
Five Days to Die. D. Linton
Five Days to Kill. R. Wilkes-Hunter
Five Days to Oblivion. D. O. Woodbury
Five Dead Men. A. Skene
Five Deceivers. F. Armitage
Five Devils of Kilmainham. E. M. McCullough
Five Diamonds. W. M. Graydon
5.18 Mystery. J. J. Farjeon
Five Faces of Murder. J. Flynn
Five Fatal Days. J. Woodford
Five Fatal Letters. Dana Scott
Five Fatal Words. E. Balmer
Five Fathoms Dead. K. Robeson
Five Fingers. G. Rivers
Five Flamboys. F. Beeding
Five Floors Down. E. S. Porter
Five for Bridge. Ernest Ward
Five for One. L. Allan
5:45 to Suburbia. V. Packer
Five Fowlers. E. Morris
Five Fragments. G. Dyer
Five Frontiers. W. H. Murray
Five Gates to Armageddon. J. Christian
Five Hours from Isfahan. W. Copeland
520%. B. North
$500. H. Alger
Five Hundred Keys. M. Carin
Five Hundred Pounds Reward. Anonymous
Five Hundred Pounds Reward. A. O. Cooke

500 Pounds Reward. D. Vane
Five in Fear. G. H. Teed
Five in Judgment. Douglas Taylor
Five Inns. R. Inchbald
Five Keys to Mystery. Francis Moore
Five Knots. F. M. White
Five-Leafed Clover. James Fraser
Five Little Pigs. A. Christian
Five Little Rich Girls. C. Harrison
Five Man War. C. Belanger
Five Matchboxes. H. Blayn
Five Men Go to Prison. R. Straus
Five Million Dollar Prince. M. Butterworth
Five Million Francs. G. Schleifer
Five Million in Cash. O. B. King
Five-Minute Marriage. Joan Aiken
5 Minute Mysteries. M. Avallone
Five-Minute Mysteries for the Armchair Detective. K. Weber
Five Minutes, Sir Matthew. T. C. Worsley
Five Minutes to Midnight. S. H. Shabtai
Five Minutes with a Stranger. M. Tripp
Five Murderers. R. Chandler
Five Mutineers. J. Spenser
Five Nights in Singapore. M. Derby
Five O'Clock Lightning. W. L. DeAndrea
Five of Hearts. V. Yorke
Five of My Best. M. G. Eberhart
Five of Spades. P. C. De Crispigny
Five Old Maids. G. Warden
Five Passengers from Lisbon. M. G. Eberhart
Five Pieces of Jade. J. Ball
Five Plays. J. Mortimer
Five Plus Four. C. S. Abraham
Five Ports to Danger. V. Connolly
Five Red Fingers. B. Flynn
Five Red Herrings. D. L. Sayers
Five Red Stars. B. Bolt
Five Rings of Fire. D. Stivers
Five Rivers to Death. M. A. Casberg
Five Roads Inn. R. Goyne
Five Roads to Death. J. Philips
Five Roads to S'Agaro. K. G. Ballard
Five Roundabouts to Heaven. J. Bingham
Five Signs from Ruby. H. C. McDonald
Five Silver Buddhas. H. S. Keeler
Five Sinister Characters. R. Chandler
Five Star Final. L. Weitzenkorn
Five Star Fugitive. J. D. MacDonald
Five Survive. C. Graves
Five Suspects. R. A. J. Walling
Five Tales. J. Galsworthy
Five Television Plays. D. Mamet
Five Thousand a Year. H. Wood
$5000 Reward. G. Fleming
Five Thousand Dollars Reward. A. F. Pinkerton
5,000 Trojan Horses. L. T. White
Five Times Maigret. G. Simenon
Five to Five. D. E. Muir
Five to Kill. M. Halliday
Five Ways to Die. Richard Grant
Five Were Doomed. D. Dayle
Five Were Murdered! T. A. Plummer
Five Who Saw Too Much! Anonymous
Five Who Vanished. G. F. Worts
Five Years! F. H. Evans
Five Years After. W. M. Graydon
Fives Wild. W. Winward
Fix. A. Capelli
Fix. L. Clancy
Fix. D. Fliegel
Fix. J. Gannold
Fix. J. Usher
Fix Like This. K. C. Constantine
Fixation. J. Pulman
Fixed Alibi. Nicholas Carter
Fixer. M. B. Dix
Fixes. Eugene Kennedy
Fixing Yellow Face and other stories. J. McCarter
Fjord of Silent Men. P. L. Brown
Flag for Sunrise. R. Stone
Flag in the City. C. Landon
Flagdown. M. Muller
Flagellator. Carter Brown

Flags at Doney. H. Greene
Flags of Nada. Michael Barrett
Flail and the Fish. F. Gerard
Flair for Affairs. H. Brand
Flame. L. P. Greene
Flame. J. Lutz
Flame. H. Zore
Flame and the Wind. J. Blackburn
Flame Breathers. K. Robeson
Flame Dancer. F. A. Mathews
Flame Eternal and the Maharajah's Son. W. E. Roys
Flame from Persepolis. J. Griffin
Flame in the Air. A. Prior
Flame in the Heather. Agnes Russell
Flame in the Mist. P. Audemars
Flame in the Snow. V. Black
Flame Lily. C. K. MacKinnon
Flame of Evil. D. M. Disney
Flame of Folly. L. Noel
Flame of Murder. M. Neville
Flame of the Forest. A. Broome
Flame of the Khan. M. B. Dix
Flame Too Hot. K. Kramer
Flame Was Fatal. M. Brody
Flamenco and Orange Blossoms. M. Vernon
Flameout. Basil Jackson
Flameout. C. D. Peel
Flames Burn High. G. Usher
Flames of Velvet. M. Dekobra
Flames of Vengeance. M. S. Jones
Flames on the Bosphorus. L. Motta
Flames Over the Castle. D. La Pointe
Flaming Belt. H. H. C. Gibbons
Flaming Crescent. O. Binns
Flaming Falcons. K. Robeson
Flaming Forest. J. O. Curwood
Flaming Frontier. J. Brearley
Flaming Jewel. R. W. Chambers
Flaming Man. M. E. Chaber
Flaming Passions. A. Lamour
Flaming Tree. P. A. Whitney
Flaming Wilderness. R. Cullum
Flamingo. J. Gardner
Flamingo. B. Reiss
Flamingo Lake. J. D. White
Flamingo Road. R. Wilder
Flamstock Mystery. J. S. Fletcher
Flanagan Boy. M. Catto
Flander's Folly. S. Christy
Flanders Spy. A. O. Pollard
Flannelfoot, Phantom Crook. Jack Henry
Flannery. Robert Campbell
Flash. J. Ruegg
Flash Casey, Detective. G. H. Coxe
Flash Casey—Hardboiled Detective. G. H. Coxe
Flash D 13. V. K. Kaledin
Flash—Hold for Murder. P. Whelton
Flash of Green. J. D. MacDonald
Flash of Light. C. Frisbie
Flash of Lightning. J. Adye
Flash of Splendour. A. Stevenson
Flash Point. J. Bruce
Flash Point. M. S. Craig
Flash Point. M. Gilbert
Flash Point. D. Pendleton
Flashback. H. Carmichael
Flashback. R. Dooley
Flashback. Michael Palmer
Flashpoint. H. Blayn
Flashpoint. M. Duke
Flashpoint. H. Janson
Flashpoint. G. La Fountaine
Flashpoint. D. J. Marlowe
Flashpoint. A. A. Randall
Flashpoint for Treason. D. Reid
Flask for the Journey. F. L. Green
Flat Aback. A. L. Long
Flat Beneath. B. Delannoy
Flat No. 4. W. J. Bayfield
Flat 2. E. Wallace
Flat Tyre in Fulham. Josephine Bell
Flats Fixed—Among Other Things. D. Tracy
Flattering Tales. A. E. Hake
Flaunting Moll and other stories. R. A. J. Walling

Flaunting Moon. C. Darby
Flaw. J. Laflin
Flaw. A. Samarakis
Flaw in the Crystal. Godfrey Smith
Flaw in the Sapphire. C. M. Snyder
Flaw in the System. R. B. Dominic
Flawed Blades. P. C. Wren
Flawless. B. Hirschfeld
Flawless Execution. J. Logue
Flaxborough Crab. Colin Watson
Fledgling. D. Lee
Flee from Terror. Martin Brett
Flee from the Past. C. G. Hart
Flee the Night in Anger. D. Keller
Fleeced. Stuart Buchan
Fleet Hall Inheritance. R. Keverne
Fleeting Hour. Rona Randall
Fleetwood Mansions Mystery. M. B. Dix
Flemish Shop. G. Simenon
Flesh. G. Weill
Flesh and Blood. T. H. Cook
Flesh and Blood. J. Foss
Flesh and Blood. B. Palmer
Flesh and Blood. D. Pendleton
Flesh and Fire. G. Arnaud
Flesh and Mr. Rawlie. Morton Cooper
Flesh and the Devil. Elbur Ford
Flesh for Sale. D. Haring
Flesh Game. H. Spencer
Flesh Market. G. Cassidy
Flesh of the Orchid. J. H. Chase
Flesh Peddlers. F. Boyd
Flesh Traders. Morton Cooper
Flesh Was Cold. B. Fischer
Flesh Wounds. D. Pendleton
Fleshwound. F. W. Belland
Fletch. G. Mcdonald
Fletch and the Man Who. G. Mcdonald
Fletch and the Widow Bradley. G. Mcdonald
Fletch Too. G. Mcdonald
Fletch Won. G. Mcdonald
Fletch's Fortune. G. Mcdonald
Fletch's Moxie. G. Mcdonald
Fleur. S. Nichols
Fleur de Lys. J. G. Sarasin
Fleur de Lys Affair. H. Ross
Flex. M. Rubel
Flic Story. R. Borniche
Flick of a Fin. G. Peters
Flickering Death. Robert MacLeod
Flier. M. Spillane
Flies. B. Von Hutten
Flies in the Web. F. Hume
Flies on the Wall. Alex Hamilton
Flight. A. Omre
Flight by Night. D. Keene
Flight 800. D. Fulani
Flight Errant. Laurence Kirk
Flight 409. S. Frazee
Flight from a Dark Equator. N. Lewis
Flight from a Firing Wall. B. Kendrick
Flight from a Throne. M. Richmond
Flight from Barcelona. N. Vida
Flight from Bucharest. R. T. Stevens
Flight from Eden Key. Dorinne Moore
Flight from Fear. M. Blake
Flight from Fear. H. Janson
Flight from Fear. Ray Owen
Flight from Montego Bay. A. Haig
Flight from Paris. R. MacLeod
Flight from Riversedge. M. K. Simmons
Flight from the Grave. R. J. Hogan
Flight from the Hunter. S. Stander
Flight Hostess. E. Thorne
Flight in Darkness. S. Harvester
Flight Instructor Murders. G. Redder
Flight Into Danger. J. Castle
Flight Into Danger. J. England
Flight Into Darkness. P. Clark
Flight Into Fear. J. Ames
Flight Into Fear. C. Dekker
Flight Into Fear. F. Gerard
Flight Into Fear. D. Kyle
Flight Into Fear. P. Saxon

Flight Into Horror. P. Valdez
Flight Into Love. J. Blackmore
Flight Into Peril. R. Roleine
Flight Into Peril. D. Rutherford
Flight Into Terror. D. Keene
Flight Into Terror. L. White
Flight 902 Is Down! F. Fishman
Flight of a Dragon. L. K. Bobker
Flight of a Fallen Angel. D. Winston
Flight of a Witch. Ellis Peters
Flight of an Angel. V. Chute
Flight of an Angel. J. F. W. Hannay
Flight of Chariots. J. Cleary
Flight of Dutchmen. N. Tranter
Flight of Faviel. R. E. Vernede
Flight of Hawks. M. Eden
Flight of Lies. Gavin Scott
Flight of Lord Rhincrew. G. Villiers-Stuart
Flight of the Archangel. I. Holland
Flight of the Bamboo Saucer. F. Gordon
Flight of the Bat. Donald Gordon
Flight of the Cormorants. R. W. Howe
Flight of the Duchess, and other stories. B. Reynolds
Flight of the Falcon. D. Du Maurier
Flight of the Intruder. S. Coonts
Flight of the Phoenix. J. Rosenberger
Flight of the Phoenix. E. Trevor
Flight of the Raven. R. Charles
Flight of the Raven. Rebecca York
Flight of the Shadows. N. Herbert
Flight of the Stiff. Michael Brett
Flight of the Wild Dog. Dale Brown
Flight One. C. Carpenter
Flight Signals. R. Tralins
Flight 685 Is Overdue. Edward Moore
Flight to a Finish. Valentine
Flight to Afar. W. L. Andersch
Flight to Darkness. G. Brewer
Flight to Fear. P. Conway
Flight to Takla-Ma. T. Thomey
Flight to the Sea. J. Pattinson
Flight to the Villa Mistra. V. Maxwell
Flight to Yesterday. V. Johnston
Flight Without Wings. M. Latham
Flighty Phyllis. R. A. Freeman
Flip of the Coin. C. Dekker
Flip-Side. B. Copper
Flip Side. T. N. Robb
Flip Side of Life. J. E. Martin
Flippant Fiction. P. O'Farrell
Flirting with Disaster. C. Jerina
Flittermouse. D. Kartun
Flittermouse. J. G. Sarasin
Floater. B. Cassiday
Floater. J. Koenig
Floating Admiral. Detection Club
Floating Care, and other stories. Margery Lawrence
Floating Dutchman. N. Bentley
Floating Fancies Among the Weird and Occult. C. H. Holmes
Floating Game. J. Garforth
Floating Head. Old Sleuth
Floating on an Ice Cloud. N. Gulliver
Floating Peril. E. P. Oppenheim
Floating Prison. G. Leroux
Flock of Ships. B. Callison
Flockmasters. N. Tranter
Flood. Lionel Black
Flood. J. Creasey
Flood. I. Rankin
Flood. A. H. Vachss
Flood Light. C. Massie
Flood of Fate. W. C. Tuttle
Flood Tide. Ian Stuart
Floodgate. Alistair MacLean
Flood's First Case. M. O'Driscoll
Floods of Fear. J. Hawkins
Floodtide 2. Roger Mark
Floodwater. P. Meredith
Floosie for Hire. Rex Richards
Floosie Goes Astray. W. Standish
Floosie on the Run. S. Vincent
Floosie on the Spot. W. Standish
Floosie Out of Focus. Carter Brown

Floosie Passes By. W. Standish
Floosie Takes a Fall. W. Standish
Floozie Takes Lawman. B. Sarto
Floral Tribute. C. E. Vulliamy
Florence. E. A. Dupuy
Florentine Dagger. B. Hecht
Florentine Finish. C. Hirschberg
Florentine Madonna. J. Griffin
Florentine Ring. Jackson Stanley
Florentine Win. H. La Barre
Florian Signet. H. Esmond
Florian Slappey. O. R. Cohen
Florian Slappey Goes Abroad. O. R. Cohen
Florida Burn. S. Grave
Florida Firefight. C. Ramm
Florida Is Closed Today. J. D. Hunter
Flotsam of the Line. O. Binns
Flow My Tears, the Policeman Said. P. K. Dick
Flower and Weed. M. E. Braddon
Flower-Bed Murder. C. P. Cleary
Flower-Covered Corpse. M. Avallone
Flower Forbidden. A. M. Williamson
Flower Gang. G. Radcliffe
Flower in the Desert. M. Richmond
Flower of Crime. A. Belot
Flower of Desire. H. Janson
Flower of Desire. A. Wood
Flower of Evil. D. Lyons
Flower of the Forest. O. Bradbury
Flower of the Forest. C. Gibbon
Flower of the Gods. E. Phillpotts
Flower of the Gorse. L. Tracy
Flower of the Judas. C. Randell
Flower o' the Orange, and other stories. A. Castle
Flower o' the Peach. W. A. MacKenzie
Flowered Box. T. J. Green
Flowering. A. S. Turnbull
Flowering Death. A. MacVicar
Flowers by Request. L. Holton
Flowers for a Dead Witch. M. Butterworth
Flowers for Lillian. Anna Gilbert
Flowers for Teacher. Margaret Archer
Flowers for the Executioner. B. Tebeira
Flowers from Berlin. N. Hynd
Flowers in the Attic. V. C. Andrews
Flowers of Darkness. E. Barr
Flowers of Evil. John Sherwood
Flowers of the Forest. J. Hone
Flowers of Vengeance. M. A. Willis
Fluke. J. Herbert
Flush As May. P. M. Hubbard
Flutter in Kings. D. Whitelaw
Fluttered Dovecote. G. M. Fenn
Flux. R. Goulart
Fly Away Death. P. Malloch
Fly Away Home. M. Percy
Fly Away, Jill. M. Byrd
Fly Away, Paul. V. Canning
Fly by Night. M. Afford
Fly by Night. C. M. Wallace
Fly-by-Nights. Charles Ross
Fly Country. Anthony Lang
Fly from Evil. F. Free
Fly in the Cobweb. F. Parrish
Fly Leaves. Mrs. H. Dudeney
Fly Me a Killer. F. Lester
Fly on the Wall. T. Hillerman
Fly Paper. M. A. Collins
Fly South to Danger. S. Clausse
Flyaway. D. Bagley
Flyaway Ned. Old Sleuth
Flyaway Peter. D. Rhodes
Flying Argosy. A. J. Reeds
Flying Armada. D. T. Lindsay
Flying Armada. J. Tregellis
Flying Arrow. M. Mizzen
Flying Beast. W. S. Masterman
Flying Beetle. G. E. Rochester
Flying Blind. Alice Campbell
Flying Blood. T. Burtis
Flying Camel. A. Aricha
Flying Chinaman. H. H. Fein
Flying Club Murder. W. Stanley
Flying Clues. C. J. Dutton

F

Flying Cowboys. G. E. Rochester
Flying Cross. J. D. Hunter
Flying Crusader. D. T. Lindsay
Flying Dagger Murder. J. Cowdroy
Flying Death. S. H. Adams
Flying Death. E. Balmer
Flying Doctor Disappears. K. Miller
Flying Dutchman. M. Arlen
Flying Dutchman. W. C. Russell
Flying Elbows. E. Lockridge
Flying Eye. B. McKnight
Flying Fifty-Five. E. Wallace
Flying Finish. D. Francis
Flying Firs. A. M. Westwood
Flying Girl. R. Marsh
Flying Goblin. K. Robeson
Flying Headhunter. T. Wallace
Flying Hooligans. Martin Kent
Flying Horse. S. Harvester
Flying Horseman. J. H. Robinson
Flying Kidnappers. Martin Kent
Flying Palatine, and other stories. J. G. Sarasin
Flying Peter. P. Trent
Flying Porcupine. R. Haligon
Flying Red Horse. F. Crane
Flying Saucer. B. Newman
Flying Saucer Gambit. L. Maddock
Flying Shots. W. Hutchison
Flying Spy. G. E. Rochester
Flying Squad. E. Wallace
Flying Squad Tragedy. W. J. Bayfield
Flying Terror. Ian Anderson
Flying Terror. G. E. Hopcroft
Flying Time. A. Lovell
Flying to Nowhere. J. Fuller
Flying Too High. K. Greenwood
Flying Visitor. A. Kennington
Flying with the Mounties. J. Cahill
Flynn. G. Mcdonald
Flynn, A.B. E. L. Long
Flynn of the "Martagon". E. L. Long
Flynn's Inn. G. Mcdonald
Flynn's Sampler. E. L. Long
Flypaper War. R. Starnes
Flywheel, Shyster, and Flywheel. Anonymous
Foam on the River. Sheila Ross
Focus on Murder. Dale Clark
Focus on Murder. G. H. Coxe
Foe-Farrell. A. T. Quiller-Couch
Foe in the Family. N. Cay
Foe in the Shadow. C. E. Pearce
Foe of Barnabas Collins. Marilyn Ross
Foe to Sleep. E. Cannon
Foes of Justice. H. Hill
Fog. Elizabeth Ford
Fog. J. Herbert
Fog. J. Remenham
Fog. V. Williams
Fog Comes. Mary Collins
Fog for a Killer. B. Graeme
Fog Hides the Fury. P. Minton
Fog Is a Shroud. M. Malmar
Fog Island. D. Osborne
Fog Island. Marilyn Ross
Fog Island Secret. Marilyn Ross
Fog Maiden. J. Toombs
Fog of Doubt. C. Brand
Fog Off Weymouth. H. Clandon
Fog on the Mountain. F. De Laguna
Fog on the Mountain. Tim Kelly
Fog Over Fundy. L. A. Cunningham
Fog Princess. F. Warden
Fog Sinister. M. Lovell
Fogarty and Co. J. Flaherty
Fogbound. Clarissa Ross
Foggerty's Fairy and other tales. W. S. Gilbert
Foggy, Foggy Death. R. Lockridge
Foggy, Foggy Dew. C. Blackstock
Foggy Foggy Dew. A. Dean
Foggy, Foggy Dew. Joel Lane
Foggy Night at Offord. H. Wood
Foghorn. G. Atherton
Foiled. Anonymous
Foiled. T. W. Speight

Foiled Again! B. J. Burtin
Foiled by an Innocent Mind. F. Carmichael
Foiling a Counterfeiter. E. C. Derby
Folded Paper Mystery. H. Footner
Folio Forty-One. Michael Sinclair
Folio on Florence White. W. Oursler
Folk Afield. E. Phillpotts
Follow a Dame. D. Haring
Follow a Shadow. G. Greenaway
Follow a Shadow. J. Marshall
Follow a Shadow. W. Reyburn
Follow, As the Night. P. McGerr
Follow Inspector Foster. Anonymous
Follow McLean. G. Goodchild
Follow Me. H. Reilly
Follow Me Down. S. Foote
Follow My Leader. G. Greenaway
Follow That Blonde. Joan Smith
Follow That Hearse! J. Gonzales
Follow the Blue Car. R. A. J. Walling
Follow the Lady. B. Gray
Follow the Leader. L. DuBreuil
Follow the Leader. J. Logue
Follow the Little Pictures. Alan Graham
Follow the Saint. L. Charteris
Follow the Sharks. W. G. Tapply
Follow the Toff. J. Creasey
Follow This Fair Corpse. L. D. Smith
Follow Your Heart. A. Maybury
Followed Man. T. Williams
Follower. H. Bromell
Follower. S. Gallagher
Follower. P. Quentin
Following a Chance Clew. Nicholas Carter
Following Ann. K. R. G. Browne
Following Feet. E. C. Vivian
Following Footsteps. J. J. Farjeon
Folly. D. Anne
Folly Hall. Lynna Cooper
Folly Morrison. F. Barrett
Folly of Fear. K. C. Groom
Folly of the Wise. S. Paternoster
Folly's Gold. L. Scott
Fond Fancy, and other stories. Marjorie Bowen
Fontego's Folly. A. Garve
Fontenay, the Swordsman. F. Du Boisgobey
Foo Dog. T. Wells
Food for Felony. B. Cobb
Food for Fishes. R. Wills
Fool and His Money. E. Colles
Fool Beloved. J. Farnol
Fool Errant. P. Wentworth
Fool for a Client. Roy Lewis
Fool for Murder. M. Babson
Fool from Down Under. R. Wilkes-Hunter
Fool Killer. H. Eustis
Fool of Fortune. B. Schwarz
Fool of Nature. J. Hawthorne
Fool of the "Yard." T. A. Plummer
Fool the Toff. J. Creasey
Fool with Women. F. Whishaw
Fooled by a Woman. E. Kennard
Foolish Cargo. N. Karta
Foolish Margaret. T. W. Speight
Foolish Virgin. N. Karta
Foolish Virgin Returns. N. Karta
Foolish Virgin Says No! N. Karta
Foolproof. P. Daniels
Foolproof Murder. Walter Blake
Fool's Apple. S. Cardiff
Fool's Bet. M. K. Douglas
Fool's Blooding. P. Pike
Fools Die on Friday. A. A. Fair
Fool's Fair. C. Campbell
Fool's Flight. W. B. Murphy
Fool's Gamble. S. Gibbons
Fool's Gold. D. Hitchens
Fool's Gold. W. B. Murphy
Fools' Gold. S. H. Page
Fool's Gold. Ted Wood
Fools in Town Are on Our Side. Ross Thomas
Fool's Mate. Ritchie Perry
Fool's Mercy. H. Allen
Fools' Parade. D. Grubb

Fool's Proof. A. S. Carter
Fool's Run. J. Camp
Fools Walk In. B. Fischer
Foot in the Grave. E. Ferrars
Foot in the Grave. Bruce Marshall
Football Crooks. Hedley Scott
Football Detective. Maxwell Scott
Football Detective. E. Yare
Football for the Brigadier, and other stories. R. Croft-Cooke
Football Pool Murders. G. Verner
Football Pools Mystery. W. D. Maydwell
Football Racket. W. D. Maydwell
Football Racketeers. F. W. Gumley
Football Spy. J. Hunter
Footbridge to Death. K. M. Knight
Footfall in the Mist. V. Black
Foothills of Fear. J. Creasey
Footlight Glare. A. Askew
Footlights. A. Applin
Footlights. M. McGrath
Footlight's Call. G. Goodchild
Footnote to Murder. L. A. Taylor
Footpath. L. Meynell
Footpath Murder. M. Bringle
Footprints. K. Bradford
Footprints. K. C. Strahan
Footprints in the Sand. W. J. Elliott
Footprints in the Sand. W. Richmond
Footprints in the Snow. Dora Russell
Footprints of Death. N. MacKenzie
Footprints of Satan. N. Berrow
Footprints on the Ceiling. C. Rawson
Footsteps. T. Du Bois
Footsteps at the Lock. R. A. Knox
Footsteps Behind Her. M. A. Wilson
Footsteps Behind Me. Anthony Gilbert
Footsteps Behind Them. S. Truss
Footsteps in the Air. S. Wells
Footsteps in the Blood. Jennie Melville
Footsteps in the Dark. G. Heyer
Footsteps in the Dark. L. Mearson
Footsteps in the Fog. P. Bennetts
Footsteps in the Night. C. Fraser-Simson
Footsteps in the Night. D. Hitchens
Footsteps in the Park. M. Joseph
Footsteps of Death. V. Gunn
Footsteps of the Cat. L. A. Olmsted
Footsteps on the Stairs. L. Ford
Footsteps on the Stairs. J. Potts
Footsteps That Follow. M. Farnsworth
Footsteps That Stopped. A. Fielding
Footwork. I. McMahan
For a Girl Called Isaiah. J. Shelynn
For a Madman's Millions. Nicholas Carter
For a Noble Cause. P. Boulle
For a Pawned Crown. Nicholas Carter
For a Woman's Honour. Christopher Wilson
For a Young Queen's Bright Eyes. R. H. Savage
For Better or Worse. C. H. Bullivant
For Cash Only. J. Payn
For Chaps and Chits. Mackenzie Lee
For Conduct Unbefitting. D. Whitelaw
For Crying Out Shroud. O. Blakeston
For Dying You Always Have Time. S. M. Singer
For England. M. Gerard
For Ever Beloved. M. Richmond
For Ever You'll Be Mine. K. Lindsay
For Fear of Little Men. J. Blackburn
For France. M. Gerard
For Gain Not Glory. J. W. McGaw
For Godmother and Country. R. T. Larkin
For Goodness' Sake. C. Wells
For Greed of Gold. Anonymous
For Her C-h-e-ild's Sake. P. Loomis
For Her Dear Sake. M. C. Hay
For Her Life. R. H. Savage
For Her Sister's Sake. M. E. Cooke
For Her to See. J. Shearing
For Himself Alone. T. W. Speight
For His Brother's Crime. C. E. Blaney
For His Brother's Crime. L. Price
For His Friend's Honor. S. Norris
For Honour and Life. W. Westall

For Honour or Death. D. Donovan
For Information Received. E. Wallace
For Jacques' Sake. J. Claretie
For Kicks. D. Francis
For Lack of Gold. C. Gibbon
For Liberty. H. Nisbet
For Life. S. Rudd
For Life and After. G. R. Sims
For Life and Love. R. H. Savage
For Love and Duty. E. Garth-Thornton
For Love and Honour. F. Barrett
For Love of a Bedouin Maid. Le Voleur
For Love of Audrey Rose. F. De Felitta
For Love of Her. G. Boothby
For Love of Imabelle. C. Himes
For Love or Crown. A. W. Marchmont
For Love or Money. M. Leighton
For Love or Money. M. J. Rodgers
For Maimie's Sake. G. Allen
For Murder I Charge More. F. McAuliffe
For Murder Will Speak. J. J. Connington
For Nina's Sake. N. Lazenby
For Old Crime's Sake. D. Ames
For One Season Only. R. Jocelyn
For Pete's Sake. B. Street
For Pete's Sake! G. Usher
For Reasons of State. A. Beevor
For Reasons Unknown. G. Goodchild
For Richer, for Poorer, Til Death. P. McGerr
For Richer for Richer. Dulcie Gray
For Sale—Murder. W. Levinrew
For Sale—with Corpse. J. M. Gregson
For So Little. Helen Davis
For Special Services. J. Gardner
For the Asking. H. R. Daniels
For the Cause. S. J. Weyman
For the Defence: Dr. Thorndyke. R. A. Freeman
For the Defense. B. L. Farjeon
For the Defense. W. Harrington
For the Defense. F. Hume
For the Defense. J. Reach
For the Eyes of the President Only. P. Salinger
For the Good of the State. Anthony Price
For the Hangman. J. S. Strange
For the Love of Mike. H. F. Maltby
For the Love of Murder. M. Scherf
For the President's Eyes Only. R. Sale
For the Queen. E. P. Oppenheim
For the Sake of Revenge. Nicholas Carter
For the Sake of the Family. M. Crommelin
For the Silverfish. R. Thurston
For Them That Trespass. E. Raymond
For Those in Peril. M. Richmond
For Those Were Stirring Times. J. S. Fletcher
For Us the Living. H. Chevalier
For Valour. F. R. Adams
For Value Received. T. Cobb
For Very Life. Hamilton Marshall
For Woman's Love. E. Southworth
For You, I Commit Murder. D. R. Sperduti
For Your Eyes Only. I. Fleming
For Your Eyes Only: Read and Destroy. L. Honig
Forbidden. A. Mayburry
Forbidden Area. P. Frank
Forbidden by Law. B. Cottingham
Forbidden by Law. A. Griffiths
Forbidden Cargo. S. Box
Forbidden Castle. W. E. D. Ross
Forbidden Cave. A. Furness
Forbidden Door. Herman Landon
Forbidden Door. E. C. Vivian
Forbidden Frontiers. L. Noel
Forbidden Frontiers. S. Maddock
Forbidden Garden. U. Curtiss
Forbidden Hour. M. Crossley
Forbidden Island. R. C. Payes
Forbidden Land. D. Cushman
Forbidden Love. C. May
Forbidden Mansion. R. N. Winstead
Forbidden Places. M. Napier
Forbidden Road. V. Canning
Forbidden Road. J. K. Morton
Forbidden Room. Jaclen Steele
Forbidden Room. R. Thorndike
Forbidden Shrine. C. Dawe
Forbidden Territory. "Capstan"
Forbidden Territory. D. Wheatley
Forbidden Tower. E. Cook
Forbidden Valley. L. P. Greene
Forbidden Valley. W. B. Mowery
Forbidden Wine. F. A. Kummer
Forbidden Word. W. LeQueux
Forbidden Years. Wadsworth Camp
Forbidden Zone. I. Slater
Force. A. Radnor
Force Nine. Robin Moore
Force of Innocence. J. Weatherhead
Force of Nature. S. Solomita
Force Play. Anthony Stuart
Force Red. M. R. Bass
Force 10 from Navarone. Alistair MacLean
Forced Apart. M. Redwing
Forced Entry. S. Solomita
Forced Landing. T. H. Block
Forced Landing. G. Goodchild
Fordham's Feud. B. Mitford
Ford's Folly, Ltd. A. Griffiths
Forecast—Murder. A. Tack
Foreign Affair. Graeme Douglas
Foreign Affairs. H. Fleetwood
Foreign Bodies. R. Petrie
Foreign Bodies. S. Truss
Foreign Body. Moira Field
Foreign Exchange. J. Sangster
Foreign Harry Complot. G. Hertz
Foreign Matter. C. Byron
Foreign Object. R. Base
Foreign Secretary Who Vanished. H. G. Hutchinson
Foreign Squad. G. Kent
Forest. J. Wainwright
Forest Affair. J. N. Chance
Forest and the Damned. R. Severn
Forest Exile. O. Binns
Forest Fire. T. Thurston
Forest Gold. R. Whitley
Forest Hills. R. McDowell
Forest Inn. H. L. V. Fletcher
Forest Mystery. N. Burnaby
Forest of Death. Jon Barton
Forest of Eyes. V. Canning
Forest of Fear. A. G. Bennett
Forest of Fear. A. Rundle
Forest of Fortune. W. W. Sayer
Forest Officer. F. E. Penny
Forest Ranger. B. Bolt
Forests of the Night. Elliott Arnold
Forests of the Night. J. Cleary
Forests of the Night. I. R. G. Hart
Forests of the Night. Margaret Moore
Foretelling. C. Crane
Forever Beat. J. Cline
Forever Evil. H. Whittington
Forever Forbidden. Carter Brown
Forever Francy. H. Zore
Forever Is Today. Raymond Mason
Forever Love. Marie Greene
Forever McLean. G. Goodchild
Forever Timeless. D. Rochester
Forever Wilt Thou Die. B. N. Byfield
Forfeit. R. Cullum
Forfeit. D. Francis
Forge and Furnace. F. Warden
Forged Check. F. Gardner
Forged Evidence. A. O. Pollard
Forged Note. H. M. Jones
Forged Note. O. Micheaux
Forged Will. Emerson Bennett
Forger. E. Wallace
Forgers and Confidence Men. G. S. McWatters
Forger's Wife. J. Lane
Forget-Me-Not. J. Shearing
Forget My Fate. R. S. Wallis
Forget What You Saw. J. Ashford
Forging the Blades. B. Mitford
Forging the Links. J. K. Stafford
Forgive Me. Lovely Lady. N. Easton
Forgive the Executioner. A. Lane
Forgive Them Their Trespasses. K. Lorraine
Forgiven Not Forgotten. Anonymous
Forgotten Fleet Mystery. G. Coffin
Forgotten Hills. M. L. Tyrrell
Forgotten Honeymoon. D. Durham
Forgotten Island. A. O. Friel
Forgotten Love. Lynna Cooper
Forgotten Mission. G. Leodas
Forgotten Murders. J. Wainwright
Forgotten of Allah. G. Radcliffe
Forgotten Place. J. Fores
Forgotten Road. S. Harvester
Forgotten Story. Winston Graham
Forgotten Terror. Constance Rutherford
Forked Lightning. M. Durham
Forked Tongue. R. L. De Havilland
Forlorn Hope. E. Yates
Form of Release. G. Petrie
Formula. S. Horler
Formula. G. Sager
Formula. S. Shagan
Formula for Crime. Richard Grant
Formula for Murder. B. S. Ballinger
Formula for Murder. Gordon Kay
Formula for Murder. Adrian Reynolds
Formula for Murder. Granville Wilson
Formula One. Bob Judd
Forsaken. T. Kingsley-Smith
Forsaken. R. Kleiner
Forsaken. D. Ransom
Forsaken Inn. A. K. Green
Forsaking All Others. J. Breslin
Forsythia Finds Murder. R. C. Payes
Fort. J. Hale
Fort Apache, the Bronx. H. Gould
Fort Minster, M.P. E. J. Reed
Fort Terror. Ian Anderson
Fort Terror Murders. V. W. Mason
FORTEC Conspiracy. R. M. Garvin
Fortenberry Rites. M. Ogan
Fortescue Candle. B. Flynn
Fortieth Birthday Party. V. Wolzien
Fortieth Victim. C. Franklin
Fortnight by the Sea. Emma Page
Fortnight of Fear. S. Drew
Fortnightly Club. H. G. Hutchinson
Fortress. David Drake
Fortress. Gabrielle Lord
Fortress at One Dallas Center. Ron Lawrence
Fortress London. Z. Hughes
Fortress of Ashes. A. Pelham
Fortress of Solitude. K. Robeson
Fortress of the Maquis. Stagg Green
Fortress of Yadasara. C. Lys
Fort's Law. J. L. Hensley
Fortunate Island. E. S. Russell
Fortunate Miss East. L. Meynell
Fortunate Mistress. D. Defoe
Fortunate Prisoner. M. Pemberton
Fortunate Wayfarer. E. P. Oppenheim
Fortune. M. Korda
Fortune A-Begging. T. Gallon
Fortune Cheats. N. Wray
Fortune Favors Fools. R. Arnold
Fortune for a Falcon. C. Darby
Fortune for Four. D. H. Barber
Fortune for the Taking. C. Dixon
Fortune Hunters. Joan Aiken
Fortune Hunters and others. C. N. Williamson
Fortune in Death. L. St. Clair
Fortune in Peril. R. M. Wells
Fortune in the Sky. J. Pattinson
Fortune Is a Woman. Winston Graham
Fortune Must Follow. D. G. Waring
Fortune of a Spendthrift. R. Andom
Fortune of Bridget Malone. M. B. Lowndes
Fortune Road. J. McCague
Fortune Seeker. E. Southworth
Fortune Spins Auburn. Raoul
Fortune Teller. M. Norman
Fortunes and Misfortunes of the Famous Moll Flanders. D. Defoe
Fortune's Apprentice. L. Cargill
Fortune's Favourites. G. Cornwallis-West

Fortune's Finger. P. Bottome
Fortune's Fingers. A. E. Wickham
Fortune's Fool. J. Hawthorne
Fortune's Fool. F. E. Wynne
Fortunes of Captain Blood. R. Sabatini
Fortunes of Conrad. S. Cobb
Fortunes of Fifi. M. E. Seawall
Fortunes of Flynn. E. L. Long
Fortunes of Hugo. D. MacKail
Fortune's Sport. A. M. Williamson
Fortune's Tangled Skein. J. H. Walworth
Fortune's Wheel. M. Gerard
Fortune's Wheel. George Long
Forty Days. O. Wynd
48 Hours. H. Janson
Forty-Eight Short Stories. E. Wallace
Forty-First Passenger. K. Hopkins
Forty-First Thief. E. A. Pollitz
'44 Vintage. A. Price
Forty-Minute War. J. Morris
Forty-Nine Chances. J. Rhys-Williams
49 Days of Death. B. S. Ballinger
Forty Pieces of Alloy. P. Carlon
Forty Thieves. R. Wallace
Forty-Three Candles for Mr. Beamish. P. Barrington
42 Days for Murder. R. Torrey
Forty Whacks. G. Homes
Forty Years On. J. Owen
Forward from Youth. L. A. Pavey
Forza Trap. K. Davis
Foss River Ranch. R. Cullum
Foucault's Pendulum. U. Eco
Foughilotra. W. R. MacDermott
Fought to the Finish. T. Worthing
Foul Deeds. Susan James
Foul Deeds Will Arise. Mark Cross
Foul Deeds Will Rise. R. Harrison
Foul Hawsers. E. L. Long
Foul Matter. J. Aiken
Foul Play. J. Potter
Foul Play. C. Reade
Foul Play. J. C. Rogers
Foul Play. T. Worthing
Foul Play at Brown's. R. W. Frampton
Foul Play at Lentwood. H. Leyford
Foul Play Suspected. John Beynon
Foul Play Suspected. M. Halliday
Foul Shot. D. Hornig
Foul Up. Ritchie Perry
Foul Weather. G. F. Gibbs
Found—Adventure. R. Hardinge
Found and Fettered. D. Donovan
Found Dead. C. Brooks
Found Dead. J. Payn
Found Dead. Hero Strong
Found Drowned. M. Burton
Found Drowned. E. Phillpotts
Found Floating. F. W. Crofts
Found Guilty. F. Barrett
Found in Possession. P. Urquhart
Found in the Jungle. Nicholas Carter
Found in the Street. P. Highsmith
Found Money. G. A. Birmingham
Found on the Beach. Nicholas Carter
Found on the Road. Gret Lane
Found Out. H. B. Mathers
Found Shot. H. Willett
Founder Member. J. Gardner
Foundered Galleon. W. Chesney
Foundling. P. Trent
Fountain at Marlieux. C. Aveline
Fountain of Beauty. L. T. Meade
Fountain of Death. H. L. Nelson
Fountain of Green Fire. P. Brebner
Fountain of Youth. R. Standish
Four Against the Mob. O. Fraley
Four Against the World. Hedley Scott
Four-and-Twenty Blackbirds. H. V. O'Brien
Four and Twenty Virgins. J. McClure
Four Answers. J. Cobnor
Four Armourers. F. Beeding
Four at Bay. Mark Cross
Four Blind Mice. C. C. Lowis
Four Boys, a Girl and a Gun. W. Wiener

Four Boys and a Gun. W. Weiner
Four Brains. W. J. Makin
Four Callers in Razor Street. S. Fowler
Four Came Back. M. Caidin
Four Chambered Villain. G. Madderom
Four Conditions. G. W. Campbell
Four Cornered Story. F. A. Chittenden
Four Corners. C. S. Raymond
Four Corners of the World. A. E. W. Mason
Four Corpses in a Million. J. Robb
Four Dames Named Sin. M. Reed
Four Days. J. Buell
Four Days. Harold King
Four Days in a Lifetime. G. Simenon
Four Days in June. Elizabeth Ford
Four Days to the Fireworks. P. Purser
Four Days' Wonder. A. A. Milne
Four Dead Men. S. Simpson
Four Dead Mice. T. B. Black
Four Defences. J. J. Connington
Four Doors to Death. J. Courage
Four Extra Daughters. J. Maconechy
Four Faces. W. LeQueux
Four Faces of Siva. R. J. Casey
Four False Weapons. J. D. Carr
Four Fautless Felons. G. K. Chesterton
Four Feet in the Grave. A. R. Long
4:50 from Paddington. A. Christie
Four Find Danger. M. Halliday
Four-Fingered Glove. Nicholas Carter
Four Fingers. F. M. White
Four for the Money. D. J. Marlowe
Four Frightened Sisters. W. Spence
Four Frightened Women. G. H. Coxe
Four Get Going. Mark Cross
Four Green Fish. E. Jepson
Four Guns to Carson City. Dan Morgan
Four Hoodoo Charms. Nicholas Carter
Four Horses. C. Pincher
Four Hours. M. Brenner
Four Hours to Fear. F. Lockridge
Four Hundred. S. Sheppard
Four Hundred. B. Vane
400 Brattle Street. G. Wolk
Four in a Fairlead. E. L. Long
Four-in-Hand. T. A. Fitzgerald
Four in Hand. J. Middlemass
Four-in-Hand. J. B. Priestley
Four Jealous Men. M. Frazer
Four Johns. E. Queen
Four Just Men. E. Wallace
Four Kings in the Street of Gold. F. H. Rose
Four Knocks on the Door. J. P. Seabrooke
Four Last Things. T. Hallinan
Four Letter Crowd. P. Leslie
Four Liars. E. Murray
Four Lost Ladies. S. Palmer
Four Lost Ships. E. Spencer
Four Mad Monarchs. R. E. Cooke
Four Make Holiday. Mark Cross
Four Marked for Murder. R. A. Braun
Four Marys. Rinalda Roberts
Four Men and a Prayer. D. Garth
Four Men Called John. E. Queen
Four Million. O. Henry
Four Million a Year. C. Collins
Four More Sherlock Holmes Plays. Michael Hardwick
Four Motives for Murder. B. Hope
Four O'Clock. M. Borden
Four of a Kind. Dan Morgan
Four of Hearts. E. Queen
Four of Us Meet Again. L. Barbee
Four on the Floor. R. McInerny
4 P.M. Express. F. Hume
Four Past Four. Roy Vickers
Four Philanthropists. E. Jepson
Four Pitiful People. A. Wood
Four Plays for Course Actors. M. Green
Four Plus One. J. H. Hurst
Four-Ply Yarn. M. Burton
Four Pools Mystery. Anonymous
Four-Pools Mystery. J. Webster
Four Red Nightcaps. W. Chesney

Four Roads to Death. B. Appel
Four Sherlock Holmes Plays. Michael Hardwick
Four Square Jane. E. Wallace
Four Stars for Danger. Jonathan Burke
Four Steps to Death. D. Ramsay
Four Stragglers. F. Packard
Four Strange Women. E. R. Punshon
Four Strike Home. Mark Cross
Four-Time Loser. D. Lynch
Four Times a Widower. A. Bliss
Four Tragedies of Memworth. Ernest Hamilton
Four Trails. W. M. Graydon
Four Unfaithful Servants. G. Bellairs
Four Walls. D. Burnet
Four Way Proof. R. A. Henriquez
Four Winds. H. Adams
Four Winds. A. Atkinson
Four Winds. S. Gluck
Four Winds. R. Pertwee
Four Winds Mystery. Norman Lee
Four Witnesses. M. Reisner
Four Women in the Case. Annie Thomas
Four Women Went. O. Cecil
Fourfingers. L. Brock
Fourflush Island. L. C. Douthwaite
Fourflusher. E. Westward
Foursome. Lionel Black
Foursquare Murder. David Hume
14 Bellchamber Tower. M. Valentine
Fourteen Dilemma. H. Pentecost
Fourteen Points. A. B. Reeve
14 Seconds to Hell. Nick Carter
Fourteen Years After! J. Hunter
14th Agent. D. C. Cooke
Fourteenth Key. C. Wells
Fourteenth Trump. J. Philips
Fourth Agency. J. Fredman
Fourth Angel. R. Hunter
Fourth Arm. J. Brason
Fourth at Junction. J. Barker
Fourth Bomb. J. Rhode
Fourth Challenge. R. H. Hutchinson
Fourth Chamber. G. R. Preedy
Fourth Codex. R. Houston
Fourth Crow. D. W. Smith
Fourth Dagger. L. Allan
Fourth Day of Fear. Berrie Davis
Fourth Deadly Sin. Lawrence Sanders
Fourth Degree. K. S. Daiger
Fourth Dimension Is Death. Samuel Holt
Fourth Down, Death. M. T. Hinkemeyer
Fourth Down to Death. B. Halliday
Fourth Durango. Ross Thomas
Fourth Finger. A. Wynne
Fourth Floor. John Burke
Fourth Funeral. C. L. Leonard
Fourth Gambler. D. Castle
Fourth Generation. W. Besant
Fourth Grave. J. Boland
Fourth Horseman. G. Bocca
Fourth King. H. S. Keeler
Fourth Letter. F. Gruber
Fourth Man. A. H. Brown
Fourth Man. W. McCarthy
Fourth Man. H. Mitchell
Fourth Man. Lou Smith
Fourth Man on the Rope. E. Berckman
Fourth Monkey. R. Parkes
Fourth Murder. D. M. Clew
Fourth of Forever. B. S. Ballinger
Fourth of July War. A. Topol
Fourth Plague. E. Wallace
Fourth Postman. C. Rice
Fourth Protocol. F. Forsyth
Fourth Reich. M. Hale
Fourth Reich. J. Rosenberger
Fourth Reich Death Squad. A. Kilgore
Fourth Road. F. Hird
Fourth Seal. P. Groom
Fourth Shadow. R. Charles
Fourth Shot. L. C. Balling
Fourth Side of the Triangle. E. Queen
Fourth Stage of Gainsborough Brown. Clarissa Watson

Fourth Star. R. Burke
Fourth Theory. W. J. Bayfield
Fourth Victim. P. Barrington
Fourth Wall. A. A. Milne
Fourth Wall. B. Paul
Fourth Widow. Harold Adams
Fowl Murder. R. H. Lindsay
Fowl Play. T. Du Bois
Fowler Formula. H. Dalmas
Fowlhaven Werewolf. V. Andrews
Fox. B. Pascoe
Fox from His Lair. E. Cadell
Fox from His Lair. John Harris
Fox in the Night. Roy Hart
Fox in the Sea. R. Magowan
Fox-Magic Murders. R. Van Gulik
Fox of Maulen. H. H. Kirst
Fox on the Run. Charles Bennett
Fox Potential. K. Hagenbach
Fox Prowls. V. Williams
Fox Trap. R. A. Smith
Fox Valley Murders. J. H. Vance
Foxbat. P. Cave
Foxbat Spiral. M. Karman
Foxcatcher. W. Hallahan
Foxes' Moon. Michel Russell
Foxfire Cove. K. Ostrander
Foxglove Country. Linden Howard
Foxglove Manor. R. Buchanan
Foxglove Summer. N. Grey
Foxhole. K. Blake
Foxhole. M. Urquhart
Foxhole in Cairo. L. O. Mosley
Foxhunt. B. Denham
Fracas in the Foothills. Elliot Paul
Fractured Silence. F. Cowen
Fragile Empires. J. Crown
Fragment of Fear. J. Bingham
Fragment of Glass. F. L. Green
Fragrant Death. C. Blake
Frail Ghost. M. Maurice
Frail on North Circular. M. Urquhart
Frail's a Phoney. N. Perrelli
Frails Can Be So Tough. H. Janson
Frailties. N. Geyer
Frame. J. Harvey
Frame and Fortune. H. Janson
Frame for Murder. K. Mechem
Frame for Murder. R. Simons
Frame Is Beautiful. Carter Brown
Frame on the Front Page. M. Brody
Frame the Baron. Anthony Morton
Frame-Up. J. G. Brandon
Frame-Up. C. Brooks
Frame-Up. A. Garve
Frame-Up. Neill Graham
Frame-Up. Stephan Gregory
Frame Up. Johnny Mack
Frame-Up. D. Whitelaw
Framed. E. Ellison
Framed. H. Janson
Framed Evidence. J. Cowdroy
Framed for Hanging. G. Cullingford
Framed in Blood. B. Halliday
Framed in Guilt. D. Keene
Framed in Guilt. J. Slate
Framework. S. M. Krauzer
Framework of Fate. Nicholas Carter
Framing of Carol Woan. B. Cobb
Frampton—of "the Yard"! T. A. Plummer
Frampton Sees Red. T. A. Plummer
France Security. S. Gandolfi
Frances. N. Baroni
Frances. F. F. Kelly
Frances Hildyard. H. Wood
Francesca. S. Marlowe
Francesca. L. Snow
Franchise Affair. J. Tey
Francine. S. Shelley
Francis Quarles Investigates. J. Symons
Francois the Valet. G. W. Appleton
Frangipangi. N. Easton
Frank James in St. Louis. W. B. Lawson
Frank Redland, Recruit. Mrs. C. Kernahan

Frank Rivers. J. H. Ingraham
Frankenstein. D. Campton
Frankenstein. V. Gialanella
Frankenstein. T. J. Kelly
Frankenstein. J. Mattera
Frankenstein. A. Nowlan
Frankenstein. M. W. Shelley
Frankenstein. P. Webling
Frankenstein Factory. E. D. Hoch
Frankenstein Lives Again. D. F. Glut
Frankenstein Meets Dracula. D. F. Glut
Frankenstein's Children. D. Mace
Frankincense and Murder. B. Kendrick
Frankincense Trail. F. J. Kenmore
Franks: Duellist. A. Pratt
Frantic. N. Calef
Franzie. P. Pannier
Fraser Butts In. H. Clevely
Frass. J. Chancellor
Fraternally Yours. H. Von Rhau
Fraternity of the Stone. D. Morrell
Fratricide Is a Gas. L. Gutteridge
Fratricides. M. Edelman
Fraud. Mrs. C. Kernahan
Frauds. M. Hastings
Fraudulent Broad. J. L. Rubel
Fraulein. J. McGovern
Fraulein Is Feline. Carter Brown
Fraulein Lili Marlene. J. W. Burke
Fraulein Spy. Nick Carter
Frazer Acquittal. S. Ransome
Freak. M. Collins
Freak Island Murders. R. Verron
Freak Museum. R. R. Ryan
Freak of Fate. E. F. Spence
Freak of St. Freda's! G. E. Rochester
Freak-Out. M. Arrighi
Freak Racket. W. J. Elliott
Frank Show Murders. Fredric Brown
Freak Show Murders. W. B. Gibson
Freaked Out Stranger. P. Morgan
Freaks of Imagination. J. Steelnib
Freaky Deaky. E. Leonard
Freckled Shark. K. Robeson
Fred Bennett, the Mormon Detective. F. E. Bennett
Fred Danford, the Skillful Detective. H. Rockwood
Fred in Situ. G. Hammond
Fred Travis, A.B. Taffrail
Freddie and the Flappers. G. M. Bowman
Freddie the Flirt. G. M. Bowman
Freddy. L. Barbee
Frederick and Sophia. L. Watkins
Frederick Hazzleden. H. Westbury
Frederick Lonton. D. W. Croft
Frederika and the Convict. L. M. Robertson
Free Agent. P. Murray
Free Agent. F. Wakeman
Free Are the Dead. S. Friedman
Free As Air. E. Kyle
Free Draw. S. Singer
Free Fall. J. Cresswell
Free Fall. J. D. Reed
Free Fall in Crimson. J. D. MacDonald
Free Flight. D. Terman
Free Hand. B. A. Clarke
Free Heart. E. C. Reed
Free-Lance Murder. V. Rodell
Free-Lance Spy. V. Armstrong
Free Lovers. R. W. Kauffman
Free Range Wife. M. Kenyon
Free Ride. J. M. Fox
Freebie and the Bean. P. B. Ross
Freebody Heiress. E. Gordon
Freebooters. N. Tranter
Freebooty. J. Foxx
Freedman. J. Pattinson
Freedom. A. Askew
Freedom for Two. J. Carr
Freedom from Fear. I. Perrot
Freedom Trap. D. Bagley
Freedom Trail to Greystone. L. Bronte
Freefall Factor. N. Geraghty
Freelance Death. Andrew Taylor
Freelance Spy. J. M. Walsh

Freeloaders. E. Lacy
Freemartin. D. K. Cohler
Freemason. J. P. Hart
Freer's Cove. E. Gordon
Freeway. D. Barkley
Freeway to Murder. W. Sproule
Freeze Frame. R. Chudley
Freeze Frame. M. Dorner
Freeze-Frame. A. Hansl
Freeze Frame. R. R. Irvine
Freeze Thy Blood Less Coldly. J. Wainwright
Freezing Peril Strikes. B. Luigi
French Atlantic Affair. E. P. Lehman
French Connection II. Robin Moore
French Deal. W. Hughes
French Decision. D. Osborn
French Doctor. L. Royer
French Doll. V. McConnor
French Entrapment. N. Cort
French Farce. E. Greenwood
French Finish. Robert Ross
French for Floosie. W. Standish
French for Murder. B. Mara
French for Trouble. L. T. Shortell
French Girl. A. Mills
French Hazard. W. Mills
French Inheritance. A. Stevenson
French Key. F. Gruber
French Killing. J. P. Cody
French Kiss. P. Israel
French Kiss. E. V. Lustbader
French Kiss. J. J. Montague
French Master. A. W. Barrett
French Ordinary Murder. R. Harrison
French Powder Mystery. E. Queen
French Quarter Killers. J. Dillman
French Strikes Oil. F. W. Crofts
Frenchman. V. Johnston
Frenchman Must Die. K. Boyle
Frenchman's Blood. M. K. Shuman
Frenchwoman. B. Paul
Frenzied Fiction. S. Leacock
Frenzy. J. O. Causey
Frenzy! L. Della
Frenzy. A. La Bern
Frenzy. Rex Miller
Frenzy in the Flesh. D. Reid
Frenzy in Yellow. C. Dekker
Frenzy of Evil. H. Kane
Frenzy of Merchantmen. B. Callison
Frequent Flier. K. Friedman
Frequent Hearses. E. Crispin
Fresh Air. G. Hughes
Fresh Waters and other stories. R. W. Child
Friarsmead. Laura Smith
Friday Before Bank Holiday. George Davis
Friday for Death. L. Lariar
Friday Harbor Murders. D. Weeks
Friday Is a Killing Day. J. A. Howard
Friday Market. C. Meadows
Friday Run. J. Wood
Friday the Rabbi Slept Late. H. Kemelman
Friday the 13th. J. J. Farjeon
Friday the 13th, Part I. S. Hawke
Friday to Monday. W. Garrett
Friday's Feast. D. Pendleton
Friedrich Harris: Shooting the Hero. P. Purser
Friend. D. Henstell
Friend in Deed. R. Jagoda
Friend in the Police. J. Givens
Friend of Mary Rose. Elizabeth Fenwick
Friend or Foe. R. Cawley
Friendless Millionaire. H. L. Phillips
Friendless Spy. A. Shenton
Friendly Fiends. P. Muller
Friendly Place to Die. M. P. Faur
Friends. T. Hauser
Friends. H. Herlin
Friends. Godfrey Smith
Friends at Court. H. Cecil
Friends in High Places. J. Weitz
Friends of Eddie Coyle. G. V. Higgins
Friends of Lucifer. D. Sinclair
Friends of Valerie Lane. D. Parson

Friends, Russians, and Countrymen. Hampton Howard
Friends Till the End. G. Dank
Friend's Victim. A. Hurlba
Friendship of Veronica. T. Cobb
Friendships, Secrets and Lies. B. H. Deal
Fright. G. Hopley
Fright. J. Reach
Frightened Amazon. A. M. Stein
Frightened Angels. J. Cannan
Frightened Bowerbird. F. Y. McHugh
Frightened Brides. M. Cumberland
Frightened Chameleon. L. Gribble
Frightened Child. D. Lyon
Frightened Dove. P. Hardin
Frightened Eyes. Roland Daniel
Frightened Fiancee. G. H. Coxe
Frightened Fingers. S. Dean
Frightened Fisherman. J. N. Chance
Frightened Girl. M. Crombie
Frightened Heart. J. Ames
Frightened Ladies. B. Benson
Frightened Lady. W. H. Baker
Frightened Lady. E. Wallace
Frightened Man. D. Chambers
Frightened Man. L. Meynell
Frightened Man. G. Verner
Frightened Murderer. N. Rutledge
Frightened One. F. Gamble
Frightened Ones. M. Marlette
Frightened People. J. T. Story
Frightened Pigeon. R. Burke
Frightened Sailor. D. Sharp
Frightened Stiff. K. Roos
Frightened to Death. Hilary Gray
Frightened Village. N. Edwards
Frightened Virgin. N. W. Firth
Frightened Widow. Bernice Carey
Frightened Widow. Colin Robertson
Frightened Wife. M. R. Rinehart
Frightened Wife. M. Tripp
Frighteners. R. Busby
Frighteners. Donald Hamilton
Frighteners. P. Leslie
Frightening Talent. L. Golding
Frightful Sin of Cisco Newman. G. A. Ralston
Frightline. R. Byers
Frigor Mortis. R. McInerny
Frigorific Ghost. H. Van Scofield
Fringe of the Law. C. H. Bullivant
Frisco Blues. G. De Marco
Frisco Boys. J. Hart
Frisco Detective. Anonymous
Frisco Doll. F. Foden
Frisco Hi-Jack. A. Capelli
Frisco Rock. D. Spade
Fritz, the Bound Boy Detective. E. L. Wheeler
Fritz, the German Detective. T. Pastor
Fritz to the Front. E. L. Wheeler
Fritzi. A. Kennington
Friulan Plot. E. Webster
Frivolities. R. Marsh
Frog and the Scorpion. A. E. Maxwell
Frog in the Moonflower. I. Drummond
Frog in the Throat. E. Ferrars
Frog King. F. McConnell
Frog Murders. L. Serrester
Frog Was Yellow. F. Vivian
Frogman Assassination. J. Seward
Frogmouth. William Marshall
Frogs at the Bottom of the Well. K. Edgar
Frogs Don't Grow Feathers. B. L. Jacot
Froler Case. J. L. Jacolliot
Frolic Welcome. F. Streeten
From a Dark Place. L. Charbonneau
From a Dartmoor Cot. W. Crossing
From a High Place. E. Mathis
From a High Tower. T. Newman
From a Prison Cell. Nicholas Carter
From a Surgeon's Diary. C. Ashdown
From A to Z. San Antonio
From All Blindness. H. Gibbs
From Behind the Arras. P. C. De Crespigny
From Clew to Clew. Nicholas Carter

From Clue to Capture. D. Donovan
From Clue to Climax. W. N. Harben
From Clue to Clue. W. M. Graydon
From Cuba with Love. Gordon Davis
From Dance Hall to Opium Den. Griff
From Death to Life. Old Sleuth
From Despair to Triumph. W. G. Forbes
From Director, CIA: Burn Scorpio. M. Roote
From Doon with Death. R. Rendell
From Door to Door. B. Capes
From Dusk Till Dawn. W. Garrett
From Eternity to Here. M. Sellers
From Evil's Pillow. B. Copper
From Exile. J. Payn
From Father to Son. P. Trent
From Hex to Hemlock. E. Harris
From Information Received. D. Donovan
From Information Received. C. F. Gregg
From Information Received. E. Radford
From Lake to Wilderness. W. M. Graydon
From Laughter to Death. J. Sandys
From London Far. M. Innes
From Love's Ashes. F. P. Stratham
From Midnight to Morning. M. Leblanc
From Natural Causes. Josephine Bell
From 9 O'Clock to Jamaica Bay. D. Broun
From Now On. F. Packard
From Out the Vasty Deep. M. B. Lowndes
From Outer Space. H. Clement
From Paris with Love. Lynna Cooper
From Peril to Peril. Nicholas Carter
From Place to Place. I. S. Cobb
From Post to Finish. H. Smart
From Russia, with Love. I. Fleming
From Satan, with Love. V. Coffman
From Scenes Like These. Gordon M. Williams
From Secret Places. M. Lynch
From Shadow to Light. G. Campbell
From Sing Sing to Liberty. H. C. Blaney
From Six to Six. W. B. Foster
From Street to Mansion. F. H. Stauffer
From the Bosom of the Deep. J. E. Muddock
From the Broad Acres. J. S. Fletcher
From the Cliffs of Croaghaun. R. Cromie
From the Front. Anonymous
From the Frontier. F. Boyle
From the Grave to the Cradle. C. Joyce
From the Hand of the Hunter. L. T. Meade
From the House of Bondage. R. Rodd
From the Land of the Wombat. W. S. Walker
From the Memoirs of a Minister of France. S. J. Weyman
From the Peasantry to the Peerage. Anonymous
From the Scourge of the Tongue. B. Marchant
From the Valley of the Missing. Grace M. White
From Thief to Detective. F. Hume
From This Dark Stairway. M. G. Eberhart
From This Day Forth. Laura Smith
From This Death Forward. R. Bloomfield
From Thunder Bay. A. Maling
From Veldt Camp Fires. H. A. Bryden
From Violent Men. D. Curzon
From Whose Bourne. L. Sharp
Front Door Key. J. Brophy
Front for Murder. G. Emery
Front Man. M. Sellar
Front Man. F. Wallace
Front of Brass. F. M. White
Front Page Murder. John Bentley
Front Page Murder. John Powers
Front Page Murder. R. Trevor
Front Page Mystery. G. M. Dean
Frontier. M. Leblanc
Frontier. P. Tabori
Frontier Detective. E. L. Wheeler
Frontier Detective. L. D. Willoughby
Frontier Incident. S. B. Hough
Frontier Mystery. B. Mitford
Frontier Mystery. J. Mowbray
Frontier of Fear. I. R. G. Hart
Frontier of Fear. M. Hartland
Frontiers. B. Ledwidge
Frontiers of Death. J. Turner
Frontiers of Fear. J. Sanders

Frontiers of Violence. C. Leader
Frontiersman. H. Bindloss
Frontiersmen. H. Bindloss
Frost. Andrew Hall
Frost at Christmas. R. Wingfield
Frost on the Moon. C. Darby
Frosted Death. K. Robeson
Frozen Assets. J. Leasor
Frozen Death. Winifred Graham
Frozen Death. A. Weymouth
Frozen Deep. W. Collins
Frozen Fire. H. Hawton
Frozen Flame. M. E. Hanshew
Frozen Franklin. S. Hanlon
Frozen Gold. A. J. Small
Frozen Ground. N. Hoult
Frozen Hearts. G. W. Appleton
Frozen Humor. R. P. Woodward
Frozen Inlet Post. J. B. Hendryx
Frozen Secrets. W. Warnock
Frozen Slippers. A. M. Williamson
Frozen Stare. R. B. Schwartz
Frozen Stiff. R. Chapman
Frozen Trail. A. J. Small
Fruit of Folly. L. Bennet-Thompson
Fruit of Indiscretion. W. Magnay
Fruit of the Poppy. R. Wilder
Fruit of the Tree. G. S. Donisthorpe
Fruits of Deception. Marian Murray
Fruits of Folly. Anonymous
Fu Manchu's Bride. S. Rohmer
Fuehrer Dies. H. Desmond
Fuel-Injected Dreams. J. R. Baker
Fugitive. W. H. Baker
Fugitive. R. Bridges
Fugitive. R. L. Fish
Fugitive. G. Simenon
Fugitive Affair. R. Gatenby
Fugitive City. W. P. Wood
Fugitive Countess. Sarah Wilkinson
Fugitive Eye. C. Jay
Fugitive Feet. R. Burroughs
Fugitive from Fear. T. E. Wilson
Fugitive from Murder. M. V. Heberden
Fugitive Men. R. Goyne
Fugitive Millionaire. A. Carlyle
Fugitive Pigeon. D. E. Westlake
Fugitive Sleuth. H. Footner
Fugitive Three. G. A. McPherson
Fugitives. W. Hackett
Fugitives. Morley Roberts
Fugitives. N. Sligh
Fugitives. Alan Thomas
Fugitives of Pearl Hill. E. A. Young
Fugitive's Road. A. MacVicar
Fugitive's Road. P. Malloch
Fuhrer Seed. G. Weill
Fulfilling of the Law. E. Gwynne
Fulfillment. Elsie Lee
Full Cargo. W. D. Steele
Full Circle. A. Brandon
Full Circle. H. Cecil
Full Cleveland. Les Roberts
Full Contact. R. J. Randisi
Full Coverage. J. M. Ullman
Full Crash Dive. A. R. Bosworth
Full Cry. T. Tone
Full Fare for a Corpse. T. Davis
Full Fathom Five. H. S. Davies
Full Fathom Five. Bart Davis
Full Fathom Five. G. V. Galwey
Full Fury. R. Ormerod
Full Hand! D. Haring
Full House. Frederick Jackson
Full House. Shelley Singer
Full Moon. T. Mundy
Full Moon. W. Spence
Full Moon for Murder. J. M. Spender
Full Stop. G. Mitcham
Full Term. P. Spencer
Full Treatment. R. S. Thorn
Fuller's Earth. C. Wells
Fullerton Case. R. Doubleday
Fully Dressed and in His Right Mind. M. Fessier

Title Index

Fully Ripe. P. H. Irving
Fun and Deadly Games. D. Tracy
Fun City. H. Barron
Fun Fair. H. W. Lee
Fun House. P. Reid
Fun of the Fair. E. Phillpotts
Fun with Dick and Jane. S. Stewart
Funeral for a Commissar. R. Magowan
Funeral for a Physicist. P. Bloxham
Funeral for Five. J. Stagge
Funeral Games. Jessica Mann
Funeral in Berlin. L. Deighton
Funeral in Eden. P. McGuire
Funeral March. F. De Felitta
Funeral March for Siegfried. A. Williamson
Funeral March of a Marionette. Winifred Duke
Funeral March of the Marionettes. F. De Felitta
Funeral of Figaro. Ellis Peters
Funeral Rites. J. Hedges
Funeral Urn. Jane Drummond
Funeral Was in Spain. E. McGirr
Funerals Are Fatal. A. Christie
Funhouse. B. Appel
Funhouse. O. West
Funland. R. Laymon
Funnelweb. R. Braddon
Funnelweb. Charles West
Funniest Killer in Town. Hampton Stone
Funny Bob. Old Sleuth
Funny Bone. J. MacLaren-Ross
Funny, Jonas, You Don't Look Dead. M. McMullen
Funny Money. R. Sapir
Funny Place to Hold a War. John Harris
Fur-Bringers. H. Footner
Fur Raiders. H. H. C. Gibbons
Furioso. V. Lestienne
Furious Old Women. L. Bruce
Furnace for a Foe. C. Rushton
Furnished for Murder. R. Barth
Furnished for Murder. E. Ferrars
Furnished Room. L. Del Rivo
Further Adventures of a Cowboy Detective. C. A. Sirengo
Further Adventures of Batman. Bob Kane
Further Adventures of Captain Kettle. C. J. C. Hyne
Further Adventures of Doctor Syn. R. Thorndike
Further Adventures of Jimmie Dale. F. Packard
Further Adventures of Quincy Adams Sawyer. C. F. Pidgin
Further Adventures of Romney Pringle. C. Ashdown
Further Adventures of Solar Pons. B. Copper
Further Adventures of the Black Pilgrim. G. Stanley
Further Evidence. A. Brock
Further Exploits of Nick Carter, Detective. Nicholas Carter
Further Foolishness. S. Leacock
Further Outlook Unsettled. H. Clevely
Further Secrets of Potsdam. W. LeQueux
Further Side of Fear. H. McCloy
Further Stir of Porridge. Paul Victor
Further Tabloid Tales. L. Heilgers
Furthest Fury. C. Wells
Furtive Flame. H. Janson
Furtive Men. L. Spencer
Fury. J. Farris
Fury. W. Standish
Fury at Fenlon. J. T. Osborne
Fury Bombs. G. Wilson
Fury of Rachel Monnet. P. Abrahams
Fury on Sunday. R. Matheson
Fury on the Pampas. L. Robin
Fury with Legs. G. Lawrence
Fury Within. R. St. Clair
Fuse. T. Keene
Futile Alibi. F. W. Crofts
Future Crime. B. Bova
Future Mrs. Dering. T. Cobb
Fuzz. E. McBain

G.B. W. F. Morris
G.B.H. T. Lewis
GG-2 Deception. C. R. Duggan
G Is for Ghoul. M. Hervey
G Is for Gumshoe. S. Grafton
G Man. C. F. Coe
G Man at the Yard. P. Cheyney
G-Men. H. K. Long
G-Men of the Ranges. A. Ford
G Men on Murder Island. L. Jamieson
G.O.B.: Goods on Board. S. Mayle
G-String Murders. G. R. Lee
Gabbart Destiny. E. L. Long
Gables Mystery. C. E. Perry
Gaboreau. P. Steward
Gaboreau the Terrible. P. Steward
Gabriel. L. Tuttle
Gabriel Comes to 24. R. Braddon
Gabriel Hounds. Mary Stewart
Gabriel Praed's Castle. A. Jones
Gabriel Samara. E. P. Oppenheim
Gabriel Samara, Peacemaker. E. P. Oppenheim
Gabriel Set-Up. P. O'Donnell
Gabriel Sounds for Africa. C. Edwards
Gabriella. A. Maybury
Gabrielle. J. Maas
Gabrielle. K. Norris
Gabrielle de Vergy. Anonymous
Gabrielle's Gamble. C. Dunn
Gabrielle's Way. A. Hunter
Gabriel's Flight. H. Bostrom
Gad. S. Geller
Gadget. N. Freeling
Gaff Lee, Detective. W. T. Stewart
Gage. D. Chako
Gaijin. M. Olden
Gainst Chink and Gunman. T. Lloyd
Gala. William Lewis
Galactic Effectuator. J. Vance
Galactic Sue Blue. R. G. Brown
Galahad Club. M. Tyler
Galahad of the Air. T. Wallace
Galahad of the Creeks. S. Levett-Yeats
Galatea. J. M. Cain
Galaxy Girl and other stories. L. Springfield
Galaxy Jane. R. Goulart
Gale Force. G. Black
Gale Gallyon Takes a Hand. Spike Gordon
Gale of the World. Laurence Kirk
Gale Warning. H. Innes
Gale Warning. D. Yates
Gallagher Plot. Nick Carter
Gallant. C. Blackstone
Gallant Adventuress. Therese Benson
Gallant Affair. Hank Hobson
Gallant Tom. T. P. Prest
Gallegher. R. H. Davis
Galleon Gold. M. Drake
Galleon Rock. G. Volk
Galleon Treasure. A. B. Sherlock
Galleon's Gold. R. W. Sneddon
Galleon's Gold. G. W. Wicking
Galleys of St. John. E. L. Long
Galloping Dick. H. B. M. Watson
Galloping Gold. D. Learmonth
Galloping Gold. W. C. Tuttle
Gallops and Gossips in the Bush of Australia. S. Sidney
Galloway Case. A. Garve
Gallowglass. B. Vine
Gallows Alley. A. Skene
Gallows Are High. H. Spencer
Gallows Are Waiting. J. York
Gallows Bait. S. Truss
Gallows-Bird. L. Storm
Gallows-Child. P. G. Winslow
Gallows' Foot. V. Gielgud
Gallows for a Fool. C. Franklin
Gallows for the Groom. D. B. Olsen
Gallows' Fruit. H. Desmond
Gallows Garden. M. E. Chaber
Gallows Land. B. Pronzini
Gallows Orange. H. Holt
Gallows in My Garden. R. Deming
Gallows in My Garden. Joan Fleming
Gallows Inn. E. P. Thorne
Gallows March. G. Norham
Gallows of Chance. E. P. Oppenheim
Gallows Orchard. C. Spencer
Gallows Parade. F. Tyler
Gallows Rock. T. M. Longstreth
Gallows Seed. P. Troubetzkoy
Gallows Set. W. Rutherford
Gallows Stands in Salem. A. Bretonne
Gallows View. Peter Robinson
Gallows Wait. J. Corbett
Gallows Waits. J. Budd
Gallows Way. D. Winston
Gallowsbird's Song. T. Nielsen
Galmart Affair. S. Westall
Galton Case. R. Macdonald
Galveston Gunman. B. Crider
Gambit. L. Kendall
Gambit. K. Lane
Gambit. R. Stout
Gambit for Mr. Groode. C. Griswold
Gamble My Last Game. R. W. Krepps
Gamble of Life. A. Applin
Gamble with Death. L. Robin
Gamble with Hearts. A. Carlyle
Gambler. C. Burdette
Gambler. A. Gray
Gambler. O. Hogstrand
Gambler. W. Krasner
Gambler of the West. O. Harper
Gambler, the Minstrel, and the Dance Hall Queen. W. Downing
Gamblers. C. Klein
Gamblers. W. LeQueux
Gamblers. E. Woodward
Gambler's Choice. J. B. Hendryx
Gambler's Girl. J. Tanner
Gambler's Girl. K. Welles
Gambler's Gold. A. Wright
Gambler's Last Throw. Anonymous
Gambler's Syndicate. Nicholas Carter
Gambler's Throw. E. L. Adams
Gambler's Wax Finger and other startling detective experiences. G. S. McWatters
Gambles with Destiny. G. Griffith
Gambling Man. C. Cookson
Gambling with Fire. D. Montrose
Game. G. Hammond
Game. M. Hastings
Game. S. W. Powell
Game and the Candle. E. M. Ingram
Game and the Candle. K. Roche
Game at Chess. J. Fogerty
Game Bet. Stockton Woods
Game Called Murder. J. Ingerson
Game for Eagles. O. M. Hall
Game for Hawks. R. Severn
Game for Heroes. J. Graham
Game for the Living. P. Highsmith
Game for Three Losers. E. Lustgarten
Game for Vultures. M. Hartmann
Game Keeper's Secret. W. M. Graydon
Game Men Play. V. Bourjaily
Game of Chance. Anthony Ferguson
Game of Checkers. J. J. Abraham
Game of Consequences. Shelley Smith
Game of Craft. Nicholas Carter
Game of Danger. Lois Duncan
Game of Death. W. T. Ballard
Game of Death. J. H. Barry
Game of Draw. Dick Stewart
Game of Eyes Only. G. de Villiers
Game of Falcons. C. Darby
Game of Flesh. J. Trinian
Game of Hazard. P. Allardyce
Game of Honor. N. Babcock
Game of Liberty. E. P. Oppenheim
Game of Life. Waters
Game of Life and Death. L. Colcord
Game of Love. G. Warden
Game of Murder. P. Barrington
Game of Murder. F. Durbridge
Game of Plots. Nicholas Carter
Game of Secrets. T. Wiseman
Game of Shadows. M. Ruuth
Game of Soldiers. S. Jackman
Game of Soldiers. J. Shannon
Game of Statues. A. Stevenson

G

Game of Sudden Death. D. Rutherford
Game of Terror. J. Messmann
Game of the Golden Ball. Elizabeth Johnson
Game of the Silence. R. Sauer
Game of Titans. G. A. Ruse
Game of Troy. J. M. White
Game of X. R. Sheckley
Game, Set and Danger. A. Clarke
Game Show Girls. J. P. Radford
Game Well Played. Nicholas Carter
Game Without Rules. M. Gilbert
Game Without Winners. Dorothy Bennett
Gamecock. M. Baldwin
Gamecock Murders. F. Gruber
Gamekeeper's Gallows. J. B. Hilton
Gamelord. R. Parkes
Gamemaker. D. K. Cohler
Gameplan. L. Waller
Games. H. Ellson
Games. B. Mochan
Games. B. Pronzini
Game's Afoot. M. Hardwick
Games Murderers Play. C. Carpenter
Games of Chance. P. Delacorte
Games of Chance. T. Hinde
Games of Chance with Strangers. M. Redfield
Games of Choice. M. Gee
Games of 80. W. H. Mefford
Games to Keep the Dark Away. M. Muller
Gaming for Gold. A. Wright
Gamma Option. J. Land
Gamma Ray Murders. P. Yorke
Gammon. S. Bosak
Gammon and Espionage. N. Bentley
Gamov Factor. D. Bannerman
Gan Waga's Island. S. Drew
Gang. H. Kastle
Gang. D. Whitelaw
Gang Against Guzir. Anonymous
Gang Buster. K. Roe
Gang Girl. Wenzell Brown
Gang Girl. A. L. Quandt
Gang Girls. C. Bingham
Gang Law. H. Clevely
Gang Moll. A. L. Quandt
Gang Rumble. E. Ronns
Gang Smasher. H. Clevely
Gang Smasher Again. H. Clevely
Gang Smashers. J. Kelso
Gang That Couldn't Shoot Straight. J. Breslin
Gang War. J. G. Brandon
Gang War. F. Colter
Gang War. G. H. Teed
Gangdon's Doom. M. Grant
Ganges Mud. E. P. Thorne
Gangland. W. P. Wood
Gang's Deserter. C. Brisbane
Gang's Orders. M. Poole
Gang's Prisoners. L. Bidston
Gangster. Roland Daniel
Gangster and the Private Eye. Dale Clark
Gangster Chronicles. M. Lasker
Gangster Girl. R. Campert
Gangster Girl. J. Lait
Gangster in the Desert. C. H. Snow
Gangster Payoff. N. W. Firth
Gangster War on Bar "G". G. C. Shedd
Gangsters. D. Chandler
Gangsters. P. Martin
Gangsters #2. P. Martin
Gangsters All. G. Stanley
Gangster's Daughter. Roland Daniel
Gangster's Deputy. S. Drew
Gangster's Girl. J. Hunter
Gangster's Girl. R. Starr
Gangster's Glory. E. P. Oppenheim
Gangster's Isle. J. Brooke
Gangster's Lady. B. Sarto
Gangster's Lair. A. Reubens
Gangster's Last Shot. Roland Daniel
Gangster's National. H. L. Hambling
Gangsters of the Air. J. Noy
Gangsters Parade. G. Stanley
Gangster's Revenge. G. N. Philips

Gangway! D. E. Westlake
Gangway for Ghosts. J. Tobias
Gannon's Line. J. Whitlach
Gantry Episode. June Drummond
Gants. R. K. Abshire
Gaol Birds at Large. James Greenwood
Gaol Breaker. E. Wallace
Gaol Gates Are Open. David Hume
Gaol in Conflict. James Preston
Gap in the Curtain. J. Buchan
Gap in the Records. J. McKemmish
Garb of Truth. I. Stuart
Garbage. S. Dixon
Garbage Boy. E. Forrest
Garbage Collector. A. M. Stein
Garde Save the World. J. La Plante
Garden. C. Brenchley
Garden at No. 19. E. Jepson
Garden City Crime. Donald Stuart
Garden Club Murders. D. Van Deusen
Garden Court Mystery. B. Delannoy
Garden Game. J. M. White
Garden House. Martin Long
Garden in Asia. M. D. Post
Garden Murder Case. S. S. Van Dine
Garden o' Dreams. F. M. White
Garden of Cucumbers. P. Tyler
Garden of Evil. R. Calif
Garden of Evil. B. Stoker
Garden of Ghosts. Marilyn Ross
Garden of Grief. H. Arvonen
Garden of Malice. S. Kennedy
Garden of Memories. M. Richmond
Garden of Mystery. R. Marsh
Garden of Satan. C. Vincent
Garden of Shadows. V. C. Andrews
Garden of Shadows. V. Coffman
Garden of Silent Beasts. Gavin Holt
Garden of Swords. M. Pemberton
Garden of the Gods. E. M. Keate
Garden of the Sun. Joyce Bell
Garden of Weapons. J. Garden
Gardenia. B. Vane
Gardenias Bruise Easily. J. P. Carstairs
Gardens of Moontower. G. Workman
Gargantua Falls. P. Bair
Gargoni Girdle. Nicholas Carter
Gargoyle Conspiracy. M. Albert
Gargoyle of Polgelly. R. Hardinge
Gargrave Mystery. H. C. Davidson
Garlands of Sylvia. Gavin Holt
Garlic, Grapes and a Pinch of Heroin. Elaine Turner
Garlic Town. Mulvey Dawson
Garment. C. Cookson
Garment of Immortality. A. Askew
Garments of Repentence. D. Whitelaw
Garmiscath. J. S. Clouston
Garnered. R. Marsh
Garnett Bell, Detective. C. H. Bullivant
Garonsky Missile. A. Caillou
Garrison Tales from Tonquin. James O'Neill
Garrity. Alan Nixon
Garston Murder Case. H. C. Bentley
Garstons. H. C. Bailey
Garth. J. Hawthorne
Garthoyle Gardens. E. Jepson
Garvey's Code. R. Busby
Garvock. C. Gibbon
Gas. B. Hirschfeld
Gas Light. P. Hamilton
Gas Mask Gang. H. Pink
Gas-Mask Murder. J. R. Warren
Gascoyne. S. Crawford
Gaslight. W. Drummond
Gaspar Trenchard. B. Hemyng
Gasparoni Detective. Anonymous
Gaston de Blondeville. A. Radcliffe
Gastronomic Murder. A. Roudybush
Gat Heat. R. S. Prather
Gate. P. S. McCoy
Gate Fever. J. B. O'Sullivan
Gate of Honor. D. Emerson
Gate of Ivory, Gate of Horn. Philip Craig
Gate of Sinners. Mrs. C. Kernahan

Gate of Temptation. P. Brebner
Gated River. L. Ferriss
Gates of Birth. R. Bridges
Gates of Brass. F. J. Kelly
Gates of Chance. V. Sutphen
Gates of Dawn. F. Hume
Gates of Death. J. Hedges
Gates of Doom. E. J. Jenkinson
Gates of Exquisite View. J. Trenhaile
Gates of Flame. R. R. Hobbs
Gates of Hell. S. Seaton
Gates of Life. B. Stoker
Gates of Montrain. W. D. Roberts
Gates of Paradise. V. C. Andrews
Gates of Sagittarius. R. Cutler
Gates of Sorrow. M. Leighton
Gates of Tien T'ze. L. H. Gordon
Gateway. J. Jenkins
Gateway to Escape. N. Deane
Gateway to Hell. D. Wheatley
Gateway to the Grave. M. Lynch
Gatherer. O. Brookes
Gathering at Greystone. L. Bronte
Gathering of Eagles. E. Lindall
Gathering of Evil. Marilyn Ross
Gathering of Ghosts. R. Lewis
Gathering of Gunmen. H. R. Simpson
Gathering of Moondust. P. Morton
Gathering of Old Men. E. J. Gaines
Gathering Place. J. L. Breen
Gathering Storm. G. Glennon
Gathering Storm. F. A. M. Webster
'Gator. G. Ford
Gatsby's Vineyard. A. E. Maxwell
Gaudi Afternoon. Barbara Wilson
Gaudy Night. D. L. Sayers
Gaudy Shadows. J. Brunner
Gauge of Deception. K. G. Ballard
Gauges Steady. E. L. Long
Gaunt Stranger. E. Wallace
Gaunt Woman. J. Blackburn
Gauntlet. M. Butler
Gauntlet of Alceste. H. Moorhouse
Gautran. B. L. Farjeon
Gay Adventure. A. Applin
Gay Adventures. W. Hackett
Gay Captain. M. V. Victor
Gay-Cat. P. Casey
Gay Conspirators. P. Curtiss
Gay Deceiver. P. Leslie
Gay Deceivers. Arthur Moore
Gay Deception. R. Harding
Gay Desperado. B. Gray
Gay Detective. L. Rand
Gay Dragoon. E. F. Harding
Gay Gallant. V. Blake
Gay Ghastly Holiday. S. Blayne
Gay Head Conspiracy. C. Baker
Gay Little Woman. J. S. Winter
Gay Lord Waring. H. Townley
Gay Mortician. M. M. Raison
Gay of Heart. A. Maybury
Gay Phoenix. M. Innes
Gay Pilgrimage. B. Bolt
Gay Triangle. W. LeQueux
Gay World. J. Hatton
Gayden. M. McLaughlin
Gaynor Women. V. Coffman
Gaynor's Passion. N. Garbo
Gaza Intercept. H. Hunt
Gazebo. Alec Coppel
Gazebo. P. Wentworth
Geek Interpreter. J. Ruyle
Gees' First Case. Jack Mann
Gelignite. W. Marshall
Gelignite Gang. J. Creasey
Gem of a Murder. C. Keith
Gemina. I. J. Miller
Gemini. Domini Taylor
Gemini Contenders. R. Ludlum
Gemini in Darkness. Clarissa Ross
Gemini Man. S. Kelly
Gemini Revenged. Charlotte Hunt
Gemini Rising. J. S. Filbrun

Gemini Run. M. Kerr
Gemini Smile, Gemini Kill. R. Lory
Gemini Trip. J. Law
Gendarme's Report. G. Simenon
General Besserley's Puzzle Box. E. P. Oppenheim
General Besserley's Second Puzzle Box. E. P. Oppenheim
General Crack. G. R. Preedy
General Died at Dawn. C. G. Booth
General Goes Too Far. L. Robinson
General Murders. L. D. Estleman
Generals. P. Wahloo
Generals Died Together. J. Bedford
Generation. A. Macallan
Generous Death. N. Pickard
Generous Heart. K. Fearing
Genesis. W. A. Harbinson
Genesis Experiment. M. Carson
Genesis Files. B. Biderman
Genesis 38. Brian Cooper
Genesta. A. Griffin
Geneva Accord. J. Whitman
Geneva Crisis. M. Golan
Geneva Force. J. Rosenberger
Geneva Mystery. F. Durbridge
Geneva Touch. L. Hitchcock
Geneva Transfer. F. Geron
Genghis Coppersmith. R. J. Griffin
Genial Stranger. D. MacKenzie
Genius in Murder. E. R. Punshon
Genocide Express. J. Arnett
Genteel Little Murder. P. Daniels
Gentle Albatross. E. Foote-Smith
Gentle Assassin. C. Richards
Gentle Betrayal. L. Erickson
Gentle Binns. E. Jepson
Gentle Giant. A. Eichler
Gentle Grafter. A. Henry
Gentle Hangman. J. M. Fox
Gentle Hearts and Murder. T. Taggart
Gentle Highwayman. P. Allardyce
Gentle Hook. F. Durbridge
Gentle Killer. P. Barrington
Gentle Kiss of Murder. A. Barron
Gentle Murderer. D. S. Davis
Gentle Obsession. F. Cowen
Gentle People. Irwin Shaw
Gentle Rain. Margaret Archer
Gentle Sex. Angus Hall
Gentle Thespians. R. M. Gilchrist
Gentleman Anonymous. M. B. Lowndes
Gentleman Called. D. S. Davis
Gentleman Crook. M. Crombie
Gentleman-Crook. Sheilah Graham
Gentleman for the Gallows. S. Horler
Gentleman from Chicago. J. Cashman
Gentleman from Nowhere. G. Thorne
Gentleman from Portland. C. R. Gull
Gentleman Garnet. H. B. Vogel
Gentleman George. A. W. Aiken
Gentleman George. J. G. Rowe
Gentleman Hangs. J. Dolland
Gentleman in Pajamas. C. N. Buck
Gentleman-in-Waiting. S. Horler
Gentleman Junkie and other stories of the Hung-Up Generation. H. Ellison
Gentleman Juror. C. L. Marsh
Gentleman Lover. C. H. Bullivant
Gentleman of France. S. J. Weyman
Gentleman of London. M. Gerard
Gentleman of Quality. D. Gilfillan
Gentleman of Rio. A. Mills
Gentleman of the Road. H. Bleackley
Gentleman of Virginia. P. Brebner
Gentleman Pirate. Janette Radcliffe
Gentleman Thorne. Old Sleuth
Gentleman Traitor. Alan Williams
Gentleman Tramp. G. Wintle
Gentleman Who Vanished. F. Hume
Gentleman with the Walrus Mustache. G. Gilpatric
Gentleman's Agreement. B. Von Hutten
Gentleman's Club. R. Gordon
Gentleman's Daughters. M. Masterman
Gentleman's Fate. K. U. P.

Gentleman's Gentleman. M. Pemberton
Gentleman's Mafia. L. M. Shakespeare
Gentlemen at Large. J. Boland
Gentlemen at Large. E. Woodward
Gentlemen Go By. L. Meynell
Gentlemen in Hades. F. A. Kummer
Gentlemen March. R. Pertwee
Gentlemen of Crime. A. Gask
Gentlemen of the Jury. H. Leyford
Gentlemen of the Night. S. Maddock
Gentlemen of the Sea. P. Trent
Gentlemen Reform. J. Boland
Gently at a Gallop. A. Hunter
Gently Between Tides. A. Hunter
Gently in an Omnibus. A. Hunter
Gently in Another Omnibus. A. Hunter
Gently Into Night. K. Coffaro
Gently by the Shore. A. Hunter
Gently Coloured. A. Hunter
Gently Continental. A. Hunter
Gently Does It. Janet Green
Gently Does It. A. Hunter
Gently Down the Stream. A. Hunter
Gently Dust the Corpse. S. H. Courtier
Gently Floating. A. Hunter
Gently French. A. Hunter
Gently Go Man. A. Hunter
Gently in the Highlands. A. Hunter
Gently in the Sun. A. Hunter
Gently in Trees. A. Hunter
Gently Instrumental. A. Hunter
Gently North-West. A. Hunter
Gently Sahib. A. Hunter
Gently Scandalous. Alan Hunter
Gently Through the Mill. A. Hunter
Gently Through the Woods. A. Hunter
Gently to a Sleep. A. Hunter
Gently to the Summit. A. Hunter
Gently Where the Birds Are. A. Hunter
Gently Where the Roads Go. A. Hunter
Gently with Love. A. Hunter
Gently with the Innocents. A. Hunter
Gently with the Ladies. A. Hunter
Gently with the Millions. Alan Hunter
Gently with the Painters. A. Hunter
Genuine Article. A. B. Guthrie
Geoffrey Hamlyn. H. Kingsley
Geoffrey Sterling. Mrs. Leith-Adams
George and Georgina. E. Phillpotts
George Canterbury's Will. H. Wood
George Caulfield's Journey. M. E. Braddon
George Elvaston. Mrs. Lodge
George St. George Julian, the Prince of Swindlers. H. Cockton
George W. Washington. M. T. Baldwin
Georgia Detective. Anonymous
Georgie's Broads. J. C. Ryer
Georgina and Georgette. M. Hutton
Gerald's Party. R. Coover
Geraldine. T. P. Prest
Geraldine Walton—Woman! M. Leighton
Geranium Case. O. Stone
Geranium Kiss. J. Harvey
Gerard. M. E. Braddon
German Helmet. P. McCutchan
German Spy. W. LeQueux
German Spy. B. Newman
German Spy System from Within. W. LeQueux
Germany Company. N. Lewis
Gerrard Street Mystery and other weird tales. J. C. Dent
Gerry North Collects. Gerry North
Gertrude Haddon. E. Southworth
Gertrude of the Rock. T. P. Prest
Gervase Castonel. H. Wood
Gestapo Dormous. Frank King
Gestapo File. D. Cory
Gestapo Fugitive. A. O. Pollard
Gestapo Gauntlet. L. Cargill
Gestapo Trial. J. Petersen
Gestures. H. S. Bhabra
Get a Load o' Dis. R. Drayton
Get a Load of This. J. H. Chase
Get Carter. T. Lewis

Get Clutha. H. Munro
Get Down There and Die. J. Lash
Get Dumm! J. Brewer
Get Garrity. Allan Nixon
Get Going, Sister! D. Hudson
Get Me Headquarters. A. Capelli
Get Me Homicide! D. Haring
Get Nookie. R. Webb
Get Off at Babylon. M. H. Albert
Get Out and Stay Out. R. Angel
Get Out of Town. P. Connolly
Get Out of Town. H. V. Dixon
Get Out the Cuffs. David Hume
Get Ready to Die. B. Gray
Get-Rich-Quick Wallingford. G. R. Chester
Get Shorty. E. Leonard
Get Smart! W. Johnston
Get Smart. C. Sergel
Get Smart Once Again! W. Johnston
Get Sonja. B. Griffiths
Get That Man. R. Drayton
Get This Straight. C. Borelli
Get Wallace! A. Wilson
Get Wise on Dames. H. Vogel
Get Your Man. E. Dorrance
Get Your Man. B. Dyker
Getaway. L. Charteris
Getaway. J. Harris
Getaway. O. John
Getaway. J. Thompson
Getaway Blues. William Murray
Getaway Gang. D. J. Gammon
Getbacks of Mother Superior. D. Lehman
Geth Straker. B. Mather
Getting a Way with Murder. R. McInerny
Getting Along Famously. M. Jacobs
Getting Away with Murder. A. D. Burke
Getting Away with Murder. Armine Campbell
Getting Away with Murder. A. Morice
Getting Even. E. Behr
Getting Rid of Anne. T. Cobb
Getting the Boy. William Scott
Getting Up with Fleas. W. B. Murphyy
Ghost. A. Bennett
Ghost and the Garnet. Marilyn Ross
Ghost at Punkin Holler. L. Rose
Ghost at Ravenkill Manor. P. Warren
Ghost at Stagmere. Alice Brennan
Ghost at the Wedding. Elna Stone
Ghost Blonde. M. Derby
Ghost Breaker. C. W. Goddard
Ghost Breaker. R. Goulart
Ghost Car. B. Knox
Ghost City. R. St. Clair
Ghost City Killings. W. Martyn
Ghost Comes Knocking. Marilyn Ross
Ghost Counts Ten. R. Trevor
Ghost Dancers. Angela Gray
Ghost Dancing. J. Magnuson
Ghost Does a Richard III. R. B. Saxe
Ghost-Farm. J. Tippette
Ghost Fingers. Colin Robertson
Ghost Flowers. M. Summerton
Ghost from Outer Space. L. Greth
Ghost from the Past. Colin Hope
Ghost from the Past. A. M. Meadows
Ghost Girl. E. E. Saltus
Ghost Girl. H. K. Webster
Ghost Guns. W. C. Tuttle
Ghost House. N. Berrow
Ghost House. F. Daingerfield
Ghost House. R. St. Clair
Ghost House. G. Verner
Ghost-Hunter and His Family. O'Hara Family
Ghost Hunters. R. Aiken
Ghost Hunters. C. Brooks
Ghost Hunters. G. Meyrick
Ghost Hunters. A. Tofte
Ghost in Green Velvet. Elizabeth Peters
Ghost in the Bank of England. Anonymous
Ghost in the Belfrey. P. Pray
Ghost in the Glass. R. St. Clair
Ghost in the Making. N. Fitzgerald
Ghost in the Wall. R. St. Clair

G

Ghost Knows His Greengages. R. B. Saxe
Ghost Lane. E. P. Hoyt
Ghost Lover. D. M. Clausen
Ghost Makers. M. Grant
Ghost Man. G. Verner
Ghost Mesa. T. Craig
Ghost Murder. L. Allan
Ghost of a Cardinal. J. Maske
Ghost of a Chance. K. Roos
Ghost of a Chance. F. Usher
Ghost of a Clue. C. Barry
Ghost of a Clue. O. Mills
Ghost of an Idea. M. Challis
Ghost of Archie Gilroy. P. Allardyce
Ghost of Castle Kilgarron. J. Edwards
Ghost of Cemetery Ridge. L. Greth
Ghost of Channing House. Genevieve St. John
Ghost of Coquina Key. J. Bellamy
Ghost of Dark Harbor. C. Ross
Ghost of Downhill. E. Wallace
Ghost of Gaston Revere. M. Hansom
Ghost of Glen George. Grace M. White
Ghost of Grand Canyon. R. H. Wilkinson
Ghost of Graveyard Hill. P. W. Fairman
Ghost of Greystone Grange. A. W. A'Beckett
Ghost of Harcourt. Anonymous
Ghost of Lost Lover's Lake. J. A. Blackwood
Ghost of Megan. M. Lovell
Ghost of Oaklands. W. E. D. Ross
Ghost of Passy. G. Z. Fighton
Ghost of Roaring Pines. P. S. McCoy
Ghost of Rupert Forbes. E. Semphill
Ghost of Sherlock Holmes. L. Halliwell
Ghost of Staghorn. Auriel Douglas
Ghost of the Air. R. St. Clair
Ghost of the Assassins. I. Todd
Ghost of the Dunsany. E. L. Long
Ghost of Thomas Penry. Kenneth O'Hara
Ghost of Truth. J. N. Chance
Ghost of Veronica Gray. K. Eulo
Ghost of Windy Hill. E. B. Cook
Ghost on the Balcony. D. Marfield
Ghost on the Loose. A. M. Halff
Ghost Party. H. Clandon
Ghost Pilot. A. Emmerton
Ghost Plane. P. Conde
Ghost Plane. J. Corbett
Ghost Plane. N. Fleming
Ghost Plane. A. Stringer
Ghost Pulls the Jackpot. R. B. Saxe
Ghost River. C. Hale
Ghost River Inn. C. Van Hazinga
Ghost Road. B. Johnson
Ghost Ship of Fog Island. Marilyn Ross
Ghost Song. D. Daniels
Ghost Squad. G. Verner
Ghost Stories. K. Prichard
Ghost Stories and Mysteries. J. S. Le Fanu
Ghost Stories and Tales of Mystery. J. S. Le Fanu
Ghost Town. C. Blackstock
Ghost Trail. L. C. Douthwaite
Ghost Trails. W. C. Tuttle
Ghost Train. Ruth Alexander
Ghost Train. A. Ridley
Ghost Train. D. Stivers
Ghost Trap. B. Woffington
Ghost Voice. M. Hervey
Ghost Walks. C. Brogan
Ghost Walks. N. MacKenzie
Ghost Walks. W. E. Wright
Ghost Wanted. G. Le Pelley
Ghost Wanted. F. McDermid
Ghost Warriors. M. McGann
Ghost Wore Black. F. Y. McHugh
Ghost Writer. D. Carter
Ghostflight. W. Katz
Ghosting. R. Goulart
Ghostly Fingers. W. Spence
Ghostly Jewels. W. E. D. Ross
Ghostly Passenger. M. Crosby
Ghostly Quarantine. R. St. Clair
Ghostly Strength. Winifred Graham
Ghosts. P. Auster
Ghosts. A. Crabb

Ghosts. E. McBain
Ghosts. K. Prichard
Ghosts and Gold. Anonymous
Ghosts Can't Kill. M. V. Heberden
Ghosts Don't Kill. P. Valdez
Ghosts, Ghouls and Gallows. G. F. Marson
Ghosts' Gloom. I. G. Holmes
Ghosts' High Noon. J. D. Carr
Ghosts' High Noon. C. Wells
Ghosts I Have Met and Some Others. J. K. Bangs
Ghosts Never Die. R. Heed
Ghosts of Ardnamore. A. Andre
Ghosts of Ballyduff. K. Ostrander
Ghosts of Chambord Affair. H. Catalan
Ghosts of Grantmeer. Clarissa Ross
Ghosts of Harrel. W. D. Roberts
Ghosts of Kings. A. Pritchett
Ghosts of Perranprah. H. Lea
Ghosts of Rhodes Manor. J. L. Latham
Ghosts of Sin-Chang. A. Gervais
Ghosts of Slave Driver's Bend. H. H. Kroll
Ghosts of Society. A. Partridge
Ghost's Retreat. C. R. Averell
Ghosts Returning. H. Steele
Ghost's Revenge, and other stories of modern Paris. R. H. Sherard
Ghost's Touch and other stories. W. Collins
Ghostwater. E. Phillpotts
Ghostway. T. Hillerman
Ghostwind. R. A. Payne
Ghoul. Frank King
Ghoul. M. Ronson
Ghoul. M. Slade
Ghoul Friend. G. Donovan
Ghoul Goalie. F. W. Gumley
Ghouls in My Grave. J. Ray
Giant Athlete. Old Sleuth
Giant City Swindle. Anonymous
Giant City Swindle. G. N. Phillips
Giant Detective. Anonymous
Giant Detective. Old Sleuth
Giant Detective Among the Cowboys. Old Sleuth
Giant Detective Among the Italian Brigands. Old Sleuth
Giant Detective in France. Old Sleuth
Giant Detective in Ireland. Anonymous
Giant Hunchback. H. J. Wurr
Giant Kill. K. Platt
Giant Killer. T. Hyman
Giant Killer. R. Vasquez
Giant Rat of Sumatra. R. L. Boyer
Giantkiller. C. Pincher
Giant's Chair. Winston Graham
Giant's Gate. M. Pemberton
Giants of Darkness. N. Thurley
Giant's Shadow. T. Bontly
Gibraltar Conspiracy. D. Betteridge
Gibraltar Prisoner. B. Perowne
Gibraltar Road. P. McCutchan
Giddy Life. C. H. Bovill
Gideon Drexel's Millions. Nicholas Carter
Gideon Drexel's Millions and other stories. Nicholas Carter
Gideon of Scotland Yard. J. J. Marric
Gideon's Art. J. J. Marric
Gideon's Badge. J. J. Marric
Gideon's Day. J. J. Marric
Gideon's Fear. W. V. Butler
Gideon's Fear. J. Creasey
Gideon's Fire. J. J. Marric
Gideon's Fog. J. J. Marric
Gideon's Force. W. V. Butler
Gideon's Law. W. V. Butler
Gideon's Lot. J. J. Marric
Gideon's March. J. J. Marric
Gideon's Men. J. J. Marric
Gideon's Month. J. J. Marric
Gideon's Night. J. J. Marric
Gideon's Power. J. J. Marric
Gideon's Press. J. J. Marric
Gideon's Raid. W. V. Butler
Gideon's Ride. J. J. Marric
Gideon's Risk. J. J. Marric
Gideon's River. J. J. Marric

Gideon's Sport. J. J. Marric
Gideon's Staff. J. J. Marric
Gideon's Vote. J. J. Marric
Gideon's Way. W. V. Butler
Gideon's Week. J. J. Marric
Gideon's Wrath. J. J. Marric
Gift from a Stranger. I. Valdes
Gift from Berlin. A. Barker
Gift Horse. M. R. Douglas
Gift Horse. M. McMullen
Gift Horse's Mouth. Robert Campbell
Gift in the Gauntlet. B. Reynolds
Gift of a Falcon. K. Harrington
Gift of Artemis. Douglas Scott
Gift of Death. E. Ronns
Gift of Evil. E. K. Buzzelli
Gift of Hermes. C. W. Whitaker
Gift of Life. H. Denker
Gift of Murder. G. Batson
Gift of the Desert. R. Parrish
Gift of the Gods. Nicholas Carter
Gift of the Sea. R. M. Sears
Gift Shop. C. Armstrong
Gift Supreme. G. A. England
Gig. S. J. Baker
Gigantic Shadow. J. Symons
Giggling Ghosts. K. Robeson
Gigins Court. B. Graeme
Giglamps. Will Scott
Gilbert the Ghost. R. R. King
Gilbert's Last Toothache. M. Scherf
Gilchrist Case. J. Barclay
Gilded Cage. G. Ferrand
Gilded Canary. B. Latham
Gilded Cobweb. D. Haring
Gilded Fleece. N. Tranter
Gilded Fly. H. Payne
Gilded Frame. M. Ashton
Gilded Hideaway. P. Twist
Gilded Kiss. D. Enefer
Gilded Lady. W. M. Clemens
Gilded Lil. B. Vane
Gilded London. A. Askew
Gilded Man. Carter Dickson
Gilded Needles. M. McDowell
Gilded Nightmare. H. Pentecost
Gilded Sarcophagus. Charlotte Hunt
Gilded Serpent. D. Donovan
Gilded Snatch Caper. J. D. Lawrence
Gilded Spurs. G. Ingram
Gilded Witch. J. Webb
Gilead Balm, Knight Errant. B. Capes
Gilgamesh. J. Bannister
Gillespie Suicide Mystery. L. Gribble
Gillian's Chain. M. S. Craig
Gillingham Rubies. E. Jepson
Gilt Edge. K. A. Saddler
Gilt-Edge Mystery. E. M. Channon
Gilt-Edge Tom, Conductor. E. L. Coolidge
Gilt-Edged Cockpit. D. Rutherford
Gilt-Edged Guilt. C. Wells
Gilt-Edged Traitor. M. Eden
Gilt Feather. D. Polk
Gilt Kid. J. Curtis
Gimmel Flash. Douglas Clark
Gin and Daggers. Jessica Fletcher
Gin and Ginger. J. F. W. Hannay
Gin and Murder. J. Pullein-Thompson
Ginger Cat. C. Reeve
Ginger Cat Mystery. R. Forsythe
Ginger Flower. H. L. Stuart
Ginger Fox, Detective. W. M. Graydon
Ginger Horse. J. F. Straker
Ginger Jar. Jeffrey Robinson
Gingerbread House. M. Dobner
Gingerbread Man. R. Parker
Ginkgo Tree. C. Jarrett
Ginny. Morton Cooper
Ginzberg Circle. A. O'Neill
Gioconda Smile. A. Huxley
Gipsey Chief. H. M. Jones
Gipsey Girl. H. M. Jones
Gipsey Mother. H. M. Jones
Gipsies Don't Have Them. G. M. Wilson

Title Index

Gipsy Blair, the Western Detective. J. R. Taylor
Gipsy Boy. T. P. Prest
Gipsy in Evening Dress. W. J. Making
Gipsy of the North. O. Binns
Gipsy or Gentleman? W. M. Graydon
Gipsy Queen's Vow. M. A. Fleming
Gipsy Reno, the Detective. Old Sleuth
Gipsy Reno, the Female Detective. Old Sleuth
Gipsy's Prophecy. H. Southworth
Gipsy's Warning. E. A. Dupuy
Giri. M. Olden
Girl, a Man and a River. J. Hawkins
Girl Alone. J. Blackmore
Girl Alone. Howel Evans
Girl and the Bill. B. Merwin
Girl and the Detective. C. E. Blaney
Girl and the Miracle. R. Marsh
Girl at Central. G. Bonner
Girl at Pine Creek. G. Goodchild
Girl at Riverfield Manor. P. Primm
Girl at Sea. A. Hunt
Girl at the 'Bacca' Shop and other tales. C. Garvice
Girl Behind the Keys. T. Gallon
Girl Between. B. Fischer
Girl by the Roadside. Roland Daniel
Girl by the Roadside. V. Vanardy
Girl Cage. J. Ehrlich
Girl Called Ann. Rona Randall
Girl Called Fathom. L. Forrester
Girl Champion. Old Sleuth
Girl Chase. D. Enefer
Girl Died Laughing. V. Paradise
Girl Died Singing. N. Morland
Girl Factory. R. F. Murphy
Girl for Danny. W. Ard
Girl for Hire. B. Vane
Girl Found Dead. M. Underwood
Girl Friday. D. Whitelaw
Girl from Addis. T. Allbeury
Girl from Alsace. B. E. Stevenson
Girl from Belfast. V. Bridges
Girl from Easy Street. R. Foster
Girl from Farris's. E. R. Burroughs
Girl from H.A.R.D. J. Moffat
Girl from Hateville. G. Brewer
Girl from Las Vegas. J. M. Flynn
Girl from Malta. F. Hume
Girl from Midnight. Wade Miller
Girl from Moscow. M. Corrigan
Girl from Nippon. C. Dawe
Girl from Nowhere. E. Bond
Girl from Nowhere. R. Foley
Girl from Nowhere. P. Minton
Girl from Outer Space. Carter Brown
Girl from Paris. J. Aiken
Girl from Peking. G. B. Mair
Girl from Scotland Yard. M. McGrath
Girl from Scotland Yard. E. Wallace
Girl from Taiping. H. C. James
Girl from Texas. C. E. Blaney
Girl from the Candle-Lit Bath. Dodie Smith
Girl from the East. D. Whitelaw
Girl from the Mimosa Club. L. Ford
Girl from the Sea. R. Abbey
Girl from the Sea. F. Struan
Girl from Tiger Bay. R. Vane
Girl from Toronto. H. Clevely
Girl from Yesterday. Wade Wright
Girl He Left Behind Him. H. F. Moulton
Girl He Loved. C. H. Bullivant
Girl Hunt. L. D. Smith
Girl Hunters. M. Spillane
Girl in a Big Brass Bed. P. Rabe
Girl in a Hurry. T. A. Plummer
Girl in a Jam. James Savage
Girl in a Mask. H. K. Maxwell
Girl in a Million. D. Enefer
Girl in a Net. John Marsh
Girl in a Shroud. Carter Brown
Girl in a Thousand. J. Middlemass
Girl in Arms. D. Enefer
Girl in Asses' Milk. W. H. Baker
Girl in Black. V. Bridges
Girl in Black Velvet. L. De Jean

Girl in Blue Pants. R. Nettell
Girl in Cabin B54. L. Fletcher
Girl in Green. A. Carr
Girl in Hand. H. Janson
Girl in His House. H. McGrath
Girl in His Past. G. Simenon
Girl in Love. C. Garvice
Girl in Love. Rona Randall
Girl in My Grave. H. Davie-Martin
Girl in 906. D. Hall
Girl in Ocean View. M. Symons
Girl in Question. L. C. V. Houk
Girl in Shadow. C. Franklin
Girl in the Blue Dress. R. Marsh
Girl in the Cage. B. Benson
Girl in the Cage. C. Fitzsimmons
Girl in the Case. R. Barr
Girl in the Case. Nicholas Carter
Girl in the Cellar. P. Wentworth
Girl in the Cheongsam. S. Yorke
Girl in the Cockpit. M. Avallone
Girl in the Cop's Pocket. Robert Turner
Girl in the Crime Belt. J. N. Chance
Girl in the Crimson Cloak. R. Trevor
Girl in the Dark. Roland Daniel
Girl in the Dark. A. Hunt
Girl in the Dark. E. C. Vivian
Girl in the Death Seat. F. Nichols
Girl in the Diamond-Studded Bed. W. R. Bentley
Girl in the Fog. J. Gollomb
Girl in the Frame. W. Fuller
Girl in the Gilded Cage. T. Berkley
Girl in the Green Beret. N. Penley
Girl in the Killer's Bed. A. Curry
Girl in the Mask. DeWitt MacKenzie
Girl in the Mirror. E. Jordan
Girl in the News. Roy Vickers
Girl in the Other Seat. A. R. Weekes
Girl in the Photograph. D. V. Baker
Girl in the Plain Brown Wrapper. J. D. MacDonald
Girl in the Punchbowl. T. B. Dewey
Girl in the Rain. J. Reach
Girl in the Red Dress. R. Cargoe
Girl in the Red Jaguar. J. Manor
Girl in the River. V. B. Miller
Girl in the Scarlet Mask. C. Brookes
Girl in the Secret. A. M. Williamson
Girl in the Spy Racket. W. J. Blackledge
Girl in the Telltale Bikini. P. Morgan
Girl in the Tiffany Dress. M. Eyre
Girl in the Tower. J. Corby
Girl in the Train. B. Bolt
Girl in the Trunk. B. Cassiday
Girl in the Wall. R. Hampton
Girl in the Web. Mark Allerton
Girl in the Wet-Look Bikini. S. Mitchell
Girl in the White Mercedes. J. Usher
Girl in 304. H. R. Daniels
Girl in Waiting. A. Eyre
Girl in Waiting. G. Simenon
Girl in White. J. Ellis
Girl Known As D 13. S. Kyle
Girl Like Wigan. J. F. Leeming
Girl Meets Body. J. Iams
Girl Missing. E. Sherry
Girl Named Marcia. M. Brucker
Girl Nobody Knows. M. McShane
Girl of Ghost Mountain. J. A. Dunn
Girl of Grit. A. Griffiths
Girl of Lost Island. W. H. Osborne
Girl of the Guard Line. C. C. Waddell
Girl of the Islands. J. M. Walsh
Girl of the Passion Play. A. M. Williamson
Girl of the Yellow Diamonds. M. Leighton
Girl on a High Wire. R. Foley
Girl on a Slay Ride. L. Trimble
Girl on Crown Street. D. Karp
Girl on the Beach. M. Cronin
Girl on the Beach. A. Holden
Girl on the Beach. V. Johnston
Girl on the Best Seller List. V. Packer
Girl on the Left Bank. Joan Shepherd
Girl on the Loose. G. G. Fickling
Girl on the M6. D. Enefer

Girl on the Prowl. G. G. Fickling
Girl on the Run. E. S. Aarons
Girl on the Run. E. Hunt
Girl on the Run. J. Sibly
Girl on the Run. H. Waugh
Girl on the Volkswagen Floor. W. A. Clark
Girl on the Waterfront. M. Urquhart
Girl on Zero. B. Perowne
Girl Out Back. C. Williams
Girl Out in Corsica. A. Philips
Girl Possessed. Dean Owen
Girl Prisoner. Nicholas Carter
Girl Raffles. C. E. Blaney
Girl Running. Adam Knight
Girl, the City, and the Soldier. W. H. Baker
Girl, the Gold Watch and Everything. J. D. MacDonald
Girl Watcher's Funeral. H. Pentecost
Girl Who Cried Wolf. H. Waugh
Girl Who Dared. D. Durham
Girl Who Dared. G. C. Thompson
Girl Who Didn't Die. R. Jensen
Girl Who Died. K. Hopkins
Girl Who Failed Him. G. Goodchild
Girl Who Had Everything. R. Foley
Girl Who Had Nothing. A. M. Williamson
Girl Who Had to Die. E. S. Holding
Girl Who Kept Knocking Them Dead. Hampton Stone
Girl Who Killed Things. T. Powell
Girl Who Knew Too Much. J. G. Brandon
Girl Who Never Was. Jan Alexander
Girl Who Never Was. T. B. Dewey
Girl Who Passed for Normal. H. Fleetwood
Girl Who Saw Too Much. D. Reid
Girl Who Stopped the War. C. H. Bullivant
Girl Who Wanted Experience. L. Shippey
Girl Who Was Clairvoyant. M. Warner
Girl Who Was Possessed. Carter Brown
Girl Who Wasn't There. T. B. Dewey
Girl Who Wasn't There. W. D. Roberts
Girl Who Wouldn't Talk. R. Vickers
Girl with a Golden Bar. Brenda Conrad
Girl with a Secret. C. Armstrong
Girl with a Squint. G. Simenon
Girl with a Symphony in Her Fingers. M. G. Coney
Girl with Money. F. Warden
Girl with No Place to Hide. N. Quarry
Girl with Red Hair. Giles Gordon
Girl with Red Suspenders. B. Whitehead
Girl with Six Fingers. H. Pentecost
Girl with the Bright Head. R. Leigh
Girl with the Dynamite Bangs. L. Cameron
Girl with the Frightened Eyes. L. Lariar
Girl with the Golden Eyes. H. Balzac
Girl with the Golden Yo Yo. E. Schiddel
Girl with the Green Eyes. M. Leblanc
Girl with the Haunting Eyes. F. Warden
Girl with the Hole in Her Head. Hampton Stone
Girl with the Key. M. K. Simmons
Girl with the Leopard-Skin Bag. M. Halliday
Girl with the Long Green Heart. Lawrence Block
Girl with the Sweet Plump Knees. T. B. Dewey
Girl with the X-ray Eyes. M. O'Nair
Girl with Two Faces. J. Kendall
Girl Without a Name. K. Slattery
Girls. J. Bowen
Girls Are Missing. C. Crane
Girls at Lighthouse Point. B. Gasner
Girls at the Grange. F. Warden
Girls for Sale. N. Baroni
Girl's Head. E. Jepson
Girls in Bondage. P. Caval
Girls in 5J. R. S. Bernhard
Girls in White. Rona Randall
Girl's Number Doesn't Answer. T. Powell
Girls on the Row. C. Banks
Girls on the 10th Floor. Steve Allen
Girl's Temptation. S. Warwick
Girls Who Came to Murder. K. Carr
Girls Will Be Girls. F. Warden
Gironde Incident. M. Hughes
Giselle. Brian Cooper
Give a Corpse a Bad Name. E. Ferrars

G

G

Give a Man a Gun. J. Creasey
Give a Man a Rope. Gavin Holt
Give Daddy the Knife, Darling. J. Lymington
Give Death a Name. Anthony Gilbert
Give 'Em the Ax. A. A. Fair
Give It to Me Straight. S. Morelli
Give Me a Gun. R. Angel
Give Me a Little Something. W. L. Rohde
Give Me a Ship! C. Edwards
Give Me Back Myself. L. P. Davies
Give Me Death. I. B. Myers
Give Me Liberty. J. Kent
Give Me Murder. G. Ashe
Give Me That Man. E. G. Cousins
Give Me the Knife. L. Meynell
Give Me the Lowdown. D. Linton
Give Me the Rocket Range. R. Mendham
Give Me This Woman. W. Ard
Give Me Tonight. L. Kleypas
Give Me Yesterday. G. Vaizey
Give Thanks to Death. H. Bailey
Give the Boys a Great Big Hand. E. McBain
Give the Devil His Due. P. Graaf
Give the Girl a Gun. R. Deming
Give the Lady a Camel. W. J. Blackledge
Give the Little Corpse a Great Big Hand. G. Bagby
Give Up the Body. L. Trimble
Give Up the Ghost. M. Erskine
Give Us the World. F. L. Green
Giveaway Girl. V. Whisenand
Given Day. R. Van Gulik
Given the Ammunition. H. Gilbert
Giver in Secret. T. Cobb
Giver of Song. S. M. Singer
Glacier Run. P. Barstow
Glad Eye. C. R. Gull
Glad Manor Murder. E. Lemarchand
Glad Summer. J. Farnol
Gladiator-at-Law. F. Pohl
Gladstone Bag. C. MacLeod
Glamour. C. H. Bullivant
Glamour. C. Priest
Glamour Girl. K. Lindsay
Glare. C. Dawe
Glass Alibi. L. Gribble
Glass Arrow. G. Verner
Glass Bottom Boat. B. Street
Glass Cage. E. Ronns
Glass Cage. G. Simenon
Glass Cage. Colin Wilson
Glass Cell. P. Highsmith
Glass Centipede. T. Painter
Glass Cipher. P. Winston
Glass Dagger. J. G. Brandon
Glass Dagger. C. J. C. Hyne
Glass Facade. J. B. Watney
Glass Fish. G. Stuart
Glass Flame. P. A. Whitney
Glass Heart. M. Holland
Glass Highway. L. D. Estleman
Glass House. Jan Alexander
Glass House. M. Charlesworth
Glass Houses. E. Thompson
Glass Interval. J. Turner
Glass Jaw. R. W. Tullipan
Glass Key. D. Hammett
Glass Knife. L. Thayer
Glass Ladder. P. W. Fairman
Glass Lady. A. Bordages
Glass Man. R. Robeson
Glass Mask. L. G. Offord
Glass Mountain. K. Robeson
Glass of Red Wine. M. Tripp
Glass on the Stairs. M. Scherf
Glass Painting. Jan Alexander
Glass Pearls. E. Pressburger
Glass Play Pen. E. Fadiman
Glass Room. E. Rolfe
Glass-Sided Ants' Nest. P. Dickinson
Glass Slipper. M. G. Eberhart
Glass Spear. S. H. Courtier
Glass Too Many. Jack Mann
Glass Totem. D. Chandler
Glass Tower. D. Osborne

Glass Triangle. G. H. Coxe
Glass Village. E. Queen
Glass Virgin. C. Cookson
Glass Zoo. J. McNeish
Glasshouse. M. Charlesworth
Glassy Pond. F. W. Moxley
Gleam of Sapphire. D. Tower
Gleaming Blade. K. Kane
Gleaming Rails. G. M. Dean
Gleave Mystery. L. Tracy
Glen Hazard. Maristan Chapman
Glenbeg Mystery. C. S. Lamont
Glencairly Castle. H. G. Hutchinson
Glencannon Afloat. G. Gilpatric
Glendower Legacy. T. Gifford
Glendraco. Laura Black
Glenlitten Murder. E. P. Oppenheim
Glenmove Abbey. Mrs. Isaacs
Glenna Powers Case. H. Waugh
Glenrannoch. Rona Randall
Glenvirgin's Ghost. Winifred Graham
Glimpse Into Terror. Clarissa Ross
Glimpse of Death. R. Ormerod
Glimpse of Evil. T. Irving-James
Glimpse of Forever. C. D. Peel
Glimpse of Paradise. A. Hale
Glimpse of Paradise. John Marsh
Glimpses of the Moon. E. Crispin
Glint of Death. John Mitchell
Glint of Spears. A. Lejeune
Glitch! David Cook
Glitter and Ash. Dennis Smith
Glitter Dome. J. Wambaugh
Glitter-Dust. A. Dwyer-Joyce
Glitter Girl. Joy Carroll
Glitter-Gold Mountain. D. C. Steele
Glitter of Diamonds. J. K. Egerton
Glitter Street. T. Sullivan
Glitterburn. H. Gould
Glittering Desire. E. R. Punshon
Glittering Hour. A. Hodges
Glittering Isle. W. Collison
Glittering Prizes. B. Flynn
Glittering Road. W. A. MacKenzie
Glitz. E. Leonard
Global Globules Affair. S. Latter
Globe Hollow Mystery. G. W. Wicking
Globe Probe. H. Janson
Gloomy Fanny and other stories. Morley Roberts
Gloria. E. Southworth
Glorious East Wind. K. G. E. Konkel
Glorious Masquerade. K. Lindsay
Glorious Morning, Comrade. M. Gee
Glory. Jack Curtis
Glory Box Mystery. G. W. Wicking
Glory Boys. G. Seymour
Glory Days. Rosie Scott
Glory Hand. P. Boorstin
Glory Hole Murders. T. Fennelly
Glory Hound. J. R. Riggs
Glory Hunter. J. Burmeister
Glory Trap. S. Williamson
Glove in Hand. M. Sproxton
Gloved Hand. L. Bryson
Gloved Hand. Nicholas Carter
Gloved Hand. B. E. Stevenson
Gloved Saskia. W. C. MacDonald
Glover. F. Pollini
Glover Undercover. G. Blumberg
Glow. B. Stanwood
Glow Job. H. Kane
Glow-Worm Tales. J. Payn
Glowering Gables. L. Churchill
Glowing Dark. M. McGregor
Glowing Emeralds. F. I. Bennett
Gloyne Murder. C. Clausen
Glut of Red Herrings. J. Bude
Glut of Virgins. B. Strutton
Glyphs of Gold. P. Edwards
Gnat. L. H. Brooks
Gnome Mine Mystery. P. De Mar
Go Ahead with Murder. M. Halliday
Go Away Death. J. Creasey
Go Away to Murder. J. Creasey

Go Back for Murder. A. Christie
Go-Between. Mrs. C. Kernahan
Go-Between. A. Maling
Go-Between. L. Starr
Go Die in Afghanistan. S. Jason
Go Down Dead. S. Stevens
Go Down, Death. S. B. Hays
Go Find a Shadow. K. Hewitt
Go for Broke. J. Welcome
Go for Garrity. Allan Nixon
Go for Out. F. Webb
Go for the Body. E. Lacy
Go Gently, Gaijin. James Melville
Go Go for Broke. D. Haring
Go Home, Stranger. C. Williams
Go, Honeylou. T. B. Dewey
Go, Lovely Rose. J. Potts
Go, Man, Go. E. De Roo
Go South, Go Crazy. K. Howard
Go to Sleep, Jennie. T. B. Dewey
Go to Thy Death Bed. S. Forbes
Go West, Inspector Ghote. H. R. F. Keating
Go with a Jerk. H. Janson
Goat. J. F. Straker
Goat Island. W. Fuller
Gobblecock Mystery. L. Austen-Leigh
Gobelin Grange. H. Drummond
Goblin Market. H. McCloy
Goblin Tree. R. Anzelon
Goblins. K. Robeson
God and All His Angels. Graham Lord
God Bless America. Stanley Johnson
God Cell. W. Bradbury
God for Tomorrow. M. Dibner
God Is an Executioner. T. Barling
God Keepers. E. R. Johnson
God Machine. M. Caidin
God of the Forest. N. Dorer
God of the Labyrinth. Colin Wilson
God Player. E. Constantine
GOD Project. Stan Lee
God Project. J. Saul
God Save the Child. R. B. Parker
God Save the Mark. D. E. Westlake
God Save the Queen! A. Upward
God-Seeker. John Williams
God Speed the Night. D. S. Davis
God Spigo. A. Tibble
God Squad Bod. M. Kenyon
God with Four Arms and other stories. H. T. W. Bousfield
Godchildren. C. C. Martin
Goddess. R. Marsh
Goddess Game. H. Barron
Goddess Gone Bad. Carter Brown
Goddess of Death. M. Underwood
Goddess of Evil. J. Huslig
Goddess of Terror. P. Gale
Goddess on the Gate. A. McKenna
Goddesses Never Die. G. B. Mair
Godfather. M. Puzo
Godfather Killer. D. Brennan
Godfather Must Live. T. Halstead
Godfires. W. Hoffman
Godkillers. T. Journet
Godmother. H. Fleetwood
Godmother. R. T. Larkin
Godmother. R. Smitten
Godmother Caper. J. D. Lawrence
Godolphin. E. Bulwer-Lytton
Godplayer. R. Cook
God's Back Was Turned. H. Whittington
God's Children. S. F. Friend
God's Clay. A. Askew
God's Defector. J. Bingham
God's Gift to All Women. T. Rome
God's Gift to the Sherlock Business. R. L. Bellem
Gods in Green. W. D. Roberts
Gods of the Lightning. Maxwell Anderson
God's Playthings. Marjorie Bowen
God's Pocket. P. Dexter
God's Prodigal. A. J. Russell
Gods, the Little Guys and the Police. H. Costantini
God's Winepress. A. Jenkinson

Godsend. Bernard Taylor
Godson. R. G. Barrett
Godwin Sideboard. J. Malcolm
Godwulf Manuscript. R. B. Parker
Goering Testament. G. Markstein
Goering Treasure. Gordon Davis
Goggle-Box Affair. V. Gielgud
Goggle-Eyed Pirates. L. Falk
Going Crooked. Winchell Smith
Going Down. D. Markson
Going Down of the Sun. J. Bannister
Going Down River. M. Mwangi
Going for the Gold. E. Lathen
Going, Going, Gone. E. G. C. Collins
Going, Going, Gone. C. Hale
Going, Going, Gone. P. A. Taylor
Going in Style. R. Grossbach
Going It Alone. M. Innes
Going Out in Style. G. Dank
Going Public. D. Westheimer
Going Solo. M. Tripp
Going Straight. Paul Victor
Going to St. Ives. Colver Harris
Going to Jerusalem. R. Dixon
Going to the Bad. E. Yates
Going to the Dogs. D. Kavanagh
Going West. J. Potter
Going Wrong. R. Rendell
Golconda Necklace. H. St. J. Cooper
Gold. L. Daintrey
Gold. D. Delamaide
Gold. K. Perkins
Gold and Copper Delamonds. A. Autumn
Gold and Flesh. B. Appel
Gold and Gaiters. C. A. Alington
Gold and Glory. F. A. M. Webster
Gold and Guns on Halfaday Creek. J. B. Hendryx
Gold—and the Mounted. J. B. Hendryx
Gold and Thorns. M. Rittenberg
Gold and Wine. Roy Vickers
Gold at K-BAR-T. W. C. Tuttle
Gold Bag. C. Wells
Gold Bait. W. J. Sheldon
Gold Ballast. E. L. Long
Gold Bomb. K. Laumer
Gold Brick Cassie. D. G. Loth
Gold Brick Island. J. J. Connington
Gold Bug. W. B. Hare
Gold Bullets. C. G. Booth
Gold by Gemini. J. Gash
Gold Cat. A. Mills
Gold Coast. N. De Mille
Gold Coast. E. Leonard
Gold Coast Nocturne. H. Nielsen
Gold Comes in Bricks. A. A. Fair
Gold Comfit Box. V. Williams
Gold Connection. Robin Moore
Gold Crew. T. N. Scortia
Gold Cup Murder. F. Duke
Gold Curse. H. Resnicow
Gold Deadline. H. Resnicow
Gold Digger, and fourteen other short stories. M. Hervey
Gold Door. Ardath Wise
Gold Drain. Stanley Johnson
Gold Dust Darrell. B. Brentford
Gold Express. J. Budd
Gold Flame. E. E. Rose
Gold Foil. R. Pennant-Rea
Gold for My Girl. J. Blackmore
Gold for Prince Charlie. N. Tranter
Gold for the Bank of England. Ernest H. Robinson
Gold Frame. H. Resnicow
Gold from Gemini. J. Gash
Gold Gamble. H. Resnicow
Gold Game. Roy Vickers
Gold Gap. F. Gruber
Gold Girl. J. B. Hendryx
Gold, Gore and Gehenna. G. A. Birmingham
Gold Hijack. C. Eland
Gold Hunters. J. O. Curwood
Gold-Hunters' Adventures. W. H. Thomes
Gold-Hunter's Adventures Between Melbourne and Ballarat. W. H. Thomes
Gold-Hunters in Europe. W. H. Thomes
Gold in Every Grave. H. L. Nielsen
Gold Is King. O. Binns
Gold Is the Color of Blood. J. M. Patterson
Gold Is Where You Find It. J. B. Hendryx
Gold Is Where You Find It. H. C. James
Gold Island. N. West
Gold Key. C. Payton
Gold-Killer. J. Prosper
Gold Machine. Martin Davies
Gold Makers. N. P. McCoy
Gold Maker's Secret. E. C. Derby
Gold Marked Charm. B. Marchant
Gold Medal Murder. J. Jenkins
Gold of Cathay. G. Wintle
Gold of Gabria. S. C. Mason
Gold of Lubra Rock. Michael Barrett
Gold of Malabar. B. Mather
Gold of Ophir. E. J. Lysaght
Gold of St. Matthew. D. Hart-Davis
Gold of the Gods. A. B. Reeve
Gold of the Sunset. F. Sleath
Gold of Troy. R. L. Fish
Gold of Vale. G. V. Morris
Gold Ogre. K. Robeson
Gold Out of China. G. Volk
Gold Pistol. James Warren
Gold Plated Hearse. J. Hedges
Gold-Plated Sewer. O. Demaris
Gold Point and other strange stories. C. L. Jackson
Gold Poison. P. Trent
Gold Run. J. Baddock
Gold Run. D. Bickerton
Gold Scoop. S. Gall
Gold Seekers. Anonymous
Gold Shield. M. Castoire
Gold Skull Murders. F. Packard
Gold Slippers. F. P. Keyes
Gold Solution. H. Resnicow
Gold-Spinner. D. Donovan
Gold Star Detective from Kentucky. Anonymous
Gold Star Line. L. T. Meade
Gold Test. Seamark
Gold the God and other tales. G. W. Murdoch
Gold Train. W. Duranty
Gold Train. William Grant
Gold Trap. A. Applin
Gold-Trackers. D. Hart-Davis
Gold Treasure Mystery. J. Laurence
Gold Was Our Grave. Henry Wade
Gold Without Glitter. B. O'Keefe
Gold Worshippers. J. B. Harris-Burland
Golden Alaskan. J. Dorrance
Golden Angel. N. Brent
Golden Angel. M. Corrigan
Golden Ape. H. Adams
Golden Apple. R. Shea
Golden Arrow. D. Clarke
Golden Arrow. C. Stoddard
Golden Ashes. F. W. Crofts
Golden Ball. L. Bennet-Thompson
Golden Ball and other stories. A. Christie
Golden Ballast. A. Hodgson
Golden Ballast. H. D. Stacpoole
Golden Barrier. A. M. Burrage
Golden Bat. F. M. White
Golden Bauble. G. Slear
Golden Beast. E. P. Oppenheim
Golden Belts. A. Murray
Golden Boats of Taradata Affair. S. Latter
Golden Bough. G. F. Gibbs
Golden Bowl. A. Joscelyn
Golden Box. F. Crane
Golden Buddha. M. Everard
Golden Buddha. A. O. Pollard
Golden Bull. I. Brook
Golden Bull. N. Carter
Golden Bullet. P. Denver
Golden Calf. M. E. Braddon
Golden Carpet. A. M. Williamson
Golden Casket. F. A. Symonds
Golden Cat. H. Long
Golden Cat. D. Newton
Golden Chalice. K. L. Meredith
Golden Child. G. C. Chesbro
Golden Child. Penelope Fitzgerald
Golden Circle. M. H. Albert
Golden Circle. L. Falk
Golden Clew. B. Wayde
Golden Cockatrice. G. Black
Golden Creep. G. Bagby
Golden Crucible. J. Stubbs
Golden Crystal. F. Hird
Golden Dagger. E. R. Punshon
Golden Dart. S. Jepson
Golden Dawns the Sun. E. Messenger
Golden Death. N. Deane
Golden Deed. A. Garve
Golden Door. B. Spicer
Golden Dress. I. Montgomery
Golden Drum. B. Freestone
Golden Duck. V. Wayman
Golden Dwarf. R. N. Silver
Golden Earnest. A. Bright
Golden Earrings. Y. Foldes
Golden Enchantress. M. Clare
Golden Express. D. Lambert
Golden-Eyed Venus. M. Dekobra
Golden Eyes. C. Gale
Golden-Eyes. S. Jepson
Golden Face. W. LeQueux
Golden Face. B. Mitford
Golden Fear. S. Harvester
Golden Fig. N. T. Smith
Golden Fleece. J. Becklund
Golden Fleece. J. Boland
Golden Fleece. J. Hawthorne
Golden Fleece. N. Lofts
Golden Fleece. Ernest Paul
Golden Fleece. R. J. Sawyer
Golden Fleecing. R. Upton
Golden Fluid. M. B. Dix
Golden Fool. D. Divine
Golden Foundling. S. Murray
Golden Fox. Wilbur Smith
Golden Frame. J. Chadwick
Golden Frame. M. Wolf
Golden Galatea. Florence Stevenson
Golden Gate. Alistair MacLean
Golden Girl. A. Askew
Golden Girl. I. Flanders
Golden Girl. D. Haring
Golden Girl. P. Warren
Golden Girl and All. R. Dennis
Golden Girls. S. Box
Golden Gizmo. J. Thompson
Golden Glory. E. M. Channon
Golden Gloves. J. Ingersol
Golden God. Ralph Hayes
Golden Goddess. H. E. Hill
Golden Goddess Gambit. L. Maddock
Golden Goose. F. Mahannah
Golden Goose. E. Queen
Golden Goose Murders. A. McRoyd
Golden Grin. Colin Lewis
Golden Guilt. F. Gerard
Golden Hades. E. Wallace
Golden Harvest. H. H. Hill
Golden Heel. W. Newbauer
Golden Helmet. H. Bogue
Golden Heron. H. Borrie
Golden Hoard. E. Balmer
Golden Hoard. Robert Morgan
Golden Hole. J. Blyth
Golden Hooligan. T. B. Dewey
Golden Hooves. Scarlet Grey
Golden Horn. B. Davidson
Golden Horse. A. Kennington
Golden Horseshoes. R. Aitken
Golden Idol. H. J. S. Anderton
Golden Imp. J. H. Chase
Golden Isle. H. H. Hill
Golden Kangaroo. A. Pratt
Golden Keel. D. Bagley
Golden Key. T. C. Bridges
Golden Key. W. O'Farrell
Golden Kill. M. Olden
Golden Knot. C. Gibbon

G

Golden Lady. B. Atkey
Golden Lady. J. Ramsay
Golden Land. B. L. Farjeon
Golden Lantern. T. Warriner
Golden Legacy. Old Sleuth
Golden Lion and the Sun. Y. Hamizrachi
Golden Lives. F. Wicks
Golden Lode. A. Davidson
Golden Lotus. A. W. Barrett
Golden Lotus. G. E. Locke
Golden Lotus. J. L. Roberts
Golden Lure. J. Davison
Golden Lure. C. Leader
Golden Man. P. K. Dick
Golden Man. F. Lockridge
Golden Man. K. Robeson
Golden Master. W. B. Gibson
Golden Mile. J. Sherlock
Golden Milestone. Scott Graham
Golden Milestone. K. Hewitt
Golden Monkey. V. Gunn
Golden Murder. F. Lester
Golden Nightmare. W. Snow
Golden Obsession. G. Cogswell
Golden Orange. J. Wambaugh
Golden Oriole. P. Traill
Golden Oyster. Donald Gordon
Golden Packet. Angela Gray
Golden Panther. S. Gluck
Golden Passage. J. Savage
Golden Pebble. M. Bennett
Golden Peril. K. Robeson
Golden Pheasant Mystery. Maurice Worth
Golden Pig. F. Du Boisgobey
Golden Pin. H. Seymour
Golden Plough. P. Merritt
Golden Precipice. H. B. M. Watson
Golden Quest. A. Askew
Golden Rain. Douglas Clark
Golden Rapids of High Life. R. H. Savage
Golden Rat. P. Trent
Golden Reef. J. Pattinson
Golden Rendezvous. Alistair MacLean
Golden Room. Irving Wallace
Golden Rope. J. W. Brodie-Innes
Golden Rose. F. M. White
Golden Sabre. J. Cleary
Golden Salamander. V. Canning
Golden Scarab. J. Adye
Golden Scarab. P. Goulden
Golden Scarab. H. Moorhouse
Golden Sceptre. G. H. Thornhill
Golden Scorpion. K. Rohmer
Golden Secret. P. Kingsland
Golden Sentinals. R. M. Sears
Golden Serpent. Nick Carter
Golden Shadow. L. T. Meade
Golden Shaft. C. Gibbon
Golden Shaft. J. Nazel
Golden Shroud. H. Arre
Golden Sickle. D. Grubb
Golden Sinner. Jim Thompson
Golden Slipper and Other Problems for Violet Strange. A. K. Green
Golden Snail, and other stories. Countess Barcynska
Golden Snare. J. O. Curwood
Golden Soak. H. Innes
Golden Spaniard. D. Wheatley
Golden Spiders. R. Stout
Golden Spike. H. Ellson
Golden Spur. J. S. Fletcher
Golden Stag. B. Heatter
Golden Statuette. J. Pendower
Golden Stone. D. A. G. Pearson
Golden Stranger. Robin Temple
Golden Swan Murder. D. C. Disney
Golden Sword. J. B. Harris-Burland
Golden Teddybear. John Marsh
Golden Temptress. H. Hill
Golden Thistle. J. L. Roberts
Golden Thread. E. Carballido
Golden Thread. T. Gallon
Golden Three. W. LeQueux
Golden Tiger. R. Whitley

Golden Tooth. J. M. Cobban
Golden Torrent. J. Davison
Golden Torrent. Alan Graham
Golden Trail. S. Drew
Golden Trap. H. Pentecost
Golden Tress. F. Du Boisgobey
Golden Triangle. P. Bonnecarrere
Golden Triangle. M. Leblanc
Golden Triangle. P. McCurtin
Golden Triangle. F. M. Proud
Golden Triangle. Colin Robertson
Golden Unicorn. P. A. Whitney
Golden Urchin. M. Brent
Golden Urge. R. Kyle
Golden Valley. D. Winston
Golden Venture. J. S. Fletcher
Golden Venus Affair. A. MacVicar
Golden Violet. J. Shearing
Golden Virgin. A. Dipper
Golden Virgin. J. Rossiter
Golden Wang-Ho. F. Hume
Golden Web. E. P. Oppenheim
Golden Widow. F. Mahannah
Golden Witch. Gavin Holt
Golden Woman. R. Cullum
Golden Woman. E. Hatch
Golden Years Caper. R. Carson
Goldenboy. M. Nava
Goldfinger. I. Fleming
Goldfish Bowl. L. Gough
Goldfish Have No Hiding Places. J. H. Chase
Goldfish Murders. W. Mitchell
Goldhawk. B. Hayles
Goldilocks. A. Coburn
Goldilocks. Sheila Johnson
Goldilocks. Ed McBain
Goldman's. S. Siwertz
Goldmine—London W.1. Philip Daniels
Goldship. F. Ross
Goldsmith's Row. Sheila Bishop
Golem. B. Anson
Golem 100. A. Bestor
Golestan Episode. J. Scotter
Golf Club Murder. O. F. Jerome
Golf-Course Murder. O. F. Jerome
Golf Course Mystery. C. K. Steele
Golf House Murder. H. Adams
Golf Links Mystery. P. Quiroule
Golficide and other tales. W. G. V. Sutphen
Golgotha. J. Gardner
Goliath. P. Geddes
Goliath. W. J. Weatherby
Goliath Scheme. W. Arden
Gondez the Monk. W. H. Ireland
Gondola Scam. Jonathan Gash
Gondreville Mystery. H. Balzac
Gone Away. Hazel Holt
Gone Man. B. Solomon
Gone Missing. C. Egleton
Gone, No Forwarding. J. Gores
Gone Shots. Kelly Lawrence
Gone to Earth. R. Boyer
Gone to Glory. R. Irvine
Gone to Ground. T. H. White
Gone to Her Death. P. Audemars
Gone to Her Death. J. McGown
Gone Tomorrow. F. C. Davis
Gone Up in Smoke. G. Reid
Gonzaga's Woman. J. Jakes
Good and Dead. J. Langton
Good and Evil. W. Reyburn
Good and the Bad. Joan Fleming
Good Axe. W. Kerr
Good Bad Man. B. Reed
Good Behavior. D. E. Westlake
Good Book. David Thoreau
Good Books. R. Philmore
Good by Stealth. H. Clandon
Good-Bye and Amen. F. Clifford
Good-Bye to Life. David Hume
Good-Bye to Market. R. M. Gilchrist
Good-Bye Tomorrow. Griff
Good Children Don't Kill. L. Thomas
Good Citizens. J. Boland

Good Copy. F. B. Harrison
Good Day to Die. T. Blackburn
Good Day to Die. Jim Harrison
Good Day to Die. J. A. Hoffman
Good Death. P. Ross
Good Evans! E. Wallace
Good Evening, Everyone. A. J. Alan
Good Fight. J. Ahern
Good Fight. L. Matera
Good for One More Ride. W. I. Frank
Good Gestes. P. C. Wren
Good Girls Don't Get Murdered. P. S. Parker
Good Guys Wear Black. M. Franklin
Good Intentions. B. Deighton
Good King Sauerkraut. Barbara Paul
Good Knight, Sailor. T. C. H. Jacobs
Good Luck, Mr. Cain. B. Freeborn
Good Luck, Sucker. R. Telfair
Good Luck to the Corpse. Max Murray
Good Men and Bad. J. B. Hendryx
Good Men and True. S. Harvester
Good Men Do Nothing. J. Brunner
Good Morning, Mavis. Carter Brown
Good-Natured Lady. J. E. Buckrose
Good Neighbor Murder. E. Pierson
Good Night and Goodbye. Timothy Harris
Good Night for Murder. P. Ketchum
Good Night, Garrity. Allan Nixon
Good Night, Irene. J. M. Ullman
Good Night, Kathy. N. J. Krinkel
Good Night, Ladies. V. Siller
Good Night, Little Spy. E. Koch
Good Night, Mr. Holmes. C. N. Douglas
Good Night, Sheriff. H. R. Steeves
Good Night, Sweet Prince. Carole Berry
Good Night to Kill. L. O'Donnell
Good Old Anna. M. B. Lowndes
Good Old Boys. W. L. Heath
Good Old Charlie. J. Bingham
Good Old Potts! C. N. Boyle
Good Old Stuff. J. D. MacDonald
Good One. G. Tabori
Good Place for Murder. C. Mullen
Good Place to Die. B. Copper
Good Place to Die. R. Gaulden
Good Place to Hide. A. Cullimore
Good Place to Work and Die. W. Van Atta
Good Recovery. A. Wright
Good Riddance. B. Abercrombie
Good Roads. L. V. V. Armstrong
Good Ship "Dove". F. Warden
Good Ship Rajah. E. L. Long
Good Spies Don't Grow on Trees. M. Lovell
Good Spy. J. Griffiths
Good Terrorist. D. Lessing
Good Thief. R. Rosenblum
Good Time Charlie's Back in Town Again. A. Silver
Good-Time Girl. M. Richmond
Good Time Lady. N. W. Firth
Good Time Lips. B. Vane
Good Weekend for Murder. Jennifer Jordan
Good Year for Dwarfs? Carter Brown
Good Year for Murder. A. E. Eddenden
Good Year for the Roses. M. Timlin
Goodbye. W. H. Manville
Goodbye, Aunt Charlotte! J. F. Straker
Goodbye, Aunt Elva. Elizabeth Fenwick
Goodbye Baby Blue. Frank Ryan
Goodbye Blonde. D. Enefer
Goodbye California. Alistair MacLean
Goodbye Chairman Mao. C. New
Goodbye Charlie. M. H. Albert
Goodbye, Chicago. W. R. Burnett
Goodbye, Dear Elizabeth. G. Hoster
Goodbye, Dr. Thorndyke. N. Donaldson
Goodbye, Friend. S. Japrisot
Goodbye, Gemini. Jenni Hall
Goodbye, Gillian. Jonathan Burke
Goodbye Goliath. E. Chaze
Goodbye Gorgeous. Keith Campbell
Goodbye Honey. B. Vane
Goodbye Is Forever. M. Carroll
Goodbye Is Not Worthwhile. W. Mole
Goodbye, Julie Scott. A. Abbott

Goodbye, L.A. Murray Sinclair
Goodbye Look. R. Macdonald
Goodbye, Miss Lizzie Borden. L. De La Torre
Goodbye, Mr. Shaft. E. Tidyman
Goodbye, Nanny Gray. J. Staynes
Goodbye Piccadilly. T. Barling
Goodbye Piccadilly, Farewell Leicester Square. A. La Bern
Goodbye, Pussy. S. Kemp
Goodbye, Shirley. P. Muller
Goodbye, Stranger. D. Heyes
Goodbye, Sweet William. P. Flower
Goodbye to an Old Friend. B. Freemantle
Goodbye to Istanbul. J. Banning
Goodbye to Murder. D. Henderson
Goodey's Last Stand. C. Alverson
Goodhues of Sinking Creek. W. R. Burnett
Goodknife Sweetheart. Carter Brown
Goodnight Moon. J. MacLane
Goodnight, Sweet Prince. Alan Hunter
Goods. Arthur Douglas
Goose and Tomtom. D. Rabe
Goose Is Cooked. E. Hogarth
Goose Woman. R. Beach
Gooseberry Fool. J. McClure
Goosefoot. P. McGinley
Gopi. H. Sherring
Gordon Dock Mystery. H. A. Ashton
Gordon Liddy Is My Muse by Tommy "Tip" Paine. J. C. Batchelor
Gore of the Guides. A. G. Hales
Gorgeous Ghoul. D. V. Babcock
Gorgeous Ghoul Murder Case. D. V. Babcock
Gorgeous Lovers. Margery Bowen
Gorgon. J. L. Hamilton
Gorgon's Head. Ladbroke Black
Gorgon's Head. F. Hurd
Gorgonzola, Won't You Please Come Home? C. Ames
Gorilla. R. Spence
Gorilla's Moll. B. Sarto
Goring Mystery. E. A. Treeton
Goring's First Case. P. Kippax
Gorky Park. M. C. Smith
Gory Details. D. Elias
Gory Dew. G. Mitchell
Gory Knight. M. R. Larminie
Gory Story. J. Kirkpatrick
Gospel According to Judas. Cecil Lewis
Gospel Lamb. J. S. Scott
Gospel of Death. W. Harrington
Gospel of Death. M. Judd
Gossamer Thread. A. Lowing
Gossip. M. Olden
Gossip to the Grave. Jonathan Burke
Gossip Truth. Joanthan Burke
Gotham Gore. S. Jason
Gothic Pursuit. J. Malcolm
Gothic Romance. E. Carrere
Gothic Story of Courville Castle. Anonymous
Gotland Deal. N. J. Crisp
Gouffe Case. J. Maass
Goulden Fleece. R. Obstfeld
Gourmet. J. Nisbet
Gourmet Killings. J. Post
Governess. E. Cromwell
Governess. E. Hervey
Government Contract. B. Stanley
Government Special Detective. Anonymous
Government Spy. Lieut. Carlton
Government Trust. B. Wayde
Government's Man. E. C. Derby
Governor. J. S. Knapp
Governor. Alan Thomas
Governor of Chi-Foo. E. Wallace
Governor of Kattowitz. G. Seton
Governors. E. P. Oppenheim
Gown and Shroud. K. Freeman
Gowns and Gunsels. J. Dekker
Gownsman's Gallows. K. Farrer
Grab. P. Aalben
Grab. J. P. Heggy
Grab. P. Malloch
Grab. Zeno

Grab Bag. C. MacLeod
Grab Operators. J. N. Chance
Grabbers. L. S. Traube
Grace. M. Gee
Grace. Michael Stewart
Grace Darling. G. W. M. Reynolds
Grace for the Dead. D. E. Fisher
Grace O'Malley, Princess and Pirate. R. Machray
Grace Walter. T. P. Prest
Graceful Exit. R. Kashner
Gracie Allen Murder Case. S. S. Van Dine
Gracious Lily Affair. V. W. Mason
Graffiti. P. Van Greenaway
Graffiti Gambit. A. Wingard
Grafin Rinsky. Hilarion
Graft Town. Neill Graham
Grafter. J. Cassells
Grafters. Nicholas Carter
Grafters. F. Lynde
Grail Tree. J. Gash
Grain of Salt. R. Goodchild
Grammarian's Funeral. E. Acheson
Grand Assize. H. Carton
Grand Babylon Hotel. A. Bennett
Grand Catch. G. Buhet
Grand Cayman Slam. R. Striker
Grand Central Murder. S. MacVeigh
Grand Central Murders. S. McGurk
Grand Cham's Diamond. A. Monkhouse
Grand Duchess. A. Duffield
Grand Duke. C. Dawe
Grand Duke's Finances. F. Heller
Grand Graft Hotel. B. Sarto
Grand Guignol. F. C. Witney
Grand Guignol Stories. M. Level
Grand Jury. R. Liebman
Grand Jury. E. Rose
Grand Man. C. Cookson
Grand Modena Murder. L. Gribble
Grand National. J. Welcome
Grand National Conspiracy. H. Graham
Grand National Mystery, and other tales. T. S. Denham
Grand National Night. D. Christie
Grand Ole Opry Murders. M. Kaye
Grand Opening. B. Glemser
Grand Prix Murders. D. Rutherford
Grand Scam. P. Stein
Grand Slam. Ritchie Perry
Grand Street Collector. J. Arleo
Grandfather Medicine. J. Hager
Grandma's Best Years. E. L. Russell
Grandmaster. W. B. Murphy
Grandmother. M. Masterman
Grandmother. G. Simenon
Grandmother Martin Is Murdered. J. Courtney
Grandmother's House. J. B. Herman
Granduca. M. Brand
Grange Mystery. A. W. Bradley
Grangerfjord Monks. R. M. Sears
Granite Folly. C. Farr
Granite Shadows. M. Warrick
Grant McKenzie. Old Sleuth
Grantham Mystery. M. Danvers
Grant's Overture. F. N. Miller
Granville Crypt Murders. Melville Burt
Grape from a Thorn. J. Payn
Grape Vine. H. Janson
Grapevine. Jonathan Starr
Graphics. H. M. Lyon
Grasp at Straws. J. Y. Dane
Grasp of the Sultan. Anonymous
Grass. P. Nash
Grass and Supergrass. P. Nash
Grass in Idleness. P. Nash
Grass Makes Hay. P. Nash
Grass Rain. E. Garrigues
Grass Roots. Stuart Woods
Grass Spinster. C. C. Lewis
Grass Widow. H. Janson
Grass Widow. R. McInerny
Grass-Widow's Tale. Ellis Peters
Grasshopper Summer. J. L. Cooper
Grassleyes Mystery. E. P. Oppenheim

Grass's Fancy. P. Nash
Grasville Abbey. G. Moore
Gratitude. G. M. Savage, Jr.
Grave Affair. Shelley Smith
Grave Between Them. C. Boutelle
Grave Can Wait. H. B. Kaye
Grave Case of Murder. R. Bax
Grave Consequences. B. Comfort
Grave Consequences. M. Cumberland
Grave Danger. F. Kane
Grave Danger. K. Roos
Grave Descend. J. Lange
Grave Desire. M. A. Kahn
Grave-Digger of Monks Arden. A. Gask
Grave-Digger's Apprentice. V. M. Grayland
Grave Doubt. I. Baker
Grave Error. S. Greenleaf
Grave Error. M. Warner
Grave for a Russian. C. G. Vance
Grave for Coyotes. S. D. Frances
Grave for Madam. P. Cagney
Grave for Miss Carling. D. W. F. Hardie
Grave for Two. H. Carmichael
Grave Gives Up. P. MacCormack
Grave Goods. Jessica Mann
Grave Is Waiting. A. MacKenzie
Grave Journey. M. Hebden
Grave Lady Jane. F. Warden
Grave-Maker's House. R. Weber
Grave Matter. L. Vardre
Grave Matters. J. Rhode
Grave Matters. M. Yorke
Grave Murder. Al Guthrie
Grave Must Be Deep. T. Roscoe
Grave of Green Water. J. Roffman
Grave of Heroes. J. Cross
Grave of Sand. D. Graham
Grave of Truth. Evelyn Anthony
Grave Responsibility. J. Staynes
Grave Undertaking. J. McCahery
Grave Undertaking. Lionel White
Grave Without Flowers. M. McMullen
Grave Without Grass. D. C. Cameron
Grave Witness. P. Levi
Gravedigger. Joseph Hansen
Gravedigger's Funeral. A. Arent
Gravel Patch. R. Goyne
Gravelhanger. V. Gielgud
Graven Image. D. G. Finlay
Graven Image. J. D. Fitz
Graven Image. Mrs. C. Kernahan
Graven Image. Ann Paris
Grave's Company. S. Nichols
Graves Ghost. A. W. Clark
Graves, I Dig! Carter Brown
Graves in Academe. S. Kennedy
Grave's in the Meadow. M. L. Stokes
Grave's Retreat. E. Gorman
Graveswood. S. Lloyd
Gravetide. C. McKnight
Graveyard. P. M. Hubbard
Graveyard for Lunatics. R. Bradbury
Graveyard Never Closes. F. C. Davis
Graveyard of My Own. R. Goulart
Graveyard Plot. M. Erskine
Graveyard Plots. B. Pronzini
Graveyard Rolls. M. Procter
Graveyard Rules. Gary Cook
Graveyard Shift. U. Curtiss
Graveyard Shift. Harry Patterson
Graveyard to Let. Carter Dickson
Graveyard Watch. A. D. Divine
Graveyard Watch. J. Esteven
Gravy Train. W. Masterman
Gravy Train Hit. Curtis Stevens
Gray Amber. Basil Carey
Gray Canaan. D. Garth
Gray Charteris. Robert Simpson
Gray Countess. Theo Douglas
Gray Creatures. Zorro
Gray Dawn. S. E. White
Gray Dusk. O. R. Cohen
Gray Eagles. D. Unkefer
Gray Eyes. S. Friedman

G

Gray Fist. M. Gray
Gray Flannel Shroud. H. Slesar
Gray Gull. H. F. Granger
Gray Magic. Herman Landon
Gray Man Walks. H. Bellamann
Gray Mask. Wadsworth Camp
Gray Monk Walks. G. Reed
Gray Overcoat. W. R. Randall
Gray Phantom. Herman Landon
Gray Phantom's Return. Herman Landon
Gray Stranger. F. Crane
Gray Terror. Herman Landon
Graymists. M. Lynch
Grayson Affair. S. Waldron
Great Abduction. A. S. Roche
Great Abduction Mystery. W. M. Graydon
Great Adams Express Robbery. A. F. Pinkerton
Great Adventure and Out of a Dark Sky. S. Horler
Great Aeroplane Mystery. J. Laurence
Great Affair. V. Canning
Great Air Swindle. J. Creasey
Great Airport Racket. J. Hunter
Great Airways Plot. J. Noy
Great Alone. G. Goodchild
Great Alternative. C. H. Bullivant
Great Amherst Mystery. W. Hubbell
Great Art-Gallery Crime. M. Osborne
Great Australian Snake Exchange. Duncan Ball
Great Autumn Double. P. Trent
Great Awakening. E. P. Oppenheim
Great Bank Mystery. N. Ned
Great Bank Robbery. J. Hawthorne
Great Bank Robbery. Old Sleuth
Great Baruma Mystery. W. P. Brown
Great Bear. E. P. Oppenheim
Great Becklesthwaite Mystery. H. Herman
Great Berwyck Bank Burglary. J. G. Bethune
Great Betrayal. H. Wintle
Great Big Laughing Hannah. W. Rutherford
Great Big Trench Coat in the Sky. M. Lovell
Great Billy. Old Sleuth
Great Black Kanba. Constance Little
Great Bluff. H. Hill
Great Boy. Old Sleuth
Great Brain Robbery. K. A. Saddler
Great Bridge Conspiracy. T. Quinn
Great Brighton Mystery. J. S. Fletcher
Great Bullion Drama. G. Prout
Great Bullion Mystery. Stockton Heath
Great Buxton Mystery. Anonymous
Great Canal Plot. G. H. Teed
Great Capture. Old Sleuth
Great Cases of the Thinking Machine. J. Futrelle
Great Chin Episode. P. Cushing
Great Circus Mystery. Anonymous
Great Circus Mystery. E. J. Murray
Great Circus Mystery. N. Ridley
Great Conspiracy. Nicholas Carter
Great Conspiracy. A. Soutar
Great Court Scandal. W. LeQueux
Great Craneboro' Conspiracy. J. Oakley
Great Crime of Grapplewick. E. Sykes
Great Cronin Mystery. Anonymous
Great Currency Racket. G. Chester
Great Dandelion. J. L. Cooper
Great Day for Dying. J. Dillon
Great Deception. M. K. Douglas
Great Deliverance. E. George
Great Detective Puzzle Book. E. R. Emmet
Great "Detectives". T. Mathieson
Great Detectives: Seven Original Investigations. J. Symons
Great Diamond Bluff. J. W. Bobin
Great Diamond Robbery. J. Minahan
Great Diamond Robbery. S. O'Donnell
Great Diamond Syndicate. Nicholas Carter
Great Dinosaur Robbery. D. Forrest
Great Divide. F. M. Robinson
Great Dollar Fraud. A. Parsons
Great Dumping Mystery. W. Jardine
Great Dusk. P. Traill
Great Elk. E. G. Cousins
Great Enigma. Nicholas Carter
Great Explosion. A. Murray

Great Express Robbery. Grace M. White
Great Fear. M. Cherkas
Great Fear. R. Goyne
Great Feast. H. Wood
Great Flood. Louise Collis
Great Fog and other weird tales. H. F. Heard
Great Football Mystery. J. Durston
Great Free Enterprise Gambit. J. Barr
Great Gamble. Anonymous
Great Game. H. C. Bailey
Great Gift. S. Paternoster
Great God Gold. W. LeQueux
Great Gold Mystery. Max Foster
Great Gold Rush. W. H. P. Jarvis
Great Gorme. Colleen Cairus
Great Grave Robbery. J. Minahan
Great Green Diamond. I. Stark
Great Green God. F. Whishaw
Great Harvard Robbery. J. Minahan
Great Hesper. F. Barrett
Great Hijack. A. Tack
Great Hold-Up Mystery. W. Usher
Great Hotel Murder. V. Starrett
Great Hotel Robbery. J. Minahan
Great House in the Park. A. Burr
Great Hush-Hush Mystery. M. B. Dix
Great Impersonation. E. P. Oppenheim
Great Indian Scout Detective. Old Sleuth
Great Insurance Murders. M. Propper
Great Ivory Swindle. G. H. Teed
Great Jade Seal. S. W. Powell
Great Jekyll Diamond. J. L. Owen
Great Jester. Morley Roberts
Great Jewel Mystery. F. Du Boisgobey
Great Journey and other stories. M. E. Braddon
Great K & A Train Robbery. P. L. Ford
Great Ling Plot. W. Martyn
Great London Mystery. S. Gluck
Great London Mystery. C. Kingston
Great Magor Diamond, and The Creaking Door. H. C. McNeile
Great Mail Racket. G. Dilnot
Great Mail Robbery. C. B. Kelland
Great Marl-Pit. G. Ohnet
Great Merlini. C. Rawson
Great Mill Street Mystery. A. Sergeant
Great Mine Mystery. F. Ferrars
Great Mining Swindle. G. H. Teed
Great Mistake. M. R. Rinehart
Great Mogul. L. Tracy
Great Money-Mail Mystery. Margaret Douglas
Great Money Order Swindle. Nicholas Carter
Great Museum Mystery. H. E. Hill
Great Mystery Solved. G. Vase
Great Newmarket Mystery. C. Rae-Brown
Great Opium Case. Nicholas Carter
Great Orme Terror. G. Radcliffe
Great Pearl Mystery. L. Phillips
Great Pearl Secret. C. N. Williamson
Great Pebble Affair. B. Shelby
Great Pimlico Mystery. K. Kingston
Great Pirate Syndicate. George Griffith
Great Plot. W. LeQueux
Great Porter Square. B. L. Farjeon
Great Portrait Mystery. R. A. Freeman
Great Pretender. J. Deane
Great Prince Shan. E. P. Oppenheim
Great "Push" Experiment. A. Pratt
Great Pyramid Robbery. J. Minahan
Great Radio Mystery. C. K. Steele
Great Railway Mystery. Anonymous
Great Renunciation. H. Bourchier
Great Revenge. S. M. Sitwell
Great Revue Mystery. H. H. C. Gibbons
Great River Mystery. Old Sleuth
Great Ruby. T. W. Hanshew
Great Ruby Mystery. Anonymous
Great Safe Mystery. Anonymous
Great Salvage Swindle. H. H. C. Gibbons
Great Scot, the Chaser, and other sporting stories. G. G.
Great Secret. Roland Daniel
Great Secret. E. P. Oppenheim
Great Security. Bartimeus

Great Shakes. E. Moodie
Great Shipyard Mystery. J. Ascott
Great Skene Mystery. B. Capes
Great Snake Murder. L. D. Stranger
Great Southern Mystery. G. D. H. Cole
Great Spy Race. A. Diment
Great Stone Heart. M. Farnsworth
Great Stores Crime. W. Edwards
Great Stores Mystery. W. Edwards
Great Syndicate. George Griffiths
Great Taxi-Cab Mystery. J. H. Collins
Great Taxi-Cab Ramp. J. G. Brandon
Great Temptation. R. Marsh
Great Temptation. S. Warwick
Great Tontine. H. Smart
Great "Tote" Fraud. J. W. Bobin
Great Train Hijack. W. Masterson
Great Train Robbery. M. Crichton
Great Travers Case. M. Merrick
Great Trunk Mystery. R. H. Poole
Great Trunk Tragedy. M. Redwing
Great Tunnel Mystery. A. Blair
Great Turf Fraud. D. J. Belgrave
Great Turf Fraud. A. Blair
Great Turf Fraud, and Other Notorious Crimes. D. Donovan
Great Turf Mystery. C. Frisbie
Great Tyneside Mystery. J. Kelso
Great Unknown. Maxwell Scott
Great Van Suttart Mystery. G. A. Chamberlain
Great Victorian Mystery. P. Menegas
Great Waltz. A. Rothberg
Great Wash. G. Kersh
Great Waxworks Crime. Gwyn Evans
Great White Army. M. Pemberton
Great Yant Mystery. A. B. Cunningham
Great Year for Dying. B. Copper
Greater Call. R. E. Salwey
Greater Claim. A. Applin
Greater Crime. G. A. England
Greater Punishment. S. Chalmers
Greatest Batman Stories Ever Told. Bob Kane
Greatest Crime. Sloan Wilson
Greatest Fool. G. Hackforth-Jones
Greatest Game. C. L. Reid
Greatest Gift. A. W. Marchmont
Greatest Joker Stories Ever Told. Anonymous
Grecian Bloodbath. S. Jason
Gredos Reckoning. C. Rougvie
Greed. M. Leighton
Greedy Fingers. T. Roan
Greedy Killers. E. Radford
Greedy Ones. V. Kelly
Greek Affair. F. Gruber
Greek Coffin Mystery. E. Queen
Greek Fire. Winston Graham
Greek Fire. J. Kirton
Greek Girl. Dorothea Bennett
Greek God Affair. R. Deming
Greek Key. C. Forbes
Greek Position. R. Roderick
Greek Revival. F. Haring
Greek Summit. Nick Carter
Greek Tragedy. G. D. H. Cole
Greek Wedding. J. A. Hodge
Green Ace. S. Palmer
Green Archer. T. J. Kelly
Green Archer. Margery Lawrence
Green Archer. E. Wallace
Green Arrow. B. Bolt
Green Bag. J. P. Seabrooke
Green Beetle. Elizabeth Ford
Green Blot. S. Gluck
Green Bondage. F. Ogilvie
Green Bough. Margery Lawrence
Green Bracken. D. Lee
Green Bungalow. F. M. White
Green Bushes. O. Allan
Green Bushes. J. B. Buckstone
Green Cape. S. Richardson
Green Cat. S. Guise
Green Circle. Mark Cross
Green Circle. C. Massie
Green Cloak. Y. Davis

Green Complex. H. MacGrath
Green Coral. H. D. Stacpoole
Green Cross. A. R. Weekes
Green Curtain. M. E. Braddon
Green Death. Elaine Hamilton
Green Death. K. Robeson
Green Death and other stories. B. Hutton
Green December Fills the Graveyard. M. Sarsfield
Green Diamond. Arthur Morrison
Green Diamond Mystery. F. Grierson
Green Diamonds. Colin Robertson
Green Domino. K. Lindsay
Green Dragon. J. J. Farjeon
Green Dragon Emerald. L. A. Cuddy
Green Drift. J. Lymington
Green Eagle. K. Robeson
Geren Eagle Score. R. Stark
Green Evil. F. Grierson
Green Eye of Death. J. Sandys
Green Eye of Goona. Arthur Morrison
Green-Eyed Monster. G. Bronson-Howard
Green-Eyed Monster. P. Quentin
Green Eyes. E. S. Brooks
Green Eyes. M. Grant
Green Eyes Are Dangerous. E. L. MacKeag
Green Eyes of Bast. S. Rohmer
Green Fancy. G. B. McCutcheon
Green Fields of Eden. F. Clifford
Green Fire. G. Hughes
Green Fire. F. Jameson
Green Fire. A. Maybury
Green Fire. R. Standish
Green Flag and other stories of war and sport. A. C. Doyle
Green Flames of Aries. R. Lory
Green Flash. Winston Graham
Green Flash and other tales of horror, suspense and fantasy. Joan Aiken
Green for a Grave. M. L. Stokes
Green for a Season. P. H. Irving
Green for Danger. C. Brand
Green for Danger. Gavin Holt
Green for Danger. P. Johnson
Green Frontier. J. B. Hilton
Green Gene. P. Dickinson
Green Ghost. Stuart Martin
Green Ghost. J. Reach
Green Ghost Murder. J. Ronald
Green Ginger. Arthur Morrison
Green Glare Murders. R. Wallace
Green Glove. J. L. Linklater
Green God. F. A. Kummer
Green Goddess. P. Edwards
Green Gold. Frank King
Green Goods Speculator. Dick Stewart
Green Grass. M. Kenyon
Green Grassy Slopes. W. A. Ballinger
Green Grow the Dollars. E. Lathen
Green Grow the Graves. M. E. Chaber
Green Grow the Tresses-O. S. Hyland
Green Hazard. M. Coles
Green Hell. P. McCurtin
Green Hell Rampage. Dan Morgan
Green Hell Treasure. R. L. Fish
Green Ice. G. A. Browne
Green Ice. R. Whitfield
Green Ice Murders. R. Whitfield
Green Ink. J. S. Fletcher
Green Jacket. Jennette Lee
Green Jade Buddha. J. Gibbons
Green Jade God. Roland Daniel
Green Jade Hand. H. S. Keeler
Green Jade Necklace. J. H. Chase
Green Killer. C. Dawe
Green Killer. K. Robeson
Green King. P. L. Sulitzer
Geren Knife. A. Wynne
Green Knight. W. M. Duncan
Green Lady. L. Ellis
Green Lama Mystery. J. Kains
Green Lane. Alec Brown
Green Lantern. B. Bolt
Green Lantern. Augustus Muir
Green Light. L. Landon

Green Light. R. Mooney
Green Light. R. St. Clair
Green Light. R. C. Schimmel
Green Light for Death. F. Kane
Green Light, Red Catch. F. Ryck
Green Lightning. R. Stillman
Green Lipstick. G. C. Foster
Green Mandarin Mystery. G. Malcom
Green Mask. A. Skene
Green Mask. G. Verner
Green Master. K. Robeson
Green Monday. M. M. Thomas
Green Moth. G. E. Mitton
Green Mountain Murder. B. Comfort
Green Mountain Murders. C. Culley
Green Mummy. F. Hume
Green Murder. V. Barlow
Green Murder. Keith Miles
Green Opal. H. C. James
Green Oranges. R. Masson
Green Orb. C. Massie
Green Overcoat. H. Belloc
Green Pack. Robert (G.) Curtis
Green Pack. E. Wallace
Green Parrot. B. Capes
Green Pastures. U. L. Silberrad
Green Phantom. G. Meyrick
Green Phantom. W. Spence
Green Plaid Pants. M. Scherf
Green Plush. J. E. Middleton
Green Ray. W. LeQueux
Green Ray. D. T. Lindsay
Green Ray. V. Thompson
Green Reapers. R. W. Jones
Green Ribbon. E. Wallace
Green Ripper. J. D. MacDonald
Green River High. D. Kyle
Green Room Crime. G. Chester
Green Rope. J. S. Fletcher
Green Rust. E. Wallace
Green Scandals. C. C. Lewis
Green Scarab. G. Hughes
Green Scarf. P. Fry
Green Scorpion. H. Hawton
Green Seal. C. E. Walk
Green Shade. H. Hill
Green Shadow. J. E. Grant
Green Shadow. Herman Landon
Green Shadows. L. V. Stevens
Green Ship. G. Volk
Green Shiver. C. B. Clason
Green Shutters. E. Addyman
Green Silence. M. Hastings
Green Stone. S. Blanc
Green Stone. H. MacGrath
Green Stones of Evil. M. Peterson
Green Suns. Henry Ward
Green Swallows. F. Sleath
Green Tablets. B. Goldie
Green Tabloids. B. Goldie
Green Talons. Gavin Holt
Green Tea. J. S. Le Fanu
Green Thermos. G. Simenon
Green Thoughts and other strange tales. J. Collier
Green to Pagan Street. J. T. Story
Green Toad. W. S. Masterman
Green Train. H. Lieberman
Green Tree Mystery. R. Doubleday
Green Triangle. Anonymous
Green Triangle. W. M. Duncan
Green Triangle Mystery. H. Pink
Green Trigger Fingers. J. Sherwood
Green Tunnel. C. C. Lewis
Green Turban. W. M. Graydon
Green Turbans. J. M. Cobban
Green Willows. Jan Alexander
Green Windmill. I. Mercer
Green Wolf Connection. Nick Carter
Green Wood Burns Slow. M. Brice
Green Wound. P. Atlee
Green Wound Contract. P. Atlee
Green Wounds. P. P. Muir
Greene Murder Case. S. S. Van Dine
Greenface. Frank King

Greenfield Mystery. G. F. Worts
Greenfinger. J. Rathbone
Greenfly. P. McCutchan
Greengage Summer. Ruth Perry
Greengirl. V. Black
Greenhouse. A. Lamb
Greenland Mystery. J. Rosenberger
Greenmantle. J. Buchan
Greenmask. J. J. Farjeon
Greenmask. E. Linington
Greensea Island. V. Bridges
Greenstone Door. W. Satchell
Greenstone Griffins. G. Mitchell
Greenwell Mystery. E. C. R. Lorac
Greenwell's Glory Case. H. G. Hutchinson
Greenwich Apartments. P. Corris
Greenwich Killing Time. K. Friedman
Greenwood. J. Phillips
Grell Mystery. F. Froest
Gremlin's Grampa. R. L. Pike
Grenelle. I. Holland
Grenencourt. I. Charles
Grenfell Legacy. M. McEvoy
Grenson Murder Case. T. C. H. Jacobs
Gresham Ghost. W. D. Roberts
Greta Dey's Confession. G. Goodrich
Gretna Green. H. M. Jones
Grey Affair. J. Weeks
Grey Bat. S. Warwick
Grey Beginning. B. Michaels
Grey Brother. D. Conyers
Grey Castle Mystery. A. O. Tibbits
Grey Cat. J. B. Harris-Burland
Grey Doctor. F. Hume
Grey Domino. P. C. De Crespigny
Grey Face. J. Cassells
Grey Face. S. Rohmer
Grey Fair. M. Gerard
Grey Fish. W. V. Cook
Grey Friar and the Black Spirit of the Way. J. English
Grey Gables. G. E. Locke
Grey Ghost. J. Cassells
Grey Ghost. P. A. Clarke
Grey Ghost. M. A. Pollexfen
Grey Ghyll. A. Rundle
Grey Magic. S. Dreher
Grey Man. M. Urquhart
Grey Manor Ghost. T. S. King
Grey Mask. P. Wentworth
Grey Mask Gang. J. A. Jordan
Grey Mask Murders. Hugh C. McDonald
Grey Messengers. M. Storme
Grey Mist Murders. Constance Little
Grey Monk. T. W. Speight
Grey Moth. F. Warden
Grey Phantom. H. Landon
Grey Phantom's Return. H. Landon
Grey Phantom's Triumphs. Herman Landon
Grey Pilgrim. J. M. Hayes
Grey Rat. O. Binns
Grey Room. E. Phillpotts
Grey Seas. R. Clements
Grey Sentinels. B. Knox
Grey Shadow. G. E. Rochester
Grey Shadow's Partner. G. E. Rochester
Grey Shapes. Jack Mann
Grey Shepherds. A. MacVicar
Grey Sisters. M. D. Anderson
Grey Sombrero. P. Fry
Grey Studio. A. Scudder
Grey Terror. H. Landon
Grey Terror. A. G. Pearson
Grey Timothy. E. Wallace
Grey Wig. I. Zangwill
Grey Wolf. M. Allington
Grey Wolf's Daughter. G. Warden
Grey Woman. F. M. White
Greybreek. A. MacVicar
Greygallows. B. Michaels
Greyhound Murder Mystery. W. D. Maydwell
Greyhound Stadium Plot. E. T. Woodhall
Greymarsh. A. J. Rees
Greyslaer. Anonymous

G

Greystone Heritage. L. Bronte
Greystone Tavern. L. Bronte
Greystones. A. Lamb
Greystones. H. Leigh
Greythorn Woman. J. Brennan
Greythorne. J. Trevelyan
Greyvale School Mystery. P. Manton
Grid Murder. E. Snell
Grief Before Night. P. Loring
Grierson Mystery. L. Osbourne
Grieve for the Past. S. Forbes
Grievous Bodily Harm. T. Lewis
Grif. B. L. Farjeon
Griff. R. Weverka
Griffin Towers. J. Winslow
Griffith Case. John Bentley
Grifters. J. Thompson
Grim Caretaker. E. Ascher
Grim Chancery. W. Mills
Grim Death. G. Verner
Grim Death and the Barrow Boys. Joan Fleming
Grim Discovery. T. E. B. Clarke
Grim Game. S. Horler
Grim Grow the Lilacs. M. Randolph
Grim Inheritance. H. Leyford
Grim Joker. G. Verner
Grim Justice. Rita
Grim Maiden. B. Flynn
Grim Pickings. J. Rowe
Grim Reaper. O. Denoux
Grim Reaper. Duncan Long
Grim Rehearsal. R. Fenisong
Grim Smile of the Five Towns. A. Bennett
Grim Souvenir. J. Rowland
Grim Tales. E. Nesbit
Grim Tomorrow. M. Richmond
Grim Vengeance. J. J. Connington
Grime and Punishment. J. Churchill
Grimm Death. D. F. Brown
Grin and Dare It. R. Drayton
Grinder's Wheel. Morley Roberts
Grindle Nightmare. Q. Patrick
Grinning Avenger. E. Jepson
Grinning Ghoul. L. Churchill
Grinning Gismo. S. W. Taylor
Grinning Pig. N. Lombard
Grip. J. S. Winter
Grip Finds the Lady. J. Dory
Grip of Fear. S. H. Burchell
Grip of Fear. V. Hansen
Grip of Fear. I. Lambot
Grip of Fear. M. Level
Grip of Fear. R. Ritchie
Grip of Gold. R. Halifax
Grip of Sin. A. Askew
Grip of the Bookmaker. Percy White
Grip of the Four. Mark Cross
Grip of the Law. J. W. Bobin
Grip of the Strangler. J. C. Cooper
Grip of the Wolf. M. Gerard
Gripped. S. Hocking
Gripped by Drought. A. W. Upfield
Grishin. H. Herlin
Gristmill. G. S. Caldwell
Grizzly Trail. G. Moffat
Groaning Spinney. G. Mitchell
Groom Lay Dead. G. H. Coxe
Groomed for Murder. V. Rhodes
Groota. J. A. Jackson
Groote Park Murder. F. W. Crofts
Groovy Way to Die. R. Deming
Gross Carriage of Justice. R. L. Fish
Grossbeak Mansion. N. Buntline
Grosvenor Square Goodbye. F. Clifford
Grotesque. P. McGrath
Grotto of Tiberius. F. E. Smith
Ground for Suspicion. M. Burton
Ground Money. Rex Burns
Ground Zero. R. Cox
Grounds for Indecency. M. H. Gropper
Grounds for Murder. J. Appleby
Grounds for Murder. T. D. Carroll
Grounds for Murder. V. Van Urk
Groundstar Conspiracy. L. P. Davies

Group Flashing Two. D. Howarth
Grouse Moor Murder. J. Ferguson
Grouse Moor Mystery. J. Ferguson
Grouser Investigates. E. S. Brooks
Grove of Doom. M. Grant
Grow Cold Along with Me. M. Lynch
Grow Grey with Fear. N. Thurley
Grow Young and Die. W. O'Farrell
Growing Concern. I. Stuart
Growing Evil. E. Messenger
Grub-and-Stakers Move a Mountain. Alisa Craig
Grub-and-Stakers Pinch a Poke. Alisa Craig
Grub-and-Stakers Quilt a Bee. Alisa Craig
Grub-and-Stakers Spin a Yarn. Alisa Craig
Grub Street Night's Entertainment. J. C. Squire
Grubstake Gold. J. B. Hendryx
Grudge. P. Chevalier
Grudge. B. Hitchens
Grudge Mountain. A. P. Terhune
Grue of Ice. G. Jenkins
Gruesome Grange. Robert Marshall
Grumpy. H. Hodges
Guadalajara. E. H. Hunt
Guaranteed to Fade. G. Bagby
Guard the Girl. R. Clifford
Guarded Pearls. Vince Kelly
Guarded Room. J. S. Fletcher
Guarded Soul. A. Dare
Guarded Trust. M. Dunlop
Guarded Woman. C. Cannell
Guardian. C. Dilke
Guardian. D. Greenburg
Guardian. J. Hough
Guardian Angel. A. Cohen
Guardian Angel. J. Garwood
Guardian Angel in the Underworld. J. Wall
Guardian at the Gate. K. A. Shoesmith
Guardian in Black. G. W. Jones
Guardian of the Cup. C. Cannell
Guardian of Willow House. D. Daniels
Guardian Spectre. M. Lovell
Guardians. W. H. Baker
Guardians. S. Brackeen
Guardians. R. Parkes
Guardian's Mystery. C. Faber
Guardians of the Prince. Reginald Hill
Guardians of the Treasure. H. C. McNeile
Guaymas Assignment. L. Lambert
Guerrilla Attack. Jon Hart
Guerrilla Games. G. Wilson
Guerrilla Girls. H. Whittington
Guess Who's Coming to Kill You? E. Queen
Guest at Gladehaven. V. Smiley
Guest in the House. P. MacDonald
Guest of Honor. Irving Wallace
Guest with the Scythe. Gret Lane
Guests at the Villa. A. Hesse
Guests of Chance. J. L. Rickard
Guild. E. Gorman
Guile. H. Hill
Guile Wears a Coronet. G. Vaizey
Guilt. H. J. Forman
Guilt by Association. M. J. Costello
Guilt Edged. W. J. Burley
Guilt Edged. J. B. O'Sullivan
Guilt Edged. T. Thayer
Guilt-Edged Cage. Carter Brown
Guilt-Edged Frame. F. Kane
Guilt-Edged Murder. L. Thayer
Guilt for Innocence. C. Franklin
Guilt Is Plain. D. Frome
Guilt Is Where You Find It. L. Thayer
Guilt Merchants. R. Harwood
Guilt of Innocence. M. Halliday
Guilt on the Lily. R. Ormerod
Guilt with Honour. J. Ashford
Guilt Without Proof. P. Alding
Guilty? J. W. Arctander
Guilty! L. Thayer
Guilty! D. Walshe
Guilty Answer. A. Livingston
Guilty Are Afraid. J. H. Chase
Guilty As Charged. E. Hanley
Guilty As Hell. B. Halliday

Guilty Be Damned. G. J. Barrett
Guilty Bonds. W. LeQueux
Guilty, But—. S. Kyle
Guilty, But Insane. Donald Stuart
Guilty But Not Insane. J. C. Lenehan
Guilty Bystander. Mike Brett
Guilty Bystander. Wade Miller
Guilty Conscience. H. O. Cooke
Guilty Conscience. R. Levinson
Guilty Gold. H. Hill
Guilty Governor. Nicholas Carter
Guilty Hands. J. A. Jordan
Guilty House. F. Hume
Guilty House. C. Kingston
Guilty Knowledge. L. Grant-Adamson
Guilty Man. F. Coppee
Guilty, My Lord. M. Peterson
Guilty, My Lord. I. Stefan
Guilty of Love. M. Cambards
Guilty Ones. D. Telfer
Guilty or Innocent? M. Leighton
Guilty or Not Guilty? M. M. Bodkin
Guilty, or Not Guilty? W. G. Hamley
Guilty or Not Guilty? N. Ridley
Guilty or Not Guilty. G. Smythies
Guilty or Not Guilty. M. V. Victor
Guilty Parties. B. Riley
Guilty Party. M. Babson
Guilty Party. John Burke
Guilty Party. R. Dolphin
Guilty Party. T. Herd
Guilty Party. George Ross
Guilty River. W. Collins
Guilty Secret. M. Pemberton
Guilty Silence. S. Warwick
Guilty Thing Surprised. R. Rendell
Guilty Until Proven Guilty. B. McNaughton
Guilty Witness. J. N. Chance
Guilty Witness. M. Hershman
Guilty You Must Be. C. Franklin
Guinea Pigs. L. Vaculik
Guinea Pigs Tail. F. Hope
Guinevere's Gift. N. St. John
Guinguette by the Seine. G. Simenon
Gulag. S. Flannery
Gulag War. J. Hild
Gulf. David Poyer
Gulf Attack. R. Mackin
Gulf Coast Girl. C. Williams
Gulf Coast Run. D. Thomas
Gulf of Fire. Gar Wilson
Gulf Scenario. R. Bulliet
Gulf Stream. C. P. McDonald
Gull Cove Murders. E. Colter
Gull Yard. Margaret Archer
Gulls Fly Low. V. Bridges
Gull's Kiss. P. Graaf
Gully of Bluemansdyke. A. C. Doyle
Gumshoe. N. Smith
Gumshoe. Josiah Thompson
Gun. M. T. Kaufman
Gun and Mr. Smith. J. Godey
Gun at My Back. A. Capelli
Gun Before Butter. N. Freeling
Gun-Brand. J. B. Hendryx
Gun Business. G. Dickson
Gun Business. V. B. Miller
Gun Cotton. Rupert Grayson
Gun Cotton—Ace High. Rupert Grayson
Gun Cotton—Adventure Nine. Rupert Grayson
Gun Cotton—Adventurer. Rupert Grayson
Gun Cotton at Blind Man's Hood. Rupert Grayson
Gun Cotton Goes to Russia. Rupert Grayson
Gun Cotton in Hollywood. Rupert Grayson
Gun Cotton in Mexico. Rupert Grayson
Gun Cotton—Murder at the Bank. Rupert Grayson
Gun Cotton—Outside the Law. Rupert Grayson
Gun Cotton, Secret Agent. Rupert Grayson
Gun Cotton—Secret Airman. Rupert Grayson
Gun Feud. W. C. Tuttle
Gun for a God. N. Morland
Gun for Company. A. Bocca
Gun for Delilah. Surrey Smith
Gun for Hire. J. Sherman

Title Index

Gun for Honey. G. G. Fickling
Gun for Inspector West. J. Creasey
Gun for My Baby. D. Haring
Gun for Sale. G. Greene
Gun for Sale. D. Spade
Gun Garden. P. Stanton
Gun Girl. D. Haring
Gun Graduate! D. Haring
Gun in Daniel Webster's Bust. M. Scherf
Gun in His Hand. V. Rosen
Gun in My Back. B. Edmunds
Gun-Men's Wake. Max Anthony
Gun Merchants. G. Harding
Gun Moll for Hire. H. Janson
Gun Play. R. B. Phillips
Gun Play. Y. M. Udoff
Gun Rule. P. Urquhart
Gun Runner. R. Meade
Gun-Runner. B. Mitford
Gun-Runner. A. Stringer
Gun Runners. G. A. Birmingham
Gun Runners. J. Crosbie
Gun-Running in the Gulf, and other adventures. H. H. Austin
Gun Smoke. N. W. Firth
Gun Street Girl. M. Timlin
Gun to Play With. J. F. Straker
Gun, Waiting. D. Haring
Gunblast. A. Capelli
Gunboat Mystery. J. G. Brandon
Gunboat Mystery. J. A. Jordan
Gungu Sahib. T. Mundy
Gunman. C. F. Coe
Gunman at Large. George Douglas
Gunman of Gozo. H. C. Davis
Gunman's Bluff. E. Wallace
Gunman's Holiday. M. Knight
Gunmen Die Hard. D. Rogan
Gunmen, Gallants, and Ghosts. D. Wheatley
Gunner. E. Wallace
Gunner Kelly. A. Price
Gunners. G. H. Teed
Gunner's Island. A. Glanville
Gunning in England. W. J. Elliott
Gunpowder Alley. J. Rowland
Gunpowder Treason and Plot. Moira Field
Gunpower. M. Schorr
Gunrunners. J. Murphy
Guns. E. McBain
Guns Across Los Pecos. B. Harding
Guns and Gamblers. J. Dekker
Guns Covered with Flowers. S. Jackman
Guns for Achin. M. Leinster
Guns in the Desert. B. Netton
Guns in the Heather. L. Amerman
Guns of Darkness. F. Clifford
Guns of Heaven. P. Hamill
Guns of Mazatlan. L. Parker
Guns of Navarone. Alistair MacLean
Guns of Palembang. P. McCurtin
Guns of the Gods. T. Mundy
Guns Over the Border. S. Brydon
Gunship. J. J. Savarin
Gunshot Grand Prix. D. Rutherford
Gunsmoke Haze. R. Wilkes-Hunter
Gunsmoke in Her Eyes. H. Janson
Gunston Cotton. Rupert Grayson
Gunther Heritage. J. L. Roberts
Gup Bahadur. T. Mundy
Guru Docket. S. Dave
Guru's Ring, and other stories. G. F. Hall
Gusher. J. Boland
Gutenberg Murders. G. Bristow
Gutter Gang. Jay De Bekker
Gutter Tragedies. S. Paternoster
Guttersnipe. G. Kersh
Guvnor. G. F. Newman
Guv'nor. E. Wallace
Guv'nor and other stories. E. Wallace
Guy Deverell. J. S. Le Fanu
Guy Fawkes. Anonymous
Guy Fawkes Murder. E. C. Lester
Guy Garrick. A. B. Reeve
Guy Gets His. J. Cello

Guy Must Live. Johnny Dark
Guy Named Judas. N. Karta
Guy with a Gun. D. Andrews
Guys and Dolls. D. Runyon
Gwen-Amyia. D. Le Litt
Gwen John Sculpture. J. Malcolm
Gwendoline's Harvest. J. Payn
Gwenyth. R. Carol
Gwythyn Clay Mystery. M. Poole
Gyfford of Weare. J. Farnol
Gyp, the Heiress. L. L. Ware
Gypsies and the Detectives. A. Pinkerton
Gypsum Flower. P. Bair
Gypsy Detective. Anonymous
Gypsy Detective. Old Sleuth
Gypsy, Go Home. W. O'Farrell
Gypsy Grove. M. K. Simmons
Gypsy in Amber. Martin Smith
Gypsy's Curse. R. Carol
Gypsy's Luck. J. Fairfax-Blakeborough
Gypsy's Warning. G. Kent
Gyrth Chalice Mystery. M. Allingham

H As in Hangman. L. Treat
H As in Hunted. L. Treat
H-Bomb for Alice. I. Stuart
H. L. Mencken Murder Case. D. Swaim
H.M.S. Anonymous. Taffrail
Ha-Ha Case. J. J. Connington
Habeas Corpus and other stories. P. Green
Habit of Fear. D. S. Davis
Habit of Homicide. K. Lewis
Habit of Loving. J. Thomson
Habit of the Blood. L. Battle
Habits of Command. J. Rosner
Hacienda on the Hill. R. H. Savage
Hacienda Triste. F. Swann
Hacker. C. Day
Had. R. Gehman
Had I But Groaned. Carter Brown
Haddon Hall Mystery. Beulah King
Hades and Hocus Pocus. L. Dent
Hades Belle. C. McManus
Hades Hello. W. Wright
Hadfield Mystery. M. E. Cooke
Hadleigh Inheritance. A. Hunt
Hadrian Ransom. A. Duane
Haelstrom Manor. S. J. Treibich
Hag Wood. J. Shrog
Hagar. E. Southworth
Hagar, Called Hannah. A. Soutar
Hagar of the Pawn-Shop. F. Hume
Hagar's Castle. Clayton Matthews
Haggard's Cove. M. K. Simmons
Haggard's Manor. E. Hayworth
Hag's Nook. J. D. Carr
Hahnemann Sequela. H. King
Haigerloch Project. I. Melchior
Haight Is the Killer. J. K. Lucas
Haiku for Hanae. James Melville
Hail, Hail, the Gang's All Here! E. McBain
Hail Hibbler. R. Goulart
Hail McLean! G. Goodchild
Hail to the Chief. L. D. Klausner
Hail to the Chief. E. McBain
Hail, Victor, Hail! Michael Kent
Hailey Street Murder. W. Jardine
Hailing Sign. S. Fink
Hailstone. T. Baxter
Hair Divides. C. Houghton
Hair of the Dog. Jean Leslie
Hair of the Dog. D. Whitelaw
Hair of the Sleuthhound. J. L. Breen
Hairpin Mystery. J. M. Walsh
Hair's Breadth. L. Thayer
Hairy Arm. E. Wallace
Haiti Circle. Marilyn Ross
Haitian Hit. D. Pendleton
Haitian Legacy. S. Wagner
Haitian Vendetta. Don Smith
Hal Hazard. F. G. Andrews
Halcyon Way. F. McShane
Haldane Station. F. E. Randall
Half a Bag of Stringer. P. McCutchan

Half a Chance. F. S. Isham
Half a Clew. R. H. Watkins
Half a Clue. J. R. Warren
Half a Corpse. R. Millar
Half a Glass of Moonshine. G. D. Martin
Half a Kick from Home. C. T. Westcott
Half a Million Insurance. H. W. Vrooman
Half a Mind. W. Hornsby
Half a Minute's Silence, and other stories. Maurice Baring
Half a Truth. Rita
Half Ace. J. M. Walsh
Half Angel. B. Jefferis
Half Brothers. E. P. Frankland
Half-Caste. A. Murray
Half-Crown Bob and tales of the Riverine. P. Warung
Half Devil, Half Tiger. R. J. Fletcher
Half-God. A. Dorrington
Half-Haunted Saloon. R. Shattuck
Half Hours of a Blind Man's Holiday. W. W. Fenn
Half Hunter. J. Sherwood
Half Interest in Murder. J. Creighton
Half-Life. Sharon Webb
Half Mast. P. Traill
Half-Mast for the Deemster. G. Bellairs
Half-Mast Murder. M. Kennedy
Half Moon Street. J. J. Lydecker
Half Moon Street. P. Theroux
Half-Mother. E. Tennant
Half-Open Door. B. Gray
Half-Past Mortem. J. A. Saxon
Half-Seas Over. G. Gilpatric
Half-Sister's Secret. F. Du Boisgobey
Half-Smart Set. F. Warden
Half-Way East. D. Footman
Half-Way to Murder. S. Troy
Halford's Adventure. H. Bindloss
Halfway House. E. Queen
Halfway to Hell. H. Whittington
Halfway to Horror. David Hume
Halfway to Paradise. Laurence Kirk
Hall of Death. N. Tyre
Hallam Moor Mystery. C. H. Barker
Hallapoose. R. N. Peck
Hallelujah Corner. J. Harris
Hallowed Murder. Ellen Hart
Halloween. L. Burgess
Halloween. B. Greer
Halloween. Curtis Richards
Hallowe'en Homicide. L. Thayer
Halloween Murder. D. M. Disney
Halloween Murders. J. N. Chance
Hallowe'en Party. A. Christie
Halloween II. J. Martin
Hallowes' Hell. N. Steed
Hallowing. F. Yariv
Hallowmass Abbey. Winifred Graham
Halo for a Lady. B. Schwarz
Halo for My Honey. D. Haring
Halo for Nobody. H. Kane
Halo for Satan. John Evans
Halo Heel. D. Haring
Halo Highway. Rafe Bernard
Halo in Blood. John Evans
Halo in Brass. John Evans
Halo Jump. Alistair Hamilton
Halo of Sin. M. Tadrack
Halo Parade. Bill James
Halo Solution. N. Neebel
Hal's Own Murder Case. Lee Martin
Halsey and the Dead Ringer. C. Martell
Halsey and the Fine Art of Murder. C. Martell
Halves. J. Payn
Ham Reporter. R. J. Randisi
Hambro's Itch. H. Robens
Hamburg Switch. Angus Ross
Hamish Munro's Experiment. V. George
Hamlet Problem. Bradshaw Jones
Hamlet, Revenge! M. Innes
Hamlet Trap. K. Wilhelm
Hamlet Ultimatum. Leonard Sanders
Hamlet Warning. Leonard Sanders
Hamlet's First Case. P. Sangster

Hammer. J. Trench
Hammer in His Hand. W. Masterson
Hammer Island. S. Styles
Hammer Me Home. R. R. Werry
Hammer of Doom. F. Everton
Hammer of God. C. H. Bullivant
Hammer of God. N. De Mille
Hammer of Justice. S. Milne
Hammer of Thor. Carter Brown
Hammer Strike Solution. V. Fields
Hammer the Toff. J. Creasey
Hammered Gold. W. O. Johnson
Hammerhead. D. Cory
Hammerhead. J. Mayo
Hammerhead. J. J. Savarin
Hammerhead Reef. K. Conway
Hammerhead Reef. D. Pendleton
Hammerheads. Dale Brown
HammerLocke. J. Barnao
Hammer's Eye. R. A. Scotti
Hammers of Fingal. A. MacVicar
Hammers of Hate. G. Thorne
Hammersleigh. R. Ellerbeck
Hammersmith Maggot. W. Mole
Hammersmith Murders. D. Frome
Hammerstrike. W. Winward
Hammerword Technique. M. Spouse
Hammett. J. Gores
Hammett Homicides. D. Hammett
Hampstead Mystery. F. Marryat
Hampstead Mystery. J. R. Watson
Hampton Classic. J. Foxe
Hampton Heat. I. Weinman
Hampton Mystery. Mrs. H. Lewis
Hampton Sisters. B. F. Conners
Hampton Stories. M. Hampton
Hamptons. L. Harris
Hamydal, the Vagabond Philosopher. M. Dekobra
Hand. Y. Aleshkovsky
Hand. M. Brandel
Hand. J. Farrington
Hand. T. F. W. Hickey
Hand Against Him. J. B. Galloway
Hand and Land. George Long
Hand and Ring. A. K. Green
Hand in Glove. M. G. Eberhart
Hand in Glove. N. Marsh
Hand in Glove. Anne Stuart
Hand in Murder. C. Dixon
Hand in Red. I. Stark
Hand in the Dark. A. J. Rees
Hand in the Game. G. Hunting
Hand in the Glove. R. Stout
Hand Me a Crime. C. M. Russell
Hand Me a Fig. J. H. Chase
Hand of a Killer. M. Seuffert
Hand of a Thousand Rings. R. Bachmann
Hand of Allah. W. LeQueux
Hand of Cain. Martin Thomas
Hand of Death. M. Yorke
Hand of Doom. Anonymous
Hand of Doom. J. M. Walsh
Hand of Evil. J. T. Osborne
Hand of Fate. M. Underwood
Hand of Fatima. R. Rothstein
Hand of Fear. G. Verner
Hand of Fu-Manchu. S. Rohmer
Hand of Ganz. I. Haiblum
Hand of Glass. Jennie Melville
Hand of Glory. J. Fairfax-Blakeborough
Hand of Horror. O. F. Jerome
Hand of Ireland and other stories. D. Byrne
Hand of Justice. F. Duncan
Hand of Lazarus. W. B. Murphy
Hand of Mary Constable. P. Gallico
Hand of Peril. A. Stringer
Hand of Power. E. Wallace
Hand of Seeta. J. G. Brandon
Hand of Solange. M. Rippon
Hand of the Chimpanzee. R. Hare
Hand of the Four. Mark Cross
Hand of the Imposter. P. Minton
Hand of the Lion. C. Coker
Hand of the Mafia. J. Baynes

Hand of the Spoiler. S. Paternoster
Hand of the Unseen. M. Leighton
Hand of the Waverleys. B. Goldie
Hand of Vengeance. H. Desmond
Hand of Vengeance. G. H. Teed
Hand of Vengeance. G. F. Underhill
Hand on the Alibi. J. Bude
Hand on the Cobbler's Safe. S. Bailey
Hand on the Latch. M. Cholmondeley
Hand on the Strings. R. Rodd
Hand on the Web. R. E. Salwey
Hand on the Window Sill. B. Wayde
Hand Out. J. Rathbone
Hand Over Mind. M. Lovell
Hand Painted. Countess Barcynska
Hand-Picked for Murder. Robert Martin
Hand-Picked to Die. R. Deming
Hand-Print Mystery. S. Fowler
Hand That Hid in Darkness. W. M. Graydon
Hand That Won. Nicholas Carter
Hand to Burn. J. Cannan
Hand to Execute. R. L. Eickhoff
Hand to Hand. Nicholas Carter
Hand Without Mercy. J. Sandys
Handcuff Wizard. Nicholas Carter
Handful of Dominoes. J. L. Johnson
Handful of Fire. N. R. Nash
Handful of Homicide. D. Haring
Handful of Murder. F. Findley
Handful of Silver. V. Canning
Handful of Silver. J. S. Strange
Handful of Sinners. C. Franklin
Handful of Stars. E. V. Zukas
Handful of Trumps. J. J. Hewson
Handkerchief Clue. H. Rockwood
Handle. R. Stark
Handle of Sin. E. Metcalfe
Handle with Care. H. Lugar
Handle with Care. Rick Madison
Handle with Care. Cassie Miles
Handle with Fear. T. B. Dewey
Hands in the Dark. M. Grant
Hands in the Darkness. A. Golsworthy
Hands of a Stranger. R. Daley
Hands of Clay. E. R. Beach
Hands of Compulsion. A. E. Barr
Hands of Death. A. Colin
Hands of Death. D. Winston
Hands of Death. Eric Wood
Hands of Doom! T. Mayne
Hands of Eddy Loyd. E. R. Johnson
Hands of Fate. A. L. Thompson
Hands of Healing Murder. B. D'Amato
Hands of Innocence. J. Ashford
Hands of Justice. B. Flynn
Hands of Justice. F. W. Robinson
Hands of Orlac. M. Renard
Hands of Terror. J. Crecy
Hands of the Enemy. M. Medoff
Hands of the Ripper. E. S. Shew
Hands of the Shadow. S. Truss
Hands of Wan Lu. B. L. Jacot
Hands Off Bulldog Drummond. G. Fairlie
Hands Off the Lady. Carter Brown
Hands Off the Lovely. Kane
Hands Unseen. Herman Landon
Hands Up! J. G. Bethune
Hands Without Healing. P. Conway
Handsome, But Dead. A. H. Wahl
Handsome Jack and other stories. James Greenwood
Handsome Phil, and other stories. J. H. Riddell
Handwriting on the Wall. D. Fox
Handwriting on the Wall. M. Propper
Handy Death. R. L. Fish
Handyman. Stephen Robertson
Handyman. G. Suster
Hang by Your Neck. H. Kane
Hang Dead Hawaiian Style. P. Morgan
Hang Glider. P. Somerville-Large
Hang Loose. B. Copper
Hang Me in Hong Kong. E. Norman
Hang on a Minute, Mate. B. Crump
Hang the Consequences. M. R. D. Meek
Hang the Hangman. M. L. Stokes

Hang the Little Man. J. Creasey
Hang the Man High. G. Household
Hang-Up. Sam Ross
Hang-Up Kid. Carter Brown
Hanged by a Thread. D. Haddow
"Hanged by the Neck." F. G. Layton
Hanged for a Sheep. R. Gatenby
Hanged for a Sheep. F. Lockridge
Hanged I'll Be! R. Goyne
Hanged Man. Douglas Scott
Hanged Man. Edmund Ward
Hanged Man's House. E. Ferrars
Hanged Men. D. Harper
Hanging. L. Halegua
Hanging Captain. Henry Wade
Hanging Doll Murder. R. Ormerod
Hanging Heiress. R. Wormser
Hanging Judge. Gwyn Evans
Hanging Judge. B. Hamilton
Hanging Matter. M. H. Bradley
Hanging of Constance Hillier. S. Fowler
Hanging On. D. R. Koontz
Hanging Rope. Martin Kent
Hanging Sword! A. Soutar
Hanging Tree. B. Knox
Hanging Valley. Peter Robinson
Hanging Waters. K. West
Hanging Woman. J. Rhode
Hanging Woman. J. Roffman
Hangings. B. Pronzini
Hanging's Too Good. J. Ronald
Hanging's Too Good. L. Thayer
Hangman. P. Geddes
Hangman. G. Verner
Hangman for Paradise. J. Canon
Hangman Is a Woman. D. Glinto
Hangman Never Waits. M. Dekobra
Hangman Waits. Roland Daniel
Hangman Waits. H. Desmond
Hangman's Child. A. Wood
Hangman's Choice. C. Knight
Hangman's Cliff. R. Neill
Hangman's Creek. P. Logan
Hangman's Crusade. J. Barwick
Hangman's Curfew. G. Mitchell
Hangman's Daughter. W. Tyrer
Hangman's Dozen. David Alexander
Hangman's Guests. Stuart Martin
Hangman's Hands. C. Wogan
Hangman's Handyman. Hake Talbot
Hangman's Harvest. M. E. Chaber
Hangman's Harvest. D. Linton
Hangman's Harvest. Austin Stone
Hangman's Hat. P. Ernst
Hangman's Hill. F. Pell
Hangman's Holiday. D. L. Sayers
Hangman's Honeymoon. C. H. Barker
Hangman's Isle. G. Griffith
Hangman's Knot. A. Gask
Hangman's Loose. R. L. Sweeney
Hangman's Moon. L. Gribble
Hangman's Noose. G. Batson
Hangman's Noose. D. D. Green
Hangman's Row. A. M. Stein
Hangman's Springs. John Reese
Hangman's Tide. J. B. Hilton
Hangman's Tie. C. Hale
Hangman's Tree. D. C. Disney
Hangman's Whip. M. G. Eberhart
Hangover House. S. Rohmer
Hangover Murders. A. Hobhouse
Hangover Square. P. Hamilton
Hangsaman. S. Jackson
Hank of Hair. C. Jay
Hank Tries the Sidewalk. Griff
Hankow Return. C. S. Archer
Hanky Panky. L. Jarreau
Hannah Massey. C. Cookson
Hannah Says Foul Play. D. V. Babcock
Hanneman's War. T. Hauser
Hannie Richards. H. Bailey
Hanno's Doll. E. Piper
Hanoi. Nick Carter
Hanoi Deathgrip. J. Buchanan

Hanoi Hellground. J. Lansing
Hans, Who Goes There? F. Helitzer
Hantu. J. Halkin
Happening. E. Curry
Happiest Ghost in Town. L. Malloy
Happy Alienist. W. Smith
Happy Anniversary, Harrison High. J. Farris
Happy Are the Clean of Heart. A. M. Greeley
Happy Are the Meek. A. Greeley
Happy Are Those Who Thirst for Justice. A. M. Greeley
Happy Chase. Mountford Williams
Happy Deathday. P. D. Westbrook
Happy Ending. Fredric Brown
Happy English Child. U. Zilinsky
Happy Ever After. L. J. Beeston
Happy Exile. F. M. White
Happy Ghost. H. H. Bashford
Happy Harvest. J. Farnol
Happy Highwayman. L. Charteris
Happy Holiday! T. O'Finn
Happy Hostage. V. Brome
Happy Hunting Ground. L. Greth
Happy Killers. K. Robeson
Happy Man. E. C. Higgs
Happy Murderers. V. Bridges
Happy New Year, Herbie and other stories. E. Hunter
Happy Nightmare. P. Buranelli
Happy Now I Go. T. Charles
Happy Prodigal. E. Denny
Happy Quest. A. Wood
Happy Returns. F. Gaite
Happy Spring. A. Preston
Happy Thieves. R. Condon
Harani Trail. A. G. Christian
Harassed Hero. E. Dudley
Harbinger. M. Graham
Harbinger Effect. S. K. Wolf
Harbingers of Fear. D. Simpson
Harbor of the Little Boats. W. E. Huntsberry
Harbour. P. MacDonald
Harbour of Refuge. F. M. White
Hard and Fast. U. S. Andersen
Hard and Fast. R. Dudgeon
Hard Bargains. J. Grady
Hard-Boiled. R. DiChiara
Hard-Boiled Defective Stories. C. Burns
Hard Candy. A. Vachss
Hard Cash. M. A. Collins
Hard Cash. C. Reade
Hard Contact. B. Copper
Hard Corps. C. Bainbridge
Hard Edge. A. Destefano
Hard Hit. J. Wainwright
Hard Kill. L. Grex
Hard Kill. D. Stivers
Hard Knocker's Luck. W. Murray
Hard Knot. C. Gibbon
Hard Line. M. Z. Lewin
Hard Lines. H. Smart
Hard Liver. A. Weymouth
Hard Luck. A. W. A'Beckett
Hard Luck Money. G. Tippette
Hard Man. L. Katcher
Hard Man. W. J. White
Hard Man to Kill. Ritchie Perry
Hard Men. J. Burmeister
Hard Men. A. Kilgore
Hard Money. M. M. Thomas
Hard Option. G. Moffat
Hard Pressed. Glenys Roberts
Hard Pressed. F. M. White
Hard Racket. D. Haring
Hard Rain. P. Abrahams
Hard Rain. N. Hartley
Hard Rain. J. Van de Wetering
Hard Rock Man. J. B. Hendryx
Hard Sell. W. Haggard
Hard Sell. R. Merwin
Hard to Get. A. S. Roche
Hard to Handle. J. Welcome
Hard to Kill. J. Marcott
Hard Trade. Arthur Lyons

Hard Trip. A. Dipper
Hard Way. J. Ahern
Hardball. B. D'Amato
Hardball. D. Hornig
Hardball. J. Sangster
Hardcover. W. Warga
Hardenbrass and Harverill. Anonymous
Harden's Escape. H. Bindloss
Harder Than Steel. G. Thorne
Harder They Come. M. Thelwell
Harder They Fall. A. Bocca
Harder They Fall. Tom Logan
Harder They Hit. R. Kantner
Harder Thing Than Triumph. B. N. Byfield
Hardican's Hollow. J. S. Fletcher
Hardiman's Landing. P. Malloch
Harding Mystery. A. J. Alderson
Harding Scandal. F. Barrett
Hardliners. W. Haggard
Hardly a Man Is Now Alive. H. Brean
Hardly a Man Is Now Alive. J. Ridgway
Hardman. D. Karp
Hardship Our Garment. L. Wood
Hardway Diamonds Mystery. M. Burton
Hardwick Mystery. F. Prentice
Hare in March. V. Packer
Hare Sitting Up. M. Innes
Harem. L. Royer
Harem Captive. A. Lamour
Harem Games. E. Tokson
Harem Mystery. A. Parsons
Hargrave Deception. H. Hunt
Harjunpaa and the Stone Murders. M. Joensuu
Hark, Hark, the Watchdogs Bark. T. Wells
Harker File. N. Hollander
Harker File. M. Olden
Harlan Legacy. J. A. Creighton
Harlem Hit. R. Mallory
Harlem Is My Heaven. I. Gordon
Harlem Showdown. M. Barry
Harlem Underground. E. Lacy
Harlequin. M. L. West
Harlequin House. L. Hayes
Harlequin of Death. S. Horler
Harlequin of Doom. J. Sandys
Harlequin Opal. F. Hume
Harley Greenoak's Charge. B. Mitford
Harlingham case. F. Warden
Harlot of Jericho. M. Molloy
Harlot's Daughter. P. Hastings
Harlot's House. E. G. Cousins
Harm in Trying. M. Dedina
Harm Intended. R. Parker
Harmattan. T. Klop
Harmful Intent. Robin Cook
Harmless Ghosts. J. A. Solmonson
Harmonetics Investigation. G. M. Heldman
Harmony. S. T. Chehak
Harmony in Autumn. K. Hewitt
Harms Way. C. Aird
Harne Grange Mystery. Colin Hope
Harness Bull. L. T. White
Harness of Death. W. S. Sykes
Harp for a Honey. B. Schwarz
Harp of Life. F. H. Rose
Harper. John Macdonald
Harper's Folly. M. Aylward
Harper's Luck. M. Aylward
Harpinger's Hunch. H. Carstairs
Harpoon. F. Ponthier
Harpoon of Death. W. O'Farrell
Harrier! D. MacKenzie
Harrier Hijack. M. D. Morrison
Harriet. Elizabeth Jenkins
Harriet Farewell. M. Erskine
Harriet Said . . . B. Bainbridge
Harriet, the Haunted. K. Kimbrough
Harrigan's File. A. Derleth
Harringay's Last Gamble. O. Williams
Harrington Street Mystery. W. P. Kelly
Harris in Wonderland. P. Reid
Harrison Affair. G. Seymour
Harrison Keith and the Phantom Heiress. Nicholas Carter

Harrison Keith at Bay. Nicholas Carter
Harrison Keith, Magician. Nicholas Carter
Harrison Keith, Sleuth. Nicholas Carter
Harrison Keith—Star Reporter. Nicholas Carter
Harrison Keith's Abduction Tangle. Nicholas Carter
Harrison Keith's Battle of Nerve. Nicholas Carter
Harrison Keith's Big Stakes. Nicholas Carter
Harrison Keith's Cameo Case. Nicholas Carter
Harrison Keith's Chance Clue. Nicholas Carter
Harrison Keith's Chance Shot. Nicholas Carter
Harrison Keith's Close Quarters. Nicholas Carter
Harrison Keith's Crooked Trail. Nicholas Carter
Harrison Keith's Cyclone Clue. Nicholas Carter
Harrison Keith's Danger. Nicholas Carter
Harrison Keith's Death Compact. Nicholas Carter
Harrison Keith's Death Watch. Nicholas Carter
Harrison Keith's Diamond Case. Nicholas Carter
Harrison Keith's Dilemma. Nicholas Carter
Harrison Keith's Double Cross. Nicholas Carter
Harrison Keith's Double Mystery. Nicholas Carter
Harrison Keith's Drag Net. Nicholas Carter
Harrison Keith's Dual Role. Nicholas Carter
Harrison Keith's Fight for Life. Nicholas Carter
Harrison Keith's Greatest Task. Nicholas Carter
Harrison Keith's Green Diamond. Nicholas Carter
Harrison Keith's Haunted Client. Nicholas Carter
Harrison Keith's Labyrinth. Nicholas Carter
Harrison Keith's Lucky Strike. Nicholas Carter
Harrison Keith's Mummy Case. Nicholas Carter
Harrison Keith's Mystic Letter. Nicholas Carter
Harrison Keith's Oath. Nicholas Carter
Harrison Keith's Padlock Mystery. Nicholas Carter
Harrison Keith's Perilous Contact. Nicholas Carter
Harrison Keith's Poison Problem. Nicholas Carter
Harrison Keith's Queer Clue. Nicholas Carter
Harrison Keith's River Front Ruse. Nicholas Carter
Harrison Keith's River Mystery. Nicholas Carter
Harrison Keith's Sparkling Trail. Nicholas Carter
Harrison Keith's Strange Summons. Nicholas Carter
Harrison Keith's Struggle. Nicholas Carter
Harrison Keith's Studio Crime. Nicholas Carter
Harrison Keith's Tact. Nicholas Carter
Harrison Keith's Time Lock Case. Nicholas Carter
Harrison Keith's Triple Tragedy. Nicholas Carter
Harrison Keith's Triumph. Nicholas Carter
Harrison Keith's Wager. Nicholas Carter
Harrison Keith's Warning. Nicholas Carter
Harrison Keith's Weird Partner. Nicholas Carter
Harrison Keith's Wireless Message. Nicholas Carter
Harrowing. A. Skinner
Harry Ambler. S. Marlow
Harry Ambler and How He Saved the Homestead. S. Marlow
Harry and the Bikini Bandits. B. Heatter
Harry Blount, the Detective. T. J. Flanagan
Harry Hogbin. D. W. MacArthur
Harry-O. L. Hays
Harry-O #2. L. Hays
Harry Pinkurton, the Boy Detective. H. Rockwood
Harry Pinkurton, the King of Detectives. H. Rockwood
Harry Roughton. L. J. F. Hexham
Harry Sharpe, the New York Detective. H. Rockwood
Harry Williams, the New York Detective. F. L. Broughton
Harry's Game. G. Seymour
Harsh Evidence. P. Fry
Harsh Evidence. R. Sheldon
Harsh Heritage. N. Tranter
Hart to Hart. R. Bowdler
Hartinger's Mouse. P. McCutchan
Hartington's Luck. D. Walshe
Hartland Case. John Bentley
Hartman's Game. Richard Cox
Hartness Millions. G. Norsworthy
Hartwell Case. R. L. Goldman
Harvard Has a Homicide. T. Fuller
Harvest Bride. Tony Richards
Harvest for Harpies. H. Lugar
Harvest Home. T. P. Prest
Harvest Moon. J. S. Fletcher
Harvest Moon. J. M. Forman
Harvest Murder. J. Rhode

H

Harvest of Death. Ray Harrison
Harvest of Death. G. Hart
Harvest of Deceit. K. Lindsay
Harvest of Deceit. C. Pemberton
Harvest of Guile. S. Warwick
Harvest of Hate. R. Goyne
Harvest of Hate. H. Leyford
Harvest of Javelins. B. Atkey
Harvest of Love. C. R. Gull
Harvest of Mischief. D. W. Burbridge
Harvest of Sin. M. Leighton
Harvest of Tares. V. Clavering
Harvest of Tares. M. Dalton
Harvest of Terror. A. Gale
Harvest of Violence. S. Brydon
Harvesting. J. Bishop
Harvey Garrard's Crime. E. P. Oppenheim
Has Anybody Here Seen Abby? C. Joyce
Has Anyone Seen Jean? W. B. Hare
Hash. N. Fleming
Hashimi's Revenge. K. Royce
Hashish. T. King
Hashknife of Stormy River. W. C. Tuttle
Hashknife of the Canyon Trail. W. C. Tuttle
Hashknife of the Double Bar 8. W. C. Tuttle
Hasington. E. Fyhrlund
Hastings Conspiracy. Alfred Coppel
Hasty Heiress. P. Muller
Hasty Wedding. M. G. Eberhart
Hat of Authority. John Sanders
Hat-Pin Murder. G. Dilnot
Hatanee. A. Eggar
Hatchet Job. J. E. Neighbors
Hatchet Man. M. Arrighi
Hatchet Man. J. Cassells
Hatchet Man. W. Marshall
Hatchet Man. San Antonio
Hatchet Man. W. Van Atta
Hatchet Men. D. Hartman
Hatchet Murders. N. Morland
Hatchetman. D. Dodge
Hatchett. L. McGraw
Hatchie, the Guardian Slave. W. J. Ashton
Hatchment. R. B. C. Graham
Hatch's Conspiracy. D. Merritt
Hatch's Island. D. Merritt
Hatch's Mission. D. Merritt
Hate! R. Gar
Hate. H. Janson
Hate Alley. M. L. Weiss
Hate Begins at Home. Joan Aiken
Hate Finds a Way. M. Cumberland
Hate for Eight. D. Thurlow
Hate for Sale. M. Cumberland
Hate Genius. K. Robeson
Hate Is for the Hunted. S. D. Frances
Hate Is My Livery. M. Durham
Hate Is Thicker Than Blood. B. Latham
Hate Island. A. West
Hate Killer. B. Walton
Hate Master. K. Robeson
Hate of Evil. K. Snowden
Hate of Man. H. Hill
Hate Ship. B. Graeme
Hate That Kills. Nicholas Carter
Hate, the Destroyer. R. N. Silver
Hate Thy Neighbor. M. Lynch
Hate Thy Neighbor. John Marsh
Hate to Kill. M. Halliday
Hate Will Find a Way. M. Cumberland
Hated by All! J. Drummond
Hated Eight. P. Quiroule
Hated One. D. Tracy
Hated Therewith. D. G. Waring
Hateful Voyage. M. Neville
Haters. T. Strauss
Hatfield-McCoy Feud. W. B. Lawson
Hatpin Misused. A. Hesse
Hatred's Web. P. Nottingham
Hats Off! A. H. Veysey
Hatteras Blue. D. C. Poyer
Hatterask Incident. J. D. Randall
Hatter's Ghosts. G. Simenon
Hatter's Phantoms. G. Simenon

Hatton Garden Mystery. F. Marlowe
Haughton Diamond Robbery. Roland Daniel
Haunt of the Nightingale. J. R. Riggs
Haunt of the "Queer" Makers. Lieut. Carlton
Haunted. Janice Bennett
Haunted. C. G. Kurtz
Haunted. G. Warden
Haunted Abbey. H. Leyford
Haunted and Hunted. E. O'Donnell
Haunted Bells. M. S. Buchanan
Haunted Bookshop. C. Morley
Haunted Bookshop. L. Rose
Haunted Castle. O. Bradbury
Haunted Castle. George Walker
Haunted Cavern. J. Palmer
Haunted Chair. G. Leroux
Haunted Chair. J. F. Stone
Haunted Chamber. Duchess
Haunted Farm. L. Austen-Leigh
Haunted Garden. W. E. D. Ross
Haunted Hammock. E. Lockwood
Haunted Harbor. D. Douglas
Haunted Hat. R. Knight
Haunted Heart. T. Brun
Haunted Heart. Claudette Nicole
Haunted Heirloom. M. Eatock
Haunted Hills. B. M. Bower
Haunted Hollow. B. Symons
Haunted Homestead. E. Southworth
Haunted Honeymoon. J. Troy
Haunted Honeymoon. S. Wagner
Haunted Hotel. W. Collins
Haunted Hotel Mystery. A. Skene
Haunted House. H. Belloc
Haunted House. A. Bernede
Haunted House. Owen Davis
Haunted House. Sharon Green
Haunted House at Kew. G. Warden
Haunted House on Berkeley Square. E. Vredenburg
Haunted Ice Rink. E. R. Home-Gall
Haunted Island. H. Bourne
Haunted Lady. M. R. Rinehart
Haunted Lake and other stories. J. J. Farjeon
Haunted Landscape. I. Bromige
Haunted Light. E. Price
Haunted Lives. J. S. Le Fanu
Haunted Looking Glass. G. Darrell
Haunted Man. J. Gaunt
Haunted Mesa. L. L'Amour
Haunted Monastery. R. Van Gulik
Haunted Ocean. K. Robeson
Haunted Pajamas. F. P. Elliott
Haunted Palace. Mrs. R. M. P. Yorke
Haunted Place. V. Coffman
Haunted Portrait. A. Ashton
Haunted Priory. S. Cullen
Haunted Rectory. H. C. McNeile
Haunted Rock. R. C. Finney
Haunted Sea. J. Pattinson
Haunted Seventh. Charles Ross
Haunted Ship. Seafarer
Haunted Shore. M. Gerard
Haunted Station, and other stories. H. Nisbet
Haunted Strangler. J. C. Cooper
Haunted Suit. N. Mapple
Haunted Summer. Anne Edwards
Haunted Theatre. J. Randall
Haunted Tower. B. Cane
Haunted Tower. H. Wood
Haunted Wing. T. Walton
Haunted Woman. Melissa Napier
Haunted Wood Hollow. V. Silliman
Haunting at Lost Lake. E. Oliphant
Haunting at Waverly Falls. H. C. Rae
Haunting Cavalier. M. Thum
Haunting Fingers. Herman Landon
Haunting Hand. W. A. Roberts
Haunting Image. S. Clausse
Haunting Kisses. J. T. Osborne
Haunting Lights. T. A. Plummer
Haunting Me. P. Allardyce
Haunting of Abbotsgarth. E. Lyons
Haunting of Alan Mais. P. Saxon
Haunting of Bally Moran. H. S. Nuelle

Haunting of Cliffside. J. Letton
Haunting of Clifton Court. Dana Ross
Haunting of Drumroe. Claudette Nicole
Haunting of Fog Island. Marilyn Ross
Haunting of Helen Farley. F. Cowen
Haunting of Helen Wren. Jan Alexander
Haunting of Hill House. S. Jackson
Haunting of Hill House. F. Andrew Leslie
Haunting of Kathleen Saunders. Reginald Campbell
Haunting of Low Fennel. S. Rohmer
Haunting of Sara Lessingham. P. Bennetts
Haunting of Toby Jugg. D. Wheatley
Haunting of Villa Gabriel. Clarissa Ross
Haunting Possibility. S. Fletcher
Haunting Shadow. J. A. Jordan
Haunting Shadow. Old Sleuth
Haunting Shadows. M. F. Hutchinson
Haunts. John Douglas
Haunts of Men. R. W. Chambers
Hauser's Memory. C. Siodmak
Havana. P. Metier
Havana Hit. M. Barry
Havana Hotel Murders. F. Dudley
Havana Mystery. W. W. Sayer
Havana X. S. Gross
Have a Change of Scene. J. H. Chase
Have a Lovely Funeral. A. T. Hopkins
Have a Nice Night. J. H. Chase
Have Gat—Will Travel. R. S. Prather
Have His Carcase. D. L. Sayers
Have Mercy. J. Mangut
Have Mercy Upon Us. T. Wells
Have Nude, Will Travel. C. Allison
Have Patience, Delaney! B. Singer
Have This One on Me. J. H. Chase
Have You Seen My Son? J. Olsen
Have You Seen This Man? G. Hurley
Haven for the Damned. S. Mitchell
Haven for the Damned. H. Whittington
Haven of Deceit. C. Virmonne
Haven of Fear. P. Ponder
Haven of St. Garth. E. L. Long
Haven of Unrest. G. Collins
Havenhurst. S. Wagner
Havenhurst Affair. A. O. Pollard
Havering Plot. R. Keverne
Haversham Legacy. D. Winston
Haviland's Chum. B. Mitford
Having No Hearts. G. Goodchild
Having Wonderful Crime. C. Rice
Havoc! James Dark
Havoc. E. P. Oppenheim
Havoc. F. F. Van De Water
Havoc by Accident. G. Simenon
Havoc for Sale. J. Jakes
Hawaii. Nick Carter
Hawaii Five-O. M. Avallone
Hawaii for Danger. N. A. Hintze
Hawaiian Cruise. T. Lester
Hawaiian Eye. F. Castle
Hawaiian Hellground. D. Pendleton
Hawaiian Takeover. D. Streib
Hawaiian Trackdown. L. Derrick
Hawk. R. Hardwick
Hawk. S. Kyle
Hawk. R. Legge
Hawk. P. Ransley
Hawk. M. J. Shapiro
Hawk and Fisher. Simon Green
Hawk Island. H. I. Young
Hawk of Rede. H. Harding
Hawk of the Desert. G. E. Mitton
Hawk Over Hollyhedge Manor. D. K. Dowdell
Hawk Shadow. M. Heath
Hawk Watch. B. Bird
Hawkeland Cache. E. Fitzmaurice
Hawkline Monster. R. Brautigan
Hawkmoor Mystery. W. H. L. Crauford
Hawkridge. J. Blackmore
Hawks. J. J. Amiel
Hawk's Nest. W. Gunning
Hawks of Glenaerie. Ruth MacLeod
Hawksbill Manor. A. Grace
Hawkshaw. R. Goulart

Title Index

Hawkshaw the Detective. T. J. Kelly
Hawkshead. J. Flores
Hawksmoor. P. Ackroyd
Hawkstone. W. Sewell
Hawkwood. A. P. O'Rourke
Hawl. J. Peacock
Hawser Pirates. O. Wynd
Hawthorn Conspiracy. S. Hesla
Hawthorn Hill. Doris Shannon
Hawthorn Wood. Jane Fleming
Hawthorne. R. Wolff
Hay Fever. W. H. Pollock
Hayduke Lives! E. Abbey
Hayes Ball Affair. W. Hunt
Haygarth Detective. Jack North
Hazard. G. A. Browne
Hazard. R. Chanslor
Hazard Chase. J. Potter
Hazard House. P. Warren
Hazard Island. P. Tabori
Hazard of the Snows. O. Binns
Hazardous Duty. David St. John
Hazardous Holiday. E. Nisot
Haze of Evil. K. Lowe
Hazel Fane. B. Roosevelt
Hazel Verne. A. L. Halstead
Hazelhurst Mystery. J. S. Lloyd
Hazell and the Menacing Jester. P. B. Yuill
Hazell and the Three Card Trick. P. B. Yuill
Hazell Plays Solomon. P. B. Yuill
Hazzard. R. D. Brown
He and She on the B-Bar-B. W. C. Platts
He Arrived at Dusk. R. C. Ashby
He Came by Night. Anthony Gilbert
He Could Not Have Slipped. F. Beeding
He Could Stop the World. K. Robeson
He Couldn't Refuse. G. Blumberg
He Dared Not Look Behind. Cledwyn Hughes
He Didn't Mind Danger. M. Gilbert
He Didn't Mind Hanging. N. B. Mavity
He Died Laughing. Rip Connolly
He Died Laughing. L. Larier
He Died of Murder! Shelley Smith
He Died Thrice. M. G. Hugi
He Died Twice. G. J. Barrett
He Died Twice. M. Hadley
He Died with His Eyes Open. D. Raymond
He Dies and Makes No Sign. M. Thynne
He Done Her Wrong. Milt Gross
He Done Her Wrong. S. M. Kaminsky
He Fell Among Thieves. D. C. Murray
He Fell Down Dead. V. Perdue
He Found Himself Murdered. D. Ames
He Had It Coming to Him. F. Grierson
He Had to Die. A. Hocking
He Hanged His Mother on Monday. N. Morland
He Huffed and He Puffed. Barbara Paul
He Isn't Dead Yet. R. A. Anderson
He Knew He Was Right. A. Trollope
He Laughed at Murder. R. Keverne
He Liked Them Murderous. L. Dundas
He Loved Freedom. S. Fairway
He Met Mr. Moon. W. J. Elliott
He Moved Away. B. Vane
He Never Came Back. H. McCloy
He Never Came Back. P. Tabori
He Ought to Be Shot. Joan Fleming
He Ran All the Way. Sam Ross
He Rather Enjoyed It. P. G. Wodehouse
He Said, What's Blue? R. L. Finn
He Shot to Kill. P. Drax
He Should Have Been King. K. Lindsay
He Should Have Died Hereafter. C. Hare
He Travels Alone. P. Loring
He Troups to Conquer. L. W. Diegre
He Walked in Her Sleep. P. Cheyney
He Walked in Her Sleep and other stories. P. Cheyney
He Walks by Night. F. Nichols
He Was Found in the Road. A. Armstrong
He Who Digs a Grave. D. Delman
He Who Fights . . . L. Gorell
He Who Hesitates. E. McBain
He Who Walked in Scarlet. N. Tom-Gallon

He Who Whispers. J. D. Carr
He Won't Need It Now. J. L. Docherty
He Would Provoke Death. C. G. Jarvis
He Wouldn't Kill Patience. Carter Dickson
He Wouldn't Stay Dead. F. C. Davis
He Wouldn't Talk. M. Adams
Head. D. Cory
Head Case. L. Cody
Head Crusher. B. Rossi
Head First. William Marshall
Head for Death. N. Longmate
Head Held High. C. B. Bass
Head Hunter. A. P. Morris
Head Hunters. J. Luceno
Head Hunter's Secret. A. Murray
Head in the Soup. P. Levi
Head Man. D. Haring
Head Men. R. Sapir
Head of a Girl. E. O'Duffy
Head of a Traveler. N. Blake
Head of Medusa. A. Grace
Head of Pasht. W. B. Allen
Head of State. R. Hoyt
Head of State. J. Watts
Head of the Force. J. Barnett
Head of the House. A. Zuckerman
Head of the Household. T. Cobb
Head On! J. W. Thomas
Head on the Sill. M. Neville
Head Over Heels in Murder. I. S. Shriber
Headcrash. Howard Baker
Headed for a Hearse. Jonathan Latimer
Headhunter. F. Scarpetta
Headhunter. M. Slade
Heading for a Wreath. David Hume
Heading West. D. Betts
Headland House Affair. W. Martyn
Headless Beings. M. Malcolm
Headless Ghost. T. S. King
Headless Girl of the North River. Old Sleuth
Headless Hound, and other stories. R. H. Mottram
Headless Lady. C. Rawson
Headless Man. G. M. Wilson
Headless Men. K. Robeson
Headless Mystery. Old Sleuth
Headless Roommate and other stories. D. Cohen
Headless Victory. D. S. Lifson
Headline for Murder. E. Lanham
Headline for Rusty Brown. C. Regan
Headline—Murder! G. Rayne
Headlined for Murder. E. Lanham
Headliners for the Campus. K. Kester
Headlines. G. Masterton
Headlines for a Hussy. M. Brody
Headlines from Paradise. W. Grotyohann
Headlines Make Murder. O. Mills
Headlong. James Underwood
Headlong for Murder. M. Mace
Headlong from Heaven. M. Valbeck
Headmaster. D. H. Landels
Headmaster's Secret. R. Hardinge
Headquarters Budapest. Robert Parker
Heads. D. Osborn
Heads. E. Stewart
Heads for Death. L. Johnson
Heads I Win. Q. Downes
Heads Off at Midnight. F. Beeding
Heads or Tails. S. Jepson
Heads You Die. L. Gribble
Heads You Live. David Hume
Heads You Lose. C. Brand
Heads You Lose. L. Cargill
Heads You Lose. R. Gillespie
Heads You Lose. B. Halliday
Heads You Lose. B. Shannon
Heads You Lose. W. Standish
Heads You Lose. Jimmy Starr
Headsman. Austin Stone
Headsman's Holiday. D. Hawkins
Healing Hands of Death. P. Audemars
Healing Heart. Magali
Health Farm Murders. Tom Howard
Healthy Body. G. Linscott
Healthy Grave. M. Leek

Healthy Way to Die. Lionel Black
Healthy Way to Die. M. Kenyon
Heap of Trouble. E. Messenger
Hear No Evil. N. Bowen
Hear No Evil. M. Carroll
Hear No Evil. S. Ransome
Hear Not My Steps. L. S. Thompson
Hear the Children Cry. R. J. Hendrickson
Hear the Stripper Scream. P. Cagney
Hear the Wind Blow. D. M. Pierce
Heard in the Dark. Nicholas Carter
Heard Tell. A. Dunnett
Hearken to the Evidence. H. R. Wakefield
Hearse. Henry Clement
Hearse Class Male. F. Kane
Hearse for Cinderella. H. Howard
Hearse for Dark Harbor. Clarissa Ross
Hearse for McNally. G. J. Barrett
Hearse for the Boss. A. Eichler
Hearse Horse Snickered. Carolyn Thomas
Hearse in May-Day. G. Mitchell
Hearse of a Different Color. M. Constiner
Hearse of Another Color. M. E. Chaber
Hearse Waiting. W. Wright
Hearse with Horses. E. McGirr
Hearsed in Death. M. Cumberland
Hearses Don't Hurry. S. Ransome
Heart and Science. W. Collins
Heart Beat. E. Dong
Heart Cut Diamond. S. Horler
Heart in Bondage. Anthony Allen
Heart in Exile. R. Garland
Heart in the Box. F. Grierson
Heart in the Highlands. N. Kennedy
Heart Merchants. L. Goldman
Heart of a Gangster. D. Sherridane
Heart of a Girl. F. Warden
Heart of a Hero. M. Gerard
Heart of a Man. G. Simenon
Heart of a Mystery. T. W. Speight
Heart of a Princess. W. LeQueux
Heart of a Woman. Baroness Orczy
Heart of Deception. C. Jauniere
Heart of Delilah. Christopher Wilson
Heart of Gold. R. H. Greenan
Heart of Ice. F. Hume
Heart of Marble. N. Buckingham
Heart of Noel. F. Whishaw
Heart of Oak Detective. E. A. St. Mox
Heart of Penelope. M. B. Lowndes
Heart of Stone. J. Haworth
Heart of Stone. G. Warden
Heart of the Dancer. Percy White
Heart of the Dog. T. A. Roberts
Heart of the Harbor. K. Blickle
Heart of the Matter. G. Greene
Heart of the Night. B. Delinsky
Heart of the North. W. B. Mowery
Heart of the Underworld. Nicholas Carter
Heart of the West. O. Henry
Heart of Unaga. R. Cullum
Heart of Winter. J. J. Toombs
Heart Payments. G. J. Goldberg
Heart Possessed. K. Sutcliffe
Heart Specialist. P. Trent
Heart to Heart. P. Boileau
Heart to Heart. D. Pendleton
Heartache. H. Janson
Heartbeat. J. Jenkins
Heartbreak Hits the News. C. Regan
Heartland. D. Hagberg
Heartland. K. Heelan
Heartlanders. M. Dixon
Heartless. S. P. Cohen
Heartless Light. G. Green
Hearts. D. C. Murray
Hearts and Flowers. H. Rowland
Hearts by the Tower. O. Sinclair
Heart's Delight. C. Gibbon
Heart's Delight. L. Tracy
Hearts Ease in Death. James Fraser
Heart's Grown Brutal. D. Brewster
Hearts in the Highlands. Lynna Cooper
Hearts in Turmoil. M. Richmond

H

Hearts of Gold. C. Sinclair
Hearts of Gold and Hearts of Steel. H. Herman
Hearts of Stone. G. A. Larson
Hearts or Diamonds. I. D. Hardy
Heart's Problem. C. Gibbon
Heart's Ransom. C. Gayet
Heart's Revenge. C. Jauniere
Heartsearch. Patricia Wright
Heartstones. R. Rendell
Heartstone. P. Margolin
Hearty Laughs. Le Roy Stahl
Heat. W. Goldman
Heat. E. McBain
Heat from Another Sun. D. L. Lindsey
Heat Lightning. R. F. Carroll
Heat Lightning. J. Lantigua
Heat Lightning. W. Shaw
Heat Not a Furance. H. Kemp
Heat of Night. H. Whittington
Heat of the Day. E. Bowen
Heat of the Sun. M. Birmingham
Heat of Winter. H. Hirt
Heat Wave. Timothy Harris
Heath Hover Mystery. B. Mitford
Heathcliff. J. Caine
Heather. M. Dobner
Heather-Bells. R. Gover
Heather Mixture. M. Gerard
Heather Mystery. M. Gerard
Heatherton Heritage. Pamela Hill
Heat's On. J. Cairo
Heat's On. R. Drayton
Heat's On! D. Haring
Heat's On. C. Himes
Heatwave. Caesar Smith
Heatwave. T. Stapleton
Heaven and Hell. A. Altman
Heaven-Kissed Hill. J. S. Fletcher
Heaven Ran Last. W. P. McGivern
Heaven-Sent Witness and other stories. J. S. Fletcher
Heaven Will Be Ours. E. Lindsay
Heavenly Bodies. T. Warriner
Heavenly Body. G. Morgan
Heavenly Heel. D. Haring
Heaven's Empire. Simon Bell
Heaven's Prisoners. J. L. Burke
Heaviest Pipe. A. M. Patterson
Heavy As Lead. M. Torrie
Heavy Connections. C. Ellingson
Heavy Gilt. D. Klaich
Heavy, Heavy Hangs. D. M. Disney
Heavy Iron. B. Copper
Heavy Stakes. M. K. Douglas
Heberden's Seat. Douglas Clark
Hebrew Maiden. T. P. Prest
Hec Ramsey. D. Owen
Hecatomb. B. Palmer
Heck. M. Renek
Heckler. E. McBain
Hector Duval. H. Collinson
Hector Tumbler Investigates. S. Crabtree
He'd Rather Be Dead. G. Bellairs
Hedgerow. F. E. Randall
Hedonists. Colin Wilson
Hedri. H. B. Mathers
Hedy—Like Wine! B. Carson
Heel. W. L. Rohde
Heel of Achilles. L. H. Fox
Heel of Achilles. E. Radford
Heel of Achilles. G. Verner
Heel of Spring. F. Rooney
Height of Day. D. Cory
Heights of Havenrest. V. Subond
Heights of Rimring. D. Hart-Davis
Heights of Zervos. C. Forbes
Heil Britannia. P. Long
Heil Harris! J. Garforth
Heil! Hollywood. Jack Preston
Heir. C. Keane
Heir Apparent. E. L. Withers
Heir-at-Law, and other tales. Waters
Heir Hunters. B. S. Ballinger
Heir of Ashly. H. Wood
Heir of Beech Hall. S. E. Rookes

Heir of Douglas. L. De La Torre
Heir of Frinton Park. F. M. Long
Heir of Grangerfjord Castle. R. M. Sears
Heir of Greymount. J. E. Cooke
Heir of Kings. WInifred Duke
Heir of Starvelings. E. Berckman
Heir of the Ages. J. Payn
Heir to Lucifer. M. Burton
Heir to Murder. M. Burton
Heir to Murder. M. Halliday
Heir to the Throne. A. W. Marchmont
Heiress Apparent. L. Conway
Heiress of Bayou Vache. Harriet Stone
Heiress of Bellefonte. Emerson Bennett
Heiress of Densley Wold. F. Warden
Heiress of Fear. C. Farr
Heiress of Fear. J. T. Osborne
Heiress of Frascati. J. Shearing
Heiress of Glen Gower. M. A. Fleming
Heiress of Haddon. W. E. Doubleday
Heiress of Montalde. A. Ker
Heiress of the Season. W. Magnay
Heiress to Corsair Keep. C. Farr
Heiress to Crag Castle. M. Rosetti
Heiress to Evil. S. O'Brien
Heiress to Wolfskill. K. Kimbrough
Heirloom. W. Haggard
Heirloom of Tragedy. E. Noone
Heirs of Cain. A. Rothberg
Heirs of Darkness. Z. K. Snyder
Heirs of Merlin. P. Atkey
Heirs of Reuben. C. Healy
Heirs of the Kingdom. K. Hudner
Heirs to Kildrennan. A. Foxe
Heist Me Higher. B. S. Ballinger
Heisters. R. P. Jones
Held Apart. R. N. Silver
Held for Ransom. N. M. Murray
Held for Trial. Nicholas Carter
Held in Suspense. Nicholas Carter
Held in the Toils. J. K. Leys
Held in Thrall. B. Hemyng
Held in Trust! W. M. Graydon
Held Open for Death. E. Payne
Held to Ransom. R. Gover
Helen. E. V. Cunningham
Helen All Alone. W. Buchan
Helen Elwood, the Female Detective. B. and R.
Helen of London. J. Goodwin
Helen of Man o' War Island. B. Grimshaw
Helen of the Moor. A. Askew
Helen Passes By. E. R. Punshon
Helen Vardon's Confession. R. A. Freeman
Helen Whitney's Edding, and other stories. H. Wood
Helena. H. S. Irwin
Helen's Lovers. G. Bullett
Helga's Web. J. Cleary
Helix File. W. D. Blankenship
Hell Ain't So Hot. T. Trenton
Hell and High Water. R. Drayton
Hell and High Water. R. Garland
Hell Below. K. Robeson
Hell-Bent for Danger. W. Grove
Hell-Bent for Election. Jack Livingston
Hell Bent for Heaven. S. OCork
Hell-Black Night. S. Fisher
Hell-Bomb Floozies. Griff
Hell-Bound Express. Nick Carter
Hell Brood. H. Janson
Hell Can Wait. H. Whittington
Hell Candidate. T. Luke
Hell Cop. P. J. Wolfson
Hell Divers. K. Ford
Hell for Heather. P. Flower
Hell for Leather. A. Wood
Hell for Tomorrow. P. Leslie
Hell Gate. James Dawson
Hell Gate. D. Stout
Hell-Gate Tides. L. Thayer
Hell Has No Exit. J. L. Gilmer
Hell Hath No Fury. L. Eby
Hell Hath No Fury. R. Marlowe
Hell Hath No Fury. M. Richmond

Hell Hath No Fury. M. Sinton
Hell Hath No Fury. C. Williams
Hell House. R. Matheson
Hell in Harness. J. Auslander
Hell in Hindu Land. J. Rosenberger
Hell in the Afternoon. W. Sproule
Hell Is a City. W. Ard
Hell Is a City. M. Procter
Hell Is Always Today. Harry Patterson
Hell Is Empty. J. F. Straker
Hell Is Forever. J. L. Gilmer
Hell Is My Destination. J. Conway
Hell Is Sold Out. M. Dekobra
Hell Is Too Crowded. Harry Patterson
Hell Is Where You Find It. J. Welcome
Hell Island. E. L. Adams
Hell Let Loose. F. Beeding
Hell Let Loose. A. Carson
Hell-Makers. P. O'Donnell
Hell Nest. M. Mandell
Hell of a Dame. H. Janson
Hell of a Murder. W. Carrier
Hell of a Spot. B. Scott
Hell of a Woman. J. Thompson
Hell of Make Believe. F. Wiles
Hell on Friday. W. Bogart
Hell on the Way. J. M. Fox
Hell on Wheels. A. Lassiter
Hell Ride. P. Hofrichter
Hell! Said the Duchess. M. Arlen
Hell Seed. C. D. Peel
Hell Ship of Many Waters. E. O'Donnell
Hell Ship to Kuma. C. Clements
Hell Shot. J. Poyer
Hell Street. M. Franklin
Hell Strip. Lee Richards
Hell to Pay! H. Clevely
Hell to Pay. W. R. Cox
Hell Week. K. Reynolds
Hell Wind in Burma. J. Rosenberger
Hell with Elaine. V. Siller
Hellbinder. D. Pendleton
Hellbirds. A. Mitcheson
Hellblazer 1. J. Delano
Hellblazer 2. J. Delano
Hellblazer 3. J. Delano
Hellblazer 4. J. Delano
Hellbomb Flight. L. Derrick
Hellbomb Theft. J. Rosenberger
Hellbottom. E. Corder
Hellbound. S. Brandon
Hellcat. Carter Brown
Hellcat. H. Janson
Hellcat. M. Logan
Hellcats of Prohibition. R. Pereira
Helldorado. H. Janson
Helldust Cruise. D. Pendleton
Heller's Leap. Ian Wallace
Hellfire. J. Saul
Hellfire. T. Tyger
Hellfire Conspiracy. Ralph Hayes
Hellfire Crusade. D. Pendleton
Hellfire Files of Jules de Grandin. Seabury Quinn
Hellfire Heritage. W. D. Roberts
Hellfire in Haiti. Jim Case
Hellflower. G. O. Smith
Hellgate. W. C. MacDonald
Hellgate Plantation. F. Swann
Hellhole. S. Grave
Hellinger's Law. J. Barr
Hellions. R. T. Bickers
Hellish Smart. F. Kenny
Hellmouth Horror. B. E. M. Ward
Hello Cruel World, Goodbye. J. Goodman
Hello Dolly . . . Goodbye. D. Haring
Hello, Lemuria, Hello. R. Goulart
Hellrider. D. Kellerman
Hell's Above Us. Henry Ward
Hell's Acre. F. H. Rose
Hell's Angel. Antheo Cohen
Hell's Angel. H. Janson
Hell's Angel Kidnapping. P. A. Foxall
Hell's Arena. C. D. Pell
Hell's Belle. Joan Fleming

Hell's Belles! R. Drayton
Hell's Belles. H. Janson
Hell's Brew. S. Horler
Hell's Full. William Harrison
Hell's Gate. D. Pendleton
Hell's Harbour. H. P. Lee
Hell's Harvest. H. S. Banner
Hell's Highway. D. Haring
Hell's Hostages. L. Derrick
Hell's Kitchen. B. Appel
Hell's Kitchen Connection. R. B. Gillespie
Hell's Little Angel. D. Haring
Hell's Loose. R. Pertwee
Hell's Only Half Full. R. Kantner
Hell's Our Destination. G. Brewer
Hell's Wenches. V. Norwood
Hellspout. B. Knox
Hellstar. J. M. Reaves
Help from the Baron. Anthony Morton
Help I Am Being Held Prisoner. D. E. Westlake
Help, Please. E. Bahr
Help the Poor Struggler. M. Grimes
Help Wanted—for Murder. W. L. Rohde
Help Wanted: Orphans Preferred. E. W. Emerson
Help Yourself to Happiness. F. R. Adams
Helping Hand. C. Dale
Helping Hand and other stories. Robert Barr
Helping Hersey. Baroness Von Hutten
Helping with Enquiries. C. Dale
Helsinki Affair. M. Sariola
Hemingway Hoax. J. Haldemann
Hemingway's Notebook. B. Granger
Hemlock. R. A. Nicholls
Hemlock Avenue Mystery. R. Doubleday
Hemlock for Eight. C. Bax
Hemlock Galore. A. Kennington
Hemlock Option. M. Vinter
Hemlock Swamp. E. L. Whittlesey
Hemlock Tree. E. Lottman
Henbane. C. Meadows
Henchman. K-O. Bornemark
Hendon's First Case. J. Rhode
Hennessy. M. Franklin
Henrietta Who? C. Aird
Henry. M. A. Kay
Henry Broch, Old Sleuth's Assistant. Old Sleuth
Henry Cassland. H. Druce
Henry Dunbar. M. E. Braddon
Henry in a Silver Frame. J. Eastwood
Henry McGee Is Not Dead. B. Granger
Henry Massinger. R. Jocelyn
Henry Northcote. J. C. Snaith
Henry Prince in Action. C. F. Gregg
Henry the Sheriff. W. C. Tuttle
Hephzibah. S. M. Stratham
Hepsworth Millions. C. Lys
Heptameron. H. Phillips
Her Assigned Husband. A. Pratt
Her Column's a Killer. M. Brody
Her Convict. M. E. Braddon
Her Convict Husband. Ladbroke Black
Her Convict Husband. M. Leighton
Her Crooked Lover. B. Delane
Her Dangerous Memory. N. Norman
Her Death of Cold. R. McInerny
Her Demon Lover. L. Bronte
Her Demon Lover. J. L. Roberts
Her Empty Triumph. A. Askew
Her Fairy Prince. G. Warden
Her Faithful Knight. G. Warden
Her Fatal Beauty. W. Braun
Her Fatal Sin. M. E. Holmes
Her Fate and His. M. Leighton
Her Father's Crime. G. Bruce
Her Father's Daughter. A. Askew
Her Father's Daughter. W. J. Coughlin
Her Foreign Conquest. R. H. Savage
Her Fugitive. C. Stanton
Her Garden of Eden. J. Chancellor
Her Grace at Bay. H. Hill
Her Great Idea and other stories. L. B. Walford
Her Great Moment. E. Balmer
Her Great Surprise. H. P. Halsey
Her Halo in Headlines. M. Brody

Her Happy Face. L. T. Meade
Her Heart in Her Throat. Ethel L. White
Her Heart's Awakening. M. Leighton
Her Heart's Desire. Lynna Cooper
Her Heart's Gift. O. Kent
Her Hidden Crime. W. J. Elliott
Her Hidden Past. B. M. Clay
Her Highness. F. Whishaw
Her Highness's Secretary. C. Dawe
Her Honor. W. J. Coughlin
Her Honour. R. Machray
Her Husband's Watch. B. King
Her Ladyship. T. W. Speight
Her Ladyship's Jewels and What Became of Them. R. H. Gooch
Her Ladyship's Secret. W. Westall
Her Ladyship's Silence. M. Leighton
Her Last Appearance. A. N. Robertson
Her Lips Betrayed. D. Walshe
Her Little Game. G. Goodchild
Her Love, Her Ruin. A. Belot
Her Lover's Peril. A. Eadie
Her Loving Slave. H. Nisbet
Her Mad Marriage. G. M. White
Her Majesty the Queen. J. E. Cooke
Her Majesty's Hit Man. A. Prior
Her Majesty's Minister. W. LeQueux
Her Marriage Lines. M. Leighton
Her Month of Freedom. P. Trent
Her Mother's Child. A. Askew
Her Mother's Husband. M. Anderson
Her Night of Terror. M. O'Regan
Her Own Affair. T. A. Plummer
Her Private Murder. J. Corbett
Her Private Passions. M. Holland
Her Reputation. T. Mundy
Her Right Divine. O. Kent
Her Royal Highness. W. LeQueux
Her Royal Highness's Love Affair. J. M. Cobban
Her Sacrifice. A. Applin
Her Second Murder. J. Corbett
Her Second Self. A. Wood
Her Secret Life. R. Machray
Her Senator. A. C. Gunter
Her Sentinel. A. W. Marchmont
Her Splendid Sin. H. Hill
Her Stepfather's House. J. Wetherell
Her Two Millions. W. Westall
Her Ways Are Death. J. Mann
Her Weapon Was Passion. H. Janson
Her Wedding Night. M. Pemberton
Her Wild Oats. P. Trent
Heracles Commando. E. McGhee
Herald. M. Shaara
Herald of Death. M. Dalman
Herald of Doom. G. Ashe
Herald Personal and other stories. Nicholas Carter
Herapath Property. J. S. Fletcher
Herbs of Death. Norman Russell
Hercule and the Gods. P. Audemars
Hercule Poirot's Casebook. A. Christie
Hercule Poirot's Christmas. A. Christie
Hercule Poirot's Early Cases. A. Christie
Hercules and the Marionettes. R. M. Gilchrist
Hercules, Esq. Gwyn Evans
Hercules—Sportsman. B. Atkey
Here Be Monsters. A. Price
Here Come the Dead. R. P. Koehler
Here Comes a Candle. F. Brown
Here Comes a Candle. J. A. Hodge
Here Comes a Chopper. G. Mitchell
Here Comes a Hero. Lawrence Block
Here Comes Charlie M. B. Freemantle
Here Comes the Bribe. B. Johns
Here Comes the Copper. Henry Wade
Here Comes the Corpse. G. Bagby
Here Comes the Corpse. G. Brandon
Here Comes the Lady. M. P. Shiel
Here Comes the Toff. J. Creasey
Here Comes Trouble. B. Channing
Here in Eden. K. Lindsay
Here Is an S.O.S. S. Horler
Here Is Danger. G. Ashe
Here Is the Evidence. P. Vane

Here Lies. D. M. Disney
Here Lies Blood. M. M. Mannon
Here Lies Georgia Linz. P. Mason
Here Lies Gloria Mundy. G. Mitchell
Here Lies My Wife. E. McGirr
Here Lies Nancy Frail. Jonathan Ross
Here Lies the Body. R. Burke
Here Lies the Shadow. R. Foxall
Here There Be Dragons. R. Bentley
Here to Die. M. Sadler
Here to Get My Baby Out of Jail. L. Shivers
Here Today. Z. Fairbairns
Here Today and Gone Tomorrow. L. Bromfield
Here Today—Dead Tomorrow. J. W. Hornby
Here Today, Dead Tomorrow. E. Lewis
Here's a Villain! J. Mitchell
Here's Blood in Your Eye. Manning Long
Here's Luck. S. F. Whitman
Here's Misery. E. V. Knox
Here's Murder Done. C. Ashton
Here's Why. F. Collins
Heresy. L. Snelling
Heretic. M. L. West
Heretic's Apprentice. Ellis Peters
Herewith the Clues! D. Wheatley
Heritage. P. Driscoll
Heritage. L. Orde
Heritage in Trust. C. Davy
Heritage of Cain. I. Ostrander
Heritage of Danger. M. Lynch
Heritage of Evil. J. L. Finn
Heritage of Fear. E. Bond
Heritage of Folly. C. Marchant
Heritage of Kid McCleod. H. Pink
Heritage of Mercy. P. Tabori
Heritage of Peril. A. W. Marchmont
Heritage of Shadows. M. Brent
Heritage of Shadows. J. S. May
Heritage of Strangers. M. L. Roby
Heritage of the Horned Steer. R. Wilkes-Hunter
Heritage of Trouble. Nicholas Carter
Heritage Perilous. J. Farnol
Herlock's One Mistake. H. A. Hering
Hermes and the Golden Thinking Machine. A. Tzonis
Hermit Island. S. W. Powell
Hermit of Eyton Forest. Ellis Peters
Hermit of Turkey Hollow. A. Train
Hermitage. M. K. Simmons
Hermitage Bell. M. McEvoy
Hermitage Hill. D. Daniels
Hermit's Island. J. Phillips
Herne Lodge. W. U. O. Cuffe
Herne Lodge Mystery. W. U. O. Cuffe
Hero. P. Haining
Hero and the Terror. M. Blodgett
Hero at Large. A. J. Carothers
Hero by Proxy. H. Tolman
Hero for Leanda. A. Garve
Hero Game. W. H. Baker
Hero in His Time. A. A. Cohen
Hero in the Tower. H. H. Kirst
Hero of a Summer's Day. J. Pudney
Hero of New York. T. G. Coughlin
Hero of Romance. R. Marsh
Hero of the Pelican. P. DeLisle
Hero Rat. W. Charleston
Herod Conspiracy. Russell Rhodes
Herod's Peal. R. Thorndike
Heroes. D. Hagberg
Heroes Also Die. M. Geller
Heroes No More. J. Wainwright
Heroes of Yuca. Michael Barrett
Heroin Annie. P. Corris
Heroin Connection. J. Rosenberger
Heroin Merchants. V. Phillips
Heroin Triple Cross. J. Weisman
Heroine. E. S. Barrett
Heroine of the Desert. A. Eadie
Heron Tree. E. Kyle
Heronbrook. A. Rundle
Heron's Nest. Elizabeth Ford
Heronstroke Mystery. E. Everett-Green
Hero's Lust. K. Jaediker

H

Herr Nightingale and the Satin Woman. W. Kotzwinkle
Hers Is a Hearse. M. Brody
Herzog Affair. R. D. Steeley
He's Dead All Right. J. Gainfort
He's Dead—She's Dead: Details at Eleven. J. B. Tucker
He's Late This Morning. C. Hale
Heseltine Mystery. H. E. Chapman
Hesitant Heart. J. Edwards
Hess Cross. J. S. Thayer
Hester and I. P. C. De Crespigny
Hester Strong's Life Work. E. Southworth
Heston House Horror. V. Leigh
Hetty and other stories. H. Kingsley
Hex. K. Robeson
Hex Marks the Spot. J. Dekker
Hex Murder. F. Hazard
Heydrich Deception. D. S. Gray
Hi-Fi Fadeout. Carter Brown
Hi-Fi Homicide! D. Haring
Hi-Jack! G. N. Smith
Hi-Jack! D. Spade
Hi-Jack for Jill. Carter Brown
Hi-Jack That Dame. Griff
Hi-Jacker's Holiday. Hank Richards
Hi-Jacker's Lady. B. Sarto
Hi-Spy-Kick-the-Can. V. MacClure
Hibernation of Ginger Scrubb. A. Gardner
Hick Town Dame. F. Foden
Hickey and Boggs. P. Rock
Hickory Dickory Death. A. Christie
Hickory Dickory Dock. A. Christie
Hickory Hall. E. Southworth
Hidden. H. C. Armstrong
Hidden Agenda. L. Matera
Hidden Agenda. A. Porter
Hidden and the Hunted. H. Swiggert
Hidden Answer. John Marsh
Hidden Blood. W. C. Tuttle
Hidden Book. M. L. Roby
Hidden Chain. Dora Russell
Hidden Chapel. L. Ames
Hidden Cipher. A. O. Pollard
Hidden Clue. E. D. Pierson
Hidden Clues. D. Deane
Hidden Death. C. Goodall
Hidden Death. M. Grant
Hidden Death. E. W. Terris
Hidden Depths. Anonymous
Hidden Door. A. Gask
Hidden Door. F. Packard
Hidden Doors. N. M. Gunn
Hidden Enemy. V. Lloyd
Hidden Eyes. E. Levison
Hidden Face. V. Canning
Hidden Faces. P. May
Hidden Fear. J. Blyth
Hidden Fires. Laura Jordan
Hidden Flame. R. Dowling
Hidden Foe. G. A. Henty
Hidden Foes. Nicholas Carter
Hidden Fury. J. T. Osborne
Hidden Gang. D. T. Hughes
Hidden Gold. W. Anthony
Hidden Gold. F. Barrett
Hidden Gold. P. Longhurst
Hidden Gold. Maxwell Scott
Hidden Grave. P. Hardin
Hidden Guest. M. Short
Hidden Hand. C. J. Daly
Hidden Hand. S. Horler
Hidden Hand. E. Phillpotts
Hidden Hand. E. Southworth
Hidden Hands. M. Leighton
Hidden Hands. W. LeQueux
Hidden Hills. J. Carlshon
Hidden Hoard. J. Creasey
Hidden Horror. M. Richmond
Hidden Hour. J. B. Harris-Burland
Hidden Hour. S. Ransome
Hidden House. J. C. Dane
Hidden Island. A. Rutherford
Hidden Key. G. H. Coxe

Hidden Kingdom. F. Beeding
Hidden Lake. T. Janeschutz
Hidden Light. M. Dalman
Hidden Lives. C. H. Merritt
Hidden Lives. E. R. Punshon
Hidden Louisa May Alcott. L. M. Alcott
Hidden Malice. E. Berckman
Hidden Man. C. F. Pidgin
Hidden Man. M. Underwood
Hidden Mask. C. G. Mitford
Hidden Meanings. M. Snelgrove
Hidden Men. S. Truss
Hidden Menace! J. W. Bobin
Hidden Menace. Donald Stuart
Hidden Message. A. Murray
Hidden Million. P. Merritt
Hidden Millions. C. Hayter
Hidden, Not Lost. Anonymous
Hidden Out. H. Fielding
Hidden Paths. W. S. King
Hidden Perils. M. C. Hay
Hidden Player. A. Noyes
Hidden Portal. Garnett Weston
Hidden Record. E. W. Blaisdell
Hidden River. R. Goertz
Hidden River. S. Jameson
Hidden Scar. J. R. Adamson
Hidden Sin. E. A. Dupuy
Hidden Spring. E. A. Hill
Hidden Spring. C. B. Kelland
Hidden Submarine. C. Holland
Hidden Target. Helen MacInnes
Hidden Terror. Anonymous
Hidden Valley. D. C. Percy
Hidden Ways. F. F. Van De Water
Hidden Will. Maxwell Scott
Hidden Witness. H. C. McNeile
Hidden Woman. J. Hay
Hidden Wrath. Stella Phillips
Hide and Go Die. Nick Carter
Hide and Go Seek. A. Garve
Hide and Go Seek. Colver Harris
Hide and Kill. J. York
Hide and Seek. B. Berg
Hide and Seek. W. Collins
Hide and Seek. E. Devlin
Hide and Seek. L. Havard
Hide and Seek. L. Maracotta
Hide and Seek. Cassie Miles
Hide and Seek. Jacqueline Wilson
Hide Away. N. Bond
Hide Her from Every Eye. H. Pentecost
Hide in Hell. F. Cannon
Hide in the Dark. F. N. Hart
Hide My Body. F. Lester
Hide My Eyes. M. Allingham
Hide-Out. L. Holden
Hide the Baron. Anthony Morton
Hide the Body! M. Propper
Hide the Children. V. Miller
Hide Those Diamonds. Roy Vickers
Hideaway. N. Content
Hideaway. J. Gardner
Hideaway. M. Procter
Hideout. S. Markham
Hiding Place. J. R. Janes
Hiding Place. C. Keith
Hiding Place. C. Wilcox
Hiding Places. R. Berliner
Hiding to Nothing. Ken Blake
Hideout. S. Markham
High Adventure. J. Farnol
High Adventure. P. Groom
High Adventure. D. E. Westlake
High and Outside. L. A. Due
High Anxiety. R. H. Pilpel
High Art. R. Fonseca
High Ballin'. Richard Robinson
High Bid for Murder. A. O'Neill
High-Bouncing Lover. Angus Hall
High Bright Sun. I. S. Black
High Castle. R. Steiber
High Citadel. D. Bagley
High-Class Kill. J. Wainwright

High Class Swindler. Old Spicer
High Command. A. Emmerton
High Command Murder. J. Rosenberger
High Commissioner. J. Cleary
High Corniche. D. Dodge
High Cost of Living. L. Hays
High Cost of Murder. H. Barron
High Crimes. W. Deverell
High Crimes. J. Westermann
High Crimes and Misdemeanors. J. Greenberg
High Crystal. M. Caidin
High Danger. D. Haring
High Disaster. L. Derrick
High Dive. F. O'Rourke
High Doom. J. L. Morrissey
High Dudgeon. A. C. Frost
High Encounter. B. Wohl
High Explosive. N. Mapple
High Explosive. G. Phillips
High Fashion in Homicide. Carter Brown
High Game. P. Geddes
High Game. S. Horler
High Ground. C. Hastings
High Hand. J. Futrelle
High Hazard. S. Horler
High Heel Homicide. F. C. Davis
High Heels. M. Tripp
High Heels and Homicide. D. Reid
High Hostage. V. Maxwell
High Jacker. H. E. O. Whitman
High Jinx. W. F. Buckley, Jr.
High Jinx. D. E. Westlake
High Jump. V. Gielgud
High Kill. P. Ordway
High Life in the Far East. J. Dalziel
High Litre Lolita. Jason
High, Low and Wide Open. R. F. James
High Midnight. S. M. Kaminsky
High-Minded Murder. C. Sykes
High Noon at Midnight. M. Avallone
High Noon to High Noon. E. L. Long
High on a Hill. F. Y. McHugh
High Pastures. H. L. V. Fletcher
High Pavement. E. Bonett
High Place. G. Household
High Places. P. Ferris
High Priest. W. B. Murphy
High Priest of California. C. Willeford
High Red for Dead. W. L. Rohde
High Rendezvous. K. M. Knight
High Requiem. D. Cory
High Road. A. C. Martens
High Road to China. J. Cleary
High Road to Hell. H. L. Gates
High Roller. F. Du Boisgobey
High San Juan. K. Franklin
High School Confidential. Morton Cooper
High School Mystery. R. St. Clair
High Seas Murder. P. Drax
High Season. E. Kyle
High Sheriff. Henry Wade
High Sierra. W. R. Burnett
High Slaughter. Jon Hart
High Speed. C. H. Stagg
High Spirits. J. Payn
High Spirits. N. Tranter
High Spot. N. Baroni
High Spy. R. Trevor
High Stakes. L. Dent
High Stakes. J. Fischer
High Stakes. D. Francis
High Stakes. S. Horler
High Stakes. L. L. Lynch
High Stakes. C. Riess
High Stakes. C. Edwards
High Stand. H. Innes
High Stepping Jezebel. P. Garroway
High Strung. J. Ellery
High Summer Homicide. A. Kirby
High Tension. E. H. Clements
High Tension. T. Du Bois
High Tension. Alex Fraser
High Terrace. V. Coffman
High Terror. I. A. Greenfield

Title Index   HITLER'S DAUGHTER / 1021

High Tide. A. F. Daniels
High Tide. P. M. Hubbard
High Tide at Midnight. R. Cocking
High Tide for Hanging. G. Compton
High Tide Temptress. M. Brody
High Toby. H. B. M. Watson
High Treason. J. Bruce
High Treason. L. A. Knight
High Treason. A. Upward
High Valley. J. North
High Voltage. T. Chastain
High Walk to Wandlemere. P. Sibley
High Wall. A. R. Clark
High Wall. B. Copper
High Wall. S. Truss
High Water at Four. J. Tickell
High Water Mark. R. Dowling
High Water Mark. F. Hume
High, Wide and Ransom. D. Tracy
High Wind in Brittany. C. Gayet
High Window. R. Chandler
High Window. V. Powers
High Wire. W. Haggard
High Wray. K. Hughes
High Yellow. W. Standish
High Yield in Death. Nick Carter
Highbinders. O. Bleeck
Higher Animals. H. E. F. Donohue
Higher They Fly. C. Hodder-Williams
Highest Ground. David Mace
Highest References. F. Warden
Highflight to hell. C. H. Wallace
Highgate Mystery. C. Kingston
Highgrade Murder. C. H. Snow
Highland Fire. A. Clements
Highland Fling. M. MacKintosh
Highland Gathering. J. Wood
Highland Homicide. J. Austwick
Highland Laddie Gone. S. McCrumb
Highland Masquerade. M. Elgin
Highland Vengeance. A. Venters
Highly Explosive Case. P. Chambers
Highly Inflammable. M. Saltmarsh
Highly Unsafe. M. Saltmarsh
Highway of Fear. Donald Moore
Highway Robber's Derby. F. Johnston
Highway Through Hell. C. Whiting
Highway to Hell. D. Forde
Highway to Murder. H. Howard
Highway Warriors. B. Ham
Highwayman. G. Rawlence
Highwayman's Daughter. K. A. Shoesmith
Highways of Death. H. Desmond
Hijack. E. Wellen
Hijack. L. White
Hijacked. D. Harper
Hijacker's Morgue. L. Mantz
Hijacking Manhattan. L. Derrick
Hiker's Secret. W. Edwards
Hilary. J. Jenkins
Hilary's Terms. H. Janson
Hilda, Take Heed. M. Halliday
Hilda Wade. G. Allen
Hildegarde Withers Makes the Scene. S. Palmer
Hill Fog. J. N. Chance
Hill Girl. C. Williams
Hill Is Mine. M. Walsh
Hill of Ashes. L. Ames
Hill of Riches. F. A. M. Webster
Hill of the Crows. F. Sleath
Hill of the Terrified Monk. G. Homes
Hill of the Wild Cat. Agnes Russell
Hillbilly in High Heels. J. Bogar
Hiller Weapon. J. N. Chance
Hillerway Letters. T. Cobb
Hilliare Henderson. N. Buntline
Hillman. E. P. Oppenheim
Hills of Fire. D. Daniels
Hills of Homicide. L. L'Amour
Hills Sleep On. J. Cannan
Hills Were Higher Then. H. M. Kahler
Hilltop. J. Letton
Hilltop Murders. M. Baker
Hilma. W. T. Eldridge

Himalayan Assignment. V. M. Mason
Himalayan Concerto. J. Masters
Himitsu Attack. W. Barker
Himmler Equation. W. P. Kennedy
Himmler Plaque. Jackson Collins
Himmler Ploy. J. Semyonov
Himself Again. R. E. Pickering
Hindmost. William Paul
Hindoo Khan. M. J. Pemberton
Hindsight. P. Dickinson
Hindu Kush. Y. L. Harris
Hindu Trinity Caper. J. Rosenberger
Hinges of Hell. S. Sterling
Hint of Murder. N. Kent
Hip Deep in Alligators. Robert Campbell
Hippo's Coup. Sean Graham
Hippy Cult Murders. R. Stanley
Hire Me a Hearse. P. Marlowe
Hire Me a Rope. B. Sarto
Hire Purchase Crime. G. Chester
Hire-Purchase Fraud. W. Tyrer
Hire This Killer. F. Findley
Hired Girl. Mrs. C. Kernahan
Hired Girl's Millions. C. E. Blaney
Hired Target. W. Tucker
Hired Wife. Lynna Cooper
His Aunt Came Late. L. Meynell
His Beautiful Client. George Griffith
His Best Girl. M. Bardon
His Better Half. George Griffith
His Bones Are Coral. V. Canning
His Book of Stories. Royston Hughes
His Brother's Keeper. M. E. Bodkin
His Brother's Keeper. E. Phillpotts
His Burial Too. C. Aird
His Chinese Concubine. M. Dekobra
His Crooked Highness. K. Lindsay
His Cuban Sweetheart. R. H. Savage
His Dainty Whim. C. G. Mitford
His Darling Sin. M. E. Braddon
His Double Self. S. Campbell
His Downward Path. Harry Mills
His Eminence, Death. Simon Quinn
His Evil Eye. H. I. Hancock
His Excellency, Governor Wallace. A. Wilson
His Excellency Regrets . . . H. Marchant
His Excellency's Secret. A. Murray
His Fabulous Fortune. Rupert Hughes
His Fatal Success. M. Bell
His Father's Crime. W. M. Graydon
His Father's Crime. E. P. Oppenheim
His Father's Ghost. Stratford Davis
His Father's Honour. D. C. Murray
His Father's Son. B. Matthews
His Father's Wife. D. Keene
His Final Arrow. R. C. Lehmann
His Final Choice. A. Applin
His First Affair. D. Walshe
His First Offense. J. S. Clouston
His Fortunate Foe. A. S. Arnold
His Foster Sister. Albert Ross
His Friend the Enemy. W. W. Cook
His Grace Gets Going. R. K. Wylie
His Great Revenge. F. Du Boisgobey
His Greatest "Shadow". Old Sleuth
His Hand Betrays. P. Conway
His Helpmeet. F. Barrett
His Heritage. L. Gardiner
His Highness Commands Pendragon. R. Trevelyan
His Honor. E. Cleveland
His Kind of Woman. Michael Morgan
His Last Bow. A. C. Doyle
His Last Vow. J. Ruyle
His Lawful Wife. J. Middlemass
His Lordship the Crook. E. Louis
His Lordship the Judge. D. H. Landels
His Lordship's Arsenal. Christopher Moore
His Love or His Life. R. Marsh
"His Majesty." A. W. Marchmont
His Majesty—the Crook. Gwyn Evans
His Majesty's Agent. D. Shahar
His Majesty's Peacock. W. A. MacKenzie
His Mascot. L. T. Meade
His Master's Voice. I. Low

His Mexican Wife. A. Applin
His Name Was Death. F. Brown
His Natural Life. M. Clarke
His One Talent. H. Bindloss
His Other Self. R. W. Cole
His Other Self. E. J. Goodman
His Own Accuser. S. Hocking
His Own Accuser. H. Townley
His Own Appointed Day. D. M. Devine
His Own Executioner. D. Haring
His Own Funeral. G. J. Barrett
His Own Ghost. D. C. Murray
His Own Law. F. Barrett
His Patients Died. C. Lillingston
His Prey Was Man. A. Gask
His Reverence the Rogue. H. Desmond
His Robe of Honor. E. Dorrance
His Royal Highness. George Hastings
His Secret. M. E. Braddon
His Silence. I. D. Hardy
His Sin and Hers. Anonymous
His Son's Honour. J. W. Bobin
His Terrible Secret. C. E. Blaney
His Unknown Wife. L. Tracy
His Weight in Gold. M. Procter
His Wife's Revenge. G. R. Sims
His Wife's Soul. J. F. Molloy
Histoire des Treize. H. D. Balzac
Historical Nights' Entertainment. R. Sabatini
Historical Nights' Entertainment. 2nd Series. R. Sabatini
Historical Nights' Entertainment. 3rd Series. R. Sabatini
Historical Vignettes. B. Capes
History and Remarkable Life of the Truly Honourable Col. Jacque. D. Defoe
History and Story. W. F. Lloyd
History of a Walking Stick. R. Le Free
History of Edward Brown. E. C. Reed
History of Godfrey Kinge. W. C. Dawe
History of Luminous Motion. S. Bradfield
History of St. Giles and St. James. D. Jerrold
Hit. R. Deming
Hit. B. Garfield
Hit. P. McCurtin
Hit. J. Mayfield
Hit and Misdemeanor. W. Gleason
Hit and Run. J. Ashford
Hit and Run. J. Creasey
Hit and Run. R. Deming
Hit and Run. V. Kathrens
Hit and Run. D. Klein
Hit and Run. Raymond Marshall
Hit and Run. A. D. Miller
Hit and Run. R. M. Morris
Hit and Run. M. O'Callaghan
Hit and Run. L. Pender
Hit and Run. D. Stivers
Hit and Run, Run, Run. A. Bodelsen
Hit Girl. A. Johns
Hit It Rich. M. Bardsley
Hit Man. J. N. Chance
Hit Man. J. Fairburn
Hit Man. R. J. Flood
Hit Man. D. Haring
Hit Man. B. Rossi
Hit Man Cometh. R. Ray
Hit Me Hard. Neill Graham
Hit #29. Joey
Hit Parade. R. Rainey
Hit Squad. H. Kastle
Hit the Jackpot. Rick Madison
Hit Them Where It Hurts. J. H. Chase
Hit Woman. G. Blumberg
Hitch-Hike Murders. M. Bryson
Hitch in Time. C. Joyce
Hitchhike Killer. Paul Ross
Hitchhike to Hell. B. Grant
Hitchhiker. G. Simenon
Hitler Diamonds. D. Cory
Hitler Has Won. F. Mullally
Hitler Needs You. J. T. Story
Hitler's Bomb. C. Scott
Hitler's Daughter. T. B. Benford

Hitler's Diaries. R. Hugo
Hitler's Legacy. D. Alexander
Hive of Glass. E. Woodward
Hive of Glass. P. M. Hubbard
Hive of Suspects. S. Pim
Hoa-Tien Killers. J. Lansing
Hoax. L. Lawrence
Hobbema Prospect. J. B. Hilton
Hobgoblin Murder. K. C. Strahan
Hochmann Miniatures. R. L. Fish
Hodak. T. Pendleton
Hoffman Episode. J. Dell
Hoffman File. B. Utermahlen
Hoffman's Row. W. H. Carnahan
Hog Murders. W. L. DeAndrea
Hogan's Last Case. W. Charles
Hogdown Farm Mystery. M. Butcher
Hog's Back Mystery. F. W. Crofts
Holbein Mystery. A. Wynne
Holcroft Covenant. R. Ludlum
Hold Back the Night. D. Leslie
Hold Back the Night. B. Sommers
Hold Everything. D. Linton
Hold Out. E. Bruton
Hold That Tiger. D. Ambler
Hold the Back Page! S. Hey
Hold-Up. Jack Davies
Hold-Up. W. F. Morris
Hole in Space. L. Niven
Holden with the Cords. W. L. M. Jay
Holding Pattern. Alistair Hamilton
Holding the Aces. J. Du Crane
Hole and Corner. P. Wentworth
Hole and Corner Marriage. F. Warden
Hole in the Ground. Josephine Bell
Hole in the Ground. A. Garve
Hole in the Mountain. "Capstan"
Hole in the Vault. Nicholas Carter
Hole in the Wall. F. MacIsaac
Hole in the Wall. Arthur Morrison
Holes in the Wall. J. Bahr
Holiday Adventures of Mr. P. J. Davenant. F. S. Hamilton
Holiday Arrangement. Elizabeth Ford
Holiday at Half-Mast. J. J. Farjeon
Holiday Camp Murder. B. Francis
Holiday Camp Mystery. W. Tyrer
Holiday Express. J. J. Farjeon
Holiday for a Spy. B. Graeme
Holiday for Inspector West. J. Creasey
Holiday for Murder. A. Christie
Holiday for Murder. J. B. Hilton
Holiday Homicide. R. King
Holiday in a Manor House. E. Everett-Green
Holiday in Gaol. F. Martyn
Holiday in Hell. Nick Carter
Holiday in Hell. S. S. Taylor
Holiday of Fear. Gretchen Travis
Holiday with a Vengeance. Ritchie Perry
Holiday with Danger. E. Wilmot
Holiday with Murder. G. Carr
Holiday with Violence. E. Pargeter
Holladay Case. B. E. Stevenson
Holland Suggestions. J. Dunning
Hollow. A. Christie
Hollow Ash Hall. M. Blount
Hollow Chest. A. Tilton
Hollow Crown Affair. D. McDaniel
Hollow House. U. Curtiss
Hollow Hub. K. West
Hollow Land. N. A. Temple-Ellis
Hollow Man. J. D. Carr
Hollow Man. J. Roeburt
Hollow Men. S. Flannery
Hollow Mountain. Alec Brown
Hollow Needle. G. H. Coxe
Hollow Needle. M. Leblanc
Hollow Sea. G. Jenkins
Hollow Shell. J. Farrimond
Hollow Skin. V. Swain
Hollow Stump Mystery. C. H. Snow
Hollow Sunday. R. Harling
Hollow Target. P. Bryers
Hollow Triumph. M. Forbes

Hollow Vengeance. A. Morice
Hollow Woman. S. Ritchie
Hollowpoint Hell. J. Cain
Hollwood Mystery. Anonymous
Holly Ash. S. Youd
Hollywood and LeVine. A. Bergman
Hollywood Assassin. S. Jason
Hollywood Czar. D. Scanlon
Hollywood Detective: Garrison. J. Rovin
Hollywood Detective: The Wolf. J. Rovin
Hollywood Gothic. T. Gifford
Hollywood Hell. D. Pendleton
Hollywood Heroes. H. T. Caine
Hollywood Hit Man. V. Saxon
Hollywood Hoax. R. C. Frazer
Hollywood Love. A. M. Williamson
Hollywood Murder. P. B. Myers
Hollywood Murder Mystery. H. Crooken
Hollywood Mystery! B. Hecht
Hollywood Number. Anonymous
Hollywood Takes. M. De Larrabeiti
Hollywood Troubleshooter. W. T. Ballard
Hollywood Wives. J. Collins
Holm Oaks. P. M. Hubbard
Holmes-Dracula File. F. Saberhagen
Holocaust. A. McCall
Holocaust Auction. P. Edwards
Holofernes. Michael Baldwin
Holy Disorders. E. Crispin
Holy Father's Navy. P. Purser
Holy of Holies. Alan Williams
Holy Secrets. S. Shubin
Holy Spirit. P. Leslie
Holy Terror. L. Charteris
Holy Terror. R. Sapir
Hombre from Sonora. W. Charles
Home. D. Lippincott
Home Again. D. Wiltse
Home and Murder. A. M. Stein
Home at Seven. R. C. Sherriff
Home Before Dark. E. Bassing
Home Court and four one-act plays. T. G. Mitchell
Home for Stray Cats. J. Kirkpatrick
Home for the Heart. H. Goodwin
Home Guard Mystery. B. Cobb
Home in the Dark. W. Perry
Home Is the Hangman. R. Sale
Home Is the Heart. A. Meredith
Home Is the Hunter. J. Wainwright
Home Is the Prisoner. J. Potts
Home Is the Sailor. D. Keene
Home Is Where the Quick Is. William Johnston
Home of His Chilren. W. J. Bayfield
Home of Silence. L. T. Meade
Home of the Inquisitor. Maxine Reynolds
Home Run. Joan Butler
Home Run. G. Seymour
Home Secretary Affair. C. Franklin
Home Secretary Will See You Now. G. Ison
Home Sweet Home. R. J. Jensen
Home Sweet Homicide. D. Haring
Home Sweet Homicide. Ann Reynolds
Home Sweet Homicide. C. Rice
Home Sweet Homicide. J. T. Story
Home Sweet Suicide. D. Haring
Home Through the Dark. Anthea Fraser
Home to Cypresswood. L. V. Stevens
Home to Our Valley. D. Lee
Home to Roost. A. Garve
Home to Roost. K. Hammond
Home to the Highlands. J. Eliot
Home to the Night. J. Thatcher
Home Town. G. Simenon
Homeboy. Seth Morgan
Homecoming. R. O'Neil
Homecoming. J. Pattinson
Hometown Heroes. S. McShea
Homeward Tide. J. MacKenzie
Homeward Trail. G. Goodchild
Homicidal Colonel. R. Player
Homicidal Holiday. G. Brandon
Homicidal Horse. H. Pentecost
Homicidal Lady. D. Keene
Homicidal Spy. A. O. Pollard

Homicidal Virgin. B. Halliday
Homicide. M. Charlton
Homicide. C. W. Sasser
Homicide. L. T. White
Homicide at Saxondale. E. Wilmot
Homicide at Yuletide. H. Kane
Homicide Blonde. M. Procter
Homicide Blues. D. Reid
Homicide Call. S. A. Krasney
Homicide Club. Gwyn Evans
Homicide Dragnet. R. Marlowe
Homicide for Hannah. D. V. Babcock
Homicide Handicap. B. McKnight
Homicide Harem. Carter Brown
Homicide Harem and Felon Angel. Carter Brown
Homicide Haven. J. V. Turner
Homicide Hell. D. Haring
Homicide Honeymoon. R. Fenisong
Homicide Honeymoon. D. B. Hobart
Homicide Hotel. Joe Barry
Homicide House. D. Frome
Homicide Hoyden. Carter Brown
Homicide Hussy. A. McGuire
Homicide Is My Game. S. Marlowe
Homicide Johnny. S. Gould
Homicide Lost. W. Vance
Homicide Racket. C. Rank
Homicide Reporter. Anonymous
Homicide Sanitarium. Fredric Brown
Homicide Suites. D. Haring
Homicide Trinity. R. Stout
Homicide West. S. A. Krasney
Homicide with Charm. E. Ryley
Homicide Zone Four. N. Christian
Homing. J. Campbell
Honduras Double Cross. K. Edgar
Hone Keep Mystery. Anonymous
Honest Crook. A. S. Roche
Honest Davie. F. Barrett
Honest Dealer. F. Gruber
Honest Lawyer. G. V. McFadden
Honest Reliable Corpse. G. Bagby
Honest Rogue. M. Park
Honestly, Now! J. Sharkey
Honesty Will Get You Nowhere. J. Sherwood
Honey Ain't So Sweet. M. Shane
Honey Ant. Duncan Kyle
Honey Blonde Blues! D. Haring
Honey Don't Dare. Pete Costello
Honey Drop Dead. C. Carter
Honey Drop That Weed. J. Kellan
Honey for the Bears. A. Burgess
Honey for the Marshal. E. H. Clements
Honey Harlot. C. Brand
Honey, Here's Your Hearse! Carter Brown
Honey, Hold That Scream. T. Angelo
Honey in the Flesh. G. G. Fickling
Honey, Not Now. S. Markham
Honey on Her Tail. G. G. Fickling
Honey Seems Bitter. B. Kiely
Honey Siege. G. Buhet
Honey—Stay Blonde. J. Bogar
Honey Take Me. H. Janson
Honey, Take My Gun. H. Janson
Honey—Warm and Hungry. D. Haring
Honey, You Slay Me. D. Spade
Honeybath's Haven. M. Innes
Honeybuzzard. A. Carter
Honeycomb Bid. B. Sandberg
Honeycombers. J. Laing
Honeyfall. W. Searle
Honeymoon Caper. J. Pattinson
Honeymoon Hate. A. M. Williamson
Honeymoon in Shanghai. M. Dekobra
Honeymoon Killers. Paul Buck
Honeymoon Murder. R. C. Finney
Honeymoon Mystery. J. Laurence
Honeymoon to Nowhere. A. Takagi
Honeymoon with Death. H. Pentecost
Honeymoon with Murder. C. G. Hart
Honeysuckle Rogue. R. M. Gilchrist
Honfleur Decision. A. Hunter
Hong Kong. Clayton Matthews
Hong Kong Aftermath. Wenzell Brown

Title Index

Hong Kong Airbase Murders. V. W. Mason
Hong Kong Caper. Carter Brown
Hong Kong Club. A. Whittle
Hong Kong Edge. Justin Scott
Hong Kong Hit. Nick Carter
Hong Kong Hit List. D. Pendleton
Hong Kong Incident. James Dark
Hong Kong Kill. Bryan Peters
Hong Kong Massacre. J. Rosenberger
Hong Kong Mystery. Charles Cooper
Hong Kong Nightstop. N. Shore
Hong Kong Papers. M. S. Rossi
Honky in the Woodpile. J. Brunner
Honky Tonk Homicide. Carter Brown
Honolulu Murder Story. L. Ford
Honolulu Murders. L. Ford
Honolulu Red. L. Zimmelman
Honolulu Slay Ride. Jason
Honolulu Snatch. M. Corrigan
Honolulu Story. L. Ford
Honor. R. W. Campbell
Honor Bound. R. Harris
Honor Legion. E. F. Droge
Honor of a Black Sheep. S. Campbell
Honor of Peter Kramer. A. Ferrera
Honor of the Name. E. Gaboriau
Honor the Godfather. N. Meglin
Honor Thy Godfather. T. P. Mulkeen
Honor Thy Godmother. R. T. Larkin
Honorable Gentleman and Others. A. Abdullah
Honorary Consul. G. Greene
Honour Among Thieves. H. C. Bailey
Honour Lost, All Lost. E. V. De Fontmell
Honour of His House. F. M. White
Honour of Ravensholme. C. Stafford
Honour of the Family. P. Trent
Honour of the Flag. W. C. Russell
Honour of the Yorkshire Light Artillery. G. Lientz
Honour of Thieves. C. J. C. Hyne
Honour—or Not? M. Alma
Honour Thy Father. L. Glaister
Honourable Algernon Knox, Detective. E. P. Oppenheim
Honourable Assassins. Geoffrey Davison
Honourable Bill. F. Russell
Honourable Detective. J. Ashford
Honourable Mr. Tawnish. J. Farnol
Honourable Pursuit. P. Wynnton
Honourable Roger. C. A. Brandreth
Honourable Schoolboy. J. Le Carre
Honours Easy. R. Pertwee
Hooch! C. F. Coe
Hood. D. Scannell
Hood for a Honey. M. Brody
Hood of Death. Nick Carter
Hooded Asp. J. A. McManis
Hooded Man. W. M. Duncan
Hooded Monster. W. S. Masterman
Hooded Raider. Donald Stuart
Hooded Riders. J. W. Bobin
Hooded Skull. P. Monnow
Hooded Snake. W. Phillips
Hooded Stranger. Harrington Strong
Hooded Stranger. G. Verner
Hooded Terror. Donald Stuart
Hooded Vulture Murders. R. P. Koehler
Hoodlum. E. Lipsky
Hoodlum. Charley Robertson
Hoodlum Alley. A. E. Ullman
Hoodlum Was a Honey. Carter Brown
Hoodlums. J. Eagle
Hoodman's Bait. J. Bogar
Hoodoo Half-Back. F. W. Gumley
Hoodoo Horror. S. Jason
Hoods. H. Grey
Hoods Come Calling. N. Quarry
Hoods Incorporated. P. J. Andrews
Hoods Ride In. Wenzell Brown
Hoods Take Over. O. Demaris
Hoodwink. P. Gosling
Hoodwink. B. Pronzini
Hoodwink. Robin Temple
Hoodwinked. T. W. Speight
Hoof. P. McCutchan

Hook. D. J. Cleary
Hook. B. Copper
Hook. A. Page
Hook, Line and Sinker. K. Nicholson
Hooker-Smash Operation. J. Rosenberger
Hookers Don't Go to Heaven. L. V. Roper
Hooky and the Crock of Gold. L. Meynell
Hooky and the Prancing Horse. L. Meynell
Hooky and the Villainous Chauffeur. L. Meynell
Hooky Catches a Tartar. L. Meynell
Hooky Gets the Wooden Spoon. L. Meynell
Hooky Goes to Blazes. L. Meynell
Hooky Hooked. L. Meynell
Hooky on Loan. L. Meynell
Hooligan. D. Dodge
Hooligan. C. Dunne
Hooligan Nights. C. Rook
Hooligans. W. Diehl
Hooligans. P. Quinn
Hooligan's Rant. I. Blair
Hooray for Homicide. James Anderson
Hop Thief. O. Blakeston
Hope Against Hope. Susan Kelly
Hope of Her Heart. A. M. Burrage
Hope Strange Mystery. E. Short
Hope to Die. H. Waugh
Hopeless Case. E. Fawcett
Hopjoy Was Here. Colin Watson
Hopkinson and the Devil of Hate. P. McCutchan
Hopscotch. B. Garfield
Horace Steps Out. D. Whitelaw
Horatio and Camilla. Anonymous
Hordern Mystery. E. Finn
Hordes of the Red Butcher. G. Stockbridge
Horizon. Helen MacInnes
Horizontal Hold. R. R. Irvine
Horizontal Lieutenant. G. Cotler
Horizontal Man. H. Eustis
Horn. B. Flynn
Horn of Roland. Ellis Peters
Horned Cat. J. M. Cobban
Horned Owl. W. B. Cooke
Hornet's Nest. E. Bond
Hornet's Nest. B. Fischer
Hornet's Nest. J. R. Holden
Hornet's Nest. C. Landon
Hornet's Nest. W. Woodrow
Horns for the Devil. L. Malley
Horns of Truth. T. B. Morris
Horrible Dummy and other stories. G. Kersh
Horrible Hat. R. Savage
Horrible Man. M. Avallone
Horrible Man in Heron's Wood. B. Cobb
Horrible Revenge. Anonymous
Horrible Revenge. I. Crookenden
Horrible Suspicion. A. Eje
Horrid Mysteries. K. F. A. Grosse
Horror at Gull House. P. Brisco
Horror at the Hacienda. B. Y. Mosler
Horror at the Moated Mill. H. Desmond
Horror at Wardens Hall. C. Wogan
Horror Castle. R. Sharp
Horror Chambers of Jules de Grandin. Seabury Quinn
Horror Comes to Thripplands. G. Collins
Horror Expert. F. B. Long
Horror from the Tombs. F. Stevenson
Horror Hall. F. W. Irwin
Horror High. T. J. Kelly
Horror House. L. C. Douthwaite
Horror House. P. Warren
Horror House. C. Wells
Horror in Hawaii. M. I. H. Rogers
Horror in the Dark. N. MacKenzie
Horror Medley. M. Hervey
Horror of Beacon Grange. J. Wylde
Horror of Fog Island. Marilyn Ross
Horror of the Juvenal Manse. K. Perkins
Horror on the Loch. D. Whitelaw
Horror on the Ruby X. F. Crane
Horror Parade. R. T. Hopkins
Horror-7. R. Bloch
Horror Story. O. McNab
Horror Tales. James Dark

Horror Walks. J. S. Knapp
Horror's Head. S. Horler
Horrors of Oakendale Abbey. Mrs. Carver
Horrors of Smiling Manor. M. B. Gardner
Horrors of the Secluded Castle. Anonymous
Horse Latitudes. R. Ferrigno
Horse of Darius. J. Cartwright
Horse-Shoe Luck. W. C. Tuttle
Horse Under Water. L. Deighton
Horse with the Delicate Air and other stories. George Joseph
Horsehair Santa Claus and other stories. R. J. McLaughlin
Horsemen in Scarlet. J. W. Chalmers
Horsemen of Death. A. Wynne
Horsemen of the Law. F. F. Van De Water
Horses. J. Helvick
Horse's Head. E. Hunter
Horses I Have Known. G. G.
Horses of Winter. A. A. T. Davies
Horstmann Inheritance. B. Healey
Hospital Homicides. E. S. De Puy
Hospital Horror. O. O. Binder
Hospital Murders. Means Davis
Hospital Thief. T. A. Plummer
Hospitality for Murder. Gerard Fisher
Hospitality of Miss Tolliver and other stories. G. Kersh
Hospitality of the House. D. M. Disney
Host for Dying. P. Audemars
Host of Extras. J. Leasor
Hostage. P. Cave
Hostage. E. Garth
Hostage. Charles Henry
Hostage. S. Horler
Hostage. M. McShane
Hostage. Colin Mason
Hostage. R. T. Stevens
Hostage. R. Wilkes-Hunter
Hostage for a Hood. L. White
Hostage Heart. Gerald Green
Hostage in Illyria. C. Leonard
Hostage in Tokyo. G. DeVilliers
Hostage: London. G. Household
Hostage of Evil. W. Winthrop
Hostage of the Damned. P. A. Foxall
Hostage One. D. Fisher
Hostage to Death. J. Ashford
Hostage to Death. H. Desmond
Hostage Tower. J. Denis
Hostaged Island. D. Stivers
Hostaged Vatican. Gar Wilson
Hostages. George Fisher
Hostages. S. Heym
Hostages. C. Israel
Hostages. G. R. Lomas
Hostages. C. Stratton
Hostages of Hell. Ralph Hayes
Hostages to Fortune. M. E. Braddon
Hostages to Fortune. P. Conway
Hostess to Death. H. R. Wakefield
Hostess to Murder. E. S. Holding
Hostile Fire. D. Stivers
Hostile Takeover. W. B. Murphy
Hostile Valley. B. A. Williams
Hostile Witness. J. Roffey
Hosts of Midian. P. Capon
Hosts of the Flaming Death. C. Steele
Hot. F. Lorenz
"Hot Air" Clew. Nicholas Carter
Hot and Cold. C. H. Ross
Hot As Fire, Cold As Ice. H. Whittington
Hot Blood—Cold Blood. J. W. Mason
Hot-Blooded Blonde. N. Neitzel
Hot Body. M. Avallone
Hot Bullets for Love. G. Nyland
Hot Car. L. Cameron
Hot Cargo. S. Coburn
Hot Cargo. G. H. Otis
Hot Chariot. J. M. Flynn
Hot Chestnuts and other stories. R. Standish
Hot Dam. N. MacNeil
Hot Dames—Cold Lead. C. Wheatley
Hot Dames Die Cold. B. Sarto

Hot Dames on Cold Slabs. M. Storme
Hot Day Hot Night. C. Himes
Hot Diary. H. J. Olmsted
Hot Dilemma. R. Vane
Hot Dough, Honey! D. Haring
Hot End of the Stick. A. Nuttall
Hot Fire. J. McKimmey
Hot-Foot. Bill Turner
Hot Freeze. Martin Grett
Hot Gold. F. MacIsaac
Hot Half-Million. R. Chapman
Hot House. H. Janson
Hot Ice. R. Angel
Hot Ice. R. J. Casey
Hot Ice. A. W. Clark
Hot Ice. L. Grex
Hot Ice. Nora Roberts
Hot Ice. H. Seymour
Hot Ice. R. D. Steeley
Hot Ice. S. Waldron
Hot Lead. D. Haring
Hot-Line. J. Bruce
Hot Line. H. Janson
Hot Line—Capricorn. D. E. Mandeville
Hot Line for a Honey. M. Brody
Hot Mods. Garrity
Hot Money. Dick Francis
Hot Money. R. Hausfeld
Hot Money Can Cook Your Goose. J. M. Glazner
Hot News. E. Gauvreau
Hot Oil. M. Carlton
Hot Oil. G. P. Putnam
Hot Pick-Up. J. T. Crawford
Hot Pot. F. Francis
Hot Potato. R. Esser
Hot Prowl. H. D. Kastle
Hot Pursuit. F. Earley
Hot Pursuit. L. Katcher
Hot Pursuit. R. Kent
Hot Pursuit. Gavin Scott
Hot Rain. C. Lewis
Hot Rain. H. Portnoy
Hot Red Money. B. Kendrick
Hot Rock. D. E. Westlake
Hot Rod. N. Karta
Hot Rod Gang Rumble. M. Dolinsky
Hot Season. G. Merrick
Hot Seat. D. Haring
Hot Seat. D. Weir
Hot Seat for a Honey. Carter Brown
Hot Seat's Cold. N. Karta
Hot Shot. D. Appell
Hot-Shot Rita. Griff
Hot Shots. L. Gough
Hot Siberian. G. A. Browne
Hot Spot. M. Davidson
Hot Spot. C. Williams
Hot Streak. J. Barkin
Hot Stuff. S. Koperwas
Hot Sugar. M. T. Dallas
Hot Summer, Cold Murder. G. Dold
Hot Summer Killing. J. Philips
Hot Swag. H. Kaner
Hot Tamale! D. Haring
Hot 30. J. Sakol
Hot Tickets. J. W. Rider
Hot Time in Old Town. M. McQuay
Hot Times. W. R. Cox
Hot Tip. J. Dolph
Hot Town. F. Malachy
Hot Type. M. Lipsyte
Hot Water. Randy Russell
Hot Water. P. G. Wodehouse
Hot Wind from Hell. H. McCutcheon
Hot Zone. B. Sloane
Hotel at Tarasco. J. Horton
Hotel Berlin. V. Baum
Hotel Cosmos. John Burke
Hotel Cremona Mystery. Gret Lane
Hotel de Luxe. Rona Randall
Hotel for Scandal. R. Lacroix
Hotel Geneva. J. Notley
Hotel Homicide. A. Parsons
Hotel Motel. Stuart Hall
Hotel Murders. S. Sterling
Hotel Orgy. Stuart Hall
Hotel Richelieu Murders. A. Blackmon
Hotel Sinister. D. Whitelaw
Hotel Tallyrand. P. H. Bonner
Hotel X. W. LeQueux
Hotels with Empty Rooms. H. Gilbert
Hotshot. F. Flora
Hotspur. M. T. Walworth
Hotsy, You'll Be Chilled. H. Janson
Hound and the Fox and the Harper. S. Herron
Hound from the North. R. Cullum
Hound Island. Mountford Williams
Hound of Death. J. Corbett
Hound of Death and other stories. A. Christie
Hound of Heaven. J. D. White
Hound of Heaven. G. Wright
Hound of the Baskervilles. A. C. Doyle
Hound of the Baskervilles. T. J. Kelly
Hound of the Baskervilles. F. A. Leslie
Hounded. D. Linton
Hounded! M. Richmond
Hounded Down. D. Durham
Hounded Man. F. Carco
Hounded to Death. Nicholas Carter
Hounds. V. Coffman
Hounds and Jackals. Barbara Wood
Hounds Are Restless Tonight. L. T. Shortell
Hounds of Carvello. F. Cowen
Hounds of Justice. R. Forsythe
Hounds of Sparta. Barry Norman
Hounds of Spring. A. Lawman
Hounds of the Moon. E. O. Allen
Hounds of the Vatican. G. R. Holms
Hounds of Vengeance. J. Creasey
Hound's Tooth. R. E. McDowell
Houndsditch Day by Day. A. M. Binstead
Houndstooth. G. A. Ruse
Hour After Westerley. R. M. Coates
Hour Before Midnight. V. Johnston
Hour Before Midnight. J. Salisbury
Hour Before Moonrise. N. Buckingham
Hour Before the Dawn. W. S. Maugham
Hour Before Zero. S. Harvester
Hour-Glass. Winifred Duke
Hour-Glass Mystery. H. Hill
Hour-Glass to Eternity. M. Hastings
Hour Is Forever. E. H. Blackledge
Hour of Blue. R. Froese
Hour of Death. L. Morningstar
Hour of Destiny. M. Richmond
Hour of Evil. A. Grace
Hour of Justice. R. Milne
Hour of Maximum Danger. J. Barlow
Hour of Recognition. P. Quiroule
Hour of the Argentine. B. Langley
Hour of the Assassins. A. Kaplan
Hour of the Bishop. W. M. Duncan
Hour of the Blue Fox. H. C. McDonald
Hour of the Cat. J. De Weese
Hour of the Clown. A. Aricha
Hour of the Dog. B. Mather
Hour of the Fox. R. Rohmer
Hour of the Gaucho. B. Langley
Hour of the Harp. Lynna Cooper
Hour of the Hyenas. J. Sherwood
Hour of the Lily. J. Kruse
Hour of the Oxrun Dead. C. L. Grant
Hour of the Scorpion. Anthony Taylor
Hour of the Unicorn. J. Parish
Hour of the Wolf. Nick Carter
Hour of the Wolf. R. Charles
Hour of Truth. D. Egerton
Hour Struck. D. E. L. Patch
Hour Worth Living. C. G. Addy
Hourglass Crisis. L. Hoklin
Hours After Midnight. J. Hayes
Hours Before Dawn. C. Fremlin
Hours to Kill. U. Curtiss
House. Stuart Hall
House. H. Lawrence
House Above Hollywood. V. Johnston
House Above the River. Josephine Bell
House Across the Park. Max Barrett
House Across the River. M. Bonham
House Across the Street. Nicholas Carter
House Across the Water. H. Bourne
House Across the Way. F. Daingerfield
House Across the Way. K. Kavanaugh
House and the Raven. Tim Kelly
House and the Tower. F. S. Smith
House Arrest. Martin Russell
House at Ballyslane. C. E. R. Sinclair
House at Balnesmoor. H. C. Rae
House at Canterbury. F. Kent
House at Fern Canyon. W. D. Roberts
House at Gray Eagle. Elizabeth MacDonald
House at Hag's Curtain. P. Motte
House at Hawk's End. Claudette Nicole
House at Kilgallen. M. L. Roby
House at Lake Taupo. M. McGregor
House at Landsdowne. C. Farr
House at Luxor. F. Stevenson
House at Norwood. W. P. Kelly
House at Parson's Landing. C. Connell
House at Pluck's Gutter. M. Coles
House at River's Bend. R. J. Jensen
House at Rose Point. Jan Alexander
House at Sandalwood. V. Coffman
House at Satan's Elbow. J. D. Carr
House at Serraville. R. Bagot
House at Swansea. A. Grace
House at the Corner. A. M. Meadows
House at the Crossroads. N. Bell
House at the Estuary. A. MacKenzie
House at Thunder Cove. M. Y. Thomas
House at Waterloo. E. S. Brooks
House at Windridge. E. A. Rife
House Behind the Mint. L. Huffman
House Between the Trees. J. Russell Lane
House-Boat Mystery. J. K. Leys
House by Exmoor. C. Stafford
House by the Bay. J. Wetherell
House by the Bridge. M. G. Easton
House by the Bridge. Melissa Napier
House by the Canal. K. Hewitt
House by the Canal. G. Simenon
House by the Church-Yard. J. S. Le Fanu
House by the Common. T. Cobb
House by the Lake. Hugh Mills
House by the Lock. A. M. Williamson
House by the River. A. P. Herbert
House by the River. F. Warden
House by the Road. C. J. Dutton
House by the Sea. M. G. Eberhart
House by the Sea. M. B. Lowndes
House by the Tarn. R. Abbey
House Called Edenhythe. N. Buckingham
House Called Whispering Winds. M. M. Fletcher
House Cried Murder. F. Nash
House Dick. B. Copper
House Dick. Gordon Davis
House for Sale. E. C. Vivian
House for Sale Haunted. J. Tobias
House Guest. F. Durbridge
House in Belmont Square. M. Erskine
House in Brook Street. R. Cocking
House in Candle Square. P. Bennetts
House in Cavendish Square. D. Whitelaw
House in Charlton Crescent. A. Haynes
House in Gowerdale. T. Lang
House in Green Street. S. Horler
House in Grey Peril. J. Truby
House in Half Moon Street, and other stories. H. Bolitho
House in Harlem. M. S. Michel
House in Hook Street. M. Erskine
House in Lordship Lane. A. E. W. Mason
House in Marsh Road. L. Meynell
House in Munich. D. K. Dowdell
House in Naples. P. Rabe
House in Paris. D. Ward
House in Pindar's Passage. H. R. De Vigne
House in Queen Anne Square. W. D. Lyell
House in Ralston Place. A. B. Moody
House in Sinister Lane. T. A. Plummer
House in Spitalfields. G. Wolfenden
House in Spite Street. W. M. Duncan

House in Spring Gardens. A. Griffiths
House in the Country. D. M. Low
House in the Crescent. A. Sergeant
House in the Fog. L. Geumlek
House in the Forest. M. Cumberland
House in the Hills. L. Meynell
House in the Hills. F. Warden
House in the Hollow. E. Lockwood
House in the Kasbah. Maxine Reynolds
House in the Mist. A. K. Green
House in the Shadows. C. McKnight
House in the Way. Colin Hope
House in the Wood. G. Chester
House in the Woods. J. Drummond
House in the Woods. L. Lance
House in Tuesday Market. J. S. Fletcher
House in White Mist. Melissa Napier
House Is Dark. Rebecca James
House Is Falling. N. Fitzgerald
House Is Just a House. J. Lindsay
House Malign. J. Wellsley
House Next Door. A. Askew
House Next Door. L. Rose
House Next Door. A. R. Siddons
House Next Door. B. E. Stevenson
House Next Door. L. White
House Nobody Lived In. R. Dumkey
House of a Hundred Eyes. P. Urquhart
House of a Thousand Candles. Meredith Nicholson
House of a Thousand Desires. Mark Reed
House of a Thousand Lanterns. V. Holt
House of Animals. Anonymous
House of Anna. A. J. Evans
House of Assignation. A. Robbe-Grillet
House of Athena. Janice Bennett
House of Black Magic. L. T. Meade
House of Blight. Mrs. C. Kernahan
House of Blue Lights. R. J. Bowman
House of Brass. E. Queen
House of Broken Dolls. D. Daniels
House of Cabra. J. Wetherell
House of Cain. S. Roberts
House of Cain. A. W. Upfield
House of Caine. K. Eulo
House of Candles. P. Brisco
House of Cards. P. Cave
House of Cards. S. Ellin
House of Cards. H. Gartland
House of Cards. Conall Ryan
House of Cards. J. M. Ullman
House of Cards. P. Wilde
House of Care. W. J. Burley
House of Carson. A. Mallory
House of Cellars. G. H. Teed
House of Certain Death. A. Cossery
House of Clouds. H. L. Poole
House of Clystevill. B. Atkey
House of Cobwebs. M. Reisner
House of Counted Hatreds. S. Jennifer
House of Creeping Horror. G. F. Worts
House of Crimson Shadows. H. D. Stacpoole
House of Crystal. H. Kades
House of Curtains. G. H. Teed
House of Dark Illusions. C. Farr
House of Dark Laughter. Melissa Napier
House of Dark Secrets. G. M. Allen
House of Dark Shadows. Marilyn Ross
House of Darkness. J. Hunter
House of Darkness. K. Laing
House of Darkness. A. MacKinnon
House of Darkness. J. Phillips
House of Deadly Calm. M. Farnsworth
House of Deadly Night. I. Barry
House of Dearth. V. MacClure
House of Death. E. J. Capocy
House of Death. C. Goodall
House of Death. L. Groc
House of Death. K. Robeson
House of Delusion. R. S. Holland
House of Destiny. C. Farr
House of Disappearance. J. J. Farjeon
House of Disappearance. C. K. Steele
House of Discord. M. E. Hanshew
House of Distant Voices. E. Bond

House of Dr. Edwardes. F. Beeding
House of Dogs. R. Elliott
House of Doom. Nicholas Carter
House of Doom. S. Wagner
House of Dread. R. Dorien
House of Echoes. John Marsh
House of Elnora Garland. W. Luttrell
House of En-Dor. A. Hocking
House of Eve. S. Somers
House of Evil. H. Clevely
House of Evil. W. LeQueux
House of Evil. C. Lipman
House of Evil. M. Lynch
House of Evil. J. Trinian
House of Evil Winds. M. J. Ragosta
House of Exile. J. E. Coyne
House of Faith. M. G. Kiddy
House of False Faces. H. G. Weston
House of Fand. K. Troy
House of Fatal Mirrors. F. W. Gumley
House of Fear. Wadsworth Camp
House of Fear. M. Dalton
House of Fear. Jack Lewis
House of Fear. Frank Richards
House of Fear. R. W. Service
House of Fear. W. Spence
House of Fears. J. England
House of Flesh. B. Fischer
House of Fools. Jan Alexander
House of Fortune. M. Pemberton
House of Four Windows. D. Lyons
House of Fury. J. A. Creighton
House of Gair. E. Linklater
House of Games. D. Mamet
House of Ghosts. L. H. Brooks
House of Ghosts. W. B. Gibson
House of Ghosts. Marilyn Ross
House of Giants. Y. Everett
House of Glass. G. Ferrand
House of Glass. M. Marcin
House of Godwinsson. E. R. Punshon
House of Gold. Ann Anderson
House of Greed. R. St. Clair
House of Green Dragons. Rosa Hill
House of Green Turf. Ellis Peters
House of Haddon. L. Ames
House of Halliwell. H. Wood
House of Happy Mayhem. W. J. Sheldon
House of Hate. J. Bowman
House of Hate. J. E. Ferris
House of Hate. Dorothy Fletcher
House of Hate. H. Mace
House of Hate. W. C. Thomas
House of Horror. M. Crombie
House of Horror. R. Halifax
House of Horror. T. C. H. Jacobs
House of Horror. N. MacKenzie
House of Horror. Donald Ross
House of Horrors. P. A. Clarke
House of Horrors. J. Reach
House of Illusion. N. Devon
House of Illusion. D. Quentin
House of Illusions. R. J. Jenson
House of Imposters. W. D. Roberts
House of Intrigue. L. Hoffman
House of Intrigue. T. Irving-James
House of Intrigue. Colin Roberson
House of Intrigue. A. Stringer
House of Intrigue. Percy White
House of Iron Men. Jack Steele
House of Jackals. S. Horler
House of Janus. Donald James
House of Jeffreys. R. Thorndike
House of Lies. J. Audrenn
House of Lies. Austin Moore
House of Lies. S. Warwick
House of Living Death. T. Blore
House of Lyes. C. W. Whitaker
House of Mad Children. R. Timperley
House of Madame Jacqueminet. B. L. Jacot
House of Make Believe. H. Bridges
House of Malory. H. McElroy
House of Mammon. F. M. White
House of Many Doors. D. Daniels

House of Many Mirrors. V. Hunt
House of Many Shadows. B. Michaels
House of Many Voices. B. Capes
House of Marney. J. Goodwin
House of Masks. Barbara Cooper
House of Masques. F. Kent
House of Men. C. Marchant
House of Menace. A. Furness
House of Merrilees. A. Marshall
House of Mirror Images. D. Winston
House of Mist. M. L. Bombal
House of Montague. T. Lee
House of Moreys. P. Bentley
House of Murder. H. L. Gates
House of Murder. J. H. Wallis
House of Mystery. M. Arden
House of Mystery. Will Irwin
House of Mystery. Hilary Lang
House of Mystery. R. Marsh
House of Mystery. W. J. Newton
House of Mystery. M. Royal
House of Mystery. Grace M. White
House of Night. L. H. Gordon
House of Numbers. J. Finney
House of Ogilvie. Winifred Duke
House of Peril. M. B. Lowndes
House of Peril. L. Tracy
House of Rancour. S. Nichols
House of Ravensbourne. M. A. Gibbs
House of Retrogression. C. Patrick
House of Rhinestad. D. M. Parish
House of Riddles. D. Gerard
House of Rising Water. Melissa Napier
House of Rogues. C. B. Booth
House of Sand. B. Rowan
House of Scorpio. P. Wallace
House of Scorpions. J. Sherman
House of Seclusion. M. Harvey
House of Secrets. E. Ames
House of Secrets. C. Farr
House of Secrets. S. Horler
House of Secrets. W. Martyn
House of Secrets. D. Noel
House of Secrets. S. Noel
House of Secrets. H. Peters
House of Secrets. H. L. Phillips
House of Secrets. J. Wellsley
House of Shade. M. Home
House of Shade. M. M. Kaye
House of Shadows. A. Adams
House of Shadows. Marsha Alexander
House of Shadows. E. Bond
House of Shadows. Renate Chapman
House of Shadows. J. J. Farjeon
House of Shadows. F. Hurd
House of Shadows. D. Martyn
House of Shadows. C. Randell
House of Shayle. John Alexander
House of Silence. C. Collins
House of Silence. D. Daniels
House of Silence. H. W. Jarvis
House of Silence. J. H. Robinson
House of Silence. D. Streib
House of Silence. G. H. Teed
House of Silence. L. Tracy
House of Silence. R. Trevor
House of Silence. C. N. Williamson
House of Silent Footsteps. Armine Grace
House of Sin. B. Sarto
House of Sin. A. Upward
House of Sinister Shadows. Cynthia Hyde
House of Sleep. Michael Burt
House of Sleep. Frank King
House of Soldiers. J. Garve
House of Sorcery. Carter Brown
House of Sorrows. F. M. White
House of Souls. A. Machen
House of Stairs. B. Vine
House of Stolen Memories. D. Daniels
House of Storm. M. G. Eberhart
House of Storms. H. Bridges
House of Strange Adventure. G. Goodchild
House of Strange Guests. N. Brady
House of Strange Music. A. L. Thompson

House of Strange Secrets. A. E. Bayly
House of Strange Victims. B. Atkey
House of Strangers. Jennifer Hale
House of Strangers. M. Padget
House of Sudden Sleep. J. Hawk
House of Tarot. R. C. Payes
House of Tears. E. Downey
House of Terror. Anonymous
House of Terror. E. Berckman
House of Terror. G. Biss
House of Terror. F. Swann
House of Terror. E. Woodward
House of the Apricots. H. Imber
House of the Arrow. A. E. W. Mason
House of the Bears. J. Creasey
House of the Black Ring. F. L. Pattee
House of the Cat. A. Roudybush
House of the Crimson Lantern. R. Willey
House of the Damned. A. M. Rud
House of the Dancing Dead. A. Vandergriff
House of the Darkest Death. A. Grace
House of the Dead Ones. J. N. Chance
House of the Deadly Nightshade. L. B. Long
House of the Enchantress. M. Erskine
House of the Fiery Cauldron. Alice Brennan
House of the Flashing Light. J. C. McMullen
House of the Four Winds. J. Buchan
House of the Fragrant Lotus. E. P. Thorne
House of the Hatchet and other tales of horror. R. Bloch
House of the Hawk. W. C. Tuttle
House of the Hunter. F. Taylor
House of the Lost. B. Gray
House of the Lost Court. M. D'Alpins
House of the Lost Woman. Louise O'Flaherty
House of the Missing. S. Gluck
House of the Moving Room. J. J. Chichester
House of the Opal. Jackson Gregory
House of the Pines. J. Tempest
House of the Purple Stairs. J. Helm
House of the Roses. C. Baker
House of the Secret. C. Farrere
House of the Seven Courts. D. Daniels
House of the Seven Flies. V. Canning
House of the Seven Keys. M. E. Hanshew
House of the Siren. J. Selborne
House of the Soul. J. B. Harris-Burland
House of the Spaniard. A. Behrend
House of the Strange Woman. M. Heath
House of the Swinging Lantern. K. Morris
House of the Sword. D. G. Browne
House of the Talisman. H. H. Ross
House of the Third Sense. L. Holt
House of the Three Ganders. I. A. Bachellor
House of the Twelve Caesars. P. Hastings
House of the Uneasy Dead. S. Horler
House of the Unicorn. L. Harper
House of the Vanishing Goblets. L. Edgley
House of the Weeping Women. Coningsby Dawson
House of the Whispering Pines. A. K. Green
House of the White Shadows. B. L. Farjeon
House of the Wicked. W. LeQueux
House of the Winds. C. Hodge
House of the Winds. J. G. Sarasin
House of the Wolf. S. J. Weyman
House of the Yellow Door. Nicholas Carter
House of Three Eagles. C. Miron
House of Thunder. L. Nichols
House of Tombs. C. Farr
House of Torment. C. R. Gull
House of Torture. L. C. Douthwaite
House of Tragedy. A. J. Fitzgerald
House of Treachery. C. Farr
House of Treason. D. Allan
House of Two Green Eyes. S. Chalmers
House of Two Wives. D. Locke
House of Tynian. George Walker
House of Valhalla. C. Farr
House of Vandekar. Evelyn Anthony
House of Vengeance. A. L. McAllister
House of Vengeance. R. St. Clair
House of Wailing Winds. W. M. Duncan
House of Whipplestaff. E. F. Boyd
House of Whispering Aspens. A. Ainsley

House of Whispering Death. M. Farnsworth
House of Whispers. J. Baer
House of Whispers. Nicholas Carter
House of Whispers. W. A. Johnston
House of Whispers. W. LeQueux
House of Women. L. K. Scott
House of Wraith. E. J. Millward
House of Yesteryear. M. Lynch
House on Black Bayou. M. Sellars
House on Bostwick Square. V. Johnston
House on Cabra. J. Wetherell
House on Carroll Street. M. Gregory
House on Charles Street. A. Burr
House on Cheyne Walk. P. Organ
House on Circus Hill. D. Daniels
House on Curtin Street. M. J. Ragosta
House on Doubloon Inlet. J. A. Dunn
House on Eagle Ledge. A. Mallet
House on Gannet's Point. C. Van Hazinga
House on Greenapple Road. H. R. Daniels
House on Hay Hill. D. Eden
House on Hibiscus Hill. J. T. Osborne
House on K Street. L. White
House on Key Diablo. J. Vance
House on Lily Street. J. Vance
House on Lime Street. W. E. D. Ross
House on Malador Street. P. Hastings
House on Mount Vernon Street. W. E. D. Ross
House on 92nd Street. Alex Morrison
House on 9th Street. J. S. Strange
House on Octavia Street. J. La Tourrette
House on Plymouth Street. U. Curtiss
House on Q Street. R. Dietrich
House on Quai Notre Dame. G. Simenon
House on Rainbow Leap. R. M. Vale
House on Russian Hill. F. Hurd
House on Sixteenth Street. E. Thorne
House on Sky High Road. I. S. Way
House on Smith Square. A. Burr
House on Somber Lake. A. De Marquand
House on Telegraph Hill. D. Lyon
House on the Bay. Arthur MacLean
House on the Beach. E. E. Cameron
House on the Beach. E. L. Withers
House on the Black Moor. D. Polk
House on the Broads. Wilfrid Robertson
House on the Cliff. G. Batson
House on the Cliff. L. Meynell
House on the Cliffs. G. Chester
House on the Cliffs. C. Farr
House on the Downs. J. Hunter
House on the Downs. G. E. Locke
House on the Dunes. R. M. Sears
House on the Drive. B. Kingsley
House on the Fen. C. Rayner
House on the Fens. C. Cookson
House on the Fens. A. Gask
House on the Hard. A. Wynne
House on the Hill. J. Drummond
House on the Hill. J. Whitehead
House on the Hudson. F. Powell
House on the Island. A. Gask
House on the Lake. J. Reach
House on the Left Bank. V. Johnston
House on the Mall. E. Jepson
House on the Marsh. J. J. Farjeon
House on the Marsh. N. Jackson
House on the Marsh. H. R. Martin
House on the Marsh. F. Warden
House on the Moat. V. Coffman
House on the River. J. Drummond
House on the Rocks. T. Charles
House on the Roof. M. G. Eberhart
House on the Saltings. V. Bridges
House on the Strand. D. Du Maurier
House on the Thames. G. W. Appleton
House on Thunder Hill. S. Somers
House on Tollard Ridge. J. Rhode
House on Trevor Street. F. Hurd
House on Twyford Street. C. Gluyas
House on Vickers' Island. J. St. Clair
House on Washington Place. P. G. Demarest
House on Wathmoor. M. Stephenson
House on Windswept Ridge. K. Kimbrough

House on Wolf Trail. Lanora Miller
House Opposite. J. J. Farjeon
House Opposite. E. Kent
House Opposite. P. Landon
House Over Hell Valley. V. Subond
House Over the Tunnel. J. J. Farjeon
House Over the Way. A. W. Barrett
House Party Murder. Colin Ward
House Party Murders. E. A. Poe
House-Party Mystery. G. Norsworthy
House Possessed. C. Blackstock
House Possessed. L. Paige
House 'Round the Corner. Gordon Holmes
House Sinister. H. Newte
House-Surgeon. I. Jefferies
House Surgeon at Luke's. Rona Randall
House Terrible. A. Towner
House That Berry Built. D. Yates
House That Chak Built. K. West
House That Died. H. Bordeau
House That Died. Josephine Gill
House That Fear Built. C. Knye
House That Hate Built. S. E. Mason
House That Hated People. V. Black
House That Jack Built. E. Dewhurst
House That Jack Built. E. McBain
House That Samael Built. R. Jenson
House That Stood Still. A. E. Van Vogt
House That Waited. C. Reeve
House That Whispered. S. Emery
House Upstairs. C. Rodda
House with a Bad Name. P. P. Sheehan
House with a History. F. Warden
House with a Past. J. Courage
House with Black Blinds. H. Bridges
House with Blind Eyes. H. Jobson
House with Crooked Walls. B. Graeme
House with Green Shudders. A. R. Long
House with Green Shutters. A. R. Long
House with No Address. E. M. Channon
House with No Address. E. Nesbit
House with Steel Shutters. A. Parsons
House with the Blue Door. H. Footner
House with the Double Moat. E. S. Brooks
House with the Green Shutters. George Douglas
House with the High Wall. A. Gask
House with the Iron Door. M. M. Jensen
House with the Light. S. Horler
House with the Myrtle Trees. Elizabeth Ford
House with the Red Blinds. T. C. Wignall
House with the Stained Glass Windows. Winston Graham
House with the Watching Eyes. N. A. Hintze
House with Two Faces. Sheila Bishop
House Without a Door. T. Sterling
House Without a Key. E. D. Biggers
House Without a Key. J. L. Latham
House Without a Number. W. C. Johnstone
House Without Locks. Anonymous
House Without the Door. E. Daly
House Without Windows. L. Constable
House Without Windows. R. Reich
Houseboat Enigma. R. R. Hillman
Houseboat Killings. R. Simons
Houseboat Mystery. J. Edwards
Housebound. W. Appel
Housebreaker. D. Linzee
Houseguest. T. Berger
Household Gods. J. Thurley
Household of Hertz. W. J. Newton
Household Skeleton. G. L. Aiken
Household Traitors. J. Blackburn
Householders. Margery Henry
Housekeeper's Daughter. D. H. Clarke
Housekeeper's Secret. H. Fielding
Houseparty. K. P. Britton
Houses of Glass. W. Lloyd
Houses Without Doors. P. Straub
Housesitter. L. Karr
Housespy. M. Duffy
Housewife and the Assassin. S. Trott
Houston Attack. C. Ramm
Houston Hellground. C. Cunningham
Houston in the Rearview Mirror. S. R. Cooper

Hovering Darkness. E. Berckman
Hovey's Deception. Philip Ross
How Amusing! and a lot of other fables. D. MacKail
How Are You, Johnnie? P. King
How Awful About Allan. H. Farrell
How Bad Can They Be? N. Leslie
How Betty Butted In. W. Spence
How Briggs Died. D. E. Harding
How Came He Dead? J. F. Molloy
How Cold the Night. B. Schwarz
How Could They? C. N. Boyle
How Dark Are the Dunes? C. Herbert
How Dead Can You Be? D. Linton
How Dead My Love. D. Keene
How Did Elmer Die? G. P. West
How Doth the Little Crocodile? P. Antony
How Evil the Word. H. G. Farrar
How Far Can You Go? D. Spade
How Far to the Top? D. Haring
How German Is It. W. Abish
How Goes the Murder? E. Queen
How Good a Detective Are You? A. Ripley
How Green Was My Apple. M. Lovell
How Hard to Kill. T. B. Dewey
How He Did It. E. A. Dupuy
How He Won Her. E. Southworth
How He Won Her, and A False Friend. G. Fleming
How I Dished the Don and other stories. J. Vanny
How I Found the Five Pound Note and What Came of It. G. S. Jealous
How I Made a Million Dollars. A. F. Taylor
How Like an Angel. M. Millar
How Many Cards? I. Ostrander
How Many Coupons for a Shroud? N. Morland
How Many to Kill? M. Halliday
How Murder Speaks. R. S. Holland
How Now, McLean? G. Goodchild
How Sleeps the Beast. D. Tracy
How Slow the Snooth. C. Herbert
How Still My Love. D. Siegel
How Strange a Thing. Dorothy Bennett
How the Dead Live. Derek Raymond
How the Old Woman Got Home. M. P. Shiel
How to Kill a Man. T. Wells
How to Live Dangerously. Joan Fleming
How to Murder Your Wife. Henry Williams
How to Steal a Million. Michael Sinclair
How to Succeed at Business Spying by Trying. S. Mead
How to Succeed at Murder Without Really Trying. D. Von Elsner
How to Trap a Crook. J. Symons
How Town. M. Nava
How 'Twas. S. Reynolds
How Tyson Came Home. W. H. Rideing
How Was It Done? Mark Cross
Howard Hughes Affair. S. M. Kaminsky
Howards of Saxondale. Rona Randall
Howard's Price. Tom Howard
Howling. G. Brandner
Howling Dog. R. Drayton
Howling in the Woods. V. Johnston
Howling III. G. Brandner
Howling II. G. Brandner
Hoxton Mystery. T. W. Hanshew
Hoyland Intervenes. P. C. Williams
Hoyland Steps Out. P. C. Williams
Hub. R. Herring
Hubberthwaite Horror. J. Austwick
Hubert de Sevrac. Mary Robinson
Hubert Phillips Annual 1951. H. Phillips
Hubschmann Effect. T. P. McMahon
Huckleberry Fiend. Julie Smith
Hucksters of Holiness. R. Gorton
Huddersfield Job. Angus Ross
Huddle. C. Wells
Hue and Cry. T. B. Dewey
Hue and Cry. B. Hamilton
Hue and Cry. J. B. O'Sullivan
Hue and Cry. P. Wentworth
Hugger-Mugger in the Louvre. Elliot Paul
Human Bacillus. R. Eustace
Human Bloodhound. E. S. Brooks
Human Cat. Dick Stewart

Human Chase. E. P. Oppenheim
Human Element. J. Fores
Human Equation. C. E. Bowman
Human Factor. G. Greene
Human Factor. Simon Quinn
Human Fiend. Nicholas Carter
Human Mole. C. Collins
Human Nature. M. Leighton
Human Question Mark. Dick Stewart
Human Salvage. W. J. Carroll
Human Time Bomb. Nick Carter
Human Toll. B. Baynton
Human Vampire. T. F. Elstow
Human Vultures. Roland Daniel
Human Zero. E. S. Gardner
Humbert Castle. Anonymous
Humdrum House. M. Foster
Humming Box. H. Whittington
Humming Cliff. M. Tannock
Humming Precipice. M. Sheppard
Humming Top. D. Spicer
Humorous Stories and Sketches. D. MacFadyen
Humour in Our Town. B. Bowyer
Humours and Oddities of the London Police Courts. Dogberry
Humours of Glenbruar. F. MacKenzie
Hump's First Case. R. Dennis
Hunch. R. Humphreys
Hunchback House. D. B. Hobart
Hunchback of Hatton Garden. G. Bowman
Hunchback of Hatton Garden! H. E. Hill
Hunchback of Soho. Roland Daniel
Hunchback of Westminster. W. LeQueux
Hundred and First. K. Cameron
Hundred Days. T. Mundy
Hundred-Dollar Girl. W. C. Gault
Hundred Per Cent. H. C. McNeile
Hundred Percent Squad. E. W. Count
Hundred Thousand Guineas. E. Jepson
Hundredth Acre. J. Campden
Hundredth Door. R. Foley
Hung by an Eyelash. L. Anson
Hung in the Balance. R. Ormerod
Hung Jury. D. O. Woodbury
Hung Until Dead. P. Johnson
Hung Up to Die. Martin Meyers
Hungarian Game. Roy Hayes
Hunger. E. M. Moses
Hunger and other stories. C. Beaumont
Hunger and the Hate. H. V. Dixon
Hunger for Heroes. C. Yaeger
Hungering Shame. R. V. Cassill
Hungry Dog. F. Gruber
Hungry Dog Murders. F. Gruber
Hungry Ghost. S. Leather
Hungry Goblin. J. D. Carr
Hungry Heart. H. B. Kaye
Hungry House. L. Lauferty
Hungry Killer. M. O'Brine
Hungry Killer. E. Radford
Hungry One. G. Brewer
Hungry Sea. L. Ames
Hungry Spider. S. Jepson
Hungry Women. Stuart Hall
Hunslett's Yard. E. L. Long
Hunt. A. Alvarez
Hunt. W. Carrier
Hunt and Kill. R. T. Bickers
Hunt at Desolation. Michael Barrett
Hunt Ball Murder. F. W. Crofts
Hunt Ball Mystery. W. Magnay
Hunt Club. N. Daniels
Hunt for Danger. A. Curry
Hunt for Red October. T. Clancy
Hunt for Richard Thorpe. J. Tickell
Hunt in the Highlands. H. J. Wurr
Hunt Is Up. A. Hocking
Hunt the Body. P. Flower
Hunt the Evidence. R. Clifford
Hunt the Killer. D. Keene
Hunt the Lady! D. Reid
Hunt the Man. W. Pearson
Hunt the Man Down. D. Haring
Hunt the Man Down. W. Pearson

Hunt the Slipper. H. Cecil
Hunt the Spy. M. McKenna
Hunt the Tiger. H. A. Hering
Hunt the Toff. J. Creasey
Hunt the Tortoise. E. Ferrars
Hunt to Kill. M. Russell
Hunt with the Hounds. M. G. Eberhart
Hunted. G. F. Gibbs
Hunted. M. Hartmann
Hunted. E. Leonard
Hunted. M. Millard
Hunted! T. A. Plummer
Hunted. M. Reisner
Hunted. Jeremy Scott
Hunted and Haunted. I. Stark
Hunted Down. C. Dickens
Hunted Down. R. Dudgeon
Hunted Down. M. Hillary
Hunted Down. J. M'Govan
Hunted Down. R. H. Rohde
Hunted Down. R. A. Wainwright
Hunted Man. W. S. Masterman
Hunted to Death. W. S. Hayward
Hunted Woman. M. Albrand
Hunted Woman. J. O. Curwood
Hunted Woman. J. Pendower
Hunter. R. Busby
Hunter. Nick Carter
Hunter. R. Holland
Hunter. J. Maudsley
Hunter. E. Sauter
Hunter. R. Stark
Hunter and the Ikon. E. Sauter
Hunter and the Raven. E. Sauter
Hunter and the Trapped. Josephine Bell
Hunter at Large. T. B. Dewey
Hunter Equation. H. Gibbons
Hunter for Hire. W. Spann
Hunter Hunted. Ken Blake
Hunter Hunted. H. Treece
Hunter, Hunter, Get Your Gun. D. Macomber
Hunter in the Dark. E. Thompson
Hunter in the Shadows. Jennie Melville
Hunter Is the Hunted. A. B. Cunningham
Hunter-Killer. G. Jenkins
Hunter of Men. Nicholas Carter
Hunter of Men. C. H. Guenter
Hunter of the Blood. W. Masterson
Hunter Squadron. R. Jackson
Hunter/Victim. R. Sheckley
Hunters. J. Ambler
Hunters. Peter Hill
Hunters. Clark Howard
Hunters and the Hunted. L. Egan
Hunter's Blood. J. Cunningham
Hunter's Green. P. A. Whitney
Hunter's Mate. J. Blackmore
Hunter's Moon. N. Benchley
Hunters of Humans. V. M. Steele
Hunters of the Lost Ashes. A. Synge
Hunter's Orange. R. Lundeen
Hunters Point. G. Sims
Hunter's Run. G. Rivers
Hunter's Walk. Ted Hart
Hunter's Way. C. Reeve
Hunterstone Outrage. S. Truss
Hunting and Hunted. D. Conyers
Hunting for Gold. H. Nisbet
Hunting-Ground. F. Clifford
Hunting Ground. M. Sutherland
Hunting of Hillary. E. Winch
Hunting of Mr. Exe. J. N. Chance
Hunting of Mr. Gloves. P. Daniels
Hunting Party. G. Landers
Hunting Party. J. Millard
Hunting Season. J. Coyne
Hunting Season. J. K. Mayo
Hunting Shack. G. Landers
Huntingtower. J. Buchan
Huntress. H. Footner
Huntress. Williams Forrest
Huntress. C. C. Lewis
Huntress. M. A. Wilson
Huntress Is Dead. B. Benson

H

Huntress of Death. S. Horler
Huntsman. G. Verner
Hurricane. J. D. MacDonald
Hurricane Alley. R. H. Dickinson
Hurricane Drift. J. N. Chance
Hurricane House. R. St. Clair
Hurricane Is a Blonde. C. Dekker
Hurricane Island. H. B. M. Watson
Hurricane Season. M. Friedman
Hurricane Squadron. R. Jackson
Hurricane Tex. G. Goodchild
Hurricane Wake. R. Ashe
Hurricane Warning! Richard Williams
Hurricane Williams' Vengeance. Gordon Young
Hurry the Darkness. M. Procter
Hurrying Feet. F. F. Van De Water
Hurt Me No More. I. Batista-Oliviera
Hurton Treasure Mystery. F. Hume
Husband. V. Caspary
Husband and Wife. M. Leighton
Husband of the Corpse. M. Judd
Husband's Secret. R. Dowling
Husband's Story. N. Collins
Hush-a-Bye Murder. David Alexander
Hush, Gabriel! V. P. Johns
Hush Hush Johnson. N. Gates
Hush-Hush Murder. A. Murphy
Hush-Hush Murders. M. T. Yates
Hush, It's a Game. P. Carlon
Hush Little Baby. J. Miller
Hush Little Darlings. J. Kelman
Hush Money. M. A. Collins
Hush, Money. J. Femling
Hush Money. P. Israel
Hush Money. J. Middlemass
Hush, Winifred Is Dead. A. P. Johnson
Hushabye Death. A. Wood
Hushed Up! W. LeQueux
Hushed Up at German Headquarters. W. LeQueux
Husky Voice. Roland Daniel
Hustle. S. Shagan
Hustle Into Death. S. Arroyo
Hustler Paul. J. Cleveland
Hustlers. C. Megahy
Hustlers. Sam Ross
Hut. L. Meynell
Huysman's Pets. K. Wilhelm
Hyacinth Spell. F. Y. McHugh
Hyde and Seek. B. Wolff
Hyde in Deep Cover. B. Wolff
Hyde Park Corner. W. Hackett
Hyde Park Murder. E. Roosevelt
Hyde Place. V. Coffman
Hyde Side Up. B. Travers
Hydra. A. Heal
Hydra Conspiracy. P. Kirk
Hydra Head. C. Fuentes
Hydra-Head. S. Noel
Hydra Monster. L. Falk
Hydra with Six Heads. Josephine Bell
Hyena Dawn. C. Sherlock
Hyena Run. David Morton
Hymn Tune Mystery. G. A. Birmingham
Hypnotic Death. P. Valdez
Hypnotic Demon. M. E. Cooke
Hypnotic Tales. J. L. Ford
Hypnotism. J. Claretie
Hypnotist Detective. Anonymous
Hypnotist of Hilary Mansion. Susan James
Hypnotized. M. Brandon
Hypocrite. C. R. Gull
Hypocrite. W. Le Pretre

I Accuse. C. Kingston
I Am a Smuggler. C. Evelyn
I Am Afraid. E. K. Lobaugh
I Am Being Poisoned. L. Phraile
I Am Death. R. Conner
I Am Death. G. Verner
I Am Gabriella! A. Maybury
I Am Jonathan Scrivener. C. Houghton
I Am Maud Latimer. J. Shard
I Am Saxon Ashe. S. Ashe
I Am the Captain. G. Hackforth-Jones

I Am the Cat. R. Kutak
I Am the Only Running Footman. M. Grimes
I Am the Withered Man. N. Deane
I Am Vidocq. V. McConnor
I, and I Alone. J. Weidman
I and My True Love. Helen MacInnes
I Asked No Other Thing. C. Jarrett
I Came to a Castle. V. Johnston
I Came to Kill. Gordon Davis
I Came to the Highlands. V. Johnston
I Can Cope. M. Cronin
I Can Take It. M. Risco
I Cannot Afford the Halo. Elizabeth Williams
I Can't Die Here. J. C. Nolan
I Can't Stop Running. E. Ronns
I Charge You Both. A. M. Meadows
I Come to Kill You. B. Halliday
I Confess. J. M. Simmel
I Could a Tale Unfold. D. Whitelaw
I Could Be Good to You. C. Keppel
I Could Have Died. G. Bagby
I Could Murder Her. E. C. R. Lorac
I Cover the Waterfront. Max Miller
I Crown Thee King. M. Pemberton
I.D.B. E. W. T.
I.D.B. in South Africa. L. V. Sheldon
I Did It! Garret Smith
I Did Not Kill Osborne. V. Bridges
I Die Possessed. J. B. O'Sullivan
I Die Slowly. K. Millar
I Died Yesterday. K. Robeson
I Do Not Think So. J. B. Morton
I Don't Die Easy. R. Drayton
I Don't Get It. Spike Gordon
I Don't Like Cats. L. Anson
I Don't Scare Easy. B. Dougall
I Don't Scare Easy. M. Hampton
I Escape. J. L. Hardy
IFO Report. T. J. Sagnier
I Fear the Greeks. A. M. Stein
I Fear You Not. B. Kerr
I Fell Among Thieves. B. Cobb
I for Intrigue. H. Janson
I Forbid. W. Standish
I Forbid the Banns. F. Frankfort Moore
I Found Him Dead. G. Gallagher
I Gave at the Office. D. E. Westlake
I Get What I Want. Larry Heller
I Give You Five Days. C. Curzon
I Had to Kill Her. E. Connell
I Hardly Knew You. E. O'Brien
I Hate Actors! B. Hecht
I Hate Blondes. V. Kaufman
I Hate Thee. M. Baroni
I Hate You to Death. K. Edgar
I Have Gloria Kirby. R. Himmel
I Have Killed a Man! C. F. Gregg
I Heard the Death Bell. C. M. Russell
I Hide, We Seek. R. M. Stern
I Hold the Four Aces. J. H. Chase
I Joined the Racketeer's Gang. Anonymous
I Keep My Word. J. M. Scott
I, Keturah. R. Wolff
I Kill 'Em Inch by Inch. B. Sarto
I Killed My Burglar. Gordon Miller
I Killed Stalin. S. Noel
I Killed the Count. Alec Coppel
I Knew MacBean. M. Erskine
I Knew Mrs. E. J. Barnett
I Know a Secret. P. Hambledon
I Know a Trick or Two. Samuel Holt
I Know My Love. F. Nichols
I Know What It's Like to Die. Jonathan Ross
I.L.F. D. Dallas
I Let Him Go. J. Brophy
I Like a Good Murder. M. Magill
I Like Danger. M. Corrigan
I Like 'Em Tough. C. Cannon
I Like It Cool. Michael Lawrence
I Like It Tough. J. A. Howard
I Like My Women Tough. W. Standish
I Love, I Kill. J. Bingham
I Love the Night. H. Vogel
I Love You Again. O. R. Cohen

I, Lucifer. P. O'Donnell
I Married a Dead Man. W. Irish
I Married a Doctor. Rona Randall
I Married Mr. Richardson. J. Ames
I, Martha Adams. P. G. Winslow
I Met a Man. M. Blankfort
I Met Murder. E. Ferrars
I Met Murder. S. Jepson
I Met Murder on the Way. C. Blackstock
I Met Murder on the Way. M. Echard
I Never Killed. Max Gordon
I Never Miss Twice. B. Cobb
I.O.U. Murder. T. B. Dewey
I.O.U.—Murder. W. Francis
I Plotted in Vain. Anonymous
I Prefer Murder. B. Norton
I Ring Doorbells. R. Birdwell
I Said I Was Sorry. M. Dines
I! Said the Demon. G. Baxt
I, Said the Fly. E. Ferrars
I, Said the Sparrow. C. Murphy
I, Said the Spy. D. Lambert
I, Savarin! D. Newton
I Saw Him Die. June Drummond
I Saw Murder. G. Cobden
I Saw Three Ships, and other winter's tales. Q
I Say "No". W. Collins
I See Red. S. Noel
I See You. C. Armstrong
I Shall Avenge. J. Robb
I, Sherlock Holmes. M. Harrison
I Shot My Bridge Partner. M. Granovetter
I Shot to Kill. Anonymous
I Should Have Sold Petunias. D. Honig
I Should Have Stayed Home. H. McCoy
I Sit in Hanger Lane. J. T. Story
I Smell a Cop. G. Usher
I Smell the Devil. C. Magoon
I Speak for the Dead. J. J. Maloney
I Spit on Your Grave. Griff
I Spit on Your Grave. Vernon Sullivan
I Spy. N. S. Lincoln
I, Spy. D. MacKenzie
I Spy. K. Medusa
I, Spy. S. Stone
I Spy. J. Tiger
I Spy, You Die. Hosanna Brown
I Start Counting. A. E. Lindop
I Stood in the Shadow of the Black Cap. J. Budd
I Take This Stranger. P. Warren
I Take This Woman. G. Simenon
I Thank a Fool. A. E. Lindop
I, the Criminal. D. Sharp
I, the Damned. M. Boone
I, the Executioner. S. Ransome
I, the Hangman. W. A. Ballinger
I, the Jury. M. Spillane
I Thought I'd Die. D. V. Reed
I Tried for the Roses. D. Collenette
I, Victoria Strange. R. Willock
I Wake Up Screaming. S. Fisher
I Want a Nurse. J. Randall
I Want a Policeman! R. King
I Want Out. T. Thomey
I Want to Be a Lady. M. Foster
I Want to Go Home. R. Lockridge
I Want to Go to Moscow. M. Duffy
I Want to Live. T. Rawson
I Wanted the Killer. A. Howe
I Wanted to Murder. C. F. Cushman
I Was a Blackmailer. Anonymous
I Was a Spy. John Arnold
I Was a Spy in Britain. G. Usher
I Was Alone. K. David
I Was Being Poisoned! Anonymous
I Was Dora Suarez. Derek Raymond
I Was Following This Girl. D. Skirrow
I Was Going Anyway. R. Switzer
I Was Murdered. M. E. Longman
I Was Murdered. G. M. Wilson
I Was the Kid with the Drum. T. Roscoe
I Was Walking Down Below. T. Gates
I Will Be Faithful. K. Shepard
I Will Kill. C. Borelli

Title Index

I Will Repay. Baroness Orczy
I Will Sing a New Song. L. T. Meade
I Will Speak Daggers. M. Procter
I Wish He Would Not Die. J. Aldridge
I Wonder What Happened to Tom? B. Reade
I Won't Promise Honey. D. Haring
I Would Rather Stay Poor. J. H. Chase
I Wouldn't Be in Your Shoes. W. Irish
Ibiza Syndicate. B. Reade
Icarus. M. Koepf
Icarus. P. Way
Icarus Agenda. R. Ludlum
Icarus Seal. C. Hyde
Icarus Threat. H. McLeave
Ice. J. Follett
Ice. E. McBain
Ice-Axe Murders. G. Carr
Ice Before Killing. M. Strobel
Ice Blues. R. Stevenson
Ice Bomb Zero. Nick Carter
Ice Castles. E. Wolfe
Ice Cathedral. G. Leonard
Ice-Cold in Alex. C. Landon
Ice Cold in Ermine. Carter Brown
Ice Cold Kill. D. Pendleton
Ice-Cold Nude. Carter Brown
Ice for the Eskimo. W. R. Philbrick
Ice Forest. V. Coffman
Ice Goddess. P. Edwards
Ice in Her Eyes. L. Como
Ice in the Bedroom. P. G. Wodehouse
Ice in the Sun. D. Enefer
Ice King. Michael Scot
Ice Maiden. J. Vicary
Ice Maidens. J. N. Chance
Ice Man. W. L. Morgan
Ice Pick. J. Baldwin
Ice Pilot. H. Leverage
Ice Planet. P. Casciani
Ice Pond Mystery. J. Kipley
Ice Raid. R. Cox
Ice Station Zebra. Alistair MacLean
Ice Trap. D. Haysom
Ice Trap Terror. Nick Carter
Ice Wolf. D. Pendleton
Ice, Wind and Fire. M. Keegan
Iceberg. C. Cussler
Icebound. R. Spencer
Icebreaker. J. Gardner
Iced Tea and Ignorance. H. L. Russell
Icefire. R. C. Wilson
Icekill. P. Lund
Iceman. Rex Miller
Iceman. M. E. Morris
Icepick. A. Fletcher
Icepick. F. Scarpetta
Icepick in Ollie Birk. E. Sudak
Icepick in the Spine. F. Scarpetta
Iceworld. H. Clement
Iciest Sin. H. R. F. Keating
Icing of Balthazar. J. Goldsmith
Icons. C. Winthrop
Icy Clutches. A. J. Elkins
I'd Crowns Resign. J. M. Cobban
Ideal Crime. J. Ashford
Ideal Genuine Man. Don Robertson
Identical Strangers. V. Hawthorne
Identification Parade. P. N. Walker
Identity. Winifred Graham
Identity Crisis. L. Latham
Identity Plunderers. I. Haiblum
Identity Unknown. T. C. H. Jacobs
Identity Unknown. Lorena
Identity Unknown. R. Marlowe
Identity Unwanted. Jean Marsh
Ides of March Conspiracy. Clyde Matthews
Ides of November. F. Stevenson
Idiot Played Rachmaninov. Michael Brown
Idle Island. E. Hueston
Idol Hunter. B. Unsworth
Idol of Last Chance. Anonymous
Idol of the Blind. T. Gallon
Idol of the Town. W. LeQueux
Idols. R. DeNavery

Idol's Eye. H. E. Hill
If a Body. G. W. Yates
If a Body Kill a Body. P. Mortimer
If a Body Meet a Body. P. Clapp
If a Body Meet a Body. G. Malcolm-Smith
"If All Tales..." E. M. C. Balfour-Browne
If Anything Happens to Hester. Anthony Morton
If Anything Should Happen. Kevin O'Hara
If Anything Should Happen to Me. A. Barker
If Death Ever Slept. R. Stout
If Dying Was All. R. Goulart
If Ever I Return, Pretty Peggy-O. S. McCrumb
If Hate Could Kill. J. Bradley
If I Die Before I Wake. Sherwood King
If I Die—It's Murder. M. Ervin
If I Don't Tell. D. Olson
If I Kill Him. J. Hawkins
If I Knew What I Was Doing. Albert Ross
If I Live to Dine. H. Waugh
If I Should Die. P. Bannon
If I Should Die. M. R. Henderson
If I Should Die. A. Sewart
If I Should Die Before I Die. Peter Israel
If I Should Die Before I Wake. W. Irish
If I Should Die Before I Wake. J. A. Potter
If I Should Lose You. M. Richmond
If I Should Murder. P. Laing
If It Please You. Richard Marsh
If It Weren't for Sex . . . I'd Have to Get a Job. James Burke
If Laurel Shot Hardy the World Would End. S. Forbes
If Love Be Ours. K. Lindsay
If Murder Interferes with Business. A. Spiller
If She Should Die. M. L. Roby
If She Should Die. F. Rydell
If Sherlock Holmes Were a Woman. T. J. Kelly
If Sinners Entice Thee. W. LeQueux
If the Coffin Fits. D. Keene
If the Price Is Right. W. Newton
If the Reaper Ride. Elizabeth Norman
If the Shoe Fits. Lee Roberts
If the Shroud Fits. P. Kruger
If the Shroud Fits. K. Roos
If There Be Thorns. V. C. Andrews
If They Fall—. V. MacClure
If This Be Murder. R. Darby
If This Be Treason. M. Echard
If Thoughts Could Kill. G. F. Bale
If Today Is the First Day of the Rest of My Life, I'm in Real Trouble. J. L. Seay
If Tomorrow Comes. Sidney Sheldon
If Truth Be Known. P. Werner
If Two of Them Are Dead. S. Forbes
If Two of Them Are Dead. M. Gregory
If Wishes Were Hearses. J. H. Bond
If Wishes Were Hearses. G. Cullingford
If You Believe the Soldiers. A. Cordell
If You Can't Be Good. E. Cannon
If You Can't Be Good. Ross Thomas
If You Have Tears. John Evans
If You Should Ever Need Me. B. Treynor
If You Want a Murder Well Done. M. Scherf
If You Want to See Your Wife Again. John Craig
If Your Cover Is Blown. J. Browning
Ifs and Ans. H. B. M. Watson
Ikon. G. Masterton
Ilene, the Superstitious. K. Kimbrough
Ilion Like a Mist. J. Mitchell
I'll Always Remember. M. Richmond
I'll Be Back Before Midnight. P. Colley
I'll Be Glad When You're Dead. D. Lyon
I'll Be Judge, I'll Be Jury. E. Hely
I'll Be Judge, I'll Be Jury. M. Kennedy
I'll Be Wearing a White Carnation. J. Miller
I'll Blackmail the World. A. Wood
I'll Bring Her Back. P. Cheyney
I'll Bury My Dead. J. H. Chase
I'll Come Quietly. T. McCoy
I'll Cry When I Kill You. Peter Isreal
Ill Deeds Done. A. Hocking
I'll Die for You. S. Ransome
I'll Die Tonight. J. Laffin
I'll Die Too Soon. D. Boyce

I'll Do Anything. D. Bateson
I'll Eat You Last. H. C. Branson
I'll Find You. R. Himmel
I'll Fix You. H. Ellson
I'll Fix You Lady! J. Bodini
I'll Fry Yet. R. Angel
I'll Get By. F. Hanson
I'll Get By. B. Sarto
I'll Get Mine. Thurston Scott
I'll Get You for This. J. H. Chase
I'll Get You Yet. J. A. Howard
I'll Go Anywhere. D. Bateson
Ill Gotten Gains. A. Murray
I'll Grind Their Bones. T. Roscoe
I'll Hate Myself in the Morning, and Summer in December. Elliot Paul
I'll Hire the Hearse. M. Lisle
I'll Kill You Last. H. C. Branson
I'll Kill You Next! Adam Knight
Ill Met by a Fish Shop on George Street. M. McShane
Ill Met by Moonlight. L. Ford
Ill Met in Mexico. C. M. Russell
I'll Never Go There Anymore. J. Weidman
I'll Never Leave You. E. Lustgarten
I'll Never Let You Go. F. Nichols
I'll Never Like Friday Again. S. Maddock
I'll Never Tell. Roy Vickers
I'll Say She Does! P. Cheyney
I'll See You in Hell. J. McPartland
I'll Sing at Your Funeral. H. Pentecost
I'll Sing You the Death of Bill Brown. B. Dexter
I'll Take Blondes. S. Markham
I'll Take Homicide. C. McGill
I'll Take the Body. B. Rigan
I'll Take What's Mine. N. Jones
I'll Tell You Everything. J. B. Priestley
Ill-Tempered Clavicord. S. J. Perelman
Ill Wind. H. Brinton
Ill Wind. R. Fenisong
Ill Wind. M. Fitt
Ill Wind. W. L. Heath
Ill Wind Contract. P. Atlee
Illegal Entry. R. Bernard
Illegal Entry. R. Hayes
Illegal Procedure. Brian Michaels
Illegal Solution. J. Ashford
Illegal Tender. D. M. Devine
Illegal Tender. E. C. Vicar
Illegitimate Spy. R. Silverwood
Illicit Cargo. R. Lacroix
Illusion. F. Keinzley
Illusion. A. Neiderman
Illusion. M. Warner
Illusion at Haven's Edge. D. Daniels
Illusionist. S. D. Frances
Illustrious Corpse. T. Thayer
Illustrious Prince. E. P. Oppenheim
I'm Afraid I'll Live! K. S. Cole
I'm Cannon—for Hire. C. Cannon
I'm King of the Castle. Susan Hill
I'm No Hero. H. Howard
I'm No Murderer. B. Perowne
I'm Trying to Give It Up. D. Skirrow
I'm Waiting. S. Reese
Image. C. Paul
Image in the Dust. Warwick Scott
Image in the Mirror. D. L. Sayers
Image Job. C. Platt
Image Killer. W. Maner
Image Maker. P. Hastings
Image Makers. B. V. Dryer
Image of a Ghost. D. Daniels
Image of a Murder. P. Capon
Image of Death. O. Kensch
Image of Evil. W. Beechcroft
Image of Evil. R. A. Crawford
Image of Hell. S. Fisher
Image of Man. M. Tripp
Image of Stephanie. S. Sloan
Image of the Beast. P. J. Farmer
Image of Truth. S. Somers
Image Seller. K. Ostrander
Images of Death. Lawrence Williams

Images of Han. J. M. Walsh
Images of Rose. Anna Gilbert
Imagine a Man. N. Fitzgerald
Imagine a Man in a Box. H. R. Wakefield
Imbroglio. R. O. Collin
Imitation Thieves. M. Lovell
Immaculate Murders. K. Brooks
Immaterial Murder Case. J. Symons
Immediate Action. R. Neebel
Immediate Jewel. A. Applin
Immediate Prospect of Being Hanged. Walter Walker
Immediate Release. W. Mathewson
Immoralist. A. Gide
Immortal Blood. B. Hambly
Immortal Coil. P. Van Greenaway
Immortals of the Mountain. C. V. Gheorghiu
Imp. A. Neiderman
Impact. B. Copper
Impact. J. Dark
Impact. S. Greenleaf
Impact. H. Olesker
Impact of Evidence. C. Carnac
Impact-20. W. F. Nolan
Impartial Eye. P. Boulle
Impatient Miss Blackett. Blair Edwards
Impeached! B. Graeme
Impeccable People. Elizabeth Fenwick
Impending Sword. H. A. Vachell
Impending Sword. E. Yates
Impenetrable Mystery of Zora Burns. Anonymous
Impenetrable Secret. F. Lathom
Imperator Plot. S. G. Spruill
Imperfect Alibi. H. Hervey
Imperfect Crime. B. Graeme
Imperfect Imposter. N. Venner
Imperfect Lover. R. Gore-Brown
Imperfect Lover. A. Soutar
Imperial Agent. T. N. Murari
Imperial Blue. E. Bond
Imperial Express. J. Bellah
Imperial Marriage. A. W. Marchmont
Imperial 109. R. Doyle
Imperial Treasure. V. Gielgud
Imperial Way. James Melville
Impersonal Attractions. S. Shankman
Impersonators. E. S. Brooks
Imperturbable Duchess and other stories. J. D. Beresford
Impetuous Mistress. G. H. Coxe
Implacable Hunter. G. Kersh
Implied Immunity. D. F. Holmes
Implosion. J. Montgomerie
Implosion Effect. G. Paulsen
Import of Evil. J. N. Chance
Importance of Being Murdered. C. Wells
Important Man and others. W. P. Ridge
Impossible Apollo. T. Cobb
Impossible Caper. D. Haring
Impossible Chance. J. Hunter
Impossible Crime. E. C. Vivian
Impossible Dream. L. Hoffman
Impossible Guest. J. J. Farjeon
Impossible Husband. F. Warden
Impossible Lover. B. Bolt
Impossible Spy. K. Carr
Impossible Virgin. P. O'Donnell
Impossibles. Mark Phillips
Imposter. W. H. Baker
Imposter. M. Cumberland
Imposter. J. Jakes
Imposter. E. Keeley
Imposter. K. Steel
Imposter. D. Whitelaw
Imposters. G. V. Higgins
Impostor. H. McCloy
Imprint. Michael Bradley
Improbable Cause. J. A. Jance
Improbable Fiction. Sara Woods
Impromptu Imposter. V. Vicas
Impulse. C. Coulter
Impulse. I. Ostrander
In a Bad Man's Grip. S. Warwick
In a Dark Dream. C. L. Grant

In a Dark Time. L. Watson
In a Deadly Vein. M. Culpan
In a Deadly Vein. B. Halliday
In a Fair Ground. L. G. Moberly
In a Glass Darkly. J. Caird
In a Glass Darkly. J. S. Le Fanu
In a House Unknown. D. Hitchens
In a Little House. T. Gallon
In a Lonely Place. D. B. Hughes
In a Place Dark and Secret. P. Finch
In a Silver Sea. B. L. Farjeon
In a Steamer Chair and other shipboard stories. Robert Barr
In a Telephone Cabinet. G. D. H. Cole
In a Turkish Garden. A. B. Gwyn
In a Vain Shadow. Raymond Marshall
In a Vanishing Room. R. Colby
In a Wild Sanctuary. William Harrison
In Accordance with the Evidence. O. Onions
In After Years. J. K. Stafford
In All Shades. G. Allen
In All Simplicity. P. Capon
In an Alpine Valley. G. M. Fenn
In an Ancient Mirror. H. Flowerdew
In an Iron Grip. L. T. Meade
In and Out. Edgar Franklin
In Another Man's Shoes. M. L. Eades
In Any Case. R. G. Stern
In at the Death. F. Duncan
In at the Death. D. Frome
In at the Death. G. F. Underhill
In at the Kill. E. Ferrars
In at the Kill. B. Knox
In at the Kill. E. McDowell
In Australia. S. Rudd
In Bad Company. R. Boldrewood
In Bad with Sinbad. A. Stringer
In Barracks and Wigwam. W. M. Graydon
In-Between Spy. P. Fuller
In Black & Whitey. E. Lacy
In Blue Waters. H. D. Stacpoole
In Brighton Waters. G. Volk
In Calvert's Valley. M. P. Montague
In Camera. John Gloag
In Camera. C. G. Mitford
In Case of Emergency. G. Simenon
In Chambers. E. O. Jones
In Chinatown. T. Burke
In Cold Blood. G. Bagby
In Cold Blood. T. Capote
In Cold Blood. A. Livingston
In Cold Pursuit. U. Curtiss
In Comes Death. P. Whelton
In Connection with Kilshaw. P. Driscoll
In Council Rooms Apart. John Craig
In Court. F. Andreas
In Crime's Disguise. F. C. Milford
In Cupid's Wars. C. Gibbon
In Dark Places. J. Russell
In Darkest Madras. H. E. Hill
In Deacon's Orders. W. Besant
In Deadly Peril. E. Gaboriau
In Deadly Peril. D. Lechmere
In Death We Trust. D. Moreau
In Death's Grip. Nicholas Carter
In Deep. D. Kyle
In Deep Abyss. G. Ohnet
In Deep Water. M. Richmond
In Defense of Judges. A. W. Gray
In Defense of Mrs. Maxon. G. A. Chamberlain
In Direst Peril. D. C. Murray
In Double Disguise. W. M. Graydon
In Dread of the Law. A. Adderley
In Durance Vile. Mrs. Hungerford
In Enemy Hands. R. Sapir
In Extremis. Mrs. Greenough
In Face of the Verdict. J. Rhode
In False Attire. G. Norway
In Fear of a Woman. Winifred Graham
In Fear of the Hangman. M. Richmond
In Fear of the Night. H. Desmond
In for a Penny. D. Mardon
In for Life. Suzanne Mayer
In for the Kill. D. Benfield

In Fort and Prison. W. M. Graydon
In Friendship's Guise. W. M. Graydon
In Full Commission. E. L. Long
In Full Cry. J. Goodwin
In Full Cry. R. Marsh
In Garde We Trust. J. La Plante
In God's Good Time. M. Leighton
In Great Danger. N. MacKenzie
In Great Waters. M. E. Braddon
In Harm's Way. Geoffrey Jenkins
In Her Garden. J. Godden
In Her Own Right. J. R. Scott
In High Places. M. E. Braddon
In His Blood. H. R. Daniels
In His Grip. D. C. Murray
In Honour Bound. C. Gibbon
In Honour Bound. G. Seymour
In Hot Blood. M. B. Cook
In Hot Blood. P. Popescu
In Hot Pursuit. N. Cay
In Jeopardy. V. Sutphen
In Jeopardy, and other stories of peril. G. M. Fenn
In Justice's Prison. R. Thurston
In King's Byways. S. J. Weyman
In La-La Land We Trust. Robert Campbell
In Lands of Terror. D. Lenton
In-Laws. D. Rogers
In-Laws and Outlaws. Barbara Paul
In League with Counterfeiters. E. C. Derby
In League with Murder. M. B. Dix
In League with Satan. I. Stark
In Letters of Fire. Nicholas Carter
In Life's Byways. C. S. Bradford
In Lightning and Rain. T. M. Longstreth
In Like Flint. B. Street
In London's Heart. G. R. Sims
In Love and War. C. Gibbon
In Lover's Lane. A. Askew
In Loving Memory. Emma Page
In Male Attire. J. Hutton
In Market Overt. J. Payn
In Memory of Murder. D. Hawkins
In Memory of Sarah Bailey. Louise Cooper
In Mid-Atlantic. B. Delannoy
In Minden Town. M. A. Curtois
In Muffled Night. D. E. Muir
In My Enemy's Arms. R. T. Stevens
In My Father's Den. M. Gee
In My Father's Name. W. Oberman
In Other Words. G. Robey
In Our Hours of Ease. F. F. Moore
In Our Town. D. Runyon
In Pale Batallions. R. Goddard
In Pastures Green and other stories. C. Gibbon
In Peril of His Life. G. D. H. Cole
In Peril of His Life. E. Gaboriau
In Place of Reason. John Fraser
In Pursuit of a Million. F. Marlowe
In Pursuit of Evil. Hugh Mills
In Quarters. J. S. Winter
In Queer Quarters. Nicholas Carter
In Queer Street. F. Hume
In re Sherlock Holmes. A. Derleth
In Record Time. Nicholas Carter
In Remembrance of Rose. M. R. D. Meek
In Safe Hands. J. Capperton
In Safe Hands. J. Sandford
In Satan's Bonds. C. E. Perry
In Savage Hayti. R. C. Armour
In Savage Surrender. W. Chambers
In Scarlet and Plain Clothes. T. M. Longstreth
In Search of a Villain. R. Gore-Brown
In Search of Eagles. C. Sloan
In Search of Emily Crew. A. Furness
In Search of Enemies. J. Stockwell
In Search of Himself. Nicholas Carter
In Search of Stephanie. K. Rhodes
In Search of Sybil. Magali
In Search of the Dove. Rebecca York
In Secret. R. W. Chambers
In Secret. W. LeQueux
In Secret Places. S. Truss
In Secret Service. J. Rosmer
In Shadows. T. Janeschutz

In Shadows of Desire. James Stevens
In Sheep's Clothing. H. Nisbet
In Sickness and in Health. R. Rendell
In Sin or Folly? A. Nestorien
In Slippery Places. Herbert Maxwell
In Spite of Thunder. J. D. Carr
In Spite of the Czar. G. Boothby
In Storm and Strife. J. Middlemass
In Strange Company. G. Boothby
In Strange Shoes. A. Askew
In Strict Confidence. B. M. Forester
In Such a Night . . . V. Gielgud
In Suspicion's Shadow. Nicholas Carter
In Tent and Bungalow. Anonymous
In Terror's Grasp. Warren Miller
In That Rich Earth. A. Sewart
In the Absence of a Body. G. Bromley
In the Absence of Mrs. Peterson. N. Balchin
In the Balance. P. Wentworth
In the Beginning. P. O'Donnell
In the Best Families. R. Stout
In the Bishop's Carriage. M. Michelson
In the Bleak Midwinter. Jean Fraser
In the Blood. R. L. Duncan
In the Blood. L. Lamensdorf
In the Blood. A. Soutar
In the Bride's Mirror. M. Turnbull
In the Brooding Wild. R. Cullum
In the Cause of Freedom. A. W. Marchmont
In the Clutch of the Law. J. K. Stafford
In the Company of Spies. S. Barlay
In the Company of Strangers. J. Freeman
In the Country of the Blind. Michael Flynn
In the Dark. S. Horler
In the Dark. D. Richberg
In the Dark. Esme Stuart
In the Dark Night. M. P. Hood
In the Days of Gold. J. B. Hendryx
In the Days of Marlborough. George Long
In the Days of My Youth. A. B. Edwards
In the Days That Are Dead. H. Clifford
In the Dead of Night. Mark Cross
In the Dead of Night. J. T. MacIntyre
In the Dead of Night. T. W. Speight
In the Dead of the Night. M. L. Roby
In the Death of a Man. L. Egan
In the Deep Woods. N. Conde
In the Dentist's Chair. A. Armstrong
In the Depths of the First Degree. J. Doran
In the Distance. G. P. Lathrop
In the Emperor's Villa. R. H. Savage
In the Enemy Camp. R. L. Duncan
In the Esbekieyeh Gardens, and other stories. R. H. Savage
In the Event of My Death. H. Bourne
In the Eye of the Law. L. Hagen
In the Eye of the Law. W. D. Lyell
In the Face of Evidence. Nicholas Carter
In the Face of Night. D. Donovan
In the Face of the Enemy. H. Allix
In the Face of the Enemy. Douglas Scott
In the Face of the Verdict. J. Rhode
In the First Degree. R. Scarlett
In the First Watch and other engine-room stories. J. Dalziel
In the Flashlight. O. Binns
In the Fog. R. H. Davis
In the Force. Anonymous
In the Force. B. Hemyng
In the Foxes' Lair. B. Carlton
In the Frame. D. Francis
In the Gloom of Night. Nicholas Carter
In the Grip of a Demon. W. J. Weedon
In the Grip of a Lie. M. Leighton
In the Grip of Destiny. C. E. Sterrey
In the Grip of Fate. Nicholas Carter
In the Grip of the Brute. G. Radcliffe
In the Grip of the Demon. M. Richmond
In the Grip of the Gestapo. S. Hope
In the Grip of the Kidnappers. N. Ridley
In the Grip of the Law. D. Donovan
In the Grip of the Tong. J. W. Bobin
In the Gun-Room. H. K. Horsefield
In the Hag's Hands. C. C. Lowis

In the Halls of Evil. T. A. Waters
In the Hand of the Riffs. W. M. Graydon
In the Hands of Head-Hunters. C. Hayter
In the Hands of Spies. J. G. Brandon
In the Hands of the Enemy. R. Sharp
In the Heat of the Night. J. Ball
In the Heat of the Summer. J. Katzenbach
In the Highest Tradition. E. F. Droge
In the Hollow of Her Hand. G. B. McCutcheon
In the Hour Before Midnight. J. Higgins
In the House of Another. B. Mantle
In the House of Dark Music. F. Lynch
In the House of Night. W. B. Huie
In the House of Secret Enemies. G. C. Chesbro
In the House of the Enemy. B. Carlton
In the House of the Eye. W. A. MacKenzie
In the Key of Black. P. Broadley
In the King's Name—! H. D. Dearden
In the Labyrinth. A. Robbe-Grillet
In the Lake of the Moon. D. Lindsey
In the Lamb White Days. F. H. Hall
In the Land of the Dead. K. W. Jeter
In the Lap of Danger. Nicholas Carter
In the Lap of Fortune. J. Hatten
In the Last Act. R. Goyne
In the Last Analysis. A. Cross
In the Lion's Den. J. Cotton
In the Long Run. N. J. Crisp
In the Long Run We Are All Dead. M. Wolfson
In the Mayor's Parlour. J. S. Fletcher
In the Meshes. F. Severne
In the Middle Watch. W. C. Russell
In the Midnight Express. A. Murray
In the Midst of Death. Lawrence Block
In the Midst of Death. H. Luce
In the Minds of Men. Max Owen
In the Mist. A. Gittins
In the Money. A. S. Roche
In the Name of a Woman. A. W. Marchmont
In the Name of Liberty. F. Marryat
In the Name of the Father. A. J. Quinnell
In the Name of the Law. C. Lachman
In the Name of the Law. Dick Stewart
In the Name of the People. A. W. Marchmont
In the Name of the Tzar. J. B. Dayne
In the National Interest. M. Kalb
In the Net. P. Wilde
In the Next Room. E. R. Belmont
In the Nick of Time. Nicholas Carter
In the Nick of Time. N. Ridley
In the Night. L. Gorell
In the Night. J. Sutherland
In the Night Watch. E. S. Brooks
In the Nude. R. Seth
In the Old Chateau. R. H. Savage
In the Onyx Lobby. C. Wells
In the Plotter's Web. M. Leighton
In the Portion of Jezreel. J. L. Cowper
In the Potter's House. G. D. Eldridge
In the Presence of Enemies. W. J. Coughlin
In the Province of Darkness. P. Morton
In the Queen's Service. D. Donovan
In the Red. C. Egleton
In the Red. Joan Fleming
In the Russian Secret Service. Old Sleuth
In the Secret State. R. McCrum
In the Secret Vault. B. Wayde
In the Serpent's Coils. F. Du Boisgobey
In the Service of Love. R. Marsh
In the Shade. V. Hawtrey
In the Shadow. Old Spicer
In the Shadow of Death. G. Campbell
In the Shadow of Fear. Nicholas Carter
In the Shadow of Gold. P. Studer
In the Shadow of Guilt. M. Leighton
In the Shadow of Kings. N. Kelly
In the Shadow of Night. E. W. Alais
In the Shadow of Pa-Menkh. D. Langlois
In the Shadow of the Bush. John Bell
In the Shadow of the Cheka. J. D. Kennedy
In the Shadow of the Dragon. P. A. Crisp
In the Shadow of the Guillotine. J. W. Bobin
In the Shadow of the Hills. G. C. Shedd
In the Shadow of the Pyramids. R. H. Savage

In the Shadow of the Scaffold. W. P. Naish
In the Shadow of the Tower. R. M. Sears
In the Shadow of the Wind. A. Hebert
In the Shadow of Tyburn. Rachelle Edwards
In the Shadows. D. Daniels
In the Shadows. N. Harris
In the Still of the Night. H. Seymour
In the Street of the Angel. P. J. Stead
In the Swim. R. H. Savage
In the Teeth of Adversity. M. Babson
In the Teeth of the Evidence. D. L. Sayers
In the Tenth Moon. S. Williams
In the Thraldom of Fear. Maurice Scott
In the Tiger's Cage. C. Wells
In the Tilt-Yard of Life. H. Newell
In the Toils. J. T. MacIntyre
In the Toils. F. Trent
In the Toils of Fear. Nicholas Carter
In the Tsar's Dominions. Le Voleur
In the Village of the Man. L. Little
In the Wake of a Stranger. I. S. Black
In the Wake of Shark Gotch. A. R. Wetjen
In the Web. W. W. Cook
In the Web. D. Miall
In the Web of the Nazi Spider. Anonymous
In the Whirl of the Rising. B. Mitford
In the Wink of an Eye. K. Cherry
In the Winter Dark. T. Winton
In the Wrong Box. F. Russell
In the Wrong Paradise. Andrew Lang
In the Year of Waiting. Anonymous
In Those Dark Woods. D. Ince
In Tight Places. A. Griffiths
In Time for Murder. R. A. J. Walling
In Times Square. D. L. Mitchell
In Too Deep. D. Haring
In Triple Disguise. W. M. Graydon
In 25 Words—or Death. N. Mitzman
In Two Latitudes. G. Simenon
In Walks Murder. C. Ryland
In What Strange Land? P. Very
In White Raiment. W. LeQueux
In Whose Dim Shadow. J. J. Connington
Inca Death Squad. Nick Carter
Inca File. J. Rosenberger
Inca Gold. N. Johnson
Inca Gold Hijack. L. Derrick
Ince Affair. J. Morella
Ince Murder Case. E. J. Pond
Incendiary. W. A. Leahy
Incendiary Blonde. K. Edgar
Incense of Death. N. Deane
Inch of the C.I.D. J. Templeton
Inch of Time. James Norman
Incident. M. Avallone
Incident. A. Rives
Incident. E. Warman
Incident at a Corner. C. Armstrong
Incident at Badamya. D. Gilman
Incident at Hendon. J. Letton
Incident at Horcado City. W. C. MacDonald
Incident at La Junta. O. Lange
Incident at Naha. M. J. Bosse
Incident at 125th Street. J. E. Brown
Incident at Parga. Nancy Livingston
Incident at the Merry Hippo. E. Huxley
Incident at Villa Rahmana. A. Eliot
Incident Closed. H. J. Dellar
Incident in Ireland. Robert MacLeod
Incident on a Summer's Day. D. Raymond
Incidental Bishop. G. Allen
Incidental Murder. J. Champion
Incidental Murder. C. Joyce
Incitement to Murder. R. Amberley
Inclination to Murder. R. Ellerbeck
Inclination to Murder. H. Hunter
Inclining to Crime. A. Kent
Incognito. N. R. Nusbaum
Income Tax Conspiracy. A. Parsons
Incomer. G. Gaunt
Incomparable Bellairs. A. Castle
Incomparable Doll. K. Lindsay
Inconsistent Villains. N. A. Temple-Ellis
Inconvenient Bride. J. M. Fox

Inconvenient Corpse. P. Daniels
Inconvenient Corpse. E. P. Fenwick
Inconvenient Corpse. D. Sharp
Inconvenient Woman. D. Dunne
Incorporated. W. Ash
Incredible Adventure. M. Richmond
Incredible Adventures of Dennis Dorgan. R. E. Howard
Incredible Adventures of Rowland Hern. N. Olde
Incredible Crime. L. Austen-Leigh
Incredible Elopement of Lord Peter Wimsey. D. L. Sayers
Incredible Murder of Cardinal Tosca. A. Nowlan
Incredible Schlock Homes. R. L. Fish
Incredible Theft. A. Christie
Incredible Truth. C. Massie
Incredulity of Father Brown. G. K. Chesterton
Incubated Girl. F. T. Jane
Incubus. Ray Russell
Incubus. D. Thurlow
Incumbent. Pamela Hill
Incursion. Dirk Hanson
Indecent Behavior. C. Rivers
Indecent Exposure. E. Berckman
Indecent Relations. K. R. McKay
Indemnity Only. S. Paretsky
Independent. T. Newman
Independent Detective. Anonymous
Independent Means. F. Singleton
Independent Witness. H. Cecil
India. E. Southworth
India Fan. Victoria Holt
India-Rubber Men. E. Wallace
Indian Bangle. F. Hume
Indian Detective Stories. S. B. Banerjea
Indian Drum. W. MacHarg
Indian Dust. O. Rothfeld
Indian Idol Mystery. H. J. Andrews
Indian Love Lyrics. M. Richmond
Indian Lullaby. M. Richmond
Indian Mystery. G. Allen
Indian Point Conspiracy. R. Felber
Indian Police. Richard Fisher
Indian Princess. A. M. Williamson
Indian Vengeance. I. Gregory
Indian Wants the Bronx. I. Horovitz
Indian Wizard. A. Lillie
Indiana Jones and the Last Crusade. R. McGregor
Indictment. J. B. Matthews
Indigo. N. Carnac
Indigo Death. M. Saltmarsh
Indigo Necklace. F. Crane
Indigo Necklace Murders. F. Crane
Indiscretions of a Lady's Maid. W. LeQueux
Indiscretions of Dr. Carstairs. A. De O
Indiscretions of Lady Asenath. Basil Thomson
Induna's Wife. B. Mitford
Industrious Chevalier. S. S. Sprigge
Inevitable Crime. H. Leyford
Inevitable Fatality. Roy Lewis
Inevitable Hour. M. Boggan
Inevitable Law. F. E. Penny
Inevitable Millionaires. E. P. Oppenheim
Inexpendable. W. H. Baker
Infallible System. C. Kingston
Infallible Witness. P. Luck
Infamous Conduct. H. A. Wrenn
Infamous Fame. E. C. Vivian
Infamous Gentleman. G. Goodchild
Infamous Princess Mari. Roberta Murphy
Infant. F. Wicks
Infant of Prague. B. Granger
Infernal Device. M. Kurland
Inference of Guilt. H. Greene
Infernal Desire Machines of Doctor Hoffman. A. Carter
Infernal Idol. H. Seymour
Infernal Light. E. Friend
Inferno. J. Creasey
Inferno. R. Dundee
Infidel. M. E. Braddon
Infiltrate! Steve Mackenzie
Infiltration. H. Janson
Infiltrator. J. Ahern

Infiltrator. M. Hughes
Infiltrator. Martin Walker
Infiltrator. A. York
Infiltrators. D. Hamilton
Infinite Morning. D. Newton
Infinite Number of Monkeys. Les Roberts
Infinity of Mirrors. R. Condon
Influenza Mystery. Sutherland Scott
Informant. The Gordons
Informant. M. Olden
Information Man. C. Joyce
Information Received. E. R. Punshon
Information Received and other stories. P. Cheyney
Informed Consent. H. L. Klawans
Informed Sources. L. Kamarck
Informer. Ladbroke Black
Informer. J. McGreevey
Informer. Liam O'Flaherty
Informer. A. Takagi
Informer. F. Whishaw
Infra Blood. P. D. Westbrook
Ingenious Captain Cobbs. G. W. Appleton
Ingenious Mr. Stone. R. Player
Ingenious Strategem. Nicholas Carter
Ingram Intervenes. A. Michaelis
Inherit the Darkness. W. D. Roberts
Inherit the Mirage. J. Thatcher
Inherit the Shadows. J. Lovesmith
Inherit the Stars. J. P. Hogan
Inherit the Wind. G. Vaizey
Inheritance. O. Brookes
Inheritance. P. J. Cooper
Inheritance. Stuart Martin
Inheritance. D. Winston
Inheritor. M. Z. Bradley
Inheritors. J. Messmann
Initials Only. A. K. Green
Initiates. P. Virdell
Initiation. W. W. Johnstone
Injudicious Judge. Michael Underwood
Injured. T. Grainer
Injured Lover. M. B. Lowndes
Injury Time. B. Bainbridge
Injustice for All. J. A. Jance
Ink Street Murder. F. Grierson
Inkosi-Carver Investigates. "Capstan"
Inland Passage. G. H. Coxe
Inn at the Red Oak. L. Griswold
Inn by the Shore. T. B. Reagan
Inn Closes for Christmas. Cledwyn Hughes
Inn of Evil. J. A. Creighton
Inn of the Thirteen Swords. D. Graeme
Inn-Side Murder. C. C. Garner
Inn with the Wooden Door. N. MacSwan
Inner Circle. J. Fast
Inner Circle. M. Harvey
Inner Circle. E. C. Mayne
Inner City Hoodlum. D. Goines
Inner Number. F. C. Williams
Inner Ring. M. Gagnon
Inner Room. P. H. Irving
Inner Steps. S. Cardiff
Innocence Lost. C. Stowers
Innocence of Father Brown. G. K. Chesterton
Innocence of Rosamond Prior. A. Dick
Innocent. Josephine Bell
Innocent. I. McEwan
Innocent. E. Piper
Innocent Abroad. M. Carr
Innocent Accomplice. B. Reynolds
Innocent Amusements. B. Pain
Innocent and Willing. Morton Cooper
Innocent Blood. P. D. James
Innocent Bottle. Anthony Gilbert
Innocent Bystander. G. Bagby
Innocent Bystander. B. Frost
Innocent Bystander. M. F. Page
Innocent Bystander. C. Rice
Innocent Bystanders. J. Munro
Innocent Criminal. J. D. Beresford
Innocent Deception. L. Shaw
Innocent Fear. R. W. Hunter
Innocent Flower. C. Armstrong
Innocent Guilt. E. C. Vivian

Innocent Gunman. J. P. Lacroix
Innocent House. F. Lockridge
Innocent Imposter and other stories. M. Grey
Innocent in Eden. M. Way
Innocent Journey. S. Natsuki
Innocent Madness. D. Hollyock
Innocent Mrs. Duff. E. S. Holding
Innocent Murder. L. D. Allen
Innocent Murderers. W. A. Johnston
Innocent One. J. Reach
Innocent Sinner. A. M. Meadows
Innocents. W. Archibald
Innocents. R. Savage
Innocents. G. Simenon
Innocents at Home. J. B. Hilton
Innocents on Broadway. E. E. Saks
Innocents on the Broads. E. R. Suffling
Innoculate! N. Bayne
Inquest. M. Barringer
Inquest. H. Clandon
Inquest. R. Neumann
Inquest. M. K. Ozaki
Inquest. P. Wilde
Inquest—Eleven Thirty. S. Darrell
Inquest on a Lady. T. J. R. Sennocke
Inquest on a Mistress. T. J. R. Sennocke
Inquests Bewraying. T. J. R. Sennocke
Inquests on the Deceased. T. J. R. Sennocke
Inquiries by the Yard. A. Brock
Inquisition. M. Olden
Inquisitors. D. Lyle
Inquisitory. R. Pinget
Insanity Mahcine. Peter Maxwell
Inscrutable. Esme Stuart
Inscrutable Charlie Muffin. B. Freemantle
Inscrutable Miss Stone. A. Askew
Inside. R. Timperley
Inside Information. N. Bentley
Inside Job. S. Allan
Inside Job. N. Brady
Inside Job. J. Boland
Inside Left's Double. J. G. Rowe
Inside Lester. F. Carmichael
Inside Man. G. H. Coxe
Inside Man. E. R. Johnson
Inside Out. William Hughes
Inside Out! G. Ludlow
Inside Out. David Miles
Inside-Out Heist. T. B. Reagan
Inside Out Man. F. Cockain
Inside Passage to Death. M. Lanford
Inside the Lines. E. D. Biggers
Inside Track. G. Dilnot
Insider. G. Joseph
Insider Out. C. Hudson
Insiders. S. Morrow
Insiders. M. Pflaum
Insidious Dr. Fu-Manchu. S. Rohmer
Insoluble. F. Everton
Insomnia Street. D. Bateson
Inspector. J. De Hartog
Inspector Answers. N. P. Hart
Inspector Bedison and the Sunderland Case. T. Cobb
Inspector Bedison Risks It. T. Cobb
Inspector Burmann's Black-Out. B. Cobb
Inspector Burmann's Busiest Day. B. Cobb
Inspector Calls. J. B. Priestley
Inspector Cole. R. Batchelor
Inspector Derben and the Widow Maker. P. A. Foxall
Inspector Derben's War. P. A. Foxall
Inspector Dickins Retires. E. P. Oppenheim
Inspector Drake's Last Case. D. Tristam
Inspector Flagg and the Scarlet Skeleton. J. Cassells
Inspector French and the Cheyne Mystery. F. W. Crofts
Inspector French and the Starvel Tragedy. F. W. Crofts
Inspector French's Greatest Case. F. W. Crofts
Inspector Frost and Lady Brassingham. H. M. Smith
Inspector Frost and the Waverdale Fire. H. M. Smith

Inspector Frost and the Whitbourne Murder. H. M. Smith
Inspector Frost in Crevenna Cove. H. M. Smith
Inspector Frost in the Background. H. M. Smith
Inspector Frost in the City. H. M. Smith
Inspector Frost's Jigsaw. H. M. Smith
Inspector Ghote Breaks an Egg. H. R. F. Keating
Inspector Ghote Caught in Meshes. H. R. F. Keating
Inspector Ghote Draws a Line. H. R. F. Keating
Inspector Ghote Goes by Train. H. R. F. Keating
Inspector Ghoste, His Life and Crimes. H. R. F. Keating
Inspector Ghote Hunts the Peacock. H. R. F. Keating
Inspector Ghote Plays a Joker. H. R. F. Keating
Inspector Ghote Trusts the Heart. H. R. F. Keating
Inspector Ghote's Good Crusade. H. R. F. Keating
Inspector Henderson, the Central Office Detective. H. I. Hancock
Inspector Higgins Goes Fishing. C. F. Gregg
Inspector Higgins Hurries. C. F. Gregg
Inspector Higgins Sees It Through. C. F. Gregg
Inspector Hornleigh Investigates. H. W. Priwin
Inspector Imanishi Investigates. S. Matsumoto
Inspector Jackson Goes North. D. T. Lindsay
Inspector Jackson Investigates. D. T. Lindsay
Inspector McLean's Casebook. G. Goodchild
Inspector McLean's Holiday. G. Goodchild
Inspector Maigret and the Burglar's Wife. G. Simenon
Inspector Maigret and the Dead Girl. G. Simenon
Inspector Maigret and the Killers. G. Simenon
Inspector Maigret and the Strangled Stripper. G. Simenon
Inspector Maigret in New York's Underworld. G. Simenon
Inspector Maigret Investigates. G. Simenon
Inspector Malone Sails In. D. J. Murphy
Inspector Manson's Success. E. Radford
Inspector Morgan's Dilemma. J. Bingham
Inspector Queen's Own Case. E. Queen
Inspector Richardson C.I.D. B. Thomson
Inspector Rusby's Finale. V. Markham
Inspector Saito's Small Satori. J. Van De Wetering
Inspector Treadgold Investigates. A. Weymouth
Inspector West Alone. J. Creasey
Inspector West at Bay. J. Creasey
Inspector West at Home. J. Creasey
Inspector West Cries Wolf. J. Creasey
Inspector West Kicks Off. J. Creasey
Inspector West Leaves Town. J. Creasey
Inspector West Makes Haste. J. Creasey
Inspector West Regrets. J. Creasey
Inspector West Takes Charge. J. Creasey
Inspector Wilkins Reads the Proofs. Murray Thomas
Inspector Wilkins Sees Red. Murray Thomas
Inspector's Holiday. R. Lockridge
Inspector's Opinion. M. Reybold
Inspector's Puzzle. C. Matthew
Instant Dead. S. Jason
Instant Enemy. R. Macdonald
Instant Replay. D. Everson
Instar. R. Brady
Instead of Murder. J. Goodman
Instigator. E. A. Treeton
Instinct at Fault. Nicholas Carter
Instinctive Criminal. G. Coleridge
Institute. J. M. Cain
Instrument. P. Everett
Instrument. V. Thorpe
Instrument of Destiny. J. D. Beresford
Instrument of Vengeance. H. McCutcheon
Instruments of Darkness. S. Horler
Instruments of Death. W. A. Harbinson
Insufficient Evidence. M. Hervey
Insulators. J. Creasey
Insult to Injury. B. I. Raizner
Insurgent Love. M. Richmond
Insurrection! D. Brennan
Insurrection of Hippolytus Brandenberg. R. Friedman
Insurrectionist. A. McCoy
Intelligence. M. Goldberg

"Intelligence" Game of Secret Service Cases and Problems. R. McKay
Intelligence Quotient. G. C. Leppanen
Intensive Care. P. Dunant
Intensive Fear. N. Christian
Intent to Kill. M. Bryan
Intent to Kill. H. Desmond
Intent to Murder. N. Deane
Intent to Murder. L. Sands
Intercept. K. Bernstein
Intercept. N. Morrison
Intercom Conspiracy. E. Ambler
Intercontinental Knot. J. Semyonov
Interface. J. Gores
Interface Assignment. W. Rayner
Interface for Murder. L. Biggle, Jr.
Interface Man. Bill Knox
Interference. R. Pertwee
Interloper. Gwendoline Butler
Interloper. E. P. Oppenheim
Interloper. R. M. Stern
Interlopers. D. Hamilton
Interlude. S. P. B. Mais
Intermind. R. Luther
Intermission. M. Albrand
Internal Affairs. J. Oster
International Affair. B. Graeme
International Commando. J. Courage
International Crook League. Nicholas Carter
International Sin. A. Whicker
International Spy. A. Upward
Interpreter's House. B. P. Neuman
Interrogators. A. Prior
Interrupted Honeymoon. A. Swift
Interrupted Kiss. R. Marsh
Interrupted Wedding. L. T. Barnard
Interrupted Wedding. M. Gerard
Intersteller Espionage. A. Del Martia
Interventions. P. Breslin
Interview. H. C. Rae
Interview and other stories. E. McBain
Interviewing's Killing. A. Tack
Interworld. I. Haiblum
Intimate Evil. P. Reidinger
Intimate Journal of Warren Winslow. Jean Leslie
Intimate Kill. M. Yorke
Intimate Relations. Frederick Jackson
Intimate Stranger. W. Lynch
Intimate Stranger. E. Thomas
Intimate Victims. V. Packer
Intimidators. D. Hamilton
Into a Dark Mirror. K. Orvis
Into His Own Trap. J. K. Stafford
Into My Parlour. P. Dallas
Into Nick Carter's Web. Nicholas Carter
Into the Blue. R. Goddard
Into the Darkness. Barbara Michaels
Into the Fog. Winston Graham
Into the Jaws of Death. W. G. Forbes
Into the Maze. D. Stivers
Into the Night. F. N. Greene
Into the Night. Jan Michaels
Into the Night. C. Woolrich
Into the Shade, and other stories. M. C. Hay
Into the Valley of Death. E. Hervey
Into Temptation. K. Lindsay
Into the Arena. E. Darby
Into the Void. F. Converse
Into Thin Air. H. Carmichael
Into Thin Air. J. Iams
Into Thin Air. G. Vaizey
Into Thin Air. H. Winslow
Into This Universe. Fredrick Jackson
Into Thy Hands. A. Applin
Intrigue. D. Cory
Intrigue. Clive Desmond
Intrigue. W. Hackett
Intrigue. P. Renin
Intrigue. G. Usher
Intrigue and Matrimony. D. Vane
Intrigue for Empire. K. M. Knight
Intrigue in Morocco. Coriola
Intrigue in Paris. S. Noel
Intrigue in Rome. E. Morley

Intrigue in Tangier. H. Seymour
Intrigue Island. A. Mills
Intrigue on Halfaday Creek. J. B. Hendryx
Intrigue on the Upper Level. T. T. Hoyne
Intriguer. Maude Parker
Intriguers. T. Cobb
Intriguers. D. Hamilton
Intriguers. W. LeQueux
Intrigues of a Prisoner. E. Gaboriau
Introducing C. B. Greenfield. L. Kallen
Introducing Dr. Zodiac. L. De Wohl
Introducing Inspector Maigret. G. Simenon
Introducing Mr. Brandon. Anthony Morton
Introducing Mr. Phreet. N. H. Perrin
Introducing Mr. Robinson. Rupert Grayson
Introducing the Super. R. Goyne
Introducing the Toff. J. Creasey
Introducing William Allison. W. Hewlett
Intruder. T. Altman
Intruder. L. Charbonneau
Intruder. O. R. Cohen
Intruder. M. Cronin
Intruder. C. Farr
Intruder. H. Horn
Intruder. S. Laforest
Intruder. Hadley Lawrence
Intruder. M. K. Lawrence
Intruder. D. M. Low
Intruder. R. Maugham
Intruder. A. Myrer
Intruder. G. Tindall
Intruder at Maison Benedict. S. Richard
Intruder from the Sea. G. McDonell
Intruder in the Dark. G. Bellairs
Intruder in the Dust. W. Faulkner
Intruder in the Wind. Jess Carr
Intruders. P. Montandon
Intrusion. E. McCrae
Intrusive Tourist. B. Reynolds
Invader. R. Wormser
Invaders. E. P. Frankland
Invaders. W. Kempley
Invaders from the Dark. G. La Spina
Invasion. H. Janson
Invasion. J. Wallace
Invasion Coast. J. G. Sarasin
Invasion of Privacy. H. Kurnitz
Invasion of the Clones. J. Rosenberger
Invasion of the Nymphomaniacs. S. O'Shea
Invasion of the Yellow Warlords. C. Steele
Invasion U.S.A. J. Frost
Invasion U.S.S.R. J. Buchanan
Invasions. E. Izzi
Inverness Murder. C. A. Byers
Inverted Crime. L. Gribble
Investigation. S. Lem
Investigation. E. Saunders
Investigation. D. Uhnak
Investigation. M. Urquhart
Investigation at Holman Square. N. M. Hopkins
Investigations Are Proceeding. J. Ashford
Investigations of Colwyn Grey. A. J. Rees
Investigations of Geoffrey Page. V. L. Whitechurch
Investigations of John Pym. D. C. Murray
Investigative Eye of Albert Ward. F. Greco
Investigators. J. S. Fletcher
Investment in Crime. J. C. Crowley
Invisibility Affair. Thomas Stratton
Invisible Assassins. D. Pendleton
Invisible Boarder. Mildred Davis
Invisible Box Murders. K. Robeson
Invisible Bridge. F. Allan
Invisible Companion and other stories. J. J. Farjeon
Invisible Cord. V. Castang
Invisible Cord. C. Cookson
Invisible Darkness. P. Paul
Invisible Death. B. Flynn
Invisible Empire. G. Steele
Invisible Enemy. T. P. Lathy
Invisible Enemy. G. C. Shedd
Invisible Evidence. P. Winn
Invisible Evil. R. Gaines
Invisible Eye. P. Tabori
Invisible Flamini. Carter Brown

Invisible Foe. L. J. Miln
Invisible Green. J. Sladek
Invisible Hand. R. Dark
Invisible Host. G. Bristow
Invisible Image. F. Chabrey
Invisible Line. V. C. Chadwick
Invisible Man. H. G. Wells
Invisible Man Murders. R. Foster
Invisible Pickpocket. J. M'Govan
Invisible Raider. S. Drew
Invisible Red. Maude Parker
Invisible Scarlet O'Neil. R. Stamm
Invisible Ships. Sea Lion
Invisible Trap. Genevieve St. John
Invisible Verdict. R. Goyne
Invisible Weapons. J. Rhode
Invisible Worm. M. Millar
Invisibles. E. E. Christopher
Invisibles. James Dark
Invitation. C. Cookson
Invitation to a Ball. P. Meredith
Invitation to a Dynamite Party. P. Lovesey
Invitation to a Funeral. T. Harknett
Invitation to a Murder. R. King
Invitation to a Murder. J. T. Story
Invitation to a Strangling. R. L. Brent
Invitation to Adventure. G. Ashe
Invitation to an Inquest. R. Hull
Invitation to Danger. D. Mai
Invitation to Danger. F. Murray
Invitation to Danger. P. Phillips
Invitation to Death. Nick Carter
Invitation to Death. A. R. Long
Invitation to Death. A. O. Pollard
Invitation to Die. F. French
Invitation to Evil. W. D. Roberts
Invitation to Kill. G. Low
Invitation to Kill. V. Warren
Invitation to Mather. B. Graeme
Invitation to Murder. Robert (G.) Curtis
Invitation to Murder. L. Ford
Invitation to Murder. Manning Long
Invitation to Murder. I. S. Shriber
Invitation to Murder. R. Stout
Invitation to Murder. R. Trevor
Invitation to Paradise. Lesley Howard
Invitation to Terror. P. Hambledon
Invitation to the Grave. David Hume
Invitation to Vengeance. K. M. Knight
Invitation to Violence. L. White
Invited. Z. Davis
Involved. Johnny Morgan
Involvement in Austria. J. N. Chance
Involvement of Arnold Wechsler. J. A. Graham
Inward Eye. P. Bacon
Inward Glance. L. Robinson
Ipcress File. L. Deighton
Ippletree Manor Mystery. D. W. Spurgeon
Iranian Hit. D. Pendleton
Iras. T. Douglas
Irena. J. Land
Irene. T. Alexander
Irene. B. Vane
Irene, Good Night. D. R. Bensen
Irina. Gavin Holt
Iris the Avenger. F. Marryat
Iris, the Bewitched. K. Kimbrough
Irish Affair. Andrea Harris
Irish Beauty Contract. P. Atlee
Irish Detective. Anonymous
Irish Detective. Old Sleuth
Irish Game. J. R. Lowell
Irish Holidays. R. Thynne
Irish Monte Cristo Abroad. A. Robertson
Irish Monte Cristo's Search. A. Robertson
Irish Monte Cristo's Trail. A. Robertson
Irish Police Officer. Robert Curtis
Irish Signorina. J. O'Faolain
Irish Stew. D. Conyers
Irish Wine. D. Wimmer
Irish Witch. D. Wheatley
Iron Apple. G. Bowman
Iron Box. C. R. Gull

Iron Burgess, the Government Detective. Anonymous
Iron Burgess, the Goverment Detenctive. Old Sleuth
Iron Butterflies. A. Norton
Iron Chalice. O. R. Cohen
Iron Chest. G. Colman
Iron Claw. F. A. Symonds
Iron Claymore. Gar Wilson
Iron Cobweb. A. Tilton
Iron Cross. S. Cobb
Iron Cross. R. H. Sherard
Iron Curtain. A. O. Pollard
Iron Door. O. Martin
Iron Egg. D. W. F. Hardie
Iron Facade. C. Marchant
Iron Gates. M. Millar
Iron God. P. O'Donnell
Iron God. D. Stivers
Iron Grip. E. Wallace
Iron Hand. J. M. Cobban
Iron Hand. Howard Dean
Iron Hand. A. Tilton
Iron Hand. F. Warden
Iron Horse. R. M. Ballantyne
Iron Horse. William Grant
Iron Maiden. Carter Brown
Iron Man and other tales of the ring. R. E. Howard
Iron Man and the Tin Woman. S. Leacock
Iron Mask. F. Du Boisgobey
Iron Mask. Gwyn Evans
Iron Mask. J. G. Sarasin
Iron Master. Anonymous
Iron Orchid. John Bentley
Iron Pirate. M. Pemberton
Iron Ring. H. S. Keeler
Iron Sanctuary. Robert MacLeod
Iron Shroud. W. Mudford
Iron Skull. K. Robeson
Iron Skull. Maxwell Scott
Iron Spiders. B. Kendrick
Iron Spiders Murder. B. Kendrick
Iron Spy. A. Edgar
Iron Staircase. G. Simenon
Iron Swastika Plot. J. Rosenberger
Iron Tiger. Harry Patterson
Iron Tiger. M. L. Stokes
Iron Virgin. J. M. Fox
Iron Way. C. M. Hincks
Iron Web. K. Crowder
Iron Will. C. N. Buck
Ironies. R. Connell
Ironing Board. C. Morley
Ironman. D. Stivers
Ironmaster's Daughter. P. Trent
Ironmouth. C. Stanton
Ironside. J. Thompson
Ironsides Abroad. Anonymous
Ironsides' Lone Hand. V. Gunn
Ironsides of the Yard. V. Gunn
Ironsides on the Spot. V. Gunn
Ironsides Sees Red. V. Gunn
Ironsides Smashes Through. V. Gunn
Ironsides Smells Blood. V. Gunn
Ironwood. Jennie Melville
Irralie's Bushranger. E. W. Hornung
Irregular Marriage. S. Warwick
Irrepressible Peccadillo. F. Flora
Irresistable Stranger. A. Applin
Irresponsibles. Elizabeth Ford
Irving Solution. L. Simon
Is and Was. H. Hewlett
Is He Dead, Miss Ffinch? J. N. Smith
Is He the Man? W. C. Russell
Is Money Everything? J. J. McCall
Is My Flesh of Brass. P. J. Wolfson
Is No One Innocent? M. H. Gropper
Is She Dead Too? Anthony Gilbert
Is Skin Deep, Is Fatal. H. R. F. Keating
Is There a Traitor in the House? P. McGerr
Is There Any Body There? P. Sneal
Is This Coffin Taken? J. F. Webb
Is This Revenge? L. Gribble
Is This the End? C. Sargent
Isa. Anonymous

Isa. A. W. Marchmont
Isaac Quartet. J. Charyn
Isabel Broderick—"Bubbles We Buy." A. Jones
Isabelle. A. Gide
Isabelle, the Frantic. K. Kimbrough
Iselane. J. L. Van Wijk
Ishmael. M. E. Braddon
Ishmael. E. Southworth
Ishmaelite. M. E. Braddon
Ishmael's Wife. Roy Vickers
Iskra Incident. J. H. Butler
Island. Mildred Nelson
Island. Thomas Perry
Island. T. M. Wright
Island Alert. J. M. Walsh
Island and other stories. D. Vernon
Island Deathtrap. D. Pendleton
Island Doctor. Rona Randall
Island Emperor. B. Priestley
Island Feud. S. M. Parkman
Island Gold. V. Williams
Island Heirs. J. Judson
Island in the Sun. A. Waugh
Island in Waiting. Anthea Fraser
Island Interlude. Jane Edwards
Island Intrigue. P. McAdam
Island Murder. T. Stevenson
Island Murder. P. Trent
Island Mystery. G. A. Birmingham
Island Mystery. J. W. Bobin
Island Mystery. J. Bolton
Island Mystery. T. Lester
Island of Atonement. H. Leyford
Island of Bitter Memories. D. Daniels
Island of Crimea. V. Aksyonov
Island of Dangerous Men. A. Drummond
Island of Death. A. Broome
Island of Death. D. Seaman
Island of Deceit. A. Andrew
Island of Deceit. E. Habersham
Island of Desire. J. L. Roberts
Island of Despair. Robert Harding
Island of Destiny. A. J. Rees
Island of Disaster. Michael Lewis
Island of Dogs. L. Falk
Island of Eden. B. Mitford
Island of Escape. H. L. Nelson
Island of Evil. D. Daniels
Island of Evil. C. Farr
Island of Fear. F. Bream
Island of Fear. J. D. Conway
Island of Fear. R. Dent
Island of Fear. Domenica
Island of Fear. H. Footner
Island of Fog. M. Kingsbury
Island of Fu Manchu. S. Rohmer
Island of Galloping Gold. E. Wallace
Island of Ghosts. O. Sackville
Island of Gold. James Grant
Island of Intrigue. I. Ostrander
Island of Mystery. A. Hale
Island of Peril. J. Creasey
Island of Romance. D. Whitelaw
Island of Secrets. S. Drew
Island of Sheep. J. Buchan
Island of Silence. C. B. Norris
Island of Slaves. S. Hope
Island of Spies. J. M. Walsh
Island of Steel. S. P. Cohen
Island of Surprises. W. B. M. Ferguson
Island of Terror. H. C. McNeile
Island of Terror. E. W. Strother
Island of Test. A. Soutar
Island of the Accursed. W. Winthrop
Island of the Damned. P. J. Clancy
Island of the Damned. J. Rosenberger
Island of the Guilty. G. H. Teed
Island of the Lost Rubies. P. Werner
Island of the Pit. V. James
Island of the Seven Hills. Z. Cass
Island of Unrest. J. G. Sarasin
Island Princess. E. Southworth
Island Quarry. E. Herndon
Island Rescue. J. Tickell

Title Index

Island Schooner. G. Volk
Island Secret. W. M. Graydon
Island Twilight. N. Tranter
Island Where Time Stands Still. D. Wheatley
Islands of the Condemned. F. A. M. Webster
Isle for a Stranger. D. W. Low
Isle of Blood. Nick Carter
Isle of Confusion. Douglas Christie
Isle of Crooks. Anonymous
Isle of Desire. Basil Carey
Isle of Desire. Douglas Christie
Isle of Desire. B. K. Seton
Isle of Dragons. Robert MacLeod
Isle of Enchantment. A. Wood
Isle of Fire Murder. B. Y. Witten
Isle of Hate. A. Dare
Isle of Horror. G. H. Teed
Isle of Illusion. G. Gibbs
Isle of Innocence. L. Noel
Isle of Men. G. Volk
Isle of Peril. S. Blake
Isle of Peril. A. Wade
Isle of Stife. G. C. Shedd
Isle of Surrey. R. Dowling
Isle of the Dolphins. J. L. Roberts
Isle of the Drums. J. A. Dunn
Isle of the Seventh Sentry. F. Kent
Isle of the Snakes. R. L. Fish
Isle of the Undead. V. Coffman
Isobel. J. O. Curwood
Isotope Man. C. E. Maine
Isoworg. H. Bentinck
Israel Rank. R. Horniman
Issac Docket. S. Dave
Issue. E. Noble
Issue of the Bishop's Blood. T. P. McMahon
Istanbul. Nick Carter
Istanbul Decision. Nick Carter
Istanbul Elopment. D. T. Hughes
Istanbul Nights. Clarissa Ross
It. R. Hawkey
It. Stephen King
It Adds Up to Trouble. A. Nuttall
It Ain't Hay. D. Dodge
It Always Happens. Robin Temple
It Always Rains on Sunday. A. La Bern
It Began in New York. M. Kennedy
It Began in Singapore. G. P. Willis
It Began in Vauxhall Gardens. K. Kellow
It Blows Up in Your Face. S. Finnegan
It Boils Down to Murder. P. D. Westbrook
It Came to Pass. S. Fairway
It Came to Pass. G. M. Fenn
It Can't Always Be Caviar. J. M. Simmel
It Can't Be My Grave. S. F. X. Dean
It Comes by Night. Clarissa Ross
It Could Happen to You. A. Booth
It Could Happen to You. J. B. O'Sullivan
It Couldn't Be Caroline. D. Egerton
It Couldn't Be Murder. H. Austin
It Couldn't Be Murder. Mark Cross
It Couldn't Be Murder. R. B. Sinclair
It Couldn't Be Suicide. Caroline Francis
It Couldn't Happen to Me. J. Blackmore
It Couldn't Matter Less. P. Cheyney
It Doesn't Add Up. R. Drayton
It Doesn't Matter When You're Dead. Max James
It Had to Be You. V. Siller
It Happened at Midnight. J. Reach
It Happened at Night. Roland Daniel
It Happened at the Cape. K. Lindsay
It Happened at the Lake. J. T. Shaw
It Happened in Boston. R. H. Greenan
It Happened in Cairo. K. Rhodes
It Happened in Essex. V. Bridges
It Happened in Hamburg. W. H. Baker
It Happened in Melgrove Square. J. Hunter
It Happened in Vienna. T. B. Marlowe
It Happened in Wayland. F. Shroyer
It Happened Like That. E. Phillpotts
It Happened on Halfaday Creek. J. B. Hendryx
It Happened to Susan. J. Blackmore
It Howls at Night. N. Berrow
It Is Expedient . . . . K. Ingram

It Is Never Too Late to Mend. C. Reade
It Is No Wonder. J. F. Molloy
It Is Not Safe to Know. B. Reynolds
It Isn't Done. C. Glick
It Leads to Murder. Wade Wright
It Leaves Them Cold. Kevin O'Hara
It Makes a Nice Change. John Gloag
It Makes You Think. A. E. Jones
It Means Mischief. R. Pertwee
It Might Have Been. P. Trent
It Might Have Meant Murder. L. Cargill
It Might Lead Anywhere. E. R. Punshon
It Never Comes Easy. W. Newton
It Never Rains. J. M. Allison
It Never Rains—. V. Bridges
It Never Rains in Los Angeles. C. Flowers
It Only Hurts a Minute. D. M. Mankiewicz
It Pays to Die. C. M. Wills
It Prowls at Dark. H. R. Taunton
It Rained That Friday. G. M. Wilson
It Seemed Like a Good Idea at the Time. D. R. Stieper
It Shouldn't Happen to a Dog. E. Lanham
It Shouldn't Happen to a Dog. Colin Watson
It Started with Queenie. Lloyd Williams
It Takes a Thief. D. Billany
It Walks at Midnight. J. Reach
It Walks by Night. J. D. Carr
It Walks the Woods. Alan Grant
It Was a Dark and Stormy Night. Tim Kelly
It Was Christmas Every Day. A. La Bern
It Was Locked. J. Hawk
It Was Murder, They Said. John Bentley
It Wasn't a Nightmare. L. F. Hay
It Wasn't Me! I. Jefferies
It Will Be All Right! T. Gallon
It Will Be Warmer When It Snows. A. La Bern
It Won't Get You Anywhere. D. Skirrow
Italian. A. Radcliffe
Italian Assets. Richard Butler
Italian Bandit. Old Sleuth
Italian Banditti. I. Crookenden
Italian Called Mario. P. H. Irving
Italian Connection. Robin Moore
Italian Gadget. H. Calvin
Italian Job. T. K. Martin
Italian Maze. E. Lascelles
Italian Mysteries. F. Lathom
Italian Villa. H. La Barre
Item 7. Alan Nixon
It's a Battlefield. G. Greene
It's a Crime. R. Ellington
It's a Frame. D. Haring
It's a Free Country. L. Brain
It's a Sin. H. Zore
It's a Sin to Kill. D. Keene
It's a Wise Child. T. Curley
It's About Crime. M. Kantor
It's Alive. R. Woodley
It's All in the Game. W. T. Tilden
It's All Yours. R. Angel
It's Always Eve That Weeps. H. Janson
It's Always Too Late to Mend. P. V. Stern
It's An Ill Wind. D. Mayor
It's Bedtime, Baby! H. Janson
It's Cold Next Door. P. De Polnay
It's Death, My Darling! A. R. Long
It's Different Abroad. H. Calvin
It's Different in July. K. Fitzgerald
It's Easier for Homicide. K. David
It's Easy Money. A. Morelli
It's Easy to Kill. A. Wood
It's Good to Be Alive. K. David
It's Hard to Be a Russian Spy. A. Korotykov
It's Her Own Funeral. C. Carnac
It's in the Bag. A. Spiller
It's Later Than You Think. M. M. Kaye
It's Loaded, Mr. Bauer. J. P. Marquand
It's Locked in with You. G. Mayo
It's Lonely on the Sidewalk. D. Bogard
It's Murder. R. Drayton
It's Murder! T. T. Flynn
It's Murder If You Say So! A. Aldous
It's Murder, McHugh. J. Flynn

It's Murder, Maguire. R. Himmel
It's Murder, Miss King. I. Waitt
It's Murder, Mr. Potter. R. Foley
It's Murder, Senorita. D. Bateson
It's Murder She Says. R. Angel
It's Murder to Live. E. Radford
It's Murder with Dover. J. Porter
It's My Funeral. P. Rabe
It's My Own Funeral. D. Lyon
It's Never Too Late to Mend. O. Harper
It's Not Easy to Die. S. Markham
It's Only Saps That Die. B. Toler
It's Quiet in the Country. H. Willett
It's Raining Violence. T. Du Bois
It's Safe in England. K. Fitzgerald
It's Up to You. E. L. G. Watson
It's Your Funeral. A. Bocca
It's Your Funeral. Kevin O'Hara
It's Your Turn to Die. Gerard Fisher
Ivan Greet's Masterpiece. G. Allen
Ivan the Serf. S. Cobb
I've Found My Love. M. Richmond
I've Got Viktor Schalkenburg. W. Mulvihill
I've Got You Covered. P. Denver
Ivor's Chance. P. Trent
Ivorstone Manor. E. Cromwell
Ivory Ball. C. C. Hotchkiss
Ivory Box. Anonymous
Ivory Dagger. P. Wentworth
Ivory Disc. P. Brebner
Ivory God. J. S. Fletcher
Ivory Goddess. W. H. L. Crauford
Ivory Grin. J. R. Macdonald
Ivory Ladies. Gavin Holt
Ivory Locket. M. Alan
Ivory Penguin. John Morgan
Ivory Queen. N. Hurst
Ivory Screen. G. H. Teed
Ivory Slave. A. Hutton
Ivory Snuff Box. A. Fredericks
Ivory Tower. M. Eatock
Ivory Trail. T. Mundy
Ivory Tusk. R. Hardinge
Ivory Valley. C. J. C. Hyne
Ivy Halls. B. H. Hyatt
Ivy Tree. Mary Stewart
Ixion's Wheel. V. Basevi

J. Alfred Prufrock Murders. C. H. Sawyer
J.B.'s Daughter. J. Sherlock
J for Jennie Murders. T. A. Plummer
J for Jupiter. T. Fuller
J. P. Dunbar. W. C. Hudson
Jacaranda Murders. H. Desmond
Jacintha. S. Hylton
Jack-All-Alone: His Cruises. F. Cowper
Jack Allyn's Friends. G. W. Appleton
Jack and Gil. Old Sleuth
Jack and Susan in 1913. M. McDowell
Jack and Susan in 1933. M. McDowell
Jack and Susan in 1953. M. McDowell
Jack and the Beanstalk. E. McBain
Jack Breakaway. Old Sleuth
Jack Carstairs of the Power House. S. Sandys
Jack Carter and the Law. T. Lewis
Jack Carter and the Mafia Pigeon. T. Lewis
Jack Carter's Law. T. Lewis
Jack Chanty. H. Footner
Jack Crews. M. F. Boggs
Jack Curzon. A. C. Gunter
Jack Gordon, Night Errant, Gotham 1883. W. C. Hudson
Jack-in-the-Box. J. J. Connington
Jack Junk. T. P. Prest
Jack Lane's Browning. D. Gethin
Jack O'Judgment. E. Wallace
Jack O'Lantern. G. Goodchild
Jack O'Lantern. K. A. Shoesmith
Jack o' the Cudgel. Anonymous
Jack of Clubs. J. Ironside
Jack of Hearts. D. Von Elsner
Jack on the Gallows Tree. L. Bruce
Jack Ranworth. J. Blyth
Jack Shepard, the Bandit King. Anonymous

J

Jack Sheppard. W. H. Ainsworth
Jack Sheppard. J. B. Buckstone
Jack Sheppard, the Bandit King. O. Harper
Jack Spot. H. Janson
Jack the Juggler. Old Sleuth
Jack the Juggler's Ordeal. Old Sleuth
Jack the Juggler's Trial. Old Sleuth
Jack the Knife. O. Tupper
Jack the Outlaw. K. Snowden
Jack the Rascal. G. M. Fenn
Jack the Ripper. M. Daniel
Jack the Ripper. Stuart James
Jack the Ripper. Richard Gordon
Jack the Ripper. R. Pember
Jack the Ripper. B. Reader
Jack the Ripper Walking Tour Murder. A. Borowitz
Jack Vinton, the Boy Detective. Anonymous
Jack Warleigh. D. J. Belgrave
Jackal. D. Whitelaw
Jackal Helix. G. V. Basile
Jackals. C. Kernahan
Jackals and others. F. E. Penny
Jackal's Head. Elizabeth Peters
Jackals of the Secret Service. Operator 1384
Jackanapes Jacket. E. M. Keate
Jackdaw. C. Hill
Jackdaw Mystery. F. Grierson
Jackey. A. J. Palmerio
Jackie. S. Ready
Jackie Lantern's Hallowe'en Revenge. Bernard Cohen
Jackpot. B. Pronzini
Jackpot! R. D. Ridyard
Jack's Father, and other stories. W. E. Norris
Jack's Mother. Anonymous
Jack's Return Home. Ted Lewis
Jacob Niemand. R. H. Sherard
Jacob Street Mystery. R. A. Freeman
Jacob's Ladder. E. P. Oppenheim
Jacob's Ladder. J. A. Williams
Jacob's Ladder, and other stories. W. B. Maxwell
Jacobs Park Killings. William Camp
Jacoby's First Case. J. C. S. Smith
Jacqueline of Olzenburg. H. Somerset
Jacqueminot. K. Rich
Jacqui. P. Loughran
Jade and Fire. R. J. Barnett
Jade; and other stories. H. Wiley
Jade Box. N. Faulkner
Jade Cat. G. L. Mair
Jade Dragon. N. Buckingham
Jade Dragon. W. B. Gibson
Jade Elephant. E. Fraser
Jade Elephants. T. Allen
Jade Eye. F. Hume
Jade Eye. J. Ingersol
Jade-Eyed Jinx. Carter Brown
Jade-Eyed Jungle. Carter Brown
Jade Figurine. J. Foxx
Jade Figurines. Jan Alexander
Jade for a Lady. M. E. Chaber
Jade God. W. E. Barry
Jade God. A. Sullivan
Jade Green. D. Daniels
Jade Green Cats. E. Blake
Jade-Green Garter. D. Newton
Jade Green Judy. D. Enefer
Jade Hatpin. M. G. Kiddy
Jade in Aries. T. Coe
Jade Lizard. Taffrail
Jade Necklace. M. Short
Jade of Death. R. Gar
Jade of Destiny. J. Farnol
Jade Pagoda. B. H. Hyatt
Jade Pavilion. M. Booth
Jade Princess. Clarissa Ross
Jade Rabbit. A. Blood
Jade Tiger. C. Thomas
Jade Unicorn. J. Halpern
Jade Vendetta. F. J. Roberts
Jade Venus. G. H. Coxe
Jade Wind. J. Harris
Jade Woman. Jonathan Gash
Jaded by Choice. R. Victor

Jade's Progress. J. S. Clouston
Jadoo. N. Newnham-Davis
Jagged Steele. J. D. Masters
Jaggers at Bay. J. Templar
Jaggers, Air Detective. J. Templar
Jaggers Swoops Again. J. Templer
Jaguar. L. Durand
Jaquar Lives. Y. Yablonsky
Jail and Farewell. M. Shane
Jail Bait! R. Angel
Jail Bait. P. Chambers
Jail Bait. S. Chayes
Jail Bait. Stuart Hall
Jail Bait. J. W. Mason
Jail Break. D. Barton
Jail-Breakers. B. Newman
Jail Gates Are Open. David Hume
Jailbait Jungle. Wenzell Brown
Jailbait Street. H. Ellson
Jailbreak. D. Andrews
Jailbreak. L. White
Jailer, My Jailer. M. Gavin
Jailer's Pretty Wife. F. Du Boisgobey
Jakarta Coup. M. K. Roberts
Jake and Sadie. B. Solomon
Jake Canuke. J. Templeton
Jake of Diamonds. D. Von Elsner
Jamaica Inn. D. Du Maurier
Jamaica Kill. T. Philbin
Jamaica Run. Clifford Mason
Jamaican Exchange. Nick Carter
Jamaican Midnight. Sherryl Woods
James Ballingray, Murderer. J. Maconechy
James Bond and Moonraker. Christopher Wood
James Bond, the Spy Who Loved Me. Christopher Wood
James Cope. C. Barmby
James Joyce Murder. A. Cross
James Knowland: Deceased. H. Carmichael
James Tarrant, Adventurer. F. W. Crofts
James Whitaker's Dukedom. E. Jepson
Jamintha. Beatrice Parker
Jamo and the Bent Playboy. J. Vaughan
Jane. P. Bottome
Jane Carberry and the Laughing Fountain. B. Symons
Jane Carberry: Detective. B. Symons
Jane Carberry Investigates. B. Symons
Jane Carberry's Week End. B. Symons
Jane Shore. T. P. Prest
Jane, the Courageous. K. Kimbrough
Jane the Ripper. W. Tyrer
Jane Ventures. P. Trent
Jane with Green Eyes. H. Janson
Janell. J. Jenkins
Janissary. A. L. Gelb
Janitor. J. Minahan
Janson, Go Home. H. Janson
January Zone. P. Corris
Janus Imperative. Evelyn Anthony
Janus Man. C. Forbes
Janus Murder. J. N. Datesh
Janus Murder Case. C. Wilson
Janus Pope. G. Marton
Japanese Corpse. J. Van De Wetering
Japanese Girl. Winston Graham
Japanese Jeopardy. P. Tabori
Japanese Mistress. R. Neely
Japanese Revenge. L. Tracy
Japanese Ronin. W. T. Stewart
Japanese Tales of Mystery and Imagination. E. Rampo
Japanese Umbrella and other stories. Francis King
Jarrah Tree. M. Kistler
Jarvis. R. W. Kauffman
Jarvis of Harvard. R. W. Kauffman
Jarwick the Prodigal. T. Gallon
Jasius Pursuit. D. Orgill
Jasmine for My Grave. Sara North
Jasmine Sloop. F. J. Kenmore
Jasmine Trail. H. J. Hagerty
Jason Affair. J. N. Chance
Jason and the Sleep Game. J. N. Chance
Jason Burr's First Case. D. Kent

Jason Goes West. J. N. Chance
Jason King. R. Miall
Jason Murders. J. N. Chance
Jasper Dane's Secret. M. E. Braddon
Jassy. N. Lofts
Jaubert Ring. W. D. Roberts
Jaunty Jock and other stories. N. Munro
Java Edge. J. E. Newton
Java Jack. O. Binns
Java Sea Mystery. F. Nunn
Javelin for Jonah. G. Mitchell
Jaws of Circumstance. C. Clausen
Jaws of Darkness. Mark Cross
Jaws of Death. G. Allen
Jaws of Death. L. Thayer
Jaws of Doom. B. Ludwig
Jaws of the Watchdog. I. Drummond
Jaws That Bite, the Claws That Catch. M. G. Coney
Jazz Jungle. H. Janson
Jealous in Honour. T. Heald
Jealous One. C. Fremlin
Jealous Woman. J. M. Cain
Jealousy. N. Karta
Jealousy. A. Robbe-Grillet
Jealousy. E. Walter
Jealousy Pulls the Trigger. M. E. Corne
Jean of the Lazy J Ranch. H. Pink
Jeanne of the Marshes. E. P. Oppenheim
Jeannie with the Light Brown Corpse. J. Cello
Jedcrow. Mark Elder
Jeff Clayton and the Outlaws. W. Ward
Jeff Clayton at Bay. W. Ward
Jeff Clayton in the Heart of Trouble. W. Ward
Jeff Clayton's Blind Trail. W. Ward
Jeff Clayton's Brigand Foe. W. Ward
Jeff Clayton's Dancing Bubble. W. Ward
Jeff Clayton's Daring Leap. W. Ward
Jeff Clayton's Deal with Death. W. Ward
Jeff Clayton's Decoy. W. Ward
Jeff Clayton's Demon Pursuer. W. Ward
Jeff Clayton's Discovery. W. Ward
Jeff Clayton's Fatal Shot. W. Ward
Jeff Clayton's Golden Ladder. W. Ward
Jeff Clayton's Invisible Hand. W. Ward
Jeff Clayton's Last Bullet. W. Ward
Jeff Clayton's Long Chase. W. Ward
Jeff Clayton's Lost Clue. W. Ward
Jeff Clayton's Lost Ship. W. Ward
Jeff Clayton's Man-Trap. W. Ward
Jeff Clayton's Masked Foe. W. Ward
Jeff Clayton's Master Stroke. W. Ward
Jeff Clayton's Mexican Plot. W. Ward
Jeff Clayton's Pursuit. W. Ward
Jeff Clayton's Puzzle. W. Ward
Jeff Clayton's Red Mystery. W. Ward
Jeff Clayton's Riddle. W. Ward
Jeff Clayton's Strange Quest. W. Ward
Jeff Clayton's Strong Arm. W. Ward
Jeff Clayton's Surprise. W. Ward
Jeff Clayton's Thunder Bolt. W. Ward
Jeff Clayton's Triumph. W. Ward
Jeff Clayton's White Mission. W. Ward
Jeff Clayton's Wild Ride. W. Ward
Jeff Clayton's Winged Flight. W. Ward
Jeff Utter. C. C. Hamilton
Jefferson Boone, Handyman. J. Messmann
Jefferson Secret. R. Blaker
Jehovah Contract. V. Koman
Jekyll, Alias Hyde. Donald Thomas
Jekyll and Hyde. L. H. Caddy
Jekyll Hydes Again! J. Sharkey
Jekyll Legacy. R. Bloch
Jem: Memoirs of an Ottoman Secret Agent. R. C. Morris
Jemima Shore Investigates. Antonia Fraser
Jemima Shore's First Case. Antonia Fraser
Jenkin's Green. R. Arnold
Jennerton & Co. E. P. Oppenheim
Jennie Barlowe, Adventuress. E. O'Donnell
Jennie Baxter, Journalist. R. Barr
Jennifer. J. Goodwin
Jennifer by Moonlight. Clarissa Ross
Jennifer Disappears. M. O'Nair
Jennifer Hale. R. Eden

Title Index

Jennifer Pontefracte. A. Askew
Jenny and I. J. Letton
Jenny Be Good. W. F. Fauley
Jenny Kissed Me. R. Fenisong
Jenny Newstead. M. B. Lowndes
Jenny Nobody. M. Hutton
Jenny Wren. R. Kirkbridge
Jenny's Case. E. F. Pinsent
Jensen Scenario. W. Fennerton
Jeopardy. M. Conte
Jeopardy. W. Standish
Jeopardy Is My Job. S. Marlowe
Jeremiah and the Princess. E. P. Oppenheim
Jeremiah Painter. G. Wolk
Jeremy Takes a Hand. C. K. Rathbone
Jericho Commandment. J. Patterson
Jericho Day. W. P. Murphy
Jericho Falls. C. Hyde
Jericho Gun. A. C. H. Smith
Jericho Man. J. Lutz
Jericho Mosaic. E. Whittemore
Jericho Rumble. C. Murphy
Jericho Scan. John Raymond
Jerry Abershaw. Anonymous
Jerry the Lag. P. Baron
Jersey Guns. D. Pendleton
Jersey Plunder. J. Chancellor
Jersey Tomatoes. J. W. Rider
Jerusalem Camp. Cameron Judd
Jerusalem Code. H. L. Klawans
Jerusalem Conspiracy. I. McFarlane
Jerusalem Conspiracy. D. A. Riis
Jerusalem Diamond. Noah Gordon
Jerusalem File. Nick Carter
Jerusalem Inn. M. Grimes
Jesmond Mystery. H. Hill
Jess. M. G. Lowe
Jessamy Court. A. Maybury
Jesse James, and His Band of Notorious Outlaws. W. Gordon
Jesse James at Coney Island. W. B. Lawson
Jesse James at Long Branch. W. B. Lawson
Jesse James' Double. W. B. Lawson
Jesse James in New York. W. B. Lawson
Jesse James' Oath. W. B. Lawson
Jessue James, Rube Burrows & Co. W. B. Lawson
Jesse James' Shadow. W. B. Lawson
Jesse James' Successor. W. B. Lawson
Jessica. A. Maybury
Jessie Trim. B. L. Farjeon
Jessie Vandeleur. E. C. Mayne
Jessop Bequest. A. Burr
Jest of Darkness. V. M. Grayland
Jesus Factor. E. Corley
Jesus Man. R. Casey
Jesus II. F. Riley
Jet and Ivory. R. Thorndike
Jet-Lag. B. Copper
Jet Race. J. B Lynne
Jet Stream. Austin Ferguson
Jethro Hammer. M. Venning
Jetsam. V. Bridges
Jetsam. Owen Hall
Jew Detective. Anonymous
Jew of Prague. A. W. Barrett
Jewel in the Crypt. O. Baster
Jewel Island. Andrea Hill
Jewel Mysteries from a Dealer's Notebook. M. Pemberton
Jewel Mysteries I Have Known. M. Pemberton
Jewel of Death. E. Berckman
Jewel of Death. H. Mee
Jewel of Death. L. Tracy
Jewel of Desire. Wade Shaw
Jewel of Destiny. G. Davison
Jewel of Doom. Nick Carter
Jewel of Seven Stars. B. Stoker
Jewel of the Java Sea. D. Cushman
Jewel of the Nile. Joan Wilder
Jewel of the Seas. J. Kaufman
Jewel Robbery. L. Fodor
Jewel Thief. A. Mills
Jewel: Undercover Cop. G. Fogelson
Jeweled Cat. L. Rutland

Jeweled Dagger. J. Ellis
Jeweled Daughter. A. Maybury
Jeweled Eye. D. Clark
Jeweled Hand. C. George
Jeweled Mummy. Nicholas Carter
Jeweled Secret. E. St. Clair
Jewelled Belt. P. E. Quinn
Jewelled Darkness. V. Coffman
Jewels. R. Perrin
Jewels for a Shroud. W. De Steiguer
Jewels Go Back. E. C. Vivian
Jewels in Jeopardy. Ernest Paul
Jewels of Death. R. Halifax
Jewels of Death. M. Richmond
Jewels of Prince de Janville. Almhain
Jewels of Sin. B. Bolt
Jewels of Terror. J. L. Roberts
Jewels of Wu Ling. Jack Lewis
Jewels That Got Away. G. Madderom
Jewess of Hull. R. Glossop
Jew's House. F. Hume
Jews Pellegrini. B. Sarto
Jews Without Jehovah. G. Kersh
Jezebel's Daughter. W. Collins
Jian. E. V. Lustbader
Jig. Campbell Armstrong
Jig-Saw. E. Phillpotts
Jig-Saw Murder Case. R. Wallace
Jig-Saw Puzzle Murder. W. F. Eberhardt
Jig-Time Murders. G. Givens
Jigger Moran. J. Roeburt
Jigsaw. D. Hoddinott
Jigsaw. Mollie Gregory
Jigsaw. E. McBain
Jigsaw. J. St. George
Jigsaw. Robin Sherman
Jigsaw. H. Waugh
Jigsaw John. A. Martinez
Jigsaw Man. Dorothea Bennett
Jihad. G. Clarkson
Jihad. J. Hild
Jihad Ultimatum. J. D. Randall
Jill. T. St. Martin
Jill Fell Down. J. Tickell
Jill Rips. F. Lindsay
Jilt. C. Reade
Jim. R. W. Kauffman
Jim Barnett Intervenes. M. Leblanc
Jim Brent. H. C. McNeile
Jim Crowshaw's Mary. F. M. White
Jim Cummings. E. Ferrars
Jim Cummings. A. F. Pinkerton
Jim Goes North. G. Goodchild
Jim Hanvey, Detective. O. R. Cohen
Jim Maitland. H. C. McNeile
Jim the Penman. C. H. Bullivant
Jim the Penman. D. Donovan
Jim the Penman. W. Gordon
Jim the Penman. C. L. Young
Jim Trelawney. O. Binns
Jim Trent. R. W. Kauffman
Jim Twelves and Trained Man. W. F. Shannon
Jimgrim. T. Mundy
Jimgrim and Allah's Peace. T. Mundy
Jimgrim Sahib. T. Mundy
Jimmie Colt: Airborne Investigator. Maurice Chapman
Jimmie Dale and the Blue Envelope Murder. F. Packard
Jimmie Dale and the Missing Hour. F. Packard
Jimmie Dale and the Phantom Clue. F. Packard
Jimmie Rezaire. A. Armstrong
Jimmy. J. S. Winter
Jimmy Brocket. D. Stivens
Jimmy Mack, Detective. Jack North
Jimmy the Kid. D. E. Westlake
Jink. T. P. McMahon
Jinx Theatre Murder. Alexander Williams
Jittery Dame. H. Vogel
Jiu San. K. Robeson
Jo Crupper, Bus Conductor. T. Le Breton
Joan Danvers. F. Stayton
Joan in Jeopardy. R. R. King
Joan in Jeopardy. D. Nicol

Joan Mar, Detective. M. Leighton
Joan of the Hills. T. B. Clegg
Joan, the Curate. F. Warden
Joanna. J. Blackmore
Joanna Sets to Work. T. Cobb
Job Abroad. G. Bartram
Job Lot Sketches and Stories. J. P. Marsden
Job of Murder. F. Gruber
Jock MacKay, Crook. Scarlet Grey
Jockey. G. Verner
Jockey Club Stories. F. Barrett
Jockey Died First. A. Mills
Jockey's Revenge. N. Gould
Joe Jenkins' Case Book. P. Rosenhayn
Joe Jenkins: Detective. P. Rosenhayn
Joe Leslie's Wife. A. Robertson
Joe Muller, Detective. G. I. Colbron
Joe Nix Is Dead. M. McClintick
Joe Phoenix, Private Detective. A. W. Aiken
Joe Phoenix Puzzled. Anonymous
Joe Phoenix, the Police Spy. A. W. Aiken
Joe Quinney's Jodie. H. A. Vachell
Joe's Bar. C. Sampayo
Joey Collects. Joey
Joey Kills. Joey
Joey's Case. K. C. Constantine
Joggers. A. Stratton
Jogger's Moon. J. Messmann
Johanna, the Unpredictable. K. Kimbrough
John Allard. E. M. Ingram
John Ames, Native Commissioner. B. Mitford
John and Son. P. Trent
John Armiger's Revenge. P. H. Hunter
John Boddy. T. Thurston
John Bodwin's Testimony. M. H. Foote
John Brand, Fugitive. J. Creasey
John Brand's Will. H. Adams
John Brown & Larry Lohengrin. W. Westall
John Brown's Body. E. C. R. Lorac
John Carruthers: Indian Policeman. E. C. Cox
John Carstairs, Space Detective. F. B. Long
John Chilcote, M.P. K. C. Thurston
John Clutterbuck. J. Ruegg
John Collier Reader. J. Collier
John Dene of Toronto. H. Jenkins
John Dighton, Mystery Millionaire. M. Pemberton
John Doe—Murderer. W. Dale
John Fanning's Legacy. N. Royde-Smith
John Ford. F. Barrett
John Gather's Garden. F. R. Stockton
John Hazell's Vengeance. W. S. Hayward
John Heriot's Wife. A. Askew
John Horsleydown. T. L. Holt
John Ingerfield and other stories. J. K. Jerome
John Jasper's Gatehouse. Edwin Harris
John Jasper's Secret. Anonymous
John Jasper's Secret. E. Jones-Evans
John Jenkin, Public Enemy. B. Graeme
John Jeremy—Cracksman. Jeffrey Montague
John Kyleing Died. E. Radford
John Lillibud. F. G. Hurrell
John Lisbon, Agent. J. Budd
John Macnab. J. Buchan
John Marchmont's Legacy. M. E. Braddon
John Moe, Double Agent. J. Moen
John Montcalm. M. Gerard
John Needham's Double. J. Hatton
John o' the Green. J. Farnol
John O'Howgate. Mac
John Parmelee's Curse. J. Hawthorne
John Quinton's Secret. Michael Poole
John Riddell Murder Case. J. Riddell
John Rutland's Romance. J. P. Bessell
John Saint. P. Brebner
John Silence. A. Blackwood
John Smith Hears Death Walking. W. Blassingame
John Solomon, Incognito. A. Hawkwood
John Thorndyke's Cases. R. A. Freeman
John Topp, Pirate. W. Chesney
John Traile: Smuggler. A. Salcroft
John Vale's Guardian. D. C. Murray
John Webb's End. F. Adams
Johnnie. D. B. Hughes
Johnnie Madison. J. Haslette

Johnny Belinda. E. B. Harris
Johnny Blood. P. Malloch
Johnny Come Deadly. P. Race
Johnny Come Lately. F. Kane
Johnny Counterfeit. M. Y. Shapleigh
Johnny Danger. P. Allardyce
Johnny Death. W. Schnurr
Johnny Get Your Gun. J. Ball
Johnny Gets His! D. Ambler
Johnny Goes East. D. Cory
Johnny Goes North. D. Cory
Johnny Goes South. D. Cory
Johnny Goes West. D. Cory
Johnny Havoc. J. Jakes
Johnny Havoc and the Doll Who Had "It". J. Jakes
Johnny Havoc Meets Zelda. J. Jakes
Johnny, I Hardly Knew You. E. O'Brien
Johnny Liddell's Morgue. F. Kane
Johnny Lost. P. Jones
Johnny Ludlow. H. Wood
Johnny Ludlow. Fifth Series. H. Wood
Johnny Ludlow. Fourth Series. H. Wood
Johnny Ludlow. Second Series. H. Wood
Johnny Ludlow. Sixth Series. H. Wood
Johnny Ludlow. Third Series. H. Wood
Johnny on the Spot. A. Dell
Johnny Purple. J. Wyllie
Johnny Sanger No. 1. "Delany"
Johnny Saxon. W. Bogart
Johnny Staccato. F. Boyd
Johnny Under Ground. P. Moyes
Johnson's Bird. A. Fullerton
Johnstown Stage, and other stories. R. H. Fletcher
JoJo and the Private Eye. L. Malloy
Joker. H. Osborne
Joker. E. Wallace
Joker Deals with Death. W. M. Duncan
Joker in a Stacked Deck. J. Shelynn
Joker in the Deck. R. S. Prather
Joker in the Pack. J. H. Chase
Joker in the Pack. John Hunt
Joker Takes Queen. B. Munslow
Jokers. M. Sands
Jolly Jess. Old Sleuth
Jolly Roger Mystery. P. Lancaster
Jonah. J. Herbert
Jonah and Co. Dornford Yates
Jonah Game. J. S. Abel
Jonah Kit. I. Watson
Jonah's Luck. F. Hume
Jonas Haggerley. J. J. Wray
Jonathan Bradford. T. P. Prest
Jonathan Guest. Margaret Archer
Jones, A., Finds the Body. H. McEvoy
Jones Men. V. E. Smith
Jones '38. D. Ogden
Jones's Little Murders. E. Radford
Jordan Intercept. J. A. MacKenzie
Jordans Murder. S. Fowler
Jorkens Borrows Another Whiskey. Lord Dunsany
Jorkens Has a Large Whiskey. Lord Dunsany
Joseph File. Alfred Harris
Joseph Prickett, the Scotland Yard Detective. I. Murray
Joseph Proctor's Money. W. H. L. Crauford
Joseph Stone. J. La Tourrette
Joseph's Coat. D. C. Murray
Joshua Factor. D. D. Clayton
Joshua Haggard's Daughter. M. E. Braddon
Joshua Humble. E. R. Reach
Joshua Sequence. F. D. Huebner
Joss. R. Marsh
Josselin Takes a Hand. A. C. Brown
Josselyn's Wife. K. Norris
Journey Downstairs. R. Philmore
Journey from Baghdad. David Roberts
Journey from Flesh. N. Yermakov
Journey in the Dark. J. Ames
Journey Into Danger. D. Faber
Journey Into Danger. J. M. Fox
Journey Into Danger. Beatrice Taylor
Journey Into Darkness. I. Mercer
Journey Into Death. Jack Jones
Journey Into Fear. E. Ambler

Journey Into Fear. V. Norwood
Journey Into Fear. M. Ruuth
Journey Into Stone. A. E. Lindop
Journey Into Terror. D. Daniels
Journey Into Terror. P. Rabe
Journey Into Twilight. M. Lynch
Journey Into Violence. D. Orgill
Journey Into Violence. H. Whittington
Journey of Fear. C. Jauniere
Journey Past Repentence. G. Arnaud
Journey to a Safe Place. I. S. Black
Journey to Cuzco. M. R. Myers
Journey to Genoa. F. D. Fawcett
Journey to Happiness. M. Richmond
Journey to Love. Rona Randall
Journey to Murder. R. P. Koehler
Journey to Nowhere. N. Tyre
Journey to Orassia. A. Caillou
Journey to Romance. L. Ames
Journey to the Hangman. A. W. Upfield
Journey Toward Death. A. Aricha
Journey with a Stranger. The Gordons
Journeying Boy. M. Innes
Journey's End. E. Berckman
Journey's Eve. E. Cadell
Joy House. D. Keene
Joy Ride. J. G. Brandon
Joy Ride. A. Prior
Joy Street Massacre. Tom Logan
Joy Wheel. P. W. Fairman
Joyce Harrington's Trust. B. Marchant
Joyce Pleasantry and other stories. G. R. Sims
Joyce, the Beloved. K. Kimbrough
Joyful Jays. J. C. Lenehan
Joyous Adventures of Aristide Pujol. W. J. Locke
Joyous Conspirator. G. F. Gibbs
Juanita Carrington. R. Jocelyn
Judah Lion Contract. P. Atlee
Judas. E. R. Johnson
Judas! P. Van Greenaway
Judas and other stories. J. Metcalfe
Judas C.I.D. F. Grierson
Judas Cat. D. S. Davis
Judas Cloak. W. Winward
Judas Code. D. Lambert
Judas Conspiracy. J. Ballem
Judas Country. G. Lyall
Judas Cross. J. M. Wallmann
Judas Diary. W. H. Baker
Judas Factor. T. Allbeury
Judas Factor. J. Shelynn
Judas Figures. A. E. Lindop
Judas Flight. T. Beattie
Judas Freak. H. Pentecost
Judas Gene. J. Klainer
Judas Goat. B. Cleeve
Judas Goat. L. Edgley
Judas Goat. R. B. Parker
Judas Gospel. R. Van Greenaway
Judas Hour. Howard Hunt
Judas, Incorporated. K. Steel
Judas Journey. Lee Roberts
Judas Judge. S. Jason
Judas Kiss. H. Adams
Judas Kiss. J. J. Dratler
Judas Kiss. V. Holt
Judas Kiss. J. J. Montague
Judas Mandate. C. Egleton
Judas Pair. J. Gash
Judas Scrolls. J. Rosenberger
Judas Sheep. Jan Roberts
Judas Soldiers. F. Garrett
Judas Spies. Colin Robertson
Judas Spy. Nick Carter
Judas Squad. J. N. Rose
Judas Voice. Anthony John
Judas Way. C. Whitton
Judas Window. Carter Dickson
Judd for the Defense. L. Goldman
Judge. E. W. Peattie
Judge. Alan Thomas
Judge and Be Damned. J. Edmonds
Judge and His Hangman. F. Duerrenmatt
Judge and the Hatter. G. Simenon

Judge Anderson Book I. John Wagner
Judge Anderson Book II. John Wagner
Judge Dee at Work. R. Van Gulik
Judge Is Reversed. F. Lockridge
Judge Me Not. Joe Cannon
Judge Me Not. J. D. MacDonald
Judge Me Tomorrow. H. Jobson
Judge Not. C. H. Bullivant
Judge of Men. J. A. Ford
Judge Priest Turns Detective. I. S. Cobb
Judge Robinson Murdered! R. L. Goldman
Judge Speaks. R. Monroe
Judge Sums Up. J. J. Farjeon
Judge Will Call It Murder. S. M. Lott
Judgement by Fire. T. Philo
Judgement Day. P. G. Winslow
Judgement in Stone. R. Rendell
Judgement of Death. B. Biderman
Judgement Postponed. G. Wark
Judge's Chair. E. Phillpotts
Judge's Daughters. G. E. Mitton
Judge's Dilemma. S. Kyle
Judges of Hades, and other Simon Ark stories. E. D. Hoch
Judge's Story. C. Morgan
Judgment. H. E. Goldfluss
Judgment. T. Wicker
Judgment by Fire. F. D. Huebner
Judgment Castle. A. Wood
Judgment Day. E. L. Rice
Judgment Day. R. Sapir
Judgment Day Archives. A. Moscovit
Judgment Deferred. G. Braddon
Judgment in Berlin. H. J. Stern
Judgment in Blood. J. D. Hunter
Judgment in St. Peter's. A. N. Rotsstein
Judgment in Suspense. G. Bullett
Judgment Night. D. Honig
Judgment of a Dame. Carter Brown
Judgment of Ann. P. Trent
Judgment of Death. A. Mills
Judgment of Death. M. Richmond
Judgment of Deke Hunter. G. V. Higgins
Judgment of Helen. T. Cobb
Judgment of Larose. A. Gask
Judgment on Deltchev. E. Ambler
Judgment Rock. L. A. Knight
Judicial Body. M. Scherf
Judith Bolero. W. J. Dawson
Judith Lee. R. Marsh
Judson Murder Case. A. B. Leonard
Judy—and the Philosopher. T. Gallon
Judy Ashbane, Police Decoy. M. O'Mair
Judy of Bunter's Buildings. E. P. Oppenheim
Judy the Torch. A. P. Hankins
Juffie Kane. Beverly Martin
Jugged Journalism. A. B. Cox
Jugger. R. Stark
Juggernaut. D. Bagley
Juggernaut. Alice Campbell
Juggernaut. A. Hine
Juggler. I. K. Martin
Juggler of Nankin. S. Cobb
Juggling Fortune. T. W. Speight
Juice. S. Becker
Juice. Robert Campbell
Juice Town. D. Owen
Juju. D. Onyeama
Juke Box King. F. Kane
Julia. P. Straub
Julia Ballantyne. G. R. Preedy
Julia Bicknell. O. Bradbury
Julia Clark. Anonymous
Julian Karslake's Secret. Mrs. J. H. Riddell
Julian Solo. S. Reuben
Julian's House. Judith Hawkes
Julie. Florence Stevenson
Julie. A. L. Stone
Juliet. Anonymous
Juliet Bravo 1. Mollie Hardwick
Juliet Bravo 2. Mollie Hardwick
Juliet Dies Twice. Lange Lewis
Juliet Effect. J. Slattery
Juliet Room. G. Hall

Julius Caesar Is Alive and Well. I. A. Greenfield
Julius Caesar Murder Case. Wallace Irwin
Julius Vernon. P. L. MacDermott
July at Fritham. M. Home
July 14 Assassination. B. Abro
July 7th. J. McCorkle
Jump Cut. R. R. Irvine
Jump for Glory. G. McDonell
Jump Into the Sun. P. Gregor
Jump the Gun. M. Cronin
Jump the High Wall. C. Richardson
Jumpers. T. Stoppard
Jumping Joan. C. H. B. Kitchin
Jumpin' Jupiter. K. Gordon
Jumping Double. C. E. Sayers
Jumping Jenny. A. Berkeley
Jumping the Cracks. R. O'Rourke
Jumpmaster. H. R. Simpson
June Jeopardy. I. H. Gillmore
June Mail. J. Warmbold
June, Moon, and Murder. C. M. Russell
June 13. F. Vreeland
Jungle. M. Brett
Jungle Blitz. L. Derrick
Jungle Crime. L. Allan
Jungle Goddess. O. Sackville
Jungle Harvest. T. Gill
Jungle Heat. D. Wilmer
Jungle Hitler. Anonymous
Jungle Hut. E. P. Thorne
Jungle Jest. T. Mundy
Jungle Kids. E. Hunter
Jungle Maid. D. Collins
Jungle Manhunt. J. Laffin
Jungle Murder. A. Amos
Jungle Murders. P. Richmond
Jungle of Stars. J. L. Chalker
Jungle of Steel and Stone. G. C. Chesbro
Jungle She. D. Cushman
Jungle Sweep. Gar Wilson
Jungle Terror. H. Wickham
Junior League Murders. C. Canyon
Junior Year Abroad. H. R. Simpson
Juniper. James Murphy
Juniper Hill. D. Daniels
Juniper Rock. P. Atkey
Junk Market. H. Janson
Junk Run. J. Pattinson
Junk on the Hill. J. Pikser
Junkie! Jonathan Craig
Junkyard Angel. J. Harvey
Junkyard Dog. Robert Campbell
Junta. June Drummond
Jupiter Crisis. W. Harrington
Jupiter Missile Mystery. E. Beatty
Juror. Parnell Hall
Juror. H. Jacobs
Juror. M. Underwood
Juror in Waiting. H. Cecil
Juror No. 17. C. C. Waddell
Jurors. B. Siegal
Jury. G. Bullett
Jury. D. Haring
Jury. E. Phillpotts
Jury Disagree. G. Goodchild
Jury Is Out. D. W. Rimel
Jury of Angels. B. Strutton
Jury of Death. R. C. Washburn
Jury of Four. G. Vallings
Jury of Her Peers. S. Glaspell
Jury of His Peers. J. Pearl
Jury of One. M. G. Eberhart
Jury People. J. Wainwright
Jury Retires. R. Wild
Jury-Room Tales and other stories. Anonymous
Juryman. F. Galbally
Juryman. D. MacKenzie
Juryman. E. E. Sumner
Just a Corpse at Twilight. Robert Martin
Just a Face in the Dark. M. McShane
Just a Matter of Time. J. H. Chase
Just a Shot Away. J. Grady
Just a Song at Twilight. J. Lodwick
Just an Ordinary Case. B. Graeme

Just and the Unjust. Nicholas Carter
Just and the Unjust. J. G. Cozzens
Just Another Angel. Mike Ripley
Just Another Day in Paradise. A. E. Maxwell
Just Another Murder. D. Furber
Just Another Sucker. J. H. Chase
Just Around the Corner. Elizabeth Ford
Just Around the Coroner. S. Brock
Just Around the Coroner. J. Starr
Just As I Am. M. E. Braddon
Just Before Dawn. D. Shields
Just Before Daybreak. A. Couloumbis
Just Causes. M. McConnell
Just Desserts. T. Heald
Just Desserts. R. Jeffries
Just Enough Light to Kill. A. E. Maxwell
Just Fate. G. Long
Just for the Bread. R. Kelly
Just for the Bride. D. P. Clark
Just for the Hell of It. D. Haring
Just Killing Time. R. Ellington
Just Let Me Be. J. Cleary
Just Like a Dame. W. Standish
Just Men of Cordova. E. Wallace
Just Murder, Darling. J. A. Brussel
Just Not Making Mayhem Like They Used To. D. Von Elsner
Just One Slip. Nicholas Carter
Just Sheaffer, or Storms in the Troubled Heir. I. Mowatt
Just the Way It Is. Raymond Marshall
Just to Remind You. Owen Davis
Just Vengeance. L. P. Greene
Just What the Doctor Ordered. Colin Watson
Justice. J. Galsworthy
Justice! C. F. Gregg
Justice. G. Simenon
Justice Astray. S. Warwick
Justice Be Damned. A. Hilliard
Justice by Accident. V. Lester
Justice by Fire. D. Stivers
Justice by Midnight. J. Farnol
Justice by Proxy. G. H. Davies
Justice-Clerk. W. D. Lyell
Justice Denied. J. Ahern
Justice Ends at Home. R. Stout
Justice Enough. H. Carmichael
Justice for a Dead Spy. J. Moffatt
Justice for a Jinx. M. Brody
Justice for Judas. I. Baker
Justice for Judy. C. E. Vulliamy
Justice for Julia. M. Richmond
Justice Game: The Lady from Rome. Peter Turnbull
Justice Has No Sword. M. Franklin
Justice Hunt. M. Turner
Justice in Jeopardy. C. M. Wills
Justice, Inc. K. Robeson
Justice Is Done. A. Soutar
Justice Is Mine. E. P. Thorne
Justice Limited. F. Duncan
Justice Never Sleeps. O. Williams
Justice of Revenge. George Griffith
Justice of Sanders. F. Gerard
Justice of the Duke. R. Sabatini
Justice on Halfaday Creek. J. B. Hendryx
Justice on the Rocks. B. Knox
Justice Peeps Over the Handkerchief. C. Herbert
Justice Returns. F. Duncan
Justice—Suspended. R. Marsh
Justification of Andrew Lebrun. F. Barrett
Justified Sinner. J. F. Molloy
Justin Bayard. J. Cleary
Justine. W. Calvert
Justus Wise. A. W. Barrett
Juve in the Dock. M. Allain
Juvenile Delinquent. R. Deming
Juvenile Delinquents. L. Kaufman
Juvenile Delinquents. R. Vane
Juvenile Hoods. J. Shallit
Juvenile Jungle. F. Counsel
Juvies. H. Ellison

K. L. Waller
K Assignment. L. Waller

K Code Plan. G. Seton
KG 200. J. D. Gilman
KGB Candidate. O. Sela
KGB Directive. R. Cox
KGB Doublecross. M. J. Costello
KGB Frame. J. Rosenberger
KGB Is Here. C. Franklin
KGB Kill. James Mitchell
KKK. P. E. Walsh
K.O. for Keeps. R. Angel
K Section. T. Lilley
K605. C. Clarke
Ka of Gifford Hillary. D. Wheatley
Kabaka. C. Johnston
Kabbalah. D. S. Milton
Kabul Contract. Ian Mitchell
Kaddish in Dublin. J. Brady
Kaduna Memories. J. McKinney
Kago. C. Wood
Kahawa. D. E. Westlake
Kahuna Killer. J. Sheridan
Kaiser or King. J. Tregellis
Kaiser's Beautiful Spy. C. H. Bullivant
Kaiser's Blonde Spy. G. Ladoux
Kak-Abdullah Conspiracy. M. Macao
Kalahari. H. Kolarz
Kalahari. P. McCurtin
Kalahari Kill. S. Dembo
Kalee's Shrine. G. Allen
Kaleidoscope. M. Avallone
Kaleidoscope. Joyce Porter
Kali Death Cult. Nick Carter
Kali-Flower! Barreaux
Kaligarh Fault. P. Roadarmel
Kama Satra Tango. J. F. Burke
Kamakaze Assignment. A. Sugar
Kamal. G. Arathorn
Kamchatka Incident. R. L. McKinney
Kamikaze Legacy. J. Ahern
Kanaga. K. R. Butler
Kane. D. Borton
Kane and Abel. J. Archer
Kane and Miss Able. Tod Conrad
Kane and Miss Able. Kane
Kane's War. Nick Stone
Kanesbrake. J. Blair
Kang-He Vase. J. S. Fletcher
Kangaroo Court. J. Jost
Kangaroo Shoots Man. A. Scobie
Kansas. J. Springs III
Kara. J. Ellis
Kara Yerta Tragedy. J. E. Harrison
Karadac, Count of Gerzy. K. Prichard
Karamanov Equations. M. Goldberg
Karamour. A. Pritchett
Karate Killers. D. Streib
Karl, the Lion. S. Cobb
Karlyn. J. Jenkins
Karma. S. Dunlap
Karpov's Brain. G. Green
Kashmiri Love Song. M. Richmond
Kashmiri Passions. Clarissa Ross
Kastle Krags. A. Martin
Kat and Copy-Cat. E. E. Steven
Kat Strikes. N. Spain
Kataki. H. Searls
Katana. G. MacBeth
Katana. M. Olden
Katapult. K. Kijewski
Kate Hannigan. C. Cookson
Kate Meredith, Financier. C. J. C. Hyne
Kate, Plus Ten. E. Wallace
Kate Scott, the Decoy Detective. Anonymous
Kate, the Curious. K. Kimbrough
Kath. K. Henshaw
Katharine Beresford. H. M. Jones
Katherine and the Dark Angel. M. Reisner
Kathleen. T. P. Prest
Kathrine, the Returned. K. Kimbrough
Katie. M. McDowell
Katie Mulholland. C. Cookson
Katie's Terror. D. E. Fisher
Katmandu Affair. P. Davidson
Katmandu Contract. Nick Carter

Katrina. R. Kirkbridge
Katwalk. K. Kijewski
Kaufman Snatch. Robin Moore
Kavalu Lion. J. Pattinson
Kay Assignation. H. Janson
Kazan. J. O. Curwood
Keane of Kalgoorlie. A. Wright
Kearny Died Twice. K. Howard
Keeban. E. Balmer
Keegan. B. Ball
Keegan: The No-Option Contract. B. Ball
Keegan: The One-Way Deal. B. Ball
Keep. J. Schubert
Keep. F. P. Wilson
Keep Away. B. Casson
Keep Away from Water! Alice Campbell
Keep Back the Dark. A. McElfresh
Keep Cool, Mr. Jones. T. Fuller
Keep It a Secret. Philip Chambers
Keep It Crisp. S. J. Perelman
Keep It Quiet. R. Hull
Keep It Simple. L. Johnson
Keep Moving, Bud. D. Linton
Keep Murder Quiet. S. Jepson
Keep Running. K. Vining
Keep the Baby, Faith. P. DeGrave
Keep the Coffins Coming. J. Long
Keep the Giraffe Burnig. J. Sladek
Keep This Door Shut. A. M. Williamson
Keep Your Fingers Crossed. S. Maddock
Keep Your Fingers Crossed. Kevin O'Hara
Keeper. M. Garrett
Keeper. H. Le Roy
Keeper. R. A. Smith
Keeper of Black Hounds. Nicholas Carter
Keeper of Red Horse Pass. W. C. Tuttle
Keeper of the Children. W. H. Hallahan
Keeper of the City. G. DiPego
Keeper of the Keys. E. D. Biggers
Keeper of the Keys. F. W. Robinson
Keeper of the Waters. M. Roberts
Keepers. R. H. Greenan
Keepers. Sam Ross
Keepers of Death. S. Jason
Keepers of the King's Peace. E. Wallace
Keepers of the Secret. Barnaby Conrad
Keepers of the Walls. F. D. Richardson
Keeping Time. D. Bear
Keeps Death His Court. M. Durham
Keepsake. P. Huson
Keerboskloof. N. Giles
Kefton, the Detective. Old Sleuth
Kek Huuygens, Smuggler. R. L. Fish
Keller's Bomb. L. Dunning
Kelleway's Luck. R. Richmond
Kellogg Junction. B. Spicer
Kelly. Eric Lambert
Kelly Among the Nightingales. J. F. Burke
Kelly Gang. E. T. Woodhall
Kelpie's Burn. John Latimer
Kemmler. Hawkshaw
Kennedy for the Defense. G. V. Higgins
Kennedy's Killing. A. Venter
Kennel Murder Case. S. S. Van Dine
Kennels Crime. M. Osborne
Kensei. S. Schlossstein
Kensington Gore. P. Fox
Kentish Manor Murders. J. Symons
Kentucky Detective. Anonymous
Kentucky Moonshiner. I. Stark
Kenya Mystery. C. T. Stoneham
Kenya Tragedy. Roland Daniel
Kenyatta's Escape. A. C. Clark
Kenyatta's Last Hit. A. C. Clark
Kept Women Can't Quit. A. A. Fair
Kermanshah Transfer. E. Sigel
Kerrell. Taffrail
Kessler. J. Brason
Kessler Alliance. T. Horstman
Kessler Legacy. R. M. Stern
Kestrel. R. E. Salwey
Kestrel House Mystery. T. C. H. Jacobs
Kestrel Syndicate. Jack Lewis
Kestrel's Clue. Jack Lewis

Kestrel's Conspiracy. Jack Lewis
Kettel Mill Mystery. I. Oellrichs
Kettle of Fish. R. Duncan
Kettle of Fish. N. Tranter
Kew for Murder. C. Cruikshank
Key. M. Aldanov
Key. R. Flanders
Key. B. Kevern
Key. M. B. Lowndes
Key. M. McClintick
Key. L. Thayer
Key. P. Wentworth
Key Diablo. D. Daniels
Key Largo. M. Anderson
Key Major. T. S. Strachan
Key Man. C. B. Kelland
Key Man. V. Williams
Key Man. A. Feist
Key of Corruption. R. Crane
Key of the Chest. N. M. Gunn
Key of the Mystery. W. M. Sabelberg
Key Ring Clew. Nicholas Carter
Key to Death. F. Lockridge
Key to Hawthorn Heath. A. P. Huff
Key to Karen. D. Haring
Key to Midnight. L. Nichols
Key to Murder. Stewart Burke
Key to Murder. R. D. Cross
Key to Murder. L. Marshall
Key to Nicholas Street. S. Ellin
Key to Rebecca. K. Follett
Key to the Case. K. Orbison
Key to the Morgue. H. Howard
Key to the Morgue. Robert Martin
Key to the Suite. J. D. MacDonald
Key to Yesterday. C. N. Buck
Key West. B. Hirschfeld
Key West Connection. R. Striker
Key Without a Door. A. Lejeune
Key Without a Lock. Jack Lloyd
Key Witness. M. Brett
Key Witness. F. Kane
Key Witness. W. D. Roberts
Keyhole Peeper. J. De Bekker
Keys for the Criminal. P. Hambledon
Keys from a Window. E. Berckman
Keys of Chance. Winston Graham
Keys of Death. G. Sims
Keys of Freedom. Robert Harding
Keys of Hell. M. Fallon
Keys of Hell. L. Osborne
Keys of My Prison. F. S. Wees
Keys of the Flat. E. C. Vivian
Keys to Billy Tillo. E. Blau
Keys to Crime. Richard Martin
Keys to Queenscourt. J. Hines
Keys to the House. E. Marion
Keys to Tulsa. B. F. Berkey
Keystone. P. Lovesey
Khaki Mafia. Robin Moore
Khamsin. M. Portugais
Khan's Tale. J. B. Fraser
Kharduni. A. Soutar
Khufra Run. J. Graham
Khymer Gold. H. McCaffrey
Kiai. P. Anthony
Kibbutz. Alan White
Kick-In. W. Mack
Kick-In. D. Torbett
Kick Start. D. Rutherford
Kickback. A. Harrell
Kickback. P. Malloch
Kicked to Death by a Camel. C. J.-L. Jackson
Kid. P. McCutchan
Kid from Riga. M. Molloy
Kid Galahad. Francis Wallace
Kid Glove Charlie. J. Cashman
Kid McGhie. S. R. Crockett
Kid Was a Killer. C. Chessman
Kid Was Last Seen Hanging Ten. Hampton Stone
Kid Who Came Home with a Corpse. Hampton Stone
Kid with a Gun. R. Wilkes-Hunter
Kidd. T. Seligson

Kiddy. T. Gallon
Kidnap. J. Boland
Kidnap. P. Bowland
Kidnap. I. Morris
Kidnap Castle. S. Styles
Kidnap Club. A. B. Reeve
Kidnap Cutie. D. Haring
Kidnap Hotel. S. Andrews
Kidnap in Rio. F. G. Wood
Kidnap Island. Roy Vickers
Kidnap Murder Case. S. S. Van Dine
Kidnap Murders. E. T. Woodhall
Kidnapped. A. S. Manley
Kidnapped Again. J. Crozier
Kidnapped Bridegroom. D. Williamson
Kidnapped Child. G. Ashe
Kidnapped Child. J. Creasey
Kidnapped Damozel, The Oval Diamond, Alrashid in Petticoats. D. S. Foster
Kidnapped for a Million. D. Dayle
Kidnapped for Revenge. C. E. Blaney
Kidnapped Heiress. Old Sleuth
Kidnapped King. R. Arnold
Kidnapped Millionaire. R. A. Wainwright
Kidnapped Millionaires. F. U. Adams
Kidnapped President. G. Boothby
Kidnapped Prince. T. S. King
Kidnapped School. E. S. Brooks
Kidnapped Scientist. M. B. Dix
Kidnapped Squatter and other Australian tales. Andrew Robertson
Kidnapped Wife. Roland Daniel
Kidnapped Witness. A. Blair
Kidnapper. C. Bishop
Kidnapper. R. Bloch
Kidnapper, and Railway Line Murder. W. G. Mack
Kidnapper of Women. M. J. Pemberton
Kidnapper Wears Curves. Carter Brown
Kidnappers. W. Kiefer
Kidnappers. Jack North
Kidnappers. B. Thomson
Kidnappers. A. E. Ullman
Kidnapper's Victim. R. Goyne
Kidnapping of Lincoln and other war detective stories. J. C. Harris
Kidnapping of Madame Storey. H. Footner
Kidnapping of the President. C. Templeton
Kidnapping Sydnicate. C. B. Booth
Kidneyed Caper. Alan Chase
Kiet and the Golden Peacock. G. Alexander
Kiet and the Opium War. G. Alexander
Kiev Footprint. C. A. Posey
Kif. G. Daviot
Kigi Sets a Trap. R. St. Clair
Kiki. John Gill
Kilbourne Connection. G. P. Larsen
Kildallon Affair. D. Vallance
Kilgaren. I. Holland
Kill! D. Haring
Kill. D. Heyes
Kill. A. Ryan
Kill! F. Scarpetta
Kill a Wicked Man. K. Hunt
Kill All the Young Girls. B. Halliday
Kill and Be Damned. M. Carrel
Kill and Desire. D. Linton
Kill and Kill Again. H. Pentecost
Kill and Tell. W. X. Kienzle
Kill and Tell. H. Rigsby
Kill As Directed. E. Queen
Kill at Dusk. P. Ketchum
Kill-Box. M. Stark
Kill City. A. Sugar
Kill Claudio. P. M. Hubbard
Kill Crazy. W. Hart
Kill Cue. L. Crews
Kill Cure. J. Rathbone
Kill Deadline. A. Sugar
Kill Dog. J. George
Kill 'Em All. A. G. Ball
Kill 'Em with Kindness. F. Dickenson
Kill Factor. R. Harper
Kill Fee. B. Paul
Kill Fee. G. Paulsen

Title Index

Kill Flash. T. J. MacGregor
Kill for It. R. Hawkes
Kill for the Millions. H. Kane
Kill Gently, But Sure. S. Jason
Kill Her If You Can. H. Janson
Kill Her with Passion. H. Janson
Kill Her—You'll Like It! M. Avallone
Kill Him Gently. P. Valdez
Kill Him Gently, Nurse. K. Fitzgerald
Kill Him Quickly, It's Raining. Michael Brett
Kill Him Tonight. J. Lane
Kill Him Twice. R. S. Prather
Kill Hitler. Jon Barton
Kill Hitler. M. Stall
Kill Huggy Bear. M. Franklin
Kill in the Ring. V. Loder
Kill Is a Four-Letter Word. A. M. Stein
Kill Jason King. R. Miall
Kill Joy. E. S. Holding
Kill Kissinger. G. De Villiers
Kill Me a Fortune. R. Colby
Kill Me a Little. D. Haring
Kill Me a Priest. J. Farrimond
Kill Me Again. John Bentley
Kill Me and Live. C. Franklin
Kill Me for Kicks. H. Janson
Kill Me Gently, Darling. B. Faith
Kill Me in Atami. Earl Norman
Kill Me in Roppongi. Earl Norman
Kill Me in Shimbashi. Earl Norman
Kill Me in Tokyo. Earl Norman
Kill Me in Yokohama. Earl Norman
Kill Me in Yoshiwara. Earl Norman
Kill Me Manana. D. Keene
Kill Me on the Ginza. Earl Norman
Kill Me Quick. D. Haring
Kill Me Quick. M. Mwangi
Kill Me Softly. E. King
Kill Me, Sweet. J. Wilcox
Kill Me Tomorrow. R. S. Prather
Kill Me with Kindness. J. H. Bond
Kill My Love. K. Hunt
Kill Now—Pay Later. L. Grex
Kill Now, Pay Later. R. Kyle
Kill of Small Consequences. J. Wainwright
Kill-Off. J. Thompson
Kill Once, Kill Twice. K. Hunt
Kill 1 Kill 2. W. W. Anderson
Kill One, Kill Two. R. Kelston
Kill or Be Killed. G. Ashe
Kill or Be Killed. V. J. Santiago
Kill or Cure. E. Ferrars
Kill or Cure. Joan Fleming
Kill or Cure. W. Francis
Kill or Cure. R. Sapir
Kill or Cure. J. Sutton
Kill Orbit. D. Stivers
Kill Patton. C. Whiting
Kill Petrosino! Frederick Nolan
Kill Quick or Die. S. Jason
Kill Riff. D. J. Schow
Kill School. D. Stivers
Kill Squad. W. Bond
Kill Squad. M. Cruz
Kill, Sweet Charity, Kill. J. L. Potter
Kill the Beloved. L. Kauffman
Kill the Boss Good-By. P. Rabe
Kill the Bull! J. Breslin
Kill the Clown. R. S. Prather
Kill the Competition. A. Shovald
Kill the Dragon. R. Hawkes
Kill the Girls and Make Them Cry. J. Wainwright
Kill the Hack! Michael Bradley
Kill the Messenger. E. D. Squire
Kill the Reporter. M. Olden
Kill the Toff. J. Creasey
Kill Them All. F. Scarpetta
Kill Them Silently. S. Jason
Kill This Man. H. Janson
Kill 3. M. Shulman
Kill Time. S. Jason
Kill to Fit. B. Fischer
Kill Trap. D. Pendleton
Kill Two Birds. P. Levene

Kill with Care. H. L. Nelson
Kill with Kindness. R. Bloomfield
Kill with Kindness. Dell Shannon
Kill with Style. H. Gulliver
Kill Your Darlings. M. A. Collins
Kill Your Own Snakes. A. Seifert
Kill Zone. L. D. Estleman
Kill Zone. D. Pendleton
Killbride Mystery. K. M. Harwell
Killed by Scandal. S. Nash
Killed in Paradise. W. L. DeAndrea
Killed in the Act. W. L. DeAndrea
Killed in the Ratings. W. L. DeAndrea
Killed on the Ice. W. L. DeAndrea
Killed on the Rocks. W. L. DeAndrea
Killed with a Passion. W. L. DeAndrea
Killer. A. Cowles
Killer. Roland Daniel
Killer. L. C. Douthwaite
Killer. E. Ionesco
Killer. H. Janson
Killer. Wade Miller
Killer. R. Parker
Killer. J. Pattinson
Killer. P. Tonkin
Killer. C. Wells
Killer. Colin Wilson
Killer Aboard. G. H. Teed
Killer Among Us. Robert Martin
Killer Among Us. Ben Ames Williams
Killer and His Star. H. M. Stephenson
Killer and the Slain. H. Walpole
Killer Angel. Doug Masters
Killer at His Back. J. Godey
Killer at Large. D. Bannon
Killer at Large. Ladbroke Black
Killer at Large. N. MacKenzie
Killer at Large. M. Procter
Killer at Scotland Yard. G. Davison
Killer at the Wheel. C. E. Morse
Killer Back Stage. J. Willard
Killer Bait. D. Linton
Killer Be Killed. K. Chase
Killer Blizzard. D. Jorgensen
Killer Boy Was Here. G. Bagby
Killer Breath. J. Wyllie
Killer Budgies. M. Harding
Killer by Night. H. Keyworth
Killer by Night. P. Valdez
Killer by Proxy. S. Jepson
Killer Came Naked. J. Tanner
Killer Came Riding. James Preston
Killer Chromosomes. R. Sapir
Killer Cinderella. Simon Shaw
Killer Cola. G. Shervell
Killer Conference. J. Carrick
Killer Conquest. B. Gray
Killer Cop. F. Findley
Killer Cop. D. Gober
Killer Cops. E. D. Krell
Killer Corps. P. Leslie
Killer Cruise. Nick Stone
Killer Dies Twice. L. R. Banks
Killer Dolphin. N. Mash
Killer Elite. R. Rostand
Killer for a Song. J. Gardner
Killer for Kicks. D. Haring
Killer for the Chairman. M. Hebden
Killer from Queer Street. J. Brullete
Killer from the Grave. F. J. Lowe
Killer Genesis. A. Kilgore
Killer Grew Tired. George Davis
Killer in Canvas Jeans. M. McCracken
Killer in Dark Glasses. H. Treece
Killer in Love. B. Sarton
Killer in My Mind. G. Blumberg
Killer in Paradise. John Leslie
Killer in Silk. H. V. Dixon
Killer in the Chorus. K. T. McCall
Killer in the Crowd. G. Daviot
Killer in the House. B. Deal
Killer in the Kitchen. F. James
Killer in the Rain. R. Chandler
Killer in the Shade. P. Marlowe

Killer in the Straw. R. Lockridge
Killer in the Street. H. Nielsen
Killer in White. T. Thomey
Killer Inside Me. J. Thompson
Killer Instinct. D. Boggis
Killer Instinct. M. Mandell
Killer Is Kissable. Carter Brown
Killer Is Loose. G. Brewer
Killer Is Loose. C. Nicolai
Killer Is Loose Among Us. R. Terrall
Killer Is Mine. T. Powell
Killer Kay. E. Wallace
Killer Keep. W. M. Duncan
Killer Loose! G. Holden
Killer Mine. H. Innes
Killer Mine. M. Spillane
Killer Moon. G. Black
Killer Mountain. M. Hammond
Killer of Fort Norman. C. Stoddard
Killer of Sheep River. C. Stoddard
Killer on the Catwalk. J. Philips
Killer on the Heights. M. Jahn
Killer on the Keys. M. Avallone
Killer on the Line. A. Hyde
Killer on the Prowl. F. Scarpetta
Killer on the Road. J. Ellroy
Killer on the Run. B. Toler
Killer on the Track. D. Rutherford
Killer on the Turnpike. W. P. McGivern
Killer Pack. W. McNeilly
Killer Passion. J. Stark
Killer Patrol. G. Fennell
Killer Pine. L. Gutteridge
Killer Reaction. J. N. Chance
Killer Road. M. Hastings
Killer Satellites. P. Kirk
Killer See, Killer Do. Jonathan Wolfe
Killer Squad. J. Creasey
Killer Stalk. V. Robinson
Killer Stalks. C. Sodaro
Killer Steele. J. D. Masters
Killer Take All. J. O. Causey
Killer Take All. M. Hampton
Killer Take All. P. Race
Killer Take All. B. Rigan
Killer That's Dead! Carl L. Brown
Killer to Come. Sam Merwin
Killer Touch. E. Queen
Killer Virus. P. Kirk
Killer Waiting. W. Sproule
Killer Warrior. M. Olden
Killer Watches the Manhunt. A. B. Cunningham
Killer Wind. R. Hiscock
Killer with a Badge. W. Masterson
Killer with a Golden Touch. A. Riefe
Killer with a Key. D. J. Marlowe
Killers. W. H. Fear
Killers Are My Meat. S. Marlowe
Killers Are on Velvet. Neill Graham
Killers at Sea. A. Joseph
Killers at Sea. J. Messmann
Killer's Bargain. D. Owen
Killer's Blade. P. Malloch
Killers Cannot Live. A. Kinlay
Killer's Caress. C. Moran
Killer's Cargo. S. Jason
Killer's Carnival. T. Field
Killer's Category. J. Armour
Killer's Choice. S. Brock
Killer's Choice. E. McBain
Killer's Choice. Wade Miller
Killers Come Cheap. E. I. English
Killer's Conscience. J. Ingersol
Killer's Contract. T. C. Bridges
Killer's Cookbook. N. S. Gray
Killers Don't Care. R. Cameron
Killers Don't Cry. M. Brody
Killers End. H. Lugar
Killers for Hire. F. Colter
Killers from the Keys. B. Halliday
Killer's Game. E. Hudiburg
Killer's Highway. M. Avallone
Killers in the Sun. J. E. Dixon
Killer's Ink. M. S. Karl

K

Killer's Kingdom. W. L. Rohde
Killer's Kiss. H. Ellson
Killer's Kiss. H. Kane
Killer's Laughter. I. Lambot
Killer's Manual. John Morgan
Killer's Mask. Colin Robertson
Killer's Moon. H. McCutcheon
Killers Must Die. Roland Daniel
Killers Must Eat. M. O'Brine
Killers of Innocence. J. Creasey
Killers of Karawala. E. Lindall
Killers of Starfish. J. Gillis
Killer's Payoff. E. McBain
Killers Play Rough. A. Ring
Killer's Playground. E. Harrison
Killer's Progress. F. Griffin
Killer's Rights. N. Hamilton
Killer's Rope. J. Cassells
Killer's Town. L. Falk
Killer's Wake. B. Cornwell
Killer's Wedge. E. McBain
Killfactor Five. Peter Maxwell
Killigrew. A. Dare
Killing. L. Swaim
Killing. L. White
Killing. David Wilson
Killing a Mouse on Sunday. E. Pressburger
Killing Affair. P. Baker
Killing Anniversary. I. St. James
Killing at the Big Tree. D. McCarthy
Killing Bone. P. Saxon
Killing Bottle Murder. L. A. Fenn
Killing Business. A. Tack
Killing Chase. R. Simons
Killing Circle. C. Wiltz
Killing Cold. T. Wood
Killing Comes Easy. P. Chester
Killing Connection. D. Hartman
Killing Cousins. F. Flora
Killing Cousins. Alanna Knight
Killing Cousins. G. Stratton
Killing Cup. P. Van Greenaway
Killing Doll. R. Rendell
Killing Edge. R. Forrest
Killing Experiment. J. N. Chance
Killing Eyes. J. Miglis
Killing Floor. A. Lyons
Killing for Charity. Arthur Kaplan
Killing for the Hawks. F. E. Smith
Killing Frost. E. Burgess
Killing Frost. M. Catto
Killing Frost. C. Leach
Killing Frost. D. Lynch
Killing Game. P. Cheyney
Killing Game. R. Faust
Killing Game. M. R. Henderson
Killing Game. B. Knox
Killing Game. L. Peters
Killing Games. Nick Carter
Killing Gift. Bari Wood
Killing Ground. Nick Carter
Killing Ground. D. Gober
Killing Ground. S. Linakis
Killing House. G. Rivers
Killing in Antiques. B. Knox
Killing in Black and White. M. Hastings
Killing in Dreamland. J. N. Frey
Killing in Gold. J. L. Hensley
Killing in Hats. J. Davey
Killing in Kluane. J. Lotz
Killing in Malta. Robert MacLeod
Killing in Real Estate. Rudd Brown
Killing in Real Estate. F. Orenstein
Killing in Real Estate. R. Upton
Killing in Rome. R. Rostand
Killing in Swords. R. Bretnor
Killing in the Market. J. Ball
Killing in the Market. N. Daniels
Killing in the Market. G. Goodman
Killing in the Real World. C. A. Bohjalian
Killing in Venture Capital. M. Logan
Killing in Xanadu. B. Pronzini
Killing Is Easy. M. Cronin
Killing Jar. E. M. Beeckman

Killing Jazz. C. B. Booth
Killing Kin. A. Hocking
Killing Kind. M. Franklin
Killing Kind. Elliott West
Killing Kindness. R. Hill
Killing Machine. B. Rossi
Killing Machine. J. Vance
Killing Man. M. Spillane
Killing Mask. M. Stall
Killing Match. R. Severn
Killing Matter. P. Mallory
Killing Mister Watson. P. Matthiessen
Killing Moon. Bill Kelly
Killing No Murder. Colin Howard
Killing No Murder. M. G. Kiddy
Killing No Murder. F. A. M. Webster
Killing of Alquin Judd. P. Monnow
Killing of Ezra Burgoyne. P. Luck
Killing of Francie Lake. J. Symons
Killing of Idi Amin. Leslie Watkins
Killing of Judge MacFarlane. M. Plum
Killing of Katie Steelstock. M. Gilbert
Killing of Kings. R. W. Campbell
Killing of Paris Norton. R. Garnett
Killing of Quemada. M. Cronin
Killing of R.F.K. D. Freed
Killing of the Fallow Deer. T. H. Cook
Killing of the Golden Goose. R. J. Black
Killing of the King. D. R. Slavitt
Killing of Yesterday's Children. M. S. Power
Killing on the Exchange. P. Ableman
Killing Orders. S. Paretsky
Killing Pace. L. H. Whitten
Killing Peace. J. Whitman
Killing Place. T. Richards
Killing Run. M. Barry
Killing Season. J. Redgate
Killing Star. M. Avallone
Killing Strike. J. Creasey
Killing the Blues. Paul Johnson
Killing the Goose. F. Lockridge
Killing Time. T. Berger
Killing Time. R. J. Conley
Killing Time. J. T. Crawford
Killing Time. D. Laiken
Killing Time. W. B. Murphy
Killing Time. D. E. Westlake
Killing Time in Buffalo. D. Laiken
Killing Time in St. Cloud. J. Guest
Killing to Hide. John Penn
Killing Touch. W. Burke
Killing Touch. W. Murray
Killing Trade. W. Boyles
Killing Trade. M. Judge
Killing Urge. D. Pendleton
Killing Wedge. J. Ahern
Killing Wind. John Lee
Killing with Kindness. A. Morice
Killing Wonder. D. Bryant
Killing Zone. Rex Burns
Killings. Clark Howard
Killings at Badger's Drift. Caroline Graham
Killings in Carter Cave. K. Whipple
Killing's No Murder. N. MacKenzie
Killings on Kersivay. A. MacVicar
Killjoy. E. Leonard
Killraven. M. Bishop
Killshot. T. Alibrandi
Killtest. G. King
Killtown. R. Stark
Killy. D. E. Westlake
Kilman's Landing. W. Judson
Kilmeny in the Dark Wood. Florence Stevenson
Kilo Forty. M. Tripp
Kilroy Gambit. I. R. Blacker
Kilternan Legacy. A. McCaffery
Kim. R. Colby
Kim Ruff. R. Gover
Kimberley Killing. P. Corris
Kimono for a Corpse. James Melville
Kimura. Robert Davis
Kin Dread. T. J. MacGregor
Kind Lady. E. Chodorov
Kind Man. H. Nielsen

Kind of Anger. E. Ambler
Kind of Courage. J. Harris
Kind of Healthy Grave. Jessica Mann
Kind of Justice. R. Gaines
Kind of Misfortune. R. Parker
Kind of Nightmare. E. Cannon
Kind of Prisoner. J. Creasey
Kind of Sleep. C. Ould
Kind of Treachery. P. Roberts
Kind of Treason. R. S. Elegant
Kind of Treason. G. MacBeth
Kind Uncle Buckby. John Gloag
Kinder Garden. Frederick Taylor
Kinderkill. Richard Harper
Kindest Use a Knife. L. Revell
Kindly Dig Your Grave, and other wicked stories. S. Ellin
Kindness of Dr. Avicenna. J. Pearson
Kindness of Strangers. B. Taylor
Kindness of Strangers. P. G. Winslow
Kindness of the Celestial and other stories. B. Payn
Kindred Crimes. J. Dawson
Kindred Passions. Rosamund Smith
Kindred Spirits. L. T. Meade
Kinds of Love, Kinds of Death. T. Coe
King Against Anne Bickerton. S. Fowler
King Among Crooks. J. K. Stafford
King and Castle. John Burke
King and Joker. P. Dickinson
King and the Corpse. Max Murray
King and Two Queens. M. MacKintosh
King Billy of the Ballaret and other stories. Morley Roberts
King, Bishop, Knight. R. Emmett
King Blood. J. Thompson
King by Night. E. Wallace
King Cobra. M. Channing
King Cobra. F. Dudley
King Cobra. W. C. Mathews
King Comes Back. V. Bridges
King Coppersmith. R. J. Griffin
King Crook. Gwyn Evans
King Dan, the Factory Detective. G. W. Goode
King Diamond. E. Bruton
King Diamond. F. M. White
King Edward Intervenes. A. Kenealy
King Edward Plot. R. L. Hall
King Fisher Lives. J. Rathbone
King Fritz's A.D.C. F. Hird
King in Bohemia. H. Herman
King in Check. T. Mundy
King in Jeopardy. Eva McDonald
King in Yellow. E. A. St. George
King Is Dead. E. Queen
King Is Dead on Queen Street. F. Bonnamy
King Jaguar. D. Sherman
King Joe Cay. K. Robeson
King John's Treasure. M. J. Ragosta
King Killers. T. B. Dewey
King Maker. K. Robeson
King Murder. C. R. Jones
King of Anarchists. B. Wayde
King of Bigamists. O. Harper
King of Blue Grass Valley. W. C. Tuttle
King of Crooks. W. H. Ainsworth
King of Crooks. C. H. Bullivant
King of Dancing Valley. W. C. Tuttle
King of Detectives. Anonymous
King of Diamonds. J. J. Chichester
Kind of Diamonds. C. Hand
King of Diamonds. T. Thackrey, Jr.
King of Fun. Old Sleuth
King of Gold. N. Ned
King—of Kearsarge. A. O. Friel
King of Kingston. Steve White
King of Satan's Eyes. G. Marsh
King of Scamps. Dick Stewart
King of Spain's Daughter. E. Spencer
King of Terror. K. Robeson
King of Terrors. R. Bloch
King of Terrors. J. D. Spooner
King of the Broncos and other stories of New Mexico. C. F. Lummis
King of the Castle. G. M. Fenn

Title Index

King of the Castle. V. Holt
King of the Clouds. P. Barr
King of the Detectives. Old Sleuth
King of the Golden Valley. A. Scholefield
King of the Highbinders. T. Champlin
King of the Hustlers. E. Izzi
King of the Khyber Rifles. T. Mundy
King of the Mountain. A. Lassiter
King of the Nightcap. William Murray
King of the Opium Ring. C. E. Blaney
King of the Opium Ring. Grace M. White
King of the Peak. S. Cranbrook
King of the Rainy Country. N. Freeling
King of the Rocks. A. Pratt
King of the Roses. U. S. Andersen
King of the Roses. Virginia Anderson
King of the Sea. D. Bickerton
King of the Shadows. Scott Richardson
King of the Underworld. Nicholas Carter
King of the Underworld. Gwyn Evans
King of the World. G. Morton
King of Tiger Bay. J. M. Walsh
King of White Lady. R. L. Hill
King on Queen. F. W. Paul
King Pin. H. Miller
King Rat. S. Heinkel
King Silky. L. Rosten
King-Sized Murder. W. Herber
King Spiv. L. Grex
King Vagabond. A. Wood
King Versus Wargrave. J. S. Fletcher
King Waits. M. Gerard
King Who Preferred Moonlight. A. Weigall
King Zub and other stories. W. H. Pollock
Kingdom and the Wall, and other tales. B. Reynolds
Kingdom at Stake. Anonymous
Kingdom Come. M. Pye
Kingdom Lost. P. Wentworth
Kingdom of Death. M. Allingham
Kingdom of Death. C. Leader
Kingdom of Death. Doug Masters
Kingdom of Death. H. Pentecost
Kingdom of Earth. A. Partridge
Kingdom of Hate. T. Gallon
Kingdom of Johnny Cool. J. McPartland
Kingdom of the Blind. E. P. Oppenheim
Kingdom's Castle. D. Winston
Kingdoms of the World. L. Osbourne
Kingfisher. G. Seymour
Kingfisher Scream. A. Fox
Kingmakers. B. E. Stevenson
Kingpin. B. Hirschfeld
King's Assegai. B. Mitford
King's Castle. L. Ames
King's Club Murder. I. Greig
King's Coil. C. B. Pallen
King's Commissar. D. Kyle
King's Counsel. F. Richardson
King's Crew. F. R. Adams
King's Curse. R. Sapir
King's Detective. Old Sleuth
Kings Die Hard. C. G. Booth
King's Elm Mystery. J. Goodwin
King's Enemies. Reginald Campbell
King's Enemies. J. M. Walsh
King's Falcon. C. Darby
King's Friends. J. Tucker
King's Gambit. G. Chesbro
King's Highway. H. B. M. Watson
Kings in Adversity. E. S. Van Zile
Kings in the Counting House. H. Mitgang
King's Incognito. W. LeQueux
King's Justice. L. Galletley
King's Mate. R. F. Murphy
King's Messenger. J. M. Walsh
Kings of Capital and Knights of Labor. J. M. Leavitt
Kings of Crime. M. Grant
King's Pawn. W. D. Roberts
King's Point. P. L. Sandberg
King's Prisoner. Nicholas Carter
King's Ransom. Ralph Hayes
King's Ransom. E. McBain
King's Ransom. G. Pierce
King's Red-Haired Girl. S. Jepson

King's Secret. H. H. C. Gibbons
King's Secret. R. H. Poole
King's Secret. R. H. Savage
King's Signature. A. Askew
King's Signet. M. Gerard
King's Stockbroker. A. C. Gunter
King's Strategem. S. J. Weyman
King's Talisman. S. Cobb
Kingsclere Mystery. M. Dalton
Kingsford Mark. V. Canning
Kingsley, the Detective. Old Sleuth
Kingsley's Touch. J. Collee
Kingsroads Legacy. D. Kamm
Kingston Black. R. East
Kingston Carnage. Gar Wilson
Kingston Papers. R. S. Silverman
Kink. L. Brock
Kinks. A. Ambrose
Kinsman to Death. B. Cottingham
Kinsmen. W. Haggard
Kirby's Last Circus. R. H. Spencer
Kiriov Tapes. O. Sela
Kirkby's Changeling. M. Brent
Kirke Webbe, the Privateer Captain. Waters
Kirkland Revels. V. Holt
Kirkwood Fires. Deborah Lewis
Kirov Affair. A. Ulam
Kirsty Affair. D. Hall
Kisaeng. M. Olden
Kiss. J. Lutz
Kiss a Day Keeps the Corpses Away. J. Yardley
Kiss a Stranger. G. Finley
Kiss and Kill. Joe Barry
Kiss and Kill. Carter Brown
Kiss and Kill. R. Deming
Kiss and Kill. Adam Knight
Kiss and Kill. R. McCary
Kiss and Kill. Martin Meyers
Kiss and Kill. R. W. Porter
Kiss and Kill. E. Queen
Kiss and Kill. M. Strobel
Kiss Before Dying. I. Levin
Kiss Before Dying. F. Winter
Kiss—But Never Tell. C. Linden
Kiss Daddy Goodbye. T. Altman
Kiss for a Killer. C. C. Fickling
Kiss for a Killer. D. B. Hughes
Kiss for a Killer. Stephen James
Kiss for a Killer. B. Sanders
Kiss for a Killer. E. F. Stafford
Kiss for a Kingdom. Bernard Hamilton
Kiss from a Killer. C. Dekker
Kiss Her Goodbye. Wade Miller
Kiss in the Dark. C. Dekker
Kiss/Kill. R. Sorrele
Kiss Kiss. R. Dahl
Kiss! Kiss! Kill! Kill! H. Kane
Kiss Life Goodbye. Carter Brown
Kiss Me Again, Stranger. D. Du Maurier
Kiss Me As You Go. D. Spade
Kiss Me Deadly. Carter Brown
Kiss Me, Deadly. M. Spillane
Kiss Me Hard. T. Brandt
Kiss Me, Kill Me. K. Cameron
Kiss Me, Kill Me. B. Sarto
Kiss Me, Killer! D. Haring
Kiss Me Once. Thomas Maxwell
Kiss Me Quick. K. Kramer
Kiss Me Twice. Thomas Maxwell
Kiss Michelle Goodbye. Carter Brown
Kiss Mommy Goodbye. J. Fielding
Kiss My Fist! J. H. Chase
Kiss of Death. L. P. Bachmann
Kiss of Death. C. Birkin
Kiss of Death. D. Haring
Kiss of Death. Malcolm Knight
Kiss of Death. E. Lipsky
Kiss of Death. F. Rhodes
Kiss of Death. F. Scarpetta
Kiss of Fire. M. Togawa
Kiss of Hot Sun. N. Buckingham
Kiss of Judas. R. A. Scotti
Kiss of the Damned. S. Harragan
Kiss of the Enemy. H. Hill

Kiss of the Raven. J. Cox
Kiss of Vengeance. R. Roleine
Kiss Off. J. Cirni
Kiss-Off. D. Heyes
Kiss Off the Dead. Garrity
Kiss on Each Cheek. D. De Simone
Kiss That Failed. G. Leroux
Kiss the Babe Goodbye. B. McKnight
Kiss the Blonde Goodbye. F. McDermid
Kiss the Blood off My Hands. Gerald Butler
Kiss the Book. A. Spiller
Kiss the Boss Goodbye. R. Crawford
Kiss the Boys and Make Them Die. J. Yardley
Kiss the Corpse Goodbye. M. Storme
Kiss the Girls and Make Them Die. C. W. Runyon
Kiss the Killer. J. Shallit
Kiss the Tiger. F. M. Davis
Kiss the Toff. J. Creasey
Kiss Tomorrow Goodbye. Griff
Kiss Tomorrow Goodbye. H. McCoy
Kiss Your Ass Goodbye. C. Willeford
Kiss Your Elbow. A. Handley
Kiss Yourself Goodbye. T. Fennelly
Kissed Corpse. A. Baker
Kissed Corpse. W. J. Elliott
Kisses Can Kill. Donnell Carey
Kisses from Satan. G. B. Mair
Kisses Leave No Fingerprints. M. Fredman
Kisses of Death. H. Kane
Kissing Covens. Colin Watson
Kissing Gourami. K. Platt
Kissing the Rod. E. Yates
Kissinger Noodles. M. Wilk
Kit. J. Payn
Kit Wyndham. F. Barrett
Kitchen Cake Murder. C. Bush
Kitchener's Gold. P. MacAlan
Kitten for Keeps! D. Haring
Kitten with a Whip. Wade Miller
Kitten with Blue Eyes. J. Godden
Kitten You're a Killer. M. Brody
Kitten's Necklace. K. O'Neill
Kitty and Others. A. Castle
Kitty Atherton. M. Blount
Kitty Brown's Princess. E. Jepson
Kitty Holden. A. Sergeant
Kitty Shafton—Swindler. A. Askew
Kitty the Madcap. M. M. Bodkin
Kitty's Engagement. F. Warden
Kitty's Father. F. Barrett
Kiwi Club. N. Leslie
Kiwi Contract. P. Atlee
Kiwi Target. J. Ball
Kleber Flight. H. Koning
Kleinert Case. Jack Mann
Klondike Claim. Nicholas Carter
Klondike Kalamity. G. Peterson
Klondyke Kit's Revenge. G. Goodchild
Klondyker. B. Knox
Klute. W. Johnston
Knave and the Game. L. M. Janifer
Knave of Diamonds. J. Karney
Knave of Diamonds. Percy Marks
Knave of Diamonds. Keith Robertson
Knave of Eagles. R. Wade
Knave of Hearts. Dell Shannon
Knave Takes Queen. P. Cheyney
Knaves & Co. S. Horler
Knaves' Castle. Colin Robertson
Knaves in High Places. Nicholas Carter
Knaves of Diamonds. George Griffith
Knaves Rampant. W. Mills
Knavish Crows. Sara Woods
Knee-Deep in Death. B. Fischer
Knife. H. Adams
Knife. H. Ellson
Knife. V. Wallace
Knife at My Back. Adam Knight
Knife at the Opera. J. Staynes
Knife Behind the Curtain. V. Williams
Knife Behind You. J. Benet
Knife Between the Ribs. J. S. Scott
Knife Edge. W. Ellis
Knife Edge. D. MacKenzie

K

Knife-Edged Thing. S. Mitchell
Knife for Celeste. E. Burgess
Knife for Harry Dodd. G. Bellairs
Knife for the Juggler. M. Coles
Knife for the Killer. N. Morland
Knife for the Toff. J. Creasey
Knife for Your Heart. P. Marlowe
Knife in My Back. Sam Merwin
Knife in the Dark. G. D. H. Cole
Knife in the Night. W. M. Duncan
Knife Is Feminine. C. Jay
Knife Is Silent. D. Kent
Knife Terror. A. West
Knife Will Fall. M. Cumberland
Knifed in the Back. Chet Moore
Knifeman. D. Craig
Knifer. W. J. Elliott
Knight and the Castle. J. N. Chance
Knight at Arms. S. Horler
Knight Errant. E. Jepson
Knight Fall. Laurence Payne
Knight in Red Armor. D. Daniels
Knight Missing. S. Stone
Knight Must Fall. T. Wender
Knight of Evil. D. Donovan
Knight of the Nineteenth Century. E. P. Roe
Knight of the North. W. Campbell
Knight of the Silver Star. C. Lys
Knight on the Bridge. W. Watson
Knight Reluctant. C. Headlam
Knight Rider. G. A. Larson
Knight Sinister. S. Rattray
Knight Takes Queen. G. Goodchild
Knight Templar. L. Charteris
Knightfall. G. Linscott
Knight's Gambit. G. Dickson
Knight's Gambit. W. Faulkner
Knight's Keep. Rona Randall
Knight's Move. F. L. Cary
Knights of Arabia. San Antonio
Knights of Calatrava. Sarah Wilkinson
Knights of the Limits. B. Bayley
Knightsbridge Affair. C. Dawe
Knit One, Drop Two. P. Levi
Knives Go Deep. J. Diamond
Knives Have Edges. S. Woods
Knock and Come In. G. Goodchild
Knock and Wait a While. W. R. Weeks
Knock at a Venture. E. Phillpotts
Knock at Midnight. C. Blackstock
Knock at Midnight. J. Reston
Knock Down. D. Francis
Knock 'Em Dead. J. Karney
Knock, Knoc, Who's There? J. Boyle
Knock, Knock! Who's There? J. H. Chase
Knock, Knock, Who's There? Anthony Gilbert
Knock, Murderer, Knock! H. Rutland
Knock-Off. Christopher Newman
Knock on Any Door. W. Motley
Knock on Any Head. F. S. Miller
Knock on the Door. K. D. Woodward
Knock on Wood. G. Hughes
Knock-Out. H. C. McNeile
Knock Out. Richard Russell
Knock-Out Kavanagh. Brian Stuart
Knock Softly on Death's Door. T. E. Wilson
Knock Three-One-Two. F. Brown
Knock Twice. H. J. Greenwald
Knockdown. D. Pendleton
Knocked for a Loop. C. Rice
Knocked Out. Anonymous
Knocker on Death's Door. Ellis Peters
Knocknagow. C. Kickham
Knockout. C. F. Coe
Knockover. N. Thornburg
Knot Garden. G. Nicholson
Knot Garden. G. R. Preedy
Knots and Crosses. I. Rankin
Knots in the Noose. Nicholas Carter
Knots Untied. G. S. McWatters
Knotted Silk. Monte Barrett
Knotted Skein. C. A. Neggers
Knotted Yarns. A. Sterne
Know Then Thyself. H. Gibbs

Known as Z.1. G. Goodchild
Known Homosexual. J. Colton
Knuckle. D. Hare
Knuckles. C. B. Kelland
Knutsford Mystery. D. Donovan
Koba. P. Straub
Koberg Link. A. Maling
Kobra Manifesto. Adam Hall
Kocska Formula. F. Riley
Koheleth. L. A. Storrs
Kojak. Abby Man
Kokoda Trail. R. Wilkes-Hunter
Kolchak's Gold. B. Garfield
Kolwezi. Ritchie Perry
Komani Mystery. V. Sampson
Komespi Affair. Ernest Paul
Kondrasher Chase. J. Rosenberger
Konigsberg Assignment. D. Kydd
Konigsmark. P. Benoit
Kono Diamond. N. Daniels
Kontrol. E. Snell
Korea Kill. Michael Newton
Korean Carnage. Mark Roberts
Korean Combat. R. Jackson
Korean Conspiracy. M. S. Weiss
Korean Kill. Nick Carter
Korean Killground. G. Wilson
Korean Tiger. Nick Carter
Kosygin Is Coming. T. Ardies
Kota. R. Forsythe
Kowloon Contract. P. Atlee
Krakatao Cult. J. Prescot
Kramer Project. R. A. Smith
Kramer's War. Derek Robinson
Krazny Connection. P. Lauben
Kregoff Necklace. Nicholas Carter
Kremlin Armoury. Matthew Hunter
Kremlin Conspiracy. S. Flannery
Kremlin Conspiracy. H. Hunt
Kremlin Contract. J. Barwick
Kremlin Contract. N. C. Weyl
Kremlin Control. O. Sela
Kremlin Correction. J. Evans
Kremlin Devils. J. Hild
Kremlin Directive. J. Midgley
Kremlin File. Nick Carter
Kremlin Kill. Nick Carter
Kremlin Kiss. B. Freemantle
Kremlin Letter. N. Behn
Kremlin Watcher. W. Perry
Kreutzman Formula. V. Scott
Kreuzeck Coordinates. P. Ross
Kriegspeil. F. H. Deane
Kris-Girl. B. Grimshaw
Kristiana Killers. H. Burland
Krone Experiment. J. C. Wheeler
Kronos Plot. J. Rosenberger
Kronstadt. M. Pemberton
Kronstadt 21. G. M. Thomson
Kruger's Gold. P. Webster
Kruger's Wagon. F. H. Rose
Krumnagel. P. Ustinov
Krush. H. Janson
Krushchev Objective. N. Hynd
Krysalis. J. Trenhaile
Kubla Khan Caper. R. S. Prather
Kukri Killer. R. Gilmour
Kumbh Docket. S. Dave
Kummersdorf Connection. E. Ramsey
Kundu. M. L. West
Kung Fu Avengers. M. Minick
Kyd for Hire. Timothy Harris
Kyle Contract. D. MacKenzie
Kyriakos and the Toad. A. Sewart

L.A. Confidential. J. Ellroy
L.A. Gang War. J. Buchanan
L.A. Massacre. N. Winski
L.A. Wars. C. Ramm
L for Murder. M. Stand
L Mystery. Dick Stewart
L.P.M. The End of the Great War. J. S. Barney
LSD Dossier. Roger Harris
L.2002. E. Jepson

La Bella and other stories. E. Castle
La Belle Dame. A. A. Methley
La Belle Laurine. B. Graeme
La Bonita Cigarera. J. H. Ingraham
La Bora. P. Jones
La Brava. E. Leonard
La Casa Dorada. J. L. Roberts
La Fenton. G. D. Galton
La Masque. C. M. Carleton
La Mattanza: The Sicilian Madness. C. Carmello
Label It Murder. Neill Graham
Laboratory Murder and other stories. N. Morland
Labour of Hercules. M. B. Lowndes
Labours of Hercules. A. Christie
Labrador Trust. T. Rook
Laburnum Grove. R. Holland
Laburnum Grove. J. B. Priestley
Labyrinth. R. M. Gilchrist
Labyrinth. J. Land
Labyrinth. E. MacKenzie-Lamb
Labyrinth. B. Pronzini
Labyrinth. Diane Stevens
Labyrinth Makers. A. Price
Labyrinth of Dreams. J. L. Chalker
Labyrinthine Ways. G. Greene
Labyrinths. J. L. Borges
Lace Curtain Murders. S. Belfort
Lace in the Mews. R. Glover
Lacey and His Friends. David Drake
Lacey Lashes Out and other crook plays. T. Doran
LaChance Mine Mystery. S. Carleton
Lachlan's Woman. A. Dwyer-Joyce
Lackey and the Lady. T. Gallon
Lacquer Screen. R. Van Gulik
Lad of London. G. Haw
Lad of Mettle. N. Gould
Ladder of Cards. J. Chancellor
Ladder of Death. B. Flynn
Ladies Always Talk. S. Truss
Ladies and Gentlemen. I. S. Cobb
Ladies and Gentlemen. B. Hecht
Ladies' Bane. P. Wentworth
Ladies' Bar. W. Dinner
Ladies Beware. P. Swift
Ladies Can Be Dangerous. L. Marshall
Ladies First. R. Crompton
Ladies in Boxes. G. Burgess
Ladies in Danger. J. Carlton
Ladies in Danger. E. Verity
Ladies in Ermine. Gavin Holt
Ladies in Ermine. F. A. Kummer
Ladies in Retirement. E. Percy
Ladies in Retreat. B. Perowne
Ladies in the Case. E. C. Vivian
Ladies in the Dark. M. Neville
Ladies in Waiting. C. Campion
Ladies' Juggernaut. A. C. Gunter
Ladies Leave the Castle. A. Athen
Ladies Love Murder. L. Halward
Ladies' Man. Rupert Hughes
Ladies' Night. E. Bowers
Ladies of Holderness. D. Fowler
Ladies of Iniquity. D. Appleford
Ladies of Lambton Green. L. Shepherd
Ladies of Locksley. F. Vivian
Ladies of the Jury. J. F. Ballard
Ladies of the Red Lamp. R. Vane
Ladies Only. M. Box
Ladies Prefer Bruisers. A. Applin
Ladies Sleep Alone. L. Della
Ladies Won't Wait. P. Cheyney
Lady. C. Massie
Lady. T. Tryon
Lady Adlaide's Oath. H. Wood
Lady Afraid. L. Dent
Lady All Alone. L. Noel
Lady and Her Doctor. E. Piper
Lady and Leader. J. G. Sarasin
Lady and the Arsenic. J. Shearing
Lady and the Burglar. Edgar Turner
Lady and the Cheetah. J. Flagg
Lady and the Giant. C. B. Kelland
Lady and the Pirate. P. Allardyce
Lady and the Prowler. J. Roeburt

Lady and the Snake. J. Farr
Lady and the Unicorn. P. H. Irving
Lady Anne's Trustee, and other stories. F. Warden
Lady at Bay. E. Maas
Lady Audley's Secret. M. E. Braddon
Lady Audley's Secret. B. J. Burton
Lady Audley's Secret. C. Cox
Lady Bachelor. H. P. Halsey
Lady, Be Bad. B. Halliday
Lady Be Bad. F. Hanson
Lady Be Bad. H. Zore
Lady, Be Careful. C. Reeve
Lady, Behave! P. Cheyney
Lady Behind Bars. B. Carson
Lady Beware. P. Cheyney
Lady Beware. M. Lavelle
Lady Bites. B. Sarto
Lady Bites the Dust. M. Shane
Lady Borrodale's Ordeal. A. Askew
Lady Bramber's Ghost. C. Charrington
Lady Bug. F. Nordstrom
Lady Called Nita. E. Wallace
Lady Came by Night. B. Halliday
Lady Came to Kill. M. E. Chaber
Lady Can Do. S. Merwin
Lady Can Lose. H. Lugar
Lady Christ. D. MacGregor
Lady Clara. F. M. White
Lady Cop. J. Ravel
Lady Cries Murder. J. W. See
Lady Death. G. Braddon
Lady Detective. Anonymous
Lady Detective. Rebecca Marsh
Lady Detective. Old Sleuth
Lady Doctor—Woman Spy. B. Newman
Lady, Don't Die on My Doorstep. J. Shallit
Lady, Don't Shroud Me! M. Brody
Lady—Don't Turn Over. D. Glinto
Lady Dorothy's Indiscretion. A. Applin
Lady Doth Protest. B. Graeme
Lady Dracula. T. J. Kelly
Lady, Drop Dead. L. Treat
Lady Eleanor, Lawbreaker. R. Barr
Lady Electra. Robert Barr
Lady Elverton's Emeralds. D. Conyers
Lady Ethel's Whim and other stories. C. Braeme
Lady Evelyn. M. Pemberton
Lady Fell in Love. E. Woodward
Lady Finger. G. Malcolm-Smith
Lady for Botany Bay. K. Lindsay
Lady for Hire. A. Lamour
Lady for Sale. N. Daniels
Lady Forgot. M. S. Marble
Lady from Boston. T. McHale
Lady from Hades. J. Bogar
Lady from Hamburg. V. Hill
Lady from Lisbon. V. Blake
Lady from Long Acre. V. Bridges
Lady from Nowhere. F. Hume
Lady from Shanghai. Sherwood King
Lady from the Air. C. N. Williamson
Lady from Tokyo. M. Corrigan
Lady Gambles. R. Fuller
Lady, Get Your Gun. P. Ernst
Lady Gets Wise. Rick Madison
Lady Gift. J. Crecy
Lady Glenroy. G. McKeand
Lady Go Careful. N. W. Firth
Lady Gone Astray. K. Hewitt
Lady Got Burnt. A. Lamour
Lady Grace and other stories. H. Wood
Lady Grace's Mistake. C. Gibbon
Lady Gwendoline. T. Cobb
Lady Had a Gun. N. Morland
Lady Had a Tiger. G. Brodie
Lady Has a Scar. H. Janson
Lady Has Claws. H. Desmond
Lady Has No Convictions. Carter Brown
Lady Helena. G. Leroux
Lady, Here's Your Wreath. Raymond Marshall
Lady Holds a Gun. D. Spade
Lady in a Cage. R. Durand
Lady in a Frame. J. N. Chance
Lady in a Million. S. Shane

Lady in a Veil. G. R. Preedy
Lady in a Wedding Dress. S. Shane
Lady in Armour. O. R. Cohen
Lady in Black. A. Clarke
Lady in Black. B. Graeme
Lady in Black. F. Warden
Lady in Blue. A. Groner
Lady in Blue. F. M. White
Lady in Cement. A. Rome
Lady in Danger. M. Afford
Lady in Danger. S. Shane
Lady in Danger. Jack Williamson
Lady in Darkness. E. Bond
Lady in Darkness. K. Booton
Lady in Distress. M. Richmond
Lady in Distress. Martin Thomas
Lady in Dread. R. Johnson
Lady in Furs. F. Warden
Lady in Green and other stories. P. Cheyney
Lady in Leicester Square. N. W. Firth
Lady in Lilac. S. Shane
Lady in Mink. V. Caspary
Lady in No. 4. R. Keverne
Lady in Peril. L. Dent
Lady in Peril. H. Desmond
Lady in Peril. B. A. Williams
Lady in Sables. G. W. Appleton
Lady in Scarlet. Roland Daniel
Lady in Shadows. A. Lamb
Lady in Tears and others tories. P. Cheyney
Lady in the Black Mask. T. Gallon
Lady in the Blue Veil. L. Clarke
Lady in the Car. W. LeQueux
Lady in the Car with Glasses and a Gun. S. Japrisot
Lady in the Case. J. Futrelle
Lady in the Lake. R. Chandler
Lady in the Lightning. K. Tobias
Lady in the Mist. T. Charles
Lady in the Morgue. Jonathan Latimer
Lady in the Tapestry. Deborah Lewis
Lady in the Tower. K. N. Burt
Lady in the Tower. M. Ritter
Lady in the Veil. A. Abdullah
Lady in the White Veil. R. C. O'Neill
Lady in the Wood. J. Dellbridge
Lady-in-Waiting. W. LeQueux
Lady Incognito. J. M. Walsh
Lady Ingram's Retreat. J. Tattersall
Lady Ingram's Room. J. Tattersall
Lady Is a Killer. Carter Brown
Lady Is a Spitfire. B. Carson
Lady Is a Spy. Lionel Black
Lady Is a Tiger. N. Perrelli
Lady Is a Tramp. H. Zore
Lady Is a Vamp. M. Dekobra
Lady Is Afraid. G. H. Coxe
Lady Is Available. Carter Brown
Lady is Chased. Carter Brown
Lady Is Dead. P. Laing
Lady Is in Danger. R. A. Eames
Lady Is Lethal. P. Muller
Lady Is Lethal. E. Saint
Lady Is Lost. D. Boyce
Lady Is Murder. Carter Brown
Lady Is Not Available. Carter Brown
Lady Is Not Fooling. A. Redwood
Lady Is Poison. B. Gray
Lady Is the Tiger. P. Coggins
Lady Is Transparent. Carter Brown
Lady Is Waiting. J. Mitchell
Lady Jade. L. O'Grady
Lady Jezebel. F. Hume
Lady Jim of Curzon Street. F. Hume
Lady Joan's Companion. F. Warden
Lady Judas. F. Barrett
Lady Kate, the Dashing Female Detective. Anonymous
Lady Killer. G. H. Coxe
Lady Killer. Anthony Gilbert
Lady Killer. W. Hardy
Lady Killer. E. S. Holding
Lady Killer. E. McBain
Lady Killer. M. Togawa
Lady Killer. H. Waugh

Lady Killer Affair. J. Arliss
Lady Killers. J. Kirkpatrick
Lady Killers. A. Riefe
Lady Kills. B. Fischer
Lady, Lady, I Did It! E. McBain
Lady Lawyer. T. Holloway
Lady Lee. F. Warden
Lady, Lie Low. H. Janson
Lady Likes to Sin. D. Spade
Lady Lisle. M. E. Braddon
Lady Living Alone. P. Curtiss
Lady Lost. D. Cory
Lady Lost Her Head. J. Starr
Lady Lost Her Head. M. L. Stokes
Lady Loved Too Well. J. Donahue
Lady MacBeth. N. Freeling
Lady Make-Believe. K. Lindsay
Lady Makes News. V. Kathrens
Lady Marked for Murder. P. Bacon
Lady Mary of the Dark House. A. M. Williamson
Lady Mary's Experiences. R. Jocelyn
Lady Maude's Mania. G. M. Fenn
Lady Mechante or Life As It Should Be. G. Burgess
Lady Middletower and the Red Dagger. J. K. Muir
Lady, Mind That Corpse. H. Janson
Lady Mislaid. K. Horne
Lady Mislaid. C. Rayner
Lady Moliy of Scotland Yard. B. Orczy
Lady Muriel's Secret. J. Middlemass
Lady Needs Help. J. Dark
Lady Noggs, Peeress. E. Jepson
Lady of a Thousand Sorrows. L. W. Mason
Lady of Arlac. S. Shulman
Lady of Ascot. E. Wallace
Lady of Balmerino. M. Leighton
Lady of Burlesque. Gypsy Rose Lee
Lady of Chantry Glades. S. Farrant
Lady of China Street. M. Corrigan
Lady of Despair. F. Grierson
Lady of Doom. G. Verner
Lady of Drawbridge Court. S. Farrant
Lady of Glenwith Grange. W. Collins
Lady of Kalamaria. R. Vickers
Lady of Little Hell. E. Wallace
Lady of Longbourne. P. Trent
Lady of Lyon House. E. Marlow
Lady of Mallow. D. Eden
Lady of Mariner's Mead. S. Farrant
Lady of Monkswood Manor. S. Farrant
Lady of Mystery House. G. C. Shedd
Lady of Night. Jerome Barry
Lady of No Compassion. P. Malloch
Lady of Ravensedge. Jack Lewis
Lady of Resource. A. S. Roche
Lady of Regan's Tower. S. Farrant
Lady of Shadows. Nicholas Carter
Lady of Stantonwyck. Maye Barrett
Lady of Storm House. E. Bond
Lady of the Barge. W. W. Jacobs
Lady of the Blue Motor. S. Paternoster
Lady of the Cameo. T. Gallon
Lady of the Guns. Andrew Murray
Lady of the Hundred Dresses. S. R. Crockett
Lady of the Ice. J. De Mille
Lady of the Island. G. Boothby
Lady of the Isle. E. Southworth
Lady of the Labyrinth. C. Llewellyn
Lady of the Lens. F. C. Long
Lady of the Leopard. C. L'Epine
Lady of the Lilacs. E. D. Pierson
Lady of the Miniature. O. Binns
Lady of the Moor. P. Phillips
Lady of the Night. S. Horler
Lady of the Night. B. Swift
Lady of the Night. V. Vanardy
Lady of the North Star. O. Binns
Lady of the Rifle. F. E. Penny
Lady of the Shadows. D. Daniels
Lady of the Shroud. B. Stoker
Lady of the Swamp. C. A. Brandreth
Lady of Wildersley. J. Edgar
Lady of Winston Park. S. Farrant
Lady on a Short Fuse. D. Haring
Lady on a Train. L. Charteris

Lady on Fire. J. M. Ullman
Lady on Loan. E. Ellison
Lady on Platform One. L. Meynell
Lady on the Lam. Kane
Lady on the Line. T. Tone
Lady, or the Tiger, and other stories. F. R. Stockton
Lady Ottoline. Mrs. Lodge
Lady Pamela's Pearls. J. Ironside
Lady—Pass My Gat! J. Bogar
Lady Passenger. A. W. Marchmont
Lady Pays. S. Coburn
Lady Prefers Murder. H. A. Wrenn
Lady Q. M. Baillee-Saunders
Lady Refused. W. Standish
Lady Regrets. J. M. Fox
Lady Richly Left. M. B. Dix
Lady Rodway's Ordeal. F. Warden
Lady Said No. A. Allyson
Lady Sativa. F. Lauria
Lady Saw Red. A. R. Long
Lady Says No. S. Markham
Lady Says When. D. Ambler
Lady Scorpio. D. Haring
Lady Screams. H. Kaner
Lady Shadower. Old Sleuth
Lady Sharlow's Secret. W. M. Graydon
Lady Sheba's Last Stunt. W. Caine
Lady, Shed Your Head. D. Foster
Lady Silverdale's Sweetheart. William Black
Lady Sinister. P. Warren
Lady So Silent. L. Dent
Lady Sylvia's Imposter. T. Cobb
Lady, Take Care. G. Goodchild
Lady, Take Care! I. B. Kershaw
Lady Takes a Flyer. E. Ronns
Lady Takes Care. G. Goodchild
Lady, That's My Skull. C. Shannon
Lady—This Is It! H. Lugar
Lady, This Is Murder. Peter Chambers
Lady, Throw Me a curve. Gene Ross
Lady to Kill. L. Dent
Lady, Toll That Bell. H. Janson
Lady True's Gate. M. L. Thomas
Lady Turned Traitor. Roland Daniel
Lady Turpin. H. Herman
Lady Unknown. W. Massey
Lady Ursula's Husband. F. Warden
Lady Vanishes. Ethel L. White
Lady Varley. D. Vane
Lady Velvet. Nicholas Carter
Lady View the Body. B. Schwarz
Lady Was a Spy. Roland Daniel
Lady Was a Tramp. H. Whittington
Lady Was Disturbed. James Warren
Lady Was Elusive. L. Cargill
Lady Was Loaded. M. Horgan
Lady Was Warned. K. Rhodes
Lady Wept Alone. C. B. Dawson
Lady, What Now! T. McCoy
Lady, What's Your Game? T. C. H. Jacobs
Lady, Where Are You? H. Desmond
Lady Who Never Was. P. Chambers
Lady with a Cool Eye. G. Moffat
Lady with a Gun. E. P. Thorne
Lady with a Rose. F. Hay
Lady with the Dice. J. T. Rogers
Lady with the Limp. S. Horler
Lady Without Mercy. R. McDougall
Lady Wore Nylons. Carter Brown
Lady Yesterday. L. D. Estleman
Lady, You Slay Me. D. Haring
Lady, Your Gun's Showing. T. Trenton
Lady, You're Killing Me. Peter Chambers
Lady, You're Lethal. M. Brody
Lady, You're Loaded. D. Haring
Lady Zia. P. Wynnton
Ladybirds Are In. H. Janson
Ladycat. N. Greenwald
Ladye Annabel. Anonymous
Ladyfingers. Jackson Gregory
Ladyfingers. S. Rifkin
Ladygrove. John Burke
Ladykiller. T. Mallanson
Ladykiller. L. O'Donnell

Lady's a Decoy. K. T. McCall
Lady's Alive. Carter Brown
Lady's Eyes Were Green. A. Aldous
Lady's for Killing. B. Shannon
Lady's in Danger. N. Berrow
Lady's Mile. M. E. Braddon
Lady's Not for Burning. C. Fry
Lady's Not for Living. D. St. Clair
Lady's Out of Circulation. M. Brody
Lagden's Luck. T. Gallon
Lago. John Lee
Lagrange Five. M. Reynolds
Lagrangists. M. Reynolds
Laguna Contracts. E. C. Allen
Laguna Heat. T. J. Parker
Laid Dead. B. Cork
Laid Up in Lavender. S. J. Weyman
Laidlaw. W. McIlvanney
Laidlaw's Wife. F. Warden
Lair. L. Charbonneau
Lair. J. Herbert
Lair of the Fox. D. Pollock
Lair of the Vampire. G. E. Rochester
Lair of the White Worm. B. Stoker
Laird. Winifred Duke
Laird and the Lady. Joan Grant
Laird of Evil. Martin Thomas
Laird's Deed of Settlement. J. M. Kippen
Laird's Luck and other fireside tales. A. T. Quiller-Couch
Lairds of Turriff Hall. A. Jamison
Lair's Dice. M. McGann
Lake District Murder. J. Bude
Lake Frome Monster. A. W. Upfield
Lake House. J. Rhode
Lake Isle. N. Freeling
Lake Loot. H. Janson
Lake Lovers. G. Wagner
Lake Mystery. M. Dana
Lake of Darkness. F. Cowen
Lake of Darkness. R. Rendell
Lake of Fire. L. Houser
Lake of Fury. Robert MacLeod
Lake of Ghosts. R. Bell
Lake of the Dead. L. P. Greene
Lake of the Diamond. J. Lee
Lake of the Wind. Lynn Williams
Lake of Wine. B. Capes
Lakeland Tragedy. J. Courage
Lakeside Murder. C. H. Snow
Lakeside Mystery. G. W. Jones
Lakeside Zero. D. Enefer
Lallie. G. Sinclair
Lalru Murders. E. N. Mangat Rai
Lam to Slaughter. D. Sanderson
Lam to the Slaughter. A. A. Fair
Lamaar Ransom—Private Eye. D. Galloway
L'Amante Anglais. M. Duras
Lama's Secret. W. M. Graydon
Lamastre. M. Strong
Lamb to the Slaughter. D. Eden
Lambert's Son. A. Maling
Lambs of Fire. P. Gascar
Lame Dog Murder. M. Halliday
Lament for a Blonde. B. Banarto
Lament for a Lady Laird. M. Arnold
Lament for a Lonesome Corpse. Ruth Reeves
Lament for a Lousy Lover. Carter Brown
Lament for a Lovely. M. Brody
Lament for a Lover. P. Highsmith
Lament for a Lover. H. Janson
Lament for a Maker. M. Innes
Lament for a Virgin. L. White
Lament for Four Brides. E. Berckman
Lament for Julie. R. Colby
Lament for Leto. G. Mitchell
Lament for Lost Lovers. Alanna Knight
Lament for the Bride. H. Reilly
Lament for William. C. M. Russell
Lamia. T. Travis
Lammas Grove. C. Dawe
Lammas Night. K. Kurtz
Lamontane. S. Blackwood
Lamp Burns Blood. Leslie Carroll

Lamp of God. E. Queen
Lamp-Post 592. S. Maddock
Lamplighter. J. Simmons
Lampton Dreamers. L. P. Davies
Lanagan, Amateur Detective. E. H. Hurlbut
Lancaster Triple Thousand. W. B. Woods
Lance for the Devil. R. Charles
Lance of God. A. McCoy
Lancer Spy. M. McKenna
Land at Last. E. Yates
Land from the Sea. S. Styles
Land God Gave to Cain. H. Innes
Land God Made in Anger. J. G. Davis
Land of Big Things. L. H. Gordon
Land of Day-Dreams. G. V. Stuart
Land of Eldorado. G. Goodchild
Land of Eucalyptus. G. Ferrand
Land of Fear. K. Robeson
Land of Gold. M. A. Hammond
Land of Leys. L. P. Davies
Land of Long Juju. K. Robeson
Land of Mirrors. A. Coppel
Land of Mystery. A. G. Pearson
Land of No Escape. G. Horne
Land of Promises. S. P. Hyatt
Land of Shadows. F. C. Matranga
Land of Terror. K. Robeson
Land of Terror. D. Storm
Land of the Blue Veil. A. Worsley
Land of the Dawning. R. D.
"Land of the Free." W. Slater
Land o' the Leal. H. B. Mathers
Land of the Lost. W. Satchell
Land Pirate. J. Bogar
Land Where Our Fathers Died. H. S. Nuelle
Land Without Heroes. G. F. Green
Land Without Shadow. M. Mewshaw
Landed at Last. N. Gould
Landed Gently. A. Hunter
Landfall. D. W. MacArthur
Landfall Finesse. D. Da Cruz
Landfall in Sefton Carey. J. Escott
Landing. H. Simons
Landlady. C. Rauch
Landlord of "The Sun". W. Gilbert
Landor Case. John Bentley
Landover Legacy. V. Holt
Landru. W. LeQueux
Landru. R. Masson
Land's End, and other stories. W. D. Steele
Landscape of Darkness. J. M. Blair
Landscape of Lies. Peter Watson
Landscape of the Body. J. Guare
Landscape with Corpse. D. Ames
Landscape with Corpses. M. Barnes
Landscape with Dead Dons. Robert Robinson
Landscape with Violence. J. Wainwright
Landsend Terror. J. Trevelyan
Landshark. I. Zacharia
Landslide. D. Bagley
Lane of Darkness. M. Clare
Langley Murder Case. Roland Daniel
Language of Cannibals. G. C. Chesbro
Lanier Riddle. D. Daniels
Lansing Legacy. A. Hyman
Lantern for Diogenes. S. Harvester
Lantern Hill. B. Worsley-Gough
Lantern House Affair. Gret Lane
Lantern Lecture. A. Mars-Jones
Lantern Network. T. Allbeury
Lantern of Luck. R. Aitkin
Lantern of Luck. H. Douglas
Lao-Ti the Celestial. M. Bird
Lapis. H. Hamman
Lapse of the Bishop. G. Thorne
Larceny for a Lovely. M. Brody
Larceny in Her Heart. L. Grex
Larceny Was Lovely. Carter Brown
Large Sapphire. Ronald Duncan
Large Type Killer. Richard Williams
Largely Luck. Evelyn Harris
Largely Trouble. Evelyn Harris
Lark. R. Forrest
Larksong at Dawn. Agnes Russell

Title Index

Larkspur. S. Simonson
Larkspur Conspiracy. J. Philips
Larrabee Heiress. D. Daniels
Larry Lohengrin. W. Westall
Las Vegas. Arthur Moore
Las Vegas Strip. M. Renek
Las Vegas Vengeance. B. Rossi
Laser Shuttle. P. Kirk
Laser War. J. Rosenberger
Lashed But Not Leashed. M. McShane
Lasko Tangent. R. N. Patterson
Last Act. J. A. Hodge
Last Act in Bermuda. D. Burnham
Last Adventure. J. Fores
Last Adventure. E. Wallace
Last Adventure of Christian Doom: Private I. R. Kenny
Last Alchemist. W. B. Murphy
Last Alive. J. M. Cobban
Last and Greatest Art. W. Winward
Last Annual Slugfest. Susan Wolfe
Last Appointment. H. Howard
Last Assassin. D. Easterman
Last Assignment. N. Fisher
Last Battle. R. Jackson
Last Best Friend. G. Sims
Last Believers. D. Karp
Last Breath. H. Q. Masur
Last Bridge. B. Garfield
Last Bridge. D. Mariner
Last Bridge Home. I. Johansen
Last Buccaneer. J. Wainwright
Last Bus to Woodstock. C. Dexter
Last Cab on the Rank. H. Grisewood
Last Caesar. E. McGhee
Last Call. Nicholas Carter
Last Call. R. Dowling
Last Call. R. Sapir
Last Call for Lissa. D. Mayor
Last Call of Mourning. C. L. Grant
Last Card. H. H. Kirst
Last Card. Mark Ross
Last Chance. B. Schwarz
Last Chance Country. G. Moffat
Last Checkpoint. J. Quigley
Last Chronicles of Ballyfungus. M. Manning
Last Chukka. A. Waugh
Last Clear Chance. B. Wilkinson
Last Clue. W. J. Bayfield
Last Clue. Eugene Jones
Last Coincidence. R. Goldsborough
Last Cold-War. J. P. Sloan
Last Command. D. B. Dodson
Last Command. C. Houghton
Last Commandment. G. H. Coxe
Last Concubine. F. S. Wees
Last Contract. Clark Howard
Last Cop Out. M. Spillane
Last Coup. H. Smart
Last Crime. J. Domatilla
Last Cruise of the "Majestic". G. Goodchild
Last Dance. J. Briley
Last Dance at Redondo Beach. M. J. Katz
Last Day in Limbo. P. O'Donnell
Last Day of Lincoln Charles. Gordon M. Williams
Last Day of Summer. E. Burfield
Last Days at St. Saturn's. E. Apffel
Last Days of America. P. Erdman
Last Days of Berlin. P. Saxon
Last Days of Horse-Shy Halloran. B. Pronzini
Last Days of Louisiana Red. I. Reed
Last Days of Miss Jenkinson. N. Hoult
Last Days of New York. C. Mandeville
Last Deadly Lie. C. Pirtle, III
Last Deal. L. Gonzales
Last Decathalon. J. Redgate
Last Deception. H. Howard
Last Deserter. J. Robb
Last Ditch. R. Bradford
Last Ditch. G. Goodchild
Last Ditch. V. Hunt
Last Ditch. M. McGrath
Last Domino Contract. P. Atlee
Last Door. O. Binns

Last Door. D. Enefer
Last Doorbell. Joseph Harrington
Last Doorbell. J. K. Vedder
Last Draw. E. Petersen
Last Drop. B. Cobb
Last Drop. W. B. Murphy
Last Drop of '68. Anonymous
Last Embrace. M. T. Bloom
Last Enemy. Keith Ayling
Last Enemy. I. Barry
Last Enemy. V. M. Methley
Last Enemy. B. Roueche
Last Escape. E. C. R. Lorac
Last Escape. M. Walker
Last Exit. F. P. Yariev
Last Express. B. Kendrick
Last Fathom. M. Caidin
Last Ferry from the Lido. B. Healey
Last Film of Emile Vico. T. Gavin
Last First. R. Hull
Last Flight. M. Land
Last Flight to Moscow. Nick Carter
Last Flowers. Michael Barrett
Last Flying Tiger. D. E. Fisher
Last Forty-Eight Hours. N. G. Bailey
Last Frame. Jim Wright
Last Frontier. Alistair MacLean
Last Galley. A. C. Doyle
Last Gambit. D. Delman
Last Gamble. J. Fairfax-Blakeborough
Last Gamble. R. Foley
Last Gamble. H. Q. Masur
Last Gasp. T. Hoyle
Last Generation. Tom Howard
Last Good Kiss. J. Crumley
Last Grand Master. J. M. White
Last Great Death Stunt. Clark Howard
Last Hero. L. Charteris
Last Heroes. John Gill
Last Heroes of Merriott Manor. P. Pacotti
Last Hope House. Wilma Forrest
Last Hour. C. Bennett
Last Hours Before Dawn. R. Gadney
Last House. G. Dessart
Last House. M. Maurice
Last House Party. P. Dickinson
Last Hunt. Lake Short
Last Hunter. F. Cederberg
Last Indictment. M. Cronin
Last Innocent Man. P. M. Margolin
Last Journey. Keith Campbell
Last Judgement. R. Hugo
Last Judgment. A. Clarke
Last Kamikaze. M. E. Morris
Last Karkawber and other stories. H. Beswick
Last Kill. Charlie Wells
Last King of Yewle. P. L. MacDermott
Last Known Address. Joseph Harrington
Last Lady. H. Janson
Last Lap. G. B. Savi
Last Laugh. C. Einstein
Last Laugh. Winifred Graham
Last Laugh. J. R. Riggs
Last Laugh and No Pictures for Cathy. P. Denver
Last Laugh for the Baron. Anthony Morton
Last Laugh, Mr. Moto. J. P. Marquand
Last Leap. D. Enefer
Last Liberator. J. Clive
Last Link. M. Gerard
Last Lord Avanley. G. Maxwell
Last Magic. N. R. Nash
Last Man at Arlington. J. Di Mona
Last Man Club. E. Queen
Last Man on the List. B. Randall
Last Man Out of Saigon. C. Mullin
Last Mandarin. S. Becker
Last Man's Head. Jessica Anderson
Last Mayday. K. Wheeler
Last Meeting. B. Matthews
Last Member of the Family. L. A. Sunagel
Last Message to Berlin. P. Van Rjndt
Last Mile. J. Wexley
Last Minute Clue. Vince Kelly
Last Mission. C. Whiting

Last Move in the Game. Nicholas Carter
Last Movement. Joan Aiken
Last Mystery of Edgar Allan Poe. Manny Meyers
Last Nazi. Max Lamb
Last Night. J. McPartland
Last Night on Masada. Gavin Douglas
Last Note for a Lovely. Carter Brown
Last of Days. M. Farhi
Last of Lysandra. Elizabeth Fenwick
Last of Mr. Moto. J. P. Marquand
Last of Mrs. Cheyney. G. Fowler
Last of Mrs. Cheyney. D. G. Herriot
Last of Mrs. Cheyney. F. Lonsdale
Last of Philip Banter. J. F. Bardin
Last of Sheila. Alexander Edwards
Last of Sherlock Holmes. T. J. Kelly
Last of the Armageddon Wars. R. Dennis
Last of the Boatriders. D. MacKenzie
Last of the Burrows Gang. W. B. Lawson
Last of the Bushrangers. R. Whitley
Last of the Country House Murders. E. Tennant
Last of the Crazy People. T. Findley
Last of the Cybernauts. P. Cave
Last of the Darrells. C. E. Pearce
Last of the Dog Team. W. W. Johnstone
Last of the Grenvilles. B. Copplestone
Last of the Honeywells. R. B. Gillespie
Last of the Mansions. D. Daniels
Last of the Pleasure Gardens. Francis King
Last of the Ruthvens. L. Barbee
Last of the Van Slacks. E. S. Van Zile
Last Offence. F. Keast
Last One. Dion Henderson
Last One Kills. W. Masterson
Last Page. J. H. Chase
Last Page. B. Fenster
Last Parable. Alex Coppel
Last Patriot. J. N. Frey
Last Place God Made. J. Higgins
Last Place Left. M. Pugh
Last Plane from Nice. Clarissa Watson
Last Plane from Uli. C. Kearey
Last Portrait of the Duchess of Alba. A. Larreta
Last Post for a Partisan. C. Egleton
Last President. M. Kurland
Last Prisoner. J. Robson
Last Private Eye. J. Birkett
Last Private Eye in Dublin. Mike Shelley
Last Quarter Hour. J. Bruce
Last Ranger. C. Sargent
Last Raven. Craig Thomas
Last Recruit of Clare's. S. R. Keightley
Last Redoubt. G. Goodchild
Last Refuge of a Scoundrel and other stories. W. Howard
Last Resort. V. Siller
Last Respects. C. Aird
Last Reunion. V. Andrews
Last Ride. D. Haring
Last Ride for Lola. S. Brandon
Last Rights. D. L. Dawson
Last Rights. H. H. Dooley
Last Rights. A. Douglas
Last Rites. R. Bloch
Last Rites. J. Saralegui
Last Rites. P. M. Smith
Last Rites. P. Spike
Last Rites for the Vulture. Simon Quinn
Last Run South. R. Hiscock
Last Safari. Richard Rhodes
Last Safari. Alan Scholefield
Last Samurai. Nick Carter
Last Scam. D. Harris
Last Score. E. Queen
Last Scourge. W. Martyn
Last Seance. M. Lovell
Last Secret. D. Chambers
Last Secret. G. Goodchild
Last Seen Alive. W. G. Duncan
Last Seen Alive. J. McCormick
Last Seen Alive. A. Mills
Last Seen Alive. D. Simpson
Last Seen Hitchhiking. B. Halliday
Last Seen in London. Anna Clarke

L

Last Seen in Samarra. J. G. Vermandel
Last Seen Wearing. Veronica Black
Last Seen Wearing. C. Dexter
Last Seen Wearing—. H. Waugh
Last Sentence. J. Goodman
Last Sentence. Maxwell Gray
Last Set. J. Ellery
Last Seven Hours. J. N. Chance
Last Shaft. E. Tidyman
Last Sherlock Holmes Story. M. Dibdin
Last Shot. C. Duggan
Last Shot. P. Loraine
Last Shot. L. Thayer
Last Shot and other stories. R. Goyne
Last Signal. Dora Russell
Last Smile. M. H. Albert
Last Spin and other stories. E. Hunter
Last Spring in Paris. H. Herlin
Last Starship from Earth. J. Boyd
Last Stop. I. K. Davis
Last Stop. W. Tucker
Last Stop Camp 7. H. H. Kirst
Last Straw. D. M. Disney
Last Straw. F. Hume
Last Straw. I. S. Shriber
Last Stroke. L. L. Lynch
Last Stronghold. J. Pattinson
Last Supper. S. Hardie
Last Supper. C. McCarry
Last Surprise. William Moore
Last Survivor. E. Dale
Last Survivor. R. Myers
Last Suspect. J. Rhode
Last Temple. R. Sapir
Last Temptation. D. Mure
Last Tenant. B. L. Farjeon
Last Things. Madison Jones
Last Throes. A. Lykiard
Last Tiger. W. A. Ballinger
Last Time. L. Dowsett
Last Time I Saw Hell. Simon Quinn
Last Time I Saw Mary. G. Corbin
Last Tomb. J. Lange
Last Touches. W. K. Clifford
Last Train from Berlin. B. Blagowidow
Last Train Out. E. P. Oppenheim
Last Train to Limbo. J. N. Chance
Last Train to Rock Ferry. D. Enefer
Last Traitor of Long Island. R. H. Savage
Last Trap. S. Gluck
Last Trick. D. Enefer
Last Trump. J. Gardner
Last Trump. L. Thayer
Last Trumpet. T. Downing
Last Twist of the Knife. M. Bonner
Last Two Weeks of Georges Rivac. G. Household
Last Vanity. H. Howard
Last Victim. A. Dramann
Last Voyage. A. Clarke
Last Voyage. R. Kytle
Last Walk Home. E. Page
Last War Dance. R. Sapir
Last Warning. Wadsworth Camp
Last Warning. T. Fallon
Last Warning. G. Verner
Last Wednesday. B. Bannerman
Last White Man. F. D. Barber
Last White Man in Panama. W. Gough
Last Will and Testament. G. D. H. Cole
Last Will and Testament. E. Ferrars
Last Witness. W. Collison
Last Witness. L. Silbersky
Last Witness. S. G. Sykes
Last Woman. R. Beeckman
Last Woman in His Life. E. Queen
Last Word. J. Popplewell
Last Word and other stories. G. Greene
Last Words. Stephen Crane
Last Words of Dutch Schultz. W. Burroughs
Last Year's Blood. H. C. Branson
Last Year's Snow. D. Tracy
Last Year's Wife. A. M. Williamson
Lastingham Murder. L. Tracy
Latacumba Assignment. John Newton

Latchkey Kids. A. Launay
Late and Cold. M. Torrie
Late Bill Smith. A. Garve
Late Boy Wonder. Angus Hall
Late Bride. T. Du Bois
Late Candidate. Mike Phillips
Late Clara Beame. T. Caldwell
Late Contessa. Dorothy Fletcher
Late Delivery. J. R. L. Anderson
Late Demented. B. Carson
Late Edwina Black. W. Dinner
Late Final Blonde. M. Brody
Late for the Funeral. D. Stapleton
Late Gentleman. S. Cameron
Late Harvest. K. Sunderland
Late Into the Night. H. Bigden
Late Knight. Laurence Payne
Late Lamented. F. Brown
Late Lamented. A. A. Thomson
Late, Lamented Lady. M. Blizard
Late Last Night. J. Reach
Late, Late in the Evening. G. Mitchell
Late Miss Cordell. P. Johnson
Late Miss Trimming. C. Carnac
Late Mr. Beverly. T. Cobb
Late Mrs. D. H. Waugh
Late Mrs. Five. R. Wormser
Late Mrs. Fonsell. V. Johnston
Late Mrs. Lane. Rona Randall
Late Night Revel. H. Janson
Late of London Wall . . . Bruce Norman
Late Payments. M. Z. Lewin
Late Phoenix. C. Aird
Late Recovery. S. Fairway
Late Repentance. T. W. Speight
Late Tenant. Gordon Holmes
Late Uncle Max. M. Fitt
Late Unlamented. C. N. Boyle
Late Unlamented. H. Carmichael
Late Unlamented. D. L. Mathews
Late Unlamented. R. A. J. Walling
Lately Deceased. B. Picton
Later Than You Think. M. M. Kaye
Latest Mrs. Adams. G. Tibbles
Latigo. F. O'Rourke
Latimer Mercy. R. Richardson
Latter End. P. Wentworth
Lattimore Arch. Angela Gray
Laugh? I Nearly Went to Miami. M. Tredinnick
Laugh of Death. K. Robeson
Laugh Was on Lazarus. J. Garforth
Laughing Bacchante. D. Yates
Laughing Bill Hyde and other stories. R. Beach
Laughing Buddha. C. Glick
Laughing Buddha. V. Starrett
Laughing Buddha Murders. R. Foster
Laughing Cat. S. Toye
Laughing Death. W. C. Brown
Laughing Death. P. Edwards
Laughing Death. D. Haring
Laughing Dog. D. Lochte
Laughing Dog. F. Vivian
Laughing Dragon Mystery. J. Kains
Laughing Fish. L. Bell
Laughing Fish. S. Jepson
Laughing Fox. F. Gruber
Laughing Gangster. D. Newton
Laughing Ghost. D. Eden
Laughing Ghost. L. Rose
Laughing Ghosts. A. E. Southon
Laughing Girl. R. W. Chambers
Laughing Girl. G. F. Worts
Laughing Grave. V. Gunn
Laughing Horseman and other tales. Anonymous
Laughing Lightweight. P. Gill
Laughing Loon. J. E. Greene
Laughing Malefactor. Carol West
Laughing Man. M. Daniel
Laughing Man. Stockton Woods
Laughing Mask. Cosmo Hamilton
Laughing Men. T. C. H. Jacobs
Laughing Mill and other stories. J. Hawthorne
Laughing Mountains. K. Lynn
Laughing Peril. H. L. Gates

Laughing Policeman. E. Bruton
Laughing Policeman. M. Sjowall
Laughing Priory. M. Meeke
Laughing Rider. L. Y. Erskine
Laughing Whitefish. R. Traver
Laughing Widow. C. Warren
Laughter and Fear. D. Campton
Laughter Came Screaming. H. Kane
Laughter in the Alehouse. H. Kane
Laughter in the Night. F. Ford
Laughter in the Ranks. M. Hervey
Laughter Trap. J. Philips
Launch. E. Stewart
Launching of Roger Brook. D. Wheatley
Laundryman. J. Evans
Laura. V. Caspary
Laura Possessed. Anthea Fraser
Laura Sarelle. J. Shearing
Laura, the Emperiled. K. Kimbrough
Laurel and Hardy Murders. Marvin Kaye
Laurell'd Captains. G. R. Preedy
Laurels Are Poison. G. Mitchell
Laurels for McLean. G. Goodchild
Laurels for the Dreamer. W. M. Duncan
Laurie's Legacy. J. Aeby
Laurine. B. Graeme
Lautrec. N. Zollinger
Lava. H. M. E. Clamp
Lava Flow Murders. Max Long
Lavender Dagger. D. C. Calthrop
Lavender Gripsack. H. S. Keeler
Lavender's Inheritance. A. Askew
Lavenham Mystery. B. Bolt
Lavish of Sin. C. E. Morse
Law. B. S. Ballinger
Law and Order. G. F. Newman
Law and Order. D. Uhnak
Law and Order on Halfaday Creek. J. B. Hendryx
Law and Order, Unlimited. W. C. MacDonald
Law and the Lady. W. Collins
Law Breakers. R. Cullum
Law-Breakers. P. Gibbs
Law-Breakers and other stories. Robert Grant
Law Bringers. G. B. Lancaster
Law Courts Mystery. A. Blair
Law Not Justice. F. Warden
Law of Love. C. Jauniere
Law of Nemesis. A. Carlyle
Law of Probability. M. Sharman
Law of the Bolo. S. P. Hyatt
Law of the Forgotten Men. A. Edgar
Law of the Four Just Men. E. Wallace
Law of the Gun. R. Cullum
Law of the Hills. O. Binns
Law of the Knife. C. Dawe
Law of the Land. G. Broadhurst
Law of the Land. F. M. White
Law of the Lion. Nick Carter
Law of the River. F. Gerard
Law of the Streets. A. Le Breton
Law of the Talon. L. Tracy
Law of the Three Just Men. E. Wallace
Lawful Pursuit. M. Underwood
Lawless. C. Dawe
Lawless Hand. W. LeQueux
Lawless Justice. A. Edgar
Lawless Lady. D. Haring
Lawless Voyage. A. D. Divine
Lawrence Barclay File. B. Musto
Laws Be Their Enemy. F. E. Smith
Law's Delay. Sara Woods
Lawton Mystery. W. J. Burns
Lawyer and the Carpenter. E. Thompson
Lawyer Bell from Boston. R. L. Tyler
Lawyer-Detective. W. Warner
Lawyer Man. M. Trell
Lawyer Manton of Chicago. Le Jemlys
Lawyers Don't Hang. G. M. Barnes
Lawyer's Purpose. J. Leitch
Lawyer's Secret. M. E. Braddon
Lawyer's Secret. J. K. Leys
Lawyer's Secret. H. Lloyd
Lawyer's Story. J. A. Maitland
Lawyer's Wife. W. N. Geary

Title Index

Laxham Haunting. J. Lymington
Lay Down and Die. M. Reed
Lay Down Dead. Matthew Bradley
Lay Down, You're Dead. T. Taggart
Lay Her Among the Lilies. J. H. Chase
Lay Low, My Lovely. C. Dekker
Lay On, MacDuff! C. Armstrong
Lay Out My Lady. M. Brody
Lay-Over Town. D. Brennan
Lay That Pistol Down. R. Powell
Lay the Dame on Ice. D. Bogard
Layers of Deceit. R. Jeffries
Layers of Deceit. Bradshaw Jones
Laying On of Hands. A. Arent
Laying of the Noone Walker. R. Ashe
Laying Out of Gussie Hoot. Margot Fraser
Layoff. R. G. Dean
Layout for a Corpse. G. Goldsmith
Layout for Murder. J. Karney
Layton Court Mystery. A. Berkeley
Layton Hall. M. Lemon
Lazarus. Morris West
Lazarus Fule. S. Prebble
Lazarus in London. F. W. Robinson
Lazarus in Vienna. A. Slote
Lazarus Inheritance. N. V. Carter
Lazarus Lie. P. Van Greenaway
Lazarus Man. J. Lutz
Lazarus Murder Seven. R. Sale
Lazarus #7. R. Sale
Lazy Detective. G. Dilnot
Lazy Lawrence Murders. T. Downing
Le Pere Goriot. H. D. Balzac
Lead Astray. Carter Brown
Lead Bites Deep. V. J. Hanson
Lead for a Lovely. D. Haring
Lead Her Gently to the Grave. D. Bogard
Lead Him to Death. H. Windsor
Lead-Lined Coffin. E. McGirr
Lead Me Into Temptation. F. Heller
Lead Me to the Gallows. F. Lester
Lead Me to the Slaughter. G. Ison
Lead On, McLean! G. Goodchild
Lead with Your Left. E. Lacy
Leaden Bubble. H. C. Branson
Leader and the Damned. C. Forbes
Leading Lady. G. Bonner
Leading Lady. H. Herman
Leading Lady. R. Mills
Leading Lady. Rex Richards
Leaf of a Lime Tree. P. Tabori
League of Counterfeiters. Old Sleuth
League of Crime. F. Balfour
League of Dark Men. J. Creasey
League of Death. H. J. S. Anderton
League of Discontent. F. Beeding
League of 89. M. Hebden
League of Five. D. Lenton
League of Frightened Men. R. Stout
League of Gentlemen. J. Boland
League of Guilt. I. Murray
League of Hawks. A. Caillou
League of Justice. F. Duncan
League of Liars. M. Pick
League of Life. M. Gerard
League of Light. J. Creasey
League of Matthias. B. Flynn
League of Missing Men. J. M. Walsh
League of Nameless Men. J. Cassells
League of Night and Fog. D. Morrell
League of St. Louis. D. Whitelaw
League of Seven. M. Everard
League of Terror. B. Granger
League of the Lotus. A. Eadie
League of the Ring and Torn Apart. M. O'Brien
League of the Scarlet Pimpernel. Baroness Orczy
League of the Triangle. L. Lurgan
League of the Twisted Horseshoe. Anonymous
League of the White Hand. O. Crawford
League of the Yellow Skull. H. J. S. Anderton
League of Three. Old Sleuth
League of Twelve. G. Boothby
League of Twelve. G. Stanley
Leah Kleschna. C. M. S. McLellan

Lean Years. H. Bindloss
Leaning Man. C. Bush
Leap Before You Look. S. Waldron
Leap for the Sun. M. Hartmann
Leap in the Dark. Donald Gordon
Leap in the Dark. A. McCandless
Leap in the Dark. W. Massey
Leap in the Dark. L. G. Moberly
Leap in the Dark. Rona Randall
Leap in the Dark. M. Richmond
Leap in the Dark. E. Southworth
Leaps and Bounds. W. P. Ridge
Learning Tree. G. Parks
Lease of Convict 308. E. W. Alais
Leases of Death. M. B. Gaunt
Least of All Evils. H. Arvonen
Leather Albatross. W. C. Odell
Leather Duke. F. Gruber
Leather Man. L. Treat
Leather Mask. A. Pratt
Leatherface. E. Dudley
Leatherface Lonergan Stakes a Claim. P. Renwick
Leatherjacket. Arthur Wise
Leathermouth. C. Dawe
Leathermouth's Luck. C. Dawe
Leave a Message for Willie. M. Muller
Leave Everything to Me. O. F. Jerome
Leave Her to Heaven. Ben Ames Williams
Leave Her to Hell! F. Flora
Leave It to Amanda. H. K. Maxwell
Leave It to Conquest. B. Gray
Leave It to Me. M. Cronin
Leave It to Me. G. Joseph
Leave It to Me. H. Lugar
Leave It to the Hangman. B. Knox
Leave It to the Toff. J. Creasey
Leave Murder to Me. R. Powell
Leave of Absence. Eric Bailey
Leave the Dead Behind Us. P. McCutchan
Leaven of Malice. Clare Curzon
Leavenworth Case. A. K. Green
Leavenworth Case. B. Ring
Leavenworth Irregulars. W. D. Blankenship
Leaves from an Old Portfolio. E. M. Barron
Leaves from Arcady. H. A. Vachell
Leaves from the Diary of a Law-Clerk. Waters
Leaves from the Journal of a Custom-House Officer. W. Russell
Leaves from the Note Book of a Chief of Police. A. Hughes
Leaves from the Note-Book of a New York Detective. J. B. Williams
Leaves from the Notebook of a New York Detective. Anonymous
Leavetaking. Anna Gilbert
Leavetaking. G. Milner
Leaving Mt. Venus. W. Hanley
Lebanon Paradise. E. Atiyah
Lecherous Academician. L. Mengchu
Lecoq, the Detective's Daughter. W. Busnach
Lecretia. F. Chamberlain
Led to the Light. M. A. Denison
Ledge. G. Schweitzer
Ledger. D. Uhnak
Ledger Is Kept. R. Postgate
Leech Club. G. W. Owen
Leeds Fiasco. Angus Ross
Leering House. B. Symons
Lees and Leaven. E. W. Townsend
Leffert's Disease. P. A. Lake
Left for Dead. Basil Carey
Left for Dead. D. Haring
Left Hand Left. M. Massey
Left Hand of God. J. Lane
Left-Handed Death. R. Hull
Left-Handed Murder. A. Carruthers
Left-Handed Passenger. F. Riesenberg
Left-Handed Policeman. R. Westbrook
Left-Handed Shell. James Grant
Left-Handed Sleeper. T. Willis
Left Leg. A. Tilton
Left of North. J. Friel
Left, Right and Centre. R. Brandon
Lefty Cuts Loose. B. Shannon

Lefty Hands It Out. B. Shannon
Lefty O'Connor Moves In. B. Shannon
Lefty Takes Over. B. Shannon
Legacy. A. Askew
Legacy. D. Bagley
Legacy. F. Hurd
Legacy. J. A. Krentz
Legacy. J. H. Schmitz
Legacy from Tenarife. R. MacLeod
Legacy in Blood. M. Allingham
Legacy in Green. D. Whitelaw
Legacy Lady. D. Haring
Legacy Lenders. H. Q. Masur
Legacy of a Spy. H. S. Maxfield
Legacy of Cain. W. Collins
Legacy of Danger. A. Andre
Legacy of Danger. Richard Grant
Legacy of Danger. P. McGerr
Legacy of Death. M. Burton
Legacy of Death. R. A. J. Walling
Legacy of Demons. P. Molloy
Legacy of Doon. E. J. Murray
Legacy of Emeralds. Dorinne Moore
Legacy of Evil. A. Clarke
Legacy of Evil. Lydia Belknap Long
Legacy of Evil. A. Pritchett
Legacy of Fear. K. T. Anders
Legacy of Fear. V. Coffman
Legacy of Fear. F. D. Hancock
Legacy of Fear. J. Lovesmith
Legacy of Fear. A. Skene
Legacy of Fear. Garnett Weston
Legacy of Hate. Nicholas Carter
Legacy of Hate. T. Douglas
Legacy of Hate. R. Hardinge
Legacy of Ladysmith. J. K. Crane
Legacy of Lanshore. F. Howe
Legacy of Lehr. K. Kurtz
Legacy of Lillian Parker. L. Holden
Legacy of Loneliness. S. Wagner
Legacy of Mendoubia. J. Reddoch
Legacy of Merton Manor. D. B. Francis
Legacy of Peril. W. M. Graydon
Legacy of Redfern. J. Judson
Legacy of Shadows. R. Batchelor
Legacy of Shame. J. W. Bobin
Legacy of Terror. K. Cameron
Legacy of Terror. D. Dwyer
Legacy of the Golden Key. W. H. Brown
Legacy of the Granite Hills. B. Mitford
Legacy of the Lake. M. A. Smith
Legacy of the Lost. J. Wetherell
Legacy of the Wolf. J. Raynes
Legacy of Vengeance. J. W. Bobin
Legacy of Vengeance. P. Trent
Legacy of Winterwyck. C. Morland
Legal Fiction. E. Ferrars
Legal Fire. O. Stanley
Legal Practitioner. C. Tearle
Legal Settlement. Harrington Strong
Legal Wreck. W. Gillette
Legatee. J. Pattinson
Legend. Evelyn Anthony
Legend. N. Conde
Legend in Blue Steel. S. Page
Legend in Green Velvet. Elizabeth Peters
Legend of Baverstock Manor. N. Buckingham
Legend of Blackhurst. M. Heath
Legend of Crownpoint. M. Heath
Legend of Death. D. Daniels
Legend of Fyrie Castle. K. G.
Legend of Hatred. A. Andre
Legend of Holderly Hall. K. Cameron
Legend of Joseph Nokato. L. P. Bachmann
Legend of Lizzie. Reginald Lawrence
Legend of Lostwithiel. E. F. Wells
Legend of Molly Moor. L. Du Breuil
Legend of Monk's Court. Dorinne Moore
Legend of Piper's Hole. P. Farmer
Legend of Raikes Cross. S. Ready
Legend of the Grey Castle. R. Eldridge
Legend of the Loch. Alanna Knight
Legend of the Seventh Virgin. V. Holt
Legend of the Slain Soldiers. M. Muller

L

Legend of the Thirteenth Pilgrim. J. North
Legend of Witchwind. J. Hines
Legends of a Nunnery. E. Montague
Legends of My Bungalow. F. Boyle
Legion. W. P. Blatty
Legion of the Living Dead. C. J. Daly
Legion of the Lost. J. Creasey
Legionnaire. J. D. Newsom
Legionnaire Spy. W. B. Bannerman
Legions of the Death Master. C. Steele
Legions of the Kaiser. J. Tregellis
Legislative Body. J. L. Hensley
Legs. W. Kennedy
Leighton Court. H. Kingsley
Leighton Grange. M. E. Braddon
Leila and Her Lover. M. Pemberton
Leipzig Affair. J. D. White
Leipzig Manuscript. Angus Ross
Leisure Dying. L. O'Donnell
Leland Case. H. Somerville
Leland Legacy. D. Daniels
Lemmings. C. Blackstock
Lemon Garden. E. Rossiter
Lemon in the Basket. C. Armstrong
Lemons Never Lie. R. Stark
Lemoyne Heritage. L. B. Long
Lena Hates Men. M. Neville
Lend a Hand. J. S. Blazer
Lend a Hand to Murder. M. Halliday
Lend Me a Rod. D. Linton
Lend Me Your Ears. A. M. Stein
Lenient Beast. F. Brown
Lenore. M. E. Edward
Leo Conversion. David Smith
Leo Wyoming Caper. J. Mandelkau
Leonard Harlowe. Waters
Leonardo and Others. Michael Sellers
Leonardo Touch. J. Eyerly
Leonardo's Law. W. B. Murphy
Leonora. W. V. Herbert
Leopard. R. A. Smith
Leopard and the Cliff. W. Breem
Leopard Cat's Cradle. Jerome Barry
Leopard Died Too. N. Brent
Leopard Hunts in Darkness. Wilbur Smith
Leopard in the Grass. Desmond Stewart
Leopard Lady. E. C. Carpenter
Leopard Man. R. C. Armour
Leopard-Paw Orchid. K. Allsop
Leopard Valley. C. K. MacKinnon
Leopard with a Thin Skin. J. B. Watney
Leopard's Prey. Rogayle Franklin
Leopard's Spots. A. Soutar
Leopard's Spots. F. M. White
Leopold Contract. G. Wolk
Leopold's Way. E. D. Hoch
Leper of St. Giles. Ellis Peters
Leper's Bell. M. Sparroy
Lepke. J. Pearl
Leprechaun Murders. Adrian Reynolds
Lerouge Case. E. Gaboriau
Lesko's Ghost. J. R. Maxim
Less Black Than We're Painted. J. Payn
Less Than the Dust. L. Crichton
Less Than the Dust. K. Lindsay
Lesser Antilles Case. R. King
Lesser Evil. R. Chambers
Lesser Evil. I. D. Hardy
Lessing Murder Case. S. Horler
Lessinger Comes Back. R. Essex
Lessinger Laughs Last. R. Essex
Lessinger's Lapse. R. Essex
Lesson in Crime. G. D. H. Cole
Lesson in Crime and other stories. G. D. H. Cole
Lesson in Dying. A. Cleeves
Lesson in Love. C. Virmonne
Lesson in Murder. S. Claydon
Lesson in Murder. J. B. Hilton
Lesson Is Murder. J. Hoppe
Lesson Time. A. Bayes
Lessons in Murder. C. McNab
Lester Affair. A. Garve
Lester Grayling, K.C. L. J. Lynwood
Lester's Secret. M. C. Hay

Lestrade and the Brother of Death. M. J. Trow
Lestrade and the Deadly Game. M. J. Trow
Lestrade and the Guardian Angel. M. J. Trow
Lestrade and the Hallowed House. M. J. Trow
Lestrade and the Leviathan. M. J. Trow
Lestrade and the Ripper. M. J. Trow
L'Estrange Case. John Bentley
Let Dead Enough Alone. R. Lockridge
Let Him Die. E. H. Clements
Let Him Go Hang. B. Clifton
Let Him Go, Let Him Tarry. M. Penoyre
Let Him Have Judgment. B. Hamilton
Let Him Stay Dead. T. C. H. Jacobs
Let It Go at That. E. Dane
Let It Lie. J. Goodwin
Let Justice Be Done. Mark Allerton
Let Justice Be Done! M. Poole
Let Me Kill You, Sweetheart. K. Carr
Let Me Kill You, Sweetheart. F. Flora
Let My People Be. D. Reid
Let No Man Write My Epitaph. W. Motley
Let Not Thy Left Hand. L. Gorell
Let or Hindrance. E. H. Clements
Let or Hindrance. E. Lemarchand
Let Sleeping Afghans Lie. M. Thall
Let Sleeping Dogs Lie. T. Heald
Let Sleeping Dogs Lie. J. R. Riggs
Let Sleeping Girls Lie. J. Mayo
Let the Bastards Freeze in the Dark. D. Simmons
Let the Crags Comb Out Her Dainty Hair. J. Marten
Let the Dead Past—. J. S. Strange
Let the Dead Sleep On. D. Bogard
Let the Dead Sleep On. B. Channing
Let the Lady Die. B. Winter
Let the Man Die. S. H. Courtier
Let the Night Cry. Charlie Wells
Let the Skeletons Rattle. F. C. Davis
Let the Tiger Die. M. Coles
Let the Witness Die. I. Lambot
Let Them Eat Bullets. H. Schoenfeld
Let Them Pray. S. Harvester
Let Tomorrow Come. A. J. Barr
Let Us Prey. Gerald Hammond
Let Us Prey. M. Quill
Let Well Alone. E. C. R. Lorac
Let X Be the Murderer. C. Witting
Let X Equal Murder. E. Healey
Lethal Assault. F. Garrett
Lethal in Love. Carter Brown
Lethal Injection. J. Nisbet
Lethal Lady. R. King
Lethal Lady. J. McPartland
Lethal Lovely. D. Haring
Lethal Orders. J. Pattinson
Lethal Playground. D. Franklin
Lethal Prey. Nick Carter
Lethal Trade. D. Stivers
Lethal Vintage. M. Sylvester
Lethal Weapon. J. Norst
Lethbridge of the Moor. M. Drake
Letitia, the Dreamer. R. Kimbrough
Let's Ask Aunt. M. Godwyn
Let's Choose Executioners. Sara Woods
Let's Count Our Dead. H. Whittington
Let's Face It. A. Bocca
Let's Go. Snip Taylor
Let's Go Play at the Adams'. M. W. Johnson
Let's Hear It for the Deaf Man. E. McBain
Let's Kill Again. R. Dudgeon
Let's Kill Agatha Christie. A. Hinds
Let's Kill Ames. K. Robeson
Let's Kill George. L. Cores
Let's Kill Uncle. R. O'Grady
Let's Kill Uncle Lionel. J. York
Let's Murder Marsha. M. Ferris
Let's Not Get Smart. A. Bocca
Let's Pretend. Jacqueline Wilson
Let's Rob Roy. G. Kraft
Let's Shoot This Out. R. Angel
Let's Talk of Graves, of Worms, and Epitaphs. R. Player
Let's Talk of Wills. S. J. Mason
Letter. W. S. Maugham

Letter-Box Man. A. Sewart
Letter E. W. LeQueux
Letter for Obi. J. F. Straker
Letter from a Stranger. L. Robin
Letter from Kiev. H. C. McDonald
Letter from Spain. F. P. Keyes
Letter from the Dead. A. Clarke
Letter of Intent. U. Curtiss
Letter of the Law. Carole Berry
Letter to a Dead Girl. S. Jepson
Letter to a Ghost. A. Furness
Letters for a Spy. A. C. Ley
Letters of a Shanghai Griffin. J. Denby
Letters of Discredit. P. Harris
Letters of Marque. A. P. Terhune
Letting Blood. R. Platt
Letty Lynton. M. B. Lowndes
Levanter. E. Ambler
Levantine. P. Delacorte
Levantine Trade. J. Pattinson
Level Five. D. Hart-Davis
Level with Me. D. Haring
Lever's Folly. B. Care
Leviathan. R. Shea
Levine. D. E. Westlake
Levity Hicks. T. Gallon
Levy Caper. D. Shaw
Lew Archer, Private Investigator. R. Macdonald
Lewker in Norway. G. Carr
Lewker in Tirol. G. Carr
Lexicon Murders. D. Whitelaw
Lezaire Mystery. A. Griffiths
Li Kwang's Dagger. F. Johnston
Li Ting of London and other stories. G. R. Sims
Liability Limited. J. A. Saxon
Liar Dice. J. S. Mosher
Liars. Peter Hill
Liars and Tyrants and People Who Turn Blue. B. Paul
Liar's Dice. C. A. Charles
Liar's League. D. Delman
Libel. E. Wooll
Libel Was a Blonde. M. Brody
Liberation. I. Ostrander
Liberation of Lord Byron Jones. J. H. Ford
Liberators. J. Cleary
Liberators. J. Pattinson
Libertines. Douglas Clark
Libertines. H. Clewes
Liberty Bar. G. Simenon
Liberty Corps. Mark Roberts
Liberty Two. R. Lypsyte
Liberty Watch. M. Gregory
Libra. D. Delillo
Library of Alex Brandt. C. St. John
Library of Death. R. S. L. Harding
Library of Fiction. Anonymous
Libya Connection. D. Pendleton
Libyan Contract. Paul Mann
Libyan Kill. W. O'Neill
Libyan Warlord. R. Skimin
License Renewed. J. Gardner
License to Kill. N. Daniels
License to Murder. E. Morgan
Licensed for Murder. J. Rhode
Lid Off. John Aiken
Lidless Eye. P. Romsey
Lidy Takes Plenty. B. Sarto
Lie a Little, Die a Little. Michael Brett
Lie Direct. Sara Woods
Lie Down, I Want to Talk to You. W. P. McGivern
Lie Down in Darkness. H. R. Hays
Lie Down, Killer. R. S. Prather
Lie Down with Lions. K. Follett
Lie Fallow My Acre. G. Joseph
Lie Like a Lady. C. S. Cody
Lie Quiet in Your Grave. M. L. Roby
Lie to Me. David Martin
Lie Witnesses. W. V. Butler
Liege-Killer. C. Hinz
Liers in Wait. Raymond Lawrence
Lies. R. Neely
Lies of Silence. Brian Moore
Lieutenant and Others. H. C. McNeile

Lieutenant Barnabas. F. Barrett
Lieutenant Bones. E. Wallace
Lieutenant Flynn, R. N. E. L. Long
Lieutenant Must Be Mad. H. H. Kirst
Lieutenant of the King. M. Gerard
Lt. Pascal's Tastes in Homicide. H. Pentecost
Lieutenant What's-His-Name. M. Futrelle
Life. D. Torbett
Life Adjuster. E. Cannon
Life, Adventure and Opinions of a Liverpool Policeman and His Contemporaries. Anonymous
Life—and a Fortnight. M. Peterson
Life and Adventures of George St. Julian, the Prince of Swindlers. H. Cockton
Life and Adventures of Roxana. D. Defoe
Life and Adventures of William Thornley in Old Van Diemen's Land. C. Rowcroft
Life and Crimes of Harry Lavender. Marele Day
Life and Death in the Country. C. A. Moreton
Life and Death of a Tough Guy. B. Appel
Life and Death of Lilian Faulds. H. McLeave
Life and Death of Peter Wade. Lionel Black
Life at Stake. P. Andreae
Life at Stake. I. Stark
Life Between. Roy Vickers
Life Cycle. H. Carmichael
Life Experiences of a Detective. A. W. Scott
Life Fashionable. P. Traill
Life for a Death. G. Ashe
Life for a Life. A. Bloomfield
Life for a Life. H. Fanger
Life for a Life. M. M. Murray
Life for Ruth. W. Drummond
Life for Sale. S. Horler
Life Goes On Forever. D. Selves
Life Has No Price. D. O'Neill
Life He Stole. S. Kyle
Life in America. W. G. Simms
Life in London. Anonymous
Life in New York. Old Sleuth
Life in Paris. Vidocq
Life in the Bush. Anonymous
Life in the Far West. C. H. Simpson
Life in the Mines. C. H. Simpson
Life Is Like That. A. E. Coppard
Life Is No Bargain. P. Graham
Life Is Short. L. Della
Life Line. Rebecca York
Life Must Go On. M. Crombie
Life of a Nobody. Winifred Graham
Life of Anson Bunker, "The Bloody Hand." Anonymous
Life of Colonel Jack. D. Defoe
Life of Ease. P. De Polnay
Life of Her Own. M. Brandel
Life of Sweeney Todd, the Demon Barber of Fleet Street. Anonymous
Life of the Party. E. Jordan
Life on the Bowery. T. J. Kelly
Life on the Nile. J. Elliott
Life on the Ocean Wave. G. Hackforth-Jones
Life Penalty. J. Fielding
Life Perilous. C. Dawe
Life-Preserver. J. Pattinson
Life Scenes in Our Great Cities and other strange and wonderful tales. J. C. Vail
Life Sentence. H. C. Bailey
Life Sentence. W. W. Burgess
Life Sentence. M. A. Hamilton
Life Sentence. O. Hesky
Life Sentence. A. Sergeant
Life Story of Madame Zelle, the World's Most Beautiful Spy. H. De Halsalle
Life That Kills. Grace M. White
Life to Life. D. Pendleton
Life to Lose. L. Hammond
Life We Live. G. R. Sims
Lifeblood. P. N. Elrod
Lifeline. P. Bottome
Lifer. J. Phelan
Life's Arrears. F. Warden
Life's Assize. J. H. Riddell
Life's Atonement. D. C. Murray
Life's Easy, Huh? D. Haring

Life's Golden Web. J. B. Harris-Burland
Life's Reminiscences of Scotland Yard. A. Lansdowne
Life's Secret. H. Wood
Life's Wheel. L. Morley
Life's Work. J. Valin
Lift and the Drop. G. V. Galwey
Lift High the Flag. B. Schwarz
Lift Murder. R. Francis Foster
Lift-Off at Satan. Richard Butler
Lift Shaft Crime. W. Jardine
Lift up the Lid. Anthony Gilbert
Lifted Curtains. E. Noble
Lifted Latch. T. Frank
Lifting of the Shadow. O. Binns
Light Above the Crossroads. J. L. Rickard
Light and a Dark Christmas. H. Wood
Light and Darkness. Mrs. C. Crowe
Light and the Shadows. R. W. Howe
Light Beyond. E. P. Oppenheim
Light Cavalry Action. J. Harris
Light Fingered Ladies. A. Livingston
Light-Fingered Lady. L. Barbee
Light-Fingered Lady. S. Rabe
Light Freights. W. W. Jacobs
Light from a Lantern. J. Stagge
Light from a Lone Star. J. Vance
Light in Dends Wood, and other stories. T. Dagless
Light in the Swamp. V. Johnston
Light in the Tower. M. Lynch
Light in the Tower. Marilyn Ross
Light in the Upper Storey. F. Warden
Light in the Window. M. Lynn
Light of Day. E. Ambler
Light on Murder. E. Messenger
Light Refreshment. W. P. Ridge
Light Side of the Law. G. A. MacDonald
Light That Jailed. Charles Bell
Light That Lies. J. L. Rickard
Light That Lures. P. Brebner
Light Thickens. N. Marsh
Light Through Glass. E. Lemarchand
Light Woman. C. Gavin
Lightbody on Liberty. N. Balchin
Lighted Match. C. N. Buck
Lighted Room. L. Cooper
Lighted Way. E. P. Oppenheim
Lighter of Candles. O. Cecil
Lighthearted Quest. A. Bridge
Lighthouse. B. Pronzini
Lighthouse. M. J. Ragosta
Lighthouse Mystery. R. A. Armour
Lighthouse Mystery. G. Volk
Lighthouse of the Gannets. Anonymous
Lighting Seven Candles. C. Lombardi
Lightly Lost. H. Smart
Lightning. D. R. Koontz
Lightning. E. McBain
Lightning Conductor Comes Back. A. M. Williamson
Lightning Crime. B. Luigi
Lightning May Strike Anywhere. M. Eldridge
Lightning Over Mayfair. J. Monmouth
Lightning Sketches. G. Baillee
Lightning Strikes. Jon Barton
Lightning Strikes Twice. J. Potts
Lightning Strikes Twice. L. Thayer
Lightning Tree. Joan Aiken
Lightning Tree. J. Crecy
Lightning's Eye. R. Savage
Lights Are Warm and Coloured. W. Norfolk
Lights, Camera, Death. E. Fulton
Lights, Camera, Murder. John Shepherd
Lights, Camera . . . Murder. D. Snell
Lights of Skaro. D. Dodge
Lights Out. J. Cello
Lights Out. P. S. McCoy
Lights That Did Not Fail. M. Annesley
Lightship. S. Lenz
Lightship Murders. N. Wray
Lightsource. Bari Wood
Ligny's Lake. S. H. Courtier
Like a Guilty Thing. B. Cobb
Like a Hole in the Head. J. H. Chase

Like a Lamb to the Slaughter. L. Block
Like a Man. J. Lane
Like a Rose. M. Peterson
Like an Evening Gone. J. Burrows
Like and Unlike. M. E. Braddon
Like Another Helen. G. Horton
Like Any Other Fugitive. J. Hayes
Like Crazy. H. Janson
Like Father, Like Son. J. Payn
Like Hell I Hate. H. Vogel
Like Ice She Was. W. Ard
Like Lethal. H. Janson
Like Love. E. McBain
Like Men Betrayed. John Mortimer
Like Poison. H. Janson
Like Shadows on the Wall. W. B. Maxwell
Like Unto a Merchant. M. A. Gray
Like Water. I. R. G. Hart
Likely to Die. J. Roffman
Lil. J. Middlemass
Lil of the Slums. D. Donovan
Lila My Lovely. Dudley Dean
Lilac Bride Mysterh. M. Crossley
Lilac Is for Sharing. J. Blackmore
Lilac Mansion. E. Hehl
Lilac Night. M. T. Hinkemeyer
Lilies for Laura. S. Markham
Lilies for Madame. H. Austin
Lilies for My Lovely. H. Janson
Lilies in Her Garden Grew. F. C. Davis
Lilies That Fester. I. Wilson
Lilith. K. Kellow
Lilith. E. Southworth
Lilith. F. Warden
Lilla Hart. C. Burdette
Lilli Marlene. K. Lindsay
Lillian's Vow. Mrs. E. B. Collins
Lily and the Devil. A. Askew
Lily Dale. P. Tabori
Lily Field. Constance Rutherford
Lily Hand and other stories. E. Pargeter
Lily Henry. M. K. Cooper
Lily in Her Coffin. B. Benson
Lily Pond. D. Daniels
Lily-Pond Mystery. G. Davison
Lily, the Felon's Daughter. T. Taggart
Limb of Satan. P. Souvestre
Limbo. J. P. DeSario
Limbo. J. Hammil
Limbo. J. Lara
Limbo. V. McConnor
Limbo Affair. A. Firth
Limbo City. E. B. Self
Limbo Connection. D. Quinn
Limbo Line. V. Canning
Limbo Lover. H. Janson
Limbo Touch. J. Weeks
Lime Pit. J. Valin
Limehouse Incident. J. A. Jordan
Limehouse Nights. T. Burke
Limelight. T. Feely
Limelight for Jane. Elizabeth Ford
Limericks of Lachasse. J. Sherwood
Lime's Crisis. R. Bass
Limey. J. Spenser
Limey Breaks In. J. Spenser
Limit. P. Lacey
Limit Bid! Limit Bid! C. B. Clement
Limited Hold-Up. Nicholas Carter
Limited Liability. H. H. C. Gibbons
Limited Options. P. Harcourt
Limited Partner. M. Lupica
Limited Partnerships. L. Zeidner
Limited Vision. R. Lewis
Limits and Renewals. R. Kipling
Limits of Pain. K. A. Blom
Limmerston Hall. H. W. Chapman
Limner. P. D. Boles
Limping Death. A. Stapleton
Limping Goose. F. Gruber
Limping Man. M. Erskine
Limping Man. F. Grierson
Limping Sailor. J. Brooke
Lincoln Diddle. B. Steward

Lincoln Highwayman. P. Dickey
Lincoln McKeever. E. Lipsky
Lincoln's Inn Tragedy. W. J. Bayfield
Lincoln's Inn Tragedy. A. Blair
Linda Walked Alone. J. MacKenzie
Lindbergh's Son. J. Vernon
Linden Affair. M. Albrand
Linden Tree. H. Rowan
Linden Walk Tragedy. F. Daingerfield
Lindsey. J. Jenkins
Line Between. S. Toye
Line by Line. A. Schor
Line Engaged. J. De Leon
Line of Duty. E. Tidyman
Line of Fire. D. Hamilton
Line of Fire. R. Parkes
Line of Fire. D. Pendleton
Line of Succession. B. Garfield
Line of Succession. W. B. Murphy
Line on Ginger. R. Maugham
Line-Up. F. Kane
Line Up. H. Lugar
Line-Up. H. Reilly
Line Up for Murder. M. Babson
Line-Up for Murder. F. C. Ticknor
Lines and Shadows. J. Wambaugh
Lingala Code. W. Kiefer
Link. C. Henry
Linked Lives. D. K. Roy
Linton Porcupine. R. Laidlaw
Linz Tattoo. N. Guild
Linz Testament. L. Perdue
Linz Trust. R. Pennington
Ligard. Colin Wilson
Lingo Dan. P. Pollard
Link. H. Carmichael
Link. P. MacDonald
Link. R. Maugham
Link by Link. J. W. Bobin
Link by Link. C. Courtenay
Link by Link. D. Donovan
Link by Link. N. D. Urner
Linked by Peril. B. Bolt
Linked to Crime. B. North
Linked with Fate. J. L. Berry
Linkram Jewels. J. Laurence
Links in the Chain. S. Campbell
Links in the Chain. H. Hill
Links in the Chain. J. Rhode
Linnet. G. Allen
Linnet Estate. D. Polk
Linnet Singing. D. Eden
Linnet's Folly. J. Aeby
Lint House Mystery. N. Oakley
Linton Memorial. L. Lloyd
Lion Against Bear. S. Drew
Lion and the Jackal. W. T. Tyler
Lion and the Lamb. E. P. Oppenheim
Lion and the Lizard. J. Rawlinson
Lion and the Mouse. A. Hornblow
Lion and the Unicorn. R. H. Davis
Lion at the Door. N. Thornberg
Lion by the Mane. Eva Dane
Lion Game. J. H. Schmitz
Lion in the Cellar. P. Branch
Lion in the Valley. Elizabeth Peters
Lion in Wait. D. Gardiner
Lion Is Rampant. R. Laidlaw
Lion Men. J. Crosbie
Lion Murders. Elwood Brown
Lion of Cooling Bay. P. Paul
Lion of Delos. A. Worboys
Lion of Petra. T. Mundy
Lion of the Law. S. Campbell
Lion? or Murder? D. Gardiner
Lion Rampant. William Paul
Lion Trimphant. P. Carr
Lions at Night. R. Himmel
Lions at the Kill. S. Kent
Lion's Cage. J. Clive
Lion's Claw. J. B. Harris-Burland
Lion's Claws. F. Delmere
Lion's Fire. W. Barker
Lion's Gate. Jan Alexander

Lion's Mouse. C. N. Williamson
Lion's Mouth. J. Corbett
Lions of Judah. T. Willis
Lion's Ransom. P. Loraine
Lion's Run. C. Thomas
Lion's Share. J. Man
Lion's Share. O. Thanet
Lion's Way. L. Orde
Lip-Service. L. J. Vance
Lips of Death. D. Linton
Lips of Death. David Steel
Lips That Died. Aileen Grey
Lipstick Clue. R. Goyne
Lipstick Larceny. Carter Brown
Liquid Death. Griff
Liquid Jungle. G. Janes
Liquid Terror. E. Graves
Liquidated and The Seer. R. Lindau
Liquidator. R. L. Brent
Liquidator. Nick Carter
Liquidator. J. Gardner
Liquor Is Quicker. H. Janson
Lisa Bastian. J. Wood
Lisping Man. F. Rawlings
List. Nick Carter
List. G. F. Newman
List of Adrian Messenger. P. MacDonald
Listen for a Stranger. S. Devine
Listen for the Click. J. L. Breen
Listen for the Whisperer. P. A. Whitney
Listen, Lovely. Keith Campbell
Listen, Please Listen. N. A. Hintze
Listen to Danger. D. Eden
Listen to the Children. Jennie Melville
Listen to the Mocking Bird. S. H. Courtier
Listener. A. Blackwood
Listener. T. Du Bois
Listener. John Gill
Listening Boy. P. Hambledon
Listening Eye. P. Wentworth
Listening House. M. Seeley
Listening In. C. Moore
Listening in the Dusk. C. Fremlin
Listening Man. J. A. Moroso
Listening Silence. H. Lillie
Listening Walls. M. Millar
Listening Woman. T. Hillerman
Listening Woman. M. Sparrow
Lister Legacy. J. Drabek
Listerdale Mystery. A. Christie
Litany of Evil. Alice Brennan
Literary Melange. S. Whiting
Literary Upshots or Split Reading. R. Mallett
Litmore Snatch. Henry Wade
Little Anarchist. A. W. Marchmont
Little Angie. E. Cave
Little Aversion and other stories. M. C. Hay
Little Big Shot. D. Haring
Little Black Book. M. Avallone
Little Blue Goddess. W. LeQueux
Little Boxes of Bewilderment. J. Ritchie
Little Boy Blue. E. Bunker
Little Boy Laughed. J. Dow
Little Boy Lost. L. Egan
Little Boy Lost. J. Ludwig
Little Boy Lost. D. Wolman
Little Bronze Man. Anonymous
Little Brother. B. Eidson
Little Brother. J. McNeil
Little Brother Fate. M. C. Roberts
Little Brother of God. L. H. Gordon
Little Brother Sherlock. L. Turner
Little Brothers. D. S. Davis
Little Caesar. W. R. Burnett
Little Caesars. E. De Roo
Little Captain. H. C. Bailey
Little Class on Murder. C. G. Hart
Little Clews. W. E. Hingston
Little Colonel. Old Sleuth
Little Company. M. Elmblad
Little Comrade. B. E. Stevenson
Little Cowboy. Old Sleuth
Little Cowboy in New York. Old Sleuth
Little Crime. J. N. Chance

Little Cuba. G. L. Barclay
Little Czar of Chicago. A. Capelli
Little Darling, Dead. J. S. Scott
Little David. E. Chaze
Little Dead-Sure. Old Sleuth
Little Death. M. Nava
Little Death Music. Joan Higgins
Little Doctor. G. Simenon
Little Dog Barked. A. Rowe
Little Dog Laughed. Joseph Hansen
Little Dog Laughed. L. Merrick
Little Dog's Day. J. T. Story
Little Doll. P. Garrod
Little Doves of Destruction. G. Wolfenden
Little Dragon from Peking. J. Eastwood
Little Drops of Blood. B. Knox
Little Drummer Girl. J. Le Carre
Little Entertainments. B. Pain
Little Ferret. R. Foxall
Little Fishes. Arthur Wise
Little Fortune. A. Fredericks
Little Game. F. Farrington
Little Gentle Sleuthing. B. Rowlands
Little Gentleman from Okehampstead. E. P. Oppenheim
Little Giant. Old Sleuth
Little Girl in a Big City. J. K. McCurdy
Little Girl Lost. C. Bolton
Little Girl Who Lives Down the Lane. L. Koenig
Little Girls Lost. Doris Shannon
Little God Ben. J. J. Farjeon
Little Gold Ring and other stories. Cosmo Hamilton
Little Green Man. E. Wallace
Little Grey Man. W. Bouchier
Little Grey Mouse. F. Warden
Little Grey Shoe. P. Brebner
Little Hanging Men. P. Groom
Little Hangman. M. Elwin
Little Heiress. F. Cowen
Little Hercules. F. Gruber
Little Hercules. F. Wallace
Little Hour of Peter Wells. D. Whitelaw
Little Killer. G. Paul
Little Lady Killing. J. Webb
Little Lady Linton. F. Barrett
Little Lady of Arrock. D. Whitelaw
Little Lady of Lagunitas. R. H. Savage
Little Lady of the Shot-Gun. L. H. Gordon
Little Learning. B. Deighton
Little Less Than Kind. C. Armstrong
Little Lie. J. Potts
Little Life Stories. H. Johnston
Little Lightning, the Shadow Detective. Police Captain James
Little Local Murder. R. Barnard
Little Lost Lady. W. Morton
Little Madness. L. Kallen
Little Man Blues. E. Mathis
Little Man from Archangel. G. Simenon
Little Man Murders. V. Loder
Little Man Who Wasn't There. Mildred Gordon
Little Matter of Arson. L. Meynell
Little Medicine Bottle. A. Turpin
Little Men, Big World. W. R. Burnett
Little Miner. Old Sleuth
Little Miss Christie. T. J. Kelly
Little Miss David—and Goliath. M. Croll
Little Miss Murder. M. Avallone
Little Miss Murder. Howard Hunt
Little Miss Prim. F. Warden
Little Murder. M. Stone
Little Murder Music. D. Ramsay
Little Murders. J. Feiffer
Little Mysteries. K. Mikolowski
Little Ned's Engagement. E. Southworth
Little Neighborhood Murder. A. J. Orde
Little Novels. W. Collins
Little Novels of Nowadays. P. Gibbs
Little Nugget. P. G. Wodehouse
Little Odessa. J. Koenig
Little Old Ladies. T. Roscoe
Little Old Lady. Roland Daniel
Little Old Man of the Batignolles. E. Gaboriau
Little People. J. Christopher

Little People. H. J. Kennedy
Little Pig-Alle. Y. Audouard
Little Red Captain. C. J. C. Hyne
Little Red Monkey. E. Maschwitz
Little Red Phone. H. Kane
Little Red Shoes. D. C. Spence
Little Red Speck, and other south sea stories. B. Grimshaw
Little Rosebud's Lovers. L. J. Libbey
Little Saigon. T. J. Parker
Little Saint. G. Simenon
Little Sally Does It Again. R. Gillespie
Little Shot. P. Wilde
Little Sin. W. Hardy
Little Sister. R. Chandler
Little Sister. P. J. MacDonald
Little Sister. Lee Roberts
Little Spot of Bother. M. Polland
Little Squaw Big Hurry. S. F. Griffin
Little Stranger. C. McWilliam
Little Tales of Misogyny. P. Highsmith
Little Tales of Smethers, and other stories. Lord Dunsany
Little Terror. C. E. Blaney
Little Time to Stay. J. Garden
Little to the East. R. Cenedella
Little Tragedy at Tien-Tsin. F. A. Mathews
Little Tramp. G. Brewer
Little Treachery. P. Paul
Little Victim. T. P. McMahon
Little Victim Play. A. Hocking
Little Victims. R. Barnard
Little Walls. Winston Graham
Little Wax Doll. P. Curtis
Little White God. E. Brock
Little White Hag. F. Beeding
Little White Hen. Robin Temple
Little White Nun. A. M. Williamson
Little Widow Murder. A. Wood
Little Windows. S. Aumonier
Little Woman in Black. M. E. Braddon
Little Zetta—Killer. N. Rosso
Littlejohn on Leave. G. Bellairs
Live Again, Love Again. D. Keene
Live and Let Die. I. Fleming
Live Bait. B. Knox
Live Bait. A. Mills
Live Bait. Bill Walsh
Live Bait. R. Wills
Live Bait. T. Wood
Live Bait for Murder. W. Herber
Live Cartridge. C. Dawe
Live Dangerously. A. Kielland
Live Flesh. R. Rendell
Live Gold. R. Sheckley
Live It Down. J. C. Jeaffreson
Live Like a Hero. Angus Hall
Live, Love, and Cry. G. B. Mair
Live Lumber. E. L. Long
Live Men's Shoes. R. Marsh
Live Now, Pay Later. J. T. Story
Live Oaks Also Die. R. Gilligan
Live On. M. Dunstan
Live Till You Die. R. Angel
Live to Remember. Lon Davis
Live Wire. Austen Allen
Live Wire. J. Bruce
Live Wire Clew. Nicholas Carter
Lively Corpse. M. Millar
Lively Dead. P. Dickinson
Lively Form of Death. E. Lindall
Lively Form of Death. Kay Mitchell
Lively Game of Death. Marvin Kaye
Lively Luke. Old Sleuth
Lively Peggy. S. J. Weyman
Lives and Times of Bernardo Brown. G. Household
Lives in a Box. Richard Grant
Lives of Harry Lime. O. Welles
Lives of the Twins. Rosamund Smith
Lives to Give. S. De Gramont
Living Alibi. S. Truss
Living and the Dead. P. Boileau
Living Bomb. M. Avallone
Living Capsule. A. S. Withanage

Living Clue. Anonymous
Living Come First. J. Danvers
Living Dangerously. F. E. Penny
Living Dangerously. R. Simpson
Living Dead. M. Waugh
Living Dead Man. L. Scott
Living Death. Nick Carter
Living Demons. R. Block
Living Dog. P. Somerville-Large
Living End. F. Kane
Living Fire Menace. K. Robeson
Living Image. G. S. Gallant
Living in Fear. A. Parsons
Living Link. J. De Mille
Living Mask. Nicholas Carter
Living Mummy. A. Pratt
Living or Dead. H. Conway
Living Shadow. M. Grant
Living Shadow. W. W. Sayer
Living Skeleton. W. J. Fraser
Living Strong-Box. F. Mauzens
Living Things. J. Russo
Living Too Fast. W. T. Adams
Living's a Dying Game. R. Hamilton
Livingston Heirs. H. K. Maxwell
Liz. F. Kane
Liz Assignation. H. Janson
Lizard in the Cup. P. Dickinson
Lizard's Tail. M. Brandel
Lizzie. E. Hunter
Lizzie. S. Jackson
Lizzie and Caroline. Ruth Moore
Lizzie Borden. M. B. Lowndes
Lizzie Borden of Fall River. T. J. Kelly
Lizzie Leigh. E. Gaskell
Llewellin. Anonymous
Lo Sweeny Gang. Roland Daniel
Loaded Dice. E. H. Clark
Loaded Dice. M. Cumberland
Loaded Dice. E. Fawcett
Loaded Dice. P. Marlowe
Loaded Gun. F. Ryck
Loaded Orange. G. Jerome
Loaded Questions. P. Loraine
Loadstone of Love. J. Middlemass
Loan Shark. J. W. O'Dell
Loanshark. P. McCurtin
Loaves and Fishes. B. Capes
Lobelia Grove. A. Rolls
Lobster Guerrillas. W. Mole
Lobster Pick Murder. M. V. Heberden
Lobster Pot. G. Volk
Local Call. M. P. Berthold
Local Color. J. A. Rice
Local Lads. J. S. Scott
Local Matter. J. M. Bennett
Local Murder. P. Whalley
Local Talent. W. Fuller
Local Talent. H. M. Kahler
Location Shots. J. F. Burke
Loch. J. Caird
Loch Sinister. Marilyn Ross
Loch Spy. D. Duff
Lock and Key. A. M. Stein
Lock and the Key. F. Gruber
Lock at Charenton. G. Simenon
Lock the Door, Mademoiselle. T. C. H. Jacobs
Locked Book. F. Packard
Locked Corridor. Marilyn Ross
Locked Door. P. Hawk
Locked Doors. M. R. Rinehart
Locked Room. Herbert Ashton, Jr.
Locked Room. M. Sjowall
Locked Room. W. Spence
Locked Tower. C. Carfax
Locked Up. A. Griffiths
LockeStep. J. Barnao
Locket for Tawi. J. Kinney
Loco-Motion, Commotion, Dr. Gorilla and Me. T. J. Kelly
Locust in the Wind. R. Collin
Lodestar. M. Pemberton
Lodestar. E. Wooll
Lodestar Legacy. Doris Shannon

Lodestar of Death. J. Sandys
Lodestar Project. D. Bradley
Lodge Sinister. Dana Ross
Lodger. M. B. Lowndes
Lodger. G. Simenon
Lodging-House Mystery. R. Hardinge
Lofoton Run. R. Middlemiss
Log Across the Road. Sheila Ross
Logan. A. Joseph
Logan. J. Neal
Logic of the Heart. P. Veryan
Lohengrin. A. Melville-Ross
Lola. Delacorta
Lola Brought Her Wreath. H. Janson
Lola of the Isles. D. W. MacArthur
Lolita Lovers. John Clarke
Lolita Man. Bill James
Lombard Cavalcade. V. Coffman
Lombard Heiress. V. Coffman
Lombard Street Mystery. A. Blair
Lombard Street Mystery. Muirhead Robertson
Lona. John Evans
London. G. Brandner
London Adventures of Mr. Collin. F. Heller
London Affair. Anthony Stuart
London After Midnight. M. Coolridge-Rask
London Assignment. Angus Ross
London Belongs to Me. N. Collins
London, Bloody London. M. Avallone
London Bridge Mystery. J. Arnold
London by Night. Anonymous
London by Night. C. Selby
London Calling. V. Gielgud
London Calling North Pole. H. J. Giskes
London Cobweb. C. Lys
London Connection. Robin Hunter
London Connection. Robin Moore
London Crimes. C. Dickens
London Deal. N. J. Crisp
London Embassy. P. Theroux
London Fields. M. Amis
London Fields. J. Milne
London Gun. B. Heatter
London Lamb. W. B. M. Ferguson
London Lights of Belsize. V. Rendell
London Lovers. D. MacKail
London Match. L. Deighton
London Merchant. G. Lillo
London, 1913. M. Stacpoole
London Only. W. P. Ridge
London Particular. C. Brand
London Plot. C. Dawe
London Pride. M. E. Braddon
London Spy Murders. P. Cheyney
London Switch. Robin Moore
London's Heart. B. L. Farjeon
Lone Commando. J. Sandys
Lone Cottage. T. P. Prest
Lone Crook Murders. C. Ryland
Lone Cross Manor Mystery. M. Danvers
Lone Hand. H. Bindloss
Lone Hand. S. Warwick
Lone House by the Sea. Old Sleuth
Lone House Mystery. E. Wallace
Lone Inn. F. Hume
Lone Isle. E. C. Vivian
Lone Kiwi. F. N. Millar
Lone Lodge Mystery. J. Hawk
Lone Trail. L. Allan
Lone Vendetta. Jean Fraser
Lone Wolf. W. C. Tuttle
Lone Wolf. L. J. Vance
Lone Wolf Returns. L. J. Vance
Lone Wolf's Last Prowl. L. J. Vance
Lone Wolf's Son. L. J. Vance
Loneliest Girl in the World. K. Fearing
Lonely Astronomer. V. Gridban
Lonely Beat. W. Keenan
Lonely Breeze. V. Sillar
Lonely Bungalow. Taffrail
Lonely Cage. F. Usher
Lonely Church. F. Hume
Lonely God. C. Kernahan
Lonely Graves. C. Monig

Lonely Hearts. John Harvey
Lonely Heritage. A. Furness
Lonely Hollow Mystery. T. A. Plummer
Lonely House. J. Blackmore
Lonely House. A. Gask
Lonely House. M. B. Lowndes
Lonely House. A. Streckfuss
Lonely Hunter. C. Wilcox
Lonely Inn Mystery. L. Grex
Lonely Is the Grave. G. J. Barrett
Lonely Island. H. L. V. Fletcher
Lonely, Lovely Lady. J. Monmouth
Lonely Magdalen. Henry Wade
Lonely Man. G. Frankau
Lonely Man. J. T. Phillifent
Lonely Margins. P. Kelly
Lonely Pathway. John Marsh
Lonely Place. B. Copper
Lonely Place. D. Daniels
Lonely Place. R. M. Sears
Lonely Place to Die. W. Ebersohn
Lonely Place to Die. Colin Robertson
Lonely Road. J. Farnol
Lonely Road. N. Shute
Lonely Road Murder. E. Westward
Lonely Russian. N. Shore
Lonely Sea. A. MacLean
Lonely Shore. G. Volk
Lonely Shroud. S. Mitchell
Lonely Side of the River. D. MacKenzie
Lonely Silver Rain. J. D. MacDonald
Lonely Skier. H. Innes
Lonely Sky. E. Couper
Lonely Steeple. Victor Wolfson
Lonely Subaltern. F. Hume
Lonely Target. H. Pentecost
Lonely Terror. S. Mayfield
Lonely the Man Without Heroes. M. S. Power
Lonely Toys. M. Lynch
Lonely Vigils. M. W. Wellman
Lonely Voyage. J. Harris
Lonely Walk. M. E. Chaber
Lonely Water. N. Thurley
Lonely Way to Die. A. Bourgeau
Lonely Way to Die. H. Debrett
Lonely Years. Alan Thomas
Lonelyheart 4122. Colin Watson
Loner. O. Friedrich
Loner. F. Nichols
Lonesome Badger. F. Gruber
Lonesome Road. P. Wentworth
Lonesome Town. E. Dorrance
Lonesome Traveler. J. W. Corrington
Long After Midnight. R. Bradbury
Long and Living Shadow. D. Winston
Long Arm. H. Cecil
Long Arm. S. M. Gardenhire
Long Arm. Alick Harvey
Long Arm. H. Janson
Long Arm. E. P. Oppenheim
Long Arm of Fantomas. P. Souvestre
Long Arm of Gil Hamilton. L. Niven
Long Arm of Mannister. E. P. Oppenheim
Long Arm of Murder. F. Gruber
Long Arm of the Funny Men. M. Tait
Long Arm of the Mounted. J. Dorrance
Long Arm of the Mounted. W. B. Mowery
Long Arm of the Prince. E. Berckman
Long Baffled Capture. I. Stark
Long Beaches, and other south sea stories. B. Grimshaw
Long Body. H. McCloy
Long Bow and Broad Arrow. W. P. Drury
Long Branch Detective. Anonymous
Long Chain of Death. Sarah Wolf
Long Chance. D. Enefer
Long Chase. J. M. Eshleman
Long Chase. J. B. Hendryx
Long Coffin. N. Tranter
Long Cool Day in Hell. G. Kersh
Long Corridor. C. Cookson
Long Corridor. K. Royce
Long Count. R. Faust
Long Dark Night. J. Hayes

Long Dark Night of Baron Samedi. J. Wyllie
Long Dark Night of the Soul. J. Ellis
Long, Dark Tea-Time of the Soul. Douglas Adams
Long Day's Dying. K. Doherty
Long Day's Dying. Alan White
Long Day's Nightmare. N. Robertson
Long Deadly Summer. P. Barnaby
Long Death. G. Dyer
Long Death. D. Hartman
Long Distance. J. A. Dale
Long Distance—Wrong Number. N. Gifford
Long Divorce. E. Crispin
Long Drop. Alan White
Long Echo. K. Hughes
Long Echo. D. Rutherford
Long Echo. R. Severn
Long Escape. D. Dodge
Long Exile. G. Simenon
Long Farewell. M. Innes
Long Fast Ride. A. F. Libby
Long Firm. J. Riley
Long Fuse. Alan White
Long Good Friday. R. Claughton
Long Goodbye. R. Chandler
Long Goodnight. C. D. Burton
Long Green. B. Spicer
Long Green Gaze. V. Fuller
Long-Haired Bill. J. A. Dunn
Long Hand. W. Magnay
Long Hand of Death. Alan White
Long Hard Cure. D. Anthony
Long Hard Look. M. Gair
Long Hate. S. Forbes
Long Haul. A. I. Bezzerides
Long Haul. M. Mills
Long Hot Night. D. Enefer
Long Island Murders. M. W. Glidden
Long Journey Home. M. F. Ford
Long Journey Home. M. Gilbert
Long Journey Home. Mary Raymond
Long Kill. D. Haring
Long Kill. P. Ruell
Long Knife. E. S. De Puy
Long Lane. P. Trent
Long Lane's Turning. H. E. Rives
Long Lankin. J. Banville
Long Lavender Look. J. D. MacDonald
Long Leaf. R. Brock
Long Lines. R. Sutton
Long Live the Dead. J. Kruse
Long Live the King. G. Boothby
Long Live the King. J. Rowe
Long Live the Spy. Charles Russell
Long Masquerade. M. Brent
Long Memory. H. Clewes
Long Memory. M. Cronin
Long Midnight. Alan White
Long Night. F. R. Adams
Long Night. O. Demaris
Long Night. P. B. Gallagher
Long Night. B. Graeme
Long Night. D. Haring
Long Night. H. Howard
Long Night. A. Lyttle
Long Night. S. Truss
Long Night. B. Walton
Long Night of Fear. Marilyn Ross
Long Night Through. H. McCutcheon
Long Nightmare. J. Roebuck
Long Night's Journey. I. MacKersey
Long Night's Walk. Alan White
Long Odds. Gilbert Chester
Long Odds. M. Clarke
Long Odds. H. Smart
Long Orbit. M. Farren
Long Overcoat. P. Fry
Long Patrol. H. A. Cody
Long Patrol. A. M. Treynor
Long Portage. N. Bindloss
Long Pursuit. J. Cleary
Long Reach. K. Hayles
Long Reconnaissance. J. Murphy
Long Rest. B. Copper
Long Revenge. B. Schwarz

Long Revenge. J. Thomson
Long Ride. J. McKimmey
Long Ride Out. V. James
Long Road. A. Furness
Long Run South. Alan Williams
Long Saturday Night. C. Williams
Long Search. G. Ashe
Long Search. S. L. Bell
Long Search. I. Holland
Long Shadow. F. Bryan
Long Shadow. J. Cleary
Long Shadow. C. Fremlin
Long Shadow. Anna Gilbert
Long Shadow. Anthony Gilbert
Long Shadow. J. Pendower
Long Shadow. H. W. Thomas
Long Shadows. J. Cannan
Long Shadows. C. Carnac
Long Shadows. Camilla Hope
Long Shadows. A. D. Sanderson
Long Short Cut. A. Garve
Long Shot. Ken Blake
Long Shot. E. Hely
Long Shot. W. Massey
Long Shot. P. Monette
Long Silence. Paul Costello
Long Silence. N. Freeling
Long Silence. J. R. Gould
Long Silence. Alan White
Long Skeleton. F. Lockridge
Long Sleep. A. Bocca
Long Spoon. C. Bryce
Long Spoon. J. B. O'Sullivan
Long Straight Road. G. Horton
Long Summer. Alan White
Long Teeth. M. H. Albert
Long Thrill. M. Boone
Long Thrill. O. L. Rosmanith
Long Time Dead. P. Chambers
Long Time No Leola. Carter Brown
Long Time No See. E. McBain
Long Time Sleeping. Michael Sinclair
Long Time to Hate. W. D. Roberts
Long Tunnel. S. Fairway
Long Vendetta. J. Gant
Long Wait. M. Spillane
Long Walk Home. M. O'Donnell
Long Walk to Wimbledon. H. R. F. Keating
Long Watch. Alan White
Long Way Down. Elizabeth Fenwick
Long Way Down. D. Hall
Long Way Down. C. Wilcox
Long Way Home. V. Norwood
Long Way Round. M. Maurice
Long Way to Die. J. N. Frey
Long Way to Fall. Angus Hall
Long Way to Go. B. Deal
Long Way to Pitt Street. D. Enefer
Long Way to Shiloh. L. Davidson
Long Week. P. Doncaster
Long White Con. R. Beck
Long Window. J. M. Eshleman
Longbow Murder. V. Luhrs
Longbridge Murders. M. Dalton
Longer Bodies. G. Mitchell
Longer Shadows. B. L. Jacot
Longer the Thread. E. Lathen
Longest Odds. B. Sheinkopf
Longest Pleasure. D. Clark
Longest Pleasure. C. Nicole
Longest Second. B. S. Ballinger
Longshot. Dick Francis
Longshot. D. Mark
Longstreet Legacy. D. Ashe
Loo Loo's Legacy. D. Dodge
Loo Sanction. Trevanian
Look Alive. M. Burton
Look at Me! D. Haring
Look at Murder. N. Deane
Look Back on Death. L. Egan
Look Back on Murder. D. M. Disney
Look Back on Murder. Malcolm Gray
Look Back to Love. V. Packer
Look Behind You. J. Barbette

Title Index

Look Behind You, Lady. M. Erskine
Look Behind You, Lady. A. S. Fleischman
Look Down for Mercy. Max Gordon
Look Down on Her Dying. D. Tracy
Look for the Body. M. F. Christopher
Look in Any Doorway. N. Morland
Look in at Murder. E. Radford
Look Into My Eyes. W. B. Murphy
Look Long Upon a Monkey. James Curtis
Look, No Hans! John Chapman
Look of Innocence. Anna Gilbert
Look Out Behind You. K. Lewis
Look Out for Lonella. Rick Madison
Look Out for Lucifer! E. Dudley
Look Out for Space. W. F. Nolan
Look Over Your Shoulder. A. McAllister
Look Three Ways at Murder. J. Creasey
Look to the Dawn. M. Richmond
Look to the Lady. M. Allingham
Look to the Lady! J. L. Bonney
Look Upon the Prisoner. H. Desmond
Look Who's Talking. R. Adam
Look Your Last. J. S. Strange
Looker. J. Saralegui
Looker-On. W. LeQueux
Looking for a Kidnapper. C. I. Hammons
Looking for Ginger North. J. Dunning
Looking for Rachel Wallace. R. B. Parker
Looking for Sampson. J. N. Chance
Looking for Zoe. D. B. Dodson
Looking-Glass. V. Coffman
Looking-Glass Murder. Anthony Gilbert
Looking-Glass Murders. D. G. Browne
Looking Glass Murders. P. Lore
Looking Glass War. J. Le Carre
Looking Out for #1. M. Monsky
Lookout Cartridge. J. McElroy
Looks That Kill. W. B. Gibson
Loom. J. Remenham
Loom and the Web. C. Gibson-Jarvie
Loom of Justice. E. Lothar
Loom of Mystery. H. R. De Vigne
Loom of Tancred. D. Pearson
Loom of Terror. P. Minton
Loom of the Law. Anonymous
Loop. R. Eden
Loop. W. Hildick
Loop Current. A. Sewart
Loop of String. M. A. Kay
Loophole. A. Maling
Loophole. R. Pollock
Loose Connection. M. Brooks
Loose End. M. Cronin
Loose End. H. Kane
Loose Ends. P. Warner
Loose Lady Death. L. Marshall
Loose Rib. Austen Allen
Loose Screw. G. Hammond
Loose Women. Stuart Hall
Loot! A. Murray
Loot. J. Orton
Loot. A. S. Roche
Loot! A. P. Terhune
Loot Curran, R.N. E. L. Long
Loot from the Temple of Fortune. H. A. Vachell
Loot of Cities. A. Bennett
Loot of France. A. Parsons
Loot of Nana Sahib. H. E. Hill
Loot of Pakistan. A. Parsons
Loot of the Lazy F. W. C. Tuttle
Looted Gold. G. E. C. Webster
Looter from Cell 13. Anonymous
Looters. Albert Conroy
Looters. J. Reese
Lop-Eared Dick. G. F. Monckton
Lopsided Man. B. S. Ballinger
Lord Alistair's Rebellion. A. Upward
Lord and Mary Ann. C. Cookson
Lord Arthur Savile's Crime. C. Cox
Lord Arthur Savile's Crime, and other stories. O. Wilde
Lord Blackshirt. B. Graeme
Lord Cobleigh Disappears. J. C. Snaith
Lord Darcy Investigates. R. Garrett

Lord Edgware Dies. A. Christie
Lord Emsworth and others. P. G. Wodehouse
Lord Have Mercy. Shelley Smith
Lord Heathbury's Revenge. Rachelle Edwards
Lord High Admiral. L. C. Cornford
Lord, I Was Afraid. N. Balchin
Lord John in New York. C. N. Williamson
Lord Lynmore's Life. I. Roy
Lord Mayor of Death. M. Babson
Lord Mayor's Gold. Anonymous
Lord Mayor's Show Mystery. A. Blair
Lord Mullion's Secret. M. Innes
Lord Oakburn's Daughters. H. Wood
Lord of High Cliff Manor. I. M. Pascoe
Lord of Irongray. J. B. Harris-Burland
Lord of Lost Island. Hedley Scott
Lord of Ravensley. C. Heaven
Lord of Terror. M. Allain
Lord of Terror. S. Horler
Lord of the Dead. R. E. Howard
Lord of the Dyke. W. Wood
Lord of the Falcons. L. Harper
Lord of the Far Island. V. Holt
Lord of the Gallows. J. Neil
Lord of the Hollow Dark. R. Kirk
Lord of the Manor. J. Blackmore
Lord of the Manor. F. M. White
Lord of the Sorcerers. Carter Dickson
Lord Penworth's Daughter. F. Warden
Lord Peter. D. L. Sayers
Lord Peter Goes A-Wooing. J. Ronald
Lord Peter Views the Body. D. L. Sayers
Lord Quare's Visitor. F. Warden
Lord Roscoe's Heir. C. H. Bullivant
Lord Satan. L. Bronte
Lord Stranleigh, Philanthropist. Robert Barr
Lord Tony's Wife. Baroness Orczy
Lord Wastwater. S. Bolton
Lords and Ladies. R. M. Gilchrist
Lords of Akchasaz. Y. Kemal
Lords of Castle Weirwyck. E. F. Wells
Lords of Dair. H. Wieselberg
Lords of Human Kind. J. D. White
Lords of the Earth. W. B. Murray
Lords of the Fo'c'sle. Morley Roberts
Lordship, the Passen, and We. F. T. Jane
Lorelei. L. P. Bachmann
Lorelei. D. Rico
Lorena Veiled. M. J. Ragosta
Lori. R. Bloch
Lorie. Old Sleuth
Loring Affair. J. Sherry
Loring Mystery. J. Farnol
Lorrimer's Legacy. Maxwell Scott
Lorry. P. Wahloo
Los Alamos Contract. A. Mather
Los Angeles Be Damned. N. Karta
Los Angeles Holocaust. M. Barry
Los Angeles Number. Anonymous
Los Huecos Mystery. E. T. Sawyer
Lose This Gun. H. Janson
Loser by a Head. H. Giddings
Loser Takes All. G. Greene
Loser Takes Nothing. M. Cronin
Losers. Clifford Irving
Loser's Blues. P. Harcourt
Losers Keepers. A. Mason
Losers Take All. J. J. Lamb
Losers, Weepers. E. Queen
Losers, Weepers. E. Silberstang
Losing Bet. M. Chernenok
Losing Game. F. W. Crofts
Losing Game. H. Nisbet
Losing Game. W. Payne
Loss of a Head. J. Bude
Loss of Heart. R. McCrum
Loss of Innocence. Magali
Loss of Patients. R. McInerny
Loss of the Culion. J. Ashford
Loss of the Jane Vosper. F. W. Crofts
Loss of the "Malpasia" and other stories. J. S. A. Jewell
Lost. G. Devon
Lost. W. Stephens

Lost! A Day. F. C. Milford
Lost Adventures of Sherlock Holmes. K. Greenwald
Lost Ambassador. E. P. Oppenheim
Lost American. B. Freemantle
Lost American. A. C. Gunter
Lost and Found Man. N. Guild
Lost and the Damned. W. Carrier
Lost Angels. D. J. Schow
Lost Armies. W. Karlin
Lost Bank Note. H. Wood
Lost Bride. C. Augusta
Lost Bride. E. Southworth
Lost Caesar. R. Fenisong
Lost Casket. F. Du Boisgobey
Lost Cause. Winifred Duke
Lost Cavern. H. F. Heard
Lost Chittendens. Nicholas Carter
Lost Clue. C. A. Walton
Lost Countess Falka. R. H. Savage
Lost Daughter. M. Cormany
Lost Despatch. N. S. Lincoln
Lost Diamond. D. G. Adee
Lost Diamonds. F. Marryat
Lost Diaries. M. Baring
Lost Diary. H. Bleackley
Lost Diary. J. Sheban
Lost Discovery. B. Reynolds
Lost Duchess. J. G. Sarasin
Lost Duchess of Greyden Castle. N. C. Pykare
Lost Eden. R. Beauderae
Lost Eden. M. E. Braddon
Lost Emeralds of Zarinthia. H. Beauchamp
Lost Endeavor. G. Boothby
Lost Expedition. W. W. Sayer
Lost for Love. M. E. Braddon
Lost Fraulein. R. Meade
Lost Friday. E. J. Fredericks
Lost Gallows. J. D. Carr
Lost Garrison. J. Robb
Lost Generation. P. Trent
Lost Generations. J. Irungu
Lost Giant. K. Robeson
Lost Girl. J. Boswell
Lost Golfer. H. G. Hutchinson
Lost Half Hour. L. Meynell
Lost Hat. E. Percy
Lost Heir. S. Cobb
Lost Heir. G. A. Henty
Lost Heir. G. Lientz
Lost Heir of Linlithgow. E. Southworth
Lost Heiress. E. Southworth
Lost Heiress of Hawkescliffe. J. C. Ware
Lost Heritage. J. Herbrand
Lost Heroes. A. Baldwin
Lost Honeymoon. C. Jauniere
Lost House. F. S. Wees
Lost House Mystery. L. West
Lost Hyena. C. K. MacKinnon
Lost Identity. D. Hennessey
Lost Idol. A. Askew
Lost in Cambodia. W. M. Graydon
Lost in Space and the Mortgate Due. T. J. Kelly
Lost in the Post, and other tales. H. Wood
Lost in the Slave Land. W. M. Graydon
Lost Inheritance. Scott Graham
Lost Island. P. A. Whitney
Lost Jewel. H. Spofford
Lost Jewel of the Mortimers. A. T. Sadlier
Lost Judge. C. R. Gull
Lost Kachina. R. Potts
Lost Karim. E. Kyle
Lost Key. Forfex et Hesta
Lost Kingdom. J. G. Sarasin
Lost Ladies of the Windswept Moor. B. C. Warren
Lost Lady. O. R. Cohen
Lost Lady. D. Haring
Lost Lake. R. Kirk
Lost Lawyer. G. A. Birmingham
Lost Leader. E. P. Oppenheim
Lost Legacy. Renate Chapman
Lost Letter. P. Phelps
Lost Liner. R. Cromie
Lost Link. Thomas Hood
Lost Lotus. A. Rundle

L

Lost Madonna. I. Holland
Lost Man's Lane. Anonymous
Lost Man's Lane. A. K. Green
Lost Mark. P. Wynnton
Lost Million. W. Alden
Lost Million. W. LeQueux
Lost Mr. Linthwaite. J. S. Fletcher
Lost Moorings. G. Simenon
Lost Name. J. S. Le Fanu
Lost Naval Papers. B. Copplestone
Lost Oasis. K. Robeson
Lost Oasis. H. H. Ross
Lost One. F. Cowen
Lost One. A. Kennington
Lost One. D. Lyon
Lost Paradise. F. A. Kummer
Lost Parchment. F. Hume
Lost Pearl. F. Grierson
Lost Person. V. White
Lost Pibroch. N. Munro
Lost Provinces. S. Glazier
Lost Rapture. B. Poynter
Lost Road. R. H. Davis
Lost Roses of Ganymede House. Constance Walker
Lost Sir Brian. F. Whishaw
Lost Sir Massingberd. J. Payn
Lost Souls in Bohemia. W. J. Elliott
Lost Squadron. G. E. Rochester
Lost Square. L. T. Meade
Lost Stradivarius. J. M. Falkner
Lost Summer. M. Boone
Lost Tale. D. Estey
Lost Trooper. F. H. Dimmock
Lost Trooper. T. Mundy
Lost Underworld. B. Luigi
Lost Valley of Iskander. R. E. Howard
Lost Vengeance. C. Portway
Lost Victim. T. A. Waters
Lost Victory. P. Bonnecarrere
Lost Viol. M. P. Shiel
Lost Will. Maxwell Scott
Lost Will. H. Wood
Lost Without Trace. B. Cobb
Lost Witness. L. L. Lynch
Lost Wives of Dunwick. B. C. Warren
Lost World. E. McDowell
Lost World. L. K. Vincent
Lost Yesterday. W. B. Murphy
Lot 41—Dead Auctioneer. M. Symons
Lotteries. D. Winston
Lottery. B. Duffield
Lottery. S. Jackson
Lottery Ticket. F. Du Boisgobey
Lottery Ticket Man. F. G. Wood
Lottie, the Poor Saleslady. C. E. Blaney
Lotus Affair. T. Wells
Lotus Deception. W. Flohr
Lotus for Miss Quon. J. H. Chase
Lotus Leaves and Larceny. Philip Chambers
Lotus Vellum. Charlotte Hunt
Loudwater Mystery. E. Jepson
Loudwater Tragedy. T. W. Speight
Louis Beretti. D. H. Clarke
Louisa. G. D. Hernon
Louisa Reignier. R. Watson
Louise. J. Dering
Louise Martin, the Village Maiden. O. Bradbury
Louise, the Restless. K. Kimbrough
Louisiana Firestorm. M. McCray
Louisiana Jesse James. W. B. Lawson
Loup-Garou. E. Phillpotts
Louse for the Hangman. L. Bruce
Lovable Man. David Fletcher
Lovable Stranger. A. Duffield
Love-a-Duck and other stories. S. Aumonier
Love After Five. Raymond Mason
Love Against the World. W. S. Hayward
Love-All. J. Leasor
Love Among Thieves. Leon Brock
Love and a Title. H. Flowerdew
Love and Bullets. J. Heddon
Love and Death. R. Timperley
Love and Death in a Barn. Anonymous
Love and Desire and Hate. Neil Bell

Love and Desire and Hate. Joan Collins
Love and Dr. Hawkins. S. Gainsley
Love and Dr. Maynard. Rona Randall
Love, and Extras. Frank Richardson
Love and Forget. J. W. Drawbell
Love and Hatred. M. B. Lowndes
Love—and Helen. S. Jepson
Love and I. E. Aiken
Love and Life. L. Heilgers
Love and Lordship. F. Warden
Love and Murder. P. Whalley
Love and Terror. W. Herrick
Love and the Land Beyond. J. Leasor
Love and the Law. H. Curties
Love and the Spy. C. N. Williamson
Love and the Whirlwind. H. P. Lewis
Love and Treason. D. Osborn
Love Avalon. Steve Wright
Love Bade Me Welcome. J. Lodwick
Love Besieged. C. E. Pearce
Love, Blood and Tears. N. Weaver
Love Calling. M. Dekobra
Love Camp. L. Royer
Love Can Be Dangerous. O. R. Cohen
Love Child. T. B. Clegg
Love Child. A. Neiderman
Love Child. T. P. Prest
Love Clinic. M. Dekobra
Love Clouds. J. Latey
Love Comes Flying. R. Eden
Love Comes Lethal. L. Della
Love Cruisers. P. Trent
Love-Death Thing. T. B. Dewey
Love Denied. R. Vane
Love for Sale. M. Corrigan
Love for the Baron. Anthony Morton
Love for the Night. R. Vane
Love Forbidden. J. Blackmore
Love from a Stranger. F. Vosper
Love from Elizabeth. M. Fitt
Love from Las Vegas. H. Vogel
Love Gelds the Scene and Women Guide the Plot. A. Castle
Love Has No Alibi. O. R. Cohen
Love-Hate Relationship. J. N. Chance
Love Hath an Island. C. Randell
Love Hunter. J. Hassler
Love in a Mist. L. V. Stevens
Love in Amsterdam. N. Freeling
Love-In and Lamentation. H. Janson
Love in Burma. R. Carr
Love in Danger. C. Talbot
Love in Fetters. R. Marsh
Love in Jeopardy. Magali
Love in Lilac-Land. C. G. Mitford
Love in Peril. S. Jepson
Love in Suburbia. J. Conway
Love in the Purple. M. Gerard
Love Insurance. E. D. Biggers
Love Is a Deadly Weapon. P. Quentin
Love Is a Fiend. E. Woodward
Love Is a Flame. M. B. Lowndes
Love Is a Racket. R. James
Love Is a Spirit. J. Hawthorne
Love Is Enough. M. Peterson
Love Is for Hating. D. Telfer
Love Is for the Living. E. Kyle
Love Is Hell, Baby! D. Haring
Love Is Just a Word. J. M. Simmel
Love Is King. R. Sharp
Love Is Murder. E. C. Barcelo
Love Is the One with Wings. P. V. Stern
Love Is the Victim. John Lawrence
Love Kills. Dan Greenberg
Love Letters. C. Massie
Love Lies Bleeding. E. Crispin
Love Lies Slain. L. L. Blackmur
Love Like an Arrow. F. Y. McHugh
Love Like That. D. Garth
Love, Lust and Larceny. Sam Evans
Love Makers. H. Janson
Love Me and Die. D. Haring
Love Me and Die. D. Keene
Love Me and Die. L. Trimble

Love Me, Hurt Me. N. Karta
Love Me in Death. D. B. Olsen
Love Me Killer. D. Haring
Love Me Now. J. McPartland
Love Me Now. F. Nichols
Love Me to Death. F. Diamond
Love Me to Death. P. Kirk
Love Murders. A. Goddard
Love, Mystery, and Misery! A. F. Holstein
Love Nest. A. Coburn
Love Not Denied. K. Lindsay
Love of Brothers. Katharine Tynan
Love of Dust. S. Ram
Love of Lucifer. D. Winston
Love of Money. L. A. Taylor
Love on the Run. F. MacIsaac
Love on the Set. A. Kennington
Love—or a Name. J. Hawthorne
Love or Kill Them All. N. Weaver
Love or Whatever It Is. W. Leslie
Love, Pain and the Whole Damn Thing. D. Dorrie
Love Racket. B. K. Burns
Love Remembered. E. Beresford
Love Rides the Rails. M. Cary
Love Secretaries. H. Janson
Love Song. A. M. Greeley
Love Song. A. Kennedy
Love Song. J. L. Roberts
Love Spell. Anonymous
Love Spy, Love. R. C. Kasper
Love Stone. A. Askew
Love Stories. M. R. Rinehart
Love Story of a Mormon. Winifred Graham
Love Street. H. Zore
Love Talker. Elizabeth Peters
Love Tap. L. Brady
Love Test. J. A. Jordan
Love That Believeth. O. Binns
Love That Kills. C. Stanton
Love That Lasts. F. Warden
Love That Spy. T. A. Waters
Love the Bright Foreigner. A. Burgh
Love the Criminal. J. B. Harris-Burland
Love, the Fiddler. L. Osbourne
Love, the Foe. F. M. White
Love the Harvester. M. Pemberton
Love the Jester. A. Askew
Love the Rogue. Anonymous
Love, the Sorcerer. A. L. Thompson
Love the Sportsman. S. Horler
Love, the Thief. H. B. Mathers
Love Thieves. P. Packer
Love Thing. H. Barron
Love to Cherish. Clarissa Ross
Love Traffic. G. Lamond
Love Trap. L. White
Love Under Smoke. T. Craig
Love Waits at Penrhyn. P. Phillips
Love Was Married. S. Kyle
Love with a Gun and other stories. P. Cheyney
Love Without Honour. M. Richmond
Love You to Death. Jack Savage
Lovecraft's Book. R. A. Lupoff
Loved and the Loving. N. Sligh
Loved and the Unloved. T. H. Phillips
Loved Enemy. S. Coulter
Loveday Brooke. C. L. Pirkis
Lovehead. Jackie Collins
Lovel Castle. Anonymous
Loveless Die First. D. Bogard
Loveless Isle. N. Penley
Lovelies Are Never Lonely. M. Storme
Lovels of Arden. M. E. Braddon
Lovely and Lethal. F. Castle
Lovely and Lethal. D. Haring
Lovely and the Damned. R. Collier
Lovely But Cold. D. Haring
Lovely But Dangerous. Roland Daniel
Lovely But Deadly. Dave Steel
Lovely—But Lethal! P. Saxon
Lovely Corpse. M. Cumberland
Lovely Day to Die. C. Fremlin
Lovely in Death. W. O'Farrell
Lovely in Her Bones. S. McCrumb

Title Index

LUXURY MERCHANTS / 1057

Lovely Ladies. N. Freeling
Lovely Lady. M. Corrigan
Lovely Lady, Pity Me. R. Huggins
Lovely Mask for Murder. Gerry Travis
Lovely Mrs. Blake. R. Marsh
Lovely Mrs. Pembroke. F. Warden
Lovely Night to Kill. D. M. Morgan
Lover. Carter Brown
Lover. H. Janson
Lover and Thief. A. Maling
Lover Come Home. D. Lee
Lover, Don't Come Back! Carter Brown
Lover for Cindy. H. V. Dixon
Lover, Let Me Live. H. Daniels
Lover Man. Dallas Murphy
Lover—Say It with Mink. Norma Lee
Lover Scorned. I. Holland
Lover, That's Lethal. D. Haring
Lover Too Many. Roy Lewis
Lover Who Lost Himself. D. Newton
Lovers and Heretics. John Hall
Lovers and Other Killers. James Anderson
Lovers Are Losers. Howard Hunt
Lovers at Fault. F. Whishaw
Lover's Feud. R. C. Finney
Lovers in a Winter Circle. J. Kirsch
Lovers in the Dark. J. Ames
Lovers in Waiting. D. Whitelaw
Lovers, Make Moan. G. Mitchell
Lovers of Astrea. J. G. Sarasin
Loves and Liars. A. M. Diehl
Love's Atonement. K. Lindsay
Love's Captain. L. Robin
Love's Challenge. J. Templeton
Love's Deadly Silhouette. L. Richards
Love's Enemy. A. J. Small
Love's Fiery Dagger. F. Hurd
Love's Great Surrender. C. H. Bullivant
Love's Harvest. B. L. Farjeon
Love's Illusion. K. Sutcliffe
Love's Labor Won. E. Southworth
Love's Last Reward. Countess Barcynska
Love's Legacy. R. Ashe King
Love's Lovely Counterfeit. J. M. Cain
Love's Lunatic. J. McCarter
Loves of Harry Dancer. Lawrence Sanders
Loves of the Harem. G. W. M. Reynolds
Loves Old and New. J. Middlemass
Love's Ordeal. D. Dayle
Love's Prisoner. R. C. Finney
Love's Privilege. S. M. During
Love's Rebel. D. Noel
Love's Revenge. M. B. Lowndes
Love's Sentinel. F. Warden
Love's Service. M. Peterson
Love's Tender Promise. Kathleen Fraser
Love's Testimony. M. Andrau
Love's the Only Guide. M. Richmond
Love's Triumph. F. Du Boisgobey
Love's Victory. B. L. Farjeon
Love's Young Dream. E. A. Rowlands
Lovespell. A. Parnell
Loving a Dream, and One of His Inventions. C. Gibbon
Loving and the Dead. Carter Brown
Loving Brothers. L. Golding
Loving Cup. A. Prior
Loving Cup. A. Wynne
Loving Elms. P. Cargill
Loving Sands, Deadly Sands. C. Keppel
Loving, Yet Unloved. C. H. Bullivant
Low Angles. J. Stinson
Low Bite. S. Siracco
Low Company. H. Atkinson
Low Company. M. Benney
Low Company. D. Fuchs
Low Dive for Lola. M. Brody
Low Road. H. Morrison
Low Treason. L. Tourney
Lowdown. R. Chanslor
Lowdown. R. Jessup
Lowdown Lady. A. Trelawny
Lowdown on G. Men. K. Medusa
Lower Part of the Sky. L. Kaufman

Lower Underworld. A. R. L. Gardner
Lowest Rung. M. Cholmondeley
Lowly Lover. F. Warden
Loxfinger. S. Weinstein
Loyal and Dedicated Servant. J. Griffiths
Loyal Lady. K. Lindsay
Loyalties. G. C. Dukes
Loyalties. G. Esler
Loyalties. J. Galsworthy
Loyalties. Raymond Williams
Loyalty of Peter Drayton, and Mrs. Peter Skeffington's Revenge. H. C. McNeile
Lubyanka. J. Burch
Luciano's Luck. J. Higgins
Lucienne. M. Pemberton
Lucien's Tombs. M. Rippon
Lucifer and Partner. Jack Henry
Lucifer at Ponsfordville. J. Workman
Lucifer at Sunset. S. Harvester
Lucifer Cell. W. Fennerton
Lucifer Cult. I. Benedict
Lucifer Directive. J. Land
Lucifer Key. M. MacPherson
Lucifer Mask. K. Rich
Lucifer Was Tall. E. Gresham
Lucifer Wine. Irma Walker
Lucifer's Dream. J. L. Curtis
Lucifer's File. D. Haring
Lucifer's Lady. D. Haring
Lucifer's Lodge. J. Tobias
Lucifer's Weekend. W. B. Murphy
Lucile Clery. J. Shearing
Lucile Dare, Detective. M. Leighton
Lucinda. H. Rigsby
Lucius Davoreen. M. E. Braddon
Luck and a Lady. J. A. Dunn
Luck and other new stories. Lord Gorell
Luck Is No Lady. D. Haring
Luck of Bella Barton. G. W. Appleton
Luck of Gerard Ridgeley. B. Mitford
Luck of Jocelyn Pinner, R.N. Bruce Norman
Luck of Life. C. H. Bullivant
Luck of Luce. D. Deane
Luck of Norman Dale. B. Pain
Luck of St. Boniface. L. C. Douthwaite
Luck of the Czar. E. Swan
Luck of the Darrells. A. Murray
Luck of the Darrells. J. Payn
Luck of the Golden Star. H. J. Andrews
Luck of the Irish. H. MacGrath
Luck of the Kid. R. Cullum
Luck of the Mounted. R. S. Kendall
Luck of the Secret Service. W. LeQueux
Luck of the Strong. W. H. Hodgson
Luck of the Vails. E. F. Benson
Luck of Udaipur. J. I. Emery
Luck Runs Out. C. MacLeod
Luck Was No Lady. Carter Brown
Luckless Lady. George Douglas
Lucky Devil. A. Maling
Lucky Dip. Neil Bell
Lucky Dollar, Private Eye. Tim Kelly
Lucky Dollar—The Musical. Tim Kelly
Lucky Ham. S. McCarthy
Lucky Jane. D. Ames
Lucky Lacey. K. Reynolds
Lucky, Lucky Hudson and the 12th St. Gang. T. J. Kelly
Lucky Mishap. F. Ferrars
Lucky Mr. Loder. G. Thorne
Lucky Partners. W. C. Tuttle
Lucky Pierre. M. Endfield
Lucky Policeman. R. Penny
Lucky Shot. E. W. Elkington
Lucky Stiff. C. Rice
Lucky Streak. J. Raymond
Lucky to Be Alive? A. Cromie
Lucretia. E. Bulwer-Lytton
Lucy and the Dark Gods. E. Jepson
Lucy's Cottage. M. James
Ludi Victor. J. Leigh
Ludus Amoris. H. Swift
Luger for a Lady. D. Haring
Luger Lullaby. R. Angel

Lugger Audace. E. L. Long
Lugs O'Leary. A. Kimmins
Luigi of Catanzaro. L. Golding
Luke Darby, the "World" Detective. E. A. Young
Luke Leighton, the Government Detective. H. Rockwood
Luke Martin Diamonds. B. N. F. Wilce
Luke's Summer. D. Lee
Lukundoo, and other stories. Edward L. White
Lullaby. E. McBain
Lullaby and Goodnight. V. T. Bugliosi
Lullaby of Murder. D. S. Davis
Lullaby with Lugers. J. Crockett
Lulu. B. Vane
Lulu. M. T. Walworth
Lumber Ship. E. L. Long
Luminous Face. C. Wells
Lumley Wood Mystery. G. W. L. Banbury
Lumsden Baby. C. F. Roe
Luna. Delacorta
Lunatic at Large. J. S. Clouston
Lunatic at Large Again. J. S. Clouston
Lunatic Fringe. W. L. De Andrea
Lunatic in Charge. J. S. Clouston
Lunatic in Love. J. S. Clouston
Lunatic Still at Large. J. S. Clouston
Lunatic, the Lover. B. Cobb
Lunatic, the Lover and the Poet. R. L. Finn
Lunatic Time. J. Roeburt
Lunatic View. D. Campton
Lunatics at Large. J. Reach
Lunch Basket. W. P. Ridge
Lunge Wire. J. B. O'Sullivan
Lupe. G. Thompson
Lure. C. Cavendish
Lure. H. R. Hailey
Lure. F. Picano
Lure. G. Scarborough
Lure of Contraband. J. Wear-Gifford
Lure of Gold. Nicholas Carter
Lure of Love. W. LeQueux
Lure of Mammon. Dick Stewart
Lure of Sweet Death. S. Kemp
Lure of the Black Pool. Old Sleuth
Lure of the Bush. A. W. Upfield
Lure of Thunder Island. L. Walmsley
Lured by Greed. A. Andre
Lured from Home. Grace M. White
Lures of Death. P. Whelton
Lures of London. C. H. Bullivant
Lurker. J. V. Smith, Jr.
Lurking Death. F. W. Gumley
Lurking Man. Gerald Butler
Lurking Policeman. G. Kent
Lurking Shadow. A. Askew
Lurking Shadow. J. Remenham
Lurking Terror. A. Peverett
Lurking Terror. E. Wilmot
Lush. P. Benchley
Lush Valley. P. Campbell
Lushington Mystery. Philippa Tyler
Lussington Abbey. H. Rouviere
Lust for Innocence. D. Doubtfire
Lust for Murder. H. Klinger
Lust for Vengeance. R. Bloomfield
Lust for Vengeance. H. Janson
Lust Hungry. Stuart Hall
Lust Is No Lady. M. Avallone
Lust Killer. A. Stack
Lust of Hate. G. Boothby
Lust of Power. H. Kane
Lust of Power. B. Selwyn
Lust of Treasure. H. C. Marksman
Lust to Kill. Edward Lee
Lustful Ape. R. Gray
Lustful Summer. R. V. Cassill
Lusting Drive. O. Demaris
Lustre Jug. F. Hird
Lusty Men. W. R. Cox
Lute and the Glove. K. W. Eyre
Luther Wing. M. Maurice
Luxembourg Run. S. Ellin
Luxembourg Run. A. Ross
Luxury Merchants. A. Richards

L

L

Luxury Tour. L. Handley
Lycanthia. F. Layland-Barratt
Lycanthrope, the Mystery of Sir William Wolf. E. Phillpotts
Lychgate Hall. M. E. Francis
Lyddon House Mystery. G. Ellinger
Lydia. E. V. Cunningham
Lydia Trendennis. F. E. Smith
Lying at Death's Door. M. Cumberland
Lying Down Below. H. Carstairs
Lying in State. J. Rathbone
Lying Jade. L. Ford
Lying Ladies. R. Finnegan
Lying Lips. W. LeQueux
Lying Lips. T. A. Plummer
Lying Three. R. McInerny
Lying Voices. E. Ferrars
Lynch Town. W. B. Murphy
Lynch Years. T. P. O'Mahony
Lynching of John Hanson. Scott Wright
Lynching of Orin Newfield. G. J. Goldberg
Lynch's Law. J. Balnave
Lyndley Waters. G. R. Preedy
Lyndwood Affair. U. L. Silberrad
Lynmara Legacy. C. Gaskin
Lynne Court Spinney. J. S. Fletcher
Lynx. J. J. Savarin
Lynx, Counter Spy. Vigilant
Lynx, Spyflyer. Vigilant
Lynx, V. C. Vigilant
Lynx, V. C., Flies Again. Vigilant
Lyona Grimswood, Spinster. L. Higgin
Lyonesse Abbey. J. Tattersall
Lyonhurst. Rona Randall
Lyon's Mail. G. Rowell
Lyons Mail. R. H. Sherard
Lyssa. J. Jenkins
Lyssa Syndrome. C. Fahy
Lyttleton Case. R. A. V. Morris
Lytton's Diary. R. Connolly

MacAlastair Looks On. A. Dick
MacAlester. Ritchie Perry
Macall Gets Curious. G. Fairlie
McAllister and His Double. A. Train
Macaterick's Revenge. A. Venters
McBain Brief. E. McBain
McBain's Ladies. E. McBain
McBain's Ladies Too. E. McBain
McCabe. E. Naughton
McCabe and Mrs. Miller. E. Naughton
McCallum. A. McGregor
McCallum Again. A. McGregor
McCann of the Legion. Operator 1384
McCarthy, C.I.D. J. G. Brandon
McCarthy's List. M. Mackey
McCarty, Incog. I. Ostrander
McCloud. C. Wilcox
McCool. P. McCurtin
McCreary Moves In. M. East
McDermott's Sky. R. Serling
McGarr and the Legacy of a Woman Scorned. B. Gill
McGarr and the Method of Descartes. B. Gill
McGarr and the P.M. of Belgrave Square. B. Gill
McGarr and the Politician's Wife. B. Gill
McGarr and the Sienese Conspiracy. B. Gill
McGarr at the Dublin Horse Show. B. Gill
McGarr on the Cliffs of Moher. B. Gill
MacGilleroy's Millinos. I. D. Hardy
McGregor's Island. O. John
McGuffin. J. Bowen
McHugh. J. Flynn
McInnes of the N.I.D. Sea-Wrack
MacIntyre Plot. P. M. Walker
McIver's Secret. L. Grimes
McKain's Dilemma. Chet Williamson
McKee of Centre Street. H. Reilly
Mackenzie Break. S. Shelley
Mackenzie's Glen. Janis Dawson
Mackintosh Man. D. Bagley
McLean at the Golden Owl. G. Goodchild
McLean Carries On. G. Goodchild
McLean Deduces. G. Goodchild
McLean Disposes. G. Goodchild
McLean Excels. G. Goodchild
McLean Finds a Way. G. Goodchild
McLean Incomparable. G. Goodchild
McLean Intervenes. G. Goodchild
McLean Investigates. G. Goodchild
McLean Invincible. G. Goodchild
McLean Keeps Going. G. Goodchild
McLean Knows Best. G. Goodchild
McLean Knows the Answers. G. Goodchild
McLean: Non-Stop. G. Goodchild
McLean of Scotland Yard. G. Goodchild
McLean Plays a Hand. G. Goodchild
McLean Predominant. G. Goodchild
McLean Prevails. G. Goodchild
McLean Remembers! G. Goodchild
McLean Scores Again. G. Goodchild
McLean Sees It Through. G. Goodchild
McLean Solves It. G. Goodchild
McLean Steps In. G. Goodchild
McLean Takes a Holiday. G. Goodchild
McLean Takes Charge. G. Goodchild
McLean Takes Over. G. Goodchild
McLean the Magnificent. G. Goodchild
McLean to the Dark Tower Came. G. Goodchild
McLoon of the South Seas. O. Sackville
Maclure Mystery. A. S. Swan
MacLurg Goes West. R. Petrie
McNeills Chase a Ghost. T. Du Bois
McQ. Alexander Edwards
McQuaid. S. Rifkin
McQuaid in August. S. Rifkin
MacStodger's Affinity. D. Whitelaw
McSullivan's Beach. K. Dewhurst
MacTaggart's War. R. Dennis
MacTavish. P. Cheyney
McTodd. C. J. C. Hyne
M. L. Falkner
M.D.—Doctor of Murder. F. MacIsaac
M.F.H.'s Daughter. R. Jocelyn
M for Murder. J. G. Brandon
M.I.A. Ransom. M. McQuay
M-MM-Minx. K. T. McCall
M.O.T.H.E.R. Versus Mafia. R. Santini
M.R.C.S. B. Delannoy
M.S. Bradford, Special. A. C. Gunter
M-Squad. D. Saunders
MW-XX.3. R. Pertwee
Mabel Seymour. C. Matthew
Mabelle Rivers, Girl Detective. A. Millard
Macabre Manor. E. Grayson
Macabre Mansion. L. Churchill
Macamba Project. M. Cronin
Macao. Nick Carter
Macao Massacre. Nick Carter
Macau. D. Carney
Maccat. A. McColl
Mace! J. Grant
Macedonian Mixup. John Bentley
Mace's Luck. J. Grant
Machete. Greg Walker
Machinations of Dr. Grue. H. M. Raleigh
Machinations of the Myo-ok. C. C. Lowis
Machine. D. Hamill
Machine Gun McCann. O. Demaris
Machine Gun Murder. Jacques Thomas
Machine to Kill. G. Leroux
Mackin Cover. D. K. Shah
Macking Gangster. C. A. Harris
Macomber Menace. W. D. Roberts
Macon Moore, the Southern Detective. J. R. Taylor
Macowen Murder. E. Y. Miller
Maculan's Daughter. S. Gainham
Mad. G. M. Fenn
Mad Annual. E. F. Benson
Mad Baxter. Wade Miller
Mad Blood. D. Nemec
Mad Death. N. Slater
Mad Doctor. F. J. Thwaites
Mad Doctor in Harley Street. F. J. Thwaites
Mad Dog Coll. S. Thurman
Mad Eyes. K. Robeson
Mad Hatter Murder. F. Grierson
Mad Hatter Mystery. J. D. Carr
Mad Hatter Summer. D. Thomas
Mad Hatter's Holiday. P. Lovesey
Mad Hatter's Rock. V. Gunn
Mad Interlude. A. L. Martin
Mad Lorrimer. Finch Mason
Mad Mesa. K. Robeson
Mad Mike. G. Goodchild
Mad Minute. J. Cain
Mad Monk. R. T. M. Scott
Mad Murder. R. H. Wilkinson
Mad Scientist. Raymond McDonald
Mad Scientist Affair. J. T. Phillifent
Mad Shepherdess. H. Brooke
Mad Sir Geoffrey. F. Warden
Mad Virgins. V. B. Ibanez
Mad with Much Heart. Gerald Butler
Madam. G. Cherrell
Madam Ambassador. N. Calmer
Madam and Eve. M. Corrigan
Madam Blood. D. Haring
Madam Captain. E. L. Long
Madam Crowl's Ghost, and other tales of mystery. J. S. Le Fanu
Madam Is Dead. R. Terrall
Madam Julia's Tale and other queer stories. N. Royde-Smith
Madam Tic-Tac. F. L. Cary
Madam Will Not Dine Tonight. H. Waugh
Madam, Will You Talk? Mary Stewart
Madam, Will You Walk? B. Ellis
Madam, You Must Die. C. Keppel
Madam You're Mayhem. Carter Brown
Madame. E. P. Oppenheim
Madame and Her Twelve Virgins. E. P. Oppenheim
Madame Aubrey and the Police. H. Travers
Madame Aubrey Dines with Death. H. Travers
Madame Baltimore. H. Knowland
Madame Bluebeard. B. Sanders
Madame Eddie's Chamber of Horrors. Mike Shelley
Madame Flirt. C. E. Pearce
Madame Holle. Margery Lawrence
Madame Judas. M. Turnbull
Madame Knits. R. Rodd
Madame Lies Murdered. G. Wishart
Madame Lucien. A. Hodges
Madame Maigret's Friend. G. Simenon
Madame Maigret's Own Case. G. Simenon
Madame Merlin. G. Beardmore
Madame Midas. F. Hume
Madame "Q". Nicholas Carter
Madame Shadow. F. Grierson
Madame Sly. M. Corrigan
Madame Spy. B. Graeme
Madame Storey. H. Footner
Madame X. M. Avallone
Madame X. J. W. MacConaughy
Madame You're Morgue-Bound. Carter Brown
Madame's Girls. M. Bentine
Madball. F. Brown
Madcap Betty. D. Whitelaw
Maddening Scar. D. R. Clinton
Maddon's Rock. H. Innes
Made for Murder. Elizabeth Anthony
Made for Murder. F. McGrew
Made for TV. R. Breen
Made in America. P. Maas
Made in Beverly Hills. R. Kaiser
Made in Detroit. R. Kantner
Made to Murder. J. Courage
Made Up for Murder. K. Roos
Made Up to Kill. K. Roos
Madelaine. J. Louis
Madeleine. C. Campion
Madeleine. Bernard Taylor
Madeleine. P. E. West
Madeleine Smith. Winifred Duke
Madeline. I. Kelly
Madeline Brown's Murderer. F. Adams
Madeline Payne, the Detective's Daughter. L. L. Lynch
Madeline Power. A. W. Marchmont
Madeline's Miracles. W. Adler
Mademoiselle B. M. Pons
Mademoiselle from Armentieres. J. Rhode

Title Index

Mademoiselle Josephine's Fridays. M. Betham-Edwards
Mademoiselle of Monte Carlo. W. LeQueux
Madgwick Affair. D. Whitelaw
Madhouse. Angus Hall
Madhouse in Washington Square. David Alexander
Madhouse on the Moors. F. Maule
Madigan. R. Dougherty
Madigan's Women. J. Conway
Madison Avenue Murder. Liza Bennett
Madison Murder. L. Grex
Madman. M. Hansom
Madman at My Door. H. Waugh
Madman of Bergerac. G. Simenon
Madman of the Marshes. W. Jardine
Madman on a Drum. N. R. De Mexico
Madman Theory. E. Queen
Madman's Bend. A. W. Upfield
Madman's Buff. K. Steel
Madman's Holiday. Fredric Brown
Madman's Manor. C. Rushton
Madman's Mansion. C. Sargent
Madman's Millions! Anonymous
Madman's Secret. Anonymous
Madman's Whisper. Richard Grayson
Madman's Will. J. N. Chance
Madmen Die Alone. J. E. Greene
Madness at the Castle. S. Claudia
Madness from Mars. D. Summers
Madness of a Seduced Woman. S. F. Schaeffer
Madness of Charlie Pierce. H. C. James
Madness of Gloria. F. Whishaw
Madness of the Heart. R. Neely
Madness of the Heart. F. Sandstrom
Madness of the People. R. Cassilis
Madness on Madonna Drive. L. Flynn
Madonna Creek Witch. J. La Tourrette
Madonna in Hollywood. M. Dekobra
Madonna of Avenue A. M. Canfield
Madonna of Hell. K. Lindsay
Madonna of the Beech Woods and other stories. Morley Roberts
Madonna of the Black Market. E. Webster
Madonna of the Music Halls. W. LeQueux
Madonna of the Poor. C. Holland
Madonna of the Seven Moons. Margery Lawrence
Madonna of the Sleeping Cars. M. Dekobra
Madonna Red. J. P. Carroll
Madrid Underground. D. Serafin
Madrigal. J. Gardner
Madrigal for Charlie Muffin. B. Freemantle
Madrone Tree. D. Duncan
Maelstrom. M. J. Bird
Maelstrom. F. Froest
Maelstrom. R. Haney
Maelstrom. Howard Hunt
Maelstrom. W. H. Murray
Maestro Murders. F. S. Wees
Mafalda. J. Goodwin
Mafia. N. Clad
Mafia Death Watch. B. Rossi
Mafia Diaries. J. R. Nash
Mafia Fix. R. Sapir
Mafia Kiss. P. Loraine
Mafia Man. R. Posner
Mafia Massacre. F. Scarpetta
Mafia Vendetta. L. Sciascia
Mafia Wipe-Out. F. Scarpetta
Mafia Women. J. Cenni
Mafia's Victim. I. Stark
Mafioso. P. McCurtin
Magda. Lisa Wells
Magdalene Scrolls. Barbara Wood
Magenta Moth. J. Patrick
Maggie? F. Barrett
Maggie. J. Tremaine
Maggie Rowan. C. Cookson
Maggot. J. Fowles
Magic. W. Goldman
Magic Casket. R. A. Freeman
Magic Change Detective. Anonymous
Magic Cottage. James Herbert
Magic Dick, a Boy Detective. Old Sleuth
Magic Eardrums. H. S. Keeler

Magic for Murder. A. Livingston
Magic Forest. K. Robeson
Magic Grandfather. D. M. Disney
Magic Island. K. Robeson
Magic Lantern Murders. Carter Dickson
Magic Makes Murder. H. R. Campbell
Magic Man. D. Bannerman
Magic Man. H. E. Rives
Magic Mirror. A. Blackwood
Magic Mirror. M. Friedman
Magic Necklace. Nicholas Carter
Magic of Chez Finnie. C. E. Elvy
Magic of To-Morrow. C. Seymour
Magic Ring. D. Daniels
Magic Valley. W. E. D. Ross
Magic Year. J. Maas
Magician. F. L. Green
Magician. G. Simenon
Magician. S. Stein
Magician and the Widow. G. Simenon
Magician Kills and The Coffin Mystery. John Reid
Magicians. James Gunn
Magician's Daughter. M. Granbeck
Magician's Wife. J. M. Cain
Maginot Line Murder. B. Newman
Magistrate's Own Case. B. P. Rosenkrantz
Magnate Detective. Anonymous
Magnet. A. O. Crozier
Magnet Detective Book One. W. Ecke
Magnet Detective Book Two. W. Ecke
Magnet for Danger. M. Richmond
Magnet for Murder. M. E. Corne
Magnet for Murder. B. Symons
Magnet of Doom. G. Simenon
Magnetic Fields. R. Loewinsohn
Magnetic Girl. R. Marsh
Magnetic Man. N. Daniels
Magnetic Peril. W. Herscholt
Magnetism and Mystery. L. Creswicke
Magnetism of Sin. Aesculapius
Magnificent Hoax. E. P. Oppenheim
Magnificent Hobo. A. Wilson
Magnificent Mirabelle. Lydia Lee
Magnificent Moll. J. Gonzales
Magnolia Curse. L. Murfi
Magnolia Murder. W. Bell
Magnolias. J. Ellis
Magnum for Schneider. J. Mitchell
Magnum Force. M. Valley
Magnum P.I. R. Bowdler
Magnum P.I. D. Zadra
Magpie House. A. Soutar
Magpie Murder. G. Coverack
Magpie on the Gallows. J. G. Sarasin
Magwitch. M. Noonan
Magyar Massacre. G. St. Germain
Maharajah and other stories. T. H. White
Maharajah's Belt. D. Storm
Mahatma's Pupil. R. Marsh
Mahdi. A. J. Quinnell
Mahjong Spies. J. Trenhaile
Mahme Nousie. G. M. Fenn
Mahogany House. J. Wetherell
Mahogany Murder. Lee Roberts
Maid for Murder. Carter Brown
Maid for Murder. C. Franklin
Maid for Murder. M. K. Ozaki
Maid for the Morgue. M. Brody
Maid from Norway. A. Munch
Maid in Armour. W. A. Locks
Maid in Paris. F. Kane
Maid Indomitable. L. T. Meade
Maid of Athens. M. Richmond
Maid of Honour. R. Aitken
Maid of Honour. P. Sabre
Maid of Mansfield. P. Trent
Maid of Mystery. L. T. Meade
Maid of Sussex. G. Volk
Maid of the Mountain. J. Gregory
Maid of the Silver Sea. J. Oxenham
Maid of the Village. Mrs. Kentish
Maid to Kill. Stephen James
Maid to Murder. Roy Vickers
Maid-Up for Murder. M. Brody

Maid with the Goggles. L. T. Meade
Maiden Armour. John Marsh
Maiden Fair and other stories. C. Gibbon
Maiden Flight That Never Was. M. D. Morrison
Maiden of Glory Island. J. Wetherell
Maiden Possessed. J. N. Chance
Maiden Widow. E. Southworth
Maiden You Slay Me. Jason
Maiden's End. J. Boyle
Maiden's Prayer. Joan Fleming
Maiden's Stakes. Dornford Yates
Maids and Deathwatch. J. Genet
Maigret Abroad. G. Simenon
Maigret Afraid. G. Simenon
Maigret and Monsieur Charles. G. Simenon
Maigret and Monsieur Labbe. G. Simenon
Maigret and the Apparition. G. Simenon
Maigret and the Black Sheep. G. Simenon
Maigret and the Bum. G. Simenon
Maigret and the Burglar's Wife. G. Simenon
Maigret and the Calame Report. G. Simenon
Maigret and the Concarneau Murders. G. Simenon
Maigret and the Coroner. G. Simenon
Maigret and the Dead Girl. G. Simenon
Maigret and the Death of a Harbor-Master. G. Simenon
Maigret and the Dosser. G. Simenon
Maigret and the Enigmatic Lett. G. Simenon
Maigret and the Flea. G. Simenon
Maigret and the Flemish Shop. G. Simenon
Maigret and the Fortune Teller. G. Simenon
Maigret and the Gangsters. G. Simenon
Maigret and the Ghost. G. Simenon
Maigret and the Headless Corpse. G. Simenon
Maigret and the Hotel Majestic. G. Simenon
Maigret and the Hundred Gibbets. G. Simenon
Maigret and the Informer. G. Simenon
Maigret and the Killer. G. Simenon
Maigret and the Lazy Burglar. G. Simenon
Maigret and the Loner. G. Simenon
Maigret and the Madwoman. G. Simenon
Maigret and the Man on the Bench. G. Simenon
Maigret and the Man on the Boulevard. G. Simenon
Maigret and the Millionaires. G. Simenon
Maigret and the Minister. G. Simenon
Maigret and the Nahour Case. G. Simenon
Maigret and the Old Lady. G. Simenon
Maigret and the Reluctant Witnesses. G. Simenon
Maigret and the Saturday Caller. G. Simenon
Maigret and the Spinster. G. Simenon
Maigret and the Sunday Caller. G. Simenon
Maigret and the Tavern by the Seine. G. Simenon
Maigret and the Toy Village. G. Simenon
Maigret and the Wine Merchant. G. Simenon
Maigret and the Yellow Dog. G. Simenon
Maigret and the Young Girl. G. Simenon
Maigret at the Coroner's. G. Simenon
Maigret at the Crossroads. G. Simenon
Maigret at the Gar-Moulin. G. Simenon
Maigret Bides His Time. G. Simenon
Maigret Cinq. G. Simenon
Maigret Goes Home. G. Simenon
Maigret Goes to School. G. Simenon
Maigret Has Doubts. G. Simenon
Maigret Has Scruples. G. Simenon
Maigret Hesitates. G. Simenon
Maigret in Court. G. Simenon
Maigret in Exile. G. Simenon
Maigret in Holland. G. Simenon
Maigret in Montmartre. G. Simenon
Maigret in New York's Underworld. G. Simenon
Maigret in Retirement. G. Simenon
Maigret in Society. G. Simenon
Maigret in Vichy. G. Simenon
Maigret Keeps a Rendezvous. G. Simenon
Maigret Loses His Temper. G. Simenon
Maigret Meets a Milord. G. Simenon
Maigret Mystified. G. Simenon
Maigret Omnibus. G. Simenon
Maigret on Holiday. G. Simenon
Maigret on the Defensive. G. Simenon
Maigret on the Riviera. G. Simenon
Maigret Quartet. G. Simenon
Maigret Rents a Room. G. Simenon

M

Maigret Returns. G. Simenon
Maigret Right and Wrong. G. Simenon
Maigret Sets a Trap. G. Simenon
Maigret Sits It Out. G. Simenon
Maigret Stonewalled. G. Simenon
Maigret Takes a Room. G. Simenon
Maigret Takes the Waters. G. Simenon
Maigret to the Rescue. G. Simenon
Maigret Travels South. G. Simenon
Maigret Trio. G. Simenon
Maigret's Boyhood Friend. G. Simenon
Maigret's Christmas. G. Simenon
Maigret's Dead Man. G. Simenon
Maigret's Failure. G. Simenon
Maigret's First Case. G. Simenon
Maigret's Little Joke. G. Simenon
Maigret's Memoirs. G. Simenon
Maigret's Mistake. G. Simenon
Maigret's Pickpocket. G. Simenon
Maigret's Pipe. G. Simenon
Maigret's Revolver. G. Simenon
Maigret's Rival. G. Simenon
Maigret's Special Murder. G. Simenon
Maigret's War of Nerves. G. Simenon
Mail for McNair. S. Lock
Mail Robber. J. E. Stewart
Mail Robbers' Syndicate. E. C. Derby
Mail Train. K. A. Dobson
Mail Van Mystery. J. G. Brandon
Mailed Fist. J. Tregellis
Main. Trevanian
Main Attraction. S. Michaels
Main Chance. Edmund Ward
Main Drag. H. Vogel
Main Experiment. C. Hodder-Williams
Main Highway. J. Stratton
Main Line Kill. R. Busby
Main Offensive. Gar Wilson
Main Street Morgue. Griff
Maine Girl. E. L. Coolidge
Maine Massacre. J. Van De Wetering
Mainline Plot. J. Rosenberger
Maitland Conspiracy. M. Hollander
Maitland Inheritance. Laura Smith
Maitland Street Murder. Mark Allerton
Maitland's Master Mystery. M. Severy
Maitre Adam. A. Dumas
Majendie's Cat. F. V. Foulkes
Majestic Mystery. R. Mackail
Majesty of the Law. M. Danning
Majii. K. Robeson
Major. John Ross
Major. F. Warden
Major Adventures. L. P. Greene
Major Crime. O. Keystone
Major Deception. L. Amey
Major Developments. L. P. Greene
Major—Diamond Buyer. L. P. Greene
Major Enquiry. L. Henderson
Major Exploits. L. P. Greene
Major Has Seven Guests. C. Wagner
Major Hazards. L. P. Greene
Major Incident. P. N. Walker
Major—Knight Errant. L. P. Greene
Major League Murder. M. Geller
Major Occasions. L. P. Greene
Major Owen, and other tales. C. N. Johnston
Major Steps Out. John Ross
Major Washington. E. A. Shaffer
Majorca. S. Dodson
Majorettes. J. Russo
Major's Mascot. N. Gould
Makariri Gold. B. Priestley
Makassar Strait Contract. P. Atlee
Make a Killing. H. Q. Masur
Make a Killing. B. Williams
Make-and-Mend. Bartimeus
Make Believe. P. DePolnay
Make-Believe Man. Elizabeth Fenwick
Make Death Love Me. R. Rendell
Make Do with Spring. E. Bonett
Make Every Kiss Count. Ronald Simpson
Make Fame a Monster. E. H. Clements
Make Haste to Die. R. Watkins

Make Haste to Live. The Gordons
Make It Fast. D. Haring
Make It Lethal. R. Drayton
Make It Look Like an Accident. J. R. Nolan
Make It Murder. J. Last
Make It Nylons. J. P. Heggy
Make Me a Murderer. Gwendoline Butler
Make Me a Widow. D. Ellis
Make Me Rich. P. Corris
Make Mine a Corpse. M. Storme
Make Mine a Harlot. M. Storme
Make Mine a Redhead. M. Storme
Make Mine a Shroud. M. Storme
Make Mine a Virgin. M. Storme
Make Mine Beautiful. M. Storme
Make Mine Dangerous. M. Storme
Make Mine High. B. Vane
Make Mine Maclain. B. Kendrick
Make Mine Mavis. W. Ard
Make Mine Mayhem. P. Muller
Make Mine Mink. H. Janson
Make Mine Murder. R. S. Bowen
Make Mine Murder. Neill Graham
Make Mine Murder. M. Hervey
Make Mine Murder. B. Winter
Make Mine Vengeance. R. Colby
Make My Bed in Hell. J. Sanford
Make My Bed Soon. J. S. Strange
Make My Bed Soon. J. Webb
Make My Coffin Big. J. B. O'Sullivan
Make My Coffin Strong. W. R. Cox
Make Out with Murder. C. Harrison
Make Room! Make Room! Harry Harrison
Make Sure I'm Dead. D. Bogard
Make the Corpse Walk. Raymond Marshall
Make Them Pay. I. Ludlow
Make-Up for Murder. J. Wright
Make-Up for the Toff. J. Creasey
Make Way for a Sailor. Seafarer
Make Way for Murder. A. A. Marcus
Make Way for Murder. N. C. Rosenthal
Make Way for the Mourners. David Hume
Make with the Brains, Pierre. Dana Williams
Makeover. M. Biederman
Makepeace Not War. J. C. Martindale
Maker of Frocks. E. C. Davies
Maker of History. E. P. Oppenheim
Maker of Mischief. S. P. Hyatt
Maker of Nations. E. Boothby
Maker of Opportunities. G. F. Gibbs
Maker of Pearls. S. W. Powell
Maker of Secrets. W. LeQueux
Maker of Shadows. Jack Mann
Maker of Ware. S. Edge
Making a Killing. J. Nassivera
Making Crime Pay. P. Cheyney
Making Good Again. L. Davidson
Making Good Blood. Jennie Melville
Making Hate. Jacqueline Wilson
Making It. O. Lange
Making It Big. J. Jakes
Making of Peter Dunn. W. A. Kennedy
Making Progress. A. Bailey
Makra Mystery. H. Campbell
Malabang Pearl. F. Archer
Malabar Magician. F. E. Penny
Malachi Breen Times Two. L. Pope
Malachite Jar. J. S. Fletcher
Malady in Madeira. A. Bridge
Malago's Visit. C. Salcido
Malaret Mystery. O. Hartley
Malaspiga Exit. Evelyn Anthony
Malay Manhunt. A. S. Fleischman
Malay Woman. A. S. Fleischman
Malayan Mystery. Anonymous
Malayan Rose. M. Derby
Malayan Story. G. Sheen
Malcolm. Old Sleuth
Malcolm Sage, Detective. H. Jenkins
Malcolm the Wonder. Old Sleuth
Malcontents. S. Franklin
Male Order. C. E. Bowman
Malefactor. E. P. Oppenheim
Malefactors. C. Blair

Malice Aforethought. F. Iles
Malice and the Maternal Instinct. M. Tripp
Malice Domestic. E. Cameron
Malice Domestic. P. Capon
Malice Domestic. R. Foley
Malice Domestic. Mollie Hardwick
Malice Domestic. W. M. Hardy
Malice Domestic. Sara Woods
Malice in Camera. L. Payne
Malice in Maggody. Joan Hess
Malice in Wonderland. N. Blake
Malice in Wonderland. R. King
Malice Matrimonial. Joan Fleming
Malice of Monday. E. Burgess
Malice with Murder. N. Blake
Malicious Madonna. D. Romaine
Malicious Mischief. L. Egan
Maliday Mystery. A. Mills
Malignant Heart. C. Sibley
Malignant Snowman. K. Laing
Malignant Stars. Jerome Barry
Malinsay Massacre. D. Wheatley
Mall. S. Kahn
Mall. Sara King
Mallabec. D. Walker
Mallen Girl. C. Cookson
Mallen Litter. C. Cookson
Mallen Lot. C. Cookson
Mallen Streak. C. Cookson
Mallion's Pride. C. Salisbury
Mallison Mystery. T. W. Hanshew
Mallore Affair. W. McCloskey
Mallory. Raymond Marshall
Mallory Case. L. Barbee
Mallory Grange. C. Randell
Mallory of the Royal Mounted. C. Stoddard
Mallory's Gambit. L. C. Balling
Mallory's Luck. K. A. Shoesmith
Malloy's Subway. R. W. Campbell
Malloy's Tryst. P. C. De Crespigny
Mally Lee. E. Kyle
Malpas Legacy. A. Pritchett
Malpractice. J. R. Feegel
Malta Conspiracy. F. Mullally
Malta Mystery. S. G. Hedges
Malta Victory. R. Jackson
Maltese Cross. E. T. Sawyer
Maltese Falcon. D. Hammett
Maltese Mob. S. Markham
Maltese Vengeance. J. Cutter
Maluti Murder. E. Haldane
Malvern Link. W. Wynne-Owen
Malverne Hall. R. C. Payes
Malverne Manor. H. York
Malvery Hold. J. S. Fletcher
Malvie Inheritance. Pamela Hill
Malvina. H. S. Edwards
Malvina of Brittany. J. K. Jerome
Mama Black Widow. R. Beck
Mama Doll. M. Woodhouse
Mambo. Campbell Armstrong
Mambo to Murder. Dale Clark
Mamigon. J. Hashian
Mamizelle Bon Voyage. G. Buhet
Mammon. P. C. Wren
Mammon on Righteousness. P. C. Wren
Mammon's Daughter. N. Tranter
Mammoth. S. P. Hyatt
Mammoth Hunters. C. Hayter
Mammoth Mansions Mystery. H. Hill
Mamo Murders. J. Sheridan
M'amselle It's Murder. K. T. McCall
Mamur Zapt and the Donkey-Vous. Michael Pearce
Mamur Zapt and the Night of the Dog. Michael Pearce
Mamur Zapt and the Return of the Carpet. Michael Pearce
Mam'zelle Guillotine. Baroness Orczy
Man. M. Dinelli
Man. Will Scott
Man. B. Stoker
Man About a Dog. Alec Coppel
Man About Broadway. H. Crooker
Man About the House. F. B. Young

Man About Town. C. Campion
Man About Town. D. Clift
Man About Town. W. LeQueux
Man Above Suspicion. J. Mayo
Man Against Fear. Mike Brewer
Man Against Man. Nicholas Carter
Man Alive. M. Cronin
Man Alone. Anthony Grey
Man Alone. Shelley Smith
Man Alone. E. C. Vivian
Man and a Half. F. Gamble
Man and His Kingdom. E. P. Oppenheim
Man and His Money. F. S. Isham
Man and His Price. Nicholas Carter
Man and Master. L. L. Lynch
Man and the Crime. H. Rockwood
Man and Two Gods. Jean Morris
Man and Wife. W. Collins
Man at Large. M. Cronin
Man at Six. J. Celestin
Man at Six. J. De Leon
Man at the Carlton. E. Wallace
Man at the Manor. O. Sinclair
Man at the Wheel. M. Kenyon
Man at the Window. Nicholas Carter
Man at Willow Ranch. H. Bindloss
Man at Windmere. V. Johnston
Man-Bait. A. Capelli
Man Bait. J. Liston
Man Beguiled. R. Rodd
Man Behind. A. Dax
Man Behind. J. Hunter
Man Behind Me. J. N. Chance
Man Behind Murder. G. W. Jones
Man Behind the Badge. M. I. Snider
Man Behind the Chair. Winifred Graham
Man Behind the Curtain. A. Murray
Man Behind the Curtain. N. Tranter
Man Behind the Curtain. J. M. Walsh
Man Behind the Curtain. D. Walshe
Man Behind the Door. A. C. Gunter
Man Behind the Face. J. March
Man Behind the Mask. G. M. Cooke
Man Behind the Mask. J. Veitch
Man Behind the Scenes. Hedley Scott
Man Behind the Screen. A. Skene
Man Behind the Tinted Glasses. Diana Forbes
Man Between. W. A. Frost
Man Called Black. W. Manson
Man Called Eighty-Eight. R. W. Hinds
Man Called Gillray. F. M. White
Man Called Harry Brent. F. Durbridge
Man Called Jones. J. Symons
Man Called Jordan. A. Aricha
Man Called Kyril. J. Trenhaile
Man Called Lenz. George Young
Man Called Scavener. P. Van Greenaway
Man Called Spade. D. Hammett
Man Called Tempest. W. Shand
Man Condemned. P. Alding
Man Could Get Killed That Way. Weldon Hill
Man Crazy. A. Wallace
Man Dead. S. Jepson
Man Destroyed. Stuart Kay
Man Died Here. G. Dessart
Man Died Talking. R. Garnett
Man Dormant. J. Lodwick
Man Drowning. H. Kuttner
Man Eater. H. M. Rideout
Man Eater of Jassapur. D. Hart-Davis
Man Everybody Was Afraid Of. J. Hansen
Man for Me. T. Charles
Man from Algiers. W. Jardine
Man from Arnheim. L. Jackson
Man from Atlantis. K. Robeson
Man from Australia. F. A. Symonds
Man from Australia. W. L. Whitehouse
Man from AVON. M. Avallone
Man from Bar Harbour. G. Mitcham
Man from Blankleys. Anonymous
Man from Butler's. C. Landstone
Man from Checkmate. W. R. Bennett
Man from Chicago. L. C. Douthwaite
Man from China. A. Parsons

Man from Chun King. R. Hardinge
Man from Dartmoor. Gwyn Evans
Man from Destiny. I. MacKintosh
Man from Dieppe. H. King
Man from Downing Street. W. LeQueux
Man from Dublin. A. Blair
Man from Egypt. H. Hill
Man from Everywhere. G. Simenon
Man from Fleet Steret. J. Creasey
Man from Greek and Roman. J. Goldman
Man from Holland. R. Hardinge
Man from India. Nicholas Carter
Man from Internal Affairs. N. Hentoff
Man from Italy. J. G. Brandon
Man from Kabul. G. De Villiers
Man from Kenya. A. Parsons
Man from Kura-Kura. A. Murray
Man from Lias River. R. Cullum
Man from Limbo. G. Endore
Man from Lisbon. T. Gifford
Man from London. Nicholas Carter
Man from M.O.D. W. B. Day
Man from Madagascar. F. Grierson
Man from Madrid. P. Meriton
Man from Maloba. O. Binns
Man from Manchester. D. Donovan
Man from Manhattan. L. Grex
Man from Maybrick Road. A. Parsons
Man from Mexico City. D. Whitelaw
Man from Michigan. B. Graeme
Man from Mongolia. R. Hardinge
Man from Morocco. E. Wallace
Man from Moscow. G. Chester
Man from Moscow. P. McCutchan
Man from Moscow. F. Usher
Man from MOTHER. Harry Gregory
Man from Norway. G. Chester
Man from Nowhere. V. Bridges
Man from Nowhere. J. Ellin
Man from Nowhere. Joan Fleming
Man from Nowhere. E. Huxley
Man from Occupied France. J. March
Man from Odessa. G. Wynne
Man from Outside. L. C. Douthwaite
Man from Pansy. D. Rico
Man from Paris. Roland Daniel
Man from Paris. L. Royer
Man from Pecos. D. Reid
Man from Persia. L. Jackson
Man from Pretoria. H. Mg'weno
Man from Prison. Roland Daniel
Man from Rome and other stories. M. Van Vorst
Man from St. Petersburg. K. Follett
Man from Scapa Flow. Taffrail
Man from Scotland Yard. D. Frome
Man from Scotland Yard. S. Horler
Man from Sing Sing. E. P. Oppenheim
Man from Singapore. J. G. Brandon
Man from Space. R. Hardinge
Man from Texas. B. Wayde
Man from the Bomb. R. Chetwynd-Hayes
Man from the Chamber of Horrors. John Ross
Man from the Clouds. J. S. Clouston
Man from the Diner's Club. S. Baol
Man from the Far East. J. Hunter
Man from the Gallows. E. L. McKeag
Man from the Jungle. R. Hardinge
Man from the Mist. M. Elgin
Man from the Norlands. J. Buchan
Man from the Past. S. P. Hyatt
Man from the Rhine. L. Cargill
Man from the River. G. D. H. Cole
Man from the Rock. D. Bateson
Man from the S.A.S. J. B. Coyle
Man from the Sea. M. Innes
Man from the South. J. R. Taylor
Man from the Turkish Slave. V. Canning
Man from the West. Anonymous
Man from the West. G. Goodchild
Man from the West, and other stories of adventure.
  G. Goodchild
Man from Tibet. C. G. Clason
Man from Toyko. W. Jardine
Man from Troy. J. G. Sarasin

Man from White Hat. S. Jason
Man from Whitehall. J. M. Walsh
Man from Yesterday. D. Daniels
Man from Yesterday. G. Markstein
Man Gets Into His Tomb. L. Mercer
Man Himself. A. M. Williamson
Man; His Mark. W. C. Morrow
Man Hunt. G. Bettany
Man Hunt. O. Cameron
Man Hunt! L. Como
Man Hunt. T. Gallon
Man Hunt. G. Household
Man Hunt. L. A. Knight
Man-Hunter. D. Donovan
Man-Hunter. M. O. Rolfe
Man I Didn't Kill. N. Deane
Man I Killed. M. Halliday
Man I Killed. S. Walker
Man in a Black Hat. T. Thurston
Man in a Mist. L. Lamb
Man in a Net. W. Butler
Man in a Net. P. Garrod
Man in a Wire Cage. M. Perakh
Man in Ambush. M. Procter
Man in Aspic. Andrew Hall
Man in Black. S. J. Weyman
Man in Blue. M. A. Denison
Man in Brown. W. Edwards
Man in Brown. M. Walsh
Man in Charge. R. Jessup
Man in Danger. M. Brewer
Man in Evening Clothes. J. R. Scott
Man in Gray. F. Crane
Man in Gray. B. Orczy
Man in Gray. E. C. Vivian
Man in Half Moon Street. B. Lyndon
Man in High Castle. P. K. Dick
Man in Lower Ten. M. R. Rinehart
Man in Motion. C. Williams
Man in Motley. T. Gallon
Man in My Chair. H. B. Kaye
Man in My Grave. W. Tucker
Man in My Shoes. J. N. Chance
Man in No. 3. J. S. Fletcher
Man in Question. J. Godey
Man in Ratcatcher, and other stories. H. C. McNeile
Man in Room 3. A. Carr
Man in Stripes. Lieut. Carlton
Man in the Auto. Nicholas Carter
Man in the Basement. B. P. Rosenkrantz
Man in the Bird Cage. K. MacLean
Man in the Blue Mask. Anthony Morton
Man in the Bottle. B. Knox
Man in the Box. N. Worth
Man in the Brown Derby. W. S. Hastings
Man in the Brown Suit. A. Christie
Man in the Button Boots. Anthony Gilbert
Man in the Cage. J. H. Vance
Man in the Cape. H. C. Bailey
Man in the Car. A. Raleigh
Man in the Check Suit. T. W. H. Delf
Man in the Cloak. S. Horler
Man in the Coach. E. C. Derby
Man in the Corner. B. Orczy
Man in the Dark. W. Cook
Man in the Dark. J. Ferguson
Man in the Dark. D. Orgill
Man in the Dark. S. Scarlett
Man in the Dark. Donald Stuart
Man in the Dark. A. P. Terhune
Man in the Dark Suit. D. R. Caro
Man in the Driver's Seat. Ira Walker
Man in the Flypaper Hat. J. C. Walls
Man in the Fog. H. Tighe
Man in the Fur Coat. J. S. Fletcher
Man in the Garden. P. Mason
Man in the Gray Flannel Shroud. F. Orenstein
Man in the Green Chevy. S. R. Cooper
Man in the Green Hat. M. Coles
Man in the Grey Cowl. A. Murray
Man in the Hood. S. Horler
Man in the Jury Box. R. O. Chipperfield
Man in the Lane. T. Neild
Man in the Lubianka. D. Vallance

M

Man in the Mail. L. Carlton
Man in the Mews. J. Packer
Man in the Middle. H. Atkinson
Man in the Middle. M. E. Chaber
Man in the Middle. F. Findley
Man in the Middle. A. Heal
Man in the Middle. N. Lewis
Man in the Middle. D. Wagoner
Man in the Mirror. F. Ayer
Man in the Mirror. H. Douglas
Man in the Mist. F. Bonnamy
Man in the Monkey Suit. A. Hathaway
Man in the Moon. F. Norwood
Man in the Moonlight. R. S. Holland
Man in the Moonlight. H. McCloy
Man in the Moss-Colored Trousers. M. Bringle
Man in the Net. P. Quentin
Man in the Night Mail Train. A. Philips
Man in the Pig Mask. C. T. Stoneham
Man in the Portrait. F. A. M. Webster
Man in the Purple Gown. C. Haddon
Man in the Queue. G. Daviot
Man in the Red Hat. R. Keverne
Man in the Red Mask. Roy Vickers
Man in the Rolls Royce. Ilian Stuart
Man in the Sandhills. A. Marsden
Man in the Shadow. R. Foley
Man in the Shadow. S. Kyle
Man in the Shadow. H. Whittington
Man in the Shadows. C. Bidmead
Man in the Shadows. P. Corris
Man in the Shadows. Caroline Crane
Man in the Shadows. C. J. Daly
Man in the Shadows. S. Horler
Man in the Shadows. K. Slattery
Man in the Sopwith Camel. M. Butterworth
Man in the Spike. Michael Barrett
Man in the Tricorn Hat. D. Ames
Man in the Trilby Hat. R. Goyne
Man in the Turkish Bath. H. F. Moulton
Man in the Twilight. R. Cullum
Man in the Water. R. Sheckley
Man in the White Raincoat. R. Lebherz
Man in the White Slicker. L. H. Nason
Man in Wax. Anonymous
Man in White. S. Horler
Man in Yellow, and The Empty House. H. C. McNeile
Man Inside. M. E. Chaber
Man Inside. N. S. Lincoln
Man-Killer. T. Powell
Man Lay Dead. N. Marsh
Man, Let's Go On. P. McCutchan
Man Made Angry. H. Brooke
Man Made Law. C. Stanton
Man Made of Tin. Shane Martin
Man Made Woman. R. F. Murphy
Man Missing. M. G. Eberhart
Man Must Live. H. Holland
Man Named Seraphin. R. Ray
Man Named Thin. D. Hammett
Man Next Door. M. G. Eberhart
Man No One Knew. L. Meynell
Man Nobody Knew. D. T. Lindsay
Man Nobody Knows. B. Trave
Man Nobody Saw. P. Cheyney
Man of a Hundred Faces. G. Leroux
Man of a Hundred Masks. G. Leroux
Man of Affairs. S. Horler
Man of Bronze. K. Robeson
Man of Character. D. H. Landels
Man of Cold Rages. Jordan Park
Man of Dangerous Secrets. M. March
Man of Dartmoor. O. Binns
Man of Death. A. Gask
Man of Double Deed. L. Daventry
Man of Evil. S. Horler
Man of Forty. G. Bullett
Man of Glass. D. Zochert
Man of Gold. E. Hervey
Man of Iron. Nicholas Carter
Man of Last Resort. M. D. Post
Man of Law. J. Wainwright
Man of Little Evils. S. Dobyns

Man of Many Colours. D. Braza
Man of Many Faces. Nicholas Carter
Man of Many Minds. E. E. Evans
Man of Millions. S. R. Keightley
Man of Miracles. M. Leblanc
Man of Mystery. Anonymous
Man of Mystery. Nicholas Carter
Man of Mystery. Leon Lewis
Man of Mystery. Old Sleuth
Man of No Sorrows. C. Kernahan
Man of Power. J. Blackmore
Man of Respect. D. London
Man of Riddles. Nicholas Carter
Man of Sentiment. T. Cobb
Man of Silver Mount. M. Pemberton
Man of Steel. W. J. Elliott
Man of Substance. A. Hodges
Man of Talent. E. Kyle
Man of the Avenue. F. Dark
Man of the Crag. G. Boothby
Man of the Forty Faces. T. W. Hanshew
Man of the Hour. W. Magnay
Man of the Islands. H. D. Stacpoole
Man of the Moment. M. Gerard
Man of the North. J. B. Hendryx
Man of the River. O. Sinclair
Man of Two Tribes. A. W. Upfield
Man of Wrath. P. Allardyce
Man on a Horse. H. Clewes
Man on a Leash. C. Williams
Man on a Nylon String. W. Masterson
Man on a Rope. G. H. Coxe
Man on a Short Leash. O. Jacks
Man on a String. M. Wolfe
Man on a Tight Rope. N. Paterson
Man on All Fours. A. Derleth
Man on Fire. A. J. Quinnell
Man on His Shoulder. K. Methold
Man on Horseback. A. Abdullah
Man on the Balcony. M. Sjowall
Man on the Bench in the Barn. G. Simenon
Man on the Box. H. MacGrath
Man on the Bridge. I. S. Black
Man on the Camel. H. M. Sachar
Man on the Cliff. J. N. Chance
Man on the Crater's Edge. J. Gerson
Man on the Dole. P. Urquhart
Man on the Dover Road. D. Whitelaw
Man on the End of the Rope. Paul Townend
Man on the Landing. F. Jones
Man on the Left. W. J. Gardiner
Man on the Marsh. D. Leach
Man on the Raffles Verandah. Lydia Kirk
Man on the Run. M. Brewer
Man on the Run. M. Cronin
Man on the Run. M. Halliday
Man on the Run! A. Kirby
Man on the Run. C. Williams
Man on the Spot. S. C. Mason
Man on the Stairs. Carnaby Brown
Man on the Terrace. M. Hacker
Man on the Tower. C. Hubold
Man on the Train. W. J. Chaput
Man on the Twenty-Fourth Floor. L. Allan
Man on Watch. T. Filer
Man Out of Nowhere. L. P. Davies
Man Out of the Rain. P. MacDonald
Man Outside. S. Campbell
Man Outside. W. Martyn
Man Outside. Donald Stuart
Man Overboard! F. W. Crofts
Man Overboard. A. MacKinnon
Man Overboard! F. Metcalfe
Man Pays. A. Applin
Man Peter. G. Goodchild
Man Pinches Bottom. J. T. Story
Man Responsible. S. Robinett
Man Running. S. Jepson
Man Running. E. West
Man Scent. S. A. White
Man That Corrupted Hadleyburg. M. Twain
Man That I Love. D. Egerton
Man the Devil Didn't Want. P. C. Wren
Man They Could Not Convict. R. Hardinge

Man They Could Not Kill. C. H. Barker
Man They Could Not Kill. J. Corbett
Man They Couldn't Arrest. A. J. Small
Man They Couldn't Buy. Gilbert Chester
Man They Couldn't Escape. M. Fiaschetti
Man They Couldn't Hang. O. Martyn
Man They Couldn't Kill. R. L. Meyers
Man They Feared. T. A. Plummer
Man They Held Back. Nicholas Carter
Man They Put Away. T. A. Plummer
Man to Be Feared. Nicholas Carter
Man to Match the Hour. S. Truss
Man Trap. Anonymous
Man Trap. J. A. Dunn
Man-Trap. J. D. MacDonald
Man-Trap. W. Magnay
Man Trap. H. Vogel
Man-Trapper. Old Sleuth
Man Under the Window. G. T. Ockley
Man Underground. K. Cook
Man Upstairs. P. Hamilton
Man Who Asked Why. Jessica Ryan
Man Who Awoke. M. I. Taylor
Man Who Backed Out! A. Parsons
Man Who Bailed Out. G. Chester
Man Who Bombed the World. J. Milton
Man Who Bought London. E. Wallace
Man Who Broke the Bank at Monte Carlo. M. Butterworth
Man Who Buried Jesus. J. E. Walsh
Man Who Butted In. V. Bridges
Man Who Called Himself Devlin. W. M. Green
Man Who Called Too Soon. A. M. Griffin
Man Who Came Back. J. Bryan
Man Who Came Back. W. M. Graydon
Man Who Came Back. M. Hastings
Man Who Came Back. E. Jepson
Man Who Came Back. H. W. Leggett
Man Who Came Back. J. Rossiter
Man Who Came Back. A. Wood
Man Who Came Back from the Dead. G. Leroux
Man Who Cannot Kill. J. F. Straker
Man Who Caught the 4:15. A. Spiller
Man Who Changed Faces. Nicholas Carter
Man Who Changed His Face. T. A. Plummer
Man Who Changed His Name. Robert (G.) Curtis
Man Who Changed His Name. E. Wallace
Man Who Changed His Name. Eric Wright
Man Who Changed His Plea. E. P. Oppenheim
Man Who Chose Death. E. Allen
Man Who Convicted Himself. D. Fox
Man Who Could Cheat Death. J. Sangster
Man Who Could Not Lose. R. H. Davis
Man Who Could Not Shudder. J. D. Carr
Man Who Could Read Cards. R. L. Broyles
Man Who Could Still Laugh. C. Houghton
Man Who Could Stop War. W. Penmare
Man Who Couldn't Sleep. C. E. Maine
Man Who Couldn't Sleep. A. Stringer
Man Who Covered Mirrors. M. Cumberland
Man Who Crawled Away. L. Butler
Man Who Cried All the Way Home. D. Hitchens
Man Who Dealt in Blood. G. Wolk
Man Who Defied the World. J. Andrews
Man Who Did Not Die. T. Harknett
Man Who Did Not Hang. S. Horler
Man Who Didn't Answer. I. Oellrichs
Man Who Didn't Count. G. M. Glaskin
Man Who Didn't Die. Anonymous
Man Who Didn't Exist. G. Homes
Man Who Didn't Exist. A. West
Man Who Didn't Fly. M. Bennett
Man Who Didn't Mind Hanging. N. B. Mavity
Man Who Died Laughing. D. Handler
Man Who Died on Friday. M. Underwood
Man Who Died Too Soon. G. H. Coxe
Man Who Died Twice. G. H. Coxe
Man Who Died Twice. M. Dekobra
Man Who Died Twice. S. Horler
Man Who Died Twice. L. Paxton
Man Who Died Twice. S. A. Peeples
Man Who Disappeared. E. Bohle
Man Who Disappeared. R. Pyke
Man Who Dressed to Kill. A. Spiller

Man Who Drove On. W. M. Graydon
Man Who Drove the Car. M. Pemberton
Man Who Ended War. Hollis Godfrey
Man Who Escaped. S. Bedford
Man Who Fainted. Nicholas Carter
Man Who Feared. P. Forsyth
Man Who Feared. W. F. Jenkins
Man Who Fell. M. Eden
Man Who Fell Through the Earth. C. Wells
Man Who Fell Up. K. Robeson
Man Who Finally Died. John Burke
Man Who Followed Women. B. Hitchens
Man Who Forgot. R. C. Armour
Man Who Forgot. H. Holt
Man Who Forgot. J. Mackie
Man Who Found Himself. M. Stacpoole
Man Who Found His Way. F. O'Rourke
Man Who Got Away. S. L. Elliott
Man Who Got Away with It. Bernice Carey
Man Who Grew Bulbs. J. M. Walsh
Man Who Grew Tomatoes. G. Mitchell
Man Who Guided Missiles. P. Denman
Man Who Had to Quit. A. Parsons
Man Who Had Too Much to Lose. Hampton Stone
Man Who Haunted Himself. Ralph Martin
Man Who Heard Too Much. B. Granger
Man Who Heard Too Much. Stockton Woods
Man Who Held Five Aces. Jean Leslie
Man Who Held the Queen to Ransom and Sent Parliament Packing. P. Van Greenaway
Man Who Hid. Dick Stewart
Man Who Japed. P. K. Dick
Man Who Killed. C. Farrere
Man Who Killed Fortescue. J. S. Strange
Man Who Killed Himself. J. Symons
Man Who Killed His Brother. Reed Stephens
Man Who Killed Hitler. R. P. Jones
Man Who Killed Me. Arthur MacLean
Man Who Killed the King. D. Wheatley
Man Who Killed Too Soon. M. Underwood
Man Who Knew. H. Leyford
Man Who Knew. M. O. Rolfe
Man Who Knew. E. Wallace
Man Who Knew. F. A. M. Webster
Man Who Knew All. M. Leighton
Man Who Knew Hammett. V. McConnor
Man Who Knew the Date. S. Kerr
Man Who Knew Too Much. Ruth Alexander
Man Who Knew Too Much. W. H. Baker
Man Who Knew Too Much and other stories. G. K. Chesterton
Man Who Laughed. G. Fairlie
Man Who Laughed at Murder. G. Ashe
Man Who Laughed Too Soon. Anonymous
Man Who Left Home. L. Jackson
Man Who Left Well Enough. M. McShane
Man Who Liked Slow Tomatoes. K. C. Constantine
Man Who Liked to Look at Himself. K. C. Constantine
Man Who Limped. V. Bridges
Man Who Limped. O. A. Kline
Man Who Lived at the Ritz. A. E. Hotchner
Man Who Lived by Night. D. Handler
Man Who Lived Twice. H. Shaw
Man Who Looked Back. Joan Fleming
Man Who Looked Death in the Eye. Hampton Stone
Man Who Looked Like Howard Cosell. J. B. Tucker
Man Who Lost an Hour. F. Marlowe
Man Who Lost Everything. P. Kuttner
Man Who Lost His Memory. A. Skene
Man Who Lost His Shadow. B. Denham
Man Who Lost His Way. W. E. Johns
Man Who Lost His Wife. J. Symons
Man Who Lost the War. W. T. Tyler
Man Who Loved Chocolates. D. Batchelor
Man Who Loved Dirty Books. D. Guy
Man Who Loved His Wife. V. Caspary
Man Who Loved Lions. Ethel L. White
Man Who Loved Mata Hari. D. Sherman
Man Who Loved Normandie. Justin Scott
Man Who Loved Spiders. S. Horler
Man Who Loved to Blow Up Trains. P. Stafford
Man Who Loved Zoos. M. J. Bosse
Man Who Made a King. R. Ladline
Man Who Made Diamonds. Warren Miller
Man Who Made Good. P. Trent
Man Who Made Money. B. Wayde
Man Who Made Monsters. J. Ronald
Man Who Made Roubles. J. Ingersol
Man Who Made the Devil Glad. D. McCaig
Man Who Met Himself. E. Crawshay-Williams
Man Who Met the Train. Harold Adams
Man Who Mislaid the War. S. Horler
Man Who Missed the War. D. Wheatley
Man Who Murdered God. J. L. Reynolds
Man Who Murdered Goliath. G. Homes
Man Who Murdered Himself. G. Homes
Man Who Must Not Die. Kenneth Way
Man Who Needed Action. M. Geller
Man Who Never Blundered. S. Gluck
Man Who Never Came Back. T. Worthing
Man Who Never Laughed. A. Hare
Man Who Never Slept! Gwyn Evans
Man Who Never Was. S. Picard
Man Who Owned New York. J. J. Osborn, Jr.
Man Who Paid. Nicholas Carter
Man Who Paid His Way. W. J. Sheldon
Man Who Played Patience. S. Truss
Man Who Played Thief. Don Smith
Man Who Plundered the City. S. Elvestad
Man Who Preferred Cocktails. S. Horler
Man Who Pulled the Strings. J. Haslette
Man Who Raised Hell. R. Sale
Man Who Ran Away. D. B. Dodson
Man Who Rang the Bell. M. Kennedy
Man Who Reaps. Katharine Jones
Man Who Risked His Partner. Reed Stephens
Man Who Rocked the Boat. W. J. Keating
Man Who Said No. W. Grove
Man Who Saw the Devil. J. Corbett
Man Who Saw Through Heaven. W. D. Steele
Man Who Saw Wrong. J. Fisher
Man Who Seduced a Bank. T. E. B. Clarke
Man Who Shook the Earth. S. Horler
Man Who Shook the Earth. K. Robeson
Man Who Shook the World. J. Creasey
Man Who Shot Birds and other tales. M. Fitt
Man Who Shot Lewis Vance. S. M. Kaminsky
Man Who Shot Rob Muldoon. J. Calder
Man Who Slept All Day. M. Venning
Man Who Sold Death. Nick Carter
Man Who Sold Death. J. Munro
Man Who Sold Secrets. Roland Daniel
Man Who Sought Trouble. Roland Daniel
Man Who Squealed. G. N. Philips
Man Who Stayed Alive. G. Ashe
Man Who Stayed at Home. J. E. H. Terry
Man Who Stayed at Home. B. Tinker
Man Who Stole Heaven. J. Ingersol
Man Who Stole Millions. Nicholas Carter
Man Who Stole Millions and other stories. Nicholas Carter
Man Who Stole the Crown Jewels. Augustus Muir
Man Who Stole the Earth. W. Holt-White
Man Who Stole the Mona Lisa. Martin Page
Man Who Stole the Sun. G. Fraser
Man Who Stood Alone. P. Trent
Man Who Thought He Was a Pauper. E. P. Oppenheim
Man Who Tried to Get Away. R. Stephens
Man Who Turned King's Evidence. J. Hunter
Man Who Understood Women and other stories. L. Merrick
Man Who Used Perfume. S. Horler
Man Who Vanished. V. Bridges
Man Who Vanished. Nicholas Carter
Man Who Vanished. F. Hume
Man Who Vanished. Old Sleuth
Man Who Vanished. J. T. Smith
Man Who Walked Away. C. Jay
Man Who Walked Like a Bear. S. M. Kaminsky
Man Who Walked Like a Dancer. R. Brennan
Man Who Walked on Diamonds. J. Quartermain
Man Who Walked Through Walls. J. Swain
Man Who Walked with Death. S. Horler
Man Who Wanted Seven Wives. L. Lyle
Man Who Wanted to Die. A. MacKenzie
Man Who Wanted to Murder Sherlock Holmes. Oriel Gray
Man Who Wanted Tomorrow. B. Freemantle
Man Who Was Bormann. Derek Boyd
Man Who Was Chief. G. Horne
Man Who Was Cursed. Nicholas Carter
Man Who Was Dead. A. W. Marchmont
Man Who Was Dead. W. S. Sykes
Man Who Was Guilty. F. H. Loughead
Man Who Was Left Behind. R. Ingalls
Man Who Was London. J. K. Keith
Man Who Was Murdered Twice. R. H. Leitfred
Man Who Was Nobody. E. Wallace
Man Who Was Not Himself. J. Graffy
Man Who Was Not Himself. M. Halliday
Man Who Was Not There. Ethel L. White
Man Who Was Saturday. D. Lambert
Man Who Was Scared. K. Robeson
Man Who Was Ten Years Late for Breakfast. C. Herbert
Man Who Was There. D. G. Barron
Man Who Was There. N. A. Temple-Ellis
Man Who Was Three Jumps Ahead. Hampton Stone
Man Who Was Thursday. G. K. Chesterton
Man Who Was Too Clever. Anthony Gilbert
Man Who Was Too Much. A. Gardner
Man Who Was Two. F. M. White
Man Who Wasn't. G. Goodchild
Man Who Wasn't Himself. L. Cargill
Man Who Wasn't There. Anthony Gilbert
Man Who Wasn't There. R. MacLeish
Man Who Wasn't There. J. Sandys
Man Who Wasn't There. J. Wainright
Man Who Wasn't There. B. Whitaker
Man Who Watched the Trains Go By. G. Simenon
Man Who Went Away. K. David
Man Who Went Up in Smoke. M. Sjowall
Man Who Went Wrong. L. Jackson
Man Who Won. C. T. Brady
Man Who Would Be F. Scott Fitzgerald. D. Handler
Man Who Would Do Anything. I. T. Ross
Man Who Would Not Swim. B. E. Wallace
Man Who Wouldn't Quit. G. Chester
Man Who Wouldn't Talk. Q. Reynolds
Man Whose Dreams Came True. J. Symons
Man Will Be Kidnapped Tomorrow. J. Ashford
Man with a Background of Flames. R. Johns
Man with a Calico Face. Shelley Smith
Man with a Crutch. Nicholas Carter
Man with a Double. Nicholas Carter
Man with a Grievance. W. Jardine
Man with a Gun. Lieut. Carlton
Man with a Gun. R. Daley
Man with a Load of Mischief. M. Grimes
Man with a Monocle. C. F. Gregg
Man with a Nose and other uncollected short stories of H. G. Wells. H. G. Wells
Man with a Number. S. Blakesley
Man with a Paper Skull. D. Marfield
Man with a Past. R. Patterson
Man with a Scar. E. C. Vivian
Man with a Secret. F. Hume
Man with a Shadow. G. M. Fenn
Man with a Thumb. W. C. Hudson
Man with a Weak Heart. G. Gardiner
Man with Bated Breath. J. B. Carr
Man with Bogart's Face. A. J. Fenady
Man with Dry Hands. S. Horler
Man with Expensive Tastes. E. Percy
Man with Fifty Complaints. M. McMullen
Man with Five Enemies. R. Hardinge
Man with Good Intentions. J. Barlow
Man with Half a Face. G. Davison
Man with His Back to the East. H. H. Ross
Man with Jitters. J. G. Brandon
Man with My Face. S. W. Taylor
Man with Nine Lives. J. Corbett
Man with Nine Lives. R. Marsh
Man with No Bones. P. Helm
Man with No Face. M. Armstrong
Man with No Face. J. N. Chance
Man with No Face. D. L. Sayers

M

Man with No Shadow. S. Marlowe
Man with Odd Shoulders. P. Haraday
Man with Talent. G. Fairlie
Man with the Amber Eyes. E. Jepson
Man with the Amber Eyes. F. Warden
Man with the Big Head. M. Scrope
Man with the Black Cord. A. Groner
Man with the Black Feather. G. Leroux
Man with the Black Patch. F. E. Verney
Man with the Black Wallet. W. W. Sayer
Man with the Black Worrybeads. G. N. Rumanes
Man with the Brooding Eyes. J. Goodwin
Man with the Brown Paper Face. I. Hamilton
Man with the Cane. J. Potts
Man with the Chocolate Egg. J. Noone
Man with the Clubfoot. D. Valentine
Man with the Crimson Box. H. S. Keeler
Man with the Crooked Arm. T. A. Plummer
Man with the Dark Beard. A. Haynes
Man with the Getaway Face. R. Stark
Man with the Glaring Eyes. A. Barclay
Man with the Glaring Eyes. A. Blair
Man with the Glass Eye. N. Leslie
Man with the Gloved Hand. J. McKimmey
Man with the Golden Gun. I. Fleming
Man with the Green Eyes. N. Goddard
Man with the Iron Chest. Richard Williams
Man with the Little Dog. G. Simenon
Man with the Lumpy Nose. L. Lariar
Man with the Magic Eardrums. H. S. Keeler
Man with the Magnetic Eyes. Roland Daniel
Man with the Mask. R. Dehan
Man with the Million Pounds. R. M. Newman
Man with the Monocle. Garnett Weston
Man with the Opals. A. W. Barrett
Man with the Painted head. H. Reilly
Man with the Parrots. A. E. Bayly
Man with the President's Mind. T. Allbeury
Man with the Purple Eyes. Anonymous
Man with the Rake. M. B. Lee
Man with the Red Beard. P. Cheyney
Man with the Red Beard. D. Whitelaw
Man with the Scar. J. Lomas
Man with the Scarlet Skull, and other tales. Gwyn Evans
Man with the Scarred Face. Anonymous
Man with the Scarred Hand. H. K. Webster
Man with the Seared Hand. J. G. Rowe
Man with the Squeaky Voice. R. A. J. Walling
Man with the Tattooed Face. M. Burton
Man with the Tiny Head. I. Drummond
Man with the Twisted Face. G. Davison
Man with the Vandyk Beard. F. M. White
Man with the Wax Face. R. Wormser
Man with the White Face. M. Gerard
Man with the Wooden Spectacles. H. S. Keeler
Man with the Yellow Eyes. A. S. Burrage
Man with Three Chins. D. Ames
Man with Three Jaguars. D. Ames
Man with Three Names. H. MacGrath
Man with Three Passports. D. Ames
Man with Three Witches. J. N. Chance
Man with Tin Trumpet. F. Mullally
Man with Two Clocks. W. Masterson
Man with Two Faces. S. Horler
Man with Two Heads. J. N. Chance
Man with Two Lives. J. Andrews
Man with Two Shadows. R. Maugham
Man with Two Souls. P. Quiroule
Man with Two Ties. H. Van Rensburg
Man with Two Wives. P. Quentin
Man with Two Wives and other stories. P. Cheyney
Man with Yellow Eyes. B. Atkey
Man with Yellow Eyes. A. Heckstall-Smith
Man Within. G. Greene
Man Without a Conscience. Nicholas Carter
Man Without a Face. A. Boissiere
Man Without a Face. J. E. Hasty
Man Without a Face. C. Robbins
Man Without a Head. J. Bowen
Man Without a Head. T. De Saix
Man Without a Head. W. S. Masterman
Man Without a Memory. A. W. Marchmont
Man Without a Mouth. J. Charles

Man Without a Name. S. Kyle
Man Without a Name. M. Russell
Man Without a Passport. A. Parsons
Man Without a Will. Nicholas Carter
Man Without Friends. M. Echard
Man Without Friends. M. Tripp
Man Without Nerves. E. P. Oppenheim
Man Without Pity. S. Truss
Man-Wolf. Erckmann-Chatrian
Man, Woman and Sin. E. Jepson
Man You Sleep With. D. E. Fisher
Manacle. M. J. Sagola
Manacle and Bracelet. E. C. Strong
Manasco Road. V. Canning
Manana. B. Vane
Manana Man. Christopher Newman
Manaton Disaster. Philippa Tyler
Manchester Thing. Angus Ross
Manchu Blood. H. Wiley
Manchu Cloud. James Bennett
Manchu Jade. S. Jepson
Manchurian Candidate. R. Condon
Mandarin Cypher. Adam Hall
Mandarin's Bell. E. Noble
Mandarin's Bride. M. Richmond
Mandarin's Dagger. L. Crichton
Mandarin's Fan. F. Hume
Mandarin's Pearl. Jeffrey Montague
Mandarin's Sapphire. D. Marfield
Mandarin's Seal. A. Murray
Mandate for Murder. J. A. S. McCombie
Mandelbaum Gate. M. Spark
Manderley Mystery. B. Ketterer
Mandragora. J. Palmer
Mandrake. D. Sherry
Mandrake in Granada. J. Haythorne
Mandrake in the Monastery. J. Haythorne
Mandrake the Magician. H. Ashman
Mandrakes in the Cupboard. T. B. Morris
Mandura Mystery. I. Barry
Maneuvers. F. Neuman
Manfac. M. Caidin
Manfred the Magic Trick Detective. Anonymous
Manfredi, Baron St. Osmond. S. Lansdell
Manfrone. M. Radcliffe
Mangrove Murder. Mary Scott
Manhandled. W. Chambers
Manhandled. A. Stringer
Manhattan Bombshell. N. W. Firth
Manhattan Cowboy. Carter Brown
Manhattan File. I. K. Martin
Manhattan 5-5742. D. Haring
Manhattan Gambit. B. Stein
Manhattan Ghost story. T. M. Wright
Manhattan Gothic. M. Arrighi
Manhattan Honey. N. Baroni
Manhattan Is My Beat. J. W. Deaver
Manhattan Love Song. C. Woolrich
Manhattan Masquerade. F. A. Kummer
Manhattan Massacre. C. Cunningham
Manhattan Massacre. J. Grecco
Manhattan Massacre. P. McCurtin
Manhattan Murder. A. Train
Manhattan Night. W. A. Wolff
Manhattan North. M. Albrand
Manhattan Number. Anonymous
Manhattan Revenge. J. Cutter
Manhattan Terrors. B. Sarto
Manhattan Underworld. J. Roeburt
Manhattan Wipeout. J. Rosenberger
Manhood Ceremony. R. Berliner
Manhunt. D. MacKenzie
Manhunt. Mark Ross
Manhunt. P. V. Stern
Manhunt in Manhattan. J. Dekker
Manhunt in Murder. W. Martyn
Manhunt in Sicily. S. Brydon
Manhunt Is My Mission. S. Marlowe
Manhunter. T. Harris
Manhunting. D. Sliman
Mania for Blondes. S. A. Krasney
Mania for Murder. Dixon Rice
Maniac. A. MacVicar
Maniac Bride. M. Blount

Maniac Father. T. P. Prest
Maniac Murders. P. Valdez
Maniac Rendezvous. M. Brandel
Maniac Responsible. R. Gover
Maniac's Dream. F. H. Rose
Manila Bay. William Marshall
Manila Espionage. Claire Phillips
Manila Hemp. Elinor Chamberlain
Manila Masquerade. D. Garth
Manila Stranger. F. Crisp
Manipulator. L. Crook
Manipulators. H. Atkinson
Manipulators. G. V. Basile
Manipulators. W. Garner
Manipulators. R. W. Jones
Manipulators. J. Rossiter
Manitou Island. M. G. McClelland
Mankill Sport. L. Derrick
Mankiller. C. Wilcox
Manna Enzyme. R. Hoyt
Mannequin. R. Byrne
Mannequin. V. Williams
Mannequin Doll. D. Glinto
Manning-Burke Murder. L. Tracy
Mannix. M. Avallone
Manoeuvres of Celeste. M. E. G.
Manor House Menace. J. Drummond
Manor House Mystery. J. S. Fletcher
Manor Inn. G. H. R. Dabbs
Manordale Mystery. Old Sleuth
Manrissa Man. P. Van Greenaway
Man's Blessing. L. Sciascia
Man's Enemies. L. Thayer
Man's Estate. J. Cleary
Man's Estate. N. Tranter
Man's Illegal Life. K. Heller
Man's Loving Family. K. Heller
Man's Shadow. R. W. Buchanan
Man's Shadow. W. H. L. Crauford
Man's Storm. K. Heller
Mansel Disappearance Mystery. G. Comley
Mansfield Mystery. J. C. Lenehan
Mansion House Mystery. S. Drew
Mansion in Miniature. E. St. Clair
Mansion Malevolent. C. Farr
Mansion of Dark Mists. E. Zumwalt
Mansion of Deadly Dreams. G. Corren
Mansion of Evil. C. Farr
Mansion of Evil. J. Millard
Mansion of Lost Memories. D. Daniels
Mansion of Menace. C. Farr
Mansion of Mystery. V. Smiley
Mansion of Mystery. C. K. Steele
Mansion of Peril. C. Farr
Mansion of Shadows. E. J. Murray
Mansion of Smiling Masks. D. Winston
Mansion of the Golden Windows. Elsie Lee
Mansion on the Moor. J. Purley
Mansion on the Moors. W. E. D. Ross
Mansion to Menace. M. Rosetti
Manslaughter. A. D. Miller
Manson Curse. Dell Shannon
Mantis. P. Fox
Mantis and the Moth. M. Weatherly
Mantle of Ishmael. J. S. Fletcher
Mantle of Methuselah. L. Reed
Mantle of the Emperor. Ladbroke Black
Mantouche Factor. Michael Bradley
Mantrackers. W. Mulvihill
Mantrap. J. N. Chance
Mantrap. A. Evans
Mantrap. D. Haring
Mantrap. P. Reakes
Mantrap. D. Yarnell
Mantrap Garden. John Sherwood
Mantrap Manor. Anonymous
Mantrapper. Anonymous
Manufacturer's Daughter. A. C. Gunter
Manuscript for Murder. R. M. Stern
Manuscript Murder. L. Robinson
Manuscript Murders. R. H. Lewis
Manuscript of Murder. P. J. Coyne
Manuscripts from the Diary of a Physician. T. P. Prest

Manville Murders. C. Fitzsimmons
Manx Cat. F. Levon
Manx Tales of Horror. A. J. Lert
Many a Monster. R. Finnegan
Many a Murder. D. Van Deusen
Many a Slip. F. W. Crofts
Many a Slip. O. Mills
Many Brace Hearts. D. M. Douglas
Many Cargoes. W. W. Jacobs
Many-Coloured Thread. L. Allan
Many Deadly Returns. P. Moyes
Many Engagements. J. S. Fletcher
Many Happy Returns. Justin Scott
Many-Headed Monster. G. Lett
Many Murders. I. H. Irwin
Many Parts. John Marsh
Many Thanks, Ben Hassett. H. De Hamel
Many Ways of Death. F. Didelot
Many Worlds of Magnus Ridolph. J. Vance
Maori Murder Case. A. L. Albert
Map of Mistrust. A. MacKinnon
Maple Hall Mystery. E. Parmer
Maple Sugar Murders. Stever Sherman
Maplethorpe Tangle. Elliot Bailey
Maracaibo Massacre. Mark Roberts
Maracaibo Mission. V. W. Mason
Marakano Formula. J. Pattinson
Maras Affair. E. Reed
Maraskar Bound. R. T. Bickers
Marathon Man. W. Goldman
Marathon Murder. J. Moffatt
Marathon Mystery. B. E. Stevenson
Marauders. M. McGann
Marauders by Night. A. Gask
Marbeau Cousins. Harry S. Edwards
Marble Angel. D. Daniels
Marble Arch Mystery. W. J. Bayfield
Marble Forest. T. Durrant
Marble Heart. H. Luger
Marble Hills. D. Daniels
Marble Jungle. C. Richards
Marble Leaf. D. Daniels
Marble Orchard. B. Copper
Marble Tomb Mystery. Colin Robertson
Marburg Virus. Stanley Johnson
Marcadia. K. Ashby
Marceau Case. H. S. Keeler
Marcel Levignet. E. Barron
March Fence. Matthew Yorke
March Hare Murders. E. Ferrars
March of Fate. B. L. Farjeon
March of the Flame Marauders. C. Steele
March of the Legion. J. Robb
March of the Long Shadows. Norman Lewis
March to the Gallows. M. Kelly
March Violets. P. Kerr
Marchand Woman. J. Ives
Marches of Honour. Ganpat
Marchester Royal. J. S. Fletcher
Marching Home. D. Honig
Marchington Inheritance. I. Holland
Marchmont. Catharine Smith
Marcia, the Innocent. K. Kimbrough
Marco. S. Cobb
Marco Polo, If You Can. W. F. Buckley, Jr.
Marcus Device. I. Melchior
Marcus Hay. S. P. Hyatt
Marcus Holbeach's Daughter. A. Jones
Mardi. K. Hewitt
Mardi Gras Massacre. L. Derrick
Mardi Gras Murders. G. Bristow
Mardi Gras Mystery. H. Bedford-Jones
Mare's Nest. C. Coffin
Margaret Benson's Vow. T. A. Plummer
Margaret Carmichael. C. Gibbon
Margaret Forster. G. A. Sala
Margaret Rutland. T. Cobb
Margaret, the Faithful. K. Kimbrough
Margaret, the Peacemaker. W. Wood
Margate Murder Mystery. B. Delannoy
Marge. K. Fitzgerald
Margery Redford and Her Friends. Mrs. M. H. Spielman
Margiana. Mrs. S. Sykes

Margie. E. V. Cunningham
Margie and the Wolf Man. R. St. Clair
Margin. Ian Stuart
Margin for Doubt. M. Borgenicht
Margin for Error. Clare Booth
Margin for Murder. Kane
Margin for Terror. F. Kane
Margin of Error. P. Henissart
Margin of Terror. P. Capon
Margin of Terror. W. P. McGivern
Margo. J. Jenkins
Margo's Reunion. J. Jenkins
Margot—and Her Judges. R. Marsh
Margot Leck. P. Piper
Margravine. L. Hiscott
Maria. Brian Cooper
Maria. B. Vane
Maria Be Mine. Pete Costello
Maria Canossa. S. Paretti
Maria Marches On. J. Slate
Maria Marten. Anonymous
Marianna. N. Buckingham
Marianne. J. Dering
Marianne. F. Mullally
Marianne the Outcast. Anonymous
Marianne's Kingdom. P. J. Cooper
Maribor Remembered. P. Laric
Maridu. S. Wagner
Marie Arnaud, Spy. B. Graeme
Marie de Brinvilliers. E. Gaboriau
Marie Halkett. R. W. Chambers
Marie-Rose. F. Du Boisgobey
Marie, the Dancing Girl. Old Sleuth
Marie Vee. D. Newton
Mariella—Spy! C. Davy
Mariette. T. P. Prest
Marigot Run. J. Ballem
Marihuana. W. Irish
Marijuana Girl. N. R. De Mexico
Marijuana Mob. J. H. Chase
Marijuana Murder. M. Stimson
Marilyn K. L. White
Marilyn the Wild. J. Charyn
Marine Corpse. W. G. Tapply
Marine Residence, and other stories. J. Payn
Mariner's End. E. B. Selig
Marinova of the Secret Service. R. Essex
Mario. J. Carrick
Mario on the Beach, and other tales. L. Golding
Marion. J. Bingham
Marion Darche. F. M. Crawford
Marionette. P. Bennetts
Marji and the Kidnap Plot. John Benton
Marjorie Daw and Other People. T. B. Aldrich
Marjorie Daw and other stories. T. B. Aldrich
Marjorie Daw and other tales. T. B. Aldrich
Mark. P. C. De Crespigny
Mark. C. E. Israel
Mark. J. Stone
Mark Castle—Cable Address: Roma. C. Marcus
Mark Danver's Sin, and The Madman of Coral Reef Lighthouse. H. C. McNeile
Mark Heffron. A. W. Bailey
Mark It for Murder. D. Sanderson
Mark Kilby and the Manhattan Murders. R. C. Frazer
Mark Kilby and the Miami Mob. R. C. Frazer
Mark Kilby and the Secret Syndicate. R. C. Frazer
Mark Kilby Solves a Murder. R. C. Frazer
Mark Kilby Stands Alone. R. C. Frazer
Mark Kilby Takes a Risk. R. C. Frazer
Mark Magic, the Detective. A. P. Morris
Mark Maturin, Parson. F. C. Whitehouse
Mark of a Buoy. G. Peters
Mark of a Witch. H. Kemp
Mark of Cain. S. A. Key
Mark of Cain. Andrew Lang
Mark of Cain. C. Wells
Mark of Cosa Nostra. Nick Carter
Mark of Displeasure. E. Hely
Mark of Kane. C. Franklin
Mark of Lucifer. E. P. Green
Mark of Merlin. A. McCaffrey
Mark of Murder. Dell Shannon

Mark of Pak San Ri. W. Stroup
Mark of Satan. A. Loring
Mark of the Beast. R. W. Kauffman
Mark of the Broad Arrow. Maurice Scott
Mark of the Cobra. V. Alily
Mark of the Crescent. J. Creasey
Mark of the Crimson Cross. Hedley Scott
Mark of the Dead. The Aresbys
Mark o' the Deil. H. Pease
Mark of the Dragon. M. Richmond
Mark of the Four. Mark Cross
Mark of the Hand. C. Armstrong
Mark of the Leech. J. Cassells
Mark of the Moccosin. K. Perkins
Mark of the Moon. F. Gerard
Mark of the Paw. Gavin Holt
Mark of the Rat. A. Fredericks
Mark of the Red Diamond. J. H. Chase
Mark of the Rope. M. Lynch
Mark of the Shadow. M. Grant
Mark of the Tong. J. G. Brandon
Mark of the Vulture. R. J. Hogan
Mark of the Vulture. M. Macao
Mark of Treachery. C. B. Kelland
Mark of Yekel. E. Y. Miller
Mark One: The Dummy. J. Ball
Mark Peterson's Daughter. M. Hutton
Mark Ryder's Vow. P. Trent
Mark Sutherland. E. Southworth
Mark the Sparrow. Clark Howard
Mark Three for Murder. R. P. Hansen
Mark Twain Murder. E. Skom
Mark Twain's A Double Barrelled Detective Story. R. St. Clair
Marked! B. Bristow
Marked "Cancelled". N. S. Lincoln
Marked Cards. J. Addiscombe
Marked Dangerous. E. Y. Miller
Marked Down for Murder. S. Dean
Marked for a Victim. S. C. Cumberland
Marked for Death. Nicholas Carter
Marked for Death. Insp. Pietro
Marked for Death. D. Plantz
Marked for Destruction. J. Barnett
Marked for Life. A. F. Pinkerton
Marked for Murder. Ronald Campbell
Marked for Murder. B. Halliday
Marked for Murder. C. R. Jones
Marked for Murder. W. X. Kienzle
Marked for Murder. J. R. Macdonald
Marked for Murder. V. B. Miller
Marked for Murder. W. Reed
Marked for Murder. R. O. Saber
Marked Hand. Nicholas Carter
Marked Lady. D. Haring
Marked Man. C. Barling
Marked Man. H. Carmichael
Marked Man. W. LeQueux
Marked Man. Hedley Scott
Marked Men. H. C. Wire
Marked Men. C. N. Buck
Marked "Personal". A. K. Green
Marked Pistol. J. C. Lenehan
Marked to Die. M. Cronin
Marked with a Cross. G. Monro
Marked Woman. G. Lamond
Marked Woman. M. Leighton
Marked Woman. D. Newton
Marked Woman. Grace M. White
Markenmore Mystery. J. S. Fletcher
Marker Calls the Tune. A. Marriott
Markers. S. Zion
Market for Murder. F. Gruber
Market for Murder. C. M. Russell
Market of Venus. M. Richmond
Markets of Treason. G. W. Jones
Markham Affair. S. P. Hyatt
Marksman. M. Cronin
Marksman. H. C. Rae
Marksman. S. Yuryenen
Marl-Pit Mystery. G. Ohnet
Marlborough Street. R. Bowker
Marley's Empire. P. McCutchan
Marloe Mansions Murder. A. G. MacLeod

Marlowe. R. Chandler
Marnie. Winston Graham
Maroc 7. M. Sands
Marooned. M. Maurice
Marooned! A. Murray
Marooned in Real Time. V. Vinge
Marooned with Murder. R. A. J. Walling
Marozia. A. G. Hales
Marquis. C. Garvice
Marquis. A. Soutar
Marquis of Loveland. C. N. Williamson
Marquis of Murray Hill. Baron
Marquis of Putney. R. Marsh
Marquise de Brinvilliers. E. Gaboriau
Marrakesh One-Two. R. Grenier
Marrendon Mystery, and other stories of crime and detection. J. S. Fletcher
Marriage and Murder. D. Sharp
Marriage at a Venture. E. Gaboriau
Marriage Bed. H. V. Dixon
Marriage-Broker. M. B. Lowndes
Marriage Broker. F. Warden
Marriage Bureau Murders. J. Bingham
Marriage by Capture. A. Stringer
Marriage by Mistake. W. Carter
Marriage Cage. W. Johnston
Marriage Chest. D. Eden
Marriage for the Defence. Roy Vickers
Marriage for Two. A. S. Roche
Marriage Has Been Arranged. P. Allardyce
Marriage Is Murder. N. Pickard
Marriage Lines. J. S. Fletcher
Marriage Mystery. F. Hume
Marriage of Adventure. E. Gaboriau
Marriage of Captain Kettle. C. J. C. Hyne
Marriage of Esther. G. Boothby
Marriage of Inconvenience. T. Cobb
Marriage of Inconvenience. J. L. Roberts
Marriage of Kettle. C. J. C. Hyne
Marriage of Margot. A. Applin
Marriage of Meldrum Strange. T. Mundy
Marriage of Yussuf Khan. F. Heller
Marriage Pact. L. Cheatham
Marriage Was Not for Her. Margaret Lang
Marriages of Mayfair. E. K. Chatterton
Married at Midnight. Anonymous
Married Beneath Him. J. Payn
Married by Stealth. F. Warden
Married for Love. F. Du Boisgobey
Married in Haste. M. E. Braddon
Married in Mask. M. T. Walworth
Married Into Murder. Reginald Campbell
Married Man. P. P. Read
Married or Trapped. T. Walton
Married People. M. R. Rinehart
Married to a Spy. R. Starr
Married to a Spy. A. Waugh
Married to Murder. E. Radford
Married to Murder. H. Whittington
Marriott Hall. D. Daniels
Marrowby Myth. W. Martyn
Marry in Haste. J. A. Hodge
Marry in May. M. Richmond
Marry Into Danger. C. Jauniere
Marrying Beneath Your Station. H. Wood
Marrying Kind. G. Finley
Marsanne. V. Coffman
Marseilles. A. Caillou
Marseilles Connection. B. Peterson
Marseilles Enforcer. Don Smith
Marsh. E. Raymond
Marsh Blood. J. Marcus
Marsh Gang. H. N. Field
Marsh House. M. L. Roby
Marshal. D. St. Pierre
Marshal and the Madwoman. M. Nabb
Marshal and the Murderer. M. Nabb
Marshal's Own Case. M. Nabb
Marshfield the Observer & The Death-Dance. E. Castle
Marshmallow Pie. Graham Lord
Marshmead Murders. S. Taylor
Marshwood. M. Heath
Marston Murder Case. W. A. Stowell

Marta. Marilyn Ross
Martello Tower. W. Haggard
Martello Tower Mystery. G. H. Teed
Marten Mystery. J. Ironside
Martha the Medium. J. Champion
Martha Willis. T. P. Prest
Martha's Vineyard Affair. S. Hart
Marthe and the Madman. J. De. Bosschere
Martin Claims Damages. H. Baron
Martin Faber, The Story of a Criminal. W. G. Simms
Martin Hewitt, Investigator. Arthur Morrison
Martin Speed Versus "The Snatcher". M. G. Hugi
Martineau Murders. R. Hull
Martini Murders. Roger Fuller
Martinis and Murder. J. Kane
Martyn Ware's Temptation. H. Wood
Martyr. J. Petschull
Martyr or Criminal? I. L. Cassilis
Martyred Fool. D. C. Murray
Marune: Alastor 933. J. Vance
Marvellous Coincidence. K. Cornwallis
Marvelous Boy. P. Corris
Marvelous Escape. Old Sleuth
Marvels and Mysteries. R. Marsh
Marworth Mystery. W. A. Frost
Mary. M. E. Braddon
Mary Barton. E. Gaskell
Mary Clifford. T. P. Prest
Mary Deare. H. Innes
Mary Elizabeth—Adventuress. R. Starr
Mary-Jane. R. Sickelmore
Mary Jane Married. George R. Sims
Mary Jane's Memoirs. George R. Sims
Mary Regan. L. Scott
Mary Reilly. Valerie Martin
Mary Roberts Rinehart's Crime Book. M. R. Rinehart
Mary Swann. C. Shields
Maryjane Tonight at Angels Twelve. M. Caidin
Marylebone Miser. E. Phillpotts
Mary's Grave. M. McClintick
Ma's Bar. P. Hallifax
Masada Plan. Leonard Harris
Masakado Lesson. W. P. Kennedy
Mascarada Pass. W. C. MacDonald
Masculine Ending. Joan Smith
Masinglee Murders. M. B. Dix
Mask. J. Cowdroy
Mask. F. DiFiore
Mask. A. Hornblow
Mask. W. LeQueux
Mask. Will Scott
Mask. O. West
Mask and the Man. P. Andreae
Mask and the Man. Alan Thomas
Mask and the Moonflower. P. A. Whitney
Mask for Crime. Marion Roberts
Mask for Murder. M. Dalman
Mask for Murder. H. Kane
Mask for Murder. A. M. Stein
Mask for the Toff. J. Creasey
Mask of Abraham Morgenstern. D. Panger
Mask of Alexander. M. Albrand
Mask of Danger. M. Clare
Mask of Death. A. Bachelin
Mask of Destiny. M. Andrau
Mask of Dimitrios. E. Ambler
Mask of Evil. C. Armstrong
Mask of Evil. J. A. Creighton
Mask of Evil. D. M. Disney
Mask of Evil. Marilyn Ross
Mask of Fear. Ross Alexander
Mask of Fu Manchu. S. Rohmer
Mask of Fury. Arthur MacLean
Mask of Glass. H. Roth
Mask of Gold. A. S. Swan
Mask of Guilt. D. B. Hughes
Mask of Love. J. Thatcher
Mask of Medusa. P. Minton
Mask of Memory. V. Canning
Mask of Mephisto. W. B. Gibson
Mask of Mephisto. M. Grant
Mask of Murder. D. Campbell

Mask of Murder. E. Radford
Mask of Pursuit. J. N. Chance
Mask of Shadows. Ray Owen
Mask of Silence. S. McErlean
Mask of Terror. H. Desmond
Mask of the Andes. J. Cleary
Mask of the Clown. William Taylor
Mask of the Enchantress. V. Holt
Mask of the Jaguar. J. North
Mask of Treason. A. Stevenson
Mask of Violence. M. Hebden
Mask of Words. J. Roffman
Masked Alibi. M. A. Clune
Masked Ball. A. Lowing
Masked Ball Murder. D. Fairfax
Masked Blackmailer. J. C. Lenehan
Masked Dancer. W. J. Bayfield
Masked Dancer. B. Bolt
Masked Death. J. Sylvester
Masked Detective. Anonymous
Masked Detective. H. P. Halsey
Masked Dictator. W. M. Graydon
Masked Dog. R. Obstfeld
Masked for Murder. H. Kuttner
Masked Forgers. W. J. Bayfield
Masked Gunman. G. Ashe
Masked in Mystery. S. Rathborne
Masked Invasion. C. Steele
Masked Judgment. D. T. Lindsay
Masked Killer. G. H. Teed
Masked Lady. M. M. Murray
Masked Man. G. Leroux
Masked Man of the Desert. C. Brisbane
Masked Marauder. R. M. Graydon
Masked Motorist. Anonymous
Masked Murder. M. Alan
Masked Raiders. R. C. Armour
Masked Slayer. R. Hardinge
Masked Stranger. L. Allan
Masked Terror. H. Pink
Masked Terror. M. Richmond
Masked Venus. R. H. Savage
Masked Woman. J. McCulley
Masked Women. R. Beach
Masks. B. Fleming
Masks. A. Skene
Masks and Faces. P. Bottome
Masks and Faces. C. Curzon
Masks of Malevolence. L. Amino
Masks of Rome. C. Llewellyn
Masks of Thespis. M. Richardson
Masks Off at Midnight. V. Williams
Mason Codex. J. Bannister
Masque. S. Holland
Masque by Gaslight. V. Coffman
Masque of a Savage Mandarin. P. Robinson
Masque of Enchantment. C. Cross
Masque of Mutiny. C. L. Reid
Masque of Satan. V. Coffman
Masque of the Red Death. Elsie Lee
Masque World. A. Panshin
Masquerade. J. Daley
Masquerade. W. X. Kienzle
Masquerade. W. Morton
Masquerade. M. Pereira
Masquerade. Clarissa Ross
Masquerade. C. Sternberg
Masquerade at Monfalcone. Dorinne Moore
Masquerade in Blue. G. M. Barnes
Masquerade in Venice. V. Johnston
Masquerade Into Madness. Samuel Merwin
Masquerade Mystery. F. Hume
Masquerade of Evil. E. Zumwalt
Masquerade of Vengeance. A. C. Ley
Masquerader. R. M. Graydon
Masquerader. K. C. Thurston
Masquerades. Shane Leslie
Masques. B. Pronzini
Masques and Phases. Robert Ross
Mass. Jack Fuller
Mass for a Dead Witch. A. Grace
Mass Radiography Murders. Sutherland Scott
Massacre at Metz. C. Whiting
Massacre at Russian River. D. Hartman

Massacre at Umtali. P. McCurtin
Massacre in Milan. Nick Carter
Massacre in Rome. J. Rosenberger
Massingham Affair. E. Grierson
Massingham Butterfly. J. S. Fletcher
Massy's Game. J. Olsen
Master. M. Braly
Master. Carter Brown
Master and Maid. Frank Jones
Master and Man. A. Askew
Master Assassin. Nick Carter
Master Crime. J. Lyons
Master Criminal. Nicholas Carter
Master Criminal. J. J. Farjeon
Master Criminal. S. Paternoster
Master Cure. C. H. Buck
Master Detective. P. Brebner
Master Dudley. P. Johnson
Master File. R. Elliott
Master Hand. R. Dallas
Master Hand. J. Futrelle
Master Key. W. Massey
Master Key. A. Soutar
Master Key. M. Togawa
Master-Key. F. Warden
Master Manhunters. J. Gollomb
Master Mind. M. Dana
Master-Mind. F. Hume
Master Mind. H. Janson
Master Mind. C. Moffett
Master-Mind Menace. B. Luigi
Master Mummer. E. P. Oppenheim
Master Murderer. C. Wells
Master Must Die. V. Gridban
Master Mystery. L. Dowsett
Master Mystery. A. B. Reeve
Master Mystery. Seamark
Master of Aysgarth. M. Mayhew
Master of Beechwood. A. Sergeant
Master of Blacktower. B. Michaels
Master of Blue Cone. V. Coffman
Master of Broken Men. C. Steele
Master of Charteris Towers. W. M. Graydon
Master of Crime. C. Williams
Master of D.E.A.T.H. J. Ahern
Master of Deception. R. Marsh
Master of Destinies. R. Bentinck
Master of Deviltry. Nicholas Carter
Master of Evil. H. Long
Master of Evrington. V. Blake
Master of Fear. C. Rushton
Master of Fortune. C. J. C. Hyne
Master of Foxhallow. S. Claudia
Master of Frinton Park. F. M. Long
Master of Graylands. H. Wood
Master of Greystone. G. Carrington
Master of High Beck. John Marsh
Master of His Fate. J. M. Cobban
Master of Jethcart. A. Dwyer-Joyce
Master of Malcarew. V. Black
Master of Men. E. P. Oppenheim
Master of Merlains. D. Whitelaw
Master of Merripit. E. Phillpotts
Master of Millions. G. C. Lorimer
Master of Money. F. Lady
Master of Montrolfe Hall. R. O'Grady
Master of Murder. T. Robbins
Master of Mysteries. Anonymous
Master of Mysteries. L. T. Meade
Master of Palowar. Magali
Master of Penrose. J. A. Hodge
Master of Phoenix Hall. E. Marlow
Master of Rathkelly. H. Smart
Master of Revels. R. H. Watkins
Master of Roxton. E. Barr
Master of Secrets. G. Bartram
Master of Shadows. Margery Lawrence
Master of Solitaire. J. L. Latham
Master of Souls. M. Hansom
Master of the Ceremonies. G. M. Fenn
Master of the Dark. J. Cassells
Master of the Day of Judgment. L. Perutz
Master of the Death Madness. G. Stockbridge
Master of the Microbe. R. W. Service

Master of the Moor. R. Rendell
Master of the Priory. A. Haynes
Master of the Skies. P. Trent
Master of Trenance. T. W. Speight
Master of Venom. S. Horler
Master Passion. Anonymous
Master Plan. B. J. Freshman
Master Plan. I. Stuart
Master Planner. N. Brady
Master Plot. Lou Smith
Master Rogue. D. G. Phillips
Master Rogue. C. Somerville
Master Schemer. V. Campbell
Master Scoundrel. H. Thurlow
Master Sniper. S. Hunter
Master Spirit. W. Magnay
Master Spy. R. J. Buckley
Master Spy. A. Gask
Master Spy. J. Pendower
Master Spy. G. E. Rochester
Master Stroke. E. C. Derby
Master Theron. C. Lawton
Master Villain. Nicholas Carter
Master Vorst. A. J. Small
Masterclass. Morris West
Masterful Voice. H. Buchanan
Masterly Trick. Nicholas Carter
Masterman's Mistake. T. Cobb
Mastermind Wears Mink. M. Brody
Masterpiece. T. Hoving
Masterpiece Affair. K. Royce
Masterpiece in Murder. R. Powell
Masterpiece of Crime. Nicholas Carter
Masterpiece of Nice Mr. Breen. H. Hunvald
Masterpieces of Crime. A. D. Vandam
Masterpieces of Mystery. A. K. Green
Masterplayers. Michael Sinclair
Masters Affair. B. Hirschfeld
Master's Challenge. W. B. Murphy
Masters Connection. D. Chandler
Masters of Kaolina. E. L. Long
Masters of the Parachute Mail. J. Carr
Masterstroke. T. Heald
Masterstroke. Douglas Payne
Masterstroke. M. Sharp
Masterstroke. J. Tiger
Masterwork. J. Miglis
Masterworks of Crime and Mystery. A. C. Doyle
Matador Dies. J. Peyre
Matador of the Five Towns. Arnold Bennett
Matador's Fortune. J. W. Bobin
Matapan Affair. F. Du Boisgobey
Matapan Jewels. F. Du Boisgobey
Matarese Circle. R. Ludlum
Match for a Murderer. D. Halliday
Match Point for Murder. K. Platt
Matched with Mystery. J. A. Jordan
Matchless Detective. Anonymous
Mate Swap. R. Raczyk
Material Witness. E. Messenger
Maternity of Harriott Wicken. Mrs. H. Dudeney
Mathematician. W. Manson
Mathematics of Guilt. I. Ostrander
Mathematics of Murder. K. Bedford
Mather Again. B. Graeme
Mather Investigates. B. Graeme
Matheson Fever. J. Easton
Matheson Formula. J. S. Fletcher
Matheson Money. F. Warden
Matilda Hunter Murder. H. S. Keeler
Matilda, My Darling. N. Krauth
Matilda Shouted Fire. J. Green
Matinee. R. Steiner
Matinee Idol. R. Base
Mating Call. W. Shaw
Mating Cry. A. E. Van Vogt
Mating in the Wilds. O. Binns
Mating of the Blades. A. Abdullah
Matlock Paper. R. Ludlum
Mato Grosso Horror. J. Rosenberger
Matorni's Vineyard. E. P. Oppenheim
Matravers Hall. E. Kellier
Matrimonial Country and other stories. Austin Phillips

Matrimonial Mixture. C. J. C. Hyne
Matrimony by Advertisement. C. G. Payne
Matrimony Most Murderous. L. Cargill
Matrix Man. W. C. Dietz
Matsu Dossier. W. Dainton
Matt. R. Buchanan
Matt. A. Hyder
Matter of Accent. D. Keith
Matter of Assassination. P. Raymond
Matter of Blood. B. Whitaker
Matter of Business and other stories. J. Farnol
Matter of Concealment. D. S. Copp
Matter of Confidence. B. Williams
Matter of Conscience. P. Harcourt
Matter of Conscience. E. P. Hoyt
Matter of Conviction. E. Hunter
Matter of Degree. T. Philbin
Matter of Diplomacy. W. Tute
Matter of Fact. H. Brean
Matter of Honour. J. Archer
Matter of Honor. W. P. McGivern
Matter of Intelligence. G. Wittman
Matter of Iodine. D. Keith
Matter of Love and Death. T. Wells
Matter of Luck and other stories. P. Cheyney
Matter of Mandrake. Barry Norman
Matter of Millions. W. J. Bayfield
Matter of Millions. A. K. Green
Matter of Millions. F. M. White
Matter of Motive. G. Montrose
Matter of Murder. Neill Graham
Matter of Nerves. R. Hull
Matter of Opportunity. C. Arley
Matter of Paradise. B. Meggs
Matter of Policy. Sam Merwin
Matter of Record. Malcolm Gray
Matter of Record. D. Morrison
Matter of Revenge. C. Demaine
Matter of Scents. T. Fitzgerald
Matter of Sixpence. J. La Tourrette
Matter of Size. H. Homewood
Matter of Skill. Nicholas Carter
Matter of Tar. H. C. McNeile
Matter of Taste. R. Lockridge
Matter of Taste. F. Saberhagen
Matter of Thousands. Old Spicer
Matter of Time. G. Cook
Matter of Time. Deborah Joyce
Matter of Witchcraft. Alice Brennan
Matters of Suspense. R. Rendell
Matthew Sharpin—Detective. Wilkie Collins
Matthew's Hand. C. Larson
Matzohball. S. Weinstein
Mau Len Death Zone. J. Lansing
Maud Blackstone, the Millionaire's Daughter. R. R. Johnston
Maud Talbot. Holme Lee
Maui Mystery. W. Rotsler
Maulever Hall. J. A. Hodge
Mauleverer Murders. A. C. Fox-Davies
Mauleverer's Millinos. T. W. Reid
Maumbury Rings. G. V. McFadden
Maunaloa Curse. Irma Walker
Maundy. Julian Gloag
Maureen of the Island. Robin Temple
Maureen Versus Fate. R. Rodd
Maurice Mystery. J. E. Cooke
Maurizius Case. J. Wasserman
Mausoleum Key. N. Daniels
Mauve Front Door. L. Meynell
Mavde Baxter. C. C. Hitchkiss
Mawpeth Millions. W. Reynolds
Max. Mrs. G. Sheldon
Max Carrados. E. Bramah
Max Carrados Mysteries. E. Bramah
Max Fargus. O. Johnson
Max Logan. P. Trent
Max Smart and the Ghastly Ghost Affair. W. Johnston
Max Smart and the Perilous Pellets. W. Johnston
Max Smart Loses Control. W. Johnston
Max Smart—The Spy Who Went Out to the Cold. W. Johnston

M

Max Trueblood and the Jersey Desperado. Teri White
Maxa. R. Elson
Maximilian and Selina. Anonymous
Maxims by a Man of the World. J. Payn
Maximum Credible Accident. J. Howlett
Maximum Game. E. Naughton
Maximum Zone. C. Keane
Maxine. P. Trent
Max's Marriage. E. Gaboriau
Maxwell Mystery. C. Wells
Maxwell's Train. C. Hyde
May Berresford, Typist. C. H. Bullivant
May Day in Magadan. A. Olcott
May Day Mystery. O. R. Cohen
May Fair. M. Arlen
May Grayson. T. P. Prest
May We Borrow Your Husband? G. Greene
May We Come Through? and other stories. R. Pertwee
May-Week Murders. D. G. Browne
May You Die in Ireland. M. Kenyon
Maya Stone Murders. M. K. Shuman
Maya Temple. D. Daniels
Mayan Connection. Nick Carter
Maybe a Trumpet. S. Harvester
Maybe He's Dead. S. Oakroyd
Maybe I'll Call Anna. W. B. Spencer
Maybe It's Murder. A. Barron
Mayday. C. Cussler
Mayday. T. P. McMahon
Mayday from Malaga. R. MacLeod
Mayday Man. W. Beecher
Mayday Over Manhattan. S. Jason
Mayeroni Myth. D. Winston
Mayfair Lou. A. Hurry
Mayfair Magician. G. Griffith
Mayfair Murder. H. Holt
Mayfair Mystery. L. Clarke
Mayfair Mystery. H. Holt
Mayfair Mystery. F. Richardson
Mayfair Nights. H. Duval
Mayfair Slayride. H. Janson
Mayhem for Milady. D. Haring
Mayhem in B-Flat. Elliot Paul
Mayhem in Greece. D. Wheatley
Mayhem in Magic. D. Haring
Mayhem in Manhattan. L. Wein
Mayhem in Mexico. D. Haring
Mayhem in Morton Episcopi. D. Lees
Mayhem in Parva. Nancy Livingston
Mayhem, It's Marvelous. D. Haring
Mayhem Madchen. J. N. Chance
Mayhem on the Coney Beat. M. Geller
Maynard Hayes Affair. Dorothea Bennett
Maynard's Wives. H. Flowerdew
Mayor Harding of New York. S. Endicott
Mayor on Horseback. E. P. Oppenheim
Mayor's Wife. A. K. Green
May's New Fangled Mirth. M. J. Adamson
Mazaroff Murder. J. S. Fletcher
Mazaroff Mystery. J. S. Fletcher
Mazatlan. E. H. Hunt
Maze. Larry Collins
Maze. A. H. Garnet
Maze. P. MacDonald
Maze. E. Orford
Maze of Crime. Anonymous
Maze of Death. P. K. Dick
Maze of Justice. T. El Hakim
Maze of Motives. Nicholas Carter
Maze of the Past. Magali
Mazeppa. T. P. Prest
Mazeppa. F. Whishaw
Mazeway. Jack Williamson
Mazurka. Campbell Armstrong
Me and Brenda. Philip Israel
Me and My Ghoul. M. Storme
Me and Rudolph. W. C. Tuttle
Me, Detective. L. T. White
Me—Gangster. C. F. Coe
Me, Hood! M. Spillane
Me Tanner, You Jane. Lawrence Block
Mea Culpa. S. Luska

Meadowlark Connection. Ken Mitchell
Meadows of Tallon. E. Thompson
Meadowsweet. Gwendoline Butler
Meagham. J. Jenkins
Mean Streets. T. B. Dewey
Mean Streets. D. Stivers
Mean Time. C. T. Leland
Meandering Corpse. R. S. Prather
Means of Escape. S. Dunleavy
Means of Evil. R. Rendell
Meanwhile Back at the Morgue. M. Avallone
Measure for Murder. C. Witting
Measure of Deceit. C. Burnes
Measure of Fear. L. Demestrichas
Measured for Murder. Babs Lee
Measures for a Coffin. K. Robeson
Meat for Murder. Lange Lewis
Meat Man. M. Mallowe
Mecca for Murder. S. Marlowe
Mechanic. L. J. Carlino
Mechanic's Son. Old Sleuth
Med. David Poyer
Medal from Pamplona. C. Rougvie
Medallion. L. Johnson
Medallion. G. Sereny
Medbury Fort Murder. G. Limnelius
Meddle with the Mafia. Fiona Sinclair
Meddler and Her Murder. J. Porter
Meddlers. C. Rayner
Medea Legend. E. York
Median Line. W. Haggard
Medical Center Murders. L. Drake
Medical Examiner. W. H. A. Carr
Medical Witness. Richard Gordon
Medici Ring. N. St. John
Medicine Dog. Geoff Peterson
Medicine Lady. L. T. Meade
Medicine Maker. W. C. Tuttle
Medicine Man. L. Reznek
Medicine-Man. W. C. Tuttle
Mediterranean Adventure. P. Phillips
Mediterranean Caper. L. Bouma
Mediterranean Caper. G. Brewer
Mediterranean Caper. C. Cussler
Mediterranean Maneuver. R. J. Szilagye
Mediterranean Murder. A. Hocking
Mediterranean Murder. Rosa Lambert
Mediterranean Mystery. S. G. Hedges
Mediterranean Mystery. F. E. Wynne
Mediterranean Nights. D. Wheatley
Medium for Murder. G. Compton
Medium for Murder. Evelyn Harris
Medium for Murder. M. Warner
Medley of Mystery. Lynn Williams
Medusa. H. Innes
Medusa. E. H. Visiak
Medusa Complex. M. H. Albert
Medusa Connection. F. Cowen
Medusa Conspiracy. E. I. Shedley
Medusa Emerald. G. F. Gibbs
Medusa Kiss. M. Woodman
Medusa Syndrome. Ron Cutler
Medusa Touch. P. Van Greenaway
Medusa's Head. J. D. Bacon
Meet a Body. Carter Brown
Meet a Body. J. Decrest
Meet a Body. J. Hinton
Meet a Body. F. Launder
Meet a Body. D. Rutherford
Meet a Dark Stranger. L. Belvedere
Meet a Dark Stranger. T. E. Huff
Meet Bill Speed. J. B. Donovan
Meet Desmond Drake. Sea Lion
Meet Doctor Death. R. Trevor
Meet Dr. Morelle. E. Dudley
Meet Dr. Morelle Again. E. Dudley
Meet Gerry North. Gerry North
Meet Helga Rolfe. J. H. Chase
Meet in Darkness. S. Ransome
Meet Inspector Bourne. R. C. Finney
Meet Me at Philippi. C. Connell
Meet Me at the Morgue. J. R. Macdonald
Meet Me in Darkness. R. E. Banks
Meet Me in the Green Glen. R. P. Warren

Meet Me Tonight. M. Albrand
Meet Mike Desmond. J. V. Nolan
Meet Miss Mayhem. Carter Brown
Meet Mr. Callaghan. G. Verner
Meet Mr. Fortune. H. C. Bailey
Meet Morocco Jones. J. Baynes
Meet Morocco Jones in the Case of the Sydnicate Hoods. J. Baynes
Meet Murder, My Angel. Carter Brown
Meet My Friends. L. Beresford
Meet Nero Wolfe. R. Stout
Meet Tango Crawford. E. Gunton
Meet the Baron. Anthony Morton
Meet the Don. B. Gray
Meet the Dragon. David Hume
Meet the Dreamer. W. M. Duncan
Meet the Falcon. D. J. Gannon
Meet the Picaroon. J. Cassells
Meet the Rev. G. Pedrick
Meet the Tiger. L. Charteris
Meet You in Munich. R. Jansson
Meeting at Midnight. J. Jenkins
Meeting by Moonlight. R. Knotts
Meeting Her Fate. M. E. Braddon
Meeting in Casa. J. Kershaw
Meeting in Madrid. Dorothy Fletcher
Meeting in Spring. Elizabeth Ford
Meeting Place and other stories. J. D. Beresford
Meeting with Murder. M. Lynch
Meg. D. Daniels
Meg the Lady. T. Gallon
Megacull. D. Hart-Davis
Megadeath. Peter Evans
Megadeath Option. P. Buck
Megan. M. K. Simmons
Megawind Cancellation. B. Boucher
Megeve Mystery. J. Mowbray
Megiddo. D. Kartun
Megstone Plot. A. Garve
Meirovity Plan. H. Arvay
Mekong Massacre. J. Lansing
Melamare Mystery. M. Leblanc
Melancholy Virgin. A. Laine
Melander's Millions. C. F. Gregg
Melbourne Mystery. J. G. Brandon
Melbourne Mystery. S. J. Stutley
Melinite, the Lady's Maid. A. Belot
Mellbridge Mystery. A. O. Cooke
Mellone. K. Krause
Malmoth. C. R. Maturin
Melodramas for Madame. S. S. Simon
Melody Man. H. J. Green
Melody Murders. R. Wallace
Melody of Death. T. A. Plummer
Melody of Death. E. Wallace
Melody of Malice. S. Hufford
Melody of Murder. Dina Allan
Melody of Terror. S. Forbes
Melon in the Cornfield. C. Blackstock
Melora. M. G. Eberhart
Meltdown. R. Kytle
Meltdown. D. Pendleton
Melting Man. V. Canning
Melting Point. Kenn Davis
Melwood Mystery. J. Hay
Melyonen. A. Lowing
Member of Tattersall's. H. Smart
Member of the Club. P. Niesewand
Member's Lobby. K. Thompson
Members of the Jury. S. Ready
Members Only. P. Welles
Memento Mori. M. Spark
Memo for Murder. D. Wilmer
Memo to a Firing Sqauad. F. H. Brennan
Memoirs to a Bow Street Runner. Henry Goddard
Memoirs of a Landlady. G. R. Sims
Memoirs of a Russian Punk. E. Limonov
Memoirs of a Veteran Detective. M. Canler
Memoirs of an Aberdeen Detective. R. Woodcroft
Memoirs of an Inspector. G. Griffith
Memoirs of an Invisible Man. H. F. Saint
Memoirs of Arsene Lupin. M. Leblanc
Memoirs of Constantine Dix. B. Pain
Memoirs of J. (Paddy) MacDowell. M. J. Hobbs

Memoirs of Jane Cameron, Female Convict. F. W. Robinson
Memoirs of Monsieur Claude. M. Claude
Memoirs of Murder. R. C. Payes
Memoirs of Professor Moriarty. C. Brooks
Memoirs of Schlock Homes. R. L. Fish
Memoirs of Sherlock Holmes. A. C. Doyle
Memoirs of Solar Pons. A. Derleth
Memoirs of Vidocq. Vidocq
Memoirs of Villain. I. Crookenden
Memorandum of a Murder. J. E. Wright
Memorial Hall Murder. J. Langton
Memories of Dying. David Hughes
Memories of Midnight. S. Sheldon
Memory Blank. J. E. Stith
Memory Boy. V. Canning
Memory Lane. V. Munn
Memory Man. J. Griffiths
Memory Man. D. Lambert
Memory Man. C. W. Sanders
Memory of a Scream. D. X. Manners
Memory of Darkness. M. Summerton
Memory of Eva Ryker. D. Stanwood
Memory of Evil. Marilyn Ross
Memory of Megan. M. Lovell
Memory of Murder. R. Bradbury
Memory of Murder. H. Pentecost
Memory of Passion. G. Brewer
Memory of Treason. H. Hossent
Memory of You. M. Richmond
Memory Trap. Anthony Price
Memory's Dancer. S. W. Goss
Memory's Geese. P. Traill
Memos from Purgatory. H. Ellison
Men and the Mirror. R. Rocklynne
Men and Women. Mrs. C. Crowe
Men Are Strange Lovers. A. Rowe
Men Are What Women Make Them. A. Belot
Men at Arms. W. P. Drury
Men Die at Cyprus Lodge. J. Rhode
Men for Counters. G. Fairlie
Men for Pieces. B. Flynn
Men from the Boys. E. Lacy
Men in Arms. J. Crosby
Men in Blue Glasses. S. P. B. Mais
Men in Chains. M. Clarke
Men in Her Death. M. Blizard
Men in Her Death. P. Marlowe
Men in Her Death. A. Morice
Men in Her Death. S. Ransome
Men in Her Life. W. Fabian
Men in Knots. Richard Grant
Men, Maids and Murder. J. Creasey
Men, Maids and Mustard Pot. G. Frankau
Men Must Live. H. Bridges
Men of Affairs. R. Pertwee
Men of Career. J. Lorraine
Men of Fear. K. Robeson
Men of Marlowe's. Mrs. H. Dudeney
Men of Mystery. W. Anthony
Men of Silence. L. Forgione
Men of Subtle Craft. Roy Lewis
Men of the Bureau. E. Gaboriau
Men of the Mist. G. Stanley
Men on Foot. F. R. Adams
Men on the Dead Man's Chest. C. S. Raymond
Men That God Made. W. A. Ballinger
Men v. Devils. T. K. Clarke
Men Vanished. K. Robeson
Men, Women and Things. Austin Philips
Men Who Die Twice. P. Heath
Men Who Died Laughing. J. Creasey
Men Who Explained Miracles. J. D. Carr
Men Who Robbed the Bank of England. C. Branson
Men Who Smiled No More. K. Robeson
Men Who Wrought. R. Cullum
Men with Tangle. A. Ross
Men with the Double Faces. V. Loder
Men with the Guns. G. F. Newman
Men with Three Eyes. L. Revell
Men Without Bones and other stories. G. Kersh
Men Without Faces. W. Martyn
Men Without Women. E. Hemingway
Men, Women and Beasts. H. D. Stacpoole

Men, Women and Guns. H. C. McNeile
Menace. L. G. Blochman
Menace. A. Carson
Menace! J. Creasey
Menace. The Gordons
Menace. R. Hausfeld
Menace. S. Horler
Menace. H. Janson
Menace. R. Keverne
Menace. P. MacDonald
Menace. A. Van Hassen
Menace at Brackstone. J. T. Osborne
Menace at the Gate. J. T. Osborne
Menace for Dr. Morelle. E. Dudley
Menace from the East. D. Holden
Menace in Siam. M. Corrigan
Menace of Death. E. Churchill
Menace of Li-Sin. N. Vane
Menace of Marble Hill. M. Farnsworth
Menace of the Silent Death. E. J. Murray
Menace of X. A. Kahn
Menace on the Downs. M. Burton
Menace to Mrs. Kershaw. Austen Allen
Menace Within. U. Curtiss
Menacers. D. Hamilton
Menaces, Menaces. M. Underwood
Menacing Darkness. S. Shulman
Menacing Groves. John Sherwood
Menage. A. Mancini
Menagerie. C. Cookson
Mendelov Conspiracy. M. Caidin
Mender of Images. N. Lorimer
Mendip Mystery. L. Brock
Mendocino Menace. Ruth MacLeod
Mendon Mystery. J. Mary
Mendoza File. Clayton Matthews
Mendoza Manuscript. Nick Carter
Mendoza's Treasure. V. Daniels
Mene Tekel. A. Groner
Menehune Murders. M. Arnold
Menfreya. V. Holt
Menfreya in the Morning. V. Holt
Menorah Men. L. Davidson
Mensa Murders. Lee Martin
Mental Fireworks. G. Robey
Mental Marvel. F. MacIsaac
Mental Monster. K. Robeson
Mental Wizard. K. Robeson
Mentons. C. F. R. Hayward
Menu Cypher. R. Elman
Mephiste the Menace. Marg Douglas
Mephisto Waltz. F. M. Stewart
Mercenaries. J. Harris
Mercenaries. G. Tippette
Mercenaries. D. E. Westlake
Mercenary. H. Barron
Mercenary. J. Freytag
Mercenary. A. Marsden
Mercenary Calling. Martin Walker
Mercenary Justice. C. Bainbridge
Mercenary Kill. J. Quinn
Mercenary Mountain. Nick Carter
Merchandise Murders. A. Richards
Merchant of Menace. K. Bedford
Merchant of Menace. J. Stevenson
Merchant of Murder. S. Dean
Merchants of Death. P. Chase
Merchants of Disaster. K. Robeson
Merchant's Secret. J. W. Bobin
Merciless Ladies. Winston Graham
Mercy. D. Lindsey
Mercy at the Manor Manor. H. J. Mundis
Mercy Flight. A. MacVicar
Mercy Killer. H. Fleetwood
Mercy Man. R. McDowell
Mercy of the Court. M. E. Porter
Mercy Trap. J. E. Martin
Mere Cypher. M. A. Dickens
Mere Murder. C. M. Wills
Mere Shakings. J. F. Keane
Meredith Legacy. S. A. Salvato
Meredith Mystery. N. S. Lincoln
Merely Man. G. Warden
Merely Michael. M. Somers

Merely Murder. G. Heyer
Merely Murder. G. Paxton
Merely Players. J. F. Molloy
Mericas. Clementina Black
Merindol. F. Du Boisgobey
Meritocrats. W. Haggard
Merivale. J. Robertshaw
Meriweather Mystery. K. C. Strahan
Merlake Towers. Mary Williams
Merlewood Mystery. Mrs. J. O. Arnold
Merlin's Forest. M. Wallenstein
Merlin's Furlong. G. Mitchell
Merlin's Keep. M. Brent
Merlin's Web. S. Mayse
Mermaid. O. Martin
Mermaid Murmurs Murder. Carter Brown
Mermaid of Dark Mountain. Melissa Napier
Mermaid on the Rocks. B. Halliday
Mermaids in the Dining Area. L. Tattersall
Mermaids on the Golf Course. P. Highsmith
Merrily to the Grave. K. Sully
Merrivale Mystery. J. Corbett
Merriweather File. L. White
Merrlyn Mystery. E. Semphill
Merry Andrews. Rona Randall
Merry Christmas, Murdock. R. Ray
Merry Devils. E. Marston
Merry Garden and other stories. Q
Merry-Go-Round. J. Cowdroy
Merry-Go-Round. G. Sklar
Merry Go Round. R. M. Stern
Merry-Go-Round of Murder. J. F. Dinneen
Merry Hippo. E. Huxley
Merry Jack Jugg—Highwayman. D. Suddaby
Merry Men and other tales. R. L. Stevenson
Merry Mug. H. M. Raleigh
Merry Murder. S. Rubenstein
Merry Murders at Montmarie. T. J. Kelly
Merry Oasis. R. Landau
Merry Virgin. N. Karta
Merry Widower. Joan Fleming
Merrylees Mystery. R. Goyne
Meryl. W. T. Eldridge
Mesalliance. W. F. Fauley
Mesh. J. Haslette
Meshes of Fear. H. Richards
Meshes of Mischance. G. Wintle
Mesmerists. B. L. Farjeon
Mesmerist's Secret. D. Dormer
Message. H. C. McNeile
Message. L. Tracy
Message Ends. D. Craig
Message from a Corpse. Sam Merwin
Message from a Ghost. Marilyn Ross
Message from a Spy. D. Helwig
Message from Absalom. A. A. Thompson
Message from Hong Kong. M. G. Eberhart
Message from John. W. Spence
Message from Julie. Sara North
Message from Malaga. Helen MacInnes
Message from Marise. P. Kruger
Message from Sirius. C. Jenkins
Message in Blood. Vera Wallace
Message of the Mute Dog. C. M. Russell
Messenger. E. Robins
Messenger. Mona Williams
Messenger Boy Detective. Anonymous
Messenger 48. J. Otis
Messenger from Munich. N. Pierce
Messenger from the Unknown. J. Hawthorne
Messenger Must Die. K.-O. Bornemark
Messengers of Death. A. West
Messengers of Evil. P. Souvestre
Messiah Stone. M. Caidin
Messiter's Dream. Brian Cooper
Metal Box. T. Cobb
Metal Flask. B. Thomson
Metal Green Mercedes. T. Williams
Metal Monster. K. Robeson
Metamorphosis. R. Marsh
Metcalfe Mystery. Elliot Bailey
Meteor Men. A. LeBaron
Meteor Menace. K. Robeson
Meteoric Affair. J. Tabler

M

Meter Maid. F. Shepard
Meteren Road. V. Thomas
Methinks the Lady—. G. Endore
Method in His Murder. T. Warriner
Method in Madness. D. M. Disney
Method of Murder. Whyte Hall
Methods of Dr. Scarlett. A. Laing
Methods of Madness. R. Garton
Methods of Maigret. G. Simenon
Methods of Mr. Ames. F. Carrel
Methods of Sergeant Cluff. G. North
Methods of Uncle Abner. M. D. Post
Methuselah Enzyme. F. M. Stewart
Methuselah Factor. J. Rosenberger
Methylated Murder. C. Robbins
Metrophage. R. Kadrey
Metropolitan Opera Murders. H. Traubel
Metzger's Dog. T. Perry
Mexican Adventure. L. Oliver
Mexican Affair. C. W. Burleson
Mexican Assassin. Hartshorne
Mexican Bill, the Cowboy Detective. N. Ned
Mexican Brown. L. Derrick
Mexican Connection. A. Mason
Mexican Hit. J. Rosenberger
Mexican Kill. D. Hartman
Mexican Mourning. J. Hedges
Mexican Slay Ride. N. MacNeil
Mexican Slay Ride. S. Weintraub
Mexican Slayride. T. B. Dewey
Mexican Stand-Off. M. Cronin
Mexican Standoff. Bruce Cook
Mexico Deadline. J. Grecco
Mexico Run. L. White
Mexico Set. L. Deighton
Mexico 21. Mark Joseph
Meyringen Papers. Allen Sharp
Mezzoni, the Brigand. M. M. Murray
Miami Blues. C. Willeford
Miami Crush. D. Stivers
Miami 59. D. Keene
Miami for Murder. B. Sarto
Maimi Golden Boy. H. Kastle
Miami Marauder. M. Barry
Miami Massacre. D. Pendleton
Miami Mayhem. A. Rome
Miami Midnight. Maggie Davis
Miami Mob and Mark Kilby Stands Alone. R. C. Frazer
Miami Murder-Go-Round. M. La France
Miami Number. Anonymous
Miami One-Way. M. Winters
Miami Undercover. E. L. Heyman
Miami War Zone. J. Buchanan
Miamigrad. J. Ahern
Miasma. E. S. Holding
Micah Faraday, Adventurer. L. T. Meade
Mice Are Not Amused. K. Hewitt
Michael. A. J. Spivey
Michael and All Angels. N. Lofts
Michael Anonymous. J. M. Scott
Michael Bray. Taffrail
Michael Carmichael. M. Sandys
Michael Cassidy, Sergeant. H. C. McNeile
Michael Dred, Detective. M. Leighton
Michael Durrant. P. Trent
Michael Intervenes. G. Clifford
Michael Shayne Investigates. B. Halliday
Michael Shayne Takes a Hand. B. Halliday
Michael Shayne's 50th Case. B. Halliday
Michael Shayne's Long Chance. B. Halliday
Michael Shayne's Triple Mystery. B. Halliday
Michaelmas Girls. J. B. Barry
Michael's Crag. G. Allen
Michael's Evil Deeds. E. P. Oppenheim
Michael's Wife. M. Millhiser
Michigan Roll. T. Kakonis
Michiko. D. Hann
Mick Cardby Works Overtime. David Hume
Micky's Hide. B. Sarto
Micro Kill. H. Janson
Microbe Murders. F. G. Eberhard
Microbe of Crime. Nicholas Carter
Microbe's Kiss. G. Braddon

Microbes of Power. A. Wilson
Microwave Factor. N. Brady
Microwave Factor. A. Fletcher
Mid-Atlantic. Taffrail
Mid-Ocean Tragedy. J. Hawk
Mid the Thick Arrows. M. Pemberton
Midas. P. Kelaart
Midas Coffin. Simon Quinn
Midas Kill. P. Kirk
Midas Man. K. Robeson
Midas Men. J. Evans
Midas Monkhouse, M.F.H. E. Woodward
Midas Touch. J. Boland
Midas Touch. W. Winward
Midday Moon. D. Daniels
Middle Class Murder. B. Hamilton
Middle Distance. O. Martin
Middle East Massacre. Nick Carter
Middle Kingdom. W. Marshall
Middle Link. Nicholas Carter
Middle of Midnight. W. G. Beymer
Middle of Nowhere. M. Brenner
Middle of Things. J. S. Fletcher
Middle Temple Murder. J. S. Fletcher
Middle Wall. Edward Marshall
Middlefold Murders. E. Radford
Midge. P. MacTyre
Midget Marvel. P. Manton
Midnight. O. R. Cohen
Midnight. G. Hughes
Midnight. D. R. Koontz
Midnight. J. A. Russo
Midnight. M. Strange
Midnight Admirals. D. Muir
Midnight Adventure and other stories. J. J. Farjeon
Midnight Alibi. E. Ellison
Midnight and Percy Jones. V. Starrett
Midnight at Mallyncourt. T. E. Huff
Midnight at Mallyncourt. E. Marlow
Midnight at Mears House. H. J. Holt
Midnight Avenger. F. Dille
Midnight Bell. F. Latham
Midnight Call. Gordon Morris
Midnight Cavalier. R. Armstrong
Midnight City. R. Tine
Midnight Club. J. Patterson
Midnight Cry. J. M. Parker
Midnight Dancers. A. Maybury
Midnight Examiner. M. Kotzwinkle
Midnight Eye. M. Roscoe
Midnight Ferry to Venice. B. Healey
Midnight Guest. F. M. White
Midnight Gun. B. Mather
Midnight Hag. Joan Fleming
Midnight Haul. M. A. Collins
Midnight Hazard. B. Sanders
Midnight Heather of Bridee Castle. B. C. Warren
Midnight Heiress. K. Frederick
Midnight Horrors. Anonymous
Midnight Hostess. Griff
Midnight House. Ethel L. White
Midnight House and other tales. W. F. Hervey
Midnight Intruder. G. Roper
Midnight Intruder. T. C. P. Webb
Midnight King. G. Delamare
Midnight Lace. W. Drummond
Midnight Lace. E. Kary
Midnight Lady. G. Leroux
Midnight Lady. H. Parker
Midnight Lady and the Mourning Man. D. Anthony
Midnight Lightning. K. Sherrill
Midnight Line. T. Savage
Midnight Lorry Crime. E. S. Brooks
Midnight Mail. H. Holt
Midnight Male. R. Drayton
Midnight Man. L. D. Estleman
Midnight Man. Kane
Midnight Man. W. B. Murphy
Midnight Masquerade. Jean Smith
Midnight Men. A. E. Fisher
Midnight Men. N. Vane
Midnight Message. Nicholas Carter
Midnight Minute. C. Herbert

Midnight Monitor. Anonymous
Midnight Moon. Jeanne Montague
Midnight Murder. P. Herring
Midnight Murder. John Morgan
Midnight Murder. K. Robeson
Midnight Murder. R. Rodd
Midnight Murder. Donald Stuart
Midnight Mystery. Anonymous
Midnight Mystery. B. Atkey
Midnight Mystery. R. Hardinge
Midnight Mystery. F. Hume
Midnight Never Comes. M. Fallon
Midnight Oak. J. Tattersall
Midnight Oil. P. Traill
Midnight on the Place Pigalle. M. Dekobra
Midnight Passenger. R. H. Savage
Midnight Patient. E. Hostovsky
Midnight Pleasures. R. Bloch
Midnight Plumber. M. Procter
Midnight Plus One. G. Lyall
Midnight Queen. Anonymous
Midnight Queen. May Carleton
Midnight Quest. Old Sleuth
Midnight Rendezvous. R. Kleiner
Midnight Road. A. Wood
Midnight Sailing. L. G. Blochman
Midnight Sailing. S. Hufford
Midnight Sins. Ellen Hall
Midnight Sister. M. H. Albert
Midnight Sister. H. Lugar
Midnight Sleep. Frank King
Midnight Special. B. Delannoy
Midnight Sun. K. Sundelof-Asbrand
Midnight Surrender. E. Nepean
Midnight Tales. W. F. Harvey
Midnight Terror. Anonymous
Midnight to High Noon. C. C. Waddell
Midnight Treasure. W. Rollins
Midnight Vigil. Warren Miller
Midnight Visitor. L. Dartey
Midnight Walker. Rona Randall
Midnight Walkers. K. Laing
Midnight Walking. J. Simmons
Midnight Waltz. J. Blake
Midnight Water. G. Norman
Midnight Webs. G. M. Fenn
Midnight Whispers. P. Matthews
Midnight Wireless. C. A. Alington
Midst Balkan Perils. E. S. Brooks
Midsummer. M. J. Costello
Midsummer Killing. Trevor Barnes
Midsummer Knight. J. Glyder
Midsummer Loki. E. Wuorio
Midsummer Madness. R. Buxton
Midsummer Madness. Langdon Dodge
Midsummer Madness. Morley Roberts
Midsummer Malice. N. Fitzgerald
Midsummer Masque. J. Tattersall
Midsummer Mink. P. Coke
Midsummer Mischief. N. Mapple
Midsummer Murder. C. M. Wills
Midsummer Murder. C. Witting
Midsummer Mystery. G. H. Gerould
Midsummer Nightmare. C. Hale
Midsummer Night's Crime. G. Bromley
Midsummer Night's Murder. R. F. Baylus
Midsummer Night's Murder. L. Crosby
Midsummer Slay Ride. L. Gribble
Midsummer's Nightmare. E. Shenkin
Midtown Aces. J. G. Bodyan
Midtown North. Mike Curtis
Midtown South. Christopher Newman
Midway to Murder. M. T. Yates
Midwinter Madness. Anthony Stuart
Miernik Dossier. C. McCarry
Might As Well Be Dead. R. Stout
Might of a Wrongdoer. S. Brice
Mighty Arm. C. Dawe
Mighty Blockhead. F. Gruber
Mighty Hunters. A. Russan
Mignon. J. M. Cain
Mignon. Chris Hunt
Mignonette. G. Norway
Mignonette. J. Shearing

Mignon's Peril. J. Middlemass
Mikado Jewel. F. Hume
Mike Dime. B. Fantoni
Mike Elder's Boy. S. P. Herron
Mike Mist Case Book. M. A. Collins
Miklos Alexandrovitch Is Missing. Anne Edwards
Miko. E. V. Lustbader
Milady Charlotte. K. Kellow
Milady Took the Rap. H. Janson
Milan Grill Room. E. P. Oppenheim
Mild Case of Murder. G. Brandon
Mildred Arkell. H. Wood
Mildred Pierce. J. M. Cain
Mile-Away Murder. A. Armstrong
Mile Deep Grave. J. Hedges
Mile High. R. Condon
Mile High. H. C. Rowland
Mile Zero. T. Sanchez
Milesian Chief. D. J. Murphy
Military Crime. F. M. Peacock
Milk and Honey. F. Kellerman
Milk Churn Murder. M. Burton
Milk of Human Kindness. E. Ferrars
Milkmaid's Millions. H. Austin
Mill. Mark Allerton
Mill House Murder. J. S. Fletcher
Mill House Mystery. F. Warden
Mill-Lass of Idderleigh. H. E. Inman
Mill Master's Secret. J. G. Jones
Mill Mystery. A. K. Green
Mill of Fear. L. Bidston
Mill of Many Windows. J. S. Fletcher
Mill of Silence. B. Capes
Mill Pond Mystery. H. E. Hill
Mill Reef Hall. A. Pritchett
Mill Street Mystery. A. Sergeant
Millbank Case. G. D. Eldridge
Miller and His Men. T. P. Prest
Miller's Deal. A. Gooch
Miller's Maid. T. P. Prest
Millie. D. H. Clarke
Millie. E. V. Cunningham
Millie Lynn, Shop Investigator. C. H. Bullivant
Millijoy, the Determined. K. Kimbrough
Milliner's Hat Mystery. B. Thomson
Million a Minute. H. Douglas
Million Cut. A. Heal
Million Dollar Babe. C. Borelli
Million Dollar Babe. Carter Brown
Million Dollar Baby. D. Haring
$1000000.00 Broad. Hal Kantor
Million Dollar Dames. C. Macey
Million Dollar Danger. D. Haring
Million-Dollar Diamond. J. S. Fletcher
Million Dollar Gamble. F. Johnston
Million Dollar Handle. B. Halliday
Million Dollar Hit. L. Starr
Million Dollar Lift. R. E. Crighton
Million Dollar Massacre. W. Barker
Million Dollar Mayhem. K. T. McCall
Million Dollar Murder. T. B. Black
Million Dollar Murder. E. Ronns
Million Dollar Murder. B. Sarto
Million Dollar Mystery. H. MacGrath
Million Dollar Snapshot. H. Howard
Million Dollar Snatch. J. Grecco
Million Dollar Stand-In. E. Webster
Million Dollar Story. E. Wallace
Million Dollar Suitcase. A. MacGowan
Million Dollar Tramp. W. C. Gault
Million Dollar Wound. M. A. Collins
Million Heiress. P. Trent
Million in Diamonds. Nicholas Carter
Million in Diamonds. Old Sleuth
Million in Jewels. Old Sleuth
Million Lives at Stake. A. H. Parr
Million of Money. A. M. Meadows
Million Pound Bus Fare. D. Weldon
Million Pound Cipher. R. Pertwee
Million Pound Deposit. E. P. Oppenheim
Million Pounds Reward. F. Lady
Million Tears. Sheila Lawrence
Million to Burn. M. S. Jones
Millionaire and Crook. E. Dower

Millionaire and the Lady. G. Warden
Millionaire and the Policeman's Wife. O. Harper
Millionaire Baby. A. K. Green
Millionaire Crook. Roland Daniel
Millionaire Detective. C. E. Blaney
Millionaire Gangster. J. Wallace
Millionaire Girl. A. W. Marchmont
Millionaire Girl and other stories. Rita
Millionaire Mystery. F. Hume
Millionaire Mystery. A. W. Marchmont
Millionaire of Yesterday. E. P. Oppenheim
Millionaire Partner. Nicholas Carter
Millionaire Sportsman. S. Drew
Millionaire Tramp. S. C. Trebor
Millionaires. H. D. Kastle
Millionaire's Crime. J. K. Stafford
Millionaire's Daughter. D. Eden
Millionaire's Fate. F. Du Boisgobey
Millionaire's Folly. Le Jemlys
Millionaire's Folly. L. E. Smyles
Millionaire's Island. M. Pemberton
Millionaire's Love Story. G. Boothby
Millionaire's Mania. Nicholas Carter
Millionaire's Nest Egg. A. Parsons
Millionaire's Revenge. O. Harper
Millionaire's Son. F. Warden
Millionairess. J. Ralph
Millions at Stake and other stories. Nicholas Carter
Millions for a Murderer. G. W. Jones
Millions for Murder. F. MacIsaac
Millions of Mischief. H. Hill
Millions of Money. L. Clarke
Mills. M. O'Brine
Mills Bomb. C. Egleton
Mills of God. E. Lothar
Mills of the Gods. D. Winston
Mills of the Law. Nicholas Carter
Millstone Man. B. Healey
Milly Darrell and other tales. M. E. Braddon
Milly the Actress. J. Askew
Milmorra House. Renata Chapman
Milngravie Collection. D. Vallance
Mimi. R. W. Taylor
Mimic a Murderer. S. H. Courtier
Mind Benders. J. Kennaway
Mind Breaker. A. Mather
Mind Breakers. D. Streib
Mind Brothers. Peter Heath
Mind-Force Warrior. D. Peters
Mind Games. A. Rule
Mind How You Go. D. Nolan
Mind Killers. Nick Carter
Mind Killers. Martin Thomas
Mind-Masters. J. F. Rossmann
Mind Murders. J. Van De Wetering
Mind My Innocence. H. Zore
Mind My Shroud. C. Rank
Mind of a Miller. J. Kirkpatrick
Mind of Dr. Morelle. E. Dudley
Mind of John Meredith. F. Gerard
Mind of Max Duvine. E. Trevor
Mind of Mr. J. G. Reeder. E. Wallace
Mind of Mr. Mosley. John Greenwood
Mind Over Mayhem. J. P. Duff
Mind Over Murder. R. S. Hastings
Mind Over Murder. W. X. Kienzle
Mind Over Murder. C. Noone
Mind Palace. S. R. Pieczenik
Mind Poisoners. Nick Carter
Mind Reader. M. Rittenberg
Mind Reader. W. A. Roberts
Mind Readers. M. Allingham
Mind to Mind. D. Pendleton
Mind to Murder. A. Clarke
Mind to Murder. P. D. James
Mind Traders. J. M. Holly
Mind Twisters. D. Streib
Mind-Twisters Affair. Thomas Stratton
Mind War. G. Snyder
Mind Wreckers, Limited, and Other Adventures of Barrow—Ace Insurance Detective. F. J. Price
Mind Your Own Murder. Y. Foldes
Mindanao Pearl. A. Caillou
Mindbend. R. Cook

Mindbender. James Cohen
Mindbenders. J. Quinn
Mindblock. G. W. Names
Minder. A. Masters
Minder Back Again. A. Masters
Minder—Yet Again. A. Masters
Mindfield. W. Deverell
Mindflight. S. Holdin
Mindless Monsters. K. Robeson
Mindreader. C. T. Cline
Mind's Eye. A. Skinner
Mindscream. R. D. Zimmerman
Mindspell. K. N. Smith
Mindwarpers. E. F. Russell
Mindy Lindy May Surprise. M. Erlanger
Mine. R. Jeffery
Mine. R. R. McCammon
Mine Enemy My Friend. T. B. Morris
Mine Ferret. F. Ferrars
Mine in the Desert. D. Footman
Mine Is the Power. J. Lukens
Mine of Ill Omen. H. Lea
Mine Own Executioner. N. Balchin
Mine Sinister Host. W. W. Sayer
Mine to Avenge. T. Wills
Miner Detective. Anonymous
Miner's Right. R. Boldrewood
Minerva Castle. Jane Harvey
Minerva Stone. A. Maybury
Ming Vase Mystery. R. Dark
Ming Yellow. J. P. Marquand
Mingled with Venom. G. Mitchell
Mingled Yarn. Shalimar
Mini-Murders. Carter Brown
Mini-Mysteries. J. R. Piggin
Mini-Skirt Murders. Martin Thomas
Miniature Murder Mystery. P. Chambers
Miniatures Frame. K. Royce
Minigods. K. Saint-John
Minimum Man. A. Marvell
Minion of the Moon. T. W. Speight
Minister of Evil. W. LeQueux
Minister of Injustice. M. Culpan
Minister of Police. H. Mountjoy
Ministering Angel. Anthea Cohen
Ministers of Vengeance. R. E. Conot
Ministers Too Are Mortal. F. Duncan
Ministry Murder. C. Dixon
Ministry of Death. J. Bingham
Ministry of Fear. G. Greene
Mink. J. Springs III
Mink and Murder. H. Holt
Mink for Miss Marchant. E. Ellison
Mink for My Lady. B. Banarto
Mink-Lined Coffin. Jonathan Latimer
Mink Makes a Shroud. E. Ellison
Mink Minx. D. Haring
Mink Steel. M. Dedina
Minkie. L. Tracy
Minnesota Gothic. W. O'Meara
Minnesota Strip. Michael Collins
Minnesota Strip. P. McCurtin
Minnie's Bishop and other stories. G. A. Birmingham
Minnie Santangelo and the Evil Eye. A. Mancini
Minnie Santangelo's Mortal Sin. A. Mancini
Minnie Swan. P. Baker
Minor in Possession. J. A. Jance
Minor Murder. R. Denham
Minor Murders. J. L. Hensley
Minor Operation. J. J. Connington
Minor Operations. Taffrail
Minority. F. T. Hill
Minos Magnificent. G. Seton
Minotaur. S. Coonts
Minotaur. J. Farris
Minotaur. B. Tammuz
Minotaur Country. H. McCloy
Minotaur Factor. S. Stern
Minotaur Garden. L. Hosegood
Minot's Folly. R. S. Holland
Minstrel Code. W. Nelson
Minstrel's Fire. A. Harrell
Minstrel's Leap. V. Black

M

Mint Mystery. W. J. Bayfield
Minuet and Foxtrot. A. Castle
Minus a Shamus. Anthony Graham
Minus Man. R. Maxwell
Minus One Corpse. J. Cleveland
Minus Pool. W. Stovall
Minus X. S. Gluck
Minute for Murder. N. Blake
Minute Mysteries. A. Ripley
Minute to Pray, a Second to Die. A. Destefano
Minuteman Murder. J. Langton
Minutes. A. R. Williams
Minutes of a Murder. M. Polland
Minutes to Impact. Michael Gray
Minutes to Murder. N. Spain
Minx Goes to the Front. C. N. Williamson
Minx Is Murder. Carter Brown
Minx Manx. D. Haring
Mira. D. Winston
Mirabilis Diamond. J. Odlum
Mirabil's Island. L. Tracy
Miracle at St. Bruno's. P. Carr
Miracle Gold. R. Dowling
Miracle in the Drawing Room. E. Greenwood
Miracle Man. F. Packard
Miracle Mission. J. Rosenberger
Miracle of Revenge. W. B. Longley
Miracles Take a Little Longer. R. H. Lewis
Miracleworker. J. Bickham
Mirador Collection. B. Flynn
Mirage. W. Ericson
Mirage. J. Follett
Mirage. P. P. Muir
Mirage. M. Serrian
Miramar Seduction. K. Jordan
Miranda. J. Blackmore
Miranda. M. E. Braddon
Miranda. C. Larner
Miranda Clair. Phyllis Ross
Miranda Must Die. H. Calvin
Miranda Said Murder. M. Carroll
Miranda's Curse. Dorinne Moore
Miranda's Folly. Rachelle Edwards
Miriam Lemaire, Money Lender. C. Stanton
Miriam Rozella. B. L. Farjeon
Mirk Abbey. J. Payn
Miro. S. Herron
Miro Papers. S. Herron
Mirror. E. C. Reed
Mirror and Knife. J. Rosenberg
Mirror Crack'd. A. Christie
Mirror Crack'd from Side to Side. A. Christie
Mirror Dance. E. Kyle
Mirror Image. P. Conway
Mirror Image. L. Du Breuil
Mirror Image. L. Fletcher
Mirror Image. S. Harper
Mirror Image. M. Sadler
Mirror Lies. G. Vaizey
Mirror Maze. J. P. Hogan
Mirror, Mirror on the Wall. S. Ellin
Mirror, Mirror on the Wall. B. Freeman
Mirror Murder. L. Z. Adams
Mirror of a Dead Lady. H. D. Irvine
Mirror of Darkness. C. Gayet
Mirror of Darkness. M. Hara
Mirror of Death. J. Wylde
Mirror of Delusion. M. Reisner
Mirror of Hell. L. Holton
Mirror of Shadows. D. Daniels
Mirror of Silver. R. Bridges
Mirror Room. C. Landon
Mirror Train. J. N. Chance
Mirrored Murder. A. W. Eyles
Mirrors. Patricia Matthews
Mirrors of the Apocalypse. D. L. Moore
Mirth and Mayhem. Peter Walker
Mirthful Nine. Morley Roberts
Mis-Rule of Three. F. Warden
Misadventures of Athelstan Digby. W. F. Harvey
Misadventures of Mr. Larkin. D. Lynn
Miscalculation. H. Bowra
Miscarriage of Justice. Anonymous
Miscarriage of Justice. Nicholas Carter
Miscarriage of Justice. C. Kingston
Miscarriage of Murder. J. F. Straker
Miscast for Murder. R. Fenisong
Miscellanea. J. H. Ewing
Miscellany. E. Trevor
Miscellany of Tales and Verse. B. Norgate
Mischief. C. Armstrong
Mischief. B. A. Williams
Mischief at Frinton Park. F. M. Long
Mischief in Maggody. Joan Hess
Mischief in the Air. M. Afford
Mischief in the Lane. A. Derleth
Mischief in the Offing. C. Witting
Mischief-Maker. E. P. Oppenheim
Mischief Makers. W. Haggard
Mischief of a Glove. P. C. De Crespigny
Mischief Past. E. Thompson
Miser. L. Egan
Miser Farebrother. B. L. Farjeon
Miser Hoadley's Secret. A. W. Marchmont
Miser Is Murdered. A. Beaton
Miser of Maida Vale. B. Orczy
Miser of Shoreditch. T. P. Prest
Misercordia Drop. F. Greenland
Miser's Money. E. Phillpotts
Miser's Ward. K. A. Shoesmith
Miser's Will. F. Hume
Misery. Stephen King
Misfire. Jonathan Evans
Misfit. G. B. Savi
Misfits. G. F. Forrest
Misfortunes of Mr. Teal. L. Charteris
Misguided Angel. R. Angel
Misguided Lives. A. Elkann
Misguided Missile. O. Mills
Misleading Lady. A. Wood
Mismatch. L. Pye
Misplaced Corpse. A. E. Martin
Misplaced Corpse. S. Rider
Misprison of Felony. Seaforth
Miss Agatha. H. L. V. Fletcher
Miss Agatha Doubles for Death. H. L. V. Fletcher
Miss Armstrong's and Other Circumstances. J. Davidson
Miss Arnott's Marriage. Richard Marsh
Miss Astbury and Milordo. I. Northan
Miss Bantling Is Missing. J. W. Meagher
Miss Bede Is Staying. Anna Gilbert
Miss Beresford's Mystery and other stories. P. B. Marston
Miss Blake's Husband. E. Jordan
Miss Bones. Joan Fleming
Miss Bracegirdle and others. S. Aumonier
Miss Brandt. Margery Lawrence
Miss Brown. R. B. Brough
Miss Brown of X.Y.O. E. P. Oppenheim
Miss Cadogna. J. Hawthorne
Miss Callaghan Comes to Grief. J. H. Chase
Miss Called Murder. Carter Brown
Miss Cayley's Adventures. G. Allen
Miss Charley. C. Blacksmith
Miss Deadly. C. Dekker
Miss Devereux of the Mariquita. R. H. Savage
Miss Dividends. A. C. Gunter
Miss Doll, Go Home. D. Markson
Miss Dynamite. B. Gray
Miss Fannie's Bomb. Mary Thompson
Miss Fenny. C. Blackstock
Miss Ferriby's Clients. F. Warden
Miss Finney Kills Now and Then. A. Dempsey
Miss Francis Baird, Detective. R. W. Kauffman
Miss from S.I.S. R. Tralins
Miss Gloria Gets Wise. E. Ellison
Miss Hamblett's Ghost. A. Brock
Miss Hawkins: The Ocean Boarder. E. Burgess
Miss Hogg and the Bronte Murders. A. Lee
Miss Hogg and the Covent Garden Murders. A. Lee
Miss Hogg and the Dead Dean. A. Lee
Miss Hogg and the Missing Sisters. A. Lee
Miss Hogg and the Squash Club Murder. A. Lee
Miss Hogg Flies High. A. Lee
Miss Hogg's Last Case. A. Lee
Miss Hurd. A. K. Green
Miss Information. C. George
Miss Ivory White. R. Haggard
Miss Jessica's Stick. Aylmer Hunter
Miss Lizzie. W. Satterthwait
Miss Mabel. R. C. Sherriff
Miss Madelyn Mack, Detective. H. C. Weir
Miss Maitland, Private Secretary. G. Bonner
Miss Maitland's Spy. G. A. Birmingham
Miss Malevolent. C. R. Gull
Miss Marple. A. Christie
Miss Marple and the Thirteen Problems. A. Christie
Miss Marple's Final Cases. A. Christie
Miss Martha Mary Crawford. C. Marchant
Miss Mary's Husbands. D. Carlson
Miss Melbourn's Million. N. Penley
Miss Melville Regrets. E. E. Smith
Miss Melville Returns. E. E. Smith
Miss Melville's Revenge. E. E. Smith
Miss Mephistopheles. F. Hume
Miss Merewether's Money. T. Cobb
Miss Middleton's Lover. L. J. Libbey
Miss Milverton. A. Hocking
Miss Mitchell. H. Brooke
Miss Mystery. S. Horler
Miss Nobody of Nowhere. A. C. Gunter
Miss or Mrs? W. Collins
Miss Ormerod's Protege. F. C. Philips
Miss Osborne Misbehaves. M. Devon
Miss Otis Blows Town. B. Sarto
Miss Otis Comes to Piccadilly. B. Sarto
Miss Otis Desires. B. Sarto
Miss Otis Gets Fresh. B. Sarto
Miss Otis Goes French. B. Sarto
Miss Otis Goes Up. B. Sarto
Miss Otis Has a Daughter. B. Sarto
Miss Otis Hits Back. B. Sarto
Miss Otis Makes a Date. B. Sarto
Miss Otis Makes Hay. B. Sarto
Miss Otis Moves In. B. Sarto
Miss Otis Plays Ball. B. Sarto
Miss Otis Plays Eve. B. Sarto
Miss Otis Relents. B. Sarto
Miss Otis Says Yes. B. Sarto
Miss Otis Takes the Rap. B. Sarto
Miss Otis Throws a Come-Back. B. Sarto
Miss Pauline of New York. St. George Rathborne
Miss Pegham. P. Conway
Miss Pell Is Missing. L. Gershe
Miss Permissive. D. Haring
Miss Pink at the Edge of the World. G. Moffat
Miss Pink Pays Off. B. Vane
Miss Pinkerton. M. R. Rinehart
Miss Pinnegar Disappears. Anthony Gilbert
Miss Private Eye. G. Batson
Miss Pym Disposes. J. Tey
Miss Rayburn's Diamonds. R. Jocelyn
Miss Rolling Stone. P. Loring
Miss Schuyler's Alias. G. Horton
Miss Seeton at the Helm. H. Charles
Miss Seeton Bewitched. H. Carvic
Miss Seeton, By Appointment. H. Charles
Miss Seeton Draws the Line. H. Carvic
Miss Seeton Sings. H. Carvic
Miss Shumway Waves a Wand. J. H. Chase
Miss Silver Comes to Stay. P. Wentworth
Miss Silver Deals with Death. P. Wentworth
Miss Silver Intervenes. P. Wentowrth
Miss Silver's Past. J. Skvorecky
Miss Strangeways. A. M. Diehl
Miss Susan Regrets. B. Vane
Miss Swinford Remembers. S. Margetson
Miss Turquoise. G. B. Mair
Miss Two-Time. D. Haring
Miss Undine's Living Room. James Wilcox
Miss White of Mayfair. G. W. Appleton
Miss Withers Regrest. S. Palmer
Miss X. S. Kyle
Missed It by That Much. W. Johnston
Misserrimus. F. M. Reynolds
Missile. A. MacKenzie
Missile Menace. Gar Wilson
Missile Mob. H. Janson
Missing! M. Avallone
Missing. M. Halliday

Missing. E. Hostovsky
Missing! S. Kyle
Missing! F. E. Penny
Missing. S. Windham
Missing—A Lady. N. MacKenzie
Missing—A Young Girl. F. Warden
Missing Ace. W. H. L. Crauford
Missing Agent. M. Annesley
Missing Airman. Anonymous
Missing! and other tales. M. C. Hay
Missing . . . and Presumed Dead. J. Hayes
Missing and the Dead. J. Lynch
Missing Archduke. G. Leroux
Missing at Lloyds. G. H. Teed
Missing Aunt. G. D. H. Cole
Missing Background. L. Cargill
Missing Bank Manager. M. Poole
Missing Banker. C. Brandon
Missing Baronet. G. D. H. Cole
Missing Beauties. E. Saint
Missing—Believed Dead. D. Andrews
Missing, Believed Dead. N. MacKenzie
Missing Bishop. R. H. Spencer
Missing Body. Roland Daniel
Missing Book-Keeper. C. Keith
Missing Bracelet. I. Stark
Missing Bride. E. Southworth
Missing Bridegroom. J. K. Leys
Missing Bronte. R. Barnard
Missing Bullet. Warren Miller
Missing Bureaucrat. H. Scherfig
Missing by Choice. R. Victor
Missing Cashier. E. D. Pierson
Missing Centre-Forward. Anonymous
Missing Chancellor. J. S. Fletcher
Missing Chauffeur. H. C. McNeile
Missing Clue. Anonymous
Missing Clue. C. Dawe
Missing Cotton King. Nicholas Carter
Missing Cyclist and other stories. B. Delannoy
Missing Delora. E. P. Oppenheim
Missing Deputy Chief. Nicholas Carter
Missing Doctor. R. J. Fletcher
Missing Elizabeth. A. Sergeant
Missing Film Star. Anonymous
Missing Finger. A. Boissiere
Missing Formula. J. Decrest
Missing from Her Home. Anthony Gilbert
Missing from His Home. Mark Cross
Missing from His Home. C. Hosken
Missing from His Home. J. R. Warren
Missing from Home. S. Green
Missing from Home. J. Halliday
Missing from Home. P. Johnson
Missing from Home. P. N. Walker
Missing from Monte Carlo. B. Malim
Missing from the Record. C. Egleton
Missing from the Shelf. M. Salkeld
Missing Gates. R. Francis Foster
Missing Grandfather. F. Y. McHugh
Missing Grave. M. Dalman
Missing Heir. Maxwell Scott
Missing Heiress. Bernice Carey
Missing Heiress. Roland Daniel
Missing Hoard. J. Creasey
Missing Hour. J. Blackmore
Missing Husband and other tales. G. R. Sims
Missing in Mexico. J. N. Pentelow
Missing Initial. N. S. Lincoln
Missing Lady. Roland Daniel
Missing Letter. H. Wood
Missing Link. K. Farrer
Missing Link. W. B. Murphy
Missing Link. C. Varney
Missing Link. C. Wells
Missing Madonna. C. O'Marie
Missing Man. B. Cane
Missing Man. Nicholas Carter
Missing Man. H. Sutherland Edwards
Missing Man. M. R. Hatch
Missing Man. K. MacLean
Missing Man. R. M. Stern
Missing Man. H. Waugh
Missing Masterpiece. H. Belloc

Missing Matisse. B. Levy
Missing Mayor. T. S. King
Missing Men. G. Leroux
Missing Men. A. Skene
Missing Million. A. Askew
Missing Million. E. H. Burrage
Missing Million. G. W. Jones
Missing Million. G. Stanley
Missing Million. E. Wallace
Missing Millionaire. Christopher Wilson
Missing Miniature. E. Kastner
Missing Minx. R. Goyne
Missing Miss Randolph. M. Leighton
Missing Mr. Mosley. J. Greenwood
Missing Money-Lender. W. S. Sykes
Missing Moon. H. Adams
Missing Note. Mrs. G. Corbett
Missing or Dead. G. Ashe
Missing or Murdered. R. Forsythe
Missing Partner. J. M. Cobban
Missing Partner. H. M. Stephenson
Missing Partners. Henry Wade
Missing Person. P. Brooks
Missing Person. O. Millard
Missing Person. N. Modiano
Missing Persons. C. T. Cline
Missing Persons. J. Olsen
Missing Piece. P. C. De Crispigny
Missing, Presumed Dead. C. Keith
Missing, Presumed Dead. J. V. Gordon
Missing Queen. Anonymous
Missing Rajah. R. Gilmour
Missing Reel. C. Rawlence
Missing Rope. C. Carnac
Missing Rubies. F. Du Boisgobey
Missing Scapegoat. B. Cobb
Missing Ships. A. Murray
Missing Spy. W. W. Sayer
Missing Treaty. C. Dawe
Missing Two. B. Reynolds
Missing Tycoon. B. H. Taylor
Missing Widow. Anthony Gilbert
Missing Will. H. Conway
Missing Witness. F. Barrett
Missing Witness. M. E. Braddon
Missing Witness. I. Cabot
Missing Witness. N. Daniels
Missing Witness. J. M. Hickman
Missing Witness. J. Reach
Missing Witness. D. W. Spurgeon
Missing Woman. M. Lewin
Missing Woman. E. Page
Mission Accomplished. J. Walker
Mission Bay Murder. P. C. Williams
Mission Berlin. T. Allbeury
Mission Code: Acropolis. B. Swift
Mission Code: Granite Island. B. Swift
Mission Code: King's Pawn. B. Swift
Mission Code: Monotaur. B. Swift
Mission Code: Scorpion. B. Swift
Mission Code: Snow Queen. B. Swift
Mission Code: Springboard. B. Swift
Mission Code: Survival. B. Swift
Mission Code: Symbol. B. Swift
Mission Code: Track and Destroy. B. Swift
Mission Code: Volcano. B. Swift
Mission Deadly Snow. J. Rosenberger
Mission for Betty Smith. Brian Cooper
Mission for Delta. L. H. Burruss
Mission for Eagles. J.-A. Price
Mission for Vengeance. P. Rabe
Mission House Murder. Hank Hobson
Mission Impossible. J. Tiger
Mission in Black. G. Cotler
Mission in Guemo. S. B. Hough
Mission in Sparrow Brush Lane. A. Stanford
Mission in Tunis. J. Pendower
Mission Into Auschwitz. K. Netzen
Mission M.I.A. J. C. Pollock
Mission of Death. M. T. Walworth
Mission of Doom. Gwyn Evans
Mission of Fear. R. M. Stern
Mission of Menace. R. Hardinge
Mission of Mercy. J. Robb

Mission of Mercy. D. Torr
Mission of Murder. R. Charles
Mission of Vengeance. R. Hardinge
Mission: Police Action. M. Kurland
Mission Revenge. F. Garrett
Mission River Justice. W. C. Tuttle
Mission: Tank War. M. Kurland
Mission: Third Force. M. Kurland
Mission to Beirut. E. Mannin
Mission to Burundi. J. M. Bernier
Mission to Majorca. I. Mercer
Mission to Malaspiga. Evelyn Anthony
Mission to Mexico. Arthur MacLean
Mission to Moscow. A. Bonnard
Mission to Murder. R. Glendinning
Mission to Siena. Raymond Marshall
Mission to Venice. Nick Carter
Mission to Venice. Raymond Marshall
Mission to Warsaw. L. Wacht
Mission: Tori. J. M. Bolton
Missionary Stew. R. Thomas
Missioner. E. P. Oppenheim
Mississippi Burning. J. Norst
Mississippi Outlaws and the Detectives. A. Pinkerton
Mississippi Run. P. D. Boles
Missouri Deathwatch. D. Pendleton
Missouri Legend. E. B. Ginty
Mist from Yarrow. A. J. B. Paterson
Mist in the Valley. D. Craig
Mist of Darkness. V. Coffman
Mist of Error. M. A. Dickens
Mist of Evil. P. Brisco
Mist of Milwood. M. Hara
Mist on the Saltings. Henry Wade
Mist on the Waters. F. L. Green
Mist Over Morro Bay. C. G. Page
Mist Over Talla. A. E. Lindop
Mistake Me Not. N. Easton
Mistaken Identity. R. Buckley
Mistaken Identity. V. L. Scott
Mistaken Identity. B. Sommers
Mistaken Manoeuvres. H. P. Raimes
Mistakenly in Mallorca. R. Jeffries
Mr. Ace. H. Christy
Mr. Allen. H. A. Vachell
Mr. & Mrs. North. Owen Davis
Mr. & Mrs. North and the Poisoned Playboy. F. Lockridge
Mr. & Mrs. North Meet Murder. F. Lockridge
Mr. Angel Comes Aboard. C. G. Booth
Mr. Apology. C. Black
Mr. Appleton Awakes. L. Beresford
Mr. Arkadin. O. Welles
Mr. Armitage Isn't Back Yet. Mervyn Jones
Mr. Babbacombe Dies. M. Burton
Mr. Balkram's Band. Frank King
Mr. Ball of Fire. B. Gray
Mr. Barnes, American. A. C. Gunter
Mr. Barnes of New York. A. C. Gunter
Mr. Bazalgette's Agent. L. Merrick
Mr. Benson's Business. Elliot Bailey
Mr. Big. M. Kenyon
Mister Big. G. Verner
Mr. Billingham, the Marquis and Madelon. E. P. Oppenheim
Mr. Birdsall Breezes Through. W. H. Mack
Mr. Blessington's Imperialist Plot. J. Sherwood
Mr. Blessington's Plot. J. Sherwood
Mr. Bobadil. F. Beeding
Mr. Bowling Buys a Newspaper. D. Henderson
Mr. Braddy's Bottle and other humorous tales. R. Connell
Mr. Brading's Collection. P. Wentworth
Mister Brown's Bodies. J. Blackburn
Mr. Buckby Is Not at Home. John Gloag
Mr. Budd Again. G. Verner
Mr. Budd Investigates. G. Verner
Mr. Buffum. H. De Selincourt
Mr. Burnside's Responsibility. T. Cobb
Mr. Byculla. E. Linklater
Mr. Calder and Mr. Behrens. M. Gilbert
Mr. Campion and others. M. Allingham
Mr. Campion: Criminologist. M. Allingham

Mr. Campion's Falcon. Y. Carter
Mr. Campion's Farthing. Y. Carter
Mr. Campion's Lady. M. Allingham
Mr. Campion's Lucky Day and other stories. M. Allingham
Mr. Campion's Quarry. Y. Carter
Mr. Capon. Jenni Hall
Mr. Caution—Mr. Callaghan. P. Cheyney
Mr. Chang of Scotland Yard. A. E. Apple
Mr. Chang's Crime Ray. A. E. Apple
Mr. Christopoulos. C. Blackstock
Mr. Clackworthy. C. B. Booth
Mr. Clackworthy, Con Man. C. B. Booth
Mr. Clerihew: Wine Merchant. W. Allen
Mr. Clunk's Text. H. C. Bailey
Mr. Coleman, Gent. E. M. Dennis
Mr. Collin Is Ruined. F. Heller
Mr. Commissioner Sanders. E. Wallace
Mr. Cooper's Frederika. L. M. Robertson
Mr. Coroner Presides. S. Truss
Mr. Craw. J. J. Bell
Mr. Cromwell Is Dead. L. Ford
Mr. Cronk's Cases. W. A. Darlington
Mr. Crook Lifts the Mask. Anthony Gilbert
Mr. Crumblestone's Eden. A. S. Well
Mr. Daddy-Detective. C. Brooks
Mr. Dass. B. Atkey
Mr. Deadly. D. Haring
Mr. Death. C. Wallace
Mr. Death Walks Abroad. C. Wallace
Mr. Denning Drives North. Alec Coppel
Mr. Diabolo. A. Lejeune
Mr. Digweed & Mr. Lumb. E. Phillpotts
Mr. Dorillon. J. Middlemass
Mr. Dovecourt's Decoy. H. Tuite
Mr. Dunton's Invention, and other stories. J. Hawthorne
Mr. Essington in Love. J. S. Clouston
Mr. Evans. C. A. Alington
Mr. Fairlie's Final Journey. A. Derleth
Mr. Faraday's Formula. D. O. Woodbury
Mr. Fortescue. W. Westall
Mr. Fortune Explains. H. C. Bailey
Mr. Fortune Finds a Pig. H. C. Bailey
Mr. Fortune Here. H. C. Bailey
Mr. Fortune Objects. H. C. Bailey
Mr. Fortune, Please. H. C. Bailey
Mr. Fortune Speaking. H. C. Bailey
Mr. Fortune Wonders. H. C. Bailey
Mr. Fortune's Case Book. H. C. Bailey
Mr. Fortune's Practice. H. C. Bailey
Mr. Fortune's Trials. H. C. Bailey
Mister Forty-Five. R. Angel
Mr. Fothergill's Murder. P. O'Donnell
Mr. Fred. J. B. Hilton
Mr. Glencannon. G. Gilpatric
Mr. Grantley's Idea. J. E. Cooke
Mr. Grex of Monte Carlo. E. P. Oppenheim
Mr. Guelpa. V. Thompson
Mr. Hamish Gleave. R. Llewellyn
Mr. Hedley's Private Hell. P. Barrington
Mr. Hercules. Gwyn Evans
Mr. Hire's Engagement. G. Simenon
Mr. Hobby. H. Kellock
Mr. Holmes and the Fair Armenian. C. V. Bark
Mr. Holmes and the Love Bank. C. V. Bark
Mr. Holmes at Sea. C. V. Bark
Mr. Holmes Goes to Ground. C. V. Bark
Mr. Holroyd Takes a Holiday. W. Stanley
Mr. Horrocks, Purser. C. J. C. Hyne
Mr. Hoyland Looks Round. P. C. Williams
Mr. Huffam and other stories. H. Walpole
Mr. Hunter. S. Ready
Mr. Hyde. H. Arnott
Mr. Incoul's Misadventure. E. E. Saltus
Mr. J. G. Reeder Returns. E. Wallace
Mr. Jackson. H. Green
Mr. Jardyne. Gwen John
Mr. Jelly's Business. A. W. Upfield
Mr. Jeremy, Detective. J. B. Whitton
Mr. Jorkens Remembers Africa. Lord Dunsany
Mr. Justice. A. Wilson
Mr. Justice Maxell. E. Wallace
Mr. Justice Philbank. P. Trent
Mr. Justice Raffles. E. W. Hornung
Mr. Kettle, Third Mate. C. J. C. Hyne
Mr. Kilmer Sees Red. P. Urquhart
Mr. Laxworthy's Adventures. E. P. Oppenheim
Mr. Lessingham Goes Home. E. P. Oppenheim
Mr. Loveday's Little Outing. E. Waugh
Mr. Lucky. Albert Conroy
Mr. Lyndon at Liberty. V. Bridges
Mr. Majestyk. E. Leonard
Mr. Malcolm Presents. G. Fairlie
Mr. Manley. G. I. Whitham
Mr. Marlow Chooses Wine. John Bentley
Mr. Marlow Stops for Brandy. John Bentley
Mr. Marlow Takes to Rye. John Bentley
Mr. Marx's Secret. E. P. Oppenheim
Mr. Mason. J. Last
Mr. Meeson's Will. H. R. Haggard
Mr. Merston's Money. J. Welcome
Mister Midas. M. Catto
Mr. Midnight. G. Verner
Mr. Mirakel. E. P. Oppenheim
Mr. Moon's Last Case. B. Patten
Mr. Mortimer Gets the Jitters. B. Gray
Mr. Moto Is So Sorry. J. P. Marquand
Mr. Moto Takes a Hand. J. P. Marquand
Mr. Munt Carries On. H. Clevely
Mr. Murray and the Boococks. W. F. Harvey
Mr. Nemesis. J. H. Vahey
Mr. Nice Guy. D. Haring
Mr. Nobody of England. A. Soutar
Mr. Parker Pyne, Detective. A. Christie
Mr. Passingham. T. Cobb
Mr. Pendlebury and the Suicide Club. A. Webb
Mr. Pendlebury Makes a Catch. A. Webb
Mr. Pendlebury's Hat Trick. A. Webb
Mr. Pendlebury's Second Case. A. Webb
Mr. Pennington Barges In. J. G. Brandon
Mr. Pennington Comes Through. J. G. Brandon
Mr. Pennington Goes Nap. J. G. Brandon
Mr. Pennington Sees Red. J. G. Brandon
Mr. Penny. M. Moiseiwitsch
Mr. Penny at War. M. Moiseiwitsch
Mr. Pepper, Investigator. B. Thomson
Mr. Perkins of New Jersey. G. Parker
Mr. Perkins of Portland. E. P. Butler
Mr. Peters. Riccardo Stephens
Mr. Pidgeon's Island. A. Berkeley
Mr. Pinkerton and the Old Angel. D. Frome
Mr. Pinkerton at the Old Angel. D. Frome
Mr. Pinkerton Finds a Body. D. Frome
Mr. Pinkerton Goes to Scotland Yard. D. Frome
Mr. Pinkerton Grows a Beard. D. Frome
Mr. Pinkerton Has the Clue. D. Frome
Mr. Pinkerton: Passage for One. D. Frome
Mr. Polton Explains. R. A. Freeman
Mr. Pond of Borneo. P. Blundell
Mr. Poskitt. J. S. Fletcher
Mr. Poskitt's Nightcaps. J. S. Fletcher
Mr. Potter of Texas. A. C. Gunter
Mr. Pottermack's Oversight. R. A. Freeman
Mr. Pottinger. S. Ready
Mr. Preed Investigates. Ladbroke Black
Mr. Preed's Gangster. Ladbroke Black
Mr. Preston's Daughter. T. Cobb
Mr. Priestley's Problem. A. B. Cox
Mr. Punch's Prize Novels. R. C. Lehmann
Mr. Punt of Chelsea. H. G. Hutchinson
Mister Q33. G. Goodchild
Mr. Quentin Investigates. Anthony Morton
Mr. Quixley of the Gate House. P. Brebner
Mr. Ramosi. V. Williams
Mr. Reeder Returns. E. Wallace
Mr. Right. C. Banks
Mr. Sandeman Loses His Life. E. P. Healey
Mister Scorpio. T. Gates
Mr. Sefton, Murderer. F. W. Crofts
Mr. Silver. H. Agg
Mr. Simpson Finds a Body. D. Frome
Mr. Smith's Hat. H. Reilly
Mr. Snoop Is Murdered. J. Reach
Mr. South Burned His Mouth. G. Nyland
Mr. Spenyard's Two Experiments. T. W. Speight
Mr. Splitfoot. H. McCloy
Mr. Standfast. J. Buchan
Mr. Stimpson and Mr. Gorse. P. Hamilton
Mr. Strang. C. J. Daly
Mr. Sun. P. O'Donnell
Mr. Surie. O. K. Joshee
Mister Target. W. Harrington
Mr. Three. W. Butler
Mr. Tolefree's Reluctant Witnesses. R. A. J. Walling
Mr. Tough. D. Haring
Mr. Treadgold Cuts In. V. Williams
Mr. Trouble. W. Ard
Mr. Tutt at His Best. A. Train
Mr. Tutt Comes Home. A. Train
Mr. Tutt Finds a Way. A. Train
Mr. Tutt Takes the Stand. A. Train
Mr. Tutt's Case Book. A. Train
Mister Violence. V. Warren
Mr. Wakefield's Crusade. B. Rubens
Mr. Walker Wants to Know. E. Dudley
Mr. Watson Intervenes. D. Gardiner
Mr. Westerby Missing. M. Burton
Mr. Whimset Buys a Gun. B. Graeme
Mr. Whipple Explains. G. Verner
Mr. Wingrave, Millionaire. E. P. Oppenheim
Mr. Wray's Cash Box. W. Collins
Mr. Wu. L. J. Miln
Mr. X. C. Brooks
Mr. Yesterday. E. Chaze
Mr. Zero. P. Wentworth
Misterioso. A. Plater
Mistigris. B. G. Quin
Mistress. Carter Brown
Mrs. Anstruther's Diamonds. R. D. Watson
Mrs. Balfame. G. Atherton
Mrs. Barthelme's Madness. S. Claudia
Mrs. Belfort's Stratagem. T. Cobb
Mrs. Blarney from Ireland. C. E. Blaney
Mrs. Brown on the Tichborne Case. A. Sketchley
Mrs. Brown's Pearls. A. Crabb
Mrs. Burlington. M. Isdale
Mrs. Carteret Receives. L. P. Hartley
Mrs. Christopher. E. Myers
Mrs. Craggs: Crimes Cleaned Up. H. R. F. Keating
Mistress Devon. V. Coffman
Mrs. Dimmock's Worries. B. L. Farjeon
Mrs. Donald Dyke, Detective. H. Rockwood
Mistress Dorothy Marvin. J. C. Snaith
Mrs. Druse's Case, and Maggie Houghtaling. Anonymous
Mrs. Dunbar's Secret. A. St. Aubyn
Mrs. Erricker's Reputation. T. Cobb
Mrs. Fuller. Marguerite Bryant
Mrs. Gainsborough's Diamonds. J. Hawthorne
Mrs. Gaskell's Tales of Mystery and Horror. E. C. Gaskell
Mrs. Gray's Past. H. Flowerdew
Mrs. Greet's Story of the Golden Owl. Mrs. Greet
Mrs. Greystone—Murdered. Roland Daniel
Mrs. Grundy's Victim. G. Corbett
Mrs. Gunness Mystery. Anonymous
Mrs. Halliburton's Troubles. H. Wood
Mrs. Homicide. D. Keene
Mrs. Inspector Jones. James Parish
Mrs. Isaac. B. L. Farjeon
Mrs. John Foster. C. Granville
Mrs. Jonathan Abroad. George Hastings
Mrs. Keith Hamilton M.B. A. S. Swan
Mrs. Keith's Crime. W. K. Clifford
Mrs. Knox's Profession. Jessica Mann
Mrs. Latham's Extravagance. T. Cobb
Mrs. Lygon's Husband. A. Sergeant
Mrs. McGinty's Dead. A. Christie
Mrs. McThing. M. Chase
Mrs. Maitland's Affair. M. Lynn
Mrs. Mallory Investigates. Hazel Holt
Mrs. Marden's Ordeal. J. Hay
Mrs. Meeker's Money. D. M. Disney
Mistress Mine. W. Standish
Mrs. Munck. E. Leffland
Mistress Murder. P. Cheyney
Mistress Murder. B. Picton
Mrs. Murdock Takes the Case. G. H. Coxe
Mrs. Murphy's Underpants. F. Brown
Mrs. Musgrave—and Her Husband. R. Marsh

Mistress of Bonaventure. H. Bindloss
Mistress of Cain. D. Haring
Mistress of Corey's Landing. M. Harmon
Mistress of Death. P. Anthony
Mistress of Destiny. B. Kingsley
Mistress of Devil's Manor. F. Stevenson
Mistress of Erebus. M. Ogan
Mistress of Evil. M. Tadrack
Mistress of Falcon Court. R. Calif
Mistress of Falcon Hill. D. Daniels
Mistress of Farrondale. D. Nile
Mistress of Fear. H. Janson
Mistress of Ghosthaven. J. Bellamy
Mistress of Harrowgate. J. Laurie
Mistress of Horror House. W. Woody
Mistress of Lost River. M. Craig
Mistress of Mellyn. V. Holt
Mistress of Mellyn. M. C. Kuner
Mistress of Moontide Manor. Lee Karr
Mistress of Moorwood Manor. Marilyn Ross
Mistress of Mount Fair. Jane Gordon
Mistress of Orion Hall. Claudette Nicole
Mistress of Quest. A. Sergeant
Mistress of Ravenstone. M. Heath
Mistress of Ravenswood. Clarissa Ross
Mistress of Ravenswood. Marilyn Ross
Mistress of Shades. N. McFather
Mistress of Soundcliff Manor. D. Wood
Mistress of Tara. C. Laffeaty
Mistress of the Damned. J. Davidson
Mistress of the Moor. A. Clements
Mistress of the Moor. E. Lockwood
Mistress on a Deathbed. N. Daniels
Mrs. Pargeter's Package. S. Brett
Mrs. Pollifax and the Golden Triangle. D. Gilman
Mrs. Pollifax and the Hong Kong Buddha. D. Gilman
Mrs. Pollifax and the Whirling Dervish. D. Gilman
Mrs. Pollifax on China Station. D. Gilman
Mrs. Pollifax on Safari. D. Gilman
Mrs. Pollifax, Spy. D. Gilman
Mrs. Pomeroy's Reputation. T. Cobb
Mrs. Porter's Letter. V. McConnell
Mrs., Presumed Dead. S. Brett
Mrs. Pym and other stories. N. Morland
Mrs. Pym of Scotland Yard. N. Morland
Mrs. Raffles. J. K. Bangs
Mrs. Snagg—Detective. O. M. Popplewell
Mrs. Snow and the Colonel. Julian Day
Mrs. Sparks of Paris. A. C. Bond
Mrs. Starr Lives Alone. J. Godden
Mrs. Tenterden. Margerie Scott
Mistress to Murder. R. Dietrich
Mrs. Vanderstein's Jewels. C. Bryce
Mrs. Vannock. A. Griffin
Mrs. Waldegrave's Will and other tales. Inspector F
Mrs. Warrender's Profession. G. D. H. Cole
Mrs. Webster and others. Mrs. W. K. Clifford
Mrs. Whiston's Party. T. Cobb
Mrs. White. M. Tracy
Mrs. William Jones and Bill. Edgar Wallace
Mrs. Winterton's Rebellion. J. Dering
Mrs. W's Last Sandwich. E. Denby
Mrs. Wylde. L. Gardiner
Mists Came Down. E. Backhouse
Mists of Danger. B. J. Hoff
Mists of Dark Harbor. C. Ross
Mists of Fear. J. Creasey
Mists of Memory. C. Marchant
Mists of Mourning. S. Somers
Mists of Ravensfall. V. F. Wake
Mists of Revilla. J. T. Osborne
Mists of Treason. J. N. Chance
Mists Over Mosley. John Greenwood
Misty Curtain. L. Cores
Misty Pathway. H. Desmond
Mitch. Roger Mark
Mitcham Murder Mystery. G. H. Teed
Mittenwald Syndicate. F. Nolan
Mitzi. N. Baroni
Mix Me a Murder. L. Grex
Mix Me a Person. J. T. Story
Mix Yourself a Redhead. C. Williams
Mixed Bags. S. C. Westerham

Mixed Cargoes. L. R. Bourne
Mixed Grill. W. P. Ridge
Mixed Pack. D. Conyers
Mixed Pickles. Neil Bell
Mixed Relations. V. L. Whitechurch
Mixed-Up Mess. Nicholas Carter
Mixer. E. Wallace
Mixture As Before. W. S. Maugham
Mixture of Plays. I. Gass
Mizmaze. M. Fitt
Moab Is My Washpot. E. G. Cousins
Moat Farm Mystery. M. E. Cooke
Moat House Mystery. B. M. Clay
Moat House Msytery. R. Francis Foster
Moated Grange. K. Tynan
Mob Says Murder. Albert Conroy
Mob War. F. Garrett
Mobile Library Murders. J. Austwick
Mobius Man. M. S. Karl
Mobius Trip. W. Garner
Mobsmen on the Spot. M. Grant
Mobster. F. Arrigio
Mobster. J. Roeburt
Moccasin Men. J. Ross
Moccasin Murders. K. Perkins
Mockery in Arms. J. Aldridge
Mocking Bird. T. Browning
Mocking Bird. E. Pugh
Mocking Face of Murder. S. Horler
Moday Mystery. M. E. Hively
Model Body. R. Reinsmith
Model Corpse. M. B. Clark
Model Father. D. C. Murray
Model for Murder. Carter Brown
Model for Murder. P. Campion
Model for Murder. J. Fast
Model for Murder. R. Kyle
Model for Murder. S. Marlowe
Model for Murder. R. O. Saber
Model for Murder. M. Warden
Model for Murder. Jeanne Wilson
Model for the Toff. J. Creasey
Model in Mayhem. H. Janson
Model Is Murdered. Babs Lee
Model Killer. Kane
Model Murder. R. Hausfeld
Model Murders. J. H. Demarest
Model of No Virtue. Carter Brown
Model Town and the Detectives. A. Pinkerton
Modeled in Murder. Manning Long
Moderate Murderer and The Honest Quack. G. K. Chesterton
Modern Cameos. A. Mills
Modern Circe. Maurice Scott
Modern Corsair. R. H. Savage
Modern Delilah. B. Bolt
Modern Dick Whittington. J. Payn
Modern Love. E. Willie
Modern Magician. J. F. Molloy
Modern Man-Hunt. P. H. Lockwood
Modern Mercenary. K. Prichard
Modern Othello. Anonymous
Modern Portia. P. Trent
Modern Prometheus. E. P. Oppenheim
Modern Quixote. August Berkeley
Modern Robyn Hood. M. M. Bodkin
Modern Sorceress. T. Mayne
Modern Sorceress. I. Stark
Modern Ulysses. J. M. Forman
Modern Ulysses. J. Hatton
Modern Wizard. R. Ottolengui
Modesty Blaise. P. O'Donnell
Modesty Blaise: Series 1. P. O'Donnell
Modesty Blaise: Series 2. P. O'Donnell
Modesty Blaise: Series 3. P. O'Donnell
Modesty Blaise: Series 4. P. O'Donnell
Modesty Blaise: Series 5. P. O'Donnell
Modesty Blaise: Series 6. P. O'Donnell
Modesty Blaise: Series 7. P. O'Donnell
Modesty Blaise: Series 8. P. O'Donnell
Modesty Blaise's The Black Pearl. P. O'Donnell
Modigliani Scandal. Z. Stone
Mods for Murder. D. Haring
Mogul Men. P. Leslie

Mohave City Cleans Up. D. Forde
Mohawks. M. E. Braddon
Mohembo Crossing. M. Bagley
Mohune's Nine Lives. P. Groom
Moina. L. L. Lynch
Mole. D. Sherman
Molehill File. M. Kenyon
Moles of Death. J. Dellbridge
Moll Flanders. D. Defoe
Moll for the Morgue. Pete Costello
Mollie the Handful. F. Warden
Molls Mean Murder. Griff
Molly. S. Gray
Molly and the Confidence Man. S. Overholser
Molly and the Gambler. S. Overholser
Molly and the Gold Baron. S. Overholser
Molly and the Indian Agent. S. Overholser
Molly and the Railroad Tycoon. S. Overholser
Molly Maguires. James O'Neill
Molly Maguires and the Detectives. A. Pinkerton
Molly on the Outlaw Trail. S. Overholser
Molly on the Spot. Frank King
Molly's Aunt at Angmering. H. C. McNeile
Molly's Husband. R. Marsh
Molting Season. C. Ferguson
Mom Meets Her Maker. J. Yaffe
Moment. E. Davies
Moment After. R. Buchanan
Moment After. V. Tracy
Moment for Murder. A. Eichler
Moment for Murder. L. Marshall
Moment in Time. J. Bedford
Moment in Time. J. Wellard
Moment More. J. Laing
Moment of Danger. D. MacKenzie
Moment of Decision. S. B. Hough
Moment of Fiction. D. Estow
Moment of Madness. C. J. Bellamy
Moment of Need. M. Coombs
Moment of Silence. D. Estow
Moment of the Predator. G. Bernard
Moment of Truth. K. A. Blom
Moment of Truth. W. M. Goeney
Moment of Truth. Magali
Moment of Truth. L. Snow
Moment of Untruth. E. Lacy
Moment of Violence. G. H. Coxe
Moment on Ice. N. Easton
Moment to Moment. Alec Coppel
Moment to Prey. H. Whittington
Momentary Stoppage. A. F. Grey
Moment's Error. A. W. Marchmont
Mona. Lawrence Block
Mona Intercept. D. Hamilton
Mona Lethal. D. Haring
Mona Lisa. J. L. Novak
Monarchs Are Flying. M. Foster
Monastery Mystery. G. Chester
Monastery Nightmares. R. H. Spencer
Moncasket Mystery and How Tom Hardy Solved It. S. Marlow
Moncrieff. I. Holland
Monday in Summer. Dorothy Sanders
Monday Never Came. C. Ryland
Monday Night. K. Boyle
Monday Night Murder. R. Trevor
Monday the Rabbi Took Off. H. Kemelman
Monday Theory. D. Clark
Monday, Tuesday, Wednesday! R. Houston
Monday's Child. Patricia Wallace
Monday's Mob. D. Pendleton
Mondo. A. De Stefano
Moneta Papers. J. Messmann
Money. M. Leighton
Money. P. L. Sulitzer
Money Barons. J. H. Vahey
Money Burn. T. Foster
Money Busy Everything. Roy Vickers
Money by Menaces. S. Adams
Money-Doublers. M. Sotabinda
Money for Murder. H. Carmichael
Money for Murder. Neill Graham
Money for Nothing. J. Harman
Money for the Taking. D. M. Disney

Money from Holme. M. Innes
Money from Home. D. Runyon
Money from Rome. R. Holt
Money Goes Round and Round. J. T. Story
Money Harvest. Ross Thomas
Money in the Air. M. Franklin
Money Jugglers. B. Wayde
Money Leads to Murder. D. M. Morgan
Money Lender. B. Delannoy
Money-Lender in Gloves. F. Blane
Money Means Murder. L. Marshall
Money Men. W. Haggard
Money Men and One-Shot Deal. G. Petievich
Money Money Money. D. Wagoner
Money Moon. J. Farnol
Money Mountain. R. MacLeod
Money Movers. D. Minchin
Money Murder. J. Ingersol
Money, Murder and the McNeills. T. Du Bois
Money Murders. Eugene Franklin
Money Musk. C. Wells
Money Musk. B. A. Williams
Money on Murder. H. Gardiner
Money on the Black. A. MacKinnon
Money Order Murder. Stafford Edwards
Money People. L. Katcher
Money Plays. M. Beckner
Money Sense. P. Trent
Money Soldiers. Martin Walker
Money Spider. M. Leighton
Money-Spider. W. LeQueux
Money Spinners. S. Murray
Money Spinners and other stories. A. Soutar
Money Stones. I. St. James
Money That Money Can't Buy. J. Munro
Money to Burn. W. Douglas
Money to Burn. M. Hendricks
Money to Burn. R. W. Kauffman
Money to Burn. H. Woodward
Money Trail. W. Jovanovich
Money Trap. L. White
Money Trouble. W. J. Reynolds
Money Walks. J. J. Farjeon
Money War. T. L. Smith
Money with Menaces. R. Dacre
Money with Menaces and To the Public Danger. P. Hamilton
Moneymaster. R. Spencer
Money's Worth of Murder. C. Conrad
Mongol Mask. David St. John
Mongolian Interlude. L. Oliver
Mongolian Mystery. G. Collins
Mongoose, R.I.P. W. F. Buckley, Jr.
Mongo's Back in Town. E. R. Johnson
Monimbo. A. De Borchgrave
Monique. D. Blankfort
Monitor Affair. C. B. Kelland
Monitor Found in Orbit. M. G. Coney
Monk. M. G. Lewis
Monk of Cruta. E. P. Oppenheim
Monk of Udolpho. T. C. H. Curties
Monkey and the Tiger. R. Van Gulik
Monkey Boat. N. Trott
Monkey Business. L. Isom
Monkey Game. G. Kent
Monkey Handlers. G. G. Liddy
Monkey Murder, and other Hildegarde Withers stories. S. Palmer
Monkey on a Chain. C. Blackstock
Monkey on a Chain. E. Lanham
Monkey on a Stick. J. Hubner
Monkey Puzzle. P. Gosling
Monkey-Puzzle. B. Von Hutten
Monkey Rope. Stephen Lewis
Monkey See, Monkey Do. T. Roscoe
Monkey-Shines. M. Stewart
Monkey Suit. K. Robeson
Monkey Trick. J. E. Gurdon
Monkey Wrench. J. Griffith
Monkey Wrench Gang. E. Abbey
Monkey's Raincoat. R. Crais
Monkhurst Case. A. Stanley
Monkhurst Murder. F. Grierson
Monk's Bridge Murder. W. G. Borth

Monk's Court. K. W. Eyre
Monk's Croft Mystery. T. S. King
Monk's Hollow. John Marsh
Monk's Hood. Ellis Peters
Monk's Hood Murders. L. Edgley
Monk's Retreat. Susannah Curtis
Monk's Terasure. G. Horton
Monksglade Mystery. H. Hill
Monkshood. E. Phillpotts
Monocled Man. J. Ronald
Monocled Monster. H. S. Keeler
Monocolo. Theodore Taylor
Monomark Mystery. L. Carlton
Monopoly. Jonathan Evans
Monopoly Menace. J. Hunter
Monopoly on Terror. B. Buck
Monopoly to Murder. R. Magowan
Monsieur Blackshirt. D. Graeme
Monsieur Brunner. D. A. Grant
Monsieur Faux-Pas. Rosa Lambert
Monsieur Jonquelle, Prefect of Police. M. D. Post
Monsieur Judas. F. Hume
Monsieur la Souris. G. Simenon
Monsieur Lecoq. E. Gaboriau
Monsieur Maurice. A. B. Edwards
Monsieur Monde Vanishes. G. Simenon
Monsieur Pamplemousse. Michael Bond
Monsieur Pamplemousse Aloft. Michael Bond
Monsieur Pamplemousse and the Secret Mission. Michael Bond
Monsieur Pamplemousse en Fete. Michael Bond
Monsieur Pamplemousse Investigates. Michael Bond
Monsieur Pamplemousse on the Spot. Michael Bond
Monsieur Pamplemousse Takes the Cure. Michael Bond
Monsieur X. R. W. Sneddon
Monsieur Zenith. R. King
Monsieur Zero. N. Tom-Gallon
Monsoon Murder. Brian Cooper
Monster. G. Fraser
Monster. H. Hext
Monster. E. Saltus
Monster Club. R. Chetwynd-Hayes
Monster in the Pool. A. Livingston
Monster of Dagenham Hall. J. Corbett
Monster of Grammont. G. Goodchild
Monster of Lazy Hook. Thorne Lee
Monster of Mu. O. Rutter
Monster of Snowdon Hall. Grove Wilson
Monster of the Lagoon. G. F. Worts
Monster Unto Many. P. Giles
Monster Wheel Affair. D. McDaniel
Monsters. K. Robeson
Monstrous Enemy. C. R. Gull
Monstrous Regiment. J. N. Chance
Monstrous Regiment. G. Petrie
Montana Man. W. C. Tuttle
Montauk Fault. M. Mitgang
Monte Carlo. D. Daniels
Monte Carlo. S. Sheppard
Monte Carlo Mission. V. Connell
Monte Carlo Stories. J. Barrett
Monte Cristo Cover-Up. J. M. Simmel
Monte Cristo in Khaki. R. H. Savage
Montenegrin Gold. B. Ball
Monterant Affair. Richard Grayson
Monterey. J. Lynch
Montezuma's Revenge. H. Harrison
Month of the Evil Moon. R. Pitt
Month of the Falling Leaves. B. Marshall
Month of the Mangled Models. R. Player
Month of the Pearl. P. Jones
Montmartre Murders. R. Grayson
Monument of Terror. V. Jones
Monza Protest. A. Neilson
Mood for Murder. F. Gruber
Mood for Murder. V. Siller
Moods and Tenses. W. F. Harvey
Moody Man. John Milne
Moon. James Herbert
Moon Cat. E. Neely
Moon Chapel. Lynna Cooper
Moon Country. G. Johnson
Moon Dance. E. P. Thorne

Moon Dancers. S. Nichols
Moon Endureth. J. Buchan
Moon Express. N. Daniels
Moon-Face and other stories. Jack London
Moon Fire. L. Benedict
Moon for Killers. G. Black
Moon Garden. Jan Alexander
Moon Gate. C. C. Estes
Moon Hill. M. Woodhouse
Moon in Pisces. C. Darby
Moon in Shadows. A. Westminster
Moon in the Gutter. D. Goodis
Moon Is Red. S. Rohmer
Moon Killer. J. Corbett
Moon Killer. R. Verron
Moon Madness. D. Haring
Moon Marriage. A. Rundle
Moon Murders. N. Morland
Moon of Darkness. M. Lynch
Moon of Death! R. Gar
Moon of Joy. Camilla Hope
Moon of Madness. S. Rohmer
Moon of the Wolf. L. H. Whitten
Moon of Valleys. D. Whitelaw
Moon of Violence. E. Douglas
Moon Over Miami. J. Deane
Moon Over the Danube. M. McEvoy
Moon Over the Water. M. Greig
Moon Over Willow Run. D. E. L. Patch
Moon Returns. Rona Randall
Moon Rock. A. J. Rees
Moon Saw Murder. G. Oliver
Moon Shadow. K. Allyson
Moon Shadows. A. Boyle
Moon-Spinners. Mary Stewart
Moon Was Made for Murder. N. Morland
Moon Was Red. D. Sage
Moonbathers. R. Miles
Moonbeams. R. V. Beste
Moonblood. P. J. Cooper
Mooncalf Murders. N. V. Carter
Moondreamer. Z. Kamitses
Moondrop to Murder. J. B. Hilton
Moondyne. J. B. O'Reilly
Mooney Moves Around. K. O'Neil
Moonflete. V. Black
Moonflower. B. Nichols
Moonflower. P. A. Whitney
Moonflower Murder. B. Nichols
Moonflowers. M. Peterson
Moonhaunt. U. Nightingale
Moonhill Mystery. W. Woodrow
Moonlake Manor. L. Churchill
Moonlight and Murder. J. E. Davis
Moonlight at Greystone. L. Bronte
Moonlight Can Betray. L. Harper
Moonlight Flitting. M. Procter
Moonlight Gondola. Janette Radcliffe
Moonlight Jewelers. A. Vidalie
Moonlight Madness. E. Nepean
Moonlight Path. K. Lindsay
Moonlight Red. D. Morel
Moonlight Variations. F. Stevenson
Moonlighter. H. Kane
Moonlighters. S. Morrow
Moonlit Door. A. Maybury
Moonlit Trap. R. Willock
Moonlit Way. R. W. Chambers
Moonlit Way. A. Dwyer-Joyce
Moonmilk and Murder. A. M. Stein
Moonmist. G. Ferrand
Moonraker. I. Fleming
Moonrakers and Mischief. G. J. Feakes
Moonraker's Bride. M. Brent
Moonrise. T. Strauss
Moonrock. R. Weverka
Moons in Gold. C. S. Montanye
Moonshadow Mountain. T. R. Bernard
Moonshell. B. Carlton
Moonshine. R. Carr
Moonshine Blade. A. Cockrell
Moonshine Momma. Carter Brown
Moonshine Mountain. C. Glore
Moonshine War. E. Leonard

Title Index
MOTHER NIGHT / 1077

Moonshiners. J. Carr
Moonshiner's Dupe. Lieut. Carlton
Moonspender. Jonathan Gash
Moonstalker. F. Wrixon
Moonstone. W. Collins
Moonstone. M. Stone
Moonstone Jungle. S. Harvester
Moonstone Mystery. A. Marsden
Moonstone Spirit. J. Deweese
Moontide. Willard Robertson
Moonwater. Claudia Nicole
Moonwind. S. Wagner
Moor. D. Whitelaw
Moor Barn Mystery. H. L. Phillips
Moor Fires Mystery. H. R. Campbell
Moor House Murders. G. Verner
Moorcroft Manor Mystery. R. Trevor
Moorhaven. D. Winston
Moorland Mystery. A. S. Falkner
Moorland Terror. H. Broadbridge
Moorland Tragedy. B. Orczy
Moorlands Murder. C. Jude
Moorsend Manor. F. Hurd
Moorwood Legacy. I. Foster
Moose Murders. A. Bicknell
Moot Point. P. De Polnay
Morag's Flying Fortress. J. T. Story
Morals and Millions. F. Warden
Morals and Mysteries. H. Aide
Morals Squad. S. A. Krasney
Moran Chambers Smiled. E. P. Oppenheim
Moran's Woman. D. Keene
Morbid Symptoms. G. Slovo
Morbid Taste for Bones. Ellis Peters
Mord Em'ly. W. P. Ridge
Mordida Man. R. Thomas
More About P.J., the Secret Service Boy. F. S. Hamilton
More Adventures of Captain Kettle. C. J. C. Hyne
More Adventures of Ellery Queen. E. Queen
More Beautiful Than Murder. O. R. Cohen
More Bitter Than Death. K. Wilhelm
More Bunkum. Frank Richardson
More by Corwin. N. Corwin
More Cargoes. W. W. Jacobs
More Crook Stuff. R. Keverne
More Dangerous Than the Moon. Richard Butler
More Dead Than Alive. R. Ormerod
More Deadly Than the Male. Amborse Grant
More Deadly Than the Male. L. Meynell
More Deaths for Sergeant Cluff. G. North
More Deaths Than One. S. Engstrand
More Deaths Than One. B. Fischer
More Deaths Than One. R. Stout
More Doctors' Tales. W. Hywel
More Educated Evans. E. Wallace
More Exploits of Sherlock Holmes. Adrian Conan Doyle
More Good Old Stuff. J. D. MacDonald
More Goon Show Scripts. S. Milligan
More Guys and Dolls. D. Runyon
More Knaves Than One. F. Packard
More Lasting Than Bronze. D. W. Burbidge
More Limehouse Nights. T. Burke
More Lives Than One. C. Houghton
More Lives Than One. C. Wells
More Murder in a Nunnery. E. Shepherd
More Mysteries of a Great City. W. LeQueux
More News from Middle East. Robert Mason
More Nightmares. R. Bloch
More Perfect Union. J. A. Jance
More Perfect Union. R. Stapp
More Secrets of Potsdam. W. LeQueux
More Stories from Thriller. Ted Hart
More Tabloid Tales. L. Heilgers
More Tales of Our Village. Mrs. C. Kernahan
More Tales of Temptation. M. Strickland
More Tales of the Black Widowers. I. Asimov
More Tales of the Uneasy. V. Hunt
More Tales of the Unexpected. R. Dahl
More Tales of the West Riding. P. Bentley
More Than a Hunch. Vickie York
More Than All. M. Warby
More Than Flesh. L. A. Brennan

More Than Kisses, Baby. S. Morelli
More Than Once Upon a Time. G. Kersh
More Than One Serpent. R. A. J. Walling
More Than Somewhat. D. Runyon
More Things in Heaven . . . W. Owen
More Tish. M. R. Rinehart
More to Be Pitied Than Scorned. C. E. Blaney
More Trouble for Archer. H. Clevely
More Two-Minute Mysteries. D. J. Sobel
More Work for the Undertaker. M. Allingham
Moreton Abbey. H. Chilcot
Moreton Mystery. E. Dejeans
Morgan of the Mounted. S. A. White
Morgan the Dauntless. J. K. Stafford
Morgan Trail. W. C. Tuttle
Morganatic Marriage. C. Dawe
Morganatic Marriage. M. Leighton
Morganatic Wife. L. Tracy
Morgan's Castle. J. Hilliard
Morgan's Horror. G. M. Fenn
Morgan's Mountain. A. Mayse
Morgan's Wife. V. James
Morgue Amour. Carter Brown
Morgue Is Always Open. J. Odlum
Morgue Has Guests. V. J. Hanson
Morgue Mate. D. Haring
Morgue the Merrier. Kane
Morgue the Merrier. J. Truesdell
Moriarty. J. Gardner
Morituri. W. J. Luddecke
Morlo. L. A. Knight
Morning After. E. Lottman
Morning After. J. B. Weiner
Morning After Death. N. Blake
Morning for Flamingos. J. L. Burke
Morning Morning True. E. Herndon
Morning of the Tiger. D. J. Fretland
Morning Ran Red. S. Bowman
Morning Walk. L. P. Davies
Moro. P. McCurtin
Moro Affair & The Mystery of Majorana. L. Sciascia
Moroccan. C. A. Haddad
Morocco Episode. W. P. Brothers
Morocco Jones and the Case of the Golden Angel. J. Baynes
Moron. M. Brandel
Morosco. R. Pertwee
Morris Hume, Detective. William Robertson
Morrison's Machine. J. S. Fletcher
Morrissey. E. Downey
Morry. R. Elson
Mort Castle. Anonymous
Mortal Affair. Anonymous
Mortal Belladaywick. M. Christensen
Mortal Coils. A. Huxley
Mortal Encounter. P. Sargent
Mortal Fear. Robin Cook
Mortal Fire. H. Gibbs
Mortal Games. P. Salinger
Mortal Gods. J. Fast
Mortal Remains. M. Yorke
Mortal Ruin. J. Malcolm
Mortal Sins. Anna Porter
Mortal Stakes. R. B. Parker
Mortal Storm. P. Bottome
Mortal Term. J. Penn
Mortal Words. K. L. Knight
Mortallone and Aunt Trinidad. A. T. Quiller-Couch
Mortdecai's Endgame. K. Bonfiglioli
Mortgage for Murder. Paul Costello
Mortgaged Lives. P. Trent
Mortician's Birthday Party. P. Whalley
Mortimer Story. P. Barrington
Mortimore Castle. Anonymous
Mortissimo. P. E. H. Durston
Mortlake. Griffin Taylor
Mortmain. H. C. Asterley
Mortmain. A. Train
Morton Mystery. E. D'Arcy
Mortover Grange Affair. J. S. Fletcher
Mortover Grange Mystery. J. S. Fletcher
Morwenna. A. Goring
Mosaic. J. Bannister
Mosaic Earring. C. Boyer

Mosaic of Death. W. Keenan
Moscow. Nick Carter
Moscow at High Noon Is the Target. P. Richards
Moscow by Nightmare. J. L. Shub
Moscow Coach. P. McCutchan
Moscow Crossing. S. Flannery
Moscow File. E. P. Thorne
Moscow 500. David Grant
Moscow Gold. J. Salisbury
Moscow Intercept. H. Arvay
Moscow Interlude. C. W. Thayer
Moscow Magician. J. Moody
Moscow Manhunt. Philip Chambers
Moscow Massacre. D. Pendleton
Moscow Maze. D. Ross
Moscow Metal. R. Boyer
Moscow Mists. Clarissa Ross
Moscow Murder. B. Newman
Moscow Mystery. I. Low
Moscow 1980. R. Vacha
Moscow Papers. J. M. White
Moscow Quadrille. T. Allbeury
Moscow Requiem. J. Simpson
Moscow Road. S. Harvester
Moscow Rules. R. Moss
Moscow Sacrament. A. Hernandez
Moscow Tape. J. N. Datesh
Moses Bottle. R. Mead
Mosley by Moonlight. J. Greenwood
Mosley Receipt. K. Royce
Mosley Went to Mow. J. Greenwood
Mosque of the Mahdi. A. Murray
Mosquito Net. G. B. Savi
Mosquito Serenade. N. McGuire
Mosquito Squadron. R. Jackson
Mosquitoes Don't Kill. R. Hamilton
Moss Cliff Abbey. M. J. Young
Moss Mystery. C. Wells
Moss Rose. J. Shearing
Mossbank Murder. Harry Mills
Mosshaven. S. Hancock
Most Beautiful Girl in the World. T. Willis
Most Beautiful Lady. D. Brande
Most Contagious Game. C. Aird
Most Contagious Game. Samuel Grafton
Most Cunning Workmen. R. Lewis
Most Dangerous Game. G. Lyall
Most Deadly Hate. H. Carmichael
Most Deadly Hate. Sara Woods
Most Delicious Poison. C. Connell
Most Grievous Murder. Sara Woods
Most Happy Con Man. J. P. Radford
Most Immoral Murder. H. Ashbrook
Most Likely Suspects. A. Bourgeau
Most Likely to Love. F. Flora
Most Men Don't Kill. David Alexander
Most Private Intrigue. L. Rosten
Most Sacred of All. J. Farnol
Most Savage Animal. H. Atkinson
Most Secret. J. D. Carr
Most Secret . . . Most Immediate. H. Swiggett
Most Unnatural Murder. Fiona Sinclair
Most Wanted. G. Bagby
Mostly by Moonlight. D. Daniels
Mostly Murder. F. Brown
Mostly Nasty. Andrew Graham
Mostly True. G. Fleming
Mote House Mystery. H. A. Vachell
Motel Girl. Paul Daniels
Moteley's Concession. C. N. Boyle
Moth. J. M. Cain
Moth and the Footlights. G. Warden
Moth in a Rag Shop. R. Chambers
Moth Murder. L. Blow
Moth-Watch Murder. M. Burton
Moth-Woman. F. Hume
Mother Finds a Body. G. R. Lee
Mother Goose Murders. W. B. Gibson
Mother Hunt. R. Stout
Mother-in-Law. E. Southworth
Mother Love. Domini Taylor
Mother Mandarin. F. Hume
Mother Murders. D. L. Gilbert
Mother Night. K. Vonnegut

Mother of Gold. D. Creed
Mother of Jack the Ripper. J. Kirkpatrick
Mother of the Year. B. B. Johnson
Mother Russia. R. Littel
Mother Shadow. M. J. Howe
Mother's Boy. Bernard Taylor
Mother's Boys. R. Barnard
Mothers Cry. H. G. Carlisle
Mother's Day. J. M. Ryan
Mother's Murder. B. K. Stevens
Mother's Sacrifice. C. Faber
Mother's Secret. E. Southworth
Moths. R. Ashe
Motion Menace. K. Robeson
Motive. H. Carmichael
Motive. M. B. Lowndes
Motive. E. Piper
Motive for a Kill. J. N. Chance
Motive for Murder. C. Barling
Motive for Murder. S. Bate
Motive for Murder. N. Brent
Motive for Murder. Neill Graham
Motive for Murder. A. Griffin
Motive for Murder. E. T. Hamill
Motive for Murder. B. Manningham
Motive for Murder. W. Reed
Motive for Murder. D. W. Rimel
Motive for Revenge. S. Clausse
Motive for Revenge. P. Conway
Motive for the Crime. A. Soutar
Motive in Shadow. L. Egan
Motive Key. J. Woodward
Motive Not the Deed. A. Arden
Motive on Record. Dell Shannon
Motives for Murder. G. Croudace
Motives of Nicholas Holtz. T. Painter
Motley and Murder. H. Holt
Motley Menace. L. Cargill
Motor Bus Murder. Donald Stuart
Motor City Blue. L. D. Estleman
Motor Coach Murder. L. Bidston
Motor Coach Mystery. A. Murray
Motor Coach Mystery. W. Tyrer
Motor Cracksman. Charles Carey
Motor-Gun. H. C. McNeile
Motor Horn Mystery. T. S. King
Motor Pirate. S. Paternoster
Motor Rally Mystery. J. Rhode
Motor Show Mystery. H. H. C. Gibbons
Motor Show Mystery. R. Hardinge
Motor Wizard's Mystery. B. L. Standish
Motormaniacs. L. Osbourne
Mottled Death. J. Creasey
Motto for Murder. M. Mace
Mouche. Demouzon
Mouls Hous Mystery. C. Barry
Mound Hill Mystery. Max Burton
Mount Desolation. C. Dawe
Mount Despair, and other stories. D. C. Murray
Mount Eden. F. Marryat
Mount Royal. M. E. Braddon
Mountain Cabin Mystery. C. Bussell
Mountain Cat. R. Stout
Mountain Cat Murders. R. Stout
Mountain Death. H. Braddock
Mountain Decameron. J. Downes
Mountain Fires. M. Sutherland
Mountain Gold. Basil Carey
Mountain Gold. G. Goodchild
Mountain House Mystery. R. St. Clair
Mountain Inn Mystery. N. Ridley
Mountain Justice. C. N. Buck
Mountain Limited. E. L. Coolidge
Mountain Madness. L. Ford
Mountain Man. H. C. Wire
Mountain Massacre. J. Buchanan
Mountain Meadow. J. Buchan
Mountain Monster. K. Robeson
Mountain Murder. J. T. Adams
Mountain Murder Case. C. H. Snow
Mountain Mystery. J. J. Farjeon
Mountain Mystery. L. L. Lynch
Mountain of Fear. W. Barker
Mountain of Fear. Rona Randall

Mountain of Terror. H. S. Banner
Mountain of the Blind. J. Creasey
Mountain Rampage. D. Pendleton
Mountain Terror. M. E. Cooke
Mountain, the Miner, and the Lord. H. M. Caudill
Mountaineer Detective. Anonymous
Mountaineer Detective. C. W. Cobb
Mountaineers. H. Bindloss
Mountainhead. D. Cory
Mountains Have a Secret. A. W. Upfield
Mountains Have No Shadow. O. Cameron
Mountains of Fears. H. C. Rowland
Mountains West of Town. W. Downing
Mounted Justice. K. Mayo
Mountford Show. Elizabeth Ford
Mountie on Trial. O. Olson
Mountie Patrol. A. Macmillan
Mounties: Great March West. T. Dicks
Mounties: Massacre in the Hills. T. Dicks
Mounties: Wardrums of the BLackfoot. T. Dicks
Mounty in a Jeep. T. M. Longstreth
Moura. V. Coffman
Mourn the Hangman. H. Whittington
Mourned on Sunday. H. Reilly
Mourner. R. Stark
Mourner's Voyage. Shane Martin
Mournful Demeanor of Lieutenant Boruvka. J. Skvorecky
Mourning After. T. B. Dewey
Mourning After. Z. Johnson
Mourning After. F. Kane
Mourning After. H. Q. Masur
Mourning Before Murder. Robert Turner
Mourning Brooch. H. Miller
Mourning Glory. D. Haring
Mourning of the Dove. I. Betz
Mourning Raga. Eliis Peters
Mourning Tree. V. Johnston
Mouse in Eternity. N. Tyre
Mouse in the Mountain. N. Davis
Mouse Trap. M. Messer
Mouse Who Wouldn't Play Ball. Anthony Gilbert
Mouse with Red Eyes. E. Eastman
Mouseback. J. C. Woodiwiss
Mousetown and The Violinist and The Flower Girl. H. Alianak
Mousetrap. A. Christie
Mousetrap and Other Plays. A. Christie
Mouth of the Wolf. W. Murray
Mouthful of Sand. M. R. D. Meek
Mouthpiece. Robert (G.) Curtis
Move. G. Simenon
Move Along. F. Castle
Move Fast, Brother! D. Spade
Move in the Dark. Nicholas Carter
Move On, Miss Mayhem. M. Brody
Movement Toward Eden. Clark Howard
Moves on an Old Board. C. Hilton
Movie Mystery. R. C. Armour
Moving Day. Charles Henry
Moving Eye. M. E. Cooke
Moving Finger. J. H. Barrington
Moving Finger. M. Bass
Moving Finger. A. Christie
Moving Finger. C. Fitzsimmons
Moving Finger. M. Gaunt
Moving Finger. N. S. Lincoln
Moving Finger. A. E. Meagher
Moving Finger. E. P. Oppenheim
Moving Graveyard. M. Avallone
Moving House of Foscaldo. C. Chadwick
Moving Pageant. L. A. Pavey
Moving Picture Boys. M. Wilk
Moving Picture Mystery. Nicholas Carter
Moving Picture Writes. P. Chambers
Moving Target. F. Earley
Moving Target. J. McClenaghan
Moving Target. John Macdonald
Moving Target. D. Pendleton
Moving Targets. W. J. Reynolds
Moving Toyshop. E. Crispin
Mowbray Mystery. B. Bolt
Mox. M. Grant
Mozart Fiddle. K. Bird

Mozart Leaves at Nine. H. Greene
Mozart Score. E. Leather
Ms. Tree. M. A. Collins
M'Sango, the Witch Doctor. F. A. M. Webster
Much Ado About Maggody. Joan Hess
Much Ado About Murder. F. Levon
Much Ado About Something. B. Graeme
Much Darker Days. A. H. Longway
Much in Evidence. H. Cecil
Muck Rakers. D. Haring
Mud in His Eye. G. Hammond
Muddles of Solon Mudhed, the Blacksmith Detective. Anonymous
Muddy Leaf Mystery. T. B. Morris
Mudflats of the Dead. G. Mitchell
Mudland. M. Adams
Muertalma. M. Dey
Muffled Man. G. Ingram
Mufti. H. C. McNeile
Mugger. E. McBain
Mugger's Day. G. Bagby
Mugs, Molls and Dr. Harvey. G. Malcolm-Smith
Muir's Blood. C. Larson
Mulberry Wharf. H. B. M. Marriott
Mule on the Minaret. A. Waugh
Mullenthrope Thing. C. Hood
Mulligan. A. J. Fenady
Mulligan Stew. G. Sorrentino
Mulligan's Pirates. D. Stanford
Mulligan's Seed. H. Burkholz
Multi-Million-Dollar Murders. V. W. Mason
Multi-Millionaire. A. Hodges
Multiple Man. B. Bova
Multiple Murder. T. Macrae
Multiplicity of Mrs. Browns. A. Sewart
Multitude of Shadows. A. Calin
Multitude of Sins. M. K. Wren
Mumberley Inheritance. W. Graves
Mumbo-Jumbo. J. Barnard
Mumbo Jumbo. I. Reed
Mummy. Riccardo Stephens
Mummy Case. D. Morrah
Mummy Case. Elizabeth Peters
Mummy Case Mystery. D. Morrah
Mummy Comes to Life. V. Van Der Elst
Mummy Moves. M. Gaunt
Mummy Sea, Mummy Do. C. Sodaro
Mummy Walks. B. Luigi
Mummy's Boy. William Paul
Mummy's Curse. T. S. King
Mummy's Hand. Mrs. C. Kernahan
Mum's the Word. D. Cannell
Mum's the Word for Murder. A. Baker
Mumsy, Nanny, Sonny, and Girly. B. Comport
Mungo. G. Woden
Mungwe Affair. J. D. Powell
Munich Involvement. F. Mullally
Munich 10. L. Orde
Munitions Master. K. Robeson
Munitions Ship Murders. V. W. Mason
Mura, the Western Detective. Old Sleuth
Mura, the Western Lady Detective. Anonymous
Murder. H. Adams
Murder! John Arnold
Murder. S. Brody
Murder!! M. Crombie
Murder. Parnell Hall
Murder. H. Janson
Murder. Evelyn Johnson
Murder a Day! R. Avery
Murder a la Mode. P. Moyes
Murder a la Mode. E. K. Sellars
Murder a la Mozambique. A. Scobie
Murder a la Richelieu. A. Blackman
Murder a la Stroganoff. C. Brahms
Murder a Mile High. E. Dean
Murder, a Mystery, and a Marrage. M. Twain
Murder Abroad. W. C. Harvey
Murder Abroad. E. R. Punshon
Murder, Absolutely Murder. H. Cloutier
Murder Across and Down. H. Resnicow
Murder Adrift. G. Bellairs
Murder Afoot. E. Westward
Murder After a Fashion. S. Dean

Title Index

Murder After a Fashion. V. Hinkle
Murder After Christmas. R. Latimer
Murder After Dark. J. Gannett
Murder After Hours. A. Christie
Murder After the Blitz. P. Piper
Murder After Tea Time. L. Cutter
Murder After the Fact. A. Ashforth
Murder After the Holidays. A. Arncliffe
Murder Against the Grain. E. Lathen
Murder Ahead. N. Deane
Murder Ahead. D. Keene
Murder al Fresco. Jennifer Jones
Murder All Over. C. F. Adams
Murder Amid Proofs. M. Bremner
Murder Among Children. T. Coe
Murder Among Friends. B. Barry
Murder Among Friends. I. E. Cox
Murder Among Friends. E. Ferrars
Murder Among Friends. Lange Lewis
Murder Among Friends. F. McConnell
Murder Among Friends. Simon
Murder Among Members. C. Carnac
Murder Among the Angells. R. Scarlett
Murder Among the Dying. G. W. Jones
Murder Among the Nudists. P. Hunt
Murder Among the Personal Ads. C. K. Cambray
Murder Among the Well-To-Do. E. Godfrey
Murder Among Thieves. P. Alding
Murder Among Those Present. H. Mace
Murder and Acquisitions. Haughton Murphy
Murder—and Ariadne. I. Wray
Murder and Blueberry Pie. F. Lockridge
Murder and Chips. L. Mantell
Murder & Co. B. Gray
Murder and Gardenias. M. Neville
Murder and Magic. R. Garrett
Murder and Marigold. G. Brandon
Murder and Miss Ming. P. Hambledon
Murder and Music. G. Lee
Murder and Mystery. Evelyn Johnson
Murder and Poor Jenny. M. Neville
Murder and the First Lady. E. Roosevelt
Murder and the Married Virgin. B. Halliday
Murder and the Red-Haired Girl. H. Balfour
Murder and the Secret Weapon. G. F. Worts
Murder and the Shocking Miss Williams. H. J. Kennedy
Murder and the Wanton Bride. B. Halliday
Murder Anonymous. Anthony Gilbert
Murder Arranged. J. Philips
Murder Arranged. B. Thomson
Murder As a Fine Art. F. Bonnamy
Murder As a Fine Art. C. Carnac
Murder As Advertised. M. Boone
Murder As an Ornament. M. Boniface
Murder As Arranged. Mark Cross
Murder As Usual. O. F. Jerome
Murder As Usual. H. Pentecost
Murder As the Curtain Rises. J. Philips
Murder Assured. T. Clayton
Murder Assured. M. Halliday
Murder at a Cottage. Roland Daniel
Murder at a Dog Show. D. F. Gardiner
Murder at a Police Station. A. Swift
Murder at Arondale Farm. J. Hawk
Murder at Arroways. H. Reilly
Murder at Auction. E. Beatty
Murder at Avalon Arms. O. F. Jerome
Murder at Bador. S. C. Mason
Murder at Barclay House. K. McKay
Murder at Bayside. R. Robins
Murder at Bean and Beluga. D. Mayo
Murder at Belle Butte. T. M. Longstreth
Murder at Belle Camille. Monte Barrett
Murder at Benfleet. G. Bettany
Murder at Bill's O'Jacks. J. Davenport
Murder at Brambles. G. Collins
Murder at Bratton Grange. J. Rhode
Murder at Bridge. Anne Austin
Murder at Brownhill. T. A. Plummer
Murder at Bubble Springs. F. Foden
Murder at Buckingham Palace. T. E. B. Clarke
Murder at Buzzards Bay. A. Abbot
Murder at Calamity House. A. Cardwell

Murder at Cambridge. Q. Patrick
Murder at Castle Deeping. W. E. Johns
Murder at Charters. J. Fethaland
Murder at Chartres Towers. M. Beard
Murder at City Hall. Dan Ross
Murder at Cloud Hospital. M. Stand
Murder at Coney Island. J. D. O'Hanlon
Murder at Constantia. C. M. Linday
Murder at Cost Price. L. H. Hart
Murder at Covent Garden. W. J. Makin
Murder at Crawford Notch. M. L. Burns
Murder at Crome House. G. D. H. Cole
Murder at Cypress Hall. O. Stacey
Murder at Dawn. L. O. Johnson
Murder at Daybreak. G. A. Mayhew
Murder at Deem House. S. Bate
Murder at Deer Lick. A. B. Cunningham
Murder at Derivale. J. Rhode
Murder at Drake's Anchorage. E. L. Waddell
Murder at Eastover. A. Rutter
Murder at Eight. S. Bate
Murder at Eight Bells. E. L. McReay
Murder at Elaine's. R. Rosenbaum
Murder at Elstree. T. Burke
Murder at End House. M. Halliday
Murder at Endor. W. A. Wolff
Murder at Exbridge. V. L. Whitechurch
Murder at Fenwold. C. Bush
Murder at Fleet. E. B. Young
Murder at Four Dot Ranch. F. L. Gregory
Murder at Full Moon. W. J. Makin
Murder at Glen Athol. N. Lippincott
Murder at Government House. E. Huxley
Murder at Grand Bay. W. D. Roberts
Murder at Grassmere Abbey. M. B. Dix
Murder at H.Q. H. Hawton
Murder at Hazelmoor. A. Christie
Murder at Hermit's Cottage. R. Hardinge
Murder at Hide and Seek. E. O'Donnell
Murder at High Noon. P. McGuire
Murder at High Noon. Edgar Roberts
Murder at High Tide. C. G. Booth
Murder at Hobcaw Barony. E. Roosevelt
Murder at Horsethief. J. D. O'Hanlon
Murder at King's Kitchen. M. Halliday
Murder at La Marimba. C. Wolfe
Murder at Le Touquet. R. Lacroix
Murder at Lancaster Gate. F. Grierson
Murder at Landred Hall. J. Turner
Murder at Lantern Corner. T. A. Plummer
Murder at Large. L. Frost
Murder at Leisure. J. G. Edwards
Murder at Leisure. M. Monteilhet
Murder at Liberty Hall. A. Clutton-Brock
Murder at Lilac Cottage. J. Rhode
Murder at Linpara. H. Horn
Murder at Lintercombe. J. Greig
Murder at Little Malling. Roland Daniel
Murder at Lover's Lake. M. Brucker
Murder at Madingley Grange. Caroline Graham
Murder at Maison Manche. H. Burleigh
Murder at Malibu. J. D. O'Hanlon
Murder at Maneuvers. R. Howes
Murder at Manor House. L. Gorell
Murder at Manson's. R. E. Young
Murder at Marble Arch. Gavin Holt
Murder at Markenden Court. H. H. Stanners
Murder at Markham. P. H. Sprinkle
Murder at Marks Caris. W. M. Duncan
Murder at Marlington. T. A. Plummer
Murder at Marston Manor. R. Forsythe
Murder at Mavering. L. Gorell
Murder at Melton Peveril. C. Ashton
Murder at Mid-Day. A. Hocking
Murder at Midday. F. Langhorn
Murder at Midnight. L. Allan
Murder at Midnight. J. Blackburn
Murder at Midnight. M. Cumberland
Murder at Midnight. H. Desmond
Murder at Midnight. C. F. Gregg
Murder at Midnight. P. Hoar
Murder at Midnight. R. Sale
Murder at Midnight. R. A. J. Walling
Murder at Midnight. H. Whittington

Murder at Midyears. Marion Mainwaring
Murder at Mrs. Loring's. S. S. Simon
Murder at Mocking House. W. C. Brown
Murder at Monk's Barn. C. Waye
Murder at Montauk. D. Wheelock
Murder at Monte Carlo. E. P. Oppenheim
Murder at Moose Jaw. T. Heald
Murder at Moreby. A. Cartlidge
Murder at Morning Prayers. Hilary Landon
Murder at Mornington. C. Carnac
Murder at Mt. Fuji. S. Natsuke
Murder at Mulberry Cottage. G. Norsworthy
Murder at Musket Beach. Bernie Lee
Murder at Night. J. Corbett
Murder at Nightfall. E. Sherry
Murder at No. 3. L. G. Horsefield
Murder at Our House. C. J. Daly
Murder at Out-Patients. A. W. Eyles
Murder at Pirate's Head. I. Waitt
Murder at Plenders. F. Everton
Murder at Plums. Amy Myers
Murder at Pringlehurst. J. Corbett
Murder at Prospect, Kentucky. A. W. Lyons
Murder at Puck's Cottage. M. Alan
Murder at Quay Cottage. S. Amberley
Murder at Radio City. N. Morland
Murder at Raven Rock. M. F. Ballard
Murder at Red Grange. J. Corbett
Murder at Red Pass. The Aresbys
Murder at Red Rock Ranch. D. Tell
Murder at Rutherford House. T. Chiodo
Murder at St. Dennis. M. A. Hubbard
Murder at San Simeon. R. L. Hall
Murder at School. G. Trevor
Murder at Scotland Yard. G. Dilnot
Murder at Sea. R. Connell
Murder at Sea. Leydon Holt
Murder at Shirttail Flats. K. Franklin
Murder at Stone House. E. Howie
Murder at Sundown. James Preston
Murder at Sunset Gables. D. Heffernan
Murder at Sunset Rock. D. P. Neely
Murder at Tall Tip. E. G. Gless
Murder at 10,000 Feet. P. Conde
Murder at the ABA. I. Asimov
Murder at the Academy Awards. J. Hyams
Murder at the Admiralty. Eric Bennett
Murder at the Angel. H. McCutcheon
Murder at the Arab Stud. S. Miles
Murder at the Bar. T. Stevenson
Murder at the Belle Vue. H. Lindsay
Murder at the Big Store. D. Mayo
Murder at the Black Crook. C. H. Matschat
Murder at the "Black Swan". N. Walthew
Murder at the Blue Garter. C. Wheatley
Murder at the Blue Owl. Lee Martin
Murder at the Boarding House. A. S. Bradshaw
Murder at the Bookstall. H. Holt
Murder at the Bridge Table. M. Granovetter
Murder at the Bugginses. M. Constanduros
Murder at the Casino. C. Wells
Murder at the Cat Show. M. Babson
Murder at the Cheatin' Heart Motel. A. Bourgeau
Murder at the Class Reunion. C. Andrews
Murder at the Club. L. Allan
Murder at the Coffee Stall. Ben Rogers
Murder at the College. V. L. Whitechurch
Murder at the Cookout. G. De Fraga
Murder at the DeSoto. J. Rand
Murder at the Diogenes Club. G. Lientz
Murder at the Dome. G. Burgess
Murder at the Eclipse. John Alexander
Murder at the Eisteddfod. J. E. Williams
Murder at the F.B.I. M. Truman
Murder at the Festival. V. Lucas
Murder at the Final Four. C. C. Risenhoover
Murder at the Flea Club. M. Head
Murder at the Flood. M. E. Allan
Murder at the Flower Show. M. Beckett
Murder at the Frankfurt Book Fair. H. Monteilhet
Murder at the Fringe. G. Demarco
Murder at the Gallop. A. Christie
Murder at the Gardner. J. Langton
Murder at the Howard Johnson's. R. Clark

M

Murder at the Hunting Club. M. Plum
Murder at the Inn. L. Brock
Murder at the Inn. R. Goyne
Murder at the Kennedy Center. M. Truman
Murder at the Kentucky Derby. C. Parmer
Murder at the Keyhole. R. A. J. Walling
Murder at the Mardi Gras. E. M. Stone
Murder at the Margin. M. Jevons
Murder at the Marina. A. Sharpe
Murder at the Met. D. Black
Murder at the Met. F. G. Jarvis
Murder at the Microphone. D. Hogg
Murder at the "Mike". Margaret Douglas
Murder at the Mike. C. Saxby
Murder at the Mill. J. Sumner
Murder at the Ministry. A. A. Thomson
Murder at the Miramar. E. Snell
Murder at the Monk's Promise. A. Spence
Murder at the Moorings. M. Burton
Murder at the Motel. V. Gunn
Murder at the Motor Show. J. Rhode
Murder at the Movies. M. Hervey
Murder at the Munition Works. G. D. H. Cole
Murder at the Murder at the Mimosa Club. Joan Hess
Murder at the National Cathedral. M. Truman
Murder at the New York's World Fair. Freeman Dana
Murder at the Nightwood Bar. K. V. Forrest
Murder at the 1984 Summer Games. S. Fawcette
Murder at the Nineteenth. J. M. Gregson
Murder at the "98" Club. A. Rhode
Murder at the Nook. A. Fielding
Murder at the Old Stone House. C. M. Russell
Murder at the Old Vicarage. J. McGown
Murder at the Open. A. MacVicar
Murder at the PTA Luncheon. V. Wolzien
Murder at the Pageant. V. L. Whitechurch
Murder at the Palace. J. Corbett
Murder at the Palace. E. Roosevelt
Murder at the Party. H. Willett
Murder at the Piano. G. Bagby
Murder at the Play. J. Corris
Murder at the Playhouse. B. E. M. Ward
Murder at the Polls. M. Propper
Murder at the Priory. Bernard Taylor
Murder at the Red Cockatoo. A. Parsons
Murder at the Red October. A. Olcott
Murder at the Savoy. M. Sjowall
Murder at the Schoolhouse. A. B. Cunningham
Murder at the "Signal". M. Byrne
Murder at the Spa. S. Matteson
Murder at the Stadium. A. Parsons
Murder at the Super Bowl. F. Tarkenton
Murder at the U.N. W. Perry
Murder at the Varsity. F. L. Cary
Murder at the Varsity. Q. Patrick
Murder at the Vicarage. M. Charles
Murder at the Vicarage. A. Christie
Murder at the War. M. M. Pulver
Murder at the Wedding. F. Grierson
Murder at the Wedding. David Martin
Murder at the White Tulip. D. Cole
Murder at the Wishing Well. A. Wood
Murder at the Women's City Club. Q. Patrick
Murder at the World's Fair. M. Plum
Murder at the Yard! J. G. Brandon
Murder at 300 to 1. J. D. O'Hanlon
Murder at Tomorrow. K. George
Murder at 28:10. N. Gayle
Murder at Vassar. E. A. Taylor
Murder at Vista Point? N. Fenton
Murder at Willow Run. Michelle Collins
Murder at Wrides Park. J. S. Fletcher
Murder Backstairs. Anne Austin
Murder Bait. W. Daemer
Murder Bait. D. Yarnell
Murder Bangs a Big Drum. Sean Gregory
Murder Be My Mistress. Max Storm
Murder Beacon. L. P. Greene
Murder Beat. R. Drennen
Murder Beat. A. Lenton
Murder Before Breakfast. L. G. Offord
Murder Before Dinner. C. Franklin

Murder Before Marriage. M. Neville
Murder Before Matins. J. Reeves
Murder Before Midnight. A. B. Cunningham
Murder Before Tuesday. Elaine Hamilton
Murder Began Yesterday. L. Johnson
Murder Begets Murder. J. Corbett
Murder Begets Murder. M. G. Hugi
Murder Begets Murder. J. Jeffries
Murder Begins at Home. D. Ames
Murder Begins at Home. D. L. Gilbert
Murder Behind Bars. J. Jenkins
Murder Behind Closed Doors. P. Lore
Murder Behind Locked Doors. E. Godfrey
Murder Behind the Mask. Adrian Dale
Murder Behind the Mike. R. L. Goldman
Murder Being Once Done. R. Rendell
Murder Belongs to Me! Roderick Wilkinson
Murder Below Wall Street. R. Delancey
Murder Beneath the Trees. C. Coram
Murder Besieged. D. Whitelaw
Murder Between Dark and Dark. Max Long
Murder Between Drinks. A. Gibbs
Murder Beyond the Pale. M. Neville
Murder Bicarb. D. Van Duesen
Murder, Bless It! N. Spain
Murder Blues. B. Edwards
Murder Bound. Poul Anderson
Murder Box. F. Gruber
Murder Breaks Trail. E. M. Boyd
Murder Breeds Murder. A. Willsdon
Murder Brewing. A. W. Eyles
Murder Business. P. C. Herring
Murder But Gentley. F. Duncan
Murder—But Natch. M. Hagan
Murder Buttoned Up. P. A. Holmes
Murder by a Maniac. S. M. Richmond
Murder by Accident. L. Mason
Murder by Air. W. E. Johns
Murder by an Aristocrat. M. G. Eberhart
Murder—by an Idiot. T. A. Plummer
Murder by Appointment. E. Browne
Murder by Appointment. J. Paul
Murder by Appointment. Frank Wiliams
Murder by Arrangement. W. G. Beyer
Murder by Arrangement. E. Roberts
Murder by Bamboo. D. Sabre
Murder by Bequest. R. Foley
Murder by Burial. S. Casson
Murder by Chance. P. Drax
Murder by Contract. Griff
Murder by Dart. B. Tempest
Murder by Death. H. Keating
Murder by Deception. D. R. Meredith
Murder by Decree. R. Weverka
Murder by Degrees. J. B. Fearnley
Murder by Degrees. A. Pearson
Murder by Design. R. Simons
Murder by Experiment. L. A. Knight
Murder by Experts. Anthony Gilbert
Murder by Formula. J. H. Wallis
Murder by Gaslight. Raymond Paul
Murder by Gemini. R. Gallagher
Murder by Impulse. D. R. Meredith
Murder by Inches. S. Hopkins
Murder by Inspiration. E. H. Bierstadt
Murder by Installment. M. Hervey
Murder by Invitation. R. Hull
Murder by Invitation. A. C. MacLean
Murder by Jury. R. B. Sanborn
Murder by Latitude. R. King
Murder by Legacy. W. A. Sweeney
Murder by Magic. J. Creasey
Murder by Magic. M. J. Freeman
Murder by Magic. W. B. Gibson
Murder by Magic. M. Grant
Murder by Magic. A. R. Long
Murder by Mail. F. McGrew
Murder by Mail, and Keep It Clean. K. Slattery
Murder by Mandate. A. V. Elston
Murder by Marriage. R. G. Dean
Murder by Matchlight. E. C. R. Lorac
Murder by Mathematics. H. Hawton
Murder by Membership Only. T. Hischak
Murder by Microphone. J. Reeves

Murder by Miss-Demeanour. Carter Brown
Murder by Mistake. P. Urquhart
Murder by Moonlight. M. Grant
Murder by Moonlight. D. Reid
Murder by Morning. J. A. Henton
Murder by Morning. Irving Wallace
Murder by Multiplication. M. Durham
Murder by Nail. J. Farnol
Murder by Natural Causes. T. J. Kelly
Murder by Neglect. Elizabeth Jenkins
Murder by Night. J. L. Rickard
Murder by Numbers. J. Phelan
Murder—by Persons Unknown. J. Rowland
Murder by Precedent. R. Petrie
Murder by Prescription. J. Stagge
Murder by Proxy. B. Boyer
Murder by Proxy. H. Carmichael
Murder by Proxy. P. Drax
Murder by Proxy. B. Halliday
Murder by Proxy. Colver Harris
Murder by Proxy. A. Morice
Murder by Proxy. H. Nielsen
Murder by Proxy. G. Ogan
Murder by Proxy. J. Spruill
Murder by Proxy. Richard Williams
Murder by Reflection. H. F. Heard
Murder by Remote Control. J. Van de Wetering
Murder by Request. B. Nichols
Murder by Schedule. J. Hinckley
Murder by Scripture. A. R. Long
Murder by Stealth. J. W. Booth
Murder by Suggestion. E. Acheson
Murder by Telecopter. D. T. Hughes
Murder by Telephone. B. Herbert
Murder by the Arch. H. W. Higginson
Murder by the Book. H. Arre
Murder by the Book. L. Hays
Murder by the Book. F. Lockridge
Murder by the Book. J. Rowe
Murder by the Book. N. Schier
Murder by the Book. R. Stout
Murder by the Book. P. Welch
Murder by the Clock. R. King
Murder by the Day. V. P. Johns
Murder by the Dozen. H. Wiley
Murder by the Lake. C. Coram
Murder by the Law. P. McGuire
Murder by the Mile. M. Russell
Murder by the Minute. A. Wood
Murder by the Pack. C. G. Hodges
Murder-by-the-Sea. L. Littlepage
Murder by the Tale. Dell Shannon
Murder by the Way. M. Halliday
Murder by the Yard. M. T. Yates
Murder by Touch. K. Jorephani
Murder by Treason. A. R. Long
Murder by Twenty-Five. C. Robbins
Murder by Warrant. E. T. Collis
Murder by Wash of Light. G. De Fraga
Murder C.O.D. F. MacIsaac
Murder Calling. D. Whitelaw
Murder Calling "50". G. Bagby
Murder Calls Dr. Hailey. A. Wynne
Murder Calls the Tune. W. M. Duncan
Murder Calls the Tune. R. Verron
Murder Came Late. J. York
Murder Came Tumbling. Martin Brett
Murder Can Be Fun. F. Brown
Murder Can Be Such Fun! L. Beresford
Murder Cancels All Debts. M. V. Heberden
Murder Can't Stop. W. T. Ballard
Murder Can't Wait. R. Lockridge
Murder Can't Wait. M. L. Stokes
Murder Caravan. T. T. Flynn
Murder Case Number 33. L. Cornell
Murder Cave. H. Hawton
Murder Challenges Valcour. R. King
Murder Charge. Wade Miller
Murder Chase. E. Elton
Murder Cheats the Bride. Anthony Gilbert
Murder Children. J. Ball
Murder, Chop Chop. James Norman
Murder Circus. M. Litchfield
Murder City. O. M. Hall

Title Index

Murder City. A. Lenton
Murder Clear, Track Fast. J. Philips
Murder Club. Howel Evans
Murder Club. I. Zacharia
Murder Column. C. Franklin
Murder Comes at Night. I. Oellrichs
Murder Comes Back. H. Ashbrook
Murder Comes Calling. Malcolm Douglas
Murder Comes Calling! D. Reid
Murder Comes Easy. Sean Gregory
Murder Comes First. F. Lockridge
Murder Comes High. H. L. Nelson
Murder Comes Home. M. Chappell
Murder Comes Home. N. Child
Murder Comes Home. Anthony Gilbert
Murder Comes Home. M. Halliday
Murder Comes in Threes. M. Sprague
Murder Comes Smiling. G. Brandon
Murder Comes to Dinner. Robert Fleming
Murder Comes to Eden. L. Ford
Murder Comes to Rothesay. J. Cassells
Murder Coming. James Powell
Murder Could Not Kill. G. Baxter
Murder, Country Style. M. F. Ford
Murder Cries Out. A. Hocking
Murder Cruise. M. Keyes
Murder Cum Laude. J. Y. Dane
Murder Curve. A. B. Ross
Murder Day by Day. I. S. Cobb
Murder Deals in Ersatz. G. W. Jones
Murder Deferred. S. Ready
Murder Defies the Roman Emperor. C. E. Gray
Murder Delayed. D. Greenwood
Murder DeLuxe. R. King
Murder Disqualifies. Alan Graham
Murder Does Light Housekeeping. M. Bardon
Murder Doesn't Always Out. F. C. Davis
Murder Doll. D. Haring
Murder Doll. M. K. Ozaki
Murder Doll. R. O. Saber
Murder, Double Murder. Neill Graham
Murder Down Below. J. Stagg
Murder Down South. L. Ford
Murder Down Under. A. W. Upfield
Murder Draws a Line. W. A. Barber
Murder Each Way. J. Brown
Murder En Route. B. Flynn
Murder Ends the Song. A. Meyers
Murder Enters the Picture. W. A. Barber
Murder Every Monday. P. Branch
Murder Expert. R. P. Koehler
Murder—Extra Special. M. Brody
Murder Extravaganza. J. W. Heming
Murder Fantastical. P. Moyes
Murder First Class. R. Ellis
Murder First Class. L. Gribble
Murder First Class. R. Simons
Murder—First Class. T. Garrett
Murder Flies the Atlantic. S. H. Page
Murder Flight. K. Hemingway
Murder Follows Desmond Shannon. M. V. Heberden
Murder for a Hollow Shell. A. L. Albert
Murder for a Million. J. G. Brandon
Murder for a Million. C. B. Kelland
Murder for a Million. Roy Vickers
Murder for a Wanton. W. Chambers
Murder for Art's Sake. R. Lockridge
Murder for Breakfast. P. Hunt
Murder for Cash. J. Ronald
Murder for Charity. O. Dudley
Murder for Charity. P. Ponder
Murder for Charity. G. West
Murder for Christmas. A. Christie
Murder for Christmas. F. Duncan
Murder for Christmas. E. Howie
Murder for Empire. K. M. Knight
Murder for Fun. R. Savage
Murder for Hannah. D. V. Babcock
Murder for Her Birthday. G. Cobden
Murder for His Money. G. Cobden
Murder for Love. A. C. Bell
Murder for Love. D. E. Boocock
Murder for Love. S. Salt

Murder for Lunch. Haughton Murphy
Murder for Madame. Adam Knight
Murder for Millions. N. Rutledge
Murder for Missemily. J. F. Straker
Murder for Money. Jay Bennett
Murder for Money. H. Liggett
Murder for Real. M. Bardon
Murder for Sale. M. Bardsley
Murder for Sale. N. W. Firth
Murder for Sale. S. Horler
Murder for Tea. E. Howie
Murder for the Asking. D. Benfield
Murder for the Asking. G. H. Coxe
Murder for the Bride. J. D. MacDonald
Murder for the Bride. J. Reach
Murder for the Holidays. H. Rigsby
Murder for the Million. R. Chapman
Murder for the Millions. H. Kane
Murder for Treasure. D. Williams
Murder for Two. G. H. Coxe
Murder for Two. N. MacKenzie
Murder for Two Pins. R. Trevor
Murder for What? K. Steel
Murder Forestalled. P. Chester
Murder, Four Miles High. R. A. Braun
Murder from Beyond. R. Francis Foster
Murder from Heaven. P. Palmer
Murder from the East. C. J. Daly
Murder from the Grave. W. Levinrew
Murder from the Grave. Eric Wood
Murder from the Mind. P. Laing
Murder from Three Angles. V. Loder
Murder from Three Angles. J. R. Warren
Murder Game. R. Batchelor
Murder Game. C. Cox
Murder Game. J. Flanagan
Murder Game. D. Ross
Murder Game. J. S. Strange
Murder Games. L. Davidson
Murder Gang. Roland Daniel
Murder Germ. A. O. Pollard
Murder Gets a Degree. J. Wender
Murder Gets Around. R. S. Bowen
Murder Gives a Lovely Light. J. S. Strange
Murder Gives Notice. P. Valdez
Murder-Go-Round. Jay Christopher
Murder-Go-Round. C. P. Donnel
Murder Goes Astray. M. V. Heberden
Murder Goes Fishing. T. Brace
Murder Goes Free. Roland Daniel
Murder Goes in a Trailer. T. Brace
Murder Goes Mumming. A. Craig
Murder Goes Nap. R. Dolphin
Murder Goes Rolling Along. H. F. S. Moore
Murder Goes Round and Round. H. Pentecost
Murder Goes South. A. R. Long
Murder Goes to Bank Night. W. C. Clark
Murder Goes to College. K. Steel
Murder Goes to Press. Cicely Cairns
Murder Goes to Press. N. Loomis
Murder Goes to School. H. Farrar
Murder Goes to School. R. Savage
Murder Goes to Sea. A. R. Bosworth
Murder Goes to the Dogs. T. Brace
Murder Goes to the World's Fair. T. Brace
Murder Goes Underground. Granville Wilson
Murder Goes West. L. C. Douthwaite
Murder Gone Mad. G. Bellairs
Murder Gone Mad. P. MacDonald
Murder Gone Mad. S. Stone
Murder Gone Minoan. C. B. Clason
Murder Gone to Earth. J. Stagge
Murder Greets Jean Holton. K. M. Knight
Murder Grows Roots. S. Taylor
Murder Half Baked. G. Bagby
Murder Happens. A. Ridley
Murder Has a Motive. F. Duncan
Murder Has a Pretty Face. Jennie Melville
Murder Has an Echo. J. Notley
Murder Has Been Arranged. R. Trevor
Murder Has Been Arranged. Emlyn Williams
Murder Has Been Done. Neill Graham
Murder Has Its Points. F. Lockridge
Murder Has Many Faces. W. Grew

Murder Has No Friends. Bradshaw Jones
Murder Has No Name. W. Dale
Murder Has No Tongue. Anthony Gilbert
Murder Has Three Dimensions. A. Spiller
Murder Has Wings. O. Kensch
Murder Has Your Number. H. Garner
Murder Hath Charms. M. Durham
Murder Helps. I. Oellrichs
Murder Hide-and-Seek. A. O. Pollard
Murder Hole Road. A. Douglas
Murder Honeymoon. R. O. Saber
Murder House. T. A. Plummer
Murder Humane. H. Kemp
Murder Hunt. R. Dudgeon
Murder Hunt. P. Stadley
Murder I Don't Remember. P. Valdez
Murder, I Presume. G. Linscott
Murder in a Barge. P. Street
Murder in a Blue Room. M. Neville
Murder in a Church. A. Wynne
Murder in a Cold Climate. Scott Young
Murder in a Dark Room. M. Neville
Murder in A-Flat. D. Flynn
Murder in a Haystack. D. Aldis
Murder in a Hurry. F. Lockridge
Murder in a Library. C. J. Dutton
Murder in a Lighter Vein. M. M. Raison
Murder in a Locked Box. A. Robbins
Murder in a Manner of Speaking. H. W. Jones
Murder in a Maze. M. Alan
Murder in a Muffler. G. Davison
Murder in a Mummy Case. K. K. Beck
Murder in a Nunnery. E. Lavery
Murder in a Nunnery. E. Shepherd
Murder in a Pug's Parlour. Amy Myers
Murder in a Road Gang. M. Cresswell
Murder in a Shell. M. Beam
Murder in a Small Town—Perhaps. H. B. Fox
Murder in a Walled Town. K. Woods
Murder in Absence. M. Burton
Murder in Advent. D. Williams
Murder in Amber. Colver Harris
Murder in Angel Yard. F. Vivian
Murder in Any Degree. O. Johnson
Murder in Any Language. K. Roos
Murder in Baracoa. P. E. Walsh
Murder in Bavaria. C. Rushton
Murder in Beacon Street. W. Martyn
Murder in Berkeley Square. R. Dark
Murder in Berlin. Harold Trembath
Murder in Bermuda. W. Sharp
Murder in Bethnel Square. S. Fowler
Murder in Black. Mark Cross
Murder in Black. F. Grierson
Murder in Black and White. David Alexander
Murder in Black and White. E. Elder
Murder in Black Letter. Poul Anderson
Murder in Bloom. T. Hischak
Murder in Blue. C. Witting
Murder in Blue Street. F. Crane
Murder in Bostall. P. McGuire
Murder in Brass. L. Padgett
Murder in Brief. M. Trask
Murder in Bright Red. F. Crane
Murder in Broad Daylight. G. D. H. Cole
Murder in Burgos. L. Foley
Murder in Burgundy. Audrey Peterson
Murder in C Major. S. H. Frommer
Murder in Camera. W. A. Ballinger
Murder in Canton. R. Van Gulik
Murder in Cardigan Square. N. MacKenzie
Murder in Chelsea. E. C. R. Lorac
Murder in China. C. Epstein
Murder in Church. Babette Hughes
Murder in College. J. Y. Dane
Murder in Company. P. King
Murder in Cowboy Bronze. C. McCormick
Murder in Crown Passage. M. Burton
Murder in Dawson City. Roland Daniel
Murder in Devil's Hollow. L. N. Morgan
Murder in Disguise. C. Kingston
Murder in Duplicate. P. Conway
Murder in Duplicate. H. L. Victor
Murder in E Minor. R. Goldsborough

M

Murder in Earl's Court. Neil Gordon
Murder in False Face. G. Childerness
Murder in False-Face. R. Lockridge
Murder in Fancy Dress. I. H. Irwin
Murder in Fancy Dress. L. Mantell
Murder in Fiji. J. W. Vandercook
Murder in Five Columns. F. Diamond
Murder in Flat 14. A. G. E. Cromwell
Murder in Focus. D. Halliday
Murder in Focus. R. Julian
Murder in Focus. Medora Sale
Murder in Four Degrees. J. S. Fletcher
Murder in Full Flight. M. Magill
Murder in Full View. J. D. Forbes
Murder in G-Sharp. K. Steel
Murder in Gay Ladies. J. Ronald
Murder in Georgetown. M. Truman
Murder in Good Measure. Margaret Moore
Murder in Gray and White. C. H. Sawyer
Murder in Haiti. J. W. Vandercook
Murder in Haste. E. P. Fenwick
Murder in Haste. H. Gardiner
Murder in Haste. B. Halliday
Murder in Haste. P. McGuire
Murder in Haste. Michael Wallace
Murder in Haste. Garnett Weston
Murder in Havana. G. H. Coxe
Murder in Hawthorn. J. Armour
Murder in Her Big Blue Eyes. J. Long
Murder in High Place. R. B. Dominic
Murder in High Places. H. Pentecost
Murder in Hollywood. Steve Allen
Murder in Hollywood. W. Braun
Murder in Hollywood. C. Gibbons
Murder in Hospital. Josephine Bell
Murder in Hospital. A. W. Eyles
Murder in Jackson Hole. Maude Parker
Murder in Las Vegas. J. Waer
Murder-in-Law. P. Engleman
Murder in Lima. R. A. Levey
Murder in Little Egypt. Darcy O'Brien
Murder in Luxury. H. Pentecost
Murder in Majengo. M. Oludhe-Macgoye
Murder in Majorca. M. Bryan
Murder in Majorca. P. Tabori
Murder in Make-Up. C. Ashton
Murder in Makeup. Lorenz Heller
Murder in Mallorca. W. Angus
Murder in Man. F. Duncan
Murder in Manchuria. G. H. Teed
Murder in Manhattan. Steve Allen
Murder in Manhattan. A. Procter
Murder in Manhattan. J. Roeburt
Murder in Manuscript. R. Strevens
Murder in Manuscript. G. Verner
Murder in Marble. J. Philips
Murder in Marrakech. C. Leader
Murder in Married Life. A. Morice
Murder in Marseilles. C. Lefevre
Murder in Maryland. L. Ford
Murder in Mayfair. J. G. Brandon
Murder in Mayfair. Henry Duval
Murder in Mayfair. F. Goldsmith
Murder in Mayfair. R. J. Lawrence
Murder in Mayfair. D. Robins
Murder in Mayfair. W. West
Murder in Maytime. G. Brandon
Murder in Medora Mansions. J. S. Fletcher
Murder in Melancholy. W. Keenan
Murder in Melbourne. Dulcie Gray
Murder in Mendocino. M. Kittredge
Murder in Mesopotamia. A. Christie
Murder in Mid-Air. D. Dayle
Murder in Mid-Atlantic. E. Antill
Murder in Midsummer. M. M. Atwater
Murder in Millenium VI. C. Gray
Murder in Mimicry. A. Morice
Murder in Mind. T. Feely
Murder in Mind. R. Fuller
Murder in Mind. Dulcie Gray
Murder in Mind. R. Hartley
Murder in Mind. J. A. Howard
Murder in Miniature. E. Mack
Murder in Miniatures. S. Merwin, Jr.

Murder in Mink. Pete Costello
Murder in Mink. R. G. Dean
Murder in Mink. B. Iles
Murder in Mocking Valley. W. Crowell
Murder in Monaco. J. Flagg
Murder in Montana. Muriel Bradley
Murder in Montmartre. N. Vexin
Murder in Montparnasse. J. Bude
Murder in Mortimer Square. F. Grierson
Murder in Moscow. A. Garve
Murder in Motley. I. D'Abbes
Murder in Motley. D. Whitelaw
Murder in Mount Holly. P. Theroux
Murder in Mozambique. David Wilson
Murder in New Guinea. J. W. Vandercook
Murder in Newport. G. B. Lambert
Murder in November. M. Alan
Murder in Ocean Drive. Roland Daniel
Murder in Odd Sizes. H. J. Hultman
Murder in Oil. J. Avrach
Murder in Oils. J. N. Chance
Murder in Okefenokee. C. H. Matschat
Murder in Outline. A. Morice
Murder in Paradise. A. Cleeves
Murder in Paradise. R. Dana
Murder in Paradise. J. Davey
Murder in Paradise. G. Joseph
Murder in Paradise. J. Laffin
Murder in Paradise. J. Shill
Murder in Paris. Alice Campbell
Murder in Pastiche. Marion Mainwaring
Murder in Peking. V. Starrett
Murder in Piccadilly. Roland Daniel
Murder in Piccadilly. C. Kingston
Murder in Pimlico. J. G. Brandon
Murder in Plain Sight. G. Brown
Murder in Port Afrique. B. V. Dryer
Murder in Print. R. Sonin
Murder in Public. J. Crozier
Murder in Queer Street. C. Ryland
Murder in Red. F. Castle
Murder in Rehearsal. A. Goetz
Murder in Retrospect. A. Christie
Murder in Reverse. W. Kerr
Murder in Reverse. A. Webb
Murder in Rockwater. M. Neville
Murder in Romney Marsh. E. Jepson
Murder in Room 700. M. H. Bradley
Murder in Room 13. Albert Conroy
Murder in Rosemary Lane. H. M. Keynes
Murder in Rosslare. K. Platt
Murder in St. John's Wood. E. C. R. Lorac
Murder in Season. O. R. Cohen
Murder in Shinbone Alley. H. Reilly
Murder in Silence. G. Selmark
Murder in Silk. R. Trevor
Murder in Soho. J. G. Brandon
Murder in SoHo. H. Shapiro
Murder in Space. D. V. Reed
Murder in Space. F. X. Woolf
Murder in Stained Glass. M. Armstrong
Murder in State. E. H. Hunt
Murder in Store. D. C. Brod
Murder in Store. R. Rooke
Murder in Strange Houses. R. Peckham
Murder in Striplicate. Kane
Murder in Style. E. L. Fetta
Murder in Style. D. Hoddinott
Murder in Style. R. Stout
Murder in Suffolk. A. Fielding
Murder in Sussex. G. Norsworthy
Murder in Switzerland. E. Snell
Murder in Sydney. L. Mann
Murder in Texas. A. E. Lingo
Murder in the Act. E. St. Clair
Murder in the Air. C. Brisbane
Murder in the Air. Mark Cross
Murder in the Air. J. Hunter
Murder in the Air. A. O. Pollard
Murder in the Air. D. L. Teilhet
Murder in the Atlantic. Carter Dickson
Murder in the Balance. D. B. Francis
Murder in the Ballroom. K. Hewitt
Murder in the Bank. R. Essex

Murder in the Basement. A. Berkeley
Murder in the Bath. F. Didelot
Murder in the Bazaar. D. Lynn
Murder in the Bedroom. G. Leroux
Murder in the Blackout. J. R. Warren
Murder in the Blue Room. E. Roosevelt
Murder in the Bookshop. C. Wells
Murder in the Borough Library. J. Austwick
Murder in the Brownstone House. W. Collison
Murder in the Bud. P. Bottome
Murder in the CIA. M. Truman
Murder in the Calais Coach. A. Christie
Murder in the Camp. M. Stand
Murder in the Cellar. L. Eppley
Murder in the Central Committee. M. V. Montalban
Murder in the Charleston Manner. P. H. Sprinkle
Murder in the Clinic. Edmond Hamilton
Murder in the Coalhole. M. Burton
Murder in the Cockpit. P. Conde
Murder in the Collective. B. Wilson
Murder in the Consulting Room. M. S. Michel
Murder in the Cotswolds. A. B. Guthrie, Jr.
Murder in the Dark. J. Braydon
Murder in the Dark. C. J. Dutton
Murder in the Delhi Mail. K. P. Bahadur
Murder in the Dentist Chair. M. Thynne
Murder in the Embassy. Diplomat
Murder in the English Department. V. Miner
Murder in the Family. M. H. Bradley
Murder in the Family. M. Brandel
Murder in the Family. D. Delman
Murder in the Family. D. Emerson
Murder in the Family. M. Leinster
Murder in the Family. D. M. MacDonald
Murder in the Family. J. Ronald
Murder in the Family. L. Stephan
Murder in the Family. J. York
Murder in the Family Way. Carter Brown
Murder in the Ferris-Wheel. G. George
Murder in the Fifth Column. R. Trevor
Murder in the Fine Arts. C. Nicolai
Murder in the First Person. S. Adams
Murder in the Flagship. P. W. Taylor
Murder in the Fog. H. L. Gates
Murder in the Fog. Elaine Hamilton
Murder in the Fog. P. Thorne
Murder in the Fog. R. Worth
Murder in the French Room. H. J. Hultman
Murder in the Game Reserve. P. W. Taylor
Murder in the Garden. F. Grierson
Murder in the Garden. Jenie Melville
Murder in the Gilded Cage. S. Spewack
Murder in the Green Sedan. R. P. Koehler
Murder in the Gunroom. H. B. Piper
Murder in the Harem Club. Carter Brown
Murder in the Haunted Sentry-Box. N. Gayle
Murder in the Hellfire Club. D. Zochert
Murder in the Highlands. P. Manton
Murder in the Home Guard. R. Adam
Murder in the Hotel. H. P. Hanshew
Murder in the House of Commons. M. A. Hamilton
Murder in the House with the Blue Eyes. J. N. Darby
Murder in the Hurricane. E. L. Adams
Murder in the Key Club. Carter Brown
Murder in the King's Road. J. Boyd
Murder in the Kitchen. F. Halliday
Murder in the Laboratory. K. Brooks
Murder in the Laboratory. T. L. Davidson
Murder in the Lady Chapel. S. Toye
Murder in the Limelight. Amy Myers
Murder in the Mackenzie. J. Lotz
Murder in the Madhouse. Jonathan Latimer
Murder in the Madhouse. C. B. Molyneaux
Murder in the Magnolias. T. J. Kelly
Murder in the Making. H. Petersen
Murder in the Map Room. F. Bream
Murder in the Markets. A. McKee-Wright
Murder in the Maze. J. J. Connington
Murder in the Melody. N. Berrow
Murder in the Mews. A. Christie
Murder in the Mews. H. Reilly
Murder in the Mill-Race. E. C. R. Lorac

Murder in the Mills. H. S. Keeler
Murder in the Mind. K. T. Knoblock
Murder in the Mirror. W. W. Masters
Murder in the Mirror. L. Thayer
Murder in the Mist. W. Chambers
Murder in the Mist. H. L. Gates
Murder in the Mist. Z. Popkin
Murder in the Mobile Unit. Sutherland Scott
Murder in the Moonlight. F. Brown
Murder in the Moor. T. Kindon
Murder in the Morning. P. Duff
Murder in the Morning. G. Pahlow
Murder in the Morning. Colin Robertson
Murder in the Morning. A. Wynne
Murder in the Museum. F. W. Gumley
Murder in the Museum. E. Heath
Murder in the Museum. J. Rowland
Murder in the Navy. R. Marsten
Murder in the Neighborhood Watch. S. Burke
Murder in the News Room. H. C. Beck
Murder in the Newspaper Guild. H. C. Beck
Murder in the Night. A. Gask
Murder in the North-West. C. W. Sanders
Murder in the O.P.M. L. Ford
Murder in the Old Jail. Michael Henry
Murder in the Opera House. Q. Mario
Murder in the Outlands. J. B. Hendryx
Murder in the Oval Office. E. Roosevelt
Murder in the Pallant. J. S. Fletcher
Murder in the Park. C. F. Gregg
Murder in the Pool. Mark Cross
Murder in the Procession. L. Cargill
Murder in the Queen's Armes. A. J. Elkins
Murder in the Radio Department. A. Eichler
Murder in the Rain. W. Collison
Murder in the Rain Forest. N. MacKenzie
Murder in the Raw. B. Fischer
Murder in the Raw. W. C. Gault
Murder in the Raw. B. Grant
Murder in the Rose Garden. E. Roosevelt
Murder in the Rough. L. Allen
Murder in the Round. D. Halliday
Murder in the Rue Royale. M. Harrison
Murder in the Ruins. N. A. Temple-Ellis
Murder in the Sacristy. D. A. Lord
Murder in the Sanctuary. L. Grex
Murder in the Senate. G. Coffin
Murder in the Smithsonian. M. Truman
Murder in the Snow. Betty Smith
Murder in the Square. Johnston Smith
Murder in the Squire's Pew. J. S. Fletcher
Murder in the Stacks. M. Boyd
Murder in the Stars. M. Halliday
Murder in the Stars. J. Stagge
Murder in the State Department. Diplomat
Murder in the Stork Club. V. Caspary
Murder in the Stratosphere. G. Eldredge
Murder in the Stratosphere. J. Laurence
Murder in the Submarine Zone. Carter Dickson
Murder in the Suez Canel. P. W. Taylor
Murder in the Sun. H. Footner
Murder in the Sun. J. T. Story
Murder in the Supreme Court. M. Truman
Murder in the Surgery. J. G. Edwards
Murder in the Taj Mahal. P. W. Taylor
Murder in the Telephone Exchange. J. Wright
Murder in the Temple. J. Brooke
Murder in the Theatre. E. M. McDuff
Murder in the Title. S. Brett
Murder in the Tomb. L. A. Osgood
Murder in the Top Drawer. E. G. Cousins
Murder in the Town. M. Richert
Murder in the Tropic Night. F. Arthur
Murder in the Vestry. M. Crossley
Murder in the Village. T. A. Plummer
Murder in the Village. J. Skinner
Murder in the WPA. Alexander Williams
Murder in the Walls. R. M. Stern
Murder in the White House. M. Truman
Murder in the Willett Family. R. King
Murder in the Wind. J. D. MacDonald
Murder in the Wind. G. Ogan
Murder in the Wind. V. Roser
Murder in the Wings. E. Gorman

Murder in the Zoo. E. Balneaves
Murder in the Zoo. Babette Hughes
Murder in Thin Air. A. Wynne
Murder in Three Acts. A. Christie
Murder in Three Moves. R. Watters
Murder in Time. L. Day
Murder in Time. E. Ferrars
Murder in Touraine. B. E. Wallace
Murder in Tow. C. Hale
Murder in Transit. W. R. Hutton
Murder in Trinidad. J. W. Vandercook
Murder in Triplicate. H. Austin
Murder in Triplicate. L. Marshall
Murder in 25 Words or Less. Irma Walker
Murder in Two Acts. D. G. Deutsch
Murder in Two Flats. Roy Vickers
Murder in Vain. L. Mantell
Murder in Vain. Michael Wallace
Murder in Vegas. W. R. Cox
Murder in Venice. Anne-Mariel
Murder in Venice. T. Sterling
Murder in Vienna. E. C. R. Lorac
Murder in Vision. K. Bird
Murder in Waiting. M. G. Eberhart
Murder in Wardour Street. N. Morland
Murder in Washington. M. Truman
Murder in Wax. P. Baron
Murder in White. H. Zachary
Murder in White Pit. J. H. Barrington
Murder in Whitehall. T. Hyde
Murder in Windy Coppice. T. A. Plummer
Murder in Wonderland. G. Bagby
Murder in Writing. Anna Clarke
Murder in Y Division. J. G. Brandon
Murder in Yiddish. I. Haiblum
Murder in Your Home. E. Cobb
Murder Incidental. M. Cronin
Murder Incidental. K. Trask
Murder Included. J. Cannan
Murder Incognito. M. Dare
Murder Inc. J. Eastwood
Murder Indicated. R. Verron
Murder Inherited. G. Cobden
Murder Insoluble. E. Wilmot
Murder, Inspector. M. Mangan
Murder Intended. F. Beeding
Murder Intended. A. Jagger
Murder Is a Best Seller. M. Judd
Murder Is a Broad. Carter Brown
Murder Is a Collector's Item. E. Dean
Murder Is a Furtive Thing. R. Boyd
Murder Is a Gamble. G. M. Barnes
Murder Is a Gentle Kiss. A. Barron
Murder Is a Habit. B. Halliday
Murder Is a House Guest. I. Cabot
Murder Is a Kill-Joy. E. S. Holding
Murder Is a Maiden's Handicap. M. Brody
Murder Is a Package Deal. Carter Brown
Murder Is a Pendulum. C. Joyce
Murder Is a Serious Business. E. Dean
Murder Is a Shady Business. A. Spiller
Murder Is a Witch. J. Bingham
Murder Is Absurd. P. McGerr
Murder Is Academic. P. M. Carlson
Murder Is an Art. A. B. Correll
Murder Is an Art. M. Innes
Murder Is an Evil Business. M. Bramhall
Murder is Announced. A. Christie
Murder Is Announced. L. Darbon
Murder Is Catching. M. Ainsworth
Murder Is Cheap. Anthony Gilbert
Murder Is Contagious. M. Bramhall
Murder Is Dangerous. S. Levinson
Murder Is Easy. A. Christie
Murder Is Easy! A. Livingston
Murder Is for Keeps. D. Belsky
Murder Is for Keeps. Peter Chambers
Murder Is Forgetful. W. Bogart
Murder Is Fun! C. Blankenship
Murder Is Grim. S. Rogers
Murder Is Incidental. D. Rutherford
Murder Is Infectuous. Sutherland Scott
Murder Is Insane. G. M. Barnes
Murder Is Its Own Reward. P. Chambers

Murder Is Justified. H. Desmond
Murder Is Like Cavair. Mary Drake
Murder Is Lonely. U. Rothwell
Murder Is Murder Is Murder. S. M. Steward
Murder Is Mutuel. J. Dolph
Murder Is My Business. B. Halliday
Murder Is My Business. J. Reach
Murder Is My Business. V. Siller
Murder Is My Dish. S. Marlowe
Murder Is My Fashion. M. Brody
Murder Is My Mistress. Carter Brown
Murder Is My Mistress. H. Whittington
Murder Is My Racket. R. H. Leitfred
Murder Is My Shadow. C. Nash
Murder Is My Weakness. Neill Graham
Murder Is No Accident. Jerome Barry
Murder Is Not Enough. B. E. Wallace
Murder Is Not Enough. S. Wells
Murder Is Not Mute. A. Newell
Murder Is Only Skin Deep. L. V. Sims
Murder Is Out. L. Thayer
Murder Is Pathological. P. M. Carlson
Murder Is Relative. K. Saum
Murder Is Ruby Red. E. Radford
Murder Is Served. F. Lockridge
Murder Is So Easy. W. D. Roberts
Murder Is So Nostaligic! Carter Brown
Murder Is So Simple. S. Horler
Murder Is So Unpleasant. F. Struan
Murder Is Staged. A. Tack
Murder Is Suggested. F. Lockridge
Murder Is Suspected. P. Alding
Murder Is Swift. C. Fitzsimmons
Murder Is the Message. Carter Brown
Murder Is the Pay-Off. L. Ford
Murder Is the Reason. L. Marshall
Murder Is Too Permanent. Sean Gregory
Murder Is Where You Find It. R. P. Hanson
Murder Is Where You Find It. A. Rutter
Murder Island. L. Jamieson
Murder Island. W. Martyn
Murder Isn't Cricket. E. Radford
Murder Isn't Cricket. P. Weathers
Murder Isn't Easy. R. Hull
Murder Isn't Enough. D. Flynn
Murder Isn't Funny. J. H. Bond
Murder Isn't Private. J. Garden
Murder Jigsaw. E. Radford
Murder Joins the Chorus. R. Simons
Murder Keeps a Secret. Haughton Murphy
Murder Kick. Wenzell Brown
Murder Knows No Master. S. Miles
Murder Lady. N. Chambers
Murder Lands the Odds. R. Verron
Murder Las Vegas Style. W. T. Ballard
Murder Laughs Last. J. Ford
Murder Lays a Golden Egg. E. T. Hull
Murder Lays the Odds. J. Letherby
Murder League. R. L. Fish
Murder Leaves a Ring. F. G. Stanley
Murder Lies in Waiting. Neill Graham
Murder Lifts the Veil. R. Verron
Murder Limited. C. R. Gull
Murder Limps By. T. A. Plummer
Murder Line. P. Alding
Murder Link. H. T. Johnson
Murder Listens In. E. Daly
Murder, London-Australia. J. Creasey
Murder, London-Miami. J. Creasey
Murder, London-New York. J. Creasey
Murder, London-South Africa. J. Creasey
Murder Looks Back. M. Alan
Murder: Love Story. W. S. Ruben
Murder Loves Company. J. Mersereau
Murder, M.A. A. Kennington
Murder M.D. M. Burton
Murder Machine. P. A. Foxall
Murder Machine. F. Scarpetta
Murder Made Absolute. M. Underwood
Murder Made Easy. R. Goyne
Murder Made Easy. Neill Graham
Murder Made Easy. D. Reid
Murder Madness. R. Hausfeld
Murder Madness. M. Leinster

M

Murder, Maestro, Please. D. Ames
Murder, Maestro, Please. J. Sharkey
Murder Magnet. B. Fischer
Murder Magnified. E. Radford
Murder Makers. J. N. Chance
Murder Makers. J. Rossiter
Murder Makes a Call. F. C. Tickner
Murder Makes a Date. Neill Graham
Murder Makes a Deadline. S. Fuller
Murder Makes a Man. W. T. Walsh
Murder Makes a Marriage. S. Broocks
Murder Makes a Merry Widow. R. G. Dean
Murder Makes a Racket. M. V. Heberden
Murder Makes a Villain. Denis Scott
Murder Makes an Entrance. C. B. Kelland
Murder Makes By-Lines. K. Secrist
Murder Makes Haste. J. Creasey
Murder Makes It Certain. Neill Graham
Murder Makes Its Mark. M. Judd
Murder Makes Me Laugh. J. Jackson
Murder Makes Me Mad. F. Findley
Murder Makes Me Mad. S. R. Robertson
Murder Makes Me Nervous. M. Scherf
Murder Makes Merry. F. W. Irwin
Murder Makes Mistakes. G. Bellairs
Murder Makes Mockery. Sean Gregory
Murder Makes Murder. H. Ashbrook
Murder Makes Murder. M. Halliday
Murder Makes the Corpse. Sean Gregory
Murder Makes the Mare Go. J. Dolph
Murder Makes the News. Neill Graham
Murder Makes the Wheels Go Round. E. Lathen
Murder Makes Tracks. G. Linscott
Murder Makes Us Gay. I. Oellrichs
Murder Man. W. Bogart
Murder Man. W. M. Duncan
Murder Manana. S. Bandolier
Murder Maniac. R. S. L. Harding
Murder Manor. A. Eadie
Murder Manor. P. Manton
Murder Mansion. J. H. Barry
Murder Mansion. Herman Landon
Murder Mansion. O. Snapp
Murder Mansion. J. H. Wallis
Murder Mansion. A. Wilson
Murder Maritime. C. Cranston
Murder Market. T. C. H. Jacobs
Murder Market. C. Rushton
Murder Market. M. Strongman
Murder Mars the Tour. M. Fitt
Murder Mask. G. Begbie
Murder Mask. S. Horler
Murder Mask. J. A. Jordan
Murder Masks Miami. R. King
Murder Masquerade. G. Bellairs
Murder Masquerade. G. Dilnot
Murder Masquerade. I. H. Irwin
Murder Matinee. B. Carson
Murder Matinee. D. Haring
Murder Matrix. E. J. Fredericks
Murder May Follow. S. Morrow
Murder May Pass Unpunished. F. Everton
Murder Mayhem. R. Stahl
Murder Maze. D. Haring
Murder Maze. H. Liggett
Murder Me for Nickels. P. Rabe
Murder Me, Murder Me Not. W. J. Springer
Murder Me Never. C. Shannon
Murder Medley. M. Hervey
Murder Meets Mephisto. Q. Mario
Murder Melody. K. Robeson
Murder Melody. K. Secrist
Murder Memo to the Commissioner. W. Oursler
Murder: Men Only. B. Cobb
Murder Menagerie. J. Lane
Murder Merchant. D. Haring
Murder Mill. C. T. Gardner
Murder Minus Motive. J. Corbett
Murder Mirage. K. Robeson
Murder Mislaid. M. Cronin
Murder Misread. P. M. Carlson
Murder Mission! Al Conroy
Murder Mission. F. W. Irwin
Murder Mistaken. Janet Green

Murder, Mr. Mosley. J. Greenwood
Murder Mistress. R. Colby
Murder Money. Jay Bennett
Murder Money. E. Ronns
Murder Money. R. Wallace
Murder Moon. P. H. Dobbins
Murder Moon. H. Leyford
Murder Most Artistic. W. Gore
Murder Most Black. R. Verron
Murder Most Distressing. L. Stephan
Murder Most Fair. J. G. Vermandel
Murder Most Familiar. M. Bremner
Murder Most Fashionable. J. Carroll
Murder Most Foul. G. Ashe
Murder Most Foul. K. B. Coxe
Murder Most Foul. H. Hawton
Murder Most Fouled Up. T. Wells
Murder Most Gentrified. M. Bringle
Murder Most Ingenious. K. Chase
Murder Most Intimate. W. H. Baker
Murder Most Ironic. Greg Howe
Murder Most Irregular. H. P. Jeffers
Murder Most Just. Herbert Adams
Murder Most Monstrous. R. Verron
Murder Most Opportune. R. G. Dean
Murder Most Strange. Dell Shannon
Murder Most Strange. Christine Smith
Murder Moves In. E. Ferrars
Murder Moves In. A. M. Pyle
Murder Moves On. J. Dall
Murder Movie. J. McGown
Murder! Murder! J. Symons
Murder! Murder! L. Vail
Murder, Murder, Little Star. M. Babson
Murder Muscles In. M. Franklin
Murder Must Advertise. D. L. Sayers
Murder Must Wait. J. Creasey
Murder Must Wait. A. W. Upfield
Murder Mutuel. B. McKnight
Murder, My Love. E. Atiyah
Murder, My Sweet. M. Holt
Murder Mystery. G. Thompson
Murder, Mystery and Mayhem. J. Carnell
Murder Needs a Face. R. Fenisong
Murder Needs a Name. R. Fenisong
Murder Next Door. M. Alan
Murder Next Door. Jean Marsh
Murder Next Year. B. J. Farmer
Murder—Nine and Out. J. V. Turner
Murder '97. F. Gruber
Murder No Object. W. Massey
Murder Noon and Night. K. Roos
Murder Now and Again. J. A. Knipe
Murder Now and Then. H. Brean
Murder Now, Pay Later. F. Bosworth
Murder Observed. E. Boylan
Murder of a Bad Man. H. Footner
Murder of a Banker. J. S. Fletcher
Murder of a Black Cat. Neill Graham
Murder of a Bookmaker. Roland Daniel
Murder of a Chemist. M. Burton
Murder of a Cop. W. M. Duncan
Murder of a Dead Man. W. H. L. Crauford
Murder of a Dead Man. K. Steel
Murder of a Diplomat. A. O. Pollard
Murder of a Film Star. H. Holt
Murder of a Headmistress. E. Pickering
Murder of a Lady. L. Marshall
Murder of a Lady. A. Wynne
Murder of a Magnate. M. Beckett
Murder of a Man Afraid of Women. A. Abbot
Murder of a Marriage. R. Armstrong
Murder of a Martinet. E. C. R. Lorac
Murder of a Matriarch. H. Austin
Murder of a Midget. M. J. Freeman
Murder of a Missing Man. A. M. Chase
Murder of a Mistress. H. Kuttner
Murder of a Mistress. J. Sherwood
Murder of a Moderate Man. J. Howlett
Murder of a Mouse. M. Fitt
Murder of a Musician. "Capstan"
Murder of a Mystery Writer. J. Hawk
Murder of a Mystery Writer. E. Heath
Murder of a Novelist. S. Wood

Murder of a Nymph. M. Neville
Murder of a Painted Lady. Harold Ward
Murder of a Professor. J. Miller
Murder of a Quack. G. Bellairs
Murder of a Redhaired Man. M. Plum
Murder of a Snob. Roy Vickers
Murder of a Startled Lady. A. Abbot
Murder of a Student. P. Malloch
Murder of a Stuffed Shirt. M. V. Heberden
Murder of a Suicide. E. Ferrars
Murder of a Wanton. Dorothea Gray
Murder of a Wife. H. Kuttner
Murder of Alonzo. P. Cheyney
Murder of an Initiate. M. Propper
Murder of an M.P. R. Gore-Brown
Murder of an M.P. B. H. Homersham
Murder of an Old Man. D. Frome
Murder of an Old-Time Movie Star. T. Kingsley-Smith
Murder of an Owl. G. Carr
Murder of an Unpopular Man. D. R. Forbes
Murder of Ann Avery. H. Kuttner
Murder of Auguste Dupin. J. B. Tarver
Murder of Augustin Dench. E. Jepson
Murder of Bishop Conrad. L. Hebach
Murder of Busy Lizzie. G. Mitchell
Murder of Caroline Bundy. Alice Campbell
Murder of Cecily Thane. H. Ashbrook
Murder of Christine Wilmerding. W. Morton
Murder of Colonel Neville. J. Kelso
Murder of Constable Cartwright. A. Blair
Murder of Convenience. R. G. Dean
Murder of Crows. P. Buchanan
Murder of Crows. M. Duffy
Murder of Dave Brandon. T. Lund
Murder of Doctor Grey. T. A. Plummer
Murder of Edwin Drood. P. T. Carden
Murder of Eleanor Pope. H. Kuttner
Murder of Estelle Cantor. C. F. Gregg
Murder of Eve. M. Dalton
Murder of Frau Schultz. J. M. Davis
Murder of Geraldine Foster. A. Abbot
Murder of Guy Thorpe. Roland Daniel
Murder of Harvey Blake. R. L. Goldman
Murder of Jacob Canansey. P. Capon
Murder of Lalla Lee. H. Burnham
Murder of Lawrence of Arabia. M. Eden
Murder of London Lew. H. S. Keeler
Murder of Love. Dulcie Gray
Murder of Lydia. J. Cowdroy
Murder of Margaret. C. Ryland
Murder of Margot Midnight. P. Herring
Murder of Maria Marten. B. J. Burton
Murder of Marion Mason. T. B. Dewey
Murder of Martin Fotherill. E. C. Lester
Murder of Mary Steers. Brian Cooper
Murder of Me. J. F. W. Hannay
Murder of Me. M. S. Michel
Murder of Me. F. A. Symonds
Murder of Miranda. M. Millar
Murder of Miss Betty Sloan. S. Williams
Murder of Mr. Mallabee. Winifred Duke
Murder of Mrs. Davenport. Anthony Gilbert
Murder of Monsieur Fualdes. A. Praviel
Murder of Munsden. C. Brisbane
Murder of My Aunt. R. Hull
Murder of My Patient. M. G. Eberhart
Murder of My Wife. Reginald Campbell
Murder of No Consequence. R. Verron
Murder of Olympia. M. Neville
Murder of Paul Rougier. V. Sampson
Murder of Quality. J. Le Carre
Murder of Roger Ackroyd. A. Christie
Murder of Santa Klaus. T. La Cour
Murder of Sherlock Holmes. James Anderson
Murder of Sigurd Sharon. H. Ashbrook
Murder of Sir Edmund Godfrey. J. D. Carr
Murder of Some Importance. B. Graeme
Murder of Steven Kester. H. Ashbrook
Murder of Suzy Pommier. E. Bove
Murder of the Admiral. S. Gould
Murder of the Circus Queen. A. Abbot
Murder of the Clergyman's Mistress. A. Abbot
Murder of the Dainty-Footed Model. F. E. Hewens

Title Index

Murder of the Fifth Columnist. L. Ford
Murder of the Honest Broker. W. Sharp
Murder of the Lawyer's Clerk. J. S. Fletcher
Murder of the Maharajah. H. R. F. Keating
Murder of the Man Next Door. P. Malloch
Murder of the Missing Link. Vercors
Murder of the Night Club Lady. A. Abbot
Murder of the Ninth Baronet. J. S. Fletcher
Murder of the Only Witness. J. S. Fletcher
Murder of the Park Avenue Playgirl. H. Kane
Murder of the Pigboat Skipper. S. Fisher
Murder of the Prime Minister. L. Clark
Murder of the Secret Agent. J. S. Fletcher
Murder of the U.S.A. W. F. Jenkins
Murder of the Well-Beloved. M. Neville
Murder of Three Ghosts. E. Radford
Murder of Whistler's Brother. David Alexander
Murder Off Broadway. L. Falkner
Murder Off Broadway. H. Klinger
Murder Off Key. K. Sproul
Murder Off Miami. D. Wheatley
Murder Off Stage. Monte Barrett
Murder Off Stage. A. Eichler
Murder Off the Glass. M. J. Katz
Murder Off the Record. J. Bingham
Murder on a Bad Trip. June Drummond
Murder on a Monument. E. C. R. Lorac
Murder on a Mystery Tour. M. Babson
Murder on a Quiet Street. R. H. Peck
Murder on a Saturday. Dulcie Gray
Murder on a Shoestring. A. Spiller
Murder on a Tangent. D. M. Disney
Murder on Alternate Tuesdays. T. Davis
Murder on Angler's Island. H. Reilly
Murder on Arrival. G. Batson
Murder on "B" Deck. V. Starrett
Murder on Bag Hill. C. Ryland
Murder on Beacon Hill. G. Brown
Murder on Both Sides. A. Sideman
Murder on Broadway. H. Q. Masur
Murder on Cape Cod. F. Shay
Murder on Capitol Hill. M. Truman
Murder on Center Stage. J. L. Twedt
Murder on Clam Pond. D. Kiker
Murder on Coney Island. Dan Morgan
Murder on Cue. J. Dentinger
Murder on Delivery. S. Dean
Murder on Demand. Neill Graham
Murder on Demand. R. Verron
Murder on Display. C. Hale
Murder on Duty. M. Burton
Murder on Embassy Row. M. Truman
Murder on Every Floor. A. Demarest
Murder on Fifth Avenue. C. Cranston
Murder on Fire. M. Bardsley
Murder on Flight 354. John Laffin
Murder on 47th Street. B. Poynter
Murder on French Leave. A. Morice
Murder on Friday. H. Ashbrook
Murder on Ghost Tree Island. K. S. Daiger
Murder on Halfaday Creek. J. B. Hendryx
Murder on Her Mind. R. Dietrich
Murder on Her Mind. Vechel Howard
Murder on Her Mind. S. Steiner
Murder on High. Carter Brown
Murder on High. G. Kennedy
Murder on High Heels. R. Burke
Murder on His Mind. G. Goldsmith
Murder on Holiday. B. Malim
Murder on Honeymoon. Dulcie Gray
Murder-on-Hudson. Jennifer Jones
Murder on Ice. M. Bardsley
Murder on Ice. V. Gunn
Murder on Ice. T. Wood
Murder on Largo Island. C. Hogarth
Murder on Leave. G. V. Galwey
Murder on Location. H. Engel
Murder on Location. G. Kennedy
Murder on Location. L. Thayer
Murder on Madison Avenue. F. Orenstein
Murder on Manoeuvres. S. C. Mason
Murder on Margin. R. G. Dean
Murder on Martha's Vineyard. D. Osborn
Murder on Martha's Vineyard. K. Roos

Murder on Mike. H. P. Jeffers
Murder on Mitcham Common. R. Simmat
Murder on Monday. G. Barnett
Murder on Monday. C. Barry
Murder on Monday. R. P. Wilmot
Murder on Monday. G. M. Wilson
Murder on Mondays. C. Bush
Murder on Monk's Wood. H. G. Hutchinson
Murder on Mount Capita. L. W. Martin
Murder on My Conscience. E. Radford
Murder on My Hands. C. Franklin
Murder on My Hands. Neill Graham
Murder on My Mind. J. T. Story
Murder on My Street. E. Lanham
Murder on Page Three. E. Griffiths
Murder on Parade. C. Wells
Murder on Paradise Island. R. Forsythe
Murder on Playboy Island. M. Franklin
Murder on Polopel. M. Wright
Murder on Queer Street. Gene Evans
Murder on Route 40. H. J. Hultman
Murder on Russian Hill. L. G. Offord
Murder on Safari. E. Huxley
Murder on Safari. H. Waugh
Murder on St. Mary Street. Timothy Green
Murder-on-Sea. R. Harrison
Murder on Shadow Island. Garnett Weston
Murder on Shark Island. J. De Witt
Murder on Show. M. Babson
Murder on Stage. Sutherland Scott
Murder on Stilts. G. Dean
Murder on Sundays. E. Gilzean
Murder-on-Thames. D. Fearon
Murder on the Air. R. Warner
Murder on the Aisle. E. Gorman
Murder on the Aphrodite. R. B. Sanborn
Murder on the Appalachian Trail. J. Carr
Murder on the Beam. G. Brandon
Murder on the Blackboard. S. Palmer
Murder on the Bluff. E. Tyler
Murder on the Boat Express. R. Hardinge
Murder on the Brain. A. Heckstall-Smith
Murder on the Brain. E. M. Poate
Murder on the Brampton. G. Camacho
Murder on the Bridge. L. Brock
Murder on the Broads. G. Chester
Murder on the Burrows. E. C. R. Lorac
Murder on the Bus. C. F. Gregg
Murder on the Camp. J. H. Waring
Murder on the Cattle Ranch. C. H. Snow
Murder on the Cliff. C. Ryland
Murder on the Common. C. Ryland
Murder on the Costa Brava. J. Bonett
Murder on the Day of Judgment. V. Rath
Murder on the Downbeat. R. Avery
Murder on the "Duchess". Neill Graham
Murder on the Eastern Shore. D. Osborn
Murder on the Eighteenth Hole. C. Miron
Murder on the "Enriqueta". M. Thynne
Murder on the Face of It. E. L. Fetta
Murder on the Fell. H. D. Stacpoole
Murder on the Fourth Floor. J. G. Brandon
Murder on the Glass Floor. V. B. Shore
Murder on the Glitter Box. Steve Allen
Murder on the High Seas. J. G. Brandon
Murder on the High Seas. R. H. Wilkinson
Murder on the Hudson. D. Flynn
Murder on the Ice Rink. J. G. Brandon
Murder on the Left Bank. Eliott Paul
Murder on the Line. J. Creasey
Murder on the Line. W. L. Rohde
Murder on the Links. A. Christie
Murder on the List. Neill Graham
Murder on the Loire. T. B. Morris
Murder on the Long Straight. C. Yarborough
Murder on the Loose. G. W. Jones
Murder on the Marsh. J. Ferguson
Murder on the Marshes. G. Chester
Murder on the Matterhorn. G. Carr
Murder on the Menu. B. Byrne
Murder on the Merry-Go-Round. Josephine Bell
Murder on the Mistral. V. G. Malo
Murder on the Monte. Ross Richards
Murder on the Moon. C. MacDaniel

Murder on the Moor. H. Desmond
Murder on the Moor. W. Edwards
Murder on the Moors. C. Campbell
Murder on the Mountain. C. N. Govan
Murder on the Mountain. A. H. Hill
Murder on the Mountain! F. W. Irwin
Murder on the Mountain. N. Rutledge
Murder on the Night Ferry. B. E. Wallace
Murder on the Nile. A. Christie
Murder on the Nose. G. Bagby
Murder on the Orient Express. A. Christie
Murder on the Pacific. D. K. Patton
Murder on the Pacific. L. Thayer
Murder on the Palisades. W. Levinrew
Murder on the Pier. G. Chester
Murder on the Pike. A. Nonweiler
Murder on the Program. M. M. Mannon
Murder on the Prowl. J. M. Spender
Murder on the Purple Water. F. Crane
Murder on the Ranch. F. C. Ryan
Murder on the Rerun. F. Carmichael
Murder on the River. R. Gar
Murder on the Rocks. R. Dietrich
Murder on the Roof. E. J. Doherty
Murder on the Rue du Bac. T. Foster
Murder on the Run. Medora Sale
Murder on the S-23. S. Fisher
Murder on the Salem Road. K. M. Roof
Murder on the Second Floor. C. Bishop
Murder on the Second Floor. F. Vosper
Murder on the Side. D. Keene
Murder on the Sixth Hole. D. Frome
Murder on the Square. D. Frome
Murder on the Stage. J. G. Brandon
Murder on the Stairs. Dulcie Gray
Murder on the Ten-Yard Line. J. S. Strange
Murder on the Terrace. H. Waugh
Murder on the Thirty-First Floor. P. Wahloo
Murder on the Tropic. T. Downing
Murder on the Underground. W. Boggs
Murder on the Veld. R. Hardinge
Murder on the Way! T. Roscoe
Murder on the Wild Side. J. Jacks
Murder on the Wing. A. Eadie
Murder on the Yacht. R. King
Murder on the Yellow Brick Road. S. M. Kaminsky
Murder on Their Minds. G. H. Coxe
Murder on Tour. Dick Clark
Murder on Tour. T. Downing
Murder on Trial. M. Underwood
Murder on Trust. C. Rushton
Murder on Tuesday. Mary Taylor
Murder on Usher's Planet. A. A. Noel
Murder on Vacation. Ruth MacLeod
Murder on Wall Street. J. B. Ethan
Murder on Wheels. S. Palmer
Murder on Wheels. K. Robeson
Murder on Wheels. L. Warden
Murder on Whispering Sands. V. Gunn
Murder Once Done. M. L. Bennett
Murder Once Removed. I. G Neiman
Murder One! M. E. Cohane
Murder One. B. Copper
Murder One. F. Gruber
Murder One. D. Haring
Murder One. H. Howard
Murder One. E. Lipsky
Murder: One, Two, Three. J. Creasey
Murder or Accident. Aimee Stewart
Murder or Manslaughter. H. B. Mathers
Murder or Mercy. J. Stagge
Murder or Not. L. Stephan
Murder or Three. L. Mantell
Murder Out of Class. H. C. Davis
Murder Out of Commission. R. B. Dominic
Murder Out of Court. J. Cowdroy
Murder Out of Court. R. B. Dominic
Murder Out of Mind. K. F. Crossen
Murder Out of School. M. Burton
Murder Out of School. I. T. Ross
Murder Out of Season. L. Gribble
Murder Out of the Past. J. Creasey
Murder Out of Tune. F. L. Cary
Murder Out of Tune. M. Magill

Murder Out of Tune. C. Rushton
Murder Out of Tune. Simon Shaw
Murder Out of Turn. F. Lockridge
Murder Out of Wedlock. H. Pentecost
Murder Over Broadway. F. Malina
Murder Over Dorval. D. Montrose
Murder Over Karmak. N. MacKenzie
Murder Over Miami. J. Reach
Murder—Paris Fashion. Carter Brown
Murder Party. H. Bordeaux
Murder Party. F. L. Cary
Murder Paves the Way. S. Truss
Murder Pays a Call. Ben Rogers
Murder Pays No Dividends. C. Cookson
Murder Picks the Jury. Harrison Hunt
Murder Pie. J. L. Rankin
Murder, Plain and Fancy. Garland Lord
Murder Plan Six. J. Bingham
Murder Play. B. J. Burton
Murder Play. G. S. Carlisle
Murder Plays an Ugly Scene. L. A. G. Strong
Murder Pluperfect. K. Giles
Murder Plus. C. Wells
Murder Point. Coningsby Dawson
Murder Points a Finger. David Alexander
Murder Points East. R. Verron
Murder Pool. E. Heath
Murder Post-Dated. A. Morice
Murder Premeditated. P. H. Powell
Murder Proof. J. B. O'Sullivan
Murder Prophet. G. W. Jones
Murder—Queen High. B. Wade
Murder R.F.D. H. Petersen
Murder R.F.D. L. Stephan
Murder Recalls Van Kill. S. Bayne
Murder Red-Handed. Richard Grayson
Murder Reflected. J. Caird
Murder Rehearsal. R. East
Murder Rehearsal. B. G. Quin
Murder Remote. J. Caird
Murder Rents a Room. S. E. Mason
Murder, Repeat Murder. A. MacKinnon
Murder Rides a Rocket. F. Diamond
Murder Rides Express. C. Dekker
Murder Rides the Campaign Train. The Gordons
Murder Rides the Express. H. Reilly
Murder Rings the Bell. Neill Graham
Murder Rings Twice. H. J. Hultman
Murder Road. G. J. Barrett
Murder Road. Arthur Moore
Murder Room. J. Sharkey
Murder Room. P. E. Walsh
Murder Rose. A. McKee-Wright
Murder Round the Clock. H. Pentecost
Murder Round the Corner. N. MacKenzie
Murder Roundabout. R. Lockridge
Murder Run Riot. J. Courage
Murder Run Wild. H. Desmond
Murder Runs a Fever. R. Fenisong
Murder Runs in the Family. H. Footner
Murder Runs Riot. S. Forbes
Murder Runs Wild. N. Morland
Murder Sails at Midnight. M. Babson
Murder Sails at Midnight. K. Gordon
Murder Scholastic. J. Caird
Murder Secretary. W. G. Beyer
Murder Seeks an Agent. Wenzell Brown
Murder Sees the Light. H. Engel
Murder Set to Music. H. R. Campbell
Murder Sets the Pace. E. W. Freeman
Murder, She Said. A. Christie
Murder! She Says. Carter Brown
Murder She Says! Reginald Campbell
Murder She Says. A. C. Headley
Murder, She Says! J. Reach
Murder Ship. G. H. Teed
Murder Sits Pretty. Colin Robertson
Murder So Real. A. Bird
Murder—So What! R. Dudgeon
Murder!—So What? B. Shannon
Murder Solves a Problem. M. Bramhall
Murder, Somewhere in This City. M. Procter
Murder Sonata. F. Fletcher
Murder Song. J. Cleary

Murder Speaks. E. Radford
Murder Special. F. MacIsaac
Murder—Special Edition! M. Brody
Murder Specialist. B. Clifton
Murder Spins the Wheel. B. Halliday
Murder Spoils Everything. J. Lane
Murder Squad. E. Meade
Murder Squad. T. Tullett
Murder Stalks a Billion. R. Wallace
Murder Stalks the Bay. E. Messenger
Murder Stalks the Circle. L. Thayer
Murder Stalks the Mayor. R. T. M. Scott
Murder Stalks the Wakely Family. A. Derleth
Murder Starts from Fishguard. H. C. Davis
Murder Steals the Show. L. Hirsch
Murder Steps In. C. M. Russell
Murder Steps Out. C. Reeve
Murder Stops the Clock. C. Rice
Murder Story. L. Kennedy
Murder Story. L. A. Knight
Murder Straight Up. E. Gorman
Murder Strikes an Atomic Unit. T. Du Bois
Murder Strikes at Dawn. H. Desmond
Murder Strikes North. N. Thurley
Murder Strikes Pink. J. Pullein-Thompson
Murder Strikes Three. D. MacDuff
Murder Strikes Thrice. C. G. Booth
Murder Strikes Twice. M. B. Dix
Murder Strikes Twice. J. V. Nolan
Murder, Sunny Side Up. R. B. Dominic
Murder Sweet and Sour. H. Pentecost
Murder Sweet Murder. Carter Brown
Murder Swings High. N. Brent
Murder Syndicate. J. Chancellor
Murder Takes a Holiday. T. J. Kelly
Murder Takes a Honeymoon. E. Fleming
Murder Takes a Partner. Haughton Murphy
Murder Takes a Wife. J. A. Howard
Murder Takes No Holiday. B. Halliday
Murder Takes Over. A. Tack
Murder Takes the Baths. L. Priestley
Murder Takes the Stage. J. Reach
Murder Takes the Veil. M. A. Hubbard
Murder That Had Everything. H. Footner
Murder That Wouldn't Stay Solved. Hampton Stone
Murder, They Say. R. St. Clair
Murder Through Room 45. T. A. Plummer
Murder Through the Looking Glass. R. G. Dean
Murder Through the Looking Glass. M. Venning
Murder Through the Window. F. Everton
Murder Thy Neighbor. M. Hervey
Murder Times Five. R. Colby
Murder Times 4. C. Neutzel
Murder Times Three. A. R. Long
Murder Times Two. Haughton Murphy
Murder Tips the Scales. J. Creasey
Murder to an Audience. Gerald Brown
Murder to Burn. L. Mantell
Murder to Follow. K. Field
Murder to Go. E. Lathen
Murder to Hounds. E. Acheson
Murder to Make You Grow Up Little Girl. L. Oriol
Murder to Measure. Robert Mason
Murder to Music. G. Burne
Murder to Music. G. Chester
Murder to Music. P. Colson
Murder to Music. W. H. L. Crauford
Murder to Music. L. Edgley
Murder to Music. J. Kilgore
Murder to Music. M. Newman
Murder to Order. L. Marshall
Murder to Type. A. R. Long
Murder to Welcome Her. M. Neville
Murder Today, Money Tomorrow. J. Messmann
Murder Too Late. G. Ashe
Murder Too Many. E. Ferrars
Murder Town. L. Marshall
Murder Trail. M. Grant
Murder Trail. C. W. Sanders
Murder Trail. R. Wallace
Murder Train. Gavin Holt
Murder Trap. D. Campbell
Murder Trap. Howel Evans

Murder Trap. J. A. Jordan
Murder Trap. A. Livingston
Murder Trapp. Eugene Franklin
Murder Tree. L. McFarlane
Murder Trial. S. Box
Murder Triangle. Lawrence Williams
Murder Trouble. L. Trimble
Murder Tunes In. C. Kingston
Murder Twice Removed. Muriel Bradley
Murder Twice Told. D. Hamilton
Murder Uncensored. Jason
Murder Under Construction. P. MacTyre
Murder Under the Big Top. R. Wallace
Murder Under the Mistletoe. Jennifer Jordan
Murder Under the Sun. L. O'Donnell
Murder Underground. W. Arden
Murder Underground. M. D. Hay
Murder Unleashed. Dorothy Bennett
Murder Unlimited. Nicholas Carter
Murder Unlimited. M. V. Heberden
Murder Unmourned. George Douglas
Murder Unplanned. E. A. St. Clair
Murder Unprompted. S. Brett
Murder Unrecognized. M. Burton
Murder Unrenovated. P. M. Carlson
Murder Unseen. J. York
Murder Unsolved. S. Adams
Murder Unsuspected. J. Cowdroy
Murder up My Sleeve. E. S. Gardner
Murder up the Glen. C. Campbell
Murder Upstairs. A. Bliss
Murder—Very Dry! S. S. Baker
Murder Waiting to Happen. L. A. Taylor
Murder Walks Alone. J. V. Nolan
Murder Walks Alone. C. Ripley
Murder Walks on Tiptoe. Neill Graham
Murder Walks the Corridors. J. D. Perry
Murder Walks the Deck. W. Martyn
Murder Walks the Stairs. G. M. Barnes
Murder Ward. R. Sapir
Murder Was My Neighbor. G. Cobden
Murder Was Never Bolder. L. G. Redmond-Howard
Murder Was Their Medicine. G. Cobden
Murder Wears a Friendly Face. V. M. Perry
Murder Wears a Mantilla. Carter Brown
Murder Wears a Mummer's Mask. B. Halliday
Murder Wears Mukluks. E. M. Boyd
Murder Week-End. M. Halliday
Murder Well Begun. S. Adams
Murder Well Done. I. S. Shriber
Murder Well Rehearsed. J. R. Carroll
Murder When Necessary. P. Levene
Murder While You Wait. J. Corbett
Murder While You Wait. Michael Wallace
Murder While You Work. S. Scarlett
Murder Will. E. Wilmot
Murder Will Be Committed. G. Goodchild
Murder Will In. C. Wells
Murder Will Out. E. M. Bowen
Murder Will Out. L. M. Elwyn
Murder Will Out. M. Leinster
Murder Will Out. H. Leyford
Murder Will Out. G. E. Minot
Murder Will Out. Jeannette Covert Nolan
Murder Will Out. Frank Scott
Murder Will Out. D. Sterling
Murder Will Out. R. Vickers
Murder Will Out. P. C. Williams
Murder Will Speak. G. Bellairs
Murder Will Speak. J. J. Connington
Murder Will Speak. Mark Cross
Murder with a Kiss. V. Gunn
Murder with a Past. E. Queen
Murder with a Theme Song. V. Rath
Murder with a Vengeance. R. Quest
Murder with Gloves. B. Huber
Murder with Grace. W. Wall
Murder with Impatience. R. Verron
Murder with Long Hair. H. D. Spatz
Murder with Love. F. Durbridge
Murder with Love. Vechel Howard
Murder with Love. Garland Lord
Murder with Love. Dell Shannon
Murder—with Love. J. T. Story

Murder with Magic. R. St. Clair
Murder with Malice. M. Underwood
Murder with Menaces. V. Hansen
Murder with Minarets. C. Forsyte
Murder with Mirrors. A. Christie
Murder with Mushrooms. G. Ashe
Murder with Music. G. Riddell
Murder with Muskets. J. Reeves
Murder with Orange Blossoms. R. Darby
Murder with Pictures. G. H. Coxe
Murder with Relish. C. L. Taylor
Murder with Roses. A. McElfresh
Murder with Southern Hospitality. L. Ford
Murder with Variety. W. Arthur
Murder with Your Malted. Jerome Barry
Murder Within Murder. F. Lockridge
Murder Without a Corpse. Dave Logan
Murder Without Alibis. S. McPhellamy
Murder Without Clues. J. L. Bonney
Murder Without Clues. E. Pierson
Murder Without Crime. B. Healey
Murder Without Crime. J. Lee Thompson
Murder Without Icing. E. Lathen
Murder Without Makeup. E. Benjamin
Murder Without Malice. R. Plomley
Murder Without Malice. A. Spiller
Murder Without Men. T. B. Morris
Murder Without Morals. M. M. Marshall
Murder Without Motive. M. Carrel
Murder Without Motive. R. L. Goldman
Murder Without Mourners. Sutherland Scott
Murder Without Mystery. J. Playfair
Murder Without Regret. E. L. Cushing
Murder Without Regret. R. Trevor
Murder Without Risk. H. Adams
Murder Without Tears. L. Lupton
Murder Without Weapon. Means Davis
Murder Without Weapons. A. B. Cunningham
Murder Won't Out. P. Hobson
Murder Won't Wait. C. J. Daly
Murder Won't Wait. R. S. O'Connor
Murder Wore Green. R. P. Koehler
Murder Yacht. Anonymous
Murder Yet to Come. I. B. Myers
Murdercon. R. Purtill
Murdered Alive! W. Braun
Murdered But Not Dead. Anne Austin
Murdered Cliche. J. Samuel
Murdered Envoy. Marg Douglas
Murdered Man's Derby. E. A. St. Clair
Murdered Manservant. C. F. Gregg
Murdered Mathematician. H. S. Keeler
Murdered Millionaire. D. Hille
Murdered Millionaire. E. Queen
Murdered Mistress. Joy Brown
Murdered: One by One. F. Beeding
Murdered Sleep. G. Braddon
Murderer. J. Bounden
Murderer. R. A. K. Heath
Murderer. W. Morton
Murderer. A. Shaffer
Murderer. G. Simenon
Murderer Among Us. Carter Brown
Murderer at Large. W. A. Ballinger
Murderer at Large. D. Henderson
Murderer at Large. S. Horler
Murderer in the Garden. Eliaabeth Howard
Murderer in the House. K. Clugston
Murderer in This House. R. King
Murderer Invisible. P. Wylie
Murderer Is a Fox. E. Queen
Murderer Next Door. R. Yglesias
Murderer of New Orleans. W. Ward
Murderer of Sleep. M. Kennedy
Murderer Returns. E. D. Torgerson
Murderer Vine. S. Rifkin
Murderer Who Wanted More. B. Kendrick
Murderers. F. Brown
Murderers Are Silent. R. Clarke
Murderer's Bluff. F. Duncan
Murderer's Bride. H. Desmond
Murderer's Challenge. H. Footner
Murderer's Choice. A. M. Wells
Murderer's Derby. H. Graham

Murderers Don't Smile. John Morgan
Murderer's Fen. A. Garve
Murderer's Holiday. D. H. Clarke
Murderers' Houses. Jennie Melville
Murderer's Island. Y. Tregarron
Murderer's Luck. H. Holt
Murderers Make Mistakes. F. W. Crofts
Murderer's Mansion. Irene Shaw
Murderer's Maze. R. Glover
Murderer's Maze. John Marsh
Murderers' Medicine. A. Train
Murderers Meet. Gwyn Evans
Murderer's Mistake. E. C. R. Lorac
Murderer's Moon. R. Dana
Murderer's Moon. R. Goyne
Murderer's Moon. G. Morgan
Murderers of Monty. R. Hull
Murderer's Row. R. Batchelor
Murderer's Row. D. Hamilton
Murderer's Stand-In. J. G. Brandon
Murderers Three. F. C. Tickner
Murderer's Trail. J. J. Farjeon
Murderer's Vanity. H. Footner
Murderer's Wench. P. Hoyt
Murderess. P. Bellairs
Murdering Kind. Gwendoline Butler
Murdering Mr. Velfrage. Roy Vickers
Murderous Journey. E. McGirr
Murderous Move. C. Plumb
Murderous Remedy. Stella Shepherd
Murderous Suspense. G. M. Barnes
Murderous Welcome. J. Irwin
Murder's a Bad Habit. D. E. Roberts
Murder's a Must. J. R. Fearn
Murder's a Swine. N. Lombard
Murder's a Waiting Game. Anthony Gilbert
Murder's Always Final. Neill Graham
Murders Anonymous. E. Ferrars
Murders at Crossby. E. P. Frankland
Murders at Hibiscus Key. V. Siller
Murders at Highbridge. R. Slingsby
Murders at Impasse Louvain. Richard Grayson
Murders at Loon Lake. K. Whipple
Murders at Moon Dance. A. B. Guthrie
Murders at Scandal House. P. Hunt
Murders at the Crab Apple Cafe. G. Manners
Murders at the Lakes. G. L. Jennings
Murders at the Manor. C. Ryland
Murders at Turbot Towers. S. J. Peskett
Murder's Burning. S. H. Courtier
Murders by Moonlight. A. Hyde
Murder's Coming. D. C. Cameron
Murder's End. R. Kelston
Murders for Sale. A. Weston
Murder's for the Birds. Frank S. Miller
Murders Form Fours. David Hume
Murders in a Good Cause. Medora Sale
Murders in Lovers' Lane. J. G. Dunton
Murders in Praed Street. J. Rhode
Murders in Sequence. M. Propper
Murders in Silk. M. Teagle
Murders in Surrey Wood. John Arnold
Murders in the Dispensary. J. Carr
Murders in the Mortuary. Austin Stone
Murders in the Rue Morgue. R. Brome
Murders in Volume 2. E. Daly
Murders I've Seen. P. Mechem
Murder's Just for Cops. L. Marshall
Murder's Little Helper. G. Bagby
Murder's Little Helper. Garland Lord
Murder's Little Sister. P. Branch
Murder's Money. G. A. Ralston
Murders Near Mapleton. B. Flynn
Murder's No Accident. A. S. Fleischman
Murder's No Accident. P. Orpet
Murder's No Picnic. E. L. Cushing
Murder's No Picnic. P. Hambledon
Murder's No Picnic. P. Muat
Murder's Not an Odd Job. R. Dennis
Murders of Miriam. W. Kerr
Murders of Richard III. ELizabeth Peters
Murders on Fox Island. M. P. Hood
Murders on the Square. T. George
Murder's Out of Season. L. Marshall

Murder's Out of Tune. S. Woods
Murder's Playground. G. W. Jones
Murder's Rock. D. Reid
Murder's Shield. R. Sapir
Murder's So Permanent. E. Howie
Murder's Web. Dorothy Dunn
Murders While You Wait. Claude Hunter
Murdoch Legacy. Irma Walker
Murdock. G. Simmons
Murdock for Hire. R. Ray
Murdock's Acid Test. G. H. Coxe
Murgunstrumm and others. H. B. Cave
Muriel Wins Through. G. Thorne
Murillo Mystery. A. Eadie
Murillo Mystery. B. Poynter
Murky Shallows. O. Low
Murmansk Assignment. J. Pattinson
Murmur of Mutiny. M. Pugh
Murmuring Willow. Rona Randall
Murmurs in the Rue Morgue. M. Cumberland
Murphy. G. Paulsen
Murphy Gang. Roland Daniel
Murphy's Fault. S. Womack
Murphy's Game. M. Tarmey
Murphy's Master, and other stories. J. Payn
Murray Hill Mystery. Nicholas Carter
Murray of the Scots Greys. L. Clarke
Murray, the Detective. Old Sleuth
Muscatel Ritual. J. Ruyle
Muscle and Blood. G. Dold
Muscle Beach Party. Elsie Lee
Muscle Boy. B. Clifton
Muscle for the Wing. D. Woodrell
Muse Theatre Murder. T. A. Plummer
Museum Murder. J. T. MacIntyre
Museum Mystery. A. Soutar
Museum Piece No. 13. R. King
Mush and Poke, Detectives. A. L. Kaser
Mushalong. G. Goodchild
Mushroom Cave. R. Rosenblum
Mushrooms on Toast. Laurence Kirk
Music and Crime. J. R. Creech
Music for Chameleons. T. Capote
Music from Another Room. J. Kelly
Music from the Past. K. Cameron
Music Gallery Murder. R. Francis Foster
Music Master. Dorothy Fletcher
Music of Aquarius. Canella Lewis
Music Room. Martin Long
Music Room. W. E. D. Ross
Music Tells All. E. R. Punshon
Music to Murder By. V. Hinkle
Music to Murder By. D. Pownall
Music Wars. G. Pape
Music When Sweet Voices Die. C. Q. Yarbro
Musical Comedy Crime. Anthony Gilbert
Musical Comedy Murders of 1940. J. Bishop
Muskrat Ramble. L. Maddox
Mussolini Murder Plot. B. Newman
Muster of the Vultures. G. Fairlie
Mustering of the Hawks. J. Harris
Mutable Many. R. Barr
Mutants. P. Van Greenaway
Mutants Are Coming. I. Haiblum
Mutation. Robin Cook
Mutation Mink. P. Traill
Mutatis Mutandis. D. Campton
Mute Witness. R. L. Pike
Muted Murder. S. Sinclair
Mutilator. B. Heatter
Mutilators. M. Casey
Mutiny. F. R. Bechdolt
Mutiny of the Saturn and other sea stories. Lt. Warneford
Mutt. A. W. Tillinghast
Mutton Dressed as Lamb, and Live. J. M. Walsh
Muzzle Blast. B. Rossi
Muzzled Ox. C. Stanton
My Adventures in the Flying Scotsman. E. Phillpotts
My Atlantic Bride. H. Russell
My Aunt Agatha. M. Brenner
My Baby Was Blasted. M. Brody
My Bad Boy. M. Neville
My Body. R. Dietrich

M

My Bones Will Keep. G. Mitchell
My Bonny Lies Under the Sea. R. Alan
My Brother. Vincent Brown
My Brother, Cain. V. Thiessen
My Brother, the Druggist. Marvin Kaye
My Brother's Executioner. J. Laffin
My Brother's Killer. D. M. Devine
My Brother's Killer. J. Potts
My Brother's Killer. J. York
My Brother's Wife. Harry Davis
My Brow Is Wet. K. Leopold
My Business Is Murder. H. Kane
My Caravaggio Style. D. L. Moore
My Child and I. F. Warden
My Coat Is Travel-Stained. F. Gamble
My Confessions. M. N. Newton
My Cousin Caroline's Wedding. H. Wood
My Cousin Cynthia, and others. P. C. De Crespigny
My Cousin Death. M. McMullen
My Cousin Gary. G. M. Wilson
My Cousin, My Gastroenterologist. M. Leyner
My Cousin Rachel. D. Du Maurier
My Cousin Rachel. Diana Morgan
My Cutie's a Corpse. Pete Costello
My Darlin' Evangeline. H. Kane
My Darling Is Deadpan. Carter Brown
My Darling's Ransom. R. Dowling
My Dead Body. G. Bagby
My Dead Brother. Rex Anderson
My Dead Wife. W. Worley
My Deadly Angel. J. Chelton
My Dear Heart. K. Lindsay
My Dear Miss Emma. P. Allardyce
My Dearest Elizabeth. A. Maybury
My Dearest Holmes. R. Piercy
My Death Is a Mockery. D. G. Baber
My Enemies Have Sweet Voices. N. McCallum
My Enemy Came Nigh. R. T. Bickers
My Enemy Jones. Robert Barr
My Enemy—My Wife. A. Haden
My Enemy's Friend. H. Osborne
My Face Beneath the Stone. J. Crecy
My Fair Lady. Georgius
My Father Sleeps. G. Mitchell
My First and Last Appearance. E. F. Turner
My First Crime. G. Mace
My First Murder. Susan Baker
My First Offer, and other stories. M. C. Hay
My Flesh Is Sweet. D. Keene
My Foe Outstretch'd Beneath the Tree. V. C. Clinton-Baddeley
My Friend Charles. F. Durbridge
My Friend Ching and other tales. Anonymous
My Friend Judas. P. Barrington
My Friend Maigret. G. Simenon
My Friend Pasquale and other stories. J. S. Tait
My Friend the Murderer and other mysteries and adventures. A. C. Doyle
My Friend Tony. W. Johnston
My Giddy Aunt. R. Cooney
My God How the Money Rolls In. J. Ripley
My Grand Enemy. J. Stubbs
My Grave Is for the Living. S. Connor
My Guess Was Murder. G. Cobden
My Gun for Hire. N. Rosso
My Gun, Her Body. J. Bogar
My Gun Is Quick. M. Spillane
My Hate Lies Bleeding. A. Sewart
My Heart and Stephanie. R. W. Kauffman
My Heart Went Dead. A. McElfresh
My Honey Says Homicide. Carter Brown
My Husband's First Love. H. Wood
My Invisible Partner. T. S. Denison
My Japanese Prince. A. C. Gunter
My Killer Doesn't Understand Me. T. P. Mulkeen
My Kind of Game. A. Rome
My Kind of Knack. D. Haring
My Kingdom for a Hearse. C. Rice
My Lady Bountiful. F. M. White
My Lady Caprice. J. Farnol
My Lady Cinderella. A. M. Williamson
My Lady Dangerous. S. Horler
My Lady Evil. P. J. Cooper
My Lady Mischief. J. L. Roberts
My Lady of the Yellow Domino. A. W. Marchmont
My Lady of Whims. F. Warden
My Lady Ruby and John Basileon, Chief of Police. G. F. Monkshood
My Lady Vamp. G. W. Gough
My Lady's Bath. G. W. Gough
My Lady's Diamonds. A. Sergeant
My Lady's Garter. J. Futrelle
My Lady's Money. W. Collins
My Late Espoused Saint. F. Durham
My Late Wives. Carter Dickson
My Laugh Come Last. J. H. Chase
My Life Is Done. Sara Woods
My Life Is My Own. W. Standish
My Little Husband. F. C. Philips
My Lodger's Legacy. R. W. Hume
My Lord Conceit. Rita
My Lord Duke. E. W. Hornung
M'Lord, I Am Not Guilty. F. S. Wees
My Lord Murderer. E. Mansfield
My Lord of Wrybourne. J. Farnol
My Lord the Felon. H. Hill
My Lost Self. A. W. Marchmont
My Love Has a Secret. A. Maybury
My Love Is Stone. C. Massie
My Love Is Violent. T. B. Dewey
My Love Johnny. M. McEvoy
My Love Noel. H. Nisbet
My Love Wears Black. O. R. Cohen
My Lovely Executioner. P. Rabe
My Master Spy. M. McKenna
My Masters. R. E. Salwey
My Mermaid Murmurs Murder. Carter Brown
My Merry Rockhurst. A. Castle
My Miscellania. W. Collins
My Mother Was Hanged. E. S. Willards
My Mysterious Clients. H. Scribner
My Name Is Black! J. Nazel
My Name Is Celia. R. Kruger
My Name Is Clary Brown. C. Keppel
My Name Is Death. C. Birkin
My Name Is Death. L. Egan
My Name Is Legion. R. Zelazny
My Name Is Love. J. Maclaren-Ross
My Name Is Michael Sibley. J. Bingham
My Name Is Morgan. W. Woolfolk
My Name Is Norval. T. D. White
My Neighbor's Wife. D. M. Disney
My Official Wife. R. H. Savage
My Old Man's Badge. F. Findley
My Only Murder, and other tales. E. Favenc
My Own Murderer. R. Hull
My Pal, the Killer. C. Warwick
My Particular Murder. D. Sharp
My Path Belated. N. Ames
My Patients. G. M. Fenn
My Peril in a Pullman Car and other tales. A. Griffiths
My Poll and My Partner. T. P. Prest
My Price Is Murder. R. Dudgeon
My Private Hangman. N. Herries
My Rubies Are Blood Red. J. C. Crawley
My Search for Ruth. A. Clarke
My Shadow. P. Malloch
My Sister Erica. J. Blackmore
My Sister, Good Night. G. McDonell
My Sister in This House. W. Kesselman
My Sister, My Friend. Katherine Blake
My Sister Ophelia. A. Kosner
My Sister's Confession and other stories. M. E. Braddon
My Sister's Keeper. D. Merritt
My Son, the Druggist. Marvin Kaye
My Son, the Murderer. P. Quentin
My Soul to Keep. E. Davis
My Strangest Case. G. Boothby
My Sweet Andrina. V. C. Andrews
My Tattered Loving. G. R. Preedy
My Terrible Twin. F. Whishaw
My Three Angels. S. Spewack
My Time or Yours. W. D. Blake
My Tom-Boy Girl. C. E. Blaney
My Treasure, My Love. Lynna Cooper
My True Love Lies. L. G. Offord
My Turn Next. Winston Graham
My Turn Now. Janet Green
My Turn to Die. K. Royce
My Two Wives and other stories. G. R. Sims
My Uncle Charles. N. Balchin
My Undiscovered Crimes. F. Wicks
My Vision's Enemy. Robin Chapman
My Weird Wooing. T. V. Foote
My Wickedness. Anonymous
My Wife Melissa. F. Durbridge
My Wife's Lover. J. Courage
My Word You Should Have Seen Us. J. Ripley
Mycroft Memorandum. R. Walsh
Mycroft Murder Case. A. Marsden
Myer for Hire. L. S. Taube
Mynns' Mystery. G. M. Fenn
Myopic Mermaid. Carter Brown
Myrimidon Project. C. Scarborough
Myrtle Fens. J. D. Clifton
Mysie, and other stories. I. B. P. Bird
Mysteries. W. LeQueux
Mysteries and Adventures. A. C. Doyle
Mysteries and Miseries of New Orleans. N. Buntline
Mysteries and Miseries of New York. N. Buntline
Mysteries and Miseries of New York. Old Sleuth
Mysteries Elucidated. A. M. Mackenzie
Mysteries for Radio. W. Weathers
Mysteries of a Great City. W. LeQueux
Mysteries of Algiers. R. Irwin
Mysteries of Ann. Alice Brown
Mysteries of Berlin. Anonymous
Mysteries of Black Valley. A. Mallory
Mysteries of Blair House. R. O. Eastman
Mysteries of Chicago. Anonymous
Mysteries of City Life. J. Rees
Mysteries of Crime, as Shown in Remarkable Capital Crimes. Anonymous
Mysteries of Ferney Castle. G. Lambe
Mysteries of Florence. G. Lippard
Mysteries of Heron Dyke. T. W. Speight
Mysteries of Hungary. Edward Moore
Mysteries of London. G. W. M. Reynolds
Mysteries of Modern London. G. R. Sims
Mysteries of Myra. C. H. Bullivant
Mysteries of Nashua. Anonymous
Mysteries of New Orleans. Anonymous
Mysteries of New Paris. F. Du Boisgobey
Mysteries of New York. Anonymous
Mysteries of New York. Old Sleuth
Msyteries of Oakendale Abbey. Anonymous
Mysteries of Paris. E. Sue
Mysteries of Ryeburn Manor. J. Laurence
Mysteries of the Castle. M. P. Andrews
Mysteries of the Castle. J. B. White
Mysteries of the City. J. M'Levy
Mysteries of the Court of London. G. W. M. Reynolds
Mysteries of the Riviera. E. P. Oppenheim
Mysteries of Udolpho. A. Radcliffe
Mysteries of Winterthurn. J. C. Oates
Mysterious Abduction. G. S. Goodman
Mysterious Affair at Styles. A. Christie
Mysterious Ambassador. L. Falk
Mysterious Aviator. N. Shute
Mysterious Baron. E. Ratcliffe
Mysterious Beggar. A. A. Day
Mysterious Bohemian. A. M. Diehl
Mysterious Burglar. G. E. Walsh
Mysterious Cane of Dr. Chang. R. St. Clair
Mysterious Card. C. Moffett
Mysterious Case. K. F. Hill
Mysterious Castle. Nicholas Carter
Mysterious Cavern. Nicholas Carter
Mysterious Chinaman. J. S. Fletcher
Mysterious Chinese Mandrake, and other stories. I. D. Ekbergh
Mysterious Commission. M. Innes
Mysterious Crime at Burleigh Mansion. Anonymous
Mysterious Dagger. Anonymous
Mysterious Disappearance. L. Tracy
Mysterious Disappearance of a Bride. M. Danvers
Mysterious Disappearance of Helen St. Vincent. J. J. Flinn
Mysterious Disappearances. G. M. Winsor

Mysterious Dr. Oliver. J. B. Ellis
Mysterious Ebony Carver. U. Ibezubge
Mysterious Foe. Nicholas Carter
Mysterious Free Booter. F. Lathom
Mysterious "Graft". Nicholas Carter
Mysterious Hand. A. J. Crandolph
Mysterious Husband. J. Meeke
Mysterious Inheritance. B. Marchant
Mysterious Journey. M. L. Tyrrell
Mysterious Juror. F. Du Boisgobey
Mysterious Madame. S. D'Erigny
Mysterious Mademoiselle. F. Grierson
Mysterious Mail Robbery. Nicholas Carter
Mysterious Marksman. Anonymous
Mysterious Marriage. E. Southworth
Mysterious Martin. T. Robbins
Mysterious Message. Anonymous
Mysterious Mickey Finn. Elliot Paul
Mysterious Millionaire. N. West
Mysterious Miss Cass. G. W. Appleton
Mysterious Miss Death. Gwyn Evans
Mysterious Miss Morrisot. V. Williams
Mysterious Missile. C. H. Snow
Mysterious Mr. Badman. W. F. Harvey
Mysterious Mr. Brent. G. Davison
Mysterious Mr. Campion. M. Allingham
Mysterious Mr. Frame. M. Merrick
Mysterious Mr. Garland. W. Martyn
Mysterious Mr. I. H. S. Keeler
Mysterious Mr. Jarvis. F. R. Giles
Mysterious Mr. Maynard. J. Hunter
Mysterious Mr. Miller. W. LeQueux
Mysterious Mr. Montague. B. Weston
Mysterious Mr. Pickering. P. E. Curtiss
Mysterious Mr. Quin. A. Christie
Mysterious Mr. Reece. R. M. Graydon
Mysterious Mr. Rocco. J. Creasey
Mysterious Mr. Sabin. E. P. Oppenheim
Mysterious Mrs. Nutford. B. M. Clay
Mysterious Mrs. Wilkinson and other stories. W. E. Norris
Mysterious Monsieur Moray. Brian Stuart
Mysterious Murder. I. Crookenden
Mysterious Murder. G. L.
Mysterious Murder of Pearl Bryan. Anonymous
Mysterious Murder of the Blonde Playgirl. A. Abbot
Mysterious Novice. S. Wilkinson
Mysterious Office. Jennette Lee
Mysterious Partner. A. Fielding
Mysterious Presence, and other stories. L. Hibberd
Mysterious Seal. W. C. Proby
Mysterious Stranger. C. H. Thorburn
Mysterious Suspect. J. Rhode
Mysterious Three. W. LeQueux
Mysterious Traders. S. Mukerji
Mysterious Valley. G. W. Wicking
Mysterious Warning. Mrs. Parsons
Mysterious Way. J. Boland
Mysterious Waye. P. C. Wren
Mysterious Wife. Grove Wilson
Mysterious Yankee. Old Sleuth
Mysteriouser and Mysteriouser. G. Bagby
Mystery. Anonymous
Mystery. G. S. Crosby
Mystery. F. Lathom
Mystery. P. Paris
Mystery. P. Straub
Mystery. S. E. White
Mystery. H. Wood
Mystery and Minette. H. Adams
Mystery and More Mystery. R. Arthur
Mystery and other stories. Annie Thomas
Mystery at a Country Inn. P. Owen
Mystery at Angel's End. J. Chancellor
Mystery at Arden Court. E. C. Holt
Mystery at Blackwater. D. Sutherland
Mystery at Butlin's. M. O'Nair
Mystery at Chillery. R. Francis Foster
Mystery at Crowstone. Colin Hope
Mystery at Folly Mill. J. Brooke
Mystery at Friar's Pardon. M. Porlock
Mystery at Furze Acres. D. Whitelaw
Mystery at Geneva. R. Macaulay

Mystery at Greenfingers. J. B. Priestley
Mystery at Greycombe Farm. J. Rhode
Nystery at Greystones. K. Lindsay
Mystery at Grimsdale. E. P. Frankland
Mystery at Hardacres. G. Morton
Mystery at Hermit's End. G. Morton
Mystery at Hidden Harbor. C. Fitzsimmons
Mystery at King's Grant. A. E. D.
Mystery at Lonesome End. M. Lockwood
Mystery at Lover's Cave. A. Berkeley
Mystery at Lynden Sands. J. J. Connington
Mystery at Manby House. J. Creasey
Mystery at Merrilees. M. Poole
Mystery at Moor Street. C. F. Gregg
Mystery at Newton Ferry. L. Meynell
Mystery at October House. Marjory Hall
Mystery at Olympia. J. Rhode
Mystery at Peak House. A. J. Rees
Mystery at Ramshackle House. H. Footner
Mystery at Spanish Hacienda. Jackson Gregory
Mystery at Stowe. V. Loder
Mystery at the Blue Villa. M. D. Post
Mystery at the Carrol Ranch. C. L. Kingsbury
Mystery at the Inn. J. H. Vahey
Mystery at the JHC Ranch. W. C. Tuttle
Mystery at the Rectory. A. Fielding
Mystery at the Ski Lodge. A. C. Martens
Mystery at Tudor Arches. L. Gribble
Mystery at Vellum. L. G. Horsefield
Mystery at Wadham Close. L. Souberge
Mystery Blues and other stories. P. Cheyney
Mystery Box. W. W. Sayer
Mystery Car. M. Gerard
Mystery Castle. Elsie Lee
Mystery Chain. L. G. Moberly
Mystery Cruise. K. Langmaid
Mystery Cruise. Taffrail
Mystery DeLuxe. R. King
Mystery Evans. B. Baker
Mystery Flier. E. T. Woodhall
Mystery Flight. John Davies
Mystery for Mary. V. Hanson
Mystery from the Air. J. Laurence
Mystery Gangster. G. Chester
Mystery Girl. C. Wells
Mystery Hand. B. Bolt
Mystery House. P. Hobson
Mystery House. K. Norris
Mystery House. J. M. Walsh
Mystery in Blue. G. E. Mallette
Mystery in Blue. W. Spence
Mystery in Glass. E. Kilvington
Mystery in Green. A. Vinton
Mystery in Hawaii. R. St. Clair
Mystery in Kensington Gore. M. Porlock
Mystery in Mdina. A. Hunt
Mystery in Minchin Mews. R. Gar
Mystery in Red. F. Grierson
Mystery in Red. S. Williams
Mystery in St. James Square. G. Collins
Mystery in the Channel. F. W. Crofts
Mystery in the Drood Family. M. Saunders
Mystery in the English Channel. F. W. Crofts
Mystery in the Mist. C. Kingston
Mystery in the Ritsmore. W. A. Johnston
Mystery in the Snow. G. Darwent
Mystery in the Woodshed. Anthony Gilbert
Mystery in White. J. J. Farjeon
Mystery Island. E. H. Hurst
Mystery Island. K. Robeson
Mystery Island. D. Storm
Mystery Island. F. Whishaw
Mystery Island. Palmer White
Mystery Keepers. M. Fox
Mystery Killer. H. Desmond
Mystery Lady. R. W. Chambers
Mystery Lady. Anna Clarke
Mystery Lamp. M. R. Rinehart
Mystery Maker. N. Fairbanks
Mystery Maker. Seamark
Mystery Man. M. Ankrum
Mystery Man. S. Hocking
Mystery Man. C. Kellett
Mystery Man. Lawrence Miller

Mystery Man. Old Sleuth
Mystery Man. J. M. Walsh
Mystery Man in the Tower. H. Chichester
Mystery Man of Mayfair. W. Lynk
Mystery Mandarin. J. W. Bobin
Mystery Manor. L. Gribble
Mystery Mansion. L. Archer
Mystery Mansion. Herman Landon
Mystery, Mayhem, and Murder! Jed Parish
Mystery Men. W. Hawes
Mystery Message. T. C. Bridges
Mystery Mile. M. Allingham
Mystery Militiaman. Ladbroke Blake
Mystery Mind. A. B. Reeve
Mystery Mission. S. Horler
Mystery Mission. M. Strangeways
Mystery Mission and other stories. S. Horler
Mystery Money. J. Laurence
Mystery Motive. M. Halliday
Mystery of a Bungalow. W. Chesney
Mystery of a Butcher's Shop. G. Mitchell
Mystery of a Cornish Moor. Anonymous
Mystery of a Diamond. F. H. Converse
Mystery of a Hansom Cab. F. Hume
Mystery of a Madstone. Anonymous
Mystery of a Madstone. K. F. Hill
Mystery of a Millionaire. M. J. Pemberton
Mystery of a Millionaire's Grave. G. Stables
Mystery of a Moonlight Tryst. I. D. Hardy
Mystery of a Motor Cab. F. Hume
Mystery of a Motor-Car. W. LeQueux
Mystery of a Shipyard. R. H. Savage
Mystery of a Studio and other stories. R. H. Fletcher
Mystery of a Turkish Bath. Rita
Mystery of a Wheelbarrow. W. H. Ferguson
Mystery of Achnaghoulash. Dave Smith
Mystery of Airedale Hall. B. Bolt
Mystery of Alfred Doubt. W. Hay
Mystery of Allan Grale. I. F. Mayo
Mystery of Allanwold. E. Van Loon
Mystery of Aloha House. L. Roddy
Mystery of Alton Grange. E. Everett-Green
Mystery of an Omnibus. F. Du Boisgobey
Mystery of Angelina Frood. R. A. Freeman
Mystery of Arrowhead Hill. L. W. Douglas
Mystery of Ashton Hall. B. Nitsua
Mystery of Avenue Road. A. Parsons
Mystery of Bar Harbor. Alsop Leffingwell
Mystery of Barry Ingram. A. S. Swan
Mystery of Beacon Hill. L. G. Redmond-Howard
Mystery of Beaton Craig. Mark Allerton
Mystery of Beckers' Brook. A. Blair
Mystery of Belgrave Square. Curtis Yorke
Mystery of Belvoir Mansions. B. Bolt
Mystery of Bent Cove. F. D. Holmgren
Mystery of Bernard Hanson. U. L. Silberrad
Mystery of Black Pit. Anonymous
Mystery of Blackmoor Prison. J. Creasey
Mystery of Blackwater Grange. E. Miller
Mystery of Blencarrow. M. Oliphant
Mystery of Bloomsbury Crescent. Mrs. Lodge
Mystery of Bullen Point. R. C. Armour
Mystery of Burnleigh Manor. W. Livingston
Mystery of Captain Burnaby. A. S. McNalty
Mystery of Cedar Bluff. H. Weeks
Mystery of Cedar Valley. V. Henry
Mystery of Cell 13. G. H. Teed
Mystery of Central Park. N. Bly
Mystery of Choice. R. W. Chambers
Mystery of Clement Dunraven. J. Middlemass
Mystery of Cloomber. A. C. Doyle
Mystery of Clough Mills. Stuart Martin
Mystery of Colde Fell. C. M. Braeme
Mystery of Collingwood. Marilyn Ross
Mystery of "Crazy Canyon" Ranch. E. H. Ott
Mystery of Crooknose. L. W. Douglas
Mystery of Crowther Castle. G. W. H. Firmstone
Mystery of DS 24. T. Wallace
Mystery of Dagget's Bank. N. Ned
Mystery of Daria Kane. M. V. Hunt
Mystery of Dark Hollow. E. Southworth
Mystery of Dead Horse Farm. S. R. Shepherd
Mystery of Dead Man's Heath. J. J. Farjeon
Mystery of Devil's Canyon. C. H. Snow

M

Mystery of Dr. Fu-Manchu. S. Rohmer
Mystery of Dudley Horne. F. Warden
Mystery of Echo Caverns. R. C. Payes
Mystery of Edwin Drood. C. Dickens
Mystery of Edwin Drood. L. Garfield
Mystery of Enid Belairs. D. Whitelaw
Mystery of Enid Favell. J. N. Chance
Mystery of Evangeline Fairfax. E. Kunst
Mystery of Evelin Delorme. A. B. Paine
Mystery of Fell Castle. A. Gask
Mystery of Fernridge Manor. R. Bodwell
Mystery of Fifty-Two. W. S. Masterman
Mystery of Flat 60. A. J. Sarl
Mystery of Flying V Ranch. R. E. Rochester
Mystery of Fourways. F. Warden
Mystery of Frances Farrington. E. Banks
Mystery of Fury Castle. Dan Ross
Mystery of Fury Castle. Marilyn Ross
Mystery of Fyfe House. V. Nielsen
Mystery of Glyn Castle. L. H. Brooks
Mystery of Gold Digger Creek. G. H. Teed
Mystery of "Golden Lotus". L. Gerard
Mystery of Grange Drayton. E. Kerr
Mystery of Gruden's Gap. Mark Cross
Mystery of Grudge Mountain. A. P. Terhune
Mystery of Hanging Sword Alley. W. J. Bayfield
Mystery of Hartley House. C. S. Raymond
Mystery of Hawthorne. Anonymous
Mystery of Hazelgrove. G. L. Warren
Mystery of Helmsley Grange. A. Askew
Mystery of Herman Wise. Captain Dallas
Mystery of High Eldersham. M. Burton
Mystery of Holly Tavern. L. Collis
Mystery of Horseshoe Island. F. W. Gumley
Mystery of Hotel Brichet. E. Chavette
Mystery of Hunting's End. M. G. Eberhart
Mystery of Irma Vep. C. Ludlam
Mystery of Jamaica Terrace. D. Donovan
Mystery of Jeanne Marie. H. E. Barlow
Mystery of Jessie Page, and other stories. H. Wood
Mystery of Joan Marryat. Mark Cross
Mystery of John Peppercorn. T. Gallon
Mystery of Judith. C. E. Pearce
Mystery of June 13. M. Severy
Mystery of Khufu's Tomb. T. Mundy
Mystery of Killard. R. Dowling
Mystery of King Cobra. D. Marfield
Mystery of King's Everard. C. Brandon
Mystery of Knickerbocker Towers. E. Thorne
Mystery of Kun-Ja-Muck Cave. G. F. Tibbetts
Mystery of Lady Chetwynd's Spectre. H. Lewis
Mystery of Lady Isobel. E. R. Punshon
Mystery of Ladyplace. C. Lys
Mystery of Landy Court. F. Hume
Mystery of Leighton Grange. M. E. Braddon
Mystery of Lincoln's Inn. R. Machray
Mystery of Lombardy Chambers. S. Westlaw
Mystery of Lone Manor. F. Warwick
Mystery of Lostland Academy. A. M. Sholl
Mystery of Lucien Delorme. G. De Teramond
Mystery of Lynne Court. J. S. Fletcher
Mystery of Madeline Le Blanc. M. Ehrmann
Mystery of Mademoiselle. W. LeQueux
Mystery of Magdalen. Mrs. C. Kernahan
Mystery of Major Molineau, and Human Repentends. M. Clarke
Mystery of Mallowmarsh. Anonymous
Mystery of Mandeville Square. G. Campbell
Mystery of Mar Saba. J. H. Hunter
Mystery of Margaret. O. Read
Mystery of Marlborough House. Anonymous
Mystery of Martha's Vineyard. G. Dyer
Mystery of Martin Guerre. J. G. Sarasin
Mystery of Mary Anne and other stories. G. R. Sims
Mystery of Mary Hamilton. Roland Daniel
Mystery of Maybury Manor. Eric Wood
Mystery of Mayfair. J. S. Winter
Mystery of Me...? W. J. Elliott
Mystery of Mere Hall. Mrs. C. Kernahan
Mystery of Merlyn Mansions. W. Shute
Mystery of Metropolisville. E. Eggleston
Mystery of Milford Haven. Taffrail
Mystery of Mirbridge. J. Payn

Mystery of Miriam. J. W. Johnston
Mystery of Miss Motte. C. A. Mason
Mystery of Mr. Bernard Brown. E. P. Oppenheim
Mystery of Mr. Cross. C. Robbins
Mystery of Mr. E. Drood. O. C. Kerr
Mystery of Mr. Jessop. E. R. Punshon
Mystery of Mr. Mock. R. A. J. Walling
Mystery of Mr. X. S. Horler
Mystery of Mr. X. M. Porlock
Mystery of Mrs. Blencarrow. M. Oliphant
Mystery of Mitcham Common. Gwyn Evans
Mystery of Moat Farm. J. Hunter
Mystery of Monastery Farm. H. R. Naylor
Mystery of Monkswood. Mrs. Lodge
Mystery of M. Felix. B. L. Farjeon
Mystery of Monte Carlo. W. M. Graydon
Mystery of Moor Manor. F. W. Irwin
Mystery of Mortimer Strange. A. W. Marchmont
Mystery of Mostyn Manor. A. W. A'Beckett
Mystery of Mouldy Manor. T. Westgate
Mystery of Murray Davenport. R. N. Stephens
Mystery of Mynd. W. Statham
Mystery of Myrtle Cottage. O. Crawford
Mystery of Nelson's Coat. E. M. Keate
Mystery of New Orleans. W. M. H. Holcombe
Mystery of New York Bay. Old Sleuth
Mystery of Nine. W. LeQueux
Mystery of Norman's Court. J. Chancellor
Mystery of North Fortune. George Douglas
Mystery of Number Five. F. J. Whaley
Mystery of No. 47. J. S. Clouston
Mystery of No. 1. S. Horler
Mystery of No. 7 Bitton Court. P. Quiroule
Mystery of No. 13. H. B. Mathers
Mystery of No. 13 Caversham Square. P. Quiroule
Mystery of Oldham. L. Bidston
Mystery of One Night. Old Sleuth
Mystery of Orchard House. J. Coggin
Mystery of Orcival. E. Gaboriau
Mystery of Orleton Manor. R. Jewell
Mystery of Paul Chadwick. J. W. Postgate
Mystery of Pauline's Lady. M. V. Woodgate
Mystery of Philip Bennion's Death. R. Marsh
Mystery of Pine Point. K. Norris
Mystery of Rapallo. Courtenay Pollock
Mystery of Redmarsh Farm. A. Marshall
Mystery of Renille Castle. L. H. Shorey
Mystery of Roaring Meg. B. L. Farjeon
Mystery of Rodney's Cove. E. S. Brooks
Mystery of Roger Bullock. T. Gallon
Mystery of St. Dunstans. T. Wright
Mystery of St. James' Park. J. E. Bloundelle-Burton
Mystery of St. Martin's Copse. Beatrix Hughes
Mystery of St. Michael's. G. Thorne
Mystery of St. Rule's. E. F. Heddle
Mystery of Saligo Bay. M. Pemberton
Mystery of Sett. J. Cowdroy
Mystery of Sheldon Bars. I. L. Cassilis
Mystery of Sherwood Towers. D. W. Steward
Mystery of Simeon Blount. A. G. Pearson
Mystery of Spider Lake. L. McFarlane
Mystery of Squadron X. W. Tyrer
Mystery of Stephen Claverton & Co. H. Knight
Mystery of Suicide Place. A. M. Miller
Mystery of Sun Dial Court. M. Wickes
Mystery of Sunny Fowt. P. Lee
Mystery of Swordfish Reef. A. W. Upfield
Mystery of Tara Heston. J. L. Rickard
Mystery of the Abandoned Cottage. W. M. Graydon
Mystery of the Abbe Montrose. S. Elvestad
Mystery of the African Expedition. R. Hardinge
Mystery of the African Farm. R. Hardinge
Mystery of the African Mine. R. Hardinge
Mystery of the "Agony" Advert. J. W. Bobin
Mystery of the Albanian Avenger. W. W. Sayer
Mystery of the American Envoy. J. Hunter
Mystery of the Amorous Music Master. G. Woden
Mystery of the Arab Agent. W. Jardine
Mystery of the Ashes. A. Wynne
Mystery of the Aztec Chain. John Norman
Mystery of the Baghdad Chest. A. Christie
Mystery of the Bankrupt Estate. A. Parsons
Mystery of the Barranca. H. Whitaker
Mystery of the Barren Lands. R. Cullum

Mystery of the Black Abbot. T. J. Kelly
Mystery of the Black Dagger. P. Elliott
Mystery of the Black Gate. B. G. Quin
Mystery of the Black Tower. J. Palmer
Mystery of the Blackmailed Baronet. H. E. Hill
Mystery of the Blitzed Tower. A. Parsons
Mystery of the Blue Inns. E. Anstey
Mystery of the Blue Train. A. Christie
Mystery of the Body on the Cliff. R. Hardinge
Mystery of the Bombed Hotel. A. Skene
Mystery of the Bombed Monastery. A. Parsons
Mystery of the Bonanza Trail. F. J. Arkins
Mystery of the Boule Cabinet. B. E. Stevenson
Mystery of the Boxing Contest. B. Hobson
Mystery of the Brompton Road. M. M. Marshall
Mystery of the Cairo Express. A. Parsons
Mystery of the Campagna, and A Shadow on a Wave. Von Degan
Mystery of the Cape Cod Players. P. A. Taylor
Mystery of the Cape Cod Tavern. P. A. Taylor
Mystery of the Cashiered Officer. G. H. Teed
Mystery of the Castle. M. S. Boyd
Mystery of the Centre-Forward. P. Gill
Mystery of the Centre-Half. Anonymous
Mystery of the Championship Belt. A. Steffens Hardy
Mystery of the Clasped Hands. G. Boothby
Mystery of the Clock. A. Murray
Mystery of the Closed Car. K. Sproul
Mystery of the Colored Circles. L. W. Badgett
Mystery of the Common. J. Blyth
Mystery of the Condemned Cottage. G. Chester
Mystery of the Confiscated Ship. G. Chester
Mystery of the Corbin Necklace. H. K. Webster
Mystery of the Corded Box. Mark Cross
Mystery of the Crashed Air LIner. G. Chester
Mystery of the Creek. J. J. Farjeon
Mystery of the Creeping Man. F. S. Wees
Mystery of the Crested Falcon. J. Noy
Mystery of the Crime in Cabin 66. A. Christie
Mystery of the Crimson Blind. F. M. White
Mystery of the Crooked Gift. A. Parsons
Mystery of the Crooks' Contract. Anonymous
Mystery of the Crystal Skull. George M. White
Mystery of the "David M". D. W. MacArthur
Mystery of the Dead Man's Wallet. J. G. Brandon
Mystery of the Dead Police. M. Porlock
Mystery of the Demobilized Soldier. G. Chester
Mystery of the Derelict. J. G. Rowe
Mystery of the Deserted Camp. J. Drummond
Mystery of the Devil Mask. R. Hardinge
Mystery of the Diamond Belt. L. Carlton
Mystery of the Docks. W. M. Graydon
Mystery of the Dope Den. J. W. Bobin
Mystery of the Double Burglary. G. Chester
Mystery of the Dover Road. W. M. Graydon
Mystery of the Downs. J. R. Watson
Mystery of the East Wind. D. Marfield
Mystery of the Egyptian Museum. Lucy Carlton
Mystery of the Elms. S. W. Judge
Mystery of the Engraved Skull. S. Hope
Mystery of the Evil Eye. A. Wynne
Mystery of the Fairlight Diamonds. A. W. Bradley
Mystery of the Fast Mail. B. D. Adsit
Mystery of the Fiddling Cracksman. H. S. Keeler
Mystery of the Fifth Tulip. D. Deane
Mystery of the Fifth Vase. Anonymous
Mystery of the Film City. G. H. Teed
Mystery of the Five Guilty Men. J. Drummond
Mystery of the Flaming Hut. H. Best
Mystery of the Flashlight Point. A. Sharpe
Mystery of the Flying V Ranch. Hedley Scott
Mystery of the Folded Paper. H. Footner
Mystery of the Forbidden Territory. R. Hardinge
Mystery of the Four Abreast. C. R. Cooper
Mystery of the Four Fingers. F. M. White
Mystery of the Four Rooms. H. H. C. Gibbons
Mystery of the Free Frenchmen. A. Parsons
Mystery of the French Milliner. B. Thomson
Mystery of the Frightened Lady. E. Wallace
Mystery of the Furlined Cloak. C. E. Pearce
Mystery of the German Prisoner. M. Frazer
Mystery of the Girl in Blue. F. Perry
Mystery of the Girl in Green. A. Parsons

Mystery of the Glass Cullet. B. Atkey
Mystery of the Golconda. W. N. Vaile
Mystery of the Gold Box. V. Williams
Mystery of the Gold Bricks. Anonymous
Mystery of the Golden Angel. F. Grierson
Mystery of the Golden Chalice. W. M. Graydon
Mystery of the Golden Palomino. J. Jenkins
Mystery of the Golden Wings. Rosa Lambert
Mystery of the Greek Exile. G. Chester
Mystery of the Green Bottle. J. G. Brandon
Mystery of the Green Car. A. Weissl
Mystery of the Green Caterpillars. J. M. Walsh
Mystery of the Green Flash. Anonymous
Mystery of the Green Garnet Murder. P. De Waal
Mystery of the Green Heart. M. Pemberton
Mystery of the Green Idol. Anonymous
Mystery of the Green Ray. W. LeQueux
Mystery of the Gregory Kotovsky. J. Pattinson
Mystery of the Grey Car. J. W. Bobin
Mystery of the Hasty Arrow. A. K. Green
Mystery of the Hated Man. J. M. Flagg
Mystery of the Haunted Square. J. Drummond
Mystery of the Head's Wife. Anonymous
Mystery of the Heart. O. Binns
Mystery of the Hidden Room. M. Harvey
Mystery of the Hope Diamond. H. L. Gates
Mystery of the Horse with the Wrong Harness. O. L. Miller
Mystery of the House of Commons. F. Hope
Mystery of the House That Wasn't There. W. C. Platts
Mystery of the Human Bookcase. W. Morton
Mystery of the Hundred Chests. A. Murray
Mystery of the Hush-Hush Factory. G. Chester
Mystery of the Hushing Pool. J. S. Fletcher
Mystery of the Hypnotic Room. Simon
Mystery of the Indian Relic. A. Parsons
Mystery of the Inn by the Shore. F. Warden
Mystery of the Iron Man. Anonymous
Mystery of the Ironworks. D. Lenton
Mystery of the Island. H. Kingsley
Mystery of the Isle of Fortune. R. C. Armour
Mystery of the Italian Ruins. D. Long
Mystery of the Kidnapped Kid. J. B. Jenkins
Mystery of the Kidnapped Munition Worker. G. Chester
Mystery of the Kneeling Woman. M. Dalton
Mystery of the Living Shadow. W. W. Sayer
Mystery of the Locked Door. E. Baird
Mystery of the Locked Room. L. Rose
Mystery of the Locks. E. W. Howe
Mystery of the Lodge. M. D. Chellis
Mystery of the London Banker. J. S. Fletcher
Mystery of the Lorry Driver. P. Urquhart
Mystery of the Lost Battle-Ship. W. W. Sayer
Mystery of the Lost Dauphin. E. P. Bazan
Mystery of the Lost Legionnaire. M. Osborne
Mystery of the Lost Loot. H. King
Mystery of the Lotus Queen. H. H. Ross
Mystery of the Louvre. A. Bernede
Mystery of the Luminous Ray. Arthur Russell
Mystery of the Lyons Mail. F. A. Edwards
Mystery of the Mad Millionaires. W. Tyrer
Mystery of the Man from Rio. G. H. Teed
Mystery of the Mandarin's Idol. W. M. Graydon
Mystery of the Mansion Fire. H. H. C. Gibbons
Mystery of the Marbletons. M. Mackin
Mystery of the Marchers. W. Edwards
Mystery of the Marshes. P. Prout
Mystery of the Marshes. H. W. Twyman
Mystery of the Masked Man. Anonymous
Mystery of the Masked Surgeon. R. C. Armour
Mystery of the Mason's Arms. A. Parsons
Mystery of the "Medea" and The Third Attempt. A. Vaughan
Mystery of the Middle Temple. R. Machray
Mystery of the Miniature. R. K. Edwards
Mystery of the Missing Angler. W. Tyrer
Mystery of the Missing Aviator. W. W. Sayer
Mystery of the Missing Constable. A. Blair
Mystery of the Missing Corpses. G. Elliott
Mystery of the Missing Doctor. C. Brisbane
Mystery of the Missing Earl. Anonymous
Mystery of the Missing Envoy. P. Quiroule

Mystery of the Missing Formula. M. Dorrell
Mystery of the Missing Journalist. W. J. Bayfield
Mystery of the Missing Refugee. H. Scott
Mystery of the Missing Sister. J. B. Jenkins
Mystery of the Missing Witness. Anonymous
Mystery of the Mixed-Up Teacher. J. B. Jenkins
Mystery of the Moat. A. Sergeant
Mystery of the Moat House. D. Vane
Mystery of the Monkey-Gland Cocktail. R. East
Mystery of the Montauk Mills. E. L. Coolidge
Mystery of the Monument. A. Blair
Mystery of the Moor. R. Saville
Mystery of the Moor. St. John Watson
Mystery of the Moving Island. Elinor Chamberlain
Mystery of the Mud Flats. M. Drake
Mystery of the Murdered Blonde. J. G. Brandon
Mystery of the Murdered Chef. R. Hardinge
Mystery of the Murdered Ice Cream Man. J. G. Brandon
Mystery of the Murdered Sentry. J. G. Brandon
Mystery of the Myrtles. E. Jepson
Mystery of the New Tenant. J. Hunter
Mystery of the "Ocean Star". W. C. Russell
Mystery of the Old Age Pensioner. G. H. Teed
Mystery of the Old Curiosity Shop. G. Chester
Mystery of the One-Day Alibi. A. Parsons
Mystery of the "Opal". R. S. Holland
Mystery of the Open Window. Anthony Gilbert
Mystery of the Outlawed Black. R. Hardinge
Mystery of the Painted Nude. W. Gore
Mystery of the Papyrus. G. B. Vale
Mystery of the Patrician Club. A. D. Vandam
Mystery of the Peacock's Eye. B. Flynn
Mystery of the Phantom Billionaire. M. J. De Lauer
Mystery of the Phantom Blackmailer. D. W. Steward
Mystery of the Phony Murder. J. B. Jenkins
Mystery of the Platinum Nugget! W. W. Sayer
Mystery of the "Polarlys". G. Simenon
Mystery of the Pot-Bank. W. J. Bayfield
Mystery of the Priest's Parlour. G. Irons
Mystery of the Purple Cloak. H. R. De Vigne
Mystery of the Purple Cloak. E. W. Terris
Mystery of the Rabbit's Paw. S. Jepson
Mystery of the Rajah's Jewels. P. Urquhart
Mystery of the Rajah's Son. H. E. Hill
Mystery of the Ravenspurs. F. M. White
Mystery of the Raymond Mortgage. F. S. Fitzgerald
Mystery of the Red Chateau. J. Hunter
Mystery of the Red Cockatoo. A. Parsons
Mystery of the Red Flame. G. Barton
Mystery of the Red Gun. A. Spence
Mystery of the Red-Haired Valet. G. Davison
Mystery of the Red Suitcase. L. M. Day
Mystery of the Red Tower. C. Brisbane
Mystery of the Red Triangle. W. C. Tuttle
Mystery of the Reunion Dinner. R. Hardinge
Mystery of the Rio Star. W. Tyrer
Mystery of the Royal Mail. B. L. Farjeon
Mystery of the Rue de Babylone. J. N. Raphael
Mystery of the Rue Soly. H. Balzac
Mystery of the S. S. Timor. G. Grantham
Mystery of the Sabotaged Jet. J. Drummond
Mystery of the Sandal-Wood Box. M. C. Barnard
Mystery of the Sandbank. S. Drew
Mystery of the Scented Death. Roy Vickers
Mystery of the Scorpion Threat. J. B. Jenkins
Mystery of the Sea. B. Stoker
Mystery of the Sea Horse. L. Falk
Mystery of the Sealed Room. V. Andrews
Mystery of the Seaside Hotel. W. J. Bayfield
Mystery of the Second Shot. J. R. Gillies
Mystery of the Seine. G. H. Teed
Mystery of the Seven. W. Usher
Mystery of the 7 Bad Men. H. L. Gates
Mystery of the Seven Cafes. S. Horler
Mystery of the Shadow. F. Hume
Mystery of the Shadowed Footballer. M. Frazer
Mystery of the Shot P.C. G. N. Philips
Mystery of the Silent Death. A. Worthing
Mystery of the Silver-Backed Hairbrush. Burton Crane
Mystery of the Silver Dagger. R. Parrish
Mystery of the Silver Run. B. Marchant

Mystery of the Singing Walls. W. A. Stowell
Mystery of the Skating Rink. H. D. Dearden
Mystery of the Skeleton Key. B. Capes
Mystery of the Skinny Sophomore. J. B. Jenkins
Mystery of the Sleeping Car Express, and other stories. F. W. Crofts
Mystery of the Smiling Doll. H. Holt
Mystery of the Smoking Gun. C. J. Daly
Mystery of the Star Sapphire. E. Fraser
Mystery of the Stolen Despatches. A. Parsons
Mystery of the Stolen Hats. B. Graeme
Mystery of the Stolen Plans. M. Coles
Mystery of the Street Musician. J. G. Brandon
Mystery of the Suez Canal. C. H. Hillcoat
Mystery of the Summer-House. H. G. Hutchinson
Mystery of the Sunken Road. R. C. Armour
Mystery of the Swamp. W. M. Graydon
Mystery of the Swanley Viaduct. G. N. Philips
Mystery of the Swindler's Stooge. W. Tyrer
Mystery of the Sycamore. C. Wells
Mystery of the Tailor's Dummy. R. Sonin
Mystery of the Tarn. C. Wells
Mystery of the Thames. F. Warden
Mystery of the Third Gable. L. Barbee
Mystery of the Third Parrot. M. Dana
Mystery of the Thirteenth Chest. P. Urquhart
Mystery of the Thirteenth Floor. L. Thayer
Mystery of the Thousand Peaks. A. Murray
Mystery of the Three Acrobats. J. G. Brandon
Mystery of the Three B Syndicate. E. Begbie
Mystery of the Three City's. J. G. Brandon
Mystery of the Three Demobbed Men. W. Tyrer
Mystery of the Three Fingers. M. Leighton
Mystery of the Tower Room. L. Despard
Mystery of the Tramp Steamer. C. Brisbane
Mystery of the Tumbling V. D. T. Lindsay
Mystery of the Turkish Agreement. W. W. Sayer
Mystery of the Twin Rubies. A. Livingston
Mystery of the Twisted Man. L. De Bechevet
Mystery of the Two-Faced Man. F. Grierson
Mystery of the 250,000 Rupees. A. Parsons
Mystery of the Underground Factory. G. Chester
Mystery of the Unicorn. W. Magnay
Mystery of the Uninvited Guest. W. Shute
Mystery of the Unknown Victim. W. Jardine
Mystery of the Vanished Trainer. J. Hunter
Mystery of the Vanishing Aerodrome. P. Conde
Mystery of the Walled Garden. A. Salcroft
Mystery of the White Knight. C. MacLeod
Mystery of the Whitehall Bomb. A. Parsons
Mystery of the Woman in Red. Anthony Gilbert
Mystery of the Woman Overboard. W. Tyrer
Mystery of the Yellow Room. G. Leroux
Mystery of Theyne Manor. W. J. Passingham
Mystery of 31, New Inn. R. A. Freeman
Mystery of Tumbling Reef. B. Grimshaw
Mystery of Tumult Rock. C. P. Hauck
Mystery of Tunnel 51. A. Wilson
Mystery of Uncle Ballard. H. D. Stacpoole
Mystery of Vaucluse. J. H. Wallis
Mystery of Victor Grayson. R. Groves
Mystery of Villa Aurelia. B. E. Stevenson
Mystery of Villa Sineste. W. Livingston
Mystery of Vincent Dane. J. L. Rickard
Mystery of White Fell Gill. H. McKay
Mystery of Witch-Face Mountain. C. E. Craddock
Mystery of Wo-Sing. A. G. Hales
Mystery of Wolverston Grange. W. R. Sunman
Mystery of Woodcroft. Anonymous
Mystery of Woodleigh Grange. Anonymous
Mystery of X04. Jack Lewis
Mystery of X20. J. G. Brandon
Mystery on Happy Bones. K. Robeson
Mystery on Southampton Water. F. W. Crofts
Mystery on the Broads. G. H. Teed
Mystery on the Centre Court. H. Willett
Mystery on the Clyde. W. M. Duncan
Mystery on the Midway. J. B. Jenkins
Mystery on the Moor. J. J. Farjeon
Mystery on the Moors. B. Michaels
Mystery on the Mount. S. Charles
Mystery on the Queen Mary. B. Graeme
Mystery on the River. B. O'Farrell
Mystery on the Snow. K. Robeson

M

Mystery Plane. J. Bolton
Mystery Play. J. C. Van Itallie
Mystery Puzzle Book. L. Wren
Mystery Puzzles. A. Ripley
Mystery Queen. F. Hume
Mystery Reef. H. Bindloss
Mystery Road. E. P. Oppenheim
Mystery Still. F. Du Boisgobey
Mystery Stories. S. Ellin
Mystery Story. D. Pirie
Mystery Street. L. Noel
Mystery Tipster. F. Johnston
Mystery Tour. D. Rutherford
Mystery Under the Sea. K. Robeson
Mystery Underground. J. J. Farjeon
Mystery Villa. E. R. Punshon
Mystery Week-End. P. Wilde
Mystery Woman. J. U. Giesy
Mystery Woman. A. MacGowan
Mystic Castle. Mr. Singer
Mystic Diagram. Nicholas Carter
Mystic Events. F. Lathom
Mystic Idol, and other stories. J. B. Brooks
Mystic Island. Renate Chapman
Mystic Lakes. D. Musello
Mystic Manor. H. G. Weston
Mystic Mullah. K. Robeson
Mystic Number Seven. Annabel Gray
Mystic Policeman. J. P. O'Neill
Mystic Rebel. R. Syvertsen
Mystic Romances of the Blue and Grey. A. C. Branscomb
Mystic Sepulchre. John Palmer, Jr.
Mystic Serpent. S. De Havilland
Mystic Tower. Anonymous
Mystic Voices. R. Pater
Mystics. K. Thurston
Myth Is Murder. Shane Martin
Myth-ing Persons. R. Asprin
Mythmaker. S. Gainham

N or M? A. Christie
N3 Conspiracy. Nick Carter
NYPD 2025. H. Stryker
Nabob and Knave. Nicholas Carter
Nabob's Jewel. C. A. Alington
Nabob's Widow. Elsie Lee
Nadine. G. Bocca
Nail of Suspicion. F. Crisp
Nailed. M. Litchfield
Nails. R. L. Hill
Naira Power. B. Emecheta
Nairobi Nightcap. D. Fearon
Naja. J. J. Savarin
Naked and Alone. Michael Lawrence
Naked and the Damned. R. Shafer
Naked and the Innocent. W. Ard
Naked and the Lost. F. M. Davis
Naked Angel. J. Webb
Naked Bishop. M. J. Sagola
Naked Blade. P. Saxon
Naked Blade, Naked Gun. A. Kilgore
Naked Canvas. Warwick Scott
Naked City. C. Einstein
Naked City. M. Wald
Naked Cloth. L. Harper
Naked Country. M. East
Naked Crusader. F. Archer
Naked Curse. D. Haring
Naked Ebony. D. Cushman
Naked Edge. M. Ehrlich
Naked Eye. Henrietta Martin
Naked Eye. W. J. Reynolds
Naked Face. Sidney Sheldon
Naked Fear. J. Farr
Naked Five. V. France
Naked Foot. H. Kaner
Naked from a Well. W. A. Ballinger
Naked Fury. D. Keene
Naked Heart. J. Briskin
Naked Hours. Wenzell Brown
Naked Hunter. W. Woolfolk
Naked in the Dark. G. Paul
Naked in the Night. J. Cleary

Naked in the Streets. R. Johnson
Naked Island. B. Heatter
Naked Jungle. H. Whittington
Naked Kiss. S. Fuller
Naked Lady. M. Corrigan
Naked Land. H. Innes
Naked Liar. H. Adams
Naked Light. J. Moffatt
Naked Mistress. W. Deptula
Naked Morning. R. V. Cassill
Naked Murder. P. Erskine
Naked Murderer. E. Piper
Naked Nemesis. K. Conway
Naked Nuns. Colin Watson
Naked Once More. Elizabeth Peters
Naked Runner. F. Clifford
Naked She Died. D. Tracy
Naked Skier. C. Short
Naked Souls. B. Johns
Naked Spur. A. Ullman
Naked Storm. S. Eisner
Naked Streets. Paul Daniels
Naked Sun. I. Asimov
Naked Sun. T. Willis
Naked Target. D. Haring
Naked Tide. Roderic Hastings
Naked to My Enemy. H. Jobson
Naked to My Pride. H. Rigsby
Naked to My Grave. H. Carmichael
Naked Typist. J. P. Hailey
Naked Villainy. Joe Barry
Naked Villainy. C. G. Hodges
Naked Villainy. Sara Woods
Naked Villany. J. Davey
Naked When We Die. T. Martin
Nakia. L. Hays
Name for Evil. A. Lyttle
Name Is Archer. J. R. Macdonald
Name Is Chambers. H. Kane
Name Is Jordan. H. Q. Masur
Name Is Judas. R. Gaines
Name Is Malone. C. Rice
Name Is Smith. Eric North
Name My Own. C. Holicker
Name of Action. G. Greene
Name of Annabel Lee. J. Symons
Name of the Game. D. Cory
Name of the Game Is Death. D. J. Marlowe
Name of the Game Is Death. C. Richardson
Name of the Game Is Murder. E. Asinof
Name of the Rose. U. Eco
Name the Woman. A. M. Williamson
Name with a Stain. Anonymous
Name Your Poison. H. Reilly
Nameless. Ramsey Campbell
Nameless Coffin. Gwendoline Butler
Nameless Corpse. C. B. Kelland
Nameless Crime. W. S. Masterman
Nameless Dread. J. K. Stafford
Nameless Five. A. Skene
Nameless Man. F. Du Boisgobey
Nameless Man. N. S. Lincoln
Nameless One. R. Temperley
Nameless Ones. L. Egan
Nameless Ones. R. T. M. Scott
Nameless Ones. L. Vardre
Nameless Order. Dargon
Nameless Road. S. Harvester
Nameless Stranger and What Happened to Flaunce. B. Reynolds
Nameless Thing. M. D. Post
Names. D. De Lillo
Name's Death, Remember Me? S. Forbes
Name's Maguire. R. Himmel
Nana. Delacorta
Nana's Talisman. M. Ashton
Nancy. N. Baroni
Nancy Lee, Mill Lass. H. E. Inman
Nancy Manouvres. C. Gleig
Nancy, the Daring. K. Kimbrough
Nanny. D. Greenburg
Nanny. E. Piper
Nantucket Diet Murders. V. Rich
Nantucket Soap Opera. S. F. X. Dean

Nap on Nighthawk. S. Horler
Napa Valley Mystery. J. Ruyle
Napalm Bugle. E. Lacy
Naples, or Die! H. Chesham
Napoleon Boswell. H. H. Malleson
Napoleon of the Press. M. Leighton
Napoleon Ring. A. Lowing
Napoleon Smith. W. J. Arkell
NARC. R. Hawkes
Narc. S. L. Stebel
Narcissus in the Way. G. V. McFadden
Narcissus Murders. XV8
Narcs. R. Coram
Narka. G. Ramsay
Narka the Nihilist. G. Ramsay
Narracong Riddle. A. Derleth
Narrow Cell. Dale Clark
Narrow Corner. B. Copper
Narrow Escape. Annie Thomas
Narrow Exit. P. Henissart
Narrow Gauge to Murder. Carolyn Thomas
Narrow House. H. Fernsee
Narrow Margin. R. Fleischer
Narrow Road. Robin Moore
Narrow Search. A. Garve
Narrowing Circle. H. Hill
Narrowing Circle. J. Symons
Narrowing Lust. G. Baxter
Narrowing Lust. H. Kane
Narrowing Stream. John Mortimer
Nashville with a Bullet. B. Sadler
Nasty Bit of Murder. C. F. Roe
Nasty Cropper. G. F. Underhill
Nasty Name Murders. R. Howes
Nasty Piece of Work. R. Croft-Cooke
Nasty Things. A. Lovegrove
Nat Foster, the Boston Detective. H. Rockwood
Nat Wedgewood, Jockey. J. Fairfax-Blakeborough
Natalie Limited. P. Trent
Natasha. C. W. Thayer
Nathanial. J. Saul
Nation Within. F. Fytton
Nation's Missing Guest. H. Footner
Nation's Peril. Nicholas Carter
Native Son. Paul Green
Native Son. R. Wright
Native Superstition. H. C. McNeile
Natural Causes. H. Cecil
Natural Causes. T. Gallagher
Natural Causes. J. Valin
Natural Enemies. W. Adler
Natural Enemy. J. Langton
Natural Prey. E. Mathis
Natural Victims. I. Eberstadt
Natural Weapon. G. Mitchelmore
Nature of a Crime. J. Conrad
Nature of the Beast. Melvin King
Nature of the Beast. M. MacGowan
Nature's Nobility. J. Newall
Naughty But Dead. G. G. Fickling
Naughty Girls. Arthur Wise
Naughty Maid of Mitcham. D. Donovan
Naval Adventuress. P. Trent
Naval Detective's Chase. Anonymous
Naval Detective's Chase. N. Buntline
Navona 1000. M. Arrighi
Navy Colt. F. Gruber
Navy in Action. Taffrail
Navy Murders. W. Chambers
Navy Spy Murders. G. F. Eliot
Nazi Assassins. D. Cory
Nazi Hunter. M. Mandell
Nazi Hunter. B. Shaw
Nazi Overcoat. R. Lebherz
Nazi Shadows. E. L. Fleming
Nazi Speedway Plot. E. T. Woodhall
Nazi Spy in Berlin. E. Rees
Nazi Spy Murders. G. W. Jones
Nazi's Wife. P. Watson
Near Closing Time. Betty Smith
Nearest and Dearest. E. Southworth
Nearing Storm. D. Donnelly
Nearly Four. E. Coles
Nearness of Evil. C. Mills

Title Index

Neat Little Corpse. Max Murray
Neath Austral Skies. L. Becke
Neath the Southern Cross. K. Lindsay
Nebraska Nightmare. B. Ham
Nebraska Quotient. W. J. Reynolds
Nebulon Horror. H. B. Cave
Nebuly Coat. J. M. Falkner
Necessary. K. Jackson
Necessary Action. P. Wahloo
Necessary Corpse. R. C. Woodthorpe
Necessary Dealing. Roy Lewis
Necessary Doubt. Colin Wilson
Necessary End. Anthea Fraser
Necessary End. V. Gielgud
Necessary End. S. Harper
Necessary End. Peter Robinson
Necessary Evil. K. Roos
Necessity. B. Garfield
Neck and Neck. L. Bruce
Neck in a Noose. E. Ferrars
Neck of Sinners. H. Spencer
Necklace. B. Vane
Necklace and Calabash. R. Van Gulik
Necklace of Death. H. Holt
Necklace of Parmona. L. T. Meade
Necklace of Skulls. I. Drummond
Necktie for Norman. J. L. Morrissey
Necromancer. L. Flammenberg
Necropolis. B. Copper
Necroscope. B. Lumley
Ned Bachman, the New Orleans Detective. Alan Dale
Ned Kelly. C. Hayter
Need a Body Tell? B. Cobb
Need to Kill. M. Pettit
Need to Know. W. Haggard
Needful Journey. Winifred Duke
Needle. Hal Clement
Needle. H. N. Field
Needle. Francis King
Needle. J. A. Potter
Needle in a Haystack. G. Joseph
Needle That Wouldn't Hold Still. Hampton Stone
Needle Track. P. Conway
Needlepoint. S. Chase
Needles. W. Deverell
Needle's Eye. Edward Lee
Needle's Kiss. Seamark
Needles of Death. P. Edwards
Needy Nine. Nicholas Carter
Nefarious Quest. H. Janson
Negative in Blue. Carter Brown
Negative Man. R. C. Galwey
Negative of a Murder. C. E. Fitch
Negative of a Nude. C. E. Fritch
Negative Value. J. Boland
Negatives. P. Everett
Neglected Clue. I. Ostrander
Neglected Fire. H. Horn
Negotiator. F. Forsyth
Negotiator. Clayton Matthews
Negotiator. R. M. Rogers
Negro. G. Simenon
Negrohead. R. Bridges
Neighbor. L. Koenig
Neighborhood Watch. M. Lazarus
Neighbors. M. Allwright
Neighbors. G. Simenon
Neil Nelson, the Veteran Detective. H. Rockwood
Neila Sen and My Casual Death. J. H. Connelly
Neither a Candle Nor a Pitchfork. J. Porter
Neither Do I Condemn Thee. A. Soutar
Neither Five Nor Three. Helen MacInnes
Neither Had I Rest. N. Cromarty
Neither Man Nor Dog. G. Kersh
Neither the Sea Nor the Sand. G. Honeycombe
Nell. S. Nichols
Nell Alone. Jennie Melville
Nell Gwyn's Diamonds. I. Hooper
Nella. J. Godey
Nella Waits. M. Millhiser
Nellie, the Obvious. K. Kimbrough
Nellie Was a Lady. J. Kirkpatrick
Nelly Jocelyn, Widow. J. Middlemass

Nelson Lee in the Navy. Maxwell Scott
Nelson Lee's Pupil. Maxwell Scott
Nelson Lee's Rival. Maxwell Scott
Nelson Lord—One of Our Agents. G. Windsor
Nelson Touch. N. Grant
Nelson's Blood. G. Kent
Nemarluck King of the Wilds. I. L. Idriess
Nemesis. J. Bedford
Nemesis. A. Christie
Nemesis. J. M. Cobban
Nemesis. P. Davis
Nemesis. G. Lovisi
Nemesis. Rosamund Smith
Nemesis at Raynham Parva. J. J. Connington
Nemesis Club. Jenny Savage
Nemesis Club. W. W. Sayer
Nemesis Conjecture. William Cooke
Nemesis Wife. C. L. Evans
Nemesis Wore Nylons. Carter Brown
Nemo. T. Douglas
Nemo, the Shadow Detective. F. L. Broughton
Neon Caesar. M. McGarrity
Neon Flamingo. W. R. Philbrick
Neon Flamingo. Matt Taylor
Neon Graveyard. G. Baxt
Neon Haystack. J. M. Ullman
Neon Jungle. J. D. MacDonald
Neon Madman. J. Harvey
Neon Mirage. M. A. Collins
Neon Preacher. R. Chambers
Neon Rainbow. C. Terrot
Neon Tough. T. Kenrick
Neopolitan Reel. G. Dowling
Neopolitan Streak. T. Holme
Neptune. N. Gerson
Neptune's Son. R. S. Holland
Nerissa Claire Case. H. Waugh
Nero's Luck. J. Kisner
Nerve. D. Francis
Nerve Beat. J. B. O'Sullivan
Nerve Centre. H. Janson
Nerve Endings. W. Martin
Nerve of Foley, and other railroad stories. F. H. Spearman
Nervestorm. M. Sharland
Nervous Affair. K. Wilhelm
Nervous Laughter. E. W. Emerson
Nervous Miss Miles. M. Short
Nervous Wreck. Owen Davis
Nesbit's Compact. P. Trent
Nest-Egg for the Baron. Anthony Morton
Nest of Fear. H. Ellson
Nest of Hawks. J. T. Osborne
Nest of Rats. J. Wainwright
Nest of Spies. Geoffrey Davison
Nest of Spies. P. Souvestre
Nest of Traitors. G. Ashe
Nest of Vipers. T. Claymore
Nest of Vipers. Wallace Crawford
Nest of Vultures. Robert MacLeod
Net. R. Beach
Net. J. Pudney
Net. E. Ronns
Net Around Joan Ingilby. A. Fielding
Net of Cobwebs. E. S. Holding
Net of Fear. R. W. Hunter
Nether Millstone. F. M. White
Netley Abbey. Richard Warner
Nets of Fate. H. Ellson
Nets to Catch the Wind. D. Hitchens
Netta. F. M. White
Nettle. E. Wooll
Nettle Shade. J. Turner
Network. Godfrey Smith
Network. L. Staig
Network. Roderic Wilkinson
Network of Crime. Nicholas Carter
Network of Fear. A. Yudkoff
Neuromancer. W. Gibson
Neutron Beam Murder. T. J. King
Neutron Nightmare. L. Derrick
Neutron Star. L. Niven
Neutron Two Is Critical. L. Dunning
Nevada Alibi. Dan Morgan

Nevada Detective. Anonymous
Nevada Gunslinger. V. Coffman
Nevada Nightmare. N. Winski
Never a Dull Moment. P. Cheyney
Never Again! W. B. Cooke
Never Again. Francis King
Never Ask a Policeman. D. J. Olivy
Never Be Caught. J. McKimmey
Never Bet Your Life. G. H. Coxe
Never by Chance. Sylvia Tate
Never Call It Loving. D. Eden
Never Come Back. J. Mair
Never Contract. D. Gerrity
Never Cross a Vampire. S. M. Kaminsky
Never Die Alone. D. Goines
Never Die in Honolulu. I. Hamilton
Ne'er-Do-Well. D. Yates
Never-Fail Blake. A. Stringer
Never-Fail Detective. H. Holmes
Never Fight a Lady. S. Truss
Never Fire First. J. Dorrance
Never Forget, Never Forgive. C. Fox
Never Forgive, Never Forget. J. Persico
Never Give a Millionaire an Even Break. H. Kane
Never Go Dark. E. Bonett
Never Had a Chance. R. Farran
Never Had a Spanner on Her. J. Leasor
Never Hit a Lady. F. S. Tobey
Never in Vain. J. L. Hardy
Never Kill a Client. B. Halliday
Never Kill a Cop! M. Colton
Never Kill a Cop. L. Costigan
Never Kill a Cop. J. B. West
Never Kill for Sport. J. L. Richard
Never Leave My Bed. J. T. Rogers
Never Live Twice. D. J. Marlowe
Never Look Back. J. Aeby
Never Look Back. H. Carter
Never Look Back. M. G. Eberhart
Never Look Back. R. Pearson
Never Love a Stranger. H. Robbins
Never Mind the Lady. D. Garth
Never Mix Business with Pleasure. B. Graeme
Never Need an Enemy. A. M. Stein
Never Never End. H. S. Gregg
Never No Third Degree. J. W. Bayly
Never Paint a Stranger. Patricia Shaw
Never Pick Up Hitchhikers. Ellis Peters
Never Put Off Till Tomorrow What You Can Kill Today. J. Godey
Never Quite Dead. S. Shubin
Never Say Dead. E. Kennedy
Never Say Die. E. Foote-Smith
Never Say Die. M. Malmer
Never Say Die. M. K. Ozaki
Never Say Die. I. S. Shriber
Never Say Live! David Hume
Never Say No. R. Drayton
Never Say No to a Killer. J. Gant
Never Shake a Skeleton. A. Flett
Never Shoot a Lady. E. Hale
Never Smile at Children. E. T. French
Never Step on a Rainbow. W. Wolfe
Never Summer Mystery. T. Perry
Never Take Candy from a Stranger. R. Garis
Never to Die. Alice Brennan
Never Too Rich. J. Gould
Never Trust a Dame. C. Wheatley
Never Trust a Woman. Raymond Marshall
Never Turn Your Back. A. Capelli
Never Turn Your Back. M. Scherf
Never Wake a Dead Man. B. Bird
Never Walk Alone. R. King
Never Walk Behind Me. L. Summerfield
Never-Was Girl. Carter Brown
Never Wed an Old Man. H. Caswell
Nevermore. R. Boldrewood
Nevermore Affair. K. Wilhelm
Nevlo. K. Robeson
Nevsky's Demon. D. Gat
Nevsky's Return. D. Gat
New Adventures of Ellery Queen. E. Queen
New Adventures of Sherlock Holmes. A. C. Doyle
New Andromeda. C. Dawe

New Arabian Nights. R. L. Stevenson
New Blood. R. Salem
New Bodies for Old. M. Renard
New Border Tales. George Douglas
New Breed. L. Costigan
New Centurions. J. Wambaugh
New Chronicles of Don Q. K. Prichard
New Departure. K. Connor
New Detective Stories. G. Campbell
New England Gothic. A. J. Allen
New Exploits of Nick Carter. Nicholas Carter
New Face in Hell. R. Busby
New Friend. R. Eden
New Girl Friend. R. Rendell
New Guinea Gold. R. Whitley
New Gulliver and other stories. B. Pain
New Gun Runners. Neil Gordon
New Hope for the Dead. C. Willeford
New Idol. G. Leroux
New Improved Murder. E. Gorman
New Jack Sheppard. E. A. Treeston
New Jersey Showdown. R. Mallory
New Kind of Killer. Jennie Melville
New Kind of Killer, an Old Kind of Death. Jennie Melville
New Kind of War. Anthony Price
New Leaf, and other stories. J. Ritchie
New Lease of Death. R. Rendell
New Lease of Life. G. Simenon
New Lease on Life. G. Simenon
New Leash on Death. S. Conant
New Made Grave. H. Footner
New Magdalen. W. Collins
New Man in Lowuni. J. Fores
New Master. A. Golsworthy
New Mexico Connection. C. Wilcox
New Mistress. G. M. Fenn
New Mrs. Aldrich. V. Stuart
New Mrs. Ranier. E. Burfield
New Monk. R. S.
New Moon. Taffrail
New Order. M. Gerard
New Orleans Holocaust. P. McCurtin
New Orleans Knockout. D. Pendleton
New Orleans Mourning. Julie Smith
New Orleans Wildcat. S. Markham
New Othello. I. D. Hardy
New People at the Hollies. Josephine Bell
New Plays for Mummers. Glenn Hughes
New Race Diplomatist. J. B. Waterbury
New Rivers Calling. J. B. Hendryx
New Serpent in Eden. Nicholas Carter
New Shining White Murder. D. Launay
New Shoe. A. W. Upfield
New Sonia Wayward. M. Innes
New Tenant. E. P. Oppenheim
New Terror. G. Leroux
New Vigilantes. J. D. Horan
New War Book. D. Pendleton
New Year Resolution. A. Cairns
New Year's Eve at the Golden Elbow. E. Heu
New Year's Eve in Lan-Fang. R. Van Gulik
New York by Night. H. Belmar
New York Connection. Robin Moore
New York Consuelo. Anonymous
New York Dance. D. E. Westlake
New York Detective. William Marshall
New York Detective. Old Sleuth
New York Detective Police Officer. J. B. Williams
New York Mystery. E. S. Brooks
New York Necromancy. M. Macao
New York, New York. S. Kahn
New York One. Lawrence Levine
Newgate. T. P. Prest
Newhaven-Dieppe. G. Simenon
Newman Factor. J. S. Prager
News Caper. R. Jansson
News from the Duchy. A. T. Quiller-Couch
News Girl. H. Brand
News of Murder. A. Lejeune
News of Paul Temple. F. Durbridge
News Reel. R. J. Casey
News Travels by Night. B. Graeme
Newsdeath. Ray Connolly

Newshound's Nemesis. R. Kirby
Newspaper Girl. A. M. Williamson
Newspaper Murders. Joe Gash
Newspaper Seller's Secret. W. Edwards
Next. B. Randall
Next, After Lucifer. D. Rhodes
Next Best Thing. John Ralston Saul
Next Door. F. Hume
Next Door Neighbors. W. P. Ridge
Next Door to Danger. C. MacLeod
Next Door to Death. B. Cobb
Next Door to Murder. L. Cargill
Next Man. M. Z. Lewin
Next of Kin. M. G. Eberhart
Next of Kin. G. Goodchild
Next o'Kin. W. M. Graydon
Next of Kin. W. B. Murphy
Next One to Die. V. Gunn
Next, Please. J. M. Walsh
Next Saturday in Milan. W. Tute
Next Stop—the Morgue. B. Winter
Next Time I'll Pay My Own Fare. R. V. Beste
Next Time, You'll Wake Up Dead. Philip Evans
Next to Die. R. Fliegel
Next to Die. J. Godey
Next to Die. G. Verner
Next-to-Last Train Ride. C. Dennis
Next Victim. Donald Stuart
Nguy-Hiem War Zone. J. Lansing
Nhu Sting. E. Helm
Nibbled to Death by Ducks. Robert Campbell
Nic Barker I.D.B. D. Brechin
Nic Revel. G. M. Fenn
Nice and Easy. David Miles
Nice Bloke. C. Cookson
Nice Class of Corpse. S. Brett
Nice Class of People. A. La Bern
Nice Cup of Tea. Anthony Gilbert
Nice Day for a Funeral. H. Howard
Nice Day for a Murder. B. Adamson
Nice Day for a Murder. V. Gunn
Nice Day for Murder. F. Murray
Nice Derangement of Epitaphs. Ellis Peters
Nice Enough to Murder. E. S. Russell
Nice Fillies Finish Last. B. Halliday
Nice Friendly Town. H. Calvin
Nice Girl Like You. R. Wormser
Nice Girl's Story. Rosemary Harris
Nice Guy Like Me. E. Cannon
Nice Guys Don't Win. S. Mitchell
Nice Guys Finish Dead. Albert Conroy
Nice Guys Finish Last. R. Kyle
Nice Knight for Murder. P. Daniels
Nice Lady. M. Hayman
Nice Little Beach Town. E. C. Ward
Nice Little Business. E. Dewhurst
Nice Little Killing. Anthony Gilbert
Nice Murder for Mom. J. Yaffe
Nice Murderer. D. Delman
Nice Neighborhood. E. Bahr
Nice People Don't Kill. F. W. Bronson
Nice People Murder. M. H. Bradley
Nice People Poison. M. H. Bradley
Nice Place to Die. M. Culpan
Nice Place to Visit. H. Garner
Nice Quiet Girl. Philip Daniels
Nice Sound Alibi. P. Lauben
Nice Way to Die. H. Janson
Nice Way to Die. M. Warner
Nice Weekend for a Murder. M. A. Collins
Nice Young Man. W. L. Harter
Nicest Corpse. John Morgan
Nicholas Goade, Detective. E. P. Oppenheim
Nicholas Lattermole's Case. C. Barry
Nicholas Snatch. P. Malloch
Nichovev Plot. Nick Carter
Nick Bigelow. Anonymous
Nick Carter and the Green Goods Men. Nicholas Carter
Nick Carter and the Red Button. Nicholas Carter
Nick Carter, Detective. Nicholas Carter
Nick Carter Down East. Nicholas Carter
Nick Carter's Auto Trail. Nicholas Carter
Nick Carter's Chance Clue. Nicholas Carter

Nick Carter's Chinese Puzzle. Nicholas Carter
Nick Carter's Cipher. Nicholas Carter
Nick Carter's Clever Protege. Nicholas Carter
Nick Carter's Close Call. Nicholas Carter
Nick Carter's Close Finish. Nicholas Carter
Nick Carter's Convict Client. Nicholas Carter
Nick Carter's Counterplot. Nicholas Carter
Nick Carter's Death Warrant. Nicholas Carter
Nick Carter's Double Catch. Nicholas Carter
Nick Carter's Egyptian Clew. Nicholas Carter
Nick Carter's Fall. Nicholas Carter
Nick Carter's Girl Detective. Nicholas Carter
Nick Carter's Intuition. Nicholas Carter
Nick Carter's Last Card. Nicholas Carter
Nick Carter's Masterpiece. Nicholas Carter
Nick Carter's Menace. Nicholas Carter
Nick Carter's New Assistant. Nicholas Carter
Nick Carter's Persistence. Nicholas Carter
Nick Carter's Promise. Nicholas Carter
Nick Carter's Retainer. Nicholas Carter
Nick Carter's Roundup. Nicholas Carter
Nick Carter's Star Pupil. Nicholas Carter
Nick Carter's Subtle Foe. Nicholas Carter
Nick Carter's Swim to Victory. Nicholas Carter
Nick Carter's Treasure Chest Case. Nicholas Carter
Nick Carter's Wildest Chase. Nicholas Carter
Nick of the Woods. T. Taggart
Nick of Time. W. T. Hickman
Nick the Click. G. K. Wilkinson
Nick Westerman, Detective. A. L. Yates
Nickel Jackpot. J. J. Lamb
Nickel Ride. M. T. Kaufman
Nicky Nimble. Anonymous
Nicola. D. Daniels
Nicola. A. E. Lindop
Nicole. J. H. Hull
Nicolette of the Quarter. V. MacClure
Niece of Abraham Pein. J. H. Wallis
Nig-Nog. E. Wallace
Nigel Ferrard. G. M. Robins
Nigel Fortescue. W. Westall
Night-Action! S. M. Parkman
Night After Night. S. Thurman
Night After the Wedding. The Gordons
Night Air Is Dangerous. Sutherland Scott
Night and Fog. A. Gask
Night and Fog. K. Netzen
Night and Fog. G. St. Germain
Night & Green Ginger. D. Lockwood
Night and Morning. E. Bulwer-Lytton
Night and Morning. Old Sleuth
Night and No Moon. J. Odlum
Night and the City. G. Kersh
Night and the City. D. Lambert
Night and the Judgement. L. Butler
Night Angel. Kate Green
Night Assassin. M. B. Dix
Night at Club Bagdad. O. F. Jerome
Night at Hogwallow. T. Strauss
Night at Krumlin Castle. Frank King
Night at Lost End. G. A. Chamberlain
Night at Sea Abbey. V. Coffman
Night at the Mocking Widow. Carter Dickson
Night at the Vulcan. N. Marsh
Night Attack. L. Crosby
Night Bait. P. Straker
Night Beat. Arthur MacLean
Night Beat. H. Vogel
Night Before Christmas. L. Perelman
Night Before Dark. Clodagh Chapman
Night Before Dying. R. M. Coates
Night Before Murder. S. Fisher
Night Before the Wedding. The Gordons
Night-Blooming Cereus. J. Hadley
Night Boat. T. Trent
Night Boat from Puerto Vedra. Donald MacKenzie
Night Boat to Paris. R. Jessup
Night Call. P. Merriman
Night Call from a Distant Time Zone. H. Lieberman
Night Caller. B. Patrick
Night Callers. F. Crisp
Night Calls. Rex Anderson
Night Calls. Tony Miller

Title Index

Night Chant. C. Woods
Night Child. C. De Blasis
Night Chills. D. R. Koontz
Night Club. P. Cheyney
Night Club. G. Simenon
Night-Club Crime. A. Skene
Night Club Honey. Pete Costello
Night Club Lady. A. Abbot
Night Club Moll. N. Baroni
Night Club Murder. J. G. Brandon
Night Club Murder. Roland Daniel
Night Club Murder. J. A. Jordan
Night Club Mystery. E. Jordan
Night-Club Mystery. G. H. Teed
Night Coach. "Capstan"
Night Comer. Jack Wilson
Night-Comers. E. Ambler
Night Cover. M. Z. Lewin
Night Cries. T. Krueger
Night Crime. D. R. Dunn
Night Crossing. K. Kolb
Night Cry. R. Dudgeon
Night Cry. W. L. Stuart
Night Dancer. W. T. Taunton
Night Darkens the Streets. A. La Bern
Night Drop. F. C. Davis
Night Encounter. Anthony Gilbert
Night Exercise. J. Rhode
Night Express. N. Jackson
Night Express Murder. L. A. Knight
Night Extra. W. P. McGivern
Night Falls at Bitterhill. P. Warren
Night Falls on the City. S. Gainham
Night Falls Too Soon. F. Chimenti
Night Ferry to Death. P. Moyes
Night Fishers of Antibes. C. Leopold
Night Flight to Zurich. C. F. Gregg
Night Flower. W. C. Butler
Night for Evil. Jack Lewis
Night for Screaming. H. Whittington
Night for Treason. J. Jakes
Night Freight. J. M. Yates
Night Frost. B. Copper
Night Games. Collin Wilcox
Night Ghouls. R. Chetwynd-Hayes
Night Glow. Martin James
Night Has a Thousand Eyes. H. Astrup
Night Has a Thousand Eyes. G. Hopley
Night Has Another Voice. G. Colizzi
Night Has Eyes. E. Backhouse
Night Has Eyes. A. Kennington
Night Has Red Eyes. J. Millson
Night Hath Eyes. Andrea Hill
Night Haunts of Paris. R. Vane
Night Hawk. J. Brearley
Night Hawk. D. Cory
Night Hawk. J. R. Holden
Night Hawk. E. Jepson
Night Hawk. A. Stringer
Night Heat. D. Stivers
Night Hostess. P. Dunning
Night Hostess. J. Wingrave
Night Howl. A. Neiderman
Night Hunt. M. Rostov
Night Hunters. J. Crecy
Night Hunters. J. Miles
Night I Caught the Sante Fe Chief. E. Thorpe
Night I Died. W. Irish
Night in Boulogne. San Antonio
Night in Casablanca. D. Ames
Night in George Square. S. Fraser
Night in Glengyle. J. Ferguson
Night in Havana. R. Sylvester
Night in October. M. Callard
Night in Which All Cats Are Gray. W. S. New
Night Intruder. D. Noel
Night Intruder. P. Reakes
Night Is a Child. R. Llewellyn
Night Is a Time for Listening. E. West
Night Is a Time to Die. J. Wainwright
Night Is for Hunting. P. Barstow
Night Is for Screaming. Robert Turner
Night Is for Violence. D. Bateson
Night Is My Enemy. F. Carmichael
Night Is My Undoing. D. Jackson
Night Is So Short. M. Risco
Night Journey. Winston Graham
Night Judgment at Sinos. J. Higgins
Night Jump—Cuba. P. Runyon
Night Kill. D. Pendleton
Night Kills. E. Gorman
Night Lady. W. C. Gault
Night Launch. J. Garn
Night Letter. P. Spike
Night Lights. M. Pemberton
Night Lords. N. Freeling
Night Magic. K. Robards
Night Mail. Percy Fitzgerald
Night Mail. H. F. Wood
Night Mall Mystery. C. H. Ogilvie
Night Man. A. Ullman
Night Manhattan Burned. B. Jackson
Night Marchers. J. Shelynn
Night Mayor. Kim Newman
Night Moves. N. Roberts
Night Moves. A. Sharp
Night Music. L. Palmer
Night Must Fall. W. Drummond
Night Must Fall. Emlyn Williams
Night My Enemy. A. Maybury
Night Nemesis. F. C. Davis
Night Never Ends. F. Lorenz
Night Never Falls. B. Shrake
Night Nurse. D. Macy
Night of Camp David. F. Knebel
Night of Clear CHoice. D. M. Disney
Night of Crime. A. Livingston
Night of Dread. J. Creasey
Night of Error. D. Bagley
Night of Errors. M. Innes
Night of Evil. Genevieve St. John
Night of Fear. M. Dalton
Night of Fear. N. MacKenzie
Night of Four Hundred Rabbits. Elizabeth Peters
Night of Glass. P. Purser
Night of Horror. C. Buchanan
Night of Horror. A. Soutar
Night of January 16. A. Rand
Night of Love. B. E. M. Ward
Night of May Third. A. M. Wells
Night of Morningstar. P. O'Donnell
Night of Murder. C. Rushton
Night of Mystery. J. C. Ellis
Night of Peril. H. Bleackley
Night of Reckoning. F. Barrett
Night of Reckoning. S. Horler
Night of Reckoning. P. Ordway
Night of Reckoning. J. S. Strange
Night of Reunion. M. Allegretto
Night of Secrets. S. Warwick
Night of Secrets. J. Wetherell
Night of Shadows. E. Gorman
Night of Shadows. F. Lockridge
Night of Terror. Joy Brown
Night of Terror. H. Desmond
Night of Terror. R. Hausfeld
Night of Terror. R. H. Wilkinson
Night of the Assassin. Don Smith
Night of the Assassins. B. Rossi
Night of the Avenger. Nick Carter
Night of the Black Horror. V. Norwood
Night of the Black Tower. Michael Sinclair
Night of the Bonfire. J. Blackmore
Night of the Bowstring. D. B. Olsen
Night of the Candles. Patricia Maxwell
Night of the Condor. Nick Carter
Night of the Crime. H. Desmond
Night of the Crisis. J. Ingersol
Night of the Damned. L. Caine
Night of the Darkest Moon. J. Peart
Night of the Dead. Dana Ross
Night of the Dunce. F. Gagliano
Night of the Eagles. R. Collin
Night of the Emperor. G. Stanley
Night of the Enchantress. K. Troy
Night of the Fair. J. Baker
Night of the Falcon. J. Oxford
Night of the Fog. Anthony Gilbert
Night of the Fourth. J. Roffey
Night of the Fox. J. Gannold
Night of the Fox. Jack Higgins
Night of the Fox. J. Lee
Night of the Full Moon. J. N. Chance
Night of the Funeral. H. C. Davis
Night of the Garter Murder. R. Howes
Night of the Generals. H. H. Kirst
Night of the Good Children. M. Carleton
Night of the Griffin. E. Giles
Night of the Hawk. R. Raine
Night of the Hellebore. J. Reddoch
Night of the Horns. D. Sanderson
Night of the Hunter. D. Grubb
Night of the Jabberwock. F. Brown
Night of the Jackals. Ralph Hayes
Night of the Jaguar. M. McCray
Night of the Jaguar. Paula Paul
Night of the Juggler. W. P. McGivern
Night of the Kill. Breni James
Night of the Living Dead. J. Russo
Night of the Long Shadows. H. St. Thomas
Night of the Moonbow. T. Tryon
Night of the Moonrose. M. Lynch
Night of the Party. M. Cronin
Night of the Phantom. Marilyn Ross
Night of the Phoenix. N. De Mille
Night of the Picaroon. J. Cassells
Night of the Ranger. M. D. Harrell
Night of the Rape. L. White
Night of the Reaper. V. M. Grayland
Night of the Ripper. R. Bloch
Night of the Rose. H. Castillou
Night of the Ruby. L. Conway
Night of the Running Man. Lee Wells
Night of the Savage. G. Beare
Night of the Scorpion. S. O'Brien
Night of the Scorpion. L. Robin
Night of the Settlement. J. N. Chance
Night of the Shadow. M. Grant
Night of the Shooting Star. D. Vipond
Night of the Short Knives. B. Wilkinson
Night of the Sphinx. T. Leighton
Night of the Storm. J. Dallas
Night of the Storm. A. Gask
Night of the Storm. Magali
Night of the Stranger. J. Blackmore
Night of the 3rd Ult. H. F. Wood
Night of the Thirteenth. S. Warwick
Night of the Thugee. G. Wilson
Night of the Tiger. D. C. Cooke
Night of the Tiger. M. Kistler
Night of the Toads. Michael Collins
Night of the Tribolites. P. Leslie
Night of the Twelfth. M. Gilbert
Night of the 12th-13th. A. Steeman
Night of the 23rd. L. Jackson
Night of the Tyger. D. Klass
Night of the Visitor. R. Willock
Night of the Warheads. Nick Carter
Night of the Watchman. J. Creasey
Night of the Wedding. C. N. Williamson
Night of the Wolf. W. H. Baker
Night of the Wolf. C. Bryan
Night of the Wolf. J. Kersey
Night of the World. F. H. Rose
Night of Vengeance. A. S. Sherring
Night of Violence. P. Barrington
Night of Violence. L. Charbonneau
Night of Wenceslas. L. Davidson
Night of Wrath. Y. Smith
Night on Penwith. F. B. Clark
Night on the Bare mountain. J. D. White
Night on the Borders of the Black Forest. A. B. Edwards
Night on the Devil's Pathway. C. M. Russell
Night on the Island. M. M. Kaye
Night on the Killer Reef. A. MacVicar
Night on the Pathway. C. M. Russell
Night Operator. F. Packard
Night Over Fitch's Pond. C. Jarrett
Night Over Mexico. T. Downing
Night Over the Wood. H. Addis
Night Passage. M. K. Robertson

Night Patrol. Griff
Night People. J. Finney
Night People. D. Haring
Night Pieces. T. Burke
Night Pillow. H. C. Rae
Night Places. Martin Bell
Night Probe! C. Cussler
Night Prowlers. K. McCullough
Night Racket. B. Vane
Night Raider. M. Barry
Night Raiders. Glen Allen
Night Raiders. A. Skene
Night Ride. J. Farrell
Night Ride. Mark Ross
Night Ride and other journeys. C. Beaumont
Night Riders. R. Cullum
Night Riders. N. Tranter
Night Rituals. M. Jahn
Night Rituals. G. Paulsen
Night Run. Elizabeth Fenwick
Night Run from Java. G. Black
Night Runners. M. Serrian
Night Safe Mystery. L. Carlton
Night Sanctuary. M. Van Vooren
Night Scenes in New York. T. Pastor
Night Scream. Evelyn Harris
Night Screams. B. Pronzini
Night Search. J. Mangione
Night Secrets. T. H. Cook
Night Seekers. K. Royce
Night Shade. D. Daniels
Night Shadow. D. Daniels
Night Shadows. Colin Robertson
Night Shadows. Mary Sellers
Night She Died. D. Simpson
Night Sky. C. Francis
Night Soldiers. A. Furst
Night Spice. K. Keast
Night Spiders. J. Lymington
Night Squad. D. Goodis
Night Stalker. C. D. Luce
Night Stalker. J. Rice
Night Stalkers. Duncan Long
Night Stands at the Door. Katherine Blake
Night Stop. E. Trevor
Night Strangler. J. Rice
Night Strike. G. G. Vanhee
Night Surprise. F. Warden
Night Talk. R. Timperley
Night Tennis. A. Davis-Goff
Night the Fog Came Down. J. Bude
Night the Gods Smiled. E. Wright
Night, the Woman. S. Ransome
Night They Killed Joss Varran. G. Bellairs
Night They Murdered Chelsea. M. Hinxman
Night They Stole Manhattan. L. Orde
Night Thorn. I. Gordon
Night Tide. G. Carpenter
Night Tide. J. R. Wilmot
Night Train. Martin James
Night Train. K. Millar
Night Train to Mombasa. J. Farrington
Night Train to Paris. M. Coles
Night Trains. P. H. Fine
Night Trains. Barbara Wood
Night Trap. Colin Robertson
Night Vision. Frank King
Night Visitor. Patricia Matthews
Night Visitor and other stories. A. Bennett
Night Waking. K. Snow
Night Walk. E. Daly
Night Walker. S. Filson
Night Walker. D. Hamilton
Night Walker. S. Stuart
Night Was a Lady Crying. K. Slattery
Night Was Dark. J. Reach
Night Was Made for Murder. W. Cotton
Night Was Made for Murder. B. Winter
Night Was Our Friend. M. Pertwee
Night Watch. R. W. Bailey
Night Watch. L. Fletcher
Night Watch. H. McCutcheon
Night Watch. A. MacNeill
Night Watch. J. Olsen

Night Watch. T. Walsh
Night Watcher. J. F. Murphy, Jr.
Night Watches. W. W. Jacobs
Night-Watchman's Friend. M. Fitt
Night We Get Rich. W. Newton
Night Wheeler. Carter Brown
Night Whisper. Patricia Wallace
Night Whispers. C. Veley
Night Wind at Northwiding. F. Hurd
Night Winds. B. Cleeve
Night Wind's Promise. V. Vanardy
Night Wings. M. Gerard
Night Without Darkness. K. Orvis
Night Without End. F. Duncan
Night Without End. S. MacIvers
Night Without End. Alistair MacLean
Night Without Sleep. E. Noll
Night Without Stars. Winston Graham
Night-World. R. Bloch
Nightbeat. William Camp
Nightbloom. H. Lieberman
Nightbone. Michael Hardwick
Nightborn. L. Grex
Nightcap. M. Dobson
Nightcap. F. Durbridge
Nightcap. M. Marcin
Nightcap. J. C. S. Smith
Nightcap and Plume. G. R. Preedy
Nightclimber. J. M. White
Nightclub Mystery. H. Clevely
Nightcomers. M. Hastings
Nightdive. C. D. Pell
Nighteyes. G. Reeves-Stevens
Nightfall. C. Bryan
Nightfall. J. Crosby
Nightfall. D. Daniels
Nightfall. J. Farris
Nightfall. D. Goodis
Nightfall. B. Myers
Nightfighter Spy. B. Newman
Nightflier. C. Fahy
Nightflyers. G. R. R. Martin
Nightgleams. J. Thatcher
Nighthawk. W. M. Duncan
Nighthawk Mops Up. S. Horler
Nighthawk of the Northwest. S. A. White
Nighthawk Strikes to Kill. S. Horler
Nighthawk Swears Vengeance. S. Horler
Nighthawk the Mountain Detective. Anonymous
Nighthawks! J. G. Brandon
Nightingale. E. Pace
Nightingale at Noon. M. Summerton
Nightingale Trivet. R. Mead
Nightingales Never Sing. J. Courage
Nightlight. M. Bardos
Nightlight. M. Cadnum
Nightlights. B. Goldie
Nightlines. J. Lutz
Nightly Deadshade. John Aiken
Nightly Encounters. G. MacKay
Nightly She Sings. E. Olmstead
Nightmare. E. S. Aarons
Nightmare. A. Blaisdell
Nightmare. L. Brock
Nightmare. M. Dorner
Nightmare. G. Endore
Nightmare. R. H. Greenan
Nightmare. L. Greth
Nightmare. W. Irish
Nightmare. A. La Bern
Nightmare. J. L. Latham
Nightmare. Gloria Murphy
Nightmare. G. Mygatt
Nightmare. R. Owen
Nightmare. N. Robbins
Nightmare. C. Woolrich
Nightmare Abbey. T. L. Peacock
Nightmare Abbey. W. E. D. Ross
Nightmare Alley. W. L. Gresham
Nightmare and Dawn. M. Aldanov
Nightmare at Dawn. J. Philips
Nightmare at Mountain Aerie. F. Hurd
Nightmare at Noon. C. Dekker
Nightmare at Noon. S. Sterling

Nightmare at Riverview. Angela Gray
Nightmare Baby. L. Du Breuil
Nightmare Blonde. M. Wolson
Nightmare Blue. G. Dozois
Nightmare Candidate. K. Stewart
Nightmare Castle. W. Martyn
Nightmare Chase. E. Berckman
Nightmare Chessboard. T. B. Morris
Nightmare Chrysalis. R. Gatenby
Nightmare Conspiracy. Ralph Hayes
Nightmare Cottage. G. M. Wilson
Nightmare Cruise. Wade Miller
Nightmare Dance. M. Lynch
Nightmare Ends. F. Cowen
Nightmare Express. I. Haiblum
Nightmare Factor. T. N. Scortia
Nightmare Farm. Jack Mann
Nightmare Fiesta. D. Martyn
Nightmare File. Jack Livingston
Nightmare for a Nymph. D. Haring
Nightmare for Dr. Morelle. E. Dudley
Nightmare Hall. A. L. McMurdie
Nightmare Honeymoon. R. Foley
Nightmare House. R. Foley
Nightmare House. B. Gray
Nightmare House. E. B. Martin
Nightmare in Algeria. J. Rosenberger
Nightmare in Colour. R. H. Greenan
Nightmare in Copenhagen. M. Albrand
Nightmare in Darkness. F. Brown
Nightmare in Dublin. P. Loraine
Nightmare in Eden. M. Asher
Nightmare in July. C. Coleman
Nightmare in Laos. J. Lansing
Nightmare in Manhattan. T. Walsh
Nightmare in Morocco. Marian Jackson
Nightmare in Naples. J. Stagg
Nightmare in New York. D. Pendleton
Nightmare in Panama. J. Rosenberger
Nightmare in Pewter. J. DeWeese
Nightmare in Pink. J. D. MacDonald
Nightmare in Rust. P. Audemars
Nightmare Incident. S. Brydon
Nightmare Island. Ralph Hayes
Nightmare Kick. Jon Stevens
Nightmare Legacy. J. Corby
Nightmare Logic. Matthew Hall
Nightmare Machine. J. N. Datesh
Nightmare Merchants. Gar Wilson
Nightmare Network. R. Rainey
Nightmare of Eyes. D. Rico
Nightmare of Murder. Mildred Davis
Nightmare on Elm Street. Jeffrey Cooper
Nightmare on the Nile. C. Leader
Nightmare Street. H. Ellson
Nightmare Street. M. Tabor
Nightmare Time. H. Pentecost
Nightmare Town. D. Hammett
Nightmares. R. Bloch
Nightmares and Geezenstacks. F. Brown
Nightmare's End. J. James
Nightmare's Morning. M. Lynch
Nightmare's Nest. J. Arliss
Nightmare's Nest. K. O'Hara
Nightrunners. Michael Collins
Nightrunners. J. R. Lansdale
Nights and Days. M. Annesley
Night's Black Agent. J. Bingham
Night's Candles. A. Hocking
Night's Cloak. E. R. Punshon
Night's Dark Secret. J. Shearing
Night's Evil. M. McShane
Night's Moves. O. Blakeston
Nights of the Long Knives. H. H. Kirst
Nights of the Round Table. Margery Lawrence
Nights with an Old Lag. W. J. Wintle
Nights with Sasquatch. J. Cotter
Nightscape. T. Chastain
Nightshade. G. M. Allen
Nightshade. T. Collins
Nightshade. I. Foster
Nightshade. R. Gadney
Nightshade. R. Horniman
Nightshade. H. Imbert-Terry

Title Index

Nightshade. J. N. Makris
Nightshade. Derek Marlowe
Nightshade. Gloria Murphy
Nightshade. J. H. Robinson
Nightshade & Damnations. G. Kersh
Nightshade Ring. L. Hardy
Nightshades. P. Pronzini
Nightside. C. Durden
Nightside City. L. Watt-Evans
Nightsight. A. Galloway
Nightspawn. J. Banville
Nightstick. D. Royal
Nighttime Guy. T. Kenrick
Nighttown. T. E. D. Klein
Nightwalker. S. Filson
Nightwalker. J. Hager
Nightwalker. T. Tessier
Nightwalkers. B. Cross
Nightwalkers. James Norman
Nightwatcher. C. P. Wilson
Nightwatchman. B. Hannah
Nightwebs. C. Woolrich
Nightwind. S. Allis
Nightwind. M. Washburn
Nightwing. M. C. Smith
Nightwitch Devil. K. Robeson
Nightwork. Joseph Hansen
Nightwork. Irwin Shaw
Nihilist's Vengeance. E. C. Derby
Nijinsky Is Dead. Kenn Davis
Nikki. S. Friedman
Nikrova's Passion. B. Henderson
Nile Green. A. Hocking
Nile Green. D. Jordan
Nile Shadows. E. Whittemore
Nimble Dollar, with other stories. C. M. Thompson
Nimble Ike, the Detective. Old Sleuth
Nimble Ike, the Trick Ventriloquist. Old Sleuth
Nimble Ike's Mystery. Old Sleuth
Nimble Ike's Romance. Old Sleuth
Nimrod. J. Midgley
Nimrod Affair. J. Fairlawn
Nina's Peril. A. M. Millar
Nine Against New York. Albert Leffingwell
Nine—and Death Makes Ten. Carter Dickson
Nine Bears. E. Wallace
Nine Bells. K. Davies
Nine Bright Shiners. Anthea Fraser
Nine Buck's Row. T. E. Huff
Nine Club. T. Clare
Nine Coaches Waiting. G. Bolton
Nine Coaches Waiting. Mary Stewart
Nine Commandments. J. Blackmore
Nine Cuts. B. Flynn
9 Dark Hours. L. G. Offord
Nine Days. E. C. Vivian
Nine Days' Blunder. W. G. Elliott
Nine Days' Murder. A. MacKinnon
Nine Days' Panic. R. Davis
Nine Doctors and a Madman. E. M. Curtiss
Nine Dragon Man. D. De Reszke
Nine Dragons. Justin Scott
9:45. Owen Davis
Nine Girls. W. H. Pettitt
Nine Green Bottles. J. Cowdroy
9 Had No Alibi. M. Silverman
Nine Holiday Adventures of Mr. P. J. Davenant in the Year 1915. F. S. Hamilton
Nine Horrors and a Dream. J. P. Brennan
Nine Lives. M. Channing
Nine Lives Are Not Enough. J. Odlum
Nine Lives of Alphonse. J. L. Johnson
Nine Lives to Pompeii. W. Melton
Nine Men of Soho. J. MacLaren-Ross
Nine Men's Morrice. W. H. Pollock
Nine Mile Walk. H. Kemelman
Nine More Lives. Michael Morgan
Nine Nicks. J. Farmdale
Nine O'Clock Curtains. J. M. Hickman
Nine O'Clock Murder. Vince Kelly
Nine O'Clock Revue Book. Harold Simpson
Nine O'Clock Shadow. J. T. Story
Nine O'Clock Tide. M. G. Eberhart
Nine of Hearts. B. L. Farjeon

Nine of Hearts. E. C. Mayne
911. T. Chastain
Nine Pine Street. J. Colton
Nine Pointed Star. C. W. Sykes
Nine Points of the Law. H. Booth
Nine Points of the Law. W. S. Jackson
Nine Seven Juliet. L. Lafore
Nine Singing Apes. H. Hawton
Nine-Spoked Wheel. J. R. L. Anderson
Nine Strings to Your Bow. M. Walsh
Nine Tailors. D. L. Sayers
9009. J. Hopper
Nine Till Six. Aimee Stuart
Nine Times Dead. D. Bogard
Nine Times Nine. H. H. Holmes
Nine Unknown. T. Mundy
Nine Waxed Faces. F. Beeding
Nine Wrong Answers. J. D. Carr
19. Roger Hall
1988. R. Lamm
1956. S. Marlowe
Nineteen Impressions. J. D. Beresford
19 Purchase Street. G. A. Browne
19 Red Roses. T. Nielsen
Nineteen Stories. G. Greene
Nineteen Thousand Pounds. B. Delannoy
Nineteenth Century Miracle. Z. Z.
Nineteenth Hole Mystery. H. Adams
Ninety Days to Nine-O. P. Shatte
98.4 C. Hodder-Williams
95 File. J. E. Martin
90 Gramercy Park. P. Dalton
Ninety in the Shade. A. R. Weekes
Ninety Million Dollar Mouse. F. M. Nevins, Jr.
Ninety Nine. J. Ahern
99 44/100% Dead. M. Franklin
99, Dark Street. F. W. Robinson
Ninety-Second Tiger. M. Gilbert
Ninja. E. V. Lustbader
Ninja Blood. Gar Wilson
Ninja Nightmare. J. Rosenberger
Ninja's Revenge. P. Anthony
Ninon. M. Peterson
Ninth Buddha. D. Easterman
Ninth Candle. F. Ford
Ninth Car. A. R. Rooth
Ninth Circle. N. J. Crisp
Ninth Circle. H. Steele
9th Directive. Adam Hall
Ninth Dragon. E. B. Cross
Ninth Earl. J. Farnol
Ninth Earl of Whitby. N. Bell
Ninth Enemy. F. Vivian
Ninth Floor. K. O'Neil
Ninth Guest. G. Bristow
Ninth Guest. Owen Davis
Ninth Hour. B. Benson
Ninth Life. L. W. Douglas
Ninth Life. F. I. S. Eden
Ninth Life. E. Ferrars
Ninth Life. Jack Mann
Ninth Life. D. Matheson
Ninth Man. John Lee
Ninth Marquess. J. Cleary
Ninth Netsuke. James Melville
Ninth Plague. D. T. Lindsay
Ninth Tentacle. M. Rippon
Ninth Week. Irene Alexander
Nipped in the Bud. S. Palmer
Nipponese Nightmare. J. Rosenberger
Nirvana Can Also Mean Death. H. Kane
Nirvana Contracts. J. P. Wohl
Nisanit. F. Faqir
Nitroglycerine. I. Stark
Nitty Gritty. D. Haring
Nitty-Gritty Affair. G. Cross
Nixon Recession Caper. R. Maloney
No Accounting for Murder. D. Budden
No Admission. R. Winder
No Alibi. B. Cobb
No Alibi. J. York
No Alibi for Murder. A. Parsons
No Angel. Morton Cooper
No Angels for Me. W. Ard

No Answer. E. Westward
No Answer from a Corpse. R. Stahl
No Apparent Motive. E. C. Williams
No Bail for Dalton. M. Borgenicht
No Bail for the Judge. H. Cecil
No Beast So Fierce. E. Bunker
No Beast So Fierce. C. Rushton
No Better Fiend. E. McGirr
No Birds Sang. J. B. Hilton
No Blonde Is an Island. Carter Brown
No Body. N. Pickard
No Body She Knows. Carter Brown
No Bones About It. Joan Fleming
No Bones About It. R. S. Wallis
No Bouquets for Brandon. V. Warren
No Business Being a Cop. L. O'Donnell
No Business for a Lady. J. L. Rubel
No Business of Mine. Raymond Marshall
No Case for the Crown. D. McLachlin
No Case for the Police. V. C. Clinton-Baddeley
No Castle of Dreams. M. McEvoy
No Cause for Dying. K. Evans
No Cause to Kill. D. Ramsey
No Caution for Caroline. K. Slattery
No Certain Life. R. Neely
No Chance in Hell. N. Quarry
No Charge for Framing. D. Sanderson
No Charge for the Poison. B. Cobb
No Choice. E. B. D'Auvergne
No Choice for Sergeant Cluff. G. North
No City of Angels. N. Noye
No Clear Evidence. J. Heys
No Clue! J. Hay
No Clues. M. Leinster
No Clues for Dexter. B. Graeme
No Coffin for the Corpse. C. Rawson
No Coffins in China. C. Edwards
No Come-Back from Connie. D. Glinto
No Comebacks. F. Forsyth
No Condition Is Permanent. D. Fulani
No Copy. K. Clayton
No Copyright on Murder. M. Brody
No Corpus Delecti. H. Bohnstedt
No Country for Old Men. A. Schwartz
No Coupons for a Shroud. N. Morland
No Crest for the Wicked. G. Morgan
No Crime for a Lady. Z. Popkin
No Crime Is Perfect. H. E. Wheeler
No Crime Like the Present. A. Gaines
No Crime Like the Present. W. Gleason
No Crime Like the Present. M. Hervey
No Crime More Cruel. M. Halliday
No Crime So Great. Elliot Bailey
No Cure for Death. M. A. Collins
No Curtain Calls. J. Rand
No Curtains for Cora. Gavin Holt
No Dahlias for the Damned. R. Callahan
No Dame Wants to Die. M. Clinton
No Darker Crime. J. Creasey
No Deals, Mr. Bond. J. Gardner
No Diamonds for a Doll. P. Cagney
No Dice! A. Bocca
No Dice, Miss Jones! D. Haring
No Dice Sister. B. Carson
No Dignity in Death. R. Lockridge
No Doors, No Windows. H. Ellison
No Doubts After Friday. I. Waltmore
No Down Payment. J. McPartland
No Drums at Midnight. J. Troy
No Dust in the Attic. Anthony Gilbert
No Duty on a Corpse. Max Murray
No Earth for Foxes. M. O'Brine
No Easy Way Out. R. Blanchard
No Easy Way Out. Robert Mason
No End of a Rogue. F. A. Clement
No End to Danger. M. Halliday
No End to Fear. H. Hossent
No Enemy But Time. Evelyn Anthony
No Entry. M. Coles
No Epitaph for Mr. Zarke. C. I. D. Smith
No Escape. Josephine Bell
No Escape. E. Ellison
No Escape. J. Hayes
No Escape. C. B. Kelland

N

No Escape. S. Kemp
No Escape. S. Le Fanu
No Escape. M. Richmond
No Escape. R. R. Ryan
No Escape from Murder. N. MacKenzie
No Escape from Murder. P. Manton
No Evil Angel. E. Linington
No Excuse for Murder. M. Hervey
No Exit. G. Goodchild
No Exit. Winston Graham
No Exit. A. E. Redmond
No Exit. H. Scott
No Exit for a Blonde! Lewis Michael
No Exit from Brooklyn. R. J. Randisi
No Extradition. A. Safroni-Middleton
No Face for a Killer. H. Spencer
No Face in the Mirror. R. Copeland
No Face to Murder. E. Howie
No Fatherland. H. H. Kirst
No Fear or Favour. H. Cecil
No Flowers by Request. S. Palmer
No Flowers, By Request. June Thomson
No Flowers for the Dead. M. Clinten
No Flowers for the General. B. Copper
No Flowers in Brazlov. F. Usher
No Flowers on My Grave. R. Magowan
No Footprints in the Bush. A. W. Upfield
No Friendly Drop. Henry Wade
No Fury. F. Beeding
No Future Fair Lady. Carter Brown
No Future for Luana. A. Derleth
No Future for Miss Morrow. B. Schwarz
No Gentle Lady. R. Buxton
No Go on Jackson Street. M. Weiss
No Gold When You Go. Peter Chambers
No Good from a Corpse. L. Brackett
No-Good Hussy. Rex Richards
No Grave for a Lady. J. Bonett
No Grave for March. M. E. Chaber
No Greater Love. W. LeQueux
No Guest at the Villa. D. Martyn
No Halo for Hedy. Carter Brown
No Halo for Me. J. Manor
No Haloes for Hoods. Craig Cooper
No Haloes in Hell. W. Wright
No Hands on the Clock. G. Homes
No Harm. W. Hornsby
No Harm Intended. E. S. Holding
No Harp for My Angel. Carter Brown
No Head for Her Pillow. S. S. Taylor
No Hero. J. P. Marquand
No Hero. Desmond Martin
No Hiding Place. R. Foley
No Hiding Place. E. Lanham
No Higher Mountain. A. Armstrong
No Holds Barred. Michael Allen
No Holds Barred. B. Sarto
No Holiday for Crime. Dell Shannon
No Holiday for Death. L. Thayer
No Honour—. Colin Hope
No Honour Amongst Spies. H. T. Rothwell
No House Limit. S. Fisher
No Hurry to Kill. N. Deane
No Jane Is Safe. Dirk Foster
No Judges' Rules. D. MacDonald
No Kickbacks for Killers. J. Dekker
No Kisses from the Kremlin. H. T. Rothwell
No Known Grave. E. Berckman
No Lady in the House. L. Kallen
No Land Without Liberty. J. G. Sarasin
No Last Words. B. Cobb
No Law Against Angels. Carter Brown
No Law in Illyria. T. S. Strachan
No Less Renowned. G. Hackforth-Jones
No Lesser Plea. R. K. Tanenbaum
No Letters from the Grave. B. Copper
No Life for a Loser. P. A. Foxall
No Light Came On. Alice Campbell
No Light to Die By. K. Robeson
No Lilies. H. Holt
No Limit. A. Applin
No Limit for Charlie. W. A. Harbinson
No Little Enemy. O. W. Bayer
No Looking Back. G. Greenaway

No Love for Miss Stent. W. Charles
No Love for Paradise. J. Canon
No Love in a Bullet. E. Kennedy
No Love Lost. M. Allingham
No Love Lost. Robert Reeves
No Luck for a Lady. F. Mahannah
No Man Alone. Robert Henry
No Man for Murder. M. Ellis
No Man Is an Island. J. M. Simmel
No Man Pursues. H. S. Davis
No Man's Hand. J. L. Bonney
No Man's Hand. H. C. McNeile
No Man's Island. Jessica Mann
No Man's Land. Reginald Hill
No Man's Land. L. J. Vance
No Man's Land. M. Walser
No Man's Laughter. K. Laing
No Man's Money. H. M. Rideout
No Man's Street. B. Nichols
No Man's Woman. A. Boyd
No Man's World. M. Caidin
No Margin for Terror. Bradley Ross
No Marks for Trying. S. Allan
No Mask for Murder. A. Garve
No Match for Murder. J. F. Webb
No Match for the Law. O. Mills
No Mean Tartar. L. F. Hay
No Medal If I Die. J. Ward
No Medals for Murder. H. Holt
No Medals for the Major. M. Yorke
No Medicine for Murder. Jeanne Wilson
No Mercy for Margaret. B. Cobb
No Mercy in the Sky. J. Fores
No Mink in a Shroud. D. Haring
No Moon Tonight. J. Courage
No Moonlight. P. H. Powell
No More a Brother. T. Newman
No More a Corpse. L. Brent
No More A-Roving. S. Troy
No More Ancestors. L. Robinson
No More Chances. D. Spade
No More Dying Then. R. Rendell
No More Love. M. Hervey
No More Monday Mornings. C. P. Crow
No More Murders. M. Lang
No More Witnesses. R. Warthen
No Mortgage on a Coffin. D. Glinto
No Mother to Guide Her. A. Forsythe
No Motive for Murder. W. E. Jones
No Mourners Present. F. G. Presnell
No Mourning for the Matador. D. Ames
No Mourning in the Family. R. Philmore
No Murder. H. C. Bailey
No Murder of Mine. Alice Campbell
No Name. W. Collins
No Names on Their Graves. Geoffrey Davison
No Need for Violence. J. Burrows
No Need to Die. G. Ashe
No Need to Fear. A. McAllister
No News on Monday. R. Clapperton
No Next of Kin. D. M. Disney
No! No! the Woman! N. Klein
No Obelisk for Emily. S. H. Courtier
No One Knows My Name. Joyce Harrington
No One Rides for Free. L. Beinhart
No One to Worry Us. T. S. Strachan
No Opera at the Op'ry House. T. J. Kelly
No Orchids for Miss Blandish. J. H. Chase
No Orchids for Miss Blandish. R. D. MacDonald
No Ordinary Cheyney. P. Cheyney
No Other Hunger. F. Mullally
No Other Killer. J. Corbett
No Other Tiger. A. E. W. Mason
No Other Victim. C. Franklin
No Other Way. L. Tracy
No Outlet. A. M. Chase
No Paine, No Gaine. Edwina Franklin
No Paradise. K. Royce
No Part in Your Death. N. Freeling
No Past Is Dead. J. J. Connington
No Patent on Murder. A. Takagi
No Peace for Archer. H. Clevely
No Peace for the Living. M. Hervey
No Peace for the Wicked. Peter Chambers

No Peace for the Wicked. E. Ferrars
No Peace for the Wicked. Andrew Hale
No Percentage in Death. R. Angel
No Place for a Dame. M. Clinten
No Place for a Tickle. R. Cooper
No Place for Me. S. Morelli
No Place for Murder. G. H. Coxe
No Place for Strangers. W. H. Baker
No Place for the Young. E. Warman
No Place Like Home. J. B. Olesker
No Place to Be a Cop. F. Nolan
No Place to Be Somebody. C. Gordone
No Place to Hide. T. Allbeury
No Place to Hide. E. Lindall
No Place to Hide. C. Runyon
No Place to Hide. E. Ronns
No Pockets in a Shroud. H. McCoy
No Pockets in Shrouds. L. Revell
No Price Sister. N. Baroni
No Profit in Dying. O. Beeby
No Proof. L. L. Lynch
No Proud Chivalry. M. Procter
No Quarter for a Star. Dulcie Gray
No Quarter Given. B. Rossi
No Question of Murder. P. Curtis
No Questions Asked. O. Bleeck
No Questions Asked. W. A. Frost
No Questions Asked. F. Rydell
No Questions Asked. E. Sherry
No Reason for Murder. E. Radford
No Red Herrings. Mary Scott
No Refuge. J. Boland
No Regrets. N. Baroni
No Regrets for Clara. H. Janson
No Rehearsals for Murder. E. Ferrars
No Reprieve. H. Desmond
No Rest for Biggles. W. E. Johns
No Rest for the Dying. J. Kelly
No Resting Place. I. Niall
No Return Ticket. M. Russell
No-Risk Operation. J. Pattinson
No Room at the Morgue. A. Bocca
No Room for Joanna. Elizabeth Ford
No Ruined Castles. J. McGovern
No Rules, No Referee. G. Wilson
No Sabe. Elisha Cook
No Safe Place. J. Hild
No Safe Road. B. Munslow
No Sainted City. S. Bunce
No Sale. M. Cronin
No Sale for Haloes. Anthony Graham
No Sanctuary. J. Bowser
No Sanctuary. T. Harriott
No Sanctuary. J. Hild
No Scars to See. I. See
No Second Prize. B. Dale
No Second Stroke. C. Rushton
No Second Wind. A. B. Guthrie
No Sentiment. A. Dick
No Sentiment in Murder. M. Cumberland
No Shame for the Devil. B. Cobb
No Shame on Jancy. H. Zore
No-Sided Professor and other tales of fantasy, humor, mystery, and philosophy. M. Gardner
No Sign of Life. M. Delving
No Sign of Life. R. Ormerod
No Sign of Murder. W. Reed
No Sign of Murder. Alan Russell
No, Sir Jeremy. A. Weymouth
No Sky. N. Balchin
No Sleep at All. James Warren
No Sleep for Elsa. T. C. H. Jacobs
No Sleep for Macall. G. Fairlie
No Slightest Whisper. D. Evans
No Smoke No Flame. O. Downes
No Snow at Latching. M. Home
No Space for Murder. N. Brent
No Special Hurry. J. Colbert
No Stockings. A. S. Roche
No Stone. K. Blake
No Such Word. R. Pertwee
No Surrender. M. Albrand
No Survivors. J. Ahern
No Sweet Aspersion. Y. Pickering

Title Index

No Target for Bowman. H. Howard
No Tears Are Shed. Stratford Davis
No Tears at the Funeral. H. Arre
No Tears for Hilda. A. Garve
No Tears for Peggy Perle. Alixe Carter
No Tears for Shirley Minton. K. Lowe
No Tears for Susie. N. Rosso
No Tears for Teddy. Surrey Smith
No Tears for the Dead. P. Audemars
No Tears for the Dead. S. Deane
No Tears for the Dead. R. Foley
No Tears for the Dead. S. Vincent
No Tears from the Widow. Carter Brown
No Tears Shed. A. B. Caldwell
No Thanks for the Shroud. J. P. Carstairs
No Thanks to the Duke. A. Dunnett
No Thoroughfare. D. Egerton
No Through Road. B. Hector
No Through Road. M. Russell
No Time at All. C. Einstein
No Time for Corpses. R. Carni
No Time for Crime. C. M. Russell
No Time for Death. P. Capon
No Time for Love. H. Meenan
No Time for Terror. P. MacDonald
No Time to Die. L. Edgley
No Time to Die. R. Pape
No Time to Kill. J. Bonett
No Time to Kill. G. H. Coxe
No Time to Laugh. J. Norwood
No Time to Live. W. H. Baker
No Time to Live. L. T. Maxim
No Time to Play. K. Hewitt
No Time to Wait! W. Standish
No Traveller Returns. D. Ames
No Traveller Returns. A. Dean
No Trespassing. D. Tracy
No Trial—No Error. Colin Robertson
No Turning Back. W. F. Morris
No Turning Back. L. Robin
No Useless Coffin. R. Watkins
No Vacation for Maigret. G. Simenon
No Vacation from Murder. E. Lemarchand
No Vindication. Mrs. C. Kernahan
No Walls of Jasper. J. Cannan
No Way Back. K. Royce
No Way Back from Prague. P. Brent
No Way Home. P. J. MacDonald
No Way Home. G. R. Preedy
No Way Out. O. Davis
No Way Out. K. Fearing
No Way Out. D. Haring
No Way Out. W. McNeilly
No Way Out. B. Musto
No Way Out. R. O. Saber
No Way Out. A. Thornton
No Way to Treat a Lady. H. Longbaugh
No Weeds for the Widow. M. M. Raison
No Will to Die. W. Ellis
No Wind of Blame. G. Heyer
No Winding Sheet. G. Mitchell
No Wings on a Cop. C. F. Adams
No Witness! C. Fitzsimmons
No Woman Was Safe. G. Lamond
No Wooden Overcoat. J. P. Carstairs
No Word from Winnifred. A. Cross
No Wreath from Manuela. A. MacKinnon
No Wreaths for the Duchess. F. Grierson
Noah's Ark Murders. A. Douglas
Nobask. M. Creagh
Nobbler. J. Royale
Nobby the "Shooting Star". Hedley Scott
Noble Blood. J. Hawthorne
Noble Enemy. C. Fox
Noble Error. M. L. Tyrrell
Noble Forger. C. C. Bergius
Noble House. J. Clavell
Noble Lord. P. Lauder
Noble Lord. E. Southworth
Noble Pirate. R. Foxall
Noble Profession. P. Boulle
Nobleman's Wife. H. Wood
Noblest Experiment in the Galaxy. L. Trimble
Nobody. L. J. Vance

Nobody Answered the Bell. R. Davies
Nobody Cared for Kate. G. Thompson
Nobody Died for Johnnie. D. Bogard
Nobody Dies in Chinatown. M. Lockhart
Nobody Heard the Shot. D. B. Chidsey
Nobody Here by That Name. Donald Mackenzie
Nobody Is Safe. M. Cumberland
Nobody Knew They Were There. E. Hunter
Nobody Knows the Dead. D. Bogard
Nobody Lives Forever. E. Buchanan
Nobody Lives Forever. W. R. Burnett
Nobody Lives Forever. Peter Chambers
Nobody Lives Forever. J. Gardner
Nobody Loves a Dead Man. M. M. Raison
Nobody Loves a Loser. H. Kane
Nobody Loves Me. E. Cannon
Nobody Needs a Corpse. M. Cronin
Nobody on the Road. G. Rose
Nobody Shoots Forever. S. A. Curtis
Nobody Sleeps. G. Le Pelley
Nobody Stops Me. Eric North
Nobody Wins. G. P. Kenneally
Nobody Wore Black. D. Ames
Nobody's Dames. B. Vane
Nobody's Daughter. C. Augusta
Nobody's Fault. N. Holmes
Nobody's Fool. M. Claridge
Nobody's Fortune. E. Yates
Nobody's Girl. P. Bruce
Nobody's Home. M. Short
Nobody's Man. E. P. Oppenheim
Nobody's Perfect. Douglas Clark
Nobody's Perfect. K. Reinsmith
Nobody's Perfect. D. E. Westlake
Nobody's Sorry He Got Killed. A. D. Goldstein
Nobody's Supposed to Murder the Butler. J. N. Chance
Nobody's Vineyard. H. C. Bailey
Nobody's Widow. G. Warden
Nocturnal. K. Eulo
Nocturnal Assassin. I. Crookenden
Nocturnal Minstrel. E. Sleath
Nocturne for the General. J. Trenhaile
Nocturne Murder. Audrey Peterson
Nodding Canaries. G. Mitchell
Nodding Towers. Sam Hill
Noise in the Night. S. Jepson
Nomad's Land. M. R. Rinehart
Nomads of the Night. G. Leroux
Nomads of the North. J. O. Curwood
Nominative Case. E. Mackin
Non-Murder. J. Ingersol
Nonconformist Parson. R. Horniman
None But the Lethal Heart. Carter Brown
None Dare Call It Treason. C. Gavin
None of Maigret's Business. G. Simenon
None of My Business. D. Sharp
None of Us Cared for Kate. J. Haythorne
None Shall Know. M. Albrand
None Shall Sleep Tonight. H. McCutcheon
None Should Look. R. Kingston
None So Blind. M. A. Wilson
Nonsense Novels. S. Leacock
Noon Balloon to Rangoon. J. Haase
Noon Jury. Mark Ross
Noonday and Night. G. Mitchell
Noonday Devil. U. Curtiss
Noonday Devil. R. McInerny
Noonday Devils. W. Martyn
Nooriabad File. G. Watson
Noose. P. MacDonald
Noose for a Lady. H. Carmichael
Noose for a Lady. G. Verner
Noose for Her. E. Crispin
Noose Is Drawn. W. A. Barker
Noose of Emeralds. B. Winter
Noose of Red Beads. T. J. King
Noose of Sin. F. Carco
Noose of Time. Stephen Murray
Nor All Your Tears. L. Charbonneau
Nor Evil Dreams. Rosemary Harris
Nor Iron Bars. S. Dannett
Nor Live So Long. Sara Woods
Nor Spell Nor Charm. Alicen White

Nora Prentiss. Alex Morrison
Nora's Love Test. M. C. Hay
Norgil: More Tales of Prestidigitection. M. Grant
Norgil the Magician. M. Grant
Norine's Revenge, and Sir Noel's Heir. M. A. Fleming
Norma Danton. Anonymous
Normandie Affair. E. Villiers
Normandie Triangle. Justin Scott
Normandy Code. Nick Carter
Norroy, Diplomatic Agent. G. Bronson-Howard
Norslag. Michael Sinclair
North. J. B. Hendryx
North Beach Girl. J. Trinian
North Beat. J. Wood
North Cape. J. Poyer
North for Danger. Colin Robertson
North from Rome. Helen MacInnes
North from Singapore. D. Nabarro
North from Thursady. J. Cleary
North Kill. J. Wood
North of Bushman's Rock. G. Harding
North of 55 Degrees. A. Murray
North of Delhi, East of Heaven. J. Sparling
North of the Border. J. Van Gieson
North of the Border. S. A. White
North of the Law. S. A. White
North of the Stars. C. Stoddard
North of Welfare. W. Krasner
North Sea Hijack. Jack Davies
North Sea Mistress. K. Blickle
North Sea Mystery. H. Edmonds
North Sea Patrol. G. E. Rochester
North Shore Mystery. H. Fletcher
North Slope. Michael Parker
North Star. H. Innes
North Star Crusade. W. Katz
North to Rabaul. Christopher Wood
North Walk Mystery. W. N. Harben
North Wing. Marion Ward
Northern Exposure. M. Kilian
Northern Lights. Gilbert Parker
Northern Mission. J. Wood
Northing Tramp. E. Wallace
Northlight. Adam Hall
Norths Meet Murder. F. Lockridge
Northward the Coast. E. Lindall
Northwater. C. Crowe
Northwest! H. Bindloss
Northwest Contract. L. Derrick
Northwest Crossing. S. A. White
Northwest Law. S. A. White
Northwest Patrol. S. A. White
Northwest Trouble. C. Stoddard
Norval, the Detective. Old Sleuth
Norwegian Spring, 1940. S. Engstrand
Norwegian Typhoon. Nick Carter
Norwich Victims. F. Beeding
Norwood Mystery. J. K. Blades
Nose for It. A. M. Stein
Nose of Papa Hilaire. K. MacNichol
Nose on My Face. L. Payne
Nostalgia Kills. R. Westbrook
Nostradamus Horoscope. Graham Lord
Nostradamus Traitor. J. Gardner
Not a Bad Man. J. Miglis
Not a Bad Show. F. Beeding
Not a Blessed Thing! M. Quill
Not a Clue. A. De Mirjian
Not a Creature Was Stirring. J. Haddam
Not a Dog's Chance. W. R. Hutton
Not a Leg to Stand On. M. Burton
Not a Nice Murder! E. Wilmot
Not a Penny More, Not a Penny Less. J. Archer
Not a Stranger. J. R. Feegel
Not a Through Street. E. Larsen
Not After Midnight. D. Du Maurier
Not As Far As Velma. N. Freeling
Not Comin' Home to You. P. Kavanagh
Not Dead Enough. Clay Henry
Not Dead, Only Resting. S. Brett
Not Dead Yet. D. Banko
Not Enough Horses. Les Roberts
Not Even a Mouse. B. Stellenach

Not Everybody Died. Danny Stephens
Not Exactly a Brahmin. S. Dunlap
Not Exactly Ghosts. A. Caldecott
Not Expected to Live. M. Cumberland
Not Fade Away. J. Dodge
Not Far from the Gioconda Tree. Tim Kelly
Not for a Curse. K. Kramer
Not for Export. M. Coles
Not for Sale. K. Gordon
Not for Sale. G. Isaacs
Not for the Squeamish. D. Scott-Moncrieff
Not Guilty. Anonymous
Not Guilty. W. E. Norris
Not Guilty. W. Phillips
Not Guilty. H. St. John
Not Guilty, My Lord. H. Desmond
Not Herbert. H. I. Young
Not I, Said the Sparrow. R. Lockridge
Not I, Said the Vixen. B. S. Ballinger
Not in Israel. Guy Thorne
Not in the Book. A. Watkyn
Not in the Contract. N. W. Hooke
Not in the Newspapers. John Gloag
Not in the Script. J. Bonett
Not in Utter Nakedness. D. Ames
Not in Vain. Gerald Green
Not Killed, Just Dead. D. Ambler
Not Long for This World. G. A. Haywood
Not Long to Live. Mark Cross
Not Me, Inspector. H. Reilly
Not Mentioned . . . A. Soutar
Not My Murder. John Marsh
Not My Thing. J. H. Chase
Not Negotiable. M. Coles
Not Nice People. H. Clevely
Not on the Agenda. N. Gilbert
Not on the Records. Nicholas Carter
Not One of Us. J. Thomson
Not Our House. W. W. Prior
Not Proven. A. Askew
Not Proven. J. Dering
Not Proven. B. Graeme
Not Proven. P. Traill
Not Proven Castle. A. Wood
Not Quite Dead Enough. R. Stout
Not Quite So Black. D. G. Waring
Not Ready to Die. J. Monmouth
Not Safe to Be Free. J. H. Chase
Not Scot Free. Duncan Macmillan
Not Single Spies. D. Betteridge
Not Sleeping, Just Dead. C. Alverson
Not So Dumb. Clive Blake
Not So Evil As Eve. J. Creighton
Not So Quickly. K. Fitzgerald
Not Sufficient Evidence. J. L. Rickard
Not That Kind of Place. F. Fyfield
Not the Glory. P. Boulle
Not Till a Hot January. M. J. Adamson
Not to Be Opened. L. Osbourne
Not to Be Taken. A. Berkeley
Not to the Swift. H. Gibbs
Not to the Swift. L. Harrison
Not Too Narrow—Not Too Deep. R. Sale
Not Wanted. F. Hume
Not Wanted on Voyage. N. Spain
Not with a Bang. C. Pincher
Not with My Neck. T. Van Dycke
Not Wooed, But Won. J. Payn
Not Working. G. Szanto
Not Yours the Island. D. Nash
Notch on the Knife. W. Haggard
Notched Hairpin. H. F. Heard
Note of Enchantment. E. H. Clements
Notebooks. S. Picard
Notebooks of Raymond Chandler and English Summer. R. Chandler
Notes of an Itinerant Policeman. J. Flynt
Nothing Bared. Johnny Morgan
Nothing But Blood. P. C. Smith
Nothing But Foxes. Roy Lewis
Nothing But the Night. J. Blackburn
Nothing But the Night. J. Yaffe
Nothing But the Truth. P. Orum
Nothing But the Truth. J. Rhode

Nothing Can Rescue Me. E. Daly
Nothing Counterfeit. D. Haring
Nothing Ever Happens. M. Lincoln
Nothing Ever Happens Here. A. McMaster
Nothing for Nothing. N. Easton
Nothing Happens to Children in Beverly Hills. Vi Wolfson
Nothing Hid. A. Marshall
Nothing in Her Way. C. Williams
Nothing Irredeemable. D. G. Waring
Nothing Is for Free. W. Newton
Nothing Is the Number When You Die. Joan Fleming
Nothing Lasts Forever. R. Thorp
Nothing Like Blood. L. Bruce
Nothing Man. J. Thompson
Nothing Matters. H. B. Tree
Nothing More Than Murder. J. Thompson
Nothing Natural. J. Diski
Nothing New. Anonymous
Nothing New. Mrs. Craik
Nothing Personal. Peter Chambers
Nothing Personal. S. Wishman
Nothing to Declare. M. Coles
Nothing to Declare. R. Mann
Nothing to Do with the Case. E. Lemarchand
Nothing to Hide. N. Perrelli
Nothing to Hide. D. Spade
Nothing to Lose. R. Charles
Nothing to Lose. R. Drayton
Nothing to Lose But My Life. L. Trimble
Nothing to Pretend. E. Thorne
Nothing to Report. R. McLaughlin
Nothing Venture. P. Wentworth
Nothing's Certain But Death. M. K. Wren
Notice of Death. J. Penn
Notice to Quit. J. Quince
Notorious. D. Keene
Notorious Landlady. I. Shulman
Notorious Miss Lisle. B. Reynolds
Notorious Miss Walters. S. Kyle
Notorious Sophie Lang. F. I. Anderson
Notting Hill Murder. C. Ryland
Notting Hill Mystery. C. Felix
Noughts and Crosses. Q
Noughts and Crosses. E. Woodward
Noumea. Richard Hall
Novel Novel. Lady Constance Howard
November. G. Simenon
November Joe, Detective of the Woods. H. Prichard
November Man. B. Freemantle
November Man. B. Granger
November 9th at Kersea. A. Swift
November Reef. R. Maugham
November Wind. P. Geddes
Novena for Murder. Sister C. A. O'Marie
Now and for Never. H. A. Hoare
Now and Then, Amen. J. Cleary
Now Barrabas. W. D. Home
Now Dead Is Any Man. P. Audemars
Now For It! G. Usher
Now, Gentlemen, Please. H. Fernee
Now I Lay Me Down to Die. E. Tebbetts-Taylor
Now Is the Time. L. Katcher
Now It's My Turn. M. E. Chaber
Now Let's Talk of Graves. S. Shankman
Now Like to Die. H. Brinton
Now Lying Dead. O. Norton
Now Lying Dead. P. H. Powell
Now or Never. M. Coles
Now Seek My Bones. S. H. Courtier
Now Trixie. E. M. Gall
Now Try the Morgue. T. D. Smith
Now We Are Free. K. David
Now Will You Try for Murder? H. Olesker
Now You Don't. R. Greth
Now You See It-Him-Them. G. DeWeese
Nowhere. T. Berger
Nowhere? A. M. Stein
Nowhere Fast. V. Wallen
Nowhere Man. J. Oster
Nowhere Man. Ritchie Perry
Nowhere Place. J. Lymington
Nowhere to Go. D. MacKenzie

Nowhere Weapon. Nick Carter
Nuclear Letters. G. Lancaster
Nude in Mink. S. Rohmer
Nude in Nevada. T. B. Dewey
Nude in Nylon. R. Dudgeon
Nude Nymph. D. Haring
Nude on the Rocks. Clay Henry
Nude on Thin Ice. G. Brewer
Nude on Thin Ice. C. Williams
Nude Stranger. M. Reed
Nude Was Framed. R. Drayton
Nude—with a View. Carter Brown
Nudist Murder. T. Stevenson
Nugget. R. Potts
Nuggets in the Devil's Punch Bowl. A. Robertson
Nuke Hill. S. Spetz
Number. A. P. Carter
Number 18. C. M. Wills
Number 87. H. Hext
Number Fifteen. D. Whitelaw
Number 9 Belmont Square. J. Erskine
Number Nineteen. J. J. Farjeon
No. 19. E. Jepson
No. 19 State Street. D. G. Adee
No. 99. A. Griffiths
Number Nought. S. Truss
Number One. R. Masson
No. 101. Wymond Carey
Number 1-2-3. F. Gerard
Number One with a Bullet. E. Jesmer
Number One's Last Crime. M. E. Cooke
Number Seven Queer Street. Margery Lawrence
No. 7, Saville Square. W. LeQueux
No. 17. J. J. Farjeon
Number Seventeen. L. Tracy
Number Seventy-Three. S. Kyle
Number Six. E. Wallace
Number 13. F. M. White
No. 13, Rue de Bon Diable. Arthur Sherburne Hardy
No. 13 Rue Marlot. R. De Pont-Jest
No. 13 Toroni. J. Regis
No. 13 Washington Square. L. Scott
No. 3. L. K. Vincent
No. 3 the Square. F. Warden
Number to Call Is . . . R. Thomspon
Number Two, North Steps. J. Dering
Numbered Account. A. Bridge
Numbers for Lovers. A. J. Fitzgerald
Numbers Man. D. J. Gerrity
Nun in the Closet. D. Gilman
Nun in the Cupboard. D. Gilman
Nun of Misericordia. Sophia Frances
Nun of the Above. M. Quill
Nun's Castle. Jennie Melville
Nuns of the Desert. E. DeActon
Nuplex Red. Simon Quinn
Nuremburg Gift. R. Conot
Nurse. A. Askew
Nurse Alice in Love. T. Charles
Nurse at Brooding Mansion. P. Warren
Nurse at Danger Mansion. P. Daniels
Nurse at the Castle. J. Holden
Nurse Elisia. G. M. Fenn
Nurse Hanson's Strange Case. G. Richmond
Nurse Lester's First Case. A. M. Griffin
Nurse on Nightmare Island. L. Eby
Nurse on Terror Island. Doris Knight
Nurse Revel's Mistake. F. Warden
Nurse Stacey Comes Aboard. Rona Randall
Nurse to Dives. P. Trent
Nursemaid Who Disappeared. P. MacDonald
Nursery. D. Lippincott
Nursery. D. Shlian
Nursery Crimes. B. M. Gill
Nursery Rhyme Murders. G. Verner
Nursery Tea and Poison. A. Morice
Nursing Home. A. Applin
Nursing Home Murder. N. Marsh
Nut-Browne Mayd. G. Warden
Nut Case. P. Conway
Nuts. T. Topor
Nuts and Nylons. J. Dekker
Nylon Nightmare. Clayton Matthews

Nylon Pirates. N. Monsarrat
Nyloned Avenger. H. Janson
Nymph at Bay. E. P. Frankland
Nymph Corps. D. Haring
Nymph in the Night. H. Janson
Nymph Island Affair. S. O'Shea
Nymph to the Slaughter. Carter Brown
Nympho Named Silvia. H. Janson
Nymphs and Satires. R. Ferguson

O As in Omen. L. Treat
O Charitable Death. R. C. Payes
O Clouds Unfold. P. Capon
O.D. at Sweet Claude's. M. Gattzden
O Huge Angel. H. Baer
OPEC Objective. M. Hammonds
O.P.E.C. Project. R. Vacha
O, Susannah! K. Wilhelm
O Sweet McTavish. C. Brooks
O-Zone. P. Theroux
Oak and Iron. J. B. Hendryx
Oakdale Affair. E. R. Burroughs
Oaks of Bashan. R. P. Pond
Oasis. J. Creasey
Oasis. P. Meredith
Oasis Nine. V. Canning
Oasis of Fear. K. Evans
Oasis of Tears. M. Richmond
Oath of Fear. W. J. Bayfield
Oath of Office. S. J. Kirsch
Oath of Seven. G. A. Glay
Oath of Vengeance. J. K. Stafford
Obeah Murders. H. Footner
Obedience. Joseph Hansen
Obelisk Conspiracy. G. Marton
Obelists at Sea. C. D. King
Obelists en Route. C. D. King
Obelists Fly High. C. D. King
Oberst. W. Harrington
Obi. Anonymous
Obit. D. Paisner
Obit Deferred. L. Trimble
Obit Delayed. H. Nielsen
Obituary Arrives at 2:00. S. Natsuki
Obituary Blonde. M. Brody
Obituary Club. H. Pentecost
Object of Jealousy. A. Rutledge
Object of the Exercise. P. Ordway
Obligation. R. Neely
Obligations of Hercule. P. Audemars
Obliging Corpse. J. Courage
Obliging Husband. F. Barrett
Oblivion Tapes. T. Murari
Oblivious Host. B. Myers
Oblong Circle. H. P. Rednour
Obole of Paradise. Agnes Miller
Obols for Charon. S. Harvester
Obscure Grave. Sara Woods
Obsequies at Oxford. E. Crispin
Observations of Henry. J. K. Jerome
Observer Corpse Mystery. R. Hardinge
Obsessed. G. Schweitzer
Obsession. Alec Coppel
Obsession. H. Janson
Obsession. S. Mitchell
Obsession. M. Tripp
Obsession. L. White
Obsession for Two. John Bentley
Obsession to Kill. M. Shane
Obsessions. T. Gurr
Obsessions. L. St. Clair
Obsidian. Dianne Day
Obsidian and other stories. Kelvin T. Jones
Obstacle Course. V. Montgomery
Obstinate Captain Samson. Gavin Douglas
Obstinate Girl. E. Jepson
Obstinate Murderer. E. S. Holding
Obstinate Virgin. S. Murray
Obvious Solution. C. F. Gregg
Occidental Sketches. B. C. Truman
Occupational Hazards. H. H. Roberts
Occupying Power. Evelyn Anthony
Ocean Knight. F. Du Boisgobey
Ocean of Fire. A. J. Griffin

Ocean Prize. J. Pattinson
Ocean Road. Jack Bennett
Ocean Secret. G. Boothby
Ocean Secret. Waters
Ocean Sleuth. M. Drake
Ocean Tragedy. W. C. Russell
Ocean Tramps. H. D. Stacpoole
Ocean's 11. G. C. Johnson
Octagon Crystal. P. Foley
Octagon House. P. A. Taylor
Octangle. E. N. Sachs
Octavia's Hill. M. Dickson
October Cabaret. E. Quest
October Circle. R. Littell
October Heat. G. De Marco
October House. K. C. Strahan
October Kill. R. Rostand
October Letters. C. H. Yaeger
October Man. E. Britton
October Men. John Mills
October Men. A. Price
October Plot. C. Egleton
October Witch. Alanna Knight
Octopus of Crime. B. House
Octopus of Paris. G. Leroux
Octopus' Shadow. M. Carrel
Octopussy. I. Fleming
Octopossy and The Living Daylights. I. Fleming
Octoroon. D. Boucicault
Octoroon. M. E. Braddon
Odd—But Even So. P. C. Wren
Odd Craft. W. W. Jacobs
Odd Flamingo. N. Bawden
Odd Issues. S. S. Sprigge
Odd Job. P. Flower
Odd Job Man. N. J. Crisp
Odd Job No. 101, and other future crimes and intrigues. R. Goulart
Odd Man In. L. A. G. Strong
Odd Man In. M. C. Tutt
Odd Man Out. F. L. Green
Odd Man Pays. D. L. Teilhet
Odd Number. G. Sorrentino
Odd One Out. L. D. Stranger
Odd Pairs. L. Housman
Odd People in Odd Places. James Greenwood
Odd Stories. F. Forbes-Robertson
Odd Trick. A. M. Meadows
Odd Woman Out. George Douglas
Odd Woman Out. S. Fox
Odd Woman Out. J. L. Linklater
Oddest of Courtships. J. W. De Forrest
Oddfather. S. Weinstein
Oddities of Short-Hand. J. B. Carey
Odds. E. M. Dell
Odds Against. D. Francis
Odds Against Her. A. Wood
Odds Against Linda. S. Ward
Odds Against Tomorrow. W. P. McGivern
Odds and Ends. B. M. Croker
Odds Are Murder. M. McQuay
Odds End. T. Wynne-Jones
Odds On. J. Lange
Odds on Bluefeather. L. Meynell
Odds on Death. C. Drummond
Odds on Gold. W. Hughes
Odds on Miss Seaton. H. Carvic
Odds-on-Murder. J. Dolph
Odds on Murder. M. Levien
Odds on the Hot Seat. J. Philips
Odds Run Out. H. Waugh
Oddways. H. Adams
Odean Theatre Mystery. D. Whitelaw
Odessa Beach. B. Leuci
Odessa File. F. Forsyth
Odious Ones. J. Sohl
Odor of Bitter Almonds. J. G. Edwards
Odor of Violets. B. Kendrick
Odour of Decay. M. Jenson
Odyssey of Husky Hillier. F. A. M. Webster
Odyssey Project. L. De Marino
Of a Fool and His Folly. Wilfred North
Of All the Bloody Cheek. F. McAuliffe
Of Demons and Darkness. J. Collier

Of Dope and Dervishes. L. Gainsborough
Of Good and Evil. E. K. Gann
Of Graves, Worms and Epitaphs. Tobias Wells
Of Hidden Depths. A. Windsor-Richards
Of High Degree. C. Gibbon
Of High Descent. G. M. Fenn
Of Ladies Dead. A. Hasluck
Of Love and Danger. J. MacLaren-Ross
Of Love and Intrigue. V. Coffman
Of Love and Shadows. I. Allende
Of Malicious Intent. L. Meynell
Of Masks and Minds. F. E. Smith
Of Mice and Murder. B. Whitaker
Of Midnight Honor. J. G. Vermandel
Of Missing Persons. D. Goodis
Of Our Time. J. Gordon
Of Royal Blood. W. LeQueux
Of Singular Purpose. Roy Lewis
Of Six Suspects. D. Newton
Of Tender Sin. D. Goodis
Of the Deepest Dye. C. Larking
Of This Death. V. Campbell
Of Unsound Mind. H. Carmichael
Of Wilful Intent. Sheila Johnson
Of Wind and Fire. J. Blackmore
Ofanu. G. Forve
O'Farrell's Law. B. Freemantle
O'Fear. P. Corris
Off Duty. A. Coburn
Off-Islanders. N. Benchley
Off Lands End. W. Reid
Off Limits. N. Cain
Off Shore. Taffrail
Off the Beaten Track. F. St. Mars
Off the Record. Joe Joyce
Off the Track. J. Aanrooy
Off the Track. H. Juta
Off the Track in London. G. R. Sims
Off to the Wilds. G. M. Fenn
Off with Her Head! G. D. H. Cole
Off with His Head. N. Marsh
Off with His Head. J. L. Morrissey
Offense Against the Persons. H. Gilbert
Offer of Marriage. Lynna Cooper
Offering. M. Bolton
Offering. James Reid
Office Party. M. A. Gilbert
Office Party—and After. R. Timperley
Office Scandal. F. A. Edwards
Office Secret. W. LeQueux
Officer! H. Footner
Officer and a Gentleman? and other stories. G. Thorne
Officer Factory. H. H. Kirst
Officer from Special Branch. T. Lilley
Officer 666. B. Currie
Officer 666. A. McHugh
Officer, That's Your Man. P. G. Larbalestier
Official Chaperon. N. S. Lincoln
Official Secret. A. Duncan
Official Secrets. J. Dell
Offshore! S. Coulter
Offshore Conspiracy. J. N. Chance
Ogden Enigma. G. Snyder
Ogilvie, Tallant & Moon. C. Q. Yarbro
Ogre. M. Ronson
Oh, Bury Me Not. M. K. Wren
Oh! Hugh Pecker. M. Clinten
Oh, Joshua! Taffrail
Oh, Murderer Mine. N. Davis
Oh, No, You Don't. H. Carstairs
Oh Shepherd, Speak! U. Sinclair
Oh! Where Are Bloody Mary's Earrings? R. Player
Oh, Wicked Wanda. F. Mullally
O'Houlihan's Jest. R. O'Grady
Oil Bastards. P. McCutchan
Oil by Murder. J. Paul
Oil Heist. W. A. Harbinson
Oil on the Rift. J. Stonehouse
Oil Pirates. L. O. Johnson
Oil Rig. F. Roderus
Oil Slick. R. Sapir
Oil Strike. J. Wingate
Oil Under the Window. N. Berrow

O

Okay, Shoot It! D. Haring
Okewood of the Secret Service. D. Valentine
Oklahoma Firefight. L. Derrick
Oklahoma Justice. Dean Morgan
Oklahoma Punk. L. D. Estleman
Oktober. S. Gallagher
Oktoberfest. F. De Felitta
Old Acquaintance. N. Guild
Old Admiral Death. R. Bridges
Old Age of Lecoq, the Detective. F. Du Boisgobey
Old Age of Monsieur Lecoq. F. Du Boisgobey
Old Anthony's Secret. W. J. Shaw
Old Bailey Mystery. A. Blair
Old Bank. W. Westall
Old Battle Ax. E. S. Holding
Old Bill. Patrick Quinn
Old Blazer's Hero. D. C. Murray
Old Bones. A. J. Elkins
Old Bones. H. Petersen
Old Bull Inn of Silver Street, Edmonton. Thomas Lee
Old Cantonment, with other stories of India. B. M. Croker
Old Corcoran's Money. R. Dowling
Old Country House. Anonymous
Old Dark House. J. B. Priestley
Old Detective's Pupil. Anonymous
Old Detective's Pupil. Nicholas Carter
Old Dick. L. A. Morse
Old Die Young. R. Lockridge
Old Ebbie. F. A. M. Webster
Old Ebbie Returns. F. A. M. Webster
Old Electricity, the Lightning Detective. Anonymous
Old Electricity, the Lightning Detective. Old Sleuth
Old English Baron. Clara Reeve
Old English Peep Show. P. Dickinson
Old Evil House. L. F. Brooks
Old Factory. W. Westall
Old-Fashioned Christmas. A. Dick
Old-Fashioned Murder. M. McIntire
Old-Fashioned Mystery. R. Fairleigh
Old-Fashioned War. W. B. Murphy
Old Fears. R. Wolfe
Old Fires and Profitable Ghosts. A. T. Quiller-Couch
Old Fox. W. Fennerton
Old Fox Deceiv'd. M. Grimes
Old Friend. V. Siller
Old Friends. Andrew Lang
Old Ghosts Never Die. M. Warner
Old Gibbet. E. Thornton
Old Goat. E. Greenwood
Old Gold Road. Ian Mitchell
Old Goriot. H. Balzac
Old Granstock. J. Easton
Old Gumber's Mill. E. J. Kyle
Old Hall, New Hall. M. Innes
Old Harry Hawks. Anonymous
Old House at Sandwich. J. Hatton
Old House at the Corner. F. Warden
Old House by the Sea. S. E. Phipps
Old House of Fear. R. Kirk
Old House of Rayner. Grimley Hill
Old House of West Street. T. P. Prest
Old Ironsides Among the Italian Brigands. Old Sleuth
Old Isaacs from the Bowery. C. E. Blaney
Old Jess. Jennifer Johnston
Old Jew Mystery. H. Adams
Old Judge Priest. I. S. Cobb
Old King Cole. S. P. B. Mais
Old King Cole. E. Shanks
Old Lady Dies. Anthony Gilbert
Old Lattimer's Legacy. J. S. Fletcher
Old Lover's Ghost. L. Ford
Old Loves Die Hard. J. C. Faust
Old McBein. W. Westrup
Old Madhouse. W. F. De Morgan
Old Maid's Secret. E. Marlitt
Old Maid's Vengeance. F. Powell
Old Mam'selle's Secret. E. Marlitt
Old Man Curry. C. E. Van Loan
Old Man Dies. G. Blundell

Old Man Dies. G. Simenon
Old Man Goriot. H. Balzac
Old Man in the Corner. B. Orczy
Old Man in the Corner Unravels the Mystery of the Fulton Gardens Mystery, and The Moorland Tragedy. B. Orczy
Old Man in the Corner Unravels the Mystery of the Pearl Necklace, and The Tragedy in Bishop's Road. B. Orczy
Old Man in the Corner Unravels the Mystery of the Russian Prince, and of Dog's Tooth Cliff. B. Orczy
Old Man in the Corner Unravels the Mystery of the White Carnation, and The Montmartre Hat. B. Orczy
Old Man Mystery. J. J. Farjeon
Old Man of the Moors. W. Jardine
Old Man Savarin and other stories. E. W. Thomson
Old Man Tutt. A. Train
Old Manor. C. F. Gregg
Old Manor Crime. W. Martyn
Old Manor House. Charlotte Smith
Old Man's Money. J. Reach
Old Margaret and other stories. H. Kingsley
Old Masters. W. Haggard
Old Mill. P. W. Wilson
Old Mill Mystery. A. W. Marchmont
Old Miser's Mystery. Old Sleuth
Old Miser's Ward. Old Sleuth
Old Mr. Davenant's Money. F. Powell
Old Mrs. Camelot. E. Bonett
Old Mrs. Fitzgerald. H. Hocking
Old Mrs. Ommanney Is Dead. M. Erskine
Old Mrs. Warren. F. Wolseley
Old Money. L. Fosburgh
Old Mortality, King of Detectives. Y. Baxter
Old Murders. P. Whalley
Old Murders Never Die. N. Carlson
Old Must Die. A. Gaines
Old Myddelton's Money. M. C. Hay
Old Neighborhood and New Settlements. E. D. E. N. Southworth
Old New York. H. Zore
Old Offenders and a Few Old Scores. E. W. Hornung
Old Patch's Medley. M. Bowen
Old Phenomenal. Anonymous
Old Puritan, the Old Time Detective. Anonymous
Old Quartz, the Nevada Detective. E. T. Sawyer
Old Reliable. P. G. Wodehouse
Old Rogue's Tragedy. Rita
Old Rowley. M. M. Bodkin
Old Sailors Never Die. H. D. Stacpoole
Old Saxon Blood. L. Tourney
Old School Tie. Andrew Taylor
Old Scores to Settle. C. Heath
Old Silent. M. Grimes
Old Sinners Never Die. D. S. Davis
Old Sins Have Long Shadows. J. L. Rickard
Old Sleuth, the Avenger. Old Sleuth
Old Sleuth, the Detective. Old Sleuth
Old Sleuth, the Protean Detective. Anonymous
Old Sleuth to the Rescue. Old Sleuth
Old Sleuth's Greatest Case. Old Sleuth
Old Sleuth's Trimph. Old Sleuth
Old Sleuth's Winning Hand. Old Sleuth
Old Sleuth's Wonderful Revelation. Old Sleuth
Old Specie, the Treasury Detective. M. Manly
Old Specie, the Treasure Detective. A. Robertson
Old Stone House and other stories. A. K. Green
Old Stonewall, the Colorado Detective. J. R. Taylor
Old Stonewall, the "Shadower". Anonymous
Old Students Never Die. I. T. Ross
Old Style's. H. Spicer
Old Terrible. Old Sleuth
Old Terrible, the Iron Arm Detective. Anonymous
Old Time Before Them. E. Phillpotts
Old Tin Sorrows. Glen Cook
Old Tollgate Mystery. W. J. Bayfield
Old Trade of Killing. J. Harris
Old Transform, the Secret Special Detective. Anonymous
Old Ugly Face. T. Mundy
Old Vengeful. A. Price

Old Wars. D. Helwig
Oldest Confession. R. Condon
Oldest Profession. B. Sarto
Oldest Road. D. G. Waring
Olga Nazimov and other stories. W. L. George
Olga Knaresbrook, Detective. H. Campbell
Olga, the Disillusioned. K. Kimbrough
Olga's Crime. F. Barrett
Olive Varcoe. Anonymous
Oliver Goldfinch. Emerson Bennett
Oliver Iverson. A. Devoore
Oliver Quendon's First Case. Cowdray Browne
Oliver Twisted. T. J. Kelly
Olivia. Gwendoline Butler
Olivia's Story. A. Winter
Olmec Head. D. Westheimer
Olura. G. Household
Olympiad. N. Frith
Olympic Mission. P. Ferguson
Olympic Sleeper. T. Barling
Om. T. Mundy
Omar, Fats and Trixie. J. Reese
Omega Assignment. David Lewis
Omega Command. J. Land
Omega Deception. C. Robertson
Omega Document. J. A. MacKenzie
Omega Factor. J. Gerson
Omega-Minus. T. Allbeury
Omega Operation. N. Conway
Omega Terror. Nick Carter
Omega Threat. M. Washburn
Omelet Murder Case. T. J. Kelly
Omen. M. Eyre
Omen of the Owls. M. Bernier
Omerta. P. McCurtin
Ominous Star. R. Foley
Omit Flowers. S. Palmer
Omit Flowers, Please. A. Gaines
Omni Strain. C. Patton
Omnibus Mystery. F. Du Boisgobey
Omnipotent Avenger. Old Sleuth
On a Blind Trail. J. K. Stafford
On a Crimson Trail. Nicholas Carter
On a Dead Man's Chest. J. M. T. Miller
On a False Charge. S. W. Hopkins
On a Fated Night. D. Malm
On a Field of Black. G. Tomlinson
On a Million-Dollar Trail. Nicholas Carter
On a Still Night. C. D. Peel
On Account of Murder. E. Powers
On Any Given Sunday. P. Toomey
On Appeal. P. Dewdney
On Circumstantial Evidence. F. Marryat
On Company's Service. W. P. Ridge
On Compassionate Leave. L. Jackson
On Course for Murder. P. A. Foxall
On Dangerous Ground. E. S. Drewry
On Death's Trail. Dick Stewart
On Desperate Seas. J. Pattinson
On Executive Orders. Rianna Craig
On Forsyte 'Change. J. Galsworthy
On Fortune's Wheel. R. M. Wells
On Government Service. F. A. M. Webster
On Hazardous Duty. David St. John
On Helle's Wave. H. Imber
On Her Majesty's Secret Service. Anonymous
On Her Majesty's Secret Service. I. Fleming
On Her Majesty's Service. A. Upward
On His Majesty's Service. R. Bridges
On His Majesty's Service. Maxwell Scott
On Ice. R. G. Dean
On Ice. T. J. MacGregor
On Land and Sea. G. Simenon
On Murder's Skirts. T. Adler
On My Honor. Malacai Black
On Schedule. E. L. Long
On Secret Air Service. L. L. T. Driggs
On Secret Service. R. Arnold
On Secret Service. J. Mowbray
On Secret Service. Hedley Scott
On Secret Service. W. N. Taft
On Such a Night. A. Quayle
On Suspicion. David Fletcher
On Swan River. H. Footner

Title Index

On Target. J. O. Mayo
On the Bed of the Ocean. E. S. Brooks
On the Borderland. F. B. Austin
On the Borderland. F. Boyle
On the Bridge at Midnight. Bruce Brandon
On the Brink. D. Batchelor
On the Brink. M. Endfield
On the Brink of a Chasm. L. T. Meade
On the Brink of Ruin. Old Spicer
On the Danger Line. G. Simenon
On the Danger List. M. Cumberland
On the Day of the Shooting. C. Franklin
On the Dead Run. W. B. Murphy
On the Double. Roger Fuller
On the Edge. R. Doliner
On the Edge. P. Lovesey
On the Edge. E. Naha
On the Edge of Empire. E. Jepson
On the Edge of the Sea. F. L. Green
On the 8th Day. L. E. Okun
On the 11:40 Down. H. King
On the Embankment. R. Dowling
On the Eve of Triumph. Nicholas Carter
On the Fringe. T. W. Speight
On the Highest Hill. H. M. Stephenson
On the Hook. R. Powell
On the Inside. F. F. Kelly
On the Inside. Ted Wood
On the Instructions of My Government. P. Salinger
On the Jury. R. Marsh
On the Jury. W. Phillips
On the Lightship. H. K. Viele
On the Line and Danger Signal. B. Hemyng
On the Loose. E. V. Adams
On the Make. J. D. MacDonald
On the Midnight Beat. J. G. Brandon
On the Night Express! H. H. C. Gibbons
On the Night Express. F. M. White
On the Night in Question. C. M. Wills
On the Night of the 18th . . . L. Meynell
On the Night of the Fire. F. L. Green
On the Night of the 14th. Mark Cross
On the Night of the Ninth. R. Trevor
On the Night of the Seventh Moon. V. Holt
On the Other Hand. R. Stevenson
On the Prime Minister's Account. O. Hogstrand
On the Rack. W. C. Hudson
On the Ragged Edge. Nicholas Carter
On the Rank. B. Hemyng
On the Right Wrists. A. Livingston
On the Rim of the Arctic. J. B. Hendryx
On the Road. B. Hemyng
On the Road. K. Okpi
On the Run. E. M. Bowen
On the Run. M. Constanduros
On the Run. Roland Daniel
On the Run. L. Daniels
On the Run. Angus Hall
On the Run. L. L. McCall
On the Run. J. D. MacDonald
On the Scent. Anonymous
On the Secret Service of His Majesty, the Queen. S. Weinstein
On the Shady Side. F. Swinnerton
On the Shores of Night. A. Mans
On the Spot. E. Wallace
On the Stairs. W. J. Hurlbut
On the Stretch. J. Welcome
On the Stroke of Midnight. M. O. Rolfe
On the Stroke of Nine. A. Parsons
On the Stroke of 12. J. LeBrandt
On the Third Day. M. Delahaye
On the Track. H. Lawson
On the Track of Death. D. Rutherford
On the Trail of "Big Finger". S. Campbell
On the Trail of Blood. A. Robbins
On the Trail of Justice. G. Wallace
On the Waterfront. B. Schulberg
On the Way Out. John Williams
On the Wing. Old Sleuth
On the Wing of Occasions. J. C. Harris
On the Wings of Truth. J. B. Boydstun
On the Yard. M. Braly
On Their Track. Old Sleuth

On Ticket of Leave. S. Blake
On Ticket of Leave. J. G. Brandon
On Toast. W. P. Ridge
On Trial. E. L. Reizenstein
On Trail. D. Torbett
On Trial for His Life. O. Harper
On Trust. T. Cobb
On Winding Waters. W. M. Graydon
Once! Curtis Yorke
Once a Copper. W. Terry
Once a Crook. E. Price
Once a Mutt. W. B. Murphy
Once a Prostitute. A. Hunter
Once a Spy. R. Airth
Once a Spy. R. Footman
Once a Thief. Z. Marko
Once a Thief. J. Trinian
Once a Week. A. A. Milne
Once a Widow. Lee Roberts
Once a Year Man. M. Tripp
Once Acquitted. A. R. Long
Once and Always Murder. O. Papazoglu
Once and Future Spy. R. Littell
Once, and Then the Funeral. B. J. Farmer
Once Bit, Twice Hit. H. C. McNeile
Once Bitten, and What Ensued. G. M. Winsor
Once Bitten, Twice Bitten. N. Karta
Once Dying, Twice Dead. R. Lewis
Once for All. M. Hillary
Once I Was Blind. Andrew Stewart
Once in a Lifetime. J. Mayo
Once in a Red Moon. J. T. Rogers
Once in Aleppo. D. R. Barton
Once in Tiger Bay. J. M. Walsh
Once More the Saint. L. Charteris
Once Off Guard. J. H. Wallis
Once Over Deadly. F. Gruber
Once Over Deadly. E. McNamara
Once Over Lightly. K. Robeson
Once There Was a Giant. K. Laumer
Once Too Often. W. Chambers
Once Too Often. Mark Cross
Once Too Often. R. Lait
Once Too Often. F. Warden
Once Upon a Christmas Time. G. R. Sims
Once Upon a Crime. Mark Cross
Once Upon a Crime. Michael Hall
Once Upon a Crime. M. Kerrigan
Once Upon a Crime. C. Monig
Once Upon a Crime. R. Selman
Once Upon a Fairy Tale. M. McShane
Once Upon a Friday. P. Moore
Once Upon a Midnight. J. Reach
Once Upon a Murder. R. J. Randisi
Once Upon a Nightmare. Lynn Williams
Once Upon a Private Eye. P. Quinn
Once Upon a Time. R. H. Davis
Once Upon a Time. E. Phillpotts
Once Upon a Time in America. L. Hays
Once Upon a Tombstone. E. Salter
Once We Were Men. G. Nimse
Once You Stop, You're Dead. E. K. Goldthwaite
Ondine. Shannon Drake
Ondine. C. Kozloff
One. D. Karp
1-A Stranger. A. Guirdham
One Across, Two Down. R. Rendell
One Against the Earth. D. Mainwaring
One Against the Odds. N. Fagan
One Alone. V. Siller
One Among None. R. Stratton
One Angel Less. H. W. Roden
One Angry Man. N. Daniels
One-Armed Murder. R. Gallagher
One Away. A. Prior
One Bang-Up Job. G. Laurence
One Between. F. Cowen
One Black Summer. B. Jefferis
One Blonde Body. Stephen James
One Blonde Died. L. Edgley
One Bright Day. E. S. Miller
One Bright Summer Morning. J. H. Chase
One by One. Linda Lee
One by One. F. Nichols

One by One They Disappeared. M. Dalton
One Clear Call. F. N. Greene
One Clear Call. U. Sinclair
One Coffee With. M. Maron
One Corpse Missing. Z. H. Ross
One Corpse Too Many. Ellis Peters
One Cried Murder. S. H. Courtier
One Cried Murder. Jean Leslie
One Cried Murder. D. C. Wall
One Crime Too Many. J. Guil
One Damn Thing After Another. N. Freeling
One Dark Night. P. Bennetts
One Day I Will Tell You. S. K. Aburish
One Day in Hell. H. Zachary
One Dead Dean. B. Crider
One Dead Debutante. H. Gould
One Deadly Dawn. H. Whittington
One Deadly Summer. S. Japrisot
One Death in the Red. E. Mazzaro
One Deathless Hour. R. Ormerod
One Dip Dead. A. M. Stein
One Dollar Death. R. Barth
One-Dollar Rip-Off. R. Dennis
One Down. A. Bodelsen
One Down and Two to Slay. H. Brinton
One Dreadful Night. R. S. L. Harding
One Drop of Blood. Anne Austin
One Easy Piece. D. Merritt
One Enchanted Evening. M. Richmond
One Enchanted Summer. A. Brooks
One Endless Hour. D. J. Marlowe
One Evening I Shall Return. Anne-Mariel
One-Eyed King. E. Fadiman
One-Eyed Knave. Ganpat
One-Eyed Mystic. K. Robeson
One-Faced Girl. C. Armstrong
One Fair Enemy. C. Dawe
One False Move. R. Drayton
One False Move. K. Roos
One Fearful Yellow Eye. J. D. MacDonald
One Fell Sloop. S. Kenney
One Fifty Three Oakland Street. D. Highland
One Fine Day. Elizabeth Ford
One Fine Day. M. Richmond
One Fine Day the Rabbi Bought a Cross. H. Kemelman
One Foot in Hell. Wilene Shaw
One Foot in the Grave. M. Cumberland
One Foot in the Grave. P. Dickinson
One Foot in the Grave. D. Grubb
One for My Dame. J. Webb
One for My Money. E. Chaze
One for Sleep. F. Bonham
One for the Book. Neill Graham
One for the Books. L. A. Taylor
One for the Death House. J. M. Flynn
One for the Devil. E. Leroux
One for the Money. D. Belsky
One for the Money. E. Chaze
One for the Road. J. Beckett
One for the Road. F. Brown
One for the Road. P. Conway
One for the Road. R. Dietrich
One for the Road. B. Grant
One for the Road. W. J. White
144 Piccadilly. S. Fuller
One Frail Woman and Four Queer Men. E. Staley
One Girl in a Million. L. Tracy
One Glorious Spring. M. Richmond
One Good Death Deserves Another. Ritchie Perry
One Good Turn. N. Easton
One Got Away. H. Whittington
One Grave Too Many. R. Goulart
One Half of the World. J. Barlow
One Hand Clapping. J. Kell
One Helluva Blow. G. Werner
One Horrible Night. E. Hayford
One Horse Race. T. H. Stone
One Hour to Kill. G. H. Coxe
100 Kilo Club. S. Gandolfi
100 Megaton Kill. Ralph Hayes
100 Mysteries for Arm-Chair Detectives. J. C. Cannell
180 Degrees Murder. G. Larsen

O

$106,000 Blood Money. D. Hammett
120-Hour Clock. F. M. Nevins, Jr.
$100,000 Kiss. Nicholas Carter
100,000 Pound Insurance Swindle. W. W. Sayer
100,000 Pounds Versus Ghosts. R. Jocelyn
100,000 Welcomes. M. Kenyon
One If by Night. M. Steeber
One in Five. J. W. Lee
One Is a Lonely Number. B. Elliott
One Is One. A. Dick
One Is One. M. Tripp
One Jump Ahead. A. Armstrong
One Jump Ahead. R. Chapman
One Jump Ahead. M. Cronin
One Just Man. James Mills
One Kind and Another. B. Pain
One Last Chance. L. Noel
One Last Mad Embrace. J. T. Story
One Last Time. M. Carrel
One Lethal Night. R. Lynford
One Life Between. A. M. Meadows
One Life, One Love. M. E. Braddon
One Live Blonde. D. Haring
One Lives, One Dies. D. Brierley
One Lonely Night. M. Spillane
One Louisburg Square. W. E. D. Ross
One Love Is Too Many for an Agent. J. Mirkarimi
One Lover Too Many. M. Tripp
One Mad Night. J. Reach
One Maid's Mischief. G. M. Fenn
One-Man Army. J. Cutter
One Man Came Back. L. Y. Erskine
One Man in His Time. S. D. Frances
One Man in the World. J. Barlow
One-Man Jury. S. Ransome
One Man Must Die. A. B. Cunningham
One Man Saw Them Die. A. Webb
One Man Show. M. Innes
One Man Too Many. V. Coffman
One Man's Awe. V. Carrington
One Man's Crime. L. W. Brent
One Man's Death. S. Truss
One Man's Enemies. S. Truss
One Man's Justice. P. Alding
One Man's Meat. W. H. L. Crauford
One Man's Meat. Colin Watson
One Man's Muddle. E. B. Quinn
One Man's Murder. D. Delman
One Man's Poison. C. Fitzsimmons
One Man's Poison. S. Fox
One Man's Reality. C. Cornwall
One Man's Secret. Stratford Davis
One Man's Secret. A. Mills
One Man's War. B. Bavin
One Man's Wars. G. Hackforth-Jones
One Man's Woman. K. Hewitt
One Million Carats. L. D. Klausner
$1,000,000 in Corpse. E. Ronns
One Million Francs. A. Fredericks
1,000,000 Pound Film Murder. Donald Stuart
1,000,000 Pound Plot. A. Skene
1,000,000 Pound Secret. J. Andrews
1,000,000 Pounds. W. J. Elliott
One Minus One. R. D. MacDougall
One-Minute Murder. J. Byrne
One Minute Past Eight. G. H. Coxe
One Minute to Eternity. R. Weverka
One Monday We Killed Them All. J. D. MacDonald
One More Bridge to Cross. A. Hale
One More for the Road. D. Haring
One More Nice White Body. D. Glinto
One More River. Laurence Kirk
One More Time. M. Avallone
One More Time. Jay Bell
One More Unfortunate. E. Lustgarten
One More Waltz, Vienna. E. McCarthy-Houck
One Murder Too Many. G. H. Coxe
One Murder Too Many. F. C. Davis
One Murder Too Many. E. Lanham
One Murder Too Many. J. C. Lenehan
One Murdered, Two Dead. M. Propper
One Must Survive. R. Charles
One Night in Styria. D. Howarth

One Night in Winter. A. Massie
One Night Mystery. Old Sleuth
One Night of Fear. A. Crane
One Night of Murder. H. Boyd
One Night of Terror. M. Carleton
One Night Stand. C. Bolt
One Night Stand. W. B. Murphy
One Night to Kill. C. Franklin
One Night with Nora. B. Halliday
One Night's Mystery. M. A. Fleming
119 Great Porter Square. B. L. Farjeon
One Object in Life. Nicholas Carter
One O'Clock. M. G. Lewis
One O'Clock at the Gotham. R. Foley
One of God's Dilemmas. A. Upward
One of Marlborough's Captains. M. Gerard
One of My Sons. A. K. Green
One of Our Agents Is Missing. David St. John
One of Our Dinosaurs Is Missing. D. Forrest
One of Our Dinosaurs Is Missing. John Harvey
One of Our H-Bombs Is Missing. F. H. Brennan
One of Our Pigeons Is Missing. R. Holdstock
One of Seven. R. Hardinge
One of the Best. S. Hicks
One of the Bevans. R. Jocelyn
One of the Eleven. W. Tyrer
One of the Family. J. Payn
One of the Flying Squad. W. M. Graydon
One of the Guilty. W. L. George
One of the Ones. J. C. Snaith
One of These Seven. C. Logan
One of Those Things. P. Cheyney
One of Those Ways. M. B. Lowndes
One of Three. C. S. Raymond
One of Two. H. Friswell
One of Us. B. Crump
One of Us. C. Emery
One of Us Is a Murderer. A. Le May
One of Us Is Wrong. Samuel Holt
One of Us Must Die. A. Clarke
One of Us Works for Them. J. D. Hunter
One-Off Job. A. Willsdon
One-One-One. G. Hackforth-Jones
One Page Missing. A. Souter
One Police Plaza. W. J. Caunitz
One Remained Seated. J. Slate
One Rose Less. P. Flower
One Sane Man. B. Beeding
One Shall Be Taken. A. Hocking
One Shipwreck Too Many. Nicholas Carter
One Shot. R. P. Greenfield
One Shot for Sadie. M. Brody
One-Shot War. B. O'Connor
One Small Step. Reginald Hill
One Step Ahead. R. Forest
One Step at a Time. Brian Todd
One Step from Murder. L. Meynell
One Step to Death. R. Hausfeld
One Step Too Far. Nicholas Carter
One Sunny Day. Joan Alexander
One Sword Less. C. D. Peel
One Tear for My Grave. M. Roscoe
One That Got Away. H. McCloy
One Thing Constant. V. B. Harris
One Thing Needful and Cut by the County. M. E. Braddon
1001 Afternoons in New York. B. Hecht
1001 Temple Avenue. R. T. Albanese
1199. Charles Rogers
1713 Madison Avenue. D. Haring
One Thrilling Night. N. Berrow
One Thrilling Night. M. K. Douglas
One-Time Champ. Duff Johnson
One to Jump. George Douglas
One to Play. H. Adams
One Too Many. Stuart Hall
One Too Many. T. Kendrick
One Touch of Blood. S. S. Baker
One Touch of Murder. H. Fraser
One Tough Cop. B. Dietl
One Traveller Returns. D. C. Murray
One Tropic Night. E. C. Vivian
One, Two, Buckle My Shoe. A. Christie
One-Two-Three Die. L. Starr

1-2-3 Murders. F. Gerard
One-Way Cemetery. M. Hinxman
One Way Only. L. A. Knight
One Way or Another. L. Sciascia
One Way Out. G. H. Coxe
One Way Out. G. Simenon
One Way Split. H. Janson
One Way Street. P. H. Irving
One Way Street. D. Keller
One Way Street. N. Marino
One Way Street. Peter Mason
One-Way Ticket. B. Hitchens
One-Way Ticket. H. Howard
One-Way Ticket. H. Lugar
One Way Ticket. R. Marlowe
One Way Ticket. A. Thackeray
One-Way Ticket. Ethel Turner
One Way to Venice. J. A. Hodge
One-Way Trail. R. Cullum
One-Way Trip. R. Angel
One Who Kills. R. Cullum
One Who Passed By. T. Cobb
One Who Saw. H. Hill
One Wife's Ways. G. F. Fox
One Woman. T. Thayer
One Woman Lost. A. McCarthy
One Wonderful Night. L. Tracy
One Wreath with Love. J. Roffman
O'Neil McDarragh. Anonymous
O'Neil McDarragh, the Detective. T. Pastor
Oni. M. Olden
Onion Field. J. Wambaugh
Onlooker. Sheila Bishop
Only a Bullet. J. K. Stafford
Only a Clod. M. E. Braddon
Only a Flirt. R. Jocelyn
Only a Girl's Heart. E. Southworth
Only a Headless Nail. Dick Stewart
Only a Horse Dealer. R. Jocelyn
Only a Love Song. M. Richmond
Only a Love Story. R. Jocelyn
Only a Matter of Time. V. C. Clinton-Baddeley
Only a Photograph. Old Sleuth
Only a Shadow. D. C. Murray
Only a Woman. M. E. Braddon
Only a Woman's Heart. E. A. Young
Only an Orphan Girl. H. Nelms
Only at Sunset. D. Martyn
Only by Mistake. P. J. Kavanagh
Only Children. David Fletcher
Only Couples Need Apply. D. M. Disney
Only Gentlemen Can Play. H. McLeave
Only Girl in the Game. J. D. MacDonald
Only Good Apple in a Barrel of Spies. M. Lovell
Only Good Body's a Dead One. T. Kenrick
Only Good German. T. Allbeury
Only Good Secretary. J. Potts
Only Half a Hoax. L. A. Taylor
Only Half Pure! D. Larson
Only Half the Doctor Died. Frank King
Only Her Hairdresser Knew . . . C. Carpenter
Only Human. D. Wade
Only in L.A. Murray Sinclair
Only in New England. T. Roscoe
Only Make Believe. Clarissa Ross
Only Men on Board. Cameron Blake
Only Mugs Die Young. Griff
Only Mugs Work. W. Grenwood
Only on Tuesdays. T. B. Dewey
Only Problem. M. Spark
Only Security. Jessica Mann
Only Seven Were Hanged. Stuart Martin
Only Some Had Guns. R. Parker
Only Son. J. W. Bobin
Only the Dead Know Brooklyn. T. Boyle
Only the Good. Mary Collins
Only the Good Die. W. Barker
Only the Guilty. A. M. Stein
Only the Hyenas Laughed. Robin Moore
Only the Losers Win. G. M. Barnes
Only the Rich Die Young. H. Pentecost
Only the Ruthless Can Play. Jonathan Burke
Only the Strong. M. Minehan
Only the Unafraid. R. Kirkbridge

Only the Very Rich. Carter Brown
Only Three Died. P. H. Powell
Only When I Larf. L. Deighton
Only When I Laugh. L. Deighton
Only When She Cries. E. Mathis
Only with a Bargepole. J. Porter
Only Witness. E. J. Goodman
Only Witness. Jan Michaels
Onyxx. T. Chiu
Oonah. G. Payne
Opal-Eyed Fan. A. Norton
Opal Heart. M. Leighton
Opal Legacy. F. Kent
Opal Murder Case. B. Symons
Opal Pendant. E. Barr
Opal Pin. J. R. Gillies
Opal Serpent. F. Hume
Opal Street. J. Wetherell
Open and Shut Case. J. Mattera
Open City. H. Miller
Open Contract. F. Scarpetta
Open Cut. J. M. O'Neill
Open Day at the Manor. Elizabeth Ford
Open Door. L. Meynell
Open Door. E. A. Walcott
Open Door. F. M. White
Open Foe. A. Sergeant
Open House. M. Innes
Open House. W. Katz
Open Mouth. M. Urquhart
Open Prison. Lady A. Scott
Open Prison. J. I. M. Stewart
Open Question. J. De Mille
Open Roadsteads. E. L. Long
Open Season. A. Mayor
Open Season. N. O'Donohoe
Open Season. D. Osborn
Open Season. B. Thielen
Open Secret. T. Cobb
Open Secret. J. Leasor
Open, Sesame! B. Reynolds
Open Shadow. B. Solomon
Open Skies. T. Block
Open Verdict. M. E. Braddon
Open Verdict. F. L. Cary
Open Verdict. R. Cooper
Open Verdict. R. Keverne
Open Verdict. W. LeQueux
Open Verdict. J. Rhode
Open Window. J. Fuller
Open Window. R. Ormerod
Open Your Hand and Close Your Eyes. P. Bair
Opener of the Way. R. Bloch
Openers of the Gate. L. A. Beck
Opening Door. H. Reilly
Opening Night. N. Marsh
Opening of a Door. W. Spence
Opera House Murders. D. Billany
Opera House Murders. D. Hanna
Opera Murders. K. Williams
Operation Afrika. C. Whiting
Operation Alcestis. M. Rennert
Operation: Alpha Death. N. Conway
Operation Aphrodite. J. Commings
Operation Apricot. C. A. Haddad
Operation Artemis. Douglas Scott
Operation Atlantis. M. G. Braun
Operation Atlantis. G. Ludi
Operation Backlash. L. McManus
Operation Bad Apple. G. F. Newman
Operation Ballerina. Selwyn
Operation Barbarossa. B. Newman
Operation Black Sea. W. X. Davies
Operation Bourdoir. S. O'Shea
Operation Breakthrough. D. J. Marlowe
Operation Bright Eyes. J. P. Sinor
Operation Burning Candle. Blyden Jackson
Operation Calpurnia. M. Rennert
Operation Carlo. J. Pendower
Operation Caroline. C. H. Gibbs-Smith
Operation Castanets. D. Martyn
Operation Catcher. S. Jackman
Operation Caucasian Fox. C. Whiting
Operation Cervantes. H. Young

Operation Che Guevara. Nick Carter
Operation Checkmate. D. J. Marlowe
Operation Choke Point. W. X. Davies
Operation Cicero. L. C. Moyzisch
Operation Cleansweep. D. Graham
Operation Cobra. A. Bodelsen
Operation Cocaine. Don Romano
Operation Code-Name Cavaller. M. D. Morrison
Operation Conquest. B. Gray
Operation Countdown. D. Streib
Operation Counterpunch. D. J. Marlowe
Operation Cuttlefish. D. R. Mounce
Operation Damascus. J. Levy
Operation Dancing Dog. J. M. Fox
Operation—Deadline. M. Dines
Operation: Death Ray. S. Cunningham
Operation Deathmaker. D. J. Marlowe
Operation Deep Six. K. Stanton
Operation Delta. A. McCall
Operation Desert Sun. C. Heath
Operation Destruct. C. Nicole
Operation Diamond. "Capstan"
Operation Diver. R. Jackson
Operation Doctors. H. Roth
Operation Dragnet. E. P. Thorne
Operation Drumfire. D. J. Marlowe
Operation Emerald. D. McCartan
Operation Endless Hour. D. J. Marlowe
Operation: Evangeline. C. W. Burleson
Operation Faust. F. Neznansky
Operation Fireball. D. J. Marlowe
Operation Fireball. Sea Lion
Operation Firedog. R. Jackson
Operation Flashpoint. D. J. Marlowe
Operation Fox Hunt. C. Whiting
Operation Getaway. R. Seth
Operation Godiva. J. Miller
Operation Goldkill. B. Cassiday
Operation Halter. Frank King
Operation Hammerlock. D. J. Marlowe
Operation Heartbreak. A. D. Cooper
Operation Hercules. J. Scotter
Operation Hijack. Don Romano
Operation Hit Man. Don Romano
Operation Homicide. E. Adams
Operation Honeymoon. Frank King
Operation Hong Kong. P. McCurtin
Operation Ice Cap. James Dark
Operation Icicle. P. Buck
Operation Il Duce. C. Whiting
Operation Intrigue. W. Hermann
Operation Iscariot. B. Marshall
Operation Jealousy. M. G. Braun
Operation Jet. Glen Allen
Operation K. N. Daniels
Operation Kill Ike. C. Whiting
Operation—Kill or Be Killed. M. Dines
Operation Kuwait. H. Arvay
Operation Lila. M. H. Albert
Operation Loan Shark. Don Romano
Operation "M.O." Taffrail
Operation: McMurdo Sound. Nick Carter
Operation Malacca. J. Poyer
Operation Manhunt. M. Coles
Operation Manhunt. C. Nicole
Operation Megali. M. Dekobra
Operation Mermaid. K. Stanton
Operation Midas. E. Ogilvie
Operation Midnight Climax. N. Bell
Operation Mind-Murder. J. Rosenberger
Operation MissSat. J. Dark
Operation Moon Rocket. Nick Carter
Operation Mora. Christopher King
Operation—Murder. L. White
Operation N. N. Daniels
Operation Nazi-U.S.A. J. Gilman
Operation Neptune. C. Nicole
Operation New York. G. De Villiers
Operation Night Hawk. J. A. Price
Operation Nightfall. J. Miles
Operation Nightmare. G. Fredrics
Operation Norfolk. C. Ramm
Operation North Africa. W. X. Davies
Operation Nuke. M. Caidin

Operation Obliterate. H. Janson
Operation Octopus. James Dark
Operation Orbit. K. Luna
Operation Overkill. H. Gantzer
Operation Overkill. D. J. Marlowe
Operation Overkill. J. Rosenberger
Operation Parrot. H. Vernes
Operation Parterre. G. Blagowidow
Operation Patch. J. Lucarotti
Operation Pax. M. Innes
Operation: Perfidia. L. Jordan
Operation Persian Gulf. W. X. Davies
Operation Petrograd. Nick Carter
Operation Piracy. P. Somers
Operation Porno. Don Romano
Operation Prophet. R. B. Asprey
Operation Q-018. G. Ludi
Operation Raven. Stuart White
Operation Red Carpet. J. Boland
Operation Red Poppy. J. N. Smith
Operation Redhead. D. Haring
Operation Royal Family. G. Null
Operation S-L. N. Daniels
Operation S.N.A.R.E. E. Gladstone
Operation Scorpio. D. Mariner
Operation Scuba. James Dark
Operation Sea Monster. K. Stanton
Operation Sharkbite. Nick Carter
Operation Sky Drop. D. Brennan
Operation Skyhook. J. Rosenberger
Operation Smokescreen. M. Judge
Operation Snake. Nick Carter
Operation Snatch. John Marsh
Operation Stalag. C. Whiting
Operation Starvation. Nick Carter
Operation Steal. J. W. R. Morrison
Operation Steel Band. G. H. Stine
Operation Steelfish. K. Stanton
Operation Stranglehold. D. J. Marlowe
Operation: Super Ms. A. Offutt
Operation Superman. H. Hawton
Operation Susie. K. Blake
Operation T. N. Daniels
Operation Ten. H. Scott
Operation Terror. The Gordons
Operation Thunderbolt. J. Rosenberger
Operation Tibet. P. Mondol
Operation—To Kill a Man. M. Dines
Operation Tokyo. T. Middleton
Operation Trigeminal. J. Bedford
Operation Urgent. Sutherland Scott
Operation VC. N. Daniels
Operation V.I.P. George Fisher
Operation Vendetta. Nick Carter
Operation Vengeance. R. Crane
Operation Weatherkill. P. Edwards
Operation Werewolf. C. Whiting
Operation Whiplash. D. J. Marlowe
Operation: World War Three. J. Milton
Operation Zenith. J. Pattinson
Operation Zimmerman. F. Geron
Operative. J. Covington
Operative. J. B. Jenkins
Operator. Stuart Hall
Operator. D. Honig
Operator. D. E. Westlake
Operator. C. Williams
Operator from Chicago. Duff Johnson
Operator No. 19. G. Goodchild
Operator X. Mark Ross
Operators. A. Prior
Ophelia. F. Stevenson
Ophelia, the Anxious. K. Kimbrough
Opium. T. Cohan
Opium Clipper. E. L. Long
Opium Flower. D. Cushman
Opium Hunter. A. Kilgore
Opium Murders. P. Baron
Opium Smugglers of Frisco. O. Harper
Opium Stratagem. H. Downs
Opperman Case. John Bentley
Opportunist. S. Youd
Opportunity. A. Soutar
Opposite Sex. M. Turni

Opposite the Jail. M. A. Denison
Option on Death. M. W. Sherer
Option to Die. L. Crews
Or All the Seas with Oysters. Avram Davidson
Or Be He Dead. J. Byrom
Or by Default. G. Vaizey
Or Give Me Death! E. Spencer
Or Murder for Free. J. L. Potter
Or the Bambino Dies. P. Inchbald
Or Was He Pushed? R. Lockridge
Oracle of Maddox Street. L. T. Meade
Orange. J. Howlett
Orange Air. R. Doliner
Orange Axe. B. Flynn
Orange Blossoms. J. Shearing
Orange Colored Necktie. A. B. Curtis
Orange Divan. V. Williams
Orange Girl. B. Hemyng
Orange Necktie. P. Fry
Orange Ray. M. G. Kiddy
Orange-Tree Mystery. J. Rowland
Orange Wednesday. Leslie Thomas
Orange-Yellow Diamond. J. S. Fletcher
Orator. E. Wallace
Orbit. T. H. Block
Orbiting Omega. D. Pendleton
Orchard Close. A. Askew
Orchard of Tears. S. Rohmer
Orchid Limousine. W. Braun
Orchid Tree. V. Coffman
Orchids. T. H. Cook
Orchids for Biggles. W. E. Johns
Orchids for Mother. A. Latham
Orchids to Murder. T. B. Morris
Orchids to You. H. Janson
Ordeal. D. Collins
Ordeal. Roger Fuller
Ordeal. The Gordons
Ordeal by Fire. A. Upward
Ordeal by Innocence. A. Christie
Ordeal by Moonlight. H. Kaner
Ordeal by Touch. Mrs. Colonel Grey
Ordeal of Alick Hillersdon. W. M. Graydon
Ordeal of Ann Curtis. A. Askew
Ordeal of Esther Gray. L. Tracy
Ordeal of Major Grigsby. J. Sherlock
Ordeal of Mark Bannister. H. Leyford
Ordeal of Mrs. Snow. P. Quentin
Order a Coffin. T. McCoy
Order of Battle. I. Melchior
Order of Death. B. Bearshaw
Order of Death. H. Fleetwood
Order of the Arrow. M. T. Hinkemeyer
Order of the Octopus. S. Horler
Ordered South. A. M. Williamson
Orders to Kill. D. Downes
Orders to Kill. C. Whiting
Orders Under Seal. L. Carlton
Ordinary Accident. R. Amberley
Ordinary Day. H. Brinton
Ordinary Decent Criminals. L. Shriver
Ordinary Lunacy. Jessica Anderson
Ordinary Man. M. Arrighi
Ordinary Murder. D. Flynn
Oregon Grab. B. Harding
Organ Grinder's Monkey. R. Fliegel
Organ Speaks. E. C. R. Lorac
Organization. D. Anthony
Organization. A. D. Brent
Organization. O. Demaris
Organized Crimes. N. Von Hoffman
Organizer. D. MacDonald
Orient Express. G. Greene
Orient Express. P. Remy
Origin of a Vendetta. J. Ahern
Origin of Evil. E. Queen
Original Carcase. G. Bagby
Original Penny Christmas Readings. G. M. Fenn
Original Penny Readings. G. M. Fenn
Original Penny Readings. Second Series. G. M. Fenn
Original Penny Readings. Third Series. G. M. Fenn
Original Sin. G. Tabori
Orion Line. N. Luard

Orion, the Gold Beater. S. Cobb
Orion Was Rising. R. Palmer
Orion's Belt. J. Michelet
Orion's Shroud. W. P. Cooke
Orlando Figgins and other stories. Mrs. A. Marks
Orloff Diamond. G. H. Teed
Ormerod's Landing. Leslie Thomas
Ormond. C. B. Brown
O'Rourke Affair. J. Calder
Orphan Ann. H. C. Bailey
Orphan Army. L. Derrick
Orphan-Monger. S. Paternoster
Orphan of Mars. J. Cannan
Orphan of the Rhine. E. Sleath
Orphan of the Shadows. P. Minton
Orphan Seamstress. Anonymous
Orphan Soldier. I. Ruff
Orphans. Lyle Kessler
Orphans. G. Pearce
Orphans of Brandenburg. H. Edmonds
Orpheus Circle. E. McGhee
Orpheus in Mayfair and other stories. Maurice Baring
'Orrible Murder. B. Trice
Orrie's Story. T. Berger
Orville College. H. Wood
Orvington's Bank. S. J. Weyman
Osage Bow. W. C. MacDonald
Oscar Betrand. M. E. Braddon
Oscar Montague—Paranoiac. G. L. Walton
Oscar Mooney's Head. W. E. Huntsberry
Oscar, the Detective. Old Sleuth
Oshawa Project. F. Nolan
Oslo Intrigue. H. Astrup
Osprey Dilemma. Steve Hayes
Osrick. R. Sickelmore
Osiris Died in Autumn. L. Langley
Ossian's Ride. F. Hoyle
Ossington Mystery. H. Richards
Ostenders. G. Simenon
Osterman Weekend. R. Ludlum
Ostrekoff Jewels. E. P. Oppenheim
Ostrich Man. A. Soutar
Oswald Gray. H. Wood
Otan Plot. B. Newman
Othello's Occupation. L. A. G. Strong
Other. C. Carr
Other. P. Lindau
Other. T. Tryon
Other Anne Fletcher. S. Jaffe
Other Assassin. B. Sloan
Other Body in Grant's Tomb. R. Starnes
Other Brother. S. Claudia
Other Brown. A. Luehrmann
Other Bullet. N. B. Mavity
Other Cathy. N. Buckingham
Other Child. M. Chittenden
Other Cousin. L. Farrell
Other David. C. Coker
Other Devil's Name. E. Ferrars
Other End. R. E. Roberts
Other Folks' Money. W. B. M. Ferguson
Other Gods. E. C. Vivian
Other Half. C. F. Coe
Other Half. Hunter Davies
Other Half of the Orange. J. M. Scott
Other House. Henry James
Other House. C. Massie
Other Island. E. H. Clements
Other Juliet. A. Maybury
Other Karen. V. Johnston
Other Kinds of Treason. T. Allbeury
Other Man. F. Durbridge
Other Man. A. MacVicar
Other Man. E. Wallace
Other Man's Danger. M. March
Other Maritha. C. Leonard
Other Men's Lives. J. Chapman
Other Men's Shoes. A. Soutar
Other Men's Wives. W. Hackett
Other Miss Evans. E. Kyle
Other Mr. North. L. Beresford
Other Mother. J. Blackmore
Other One. C. Turney

Other Passenger. J. K. Cross
Other Paths to Glory. A. Price
Other People. M. Amis
Other People. S. Stein
Other People's Business. S. Pim
Other People's Houses. S. R. Cooper
Other People's Money. E. Gaboriau
Other People's Money. Arthur Lyons
Other Person. F. Hume
Other Richard Graham. F. Chatterton
Other Romilly. E. P. Oppenheim
Other Room. J. Blackmore
Other Shoe. M. McMullen
Other Shore of Time. P. DePolnay
Other Side. D. Henstell
Other Side of Midnight. S. Sheldon
Other Side of Silence. T. Allbeury
Other Side of Summer. V. Maxwell
Other Side of the Door. L. Chamberlain
Other Side of the Door. H. Howard
Other Side of the Door. L. O'Donnell
Other Side of the Tunnel. C. Kendall
Other Side of the Wall. H. C. McNeile
Other Side of the Wall. S. Truss
Other Side of the World. A. Hale
Other Side of Time. K. Laumer
Other Sins Only Speak. H. Kane
Other Than Natural Causes. Mark Cross
Other Three. B. Bolt
Other Woman. O. R. Cohen
Other Woman. R. Foley
Other World. K. Robeson
Others. G. Simenon
Otis Dunn: Manhunter. N. Richards
Otley. M. Waddell
Otley Forever. M. Waddell
Otley Pursued. M. Waddell
Otley Victorious. M. Waddell
Ottawa Allegation. P. Geddes
Otto's Boy. W. Wager
Ouija. A. Laurance
Ouija Board. T. Lester
Ould Flynn. E. L. Long
Our Admirable Betty. J. Farnol
Our Adversary. M. E. Braddon
Our Agent in Rome Is Missing. Nick Carter
Our Beautiful Heroine. J. Roubaud
Our Doom Is Gone. R. Harrison
Our Earth Here . . . D. Wyllarde
Our Father's Lies. Anthony Taylor
Our Father's Shadows. Jack Fuller
Our Feather Farm and other tales. Anonymous
Our First Murder. T. Chanslor
Our Friends from Frolix 8. P. K. Dick
Our Island. Anonymous
Our Jubilee Is Death. L. Bruce
Our Lady of Darkness. B. Capes
Our Lady of Pain. J. Blackburn
Our Lady's Inn. J. S. Clouston
Our Lives Are Swiss. P. Chamberlain
Our Man Flint. J. Pearl
Our Man in Camelot. A. Price
Our Man in Havana. G. Greene
Our Man in Mongoa. A. Alben
Our Man in Morton Episcopi. D. Lees
Our Member Mr. Muttlebury. J. S. Clouston
Our Missile's Missing. Robin Moore
Our Mother's House. Julian Gloag
Our Mysterious Passenger, and other stories. R. H. Savage
Our Second Murder. T. Chanslor
Our Share of Love. W. E. D. Ross
Our Spacecraft Is Missing! P. Richards
Our Very Best People. C. S. Raymond
Our Widow. F. Warden
Our Wills and Fates. K. Wylde
Ourselves Alone with The Long March and A Woman Calling. A. Devlin
Ouster Conspiracy. Nick Carter
Out. Max Austin
Out. P. Rey
Out Are the Lights. R. Laymon
Out Brief Candle. J. Rosenberg
Out, Brief Candle! L. Thayer

Title Index

Out by the River. L. Peters
Out, Damned Tot! N. Spain
Out for a Killing. J. W. Vandercook
Out for Kicks. W. Shaw
Out for the Count. N. W. Firth
Out for the Kill. Anthony Gilbert
Out for Vengeance. Nicholas Carter
Out from Shanghai. S. M. Parkman
Out from the Night. A. M. Meadows
Out from the Shadows. A. Davidson
Out Goes She. R. Stout
Out in the Shadows. D. Stein
Out Is Death. P. Rabe
Out of a Dark Sky. S. Horler
Out of Asia Alive. M. Derby
Out of Body, Out of Mind. R. Brandon
Out of Bounds. A. Watkyn
Out of Chaos. R. M. Wells
Out of Circulation. A. Bell
Out of Control. J. Ahern
Out of Control. B. Kendrick
Out of Control. G. G. Liddy
Out of Crime's Depths. Nicholas Carter
Out of Death's Shadow. Nicholas Carter
Out of Evil. Richard Fisher
Out of Evil. Ganpat
Out of Evil. D. G. Waring
Out of Focus. Peter Townend
Out of His Head. T. B. Aldrich
Out of It All. C. Saxby
Out of Order. P. A. Taylor
Out of Prison. M. A. Denison
Out of Reach of the Law. J. W. Bobin
Out of Satan's Grip. C. Frisbie
Out of Season. M. Kenyon
Out of Season. M. Lewin
Out of Shape. L. Greenbaum
Out of Sight—Out of Murder. F. Carmichael
Out of Sync. I. Haiblum
Out of the Ashes. F. Grierson
Out of the Ashes. E. W. Mumford
Out of the Blackout. R. Barnard
Out of the Blue. F. Archer
Out of the Blue. J. McManus
Out of the Blue. H. C. McNeile
Out of the Blue. J. Milne
Out of the Dark. U. Curtiss
Out of the Dark. G. F. Gibbs
Out of the Dark. G. Knevels
Out of the Dark. Seamark
Out of the Darkness. C. J. Dutton
Out of the Darkness. P. Fendall
Out of the Deep. H. Wood
Out of the Depths. R. L. Finn
Out of the Depths. L. Holton
Out of the Desert. A. Dare
Out of the Dog House. Charles North
Out of the Dusk. B. Flynn
Out of the East. W. M. Hills
Out of the Fire. H. Howard
Out of the Foam. J. E. Cooke
Out of the Fog. J. C. Lincoln
Out of the Fog. Clarissa Ross
Out of the Fog. F. A. Symonds
Out of the Frying Pan. C. N. Boyle
Out of the Jaws of Death. F. Barrett
Out of the Labyrinth. L. L. Lynch
Out of the Mouths of Graves. R. Bloch
Out of the Net. A. Clare
Out of the Night. M. Andrau
Out of the Night. R. Brome
Out of the Night. E. B. James
Out of the Night. B. Reynolds
Out of the Night. Dan Ross
Out of the Night. R. O. Saber
Out of the Night. M. White
Out of the Past. P. Wentworth
Out of the Past. M. Carr
Out of the Past. F. Hutchinson
Out of the Running. A. Askew
Out of the Shadow. A. Glanville
Out of the Shadows. H. Curties
Out of the Shadows. M. Halliday
Out of the Shadows. E. Mathis

Out of the Storm. R. Braddon
Out of the Underworld. I. Stark
Out of the War? M. B. Lowndes
Out of the Whirlwind. W. T. Walsh
Out of the Wreck. Ethel George
Out of This World. M. Cumberland
Out of This World. A. Goetz
Out of This World. J. Pendower
Out of Time. R. Crane
Out of Time. C. Franklin
Out of Time. M. Lewin
Out of Wild Hills. C. Campbell
Out of Yesterday. F. R. Smith
Out on Bail. R. L. Goldman
Out on the Cutting Edge. L. Block
Out on the Rim. Ross Thomas
Out There. D. Donovan
Out to Win. J. A. Jordan
Out to Win. R. Pertwee
Out to Win. Maxwell Scott
Out Went the Taper. R. C. Ashby
Out with the Tide. Nicholas Carter
Outback. A. Fletcher
Outback Ghosts. Nick Carter
Outbanker. T. A. Madden
Outbid. D. Hume
Outbreak. Lionel Black
Outbreak. Robin Cook
Outbreak! R. DeMaria
Outbreak. M. Ruuth
Outcast. M. E. Braddon
Outcast. P. Cornford
Outcast. H. Janson
Outcasts. J. L. Hensley
Outcasts. A. Murray
Outcrop. Colin Cooper
Outer Darkness. R. H. Wright
Outer Edges. C. R. Jackson
Outer Gate. O. R. Cohen
Outer Ring. A. E. Lindop
Outerworld. I. Haiblum
Outfit. R. Stark
Outlaw. D. Hennessey
Outlaw. W. Kiefer
Outlaw. G. Simenon
Outlaw and Lawmaker. C. Praed
Outlaw Breed. W. B. Mowery
Outlaw Empire. W. C. Tuttle
Outlaw Island. A. R. Hilliard
Outlaw Jess. A. Askew
Outlaws. G. V. Higgins
Outlaws. Clarke Little
Outlaw's Bride. H. M. Jones
Outlaw's Oath. E. C. Derby
Outlaws of Halfaday Creek. J. B. Hendryx
Outlaws of the Air. George Griffith
Outlaws of the Blue. Nicholas Carter
Outlaws of Yugo-Slavia. W. W. Sayer
Outpost of Eternity. H. Arvonen
Outrage. H. Denker
Outrage. M. Tarmey
Outrage in Manchukuo. V. Gielgud
Outrage on Gallows Hill. G. Bellairs
Outrageous Exposures. John Penn
Outrageous Fortune. M. Elmblad
Outrageous Fortune. Elizabeth Ford
Outrageous Fortune. M. L. Machin
Outrageous Fortune. P. Wentworth
Outrageous Lady Caroline. Rachelle Edwards
Outrider. R. Harding
Outrun the Constable. S. Jepson
Outrun the Dark. C. Bartholomew
Outside Eden. J. C. Squire
Outside In. M. Z. Lewin
Outside Job. A. Brede
Outside Man. J. Kern
Outside Man. R. N. Patterson
Outside the Law. J. Barnes
Outside the Law. T. Browning
Outside the Law. A. Crawford
Outside the Law. W. Dale
Outside the Law. A. Forrester
Outside the Law. H. Leyford
Outside the Law. P. Loraine

Outside the Law. M. McGrath
Outside the Radius. W. P. Ridge
Outsider. L. Cameron
Outsider. I. Cleaton
Outsider. M. K. Douglas
Outsider. J. Letherby
Outsider. E. R. Sabato
Outsider. H. Smart
Outsider in Amsterdam. J. Van De Wetering
Outsiders. A. E. Martin
Outsider's Year. F. Warden
Outward Walls. John Burke
Outwitted. O. Bland
Outwitted. R. Marsh
Outwitted at Last. S. A. Gardner
Oval Table. J. J. Farjeon
Oven. G. Thorne
Over and Above. J. E. Gurdon
Over and Done With. E. H. Clements
Over Her Dead Body. R. S. Prather
Over My Dead Body. R. Angel
Over My Dead Body. F. Mayfair
Over My Dead Body. S. Mitchell
Over My Dead Body. M. Risco
Over My Dead Body. R. Stout
Over My Dead Body. P. Williams
Over My Shoulder. Margery Lawrence
Over My Shoulder. I. Valdes
Over the Border. R. Barr
Over the Border. H. Whitaker
Over the Cliffs. C. Chanter
Over the Edge. J. Kellerman
Over the Edge. S. Kemp
Over the Edge. David Miles
Over the Edge. L. Treat
Over the Edge. D. Westheimer
Over the Edge of the World. Nicholas Carter
Over the Garden Wall. C. Carnac
Over the High Side. N. Freeling
Over the Hill. T. Thurston
Over the Hills. J. Farnol
Over the Hump. E. S. Gardner
Over the Line. Alec Coppel
Over the Sea to Death. G. Moffat
Over the Sea to Die. R. Grindal
Over the Top. D. Newton
Over the Tunnel. A. Rives
Over the Wall. T. D. Smith
Over to You. R. Dahl
Overboard. G. F. Worts
Overdose of Death. A. Christie
Overdrive. Mike Curtis
Overdrive. M. Gilbert
Overdue. F. Clifford
Overdue for Death. Z. H. Ross
Overflowing Rain. R. Stohlman
Overheard. S. Aumonier
Overkill. N. Daniels
Overkill. W. Garner
Overkill. J. Lange
Overkill. M. Schorr
Overload. D. Cory
Overload. C. Kearey
Overloap of Hope. J. Fores
Overlook House. W. Payne
Overlooked. B. Hawker
Overlord. O. Demaris
Overlord of the Damned. G. Stockbridge
Overlords. N. Sligh
Overlords. W. Woolfolk
Overnight. R. Goyne
Overnight Escapade. D. Mark
Overnight Express. P. McCutchan
Overpassionate Blonde! N. Neitzel
Overture in Venice. H. Rowan
Overture to Death. H. Desmond
Overture to Death. N. Marsh
Overture to Trouble. S. Maddock
Owen Castle. M. A. Sullivan
Owl. R. Forward
Owl. J. Gray
Owl. Frank King
Owl and the Pussycat. O. Cameron
Owl Flies Home. B. Rodney

Owl Hoots. B. Rodney
Owl in the Cellar. M. Scherf
Owl Is Abroad. R. Bridges
Owl Meets the Devil. B. Rodney
Owl of Darkness. M. Afford
Owl Sang Three Times. V. Kelsey
Owl Taxi. H. Footner
Owlers. M. Mayhew
Owlhoot Express. W. Grant
Owls Don't Blink. A. A. Fair
Owl's Warning. Herman Landon
Owner Lies Dead. T. Perry
Ownley Inn. J. C. Lincoln
Ox. J. Brothers
Oxford Blood. Antonia Fraser
Oxford Gambit. J. Hone
Oxford Murders. A. Broome
Oxford Mystery. G. D. H. Cole
Oxford Tragedy. J. C. Masterman
Oyster-Bed Mystery. A. Murray
Ozark Flats. Bob Williams
Ozark Payback. B. Ham
Ozmar the Mystic. E. Hulme-Beaman

P.A. to Murder. A. Tack
P As in Police. L. Treat
P.C. Richardson's First Case. B. Thomson
P.J., the Secret Service Boy. F. S. Hamilton
PK Factor. C. H. Martin
P. Moran, Oeprative. P. Wilde
P.O. Detective. B. D. Adsit
P.O.W. D. E. Zlotnik
P.P.C. N. S. Lincoln
P's Progress. F. O'Rourke
P.S. Your Cat Is Dead. J. Kirkwood
P.S. Your Shrink Is Dead. J. Reisman
Pace. L. Allan
Pace Grows Hotter. B. Sarto
Pace That Kills. W. Fuller
Pace That Kills. Kevin O'Hara
Pace That Kills. E. Saltus
Pace That Thrills. R. Weber
Pacific Blue. C. Dawe
Pacific Cavalcade. V. Coffman
Pacific Clipper. P. Doyle
Pacific Edge. S. Smoke
Pacific Flight. T. Block
Pacific Hideout. R. O'Hanna
Pacific Interlude. L. Gentle
Pacific North-West. D. Enefer
Pacific Payload. J. Hild
Pacific Pearl. M. Cronin
Pacific Tales. L. Becke
Pacific Vortex. C. Cussler
Pack Bay. W. Martin
Pack of Lies. G. Ashe
Package Deal. E. Hely
Package Holiday Spy Case. D. Betteridge
Package Included Murder. J. Porter
Package to Spain. M. Polland
Packard Case. W. Merrick
Packed for Murder. J. Blackburn
Packet of Death. H. Metcalfe
Packet of Trouble F. U. Ashford
Pact. J. A. Brown
Pact. C. Connolly
Pact of Love. Magali
Pact with Satan. L. Holton
Pact with the Devil. H. Desmond
Padded Cell. P. Conway
Padded Door. B. Flynn
Paddington Mystery. J. Rhode
Paddy's Puzzle. F. Kidman
Padgate Mystery. E. C. Reed
Padrone. Don Smith
Paduan Conspiracy. M. Walton
Pagan. W. F. Morris
Pagan Joe. T. A. Plummer
Pagan Madonna. H. MacGrath
Pagan Pagoda. M. Mundy
Pagan Perilous. Carter Brown
Pagans. A. Soutar
Pagan's Cup. F. Hume
Page Me a Pin-Up. M. Brody

Page Mr. Pomeroy. E. Jordan
Page Mr. Tutt. A. Train
Page Three Murder. L. Beghel
Pageant, and other stories. E. H. W. Meyerstein
Pageant of Murder. G. Mitchell
Pagett Calling. W. P. Drury
Paging Blackshirt. R. Graeme
Paging the Saint. L. Charteris
Pagoda. R. K. Largent
Pagoda. J. A. Phillips
Pagoda Mystery. Maurice Worth
Pagoda Tree. B. Mather
Paid. M. Dana
Paid in Full. R. Bay
Paid in Full. M. Cronin
Paid in Full. E. Ellison
Paid in Full. J. Godwin
Paid in Full. L. Meynell
Paid in His Own Coin. E. J. Goodman
Paid Out. J. P. Bessell
Paid Piper. C. S. Forester
Paid with Death. Nicholas Carter
Paige. J. Jenkins
Paignton Honour. A. Askew
Pain of Death. P. Ordway
Painful Predicament of Sherlock Holmes. W. Gillette
Painkiller. S. Spruill
Painless Death. S. Rena
Painswick Line. H. Cecil
Paint, Gold and Blood. M. Gilbert
Paint Her Face Dead. Jane Johnston
Paint It Black. W. R. Philbrick
Paint Me a Million. D. L. Goodrich
Paint Me a Murder. T. Brady
Paint Out. Robert Wallace
Paint-Stained Flannels. P. Fry
Paint the Town Black. David Alexander
Paint the Town Red. H. Adams
Painted Angel. G. R. Preedy
Painted Castle. Jennie Melville
Painted Dagger. J. Drummond
Painted Deal Locker. R. S. Freeman
Painted Death. D. Enefer
Painted Death. P. Quiroule
Painted Devil. J. Welcome
Painted Dog. V. Gunn
Painted Doll Affair. A. MacVicar
Painted Face. J. Stubbs
Painted Faces. Colin Robertson
Painted for the Kill. L. Cores
Painted Honeymoon. S. H. Webb
Painted Lady. J. Boland
Painted Mask. M. Erskine
Painted Monster. A. Rowe
Painted on a Donkey Cart. J. Bogar
Painted Rock. Morley Roberts
Painted Window. Lady A. Scott
Painted Woman. F. A. Kummer
Painted Woods. N. Henshaw
Painter of Flowers. H. Fleetwood
Painter of Parma. S. Cobb
Painting the Darkness. R. Goddard
Pair of Dueces. J. Reese
Pair of Knaves. M. Cronin
Pair of Knaves and A Few Trumps. M. D. Flattery
Pair of Rogues. H. Graham
Pairs and Losers. D. Niland
Pakistan Kill Ground. J. Rosenberger
Pakistani Agent. P. Robinson
Palace. D. G. Compton
Palace. P. Erdman
Palace and Prison. F. H. Rose
Palace Guard. C. MacLeod
Palace of Chance. Old Spicer
Palace of Enchantments. D. Hurd
Palace of Love. J. Vance
Palace of Mirrors. C. Rigdon
Palace of Spies. H. Compton
Palace of Terror. E. J. Murray
Palace Tales. H. Fielding
Paladin. B. Garfield
Palais de Danse Tragedy. G. Chester
Pale Ape. M. P. Shiel

Pale Betrayer. D. S. Davis
Pale Blue Nightgown. L. Golding
Pale Criminal. P. Kerr
Pale Door. Lee Roberts
Pale Ghost at Graves End. L. Richards
Pale Grey for Guilt. J. D. MacDonald
Pale Hand of Danger. M. Lynch
Pale Horse. A. Christie
Pale Kings and Princes. R. B. Parker
Pale Moon Rising. M. O'Brine
Pale Pink House. F. Y. McHugh
Palermo Affair. C. Forbes
Palermo Ambush. C. Forbes
Palgrave Mummy. F. M. Pettee
Palimpsest. M. E. Atkins
Palindrome. P. Conway
Paliser Case. E. Saltus
Pall for a Painter. E. C. R. Lorac
Pallard the Punter. E. Wallace
Palludia. A. Burr
Palm for Mrs. Pollifax. D. Gilman
Palm Springs. T. Ardies
Palmprint. J. Barnett
Palomino Blonde. T. Allbeury
Pals First. L. W. Dodd
Palzer Experiment. A. Murray
Pam Slipped Up. Dirk Foster
Pamela and Her Lion Man. M. Peterson
Pamela's Honeymoon. R. Jocelyn
Pamela's Palace. A. J. Fitzgerald
Pamplona Affair. Nick Carter
Panama Dead. J. Arnett
Panama Gold. R. Harlan
Panama Paradox. M. Wolfe
Panama Plot. A. B. Reeve
Panama Portrait. S. Ellin
Panama Power Play. L. Derrick
Panama Red. S. Diamond
Panchronicon Plot. R. Goulart
Panda Bear Is Critical. F. Michaels
Panda One Investigates. P. N. Walker
Panda One on Duty. P. N. Walker
Pandemic. T. Ardies
Pandora. P. Kaufman
Pandora. A. B. Reeve
Pandora by Holly Hollander. G. Wolfe
Pandora Feature. I. Baker
Pandora Man. K. Newcomb
Pandora Option. J. Rathbone
Pandora Plague. L. A. Matthias
Pandora Secret. A. Forrest
Pandora's Box. T. Chastain
Pandora's Box. R. Dundee
Pandora's Box. Elizabeth Gage
Pandora's Box. S. McKenna
Panel Patient. J. Glyder
Panelled Room. R. S. Holland
Pangersbourne Murders. J. Sturrock
Pangolin. P. Driscoll
Panic! J. Creasey
Panic. H. McCloy
Panic! B. Pronzini
Panic Blood. C. Texier
Panic Button. T. Beattie
Panic in Box C. J. D. Carr
Panic in Needle Park. James Mills
Panic in Paradise. A. Amos
Panic in Philly. D. Pendleton
Panic in Pursuit. S. Dewes
Panic in the Night. J. Stagg
Panic in the Solomons. K. M. Stevens
Panic in the Streets. S. D. Frances
Panic of '89. P. Erdman
Panic on Page One. L. Stewart
Panic Party. A. Berkeley
Panic-Stricken. M. A. Wilson
Panic Walks Alone. W. L. Rivera
Panjong Incident. Charles Ryan
Panther. H. J. S. Anderton
Panther Face. E. Woodward
Panther Jones for President. Stanley Johnson
Panther Throne. T. Murphy
Panther's Claw. A. Goetz
Panther's Moon. V. Canning

Title Index

Pantomime Girl. A. Applin
Pantomime Man. R. Middleton
Pantoufle. Fredrick Jackson
Papa. A. M. Williamson
Papa La-Bas. J. D. Carr
Papa Legacy. J. R. Pici
Papa Pontivy and the Maginot Murder. B. Newman
Papa San Files. H. Henn
Paper Albatross. R. Croft-Cooke
Paper Bag. J. Rhode
Paper Boat. Palinurus
Paper Bullet. O. Carney
Paper Chain. F. L. Cary
Paper Chase. Bob Cook
Paper Chase. H. Balfour
Paper Chase. O. W. Bayer
Paper Chase. L. Egan
Paper Chase. R. Esser
Paper-Chase. A. Fielding
Paper Chase. W. Garner
Paper Chase. J. Kennedy
Paper Chase. J. McNally
Paper Chase. M. Saxton
Paper Chase. J. Symons
Paper Chase. R. Watkins
Paper-Chase Mystery. A. Fielding
Paper Circle. B. Fischer
Paper Coffin. L. Lamensdurf
Paper Cuts. B. Biderman
Paper Doll. C. Dekker
Paper Doll. J. Lennox
Paper Dolls. L. P. Davies
Paper Ghost. E. Lindall
Paper Gold. M. Goodkin
Paper Gun. H. Browne
Paper Mask. J. Collee
Paper Mistress. D. Malm
Paper Money. Z. Stone
Paper Orchid. A. La Bern
Paper Palace. R. Harling
Paper Phoenix. M. Friedman
Paper Pistol Contract. P. Atlee
Paper Prison. P. C. Wren
Paper Products. Jim Hall
Paper Salvage Crime. G. Chester
Paper Thunderbolt. M. Innes
Paper Tomb. S. Donati
Paperback Thriller. Lynn Meyer
Paperbag. Richard Russell
Paperchase Murder. H. Seymour
Papers Mean Peril. Noel Lee
Papers of Andrew Melmoth. H. S. Davies
Papers of Tony Veitch. W. McIlvanney
Papersnake. L. Meynell
Papier Mache. Charles Allen
Papyrus Murders. T. B. Morris
Par for the Corpse. J. Sharkey
Parachute Murder. L. Mitchell
Parachutists. Ed Klein
Parade of Cockeyed Creatures. G. Baxt
Parade of the Empty Boots. C. A. Seltzer
Paradigm Red. Harold King
Paradine Case. R. Hichens
Paradine's Gauntlet. D. Pendleton
Paradise. H. Fleetwood
Paradise Coal-Boat, and other tales. C. J. C. Hyne
Paradise Conspiracy. G. Tracey
Paradise County. R. Sparkia
Paradise Court. J. S. Fletcher
Paradise Eater. J. R. Saul
Paradise for Two. M. Richmond
Paradise Formula. A. Dipper
Paradise Garden. G. F. Gibbs
Paradise Gun. J. Flagg
Paradise in Flames. Joseph Brandon
Paradise in the Sun. J. Pattinson
Paradise Island. M. Caywood
Paradise Man. J. Charyn
Paradise Men. S. Harvester
Paradise Motel. E. McCormack
Paradise Mystery. J. S. Fletcher
Paradise of Death. F. Orenstein
Paradise of Fools. D. Vane
Paradise Party. E. Hunter

Paradise Plot. E. Nahe
Paradise Road. D. S. Milton
Paradise Smith. R. Johnston
Paradise Spells Danger. G. B. Mair
Paradise Trail. W. B. Mowery
Paradise Trap. R. Crane
Paradiso. A. Prior
Paradiso County. P. Durst
Paradox Planet. S. Spruill
Paradoxes of Mr. Pond. G. K. Chesterton
Paragon. R. Pertwee
Paragon. E. Trevor
Paragon Man. C. Garrison
Paragon Walk. A. Perry
Parajacker. J. Jack
Parallax View. O. Singer
Parallelogram. T. Caplan
Paramilitary Plot. D. Pendleton
Paramount Kill. G. Larsen
Parasite. O. Demaris
Parasite Person. C. Fremlin
Parasites. T. E. Wilson
Parcel of Fortune. E. H. Clements
Parcel of Their Fortunes. B. N. Byfield
Parcel Post Murder. B. Herbert
Parcels for Inspector West. J. Creasey
Parchment Key. S. Hopkins
Pardon My Blood. P. Whelton
Pardon My Body. P. Bogard
Pardon My Goulish Laughter. F. Brown
Pardon My Gun. Keith Campbell
Pardon My Gun. J. P. Carstairs
Pardon My Gun. Roscoe King
Pardon My Pistol. B. Casson
Pardon My Return. D. Leslie
Parental Murder. Anonymous
Pariah. Collin Wilcox
Paris After Dark. M. Lavelle
Paris Agent. A. Mills
Paris Bit. I. Marder
Paris by Night. David Hare
Paris Calling. L. Golding
Paris Drop. A. Furst
Paris in September. E. Randolph
Paris Kill. P. Kirk
Paris Kill-Ground. J. Rosenberger
Paris One. James Brady
Paris Puzzle. V. McConnor
Paris Trap. J. Hone
Paris Trout. P. Dexter
Paris 2005. C. Zezza
Parisian Adventure. L. H. Brenning
Parisian Affair. Nick Carter
Parisian Detective. F. Du Boisgobey
Parisian Love. L. H. Brenning
Parisian Nights. R. Goyne
Parisian Pigeon Drop. J. P. Radford
Park. D. Gold
Park Avenue. W. V. Cole
Park Avenue Executioner. David Wilson
Park Avenue Girl. F. Shaw
Park Avenue Murder! Nicholas Carter
Park Avenue Tramp. F. Flora
Park Is Mine. S. Peters
Park Lane Mystery. J. Hatton
Park Lane Mystery. L. Tracy
Park Lane South, Queens. M. A. Kelly
Park Mystery. H. L. Phillips
Parker Case. J. Courage
Parker Pyne Investigates. A. Christie
Parkwater. H. Wood
Parliament of Owls. P. Buchanan
Parlor Games. R. Marasco
Parody Murder Case. C. Bonsack
Parole. J. Ehrlich
Parrish for the Defense. H. Waugh
Parrot & Co. H. MacGrath
Parrot Faced Man. C. R. Gull
Parrot Man. R. Middlemiss
Parsifal Mosaic. R. Ludlum
Parson o' Dumford. G. M. Fenn
Parson Thring's Secret. A. W. Marchmont
Parson's House. E. Cadell
Parson's Pleasure. Mollie Hardwick

Part for a Poisoner. E. C. R. Lorac
Part for a Policeman. J. Creasey
Part of Virtue. Roy Lewis
Part 35. J. N. Iannuzzi
Parted by Fate. L. J. Libbey
Parted on Her Wedding Morn. L. Price
Parting Breath. C. Aird
Partisan. M. Urquhart
Partisan Demolition. N. Cort
Partisans. A. MacLean
Partisans Die Alone. R. Wilkes-Hunter
Partners. W. Harrington
Partners. J. Martel
Partners in Crime. A. Christie
Partners in Crime. R. Hinojoso
Partners in Crime. H. King
Partners in Peril. Nicholas Carter
Partners in Time. Paula Simpson
Partners of the Night. L. Scott
Partridge Kite. Michael Nicholson
Parts Unknown. Rex Burns
Party. D. Telford
Party at No. 5. Shelley Smith
Party at the Penthouse. A. M. Chase
Party Every Night. F. Lorenz
Party for Lawty. M. Sarsfield
Party for the Shooting. L. Revell
Party Games. H. H. Kirst
Party Girl. M. Albert
Party in Dolly Creek. C. Blackstock
Party Killer. H. Pentecost
Party Man. C. B. Kelland
Party Murder. F. MacIsaac
Party of Eight. L. Meynell
Party of the Year. J. Crosby
Party to Murder. O. Chase
Party to Murder. M. Underwood
Party to Murder. R. Verron
Party to Murder. L. White
Party Was the Pay-Off. E. S. Holding
Pas de Deux. O. Beer
Pasang Run. E. Trevor
Pascali's Island. B. Unsworth
Pascal's Mill. B. A. Williams
Pascoe's Ghost. R. Hill
Pasha's Web. H. Bradshaw
Pasquinado. J. S. Fletcher
Pass. R. G. Hubler
Pass Along, Madam! A. Webb
Pass Beyond Kashmir. B. Mather
Pass Key to Murder. B. Reed
Pass the Aspirin. C. L. Pancoast
Pass the Body. C. S. Sprigg
Pass the Gravy. A. A. Fair
Pass Word. G. Barcelone
Passage. D. Fuller
Passage. B. Nicolaysen
Passage by Night. H. Marlowe
Passage in Park Lane. J. D. Rowley
Passage of Arms. E. Ambler
Passage Through Bohemia. F. Warden
Passage Through Midnight. U. Hall
Passage to Danger. E. Lanham
Passage to Jamaica. C. Jauniere
Passage to Samoa. D. Keene
Passage to Terror. E. Ronns
Passage to Violence. S. Kennedy
Passages from the Diary of a Late Physician. S. Warren
Passenger. F. Durbridge
Passenger. Elizabeth Fenwick
Passenger from Calais. A. Griffiths
Passenger from Scotland Yard. H. F. Wood
Passenger List. O. L. Rosmanith
Passenger on the U. C. Aveline
Passenger to Folkestone. J. S. Fletcher
Passenger to Frankfurt. A. Christie
Passenger to Nowhere. Anthony Gilbert
Passengers for Painted Rock. W. C. Tuttle
Passerman's Hollow. Jane Stuart
Passers-By. A. Partridge
Passing Advantage. M. McGarrity
Passing Game. S. Tesich
Passing Madness. F. Marryat

P

P

Passing of a Race. D. W. Higgins
Passing of Charles Lanson. L. Tracy
Passing of Evil. M. McShane
Passing of Fan Chu Fang. T. Mayne
Passing of Gloria Monday. J. Garforth
Passing of Mr. Quinn. G. R. McRae
Passing of Night. J. F. Bradley
Passing of the Flagship. W. P. Drury
Passing of Third Floor Back. C. Houghton
Passing of Third Floor Back. J. K. Jerome
Passing of Tony Blount. S. M. Parkman
Passing Show. R. H. Savage
Passing Strange. C. Aird
Passing Strange. R. Sale
Passing Stranger. M. Cody
Passing Stranger. L. Hoffman
Passing Time. M. Butor
Passion. R. Manvell
Passion and the Pity. E. Trevor
Passion at Pistol-Point! Anonymous
Passion Flower Puzzle. D. Rico
Passion for Treason. R. Nicholson
Passion Game. N. Geyer
Passion in the Peak. J. B. Hilton
Passion Lighting the World. M. Dekobra
Passion Madman. A. Shole
Passion Murders. D. Keene
Passion of Dracula. B. Hall
Passion of Gabrielle. M. S. Boylan
Passion of Kathleen Duveen. L. T. Meade
Passion of Molly T. Lawrence Sanders
Passion of New Eve. Angela Carter
Passion of the Beast. J. Lamarre
Passion of the President. J. Haslette
Passion of Women. S. Japrisot
Passion Pact. H. Janson
Passion Play. W. E. Blain
Passion Pulls the Trigger. A. Wallace
Passion the Plaything. R. M. Gilchrist
Passion Trap. G. D. Robinson
Passionate. Carter Brown
Passionate Adventure. F. Stayton
Passionate Atonement. M. Richmond
Passionate City. I. S. Black
Passionate City. J. L. Rickard
Passionate Invaders. J. Clare
Passionate Killer. F. Winter
Passionate Land. G. Wagner
Passionate Pagan. Carter Brown
Passionate Particles. M. Peterson
Passionate Playmate. H. Janson
Passionate Plaything. Mark Randolph
Passionate Quest. E. P. Oppenheim
Passionate Sin. R. M. Stewart
Passionate Stranger. C. Gayet
Passionate Strangers. G. Wagner
Passionate Trail. A. Hillgarth
Passionate Victims. Lange Lewis
Passionate Waif. H. Janson
Passionate Youth. E. C. Reed
Passionate Youth. R. Vane
Passionless Quest. C. Cannell
Passion's Aftermath. J. M. Foster
Passion's Not for Noon. H. Zore
Passions of Medora Graeme. Elsie Lee
Passion's Victim. H. Duval
Passive Crime, and other stories. The Duchess
Passover Commando. I. R. Cohen
Passport. R. Bagot
Passport. E. Voute
Passport for a Pilgrim. J. Leasor
Passport for a Renegade. K. Bennett
Passport in Suspense. J. Leasor
Passport Into Fear. W. H. Baker
Passport Invisible. G. C. Shedd
Passport to Danger. J. Paull
Passport to Danger. M. Richmond
Passport to Danger. J. Stagg
Passport to Death. B. Home
Passport to Murder. E. Allen
Passport to Murder. Neill Graham
Passport to Oblivion. J. Leasor
Passport to Oblivion. Babs Lee
Passport to Panic. E. Reed

Passport to Paradise. C. Houghton
Passport to Peril. P. Buck
Passport to Peril. R. Dudgeon
Passport to Peril. Anna C. Clarke
Passport to Peril. A. Hutton
Passport to Peril. J. Leasor
Passport to Peril. S. Marlowe
Passport to Peril. Robert Parker
Passport to Terror. M. Daniels
Passport to Treason. M. O'Brine
Passports to Murder. P. Hambledon
Password. D. Kim
Past All Dishonor. J. M. Cain
Past Caring. R. Goddard
Past Dies Hard. D. W. MacArthur
Past Finding Out. D. E. L. Patch
Past Is Dead. W. Ainslie
Past Master of Crime. D. J. MacKenzie
Past Murder Imperfect. B. Barton
Past Praying For. Sara Woods
Past, Present and Murder. H. Pentecost
Past Reckoning. June Thomson
Past Regret. M. Babson
Past Tense. I. Lambot
Past Tense. T. Vasilos
Past Won't Die. M. Malmer
Pastime. A. Fowles
Pastor and Prelate. R. Tellet
Pastourel. F. Soulie
Pat. T. Cobb
Pat o'Nine Tales. M. M. Bodkin
Patch. C. P. McDonald
Patch Unit. N. G. Bailey
Patched-Up Affair. F. Warden
Patchwork. C. Banks
Patchwork Girl. L. Niven
Patchwork Man. D. Harper
Patchwork of Death. P. Nichols
Patchwork Palace. M. L. Tyrrell
Paternoster Ruby. C. E. Walk
Path of a Hundred Deaths. C. R. Gull
Path of a Star. A. Applin
Path of Fear. W. M. Graydon
Path of Ghosts. Robert MacLeod
Path of Ivory. W. R. Foran
Path of Lies. A. Askew
Path of the Spendthrift. Nicholas Carter
Path of Virtue. G. Warden
Path to Glory. S. Styles
Path to the Bridge. Brian Cooper
Pathet Vengeance. M. K. Roberts
Pathless Trail. A. O. Friel
Paths of the Dead. H. Nisbet
Pathway of Adventure. R. Tyrrell
Pathway to Fame. P. Trent
Patience of a Saint. A. M. Greeley
Patience of Maigret. G. Simenon
Patience Pettigrew's Perplexities. C. Augusta
Patient. A. Christie
Patient. G. Simenon
Patient in Cabin C. M. G. Eberhart
Patient in 4b. A. F. Daniels
Patient in Room 18. M. G. Eberhart
Patient Is the Hunter. R. Wilkes-Hunter
Patmos Conspiracy. Bruce Merritt
Paton Street Case. J. Bingham
Patricia Lancaster's Revenge. Beatrice Chase
Patricia, the Beautiful. K. Kimbrough
Patrick Butler for the Defense. J. D. Carr
Patrick, Undergraduate. Anthony Armstrong
Patriot. C. Durbin
Patriot. R. Seth
Patriot. A. E. Walter
Patriot for Hire. A. Sinclair
Patriot Game. J. De St. Jorre
Patriot Game. G. V. Higgins
Patriot Games. T. Clancy
Patriotic Murders. A. Christie
Patriots. J. Barlow
Patriots. June Drummond
Patriots. K. Royce
Patriots. G. C. Seeber
Patriots. S. Sohmer
Patriots. F. Whishaw

Patriot's Dream. B. Michaels
Patrol Car. R. Jeffries
Patrol of the Sun Dance Trail. R. Connors
Patrol to Zaruse. J. Robb
Patron Saint and other stories. C. R. Gull
Patsy. D. Haring
Patsy. B. Vane
Patsy Prize. R. Cooper
Pattern. M. G. Eberhart
Pattern Crimes. W. Bayer
Pattern for Destruction. P. W. Fairman
Pattern for Murder. D. Knight
Pattern for Murder. I. S. Shriber
Pattern for Murder. E. Warman
Pattern for Panic. R. S. Prather
Pattern for Perfidy. John Bentley
Pattern for Terror. H. Pentecost
Pattern in Beads. D. M. Bumpus
Pattern in Black and Red. F. Keene
Pattern in Poison-Ivy. G. Bowman
Pattern in Yellow. K. Hewitt
Pattern Is Murder. Jean Marsh
Pattern of Chalk. Dennis Miles
Pattern of Chance. G. Gardiner
Pattern of Conquest. K. Thompson
Pattern of Death. P. George
Pattern of Guilt. Gavin Holt
Pattern of Life. S. D. Frances
Pattern of Love. W. E. D. Ross
Pattern of Murder. M. G. Eberhart
Pattern of Murder. M. Symons
Pattern of Rape. H. Janson
Pattern of Terror. Ayresome Johns
Pattern of Violence. R. Busby
Patterns in the Dust. L. Grant-Adamson
Patterns of Abuse. John Taylor
Patterson's Volunteers. John Smith
Patty's Partner. J. Middlemass
Paul Beck, Detective. M. M. Bodkin
Paul Beck, the Rule of Thumb Detective. M. M. Bodlin
Paul Burdon. W. Magnay
Paul Campenhaye, Specialist in Criminology. J. S. Fletcher
Paul Clifford. E. G. Bulwer-Lytton
Paul Clifford. T. P. Prest
Paul Deverell. Anonymous
Paul Ferroll. Anonymous
Paul Jones's Alias. D. C. Murray
Paul Pry's Poison Pen. E. Baird
Paul Quentin. F. M. White
Paul Richards—Detective. D. Dallas
Paul Temple and the Conrad Case. F. Durbridge
Paul Temple and the Front Page Men. F. Durbridge
Paul Temple and the Harkdale Robbery. F. Durbridge
Paul Temple and the Kelby Affair. F. Durbridge
Paul Temple and the Madison Case. F. Durbridge
Paul Temple and the Margo Case. F. Durbridge
Paul Temple Intervenes. F. Durbridge
Paul, the Sage. F. M. White
Paul Vargas, a Mystery, and other tales. F. J. Fargus
Paula. D. Kingery
Paulette. K. Lindsay
Pauline. J. Hawthorne
Pauline—A Mystery. Nicholas Carter
Pauline's Affair. R. Carstairs
Pauline's Lady. M. V. Woodgate
Paul's Apartment. V. Siller
Paulton Plot. H. Adams
Pauper Millionaire. A. Fryers
Pauper of Park Lane. W. LeQueux
Pavement Artist Mystery. W. Jardine
Pavilion. Hilda Lawrence
Pavilion at Monkshood. A. Maybury
Pavilion by the Lake. A. J. Rees
Pavilion of Honour. G. R. Preedy
Pavilion on the Links. R. L. Stevenson
Paw in the Bottle. Raymond Marshall
Pawn. L. A. Knight
Pawn. F. Nichols
Pawn. N. P. Sutherland
Pawn in Jeopardy. E. Gresham
Pawn in Jeopardy. S. Rattray

Pawn in the Game. J. L. Hardy
Pawn of Evil. A. Leech
Pawn to King Three. M. Sipra
Pawn to King's Cross. E. Mazzaro
Pawn to Queen. P. Dobie
Pawned. F. Packard
Pawnee Tom. Old Sleuth
Pawns. D. L. Soderberg
Pawns and Kings. Seamark
Pawns Count. E. P. Oppenheim
Pawns of Fate. P. E. Bowers
Pawns of Fear. J. Manor
Pawns of Murder. W. Woodrow
Pawnshop Murder. J. G. Brandon
Paxos Tiger. T. Simon
Paxton Plot. C. G. Mitford
Pay Any Price. T. Allbeury
Pay As You Die. R. Crawford
Pay Day. R. E. Howard
Pay-Day. H. Osborne
Pay-Grab Murders. P. Chester
Pay Off. N. Baroni
Pay-Off. Joe Barry
Pay-Off. J. C. Barton
Pay Off. Neill Graham
Pay Off. K. Laing
Pay Off. S. Leather
Pay Off. Johnny Mack
Pay Off. A. W. Sherring
Pay-Off. D. Wiles
Pay-Off for a Dumb Dame. F. Duggan
Pay-Off for Desire. M. Lavelle
Pay-Off in Blood. B. Halliday
Pay-Off in Calcutta. R. Collier
Pay on the Way Out. J. Murphy
Pay Out. P. Elliott
Pay the Devil. D. Alexander
Pay the Devil. Harry Patterson
Pay to Bearer. M. S. Jones
Payback. J. C. Pollock
Payback. Sam Stewart
Paybacks. C. Britton
Payday. Robert Wallace
Paydirt. L. Durie
Paydirt. B. J. Rockliff
Paying Guest. P. Assinder
Paying Guest. L. A. Knight
Paying the Piper. S. McCrumb
Paying the Price. Nicholas Carter
Payment Deferred. J. Dell
Payment Deferred. C. S. Forester
Payment Down. J. H. Vahey
Payment for Silence. A. Rivers
Payment in Blood. E. George
Payment in Full. J. W. Bobin
Payment in Lead. G. Franklin
Payment Suspended! J. W. Bobin
Payoff. G. Brewer
Payoff. H. Howard
Payoff. N. Karta
Payoff. Ronald Owen
Payoff. Mike Phillips
Payoff. Don Smith
Payoff. A. Veraldi
Payoff for Paula. J. Bogar
Payoff for the Banker. F. Lockridge
Payoff in Black. W. G. Schofield
Payoff in Switzerland. Robert MacLeod
Payoff on Fever Street. J. Wolf
Payola! G. Cagle
Payola. D. Keene
Payroll. D. Bickerton
Payroll of Fate. W. C. Tuttle
Pazenger Problem. J. Plain
Peabody Experience. C. Carpenter
Peace Among the Pelicans. G. C. Foster
Peace and Peter Lamont. N. Harman
Peace Bridge. W. A. Low
Peace Maker. M. J. Livingstone
Peace on Earth. Gordon Stevens
Peacekeepers. B. Bova
Peacemaker. J. Remenham
Peacemaker. P. Trent
Peacock. S. Gibbons

Peacock Fan. H. S. Keeler
Peacock Feather Murders. Carter Dickson
Peacock House and other mysteries. E. Phillpotts
Peacock Is a Bird of Prey. R. Foley
Peacock of Jewels. F. Hume
Peacock Season. O. Bigelow
Peacock's Feather. S. Esmond
Peak House. A. J. Rees
Peak of Frenzy. H. Brand
Peak Performance. I. Baker
Peal of Ordnance. J. Lodwick
Peanut Butter & Jelly Is Not for Kids. B. Kelly
Pear-Tree. W. Hewlett
Pearl and Plain. A. Griffin
Pearl Choker. R. East
Pearl Divers of Rencador Reef, and other stories. L. Becke
Pearl-Headed Pin. D. Durham
Pearl Island. H. C. Rowland
Pearl Necklace. A. Applin
Pearl of Blood. K. Netzen
Pearl of Great Price. A. Askew
Pearl of Oyster Island. H. Davie-Martin
Pearl of the Orient. C. Nicole
Pearl Poachers. S.Drew
Pearl Seekers. C. Hayter
Pearl Thief. B. Ruck
Pearlhanger. Jonathan Gash
Pearlkillers. R. Ingalls
Pearls and Perjury. H. H. Lewis
Pearls Are a Nuisance. R. Chandler
Pearls Before Swine. M. Allingham
Pearls of Cheong Tah. S. W. Powell
Pearls of Death, and other stories. A. Govan
Pearls of Desire. A. J. Small
Pearls of Doom. G. H. Teed
Pearls of Pilolu. Alys Brown
Peccadilloes. F. Keene
Peccavi. E. W. Hornung
Peccavi. C. Massie
Peck of Salt. K. Royce
Peckover Holds the Baby. M. Kenyon
Peculiar Exploits of Brigadier Ffellowes. S. E. Lanier
Peculiarly Passionate Pair. R. Weldon
Peddler. D. Ring
Peddler. H. C. Rowland
Pedestal. G. Lanning
Pedigree. G. Simenon
Pedigree in Pawn. A. H. Veysey
Pedigreed Murder Case. J. S. Fletcher
Pedlar's Acre. T. P. Prest
Pedlar's Pack. M. E. Mann
Pedlar's Pack. O. Onions
Peel Me a Peach. D. Haring
Peel Rocke—Black Sheep. H. H. Ross
Peeper. W. Brinkley
Peeper. L. D. Estleman
Peeping Thomas. R. Reeves
Peeping Tom Murders. J. Baynes
Peer and His Plunder. H. Hill
Peer and the Woman. E. P. Oppenheim
Peerage in Peril. R. E. Salwey
Pegged for Murder. N. Kelvin
Peggy Paradine, House Agent. M. O'Nair
Peggy, the Concerned. K. Kimbrough
Peggy's Dilemma. T. Cobb
Pekin Target. Adam Hall
Peking Agent. J. D. Horan
Peking Connection. Don Smith
Peking Dimension. N. Calmer
Peking Dossier. Nick Carter
Peking Duck. R. L. Simon
Peking Incident. G. Atcheson
Peking Man Is Missing. C. Taschjian
Peking Mandate. P. Siris
Peking Payoff. I. Stewart
Peking Plot. Ralph Hayes
Peking Switch. J. J. Marsh
Peking Target. Adam Hall
Peking/The Tulip Affair. Nick Carter
Pekoe Reef. F. Knight
Pel Among the Pueblos. M. Hebden
Pel and the Bombers. M. Hebden
Pel and the Faceless Corpse. M. Hebden

Pel and the Missing Person. M. Hebden
Pel and the Paris Mob. M. Hebden
Pel and the Party Spirit. M. Hebden
Pel and the Picture of Innocence. M. Hebden
Pel and the Pirates. M. Hebden
Pel and the Predators. M. Hebden
Pel and the Prowler. M. Hebden
Pel and the Staghound. M. Hebden
Pel and the Touch of Pitch. M. Hebden
Pel Is Puzzled. M. Hebden
Pel Under Pressure. M. Hebden
Pelham. E. Bulwer-Lytton
Pelham Affair. L. Tracy
Pelham Murder Case. Monte Barrett
Pelican Island. A. D. Divine
Pelican Strikes Back. R. Arnold
Pelican's Clock. R. Middlemiss
Pelota Murder. J. Daymont
Peloton, Detective. H. A. Cartledge
Pembroke Mason Affair. G. Barton
Pemex Chart. Nick Carter
Pen-Friend. A. Wykes
Pen Is Deadlier. F. Carmichael
Penal Settlement. C. C. Lowis
Penalty Is Death! V. G. Kennedy
Penalty of Fate. M. E. Braddon
Penance for Jerry Kennedy. G. V. Higgins
Penance of Brother Alaric. B. Graeme
Penance Was Dath. L. B. McNamara
Penarth. D. C. Parkinson
Pencarnan. J. Rigg
Pencil Points to Murder. W. A. Barber
Pending Investigation. R. McLaughlin
Pendragon. M. Howe
Pendragon, Late of Prince Albert's Own. R. Trevelyan
Pendragon, Seeds of Mutiny. R. Trevelyan
Pendragon, the Illusionist. R. Trevelyan
Pendragon, the Montenegran Plot. R. Trevelyan
Pendulum. J. Christopher
Pendulum. R. Eastman
Penelope. E. V. Cunningham
Penelope Brandling. V. Lee
Penelope of the Polyantha. E. Wallace
Penelope, the Damp Detective. W. C. Anderson
Penelope's Daughter. Dair Alexander
Penelve. R. H. Thomas
Penetrators. Anthony Gray
Pengard Awake. R. Straus
Penguin Island Murders. M. MacElwain
Penguin Pool Murder. S. Palmer
Penhallow. G. Heyer
Penknife in My Heart. N. Blake
Penman's Progress. S. Brydon
Penmarric. S. Howatch
Pennhaven. H. York
Pennies for His Eyes. W. M. Duncan
Pennies from Hell. David Alexander
Pennies on Her Eyes. M. L. Roby
Pennies on Her Eyes. N. Rosso
Penniless Millionaire. D. C. Murray
Pennington Case. R. H. Wilkinson
Penny Black. S. Moody
Penny Dreadful. S. Moody
Penny Ferry. R. Boyer
Penny for the Guy. J. Roffman
Penny in the Fountain. D. Collenette
Penny Murders. Lionel Black
Penny of Top Hill Trail. B. K. Maniates
Penny Pinching. Susan Moody
Penny Post. Susan Moody
Penny Royal. Susan Moody
Penny to Spend. Edward Brown
Penny Whipp. C. Massie
Penny Wise. Susan Moody
Pennycross Murders. M. Procter
Pennygreen Street. A. La Bern
Pennyworth of Murder. G. Meyrick
Penrose Mystery. R. A. Freeman
Pension for Death. R. H. Lewis
Pentagon. H. Searls
Pentagon Case. V. J. Fox
Pentagon Tapes. C. Mackenzie
Pentallion. V. Blake

Pentecost Project. T. Breton
Penthouse. A. S. Roche
Penthouse. E. Trevor
Penthouse Conspirators. C. Pincher
Penthouse Killings. H. Brown
Penthouse Murders. R. P. Holden
Penthouse Mystery. E. Queen
Penthouse Passout. Carter Brown
Penthouse Preview. M. Brody
Penultimate Problem of Sherlock Holmes. J. Nassivera
People Against Nancy Preston. J. A. Moroso
People Against O'Hara. E. Lipsky
People Apart. L. T. Shortell
People Ask Death. G. Dyer
People Exchange. R. F. Baylus
People from the Sea. V. Johnston
People in Cages. H. Ashton
People in Glass House. June Drummond
People in Glass Houses. E. Lewis
People in Trouble. S. Schulman
People Like Us. D. Dunne
People Like Us. F. Vosper
People Next Door. Caroline Crane
People of Darkness. T. Hillerman
People of the Night. V. Russell
People of the River. E. Wallace
People on the Hill. V. Johnston
People vs. Kirk. R. Traver
People vs. Maxine Lowe. L. B. McMahon
People vs. Withers and Malone. S. Palmer
People Who Knock on the Door. P. Highsmith
People Will Talk. E. C. R. Lorac
People's Man. E. P. Oppenheim
People's Republic. P. F. Amor
Peplow's Paper-Chase. T. Gallon
Pepper Pike. Les Roberts
Pepper-Pot Problem. O. Cecil
Perahera. Julia Leslie
Perchance of Death. E. Linington
Perchance to Kill. S. W. Edgar
Perchance to Kill. C. Franklin
Perdida. F. W. Pangborn
Perdita's End. P. Tabori
Perdition Express. B. Lang
Pere Goriot. H. Balzac
Peregrination 22. P. Purser
Peregrine. W. Bayer
Peregrine Dream. R. H. Ring
Peregrine House. J. Flores
Peregrine's Progress. J. Farnol
Perennial Boarder. P. A. Taylor
Perestroika Christi. J. Hands
Perfect Alibi. J. Laurence
Perfect Alibi. A. A. Milne
Perfect Alibi. C. S. Sprigg
Perfect Assignment. J. Moffatt
Perfect Carrier. Sheila Ross
Perfect Corpse. L. R. Wright
Perfect Crime. H. Kane
Perfect Crime. E. Queen
Perfect Crime, or Two. H. Monteilhet
Perfect Criminal. G. Furnivall
Perfect Demon! Allen Carter
Perfect End. W. Marshall
Perfect Family. D. Husted
Perfect Fool. F. Warden
Perfect Fools. E. P. Green
Perfect Frame. W. Ard
Perfect Frame. John Morgan
Perfect Gallows. P. Dickinson
Perfect Little Angels. A. Neiderman
Perfect Match. J. McGown
Perfect Murder. J. Atholl
Perfect Murder. S. Devi
Perfect Murder. Mike Johnson
Perfect Murder. H. R. F. Keating
Perfect Murder Case. C. Bush
Perfect Pigeon. R. Wormser
Perfect Place. S. Kohler
Perfect Plot. G. Canary
Perfect Poison. A. Campsie
Perfect Round. H. Adams
Perfect Score. R. E. Cummins

Perfect Spy. J. Le Carre
Perfect Thief. R. J. Bass
Perfect Trap. D. Thurlow
Perfect Treasure. J. Payn
Perfect Victim. Marina Campbell
Perfect Victim. J. McKimmey
Perfect Victim. Carla Norton
Perfect Weapon. B. Michelson
Perfect Wife. J. Pendower
Perfectionist. L. Kauffmann
Perfidious Lydia. F. Barrett
Performance. D. Clark
Perfume of the Lady in Black. G. Leroux
Perfume: The Story of a Murderer. P. Suskind
Perfumed Lure. M. St. Dennis
Perfumed Poison. Carter Brown
Perfumes of Arabia. E. Dewar
Perhaps a Little Danger. E. H. Clements
Perhaps I Look Simple. R. B. Amos
Perhaps the Prodigal. J. Courage
Perhaps to Kill. H. C. Davis
Peril. S. Horler
Peril. L. Osbourne
Peril Ahead. J. Creasey
Peril at Cranbury Hall. J. Rhode
Peril at Dorrough. J. T. Osborne
Peril at Dune's Edge. D. Quick
Peril at End House. A. Christie
Peril at End House. A. Ridley
Peril at Journey's End. Norman Lee
Peril at Midnight. Elaine Hamilton
Peril at Polvellyn. M. McEvoy
Peril at Stone House. J. Corby
Peril at the Spy Nest. A. M. Chase
Peril in Darkness. H. Willett
Peril in Mayfair. B. Woodhouse
Peril in Persia. J. Andrews
Peril in Provence. R. Hugill
Peril in the North. K. Robeson
Peril in the Pyrenees. J. J. Farjeon
Peril is My Pay. S. Marlowe
Peril Island. P. Brebner
Peril of an Empire. Robert Johnson
Peril of Barnabas Collins. Marilyn Ross
Peril of Helen Marklove and other stories. W. LeQueux
Peril of Oliver Sargent. E. J. Bliss
Peril of Richard Pardon. B. L. Farjeon
Peril of the Course. M. K. Douglas
Peril of the Prince! S. S. Brooks
Peril of the Prince. H. Hill
Peril Pit. J. Andrews
Peril Under the Palms. K. K. Beck
Perilous Adventure. M. Richmond
Perilous Assignment. R. Marlowe
Perilous Country. J. Creasey
Perilous Crossways. J. S. Fletcher
Perilous Discovery. G. Johnston
Perilous Elopement. J. L. Rickard
Perilous Errand. M. Sutherland
Perilous Hazard. Mark Cross
Perilous Holiday. Don Smith
Perilous Love. M. Turner
Perilous Parole. Nicholas Carter
Perilous Passage. A. Mayse
Perilous Passage. B. Nicolaysen
Perilous Passport. E. Allen
Perilous Promises. J. Rossetta
Perilous Quest. J. Ames
Perilous Quest. T. A. Niccolls
Perilous Quest. Maxwell Scott
Perilous Sanctuary. D. J. Hall
Perilous Secret. D. Peacock
Perilous Secret. C. Reade
Perilous Sky. D. Rutherford
Perilous Transactions of Mr. Collin. F. Heller
Perilous Voyage. D. Quentin
Perilous Voyage. R. St. Clair
Perilous Waters. J. Blackmore
Perilous Waters. E. Nepean
Perilous Way. M. Cumberland
Perils and Adventures of Mr. William Thornely. C. Rowcroft
Perils in Persia. J. Bolton

Perils of Josephine. Ernest Hamilton
Perils of Pekin. W. M. Graydon
Perils of Petrograd. W. M. Graydon
Perils of the Red Box. H. Hill
Perimeter Fence. A. Crockett
Period of Evil. M. Halliday
Period Stuff. D. Yates
Peripheral Spy. B. Peterson
Periscope Red. R. Rohmer
Perish by the Sword. Poul Anderson
Perish in July. Mollie Hardwick
Perish the Thought. J. Bonett
Perishable Goods. D. Yates
Periwinkle. Arnold Gray
Periwinkle Brooch. K. Frederick
Perjured Alibi. W. S. Masterman
Perkins of Portland: Perkins the Great. E. P. Butler
Permanent Eclipse. M. Maurice
Permanent Wave. Virginia Sullivan
Perpetrators. Anthony Gray
Perpetua. D. Calthrop
Perpetual Check. C. Haynes
Perpignon Exchange. W. Kiefer
Perrin Murder Case. G. Morton
Perrine. D. Daniels
Perris of the Cherry Tree. J. S. Fletcher
Persecuted. F. Whishaw
Persecutor. I. Hamilton
Persian Bride. H. Janson
Persian Cat. J. Flagg
Persian Death-Trap. J. Christian
Persian Peril. D. Hoys
Persian Price. Evelyn Anthony
Persian Ransom. Evelyn Anthony
Persian Tassel. O. S. Cornelius
Persimmon Tree. William Taylor
Person Called "Z". J. J. Farjeon
Person of Some Importance. L. Osbourne
Person Shouldn't Die Like That. A. D. Goldstein
Persona Non Grata. Timothy Williams
Personal. C. K. Cambray
Personal Adventures of a Detective. A. Carmichael
Personal Appearance of a Lioness. V. Tracy
Personal Call and other stories. Celia Dale
Personal Effects. Rex Reed
Personal Justice. A. Hilborn
Personal Possessions. Jeanne Hart
Personal Recollections of Peter Stonner, Esq. C. Blatherwick
Personal War. B. Ham
Personality Surgeon. Colin Wilson
Persons Unknown. P. MacDonald
Persons Unknown. G. Moffat
Persons Unknown. H. Sutcliffe
Persons Unknown. L. Thayer
Persons Unknown. V. Tracy
Persuader. D. Haring
Persuaders #1. F. E. Smith
Persuaders #2. F. E. Smith
Persuaders #3. F. E. Smith
Persuaders Again! F. E. Smith
Persuaders at Large. F. E. Smith
Perth Amboy Mystery. C. Clinch
Perturbing Spirit. J. Caird
Peruvian Contracts. F. Fowlkes
Peruvian Nightmare. M. Barry
Peruvian Printout. A. Haig
Perversions in the Sand. R. Weldon
Perversity. F. Carco
Perverted Village. A. Soutar
Pest. A. P. Terhune
Pester Finger. H. B. M. Watson
Pestis 18. Sharon Webb
Pet. C. L. Grant
Pet Peeves. T. McCafferty
Petals of Blood. Ngugi Wa Thiong'o
Petals on the Wind. V. C. Andrews
Peter Called Simon and other stories. Kobold Knight
Peter Cornish's Revenge. H. C. McNeile
Peter Cotterell's Treasure. R. S. Holland
Peter Darington. Dougals V. Duff
Peter Fry at Exit. Christopher John
Peter Grayleigh Flies High. Colin Robertson
Peter Gunn. H. Kane

Peter Hyde, M.P. P. Trent
Peter in Peril. V. Bridges
Peter Intervenes. E. Jepson
Peter Krimsov. L. S. Taube
Peter Ruff. E. P. Oppenheim
Peter Ruff and the Double-Four. E. P. Oppenheim
Peter Rugg, the Missing Man. W. Austin
Peter the Brazen. G. F. Worts
Peterbilt to Laredo. J. Shaffer
Peter's Pence. J. Cleary
Peter's Profession. C. L. Reid
Petersburg-Cannes Express. H. Koning
Petersburg Tales. O. Garnett
Petrella at Q. M. Gilbert
Petrified Eye. W. P. Drury
Petrified Forest. R. E. Sherwood
Petrodollar Takeover. P. Tanous
Petrograd Consignment. O. Sela
Petronella and Madame Ponowski. M. C. Rowsell
Petronov Plan. J. Pattinson
Petrovka 38. J. Semyonov
Petrus Borel Stories. T. Ahern
Petticoat Lane. G. Goodchild
Petticoat Lane Murders. V. Gunn
Pew Group. A. Oliver
Phantasmagoria. Anonymous
Phantasmagoia. P. Wiat
Phantasms. W. Gerrare
Phantom. L. Gilbert
Phantom. J. Sylvester
Phantom Airman. R. Walker
Phantom Alibi. H. Leverage
Phantom and Barnabas Collins. Marilyn Ross
Phantom Army. M. Pemberton
Phantom at Lost Lake. D. Lyons
Phantom Bat. R. C. Elliott
Phantom Bells. R. St. Clair
Phantom Bride. L. Ames
Phantom Bride. M. M. Brown
Phantom Bus. R. St. Clair
Phantom Canoe. W. B. Mowery
Phantom Car. F. M. White
Phantom Circus. A. Spiller
Phantom City. K. Robeson
Phantom Clue. G. Leroux
Phantom Conspiracy. M. Barak
Phantom Cottage. V. Johnston
Phantom Crime. S. Strand
Phantom Death, and other stories. W. C. Russell
Phantom Dirigible. R. St. Clair
Phantom Drummer. A. Ridgway
Phantom Empire. R. M. Sears
Phantom-Fighter. Seabury Quinn
Phantom Figures. F. Dickberry
Phantom Filly. C. Burnes
Phantom Fingers. J. J. Farjeon
Phantom Fingers. L. Mearson
Phantom Flame of Wind House. K. Kimbrough
Phantom Fleet. Sea Lion
Phantom Foe. J. Brearley
Phantom Footballer. F. W. Gumley
Phantom Fortune. M. E. Braddon
Phantom Fortune. K. C. Groom
Phantom Forward. S. Horler
Phantom Gentleman. J. Hershey
Phantom Gondola. M. Dekobra
Phantom Greyhound. F. W. Gumley
Phantom Gunman. N. Morland
Phantom Holiday. M. Russell
Phantom Hollow. G. Verner
Phantom in the House. A. Soutar
Phantom in the Rainbow. S. La Master
Phantom in the Wings. Michael Elder
Phantom Island. E. S. Brooks
Phantom Island. R. Walker
Phantom Isle. S. Warwick
Phantom Killer. Colin Hope
Phantom Killer. H. Taylor
Phantom Lady. Carter Brown
Phantom Lady. W. Irish
Phantom Leg. F. Du Boisgobey
Phantom Light. E. Price
Phantom Lover. A. Eadie
Phantom Lover. E. Mansfield

Phantom Manor. Marilyn Ross
Phantom Millionaire. M. E. Longman
Phantom Miner. R. St. Clair
Phantom Murderer. Anonymous
Phantom Murderer. B. G. Quin
Phantom Musketeer. C. Brandon
Phantom of Belle Acres. Marilyn Ross
Phantom of Dark Harbor. Clarissa Ross
Phantom of Edgewater Hall. W. E. D. Ross
Phantom of Fog Island. Marilyn Ross
Phantom of Fonthill Park. K. R. Vernon
Phantom of Forty-Second Street. M. M. Raison
Phantom of Glencourt. Clarissa Ross
Phantom of Harley Grange. Lilian Barnes
Phantom of Meadow Creek. Old Sleuth
Phantom of Scotland Yard. B. Weston
Phantom of the Creek. G. H. Teed
Phantom of the Dogger Bank. Anonymous
Phantom of the Films. A. Eadie
Phantom of the High School. A. C. Martens
Phantom of the Mill. L. Bidston
Phantom of the Opera. G. Leroux
Phantom of the Opera. G. Traylor
Phantom of the Op'ry. Tim Kelly
Phantom of the Pacific. W. W. Sayer
Phantom of the Sacred Well. P. Leonard
Phantom of the Snow. Marilyn Ross
Phantom of the Soap Opera. Judi Miller
Phantom of the Swamp. Marilyn Ross
Phantom of the Temple. R. Van Gulik
Phantom of the Thirteenth Floor. Marilyn Ross
Phantom Passenger. Mansfield Scott
Phantom Pilot. P. Conde
Phantom Pilot. K. Kavanaugh
Phantom Pirate. M. Everard
Phantom 'Plane. A. O. Pollard
Phantom Plot. K. Kavanaugh
Phantom President. G. F. Worts
Phantom Raider. R. Trevor
Phantom Railway. A. Wood
Phantom Reflection. A. Ashton
Phantom Room. E. E. Mande
Phantom Scarlet. W. Mills
Phantom Seven. T. Worthing
Phantom Ship. Capt. Marryat
Phantom Slayer. D. Steele
Phantom Spy. Anonymous
Phantom Spy. M. Brand
Phantom Spy. F. Russell
Phantom Stockman. G. Boothby
Phantom Tiger. R. St. Clair
Phantom Torpedo-Boats. A. Upward
Phantom Tourer. G. Collins
Phantom Train. D. Timins
Phantom Violin. J. Renaud
Phantom Wedding. Marilyn Ross
Phantom Wedding. E. Southworth
Phantom Wife. M. V. Victor
Phantom Wires. A. Stringer
Phantom Wreck. Old Sleuth
Phantoms of a Physician. Alan Miller
Phantoms of the Cloister. I. H.
Phantoms Over Potsdam. R. Vacha
Pharaoh and His Waggons and other stories. R. Croft-Cooke
Pharaoh's Crown. F. H. Rose
Pharaoh's Daughter and other stories. W. W. Astor
Pharaoh's Ghost. K. Robeson
Pharaoh's Turquoise. A. M. Judd
Pharisees Unveiled. Mrs. G. Corbett
Pharos, the Egyptian. G. Boothby
Phase of Darkness. Robin Moore
Phil and Me. M. Woodhouse
Phil Conway. A. C. Gunter
Phil Fenn—Boy International. J. Durston
Phil Scott, the Detective. J. R. Taylor
Phil Scott, the Indian Detective. J. R. Taylor
Philadelphia Blow-Up. M. Barry
Philadelphia Fire. J. E. Wideman
Philadelphia Murder Story. L. Ford
Philadelphian. L. J. Jennings
Philanthropic Burglar. Rita
Phileas Fox, Attorney. A. T. Sadlier
Philip Bennion's Death. R. Marsh

Philip Derby, Reporter. W. J. Abbot
Philip Henson M.D. George Hastings
Philip Loveluck. Charles Owen
Philip Mordant's Ward. Marianne Kent
Philip, the Draftsman. F. X. J. Coleman
Philipp Steele of the Royal Northwest Mounted Police. J. O. Curwood
Philippa Sees It Through. D. Maule
Philippine Hardpunch. Jim Case
Phillida. T. Cobb
Phillip and the Flappers. D. Newton
Phillip in Particular. D. Newton
Philly. Dan Greenburg
Philly Stakes. Gillian Roberts
Philo Gubb, Correspondence School Detective. E. P. Butler
Philomel Foundation. J. Gollin
Philopena. H. K. Webster
Philosopher's Hemlock. M. Cranston
Philosopher's Murder Case. J. R. Crawford
Philosopher's Pendulum and other stories. R. Lindau
Philosopher's Stone. Colin Watson
Philosophy of the Marquise. M. B. Lowndes
Phineax Redux. A. Trollope
Phoebe, the Miller's Daughter. T. P. Prest
Phoebe's Knee. B. Comfort
Phoenix. A. Aricha
Phoenix. L. P. Bachmann
Phoenix. S. Brust
Phoenix Assault. J. Kerrigan
Phoenix Formula. T. Leighton
Phoenix from the Ashes. H. Monteilhet
Phoenix from the Gutter. P. Motte
Phoenix in Castile. J. G. Sarasin
Phoenix in Flames. G. Wilson
Phoenix in the Blood. Harry Patterson
Phoenix Inferno. M. Barry
Phoenix Man. J. Sherman
Phoenix Nest. M. Hermes
Phoenix No More. E. Gage
Phoenix Pact. M. Hartmann
Phoenix Reaction. L. Phillips
Phoenix Sings. D. Cory
Phoenix Sword. W. Barker
Phoenix Tree. J. Cleary
Phoenix with Oily Feathers. L. G. Shreve
Phone Booth Mystery. J. Ironside
Phone Call. J. Messmann
Phone Calls. L. O'Donnell
Phone for a Hearse. B. Carson
Phoney Hitman. J. R. Pici
Phonies. W. B. M. Ferguson
Phonographic Mystery. L. Madreyhijo
Photo Crimes. Anonymous
Photo Finish. J. Bruce
Photo Finish. Howard Mason
Photo Game. Jack Lang
Photocrimes. M. Horton
Photogenic Soprano. D. Halliday
Photographer. P. Boulle
Photographer's Evidence. Nicholas Carter
Photographic Pleasures. C. Bede
Photographs Have Been Sent to Your Wife. P. Loraine
Phreak-Out! Carter Brown
Phryne. M. Dekobra
Phyllis. E. V. Cunningham
Phyllis, the Cautious. K. Kimbrough
Physalia Incident. A. Spikol
Physical Attraction. H. Janson
Physical Evidence. T. T. Noguchi
Physician, Heal Thyself! E. Phillpotts
Physician's Fare. C. G. Learoyd
Physiognomist, and other tales. H. M. Budgett
Pianist Shoots First. G. Fairlie
Piano Bird. L. Kallen
Piano Box Mystery. Nicholas Carter
Picaroon. E. Dudley
Picaroon and the Burglar Tools. Herman Landon
Picaroon Collects. J. Cassells
Picaroon Does Justice. Herman Landon
Picaroon Gets the Run-Around. J. Cassells
Picaroon Goes West. J. Cassells
Picaroon in Pursuit. Herman Landon

Picaroon: Knight Errant. Herman Landon
Picaroon Laughs Last. J. Cassells
Picaroon Resumes Practice. Herman Landon
Picaroons. G. Burgess
Piccadilly Ghost. E. Spencer
Piccadilly Jim. P. G. Wodehouse
Piccadilly Murder. A. Berkeley
Piccadilly Puzzle. F. Hume
Pick and Run. J. Farrimond
Pick-Me-Ups. N. Gubbins
Pick Up. J. B. O'Sullivan
Pick Up. Bill Ryan
Pick-Up. C. Willeford
Pick-Up on Noon Street. R. Chandler
Pick Up Sticks. E. Lathen
Pick Up the Pieces. J. F. Straker
Pick Your Victim. P. McGerr
Picked Up. A. Applin
Pickled Poodles. Larry Harris
Pickup. Raymond Marshall
Pickup Alley. E. Ronns
Picnic at Nearside. J. Varley
Picnic in November. E. Amshey
Picture Frame. L. Lamb
Picture Her Missing. Lynn Williams
Picture Him Dead. F. A. Clement
Picture Miss Seeton. H. Carvic
Picture Mommy Dead. Robert Sherman
Picture of Death. K. Giles
Picture of Death. D. La Pointe
Picture of Death. E. C. R. Lorac
Picture of Death. R. Simons
Picture of Defeat. John Harris
Picture of Guilt. M. Innes
Picture of Innocence. H. Fleetwood
Picture of Millie. P. M. Hubbard
Picture of Murder. S. Curtis
Picture of the Victim. J. S. Strange
Picture of the Year. C. Egleton
Picture on the Wall. J. B. Ellis
Picture-Perfect Murders. T. Chastain
Picture Postcard. F. D. Huebner
Pictures in a Mirror. W. M. Thomas
Pictures in the Dark. Ian Stuart
Pictures in the Fire. J. Collier
Pictures of Death. K. Robeson
Pictures on the Wall. J. Breckenridge Ellis
Pidgin Island. H. MacGrath
Piece by Piece. J. K. Stafford
Piece of Action. E. Cannon
Piece of Resistance. C. Egleton
Piece of Something. Harry Reed
Piece of the Moon. Robert Lambert
Piece of the Moon Is Missing. J. L. Johnson
Piece of the Silence. J. Livingston
Pieces in a Jigsaw. William Taylor
Pieces of a Hero. W. Overgard
Pieces of Cream. R. Hilary
Pieces of Death. J. Lynch
Pieces of Gold and other south sea stories. B. Grimshaw
Pieces of Modesty. P. O'Donnell
Pieces of the Game. L. Gifford
Pied Piper. R. Paier
Pied Piper of Dipper Creek and other tales. T. H. Raddall
Pied Piper of Helfenstein. E. V. McCarthy
Piedouche, a French Detective. F. Du Boisgobey
Pier. R. Heppenstall
Pierce the Gloom. M. Clare
Pierce with a Pin. K. Hopkins
Pierced Ear Murders. T. A. Plummer
Pierhead 627. D. Enefer
Pierre and Adeline. D. F. Haynes
Pierre and His People. Gilbert Parker
Pierrotechnics. H. C. Sargeant
Pierrots on the Pier. P. Herring
Pietrov and Other Games. Jeffrey Robinson
Pietrov Game. Jeffrey Robinson
Pig in a Poke. L. Thayer
Pig Is Fat. L. M. Maynard
Pig-Tail Murder. F. Durbridge
Pig That Got Up and Slowly Walked Away. J. Ripley

Pigeon Among the Cats. Josephine Bells
Pigeon Blood. G. Alexander
Pigeon Blood Rubies. M. M. Bodkin
Pigeon House. V. Williams
Pigeon Loft Crime. J. G. Brandon
Pigeon Parade. Maz
Pigeon Pie. N. Mitford
Pigeon Project. Irving Wallace
Pigeon Shoot. J. Crumley
Pigeon Wins. E. Woodward
Pigeon's Blood. M. Pereira
Pigs Get Fat. W. B. Murphy
Pigs Have Wings. P. G. Wodehouse
Pigskin and Willow. B. Webber
Pigskin Bag. B. Fischer
Pilate Plot. Martin Page
Pilditch Puzzle. W. Morton
Pilebuck. J. Hawkins
Pilgrim at the Gate. D. Cory
Pilgrim Came Late. M. Purcell
Pilgrim Come Home. C. Rodda
Pilgrim of Desire. V. Black
Pilgrim of Hate. Ellis Peters
Pilgrim on the Island. D. Cory
Pilgrim's End. L. B. McNamara
Pilgrims Meet Murder. Dexter Muir
Pilgrim's Rest. P. Wentworth
Pilkington. W. Caine
Pillar of Fire. M. Clare
Pillar of Light. L. Tracy
Pillars of Fire. S. Shagan
Pillars of Hell. R. Chester
Pillars of Salt. A. Mills
Pilloried! Sewell Stokes
Pillory. B. Fleming
Pillow Killer. Peter Israel
Pillow of the Community. R. Hilary
Pilot Error. B. Knox
Pilot's Graveyard. P. Conde
Pimlico Plot. M. McMullen
Pimp for the Dead. R. Dennis
Pimpernel and Rosemary. Baroness Orczy
Pimpernel 60. P. Kinsley
Pin a Rose on Me! Gordon Berry
Pin It on the Doll. C. Dekker
Pin Men. R. East
Pin to See the Peepshow. F. T. Jesse
Pinball Murders. T. B. Black
Pinch of Poison. F. Lockridge
Pinch of Snuff. R. Hill
Pinch of Snuff. M. Underwood
Pinchbeck Masterpiece. P. Cleife
Pincher in Peace and War. C. M. Hincks
Pincher Martin, O.D. Taffrail
Pinday and the "White Slaver". B. Sarto
Pine-Top Jones: Fugitive. B. Harding
Pine-Top Jones: Renegade. B. Harding
Pine-Top Jones: Vigilante. B. Harding
Pinecastle. I. Manchester
Pinehurst. J. Rhode
Pink and the Brown. H. Atkinson
Pink Cadillac. T. Strasser
Pink Camellia. L. Bergstrom
Pink Carrara. Harris Evans
Pink Castle. C. Vincent
Pink Film. J. Bogar
Pink Lady. K. Robeson
Pink Panther. M. Albert
Pink Panther Strikes Again. W. Gleason
Pink Panther Strikes Again. F. Waldman
Pink Ribbon, As Told to the Police. O. Blakeston
Pink Shop. F. Hume
Pink Silk Alibi. B. Sanders
Pink String and Sealing Wax. R. Pertwee
Pink Triangle. R. Raftery
Pink Umbrella. F. Crane
Pink Umbrella Murder. F. Crane
Pinkerton. F. Cordelli
Pinkerton Ferret. C. Morris
Pinnacle of Ice. J. Raven
Pinned Man. G. Griswold
Pins and Needles. E. Greenwood
Pint of Murder. A. Craig
Pioneer. H. Bindloss

Pioneer Jack. R. Harding
Pious Agent. J. Braine
Pious Deception. Susan Dunlap
Pipe All Hands! Sinbad
Pipe Dream. P. Ferguson
Pipe Dream. J. Symons
Pipe Dream Finesse. D. Da Cruz
Pipe Pushers. W. Martyr
Pipeline from Hell. D. Bannerman
Pipeline to Death. A. Eichler
Piper. Campbell Black
Piper in the Street Today. B. Boswell
Piper of Arristoun. B. Goldie
Piper on the Mountain. Ellis Peters
Piperock Tales. W. C. Tuttle
Pipes Are Calling. Carter Brown
Pipes of Margaree. J. Aeby
Piping a Detective. Anonymous
Piping Times. J. Farnol
Pippin's Journal. R. O'Grady
Piracies, Ltd. Bok
Piracy Wears Pink. Kane
Piraeus Plot. H. Arvay
Piranha, Piranha. I. Zacharia
Pirate Airship. J. Noy
Pirate Isle. K. Robeson
Pirate Love. M. Richmond
Pirate of Pittsburgh. H. E. O. Whitman
Pirate of the Pacific. K. Robeson
Pirate Submarine. R. Simmonds
Pirates. Taffrail
Pirate's Ghost. K. Robeson
Pirate's Gold. D. Whitelaw
Pirates of Society. W. Biddulph
Pirates of the Air. G. E. Rochester
Pirates of the Air Way. R. C. Armour
Pirates of the Main. Stuart Martin
Pirates of the Sky. S. Gaillard
Pirate's Pack. J. G. Sarasin
Pirate's Purchase. B. A. Williams
Pirate's Retreat. Lieut. Carlton
Pirdale Island. A. O. Pollard
Pistol at My Head. A. Nuttall
Pistol for Miss Preedy. H. C. Davis
Pistolero. P. Kinsley
Pistols and Pedagogues. F. Evans
Pistols for Two. G. Heyer
Pistols for Two. A. M. Stein
Pistols with Coffee. W. Du Bois
Pit. F. Merrilees
Pit. O. West
Pit and the Pendulum. L. Sheridan
Pit in the Garden. L. Meynell
Pit of Death. Breton Lee
Pit-Prop Syndicate. F. W. Crofts
Pit Town Coronet. C. J. Wills
Pitch Dark. R. Adler
Pitchblende Quarry. A. Gordon
Pitfall. F. L. Cary
Pitfall. J. J. Dratler
Pitfall. P. Ritchie
Pitfall. W. Magnay
Pitfall in August. H. Roman
Pitiful Rebellion. M. Peterson
Pitiless As Death. Anonymous
Pity for Pamela. M. Fitt
Pity Him Afterwards. D. E. Westlake
Pity It Wasn't George. J. F. Straker
Pity My Love. D. Winston
Pity My Simplicity. C. Massie
Pity the Honest. E. Lacy
Pity Us All. J. Reese
Pixie at the Wheel. D. Sturrock
Pizza House Crash. D. Danks
Place. T. M. Wright
Place at Whitten. T. Keneally
Place Called Purgatory. J. Shelynn
Place Called Skull. J. N. Chance
Place for a Poisoner. E. C. R. Lorac
Place for Murder. E. Lathen
Place for Outlaws. A. Wier
Place for the Mighty. H. Denker
Place for the Wicked. E. Trevor

Place in the Country. S. Gainham
Place Like Hessberg. C. Fleet
Place of Devils. Lucinda Baker
Place of Dreams. W. Barry
Place of Execution. A. Curry
Place of Execution. M. Vinter
Place of Judgment. B. Levy
Place of Little Birds. M. Home
Place of Many Stars. A. Preston
Place of Mischief. E. E. Cameron
Place of Mists. Robert MacLeod
Place of Sapphires. F. E. Randall
Place of Shadows. K. Booton
Place of Stones. C. Heaven
Place of the Dawn. Gordon Taylor
Place of the Dragons. W. LeQueux
Place on Dark Island. G. Corren
Place Taker. P. Earlston
Place to Hide. Evelyn Anthony
Place to Hide. Clifford King
Place to Stand. A. Bridge
Place with Two Faces. Josephine Mann
Plagiarist. W. Myrtle
Plague Court Murders. Carter Dickson
Plague Makers. J. Pattinson
Plague of Demons. G. Ashe
Plague of Dragons. J. M. Brett
Plague of Sailors. B. Callison
Plague of Silence. J. Creasey
Plague of Spies. M. Kurland
Plague of Violence. H. Pentecost
Plague on Both Your Causes. J. Brunner
Plague on Both Your Houses. M. Ashton
Plague Over London. T. Craig
Plague Panic. S. G. Hedges
Plague Spot. B. Tutton
Plague Stone. Gill White
Plague Summer. Hugh Cook
Plaid Shroud. Marc Miller
Plain Case of Murder. L. Thayer
Plain Man. J. Symons
Plain Miss Cray. F. Warden
Plain Murder. C. S. Forester
Plain Murder. R. Greth
Plain Old Man. A. MacLeod
Plain Sailing. Douglas Clark
Plain Tales of the City and Suburbs. D. Levenax
Plain Unvarnished Murder. K. Klein
Plains of Fire. J. Hild
Plains of Silence. A. Askew
Plan for Escape. A. Bioy-Casares
Plan 79. C. F. Maxwell
Plan XVI. D. G. Browne
Planet X. G. Hunt
Planetary Journeys and Earthly Sketches. G. Raffalovich
Planetoid 127 and The Sweizer Pump. E. Wallace
Planned Coincidence. B. Mortlock
Planning for Murder. A. Morice
Plans for Departure. N. Sahgal
Plant Me Now. M. Hagen
Plant Poppies on My Grave. A. Kent
Plantation Inn. Patricia Maxwell
Plantation Murder. C. N. Govan
Planter. H. Whitaker
Planter's Ward. N. Buntline
Plaster Saints. F. A. Kummer
Plaster Sinners. Colin Watson
Plastic Kind of Death. T. D. Carroll
Plastic Magicians. P. Leslie
Plastic Man. D. J. Gerrity
Plastic Nightmare. R. Neely
Plate of Ladies. G. Fraser
Plate of Red Herrings. R. Lockridge
Platinum Ass. A. Storey
Platinum Bullet. R. L. Graves
Platinum Cat. M. Burton
Platinum High School. I. Shulman
Platinum Jag. A. Storey
Platinum Smugglers. R. C. Armour
Platypus of Doom and other nihilists. A. B. Cover
Play Dead. H. Coben
Play for Keeps. H. Whittington
Play for Millions. Nicholas Carter
Play for Murder. N. Deane
Play It Casual. H. Janson
Play It Cool. J. Gerstine
Play It Hard. G. Brewer
Play It Quiet. H. Janson
Play It Smart. S. Markham
Play It Solo. Neill Graham
Play It to a Bust. Dave Greenberg
Play It Your Way. A. Capelli
Play Melancholy Baby. J. Daniel
Play Misty for Me. P. J. Gillette
Play Now—Kill Later! Carter Brown
Play or Pay. H. Smart
Play-Room. Gloria Murphy
Play Rough! R. Wayne
Play the Roman Fool and Die. Richard Grayson
Play with Death. C. Franklin
Play with Fire. E. Lamartine
Play with Fire. E. Percy
Play with Knives. J. Maiden
Play with Matches. F. Ford
Playback. R. Chandler
Playback. The Gordons
Playboy. P. W. Fairman
Played the Hard Way. Griff
Played to a Finish. Nicholas Carter
Player. W. Downing
Player. M. Tolkin
Player and the Guest. G. F. Newman
Player on the Other Side. E. Queen
Players. W. Magnay
Players and the Game. J. Symons
Players' Boy is Dead. L. Tourney
Players Come Again. A. Cross
Players in a Dark Game. S. Coulter
Player's Tragedy. H. H. Fyfe
Playgirl. D. Haring
Playgirl. H. Janson
Playgirl for Keeps. K. T. McCall
Playgirl Wanted. Roy Vickers
Playground of Death. J. B. Hilton
Playhouse. R. Levinson
Playing a Bold Game. Nicholas Carter
Playing a Lone Hand. Nicholas Carter
Playing Catch-Up. A. B. Guthrie, Jr.
Playing for a Fortune. Nicholas Carter
Playing for Keeps. J. Kendall
Playing for Keeps. J. Waterhouse
Playing for Time. R. Rand
Playing God. B. Whitehead
Playing Safe. E. Dewhurst
Playing Square. J. Wilder
Playing the Dozens. W. D. Pease
Playing the Knave. F. Warden
Playing the Mischief. J. W. De Forrest
Playing with Fire. J. Bloom
Playing with Fire. Susan Moody
Playing with Fire. G. Sampson
Playing with Fire. B. Veder
Playmates. A. Neiderman
Playmates. R. B. Parker
Playroom. M. Drayton
Plays. Steve Carter
Play's Afoot! B. Barton
Plays of Evil and Suspense. P. Groves
Plaything of Fate. Nicholas Carter
Plaza Mystery. Maurice Worth
Plea for Justice. Nicholas Carter
Pleasant Dreams—Nightmares. R. Bloch
Pleasant Grove Murders. J. H. Vance
Pleasant Husband, and other stories. Marjorie Bowen
Pleasant Rogue. L. Keith
Pleasantries of Old Quong. T. Burke
Please Communicate. M. Oldfield
Please . . . Don't Kill Me. W. C. Dear
Please Kill My Cousin. G. Fairlie
Please Omit Funeral. H. Dolson
Please Pass the Guilt. R. Stout
Pleasure Business. Patrick Anderson
Pleasure Buyers. A. S. Roche
Pleasure Cruise Murder. W. Jardine
Pleasure Cruise Mystery. R. Forsythe
Pleasure Dome. E. Kyle
Pleasure-Dome. D. Madden
Pleasure Girl. B. Sarto
Pleasure House. P. Tabori
Pleasure Island. F. R. Adams
Pleasure Island. Nick Carter
Pleasure of Your Death. M. Farhi
Pleasure Principle. P. McCurtin
Pleasure Seekers. H. V. Dixon
Pleasure's Daughter. Marilyn Ross
Pleasuring of Rory Malone. C. Panati
Pledge. F. Duerrenmatt
Pledge of Hatred. A. Andre
Pledged to the Dead. E. M. Poate
Plekhanov Original. J. Burmeister
Plekhov Place. William Taylor
Plender. T. Lewis
Plenty Under the Counter. K. Hewitt
Plight of the Innocents. A. Sewart
Plot. E. Hostovsky
Plot. K. P. Kelley
Plot. E. Piper
Plot. Irving Wallace
Plot Against a Widow. R. C. Ashby
Plot Against Roger Rider. J. Symons
Plot and Counterplot. Anonymous
Plot and Counterplot. Old Sleuth
Plot Counter-Plot. A. Clarke
Plot for a Warship. Nicholas Carter
Plot for an Empire. Nicholas Carter
Plot for Millions. S. Campbell
Plot for Murder. F. Brown
Plot for the Fourth Reich. Nick Carter
Plot in Private Life, and other tales. W. Collins
Plot It Yourself. R. Stout
Plot-Maker. W. Hewlett
Plot of the Yellow Emperor. A. Parsons
Plot That Failed. Nichoals Carter
Plot to Kill the President. J. Pearl
Plot to Kill Wallace Simpson. G. Fisher
Plot Uncovered. Nicholas Carter
Plot Within a Plot. Nicholas Carter
Plots. B. Capes
Plots and Counterplots. L. M. Alcott
Plotters. A. Caillou
Plotters. R. Hardwick
Plotters. T. W. Speight
Plotters of Paris. E. Mitchell
Plotters of Peking. C. Dawe
Plowing Up a Snake. M. Drown
Pluck. Jonathan Webb
Plucked. H. Smart
Plucking the Crow. P. Crobyn
Plucky Bob. Old Sleuth
Plucky Girl. Old Sleuth
Plugged Nickel. Robert Campbell
Plugged Nickel. P. Sherwood
Plum Blossoms and Blue Incense. J. W. Bennett
Plum Thicket. J. Giles
Plumb. M. Gee
Plume of Smoke. E. Morris
Plumly Inheritance. C. Bush
Plunder. B. Appel
Plunder. R. Goulart
Plunder. P. Meriton
Plunder. A. S. Roche
Plunder. B. Travers
Plunder. F. F. Van De Water
Plunder Bar. S. M. Parkman
Plunder for the Picaroon. J. Cassells
Plunder of the Sun. D. Dodge
Plunder Pit. K. Snowden
Plunder Ship. H. Hill
Plunder Squad. R. Stark
Plundered Paradise. L. Derrick
Plunderers. F. Cowen
Plunderers. E. Lefevre
Plunderers. E. P. Oppenheim
Plunderers. Morley Roberts
Plunge. C. Brogan
Plunge Into Crime. Nicholas Carter
Plunge Into Peril. W. Spann
Plunger. H. Smart
Plush and Guilt. J. Foss
Plush-Lined Coffin. Carter Brown

Plutonium. V. Mayhew
Plutonium Conspiracy. Jeffrey Robinson
Plutonium Factor. M. Bagley
Plutonium Heist. W. M. Green
Poached Peerage. W. Magnay
Poacher. R. T. Baker
Poacher. P. Baron
Poacher. B. McNaughton
Poacher's Bag. Douglas Clark
Poacher's Wife. C. Carew
Pocket Book of Father Brown. G. K. Chesterton
Pocket Full of Clues. J. R. Langham
Pocket Full of Dead. J. Wyllie
Pocket Full of Rye. A. Christie
Pocket Hercules. E. Jepson
Pocketful of Clues. J. R. Langham
Pocock & Pitt. E. Baker
Pod, Bender & Co. G. A. England
Poe Must Die. M. Olden
Poe Papers. N. L. Zaroulis
Poellenberg Inheritance. Evelyn Anthony
Poet and the Lunatics. G. K. Chesterton
Poetic Justice. A. Cross
Poetic Justice. L. A. Taylor
Poets and Murder. R. Van Gulik
Poinciana. P. A. Whitney
Poindexter Crashes the Fifth Column. G. C. Foster
Point Blank. J. Hild
Point Blank. Jayson Livingston
Point Blank. P. Rosenberg
Point Blank. R. Stark
Point-Blank. D. Wulffson
Point of a Gun. A. MacKenzie
Point of a Thousand Spears. L. P. Greene
Point of Death. N. Dun
Point of Death. I. Lambot
Point of Honor. D. Gethin
Point of Honour. A. Scholefield
Point of Lost Souls. J. J. Toombs
Point of Murder. M. Yorke
Point of No Escape. M. Colton
Point of Peril. E. Ronns
Point of Reference. Richard Russell
Point of Violence. Lois Duncan
Point Team. J. B. Hadley
Pointed Tower. V. Thompson
Pointer to a Crime. A. Fielding
Pointers to Crime. Nicholas Carter
Pointing Finger. M. Richmond
Pointing Finger. Rita
Pointing Man. M. Douie
Points and Lines. S. Matsumoto
Poirot and the Regatta Mystery. A. Christie
Poirot Investigates. A. Christie
Poirot Knows the Murderer. A. Christie
Poirot Lends a Hand. A. Christie
Poirot Loses a Client. A. Christie
Poirot on Holiday. A. Christie
Poirot's Early Cases. A. Christie
Poison. A. Askew
Poison. D. Linton
Poison. E. McBain
Poison. L. Thayer
Poison and the Root. R. Savage
Poison at Plessis. M. Dekobra
Poison by Proxy. B. Vane
Poison Case Number 10. L. Cornell
Poison Chasers. H. Calvin
Poison Cocktail Murders. C. B. Molyneaux
Poison Cross Mystery. I. H. Irwin
Poison Cupboard. John Burke
Poison Dealer. G. Ohnet
Poison Death. Glint Green
Poison Duel. P. Dingwall
Poison Eye. M. S. Buchanan
Poison Flower. D. Daniels
Poison Fly Murder. H. Rutland
Poison for One. J. Rhode
Poison for One. E. Wilmot
Poison for Teacher. N. Spain
Poison for the Toff. J. Creasey
Poison from a Wealthy Widow. P. Haggard
Poison Gang. D. Steele
Poison Gas Robberies. J. Creasey

Poison in a Garden Suburb. G. D. H. Cole
Poison in Jest. J. D. Carr
Poison in Kensington. C. Kingston
Poison in Paradise. A. Hocking
Poison in Pimlico. Elbur Ford
Poison in Play. N. Spain
Poison in Public. C. Barry
Poison in Putney. F. M. Long
Poison in the Blood. P. Dolan
Poison in the Garden Suburb. G. D. H. Cole
Poison in the Parish. M. Kennedy
Poison in the Pen. P. Wentworth
Poison in the Shade. E. Benfield
Poison Is a Bitter Brew. A. Hocking
Poison Is Queen. J. L. Morrissey
Poison Island. A. T. Quiller-Couch
Poison Island. K. Robeson
Poison Ivy. Carter Brown
Poison Ivy. P. Cheyney
Poison Ivy. J. P. Heggy
Poison Jasmine. C. B. Clason
Poison League. J. B. Harris-Burland
Poison Lockspur. C. W. Sanders
Poison of Asps. F. Marryat
Poison of Poppies. G. Brodie
Poison on the Menu. F. Ramsdale
Poison Oracle. P. Dickinson
Poison Parsley. A. Clarke
Poison Party. M. Brucker
Poison Pen. H. Desmond
Poison Pen. R. Llewellyn
Poison-Pen at Pyford. D. Fisher
Poison Pen Playgirl. M. Brody
Poison People. W. Haggard
Poison Plague. W. Levinrew
Poison, Poker and Pistols. E. M. Stone
Poison Pool. G. Collins
Poison Ring. M. Y. Halidom
Poison Shadows. W. LeQueux
Poison Speaks Softly. D. P. Clark
Poison Summer. J. L. Hensley
Poison Trail. A. Armstrong
Poison Tree. S. Stern
Poison Unknown. M. Dalman
Poison Unknown. C. J. Dutton
Poison War. Ladbroke Black
Poison Weed. M. Richmond
Poisoned Anemones. U. Sanford
Poisoned Arrow. Lieut. Carlton
Poisoned Arrows. J. Middlemass
Poisoned Chalice. A. Hocking
Poisoned Chalice. J. Pattinson
Poisoned Chocolates Case. A. Berkeley
Poisoned Fang. K. Bruce
Poisoned Glass. S. J. Stutley
Poisoned Goblet. A. Gask
Poisoned Letter. Anonymous
Poisoned Mountain. M. Channing
Poisoned Orchard. U. Curtiss
Poisoned Paradise. Mark Roberts
Poisoned Paradise. R. W. Service
Poisoned Pen. O. Binns
Poisoned Pen. A. B. Reeve
Poisoned Relations. G. Simenon
Poisoned Sleep. B. Graeme
Poisoned Stream. H. Habe
Poisoned Web. A. Clarke
Poisoner. G. Verner
Poisoners. D. Hamilton
Poisoners. G. R. Preedy
Poisoner's Base. B. Cobb
Poisoner's Mistake. B. Cobb
Poisonous Angel. Griff
Poisonous Relations. J. Cannan
Poisons of Exili. Nicholas Carter
Poisons Unknown. F. Kane
Poker Game. F. Knebel
Poker Jim, Gentleman and other tales and sketches. G. F. Lydston
Poker King. M. Manly
Pokerface. P. Corris
Polar Assault. F. Garrett
Polar City Blues. K. Kerr
Polar Star. M. C. Smith

Polar Treasure. K. Robeson
Poldrate Street. Garnett Weston
Pole Reaction. J. Bruce
Pole Star Secret. Garnett Weston
Polferry Mystery. P. MacDonald
Polferry Riddle. P. MacDonald
Police and Detection. R. Jeffries
Police at the Funeral. M. Allingham
Police Blotter. R. L. Pike
Police Car. R. Jeffries
Police Chief. J. Ball
Police Detective. Anonymous
Police Detective Stories. L. Dexter
Police Dog. R. Jeffries
Police Matron. C. Glick
Police Murders. P. H. Powell
Police Nurse. W. Neubauer
Police Patrol Boat. R. Jeffries
Police Patrol: 2000 A.D. M. Reynolds
Police Records and Recollections. Edward Savage
Police Sergeant C21. R. Barnett
Police Station Mystery. R. Hardinge
Police Your Planet. E. Van Lhin
Policeboat Mystery. A. Blair
Policeman. Anonymous
Policeman at the Door. C. Carnac
Policeman Flynn. E. Flower
Policeman from Eton. Reginald Campbell
Policeman in Armour. R. Penny
Policeman's Dread. J. Creasey
Policeman's Evidence. R. Penny
Policeman's Gazette. H. Cole
Policeman's Holiday. R. Penny
Policeman's Lantern. James Greenwood
Policeman's Lot. C. Bond
Policeman's Lot. H. Cole
Policeman's Lot. E. Linington
Policeman's Lot. Henry Wade
Policeman's Nightmare. M. Cumberland
Policeman's Patch. H. Cole
Policeman's Patrol. H. Cole
Policeman's Progress. H. Cole
Policeman's Progress. B. Piction
Policeman's Story. H. Cole
Policeman's Travels. H. Cole
Policeman's Triumph. P. Manton
Policemen in the Precinct. E. C. R. Lorac
Policewoman. D. Uhnak
Policing the Arctic. H. Steele
Policy for Murder. J. Popplewell
Polite Pirate. "Capstan"
Political Plotter. Dick Stewart
Political Suicide. Robert Barnard
Politician. V. Torrio
Politics Is Murder. E. Lanham
Polka Dot Nude. Joan Smith
Polka-Dot Pet. D. Haring
Polkadot Murder. F. Crane
Polluted City. G. Thorne
Polly Put the Kettle On. Joan Fleming
Polly, the Worried. K. Kimbrough
Polmarran Tower. C. Massey
Polo, Anyone? J. Kennealy
Polo Ground Mystery. R. Forsythe
Polo in the Rough. J. Kennealy
Polo Solo. J. Kennealy
Polo's Ponies. J. Kennealy
Polo's Wild Card. J. Kennealy
Pomeroy. G. M. Williams
Pomeroy Abbey. H. Wood
Pomeroy, Deceased. G. Bellairs
Pomfret Mystery. A. D. Vinton
Pompeii Scroll. J. La Tourrette
Pompeii Splendor. J. La Tourrette
Pong, Ho. D. Flatau
Ponson Case. F. W. Crofts
Pontifex, Son & Thorndyke. R. A. Freeman
Pontius Pilate Papers. W. Kiefer
Poodle Springs. R. Chandler
Pool. M. R. Rinehart
Pool of Death. K. Patrick
Pool of Flame. L. J. Vance
Pool of Tears. J. Wainwright
Pool Ticket. C. Baker

Title Index PRAIRIE DETECTIVE / 1117

Pools of the Past. C. Procter
Poor Boy. R. Brissenden
Poor Butterfly. S. M. Kaminsky
Poor Dead Cricket. W. G. Duncan
Poor Devils. D. Ely
Poor Harriet. Elizabeth Fenwick
Poor Man's Shilling. K. M. Knight
Poor Millie. T. Baird
Poor Miss Finch. W. Collins
Poor Old Lady's Dead. J. S. Scott
Poor, Poor Ophelia. C. Weston
Poor, Poor Yorick. F. C. Davis
Poor Prisoner's Defense. R. Sheldon
Poor Quail. D. Skirrow
Poor Richard's Game. G. O'Toole
Poor Roger Is Dead. M. Lynch
Pop Goes the Queen. B. Wade
Pop. 1280. J. Thompson
Pope Must Die. F. Norwood
Pope of Greenwich Village. Vincent Patrick
Poppies of Death. P. Edwards
Poppies of Doom. Philip Richmond
Poppy Show. H. B. M. Watson
Porcelain Dolls Don't Bleed. C. Vail
Porcelain Fish. H. R. Campbell
Porcelain Fish Mystery. H. R. Campbell
Porcelain Mask. J. J. Chichester
Porch Climber. K. Kavanaugh
Porcupine Basin. D. Rutherford
Pork Butcher. D. Hughes
Pork City. Howard Browne
Porkchoppers. Ross Thomas
Porn Tapes. R. Rainey
Pornbroker. Carter Brown
Porridge. P. Ableman
Porridge. Jonathan Marshall
Porro Palaver. A. Broome
Porson's Flying Service. G. E. Rochester
Port Afrique. B. V. Dryer
Port Allington Stories and others. R. E. Vernede
Port and a Star Boarder. B. J. Morison
Port of Call. W. Reyburn
Port of Destination. E. L. Long
Port of Light. D. Serafin
Port of Little Ships. A. Wood
Port of London Murders. Josephine Bell
Port of Lost Cargoes. M. Hastings
Port of Missing Men. Meredith Nicholson
Port o' Missing Men. P. C. Wren
Port of No Return. P. M. Irvine
Port of No Return. R. M. Sears
Port of Seven Strangers. K. M. Knight
Port Orient. D. Cushman
Port Tropique. B. Gifford
Portal of the Wind. S. Natsuki
Portals. E. A. Mann
Portcullis Room. V. Williams
Porterfield Legacy. C. Stephens
Porth Smuggler. E. Vale
Portland Murders. C. Larson
Portland Place Mystery. C. Kingston
Portland Place Mystery. E. D. Pierson
Portly Peregrine. P. Traill
Portrait in a Dusty Frame. M. Hebden
Portrait in Black. J. V. Frost
Portrait in Black. I. Goff
Portrait in Black. Richard Vincent
Portrait in Fear. V. Henry
Portrait in Murder and Gay Colors. H. P. Jeffers
Portrait in Shadows. J. Wainwright
Portrait in Smoke. B. S. Ballinger
Portrait Invisible. J. Gollomb
Portrait of a Beautiful Harlot. H. Howard
Portrait of a Beautiful Woman. C. Massie
Portrait of a Dead Heiress. T. B. Dewey
Portrait of a Dead Lady. M. A. Taylor
Portrait of a Judge and other stories. H. Cecil
Portrait of a Killer. C. D. E. Francis
Portrait of a Man with Red Hair. H. Walpole
Portrait of a Mobster. H. Grey
Portrait of a Murderer. A. Meredith
Portrait of a Scoundrel. E. Phillpotts
Portrait of a Spy. T. Thurston
Portrait of a Victim. R. E. McDowell
Portrait of a Witch. D. Daniels
Portrait of Alison. F. Durbridge
Portrait of Barbara. R. Squire
Portrait of Death. W. Bannister
Portrait of Doubt. R. Abbey
Portrait of Emma. L. Cheatham
Portrait of Evil. Jennifer Hale
Portrait of Fear. M. Richardson
Portrait of Fear. F. Usher
Portrait of Jirjohn Cobb. H. S. Keeler
Portrait of Lilith. J. Thomson
Portrait of Love. Lynna Cooper
Portrait of Love. J. De Secary
Portrait of Murder. R. Bloomfield
Portrait of Rene. Harry Davis
Portrait of Sarah. V. Black
Portrait of Susan. G. Davies
Portrait of Terror. J. Masiello
Portrait of Terror. P. Minton
Portrait of the Accused. F. A. Symonds
Portrait of the Artist As a Dead Man. F. Bonnamy
Portraits of the Past. K. Cameron
Portrush Mystery. G. L. Curry
Portuguese Defection. G. DeVilliers
Portuguese Diamonds. G. Horne
Portuguese Escape. A. Bridge
Portuguese Fragment. O. Sela
Portuguese Silver. C. N. Buck
Poseidon Target. Nick Carter
Poseidon's Shadow. A. P. Kobryn
Position of Trust. R. Hart
Position of Ultimate Trust. W. Beechcroft
Possess and Conquer. Wenzell Brown
Possess Me Not. F. Nichols
Possess the Land. Alan White
Possessed. D. Daniels
Possessed. C. Farr
Possessed. W. Gombrowicz
Possessed. F. Hurd
Possessed. C. Moffett
Possessed. A. Radnor
Possessed. R. Powe
Possessed. G. F. Scott
Possessed. C. Turney
Possessed: The Sequel. R. Powe
Possession. L. P. Davies
Possession. C. Fremlin
Possession. Peter James
Possession. A. Rule
Possession of Elizabeth Calder. Melissa Napier
Possession of Joel Delaney. R. Stewart
Possession of Tracy Corbin. D. Daniels
Post After Post-Mortem. E. C. R. Lorac
Post-Mark Homicide. A. A. Marcus
Post Mortem. H. Carmichael
Post-Mortem. G. Collins
Post Mortem. G. Cullingford
Post-Mortem. M. Moiseiwitsch
Post Mortem. P. Whalley
Post-Mortem Effects. T. Boyle
Post-Mortem Evidence. S. Fowler
Post Mortems. C. Divine
Post No Bonds. M. Biderman
Post Office Burglars of the Shawangunk Mountains. L. A. Newcome
Post Office Case. D. M. Disney
Post Office Detective. Anonymous
Post-Office Detective. G. W. Goode
Post Road. W. D. Steele
Postage Stamp Murder. G. C. Bestor
Posted for Murder. V. Rath
Postern of Fate. A. Christie
Posthumous Papers. R. Barnard
Postman Always Rings Twice. J. M. Cain
Postman's Daughter, and other tales. H. Herman
Postman's Knock. J. F. Straker
Postmark. S. Chase
Postmark Murder. M. G. Eberhart
Postmaster of Market Deignton. E. P. Oppenheim
Postmaster's Daughter. L. Tracy
Postmortem. P. D. Cornwell
Postscript for Malpas. P. Pearson
Postscript to a Dead Letter. D. MacKenzie
Postscript to a Death. M. Cumberland
Postscript to Murder. P. Winn
Postscript to Nightmare. D. Hitchens
Postscript to Penelope. S. Gilruth
Postscript to Poison. D. Bowers
Pot au Feu. M. Pickthall
Pot Holes. E. C. Webster
Pot of Trouble. D. Tracy
Pot Shot. L. Stallworth
Potboilers. C. Marowitz
Potentate. W. Fennerton
Potman Spoke Sooth. D. Fulk
Potomac Conspiracy. D. L. Levy
Potsdam Murder Plot. D. Betteridge
Potsherds. M. C. Birchenough
Potter's Field. Ellis Peters
Potter's Wheel. F. C. Williams
Potting Shed. G. Greene
Poulter's Passage. P. McCutchan
Pound of Flesh. B. Delannoy
Pour a Swindle Through a Loophole. D. Von Elsner
Pour the Hemlock. A. J. Russell
Poverty Bay. E. W. Emerson
Powder Barrel. W. Haggard
Powder Burn. W. D. Montalbano
Powder Keg. R. Kleiner
Powder Train. W. Tute
Powdered Proof. M. S. Buchanan
Power! A. Edgar
Power. W. Harrington
Power. James Mills
Power. F. M. Robinson
Power. R. M. Stern
Power and the Glory. D. Cannan
Power and the Glory. G. Greene
Power Barons. D. Streib
Power Bug. G. Osborne
Power Cube Affair. J. T. Phillifent
Power Eaters. D. Davenport
Power Failure. James Preston
Power Gambit. Gar Wilson
Power Game. P. Mail
Power Gods. B. Clifton
Power-House. B. Appel
Power-House. J. Buchan
Power House. W. Haggard
Power in the Land. S. Prebble
Power Kill. C. Runyon
Power Killers. J. Philips
Power of a Villain. Warren Miller
Power of Command. F. H. Shaw
Power of Gold. C. Meyer
Power of Nothingness. A. David-Neel
Power of the Borgias. W. LeQueux
Power of the Bug. I. Drummond
Power of the Unknown. A. Edgar
Power of Women's Hate. N. Buntline
Power on the Scent. H. Clandon
Power Play. T. J. Culver
Power Play. The Gordons
Power Play. L. Johns
Power Play. R. Sapir
Power Plays. G. F. Walker
Power Plays. C. Wilcox
Power Sellers. P. Hall
Power to Kill. R. Hichens
Power Without Glory. M. C. Hutton
Powers. W. Bailey
Powers and Maxine. C. N. Williamson
Powers of Charlotte. J. Lazarre
Powers of Darkness. D. Miall
Powers of Darkness. M. Napier
Powers of Darkness. F. M. White
Powers of Lismara. P. Tierney
Powers of Mischief. W. Magnay
Powers That Prey. J. Flynt
Practice Makes Murder. B. Bearshaw
Practice to Deceive. G. Bradshaw
Practice to Deceive. E. Linington
Practise to Deceive. R. Lockridge
Praed Street Dossier. A. Derleth
Praed Street Papers. A. Derleth
Praetorius Point. N. Pierce
Prairie Detective. Anonymous
Prairie Detective. L. P. Richardson

P

Prairie Fire. D. Pendleton
Prairie Flowers. J. B. Hendryx
Prairie Gold. H. Bindloss
Prairie Patrol. H. Bindloss
Prairie Peril. C. Stoddard
Prairie, Snow and Sea. L. Mott
Prairie Wife. A. Stringer
Pranks. D. Higman
Pratfall. T. A. Schock
Pray for a Brave Heart. Helen MacInnes
Pray for a Miracle. A. Amos
Pray for Ricky Foster. J. Johnston
Pray for the Dawn. E. Harding
Pray Silence. M. Coles
Pray to the Hustler's God. J. Donahue
Prayer for an Assassin. I. Sentjurc
Prayer for Fair Weather. J. Broderick
Prayer for My Daughter. T. Babe
Prayer for the Dying. J. Higgins
Prayer for the Guilty. P. A. Foxall
Prayer of a Chance. L. Leibee
Praying Mantis. Edgar Johnson
Praying Mantis. H. Monteilhet
Praying Mantis. Domini Taylor
Praying Monkey. Gavin Holt
Preach No More. R. Lockridge
Preacher. T. Thackrey, Jr.
Preacher of the Lord. A. Askew
Preaching Jim. D. Donovan
Precinct 19. T. L. Adcock
Precinct #1: Siberia. T. Philbin
Precinct Siberia. T. Philbin
Precious Cargo. J. Pattinson
Precious Company. J. Budd
Precious in His Sight. M. E. Hughes
Precious Objects. D. G. Devon
Precious Procelain. N. Bell
Precipice. F. Warden
Predator. R. Braddon
Predator. D. Flint
Predator. Anthony John
Predator. P. Monette
Predator. D. Pitts
Predator. A. York
Predators. E. Sauter
Predators. D. Streib
Predator's Waltz. J. Brandon
Prediction. J. Hyde
Preened for Paradise. D. Haring
Preface to a Killing. N. Ashe
Prelude for War. L. Charteris
Prelude in Prague. S. F. Wright
Prelude to a Certain Midnight. G. Kersh
Prelude to a Killing. N. Ashe
Prelude to Blue Mountains. A. Hyder
Prelude to Crime. J. J. Farjeon
Prelude to Darkness. M. Naismith
Prelude to Horror. W. B. M. Ferguson
Prelude to Murder. G. C. Bestor
Prelude to Murder. Anthony Gilbert
Prelude to Murder. N. Leslie
Prelude to Murder. S. Noel
Prelude to Passion. H. Lugar
Prelude to Peril. J. Sohl
Prelude to Peril. S. Toye
Prelude to Terror. Helen MacInnes
Prelude to Trouble. John Bentley
Premature Burial. M. H. Danne
Premedicated Murder. Douglas Clark
Premeditated Murder. P. Cheyney
Premier. G. Simenon
Premiere at Willow Run. Michelle Collins
Premier's Daughter. A. Askew
Premium on Death. Roy Lewis
Prenatal Entreaty. J. Ruyle
Prep School for Heaven. E. Dickey
Preparatory School Murder. R. Macnaughtan
Prepare for Action. J. Creasey
Prescription for Death. Desmond Martin
Prescription for Justice. V. Wartofsky
Prescription for Murder. H. Lees
Prescription for Murder. S. Miles
Prescription for Murder. David Williams
Prescription: Murder. D. M. Disney
Prescription: Murder. W. Link
Presence. M. Eyre
Presence in an Empty Room. V. Johnston
Presence in the House. M. Lovell
Presence of Evil. I. Moffitt
Present Danger. W. J. Buchanan
Present from Hugo. A. Paul
Present from Peking. D. Lampard
Present from Santa. James Burke
Presenting Inspector Flagg. J. Cassells
Presenting Moonshine. J. Collier
Presenting the Dreamer. W. M. Duncan
President Fu Manchu. S. Rohmer
President Has Been Kidnapped! P. Richards
President Is Coming to Lunch. Nan Lyons
President Is Dead. P. Alexandre
President Is Dead. K. Royce
President Is Missing! H. A. Milton
President Kettle. C. J. C. Hyne
President Must Die. R. Raphael
President Plan. D. Meiring
President Vanishes. Anonymous
Presidential Agent. U. Sinclair
Presidential Emergency. W. Stovall
Presidential Mission. U. Sinclair
Presidential Plot. Stanley Johnson
President's Agent. J. Hilton
President's Brother. W. H. Mefford
President's Child. F. Weldon
President's Doctor. W. Woolfolk
President's Grass Is Missing. P. Breen-Bond
President's Man. N. Guild
President's Mistress. Patrick Anderson
President's Mystery Story. F. D. Roosevelt
President's Plane Is Missing. R. J. Serling
President's Ransom. H. Gantzer
President's Son. K. Kraus
President's Team. E. Meade
Presidio. M. Cogan
Press Agent for Murder. M. Ryerson
Press Gang. Richard Wilson
Press of Suspects. A. Garve
Pressing Peril. Nicholas Carter
Pressing Problems. V. Bird
Pressure. C. F. Coe
Pressure Drop. P. Abrahams
Pressure-Gauge Murder. F. W. B. Von Linsingen
Pressure Man. Zach Hughes
Pressure Man. Roderick Wilkinson
Pressure Point. L. Agniel
Pressure Point. H. Bostrom
Pressure Point. Nick Carter
Pressure Point. B. Copper
Preston Jayne. Old Sleuth
Presumed Dead. J. Larteguy
Presumed Dead. Ritchie Perry
Presumed Dead. P. Urquhart
Presumed Dead. D. Whitelaw
Presumed Innocent. S. Turow
Presumption of Guilt. J. Ashford
Presumption of Innocence. D. Pedneau
Presumption of Stanley Hay, M.P. N. Cay
Pretender. C. Hosken
Prettiest Girl I Ever Killed. C. Runyon
Pretty Boy. W. Cunningham
Pretty Boy Dead. J. Colton
Pretty Daredevil. G. Goodchild
Pretty Enough to Kill. A. McAllister
Pretty Fanny's Way. R. M. Gilchrist
Pretty Jailer. F. Du Boisgobey
Pretty Lady. M. Babson
Pretty Maids All in a Row. Anthea Fraser
Pretty Maids All in a Row. F. Pollini
Pretty Miss Murder. W. T. Ballard
Pretty Miss Smith. F. Warden
Pretty Ones. D. Eden
Pretty Pass. D. Footman
Pretty Peg Woffington. O. Allan
Pretty Pink Shroud. E. Ferrars
Pretty Place for a Murder. Roy Hart
Pretty Poison. S. Geller
Pretty Sinister. F. Beeding
Pretty Stenographer Mystery. Nicholas Carter
Prettybelle. Jean Arnold
Preventive Man. G. V. McFadden
Previous Lady. J. La Tourrette
Previously Reported Missing—Now? G. Chester
Prey! G. Beare
Prey. C. T. Cline
Prey. G. Douglas
Prey by Dawn. H. Kane
Prey by Night. Malcolm Douglas
Prey for a Newshawk. H. Janson
Prey for Me. T. B. Dewey
Prey for the Dreamer. W. M. Duncan
Prey for the Nightingale. H. McCutcheon
Prey for the Picaroon. J. Cassells
Prey of the Eagle. P. G. Leonard
Prey of the Falcon. R. Charles
Prey of the Strongest. Morley Roberts
Prey to Murder. A. Cleeves
Preying Mantis. N. Rutledge
Preying Streets. Ledru Baker
Price. D. Chacko
Price. A. Hornblow
Price. F. Lynde
Price. G. F. Newman
Price of a Secret. Nicholas Carter
Price of a Secret. T. W. Speight
Price of a Soul. P. Trent
Price of Admiralty. M. B. Lowndes
Price of Admiralty. S. Stone
Price of an Impulse. J. P. Bessell
Price of an Orphan. P. Carlon
Price of Death. F. Usher
Price of Delusion. W. Magnay
Price of Diamonds. G. Kelly
Price of Exile. W. J. Makin
Price of Freedom. A. W. Marchmont
Price of Heaven. S. Blackwelder
Price of Love. A. Applin
Price of Murder. J. D. MacDonald
Price of Pity. C. R. Gull
Price of Power. W. LeQueux
Price of Protection. Warren Miller
Price of Revenge. David Woods
Price of Silence. S. Barlay
Price of Silence. M. Dalton
Price of Silence. Mrs. Bagot Harte
Price of Silence. S. Kyle
Price of Silence. H. Pentecost
Price of Silence. F. Warden
Price of Silence. M. C. Weiner
Price of Things. E. Glyn
Price of Treachery. Nicholas Carter
Price Tag for Murder. S. Dean
Price Was High. G. Hackforth-Jones
Price You Pay. H. Wakefield
Priceless Pearl. D. Haring
Priceless Thing. M. S. Rawson
Pricking Thumb. H. C. Branson
Pride of Dolphins. M. Hebden
Pride of Healers. R. Hirschhorn
Pride of Heroes. P. Dickinson
Pride of Kings. Justin Scott
Pride of Life. W. Magnay
Pride of Overmoor. E. Woodward
Pride of Pigs. J. Wainwright
Pride of Race. B. L. Farjeon
Pride of Royals. Justin Scott
Pride of the Paddock. H. Smart
Pride of the Peacock. V. Holt
Pride of the Police. Andrew Gray
Pride of the Ring. B. Bolt
Pride of the Stable. E. J. Murray
Pride of the Trevallions. C. Salisbury
Pride of Women. K. Platt
Prideful Woman. H. G. Hutchinson
Priest of Piccadilly. A. Applin
Priestess of the Damned. V. Coffman
Priestly Murders. Joe Gash
Priests of the Abomination. I. Drummond
Priest's Secret. E. Finn
Priest's Secret. W. M. Graydon
Priest's Secret. A. Maxwell
Prillilgirl. C. Wells
Prim Windows. J. Chancellor
Prima Donna at Large. B. Paul

Prima Donna's Husband. F. Du Boisgobey
Primal Scene. Y. Kramer
Primary Target. M. A. Collins
Primary Target. Marilyn Wallace
Prime Cut. M. Roote
Prime Evil. J. Kelman
Prime Minister and Mrs. Grantham. C. Dawe
Prime Minister Is Dead. H. Simpson
Prime Minister Spy. Michael Spicer
Prime Minister's Boat Is Missing. J. Dyson
Prime Minister's Pencil. C. Waye
Prime Minister's Pyjamas. F. Evelyn
Prime Minister's Secret. W. Holt-White
Prime Objective. Paul Mann
Prime Roll. E. Izzi
Prime Suspect. R. D. Brown
Prime Target. J. MacAnthony
Prime Target. M. Russell
Prime Time Corpse. J. Babbin
Prime Time Crime. W. Gleason
Primeval and other stories. M. Bannerjee
Primitives. S. B. Hough
Primrose. M. Dobson
Primrose. A. Mills
Primula. G. R. Preedy
Primus. B. Street
Prince and the Perjurer. A. Hillgarth
Prince and the Suti. B. L. Van Vors
Prince and the Undertaker, and What They Undertook. Riccardo Stephens
Prince Buys the Manor. E. Huxley
Prince Cinderella. G. Alexander
Prince for Inspector West. J. Creasey
Prince Has Five Aces. Geoffrey Webb
Prince in Petrograd. E. Jepson
Prince in the Garret. A. C. Gunter
Prince Karl. M. Gerard
Prince Karl. A. C. Gunter
Prince of Balkistan. A. Upward
Prince of Berlin. D. Sherman
Prince of Blackmail. C. Bishop
Prince of Blackmailers. Anonymous
Prince of Crooks. G. Goodchild
Prince of Darkness. B. Michaels
Prince of Darkness. E. Southworth
Prince of Darkness. F. Warden
Prince of Evil. G. Stockbridge
Prince of Fraud. E. T. Sawyer
Prince of Good Fellows. R. Barr
Prince of India. L. Clarke
Prince of Liars. Nicholas Carter
Prince of Lovers. W. Magnay
Prince of Malta. J. D. Buchanan
Prince of Mischance. T. Gallon
Prince of Paradise. F. Gerard
Prince of Plunder. S. Horler
Prince of Poisoners. Ladbroke Black
Prince of Rogues. Nicholas Carter
Prince of Romance. R. Pertwee
Prince of Sinners. E. P. Oppenheim
Prince of Spies. G. Davison
Prince of Swindlers. G. Boothby
Prince of the Blood. J. Payn
Prince of the Captivity. J. Buchan
Prince of the Furies. G. Webb
Prince of the Palais Royal. M. Pemberton
Prince of Thieves. J. J. Lynx
Prince of Trouble. Colin Hope
Prince of Turf Crooks. F. Johnston
Prince of Ventriloquists. Old Sleuth
Prince of Wales's Garden Party. Mrs. J. H. Riddell
Prince of Zell. W. E. Cule
Prince or Clown. M. Dekobra
Prince Punnie. A. W. Marchmont
Prince Rupert, the Buccaneer. C. J. C. Hyne
Prince Saroni's Wife. J. Hawthorne
Prince Schamyl's Wooing. R. H. Savage
Prince Zaleski. M. P. Shiel
Prince Zaleski and Cummings King Monk. M. P. Shiel
Princely Detective. Anonymous
Princely Quartet. J. Budd
Prince's Darling. G. R. Preedy
Prince's Diamond. E. Hulme-Beaman

Princes of Peele. W. Westall
Princes of the Palais Royal. M. Pemberton
Princess. Alan Brown
Princess After Dark. S. Horler
Princess and Priest. A. S. F. Hardy
Princess and the Pilot. N. Sheraton
Princess Brinda. M. Dekobra
Princess Casamassina. H. James
Princess Galva. D. Whitelaw
Princess in Mufti. H. T. Johnson
Princess Kate. L. Tracy
Princess Maritza. P. Brebner
Princess Mazaroff. J. Hatton
Princess of Alaska. R. H. Savage
Princess of Copper. A. C. Gunter
Princess of Crime. Nicholas Carter
Princess of Darkness. I. Zacharia
Princess of Jutedom. C. Gibbon
Princess of New York. C. Hamilton
Princess of Paradise. Stuart Martin
Princess of Paris. A. C. Gunter
Princess of Persia. J. D. White
Princess of Steel. R. W. Kerr
Princess of the Purple Palace. W. M. Graydon
Princess' Own. Roland Daniel
"Princess Proxy." J. R. Warren
Princess Stakes Murder. K. Platt
Princess Thora. J. B. Harris-Burland
Princess Zara. R. Beeckman
Print-Out. B. Copper
Print-Out. R. Gillespie
Printer's Devil. Bill Barclay
Printer's Devil. C. Dane
Printer's Devil. C. D. Stevens
Printer's Error. G. Mitchell
Prinvest-London. V. Gielgud
Prior Betrothal. Elsie Lee
Priorities. Lynda Lyons
Priority for Death. P. Vane
Priority Murder. L. Ford
Priory. M. Wasser
Priory of Alba and the Castle on the Cliffs. Anonymous
Priory of St. Bernard. N. Harley
Priory of St. Clair. S. Wilkinson
Priscilla Copperwaite Case. H. Waugh
Priscilla Darling. Maz
Priscilla to the Rescue. T. Cobb
Prism. Gerrard Parker
Prison. G. Simenon
Prison at Montauban. Julia Smith
Prison at Obregon. B. Adkins
Prison Breakers. R. H. Poole
Prison Breakers. E. Wallace
Prison Feud. James Preston
Prison Girl. Wenzell Brown
Prison House. D. F. Gardiner
Prison Murder. R. Dark
Prison of Ice. D. Axton
Prison Princess. A. Griffiths
Prison Ship. M. Caidin
Prisoner. P. Boileau
Prisoner. Roland Daniel
Prisoner. T. M. Disch
Prisoner. M. Gerard
Prisoner. D. McDaniel
Prisoner. D. St. Michaels
Prisoner at the Bar. J. Ashford
Prisoner Born. C. Aveline
Prisoner Go Free. D. Lee
Prisoner in the Hold. A. Parsons
Prisoner in the Mask. D. Wheatley
Prisoner in the Opal. A. E. W. Mason
Prisoner in the Skull. D. Dye
Prisoner in the Square. D. Quentin
Prisoner #2. D. McDaniel
Prisoner #3. D. McDaniel
Prisoner #3. H. Stine
Prisoner of Ceuta. P. J. Clancy
Prisoner of Dreams. K. Ripley
Prisoner of Ellis Island. W. M. Graydon
Prisoner of Evil. D. Tower
Prisoner of Fire. E. Cooper
Prisoner of Garve. S. Shulman

Prisoner of Ingecliff. J. Bellamy
Prisoner of Lemnos. C. Gayet
Prisoner of Lost Island. J. Hunter
Prisoner of Love. H. Monteilhet
Prisoner of Love. M. Richmond
Prisoner of Malville Hall. D. Daniels
Prisoner of Ornith Farm. F. Powell
Prisoner of the Buddha. R. C. Armour
Prisoner of the Chateau. G. H. Teed
Prisoner of the Devil. Michael Hardwick
Prisoner of the Garret. B. Reynolds
Prisoner of the Kremlin. A. Murray
Prisoner of the Manor. R. Abbey
Prisoner of the Manor. R. Hardinge
Prisoner of the Mountains. W. M. Graydon
Prisoner of the Past. D. Noel
Prisoner of the Priory. C. Goodall
Prisoner of the Pyramid. F. Gerard
Prisoner of War. Grace M. White
Prisoner on the Dam. C. Coram
Prisoner on the Run. C. Coram
Prisoner Pleads "Not Guilty". L. Thayer
Prisoners. M. Cholmondeley
Prisoner's Base. C. Fremlin
Prisoner's Base. E. Gresham
Prisoner's Base. R. Stout
Prisoner's Friend. A. Garve
Prisoner's Friend. G. Goodchild
Prisoners in the Wall. G. Radcliffe
Prisoners of Devil's Claw. E. H. Hawkins
Prisoners of Fear. M. Broughton
Prisoners of Peru. Gwyn Evans
Prisoners of the Desert. S. Blake
Prisoner's Plea. H. Waugh
Prisoner's Secret. J. K. Leys
Prisoner's Tale. G. F. Newman
Prisoner's Wife. J. Holland
Prisonland. J. Frost
Prissy. C. Hanley
Private and Confidential. P. Trent
Private Anger, and Flight and Pursuit. F. O'Rourke
Private Carter's Crime. J. Creasey
Private Coles—Philosopher. S. Jarvis
Private Death. M. Urquhart
Private Detective. A. Forrester
Private Detective. J. J. Giblin
Private Detective. R. Machray
Private Detective. J. D. Shea
Private Detective No. 39. J. W. Postgate
Private Doll. B. Vane
Private Enquiry. C. H. Ross
Private Enterprise, and other stories. R. Standish
Private Eye. C. F. Adams
Private Eye. E. Dudley
Private Eye. T. N. Robb
Private Eyeful. H. Kane
Private Eyeful. N. Perrelli
Private Face of Murder. J. Bonett
Private Gallery. P. Tabori
Private I. J. Sangster
Private Inquiries. Dorothy Johnson
Private Investigation. K. Alexander
Private Killing. J. Benet
Private Killing. Kent Howard
Private Kind of War. H. A. Schofield
Private Lies. M. K. Cooper
Private Life. P. Selver
Private Life of Dr. Crippen. R. Gordon
Private Life of Dr. Watson. M. Hardwick
Private Life of Jack the Ripper. Richard Gordon
Private Life of Sherlock Holmes. M. Hardwick
Private Line. S. Maddock
Private Lives of Sherlock Holmes. M. Lambe
Private Memoirs and Confessions of a Justified Sinner. Anonymous
Private Murder. Al Guthrie
Private Party. W. Ard
Private Pavilion. J. G. Edwards
Private Pinkerton, Millionaire. H. Ashton
Private Practice of Michael Shayne. B. Halliday
Private Practices. L. Wolfe
Private Prosecution. E. Dewhurst
Private Report. K. Roberts
Private Screening. R. N. Patterson

P

Private Sector. J. Hone
Private Sector. J. Millar
Private Undertaking. H. T. Teilhet
Private Vendetta. Roderick Grant
Private Vendetta. Bradshaw Jones
Private View. M. Innes
Private Wire to Washington. H. MacGrath
Private Worlds. S. Gainham
Private Wound. N. Blake
Privateer Captain. Waters
Privateers. H. B. M. Watson
Privateer's Defiance. B. Wayde
Privateer's Peril. Waters
Privateersman's Legacy. F. Du Boisgobey
Privilege. John Burke
Privileged Character. J. Laborde
Privileged Lives. Edward Stewart
Prize. Irving Wallace
Prize Meets Murder. R. T. Edwards
Prize of Flesh. F. W. Paul
Prize of Gold. M. Catto
Prize of Traitors. D. Vallance
Prizewinner. F. Mullally
Prizzi's Family. R. Condon
Prizzi's Glory. R. Condon
Prizzi's Honor. R. Condon
Pro. B. Hamilton
Pro-Am Murders. P. Cake
Probability Broach. L. N. Smith
Probability Factor. W. Kempley
Probability Pad. T. A. Waters
Probable Cause. Ridley Pearson
Probation. M. L. Storer
Probationer! E. Price
Probe. C. N. Douglas
Probing by Fire. S. Grave
Problem at Piha. F. Bream
Problem at Pollensa Bay and Christmas Adventure. A. Christie
Problem by Rail. E. C. Vivian
Problem Club. B. Pain
Problem for Superintendent Flagg. J. Cassells
Problem for the Dreamer. W. M. Duncan
Problem in Angels. L. Holton
Problem in Ciphers. "Capstan"
Problem in Ciphers. R. Hardinge
Problem in Prague. R. MacLeod
Problem Island. D. E. R. Sinclair
Problem of Cell 13. J. Futrelle
Problem of Evil. M. D. Pohlman
Problem of Lot 99. Anonymous
Problem of the Derby Favorite. J. W. Bobin
Problem of the Green Capsule. J. D. Carr
Problem of the Purple Maculas. J. C. Iraldi
Problem of the Wire Cage. J. D. Carr
Problem of Virtue. M. D. Pohlman
Problem Parade. R. M. Lucey
Problems of Lieutenant Knap. J. Mucha
Procane Chronicle. O. Bleeck
Proceed at Will. B. Wilkinson
Proceed to Judgement. Sara Woods
Proceed with Cuation. J. Rhode
Process of Elimination. G. Baxt
Procession of the Damned. W. Tucker
Procession of Two. R. Philmore
Procession—to Prison. D. Henderson
Prochain Episode. H. Aquin
Procrastination of Sergeant Cluff. G. North
Proctor Case. S. Blakesley
Prodigal. I. Osbourne
Prodigal, and other stories. A. Soutar
Prodigal Gun. E. L. Sloane
Prodigal Soldier. F. H. Rose
Prodigals and Sons. J. Ayscough
Prodigals of Monte Carlo. E. P. Oppenheim
Prodigal's Portion. C. C. Lewis
Prodigal's Progress. F. Barrett
Prodigy. M. J. Livingston
Prodigy Plot. T. Thomey
Produce the Body. R. Goyne
Productions of Time. J. Brunner
Professional. J. D. Buchanan
Professional Guest. W. Garrett
Professional Jealousy. C. F. Gregg

Professional Prince. E. Jepson
Professional Thieves and the Detective. A. Pinkerton
Professionals. J. Harris
Professor. Roland Daniel
Professor. J. Lynn
Professor. Alan Thomas
Professor Aylmer's Experiment. A. J. Anderson
Professor Dies. J. Rowland
Professor in Peril. A. Lejeune
Professor Knits a Shroud. W. Van Arsdale
Professor on the Case. J. Futrelle
Prof. Slagg of London. D. E. Marvin
Professor's Christmas Party, and A Student of the Obvious. H. C. McNeile
Professor's Mystery. W. S. Hastings
Professor's Poison. Neil Gordon
Professor's Secret. Anonymous
Profile in Gilt. J. C. Nolan
Profile of a Murder. R. King
Profit and Sheen. J. Colbert
Profit for the Picaroon. J. Cassells
Profit Motive. W. B. Murphy
Profit Without Honor. T. Keene
Profiteers. E. P. Oppenheim
Profligate. A. Hornblow
Progeny. J. G. Maxon
Progeny of the Adder. L. H. Whitten
Programme for a Puppet. Roland Perry
Programmed for Danger. J. M. Favors
Programmed for Danger. K. G. McCullough
Programmed for Death. L. Gribble
Programmed for Terror. B. W. Battin
Programmed Man. W. D. Blankenship
Programmer. Bruce Jackson
Progress of a Crime. J. Symons
Progress of Rachel. J. Sergeant
Progress of Romance Through Times, Countries, and Manners. Clara Reeve
Project Andromeda. J. Rosenberger
Project Jael. A. Fletcher
Project Named Desire. J. W. Corrington
Project Norouz. R. Swift
Project Web. Barbara Rogers
Project X. Colin Robertson
Projects Section. T. Lilley
Prologue to Murder. M. B. Dix
Prologue to the Gallows. P. McGuire
Prom Concert Murders. A. Wood
Prometheus Operation. M. Elder
Prometheus Project. R. K. Largent
Prometheus Trap. V. Connolly
Prominent Among the Mourners. Carolyn Thomas
Promise. J. B. Hendryx
Promise for Death. J. Messmann
Promise for Tomorrow. E. Woodward
Promise of Diamonds. G. Ashe
Promise of Murder. M. G. Eberhart
Promise of the Phoenix. F. Gerard
Promise to Keep. L. A. Sunagel
Promise to Kill. P. Marlowe
Promised Land. R. B. Parker
Promise(s) of Marriage. E. Gaboriau
Promises to Keep. G. Bernau
Promises to Keep. H. Brett
Promotion of the Admiral. Morley Roberts
Promotion Tour. T. Harknett
Prompt for Murder. S. MacKellar
Proof. D. Francis
Proof, Counter Proof. E. R. Punshon
Proof of Innocence. Olive Jackson
Proof of the Poison. F. L. Cary
Proof of the Pudding. P. A. Taylor
Proof Positive. John Drummond
Proper Age for Love. C. Jauniere
Property in Cyprus. Robert MacLeod
Property of a Gentleman. C. C. Gaskin
Property of a Lady. A. Oliver
Prophecy of Duncannon. W. C. Green
Prophet. J. T. Morrow
Prophet Motive. Cleo Jones
Prophet of Fire. J. Creasey
Prophetess. J. Kidde
Prophetic Heiress. M. Blount
Prophetic Warning. Anonymous

Prophet's Mantle. F. Bland
Proprietor. G. C. Seeber
Proprietor's Daughter. Lewis Orde
Props. J. B. Lynch
Propsy. J. B. Douglas
Pros and Cons. B. Campbell
Prose Romances of Edgar A. Poe. E. A. Poe
Prose Works of Henry Lawson. H. Lawson
Prosecutor. B. Botein
Prosecutor. James Mills
Prosecutor. M. Nabb
Prosecutor. P. R. Van Zyl
Prospect of Vengeance. Anthony Price
Prospect's Dead. A. Tack
Prospero Drill. C. A. Posey
Protagonists. J. Barlow
Protection. Bill James
Protection. Jack Kelly
Protection Agent. M. McCracken
Protection for a Lady. M. Delany
Protection for a Lady. J. T. Story
Protection of Democracy. P. Chesney
Protection Payoff. S. Markham
Protector. M. Braly
Protector. Larry Harris
Protector Conclusion. J. Burmeister
Protectors. W. Haggard
Protectors. R. Miall
Protectors. W. Pine
Protege. C. Armstrong
Protege. M. MacPherson
Proteus. M. L. West
Proteus Operatin. J. P. Hogan
Proteus Pact. G. St. George
Protocol for a Kidnapping. O. Bleeck
Prototype PZ.642. K. Ford
Proud Adversary. Howard Mason
Proud Citadel. T. Charles
Prove It, Mr. Tolefree. R. A. J. Walling
Provenance. F. McDonald
Provenance House. E. St. Clair
Provenance of Death. K. Giles
Provence Puzzle. V. McConnor
Proverbial Murder Case. W. Sutherland
Providence. Geoffrey Wolff
Providence Hall. C. Rodda
Province Puzzle. V. McConnor
Provincetown. B. Hirschfeld
Provincial Crime. Lionel Black
Provincial Papers. J. Hatton
Proving. T. Szollosi
Proving Flight. D. Beaty
Proving Ground. Eric Thomas
Provo Link. D. Hayward
Prowl Cop. G. Jones
Prowl No More, Lady. James Warren
Prowler. F. Rickett
Prowler in the Night. J. Matcha
Prowler of Mount Hebron. G. H. Atwood
Prowling Terror. C. T. Stoneham
Prudence Be Damned. M. McMullen
Pruneface. C. Gould
Prussian Blue. A. Hocking
Prussian Spy. V. Valmont
Prynter's Devil. J. Wainwright
Psalm Stone. F. M. White
Psi Delegation. A. Conan
Psi Hunt. M. Kurland
Psionics War. J. Rosenberger
Psychedelic Spy. T. A. Waters
Psychiatric Murders. M. S. Michel
Psychiatrist Says Murder. L. Freeman
Psychic. M. Franklin
Psychic Detective: The Unicorn. H. W. Holzer
Psychic Trap. J. N. Chance
Psycho. R. Bloch
Psycho. P. Moore
Psycho House. R. Bloch
Psycho in Focus. L. Smith
Psycho Soldiers. J. Cutter
Psycho Squad. W. W. Crain
Psycho II. R. Bloch
Psychopath Plague. S. G. Spruill
Psychotron Plot. J. Rosenberger

Pub Crawler. M. Procter
Pub on the Pool. A. D. Divine
Public Defender. G. Goodchild
Public Enemies. A. Bracey
Public Enemy. A. Capelli
Public Enemy. H. Clevely
Public Enemy. K. Glasmon
Public Enemy—No. 1. B. Graeme
Public Faces in Private Places. J. Rosner
Public Ghost Number One. A. Soutar
Public Hating. Steve Allen
Public Mischief. S. Maddock
Public Murders. B. Granger
Public Scandal, and other stories. G. A. Birmingham
Public School Murder. R. C. Woodthorpe
Public Secrets. Nora Roberts
Publicity for Anne. A. M. Williamson
Publicity for Murder. E. Messenger
Publish and Be Killed. A. Morice
Publish and Perish. F. M. Nevins
Puck of Crooks' Hill. San Antonio
Pulitzer Prize Murders. D. Heyward
Pull Down the Blind. W. Standish
Pull the House Down. M. L. Tyrrell
Pulled Down. P. Paul
Pulling Strings. P. Conway
Pulling the Strings. F. E. Penny
Pullman Car Detective. H. C. Culver
Pulpit in the Grill Room. E. P. Oppenheim
Pulptime. P. H. Cannon
Pulse. W. R. Dantz
Pulse of Danger. J. Cleary
Pulse Persuader. D. Haring
Pulse Points. S. Topper
Puma. U. Miehe
Puma Quest. Michael Hastings
Punch and Judy Murders. Carter Dickson
Punch and Judy Murders. G. Hart
Punch with Care. P. A. Taylor
Punctual Rage. C. Black
Pungi Patrol. J. Lansing
Punish Me with Kisses. W. Bayer
Punish the Sinners. J. R. Saul
Punishment. Doris Shannon
Punitive Action. J. Robb
Punitive Damage. C. M. Oksner
Punjat's Ruby. M. J. A. Jackson
Punt Murder. A. Griffin
Punter's Luck. Arthur Russell
Puppet for a Corpse. D. Simpson
Puppet Master. Nick Carter
Puppet Master. A. McQuoid
Puppet Master. P. O'Donnell
Puppet-Masters. W. Garner
Puppet on a Chain. Alistair MacLean
Puppeteer. T. Williams
Puppets Dallying. A. Lillie
Puppets of Chance. R. P. Koehler
Puppets of Fate. S. Jepson
Puppets of Father Bouvard. W. M. Duncan
Puppet's Part. D. Carew
Purcell Papers. J. S. Le Fanu
Purchase Price. R. Cullum
Pure As the Driven Snow. P. Loomis
Pure As the Lily. C. Cookson
Pure Evil. K. Robeson
Pure Murder. A. M. Pyle
Pure Poison. H. Waugh
Pure Sweet Hell. Malcolm Douglas
Purgatory Street. R. McDougald
Puritan. Colin Watson
Puritan's Wife. M. Pemberton
Purity League. Alan Williams
Purloined Letter. R. Brome
Purloined Prince. Edgar Turner
Purloined Prince. Ian Wallace
Purloining Tiny. J. F. Bardin
Purple Aces. R. J. Hogan
Purple and the Gold. D. Daniels
Purple Ball. F. Packard
Purple Claw. H. Horn
Purple Dragon. K. Robeson
Purple Dressing Gown. P. Fry
Purple Fern. F. Hume

Purple Head. E. Pugh
Purple Jacaranda. Nancy Graham
Purple Legion. G. F. Eliot
Purple Limited. H. Leverage
Purple Love. M. Gerard
Purple Mask. L. J. Miln
Purple Mist. G. E. Locke
Purple Onion Mystery. H. Ashbrook
Purple Parrot. C. B. Clason
Purple Pearl. A. Pryde
Purple Place for Dying. J. D. MacDonald
Purple Plague. D. Steele
Purple Plant. A. Felton
Purple Pony Murders. S. E. Porcelain
Purple Pterodactyls. L. S. De Camp
Purple Rock. A. MacVicar
Purple Shadow. E. Snell
Purple Shadows. A. V. Bartram
Purple Sheba. K. Hayles
Purple Shells. R. L. Goldman
Purple Sickle Murders. F. W. Crofts
Purple-6. H. Brinton
Purple Spot. Nicholas Carter
Purple Stain. J. M. Walsh
Purple Threat. D. Dayle
Purple Trident. C. Whitton
Purple Twilight. P. Groom
Purple Zombie. K. Robeson
Purpose of Evasion. G. Dinallo
Purse Which Was Found and other stories. R. Marsh
Purser's Mate. E. L. Long
Pursue the Wind. L. Richards
Pursued. A. Mills
Pursued by the Crooked Man. S. Trott
Pursued by the Law. J. M. Cobban
Pursuer. L. Golding
Pursuer. G. Weisenborn
Pursuing Shadow. J. Laurence
Pursuit. L. G. Blochman
Pursuit. R. L. Fish
Pursuit. H. Janson
Pursuit. M. McLaren
Pursuit. R. Pertwee
Pursuit. F. Saville
Pursuit. A. Soutar
Pursuit. J. S. Thayer
Pursuit. R. Unekis
Pursuit in Peru. C. L. Leonard
Pursuit of a Parcel. P. Wentworth
Pursuit of Agent M. D. Copp
Pursuit of Arms. G. Hammond
Pursuit of Camilla. Clementina Black
Pursuit of Fear. W. Beechcroft
Pursuit of Mr. Faviel. R. E. Vernede
Pursuit of Penelope. L. T. Meade
Pursuit of the Eagle. Nick Carter
Pursuit of the House Boat. J. K. Bangs
Pursuit of the Owl. A. Howlett
Pursuit of the Phoenix. J.-A. Price
Pursuit Till Morning. A. Wykes
Pursuit to Algeria. Arthur MacLean
Push-Button Spy. L. James
Push, Meet Shove. P. Barthelme
Pushbutton Butterfly. K. Platt
Pusher. E. McBain
Pushkin Shove. P. N. Gwynne
Pushover. D. Haring
Pushover for Susie. J. Dekker
Puss in Boots. E. McBain
Pussy Cat, Pussy Cat. I. Taylor
Put Back the Clock. M. Richmond
Put In, Take Out. D. Hann
Put On by Cunning. R. Rendell
Put on the Spot. J. Lait
Put Out That Light. R. C. Woodthrope
Put Out That Star. H. Carmichael
Put Out the Light. H. Desmond
Put Out the Light. R. Foley
Put Out the Light. S. Truss
Put Out the Light. Ethel L. White
Put Out the Light. Sara Woods
Put Yourself in Her Place. M. Leighton
Putting Out. N. Ferguson
Putting the Boot In. D. Kavanagh

Puzzle. L. Thayer
Puzzle for Experts. J. Nathenson
Puzzle for Fiends. P. Quentin
Puzzle for Fools. P. Quentin
Puzzle for Inspector West. J. Creasey
Puzzle for Pilgrims. P. Quentin
Puzzle for Players. P. Quentin
Puzzle for Puppets. P. Quentin
Puzzle for Wantons. P. Quentin
Puzzle in Paint. Kootz
Puzzle in Paisley. E. Gresham
Puzzle in Parchment. E. Gresham
Puzzle in Parquet. E. Gresham
Puzzle in Pearls. G. Ashe
Puzzle in Petticoats. Kootz
Puzzle in Pewter. R. Grey
Puzzle in Poison. A. Berkeley
Puzzle in Porcelain. R. Grey
Puzzle in Pyrotechnics. J. Rowland
Puzzle Lock. R. A. Freeman
Puzzle of Five Pistols and other stories. Nicholas Carter
Puzzle of the Blue Banderilla. S. Palmer
Puzzle of the Briar Pipe. S. Palmer
Puzzle of the Happy Hooligan. S. Palmer
Puzzle of the Pepper Tree. S. Palmer
Puzzle of the Red Stallion. S. Palmer
Puzzle of the Silver Persian. S. Palmer
Puzzle Parade. Morley Adams
Puzzled Policeman. G. Woden
Puzzles of the Black Widowers. I. Asimov
Puzzling Shadow. Old Sleuth
Pyramid of Death. N. MacKenzie
Pyramid of Lead. B. Atkey
Pyramids of Snow. E. Metcalfe
Pyrenean Banditta. E. Sleath
Pyromaniac. A. B. Allen
Pyrrha. P. Grayson
Python Project. V. Canning
Pyx. J. Buell

Q & A. E. Torres
Q As in Quicksand. L. Treat
QBI: Queen's Bureau of Investigation. E. Queen
Q Clearance. P. Benchley
Q Document. J. H. Roberts
Q.E.D. L. Brock
Q.E.D. L. Thayer
QED: Queen's Experiments in Detection. E. Queen
QEII Is Missing. H. Harrison
Q Factor. P. Kirk
Q-Man. Nick Carter
"Q" Squad. G. Verner
Q's Mystery Stories. A. T. Quiller-Couch
Q33. G. Goodchild
Q33—Spy Catcher. G. Goodchild
Quade Inheritance. B. K. Wilson
Quadraphone Homicide. J. Weisman
Quadriphobia. Alan Ryan
Quaker City. Anonymous
Quaker City. G. Lippard
Quaking Terror. L. Derrick
Quaking Widow. R. Colby
Qualified Adventurer. S. Jepson
Quality Bill's Girl. C. W. Tyler
Quality of Mercy. R. Carson
Quality of Mercy. F. Kellerman
Quality of the Informant. G. Petievich
Quality Parties. D. Clarins
Quallsford Inheritance. L. Biggle, Jr.
Qualtrough. Angus Hall
Quantum Web. K. Wilkins
Quarantine. N. Hasluck
Quarantine. Josh Webster
Quark Maneuver. M. Jahn
Quarmby. R. Sharp
Quarrel. C. Houghton
Quarrel with Murder. M. Halliday
Quarrelling Room. J. B. Watney
Quarry. C. T. Cline, Jr.
Quarry. M. A. Collins
Quarry. F. Duerrenmatt
Quarry. E. Harwood
Quarry. F. A. Moroso

Q

Quarry. R. L. Pike
Quarry House. J. Ware
Quarry's Contract. Robin Hunter
Quarry's Cut. M. A. Collins
Quarry's Deal. M. A. Collins
Quarry's List. M. A. Collins
Quarter of Eight. W. B. Gibson
Quarter to Four. W. W. Cook
Quartet. E. Phillpotts
Quartet of Three. M. Tripp
Quartz Eye. H. K. Webster
Quayle of the Yard. P. Trent
Quayle's First Case. P. Trent
Que Viva Guevera. G. De Villiers
Quebec Connection. L. Derrick
Queen Against Defoe. S. Heym
Queen Against Owen. A. Upward
Queen and the Corpse. Max Murray
Queen and the Gypsy. C. Heaven
Queen Anne's Gate Mystery. R. Arkwright
Queen Bee. E. Lee
Queen City Murder. Case. W. Bogard
Queen Dies First. I. Lambot
Queen from Mars. R. St. Clair
Queen in Danger. S. Rattray
Queen Is Dead. G. Kezer
Queen of a Day. J. S. Fletcher
Queen of America. R. H. Greenan
Queen of Angels. G. Bear
Queen of Blackmailers. M. O. Rolfe
Queen of Bohemia. J. Hatton
Queen of Chance. Dick Stewart
Queen of Clubs. H. Footner
Queen of Coins. Stephanie Hall
Queen of Crookdom. M. Welford
Queen of Crooks. Detective Dunn
Queen of Crook's Harem. B. Sarto
Queen of Diamonds. Nicholas Carter
Queen of Diamonds. K. Kavanaugh
Queen of Ecuador. R. M. Manley
Queen of Hearts. W. Collins
Queen of Hearts. L. Paige
Queen of Knaves and other stories. Nicholas Carter
Queen of My Heart. M. Richmond
Queen of Night. H. Hill
Queen of Spades. H. C. Bailey
Queen of Spades. J. C. Griffiths
Queen of Spades. H. H. Henderson
Queen of Spades. M. McEvoy
Queen of Spades. T. J. Morrison
Queen of Spades. E. P. Roe
Queen of Spies. T. Coulson
Queen of the Black Hand. H. C. Davidson
Queen of the Gangsters. J. Fairfax-Blakeborough
Queen of the Highway. Old Sleuth
Queen of the Jesters. M. Pemberton
Queen of the Looking Glass. A. L. McAllister
Queen of the Meadow. C. Gibbon
Queen of the Mirage. K. Lindsay
Queen of the Night. K. Perkins
Queen of the Night Clubs. M. Strongman
Queen of the Outlaw's Camp. Anonymous
Queen of the Outlaw's Camp. O. Harper
Queen of the Riffs. Operator 1384
Queen of the Secret Seven. Anonymous
Queen of the Secret Seven. O. Harper
Queen of the South. G. Isaacs
Queen of the Stage. F. M. White
Queen of the Underworld. J. W. Booth
Queen of the White Slaves. Grave M. White
Queen of the World. George Weston
Queen Sends for Mrs. Chadwick. David Sanders
Queen Street. M. Gant
Queen Sweetheart. A. M. Williamson
Queen Vaiti. B. Grimshaw
Queen Versus Billy and other stories. L. Osbourne
Queen Victoria's Revenge. H. Harrison
Queen Wasp. J. Middlemass
Queenie. W. F. Fauley
Queenie's Terrible Secret. A. M. Miller
Queen's Advocate. A. W. Marchmont
Queen's Bush. W. M. Brown
Queen's Crossing. B. Granger
Queen's Desire. H. Nisbet

Queen's Error. H. Curties
Queen's Evidence. E. Kyle
Queen's Falcon. E. E. Blau
Queens Full. E. Queen
Queen's Gate Mystery. H. Adams
Queen's Gate Mystery. H. Curties
Queen's Gate Reckoning. L. Perdue
Queen's Grace. N. Tranter
Queen's Hall Murder. A. Broome
Queen's Hand. B. Reynolds
Queen's Harbour. Elizabeth Ford
Queens Have Died Young and Fair. Clementine Hunter
Queen's Head. E. Marston
Queen's Justice. Edwin Arnold
Queen's Mare. J. Birkett
Queen's Mate. M. Gerard
Queen's Mate. T. Hughes
Queen's Messenger. W. R. Duncan
Queen's Pawn. V. Canning
Queen's Ransom. T. Dresden
Queen's Revenge. S. Cobb
Queen's Scarf. D. C. Murray
Queen's Scarlet. G. M. Fenn
Queen's Treasure. C. Ashdown
Queensland Desperadoes. C. Grabs
Queer Affair. G. Boothby
Queer Bag of Bodies. A. Webb
Queer Face. G. Verner
Queer Fish. J. Boland
Queer Folk Next Door. G. Woden
Queer Kind of Death. G. Baxt
Queer Looking Box, and other stories. M. Hervey
Queer Mr. Quell. W. J. Makin
Queer Partners. S. Murray
Queer Patients. M. Oston
Queer Race. W. Westall
Queer Side Stories. J. F. Sullivan
Queer Sisters. S. Harragan
Queer Stories from Russia. C. Chernilo
Queer Things at Queechy. P. Gurney
Queerest Man Alive, and other stories. G. H. Hepworth
Quella. G. N. Farmer
Quenchless Fire. S. K. Hocking
Quentin, a Spy. D. Selves
Quest. N. De Mille
Quest. R. B. Sapir
Quest. N. A. Temple-Ellis
Quest, and other stories. R. Findlay
Quest for a Fortune. Philippa Tyler
Quest for Alexis. N. Buckingham
Quest for K. C. Curzon
Quest for Love. D. Faber
Quest for Superintendent Flagg. J. Cassells
Quest for the Bogeyman. F. Lockridge
Quest for the Picaroon. J. Cassells
Quest of Douglas Holms. H. E. Inman
Quest of El Dorado. A. Askew
Quest of Geoffrey Darrell. A. Sergeant
Quest of John Clare. Sea Lion
Quest of Julian Day. D. Wheatley
Quest of Juror 19. David Davidson
Quest of Krang. C. Van Horn
Quest of Mr. Sandyman. Neill Graham
Quest of Nigel Rex. Eg. Goodchild
Quest of Qui. K. Robeson
Quest of the Code Breakers. A. Baritone
Quest of the Crimson Idol. H. J. S. Anderton
Quest of the Crooked. H. Maxwell
Quest of the Doltada Diamonds. Anonymous
Quest of the Emerald. M. Seville
Quest of the Golden Skull. Anonymous
Quest of "The Lost Hope". Nicholas Carter
Quest of the Ruby Scarab. C. Hayter
Quest of the Sacred Slipper. S. Rohmer
Quest of the Seeker. J. T. Elton
Quest of the Seven Carrier. P. Albano
Quest of the Spider. K. Robeson
Quest of the "Stormalong". D. W. MacArthur
Quest of the Vanishing Star. R. Ladline
Quest of the Yellow Pearl. P. C. MacFarlane
Quest of Youth. J. Farnol
Quest of Youth. J. G. Sarasin

Quest Sinister. S. P. B. Mais
Quest to Kill. R. Severn
Questing Hound. G. Hackforth-Jones
Questing Man. M. Home
Question. M. Peterson
? Crime. R. B. Whorf
Question of Cain. Mrs. C. Hoey
Question of Character. N. Jacob
Question of Character. J. Hougron
Question of Coercion. G. Norham
Question of Degree. Roy Lewis
Question of Evidence. Old Spicer
Question of Guilt. F. Fyfield
Question of Guilt. R. Gordon
Question of Guilt. Magali
Question of Identity. H. C. McNeile
Question of Identity. J. Thomson
Question of Inheritance. Josephine Bell
Question of Judgment. T. Mix
Question of Judgment. P. B. Young
Question of Law. M. Jon
Question of Loyalty. N. Freeling
Question of Max. A. Cross
Question of Mud. H. C. McNeile
Question of Murder. Anthony Gilbert
Question of Murder. R. H. Lees
Question of Murder. Eric Wright
Question of Negligence. H. McLeave
Question of Policy. B. Wayde
Question of Principle. J. Ashford
Question of Proof. N. Blake
Question of Risk. L. M. Shakespeare
Question of Quarry. G. Bagby
Question of Queens. M. Innes
Question of Survival. E. Cannon
Question of Taste. F. Bamford
Question of Time. H. Carmichael
Question of Time. Nicholas Carter
Question of Time. F. Duncan
Question of Time. H. McCloy
Questionable Shape. M. Cumberland
Questions of Identity. Bob Cook
Questor Tapes. D. C. Fontana
Quests of Paul Beck. M. M. Bodkin
Quests of Simon Ark. E. D. Hoch
Queue Here for Murder. M. Babson
Queue Here for Murder. N. MacKenzie
Queue Up to Listen. A. Spiller
Quick and the Dead. P. Bennetts
Quick and the Dead. E. Queen
Quick and the Dead. V. Starrett
Quick Brown Fox. W. R. Burnett
Quick Change. J. Cronley
Quick Curtain. A. Melville
Quick or the Dead. Griff
Quick Red Fox. J. D. MacDonald
Quick Tempo. N. Easton
Quickie Mysteries. A. Badger
Quickly Dead. B. Cobb
Quickness of the Hand. J. Mayo
Quicksand. Elliott Arnold
Quicksand. J. Brunner
Quicksand. W. Greatorex
Quicksand. M. Land
Quicksands of Crime. Denis Boyle
Quicksands of London. C. H. Bullivant
Quicksilver. Roland Daniel
Quicksilver. M. Gallagher
Quicksilver. R. Graves
Quicksilver. N. Hartley
Quicksilver. B. Pronzini
Quicksilver Pool. P. A. Whitney
Quicksilver Solution. R. Pennington
Quickthorn. Lanora Miller
Quid Est. E. Mariner-Scarritt
Quidnunc County. R. M. Stern
Quiet American. G. Greene
Quiet As a Nun. Antonia Fraser
Quiet Assassin. T. Kirkwood
Quiet City. Mark Ross
Quiet Conspiracy. E. Ambler
Quiet Dogs. J. Gardner
Quiet Earth. Craig Harrison
Quiet Fear. M. Halliday
Quiet Game of Bambu. R. Gouze

Quiet Gentleman. G. Heyer
Quiet Horror. S. Ellin
Quiet Killer. D. MacKenzie
Quiet Mrs. Fleming. R. Pryce
Quiet Murder. V. R. Muzzey
Quiet Murder and other stories. E. M. Bailey
Quiet Ones. B. Graeme
Quiet Passion. L. Hoffman
Quiet Place in the Country. Henry Clement
Quiet River. P. M. Hubbard
Quiet River. J. D. White
Quiet Road to Death. S. Radley
Quiet Room in Hell. B. Copper
Quiet Sound of Fear. L. Paxton
Quiet Stranger. J. B. Hilton
Quiet Terror. W. Wall
Quiet Under the Sun. K. Fitzgerald
Quiet Violence. D. M. Disney
Quiet Waits the Grave. H. Janson
Quiet War. J. Browning
Quiet Woman. H. Carmichael
Quietly She Lies. E. M. D. Hawthorn
Quiller. Adam Hall
Quiller Barracuda. Adam Hall
Quiller KGB. Adam Hall
Quiller Memorandum. Adam Hall
Quiller's Run. Adam Hall
Quimby. Arthur Adams
Quincannon. B. Pronzini
Quincunx. C. Palliser
Quincunx Case. W. D. Pitman
Quincy, M. E. T. Racina
Quincy, M. E. #2. T. Racina
Quinn. N. Scanlan
Quinn and the Desert Oil. N. Scanlon
Quinneys'. H. A. Vachell
Quinney's Adventures. H. A. Vachell
Quinney's for Quality. H. A. Vachell
Quin's Hide. M. Summerton
Quinta Affair. N. Grey
Quintain. R. E. Harrington
Quintain Strikes Back. W. H. Baker
Quintana Inheritance. E. Tokson
Quinton Clyde, Private Investigator. T. McCoy
Quinton's Rouseabout, and other stories. E. S. Sorenson
Quint's World. S. Fuller
Quintus Oakes. C. R. Jackson
Quips and Cranks. Thomas Hood
Quiraing List. J. J. Savarin
Quirinal Hall Affair. B. Hambly
Quirindi. K. R. Butler
Quislings Over Paris. M. Cumberland
Quit Playing Dames. Kane
Quite by Accident. K. Booton
Quite Like Old Days. V. Bridges
Quittance in Full. T. W. Speight
Quiver of Arrows. J. Archer
Quixote of Magdalen. Mrs. C. Kernahan
Quonsett. J. F. Murphy
Quoth the Raven. B. Fischer

R Document. Irving Wallace
R. Holmes & Co. J. K. Bangs
R.I.P. P. Macdonald
R.I.S.C. R. C. Frazer
R in the Month. N. Spain
R.O.F. Murders. H. Varley
R.S.V.P. Murder. M. G. Eberhart
Ra-Ta-Plan—! D. Ogburn
Rabbi's Spell. S. C. Cumberland
Rabbi's Wife. D. Benedictus
Rabbitfoot. A. W. Grahame
Rabbit's Paw. S. Jepson
Rabble of Rebels. G. Ashe
Rabble's Curse. C. A. Fought
Rabid Brigadier. C. Sargent
Race Against the Sun. D. Rutherford
Race for a Fortune. R. S. Holland
Race for a Wife. H. Smart
Race for Life. A. F. Pinkerton
Race for Life. J. Remy
Race for Life. F. Whishaw
Race for Life and other tales. Anonymous

Race for Millions. D. C. Murray
Race for Ten Thousand. Nicholas Carter
Race for the Golden Tide. Gordons
Race Gang. E. Woodward
Race of Death. Nick Carter
Race of Life. G. Boothby
Race the Lazy River. W. J. Watkins
Race Toward Death. N. MacKenzie
Race Track Crooks. N. Ridley
Race Track Gambler. Nicholas Carter
Race with Death. Dick Stewart
Race with Ruin. H. Hill
Race with the Sun. G. Church
Race with the Sun. L. T. Meade
Racecourse Tragedy. N. Gould
Rachel. S. Nichols
Rachel Dyer. J. Neal
Rachel, the Possessed. K. Kimbrough
Rachel Weeping. Shelley Smith
Rachel Wulfoten and other stories. W. Stebbing
Racing Adventures of Barry Bromley. H. Gould
Racing and 'Chasing. A. E. T. Watson
Racing Axes. James Preston
Racing Crazy. Duff Johnson
Racing Ramp. A. J. Sarl
Racing Rubber. H. Smart
Racing Yacht Mystery. B. Graeme
Rack of This Tough World. A. Giberne
Racket. B. Cormack
Racket Boss. C. Kline
Racket Buster. Vince Kelly
Racket Busters, Incorporated. H. W. Lee
Racketeers. R. Sharp
Racketeers of the Turf. Carlton Ross
Racketeer's Will. W. P. Vickery
Rackets and Dames. B. Banarto
Rackets Incorporated. B. Banarto
Rackets Incorporated. A. D. Brent
Rackets Incorporated. Griff
Racoon Lake Mystery. N. M. Hopkins
Radar Job. J. Baddock
Radar Target. G. Vaughan
Radcliffe Case. John Bentley
Radford Shone. H. Hill
Radiance. A. Maybury
Radiance. N. R. Nash
Radiation Hit. L. Derrick
Radical Departure. L. Matera
Radical Diver. J. Cleveland
Radingham Mystery. Roy Vickers
Radio-Active General and other stories. R. Standish
Radio and Television Dramas. J. Mickel
Radio Blackmail. L. G. Redmond-Howard
Radio Blues. G. Nagy
Radio Crook. R. Hardinge
Radio Detective. A. B. Reeve
Radio Gunner. Alexander Forbes
Radio Mystery. J. Mowbray
Radio Sketches and How to Write Them. P. Dixon
Radio Studio Murder. C. Wells
Radioactive Camel Affair. P. Leslie
Radiobuster. V. G. Mathison
Radish River Caper. R. H. Spencer
Radium Profiteer. G. N. Philips
Radium Terrors. A. Dorrington
Radkin Revenge. W. D. Roberts
Radnitz. J. Nathenson
Rafferty. B. S. Ballinger
Rafferty. L. White
Rafferty and the Gold Dust Twins. Lillian Roberts
Rafferty's Rules. W. G. Duncan
Raffles. David Fletcher
Raffles. E. W. Hornung
Raffles After Dark. B. Perowne
Raffles and the Key Man. B. Perowne
Raffles' Crime in Gibraltar. B. Perowne
Raffles in Pursuit. B. Perowne
Raffles of the Albany. B. Perowne
Raffles of the M.C.C. B. Perowne
Raffles Revisited. B. Perowne
Raffles, the Amateur Cracksman. E. W. Hornung
Raffles Under Sentence. B. Perowne
Raffles vs. Sexton Blake. B. Perowne
Raft of Swords. D. Kyle

Rag and a Bone. H. Waugh
Rag Bag Clan. R. Barth
Rag Doll Murder. H. P. Jeffers
Rag Pickers. H. V. Dixon
Raga Six. F. Lauria
Rage. R. Bachman
Rage. P. Friedman
Rage. G. Moffat
Rage. J. Ramsay
Rage. L. V. Roper
Rage at Sea. F. Lorenz
Rage in Babylon. S. Mitchell
Rage in Harlem. C. Himes
Rage in Heaven. J. Hilton
Rage of Angels. S. Sheldon
Rage of Desire. Clayton Matthews
Rage of Heaven. J. Eller
Rage of the Vulture. B. Unsworth
Rage to Die. R. Jessup
Rage to Kill. B. E. Lovell
Ragged Edge. J. Karney
Ragged Edge. J. T. MacIntyre
Ragged Plot. R. Barth
Ragged Robin Murders. G. Morton
Raging Waters. D. Daniels
Ragland. J. Van Orsdell
Rags. A. Applin
Ragtime. E. L. Doctorow
Ragusa Theme. A. Quinton
Rahab Link. J. A. MacKenzie
Raid. W. E. Johns
Raid. A. Mather
Raid. J. B. O'Sullivan
Raid. J. Romanes
Raid on the Bremerton. I. Eachus
Raid on the Mint. F. Putnam
Raid on the Villa Joyosa. R. Hopkins
Raiders Moon. A. Knox
Raiders of the Southern Seas. T. Wallace
Raiders of Wyoming. R. Story
Raiders Passed! J. Hunter
Rail-Road Forger and the Detectives. A. Pinkerton
Railroad Murder Case. R. M. Laurenson
Railroad Romances. J. L. Owen
Railway Detective. Anonymous
Railway Detective. H. Rockwood
Railway Hotel Murder. A. Compton-Rickett
Railway Mystery. H. Saint Maur
Railway Stories. S. T. James
Railway Tragedy. F. Du Boisgobey
Rain. S. Gallagher
Rain. Keith Peterson
Rain Before Seven. J. August
Rain Before Seven. M. Brandel
Rain Before Seven. C. Buckley
Rain Islands. J. Wood
Rain Lover. D. Burkey
Rain of Death. J. D. Kennedy
Rain of Death. D. Stivers
Rain of Terror. Malcolm Douglas
Rain of Terror. W. B. Murphy
Rain on the Roof. G. Goodchild
Rain on the Roof. K. Lipky
Rain Rustlers. F. Roderus
Rain with Violence. Dell Shannon
Rainbird Pattern. V. Canning
Rainblast. M. Russell
Rainbow. W. H. Harding
Rainbow Coloured Hearse. K. Bird
Rainbow Coloured Shroud. J. Hedges
Rainbow Conspiracy. D. Lees
Rainbow Deaths. J. Churchward
Rainbow Drive. Roderick Thorp
Rainbow Feather. F. Hume
Rainbow Glass. A. Dwyer-Joyce
Rainbow Gold. D. C. Murray
Rainbow in Hell. David Fletcher
Rainbow in the Mist. P. A. Whitney
Rainbow Island. M. Caywood
Rainbow Island. L. Tracy
Rainbow Man. T. Pollock
Rainbow Mystery. W. LeQueux
Rainbow Nights, and other stories. A. Soutar
Rainbow Puzzle. E. C. Vivian

R

Rainbow Ribbon. Pamela Thompson
Rainbow/Seagreen Case. P. K. Palmer
Rainbow Soldiers. W. Winward
Rainbow Stories. W. T. Vollman
Rainchaser. J. Luceno
Rainbow's End. J. M. Cain
Rainbow's End. Ellis Peters
Rainbows End in Tears. David Fletcher
Rainbrother. C. Edwards
Rainsong. P. A. Whitney
Rainy City. E. W. Emerson
Rainy North Woods. V. Kohler
Raise the Dark Gambler. Mary Sellers
Raise the Devil. D. Wade
Raise the Titanic! C. Cussler
Raising the Dead. R. L. Simon
Rajah of Dah. G. M. Fenn
Rajah of Ghanapore. H. E. Hill
Rajah's Casket. Douglas Christie
Rajah's Fortress. W. M. Graydon
Rajah's Racer. N. Gould
Rajah's Revenge. A. Murray
Rajah's Ruby. L. Barbee
Rajah's Ruby. Nicholas Carter
Rajah's Sapphire. M. P. Shiel
Rajah's Second Wife. H. Hill
Rakehell. A. Rundle
Raker. Don Scott
Raking for the Moon. M. G. Lowe
Rale McCoy. M. J. J. McKeown
Rally to Kill. B. Knox
Rally to the Death. D. Rutherford
Ralph. N. Crabb
Ralph. J. Stonehouse
Ralph Norbreck's Trust. W. Westall
Ralph Rashleigh. J. Tucker
Ralph Ryder of Brent. F. Warden
Ralph the Bailiff and other tales. M. E. Braddon
Ralph Wildhawk. Anonymous
Ram Dass. C. Felix
Rambo: First Blood Part II. D. Morrell
Rambo III. D. Morrell
Ramona. M. Risco
Rampage. B. Haning
Rampage. Justin Scott
Rampage. W. P. Wood
Rampage in Rio. L. Derrick
Ramsden. T. Mundy
Ramsden Case. D. Chandler
Ramsey, the Detective. Old Sleuth
Ramsey's Best: Collector of the Badges. J. L. Foster
Ramshackle House. H. Footner
Ramshackle Inn. G. Batson
Rancho Maria. J. Oster
Randolph Mason, Corrector of Destinies. M. D. Post
Randolph Mason: The Clients. M. D. Post
Randolph Mason: The Strange Schemes. M. D. Post
Random Access Murder. Linda Grant
Random Army. M. Polland
Random Death. L. Egan
Random Factor. L. J. LaRosa
Random Killer. H. Pentecost
Random Track. Austin Ferguson
Random Track to Peking. Austin Ferguson
Random Walk. L. Block
Randy Inheritance. J. N. Chance
Raneslough. M. Heath
Range Justice. R. Wilkes-Hunter
Ranger of the Susquehannock. R. W. Kauffman
Ranger of the Tomb. Wilhelmina Johnson
Ranger of the Tomb. T. P. Prest
Ranger Spy. Anonymous
Ranger's Recruit. Hedley Scott
Rangoon Man. Nick Carter
Rank Outsider. J. Fairfax-Blakeborough
Rank Outsider. N. Gould
Rankin: Enemy of the State. J. Osier
Ranks of the Black Order. P. Christian
Ransom. J. Cleary
Ransom. C. F. Coe
Ransom. L. Crawford
Ransom. M. Denning
Ransom. C. Hume

Ransom! J. Messmann
Ransom! A. S. Roche
Ransom. R. K. Smith
Ransom. P. Wheeler
Ransom Castle. M. Farnsworth
Ransom Commando. James Grant
Ransom for a Nude. Lionel Black
Ransom for London. J. S. Fletcher
Ransom for Miss Le Grun. B. Schwarz
Ransom for the First Lady. D. Thurlow
Ransom Game. H. Engel
Ransom Game. J. B. Hilton
Ransom in Jade. F. Earley
Ransom of Black Stealth One. D. Ing
Ransom of Red Chief. A. G. Smith
Ransom of the Angel. D. Dodge
Ransom Racket. L. Thayer
Ransom Run. M. Dibner
Ransom Town. P. Alding
Ransomed Madonna. L. White
Ranson's Folly. R. H. Davis
Raoul: Gentleman of Fortune. H. C. Bailey
Rap. E. Brawley
Rape. L. Trevor
Rape of a Quiet Town. D. Lees
Rape of a Town. N. Daniels
Rape of Aphrodite. A. Winch
Rape of Berlin. W. H. Baker
Rape of Europe. G. Sager
Rape of Sun Lee Fong. M. Macao
Rape of the Nicollet Mall Mannequin. Steve Hall
Rape of Venice. D. Wheatley
Rape One. F. Canavor
Rape Squad. S. Wolf
Raper. J. McCready
Raphael Affair. I. Pears
Raphael, M.D. Augustus Muir
Raphael "Resurrection". T. Newman
Rapid Fire. J. Butler
Rapidan. Jackson Gregory
Rapist. Stuart Hall
Rapist. M. Kenyon
Rapist. S. A. Krasney
Rapist. D. Logan
Rappel 1910. C. Brahms
Rapt in Glroy. E. Silberstang
Raptor. J. Van Gieson
Raptor Zone. G. Moffat
Rapture. P. Harpur
Rapture. T. Tessier
Rapture Beyond. K. N. Burt
Rare Adventure. B. Fergusson
Rare and the Lovely. M. Blake
Rare Benedictine. Ellis Peters
Rare Coin Score. R. Stark
Rare Earth. M. L. Grisanti
Rascal Money. J. R. Garber
Rascal of Quality. Nicholas Carter
Rascals and Co. Nicholas Carter
Rascal's Nerve. M. O. Rolfe
Rash Conclusions. G. W. Appleton
Rashevski Ikon. J. Pattison
Rashleigh Abbey. R. Sickelmore
Rasp. P. MacDonald
Raspberry Jam. C. Wells
Raspberry Reich. W. Mankowitz
Raspberry Tart Affair. F. Halliday
Rasprava. E. J. Harrison
Rasputin Letter. Colin Clarke
Rasputin the Rascal Monk. W. LeQueux
Rasputinism in London. W. LeQueux
Rasputin's Revenge. J. T. Lescroart
Rat. P. Bottome
Rat Alley. H. Robison
Rat Began to Knaw the Rope. C. W. Grafton
Rat Box. C. Clarke
Rat in a Trap. M. Vinter
Rat on Fire. G. V. Higgins
Rat Pack. S. Stevens
Rat Quotient. K. Hagenbach
Rat Race. A. Bester
Rat Race. D. Francis
Rat Race. J. Franklin
Rat Report. C. Fitzgibbon

Rat-Tat Papers. Anonymous
Rat Trap. W. LeQueux
Rat Trap. Craig Thomas
Ratcatcher. C. Dunne
Rather a Common Sort of Crime. J. Porter
Rather a Vicious Gentleman. F. McAuliffe
Rather Cool for Mayhem. L. G. Blochman
Rather Like. J. Castier
Ratings Are Murder. R. R. Irvine
Ratman's Notebooks. S. Gilbert
Rats. A. Christie
Rats. J. Herbert
Rats' Alley. W. Garner
Rats' Castle. H. Bridges
Rat's Nest. Charles West
Rattenbury Mystery. Conway Carr
Rattle His Bones. J. Shore
Rattle-Rat. J. Van De Wetering
Rattler. J. Cassells
Rattlers. J. Gilmore
Rattlesnake. H. Pink
Rattlesnake. K. Tynan
Rattlesnake Master. B. Cranford
Rattlesnakes and Roses. J. Oppenheimer
Rattling of Old Bones. Jonathan Ross
Ravaged. S. Friedman
Ravagers. D. Hamilton
Rave for a Roughneck. H. Janson
Ravel of Waters. G. Jenkins
Raven. M. E. Cooke
Raven. B. Goldie
Raven. W. Kinsolving
Raven. M. Lundy
Raven. Stanley Morgan
Raven. E. Sudak
Raven After Dark. D. MacKenzie
Raven and the Dove. K. Kinder
Raven and the Kamikaze. D. MacKenzie
Raven and the Paperhangers. D. MacKenzie
Raven and the Phantom. Clarissa Ross
Raven and the Ratcatcher. D. MacKenzie
Raven Club Papers. N. Nutgall
Raven Feathers His Nest. D. MacKenzie
Raven in Flight. D. MacKenzie
Raven in the Foregate. Ellis Peters
Raven Is a Blood Red Bird. D. M. Marlowe
Raven Never More. G. Marton
Raven Rock. M. F. Ballard
Raven Settles a Score. D. MacKenzie
Raven Wings. Anne Edwards
Ravenburn. Laura Black
Ravencroft Mystery. W. H. L. Crauford
Ravendon. J. Blackmore
Ravenelle Ridddle. E. B. Black
Ravenhurst. Marilyn Ross
Ravenkill. G. Janes
Ravenkill. P. Warren
Raven's Beak. H. C. Nisbet
Raven's Causeway. C. Hodge
Raven's Eye. E. Bond
Raven's Feathers. D. Carey
Raven's Forge. Jennie Melville
Raven's Longest Night. D. MacKenzie
Ravens of Rockhurst. M. Martin
Raven's Revenge. D. MacKenzie
Raven's Shadow. D. MacKenzie
Ravenscroft. D. Eden
Ravenscroft Affair. C. R. Gull
Ravenscroft Horror. C. R. Gull
Ravensdale Mystery. G. E. Locke
Ravensdene Court. J. S. Fletcher
Ravensgate. D. Rowan
Ravensgill. W. Mayne
Ravenshaw of Rietholine. B. Mitford
Ravenshoe. H. Kingsley
Ravensley Manor. Cecily Clark
Ravensley Touch. C. Heaven
Ravensmount. M. McEvoy
Ravensnest. C. Farr
Ravensridge. Jennifer Hale
Ravenswood. E. W. Gilliam
Ravenswood. J. L. Roberts
Ravenswood Hall. Angela Gray
Ravenswood Mystery. J. S. Fletcher

Title Index

Raventree. S. Sloan
Ravine. K. Young
Raving Monarchist. J. Rathbone
Ravishing Idiot. C. Exbrayat
Ravishing of Lady Mary Ware. D. Wheatley
Raw Deal. W. Wager
Raw Deal for Dames. M. Hampton
Raw Edge. B. Appel
Raw Gold. J. B. Hendryx
Raw Material. G. B. Savi
Raw Summer. J. Blackmore
Rawdon Murder Case. J. H. Acott
Rawhide Vixen. Tod Conrad
Rawson of the Mounted. E. Dorrance
Raxl, Voodoo Priestess. D. Daniels
Ray of Doom. W. S. Sykes
Raya. Frank King
Raymond Chandler's Philip Marlowe. R. Chandler
Raymond's Bride. N. Gould
Rayner Case. R. Wray
Rayner-Slade Amalgamation. J. S. Fletcher
Ray's Adventure. Old Sleuth
Rays of Darkness. L. Bamburg
Razor. B. Sadler
Razor. A. Southwell
Razor Game. J. Grady
Razor Jacques. A. Sewart
Razor Moon. P. Pairo III
Razor Sharp. M. Winters
Razorback. P. Brennan
Razor's Edge. S. Grave
Razor's Edge. R. W. Walker
Razzle-Dazzle. E. Naha
Razzmatazz. J. Early
Re-Enter Arnholt. G. Latta
Re-Enter Dr. Fu Manchu. S. Rohmer
Re-Enter Fu Manchu. S. Rohmer
Re-Enter Sir John. C. Dane
Re-Enter the Blithe Sheriff. F. R. Buckley
Reach for the Shadows. A. Dwyer-Joyce
Reach for the Sky. Cliff Rogers
Reach of Fear. D. L. Mathews
Reaching Hand. A. MacKenzie
Reader Is Warned. Carter Dickson
Ready, Aim, Die. P. Buck
Ready Cash. Joan Butler
Ready for Death. H. J. Hultman
Ready for the Tiger. Sam Ross
Ready-Made Man. A. McMaster
Ready or Not. I. S. Shriber
Ready Revenge. C. Arley
Ready to Burn. C. J. Daly
Ready to Die. J. Frederics
Real Boyd. Carter Brown
Real Charlotte. E. O. Somerville
Real Connection. E. Taillet
Real Cool Cat. J. Weil
Real Cool Corpse. D. Haring
Real Cool Killers. C. Himes
Real Detective. G. Dilnot
Real Endings. G. Duris
Real Estate Skeleton Caper. W. J. Jones
Real Gold. G. M. Fenn
Real Gone Goose. G. Bagby
Real Gone Guy. F. Kane
Real Inspector Hound. T. Stoppard
Real Killing. W. Keegan
Real Killing. J. Pattinson
Real Life. A. R. Weekes
Real Mrs. Daybrook. F. Warden
Real Murders. Charlaine Harris
Real Serendipitous Kill. Hampton Stone
Real Shot in the Arm. A. Roome
Real Thing. R. G. Barrett
Real Thing. A. Philips
Realist. H. Flowerdew
Realist and other stories. T. Thurston
Realization of Justus Moran. F. Carrel
Really Cute Corpse. Joan Hess
Realm Seven. T. Chiu
Reap the Whirlwind. M. L. Roby
Reap What You Sow. M. Allwood
Reaper. T. Allbeury
Reaper. C. T. Cline, Jr.

Reaper. G. Fairlie
Reaping. Bernard Taylor
Reaping the Whirlwind. Anonymous
Reaping the Whirlwind. Nicholas Carter
Rear Car. E. E. Rose
Rear View Mirror. C. B. Cooney
Rear Window and other stories. C. Woolrich
Reardon. R. L. Pike
Reason for Loving. A. Furness
Reason for Madness. T. S. Drachman
Reason for Murder. A. Hocking
Reason for Murder. J. Usher
Reason for Violence. D. Doubtfire
Reason to Kill. E. Zaremba
Reason to Murder. R. A. Bennett
Reason Why. M. B. Lowndes
Reasonable Doubt. Catherine Anderson
Reasonable Doubt. S. Barish
Reasonable Doubt. P. Friedman
Reasonable Doubt. Edgar Smith
Reasonable Doubt. J. S. Strange
Reasonable Madness. F. Dorf
Reasonable Man. R. Busby
Reasons of Hate. J. Welcome
Reasons of the Heart. H. Giniger
Rebecca. D. Du Maurier
Rebecca of the Snatch Racket. B. Sarto
Rebecca, the Mysterious. K. Kimbrough
Rebecca's Pride. D. N. Douglas
Rebekka Moon. M. Spence
Rebel. C. Ruhen
Rebel Chief. H. Nisbet
Rebel Heart. A. Maybury
Rebel in Spain. R. D. Pullan
Rebel Lady. K. Lindsay
Rebel Wife. Rona Randall
Rebel Woman. H. Whittington
Rebellion. W. A. Ballinger
Rebellion. N. Harman
Rebellion. S. P. B. Mais
Rebellion of Lee McGuire. C. B. Davis
Reborn. L. Simon
Rebound. I. Barclay
Rebound. D. Everson
Rebound. J. Mayo
Rebuilding Coventry. S. Townsend
Rebuilt Man. W. Beechcroft
Recall. T. P. Walker
Recalled by the Double-Four. E. P. Oppenheim
Recalled to Life. G. Allen
Receipt for Murder. Gwendoline Butler
Receivers. B. Osborne
Reception at High Tower. D. Ward
Recess. H. Grisewood
Recess. Sophia Lee
Recipe for a Crime. R. Denham
Recipe for Diamonds. C. J. C. Hyne
Recipe for Homicide. L. G. Blochman
Recipe for Murder. J. Ashford
Recipe for Murder. A. Ridley
Recipe for Murder. R. Stock
Reckers and Methodists. H. D. Lowry
Reckless. R. Angel
Reckless. Sherryl Woods
Reckless Abandon. S. S. Salinger
Reckless Angel. M. B. Lowndes
Reckless Coulson. Jack Mann
Reckless Lady. Vera Brown
Reckless Lady. R. Foley
Reckless Masquerade. Rachelle Edwards
Reckless Passage. G. D. Colman
Reckoning. H. Atkinson
Reckoning. I. Barclay
Reckoning. A. Fletcher
Reckoning. M. Logan
Reckoning. M. Pye
Reckoning. G. Simenon
Reckoning in Ice. J. R. L. Anderson
Reckoning Figure. H. Kurnitz
Reckoning Figure. Marco Page
Reclaimed. J. J. Gray
Reclining Nude. Maurice Watson
Recluse of Fifth Avenue. W. Martyn
Recoil. B. Garfield

Recoil. K. C. Groom
Recoil. J. L. Hardy
Recoil. B. How
Recoil. J. Thompson
Recoiling Vengeance. F. Barrett
Recollections of a Country Doctor. J. K. Spender
Recollections of a Detective. Waters
Recollections of a Detective-Police-Office. Waters
Recollections of a Glasgow Detective Officer. T. P. MacNaught
Recollections of a Physician. W. H. Hillyard
Recollections of a Policeman. Waters
Recollections of a Relieving Officer. E. P. Rowsell
Recollections of a Sheriff's Officer. Waters
Recollections of an Irish Police Magistrade and Other Reminiscences of the South of Ireland. H. R. Addison
Recollections of Geoffrey Hamlyn. H. Kinsley
Recollections of the Golden Triangle. A. Robbe-Grillet
Recon. G. H. Frost
Recon. Steve Mackenzie
Recon Strike. G. H. Frost
Reconnaissance. G. Gardiner
Record Mystery. R. Sage
Record No. 33. I. C. Clarke
Record of Jeffrye Cranfield. G. C. Keech
Record of Sin. J. McGown
Record of the Case. W. M. Graydon
Recorded Verdict. G. Wark
Records of Vincent Trill of the Detective Service. D. Donovan
Recount. D. Everson
Recover or Kill. L. Butler
Recovery. S. L. Thompson
Rector. V. Gay
Rector's Will. F. Whitehead
Rectory. T. C. Evans
Rectory Governess. F. Hume
Recurrent Melody. R. Pinget
Recycled Citizen. C. MacLeod
Recycled Souls. I. Ross
Red Account. V. Gielgud
Red Aces. E. Wallace
Red Agents. W. T. Stewart
Red Alert. P. Bryant
Red Alert. Harold King
Red Alert. A. MacNeill
Red Alert. E. Webster
Red Altars. J. G. Brandon
Red and White Heather. R. Buchanan
Red Anger. G. Household
Red Arrow. J. Rovin
Red Arrows in the Night. D. A. Lord
Red Bamboo. E. P. Thorne
Red Band. F. Du Boisgobey
Red Barn. R. Huish
Red Beard. Paul Costello
Red Berets. T. Biracree
Red Bicycle. F. Hume
Red Bishop. Howard Mason
Red Boomerang. J. G. Brandon
Red Boulders. P. Sebastian
Red Boulders Mystery. P. Sebastian
Red Box. R. Stout
Red Box Clue. J. B. Ellis
Red Boxes. P. Northman
Red Bridal. W. Westall
Red Bull. R. Stout
Red Burgee. Morley Roberts
Red Button. Will Irwin
Red Cadillac. R. Semon
Red Camarilla. E. J. Harrison
Red Camelia. F. Du Boisgobey
Red Canyon Mystery. W. B. Lawson
Red Carnation. Augustus Muir
Red Carnation. B. E. Stevenson
Red Carnation. P. A. Whitney
Red Carpet for the Shah. P. Ritner
Red Castle. H. C. Bailey
Red Castle Mystery. H. C. Bailey
Red Castle Women. M. Widdemer
Red Cavalier. G. E. Locke
Red Cecil, the Detective. Old Sleuth

R

Red Cent. Robert Campbell
Red Centre. Frederick Nolan
Red Chameleon. S. M. Kaminsky
Red Chameleon. C. Robertson
Red Chancellor. W. Magnay
Red Chindvit Conspiracy. H. W. Holzer
Red Christmas. P. Ruell
Red Citroen. T. Williams
Red Claws. M. Richmond
Red Club. H. R. Taunton
Red Coats Galloping. J. Welcome
Red Cobra. H. S. Branner
Red Colonel. G. Edgar
Red Colonel. G. Seton
Red Court Farm. H. Wood
Red Crab. G. Wagner
Red Crescent. A. Murray
Red Cripple. C. Bradley
Red Crystal. C. Francis
Red Curtain. Duncan Taylor
Red Dagger. J. Corbett
Red Dagger. H. Naybard
Red Dancer of Moscow. H. L. Gates
Red Danger. P. Wentworth
Red Danube. B. Marshall
Red Danube. C. A. Posey
Red Darkness. A. B. Sherlock
Red Darkness. G. F. Worts
Red Dawning. M. Richmond
Red Death. G. Collins
Red Death. M. Marlow
Red Derelict. B. Mitford
Red Desert. H. Edmonds
Red Devil. D. Saperstein
Red Devil of the Air Force. J. Noy
Red Diamond. M. Schorr
Red Diamonds. J. H. McCarthy
Red Dice. Norman Lucas
Red Dog. J. D. Buchanan
Red Dog Run. Jan Michaels
Red Doll. N. Baroni
Red Doll. J. L. Cebrian
Red Domino. W. W. Sayer
Red Dove. D. Lambert
Red Dragon. W. Curtis
Red Dragon. T. Harris
Red Dragon Operation. J. Rosenberger
Red Drums. E. A. Powell
Red Dwarf. F. A. Symonds
Red Dwarf. M. Thynne
Red Eagle. Gavin Holt
Red Eagle. J. Lucas
Red Eagles. D. Downing
Red Earth. Morley Roberts
Red Earth, White Earth. W. Weaver
Red Emerald. J. R. Scott
Red Emeralds. S. Gluck
Red Encounter. R. D. Zimmerman
Red Ending. H. Hervey
Red Escapade. R. Bax
Red Exit. J. Pattinson
Red Eye for the Baron. Anthony Morton
Red Eyes of Kali. T. C. H. Jacobs
Red Farm Mystery. J. Corbett
Red Fate. E. Forbes
Red Fathom. R. E. Alter
Red Falcons. A. Dempsey
Red File for Callan. J. Mitchell
Red Firestorm. Dan Schmidt
Red Flame of Erinpura. J. Mundy
Red Flight. Glen Allen
Red Flower Kill. W. J. Sheldon
Red Flowers of Death. C. Rudd
Red Flows the Barada. D. Weir
Red for Danger! E. Price
Red for Murder. H. Kemp
Red for Terror. R. E. Crighton
Red Fox. A. Hyde
Red Fox. G. Seymour
Red Gang. J. W. Heming
Red Gardenias. Jonathan Latimer
Red Gas. E. Topol
Red Gate. R. Burke
Red Geranium. V. Siller

Red Glen. C. Campbell
Red Glove. Douglas Grant
Red God of Tragedy. Nicholas Carter
Red Gods. D. Lindquist
Red Gods Calling. B. Grimshaw
Red Gold. M. Leighton
Red Greed. Marion Roberts
Red, Green and Amber. P. Traill
Red Guard. Nick Carter
Red Gunship. J. J. Savarin
Red Hair. S. Kyle
Red-Haired Alibi. W. Collison
Red-Haired Death. S. Horler
Red-Haired Girl. C. Wells
Red Hammer Down. J. Hild
Red Hand. S. Cobb
Red Hand. Maxwell Scott
Red-Handed. L. Thayer
Red-Handed They Came. A. Wood
Red Harvest. D. Hammett
Red Hat. W. LeQueux
Red Hazard. A. O. Pollard
Red Head Herring. B. Healey
Red Head of the Red Sea. W. J. Makin
Red Head Rhapsody. B. Carson
Red-Headed Dames and Murder. Roland Daniel
Red-Headed Man. F. Hume
Red-Headed Sinner. Jonathan Craig
Red Heart of the Incas. Jack Lewis
Red Heat. W. Katz
Red Heat. R. Tine
Red Hen Conspiracy. K. Benton
Red Heroin. W. Curtis
Red Herring. E. Acheson
Red Herring. W. Tucker
Red Herring Murder. P. D. Westbrook
Red Herrings. T. Heald
Red Herrings. C. J. C. Hyne
Red Herrings Ltd. Laurence Kirk
Red Highway. L. D. Estleman
Red Hill Tragedy. E. Southworth
Red Horse Caper. L. V. Roper
Red Horseman. K. Laing
Red, Hot and Deadly. M. Clinten
Red Hot and Deadly. D. Haring
Red Hot and Morgue Bound. M. Brody
Red Hot and Ready. D. Haring
Red Hot Dollar and other stories from "The Black Cat". H. D. Umbstaetter
Red Hot Ice. F. Kane
Red-Hot Murder. S. Levinson
Red Hotel. H. Hervey
Red House. G. A. Chamberlain
Red House. Mrs. Hungerford
Red House. Derek Lambert
Red House. E. Nesbit
Red House. M. C. Rowsell
Red House Mystery. Mrs. Hungerford
Red House Mystery. A. A. Milne
Red House Mystery. Ruth Perry
Red House on Rowan Street. R. Doubleday
Red Ice. N. Barker
Red Ice. R. L. Crossland
Red Ice. J. Dallas
Red Ice. M. J. Hutchinson
Red Ice. C. Wheatley
Red Idol. L. P. Greene
Red in the Morning. D. Yates
Red Invader. H. Edmonds
Red Is for Killing. G. Bagby
Red Is for Murder. Martin Meyers
Red Is for Murder. P. A. Whitney
Red Is for Shrouds. M. A. Taylor
Red Is the Hue of Hell. F. Brown
Red Jaguar. N. McFather
Red Jaguar. J. Manor
Red January. W. Chamberlain
Red Joker. Michael Nicholson
Red Judas. D. Newton
Red Key. C. Emery
Red Kite Clue. O. F. Jerome
Red Kill. Guy Richards
Red Knight. J. N. Chance
Red Lacquer Case. H. R. Jorgensen

Red Lacquer Case. P. Wentworth
Red Lady. K. N. Burt
Red Lady. A. Wynne
Red Lake of the Heart. M. Logue
Red Lamp. M. R. Rinehart
Red Leaf 645. W. M. Evans
Red League. Nicholas Carter
Red Ledger. F. Packard
Red Light. N. MacKenzie
Red Light Red. A. Radnor
Red Light Red Light. H. A. Schofield
Red-Light Victim. L. Kinsley
Red-Light Will, the River Detective. Anonymous
Red Lights. G. Simenon
Red Lilac. L. Gorell
Red Lion. D. Tower
Red Lion and Blue Star, with other stories. J. A. Barry
Red Lodge. V. Bridges
Red Lottery Ticket. F. Du Boisgobey
Red Mammon. D. Learmonth
Red Man Contract. M. McCray
Red Mark, and other stories. J. Russell
Red Mask. W. J. Makin
Red Masquerade. L. J. Vance
Red Mass. V. Williams
Red Meekins. W. A. Fraser
Red Menace. M. Grant
Red Menace. D. Stivers
Red Message. P. Abrahams
Red Mill Mystery. Detective Dunn
Red Mirage. P. Trent
Red Mirror Mystery. Gret Lane
Red Mist. J. Borgen
Red Mist. M. O'Toole
Red Money. F. Hume
Red Moon. J. B. Harris-Burland
Red Moon. W. B. Murphy
Red Moon. K. Robeson
Red Morn. M. Pemberton
Red Mountain. W. W. Sayer
Red Mountain, Limited. E. A. Clancy
Red Mouse. W. H. Osborne
Red Murchison. Roland Daniel
Red Murder File. C. Dixon
Red Net. T. C. H. Jacobs
Red Nights of Paris. M. F. Goron
Red Omega. J. Kruse
Red on Wight. D. Winsor
Red Owl. W. Gillette
Red Painted Box. M. Leighton
Red Paper. C. C. Hotchkiss
Red Parka. M. L. Metzger
Red Passport. J. F. Fraser
Red Paste Murders. A. Gask
Red Pavilion. M. Summerton
Red Pavilion. R. Van Gulik
Red Pawns. G. Griswold
Red Phoenix. L. Bond
Red Plague. Nicholas Carter
Red Plague in Bolivia. M. Macao
Red Poppies. E. Morrison
Red President. Martin Gross
Red Queen Club. A. Broome
Red Radio. R. L. Hadfield
Red Rafferty. H. B. Kaye
Red Raiders. D. Storm
Red Rain Mystery. H. Hill
Red Rainbow. M. C. Fagan
Red Raincoat. H. Bourne
Red Rajah. F. Whittaker
Red Rat's Daughter. G. Boothby
Red Rays. Nick Carter
Red Rebellion. Nick Carter
Red Records. A. Perrin
Red—Red—Red. A. Kent
Red, Red Rose. M. McEvoy
Red Redmaynes. E. Phillpotts
Red Revenge. C. E. Pearce
Red Revenge. G. A. Ralston
Red Rhapsody. C. Fitzsimmons
Red Riding Hood. E. Jordan
Red Right Hand. J. T. Rogers
Red Rivington. W. Westall

Title Index

Red Road. S. Harvester
Red Rocking Bird. A. Marlowe
Red Rods. Dale Clark
Red Room. W. LeQueux
Red Rope. F. Gerard
Red Rosa. Michael Collins
Red Rose for Annabel. Agnes Russell
Red Rose for Maria. D. Downes
Red Rube Barrows. W. B. Lawson
Red Rust of Death. P. Audemars
Red Ruth. L. T. Meade
Red Sap. J. Easton
Red Saunders Bites the Dust. P. Renwick
Red Scar. A. Wynne
Red Scarf. G. Brewer
Red Scorpion. Anonymous
Red Scorpion. C. Buchanan
Red Sea Nights. W. J. Makin
Red Sea Spy. W. J. Makin
Red Seal. M. Gerard
Red Seal. N. S. Lincoln
Red Serge. H. Steele
Red Shadow. P. Wentworth
Red Shadows. M. Cherkas
Red Signal. Nicholas Carter
Red Signal. G. L. Hill
Red Skull. F. Hume
Red Skull. K. Robeson
Red Sky. V. James
Red Sky in the Morning. R. Johnston
Red Slayer. E. Leslie
Red Snow. O. Lange
Red Snow. K. Robeson
Red Snow. E. Topol
Red Snow at Darjeeling. L. G. Blochman
Red Spider. E. S. Brooks
Red Spider. K. Robeson
Red Spider Web. B. Newman
Red Spinner. E. Snell
Red Spy at Night. Robert King
Red Square. E. Topol
Red Square. A. Wood
Red Stain. A. Abdullah
Red Stain. S. Campbell
Red Stain. V. Loder
Red Stain. W. Magnay
Red Staircase. Gwendoline Butler
Red Stands for Danger. R. Trevor
Red Star Mystery. C. Barry
Red Star of Night. W. A. MacKenzie
Red Star Over London. D. Roland
Red Star Run. D. Muir
Red Stefan. P. Wentworth
Red Stiletto. A. Skene
Red Stockings. P. Fry
Red Storm Rising. T. Clancy
Red Stranger. Netley Lucas
Red Streak. P. Trent
Red Sun of Nippon. H. O. Yardley
Red Sunset. J. Stockwell
Red Sweater Girl. D. Haring
Red Symbol. J. Ironside
Red Tape Murders. G. Verner
Red Tassel. D. Dodge
Red Terrors. K. Robeson
Red Threads. R. Stout
Red Thumb Mark. R. A. Freeman
Red Tide. A. Morelli
Red Tiger. R. Carr
Red Token. O. Binns
Red Tower. L. V. Stevens
Red Trail of a .41. W. C. Tuttle
Red Triangle. Nicholas Carter
Red Triangle. Arthur Morrison
Red Turrets of Orne. C. Connell
Red Van. A. St. Aubyn
Red Van Mystery. G. Chester
Red Vengeance. J. Hild
Red Vulture. F. Sleath
Red War. J. Philips
Red Warning. V. Markham
Red White and Blue. J. G. Dunne
Red Widow. W. LeQueux
Red Widow Murders. Carter Dickson

Red Wind. R. Chandler
Red Window. F. Hume
Red Wine of Rapture. Margaret Worth
Red-Winged Angel. A. Mackinnon
Red Winter. M. Cormany
Red Wolf. I. Gregory
Red Year. L. Tracy
Redbeard. L. A. Knight
Redbird Affair. L. V. Stevens
Redcap. P. McCutchan
Redding Straik. R. Aitken
Reddy Brant, His Adventures. W. C. Tuttle
Reddy or Not. I. Zacharia
Redeemed. C. R. B.
Redeemer. H. Fleetwood
Redemption. C. Hagan
Redemption. J. McGown
Redemption Factor. W. E. Chambers
Redemption of Grace Milroy. C. Dawe
Redemption of Richard. Marguerite Bryant
Redemption Range. Gavin Holt
Redeye. R. Aellen
Redfern's Miracle. E. Trevor
Redfingers. W. M. Duncan
Redhead. A. Andersch
Redhead. J. Creasey
Redhead for Danger. Arthur MacLean
Redhead for Free. K. T. McCall
Redhead for Mike Shayne. B. Halliday
Redhead from Chicago. L. Royer
Redhead from Sun Dog. W. C. Tuttle
Redhead Racket. H. Zore
Redheads. J. Spencer
Redheads Are Poison. B. Winter
Redheads Cool Fast. B. Winter
Redheads Die Young. B. Diamond
Redheads Fall Hard. B. Vane
Redheads Never Regret. W. Standish
Redivivia. M. Comyn
Redlance. W. J. Elliott
Redman Cave Murder. E. Barker
Redmaynes. G. E. Locke
Redolmo Affair. Nick Carter
Redoubtable Dexter. G. Hackforth-Jones
Redshift Rendezvous. J. E. Stith
Reduction of Staff. F. J. Whaley
Redundancy Pay. J. R. L. Anderson
Reeds in the Wind. C. Gleig
Reef of Gold. M. H. Hervey
Reef Pearlers. S. M. Parkman
Reefer Boy. H. Ellson
Reefer Girl. M. Lavelle
Reefer Man. R. T. Coughlin
Reefer Rhapsody. H. Vogel
Reel Murder. M. Babson
Reel of Death. R. Simons
Reference to Death. L. R. Davis
Reflection. A. Neiderman
Reflection of Evil. J. Roffman
Reflex. D. Francis
Reflex Action. C. Fitzsimmons
Reformation of Royce Remington. W. M. Graydon
Reformatory Girls. N. Tyre
Refrigerators. M. Fratti
Refuge. C. Brenchley
Refuge in Terror. W. J. Watkins
Regan. I. K. Martin
Regan and the Bent Stripper. J. Balham
Regan and the Deal of a Century. I. K. Martin
Regan and the High Rollers. J. Balham
Regan and the Human Pipeline. J. Balham
Regan and the Lebanese Shipment. J. Balham
Regan and the Manhattan File. I. K. Martin
Regan and the Snout Who Cried Wolf. J. Balham
Regan and the Venetian Virgin. J. Balham
Regarding Sherlock Holmes. A. Derleth
Regatta Mystery. A. Christie
Regency Buck. G. Heyer
Regency Rake. Michael Hardwick
Regency Revenge. Michael Hardwick
Regency Royal. Michael Hardwick
Regensburg Legacy. J. Bickham
Regent Street Raid. J. G. Brandon
Regent's Candlesticks. E. Kyle

Reggis Arms Caper. R. H. Spencer
Regimental Legends. J. S. Winter
Regina v Rumpole. J. Mortimer
Reginald Hetherege. H. Kingsley
Reginald Vernon. W. H. Hillyard
Register Here. David Meyer
Regression. F. Wyka
Regular Fraud. R. Jocelyn
Rehabilitated Man. Eric Lambert
Rehearsal for Death. G. Batson
Rehearsal for Death. Theodora Benson
Rehearsal for Murder. D. D. Brooke
Rehearsal for Murder. F. Bunce
Rehearsal for Murder. P. M. Carlson
Rehearsal for the Funeral. E. Colter
Reich Four. Nick Carter
Reign. Chet Williamson
Reign of Terror. H. Desmond
Reign of Terror. P. Richmond
Reimann Curse. J. Deweese
Reincarnation in Venice. M. Ehrlich
Reincarnation of Peter Proud. M. Ehrlich
Reincarnation of Reece Erikson. R. Obstfeld
Reinhard Action. H. Eisenberg
Reins of Chance. C. R. Gull
Reivaulx Abbey. N. Davison
Rejected Bride. E. Southworth
Rejected Wife. M. Blount
Rejuvenation of Mrs. Semaphore. H. Godfrey
Rejuvenators. H. Miller
Rekill. I. K. Martin
Relative Distance. R. Lewis
Relative Murder. A. Hocking
Relative Stranger. A. Stevenson
Relative to Death. S. Forbes
Relative to Murder. E. Warman
Relative to Poison. E. C. R. Lorac
Relative Values. H. C. McNeile
Relatively Dangerous. R. Jeffries
Release the Lions. R. Croft-Cooke
Release the Prisoner. A. Wood
Released for Death. Henry Wade
Relentless. B. Garfield
Relentless Current. M. E. Charlesworth
Relentless Storm. C. Lorrimer
Religion. N. Conde
Religious Body. C. Aird
Reluctant Agent. J. N. Chance
Reluctant Assassin. J. Dark
Reluctant Assassin. J. Godey
Reluctant Assassin. A. Reynaud-Fourton
Reluctant Blonde. D. Haring
Reluctant Bride. C. Laffeaty
Reluctant Cloak and Dagger Man. Ernest Paul
Reluctant Duchess. M. Richmond
Reluctant Executioner. John Marsh
Reluctant Gunman. W. H. Baker
Reluctant Hangman and other stories of crime. G. Allen
Reluctant Heiress. G. H. Coxe
Reluctant Heiress. A. Laine
Reluctant Hostess. H. Janson
Reluctant Hussy. R. Burke
Reluctant Inmate. Stuart Hall
Reluctant Lover. G. Ferrand
Reluctant Medium. L. Vardre
Reluctant Murderer. Bernice Carey
Reluctant Paragon. S. Farrant
Reluctant Prodigal. H. L. V. Fletcher
Reluctant Puritan. K. A. Shoesmith
Reluctant Rebel. M. Richmond
Reluctant Ronin. James Melville
Reluctant Sleeper. J. Wainwright
Reluctant Sleuth. F. Crane
Reluctant Spy. J. Blackburn
Reluctant Spy. T. D. Calnan
Reluctant Spy. J. Laflin
Reluctant Spy. H. Wood-Hill
Reluctant Transgressor. M. Kane
Reluctant Virgin. N. Karta
Remains to Be Seen. M. Butterworth
Remains to Be Seen. M. Cumberland
Remains to Be Seen. Roy Hart
Remains to Be Seen. H. Lindsay

Remarkable Adventures of Christopher Poe. R. C. Brown
Remarkable Case of Burglary. H. R. F. Keating
Remarkable Convictions. Anonymous
Remarkable Feat. Old Sleuth
Remarkable Murder. G. Kramer
Remarkable "Shadow". Old Sleuth
Rematch. D. Everson
Rembrandt Decisions. A. V. Badgley
Rembrandt File. O. Banks
Rembrandt Murder. H. J. Forman
Rembrandt Panel. O. Banks
Remedy. H. B. Drake
Remember! J. G. Sarasin
Remember March. M. J. Adamson
Remember Maybelle? Carter Brown
Remember Mimi. B. Vane
Remember Pearl Harbor. A. Cowles
Remember That Face. F. Findley
Remember the Shadows. D. Duncan
Remember the Summer We Lived at the Pad. A. Lamb
Remember to Kill Me. H. Pentecost
Remember with Tears. H. Arvonen
Remembered Anger. M. Albrand
Remembered Death. A. Christie
Remembering Heart. J. T. Osborne
Remembering Louise. Anna Gilbert
Remembrance of Miranda. M. Ingate
Remembrance of Threatening Green. D. McGregor
Rememory. J. Betancourt
Remind Me to Forget. C. B. Dawson
Remington Contract. R. Obstfeld
Remington Factor. R. Obstfeld
Remington Set. J. Charlton
Reminiscences of a Gentleman Horse Dealer. H. Tremayne
Reminiscences of a Raven. James Greenwood
Reminiscences of a Rogue. F. Martyn
Reminiscences of a Virginia Physician. P. S. Ruter
Reminiscences of Chief-Inspector Littlechild. J. G. Littlechild
Reminiscences of Jock Thirlstane. W. Russell
Reminiscences of Solar Pond. A. Derleth
Remittance-Woman. A. Abdullah
Remo: The First Adventure. W. B. Murphy
Remorse. W. Standish
Remote Control. H. Carmichael
Remote Control. Clyde North
Remote Journey. L. Handley
Removalists. D. Williamson
Removals Ltd. Trill
Remove the Bodies. E. Ferrars
Remover. Roland Daniel
Remover Returns. Roland Daniel
Removers. D. Hamilton
Rempal Inquest. K. McKinnon
Remus Code. S. Englander
Rena. B. Gayle
Render Unto Caesar. K. Lindsay
Rendezvous. Evelyn Anthony
Rendezvous at Live Oaks. E. W. Strother
Rendezvous at the Hallows. J. T. Osborne
Rendezvous in Amsterdam. E. Randolph
Rendezvous in Austria. W. E. D. Ross
Rendezvous in Black. C. Woolrich
Rendezvous in Haiti. S. Becker
Rendezvous in Peking. Anne-Mariel
Rendezvous in Rio. G. Fallon
Rendezvous in Rio. Vince Howard
Rendezvous in Tripoli. C. Gayet
Rendezvous in Vienna. L. Hamilton
Rendezvous in Vienna. J. Ellis
Rendezvous of Mysteries. K. S. Nakagawa
Rendezvous on an Island. T. Claymore
Rendezvous 2.2. R. D. Bennett
Rendezvous with a Dead Man. Nicholas Carter
Rendezvous with Danger. J. Corbett
Rendezvous with Danger. M. Pemberton
Rendezvous with Danger. Lynn Williams
Rendezvous with Death. John Bentley
Rendezvous with Death. J. Corbett
Rendezvous with Death. J. Paull
Rendezvous with Fear. N. Davis
Rendezvous with Fear. A. Worboys
Rendezvous with the Past. K. M. Knight
Renegade Agent. D. Pendleton
Renegade Bleu. B. Schwarz
Renegade Cop. Jonathan Craig
Renegade from Russia. H. C. Davis
Renegade Sheriff. W. C. Tuttle
Renegade Steele. J. D. Masters
Renewable Virgin. B. Paul
Renfrew Flies Again. L. Y. Erskine
Renfrew in the Valley of the Vanished Men. L. Y. Erskine
Renfrew of the Royal Mounted. L. Y. Erskine
Renfrew Rides Again. L. Y. Erskine
Renfrew Rides North. L. Y. Erskine
Renfrew Rides the Range. L. Y. Erskine
Renfrew Rides the Sky. L. Y. Erskine
Renfrew's Long Trail. L. Y. Erskine
Reno Rendezvous. L. Ford
Renshaw Fanning's Quest. B. Mitford
Renshaw Strike. Ian Stuart
Repaid in Like Coin. Nicholas Carter
Reparation. O. Williams
Repeat Performance. W. O'Farrell
Repeat the Instructions. R. V. Beste
Repent at Leisure. P. Conway
Repent at Leisure. R. Foley
Repentance of Rachel. Hedley Richards
Replay: Murder. J. Logue
Replica. R. Bowker
Reply Paid. H. F. Heard
Report for a Corpse. H. Kane
Report for Murder. V. McDermid
Report from Argyll. A. MacKinnon
Report from Group 17. R. C. O'Brien
Report to the Commissioner. James Mills
Reporter. K. Attiwill
Reporter. J. Stearn
Reporter. E. Wallace
Reporter Detective. D. J. MacKenzie
Reporter's Triumph. S. Campbell
Reporting Murder. D. Maggs
Reprieve of Roger Maine. G. McDonell
Reprisal. I. Barclay
Reprisal. Arthur Gordon
Reprisal. W. P. McGivern
Reprisal. E. Vance
Reprise. C. Rayner
Reprise. L. Stephan
Repulse Monkey. D. Cluster
Reputation Dies. A. C. Ley
Reputation for a Song. E. Grierson
Reputation of George Saxon and other stories. Morley Roberts
Requiem at Rogano. S. Knight
Requiem for a Blonde. K. Roos
Requiem for a Chase. J. Conway
Requiem for a Cop. V. B. Miller
Requiem for a Crown. R. Vacha
Requiem for a Dove. M. Eccles
Requiem for a Dream. H. Selby
Requiem for a Loser. J. Wainwright
Requiem for a Murder. S. Clausse
Requiem for a Nun. W. Faulkner
Requiem for a Rat. J. Godwin
Requiem for a Redhead. A. Bocca
Requiem for a Redhead. L. Hardy
Requiem for a Redhead. D. Haring
Requiem for a Schoolgirl. I. T. Ross
Requiem for a Spy. A. Giovannetti
Requiem for Charles. H. Carmichael
Requiem for Redheads. W. H. Baker
Requiem for Robert. M. Fitt
Requiem for Rogues. David Hume
Requiem for Two Sisters. J. Turner
Requiem in Utopia. R. Starnes
Requiem of Sharks. P. Buchanan
Rescue! Steve Mackenzie
Rescue Flight. W. E. Johns
Rescue from the Rose. J. B. Hilton
Rescuing Rupert. G. Thorne
Resemblance. A. Pombo
Reservation for Murder. J. Wright
Reservation of Fear. Louise Carter
Reservations for Death. B. Kendrick
Reserve Two for Murder. J. Randall
Resident. W. Tute
Resident Magistrate. B. Marnan
Resisting Arrest. Steven Phillips
Resolute Jack. Old Sleuth
Resolved to Be Rich. E. H. Cooper
Resort. S. Stein
Resort to Murder. W. Krasner
Resort to War. G. Revelli
Resources of Mycroft Holmes. C. Andrews
Respect. D. London
Respectable Miss Parkington-Smith. P. Allardyce
Respectable Woman. David Fletcher
Rest Hollow Mystery. R. N. Porter
Rest in Agony. I. Jorgensen
Rest in Piece. J. MacLane
Rest in Pieces. R. McInerny
Rest Is Silence. P. Barrington
Rest Is Silence. V. Coffman
Rest Must Die. R. Foster
Rest Without Peace. E. Byrd
Rest You Merry. C. MacLeod
Restless Corpse. A. Pruitt
Restless Hands. B. Fischer
Restless Natives. N. Dunnett
Restless Obsession. J. J. Toombs
Restless Quiet. D. O'Connor
Results of a Duel. F. Du Boisgobey
Resume for Murder. C. McCormick
Resurrection Day. D. Pendleton
Resurrection Day. K. Robeson
Resurrection Game. J. Midgley
Resurrection Man. T. Walsh
Resurrection Murder Case. S. H. Page
Resurrection of Candy Sterling. R. W. Martin
Resurrection of His Grace. C. Rae-Brown
Resurrection of Maltravers. A. Lernet-Holenia
Resurrection Row. A. Perry
Retake. Richard Hubbard
Retaliation. H. Flowerdew
Retaliators. D. Hamilton
Retief: Envoy to New Worlds. K. Laumer
Retired from the Yard. A. Parsons
Retreat. J. Mundis
Retreat for Death. Nick Carter
Retreat from Oblivion. D. Goodis
Retreat Into Night. R. Glendinning
Retreat of Radiance. I. Moffitt
Retribution. I. Barclay
Retribution. C. C. Caldwell
Retribution. D. Essex
Retribution. H. Fisher
Retribution. C. R. Gull
Retribution. T. P. Prest
Retribution. E. Southworth
Retrieval. C. Dunne
Return. Evelyn Anthony
Return. M. Fratti
Return. D. Winston
Return a Gain for Murder. R. Verron
Return Engagement. W. B. Murphy
Return from Cormoral. K. Robeson
Return from Darkness. N. Vida
Return from the Ashes. H. Monteilhet
Return from the Dead. M. Burton
Return from Vorkuta. David St. John
Return Load. D. Rutherford
Return Match. E. Cadell
Return of A. J. Raffles. G. Greene
Return of a Traitor. T. B. Morris
Return of Anthony Trent. W. Martyn
Return of Arsene Lupin. M. Leblanc
Return of Blackshirt. B. Graeme
Return of Blue Mask. Anthony Morton
Return of Blue Pete. L. Allan
Return of Bulldog Drummond. H. C. McNeile
Return of Cardannesley. G. Ellinger
Return of Cavannagh. Ian Anderson
Return of Clubfoot. V. Williams
Return of Colonel Pho. Ronald Simpson
Return of Dick Barton. Anonymous
Return of Dr. Fu-Manchu. S. Rohmer

Title Index

Return of Dr. Sam: Johnson, Detector. L. De La Torre
Return of Frank Clamart. H. C. Rowland
Return of Frass. J. Chancellor
Return of George Washington. L. Brent
Return of Grey Shadow. G. E. Rochester
Return of Henry Prince. C. F. Gregg
Return of Henry Starr. R. Slotkin
Return of Hercules, Esq. Gwyn Evans
Return of Jack the Ripper. Mark Andrews
Return of Jennifer. H. Upshaw
Return of Jenny Weaver. M. Turnbull
Return of Lanny Budd. U. Sinclair
Return of Lieutenant Boruvka. J. Skvorecky
Return of Mick Cardby. David Hume
Return of Mr. Benjamin. M. Short
Return of Mr. Budd. G. Verner
Return of Mr. Campion. M. Allingham
Return of Moriarty. J. Gardner
Return of Nighthawk. S. Horler
Return of Picklock Holes. R. C. Lehman
Return of Raffles. B. Perowne
Return of Raffles. P. Tremayne
Return of Sanders of the River. F. Gerard
Return of Sherlock Holmes. A. C. Doyle
Return of Skull-Face. R. E. Howard
Return of Solar Pons. A. Derleth
Return of Sumuru. S. Rohmer
Return of the Assassin. A. Tack
Return of the Black Gang. G. Fairlie
Return of the Ceteosaurus, and other tales. G. Radcliffe
Return of the Continental Op. D. Hammett
Return of the Cornish Soldier. Michael Barrett
Return of the Hood. M. Spillane
Return of the Howling. G. Brandner
Return of the Living Dead. J. Russo
Return of the Maniac. M. Johnson
Return of the Night Wind. V. Vanardy
Return of the Opium Wars. M. Macao
Return of the Pink Panther. F. Waldman
Return of the Royalist. K. A. Shoesmith
Return of the Shadow. W. B. Gibson
Return of the Shadow. M. Grant
Return of the Vagabond. G. M. Cohan
Return of Uncle Walker and other stories. D. V. Baker
Return of Van Weik. C. Evelyn
Return of Wu Fang. Roland Daniel
Return of Yesterday. K. Ingram
Return of Zingrave. E. S. Brooks
Return They Must. John Marsh
Return to Adventure. N. Deane
Return to Armageddon. G. Wilson
Return to Aylforth. A. Eliot
Return to Ballyrock. A. Furness
Return to Clerycastle. M. Heath
Return to Cottington. F. Bamford
Return to Darkness. W. D. Roberts
Return to Death Valley. J. N. Chance
Return to Foxdale. L. Dartey
Return to Glenshael. M. Elgin
Return to Gravesend. M. Eyre
Return to Hawkeston Hall. L. Whitaker
Return to Honor. D. Beason
Return to Love. J. Blackmore
Return to Murder. M. A. Taylor
Return to Octavia. D. Macomber
Return to Peril. L. A. Olmstead
Return to Sender. D. Cluster
Return to Terror. M. Albrand
Return to Terror. T. Charles
Return to Terror. F. Hurt
Return to the Alcazar. E. Kyle
Return to the River. K. Hewitt
Return to the Scene. Q. Patrick
Return to Tiger Bay. J. M. Walsh
Return to Vienna. N. Buckingham
Return to Vietnam. D. Pendleton
Return to Vikki. J. Tomerlin
Return to Violence. W. Spann
Reuben. J. E. Wideman
Reuben Foreman, the Village Blacksmith. D. Dale
Reunion. W. Kuhns

Reunion. L. V. Roper
Reunion. Richard Russell
Reunion for Death. Martin Meyers
Reunion in Eros. H. Manis
Reunion in Florida. T. Claymore
Reunion in Renfrew. W. E. D. Ross
Reunion on Gallows Hill. T. J. Kelly
Reunion with Murder. T. Fuller
Revealed by Lightning. I. Stark
Revelations. A. Lane
Revelations of a Detective. A. Forrester
Revelations of a Lady Detective. Anonymous
Revelations of a Police Court Interpreter. J. Jacobsen
Revelations of a Private Detective. A. Forrester
Revelations of a Sly Parrot. John Bennett
Revelations of Inspector Morgan. O. Crawfurd
Revelations of the Secret Service. W. LeQueux
Revellers. L. Tracy
Revenge! R. Barr
Revenge. H. Brenton
Revenge. J. Cartwright
Revenge. J. Ehrlich
Revenge. N. Hynd
Revenge. Joseph Warren
Revenge at Indy. L. Kenyon
Revenge at Nightfall. Elliot Bailey
Revenge Can Wait. Irene Alexander
Revenge Game. G. Hammond
Revenge in "The Convent". C. B. Boyd
Revenge Incorporated. Dennis Phillips
Revenge Is a Violin. E. Reynolds
Revenge of Annie Charlie. A. Fry
Revenge of Fantomas. M. Allain
Revenge of Gilbert Strange. W. Wood
Revenge of Moriarty. J. Gardner
Revenge of Taurus. R. Lory
Revenge of the Generals. Nick Carter
Revenge of the Hound. Michael Hardwick
Revenge of the Master. J. Ahern
Revenge of the Robins Family. T. Chastain
Revenge of Valerie. H. Nisbet
Revenge Shall Be Mine. J. N. Yeloushan
Revenge with a Vengeance. C. L. Reid
Revengeful Turk. I. Crookenden
Revenger. J. Messmann
Revengers. D. Hamilton
Revenue Detective. Anonymous
Revenue Detective. Police Captain James
Rev. Captain Kettle. C. J. C. Hyne
Reverend Gentleman. J. M. Cobban
Rev. Miles Latimer. L. Gardiner
Reverend Randollph and the Avenging Angel. C. M. Smith
Reverend Randollph and the Fall from Grace, Inc. C. M. Smith
Reverend Randollph and the Holy Terror. C. M. Smith
Reverend Randollph and the Modern Miracles. T. L. Smith
Reverend Randollph and the Splendid Samaritan. C. M. Smith
Reverend Randollph and the Unholy Bible. C. M. Smith
Reverend Randollph and the Wages of Sin. C. M. Smith
Reverse Negative. A. Jute
Reverse the Charges. B. Flynn
Reversible Santa Claus. Meredith Nicholson
Revised Proof. P. Conway
Revolt. H. Janson
Revolt. G. B. Lissenden
Revolt from Bondage. H. D. Dearden
Revolt in the Desert. J. Robb
Revolt of Abbe Lee. J. McBrien
Revolt of Beatrix. F. Whishaw
Revolting Development. L. R. Smith
Revolution Island. J. Fane
Revolution Script. B. Moore
Revolutionist. E. Garth
Revue Girl. A. Applin
Reward. Michael Barrett
Reward for a Defector. M. Underwood
Reward for Retief. K. Laumer
Reward for the Baron. Anthony Morton

Reward for Treason. T. C. H. Jacobs
Reward Game. G. Hammond
Rex Mundi. G. Sims
Rexworth Mystery. S. Cummings
Rhapsody in Fear. J. N. Chance
Rhea. R. De Pont-Jest
Rheingold Route. A. Maling
Rhine Replica. M. Albrand
Rhinemann Exchange. R. Ludlum
Rhino for Rosamund. D. Fearon
Rhino in the Kitchen. D. W. MacArthur
Rhino Ritz. K. Abbott
Rhoda Roberts. Harry Lindsay
Rhodesia. Nick Carter
Rhododendron Man. J. A. Tyson
Rhyme and Prose, and A Burlesque and Its History. G. Isaacs
Ria. F. C. Forrest
Ribbom for My Repute. A. Sewart
Ribs of Death. Joan Aiken
Rice Papers. H. L. Morris
Rice Wine. B. Came
Riceburner. R. Hyer
Rich and Dangerous Game. L. White
Rich and the Damned. R. Himmel
Rich Crimson Silk. J. Burn
Rich Die Hard. B. Nichols
Rich Die Young. C. G. Hart
Rich Full Life. M. Dibdin
Rich Get It All. F. Huston
Rich, Hip and Deadly. H. Paul
Rich Is the Treasure. M. Procter
Rich Man. G. Simenon
Rich Man, Dead Man. H. Waugh
Rich Man, Murder. H. Waugh
Rich Man, Poor Man. M. Foster
Rich Man's Wife. D. Donovan
Rich or Dead. M. Cormany
Rich People. Morton Cooper
Rich, Radiant Slaughter. O. Papazoglu
Rich to Die. B. Tutton
Rich Way to Die. K. Evans
Richard. Marguerite Bryant
Richard A. S. Yurick
Richard Arbour. J. Payn
Richard Barlow the Bloodhound. C. Rae-Brown
Richard Matheson: Collected Stories. R. Matheson
Richard Parker. T. P. Prest
Richard's Feet. Carey Harrison
Richardson Goes Abroad. B. Thomson
Richardson Scores Again. B. Thomson
Richardson Solves a Dartmoor Mystery. B. Thomson
Richardson's Second Case. B. Thomson
Riches and Honor. T. Hyman
Richest Corpse in Show Business. Dan Morgan
Richest Girl in the World. V. Coffman
Richest Man. E. Shanks
Richlands. A. S. Turnbull
Richmond. Anonymous
Rick. D. G. Falk
Rickerby's Folly. T. Gallon
Ricksha Clue. G. Ellinger
Rickshaw Bend. H. Arvonen
Ricochet. B. Copper
Rocochet. O. Demaris
Ricochet. J. F. Straker
Ridan the Devil, and other stories. L. Becke
Riddle. T. Hillstrom
Riddle. D. Sherman
Riddle, and other stories. W. De La Mare
Riddle in Wax. F. Pepper
Riddle Me a Murder. D. Crowley
Riddle Me This. M. Roscoe
Riddle Me This! D. N. Rubin
Riddle of a Lady. Anthony Gilbert
Riddle of Big Ben. A. Parsons
Riddle of Crocodile Creek. W. M. Graydon
Riddle of Crooked Creek. J. W. Booth
Riddle of Cubicle 7. A. Parsons
Riddle of Dead Man's Mine. M. Frazer
Riddle of Dead Man's Pit. R. C. Armour
Riddle of Double Island. M. Corrigan
Riddle of Five Needle Creek. A. Blair

Riddle of Garth. Augustus Muir
Riddle of Helena. C. Houghton
Riddle of Identities. Nicholas Carter
Riddle of John Rowe. Winston Graham
Riddle of Loch Lemman. A. O. Pollard
Riddle of Nap's Hollow. L. A. Knight
Riddle of Nine Tree Pit. Anonymous
Riddle of Rainbow Mountain. J. A. Rennie
Riddle of Riverdale. J. W. Bobin
Riddle of Samson. A. Garve
Riddle of the Amber Room. H. E. Hill
Riddle of the Amber Ship. M. E. Hanshew
Riddle of the Black Racketeers. J. Hunter
Riddle of the Blazing Bungalow. S. Blakesley
Riddle of the Bleeding Venus. P. Richmond
Riddle of the Body on the Road. E. S. Brooks
Riddle of the Book-Mark. W. J. Lomax
Riddle of the Burmese Curse. A. Parsons
Riddle of the Cambrian Venus. D. W. F. Hardie
Riddle of the Captured Quisling. A. Parsons
Riddle of the Crooked Gambler. R. Hardinge
Riddle of the Dead. L. Bamburg
Riddle of the Dead Cats. A. Blackmon
Riddle of the Dead Man's Bay. J. G. Brandon
Riddle of the Disguised Greek. A. Parsons
Riddle of the Eighth Guest. B. Wheeler
Riddle of the Emeralds. P. C. De Crispigny
Riddle of the Escaped P.O.W. A. Parsons
Riddle of the Evil Eye. P. Quiroule
Riddle of the Film Star's Jewels. L. Jackson
Riddle of the Florentine Folio. E. S. Liddon
Riddle of the Forest. E. W. Townsend
Riddle of the Forest. B. Tozer
Riddle of the French Alibi. W. Tyrer
Riddle of the Frontier. Robert Harding
Riddle of the Frozen Flame. M. E. Hanshew
Riddle of the Gambling Den. A. Parsons
Riddle of the Garage. H. H. C. Gibbons
Riddle of the Gas Meter. G. Chester
Riddle of the Golden Fingers. E. J. Murray
Riddle of the Great Art Exhibition. R. C. Armour
Riddle of the Greek Financier. J. G. Brandon
Riddle of the Green Cylinder. W. Jardine
Riddle of the Highwayman's Stone. R. Hardinge
Riddle of the Indian Alibi. A. Parsons
Riddle of the Invisible Menace. R. Hardinge
Riddle of the Italian Prisoner. J. Hunter
Riddle of the Keys. J. A. Kolbe
Riddle of the Kidnapped Pensioner. G. Chester
Riddle of the Lascar's Head. L. H. Brooks
Riddle of the Leather Bottle. J. Drummond
Riddle of the Lost Emigrant. R. C. Armour
Riddle of the Lost Ship. J. Hunter
Riddle of the Marsh. J. Blyth
Riddle of the Million Pound Bet. W. J. Bayfield
Riddle of the Missing Fire Watcher. G. Chester
Riddle of the Mummy Case. J. Drummond
Riddle of the Murdered Fisherman. G. Chester
Riddle of the Mysterious Light. M. E. Hanshew
Riddle of the Negro's Head. C. Brisbane
Riddle of the Night. T. W. Hanshew
Riddle of the Night Garage. G. Chester
Riddle of the Phantom Plague. D. W. Steward
Riddle of the Prince's Stooge. A. Parsons
Riddle of the Purple Emperor. T. W. Hanshew
Riddle of the Rail. F. M. White
Riddle of the Rajah's Curios. A. Parsons
Riddle of the Ranch. W. Jardine
Riddle of the Ravens. L. Gribble
Riddle of the Receiver's Hoard. J. Drummond
Riddle of the Red Devil Costume. T. J. Saunders
Riddle of the Red Dragon. Edmund Burton
Riddle of the Red Dragon. Gwyn Evans
Riddle of the Registry Office. H. H. C. Gibbons
Riddle of the Ring. W. LeQueux
Riddle of the River. J. Wear-Gifford
Riddle of the Roost. L. Brock
Riddle of the Rose. W. B. M. Ferguson
Riddle of the Rovers. C. M. Hincks
Riddle of the Rovers. A. B. Maurice
Riddle of the Ruins. L. Jackson
Riddle of the Runaway Cat. H. H. C. Gibbons
Riddle of the Russian Bride. A. Parsons
Riddle of the Russian Gold. G. H. Teed
Riddle of the Russian Princess. E. S. Liddon
Riddle of the Sands. E. Childers
Riddle of the Sealed Room. R. Hardinge
Riddle of the Smiling Man. J. Hunter
Riddle of the Snows. T. B. Tivey
Riddle of the Spanish Circus. M. Corrigan
Riddle of the Spinning Wheel. M. E. Hanshew
Riddle of the Straits. H. Edmonds
Riddle of the Sunken Garden. Donald Stuart
Riddle of the Third Mile. C. Dexter
Riddle of the Three Marked Men. G. N. Philips
Riddle of the Traveling Skull. H. S. Keeler
Riddle of the Turkish Baths. Gwyn Evans
Riddle of the Ugly Face. P. Quiroule
Riddle of the Uncensored Letter. J. Hunter
Riddle of the Veiled Song. C. B. MacDonald, Jr.
Riddle of the West End Hairdresser. H. H. C. Gibbons
Riddle of the Winged Death. H. P. Hanshew
Riddle of the Workman Squire. L. Jackson
Riddle of the Yellow Zuri. H. S. Keeler
Riddle of the Yukon. L. C. Douthwaite
Riddle of Three-Way Creek. R. Cullum
Riddle of Wraye. J. Laurence
Riddle Ring. Justin McCarthy
Riddles of Hildegarde Withers. S. Palmer
Riddles Read. D. Donovan
Ride. J. Wainwright
Ride a Dead Horse. B. Edmunds
Ride a High Horse. R. S. Prather
Ride a Pale Horse. H. MacInnes
Ride a Tiger. A. Booth
Ride a Tiger. H. Livingston
Ride a Tiger. D. Orgill
Ride a Tiger. A. A. Randall
Ride a White Dolphin. A. Maybury
Ride for a Fall. V. Gielgud
Ride of the Razorback. Carl Stevens
Ride on a Tiger. Dulcie Gray
Ride out the Storm. John Harris
Ride the Dark Moors. H. Stephenson
Ride the Dark Storm. N. Jones
Ride the Gold Mare. O. Demaris
Ride the Golden Tiger. Jonathan Black
Ride the Golden Tiger. C. Fast
Ride the Lightning. J. Lutz
Ride the Man Down. R. Dolphin
Ride the Nightmare. F. Dudley
Ride the Nightmare. R. Matheson
Ride the Pink Horse. D. B. Hughes
Ride the Roller Coaster. Carter Brown
Ride the Tiger. R. Emmett
Ride West of the Law. R. Wilkes-Hunter
Ride with Terror. Charles Henry
Rider in the Sky. L. A. Knight
Rider of Waroona. G. Firth Scott
Rider's Leap. F. Langbridge
Riders of the Sands. W. W. Sayer
Ridge. L. W. Cantrell
Ridgway Woman. R. Neely
Riding for a Fall. S. D. Price
Riding High. J. Francome
Rififi in New York. A. Le Breton
Rifled Gold. W. C. Tuttle
Rift. L. Cody
Rig. R. Douglas
Rig. R. Wilcox
Rig Warrior. W. W. Johnstone
Rigby File. T. Heald
Rigdale Puzzle. C. Kingston
Rigging the Evidence. C. Carnac
Right and Wrong. B. Z. Spencer
Right Church Wrong Pew. Walter Stewart
Right for Murder. L. White
Right for Trouble. N. Easton
Right Hand Opposite. R. M. Stern
Right Honourable Corpse. Max Murray
Right Jack. M. Maron
Right Kind of House. A. C. Martens
Right Moves. A. Zelman
Right Murder. C. Rice
Right of Reply. J. Harris
Right to Be Wrong. E. McCann
Right to Die. J. R. Davis
Right to Die. R. Stout
Right to Kill. R. R. Ryan
Right to Remain Silent. C. Brandt
Right to Sing the Blues. J. Lutz
Right Turn for Murder. R. Verron
Right You Are, Mr. Moto. J. P. Marquand
Righted Wrong. E. Yates
Righteous Abel. J. Remenham
Rightfully Mine. D. Mortman
Rights of Mallaroche. C. N. Boyle
Rigoletto Murder. Angus Hall
Rigoville Match. D. Walker
Riley of the Special Branch. L. Gribble
Rim-Fire, Detective. C. Ballew
Rim of Fire. Gar Wilson
Rim of Fire Conspiracy. J. Rosenberger
Rim of Heaven. Tom Howard
Rim of Terror. H. T. Teilhet
Rim of the Pit. Hake Talbot
Rim Rider. W. C. Tuttle
Rim-World Legacy. F. A. Javor
Rimers of Eldritch. L. Wilson
Rimfire Murders. Frank O'Brian
Rimualdo. W. H. Ireland
Rinaldi Rinaldini, Captain of Banditti. C. A. Vulpius
Ring. B. Tucker
Ring-a-Ding-Ding. F. Kane
Ring-a-Ding Girl. D. Rico
Ring-a-Ding UFO's. R. Tralins
Ring and the Lamp. W. Rollins
Ring and Walk In. M. Borgenicht
Ring Around a Rogue. J. M. Flynn
Ring Around a Murder. G. Bagby
Ring Around Rosa. W. C. Gault
Ring Around Rosa. J. C. McMullen
Ring Around Rosy. Gordon Davis
Ring for a Noose. Anthony Gilbert
Ring for Luck. J. Pudney
Ring in Meiji. W. Butler
Ring Master. D. Gurr
Ring o' Bells. G. R. Sims
Ring of Darkness. K. Ostrander
Ring of Dust. Nicholas Carter
Ring of Eyes. H. Footner
Ring of Fear. A. McCaffrey
Ring of Fire. B. Gavin
Ring of Fire. D. Schmidt
Ring of Innocent. B. Flynn
Ring of Iron. I. Stark
Ring of Kerry. J. Griffin
Ring of Liars. J. N. Chance
Ring of Mischief. M. Summerton
Ring of Rascals. Nicholas Carter
Ring of Roses. J. Blackburn
Ring of Roses. C. Brand
Ring of Rubies. L. T. Meade
Ring of Truth. G. H. Coxe
Ring the Bell at Zero. H. L. Nelson
Ring the Bell, Sister! L. Bell
Ring the Bell Softly. P. Bennetts
Ring Twice for Murder. A. Spiller
Ring Up Nighthawk. S. Horler
Ringara. C. Lansbury
Ringed with Fire. Alice Campbell
Ringer. Dell Shannon
Ringer. D. R. Slavitt
Ringer. J. S. Thayer
Ringer. E. Wallace
Ringer Returns. E. Wallace
Ringer 'Tec. J. Ascott
Ringing Sands. O. Binns
Ringleader. L. Dunne
Ringmaster. L. Dunne
Ringnecker. S. H. Courtier
Rings of Sand. T. McNab
Rings on Her Finger. Laurence Kirk
Rio Casino Intrigue. V. W. Mason
Rio Contract. W. Newton
Rio d'Oro. N. Tranter
Rio Pasion. J. Luceno
Rio Rustlers. J. Dorrance
Riot. F. Elli
Riot. R. Parkes

Riot Act. Will Greene
Riot Act. R. Philmore
Riot Night in Cedarville. W. Caryl
Riot '71. L. Peters
Rip-Off. Carter Brown
Rip-Off! B. J. Hurwood
Rip-Off! Jim Thompson
Rip-Off. W. C. Ulsh
Rip Van Winkle of the Kalahari. F. C. Cornell
Ripe for Development. John Gloag
Ripe for Rapture. H. Janson
Ripe Fruit. J. McPartland
Ripening. E. Clissant
Ripley Under Ground. P. Highsmith
Ripley's Game. P. Highsmith
Ripoff. A. Maling
Ripper. Mark Clark
Ripper. W. Dobson
Ripper. Mike Newton
Ripper. M. Procter
Ripper File. Elwyn Jones
Ripper Murders. M. Procter
Ripper Returns. A. Skene
Ripper's Apprentice. Donald Thomas
Ripping Yarns. M. Palin
Ripple of Murders. J. Wainwright
Ripple on the Water. D. M. Low
Rippling Ruby. J. S. Fletcher
Rise and Fall of Legs Diamond. O. H. Gaylord
Rise at Dawn. N. Fisher
Rise of Ruderick Clowd. J. Flynt
Rise of Tyne Gate. Andrew Gray
Rise with the Wind. A. C. Marin
Risen Dead. F. Marryat
Rishi. L. Giroux, Jr.
Risifi's Daughter. A. K. Green
Rising. Alison Smith
Rising of the Lark. S. Styles
Rising of the Moon. G. Mitchell
Rising Sea. M. Hastings
Rising Star. D. C. Murray
Rising Storm. D. Wheatley
Rising Sun. H. L. V. Fletcher
Rising Suns. John Gloag
Risk. L. Earl
Risk. D. Francis
Risk All for Love. M. Richmond
Risky! L. Della
Risky. G. M. Wilson
Risky Game. H. Bindloss
Risky Pleasure. J. A. Ross
Risky Way to Kill. R. Lockridge
Rissole Mystery. S. Fowler
Rita. R. Gaulden
Rita Makes a Killing. E. Ellison
Rita Takes a Ride. N. Perrelli
Rite of Expiation. D. Riley
Rite of Passage. G. Landers
Rite of Spring. A. W. Greeley
Rite of Survivorship. B. McGullion
Rite of the Damned. L. Osborne
Rite of the Dragon. J. Gluckman
Rites for a Killer. J. M. Fox
Rites of Murder. W. J. Sheldon
Rites of Sacrifice. W. Chorlton
Ritherton's Grange. S. De Havilland
Rittenhouse Square. A. P. G. Solmssen
Ritter Double-Cross. F. Nolan
Ritter's Gold. F. N. Hawkins
Ritual. W. Heffernan
Ritual. D. Pinner
Ritual Bath. F. Kellerman
Ritual Fire Dance. L. Phillips
Ritual in the Dark. Colin Wilson
Ritual Murder. S. T. Haymon
Ritual of Blood. Doug Masters
Rituals. R. Nordan
Ritz. T. McNally
Rival Claimants. E. P. Palmer
Rival Detectives. L. L. Lynch
Rival Detectives. J. W. Postgate
Rival Detectives. H. Rockwood
Rival Lovers. Anonymous
Rival Lovers. O. Bradbury

Rival Millionaires. L. Fitzhamon
Rival Stables. M. K. Douglas
Rivals. L. Meynell
Rivals. T. P. Prest
Rivard House. F. E. Lambirth
River and the Rose. S. Abbott
River Detective and the Wharf Rat's Game. Old Sleuth
River Gang. Roland Daniel
River Gets Wider. R. L. Gordon
River Girl. C. Williams
River Grown Deep. M. Pereira
River House. Mrs. Mary Armat
River House Mystery. G. Verner
River House Mystery. S. Warwick
River in the Dark. M. Latham
River in the Sun. E. Beatty
River Is Cold. D. Rimel
River Men. G. Verner
River Mystery. A. J. Rees
River of Death. A. MacLean
River of Diamonds. T. Craig
River of Diamonds. G. Jenkins
River of Fate. Michael Hastings
River of Fear. Leslie T. White
River of Fire. G. J. Breckling
River of Ice. K. Robeson
River of Life. J. Latey
River of Marriage. A. Furness
River of No Return. L. T. White
River of Pearls. R. De Pont-Jest
River of Stars. E. Wallace
River of Unrest. B. Mitford
River Passage. E. L. Long
River Patrol. R. Jeffries
River Pirate. C. F. Coe
River Pirate. A. Edgar
River Raid. E. Helm
River Rising. J. North
River Secrets. B. Hemyng
River Syndicate. C. E. Carryl
River Tragedy. Old Sleuth
River Trail. L. Y. Erskine
River Will Hide Me. A. Wood
Rivera Collection. B. Adkins
Riverfall. L. B. Porter
Rivergate House. E. Grandower
Rivermist. A. Harrell
Riverport Mail. O. Wright
River's End. J. O. Curwood
Rivers of Darkness. R. Hardy
Rivers of Flesh. J. Hild
Rivers to Cross. R. Pertwee
Riverside Club Murder. A. Skene
Riverside Mystery. J. G. Brandon
Riverside 90. D. Enefer
Riverside Villas Murder. K. Amis
Riverslea. G. Norway
Riverton Wagers. H. Collinson Owen
Rivertown. J. L. Roberts
Rivertown Risk. J. L. Hensley
Riverwood. J. Corby
Riverwood. M. Lynch
Riverworld. P. J. Farmer
Riviera Blues. J. Batten
Riviera Love Story. S. Jepson
Riviera Nights. B. Sarto
Riviera Puzzle. V. McConnor
Riviera Showdown. H. Janson
Rizzla Green Blues. P. McDowell
Roach & Co., Pirates, and other stories. H. Fuller
Road. V. Siller
Road and the Star. B. Mather
Road Back. B. M. Scott
Road Back. S. Warwick
Road Block. H. Waugh
Road End. W. Morrison
Road Floozie. D. Glinto
Road from Chilanga. D. W. MacArthur
Road Home. G. Vaizey
Road House. W. Hackett
Road House Murder. A. Skene
Road House Murders. R. P. Koehler
Road Kills. C. C. Gilmore

Road of Iron. G. St. Germain
Road Through the Wall. S. Jackson
Road to Bagdad. G. F. Gibbs
Road to Ballarat. K. Lindsay
Road to Canossa. J. Wood
Road to Desperation. M. H. Bradley
Road to Ein Harod. A. Kenan
Road to El Saida. Paul Townend
Road to Folly. L. Ford
Road to Fortune. F. A. Kummer
Road to Gandolfo. M. Shepherd
Road to Glenfairlie. D. Garth
Road to Hell. Everatt Jackson
Road to Hell. H. Monteilhet
Road to Hell. H. Vogel
Road to Las Vegas. J. Bogar
Road to London. D. S. Foster
Road to London. Edgar Wallace
Road to Marrakesh. G. Goodchild
Road to Midnight. M. Lynch
Road to Moscow. F. M. Long
Road to Murder. V. Gunn
Road to Nowhere. G. M. Glaskin
Road to Nowhere. M. Walsh
Road to Paradise. Keith Roberts
Road to Paradise Island. V. Holt
Road to Rhuine. S. Troy
Road to Romance. A. Soutar
Road to Ruin. Anonymous
Road to Ruin. M. E. Porter
Road to Shame. J. Wingrave
Road to the Coast. J. Harris
Road to the Moon. W. C. Tuttle
Road to the Snail. W. P. McGivern
Road Winds Back. P. Conway
Roadblock. M. Borgenicht
Roadhouse Girl. D. Reid
Roadhouse Mystery. J. G. Brandon
Roadknight. R. M. Gilchrist
Road's End. Albert Conroy
Roads of Destiny. O. Henry
Roadshow. W. Marshall
Roadside Murder. J. W. Heming
Roadside Night. E. N. Nistler
Roag's Syndicate. George Davis
Roanleigh. G. Mockler
Roar Devil. K. Robeson
Roar of the Ring. N. Gould
Roast Eggs. D. Clark
Rob the Lady. Jonathan Burke
Robak's Cross. J. L. Hensley
Robak's Fire. J. L. Hensley
Robak's Firm. J. L. Hensley
Robak's Run. J. L. Hensley
Robbed Blind. Roy Hart
Robber Countess. S. Cobb
Robber in a Mole Trap. P. N. Walker
Robber King. P. Tyrell
Robberies Co., Ltd. N. Lloyd
Robbers. P. Whalley
Robbers Passing By. G. M. Thomson
Robbery at Portage Bend. T. Lund
Robbery at Rudwick House. V. L. Whitechurch
Robbery Blue. R. Busby
Robbery of the Orphans. F. Du Boisgobey
Robbery Under Arms. R. Boldrewood
Robe of Lucifer. F. M. White
Robert Ainsleigh. M. E. Braddon
Robert Ashton's Wedding Day, and other stories. H. Wood
Robert Macaire. Anonymous
Robert the Devil. G. Warden
Roberta Died. G. M. Wilson
Robespierre Serial. N. Luard
Robin-a-Tiptoe. B. Merivale
Robin and the 7 Hoods. J. Pearl
Robin Grey. C. Gibbon
Robin Hood Caper. F. Carmichael
Robin Hoodwinker, V.C. G. Davison
Robin Redbreast in a Cage. Myrtle Johnston
Robineau Look. K. M. Knight
Robineau Murders. K. M. Knight
Robinson. M. Spark
Robinson Factor. J. M. White

Robocop. E. Naha
Robocop 2. E. Naha
Robot Detective. M. Billett
Robots and Empire. I. Asimov
Robots of Dawn. I. Asimov
Robthorne Mystery. J. Rhode
Rochemer Hag. L. W. King
Rock. H. Ellson
Rock! C. Stratton
Rock Ahead. E. Yates
Rock Baby. M. Woodhouse
Rock Bottom. J. Luceno
Rock Critic Murders. J. Sublett
Rock Harvest. H. C. Rae
Rock in the Baltic. R. Barr
Rock of Ages. F. H. Rose
Rock of Despair. Anonymous
Rock of Diamond. J. Quartermain
Rock of Justice. H. M. Richardson
Rock of Refuge. J. Haworth
Rock Rude. E. Stewart
Rock Sinister. K. Robeson
Rockabilly. H. Ellison
Rockabye. L. Koenig
Rockabye Baby. S. Gresham
Rockabye Contract. P. Atlee
Rockefeller Gift. P. G. Winslow
Rocket for the Toff. J. Creasey
Rocket to the Morgue. H. H. Holmes
Rockets—Operation Manhattan. H. Edmonds
Rockets Red Glare. G. Dinallo
Rockfire. C. Dillon
Rocking Chair. F. Y. McHugh
Rockingham Diamond. H. Collinson Owen
Rocklitz. G. R. Preedy
Rocks and Romance. F. B. Johnson
Rocks and Ruin. H. J. Calin
Rocksburg Railroad Murders. K. C. Constantine
Rockwell. P. McCurtin
Rocky Libido in San Francisco. L. Folder
Rocky Mountain. Duff Johnson
Rocky Rhodes. W. C. Tuttle
Rococo Coffin. Richard Brown
Rod of Anger. D. Nabarro
Rod of Justice. A. Skew
Rod of the Snake. V. Shortt
Rodent in Doubt. W. G. Tapply
Rodeo Murder Mystery. H. Pink
Roderick of Kildare. S. Cobb
Rodman the Boatsteerer, and other stories. L. Becke
Rodrigues Affair. J. Pattinson
Rogano. S. Knight
Roger Bennion's Double. H. Adams
Roger Quinney. P. H. Irving
Roger Sheringham and the Vane Mystery. A. Berkeley
Roger Sinclair's Treasure. N. Worth
Rogue. T. W. H. Crosland
Rogue. B. Mackinnon
Rogue. W. E. Norris
Rogue Aunt. J. N. Chance
Rogue Bear. Donald Seaman
Rogue by Compulsion. V. Bridges
Rogue Cop. W. P. McGivern
Rogue Cop. G. F. Newman
Rogue Diamond. J. B. Lynne
Rogue Eagle. J. McClure
Rogue Force. D. Pendleton
Rogue Haven. B. Home
Rogue Hercules. D. Pitts
Rogue in Ambush. H. Hill
Rogue in Love. T. Gallon
Rogue Justice. G. Household
Rogue Male. G. Household
Rogue of Afghanistan. W. M. Graydon
Rogue of Quality. Nicholas Carter
Rogue of Rye. W. W. Dixon
Rogue of the Racecourse. Anonymous
Rogue Ransome—Manhunter. Dan Morgan
Rogue Ransome—Racket Buster. Dan Morgan
Rogue Ransome—Triggerman. Dan Morgan
Rogue Royal. Gwyn Evans
Rogue Running. M. Procter
Rogue with a Past. R. Wesley

Rogue Worth Trapping. Nicholas Carter
Rogues. A. Sadler
Rogues. R. H. Sherard
Rogues and Company. I. A. R. Wylie
Rogues and Diamonds. S. Jepson
Rogues and Vagabonds. G. R. Sims
Rogue's Badge. C. N. Buck
Rogue's Castle. S. Stanley
Rogue's Coat. T. Du Bois
Rogue's Conscience. D. C. Murray
Rogues Fall Out. H. Adams
Rogues Fall Out. F. Warden
Rogue's Gambit. A. Caillou
Rogue's Gold. W. W. Lee
Rogue's Harbour. J. T. Story
Rogue's Harvest. N. Cromarty
Rogue's Haven. R. Bridges
Rogue's Heiress. T. Gallon
Rogue's Holiday. M. March
Rogues in Arcady. W. Magnay
Rogues in Clover. P. Wilde
Rogues in the Forest. C. T. Stoneham
Rogues' Island. B. Perowne
Rogue's Life. W. Collins
Rogues Ltd. C. R. Gull
Rogue's Luck. A. Wright
Rogues' March. G. Dilnot
Rogue's March. E. W. Hornung
Rogues' March. M. Turnbull
Rogue's March. W. T. Tyler
Rogue's Murder. W. Ard
Rogues' Nest. R. South
Rogues of Fortune. J. J. Chichester
Rogues of Ransom. G. H. Teed
Rogues of Society, and The Doctor of Duddlestone. G. F. Underhill
Rogues of the Desert. W. M. Graydon
Rogues of the North. A. M. Treynor
Rogues of the Racecourse. Andrew Gray
Rogues of the Stables. S. Hope
Rogues' Paradise. E. Pugh
Rogue's Progress. E. Oliver
Rogues Rampant. G. Ashe
Rogue's Ransom. G. Ashe
Rogue's Reach. Nicholas Carter
Rogues' Republic. G. H. Teed
Rogues' Syndicate. F. Froest
Rogue's Tragedy. B. Capes
Roker's Reef Affair. M. Cronin
Rokewood Tragedy. M. Pinkerton
Roland Yorke. H. Wood
Roles and Relations. D. Sarmiento
Roll Film Mystery. M. Poole
Roll, Jordan, Roll. D. P. Clark
Roll of Honour. J. Gardner
Roll-Top Desk Mystery. C. Wells
Rollerball. P. McCutchan
Rollercoaster. B. Wohl
Rollicking Rogue. J. McCulley
Rolling Heads. A. M. Stein
Rolling Road. B. Cable
Rolling Stone. J. Hartley
Rolling Stone. P. Wentworth
Rolling Stones. O. Henry
Rolling Thunder. John Smith
Rolling Vengeance. B. Ham
Rollo of Normandy. S. Cobb
Roman Adventure. M. MacKintosh
Roman Circus. F. O'Neill
Roman Collar Detective. G. Johnson
Roman Death. J. O'Hagan
Roman Enigma. W. F. Murphy
Roman Gold. Michael Lewis
Roman Hat Mystery. E. Queen
Roman Magic. H. Fleetwood
Roman Mystery. R. Bagot
Roman Ring. C. P. Bracken
Roman Solution. W. Henley
Roman Way. G. V. McFadden
Romance at Hillyard House. K. Norris
Romance at Random. H. B. M. Watson
Romance Comes to Scotland Yard. H. Black
Romance in Crimson. O. R. Cohen
Romance in the First Degree. O. R. Cohen

Romance of a Common Life. Waters
Romance of a Coward. M. Dekobra
Romance of a Madhouse. A. M. Meadows
Romance of a Maid of Honour. R. Marsh
Romance of a Million Dollars. E. Dejeans
Romance of a Musical Bachelor. G. Penworth
Romance of a Nautch Girl. Mrs. F. Penny
Romance of a Pretty Girl. R. De Pont-Jest
Romance of a Queen. W. Chesney
Romance of a Salvation Army Girl. Old Sleuth
Romance of a Spy. E.7
Romance of an Alter Ego. L. Bryce
Romance of Elaine. A. B. Reeve
Romance of Heelerism. A. S. Gifford
Romance of His Life. M. Cholmondeley
Romance of Lilies. C. H. Montague
Romance of Nikko Cheyne. R. Pertwee
Romance of Poisons. R. Cromie
Romance of Politics. A. Upward
Romance of Smyrna. Mrs. R. P. M. Yorke
Romance of the Castle. J. Elson
Romance of the Forest. A. Radcliffe
Romance of the Ruby. G. Campbell
Romance of the Woods. F. Whishaw
Romance of Wastdale. A. E. W. Mason
Romance on the Rhine. Elsie Lee
Romances in Red. A. Castle
Romances of Crime. J. M'Levy
Romances of Mayfair. Anonymous
Romances of the Law. W. T. E. Francillon
Romances of the Old Seraglio. H. N. Crellin
Romances of the Road. Thormanby
Romanesque. R. McInerny
Romano Castle. L. Watkins
Romanoff Jewels. M. Grant
Romanov Connection. W. M. Green
Romanov Ransom. A. A. Thompson
Romanov Succession. B. Garfield
Romantic Assignment. Elsie Lee
Romantic History of Dhoondiah. C. F. Powell
Romantic Journey. N. Buckingham
Romantic Road. G. Rawlence
Romantic Stories of Famous Families. Anonymous
Romantic Stories of the Legal Profession. R. E. Francillon
Romantics. M. R. Rinehart
Romany Curse. S. Somers
Rome Express. Ruth Alexander
Rome Express. A. Griffiths
Romelle. W. R. Burnett
Romeo Flag. C. Hougan
Romeo's Tune. M. Timlin
Rommany. F. Hurd
Rommel Plot. J. Tarrant
Rommel's Gold. Maggie Davis
Romp in Green Heat. A. Sewart
Romula, the Dedicated. K. Kimbrough
Ronald o' the Moors. G. E. Locke
Ronald Standish. H. C. McNeile
Ronald the Fusilier. F. M. Peacock
Ronin. M. Christian
Roof. Maurice Walker
Roof. D. Whitelaw
Rooftops. Tom Lewis
Rooftops. R. Tine
Rook Takes Knight. S. Palmer
Rookery. H. C. Rae
Rookery Detective. Anonymous
Rookies. C. Parker
Rook's Gambit. S. Rattray
Rook's Nest. G. W. Appleton
Rooksmiths. S. Truss
Rookwood. W. H. Ainsworth
Rookwood. G. D. Pitt
Room at the Bottom. J. L. Potter
Room at the Hotel Ambre. A. Armstrong
Room Beneath the Stairs. K. St. Clair
Room, Board and Death. Marc Miller
Room Five. H. Drummond
Room for a Body. Josephine Bell
Room for a Ghost. Winifred Duke
Room for Murder. T. B. Dewey
Room for Murder. D. M. Disney
Room 14. M. Annesley

Title Index

Room in Camden Town. David Lynn
Room in Quiver Court. J. Cassells
Room in Soho. J. Wingrave
Room in the Tower. J. Blackmore
Room in the Tower and other stories. E. F. Benson
Room Mate. J. Wein
Room Nineteen. F. Warden
Room Number 6. J. J. Farjeon
Room Number 3 and other stories. A. K. Green
Room of Mirrors. Nicholas Carter
Room of Mirrors. H. Flowerdew
Room of Secrets. C. Farr
Room of Secrets. W. LeQueux
Room on Floor One. B. E. London
Room Opposite, and other tales of mystery and imagination. F. M. Mayor
Room Service. Alan Williams
Room 13. E. Wallace
Room 37. H. Howard
Room to Die In. E. Queen
Room to Swing. E. Lacy
Room 12a. A. Marsh
Room Under the Stairs. Herman Landon
Room Upstairs. Mildred Davis
Room Upstairs. M. Dickens
Room with Dark Mirrors. V. Johnston
Room with No Escape. A. Barber
Room with the Iron Shutters. A. Wynne
Room with the Tassels. C. Wells
Room Without a Key. W. E. D. Ross
Rooming House. B. Roueche
Roommate. J. Wein
Rooms at Mrs. Oliver's. K. Kellow
Rooney. C. Cookson
Rooney's Gold. I. Lambot
Root and Branch. N. Tranter
Root of All Evil. E. Ferrars
Root of All Evil. J. S. Fletcher
Root of All Evil. F. Marryat
Root of All Evil. R. Neidhardt
Root of All Evil. Dell Shannon
Root of All Evil. M. Sproxton
Root of All Evil. I. Stark
Root of Evil. J. Cross
Root of Evil. E. K. Goldthwaite
Root of Evil. D. Haring
Root of His Evil. W. Ard
Root of His Evil. J. M. Cain
Rooted Sorrow. P. M. Hubbard
Roots of Fury. I. Shulman
Rope. P. Hamilton
Rope. A. Hitchcock
Rope Began to Hang the Butcher. C. W. Grafton
Rope Broke. D. Barr
Rope by Arrangement. H. Clandon
Rope-Dancer. V. Marchetti
Rope Enough. J. S. Strange
Rope Fodder. O. Thomas
Rope for a Convict. R. C. Woodthorpe
Rope for a Gal Called Lou. R. Buxton
Rope for a Lady. B. Sarto
Rope for a Redhead. Carter Brown
Rope for an Ape. D. Chambers
Rope for Breakfast. A. Spiller
Rope for Christmas. F. Griffin
Rope for General Dietz. J. Rossiter
Rope for the Baron. Anthony Morton
Rope for the Hanging. N. Morland
Rope for the Judge. H. Hawton
Rope of Sand. F. Bonnamy
Rope of Sand. C. Franklin
Rope of Sand. P. Traill
Rope of Slender Threads. Nicholas Carter
Rope Over Jezebel. R. Harrison
Rope to Spare. P. MacDonald
Rope Waits. L. Dean
Rope Which Hangs. G. Fairlie
Ropedancer's Fall. M. K. Lorens
Rope's End. P. Hamilton
Rope's End—Rogue's End. E. C. R. Lorac
Ropespinner Conspiracy. M. M. Thomas
Rosa at Ten O'Clock. M. Denevi
Rosalie. T. P. Prest
Rosalie Du Pont. Emerson Bennett

Rosalin. F. V. Metz
Rosalind de Tracy. E. S. Tomlins
Rosalind Runs Wild. E. Ellison
Rosaline Woodbridge. H. M. Jones
Rosalviva. G. Fletcher
Rosamunda. Marjory Hall
Rosario. M. K. Robertson
Rosario Murder Case. Roland Daniel
Rosario, the Female Monk. M. G. Lewis
Rosary Murders. W. X. Kienzle
Rosa's Dilemma. Michael Underwood
Rose and Chrysanthemum. C. Dawe
Rose and Grey. L. Heilgers
Rose and the Key. J. S. Le Fanu
Rose Bath Riddle. A. M. Rud
Rose Brocade. P. C. De Crispigny
Rose Can Kill. J. Ingersol
Rose Exterminator. W. Carney
Rose for Ana Maria. F. Yerby
Rose for This Day's Madness. A. Longfellow
Rose from the Dead. P. Ernst
Rose Garden. K. Palka
Rose Geranium. Anonymous
Rose in Darkness. C. Brand
Rose Lodge. H. Wood
Rose Medallion. James Grant
Rose-Mount Castle. M. J. Young
Rose of Algiers. C. H. Bullivant
Rose of Allandale. G. Stables
Rose of Blenheim. M. Gerard
Rose of Death. W. S. Masterson
Rose of Granada. B. Winter
Rose of Kantara. A. Richardson
Rose of Life. M. E. Braddon
Rose of Tibet. L. Davidson
Rose Petal Murders. C. G. Givens
Rose Rent. Ellis Peters
Rose, Rose, Where Are You? R. Ellerbeck
Rose Seymour. N. Buntline
Rose Tree. J. Broderick
Rose Window. S. Blanc
Roseanna. M. Sjowall
Rosebud. J. Hemingway
Rosebury. L. T. Meade
Rosecrest Cell. V. Caspary
Roseheath. K. Troy
Rosella. M. Charlton
Rosemarie. E. Kuby
Rosemary for Death. Dexter Muir
Rosemary for Remembrance. J. F. Martins
Rosemary for Remembrance. S. Nichols
Rosemary for Remembrance. J. Thomson
Rosemary King, Government Girl. T. Holloway
Rosemary's Baby. I. Levin
Rosery Folk. G. M. Fenn
Roses Are Dead. L. D. Estleman
Roses from a Haunted Garden. J. F. Webb
Rose's Last Summer. M. Millar
Roses Love Sunshine. D. M. Pierce
Roses of Constant. B. Campbell
Rosevean. I. Bromige
Rosewell Heritage. M. F. Ford
Roshanara of the Seevn Cities. W. R. Foran
Rosie Among Thorns. A. McDonald
Ross Forgery. W. H. Hallahan
Rossano. G. Lett
Rossetti and other tales. T. Thurston
Rossi Killings. M. Stall
Rostnikov's Corpse. S. M. Kaminsky
Rostron Outfit. Dan Morgan
Rostron Outfit in Chicago. Dean Morgan
Rostron Outfit in Mexico. Dean Morgan
Rostron Outfit in Rio. Dean Morgan
Rostron Outfit in Texas. Dean Morgan
Rostron Outfit—Undercover Agents. Dean Morgan
Rosy Death. T. S. King
Rosy Pastor. N. Fitzgerald
Rothby. Marilyn Ross
Rothhaven. W. E. D. Ross
Rothschild Conversion. P. Buckman
Rotten Apples. E. P. Green
Rotten Deal. Demouzon
Rotten with Honour. Derek Robinson
Rotterdam Delivery. E. A. O'Neill

Rotunda. R. R. Siegrist
Rouge. H. McFall
Rough Air. E. Haycox
Rough Cider. P. Lovesey
Rough Company. D. Hamilton
Rough Cut. N. Cain
Rough Cut. Bruce Cook
Rough Cut. E. Gorman
Rough Cut. D. Lambert
Rough Cut. A. McCullough
Rough Cut. G. McGill
Rough Deal. W. Winward
Rough Going. G. Goodchild
Rough Justice. M. E. Braddon
Rough Justice. J. Oster
Rough Justice. Keith Peterson
Rough on Rats. W. Francis
Rough Passage. Gavin Douglas
Rough Passage. G. Hackforth-Jones
Rough Passage. A. Wright
Rough Passages. A. Perrin
Rough Red. M. Sylvester
Rough Seas to Sunrise. J. Ames
Rough Shoot. G. Household
Rough Shooting. P. C. Wren
Rough Sketch. R. Sylvester
Rough Trade. A. Fowles
Rough Trade. L. Rand
Rough Treatment. John Harvey
Roughcut. E. Gorman
Roughneck. J. Thompson
Roumanian Circle. Lionel Black
Roumanian Envoy. G. N. Philips
Roumanian Operation. J. Rosenberger
Round Dozen. E. Cadell
Round Robin. G. W. Bain
Round Table Murders. P. Baron
Round Table Murders. Adrian Reynolds
Round the Block. Anonymous
Round the Clock at Volari's. W. R. Burnett
Round the Fire Stories. A. C. Doyle
Round the Next Corner. Rolf Bennett
Round the Red Lamp. A. C. Doyle
Round the World for a Quarter. Nicholas Carter
Round Tower. C. F. Barrett
Round Trip. D. Tracy
Round Trip in the Year 2000. W. W. Cook
Round Trip to Nowhere. J. T. MacCargo
Round Voyage. J. R. Wilson
Roundabout. M. Allwright
Roundhead Retreat. John Sanders
Roupell Mystery. A. Granville
Rouse the Demon. C. Weston
Rout of the Oliver Samuelsons. H. C. McNeile
Route of Evil. S. Pace
Route of the Red Gold. D. J. Marlowe
Routine Investigation. H. Howard
Roving Hearts. K. Prichard
Rowan Tree Crop. E. Pollack
Rowforest. A. Weekes
Rowforest Plot. A. Weekes
Rowleston. B. Riefe
Rox Hall Illuminated. P. Paul
Roxana. D. Defoe
Roxy by Proxy. H. Janson
Roy of Roy's Court. W. Westall
Royal Abduction. A. W. Upfield
Royal Affair and other stories. G. Boothby
Royal Alliance. C. Dawe
Royal Bed for a Corpse. Max Murray
Royal Bluejacket. F. T. Jane
Royal Box. F. P. Keyes
Royal Chase. C. Buckley
Royal Conspiracy. M. Cummings
Royal Exchange. J. M. Cobban
Royal Exchange. H. M. Raleigh
Royal Flush. M. Creighton
Royal Flush. D. Stivers
Royal Flush Murders. G. Verner
Royal Game. S. Vaughan
Royal Game. S. Zweig
Royal Heritage. R. Pertwee
Royal Hoax. F. Whishaw
Royal Indiscretion. R. Marsh

Royal Ishmael. Winifred Duke
Royal Navy Days, and Afterwards. Anonymous
Royal Outlaw. S. Cobb
Royal Pain. R. Merwin
Royal Prisoner. P. Souvestre
Royal Rascal. A. Griffiths
Royal Special, and other stories. E. Burton
Royal Street. F. Swann
Royal Thief. Nicholas Carter
Royal Twins. T. P. Prest
Royal Wrong. F. M. White
Royce of the Royal Mounted. Amos Moore
Royce Prospect. B. Hirschfeld
Royston Affair. D. M. Devine
Rub-a-Dub-Dub. R. L. Fish
Rub-Out Specialty. Griff
Rub Out the Redhead. M. Brody
Rubbed Out. R. Barnett
Rubber Band. R. Stout
Rubber Mask. F. L. Stickeny
Rubber Smugglers. G. H. Teed
Rubber Stamp, and A Matter of Voice. H. C. McNeile
Rubberface. G. Stanley
Rubberneck. B. Shannon
Rubbish. S. Barrett
Rube Burrows League. M. Manley
Rubicon. Stuart Hall
Rubicon One. D. Jones
Rubies, Emeralds and Diamonds. B. Chetwynd
Rubout at the Onyx. H. P. Jeffers
Ruby. F. Lorenz
Ruby. J. Siegal
Ruby. K. Stewart
Ruby Beyond Price. G. Campbell
Ruby Cup. L. K. Vincent
Ruby Heart of Kishgar. A. W. Marchmont
Ruby Maclaine. J. Roeburt
Ruby of a Thousand Dreams. Roland Daniel
Ruby Pin. Nicholas Carter
Ruby Red Death. Nick Carter
Ruby Sweetwater and the Ringo Kid. S. Bart
Ruby Sword. B. Mitford
Rudder Grangers Abroad and other stories. F. R. Stockton
Rude Awakening. H. Brinton
Rude Justice. L. Austen-Eligh
Rudolph and Adelaide. M. A. Marchant
Rue Bargain. R. M. Gilchrist
Rue de Bac. T. Foster
Rue the Day. M. Alan
Rue the Reservoir. Annabelle Melville
Ruffian Boy. Sarah Wilkinson
Ruffles. L. T. Meade
Rufin's Legacy. W. Gerrare
Rugged Trail. H. L. Floyd
Rugged Way. E. W. Elkington
Ruin. E. S. West
Ruined by Love. A. Lamour
Ruined Map. K. Abe
Ruins of Avondale Priory. I. Kelly
Ruins of Love. D. Mai
Ruins of Rigonda. H. Saint Victor
Rule of Night. T. Hoyle
Rule of Three. Douglas Reed
Ruled by Radio. R. L. Hadfield
Ruled off the Turf. Grace M. White
Rules Don't Apply. R. Hamilton
Rules of Engagement. B. Freemantle
Rules of Prey. J. Sandford
Rules of the Game. B. Fitzpatrick
Rules of the Game. S. Morrow
Rules of the Game. G. Simenon
Rules of the Knife Fight. Walter Walker
Rules of the Road. L. K. Truscott, IV
Ruling Passion. S. Barlay
Ruling Passion. R. Hill
Ruling Passion. Judith Michael
Ruling Passion. J. Willing, Jr.
Ruling the Planets. M. E. Burton
Ruling Vice. P. Trent
Rum Alley. A. O. Pollard
Rum and Coca-Cola Murders. Wenzell Brown
Rum Row Murders. C. R. Jones

Rum Week. N. Tranter
Rumble. H. Ellison
Rumble Murders. M. Deal
Rumble on the Docks. F. Paley
Rumbo. C. Mercati
Rumfy. V. Gordon
Rummies. P. Benchley
Rumor Hath It. C. Hale
Rumour at Nightfall. G. Greene
Rumpelstiltskin. E. McBain
Rumpole. J. Mortimer
Rumpole a la Carte. J. Mortimer
Rumpole and the Age of Miracles. J. Mortimer
Rumpole and the Golden Thread. J. Mortimer
Rumpole for the Defense. J. Mortimer
Rumpole of the Bailey. J. Mortimer
Rumpole's Last Case. J. Mortimer
Rumpole's Return. J. Mortimer
Run. M. Shedd
Run! P. Wentworth
Run a Golden Mile. C. Joyce
Run Away to Murder. J. York
Run Before the Wind. Stuart Woods
Run, Brother, Run!. T. Brandt
Run by Night. H. Innes
Run, Chico, Run. Wenzell Brown
Run Corpse, Run. G. Pember-Hiller
Run Down. Robert Garrett
Run Far, Run Fast. L. A. Goldstone
Run, Fool, Run. F. Gruber
Run for Blood. G. Warren
Run for Cover. J. Welcome
Run for Doom. H. Kane
Run for Lover. H. Janson
Run for the Money. Dale Clark
Run for the Money. R. Colby
Run for Your Death. H. Hossent
Run for Your Life. B. Abercrombie
Run for Your Life. C. Dekker
Run for Your Life. B. Fischer
Run for Your Life. R. Foley
Run for Your Life! S. Noel
Run for Your Life! M. Stark
Run for Your Money. G. Nyland
Run for Your Money. H. Seymour
Run from Death. J. P. Duff
Run from Nightmare. M. O'Callaghan
Run from the Hunter. K. Grantland
Run from the River. L. Barth
Run from the Sheep. E. Capit
Run If You Can. O. Dudley
Run If You Can. J. Madison
Run If You're Guilty. J. McKimmey
Run in Diamonds. A. Saxon
Run, Jack, Run. Tom Logan
Run, Killer, Run. N. Deemster
Run, Killer, Run. W. C. Gault
Run, Killer, Run. L. White
Run, Lady, Run! D. Haring
Run Lethal. R. Stark
Run Like a Thief. M. Niall
Run Man Run. C. Himes
Run, Mann, Run! J. Keenan
Run, Mongoose. B. Wilkinson
Run, Nurse, Run. J. Carew
Run, Robber, Run. R. A. Anderson
Run...Run...Run. F. Taubes
Run, Sara, Run. A. Worboys
Run Scared. M. G. Eberhart
Run, Shadow, Run. H. B. Cave
Run, Sheep, Run. G. Sager
Run, Spy, Run. Nick Carter
Run, Thief, Run. F. Gruber
Run, Thief, Run. J. Manchester
Run to Death. R. Kelston
Run to Death. P. Quentin
Run to Earth. M. E. Braddon
Run to Earth. Nicholas Carter
Run to Earth. P. Grayson
Run to Evil. L. Egan
Run to Ground. R. Jocelyn
Run to Ground. D. Pendleton
Run to Morning. J. Graham
Run Tough, Run Hard. C. Bingham

Run, Traitor, Run. R. Pierce
Run When I Say Go. H. Waugh
Run While You Can. W. Woolfolk
Run with the Fox. Craig Cooper
Run with the Hare. K. Abbey
Run with the Killer. J. Armour
Run with the Weasel. R. Wilkes-Hunter
Runagate. C. C. Lowis
Runagates Club. J. Buchan
Runaround. B. Freemantle
Runaround. V. Warren
Runaway. M. Halliday
Runaway. N. Holland
Runaway. Richard Hubbard
Runaway. R. Marsten
Runaway. Old Sleuth
Runaway. J. Peter
Runaway. C. Stratton
Runaway. Clarissa Watson
Runaway Bag. A. P. Terhune
Runaway Black. R. Marsten
Runaway Corpse. James Warren
Runaway from Love. Ronas Randall
Runaway Home! K. Booton
Runaway Man. E. Trevor
Runaway Match. H. Wood
Runaway Pigeon. L. Edgley
Runaway Wife. S. O'Donnell
Rundown. J. Magnuson
Rundown. F. Woods
Rung In. A. Wright
Runner in the Street. J. Grady
Runner Is Red. J. B. Kovalsky
Runner Stumbles. M. Stitt
Running. R. Shaw
Running Amok. G. M. Fenn
Running Blind. D. Bagley
Running Deep. R. Petrie
Running Dog. D. De Lillo
Running Down a Double. Anonymous
Running Duck. P. Gosling
Running Fight. W. H. Osborne
Running Fix. T. Gibbs
Running Free and other stories. Countess Barcynska
Running Hot. D. Pendleton
Running Killer. W. J. Elliott
Running Lions. J. D. White
Running Man. R. Bachman
Running Man. B. Benson
Running Man. L. Dietz
Running Man. Anthony Ferguson
Running Man. W. Goldman
Running Man. W. A. Harbinson
Running Nun. B. Flynn
Running of Beasts. B. Pronzini
Running of the Spies. J. N. Chance
Running Sand. Jonathan Wade
Running Scared. H. Brand
Running Scared. J. Burmeister
Running Scared. Craig Cooper
Running Scared. Gregory McDonald
Running Scared. B. McKnight
Running Scared. J. Mathewson
Running Skeletons. K. Robeson
Running Special. F. Packard
Running Spy. J. Milton
Running Target. S. Frazee
Running Target. G. Seymour
Running the Blockade. W. H. Thomes
Running the Gauntlet. E. Yates
Running Thursday. P. Hastings
Running Tide. J. R. Gould
Running Water. A. E. W. Mason
Running Wild. J. G. Ballard
Running Wild. A. Trew
Running Woman. P. Carlon
Runway to Death. C. M. Filgate
Runway Zero-Eight. J. Castle
Runyon First and Last. D. Runyon
Rupert Alison; or, Broken Lights. G. Forde
Rupert Godwin. M. E. Braddon
Rupert Hall. H. Wood
Ruse of the Vanished Women. V. Gielgud
Rush. K. Wozencraft

Title Index

Rush Hour Crime. A. Skene
Rush of Blood. H. T. Smith
Rush on the Ultimate. H. R. F. Keating
Rushmoreland Rubies. Wynne Smith
Russian Coward. F. Whishaw
Russian Crucifix. R. Freeborn
Russian Enigma. C. Egleton
Russian Hi-Jack. N. Shore
Russian Hide-and-Seek. K. Amis
Russian House. J. Le Carre
Russian Intelligence. M. Moorcock
Russian Interpreter. M. Frayn
Russian Judas. F. Whishaw
Russian Leave. Anthony Stuart
Russian Professor. A. Gilchrist
Russian Roulette. T. Ardies
Russian Roulette. A. Bloomfield
Russian Roulette. R. Freeborn
Russian Roulette. J. Mitchell
Russian Roulette. B. Picton
Russian Spring. D. Jones
Russian Woman. T. Hyman
Rust of Murder. J. March
Rustle of Spring. K. Lindsay
Rustler's Roost. W. C. Tuttle
Rustler's Venom. W. W. Lee
Rustling Death. K. Robeson
Rustling End. D. G. Browne
Rusty Thumbs a Ride. C. Regan
Ruth. V. Caspary
Ruth Anstey. J. Middlemass
Ruth of the U.S.A. E. Balmer
Ruth, the Unsuspecting. K. Kimbrough
Rutherford. E. Fawcett
Ruthless. Raymond Marshall
Ruthless Avenger. Mrs. Conney
Ruthless Enemy. F. Struan
Ruthless Ones. L. Moody
Rutland Mystery. C. F. Gregg
Rutland Place. A. Perry
Rx for Murder. J. Layhew
Ryan Affair. D. MacDonald
Ryan Girl. E. Goulding
Ryan's Rules. E. Leonard
Ryecroft Verdict. D. Whitelaw
Ryerson Mystery. P. Phelps
Ryfka. P. Alexander
Rynox. P. MacDonald
Rynox Murder Mystery. P. MacDonald
Rynox Mystery. P. MacDonald

S.O.S. W. W. Ellis
S.O.S. S. Horler
S.O.S. Queenie and other stories. O. Sandys
S—Portrait of a Spy. I. Adams
S.P.Q.R. P. H. Bonner
SPQR. J. M. Roberts
S.P.Y.S. T. R. Joyce
S—Portrait of a Spy. I. Adams
SS-GB. L. Deighton
S.S. Murder. Q. Patrick
S.S. Mystery. L. A. Knight
S-S-S-Sh! K. Carmel
SWF Seeks Same. J. Lutz
Saba's Treasure. D. M. Douglass
Sabath Quest. I. Foster
Sabbath Slayer. B. Heygate
Saberdene Variations. Thomas Maxwell
Saberlegs. E. Pace
Sabine. N. Freeling
Sable in the Rain. W. E. D. Ross
Sable Lorcha. H. Hazeltine
Sable Messenger. F. Vivian
Sable Night. A. Roy
Sables Spell Trouble. S. Mitchell
Sabotage. C. F. Adams
Sabotage. J. Creasey
Sabotage. R. C. Elliott
Sabotage. O. John
Sabotage. F. Knebel
Sabotage at Sea. John Davies
Sabotage at Sea. C. Lowe
Sabotage at Sea. W. R. D. McLaughlin
Sabotage Broadcast. H. Innes

Sabotage Murder Mystery. M. Allingham
Sabotage Unlimited. P. Groom
Saboteurs. June Drummond
Saboteurs. J. W. Mason
Sabre Squadron. S. Raven
Sabre-Tooth. P. O'Donnell
Sabres on the Sand. G. Household
Sac Mau, Victor Charlie. J. Cain
Sack of Monte Carlo. W. Frith
Sackcloth and Broadcloth. J. Middlemass
Sacked City. G. R. Preedy
Sacrament of Death. S. Esmond
Sacred and Profane. F. Kellerman
Sacred Cave. J. D. Powell
Sacred City. W. W. Sayer
Sacred Crescents. W. Westall
Sacred Eye. J. Creasey
Sacred Goblet. Anonymous
Sacred Herb. F. Hume
Sacred Monster. D. E. Westlake
Sacred Shaft. J. Weatherhead
Sacred Sins. Nora Roberts
Sacred Trusts. B. Atlee
Sacrife. R. P. Morrison
Sacrifice. G. Masterton
Sacrifice. C. H. Merrett
Sacrifice. Blake Mitchell
Sacrifice. F. E. Penny
Sacrifice. G. Simenon
Sacrifice. H. Sutton
Sacrifice. P. Trent
Sacrifice & Co. Winifred Graham
Sacrifice Play. C. Haynes
Sacrificial Ground. T. H. Cook
Sacrificial Pawn. F. Ryck
Sacrilege Farm. M. Hart
Sad Adventurers. M. Rutledge
Sad and Savage Dying. P. Audemars
Sad and Tender Flesh. S. D. Frances
Sad Cypress. A. Christie
Sad-Eyed Seductress. Carter Brown
Sad Road to the Sea. G. Kersh
Sad Song Singing. T. B. Dewey
Sad Sontag Plays His Hunch. W. C. Tuttle
Sad, Sudden Death of My Fair Lady. S. Forbes
Sad Variety. N. Blake
Sad Wind from the Sea. Harry Patterson
Saddle a Killer. N. Wylie
Saddle and Sabre. H. Smart
Saddle & Steel. Lord Dunalley
Saddle Tramps. Stuart Hall
Saddled with Murder. S. Miles
Saddleroom Murder. N. K. McKechnie
Sadie, Don't Cry Now. H. Janson
Sadie Plays Rough. D. Saxon
Sadie Shapiro in Maimi. R. K. Smith
Sadie Socks the Saboteurs. C. George
Sadie Swings the Blues. B. Shannon
Sadie When She Died. E. McBain
Sadist. E. T. Hamill
Safari. E. Rhodes
Safari for Spies. Nick Carter
Safari with Fear! R. Hardinge
Safari with Fear. J. York
Safe at Home. Alison Gordon
Safe Behind Bars. Andrew Hall
Safe Conduct. J. England
Safe Custody. D. Yates
Safe Haven. F. Yariv
Safe House. J. Cleary
Safe House. D. Kartun
Safe Job. D. Vallance
Safe Number Sixty-Nine. J. S. Fletcher
Safe Place. A. Rider
Safe Road. K. N. Burt
Safe Secret. H. Carmichael
Safekeeping. G. McDonald
Safely to the Grave. Margaret Yorke
Safer Dead. J. H. Chase
Safer Than Life. R. R. Petersunne
Safety Catch. J. Summers
Safety First Murders. E. Radford
Safety Last. G. Goodchild
Safety Last. J. Gray

Safety Pin. J. S. Fletcher
Saffron Robe. J. Browning
Saffron Summer. M. Summerton
Saffron's War. F. E. Smith
Saga of a Scoundrel. P. Barrington
Saga of Halfaday Creek. J. B. Hendryx
Saga of the Cliffs. E. L. Long
Sagas of the Mounted Police. W. B. Mowery
Sage-Brush Stories. F. Niven
Sagomi Gambit. J. Evans
Sahara Road. S. Harvester
Sahara Strike. D. J. Cleary
Sahara Survival. Burt Cole
Said Dr. Spendlove. Hilda Lewis
Said the Blind Man. J. Oldfield
Said the Spider to the Fly. R. Hugill
Said the Spider to the Fly. R. Shattuck
Said the Spider to the Spy. F. Carmichael
Said with Flowers. A. Nash
Saigon. Nick Carter
Saigon Commandos. J. Cain
Saigon Merchant. J. Pattinson
Saigon Singer. V. W. Mason
Saigon Slaughter. J. Buchanan
Saigon Slaughter. J. Lansing
Sail a Crooked Ship. N. Benchley
Sail Into Silence. D. Marble
Sailcloth Shroud. C. Williams
Sailor and the Widow. E. L. Long
Sailor and the Widow. Seafarer
Sailor, Take Warning. K. Roos
Sailor, Take Warning. R. Sale
Sailors Do Care. Sinbad
Sailors' Knots. W. W. Jacobs
Sailor's Leave. Brian Moore
Sailor's Luck. B. Heatter
Sailor's Rendezvous. G. Simenon
Saint Abroad. L. Charteris
Saint: Ace of Knaves. L. Charteris
Saint and Cynic. A. Simmons
Saint and Mr. Teal. L. Charteris
Saint and the Fiction Makers. L. Charteris
Saint and the Hapsburg Necklace. L. Charteris
Saint and the Last Hero. L. Charteris
Saint and the People Importers. L. Charteris
Saint and the Sizzling Saboteur. L. Charteris
Saint and the Templar Treasure. L. Charteris
Saint Around the World. L. Charteris
Saint at a Thieves' Picnic. L. Charteris
Saint at Large. L. Charteris
St. Bernard's Priory. M. Harley
Saint Bids Diamonds. L. Charteris
Saint Bodolph's Priory. T. C. H. Curties
Saint Brooklyn. S. Whalen
St. Cadix Case. E. Miller
Saint Catherine's Wheel. J. Griffin
Saint Cleans Up. L. Charteris
Saint Closes the Case. L. Charteris
St. Cloud Affair. B. Baskerville
St. Cuthbert's Tower. F. Warden
Saint Errant. L. Charteris
Saint Eustace and the Albatross. D. Ryan
Saint-Fiacre Affair. G. Simenon
St. George Manor. R. M. Sears
Saint Goes On. L. Charteris
Saint Goes West. L. Charteris
Saint: Good As Gold. L. Charteris
Saint in Action. L. Charteris
Saint in England. L. Charteris
Saint in Europe. L. Charteris
Saint in London. L. Charteris
Saint in Miami. L. Charteris
Saint in Mufti. C. Dawe
Saint in New York. L. Charteris
Saint in Pursuit. L. Charteris
Saint in the Sun. L. Charteris
Saint in Trouble. L. Charteris
Saint Intervenes. L. Charteris
St. Ives. O. Bleeck
St. Ives Murders. R. Wincor
Saint Jack. P. Theroux
St. John of Honeylea. G. I. Whitham
St. John's Baptism. W. Babula
St. Lawrence Run. S. F. Wilcox

S

S

St. Louis Showdown. D. Pendleton
St. Lucian Affair. S. Sonny
Saint Maker. L. Holton
Saint-Malo Mystery. J. Maske
St. Martin's Eve. H. Wood
St. Maur. A. Sergeant
Saint Meets His Match. L. Charteris
Saint Meets the Tiger. L. Charteris
Saint Mike. J. Oster
Saint Mudd. Steve Thayer
Saint Nicholas 'Eve and other tales. M. C. Rowsell
Saint of the Speedway. R. Cullum
Saint on Guard. L. Charteris
Saint on TV. L. Charteris
Saint on the Spanish Main. L. Charteris
Saint Overboard. L. Charteris
Saint Peter's Fair. Ellis Peters
St. Peter's Finger. G. Mitchell
Saint Peter's Plot. D. Lambert
Saint Plays with Fire. L. Charteris
Saint Returns. L. Charteris
Saint Sees It Through. L. Charteris
Saint Steps In. L. Charteris
Saint—The Brighter Buccaneer. L. Charteris
Saint—The Happy Highwayman. L. Charteris
Saint to the Rescue. L. Charteris
Saint: Two in One. L. Charteris
St. Valentine's Day Massacre. B. O'Hara
Saint Valentine's Day Murders. R. D. Edwards
St. Valentine's Night. A. M. Greeley
Saint vs. Scotland Yard. L. Charteris
Saint—Wanted for Murder. L. Charteris
Saints Are Sinister. B. Flynn
Saint's Getaway. L. Charteris
Saintsbury Affair. R. Doubleday
Sakhalin Breakout. J. Hild
Sakkara. N. Barber
Saladin! A. Osmond
Salamander. M. L. West
Salamander Chill. Roy Lewis
Salamander Sword. L. Wilkinson
Salamander Touch. Ivan Roe
Salamandra Glass. A. W. Mykel
Salang. S. Gall
Salazar Grant. E. L. Withers
Sale of Lot 236. M. Delahaye
Salekov Kill. G. Richards
Salem Chapel. Mrs. Oliphant
Salesman of Death. C. Leader
Salisbury Manuscript. W. M. Green
Sally. N. Baroni
Sally. E. V. Cunningham
Sally. W. B. M. Ferguson
Sally of Scotland Yard. L. Gribble
Sally of the Underworld. Roland Daniel
Sally's in the Alley. N. Davis
Salmon in the Soup. Meg O'Brien
Salome Syndrome. A. Sewart
Saloon Bar. F. Harvey, Jr.
Salt and Pepper. Alex Austin
Salt Cat Bank. A. Sax
Salt for the Tiger. W. C. Tuttle
Salt Is Leaving. J. B. Priestley
Salt Mine. D. Lippincott
Salt of the Earth. F. M. White
Salt Seas and Sailormen. F. W. Wallace
Salted Almonds. F. Anstey
Salter's Folly. A. Marsden
Saltmaker. B. Reiss
Saltmarsh Murders. G. Mitchell
Salty Waters. Stephen Murray
Salute Blue Mask. Anthony Morton
Salute for the Baron. Anthony Morton
Salute from a Dead Man. Donald MacKenzie
Salute Inspector Flagg. J. Cassells
Salute Mr. Sandyman. Neill Graham
Salute the Dreamer. W. M. Duncan
Salute the Picaroon. J. Cassells
Salute the Toff. J. Creasey
Salute to Bazarada and other stories. S. Rohmer
Salute to Blackshirt. R. Graeme
Salute to Murder. Neill Graham
Salute to Murder. R. P. Koehler
Salute to the Gods. Malcolm Campbell

Salute to Tomorrow. J. Nicholas
Salvage. R. S. Porteous
Salvage. H. Smart
Salvage for the Saint. L. Charteris
Salvage Job. Robert MacLeod
Salvage of the Sea. W. M. Graydon
Salvage Pirates. G. Chester
Salvation. A. Askew
Salvation of Pisco Gabar and other stories. G. Household
Salvation Peddler. J. Marcus
Salvator. P. Gibbon
Salvatore. P. Tabori
Salving of a Derelict. M. Drake
Salzberg Affair. J. D. White
Salzberg Connection. Helen MacInnes
Sam Benedict: Cast the First Stone. Elsie Lee
Sam Briggs: His Book. Richard Marsh
Sam Casanova. M. Catto
SAM 7. R. Cox
Sam Small Flies Again. Eric Knight
Samain. M. E. Atkins
Samantha. J. Carew
Samantha. E. V. Cunningham
Samantha. D. Eden
Samara. N. Lewis
Samarai Affair. A. Behrend
Samaritan. C. Brenchley
Samaritan. P. Johnson
Samaritan. P. Van Rjndt
Samarkand Dimension. D. Wise
Same Difference. H. Janson
Same Lie Twice. R. Goulart
Same Song, Next Verse. M. Steeber
Sammy. D. Enefer
Samson. E. C. Vivian
Samson Strike. T. Williamson
Samson's Deal. S. Singer
Samson's Surrender. T. Lloyd
Samuel Boyd of Catchpole Square. B. L. Farjeon
Samuel Lyle, Criminologist. A. Crabb
Samurai Kill. Nick Carter
Samurai Six. J. Stanley
Samurai Strategy. T. Hoover
San Andreas. A. MacLean
San Diego Lightfoot Sue. T. Reamy
San Diego Siege. D. Pendleton
San Francisco by Night. D. Spade
San Francisco Dame. Rex Richards
San Francisco Shakedown. D. Haring
San Francisco Surrender. Donna Fletcher
San Francisco Vendetta. R. Mallory
San Juan Inferno. Nick Carter
San Quentin. J. Lynch
Sanction. W. W. Johnstone
Sanction to Slaughter. Nick Carter
Sanctity. O. Papazoglu
Sanctuary. J. DeSario
Sanctuary. W. Faulkner
Sanctuary Club. L. T. Meade
Sanctuary Island. Robert (G.) Curtis
Sanctuary Isle. B. Knox
Sanctuary Sparrow. Ellis Peters
Sand Against the Tide. P. Bishop
Sand and Satin. S. Rohmer
Sand Castles. N. Freeling
Sand Dollar. G. Sims
Sand Dollars. R. Terrall
Sand Pit. H. Jobson
Sand Rose. M. Summerton
Sand Trap. C. B. Cooney
Sand Trap. Ian Stuart
Sandal Wood Slipper. Nicholas Carter
Sandalwood Fan. K. W. Eyre
Sandalwood Fan. T. McMorrow
Sandalwood Princess. L. Chase
Sandbaggers. I. Mackintosh
Sandbar Sinister. P. A. Taylor
Sandcastle Murders. E. St. Clair
Sandcatcher. S. Jackman
Sandcliff Mystery. Scott Graham
Sanders. E. Wallace
Sanders of the River. E. Wallace
Sanderson: Master Rogue. J. J. Chichester

Sanderson's Diamond Loot. J. J. Chichester
Sandi, the King Maker. E. Wallace
Sandlappers. A. Rutherford
Sandler Inquiry. N. Hynd
Sandling Case. L. Tracy
Sandman. L. Crockett
Sandman. M. Gibson
Sandman. W. W. Johnstone
Sandman. R. Martins
Sandman. R. Ward
Sandmouth People. R. Frame
Sandover Goes Gay. D. Lee
Sandra. D. Rome
Sandra Rifkin's Jewels. R. Doliner
Sands of Fear. Augustus Muir
Sands of Khali. M. Hastings
Sands of Lilliput. S. Dembo
Sands of Oro. B. Grimshaw
Sands of the Desert. P. Meredith
Sands of Time. S. Sheldon
Sands of Windee. A. W. Upfield
Sands Street. W. Bogart
Sandscreen. Ian Stuart
Sandstorm. L. Gough
Sandwiches Are Not My Business. B. Kelly
Sandwiches Are Waiting and other stories. Jane McClure
Sandy and others. D. Conyers
Sandy Bar with other stories. B. Harte
Sandycroft Mystery. T. W. Speight
Sanfield Scandal. R. Keverne
Sanibel. R. W. White
Sankov Confession. P. S. Donoghue
Sant of the Secret Service. W. LeQueux
Santa Ana Wind. S. Ashton
Santa Claus Bank Robbery. A. C. Greene
Santa Claus Killer. A. H. Garnet
Santa Dolores Stage. W. C. Tuttle
Santa Klaus Murder. M. D. Hay
Santa Maria. J. Fox
Santa Maria. Seafarer
Santiago. M. Resnick
Santorini. Alistair MacLean
Santos, Border Detective. W. B. Bannerman
Santubong Affair. J. M. Chin
Sapper: The Best Short Stories. H. C. McNeile
Sappers and Miners. G. M. Fenn
Sapphire. E. G. Cousins
Sapphire. A. E. W. Mason
Sapphire Conference. P. Graaf
Sapphire Cross. G. M. Fenn
Sapphire King, and other stories. R. Dowling
Sapphire Legacy. B. C. Warren
Sapphire Ring. C. Granville
Sapphires on Wednesday. M. Gair
Saraband for a Smuggler. S. Brydon
Saracen Gardens. M. K. Simmons
Saracen Shadow. Shane Martin
Sarah Brown, Detective. Anonymous
Sarah Brown, Detective. K. F. Hill
Sarah Cobb. C. M. Rae
Sarah Mandrake. M. Wadelton
Saranoff Murder. M. L. Luther
Saratoga. D. Daniels
Saratoga Bestiary. S. Dobyns
Saratoga Headhunter. S. Dobyns
Saratoga Hexameter. S. Dobyns
Saratoga Lady. F. Y. McHugh
Saratoga Longshot. S. Dobyns
Saratoga Mantrap. D. St. Clare
Saratoga Snapper. S. Dobyns
Saratoga Swimmer. S. Dobyns
Sardia. C. L. Daniels
Sardine Deception. L. Davidson
Sargasso. E. Corley
Sargasso Ogre. K. Robeson
Sargasso People. Wade Miller
Sargasso Secret. K. Stanton
Sarita, the Carlist. A. W. Marchmont
Sark Street Chapel Murder. T. Cobb
Sarnia. H. Ford
Sarsen Place. Gwendoline Butler
Sartaroe. J. A. Maitland
Sarton Kell. K. Mallory

Title Index SCARED TO DEATH / 1137

Saskatoon Patrol. G. Goodchild
Satan Black. K. Robeson
Satan Bug. I. Stuart
Satan Buys a Wreath. M. Storme
Satan Comes Across. B. Barlay
Satan Has Six Fingers. V. Kelsey
Satan in High Heels. N. Chandler
Satan in Malibu. F. Cannon
Satan in St. Mary's. P. C. Doherty
Satan in Satin. D. Haring
Satan Is a Woman. G. Baxt
Satan Is a Woman. G. Brewer
Satan Is Blonde. B. Sarto
Satan Ltd. Gwyn Evans
Satan, My Love. H. P. Holden
Satan Ring. Mike Newton
Satan Sampler. V. Canning
Satan Sanderson. H. E. Rives
Satan Stone. Ralph Hayes
Satan Strike. J. Rosenberger
Satan Takes a Hand. E. Seeley, Jr.
Satan Takes the Helm. C. Clements
Satan Touch. K. Royce
Satan Trap. Nick Carter
Satan Was a Man. E. H. Bierstadt
Satan Whispers. Clarissa Ross
Satania. D. Haring
Satanic Condition. D. Thoreau
Satanic Power. V. Van Der Elst
Satanic Sex. A. J. Fitzgerald
Satanist. M. C. Fraser
Satanist. D. Wheatley
Satan's Acres. S. Wagner
Satan's Angel. S. Fisher
Satan's Apt Pupil. Nicholas Carter
Satan's Bay. Michael Hastings
Satan's Child. P. Saxon
Satan's Children. G. Simenon
Satan's Coach. F. Du Boisgobey
Satan's Coast. Elsie Lee
Satan's Daughters. O. Peters
Satan's Death Blast. G. Stockbridge
Satan's Island. Marilyn Ross
Satan's Manor. Mark Andrews
Satan's Master. J. Nazel
Satan's Messenger. P. Fox
Satan's Mistress. B. Graeme
Satan's Mistress. D. Haring
Satan's Rock. Marilyn Ross
Satan's Sabbath. D. Pendleton
Satan's Sabbath. P. Valdez
Satan's Satellite. G. Davison
Satan's Seal. P. Rose
Satan's Secret. B. Stacey
Satan's Seed. J. Sherman
Satan's Sister. T. Angelo
Satan's Sister. R. J. Jensen
Satan's Slave. Anthony Allen
Satan's Spring. S. Nichols
Satan's Sunset. S. Hufford
Satan's Swarm. L. Derrick
Satan's Widow. H. Whittington
Satellite City. M. Reynolds
Satellite Slaughter. L. Derrick
Satin Sell-Out. D. Haring
Saturday Epic. H. C. Rae
Saturday Games. B. Meggs
Saturday Night Dead. Richard Rosen
Saturday Night Knife and Gun Club. B. P. Reiter
Saturday Night Massacre. J. Armour
Saturday Night Town. H. Whittington
Saturday of Glory. D. Serafin
Saturday Out. L. Meynell
Saturday Sterne. J. E. Reade
Saturday the Rabbi Went Hungry. H. Kemelman
Saturday to Monday. F. Whitaker
Saturn Experiment. P. Shepherd
Saturn Over the Water. J. B. Priestley
Saturn Stone. L. Osborne
Satyr. J. McKimmey
Satyr Candidate. R. M. Rose
Satyr Mask. Augustus Muir
Satyr Ring. A. Quinn
Sauce for the Pigeon. G. Hammond

Sausalito. S. Dodson
Sausalito. J. Lynch
Savage. P. Boorson
Savage. N. Clad
Savage Affair. V. Scott
Savage Breast. Manning Long
Savage Breast. J. Trinian
Savage Chase. F. Lorenz
Savage City. A. J. Merak
Savage Day. J. Higgins
Savage Day. T. Wiseman
Savage Encounter. G. Goodchild
Savage Fire. D. Pendleton
Savage Freedom. Roderick Grant
Savage Game. J. Trevor
Savage Gentlemen. P. Wylie
Savage Height. J. Trevor
Savage Holiday. R. Wright
Savage Interlude. D. Cushman
Savage Life. F. Boyle
Savage Love. Whit Harrison
Savage Night. J. Thompson
Savage Oaks. J. Ellis
Savage Place. R. B. Brown
Savage Ransom. E. Lippincott
Savage Salome. Carter Brown
Savage Season. J. R. Lansdale
Savage Sequel. H. Janson
Savage Siren. H. Zore
Savage Sisters. Carter Brown
Savage Slaughter. B. Rossi
Savage Snow. W. Holt
Savage Spirits of Seahedge Manor. D. Price
Savage Squeeze. Arthur MacLean
Savage State of Grace. Donald Mackenzie
Savage Streets. W. P. McGivern
Savage Streets. F. C. Miller
Savage Stronghold. C. Sargent
Savage Triangle. L. Royer
Savage Venture. W. A. Ballinger
Savage Way to Die. A. Shenton
Savage Woman. Mike Curtis
Savaged. V. Burgoyne
Savaged. Peter Hill
Savannah. N. Faulkner
Savannah Blue. W. Harrison
Savannah Purchase. J. A. Hodge
Savannah Score. L. Dykes
Savannah Swingsaw. D. Pendleton
Savannah Syndrome. John Davies
Savant's Vendetta. R. A. Freeman
Savaran and the Great Sand. D. Newton
Savarin's Shadow. R. Goyne
Save a Lady. W. Collison
Save a Rope. H. C. Bailey
Save Johanna! F. P. Pascal
Save Me from My Friends. E. F. Knight
Save the Children. D. Pendleton
Save the Last Dance for Me. J. Miller
Save the Witness. P. McGerr
Save Them for Violence. J. M. Fox
Save Your Pity. M. Hervey
Save Your Tears. Rick Madison
Saved at the Scaffold. A. F. Pinkerton
Saved by a Detective. Old Sleuth
Saved by a Ruse. Nicholas Carter
Saved from the Harem. F. Du Boisgobey
Saved in Time. Anonymous
Saverstall. J. Vicary
Savinelli. J. C. Molony
Saving a Rope. H. C. Bailey
Saving Clause. H. C. McNeile
Saving Face. P. Boulle
Saving Grace. R. W. Jones
Saving of Christian Sergison. E. A. Treeton
Saving the Queen. W. F. Buckley
Savings and Loam. R. McInerny
Saviour. H. Miller
Sawdust Angel. G. Bowman
Sawn Off. G. M. Fenn
Sawney Bean, the Man Eater of Midlothian. T. P. Prest
Saxon Ashe...Secret Agent. S. Ashe
Saxon's Ghost. S. Fisher

Say Au R'voir But Not Goobye. M. P. Shiel
Say It with Bullets. R. Powell
Say It with Candy. H. Janson
Say It with Flowers. G. C. Foster
Say It with Flowers. G. Mitchell
Say it with Homicide. B. Diamond
Say It with Murder. Neill Graham
Say It with Murder. E. Ronns
Say It with Violence. D. Eames
Say No to Murder. N. Pickard
Say Yes, Sugar. P. Garroway
Say Yes to Murder. W. T. Ballard
Say Your Prayer, Sister. A. Capelli
Sayle Case. T. Freeman-Hilton
Sayonara, Sweet Amaryllis. James Melville
Scaffold. Cameron Ross
Scales of Chance. H. Curties
Scales of Justice. R. Caswell
Scales of Justice. B. Delannoy
Scales of Justice. G. L. Knapp
Scales of Justice. N. Marsh
Scales of Justice. F. M. White
Scallywag. G. Allen
Scalpel. I. Corn, Jr.
Scalpel. H. McCoy
Scalps. M. Leinster
Scamp. V. Markham
Scamp Hunter. Dick Stewart
Scamp's Law. P. A. Foxall
Scandal. S. Endo
Scandal. F. Nichols
Scandal. R. W. Taylor
Scandal at High Chimneys. J. D. Carr
Scandal at School. G. D. H. Cole
Scandal at Scotland Yard. B. Cobb
Scandal at the Home Office. F. A. Clement
Scandal Has Two Faces. M. E. Campbell
Scandal in Bulimia. J. Ruyle
Scandal in Eden. G. Rogers
Scandal in the Chancery. Diplomat
Scandal-Monger. W. LeQueux
Scandal of Father Brown. G. K. Chesterton
Scandal on the Sand. J. Trinian
Scandal Point. J. Patrick
Scandal Street. W. H. Baker
Scandalize My Name. Fiona Sinclair
Scandalous Affair. Clarissa Ross
Scandalous Miss. Donna Bell
Scanner Darkly. P. K. Dick
Scapegoat. D. Du Maurier
Scapegoat. P. Orum
Scapegoat Dances. M. Benney
Scapegoats for Murder. A. Wilson
Scapescope. J. E. Stith
Scar. F. Kippax
Scar. D. Vane
Scar. D. Wright
Scar of Crime. J. Corey
Scar 77. G. Seton
Scarab. D. Creed
Scarab Clue. H. H. Ross
Scarab Murder Case. S. S. Van Dine
Scarabaeus. C. Lanza
Scaramouche. R. Sabatini
Scaramouche the Kingmaker. R. Sabatini
Scarborough Fear. D. M. Cayer
Scarborough Hall. B. Upchurch
Scarborough House. S. A. Salvato
Scarborough Romance. F. Warden
Scarbrow. G. Bettany
Scare Power. W. V. Butler
Scare Tactics. J. Farris
Scare the Gentle Citizen. I. Crawford
Scarecrow. R. T. Cusick
Scarecrow. A. Fielding
Scarecrow. E. K. Goldthwaite
Scarecrow. R. H. Morrieson
Scarecrow Creeps. J. Tobias
Scarecrow House. J. Hines
Scarecrow Murders. F. A. Kummer
Scarecrow Rides. R. Thorndike
Scared Nymph. A. Applin
Scared Stiff. P. J. Rainier
Scared to Death. G. Bagby

Scared to Death. R. Foley
Scared to Death. A. Morice
Scarf. R. Bloch
Scarf. F. Durbridge
Scarf of Passion. R. Bloch
Scarf on the Scarecrow. M. J. Freeman
Scarface. A. Trail
Scarfaced Killer. B. Rossi
Scarhaven Keep. J. S. Fletcher
Scarlatti Inheritance. R. Ludlum
Scarlet Bat. F. Hume
Scarlet Bee. Tanjong
Scarlet Bikini. G. Croudace
Scarlet Blossoms. M. Peterson
Scarlet Bride. M. Reed
Scarlet Button. Anthony Gilbert
Scarlet Car. R. H. Davis
Scarlet Circle. J. Stagge
Scarlet Cloak. P. Fry
Scarlet Clue. S. Hocking
Scarlet Cord. L. W. Sullivan
Scarlet Death. Roger Randall
Scarlet Fan. H. L. Gates
Scarlet Feather. H. Adams
Scarlet Feather. F. Gruber
Scarlet Feather. H. Townley
Scarlet Flower. T. Rourke
Scarlet Flush. Carter Brown
Scarlet Fortune. H. Herman
Scarlet Fountains. G. Milner
Scarlet Fox. E. H. Ball
Scarlet Gargoyle. T. F. Elstow
Scarlet Handkerchief. Le Jemlys
Scarlet Ikon. T. S. King
Scarlet Imperial. D. B. Hughes
Scarlet Imposter. D. Wheatley
Scarlet in Gaslight. Martin Powell
Scarlet Iris. V. Thompson
Scarlet Lady. A. St. Aubyn
Scarlet Letters. E. Queen
Scarlet Lily. N. Brent
Scarlet Livery. Rupert Grayson
Scarlet Macaw. G. E. Locke
Scarlet Mansion. A. W. Eckert
Scarlet Mask. W. E. Groves
Scarlet Mask. R. Pearsall
Scarlet Mask. C. Rodda
Scarlet Messenger. H. Holt
Scarlet Night. D. S. Davis
Scarlet on Gold. B. Schwarz
Scarlet Pimpernel. Baroness Orczy
Scarlet Reckoning. M. J. Moeller
Scarlet Riders. W. Campbell
Scarlet Runner. C. N. Williamson
Scarlet Ruse. J. D. MacDonald
Scarlet Saint. M. Sarne
Scarlet Scandals. C. Budd
Scarlet Scarab. L. C. Douthwaite
Scarlet Scarab. F. H. Mabley
Scarlet Scissors. B. Fischer
Scarlet Scourge. J. McCulley
Scarlet Scourge. Harrington Strong
Scarlet Seal. D. Donovan
Scarlet Shadow. W. Spence
Scarlet Shawl. R. Jefferies
Scarlet Ship. R. C. Finney
Scarlet Sign. W. LeQueux
Scarlet Sin. A. Askew
Scarlet Sin. F. Marryat
Scarlet Sinners. D. Donovan
Scarlet Slippers. J. M. Fox
Scarlet Spade. E. K. Goldthwaite
Scarlet Spot. Dick Stewart
Scarlet Squadron. G. E. Rochester
Scarlet Starlet. D. Warren
Scarlet Storm. M. De Moss
Scarlet Surf at Makaha. P. Morgan
Scarlet Tanager. J. A. Tyson
Scarlet Thread. Evelyn Anthony
Scarlet Thread. D. Downes
Scarlet Thread. M. P. Hood
Scarlet Thumb. J. March
Scarlet Thumb Print. G. Morton
Scarlet Tower. J. M. English

Scarlet Town. A. Askew
Scarlet Venus. C. Green
Scarlet Widow. R. Rioti
Scarlet Widow. B. Sanders
Scarlet Wreath. P. J. Carraher
Scarlet X. H. Wickham
Scarlett Gets the Kidnapper. S. Horler
Scarlett Murder. W. Martyn
Scarlett of the Mounted. M. Merington
Scarlett—Special Branch. S. Horler
Scarred Chin. W. Payne
Scarred Faces. H. Janson
Scarred Hand. E. H. Robinson
Scarred Jungle. H. Footner
Scarred Man. Philip Daniels
Scarred Man. B. Heatter
Scarred Man. Keith Peterson
Scarred Wrists. V. M. Steele
Scars of Dracula. Angus Hall
Scarsdale Peerage. F. Talbot
Scarthroat. Roland Daniel
Scarweather. A. Rolls
Scattered Death. I. Somerville
Scattered Souls. D. Henry
Scattergood Baines. C. B. Kelland
Scattergood Pulls the Strings. C. B. Kelland
Scattergood Returns. C. B. Kelland
Scattershot. B. Pronzini
Scavenger Kill. Ralph Hayes
Scavengers. B. Knox
Scavengers. Y. Montgomery
Scavengers. Allan Nixon
Scavengers. D. O'Callaghan
Scavengers at War. C. Leader
Scenario for Murder. Dana Wilson
Scend of the Sea. G. Jenkins
Scene Changing. E. Candy
Scene for Death. N. Hoult
Scene in the Ice-Blue Eyes. P. Winner
Scene of the Crime. J. Creasey
Scenes from a Subaltern's Life. C. L. Gilson
Scenes from the Show. G. R. Sims
Scenes of Crime. L. Egan
Scent from Heaven. H. Janson
Scent of Danger. R. Kyle
Scent of Danger. D. MacKenzie
Scent of Death. E. Page
Scent of Death. Morley Roberts
Scent of Fear. S. Dean
Scent of Fear. M. Yorke
Scent of Lilacs. Carolyn Wilson
Scent of Mayhem. R. T. Bickers
Scent of Mystery. K. Roos
Scent of New-Mown Hay. J. Blackburn
Scent of Roses. H. Bourne
Scent of Roses. G. Ferrand
Scent of Sandalwood. C. Coleman
Scent of the Rose. M. Peterson
Scent of Violets. R. Fabian
Scent of White Poppies. J. Christopher
Scented Danger. F. Cowen
Scented Death. A. Drummond
Scented Flesh. R. O. Saber
Schack Job. H. Kane
Schade. D. Thurlow
Schamyl, the Sultan, Warrior and Prophet of the Caucasus. T. P. Prest
Scheherazade. F. Warden
Scheme for One. A. Roberts
Schemer. W. E. Groves
Schemers. R. Fenisong
Schiller. Matthew Hunter
Schirmer Inheritance. E. Ambler
Schism. B. Granger
Schlock Homes: The Complete Bagel Street Saga. R. L. Fish
Scholars of the Night. J. M. Ford
School Afloat. D. Storm
School Days. Robert Hughes
School for Liars. O. Norton
School for Murder. R. Barnard
School for Murder. H. Carmichael
School for Murder. D. Scanlon
School for Scoundrels. A. Bracey

School for Secrets. D. Ames
School for Slaughter. P. Buck
School of Darkness. M. W. Wellman
School of English Murder. R. D. Edwards
School on Lone Island. B. E. M. Ward
School on 103rd Street. R. S. Jefferson
Schoolboys Three. W. P. Keely
Schooled to Kill. Dell Shannon
Schoolgirl Murder Case. Colin Wilson
Schoolmaster. W. J. Burley
Schoolmaster's Daughters. D. Eden
Schooner "Sybil". E. L. Long
Schroeder's Game. A. Maling
Schulsinger Affair. R. Temple
Schultz Mnoey. M. Gair
Schwartz. D. C. Murray
Sci Fi. W. Marshall
Science Traps the Criminal. J. W. Booth
Scientific Forger. Nicholas Carter
Scientific Sprague. F. Lynde
Scimitar. P. Niesewand
Scimitar. Scott C. S. Stone
Scipio. T. Gates
Scissors Cut Paper. G. Fairlie
Scissors, Paper, Stone. M. Boggs
Scobie in September. B. Craig
Scoop. Detection Club
Scoop. J. Hart
Scoop. L. Meynell
Scorch. N. Williams
Scorched Earth. C. Bainbridge
Scorched Earth. D. Stivers
Scorcher. J. Lutz
Scorcher. M. Maguire
Score. R. Stark
Score at Tea-Time. Michael Ellis
Score for Superintendent Flagg. J. Cassells
Score for the Toff. J. Creasey
Score of Arms. R. Meade
Scornful Corpse. M. Kennedy
Scornful Man. Muriel Harris
Scorpio. D. Haring
Scorpio. S. Lawson
Scorpio. M. Roote
Scorpio Cipher. R. Hayes
Scorpio 5. W. Harrington
Scorpio Letters. V. Canning
Scorpio Moon. K. Maxwell
Scorpion. D. Carey
Scorpion. Mildred Davis
Scorpion. C. Hill
Scorpion. A. Kaplan
Scorpion. W. Penmare
Scorpion. E. A. Vizetelly
Scorpion Menace. L. Falk
Scorpion of Chateau Laverria. M. M. Fletcher
Scorpion Reef. C. Williams
Scorpion Sapphire. B. Monson
Scorpion Sanction. G. Pape
Scorpion Signal. Adam Hall
Scorpion Summer. E. B. Selig
Scorpion Trap. A. Handley
Scorpion's Dance. W. B. Murphy
Scorpion's Nest. J. Angus
Scorpion's Nest. H. McCutcheon
Scorpion's Sting. E. A. Pollitz, Jr.
Scorpion's Suicide. F. Dale
Scorpion's Tale. W. Haggard
Scorpion's Trail. T. C. H. Jacobs
Scorpius. J. Gardner
Scotch and Water. G. Gilpatric
Scotch Murder. C. Cruikshank
Scotch on the Rocks. D. Hurd
Scotland Expects. J. S. Clouston
Scotland Yard. J. Gollomb
Scotland Yard Alibi. D. Betteridge
Scotland Yard Can Wait! D. Frome
Scotland Yard: Department of Queer Complaints. Carter Dickson
Scotland Yard Experiences. G. H. Greenham
Scotland Yard Photo Crimes from the Files of Inspector Black. Anonymous
Scotland Yard Takes a Holiday. L. Allan
Scots Wha Ha'e. J. S. Clouston

Title Index

Scott-Dunlap Ring. G. La Fountaine
Scottish Chieftains. H. M. Jones
Scottish Decision. A. Hunter
Scoundrel. M. Aldanov
Scoundrel at School and the Exploits of Ned Ranger. Anonymous
Scoundrel Mark. F. Dilnot
Scoundrel or Saint? G. Warden
Scoundrels & Co. C. Kernahan
Scoundrels Ltd. Howard Steele
Scoundrels Rampant. Nicholas Carter
Scourge. T. L. Dunne
Scourge of Damascus. S. Cobb
Scourge of the Desert. Operator 1384
Scourge of the Steel Mask. R. J. Hogan
Scourge of the Wizard. Nicholas Carter
Scourge of the World. Anonymous
Scourged by Fear. Nicholas Carter
Scout Grey—Detective. R. L. Bellamy
Scout's Honor. M. Black
Scouts, Spies and Detectives of the Great Civil War. L. P. Brockett
Scouts, Spies and Heroes of the Great Civil War. L. P. Brockett
Scrambled Yeggs. O. R. Cohen
Scrambled Yeggs. D. Knight
Scrap-Metal Mystery. W. Tyrer
Scrap of Black Lace. Nicholas Carter
Scrap of Paper. H. C. McNeile
Scrap of Paper. Maxwell Scott
Scratch a Lover. J. G. Vermandel
Scratch a Thief. Z. Marko
Scratch a Thief. J. Trinian
Scratch Fever. M. A. Collins
Scratch on the Dark. B. Copper
Scratch on the Surface. T. Harknett
Scratch One. J. Lange
Scratchproof. M. Maguire
Scream. D. Launay
Scream. J. Skipp
Scream and Scream Again. P. Saxon
Scream at Midnight. J. P. Brennan
Scream at Midnight. T. A. Plummer
Scream at the Sea. C. Murphy
Scream Away. Andrea Harris
Scream Bloody Murder. R. Telfair
Scream Blue Murder. R. Dacre
Scream for Sarah. V. Heley
Scream in a Cave. E. Denby
Scream in Soho. J. G. Brandon
Scream in the Dark. N. Ridley
Scream in the Night. Monte Barrett
Scream in the Night. H. Desmond
Scream in the Sky. N. McCallum
Scream in the Storm. C. Farr
Scream of Murder. G. Ashe
Scream of the Doll. S. K. Wilson
Scream of the Dove. R. Charles
Scream on the Storm. C. Farr
Scream Street. Mike Brett
Screaming Bones. P. Burden
Screaming Bride. H. T. Teilhet
Screaming Cargo. J. M. Flynn
Screaming Dead Balloons. P. McCutchan
Screaming Fog. J. N. Chance
Screaming Gull. A. MacVicar
Screaming Knife. R. E. Vardeman
Screaming Man. K. Robeson
Screaming Mimi. Fredric Brown
Screaming Orchid. D. Enefer
Screaming Portrait. F. L. Fraser
Screaming Rabbit. H. Carmichael
Screaming Skull and other stories. S. Horler
Screams from a Penny Dreadful. Joan Fleming
Screen for Murder. A. Jeffers
Screen for Murder. E. C. R. Lorac
Screen Test. S. George
Screened. F. Wolseley
Screw Loose. Edward Lewis
Screwball King Murder. K. Platt
Screwdriver. G. Kraft
Scribbler's Club. C. Garvice
Scrimshaw Millions. L. Thayer
Scroll of Benevolence. J. Trenhaile

Scrope. F. B. Perkins
Scruples. T. Cobb
Scrutinies of Simon Iff. A. Crowley
Sculptor's Daughter. F. Du Boisgobey
Scum in the Pot. W. A. Miller
Scutari. M. Zarubica
Scylla. Malden Grange Bishop
Sea Angel. K. Robeson
Sea Case. G. Volk
Sea Cave. A. Scholefield
Sea Change. E. H. Clements
Sea-Change. P. Loraine
Sea Cliff. M. T. Hinkemeyer
Sea Could Tell. A. M. Williamson
Sea-Crossed Fisherman. Y. Kemal
Sea Devil. R. P. Henrick
Sea Dogs. Morley Roberts
Sea Dust. E. L. Long
Sea Fever. A. Trew
Sea File. J. D. Scott
Sea Fog. J. S. Fletcher
Sea Fox. Nicholas Carter
Sea Fury. J. Pattinson
Sea Gate. J. Aeby
Sea Gold. J. Remenham
Sea Gold. I. Slater
Sea Gull. J. D'Astor
Sea House. M. Summerton
Sea Jade. P.A. Whitney
Sea King's Daughter. B. Michaels
Sea-Kissed. R. Bloch
Sea Lavender. R. Gover
Sea Leopard. C. Thomas
Sea Lion. F. A. Leib
Sea Loot. A. D. Divine
Sea Lord. B. Cornwell
Sea Magician. K. Robeson
Sea Monks. A. Garve
Sea Mystery. F. W. Crofts
Sea of Death. H. H. Ross
Sea of Fortune. R. Jocelyn
Sea of Green. T. L. Adcock
Sea of Savages. G. Wilson
Sea of Troubles. Sea Lion
Sea of Troubles. Janet Smith
Sea Raiders. A. B. Sherlock
Sea Range. E. L. Long
Sea-Salt and Cordite. P. Vaux
Sea Scamps. H. C. Rowland
Sea Scrape. James Dark
Sea Shall Not Have Them. J. Harris
Sea Shroud. S. Gluck
Sea Spider. G. E. Rochester
Sea, Spray and Spindrift. Taffrail
Sea Spy. E. K. Chatterton
Sea Stalk. R. Kytle
Sea Tigers. P. Saxon
Sea Tower. K. Ostrander
Sea Trails. Sea-Wrack
Sea Trap. Nick Carter
Sea Treasure. K. Bakker
Sea Treasure. E. Barr
Sea Trial. F. DeFelitta
Sea Troll. S. Blanc
Sea Urchin. A. Q. Roby
Sea Urchins. W. W. Jacobs
Sea Vengeance. R. Charles
Sea Vermin. K. Henshaw
Sea Whispers. W. W. Jacobs
Sea Wind. M. P. Dobner
Sea Wolves. M. Pemberton
Sea Wrack. R. Hitchcock
Sea Yarns. J. A. Barry
Seabird Nine. J. McVean
Seacliffe. J. W. De Forrest
Seacliffe. E. Noone
Seadrift House. C. Hamilton
Seafire. B. Knox
Seaford's Snake. B. Mitford
Seagull Crag. E. Welles
Seagull Said Murder. M. Neville
Seajet Spies. N. Rich
Seal of Confession. H. A. Bulley
Seal of Death. Nicholas Carter

Seal of Silence. Nicholas Carter
Seal of Silence. A. F. Conder
Seal Poachers. C. Hayter
Sealed and Despatched. F. Bream
Sealed Book. A. Livingstone
Sealed by a Kiss. J. Middlemass
Sealed Door. Nicholas Carter
Sealed Envelope. B. Bolt
Sealed Envelope. Lady A. Scott
Sealed Fountain. R. Roleine
Sealed Knot. Elizabeth Law
Sealed Lips. S. Campbell
Sealed Lips. F. Du Boisgobey
Sealed Lips. M. Leighton
Sealed Lips. V. Yorke
Sealed Messenger. F. Hume
Sealed Orders. A. E. Carey
Sealed Orders. Nicholas Carter
Sealed Orders. D. Goodwin
Sealed Orders. R. Gover
Sealed Orders. E. J. Lysaght
Sealed Room Murder. M. Crombie
Sealed-Room Murder. R. Penny
Sealed Trunk. H. K. Webster
Sealed Valley. H. Footner
Sealed Verdict. L. L. Lynch
Sealed Verdict. L. Shapiro
Sealed with a Loving Kill. R. Ormerod
Sealed with Blood. S. Jason
Sealer. J. Wood
Sealing. L. Webb
Seals. P. Dickinson
Seamew Abbey. F. Warden
Seance. M. McShane
Seance for Susan. L. B. Clark
Seance for the Dead. F. Hurd
Seance for Two. M. McShane
Seance on a Wet Afternoon. M. McShane
Search. M. Land
Search. Robert Mayer
Search. I. C. Smith
Search and Destroy. I. R. Blacker
Search and Destroy. J. P. Cody
Search and Destroy. Robin Moore
Search and Destroy. Gar Wilson
Search by Night. V. Lucas
Search for a Dead Nympho. P. W. Fairman
Search for a Missing Lady. Neill Graham
Search for a Motive. Dick Stewart
Search for a Scientist. C. L. Leonard
Search for a Secret. G. A. Henty
Search for a Sultan. M. Coles
Search for Anderson. I. I. Magdalen
Search for Basil Lyndhurst. R. N. Carey
Search for Bruno Heidler. S. Marlowe
Search for Elizabeth Brandt. W. Harrington
Search for Geoffrey Goring. David Wilson
Search for Joseph Tully. W. H. Hallahan
Search for Maggie Hare. E. Byrd
Search for Miss Sylvester. W. V. Cook
Search for My Great-Uncle's Head. P. Coffin
Search for Rita. Barry Cole
Search for Sara. M. Russell
Search for Sergeant Baxter. B. Cobb
Search for Simon. A. Hutton
Search for Sybil. A. C. Peniston
Search for Tabitha Carr. R. M. Stern
Search for the Blue Sedan. Gavin Douglas
Search for Tomorrow. E. Lindall
Search for Willie. W. D. Roberts
Search for X-Y-Z. H. S. Keeler
Search for Yesterday. L. Robin
Search in the Dark. A. MacKenzie
Search in the Shadows. P. Warren
Search Me. C. Sodaro
Search Party. G. A. Birmingham
Search Relentless. C. L. Skinner
Search the Dark Woods. M. Land
Search the Lady. H. Duval
Search the Seven Hills. B. Hambly
Search the Shadows. Barbara Michaels
Search Through the Mist. L. V. Stevens
Search Warrant. J. Pattinson
Search Will Find It Out. B. Harraden

Searchers. John Foster
Searchers of the Dead. Kenneth O'Hara
Searching Spectre. S. Claudia
Searchlight and the Idol. J. Moon
Searchlight on Hambledon. J. Dellbridge
Searchlight on the Throne. Anonymous
Seared Hand. J. G. Rowe
Searle of the Mounted. M. Merington
Sea's Fool. F. Knight
Seascape with Dead Figures. Roy Hart
Seaside Cafe Crime. W. Jardine
Seaside Comedy. I. Jerrold
Seaside Crime. W. Jardine
Seaside Mystery. C. B. Booth
Season for Death. Ray Harrison
Season for Death. A. Roudybush
Season for Murder. H. L. Nelson
Season for Violence. T. B. Dewey
Season in Hell. Jack Higgins
Season of Anguish. D. Noel
Season of Assassins. G. Wagner
Season of Danger. R. Gatenby
Season of Desire. A. W. Lyons
Season of Doubt. J. Cleary
Season of Evil. Jane Gordon
Season of Evil. S. Morrow
Season of Nerves. J. Mayo
Season of Snows and Sins. P. Moyes
Season of the Falcon. C. Darby
Season of the Machete. J. Patterson
Season of the Skylark. J. T. Story
Season of the Stranger. S. Becker
Season of the Strangler. Madison Jones
Season to Be Deadly. R. Hardwick
Seasons of Death. M. K. Wren
Seasons of God. Edythe Latham
Seasons of Revenge. W. Paul
Seat of the Scornful. J. D. Carr
Seatag. M. Jancath
Seattle. J. Lynch
Seaview Manor. E. Grandower
Seaward for the Foe. H. Hill
Seaway Tombstone. K. Klein
Seawaymen. J. Wingate
Seawife. J. M. Scott
Seawitch. Alistair MacLean
Sebastian Strome. J. Hawthorne
Sebastiani's Secret. S. E. Waller
Seclusion Room. F. Neuman
Second Baffle Book. L. Wren
Second Baronet. L. Tracy
Second Best. C. Stanton
Second Book of Robert E. Howard. R. E. Howard
Second Book of Tobiah. U. L. Silberrad
Second Bounce. M. Cronin
Second Bout with the Mildew Gang. S. Fowler
Second Bullet. R. O. Chipperfield
Second Bullet. C. J. Dutton
Second Bullet. L. Thayer
Second Bureau. C. R. Dumas
Second Burial. A. M. Stein
Second Case of Mr. Paul Savoy. Jackson Gregory
Second Chance. P. Trent
Second Chance. E. Trevor
Second Chance. W. Woodrow
Second Child. John Saul
Second Class Passenger and other stories. P. Gibbon
Second Confession. R. Stout
Second Contact. M. Resnick
Second Count. S. Pearson
Second Cousin Removed. S. Troy
Second Cousin Twice Removed. M. Pereira
Second Curtain. Roy Fuller
Second Dandy Chater. T. Gallon
Second Deadly Sin. Lawrence Sanders
Second Death of Ramon Mercader. J. Semprun
Second Elopement. H. Flowerdew
Second Floor Mystery. E. D. Biggers
Second Front—First Spy. B. Newman
Second Guess. W. C. Brown
Second Guest. H. Beresford
Second Half. J. Greaves
Second-Hand Death. E. E. Sumner
Second-Hand Nude. B. Fischer

Second-Hand Tomb. R. J. White
Second Horseman Out of Eden. G. C. Chesbro
Second House. Jan Alexander
Second-in-Command. G. Hackforth-Jones
Second in the Field. T. Cobb
Second Jeopardy. R. Ormerod
Second Jesse James. W. B. Lawson
Second Key. M. B. Lowndes
Second Knife. H. J. Gill
Second Lady. Irving Wallace
Second Lady Cameron. F. Thomson
Second Latchkey. C. N. Williamson
Second Life of Cecily Pride. C. Dalton
Second Longest Night. S. Marlowe
Second Love. T. W. Speight
Second Maigret Omnibus. G. Simenon
Second Mally Lee. E. Kyle
Second Man. E. Grierson
Second Midnight. Andrew Taylor
Second Mrs. Carstairs. Nicholas Carter
Secone Mrs. Locke. J. Cassells
Second Mrs. Lynton. W. Collison
Second Mrs. Savenage. H. W. Leggett
Second Officer. Taffrail
Second Oldest Profession. W. Pinkham
Second Only to Murder. S. Box
Second Opinion. R. S. Thorn
Second Plan. C. G. Hope
Second Red Dragon. C. V. Bark
Second Romance. Elsie Lee
Second Saint Omnibus. L. Charteris
Second Saladin. S. Hunter
Second Seal. D. Wheatley
Second Season. Elsie Lee
Second Secret. E. Noone
Second Seed. M. L. Polan
Second Shot. A. Berkeley
Second Shot. L. Thayer
Second Shot in the Dark. A. Roome
Second Sickle. U. Curtiss
Second Sight. C. Bartholomew
Second Sight. A. Redman
Second Sight. D. Williams
Second Storey Sinner. M. Brody
Second Storm. M. Sutherland
Second Story Peggy. K. Kavanaugh
Second String. H. Janson
Second Stroke. F. Leslie
Second Tablet. C. E. Simon
Second Thoughts. M. Le Bas
Second Thursday. Elspeth Taylor
Second Tigress. Ganpat
Second Time Is Easy. Martin Russell
Second Time Round. H. McLeave
Second Vanetti Affair. M. Lovell
Second Vespers. R. McInerny
Second Victory. M. L. West
Second Wager. H. R. Taunton
Second War of Worlds. G. H. Smith
Seconds. D. Ely
Seconds and Thirds. E. L. Long
Secrecy. Eliza Fenwick
Secrecy at Sandhurst. C. Barry
Secrecy Essential. V. Bridges
Secrecy Street. M. Crossley
Secret. L. De Breuil
Secret. E. P. Oppenheim
Secret. G. C. Wallis
Secret Adventure. O. Binns
Secret Adventure of the Thornborough Ghost. F. Sherrod
Secret Adversary. A. Christie
Secret Affairs. M. Cherkas
Secret Agenda. J. Hougan
Secret Agent. J. Conrad
Secret Agent. H. L. Hadley
Secret Agent. S. Horler
Secret Agent: Ashton-Kirk. J. T. MacIntyre
Secret Agent in Africa. Rupert Grayson
Secret Agent in Port Arthur. W. O. Greener
Secret Agent Number One. F. Frost
Secret Agent X-9. D. Hammett
Secret Agent X-9: Book Two. D. Hammett
Secret Agents of Brazil. Nicholas Carter

Secret Anniversaries. Scott Spencer
Secret Arena. E. Trevor
Secret at Jester Moor. R. Roleine
Secret at Midwinter End. M. E. Wakefield
Secret at Orient Point. P. Werner
Secret at Ravenswood. C. Farr
Secret at Sixty-Six Fathoms. S. Hope
Secret at the Abbey. A. Andre
Secret Attic. F. R. Adams
Secret Avengers. J. A. K. Curtis
Secret Baby. S. V. Ashley
Secret Barrier. C. Kingston
Secret Base. M. Strangeways
Secret Below 103rd Street. R. S. Jefferson
Secret Beyond the Door. R. King
Secret Book. Edmund Pearson
Secret Brotherhood. J. G. Brandon
Secret Brotherhood. H. Campbell
Secret Cargo. S. Esmond
Secret Cargo. J. S. Fletcher
Secret Ceremony. M. Denevi
Secret Ceremony. W. Hughes
Secret Chamber at Chad. E. Everett-Green
Secret Citadel. M. Heath
Secret City. D. Storm
Secret Command. J. Hawkins
Secret Compact. J. B. Williams
Secret Country. F. O'Neill
Secret Dancer. N. Berrow
Secret Dancer. R. Timperley
Secret Door. R. St. Clair
Secret Door. D. Vane
Secret Dragnet. B. Sanders
Secret Emerald Mines. G. H. Teed
Secret Enemy. C. Chater
Secret Enemy. E. O'Duffy
Secret Enemy. M. K. Robertson
Secret Enterprise. Basil Carey
Secret Errand. N. Deane
Secret Families. J. Gardner
Secret Fear. A. E. W. Mason
Secret Fear. W. O'Farrell
Secret Fear. R. Underwood
Secret Files of Sherlock Holmes. June Thomson
Secret Files of Solar Pons. B. Copper
Secret Foe. E. Pickering
Secret Foe. G. Warden
Secret Formula. W. LeQueux
Secret Formula. A. Peters
Secret Formula. A. O. Pollard
Secret Fortune. M. E. Cooke
Secret Front. P. Gallico
Secret Generations. J. Gardner
Secret Gold. A. M. Williamson
Secret Guest Mystery. Anonymous
Secret Guest Mystery. M. Welford
Secret Hand. Roland Daniel
Secret Hand. C. G. L. Du Cann
Secret Hand. S. Horler
Secret Hand. D. Valentine
Secret Harbour. S. A. White
Secret Heart. E. Shenkin
Secret History of Today. A. Upward
Secret: Hong Kong. F. M. Davis
Secret Hour. M. Richmond
Secret House. E. Wallace
Secret House of Death. R. Rendell
Secret Houses. J. Gardner
Secret in Seven Fathoms. M. Frazer
Secret in the Hill. B. Capes
Secret in the Sky. K. Robeson
Secret Information. R. Hichens
Secret Inheritance. B. L. Farjeon
Secret Inquest. A. Blair
Secret Inquiry. B. Cobb
Secret Isaac. J. Charyn
Secret Island. J. Fores
Secret Journal of Charles Dunbar. J. Maconechy
Secret Journey. R. Kirkbridge
Secret Judges. F. Grierson
Secret-Keeper. S. Eskapa
Secret Kills. W. Beechcroft
Secret Kingdom. F. Richardson
Secret Life of Algernon Pendleton. R. H. Greenan

Secret Life of Miss Lottinger. Neil Bell
Secret Life of Mr. Beauty. G. Kay
Secret Life of the Ex-Tsaritza. W. LeQueux
Secret Life of Heinrich Roehm. M. Barak
Secret Listeners. L. Goldman
Secret Listeners of the East. D. G. Mukerji
Secret Lives. W. Targ
Secret Lives. H. Weiss
Secret Love. D. Noel
Secret Lover. E. Nepean
Secret Lovers. C. McCarry
Secret Loving Shadows. M. E. Atkins
Secret Marriage. A. W. Barrett
Secret Masters. G. Kersh
Secret Meeting. J. Rhode
Secret Melody. P. Minton
Secret Menace. Wilfred Barclay
Secret Millionaire. H. H. C. Gibbons
Secret Ministry. D. Cory
Secret Mission. Anonymous
Secret Mission. H. Janson
Secret Mission. F. S. Smythe
Secret Mission: Angola. Don Smith
Secret Mission: Athens. Don Smith
Secret Mission: Cairo. Don Smith
Secret Mission: Corsica. Don Smith
Secret Mission: Istanbul. Don Smith
Secret Mission: Morocco. Don Smith
Secret Mission: Munich. Don Smith
Secret Mission: North Korea. Don Smith
Secret Mission of Colonel Death. J. Rapier
Secret Mission: Peking. Don Smith
Secret Mission: Prague. Don Smith
Secret Mission: The Kremlin Plot. Don Smith
Secret Mission: Tibet. Don Smith
Secret Mission to Bangkok. V. W. Mason
Secret Mountains. J. Appleby
Secret Murder. G. Ashe
Secret Net. A. Ridgway
Secret Oath. Anonymous
Secret of a Hollow Tree. N. Covertside
Secret of a Letter. G. Warden
Secret of Anna Katz. S. Swift
Secret of Annexe 3. C. Dexter
Secret of Ashton Manor House. E. Kerr
Secret of Awen Castle. F. Hurd
Secret of Ayanora. Basil Carey
Secret of Barnabas Collins. Marilyn Ross
Secret of Baron's Folly. H. M. Webster
Secret of Belledonne Room 16. A. DeVries
Secret of Benjamin Square. J. Plum
Secret of Berry Pomeroy. F. Whishaw
Secret of Bogey House. H. Adams
Secret of Bourke's Mansion. C. Moyer
Secret of Brackenwood. J. T. Osborne
Secret of Canfield House. F. Hurd
Secret of Capri. W. Jardine
Secret of Carickferneagh Castle. S. A. Turk
Secret of Castle Ferrara. C. Farr
Secret of Castle Voxzel. A. O. Pollard
Secret of Chateau Kendall. S. Richard
Secret of Chateau Laval. S. Marvin
Secret of Chauville. D. Whitelaw
Secret of Chimneys. A. Christie
Secret of Christopher Greatorex. J. Kelso
Secret of Circle 16. Reginald Kirby
Secret of Devil's Cave. Jennifer Hale
Secret of Draker's Folly. A. Murray
Secret of Dresden Farm. Genevieve St. John
Secret of Elizabeth. V. Caspary
Secret of Enoch Seal. J. B. Harris-Burland
Secret of Father Brown. G. K. Chesterton
Secret of Ferrars. R. Mattheson
Secret of Fire 5. J. Olsen
Secret of Frontellac. F. K. Scribner
Secret of Gaunt House. F. H. Dimmock
Secret of Giltham Hall. J. Cheyney
Secret of Gnome Head. B. Strong
Secret of Graytowers. E. Randolph
Secret of Greylands. A. Haynes
Secret of Harbor House. Claudette Nicole
Secret of Haverly House. C. Bauman
Secret of Hayworth Hall. F. Hurd
Secret of Hedges Hall. Lynn Williams

Secret of High Eldersham. M. Burton
Secret of Holm Peel and other strange stories. S. Rohmer
Secret of Kensington Manor. Genevieve St. John
Secret of Killer Mountain Inn. K. Brooks
Secret of Kyriels. E. Nesbit
Secret of Lonesome Cove. S. H. Adams
Secret of Love. G. Finley
Secret of Lucifer's Island. M. Lynch
Secret of Lynndale. F. Warden
Secret of MI6. L. Smith
Secret of Mallet Castle. Clarissa Ross
Secret of Marly Stones. D. Kamm
Secret of Matchams. N. Burnaby
Secret of Maxshelling. E. Everett-Green
Secret of Mirror House. Patricia Maxwell
Secret of Mohawk Pond. N. S. Lincoln
Secret of Monk's House. Rachelle Edwards
Secret of Moor House. Donald Stuart
Secret of Musterton House. G. Granby
Secret of Oil Creek. A. Parsons
Secret of Providenc Lodge. R. E. Salwey
Secret of Quarry House. C. Lorrimer
Secret of Room No. 13. C. E. Pearce
Secret of Saint Florel. J. Berwick
Secret of Sam Barlow. A. J. Fenady
Secret of San Felipe. P. Buck
Secret of Saraband. M. Floyd
Secret of Saramount. L. Cheatham
Secret of Sarek. M. Leblanc
Secret of Scotland Yard. Anonymous
Secret of Scotland Yard. A. E. Bayly
Secret of Sea-Dream House. A. P. Terhune
Secret of Secrets. J. S. Fletcher
Secret of Seven. Donald Stuart
Secret of Seven Oaks. J. Coulson
Secret of Shanghai. P. J. Clancy
Secret of Sheen. J. Laurence
Secret of Sherlock Holmes. Jeremy Paul
Secret of Shorewood Hall. D. O. Smith
Secret of Shower Tree. V. Coffman
Secret of Simon Cornell. H. Howard
Secret of Sir George Hartley. A. M. Diehl
Secret of Skull Island. Tim Kelly
Secret of Skye. A. S. Swan
Secret of Spandau. P. Lear
Secret of Stark Island. Colin Desmond
Secret of Stillwater Mere. G. Chester
Secret of Strangeways. Joyce Bentley
Secret of Superintendent Manning. B. Cobb
Secret of Sylvia. Lee Borden
Secret of Tangles. L. Gribble
Secret of Tarn-End House. C. Randell
Secret of the African Settle. R. Hardinge
Secret of the African Trader. R. Hardinge
Secret of the Armaments King. P. Quiroule
Secret of the Ashes. A. Ornstien
Secret of the Balkan Heiress. C. Brisbane
Secret of the Baltic. T. C. Bridges
Secret of the Barbican. J. S. Fletcher
Secret of the Bayou. F. Davenport
Secret of the Bird. C. Grae
Secret of the Black Mere. Anonymous
Secret of the Black Wallet. W. W. Sayer
Secret of the Blue Macaw. I. L. Forrester
Secret of the Blue Vase. H. Tuite
Secret of the Bucket Shop. J. G. Jones
Secret of the Bungalow. R. J. Casey
Secret of the Burma Road. A. Parsons
Secret of the Carpathians. H. H. C. Gibbons
Secret of the Cask. R. C. Armour
Secret of the Castle Ruins. A. Parsons
Secret of the Cavern. Mrs. Burke
Secret of the Cellar. W. Edwards
Secret of the Chateau. C. Farr
Secret of the Chateau Leval. S. Richard
Secret of the Chinese Jar. F. Hume
Secret of the Circle. P. Quiroule
Secret of the Coconut Groves. G. H. Teed
Secret of the Cove. H. L. Deakin
Secret of the Creek. V. Bridges
Secret of the Dark Room. R. J. Casey
Secret of the Dead. L. T. Meade
Secret of the Dead. I. Stark

Secret of the Dead Convict. M. B. Dix
Secret of the Dead Man. P. Urquhart
Secret of the Demolition Worker. J. Hunter
Secret of the Dental Surgeon. R. Hardinge
Secret of the Desert. R. C. Armour
Secret of the Desert. R. Hardinge
Secret of the Diamond. E. D. Pierson
Secret of the Diamonds. C. W. Greatorex
Secret of the Doubting Saint. L. Holton
Secret of the Downs. W. S. Masterman
Secret of the East Wind. C. G. Page
Secret of the Elephant. B. Scott
Secret of the Evacuee. P. Urquhart
Secret of the Everglades. B. Marchant
Secret of the Farm. G. Chester
Secret of the Fated Family. R. Hardinge
Secret of the Flames. W. M. Graydon
Secret of the Flames. R. Rodd
Secret of the Frozen North. W. W. Sayer
Secret of the Garden. A. Gask
Secret of the Ghostly Shroud. N. Buckingham
Secret of the Glacier. W. Jardine
Secret of the Glacier. A. Murray
Secret of the Glen. C. Brisbane
Secret of the Gold Locket. R. C. Armour
Secret of the Golden Horse. A. Parsons
Secret of the Grange. Mark Cross
Secret of the Grave. J. Hunter
Secret of the Graveyard. J. Addiscombe
Secret of the Green Lagoon. E. J. Murray
Secret of the Green Vase. Frances Cooke
Secret of the Grey Phantom. J. Ascott
Secret of the Haunted Tarn. Anonymous
Secret of the Hills. W. Garrett
Secret of the Hold. J. Hunter
Secret of the Hulk. A. Murray
Secret of the Hulk. Donald Stuart
Secret of the Hunger Desert. A. Murray
Secret of the Identification Parade. W. Edwards
Secret of the Indian Lawyer. A. Parsons
Secret of the Jungle. W. M. Graydon
Secret of the Jungle. R. Hardinge
Secret of the Jungle. G. Rees
Secret of the Lagoon. R. C. Armour
Secret of the Lake House. J. Rhode
Secret of the Lamp. Anonymous
Secret of the Lebombo. B. Mitford
Secret of the Little Flea. B. Munslow
Secret of the Little Gods. K. H. Taylor
Secret of the Living Skeleton. J. Drummond
Secret of the Loch. C. Brisbane
Secret of the Locket. E. St. Clair
Secret of the Lost River. S. Warwick
Secret of the Man Who Died. R. Hardinge
Secret of the Mansions. W. J. Bayfield
Secret of the Marble Mantle. Nicholas Carter
Secret of the Marionettes. E. D. Pierson
Secret of the Marsh. O. Warner
Secret of the Marshbanks. K. Norris
Secret of the Marshes. M. Richmond
Secret of the Mere. D. Peacock
Secret of the Mere. J. J. Wray
Secret of the Midway Plaza. A. E. Dramond
Secret of the Mine. A. Steffens Hardy
Secret of the Missing Checks. H. Rockwell
Secret of the Missing Convict. A. Murray
Secret of the Moat. H. Desmond
Secret of the Monastery. S. G. Shaw
Secret of the Moor. M. Gerard
Secret of the Moor Cottage. H. R. Cromarsh
Secret of the Morgue. F. G. Eberhard
Secret of the Moroccan Bazaar. A. Parsons
Secret of the Night. G. Leroux
Secret of the Oblong Chest. W. W. Sayer
Secret of the Old Lighthouse. J. G. Rowe
Secret of the Pale Lover. Clarissa Ross
Secret of the Past. W. M. Graydon
Secret of the Past. V. O. Power
Secret of the Pit. L. Meynell
Secret of the President's Daughter. G. H. Teed
Secret of the Priory. S. O. Bryan
Secret of the Priory. M. Richmond
Secret of the Raft. H. Townley
Secret of the Red Mountain. W. W. Sayer

Secret of the Reef. J. Andrews
Secret of the Ring. Maxwell Scott
Secret of the River. Dora Russell
Secret of the Roman Temple. A. Parsons
Secret of the Russian Refugees. W. M. Graydon
Secret of the Safe. A. Edgar
Secret of the Sahara. W. M. Graydon
Secret of the Sale Room. R. Hardinge
Secret of the Saltings. V. Bridges
Secret of the Sanatorium. C. Brisbane
Secret of the Sandbanks. J. Plain
Secret of the Sandhills. A. Gask
Secret of the Sandhills. F. Marlowe
Secret of the Sands. W. Tyrer
Secret of the Sands. F. M. White
Secret of the Sapphire Ring. M. V. Woodgate
Secret of the Scarlet Bomber. P. Conde
Secret of the Screen. S. Fowler
Secret of the Sea. W. Allison
Secret of the Sea. C. M. Parsons
Secret of the Sea. T. W. Speight
Secret of the Sealed Room. Donald Stuart
Secret of the Seas. D. Haywood
Secret of the Second Door. R. Colby
Secret of the Seven Sisters. John Marsh
Secret of the Seven Spiders. G. Stanley
Secret of the Shadow. Gertrude Griffiths
Secret of the Sheba. R. Hardinge
Secret of the Siding. J. Brooke
Secret of the Siegfried Line. M. B. Dix
Secret of the Silent City. D. Haywood
Secret of the Silver Ape. E. H. Robinson
Secret of the Silver Car. W. Martyn
Secret of the Six Black Dots. W. W. Sayer
Secret of the Sixty Steps. J. Drummond
Secret of the Smuggler's Cove. R. Hardinge
Secret of the Snows. G. Chester
Secret of the Snows. H. H. C. Gibbons
Secret of the Snows. J. Plain
Secret of the Snows. W. Tyrer
Secret of the Spa. C. L. Leonard
Secret of the Spectre's Nest. W. E. Groves
Secret of the Sphinx. H. Carew
Secret of the Square. W. LeQueux
Secret of the Stage. N. Ridley
Secret of the Stargazer's Club. Jack Carew
Secret of the Steps. G. Chester
Secret of the Strong Room. G. H. Teed
Secret of the Su. K. Robeson
Secret of the Sudan. W. Jardine
Secret of the Suez Canal. G. Rees
Secret of the Sunken Ships. G. Chester
Secret of the Surgery. J. W. Bobin
Secret of the Surgery. W. Jardine
Secret of the Swamp. G. Bettany
Secret of the Swinging Room. E. M. Robinson
Secret of the Ten Bales. A. Parsons
Secret of the Thames. J. Tregellis
Secret of the Thieves' Kitchen. G. H. Teed
Secret of the Tomb. W. J. Bayfield
Secret of the Tong. A. Edgar
Secret of the Tower. P. A. Clarke
Secret of the Tower. Anthony Hope
Secret of the Two Blackmailed Men. W. M. Graydon
Secret of the Vampire Actress. W. M. Graydon
Secret of the Vase. Preston James
Secret of the Vault. D. W. Steward
Secret of the Veld. R. Hardinge
Secret of the Villa Como. S. Marvin
Secret of the Vineyard. M. Heath
Secret of the Weeping Monk. B. McMikle
Secret of the White Thug. R. Francis Foster
Secret of the Willows. Elna Stone
Secret of the Woods. P. Quiroule
Secret of the Yellow Robe. P. Anson
Secret of the Zodiac. J. Sterne
Secret of Thirty-Seven Hardy Street. R. J. Casey
Secret of Thirty Years! W. W. Sayer
Secret of Thurlston Towers. L. H. Brooks
Secret of Torre Island. R. C. Armour
Secret of Trescobell. J. Hocking
Secret of Tso Feng. L. C. Douthwaite
Secret of Villa Vanesta. E. Glen

Secret of Wardale Court and other stories. Andree Hope
Secret of Weir House. F. Cowen
Secret of Windthorn. B. Carlton
Secret of Wold Hall. E. Everett-Green
Secret of Wyvern Towers. T. W. Speight
Secret Orchards. Michael Burt
Secret Orders. H. P. Jeffers
Secret Pact. A. O. Pollard
Secret Panel. Nicholas Carter
Secret Panel. A. S. Swan
Secret Paper. W. Wood
Secret Passage. F. Hume
Secret Past. A. Marmor
Secret Pathway. A. Askew
Secret Pearls. O. Binns
Secret People. H. H. C. Gibbons
Secret Pilot. G. E. Rochester
Secret Place. D. V. Baker
Secret Place. J. P. Barter
Secret Police. John Lang
Secret Power. T. C. H. Jacobs
Secret Power. V. Van Der Elst
Secret Protocol. J. M. Simmel
Secret Quest. G. M. Fenn
Secret Rage. C. Harris
Secret Road. J. Ferguson
Secret Room of Morgate House. E. Grandower
Secret Sceptre. F. Gerard
Secret Sea-Plane. G. Thorne
Secret Search. E. R. Punshon
Secret Sentence. V. Baum
Secret Servant. G. Lyall
Secret Servant. B. Newman
Secret Service. C. T. Brady
Secret Service. A. Forrester
Secret Service. W. Gillette
Secret Service. W. LeQueux
Secret Service. P. Sebastian
Secret Service: Tales of the Letter Bag. P. H. Woodward
Secret Service Girl. Roland Daniel
Secret Service Girl. J. M. Walsh
Secret Service Man. G. Dilnot
Secret Service Man. S. Horler
Secret Service Mystery. H. Pink
Secret Service Operator 13. R. W. Chambers
Secret Service Schoolboy. E. Protheroe
Secret Service Ship. C. E. Averill
Secret Service Smith. R. T. M. Scott
Secret Service Submarine. G. Thorne
Secret Service Woman. H. De Halsalle
Secret Services. G. Frankau
Secret Seven. R. Essex
Secret Shame of the Kaiser. W. LeQueux
Secret Ship. E. K. Chatterton
Secret Sin. W. LeQueux
Secret Singing. Roy Lewis
Secret Singing. R. C. Smith
Secret Sinners. B. McKnight
Secret Sister. A. Applin
Secret Six. F. Marion
Secret Society. D. Onyeama
Secret Soldier. J. Quigley
Secret Spring. P. Benoit
Secret Squadron. L. L. Driggs
Secret Squadron in Germany. G. E. Rochester
Secret Square. E. Jepson
Secret Strangers. T. Tessier
Secret Submarine. Anonymous
Secret Submarine. M. Ash
Secret Super-Charger. P. Gill
Secret Suspicion. M. O. Rolfe
Secret Syndicate. R. C. Frazer
Secret Syndicate. F. Whishaw
Secret Telephone. W. LeQueux
Secret Temple. C. Brisbane
Secret Tent. E. Addyman
Secret Terror. F. Hird
Secret That Was Kept. E. Robins
Secret Thread. E. Vance
Secret Toll. P. Thorne
Secret Tomb. M. Leblanc
Secret Tontine. R. M. Gilchrist

Secret Traffic. B. Tozer
Secret Trail. A. Armstrong
Secret Trial. L. Bedford
Secret Tunnel. R. C. Finney
Secret Understanding. Merle Miller
Secret Valley. Elliot Bailey
Secret Vanguard. M. Innes
Secret Vendetta. A. O. Pollard
Secret Voice. H. Desmond
Secret Voyage. Basil Carey
Secret War. N. Daniels
Secret War. D. Wheatley
Secret Warriors. A. Baldwin
Secret Way. J. S. Fletcher
Secret Ways. Alistair MacLean
Secret Ways. A. Soutar
Secret Weapon. F. Beeding
Secret Weapon. B. Newman
Secret Weapons. J. M. Walsh
Secret Whispers. T. Allbeury
Secret Witness. G. F. Gibbs
Secret Woman. V. Holt
Secretary. Anonymous
Secretary of Frivolous Affairs. M. Futrelle
Secretary of State for Death. H. Carstairs
Secrets. F. L. Bailey
Secrets. A. Cavendish
Secrets. B. Hastings
Secrets. B. Hirschfeld
Secrets. J. R. Lowell
Secrets. S. Wagner
Secrets Can Be Fatal. M. Heath
Secrets Can't Be Kept. E. R. Punshon
Secrets for Sale. C. L. Leonard
Secrets for Sale. J. H. Vahey
Secrets in the Snow. J. Hinchman
Secrets of a Dark Plot in New York Society. A. S. Manley
Secrets of a Private Enquiry Office. Mrs. G. Corbett
Secrets of a Private Enquiry Office. J. Peddie
Secrets of Cromwell Crossing. D. Winston
Secrets of Dr. Taverner. D. Fortune
Secrets of Harry Bright. J. Wambaugh
Secrets of Hillyard House. K. Norris
Secrets of Mabel Eastlake. D. S. Olson
Secrets of Monte Carlo. W. LeQueux
Secrets of My Office. Anonymous
Secrets of Potsdam. W. LeQueux
Secrets of Sedbury Manor. Marilyn Ross
Secrets of the Coast. S. Cobb
Secrets of the Courts of Europe. A. Upward
Secrets of the Dead-Letter Office. B. Hemyng
Secrets of the Foreign Office. W. LeQueux
Secrets of the Heart. J. Ashley
Secrets of the Past. A. Upward
Secrets of the Police. Grace M. White
Secrets of the Racecourse. A. S. Hardy
Secrets of the River. B. Hemyng
Secrets of the Turf. B. Hemyng
Secrets of the White Tsar. W. LeQueux
Secrets of Tyrone. R. Forest
Section 558. J. Hawthorne
Sector 12. R. D. Bennett
Security Risk. J. Blackwell
Security Risk. G. Hackforth-Jones
Security Risk. T. C. H. Jacobs
Security Secrets Sold Here. B. Cobb
Sedan Murder Mystery. J. Wallace
Sedona. J. Farmer
Seduce and Destroy. J. Eastwood
Seducer. F. Flora
Seducers. J. J. Jordan
Seduction. A. Bourgeau
Seduction. S. Yorke
Seduction in Berlin. W. Kotzwinkle
Seduction of a Tall Man. R. Gadney
Seduction of Peter S. Lawrence Sanders
Seductress. Carter Brown
Sedulous Ape. D. Batchelor
See Charlie Run. B. Freemantle
See How They Run. W. M. Green
See How They Run. A. Kennington
See How They Run. M. Litchfield
See How They Run. D. M. Mankiewicz

See If He Wins. R. Spong
See It Again, Sam. Carter Brown
See Naples and Die. John Davies
See Naples and Die. J. Nathenson
See Naples and Kill. G. Dowling
See No Evil. M. Eatock
See No Evil. W. Hughes
See No Evil. F. McDermid
See No Evil. E. Mathis
See No Evil. G. McGill
See No Evil. Patricia Wallace
See No Evil. K. Welles
See Nothing—Say Nothing. P. Carlon
See-Pah-Poo. K. Robeson
See Rome and Die. L. Revell
See the Kid Run. B. Ottum
See the Living Crocodiles. C. V. Bark
See the Red Blood Run. N. N. Peebles
See the Woman. D. Barnes
See Them Die. E. McBain
See Who's Dying. S. H. Courtier
See You at the Morgue. L. G. Blochman
See You Later, Alligator. W. F. Buckley, Jr.
Seed of Empire. F. M. White
Seed of Evil. P. Crawford
Seed of Suspicion. J. T. Osborne
Seed of the Falcon. C. Darby
Seed of Violence. Williams Forrest
Seed Was Kind. D. Macardle
Seedbreakers. P. V. Timlett
Seeding. D. Shobin
Seeds of Corruption. J. Knowler
Seeds of Destruction. R. V. Beste
Seeds of Destruction. J. Griffin
Seeds of Destruction. D. Nabarro
Seeds of Doom. Ralph Hayes
Seeds of Evil. M. Bingley
Seeds of Evil. D. Streib
Seeds of Hate. H. Carmichael
Seeds of Murder. V. M. Mason
Seeds of Murder. J. York
Seeds of Suspicion. J. McGreevey
Seeds of Suspicion. J. Roffman
Seeds of Treason. T. Allbeury
Seeds of Violence. M. Sharman
Seeds of Yesterday. V. C. Andrews
Seeing. W. P. McGivern
Seeing Double. E. Ferrars
Seeing Eye. Josephine Bell
Seeing Is Believing. Carter Dickson
Seeing Knife. F. Crawley
Seeing Life. E. P. Oppenheim
Seeing Life! and other stories. Marjorie Bowen
Seeing Red. T. Du Bois
Seeing Red. R. Ormerod
Seeing Red. D. J. Schow
Seek and Destroy. Ray Owen
Seek and Destroy. M. K. Robertson
Seek for Justice. R. Lewis
Seek, Strike and Destroy. K. Stanton
Seeker to the Dead. A. M. Burrage
Seen and Not Heard. Anne Stuart
Seen and the Unseen. R. Marsh
Seen Dimly Before Dawn. N. Balchin
Seen from a Windmill. Drew Miller
Seen in the Shadow. F. Hume
Seeress. G. B. Lissenden
Seersucker Whipsaw. Ross Thomas
Seesaw Millions. J. Van de Wetering
Seidlitz and the Super-Spy. Carter Brown
Seige for Panda One. P. N. Walker
Seine Fishers. J. Wood
Seine Mystery. C. Moffett
Seize a Passing Stranger. C. Joyce
Seize the Dragon. M. Schorr
Seizing of Singapore. I. Stewart
Seizing of Yankee Green Mall. Ridley Pearson
Seizure. David Fraser
Selected Great Stories. B. Hecht
Selected Plays. Lady Gregory
Selected Short Stories of Sinclair Lewis. S. Lewis
Selected Stories. D. V. Baker
Selected Stories. G. Kersh
Self-Appointed Saint. A. E. Lindop

Self-Convicted. H. Wood
Self-Doomed. B. L. Farjeon
Self-Destruct. Angus Hall
Self-Made. E. Southworth
Self-Made Thief. H. Footner
Self-Made Widow. P. Race
Self-Portrait of Murder. F. Bonnamy
Self-Portrait of Someone Else. V. Eaton
Self-Raised. E. Southworth
Selicombe Murder. N. Islay
Sellers of Death. W. W. Sayer
Selling Death Short. Fredric Brown
Selling's Murder! Ay. Tack
Sellout. D. Jewell
Selmin of Selmingfold. B. Mitford
Selsey Gold. H. C. Davis
Semi-Society. F. Richardson
Seminar for Murder. B. M. Gill
Seminar in Evil. D. Winston
Semonov Impulse. J. Meldrum
Semper Inheritance. C. Carfax
Semprinski Affair. W. S. Kuniczak
Senator's Nude. B. Goode
Senator's Plot. Nicholas Carter
Senator's Ransom. K. Bernstein
Send Another Coffin. J. Grecco
Send Another Coffin. F. G. Presnell
Send Another Hearse. H. Q. Masur
Send Bygraves. M. Grimes
Send Danger. M. Sutherland
Send for Angel. G. Montrose
Send for Mr. Robinson. J. M. White
Send for Paul Temple. F. Durbridge
Send for Paul Temple Again! F. Durbridge
Send for the Saint. L. Charteris
Send Him Victorious. D. Hurd
Send in the Lions. Eric Clark
Send Inspector West. J. Creasey
Send Me a Mink! W. Standish
Send Me No Lilies. P. Denver
Send No Flowers. Gavin Holt
Send No More Roses. E. Ambler
Send-Off. R. Hiscock
Send-Off. C. Leach
Send Superintendent West. J. Creasey
Sendai. W. Woolfolk
Sending. G. Household
Seneca, U.S.A. J. Roeburt
Senor Saint. L. Charteris
Sensation at Blue Harbour. J. L. Rickard
Sensation on Sin Street. M. Brody
Sensational Case. F. Warden
Sensational Tales. M. Clarke
Sensational Trance. F. Dawson
Sense of Danger. E. Cannon
Sense of Guilt. G. Simenon
Sense of Loyalty. J. Ashford
Sense of Reality. G. Greene
Sense of Survival. K. Casey
Senseless. J. D. Burtt
Sensitive Case. Eric Wright
Sensitive Encounter. Canella Lewis
Sensitives. H. Burkholz
Sensualists. B. Hecht
Sensuality. H. Janson
Sent to His Account. E. Dillon
Sentence Deferred. A. Derleth
Sentence for Sin. H. Janson
Sentence of Death. J. York
Sentence of Life. Julian Gloag
Sentence of the Court. H. Hill
Sentence of the Court. F. M. White
Sentence of the Judge. H. E. Barlow
Sentence of the Six-Gun. A. M. Rud
Sentence Suspended. C. Joyce
Sentenced! S. Gibney
Sentenced to Death. R. Machray
Sentenced to Life. M. A. Hamilton
Sentiment, and other stories. V. O'Sullivan
Sentimental Adventures of Jimmy Bulstrode. M. Van Vorst
Sentimental Crook. A. Wilson
Sentimental Kill. R. Clapperton
Sentimental Maria. J. S. Winter

Sentimental Season. T. Cobb
Sentimental Sex. G. Warden
Sentimental Spy. A. C. Ley
Sentimental Warrior. E. Jepson
Sentinel. J. Konvitz
Sentinel Point. N. Dorer
Sentries. E. McBain
Senty-Box Murder. N. Gayle
Separate Cases. R. J. Randisi
September Can Be Dangerous in Edinburgh. B. Craig
September Comes In. F. M. McGuire
September September. S. Foote
September Story. R. Inchbald
Septimus and the Danedyke Mystery. Stephen Chance
Septimus and the Minster Ghost. Stephen Chance
Septimus and the Minster Ghost Mystery. Stephen Chance
Septimus and the Spy Ring. Stephen Chance
Septimus and the Stone of Offering. Stephen Chance
Sepulchre. James Herbert
Sequel to a Verdict. P. Dunning
Sequel to Opposite the Jail. M. A. Denison
Sequel to Yesterday. P. A. Foxall
Sequence of Events. E. Ferrars
Sequin Syndicate. O. Hesky
Sequins Lost Their Lustre. S. Harvester
Sequoia Shootout. John Reese
Seraphim Code. R. A. Liston
Serbian Assignment. Andrew Moore
Serena. J. Aeby
Serena. J. Fitzpatrick
Serenade. J. M. Cain
Serenade for a Shylock. A. Zeiger
Serenade for Murder. A. Wood
Serenade to the Hangman. M. Dekobra
Sergeant and the Queen. R. Crane
Sergeant Bigglesworth C.I.D. W. E. Johns
Sergeant Cluff and the Day of Reckoning. G. North
Sergeant Cluff and the Madmen. G. North
Sergeant Cluff and the Price of Pity. G. North
Sergeant Cluff Goes Fishing. G. North
Sergeant Cluff Rings True. G. North
Sergeant Cluff Stands Firm. G. North
Sgt. Corbin's War. R. Crane
Sergeant Cork's Casebook. A. Swinson
Sergeant Cork's Second Casebook. A. Swinson
Sergeant Death. D. G. Browne
Sergeant Death. F. P. Grady
Sergeant Death. J. Mayo
Sergeant Dunn, C.I.D. E. Wallace
Sergeant Getulio. J. U. Ribeiro
Sergeant Gray's Crime. J. Hunter
Sgt. Hawk. P. Clay
Sergeant Horn's Murder Trap. J. O'Donoghue
Sergeant Lancey Carries On. L. P. Greene
Sergeant Lancey Reports. L. P. Greene
Sergeant Lancey Tells the Tale. L. P. Greene
Sergeant Michael Cassidy, R. E. H. C. McNeile
Sergeant O'Mara. M. Sandford
Sergeant on Trial. I. Johnston
Sergeant O'Reilly. Ian Anderson
Sergeant Ritchie's Conscience. F. Branston
Sergeant Ross in Disguise. B. Cobb
Sergeant Sir Peter. E. Wallace
Sergeant Verity and the Blood Royal. F. Selwyn
Sergeant Verity and the Cracksman. F. Selwyn
Sergeant Verity and the Imperial Diamond. F. Selwyn
Sergeant Verity and the Swell Mob. F. Selwyn
Sergeant Verity Presents His Compliments. F. Selwyn
Sergeant Von. Unknown
Sergeant Whatisname. L. P. Greene
Sergeant's Cat. J. Van de Wetering
Series of Murders. S. Brett
Serious Crimes. L. Gough
Serious Crimes. D. W. Smith
Serious Investigation. L. Egan
Serle's Secret. F. Warden
Sern Charter. F. Ryck
Serpent. R. Vane

Serpent. D. Wiltse
Serpent Among the Lilies. P. C. Doherty
Serpent and the Slave. C. H. Woodcock
Serpent-Headed Stick. J. Hawk
Serpent Heart. M. A. Taylor
Serpent in the Shadows. A. Barron
Serpent of Lilith. M. Villiers
Serpent Sleeping. E. Weismuller
Serpent Stirs. Richard Grant
Serpent Under It. E. Taylor
Serpentine Murder. L. Gribble
Serpentine Wall. J. DeBrosse
Serpent's Circle. P. Harpur
Serpent's Egg. D. Duncan
Serpent's Eye. W. Barker
Serpent's Fang. Brian Stuart
Serpent's Mark. R. L. Duncan
Serpent's Smile. O. Hesky
Serpent's Tooth. D. Kilcommons
Serpent's Tooth. S. Nichols
Serpent's Tooth. Sara Woods
Servant of Death. J. H. Wallis
Servant of Satan. L. Berard
Servants of the Goddess. H. Campbell
Servants of the Skull. B. House
Servants of Twilight. L. Nichols
Servant's Problem. V. P. Johns
Service of All the Dead. C. Dexter
Set. Gwen Davis
Set a Spy. M. McKenna
Set a Thief. G. F. Newman
Set a Thief. Martin Page
Set a Thief. E. E. Paramore
Set a Thief. L. Thayer
Set a Trap. E. G. Love
Set Fair. Joan Butler
Set of Flats. A. Griffiths
Set of Rogues. F. Barrett
Set of Six. J. Conrad
Set to Partners. G. Warden
Set-Up. J. K. Baxter
Set-Up. A. Capelli
Set-Up. R. Carni
Set-Up. L. Corradi
Set-Up. M. Franklin
Set Up. Stuart Hall
Set-Up. E. G. Love
Set-Up. B. E. Miller
Set-Up. W. Newton
Set-Up. V. Volkoff
Set-Up for a Sinner. M. Brody
Set Up for Danger. Rick Madison
Set-Up for Murder. P. Cheyney
Set-Up for Scandal. M. Brody
Seth Bond. Old Sleuth
Seth Papers. F. Lauria
Setting for Murder. E. Fulton
Settled Out of Court. H. Cecil
Settled Out of Court. R. A. Knox
Settler or Slaver. A. Murray
Settling of Accounts. C. G. Hart
Setup. F. Earley
Setup for Murder. L. A. Olmsted
Seven. Evan Hunter
Seven. J. D. MacDonald
Seven Against Greece. Nick Carter
Seven Agate Devils. K. Robeson
Seven Black Chessmen. J. Huntingdon
Seven Bloodhounds. M. Richmond
Seven Blue Diamonds. C. B. Stilson
Seven Chines. W. W. Hall
Seven Chose Murder. Roy Vickers
Seven Clues. G. Verner
Seven Clues in Search of a Crime. B. Graeme
Seven Conundrums. E. P. Oppenheim
Seven Dawns to Death. B. Gray
Seven Day Soldiers. T. Kenrick
Seven Days Before Dying. H. Nielsen
Seven Days for Hanging. J. M. Spender
Seven Days from Midnight. Rona Randall
Seven Days' Hard. S. M. Parkman
Seven Days in a Pullman Car. A. Towner
Seven Days in May. F. Knebel
Seven Day's Mystery. F. R. Burton

Seven Days' Secret. J. S. Fletcher
Seven Days to a Killing. C. Egleton
Seven Days to Death. N. MacKenzie
Seven Days to Death. J. J. Marric
Seven Days to Disaster. Jonas Flagg
Seven Days to Never. P. Frank
Seven Days to Petrograd. T. Hyman
Seven Dead. J. J. Farjeon
Seven Deadly Sins. Marjorie Bowen
Seven Deadly Sisters. P. McGerr
Seven Dials Mystery. A. Christie
Seven Died. G. Homes
711—Officer Needs Help. W. Masterson
Seven Elms Mystery. H. B. Harris
Seven File. W. P. McGivern
Seven Footprints to Satan. A. Merritt
Seven for Murder. R. Glenning
Seven Games in October. Charles Brady
Seven Gates to Nowhere. T. Willis
Seven Green Stones. P. Wentworth
Seven Guests of Fear. I. Barry
Seven Hells. C. Brooks
Seven Keys to Baldpate. E. D. Biggers
Seven Keys to Baldpate. G. M. Cohan
Seven Lamps. G. Verner
Seven Lean Years. C. Fremlin
Seven Lies South. W. P. McGivern
Seven Looked On. B. Malim
Seven Madmen. R. Arlt
Seven Men. M. Beerbohm
Seven Men. T. Roscoe
Seven Men Are Murdered. R. Wallace
Seven Miles from Sydney. Lesley Thompson
Seven Minutes Past Midnight. W. Winward
7 Murders. R. H. May
7 Must Die. J. W. Bellah
Seven Nights at the Resort. D. Enefer
Seven North. N. Ravin
Seven of Hearts. M. Leblanc
Seven of Swords. R. E. Harrington
Seven-Per-Cent Solution. N. Meyer
Seven Pillars to Hell. H. Marlowe
Seven Red-Headed Men. F. Marlowe
Seven Red Herrings. E. P. Thorne
Seven Saints. G. Stanley
Seven Schemers. Nicholas Carter
Seven Screens. G. Dickson
Seven Seas Murders. V. W. Mason
Seven Seats to the Moon. C. Armstrong
Seven Secrets. W. LeQueux
Seven Shadows. G. Stanley
Seven Silent Men. N. Behn
Seven Sins. S. Rohmer
Seven Sirens. Carter Brown
Seven Sisters. W. T. Ballard
Seven Sisters. R. Chapman
Seven Sisters. J. Lilly
Seven Slayers. P. Cain
Seven Sleepers. F. Beeding
Seven Sleepers. E. Ferrars
Seven Sleepers. J. Pattinson
Seven Sleepers. B. St. James
Seven Sons. A. Simon
Seven Sons of Mammon. G. A. Sala
Seven Stabs. J. Cameron
Seven Stars. V. Bridges
Seven Stars. Maxwell Scott
Seven Steps East. B. Benson
Seven Steps to Treason. M. Hartland
Seven Strange Tales. Kaye Drummond
Seven Suspects. G. K. Chesterton
Seven Suspects. M. Innes
Seven Suspects. F. Ryerson
Seven Tears for Apollo. P. A. Whitney
7:30 Victoria. P. McGuire
Seven Thunders. R. Croft-Cooke
Seven Thunders. M. M. Lawrence
Seven Tickets to Singapore. Ared White
Seven Times Seven. J. Creasey
Seven to Die. H. Long
7 to 12. A. K. Green
Seven-Ups. R. Posner
Seven Votes for Death. P. Bannister
Seven Were Suspect. R. Goyne

Seven Were Suspect. K. M. Knight
Seven Were Veiled. K. M. Knight
Seven Who Waited. A. Derleth
Seven Widows of Hempstead. S. Ready
Seven Witnesses. E. Trevor
Seven Wives for Dracula. T. J. Kelly
Seven Women. Winifred Duke
Seven Xmas Eves. Anonymous
Seven Year Friend. D. Huxley
Seven Year Secret. F. Hurt
Seven Years Dead. S. Truss
17 and Black. J. Waer
17 Ben Gurion. J. Hoffenberg
Seventeen Cards. E. C. Vivian
17 Farrington Way. L. H. Bank
Seventeen Moments of Spring. J. Semyonov
Seventeen Thieves of El-Kabil. T. Mundy
Seventeen Widows of San Souci. C. Armstrong
17th Letter. D. C. Disney
Seventeenth Stair. P. Paul
Seventh. R. Stark
Seventh All Hallows' Eve. R. Jensen
Seventh Avenue Murder. Liza Bennett
Seventh Chasm. O. Gard
Seventh Child. B. Stanwood
Seventh Cross. A. Seghers
Seventh Crossword. H. Resnicow
Seventh Entanglement. E. Leslie
Seventh Fury. J. Castle
Seventh Game. D. Kowet
Seventh Gate. D. Holliday
Seventh Gate. K. Leckie
Seventh Hexagram. I. McLachlan
Seventh Hunch. W. H. Hamby
Seventh Juror. F. Didelot
Seventh Man. Wilson Barclay
Seventh Man. G. Garden
Seventh Man. J. Scotland
Seventh Mask. H. Slesar
Seventh Mourner. D. Gardiner
Seventh Passenger. P. Capon
Seventh Passenger. A. MacGowan
Seventh Postcard. H. Flowerdew
Seventh Power. James Mills
Seventh Royale. D. Stanwood
Seventh Sacrament. Roland Cutler
Seventh Sanctuary. D. Easterman
Seventh Secret. Irving Wallace
Seventh Sense. H. R. Thompson
Seventh Shot. H. Coverdale
Seventh Sign. B. Flynn
Seventh Sinner. Elizabeth Peters
Seventh Station. R. McInerny
Seventh Stone. W. B. Murphy
Seventh Vial. F. Sleath
Seventh Wife of Prince Hasson. M. Dekobra
Seventy Fathom Treasure. A. D. Divine
Seventy North—70 Degrees N. Taffrail
71 Hours. M. Mason
77, Park Lane. W. Hackett
77 Rue Paradis. G. Brewer
77 Sunset Strip. R. Huggins
77 Willow Road. H. D. Irvine
77th Day. H. Possendorf
70 Sutton Place. J. Di Mona
70,000 Witnesses. C. Fitzsimmons
Seventy Times Seven. J. B. Sanford
Several Deaths Later. E. Gorman
Severed Hand. F. Du Boisgobey
Severed Hand. E. Lecale
Severed Hand. M. Serao
Severed Key. H. Nielsen
Severed Wasp. M. L'Engle
Severence. T. Cobb
Severing Line. S. Cardiff
Severith Style. D. Honig
Severn Affair. G. Warden
Sevier Secrets. D. Daniels
Seward's Folly. G. Lancaster
Sex Angle. H. Janson
Sex Castle. E. Lacy
Sex Clinic. Carter Brown
Sex Cult Murders. J. Davidson
Sex Gauntlet to Murder. Mark Shane

Title Index

Sex Is a Deadly Exercise. P. Scot-Bernard
Sex Life. B. Cook
Sex Life on the Planet Mars. F. Brown
Sex Marks the Spot. S. Browning
Sex Resort. Stuart Hall
Sex Trap. Carter Brown
Sex Trap. Bill Turner
Sex War. S. Merwin, Jr.
Sexless Spy. T. Hoyle
Sexton Blake. Anonymous
Sexton Blake and the Demon God. J. Garforth
Sexton Blake at Oxford. C. Hayter
Sexton Blake at School. C. Hayter
Sexton Blake at the 'Varsity. J. Andrews
Sexton Blake Casebook. Anonymous
Sexton Blake, Clerk. E. J. Gannon
Sexton Blake, Foreman. E. W. Alais
Sexton Blake in Siberia. W. M. Graydon
Sexton Blake in Silesia. W. M. Graydon
Sexton Blake in the Congo. W. M. Graydon
Sexton Blake in the Sixth. C. Hayter
Sexton Blake, Sixth Former. C. Hayter
Sexton Blake—Special Constable. J. W. Robin
Sexton Blake, Spy. W. M. Graydon
Sexton Blake, Steward. E. W. Alais
Sexton Blake Wins. Anonymous
Sexton Blake's Early Cases. Anonymous
Sexton Blake's Honour. N. Goddard
Sexton Blake's Quest. W. M. Graydon
Sexton Blake's Schooldays. C. Hayter
Sexton Blake's Trust. E. J. Gannon
Sexton Blake's Vow. A. Steffens Hardy
Sexton Blake's Zulu. C. Hayter
Sexton Woman. R. Neely
Sexy Vixen. H. Janson
Shabby Eagles. B. Gaston
Shack Locker. F. W. Wallace
Shack Road Girl. H. Whittington
Shack-Up. A. Curry
Shackled. M. Crossley
Shackles. B. Pronzini
Shackleton Called Sheila. D. Mariner
Shade Against the Sun. F. Greenland
Shade of Darkness. M. Torrie
Shade of the Moon. M. Carnson
Shade of Time. D. Duncan
Shades and Shadows. L. Churchill
Shades of Darkness. R. Cowper
Shades of Evil. S. Wagner
Shades of Gray. M. Denning
Shades of Greene. G. Greene
Shades of Peril. M. Cordell
Shades Will Not Vanish. H. Fowler
Shadow. H. Bedford-Jones
Shadow. G. Dare
Shadow. B. Garnett
Shadow. W. B. Gibson
Shadow. V. Kelly
Shadow. M. Level
Shadow. P. Mason
Shadow. A. Melville-Ross
Shadow. A. Stringer
Shadow. Donald Stuart
Shadow. P. Urquhart
Shadow Acres. F. Y. McHugh
Shadow Across the Sun. J. Ames
Shadow Agent. W. Martyn
Shadow, and other stories. J. Farnol
Shadow and the Blot. N. D. Lobell
Shadow and the Fear. J. Corby
Shadow and the Golden Master. W. G. Gibson
Shadow and the Stone. L. Meynell
Shadow and the Web. Mary Allerton
Shadow at Dunston Hall. E. Desmond
Shadow Before. J. N. Chance
Shadow Before. L. P. Davies
Shadow Before. W. Rollins
Shadow Behind. F. Warwick
Shadow Behind the Curtain. V. Johnston
Shadow Behind the Throne. O. Harper
Shadow Between. S. Hocking
Shadow Between. R. Pattison
Shadow Beware. M. Grant
Shadow Box. V. Coffman

Shadow Buttress. S. Styles
Shadow Cabinet. W. T. Tyler
Shadow Called Janet. J. N. Chance
Shadow Crook. A. De Brune
Shadow Crook. G. H. Teed
Shadow Crusade. W. Mills
Shadow Dance. Susan Anderson
Shadow Dance. A. Carter
Shadow Dancers. H. Lieberman
Shadow—Destination Moon. M. Grant
Shadow Detective. Old Sleuth
Shadow 81. L. Nahum
Shadow Falls. C. Lorrimer
Shadow Falls. G. Simenon
Shadow Flight. J. Weber
Shadow for a Lady. J. L. Linklater
Shadow from the Bogue. Clement Wood
Shadow from the Past. F. S. Gabbert
Shadow Game. D. Kamm
Shadow Game. M. Underwood
Shadow Glen. D. Daniels
Shadow—Go Mad! M. Grant
Shadow Guest. H. Waugh
Shadow Guests. Joan Aiken
Shadow Hall. J. P. Seabrooke
Shadow Hill. Joyce Wilson
Shadow in Pursuit. J. N. Chance
Shadow in Red. L. O'Donnell
Shadow in the Corner. M. E. Braddon
Shadow in the Courtyard. G. Simenon
Shadow in the House. S. Gluck
Shadow in the House. M. March
Shadow in the Sea. O. John
Shadow in the Sun. L. Meynell
Shadow in the Wild. W. Masterson
Shadow: Jade Dragon and House of Ghosts. W. B. Gibson
Shadow Jury. P. Hutin
Shadow Kills. W. R. Philbrick
Shadow Knows. Diane Johnson
Shadow Lady. D. Haring
Shadow Laughs! M. Grant
Shadow Line. L. Furman
Shadow Man. R. M. Ayres
Shadow Man. C. Barroll
Shadow Man. J. Goodwin
Shadow Man. J. W. Kunetka
Shadow Man. J. Lutz
Shadow Man. F. M. Parker
Shadow Man of Berlin. Anonymous
Shadow Mansion. R. Calif
Shadow Mansion. Wilma Forrest
Shadow Men. D. Richberg
Shadow Men. G. Verner
Shadow Money. G. A. Effinger
Shadow of a Broken Man. G. Chesbro
Shadow of a Cat. P. Nottingham
Shadow of a Crime. H. Caine
Shadow of a Crime. C. K. Earl
Shadow of a Crime. J. Rhode
Shadow of a Crime. Mrs. G. Sheldon
Shadow of a Dead Man. T. W. Hanshew
Shadow of a Doubt. H. Judd
Shadow of a Doubt. J. Thomson
Shadow of a Dream. R. Fernand
Shadow of a Gun. D. Spade
Shadow of a Gun. Martin Thomas
Shadow of a Hair. D. C. Meade
Shadow of a Hawk. M. Carrel
Shadow of a Hero. Allan Chase
Shadow of a Killer. W. Mole
Shadow of a Lady. H. Roth
Shadow of a Life. J. L. Hornibrook
Shadow of a Man. D. Daniels
Shadow of a Man. D. M. Disney
Shadow of a Man. E. W. Hornung
Shadow of a Past Love. W. D. Roberts
Shadow of a Sin. H. Zore
Shadow of a Spy. A. MacKenzie
Shadow of a Stranger. A. Maybury
Shadow of a Tiger. Michael Collins
Shadow of a Vendetta. A. C. Gunter
Shadow of a Witch. P. Minton
Shadow of a Witch. M. Paradise

Shadow of an Alibi. J. Rhode
Shadow of an Assassin. I. Stark
Shadow of an Unknown Woman. D. Winston
Shadow of Ashlydyat. H. Wood
Shadow of Burmah. M. Chantoon
Shadow of Cain. V. T. Bugliosi
Shadow of Christine. E. C. Vivian
Shadow of Chu-Sheng. E. Thomas
Shadow of Death. G. Ashe
Shadow of Death. Caroline Gray
Shadow of Death. W. X. Keinzle
Shadow of Death. R. Hausfeld
Shadow of Deceit. L. Loghry
Shadow of Dr. Ferrari. E. P. Thorne
Shadow of Doctor Syn. R. Thorndike
Shadow of Doom. J. Creasey
Shadow of Doubt. A. S. Roche
Shadow of Drumcarnett. A. W. Kerr
Shadow of Egypt. H. H. Ross
Shadow of Elizabeth. Michael Pearson
Shadow of Evil. M. Black
Shadow of Evil. L. Blanchet
Shadow of Evil. C. Dawe
Shadow of Evil. D. Donovan
Shadow of Evil. C. J. Dutton
Shadow of Evil. D. Romaine
Shadow of Fear. R. C. Payes
Shadow of Fear. B. Spicer
Shadow of Fu Manchu. S. Rohmer
Shadow of Gilsland. M. Gerard
Shadow of Guilt. R. Bloomfield
Shadow of Guilt. Old Spicer
Shadow of Guilt. P. Quentin
Shadow of Hampton Mead. E. Van Loon
Shadow of Himself. M. Delving
Shadow of His Crime. J. W. Bobin
Shadow of John Wallace. L. Clarkson
Shadow of Larose. A. Gask
Shadow of Li Tong Su. C. Bishop
Shadow of Lies. D. E. McQuinn
Shadow of Madness. H. Pentecost
Shadow of Malreward. J. B. Harris-Burland
Shadow of Monte Carlo and other stories. C. Kingston
Shadow of Murder. C. Blackstock
Shadow of Murder. M. F. Ford
Shadow of Murder. P. Laing
Shadow of My Brother. D. Grubb
Shadow of Peril. A. I. Zhdanov
Shadow of Popperro. F. Cowen
Shadow of Quong Lung. C. W. Doyle
Shadow of Ravenscliffe. J. S. Fletcher
Shadow of Salvador. J. Haslette
Shadow of Shadows. T. Allbeury
Shadow of Shame. Austyn Granville
Shadow of Sheila Ann. P. Wissmann
Shadow of Suspicion. W. A. Miles
Shadow of Tarleton Manor. B. M. Clay
Shadow of Terror. A. Goetz
Shadow of the Bars. E. D. Pierson
Shadow of the Bear. H. Hill
Shadow of the Beast. G. F. Di Pego
Shadow of the Caravan. S. O'Brien
Shadow of the Cat. M. Hara
Shadow of the Cliff. N. Kennedy
Shadow of the Cliff. C. E. Mallandaine
Shadow of the Cobra. D. Dalheath
Shadow of the Condor. J. Grady
Shadow of the Czar. J. R. Carling
Shadow of the Dragon. A. Kuller
Shadow of the Eagle. J. Hagar
Shadow of the Four. Mark Cross
Shadow of the Gallows. M. Richmond
Shadow of the Gestapo. W. Darrell
Shadow of the Guillotine. G. E. Rochester
Shadow of the House. J. Lindsay
Shadow of the Hunter. C. Kerr
Shadow of the Killer. J. N. Chance
Shadow of the Knife. K. R. McKay
Shadow of the Leopard. M. Hartmann
Shadow of the Lynx. V. Holt
Shadow of the Mafia. L. Malley
Shadow of the Monsoon. W. Manchester
Shadow of the Moth. E. Hawkes

S

Shadow of the Needle. L. A. Sunagel
Shadow of the Noose. Richard Cooper
Shadow of the Palms. J. Law
Shadow of the Past. M. Richmond
Shadow of the Pyramid. R. Ritchie
Shadow of the Red Barn. P. Lindsay
Shadow of the Rock. G. Hackforth-Jones
Shadow of the Rope. E. W. Hornung
Shadow of the Rope. I. Stark
Shadow of the Sun. S. Wagner
Shadow of the Tamaracks. Sara North
Shadow of the Titan. A. Fenton
Shadow of the Truth. H. Arvonen
Shadow of the Volcano. D. Rowan
Shadow of the Warmaster. J. Clayton
Shadow of the Wolf. R. A. Freeman
Shadow of the Wolf. Donald James
Shadow of the Yemen. B. Bolt
Shadow of Theale. F. Cowen
Shadow of Thirteen. J. J. Farjeon
Shadow of Time. C. Landon
Shadow of Tyburn Tree. D. Wheatley
Shadow of Wrong. C. Gibbon
Shadow on Capricorn. Clarissa Ross
Shadow on Mercer Mountain. D. Winston
Shadow on Mockways. M. Bowen
Shadow on Spanish Swamp. Genevieve St. John
Shadow on the Cliff. M. Burton
Shadow on the Course. B. Strong
Shadow on the Downs. R. C. Woodthorpe
Shadow on the Glass. C. J. Dutton
Shadow on the Hearth. F. Halsey
Shadow on the House. A. W. Barrett
Shadow on the House. F. Ford
Shadow on the House. M. Hansom
Shadow on the House. F. Stevenson
Shadow on the House. E. C. Vivian
Shadow on the Left. Augustus Muir
Shadow on the Moon. L. Churchill
Shadow on the Purple. Anonymous
Shadow on the Roof. R. Timperley
Shadow on the Sea. M. Pemberton
Shadow on the Steppe. M. Billett
Shadow on the Sun. G. Seymour
Shadow on the Threshold. M. C. Hay
Shadow on the Wall. H. C. Bailey
Shadow on the Wall. M. E. Coleridge
Shadow on the Wall. M. Dalton
Shadow on the Water. H. Ainsworth
Shadow on the Wind. A. Lowing
Shadow on the Window. G. Bagby
Shadow Over Beauclaire. S. Miles
Shadow Over Bright Star. I. M. Pascoe
Shadow Over Denby. Marilyn Ross
Shadow Over Elveron. M. J. Kingsley
Shadow Over Emerald Castle. Marilyn Ross
Shadow Over Europe. N. Leslie
Shadow Over Fairholme. S. Kyle
Shadow Over Grove House. M. L. Roby
Shadow Over Heldon Hall. N. Herbert
Shadow Over Mount Sharon. F. Y. McHugh
Shadow Over Pleasant Heath. K. Kimbrough
Shadow Over Seventh Heaven. J. Arliss
Shadow Over the Garden. C. Ross
Shadow Over the Island. J. Ames
Shadow Over Wyndham Hall. J. T. Osborne
Shadow Passes. E. Phillpotts
Shadow Passes. Y. Pickering
Shadow People. K. Laing
Shadow Play. C. Beaumont
Shadow Play. John Milne
Shadow Play. C. Phillips
Shadow Play. L. Powell
Shadow Play. M. Werlin
Shadow President. S. Katz
Shadow Prey. J. Sandford
Shadow Run. D. Lowden
Shadow Shooter. W. C. Tuttle
Shadow Show. P. Flower
Shadow Spy. N. Luard
Shadow Stalker. J. Saralegui
Shadow Strikes. M. Grant
Shadow Syndicate. C. Hosken
Shadow That Caught Fire. H. Jobson

Shadow the Baron. Anthony Morton
Shadow Tiger. Barry Taylor
Shadow Trade. A. Furst
Shadow Warriors. D. Stivers
Shadow Wife. D. Eden
Shadow Witness. F. L. Cary
Shadow World. D. Haring
Shadowbox. S. Noyes
Shadowboxer. N. Behn
Shadowboxer. M. A. Calde
Shadowchase. M. Blank
Shadowdance. A. Bushell
Shadowed! H. Belloc
Shadowed. M. Cumberland
Shadowed. B. Glynn
Shadowed by a Detective. V. Champlin
Shadowed by Danger. D. Mai
Shadowed by the C.I.D. T. A. Plummer
Shadowed by Three. L. L. Lynch
Shadowed by 2. Old Sleuth
Shadowed from Europe. Hawkshaw
Shadowed Lives. A. Applin
Shadowed Lives. W. M. Graydon
Shadowed Love. F. M. White
Shadowed Place. V. Scannell
Shadowed Millinos. M. Grant
Shadowed Porch. E. Moor
Shadowed Round the World. J. K. Stafford
Shadowed Spring. C. Salisbury
Shadowed Staircase. P. Warren
Shadowed to Europe. Le Jemlys
Shadowed to His Doom. Old Sleuth
Shadowed Victory. A. Stringer
Shadowers. D. Hamilton
Shadowfires. Leigh Nichols
Shadowhunter. G. Archer
Shadowland. Elaine Evans
Shadowless Men. Bradshaw Jones
Shadowplay. N. Hartley
Shadowplay. Linda Stevens
Shadows. Jan Alexander
Shadows. Winifred Duke
Shadows. S. Hutson
Shadows. Douglas Scott
Shadows. Will Scott
Shadows. J. Sherman
Shadows Across the Bayou. S. L. Anderson
Shadows and Dark Places. M. Lovell
Shadows and Lights. S. Heym
Shadows at Noon. M. M. Goldsmith
Shadows at Noon. K. Hess
Shadows Before. D. Bowers
Shadows by the Sea. J. J. Farjeon
Shadows Don't Bleed. W. Wright
Shadows from the Past. D. Daniels
Shadows from the Past. R. Neely
Shadows from the Thames. E. Noble
Shadows in a Hidden Land. S. Harvester
Shadows in Bronze. Lindsey Davis
Shadows in Succession. E. K. Lobaugh
Shadows in the Afternoon. R. T. Stevens
Shadows in the Fire. Eva Dane
Shadows in the Moonlight. Elizabeth Peters
Shadows in the Night. J. Reach
Shadows in the Sun. J. Edgar
Shadows in Umbria. J. La Tourrette
Shadows of a City Care Forgotten. Moses Williams
Shadows of a Great City. Anonymous
Shadows of Amanda. H. S. Nuelle
Shadows of Castle Fosse. J. Tattersall
Shadows of Cliffside. B. Lee
Shadows of Death. James Lewis
Shadows of Death. G. St. Germain
Shadows of Doubt. P. Harcourt
Shadows of Evil. G. La Spina
Shadows of Fear. K. Hess
Shadows of Fieldcrest Manor. C. Stephens
Shadows of Life. C. Meyer
Shadows of Men. J. Tully
Shadows of One Another. T. R. Cox
Shadows of Passion. P. Gallagher
Shadows of Power. J. Bacia
Shadows of Reddoch's Landing. Melissa Lee
Shadows of the Heart. F. Hurd

Shadows of the House. M. E. Atkins
Shadows of the Past. K. Cameron
Shadows of the Past. M. Craig
Shadows of the Past. G. Ferrand
Shadows of Tomorrow. D. Daniels
Shadows of Vengeance. D. Charles
Shadows of Violence. K. Evans
Shadows of Yesterday. Marjorie Bowen
Shadows on a Wall. C. E. Israel
Shadows on Abu Simbel. T. B. Morris
Shadows on the Bay. Rebecca Holland
Shadows on the Hill. M. Carleton
Shadows on the Landing. G. M. Wilson
Shadows on the Mirror. F. Fyfield
Shadows on the Moon. K. Cameron
Shadows on the Moon. N. Fairweather
Shadows on the Moon. D. Houston
Shadows on the River. A. MacKenzie
Shadows on the Sand. G. Greenaway
Shadows on the Sand. Rona Randall
Shadows on the Sceptered Isle. J. A. Stang
Shadows on the Tor. S. Brand
Shadows on the Wall. M. Reisner
Shadows on the Water. Dorothy Fletcher
Shadows or Glimpses of Society. Ernest Martin
Shadows Over Briarcliff. Marilyn Ross
Shadows Over Seascape. Lynn Williams
Shadows Over Silver Sands. M. Pemberton
Shadow's Revenge. M. Grant
Shadow's Shadow. M. Grant
Shadows Sometimes Scream. L. Della
Shadows Tonight. A. Seifert
Shadows Under White Face. A. Heald
Shadows Waiting. A. Eliot
Shadowshow. B. Strickland
Shadowtide. D. Price
Shadowtown. J. Lutz
Shadowy Thing. H. B. Drake
Shadowy Third. Marco Page
Shady Doings. V. P. Johns
Shady Lady. C. F. Adams
Shady Place to Die. John Savage
Shaft. P. Chevalier
Shaft. D. J. Schow
Shaft. E. Tidyman
Shaft Among the Jews. E. Tidyman
Shaft Has a Ball. E. Tidyman
Shaft 235. R. D. Bennett
Shaft's Big Score. E. Tidyman
Shaggy Dog and other murders. F. Brown
Shaggy Dog and other stories. F. Brown
Shaggy Planet. R. Goulart
Shah-Mak. Alan Williams
Shaitan. M. Ehrlich
Shake a Crooked Town. D. J. Marlowe
Shake Hands for Ever. R. Rendell
Shake Hands for Ever. E. Woodward
Shake Hands with the Devil. R. Conner
Shake Hands with the Devil. M. K. Ozaki
Shake-Up. H. Edmiston
Shake-Up. Breni James
Shakedown. R. Ellington
Shakedown. B. Kerr
Shakedown. J. Kwitney
Shakedown. Johnny Mack
Shakedown. J. Nazel
Shakedown. G. Petievich
Shakedown. Roney Scott
Shakedown for Murder. E. Lacy
Shakedown Hotel. E. J. Fredericks
Shakedown Kid. N. Singer
Shakedown Strip. L. Malley
Shaken Down. A. MacGowen
Shaken Leaf. D. Cory
Shakeout. K. Follett
Shakespeare Curse. J. Boland
Shakespeare Murders. Neil Gordon
Shakespeare Murders. A. R. Long
Shakespeare's Christmas. Q
Shaking Shadow. Elizabeth Stuart
Shaking Spear. B. Flynn
Shall Do No Murder. H. Alexander
Shall We Join the Ladies? J. M. Barrie
Shall We Send Flowers? P. Lauben

Shall We Tell the President? J. Archer
Shallow Grave. J. Quinn
Shallow Grave. J. S. Scott
Shallow Runs the River. Emma Moore
Shalom, My Love. H. Janson
Sham Detective. Anonymous
Shaman. F. Coffey
Shaman Tree. R. Abshire
Shamballah. J. F. Rossmann
Shambhala Strike. J. Rosenberger
Shame. R. Himmel
Shame Dance, and other stories. W. D. Steele
Shame of Arizona. W. C. Tuttle
Shame of Motley. R. Sabatini
Shame of Silence. M. Leighton
Shame the Devil. P. Appleman
Shame the Devil. A. J. Leavitt
Shamelady. J. Mayo
Shameless. J. M. Cain
Shameless. H. Vogel
Shameless Souls. J. Wingrave
Shamrock Cohen and the Amorous Doppelganger. B. Buonocore
Shamrock Smash. J. Rosenberger
Shamus. R. Giles
Shamus. Johnny Mack
Shamus, Your Slip Is Showing. Carter Brown
Shan. E. V. Lustbader
Shan Chung's Conspiracy. P. Bayne
Shandon Hall. J. L. Rickard
Shanghai. W. Marshall
Shanghai. B. J. Sussman
Shanghai Bund Murders. V. W. Mason
Shanghai Flame. A. S. Fleischman
Shanghai Gesture. J. Colton
Shanghai Honeymoon. M. Dekobra
Shanghai Incident. S. Dodge
Shanghai Jezebel. M. Corrigan
Shanghai Jim. F. Packard
Shanghai Lily. M. S. Jones
Shanghai Nights. T. Ile
Shanghai Sanctuary. V. W. Mason
Shanghai Story. N. Morland
Shanghai Surprise. T. Kenrick
Shanghai Tango. W. Overgard
Shanghai Thunder. D. Hewson
Shanghaied. F. Norris
Shanidar. Hashian
Shankill Road Contract. P. Atlee
Shannon. P. Gallagher
Shannon. J. Jenkins
Shannon. M. Parnell
Shannon Terror. T. Du Bois
Shannondale. E. Southworth
Shannonese Hustle. F. Bandy
Shanty Irish. J. Tully
Shanty Shed. H. Footner
Shape of a Stain. E. Ferrars
Shape of Danger. A. Kielland
Shape of Dread. M. Muller
Shape of Fear. Nan Hamilton
Shape of Fear. L. B. Long
Shape of Fear. H. Pentecost
Shape of Illusion. W. E. Barrett
Shape of Murder. J. F. Straker
Shape of Space. L. Niven
Shapely Lady. N. Baroni
Shapes of Sleep. J. B. Priestley
Shapes That Creep. M. Bonner
Shard at Bay. P. McCutchan
Shard Calls the Tune. P. McCutchan
Shards. J. Bannister
Shard's Rock. D. Justin
Share and Share Alike. R. W. Kauffman
Sharendal. M. Carr
Shares in Murder. J. L. Waten
Sharing. Sy Cook
Sharing Her Crime. M. A. Fleming
Shark Among Herrings. G. Milner
Shark Bait Affair. J. Arliss
Shark Fighter. N. Brady
Shark Gotch and Typhoon Bradley. A. R. Wetjen
Shark Gotch Shoots It Out, and Goes on the Last Great Adventure. A. R. Wetjen

Shark Gotch of the Islands. A. R. Wetjen
Shark River. R. Powell
Shark Run. V. Canning
Sharkbait. Richard Butler
Sharks of Society. B. Hemyng
Sharkskin Book. H. S. Keeler
Sharky's Machine. W. Diehl
Sharon Jones, Free Lance Photographer. E. Wesley
Sharp Edge. R. Himmel
Sharp Edge. W. Wright
Sharp Intake of Death. James Shannon
Sharp Night's Work. J. F. Fitts
Sharp Practice. J. Farris
Sharp Quillet. B. Flynn
Sharp Rise in Crime. J. Creasey
Sharper's Downfall. Nicholas Carter
Sharpshooter. J. Reese
Sharretts the Detective. P. H. Woodward
Shatter. J. Farris
Shattered. K. R. Dwyer
Shattered. R. Neely
Shattered. P. Trent
Shattered Affair. B. Palmer
Shattered Echoes. M. Chevalier
Shattered Eye. B. Granger
Shattered Halo. A. McElfresh
Shattered Hopes. Roland Daniel
Shattered Lullabies. Morton Reed
Shattered Masks. D. G. Devon
Shattered Moon. Kate Green
Shattered Raven. E. D. Hoch
Shattered Silk. Barbara Michaels
Shattered Steel. J. Preston
Shattered Visage. D. Motter
Shaved Fish. S. Geason
Shawnee Alley Fire. John Douglas
Shaw's War. A. Melville-Ross
Shayne Case. W. B. M. Ferguson
Shayne Dame. S. Harragan
She Ain't Got No Body. J. T. Story
She Asked for Adventure. A. Applin
She Asked for It. E. Berckman
She Asked for Murder. E. Sherry
She Ate Her Cake. B. Treynor
She Came Back. P. Wentworth
She Came by Night. J. Pendower
She Came in a Flash. M. Wings
She Came Too Late. M. Wings
She Could Take Care. S. Truss
She Couldn't Stay. B. Vane
She Deserved to Die. F. Griffin
She Devil. Robert Turner
She Didn't Like Dying. N. Morland
She Died a Lady. Carter Dickson
She Died Because . . . K. Hopkins
She Died Dancing. K. Roos
She Died Downtown. B. Carson
She Died Laughing. L. Gribble
She Died, Of Course. T. Warriner
She Died on the Stairway. K. Rhoades
She Died Without Light. N. Mathews
She Died Young. A. Kennington
She Drew the Bolt. E. Elton
She Faded Into Air. Ethel L. White
She Fell Among Actors. James Warren
She Fell Among Thieves. Gretchen Travis
She Fell Among Thieves. D. Yates
She Gave Me Hell and . . . D. Glinto
She Got What She Asked For. J. Ronald
She Had a Little Knife. J. L. Linklater
She Had It Coming—. Griff
She Had My Number. M. Delany
She Had to Have Gas. R. Penny
She Had to Kill. J. G. Henderson
She Kept on Dying. G. M. Wilson
She Left a Silver Slipper. F. Stevens
She Let Him Continue. S. Geller
She Liked It That Way. D. Spade
She Married Raffles. B. Perowne
She, Me, and Murder. Robert Martin
She Means Trouble. Spike Gordon
She Met Murder. H. Desmond
She Modelled Her Coffin. D. Launay
She Never Grew Old. Garland Lord

She Never Reached the Top. E. K. Lobaugh
She Paid 'Em Off. Griff
She Painted Her Face. D. Yates
She Posed for Death. Russell Gordon
She Ruled with a Rod. B. Sarto
She Saw the Murderer. E. M. Crawford
She Screamed Blue Murder. K. Secrist
She Sees Things. G. M. Wilson
She Sent Her Mother to the Scaffold. W. Tyrer
She Shall Die. Anthony Gilbert
She Shall Have Murder. D. Ames
She Shark. J. Farr
She Should Have Cried on Monday. E. S. Russell
She Sleeps to Conquer. H. Janson
She Stayed the Night. J. Glyder
She Sure Slipped. N. Perrelli
She Talked with a Gun. B. Sarto
She, the Accused. M. Moiseiwitsch
She Vamped a Strangler. H. Duval
She Vanished in the Dawn. Anthony Gilbert
She Walked in Fear. Roy Vickers
She Walks Alone. H. McCloy
She Walks by Night. D. Wade
She Walks in Shadow. L. Paige
She Wanted a Guy. R. Rand
She Was a Lady. L. Charteris
She Was His Secretary. A. Demarest
She Was My Beloved. K. Lindsay
She Was No Angel. B. E. M. Ward
She Was No Lady. A. Bocca
She Was Only the Sheriff's Daughter. S. Forbes
She Who Sleeps. S. Rohmer
She Who Was Helena Cass. L. Rising
She Who Will Not—. E. C. Vivian
She Woke to Darkness. B. Halliday
She Wolf. H. Janson
She Wore No Shroud. Carter Brown
She Wore Pink Gloves. M. Dekobra
She Wouldn't Say Who. D. Ames
Shear the Black Sheep. D. Dodge
Shears of Destiny. Winifred Duke
Shears of Destiny. L. Scott
Shearwater. M. Jahn
Shed a Bitter Tear. H. F. S. Moore
Shed Light on Death. L. A. Taylor
Shed No Tears. Don Martin
Sheep and the Wolves. G. Burnett
Sheep Grass. Padder Nash
Sheep in Wolf's Clothing. C. Debans
Sheep May Safely Graze. S. Harvester
Sheep's Clothing. Celia Dale
Sheep's Clothing. A. Lee
Sheep's Clothing. L. J. Vance
Sheep's-Head & Babylon. Marjorie Bowen
Sheer Bluff. John Collins
Sheer Silk. W. J. Elliott
Sheer Torture. R. Barnard
Sheerluck Jones. M. Watson
Sheets in the Wind. R. Cullum
Sheikh Bill. A. M. Williamson
Sheikh Stuff. H. M. Raleigh
Sheikh Touch, and other stories. B. Reynolds
Sheikh's Son. A. Murray
Sheiks and Adders. M. Innes
Sheik's Capture. Old Sleuth
Sheilah McLeod. G. Boothby
Shelf Life. D. Clark
Shelkagari. Harold King
She'll Be Dead by Morning. D. Chambers
Shell Game. R. Powell
Shell Game. D. Terman
She'll Get Hers. J. Plunkett
She'll Hate Me Tomorrow. R. Deming
She'll Love You Dead. C. Franklin
Shell of Death. N. Blake
Shell Scott Sampler. R. S. Prather
Shell Scott's Seven Slaughters. R. S. Prather
Shellshock. R. A. Prather
Shelter. L. Meynell
Sheltered. J. Leach
Sheltered Garden. S. Pim
Shelton Conspiracy. R. Foley
Shemerelda. P. Tinniswood
Shem's Demise. M. Underwood

Shen's Pigtail, and Other Cues of Anglo-China Life. Mr. M—
Shepherd File. C. V. Bark
Shepherd Market. T. Aldridge
Shepherd's Crook. E. C. R. Lorac
Sherbourne's Folly. N. Barry
Sheridan Road. H. T. Miller
Sheridan Road Mystery. P. Thorne
Sheriff and the Branding Iron Murders. D. R. Meredith
Sheriff and the Folsom Man Murders. D. R. Meredith
Sheriff and the Panhandle Murders. D. R. Meredith
Sheriff of Angel Gulch. C. E. Blaney
Sheriff of Bombay. H. R. F. Keating
Sheriff of Dyke Hole. R. Cullum
Sheriff of Purgatory. Jim Morris
Sheriff of Wasco. C. R. Jackson
Sheriff Olson. M. G. Shute
Sheriff's Deputy. G. V. McFadden
Sherlock Holmes. C. George
Sherlock Holmes. W. Gillette
Sherlock Holmes. T. J. Kelly
Sherlock Holmes and a Near Case of Murder. R. Mauro
Sherlock Holmes and a Theatrical Mystery. V. Andrews
Sherlock Holmes and the Arabian Princess. John North
Sherlock Holmes and the Arthritic Clergyman. V. Andrews
Sherlock Holmes and the Brighton Pavilion Mystery. V. Andrews
Sherlock Holmes and the Case of Sabina Hall. L. B. Greenwood
Sherlock Holmes and the Case of the Raleigh Legacy. L. B. Greenwood
Sherlock Holmes and the Curious Adventure of the Clockwork Prince. J. A. Hitt
Sherlock Holmes and the Curse of the Sign of Four. D. Rosa
Sherlock Holmes and the Drood Mystery. E. L. Pearson
Sherlock Holmes and the Eminent Thesian. Val Andrews
Sherlock Holmes and the German Nanny. John North
Sherlock Holmes and the Giant Rat of Sumatra. Tim J. Kelly
Sherlock Holmes and the Golden Bird. F. Thomas
Sherlock Holmes and the London Zoo Mystery. Willoughby Lane
Sherlock Holmes and the Mark of the Beast. R. C. Weyman
Sherlock Holmes and the Masquerade Murders. Frank Thomas
Sherlock Holmes and the Mysterious Friend of Oscar Wilde. Russell A. Brown
Sherlock Holmes and the Red-Headed League. J. Forster
Sherlock Holmes and the Sacred Sword. F. Thomas
Sherlock Holmes and the Thistle of Scotland. L. B. Greenwood
Sherlock Holmes and the Treasure Train. F. Thomas
Sherlock Holmes and the Wood Green Empire Mystery. W. Lane
Sherlock Holmes at Elsinore. C. Muusmann
Sherlock Holmes at Oxford. N. Utechin
Sherlock Holmes at the 1902 Fifth Test. Stanley Shaw
Sherlock Holmes, Bridge Detective. G. Gooden
Sherlock Holmes Bridge Detective Returns. F. Thomas
Sherlock Holmes Comedy Trilogy. D. Charlton
Sherlock Holmes, Consulting Detective. Kelvin Jones
Sherlock Holmes' First Case. R. H. Bibolet
Sherlock Holmes in Dallas. E. Aubrey
Sherlock Holmes in Gibraltar. S. Benady
Sherlock Holmes in New York. D. R. Bensen
Sherlock Holmes in Tibet. R. Wincor
Sherlock Holmes Investigates the Murder in Euston Square. R. Pearsall
Sherlock Holmes Meets Annie Oakley. Stanley Shaw
Sherlock Holmes Meets the Phantom. T. J. Kelly
Sherlock Holmes: My Life and Crimes. M. Hardwick
Sherlock Holmes on the Roof of the World. T. K. Miller
Sherlock Holmes Revisited. C. Brooks
Sherlock Holmes Revisited: Volume 2. C. Brooks
Sherlock Holmes' Solution. P. Hartley
Sherlock Holmes: The Adventure of the Ancient Gods. R. Vaughn
Sherlock Holmes Versus Arsene Lupin. M. Leblanc
Sherlock Holmes vs. Dracula. L. D. Estleman
Sherlock Holmes vs. Jack the Ripper. E. Queen
Sherlock Holmes Versus John Thorndyke and Reginald Fortune. A. C. Ward
Sherlock Holmes's War of the Worlds. M. W. Wellman
Sherlock's Last Case. C. Marowitz
Sherri. John Benton
Sheryl. Ralph Hayes
She's a Cop, Ain't She? I. King
She's Dynamite! J. Kellan
She's Folling Thee! J. Middlemass
She's No Lady. J. Grecco
She's Not for Sale. D. Haring
Shetland Plan. Taffrail
Shibu Discipline. W. Barker
Shibumi. Trevanian
Shield and Sword. V. Kozhevnikov
Shield for Murder. W. P. McGivern
Shield of His Honor. R. H. Savage
Shield of Love. B. L. Farjeon
Shield of Silence. E. Balmer
Shield of the Law. W. M. Graydon
Shield Project. D. R. Mounce
Shift Key. J. Brunner
Shift of Guilt. J. Bude
Shilling for Candles. J. Tey
Shills Can't Cash Chips. A. A. Fair
Shiloh Project. D. C. Poyer
Shinglo. Alex Kane
Shining Day. F. Ross
Shining Head. J. Madeley
Shining Mischief. B. Levy
Shining Through. S. Isaacs
Shining Trail. O. Binns
Shining Trap. D. Enefer
Shining with the Shiner. J. A. Lee
Shiny Night. B. Tunstall
Ship Ashore. S. M. Parkman
Ship in the Swamp and other stories. W. Townend
Ship of Death. J. Creasey
Ship of Death. R. Sapir
Ship of Gold. T. B. Allen
Ship of Gold. J. Leasor
Ship of Hate. R. Danton
Ship of Secrets. V. Loder
Ship of Spies. G. Sinstadt
Ship of the Damned. J. Hilton
Ship That Died of Shame, and other stories. N. Monsarrat
Ship to Shore Murder. T. Noice
Shipkiller. Justin Scott
Shipmates. Morgan Robertson
Ships Aflame! J. Toussaint-Samat
Ship's Company. W. W. Jacobs
Ships of Mon Desir. D. Lyall
Ships That Pass. R. L. Dearden
Ships with Wings. T. Claymore
Shipwreck Passion. W. J. Elliott
Shipwrecked. G. Greene
Shipwrecked Detective. W. M. Graydon
Shipwrecked Schoolship. John Marsh
Shipyard Menace. J. Stamper
Shirkers. C. M. S. McLellan
Shirley. E. V. Cunningham
Shirley Holmquist and Aunt Wilma: Whodunit? J. L. Martin
Shirt Front. C. Blackstock
Shivering Bough. N. Burke
Shivering Mountain. P. Somers
Shivering Sands. W. Holt
Shiwan Khan Returns. W. B. Gibson
Shoal Water. D. Yates
Shock! B. Clemens
Shock! V. Markham
Shock Corridor. M. Avallone
Shock Tactics. J. Bruce
Shock to Society. F. Warden
Shock to the System. S. Brett
Shock Treatment. J. H. Chase
Shock Treatment. W. Van Atta
Shock Value. K. Berne
Shock Value. W. B. Murphy
Shock-Wave. B. Copper
Shock Wave. D. S. Davis
Shock Waves. D. Pendleton
Shocking Nymphs. M. Tadrack
Shocking Pink Hat. F. Crane
Shocking Secret. H. Roth
Shockwave. R. Cawley
Shockwave. D. Cory
Shockwave. C. Forbes
Shoe Fits. R. Ladline
Shoemaker. O. Harper
Shoes for My Love. Jean Leslie
Shoes That Had Walked Twice. J. Toussaint-Samat
Shoestring. P. Ableman
Shoestring's Finest Hour. P. Ableman
Sholto Budd. M. Cobb
Shoot. D. Fairbairn
Shoot! B. Newman
Shoot. E. Trevor
Shoot a Sitting Duck. David Alexander
Shoot at the Moon. W. F. Temple
Shoot If You Must. R. Powell
Shoot It. P. Tyner
Shoot It Again. E. Lacy
Shoot It Again, Sam. M. Avallone
Shoot Me Dacent. A. M. Stein
Shoot-Out. B. Copper
Shoot-Out. D. Enefer
Shoot the Moon. J. Page
Shoot the Piano Player. D. Goodis
Shoot the Scene. E. Queen
Shoot the Works. R. Ellington
Shoot the Works. B. Halliday
Shoot to Kill. J. Dekker
Shoot to Kill. B. Halliday
Shoot to Kill. J. McCarter
Shoot to Kill. Wade Miller
Shoot to Live. Griff
Shoot When Ready. W. H. Baker
Shoot Your Enemies. Richard Grant
Shooter. T. N. Murari
Shooter. G. Vanhee
Shooter Man. T. Barling
Shooting Gallery. H. C. Rae
Shooting in the Dark. C. Hougan
Shooting Made Easy. K. Howard
Shooting of Dan McGrew. M. Kenyon
Shooting of Sergius Leroy. Roland Daniel
Shooting of the Green. J. Poyer
Shooting Party. A. Checkhov
Shooting Schedule. W. B. Murphy
Shooting Script. G. Lyall
Shooting Star. R. Bloch
Shooting Star. D. Brierley
Shooting Star. F. Woods
Shooting Stars. N. Coleridge
Shooting Stars. E. C. Vivian
Shop at Sly Corner. E. Percy
Shop-Girl. C. N. Williamson
Shop in Loch Street. J. Wood
Shop Window Murders. V. Loder
Shoplifter. R. H. R. Smithies
Shore House Mystery. Jean Marsh
Shorecliff. Marilyn Ross
Short and Sweet. H. N. Gittins
Short and Sweet. T. Taggart
Short Bier. F. Kane
Short Break in Venice. P. Inchbald
Short Cases of Inspector Maigret. G. Simenon
Short Circuit. H. Miller
Short Circuit. L. Oriol
Short Cruises. W. W. Jacobs
Short Cut. D. Blunt
Short Cut Brooke's First Case. Stockton Heath

Title Index

Short End of the Stick, and other stories. I. Shulman
Short Eyes. M. Pinero
Short Life. T. B. Allen
Short List. R. Philmore
Short-Lived Bushrangers. Chas. White
Short Madness. A. Manning
Short Measure. A. R. Williams
Short Night. R. Kirkbridge
Short Night. Russell Turner
Short of Murder. P. Ernst
Short of Murder. T. T. Ness
Short of Murder. W. E. Wright
Short Radio Plays. L. J. Huber
Short Reaction. J. Gale
Short Shrift. Manning Long
Short Skirts. R. Eden
Short Sorties. W. E. Johns
Short Stories. E. Bramah
Short Stories of H. G. Wells. H. G. Wells
Short Term. A. Baker
Short-Term Wife. H. Janson
Short Time to Live. Mervyn Jones
Short Time to Live. G. Moffat
Short Walk Abroad. J. Wiles
Short Walk in Williams Park. C. H. B. Kitchin
Short Walk to Death. R. A. Bennett
Short Wave. J. Bruce
Short Weekend. T. S. Strachan
Shortest Night. G. B. Stern
Shortest Way to Hades. S. Caudwell
Shortly Before Midnight . . . E. Nisot
Shorty Bill. H. C. McNeile
Shoshone Mike. F. Bergon
Shot. S. Creed
Shot at Dawn. J. Rhode
Shot at Dawn. G. M. Wilson
Shot at Night. T. A. Plummer
Shot Bolt. C. Curzon
Shot from Above. J. K. Stafford
Shot from the Dark. Philip Chambers
Shot from the Door. G. Barry
Shot in Question. M. Gilbert
Shot in the Arm. J. Sherwood
Shot in the Dark. H. Agg
Shot in the Dark. E. Fairlie
Shot in the Dark. L. Ford
Shot in the Dark. H. Kurnitz
Shot in the Dark. R. Powell
Shot in the Dark. F. Stayton
Shot in the Dark. F. Usher
Shot in the Night. B. Bolt
Shot in the Pulpit. S. M. Woodward
Shot in the Woods. O. Binns
Shot of Murder. J. Iams
Shot on Location. H. W. Jones
Shot on Location. H. Nielsen
Shot on the Downs. V. L. Whitechurch
Shot-Silk. W. J. Elliott
Shot Silk. M. Maguire
Shot That Killed Graeme Andrews. H. L. Deakin
Shot to Hell. D. Stivers
Shotgun. E. McBain
Shotgun. W. Wingate
Shotgun Gold. W. C. Tuttle
Shotgun Saturday Night. B. Crider
Should a Corpse Tell? G. Dugdale
Should Auld Acquaintance. D. M. Disney
Should She Have Left Him? W. C. Hudson
Should She Have Spoken? A. Forbes
Should She Have Spoken? E. Miller
Show Business. B. Ford
Show Business Is Murder. C. L. Ross
Show Girl. M. Pemberton
Show House—Sold. R. Thorndike
Show Me a Hero. P. Alexander
Show Me a Hero. A. Coppel
Show Must Go On. G. Verner
Show No Mercy. L. Hardy
Show of Force. C. D. Taylor
Show of Force. Gar Wilson
Show of Violence. Sara Woods
Show Red for Danger. R. Lockridge
Show-Up. C. E. Erbstein
Show-Up. R. Kasper

Showbiz Wipeout. L. Derrick
Showboat Mystery. A. W. Clark
Showdown. R. Carni
Showdown. R. Caulfield
Showdown. S. Coburn
Showdown. T. M. Longstreth
Showdown. Johnny Mack
Showdown in Sydney. D. Reid
Showman's Daughter. Scott Graham
Shown on the Screen. Nicholas Carter
Shred of Evidence. R. C. Sherriff
Shreiber. A. Boyarsky
Shrew Is Dead. Shelley Smith
Shrewsdale Exit. J. Buell
Shrewtzer Castle. Anonymous
Shriek in the Midnight Tower. K. Kimbrough
Shriek of Tyres. D. Rutherford
Shrieking Pit. A. J. Rees
Shrieking Shadow of Penporth Island. S. D. Stevens
Shrine of Kali. H. E. Hill
Shrinking. A. Lelchuk
Shrinking Pond. J. T. Osborne
Shriveling Murders. Zorro
Shroud. J. Coyne
Shroud for a Lady. E. Daly
Shroud for a Nightingale. P. D. James
Shroud for a Redhead. H. Spencer
Shroud for a Wanton. B. Schwarz
Shroud for Aquarius. M. A. Collins
Shroud for Delilah. Anthea Fraser
Shroud for Grandmama. D. Ashe
Shroud for Her Shame. K. T. McCall
Shroud for Jesso. P. Rabe
Shroud for Mr. Bundy. J. M. Fox
Shroud for My Sugar. Carter Brown
Shroud for Rowena. V. Rath
Shroud for Sharon. Kane
Shroud for Shylock. S. Ransome
Shroud for the Bride. D. B. Olsen
Shroud for the Bride. Sinclair Russell
Shroud for the Shrew. G. Janes
Shroud for Thelma. N. Rosso
Shroud for Unlac. S. H. Courtier
Shroud 9. Robert Turner
Shroud of Canvas. I. Lambot
Shroud of Darkness. E. C. R. Lorac
Shroud of Fog. W. D. Roberts
Shroud of Silence. N. Buckingham
Shroud of Snow. A. Mills
Shroud Off Her Back. S. Ransome
Shroud Society. R. Crawford
Shrouded Death. H. C. Bailey
Shrouded Tower. T. Charles
Shrouded Walls. S. Howatch
Shrouded Way. J. Caird
Shrouded Woman. M. L. Bolton
Shrouds Are Cheap. D. Linton
Shrunken Head. R. L. Fish
Shrunken Heads. J. Kellerman
Shudder Show. A. E. Martin
Shuddering Castle. W. F. Fauley
Shuddering Fair One. P. J. Cooper
Shudders. A. Abbot
Shudders. L. E. Austin
Shulamite. A. Askew
Shut Out the Sun. L. Alroy
Shutterbug Caper. R. Carberry
Shuttered House. K. Roche
Shuttered Room. C. A. Sherman
Shuttered Room. J. Withers
Shuttle of Hate. R. Harrison
Shuttle People. G. Bishop
Shuttle Showdown. David Taylor
Shuttlecock. G. Swift
Shy Moon. T. A. Roberts
Shy Plutocrat. E. P. Oppenheim
Shylock Holmes: His Posthumous Memoirs. J. K. Bangs
Shylock of the River. F. Hyme
Shyster Lawyer. L. F. Schmitt
Si-Fan Mysteries. S. Rohmer
Siamese Cat. J. Dekker
Siamese Cat. H. M. Rideout
Siamese Coup Affair. S. Weintraub

Siamese Twin Mystery. E. Queen
Siberian Alternative. A. Kilgore
Siberian Road. S. Harvester
Sibling. E. Trevor
Sibyl Falcon. E. Jepson
Sibyl Sue Blue. R. G. Brown
Sibylla Joy. J. H. Robinson
Sic Transit Gloria. M. Kennedy
Sicilian. M. Meeke
Sicilian. M. Puzo
Sicilian Affair. M. MacKintosh
Sicilian Blood. D. London
Sicilian Connection. A. Venters
Sicilian Defense. J. N. Iannuzzi
Sicilian Episode. R. H. Wyatt
Sicilian Heritage. J. Higgins
Sicilian Mysteries. J. A. K. Curtis
Sicilian Romance. A. Radcliffe
Sicilian Slaughter. Jim Peterson
Sicilian Specialist. N. Lewis
Sicilian Uncles. L. Sciascia
Sicily Street. R. Masson
Sick Fox. P. Brodeur
Sick Heart River. J. Buchan
Sick of Shadows. S. McCrumb
Sick to Death. Douglas Clark
Sickle Murders. Trill
Sickly Flame. E. Gresham
Sickness of the Soul. H. E. Fuller
Sidartha. K. Behenna
Side-Effect. R. Hawkey
Side Effects. Woody Allen
Side Effects. B. Betcherman
Side Effects. M. Palmer
Side Street. Malcolm St. Clair
Sidelights. H. W. C. Newte
Sideshow Girl. J. Clayford
Sideshow Girl. S. Harragan
Sideslip. Ted White
Sideswipe. C. Willeford
Sidewalk Caesar. D. Honig
Sidewalk Empire. D. Haring
Sidewalk Floozie. B. Sarto
Sidewalk Serenade. H. Vogel
Sidney Yorke's Friend. E. A. Bennett
Siege. P. Cave
Siege. R. Hoyt
Siege. V. B. Miller
Siege. D. Pendleton
Siege. Domini Taylor
Siege of Buckingham Palace. W. Nelson
Siege of Hampton Mall. B. Robertson
Siege of Scotland Yard. L. G. Redmond-Howard
Siege of Silence. A. J. Quinnell
Siege of Superport. J. B. Olesker
Siege of Trencher's Far. Gordon M. Williams
Siegfried Spy. B. Newman
Sierra Death Dealers. Steve White
Siesta Sister. D. Haring
Sigh for a Drum-Beat. P. Doncaster
Sigh on the Breeze. M. McGregor
Sight of Death. J. York
Sight Unseen. Kathy Clark
Sight Unseen. D. Gilroy
Sight Unseen. B. Latham
Sight Unseen. A. E. Lindop
Sight Unseen. D. Lorne
Sight Unseen. A. Neiderman
Sight Unseen, and The Confession. M. R. Rinehart
Sightings. S. Trott
Sign at Six. S. E. White
Sign in the Sky. A. Edgar
Sign of Arnim. G. Seton
Sign of Blood. P. Street
Sign of Death. B. Merrell
Sign of Evil. A. Wynne
Sign of Fear. A. Derleth
Sign of Seven. G. Stanley
Sign of Silence. W. LeQueux
Sign of the Black Feather. H. E. Hill
Sign of the Blue Dragon. J. Aeby
Sign of the Blue Triangle. S. Hope
Sign of the Burning Ship. L. A. Cunningham
Sign of the Cobra. Nick Carter

Sign of the Coin. Nicholas Carter
Sign of the Crescent. Dick Stewart
Sign of the Crossed Knives. Nicholas Carter
Sign of the Dagger. Nicholas Carter
Sign of the Dagger. H. O. Cooke
Sign of the Dagger. J. L. Jacolliot
Sign of the Death Circle. C. H. Snow
Sign of the Double Four. B. Weston
Sign of the Flying Fox. J. Grieg
Sign of the Four. A. C. Doyle
Sign of the Four. J. Hershey
Sign of the Four. W. Spence
Sign of the Glove. C. Dawe
Sign of the Golden Goose. R. Danton
Sign of the Grinning Dragon. M. Grimshaw
Sign of the Knotted String. H. Harper
Sign of the Mute Medusa. Ian Wallace
Sign of the Nine. F. Grierson
Sign of the Prayer Shawl. Nick Carter
Sign of the Ram. M. Ferguson
Sign of the Rose. G. Beban
Sign of the Saracen. Gwyn Evans
Sign of the Scorpion. B. Abbott
Sign of the Scorpion. E. Snell
Sign of the Serpent. J. Goodwin
Sign of the Serpent. W. M. Graydon
Sign of the Serpent. S. Hely
Sign of the Server. C. DeLuca
Sign of the Seven Sins. W. LeQueux
Sign of the Skull. J. A. Dunn
Sign of the Snake. D. Vane
Sign of the Spider. E. L. MacKeag
Sign of the Spider. B. Mitford
Sign of the Stranger. W. LeQueux
Sign of the Swan. M. Baillie-Saunders
Sign of the Thunderbird. R. Montana
Sign of the Tiger. O. Williams
Sign of the Triangle. J. Hocking
Sign of the Vulture. J. Chancellor
Sign on for Tokyo. A. Haig
Sign on the Door. C. Pollock
Signal. Roland Daniel
Signal for Danger. T. Harnan
Signal for Death. J. Rhode
Signal for Invasion. H. Adams
Signal Thirty-Two. M. Kantor
Signals. D. Deutschman
Signature. B. Goldie
Signature to a Crime. O. L. Rosmanith
Signed in Yellow. E. H. Loban
Signet Active. T. Page
Signet of Death. L. Grey
Signing Off. J. T. MacIntyre
Signora. P. Andreae
Signora. E. D. Lyon
Signors of the Night. M. Pemberton
Signpost to Fear. M. Drin
Signpost to Murder. M. Doyle
Signpost to Murder. D. Folliott
Signs and Omens. B. M. Forester
Silas Quelch. B. Johns
Silas Sharp, the Silent Detective. Anonymous
Silecroft Case. J. C. Lenehan
Silence. Edmond Burton
Silence. Richard Hubbard
Silence. S. Kyle
Silence! A. Soutar
Silence After Dinner. C. Witting
Silence at Salerno. F. Steegmuller
Silence for the Murderer. F. W. Crofts
Silence in Court. P. Wentworth
Silence in Crete. E. Ayrton
Silence in Hanover Close. Anne Perry
Silence in the Garden. W. Trevor
Silence Is Broken. J. Jenkins
Silence Is Deadly. L. Biggle
Silence Is Golden. Elsie Lee
Silence Observed. M. Innes
Silence of a Purple Shirt. R. C. Woodthorpe
Silence of Birds. M. Ashton
Silence of Dean Maitland. Maxwell Gray
Silence of Dr. Duveen. M. Leighton
Silence of Guilt. R. A. Bennett
Silence of Herondale. Joan Aiken

Silence of Jeremy Langton. H. H. Ross
Silence of Mrs. Harrold. S. M. Gardenhire
Silence of the Lambs. Thomas Harris
Silence of the Night. R. Ormerod
Silence Over Sinai. M. Awin
Silence So Deadly. C. Dekker
Silence Under Threat. B. Cobb
Silence with Voices. C. Carfax
Silenced. L. T. Meade
Silenced Witnesses. N. C. Rosenthal
SIlencers. D. Hamilton
Silent Accuser. A. Soutar
Silent Are the Dead. G. H. Coxe
Silent Barrier. G. Templeton
Silent Barrier. L. Tracy
Silent Battle. G. F. Gibbs
Silent Battle. A. M. Williamson
Silent Bell. Elaine Hamilton
Silent Bullet. P. Elliott
Silent Bullet. A. B. Reeve
Silent Clue. M. Leighton
Silent Conquest. M. Gerard
Silent Cousin. Elizabeth Fenwick
Silent Cracksman. J. J. Chichester
Silent Cry. H. Jobson
Silent Dead. A. Gask
Silent Death. M. Grant
Silent Death. H. Leyford
Silent Dust. B. Fischer
Silent Enemy. K. Netzen
Silent Executioner. P. Souvestre
Silent Five. T. M. Longstreth
Silent Force. Harry Goddard
Silent Four. T. A. Plummer
Silent Gate. T. Hopkins
Silent Guardian. Nicholas Carter
Silent Guests. A. E. Forrest
Silent Halls of Ashenden. D. Daniels
Silent Hostage. S. Gainham
Silent House. J. G. Brandon
Silent House. N. Deane
Silent House. F. Hume
Silent House. L. Tracy
Silent House in Pimlico. F. Hume
Silent Hunter. C. D. Taylor
Silent Informer. P. A. Foxall
Silent Jury. Gwyn Evans
Silent Killer. D. Cross
Silent Killing. Janice Robinson
Silent Kind of War. J. Laflin
Silent Knife. J. D. Powell
Silent Knives. L. Gough
Silent Liars. M. Underwood
Silent Loom. P. Inman
Silent Man. J. M. Walsh
Silent Men. C. Bidmead
Silent Menace. A. Skene
Silent Mountain. G. Bettany
Silent Murder. C. Cunningham
Silent Murders. Neil Gordon
Silent Murders. Ernest Paul
Silent, My Love. C. Randell
Silent One. O. Cameron
Silent Ones. E. Ogilvie
Silent Partner. A. Bodelsen
Silent Partner. L. Brackett
Silent Partner. Nicholas Carter
Silent Partner. J. Kellerman
Silent Partner. K. M. Knight
Silent Partner. Augustus Muir
Silent Partner. Paula Paul
Silent Passenger. G. W. Appleton
Silent Passenger. Nicholas Carter
Silent Place. R. C. Payes
Silent Pool. F. Cowen
Silent Pool. P. Wentworth
Silent Portrait. F. Cavandish
Silent Pursuit. D. J. Harrington
Silent Reach. O. White
Silent Reefs. D. Cottrell
Silent Room. F. Chimenti
Silent Salesman. M. Z. Lewin
Silent Scream. Michael Collins
Silent Scream. Jane Lake

Silent Seducers. R. Arana
Silent Seven. M. Grant
Silent Shore. J. E. Bloundelle-Burton
Silent Shot. C. H. Snow
Silent Signal. F. Hume
Silent, Silken Shadows. P. Dalton
Silent Siren. T. Sterling
Silent Sisters. Margaret Archer
Silent Six. Seamark
Silent Slain. C. Pilgrim
Silent Slaughter. P. Beere
Silent Slayer. D. W. Steward
Silent Speaker. R. Stout
Silent Stranger. H. G. Harper
Silent Street. G. Barnet
Silent Syndicate. L. Bidston
Silent Terror. L. C. Douthwaite
Silent Terror. J. Ellroy
Silent Terror. T. C. H. Jacobs
Silent Thunder. R. C. Barnes
Silent Thunder. L. D. Estleman
Silent Thunder. Rona Randall
Silent Thunder. A. Soutar
Silent Voice. S. Claudia
Silent Voyage. J. Pattinson
Silent Walls. M. L. Roby
Silent War. P. Haden
Silent Watcher. F. Stevenson
Silent Watchers. I. D. Hardy
Silent Watchers. Dora Russell
Silent Witness. Gordon Alexander
Silent Witness. G. H. Coxe
Silent Witness. J. De Leon
Silent Witness. J. Dering
Silent Witness. H. Desmond
Silent Witness. M. F. Ford
Silent Witness. R. A. Freeman
Silent Witness. J. Hunter
Silent Witness. K. S. McKinney
Silent Witness. M. D. Post
Silent Witness. J. Walworth
Silent Witness. Collin Wilcox
Silent Witness. J. Wylde
Silent Witness. E. Yates
Silent Witness. M. Yorke
Silent Witnesses. J. S. Strange
Silent Women. M. P. Hood
Silent World of Nicholas Quinn. C. Dexter
Silhouette. D. Haring
Silhouette. E. Trevor
Silhouette in Scarlet. Elizabeth Peters
Silhouette Symbol. P. Quiroule
Silhouettes. P. Patti
Silicon Valley Connection. J. Rosenberger
Silicon Valley Slaughter. J. Quinn
Silinski, Master Criminal. E. Wallace
Silk! W. J. Elliott
Silk and Cordite. D. Spade
Silk and Satin. M. Wolfson
Silk Lady. Gwen Davis
Silk Purse. J. Tickell
Silk Road. S. Harvester
Silk Rope. G. Mountford
Silk Scarf Murders. J. Addiscombe
Silk Stocking Murders. A. Berkeley
Silk Stocking Murders. G. Chester
Silk Vendetta. Victoria Holt
Silken Baroness. P. Atlee
Silken Baroness Contract. P. Atlee
Silken Divans. R. Vane
Silken Menace. H. Janson
Silken Net. Rachelle Edwards
Silken Nightmare. Carter Brown
Silken Shroud. J. Sandys
Silken Sin. R. Vane
Silken Snare. H. Janson
Silken Symphony. D. Haring
Silken Threads. G. Afterem
Silken Web. M. Lynch
Silky. L. Rosten
Silky Ones Sting. Richard Grant
Silsby. S. Nichols
Silver. G. Masterton
Silver and Death. R. Simons

Title Index

Silver Arrow. A. Wynne
Silver Arrow Murder. T. Stevenson
Silver Bag. T. Cobb
Silver Bar Mystery. W. C. Tuttle
Silver Basilisk. S. Warwick
Silver Bears. P. E. Erdman
Silver Birch, and other stories. R. Crompton
Silver Blade. C. E. Walk
Silver Bough. N. M. Gunn
Silver Bridge. H. P. Lewis
Silver Buckshot. W. C. Tuttle
Silver Bugle. G. McDonell
Silver Bullet. F. Hume
Silver Bullet. P. H. Hunter
Silver Bullet Gang. J. Miles
Silver Butterfly. W. Woodrow
Silver Canyon. G. M. Fenn
Silver Castle. E. Quest
Silver Chest. Herman Landon
Silver Circle. A. Skene
Silver City Scandal. Gerald Hammond
Silver Cobweb. B. Benson
Silver Cord. G. A. Chamberlain
Silver Cord. R. Shambrook
Silver Cup. Granville Wilson
Silver Death. G. F. Gibbs
Silver Death. M. Hervey
Silver Death. E. Mott
Silver Doll. B. Treynor
Silver Dolphin. V. Johnston
Silver Dwarf. Maxwell Scott
Silver Eagle. W. R. Burnett
Silver Falcon. Evelyn Anthony
Silver Fang. G. F. Worts
Silver Forest. B. A. Williams
Silver Fox. R. Hansard
Silver Ghost. C. MacLeod
Silver Goblet. R. Foxall
Silver Grass. G. Croudace
Silver Greyhound. B. Newman
Silver Greyhound. J. M. Walsh
Silver Guilt. L. Meynell
Silver Hair Clue. Nicholas Carter
Silver Haze. J. Ruyle
Silver Horseshoe. G. Verner
Silver Jackass. C. K. Boston
Silver Key. Griff
Silver Key. Maxwell Scott
Silver Key. E. Wallace
Silver King. A. W. Barrett
Silver King. H. A. Jones
Silver King Mystery. I. Greig
Silver Kings. P. Amos
Silver King's Vengeance, and other stories. H. Herman
Silver Ladies. M. Erskine
Silver Lady. J. Facos
Silver Leopard. Z. Cass
Silver Leopard. W. S. Masterman
Silver Leopard. H. Reilly
Silver Lever. D. C. Murray
Silver Linings. Charles Cohen
Silver Medallion. P. Brebner
Silver Mirror. M. V. Woodgate
Silver Mistress. P. O. Donnell
Silver Panther. W. J. Elliott
Silver Peril. M. Rutledge
Silver Phantom Murder. Brian Stuart
Silver Pigs. Lindsey Davis
Silver Pin. A. W. Barrett
Silver Pineapple. E. Kyle
Silver Poppy. A. Stringer
Silver Puma. A. Riefe
Silver Sandals. C. H. Stagg
Silver Scale Mystery. A. Wynne
Silver Setup. R. Blaine
Silver Shadow. L. Noel
Silver Shamrock. H. Curties
Silver Shine. J. V. Frost
Silver Shoe. H. E. A. Gingold
Silver Shroud. D. Creekmore
Silver Sickle Case. L. Brock
Silver Slave. G. Stanley
Silver Spade. L. Revell

Silver Spoon. A. Griffiths
Silver Spoon. C. B. Kelland
Silver Spoon Murders. D. W. Smith
Silver Stair. M. Leighton
Silver Star. S. Silliphant
Silver Strand. G. Hall
Silver Streak. J. C. Rogers
Silver Street. E. R. Johnson
Silver Street Killer. E. R. Johnson
Silver Threads. R. Flanders
Silver Tom, the Detective. Anonymous
Silver Tombstone. F. Gruber
Silver Tombstone Mystery. F. Gruber
Silver Tower. Dale Brown
Silver Trail. G. Templeton
Silver Unicorn. J. Blackmore
Silver Urn. F. Daingerfield
Silver Venus. H. McElroy
Silver-Voiced Murder. G. Morton
Silver Wood. D. Rowan
Silvercat. K. Franklin
Silvered Cage. H. Blayn
Silverface. H. Long
Silverface Surrenders. H. Long
Silverhill. P. A. Whitney
Silvermead. J. Middlemass
Silvernail. Jim Morris
Silver's City. M. Leitch
Silverskull. P. Edwards
Silversword. P. A. Whitney
Simba Bwana. D. W. MacArthur
Simeon Chamber. S. P. Martini
Simeon Tetlow's Shadow. Jennette Lee
Simon. J. S. Clouston
Simon Lash, Detective. F. Gruber
Simon Lash, Private Detective. F. Gruber
Simon of Hangletree. A. J. Rees
Simon Takes "the Rap". T. A. Plummer
Simon Wheeler, Detective. M. Twain
Simple Art of Murder. R. Chandler
Simple Case of Ill-Will. E. Berckman
Simple Case of Susan. J. Futrelle
Simple Justice. T. B. Morris
Simple Life. N. Balchin
Simple Pass On. J. Cannan
Simple Peter Cradd. E. P. Oppenheim
Simple Simon Smith. D. Collins
Simple Suburban Murder. M. R. Zubro
Simple Truth. E. Hardwick
Simple Way of Poison. L. Ford
Simple Way of Poison. A. Hocking
Simply to Die For. J. Christmas
Simpson of Snells. W. Hewlett
Simultaneous Eauations. L. Halley
Simultaneous Man. Ralph Blum
Sin. A. Applin
Sin. R. Vaughan
Sin Against the Odds. Stephen James
Sin and Johnny Inch. J. F. Straker
Sin and Sand. H. H. Ross
Sin and the Sinners. F. E. Smith
Sin and the Woman. D. Vane
Sin City. W. Perriam
Sin Convention. Stuart Hall
Sin Devil. Andrew Shaw
Sin File. S. Ransome
Sin for Me. G. Brewer
Sin Has No Future. J. Cello
Sin in the South. D. Gallo
Sin in Their Blood. E. Lacy
Sin in Time. J. Conway
Sin Is a Redhead. S. Harragan
Sin Is a Sideshow. R. Sterling
Sin Is Her Mantle. J. Cello
Sin Is My Shadow. N. Rosso
Sin Mark. M. P. Hood
Sin of Angels. A. M. Wells
Sin of David. M. Cumberland
Sin of Gabrielle. Mrs. C. Kernahan
Sin of Hagar. H. B. Mathers
Sin of Hong Kong. M. Corrigan
Sin of Joost Avelingh. M. Maartens
Sin of Laban Routh. A. Sergeant
Sin of Miss Bishop. N. Karta

Sin of Olga Zassoulich. F. Barrett
Sin of Preaching Jim. D. Donovan
Sin of Sacrifice. L. G. Redmond-Howard
Sin of Silence. O. Binns
Sin of Sister Betty. P. Cartrell
Sin of the Duchess. H. Townley
Sin Pit. P. Meskil
Sin Sniper. H. Garner
Sin-Stained. R. Vane
Sin Street. B. Bristow
Sin Strikes Six. F. Winter
Sin That Was His. F. Packard
Since There's No Help. A. Kennington
Sine Qua Nun. M. Quill
Sinews of War. E. Phillpotts
Sinful Cowboy. T. E. Abrams
Sinful Sisters. R. Vane
Sinful Stones. P. Dickinson
Sinful Woman. J. M. Cain
Sinfully Rich. H. Footner
Sinfully Yours. Carter Brown
Sing a Dark Song. W. D. Roberts
Sing a Song of Cyanide. N. Morland
Sing a Song of Homicide. J. R. Langham
Sing a Song of Murder. P. Drax
Sing a Song of Murder. R. P. Koehler
Sing a Song of Murder. J. R. Langham
Sing a Song of Murder. J. Michaels
Sing a Song of Murder. A. Spiller
Sing, Baby, Sing Sing. Kane
Sing, Clubman, Sing! Kevin O'Hara
Sing Me a Moon. C. Darby
Sing Me a Murder. H. Nielsen
Sing Out, Sweet Homicide. J. Roeburt
Sing Sing. D. Haring
Sing Sing Nights. H. S. Keeler
Sing Softly, Stranger. G. Greenaway
Sing Witch, Sing Death. R. Gellis
Singapore. J. Ball
Singapore. W. Bogart
Singapore Downbeat. M. Corrigan
Singapore Exile Murders. V. W. Mason
Singapore Kate. Roland Daniel
Singapore Set-Up. J. Dekker
Singapore Sling. Nick Carter
Singapore Wink. Ross Thomas
Singer Not the Song. A. E. Lindop
Singing Bone. R. A. Freeman
Singing Cave. J. Appleby
Singing Clock. V. Perdue
Singing Corpse. B. Dougall
Singing Diamonds. H. McCloy
Singing Ghost. R. St. Clair
Singing Harp. E. St. Clair
Singing Head. F. Hume
Singing in the Shrouds. N. Marsh
Singing Kid. W. C. Tuttle
Singing Lizard. J. Knowler
Singing Masons. F. Vivian
Singing Millionaire. M. Pereira
Singing River. W. C. Tuttle
Singing Room. N. Berrow
Singing Sands. J. Tey
Singing Shadows. D. Eden
Singing Soul. A. J. Foxall
Singing Spider. A. MacVicar
Singing Stones. P. A. Whitney
Singing Swans. A. Manners
Singing Sword. P. G. Larbalester
Singing Widow. W. P. Johns
Singing Wind. Jennifer Wade
Single Clue. Old Sleuth
Single Death. Eric Wright
Single File. N. Fruchter
Single Hair. H. Adams
Single Monstrous Act. K. Benton
Single Pilgrim. N. Lewis
Single Spies. Alan Bennett
Single Spies and Talking Heads. Alan Bennett
Single Ticket to Death. G. Bellairs
Single to Hong Kong. K. Boyce
Single Track. Douglas Grant
Single White Female. J. Lutz
Singled Out. S. Whitney

Singles Only. Stuart Hall
Singleton's Mill. Sinclair Buchan
Singular Case of the Multiple Dead. M. McShane
Singular Conspiracy. B. Perowne
Singular Crime. H. Nisbet
Singular Fury. H. L. Oleck
Singular Sinner. C. R. Harker
Sinister Abbey. Elsie Lee
Sinister Alibi. C. Wallace
Sinister Assignment. R. Fenisong
Sinister Cargo. M. Black
Sinister Cargo. S. H. Page
Sinister Castle. Gwyn Evans
Sinister Charade. D. Mariner
Sinister Civility. W. Croyland
Sinister Craft. R. Ladline
Sinister Crag. N. Gayle
Sinister Creek. J. Rowland
Sinister Eden. B. Cotterell
Sinister Encoutner. J. Brooke
Sinister Errand. P. Cheyney
Sinister Forces. Patrick Anderson
Sinister Forces. A. Westwood
Sinister Garden. Marilyn Ross
Sinister Gardens. W. D. Roberts
Sinister History of Ambrose Hinkle. T. McMorrow
Sinister House. C. G. Booth
Sinister House. L. C. Douthwaite
Sinister House. C. Farr
Sinister House. L. Hall
Sinister House. T. Taggart
Sinister House. G. Verner
Sinister Inn. J. J. Farjeon
Sinister Island. Wadsworth Camp
Sinister Island. S. Warwick
Sinister Island. A. Wood
Sinister Isle of Love. E. Morley
Sinister Lady. D. M. Disney
Sinister Legacy. D. Martyn
Sinister Light. Frank King
Sinister Light. Ethel L. White
Sinister Love. L. Ames
Sinister Lovely. N. Karta
Sinister Madonna. W. Jackson
Sinister Madonna. S. Rohmer
Sinister Man. E. Wallace
Sinister Mark. L. Thayer
Sinister Melody. F. Cowen
Sinister Moonlight. Colin Robertson
Sinister Murders. P. Cheyney
Sinister Playhouse. R. Armstrong
Sinister Purposes. M. Arnold
Sinister Quest. T. C. H. Jacobs
Sinister Rapture. H. Janson
Sinister Ray. L. Dent
Sinister Richard Shale. M. Verne
Sinister River. A. Soutar
Sinister Sanctuary. E. P. Thorne
Sinister Scourge. B. House
Sinister Secret. F. Gerard
Sinister Secret. A. Nettleton
Sinister Secret. A. O. Pollard
Sinister Service. W. E. Johns
Sinister Shadow. S. Hocking
Sinister Shadow. H. Holt
Sinister Shelter. C. L. Leonard
Sinister Sister. M. Brody
Sinister Smith. H. Atkins
Sinister Square. W. J. Elliott
Sinister Stars. J. Pattinson
Sinister Station. R. St. Clair
Sinister Stone. D. Winston
Sinister Stones. Jasper John
Sinister Stones. A. W. Upfield
Sinister Strangers. C. B. Kelland
Sinister Street. R. Burke
Sinister Street. S. Horler
Sinister Street. Vince Kelly
Sinister Talent. J. Pendower
Sinister Touch. J. Castle
Sinister Valley. G. Stanley
Sinister Voice. Genevieve St. John
Sinister Warning. M. S. Michel
Sinister Widow. R. Armstrong

Sinister Widow Again. R. Armstrong
Sinister Widow at Sea. R. Armstrong
Sinister Widow Comes Back. R. Armstrong
Sinister Widow Down Under. R. Armstrong
Sinister Widow Returns. R. Armstrong
Sinister Wooing. B. Sarto
Sink Me the Ship. Sea Lion
Sinkiang Executive. Adam Hall
Sinless. M. H. Yardley
Sinless Crime. G. Fleming
Sinless Season. D. Galgut
Sinless Secret. Rita
Sinless Sinner. M. H. Tennyson
Sinner. D. Linton
Sinner at Sea. P. Swift
Sinner in Black. E. Croft
Sinner or Later. M. Brody
Sinner Take All. D. Haring
Sinner Take All. Wade Miller
Sinner Takes All. A. Bocca
Sinner Takes All. M. Corrigan
Sinner Takes All. D. Holt
Sinner Takes All. R. Watkins
Sinner, You Slay Me! Carter Brown
Sinners. E. S. Aarons
Sinners. Carter Brown
Sinners. D. Torbett
Sinners and Shrouds. Jonathan Latimer
Sinners Beware. E. P. Oppenheim
Sinners' Castle. A. Wood
Sinner's Club. H. Whittington
Sinners' Game. G. Baldwin
Sinners Go Secretly. A. Wynne
Sinners in Clover. S. Toye
Sinners Never Die. A. E. Martin
Sinners of San Ramon. W. Mantalbano
Sinner's Shroud. T. Angelo
Sinners' Syndicate. C. Stanton
Sinners Twain. J. Mackie
Sinners Wild. Mark Reed
Sinnings of Seraphine. Mrs. C. Kernahan
Sino-Variant. A. Ind
Sinquake. G. Janes
Sins for Father Knox. J. Skvorecky
Sin's Half Mile. D. Linton
Sins of Billy Serene. W. Ard
Sins of Commission. H. L. Klawans
Sins of Harry Collins. Marina Campbell
Sins of Rachel Ellis. P. Caveney
Sins of Severac Bablon. S. Rohmer
Sins of Society. C. Raleigh
Sins of Sumuru. S. Rohmer
Sins of the City. W. LeQueux
Sins of the Father. J. Blackburn
Sins of the Father. Lawrence Block
Sins of the Father. Nick Taylor
Sins of the Fathers. A. Applin
Sins of the Fathers. C. Houghton
Sins of the Fathers. R. Rendell
Sins of the Fathers. T. Walton
Sins of the Flesh. M. Reed
Sins of the Past. H. S. Nuelle
Sins of the Past. L. R. Wisdom
Sins of War. J. R. Zodrow
Sinsation of a Sintury. D. O. Wilderness
Sinsation Sadie. Carter Brown
Sion Crossing. A. Price
Sir Adam Disappeared. E. P. Oppenheim
Sir Anthony. A. Sergeant
Sir Anthony's Secret. A. Sergeant
Sir Charles Danvers. M. Cholmondeley
Sir Christopher Leighton. M. L. Storer
Sir Devil. S. Styles
Sir Gregory's Silence. A. W. Marchmont
Sir Hector. R. Machray
Sir Hector's Watch. C. Granville
Sir Hilton's Sin. G. M. Fenn
Sir Jaffray's Wife. A. W. Marchmont
Sir Jasper's Tenant. M. E. Braddon
Sir John Dering. J. Farnol
Sir John Magill's Last Journey. F. W. Crofts
Sir Julian's Crime. F. Warden
Sir Morecambe's Marriage. F. Warden
Sir Penywern's Wife. F. Warden

Sir Percy Hits Back. Baroness Orczy
Sir Percy Leads the Band. Baroness Orczy
Sir Peter's Arm. M. Cobb
Sir Ralph's Secret. J. M. Cobban
Sir Richard Penniless. C. Edwards
Sir Theodore's Guest and other stories. G. Allen
Sir Vincent's Patient. H. Hill
Sir, You Bastard. G. F. Newman
Sirdar's Oath. B. Mitford
Sirdar's Sabre. L. Tracy
Sire. L. Allan
Siren. T. A. Trollope
Siren and the Centaur. Conrad Phillips
Siren in Satin. D. Walshe
Siren in the Night. L. Ford
Siren of the Snows. Stanley Shaw
Siren on the Skids. M. Brody
Siren Signs Off. Carter Brown
Siren Song. D. Beaty
Siren Stars. R. Carrigan
Sirens. E. V. Lustbader
Sirens. S. Pett
Siren's Lure. Andrea Davidson
Sirens Sang of Murder. S. Caudwell
Sirocco. A. Betteridge
Siskiyou Two-Step. R. Hoyt
Sister Act. M. F. Harris
Sister at Sea. Rona Randall
Sister Craven. S. Ready
Sister Death. P. G. Winslow
Sister Discipline. W. LeQueux
Sister, Don't Hate Me. H. Janson
Sister Don't Move. A. Capelli
Sister Earth. A. Brede
Sister Matty and Company. R. Holmes
Sister, Move Over. A. Capelli
Sister of Cain. Mary Collins
Sister on Leave. I. Roberts
Sister Satan. G. Dilnot
Sister Simon's Murder Case. M. A. Hubbard
Sister Susie—Spinster. A. Applin
Sister Theatre. G. Vaizey
Sisterhood. B. Black
Sisterhood. M. Palmer
Sisters. R. Littell
Sisters at War. L. Robin
Sisters of Sorrow. A. Vandergriff
Sisters of the Road. Barbara Wilson
Sister's Sacrifice. G. Fleming
Sister's Sin. Mrs. L. Cameron
Sit-In. G. Anderson
Sittaford Mystery. A. Christie
Sitting Duck. G. Bagby
Sitting Duck. M. Carr
Sitting Ducks. M. R. D. Meek
Sitting Emperor. E. N. Willett
Sitting Target. L. Henderson
Sitting Up Dead. A. M. Stein
Situation, Grave! H. Janson
Situation Tragedy. S. Brett
Situation Vacant. M. Burton
Situations Vacant. Norman Lucas
Six Against the Yard. Detection Club
Six and Severn. L. Rea
Six Bars at Seven. Mollie Kaye
Six Bells. Sea-Wrack
Six Black Camels. E. Lanham
Six Came to Dinner. Roy Vickers
Six Cent Sam's. J. Hawthorne
Six Curtains for Stroganova. C. Brahms
Six-Day Week. A. Gardner
Six Days of the Condor. J. Grady
Six Days to Death. P. Alding
Six Days to Die. Gus Stevens
Six Dead Men. A. Steeman
Six Deadly Dames. F. Nebel
Six Feet of Dynamite. B. Gray
Six Feet Under. D. Simpson
Six Foot Deep. H. Lugar
Six Foot of Rope. H. R. Taunton
Six for the Toff. J. Creasey
Six Gentle Criminals. Katharine Moore
Six Golden Angels. M. Brand
Six Graves to Munich. M. Cleri

Six Green Bottles. A. Hocking
Six Gun Empire. R. Wilkes-Hunter
Six-Hour Mystery. A. Marsden
600 Pound Gorilla. Robert Campbell
Six Iron Spiders. P. A. Taylor
Six Key Cut. M. Crawford
Six-Letter Word for Death. T. R. Frierson
Six Letter Word for Death. P. Moyes
Six Lines. N. A. Temple-Ellis
Six Lives and a Book. C. Houghton
Six Men. E. Radford
Six Men Died. G. Verner
Six-Mile Face. H. Gibbs
Six Minute Sketches. L. J. Huber
Six Minutes Past Twelve. Gavin Holt
Six Murders in the Suburbs. Roy Vickers
Six Nights of Mystery. W. Irish
Six Nuns and a Shotgun. Colin Watson
Six of One. P. Traill
Six Other Days. A. Meisels
Six Playlets. R. Willis
Six-Pointed Cross in the Dust. J. Roland
Six Problems for Don Isidro Parodi. J. L. Borges
Six Proud Walkers. F. Beeding
Six Proud Walkers. Anthea Fraser
Six Queer Things. C. S. Sprigg
Six Ropes for Glory. J. G. Sarasin
Six Rubies. J. M. Forman
Six Seconds of Darkness. O. R. Cohen
Six Seconds to Kill. B. Halliday
Six Sign-Post Murder. C. Robbins
Six Silver Handles. G. Homes
666. J. Anson
Six Stories. E. Everett-Green
633 Squadron. F. E. Smith
633 Squadron, Operation Rhine Maiden. F. E. Smith
Six Times Death. W. Irish
Six to Kill. B. Gray
6 to 10. J. Garden
Six Under Suspicion. C. Kingston
Six Weeks. L. Saunders
Six Weeks South of Texas. L. T. White
Six Were Present. E. R. Punshon
Six Were to Die. J. Ronald
Six Who Ran. M. E. Chaber
6XH. R. Heinlein
Sixes and Sevens. O. Henry
Sixpenny Dame. E. K. Goldthwaite
16 Beans. H. S. Keeler
Sixteen Bells. G. Hackforth-Jones
Sixteenth of September Game. R. Houston
Sixteenth Stair. E. C. R. Lorac
Sixth Column. P. Fleming
Sixth Commandment. Howel Evans
Sixth Commandment. Lawrence Sanders
Sixth Commandment. C. Wells
Sixth Day. P. Beere
Sixth Director. D. Newton
Sixth Directorate. J. Hone
Sixth Family. P. Diapoulos
Sixth Key. R. St. Clair
Sixth of October. R. Hichens
Sixth Precinct. Christopher Newman
Sixth Raid. D. Enefer
Sixth Seal. M. Wesley
Sixth Sense. R. Stewart
Sixth Sense Is Death. J. Garforth
Sixth Victim. W. M. Graydon
Sixty Days or Else. W. Richardson
Sixty Days to Live. D. Wheatley
Sixty-Fifth Tape. F. Ross
Sixty-First Second. O. Johnson
64 Thousand Murder. V. Gunn
60 Hours of Darkness. A. Sederberg
69 Babylon Park. H. Whittington
Sixty-Nine Diamonds. J. Lord
Size. A. W. Gray
Skater's Waltz. E. Kyle
Skein Well Tangled. J. K. Stafford
Skeleton. I. Crookenden
Skeleton at the Feast. C. Wells
Skeleton at the Villa Wokonsky. C. Pincher
Skeleton Clew. Dick Stewart

Skeleton Closet of Jules de Grandin. Seabury Quinn
Skeleton Coast Contract. P. Atlee
Skeleton Crew. Stephen King
Skeleton Finger. H. Hill
Skeleton in Concrete. J. E. Barry
Skeleton in Every House. Waters
Skeleton in Search of a Closet. E. Ferrars
Skeleton in Search of a Cupboard. E. Ferrars
Skeleton in the Clock. Carter Dickson
Skeleton in the Closet. A. B. Cunningham
Skeleton in the Closet. E. Southworth
Skeleton in the Cupboard. G. Goodchild
Skeleton in the Cupboard. H. Hawton
Skeleton in the Grass. Robert Barnard
Skeleton-in-Waiting. P. Dickinson
Skeleton Island. G. Mitchell
Skeleton Key. B. Capes
Skeleton Key. R. Dowling
Skeleton Key. L. G. Offord
Skeleton Key. D. Winston
Skeleton Man. Jay Bennett
Skeleton Out of the Cupboard. V. Williams
Skeleton Staff. E. Ferrars
Skeleton Talks. F. G. Eberhard
Skeleton Walks! F. Metcalfe
Skeletons. E. Sauter
Skeletons. G. Swarthout
Skeletons and Cupboards. R. Arnold
Skeleton's Clutch. T. P. Prest
Skeleton's Holiday. L. Ashley
Skeletons in the Closet. E. Ferrars
Skeletons in the Cupboard. K. Fowler
Skeleton's Secret. G. W. Jones
Sketches and Stories. M. Carmichael
Sketches in France. H. Everard
Sketches in Lavender, Blue and Green. J. K. Jerome
Sketches Light and Descriptive. W. Chambers
Sketches of Gotham. I. Swift
Ski Lift to Love. Helen Murray
Skid. M. Farrell
Skid Row. D. Spade
Skim. T. Henege
Skin and Bone. E. Greenwood
Skin Dealer. M. Tripp
Skin Deep. P. Dickinson
Skin Deep. G. Garcia
Skin Deep. J. Gautier
Skin Deep. W. Harrington
Skin Deep. S. Hufford
Skin Deep. C. D. Luce
Skin Deep. W. B. Murphy
Skin Deep. D. Wiles
Skin for Skin. Winifred Duke
Skin for Skin. D. Rutherford
Skin Game. F. Bonham
Skin Game. M. Brodin
Skin Game. D. Haring
Skin o' My Tooth. B. Orczy
Skin Swindle. W. Barker
Skin Tight. C. Hiassen
Skin Trap. W. Mole
Skinflick. J. Hansen
Skinhead Escapes. Richard Allen
Skinhead Farewell. Richard Allen
Skinman. M. Tarmey
Skinner. H. C. Rae
Skinnerball!! in Pursuit of Them. D. Joseph
Skintight Shroud. W. D. Dundee
Skinwalkers. T. Hillerman
Skipper Anne. M. Bower
Skippers and Shellbacks. J. Runciman
Skiptrace. A. Azolakov
Skirmish. C. Egleton
Skirts Bring Me Sorrow. H. Janson
Skirts of the Dead Night. W. W. Seward
Skorpion Dossier. O. Sela
Skorpion's Death. D. Brierley
Skuldoggery. F. Flora
Skulduggery. C. G. Hart
Skulduggery. M. Marshall
Skull. J. Buffer
Skull. B. J. McOwen
Skull Beneath the Eaves. H. Best
Skull Beneath the Skin. P. D. James

Skull-Face. R. E. Howard
Skull-Face and Others. R. E. Howard
Skull Mountain. D. Hawkins
Skull of Kanaima. V. Norwood
Skull of the Marquis de Sade and other stories. R. Bloch
Skull of the Waltzing Clown. H. S. Keeler
Skull Still Bone. J. Wyllie
Skulldoggery. P. Marks
Skullduggery on Halfaday Creek. J. B. Hendryx
Skull's Light. W. F. Swankler
Sky Bandits. G. E. Rochester
Sky Block. S. Frazee
Sky-Blue Life. M. Moiseiwitsch
Sky Divers. L. Cameron
Sky Fever, and other stories. W. E. Johns
Sky Fighters. K. Ford
Sky High. M. Gilbert
Sky High. W. E. Johns
Sky High. F. Ryerson
Sky-High Terror. R. Trevor
Sky Hunter. P. T. Owen
Sky Is Falling. W. B. Murphy
Sky Is Overcast. A. Booth
Sky-Jacked. S. Morgan
Sky Kill. D. Da Cruz
Sky Pirate. L. Pender
Sky Raiders. V. Norton
Sky Riders. L. Cameron
Sky-Rocket. M. Fitt
Sky Steward. K. Attiwill
Sky Tracker. J. E. Gurdon
Sky Train. P. Cruger
Sky Walker. K. Robeson
Sky Wolves. G. Radcliffe
Skyblazer. P. Allen
Skyborne Sapper. H. Chesham
Skycruiser. H. M. Brier
Skydancer. G. Archer
Skye Cameron. P. A. Whitney
Skyfall. T. Block
Skyfire. T. Page
Skyhigh Betrayers. L. Derrick
Skyjack. J. Hild
Skyjacked. D. Harper
Skylark Mission. I. MacAlister
Skylight. R. Kittredge
Skyline Message. Nicholas Carter
Skyprobe. P. McCutchan
Skyraiders. A. Marks
Skyriders. T. Wallace
Skyripper. D. Drake
Skyrocket Steele. R. Goulart
Skyrocket Steele Conquers the Universe. R. Goulart
Sky's the Limit. R. Ladline
Sky's the Limit. E. Woodward
Skyscraper. R. Byrne
Skyscraper Murder. S. Spewack
Skyship. J. Brosnan
Skyshroud. T. Keene
Skysweep. D. Pendleton
Skytip. E. Reed
Skytrap. G. Harding
Skytrap. John Smith
Skywatcher. W. Kent
Skyway Vampire. P. Conde
Skywayman. G. E. Rochester
Slab Happy. R. S. Prather
Slack Tide. G. H. Coxe
Slack Water. A. D. Divine
Sladd's Evil. P. McCutchan
Slade of the yard. R. Essex
Slade, Range Detective. G. Tuttle
Slade Scores Again. R. Essex
Slade's Marauders. S. Cade
Slag. D. McGibney
Slag. J. T. MacIntyre
Slalom to Terror. C. G. Thacker
Slam the Big Door. J. D. MacDonald
Slander. A. S. Roche
Slander of Witches. R. Gehman
Slander Villa. C. Stewart
Slane's Long Shots. E. P. Oppenheim
Slant Eye. Roland Daniel

Slashed Portrait. J. Hines
Slasher. Max Collins
Slasher. Michael Collins
Slasher. O. Demaris
Slasher. H. Desmond
Slasher. E. T. Hamill
Slate. N. Aldyne
Slate and Wyn and Blanche McBride. Georgia Savage
Slate Landscape. J. Turner
Slate Secret. Roy Burns
Slaughter. Henry Clement
Slaughter Day. Nick Carter
Slaughter Horse. M. Maguire
Slaughter in El Salvador. J. Rosenberger
Slaughter in Satin. A. Bocca
Slaughter in Satin. Carter Brown
Slaughter in September. S. Jason
Slaughter in the Sun. S. Christie
Slaughter in the Sun. D. Haring
Slaughter Run. A. Kilgore
Slaughter Street. A. Capelli
Slaughter Street. L. Falstein
Slaughter Summit. M. Mandell
Slaughter Zone. F. Garrett
Slaughtered Lovelies. D. Stanford
Slaughterhouse. F. Scarpetta
Slaughter's Big Rip-Off. A. Kane
Slave. E. Amadi
Slave Bangle. G. Leroux
Slave Brain. D. Reid
Slave Island. Gilbert Chester
Slave Junk. F. Packard
Slave Market of Mucar. L. Falk
Slave of Circumstances. E. D. Pierson
Slave of Crime. Nicholas Carter
Slave of Silence. F. M. White
Slave of the Mill. O. Harper
Slave of the Warmonger. H. Janson
Slave Safari. R. Sapir
Slave Stories in Rubber Dealing. J. W. L.
Slave Trade. C. Bainbridge
Slave Trade. H. Gold
Slavemaster. Nick Carter
Slavers. R. Telfair
Slaver's Secret. P. Quiroule
Slaves of Ishtar. Richard Grant
Slaves of Paris. E. Gaboriau
Slaves of Passion. R. Vane
Slaves of Seduction. H. Janson
Slaves of Sumuru. S. Rohmer
Slaves of the Lamp. G. Bronson-Howard
Slay at the Races. Kate Morgan
Slay Belle. C. Dekker
Slay Me a Sinner. P. Audemars
Slay Me Slow! D. Haring
Slay Me Suddenly. Antony Brown
Slay-Ride. D. Francis
Slay Ride. F. Kane
Slay Ride. Michael Newton
Slay Ride for a Lady. H. Whittington
Slay-Ride for Cutie. H. Janson
Slay the Loose Ladies. P. Quentin
Slay the Murderer. H. Holman
Slay Time. P. Muller
Slayboys. P. Kirk
Slayer. Roland Daniel
Slayer and the Slain. H. McCloy
Slayer of Souls. T. S. King
Slayground. R. Stark
Slaying in September. I. MacKintosh
Slaying of Julian Summers. Richard Williams
Slaying on the 16th Floor. Arthur MacLean
Slaying Squad. Robert Mason
Slease. L. A. Morse
Sledgehammer. Jasper Smith
Sledgehammer. W. Wager
Sleep. J. Creasey
Sleep and His Brother. P. Dickinson
Sleep, and the City Trembles. J. Garforth
Sleep Before Evening. D. Olson
Sleep for the Wicked. H. Howard
Sleep If You Dare. G. Usher
Sleep in a Ditch. M. Birmingham

Sleep in the Woods. D. Eden
Sleep Is Death. O. Kensch
Sleep Is Deep. H. L. Nelson
Sleep Is for the Rich. D. MacKenzie
Sleep Long, My Love. H. Waugh
Sleep Long, My Lovely. B. Winter
Sleep, My Love. Robert Martin
Sleep, My Love. Elizabeth Norman
Sleep My Love. L. Q. Ross
Sleep, My Pretty One. H. Howard
Sleep No More. M. Erskine
Sleep No More. F. Ryerson
Sleep No More. G. Sims
Sleep No More. S. S. Taylor
Sleep of Reason. C. P. Snow
Sleep of Spies. P. Harcourt
Sleep of the Unjust. E. Ferrars
Sleep of the Unjust. L. Meynell
Sleep off the Highway. P. J. Sherman
Sleep on Death. A. Morice
Sleep, Sugar, Sleep! D. Haring
Sleep Tight. M. J. Costello
Sleep Tight, Baby! D. Haring
Sleep-Walkers. D. Karp
Sleep Well, Christine. Alice Brennan
Sleep While I Sing. L. R. Wright
Sleep with Nightmare. D. C. Cooke
Sleep with Slander. D. Hitchens
Sleep with Strangers. D. Hitchens
Sleep with the Devil. D. Keene
Sleep with the Devil. R. McCary
Sleep Without Dreams. H. Kane
Sleep Without Morning. R. Foley
Sleeper. J. Browning
Sleeper. Eric Clark
Sleeper. B. Crowther
Sleeper. E. Dewhurst
Sleeper. M. Hughes
Sleeper. H. Roth
Sleeper Agent. I. Melchior
Sleeper Awakes. M. Hughes
Sleeper Murders. Donald Woods
Sleeper Wakes. G. F. Gibbs
Sleepers. D. Thurlow
Sleepers Can Kill. S. Jay
Sleepers East. F. Nebel
Sleepers of Erin. Jonathan Gash
Sleeping Bacchus. H. S. Saunders
Sleeping Beauty. P. Boileau
Sleeping Beauty. L. L. Greene
Sleeping Beauty. R. Macdonald
Sleeping Beauty Murders. L. O'Donnell
Sleeping Bomb. J. Moffatt
Sleeping Bride. D. Eden
Sleeping Car Murders. S. Japrisot
Sleeping Cat. I. Ostrander
Sleeping Cop. I. Ostrander
Sleeping Cupid. E. G. Whitney
Sleeping Death. G. D. H. Cole
Sleeping Dog. D. Lochte
Sleeping Dogs. E. Ferrars
Sleeping Dogs. W. Garner
Sleeping Dogs. F. Ross
Sleeping Dogs. C. Wells
Sleeping Dogs Die. Frank King
Sleeping Dogs Laugh. H. C. Danby
Sleeping Dogs Lie. Julian Gloag
Sleeping Dogs Lying. Kenneth O'Hara
Sleeping Draught. H. Adams
Sleeping Draught. C. E. Simon
Sleeping Girls Don't Lie. Hansjorg Martin
Sleeping House Party. Elisabeth Lambert
Sleeping Island. F. Vivian
Sleeping Life. R. Rendell
Sleeping Memory. E. P. Oppenheim
Sleeping Mountain. J. Harris
Sleeping Murder. A. Christie
Sleeping Partner. Winston Graham
Sleeping Salamander. C. Carfax
Sleeping Sphinx. J. D. Carr
Sleeping Spy. H. Burkholz
Sleeping Tiger. D. M. Devine
Sleeping Tiger. H. Jobson
Sleeping Tiger. M. Moiseiwitsch

Sleeping with the Enemy. Nancy Price
Sleeping Witness. M. V. Heberden
Sleepless Eye. Warren Miller
Sleepless Lunch. J. Vaizey
Sleepless Man. Gwyn Evans
Sleepless Men. E. Nisot
Sleepwalker. D. Combs
Sleepwalker. E. J. Gannon
Sleepwalker. H. McCloy
Sleepwalker. E. K. Stirling
Sleepy Death. G. Ashe
Sleepy-Eyed Blonde. J. Monmouth
Sleeve of Night. P. Traill
Sleight of Body. R. McInerny
Sleight of Hand. C. Carpenter
Slightly Deceived. P. A. Kelley
Slightly Guilty. P. A. Kelley
Slightly Invisible. P. A. Kelley
Slightly Lethal. P. A. Kelley
Slightly Murder. P. A. Kelley
Slender Chance. D. O'Connor
Slender Clue. L. L. Lynch
Slender Is the Thread. H. M. Caudill
Slender Margin. B. Francis
Slender Thread. P. J. Merrill
Slender Thread. S. Silliphant
Sleuth. A. Shaffer
Sleuth and the Liar. J. Sherwood
Sleuth Hound. G. Leroux
Sleuth o' the World. R. Rodd
Sleuth of St. James's Square. M. D. Post
Slice. Rex Miller
Slice. B. S. Mosiman
Slice of Death. B. McKnight
Slice of Hell. M. Roscoe
Slice of Life. J. Kisner
Slice of the Cake. W. Newton
Slick. C. Grae
Slick and the Dead. A. Bocca
Slick and the Dead. P. Cleife
Slick Detective Yarns. Anonymous
Slick-Fingered Kate. Roland Daniel
Slick Revenge. J. Nazel
Slickensides. J. B. Hilton
Sliding Death. K. Bruce
Sliding Scale of Life. J. M'Levy
Slight Case of Murder. H. Desmond
Slight Case of Murder. D. Runyon
Slight Mourning. C. Aird
Slightly Bitter Taste. H. Carmichael
Slightly Dead. Carter Brown
Slightly Disjointed Affair. I. L. Dunn
Slightly Imperfect. Ann Chester
Slightly Scarlet. Percy Heath
Sling and the Arrow. S. Engstrand
Slings and Arrows. C. Dawe
Slings and Arrows and other tales. F. J. Fargus
Slingshot. S. Jackman
Slinky Jane. C. Cookson
Slip-Carriage Mystery. L. Brock
Slip Coach. C. Baines
Slip of a Girl. S. Warwick
Slipknot. Angus Black
Slipperdown Chant. J. Rigg
Slippery Ann. H. C. Bailey
Slippery As Sin. P. Souvestre
Slippery Dick. H. Adams
Slippery Hitch. Gerald Butler
Slippery Staircase. E. C. R. Lorac
Slippery Step. R. Foley
Slippin'. E. Finnegan
Slippy McGee. M. C. Oemler
Slips Sees Red. P. Boyd
Slit My Throat, Gently. Michael Brett
Slitting of Mr. Crispe's Nose. E. M. Oddie
Sloane Square Mystery. H. Adams
Sloane Square Scandal and other stories. Annie Thomas
Slob. Rex Miller
Slocombe Dies. L. A. G. Strong
Sloth and Heathen Folly. E. L. Robinson
Slow. John Gloag
Slow Burn. P. Cave
Slow Burn. R. Dudgeon

Title Index

Slow Burn. J. Ehrlich
Slow Burn. J. Helgerson
Slow Burner. W. Haggard
Slow Dance in Autumn. P. L. Williams
Slow Dancer. W. R. Philbrick
Slow Death. Gar Wilson
Slow Death at Geneva. Diplomat
Slow Down the World. J. Ashford
Slow Gallows. W. Masterson
Slow Grave. W. R. Philbrick
Slow Heat in Heaven. Sandra Brown
Slow Poison. P. Barrington
Slow Poison. J. Rowland
Slow Turn. M. Marqusse
Slow Twitch. R. Enders
Slow Vengeance. J. Bude
Slowly, Slowly in the Wind. P. Highsmith
Slowly the Poison. June Drummond
Slug It Slay. E. Lanham
Slugger. P. Malloch
Slum Silhouettes. J. D. Brayshaw
Sly As a Serpent. M. Halliday
Slyboots. P. Flower
Slype. R. Thorndike
Smack Goddess. R. Stratton
Smack Man. N. De Mille
Small and Deadly. John Marsh
Small and Incidental Murder. J. W. Putre
Small Back Room. N. Balchin
Small But Deadly Wars. C. Heath
Small Change. Carnaby Brown
Small Favors. Patricia Wallace
Small Felonies. B. Pronzini
Small Gust of Wind. T. Magnuson
Small Hotel. Edward Morris
Small Hours of the Morning. M. Yorke
Small House Over the Water and other stories. M. Lemon
Small Masterpiece. T. Heald
Small Miracle. N. Krasna
Small-Part Lady, and other stories. G. R. Sims
Small Portions. A. R. Williams
Small Slain Body. P. Audemars
Small Slice of War. P. Kanto
Small Tawny Cat. V. Coffman
Small Time Crooks. K. Howard
Small Town Big Shot. Dirk Foster
Small Town Corpse. Clarence Hunt
Small-Town D.A. R. Traver
Small Town in Germany. J. Le Carre
Small Town Murder. B. W. Jefferson
Small Venom. W. Mole
Small Voice. R. Westerby
Small War Made to Order. N. Lewis
Small Wilderness. M. Summerton
Small World of Murder. E. Ferrars
Smallbone Deceased. M. Gilbert
Smaller Penny. C. Barry
Smallways Rub Along. Neil Bell
Smart-Aleck Kill. R. Chandler
Smart Bombs. P. Kirk
Smart Dame. J. Grecco
Smart Dames Play Dumb. H. Wolfe
Smart Doublecross. A. Capelli
Smart Girl. B. Vane
Smart Girls Don't Talk. H. Janson
Smart Guy. F. Kenny
Smart Guy. W. MacHarg
Smart House. K. Wilhelm
Smart Hussy. B. Vane
Smart Money. L. Matera
Smart Money Doesn't Sing or Dance. J. M. Glazner
Smart Moves. S. M. Kaminsky
Smartest Grave. R. J. White
Smash a Glass Image. K. Bird
Smash and Grab. V. McCall
Smash and Grab. C. Robbins
Smasher. J. Hunter
Smasher. T. Powell
Smashers. H. Paul
Smashers. D. E. Westlake
Smashing Bird I Used to Know. John Burke
Smashing the Drug Ring. J. Kelso

Smashing Through. J. Hunter
Smear Job. J. Mitchell
Smell of Evil. C. Birkin
Smell of Fear. R. Chandler
Smell of Fear. S. Dean
Smell of Fraud. G. Hogg
Smell of Garbage. V. Castang
Smell of Money. M. Head
Smell of Money. W. Newton
Smell of Murder. S. S. Van Dine
Smell of Peardrops. J. P. Carstairs
Smell of Smoke. M. Burton
Smell of Trouble. L. Trimble
Smile and Be a Villain. H. Jobson
Smile and Murder. F. A. Symonds
Smile Baby—Smile! R. Angel
Smile of Cheng Su. E. P. Thorne
Smile of the Stranger. Joan Aiken
Smile on the Face of the Tiger. D. Hurd
Smile Through Tears. G. Sava
Smiler Bunn Brigade. B. Atkey
Smiler Bunn, Byewayman. B. Atkey
Smiler Bunn, Crook. B. Atkey
Smiler Bunn, Gentleman-Adventurer. B. Atkey
Smiler Bunn, Gentleman-Crook. B. Atkey
Smiler Bunn, Manhunter. B. Atkey
Smiler with the Knife. N. Blake
Smiley's People. J. Le Carre
Smiling Buddha. I. Gregory
Smiling Buddha. Margaret Jones
Smiling Cadaver. J. N. Chance
Smiling Corpse. Anonymous
Smiling Corpse. H. Bailey
Smiling Death. F. Grierson
Smiling Dogs. K. Robeson
Smiling Killer. F. C. Davis
Smiling Mask. Frank King
Smiling Medusa. Jean Muir
Smiling Spider. L. Halliday
Smiling the Boy Fell Dead. M. Delving
Smiling Tiger. L. G. Offord
Smiling Trip. S. H. Courtier
Smiling Willie and the Tiger. J. Harris
Smith & Jones. N. Monsarrat
Smith and Son—Removers. M. Bentine
Smith Conspiracy. R. Neely
Smith of the Secret Service. R. T. M. Scott
Smith Slayer. "Burmar"
Smithereens. B. W. Battin
Smithfield Bargain. Rachelle Edwards
Smithfield Slayer. E. Bruton
Smith's Dream. C. K. Stead
Smith's Odyssey. G. D. Hooker
Smith's the Man. M. O'Nair
Smog. J. Creasey
Smoke. T. Barling
Smoke. G. Leeds
Smoke and Mirrors. Barbara Michaels
Smoke Detector. E. Wright
Smoke Dragon. T. Barling
Smoke-Filled Boudoir. Lawrence Williams
Smoke from the Ashes. W. W. Johnstone
Smoke Screen. C. Hale
Smoke Screen. L. Saunders
Smoke-Screen. D. Walshe
Smoke Without Fire. E. Ferrars
Smoked Out. W. B. Murphy
Smoker's Cough. A. Sewart
Smokers of Hashish. N. Berrow
Smokes of Spring. A. M. Burrage
Smokescreen. T. Allbeury
Smokescreen. D. Francis
Smokescreen. R. Kasper
Smoking Leg and other stories. J. Metcalfe
Smoking Mirror. H. McCloy
Smoky Cell. Robert (G.) Curtis
Smoldering Sea. U. S. Andersen
Smooth Face of Evil. M. Yorke
Smooth Justice. M. Underwood
Smooth Killing. W. H. L. Crauford
Smooth Runs the Water. M. Hill
Smooth Silence. M. Billett
Smouldering Fire. M. Clare

Smouldering Fire. G. Franklin
Smouldering Fuse. F. French
Smuggled Atom Bomb. P. Wylie
Smuggled Masterpiece. E. Jepson
Smuggled Sin. S. Harragan
Smuggler of King's Cove. S. Cobb
Smugglers. N. Gerson
Smugglers. F. Goldsmith
Smugglers. K. Okpi
Smuggler's Ally. B. Wayde
Smugglers at Odds. J. K. Stafford
Smuggler's Bride. R. Laker
Smuggler's Buoy. A. O. Pollard
Smuggler's Fate. E. C. Derby
Smuggler's Gate. M. K. Simmons
Smuggler's Ghost. H. Wood
Smuggler's Haunt. K. A. Shoesmith
Smugglers' Moon. Colin Robertson
Smugglers' Moon. C. Springer
Smuggler's Moon. S. Thorpe
Smuggler's Notch. J. Koenig
Smuggler's Pay for Firebrace. Seafarer
Smuggler's Secret. F. Barrett
Smuggler's Secret. H. Huntingdon
Snaggletooth. S. Jepson
Snags and Shallows. C. C. Lowis
Snail-Watcher and other stories. P. Highsmith
Snake. J. Crosby
Snake. J. Godey
Snake. J. McClure
Snake. M. Spillane
Snake and the Arrow. M. Hastings
Snake-Bite. R. Hichens
Snake Charmer. J. Griffiths
Snake Doctor. C. Garrison
Snake Doctor and other stories. I. S. Cobb
Snake Eyes. G. Dold
Snake Face. Roland Daniel
Snake Flag Conspiracy. Nick Carter
Snake Harvest. F. J. Thornton
Snake Hips. B. Sarto
Snake in the Grass. Anthony Gilbert
Snake in the Grass. J. Wellard
Snake in the Grasses. R. Hilary
Snake Is Living Yet. S. Gilruth
Snake of Luvercy. M. Renard
Snake Oil. Les Roberts
Snake on 99. S. Farrar
Snake on the Grave. G. Beare
Snake Tattoo. Linda Barnes
Snake Walk. Johnny Dark
Snake Water. Alan Williams
Snakes and Ladders. A. Broome
Snakes Have Fangs. D. Lee
Snakes in the Garden. L. S. Whiteley
Snakes of St. Cyr. W. O'Farrell
Snake's Pass. B. Stoker
Snake's Picnic. T. Herd
Snap. A. J. Quinnell
Snap. Jacqueline Wilson
Snap and Jenny. Old Sleuth
Snap Judgement. L. Denny
Snap Judgment. Anthony Stuart
Snap Shot. A. J. Quinnell
Snapdragon. F. L. East
Snapdragon. Margery Lawrence
Snapdragon Murders. B. Healey
Snappy Vendetta. H. W. Lee
Snapshot Chap. B. Lebhar
Snapshot Mystery. B. Bolt
Snare. J. A. Brown
Snare. N. Calef
Snare. G. Moffat
Snare. L. Robin
Snare. R. Sabatini
Snare and the Game. Nicholas Carter
Snare Analucian. A. M. Stein
Snare at Sycamore Grove. J. T. Osborne
Snare for Sinners. R. Fenisong
Snare for Witches. Elinor Chamberlain
Snare in the Dark. F. Parrish
Snare of Circumstance. E. E. Buckley
Snare of Serpents. Victoria Holt

Snare of the Fowler. C. R. Gull
Snare of the Hunter. Helen MacInnes
Snare of the Wicked. T. F. Moynihan
Snares of the Enemy. Pauline King
Snark. W. L. DeAndrea
Snark Was a Boojum. R. Shattuck
Snarl of the Beast. C. J. Daly
Snarl of the Lynx. R. Charles
Snarled Identities. Nicholas Carter
Snarleyow. Capt. Marryat
Snatch. R. Airth
Snatch. G. Ashe
Snatch. H. R. Daniels
Snatch. R. L. Goldman
Snatch. B. Graeme
Snatch. L. Mantz
Snatch. V. Markham
Snatch. B. Pronzini
Snatch. D. Scanlon
Snatch! R. Taylor
Snatch an Eye. H. Kane
Snatch and Grab. Rex Grayson
Snatch Game. J. G. Brandon
Snatch of Music. L. Peters
Snatch the Lady. Craig Cooper
Snatched. D. Linton
Snatched. G. Mcdonald
Snatched Dame. W. J. Elliott
Snatchers. L. White
Sneak Preview. R. Bloch
Sneaks. E. P. Green
Sneaky People. T. Berger
Sneeze on a Monday. P. Tabori
Sneeze on Monday. S. Carver
Sneeze on Sunday. A. Weston
Snide Man. Roland Daniel
Snipe Hunt. A. Dean
Sniper. N. De Mille
Sniper. Steve Mackenzie
Sniper. P. Malloch
Sniper. H. Pentecost
Sniper. W. D. Roberts
Sniper. M. Stratford
Sniper. Richard Williams
Sniper. B. Wynne
Sniper Jackson. F. Sleath
Sniper Murders. Richard Grant
Sniper's Moon. C. Stroud
Snipe's Spinster. J. Nuttall
Sno' Haven. Lee Miller
Snow. T. Kemp
Snow. J. Levin
Snow Along the Border. R. H. Sawkins
Snow Among the Stars. A. K. George
Snow and Ice. P. A. Bonds
Snow Bees. P. Cunningham
Snow Blind. A. M Treynor
Snow Falcon. Ganpat
Snow Falcon. Craig Thomas
Snow Fury. R. C. Holden
Snow Hawk. L. McFarlane
Snow Heroine. M. Gerard
Snow in Essex. J. Clappen
Snow in June. J. Blackmore
Snow in Paradise. R. H. Sawkins
Snow in Venice. Frederick Davies
Snow Job. B. Copper
Snow Job. M. Gair
Snow Job. R. Gallagher
Snow Job. D. Haring
Snow Leopard. S. Miller
Snow Leopard of Shanghai. E. Pizzey
Snow Man. R. Busby
Snow on High Ground. R. H. Sawkins
Snow on the Ben. I. Stuart
Snow Rattlers. S. Rifkin
Snow Shadow. A. Norton
Snow Storms in a Hot Climate. S. Dunant
Snow Tiger. D. Bagley
Snow Upon the Desert. J. R. Warren
Snow Vogue. D. Glinto
Snow Was Black. G. Simenon
Snow White and Rose Red. E. McBain
Snow-White Murder. L. Ford

Snowball. T. Allbeury
Snowball. J. Sangster
Snowball in Hell. A. Lassiter
Snowbird. O. Binns
Snowbird. Larry Levine
Snowbird Paradine. L. Clarke
Snowbound. B. Pronzini
Snowbound. B. Stoker
Snowboys. F. Webb
Snowdon Labyrinth. T. Barling
Snowdrift. J. B. Hendryx
Snowdrop's Message and other tales. Mrs. Chads
Snowed Up. Mrs. E. M. Stewart
Snowfall and Other Chilling Events. E. Walter
Snowfire. P. A. Whitney
Snowflake and Shaky. C. Gould
Snowline. D. Brierley
Snowline. B. Mather
Snowman. N. Bogner
Snowman. A. Maling
Snowman Cometh. D. Reid
Snows of Craggmoor. S. Harte
Snows of Offenburg. A. Andre
Snows of Yesterday. B. De Forrest
Snowshot. D. McBriarty
Snowstone. J. M. Scott
Snowtrap. C. D. Peel
So Bad a Death. J. Wright
So Blue Marble. D. B. Hughes
So Bright a Lady. M. Turner
So Cold, My Bed. S. S. Taylor
So Cold the Night. R. L. Yorck
So Dark a Heritage. F. B. Long
So Dark a Shadow. F. Hurt
So Dark the Mirror. J. Blackmore
So Dead My Love! H. Whittington
So Dead My Lovely. D. Keene
So Dead, So Sweet. D. Linton
So Dead the Rose. M. E. Chaber
So Deadly the Web. Ray Owen
So Deadly Fair. Gertrude Warden
So Deadly My Love. S. Ransome
So Deadly, Sinner! Carter Brown
So Dear, So Deadly. L. Du Breuil
So Death Came. C. Ryland
So Deep Suspicion. Elizabeth Ford
So Deep the River. D. Spade
So Dies the Dreamer. U. Curtiss
So Difficult to Die. J. Matheson
So Disdained. N. Shute
So Easy to Love. Marcie Gray
So Evil My Love. J. Shearing
So Fair, So Evil. P. Connolly
So Fair, So Evil. E. B. Stuart
So Far from God. John Harris
So Help Me God. Felix Jackson
So Help Me Hannah. L. Malloy
So Hurt and Humiliated and other stories. Francis King
So I Killed Her. L. O. Mosley
So I'm a Heel. M. Heller
So It Goes On. W. Willett
So Late, Monsieur Calone. A. Page
So Like a Woman. G. M. Fenn
So Like Sleep. J. Healy
So Little Cause for Caroline. E. Bercovici
So Little Time. S. M. Combes
So Long As You Both Shall Live. E. McBain
So Long at the Fair. A. Thorne
So Long at the Fair. J. G. Vermandel
So Long, Johnny! R. Angel
So Long, My Lady. Peter Williams
So Long, See You Tomorrow. W. Maxwell
So Long, Sucker. M. Clinten
So Long Sweetheart. F. Winter
So Lovely She Lies. Carter Brown
So Lovely to Kill. Harrison Wade
So Low, So Lonely. Curtis Lucas
So Lush, So Deadly. B. Halliday
So Many Dangers. T. B. Morris
So Many Dead. B. Shannon
So Many Doors. O. M. Hall
So Many Doors. A. Hocking
So Many Doors. L. Meynell

So Many Doors. E. R. Punshon
So Many Midnights. A. De Marquand
So Many Steps to Death. A. Christie
So Move the Body. Carter Brown
So Much Blood. Simon Brett
So Much Blood. B. Fischer
So Much Blood. Z. Popkin
So Much for Gennaro. J. Palmer
So Much in the Dark. J. Bude
So Near and Yet. C. Farr
So Near to Love. K. Lindsay
So Nude, So Dead. E. Hunter
So Pale, So Cold, So Fair. C. Birkin
So Perilous My Love. Clarissa Ross
So Pitifully Slain. A. Evans
So Pretty a Problem. F. Duncan
So Quiet a Death. N. Morland
So Rich, So Dead. G. Brewer
So Rich, So Lovely and So Dead. H. Q. Masur
So Sad, So Fresh. B. Hamilton
So Sharp the Razor. B. Graeme
So She Sent FLowers. A. Scobie
So Sits the Turtle. P. Traill
So Slender the Thread. C. Dixon
So Small a Carnival. J. W. Corrington
So Soon Done For. M. Babson
So Soon to Die. J. York
So Speed We. G. V. McFadden
So Sweet, So Deadly. D. Rico
So Sweet, So Wicked. S. Rand
So the Lady Died. E. Hale
So Thin Is the Veil. D. E. Bordeaux
So This Is Love! E. Woodward
So Violent My Love. C. Hammond
So What Happens to Me? J. H. Chase
So What Killed the Vampire? Carter Brown
So Wicked My Love. B. Fischer
So Young a Body. F. Bunce
So Young, So Cold, So Fair. J. Creasey
So Young, So Wicked. Jonathan Craig
So Young to Burn. J. Creasey
So Young to Die. G. Tree
Soap Opera Slaughters. M. Kaye
Soapy Murder Case. T. J. Kelly
Sob-Sister Cried Murder. Carter Brown
Sober As a Judge. H. Cecil
Soccer League Scandal. W. D. Maydwell
Social Buccaneer. F. S. Isham
Social Death. Renate Yates
Social Evil. P. Grayson
Social Gangster. A. B. Reeve
Social Highwayman. E. P. Train
Social Kaleidoscope. G. R. Sims
Social Sinner. R. Bacon
Social Sinners. H. Smart
Social Storming. W. Martyn
Social Vicissitudes. F. C. Philips
Socialism of Lady Jim. F. Warden
Socialist. Guy Thorne
Society Ball Murders. J. A. Anderson
Society Detective. Anonymous
Society Detective. O. Maitland
Society Editor. H. C. Beck
Society Intrigues I Have Known. W. LeQueux
Society Jezebel. F. M. White
Society Marriage. A. Askew
Society of Fear. H. Arvay
Society of Nine. Nick Carter
Society of Nobles. I. Tattersall
Society of the Dispossessed. R. Foxall
Society of the Spiders. Roland Daniel
Society Scare. F. Warden
Society's Prodigal. P. Crowe
Sock-It-to-Em Murders. R. Deming
Soeur Angele and the Bell Ringer's Niece. H. Catalan
Soeur Angele and the Embarrassed Ladies. H. Catalan
Soeur Angele and the Ghosts of Chambord. H. Catalan
Soft Arms of Death. R. Hayward
Soft As Silk. M. C. McDougall
Soft at the Centre. E. Warman
Soft Breeze from Hell. H. Miller

Soft Cargo. H. Janson
Soft Centre. J. H. Chase
Soft-Footed Moor. K. Royce
Soft Guy. V. Hill
Soft in the Middle. M. Storey
Soft Job. D. Haring
Soft Kill. C. Free
Soft Sell. J. Bruce
Soft Talkers. M. Millar
Soft Targets. D. Ing
Soft Touch. J. H. Chase
Soft Touch. D. Haring
Soft Touch. J. D. MacDonald
Soft Touch. Bradley Ross
Softcops. C. Churchill
Softcover Kill. T. Harknett
Softener. M. Bolton
Softly As I Kill You. C. Neutzel
Softly Dust the Corpse. S. H. Courtier
Softly in the Night. M. E. Chaber
Softly, Softly. Elwyn Jones
Softly—Softly. W. Standish
Softly, Softly Casebook. A. Yarrow
Softly Softly Murder Casebook. A. Yarrow
Softly Treads Danger. M. McEvoy
Softwar. T. Breton
Soho Cafe Crime. W. W. Sayer
Soho Girl. N. W. Firth
Soho Jungle. D. Bateson
Soho Pay Off. H. Jackson
Soho Racket. G. Dickson
Soho Solame. N. Perrelli
Soho Spiv. B. Sarto
Soho Spy. Colin Robertson
Solander Box Mystery. L. A. Knight
Solange Stories. F. T. Jesse
Solar Menace. Nick Carter
Sold! N. Lyons
Sold for Slaughter. D. Pendleton
Soldato! Al Conroy
Solden's Women. Bill Turner
Soldier and a Gentleman. J. M. Cobban
Soldier from the Wars Returning. J. Tickell
Soldier No More. A. Price
Soldier of Fortune. E. K. Gann
Soldier of the Legion. O. Binns
Soldier of the Legion. C. N. Williamson
Soldier on the Other Side. P. Alexander
Soldier Spies. A. Baldwin
Soldier's Love. A. W. Barrett
Soldiers of Fortune. W. McFee
Soldier's Pay. C. Fuller
Soldiers' Revolt. H. H. Kirst
Sole Agent. K. Benton
Sole Condition. V. Caudwell
Sole Survivor. L. Falstein
Sole Survivor. G. Hackforth-Jones
Sole Survivor. Gavin Holt
Sole Survivor. W. B. Murphy
Sole Survivor and The Kynsard Affair. Roy Vickers
Solemn High Murder. B. N. Byfield
Solemn Injunction. A. Musgrave
Solent Intrigue. M. Easton
Solid Gold Buddha. W. H. Canaway
Solitaire Man. B. C. Spewack
Solitary Child. N. Bawden
Solitary Farm. F. Hume
Solitary House. E. R. Punshon
Solitary Man. J. Evans
Solitary Man. J. Winchester
Solitary Terrorist. Peter Harris
Solitary Witness. R. Collier
Solitude Island. J. Brophy
Solitude Limited. J. H. Vahey
Solo. J. Higgins
Solo Blues. P. Harcourt
Solo for No Voices. W. Padden
Solo for Several Players. B. Jefferis
Solo Run. H. Herlin
Solomon Isaacs. B. L. Farjeon
Solomon's Knife. V. Koman
Solomon's Seal. H. Innes
Solomon's Story. W. J. Shaw
Solomon's Vineyard. Jonathan Latimer

Solstice Cipher. B. H. Boyer
Solstice Man. D. Quinn
Solution. L. Woody
Solution of a Mystery. J. S. Fletcher
Solve-a-Crime. A. C. Gordon
Solved in Thirty-Six Hours! H. H. C. Gibbons
Solved Mysteries. J. M'Govan
Solver of Mysteries and other stories. R. H. Todd
Solving a Mystery. D. Miall
Solving the Unsolvable. H. Mee
Somali Smashout. P. McCurtin
Somber Memory. V. Siller
Some Adventures of Samson Cogg. R. H. Clark
Some Are Born to Die. N. Rosso
Some Avenger, Rise! L. Egan
Some Beasts No More. K. Giles
Some Beckoning Wraith. P. Warren
Some Buried Caesar. R. Stout
Some Call It Love. R. James
Some Call It Perjury. L. Du Breuil
Some Cases of Sherwood Lang, Detective. C. D. Warren
Some Chose Hell. J. Hild
Some Crime Stories. C. Windust
Some Curious People. B. MacNamara
Some Dame. N. Karta
Some Dame, This One. D. Haring
Some Dames Are Deadly. Jonathan Latimer
Some Dames Die Young. D. Foster
Some Dames Do. Rex Richards
Some Dames Don't. P. Muller
Some Dames Don't. N. Perrelli
Some Dames Play Rough. S. Mitchell
Some Day I'll Kill You. D. Chambers
Some Die Eloquent. C. Aird
Some Die Hard. Stephen Brett
Some Die Hard. N. Quarry
Some Die in Their Beds. M. L. Roby
Some Die Running. N. Daniels
Some Die Slow. W. Herber
Some Die Telling. S. Cameron
Some Die Young. J. P. Duff
Some Die Young. Jeanne Hart
Some Die Young. J. Kilgore
Some Died Laughing! R. Dolphin
Some Further Adventures of Mr. P. J. Davenant. F. S. Hamilton
Some Geese Lay Golden Eggs. B. Graeme
Some Get It. B. Shannon
Some Happenings. H. A. Vachell
Some Happenings at Glendalyne. D. Conyers
Some Kind of Grace. R. Jenkins
Some Kind of Hero. J. Kirkwood
Some Lie and Some Die. R. Rendell
Some Like 'Em Shot. F. Malina
Some Like It Cool. R. Kyle
Some Like It Hot. S. Marshall
Some Like It Tough. J. Karney
Some Look Better Dead. H. Janson
Some Men and Women. M. B. Lowndes
Some Mischief Still. J. E. Hasty
Some Must Die. G. Brewer
Some Must Die. L. Moody
Some Must Watch. B. Cobb
Some Must Watch. S. Ransome
Some Must Watch. Ethel L. White
Some Names Are Dangerous. M. Latham
Some of Your Blood. T. Sturgeon
Some Other Place, the Right Place. D. Harington
Some Personal Recollections. Anonymous
Some Persons Unknown. E. W. Hornung
Some Persons Unknown. R. Trevor
Some Plain—Some Coloured. J. J. Bell
Some Poisoned by Their Wives. S. Forbes
Some Predators Are Male. M. Tripp
Some Put Their Trust in Chariots. A. Grey
Some Queer Stories. Anonymous
Some Rain Must Fall. W. A. Adler
Some Rats Have Two Legs. Griff
Some Rise by Sin. C. Houghton
Some Rise by Sin. A. Whicker
Some Rogues and Daphne. R. Tremayne
Some Run Crooked. J. B. Hilton
Some Slips Don't Show. A. A. Fair

Some Stay Dumb. D. Maddox
Some Take a Lover. P. Traill
Some Tales of the Fancy. E. Sampson
Some Tommies. M. Dekobra
Some Try Murder. R. P. Koehler
Some Unaccountable Exploits of Sherlock Holmes. C. Fisher
Some Unconventional People. R. Jebb
Some Unknown Hand. Elaine Hamilton
Some Unknown Person. S. Scoppettone
Some Village Borgia. S. H. Courtier
Some Women Won't Wait. A. A. Fair
Somebody at the Door. R. Postgate
Somebody Else and other stories. J. Symons
Somebody Has to Lose. Peter Chambers
Somebody Just Grabbed Annie. C. Dennis
Somebody Killed Kelvin. H. Clevely
Somebody Killed Milner. G. P. Willis
Somebody Killed the Messenger. Clarissa Watson
Somebody Knew. M. Montgomery
Somebody Knows. J. Van Druten
Somebody on the Phone. W. Irish
Somebody Owes Me Money. D. E. Westlake
Somebody Shot the Captain. G. Pahlow
Somebody to Kill. R. Reinsmith
Somebody Wants Me Dead. Richard Williams
Somebody's Crooked. S. Toler
Somebody's Done For. D. Goodis
Somebody's Luggage. F. J. Randall
Somebody's Sister. D. Marlowe
Somebody's Story. H. Conway
Somebody's Walking Over My Grave. R. Arthur
Someday I'll Kill You. H. Desmond
Someday the Rabbi Will Leave. H. Kemelman
Someone and Felicia Warwick. Raymond Mason
Someone at the Door. Dorothy Christie
Someone at the Door. C. Crane
Someone Else's Grave. A. Smith
Someone Else's Life. M. Philipson
Someone Else's Money. M. M. Thomas
Someone Else's War. J. Burmeister
Someone Falling. D. Ambler
Someone from the Past. M. Bennett
Someone Has to Take the Fall. W. Newton
Someone in the House. B. Michaels
Someone Is Bleeding. R. Matheson
Someone Is Killing the Great Chiefs of Europe. N. Lyons
Someone Is Watching. P. Field
Someone Killed Her Husband. C. B. Phillips
Someone Like You. R. Dahl
Someone Lying, Someone Dying. Jonathan Burke
Someone Must Die. M. Cumberland
Someone Waiting. K. Troy
Someone Waiting. Emlyn Williams
Someone Walked Over My Grave. J. B. O'Sullivan
Someone Will Die Tonight in the Caribbean. R. Puissesseau
Someone's Death. C. Larson
Someone's Sleeping in My Bed. J. Gonzales
Someone's Stolen Nellie Grey. Ira Walker
Someone's Watching. A. Neiderman
Somerset Murder Case. B. Flynn
Somerville Case. J. Corbett
Something About Midnight. D. B. Olsen
Something Attempted. J. Brampton
Something Between. M. Cockrell
Something Blue. C. Armstrong
Something Burning. N. Daniels
Something Doing. V. Vanardy
Something Else. J. B. Ellis
Something Evil. C. Crane
Something Evil. A. Hoffe
Something Evil. D. Quick
Something for Nothing. H. V. Dixon
Something for Nothing. K. Kilgore
Something for Nothing. J. T. Story
Something for the Birds. A. Dean
Something for the Birds. T. S. Drachman
Something in the Air. J. A. Graham
Something in the Air. E. Lathen
Something in the Attic. M. Raynor
Something in the City. F. Warden
Something in the Heart. J. Lodwick

Something in the Shadows. V. Packer
Something Missing. A. McColm
Something Nasty in the Woodshed. K. Bonfiglioli
Something Nasty in the Woodshed. Anthony Gilbert
Something Occurred. B. L. Farjeon
Something of the Night. M. McMullen
Something of Value. J. Pattinson
Something on the Stairs. S. Maddock
Something or Nothing. J. W. Conway
Something Rich. J. Butler
Something Rotten. Stuart Kay
Something Shady. S. Dreher
Something Terrible, Something Lovely. W. Sansom
Something the Cat Dragged In. C. MacLeod
Something to Hide. M. Burton
Something to Hide. P. MacDonald
Something to Hide. N. Monsarrat
Something to Hide. Patricia Robinson
Something to Hide. L. Sands
Something to His Advantage. W. F. Morris
Something to Kill About. D. Reid
Something Up a Sleeve. R. Lockridge
Something Wicked. E. Ferrars
Something Wicked. C. G. Hart
Something Wicked. H. McCutcheon
Something Wicked. C. Runyon
Something Worth Fighting For. R. Gadney
Something Wrong. E. Linington
Something Wrong. E. Nesbit
Something Wrong at Chillery. R. Francis Foster
Something's Afoot. James McDonald
Something's Happened to Kate. G. Holden
Sometime Wife. Carter Brown
Sometimes Life's Funny. J. J. Farjeon
Sometimes They Bite. L. Block
Sometimes You Could Die. J. Mitchell
Somewhere a Voice Is Calling. J. Lodwick
Somewhere in England. R. Gadney
Somewhere in France. R. H. Davis
Somewhere in France. L. Heilgers
Somewhere in Hamburg. M. Skinner
Somewhere in Sark. A. Philips
Somewhere in the House. E. Daly
Somewhere in the Night. Bill Barclay
Somewhere in the Night. M. Borowsky
Somewhere in the Night. J. N. McMahan
Somewhere in This City. M. Procter
Somewhere in This House. R. King
Somewhere Off Borneo. W. B. M. Ferguson
Somewhere, Out There. M. Grahame
Somewhere Quiet. G. Norham
Somewhere Within This House. J. F. Webb
Somnambulist and the Detective. A. Pinkerton
Son. G. Simenon
Son-in-Law Syndicate. F. Marlowe
Son of Blackshirt. B. Graeme
Son of Desolation. M. Y. Halidom
Son of Empire. Morley Roberts
Son of Flynn. E. L. Long
Son of His Father. R. Cullum
Son of Holmes. J. T. Lescroart
Son of Ishmael. L. T. Meade
Son of Judith. J. Keating
Son of Mars. A. Griffiths
Son of Nightingales. M. Hathaway
Son of Power. W. L. Comfort
Son of Sam. J. Breslin
Son of Sherlock Holmes. B. Preiss
Son of the Endless Night. J. Farris
Son of the Flying Tiger. M. Macao
Son of the Gods. Mrs. Lodge
Son of the Immortals. L. Tracy
Son of the Sun. M. Caldecott
Son of the Typhoon. James Bennett
Son of the White Wolf. R. E. Howard
Son of Three Fathers. G. Leroux
Son of Wallingford. G. R. Chester
Son of Wu Fang. Roland Daniel
Song at Twilight. B. Forbes
Song for a Prince. R. Foxall
Song for a Siren. V. B. Harris
Song for the Angels. F. L. Green
Song in the Morning. G. Seymour

Song of Corpus Juris. J. L. Hensley
Song of Doom. V. Markham
Song of India. M. Richardson
Song of Sixpence. F. A. Kummer
Song of the Dawn. K. Lindsay
Song of the Flea. G. Kersh
Song of the Scorpions. P. Tabori
Songs of War. K. Alexander
Sonneberg Run. G. R. Elford
Sonntag. Michael Sinclair
Sonny. T. J. Williams
Sonora Mutation. A. J. Elias
Sons and Fathers. H. S. Edwards
Sons and the Daughters. P. Gallagher
Sons of Belial. W. Westall
Sons of Earth. R. Rhodes
Sons of Fire. M. E. Braddon
Sons of Heaven. Terence Strong
Sons of Nippon. Bryan Peters
Sons of Satan. J. Creasey
Sons of Satan. W. LeQueux
Sons of Seven. C. B. Dignan
Sons of the Legion. G. E. Rochester
Sons of the Morning. J. Cassells
Sons of the Mounted Police. T. M. Longstreth
Sons of the Pioneers. J. Givens
Sons of the Wolf. B. Michaels
Sontag of Sundown. W. C. Tuttle
Soon She Must Die. A. Clarke
Sooner Spy. J. Lehrer
Sooner You Die. D. Haring
Sooper and others. E. Wallace
Sooper's Cases. N. Morland
Soothsayer. M. Dobson
Sophisticates. G. Atherton
Sophy Bunce. T. Cobb
Sorcerer of the Castle. F. Stevenson
Sorcerers. David St. John
Sorcerers. D. Winslow
Sorcerer's Broth. R. Garland
Sorcerer's Chessman. M. Hansom
Sorcerer's House. G. Verner
Sorcerers of Set. Martin Thomas
Sorcerer's Shaft. F. Gerard
Sorcerer's Stone. B. Grimshaw
Sorceress. A. Destefano
Sorceress of the Strand. L. T. Meade
Sorcery. F. C. MacDonald
Sore Temptation. J. K. Leys
Sorority House. J. Park
Sorority Mystery. J. Victor
Sorrow for Angels. H. Arvonen
Sorrow of a Secret. M. C. Hay
Sorrow of Michael. M. Ouseley
Sorry, Chief. W. Johnston
Sorry for You, Beautiful. S. Morelli
Sorry State. M. Kenyon
Sorry—Wrong Corpse. Clement Wood
Sorry Wrong Number. M. Simpson
Sorry, Wrong Number. A. Ullman
Sorry Wrong Number, and The Hitchhiker. L. Fletcher
Sorry You've Been Shot. A. Bocca
Sorry You've Been Troubled. P. Cheyney
Sorry You've Been Troubled. W. Hackett
Sort of Madness. E. B. Ronald
Sort of Samurai. James Melville
Sort of Tragedy. P. Lauben
Sort of Traitors. N. Balchin
Sorting Van Murder. Mander Ross
Soukour Deadline. A. Trew
Soul Destroyers. Nicholas Carter
Soul Eater. Robert Alexander
Soul Hit. C. Haas
Soul Hunters. G. Markstein
Soul Laid Bare. J. K. Egerton
Soul/Mate. Rosamund Smith
Soul of a Man. D. Vane
Soul of a Shop Girl. C. E. Pearce
Soul of China. L. J. Miln
Soul of Croesus. G. Villiers-Stuart
Soul of Phyllis Fabian. Mrs. C. Kernahan
Soul of the Sword. R. Bridges
Soul of the White Ant. Snoo Wilson

Soul of Viktor Tronko. D. Quamman
Soul Scar. A. B. Reeve
Soul Search Project. J. Rosenberger
Soulcatcher. J. Lara
Souls Adrift. A. Askew
Souls in Bondage. P. Gibbon
Souls in Hell. John O'Neill
Souls on Fire. L. Tracy
Sound Alibi. M. Edwin
Sound an Alarm. G. Holden
Sound Evidence. J. Thomson
Sound Like Laughter. D. Helwig
Sound Machine. E. Snell
Sound of a Voice. L. Gardiner
Sound of Dying Roses. J. De Pre
Sound of Footsteps. L. Ford
Sound of Hasty Footsteps. B. La Force
Sound of Insects. Mildred Davis
Sound of Lightning. J. Cleary
Sound of Midnight. C. L. Grant
Sound of Murder. J. Bonett
Sound of Murder. W. Fairchild
Sound of Murder. K. Fearing
Sound of Murder. M. Hinxman
Sound of Murder. R. Stout
Sound of Murder. Martin Thomas
Sound of Rain. P. Muse
Sound of Revelry. O. R. Cohen
Sound of Rowlocks. W. D. Steele
Sound of the Sea. R. Abbey
Sound of the Weir. M. Ingate
Sound of Water. M. S. Gerry
Sound of Wings. S. Dunmore
Sound of Winter. F. L. Green
Sounder of Swine. P. Buchanan
Soundless Scream. M. Butterworth
Soundless Years. H. Home
Sour Apple Tree. J. Blackburn
Sour Cream with Everything. J. Porter
Sour Grapes. H. Bindloss
Sour Lemon Score. R. Stark
Source. B. Lumley
Source of Death. H. Windsor
Source of Fear. B. S. Ballinger
Sourdough Gold. J. B. Hendryx
Sourdough Wars. Julie Smith
Souter's Lamp. H. McGregor
South African Affair. K. Okpi
South by Java Head. Alistair MacLean
South Coast Mystery. J. Drummond
South Coast Mystery. H. H. C. Gibbons
South Coast of Danger. V. Connolly
South Florida Book of the Dead. R. Merkin
South Foreland Murder. J. S. Fletcher
South of Arroyo. B. Harding
South of Heaven. J. Thompson
South of Hell's Gates. Richard Butler
South of Rio. E. L. McKeag
South of the Border. B. Machin
South of the Line. R. Stock
South of the Line. G. Volk
South of the Pagodas. A. Gilchrist
South of the Sun. Wade Miller
South Pacific Affair. E. Lacy
South Pole Terror. K. Robeson
South Sea Bubble. R. Pertwee
South Sea Buccaneer. A. Dorrington
South Sea Gold. C. Rodda
South Sea Sarah, and Murder in Paradise. B. Grimshaw
South Sea Yarns. Basil Thomson
South Street Confidential. D. Belsky
South Wind Blows. C. Porteous
Southarn Folly. P. Allardyce
Southeast of Mandalay. F. J. Kenmore
Southern Cross. Jenna Ryan
Southern Daughter. D. Keene
Southern Daughter. D. White
Southern Electric Murder. F. J. Whaley
Southern Fires. J. G. Sarasin
Southern Moon. J. Parkhurst
Southern Reporter. J. W. Corrington
Southern Seas. M. V. Montalban
Southern Tower. Anonymous

Title Index

Souvenir. P. Carlon
Souvenir. D. A. Kaufelt
Souvenir from Qam. M. Connelly
Souvenir of Monique. M. Z. Bradley
Sovereign Solution. M. M. McNamara
Soviet Marriage. P. Trent
Soviet Sources. R. Cullen
Sow Death, Reap Death. H. Pentecost
Sow the Wind. D. M. Disney
Sowing of Alderson Cree. M. P. Montague
Soyuz Affair. S. Coulter
Space Bean. J. Robb
Space for Hire. W. F. Nolan
Space Pirates. A. Del Martia
Spacehawk, Inc. R. Goulart
Spades Are Trumps. D. Spade
Spades at Midnight. S. Maddock
Spahis. M. McCracken
Spandau Quid. O. Fleming
Spandau Wager. M. Hammond
Spandau Warrant. Allan Morgan
Spangles. N. Revell
Spaniard. P. Pettit
Spaniard in the Works. J. Lennon
Spaniard's Gift. E. Welles
Spaniard's House. Robin Temple
Spaniard's Leap. H. Davie-Martin
Spaniard's Thumb. N. Berrow
Spanish Blood. R. Chandler
Spanish Cape Mystery. E. Queen
Spanish Chapel. D. Daniels
Spanish Connection. Nick Carter
Spanish Cove. L. A. Knight
Spanish Crown Affair. C. Conte
Spanish Death. E. C. G. R. Evans
Spanish Duet. F. Clifford
Spanish Galleon. N. Tranter
Spanish Gambit. S. Hunter
Spanish Harlem. D. Haring
Spanish Hawk. J. Pattinson
Spanish Heels. D. Whitelaw
Spanish House. H. Bourne
Spanish Interlude. Margery Lawrence
Spanish Jade. M. Hewlett
Spanish Lady. M. Cronin
Spanish Lady. A. Fredericks
Spanish Maze Game. R. MacLeod
Spanish Pistol and other stories. A. G. Macdonnell
Spanish Prisoner. P. C. De Crespigny
Spanish Prisoner. F. Gruber
Spanish Prisoner. F. Tilden
Spanish Season. B. Oldsey
Spanish Steps. G. Goodchild
Spanish Steps. P. McGuire
Spanking Girls. Carter Brown
Spanner. T. Chastain
Spare Men. J. Baggaley
Spare the Vanquished. M. F. Page
Spare Time for Murder. J. Gale
Spargo. J. D. Scott
Sparkling Cyanide. A. Christie
Sparrowhawk. T. A. Easton
Sparrows of Paris. M. Pei
Sparta Medallion. H. L. Lawrence
Spatchcock Plan. P. McCutchan
Spawn. R. Holles
Spawn. L. J. Key
Spawn of Satan. C. Birkin
Spawn of Space. F. Harkon
Spawn of the Desert. W. C. Tuttle
Spawn of the Hawk. P. Conde
Spawn of the Vampire. N. W. Firth
Spayde Conspiracy. J. Pattinson
Speak for the Dead. R. Burns
Speak for the Dead. M. Yorke
Speak Ill of the Dead. Peter Chambers
Speak Ill of the Dead. Richard Williams
Speak Justly of the Dead. E. C. R. Lorac
Speak No Evil. M. G. Eberhart
Speak No Evil. J. Marton
Speak No Evil. M. Warner
Speak No Evil of the Dead. M. L. Roby
Speak of the Devil. E. S. Holding
Speak Softly. L. Alexander

Speak Softly to the Dead. D. Bogard
Speak to Me of Love. D. Eden
Speaker. G. Ashe
Speaker of Mandarin. R. Rendell
Speaker to Heaven. A. A. Noel
Speakers in Silence. Ganpat
Speaking Eye. Clark Smith
Speaking of Murder. A. Roos
Speaking of Murder. V. Van Urk
Speaking Stone. K. Robeson
Speaking Stones. S. Cardiff
Spear. J. Herbert
Spear Gun Murders. B. Kendrick
Spear of Destiny. L. Rutman
Spearfield's Daughter. J. Cleary
Spearhead. F. M. Davis
Spearhead. P. Driscoll
Spearhead Death. M. Procter
Special Agent. Roland Daniel
Special Agent. N. Gerson
Special Agent. J. R. McCarthy
Special Assignment. T. C. P. Webb
Special Branch: In at the Kill. J. Eyers
Special Circumstances. B. Lysaght
Special Collection. T. Allbeury
Special Deception. A. Fullerton
Special Deliverance. A. Fullerton
Special Delivery. M. Dixon
Special Delivery. V. Gielgud
Special Delivery. J. Pattinson
Special Detective: Ashton-Kirk. J. T. MacIntyre
Special Drug Squad. I. Johnston
Special Duty. P. N. Walker
Special Dynamic. A. Fullerton
Special Edition—Murder. A. Kent
Special Flower. M. Gee
Special Guest. D. Elser
Special Kind of Nightmare. P. Geddes
Special Mission. R. Sharp
Special Murders. A. Douglas
Special Occasion. C. Curzon
Special Operations. J. K. Dugan
Special Operations Command. J. N. Pruitt
Special Orders for Commander Leigh. R. H. Savage
Special Payments. Jeremy Woods
Special Performances. W. P. Ridge
Special Providence. M. A. Hamilton
Special Relationship. W. Clark
Specialist. Jasper Smith
Specialist in Crime. G. G. Bolton
Specialists. Lawrence Block
Specialty of the House. S. Ellin
Specimen Case. E. Bramah
Speck of the Motley. F. Hume
Speckled Band. T. J. Kelly
Speckled Swan. Dexter Muir
Spectacle. R. Kruger
Spectacles of Mr. Cagliostro. H. S. Keeler
Specter of the Dunes. K. Ostrander
Spectral Bride. J. Shearing
Spectral Evidence. R. Hare
Spectral Mist. C. Ross
Spectre. Stephen Laws
Spectre. R. Weverka
Spectre Bullet. T. Mack
Spectre Chief. F. Legge
Spectre Gold. H. Hill
Spectre in Brown. H. Adams
Spectre Lover. E. Southworth
Spectre Mother. Anonymous
Spectre of Dolphin Cove. K. Kimbrough
Spectre of Lanmere Abbey. S. Wilkinson
Spectre of Maralinga. M. Hughes
Spectre of Strathannan and other stories. W. L. Norris
Spectre of the Camera. J. Hawthorne
Spectre of the Forest. J. McHenry
Spectre of the Turret. I. Crookenden
Spectres. Sarah Wilkinson
Spectre's Secret. S. Cobb
Spectrum. D. Wise
Speculations About Jakob. U. Johnson
Sped Arrow. V. Watkinson
Speech Day Murder. F. Dobbs

Speed Fever. B. Lyndon
Speed King. J. Addiscombe
Speed Mad. Gilbert Chester
Speed Queens. J. Bogar
Speedman Crook. J. Ascott
Speedo! M. Urquhart
Speedwell. T. Claymore
Speedy. R. Holman
Speedy Death. G. Mitchell
Speight Street Angle. O. Norton
Spell of Choti. Anita Allen
Spell of Sarnia. B. Reynolds
Spell of the Antilles. L. Robin
Spell of the Devil. F. E. Penny
Spell of the Hanged Man. R. Timperley
Spell of the Snow. C. G. Mitford
Spellbinder. C. Wilcox
Spellbound. F. Beeding
Spellbound. C. Vincent
Spellcaster. J. E. Ames
Spells of Evil. P. Boileau
Spence and the Holiday Murders. M. Allen
Spence at Marlby Manor. M. Allen
Spence at the Blue Bazaar. M. Allen
Spence in Petal Park. M. Allen
Spencer Blair, G-Man. Roland Daniel
Spencer's Bag. W. M. Green
Spend Game. J. Gash
Spend the Night. Grant Lane
Sphere of Death. Ray Harrison
Sphinx. F. Converse
Sphinx. R. Cook
Sphinx's Lawyer. F. Danby
Spice of Life. Neil Bell
Spice Route Contract. P. Atlee
Spicy Detective Encores #2. J. Case
Spicy Detective Encores #3. R. A. Garron
Spicy Detective Encores #4. E. H. Price
Spicy Detective Encores #5. R. L. Bellem
Spicy Detective Encores #6. C. Moran
Spicy Lady. J. A. Daley
Spicy Zeppelin Stories. Will Murray
Spider. Elliot Bailey
Spider. R. Brome
Spider. F. Hume
Spider. F. Oursler
Spider. G. Oursler
Spider. Gordon Stevens
Spider and the Fly. Graham Lord
Spider and the Fly. R. A. J. Walling
Spider at the Elvira. L. Dundas
Spider Ballet. A. G. Wilson
Spider Flies Again. J. R. Holden
Spider Game. G. Courtis
Spider Girls. D. Walshe
Spider House. V. M. Mason
Spider in the Cup. J. Shearing
Spider in the Morning. D. Hart-Davis
Spider in the Web. N. Brent
Spider Island. J. Spalding
Spider Island. T. Taggart
Spider Joe. F. Johnston
Spider Kiss. H. Ellison
Spider Lily. B. Fischer
Spider Man. T. A. Plummer
Spider Never Falls. Winifred Graham
Spider of Soho. S. Cranbrook
Spider of Truxillo. R. H. Savage
Spider on the Belly. W. Rabon
Spider Orchid. C. Fremlin
Spider Pete. C. Stuart
Spider Play. L. Killough
Spider Run Alive. B. Munslow
Spider Spinning. P. Troubetzkoy
Spider Stone. E. E. Cameron
Spider Strikes. M. Innes
Spider Strikes! R. T. M. Scott
Spider Underground. K. Royce
Spider Webs. M. Millar
Spider Woman. J. Goodwin
Spider's. Richard Lewis
Spider's Debt. J. McCulley
Spider's Den. J. McCulley
Spider's Den. Harrington Strong

Spider's Eye. C. Fayet
Spider's Eye. W. LeQueux
Spider's Fury. J. McCulley
Spiders in the Night. B. Edmunds
Spider's Parlor. Nicholas Carter
Spider's Parlour. P. Wynnton
Spider's Touch. V. Williams
Spider's Web. R. Brome
Spider's Web. A. Christie
Spider's Web. Roland Daniel
Spider's Web. Winifred Duke
Spider's Web. S. Harvester
Spider's Web. A. Helsby
Spider's Web. R. W. Kauffman
Spider's Web. J. Nazel
Spider's Web. S. Rathbone
Spider's Web. Mansfield Scott
Spiderweb. R. Bloch
Spiderweb. Alice Campbell
Spiderweb. J. E. Persico
Spiderweb Clues. P. Thorne
Spies. R. B. Sapir
Spies. S. C. S. Stone
Spies. T. Von Harbou
Spies Abounding. M. Annesley
Spies Abroad. Anonymous
Spies Against Them. C. R. Dumas
Spies Along the Severn. S. Maddock
Spies and Rebels. Operator 1384
Spies Are Abroad. J. M. Walsh
Spies Are Lonely Lovers. D. Haring
Spies Die at Dawn. H. Hossent
Spies from the Skies. J. M. Walsh
Spies Go Running. O. Quinn
Spies Have No Friends. H. Hossent
Spies in Action. M. Annesley
Spies in Amber. A. Armstrong
Spies in Ambush. J. H. Vahey
Spies in Concert. R. Stephenson
Spies in Pursuit. J. M. Walsh
Spies in Spain. J. M. Walsh
Spies in the Web. M. Annesley
Spies, Inc. J. D. Hunter
Spies Left! D. Betteridge
Spies Like Us. G. McGill
Spies Ltd. G. H. Teed
Spies Must Die. P. Christopher
Spies Never Return. J. M. Walsh
Spies of Good Intent. G. Veraldi
Spies of Peace. W. Martyn
Spies of Peenemunde. D. Betteridge
Spies of the Kaiser. W. LeQueux
Spies of the Secret Police. J. G. Rowe
Spies of the Western Front. G. E. Rochester
Spies of the Wight. H. Hill
Spies on the Roof. O. Quinn
Spies Over France. James Stewart
Spies' Vendetta. J. M. Walsh
Spies Within. B. Wynne
Spike. A. De Borchgrave
Spiked Heel. R. Marsten
Spiked Lion. B. Flynn
Spikes Gang. G. Tippette
Spill the Jackpot! A. A. Fair
Spin a Coin for Murder. V. B. Hoyd
Spin a Dark Web. A. Barron
Spin a Dark Web. M. Clare
Spin a Yarn, Sailor. Sinbad
Spin Me a Shadow. V. Black
Spin of the Coin. E. R. Punshon
Spin the Glass Web. M. Ehrlich
Spin Your Crime. J. Carol
Spin Your Web, Lady! R. Lockridge
Spinach Jade. James Bennett
Spindrift. P. A. Whitney
Spine. H. Imber
Spinner of Death. Nicholas Carter
Spinners of Life. V. Thompson
Spinning Target. J. Nazel
Spinoff. J. Sharkey
Spinsters. John Williams
Spinsters in Jeopardy. N. Marsh
Spinster's Secret. Anthony Gilbert
Spiral. Robert Garrett

Spiral. D. Lindsey
Spiral of Death. D. Masters
Spiral Path. Richard Grayson
Spiral Staircase. F. A. Leslie
Spiral Staircase. J. Wainwright
Spiral Staircase. Ethel L. White
Spiral Web. J. M. Wallmann
Spirals. W. Patrick
Spirit and the Bride. H. J. Kaplan
Spirit House. Scober
Spirit Murder Mystery. R. Forsythe
Spirit of Brynmaster Oaks. A. J. Griffin
Spirit of Cove Island. R. M. Sears
Spirit-of-Iron. H. Steele
Spirit of Melissa Norgate. E. E. Mande
Spirit of the Castle. W. C. Proby
Spirit of the Fist. Ronald Campbell
Spirit of the Hills. Dan O'Brien
Spirit of Turrettville. Anonymous
Spirit Smugglers. G. H. Teed
Spirit Stalker. N. Romberg
Spiritualists and the Detectives. A. Pinkerton
Spit in the Ocean. Shelley Singer
Spitfire Parade. W. E. Johns
Spitting Image. M. Avallone
Spiv's Mistake. J. Hunter
Spiv's Progress. A. Dotchin
Splash of Red. Antonia Fraser
Splash of Red. A. MacKenzie
Splendid Adventure of Hannibal Tod. E. Jepson
Splendid Blackguard. R. Pocock
Splendid Coward. H. Townley
Splendid Crime. G. Goodchild
Splendid Executioner. T. Downey
Splendid Exile. L. P. Greene
Splendid Hazard. H. MacGrath
Splendid Imposter. F. Whishaw
Splendid Love. H. S. Cooper
Splendid Outcast. G. F. Gibbs
Splendid Sin. G. Allen
Splendor and the Dust. H. Gibbs
Splendour Falls. K. Lindsay
Splinter of Glass. J. Creasey
Splinter of Ice. B. Marriner
Splintered Eye. B. S. Patric
Splintered Man. M. E. Chaber
Splintered Sunglasses Affair. P. Leslie
Splinters of Fear. N. W. Erickson
Split. G. F. Newman
Split. R. Stark
Split Bamboo. L. Phillips
Split Down the Middle. David Miles
Split Image. D. Pendleton
Split Images. E. Leonard
Split on Red. W. Hughes
Split Peas. H. Hill
Split Scene. F. Mullally
Split Second. D. McIntyre
Split Second. M. R. D. Meek
Spoil! E. G. Perrault
Spoil of the Desert. H. H. Hill
Spoiler. D. Stansberry
Spoiler of Men. R. Marsh
Spoilers. D. Bagley
Spoilers. J. Pattinson
Spoilers. E. Pugh
Spoilers and the Spoiled. Nicholas Carter
Spoils of Ararat. R. Katz
Spoils of Chance. Nicholas Carter
Spoils of Time. June Thomson
Spoils of War. W. B. Murphy
Spoilt Girl. F. Warden
Spoilt Kill. M. Kelly
Spoletta Story. J. D. White
Spook. S. Vance
Spook Hole. K. Robeson
Spook Legion. K. Robeson
Spook of Grandpa Eben. K. Robeson
Spook Who Sat by the Door. S. Greenlee
Spooks. R. J. Sherman
Spooks Alive. L. Rose
Spooks and Spasms. J. Tobias
Spooks Sometimes Sing. J. Courage
Spooky Hollow. C. Wells

Spooky Junction. J. F. Stone
Spooky Riders. W. C. Tuttle
Spooky Tavern. J. Tobias
Spoonful of Luger. R. Ormerod
Sport and Spangles. B. Webber
Sport for Inspector West. J. Creasey
Sport for the Baron. Anthony Morton
Sport of Chance. T. W. Speight
Sport of Fate. L. Clarke
Sport of Fate. R. Dowling
Sport of Fate. Old Spicer
Sport of Kings. A. S. Roche
Sport of the Gods. E. Miller
Sport of the Gods. Grove Wilson
Sport Royal and other stories. A. Hope
Sporting Chance. A. Askew
Sporting Deacon. C. E. Blaney
Sporting Detective. Hedley Scott
Sporting Offer. F. Warden
Sporting Proposition. J. Aldridge
Sporting Sketches. N. Gould
Sporting Stories. N. Gould
Sporting Stories and Sketches. G. G.
Sports Freak. S. OCork
Sports Stars in Danger. T. Haile
Sportsman-Detective. Mansfield Scott
Spot Marked X. B. Gray
Spot of Bother. V. Sylvaine
Spot of Murder and other stories. P. Cheyney
Spot the Lady. L. Powell
Spotlight. J. Korotkin
Spotlight. P. Wentworth
Spotlight on a Simple Case. Roberts Morgan
Spotlight on Murder. F. A. Symonds
Spotlight on Murder. Martin Thomas
Spotlight on Murder. J. Wellard
Spotted Hemlock. G. Mitchell
Spotted Men. K. Robeson
Spotted Soliders. C. E. Dibb
Spread of Sail. J. D. White
Spree. M. A. Collins
Spreewald Collection. D. MacKenzie
Sprengler Cache. M. Stall
Sprig of Sea Lavender. J. R. L. Anderson
Spriggs the Cracksman. H. Hill
Sprightly Fancies, and other odds and ends. C. C. Atchison
Spring Came Late. G. Greenaway
Spring Comes to the Crescent. Elizabeth Ford
Spring Cruise. L. A. Knight
Spring Darkness. J. Metcalfe
Spring Fire. V. Packer
Spring Harrowing. P. A. Taylor
Spring of Malice. J. Harris
Spring 1940. S. Engstrand
Spring of the Tiger. V. Holt
Spring of Violence. Dell Shannon
Spring Street. J. R. Richardson
Spring Term. B. Hamilton
Springblade. Greg Walker
Springboard. J. Fores
Springers. B. Mather
Springs of Violence. E. Lindall
Sprung. H. Janson
Spun Silk. W. J. Elliott
Spun Yarns. Morgan Robertson
Spunyarn. A. C. Barker
Spur of Danger. C. C. Hotchkiss
Spurious Note Maker. J. K. Stafford
Spurlock: Sheriff of Purgatory. Jim Morris
Spurs of Troodos. W. H. Murray
Spy. J. F. Cooper
Spy. N. Garbo
Spy. J. B. Harris-Burland
Spy. S. Horler
Spy. A. Mullin
Spy. B. Newman
Spy. P. Thomas
Spy. T. Von Harbou
Spy Against the Reich. M. Annesley
Spy and Die. Martin Meyers
Spy and the Pirate Queen. H. D. Steward
Spy and the Thief. E. D. Hoch
Spy at Angkor Wat. B. S. Ballinger

Title Index

Spy at Evening. Donald James
Spy at No. 10. B. Newman
Spy at the Gate. V. Gay
Spy at the Villa Miranda. Elsie Lee
Spy Business. J. Pendower
Spy Castle. Nick Carter
Spy Catchers. N. MacNeil
Spy Catchers. B. Newman
Spy Company. A. C. Gunter
Spy Concerto. C. Merlin
Spy Converted. P. Boulle
Spy Corner. M. Annesley
Spy-Counter Spy. M. Annesley
Spy-Counter Spy. D. Betteridge
Spy Fever. M. Hatfield
Spy Flyers. W. E. Johns
Spy for a Spy. B. Mather
Spy for Churchill. R. Vacha
Spy for England. Martin Kent
Spy for Germany. E. Gimpel
Spy for Mr. Crook. Anthony Gilbert
Spy for Napoleon. Rachelle Edwards
Spy for Sale. L. Payne
Spy from Spain. J. G. Brandon
Spy from the Grave. James Dark
Spy Game. M. Lovell
Spy Game. J. McNeil
Spy Gang. P. Sebastian
Spy Ghost. N. Daniels
Spy Hook. L. Deighton
Spy Hunt. N. Daniels
Spy Hunter. W. LeQueux
Spy Hunters. J. Bolton
Spy-In. R. Deming
Spy in Amber. M. Malgamukar
Spy in Bangkok. B. S. Ballinger
Spy in Black. J. S. Clouston
Spy in Black. C. Weston
Spy in Camera. Richard Grayson
Spy in Chancery. K. Benton
Spy in Chancery. P. C. Doherty
Spy in Damascus. N. Vange
Spy in Khaki. M. McKenna
Spy in My Bed. H. Janson
Spy in Question. T. Sebastian
Spy in the Brown Derby. B. Newman
Spy in the Deuce Court. F. DeFord
Spy in the Family. A. Waugh
Spy in the Hand. Henry Talbot
Spy in the Java Sea. B. S. Ballinger
Spy in the Jungle. B. S. Ballinger
Spy in the Navy. D. Lenton
Spy in the Nude. R. Seth
Spy in the Ointment. D. E. Westlake
Spy in the Room. D. Clift
Spy in the Tunnel. John Morgan
Spy in the Vodka. Ross Thomas
Spy in White Gloves. J. Laflin
Spy in Winter. M. Hastings
Spy Is a Dirty Word. R. Temple
Spy Is Dead. Charles Russell
Spy Is Falling. Stuart James
Spy Is Forever. R. P. French
Spy Island. M. Annesley
Spy Kill. L. W. Blanco
Spy Line. L. Deighton
Spy Me This One. J. Kirkpatrick
Spy Meets Spy. C. V. Frost
Spy Net. Ared White
Spy Next Door. L. Kessner
Spy Now, Pay Later. N. Rich
Spy No. 13. R. W. Chambers
Spy of Napoleon. Baroness Orczy
Spy of Osawatomie. M. E. Jackson
Spy of the Old School. J. Rathbone
Spy on Approval. R. Child
Spy on Riverside Drive. C. Rauch
Spy on Spider. J. N. Chance
Spy on the Centre Court. F. DeFord
Spy on the Run. M. Lovell
Spy or Die. B. Graham
Spy Paramount. E. P. Oppenheim
Spy Probe. K. Blake
Spy Puppets. Geoffrey Davison

Spy Shadow. T. Sebastian
Spy Sinker. L. Deighton
Spy Story. James Burke
Spy Story. L. Deighton
Spy Trap. W. Gilman
Spy Trap. B. Graham
Spy 222. R. Dark
Spy Was Born. M. McKenna
Spy Wednesday. William Hood
Spy Who Barked in the Night. M. Lovell
Spy Who Came . . . L. Dawson
Spy Who Came Home to Die. J. Weil
Spy Who Came in from the Cold. J. Le Carre
Spy Who Didn't. J. Laflin
Spy Who Died in Bed. G. Wolfenden
Spy Who Died of Boredom. G. Mikes
Spy Who Died Twice. M. Bar-Zohar
Spy Who Drank Blook. G. Linzner
Spy Who Fell Off the Back of the Bus. M. Lovell
Spy Who Got His Feet Wet. M. Lovell
Spy Who Got Off at Las Vegas. D. Savage
Spy Who Hated Fudge. R. L. Hershatter
Spy Who Hated Licorice. R. L. Hershatter
Spy Who Longed for Home. M. G. Spang
Spy Who Loved America. J. Laflin
Spy Who Loved Me. I. Fleming
Spy Who Never Was. Sheila Martin
Spy Who Read Latin and other stories. E. D. Hoch
Spy Who Sat and Waited. R. W. Campbell
Spy Who Spoke Porpoise. P. Wylie
Spy Who Swopped Shoes. Geoffrey Davison
Spy Who Was Three Feet Tall. P. Rabe
Spy Who Wasn't Exchanged. A. Tack
Spy Who Wouldn't Die. Stuart James
Spy with a Cold Nose. R. Galton
Spy with His Head in the Clouds. M. Lovell
Spy with the Blue Kazoo. Dagmar
Spy with the Scar. J. Rowland
Spy with Three Antlers. Donn Reed
Spycracker. G. Moxon
Spying at the Fountain of Youth. W. Butler
Spying Blind. James Dark
Spying Blind. M. McKenna
Spykiller. Nick Carter
Spylight. J. Leasor
Spylight. W. Taylor
Spymaster. A. Aricha
Spymaster. D. Freed
Spymaster. P. Freund
Spymaster. E. P. Oppenheim
Spyrocket. W. Taylor
Spy's Flight. Basil Jackson
Spy's Wife. R. Hill
Spyship. T. Keene
Spytrap. W. Crisp
Squaberry Canyon. A. Rutherford
Squad. P. Beere
Squad Room. T. J. Kelly
Squadron Scramble. R. Jackson
Squadron Without a Number. G. E. Rochester
Squall Line. Jim Hall
Square Circle. D. Carney
Square Crooks. J. P. Judge
Square Dance. J. Wainwright
Square Deal. G. Goodchild
Square Egg. H. H. Munro
Square Emerald. F. Johns
Square Emerald. E. Wallace
Square in the Middle. W. C. Gault
Square Mark. Grace M. White
Square of Many Colours. J. Blackmore
Square One. H. Janson
Square Peg. G. Malcolm-Smith
Squaring the Triangle, and other stories. H. Kaner
Squaw Point. R. H. Shimer
Squeaker. E. Wallace
Squeaking Golbin. K. Robeson
Squeal Man. M. Flusser
Squeal Squad. D. Haring
Squealer. Johnny Dark
Squealer. G. Verner
Squealer. E. Wallace
Squealer's Secret. Donald Stuart
Squeeze. G. Brewer

Squeeze. D. Craig
Squeeze Play. P. Benjamin
Squeeze Play. J. McKimmey
Squeeze Play. T. H. Stone
Squeeze Play. K. Vining
Squid. K. Horan
Squid. B. Mitcalfe
Squire Errant. R. Foxall
Squire of Death. R. Lockridge
Squire of Kilderman. F. Burdon
Squire of Landrewn. G. V. Vosper
Squire Trevlyn's Heir. H. Wood
Squire's Fatal Will. M. Danvers
Squire's Heir. E. Everett-Green
Squire's Legacy. M. C. Hay
Sssh! She's a Killer. Carter Brown
Stab in the Back. H. Adams
Stab in the Back. C. Drummond
Stab in the Back. Malcolm Gray
Stab in the Dark. L. Block
Stab in the Dark. Carter Brown
Stab in the Dark. C. Dekker
Stab in the Dark. J. Rayter
Stab in the Dark. L. Trimble
Stable Mystery, and other stories. N. Gould
Stables Crime. M. Osborne
Stables to 1,000,000 Pounds. Gordon Holt
Stacey. W. Sherman
Stacked Deck. F. Kane
Staffordshire Assassins. C. Stokes
Staffordshire Knot. J. Ruegg
Stag Dinner Death. J. Penn
Stag Party. W. Krasner
Stage Blood. C. Ludlam
Stage Door. A. Applin
Stage Door Crime. G. Chester
Stage Door Fright. Dulcie Gray
Stage Door Murder. S. Bate
Stage Plays from the Classics. J. Bland
Stage-Struck. A. Applin
Stage Struck. S. Gray
Staged for Death. P. Bird
Stages of Terror. B. Kingsley
Stain. F. Halsey
Stain of Suspicion. C. Williams
Stain on the Snow. G. Simenon
Stained Glass. W. F. Buckley
Stainless Steel Rat. H. Harrison
Stainless Steel Rat for President. H. Harrison
Stainless Steel Rat Gets Drafted. H. Harrison
Stainless Steel Rat Is Born. H. Harrison
Stainless Steel Rat Saves the World. H. Harrison
Stainless Steel Rat Wants You. H. Harrison
Stainless Steel Rat's Revenge. H. Harrison
Stainless Steel Wreath. J. Hedges
Staircase 4. H. Reilly
Staircase of Surprise. F. A. Mathews
Stairs Lead Nowhere. H. Swiggett
Stairs of Sand. E. D. Pierson
Stairway. U. Curtiss
Stairway on the Wall. A. Prescott
Stairway to an Empty Room. D. Hitchens
Stairway to Death. B. Fischer
Stairway to Murder. A. Kent
Stairway to Murder. O. Mills
Stairway to Murder. F. Usher
Stairway to Nowhere. H. Ellson
Stake. J. S. Rand
Stake in the Game. E. Berckman
Stake Out. Ken Blake
Staked Goat. J. Healy
Stalag Mites. L. Grex
Stalag 17. D. Bevan
Stalag Texas. John Lee
Stalemate. E. Berckman
Stalin Account. K. Royce
Stalk a Long Shadow. R. Severn
Stalk the Hunter. M. A. Wilson
Stalk the Killer. Steve Davis
Stalk to Kill. R. Adam
Stalked. F. Rickett
Stalked by Fear. L. Robin
Stalker. L. Cody
Stalker. B. Pronzini

Stalker. Theodore Taylor
Stalkers. P. Ketchum
Stalkers of the Sea. K. Stanton
Stalking. T. Seligman
Stalking Angel. T. Allbeury
Stalking Blind. S. Ashley
Stalking Horse. M. Delahaye
Stalking Horse. V. Gielgud
Stalking Horse. B. Howley
Stalking Horse. J. McGown
Stalking Horse. J. Pattinson
Stalking Horse. A. Rothberg
Stalking Horse. C. Wilcox
Stalking Lamb. M. Babson
Stalking Man. W. Tucker
Stalking of Adrian Lawford. Roderick Grant
Stalking Point. D. Kyle
Stalking Stranger. Colin Robertson
Stalking Terror. V. Coffman
Stalking the Angel. R. Crais
Stalking the Unicorn. M. Resnick
Stallion Gate. M. C. Smith
Stamboul Intrigue. R. Charles
Stamboul Nights. H. G. Dwight
Stamboul Train. G. Greene
Stamp-Fiend's Raid. W. E. Imeson
Stamp King. G. de Beauregard
Stamp Me Mortal. J. Lodwick
Stamped for Death. E. McDowell
Stamped for Murder. B. Benson
Stampede. L. Sieveking
Stamping Out Murder. J. R. Linck
Stand and Deliver. G. Warden
Stand By! Taffrail
Stand By for Danger. P. Manton
Stand By—London Calling. H. S. Keeler
Stand By to Shoot. E. Cannon
Stand In. B. Kingsley
Stand-In. E. Piper
Stand-In for Danger. K. Hewitt
Stand-In for Danger. R. Rayner
Stand-In for Death. M. Echard
Stand-In for Death. B. Raymond
Stand-In for Murder. L. Grex
Stand-In for Murder. L. Gribble
Stand-In for Murder. A. C. MacLean
Stand-In for Murder. D. Reid
Stand-In for Sin. M. Brody
Stand Over. F. Blague
Stand Proud. E. Kelton
Stand Up and Die. R. Lockridge
Stand Up and Fight. David Hume
Standard-Bearers. K. Mayo
Standing Into Danger. D. Briggs
Standing Into Danger. J. Griffin
Standish Gaunt Case. I. Patterson
Standish Place. I. Holland
Stanfield Place. R. D. Perrier
Stanforth Secrets. J. Beverley
Stanhope Gate Mystery. R. Machray
Stanhope of Chester. P. Andreae
Stanton Wins. E. M. Ingram
Star Above Paris. J. G. Sarasin
Star-Anchored, Star-Angered. S. H. Elgin
Star Bridge. J. Gunn
Star-Cluster Kill. L. Maddox
Star Crossed. M. Mead
Star-Crossed Love. Elsie Lee
Star-Crossed Lover. Carter Brown
Star Detective. D. Essex
Star Driver. L. Correy
Star Dust. J. Ronald
Star Fire. I. Swann
Star-Fire Prophecy. J. J. Toombs
Star-Gazers. G. M. Fenn
Star Griffin. M. Kurland
Star House. R. Newell
Star in a Mist. A. Stringer
Star Is Falling. M. Richmond
Star King. J. Vance
Star Light, Star Bright. S. Ellin
Star of Danger. Elsie Lee
Star of Death. M. Gillen
Star of Earth. O. R. Cohen

Star of Egypt. B. Sanders
Star of Evil. L. Noel
Star of Hollywood. E. Stilgebauer
Star of Ill-Omen. D. Wheatley
Star of Midnight. A. S. Roche
Star of Persia. R. Adams
Star of Sutherland. G. Breaznell
Star of the East. C. E. Pearce
Star of the Goddess. M. Clare
Star Ruby Contract. J. Garrison
Star Shot. D. Terman
Star Spangled Crunch. R. Condon
Star Stalker. R. Bloch
Star Trap. Simon Brett
Star Trap. R. Colby
Star Wars Plot. R. Pennington
Star Well. A. Panshin
Star Witness. Rick Madison
Star Witness. J. Wood
Star Wormwood. C. Bok
Starbuck. Bryan Peters
Starcrossed Road. M. Farnsworth
Stardust. R. B. Parker
Starett. A. V. Deutsch
Starfish Affair. J. N. Chance
Starfish Syndrome. E. Van Ees
Stargate. S. Robinett
Starik. J. Rovin
Staring Eyes! T. A. Plummer
Staring Man and other stories. P. Lovesey
Stark Docket. S. Dave
Stark Inheritance. E. Kyle
Stark Island. Lynna Cooper
Stark Murder. L. Thayer
Stark Naked. L. R. Bourne
Stark Truth. P. Freeborn
Starlet for a Penny. W. A. Ballinger
Starlight Motel Incident. J. Weisman
Starling Street. D. Palmtag
Starmaker. H. Denker
Starpirate's Brain. R. Goulart
Starr Bedford Dies. R. Garnett
Starrbelow. C. Thompson
Starry-Eyed Chipmonk. S. M. Schley
Starry Eyed Murder. T. A. Plummer
Stars and Stripes. M. Dekobra
Stars and Swastikas. Steve White
Stars Are Dark. P. Cheyney
Stars Cannot Tell. A. Maybury
Stars for the Toff. J. Creasey
Stars Give Warning. Brenda Conrad
"Stars I'd Give—." A. Soutar
Stars in the Heather. O. Wynd
Stars in the Water. J. Appleby
Stars My Destination. A. Bester
Stars of Doom. J. Hunter
Stars of Evil. D. E. Stitt
Stars Scream Murder. A. B. Reeve
Stars Spell Death. J. Stagge
Starshine Connection. B. Sanders
Starsky and Hutch. M. Franklin
Starstruck. E. Tidyman
Start Screaming Murder. T. Powell
Startex Assignment. R. Pope
Starting Gun. G. Bagby
Startling and Thrilling Narrative of the Dark and Terrible Deeds of Henry Madison, and His Associate and Accomplice, Miss Ella Stevens, Who Was Executed by the Vigilance Committee of San Francisco, on the 20th of September Last. S. Drury
Startling Crimes and Notorious Criminals. D. Donovan
Startling Discovery. Old Sleuth
Starvation Camp. B. Pronzini
Starvecrow Farm. S. J. Weyman
Starved. A. Thompson
Starvel Hollow Tragedy. F. W. Crofts
Stash Spots a Murder. R. Peters
State Department Cat. M. Plum
State Department Murders. E. Ronns
State of Corruption. P. Geddes
State of Emergency. B. Jackson
State of Emergency. J. Robb

State of Emergency. Sheila Ross
State of Emergency. J. Sherlock
State of Fear. M. Napier
State of Fear. D. Reid
State of Grace. R. Tine
State of Seige. E. Ambler
State Puppet. Dorothy Bennett
State Scarlet. D. Aaron
State Secret. H. Dube
State Secret, and other stories. B. M. Croker
State Secrets. W. B. Home-Gall
State Torch. J. G. Sarasin
State Trooper. N. B. Gerson
State vs. Elinor Norton. M. R. Rinehart
State vs. Elna Jepson. N. B. Mavity
State Visit. C. Egleton
Stateline. J. Van Der Zee
Stately Home Murder. C. Aird
Stately Homicide. S. T. Haymon
Stately Homicide. G. Milner
Stateroom Opposite. A. H. Veysey
State's Evidence. S. Greenleaf
Statesman's Game. J. Aldridge
Static. J. R. Lane
Station Gehenna. A. Weinder
Station in the Delta. J. Cassidy
Station Master's Secret. A. Murray
Station-to-Station Stories. W. St. Iven
Station Wagon in Spain. F. P. Keyes
Station Wagon Murder. M. Propper
Station X. G. M. Winsor
Statue. E. Phillpotts
Statue and the Lady. S. M. Wick
Status 1SQ. R. Herst
Statute of Limitations. J. Buckley
Statutory Murder. Dicey Thomas
Stay Dead, Sweetheart. R. Drayton
Stay of Execution. H. Desmond
Stay of Execution. M. Gilbert
Stay of Execution. L. Halliday
Stay of Execution. E. C. Williams
Stay Out of Menchis. B. Sarto
Stay Until Tomorrow. A. Maybury
Staying Alive. Robin Morris
Steadfast Heart. M. Richmond
Steady, Boys, Steady. J. Mitchell
Steal Away. Ramona King
Steal Big. P. Mann
Steal Big. L. White
Steal the Sun. A. E. Maxwell
Stealing Lillian. T. Kenrick
Stealing Time. N. Edwards
Stealth. G. Durham
Stealth Strike. Frank O'Brien
Stealthy Death. M. Richmond
Stealthy Steve, the Six-Eyed Sleuth. N. Newkirk
Stealthy Terror. J. Ferguson
Steam-Driven Boy. J. Sladek
Steam Pig. J. McClure
Steamboatmen. C. J. C. Hyne
Stedman Gang. Roland Daniel
Steel Balloon. H. McLeave
Steel Callaghan. M. Chesney
Steel Casket and other stories. Nicholas Carter
Steel Crown. F. Hume
Steel Eye. C. Gottfried
Steel Face. Gwyn Evans
Steel Garrotte. J. Ingersol
Steel Hit. R. Stark
Steel Killer. R. Charles
Steel Mask. M. Carrel
Steel Mirror. D. Hamilton
Steel Necklace. F. Du Boisgobey
Steel Noose. A. Drake
Steel Palace. H. Pentecost
Steel Safe. H. L. Williams
Steel Shutters. Gavin Holt
Steel Spring. P. Wahloo
Steel Tiger. S. Silliphant
Steel Trap. A. Sugar
Steele. J. D. Masters
Steele Bey's Revenge. T. Lund
Steele of the Royal Mounted. J. O. Curwood
Steeley Flies Again. W. E. Johns

Title Index

Steeltown. J. Grady
Steeltown Strangler. H. S. Keeler
Steelyard Blues. Timothy Harris
Steep Steps. K. Ingram
Steinway Collection. R. J. Randisi
Stella Buys a Shroud. M. Storme
Stella Nash. Ganpat
Stella Shall Die. H. Desmond
Stench of Poppies. I. Drummond
Stendal Raid. A. Dempsey
Step Aside to Death. S. Maddock
Step by Step. C. Collins
Step in the Dark. F. Cowen
Step in the Dark. K. Eyre
Step in the Dark. E. Lemarchand
Step in the Dark. Ethel L. White
Step in the House. R. Ramsay
Step in the Right Direction. S. Frith
Step Into Fire. C. Dekker
Step Into Murder. S. Curtis
Step Into Quicksand. L. Treat
Step Into Terror. Marilyn Ross
Step Lightly, Lady. Margery Lawrence
Step on the Stair. A. K. Green
Step Softly on My Grave. M. A. Hubbard
Step Softly, Sinner. M. Brody
Step Softly, Sweetheart. Rod Callahan
Step Up, Sucker. Gene Ross
Stepfather. C. Jay
Stepford Wives. I. Levin
Stephen Vale. P. Trent
Stepmother's House. C. Bramwell
Stepping Blindfold. T. W. Speight
Steps Going Down. Joseph Hansen
Steps Going Down. J. T. MacIntyre
Steps in Mystery. T. R. Morden
Steps in the Dark. M. Black
Steps in the Dark. M. Cumberland
Steps to Murder. R. King
Steps to Murder. R. P. Koehler
Steps to Nowhere. C. Leonard
Steps to the Grotto. C. Knye
Steps to the High Garden. C. Duckworth
Stepsons of France. P. C. Wren
Stepwives. Phillis Stevens
Stereopticon. S. R. Lucas
Sterling Standard. G. Brandner
Stern Chase. G. Hackforth-Jones
Stern Chase. Mrs. C. Hoey
Sterne of the Secret Service. J. A. Jordan
Stettin Secret. J. S. Thayer
Steve. G. Goodchild
Steve Bentley's Calypso Caper. R. Dietrich
Steve Brown's Bunyip, and other stories. J. A. Barry
Stevedore Mystery. B. North
Steward. E. Wallace
Stewardess Strangler. R. Gallagher
Stick. E. Leonard
Stick at Nothing. A. Wood
Stick 'Em Up! F. Ryerson
Stick or Bust. R. Drayton
Stick-Up, Pin-Up. D. Haring
Sticking Place. Jessica Mann
Sticking Point. K. Jackson
Stickman. B. Fantoni
Sticks and Stones. M. L. Dodge
Stiff As a Broad. G. G. Fickling
Stiff Silk. S. Milne
Stiff Upper Lip. P. Israel
Stiffs Can't Squeal. Griff
Stiffs Don't Vote. G. Homes
Stiffsons, and other stories. H. Jenkins
Stigma. B. Clendenen
Stigma. Williams Forrest
Stigma for Valor. Williams Forrest
Stiletto. B. Betcherman
Stiletto. H. Robbins
Stiletto. B. Rossi
Stiletto. Greg Walker
Stiletto Signature. J. Messmann
Still Among the Living. Z. Klein
Still and Woven Blue. R. Stookey
Still As the Grave. M. L. Roby
Still Dead. R. A. Knox

Still Life. M. Borgenicht
Still Life with Pistol. R. Ormerod
Still Missing. B. Gutcheon
Still More Adventures by a Villager. Anonymous
Still More Two-Minute Mysteries. D. J. Sobol
Still Murder. F. Moorhead
Still No Answer. L. Thayer
Still of Night. L. Powell
Still the World Is Young. K. Hewitt
Still They Smile. P. Conway
Still Water. K. N. Burt
Still Waters. Dorothy Fletcher
Still Waters. E. C. R. Lorac
Still Waters. F. F. Van De Water
Still Waters Run Deadly. I. Lambot
Still Waters Run Deep. T. Taylor
Stilled Life. M. Dunham
Stillness at Sea. A. Aasheim
Stillwatch. M. H. Clark
Stillwater Tragedy. T. B. Aldrich
Stillwell Murder. M. T. Dawson
Sting. W. LeQueux
Sting. David Rogers
Sting. R. Weverka
Sting in the Tail. B. Clemens
Sting of Death. Jessica Mann
Sting of Death. P. D. Westbrook
Sting of the Adder. Nicholas Carter
Sting of the Bee. J. Worrell
Sting of the Honeybee. F. Parrish
Sting of the Scorpion. G. V. Basile
Sting of the Wasp. Katharine Mortimer
Stingaree. E. W. Hornung
Stingaree Murders. W. S. Pleasants
Stinger. N. Gottlieb
Stinger. D. Hornig
Stinger. R. R. McCammon
Stink of Murder. W. Spann
Stinson's Reef. C. J. C. Hyne
Stir. G. Ingram
Stir Crazy. B. Shannon
Stir of Echoes. R. Matheson
Stir Train. G. Ingram
Stirring Adventures. F. A. M. Webster
Stirrup Cup. J. A. Tyson
Stitch in Snow. A. McCaffrey
Stitch in Time. E. Lathen
Stitch in Time. A. Pearson
Stoat. L. Brock
Stockade. W. C. Tuttle
Stockbroker's Wife, and other sensational tales. B. Hemyng
Stockholders in Death. K. Robeson
Stockholm Syndicate. C. Forbes
Stoenberg Affair. R. A. Goodwin
Stoke Silver Case. L. Brock
Stolen Bacillus, and other incidents. H. G. Wells
Stolen Blessings. Lawrence Sanders
Stolen Boat-Train. D. G. Browne
Stolen Brain. Nicholas Carter
Stolen Bride. J. Beverley
Stolen Bride. E. Klein
Stolen Bride of Glengarra Castle. A. Knoll
Stolen Budget. J. S. Fletcher
Stolen Car. E. J. Rath
Stolen Cellini. Alan Thomas
Stolen Christmas Box. L. de la Torre
Stolen Cipher. Sea Lion
Stolen Crown. J. W. Bobin
Stolen Death. L. Grex
Stolen Fiddle. W. H. Mayson
Stolen Flower. P. Carlo
Stolen Formula Mystery. M. E. Cooke
Stolen Girl. P. W. Batten
Stolen Gold. J. Chancellor
Stolen Goods. C. B. Kelland
Stolen Heiress. C. Merrick
Stolen Home Secretary. L. Gribble
Stolen Honeymoon. M. Leighton
Stolen Husband. R. D. Andrews
Stolen Idea. E. Godfrey
Stolen Identity. Nicholas Carter
Stolen Idols. E. P. Oppenheim
Stolen Jew. J. Neugeboren

Stolen Jewels. Old Spicer
Stolen Jockey. Bat Masters
Stolen Judge. Anonymous
Stolen Laces. J. W. Postgate
Stolen Laces. D. Simmons
Stolen Lady. A. Askew
Stolen Letter. C. Morris
Stolen Liberty Bonds. N. Ridley
Stolen Life. M. M. Bodkin
Stolen Like Magic Away. P. Audemars
Stolen Man. Mrs. C. Kernahan
Stolen March. D. Yates
Stolen Mask. W. Collins
Stolen Millionaire. S. Truss
Stolen Moments. Sherryl Woods
Stolen Name. Nicholas Carter
Stolen Necklace. Roland Daniel
Stolen Nugget of Gold. N. Ridley
Stolen or Strayed. D. Collins
Stolen Partnership Papers. J. W. Bobin
Stolen Pay Train. Nicholas Carter
Stolen Pay Train and other stories. Nicholas Carter
Stolen Pearl. G. Warden
Stolen Peer. G. Boothby
Stolen Plans. R. Gar
Stolen Race Horse. Nicholas Carter
Stolen Racer. N. Gould
Stolen Scar. Gret Lane
Stolen Signet. F. M. Smith
Stolen Singer. M. Bellinger
Stolen Souls. W. LeQueux
Stolen Spring. H. Scherfig
Stolen Squadron. C. L. Leonard
Stolen Stamps. J. B. Chittenden
Stolen Statesman. L. Gribble
Stolen Statesman. W. LeQueux
Stolen Story and other newspaper stories. J. L. Williams
Stolen Strychnine. B. Cobb
Stolen Submarine. R. Bacon
Stolen Submarine. George Griffith
Stolen Submarine. S. Hope
Stolen Submarine. Maxwell Scott
Stolen Sweets. W. LeQueux
Stolen Test-Tube. W. Jardine
Stolen Time. J. Fast
Stolen Virtue. C. Kingston
Stolen White Elephant. M. Twain
Stolen Will. W. S. Hayward
Stolen Will. M. Pinkerton
Stolen Woman. Wade Miller
Stomping Ground. Denis Hamill
Stone. Anthea Frazer
Stone. N. Tranter
Stone Angel. M. H. Albert
Stone Around Her Neck. B. McKnight
Stone Baby. B. Healey
Stone Blunts Scissors. G. Fairlie
Stone Bull. P. A. Whitney
Stone Carnation. N. A. Hintze
Stone City. Mitchell Smith
Stone Cold. J. Francome
Stone Cold Blonde. Adam Knight
Stone Cold Dead. R. Ellington
Stone Cold Dead. H. Garner
Stone Cold Dead in the Market. C. Landon
Stone-Cold-Dead in the Market Affair. P. Leslie
Stone-Cold-Dead in the Market Affair. J. Oram
Stone Dead. C. Ashton
Stone Dead. P. Laing
Stone Dead. San Antonio
Stone Dead. F. A. Symonds
Stone Dormitory. J. Turner
Stone Dragon and Other Tragic Romances. R. M. Gilchrist
Stone 588. G. A. Browne
Stone for His Head. B. Cobb
Stone Hawk. G. Moffat
Stone House. D. Daniels
Stone Junction. J. Dodge
Stone Killer. J. Gardner
Stone Killer. J. Midgley
Stone Killer. F. Scarpetta
Stone Lady. A. Ransome

Stone Leopard. C. Forbes
Stone Maiden. V. Johnston
Stone Maiden. A. Manners
Stone Man. K. Robeson
Stone Murders. M. Joensuu
Stone of Blood. J. Coulson
Stone of the Heart. J. Brady
Stone of Vengeance. V. Thorpe
Stone Offering. Stephen Chance
Stone Roses. S. Gainham
Stone Shadow. Rex Miller
Stone Veil. R. Tierney
Stone Virgin. B. Unsworth
Stone Walls. C. Heath
Stoned Cold Soldier. C. Dennis
Stonefish. Charles West
Stonehaven. E. St. Clair
Stoner McTavish. S. Dreher
Stones of Enchantment. W. Martyn
Stones of Khor. D. Whitelaw
Stones of Satan. R. Wallace
Stones of Stavros. B. Gavin
Stones of Strendleigh. G. Killoran
Stonewall Steevens Investigates. M. G. Kiddy
Stoneware Monkey. R. A. Freeman
Stony Man Doctrine. D. Pendleton
Stool Pigeon. Roland Daniel
Stool Pigeon. L. Malley
Stool Pigeon Pie. N. Rosso
Stop at Nothing. D. Rutherford
Stop at Nothing. I. Welcome
Stop-at-Nothing Man. Roland Daniel
Stop at the Red Light. A. A. Fair
Stop on the Green Light! M. Barrington
Stop-Over Danger. V. Warren
Stop Press. M. Innes
Stop, Press! E. Spencer
Stop Press—Homicide! R. Dolphin
Stop Press in Scarlet. M. Brody
Stop Press: Murder. M. T. Garba
Stop Press Murder. A. McKee-Wright
Stop Press Murder. G. Ramsey
Stop Press—Murder! P. Stirling
Stop Press Standover. M. Brody
Stop That Dame. H. Vogel
Stop That Man. C. Franklin
Stop That Man! R. Ladline
Stop Thief! G. C. Jenks
Stop Thief! Carlyle Moore
Stop This Man! P. Rabe
Stopgap. T. A. Schock
Stopover for Murder. F. Mahannah
Stopover for Murder. T. H. Stone
Stopover: Tokyo. J. P. Marquand
Stopped Clock. J. T. Rogers
Store of Wrath. S. Truss
Store up the Anger. W. Ebersohn
Storefront Lawyers. A. L. Conroy
Stories and Interludes. B. Spain
Stories and Reminiscences. Anonymous
Stories and Sketches. J. Payn
Stories Cops Only Tell Each Other. G. Radano
Stories for the Smoking Room. Anonymous
Stories from Scotland Yard. M. Moser
Stories from the Diary of a Doctor. L. T. Meade
Stories from the Note-Book of a Detective. D. Donovan
Stories Grave and Gray. Fred Davies
Stories in Black and White. G. R. Sims
Stories in Grey. B. Pain
Stories in Light and Shadow. B. Harte
Stories in the Dark. B. Pain
Stories of a World Renown Detective. Anonymous
Stories of Crime and Murder. C. K. Razdan
Stories of Darkness and Dread. J. P. Brennan
Stories of Donald Soubridge. D. Shoubridge
Stories of East and West. H. D. Stacpoole
Stories of Fear. J. McLaren
Stories of Mystery and Horror. E. C. Gaskell
Stories of Old New Spain. T. A. Janvier
Stories of Ray Bradbury. R. Bradbury
Stories of Scotland Yard. Vivien Grey
Stories of Strange Happenings. D. Wyllarde
Stories of Strange Women. J. Y. F. Cooke

Stories of the Broadmoor Patient, and the Poor Clerk. F. Wicks
Stories of the Railroad. J. A. Hill
Stories of the Railway. V. L. Whitechurch
Stories of the Rhine. Erckmann-Chatrian
Stories of the Seen and the Unseen. M. Oliphant
Stories of the South Seas. J. McLaren
Stories of the Strange and Sinister. F. Baker
Stories of Three Burglars. F. R. Stockton
Stories of Today and Yesterday. P. C. De Crespigny
Stories of West Country Folk. A. E. Horne
Stories Weird and Wonderful. J. E. Muddock
Stories Weird and Wonderful. H. Nisbet
Stories Without Tears. B. Pain
Storm. H. L. V. Fletcher
Storm. Gavin Holt
Storm. I. Slater
Storm Against the Wall. L. Meynell
Storm and the Silence. David Walker
Storm at Daybreak. B. J. Hoff
Storm Beaten. R. Buchanan
Storm-Bound. J. G. Sarasin
Storm Breaks. A. Gask
Storm Canvas. E. L. Long
Storm Castle. Jan Anderson
Storm Center. B. E. Stevenson
Storm Centre. Douglas Clark
Storm Centre. B. Musto
Storm Cloud Over Vienna. O. L. Rosmanith
Storm Clouds Over Paradise. C. G. Page
Storm Driven. A. Applin
Storm Evil. J. Robb
Storm Fear. C. Seeley
Storm Front. P. Finch
Storm Gang. Richard Grant
Storm Girl. J. C. Lincoln
Storm House. F. Hurd
Storm in a Sanctuary. K. Ingram
Storm in an Inkpot. C. Franklin
Storm in April. I. A. R. Wylie
Storm in Harbour. G. Hackforth-Jones
Storm in the Family. J. Blackmore
Storm in the Mountains. N. Buckingham
Storm in the Sand. T. B. Morris
Storm Is Rising. G. Dyer
Storm Island. K. Follett
Storm Islands. A. Quinton
Storm Knight. F. E. Smith
Storm Lady. J. H. Vahey
Storm Maiden. K. Lindsay
Storm Music. D. Yates
Storm of Deception. A. Andre
Storm of Spears. A. C. Marin
Storm of Wrath. A. Dwyer-Joyce
Storm Over Bitterhill. P. Warren
Storm Over Fox Hill. G. Addison
Storm Over Hollywood. J. Reach
Storm Over Ibiza. R. Roleine
Storm Over Minitrea. J. T. Osborne
Storm Over Paris. S. Noel
Storm Over Rockall. W. H. Baker
Storm Over Roseheath. K. Troy
Storm Over Windmere. C. Alcott
Storm Signals. R. H. Savage
Storm South. P. McCutchan
Storm Squad. P. Leslie
Storm Tarn. P. Troubetzkoy
Storm Tide. A. MacVicar
Storm Tossed. M. S. Jones
Storm-Tossed. Vince Kelly
Storm Track. R. Terpening
Storm Warning. J. Higgins
Storm Wind Rising. J. Rouverol
Storm Witch. E. Barr
Storm-Wrack. H. Hill
Stormberg Jewel Case. K. M. Sheahan
Stormcliff. M. T. Walworth
Stormhaven. Jennifer Hale
Storming Intrepid. Payne Harrison
Stormlight. J. N. Chance
Storms and Son. A. Caputi
Storm's End. Rebecca James
Stormswift. M. Brent
Stormtide. B. Knox

Stormy Night. C. Hale
Stormy Paradise. K. Lindsay
Storrington Papers. D. Eden
Story Behind the Verdict. F. Danby
Story Hunter. E. R. Suffling
Story of a Dark Crime. Hawkshaw
Story of a Dead Woman. J. Kirkpatrick
Story of a Great Sin. M. Leighton
Story of a Killer. D. Spade
Story of a Sculptor. H. Conway
Story of a Sin. H. B. Mathers
Story of a Trust. A. G. Mears
Story of Annie D. S. T. Chehak
Story of Antony Grace. G. M. Fenn
Story of Barbara. M. E. Braddon
Story of Black Bess As Told by her Owner. N. Gould
Story of Charles Strange. H. Wood
Story of Clovelly's Wife. W. J. Newton
Story of Dorothy Grape, and other tales. H. Wood
Story of Dorothy Stanfield. O. Micheaux
Story of Duciehurst. C. E. Craddock
Story of Francis Cludde. S. J. Weyman
Story of Henri Tod. W. F. Buckley, Jr.
Story of Ivy. M. B. Lowndes
Story of Joan Courage. R. Rodd
Story of Leland Gay. A. R. Weekes
Story of Mary Dunne. M. E. Francis
Story of Morella de Alto. I. Crookenden
Story of Professor X. J. Budd
Story of Rachel. R. Abbey
Story of the Beautiful Girl Who Was Hated by Her Father. Anonymous
Story of the Bells. Anonymous
Story of the Fast Mail. C. Thornton
Story of the Foss River Ranch. R. Cullum
Story of the Phantom. L. Falk
Story of the Stage. C. R. Gull
Story of the Stone. B. Hughart
Story of Two Pictures. C. Braeme
Story Teller. G. Buhet
Story-Teller. P. Highsmith
Story-Teller's Pack. F. R. Stockton
Story That Could Not Be Told. M. Albrand
Story to Tell. P. Fleming
Story with a Vengeance. A. B. Reach
Story Without a Moral. H. Malot
Story Without a Name. A. Stringer
Stout Cortez. G. Goodchild
Stowaway. R. Johnston
Stowaway. A. Mills
Stowaway. G. Simenon
Stowaway. L. Tracy
Stowaway Girl. L. Tracy
Stowaway of the S. S. Wanderer. A. Parsons
Stowaway's Quest. E. S. Brooks
Stowmarket Mystery. L. Tracy
Strad and other stories. C. Igglesden
Straight. D. Francis
Straight. S. Knickmeyer
Straight Ahead for Danger. W. M. Duncan
Straight and Crooked. M. McShane
Straight Clue. Old Sleuth
Straight Crooks. H. Fielding
Straight Cut. M. S. Bell
Straight Down the Crooked Lane. B. Runkle
Straight Furrow. Constance Rutherford
Straight Man. K. Nelson
Straight Man. R. L. Simon
Straight No Chaser. J. Batten
Straight-Out Detective. Old Sleuth
Straight Road. G. Radcliffe
Straight Shooting. W. C. Tuttle
Straight Through the Door. W. Hodge
Straight Time. E. Bunker
Straight to the Mark. Old Sleuth
Straight-Up Girl. D. Glinto
Strained Relations. A. Cairns
Stranded. E. R. Beach
Stranded. W. Norwood
Stranded in Arcady. F. Lynde
Strands of Red . . . Hair! Glint Green
Strands of War. J. A. Kemeny

Strange Adventure of Anelay Moreland. R. S. Gresson
Strange Adventures of a Magistrate. T. R. Threlfall
Strange Adventures of Bromley Barnes. G. Barton
Strange Adventures of Handel Archimedes. C. W. Sykes
Strange Adventures of James Shervinton. L. Becke
Strange Adventures of Miss Brown. R. Buchanan
Strange Adventures of Mr. Colin. F. Heller
Strange Adventures of Mr. Middleton. W. A. Curtis
Strange Adventures of Richard Conway Bowen. C. R. Benstead
Strange Affair. B. Toms
Strange Affair at Greylands. Mark Cross
Strange Affair of the Shot Gun Sniper. W. Tyrer
Strange Affair of the Widow's Diamonds. H. Clevely
Strange Affection. G. Des Cars
Strange Alibi. L. T. White
Strange and Private War. A. Lejeune
Strange Bargain. H. Whittington
Strange Bedfellow. E. Berckman
Strange Bedfellows. H. Burkholz
Strange Blue Yawl. L. Fletcher
Strange Boarders. G. Batson
Strange Boarders of Palace Crescent. E. P. Oppenheim
Strange Capers. A. Meeker
Strange Caravan. Margery Lawrence
Strange Career of Bishop Sterling. S. Endicott
Strange Career of Thomas Gander and His Friend and Tutor Doctor Quack. C. H. Ross
Strange Cargo. M. Richmond
Strange Case. Anonymous
Strange Case for Dr. Rolland. J. Judson
Strange Case of a Missing Man. C. Cregan
Strange Case of Cavendish. R. Parrish
Strange Case of Deacon Brodie. F. Bramble
Strange Case of Dr. Bruno. F. E. Daniel
Strange Case of Dr. Earle. F. W. Crofts
Strange Case of Dr. Jekyll and Mr. Hyde. R. L. Stevenson
Strange Case of Edgar Heriot. F. Grierson
Strange Case of Eleanor Cuyler. K. Crosby
Strange Case of Gunner Rawley. W. F. Morris
Strange Case of Habberton's Mile. W. J. Bayfield
Strange Case of Harriet Hall. M. Dalton
Strange Case of Henry Toplass and Capt. Shiers. J. W. Postgate
Strange Case of John R. Graham. V. Kutchin
Strange Case of Lucile Clery. J. Shearing
Strange Case of Mary Page. F. Lewis
Strange Case of Mr. Henry Marchmont. J. S. Fletcher
Strange Case of Mr. Jocelyn Thew. E. P. Oppenheim
Strange Case of Mr. Pelham. A. Armstrong
Strange Case of Mortimer Fenley. L. Tracy
Strange Case of Pamela Wilson. Mark Cross
Strange Case of Peter the Lett. G. Simenon
Strange Case of Sir Merton Quest. A. Soutar
Strange Case of the Antlered Man. E. S. Brooks
Strange Case of the End of the World As We Know It. J. Cleese
Strange Case of the Footman's Crime. G. Chester
Strange Case of the Megatherium Thefts. E. C. Roberts
Strange Case of Vincent Hume. D. Miall
Strange Case of Vintrix Polbarton. I. Marshall
Strange Case of William Cook. R. Keverne
Strange Cases of Dr. Stanchon. J. D. Bacon
Strange Cases of Magistrate Pao. L. Comber
Strange Cases of Mason Brant. N. M. Hopkins
Strange Citadel. R. Spain
Strange Clients. S. De Havilland
Strange Clues. J. M'Govan
Strange Coast. L. Pawle
Strange Code of Justice. R. K. Isley
Strange Coincidence. J. B. Phillips
Strange Conflict. D. Wheatley
Strange Corner. Mildred Davis
Strange Corpse on Murder MIle. D. Boyle
Strange Countess. E. Wallace
Strange Crime in Bermuda. E. S. Holding
Strange Crimes. W. Westall

Strange Daughter. L. De Wohl
Strange Death of a Doctor. L. Landon
Strange Death of Manny Square. A. B. Cunningham
Strange Deception. R. Coward
Strange Delilah. B. B.
Strange Destiny. S. Bray
Strange Destiny. C. Dawe
Strange Destiny. H. Janson
Strange Dilemma of Gordon Holmes. W. J. Carroll
Strange Disappearance. A. K. Green
Strange Disappearance of Eugene Comstocks. M. R. Hatch
Strange Disappearance of John Haversham. I. D. Hardy
Strange Disappearance of Lady Delia. L. Tracy
Strange Disappearance of Mary Young. M. Propper
Strange Doctor and other mystic stories. V. Van Der Elst
Strange Doings on Halfaday Creek. J. B. Hendryx
Strange Enchantment. B. L. Farjeon
Strange Enchantment. P. Webling
Strange Ending. E. R. Punshon
Strange Experiences of Mr. Verschoyle. T. W. Speight
Strange Experiment. Valentine
Strange Face of Murder. W. A. Ballinger
Strange Fate. R. S. L. Harding
Strange Fellowship of Maxwell Gale. W. Bouchier
Strange Felony. E. Linington
Strange Fish. K. Robeson
Strange Flaw. H. S. Wilcox
Strange Fortune. J. Salt
Strange Fruit. Lilian Smith
Strange Fugitive. M. Callaghan
Strange Happening. N. MacKenzie
Strange Harmony. A. Carr
Strange Heritage. M. A. Clune
Strange Heritage. L. Harper
Strange Heritage. T. Uphill
Strange Holiday. E. Gill
Strange Honeymoon. O. R. Cohen
Strange Identity. S. Turnbull
Strange Infatuation. L. Harrison
Strange Inheritance. B. Biderman
Strange Inheritance. G. Simenon
Strange Inheritance. P. Trent
Strange Instrument. N. Rennie
Strange Journeys. B. Hemyng
Strange Land. H. Innes
Strange Landing. L. Meynell
Strange Legacy. A. Barron
Strange Legacy. L. Bergstrom
Strange Legacy. E. M. Williams
Strange Legacy of Aunt Bettina. L. Crail
Strange Little Snakes. J. Turner
Strange Loop. A. Prantera
Strange Lovers. J. Trinian
Strange Luck Gully. J. Crothers
Strange Mansion. T. Rook
Strange Manuscript Found in a Copper Cylinder. J. De Mille
Strange Message. Dora Russell
Strange Money. Mark Ross
Strange Motives. R. Goyne
Strange Murder of Hatton, K. C. H. Adams
Strange Murders at Greystones. E. N. Wright
Strange Nocturne. Andrea Hill
Strange Notions and The Dark Ocean. J. Vance
Strange Occupation. J. A. Park
Strange Occurrences. Leopold Davis
Strange Pages from Family Papers. T. F. T. Dyer
Strange Papers of Dr. Blayre. C. Blayre
Strange Paradise. D. Daniels
Strange Partner. D. Lee
Strange Partners. G. Wintle
Strange Phantasy of Doctor Trintzius. A. Vitu
Strange Place for Murder. C. Barroll
Strange Prisoner. M. Hone
Strange Pursuit. N. R. De Mexico
Strange Pursuit. P. Wynnton
Strange Quartet. K. Rhodes
Strange Relations. Jerome Barry
Strange Rendezvous. H. D. Dearden
Strange Report. John Burke

Strange Return. A. B. Cunningham
Strange Ritual. H. Janson
Strange Romance. B. Herbert
Strange Salvation. K. Hewitt
Strange Sanctuary. E. Butler
Strange Schemes of Randolph Mason. M. D. Post
Strange Secrets. V. Coffman
Strange Sin. C. Kernahan
Strange Sisters. F. Flora
Strange Smell of Murder. L. Dundas
Strange Stories. G. Allen
Strange Stories. V. Sorensen
Strange Stories from a Chinese Studio. H. A. Giles
Strange Stories of a Detective. Anonymous
Strange Stories of Strange People. O. Dale
Strange Story. E. Bulwer-Lytton
Strange Story. Hilda Lewis
Strange Story in the Falconer Papers. U. L. Silberrad
Strange Story of Hester Wynne. G. Colmore
Strange Story of Linda Lee. D. Wheatley
Strange Sylvester Affair. L. Thayer
Strange Tales. E. C. Grenville-Murray
Strange Tales. M. Sproxton
Strange Tales from "Vanity Fair." Silly Billy
Strange Tales of a Nihilist. W. LeQueux
Strange Tangle. Alice King
Strange Visitor. H. Elsna
Strange Voyage. H. MacQueen
Strange Way Home. R. Easterling
Strange Welcome. F. A. Chittenden
Strange Will. H. S. Keeler
Strange Witness. D. Keene
Strange Witness. B. Symons
Strange Wooing. C. Gibbon
Strange Wooing. R. Marsh
Strange Wooing of Mary Bowler. R. Marsh
Strange World. M. E. Braddon
Strange Young Man. L. Gerard
Strangely She Died. N. Morland
Stranger. L. Barbee
Stranger. C. Dumas
Stranger. B. Forbes
Stranger. A. Veiller
Stranger and Afraid. E. Ferrars
Stranger and Afraid. M. Hardt
Stranger at Christmas. A. MacVicar
Stranger at Home. G. Sanders
Stranger at Midnight. Coriola
Stranger at My Door. M. Kistler
Stranger at Pembroke. A. Eliot
Stranger at Plantation Inn. P. Maxwell
Stranger at the Door. M. Blake
Stranger at the Gate. M. Bosse
Stranger at the Gate. J. Edgar
Stranger at the Gates. Evelyn Anthony
Stranger at the Wedding. F. Lynch
Stranger at Wildings. M. Brent
Stranger Beware. Rick Madison
Stranger by Night. M. Lynn
Stranger by the Lake. Beatrice Parker
Stranger Called the Blues. S. Coulter
Stranger Came Back. C. Franklin
Stranger Came to Dinner. A. Soutar
Stranger Case of Dr. Hide and Mr. Crushall. R. B. Stavingson
Stranger City Caper. R. H. Spencer
Stranger in a Dark Land. J. Wellsley
Stranger in Galah. Michael Barrett
Stranger in Her House. H. Arvonen
Stranger in His Grave. Dorothy Bennett
Stranger in My Arms. E. Raskin
Stranger in My Grave. M. Millar
Stranger in My Midst. V. Ross
Stranger in the Dark. H. Nielsen
Stranger in the House. A. Caballero
Stranger in the House. P. J. MacDonald
Stranger in the House. S. Mayfield
Stranger in the Kingdom. H. F. Mosher
Stranger in the Land. M. Pereira
Stranger in the Land. W. Thomas
Stranger in the Night. P. S. McCoy
Stranger in These Parts. E. F. Boyd
Stranger in Town. R. Bloomfield
Stranger in Town. B. Halliday

Stranger in Town. J. Reach
Stranger in Town. J. D. White
Stranger in Vienna. H. La Barre
Stranger Is Watching. M. H. Clark
Stranger on the Cliff. Josephine Bell
Stranger on the Highway. H. R. Hays
Stranger Than Fiction. C. Dawe
Stranger Than Fiction. H. Desmond
Stranger Than Fiction. M. L. Gamble
Stranger Than Fiction. C. George
Stranger Than Fiction. Albert Ross
Stranger Than Fiction. P. Smith
Stranger Than Truth. V. Caspary
Stranger Than Truth. H. Swaffer
Stranger Threatens. L. Dartey
Stranger to Herself. B. Williams
Stranger to Himself. J. Colton
Stranger to Myself. S. Shubin
Stranger to Town. L. P. Davies
Stranger, Tread Light. Jean Muir
Stranger with My Face. P. McGerr
Stranger Within the Gates. C. N. Boyle
Strangers. D. R. Koontz
Strangers Among the Dead. G. Bellairs
Strangers and Afraid. T. Sterling
Strangers and Pilgrims. M. E. Braddon
Strangers at Collins House. Marilyn Ross
Strangers from the Sea. A. MacVicar
Stranger's Gate. E. P. Oppenheim
Strangers in Company. J. A. Hodge
Strangers in Flight. M. G. Eberhart
Strangers in 7-A. F. Farrington
Strangers in the House. G. Simenon
Strangers in the Night. Genevieve St. John
Strangers in the Sun. M. Sheppard
Strangers Meeting. Winston Graham
Stranger's Meeting. R. Savage
Strangers of the Glen. H. M. Jones
Strangers on a Train. P. Highsmith
Strangers on Friday. H. Whittington
Strangers on the Moor. S. Thorpe
Strangest Grand National. F. Johnston
Strangest Journey of My Life and other stories. F. Pigot
Strangle Hold! Al Conroy
Strangle Hold. M. McMullen
Strangled Prose. Joan Hess
Strangled Witness. L. Ford
Stranglehold. H. Arvay
Stranglehold. H. Carmichael
Stranglehold. D. Cory
Stranglehold. J. Creighton
Stranglehold. A. Hocking
Stranglehold. G. C. Knapp
Stranglehold. D. T. Lindsay
Stranglehold. C. Posard
Stranglehold. B. Reynolds
Strangler. D. Black
Strangler. H. Desmond
Strangler. P. Hall
Strangler. L. Marshall
Strangler. T. A. Plummer
Strangler. E. C. Reed
Strangler. San Antonio
Strangler. Hampton Stone
Strangler. M. Thynne
Strangler. T. J. Williams
Strangler Fig. J. S. Strange
Strangler Who Couldn't Let Go. Hampton Stone
Strangler's Holiday. K. Steel
Strangler's Moon. C. Leader
Stranglers of Bombay. Stuart James
Strangler's Serenade. W. Irish
Strangling Man. Alan Hunter
Stranleigh's Millions. Robert Barr
Strasbourg Connection. D. Hayward
Strasbourg Legacy. W. Craig
Strasburg Collection. E. L. McGinnis
Strategem. H. Griswood
Strategic Compromise. W. Nixon
Strategies of Zeus. Gary Hart
Stratford Affair. P. Hastings
Strathgallant. Laura Black
Straus. A. Bodelsen

Strausser Transfer. Don Smith
Straw Donkey Case. A. S. Fleischman
Straw Man. D. M. Disney
Straw Virgin. A. Barker
Strawberry Blonde Jungle. Carter Brown
Strawberry Marten. P. G. Winslow
Straws in the Wind. C. Dawe
Straws in the Wind. P. C. De Crespigny
Straws in the Wind. W. C. Tuttle
Strawstack. D. C. Disney
Strawstack Murders. D. C. Disney
Stray Bullet. D. Franklin
Stray Cat. D. Matheson
Stray Shot. Gerald Hammond
Streak of Light. R. Lockridge
Streaked-Blond Slave. Carter Brown
Streaked Peril. Nicholas Carter
Streaked with Crimson. C. J. Dutton
Streaker Murders. P. Dorian
Stream Sinister. K. M. Knight
Streamlined Dragon. L. C. Goldsmith
Streamlined Murder. P. MacTyre
Street. D. Lindquist
Street Cops. W. Klasne
Street Dance. Bill Kelly
Street 8. D. Fairbairn
Street Fights. J. Martori
Street Games. Eddie Stone
Street Hawk. Jack Roberts
Street Killer. T. Philbin
Street of a Thousand Delights. J. Gelzer
Street of Dark Desires. M. Reed
Street of Desire. W. Standish
Street of Dreams. Lynn Leslie
Street of Fear. J. Fast
Street of Fortune. M. L. Tyrrell
Street of Grass. P. Audemars
Street of Hanger's End. Ladbroke Black
Street of No Return. D. Goodis
Street of Painted Lips. M. Dekobra
Street of Shadows. A. Ridgway
Street of Strange Faces. L. J. Vance
Street of the Crying Woman. G. Homes
Street of the Five Moons. Elizabeth Peters
Street of the Leopard. N. Morland
Street of the Lost. D. Goodis
Street of the Serpent. P. Beeding
Street of the Singing Fountain. Rona Randall
Street of the Small Steps. R. Willock
Street Paved with Water. Robin Temple
Street Paved with Water. A. Wood
Street Players. D. Goines
Street Singer. J. T. MacIntyre
Street That Died. W. Reyburn
Street Trick. N. Cain
Streetbird. J. Van De Wetering
Streetcar to Hell. J. Dekker
Streets of Blood. P. Rawls
Streets of Death. Dell Shannon
Streets of Fire. T. H. Cook
Streets of Shadow. L. McFarlane
Strega. A. Vachss
Strelsau Dimension. J. Haythorne
Strelson Castle Mystery. H. Pink
Strength of Straw. Esme Stuart
Strength of the Weak. Dick Stewart
Stretelli Case and other mystery stories. E. Wallace
Strethcairn. C. A. Collins
Stretton Case. H. Howard
Stretton Darknesse Mystery. M. Dalton
Stretton Street Affair. W. LeQueux
Stricken. M. J. Bosse
Strictly a Loser. E. Sherry
Strictly Amateur. T. McCormack
Strictly Business. O. Henry
Strictly Confidential. E. Crawshay-Williams
Strictly Corruptible. M. Brody
Strictly for Cash. J. H. Chase
Strictly for Felony. Carter Brown
Strictly Illegal. M. Clinten
Strictly Legitimate. M. Cronin
Strictly Poison. D. Norris
Strictly Private. Therese Benson
Strictly Private Business. M. Cronin

Strictly Wild. H. Brand
Stride. J. Pattinson
Striding Folly. D. L. Sayers
Strike Deep. A. North
Strike Fighters. T. Willard
Strike for a Kingdom. M. Gallie
Strike for Death. J. Creasey
Strike for Freedom. Nicholas Carter
Strike for Millions. E. T. Sawyer
Strike Force. D. Stivers
Strike Force 7. I. MacAlister
Strike Force Ten. H. G. Konsalik
Strike Force Terror. Nick Carter
Strike North. W. H. Baker
Strike Out Where Not Applicable. N. Freeling
Strike Terror. H. Steirman
Strike Three You're Dead. R. D. Rosen
Strike Zone. Richard Curtis
Strike Zone. Charles Robertson
Strikeback! R. Crane
Strikefast. R. Charles
Striker One Down. J. N. Pruitt
Striker Portfolio. Adam Hall
Strikers, Communists, Tramps and Detectives. A. Pinkerton
Strikezone. D. F. Nighbert
Striking Force. Douglas Christie
Striking Hours. E. Phillpotts
Striking Shadow. Hedley Scott
String Glove Mystery. H. R. Campbell
String of Chinese Peach Stones. W. A. Cornaby
String of Pearls. T. P. Prest
Strip Death Naked. N. Longmate
Strip for Murder. R. S. Prather
Strip for Murder. E. Thomas
Strip for Violence. E. Lacy
Strip Jack Naked. W. Garner
Strip Search. Rex Burns
Strip Tease. J. Bruce
Strip Tease Angel. D. Linton
Strip-Tease Macabre. L. Gribble
Strip Tease Murders. N. W. Firth
Strip-Tease Murders. G. R. Lee
Strip the Town Naked. Whit Harrison
Strip Without Tease. Carter Brown
Stripe for a Stripe. J. Sandys
Striped Majesty. Reginald Campbell
Striped Suitcase. C. Carnac
Stripped for Murder. R. Blake
Stripped for Murder. B. Fischer
Stripped to Kill. R. Drayton
Stripped to Kill. D. Haring
Stripper. Carter Brown
Stripper Strikes Out. K. T. McCall
Stripper, You're Stuck. Carter Brown
Stripper, You've Sinned. Carter Brown
Striptease. G. Simenon
Striptease for Murder. P. Denver
Striptease for Murder. B. Laster
Striving with Gods. J. Bannister
Strode Venturer. H. Innes
Stroke Counterstroke. W. Camp
Stroke of a Knife. Burnham F. Mason
Stroke of Death. Josephine Bell
Stroke of Light. J. L. Hardy
Stroke of Nine. E. O. Jones
Stroke of One. R. A. J. Walling
Stroke of Policy. Nicholas Carter
Stroke of Seven. R. Wade
Stroke of Twelve. W. M. Berger
Stroke Sinister and other stories. S. Horler
Strolling Players. A. Dwyer-Joyce
Stromboli and the Guns and other tales. F. Gribble
Strong Arm. Robert Barr
Strong-Arm. B. Copper
Strong Arm Stuff. D. Spade
Strong As Death. F. Adams
Strong Dose of Poison. H. Desmond
Strong Man. H. R. F. Keating
Strong Man's Way. C. H. Bullivant
Strong Men and True. Morley Roberts
Strong Poison. D. L. Sayers
Strong Right Arm. P. Trent
Strong Room. R. A. J. Walling

Strong Room of the Sutro. E. L. Long
Strongarm. D. J. Marlowe
Strongbox. H. Swiggett
Stronger Hand. J. Goodwin
Stronghold. S. Ellin
Stronghold. Steve Mackenzie
Strontium Code. Nick Carter
Stroud Case. E. C. Williams
Struck Dead. Anonymous
Struck Down. J. G. Rowe
Struck Down. H. Smart
Struck Dumb. P. Conway
Struggle. Gavin Douglas
Struggle to Win. Old Sleuth
Struggle with Destiny. Nicholas Carter
Strumpet's Fool. F. Griffin
Strychnine for One. T. A. Plummer
Strychnine Tonic, and A Dose of Cyanide. G. D. H. Cole
Stryker. William Crawford
Stryker. C. Scarborough
Stryker's Children. J. A. Schneider
Stuart Legacy. R. Kerr
Stubble. Winifred Duke
Stubb's Run. P. L. Sandberg
Stud Game. D. Anthony
Stud Service. J. D. Revere
Studd. A. Cullen
Studdingly Stables Mystery. B. Strong
Student Body. J. S. Borthwick
Student Body. N. Fitzgerald
Student Body. M. R. Hodgkin
Student Body. J. R. Hulland
Student Fraternity Murder. M. Propper
Studies in Black and Red. J. Forster
Studies in Brown Humanity. H. Clifford
Studies in Love and Terror. M. B. Lowndes
Studies in Wives. Mrs. B. Lowndes
Studio Crime. G. Chester
Studio Crime. I. Jerrold
Studio Love. P. Swift
Studio Model. B. Delannoy
Studio Murder Mystery. Edingtons
Studio Mystery. R. C. Armour
Studio Mystery. F. Aubrey
Studio One Murder. W. A. Ballinger
Studio Revels. N. W. Firth
Studs. Stuart Hall
Study in Lilac. M.-A. Oliver
Study in Scarlet. A. C. Doyle
Study in Sorcery. M. Kurland
Study in Suspense. A. Soutar
Study in Terror. E. Queen
Study of Death. F. Leslie
Stuff the Lady's Hatbox. C. E. Morse
Stuff to Give the Troops. J. MacLaren-Ross
Stuffed Man. J. B. O'Sullivan
Stuffed Men. A. M. Rud
Stuffed Swan. J. Appleby
Stumble on the Threshold. J. Payn
Stumble Upon the Dark Mountains. L. Woodrum
Stumbling. D. E. Smalley
Stunt Man. P. Brodeur
Sturdy Beggar, and Lady Bramber's Ghost. C. Charrington
Sturgeon's West. T. Sturgeon
Sturgis Wager. E. Morette
Sturmer. I. F. Romer
Stuttering Death. L. Como
Stuyvesant Square. M. Lewerth
Stylist. G. Cullingford
Styx. C. Hyde
Styx Complex. Russell Rhodes
Sub. Taffrail
Sub Killers. San Antonio
Sub Rosa. C. T. Murray
Sub-Zero! R. W. Walker
Subaltern, the Policeman, and the Little Girl. B. Fforde
Subject—Murder. C. Witting
Subject of Harry Egypt. D. Broun
Subjugated Beast. R. R. Ryan
Submarine. J. Wingate
Submarine at Bay. A. Mars

Submarine Flotilla. G. Hackforth-Jones
Submarine Girl. Edgar Turner
Submarine Mystery. K. Robeson
Submarine Signalled . . . Murder! A. R. Bosworth
Submarine Trail. Nicholas Carter
Submarine U-137. E. Topol
Submariner. E. Stephens
Subscription to Murder. M. V. Heberden
Substitute Bride. Lynna Cooper
Substitute Millionaire. H. Footner
Substitute Prisoner. M. Marcin
Substitute Victim. H. Pentecost
Subterranean Club. L. Geoghegan
Subterranean Passage. Sarah Wilkinson
Subtle Adversary. C. Scofield
Subtle Minotaur. A. Alderson
Subtle Trail. J. Gollomb
Suburban Saraband. R. Harrison
Suburban Vendetta. J. K. Leys
Suburbs of Hell. R. Stow
Subway in the Sky. B. Birch
Subway Murder. M. S. Buchanan
Subway Mystery. B. Bolt
Subway Stalker. L. Cameron
Subways Are for Killing. W. B. Murphy
Successful Alibi. M. E. Cooke
Successful "Shadow". Old Sleuth
Such a Gorgeous Kid Like Me. H. Farrell
Such a Nice Client. Josephine Bell
Such a Nice Family. June Drummond
Such an Enmity. R. Pertwee
Such Bitter Business. Elbur Ford
Such Bright Disguises. B. Flynn
Such Friends Are Dangerous. W. Tyrer
Such Good Neighbors. M. Bingley
Such Is Death. L. Bruce
Such Men Are Dangerous. B. Diamond
Such Men Are Dangerous. P. Kavanagh
Such Men Are Dangerous. Martin Thomas
Such Natural Deaths. L. Anson
Such Nice People. S. Scoppettone
Such Nice People. Mary Scott
Such Power Is Dangerous. D. Wheatley
Such Pretty Toys. S. F. X. Dean
Such Stuff As Screams Are Made Of. R. Bloch
Such Things Happen. J. Massey
Such Women Are Dangerous. J. Webb
Sucker Bait. J. Bogar
Sucker Bait. R. O. Saber
Sucker for a Red-Head. M. Storme
Sucker for Dames. J. Grecco
Sucker Money. R. H. Rohde
Sucker Punch. Duff Johnson
Sucker Punch. Raymond Marshall
Sucker Trap. M. Kane
Sudan Slaughter. D. Pendleton
Sudden Darkness. E. McCrae
Sudden Death! A. Bocca
Sudden Death. P. Brennan
Sudden Death. F. W. Crofts
Sudden Death. D. Delman
Sudden Death. J. Gibbins
Sudden Death. W. X. Kienzle
Sudden Death. D. Pendleton
Sudden Death. B. C. Skottowe
Sudden Death. L. Thayer
Sudden Death at Scotland Yard. G. Begbie
Sudden Death Finish. T. Halleran
Sudden Death of the M.F.H. E. Weldon
Sudden Departures. Jonathan Ross
Sudden Fear. E. Sherry
Sudden Ice. J. Leeke
Sudden Impact. J. C. Stinson
Sudden Lady. M. G. Lowe
Sudden Madness. N. Garbo
Sudden Madness. R. Hayes
Sudden Silence. C. Fitzsimmons
Sudden Squall. J. C. Nolan
Sudden Storm. V. Siller
Sudden Vengeance. E. Crispin
Suddenly a Corpse. H. Q. Masur
Suddenly a Shroud. M. Kerrigan
Suddenly a Widow. G. H. Coxe
Suddenly at His Residence. C. Brand

Suddenly at Home. F. Durbridge
Suddenly, at Singapore. G. Black
Suddenly at the Priory. J. Williams
Suddenly by Shotgun. N. Daniels
Suddenly by Violence. Carter Brown
Suddenly He Knew. W. Vinn
Suddenly in Her Sorbet. J. Christmas
Suddenly in Paris. A. Roudybush
Suddenly, in the Air. Karen Campbell
Suddenly, in Vienna. H. McCutcheon
Suddenly It's Murder. J. T. Story
Suddenly It's Sin. H. Janson
Suddenly One Night. K. Roos
Suddenly While Gardening. E. Lemarchand
Suddenly You're Dead. W. Wright
Sue for Mercy. V. Heley
Sue Me. W. B. Murphy
Sue Slate, Private Eye. L. Lynch
Suez Patrol. J. R. Holden
Suez Side Ace. J. R. Holden
Suffer a Sea Change. C. De Blasis
Suffer a Witch. N. Fitzgerald
Suffer a Witch. R. Foley
Suffer a Witch to Die. E. Davis
Suffer Little Children. Sheila Johnson
Suffer Little Children. Domini Taylor
Suffer! Little Children. P. Van Greenaway
Suffer the Children. J. Saul
Sufficient Rope. C. F. Gregg
Sugar. G. Brewer
Sugar and Spice. R. Crompton
Sugar and Spice. D. Haring
Sugar and Vice. H. Janson
Sugar Cuts the Corners. L. Marshall
Sugar Daddy's Diamonds. D. Jervis
Sugar for the Inspector. M. Kay
Sugar for the Lady. L. Marshall
Sugar Man's Dead. J. Franklin
Sugar on the Carpet. L. Marshall
Sugar on the Cuff. L. Marshall
Sugar on the Kill. L. Marshall
Sugar on the Loose. L. Marshall
Sugar on the Prowl. L. Marshall
Sugar on the Target. L. Marshall
Sugar Puss. B. Vane
Sugar Shannon. Adam Knight
Sugar, You're a Scoop! M. Brody
Sugar, You're Swell. J. Farrell
Sugarplum Staircase. R. English
Sugartown. L. D. Estleman
Suicide Academy. Daniel Stern
Suicide Alibi. J. Rowland
Suicide and Murder. E. Jones-Evans
Suicide and other one-act comedies. C. Seiler
Suicide Can Be Murder. Roland Daniel
Suicide Circle. W. J. Elliott
Suicide Clause. H. Carmichael
Suicide Club. R. Brome
Suicide Club. R. L. Stevenson
Suicide Excepted. C. Hare
Suicide Fleet. H. Desmond
Suicide Hill. J. Ellroy
Suicide House. E. Snell
Suicide in B-Flat. S. Shepard
Suicide in San Juan. S. Jason
Suicide, Inc. R. Goulart
Suicide King. Shelley Singer
Suicide Most Foul. J. Sturrock
Suicide Murders. H. Engel
Suicide Passage. A. A. Randall
Suicide Plague. E. Nahe
Suicide Season. Rex Burns
Suicide Seat. Nick Carter
Suicide Sheet. R. Dudgeon
Suicide Spies. M. Annesley
Suicide Squad. J. Cain
Suicide Squad. Richard Curtis
Suicide Squad. R. Goyne
Suicide's Grave. Anonymous
Suitable Case for Corruption. N. Lewis
Suitable Day for Dying. M. Hinxman
Suitable for Framing. M. Holbrook
Suitable for Framing. J. A. Phillips
Suitable for Framing. A. Thurlo

Suitcase Full of Money. W. C. Thompson
Suitcase in Berlin. D. Flynn
Suitor. G. Dyal
Suitor. G. E. Hatvary
Sullen Sky Mystery. H. C. Bailey
Sullivan. H. C. Rae
Sullivan's Revenge. J. Cutter
Sullivan's Sting. Lawrence Sanders
Sultan of Smut. D. Haring
Sultana. H. C. Rowland
Sultan's Daughter. D. Wheatley
Sultan's Pearls. Nicholas Carter
Sultan's Skull. W. K. Smith
Sultry Avenger. H. Janson
Sulu Sea Murders. V. W. Mason
Sumatra Seven Zero. O. Wynd
Summary Justice. S. Michaels
Summer Adventure. Alan Thomas
Summer Assassin. Jennie Melville
Summer at Raven's Roost. E. Grandower
Summer Book. M. Pemberton
Summer Camp Mystery. N. Blake
Summer Concerto. G. Ferrand
Summer Fires. B. Reiss
Summer for Witches. M. Lynch
Summer Girl. C. Crane
Summer Holiday. G. Simenon
Summer House. D. Daniels
Summer in Rome. P. H. Bonner
Summer Lightning. G. F. Hummel
Summer Moon. G. Goodchild
Summer of Deceit. L. Robin
Summer of Evil. H. Arvonen
Summer of Fear. S. Marvin
Summer of Katya. Trevanian
Summer of Sighs. P. Gallagher
Summer of Sin. Stuart Hall
Summer of the Dragon. Elizabeth Peters
Summer of the Fire Ship. N. Faulkner
Summer of the Red Wolf. M. L. West
Summer Scandal. E. Kyle
Summer School Mystery. Josephine Bell
Summer Shock. Thorne Lee
Summer Showers. H. Arthur
Summer Soldier. N. Guild
Summer Solstice. M. T. Hinkemeyer
Summer Stranger. G. Wagner
Summer Street. H. Ellson
Summer Sunday. D. Eden
Summer Velvet. F. Y. McHugh
Summerhaven. L. Masterton
Summerhouse. P. Wentworth
Summer's Cloud. J. Tattersall
Summer's Day. I. Jerrold
Summer's Lease. C. Larner
Summer's Lease. Johm Mortimer
Summerstorm. A. Cleaver
Summertime Soldiers. Susan Kelly
Summit. R. Bowker
Summit. S. Marlowe
Summit Chase. R. Sapir
Summit House Mystery. L. Dougall
Summit Kill. Clark Howard
Summitt. W. P. McGivern
Summon the Bright Water. G. Household
Summoned to Darkness. A. Sheridan
Summoning. J. Pintoro
Summons. A. E. W. Mason
Summons from Baghdad. A. MacKinnon
Summons to Adventure. A. Pelham
Sumurai Contract. M. McCray
Sumuru. S. Rohmer
Sun Blight. R. Holles
Sun Chemist. L. Davidson
Sun Dance Murders. P. McCurtin
Sun Dog Loot. W. C. Tuttle
Sun Dogs. R. O. Butler
Sun God. R. C. Armour
Sun in the Hunter's Eyes. M. Derby
Sun Is a Witness. A. M. Stein
Sun Is Bleeding. G. Bartram
Sun Place. Ray Connolly
Sun Virgin. R. Charles
Sunbeam. Mrs. T. Godfrey

Sunburned Corpse. Adam Knight
Sunburst. D. Cory
Sunburst. F. Keast
Sunday. G. Simenon
Sunday Alibi. R. Lilly
Sunday Best. B. Rubens
Sunday Evening. M. Lynn
Sunday Fix. J. Nazel
Sunday Hangman. J. McClure
Sunday Pigeon Murders. C. Rice
Sunday the Rabbi Stayed Home. H. Kemelman
Sunday Woman. C. Fruttero
Sunday's Child. E. O. Phillips
Sunflower. M. Sharp
Sunflower Plot. John Sherwood
Sundial. S. Jackson
Sundial. F. M. White
Sundial Clue. B. Bolt
Sundial Drug Mystery. J. Ronald
Sundiver. D. Brin
Sundown Gun. D. Owen
Sundry Fell Designs. O. Mills
Sunk Island. J. B. Harris-Burland
Sunk Without Trace. D. Devine
Sunk Without Trace. S. M. Parkman
Sunken Rocks. A. Pantulf
Sunken Sailor. P. Moyes
Sunlight and Gloom. G. Fleming
Sunlit Ambush. M. Derby
Sunningdale Mystery. A. Christie
Sunny. L. Madl
Sunny. B. Vane
Sunny Draper. C. Phillips
Sunny Stories, and some shady ones. J. Payn
Sunrise. P. Way
Sunset at Sheba. J. Harris
Sunset Bomber. D. Kincaid
Sunset Boulevard. W. Standish
Sunset Express. F. Marlowe
Sunset Gang. W. Adler
Sunset Gun. G. Bartram
Sunset Hour. M. Summerton
Sunset Law. J. B. Hilton
Sunset Over Soho. G. Mitchell
Sunset Patriots. C. D. Taylor
Sunset People. H. Kastle
Sunset Strip. J. Reach
Sunshine and Snow. H. Smart
Sunshine Corpse. Max Murray
Sunshine Enemies. K. C. Constantine
Sunspot. D. Lowden
Sunstrike. M. Beres
Sunstrike. P. McCutchan
Sunstroke. A. Hansl
Sup with the Devil. S. Troy
Super. J. Cornwell
Super-Barbarians. C. Dawe
Super-Celeste. P. Way
Super-Cinema Murder. L. A. Knight
Super Fly. P. Fenty
Super-Gangster. F. G. Eberhard
Super Man Chu. S. M. Sullivan
Super Spy. Carter Brown
Super Spy. W. Holt-White
Superdoll. L. August
Superdude. John Craig
Supergun Mission. L. Derrick
Superintendent Slade Investigates. L. Gribble
Superintendent Wakley's Mistake. G. D. H. Cole
Superintendent Wilson's Holiday. G. D. H. Cole
Superintendent's Room. J. Ashford
Superkill. J. Tiger
Supermind. Mark Phillips
Supernatural Clew. S. Campbell
Superantural Solution. M. Parry
Supersonic. Basil Jackson
Superstar Murder. J. P. Hudson
Supplanter. P. Trent
Suppressed Evidence. V. Yorke
Suppressed Sensations. Anonymous
Suppression. W. Hallatt
Supreme Adventure of Inspector Lestrade. M. J. Trow
Surabaya. Grant Holmes
Surakarta. W. MacHarg

Sure Thing. W. B. Murphy
Sure Thing. R. S. Prather
Surf Queen. Stuart Martin
Surfeit of Alibis. P. Lauben
Surfeit of Lampreys. N. Marsh
Surfeit of Sun. Sean Graham
Surfeit of Suspects. G. Bellairs
Surfing Samurai Robots. M. Gilden
Surfside Caper. L. Trimble
Surfside 6. J. M. Flynn
Surgeon. Alan Thomas
Surgeon of Gaster Fell. A. C. Doyle
Surgeons Adrift. E. L. Long
Surgical Strike. J. Ahern
Surinam Affair. J. Rosenberger
Surly Sullen Bell. R. Kirk
Surprise for the Four. Mark Cross
Surprise of His Life. Old Sleuth
Surprise Party. W. Katz
Surprise Party Murder. E. V. Brewster
Surprise! Surprise! A. Christie
Surprise, Surprise. H. McCloy
Surprises of an Empty Hotel. A. C. Gunter
Surprising Experiences of Mr. Shuttlebury Cobb. R. A. Freeman
Surprising Husband. R. Marsh
Surprising Sanctuary. L. Cargill
Surregar's Raft. P. Kenley
Surrender and Other Happenings. M. Gaunt
Surrender Value. J. B. Hilton
Surrendered. R. Rand
Surrey Cat. A. Sinclair
Surrey Wood Mystery. J. Arnold
Surrogate. R. B. Parker
Surrounded. B. Coffey
Survival Course. W. B. Murphy
Survival Game. P. Kerrigan
Survival of the Fittest. E. Sherry
Survival Run. R. Hoskins
Survival Zero. M. Spillane
Survivor. M. Brandel
Survivor. J. Herbert
Survivor. T. Keneally
Survivor. S. Lenz
Survivor. E. P. Oppenheim
Survivor. J. Q.
Survivor. Sydney Smith
Survivor Murders. G. W. Jones
Survivor of Darkness. V. Coffman
Survivor of Darkness. D. Daniels
Survivors. Anne Edwards
Survivors. H. Innes
Survivors. G. Simenon
Survivor's Secret. J. G. Brandon
Sus. B. Keefe
Susan Turnbull. A. C. Gunter
Susan Wooed and Susan Won. E. Brooke
Susana. B. Vane
Susanna, Don't You Cry! M. Plum
Susannah, Beware. T. E. Huff
Susannah Is Missing! J. Edwards
Susannah Screaming. C. Weston
Susannah, the Righteous. K. Kimbrough
Susie and the F.B.I. R. St. Clair
Susie Comes to Soho. B. Sarto
Susie's Girls. Susanna Sheldon
Suspect. G. Fairlie
Suspect. B. M. Gill
Suspect. Martin Meyers
Suspect. H. L. Nelson
Suspect. E. Percy
Suspect. G. Simenon
Suspect. Gertrude Walker
Suspect. L. R. Wright
Suspect Scientist. L. Meynell
Suspected. G. Dilnot
Suspected. F. P. Rathbun
Suspected. L. Stratenus
Suspected Four. W. D. Roberts
Suspected Governess. Anonymous
Suspected Six. H. Scott
Suspects. W. J. Caunitz
Suspects. D. Thomson
Suspects All. Marco Page

Suspects—Nine. E. R. Punshon
Suspended Animation. Jenna Ryan
Suspense. B. Graeme
Suspense. G. Hughes
Suspense. H. Janson
Suspense. K. Lindsay
Suspense. H. S. Merriman
Suspense. I. Ostrander
Suspense. R. M. Stern
Suspense Is Killing Me. Thomas Maxwell
Suspension of Mercy. P. Highsmith
Suspicion. P. Brebner
Suspicion. M. Hervey
Suspicion. E. J. Landon
Suspicion. V. Loder
Suspicion. C. Lys
Suspicion. F. Riddell
Suspicion. Lee Roberts
Suspicion. R. Timperley
Suspicion Aroused. D. Donovan
Suspicion in Triplicate. B. Cobb
Suspicion Was Aroused. A. Brock
Suspicions. B. Betcherman
Suspicions. P. Daniels
Suspicious Characters. D. L. Sayers
Suspicious Circumstances. P. Quentin
Suspicious Company. M. Richmond
Suspicious Death. D. Simpson
Sussex Cuckoo. B. Flynn
Sussex Downs Murder. J. Bude
Sutherland's Law. L. Galloway
Sutter House. E. Orford
Sutter's Sands. M. C. Donahue
Sutton Papers. S. Jepson
Sutton Place Murders. R. G. Dean
Suva Harbour Mystery. F. Arthur
Suvarov Adventure. D. Kyle
Svengali Plot. T. Hoyle
Swag. C. F. Coe
Swag. E. Leonard
Swallow Them Up. W. Woodrow
Swallowing the Anchor. A. G. Bee
Swallow's Fall. Collin Wilcox
Swamp Fever. B. Sarto
Swamp Fire. D. Kingery
Swamp Kill. Whit Harrison
Swamp Man. D. Goines
Swamp of Cardelli. T. Craig
Swamp of Death. Hawkshaw
Swamp Rats. L. Falk
Swamp Sanctuary. B. McKnight
Swamp Sister. R. E. Alter
Swampers. H. Nisbet
Swan Dive. J. Healy
Swan Dive. K. Korman
Swan Island Murders. V. Lincoln
Swan River Story. P. Hastings
Swan Sang Once. M. Carleton
Swan Song. T. J. Binyon
Swan Song. E. Crispin
Swan Song. H. Robertson
Swan-Song Betrayed. Josephine Bell
Swan Song for a Siren. Carter Brown
Swan Song for a Thrush. G. Joseph
Swan Song for Paolo. L. O'Brien
Swann. D. Sherman
Swann. C. Shields
Swansong for a Rare Bird. A. Draper
Swap. W. Wager
Swarthmoor Tragedy. E. P. Frankland
Swarthyface. N. Lazenby
Swashbuckler, and other tales. B. Reynolds
Swastika. R. Kail
Swastika. K. Maning
Swastika Hunt. D. Cory
Swastika Rises. C. Short
Sway of Sin. Nicholas Carter
Swaying Corpse. R. Platt
Swaying Pillars. E. Ferrars
Swaying Rock. A. J. Rees
Swayneford. F. T. Woodington
Sweat of Fear. R. C. Dennis
Swedish Mysteries. A. M. MacKenzie
Sweeney. I. K. Martin

Sweeney Todd. R. Hull
Sweeney Todd. T. J. Kelly
Sweeney Todd. A. Rosser
Sweeney Todd, the Barber. B. J. Burton
Sweeney Todd, the Demon Barber. Anonymous
Sweeney Todd, the Demon Barber of Fleet Street. H. C. Wheeler
Sweeny Todd, the Demon Barber of Fleet Street. C. G. Bond
Sweeper. G. Paulsen
Sweeps. B. Granger
Sweepstake Murders. J. J. Connington
Sweepstake Winner. E. Jepson
Sweet Adelaide. J. Symons
Sweet and Bitter Fancy. B. Bonham
Sweet and Deadly. V. Chute
Sweet and Deadly. M. Corrigan
Sweet and Deadly. D. Duncan
Sweet and Deadly. C. Harris
Sweet and Deadly. P. MacDonald
Sweet and Deadly. F. Olbrich
Sweet and Low. E. Lathen
Sweet and Low. N. Perrelli
Sweet and Low-Down. J. Waer
Sweet Bait of Money. C. Fox
Sweet Blond Trap. W. C. Gault
Sweet, Blonde and Goulish. R. Lynford
Sweet But Deadly. K. T. McCall
Sweet But Sinful. K. T. McCall
Sweet Charlie. H. Kane
Sweet Cheat. H. Crooker
Sweet Cyanide. C. Noone
Sweet Danger. M. Allingham
Sweet Deadly Passion. V. Hawthorne
Sweet Deals. B. Lysaght
Sweet Death. F. Hurt
Sweet Death, Kind Death. A. Cross
Sweet Dreams. R. Sapir
Sweet Dreams, My Darling. Anna Joseph
Sweet Enemy. Robin Temple
Sweet Epitaph. M. Lynn
Sweet Eros, and Witness. T. McNally
Sweet Evil. C. Platt
Sweet Evil. J. D. White
Sweet Familiarity. D. Winston
Sweet Fury. H. Janson
Sweet Heart. Peter James
Sweet Herbs and Bitter. Morley Roberts
Sweet Hostage. N. Benchley
Sweet Inisfail. R. Dowling
Sweet Is Revenge. J. F. Molloy
Sweet Is the Rose. H. D. Irvine
Sweet Jael. S. Farrant
Sweet Jeopardy. C. Jerina
Sweet Justice. J. Oster
Sweet Justice. Colin Robertson
Sweet La La Land. Robert Campbell
Sweet Lady Death. P. Malloch
Sweet Life of Jimmy Riley. J. Reardon
Sweet Mace. G. M. Fenn
Sweet Murder. M. S. Michel
Sweet Narcissus. M. K. Lorens
Sweet Nelly. M. Callard
Sweet Night for Murder. M. Neville
Sweet Poison. Douglas Clark
Sweet Poison. M. Fitt
Sweet Poison. T. C. H. Jacobs
Sweet Poison. R. Penny
Sweet Racket. John Gloag
Sweet Reason. R. Littell
Sweet Revenge. D. Beaird
Sweet Revenge. S. Gilruth
Sweet Revenge. T. Racina
Sweet Revenge. Nora Roberts
Sweet Revenge. J. C. Shaffer
Sweet Ride. W. Murray
Sweet Ride. R. S. Prather
Sweet Rome. A. Stainton
Sweet Sammy Is Dead. D. Haring
Sweet, Savage Death. O. Papazoglou
Sweet Secrets. E. Kidd
Sweet Shame of Fury. S. D. Frances
Sweet Short Grass. P. Inchbald
Sweet Silver Blues. Glen Cook

Sweet Sinner. H. Nisbet
Sweet Sister Death. Frederick Nolan
Sweet Sister Seduced. S. B. Hough
Sweet Smelling Death. V. Gunn
Sweet Summer. Frank Ryan
Sweet, Svelte and Sinful. M. Brody
Sweet, Sweet Poison. K. Wilhelm
Sweet, Sweet Summer. J. Gaskell
Sweet Talk. H. Janson
Sweet Taste in Venom. James Dark
Sweet Water. M. Cronin
Sweet Wild Wench. W. C. Gault
Sweet William Is Dead. L. O'Brien
Sweet Women Lie. L. D. Estleman
Sweetbriar in Town, and other tales. D. C. Murray
Sweetcrab. M. Summerton
Sweeter for His Going. S. Truss
Sweetheart. A. Coburn
Sweetheart. S. Swanton
Sweetheart and Wife. Anonymous
Sweetheart Deal. R. Rosenblum
Sweetheart, Here's Your Grave! H. Janson
Sweetheart of the Razors. P. Cheyney
Sweetheart Submarine. G. Thorne
Sweetheart, Sweetheart. Bernard Taylor
Sweetheart, This Is Homicide. Carter Brown
Sweetheart with a Wreath. M. Storme
Sweetheart You Slay Me. Carter Brown
Sweetheart, You're a Sinner. M. Brody
Sweethearts and Wives. G. Hackforth-Jones
Sweethearts Vengeance. Dirk Foster
Sweetie, Hold Me Tight. H. Janson
Sweetman Curve. G. Masterman
Sweetness of Revenge. R. H. Williamson
Sweets and Sinners. A. Griffin
Sweetsir. H. Yglesias
Sweetwater Point Motel. P. Saab
Sweetwater Ranch. G. Norman
Swell Garrick. J. Spencer
Swell-Looking Babe. J. Thompson
Swell Night for Murder! G. Brandon
Swell Style of Murder. R. Santini
Swift. J. Follett
Swift Hand of Vengeance. Clifton Yorke
Swift Solution. F. J. Whaley
Swift Summer. John Burke
Swift to Die! R. Dudgeon
Swift to Its Close. S. Troy
Swifter Than a Weaver's Shuttle. J. W. Gambier
Swiftly to Evil. B. Arthur
Swimming Frog. C. Brooks
Swimming Pool. M. R. Rinehart
Swimming Pool Murder. J. Bolton
Swindle. George Adams
Swindler, and other stories. E. M. Dell
Swindler Named Zefano. C. H. Guenter
Swing Away, Climber. G. Carr
Swing, Brother, Swing. N. Marsh
Swing High, Sweet Murder. S. H. Courtier
Swing It, Death. Gavin Holt
Swing Low, Sweet Death. R. T. Campbell
Swing Low, Sweet Harriet. G. Baxt
Swing Low, Swing Dead. F. Gruber
Swing Music Murder. Harlan Reed
Swing, Swing Together. P. Lovesey
Swinger Who Swung by the Neck. Hampton Stone
Swingers. Carter Brown
Swinging Corpse. D. Linton
Swinging Couples. Stuart Hall
Swinging Death. B. Flynn
Swinging Murder. Lionel Black
Swinging Shutter. C. Fraser-Simson
Swinging Virgin. D. Rico
Swirling Mists of Cornwall. P. Werner
Swirling Waters. M. Rittenberg
Swiss Abduction. M. Denning
Swiss Account. L. Waller
Swiss Arrangement. W. Fairchild
Swiss Conspiracy. M. Stanley
Swiss Deal. H. Arvay
Swiss Legacy. A. A. Thompson
Swiss Secret. J. Messmann
Swiss Shot. Michael Bradley
Switch. W. Bayer

Switch. M. Jahn
Switch. E. Leonard
Switch. P. Ridgeway
Switch. N. Sharman
Switch #2. M. Jahn
Switch Bitch. R. Dahl
Switchback. Catherine Anderson
Switchback City. J. R. Duncan
Switchblade. P. Rawls
Switched Out. R. Lait
Switcheroo. E. McDowell
Swooning Lady. K. Robeson
Swooning Venus. A. Marsden
Sword and Dragon. R. Pocock
Sword and the Net. W. Stuart
Sword and the Scales. H. McLeave
Sword and the Baron. Anthony Morton
Sword in the Air. A. C. Gunter
Sword in the Pool. D. Marfield
Sword of Allah. C. L. Clifford
Sword of Allah. R. Elliott
Sword of Allah. M. Olden
Sword of Damocles. A. K. Green
Sword of Fate. H. Herman
Sword of Fate. D. Wheatley
Sword of Fortune. B. Bolt
Sword of Ganelon. R. Parker
Sword of Genghis Khan. James Dark
Sword of God. A. Caillou
Sword of Harlequin. J. K. Keith
Sword of Honour. D. Beaty
Sword of Justice. F. Duncan
Sword of Mithras. C. Merlin
Sword of Monsieur Blackshirt. D. Graeme
Sword of Orley. S. Farrar
Sword of Peace. A. Askew
Sword of Samos. Tom Logan
Sword of Silk. M. Carrel
Sword of the Prophet. Jim Case
Sword of the Shaheen. M. E. Morris
Sword of Vengeance. G. Chester
Sword of Vengeance. M. Olden
Sword Point. H. Coyle
Sword Swallower. R. Goulart
Sword to the Rescue. P. Curtis
Swordlight. A. Rundle
Swords of Shahrazar. R. E. Howard
Swordsman of Fortune. L. P. Greene
Swordsman of Warsaw. T. Pastor
Sworn Foes and The Skeleton on the Hearth. Anonymous
Sworn to Silence. A. M. Miller
Sybaritic Death. A. Roudybush
Sybil Brotherton. E. Southworth
Sybil Cipher. J. M. Simmel
Sybil, Trapper of Men. M. Barbour
Sydney for Sin. M. Corrigan
Sykaos Papers. E. P. Thomson
Sylvanian Adventure. F. Wheeler
Sylvester Sound, the Somnambulist. H. Cockton
Sylvia. E. V. Cunningham
Sylvia Arden. O. Crawford
Sylvia in Flowerland. L. Gardiner
Sylvia's Chauffeur. L. Tracy
Symbol of the Cat. Neill Graham
Symbol of Vengeance. D. Mariner
Symbols at Your Door. Anthea Fraser
Sympathy for the Devil. Kent Anderson
Symphony in Murder. A. R. Long
Symphony in Two Time. A. Irving
Synapse Function. M. J. Livingston
Syncopated Love. W. J. Makin
Syndic. C. M. Kornbluth
Syndicate. R. Chestnut
Syndicate. P. McCurtin
Syndicate. A. Masters
Syndicate. Denys Rhodes
Syndicate for Sin. M. Brody
Syndicate Girl. F. Kane
Syndicate Murders. W. R. Randall
Syndicate of Crooks. Anonymous
Syndicate of Death. F. Foden
Syndicate of Death. H. E. Wheeler
Syndicate of Evil. W. R. D. McLaughlin

Syndicate of Rascals. Nicholas Carter
Syndicate of Sinners. G. Warden
Syndicate That Failed. A. Goldberg
Syndicate Wife. H. Messick
Syndrome. B. Pronin
Syndrome Equation. J. Rolt
Synonym for Murder. R. Clarke
Synthetic Gentleman. Channing Pollock
Synthetic Philanthropist. J. H. Wallis
Syrian Client. J. Pattinson
System. H. Calvin
System. T. A. Thinnes
Systems. W. T. Quick
System's Hand. M. T. Jones
Systems of Mr. M. R. Shurnas. D. Nemec

T As in Trapped. L. Treat
T.E.C. Sharp, the Football Sleuth. J. M. Howard
TNT. D. Masters
TNT. P. Rey
TNT for Two. J. Byron
T. Racksole and Daughter. A. Bennett
Tabernacle. T. H. Cook
Tabitha. A. Ridley
Table. Robert (G.) Curtis
Table d'Hote. Douglas Clark
Table d'Hote. W. P. Ridge
Table for Two. G. Hind
Table Near the Band, and other stories. A. A. Milne
Table Number Seven. H. Kingsmill
Tabley Intervening. E. T. Cocking
Tabloid Murders. Clement Wood
Tabloid Tales. L. Heilgers
Taboo Spy. W. Flohr
Tachi Tree. L. O'Donnell
Tadpole of an Archangel. W. P. Drury
Taffin. L. Mallet
Taffin's First Law. L. Mallet
Tag Murders. C. J. Daly
Tag, Rag & Co. James Greenwood
Taggart: Murder in Season. P. Cave
Tagget. I. A. Greenfield
Tail Job. H. Kane
Tail of Gold. D. Hennessey
Tail of the "Dozing Cat". E. Messenger
Tail Spin Morgan. T. Wallace
Tailor's Dummy. I. Weinman
Tailspin. J. D. Hunter
Tailspin Sammy. A. W. Clark
Tailsting. H. Janson
Tailwind to Danger. C. H. Wallace
Taint. P. Wallace
Taint of Innocence. M. Childs
Taint of Plague. Bradshaw Jones
Tainted Gold. P. Trent
Tainted Gold. H. N. Williams
Tainted Jade. R. Blaine
Tainted Man. J. Wainwright
Tainted Money. A. Manning
Tainted Power. C. J. Daly
Tainted Token. K. M. Knight
Tainted Turf. D. Learmonth
Taiwan. C. Wood
Take. E. Izzi
Take. Bill James
Take a Body. M. Halliday
Take a Chair, Assassin! D. Haring
Take a Dark Journey. M. Erskine
Take a Murder, Darling. R. S. Prather
Take a Pair of Private Eyes. J. T. McIntosh
Take a Powder. Dick Hudson
Take a Step to Murder. D. Keene
Take All You Can Get. S. Fisher
Take Any City. G. Joseph
Take-Away Girl. G. Tracey
Take Away the Lady. J. Chinn
Take Away the Lady. Gavin Holt
Take Care. N. Bond
Take Death for a Lover. W. H. Baker
Take Death for a Lover. A. Berry
Take Heed of Loving Me. H. Elsna
Take It and Like It. S. Morelli
Take It Crooked. F. Beeding
Take It Easy. M. Perrelli

Take It Easy. D. Runyon
Take It Easy—But Take It! Poyntz Tyler
Take It on the Lam. R. Drayton
Take It or Leave It. J. Dark
Take Me! D. Haring
Take Me Alive. B. Tutton
Take Me—Any Time. D. Haring
Take Me As I Am. W. H. Fielding
Take Me Home. F. Flora
Take Me to My Friend. H. D. Jordan
Take Murder . . . J. Wainwright
Take My Drum to England. H. D. Jordan
Take My Face. P. Held
Take My Life. Winston Graham
Take No Prisoners. J. Crosby
Take-Off. W. Ash
Take-Off to Murder. M. K. Ozaki
Take One Ambassador. A. Broinowski
Take One for Murder. M. E. Chaber
Take Only As Directed. J. Byrom
Take-Over. V. B. Miller
Take Over, Angel. B. Sarto
Take-Over Man. J. Wainwright
Take the D Train. Frank King
Take the Money and Die. W. Williams
Take the Money and Run. L. Payne
Take the War to Washington. P. Van Greenaway
Take Thee a Sharp Knife. R. T. Campbell
Take This Gun. R. Wilkes-Hunter
Take This Life. S. Bunce
Take This My Heart. K. Lindsay
Take This—Sweetie. H. Janson
Take Two at Bedtime. M. Allingham
Take Two Blondes. H. Janson
Take Two Popes. H. Calvin
Take Up the Bodies. K. T. Knoblock
Take What You Want. G. Nimse
Take What's Coming. B. Sarto
Take Your Choice. D. Wyllarde
Take Your Last Look. Matt Brady
Taken. D. Brennan
Taken at the Flood. G. Bonner
Taken at the Flood. M. E. Braddon
Taken at the Flood. A. Christie
Taken at the Flood. B. Newman
Taken by Assault. Morley Roberts
Taken by Force. S. Hutson
Taken by Force. K. Stellier
Taken for Dollars. Spike Gordon
Taken in Vein. J. Heys
Takeoff. C. M. Kornbluth
Takeover. Bart Davis
Takeover. G. C. Edmondson
Takeover. J. Evans
Takeover. D. Thurlow
Takeover. R. Wormser
Takeover Bid. S. Gainham
Takers. J. Ahern
Takers. M. Ehrlich
Takers. H. J. Taub
Taking Care of Mrs. Carroll. P. Monette
Taking Gary Feldman. S. Cohen
Taking Liberty. L. Dunning
Taking Life Easy. Kevin O'Hara
Taking of Agnes. Jennifer Potter
Taking of Pelham One Two Three. J. Godey
Taking of Satcon Station. B. Cohen
Taking the Fifth. J. A. Jance
Taking the Veil. J. Friel
Talatala. G. Simenon
Talbot Odyssey. N. De Mille
Talbot's Folly. W. B. Guinee
Talbott Agreement. R. M. Garvin
Talboys. D. L. Sayers
Tale for Midnight. F. Prokosch
Tale of a Physician. A. J. Davis
Tale of Copperella. C. Redmond
Tale of Fleur. E. C. Vivian
Tale of Mystery. Anonymous
Tale of Pimlico. Gavin Douglas
Tale of Sin, and other tales. H. Wood
Tale of Tangled Ladies. J. N. Chance
Tale of the Lazy Dog. Alan Williams
Tale of the Town. George Hastings

Title Index

Tale of Twenty-Five Hours. B. Matthews
Tale of Two Clocks. J. H. Schmitz
Tale of Two Murders. H. C. Asterley
Tale of Two Murders. E. Ferrars
Tale of Two Thieves. G. Beardmore
Tale of Two Tunnels. W. C. Russell
Tale Untold. E. Morrison
Talent for Destruction. S. Radley
Talent for Dying. J. A. Potter
Talent for Murder. J. L. Benton
Talent for Murder. J. Wainwright
Talent for Murder. A. M. Wells
Talent for Revenge. J. Cutter
Talent for the Invisible. R. Goulart
Talent for Violence. W. Manson
Talented Angel. C. Dekker
Talented Mr. Ripley. P. Highsmith
Tales. E. A. Poe
Tales and Sketches. F. Plant
Tales and Stories. M. W. Shelley
Tales Before Midnight. S. V. Benet
Tales by a Female Detective. A. Forrester
Tales by Three Brothers. Phil Robinson
Tales for a Stormy Night. D. S. Davis
Tales for a Winter's Night. A. C. Doyle
Tales for the Marines. R. Blatchford
Tales from a Far Riding. O. Onions
Tales from a Gilded Palace. Old Sleuth
Tales from a Rolltop Desk. C. Morley
Tales from Five Chimneys. M. Pickthall
Tales from Tahiti. S. W. Powell
Tales from the Old Reading Room. Arthur Arnold
Tales from the Terrace. W. B. Guinee
Tales from the Veldt. E. Glanville
Tales from Two Pockets. K. Capek
Tales in a Jugular Vein. R. Bloch
Tales in Eccentric Life. W. A. Hammond
Tales in Prose and Verse. T. E. Heath
Tales in Prose and Verse. D. C. Murray
Tales of a Cruel Country. G. Cumberland
Tales of a "Dug-Out". Anonymous
Tales of a Government Official. A. Griffiths
Tales of a Pilgrim. Anonymous
Tales of a Tar. Anonymous
Tales of a Tin Mine. S. Hocking
Tales of Adventure. R. H. Savage
Tales of Adventurers. G. Household
Tales of an Antiquary. Anonymous
Tales of an Ulster Detective. T. M. Albert
Tales of Australian Life. N. W. Swan
Tales of Balukek. A. Bellairs
Tales of Bandits, Robbers and Smugglers. Anonymous
Tales of Bengal. S. B. Banerjea
Tales of Changing Seas. Morley Roberts
Tales of Chinatown. S. Rohmer
Tales of East and West. S. Rohmer
Tales of Fantasy and Fact. B. Matthews
Tales of Hate. Winifred Duke
Tales of Heroism and Records of Strange and Wonderful Adventures. Anonymous
Tales of Intrigue and Revenge. S. McKenna
Tales of Known Space. L. Niven
Tales of Land and Sea. W. H. Hodgson
Tales of Life and Death. G. F. Berkeley
Tales of Love and Death. R. Aickman
Tales of Love and Hate. C. H. Crichton
Tales of Love and Hate. Adrian Conan Doyle
Tales of Love and Mystery. J. Hogg
Tales of Mean Streets. Arthur Morrison
Tales of Mynheer Amayat. H. D. Stacpoole
Tales of Mystery. F. Starr
Tales of Mystery and Crime. W. Wallace
Tales of Mystery and Horror. M. Level
Tales of Mystery and Horror. C. D. Pamely
Tales of Mystery and Revenge. N. Langley
Tales of Mystery and Romance. F. Moorhouse
Tales of Mystery and Suspense. A. Creese
Tales of Natural and Unnatural Catastrophes. P. Highsmith
Tales of Northumbria. H. Pease
Tales of Ordinary Madness. C. Bukowski
Tales of Romance and Mystery. H. Rockwood
Tales of Secret Egypt. S. Rohmer

Tales of South Africa. H. A. Brydon
Tales of Suspense. W. Collins
Tales of Temptation. M. Strickland
Tales of Terror. D. Donovan
Tales of Terror. E. Sudak
Tales of Terror and Mystery. A. C. Doyle
Tales of Terror and the Supernatural. W. Collins
Tales of the African Wild. F. W. Dodds
Tales of the Black Widowers. I. Asimov
Tales of the Cliffs. W. H. Bracewell
Tales of the Coast Guard. L. Warneford
Tales of the Coastguard and other stories. Anonymous
Tales of the Colonies. C. Rowcroft
Tales of the Divining Rod. E. W. Beaven
Tales of the Fantastic. Ahmad
Tales of the Five Towns. Arnold Bennett
Tales of the Frightened. M. Avallone
Tales of the Frontiers. Robert Harding
Tales of the Isle of Death. P. Warung
Tales of the Ivory Trade. T. A. Barns
Tales of the Long Bow. G. K. Chesterton
Tales of the Masque. J. H. Pearce
Tales of the Moor. J. Homely
Tales of the Moors. Anonymous
Tales of the Mounted. W. Brockie
Tales of the Mounted Police. W. B. Mowery
Tales of the Mysterious and Macabre. A. Blackwood
Tales of the North-West Mounted Police. H. Steele
Tales of the Old Regime. P. Warung
Tales of the Open Hazard. H. Sutcliffe
Tales of the Ozarks. W. B. Mowery
Tales of the R.I.C. Anonymous
Tales of the Rock. M. Anderson
Tales of the Scientific Crime Club. R. Cummings
Tales of the Strong Room. F. Denison
Tales of the Temple and Elsewhere. Archie Armstrong
Tales of the Tenements. E. Phillpotts
Tales of the Trains. C. Lever
Tales of the Uneasy. V. Hunt
Tales of the Unexpected. R. Dahl
Tales of the Weird and West Countree. M. St. Germain
Tales of the West Riding. P. Bentley
Tales of the Western Tropics. E. F. O. Swan
Tales of the Wild and Wonderful. Anonymous
Tales of the Wolf. Lawrence Sanders
Tales of Three Colonies. Evelyn Adams
Tales of Today. G. R. Sims
Tales of Two Continents. R. Barr
Tales Out of Court. F. T. Hill
Tales, Poems and Sketches. B. Harte
Tales—Talks and Trifles. C. W. Railton
Tales That Are Told. A. Perrin
Tales Told by Simpson. May Sinclair
Tales Told to the Magistrate. R. E. Corder
Talika, the Geisha Girl. Nicholas Carter
Talisman. C. Crowe
Talisman. J. Godey
Talisman Ring. G. Heyer
Talk of Death. Gary Evans
Talk of the Devil. F. Baker
Talk of the Town. J. Payn
Talk of the Town. C. Williams
Talk Show Murders. S. Allen
Talk to Me About England. P. Ferris
Talk with the Angels. D. Meiring
Talkative Policeman. R. Penny
Talkie Murder Mystery. W. Shute
Talking Clock. F. Gruber
Talking Clues. R. C. Finney
Talking Devil. K. Robeson
Talking Dog and other stories. R. Standish
Talking God. T. Hillerman
Talking Mysteries. T. Hillerman
Talking of Murder. L. N. Morgan
Talking Pictures Murder. G. Baxt
Talking Skull and other selected short stories grave and gay. G. H. R. Young
Talking Sparrow Murders. D. L. Teilhet
Talking to Strange Men. R. Rendell
Talking Turkey. K. A. Saddler
Tall, Balding, Thirty-Five. A. Firth

Tall Dark Alibi. C. Jerina
Tall, Dark and Dead. K. Jaediker
Tall, Dark and Deadly. H. Q. Masur
Tall Dark Man. A. Chamberlain
Tall, Dark Stranger. J. Wellsley
Tall Dead Wives. Rowland Morgan
Tall Dolores. M. Avallone
Tall Headlines. A. E. Lindop
Tall House Mystery. A. Fielding
Tall Man. Gavin Douglas
Tall Man. John Ross
Tall Man Walking. K. Wolffe
Tall Pines in Paddington. C. Edwards
Tall Timber. G. Goodchild
Tallant for Disaster. A. York
Tallant for Trouble. A. York
Tallants of Barton. J. Hatton
Talleyrand Maxim. J. S. Fletcher
Talley's Truth. Philip Ross
Tallulah Bankhead Murder Case. G. Baxt
Tallyman. B. Knox
Tallyman's Fate. L. Jackson
Talon. J. Coltrane
Talon. A. Melville-Ross
Talons of the Falcon. Rebecca York
Talons of the Hawk. J. Hines
Tamara. M. L. Dodge
Tamarind Seed. Evelyn Anthony
Tame Fox and other sketches. Finch Mason
Tame the Wild Flesh. Wilene Shaw
Tamer. N. Fokker
Tamer of Men. O. Binns
Taming a Sea-Horse. R. B. Parker
Taming of Carney Wilde. B. Spicer
Taming of Nancy. G. Goodchild
Taming of Neville Ibbetson. W. M. Graydon
Taming of Sydney Marsham. H. C. McNeile
Taming the Furies. P. A. Foxall
Tamplin's Tales of His Family. B. Pain
Tan and Sandy Silence. J. D. MacDonald
Tanagra Affair. P. Kenny
Tancred. Joseph Fox
Tancredi. L. Cameron
Tandem Rush. F. V. Huber
Tandra. Robert Mason
Tang Murders. C. Cruickshank
Tangent Factor. Lawrence Sanders
Tangent Objective. Lawrence Sanders
Tangier. W. Bayer
Tangier Assignment. C. Rougvie
Tangle. M. E. Atkins
Tangle. W. S. Masterman
Tangle. H. L. Phillips
Tangle. H. A. Wrenn
Tangle of Terror. E. J. Murray
Tangled Case. Nicholas Carter
Tangled Cord. F. Lockridge
Tangled Destinies. D. Donovan
Tangled Evidence. P. C. De Crespigny
Tangled Flags. A. C. Gunter
Tangled in Crime. Nicholas Carter
Tangled Lies. Anne Stuart
Tangled Lives. T. W. Speight
Tangled Marriage. C. Dawe
Tangled Miracle. H. Herne
Tangled Murders. R. M. Stern
Tangled Skein. Nicholas Carter
Tangled Skein. A. D. Fonblanque
Tangled Skein. G. Mewburn
Tangled Snarl. J. Rustan
Tangled Thread. Susan Leslie
Tangled Threads. Nicholas Carter
Tangled Trails. W. M. Raine
Tangled Web. M. Andrau
Tangled Web. N. Blake
Tangled Web. B. J. Hoff
Tangled Web. J. D. Levick
Tangled Web. L. G. Moberly
Tangled Web. J. Moffatt
Tangled Web. L. A. Sunagel
Tangled Web. G. Vaizey
Tangled Web. E. B. Wright
Tangles Unravelled. E. K. Johnson
Tanglewood Murder. L. Kallen

Tanglewood Mystery. C. E. Pearce
Tango. M. Atwell
Tango. Alan Judd
Tango. C. Rodda
Tango Briefing. Adam Hall
Tango Key. Alison Drake
Tango November. J. Howlett
Tania. T. Lester
Tank of Sacred Eels. I. Drummond
Tank of Serpents. J. Leasor
Tanker. R. Kruger
Tannahill Tangle. C. Wells
Tanner's Tiger. Lawrence Block
Tanner's Twelve Swingers. Lawrence Block
Tansy. N. Baroni
Tantalus. I. Cullen
Tantalus. A. Hemingway
Tantler's Sister. E. F. Turner
Tap on the Shoulder. M. Dupree
Tapestry Odyssey. P. Conway
Tapestry of Death. D. M. Bowick
Tapestry of Fear. M. Pemberton
Tapestry of Spies. Stephen Hunter
Tapestry of Terror. M. Ruuth
Tapestry Room Murder. C. Wells
Tapestry Triangle. T. P. Kelley
Tapping at the Window. L. L. McCall
Tapping on the Wall. H. Hull
Tapping the Source. K. Nunn
Taps, Colonel Roberts. H. Gibbs
Tara. M. Hutton
Tarakian. L. Peters
Tarantula Hawk. A. Mather
Tarantula Strike. Nick Carter
Target. W. W. Haines
Target. S. Hunter
Target! Steve Mackenzie
Target Amin. J. Konrad
Target Capricorn. Agnes Russell
Target: Charity Ross. J. Bickham
Target Criminal. P. N. Walker
Target Doomsday Island. Nick Carter
Target Five. C. Forbes
Target for a Gunman. M. Gorgon
Target for a Tigress. D. Haring
Target for Conquest. B. Gray
Target for Death. K. Robeson
Target for Malice. Barbara Cooper
Target for Murder. G. E. Giles
Target for Terror. M. Hershman
Target for Terror. T. C. H. Jacobs
Target for Target. S. A. Martinez
Target for Their Dark Desire. Carter Brown
Target for Tonight. R. Telfair
Target for Tragedy. J. Philips
Target in Taffeta. B. Benson
Target: Intruder. M. Tanner
Target Is H. L. Derrick
Target Manhattan. D. Mallory
Target Manhattan. D. Pitts
Target Margaret Thatcher. J. Calder
Target Mayflower. R. Hirschhorn
Target: Mike Shayne. B. Halliday
Target Norway. N. Cort
Target of Opportunity. M. Byrd
Target Plutex. P. Bryers
Target Practice. N. Meyer
Target Red Star. Nick Carter
Target Risk. J. Wingate
Target: Sahara. G. St. Germain
Target Stealth. J. Merek
Target Steele. J. D. Masters
Target: The Men They Were Once. S. Masters
Target Tobruk. R. Jackson
Target Westminster. B. M. Gull
Tarlov Cipher. Nick Carter
Tarn House. R. Brock
Tarnham Connection. W. Tute
Tarnish. A. J. Talbot
Tarnished Angel. H. Pentecost
Tarnished Dreams. M. Cherkas
Tarnished Gold. W. Mills
Tarnished Love. Gerry Travis
Tarnished Phoenix. James Melville

Tarnished Woman. V. Thompson
Tarot Cards in Thessaly. H. Latouche
Tarot Murders. M. Warner
Tarot Spell. W. D. Roberts
Tarotown. B. Jones
Tarot's Tower. Jennie Melville
Tarry and Be Hanged. Sara Woods
Tart, with a Silken Finish. P. Barthelme
Tartan and Gold. B. Webber
Tartan Murders. P. C. Williams
Tartan Rings. Jonathan Gash
Tartan Sell. Jonathan Gash
Tarzan and the Castaways. E. R. Burroughs
Tashkent Crisis. W. Craig
Task Demolition. R. Wilkes-Hunter
Task of Destruction. Michael Barrett
Taskmaster. Harold King
Tass Is Authorized to Announce. J. Semyonov
Taste for Blood. R. Hayes
Taste for Blood. J. B. West
Taste for Brilliants. N. Clad
Taste for Cognac. B. Halliday
Taste for Death. P. O'Donnell
Taste for Death. P. D. James
Taste for Honey. H. F. Heard
Taste for Murder. H. F. Heard
Taste for Murder. F. Lockridge
Taste for Treason. O. Mendels
Taste for Violence. B. Halliday
Taste of Ashes. H. Browne
Taste of Blood. D. Batchelor
Taste of Brass. R. D. Locke
Taste of Conspiracy. C. Egerton-Thomas
Taste of Death. Richard Grayson
Taste of Death. F. McGrew
Taste of Death. M. J. Rodgers
Taste of Deception. E. Gladstone
Taste of Fears. J. Millar
Taste of Fears. Sara Woods
Taste of Murder. J. Cannan
Taste of Murder. I. Lambot
Taste of Poison. R. Ullman
Taste of Power. W. J. Burley
Taste of Proof. B. Knox
Taste of Sangria. C. Keith
Taste of Sin. G. Brewer
Taste of Terror. M. Albrand
Taste of Treachery. L. Denny
Taste of Treason. A. Maling
Taste of Treason. L. Pender
Taste of Treasure. G. Ashe
Taste of Vengeance. L. R. Davis
Tasty Way to Die. J. Laurence
Tatterley. T. Gallon
Tattershall Castle. B. Gilbert
Tattoo Mystery. W. LeQueux
Tattooed Arm. I. Ostrander
Tattooed Man. T. C. H. Jacobs
Tattooed Potato and Other Clues. E. Raskin
Tattooed Triangle. J. G. Brandon
Tattooed Woman. Guy Scott
Tattooed Wrist. Old Spicer
Tau Cross Mystery. J. J. Connington
Taurus Trip. T. B. Dewey
Tavern. G. M. Cohan
Tavern and the Arrows. A. Carlyle
Tavern Wench. S. Farrant
Taverns in Terrazzo. M. J. Ragosta
Tavistocks. A. Griffin
Tawny Menace. B. Sanders
Tax Exile. G. Bellamy
Tax in Blood. B. M. Schutz
Taxed to Death. R. Simons
Taxi-Cab Murder. J. G. Brandon
Taxi Man's Quest. G. Chester
Taxi to Dubrovnik. W. Cook
Taxicab Riddle. Nicholas Carter
Te. M. Olden
Tea and Arsenic. C. Sodaro
Tea and Trickery. N. B. Chute
Tea at Four. R. H. Wilkinson
Tea at the Abbey. C. E. Vulliamy
Tea from China. F. W. Wallace
Tea on Sunday. Lettice Cooper

Tea-Shop in Limehouse. T. Burke
Tea Time Tragedy. M. Beckett
Tea Tray Murders. C. Bush
Tea with the Black Dragon. R. A. McAvoy
Teach You a Lesson. J. Hollis
Teach Yourself Treachery. Jonathan Burke
Teacher Goes Abroad. E. Randolph
Teacher's Blood. I. T. Ross
Teacher's Pet. A. Neiderman
Teacher's Pet. Domini Taylor
Teak Forest. P. Ordway
Team of Crooks. A. Steffens Hardy
Tear in the Silk. L. O'Flaherty
Tear Must Fall. R. Blanchard
Tear of Kalee. H. E. Inman
Teardown. V. Wuamett
Tearless Widow. J. Roeburt
Tears Are for Angels. P. Connolly
Tears for Jessie Hewitt. E. Sherry
Tears for the Bride. Robert Martin
Tears for Yesterday. C. Borelli
Tears in Paradise. J. Blackmore
Tears of Angels. H. Curties
Tears of Autumn. C. McCarry
Tears of Blood. M. Carrel
Tears of Flame. Samantha Harte
Tears of Hate. G. Thorne
Tears of the Moon. Gary Ross
Tears of the Tiger. C. Dickason
Tease. G. Brewer
Tease. R. H. R. Smithies
Tease the Wild Flame. M. Reed
Teaser Set to Kill. M. Brody
Teaspoon of Murder. Elizabeth Morris
Teathered Goat. J. Healy
Tech War. D. Stivers
Technicians of Death. T. Williamson
Technique for Treachery. S. Truss
Technocrats. F. W. Horton, Jr.
Teddington Tragedy. D. H. Landels
Teddy Bear. G. Simenon
Teddy Bear Did It. D. Haring
Teddy-Boy Mystery. J. Drummond
Teen-Age Cop. P. N. Walker
Teen-Age Jungle. H. Whittington
Teen-Age Mafia. Wenzell Brown
Teen-Age Mobster. B. Appel
Teen-Age Terror. Wenzell Brown
Teeth for the Brigadier. M. Hamilton
Teeth of the Dragon. M. Grant
Teeth of the Tiger. M. Leblanc
Teeth of the Wolf. A. Paris
Tefuga. P. Dickinson
Teheran Wipeout. D. Pendleton
Tejera Secrets. M. Orr
Tekwar. W. Shatner
Telefair. C. Rice
Telefon. W. Wager
Telegram from Le Touquet. J. Bude
Telegraph Clue. I. Stark
Telegraph Secrets. B. Hemyng
Telekiller. John Warwick
Telemann Touch. W. Haggard
Telephone Call. J. Rhode
Telephone Girl. A. Askew
Telephone Never Tells. M. Hinxman
Television Murders. W. A. Ballinger
Television Mystery. R. St. Clair
Television Plays. K. Parker
Tell Death to Wait. A. Boutell
Tell Her It's Murder. H. Reilly
Tell It Me Again. John Fuller
Tell It to the Birds. J. H. Chase
Tell It to the Dead. L. Vardre
Tell Me No Lies. E. Lowell
Tell Me Now, and Again. R. Llewellyn
Tell No Tales. G. Day
Tell No Tales. G. Limnelius
Tell-Tale Clock Mystery. J. Carmack
Tell-Tale Murder. P. Weathers
Tell-Tale Photographs. Nicholas Carter
Tell-Tale Tart. P. Duncan
Tell-Tale Tattoo. J. Sharp
Tell-Tale Watch. G. Hocker

Tell Them Nothing. H. Ellson
Tell Them What's-Her-Name Called. Mildred Davis
Tell You What I'll Do. H. Cecil
Teller. E. N. Westcott
Telling of Lies. T. Findley
Telling of Murder. D. Rutherford
Telling the Truth. W. Hewlett
Telltale Corpus Delicti. Bruce Sanders
Telltale Print. C. B. Booth
Telltale Telegram. H. Burnham
Telluride Smile. R. H. Ring
Telzey Toy. J. H. Schmitz
Tempania Mystery. J. M. Walsh
Temperamental Journey. P. Groom
Temperamental People. M. R. Rinehart
Tempering Steel. S. Jepson
Tempest at Dawn. A. Richmond
Tempest at Summer's End. J. Thatcher
Tempest Driven. R. Dowling
Tempest in a Tea-Cup. W. Shand
Tempest Squadron. R. Jackson
Tempest Weaves a Shroud. W. Shand
Tempestuous Petticoat. M. A. Gibbs
Tempestuous Wooer. G. T. Ockley
Temple at Ilumquh. J. Laflin
Temple Dogs. R. L. Duncan
Temple Dogs. W. B. Murphy
Temple Dogs Guard My Fate. D. Sinclair
Temple Falls. A. MacVicar
Temple, K. C. E. K. Webb
Temple Kent. D. G. Devon
Temple Murder. H. M. Richardson
Temple of Darkness. Marilyn Ross
Temple of Dawn. Colin Robertson
Temple of Death. F. Du Boisgobey
Temple of Death. E. Mitchell
Temple of Doom. Anonymous
Temple of Fear. J. Andrews
Temple of Fear. Nick Carter
Temple of Lies. J. B. Harris-Burland
Temple of Slumber. Neill Graham
Temple of the Dead. V. Norwood
Temple of the Flaming God. D. T. Lindsay
Temple of Vice. Nicholas Carter
Temple Tower. H. C. McNeile
Temple Tree. D. Beaty
Temple's Trial. E. Everett-Green
Templeton Case. V. L. Whitechurch
Templeton Memoirs. D. Daniels
Temporary A.S.P. Smith. H. L. Jones
Temporary Ghost. M. Friedman
Tempt a Tigress. Carter Brown
Tempt Me Not. A. Weymouth
Temptation. Pete Costello
Temptation in a Private Zoo. A. Dekker
Temptation of Adam. H. Gruber
Temptation of Carlton Earle. S. M. During
Temptation of Father Anthony. G. Horton
Temptation of Gideon Holt. Mrs. C. Kernahan
Temptation of Mary Gordon. S. Horler
Temptation of Selma. C. Dawe
Temptation of Tavernake. E. P. Oppenheim
Temptation Sordid. W. Phelps
Temptation Street. R. Dudgeon
Temptation to Steal. N. B. Gerson
Temptations of Hercule. P. Audemars
Temptations of Valerie. H. Whittington
Tempted of the Devil. Anonymous
Tempter. A. Bloomfield
Tempting Anne Brayton. A. Applin
Tempting Miss. Janice Bennett
Tempting of Paul Chester. A. Askew
Tempting of Tavernake. E. P. Oppenheim
Tempting Target. D. Haring
Temptress. Carter Brown
Temptress. W. LeQueux
Temptress. S. Shulman
Temptress on Trial. J. Laffin
Temptress Touch. D. Haring
Ten-a-Penny People. J. Phelan
Ten Against Nura. Michael Barrett
Ten Black Pearls. C. F. Gregg
Ten Commandments. G. R. Sims
Ten Crowded Hours. C. A. Alington

Ten Dangerous Hours. G. B. Jenkins
Ten Day Mystery. Old Sleuth
Ten Days Before the Wedding. L. Barbee
Ten Day's Leave. W. M. Graydon
Ten Days, Mr. Cain. B. Freeborn
Ten Days to Oblivion. M. Cooney
Ten Days' Wonder. E. Queen
10–8 to Heaven. Rodney Jones
Ten Faces of Cornell Woolrich. C. Woolrich
Ten Fathoms Deep. J. Templeton
Ten Grand Story. B. Carson
Ten Grand Tallulah and Temptation. Carter Brown
Ten Green Brothers. A. MacVicar
Ten Holy Horrors. F. Beeding
Ten Hours. H. S. Keeler
Ten Jewels. P. Wynnton
Ten Little Indians. A. Christie
Ten Little Niggers. A. Christie
Ten Men of Mellowbrook. M. Watling
Ten Million. M. Hellinger
Ten Million Dollar Cinch. J. Pattinson
Ten Million Dollar Girl. C. Miron
Ten Minute Alibi. A. Armstrong
Ten Minute Stories. A. Blackwood
Ten Minute Tales. G. Bullett
Ten Minutes on a June Morning. F. Clifford
Ten Peacocks. A. Wood
Ten Per Cent of Your Life. S. Winchester
Ten Percent of Life. H. Conteris
Ten Percent of Trouble. C. Heath
Ten Plays. T. Eyen
Ten Plays from O. Henry. A. G. Smith
Ten Plus One. E. McBain
Ten-Round Contest. Ronald Campbell
Ten Seconds to Hell. L. P. Bachmann
Ten Seconds to Zero. K. Stanton
Ten Star Clues. E. R. Punshon
Ten Steps to the Gallows. J. Wainwright
Ten Tales. F. Coppee
Ten Teacups. Carter Dickson
Ten—the Hard Way. K. Banks
Ten Thirteen. C. Edwards
10:30 from Marseilles. S. Japrisot
Ten-Thirty on a Summer Night. M. Duras
Ten-Thirty Sharp. H. Gibbs
10,000 Days. K. Royce
$10,000 Reward. C. B. Booth
Ten Thousand Passports to Hell. H. P. Lees
10,000 Pound Trophy Race. P. Gill
Ten Thousand Several Doors. H. L. Craig
Ten Times Dynamite. Nick Carter
Ten-Tola Bars. B. Wohl
Ten Ton Snakes. K. Robeson
Ten Trails to Tyburn. B. Graeme
Ten True Secret Service Stories. D. B. Shaw
10.12 Express. W. E. Grogan
Ten Were Missing. M. Allingham
Ten Words of Poison. B. Perowne
Ten Years After. J. W. Bobin
Ten Years Among the Mail Bags. J. Holbrook
Ten Years Beyond Baker Street. C. Van Ash
Tenacity. G. Cottar
Tenant. D. V. Baker
Tenant. John Gill
Tenant. R. Topor
Tenant for Death. C. Hare
Tenant for the Tomb. Anthony Gilbert
Tenant of Chesdene Manor. A. C. Ley
Tenant of No. 13. L. Jackson
Tenant of Sea Cottage. B. L. Ritchie
Tenant of the Grange. M. Gerard
Tenants of Malory. J. S. Le Fanu
Tendencies. T. Cohrs
Tendency to Corrupt. R. Barker
Tender Conspiracy. Eric Lambert
Tender Conspiracy. C. Virmonne
Tender Death. Annette Meyers
Tender Fate. Magali
Tender Is the Knife. Joan Shepherd
Tender Killer. S. B. Hough
Tender Leaves. Robert Mason
Tender Loving Care. A. Neiderman
Tender Offers. P. Engel
Tender Poisoner. J. Bingham

Tender Prey. S. W. Bradford
Tender Prey. J. Grice
Tender Prey. P. Roberts
Tender to Danger. E. Reed
Tender to Moonlight. E. Reed
Tenderfoot. L. Allan
Tengu. G. Masterton
Tennessee Smash. D. Pendleton
Tennessee Terror. B. Ham
Tennessee Tess. C. E. Blaney
Tennis Club Mystery. J. Reach
Tennis Murders. T. L. Welch
Tennyson Code. R. Cooper
Tension. H. Janson
Tension. J. Wainwright
Tentacles. D. Lyon
Tenth Commandment. V. Bridges
Tenth Commandment. Lawrence Sanders
Tenth Crusade. C. Hyde
Tenth Interview. J. Wainwright
Tenth Leper. F. Didelot
Tenth Life. R. Lockridge
Tenth Man. G. Greene
Tenth Point. T. Walsh
Tenth Session. R. Quilty
Tenth Street Killer. K. Slattery
Tenth Victim. R. Sheckley
Tenth Virgin. G. Stewart
Tenth Year of the Ship. N. Lewis
Tents of Shame. E. C. Reed
Tents of Shem. G. Allen
Terence O'Rourke, Gentleman Adventurer. L. J. Vance
Teresa of Watling Street. A. Bennett
Term of Silence. F. Halsey
Term of Terror. P. Flower
Term of Trial. J. Barlow
Terminal. C. Forbes
Terminal Arrangements. J. Pennycook
Terminal Connection. Robin Moore
Terminal Man. M. Crichton
Terminal Three. H. Miller
Terminal Transfer. Trevor Martin
Terminal Velocity. D. Pendleton
Terminate with Prejudice. T. Barling
Termination Interview. Lynne Murray
Termination Order. P. Friedman
Terminator. S. Hutson
Terminator. K. McKenney
Terminators. D. Hamilton
Terminators. B. Mather
Terminus. Andrew Puckett
Terms of Surrender. L. Tracy
Terms of Vengeance. Nick Carter
Terra Cotta. A. Macalilly
Terrace Suicide Mystery. L. Gribble
Terrace Terrors. Richard Allen
Terraces of Night. Margery Lawrence
Terracotta Palace. A. Maybury
Terraplane. J. Womack
Terrarium. L. Head
Terrell in Trouble. S. Blakesley
Terrible Baron, and other stories. B. Reynolds
Terrible Beauty. A. J. Roth
Terrible Choice. T. F. Moynihan
Terrible Crime. E. G. Jones
Terrible Door. B. Sims
Terrible Family. F. Warden
Terrible Game. D. T. Morse
Terrible Hand. L. F. Hay
Terrible Hobby of Sir Joseph Londe, Bt. E. P. Oppenheim
Terrible Inheritance. G. Allen
Terrible Island. B. Grimshaw
Terrible Legacy. G. W. Appleton
Terrible Night. P. Cheyney
Terrible Ones. Nick Carter
Terrible People. E. Wallace
Terrible Performance. J. Bergner
Terrible Pictures. B. Healey
Terrible Secret. G. Fleming
Terrible Secret. M. A. Fleming
Terrible Stork. K. Robeson
Terrible Temptation. C. Reade

Terrible Thing Has Happened to Miss Dupont. P. Hobson
Terrible Thirteen. Nicholas Carter
Terrible Tide. A. Craig
Terrible Time to Die. T. Scaduto
Terrible Tuesday. D. Pendleton
Terrible Youth. Old Sleuth
Terribly Wild Flowers. G. Kersh
Terrified Heart. A. Grace
Terrified Society. H. T. Teilhet
Terrified Target. A. Grace
Terriford Mystery. M. B. Lowndes
Terrifying Stories. James Dark
Territorial Rights. M. Spark
Terror. R. Bloch
Terror. J. Creasey
Terror. A. Machan
Terror. E. Wallace
Terror. R. Wilkinson
Terror Alliance. J. D. Hunter
Terror and the Lonely Widow. K. Robeson
Terror at Black Oaks. J. Reach
Terror at Boulder Dam. V. Robinson
Terror at Bramble Tor. Jean Carew
Terror at Dark Harbor. Clarissa Ross
Terror at Dearcliff House. G. Davies
Terror at Deepcliff. D. Nile
Terror at Golden Sands. R. Roleine
Terror at Hillcrest. Shannon Graham
Terror at Nelson Woods. S. Richard
Terror at Octagon House. A. Coffman
Terror at Seacliff Pines. F. Hurd
Terror at Staups House. Frank King
Terror at Tansey Hill. S. Roberts
Terror at Thor Mountain. J. T. Osborne
Terror at Tolliver Hall. J. T. Osborne
Terror at Tombstone End. Rick Foster
Terror at Tree Tops. A. Parsons
Terror at Twilight. T. Keller
Terror Below. D. Haring
Terror Brigade. D. A. Phillips
Terror by Day. G. Ashe
Terror by Design. J. Edwards
Terror by Gaslight. T. J. Kelly
Terror by Night. R. D. Bunnell
Terror by Night. R. Chetwynd-Hayes
Terror by Night. J. M. Cobban
Terror by Night. L. Crosby
Terror by Night. P. W. Fairman
Terror by Night. G. W. Gough
Terror by Night. C. R. Gull
Terror by Night. N. Klein
Terror by Night. P. Luck
Terror by Night. M. Richmond
Terror by Twilight. K. M. Knight
Terror Catches Up. H. Kaner
Terror Chronicle. B. Sang
Terror Code. Nick Carter
Terror Comes Creeping. Carter Brown
Terror Comes to London. C. Bishop
Terror Comes to Twelvetrees. S. Horler
Terror Contract. A. Kilgore
Terror Factor. E. Wuorio
Terror Farm. B. Amis
Terror Flight. Basil Jackson
Terror for Sale. D. Streib
Terror for the Toff. J. Creasey
Terror from the Sea. Anonymous
Terror-Go-Round. J. Moffatt
Terror in Algiers. E. C. Schurmacher
Terror in D.C. C. Ramm
Terror in Exton. Molly Nelson
Terror in Guyana. Gar Wilson
Terror in Room 201. T. Mitcheltree
Terror in Taormina. A. Hesse
Terror in Taos. L. Derrick
Terror in the Bay. I. F. Turek
Terror in the Fog. N. Berrow
Terror in the Navy. K. Robeson
Terror in the Night. S. Blayne
Terror in the Night. B. Carlton
Terror in the Night. Old Sleuth
Terror in the Night and other stories. R. Bloch
Terror in the Sun. M. Avallone

Terror in the Sun. R. Glendinning
Terror in the Sunlight. J. Hager
Terror in the Sunlight. A. McAllister
Terror in the Thames. A. D. Divine
Terror in the Town. E. Ronns
Terror in Times Square. A. Handley
Terror in Tokyo. N. Perrelli
Terror in Turin. Steve White
Terror Is My Trade. S. Marlowe
Terror Island. R. C. Armour
Terror Island. M. E. Longman
Terror Keep. E. Wallace
Terror Loch. W. McNeilly
Terror Love. N. Norman
Terror Lurks in Darkness. D. Hitchens
Terror Manor. M. E. Edward
Terror Merchant. R. Spencer
Terror Merchants. D. Streib
Terror of Frankenstein. D. F. Glut
Terror of Gold-Digger Creek. G. H. Teed
Terror of Her Ways. Mike Shelley
Terror of Lonely Tor. Donald Stuart
Terror of Mocking Valley. W. Crowell
Terror of Stapleton Quarry. G. Goodchild
Terror of Stormcastle. A. Leech
Terror of Tangier. G. H. Teed
Terror of the Air. W. LeQueux
Terror of the Desert. Robert Harding
Terror of the Gang. H. Clevely
Terror of the Handless Corpse. W. Dale
Terror of the Moat House. L. C. Douthwaite
Terror of the Pacific. J. G. Brandon
Terror of the Road. Vivian Grey
Terror of the Shape. C. Jude
Terror of the Tenements. A. Skene
Terror of the Theatre. W. J. Elliott
Terror of the Tongs. J. Sangster
Terror of the Triads. S. O'Callaghan
Terror of Thunder Creek. S. Hope
Terror of Tibet. E. S. Brooks
Terror of Tibet. G. H. Teed
Terror of Tongues. Roy Vickers
Terror of Torlands. T. C. H. Jacobs
Terror of Toynham Hall. H. K. McDonnell
Terror of Tregarwith. J. Sylvester
Terror on Broadway. David Alexander
Terror on Compass Lake. T. Davis
Terror on Duncan Island. C. Farr
Terror on Halfaday Creek. J. B. Hendryx
Terror on the Docks. M. Franklin
Terror on the Island. J. Ferguson
Terror on the Railroad. J. Stratton
Terror on Tip-Toe. S. Horler
Terror Over London. G. F. Fox
Terror Package. R. Chavis
Terror Rides the West Wind. Rick Madison
Terror Ship. C. Edwards
Terror Squad. R. Sapir
Terror Stalks Abroad. M. Richmond
Terror Stalks by Night. N. W. Firth
Terror Stalks the Mangroves. E. L. Adams
Terror Strikes. N. W. Firth
Terror Syndicate. E. Seaman
Terror Takes 7. K. Robeson
Terror Tales. James Dark
Terror Times Two. Nick Carter
Terror Touches Me. S. Forbes
Terror Tournament. J. M. Flynn
Terror Tower. F. W. Irwin
Terror Tower. C. Rushton
Terror Tower. G. Verner
Terror Trade. M. Lester
Terror Train. J. N. Chance
Terror Trap. J. Creasey
Terror-Trap! N. Lazenby
Terror Trap. W. D. Roberts
Terror Truckers. S. Jason
Terror Walks by Night. H. Desmond
Terror Walks Tonight. J. Kirkpatrick
Terror Watched and other stories. K. W. Hall
Terror Wave. H. S. Banner
Terror Wears a Feathered Cloak. T. W. Crawford
Terror Wears a Smile. L. Grex
Terror Wears No Shoes. K. Robeson

Terrorist. Graham Jones
Terrorist. R. Moss
Terrorist Conspiracy. R. Holloway
Terrorist Killers. G. Metcalf
Terrorist Summit. D. Pendleton
Terrorist Torment. L. Derrick
Terrorists. N. De Mille
Terrorists. M. Sjowall
Terrorist's Woman. J. Honeywood
Terrorizers. D. Hamilton
Terrors and other stories. A. Marshall
Terrors at Penharris Manor. E. J. Brown
Terror's Cradle. D. Kyle
Terrors of the Earth. S. Forbes
Terry and the G-Man. W. N. Bugbee
Terry of Tangistan. Douglas Christie
Tesla Bequest. L. Perdue
Tessacott Tragedy. C. Garvice
Test. M. M. Bodkin
Test Case. B. D. Ashe
Test Flight No. 8. Glen Allen
Test Match Murder. D. Batchelor
Test Match Murder. A. Tack
Test Match Mystery. H. Pink
Test of Anarchy. E. C. Derby
Test of Courage. Nicholas Carter
Test of Love. Gerald Moore
Test of Love. E. Southworth
Testament. D. Morrell
Testament of Cairo, 1898. R. Maugham
Testament of Caspar Schultz. M. Fallon
Testament of Death. Norman Lucas
Testament of Evil. Bradshaw Jones
Testament of John Hastings. A. C. Fox-Davies
Testament to Violence. P. A. Foxall
Tester. W. Palmer
Testimony by Silence. D. M. Disney
Testing. M. Bolton
Testing Ground. G. F. Newman
Testing of Olive Vaughn. P. Brebner
Testing of Tony. M. Cumberland
Testkill. T. Dexter
Tether's End. M. Allingham
Tetramachus Collection. P. Van Rjndt
Teville Obsession. C. Stafford
Texan. J. B. Hendryx
Texas Bank Murders. Christopher Culley
Texas by the Tail. J. Thompson
Texas Gold. J. Reese
Texas Noon. Leonard Sanders
Texas Showdown. D. Stivers
Texas Station. C. Leach
Texas Storm. D. Pendleton
Texas Wind. J. M. Reasoner
Text for Murder. P. Fielding
Texts of Dime. B. Nevitt
Thai Game. W. Woolfolk
Thai Gold. J. Schoonover
Thai Horse. W. Diehl
Thakur Pertab Singh. C. Crosthwaite
Thameside Gold. M. Welford
Thameside Pirate. Anonymous
Thanatos Syndrome. W. Percy
Thaneworth House. K. Kimbrough
Thank You, Good-Bye. J. Jenkins
Thank You, Mr. Conquest. B. Gray
Thank You, Mr. Moto. J. P. Marquand
Thank You, Mr. Pendlebury. A. Webb
Thanks for the Apple. K. Hewitt
Thanks for the Felony. L. Grex
Thanks to Dr. Molly. S. Fairway
Thanks to Murder. J. Krumgold
Thanks to the Saint. L. Charteris
Tharon of Lost Valley. V. E. Roe
That Affair at Elizabeth. B. E. Stevenson
That Affair at Portstead Manor. G. E. Locke
That Affair at St. Peter's. E. A. Brown
That Affair at the Cedars. L. Thayer
That Affair Next Door. A. K. Green
That Alien. Walter Newman
That American Girl. S. Warwick
That Awful Mess on Via Merulana. C. E. Gadda
That Brain Again. H. Janson
That Bullet Hole Has a History! H. C. McNeile

Title Index THEY FOUND EACH OTHER / 1175

That Charming Crook. Frank King
That Cold Day in the Park. R. Miles
That Dame Sal. D. Linton
That Dark Inn. S. Nichols
That Darn Cat. The Gordons
That Dinner at Bardolph's. R. A. J. Walling
That Eternal Triangle. M. Ashton
That Evening in Shanghai. P. Thorne
That Fatal Feeling. E. Kennedy
That Fatal Night. M. Richmond
That Fatal Touch. M. L. Roby
That Fatal Tree. V. Day
That Feeds on Men. I. Wilson
That Fellow MacArthur. S. Jepson
That Fiddler Fellow. H. G. Hutchinson
That Followed After. J. G. Lockhart
That French Girl. J. Hilton
That Frenchman! A. C. Gunter
That Gay Nineties Murder. F. Daingerfield
That Girl from Istanbul. M. G. Braun
That Girl in the Alley. M. Kelly
That Glover Woman. H. Ellson
That He May Die. G. Braddon
That Last Mountain. T. Strong
That Mainwaring Affair. A. M. Barbour
That Man Bolt. P. Crowcroft
That Man Gull. Anthony Stuart
That Man Returns. G. Fairlie
That Nairobi Affair. B. Leslie-Melville
That Night. J. Blackmore
That Night at Nine. D. R. Sperduti
That Night It Rained. H. Waugh
That Old Gang of Mine. Leslie Thomas
That Room in Camden Town. Griff
That Royle Girl. E. Balmer
That Strange Sylvester Affair. L. Thayer
That Summer at Bacclesea. Elizabeth Ford
That Summer, That Fall, and Far Rockaway. F. Gilroy
That Summer's Earthquake. M. Bennett
That Villain, Romeo! J. F. Molloy
That Was No Lady. Keith Campbell
That Was Yesterday. M. Home
That Washington Affair. J. Hay
That We Might Live. Alan Thomas
That Which Is Crooked. D. M. Disney
That Which Is Crooked. Warren Hill
That Which Is Hidden. R. Hichens
That Wilmslow Girl! J. Oakley
That Winslow Woman. R. Pell
That Woman. H. Moray
That Year at the Office. R. Timperley
That Yew Tree's Shadow. C. Hare
That's All I Need. D. Spade
That's Her Problem. M. Hampton
That's Mark Avery. M. L. Tyrrell
That's My Baby! D. Haring
That's No Way to Die. L. Kelley
That's Piracy, My Pet. Carter Brown
That's the House, There. L. Singer
That's the Spirit. M. V. Heberden
That's the Way the Money Goes. S. Miller
That's Where the Cat's At, Baby. B. B. Johnson
That's Your Man, Inspector! D. Frome
Theatre Crime. F. Andreas
Theatre of Life. G. R. Sims
Theban Mysteries. A. Cross
Theft from the Provincial Museum. I. Strelkova
Theft in Kind. M. Summerton
Theft of Magna Carta. J. Creasey
Theft of the Crown Jewels. E. Jepson
Theft of the Iron Dogs. E. C. R. Lorac
Theft of the Persian Slipper. E. D. Hoch
Thefts of Nick Velvet. E. D. Hoch
Their Dusty Hands. M. Carleton
Their Evil Ways. L. Wainwright
Their Flowers Were Always Black. P. Hastings
Their Great Adventure. W. M. Graydon
Their Little Lives. G. S. Marlowe
Their Majesties' Bucketeers. L. N. Smith
Their Man in the White House. T. Ardies
Their Nearest and Dearest. Bernice Carey
Their Rainbow Had Black Edges. Gerald Butler
Their Wife. D. Walshe

Theme Is Murder. M. A. De Ford
Theme Is Murder. Gavin Holt
Then Came Bronson. W. Johnston
Then Came the Police. C. M. Wills
Then Came Two Women. C. Armstrong
Then Came Violence. J. Ball
Then Hang All the Liars. A. Storey
Then There Was Murder. B. Parvin
Then There Were None. A. Morelli
Then There Were Three. G. Homes
Theodora. K. Lindsay
Theodosia. J. A. Bartlett
Theodosius de Zulvin, the Monk of Madrid. George Moore
Therapist. R. Alleman
Therapy for Murder. L. Munder
Therapy in Dynamite. V. B. Miller
There Ain't No Justice. J. Curtis
There and Back. B. Crump
There Are Crimes and Crimes. A. Strindberg
There Are Dead Men in Manhattan. J. Roeburt
There Are Giants. E. Woodward
There Are More Ways of Killing . . . M. Fitt
There Are No Ghosts in the Soviet Union. Reginald Hill
There Are No Spies. B. Granger
There Are Thirteen. F. Beeding
There Are Worse Jungles. N. Tranter
There Came Both Mist and Snow. M. Innes
There Could Be Trouble. B. Carson
There Fell a Shadow. Keith Peterson
There Goes Charlie! A. Fleming
There Goes Davy Cohen. W. Owen
There Goes Death. G. Ashe
There Goes His Ghost. J. Atholl
There Goes Shorty Higgins. J. Karney
There Goes the Bride. M. Brucker
There Goes the Bride. W. Maner
There Hangs the Knife. M. Muller
There Has Been a Murder. H. Holt
There Is a Death, Elizabeth. Gerald Butler
There Is a Destiny. R. J. Burge
There Is a Green Hill. Robert Mason
There Is a Serpent in Eden. R. Bloch
There Is a Tide . . . A. Christie
There Is a Tide— E. Wooll
There Is No Justice. R. B. Dominic
There Is No Ogpu. A. Wood
There Is No Return. A. Blackmon
There Is No Silence. M. Dolinsky
There Is No Yesterday. K. Lindsay
There Is One S.O.S. J. B. O'Sullivan
There Is Something About a Dame. M. Avallone
There Lies Your Love. Jennie Melville
There Must Be Some Mistake. M. Babson
There Must Be Victims. M. Cumberland
There None Embrace. F. Shroyer
There Sits Death. P. McGuire
There Was a Crooked Man. D. Keene
There Was a Crooked Man. K. Roos
There Was a Crooked Man. C. Witting
There Was a Crooked Man. G. W. Yates
There Was a Door. T. Mundy
There Was a Little Boy. C. R. Jacobs
There Was a Little Girl. E. Dewhurst
There Was a Little Man. C. Conrad
There Was a Witness. E. Salter
There Was an Old Woman. E. Davis
There Was an Old Woman. E. Phillpotts
There Was an Old Woman. E. Queen
There Was No Island. L. Handley
There Was No Moon. F. Hay
There Were No Asper Ladies. E. Ascher
There Were No Windows. N. Hoult
Thereby Hangs a Corpse. C. Mullen
Thereby Hangs a Tale. G. M. Fenn
Thereby Hangs a Tale. G. Robey
Therefore I Killed Him. H. Jobson
There's a Hippie on the Highway. J. H. Chase
There's a Reason for Everything. E. R. Punshon
There's Always a Dame. B. Sarto
There's Always a Murder. K. Parker
There's Always a Payoff. R. P. Hansen
There's Always a Price Tag. J. H. Chase

There's Always Juliet. J. Van Druten
There's Always Time to Die. O. R. Cohen
There's Always Tomorrow. A. Meredith
There's Been Murder Done. K. T. Knoblock
There's Death in the Churchyard. W. Gore
There's Death in the Cup. A. Hocking
There's Death, Miss Minden! A. Jackson
There's Money in Murder. G. Barnett
There's No Future in Murder. P. Valdez
There's No One in the Village. O. Rees
There's No Tomorrow. D. Haring
There's Nothing Like Leather. W. A. Everton
There's Nothing to Be Afraid Of. M. Muller
There's Something in a Sunday. M. Muller
There's Trouble Brewing. N. Blake
Theresa. T. P. Prest
Therese. T. Job
Theresa Raquin. E. Zola
Thermal Thursday. D. Pendleton
These Are Strange Tales. A. Abbot
These Arrows Point to Death. W. O'Farrell
These Charming People. M. Arlen
These Cliffs Are Dangerous. L. March
These Haunted Streets. John Burke
These Lonely, These Dead. R. Colby
These Lonely Victories. E. West
These Names Make Clues. E. C. R. Lorac
These Men and Women. S. Horler
These Small Glories. J. Cleary
These Stories. Stenson Cooke
These Tigers' Hearts. Jane Land
These Unlucky Deeds. R. M. Stern
These Within. L. K. Vincent
These Women! These Women! L. A. Biggers
Theseus Code. M. Hammond
Thespian Detective and other theatrical stories. B. Delannoy
Theta Syndrome. E. Trevor
They All Bleed Red. R. Sted
They All Came Back. J. Courage
They All Ran Away. E. Ronns
They Being Dead Yet Speak. C. Massie
They Blocked the Suez Canal. A. D. Divine
They Buried a Man. Mildred Davis
They Burn for Me. B. Sarto
They Call It Murder. Peter Chambers
They Call It Murder. Tom Hart
They Call It Murder. B. Manktelow
They Call Him Death. David Hume
They Called Him Nighthawk. S. Horler
They Came by Night. B. Lyndon
They Came by Night. S. Truss
They Came to Baghdad. A. Christie
They Came to Kill. M. Scherf
They Came to Kill. D. Stivers
They Came to London. P. Tabori
They Came to Spy. J. Brearley
They Can Only Hang You Once. D. Hammett
They Can Only Kill You Once. D. Brennan
They Can't All Be Guilty. M. V. Heberden
They Can't Hang Caroline. Roy Vickers
They Can't Hang Me! J. Mallett
They Can't Hang Me! J. Ronald
They Carry a Torch. J. Blackmore
They Could Do No Other. E. Phillpotts
They Couldn't Go Wrong. R. Armstrong
They Couldn't Lose the Body. Bruce Sanders
They Cracked Her Glass Slipper. Gerald Butler
They Deal in Death. R. Terrall
They Die Alone. H. Janson
They Died in the Spring. J. Pullein-Thompson
They Died Twice. K. Robeson
They Do It with Mirrors. A. Christie
They Do It with Mirrors. J. C. Conaway
They Don't Always Hang Murderers. B. Herbert
They Don't Dance Much. James Ross
They Don't Live Long. J. Cello
They Don't Make Them Like That Any More. J. Leasor
They Don't Shoot Cowards. John Reese
They Drive by Night. J. Curtis
They Found a Way Back. N. Sheraton
They Found Atlantis. D. Wheatley
They Found Each Other. G. Fairlie

They Found Him Dead. G. Heyer
They Gave Him a Gun. W. J. Cowan
They Hadn't a Clue. Q. Downes
They Hang Them in Gibraltar. B. Perowne
They Hanged My Saintly Billy. R. Graves
They Hunted a Fox. Alice Campbell
They Journey by Night. D. Ames
They Kidnapped Stanley Matthews. L. Gribble
They Kill by Night. K. Medusa
They Kill to Live. M. Shane
They Killed a Spy. M. Hastings
They Like 'Em Rough. B. Kemp
They Liked Entwhistle. R. A. J. Walling
They Lived with Death. H. Desmond
They Love Not Poison. Sara Woods
They Met at Mrs. Bloxom's. H. Norwood
They Never Came Back. B. Flynn
They Never Came Back. David Hume
They Never Came Back. E. P. Thorne
They Never Looked Inside. M. Gilbert
They Never Say When. P. Cheyney
They Rang Up the Police. J. Cannan
They Rubbed Him Out. J. L. Cora
They Sailed on a Friday. T. C. Paynter
They Say I'm Bad. B. Shannon
They See in Darkness. Ethel L. White
They Shall Not Die. B. Quain
They Shall Not Die. J. Wexley
They Shoot Horses, Don't They? H. McCoy
They Stand Accused. G. Braddon
They Stay for Death. Sara Woods
They Stole a Ship. C. H. Barker
They Stuck at Nothing. R. Ladline
They Talked of Poison. M. Evermay
They Tell No Tales. M. Coles
They Tell No Tales. A. Spiller
They Tell No Tales. L. Thayer
They Thought He Was Dead. S. Horler
They Used Dark Forces. D. Wheatley
They Vanish at Night. Frank King
They Voted Me to Die. J. Laffin
They Waited for the Night. V. Dale
They Walk Alone. M. Catto
They Walk by Night. Hilary Dean
They Walk in Darkness. G. Verner
They Walked in Fear. B. Amis
They Want Me Dead. P. Bannon
They Wanted Him Dead! L. Eyles
They Watched by Night. J. Rhode
They Went Thataway. D. A. Brown
They Were Seven. E. Phillpotts
They Wetted His Head. H. Fernee
They Who Sin. J. Roeburt
They Won't Believe Me. G. McDonell
They Won't Lie Down. M. Annesley
They Wouldn't Be Chessmen. A. E. W. Mason
They'll Never Find Out. F. Duncan
They're Coming to Kill You, Jane. K. Carr
They're Going to Kill Me. K. M. Knight
They're Not Home Yet. F. Rydell
They've Got Me Again. D. Linton
They've Killed Anna. N. Hollander
They've Killed Anne. M. Olden
They've Shot the President's Daughter. E. Stewart
Thick As Thieves. M. Nicole
Thick Blue Sweater. P. Fry
Thickening Light. G. Ferrand
Thicker Than Water. M. Halliday
Thicker Than Water. R. McInerny
Thicker Than Water. J. Payn
Thicker Than Water. M. Polland
Thicker Than Water. J. Sandys
Thicker Than Water. F. Tilsley
Thicker Than Water. W. C. Tuttle
Thicket. P. Gallagher
Thief. R. Croft-Cooke
Thief. M.L. Tyrrell
Thief by Night. D. Peacock
Thief in the Night. Nicholas Carter
Thief in the Night. E. W. Hornung
Thief in the Night. P. Manton
Thief in the Night. E. Wallace
Thief in the Night. T. Walsh
Thief Is an Ugly World. P. Gallico

Thief of Clubs. G. Johns
Thief of Hearts. Rachelle Edwards
Thief of Time. T. Hillerman
Thief of Time. J. Wainwright
Thief or Two. Sara Woods
Thief Taker. J. Sturrock
Thief Who Came to Dinner. T. L. Smith
Thief Who Couldn't Sleep. Lawrence Block
Thief Who Painted Sunlight. O. Bleeck
Thief Who Was Robbed. Nicholas Carter
Thieves. Aix
Thieves' Carnival. J. Anouilh
Thieves Fall Out. C. Kay
Thieves Go by Air. P. T. Owen
Thieves' Highway. Ruth Grayson
Thieves' Hole. D. Howarth
Thieves' Honour. S. Gluck
Thieves' Justice. A. Marsden
Thieves' Kitchen. J. N. Chance
Thieves Like Us. R. E. Alter
Thieves Like Us. E. Anderson
Thieves Market. A. I. Bezzerides
Thieves' Nights. H. S. Keeler
Thieves of Alexandria. J. Hunter
Thieves of Enchantment. P. Audemars
Thieves of Tumbutu. H. Greene
Thieves' Picnic. L. Charteris
Thieves' Wit. H. Footner
Thieving Fingers. F. Du Boisgobey
Thin Air. H. Brown
Thin Air. W. Marshall
Thin Air. J. Pudney
Thin Air. G. E. Simpson
Thin Edge of Mania. M. Macklin
Thin Edge of Violence. W. O'Farrell
Thin Ice. John Raymond
Thin Ice. M. Richmond
Thin Line. E. Atiyah
Thin Line. R. Doliner
Thin Man. D. Hammett
Thin Red Line. A. Griffiths
Thin-Spun Thread. A. Hocking
Thin Woman. D. Cannell
Thing at the Door. H. Slesar
Thing at Their Heels. H. Hext
Thing in the Brook. P. Storme
Thing in the Night. K. Virden
Thing in the Road. T. M. White
Thing in the Woods. Harper Williams
Thing in the Woods. Margery Williams
Thing That Happens to You. E. Berckman
Thing That Made Love. D. V. Reed
Thing That Pursued. K. Robeson
Thing to Love. G. Household
Things As They Are. W. Godwin
Things Beyond Midnight. W. F. Nolan
Things Happen. R. Glover
Things Invisible. W. J. Reynolds
Things Men Do. Raymond Marshall
Things That Are Caesar's. R. W. Kauffman
Things That No One Tells. E. C. Mayne
Things That Women Do. F. Warden
Things Undone. M. Childers
Things We Do for Love. B. M. Schutz
Think Big, Think Dirty. W. Garner
Think Fast, Mr. Moto. J. P. Marquand
Think Fast. Mr. Peters. S. M. Kaminsky
Think Fast Sister. T. Barton
Think Inc. A. Diment
Think of a Humber. A. Bodelsen
Think of Death. R. Lockridge
Thinking Machine. J. Futrelle
Thinking Machine Affair. Joel Barnard
Thinking Machine on the Case. J. Futrelle
Thinner. R. Bachman
Thinner Than Water. E. Ferrars
Thinning the Turkey Herd. Robert Campbell
Third Act. H. G. Richards
Third Alibi. M. Dalman
Third Angle. S. Lamont
Third Arm. K. Royce
Third Assassin. H. C. Davis
Third Attempt. H. E. Wheeler
Third Baffle Book. L. Wren

Third Beast. P. Loughran
Third Betrayal. M. Hartland
Third Blonde. M. S. Craig
Third Bullet. Carter Dickson
Third Bullet. A. C. Stream
Third Bullet and other stories. J. D. Carr
Third Case of Mr. Paul Savoy. Jackson Gregory
Third Child. A. Nichols
Third Circle. B. Howley
Third Crime Lucky. E. S. Brazier
Third Crime Lucky. Anthony Gilbert
Third Day. M. Delahaye
Third Day. J. Hayes
Third Deadly Sin. Lawrence Sanders
Third Degree. Joe Barry
Third Degree. M. B. Dix
Third Degree. C. Franklin
Third Degree. A. Hornblow
Third Degree. C. R. Jackson
Third Diamond. J. B. Ellis
Third Ear. C. Siodmak
Third Encounter. Sara Woods
Third Eye. E. Leroux
Third Eye. Ethel L. White
Third Figure. C. Wilcox
Third Force. H. Matheson
Third Force. D. Sinclair
Third Friday. G. Bellak
Third Fury. R. Rhodes
Third Girl. A. Christie
Third Grave. D. Case
Third Half. Mildred Davis
Third Horseman. J. B. O'Sullivan
Third Hour. G. Household
Third Identity. R. Gatenby
Third Key. H. H. C. Gibbons
Third Key. G. Verner
Third Kiss. H. Flowerdew
Third Lady. S. Natsuki
Third Letter. F. Ramirez
Third Life. Caroline Gray
Third Man. J. G. Bethune
Third Man. G. Greene
Third Man and The Fallen Idol. G. Greene
Third Messenger. P. Wynnton
Third Miracle. L. Tracy
Third Murderer. C. J. Daly
Third Mutant. L. Elliott
Third on a Seesaw. N. MacNeil
Third One. R. Mead
Third Owl. R. J. Casey
Third Party. F. A. Stanley
Third Party Risk. N. Bentley
Third Party Risk. G. Cullingford
Third Passenger. C. Crane
Third Policeman. Flann O'Brien
Third Possibility. S. Jepson
Third Robin Featherstone. L. C. Douthwaite
Third Round. H. C. McNeile
Third Seat Back. K. Sunderland
Third Shadow. D. Nile
Third Shot. F. W. Irwin
Third Side of the Coin. F. Clifford
Third Skin. J. Bingham
Third Spectre. W. E. D. Ross
Third Statue. Shane Martin
Third Time Unlucky. Mark Cross
Third Time Unlucky! L. Meynell
Third Time Unlucky. T. B. Morris
Third Tower. A. Abbott
Third Truth. M. Bar-Zohar
Third Twin. Clay Henry
Third Victim. J. J. Farjeon
Third Victim. Donald Stuart
Third Victim. L. M. Waltch
Third Victim. C. Wilcox
Third Visitor. G. Anstruther
Third Volume. F. Hume
Third Warning. Augustus Muir
Third Way. J. Warmbold
Third Wife. J. Himes
Third Woman. J. De Pre
Thirsty Evil. P. M. Hubbard
Thirsty Evil. G. Verner

Thirteen. F. B. Austin
Thirteen. H. Balzac
13. P. Loraine
13. S. Wilson
Thirteen at Dinner. A. Christie
13 Castle Walk. D. Bodeen
13 Clues for Miss Marple. A. Christie
Thirteen Days. I. Jefferies
Thirteen Detectives. G. K. Chesterton
Thirteen Doctors. Mrs. J. K. Spender
13 for Luck! A. Christie
Thirteen for the Kill. P. Buck
13 French Street. G. Brewer
Thirteen Guests. J. J. Farjeon
Thirteen in a Fog. B. Graeme
Thirteen Men. T. Thayer
Thirteen Moons. M. L. Tyrrell
Thirteen O'Clock. S. V. Benet
Thirteen O'Clock. E. Bond
Thirteen O'Clock. T. Clarke
Thirteen Paint a Portrait. P. Wrightson
Thirteen Problems. A. Christie
Thirteen Sinners. A. Marmor
Thirteen Stannergate. G. M. Wilson
Thirteen Steps. W. Chambers
13 Steps to Lime Street. D. Enefer
Thirteen Stories. R. B. C. Graham
Thirteen Strange Tales. Douglas Kennedy
13 Thirteenth Street. N. S. Lincoln
13 Times Death. D. Rome
Thirteen Towers. C. Caldwell
Thirteen Toy Pistols. E. E. Halleran
Thirteen Travellers. H. Walpole
Thirteen Trumpeteers. L. Meynell
Thirteen Ways Home. E. Nesbit
13 West Street. L. Brackett
13 White Tulips. F. Crane
Thirteen Winston Street. J. Wetherell
Thirteen Women. T. Thayer
Thirteenth Bed in the Ballroom. E. H. Fonseca
Thirteenth Brydain. M. Moule
Thirteenth Chair. B. Veiller
13th Chime. T. C. H. Jacobs
13th Code. W. Jardine
Thirteenth Day. C. George
13th Directorate. B. Chubin
13th Doll. A. Loring
Thirteenth Floor. J. F. W. Hannay
Thirteenth Guest. F. Hume
Thirteenth Guest. A. Trail
13th Hour. S. Horler
Thirteenth Hour. John Lee
Thirteenth House. C. Barry
13th Juror. H. I. Dodge
Thirteenth Juror. F. T. Hill
Thirteenth Letter. N. S. Lincoln
Thirteenth Lover. R. Clarke
13th Lover. M. Dekobra
13th Man. M. T. Bloom
Thirteenth Man. Mrs. C. Kernahan
13th Mummy. G. Radcliffe
13th Murder. F. G. Eberhard
13th Spy. Nick Carter
Thirteenth Treasure. Charlotte Hunt
Thirteenth Trick. R. Braddon
Thirty Corpses Every Thursday. F. Brown
Thirty Days. H. Wales
Thirty Days Hath July. Alice Brennan
Thirty Days Hath September. P. Capon
30 Days Hath September. D. C. Disney
Thirty Days Hath September. O. John
Thirty Days to Live. P. Conway
Thirty Days to Live. Anthony Gilbert
30 Degrees North 165 Degrees East. P. J. Stam
Thirty-Eighth Floor. Clifford Irving
Thirty Famous Chinese Stories. W. I-Ting
Thirty-First Bullfinch. H. Reilly
Thirty-First Floor. P. Wahloo
Thirty-First of February. J. Symons
30 for a Harry. R. Hoyt
Thirty-Four East. Alfred Coppel
30 Manhattan East. H. Waugh
Thirty-Nine Steps. J. Buchan
Thirty-Ninth Victim. P. Griffiths

Thirty Pieces of Silver. A. Soutar
Thirty-Second Floor. E. Dudowicz
Thirty Seconds Over New York. R. Buchard
36 Hours. C. K. Hittleman
36-24-Forty-Five. D. Haring
Thirty Years After. W. M. Graydon
This Ancient Evil. D. Daniels
This Animal Is Dangerous. Reginald Campbell
This Animal Must Die. F. Scarpetta
This Band of Spirits. Nick Carter
This Blessed Plot. M. R. D. Meek
This Body Must Die. A. Sergeant
This Business of Bumfog. M. Donne
This Chequered Floor. F. Bamford
This City Is Ours. D. Pitts
This Club Frowns on Murder. A. Borowitz
This Creeping Evil. Sea Lion
This Crowded Earth & Ladies' Day. R. Bloch
This Dame Must Die. Brad Nolan
This Dame Dies Soon. H. Janson
This Dame Spells Death. C. Wheatley
This Dark Desire. J. Conway
This Dark Monarchy. F. Leary
This Darkening Universe. L. Biggle
This Day Violence. M. Reed
This Day's Madness. D. G. Waring
This Deadly Dark. L. Wilson
This Deadly Grief. P. Power
This Death Was Murder. M. Evermay
This Delicate Murder. H. Clandon
This Doll Is Dangerous. Frank King
This Downhill Path. A. Clarke
This Drakotny—. P. McCutchan
This Evil Village. Marilyn Ross
This Fatal Writ. Sara Woods
This Fearful Paradise. J. Ames
This Fell Sergeant. D. Garner
This Fortress. M. Coles
This Frightened Lady. D. Ross
This Frightened Lady. Marilyn Ross
This Game of Murder. R. Deming
This Game of Murder. J. M. Stevens
This Ghost Business. A. W. Clark
This Girl for Hire. G. G. Fickling
This Gun for Gloria. B. Mara
This Gun for Hire. G. Greene
This Gun for Justice. V. J. Santiago
This Honey Is Mine. B. Vane
This Hood for Hire. H. Janson
This House is Burning. Mona Williams
This House is Haunted. R. Bridges
This House to Let. W. LeQueux
This Inward Horror. J. R. Warren
This Is a Mystery. G. Pardoe
This Is Death Calling. J. Sandys
This Is Dynamite. Richard Grant
This Is for Keeps. G. Joseph
This Is for Real. J. H. Chase
This Is Harry Flynn. J. Jost
This Is It. H. Ellson
This Is It, Michael Shayne. B. Halliday
This Is Jezebel. D. Cory
This Is Mr. Fortune. H. C. Bailey
This Is Murder. W. Ard
This—Is Murder! C. Fitzsimmons
This Is Murder. C. J. Kenny
This Is Murder. P. Muller
This Is Murder, Lady! N. W. Firth
This Is Murder, Mr. Herbert and other stories. D. Keene
This Is Murder, Mr. Jones. T. Fuller
This Is My Murder. M. B. Dix
This Is My Night. R. Deming
This Is My Son. C. B. Kelland
This Is the Castle. N. Freeling
This Is the House. Shelley Smith
This Is What Happened. T. Claymore
This Is Your Death. D. Devine
This Is Your Life. B. Newman
This Kill Is Mine. D. Evans
This Land Turns Evil Slowly. M. L. Roby
This Little Angel Went to Hell. P. Fenton
This Little Measure. Sara Woods
This Little World. D. C. Murray

This Man Belongs to Me. M. Richmond
This Man Dawson. H. E. Helseth
This Man Did I Kill? M. Halliday
This Man I Love. W. E. D. Ross
This Man Is a Spy. D. L. David
This Man Is a Stranger. H. B. Kaye
This Man Is Dangerous. P. Cheyney
This Man Is Death. A. Capelli
This Man Is Mine. K. Lindsay
This Man Must Die! W. A. Ballinger
This Man's Doom. L. Thayer
This Man's Wife. G. M. Fenn
This Man's World. I. S. Cobb
This Mortal Coil. G. Allen
This Mortal Coil. J. R. Warren
This Murder Comes to Mind. R. Ormerod
This Murderous Shaft. H. J. Hultman
This New Corn. D. G. Waring
This One Night. D. Robins
This Other Eden. E. V. Knox
This Outward Angel. Alanna Knight
This Passionate Land. H. Janeway
This Path Is Dangerous. F. J. Whaley
This Prize Is Dangerous. M. Prize
This Road Is Dangerous! H. D. Dearden
This Road Is Dangerous. M. Richmond
This Rough Magic. Mary Stewart
This Shrouded Night. Dana Ross
This Side Murder. J. Bonett
This Side of Hell. R. Charles
This Side of Terror. D. Bateson
This Side of the Sky. J. Barlow
This Side Up. H. Lugar
This Son of Vulcan. W. Besant
This Spy Must Die. P. Saxon
This Story of Yours. J. Hopkins
This Suitcase Is Going to Explode. T. Ardies
This Sweet Sickness. P. Highsmith
This Tangled Web. E. O. Allen
This Thing Called Sin. R. Vane
This Time for Keeps. M. Baroni
This Time Forever. A. J. Merak
This Traitor, Death. D. Cory
This Troublesome World. L. T. Meade
This Undesirable Residence. M. Burton
This Unnecessary Murder. F. S. Wees
This Was a Woman. H. Zore
This Was No Accident. J. A. Saxon
This Water Laps Gently. M. Ingate
This Way for a Shroud. J. H. Chase
This Way for Hell. Gene Ross
This Way Out. H. Dudeney
This Way Out. M. Grahame
This Way Out. S. Radley
This Way Out. J. Ronald
This Way Out. A. M. Sholl
This Way Sister. B. Carson
This Way, Sucker. D. Haring
This Way to Evil. H. P. Lees
This Wicked Sex. H. Janson
This Will Kill You. Jerome Barry
This Witch. W. Tucker
This Woman Is Dangerous. L. Mallory
This Woman Is Dangerous. Mark Ross
This Woman Is Death. S. D. Frances
This Woman Is Death. H. Janson
This Woman Is Death. M. Storme
This Woman Is Wanted. Roland Daniel
This Woman Is Wanted. G. Goodchild
This Woman to This Man. C. N. Williamson
This Woman Wanted. R. Foley
This Won't Hurt You. N. Fitzgerald
This World Is Wide Enough. G. Greenfield
This Year in Jerusalem. J. Gross
This Year—Next Year. Lionel Brown
This Year's Death. J. Godey
This Yellow Slave. L. Durie
This'll Kill You. Peter Chambers
This'll Kill You. A. Payne
This'll Kill You. M. Randolph
Thistle Sifters. C. R. Burke
Thistlewood Plot. J. G. Jeffries
Thomas Berryman Number. J. Patterson
Thomas Crown Affair. E. L. Heyman

T

Thomas Document. H. Gantzer
Thomas Shelton's Ghost. J. Brocke
Thomas Street Horror. R. Paul
Thompson the Detective. J. L. Hempstead
Thompson's Progress. C. J. C. Hyne
Thor Option. M. Benassi
Thorn in the Dust. P. Audemars
Thorne House. J. Ware
Thorne in the Flesh. R. Petrie
Thorne Theatre Mystery. Joshua Willard
Thornley Colton, Blind Detective. C. H. Stagg
Thornley Colton, Blind Reader of Hearts. C. H. Stagg
Thornyhold. Mary Stewart
Thoroughbred Vagabond. James Greenwood
Those Dark Eyes. E. M. Brez
Those in Peril. N. Freeling
Those Lake View Wives. Charles Cohen
Those on the List. A. Parsons
Those Other Days. E. P. Oppenheim
Those Seven Alibis. C. G. Booth
Those Subtle Seeds. J. A. Lordahl
Those That Have Eyes. P. Conway
Those Westerton Girls. F. Warden
Those Who Blink. William Mills
Those Who Have Come Back. P. C. MacFarlane
Those Who Hunt the Night. B. Hambly
Those Who Prey Together Slay Together. D. Von Elsner
Those Who Return. M. Level
Those Who Smiled, and other stories. P. Gibbon
Those Who Walk Away. P. Highsmith
Those Who Walk in Darkness. G. C. Shedd
Thou Art the Man. M. E. Braddon
Thou Shalt Not Kill. B. Heygate
Thou Shalt Not Kill. M. B. Lowndes
Thou Shell of Death. N. Blake
Thou Shouldst Be Living. J. Byrom
Though I Know She Lives. Sara Woods
Thoughtless Yes. H. H. Gardener
Thousand and One Afternoons in Chicago. B. Hecht
Thousand and Second Night. F. Heller
Thousand Coffins Affair. M. Avallone
Thousand Dollar Reward. W. Darrow
Thousand Doors. A. Rothberg
Thousand Faces of Night. Harry Patterson
Thousand Francs Reward. E. Gaboriau
Thousand Hands. Bruce Norman
Thousand-Headed Man. K. Robeson
Thousand Secrets. J. Selborne
Thousand Witnesses. G. Beardmore
Thousandth Case. G. Dilnot
Thousandth Woman. E. W. Hornung
Thread of Evidence. B. Picton
Thread of Proof. H. Hill
Thread o' Scarlet. J. J. Bell
Threads of Gold. L. V. Stevens
Threads of Intrigue. Lynn Williams
Threads of Love. E. Randolph
Threat. R. Jessup
Threat of Dragons. L. R. Davis
Threat of the Cloven Hand. Richard Grant
Threat of the Tattooed Spy. Anonymous
Threat Warning Red. A. Fox
Threatening Eye. L. Grant-Adamson
Threatening Eye. Colin Robertson
Threats or Promises. B. Delinsky
Three. F. Hume
Three Act Tragedy. A. Christie
Three Against Fate. M. A. Hamilton
Three Alibis. J. F. W. Hannay
Three Amateurs. Michael Lewis
Three Among Mountains. H. Slater
Three and One Make Five. R. Jeffries
Three at the Angel. M. Procter
Three at Wolfe's Door. R. Stout
Three Bad Girls. S. Harragan
Three Bad Nights. B. Buckingham
Three Bars Interval. S. Aumonier
Three Beans. M. Coles
Three Beds in Manhattan. G. Simenon
Three Bells. H. Barber
Three Black Bags. M. P. Angellotti

Three Black Dots. O. Binns
Three Blind Mice. V. Bridges
Three Blind Mice. A. Christie
Three Blind Mice. E. McBain
3 Blind Mice. A. Seifert
Three Blind Mice. J. Wood
Three Blue Anchors. O. Binns
Three Boots. W. H. Stacpoole
Three Boy Detectives. Old Sleuth
Three Brass Balls. G. R. Sims
Three Brass Elephants. Herman Landon
Three Bright Pebbles. L. Ford
Three Brothers. J. Pickersgill
Three Buccaneers. L. Lindsay
Three Candles for the Dark. Rosemary Harris
Three Cheers for the Good Guys. F. Dickens
Three Cheers for Treason! Robert Mason
Three Coffins. J. D. Carr
Three Colonels. P. Cosgrave
Three-Coloured Pencil. S. P. B. Mais
Three-Core Lead. C. Curzon
Three-Cornered Cover. G. Marton
Three-Cornered Murder. Jean Leslie
Three-Cornered Wound. G. Dyer
Three Corners to Nowhere. M. Caidin
Three Corpse Parlay. Fredric Brown
Three Corpse Trick. M. Burton
Three Couriers. C. MacKenzie
Three Cousins Die. J. Rhode
Three Cries of Terror. A. Ashton
Three Crimes. M. Burton
Three Crows. J. Hunter
Three Daggers. C. F. Gregg
Three Dan Turner Stories. R. L. Bellem
Three Dates with Death. V. Gunn
Three Daughters of Night. D. Vane
Three Day Alliance. H. R. Simpson
Three Day Break. D. Hegarty
Three Day Pass—to Kill. J. W. Burke
3-Day Terror. V. Packer
Three Days for Emeralds. M. G. Eberhart
Three Days in Hong Kong. F. Crane
Three Days in Winter. J. Jenkins
Three Days of the Condor. J. Grady
Three Days' Terror. J. S. Fletcher
Three Days Terror. P. Manton
Three Days to Live. R. Charles
Three Dead. D. Magarshack
Three Dead Men. P. McGuire
Three Dead, One Hurt. S. Mackenzie
Three Decades to Doom. D. A. Oxley
Three Devils. K. Robeson
Three Die at Midnight. J. Hunter
Three Die at Midnight. P. Meriton
Three Died Beside the Marble Pool. C. M. Chapin
Three Died for Morson. C. Ryland
Three Died That Night. Gret Lane
3 Died Variously. G. E. Giles
Three Doors to Darkness. W. Palmer
Three Doors to Death. R. Stout
Three Dots and a Dash. T. Taggart
Three Down Vulnerable. Z. H. Ross
Three Envelopes. H. Drummond
Three Exploits of M. Parent. J. Lermina
Three Faces East. A. P. Kelly
Three Faces of Death. J. Weisman
Three Fair Philanthropists. A. M. Muzzy
Three Fears. J. Stagge
Three Finger Marks. Old Spicer
Three Fingered Death. G. M. Wilson
Three Fingers in the Door. F. Metcalfe
Three Fishers. F. Beeding
Three Flights Up. J. J. Byrd
Three for a Killing. D. Leach
Three for Passion. H. Janson
Three for the Chair. R. Stout
Three for the Gallows. E. McDowell
Three for the Money. W. T. Ballard
Three for the Money. Joe Barry
Three for the Money. J. McConnaughey
Three Freaks. T. Robbins
Three Friends. G. H. Faulkner
Three Frightened Men. B. Gray

Three Gentleman from New Caledonia. R. D. Hemingway
Three Ghosts of the Forest. Alexander Thomson
3 Girls and a Killer. H. D. Spatz
Three Glass Eyes. W. LeQueux
Three Gnomes. G. Verner
Three Gold Crowns. K. Robeson
Three Gold Feathers. G. H. Teed
Three Golden Balls. H. Hazel
Three Graces. P. Hobson
Three Green Bottles. D. Devine
Three Ha-Pence to the Angel. Charles Harris
Three Hostages. J. Buchan
Three Hours to Hang. A. MacKenzie
Three Hundred Grand. J. Pattinson
361. D. E. Westlake
330 Park. S. Cohen
Three Hunting Horns. M. Fitt
Three Imposters. A. Machen
Three in a Cell. R. Croft-Cooke
Three Inquisitive People. D. Wheatley
Three Jolly Vagabonds. J. Budd
Three Judges. H. Maxwell
Three Just Men. E. Wallace
Three Keys. F. Ormond
Three Keys to Murder. M. Holloway
Three Knaves. S. L. Greenleaf
Three Knaves. E. Phillpotts
Three Knots. W. LeQueux
Three Knots. R. Parker
Three Layers of Guilt. J. Ashford
Three Lepers' Heads. P. Quiroule
Three Letters of Credit. K. Bilir
Three Letters to Pan. J. Blackmore
Three Lights Went Out. R. G. Dean
Three Little Tramps. Old Sleuth
Three Live Ghosts. F. S. Isham
Three Lost Ladies. H. R. Campbell
Three L's. Anonymous
Three Masked Men. J. N. Pentelow
Three Masks of Death. J. N. Chance
3 Megaton Gamble. D. Terman
Three Men and a God, and other stories. N. Newham-Davis
Three Men and a Maid. Robert Fraser
Three Men Die. S. G. Millin
Three Men for the Job. D. Ambler
Three Men in a Plane. C. Winchester
Three Men Murdered. A. A. Archer
Three Men—One Love. Carter Brown
Three Men Out. R. Stout
$3 Million Turn-Over. Richard Curtis
Three Millions! W. T. Adams
Three Minus Two. D. MacKenzie
Three Minutes to Midnight. Mildred Davis
Three Motives for Murder. R. Winsor
Three Must Die! D. Gregory
Three Mysteries. T. Douglas
Three Names for Murder. H. R. Campbell
Three Nights. E. Hostovsky
Three Oak Mystery. E. Wallace
Three O'Clock Handicap. Anonymous
Three of a Kind. J. M. Cain
Three of a Kind. R. Ingalls
Three of a Kind, and The Haunting of Jack Burnham. H. C. McNeile
Three of Clubs. V. Williams
Three of Diamonds. K. M. Knight
Three of Hearts. J. M. Cain
Three on the Road. S. Ryder
Three One-Act Plays. H. M. Harwood
Three Pairs of Heels. Neil Bell
Three People's Secret. G. M. Fenn
Three-Pipe Problem. J. Symons
Three Plays. J. Ashbery
Three Plays. E. De Filippo
Three Plays. J. Mortimer
Three Plots for Asey Mayo. P. A. Taylor
Three Point Murder. R. C. Finney
Three Porges Parodies and a Pastiche. A. Porges
Three Potato, Four. W. Greatorex
Three Prize Plays. N. Holland
Three Problems for Solar Pons. A. Derleth

3 Professional Ladies. G. F. Newman
Thre Quick and Five Dead. G. Mitchell
Three Racketeers. A. Giancol
Three Rainbows. K. Hewitt
Three Recruits, and the Girls They Left Behind Them. J. Hatton
Three Roads. K. Millar
Three Roads to a Star. D. Garth
"Three Rounds Rapid—." R. Hardinge
Three Rousing Cheers for the Rollo Boys. C. Ford
Three R's. Ganpat
Three Saw the Murder. H. L. Blair
Three Sentinels. G. Household
Three, Seven, Ace. V. Tendriakov
3-7-9 Murder. G. Morton
Three Sevens. P. P. Sheehan
Three Sheets in the Wind. G. Gilpatric
Three Short Biers. J. Starr
Three Short Men. F. Vivian
Three Shots. O. Gray
Three Silent Men. E. P. Thorne
Three Silver Birches. R. M. Sears
Three Sisters Flew Home. M. Fitt
Three Sisters in Black. N. Zierold
Three Sisters of No End House. M. Farnsworth
Three Slips to a Noose. Fiona Sinclair
Three Spaniards. George Walker
Three Spies for Glory. M. McKenna
Three Steps to Hell. V. Warren
Three Steps to Murder. N. MacKenzie
Three Stories. R. Rendell
Three Strangers. M. Dalman
Three Strangers. G. Joseph
Three Strangers. Alex Morrison
Three Straw Men. A. Derleth
Three Strings. N. S. Lincoln
Three Sundays to Live. Roland Daniel
Three Taps. R. A. Knox
Three Taps at Twelve. A. Saunders
Three Taps on a Wall. L. Barbee
Three Thirds of a Ghost. T. Fuller
3-13 Murders. T. B. Black
Three Thousand Dollars. A. K. Green
Three Tiers of Fantasy. N. Berrow
Three-Time Losers. G. Bagby
Three Times a Corpse. K. Robeson
Three Times a Victim. F. L. Wallace
Three Times Dead. M. E. Braddon
Three to Be Read. P. Wylie
Three to Get Ready. H. Ostrum
Three to Make Murder. Victor Patrick
Three-Toed Pussy. W. J. Burley
Three Trails. W. M. Graydon
Three Trials of Manirema. J. J. Veiga
Three Verdicts. F. I. Katzenberger
Three-Way Split. G. Brewer
Three Wayward Girls. F. Warden
Three Went In. N. A. Temple-Ellis
Three Were to Die. F. C. Ticknor
Three Who Died. A. Derleth
Three Who Paid. Donald Stuart
Three Widows. Bernice Carey
Three Wild Men. K. Robeson
Three Wise Guys. D. Runyon
Three with a Bullet. Arthur Lyons
Three—with Blood. A. M. Stein
Three Witnesses. S. Fowler
Three Witnesses. R. Stout
Three Wives. Alex Fraser
Three Women. W. Reyburn
Three Women in Black. H. Reilly
Three Women in the House. E. Thompson
Three Wooden Overcoats. H. Clevely
Three Worlds of Johnny Handsome. J. Godey
Three Yards of Cord. C. Brooks
Three Years After. N. Buntline
Three Years with Thunderbolt. A. Pratt
Threefold Cord. F. Vivian
Threefold Disappearance. Nicholas Carter
Threefold Threat. D. Miall
Threepence to Marble Arch. P. McGuire
Threepersons Hunt. B. Garfield
Three's a Crowd. D. M. Disney

Three's a Shroud. R. S. Prather
Threescore Years. P. Capon
Threshing Floor. J. S. Fletcher
Threshold. S. Coulter
Threshold. Janet Morris
Threshold of Fear. A. J. Rees
Thrice Captive. A. Griffiths
Thrice Judas. F. Grierson
Thrice Past the Post. H. Smart
Thrice Upon a Killing Spree. P. Quinn
Thrifty Abe. Old Sleuth
Thrill. B. Petty
Thrill. Patricia Wallace
Thrill a Minute with Jack Albany. J. Godey
Thrill Hungry. B. Lauren
Thrill Kids. V. Packer
Thrill Kill. B. L. Wilson
Thrill Killers. R. Novak
Thrill Machine. I. Hamilton
Thrill on the Underground. D. Shaw-Taylor
Thriller. Ted Hart
Thriller of the Year. Glyn Jones
Thrilling Adventures of a New York Detective. Anonymous
Thrilling Detective Stories. T. P. MacNaught
Thrilling Mystery. Old Sleuth
Thrilling Stories of the Railway. V. L. Whitechurch
Thrilling—Sweet and Rotten. I. Stuart
Thrilling Tales. M. Hervye
Throbbing Dark. F. Arthur
Throne of Bayonets. K. Fitzgerald
Throne of Peril. C. M. Hincks
Throne of Satan. James Dark
Through a Field Glass. G. F. Underhill
Through a Glass Darkly. Anonymous
Through a Glass Darkly. T. Blakemore
Through a Glass Darkly. V. Gielgud
Through a Glass, Darkly. H. McCloy
Through a Glass Darkly. E. Phillpotts
Through a Glass Darkly. B. Symons
Through a Glass Darkly. C. S. Wallbridge
Through an Indian Mirror. Gilbert Campbell
Through Another Gate. R. Bridges
Through Another Gate. G. Vaizey
Through Deep Waters. B. Walsh
Through Devil's Gate. D. P. Neeley
Through Fire and Water. R. C. Armour
Through Flame to Fortune. T. S. King
Through Folly's Mill. A. Askew
Through One Man's Sin. H. Orton
Through Race Glasses. F. E. Vincent
Through the Bamboo Curtain. M. Urquhart
Through the Cellar Wall. Nicholas Carter
Through the Dark and Hairy Wood. S. Herron
Through the Eye of the Needle. H. Clement
Through the Eyes of a Pig. J. Humphries
Through the Eyes of Evil. A. Blair
Through the Eyes of the Dead. M. C. Michaels
Through the Eyes of the Judge. B. Graeme
Through the Flames. D. Stein
Through the Lens. M. Massey
Through the Night. F. Ryerson
Through the Valley of Death. E. M. A. Allison
Through the Wall. C. Moffett
Through the Wall. K. Sully
Through the Wall. P. Wentworth
Through Trackless Tibet. S. Drew
Through Unknown Africa. C. Hayter
Through War to Peace. Benjamin F. Mason
Throw. A. Bloomfield
Throw Back the Little Ones. P. Colombo
Throwaway Man. P. Jarrett
Thug Executive. J. N. Chance
Thugs and Bottles. San Antonio
Thumb-Mark. Warren Hill
Thumb Stroke. F. Du Boisgobey
Thunder Above. A. J. Wallis
Thunder Ahead. Malcolm Campbell
Thunder and Lightning Man. C. Cooper
Thunder at Dawn. Alan Evans
Thunder at Dawn. H. Gibbs
Thunder at Dawn. J. Hoffenberg
Thunder at Noon. Harry Patterson
Thunder Below. H. R. Oldham

Thunder Castle. V. Smith
Thunder Dragon Gate. T. Mundy
Thunder Heights. P. A. Whitney
Thunder in Europe. J. Creasey
Thunder in the Air. L. Barbee
Thunder in the Kirk. A. Marlowe
Thunder Island. J. Hunter
Thunder Island. L. Johns
Thunder Island. G. Volk
Thunder-Maker. J. Creasey
Thunder of Crude. B. Callison
Thunder on the Roses. M. Peyrou
Thunder on Sunday. Karen Campbell
Thunder on the Right. Mary Stewart
Thunder Over South Parish. A. J. Allen
Thunder Over the Reefs. P. Minton
Thunder Rise. G. W. Miller
Thunder Rock. Anita Allen
Thunder Station. D. N. Norman
Thunderball. I. Fleming
Thunderbird. D. Garth
Thunderbird Range. W. C. Tuttle
Thunderbolt. J. M. Macdonald
Thunderbolt. J. G. Sarasin
Thunderbolt and Lightfoot. J. Millard
Thunderbolt Collects. J. McCulley
Thunderbolt's Jest. J. McCulley
Thunderclap. Jack Sheridan
Thunderstrike in Syria. Nick Carter
Thurb Revolution. A. Panshin
Thurman Lucas. H. E. Read
Thursday at Dawn. W. J. Luddecke
Thursday at Noon. W. F. Brown
Thursday Island. M. Keck
Thursday the Rabbi Walked Out. H. Kemelman
Thursday Turkey Murders. J. McGreevey
Thursday Turkey Murders. C. Rice
Thursday Woman. M. Davidson
Thursday's Blade. F. C. Davis
Thursday's Folly. J. Philips
Thurtell's Crime: The Story of a Strange Tragedy. D. Donovan
Thus Far. J. C. Snaith
Thus My Orient. H. Banner
Thus Was Adonis Murdered. S. Caudwell
Thy Arm Alone. J. Slate
Thy First Begotten. Neil Bell
Thy Guilt Is Great. C. I. D. Smith
Thy Sting, Oh Death. J. K. Drummond
Tiara. Anthony Mann
Tiberius Smith. H. Pendexter
Tibesti Assignment. D. J. Williams
Tic-Tac. D. Learmonth
Tick of Death. P. Lovesey
Tick of the Clock. H. Asbury
Tick...Tick...Tick. P. Rock
Tickencote Treasure. W. LeQueux
Ticker-Tape Murder. M. Propper
Ticket. C. Stratton
Ticket for Death. E. M. Bowen
Ticket of Leave. G. Simenon
Ticket-of-Leave Girl. A. M. Meadows
Ticket-of-Leave Man. C. H. Bullivant
Ticket-of-Leave Man. Tom Taylor
Ticket-of-Leave Man. H. C. Williams
Ticket San Diego. A. Bocca
Ticket to Buffalo. A. Dean
Ticket to Eternity. G. Shayne
Ticket to Hell. H. Whittington
Ticket to Nowhere. P. Rosemoor
Ticket to Oblivion. Robert Parker
Ticket to Ride. Ritchie Perry
Ticket to Ride. D. Potter
Ticket to the Boneyard. L. Block
Tickets for Death. B. Halliday
Ticking Clock. F. Lockridge
Ticking Heart. D. B. Olsen
Ticking Terror Murders. D. L. Teilhet
Tickled to Death. S. Brett
Tickletoby. H. Wayne
Tidal Race. G. Foy
Tidal Wave. G. Simenon
Tide Can't Wait. L. Trimble
Tide of Death. J. M. Hickman

Tide of Fortune. M. Gerard
Tide Race. H. Gilbert
Tide Rip. Robin Temple
Tide Waits for No Man. H. La Garde
Tide Watchers. S. M. Parkman
Tideless Sea. G. Volk
Tidemill. D. Daniels
Tides. P. Shelby
Tides of Sligo. L. G. Shreve
Tides of Tremannion. K. A. Shoesmith
Tides of War. D. Muir
Tideway. J. Ayscough
Tidewrack. N. Tranter
Tidings of Joy. G. Goodchild
Tidy Bit of Brass. P. M. Learoyd
Tidy Death. N. Lombard
Tie and Trick. H. Smart
Tie-Breaker. I. Nastase
Tiebreaker. J. Bickham
Tied for Murder. C. Fitzsimmons
Tied Up in Tinsel. N. Marsh
Ties of Blood. G. Slovo
Tiffany Caper. J. Purtell
Tiger Among Us. L. Brackett
Tiger at Bay. B. Picton
Tiger by the Tail. J. H. Chase
Tiger by the Tail. L. Goldman
Tiger Claws. F. Packard
Tiger Dawn. S. Jepson
Tiger from the Shadows. Bradshaw Jones
Tiger Game. W. E. Knight
Tiger-Heart. J. G. Sarasin
Tiger Hill. Ardath Wise
Tiger House. R. St. Clair
Tiger in Red Weather. J. Wyllie
Tiger in the Bed. M. Catto
Tiger in the Night. R. Kyle
Tiger in the Night. J. M. Walsh
Tiger in the North. S. Harvester
Tiger in the Smoke. M. Allingham
Tiger in the Streets. L. Malley
Tiger Kittens. A. Zuckerman
Tiger, Life. S. Gainham
Tiger Lily. G. Dilnot
Tiger Lily. C. Emery
Tiger Lily. G. M. Fenn
Tiger Lily. M. Risco
Tiger Lily. C. N. Williamson
Tiger Mark. P. Graham
Tiger Milk. D. Garth
Tiger of Baragunga. J. I. Emery
Tiger of Canton. G. H. Teed
Tiger of Cloud River. R. Cullum
Tiger of Karan. D. Lenton
Tiger of Mayfair. H. Holt
Tiger of Paris. Anonymous
Tiger on My Back. Gordons
Tiger Reef. M. Hastings
Tiger River. A. O. Friel
Tiger Rose. W. Mack
Tiger Snake. H. S. Keeler
Tiger Sniffs the Rose. H. G. Carlisle
Tiger Standish. S. Horler
Tiger Standish Comes Back. S. Horler
Tiger Standish Does His Stuff. S. Horler
Tiger Standish Has a Party. S. Horler
Tiger Standish Steps on It. S. Horler
Tiger Standish Takes the Field. S. Horler
Tiger Street. E. Trevor
Tiger Strikes Again. C. M. Wills
Tiger Ten. W. D. Blankenship
Tiger, Tiger. A. Bestor
Tiger, Tiger. G. Goodchild
Tiger Tiger. Frank Ryan
Tiger Tooth. E. Woodward
Tiger War. D. Pendleton
Tigerman of Terrahpur. E. Lecale
Tigers Are Hungry. C. Early
Tiger's Back. J. W. Mason
Tiger's Claw. W. Braun
Tiger's Claw. Lewis Orde
Tiger's Claw. A. P. Terhune
Tiger's Claws. Colin Robertson
Tiger's Coat. E. Dejeans

Tiger's Cub. E. Phillpotts
Tiger's Cub. G. Seton
Tigers Fight Alone. F. Duncan
Tigers Have Claws. B. Graeme
Tiger's Head Mystery. E. T. Sawyer
Tiger's Heart. Lewis Orde
Tiger's Millions. Anonymous
Tiger's Necklace. R. St. Clair
Tigers of Deceit. M. Hartmann
Tigers of Justice. G. Wilson
Tigers of Subtopia. J. Symons
Tigers on Tuesday. C. Rank
Tiger's Wife. Wade Miller
Tight Case. E. J. Hogan
Tight Circle. J. F. Straker
Tight Corner. B. Copper
Tight Corner. A. W. Marchmont
Tight Corner. Sam Ross
Tight Grip. R. Dudgeon
Tight Lines. Bill Walsh
Tight Rope. A. L. Burks
Tight Squeeze. R. Enders
Tight Squeeze. W. Fuller
Tightening String. A. Bridge
Tightening the Coils. Old Spicer
Tightrope. James Grant
Tightrope. J. Legaret
Tightrope. L. Marcus
Tightrope. A. Melville-Ross
Tightrope. D. Pendleton
Tightrope. Teri White
Tightrope for Three. M. Babson
Tightrope Men. D. Bagley
Tightrope Minor. T. Topor
Tightrope Walker. D. Gilman
Tigress. J. Bogar
Tigress. Carter Brown
Tigress. M. Derby
Tigress. H. Janson
Tigress Bites. N. Karta
Tigress of Brazil. B. Sarto
Tigress of the Evening. Anne-Mariel
Tijuana Bible. R. Goulart
Tijuana Traffic. Don Scott
'Til Death. E. McBain
'Til Death Do Us Part. A. Hynd
'Til Death You Do Pay. M. Davidson
Tiled House Mystery. W. M. Duncan
Till Death Do Us Part. J. D. Carr
Till Death Do Us Part. L. Trimble
Till Doomsday. Robin Temple
Till It Hurts. N. Quarry
Till Life Us Do Part. E. Petersen
Till Murder Do Us Part. W. H. L. Crauford
Till Proven Guilty. H. Simart
Till the Clock Stops. J. J. Bell
Till the Dying Day. A. Watkins
Tiller and Tideway. W. E. Alais
Tillinger Codicil. T. Beattie
Tilsit Inheritance. C. Gaskin
Tilted Moon. B. Perowne
Tim Frazer Again. F. Durbridge
Tim Frazer Gets the Message. F. Durbridge
Timbalier. C. W. Coleman
Timber and Top Dressing. A. Manning
Timber Beasts. C. Stoddard
Timber Line. W. E. Murphy
Timber Sahib. Robert Harding
Timber Wolf. J. Templeton
Timberjack. D. Cushman
Timbuktu. David Smith
Time After Time. K. Alexander
Time After Time. A. Appel
Time After Time. J. Mattera
Time and the Torture. N. Sligh
Time at Tarragon. J. Tattersall
Time and the Place. S. Yorke
Time and Time Again. B. M. Gill
Time Bargains. T. W. Speight
Time Before Genesis. L. Dawson
Time Before This. N. Monsarrat
Time Bomb. J. D. Atwater
Time Bomb. J. N. Chance
Time Bomb. H. Howard

Time Bomb. J. Kellerman
Time Bomb. W. Tucker
Time Bomb. Gar Wilson
Time Clock of Death. Nick Carter
Time Dissolver. J. Sohl
Time Enough to Die. P. Rabe
Time Exposure. J. Lutz
Time for a Murder. G. Coverack
Time for Caution. P. Cheyney
Time for Crime. P. C. Williams
Time for Dying. Jonathan Ross
Time for Frankie Coolin. B. Griffith
Time for Heroes. W. Bryant
Time for Killing. J. Rowland
Time for Legends. N. Beishir
Time for Murder. J. Kirton
Time for Murder. P. O. McGuire
Time for Murder. H. P. Martin
Time for Murder. R. O. Saber
Time for Murder. J. Stagg
Time for Passion. H. Rigsby
Time for Payment. H. H. Kirst
Time for Pirates. G. Black
Time for Scandal. H. H. Kirst
Time for Sherlock Holmes. D. Dvorkin
Time for Survival. P. McCutchan
Time for Tea. J. Coates
Time for Tempting. D. Haring
Time for Treason. P. Deane
Time for Treason. O. Hesky
Time for Truth. H. H. Kirst
Time for Vengeance. G. Osborne
Time for Violence. A. Goddard
Time Has a Door. O. Kensch
Time in the End. F. M. McGuire
Time Is an Ambush. F. Clifford
Time Is an Enemy. S. J. Baker
Time Limit. H. Denker
Time Limit. R. Sheckley
Time Lock. C. E. Walk
Time, Murderer, Please. C. Dyer
Time of Assassins. R. Batchelor
Time of Day. F. Durbridge
Time of Dreaming. J. Edgar
Time of Fine Weather. J. S. Scott
Time of Hope. Susan Kelly
Time of Illusion. R. Roleine
Time of Killing. W. Hardy
Time of Madness. R. Early
Time of Night. R. Swazee
Time of Predators. J. Gores
Time of Reckoning. P. Audemars
Time of Reckoning. W. Wager
Time of Terror. H. Pentecost
Time of Terror. L. White
Time of the Burning Mask. D. Rowan
Time of the Crime. Donald Stuart
Time of the Fire. M. Brandel
Time of the Hunter's Moon. V. Holt
Time of the Wolf. J. S. Jones
Time Off for Death. G. Braddon
Time Off for Murder. Z. Popkin
Time Out. D. Ely
Time Out for Murder. A. F. Marston
Time Out of Mind. J. R. Maxim
Time Puddles. G. P. Williams
Time Remembered, Time Lost. Rona Randall
Time Right Deadly. S. Gainham
Time Running Out. K. Booton
Time Running Out. R. Crane
Time Runs Out at the Democratic Convention. S. Fawcette
Time Terror. K. Robeson
Time Thief. P. Valdez
Time to Betray. D. Boggis
Time to Change Hats. M. Bennett
Time to Die. George Douglas
Time to Die. L. Johns
Time to Die. Hilda Lawrence
Time to Die. Frederick Nolan
Time to Embrace. Lili Palmer
Time to Hate. S. Truss
Time to Kill. C. Barling
Time to Kill. Alec Brown

Title Index

Time to Kill. A. Capelli
Time to Kill. L. Darbon
Time to Kill. R. Fleigel
Time to Kill. J. Grisham
Time to Kill. G. Household
Time to Kill. M. Lynch
Time to Kill. M. S. Michel
Time to Kill. Diana Morgan
Time to Kill. R. Ormerod
Time to Kill. D. Pendleton
Time to Kill. W. Reed
Time to Kill. Colin Robertson
Time to Kill. T. Spain
Time to Kill. J. M. Walsh
Time to Kill. G. Ward
Time to Kill. J. Weeks
Time to Kill . . . A Time to Die. J. Pearl
Time to Murder and Create. Lawrence Block
Time to Prey. F. Kane
Time to Prey. F. Keinzley
Time to Reap. M. T. Hinkemeyer
Time to Remember. S. Shapiro
Time to Retreat. Brian Cooper
Time to Run. S. Waldron
Time to Time. D. Pendleton
Time Too Soon. E. Lindall
Time-Torn Man. W. Hosegood
Time Trap Gambit. L. Maddock
Time Trial. W. B. Murphy
Time Without Shadows. T. Allbeury
Time-Worn Town. J. S. Fletcher
Timeless Serpent. Roger Fuller
Timeless Sleep. R. C. Galwey
Timelock. D. Cory
Times Have Changed. E. H. Davis
Time's Hour Glass. A. E. Carey
Time's Revenges. D. C. Murray
Times Square Connection. F. Scarpetta
Time's Witness. M. Malone
Timetable. A. Elon
Timetable for the General. B. Frizell
Timetable Murder. R. Denbie
Timid Tycoon. R. C. Frazer
Timor Mortis. W. Harriss
Timothy Files. Lawrence Sanders
Timothy Tealeaf, Business Investigator. W. W. Hill
Timothy Twill's Secret. F. J. Proctor
Timothy's Game. Lawrence Sanders
Tin Angel. P. Pines
Tin Bath Murder. M. G. Hubi
Tin Cop. F. C. Clinton
Tin Cowrie Dass. H. M. Rideout
Tin Cravat. J. D. Hunter
Tin Ear. A. J. Collins
Tin God of Twisted River. W. C. Tuttle
Tin Hats. F. MacIsaac
Tin Soldier. E. Cannon
Tin Tree. J. Quince
Tin Trumpets at Dawn. J. Appleby
Tincture of Death. Ray Harrison
Tincture of Murder. Sutherland Scott
Tinker, Tailor, Soldier, Spy . . . J. Le Carre
Tinker's Curse. J. Heys
Tinker's Kitchen. A. R. L. Gardner
Tinker's Lone Hand. A. Murray
Tinker's Pride. N. Tranter
Tinker's Schooldays. C. Hayter
Tinkletop's Crime and other tales. G. R. Sims
Tinkling Symbol. P. A. Taylor
Tinman. T. Gallon
Tinplate. N. Steed
Tinseltown Murders. J. Blumenthal
Tinsley's Bones. P. Wilde
Tinted Vapours. J. M. Cobban
Tiny Carteret. H. C. McNeile
Tiny Diamond. C. M. Russell
Tip and Run. W. Tait
Tip Off. A. W. Sherring
Tip on a Dead Crab. W. Murray
Tip on a Dead Jockey. Irwin Shaw
Tipster. Roland Daniel
Tipster. G. Verner
Tiptoe Boys. J. Follett
Tiptoe Thro' a Graveyard. M. Storme

Tirana Assignment. C. Portway
Tired Spy. D. Stone
Tis the Season to Be Dying. J. K. Drummond
Tish. M. R. Rinehart
Tish Marches On. M. R. Rinehart
Tish Plays the Game. M. R. Rinehart
Tisket, a Casket. J. L. Linklater
Titan Game. N. Busch
Titanic. T. Aspler
Titanic Hotel Mystery. J. Hawk
Titan's Duel. D. Streib
Tithe War Mystery. G. Chester
Title Is Murder. H. L. Nelson
Titled Counterfeiter. Anonymous
Titled Counterfeiter. Nicholas Carter
Titron Madness. J. Bedford
Titty's Dead. P. Hobson
To a Blindfold Lady. J. Purtell
To an Easy Grave. Alexander Law
To Any Lengths. G. Simenon
To Be a Hero. J. McCague
To Be Hanged. B. Hamilton
To Bed at Noon. V. Gielgud
To Bed at Noon. J. Shearing
To Borrow Trouble. M. Borgenicht
To Burgundy and Back. D. M. Low
To Cache a Millionaire. M. Scherf
To Call Her Mine. W. Besant
To Catch a Crooked Girl. P. W. Fairman
To Catch a Forger. Robert Wallace
To Catch a King. H. Patterson
To Catch a Rainbow. E. Thompson
To Catch a Rat. W. Harris
To Catch a Shadow. Bradshaw Jones
To Catch a Spy. A. A. Randall
To Catch a Spy. B. Sanders
To Catch a Spy. C. Scott
To Catch a Thief. M. Burton
To Catch a Thief. D. Dodge
To Catch a Thief. Daphne Sanders
To Catch a Thief. L. Thayer
To Catch a Viper. J. Wyllie
To Cease Upon the Midnight. A. Hocking
To Comfort the Signora. E. G. Cousins
To Court Danger. C. Virmonne
To Defeat the Ends of Justice. H. Compton
To Die a Little. C. Carfax
To Die a Little. H. Jobson
To Die Elsewhere. T. Wilden
To Die for a Golden Leaf. R. P. Hilldrup
To Die in Beverly Hills. G. Petievich
To Die in California. N. Thornburg
To Die or Not to Die. H. Kane
To Dream of Evil. L. Hoffman
To Dusty Death. H. McCutcheon
To Dwell in Shadows. N. G. Smith
To Each His Own. L. Sciascia
To Effect an Arrest. H. Steele
To Fear a Painted Devil. R. Rendell
To Find a Killer. L. White
To Guard the Right. H. Zachary
To Hang a Witch. P. Wissmann
To Have and to Have Not. E. Hemingway
To Have and to Hold. Macdonald Newton
To Have and to Hold. M. Richmond
To Have and to Kill. Robert Martin
To Hell for Half-a-Crown. J. Cross
To Hell in a Basket. I. R. Blacker
To Hell on Skates. S. Finnegan
To Hell Together. H. V. Dixon
To Hell with Hedda! C. Brahms
To Hell with the Law. E. Martin
To Hide a Rogue. T. Walsh
To Hinder Their Coming. C. Drummond
To His Just Deserts. O. Low
To Keep or Kill. W. Tucker
To Kill a Call Girl. P. A. Foxall
To Kill a Cat. W. J. Burley
To Kill a Cat. R. Pertwee
To Kill a Coconut. P. Moyes
To Kill a Cop. R. Daley
To Kill a Corpse. E. Ascher
To Kill a Dead Man. C. W. Runyon
To Kill a Hero. John Morgan

To Kill a House. S. Roberts
To Kill a Jogger. J. Messmann
To Kill a Judge. G. Ogan
To Kill a Killer. K. Hunt
To Kill a King. R. Cutler
To Kill a Mockingbird. H. Lee
To Kill a Mockingbird. C. Sergel
To Kill a Snowman. C. Miron
To Kill a Witch. Alice Brennan
To Kill a Witch. B. Knox
To Kill Again. R. Stout
To Kill or Be Killed. D. Linton
To Kill or Die. J. York
To Kill or to Die. J. York
To Kill the Pope. K. Wlaschin
To Kill the Potemkin. Mark Joseph
To Killashea. N. Flood
To Kiss, or Kill. D. Keene
To Know Is to Die. C. H. Guenter
To Let. B. M. Croker
To Let, Furnished. Josephine Bell
To Live and Die in Dixie. T. Roscoe
To Live and Die in L.A. G. Petievich
To Live Forever. J. Vance
To Live in Danger. B. Magee
To Love a Dark Stranger. V. Coffman
To Love a Stranger. J. Howell
To Love a Stranger. L. A. Olmsted
To Love a Stranger. B. Paul
To Love Again. A. Furness
To Love Again. D. Noel
To Love and Be Wise. J. Tey
To Love and to Perish. E. Dudley
To Love and Yet to Die. S. D. Frances
To Make a Killing. J. Thomson
To Make You Mine. M. Richmond
To Make an Underworld. Joan Fleming
To Market, to Market. A. Richards
To Meet Mr. Stanley. Dorothy Johnson
To Meet the Law. F. A. M. Webster
To Mourn a Mischief. A. Quinton
To Nick a Good Body. Barry Norman
To Play the Devil. Angus Hall
To Play the Fox. M. S. Craig
To Protect the Guilty. J. Ashford
To Prove a Villian. G. M. Townsend
To Ravish Rani. N. McGuyer
To Reach a Dream. N. C. Heard
To Ride a Tiger. M. H. Cooper
To Ripen or to Kill. Marjorie Robertson
To Run a Little Faster. J. Gardner
To Save His Life. K. Roos
To See a Stranger. M. Lynn
To Seek Where Shadows Are. M. Benedict
To Set Her Free. G. M. Robins
To Settle for Murder. S. Ready
To Shadow Our Love. L. Ames
To Slay the Dreamer. A. Cordell
To Sleep No More. R. Angel
To Sleep, Perchance to Kill. L. V. Sims
To Sleep, to Die. R. Claremont
To Speak for the Dead. P. Levine
To Spite Her Face. H. Dolson
To Stalk a Killer. C. Gayet
To Study a Long Silence. V. C. Clinton-Baddeley
To the Adventurous. E. Nesbit
To the Bitter End. M. E. Braddon
To the Bitter End. J. M. Simmel
To the Castle. Janice Bennett
To the Castle. D. Malm
To the Dark Tower. M. S. Gross
To the Dark Tower. Francis King
To the Dark Tower. L. B. Long
To the Dark Tower Came. K. O. Jones
To the Death. R. Merritt
To the Devil—a Daughter. D. Wheatley
To the Eagle's Nest. J. Di Mona
To the Ends of the Earth. Nicholas Carter
To the Gallows I Must Go. T. S. Matthews
To the Honor of the Fleet. R. H. Pilpel
To the Minute and Scarlet and Black. A. K. Green
To the Seventh Power. F. Picano
To the Tombaugh Station. W. Tucker
To the Tune of Murder. H. M. Ballard

To This End. B. Malim
To This Favour. S. Gilruth
To Venus in Five Seconds. F. T. Jane
To Wake the Dead. J. D. Carr
To Walk the Night. J. Land
To Walk the Night. J. Mangione
To Walk the Night. W. Sloan
To Wed a Stranger. C. Virmonne
To Welcome the King and other stories. W. Matchell
To What Dread End. M. V. Heberden
To What Red Hell. P. Robinson
To Win and to Lose. K. Netzen
To Win the Love He Sought. E. P. Oppenheim
To Windward. H. C. Rowland
Toady. Mark Morris
Toast Is Death! F. W. Gumley
Toast to a Corpse. David Hume
Toast to Cousin Julian. Estelle Thompson
Toast to Tomorrow. M. Coles
Toasted Blonde. C. Reeve
Tobacco Auction Murders. Robert Turner
Tobey's First Case. C. L. Burnham
Toby Jug Murders. H. A. Wrenn
Toby Scuffell. P. Capon
Toby Shed. Taffrail
Toby's Folly. M. Arnold
Tocsin. A. Askew
Tod McAlpin. A. C. Wylie
Today and Forever. P. S. Buck
Todd Dossier. C. Young
Todmanhawe Grange. J. S. Fletcher
Toff. J. Creasey
Toff Among the Millions. J. Creasey
Toff and Old Harry. J. Creasey
Toff and the Crooked Copper. J. Creasey
Toff and the Curate. J. Creasey
Toff and the Dead Man's Finger. W. V. Butler
Toff and the Deadly Parson. J. Creasey
Toff and the Deep Blue Sea. J. Creasey
Toff and the Fallen Angels. J. Creasey
Toff and the Golden Boy. J. Creasey
Toff and the Great Illusion. J. Creasey
Toff and the Kidnapped Child. J. Creasey
Toff and the Lady. J. Creasey
Toff and the Runaway Bride. J. Creasey
Toff and the Sleepy Cowboy. J. Creasey
Toff and the Spider. J. Creasey
Toff and the Stolen Tresses. J. Creasey
Toff and the Teds. J. Creasey
Toff and the Terrified Tax Man. J. Creasey
Toff and the Toughs. J. Creasey
Toff and the Trip-Trip-Triplets. J. Creasey
Toff at Butlin's. J. Creasey
Toff at the Fair. J. Creasey
Toff Breaks In. J. Creasey
Toff Down Under. J. Creasey
Toff Goes Gay. J. Creasey
Toff Goes On. J. Creasey
Toff Goes to Market. J. Creasey
Toff in New York. J. Creasey
Toff in Town. J. Creasey
Toff in Wax. J. Creasey
Toff Is Back. J. Creasey
Toff on Board. J. Creasey
Toff on Fire. J. Creasey
Toff on Ice. J. Creasey
Toff on the Farm. J. Creasey
Toff on the Trail. J. Creasey
Toff Proceeds. J. Creasey
Toff Steps Out. J. Creasey
Toff Takes Shares. J. Creasey
Together Brothers. Jim Robinson
Togo Commando. H. Arvay
Toilers of Babylon. B. L. Farjeon
Toilers of the Thams. B. Hemyng
Toils of Silence. H. S. Cooper
Token. L. Tracy
Token. G. Verner
Token of Evil. E. Grayson
Tokyo Doll. J. McPartland
Tokyo Escapade. S. Walker
Tokyo Intrigue. W. Bender
Tokyo Purple. L. Derrick

Told at Monte Carlo. A. M. Williamson
Told at the Plume. E. Phillpotts
Told by the Colonel. W. L. Alden
Told by the Taffrail. Sundowner
Told by Twilight. Douglas Stewart
Told in New England and other stories. M. C. Hay
Told in Silence. J. Storry
Told in "Tatt's". N. Gubbins
Told in the East. T. Mundy
Told in the Marketplace. F. B. Austin
Told in the Rockies. A. M. Barbour
Told in the Twilight. I. R. Allen
Told in the Twilight. H. Wood
Told in the Verandah. Anonymous
Told to the Marines. W. L. Clowes
Toledano. George Davis
Toledo Dagger. R. Brennan
Toledo Sword. M. L. Tyrrell
Toll. M. L. Fowler
Toll Call. S. Greenleaf
Toll for the Brave. Harry Patterson
Toll-Gate. G. Heyer
Toll-House Murder. A. Wynne
Toll the Bell for Murder. G. Bellairs
Tolliver Case. R. A. J. Walling
Toltec. W. Heffernan
Toltec Cup. Anonymous
Tom and Jerry. Anonymous
Tom and Jerry. T. Pastor
Tom Brown's Body. G. Mitchell
Tom Chester's Sweetheart. J. Hatton
Tom Dawson. F. Warden
Tom Flaherty's Ghost. John Shore
Tom Fox. Anonymous
Tom Gerrard. L. Becke
Tom Harris. S. Themerson
Tom Ossington's Ghost. R. Marsh
Tom Rocket. A. Fonblanque
Tom Sawyer, Detective, and other stories. M. Twain
Tom, the Young Explorer. Old Sleuth
Tom Tiddler's Island. J. J. Connington
Tomb for Mr. Lee. R. Wilkes-Hunter
Tomb of Aurora. Anonymous
Tomb of Horror. E. Ellison
Tomb of the Twelfth Iman. R. Bulliet
Tomb of T'Sin. E. Wallace
Tomb Seven. G. Snyder
Tomb with a View. N. Robbins
Tomb with a View. L. Sieveking
Tomboy. H. Ellson
Tombs of Blue Ice. R. Faust
Tombstone Cipher. I. Melchior
Tombstone for a Troubleshooter. W. C. MacDonald
Tombstone Treasure. F. Hume
Tombstones Are Free to Quitters. B. Sarto
Tommy Weston, Adventuress. W. Sheridan
Tomorrow a Stranger. E. M. Williams
Tomorrow and Yesterday. N. Sligh
Tomorrow Country. Jack Wilson
Tomorrow File. Lawrence Sanders
Tomorrow for the Roses. L. Grayson
Tomorrow I Die. J. Spillane
Tomorrow in Katmandu. Nan Hamilton
Tomorrow Is Murder. Carter Brown
Tomorrow Is Too Late. J. Hayes
Tomorrow Lies in Ambush. Bob Shaw
Tomorrow Plus X. W. Tucker
Tomorrow—the Chair. R. Angel
Tomorrow Trap. M. Borgenicht
Tomorrow We Die. K. Lindsay
Tomorrow We'll Be Sober. M. Cranston
Tomorrow Will Be Monday. M. Marlette
Tomorrow's Another Day. W. R. Burnett
Tomorrow's Crimes. D. E. Westlake
Tomorrow's Ghost. A. Price
Tomorrow's Harvest. M. Richmond
Tomorrow's Horizon. G. E. Meagher
Tomorrow's Men. M. Shea
Tomorrow's Silence. N. Goller
Tomorrow's Spectacles. W. J. Elliott
Tomorrow's Treason. P. Harcourt
Tomorrow's Vengeance. Stuart Ready
Tomorrow's Yesterday. B. Graeme
Tondeau of Chartres. G. Petrie

Tondo for Short. P. Inchbald
Tong. Bok
Tong Men and a Million. E. Kinsburn
Tongking! D. Cushman
Tongue of Treason. R. Crane
Tongue Pie. P. Belloc
Tongue-Tied Canary. N. Bentley
Tongues of Fire. P. Abrahams
Toni Diamonds. G. Latta
Tonight and Tomorrow. Michael Barrett
Tonight Is for Death. Gavin Holt
Tonight They Die to Mendelssohn. F. Gordon
Tontine Bell. E. Kyle
Tontine Treasure. H. M. Webster
Tony Rome. A. Rome
Tony, the Bootblack. O. Harper
Too Bad for Susie. B. Sarto
Too Beautiful to Die. M. Carroll
Too Black for Heaven. D. Keene
Too Busy to Die. H. W. Roden
Too Clever by Half. R. Jeffries
Too Clever by Half. L. Meynell
Too Close for Comfort. M. Carr
Too Close to the Edge. Susan Dunlap
Too Curious. E. J. Goodman
Too Dangerous to Be Free. J. H. Chase
Too Dangerous to Live. David Hume
Too Dead to Run. J. Manor
Too Dead to Talk. A. E. Jones
Too Deep Then. David Stone
Too Fast We Live. R. Glendinning
Too French and Too Deadly. H. Kane
Too Friendly, Too Dead. B. Halliday
Too Good for the Poor. N. Karta
Too Good to Be True. M. Halliday
Too Good to Be True. J. F. Hutton
Too Hard to Handle. D. Nabarro
Too High a Price. D. Haring
Too Hot for Hawaii. T. B. Dewey
Too Hot for Hell. K. Vining
Too Hot to Handle. I. Fleming
Too Hot to Handle. N. Johnson
Too Hot to Handle. D. Keene
Too Hot to Handle. S. Markham
Too Hot to Handle. F. G. Presnell
Too Hot to Handle. S. Sterling
Too Hot to Hold. D. Keene
Too Hot to Kill. S. Sterling
Too Innocent to Kill. D. M. Disney
Too Late. S. Dixon
Too Late for Death. D. Linton
Too Late for Mourning. R. Foster
Too Late for Tears. H. Carmichael
Too Late for Tears. P. Henneker
Too Late for Tears. R. Huggins
Too Late for Tears. K. Schneider
Too Late for the Funeral. R. Ormerod
Too Late to Be Good. Craig Jones
Too Late to Die. B. Crider
Too Late to Mend. T. Rainham
Too Late to Shout. R. Drayton
Too Late to Talk. Nicholas Carter
Too Late to Tell. J. Jenkins
Too Late to Weep. Rex Richards
Too Late! Too Late! The Maiden Cried. Joan Fleming
Too Like the Dead. D. Chambers
Too Like the Lightning. D. Chambers
Too Lively to Live. A. Damer
Too Long Endured. L. Thayer
Too Lovely to Live. R. Fenisong
Too Many Boats. C. L. Clifford
Too Many Bones. R. S. Wallis
Too Many Bottles. E. S. Holding
Too Many Candles. M. Eatock
Too Many Chiefs. S. Marlowe
Too Many Clients. R. Stout
Too Many Clues. C. Henderson
Too Many Cooks. R. Stout
Too Many Cousins. D. G. Browne
Too Many Crooks. R. S. Prather
Too Many Crooks. E. J. Rath
Too Many Crooks. I. Trent
Too Many Crooks Spoil the Caper. F. Norman

Title Index

Too Many Dames Spell Trouble. W. Standish
Too Many Doctors. H. Roth
Too Many Doors. L. Crosby
Too Many Enemies. W. Haggard
Too Many Ghosts. P. Gallico
Too Many Innocents. O. Beeby
Too Many Magicians. Randall Garrett
Too Many Murderers. G. Childerness
Too Many Murderers. G. Compton
Too Many Murderers. M. L. Stokes
Too Many Sinners. S. Stark
Too Many Suspects. J. Rhode
Too Many Women. D. Haring
Too Many Women. M. K. Ozaki
Too Many Women. R. Stout
Too Many Yesterdays. D. Linton
Too Many Yesterdays. K. Rogers
Too Married. A. Applin
Too-Mini Murders. P. Morgan
Too Much Ambition. E. Ellison
Too Much for Mr. Jellipot. S. Fowler
Too Much of Water. B. Hamilton
Too Much Poison. A. Rowe
Too Old a Cat. W. B. Murphy
Too Old to Die. Gretchen Travis
Too Rich to Die. H. V. Dixon
Too Rich to Live. S. Morgan
Too Sane a Murder. L. Martin
Too Scared to Live. K. Schneider
Too Sharp by Half. B. Hemyng
Too Small for His Shoes. L. Payne
Too Smart to Live. R. Callahan
Too Smart to Live. A. Capelli
Too Smart to Live. E. Ellison
Too Solid Flesh. N. O'Donohoe
Too Soon for Daisies. W. Dinner
Too Soon to Die. H. Janson
Too Soon to Die. Henry Wade
Too Strange a Hand. D. Quick
Too Sweet to Die. R. Goulart
Too Tough for a Halo. J. V. Nolan
Too Tough for Death. D. Steel
Too Tough to Die. G. Bruce
Too Tough to Die. R. Gadhart
Too Tough to Die. F. Gruber
Too Tough to Live. Griff
Too-Wise Owl. K. Robeson
Too Young to Die. O. Makoloo
Too Young to Die. R. O. Saber
Too Young to Die. L. White
Tool of the Trade. J. Haldemann
Tooth and Claw. Gabrielle Lord
Tooth and Claw. G. Wilson
Tooth and Nail. Nicholas Carter
Tooth and the Nail. B. S. Ballinger
Tooth Merchant. C. L. Sulzberger
Toothache Tree. J. Galloway
Top Assignment. G. H. Coxe
Top Bloody Secret. S. Hyland
Top Boot. M. Kennedy
Top Dog. Stuart Hall
Top Dog. F. Hume
Top End. S. L. Thompson
Top Floor Back. G. Radcliffe
Top-Floor Killing. W. A. Roberts
Top Knocker. J. F. Mills
Top Landing. P. Brebner
Top Level Death. H. Zachary
Top of the Heap. A. A. Fair
Top Secret. J. Bruce
Top Secret. L. Halliday
Top Secret Affair. V. York
Top Secret Kill. J. P. Cody
Top Secret No. 1. W. Jardine
Top Spot for Danger. R. Bentinck
Top Steal. A. Tack
Top Storey Murder. A. Berkeley
Top Ten. H. Janson
Topaz. L. Uris
Topaz for My Lady Fair. J. J. Toombs
Toper's End. G. D. H. Cole
Topkapi. E. Ambler
Topless Corpse. Mike Warden
Topless Dancer Hangup. P. Morgan

Topless Kitties. S. O'Shea
Topless Tulip Caper. C. Harrison
Toplin. M. McDowell
Topology of a Phantom City. A. Robbe-Grillet
Toppling Terror. B. Luigi
Topsy and Evil. G. Baxt
Torch. T. Biracree
Torch. G. Wright
Torch and other tales. E. Phillpotts
Torch Bearers. B. V. Dryer
Torch for a Dark Journey. L. Shapiro
Torch for a Tramp. D. Haring
Torch Murder. C. R. Jones
Torch of Venus. L. Mortimer
Torch of Violence. D. Forrest
Torhaven Mystery. J. B. Harris-Burland
Torment. H. Janson
Torment for Trixie. H. Janson
Torment Was a Redhead. Richard Williams
Torment Was a Woman. B. Carson
Tormented. D. Daniels
Tormented. F. E. Smith
Tormented. B. Swift
Tormented. C. Weston
Tormenting Memories. E. Robins
Tormenting of Lafayette Jackson. A. Rosenheim
Tormentors. G. Bellairs
Torn Branch. A. W. Upfield
Torn Curtain. R. Wormser
Torn Letter. E. Balmer
Torn-Out Page. Dora Russell
Tornado in Town. K. T. McCall
Toronado. J. T. Osborne
Torquemada Principle. J. Morgulas
Torquemada Puzzle Book. Torquemada
Torrid Affair. T. Vail
Torrid Temptress. H. Janson
Torrington Square Mystery. M. L. Eades
Torry Diamonds Mystery. M. C. Leighton
Tortoiseshell Cat. N. Royde-Smith
Tortuous Trails. H. Footner
Torture Chamber. R. H. Vose
Torture Chamber and other stories. V. Van Der Elst
Torture Contract. F. Scarpetta
Torture Island. L. R. G. Hart
Torture Machine. D. Dayle
Torture Machine. P. Tabori
Torture Trust. B. House
Tortured Angel. D. Garth
Tortured Boy. H. C. Davis
Tortured Heart. E. Southworth
Tortured Love. H. Duval
Tortured Path. K. F. Crossen
Torturer. R. Dade
Torturer. P. Saxon
Torturer's Horse. R. Inman
Torturers of Tet. J. Cain
Torus. J. Follett
Torvick Affair. M. Sariola
Toss of a Coin. Nicholas Carter
Toss of a Penny. Nicholas Carter
Total Eclipse. J. Brunner
Total Recall. Piers Anthony
Total Recall. P. Case
Total Recall. W. B. Murphy
Totem. Blyden Jackson
Totem. D. Morrell
Touch. E. Leonard
Touch a Cold Door. Carey Roberts
Touch a French Pom-Pom. J. P. Carstairs
Touch a Wild Heart. V. Munn
Touch and Go. L. Della
Touch and Go. J. Middlemass
Touch and Go. E. C. Vivian
Touch and Go. P. Wentworth
Touch Me and You'll Never Forget Me. Paul Kelly
Touch Not the Cat. Mary Stewart
Touch of a Vanishing Hand. A. Quogan
Touch of Chill. Joan Aiken
Touch of Danger. F. Durbridge
Touch of Danger. James Jones
Touch of Darkness. J. Crowe
Touch of Death. J. Creasey
Touch of Death. M. Sadler

Touch of Death. C. Williams
Touch of Drama. G. Cullingford
Touch of Evil. L. Colby
Touch of Evil. Arthur MacLean
Touch of Evil. W. Masterson
Touch of Fear. Dorothy Christie
Touch of Fear. J. Ware
Touch of Frost. R. Wingfield
Touch of Jade. A. Harrell
Touch of Jonah. L. Holton
Touch of Judas. L. Wilkinson
Touch of Magic. M. R. Myers
Touch of Malice. J. Wainwright
Touch of Murder. J. B. Cearley
Touch of Myrrh. Charlotte Hunt
Touch of Nutmeg. J. Collier
Touch of Purple. E. Trevor
Touch of Red. W. Fennerton
Touch of Stagefright. J. Davey
Touch of Terror. C. Bert
Touch of Terror. S. Farrant
Touch of the Black Widow. B. Carlton
Touch of the Child. L. M. Lion
Touch of the Child, and other stories. T. Gallon
Touch of the Nettle. J. M. Scott
Touch of the Past. J. L. Breen
Touch of the Sun. H. B. Kaye
Touch of the Witch. J. Wetherell
Touch of Thunder. Brian Cooper
Touch of Treason. S. Stein
Touch Pitch. L. Peck
Touch the Devil. J. Higgins
Touch the Lion's Paw. Derek Lambert
Touchdown. M. Russell
Touchfeather. J. Sangster
Touchfeather, Too. J. Sangster
Touching Evil. N. S. Rosen
Touchstone. E. Bradford
Touchstone. M. Dobson
Tough and the Tender. A. MacLeod
Tough Assignment. L. Paradise
Tough Baby. J. Sublett
Tough Company. C. Dawe
Tough Cop. J. Roeburt
Tough Dames Don't Die. B. Cagson
Tough Die Hard. Robert Martin
Tough Enough. W. R. Philbrick
Tough for You, Hazel. D. Foster
Tough Get Going. G. Bagby
Tough Ghosts. W. J. Elliott
Tough Guy. A. I. Bezzerides
Tough Guy. P. Clare
Tough Guys. I. Don
Tough Guys. M. Spillane
Tough Guys Don't Dance. N. Mailer
Tough Guys Fall Too. S. Vincent
Tough Hide Tenderfoot. B. Johns
Tough Justice. San Antonio
Tough Luck L.A. Murray Sinclair
Tough on a Corpse. N. Rosso
Tough on the Wops. B. Toler
Tough One to Lose. T. Kenrick
Tough Spot for Cupid and other stories. P. Cheyney
Tough Tontine. A. Sewart
Tough Town. J. Karney
Toughs Afloat. M. Hervey
Toughs Ashore. M. Hervey
Tour. D. Ely
Tour de Force. C. Brand
Tour de Force. P. Cleife
Tour of Terror. J. W. Bobin
Touring Company Crime. A. Steffens Hardy
Tourist Season. C. Hiassen
Tourist Trap. Julie Smith
Tourist Trap. Ted Stratton
Tourists. R. B. Wright
Tourists Are for Trapping. M. Babson
Tournament. J. Quirk
Tournament of Shadows. N. Carnac
Tournelles Plot. H. Drummond
Towards Tomorrow. J. Blackmore
Towards Zero. A. Christie
Towards Zero. G. Verner
Tower. P. M. Hubbard

Tower. S. Lansdell
Tower. R. M. Stern
Tower Abbey. I. Holland
Tower Hill Mystery. A. W. Barrett
Tower in the Sea. J. Thatcher
Tower Mystery. P. McGuire
Tower of Babel. M. L. West
Tower of Blood. S. Andrews
Tower of Darkness. H. Hawton
Tower of Evil. J. Rhode
Tower of Hate. F. Shroyer
Tower of Ivory. G. Atherton
Tower of Kilraven. C. Crowe
Tower of Malecombe. J. D'Astor
Tower of Monte Rado. Sheila Ross
Tower of Sand. W. D. Steele
Tower of Strength. Nicholas Carter
Tower of Terror. J. I. Lawrence
Tower of Terror. D. Stivers
Tower of the Crow. D. Polk
Tower of the Dark Light. E. E. Mande
Tower of Treason. Z. Hughes
Tower Park. E. De Vincent
Tower Room. D. Daniels
Tower Room. M. L. Roby
Tower Room. D. Spicer
Tower Room. J. Trevelyan
Tower Room Mystery. R. St. Clair
Tower Struck by Lightning. F. Arrabal
Towers of Fear. C. Farr
Towers of Love. S. Birmingham
Towers of Silence. David St. John
Towers of Terror. D. Dayle
Towers of Urbandine. G. C. Carr
Towing-Path Bess. R. Pryce
Town Cried Murder. L. Ford
Town Hall Crime. A. Blair
Town Is Full of Rumors. R. Wilson
Town Lady and Country Lass. F. Warden
Town of Masks. D. S. Davis
Town of Shadows. J. Drummond
Town of Sin. Stuart Hall
Town Parole. Alex Hamilton
Town That Saw No Evil. Harry Kantor
Town That Went Sick. S. Truss
Town Traveller. G. Gissing
Town Without Pity. M. Gregor
Town's Verdict. E. F. Heddle
Townsend Murder Mystery. O. R. Cohen
Toxic Shock. S. Paretsky
Toxin. R. Swigart
Toy. K. Booton
Toy Cupboard. Lee Jordan
Toy Lamb. B. Flynn
Toy Soldiers. W. P. Kennedy
Toy Tree. V. Mullen
Toying with Fate. Nicholas Carter
Toyland. Mark Smith
Toys of Death. G. D. H. Cole
Toys of Desperation. A. Crockett
Toys of Peace. H. H. Munro
Toyshop. Andrew Taylor
Trace. W. B. Murphy
Trace and 47 Miles of Rope. W. B. Murphy
Trace Elements. K. L. Knight
Trace of Malice. P. Modiano
Trace of Tred. E. Hannibal
Traced and Tracked. J. M'Govan
Traced Through a Dream. C. Courteney
Tracer of Lost Persons. R. W. Chambers
Traces. P. Wallace
Traces of Brillhart. H. Brean
Traces of Merrilee. H. Brean
Tracey. S. Nichols
Track of Midnight. G. F. Scott
Track of the Assassin. P. R. Rothweiler
Track of the Beast. Ralph Hayes
Track of the Slayer. B. Strong
Tracked Across the Atlantic. Nicholas Carter
Tracked Across the Seas. Wilfred Barclay
Tracked and Taken. D. Donovan
Tracked by a Female Detective. Old Sleuth
Tracked by a Pin. R. Hackstaff
Tracked by a Tattoo. F. Hume

Tracked by a Woman. "Goldey"
Tracked by a Woman. Old Sleuth
Tracked by Bushrangers, and other stories. Mrs. Chads
Tracked by Fate. F. Hume
Tracked by the Ogpu. E. Jepson
Tracked by Wireless. W. LeQueux
Tracked Down. L. Edgley
Tracked Down. H. Hill
Tracked on a Wheel. Old Sleuth
Tracked Out. A. W. A'Beckett
Tracked to Death. M. Redwing
Tracked to Doom. D. Donovan
Tracked to His Doom. J. K. Stafford
Tracked to the West. N. Ridley
Tracker. R. Stillman
Tracker of Skull Island. Michael Hastings
Tracker Tracked. G. Furnivall
Tracker Tracked. B. Wayde
Tracking of K.K. D. Grey
Tracking Trantor. G. Chater
Trackless Death. A. Livingston
Trackless Seas. J. L. Johnson
Trackless Thing. J. Atholl
Tracks in the Snow. G. R. Benson
Trackwalker. William Grant
Tracy Diamonds. M. J. Holmes
Tracy's Wartime Memories. M. A. Collins
Trade. W. H. Hallahan
Trade of Angels. Derek Parker
Trade-Off. V. B. Miller
Trade-Off. G. F. Newman
Trade Secrets. R. Garton
Trade Wind. M. M. Kaye
Trade Winds Over Kokio. L. C. Raef
Trademark of a Traitor. K. M. Knight
Trader Brook. K. Hayles
Trader Carson. John Barnett
Trader Random. O. Binns
Trader to the Stars. Poul Anderson
Traders. M. Woodhouse
Trader's Daughter. W. M. Graydon
Trader's License. J. England
Trading with Bodies. Griff
Traditional Murders. J. N. Chance
Traditions. Anonymous
Traditions of London. Waters
Trafalgar Square. Gavin Holt
Trafalgar Square Mystery. C. Brisbane
Traffic in Souls. E. H. Ball
Traffic in Souls. R. Carstairs
Traffic in Souls. G. Pardoe
Traffic with Evil. A. Johns
Traficante. F. Hilaire
Tragedies of Mr. Pip. E. Jepson
Tragedies of Oak Hurst. B. Marean
Tragedy After Tea. C. Ashton
Tragedy and Comedy in Clerical Life. T. J. Worrall
Tragedy and Strategy. Old Sleuth
Tragedy at Beechcroft. A. Fielding
Tragedy at Blue Aloes. M. Richmond
Tragedy at Cumberland Park. Arthur Russell
Tragedy at Draythorpe. L. Grex
Tragedy at Freyne. Anthony Gilbert
Tragedy at Law. C. Hare
Tragedy at Ravensthorpe. J. J. Connington
Tragedy at the Beach Club. W. A. Johnston
Tragedy at the Thirteenth Hole. M. Burton
Tragedy at the Unicorn. J. Rhode
Tragedy at Tiverton. R. Paul
Tragedy at Twelvetrees. A. J. Rees
Tragedy at Wenbley. C. F. Gregg
Tragedy Behind the Curtain and other stories. A. A. D. Bayldon
Tragedy in a Brick Box. J. Budd
Tragedy in Blue. M. Bramhall
Tragedy in E Flat. L. Gribble
Tragedy in Pewsey Chart. H. Willett
Tragedy in the Dark. Elaine Hamilton
Tragedy in the Hollow. F. W. Crofts
Tragedy in the Rue de la Paix. A. Belot
Tragedy in Turquoise. L. Trimble
Tragedy Indeed. A. Belot
Tragedy Near Tring. J. K. Ryland

Tragedy of a Flirtation. H. B. Vogel
Tragedy of an Indiscretion. J. W. Brodie-Innes
Tragedy of Andrea. E. P. Oppenheim
Tragedy of Ascot Mills. S. Campbell
Tragedy of Brinkwater. M. L. Moodey
Tragedy of Captain Harrison. R. C. J.
Tragedy of Errors. F. A. Munsey
Tragedy of Featherstone. B. L. Farjeon
Tragedy of Grub Street and other stories. S. J. A. Fitz-Gerald
Tragedy of Ida Noble. W. C. Russell
Tragedy of Josephine Maria. C. S. Brooks
Tragedy of Lime Hall. C. Braeme
Tragedy of Redmount. M. E. Holmes
Tragedy of the Bromleigh's. R. Hardinge
Tragedy of the Chinese Mine. I. Greig
Tragedy of the Great Emerald. W. Chesney
Tragedy of the Lady Palmist. W. L. Longstaff
Tragedy of the Silver Moon. A. Gask
Tragedy of the West End Actress. J. G. Brandon
Tragedy of Wild River Valley. M. Finley
Tragedy of Windyridge. R. Hardinge
Tragedy of X. B. Ross
Tragedy of Y. B. Ross
Tragedy of Z. B. Ross
Tragedy on a Trooper. J. Strange
Tragedy on the Line. J. Rhode
Tragic Case of John Renold. H. Allan
Tragic Case of the Station Master's Legacy. J. Drummond
Tragic Curtain. S. H. Page
Tragic Lesson. J. H. Vahey
Tragic Mystery. J. Hawthorne
Tragic Mystery. Old Sleuth
Tragic Quest. F. W. Irwin
Tragic Quest. Old Sleuth
Tragic Target. M. V. Heberden
Trail from Devil's Country. A. M. Treynor
Trail of a Human Tiger. Nicholas Carter
Trail of a Tramp. N. Quarry
Trail of Adventure. O. Binns
Trail of Ashes. M. Babson
Trail of Blood. J. Potter
Trail of Blood. C. Rushton
Trail of Death. W. M. Graydon
Trail of Death. G. E. Rochester
Trail of Deceit. W. C. Tuttle
Trail of Doom. R. C. Armour
Trail of Fear. A. Armstrong
Trail of Fire. C. Curzon
Trail of Fu Manchu. S. Rohmer
Trail of Raider No. 1. S. Blakesley
Trail of the Axe. G. Cullum
Trail of the Barrow. Anonymous
Trail of the Barrow. J. Mooney
Trail of the Beast. A. Abdullah
Trail of the Black King. A. Armstrong
Trail of the Borealis. E. Grey
Trail of the Catspaw. Nicholas Carter
Trail of the Cloven Hoof. A. Eadie
Trail of the Dead. B. F. Robinson
Trail of the Dope Chief. J. Hunter
Trail of the Dragon. Susan Kelly
Trail of the Fingerprints. Nicholas Carter
Trail of the Ghosts. N. Thurley
Trail of the Hunted. R. Wilkes-Hunter
Trail of the Lonely River. H. Edmonds
Trail of the Lotto. A. Armstrong
Trail of the Missing Scientist. A. Parsons
Trail of the Old Lag. W. J. Bayfield
Trail of the Poison Gang. L. Bidston
Trail of the Purple Ace. Anonymous
Trail of the Reaper. P. Fox
Trail of the Red Spider. Anonymous
Trail of the Ruby. W. Proudfoot
Trail of the Seahawks. A. Mayhar
Trail of the Serpent. M. E. Braddon
Trail of the Serpent. T. E. B. Clarke
Trail of the Serpent. E. Southworth
Trail of the Serpent. C. Worth
Trail of the Shadow. H. Bedford-Jones
Trail of the Shadow. S. M. Parkman
Trail of the Skull. Gavin Holt
Trail of the Squid. H. Wickham

Title Index

Trail of the Three Lean Men. N. Barclay
Trail of the Tiger. R. C. Armour
Trail of the Traitor. A. Edgar
Trail of the Twisted Cross. B. Sanders
Trail of the White Knight. B. Graeme
Trail of the White Turban. C. Brisbane
Trail of the Yoshiga. Nicholas Carter
Trail to Death. R. Wallace
Trail to Kingdom Come. W. C. Tuttle
Trail to Treason. C. Dixon
Trail Under the Sea. R. H. Poole
Trailed to the End. J. K. Stafford
Trailer Mystery. R. St. Clair
Trailer Park. J. Vaughn
Trailers of the North. W. L. Lockwood
Trailersnatch. A. Harrell
Trailing Death. G. Begbie
Trailing of the Picaroon. Herman Landon
Trails End. W. L. Murphy
Train. G. Simenon
Train a Fast Gun. R. Wilkes-Hunter
Train from Katanga. Wilbur Smith
Train Leaves at Midnight. W. Solski
Train of Glory. W. Grant
Train Robbers. Anonymous
Train to Hell. A. Sayle
Train Wreck! J. Jack
Trainer's Secret. A. Steffens Hardy
Trainer's Tales. N. Gould
Trains That Met in the Blizzard. R. P. Woodward
Traitor. L. Allan
Traitor! W. H. Baker
Traitor. L. Divomlikoff
Traitor. S. Horler
Traitor. G. Sheen
Traitor. D. Sherman
Traitor. H. Wouk
Traitor and Loyalist. A. R. Weekes
Traitor and Spy. A. Steffens Hardy
Traitor Betrayed. O. Mills
Traitor Blitz. J. M. Simmel
Traitor Come Home. A. Bonnard
Traitor Dragoon. W. M. Graydon
Traitor for a Cause. G. Markstein
Traitor Game. D. McLeish
Traitor in London. F. Hume
Traitor in the Fleet. E. L. MacKeag
Traitor Mask. F. A. Smith
Traitor Spy. T. C. H. Jacobs
Traitor Unmasked. G. Davison
Traitor Within. Alicen White
Traitorous Heart. Victoria Hamilton
Traitors. P. Chester
Traitors. E. P. Oppenheim
Traitor's Blood. Reginald Hill
Traitor's Bridge. N. Sligh
Traitor's Contract. Paul Mann
Traitor's Crime. R. Jeffries
Traitor's Cross. F. Grierson
Traitor's Dispatch. L. Pender
Traitor's Doom. J. Creasey
Traitor's End. Alan Hunter
Traitor's Exit. J. Gardner
Traitor's Gate. C. Gavin
Traitors' Gate. S. Harvester
Traitor's Gate. G. Osborne
Traitor's Gate. E. Wallace
Traitor's Gate. D. Wheatley
Traitor's Gate and other stories. G. M. Fenn
Traitor's Harvest. M. Richmond
Traitor's Honor. J. Kebbe
Traitor's Island. F. Hay
Traitor's Island. J. Pendower
Traitor's Market. G. Dickson
Traitor's Mask. D. Noel
Traitor's Mountain. S. Styles
Traitor's Pass. D. Duff
Traitor's Purse. M. Allingham
Traitor's Road. G. Daniels
Traitor's Rock. G. E. Rochester
Traitor's Tide. R. Goyne
Traitor's Way. B. Hamilton
Traitor's Wife. D. Montrose
Traitor's Wooing. H. Hill

Traits and Confidences. E. Lawless
Tramp. E. Wallace
Tramp in Armour. C. Forbes
Trample an Empire. W. Mole
Tramplers. J. Manor
Tramp's Evidence. E. C. Vivian
Tramp's Wallet. F. T. Read
Trance. J. Fielding
Trance. D. Lambert
Trans Mercurian. K. Lang
Trans-Siberian Express. W. Adler
Transactions of Lord Louis Lewis. R. Pertwee
Transactions of Oliver Prince. R. E. Forbes
Transatlantic Ghost. D. Gardiner
Transatlantic Puzzle. M. O. Rolfe
Transatlantic Trouble. L. Grex
Transcendental Murder. J. Langton
Transfer. T. Palmer
Transformation. J. Fielding
Transformation of Timothy. T. Cobb
Transformation Scene. C. Houghton
Transgressing the Law. F. Whittaker
Transgressions. R. Vaughan
Transgressor. F. Thompson
Transgressors. J. Thompson
Transient Guest, and Other Episodes. E. Saltus
Transister Girls. Paul Daniels
Transit of the Red Dragon, and other tales. E. Phillpotts
Transit Visa. A. Seghers
Transome Murder Mystery. P. Luck
Transparent Traitor. F. Gerard
Transparent Tree. R. Kelly
Transplant. J. Weatherhead
Transport Murders. J. G. Brandon
Transvection Machine. E. D. Hoch
Transylvania Stgation. D. E. Westlake
Trap. Jenifer Beckett
Trap. D. Billany
Trap. M. Brenner
Trap. John Burke
Trap. J. L. Cotte
Trap. D. Donovan
Trap. M. Foster
Trap. T. Hubert
Trap. George E. Jones
Trap. E. Jordan
Trap. Mrs. C. Kernahan
Trap. T. King
Trap. J. Knowler
Trap. J. Treherne
Trap. D. Winston
Trap for a Lonely Man. Robert Thomas
Trap for a Redhead. S. Palmer
Trap for Bellamy. P. Cheyney
Trap for Cinderella. S. Japrisot
Trap for Fools. A. Cross
Trap for Fools. J. Pendower
Trap for Lovers. J. Blackmore
Trap in the Tunnel. G. Ellinger
Trap Line. W. D. Montalbano
Trap Mystery. N. Karta
Trap #6. S. Ransome
Trap of Fate. I. D. Hardy
Trap of Tangled Wire. Nicholas Carter
Trap Spider. K. Royce
Trap the Baron. Anthony Morton
Trapdoor. D. Bloodworth
Trapdoor. H. Galtzner
Trapdoor. B. J. O'Keefe
Trapdoor. Keith Peterson
Trapeze. M. Catto
Trapline. T. B. Tivey
Trapped. A. Capelli
Trapped. R. Hayward
Trapped. J. Hougron
Trapped. H. Innes
Trapped. R. Jeffries
Trapped. L. Mantz
Trapped! W. Norwood
Trapped. M. L. Roby
Trapped by a Female Detective. Old Sleuth
Trapped by a Woman. Nicholas Carter
Trapped by Avarice. H. Grimshawe

Trapped in His Own Net. Nicholas Carter
Trapped Ones. L. Charbonneau
Trapper. T. York
Trapper of Rat River. C. Stoddard
Trapper's Secret. A. Armitage
Trapper's Victim. C. Brisbane
Trapping the Moonshiners. Old Sleuth
Trappings Are Gorgeous. H. D. Dearden
Trapp's Place. B. Callison
Traps. F. Duerrenmatt
Traps Need Fresh Bait. A. A. Fair
Trash Stealer. J. Potts
Trauma. R. Craig
Travel Tales of Mr. Joseph Jorkens. Lordy Dunsany
Travel the Hard Way. M. Hervey
Traveler. J. Katzenbach
Traveling Butcher. Alice Campbell
Traveling Corpse. K. Steel
Traveling Grave. L. P. Hartley
Traveling Horseman. N. Luard
Traveling Lady. H. Foote
Traveling Man. P. James
Traveling Skull. H. S. Keeler
Traveling with Sherlock Holmes and Dr. Watson. H. A. Litzinger
Traveller in the Fur Coat. S. J. Weyman
Traveller Returns. P. Wentworth
Travellers in an Antique Land. D. Creed
Traveller's Samples. Mrs. H. Dudeney
Travelling Deadman. J. Varnam
Travelling Executioners. B. Newman
Travels with a Duchess. M. Gallie
Travels with My Aunt. G. Greene
Travers. Sara Dean
Travers, a Mystery Story. R. B. Siddall
Travers Hall Mystery. J. R. C. Hamilton
Traverse of the Gods. B. Langley
Trawl Adrift. E. L. Long
Treacherous Border. N. Thurley
Treacherous Mission. D. Noel
Treacherous Road. S. Harvester
Treachery. K. Lindsay
Treachery. L. S. Stanhope
Treachery at Guadamonte. D. Martyn
Treachery Game. J. Gerson
Treachery in Trieste. C. L. Leonard
Treachery in Type. Josephine Bell
Treachery Trade. E. Cannon
Tread Gently, Death. R. P. Koehler
Tread Lightly, Angel. F. C. Davis
Tread Lightly, My Dear. E. Bercovici
Tread Softly. B. Flynn
Tread Softly. R. Laymon
Tread Softly. P. Malloch
Tread Softly. F. Rickett
Tread Softly in This Place. B. Cleeve
Tread Softly, Nurse Scott. Marilyn Ross
Tread Warily. Hilary Mason
Tread Warily at Midnight. M. Carr
Treason at Home. Mrs. Greenough
Treason by Truth. W. H. Baker
Treason-Felony. J. Hill
Treason in My Breast. Anthony Gilbert
Treason in the Egg. L. A. G. Strong
Treason Line. D. Torr
Treason of the Blood. E. Brewer
Treason Remembered. W. H. Baker
Treason Under Seal. W. V. Cook
Treasure. C. Cussler
Treasure. A. E. Hotchner
Treasure. Larry Levine
Treasure. Steve Mackenzie
Treasure at Greyladies. H. Leyford
Treasure at Loatani Point. R. W. Nolan
Treasure by Degrees. David Williams
Treasure Chest. M. L. Roby
Treasure Chest Girl. D. Haring
Treasure Divers. D. Streib
Treasure for Treasure. Justin Scott
Treasure Hidden. T. Trueblood
Treasure House of Martin Hews. E. P. Oppenheim
Treasure Hunt. Leona Karr
Treasure Hunt. T. Pace
Treasure Hunters. W. H. Baker

Treasure in Oxford. David Williams
Treasure in Roubles. David Williams
Treasure Nets. G. Fairlie
Treasure Preserved. David Williams
Treasure of Big Waters. R. Cullum
Treasure of Blackmoor Island. Francis Warwick
Treasure of Captain Scarlett. A. Sergeant
Treasure of Caricar. R. W. Hinds
Treasure of Christophe. O. Binns
Treasure of Israel. W. LeQueux
Treasure of Kamska. Anonymous
Treasure of Rodolfo Fierro. St. George Cooke
Treasure of Sainte-Foy. MacDonald Harris
Treasure of Scarland. M. B. Dix
Treasure of Seacliff Manor. Y. Norman
Treasure of the Cosa Nostra. J. Ridgway
Treasure of the Golcondas. H. Vernes
Treasure of the Manchus. R. C. Armour
Treasure of the Ragazzeo. H. Braddock
Treasure of the Sun. H. McCutcheon
Treasure of the Temple. J. Lyons
Treasure of the Yukon. T. McCoy
Treasure of Wycliffe House. J. Judson
Treasure on Camise. Alan Graham
Treasure on Earth. Laurence Kirk
Treasure on the Broads. W. G. Elliott
Treasure Royal. W. Garrett
Treasure Trail. R. Pertwee
Treasure Train. A. B. Reeve
Treasure Up in Smoke. D. Williams
Treasures. J. Kingsley
Treasures of Darkness. C. Jessey
Treasures of the Wicked. Anonymous
Treasures on Earth. W. Walden
Treasury Alarm. J. Davey
Treasury-Officer's Wooing. C. C. Lowis
Treasury's Millions. B. Wayde
Treble Chance Murder. V. Gunn
Treble Cross. H. Howard
Treble Exposure. A. Morice
Tree Frog. M. Woodhouse
Tree of Death. M. Muller
Tree of Evil. R. Morrison
Tree of Hands. R. Rendell
Tree of Heaven. E. Raymond
Tree Surgeon. R. Ray
Treen and Wild Horses. P. F. Gaye
Tregaron's Daughter. M. Brent
Tregarthen. G. Norway
Tregarthen's Wife. F. M. White
Tregear's Treasure. J. Remenham
Trek Chain. W. Westrup
Trek East. T. Mundy
Trek or Treat. E. St. Clair
Trelawny. I. Holland
Trelawny's Fell. I. Holland
Tremayne Case. Alan Thomas
Tremayne's Wife. Charlotte Hunt
Trembling Earth. F. Clifford
Trembling Earth Contract. P. Atlee
Trembling Flame. L. J. Vance
Trembling Hills. P. A. Whitney
Trembling Thread. C. Franklin
Tremendous Event. M. Leblanc
Tremlett Diamonds. A. St. Aubyn
Tremlow Murder Case. R. Dark
Tremolo. E. Borneman
Tremor of Forgery. P. Highsmith
Tremor of Intent. A. Burgess
Tremor Violet. D. Lippincott
Tremorra Towers. H. York
Trench Yarns. "Peter"
Trench's Wives. Anonymous
Trenfell Castle. H. Moray
Trent Fights Again. W. Martyn
Trent Intervenes. E. C. Bentley
Trent of the Lone Hand. W. Martyn
Trent Trail. W. Martyn
Trent's Last Case. E. C. Bentley
Trent's Own Case. E. C. Bentley
Trepidation in Downing Street. L. E. Jones
Trespass. A. Askew
Trespass. P. Finch
Trespass. F. Knebel

Trespass. N. Tranter
Trespass in the Sun. J. Pudney
Trespassers. A. Coburn
Trespassers Will Die. M. Seuffert
Trevayne. J. Ryder
Trevena's Daughter. B. Davis
Treveryan. A. Du Maurier
Trevlyn Hold. H. Wood
Trevor Case. N. S. Lincoln
Trewinnot of Guy's. Mrs. C. Kernahan
Triad. S. Bowen
Triad. D. Lambert
Triad. M. Leader
Triad. H. K. Marks
Triad. R. Rohmer
Triad Conspiracy. A. M. MacKay
Triad Imperative. Dwight Martin
Triad of Knives. Tom Cooper
Triad 21. H. Arvay
Trial. A. Booth
Trial. W. Harrington
Trial. C. Irving
Trial. D. M. Mankiewicz
Trial. D. Pendleton
Trial. C. M. Yonge
Trial and Error. A. Berkeley
Trial and Error. George Joseph
Trial and Terror. L. Treat
Trial and Triumph. Anonymous
Trial at Bannock. J. Bier
Trial by Ambush. L. Ford
Trial by Desire. K. G. Ballard
Trial by Fear. F. Kane
Trial by Fire. F. Fyfield
Trial by Fury. E. Ferrars
Trial by Fury. J. A. Jance
Trial by Fury. C. Rice
Trial by Love. M. Cambards
Trial by Murder. E. S. Holding
Trial by Murder. G. Hoster
Trial by Ordeal. O. Mills
Trial by Perjury. J. Creighton
Trial by Slander. T. Macrae
Trial by Terror. P. Gallico
Trial by Terror. R. Lockridge
Trial by Water. H. Footner
Trial by Wilderness. T. M. Longstreth
Trial from Ambush. L. Ford
Trial of Adolph Hitler. P. Van Rjndt
Trial of Alvin Boaker. J. Reywall
Trial of Bebe Donge. G. Simenon
Trial of Billy Jack. H. Liebling
Trial of Callista Blake. E. Pangborn
Trial of Gideon, and Countess Almara's Murder. J. Hawthorne
Trial of Gregor Kaska. F. Andreas
Trial of Jenny Sykes. H. Weenolsen
Trial of John and Henry Norton. R. Puccetti
Trial of Lizzie Borden and other radio plays. D. Henderson
Trial of Lobo Icheka. D. Creek
Trial of Mary Dugan. B. Veiller
Trial of Mary Dugan. W. A. Wolff
Trial of Parson Finch. S. Gibney
Trial of Scotland Yard. Stuart Martin
Trial of Soren Qvist. Janet Lewis
Trial of the Golden Girl. R. Dolphin
Trial of Vincent Doon. W. Oursler
Trial of Vivienne Ware. K. M. Ellis
Trial Run. D. Francis
Triall Case. L. Durie
Trials and Tribulations of Aaron Amsted. K. A. Lapatine
Trials of Commander McTurk. C. J. C. Hyne
Trials of Love. H. M. Jones
Trials of O'Brien. R. L. Fish
Trials of Rumpole. J. Mortimer
Trials of the Phideas. E. L. Long
Triangle. A. Lassiter
Triangle. M. Leighton
Triangle. T. White
Triangle Has Four Sides. P. Barrington
Triangle Man. G. F. Gibbs
Triangle Murder. R. Batchelor

Triangle of Death. Jon Hart
Triangle of Fear. J. N. Chance
Triangle of Terror. Gwyn Evans
Triangle of the Grey Wolf. J. Addiscombe
Triangles of Fire. J. Siler
Tribal Town. H. Munro
Tribe. Bari Wood
Tribunal. P. Bair
Tribute to Satan. J. B. Dayne
Trick Baby. I. Slim
Trick of Diamonds. A. Auswaks
Trick of the Ga Bolga. P. McGinley
Trick of the Light. S. Faulks
Trick of Time. F. Hume
Trick or Treat. C. Crane
Trick or Treat. D. M. Disney
Trick Thirteen. T. Reese
Trick, Trial and Triumph. A. Cheviot
Tricked and Trapped. I. Stark
Tricks. E. McBain
Tricks and Triumphs. Old Sleuth
Tricks of the Light. S. Smoke
Tricks of the Trade. R. L. Fish
Tricks of the Trade. Sidney Michaels
Trickshot. Randolph Harris
Tricycle. R. Rhodes
Trident Hijacking. D. Streib
Trident Tragedy. S. C. Monroe
Tried As Pure Gold, and other tales. Mrs. Chads
Tried for Her Life. E. Southworth
Tried for His Life. Anonymous
Tried for His Life. B. Hemyng
Trieste. D. Cory
Trificante Treasure. D. Winston
Trifles. S. Glaspell
Trigger. A. Melville-Ross
Trigger Finger. C. R. Cooper
Trigger Lady. P. Swan
Trigger Man. B. Copper
Trigger Man. Joe Joyce
Trigger Man. R. Posner
Trigger Man. A. Rosenfeld
Trigger Mortis. F. Kane
Trigger of Conscience. R. O. Chipperfield
Trigger Points. M. Mayer
Trigger Serenade. J. Brady
Trigger Tramp. D. Haring
Triggerman. B. Rossi
Triggerman! G. Usher
Triggers Are Trumps. W. J. Elliott
Trillion Dollar Tricks. S. A. Bassion
Trilogy in Jeopardy. H. Kane
Trimmed Lamp. O. Henry
Trinity. R. Bridges
Trinity Factor. O. Sela
Trinity Implosion. Robin Moore
Trinity in Violence. H. Kane
Trio for Blunt Instruments. R. Stout
Trio in Three Flats. E. Dewhurst
Trip to Eternity. G. Monro
Trip to Jerusalem. E. Marston
Trip Trap. J. Rathbone
Triphammer. Dan McCall
Triple. K. Follett
Triple Bite. B. Flynn
Triple Crime. Nicholas Carter
Triple Cross. Joe Barry
Triple Cross. Nicholas Carter
Triple Cross. J. Roeburt
Triple Cross. J. K. Stafford
Triple Cross Murders. A. R. Long
Triple Crown. J. L. Breen
Triple Death. C. Carnac
Triple Exposure. Peter Townend
Triple Factor. O. Sela
Triple Identity. Nicholas Carter
Triple Indemnity. J. Richards
Triple Jeopardy. R. Speight
Triple Jeopardy. R. Stout
Triple Knavery. Nicholas Carter
Triple Knock. Nicholas Carter
Triple Mirror. J. Gautier
Triple Mirror. L. James
Triple Murder. Colin Hughes

Title Index

Triple Murder. D. D. Mancini
Triple Murder. C. Wells
Triple Mystery. A. Luehrmann
Triple "O" Seven. I. R. Jamieson
Triple Quest. E. R. Punshon
Triple Scar. E. A. Barron
Triple Slay. Adam Knight
Triple Take. Jonathon Kane
Triple Terror. H. Kane
Triple Threat. K. Roos
Triple Threat. M. Wallenstein
Triple Zero. A. Whitney
Tripleship Cracksman. N. Adam
Tripletrap. W. Hallahan
Triplets. M. Gregory
Tripoli Documents. H. Kane
Triptych. R. G. Jones
Tripwire. J. Brandon
Tripwire. B. Garfield
Triton Ultimatum. L. Delaney
Triumph. C. F. Coe
Triumph for Inspector West. J. Creasey
Triumph of Elaine. A. B. Reeve
Triumph of Evil. P. Kavanagh
Triumph of Hilary Blackland. B. Mitford
Triumph of Inspector Maigret. G. Simenon
Triumph of John Kars. R. Cullum
Triumph of Love. Mrs. M. C. Toon
Triumph of McLean. G. Goodchild
Triumph of Manhood. M. Leighton
Triumph of the Rat. D. Robins
Triumph of the Scarlet Pimpernel. Baroness Orczy
Triumph of Tinker. E. Jepson
Triumphal Chariot. P. H. Irving
Triumphant Beast. Marjorie Bowen
Triumphant Defeat. B. Christianson
Triumphant Prodigal. W. Martyn
Triumphs of Eugene Valmont. R. Barr
Triumphs of Fabian Field: Criminologist. D. Donovan
Triumverate. H. Baldwin Taylor
Trixie. B. Vane
Trixie True, Teen Detective. K. Hamilton
Trixy. Mrs. G. Sheldon
Trocadero. L. Waller
Trodmore Turf Mystery. F. Johnston
Troika. C. Egleton
Troika. D. Gurr
Troika. S. Harvester
Troika. D. Montross
Trojan Cow. G. Tippette
Trojan Gold. S. Cudahy
Trojan Gold. Elizabeth Peters
Trojan Hearse. B. Callison
Trojan Hearse. C. Curzon
Trojan Hearse. R. S. Prather
Trojan Horse. H. Innes
Trojan Horse. D. Pendleton
Trojan Horses. R. Emmett
Trojan in Iran. R. Skimin
Trojan Mule. J. Drummond
Trooper and Bushranger. C. Hayter
Trooper MacLean. C. Stoddard
Trooper O'Neill. G. Goodchild
Trooper Useless. L. P. Greene
Trophies and Dead Things. M. Muller
Trophy. J. J. Savarin
Tropic Equations. D. Gordon
Tropic Gold. C. Jerina
Tropic Heat. D. Pendleton
Tropic Love. H. D. Stacpoole
Tropic Moon. G. Simenon
Tropic of Fear. John Carroll
Tropical Deathpact. Nick Carter
Tropical Freeze. Jim Hall
Tropical Heat. J. Lutz
Tropical Murder. S. Murray
Tropical Murder. Louis Williams
Tropical Tales. Howard Jones
Tropical Tales and others. D. Wyllarde
Trot. D. Ely
Trotsky's Run. R. Hoyt
Trotter. B. Fforde
Trouble. M. Gilbert

Trouble! B. Graeme
Trouble A-Brewing. J. Bude
Trouble Aboard. T. Muir
Trouble Ahead. E. Gunton
Trouble at Aquitaine. N. Livingston
Trouble at Glaye. B. Reynolds
Trouble at Hanard. V. Beynon-Harris
Trouble at Harrison High. J. Harris
Trouble at Moon Dance. A. B. Guthrie
Trouble at Number Seven. G. Bullett
Trouble at Pinelands. E. M. Poate
Trouble at Saxby's. J. Creasey
Trouble at the Gabourys'. J. Oppenheimer
Trouble at the Inn. Roland Daniel
Trouble at the JHC. W. C. Tuttle
Trouble at the Top. C. B. Flood
Trouble at Turkey Hill. K. M. Knight
Trouble at Wrekin Farm. Josephine Bell
Trouble Calling. A. Bocca
Trouble Comes Double. R. P. Hansen
Trouble Crossing the Pyrnees. G. D. Larsen
Trouble Follows Me. K. Millar
Trouble for Tallon. J. Ball
Trouble in Bugland. W. Kitzwinkle
Trouble in Burma. V. W. Mason
Trouble in College. F. J. Whaley
Trouble in Hunter Ward. Josephine Bell
Trouble in Mind. R. S. Coburn
Trouble in Muristan. J. Marlowe
Trouble in Paradise. Nick Carter
Trouble in Paradise. R. L. Fish
Trouble in the Air. K. Kay
Trouble in the Bank. H. C. Davis
Trouble in the Brasses. Alisa Craig
Trouble in Thor. J. Valentine
Trouble in Tokyo. J. Black
Trouble in Triplicate. R. Stout
Trouble in West Two. K. Fitzgerald
Trouble Is a Dame. Carter Brown
Trouble Is a Woman. R. Dudgeon
Trouble Is My Business. R. Chandler
Trouble Is My Name. R. Dolphin
Trouble Is My Name. S. Marlowe
Trouble Makers. C. Fremlin
Trouble Making Toys. A. M. Pyle
Trouble Man. J. D. Black
Trouble of Fools. Linda Barnes
Trouble on Parade. K. Robeson
Trouble on the Frontier. Douglas Christie
Trouble on the Thames. V. Bridges
Trouble on Tuesday. S. Carver
Trouble Rides Tall. H. Whittington
Trouble Shooter. W. C. MacDonald
Trouble—Texas Style. J. Bramlett
Trouble Trailer. W. C. Tuttle
Trouble Trip. W. H. Canaway
Trouble with Ava. S. Friedman
Trouble with Crime. J. Noel
Trouble with Fidelity. G. Malcolm-Smith
Trouble with Guns. J. Noel
Trouble with Harry. J. T. Story
Trouble with Murder. R. Bax
Trouble with Penelope. B. Healey
Trouble with Product X. Joan Aiken
Trouble with Ruth. R. Rayner
Trouble with Series Three. M. Kenyon
Trouble with Stephanie. J. Louis
Trouble with Tycoons. H. B. Taylor
Trouble with Women. J. P. Heggy
Troublecross. Jessica Mann
Troubled Deaths. R. Jeffries
Troubled Harvest. E. Woodward
Troubled Heritage. M. Richmond
Troubled House. K. Booton
Troubled Journey. R. Lockridge
Troubled Midnight. R. Garland
Troubled Mind. Stratford Davis
Troubled Night. R. Drayton
Troubled Star. J. August
Troubled Tranton. W. E. Norris
Troubled Waters. P. H. Fine
Troubled Waters. H. Hill
Troubled Waters. E. Lemarchand
Troublemaker. J. Hansen

Troublemaker. J. Potts
Troubles of Colonel Marwood. A. C. Fox-Davies
Troubles of Doctor Cortland. S. Friedman
Troubleshooter. D. Dodge
Troubleshooter. R. Weber
Troupe. G. Linzner
Troupe of Star-Crossed Killers. T. Journet
Trout in the Milk. H. Holman
Trout in the Milk. Roy Lewis
Trout in the Milk. M. Underwood
Trout Inn Mystery. W. Greenleaves
Trout Inn Tragedy. W. Greenleaves
Troy Dossier. Manny Meyers
Truce of the Bear. H. C. McNeile
Truck Shot. J. Stinson
Truckful of Gold. S. J. L. Zake
True. I. Blair
True Adventures of the Secret Service. C. E. Russell
True Blue, the Detective. Old Sleuth
True Bride. T. Altman
True Confessions. J. G. Dunne
True Crime. M. A. Collins
True Detective. M. A. Collins
True Detective. T. Weesner
True Detective Stories. A. L. Drummond
True Detective Stories. M. Moser
True Detective Stories from the Archives of the Pinkertons. C. Moffett
True Lies. Philip Ross
True-Life Adventure. Julie Smith
True or False. M. Borgenicht
True Son of the Beast! Carter Brown
True Stories of Crime. A. Train
True Tales of the D.C.I. K. Detzer
True Tales of Travel and Adventure. H. De Windt
True Woman. Baroness Orczy
Truly Remarkable Life of the Beautiful Helen Jewett. Anonymous
Truman's Spy. N. Hynd
Trump Card. D. Vane
Trumpets of November. W. S. Thurston
Trunch. D. Durrant
Trunk Call. J. J. Farjeon
Trunk Call Mystery. J. J. Farjeon
Trunk Call to Murder. E. Radford
Trunk Crime. E. Percy
Trunk Crime Number Three. W. Tyrer
Trust. G. V. Higgins
Trust a Woman? R. Foley
Trust and Treason. M. Birkhead
Trust Doesn't Rust. G. A. Larson
Trust McLean. G. Goodchild
Trust Me on This. D. E. Westlake
Trust-Money. W. Westall
Trust No Man. P. Swift
Trust No One at All. A. McAllister
Trust the Liar. S. Zannos
Trust the Police. P. Elliott
Trust the Saint. L. Charteris
Trust Them and Die. Jeffry Scott
Trusted Like the Fox. Raymond Marshall
Trusted Like the Fox. Sara Woods
Trusted Rogue. Nicholas Carter
Trusting Victim. D. Lyon
Trusty Servant. G. V. McFadden
Truth About Bebe Donge. G. Simenon
Truth About Belle Gunness. L. De La Torre
Truth About Claire Veryan. S. Truss
Truth About Lord Tench. Donald Stuart
Truth About Lorin Jones. A. Lurie
Truth About My Father. P. Martens
Truth About Peter Harley. James Mills
Truth About the Case. M. F. Goron
Truth About Unicorns. B. J. Reynolds
Truth Came Out. E. R. Punshon
Truth Comes Limping. J. J. Connington
Truth Game. D. Hurd
Truth of the Matter. J. Lutz
Truth or Dare. Jacqueline Wilson
Truth Will Out. Charlotte Francis
Truth with Her Boots On. H. Cecil
Truthful Lady. J. S. Clouston
Truxton Cipher. H. Gruppe
Try Anything Once. A. A. Fair

T

Try Anything Once. J. Pendower
Try Anything Twice. P. Cheyney
Try This One for Size. J. H. Chase
Try to Find a Dead Man. M. Ashton
Trying Patient. J. Payn
Tryst. M. Dibdin
Tryst for a Tragedy. E. C. R. Lorac
Tryst with Terror. W. Winthrop
Tsing-Boum. N. Freeling
Tsunami. S. Barlay
Tsurande Enterprise. M. Cronin
Tube. P. Boileau
Tuck-of-Drum and other stories. A. T. Sheppard
Tucker's People. I. Wolfert
Tudor Garden Mystery. G. Verner
Tudor Murder. E. Hyde
Tuesday Afternoon and other stories. L. A. G. Strong
Tuesday Blade. B. Ottum
Tuesday Club Murders. A. Christie
Tuesday the Rabbi Saw Red. H. Kemelman
Tug of War. L. P. Greene
Tug of War. M. W. H. Hungerford
Tularemia Gambit. S. Perry
Tule Marsh Murder. N. B. Mavity
Tule Witch. J. Toombs
Tulip Tree. H. Rigsby
Tulku. Stephen Hayes
Tumbled House. Winston Graham
Tumbledown Farm. A. Muir
Tumbleweed. J. Van De Wetering
Tumbling River Range. W. C. Tuttle
Tumult and the Shouting. H. Gibbs
Tumult in San Benito. John Arnold
Tumult in the North. G. R. Preedy
Tumulto. B. Williams
Tuna Is Not for Eating. B. Kelly
Tundra Trail. C. Stoddard
Tune In on Terror. J. Tobias
Tune in Tonight. R. Clark
Tune to a Corpse. P. Drax
Tuned for Murder. K. Robeson
Tung and Cheek. Pat Cook
Tunnel. A. Bristowe
Tunnel. R. Byrne
Tunnel. H. Friedman
Tunnel. Stanley Johnson
Tunnel. B. Kendrick
Tunnel. E. Sabato
Tunnel Dig and the Saccharin Murders. L. Montford
Tunnel for Traitors. Nick Carter
Tunnel from Calais. A. D. Divine
Tunnel Mystery. J. C. Lenehan
Tunnel Mystery and Its Solution. A. W. A'Beckett
Tunnel of Darkness. R. N. Winstead
Tunnel of Nightmare. F. Struan
Tunnel of Shadows. R. Timperley
Tunnel Terror. K. Robeson
Tunnel 13. M. M. Raison
Tunnel to Doom. R. W. Hinds
Tunnel War. J. Poyer
Tuppenny Box. C. Fitzgerald
Turbo. D. Rutherford
Turbulence. C. Hodder-Williams
Turbulent Duchess. P. Brebner
Turbulent Messiters. Elizabeth Ford
Turbulent Tales. R. Sabatini
Turf and Veldt. D. J. Belgrave
Turf Bandits. E. Woodward
Turf Conspiracy. N. Gould
Turf Crook. F. Johnston
Turf Mystery. J. Fairfax-Blakeborough
Turf Racketeers. F. Johnston
Turkey-Track Rampage. B. Haning
Turkish Bloodbath. Nick Carter
Turkish Mafia Conspiracy. Ralph Hayes
Turkish Rondo. A. Stevenson
Turkish Spy. Charles Cooper
Turkish White. M. Arrighi
Turmoil at Brede. S. Truss
Turmoil in Zion. G. Bellairs
Turn About Tales. A. H. Rice
Turn-Around. V. Volkoff

Turn Back from Death. H. Desmond
Turn Back the Clock. M. Cole
Turn Blue, You Murderers. Michael Brett
Turn Down an Empty Glass. B. Copper
Turn for the Nurse. R. Abbot
Turn Killer. B. Lecomber
Turn Left for Danger. B. Gray
Turn Left for Murder. S. Marlowe
Turn Left or Be Killed. N. Ashbaugh
Turn Loose the Dragon. G. Chesbro
Turn of a Card. Nicholas Carter
Turn of a Wheel. A. Rowe
Turn of the Screw. Henry James
Turn of the Table. J. Stagge
Turn of the Tide. F. M. White
Turn of Traitors. P. Harcourt
Turn Off the Heat! N. Karta
Turn on the Heat. A. A. Fair
Turn-Out Man. F. Roderus
Turn the Key Softly. J. Brophy
Turn the Light Out As You Go. E. Lustgarten
Turn-Up. A. Sewart
Turn Up a Stone. A. Cade
Turnabout. C. Haynes
Turnaround Jack. R. Abshire
Turncoat. Nick Carter
Turncoat. D. Creed
Turncoat. H. G. Evart
Turncoat. G. Langelaan
Turncoat. J. Lynn
Turner's Wife. N. Garbo
Turning. Justin Scott
Turning Point. H. Clevely
Turning Sword. S. Bayne
Turning Sword. G. V. McFadden
Turning Wheel. D. Donovan
Turnpike. G. E. Evans
Turnpike House. F. Hume
Turns of Fortune. R. Holmes
Turns of Time. P. Audemars
Turnstile of Night. W. Allison
Turnstile of Night. A. M. Williamson
Turquoise Clues. A. Cecil
Turquoise Dragon. D. R. Wallace
Turquoise Hazard. A. B. Caldwell
Turquoise Lament. J. D. MacDonald
Turquoise Mask. P. A. Whitney
Turquoise Shop. F. Crane
Turquoise Spike. F. Archer
Turquoise Talisman. S. Wagner
Turquoise Trail. W. C. Tuttle
Turquoise/Yellow Case. P. K. Palmer
Turret and Torpedo. J. S. Margerison
Turret Room. C. Armstrong
Tuscany Madonna. M. Canfield
Tuscany Terror. D. Pendleton
Tut, Tut! Mr. Tutt. A. Train
Tutt and Mr. Tutt. A. Train
Tutt for Tutt. A. Train
Tuxedo Park. B. Copper
Twana. A. Du Camp
Tweak the Devil's Nose. R. Deming
Tweedledum and Tweedledee. Alec Coppel
Tween Snow and Fire. B. Mitford
Twelfth Crime. S. Cross
Twelfth Juror. B. M. Gill
Twelfth Juror. M. H. Large
Twelfth Man. M. Marquis
Twelfth Mile. E. G. Perrault
Twelfth Night Murders. C. Ryland
Twelfth Night of Ramadan. K. J. Peel
Twelfth of April. R. Doliner
Twelfth of August. W. R. Morris
12th of Never. D. Heyes
Twelfth Power of Evil. J. Morgulas
Twelve Angry Men. R. Rose
Twelve Apostles. G. Verner
Twelve Chinamen and a Woman. J. H. Chase
Twelve Chinks and a Woman. J. H. Chase
12 Dandy McLean Detective Stories. G. Goodchild
Twelve Deaths of Christmas. M. Babson
Twelve Disguises. F. Beeding
12 Famous McLean Cases. G. Goodchild
12:15 A.M.: I'm Blasted. M. Horgan

Twelve Girls in the Garden. Shane Martin
Twelve Horses and the Hangman's Noose. G. Mitchell
Twelve Hours to Destiny. M. K. Robertson
Twelve Hours to Kill. R. M. Stern
Twelve in a Grave. Nicholas Carter
Twelve Maidens. S. Farrar
Twelve Midnight Street. R. Davis
12 Must Die. Zorro
Twelve on Endurance. Michael Hastings
Twelve Steps at Miramar. M. Reisner
Twelve Tales. G. Allen
Twelve Tales. G. Frankau
Twelve Tales and one other. Cardyff
Twelve Tales of Suspense and the Supernatural. D. Grubb
12:30 from Croydon. F. W. Crofts
Twelve Tin Boxes. Nicholas Carter
Twelve to Dine. E. Nisot
Twelve Trains to Babylon. A. Connable
12:20 P.M. W. G. Beymer
Twelve Wise Men. Nicholas Carter
Twentieth Day of January. T. Allbeury
20th of July. H. H. Kirst
Twenty East of Greenwich. J. Lodwick
2835 Mayfair. R. Richardson
Twenty-Fifth Hour. C. V. Gheorghiu
Twenty-Fifth Hour. M. Kelly
Twenty-First Burr. V. Lauriston
Twenty-First Century Sub. F. Herbert
Twenty-Five Cents. W. E. Harris
Twenty-Five Sanitary Inspectors. R. East
Twenty-Four Hours. L. T. Meade
24 Hours to Kill. J. McKimmey
24th Horse. H. Pentecost
24th Level. K. Benton
Twenty Innocent People. D. Gratrix
Twenty Miles to Terror. Eddie Stone
Twenty Minutes to Kill. A. M. Chase
29 Herriott Street. J. Hutton
Twenty-One Clues. J. J. Connington
Twenty-One Stories. G. Greene
Twenty Per Cent. T. Macrae
Twenty Plus Two. F. Gruber
22nd Man. D. L. Hammer
27. W. Diehl
Twenty-Seventh City. J. Franzen
27th Ride. A. D. Welton
Twenty-Six Clues. I. Ostrander
26 Three-Minute Mysteries. N. Morland
Twenty-Third Man. G. Mitchell
Twenty-Third Web. R. Himmel
20/20 Vision. Pamela West
22 Brothers. D. Sage
22 Fires. J. Agel
Twenty-Two Windows. Roland Daniel
Twenty Years of Hate. Donald Stuart
Twenty Years' Recollections of an Irish Police Magistrate. F. T. Porter
Twentymen. P. Purser
Twice a Victim. C. Joyce
Twice American. E. M. Ingram
Twice As Dead. D. Spade
Twice Broken. M. Peterson
Twice Burned. R. Gettel
Twice Checked. Graham Hastings
Twice Dead. J. Bude
Twice Dead. E. M. Channon
Twice Dead. J. B. Hilton
Twice Dead. L. D. Names
Twice Dead. J. Rhode
Twice Dead. Colin Robertson
Twice Dead. Marilyn Ross
Twice Killed. R. Smitten
Twice Lost. P. Paul
Twice Murdered. C. H. Snow
Twice Murdered Man. N. Toye
Twice Retired. R. Lockridge
Twice Round the Clock. B. Houston
Twice Shy. D. Francis
Twice So Fair. N. Tyre
Twice Ten Thousand Miles. F. Lynch
Twice Times Murder. R. Sonin
Twice-Told Tales. N. Hawthorne

Twice Tried. W. LeQueux
Twice Upon a Crime. P. Quinn
Twice Wronged! J. W. Bobin
Twickenham Peerage. R. Marsh
Twickenham Tales. Anonymous
Twig Is Bent. E. Thompson
Twilight. L. Nichols
Twilight Arrow. P. A. Cocks
Twilight at Dawn. Max Murray
Twilight at Mac's Place. Ross Thomas
Twilight at Monticello. W. H. Peden
Twilight at the Elms. D. Daniels
Twilight Eyes. D. R. Koontz
Twilight for Taurus. M. Lynch
Twilight Forest. C. Hamilton
Twilight Justice. Duncan Long
Twilight of Death. L. Langley
Twilight of Honor. A. Dewlin
Twilight of the Generals. H. H. Kirst
Twilight People. R. Batchelor
Twilight People. S. D. Frances
Twilight Return. J. Kimbro
Twilight Strangler. C. Miron
Twilight Tigress. H. Janson
Twilight Walk. A. B. Shiffrin
Twilight Web. W. E. D. Ross
Twilight Whispers. B. Delinsky
Twilight's Burning. D. Guest
Twillford Mystery. G. F. Scott
Twin Athletes. Old Sleuth
Twin Bridges Murder. A. Harrell
Twin Detectives. K. F. Hill
Twin Detectives "Which Wins". Anonymous
Twin Killing. G. Bagby
Twin Mystery. Nicholas Carter
Twin Serpents. R. S. Thorn
Twin Sisters. R. Marsh
Twin Tales. A. Stringer
Twin Tragedy. M. Carr
Twin Ventriloquists. Old Sleuth
Twinkle, Twinkle, Little Spy. L. Deighton
Twinkleface, the Merry Elf. M. Peterson
Twins. Bari Wood
Twins Murder Case. H. G. Hutchinson
Twins of Manscroft. George Harris
Twins of Skirlaugh Hall. E. Brooke
Twins of Suffering Creek. R. Cullum
Twist and other stories. J. J. Farjeon
Twist for Two. H. Janson
Twist in the Silk. Z. Cass
Twist in the Tale. J. Archer
Twist in the Trail. W. J. Bayfield
Twist of a Stick. G. Peters
Twist of Fate. J. De Secary
Twist of Fate. D. Haring
Twist of Fate. J. A. Krentz
Twist of Hate. C. Joyce
Twist of Sand. G. Jenkins
Twist of the Knife. V. Canning
Twist of the Knife. S. Solomita
Twist of the Rope. J. Bude
Twist of Yarn. E. Lookabee
Twist the Knife Slowly. K. Clugston
Twisted Cameo. K. Kimbrough
Twisted Cross. A. Pinchot
Twisted Evidence. M. B. Dix
Twisted Face. F. A. Kummer
Twisted Face Defends His Title. G. Davison
Twisted Face Strikes Again. G. Davison
Twisted Face, the Avenger. G. Davison
Twisted Foot. H. M. Rideout
Twisted Grin. A. Salcroft
Twisted Key. R. Willock
Twisted Mirror. Leonard Lee
Twisted Nerve. Peter Evans
Twisted Ones. V. Packer
Twisted Path. D. Pendleton
Twisted People. J. Phillips
Twisted Tales. L. H. Fox
Twisted Tales. Christopher Ward
Twisted Thing. M. Spillane
Twisted Thread. J. Moffat
Twisted Tongues. Jonathan Burke
Twisted Trails. W. C. Tuttle

Twisted Tree. L. Benedict
Twisted Tree. P. Harcourt
Twisted Wire. R. Falkirk
Twister. E. Wallace
Twisters. V. Hansen
Twister's Double. C. Davy
Twisting the Rope. R. A. McAvoy
Twittering Bird Mystery. H. C. Bailey
Twixt Devil and Deep Sea. A. M. Williamson
Twixt Law and Love. C. H. Bullivant
Twixt Night and Morn. I. Sousa
Twixt Sword and Glove. A. C. Gunter
Twixt the Lights. W. W. Fenn
Two. J. D. MacDonald
Two. C. Trieschman
Two After Malic. L. Peters
Two Against Scotland Yard. D. Frome
Two and Two Make Five. T. E. B. Clarke
Two and Two Make Five. B. Graeme
Two and Two Make Twenty-Two. G. Bristow
Two Apaches of Paris. A. Askew
Two Aunts and a Grandmother. T. B. Morris
Two Black Pearls. M. Leighton
Two Bottles of Relish. E. Darby
Two Bottles of Relish. R. Plomley
Two Bullets for Briggs. D. MacDonald
Two by Day and One by Night. V. Bell
Two by Tricks. E. Yates
Two Clues. E. S. Gardner
Two Conspirators. Old Sleuth
Two Conspirators. M. O. Rolfe
Two Crimes. J. Ibarguengoitia
Two Crosses. W. J. Newton
Two Dames Too Many. N. Perrelli
Two Days, Two Nights. P. O. Sundman
Two Dead. V. Loder
Two Dead Charwomen. N. Morland
Two Dead Men. J. Anker
Two Deaths for a Penny. N. Burnaby
Two Deaths Must Die. R. Himmel
Two Destinies. W. Collins
Two Died at Three. C. F. Gregg
Two Died in Singapore. J. Sherwood
Two Dude Defense. W. Walker
Two Ends in the Town. J. Bude
Two Equals One. P. Dagmar
Two-Face. E. Dudley
Two-Faced. B. Graeme
Two-Faced Death. E. Jeffries
Two-Faced Man. V. Vanardy
Two Faced Murder. Jean Leslie
Two Faces of Death. W. Wright
Two Faces of Fear. J. Wellsley
Two Faces of January. P. Highsmith
Two Faces of Love. D. Noel
Two Faces of Murder. G. Batson
Two Faces of Nemesis. A. Melville-Ross
Two False Moves. J. Middlemass
Two Fates and a Fortune. L. Crow
Two Feet from Heaven. P. C. Wren
Two-Fisted Detective. R. E. Howard
Two-Fisted Killer. K. Slattery
Two-Five to Mardon. K. Field
Two Flights Up. M. R. Rinehart
Two-Fold Inheritance. G. Boothby
Two for a Pair. D. Walshe
Two for Inspector West. J. Creasey
Two for Tanner. Lawrence Block
Two for the Grave. R. B. Houston
Two for the Money. H. Halliday
Two for the Price of One. T. Kenrick
Two Forces. E. W. Elkington
Two Gay Sleuths. H. R. Kaye
Two Gentlemen of Soho. A. P. Herbert
Two Girls and a Saint. G. Warden
Two Goodwins. R. M. Gilchrist
Two Graphs. J. Rhode
Two Gun Hedgehopper. T. Wallace
Two-Gun Sue. Douglas Grant
Two Gun Theresa. B. Diamond
Two Guns for Hire. N. MacNeil
Two Heads Are Better. Elliott Lewis
Two Hearts Apart. Jane Gordon
Two Hot to Handle. E. Lacy

Two Hours to Doom. P. Bryant
Two Houses on the Cliff. M. V. Woodgate
200% Rule. E. A. Pollitz
250 Pound Marriage Case. J. G. Brandon
Two Hundred Pounds Reward, and other tales. J. Payn
Two Hundred Rule. H. Hamilton
Two If by Sea. R. Bax
Two If by Sea. E. Savage
Two Imposters. P. Audemars
Two in a Tangle. W. LeQueux
Two in a Train. W. Deeping
Two in One. M. Gicheru
Two in Shadow. J. Blackmore
Two in the Bush. G. Bagby
Two in the Bush. G. Blumberg
Two in the Dark. G. G. Magnus
Two Kinds of Murder. D. MacDonald
Two Kings. G. Johnston
Two Kisses. H. Smart
Two Knaves and a Queen. F. Barrett
Two Knocks for Death. W. Jackson
2 L.O. W. S. Masterman
Two Ladies in Verona. Lionel Black
Two Lads and a Lass, and other stories. F. Warden
Two Legacies. Mrs. C. Kernahan
Two Little Children and How They Grew. D. M. Disney
Two Little Rich Girls. M. G. Eberhart
Two Little Sailor Boys. G. M. White
Two Little Ships. E. L. Long
Two Lives. B. Jerrold
Two Lives in Parenthesis. George Long
Two Lives of Robert Ledru. F. Oughton
Two Living and One Dead. S. Christiansen
Two Lovers Too Many. Joan Fleming
Two Lucky People. T. Kenrick
Two Magics. Henry James
Two Meet Trouble. M. Halliday
Two Men from Kimberley. H. B. Baker
Two Men from the East. T. A. Plummer
Two Men in Twenty. M. Procter
Two Men Missing. G. Ashe
Two Million. H. B. Vogel
$2,000,000 Blueprint. C. Miron
Two-Minute Mysteries. D. J. Sobol
Two Minute Warning. G. La Fountaine
Two Mrs. Camerons. W. Carter
Two Mrs. Carrolls. H. Arvonen
Two Mrs. Carrolls. M. Vale
Two Mrs. Farrells. John Marsh
Two Mrs. Grenvilles. D. Dunne
Two Mrs. Hemingways. W. Massey
Two Moods of a Man. H. G. Hutchinson
Two Much! D. E. Westlake
Two Must Die. H. Kane
Two Must Die. Colin Robertson
Two Mysteries. G. H. Teed
Two Names for Death. E. P. Fenwick
Two O'Clock Courage. G. Burgess
209 Thriller Road. Sam North
Two of a Kind. H. Horwich
Two of Diamonds. L. Brock
Two on the Trail. H. Footner
Two Pardons. H. S. Vince
Two-Piece Clue. A. Fortune
Two Pinches of Snuff. W. Westall
Two Plus Two. Nicholas Carter
Two Plus Two. A. Cochran
Two Plus Two Equals Minus Seven. J. P. Adams
Two Red Capsules. D. T. Lindsay
Two Sets to Murder. L. Peters
Two Shadows for Death. J. Wolf
Two Shadows Pass. Clifford King
Two Shots. P. Luck
Two Sisters. E. Southworth
Two Small Bodies. N. Bell
Two Smart Dames. Gene Ross
Two Songs This Archangel Sings. G. C. Chesbro
2 Spruce Lane. Gretchen Travis
Two-Star Pigeon. M. Wolfe
Two Steps from Three East. W. B. Murphy
Two Stolen Idols. F. Packard
Two Strange Adventures. K. Cornwallis

T

Two Strange Ladies. H. S. Keeler
Two Strange Men. J. S. Clouston
Two Strokes of the Bell. C. H. Montague
Two Tales of the Occult. M. Eliade
Two-Ten Conspiracy. L. Le Grand
Two Thieves and a Puma. John Reese
Two-Thirds of a Ghost. H. McCloy
Two Thousand Maniacs! H. G. Lewis
Two Thrillers. A. Christie
Two Thyrdes. B. Denham
Two Tickets Puzzle. J. J. Connington
Two Tickets to Destruction. G. S. Foster
Two Tickets to Tangier. V. W. Mason
Two Times Murder. Lanny Rogers
Two-Timing Blonde. Carter Brown
Two to Slay. H. Brinton
Two to Tangle. F. Kane
Two Undertakers. F. Beeding
Two Villains in One. Nicholas Carter
Two Way Cut. Peter Turnbull
Two-Way Frame. T. Harknett
Two-Way Mirror. D. Launay
Two-Way Witness. D. Franklin
Two Ways to Die. L. Thayer
Two Ways to Murder. E. Radford
Two Weeks Before Murder. W. Metcalfe
Two Weeks to Find a Killer. C. Davis
Two White Elephants. A. H. Veysey
Two Who Talked. Frank King
Two with a Gun. P. Malloch
Two Women. M. Pemberton
Two Women and Their Man. Mervyn Jones
Two Women in Black. J. W. Postgate
Two Women of London. E. Tennant
Two Wonderful Detectives. Old Sleuth
Two Worlds of Peggy Scott. D. Daniels
Twopence for a Rat's Tail. S. M. Lott
Twopenny Box. J. N. Chance
Two's Company. M. Kennedy
Twospot. B. Pronzini
Tycoon and the Tigress. W. R. Cox
Tycoon of Crime. R. Wallace
Tycoon's Death-Bed. G. Bellairs
Tyger at Bay. A. Riefe
Tyger by the Tail. A. Riefe
Tyger! Tyger! R. C. K. Ginn
Tyler Mystery. P. Temple
Tyneside Ultimatum. Angus Ross
Typed for a Corpse. A. Pruitt
Typescript. J. Trench
Typewritten Letter. R. H. Sherard
Typhoon. J. W. McConaughy
Typhoon Shipments. K. Klose
Typhoon's Secret. S. N. Sheridan
Tyrants of Today. C. L. Johnstone
Tyree Legend. W. Kelley
Tyro. J. Milne
Tyson Murder Case. T J. O'Connell

U-Boat in the Hebrides. A. D. Divine
U.N. Affair. S. Jason
U.N. Sabotage. R. Skimin
USSA. J. N. Frey
U.S.S.A. D. Madsen
U-700. J. Follett
UTBU. J. Kirkwood
Ubik. P. K. Dick
Ubique, the Scientific Bushranger. C. W. Martin
Ubiquitous Yank. Old Sleuth
Ugly Customer. C. F. Gregg
Ugly Face of Love and other stories. G. Kersh
Ugly Man. Anonymous
Ugly Man. E. Downey
Ugly Woman. M. Cameron
Ugly Woman. W. O'Farrell
Uist Project. J. Wood
Ukridge. P. G. Wodehouse
Ullman Code. R. Bernhard
Ulsterman. A. Lane
Ultimate. J. Lund
Ultimate Act. L. P. Bachmann
Ultimate Client. M. Avallone
Ultimate Conclusion. A. C. Fox-Davies
Ultimate Code. Nick Carter

Ultimate Deterrent. H. Janson
Ultimate Game. J. W. Cummings
Ultimate Game. R. Glendinning
Ultimate Good Luck. R. Ford
Ultimate Hostage. A. Gilchrist
Ultimate Island. L. Sieveking
Ultimate Issue. G. Markstein
Ultimate Judge. A. Howlett
Ultimate Secrets. L. V. Moore
Ultimate Sin. Stuart Hall
Ultimate Solution. E. Norden
Ultimate Terror. G. Wilson
Ultimatum. P. Bonnecarrere
Ultimatum. B. Meyer
Ultimatum. R. Rohmer
Ultimatum. A. Trew
Ultimatum: PU-94. U. Dan
Ultra Deadly. N. Randall
Ultraviolet Widow. F. Crane
Umbrella-Maker's Daughter. J. Caird
Umbrella Murder. C. Wells
Umgasi Diamonds. E. De Caire
Un Mystere. H. Greville
Unable by Reason of Death. Catherine Lewis
Unaccepted Death. H. Gilson
Unaccountable Crook. Nicholas Carter
Unafraid. Gerald Butler
Unafraid. E. M. Ingram
Unaltered Cat. A. Lewin
Unappointed Rounds. D. M. Disney
Unbalanced Accounts. K. Gallison
Unbalanced Acts. J. Raines
Unbarred Door. C. H. Bullivant
Unbecoming Habits. T. Heald
Unbegotten. J. Creasey
Unbidden. R. Chetwynd-Hayes
Unbidden Guest. Frances Cooke
Unbridled. M. Daniel
Unbriefed Mission. L. Bridgemont
Uncanny. G. C. Bachelor
Uncanny. W. Louder
Uncanny Adventures. E. Ascher
Uncanny Stories. May Sinclair
Uncanny Tales. R. T. Hopkins
Uncas Insland Murdrs. F. W. Bronson
Uncertain Agent. S. Donald
Uncertain Death. Anthony Gilbert
Uncertain Glory. H. Meadow
Uncertain Heart. Carter Brown
Uncertain Judgement. G. Mitcham
Uncertain Quest. E. Messenger
Uncertain Sound. Roy Lewis
Uncertain Treasure. D. Lee
Uncertain Trumpets. B. McGregor
Uncertain Voyage. D. Gilman
Uncharted. S. M. Parkman
Uncharted Island. S. M. Parkman
Uncharted Seas. D. Wheatley
Uncharted Waters. R. Stock
Uncivil Seasons. M. Malone
Unclaimed Daughter. Anonymous
Unclaimed Letter. A. M. Sholl
Unclaimed Million. H. Maxwell
Uncle Abner, Master of Mysteries. M. D. Post
Uncle Charles. G. Simenon
Uncle Charles Locked Himself In. G. Simenon
Uncle from India. E. D. Pierson
Uncle Happy. P. O'Donnell
Uncle Harry. T. Job
Uncle in Trouble. E. Rowan
Uncle Jack. W. Besant
Uncle James Pays a Visit. M. McNeile
Uncle James's Golf Match. H. C. McNeile
Uncle Joe's Legacy and other stories. G. Boothby
Uncle Oscar's Niece. G. Goodchild
Uncle Paul. C. Fremlin
Uncle Sagamore and His Girls. C. Williams
Uncle Sam, Detective. W. A. Dupuy
Uncle Sam's Bad Boys. B. D. Adsit
Uncle Silas. J. S. Le Fanu
Uncle Simon. M. Stacpoole
Uncle Target. G. Lyall
Uncle William and other stories. D. G. Brown
Uncle Xavier. D. H. Landels

Unclean. G. Des Cars
Unclean Bird. M. Reinhardt
Uncle's Advice. W. Hewlett
Uncle's Crime. J. H. Robinson
Uncoffin'd Clay. G. Mitchell
Uncollected Cases of Solar Pons. B. Copper
Uncollected Stories. A. C. Doyle
Uncollected Wodehouse. P. G. Wodehouse
Uncommitted Man. R. E. Pickering
Uncommon Cold. E. H. Clements
Uncommon Danger. E. Ambler
Uncommon Market. H. Janson
Uncomplaining Corpses. B. Halliday
Unconfessed. M. H. Bradley
Unconfessed. Maxwell Gray
Unconquerable. Helen MacInnes
Unconscious Crime. N. T. Oliver
Unconscious Witness. R. A. Freeman
Unconventional Beauty. V. Tremont
Uncounted Hour. W. Allen
Uncover Agent. H. Janson
Uncreated Man. A. Fryers
Uncrossed Boundary. K. Arthur
Uncrowned Prince. J. J. Farrington
Uncut Diamonds. D. Brechin
Undaunted. J. Harris
Under a Ban. Mrs. Lodge
Under a Black Veil. Nicholas Carter
Under a Cloud. J. K. Ludlum
Under a Cloud. V. Siller
Under a Cloud. T. W. Speight
Under a Mask. J. K. Leys
Under a Mask. J. B. Williams
Under a Monsoon Cloud. H. R. F. Keating
Under a Strange Mask. F. Barrett
Under a Veil. Old Sleuth
Under Blue Skies. H. D. Stacpoole
Under Bow Bells. J. Hollingshead
Under Contract. L. Cody
Under Cover. W. Martyn
Under Cover. R. C. Megrue
Under Cover. T. Philbin
Under Cover Man. J. Wilstach
Under Cover of Darkness. Donald Smith
Under Cover of Daylight. Jim Hall
Under Cover of Night. R. M. Gilchrist
Under Cover of Night. M. L. Stokes
Under Cover of Night. C. Virmonne
Under Dog and other stories. A. Christie
Under Dogs. H. Footner
Under Egyptian Skies. S. Rathbone
Under Etna. L. Cook
Under False Colors. Nicholas Carter
Under False Pretenses. A. Sergeant
Under Fate's Wheel. L. L. Lynch
Under Fire. R. C. Megrue
Under Fire. R. Parker
Under Gemini. R. Pilcher
Under Groove. A. Stringer
Under His Thumb. Anonymous
Under His Thumb. D. J. MacKenzie
Under Jekyll's Hyde. T. J. Kelly
Under Life's Key, and other stories. M. C. Hay
Under Lock and Key. T. W. Speight
Under London. V. Gielgud
Under Love's Rule. M. E. Braddon
Under Masks. H. F. Wood
Under North Star and Southern Cross. Francis Sinclair
Under Observation. Douglas Christie
Under One Flag. Richard Marsh
Under One Roof. J. Payn
Under Orders. M. Daniel
Under Orion. J. Law
Under Police Observation. G. Chester
Under Police Protection. J. G. Brandon
Under Pressure. F. Herbert
Under Proof. J. Cannan
Under St. Paul's. R. Dowling
Under Seal of the Confessional. Mrs. C. Kernahan
Under Sealed Orders. G. Allen
Under Sealed Orders. J. G. Brandon
Under Sealed Orders. H. A. Cody
Under-Secretary. W. LeQueux

Under Sentence. Mary Cross
Under Sentence of Death. Old Sleuth
Under Siege. S. Coonts
Under Suspicion. H. W. Leggett
Under Suspicion. A. MacVicar
Under Suspicion. A. Sergeant
Under Suspicion. A. O. Tibbits
Under Suspicion. R. Trevor
Under the Allies Flag. J. Tregellis
Under the Black Eagle. A. W. Marchmont
Under the Boardwalk. B. Kent
Under the Bright Lights. D. Woodrell
Under the Broad Arrow. M. Leighton
Under the Cherry Tree. P. Traill
Under the Clock. C. H. E. Brookfield
Under the Dragon Throne. L. T. Meade
Under the Eagle's Wing. G. H. Teed
Under the Eye of Night. R. E. Mills
Under the Fourth—? P. Luck
Under the Freeze. G. Bartram
Under the Goad. C. A. Brandreth
Under the Golden Bough. G. F. Gibbs
Under the Great Seal. J. Hatton
Under the Ice. R. P. Henrick
Under the Icefall. H. McLeave
Under the Influence. G. Kerr
Under the Influence. E. Travis
Under the Knife. T. Gerritsen
Under the Lake. Stuart Woods
Under the Law. J. Wilder
Under the Lens. F. B. Austin
Under the Long Barrow. C. Haddon
Under the Quiet Water. F. S. Wees
Under the Red Flag. M. E. Braddon
Under the Red Flag. M. J. Pemberton
Under the Red Star. M. Gerard
Under the Rose. H. Wood
Under the Shadow. H. L. Jones
Under the Shadow of Night. M. Pike
Under the Skin. Dorothea Bennett
Under the Spell of the Orient. C. E. Perry
Under the Street Lamp. J. Hawke
Under the Sunset. B. Stoker
Under the Surface. J. K. Stafford
Under the Tiger's Claws. Nicholas Carter
Under the Wall. Nick Carter
Under the Will, and other tales. M. C. Hay
Under the Willows. E. Van Loon
Under Three Flags. B. L. Taylor
Under Tropic Skies. L. Becke
Under Twelve Stars. H. S. Keeler
Under Two Skies. E. W. Hornung
Under Western Eyes. J. Conrad
Under-World. J. Osbourne
Undercover. S. Santiago
Undercover Agent. E. Ellison
Undercover Cat. The Gordons
Undercover Cat Prowls Again. The Gordons
Undercover Cutie. M. Brody
Undercover: El Salvador. J. Tabler
Undercover Girl. Roland Daniel
Undercover Man. H. H. Kirst
Undercover Run. L. Dykes
Undercover Woman. D. Herzog
Undercurrent. J. Bogar
Undercurrent. M. Boggan
Undercurrent. B. Jefferis
Undercurrent. B. Pronzini
Undercurrents. Ridley Pearson
Underdog. W. R. Burnett
Underdog. Mrs. Middlemass
Underground. J. S. Dutton
Underground. J. J. Farjeon
Underground. J. Hallums
Underground. Russell James
Underground. J. K. Leys
Underground. J. Raskin
Underground. M. Sloan
Underground. C. Stratton
Underground Cities Contract. P. Atlee
Underground City. H. L. Humes
Underground Connection. P. Niesewand
Underground Man. J. P. Hailey
Underground Man. R. Macdonald

Underground Men. M. Carrel
Underground Mystery. R. H. Sherard
Underground Syndicate. A. M. Williamson
Underhandover. Kenneth O'Hara
Underkill. B. Crowther
Underlay. B. N. Malzberg
Undersong. H. C. MacIlwaine
Understrike. J. Gardner
Understudy. D. H. Landels
Understudy. M. Tabor
Understudy to Murder. Dulcie Gray
Undertaker. J. Quinn
Undertaker Dies. Garnett Weston
Undertaker Wind. W. Masterson
Undertaker's Field. H. Compton
Undertaker's Gone Bananas. P. Zindel
Undertow. D. Cory
Underwood Mystery. C. J. Dutton
Underworld. Reginald Hill
Underworld. I. Wolfert
Underworld Feud. Reginald Kirby
Underworld Nights. C. Raven
Undesirable Company. F. Ryck
Undetective. B. Graeme
Undine. P. B. Young
Undiplomatic Exit. J. Sherwood
Undisclosed Client. E. Wallace
Undiscovered Crimes. Waters
Undivided Light. C. Massie
Undoing of Mrs. Cransby. H. C. McNeile
Undoubted Deed. J. Davey
Undressed to Kill. P. Cheyney
Undressed to Kill. D. Haring
Undue Influence. M. Borgenicht
Undue Influence. S. Yastrow
Undying Monster. J. D. Kerruish
Undying Serpent. T. B. Morris
Une Tenebreuse Affaire. H. D. Balzac
Unearthly. D. Daniels
Uneaseful Death. Mollie Hardwick
Uneasy Alibi. N. Karta
Uneasy Freehold. D. Macardle
Uneasy Is the Grave. J. S. Strange
Uneasy Lies. E. Zaremba
Uneasy Lies the Dead. M. E. Chaber
Uneasy Lies the Head. W. L. Rohde
Uneasy Lies the Head. R. Tine
Uneasy Money. M. Tannock
Uneasy Street. B. Chetwynd
Uneasy Street. S. Coburn
Uneasy Street. Wade Miller
Uneasy Street. A. S. Roche
Uneasy Sun. M. Butterworth
Uneasy Terms. P. Cheyney
Uneasy Virtue. Reginald Campbell
Uneasy Virtue. Dana Wilson
Uneasy Years. L. Noel
Unending Track. J. Farrimond
Unequal Match. Rachelle Edwards
Uneven Score. C. A. Neggers
Unexpected. F. Hume
Unexpected Adventure. T. F. W. Hickey
Unexpected Angel. J. B. Watney
Unexpected Corpse. E. L. Cushing
Unexpected Corpse. B. J. Oliphant
Unexpected Daughter. P. Trent
Unexpected Death. Dell Shannon
Unexpected Developments. R. B. Dominic
Unexpected Guest. A. Christie
Unexpected Legacy. E. R. Punshon
Unexpected Mrs. Pollifax. D. Gilman
Unexpected Move. S. Campbell
Unexpected Night. E. Daly
Unexpected Vacation. M. Naylor
Unexploded Man. Leslie Watkins
Unfair Exchange. M. Babson
Unfair Fare Affair. P. Leslie
Unfair Lady. G. Fairlie
Unfaithful. Alex Morrison
Unfinished Business. M. Cronin
Unfinished Business. C. Lucas
Unfinished Business. S. Robinett
Unfinished Clue. G. Heyer
Unfinished Crime. E. S. Holding

Unfinished Crime. H. McCloy
Unfinished Letter. Nicholas Carter
Unfinished Murder. E. W. Lyon
Unfinished Tapestry. Susan Leslie
Unfit to Plead. J. Dellbridge
Unfolding Years. A. Gask
Unforbidden Sin. Roy Vickers
Unforeseen. D. Macardle
Unforeseen. J. C. Snaith
Unforgettable. T. Meldal-Johnson
Unforgetting Heart. Margery Lawrence
Unforgivable Sin. A. Applin
Unforgiven. Maynah Lewis
Unforgiven. P. J. MacDonald
Unforgiving Minutes. M. M. Pulver
Unforgiving Moment. F. Cowen
Unforgiving Wind. J. Harris
Unforgotten. L. Conway
Unforgotten. D. Winston
Unfortunate Murderer. R. Hull
Unfortunate Replacement. M. Jahn
Unfortunate Rogue. Warren Miller
Unfriendly Persuasion. W. A. Ballinger
Unfunny Money. G. Alexander
Ungilded Lily. Morton Cooper
Unguarded. D. Daniels
Unguarded Hour. A. W. Marchmont
Unguarded Hour. D. Vane
Unguarded Moment. H. A. Wrenn
Unhallowed Ground. P. Guernsey
Unhallowed Murder. S. Nash
Unhandsome Corpse. S. Campion
Unhanged Man. A. Hunter
Unhappy Hooligan. S. Palmer
Unhappy Hophead. Spike Gordon
Unhappy Lady and other stories. P. Cheyney
Unhappy New Year. C. C. Estes
Unhappy Parting. Elsie Lee
Unhappy Rendezvous. A. Nash
Unhappy Returns. E. Lemarchand
Unhappy Ship. E. L. Long
Unhappy Souls. D. Rogan
Unheeded Warning. Dick Stewart
Unholy Alliance. B. Crowther
Unholy Child. C. Breslin
Unholy Communion. Richard Hughes
Unholy Crusade. D. Wheatley
Unholy Dying. R. T. Campbell
Unholy Flame. O. L. Rosmanith
Unholy Ground. J. Brady
Unholy Matrimony. J. Dillmann
Unholy Matrimony. Winifred Graham
Unholy Moses. P. Degrave
Unholy Mourning. D. Lippincott
Unholy Sanctuary. M. Higgins
Unholy Spell. C. Vincent
Unholy Terror. George Douglas
Unholy Three. T. Robbins
Unholy Trio. H. Kane
Unholy Trio. J. Ronald
Unholy Wife. J. Roeburt
Unholy Wish, and other stories. H. Wood
Unholy Writ. D. Williams
Unhung Man. A. Hunter
Unhurrying Chase. M. Markey
Unicorn. C. Goodall
Unicorn Caper. J. W. Lampp
Unicorn Group. L. R. Bobker
Unicorn Murders. Carter Dickson
Unidentified Woman. M. G. Eberhart
Uniformed Killers. R. Wallace
Uninvited. F. A. Chittenden
Uninvited. T. J. Kelly
Uninvited. D. Macardle
Uninvited Corpse. Michael Underwood
Uninvited Corpse. P. Whelton
Uninvited Ghost. L. Rose
Uninvited Guest. G. H. Coxe
Uninvited Guest. B. Kennedy
Uninvited Guests. J. J. Farjeon
Union Bust. R. Sapir
Union Club Mysteries. I. Asimov
Union Down. S. Campbell
Unique Hamlet. V. Starrett

U

Unique Mistress. Mark Randolph
Unity Penfold. M. Tabor
Universe Against Her. J. H. Schmitz
Unjust Jury. Winifred Duke
Unjustly Branded. R. H. Poole
Unkindly Cup. H. McElroy
Unkindness of Ravens. T. B. Reagan
Unkindness of Ravens. R. Rendell
Unknown. J. Barclay
Unknown. E. Southworth
Unknown Agent. M. Annesley
Unknown Assailant. P. Hamilton
Unknown Blond. L. L. Brookman
Unknown Conan Doyle. A. C. Doyle
Unknown Countess. Emerson Bennett
Unknown Enemy. Gret Lane
Unknown Foe. J. K. Stafford
Unknown Goddess. A. Philips
Unknown Hand. G. Linscott
Unknown Hand. M. Peterson
Unknown Man #89. E. Leonard
Unknown Man, Seen in Profile. Kenneth O'Hara
Unknown Menace. Donald Stuart
Unknown Mission. N. Deane
Unknown Murderer. H. Liggett
Unknown Path. Lady A. Scott
Unknown People. R. West
Unknown Quantity. M. G. Eberhart
Unknown Quantity. W. E. Johns
Unknown Quest. Ralph Scott
Unknown River. J. M. Scott
Unknown Seven. H. Coverdale
Unknown Skyjacker. S. N. Rampal
Unknown Soldier. M. Hastings
Unknown Terror. H. Holt
Unknown Tomorrow. W. LeQueux
Unknown Warrior. J. Leasor
Unknown Woman. L. Hoffman
Unlamented. D. Daniels
Unlatched Door. L. Thayer
Unlawful. C. Turner
Unlawful Justice. John Gloag
Unlawful Occasions. H. Cecil
Unlawful Occasions. P. Wentworth
Unleashed Will. Christopher Clark
Unless a Child Is Born—. B. Heygate
Unlighted House. J. Hay
Unloved. D. Birkley
Unloved Wife. E. Southworth
Unlucky Break. M. Clinton
Unlucky Break. O. Mills
Unlucky Dip. Margaret Henry
Unlucky for Some. A. Behrend
Unlucky Mark. F. E. Penny
Unlucky Number. E. Phillpotts
Unlucky Virgin. M. Storme
Unmasked at Last. H. Hill
Unmasking a King. O. Newman
Unnamed. W. LeQueux
Unnatural Break. T. Girtin
Unnatural Causes. H. Hawton
Unnatural Causes. P. D. James
Unnatural Causes. T. T. Noguchi
Unnatural Causes. M. Olshaker
Unnatural Death. M. Richmond
Unnatural Death. D. L. Sayers
Unnatural Deeds. E. Nisot
Unnatural Hazard. B. Cork
Unnatural Selection. J. Ranbern
Unneutral Murder. H. Footner
Unofficial Executor. H. F. Moulton
Unofficial Rosie. A. McDonald
Unofficial Spy. A. O. Pollard
Unorthodox Corpse. Carter Brown
Unorthodox Methods. D. Valentine
Unorthodox Murder of Rabbi Moss. J. Telushkin
Unorthodox Murder of Rabbi Wahl. J. Telushkin
Unorthodox Practices. M. Piesman
Unpardonable Crime. D. B. Miller
Unpardonable Sin. A. D. Vinton
Unpleasant Profession of Jonathan Hoag. R. A. Heinlein
Unpleasantness at the Bellona Club. D. L. Sayers

Unpossessed. W. H. Fielding
Unprofessional Spy. M. Underwood
Unprotected. I. Barry
Unpublishable Memoirs. A. S. W. Rosenbach
Unquenchable Flame. A. J. Rees
Unquiet Corpse. W. Sloan
Unquiet Dead. M. Bingley
Unquiet Grave. J. LaPierre
Unquiet Grave. J. S. Strange
Unquiet Night. P. Carlon
Unquiet Night. M. Cronin
Unquiet Sleep. W. Haggard
Unraveled Knots. B. Orczy
Unraveled Skeins. G. Gow
Unravish'd Bride. J. Hope-Simpson
Unreasonable Doubt. E. Ferrars
Unrehearsed Incident and other stories. E. Baume
Unrelenting. C. W. Dodge
Unrepentant. C. Phillips
Unrepentant Sinners. L. Royer
Unrequited Affection. H. Balzac
Unripe Gold. G. Jenkins
Unruly Son. R. Barnard
Unscheduled Flight. H. Atkinson
Unscrupulous Mr. Callaghan. P. Cheyney
Unseemly End. R. Jeffries
Unseen! A. P. Terhune
Unseen. Ethel L. White
Unseen Assassin. H. Janson
Unseen Barrier. M. Gerard
Unseen Ear. N. S. Lincoln
Unseen Enemy. C. Landon
Unseen Foes. Nicholas Carter
Unseen Hand. L. L. Lynch
Unseen Hand. C. H. New
Unseen Hand. I. Stark
Unseen Hand. Valentine
Unseen Hands. R. O. Chipperfield
Unseen Torment. K. Kimbrough
Unseen Way. D. Newing
Unseen Witness. B. Bolt
Unsheltered. D. Ward
Unsolved. B. Graeme
Unsolved Case of Sherlock Holmes. Allen Sharp
Unsolved Mysteries. V. Tweedale
Unspeakable. S. Ransome
Unspeakable Turk. G. Horton
Unspoken Word. M. Gerard
Unsuccessful Man. T. Nielsen
Unsuitable Job for a Woman. P. D. James
Unsuitable Miss Pelham. June Drummond
Ursula. K. D. King
Unsung Road. S. Harvester
Unsuspected. C. Armstrong
Unsuspected. R. Brome
Unsuspected Chasm. M. Innes
Unsuspected Conduct. E. K. Stirling
Unsuspected Evil. D. M. Disney
Unsuspecting Victim. J. F. Drexler
Untamed. H. Janson
Untamed. V. Norwood
Untaxed Whiskey. B. Wayde
Untidy Murder. F. Lockridge
Until Death. S. Somers
Until Death Do Us Part. M. McMullen
Until Proven Guilty. C. W. Calhoun
Until Proven Guilty. J. A. Jance
Until Proven Innocent. Susan Kelly
Until She Dies. W. Wright
Until She Was Dead. R. Hull
Until Temptation Do Us Part. Carter Brown
Until the Dawn. S. E. Walford
Until the Day She Dies. J. MacLaren-Ross
Until They Are Dead. John Lloyd
Until You Are Dead. H. Kane
Untimely Death. C. Hare
Untimely Frost. E. G. Cousins
Untimely Guest. M. Babson
Untimely Ripped. M. McShane
Untimely Slain. J. Gray
Untitled and other radio dramas. N. Corman
Unto Death Utterly. M. Cumberland
Unto the Grave. John Penn
Unto the Third Generation. M. P. Shiel

Untold Legend of the Bat Man. L. Wein
Untold Sequel to the Strange Case of Dr. Jekyll and Mr. Hyde. Anonymous
Untold Sherlock Holmes. W. E. Dudley
Untold Tale. L. K. Vincent
Untouchable Juli. J. Aldridge
Untouchables. M. H. Albert
Untouchables. K. Blake
Unusual Behaviour. Lettice Cooper
Unvarnished Tales. W. McKay
Unvarnished Truth. R. Ryton
Unveiled. M. A. Dickens
Unwanted Attentions. K. K. Beck
Unwanted Child. P. Conway
Unwanted Corpse. M. Burton
Unwanted Witness. George Douglas
Unwashed Gods. E. C. Vivian
Unwelcome Audience. M. Russell
Unwelcome Corpse. B. Frost
Unwelcome Presence. Malcolm Gray
Unwelcome Rapture. M. Richmond
Unwelcome Visitor. A. Corliss
Unwilling Adventurer. John Gloag
Unwilling Angel. Alan Stuart
Unwilling Bride. F. Hume
Unwilling Guest. E. Ellison
Unwilling Rebel. M. Lynch
Unwilling to Wed. M. Richmond
Unwilling Witness. T. Holloway
Unwise Guy. B. Johns
Unwise Virgin. Mrs. C. Kernahan
Unwitting Accomplice. T. Vasilos
Unwitting Witness. A. Blair
Up a Winding Stair. H. V. Dixon
Up Against It. V. Vanardy
Up and Coming Man. F. Branston
Up for Grabs. A. A. Fair
Up for Grabs. John Harris
Up from Earth's Center. K. Robeson
Up from the Grave. D. Craig
Up Hill, Down Dale. E. Phillpotts
Up Jumped the Devil. C. F. Adams
Up, McLean! G. Goodchild
Up North. T. Lund
Up North. J. H. Vahey
Up the Garden Path. M. Burton
Up the Garden Path. J. Rhode
Up the Ladder. M. M. Murray
Up the Ladder of Gold. E. P. Oppenheim
Up This Crooked Way. H. Holman
Up Tight. John Allen
Up-Tight Blonde. Carter Brown
Up to Her Neck. J. N. Chance
Up to No Good. A. M. Stein
Up to the Hilt. A. Rowe
Up Will Go Parliament. G. Jones
Up with Your Hands. G. Jones
Upas Tree. R. McMurdy
Upfold Farm Mystery. A. Fielding
Upfold Witch. Josephine Bell
Upland Mystery. M. R. Hatch
Upmarket Affair. T. Harknett
Upon Some Midnights Clear. K. C. Constantine
Upper Case. M. Merrick
Upper Hand. S. Hood
Upperdown. Stephen Cook
Upright Man. J. E. Lord
Uproar in the Village. O. Jellinek
Uprush of Mayhem. J. S. Scott
Upside Down Murders. H. Austin
Upside Down Tree. H. Kruger
Upside Downside. R. Goulart
Upstairs. J. L. Rickard
Upstairs and Downstairs. C. Carnac
Upstairs and Downstairs. R. S. Thorn
Upstairs, Downstairs. C. Carnac
Upstart. P. P. Read
Uranian Jewel Case. R. Dark
Uranium Murders. J. E. Barry
Urban District Lover. J. T. Story
Urban Prey. P. Beere
Urbane Guerilla. Stanley Johnson
Urbane Terrorist. M. Pedrick
Urge for Justice. J. Wainwright

Urgent Action. N. Forde
Urgent Conference. N. Forde
Urgent Delivery. N. Forde
Urgent Enquiry. N. Forde
Urgent Hangman. P. Cheyney
Urgent Lust. Stuart Hall
Urgent Private Affairs. H. F. Moulton
Urgent Trip. N. Forde
Urgent Wedding. N. Forde
Urn Burial. P. Ruell
Ursa Ultimatum. T. Baxter
Ursala, the Proud. K. Kimbrough
Ursula Lenorme. T. W. Speight
Ursula Vanet. A. Mills
Ursus. D. Dvorkin
Us or Them War. W. Garner
Used in Evidence. P. Froud
Usurpation. T. P. Lathy
Utmost Ebb. R. Harrison
Utmost Good Faith. L. M. Shakespeare
Utopia Affair. D. McDaniel
Uttermost Farthing. R. A. Freeman
Uttermost Farthing. M. B. Lowndes

V. T. Pynchon
V As in Victim. L. Treat
V.C. D. C. Murray
V for Vendetta. Alan Moore
V for Vengeance. D. Wheatley
V for Victim. M. Childress
V for Vitality. H. Janson
V for Vixen. D. Haring
V.I.P. W. L. Rohde
V.I.P. E. Trevor
V-J Day. A. Fields
V-Mann Papers. C. Cruickshank
V Plan. G. Seton
V-3. I. Melchior
V2 Expert. A. J. Evans
V2 Virus. E. Cannon
Vaaldorf Diamond. Eva Dane
Vacancy. P. Mann
Vacancy with Crime. M. Burton
Vacant Possession. M. Butcher
Vacant Throne. P. Hanna
Vacation with Fear. J. T. Story
Vagabond Nights. H. S. Keeler
Vagabond Sonata. L. Geoghegan
Vagabond Vamp. H. Janson
Vagabond's Honor. E. D. Pierson
Vagrant Bride. Mrs. C. Kernahan
Vagrant Duke. G. F. Gibbs
Vagrant Wife. F. Warden
Vaia's Lord. J. Middlemass
Vail. T. Hoyle
Vail's Gate. J. Cabot
Vain Ambitions. R. Gaines
Vain Citadel. B. S. Morgan
Vain Escape. E. C. Vivian
Vain Pride. C. Kingston
Vain Sacrifice. Nicholas Carter
Vain Tales from "Vanity Fair". L. Heilgers
Vaivaisukko's Bride. D. Scott-Moncrieff
Val Strange. D. C. Murray
Valago Crest. J. A. Bartlett
Valazy Family and other narratives. Waters
Valcour Meets Murder. R. King
Valdez Is Coming. E. Leonard
Valediction. R. B. Parker
Valentine Estate. S. Ellin
Valentine Vaughan Omnibus. R. T. Hopkins
Valentine Victim. D. McLeish
Valerie. S. Nichols
Valhalla. George Long
Valhalla Exchange. H. Patterson
Valhalla Testament. J. Land
Valiant. H. Hall
Valiant Jester. M. Edwin
Valiant View. T. Mundy
Valkyrie Directive. P. MacAlan
Valkyrie Mandate. R. Vaughan
Valkyrie Project. M. Kilian
Vallency Tradition. G. Merrick
Vallette Heritage. L. Bronte

Valley. Clifford Irving
Valley and the Shadow. W. H. Boore
Valley of Achor. P. C. De Crispigny
Valley of Bells. D. Whitelaw
Valley of Collares. Mrs. R. P. M. Yorke
Valley of Creeping Men. R. Crawley
Valley of Death. S. Jason
Valley of Death. Paul Ross
Valley of Doom. M. Richmond
Valley of Fear. J. Creasey
Valley of Fear. A. C. Doyle
Valley of Fear. R. Gar
Valley of Fear. F. A. Symonds
Valley of Ghosts. J. Tobias
Valley of Ghosts. E. Wallace
Valley of Green Shadows. L. A. Knight
Valley of Hanoi. I. R. Blacker
Valley of Headstrong Men. J. S. Fletcher
Valley of Lies. G. Goodchild
Valley of Lights. S. Gallagher
Valley of Lost Gold. G. Bettany
Valley of Never-Come-Back, and other stories. B. Grimshaw
Valley of Night. J. Farnol
Valley of No Escape. James Preston
Valley of No Return. C. Virmonne
Valley of Perils. A. McColl
Valley of Poppies. J. Hatton
Valley of Sapphires. M. Lindsey
Valley of Shadows. G. Colmore
Valley of Shadows. D. Lyons
Valley of Silence. C. Randell
Valley of Silent Men. J. O. Curwood
Valley of Skulls. O. Sackville
Valley of Smugglers. A. W. Upfield
Valley of Suspicion. F. Riddell
Valley of Suspicion. W. C. Tuttle
Valley of Terror. Donald Stuart
Valley of the Assassins. I. MacAlister
Valley of the Damned. V. Norwood
Valley of the Fox. J. Hone
Valley of the Ravens. N. Buckingham
Valley of the Shadow. W. LeQueux
Valley of the Shadow. M. Richmond
Valley of the Shadows. D. Daniels
Valley of the Shadows. Diane Stevens
Valley of Twisted Trails. W. C. Tuttle
Valley of Vanishing Herds. W. C. Tuttle
Valley of Vision. H. Van Dyke
Valley of Vultures. P. Edwards
Valley So Low. M. W. Wellman
Valley Vixen. B. A. Williams
Valparaiso. F. R. E. Nicolas
Valperga. M. W. Shelley
Valrose Mystery. W. LeQueux
Valse Caprice. Gavin Holt
Valse Macabre. K. M. Knight
Value for Murder. Craig Cooper
Vamp Till Ready. T. Rieman
Vamphyri. B. Lumley
Vampire. R. Hodder
Vampire. S. Horler
Vampire. J. Sherman
Vampire Abroad. M. Dalman
Vampire Affair. D. McDaniel
Vampire, and sixteen other narratives. L. H. Fox
Vampire Bat. R. St. Clair
Vampire Cameo. D. Nile
Vampire Chase. Stephen Brett
Vampire City. T. S. King
Vampire Contessa. Marilyn Ross
Vampire Curse. D. Winston
Vampire in the Shadows. M. Lovell
Vampire Man. G. Verner
Vampire Murders. R. Wallace
Vampire of N'Gobi. R. Cullum
Vampire of the Andes. H. Carew
Vampire of the Skies. J. Corbett
Vampire Tapes. A. Randolphe
Vampires and the Witch. L. Falk
Vampire's Honeymoon. C. Woolrich
Vampire's Moon. P. Saxon
Vampires of Finistere. P. Saxon
Vampires of Vengeance. J. A. Kolbe

Vampires Overhead. A. Hyder
Vampire's Trail. Nicholas Carter
Vampyre. Tim Kelly
Vampyre of Moura. V. Coffman
Van. J. Ball
Van Alstine Case. Nicholas Carter
Van Beck Will. H. W. Jessup
Van Bibber and Others. R. H. Davis
Van Dreisen Affair. H. Roth
Van Dylk Diamonds. A. Applin
Van Dyne Collection. M. D. Scott
Van Langeren Girl. Brian Cooper
Van Norton Murders. C. R. Jones
Van Peltz Diamonds. Anonymous
Van Rhyne Heritage. L. Bronte
Van Roon. J. C. Snaith
Van Suyden Sapphires. Charles Carey
Van, the Government Detective. H. P. Halsey
Van, the Government Detective. Old Sleuth
Vancenza. M. Robinson
Vandals. W. Hildick
Vandekkers. R. Thorndike
Vanderleigh Legacy. B. Caldwell
Vanderlyn's Adventure. M. B. Lowndes
Vandersley. Edward Brown
Vandor Mystery. C. F. Gregg
Vane Pursuit. C. MacLeod
Vanessa. K. Martin
Vanish. A. F. Mortimer
Vanish in an Instant. M. Millar
Vanished. M. Carleton
Vanished. F. Knebel
Vanished. W. Norwood
Vanished. B. Pronzini
Vanished Emperor. P. Andreae
Vanished Guest. O. Binns
Vanished Messenger. E. P. Oppenheim
Vanished Million. W. W. Sayer
Vanished Prospector. T. Lund
Vanished Squadron. J. R. Holden
Vanished Stamps Mystery. M. Poole
Vanished Three. R. C. Armour
Vanished Vice-Counsel. M. Annesley
Vanished Yacht. E. H. Burrage
Vanisher. K. Robeson
Vanishers. Donald Hamilton
Vanishing Act. M. Butterworth
Vanishing Act. J. Magezis
Vanishing Brands. W. C. Tuttle
Vanishing Bride. Magali
Vanishing Bridegroom. A. Sharpe
Vanishing Celebrities. A. Alington
Vanishing Cheques. B. Capes
Vanishing Clue. Anonymous
Vanishing Clue. H. K. McDonnel
Vanishing Corpse. Anthony Gilbert
Vanishing Corpse. E. Queen
Vanishing Death. W. M. Graydon
Vanishing Death. N. Vane
Vanishing Diamond. G. Campbell
Vanishing Diary. J. Rhode
Vanishing Emerald. Nicholas Carter
Vanishing Goddess. P. S. McCoy
Vanishing Gold Truck. H. S. Keeler
Vanishing Hand. E. L. Wilson
Vanishing Heiress. Nicholas Carter
Vanishing Holes Murder. P. Chambers
Vanishing Idol. G. F. Gibbs
Vanishing Ladies. R. Marsten
Vanishing Man. R. A. Freeman
Vanishing Men. R. W. Child
Vanishing Men. W. B. M. Ferguson
Vanishing Men. G. M. Winsor
Vanishing Murderer. C. J. Dutton
Vanishing of Betty Varian. C. Wells
Vanishing of Ira Bouck. J. St. David
Vanishing of Tera. F. Hume
Vanishing Point. V. Canning
Vanishing Point. Coningsby Dawson
Vanishing Point. P. Flower
Vanishing Point. A. Tabucchi
Vanishing Point. P. Wentworth
Vanishing Professor. F. MacIsaac
Vanishing Racehorse. H. L. Hambling

Vanishing Senator. J. Philips
Vanishing Shadows. J. Maconechy
Vanishing Smuggler. S. Chalmers
Vanishing Trick. H. Carmichael
Vanishing Vector. J. P. Evans
Vanishing Venus. Jason
Vanishing Vixen. R. P. Sparkia
Vanishing Yacht. E. Anstey
Vanity Box. A. M. Williamson
Vanity Case. C. Wells
Vanity Dies Hard. R. Rendell
Vanity Row. W. R. Burnett
Vanity's Daughter. H. Smart
Vantage Hall. C. Gluyas
Vantage Point. K. Rogers
Vantage Striker. H. Simpson
Vantine Diamonds. Seamark
Varanoff Trandition. O. Panbourne
Vardy. J. Harris
Variable Man. P. K. Dick
Variant. A. Engel
Variation on a Theme of Murder. C. G. Jarvie
Variations on a Theme. D. E. Fisher
Variety. R. Connell
Variety Jack. Old Sleuth
Variety of Weapons. R. King
Varkaus Conspiracy. J. Dalmas
Varney the Vampire. M. J. Rymer
Varney the Vampire. Tim Kelly
Varsity Man. I. Allen
Vase Mystery. V. Loder
Vasiliko Affair. M. Culpan
Vasty Deep. S. C. Cumberland
Vatchman Switch. P. Kinsley
Vatican Affairs. M. Valdemi
Vatican Cellars. A. Gide
Vatican Gold. J. R. Zodrow
Vatican Kill. D. Revere
Vatican Rip. Jonathan Gash
Vatican Swindle. A. Gide
Vatican Target. B. Schiff
Vatican Vendetta. Nick Carter
Vault of Doom. A. Skene
Vaults of Blackarden Castle. A. Gask
Vavel, the Wonderful Treasure Seeker. Old Sleuth
Vector. R. Swigart
Vectors. T. Krueger
Veetols. Anthony Graham
Vegas. M. Franklin
Vegas Legacy. O. Demaris
Vegas Trap. Hal Kantor
Vegas Vampire. J. Sherman
Vegas Vendetta. D. Pendleton
Vegas Vengeance. C. Ramm
Vegas Wenches. J. L. Rubel
Vegetable Duck. J. Rhode
Veil. G. C. Chesbro
Veil. E. S. Stevens
Veil of Death. R. Simons
Veil of Ignorance. M. Quill
Veil of Islam. L. Noel
Veil of Secrets. U.-M. Parker
Veil of Silence. A. Seilaz
Veil of Treachery. D. Daniels
Veil Withdrawn. B. J. Maddux
Veiled Beauty. Old Sleuth
Veiled Hand. F. Wicks
Veiled Isis. Michael Hastings
Veiled Lady. L. Falk
Veiled Lady. H. Sealis
Veiled Lady. F. Warden
Veiled Lady and The Mystery of the Baghdad Chest. A. Christie
Veiled Man. W. LeQueux
Veiled Murder. Alice Campbell
Veiled One. R. Rendell
Veiled Picture. E. J. Lysaght
Veiled Prisoner. G. Leroux
Veiled Threat. J. Jenkins
Veiled Vampire. A. Eadie
Veiled Woman. A. Abdullah
Veils of Death. N. Vane
Veils of Fear. G. Mark
Vein of Violence. W. C. Gault

Veins of Compassion. P. Audemars
Veldt Official. B. Mitford
Veldt Vendetta. B. Mitford
Vellum. B. Goldie
Velvet Ape. D. C. Holmes
Velvet Black. R. W. Child
Velvet Claw. A. Dorrington
Velvet Fleece. L. Eby
Velvet Hammer. D. Franklin
Velvet Hand. H. Footner
Velvet Hand. H. Reilly
Velvet Johnnie and other stories. P. Cheyney
Velvet Jungle. D. J. Chiodo
Velvet Lawn. C. Felix
Velvet Mask and other stories. L. Gribble
Velvet Shadows. A. Morton
Velvet Shadows of Justin Wood. A. Haley
Velvet Target. G. Holden
Velvet Trap. J. Blackmore
Velvet Vixen. Carter Brown
Velvet Vixen. K. T. McCall
Velvet Well. J. Gearon
Velvet Whip. L. Snyder
Venables. G. Wagner
Vendetta. J. Boland
Vendetta. H. Carmichael
Vendetta. J. Cutter
Vendetta. M. Dibden
Vendetta. C. Durbin
Vendetta. J. Gilmore
Vendetta. J. L. Haas
Vendetta. J. D. Humphreys
Vendetta. D. Lambert
Vendetta. P. McCurtin
Vendetta. N. Quarry
Vendetta. S. Shagan
Vendetta! Richard Williams
Vendetta. I. Zacharia
Vendetta Castle. S. Marino
Vendetta Con Brio. B. De Bilio
Vendetta Contract. J. Messmann
Vendetta for the Saint. L. Charteris
Vendetta in Spain. D. Wheatley
Vendetta in Venice. D. Pendleton
Vendettists. W. Haggard
Veneered Scamp. J. Middlemass
Venetian Affair. Helen MacInnes
Venetian Affair. Clarissa Ross
Venetian Bird. V. Canning
Venetian Blind. W. Haggard
Venetian Blonde. A. S. Fleischman
Venetian Charade. H. York
Venetian Court. C. L. Harness
Venetian Key. A. Upward
Venetian Mask. M. Friedman
Venetian Mask. Colin Robertson
Venetian Masque. R. Sabatini
Venetian Portrait. C. Virmonne
Venetian Secret. E. Bond
Venetian Spy. E. Webster
Venetian Swimmer Mystery. S. G. Hedges
Venetian Vendetta. S. Jason
Venetians. M. E. Braddon
Vengeance. J. Ahern
Vengeance. H. Janson
Vengeance. M. Marquis
Vengeance. A. Murray
Vengeance. B. Tozer
Vengeance Army. A. Kilgore
Vengeance Business. Jim Ryan
Vengeance Due. J. Sandys
Vengeance Game. S. Grave
Vengeance in the Air. Colin Hope
Vengeance in the Sun. M. Pemberton
Vengeance Is a Woman. Stuart Hall
Vengeance Is Also Mine. W. Palmer
Vengeance Is His. W. Barker
Vengeance Is Mine. S. Crawford
Vengeance Is Mine. D. Dane
Vengeance Is Mine. J. Fluke
Vengeance Is Mine. Ralph Hayes
Vengeance Is Mine. M. Leighton
Vengeance Is Mine. R. Marlowe
Vengeance Is Mine. J. Middlemass

Vengeance Is Mine. Mark Richards
Vengeance Is Mine! M. Spillane
Vengeance Is Ours. P. Saxon
Vengeance Is Thine. W. Crisp
Vengeance Man. M. Coles
Vengeance Man. D. J. Marlowe
Vengeance Mountain. J. Cutter
Vengeance, My Love. E. G. Fulton
Vengeance of ? J. Wallace
Vengeance of Blue Pete. L. Allan
Vengeance of Five. H. K. McDonnell
Vengeance of Flynn. E. L. Long
Vengeance of Henry Jarroman. Roy Vickers
Vengeance of Hurricane Williams. Gordon Young
Vengeance of Kali. I. Marshall
Vengeance of Larose. A. Gask
Vengeance of Li-Sin. N. Vane
Vengeance of Mrs. Danvers. S. Kyle
Vengeance of Monsieur Blackshirt. D. Graeme
Vengeance of Mortimer Daly. M. Locke
Vengeance of Mynheer Van Lok and other stories. H. D. Stacpoole
Vengeance of Pomoola. Anonymous
Vengeance of Science. J. Dalmaine
Vengeance of Sheevra. O. Williams
Vengeance of the Cat Goddess. J. Stephens
Vengeance of the Golden Hawk. J. Rosenberger
Vengeance of the Ivory Skull. M. Harvey
Vengeance of the Tong. Ben Rogers
Vengeance of the Tong. G. H. Teed
Vengeance of Three. W. M. Graydon
Vengeance of Valdone. B. Ferm
Vengeance Pulls the Trigger. S. M. Schley
Vengeance Run. R. Rostand
Vengeance Street. R. Bloomfield
Vengeance 10. J. Poyer
Vengeance Trail. W. B. Mowery
Vengeance Under Law. F. Castle
Vengeance with a Twist and other stories. P. Cheyney
Vengeful Flames. A. Sewart
Vengeful Sinner. H. Whittington
Vengeful Virgin. G. Brewer
Venice of the Black Sea. H. Robertson
Venice Plot. R. Rudorff
Venice Preserve Me. J. Appleby
Venice Train. G. Simenon
Venice Ultimatum. J. Raven
Venner Crime. J. Rhode
Venom. Johnny Dark
Venom. C. Falconer
Venom. A. Scholefield
Venom Business. J. Lange
Venom House. A. W. Upfield
Venom in Eden. M. Boniface
Venom in the Cup. G. Joseph
Venom of the Cobra. R. Charles
Venom Squadron. R. Jackson
Ventilated Head. A. Nuttall
Ventriloquist. E. Belasyse
Ventriloquist Detective. Old Sleuth
Ventry. D. C. Lynch
Venture. J. Cummings
Venture. R. N. Grisewood
Venturers All. L. Gorell
Venturous Lady. G. H. Coxe
Venus Afflicted. F. Mullally
Venus and the Woodman. Vincent Brown
Venus Belt. L. N. Smith
Venus Besieged. E. C. Reed
Venus Death. B. Benson
Venus Died at Dawn. L. H. Hart
Venus Disarmed. J. Dole
Venus Fly-Trap. J. Wainwright
Venus Girl. L. Beresford
Venus Had Claws. C. Dekker
Venus in Plastic. J. Mitchell
Venus Makes Three. H. Janson
Venus on Wheels. M. Dekobra
Venus Probe. David St. John
Venus Shoe. C. A. Neggers
Venus Trap. J. M. Ullman
Venus Unarmed. Carter Brown
Venus Unarmed. L. Treat

Title Index

Venus Underground. R. Rainey
Venus Venture. H. Zachary
Venus with Pistol. G. Lyall
Vera Gerard Case. J. C. Cooke
Verboten. S. Esmond
Verdict. A. Christie
Verdict. J. B. Lynne
Verdict. L. Martin
Verdict. B. Reed
Verdict Afterwards. D. Ensor
Verdict in Question. S. Jepson
Verdict of One. H. Kromer
Verdict of the Heart. C. Garvice
Verdict of Twelve. R. Postgate
Verdict of You All. Henry Wade
Verdict Suspended. H. Nielsen
Verdict Without Jury. A. Webb
Verdugo Affair. B. Hirschfeld
Vermilion. N. Aldyne
Vermilion. P. A. Whitney
Vermont Village Murder. B. Comfort
Verner's Pride. H. Wood
Veron Mystery. H. C. Bailey
Verona Passamezzo. J. Gollin
Verona's Father. D. C. Murray
Veronica Dean Case. H. Waugh
Veronica Died Monday. G. Trotta
Veronica's Room. I. Levin
Veronique. V. Coffman
Verrall Street Affair. M. E. Cooke
Verratoli Inheritance. E. Webster
Versus Inspector Maigret. G. Simenon
Versus the Baron. Anthony Morton
Versus the C.I.A. G. De Villiers
Vertigo. P. Boileau
Very Bad Thing. Ned White
Very Big Bang. P. McCutchan
Very Black Deed. W. Manson
Very Breath of Hell. G. Beare
Very British Coup. C. Mullin
Very Cagey Lady. J. Elbert
Very Cold for May. W. P. McGivern
Very Costly Escape. P. J. Scott
Very Dead of Winter. S. Nichols
Very Deadly Game. V. B. Miller
Very Dry with a Twist. D. Banko
Very Fall of the Sun. S. Hazo
Very First Lady. S. Dunleavy
Very Good Hater. M. Challis
Very Good Hater. Reginald Hill
Very Great Grandson of Sherlock Holmes. B. Majeski
Very Large Consulate. H. R. Simpson
Very Last Gambado. Jonathan Gash
Very Long Odds and A Strange Finish. C. Rae-Brown
Very Old Money. S. Ellin
Very Ordinary Murder. A. Sewart
Very Parochial Murder. J. Wainwright
Very Particular Murder. S. T. Haymon
Very Private Enterprise. E. Ironside
Very Private Island. Z. Z. Smith
Very Private Secretary. B. Reynolds
Very Proper Death. A. Juniper
Very Queer Business, and other stories. W. Westall
Very Quiet Murder. F. Crane
Very Quiet Place. A. Garve
Very Rough Diamond. F. Warden
Very Short Memory of Mr. Joseph Scorer. J. Oxenham
Very Special Agent. G. Napier
Very Thin Line. M. Borgenicht
Very Welcome Death. D. L. Mathews
Very Wicked. Clifton Adams
Very Wicked. N. Hudson
Very Wrong Number. A. Douglas
Very Young Couple. B. L. Farjeon
Vesey Inheritance. Gwendoline Butler
Vesper Bells. B. H. Hyatt
Vesper Service Murders. V. W. Mason
Vespers. E. McBain
Vespucci Papers. B. Healey
Vessel May Carry Explosives. S. Harvester
Vest Pocket Theatre. A. Armer

Vestibule Limited Mystery. M. Manley
Vestibule Limited Mystery. A. Robertson
Vestry Murder. T. A. Plummer
Vet It Was That Died. M. Silverman
Veterans. Eric Lambert
Vet's Daughter. B. Comyns
Via Berlin. C. Marriott
Viaduct Murder. R. A. Knox
Vial of Death. Nicholas Carter
Vial with the White Powder. J. B. Williams
Vibert Affair. G. M. Fenn
Vicar. J. Hatton
Vicar Done It. F. Bream
Vicar in Hell. A. Melville
Vicar Investigates. F. Bream
Vicar of Dunkerley Briggs, and other short stories. L. Golding
Vicar of Moura. V. Coffman
Vicar's Experiments. A. Rolls
Vicar's People. G. M. Fenn
Vicar's Roses. J. L. Breen
Vicar's Secret. C. E. Jeffery
Vice and Its Victim. T. P. Prest
Vice City. B. Sarto
Vice Cop. R. Deming
Vice Cop. M. Reed
Vice Czar Murders. F. Charles
Vice Inc. J. Joesten
Vice Isn't Private. B. Cleeve
Vice Merchants. R. McCary
Vice Net. M. Carey
Vice Rackets of Soho. R. Vane
Vice Ring Murders. Grant Franklin
Vice Squad. W. Rotsler
Vice Squad. H. Spencer
Vice Squad. J. Van Raalte
Vice Squad. L. T. White
Vice Squad Cop. M. Carey
Vice Town. E. Willie
Vice Trap. E. Gilbert
Vice Volcano. B. Sarto
Viceroy's Protege. G. Boothby
Vicious Breed. B. Sarto
Vicious Circle. D. Clark
Vicious Circle. A. Evans
Vicious Circle. Manning Long
Vicious Circles. Anthony Stuart
Vicious Circuit. C. G. Jarvie
Vicious Circuit. J. Langdon
Vicious Ones. D. Haring
Vicious Pattern. M. V. Heberden
Vicious Virtuoso. L. Lombard
Vicissitudes of Flynn. B. Kennedy
Vicky Van. C. Wells
Victim. Josephine Bell
Victim! Carter Brown
Victim. W. Drummond
Victim. M. Fratti
Victim. T. Journet
Victim. D. Winston
Victim Died Twice. H. Liggett
Victim for Hire. P. Morales
Victim Must Be Found. H. Engel
Victim Must Be Found. A. Hocking
Victim Needs a Nurse. J. Redfern
Victim of Black Magic. G. H. Teed
Victim of Circumstances. Nicholas Carter
Victim of Circumstances. M. Underwood
Victim of Deceit. Nicholas Carter
Victim of Fashion. H. M. Jones
Victim of His Clothes. H. Fielding
Victim of Love. N. Buckingham
Victim of Love. J. Delutry
Victim of Rape. Eddie Stone
Victim of the Aurora. T. Keneally
Victim of the Combine. G. Chester
Victim of the Crooked Hypnotist. J. Hunter
Victim of the Cult. W. Jardine
Victim of the Devil's Bowl. R. Hardinge
Victim of the Gang. G. H. Teed
Victim of the Girl Spy. M. B. Dix
Victim of the Occult. I. Stark
Victim of the Red Mask. S. Hope
Victim of the Secret Service. J. G. Brandon

Victim of the Thieves' Den. J. G. Brandon
Victim of the Waterway. G. N. Philips
Victim of Villainy. F. L. Broughton
Victim Prime. R. Sheckley
Victim Unknown. D. Reid
Victim Was Important. J. Rayter
Victims. P. Boileau
Victims. T. Gift
Victims. B. M. Gill
Victims. James Grant
Victims. S. Hutson
Victims. E. McCabe
Victims. A. Maimane
Victims. J. Pearl
Victims. J. Rossiter
Victims. S. Shea
Victims. D. Uhnak
Victims. C. Wilcox
Victim's Niece. B. Hector
Victims of Circumstance. P. Conway
Victims of Devil's Alley. P. Urquhart
Victims of the Devil's Triangle. D. Swan
Victims of Villainy. Andrew Murray
Victims Unknown. R. Clapperton
Victor. D. Kirby
Victor and Vanquished. M. C. Hay
Victor Maury, the French Detective. G. Reynolds
Victor Versus Verhasst. D. Kirby
Victoria. R. Gadney
Victoria Grandolet. H. Bellamann
Victoria Pruitt Comes to Town. R. G. Cochran
Victoria Winters. Marilyn Ross
Victorian Album. E. Berckman
Victorian Crown. E. Noone
Victoria's House. F. Carmichael
Victorine. F. P. Keyes
Victors. J. Harris
Victor's Spoils. I. Stark
Victory Murders. F. Johns
Victory Song. H. Adams
Vida. Delacorta
Video Games. J. Gooding
Video Kill. J. Fluke
Video Killer. S. Crawford
Video Vandal. F. Roderus
Video Vengeance. M. Tripp
Vidocq of New York. C. Fulton
Vidocq, the Police Spy. Vidocq
Vienna Blood. L. Payne
Vienna Elephant. E. Leather
Vienna Pursuit. A. Goddard
Vienna Summer. N. Buckingham
Viennese Love. H. Bettauer
Viennese Snuffbox. H. Drury
Viet Rampage. M. Acres
Vietnam Fallout. D. Pendleton
Vietnam Spook Show. W. Care
View from Chickweed's Window. J. Vance
View from Daniel Pike. B. Knox
View from Deacon Hill. J. S. Scott
View from the Square. J. Trenhaile
View from the Terrace. L. Meynell
View to Ransom. J. Arney
Viewless Winds. M. C. Morgan
Vignettes. Rita
Vigorous Daunt, Billionaire. A. Pratt
Viking Feast Mystery. L. A. Knight
Viking Process. N. Hartley
Viking Summer. C. A. Brady
Viking's Skull. J. R. Carling
Vile Village. C. Sargent
Vileroy. T. P. Prest
Villa Aurelia. B. E. Stevenson
Villa Fountains. V. Coffman
Villa Golitsyn. P. P. Read
Villa Head. R. D. Brown
Villa Jane. J. Laing
Villa Mimosa. J. Tickell
Villa Mystery. H. Flowerdew
Villa Nova. C. Selden
Villa of Shadows. C. Farr
Villa of the Scorpions. E. Follett
Villa on the Shore. M. Butterworth
Villa Petroff. D. Whitelaw

V

Villa Plot, Counterplot. Cameron Ross
Villa Rossignol. M. L. Storer
Village Affairs. R. Armfelt
Village Afraid. M. Burton
Village Blacksmith. D. Dale
Village Called Death. P. Motte
Village Casanova, and other stories. Neil Bell
Village Detective. V. Lipatov
Village East. R. Chambers
Village Gentleman, and The Attorney at Law. A. Duncombe
Village Hampden. E. O. Schlunde
Village Match and After. M. D. Lyon
Village Mystery. Mrs. C. Kernahan
Village Mystery. Benjamin F. Mason
Village Never Knew. B. Goldie
Village of Fear. F. Cowen
Village of Fear. M. Jenson
Village of Fear. Donald Stuart
Village of Rogues. J. Sturrock
Village of Satan. M. Bingley
Village of Stars. P. Stanton
Village Policeman. I. Niall
Village Pub Murders. F. Krull
Village Scandal. H. M. Jones
Village Tale. N. Kennedy
Village Tales and Jungle Tragedies. B. M. Croker
Village Temptress. F. Whishaw
Villain and the Virgin. J. H. Chase
Villain Foiled Again. A. L. Kaser
Villain of the Piece. Graham Fisher
Villainous Company. R. Fenisong
Villainous Saltpetre. C. Witting
Villainous Scheme. Nicholas Carter
Villains. C. Keppel
Villains. J. Rossiter
Villains. P. Whalley
Villains by Necessity. Sara Woods
Villains Galore. G. Bell
Villain's Tale. G. F. Newman
Villain's Work. Dick Stewart
Villainy. G. Bettany
Villainy at Vespers. J. Cockin
Villars-Manningham Papers. J. Shakley
Villiers Touch. B. Garfield
Villiger. J. J. Savarin
Villon of the Piece. H. Janson
Vindicator. J. J. Dalton
Vindicator. E. P. Oppenheim
Vinegar—and Cream. H. T. W. Bousfield
Vinegar in the Spice. D. Thurlow
Vines of Ferrara. C. Coker
Vines of Yarrabee. D. Eden
Vineyard Chapel. D. Daniels
Vintage. U. Keir
Vintage Murder. N. Marsh
Vintage So Evil. M. Vinter
Vintage Stuff. A. Brede
Violante. G. R. Preedy
Viola's Dilemma. T. S. King
Violated One. J. Hanley
Violator. H. Kane
Violator. John Warwick
Violators. D. Haring
Violence. C. Woolrich
Violence in Paradise. D. Buttenshaw
Violence in Quiet Places. J. T. Story
Violence Is Velvet. M. Avallone
Violence Is Golden. B. Halliday
Violence Is Golden. C. H. Thames
Violence Is My Business. S. Marlowe
Violence of Hate. H. P. Lees
Violent Air. C. Reen
Violent Breed. S. A. Curtis
Violent Brink. A. Beevor
Violent Brothers. E. Bruton
Violent City. J. Hawkins
Violent Dark. L. Gribble
Violent Dawn. C. Rudd
Violent Death. Roy Lewis
Violent Death. W. Sproule
Violent Death of a Bitter Englishman. B. Cleeve
Violent End. V. Kathrens
Violent End. E. Page

Violent Ends. G. Simenon
Violent Enemy. H. Marlowe
Violent Flame. F. T. Jane
Violent Heritage. Sheila Johnson
Violent Holiday. R. Wilkes-Hunter
Violent Hours. F. Castle
Violent Hours. P. Saxon
Violent Hours. R. Walsh
Violent Keepsake. L. Grex
Violent Lady. M. E. Knerr
Violent Man. A. E. Van Vogt
Violent Midnight. L. Gribble
Violent Night. Whit Harrison
Violent Night. R. Jackson
Violent Ones. Howard Hunt
Violent Ones. C. Ruhen
Violent Ones. P. Saxon
Violent Passions. Adam Walker
Violent Past. E. Berridge
Violent Saturday. W. L. Heath
Violent Security. G. Burnett
Violent Streets. D. Pendleton
Violent Virgin. D. Haring
Violent World of Hugh Greene. Colin Wilson
Violent World of Michael Shayne. B. Halliday
Violet Closet. G. Gottesfeld
Violet Forster's Lover. R. Marsh
Violin and Vendetta. T. I. S.
Viper. H. Footner
Viper. L. Pryor
Viper. A. Riefe
Viper Factor. G. Wilson
Viper in Her Bosom. P. Muller
Viper of Luxor. G. Seton
Viper Squad. J. B. Hadley
Viper Three. W. Wager
Viper's Bite. J. D. Fitz
Viper's Brood. B. Sarto
Viper's Game. R. Rostand
Viper's Heart. A. Hemingway
Viper's Sting. H. Desmond
Viper's Vengeance. R. Trevor
Viper's Vengeance. B. E. M. Ward
Virgel Detective. T. Richards
Virgil's Ghost. I. Weinman
Virgin and Martyr. A. Greeley
Virgin Cay. B. Heatter
Virgin Collector. D. Ambler
Virgin Fortress. M. Pemberton
Virgin Heiresses. E. Queen
Virgin Huntress. E. S. Holding
Virgin in Flames. S. Rohmer
Virgin in the Ice. Ellis Peters
Virgin Kills. R. Whitfield
Virgin Luck. L. Meynell
Virgin on the Rocks. M. Butterworth
Virgin Stealers. D. Streib
Virgin Widow. A. Matthey
Virginia. C. Dawe
Virginia. K. Lindsay
Virginia and Magdalene. E. Southworth
Virginia Box and the "Unsatisfied". J. Moffatt
Virginia's Quest. M. Caywood
Virginia's Quest. J. Templeton
Virginia's Thing. H. Woodfin
Virgins Die Lonely. Pete Costello
Virgins Die Lonely. N. Perrelli
Virgin's Vendetta. N. Perrelli
Virility Factor. H. Kane
Virtue of Necessity. Herbert Adams
Virtue Triumphant. P. Norris
Virtues of Hell. P. Boulle
Virtuous Vamp. J. S. Clouston
Virus. P. Caine
Virus Man. C. Rayner
Virus X. S. Horler
Visa for Violence. M. Risco
Visa to Death. E. Lacy
Visa to Limbo. W. Haggard
Viscount Lacklands. A. Griffiths
Visibility Nil. P. Conde
Visibility Nil. M. Elgin
Visible and Invisible. E. F. Benson
Vision. D. R. Koontz

Vision of Beauty. J. Hatton
Vision of Murder. J. M. Brillant
Vision of the Foam. J. MacEnery
Vision Sinister. N. Karta
Visions of Esmares. Elna Stone
Visions of Heydrich. P. Everett
Visions of Terror. W. Katz
Visit. F. Duerrenmatt
Visit After Dark. D. Winston
Visit from a Broad. H. Janson
Visitation. R. Amare
Visiting Hours. K. Rembo
Visiting Villain. C. Wells
Visitor. J. Cunningham
Visitor. M. Donald
Visitor. Anthony Gilbert
Visitor. Maureen Lee
Visitor. C. Randau
Visitor. K. White
Visitors for Venning. C. Ryland
Vital Statistics. T. Chastain
Vitriol Thrower. J. Du Boisgobey
Viva McHugh. J. Flynn
Vivanti. S. Horler
Vivanti Returns. S. Horler
Vivero Letter. D. Bagley
Vivia. E. Southworth
Vivian Morgan's First Case. F. Curtis
Vivienne—Gently Where She Lay. A. Hunter
Vivier of Vivier, Longman & Company, Bankers. W. C. Hudson
Vivonio. Sophia Frances
Vixen. M. E. Braddon
Vixen. Carter Brown
Vixen. L. Fitzhamon
Vixen 03. C. Cussler
Vixen's Vengeance. T. Trenton
Vodka on Ice. H. McLeave
Voice. C. Connolly
Voice. Anthony Gilbert
Voice and other stories. S. Matsumoto
Voice at Johnnywater. B. M. Bower
Voice from the Cell. A. MacKenzie
Voice from the Dark. E. Phillpotts
Voice from the Dead. B. Copper
Voice from the Grave. D. M. Disney
Voice from the Grave. Clarissa Ross
Voice from the Grave. Clifton Yorke
Voice from the Living. M. Lovell
Voice from the Night. C. E. Sterry
Voice from the Past. Nicholas Carter
Voice from the Void. W. LeQueux
Voice from Yesterday. F. Crisp
Voice in the Closet. Herman Landon
Voice in the Dark. R. Dyar
Voice in the Dark. C. Lorrimer
Voice in the Darkness. P. Bennetts
Voice in the Fog. H. MacGrath
Voice in the Light. Bart Kennedy
Voice in the Night. V. Johnston
Voice Like Velvet. D. H. Landels
Voice of Air. E. Berckman
Voice of Armageddon. D. Lippincott
Voice of Bethia. T. Cobb
Voice of Doom. G. W. Jones
Voice of Murder. M. Erskine
Voice of Vengeance. J. T. Osborne
Voice of the Charmer. L. T. Meade
Voice of the City. O. Henry
Voice of the Clown. B. B. Canary
Voice of the Corpse. Max Murray
Voice of the Crab. G. Halls
Voice of the Dolls. D. Eden
Voice of the House. M. Erskine
Voice of the Lobster. R. J. Casey
Voice of the Murderer. G. Walsh
Voice of the Night. B. Coffey
Voice of the Past. M. Leek
Voice of the Peacock. E. Salter
Voice of the Seven Sparrows. H. S. Keeler
Voice of Vice. R. Angel
Voice on the Telephone. Mildred Davis
Voice on the Wind. D. Daniels
Voice on the Wire. E. H. Ball

Voice Out of Darkness. U. Curtiss
Voice Outside. K. Grimwood
Voice Said "Good Night". R. Pertwee
Voiceless Ones. J. Creasey
Voiceless Victims. G. Thorne
Voices. G. J. Brenn
Voices. S. Shubin
Voices from the Bottom of the World. T. M. Walker
Voices from the Dust. J. Farnol
Voices in an Empty House. Joan Aiken
Voices in an Empty Room. P. Loraine
Voices in the Fog. K. Cameron
Voices in the House. P. S. Buck
Voices in the Night. S. Smoke
Voices in the Wind. E. V. Allen
Voices in the Wind. E. Anthony
Voices Long Hushed. B. A. Pauley
Voices of Doom. B. Copper
Voices of Terror. C. Virmonne
Voices of the Storm. J. Sandys
Voices on the Brink. Tom Marshall
Voices Out of Time. Deborah Lewis
Void in Hearts. W. G. Tapply
Volcano. K. Hayles
Volcano Island. A. Wood
Volcanoes Above Us. N. Lewis
Volcanoes of San Domingo. Adam Hall
Voltan Treasure. Jackson Collins
Volunteers. D. Reeman
Volunteers for Danger. R. T. Bickers
Voluptuaries. B. E. Ullman
Von Eyssen Deception. R. Hirschhorn
Von Kessel Dossier. L. Le Grand
Von Stahmer Jigsaw. P. Lovegrove
Voodoo. J. Esteven
Voodoo Death. M. Grant
Voodoo Die. R. Sapir
Voodoo Drum. P. Saxon
Voodoo Drums. V. Leigh
Voodoo Drums. E. Wilmot
Voodoo Goat. A. Gaines
Voodoo Island. G. H. Teed
Voodoo Murders. M. Avallone
Voodoo Violence. H. Janson
Voodoo'd. K. Perkins
Vorovich Affair. S. L. Stebel
Vortex. J. Cleary
Vortex. J. Land
Vortex. F. Whishaw
Vortex Assignment. A. Handley
Vote Against Poison. J. Sherwood
Vote for Death. N. Longmate
Vote for Murder. Richard Martin
Vote for the Toff. J. Creasey
Vote to Kill. D. Hurd
Vote X for Treason. B. Cleeve
Vow. P. Trent
Vow of Love. F. Y. McHugh
Vow of Silence. Veronica Black
Vow of Silence. B. J. Hoff
Vow of Vengeance. A. Carlyle
Voyage Home. Alan Graham
Voyage Into Nowhere. J. Wood
Voyage Into Peril. Seafarer
Voyage Into Violence. F. Lockridge
Voyage of Death. M. Cruz
Voyage of Fear. R. Hardinge
Voyage of the Chianti. B. J. Morison
Voyage of the "Colin Cowdrey". A. Synge
Voyage of the "San Marcos". M. Hastings
Voyage of the Secret Duchess. F. Hurd
Voyage with Murder. J. York
Voyeur. A. Robbe-Grillet
Vrouw Grobelaar and Her Leading Cases. P. Gibbon
Vrouw Grobelaar's Leading Cases. P. Gibbon
Vulcan Academy Murders. J. Lorrah
Vulcan Bulletins. S. Gullivar
Vulcan Disaster. Nick Carter
Vulcan Rising. A. Aasheim
Vulcan's Hammer. D. Da Cruz
Vulgar Boatman. W. G. Tapply
Vulnerable. D. Collins
Vulture. J. Carrick

Vulture. C. Heath
Vulture. G. Scott-Heron
Vulture. Harold Ward
Vulture in the Sun. J. Bingham
Vulture Is a Patient Bird. J. H. Chase
Vulture Strikes. Harold Ward
Vultures. I. Gregory
Vultures Gather. A. Hocking
Vultures in the Sky. T. Downing
Vultures in the Smoke. P. A. Foxall
Vultures, Ltd. B. Gray
Vultures of Desolate Island. G. E. Rochester
Vultures of Erin. N. J. Dunn
Vultures of the Dark. R. E. Enright
Vultures of the Horn. J. Hild
Vultures of the Sky. P. Conde
Vultures of the White Death. R. J. Hogan
Vulture's Prey. T. De Saix
Vulture's Vengeance. D. Pendleton
Vye Murder. I. Wray
Vyvyans. Andree Hope

W. G. Grace's Last Case. W. Rushton
W.H.O.R.E. Carter Brown
W.I.L. One to Curtis. P. Loraine
WO2. M. Drake
W.1. P. McGuire
W Plan. G. Seton
Wabash Factor. E. V. Cunningham
Waddington Cipher. W. A. Johnston
Wade House. F. Hurd
Wade Inheritance. L. V. Brown
Wager. Ladbroke Black
Wager. R. L. Fish
Wager, and The House at Fernwood. F. Oursler
Wager for Love. Rachelle Edwards
Wages of Fear. G. Arnaud
Wages of Peril. J. Bechdolt
Wages of Rascality. Nicholas Carter
Wages of Sin. M. E. Braddon
Wages of Sin. E. Yates
Wages of Zen. James Melville
Wagner the Wehrwolf. G. W. M. Reynolds
Wagon-Load of Monkeys. D. Fletcher
Wagoner's Halt Mystery. M. Poole
Waif of Destiny. L. G. Moberly
Waif of the River. J. Farnol
Waifs and Strays. O. Henry
Waifs of Circumstance. L. Tracy
Waif's Paradise. Howard Hall
Waikiki Widow. J. Sheridan
Wail for the Corpses. L. Treat
Wail of the Lonely Wench. A. J. Collins
Wailing Frail. R. S. Prather
Wailing Rock Murdrs. C. Orr
Wailing Winds of Juneau Abbey. P. Darty
Wailing Woman. D. Shattuck
Wait. E. Berckman
Wait and Hope. J. E. Reade
Wait for Death. G. Ashe
Wait for Death. J. Veitch
Wait for It, Paul. A. Bocca
Wait for Me, Wendy. J. Marie
Wait for the Corpse. Max Murray
Wait for the Dawn. M. Albrand
Wait for the End. M. Lemon
Wait for the Wake. M. Carr
Wait for the Wedding. C. Fremlin
Wait for What Will Come. B. Michaels
Wait, Just You Wait. E. Berckman
Wait Long, Wait Still. M. M. Thomas
Wait Till Dark. John Cunningham
Wait 'Till Holly Comes. R. English
Wait Until Dark. F. Knott
Wait Until Midnight. V. Pittenger
Wait Until the Evening. H. Bennett
Waiting. G. Levine
Waiting. Mary Napier
Waiting Darkness. M. Bingley
Waiting Darkness. W. D. Roberts
Waiting Eyes. E. Bond
Waiting for a Tiger. B. Healey
Waiting for Caroline. A. McAllister
Waiting for Nothing. T. Kromer

Waiting for Oliver. S. Troy
Waiting for the End of the World. M. S. Bell
Waiting for the End of the World. Andrew Taylor
Waiting for the News. L. Litwak
Waiting for the Police and other stories. J. J. Farjeon
Waiting for Thursday. H. Jobson
Waiting for Willa. D. Eden
Waiting Game. M. Powell
Waiting Game. P. Wayland
Waiting in the Shadows. Marilyn Ross
Waiting Race. E. Yates
Waiting Room Mystery. A. Blair
Waiting Sands. S. Howatch
Waiting to Hear from William. B. H. Deal
Wake All the Dead. S. Kilpatrick
Wake for a Lady. H. W. Roden
Wake for Donald. E. Hood
Wake for Mourning. Shane Martin
Wake in Darkness. D. E. McQuinn
Wake in Fright. K. Cook
Wake Not the Sleeping Wolf. T. McCoy
Wake of a Lawyer. A. Holmes
Wake of the Icarus. N. Benchley
Wake of the Setting Sun. W. A. Stowell
Wake the Sleeping Wolf. R. Foley
Wake Up and Die. C. Grey
Wake Up and Scream. M. K. Ozaki
Wake Up, Darlin' Corey. M. K. Wren
Wake Up Dead. W. Wall
Wake Up Screaming! A. Kent
Wake Up to Murder. D. Keene
Wake Up with a Stranger. F. Flora
Wakefield Witches. D. Winston
Waking Dream. C. M. Wallace
Waking of the Stone. J. Lymington
Walbury Case. A. Hilliers
Walde-Warren. Emerson Bennett
Waldo. L. Kauffmann
Waldorf. J. Goldman
Walk a Black Wind. Michael Collins
Walk a Crooked Mile. R. Deming
Walk a Crooked Mile. J. Philips
Walk a Crooked Mile. S. Truss
Walk a Tightrope. J. Ellis
Walk a Wicked Mile. R. P. Hansen
Walk a Winter Beach. Sandy Johnson
Walk Around the Square. D. Winston
Walk at a Steady Pace. N. Fisher
Walk at Night. D. Craig
Walk-In. V. Scott
Walk in Dead Man's Wood. J. S. Scott
Walk in, Death. P. Malloch
Walk in Deep Shadows. Sara Mitchell
Walk in Fear. W. H. Baker
Walk in Fear. W. T. Ballard
Walk in Shadow. J. Fast
Walk in the Dark. C. Phillips
Walk in the Dark. J. Roffman
Walk in the Jungle. G. Canary
Walk in the Paradise Garden. A. Maybury
Walk in the Shadows. R. Dolphin
Walk in the Wood. A. Gilbert
Walk Into Darkness. J. Ellis
Walk Into Murder. P. Helm
Walk Into My Parlour. D. Eden
Walk Into My Parlour. A. Hocking
Walk Into My Parlour. Rona Randall
Walk Into Yesterday. Mildred Davis
Walk of the Devil. M. Kane
Walk on the Blind Side. J. T. MacCargo
Walk Out on Death. C. Armstrong
Walk Softly. W. Sproule
Walk Softly and Beware. M. Blake
Walk Softly in Fear. M. Butterworth
Walk Softly, Men Praying. O. Wynd
Walk Softly Sweetheart. D. Haring
Walk Softly, Walk Deadly. L. Bergman
Walk Softly Witch! Carter Brown
Walk the Bloody Boulevard. A. A. Marcus
Walk the Dark Bridge. W. O'Farrell
Walk the Evil Street. D. Wade
Walk the Knife Edge. C. Dekker
Walk the Night Unseen. Lucinda Baker
Walk to the River. W. Hoffman

Walk to Your Grave. N. M. Newland
Walk with a Shadow. J. T. Osborne
Walk with Care. P. Wentworth
Walk with Danger. S. G. Rubin
Walk with Evil. R. Wilder
Walk with Me Into Darkness. J. McKelvey
Walker in Shadows. B. Michaels
Walker of the Secret Service. M. D. Post
Walking a Thin Line. I. S. Grant
Walking After Midnight. R. Nusser
Walking Corpse. G. D. H. Cole
Walking Dead. P. Dickinson
Walking Dead. M. Hervey
Walking Dead. M. Lambe
Walking Dead Man. H. Pentecost
Walking Oscars. Simon Williams
Walking Shadow. B. J. Appleton
Walking Shadow. R. Forrest
Walking Shadow. L. G. Offord
Walking Shadow. J. Pattinson
Walking Shadow. J. M. Walsh
Walking Shadows. M. Gelien
Walking Shadows. A. Noyes
Walking Shadows. F. Taylor
Walking Stick. Winston Graham
Walking Tall. D. Warren
Walking Tall: Part 2. Webster Carey
Walking the Dusk. L. J. Webb
Walking Trip. H. Buckmaster
Walking Wind. F. M. Proud
Walking Wounded. J. Laffin
Walking Wounded. W. B. Murphy
Walking Wounded. R. S. Stokes
Wall. A. Mayhar
Wall. M. R. Rinehart
Wall in the Long Dark Night. O. Wynd
Wall of Eyes. M. Millar
Wall of Glass. W. Satterthwait
Wall of Jeopardy. W. Spann
Wall of Masks. B. Coffey
Wall of Men. W. Rollins
Wall Street and the Woods. W. J. Flagg
Wall Street Blues. J. Tuccille
Wall Street Haul. Anonymous
Wall Street Haul. Nicholas Carter
Wall Street Murders. D. M. Hoffecker
Wall Street Swindlers. J. Sharp
Wall Street Wonder. D. J. MacKenzie
Wallace at Bay. A. Wilson
Wallace Intervenes. A. Wilson
Wallace of the Secret Service. A. Wilson
Walled Parrot. J. Weston
Wallingford. E. C. Savidge
Wallingford and Blackie Daw. G. R. Chester
Wallingford in His Prime. G. R. Chester
Wallington Case. M. Jon
Walls Are High. J. Van Raalte
Walls Came Tumbling Down. B. H. Deal
Walls Came Tumbling Down. J. Eisinger
Walls Have Eyes. Ganpat
Walls of Silence. D. Hawkins
Wally the Boy 'Tec. V. Norton
Walnut Door. J. Hersey
Walt Wheeler, the Scout Detective. H. Rockwood
Walter Duerell. Anonymous
Walter Graydon. F. S. Potter
Walter Syndrome. R. Neely
Walter's Word. J. Payn
Walther P.38. J. Wainwright
Walton Mystery. L. Reynolds
Waltz Across Texas. M. Crawford
Waltz in Scarlet. Muriel Bradley
Waltz Into Darkness. W. Irish
Waltz of Death. P. B. Maxon
Waltz of My Heart. M. Richmond
Wan Lee, the Pagan, and other sketches. B. Harte
Wandering Dogies. W. C. Tuttle
Wandering Knife. M. R. Rinehart
Wandering Mason. W. T.
Wandering Romanoff. B. Kennedy
Wandering Spirit. Anonymous
Wandering Widows. E. Ferrars
Wanderings of Asaf. Afghan
Want to Stay Alive? J. H. Chase

Wanted! C. Dawe
Wanted! D. Donovan
Wanted. W. M. Graydon
Wanted: A Clew. Nicholas Carter
Wanted: A Fool. P. E. Curtiss
Wanted: A Murderess. M. Holbrook
Wanted at His Office. Leonard Cooper
Wanted by the Gestapo. A. O. Pollard
Wanted by the Police. O. Harper
Wanted by Two Clients. Nicholas Carter
Wanted: Danny Fontaine. W. Ard
Wanted: Dead Men. M. E. Chaber
Wanted Dead or Alive! M. Leinster
Wanted for Killing. J. Welcome
Wanted for Murder. L. Charteris
Wanted for Murder. R. Gilmour
Wanted for Murder. H. Holt
Wanted for Murder. O. Kennard
Wanted for Murder. N. Rutledge
Wanted for Questioning. Mark Cross
Wanted for Questioning. W. McNeilly
Wanted Man. H. Cecil
Wanted on Holiday. F. Jefkins
Wanted—One Body! R. Dyer
Wanted: Someone Innocent. M. Allingham
Wanting. Campbell Black
Wanting Factor. G. DeWeese
Wanton. Carter Brown
Wanton City. O. M. Hall
Wanton for Murder. H. Klinger
Wanton Fury. J. A. Broom
Wanton Hour. Lewis Clay
Wanton Princess. D. Wheatley
Wanton Venus. M. Leblanc
Wanton Wench. J. Craig
Wanton Wife. R. Vane
Wantons Die Hard. L. Gribble
Wantons of Betrayal. A. Rivere
Wapping Butt. L. Blake
War Against Chaos. Anita Mason
War Against Charity Ross. J. Bickham
War Against the Mafia. D. Pendleton
War Born. D. Pendleton
War Cache. D. Newton
War Chariot. T. Willard
War Chest. P. A. Foxall
War Dog Stirs. H. Hastings
War from the Clouds. Nick Carter
War Game. A. Price
War God. P. F. Rogers
War in Heaven. C. Williams
War in the Desert. J. Andrews
War in the Gates. L. A. B. Cooke
War Machine. W. Marshall
War Maker. A. Hillgarth
War Moon. Tom Cooper
War of Brains. Nicholas Carter
War of Dreams. A. Carter
War of Nerves. P. Brickhill
War of Nerves. Robert Graham
War of Nerves. R. Starko
War of 1938. S. F. Wright
War of the Dons. P. Rabe
War of the Godfathers. W. F. Roemer, Jr.
War of the Raven. A. Kaplan
War of the Running Fox. B. Langley
War Patrol. A. S. Long
War Runners. W. McNeilly
War Ship. C. D. Taylor
War Story. G. McGill
War Terror. A. B. Reeve
War Toys. Hampton Howard
War Weapons. C. Sargent
War Without Frontiers. A. Osmond
Warbeck of Wolfstein. Miss Holford
Ward of Navarre. M. Gerard
Warden of the North. L. C. Douthwaite
Warden of the Wilds. L. C. Douthwaite
Wardour Street Mystery. R. Dark
Wards of Armageddon. J. N. Williams
Ware Case. G. Pleydell
'Ware Danger. G. Ashe
'Ware Wolf. E. L. Forester
Warehouse Murder. E. C. Davies

Warfield Syndrome. H. Denker
Wargamer. R. Neebel
Warhawk. J. J. Savarin
Warhead. F. R. Baker
Warkfield Castle. Jane Harvey
Warlock. J. M. Flynn
Warlock. M. Olden
Warlock. W. Tucker
Warlock's Daughter. Angel Gray
Warlock's Woman. J. De Pre
Warlord. J. Frost
Warlord! Janet Morris
Warlord of Azatlan. D. Stivers
Warlords. B. Langley
Warlord's Hill. G. Fox
Warlords of Phoenix. P. O'Donnell
Warlords Revenge. C. Sargent
Warm and Golden War. N. Luard
Warmaster. P. McCutchan
Warn That Man! V. Sylvaine
Warn the Baron. Anthony Morton
Warned by Wireless. Anonymous
Warned Off. J. Fairfax-Blakeborough
Warned Off. N. Gould
Warned Off. Andrew Gray
Warned Off! J. Hunter
Warned Off. R. S. Sievier
Warning. H. Arnston
Warning Bell. S. Ransome
Warning Bell. Grace M. White
Warning Call. R. G. Keller
Warning Shot. W. Masterson
Warning to Critics. A. Melville
Warning Wings. R. Adam
Warped in the Making. H. Ashton-Wolfe
Warrant for a Wanton. M. Gillian
Warrant for Arrest. F. Didelot
Warrant for X. P. MacDonald
Warrant No. 113. E. Gaboriau
Warrielaw Jewel. W. Peck
Warriors. B. Tillman
Warriors. S. Yurick
Warrior's Playtime. G. Hackforth-Jones
Warrior's Revenge. D. Pendleton
Wars Within Wars. Sheila Ross
Warsaw. A. Litewka
Warsaw Concerto. Dennis Jones
Warsaw Document. Adam Hall
Warsprite. J. P. Swycaffer
Wartime. A. Mitchell
Warwick. M. T. Walworth
Wary Transgressor. Raymond Marshall
Was Ever Woman in This Humor Wooed? C. Gibbon
Was He Guilty? E. A. Dupuy
Was He Severe? H. Wood
Was It a Ghost? Anonymous
Was It Coincidence? and other stories. A. Ridehalgh
Was It Montelli? L. Cargill
Was It Murder? F. Du Boisgobey
Was It Murder? G. Trevor
Was It Murder? J. H. Waring
Was Murder Done? S. Fowler
Was She Justified? F. Barrett
Was She Poison? D. Linton
Was She Worth It? M. Leighton
Was the Mayor Murdered? T. A. Plummer
Was This Murder? B. Stoner
Was This the Man? E. Wooton
Washed in the Blood. C. H. Flynn
Washermen. Peter Hill
Washington Deceased. Michael Bowen
Washington IOU. D. Pendleton
Washington Legation Murders. V. W. Mason
Washington Never Slept Here. L. Greth
Washington Payoff. Gordon Davis
Washington Square Enigma. H. S. Keeler
Washington Square Ensemble. M. S. Bell
Washington Whispers Murder. L. Ford
Washington Woman. D. Varnado
Wasp. J. Cleft-Addams
Wasp. U. Curtiss
Wasp in the Web. R. B. Amos
Wasps in the Woodpile. M. Warden

Title Index

Wasp's Nest. A. Matthews
Waste Lands. C. Dawe
Waste Remains. J. Cook
Wasted. L. Wolfe
Wasted Crime. D. C. Murray
Wasted Fires. H. Nisbet
Wasted Pride. P. Nottingham
Wasteland. M. Rowson
Wasting Assets. T. Palmer
Wastrel Goes West. J. Street
Watch, a Wallet and a Jack of Spades. L. Barbee
Watch Across the Channel. M. McKenna
Watch Below. Taffrail
Watch Dog. A. Hornblow
Watch It, Dr. Adrian. B. Litzinger
Watch McLean. G. Goodchild
Watch Mr. Moh. J. Cowdroy
Watch of Evil. P. Le Bailly
Watch on the Bridge. D. Garth
Watch on the Wall. H. Burnett
Watch Sinister. M. Blizard
Watch the Birdie. Ramsey Campbell
Watch the Wall, My Darling. J. A. Hodge
Watch Your Step. G. M. Savage
Watch Your Step, Bud. C. Defoe
Watchdogs. J. Weisman
Watchdogs of Abaddon. I. Melchior
Watched Out. E. A. Clancy
Watcher. Renate Chapman
Watcher. D. Hitchens
Watcher. J. R. Janes
Watcher. C. MacLean
Watcher. K. N. Smith
Watcher. G. Verner
Watcher. C. Wilcox
Watcher and other weird stories. J. S. Le Fanu
Watcher at the Door. G. H. Hall
Watcher by the Threshold. J. Buchan
Watcher in the Dark. D. Daniels
Watcher in the Dark. Beverly Hastings
Watcher in the Garden. A. Paar
Watcher in the Shadows. G. Household
Watcher in the Wood. M. G. Kiddy
Watcher on the Shore. I. Lambot
Watcher Within. W. Appel
Watchers. D. R. Koontz
Watchers. A. E. W. Mason
Watchers. W. D. Roberts
Watchers. V. Siller
Watchers. E. Webster
Watchers in the Hills. W. R. Foran
Watchers of the Dark. L. Biggle
Watchers of the Plains. R. Cullum
Watches of the Night. G. R. Sims
Watchful at Night. J. Fast
Watching Brief. J. Pattinson
Watching Eye. Alicen White
Watching Eyes. T. C. Bridges
Watching the Detectives. J. Rathbone
Watchmaker. G. Simenon
Wtachmaker of Everton. G. Simenon
Watchman. D. G. Finlay
Watchman. D. Grubb
Watchman. J. B. Harris-Burland
Watchman. I. Rankin
Watchman's Daughter, and other tales. Mrs. G. L. Banks
Watchman's Stone. Rona Randall
Water for the Fire. J. Fores
Water from the Moon. R. Barnes
Water Horse. Genevieve Scott
Water on the Brain. C. MacKenzie
Water Trail. J. Stark
Water Walker. Fredric Brown
Water Weed. Alice Campbell
Water Widow. E. Griffiths
Water Witch. R. Thorndike
Watercress File. A. Gilchrist
Waterfront. J. Brophy
Waterfront. F. Findley
Waterfront Cop. W. P. McGivern
Waterfront Rat. D. Spade
Waterhole. J. J. Savarin
Watering Places of Good Peace. G. Jenkins

Waterland. G. Swift
Waterman. D. Hornig
Watermead Affair. R. Barr
Waters of Centarus. R. G. Brown
Waters of Death. I. A. Greenfield
Waters of Sadness. J. Cassells
Waters of the North. L. C. Douthwaite
Watershed. N. Tranter
Watersplash. P. Wentworth
Watertown Mystery. H. Rockwood
Waterview Manor. E. Welles
Watson's Apology. B. Bainbridge
Watson's Choice. G. Mitchell
Watson's Revenge. R. Mallett
Wave. Christopher Hyde
Wave Hangs Dark. A. Dipper
Wave of Fatalities. M. Delving
Wavecrest. B. Knox
Wavelengths. D. M. Klein
Waves Behind the Boat. Francis King
Waves of Death. K. Robeson
Wax. Ethel L. White
Wax Apple. T. Coe
Wax Basket Murder. Edna Dean
Wax Flowers for Gloria. P. Flower
Wax Image. K. Rhodes
Wax Model. C. Dekker
Waxen Image. R. S. Podaca
Waxwork. P. Lovesey
Waxworks Murder. J. D. Carr
Waxworks Spies. H. C. Davis
Way Back. J. Mitchell
Way Beyond. J. Farnol
Way Home. S. Kitt
'Way Loft. E. L. Long
Way of a Maid. C. Dawe
Way of a Wanton. R. S. Prather
Way of an Eagle. D. Potter
Way of Cain. A. Dunn
Way of Deception. L. Beresford
Way of Escape. C. Stanton
Way of Life. Tom Howard
Way of Sinners. M. Leighton
Way of the Cardines. S. P. Hyatt
Way of the Four. Mark Cross
Way of the North. J. B. Hendryx
Way of the Scarlet Pimpernel. Baroness Orczy
Way of the Strong. R. Cullum
Way of the Tamarisk. V. Maxwell
Way of the Weasel. J. Mowbray
Way of the Wicked. Nicholas Carter
Way of the Wicked. W. Woolfolk
Way of the World. W. T. Adams
Way of the World. D. C. Murray
Way of These Women. E. P. Oppenheim
Way Out. B. Graeme
Way Out Wanton. H. Janson
Way Some People Die. J. R. Macdonald
Way the Cookie Crumbles. J. H. Chase
Way Through the Wood. N. Balchin
Way to Adventure, and two other stories. J. G. Dunbar
Way to Dusty Death. Alistair MacLean
Way to Get Dead. W. Newton
Way to Go, Doll Baby! W. R. Cox
Way to Gold. W. D. Steele
Way to Nowhere. M. McShane
Way to Santiago. A. Calder-Marshall
Way to the Old Sailor's Home. T. Baird
Way to Win. W. LeQueux
Way We Die Now. M. Z. Lewin
Way We Die Now. C. Willeford
Way We Love. S. Friedman
Waylaid by Wireless. E. Balmer
Waylaid in Boston. Elliot Paul
Wayland of the Guides. B. Bolt
Wayland 13. F. Shroyer
Ways and Means. H. Cecil
Ways of Darkness. J. Hayes
Ways of Death. Hans C. Owen
Ways of Men. H. Flowerdew
Ways of Miss Barbara. A. Castle
Ways of the Hour. J. F. Cooper
Ways of the Millionaire. O. Crawfurd

Ways That Are Wary. L. De Bra
Wayside. Andrul
Wayward. Carter Brown
Wayward Angel. V. Chute
Wayward Blonde. M. Corrigan
Wayward Blonde. J. Creighton
Wayward Daughters. N. Lazenby
Wayward Girl. B. Reynolds
Wayward Girl's Fate. Hawkshaw
Wayward Heart. J. MacKenzie
Wayward Madonna. V. Black
Wayward Nymph. C. H. Barker
Wayward Season. V. S. Gunn
Wayward Seeds of Grass. P. Nash
Wayward Wahine. Carter Brown
Wayward Widow. W. C. Gault
Wayward Woman. A. Griffiths
We All Killed Grandma. F. Brown
We Always Threat Women Too Well. R. Queneau
We Are for the Dark. D. Eden
We Are Holding the President Hostage. W. Adler
We Are Not Alone. J. Hilton
We Died in Bond Street. J. Ward
We Don't Want to Lose You. V. Bridges
We Have Always Lived in the Castle. S. Jackson
We Have Always Lived in the Castle. H. C. Wheeler
We Haven't Seen Her Lately. E. Ferrars
We Must Have a Trial. M. Leek
We Must Kill Toni. I. S. Black
We Never Die in the Winter. A. Manning
We Saw Him Die. A. M. Stein
We Shall See. E. Wallace
We Shot an Arrow. G. Goodchild
We, the Accused. E. Raymond
We the Bereaved. A. Clarke
We the Condemned. N. Karta
We, the Condemned. J. Robb
We, the Killers. Michael Brett
We the Unworthy. J. Courage
We Walk with Death. H. Desmond
We Who Survived. S. Noel
We Will Meet Again. J. Hawkins
Weak and the Strong. A. Kent
Weak-Eyed Bat. M. Millar
Weak-Kneed Rogue. Nicholas Carter
Weak Link. Allan Wood
Weaker Vessel. D. C. Murray
Wealth and Poverty, and other tales. Anonymous
Wealth Seeker. M. Grant
Weapon. J. Howell
Weapon. R. C. Mason
Weapon Heavy. J. Reese
Weapon of Night. Nicholas Carter
Weapons of Mystery. J. Hocking
Wear the Butcher's Medal. J. Brunner
Weasel. G. N. Roberts
Weasel Hunt. J. K. McDougall
Weather—Clearing. F. A. Warren
Weather of My Fate. P. Conway
Weather War. L. Leokum
Weatherby. J. M. T. Miller
Weathercock. E. H. Clements
Weatherel Affair. J. W. De Forrest
Weatherman Guy. J. Burmeister
Weatherhawk. H. Crowder
Weatherspy. P. Kerrigan
Weave a Rope of Sand. E. Trevor
Weave a Wicked Web. P. Kruger
Weaver Webb. Old Sleuth
Weavers. A. Askew
Weavers and Weft, and other tales. M. E. Braddon
Weaving the Web. Nicholas Carter
Weaving the Web. H. Mee
Web. Rolf Bennett
Web. H. Brooke
Web. A. Capelli
Web. C. Gibson-Jarvie
Web. F. T. Hill
Web. S. Horler
Web. F. A. Kummer
Web. M. Mallay
Web. S. Talmy
Web. F. Urquhart
Web in Childhood. Winifred Duke

Web of Allyngrood. F. Chimenti
Web of Danger. A. Allston
Web of Danger. A. Blair
Web of Deceit. C. A. Smith
Web of Deception. F. Chimenti
Web of Destiny. Seamark
Web of Dragons. M. Hartmann
Web of Dreams. V. C. Andrews
Web of Enchantment. M. Richmond
Web of Evil. Joselyn Chadwick
Web of Evil. L. Emerick
Web of Fate. T. W. Speight
Web of Fate. C. Wooff
Web of Fear. L. Linares
Web of Fear. M. Reisner
Web of Flesh. D. Haring
Web of Guilt. J. DeWeese
Web of Haefen. J. T. Osborne
Web of Hate. L. Thayer
Web of Horror. C. Farr
Web of Intrigue. E. Lamartine
Web of Love. W. E. D. Ross
Web of Murder. Seamark
Web of Murder. J. Troy
Web of Murder. J. Westerham
Web of Murder. H. Whittington
Web of Obsession. Andrea Hill
Web of Peril. D. Daniels
Web of Salvage. B. Callison
Web of Shadows. E. Backhouse
Web of Silence. J. Wainwright
Web of Spies. Nick Carter
Web of Terror. J. Cannon
Web of the City. H. Ellison
Web of the Spider. H. B. M. Watson
Web of Wan Li. L. Beresford
Web to Catch a Spider. C. Joyce
Webs in the Way. G. M. Fenn
Wed for Wealth. A. Wood
Wedded But Not a Wife. F. Warden
Wedded for a Week. M. A. Fleming
Wedderburn's Will. T. Cobb
Wedding Bargain. A. S. Turnbull
Wedding-Chest Mystery. A. Fielding
Wedding Day. C. N. Williamson
Wedding Eve Murder. B. M. Dix
Wedding Guest. D. Wiltse
Wedding Guest Sat on a Stone. R. Shattuck
Wedding Journey. M. Eatock
Wedding March Murder. Monte Barrett
Wedding Night Murder. C. Bush
Wedding of the Lady of Lovell. U. L. Silberrad
Wedding Ring. H. M. Jones
Wedding Treasure. D. Williams
Wednesday at Noon. J. Corbett
Wednesday Midnight. P. S. McCoy
Wednesday the Rabbi Got Wet. H. Kemelman
Wednesday the Tenth. G. Allen
Wednesday's Wrath. D. Pendleton
Wee Ones. K. Robeson
Weed. C. L. Cooper
Weed. J. Pattinson
Weeds. H. Imbert-Terry
Weeds of Hate. O. Binns
Week by the Sea. Elizabeth Ford
Week-End at Green Trees. M. Meynell
Week-End at Thrackley. A. Melville
Week-End Crime Book. J. M. Walsh
Week-End Murder. N. Brady
Week-End Murders. A. A. Archer
Week-End with Death. Hilary Gray
Week-Ends with Henry. H. Holland
Week of Love. J. Leasor
Week of Passion. Edward Jenkins
Week of Suspense. G. Greenaway
Week of Suspense. A. MacKenzie
Week of the Scorpion. B. Healey
Week of the Succubus. T. R. Austin
Week to Kill. D. Delman
Weekend at the Villa. D. G. Quintano
Weekend for Murder. M. Babson
Weekend Girls. Jonathan Burke
Weekend in Baghdad. R. Wadham
Weekend Mystery. R. A. Simon

Weekend of Shadows. H. Atkinson
Weekend of Terror. J. L. Purvis
Weekend to Danger. T. Vail
Weekend to Kill. H. Atkinson
Weekend to Kill. Ian Stuart
Weekend with Death. P. Wentworth
Weekend with Maxwell. E. G. Cousins
Weep for a Blonde. B. Halliday
Weep for a Wanton. L. Treat
Weep for Her. Sara Woods
Weep for Me. J. D. MacDonald
Weep for Willow Green. P. Kruger
Weep, Moscow, Weep. Gar Wilson
Weep No More, Lady. John Evans
Weep No More, My Lady. M. H. Clark
Weep Now, Die Later. D. Haring
Weeping and the Laughter. V. Caspary
Weeping Ash. Joan Aiken
Weeping Ferry and other stories. M. L. Woods
Weeping Lady. J. L. Roberts
Weeping Tower. C. Randell
Weeping Willow Murders. C. Koonce
Weighed in the Evidence. Nicholas Carter
Weight of Evidence. R. Ormerod
Weight of the Crown. F. M. White
Weight of the Evidence. M. Innes
Weighted Scales. B. Musto
Weir Boyd Mystery. S. G. Hedges
Weird Adventures of the Shadow. M. Grant
Weird Courtship. Old Sleuth
Weird Gift. G. Ohnet
Weird Idol of Penang Towers. G. Wells
Weird Legacies. M. Ashley
Weird Legacy. F. Johnston
Weird of Deadly Hollow. B. Mitford
Weird o' It. M. P. Shiel
Weird Picture. J. R. Carling
Weird Sea Mystery. Old Sleuth
Weird Sisters. R. Dowling
Weird Stories. Mrs. J. H. Riddell
Weird Tales of Terror and Detection. H. F. Heard
Weird Transformation. M. Y. Halidom
Weird Treasure. Nicholas Carter
Weird Valley. K. Robeson
Weird Wedlock. R. M. Gilchrist
Weird World of Wes Beattie. J. N. Harris
Weirdos. D. Haring
Weirdown Experiment. W. Hildick
Welcome Back to Wayland. F. Shroyer
Welcome, Danger! J. Reach
Welcome Danger. Robert Simpson
Welcome Death. G. Daniel
Welcome for a Hero. Robin Perry
Welcome Home! H. Adams
Welcome Home, Jaime. E. Lottman
Welcome Home, Lily Glow. Clay Henry
Welcome, My Dear, to Belfry House. S. Forbes
Welcome, Proud Lady. June Drummond
Welcome Sundays. N. Kiefetz
Welcome to the Feast. G. Wilson
Welcome to the Grave. M. McMullen
Welcome to the Torture Chamber. Mastero Storyteller
Welcome to Xanadu. N. Benchley
Welded Lives. G. Ingram
Welding the Chain. Dick Stewart
Welfleet Mystery. Mrs. G. Sheldon
Well, After All . . . F. F. Moore
Well-Born Corpse. E. Benjamin
Well Caught. A. Armstrong
Well Caught, McLean! G. Goodchild
Well-Dressed for Murder. Laverne Rice
Well-Dressed Skeleton. B. Williams
Well-Furnished Life. E. McCrae
Well, I'll Be . . . A. Baritone
Well, I'll Be Hanged! Kevin O'Hara
Well-Known Face. Josephine Bell
Well Now, My Pretty—. J. H. Chase
Well-Schooled in Murder. E. George
We'll Share a Double Funeral. J. H. Chase
Well-Told Lie. C. Hobhouse
Well-Wisher. P. Carder
Wellington's. M. Olden
Wells of St. Mary's. R. C. Sherriff

Wellspring. E. H. Hawkins
Welsh Courtship. F. W. West
Welsh Fargo. H. Secombe
Wench Is Dead. F. Brown
Wench Is Dead. C. Dexter
Wench Is Dead. R. Fenisong
Wench Is Wicked. Carter Brown
Wendy Picks a Winner. Duff Johnson
Wentworth Hall. A. O'Neill-Barna
Wentworth Mystery. W. Phillips
We're All Guilty. J. Reach
Were Death Denied. D. Yates
Were He a Stranger. M. Craig
Were They Justified? A. Philips
Werewolf. P. McCutchan
Werewolf. C. L. Swem
Werewolf Among Us. D. Koontz
Werewolf of Elphinstone. R. C. Armour
Werewolf of Paris. G. Endore
Werewolf Trace. J. Gardner
Werewolf Walks Tonight. M. Avallone
Werewolf's Last Raid. Anonymous
Werewolves of London. B. Stableford
WerewolveSS. J. Ahern
Wes Hardin's Gun. J. Reese
West Coast Turnaround. E. W. Rukuza
West End. J. G. Brandon
West End Horror. N. Meyer
West End People. P. Wildeblood
West End Women. A. Lamour
West Highland Spirits. C. J. C. Hyne
West of Aztec Pass. W. C. Tuttle
West of Jerusalem. G. De Villiers
West of Orange. J. Dandola
West of Rio Grande. T. Craig
West of the Moon. A. Burr
West Pier. P. Hamilton
West Point Detective. Old Sleuth
West Shore Mystery. Old Sleuth
West Side Jungle. J. Ridgway
Westbound Murder. C. S. Wallace
Western Express Robbery. N. Ridley
Western Ferret. I. Stark
Westerner. L. Allan
Westgate Mystery. Darby St. John
Westhorpe Mystery. I. D. Hardy
Westing Game. E. Raskin
Westlade Murders. T. A. Plummer
Westlakes. T. Cobb
Westland Case. Jonathan Latimer
Westminster Disaster. F. Hoyle
Westminster Mystery. Elaine Hamilton
Westminster One. T. Willis
Weston of the North-West Mounted Police. T. Lund
Westwind. I. Rankin
Westwood Mystery. C. J. Dutton
Westwood Mystery. A. Fielding
Wet Graves. P. Corris
Wet Job. M. Stall
Wet Work. C. Buckley
Wetback. W. O'Farrell
Wettermark. E. Chaze
We've Been Waiting for You. E. Thornbury
Wexford. J. Ellis
Whadda We Do Now, Butch? S. Talmy
Whale's Footprints. R. Boyer
Wharf Girl. W. Manners
Wharf Sinister. A. Grace
What a Body! A. Green
What a Gal! Barreaux
What a Man Wills. Mrs. G. D. Vaizey
What a Tangled Web. A. Hocking
What a Way to Go. D. Haring
What a Way to Go! S. O'Shea
What Are the Bugles Blowing For? N. Freeling
What Are Your Angels Now? P. Groom
What Became of Alex Bretherton? P. Harris
What Became of Eugene Ridgewood? P. James
What Became of Mr. Desmond. C. N. Boyle
What Beckoning Ghost. D. G. Browne
What Befell a Bristol Trader. J. Johnson
What Bloody Man Is That? S. Brett
What Can You Lose? R. B. Saxe

Title Index

What Changed Charley Farthing. M. Hebden
What Comes Next. H. Vogel
What Crime Is It? D. Gardiner
What Dark Secret. D. Dudley
What Did Hattie See? K. Roos
What Did I Do Tomorrow? L. P. Davies
What Do I Care? D. Linton
What Dread Hand. C. Brand
What Dread Hand. E. Gill
What Dread Hand. S. Kemp
What Else Could I Do? T. Claymore
What Ever Happened to Baby Jane? H. Farrell
What Fools Men Are! S. Murray
What Fools Women Are! D. Vane
What Gentleman Strangles a Lady? R. G. Dean
What Gives? D. Spade
What Happened at Andals? John Arnold
What Happened at Hazelwood. M. Innes
What Happened Is This. B. Von Hutten
What Happened Then? L. T. Bradley
What Happened to Forester. E. P. Oppenheim
What Happened to Hammond? H. Blayn
What Happened to Mary? R. C. Brown
What Hast Thou Done? J. F. Molloy
What Have They Done to You, Ben? B. Reade
What He Cost Her. J. Payn
What He Least Expected. Holworthy Hall
What I Tell You Three Times Is False. Samuel Holt
What Immortal Hand. J. Curtis
What Is This Mystery? M. E. Braddon
What Is Your Verdict? T. J. R. Sennocke
What Killed Christopher Scammell? P. L. Read
What Lies Beneath. B. Swift
What Makes You Tick? D. Haring
What, Me, Mr. Mosley. John Greenwood
What Mrs. McGIllicuddy Saw! A. Christie
What News of Kitty? D. Quentin
What Next? Winifred Graham
What Next? J. T. Patterson
What Nigel Knew. E. Field
What Night Will Bring. H. Bailey
What—No Body? Mary Archer
What—No Witnesses? Mary Archer
What No Woman Knows. Neil Bell
What Now My Love. F. Salas
What of Terry Conniston? B. Garfield
What Old Father Thames Said. C. Nelson
What Ought She to Do? F. Warden
What Price Adventure? B. Johns
What Price Doubloons? Frank King
What Price Murder. C. F. Adams
What Price Murder? M. Grable
What Price Paradise? A. Hillgarth
What Price Silence? D. Haring
What Really Happened. B. Halliday
What Really Happened. M. B. Lowndes
What Rhymes with Murder? J. Iams
What Rough Beast. J. Trench
What Say the Jury? C. M. Wills
What Shall I Cry. A. Binkley
What Shall It Profit? H. E. Inman
What Should a Man Do? H. G. Hutchinson
What Stranger Cause? F. Bamford
What the Dead Men Say. E. Gorman
What the Doctor Ordered. V. Bridges
What the Peeper Saw. J. Gratus
What Then Is Love. E. Loring
What Thinkest Thou, Simon? Winifred Graham
What to Do Until the Undertaker Comes. T. Wells
What Was It? and other stories. Fitz-James O'Brien
What Will the World Say? C. Gibbon
What Would You Have Done? L. Tracy
What You Pay For. C. J. Henderson
Whatever Dies. P. Woodruff
Whatever Goes Up. B. Millhauser
Whatever Happened to Aunt Alice? U. Curtiss
Whatever Happened to Ruby? W. Owen
Whatever Happened to Rosie Dunn? T. Beauford
Whatever's Been Going On at Mumblesby? Colin Watson
What's at the End? L. Beresford
What's Become of Anna? T. Tucker
What's Become of Screwloose? and other stories. R. Goulart
What's Better Than Money? J. H. Chase
What's Bred in the Bone. G. Allen
What's Bred in the Bone. R. Davies
What's Funny About Murder. Craig Cooper
What's Happening? J. N. Iannuzzi
What's in a Name? A. Spiller
What's in It for Walter? F. Tilsley
What's in the Dark? E. Queen
What's Left of Fred. W. Maner
What's the Matter with Helen? R. Deming
What's with You? D. Ambler
What's Wrong at Pyford? D. Fisher
What's Wrong with the Rovers? Hedley Scott
What's Ya Problem? H. Zore
Whatsoever a Man Soweth. W. LeQueux
Whatsoever Things Are True. S. Harvester
Wheat and Tares. P. Trent
Wheat Killing. P. Tanous
Wheatstack. J. S. Fletcher
Wheel. Alan White
Wheel Fortune. Karen Campbell
Wheel Is Fixed. J. M. Fox
Wheel o'Fortune. L. Tracy
Wheel of Circumstance. D. W. Spurgeon
Wheel of Death. R. T. M. Scott
Wheel of Fate. Mrs. B. Harte
Wheel of Fate. P. Saint-Lambert
Wheel of Fire. J. Middlemass
Wheel of Fortune. Karen Campbell
Wheel of Fortune. S. Howatch
Wheel Spins. Ehtle L. White
Wheel That Turned. K. M. Knight
Wheel Turns. E. Lemarchand
Wheelchair Corpse. W. Levinrew
Wheeler, Dealer! Carter Brown
Wheeler Fortune. Carter Brown
Wheelie! Stuart Hall
Wheeling Light. F. Hume
Wheels. J. Spenser
Wheels Beneath. G. Kelton
Wheels in the Forest. J. N. Chance
Wheels of Anarchy. M. Pemberton
Wheels of Death. Stuart Hall
Wheels of Death. W. W. Johnstone
Wheels Within Wheels. H. Mee
Wheels Within Wheels. C. Wells
When a Blonde Dies. M. Skinner
When a Man Yields. Nicholas Carter
When a Rogue's in Power. Nicholas Carter
When All Is Staked. Nicholas Carter
When and If. P. Reynolds
When Ape Is King. O. Wynd
When Beggars Choose. K. N. Burt
When Blondes Meet. B. Vane
When Brave Men Tremble. Nicholas Carter
When Can You Trust a Dame? Peter Williams
When Carruthers Laughed. H. C. McNeile
When Clews Are Hidden. Nicholas Carter
When Cold Steel Clshed. C. Frisbie
When Conscience Sleeps. W. J. Bayfield
When Crook Meets Crook. A. Spiller
When Dames Get Tough. H. Janson
When Danger Threatens. Mark Cross
When Danger Threatens. Sea Lion
When Darkness Falls. P. Zindel
When Dead Men Tell Tales. J. Goodwin
When Death Walks. J. Corbett
When Destruction Threatens. Nicholas Carter
When Dorinda Dances. B. Halliday
When Dragons Dance. B. Tokson
When Dreams Come True. E. Blair
When Duty Calls. M. I. Burke
When Eight Bells Toll. Alistair MacLean
When Elephants Forget. W. B. Murphy
When Emmalyn Remembers. E. Marlow
When Fell the Night. E. Queen
When First We Practise. W. Cheame
When Fish Begin to Smell. M. H. Cooper
When Fools Endanger Us. R. Ladline
When Footsteps Echo. B. Copper
When Gravity Fails. G. A. Effinger
When Greek Meets Greek. J. Hatton
When Greek Meets Greek. P. Trent
When Honors Fall. Nicholas Carter
When I Grow Rich. Joan Fleming
When I Say Goodbye, I'm Clary Brown. C. Keppel
When I Was Czar. A. W. Marchmont
When I Was Otherwise. S. Benatar
When in Greece. E. Lathen
When in Rome. N. Marsh
When It Was Dark. G. Thorne
When Jealousy Spurs. Nicholas Carter
When Johnny Died. C. Rougvie
When Johnny the Cleaver Took Britain. D. Webster
When Last I Died. G. Mitchell
When Last Seen . . . M. J. Herrick
When London Sleeps. H. T. Johnson
When Love Called. A. W. Marchmont
When Love Is Strong. G. Keon
When Love Was Not Enough. Clifford Mason
When Michael Calls. J. Farris
When My Ship Comes Home. C. Massie
When Necessity Drives. Nicholas Carter
When No Man Pursueth. M. B. Lowndes
When No Man Pursueth. D. Sharp
When One Door Shuts. M. Pereira
When Only the Bougainvillea Blooms. I. Charles
When Passions Rule. F. Hart
When Rich Men Die. Harold Adams
When Rogues Conspire. Nicholas Carter
When Rogues Fall Out. R. A. Freeman
When Rogues Fall Out. J. Hatton
When Satan Ruled. C. R. Gull
When Scholars Fall. T. Robinson
When Shadows Fall. N. C. Heard
When Shall I Sleep Again? N. W. Firth
When She Wakes. L. O'Brien
When She Was Bad. W. Ard
When Spy Meets Spy. R. Walker
When Strangers Came. J. Raven
When Strangers Meet. R. Bloomfield
When Summer Comes Again. B. Baskerville
When the Bells Rang. B. Graeme
When the Bough Breaks. J. Kellerman
When the Bough Breaks. S. Rosenberg
When the Case Was Opened. J. Bude
When the Cat's Away. G. Bullett
When the Cat's Away. K. Friedman
When the Century Blooms. J. Wetherell
When the Clews Point Wrong. Dick Stewart
When the Clock Strikes 13. D. Hanna
When the Dark Man Calls. S. M. Kaminsky
When the Death Penalty Came Back. G. J. Cadbury
When the Devil Drives. F. Warden
When the Devil Was Sick. C. Carnac
When the Devil Was Sick. Charles Ross
When the Dragon Dies. G. Clifton
When the Empire Crashed. A. W. Marchmont
When the Fat Man Sings. William Murray
When the Gallows Is High. P. Hastings
When the Gangs Came to London. E. Wallace
When the Gods Laughed. P. Audemars
When the Gunmen Came. J. Hunter
When the Jury Disagreed! J. Hunter
When the Killing Starts. Ted Wood
When the Lusting Began. T. Thomey
When the Moon Died. R. Savage
When the Moon Is Full. H. Shaw
When the Mopoke Calls. W. S. Walker
When the Music Stopped. E. Ogilvie
When the Nightbird Cries. L. Palmer
When the Police Failed. R. Ladline
When the Quarry Turns. I. Stark
When the Rainbow Is Pale. G. Joseph
When the Red Gods Call. B. Grimshaw
When the Sacred Ginmill Closes. L. Block
When the Sea Gives Up Its Dead. Mrs. G. Corbett
When the Sky Falls. M. Ashton
When the Sun Goes Down. C. Blackstock
When the Trail Calls. A. P. Lehner
When the Trap Was Sprung. Nicholas Carter
When the Wicked Man . . . J. F. W. Hannay
When the Wicked Man. G. Thorne
When the Wicked Prosper. Nicholas Carter
When the Wind Blows. C. Hare
When the Wind Blows. J. Saul
When the Wind Cries. Claudette Nicole
When the Witch Is Dead. M. L. Roby

When the World Was Younger. M. E. Bradden
When They Kill Your Wife. J. Crowe
When Thief Meets Thief. H. S. Keeler
When Thieves Fall Out. Mark Cross
When Thieves Fall Out. S. A. Curtis
When Thieves Fall Out. H. Graham
When Thieves Fall Out. G. Reed
When Thieves Fall Out. J. K. Stafford
When Thieves Fall Out. B. Thomson
When Threads Get Tangled. J. K. Stafford
When Three Makes Two. H. Carstairs
When Time Went Back. Anonymous
When Tragedy Grins. Grace M. White
When Trails Cross. J. K. Stafford
When Trails Were New. T. Mundy
When Trouble Beckons. M. McQuay
When Tutt Meets Tutt. A. Train
When Victims Meet. H. Roman
When We Ran. K. Leopold
When We the Dead Awaken. John Holt
When Women Love. G. M. White
When You Comin' Back, Range Rider. C. Heath
Where All the Girls Are Sweeter. Richard Butler
Where Angel Treads. G. Montrose
Where Angels Fear . . . B. Hemyng
Where Angels Fear to Tred. Morgan Robertson
Where Are the Children? M. H. Clark
Where Are You Going? A. Applin
Where Danger Lies. J. T. Osborne
Where Dead Men Walk. H. Leverage
Where Did Charity Go? Carter Brown
Where Did the Girls Go? M. Cousin
Where Eagles Dare. Alistair MacLean
Where East Is East. T. Browning
Where Every Prospect Pleases. R. Halket
Where Evil Waits. M. Lynch
Where Helen Lies. R. Foley
Where Ignorance Is Bliss. R. Greene
Where Is Barbara Prentice? M. Burton
Where Is Bianca. E. Queen
Where Is Crystal Martin? C. K. Cambray
Where Is Evie Alton? H. Bourne
Where Is Holly Carleton? S. Marvin
Where Is Jane? Lynn Williams
Where Is Janice Gantry? J. D. MacDonald
Where Is Jenny Now? F. S. Wees
Where Is Jenny Willet? W. H. L. Crauford
Where Is Mary Bostwick? R. Foley
Where Is She Now? L. Meynell
Where Is the Withered Man? N. Deane
Where Lawyers Fear to Tread. L. Matera
Where Lionel Lies. A. S. Well
Where Murder Waits. Gordon Davis
Where No Fire Burns. M. Barratt
Where No Flags Fly. F. Ayer, Jr.
Where Nobody Dies. C. Wheat
Where Nothing Ever Happens. L. Shippey
Where Peril Beckons. Nicholas Carter
Where Satan Dwells. F. Stevenson
Where Secrecy Begins. J. C. Nolan
Where Shadows Fall. J. Kelman
Where Shadows Lie. M. Lynch
Where Shadows Linger. J. S. May
Where Should He Die? Sara Woods
Where Some Men Are Men. G. F. Worts
Where Terror Stalked. C. Birkin
Where the Atlantic Meets the Land. C. Lipsett
Where the Clue Leads. I. Stark
Where the Dark Streets Go. D. S. Davis
Where the Desert Ends. W. LeQueux
Where the East Wind Blows. A. Mair
Where the Fresh Grass Grows. Brian Cooper
Where the Heart Is. A. Hale
Where the Jungle Ends. Ken Blake
Where the Lost Aprils Are. E. Ogilvie
Where the Money Is. J. Pattinson
Where the Pavement Ends. J. Russell
Where the Rail Runs Now. F. F. Moore
Where the River Bends. J. M. Scott
Where the Shoe Pinches. L. T. Meade
Where the Snow Was Red. H. Pentecost
Where the Spies Are. J. Leasor
Where the Trade-Wind Blows. Mrs. S. Crowninshield

Where the Trail Ended. W. M. Graydon
Where the Truth Lies. H. Hayes
Where There Are Vultures. A. Heckstall-Smith
Where There Is a Will . . . A. Griffin
Where There Was Smoke. B. Flynn
Where There's a Head. L. Gorell
Where There's a Will. Anne Burton
Where There's a Will. K. Chase
Where There's a Will. R. S. Hastings
Where There's a Will. Ellis Peters
Where There's a Will. E. Phillips
Where There's a Will. M. R. Rinehart
Where There's a Will. R. Stout
Where There's Smoke. C. B. Kelland
Where There's Smoke. E. McBain
Where There's Smoke. S. Sterling
Where Trojan Horses Fear to Tread. D. R. Garrett
Where Vultures Reign. Laurie Davis
Where Was Trail Murdered? T. A. Plummer
Where You Throw Blood. B. Sarto
Whereabouts Unknown. B. Reynolds
Where's Emily. C. Wells
Where's Mr. Chumley. S. Truss
Where's Mommy Now? R. M. Krich
Where's the Body? T. Jackson
Where's Zeobia.? F. Du Boisgobey
Wherever Lynn Goes. Beatrice Parker
Which Doctor? E. Candy
Which I Never. L. A. G. Strong
Which—Innocent or Guilty? E. S. Clem
Which Mrs. Bennett? A. Littlefield
Which Mrs. Torr? Maude Parker
Which of Them? P. Black
Which of Us Is Safe? M. Cumberland
Which One? R. A. Bennet
Which Side Gave In? J. Hitchins
Which the Justice, Which the Thief. W. Harrington
Which Way Came Death? F. Wolseley
Which Way to Die? E. Queen
Whiff of Death. I. Asimov
Whiff of Money. J. H. Chase
Whiff of Sulphur. G. Linscott
Whiffs from a Short Briar. Max Baring
While Angels Sleep. J. Kelman
While Guy Was in France. T. Cobb
While London Sleeps. R. Dowling
While Love Lay Sleeping. R. Neely
While Murder Waits. B. Cassiday
While Murder Waits. J. Esteven
While My Pretty One Sleeps. M. H. Clark
While of Sound Mind. S. McKenna
While She Sleeps. Ethel L. White
While Still We Live. Helen MacInnes
While the Bells Rang. C. L. Clifford
While the City Sleeps. C. Einstein
While the Coffin Waited. J. Sheridan
While the Fetters Were Forged. Nicholas Carter
While the Lights Were Out. J. Sharkey
While the Patient Slept. M. G. Eberhart
While the Wind Howled. A. Gaines
While There Is Life. W. Markall
Whilst the Crowd Roared. S. Horler
Whim to Kill. Dell Shannon
Whims. Wanderer
Whims of Erasmus. W. C. Platts
Whims of Fate. C. Jauniere
Whip. S. E. Mason
Whip. R. Parker
Whip and the Tongue. H. L. V. Fletcher
Whip Hand. V. Canning
Whip Hand. R. Crawford
Whip Hand. D. Francis
Whip Hand. I. Gordon
Whip Hand. W. F. Sanders
Whip of Hate. W. R. Scott
Whip of the Will. Mrs. C. Kernahan
Whip-Poor-Will Mystery. H. Footner
Whiplash. H. Janson
Whiplash. W. C. MacDonald
Whiplash. R. W. Taylor
Whipping Boy. B. Holmes
Whipping Boy. P. Orum
Whipping Boys. G. Cullingford
Whipping Girl. R. Rodd

Whips of Time. N. Giles
Whipsaw. D. Pendleton
Whirl of a Bird. G. Peters
Whirligig. R. L. Fish
Whirligig of Time. L. Biggle
Whirligig of Time. D. De Jong
Whirligigs. O. Henry
Whirling Death. Nicholas Carter
Whirlpool. J. L. Henderson
Whirlpool. A. Howlett
Whirlpool. D. Lamson
Whirlpool. V. Morton
Whirlpool of Thunder. W. H. Caryl
Whirlpools. J. P. McGinty
Whirlwind. J. Clavell
Whirlwind. J. Creasey
Whirlwind Beneath the Sea. K. Stanton
Whisker of Hercules. K. Robeson
Whiskered Footman. E. Jepson
Whiskers and Soda. F. Richardson
Whiskey Drips. J. J. Brooks
Whiskey River. L. D. Estleman
Whisky Johnny. C. McManus
Whisky Murders. R. Grayson
Whisper. William Marshall
Whisper Can Kill. G. Sherry
Whisper Down the Moon. C. Darby
Whisper Her Name. Howard Hunt
Whisper His Sin. V. Packer
Whisper If You Dare! A. MacKenzie
Whisper in a Lonely Place. G. Sinstadt
Whisper in the Dark. K. Troy
Whisper in the Darkness. T. E. Huff
Whisper in the Dust. Stephanie Hall
Whisper in the Forest. N. Ames
Whisper in the Glen. P. M. Hubbard
Whisper in the Gloom. N. Blake
Whisper in the Night. J. Aiken
Whisper Murder! V. Kelsey
Whisper Murder Softly. P. Bannon
Whisper of Danger. Clarissa Ross
Whisper of Darkness. M. Lynn
Whisper of Death. V. Hanson
Whisper of Death. V. Siller
Whisper of Evil. R. Gatenby
Whisper of Fear. C. Randell
Whisper of Fear. Elna Stone
Whisper of Heather. L. Benedict
Whisper of Shadows. J. L. H. Whitney
Whisper of the Axe. R. Condon
Whisper of Treason. Harshorne
Whisper on the Stair. L. Mearson
Whisper Town. J. Philips
Whisper Who Dares. T. Strong
Whisperer. W. M. Duncan
Whisperer. C. Goodrich
Whisperer. Mrs. C. Kernahan
Whisperer. J. M. Walsh
Whispering Bird. Traill Stevenson
Whispering Buddha. J. C. Cowles
Whispering Cat Mystery. J. Kains
Whispering Caverns. A. Winter
Whispering Chorus. P. P. Sheehan
Whispering City. Horace Brown
Whispering Corpse. W. P. McGivern
Whispering Cracksman. B. Perowne
Whispering Cup. M. Seeley
Whispering Dead. A. Ganachilly
Whispering Death. Fredric Brown
Whispering Death. D. Carney
Whispering Death. J. Pattinson
Whispering Death. J. Spencer
Whispering Death. J. Wylde
Whispering Ear. C. B. Clason
Whispering Echo. M. McGregor
Whispering Gables. S. Abbott
Whispering Galleries. B. Goldie
Whispering Gallery. R. H. Francis
Whispering Gallery. P. Robinson
Whispering Gallery. W. E. D. Ross
Whispering Ghost. S. Chalmers
Whispering Hill. M. Albrand
Whispering House. M. Erskine
Whispering Island. N. McFather

Whispering Knights. G. Mitchell
Whispering Lane. F. Hume
Whispering Leaves. D. Collett
Whispering Lodge. S. Murray
Whispering Man. W. M. Duncan
Whispering Man. H. Holt
Whispering Man. H. K. Webster
Whispering Master. F. Gruber
Whispering Money. Richard Bennett
Whispering Pines. R. C. Schimmel
Whispering Raider. Anonymous
Whispering Riders. W. B. Bannerman
Whispering Runes. Doris Shannon
Whispering Shadows. Herman Landon
Whispering Smith. F. H. Spearman
Whispering Steel. J. Nicholas
Whispering Tongues. Laurence Kirk
Whispering Wall. P. Carlon
Whispering Walls. E. Brennan
Whispering Walls. W. Spence
Whispering Willows. D. Osborne
Whispering Window. C. Fitzsimmons
Whispering Windows. T. Burke
Whispering Wires. H. Leverage
Whispering Wires. K. L. McLaurin
Whispering Woman. G. Verner
Whisperland. C. Hyde
Whispers. G. Colmore
Whispers. Louis Dodge
Whispers. D. R. Koontz
Whispers at Midnight. A. Parnell
Whispers from the Dark Side of Tomorrow. O. Peters
Whispers in the Dark. S. Hacker
Whispers in the Dark. J. M. Walsh
Whispers in the Night. Clarissa Ross
Whispers in the Night. W. E. D. Ross
Whispers in the Sun. M. Greig
Whispers in the Wind. Marsha Alexander
Whispers in the Wind. R. Wissman
Whispers of the Flesh. F. Flora
Whistle and I'll Come. P. McCutchan
Whistle at My Window. H. Arvonen
Whistle Blower. John Hale
Whistle for the Crows. D. Eden
Whistle in the Wind. D. Daniels
Whistle Me Over the Water. W. Leighton
Whistle of Doom. B. Ludwig
Whistle of Fate. R. Marsh
Whistle Past the Graveyard. R. Deming
Whistle Stop. M. M. Wolff
Whistle Up the Devil. Derek Smith
Whistlejacket. John Hawkes
Whistler in the Dark. J. Malcolm
Whistler's Lane. Anthea Fraser
Whistling Hangman. B. Kendrick
Whistling in the Dark. H. K. Carpenter
Whistling in the Dark. L. Gross
Whistling Key. V. Gunn
Whistling Legs. R. McDougald
Whistling Legs. M. Foster
Whistling Sands. E. Dudley
Whistling Shadow. M. Seeley
Whistling Wires. P. Groom
White Alley. C. Wells
White and Wanton. R. H. Badrig
White Angel. J. Corbett
White Angel. E. B. Cross
White Arab. E. P. Thorne
White Arrow. A. Wynne
White Audi. Timothy Williams
White August. J. Boland
White Badger. C. Talbot
White Bikini. Carter Brown
White Bird, and other stories. W. J. Newton
White Blackbird. H. Douglas
White Bride. F. M. White
White Brow. B. Lyon
White Cad Cross-Up. W. F. Nolan
White Camel. L. Allan
White Camellia. F. Grierson
White Camellias. A. T. Brooks
White Cargo. Stuart Woods
White Castello. M. McEvoy

White Cat. G. Burgess
White Chalet. L. Cross
White Cipher. H. Leverage
White Circle. C. J. Daly
White Circle. J. Shrog
White Cockatoo. M. G. Eberhart
White Cottage Mystery. M. Allingham
White Countess. F. Warden
White Cowl. F. H. Harrison
White Crash Helmet. P. Fry
White Crow. P. MacDonald
White Crown and other stories. H. D. Ward
White Cruiser. N. Buntline
White Crusaders. A. W. Halse
White Dacoit. B. Mather
White Darkness. L. Mott
White Death. Nicholas Cain
White Death. Nick Carter
White Death. W. M. Graydon
White Death. A. Neilson
White Death. R. Sheckley
White Desert. C. R. Cooper
White Dominoes. F. M. Pettee
White Dress. M. G. Eberhart
White Eagle. Roland Daniel
White Eagles Over Serbia. L. Durrell
White-Eyed Woman. E. Bowen-Rowlands
White Face. E. Wallace
White-Faced Man. Gavin Holt
White Falcon. J. McVean
White Feather Mystery. M. Williamson
White Feathers. G. I. Cervus
White Fire. D. Stivers
White Fires Burning. C. Dillon
White Flower. Philip Ross
White for a Shroud. D. C. Cameron
White for Danger. David Stevens
White Friar. Donald Stuart
White Gamma. D. Chacko
White Gas. R. Keverne
White Gauntlet. P. Brebner
White Ghost of Fenwick Hall. A. Wharton
White Girls Eastward. T. Craig
White Glove. W. LeQueux
White Glove. F. M. White
White Gold. O. Binns
White Gold. M. D. Orr
White Gorilla. H. Vernes
White Hand. J. Warmbold
White Hand and a Black Thumb. H. Spicer
White Hand and the Black. B. Mitford
White Hand Murder Mystery. M. E. Campbell
White Hand of Athene. J. Thorne
White Hands of Justice. O. Binns
White Hat and other stories. Finch Mason
White Heat. C. Bainbridge
White Heat. R. Dudgeon
White Hecatomb. W. C. Scully
White Hell. D. Tracy
White Hell. G. Wilson
White Hen. P. Traill
White Horse Inn. G. Simenon
White Horse to Banbury Cross. R. Llewellyn
White Horsemen. C. Stanton
White House. M. E. Braddon
White House Massacre. S. Victor
White House Murder Case. J. Feiffer
White House Pantry Murder. E. Roosevelt
White Is the Color of Death. J. N. Catanach
White Island. N. Lansdale
White Jade. Jan Alexander
White Jade. W. D. Roberts
White Jade Fox. A. Norton
White Khan. C. Dillon
White King of Africa. W. M. Graydon
White Knight. T. Melville
White Lady. M. Crommelin
White Lady. E. Kyle
White Lady of Khaminavatka. R. H. Savage
White Leaves of Death. P. Audemars
White Lie. G. R. Beardmore
White Lie. W. LeQueux
White Lie and No Glory. D. Mariner
White Lie Assignment. P. Driscoll

White Lie Company, and The Woman with the Green Eyes. A. Soutar
White Lie the Dead. P. Loraine
White Lies. C. Budd
White Lies. C. Hyde
White Light. Campbell Armstrong
White Line Fever. C. S. Cotelo
White Line War. D. Pendleton
White Magic. M. M. Bodkin
White Male Running. M. G. Webb
White Mamaloi and other stories. Morley Roberts
White Mandarin. D. Sherman
White Man's Chance. J. McCulley
White Man's Justice: Black Man's Grief. D. Goines
White Man's Stride. L. P. Greene
White Mask. J. M. Walsh
White Mazurka. B. Boyer
White Meat. P. Corris
White Menace. J. Rhode
White Menace. Colin Robertson
White Mercenary. P. Saxon
White Mice. R. H. Davis
White Midnight. C. Risku
White Moll. F. Packard
White Motley. M. Pemberton
White Mountain Murders. Steve Sherman
White Negro. A. Mills
White Nigger. F. A. M. Webster
White Night. F. Rosaire
White Night, Red Dawn. F. Nolan
White Ninja. E. V. Lustbader
White Owl. E. Snell
White Panthers. D. Vane
White Pavilion. V. Johnston
White Peacock. M. L. Roby
White Peril. G. Bartram
White Peril. S. Westlaw
White Phantom. M. E. Braddon
White Phantom. W. Braun
White Phantom. J. Hunter
White Pierrot. P. Barrington
White Plague. F. Herbert
White Poppy. H. Osborne
White Prior. F. Hume
White Priory Murders. Carter Dickson
White Python. V. Canning
White Raiment. C. H. Bullivant
White Raven. M. Blodgett
White Refugees. R. C. Armour
White Rider. L. Charteris
White Rook. J. M. Davis
White Rook. J. B. Harris-Burland
White Rook. H. M. Kahler
White Room. L. P. Davies
White Rose. Alanna Knight
White Rose Mystery. G. Biss
White Rose of Memphis. W. C. Falkner
White Sapphire. L. F. Hartman
White Satin. J. L. Rickard
White Savage. A. W. Upfield
White Sheep of the Family. L. du G. Peach
White Shield. B. Mitford
White Shroud. R. Nicholas
White Sin. A. Wood
White Sioux: Major Walsh of the Mounted Police. I. C. Allan
White Siren. S. Maddock
White Slave. Richard Owen
White Slave. Maxwell Scott
White Slave Racket. R. Vane
White Slaves of Many Nations. J. Wingrave
White Slaves of New Orleans. R. Vane
White Slaves of the Congo. J. Wingrave
White Slaves of the Red Lamp. R. Vane
White Snake. A. Mills
White Snake. L. Whiteson
White South. H. Innes
White Stacks. W. Hewlett
White Streak. S. Gluck
White Trails Over London. R. Wilkes-Hunter
White Taureg. Operator 1384
White Tiger. R. S. Nathan
White Vampire. A. M. Judd
White Velvet. S. Rohmer

White Violets. E. Crandall
White Virgin. G. M. Fenn
White Walls. M. Pemberton
White Wash. I. Ludlow
White Widows. S. Merwin, Jr.
White Wig. G. Verner
White Witch. F. Warden
White Witch of Mayfair. George Griffith
White Witch of the Matabele. J. Whishaw
White Witch of the South Seas. D. Wheatley
White Witch's Warning. Anonymous
White Wizard. N. Buntline
White Wolf. P. Feval
White Wolf and other fireside tales. Q
White Wolverine Contract. P. Atlee
White Yawl. J. B. Harris-Burland
White Zone. J. W. Corrington
Whitebird Murders. T. B. Black
Whitechapel Murder. F. Allen
Whitechapel Murders. A. F. Pinkerton
Whitechapel Mystery. N. T. Oliver
Whitefire. G. Wright
Whitelands Affair. Anna Clarke
Whiteoaks Murder. J. Laurence
Whiteout! D. Kyle
Whitewashed Tombs. A. R. Thurman
Whitewater. B. Knox
Whitewater VI. D. McBriarty
Whither, Barbara? J. C. Carlson
Whither Do You Wander? J. Tickell
Whither Thou Goest. W. LeQueux
Whitney Case. John Bentley
Whittington Pact. L. Le Grand
Whitton's Folly. Pamela Hill
Who? P. Baron
Who? A. Budrys
Who? E. Kent
Who? A. W. Marchmont
Who? A. J. Palermo
Who Are You, Linda Condrick? P. Carlon
Who Benefits? L. Thayer
Who Called Diamonds? G. Brodie
Who Calls the Tune. N. Bawden
Who Censored Roger Rabbit? G. K. Wolf
Who Closed the Casement? T. Cobb
Who Could Hate Percy? C. Shaw
Who Cries for a Loser? Ray Owen
Who Cut the Colonel's Throat? W. L. Hay
Who Dare to Live. R. Lucas
Who Dares? Loring Brent
Who Dialed 999? C. F. Gregg
Who Did It. Anonymous
Who Did It? N. Gould
Who Did It? Marjorie Williamson
Who Died at the Grange? M. Halliday
Who Died Last. F. Du Boisgobey
Who Dies? S. P. B. Mais
Who Dies for Me? S. H. Courtier
Who Dies Next? H. J. Wurr
Who Dies There? J. P. Duff
Who Dies There? H. Kane
Who Do Women?... M. Corrigan
Who Else But She? S. Fowler
Who Evil Thinks. R. Glendinning
Who Fired the Factory? T. A. Plummer
Who Giveth This Woman? W. LeQueux
Who Goes Hang? S. Hyland
Who Goes Home? R. Curle
Who Goes Home? E. Lemarchand
Who Goes Next? J. Wainwright
Who Goes There? B. K. Benson
Who Goes There? L. Paxton
Who Goes There? D. Vane
Who Guards a Prince. Reginald Hill
Who Has Wilma Lathrop. D. Keene
Who He? A. Bestor
Who Is Cato? G. Sims
Who Is Elissa Sheldon? D. Montross
Who Is Guilty? P. Woolf
Who Is John Noman? C. H. Beckett
Who Is Lewis Pinder? L. P. Davies
Who Is Mary Stark? L. Kropp
Who Is Melody? P. Drew
Who Is My Enemy? Barbara Cooper

Who Is My Neighbor? N. Balchin
Who Is Nemo. R. Douglas
Who Is Simon Warwick? P. Moyes
Who Is Teddy Villanova? T. Berger
Who Is the Ace? N. Anthony
Who Is the Heir? M. Collins
Who Is the Man? J. S. Tait
Who Is the Next? H. K. Webster
Who Is This Girl? H. T. Miller
Who is This Man? A. MacGowan
Who Keeps the Keys? F. Leslie
Who Kill to Live. N. Harris
Who Killed Agatha Christie? T. Gates
Who Killed Alfred Snow? J. S. Fletcher
Who Killed Amanda? G. Monro
Who Killed Ann Gage? R. St. Clair
Who Killed Aunt Caroline? G. Richards
Who Killed Aunt Maggie? Medora Field
Who Killed Beau Sparrow? Roger Fuller
Who Killed Brother Treasurer? C. M. Wills
Who Killed Caldwell? C. Wells
Who Killed Carson? H. H. C. Gibbons
Who Killed Cavelotti? A. Newell
Who Killed Charmian Karslake? A. Haynes
Who Killed Chloe? M. Allingham
Who Killed Cock Robin? M. Duffy
Who Killed Cock Robin? H. Hext
Who Killed Coralie? The Aresbys
Who Killed Corey? Rob Eden
Who Killed Diana? H. Hext
Who Killed Dick Whittington? E. Radford
Who Killed Dr. Sex? Carter Brown
Who Killed Enoch Powell. Arthur Wise
Who Killed Falstaff? T. R. Burch
Who Killed Farraby? C. H. Ogilvie
Who Killed Frankie Leash? M. Echard
Who Killed Gatton? E. C. Vivian
Who Killed Gerald Cruden? Alan Graham
Who Killed Gregory? Eugene Jones
Who Killed Henry Wickenstrom. Mark Cross
Who Killed Honeybee? Craig Cooper
Who Killed Jefferson Broome? H. M. Keynes
Who Killed Jock Ewing? R. Tine
Who Killed Lady Poynder? R. Marsh
Who Killed Lord Brisham? G. De Jeans
Who Killed Lord Henry Rollestone? J. Daye
Who Killed Lord Luxmore? M. Leighton
Who Killed Madcap Millicent? Roger Fuller
Who Killed Marie Westhoven? Eric North
Who Killed Me? J. Allan
Who Killed Merblyn Henderson. P. E. Donkor
Who Killed Mr. Fisk. J. Brooke
Who Killed Mr. Garland's Mistress. R. Forrest
Who Killed My Wife? R. Goyne
Who Killed Nancy Dormans. O. Ayton
Who Killed Netta Maul? F. Arthur
Who Killed Oliver Cromwell? L. Gribble
Who Killed Palomino Molero? M. V. Llosa
Who Killed Peter Trueman? Anonymous
Who Killed Pretty Becky Low? A. B. Cunningham
Who Killed Rebecca? M. Halliday
Who Killed Robert Prentice? D. Wheatley
Who Killed Robin Cock. B. McDermott
Who Killed Robin Cockland? P. Luck
Who Killed Roger Whitely? B. Allerton
Who Killed Rosa Gray? F. Usher
Who Killed Santa Claus. T. Feely
Who Killed Stella Pomeroy? B. Thomson
Who Killed Stephen Tennant? T. S. King
Who Killed Sweet Sue? H. Kane
Who Killed the Chauffeur? G. V. Vosper
Who Killed the Count? B. Delane
Who Killed the Crooner? R. Trevor
Who Killed the Curate? J. Coggin
Who Killed the Doctor? M. Burton
Who Killed the Doctors? A. Peters
Who Killed the Husband? H. Footner
Who Killed the Pie Man? P. Lore
Who Killed the Snowman? J. Browner
Who Killed Trainer Lincoln. A. Steffens Hardy
Who Killed Uncle? H. Javits
Who Killed Utopia? Paul Walker
Who Killed Willian Drew? Harrington Strong
Who Killed You, Cindy Castle? K. Carr

Who Knows? I. A. Greenfield
Who Knows Julie Gordon? K. Booton
Who Lies Bleeding? H. Carstairs
Who Lies Here? Ellis Peters
Who Lies There? P. Johnson
Who Maimed Spurto? J. Fairfax-Blakeborough
Who Murdered Reynard? S. Fowler
Who Murdered Westaway? G. Comley
Who Needs Enemies? G. Kent
Who Needs Forever? E. I. English
Who Opened the Door? T. Cobb
Who Owned the Jewels? M. V. Victor
Who Pays the Piper? P. Wentworth
Who Plays with Sin. A. Spiller
Who Poisoned Hetty Duncan? and other detective stories. D. Donovan
Who Put It There? Mary Scott
Who Rides a Tiger. D. M. Disney
Who Rides a Tiger? Colin Robertson
Who Rides on a Tiger. M. B. Lowndes
Who Rides the Tiger. B. Myers
Who Said Murder. M. Halliday
Who Saw Her Die? P. Moyes
Who Saw Her Die? M. Warner
Who Saw Him Die? M. Halliday
Who Saw Him Die? S. Radley
Who Saw Maggie Brown? K. Roos
Who Says a Corpse Has to Be Dull. D. Von Elsner
Who Says Murder? P. King
Who Screamed? J. Courage
Who Shall Be Victor? E. A. Dupuy
Who Shall Condemn? J. C. Shannon
Who Shall Hang? M. Magill
Who Shall Win? J. A. Loughman
Who Shot Longshot Sam? P. Engleman
Who Shot the Bull? B. Knox
Who Shot the Pianist? E. Gavin
Who Shot the Spy? Anonymous
Who Should Have Died? M. Silverman
Who Sold Australia? J. Stonehouse
Who Spies, Who Kills? E. Queen
Who Spoke Last? J. V. Turner
Who Steals My Name. James Fraser
Who Steals My Name. C. Richards
Who Stole Sassi Manoon? D. E. Westlake
Who Strikes by Night. Richard Grant
Who Sups with the Devil? P. McCartney
Who the Heck Is Sylvia? J. Porter
Who the Hell Is Ned Kelly. D. Haring
Who Told Clutha. H. Munro
Who Told the Belle? N. Perrelli
Who Took Tobi Rinaldi? G. Mcdonald
Who Walk in Fear. N. Bell
Who Walks by Moonlight? M. McEvoy
Who Walks in the Dark. Tim Kelly
Who Was Clare Jallu? P. Boileau
Who Was Ellen Smith? K. Ayling
Who Was He? P. Little
Who Was He? M. V. Victor
Who Was Lady Thurne? F. Warden
Who Was Mr. Brown? T. Worthing
Who Was That Blonde I Saw You Kill Last Night? F. Brown
Who Was That Lady I Saw You With? N. Krasna
Who Was the Jester? G. Ashe
Who Was the Killer? J. Corbett
Who Was the Killer? N. Wray
Who Was This Woman?, Two Photographs, and the King of Hearts. H. C. McNeile
Who Were You With Last Night? F. Raphael
Who Will Watch the Watchers. E. Fadiman
Who Wins. M. A. Fleming
Who Would A-Murdering Go? Walter Blake
Who'd Hire Brett? J. Brett
Who'd Shoot a Genius? S. M. Schley
Who'd Want to Kill Old George? R. Upton
Whodunit. A. C. Martens
Whodunit? A. Radnor
Whodunnit. A. Shaffer
Whoever I Am. E. Dewhurst
Whole Hog. M. Kenyon
Whole Truth. J. Ehrlichman
Whole Truth. P. Mackie
Whole Truth. Anthony Robinson

Who'll Buy My Evil? A. Caillou
Whom. Matthew Francis
Whom God Hath Sundered. O. Onions
Whom Gods Destroy. Clifton Adams
Whom Nobody Owns. A. Spiller
Whom the Gods Destroy. A. G. Bennett
Whom the Gods Would Destroy. Nicholas Carter
Whomsoever I Shall Kiss. C. Siodmak
Whore-Mother. S. Herron
Whores. J. Crumley
Whoreson. D. Goines
Who's Afraid? E. S. Holding
Who's Been Sitting in My Chair? C. Armstrong
Who's Calling? H. McCloy
Who's for Dying. M. MacQuade
Who's Got the Bastard Pope. P. A. Fulford
Who's Guilty? L. J. Huber
Who's in Charge Here? H. H. Kirst
Who's Innocent? D. Haring
Who's Kidding Who? D. Haring
Who's Next? J. Allan
Who's Next. G. Baxt
Who's on First? J. Allan
Who's on First? W. F. Buckley
Who's on First? J. Sharkey
Who's Sorry Now? D. Linton
Who's the Guy? A. J. Evans
Who's the Murderer? E. Sleath
Who's the Target? M. Carr
Who's Who in the Home. A. L. Kaser
Whose Body? D. L. Sayers
Whose Corpse? S. Ransome
Whose Dog Are You? Gerald Hammond
Whose Grandfather? D. Haring
Whose Grave Next Honey. R. Callahan
Whose Hand? V. Loder
Whose Hand? W. G. Willis
Whose Head? W. E. Huntsberry
Whose Little Girl Are You? D. Craig
Whose Millions? Joseph Montague
Whose the Hand? Diana Forbes
Whose Was the Crime? G. Warden
Whose Was the Hand? W. J. Bayfield
Whose Was the Hand? M. E. Braddon
Whose Was the Hand? J. E. Muddock
Whose Wife? C. H. Bullivant
Whoso Diggeth a Pit. C. H. Bullivant
Whoso Findeth a Wife. W. LeQueux
Whosoever Loveth. W. LeQueux
Whosoever Shall Offend . . . F. M. Crawford
Why? E. D. Bartlett
Why Aren't They Screaming? Joan Smith
Why Be Lonely? M. B. Lowndes
Why Bother, Beautiful? D. Haring
Why Call It Homicide? R. Kirby
Why Diamond Had to Die. Richard Burns
Why Did He Do It? B. Capes
Why Did She Die? J. Coggin
Why Did Trethewy Die? R. A. J. Walling
Why Didn't They Ask Evans? A. Christie
Why Isn't Becky Twitchell Dead? M. R. Zubro
Why It Happened. M. B. Lowndes
Why Jane Matcham Disappeared. M. Carane
Why Kill a Butler? P. H. Powell
Why Kill Arthur Potter? R. Harrison
Why Kill Johnny? H. Carmichael
Why Me? D. E. Westlake
Why Murder? N. Deane
Why Murder? J. Philips
Why Murder Mrs. Hope? J. Courage
Why Murder the Judge? C. S. Hammock
Why Not? George Scott
Why Pick on Me? Raymond Marshall
Why Pick on Me? P. Muller
Why Pick on Pickles? M. Durham
Why She Cries, I Do Not Know. W. Masterson
Why She Left Him. F. Warden
Why Shoot a Butler? G. Heyer
Why Should Sylvia? H. Janson
Why Slug a Postman? S. Truss
Why So Dead? E. Queen
Why Someone Had to Die. J. Roffman
Why Squeal on Me? Max Gordon

Why There Aren't No Ten Commandments. Henry Holt
Why They Married. M. B. Lowndes
Whyte Hart. P. C. Doherty
Wicked. A. Applin
Wicked Angel. T. Caldwell
Wicked As the Devil. M. Halliday
Wicked Designs. L. O'Donnell
Wicked Flee. A. Hocking
Wicked Girl. M. C. Hay
Wicked Guardian. Elsie Lee
Wicked Lord. R. Foxall
Wicked, Loving Murder. O. Papazoglou
Wicked Marquis. E. P. Oppenheim
Wicked One. F. Winter
Wicked Pack of Cards. Rosemary Harris
Wicked Pack of Cards. H. R. Williamson
Wicked Saint. E. Bruton
Wicked Shall Flourish. H. Desmond
Wicked Slice. C. Elkins
Wicked Stepmother. A. Young
Wicked Streets. Wenzell Brown
Wicked Uncle. P. Wentworth
Wicked Way to Die. J. Sturrock
Wicked Widow. Carter Brown
Wicked Woman. Anne Austin
Wicked Wynsleys. Alanna Knight
Wickedest Man. J. Millard
Wicker Man. Robin Hardy
Wide Arch. D. Stivens
Wide Boy? M. Hervey
Wide Boy. Dennis Warner
Wide Boys Never Work. R. Westerby
Wide Girl. M. Hervey
Wide Open Door. T. E. B. Clarke
Wide Sargasso Sea. J. Rhys
Widening Gyre. R. B. Parker
Widening Stain. W. B. Johnson
Wider Sea of Love. F. E. Smith
Widow. C. Blackstock
Widow. N. Freeling
Widow. Francis King
Widow. G. Simenon
Widow and the Cavalier. R. Armstrong
Widow and the Web. Robert Martin
Widow Barony. W. R. Burnett
Widow Bewitched. Carter Brown
Widow Cherry. B. L. Farjeon
Widow for Hire. L. E. Linsley
Widow from Spain. J. Pendower
Widow Gay. A. A. Marcus
Widow Had a Gun. G. H. Coxe
Widow in White. E. Bond
Widow in White. F. A. Chittenden
Widow Is Willing. Carter Brown
Widow Lerouge. E. Gaboriau
Widow Maker. F. Diamond
Widow-Makers. M. Blankfort
Widow Mortimer. T. P. Prest
Widow of Bath. M. Bennett
Widow of Desire. Justin Scott
Widow of Grange Farm. A. Marsh
Widow of Ratchets. A. Brookes
Widow of Zanzibar. R. Anthony
Widow Watchers. F. Archer
Widow, Weep for Me. Marc Miller
Widow with the Pink Gloves. M. Dekobra
Widow Wondered Why. W. J. Coughlin
Widow Wore Red. R. Wormser
Widow Wore White. C. P. Cleary
Widowed Bride of Raven Oaks. P. Darty
Widower. V. Siller
Widower. G. Simenon
Widower's Wife. T. Charles
Widowmaker. M. Fagyas
Widowmaster. L. Bergson
Widows. L. La Plante
Widow's Beads. C. Joyce
Widows' Blackmail. H. Fenisong
Widows Can Be Dangerous. N. Leslie
Widow's Club. D. Cannell
Widow's Cruise. N. Blake
Widow's Escort. B. De Bilio
Widow's Might. M. Dekobra

Widow's Mite. E. S. Holding
Widow's Necklace. E. Davies
Widows of Broome. A. W. Upfield
Widows of the Magistrate. K. West
Widows of Westwood. Marilyn Ross
Widows Ought to Weep. D. B. Olsen
Widow's Peak. J. Nicholas
Widow's Pique. B. Treynor
Widow's Plight. R. Fenisong
Widow's Son. E. Southworth
Widow's Trial. J. Ehle
Widows II. L. La Plante
Widow's Walk. Anonymous
Widow's Walk. M. Bishop
Widow's Walk. A. Coburn
Widow's Walk. T. J. Kelly
Widow's Walk. S. Nichols
Widow's Walk. C. Rabou
Widow's Walk. W. Tucker
Widow's Walk. M. Yates
Widow's War. Alan Williams
Widows Wear Weeds. A. A. Fair
Widow's Web. U. Curtiss
Widows Won't Wait. D. Hitchens
Wieland. C. B. Brown
Wife at Sea. G. Simenon
Wife by Purchase. P. Trent
Wife Found Slain. C. Crane
Wife He Never Saw. M. Marcin
Wife in the Dark. H. Desmond
Wife in Toledo. J. Budd
Wife Next Door. R. V. Cassill
Wife of Baal. M. Dalton
Wife of Elias. E. Phillpotts
Wife of Ronald Sheldon. P. Quentin
Wife of the Red-Haired Man. B. S. Ballinger
Wife or Death. E. Queen
Wife or No Wife? and A Close Shave. T. W. Speight
Wife-Smuggler. M. Tripp
Wife Who Died Twice. E. Bohle
Wife Who Disappeared. B. Flynn
Wife Who Ran Away. T. Mascott
Wife Whom God Forgot. C. H. Bullivant
Wife's Dream. T. P. Prest
Wife's Honor. E. A. Young
Wife's Tale. R. Timperley
Wife's Victory. E. Southworth
Wiggles. H. S. Carter
Wight That Wailed. E. Manfred
Wigwam and Cabin. W. G. Simms
Wigwam and the Cabin. Anonymous
Wilberforce Legacy. Josephine Bell
Wilby Conspiracy. P. Driscoll
Wild. G. Brewer
Wild About Harry. P. Pickering
Wild Abyss. John Gunn
Wild and Weird. G. Campbell
Wild Apple Orchard. D. Lee
Wild at Heart. B. Gifford
Wild Beauty. D. Donovan
Wild Bird. H. Footner
Wild Blue Berries. E. Hong
Wild Boar Wood. J. Marshall
Wild Boys of Paris. Anonymous
Wild Breed. Ted Stratton
Wild Card. P. A. Foxall
Wild Card. R. Hawkey
Wild Card. D. Pendleton
Wild Cat. Laura Black
Wild-Cat Scheme. E. M. Keate
Wild-Catters. C. J. C. Hyne
Wild Colonial Boy. J. Hynes
Wild Cry of Love. B. Paul
Wild Darrie. D. C. Murray
Wild Dreams. Michael Sinclair
Wild Duck Murders. T. Du Bois
Wild Flame. Winifred Duke
Wild Geese. D. Carney
Wild Geese II. D. Carney
Wild Georgie. J. Middlemass
Wild Girl. H. Janson
Wild Girl. D. Keene
Wild Goose Chase. F. C. Wynne
Wild Grapes. B. Jefferis

Wild Grow the Lilies. Christy Brown
Wild Horse Valley. W. C. Tuttle
Wild Hunt. J. Tattersall
Wild Is My Heart. T. Thomas
Wild Island. Antonia Fraser
Wild Justice. G. A. Birmingham
Wild Justice. F. Clifford
Wild Justice. L. Grant-Adamson
Wild Justice. T. B. Morris
Wild Justice. L. Osbourne
Wild Justice. J. Pattinson
Wild Justice. R. C. Smith
Wild Justice. Wilbur Smith
Wild Lonesome. H. Whittington
Wild Man of Cape Cod. F. MacIsaac
Wild Midnight Falls. M. E. Chaber
Wild Night. R. Foley
Wild Night. L. J. Washburn
Wild Onion. Loren Carroll
Wild Party. J. McPartland
Wild Passion. B. Stack
Wild Pitch. A. B. Guthrie
Wild Reckoning. M. Richmond
Wild Ride. W. Boyles
Wild Secret. M. Clare
Wild Sheba. A. Askew
Wild Sheep Chase. H. Murakami
Wild Sound of Murder. D. De Villiers
Wild Summer. Jack Wilson
Wild Thyme and other stories. Lord Gorell
Wild to Possess. G. Brewer
Wild Town. J. Thompson
Wild Track. Alex Hamilton
Wild Trip. M. Arrighi
Wild Turkey. R. L. Simon
Wild Type. J. I. Victoroff
Wild Violets. R. B. Field
Wild Wave. K. Hess
Wild Week-End. T. C. H. Jacobs
Wild Winds. M. Unsworth
Wild Wives and High Priest of California. C. Willeford
Wild Wooing. F. Warden
Wildcat. D. Ambler
Wildcat. Carter Brown
Wildcat. S. Gluck
Wildcat. Craig Thomas
Wildcatter. D. Meiring
Wildcatters. Bryan Cooper
Wildcliffe Bird. C. Heaven
Wilde Alliance. I. Mackintosh
Wilder and Wilder. R. J. Conley
Wilder Curse. K. Robeson
Wilderness. T. B. Clegg
Wilderness. R. Donaldson
Wilderness. R. B. Parker
Wilderness Inn. J. L. Roberts
Wilderness of Mirrors. T. Allbeury
Wilderness of Mirrors. D. Seaman
Wilderness Patrol. H. Bindloss
Wilderness Patrol. C. Stoddard
Wilderness Road. A. Davidson
Wilders Walk Away. H. Brean
Wildersmoor. C. L. Antrobus
Wildest Street. W. C. Spatari
Wildfire. Nicholas Carter
Wildfire. J. Foxx
Wildfire at Midnight. Mary Stewart
Wildfire Love. J. Blackmore
Wildtrack. B. Cornwell
Wildwater Terrace. R. E. Salwey
Wildwood. John Farris
Wiles of the Wicked. W. LeQueux
Wiles of Wilhelmina. F. Warden
Wilfred Montressor. Anonymous
Wilful and Premeditated. F. W. Crofts
Wilful Lady. J. Sturrock
Wilful-Missing. D. G. Waring
Wilful Murder. J. York
Wilful Susie. A. Applin
Wilful Ward. F. Warden
Wilful Way. H. Compton
Wilkes: His Life and Crimes. W. Schoonover

Will. R. M. Stern
Will. P. Werner
Will and Last Testament of Constance Cobble. S. Forbes
Will and the Deed. D. Ogburn
Will and the Deed. Ellis Peters
Will and the Way. B. Capes
Will and the Willful. M. Webb
Will Anyone Who Saw the Accident . . . J. Ashford
Will He Betray Her? H. Wood
Will in the Way. M. Burton
Will-o'-the Wisp. P. Wentworth
Will o' the Wisp Flashes. Donald MacDonald
Will of God! P. J. Walkowski
Will of Her Own. D. M. Day
Will of the Tribe. A. W. Upfield
Will on the Watch. Ernest H. Robinson
Will-Power. H. Janson
Will to Die. F. Anderson
Will to Kill. R. Bloch
Will to Kill. G. Brodie
Will to Kill. J. Penn
Will to Survive. E. Salter
Will Watch. H. D. Miles
Will You Walk a Little Faster. R. Braddon
Willard. S. Gilbert
Willard and His Bowling Trophies. R. Brautigan
Willfreud Curse. S. F. Griffin
William Allair. H. Wood
William Conrad. P. Boulle
William Crook—Antique Dealer. R. Keverne
William Jordan Junior. J. C. Snaith
William Pollok, and other tales. G. Grogan
Williamsburg Forgeries. J. Ballinger
Willing Hostage. M. Millhiser
Willing Sinners. R. Vane
Willing Transgressor, and other stories. A. G. Plympton
Willing Witness. B. Cobb
Willough Haven. G. Killoran
Willoughby Affair. G. W. Appleton
Willoughby Manor. J. Wetherell
Willow Grove. J. A. Bartlett
Willow Herb. Rona Randall
Willow Pattern. R. Van Gulik
Willow Pattern War. W. H. Canaway
Willow Pond. M. K. Simmons
Willow Weep. D. Daniels
Willowbrake. R. M. Albrist
Willowdene Will. H. Sutcliffe
Willowford Woods. R. M. Gilchrist
Wills of Jane Kanwhistle. S. Fowler
Willy Velvet, Homicide Detective. R. L. Wimberly
Wilson and Some Others. G. D. H. Cole
Wilson Calling. G. D. H. Cole
Wilson of the Mounted. L. E. Sandford
Wilson Young on the Run. G. Tippette
Wilson's Choice. G. Tippette
Wilson's Gold. G. Tippette
Wilson's Luck. G. Tippette
Wilson's Revenge. G. Tippette
Wilson's Woman. G. Tippette
Wilt. T. Sharpe
Wilt Alternative. T. Sharpe
Wilt on High. T. Sharpe
Wilt Thou Have This Woman? J. M. Cobban
Wilton's Silence. P. Trent
Wily Widow. A. Bouvier
Wimbledon. R. McDowell
Wimbledon Common Trap. J. Hunter
Wimbledon Poisoner. Nigel Williams
Win, Lose or Die. J. Gardner
Win, Place and Die! L. Lariar
Win Some, Lose Some. B. Halliday
Win with Sin. S. O'Shea
Wind and the Rain. J. M. Simmel
Wind and the Water. S. Mason-Parker
Wind and the Waterfall. R. Gathorne-Hardy
Wind at Winter's End. Deborah Lewis
Wind-Bells of Lovingwood. J. T. Osborne
Wind Blows Death. C. Hare
Wind Chill. N. O'Donohoe
Wind Chill Factor. T. Gifford
Wind-Chime Legacy. A. W. Mykel

Wind from Nowhere. O. Micheaux
Wind in His Fists. M. Duston
Wind in the Cypress. R. M. Sears
Wind in the East. A. Burr
Wind in the East. H. Edmonds
Wind in the Snottygobble Tree. J. T. Story
Wind of Death. G. Black
Wind of Death. G. Grellet
Wind of Death. Robert Jackson
Wind of Death. M. Wilson
Wind of Desire. K. Lindsay
Wind off the Sea. D. Beaty
Wind Over the Citadel. L. Ames
Wind Over the Citadel. W. E. D. Ross
Wind Tunnel. D. Buckingham
Wind Up. N. Steed
Wind-Up Doll. Carter Brown
Wind Was Cold. H. Clevely
Wind Without Rain. G. McDonell
Windblow Mystery. E. Gellibrand
Windfall. D. Bagley
Windfall. Andrea Harris
Windfall. A. Leslie
Windfall. M. Pflaum
Windfall Harvest. M. Edwin
Windfalls. R. Aitken
Windfellow. C. Edwards
Winding Road. C. Dawe
Winding Sheet. R. Cassilis
Winding Stair. J. A. Hodge
Winding Stair. A. E. W. Mason
Winding Way. J. S. Fletcher
Windmill. F. H. Fellows
Windmill Mystery. J. J. Farjeon
Windmills of the Gods. S. Sheldon
Windover Tales. H. Sutcliffe
Window. K. Ingram
Window. J. Reach
Window at the Inn. C. S. Brooks
Window at the White Cat. M. R. Rinehart
Window Episode. E. Geller
Window Hack. R. Standish
Window in Chungking. S. H. Courtier
Window in the Dark. E. Kilvington
Window in the Dark. F. O'Rourke
Window of Death. G. Lamond
Window on the Seine. F. Y. McHugh
Window on the Square. P. A. Whitney
Window Over the Way. G. Simenon
Window with the Sleeping Nude. R. L. Bellem
Windows. H. B. Gilmour
Windows Facing West. V. MacFadyen
Wind's End. H. Asquith
Winds of April. I. D. Baharav
Winds of Evil. A. W. Upfield
Winds of Fear. J. Ames
Winds of Fortune. J. Farnol
Winds of Midnight. J. Blackburn
Winds of Night. K. Troy
Winds of Pentecost. R. Chester
Winds of Terror. P. Hagan
Winds of Terror. P. H. Howell
Winds of the Old Days. B. Asward
Winds of the World. T. Mundy
Winds of Time. H. Gibbs
Winds of Wakefield. T. R. Bernard
Windscreen Weepers and other stories of horror and suspense. Joan Aiken
Windshear. J. J. Savarin
Windsor Knot. S. McCrumb
Windsor Plot. P. G. Winslow
Windsor Red. Jennie Melville
Windswept Farm. W. Hewlett
Windward Passage. Mark Brewer
Windy Side of the Law. Sara Woods
Wine Dark Sea. L. Sciascia
Wine-Drinker and other stories. W. J. Batchelder
Wine in a Venetian Goblet. J. McConnell
Wine, Murder & Blueberry Sundaes. C. C. Risenhoover
Wine of Life. L. Egan
Wine of the Generals. R. P. Jones
Wine of Vengeance. J. Wellsley
Wine of Violence. N. S. Boardman

Wine of Violence. L. Egan
Wine of War. E. G. Cousins
Wine on the Desert, and other stories. M. Brand
Wine Room Murder. S. Vestal
Wine with Veronica. A. Redwood
Wine, Women and Bullets. N. Spain
Wine, Women . . . and Death. W. Deptula
Wine, Women, and Murder. Desmond Martin
Wine, Women and Murder. J. Roeburt
Wine, Women and Waiters. G. Frankau
Wines of Cyprien. D. Daniels
Wingarden. Elsie Lee
Winged Adventurer. J. Brearley
Winged Dancer. C. Grae
Winged Danger. A. Foxe
Winged Death. J. R. Holden
Winged Guns. K. Ford
Winged Murderer. F. MacIsaac
Winged Mystery. A. W. Upfield
Winged Victory. N. Leslie
Winged Witnesses. H. Robertson
Winger's Landfall. S. Lauder
Wingrave Case. P. Luck
Wings Above the Claypan. A. W. Upfield
Wings Above the Diamantina. A. W. Upfield
Wings Behind Bars. P. Trent
Wings North. R. O. Case
Wings of Adventure. A. Whitehouse
Wings of Chance. M. Leinster
Wings of Darkness. P. Audemars
Wings of Darkness. E. Milburn
Wings of Death. M. Boniface
Wings of Death. C. Sloan
Wings of Desire. M. Dekobra
Wings of Destiny. W. F. Moore
Wings of Destiny. George Weston
Wings of Destiny. Christopher Wilson
Wings of Doom. G. E. Rochester
Wings of Fear. M. G. Eberhart
Wings of Love. C. R. Gull
Wings of Love. P. Trent
Wings of Madness. J. Philips
Wings of Mystery. W. Gavine
Wings of Peace. J. Creasey
Wings of Revolution. J. R. Holden
Wings of Romance. W. E. Johns
Wings of the Black Death. G. Stockbridge
Wings of the Falcon. B. Michaels
Wings of the Morning. L. Tracy
Wings of the Vulture. P. T. Owen
Wings of the Wind. Ronald Hardy
Wings of Tomorrow. P. Traill
Wings of Victory. F. M. White
Wings of War. Hedley Scott
Wings Over Africa. D. T. Lindsay
Wings Over Palestine. P. J. Clancy
Wings Over Panama. G. Church
Wings Over the Amazon. D. T. Lindsay
Wings Over the Atlantic. A. D. Divine
Wings Without Freedom. J. G. Sarasin
Wingwalker. J. Crosby
Winifred. D. M. Disney
Winifred Power. Anonymous
Wink. K. Bennett
Wink from a Witch. C. Dekker
Winking at the Brim. G. Mitchell
Winner from Scotland Yard. K. Gray
Winner Harris. I. St. James
Winner Take All. G. Fairlie
Winner Take All. J. McKimmey
Winner Take Nothing. E. Hemingway
Winner Takes All. R. Douglas
Winners. J. Mitchell
Winner's Circle. J. Hayes
Winner's Cut. P. Pairo III
Winner's Share. R. Beardwood
Winnie O'Wynn and the Dark Horses. B. Atkey
Winnie O'Wynn and the Wolves. B. Atkey
Winnifred's Way. A. Griffith
Winning a Princess. Old Sleuth
Winning Clue. J. Hay
Winning of Winifred. L. Tracy
Winning Streak. A. Grisman
Winning Through. A. Applin

Winning Through. J. Templeton
Winning Trick. N. Brand
Winnowing Winds. A. Marlowe
Winny Darling. E. Southworth
Winsome Lass. K. Lindsay
Winston Affair. H. Fast
Winston Churchill Murder. K. Netzen
Winston of the Prairie. H. Bindloss
Winter. L. Deighton
Winter. G. Horne
Winter After This Summer. S. Ellin
Winter Amid the Ice. J. Verne
Winter and the Wanderer. B. Gaston
Winter and the White Witch. B. Gaston
Winter and the Widowmakers. B. Gaston
Winter and the Wild Rover. B. Gaston
Winter at Blackfont. C. Gayet
Winter Bride. C. Salisbury
Winter by Degrees. J. Smolens
Winter Chill. J. Fluke
Winter Evening Tales Collected Among the
  Cottagers in the South of England. J. Hogg
Winter Hawk. Craig Thomas
Winter in a Dark Land. M. Lynch
Winter Keeper. J. Crecy
Winter Kill. S. Fisher
Winter Killing. F. Irwin
Winter Kills. R. Condon
Winter Landscape. N. Brand
Winter Losses. M. Probst
Winter Murder Case. S. S. Van Dine
Winter Nights. N. Drake
Winter of Discontent. G. Frankau
Winter of Fear. S. Tempest
Winter of Madness. D. Walker
Winter of the Fox. J. Roffman
Winter of the Wildcat. B. Gaston
Winter Palace. Dennis Jones
Winter Quarry. P. Henissart
Winter Reckoning. N. M. Kennedy
Winter Roses. L. Hagen
Winter Spy. P. Henissart
Winter Stalk. J. L. Stowe
Winter Touch. C. Egleton
Winter Wears a Shroud. R. Chapman
Winter Wheat. E. Woodward
Wintermute. C. Brookhouse
Winter's Flame. Marie Greene
Winter's Tale. Robert Hardy
Winterset. Maxwell Anderson
Wintershade. E. Evans
Winterton Hotel Mystery. J. Corbett
Winterwood. D. Eden
Winton Street Mystery. H. Carstairs
Wipe-Out! D. J. Cleary
Wiped Off: Gangsters! J. W. Heming
Wipeout. J. Tiger
Wire. N. Gowing
Wire Devils. F. Packard
Wire Tappers. A. Stringer
Wire Window. F. J. Kenmore
Wirecutter. J. Brizzolara
Wired. H. Hellerstein
Wired for Scandal. F. L. Wallace
Wireless Call. Mrs. C. Kernahan
Wireman. B. S. Mosiman
Wiretap! C. Einstein
Wisdom of Father Brown. G. K. Chesterton
Wisdom of Folly. E. T. Fowler
Wise and Foolish Virgin. G. Warden
Wise Child. S. Gray
Wise Dames Play Solo. N. Rosso
Wise Fool. S. Jepson
Wise Fool. E. C. Reed
Wise Man of Welby. N. Worth
Wise Thrush. F. Hutchinson
Wise Virgin. G. Goodchild
Wise Virgin. M. McGrath
Wiseguys. V. Teresa
Wiseman Originals. R. Goulart
Wish Me Dead. D. West
Wish You Were Dead. R. Chapman
Wish You Were Dead. H. McCloy
Wish You Were Here. R. M. Brown

Wish You Were Here. H. Steinberg
Wishbone. Stirling Bowen
Wishful Think. B. Newman
Wishful Thinking. F. Wyka
Wishing Smith. C. J. C. Hyne
Wisteria Cottage. R. M. Coates
Wistful Wanton. P. Muller
Witch. B. Michaels
Witch. B. St. James
Witch Alone. M. Higgins
Witch at the Funeral. F. Hurt
Witch Door. E. Ogilvie
Witch-Finder. R. Bassett
Witch Finder, the Evil at Monteine. B. Ball
Witch from the Sea. P. Carr
Witch Haven. L. Churchill
Witch Hill. M. Z. Bradley
Witch Hill Murder. P. G. Winslow
Witch House. E. Walton
Witch Hunt. Henry Duval
Witch Hunt. S. Harvester
Witch-Hunt! D. Reid
Witch Man. M. B. Houston
Witch Miss Seeton. H. Carvic
Witch of Blackbird Pond. E. G. Spear
Witch of Bralhaven. Marilyn Ross
Witch of Chelsea. O. Hartley
Witch of Goblin's Acres. W. E. D. Ross
Witch of Manhattan. Old Sleuth
Witch of Murray Hill. Stephanie Hill
Witch of Nun. D. Newton
Witch of Ravensworth. G. Brewer
Witch of the Hills. F. Warden
Witch of the Lowtide. J. D. Carr
Witch of Wykham. M. Carr
Witch or Wife. S. Rathbone
Witch Rhymes with . . . D. Haring
Witch Temple. Alan Graham
Witch Tree. L. B. Long
Witch Who Wouldn't Hang. T. J. Kelly
Witch Wood. C. Hale
Witchchild. Carole Mortimer
Witchcraft for Panda One. P. N. Walker
Witchcraft Murder. J. Ingersol
Witchdance in Bavaria. Robert MacLeod
Witcheries of Craig Isaf. W. F. Williams
Witches. Carter Brown
Witches. P. Curtis
Witches' Cove. Marilyn Ross
Witches' Holiday. M. Lynch
Witches' Ladder. L. Osborne
Witches' Moon. G. Verner
Witches of All Saints. J. Tattersall
Witches of Brimstone Hill. H. Arvonen
Witches of Notting Hill. W. A. Ballinger
Witches of Omen. A. Leech
Witches of Turnstone Bay. A. Burns
Witches of Windlake. M. Lynch
Witches' Pond. F. Hurd
Witches' Pond. S. Wells
Witches' Sabbath. P. Allardyce
Witchfinder. M. Hilliard
Witchfinder. S. F. Wright
Witching. C. John
Witching. F. Ravenswood
Witching Hill. E. W. Hornung
Witching Hour. Rona Randall
Witching Hour. F. Stevenson
Witching Hour. Augustus Thomas
Witching Murder. Jennie Melville
Witching Night. C. S. Cody
Witchline. R. MacLeod
Witchrock. B. Knox
Witch's Brew. N. Faulkner
Witch's Castle. D. Daniels
Witch's Cauldron. E. Phillpotts
Witch's Crossing. F. Stevenson
Witch's Doing. A. Dick
Witch's Hammer. C. Farr
Witch's House. C. Armstrong
Witch's Island. D. Daniels
Witch's Mark. June R. Lewis
Witch's Money. J. Collier
Witch's Moon. G. Jackson

Witch's Song. M. Lynch
Witch's Suckling. G. Hall
Witch's Tower Mystery. J. Kains
Witch's Web. D. Spicer
Witchstone. V. Graham
Witchwater. G. M. Wilson
With a Bare Bodkin. C. Hare
With a Madman Behind Me. T. Powell
With a Strange Device. E. F. Russell
With a Vengeance. G. Di Pego
With a Vengeance. Dell Shannon
With a View to Matrimony, and other stories. J. Blyth
With All John's Love. M. B. Lowndes
With Bated Breath. Alice Campbell
With Blood and Kisses. R. Shattuck
With Bullet and Steel. J. K. Stafford
With Cause Enough? S. Fowler
With Chains of Brass. I. Stark
With Clipped Wings. M. S. Boyd
With Cossack and Convict. W. M. Graydon
With Criminal Instinct. R. Hardinge
With Dead Bodies. J. Cadman
With Edged Tools. H. S. Merriman
With Extreme Prejudice. B. Mather
With Fate Conspire. Y. MacManus
With Flowers That Fell. M. R. D. Meek
With Fondest Thoughts. C. Blackstock
With Gauge and Swallow, Attorneys. A. Tourgee
With Intent. L. Henderson
With Intent to Deceive. M. Coles
With Intent to Destroy. K. Rogers
With Intent to Kill. B. Cobb
With Intent to Kill. G. H. Coxe
With Intent to Kill. H. Pentecost
With Intent to Kill. Dell Shannon
With Intent to Kill. E. C. Vivian
With Lance and Pennon. W. F. Auburn
With Links of Steel. Nicholas Carter
With Love from Rachel. S. Murray
With Malice Aforethought. G. W. Jones
With Murder for Some. H. C. Huston
With Murder in Mind. F. Bream
With Murder in Mind. E. Ferrars
With Murder in Mind. J. Roffman
With My Friends. B. Matthews
With My Knives I Know I'm Good. J. Rathbone
With My Little Eye. D. Durrant
With My Little Eye. Roy Fuller
With No Crying. C. Fremlin
With One Stone. R. Lockridge
With Option to Die. R. Lockridge
With Penalty and Interest. D. Mardon
With Shackles of Fire. Nicholas Carter
With Siberia Comes a Chill. Kirk Mitchell
With Sirens Screaming. Ernest Booth
With Soul So Dead. G. Mason
With the Gilt Off. A. S. Auburn
With the Unhanged. R. Dowling
With This Ring. M. G. Eberhart
With Time Running Out. L. W. Robinson
With What Motive? T. C. H. Jacobs
Withdraw Thy Foot. C. R. Sumner
Withdrawing Room. C. MacLeod
Withered Garland. H. Gibbs
Withered Man. N. Deane
Withered Murder. A. Shaffer
Withering Fire. M. Bowen
Within an Inch of His Life. E. Gaboriau
Within Bohemia. H. Curwen
Within Four Walls. E. Baulsir
Within Fourteen Days. W. M. Graydon
Within Sound of the Weir. T. S. Hake
Within the Bubble. J. Shearing
Within the Labyrinth. N. Lewis
Within the Law. M. Dana
Within the Law. B. Veiller
Within the Maze. H. Wood
Within the Precincts of the Prison. A. Lunn
Within the Radius. A. Kinroos
Within the Tides. Joseph Conrad
Within the Vault. L. Thayer
Within the Web. M. Weiser
Within This Circle. G. Beaumont

Within This House. F. Crisp
Within Twenty-Four Hours. H. Leyford
Without a Clew. Nicholas Carter
Without a Grave. P. Nottingham
Without a Name. Dick Stewart
Without a Trace. Catherine Anderson
Without a Trace. K. K. Beck
Without a Trace. S. Ransome
Without a Warrant. H. Brooks
Without Armour. J. Hilton
Without Blood They Die. G. W. Jones
Without Clues. J. Helm
Without Fear. M. Judge
Without Gloves. J. B. Hendryx
Without Honor. D. J. Hagberg
Without Issue. H. Cresswell
Without Judge or Jury. R. Rodd
Without Justification. J. L. Rickard
Without Lawful Authority. M. Coles
Without Love or Licence. H. Smart
Without Malice. B. Graeme
Without Mercy. G. D. Adams
Without Mercy. J. J. Dratler
Without Mercy. J. Goodwin
Without Mercy. Leonard Jordan
Without Mercy. G. Provost
Without Motive. Winston Graham
Without Motive. Colin Robertson
Without Music. G. Fox
Without Orders. M. Albrand
Without Ransom. R. Bliss
Without the Law. H. F. Moulton
Without the Option. A. Hocking
Without Trace. C. Goodall
Without Trace. Katherine John
Without Trace. W. LeQueux
Without Trumpet or Drum. John Sanders
Without Virtue. W. Standish
Without Warning. W. H. Baker
Without Witness. A. Armstrong
Witness. W. Kelley
Witness. R. G. Toepfer
Witness. D. Uhnak
Witness at Large. M. G. Eberhart
Witness at the Window. C. Barry
Witness Before the Fact. E. Ferrars
Witness Box. V. Karsland
Witness for the Crown. Richard Gordon
Witness for the Defence. A. E. W. Mason
Witness for the Prosecution. A. Christie
Witness in Peril. M. Marlette
Witness in Support. J. H. Vahey
Witness My Death. Roy Lewis
Witness of the Sun. H. S. Williams
Witness on the Roof. A. Haynes
Witness This Woman. G. F. Fox
Witness to Murder. E. Harrison
Witness to the Crime. J. Hunter
Witness to the Deed. G. M. Fenn
Witness to Treason. M. J. Ragosta
Witness Tree. H. C. Wire
Witnesses. A. Holden
Witnesses. G. Simenon
Witnesses and the Watchmaker. G. Simenon
Witnesses to Tears. G. Abubakar
Wit's End. J. R. Scafidel
Wits' End. W. Spence
Wives and Lovers. Stuart Hall
Wives to Burn. L. G. Blochman
Wizard Detective. Old Sleuth
Wizard of Berner's Abbey. M. Hansom
Wizard of Death. R. Forrest
Wizard of the Cue. Nicholas Carter
Wizard of Whitechapel. S. Hawke
Wizard Tramp. Old Sleuth
Wizard's Aunt. J. Laing
Wizard's Daughter. B. Michaels
Wizard's Spyglass. E. Kinsburn
Wobble to Death. P. Lovesey
Wodehouse on Crime. P. G. Wodehouse
Wohldorf Shipment. P. O'Hara
Wolaroi's Cup. A. Pratt
Wolf. H. Holt
Wolf. V. Weber

Wolf at the Door. F. Warden
Wolf by the Ears. Roy Lewis
Wolf Cop. R. Jessup
Wolf Creek Valley. W. C. Tuttle
Wolf Hollow Bubbles. D. H. Keller
Wolf Howls "Murder". M. L. Stokes
Wolf Hunt. M. Elder
Wolf Hunt. C. Whiting
Wolf Hunters. J. O. Curwood
Wolf in Man's Clothing. M. G. Eberhart
Wolf in Sheep's Clothing. V. Bird
Wolf in Sheep's Clothing. J. K. Leys
Wolf in Sheep's Clothing. J. R. Riggs
Wolf in the Clouds. R. Faust
Wolf in the Fold. V. Loder
Wolf-Lure. A. Castle
Wolf Man. A. Machard
Wolf Mountain. P. L. Sandberg
Wolf-Net. Winifred Graham
Wolf of Corsica. W. J. Elliott
Wolf of Texas. Steve Rogers
Wolf of the Evenings. Winifred Graham
Wolf Pack. R. Cullum
Wolf Pack of Lobo Butte. W. C. Tuttle
Wolf Plays the Joker. W. K. Watts
Wolf Shows His Teeth. B. Sarto
Wolf Swept Down. R. Ladline
Wolf That Follows. H. Clevely
Wolf Time. J. Gores
Wolf to the Slaughter. R. Rendell
Wolf Tone. L. Goldman
Wolf Tracks. D. Case
Wolf Trap. F. Nolan
Wolf Troubleth Not. B. M. Scott
Wolf Whispered Death. Barbara Moore
Wolf Winter. Clare Francis
Wolf Within. Nicholas Carter
Wolf! Wolf! Josephine Bell
Wolf Woman. A. Stringer
Wolfen. W. Streiber
Wolfe's Cloister. B. Plagemann
Wolfman. A. Bourgeau
Wolfnight. N. Freeling
Wolfrun. J. J. Savarin
Wolf's Claw. H. Holt
Wolf's Crag. D. Whitelaw
Wolf's Head. J. K. Mayo
Wolf's Hour. R. R. McCammon
Wolf's Long Howl. S. Waterloo
Wolf's Prey. T. Vasilos
Wolfsbane. Craig Thomas
Wolftrap. E. Bercovici
Wolves and the Lamb. J. S. Fletcher
Wolves and the Lamb. A. Soutar
Wolves at Cooking Lake. G. McClintock
Wolves at the Door. T. King
Wolves Come Down from the Mountain. M. Strong
Wolves of Chaos. H. MacGrath
Wolves of Craywood. Jan Alexander
Wolves of New York. A. W. Aiken
Wolves of Summer. J. Nazel
Wolves of the Border. J. Brearley
Wolves of the Deep. S. Drew
Wolves of the Night. S. Horler
Wolves of the Sea. G. Leroux
Woman. A. P. Terhune
Woman Accused. D. Durham
Woman Accused. J. Templeton
Woman Against the World. George Griffith
Woman Against Woman. M. A. Holmes
Woman Always Knows. J. Cleft-Addams
Woman Always Wins. C. H. Bullivant
Woman and Her Master. J. F. Smith
Woman and the Prowler. S. Friedman
Woman and the West. C. Marriott
Woman and the Wheel. T. B. Morris
Woman Aroused. E. Lacy
Woman at Bay. Nicholas Carter
Woman at Bay. G. H. Coxe
Woman at Dead Oaks. J. Kirkpatrick
Woman at Iron Crag. A. S. Adcock
Woman at Kensington. W. LeQueux
Woman at Point Zero. N. El Saadawi
Woman at Risk. M. Tripp

Woman at the Window. J. Jenkins
Woman at the Window. P. O'Conaire
Woman Ayisha. T. Mundy
Woman Bars the Way. M. Leighton
Woman Beware Woman. E. Tennant
Woman Cain. M. Richmond
Woman Called Omega. H. Green
Woman Called Scylla. D. Gurr
Woman Delia. P. Piper
Woman Dominant. E. C. Vivian
Woman from A.U.N.T. B. Negulesco
Woman from Outside. H. Footner
Woman from the East. E. Wallace
Woman Hater. J. N. Chance
Woman He Chose. J. H. Wallis
Woman Hunt. F. Ryck
Woman Hunter. Laura Hale
Woman in Armour. D. C. Murray
Woman in Bed. M. Tripp
Woman in Black. H. Adams
Woman in Black. M. Arden
Woman in Black. E. C. Bentley
Woman in Black. Nicholas Carter
Woman in Black. J. Ford
Woman in Black. L. Grieg
Woman in Black. M. Y. Halidom
Woman in Black. M. Heath
Woman in Black. W. Spence
Woman in Chains. E. V. Timms
Woman in Exchange. H. Buck
Woman in Grey. C. Salisbury
Woman in Grey. A. M. Williamson
Woman in Marble. C. Dekker
Woman in Mauve. G. MacMillan
Woman in 919. J. P. Seabrooke
Woman in Number Five. L. Meynell
Woman in Purple Pajamas. W. Kent
Woman in Question. J. R. Scott
Woman in Red. S. Campbell
Woman in Red. Anthony Gilbert
Woman in Red. P. Gosling
Woman in Red. R. St. Clair
Woman in Silk and Shadow. D. Daniels
Woman in the Alcove. A. K. Green
Woman in the Car. R. Marsh
Woman in the Case. Mark Allerton
Woman in the Case. C. Fitch
Woman in the Case. C. R. Gull
Woman in the Case. H. Malot
Woman in the Case. F. P. Rathburne
Woman in the Case. P. Renin
Woman in the Case. N. Thurley
Woman in the Case. Bessie Turner
Woman in the Dark. D. Hammett
Woman in the Dark. F. W. Robinson
Woman in the Firelight. O. Sandys
Woman in the Maze. M. Dobner
Woman in the Mirror. Winston Graham
Woman in the Mirror. A. G. Melross
Woman in the Moon. D. Lehmkuhl
Woman in the Picture. J. August
Woman in the Sea. Shelley Smith
Woman in the Shadow. L. J. Vance
Woman in the Wardrobe. P. Antony
Woman in the Way. W. LeQueux
Woman in the Window. D. Clarins
Woman in the Window. J. H. Wallis
Woman in the Woods. C. Blackstock
Woman in White. W. Collins
Woman in Whitehall. R. Walker
Woman Intervenes. R. Barr
Woman Involved. J. G. Davis
Woman Is Dead. R. King
Woman Missing and other stories. H. Nielsen
Woman Named Anne. H. Cecil
Woman Named Smith. M. C. Oemler
Woman of Action. P. Trent
Woman of Business. A. Griffiths
Woman of Cairo. N. Barber
Woman of Cairo. J. Flagg
Woman of Character. Julian Gloag
Woman of Consequence. S. Gottlieb
Woman of Danger. N. W. Firth
Woman of Death. G. Boothby

Woman of Death. Old Sleuth
Woman of Destiny. S. Maddock
Woman of Evil. Nicholas Carter
Woman of Fire. D. Grabien
Woman of Kronstadt. M. Pemberton
Woman of Montmartre. R. Vane
Woman of Mystery. Nicholas Carter
Woman of Mystery. A. K. Green
Woman of Mystery. M. Leblanc
Woman of Mystery. G. Ohnet
Woman of Nerve. N. T. Oliver
Woman of Nerve. R. M. Wells
Woman of Paris. G. Des Cars
Woman of Saigon. P. Saxon
Woman of Shanghai. M. L. Berges
Woman of Sorek. A. Gould
Woman of Steel. Nicholas Carter
Woman of Straw. C. Arley
Woman of the Grey House. G. Simenon
Woman of the Iron Bracelets. F. Barrett
Woman of Valor. A. Topol
Woman of Wiles. A. Munro
Woman on Her Own. J. Blackmore
Woman on the Place. H. Whittington
Woman on the Roof. M. G. Eberhart
Woman on the Roof. H. Nielsen
Woman on the Spot. J. Hunter
Woman Out of Nowhere. L. Hoffman
Woman Pays. S. Warwick
Woman Possessed. Whit Harrison
Woman Possessed. C. Randell
Woman Question. D. Malm
Woman Racket. G. Lawrence
Woman Run Mad. J. L'Hereux
Woman Slaughter. E. Ferrars
Woman Spy. H. De Halsalle
Woman Stealer. Harry Mills
Woman Tempted Him. W. Westall
Woman, the Man, and the Monster. C. Dawe
Woman, the Mystery. H. Herman
Woman: The Sphinx. F. Hume
Woman They Sent to Fight. D. Boggis
Woman Trap. A. Capelli
Woman Trap. J. Davidson
Woman Under the Mountain. R. McDougald
Woman Vanishes. C. Crane
Woman Who Dared. L. L. Lynch
Woman Who Dared. A. M. Williamson
Woman Who Held On. F. Hume
Woman Who Knew. M. Pemberton
Woman Who Knew Too Much. D. Clarins
Woman Who Saved the World. W. Holt-White
Woman Who Stole Everything and other stories. A. Bennett
Woman Who Tempted. G. Warden
Woman Who Understood. Mrs. C. Kernahan
Woman Who Waited. T. C. H. Jacobs
Woman Who Was. P. Boileau
Woman Who Was God. Francis King
Woman Who Was No More. P. Boileau
Woman Who Was Not. A. Applin
Woman Who Went Away. F. Haring
Woman Who Would Not Die. C. B. Bauman
Woman Wins. R. Barr
Woman Wins. C. H. Bullivant
Woman Wins. R. Machray
Woman with a Gun. G. H. Coxe
Woman with a Past. R. Vane
Woman with a "Record". L. Jackson
Woman with a Secret. R. Ferguson
Woman with Claws. Williams Forrest
Woman with One Hand, and Mr. Ely's Engagement. R. Marsh
Woman with the Diamonds. F. Warden
Woman with the Portuguese Basket. E. Wuorio
Woman with the Yellow Eyes. C. Dawe
Woman with the Yellow Hair and Other Modern Mysteries. Anonymous
Woman with Two Smiles. M. Leblanc
Woman Without a Name. L. M. Janifer
Woman Without a Name. G. Lenotre
Woman Worth Winning. G. M. Fenn
Womanhunt. M. Derby
Woman's Burden. F. Hume

Woman's Calvary. J. Middlemass
Woman's Courage. F. Wicks
Woman's Debt. W. LeQueux
Woman's Devotion. J. W. Postgate
Woman's Eyes. G. Weill
Woman's Face. F. Warden
Woman's Fate. E. Southworth
Woman's Footprint. E. R. Punshon
Woman's Friend. M. Storme
Woman's Hand. Nicholas Carter
Woman's Hand. J. R. Coryell
Woman's Honor. E. P. Green
Woman's Honor. E. A. Young
Woman's House. H. L. V. Fletcher
Woman's Law. M. Thompson
Woman's Loyalty. I. D. Hardy
Woman's Prerogative. G. B. Lissenden
Woman's Ransom. F. W. Robinson
Woman's Revenge. M. Pinkerton
Woman's Story. F. Warden
Woman's Tragedy. L. L. Lynch
Woman's Vengeance. M. A. Holmes
Woman's Vengeance. J. Payn
Woman's View. H. Flowerdew
Woman's World. A. Askew
Women and Ships. Morley Roberts
Women Are Dynamite. J. Hewett
Women Are Like That. T. C. H. Jacobs
Women Are Like That. E. Woodward
Women Are Skin Deep. P. Whelton
Women at Belguardo. M. Erskine
Women—Dope—and Murder. Roland Daniel
Women for Sale. J. Mangut
Women Hate Till Death. H. Janson
Women in Evidence. S. Japrisot
Women in Paradise. Stuart Hall
Women in the Case. L. Tracy
Women in White. J. Reach
Women Kill As Well. W. Parker
Women Like to Know. Kevin O'Hara
Women of London. B. Hemyng
Women of Morning. A. Sewart
Women of Paris. B. Hemyng
Women of Peasenhall. R. J. White
Women of Twilight. S. Rayman
Women Swore Revenge. I. H. Irwin
Women That Are Lost. W. Standish
Women to Love. S. Drago
Women Who Wait. E. Bissell
Women Without Men. R. Marr
Won by Magic. Nicholas Carter
Wonder Craft. E. S. Brooks
Wonder Jack. Old Sleuth
Wonderful and Thrilling Tales for Winter Evenings. Anonymous
Wonderful Bishop and other London adventures. Morley Roberts
Wonderful Career of Ebenezer Lobb. A. Upward
Wonderful Detective. Old Sleuth
Wonderful Lips of Thibong Linh. T. Roscoe
Wonderful Scheme. H. S. Keeler
Wonderful Scheme of Mr. Christopher Thorn. H. S. Keeler
Wonderful Years. G. V. Higgins
Wondering Moon. George Weston
Wood and the Trees. M. Elgin
Woodchuck Hunt. U. Becher
Woodchuck Jerry. Old Sleuth
Woodchuck Jerry, the Country Detective. Old Sleuth
Woodcutter Operation. K. Royce
Wooden Hand. F. Hume
Wooden Indian. C. Wells
Wooden Kimono. J. Floyd
Wooden Overcoat. P. Branch
Wooden Spectacles. H. S. Keeler
Wooden Wolf. John Kelly
Woodley Lane Ghost and other stories. M. V. Dahlgren
Woodsedge. Barbar Knight
Woodsman. M. F. Anderson
Woodwitch. Stephen Gregory
Wooing of a Fairy. G. Warden
Wooing of Esther Gray. L. Tracy

Wooing of Grey Eyes, and other stories. Riccardo Stephens
Wooing of Martha. C. G. Mitford
Wooing of Webster. A. M.
Woolf Sarason, Special Agent. M. Moiseiwitsch
Woolen Monkey. G. Goodchild
Woolwich Arsenal Mystery. E. J. Gannon
Word and the Will. J. Payn
Word for Word and Letter for Letter. A. J. D. Biddle
Word in Her Ear. P. Conway
Word of a Gentleman. P. Niesewand
Word of Honor. N. De Mille
Word of Honour. H. C. McNeile
Word of Six Letters. H. Adams
Word of the Sorceress. B. Mitford
Words Can Kill. K. Davis
Words for Murder Perhaps. E. Candy
Words Have Wings. N. Berrow
Words, Weather, and Wolfmen. T. Hillerman
Work for a Dead Man. S. Ritchie
Work for a Million. E. Zaremba
Work for the Hangman. B. Graeme
Work of a Fiend. J. Peddie
Work of Art. D. V. Baker
Work of Betrayal. M. Brelich
Work of Darkness. J. Karney
Work of Her Hands. A. Askew
Work of the Devil. E. Willie
Workers All. P. Trent
Working for the Man. R. Dennis
Working Man Detective. D. J. MacKenzie
Working Murder. E. Boylan
Works in Darkness. J. B. Harris-Burland
Works of the Late Edgar Allan Poe. E. A. Poe
World Bewitched. J. M. Graham
World Championship Mystery. W. J. Passingham
World Cup Murder. Pele
World Grabbers. P. W. Fairman
World in Bud. G. Bullett
World in My Pocket. J. H. Chase
World Masters. George Griffith
World of Crime. M. F. Goron
World of Sin. H. T. Johnson
World of Tim Frazer. F. Durbridge
World of Violence. Colin Wilson
World Outside. H. MacGrath
World Rapers. B. von Block
World-Shakers. D. Reid
World Stood Still. W. Holt-White
World, the Flesh, and the Devil. M. E. Braddon
World to Win. U. Sinclair
World Under Snow. D. K. Broster
World War III Game. D. Stivers
World We Live In. L. Bromfield
World Without Dreams. R. Garland
World Without End. Winifred Graham
Worldbreaker. J. Milton
Worldlings. L. Merrick
Worldly Goods. A. Soutar
Worldly Innocent. Joanna Harris
World's a Stage. K. Kellow
World's Blackmail. L. Cleeve
World's End. J. Conway
World's End. J. Wasserman
World's End and other stories. P. Theroux
World's Fair Goblin. K. Robeson
World's Fair Murders. J. Ashenhurst
World's Finger. T. W. Hanshew
World's Great Snare. E. P. Oppenheim
Worlds Made of Fire. M. Childress
World's Mercy. Maxwell Gray
Worlds Without End. D. V. Baker
Worm in the Rose. T. Stacey
Worm of Death. N. Blake
Worm of Doubt. M. R. D. Meek
Worm Turns. A. Douglas
Worms Have Eaten Them. W. J. Elliott
Worms Must Wait. J. Wainwright
Worried Widow. Gerald Hammond
Worse and More of It. N.E. Henshaw
Worse Than a Crime. Anne Burton
Worse Than a Crime. F. Crane
Worse Than Death. T. Bunn
Worse Than Death. L. Lamb
Worse Than Murder. E. Berckman
Worse Than Murder. D. Duncan
Worshippers. V. Thorpe
Worst Case on Record. Nicholas Carter
Worst Enemies. J. Scaparro
Worst Enemy. G. Hackforth-Jones
Worst Man in the World. S. Horler
Worst Man in the World. F. Richardson
Worst Squadron in France. G. E. Rochester
Worst Way to Die. B. Rossi
Worsted Viper. G. Mitchell
Worth His Weight in Gold. Anonymous
Worth More Dead. B. Sarto
Worthies of Hyben. F. Dilnot
Wotan Warhead. J. Follett
Wotan's Wedge. F. Gerard
Would You Kill Him? G. P. Lathrop
Wound and the Scar. V. Scannell
Wound of Love. R. V. Cassell
Wounded and the Slain. D. Goodis
Wounded Heart. K. Ross
Wounds of Treason. M. Vinter
Woven Web. P. Audemars
Wrack. M. Drake
Wrack and Rune. C. MacLeod
Wraith. P. MacDonald
Wraith of Olverstone. F. Warden
Wraiths and Changelings. G. Mitchell
Wraithwood. L. Churchill
Wrap It Up. A. Dean
Wrath. B. Ham
Wrath of Fu Manchu and other stories. S. Rohmer
Wrath of Garde. J. La Plante
Wrath of God. J. Graham
Wrath of the Lion. Harry Patterson
Wrath to Come. E. P. Oppenheim
Wraxton Marne. R. Ray
Wreath for a Bride. L. O'Donnell
Wreath for a Dead Angel. H. Kimberley
Wreath for a Lady. M. Baroni
Wreath for a Ragman. B. Parvin
Wreath for a Redhead. Carter Brown
Wreath for a Redhead. Peter Chambers
Wreath for a Redhead. B. Moore
Wreath for a Spy. R. Tashkent
Wreath for a Widow. B. Banarto
Wreath for America. R. Raine
Wreath for Jenny's Grave. Charlotte Hunt
Wreath for Miss Wong. C. Leader
Wreath for Rebecca. Carter Brown
Wreath for Rivera. N. Marsh
Wreath for the Bride. M. Lang
Wreath for the Lady. H. Holt
Wreath for the Springboks. J. Calder
Wreath from Bangkok. C. Leader
Wreath of Bones. J. N. Chance
Wreath of Camellias. G. B. Mair
Wreath of Cherry Blossoms. C. Leader
Wreath of Honesty. P. Burden
Wreath of Lords and Ladies. James Fraser
Wreath of Orchids. M. Shoebridge
Wreath of Poppies. C. Leader
Wreath of Roses. J. Blackburn
Wreath of Water-Lilies. P. Flower
Wreck. P. J. Cooper
Wreck of the Chinook. L. Tracy
Wreck of the Grey Cat. Winston Graham
Wreck of the Mary Deare. H. Innes
Wreck of the Redwing. B. Grimshaw
Wrecked in Port. E. Yates
Wrecker. Ruth Alexander
Wrecker. A. Ridley
Wrecker. R. L. Stevenson
Wreckers. F. Lynde
Wreckers Must Breathe. H. Innes
Wrecking Crew. D. Hamilton
Wrecking of Offshore Five. R. Johnston
Wrecking Ray. G. E. C. Webster
Wrenfield Mystery. G. Woden
Wrenwatchers. Robin Simon
Wrestler on the Shore. L. Lurgan
Wrist Mark. J. S. Fletcher
Write It Murder. H. Arre
Write Me a Murder. Amanda Carter
Write Me a Murder. F. Knott
Write Murder Down. R. Lockridge
Write-Off. P. Malloch
Write Off the Redhead. M. Brody
Write on Both Sides of the Paper. M. Kelly
Writing on the Wall. H. Adams
Written for Hitchcock. Talmage Powell
Written in Blood. Nicholas Carter
Written in Cypher. E. Gaboriau
Written in Dust. M. Burton
Written in Red. Anonymous
Written in Red. C. H. Montague
Wroclaw Dracula. M. Murdoch
Wrong Body. Anthony Gilbert
Wrong Body. V. A. Van Sickle
Wrong Box. G. Napier
Wrong Box. R. L. Stevenson
Wrong Case. J. Crumley
Wrong Envelope and other stories. Mrs. Molesworth
Wrong House. C. F. Gregg
Wrong Impression. J. Malcolm
Wrong Letter. W. S. Masterman
Wrong Man. H. C. Bailey
Wrong Man. J. H. Oliver
Wrong Man. A. V. Partipilo
Wrong Man in the Mirror. P. Loraine
Wrong Mr. Chamberlain and other stories. P. Herring
Wrong Move. A. Burr
Wrong Place, Wrong Time. W. G. Duncan
Wrong Road. A. Griffiths
Wrong Road by Hook or Crook. A. Griffiths
Wrong Saturday. E. Thompson
Wrong Side of the Sky. G. Lyall
Wrong Slant of Red. H. L. Skalland
Wrong Target. W. Kaye
Wrong Target. John Wolfe
Wrong That Was Done. John Marsh
Wrong That Was Done. F. W. Robinson
Wrong Trail. Anonymous
Wrong Turn. D. Harper
Wrong Turning. T. E. B. Clarke
Wrong Venus. C. Williams
Wrong Verdict. W. S. Masterman
Wrong Verdict. A. O. Pollard
Wrong Way Down. E. Daly
Wrong Way to Die. E. Messenger
Wrong Wife. A. S. Roche
Wrongdoer. A. Upward
Wrongly Condemned. B. Harte
Wrychester Paradise. J. S. Fletcher
Wu Fang. Roland Daniel
Wu Fang's Revenge. Roland Daniel
Wulfheim. M. Furey
Wyatt. D. Gethin
Wyatt and the Moresby Legacy. D. Gethin
Wyatt's Hurricane. D. Bagley
Wyatt's Orphan. D. Gethin
Wych Stone. M. McEvoy
Wycherly Woman. R. Macdonald
Wychford Murders. P. Gosling
Wychford Poisoning Case. A. Berkeley
Wychwood. N. St. John
Wycliffe and the Beales. W. J. Burley
Wycliffe and the Cycle of Death. W. J. Burley
Wycliffe and the Four Jacks. W. J. Burley
Wycliffe and the Pea-Green Boat. W. J. Burley
Wycliffe and the Quiet Virgin. W. J. Burley
Wycliffe and the Scapegoat. W. J. Burley
Wycliffe and the Schoolgirls. W. J. Burley
Wycliffe and the Tangled Web. W. J. Burley
Wycliffe and the Winsor Blue. W. J. Burley
Wycliffe in Paul's Court. W. J. Burley
Wycliffe-Pepin Case. A. Fane
Wycliffe's Wild-Goose Chase. W. J. Burley
Wye Valley Mystery. Essex Smith
Wylder's Hand. J. S. Le Fanu
Wyllard's Weird. M. E. Braddon
Wyndham's Pal. H. Bindloss
Wyndham's Partner. H. Bindloss
Wyndspelle. A. Vandergriff
Wyndspelle's Child. A. Vandergriff
Wynnum. D. Hennessey
Wyoming Tragedy. W. B. M. Ferguson

Title Index

Wyss Pursuit. Adam Hamilton
Wyvern Mystery. J. S. Le Fanu

X. E. Sudak
X Esquire. L. Charteris
X Factor. D. Wiles
X14. G. Lennox
X. Jones. H. S. Keeler
X. Jones of Scotland Yard. H. S. Keeler
X Marks the Spot. M. Butterworth
X Marks the Spot. Muriel Stafford
X Marks the Spot. L. Thayer
X-On. R. M. Hunt
XPD. L. Deighton
X-Rated Corpse. M. Avallone
X-Ray Menace. W. Herscholt
X-Ray Murders. M. S. Michel
X-Ray Solution. K. Voldeng
X v. Rex. M. Porlock
XX—A Fatal Clue. Anonymous
XYY Man. K. Royce
XYZ. A. K. Green
Xanadu Program. R. Carroll
Xanadu Talisman. P. O'Donnell
Xander Pursuit. Adam Hamilton
Xavier Affair. R. L. Fish
Xelucha and Others. M. P. Shiel
X's Page. N. Miller

Y. Cheung, Business Detective. H. S. Keeler
Ya Don't Say. B. Logan
Yaba Round-About Murder. C. Ekwensi
Yacht of Mystery. W. M. Graydon
Yachting Yarns. F. B. Cooke
Yakusa Tattoo. J. Ahern
Yakuza. S. Schlossstein
Yakuza. L. Schrader
Yang Meridian. J. Leasor
Yangtze. A. Fisher
Yangtze Run. P. O'Hara
Yank. A. Sugar
Yank in Fleet Street. R. McLoughlin
Yankee Doodle Detective. A. La Croix
Yankee Lawyer—The Autobiography of Ephraim Tutt. A. Train
Yankee Napoleon. J. F. Macpherson
Yankee Poodle. C. H. Gibbs-Smith
Yankey Rue, the Ex-Pugilist Detective. Old Sleuth
Yarns of a Country Attorney. L. J. Walsh
Yarns of the Yilgarn. C. E. Goode
Yaroslav Incident. D. Mariner
Yard Lengths. D. Shoubridge
Yarns of Billy Borker. F. Hardy
Yashar Pursuit. Adam Hamilton
Yasmin. A. Lowing
Yatton Murders. L. Galletley
Yawning Lion. M. Warrick
Yazoo Mystery. I. Craddock
Year and a Day. G. Thorne
Year As a Lion. E. Roman
Year of August. M. Saxon
Year of Living Dangerously. C. J. Koch
Year of Miracle. F. Hume
Year of the Ape. L. Chang
Year of the Boar. L. Chang
Year of the Dragon. L. Chang
Year of the Dragon. B. Copper
Year of the Dragon. R. Daley
Year of the Golden Ape. C. Forbes
Year of the Gun. M. Mewshaw
Year of the Horse. L. Chang
Year of the Monkey. R. Argo
Year of the Monkey. Carole Berry
Year of the Rat. L. Chang
Year of the Rat. M. Zarubica
Year of the Rooster. M. K. Simmons
Year of the Snake. L. Chang
Year of the Tiger. L. Chang
Year of the Tiger. M. Fallon
Yearbook Killer. T. Philbin
Years Between. P. Trent
Years of the Hungry Tiger. J. G. Davis
Yell Bloody Murder. J. Shallit
Yell Ruddy Murder. J. Shallit

Yellerlegs. L. C. Douthwaite
Yellow Angel. M. A. Gilbert
Yellow Angels. H. E. Helseth
Yellow Arrow Murders. V. W. Mason
Yellow Babe. A. Capelli
Yellow Badge. J. Middlemass
Yellow Beetle. A. B. Sherlock
Yellow Brand. Nicholas Carter
Yellow Brick Road. E. Cadell
Yellow Bungalow Mystery. L. Gribble
Yellow Card Mystery. P. G. Larbalestier
Yellow Cargo. N. Lazenby
Yellow Cat. H. H. C. Gibbons
Yellow Cat. C. Knight
Yellow Circle. Anonymous
Yellow Circle. P. Foley
Yellow Circle. C. E. Walk
Yellow Claw. S. Rohmer
Yellow Claw. Hedley Scott
Yellow Claws. H. J. S. Anderton
Yellow Claws of Wong. E. H. Robinson
Yellow Cloud. K. Robeson
Yellow Cord. J. Wylde
Yellow Corsair. James Bennett
Yellow Crayon. E. P. Oppenheim
Yellow Crystal. A. Wynne
Yellow Danger. M. P. Shiel
Yellow Death. U. Key
Yellow Devil. Ronald Daniel
Yellow Devil. J. J. Farjeon
Yellow Diamond. G. F. Gibbs
Yellow Diamond. A. Sergeant
Yellow Disc Murder. Nicholas Carter
Yellow Disc Murders. T. A. Plummer
Yellow Document. M. Allain
Yellow-Dog Contract. Ross Thomas
Yellow Door. D. Whitelaw
Yellow Dove. G. F. Gibbs
Yellow Dragon. D. Haring
Yellow Dragon. A. Mills
Yellow Dusk. B. Bedwell
Yellow Face. W. M. Graydon
Yellow Face. F. M. White
Yellow Fangs. T. F. Elstow
Yellow Fetish. T. W. Pierson
Yellow Fever. R. A. Shiomi
Yellow Fiend. Mrs. Alexander
Yellow Fiend. W. J. Elliott
Yellow Flag. I. S. Black
Yellow Flag. E. Yates
Yellow Gardenia. A. Mancini
Yellow Gods. J. G. Brandon
Yellow Gold of Tiryns. H. Osborne
Yellow Hand. A. Upward
Yellow Hearse. F. Mahannah
Yellow Hibiscus. J. Templeton
Yellow Hoard. K. Robeson
Yellow Holly. F. Hume
Yellow House. E. P. Oppenheim
Yellow Hunchback. F. Hume
Yellow Is for Fear and other stories. D. Eden
Yellow Jacket. E. Snell
Yellow Journalist. M. Michelson
Yellow Label. Nicholas Carter
Yellow Letter. W. A. Johnston
Yellow—Like Gold! Douglas Christie
Yellow Magic. E. Thomas
Yellow Man. C. Dawe
Yellow Mask. J. G. Brandon
Yellow Mask. W. Collins
Yellow Men and Gold. G. Morris
Yellow Mistletoe. W. S. Masterman
Yellow Munro. G. Fairlie
Yellow Music Kill. W. J. Sheldon
Yellow Overcoat. S. Acre
Yellow Paint War. W. C. Taylor
Yellow Peril. G. Hackforth-Jones
Yellow Peril. B. Kingston
Yellow Peril. M. P. Shiel
Yellow Phantom. L. Cargill
Yellow Rain. P. McCurtin
Yellow Rain. S. Spetz
Yellow Rat. F. Grierson
Yellow Ribbon. W. LeQueux

Yellow Robe Murders. Melville Burt
Yellow Robed Wago. Marion Roberts
Yellow Rock. D. Footman
Yellow Room. M. R. Rinehart
Yellow Room. G. Shipway
Yellow Satchel. F. Whishaw
Yellow Scourge. C. Steele
Yellow Seven. G. E. Rochester
Yellow Seven. E. Snell
Yellow Shadow. H. Vernes
Yellow Shadows. S. Rohmer
Yellow Shadows of Death. R. Wallace
Yellow Shop. F. MacIsaac
Yellow Skull. G. H. Teed
Yellow Snake. E. Wallace
Yellow Spider. J. C. Beecham
Yellow Spider. S. Hope
Yellow Spies. W. T. Stewart
Yellow Stockings. D. W. MacArthur
Yellow Strangler. Colin Robertson
Yellow Streak. V. Williams
Yellow Stub. E. Lynn
Yellow Taxi. J. Stagge
Yellow Terror. R. Hardinge
Yellow Ticket. V. Morton
Yellow Tiger! G. H. Teed
Yellow Triangle. Margery Lawrence
Yellow Trousers. P. Fry
Yellow Turban. C. Jay
Yellow Typhoon. H. MacGrath
Yellow Vengeance. P. Urquhart
Yellow Villa. S. Blanc
Yellow Violet. F. Crane
Yellow Viper. S. Fairway
Yellow Wagon. C. Edwards
Yellow Will Out! Warren Hill
Yellow Witch. D. Hann
Yellow Wolf. T. S. King
Yellow Yoke. A. Askew
Yellowfish. J. Keeble
Yellowleaf. Sacha Gregory
Yellowstones. G. Goodchild
Yellowthread Street. W. Marshall
Yermakov Transfer. Derek Lambert
Yes, Inspector McLean. G. Goodchild
Yesterday I Died. J. Cooper
Yesterday Is Dead. D. Barnes
Yesterday Man. D. Stringer
Yesterday Walkers. S. Harvester
Yesterday's Bones. S. Tower
Yesterday's Child. Barbara Wood
Yesterday's Enemy. W. Haggard
Yesterday's Enemy. M. Moiseiwitsch
Yesterday's Evil. L. B. Clark
Yesterday's Evil. D. Daniels
Yesterday's Love. J. L. Rickard
Yesterday's Man. J. Midgley
Yesterday's Murder. C. Rice
Yesterday's Murder. J. York
Yesterday's News. J. Healy
Yesterday's Poison. Ruth Grayson
Yesterday's Spy. L. Deighton
Yet She Must Die. H. McCutcheon
Yet She Must Die. Stella Phillips
Yet She Must Die. Sara Woods
Yetta the Magnificent. J. F. Macpherson
Yield to the Night. Joan Henry
Yield to the Night. J. Karney
Yo-Ho, and a Bottle of Rum! H. M. Stephenson
Yo-Ho-Ho and a Bottle of Ink! P. J. Willis
Yoga Mist. E. P. Thorne
Yoga Shrouds Yolande. Carter Brown
Yogi Shrouds Yolande and Poison Ivy. Carter Brown
Yokohama Hood. J. R. Fernandes
Yolan. J. Tickell
Yolan of the Plains. J. Tickell
Yonder. M. B. Houston
Yonder Grow the Daisies. W. Lipman
Yoris. R. Ingham
Yorke the Adventurer, and other stories. L. Becke
Yorkshire Moorland Murder. J. S. Fletcher
Yoshar the Soldier. W. Harrington
You and Me. A. Plater
You Asked for It. I. Fleming

You Belong to Me. Sam Ross
You Belong to Me. W. Standish
You Bet Your Life. S. M. Kaminsky
You Can Always Blame the Rain. M. Fredman
You Can Always Duck. P. Cheyney
You Can Call It a Day. P. Cheyney
You Can Deal Me In. W. Newton
You Can Go Feet First. W. Newton
You Can Help Me. M. Birmingham
You Can Keep the Corpse. Colin Robertson
You Can Only Die Once. J. Beede
You Can Run So Far. M. Barnes
You Can Say That Again. J. H. Chase
You Can't Beat Hell. J. Diamond
You Can't Beat the Law. H. H. Van Loan
You Can't Believe Your Eyes. Joan Fleming
You Can't Bring 'Em Back. K. Slattery
You Can't Call It Murder. Neill Graham
You Can't Call It Murder. D. Ramsay
You Can't Catch Me. L. Lariar
You Can't Die Here. S. Coburn
You Can't Die Laughing. A. A. Fair
You Can't Die Tomorrow. L. Gribble
You Can't Do Business with Murder. D. Von Elsner
You Can't Escape. L. M. Janifer
You Can't Escape Me. John Tyler
You Can't Gag the Dead. M. Propper
You Can't Get Away by Running. W. Chambers
You Can't Get Away with Murder! A. Spiller
You Can't Hit a Woman and other stories. P. Cheyney
You Can't Ignore Murder. R. Teague
You Can't Keep Murder Out. P. Valdez
You Can't Keep the Change. P. Cheyney
You Can't Kill a Corpse. L. Trimble
You Can't Kill a Dead Man. D. Pranger
You Can't Kill Shadows. R. Goyne
You Can't Kill the Dead. E. Bowen-Rowlands
You Can't Kill the Dead. C. Macey
You Can't Live Forever. H. Q. Masur
You Can't See Round Corners. J. Cleary
You Can't Stop Me. W. Ard
You Can't Trust Duchesses and other stories. P. Cheyney
You Could Call It Murder. L. Block
You Could Die Laughing, and The Swingers. J. Adams
You Did It. E. K. Goldthwaite
You Die, Du Man! J. Cain
You Die in Valpaso. B. Sarto
You Die Next, Jill Baby! K. Carr
You Die Today! B. Kendrick
You Diet Today. B. Kendrick
You Don't Die Twice. R. Angel
You Don't Need an Enemy. R. M. Stern
You Don't Say! H. Lugar
You Find Him—I'll Fix Him. Raymond Marshall
You Flash Bastard. G. F. Newman
You Get What You Pay For. L. Beinhart
You Gotta Be Rough. M. Fiaschetti
You Have Yourself a Deal. J. H. Chase
You Kill Me. J. D. MacDonald
You Kill Me! P. Muller
You Know the Way It Is. A. E. Jones
You Leave Me Cold! S. Rogers
You Live Once. J. D. MacDonald
You Murdered Me. R. Tarne
You Must Never Go Back. B. Cleeve
You Never Believe Me and other stories. D. Grubb
You Never Know with Women. J. H. Chase
You Never Learn. M. Cronin
You Nice Bastard. G. F. Newman
You Only Die Once. B. Copper
You Only Die Once. H. B. Kaye
You Only Hang Once. H. W. Roden
You Only Live Twice. I. Fleming
You Only Live Until You Die. S. Weinstein
You Only Lose It Once. N. Karta
You Pay for Pity. W. Mole
You Pay the Price. Griff
You Pay Your Money. M. Cronin
You Play the Black and the Red Comes Up. R. Hallas
You Remember the Case. T. Claymore

You Shall Know Them. Vercors
You Slay Me. D. Spade
You Stand Accused. D. Hughston
You Take the Rap. Spike Gordon
You Talk Too Much. B. Shannon
You the Detective. Robin Simon
You, the Jury. J. Cleary
You, the Jury. J. M. Liebeler
You, the Jury. A. C. Martens
You, the Jury. J. Reach
You Too Can Have a Body. F. Robinson
You Took Me . . . Keep Me. D. Glinto
You Want to Die, Johnny? G. Black
You Will Die Today! R. I. Wakefield
You Will Like It Here. N. Dorer
You Won't Let Me Finish. Joan Fleming
You Won't Need a Coat. E. Messenger
You Wouldn't Be Dead for Quids. R. G. Barrett
You'd Be Surprised. P. Cheyney
You'd Better Believe It. B. James
You'll Be All Right. K. Blake
You'll Be Better Off Dead. M. Storme
You'll Be Sorry! S. Rogers
You'll Be the Death of Me. M. Lynch
You'll Catch Your Death. David Hume
You'll Die, Darling. M. Grove
You'll Die Laughing. Craig Cooper
You'll Die Laughing. B. Elliott
You'll Die Laughing. M. Grove
You'll Die Laughing. J. Tobias
You'll Die Next! H. Whittington
You'll Die Now! R. Drennen
You'll Die Today. M. Grove
You'll Die Tomorrow. M. Grove
You'll Die Tonight. M. Grove
You'll Die When You Hear This. M. Grove
You'll Die Yesterday. M. Grove
You'll End Up Dead. L. H. Hart
You'll Fry Tomorrow. M. V. Heberden
You'll Get Yours. T. Wills
You'll Hang, My Love. F. Swann
You'll Have to Talk. D. Steel
You'll Hear from Us. M. Cooley
You'll Like My Mother. N. A. Hintze
You'll Live to Talk. Dave Steel
You'll Never Get Me. S. Morelli
You'll Never Get to Heaven. S. Mitchell
You'll Never See Me Again. W. Irish
You'll Never Take Me. R. D. Mead
You'll Play This Way. D. Spade
Young Accused. A. Furness
Young Adam. A. Trocchi
Young Alladin. Old Sleuth
Young and Deadly. J. Carrick
Young and Fair. N. R. Nash
Young and Violent. V. Packer
Young and Wild. Morton Cooper
Young Ann. Elizabeth Ford
Young Archduchess. W. LeQueux
Young Beck. M. M. Bodkin
Young Blood. K. Alexis
Young Blood. E. W. Hornung
Young Blood. F. Lynde
Young Buffalo in New York. C. E. Blaney
Young Can Die Protesting. T. Wells
Young Cardinaud. G. Simenon
Young Chauncey. Old Sleuth
Young Chevalier. D. W. MacArthur
Young Dash. Old Sleuth
Young Detective. R. Abbott
Young Dillinger. S. Stuart
Young Don't Cry. R. Jessup
Young Engineer. Old Sleuth
Young Eve and Old Adam. T. Gallon
Young Fair God. H. Fleetwood
Young Flynn. E. L. Long
Young Gingers. Old Sleuth
Young Girl's Bondage. J. R. Wilmot
Young Girl's Life. B. L. Farjeon
Young Harold. Old Sleuth
Young Killers. W. Wiener
Young Ladies' Room. Elizabeth Ford
Young Lady from Paris. J. Aiken
Young Lord Folliot. N. H. Romanes

Young Lord Stranleigh. Robert Barr
Young Love. J. G. Brandon
Young Lucifer. C. Blackstock
Young Magician. Old Sleuth
Young Man from Lima. J. Blackburn
Young Man, I Think You're Dying. Joan Fleming
Young Man in a Hurry. R. W. Chambers
Young Man in Question. J. L. Rickard
Young Man on a Bicycle. V. Canning
Young Man Who Stroked Cats and other stories. Morley Roberts
Young Man with a Scythe. A. Kennington
Young Men May Die. D. Craig
Young Mr. Gibbs. J. L. Rickard
Young Mr. X. E. Jordan
Young Mrs. Barter's Repentence. D. C. Murray
Young Mrs. Caudle. G. R. Sims
Young Mrs. Cavendish and the Kaiser's Men. K. K. Beck
Young Nick and Old Nick. S. R. Crockett
Young Petrella. M. Gilbert
Young Prey. H. Waugh
Young Reporter. W. Drysdale
Young Savages. E. Hunter
Young Sherlock Holmes. A. Arnold
Young Sherlock: The Adventure at Ferryman's Creek. G. Frow
Young Sherlock: The Mystery of the Manor House. G. Frow
Young Sleuth's Victory. A. Kutch
Young Vanish. F. Everton
Young Vigilance. Old Sleuth
Young Villain with Wings. R. Kruger
Young Wallingford. G. R. Chester
Young Widow. E. E. Cameron
Young Wife's Trial. F. Warden
Young Wolves. H. Janson
Younger Brothers Vow. W. B. Lawson
Younger Venus. N. Royde-Smith
Youngest Miss Brown. F. Warden
Youngest Soldier of the Grand Armee. F. Du Boisgobey
Your Alibi Is Showing. Carter Brown
Your Casket Awaits. Madame. M. Lynch
Your Daughter Will Die! J. P. Cody
Your Day in the Barrel. A. Furst
Your Deal, My Lovely. P. Cheyney
Your Eyelids Are Growing Heavy. B. Paul
Your Friendly Neighborhood Death Pedlar. J. Sangster
Your Golden Jugular. W. Squerent
Your Loving Victim. P. McGerr
Your Money and Your Life. G. Milner
Your Money and Your Wife. Ritchie Perry
Your Move, Delaney! B. Singer
Your Move Sister. Pete Costello
Your Neck in a Noose. E. Ferrars
Your Number Is Up. A. Mills
Your Red Wagon. E. Anderson
Your Royal Hostage. Antonia Fraser
Your Secret Friend. M. Torrie
Your Secret Is in a Well. Elaine Turner
Your Shot, Darling? L. Bergquist
Your Time Is Up. E. F. Hornung
Your Turn, Mr. Moto. J. P. Marquand
Your Verdict Is? A. Reubens
You're a Long Time Dead. R. Clapperton
You're Best Alone. P. Curtis
You're Better Off Dead. Peter Chambers
You're Dead, My Lovely. Gene Ross
You're Dead Right. J. Watt
You're Dead Without Money. J. H. Chase
You're Fairly Welcome. J. Ditton
You're Far Too Young! Spondee
You're Hired: You're Dead. K. Carr
You're in the Racket, Too. J. Curtis
You're Lonely When You're Dead. J. H. Chase
You're My Man! C. C. Waddell
You're My Ugly. H. Zore
You're Never Too Old to Die. A. D. Goldstein
You're No Lady. Spike Gordon
You're Welcome to Ulster! M. Gallie
You're Wrong, Delaney. B. Singer
Yours Truly, Angus MacIvor. N. Harman

Title Index

Yours Truly, from Hell. T. L. Smith
Yours Truly, Hoodlum. D. Glinto
Yours Truly, Jack the Ripper. R. Bloch
Yours Truly, Jack the Ripper. Pamela West
Youth at Bay. L. Vincent
Youth Hostel Murders. G. Carr
Youth Hostel Mystery. L. Dowsett
Youth Without Glory. B. Von Hutten
Youthful Imposter. G. W. M. Reynolds
You've Been Tumbled. Frank Hanson
You've Bet Your Life. G. Ashe
You've Got Him Cold. T. B. Dewey
You've Got It Coming. J. H. Chase
You've Had It, Girl. P. Swann
You've Had Your Chance. J. Cairo
Yu-Chu Stone. E. Snell
Yu-Malu, the Dragon Princess. T. Leslie
Yu'an Hee See Laughs. S. Rohmer
Yukon Gold. W. D. Blankenship
Yukon Kid. J. B. Hendryx
Yukon Patrol. L. C. Douthwaite
Yukon Target. Nick Carter
Yunnan Terminus. R. Neebel
Yvonne, the Confident. K. Kimbrough

Z. V. Vassilikos
Z Cars. T. K. Martin
Z Cars Again. A. Prior
Z Case. Roland Daniel
Z Document. Nick Carter
Z Effect. M. Laurens
Z for Zaborra. E. Wuorio
Z Murders. J. J. Farjeon
Z Papers. G. S. Simmons
Z Ray. E. Snell
Z-Sting. I. Wallace
Z Warning. D. Oran
Zachary. E. Pintoff
Zadda Street Affair. W. Jackson
Zadig. Voltaire
Zadok's Treasure. M. Arnold
Zahara. M. T. Walworth
Zaharan Pursuit. Adam Hamilton
Zaharoff Commission. A. Jute
Zaibatsu. John Brown
Zaibatus. L. Perdue
Zaitech Sting. J. Arnett
Zakari's Skull. Michael Barrett

Zakhov Mission. A. Gulyashki
Zakka Slaughter. W. Barker
Zalea. R. C. Garland
Zaleski's Percentage. D. MacKenzie
Zambesi Break. T. Beattie
Zambra the Detective. H. Hill
Zantelli. Old Sleuth
Zanzibar Intrigue. V. W. Mason
Zap Day. J. Lindblad
Zara. A. Randazzo
Zarahemia Vision. Gary Stewart
Zastrozzi. P. B. Shelley
Zdt. J. Rathbone
Zebra Network. S. Flammery
Zebra-Striped Hearse. R. Macdonald
Zecan Termination. Curt Lawrence
Zelda. Carter Brown
Zeluco. J. Moore
Zemba. M. Grant
Zembya Expedition. J. Rosenberger
Zen There Was Murder. H. R. F. Keating
Zenia: Spy in Togoland. C. Cameron
Zeno. J. F. Rinn
Zenobie Capitaine. F. Du Boisgobey
Zeph and other stories. G. R. Sims
Zeppelin. R. Florence
Zeppelin Destroyer. W. LeQueux
Zeppelin's Passenger. E. P. Oppenheim
Zero. E. V. Lustbader
Zero Always Wins. P. Gascoigne
Zero at the Bone. E. Ferrars
Zero Cool. J. Lange
Zero Counts Dead! D. Haring
Zero Factor. W. O. Johnson
Zero Gravity. R. Lourie
Zero Hour. L. C. Douthwaite
Zero Hour. Colin Robertson
Zero Hour Strike Force. Nick Carter
Zero in the Gate. S. Farrar
Zero Minus Nine. E. P. Thorne
Zero 08:00. B. Gaston
Zero Takes All. H. Janson
Zero the 14th. H. Clevely
Zero Time. Jack Anderson
Zero Trap. P. Harcourt
Zero Yield. H.S. Bhabra
Zhukov Briefing. A. Trew
Zia. P. Wynnton

Zig-Zag Man. J. C. Goodwin
Zig-Zag the Clown. F. Du Boisgobey
Zig Zag . . . to Armageddon. T. Foster
Ziggurat. R. Katz
Zigzag. M. Kenyon
Zilov Bombs. D. G. Barron
Zinger. L. Davidov
Zinsser Implant. L. Kamarck
Zinzin Road. F. Knebel
Zion Road. S. Harvester
Zip-Gun Angels. A. L. Quandt
Zitlaw the Cruel. S. Wilkinson
Zoboa. M. Caidin
Zodiac. D. Lees
Zodiac. N. Stephenson
Zodiac Killer. J. Weissman
Zofloya. C. Dacre
Zoharoff Commission. A. Jute
Zola's Thirteen. G. Morton
Zolar's Astrological Murder Mysteries. Zolar
Zolotov Affair. R. H. Rimmer
Zolta Configuration. D. Quammen
Zombie. T. J. Kelly
Zombie. E. Lecale
Zombie. D. Lynn
Zombie. R. St. Clair
Zombie! P. Tremayne
Zone of Fire. H. Hill
Zone of Violence. D. Dunham
Zone Zero. J. Robb
Zones of Silence. W. Garner
Zoo Gang. P. Gallico
Zoo Murder. F. Grierson
Zoo Murders. J. Farr
Zoo Ship. G. Volk
Zoom! Peter Townend
Zooman and the Sign. C. Fuller
Zoot Suit. L. Valdez
Zoot-Suit Murders. T. Sanchez
Zorn. Jonah Jones
Zukovka Experiment. N. Gottlieb
Zulu Blood. R. Skimin
Zurich/AZ 900. M. Albrand
Zurich Numbers. B. Granger
Zurich Syndicate. A. K. Robertson
Zuss Imperative. P. Cleife
Zylgrahoff. J. C. Shannon

SETTINGS INDEX

Settings Index   **ACADEMIA / 1217**

ABYSSINIA. See: Ethiopia.

ACADEMIA (Acad. School settings at all levels)
Acheson, E. Grammarian's Funeral
Adler, T. On Murder's Skirts
Aird, C. Parting Breath
Allen, I. 'Varsity Man
Anderson, R. Cover Her with Roses
Anthony, D. Midnight Lady and the Mourning Man
Apffel, E. R. Last Days at St. Saturn's
Appiah, A. Avenging Angel
Asimov, I. Death Dealers
August, J. Troubled Star
Babson, M. Past Regret
Bagby, G. Corpse with the Purple Thighs
Barnard, R. Little Victims
Barry, C. Secrecy at Sandhurst
Bell, Josephine. Death at Half-Term
    Summer School Mystery
Bell, Pauline. Dead Do Not Praise
Bidwell, M. Death and His Brother
Blackstock, C. Melon in the Cornfield
Blain, W. E. Passion Play
Blake, N. Morning After Death
    Question of Proof
Borthwick, J. S. Student Body
Bourgeau, A. Most Likely Suspect
Boyd, M. Murder in the Stacks
Brady, John. Stone in the Heart
Bramhall, M. Murder Is Contagious
Bream, F. Murder in the Map Room
Bronson, F. W. Bulldog Has the Key
Broome, A. Cambridge Murders
    Oxford Murders
Brown, R. D. Prime Suspect
Bruce, L. Death at St. Asprey's School
Brucker, M. Death in the Dormitory
Bullett, G. Judgment in Suspense
Burley, W. J. Taste of Power
Burton, M. Murder in the Coalhole
    Murder Out of School
Bush, C. Case of the Dead Shepherd
Byrom, J. Thou Shouldst Be Living
Caird, J. Murder Scholastic
Campbell, M. E. Scandal Has Two Faces
Candy, E. Words for Murder Perhaps
Cannan, J. Frightened Angels
Cape, T. Cambridge Theorem
Carlson, P. M. Audition for Murder
    Murder Is Academic
    Murder Is Pathological
    Murder Misread
Carr, J. D. Dead Man's Knock
Cassill, R. V. Dormitory Room
Chater, L. Course in Murder
Christie, A. Cat Among the Pigeons
    They Do It with Mirrors
Clark, Douglas. Golden Rain
Clemeau, C. Ariadne Clue
Clinton-Baddeley, V. C. Death's Bright Dart
Clutton-Brock, A. Murder at Liberty Hall
Cohen, O. R. May Day Mystery
Cole, G. D. H. Knife in the Dark
    Off with Her Head!
    Scandal at School
Collins, R. Case of the Philosopher's Ring
Compton, G. Disguise for a Dead Gentleman
Constantine, K. C. Blank Page
Cook, S. Upperdown
Coxe, K. B. Murder Most Foul
Crider, B. Dying Voices
    One Dead Dean
Crispin, E. Case of the Gilded Fly
    Love Lies Bleeding
Crosby, V. Fast-Death Factor
Cross, A. Poetic Justice
    Sweet Death, Kind Death
    Theban Mysteries
Curran, T. All Booked Up
Dalmas, H. both titles
Dane, J. Y. Murder Cum Laude
Davidson, T. L. Murder in the Laboratory
Davies, L. P. Paper Dolls
Davis, D. S. Shock Wave

Davis, Mildred. Tell Them What-s-Her-Name
    Called
Davis, S. Death in Seven Hours
Dean, S. F. X. By Frequent Anguish
Deighton, B. Little Learning
Delman, D. Death of a Nymph
Devine, D. M. Death Is My Bridegroom
    Devil at Your Elbow
DeWeese, G. Wanting Factor
DeWeese, J. Web of Guilt
Dickinson, P. Hindsight
Dillon, E. Death in the Quadrangle
Dwight, O. Close His Eyes
Edwards, R. D. School of English Murder
Ellis, V. Death Comes Like a Thief
Epstein, C. Murder in China
Eulo, E. Y. Ice Orchids
Eustis, H. Horizontal Man
Evans, F. Pistols and Pedagogues
Fairway, S. Long Tunnel
Farrar, H. Murder Goes to School
Farrer, K. Gownsman's Gallows
Fenwick, E. Long Way Down
Fenwick, E. P. Murder in Haste
Fiske, D. Academic Murder
    Bound to Murder
Foote-Smith, E. Gentle Albatross
Ford, L. By the Watchman's Clock
Fox, P. Kensington Gore
Freeman, K. Gown and Shroud
Fuller, T. Harvard Has a Homicide
Galbraith, R. Convenient Death
Garnet, A. H. Maze
Gilbert, M. Night of the Twelfth
Gill, B. M. Death Drop
Gilla, E. N. Cap and Gown for a Shroud
Gosling, P. Monkey Puzzle
Graaf, P. Sapphire Conference
Graham, J. A. Involvement of Arnold Wechsler
Gray, J. Untimely Slain
Greenbaum, L. Out of Shape
Gresham, E. Puzzle in Parchment
Griffiths, Sally. Winter Day in a Glasshouse
Hannah, B. Nightwatchman
Hardy, W. Lady Killer
Harrison, William. In a Wild Sanctuary
Hart, C. G. Little Class on Murder
Hawton, H. Murder by Mathematics
Hay, M. D. Death on the Cherwell
Haynes, C. Bishop's Gambit
    Perpetual Check
Heald, T. Masterstroke
Heddle, E. F. Mystery of St. Rule's
Hess, J. Strangled Prose
Hill, R. Advancement of Learning
Hillman, D. A. Fallen Nun
Hilton, J. B. Innocents at Home
Hobson, P. Titty's Dead
Hodgkin, M. R. Student Body
Holland, I. Grenelle
Hollis, J. Teach You a Lesson
Holman, H. Death Like Thunder
Holton, L. Corner of Paradise
Hopkins, K. Campus Corpse
Hoppe, J. Lesson Is Murder
Hoster, G. Goodbye, Dear Elizabeth
Howard, T. Howard's Price
Hubbard, M. A. Murder Takes the Veil
Hughes, B. Murder in the Zoo
Hull, H. Tapping on the Wall
Hulland, J. R. Student Body
Iams, J. Corpse of the Old School
Ince, D. In Those Dark Woods
Innes, M. Death at the President's Lodging
    Old Hall, New Hall
    Weight of the Evidence
Irving, A. Bitter Ending
James, P. D. Shroud for a Nightingale
James, Susan. Foul Deeds
Janeschutz, T. In Shadows
Jevons, M. Fatal Equilibrium
Johnson, W. B. Widening Stain
Johnston, W. Innocent Murderers
Jordan, C. Carol in the Dark

Karp, D. One
Keech, S. Ciphered
Kelly, M. Dead Man's Riddle
Kelly, N. In the Shadow of King's
Kelman, J. Where Shadows Fall
Kelvin, N. Pegged for Murder
Kemelman, H. Tuesday the Rabbi Saw Red
Kenney, S. Graves in Academe
Kennington, A. Bagful of Bones
Kenyon, M. Whole Hog
King, P. Snares of the Enemy
Klass, D. Night of the Tyger
Knight, K. L. Trace Elements
Koehler, R. P. Case of the Dead Cadet
Kyd, T. Blood Is a Beggar
Laing, P. Lady Is Dead
Lake, M. D. Amends for Murder
    Cold Comfort
Landels, D. H. Headmaster
Lang, B. Crockett on the Loose
Langley, L. both titles
Langton, J. Memorial Hall Murder
Lansbury, C. Felicity
La Roche, K. A. Dear Dead Professor
Larsen, G. D. 180 Degree Murder
Lathen, E. Come to Dust
Lathrop, G. P. In the Distance
Lawrence, A. Dean's Death
Le Carre, J. Murder of Quality
Lemarchand, E. Death of an Old Girl
    Light Through Glass
Leslie, Jean. One Cried Murder
    Two Faced Murder
Levin, I. Kiss Before Dying
Lewis, Catherine. Unable by Reason of Death
Lewis, Lange. Juliet Dies Twice
    Murder Among Friends
Lewis, R. Error of Judgment
Lilly, J. False Face
Lockridge, F. Drill Is Death
Lockridge, R. Twice Retired
Long, A. R. Death Looks Down
    Shakespeare Murders
Longmate, N. Head for Death
Lupica, M. Extra Credits
McCloy, H. Man in the Moonlight
    Through a Glass Darkly
McCormick, C. Resume for Murder
McDermid, V. Report for Murder
Macdonald, R. Chill
MacDuff, D. Murder Strikes Three
McGown, J. Death of a Dancer
McGregor, I. Death Wore a Diadem
McGrew, F. Taste of Death
MacKay, A. Death Is Academic
MacLeod, C. Luck Runs Out
    Rest You Merry
Macnaughtan, R. Preparatory School Murders
Mackin, E. Nominative Case
Magoon, C. I Smell the Devil
Mainwaring, M. Murder at Midyears
Mais, S. P. B. Who Dies?
Maner, W. Die of a Rose
Mann, Jessica. Captive Audience
    Only Security
Manton, P. Greyvale School Mystery
Marasco, R. Child's Play
Marin, A. C. Storm of Spears
Maron, M. One Coffee With
Martens, A. C. Phantom of the High School
Masterman, J. C. Oxford Tragedy
Melville, J. New Kind of Killer, an Old Kind of
    Death
Michaels, Barbara. Search the Shadows
Miles, Dennis. Pattern of Chalk
Millar, K. Dark Tunnel
Miller, J. Murder of a Professor
Minahan, J. Great Harvard Robbery
Miner, V. Muder in the English Department
Mitchell, G. Death at the Opera
    Laurels Are Poison
    Spotted Hemlock
Mitchell, R. E. Design for November
Moreton, C. A. Death in Practice

A

ACADEMIA

Morice, A. Murder in Outline
Morrah, D. Mummy Case
Murphy, B. Enigma Variations
Murphy, W. B. Dead Letter
Nash, S. Dead of a Counterplot
Nicholas, R. White Shroud
Nowak, J. Death at the Crossings
Olsen, D. B. Enrollment Cancelled
O'Marie, C. A. Novena for Murder
Onions, O. In Accordance with the Evidence
Owen, H. C. Ways of Death
Packer, V. Hare in March
Park, J. Sorority House
Parker, R. B. Godwulf Manuscript
Patrick, Q. Death and the Maiden
    Death Goes to School
    Murder at Cambridge
Pearson, A. Murder by Degrees
Peden, W. H. Twilight at Monticello
Penn, J. Mortal Term
Penny, R. Sweet Poison
Peters, Ellis. Black Is the Colour of My True Love's Heart
Philips, J. Nightmare at Dawn
Philmore, R. Procession of Two
Pilgrim, C. Silent Slain
Post, M. Candidate for Murder
Propper, M. Student Fraternity Murder
Queen, E. Campus Murders
    Devil's Cook
Rankin, J. L. Murder Pie
Rath, V. Ferryman, Take Him Across!
Rees, D. Cambridge Murders
Reeves, R. Doubting Thomas
Rennert, M. Circle of Death
    Operation Alcestis
Resnicow, H. Seventh Crossword
Rhodes, R. Tricycle
Risenhoover, C. C. Wine, Murder & Blueberry Sundaes
Robinson, R. Landscape with Dead Dons
Robinson, T. When Scholars Fall
Rosenheim, A. Tormenting of Lafayette Jackson
Ross, I. T. Murder Out of School
    Requiem for a Schoolgirl
    Teacher's Blood
Ruark, E. B. Campus Killings
Ryp, E. Deadly Bonds
Saber, R. O. Black Dark Murders
St. Clair, R. High School Mystery
Savage, R. Murder Goes to School
Sharpe, T. Wilt on High
Shaw, H. Death of a Don
Shepherd, E. Murder in a Nunnery
Sholl, A. M. Mystery of Lostland Academy
Silver, V. Death of a Harvard Freshman
    Death of a Radcliffe Roommate
Simmons, A. Death on the Campus
Simpson, H. R. Junior Year Abroad
Skom, E. Mark Twain Murder
Smith, Joan. Masculine Ending
Smith, Rosamund. Nemesis
Smithies, R. H. R. Academic Question
Spain, N. Death Before Wicket
    Poison for Teacher
Spencer, P. Full Term
Sprinkle, P. H. Murder at the Markham
Sproul, K. Death and the Professors
Staynes, J. Knife at the Opera
Steel, K. Murder Goes to College
Stein, A. M. Body for a Buddy
    Case of the Absent-Minded Professor
    Cradle and the Grave
Strange, M. Midnight
Strong, L. A. G. Othello's Occupation
Sutton, H. Sacrifice
Symons, J. Paper Chase
Tapply, W. G. Death at Charity's Point
Tate, R. Birds of a Bloodied Feather
Taylor, E. A. Murder at Vassar
Taylor, Edith. Serpent Under It
Tey, J. Miss Pym Disposes
Thomas, C. Prominent Among the Mourners
Timperley, R. After School Hours
Townsend, G. M. To Prove a Villain
Trevor, G. Murder at School
Varnam, J. Traveling Deadman
Vulliamy, C. E. Don Among the Dead Men
Waddell, E. L. Murder at Drake's Anchorage
Wakefield, R. I. You Will Die Today!
Wallace, F. Front Man
Wallis, J. H. Mystery of Vaucluse
Waltch, L. M. Third Victim
Waugh, H. Last Seen Wearing
Wees, F. S. Mystery of the Creeping Man
Wellman, M. W. School of Darkness
Wells, Carolyn. Mystery Girl
Wender, T. Knight Must Fall
    Murder Gets a Degree
Westbrook, P. D. Happy Deathday
Whaley, F. J. Reduction of Staff
    Trouble in College
Whitechurch, V. L. Murder at the College
Williams, D. Treasure by Degrees
Williams, G. M. Silk Rope
Wolseley, F. Which Way Came Death?
Woodbury, D. O. both titles
Woodfin, H. Virginia's Thing
Woodthorpe, R. C. Public School Murder
Wright, June. Faculty of Murder
Yaffe, J. Cliffhanger
    Nice Murder for Mom
Yorke, M. Cast for Death
Zubro, M. R. Why Isn't Becky Twitchell Dead?

ADELAIDE (See also: Australia; Melbourne; Sydney; Solomon Islands; Tasmania)

Brady, T. Paint Me a Murder
Sinclair, B. Blood Brothers

AFGHANISTAN (Afghan.)

Block, Lawrence. Here Comes a Hero
Bolt, B. Wayland of the Guides
Bolton, M. Offering
Caillou, A. Afghan Assault
Carter, Nick. Afghan Intercept
De Villiers, G. Man from Kabul
Follett, K. Lie Down with Lions
Gall, S. Salang
Griffiths, J. C. Queen of Spades
Hadley, J. B. Cobra Strike
Hamman, H. Lapis
Harris, Y. L. Hundi Kush
Harvester, S. Silk Road
Hild, J. Jihad
Innes, H. Black Tide
Jason, S. Go Die in Afghanistan
Kilgore, A. Afghanistan Penetration
Kruse, J. Hour of the Lily
Leckie, K. Seventh Gate
McCurtin, P. Yellow Rain
Morrell, D. Rambo III
Niesewand, P. Scimitar
Osborne, H. White Poppy
Pendleton, D. Appointment in Kabul
Rosenberger, J. Afghanistan Crashout
Seymour, G. In Honour Bound
Spetz, S. Yellow Rain
Trantor, N. Cable from Kabul
Willard, T. Dolomite Memorandum

AFRICA (Afr. See also: Africa, East; Africa, North; Africa, West; individual countries)

Aarons, E. S. Assignment—Black Gold
    Assignment—Golden Girl
    Assignment—Silver Scorpion
    Assignment—Star Stealers
Ahern, J. Escape
Alily, V. Mark of the Cobra
Ambler, E. Dirty Story
Amesbury, J. E. SAporting Chance
Armour, T. Blood Tells
Atlee, P. Skeleton Coast Contract
Bagley, D. Flyaway
Bainbridge, C. Mercenary Justice
Ballinger, W. A. Congo
Barber, F. D. Last White Man
Beaty, D. Excellency
Bee, D. Our Fatal Shadows
Bernier, J. M. Mission to Burundi
Bickham, J. Regensburg Legacy
Black, Lionel. Chance to Die
Block, Lawrence. Me Tanner, You Jane
Boothby, G. Sailor's Bride
Brett, J. M. Plague of Dragons
Buchanan, J. Desert Death Raid
Buck, P. Passport to Peril
Butler, K. R. Desert of Salt
Butler, Rupert. Assassin
Butler, W. Mr. Three
Calvin, H. Boka Lives!
Carstairs, J. P. Concrete Kimono
Carter, Nick. Six Bloody Summer Days
Charles, R. This Side of Hell
Cleary, D. J. Sahara Strike
Cole, B. Sahara Survival
Corrigan, M. Danger's Green Eyes
Cory, D. Height of Day
    High Requiem
Couper, E. Lonely Sky
Crawley, R. both titles
Creasey, J. Mountain of the Blind
Cullen, A. Studd
Curtis, Robert. Green Pack
Delft, J. Drums of Kufu
Dembo, S. Sands of Lilliput
Dlovu, A. Angel of Death
Dodds, F. W. Tales of the African Wild
Dryer, B. Port Afrique
Dube, H. State Secret
Edwards, C. Gabriel Sounds for Africa
Emecheta, B. Nairi Power
Essex, P. Exile
Evans, J. P. Breach of Fate
Falk, L. at least 9 titles
Farmer, P. J. Adventures of the Peerless Peer
Farrington, J. Night Train to Mombasa
Fearon, D. Rhino for Rosamund
Ferrars, E. Swaying Pillars
Forrester, L. Diamond Beach
Fuller, B. Far Place
Gall, S. Gold Scoop
Garrett, F. Lethal Assault
Gerard, F. Justice of Sanders
    Law of the River
    Return of Sanders of the River
Gibbs, G. F. Yellow Diamond
Goodchild, G. Last Secret
Grant, M. Shadow's Revenge
Grant, Richard. Legacy of Danger
Grayson, Rupert. Secret Agent in Africa
Greene, H. Thieves of Timbutu
Gwynne, P. N. Firmly by the Tail
Hall, Adam. Tango Briefing
Halliday, M. Death Out of Darkness
Hardinge, R. Beyond the Skyline
Harris, J. Old Trade of Killing
Harrison, W. Savannah Blue
Hartmann, M. Days of Thunder
    Leap for the Sun
Harvester, S. Sahara Road
Hayes, Ralph. Nightmare Conspiracy
Hild, J. Barrabas Run
    Point Blank
Horne, G. Portuguese Diamonds
Huxley, E. Merry Hippo
    Murder on Safari
Irungu, J. Lost Generations
Jackson, C. J. Kicked to Death by a Camel
Jason, S. Blood Vengeance
Jenkins, G. Bridge of Magpies
Johnston, W. Missed It by That Much
Jordan, D. Black Account
Jude, C. Terror of the Shape
Kearey, C. both titles
Keene, T. Earthrace
Kilgore, A. Bush Warfare
Kolarz, H. Kalahari
Leonard, C. L. Expert in Murder
Leslie, P. Radioactive Camel Affair
Lindsay, D. T. Wings Over Africa
Lyall, G. Wrong Side of the Sky

Settings Index

McAllister, B. Bullion Run 101
McCoy, A. Blood Ivory
McCurtin, P. Kalahari
MacLeod, R. Drum of Power
MacPherson, M. Protege
Macao, M. Kak-Abdullah Conspiracy
Mair, G. B. Miss Turquoise
Mangut, J. Blackmailers
    Women for Sale
Mason, A. Losers Keepers
Mason, A. E. W. Winding Stair
Meade, R. Lost Fraulein
Merrick, W. No One of That Name
Mills, A. Black Royalty
Milne, S. Beware the Lurking Scorpion
Mitford, B. many titles
Moore, Robin. Only the Hyenas Laughed
    Phase of Darkness
Morton, David. Hyena Run
Mundy, T. Ivory Trail
Murphy, C. Dance for a Diamond
Napier, M. Powers of Darkness
Neebel, R. Halo Solution
Norwood, E. both titles
Okpi, K. 5 titles
Oppenheim, E. P. Millionaire of Yesterday
Ordway, P. Final Safari
Parkes, R. Fourth Monkey
Pendleton, D. Anvil of Hell
    Sudan Slaughter
    Terrorist Summit
Percy, D. C. Hidden Valley
Peterson, M. Death Drum
Phil-Ebosie, P. Dead of Night
Powell, J. D. Mungwe Affair
Rabe, P. Spy Who Was Three Feet Tall
Raymond, P. Matter of Assassination
Richardson, M. Daughter of the Sacred Mountain
Robeson, K. Land of Long Juju
    Munitions Master
Rooinek. African Nights
Sadler, B. Razor
Sanders, Lawrence. Tangent Factor
    Tangent Objective
Sangster, J. Touchfeather, Too
Sapir, R. Slave Safari
    Summit Chase
Scholefield, A. Last Safari
Semyonov, J. Tass Is Authorized to Announce
Shannon, C. Fatal Footsteps
Sheraton, N. African Terror
Simenon, G. Tropic Moon
Simpson, H. R. Assignment for a Mercenary
Smith, David. Leo Conversion
    Timbuktu
Smith, Wilbur. Leopard Hunts in Darkness
Snell, E. Red Spinner
Sotabinda, M. Dangerous Waters
    Money-Doublers
Stephenson, R. Down Among the Dead Men
Telfair, R. Slavers
Thomas, R. Seersucker Whipsaw
Thorp, V. Stone of Vengeance
    Worshippers
Tippette, G. Mercenaries
Tokson, E. Desert Captive
Townend, Paul. Road to El Saida
Umelo, R. Finger of Suspicion
Vinter, I. M. African Nights
Wallace, E. 6 titles
Webster, F. A. M. Black Shadow
Wheatley, D. Secret War
Wilson, Gar. Africa Burn
Wingate, W. Bloodbath
Zeno. Grab

AFRICA, EAST (Afr., E. See also: Africa; Africa, North; Africa, West; individual countries)
Bennett, J. Ocean Road
Brown, Robin. Bloody Ivory
Canning, V. Burning Eye
Drummond, I. Frog in the Moonflower
Hayes, Ralph. Taste of Blood
Huxley, E. Death of an Aryan
MacLeod, R. Lake of Fury
Pitts, D. Rogue Hercules
Tyler, W. T. Lion and the Jackal

AFRICA, NORTH (Afr., N. See also: Africa; Africa, East; Africa, West; individual countries)
Allen, E. Death on Delivery
Bridges, A. Lighthearted Quest
Brierley, D. Skorpion's Death
Canning, V. Golden Salamander
Fielding, G. Eight Days
Foss, J. Flesh and Blood
Home, M. House of Shade
Maybury, A. Midnight Dancers
Moore, Robin. Force Nine
North, Gil. Corpse for Kofi Katt
O'Neill, F. Agents of Sympathy
Rabe, P. Box
St. Germain, G. Target: Sahara
Saul, J. Baraka
Sheckley, R. Live Gold
Swift, B. Mission Code: Symbol
Wheatley, D. Sword of Fire
William, P. Affair at Abu Mina
Williams, Alan. Barbouze
Wolf, J. Death Rides a Camel

AFRICA, WEST (Afr., W. See also: Africa; Africa, East; Africa, North; individual countries)
Bagley, D. Juggernaut
Best, H. both titles
Broome, A. 9 titles
Cameron, C. Zenia: Spy in Togoland
Ferguson, A. Running Man
Greene, G. Heart of the Matter
Harcourt, P. Twisted Tree
Head, M. Cabinda Affair
Henege, T. Skim
Huxley, E. Murder at Government House
Hyne, C. J. C. Kate Meredith, Financier
Limnelius, G. Medbury Fort Murder
McCutchan, P. Bluebolt One
Mason, S. C. Man on the Spot
Meredith, P. Crocodile Man
Robinson, L. W. General Goes Too Far
Southon, A. E. Laughing Ghosts
Strong, T. Conflict of Lions
Tabori, G. Good One
Weston, C. Danju Gig
Williams, J. A. Jacob's Ladder
Wyllie, J. all 7 Dr. Quarshie titles

AIRCRAFT (air.)
Bonnell, J. F. Death Flies West
Campbell, Karen. Suddenly in the Air
Corley, E. Air Force One
Dent, L. Dead at the Take-Off
Didelot, F. Many Ways of Death
Ferguson, Austin. Jet Stream
Field, T. Five
Harper, D. Hijacked
Kennedy, G. Murder on High
King, C. D. Obelists Fly High
LeQueux, W. Terror of the Air
Page, S. H. Murder Flies the Atlantic
Pendleton, D. Flight 741
    Vulture's Vengeance
Stevens, G. Peace on Earth
Teilhet, D. L. Death Flies High

ALABAMA (Ala. See also: Birmingham; South)
Chaze, E. three titles
Childress, M. V for Victim
Connolly, P. So Fair, So Evil
Darty, P. Widowed Bride of Raven Oaks
Deal, B. H. Walls Came Tumbling Down
Feegel, J. R. Not a Stranger
Grantland, K. Run from the Hunter
Greene, F. N. One Clear Call
Howell, P. H. Winds of Terror
Jones, M. Season of the Strangler
Knight, K. M. Robineau Look
Manly, M. Rube Burrows League
Mason, S. E. Crimson Feather
    House That Hate Built
    Murder Rents a Room
Murphy, W. B. Return Engagement
Packer, V. 3 Day Terror
Patterson, R. N. Outside Man
Russell, H. L. Iced Tea and Ignorance
Saunders, E. Investigation
Stivers, D. Cowboy's Revenge
Thompson, R. Number to Call Is . . .
Williams, C. Long Saturday Night

ALASKA
Boyd, E. M. all 3 titles
Butler, R. O. Sun Dogs
Darty, P. Wailing Winds of Juneau Abbey
De Laguna, F. Fog on the Mountain
Elkins, A. J. Icy Clutches
Granger, B. Henry McGee Is Not Dead
Hall, W. Even Jericho
Hanlon, S. all 3 titles
Haring, D. Trigger Tramp
Head, H. S. Death Below Zero
Hendryx, J. B. Connie Morgan in Alaska
Hild, J. Alaska Deception
Laforest, S. Intruder
MacLean, Alistair. Athabasca
Page, C. G. Beyond the Windswept Sea
Pendleton, D. Black Dice
    White Hell
Robeson, K. Mountain Monster
Rosenberger, J. Alaska Conspiracy
Shimer, R. H. Squaw Point
Simmons, D. Let the Bastards Freeze in the Dark
Smith, B. A. Death of an Alaskan Princess
Walker, Greg. Bowie

ALBANIA (Alb. See also: Balkans)
Baker, W. H. Departure Deferred
Daniels, N. Overkill
Driscoll, P. White Lie Assignment
Fallon, M. Keys of Hell
Gilman, D. Unexpected Mrs. Pollifax
Kinsley, P. Pimpernel 60
Martin, I. K. Rekill
Masters, Doug. Killer Angel
Napier, M. Forbidden Places
O'Brine, M. Crambo
Quayle, A. Eight Hours from England
Rosenberger, J. Albanian Connection
Wellard, J. Action of the Tiger
Zarubica, M. Scutari

ALBUQUERQUE (Albuq. See also: New Mexico; Sante Fe; Southwest)
Curtiss, U. Danger: Hospital Zone
    Don't Open the Door
    Menace Within
    Poisoned Orchard
Van Giesen, J. North of the Border

ALGERIA (See also: Algiers; Africa; Africa, North)
Appleby, J. Singing Cave
Creasey, J. Hounds of Vengeance
Driscoll, P. Heritage
Graham, James. Khutra Run
Lee, John. Assignment in Algeria
MacLean, Arthur. Pursuit to Algeria
Rosenberger, J. Nightmare in Algeria
Rutherford, D. Perilous Sky
Sellers, C. Algerian Incident
Vance, J. H. Man in the Cage
Whittington, H. Guerrilla Girls
Williams, Alan. Long Run South

ALGIERS (See also: Algeria; Africa; Africa, North)
Aarons, E. S. Assignment—Madeleine
Gluck, S. Red Emerald
Hertz, G. Foreign Harry Complot
Irwin, R. Mysteries of Algiers
Rovin, J. Destination: Algiers
Schurmacher, E. C. Terror in Algiers
Stead, P. J. In the Street of the Angel
Stokes. D. Captive in the Night

AMSTERDAM (Amst. See also: Holland)
Bhabra, H. Gestures
Carter, Nick. Amsterdam
Freeling, N. Criminal Conversation
    Long Silence
    Love in Amsterdam
    Over the High Side
Glaskin, G. M. Man Who Didn't Count
Grimsey, L. Amsterdam Connection
Guild, N. Favor
Helm, P. Death Has a Thousand Entrances
Hougan, C. Shooting in the Dark
MacLean, Alistair. Puppet on a Chain
Miglis, J. Masterwork
Miller, S. Snow Leopard
Mills, W. Shadow Crusade
Randolph, E. Rendezvous in Amsterdam
Ross, Angus. Amsterdam Diversion
Semprun, J. Second Death of Roman Mercader
Stein, A. M. Hangman's Row
Van de Wetering, J. 11 titles
Van Gulik, R. Given Day
Wallace, Robert. Paint Out
Winsor, D. Death Convention

ANDORRA
Ames, D. Murder, Maestro, Please
Appleby, J. Secret Mountains
MacKintosh, M. King and Two Queens

ANGOLA (See also: Africa)
Smith, Don. Secret Mission: Angola
Walker, Martin. Mercenary Calling

ANTARCTIC (See also: Arctic)
Carter, Nick. Operation: McMurdo Sound
    White Death
Forbes, Stephen. False Cross
Griffin, J. Antarctic Convergence
Innes, H. White South
Keneally, T. Survivor
    Victim of the Aurora
Morris, M. E. Iceman
Peters, G. Chill of a Corpse
Robeson, K. South Pole Terror
Rosenberger, J. Atlantean Horror
Wheatley, D. Man Who Missed the War

ANTWERP (See also: Brussels; Belgium)
Flynn, B. League of Matthias
MacKintosh, I. Slaying in September
Riefe, A. Tyger by the Tail
Roberts, K. Center of the Web

ARABIA. See: Saudi Arabia.

ARCTIC (See also: Antarctic)
Adams, F. R. Long Night
Carter, Nick. Ice Bomb Zero
Dark, J. Operation Ice Cap
Edwards, P. Ice Goddess
Gosling, P. Zero Trap
Harris, J. Unforgiving Wind
Johnson, J. L. Piece of the Moon Is Missing
MacLean, Alistair. Bear Island
    Ice Station Zebra
McVean, J. Seabird Nine
Perrault, E. G. Spoil!
Robeson, K. Devil Ghengis
    Lost Giant
    Polar Treasure
Rosenberger, J. Operation Mind-Murder
    Pole Star Secret
    Zembya Expedition
Swift, B. Mission Code: Snow Queen
Wood, J. Fire Rock
Wright, G. Whitefire

ARGENTINA (Arg. See also: Buenos Aires; South
    America)
Adams, I. Becoming Tania
Barrett, Michael. Reward
Benton, K. Red Hen Conspiracy

Boothby, G. Across the World for a Wife
Carter, Nick. Plot for the Fourth Reich
Constantini, H. Gods, the Little Guys and the Police
Cory, D. Johnny Goes South
Creighton, J. A. House of Fury
Galwey, R. C. Assignment Argentina
Greene, G. Honorary Consul
Hayes, R. King's Ransom
Houston R. Blood Tango
Kiefer, W. Kidnappers
Langley, B. Conquistadores
Marchant, B. Joyce Harrington's Trust
Timins, D. Extra Passenger
Wheatley, D. Gateway to Hell
Wilson, G. Argentine Deadline
Wood, C. Death on the Pampas

ARIZONA (Ariz. See also: Phoenix; Tucson;
    Southwest)
Adams, C. F. Private Eye
Austin, H. Death Has Seven Faces
Backer, J. M. Echoes from the Past
Baker, Lucinda. Place of Devils
Blankenship, W. D. Helix File
Bramwell, C. Cousin to Terror
Brown, F. One for the Dead
Bunnell, R. Terror by Night
Chavis, R. Terror Package
Clifford, F. Overdue
Clifton, B. Let Him Go Hang
Conde, N. Legend
Creighton, J. No So Evil As Eve
D'Amato, B. Eyes on Utopia Murders
Dickey, P. Brass Bandit
Dobbins, P. H. Death in the Dunes
Dreher, S. Gray Magic
Eyre, M. Absence
Foley, R. Sleep Without Morning
Ford, P. L. Great K & A Train Robbery
Forest, R. Walking Shadow
Fuller, R. Fear in a Desert Town
Garfield, B. Deep Cover
    Relentless
    Threepersons Hunt
    What of Terry Conniston?
Gluck, S. Wildcat
Gordon, M. Little Man Who Wasn't There
Gordons. Captive
    Make Haste to Live
    Ordeal
Griffiths, J. Dream House
Haring, D. Home Sweet Homicide
Harper, R. Death to the Dancing Masters
    Kill Factor
    Kinderkill
Hayes, J. M. Gray Pilgrim
Heath, C. When You Comin' Back, Range Rider
Hillerman, T. Blessing Way
    Listening Woman
Ives, J. Fear in a Handful of Dust
Janson, H. Accused
Jessey, C. Treasures of Darkness
Johnston, V. Voice in the Night
Kantor, Harry. Town That Saw No Evil
Kelland, C. B. Archibald the Great
    This Is My Son
Killoran, G. Willough Raven
Knight, C. Affair of the Painted Desert
Kuttner, H. Man Drowning
La Tourrette, J. Madonna Creek Witch
Leinster, M. Scalps
McCormick, C. Murder in Cowboy Bronze
McCurtin, P. Sun Dance Murders
MacDonald, W. C. Action of Arcanum
Millhiser, M. Michael's Wife
Moffat, G. Last Chance Country
Moore, L. Cold Waters
Murphy, W. B. Shooting Schedule
Myers, B. Evil Ever After
Names, L. D. Cowboy Conspiracy
Neban, H. Crucible of Courage
O'Hanlon, J. D. Murder at Horsethief
Olsen, D. B. Cat Wears a Mask
Page, J. Shoot the Moon

Pendleton, D. Arizona Ambush
    Border Sweep
    Orbiting Omega
    Run to Ground
Peters, Elizabeth. Summer of the Dragon
Platts, W. C. He and She on the B-Bar-B
Prather, R. S. Cockeyed Corpse
Ring, R. H. Peregrine Dream
    Telluride Smile
Robeson, K. Red Skull
    Stone Man
Rollins, W. Midnight Treasure
Roper, L. V. Death—As in Matador
Rossiter, J. Murder Makers
Rowan, D. Time of the Burning Mask
St. John, G. Death in the Desert
Savage, J. Shady Place to Die
Scherf, M. Banker's Bones
Sherwood, R. E. Petrified Forest
Simenon, G. Maigret and the Coroner
Siodmak, C. Donovan's Brain
Smith, M. C. Nightwing
Spicer, B. Long Green
Stein, A. M. Sun Is a Witness
Stratton, C. Rock!
Thomas, Augustus. Arizona
Tracy, D. Pot of Trouble
Trimble, L. Fit to Kill
    Love Me and Die
Wagner, Sharon. Satan's Acres
Waters, T. A. Centerforce
Webb, J. Make My Bed Soon
Whitney, P. A. Vermilion
Woodrow, W. Black Pearl

ARKANSAS (Ark. See also: South)
Campbell, Bethany. Roses of Constant
Cooper, Monte. Death Near the River
Giles, J. Plum Thicket
Ham, B. Ozark Payback
Herring, R. Hub
Hess, J. all 7 titles
Lambirth, F. Behind the Door
Lawson, W. B. Younger Brothers' Vow
McPartland, J. I'll See You in Hell
Madl, L. Sunny
Morgan, Speer. Assemblers
Morris, G. Delaney
Morris, Jim. Sheriff of Purgatory
Murray, M. M. Arkansas Ranger
Pendleton, D. Fiery Cross
Quinn, J. Kill Squad
Robeson, K. Crimson Serpent
Stirling, E. K. Sleepwalker

ATHENS (See also: Greece; Balkans; Crete;
    Macedonia)
Appleby, J. Captive City
Dekker, C. Venus Had Claws
De Lillo, D. Names
Doody, M. Aristotle Detective
Fenton, E. Double Darkness
Ferrand, G. Encounter in Athens
Fitzgerald, K. Dangerous to Lean Out
Greene, H. FSO-1
Highsmith, P. Two Faces of January
Hild, J. Barrabas Hit
Kenny, P. Tanagra Affair
Lowden, D. Boudapesti 3
Marlowe, D. J. Raven is a Blood Red Bird
Roberts, J. Judas Sheep
Smith, Don. Secret Mission: Athens
Stein, A. M. Body Search
    I Fear the Greeks
Tute, W. Matter of Diplomacy
Tzonis, A. Hermes and the Golden Thinking
    Machine

ATLANTA (See also: Georgia; South)
Anthony, Elizabeth. Ballet of Fear
Cook, T. H. Sacrificial Ground
Dennis, R. probably all 12 JH titles
Diehl, W. Sharkey's Machine
Dunne, T. L. Scourge

Settings Index

AUSTRALIA / 1221

Feegel, J. R. Dance Card
Ham, B. Atlanta Burn
Holden, G. Don't Go in Alone
    Down a Dark Alley
Hopkins, L. C. Candle
Keifetz, N. Welcome Sundays
Kennedy, Stetson. Passage to Violence
Lee, E. Queen Bee
Logue, J. Follow the Leader
Miller, Rex. Slice
Moore, H. F. S. Shed a Bitter Tear
Moore, R. A. Death of a Source
Pendleton, D. Dixie Convoy
Ramm, C. Atlanta Extreme
Sibley, C. Malignant Heart
Story, A. First Kill All the Lawyers
    Then Hang All the Liars
Stratham, F. P. From Love's Ashes
Webb, Sharon. Half-Life
Williams, P. L. Slow Dance in Autumn
Woods, Sherryl. Body and Soul

AUCKLAND (See also: Wellington; New Zealand)
Beam, F. Problem at Piha
Messenger, E. Growing Evil

AUSTIN (See also: Texas; Dallas; Houston; San
        Antonio; Southwest)
Sublett, J. Rock Critic Murders
    Tough Baby

AUSTRALIA (See also: Adelaide; Melbourne;
        Sydney; Solomon Islands; Tasmania)
Adams, F. all three titles
Adamson, B. Nice Day for a Murder
Ainsworth, P. Devil's Hole
Aldous, A. Danger on the Map
Aldridge, J. Sporting Proposition
    Untouchable Juli
Anonymous. Three L's
Ashe, G. Taste of Treasure
Atkinson, H. three titles
Atlee, P. Kiwi Contract
B. and R. Helen Elwood, the Female Detective
Backhouse, E. Death Came Uninvited
    Mists Came Down
    Web of Shadows
Ball, Duncan. Great Australian Snake Exchange
Barnard, R. Death of an Old Goat
Barrett, M. Gold of Lubra Rock
    Stranger in Galah
Barrett, R. G. Godson
Baynton, B. both titles
Beck, L. Tom Gerrard
Bedford, Randolph. Billy Pagan, Mining Engineer
Bennett, R. D. Shaft 235
Boldrewood, R. In Bad Company
    Miner's Right
    Nevermore
    Robbery Under Arms
Boothby, G. 8 titles
Boucher, B. Megawind Connection
Bradden, R. Gabriel Comes to 24
    Out of the Storm
Brennan, P. Razorback
Brent, M. Golden Urchin
Bridges, R. Alden Case
    Case for Mrs. Heydon
    Cloud
Brissenden, R. Poor Boy
Brown, C. Lover, Don't Come Back!
Brown, Hosanna. Death Upon a Spear
    I Spy, You Die
Bullivant, C. H. Hammer of God
Carlon, P. Crime of Silence
    Forty Pieces of Silver
Carroll, John. both titles
Carter, Nick. Day of the Dingo
    Executioners
    Outback Ghosts
Caswell, R. Scales of Justice
Clapperton, R. No News on Monday
    Sentimental Kill

Cleary, J. Justin Bayard
    Long Shadow
Clive, J. Barossa
Cook, K. Wake in Fright
Cornford, P. Outcast
Corrigan. M. Big Boys Don't Cry
    Big Squeeze
    Cruel Lady
Corris, P. Kimberley Killings
    Marvelous Boy
    O'Fear
    White Meat
Courtier, S. H. at least 20 titles
Crane, A. Bushman
Creasey, J. Toff Down Under
Crothers, J. Strange Luck Gully
D., R. Land of the Dawning
Dale, B. No Second Prize
Daniels, N. Operation T
Danvers, J. Living Comes First
Davis, Helen. "For So Little"
Dawe, C. Emu's Head
Dee, R. K. Mortgaged Years
De Fraga, G. Murder at the Cookout
    Murder by Wash of Light
De Weese, G. Charles Fort Never Mentioned
    Wombats
Denham, R. Minor Murder
Denton, K. Fiddler's Bridge
Dewhurst, K. McSullivan's Beach
Donovan, D. Out There
Dorrington, A. Children of the Cloven Hoof
Doyle, R. M. both titles
East, F. L. Snapdragon
East, M. Naked Country
Eden, D. Afternoon for Lizards
Elliott, P. Mystery of the Black Dagger
    Pay Out
    Trust the Police
Elliott, S. L. Careful, He Might Hear You
English, R. Wait 'Till Holly Comes
Farjeon, B. L. Golden Land
    Grif
Ferrars, E. Come and Be Killed
    Crime and the Crystal
Flower, P. at least 12 titles
Foote, T. V. My Weird Wooing
Foster, D. Blue Crochet Coathanger Cover
    Dog Rock
Francis, D. In the Frame
Garve, A. Boomerang
Gask, A. 7 titles
Gaunt, M. Moving Finger
Glaskin, G. M. Road to Nowhere
Glenning, R. Seven for Murder
Goode, C. E. Yarns of the Yilgarn
Gould, N. at least 6 titles
Grabs, C. Queensland Desperadoes
Graham, Nancy. both titles
Green, Evan. Alice to Nowhere
Hall, Richard. Costello
Hall, Rodney. Captivity Captive
Hall, Stuart. at least 17 titles
Hamilton, I. Man with the Brown Paper Face
Harding, W. J. Bright To-Morrow
Hardy, F. Yarns of Billy Borker
Haring, D. No Mink for a Shroud
Hawke, J. Under the Street Lamp
Hay, W. Mystery of Alfred Doubt
Hennessey, D. Australian Bush Track
    Caves of Shend
Hill, H. H. Spoil of the Desert
Hobart, R. Blood on the Lake
    Dangerous Cargoes
Hodge, H. Death in the Morning
Hornung, E. W. Boss of Taroomba
    Denis Dent
    Irralie's Bushranger
    Rogue's March
Howard, Tom. Beach-Front Murders
    Rim of Heaven
Hume, F. Madame Midas
Hunter, R. W. Innocent Savage
Idriess, I. L. Nemarluk, King of the Wilds

Infante, A. Death Among the Dunes
Innes, H. Golden Soak
Isaacs, G. Queen of the South
James, B. Loser Pays
Jay, C. Knife Is Dangerous
Jefferis, B. One Black Summer
    Solo for Several Players
    Wild Grapes
Jones, P. Johnny Lost
Jost, J. This Is Harry Flynn
Junor, C. Dead Men's Tales
Karlson, H. Atomic Death
Kelly, Vince. All Sorts
    Shadow
Keneally, T. Chant of Jimmie Blacksmith
    Fear
    Place at Whitten
Kensch, O. Murder Has Wings
    Time Has a Door
Kimmins, A. Lugs O'Leary
Krauth, N. Matilda, My Darling
Lambert, E. Ballarat
    Five Bright Stars
    Kelly
Lang, John. Botany Bay
    Forger's Wife
Leopold, K. My Brow Is Wet
Lindall, E. Gathering of Eagles
    Killers of Karawala
    Lively Form of Death
Lindsay, H. Murder at the Belle Vue
Little, C. Great Black Kanba
Livingston, N. Death in a Distant Land
Lloyd, V. Don't Tie Me Down
Lord, Gabrielle. Fortress
    Tooth and Claw
Ludwig, B. Whistle of Doom
Luigi, B. Cosmic Calamity
McCarter, J. Love's Lunatic
McCutchan, P. All-Purpose Bodies
McDaniel, D. Utopia Affair
Macdonald, J. M. Thunderbolt
MacDonnell, J. E. Doctor's Challenge
McGuire, F. M. Time in the End
MacKenzie, N. Three Steps to Murder
McShane, M. Ill Met by a Fish Shop on George
    Street
Madden, E. S. Craig's Spur
Martin, A. E. Bridal Bed Murders
    Common People
    Curious Crime
    Sinners Never Die
Martin, C. W. "Ubique," The Scientific Bushranger
Martin, L. W. Murder on Mount Capita
Mason, Colin. Copperhead Creek
Mather, A. Raid
    Tarantula Hawk
Meagher, A. E. Moving Finger
Michaelis, A. Ingram Intervenes
Moffitt, I. Death Adder Dreaming
Mooney, R. Blue Buckle
Morgan, P. Deadly Group Down Under
    Girl in the Telltale Bikini
Morton, A. Sport for the Baron
Mott, E. Silver Death
Murray, M. Right Honourable Corpse
Neville, M. at least 9 titles
Nicholls, R. A. Hemlock
Niland, D. Dadda Jumped Over Two Elephants
    Dead Men Running
Noonan, M. Magwitch
North, E. Nobody Stops Me
Nottingham, P. Wasted Pride
O'Hagan, J. Against the Grain
O'Reilly, J. B. Moondyne
Pascoe, B. Fox
Peel, C. D. Snowtrap
Perry, Roland. Faces in the Rain
Peters, G. Mark of a Buoy
    Twist of a Stick
Potter, J. Going West
Powell, S. H. Great Jade Seal
Praed, C. Outlaw and Lawmaker
Pratt, A. Golden Kangaroo

A

A

AUSTRALIA

Three Years with Thunderbolt
Wolaroi's Cup
Preston, A. Place of Many Stars
Preston, James. Axes of Hate
    Shattered Steel
Punshon, E. R. Earth's Great Lord
Rankin, J. L. Murder Pie
Renwick, P. Black Hogan Strikes Again
    Leatherface Lonergan Stakes a Claim
Richards, P. Our Spacecraft Is Missing!
Robertson, Andrew. The Kidnapped Squatter
Rothwell, U. Death on the Run
Rowe, J. Grim Pickings
Rudd, S. both titles
Russell, Arthur. Tragedy at Cumberland Park
Sabelberg, W. M. both titles
Sage, R. Record Mystery
St. Thomas, H. Night of the Long Shadows
Salter, E. There Was a Witness
    Voice of the Peacock
    Will to Survive
Sanders, Dorothy. Monday in Summer
Savarin, J. Waterhole
Sayers, C. E. Jumping Double
Schlunke, E. O. Village Hampden
Scott, G. F. Rider of Waroona
Singer, B. You're Wrong, Delaney
Smith, Spenser. Dead Don't Matter
Spence, A. Mystery of the Red Gum
Stevens, J. M. This Game of Murder
Streib, D. Down Under and Dirty
Stutley, S. J. Poisoned Glass
Thomes, W. H. Belle of Australia
    Bushrangers
    Gold Hunters' Adventures
Thompson, E. 6 titles
Thompson, S. L. Top End
Thynne, R. Boffin's Find
Tucker, J. Ralph Rashleigh
Upfield, A. W. all 34 titles
W., W. Detective's Album
Walker, T. Felonry of New South Wales
Walker, W. S. From the Land of the Wombat
    When the Mopoke Calls
Wallace, J. Invasion
    Millionaire Gangster
Waten, J. Shares in Murder
Watkins, A. Till the Dying Day
West, Charles. Funnelweb
West, Morris. Cassidy
White, O. Silent Reach
Wicking, G. W. Bales of Trouble
    Galleon's Gold
    Glory Box Mystery
Winn, P. Dead Innocent
    Fact X
    Postscript to Murder
Wood, Christopher. Dead Center
Woodhall, E. T. Kelly Gang
Wilson, Gar. Down Under Thunder
Workman, J. Contrabandits
Wright, A. Rogue's Luck
    Rung In
Yarborough, C. Murder on the Long Straight

AUSTRIA (See also: Vienna)

Albrand, M. Call from Austria
Ambler, E. Uncommon Danger
Beeding, F. Nine Waxed Faces
Blake, K. Night Stands at the Door
Bottom, P. Lifeline
Canning, V. Whip Hand
Carnac, C. Crossed Skis
Carr, G. Corpse in the Crevasse
    Lewker in Tirol
Caspary, V. Chosen Sparrow
Chance, J. N. Involvement in Austria
Christopher, J. Caves of Night
Coles, M. Basle Express
Cory, D. Dead Man Falling
Davison, J. Golden Torrent
De Villiers, G. Countess and the Spy
Dratler, J. J. Ducks in Thunder
Elliot, J. M. Danube Covenant

Esmond, H. Florian Signet
Fitt, M. Murder Mars the Tour
Gainham, S. Place in the Country
Gale, A. Angel Among the Witches
Gilbert, M. After the Fine Weather
Goddard, A. Vienna Pursuit
Goodman, G. S. Mysterious Abduction
Greene, H. "Mozart" Leaves at Nine
Groner, A. Lady in Blue
    Man with the Black Cord
Halliday, L. Smiling Spider
Hardt, M. Stranger and Afraid
Hely, E. Long Shot
Hennessey, D. Dis-Honourable
Hinxman, M. Sound of Murder
Kingsley, H. Hetty and other stories
    Mystery of the Island
Leather, E. Mozart Score
MacInnes, H. Above Suspicion
    Horizon
    Prelude to Terror
    Salzburg Connection
Magee, B. To Live in Danger
Meade, R. Danube Runs Red
Minton, P. Hand of the Imposter
Moore, Dorinne. Legacy of Emeralds
Neumann, R. Inquest
Patterson, H. Valhalla Exchange
Peters, Ellis. Horn of Roland
    House of Green Turf
    Will and the Deed
Pollard, A. O. Sinister Secret
Roberts, J. L. Dorstein Ikon
Rosenberger, J. Devil's Trashcan
Ross, Marilyn. Marta
Ross, P. Kreuzeck Coordinates
Ross, W. E. D. Forbidden Castle
Rowan, H. Snowfall
Salter, E. Once Upon a Tombstone
Steiber, R. High Castle
Stern, R. M. Kessler Legacy
    Merry Go Round
Stewart, M. Airs Above the Ground
Von Doderer, H. Every Man a Murderer
Wingate, J. Avalanche
Wolfe, E. Ice Castles
Yates, D. at least 9 titles
Yorke, M. Silent Witness

AZORES

Wheatley, D. They Found Atlantis

BAGHDAD (See also: Middle East, Mesopotamia)

Christie, A. They Came to Baghdad
Greenlee, S. Baghdad Blues
Griffith, Glyn. Fire Over Baghdad
MacKinnon, A. Assignment in Iraq
Wadham, R. Weekend in Baghdad

BAHAMAS (See also: Nassau; West Indies; Caribbean)

Abrahams, P. Pressure Drop
Bagley, D. Bahama Crisis
Carmichael, F. Double in Diamonds
Carter, Nick. Target Doomsday Island
    Trouble in Paradise
Chandler, B. Coral Kill
Cheyney, P. Dark Bahama
Connolly, R. Sun Place
Dark, J. Come Die with Me
    Invisibles
Derrick, L. Deepsea Shootout
Du Bois, W. Case of the Frightened Fish
Fleming, I. Thunderball
Ford, L. Bahamas Murder Case
Graves, R. L. Platinum Bullet
Halliday, D. Dolly and the Doctor-Bird
Heatter, B. Naked Island
Hess, K. Death Goes to the Bahamas
King, T. J. Noose of Red Beads
Perry, Ritchie. Holiday with a Vengeance
Q., J. Tournament
Upton, R. Dead on the Stick
Wilson, G. No Rules, No Referee

BALI (See also: Indonesia; Borneo; Djakarta; Java; New Guinea; Sumatra)

Conyn, C. Bali Ballet Murder
Fleischman, A. S. Danger in Paradise
Silliphant, S. Bronze Bell

BALKANS (See also: Albania; Bulgaria; Greece; Rumania; Macedonia; Turkey; Yugoslavia)

Ambler, E. Dark Frontier
    Judgment on Deltchev
Atlee, B. Black Feather
Barr, Peter. King of the Clouds
Barry, Jane. Conscience of the King
Betteridge, D. Balkan Spy
Dodge, D. Lights of Skaro
Farjeon, J. J. Black Castle
Haggard, W. Old Masters
Holt, Gavin. Irina
Linnell, G. Black Ghost of the Highway
Meynell, L. Dark Square
    Door in the Wall
    His Aunt Came Late
Oppenheim, E. P. Stranger's Gate
Peters, L. Cry Vengeance
    Out by the River
Pollard, A. O. Fifth Freedom
Poyer, J. Balkan Assignment
Reed, E. Maras Affair
Robeson, K. King Maker
Sherwood, J. Mr. Blessington's Plot
Swift, B. Mission Code: King's Pawn
Tokson, E. Cavender's Balkan Quest
Vickers, R. Lady of Kalamaria
Weir, D. Balkan Saga
Williams, D. Agent from the West
Williams, Eric. Borders of Barbarism

BALTIMORE (Balt. See also: Maryland)

Baylus, R. F. Midsummer Night's Murder
Berliner, R. Hiding Places
Bortner, N. S. both titles
Brandon, J. Tripwire
Cain, J. M. Enchanted Isle
Daly, C. J. Amateur Murder
Dykes, L. Choke Hold
Ford, L. Girl from the Mimosa Club
    Trial by Ambush
Gelb, A. L. Janissary
Grady, J. Just a Shot Away
    Razor Game
Grossbach, R. . . . And Justice for All
Harris, C. A. Macking Gangster
Harris, Cover. Going to St. Ives
McAfee, C. Climbing Tree
Morris, A. P. Cipher Detective
    Electro Pete, the Man of Fire
    Head Hunter
    Mark Magic, Detective
Papazoglou, O. Rich, Patient Slaughter
Pendleton, D. Baltimore Trackdown
    Friday's Feast
Strange, J. S. For the Hangman
Tracy, D. Criss-Cross
Warren, C. M. Deadhead
Williams, J. B. Dead Yet Living
    Under a Mask
    Vial with the White Powder
York, Rebecca. Life Line

BANGKOK (See also: Thailand; Far East)

Aarons, E. S. Assignment—Bangkok
Blackstock, C. When the Sun Goes Down
Campbell, Reginald. Bangkok Murders
Corrigan, M. Menace in Siam
Hall, Adam. 9th Directive
Kalish, R. Bloodrun
Mason, V. M. Secret Mission to Bangkok
Morse, E. Emerald Buddha
Noye, N. No City of Angels
Saul, J. R. Paradise Eater
Templeton, J. Yellow Hibiscus
Williamson, T. Technicians of Death
Wilson, Gar. Slow Death
Woolfolk, W. Thai Game

Settings Index

BARBADOS (See also: West Indies; Caribbean)
Coxe, G. H. Man Who Died Twice
    Moment of Violence
    Uninvited Guest
Fish, R. L. Green Hell Treasure
Haring, D. Nothing Counterfeit
Jepson, E. Hundred Thousand Guineas
Mole, W. Goodbye Is Not Worthwhile
Morgan, M. Darkness at Bromley Hall
Phillpotts, E. George and Georgina

BARCELONA (See also: Spain; Madrid; Canary Islands; Majorca)
Montalban, M. V. all 3 titles
Wilson, Barbara. Gaudi Afternoon

BEIRUT (See also: Lebanon; Middle East)
Alan, R. Beirut Pipeline
Bainbridge, C. Beirut Contract
Black, I. S. Journey to a Safe Place
Bradley, Michael. Blood Bargain
Carter, Nick. Turncoat
Creed, D. Travellers in an Antique Land
Cutter, J. Beirut Retaliation
Daniels, N. Operation N
Dukes, G. Draper Solution
Haworth, J. Rock of Refuge
Ignatius, D. Agents of Influence
Kramer, D. Blast Out in Lebanon
Mannin, E. Mission to Beirut
Mendels, O. Taste for Treason
Morell, J. Cry Lebanon
Morrison, Brian. Blood Brother
Norst, J. Delta Force
Pendleton, D. Beirut Playback
Stagg, J. Assignment in Beirut

BELFAST (See also: Ireland; Dublin)
Bass, M. Belfast Connection
De Villiers, G. Belfast Connection
Green, F. L. Mist on the Waters
    Odd Man Out
Holland, J. Prisoner's Wife
Moore, Brian. Lies of Silence
Power, M. S. Killing of Yesterday's Children
Rankin, I. Watchman
Seymour, G. Harry's Game
Shelley, M. Last Private Eye in Belfast
Thompson, David. Broken English

BELGIAN CONGO (Bel. Cong. See also: Africa)
Caillou, A. Congo War Cry
Canning, V. Black Flamingo
Greene, G. Burnt-Out Case
Head, M. Congo Venus
    Devil in the Bush
Hunter, R. W. Congo Mercenary Major
Iams, J. Body Missed the Boat
Kiefer, W. Lingala Code
Lejeune, A. Glint of Spears
Maggio, J. Company Man
Martyn, M. Stones of Enchantment
Pendleton, D. Ambush on Blood River
Tyler, W. T. Rogue's March
Wallace, C. H. Crashlanding in the Congo

BELGIUM (Belg. See also: Antwerp; Brussels)
Carter, Nick. Race of Death
Coles, M. House at Pluck's Gutter
    Not Negotiable
Kirk, L. Embassy Madonna
Kyle, E. Love Is for the Living
Stein, A. M. Bombing Run
Sturrock, J. Suicide Most Foul
Wheatley, D. Desperate Measures
White, Alan. Long Drop

BELGRADE (See also: Yugoslavia; Balkans; Macedonia)
Bickham, J. Tiebreaker
Bleeck, O. Protocol for a Kidnapping
Campbell, R. W. Honor
Rosenberger, J. Belgrade Battleground

BELIZE (See also: South America)
Coxe, G. H. Inside Man
    With Intent to Kill
Kenyon, M. Peckover Holds the Baby
Stivers, D. Shot to Hell
Westlake, D. E. High Adventure
Weyer, D. Assassin and the Deer

BERLIN (East and West. See also: Germany; Frankfurt; Hamburg; Munich)
Anonymous. Mysteries of Berlin
Baddock, J. Emerald
Bahr, J. Holes in the Wall
Baker, W. H. Rape of Berlin
Balling, L. C. Mallory's Gambit
Ballinger, B. S. Lopsided Man
Black, C. Death's Head
Brand, M. Phantom Spy
Buckley, W. F., Jr. Story of Henri Tod
Caine, J. Cold Room
Carter, Nick. Berlin
    Deadly Dove
    Tunnel for Traitors
    Under the Wall
Chaber, M. E. No Grave for March
    So Dead the Rose
    Splintered Man
Cleary, J. City of Fading Light
Coles, M. Green Hazard
    Not for Export
Davison, Geoffrey. Berlin Spy Trap
Dege, R. G. Decision in Berlin
Dekker, C. Murder Rides Express
    Nightmare at Noon
De Villiers, G. Checkpoint Charlie
Dobbs, M. Wall Games
Emmett, R. Beat a Distant Drum
Ferguson, J. Stealthy Terror
Fitt, M. Bulls Like Death
Flynn, Don. Suitcase in Berlin
Gainham, S. Cold Dark Night
    Tiger, Life
Hall, Adam. Berlin Memorandum
Haring, D. Darling Decoy
Hild, J. Agile Retrieval
Hughes, W. Inside Out
Hughes, Z. Adlon Link
Isaacs, S. Shining Through
Janson, H. Framed
Jones, R. P. Man Who Killed Hitler
Joseph, R. Berlin at Midnight
Kaye, M. M. Death Walked in Berlin
Kerr, Philip. March Violets
    Pale Criminal
Kerrigan, J. Phoenix Assault
Kirkwood, T. Quiet Assassin
Kirst, H. H. Twilight of the Generals
Knebel, F. Crossing in Berlin
Kotzwinkle, W. Seduction in Berlin
Lee, John. Thirteenth Hour
Lindquist, D. Berlin Tunnel 21
McEwan, I. Innocent
McGill, G. War Story
McGovern, J. Berlin Couriers
McQuoid, A. Puppet Masters
Marlowe, D. Dandy in Aspic
Marlowe, S. Drum Beat—Berlin
    Valkyrie Encounter
Miehe, U. Dead One in Berlin
Olshaker, M. Blood Race
Patrick, W. Blood Winter
Pickering, P. Blue Gate of Babylon
Raygor, L. Catherine's Twins
Revelli, G. Amanda in Berlin
Richards, D. Double Game
Romanes, J. Berlin Breakout
Saxon, P. Last Days of Berlin
Scholefield, A. Berlin Blind
Sherman, D. Prince of Berlin
Simmel, J. M. Sybil Cipher
Taylor, Frederick. Kinder Garden
Thayer, C. W. Checkpoint
Tiger, J. Superkill
Trembath, H. Murder in Berlin
Tucker, J. Blaze of Riot
Underwood, M. Unprofessional Spy
West, E. These Lonely Victories
Wilden, T. Exchange
Winnington, A. Berlin Epitaph
Winters, J. C. Berlin Fugue
Winward, W. Seven Minutes Past Midnight
Wiseman, T. Day Before Sunrise

BERMUDA
Ames, J. Fearful Paradise
    Shadow Across the Sun
Burnham, D. Last Act in Bermuda
De Blasis, C. Suffer a Sea Change
Denbie, R. Death Cruises South
Ford, F. Play with Matches
Garth, D. Bermuda Calling
Holding, E. S. Strange Crime in Bermuda
Hyde, C. Whisperland
King, C. D. Bermuda Burial
Leighton, F. As Strange a Maze
Mason, V. W. Castle Island Case
    Gracious Lily Affair
Patrick, Q. Return to the Scene
Sharp, W. Murder in Bermuda
Siller, V. Bermuda Murder
    Last Resort
Spikol, A. Physalia Incident
Thayer, L. Prisoner Pleads "Not Guilty"

BIRMINGHAM (See also: Alabama; South)
Cook, T. H. Streets of Fire
Field, B. Blood Relations

BOLIVIA (See also: South America)
Atlee, P. Irish Beauty Contract
Bainbridge, C. White Heat
Brierley, D. One Lives, One Dies
Carter, Nick. Bolivian Heat
    Operation Che Guevara
Cleary, J. Mask of the Andes
Derrick, L. City of the Dead
Dodge, R. Red Tassel
Hild, J. Barrabas Creed
Macao, M. Red Plague in Bolivia
Pendleton, D. Tropic Heat
Rockliff, B. J. Paydirt
Sage, D. Moon Was Red
Wolff, B. Hyde in Deep Cover

BOMBAY (See also: India; Calcutta; New Delhi)
Chettur, S. K. Bombay Murder
James, S. Stranglers of Bombay
Joshee, O. K. Mr. Surie
Keating, H. R. F. Dead on Time
    Iciest Sin
    Inspector Ghote Plays a Joker
    Sheriff of Bombay
Olbrich, F. all 3 titles

BORNEO (See also: Indonesia; Malaysia; Bali; Djakarta; Java; New Guinea; Sumatra)
Beecham, J. C. both titles
Black, G. You Want to Die, Johnny?
Cushman, D. Jewel of the Java Sea
Kyle, D. Green River High
MacLeod, R. Isle of Dragons
Snell, E. Crimson Butterfly
    Yu-Chi Stone
Wilkes-Hunter, R. Borneo Patrol

BOSTON (See also: Massachusetts; Cape Cod; Sumatra)
Aldyne, N. Canary
    Slate
    Vermilion
Bailey, F. L. Secrets
Banks, O. Rembrandt Panel
Barnes, L. J. Coyote
    Dead Heat
    Snake Tattoo
    Trouble of Fools
Barry, M. Boston Avenger

BOSTON

Behn, N. Big Stick-Up at Brink's!
Belfort, S. Lace Curtain Murders
Benjoya, M. Final Judgment
Benton, J. L. Art Treasure Murders
Bloom, J. Playing with Fire
Boyer, R. Billingsgate Shoal
    Daisy Ducks
    Moscow Metal
Brown, G. Murder on Beacon Hill
Bryson, M. Hitch-Hike Murders
Burgess, G. Two O'Clock Courage
Burke, A. D. Dead Wrong
    Driven to Murder
Byrd, M. Target of Opportunity
Capeto, I. Few Drops of Murder
Carleton, M. Cry Wolf
    Vanished
Carter, Nick. Revenge of the Generals
    Snake Flag Conspiracy
Casey, R. Jesus Man
Cheatham, L. Portrait of Emma
Coben, H. Play Dead
Coburn, A. Babysitter
    Off Duty
    Sweetheart
Coffman, V. Mistress Devon
Collins, E. G. C. Going, Going, Gone
Conant, S. Dead and Doggone
    New Leash on Death
Cook, R. Coma
Coolidge, E. L. Maine Girl
Cotton, W. Night Was Made for Murder
Coxe, G. H. 27 titles
Curran, T. All Booked Up
Curtiss, U. Second Sickle
Davey, J. Treasury Alarm
Dean, E. Murder Is a Collector's Item
    Murder Is a Serious Business
Derrick, L. Bloody Boston
Dobyns, S. Dancer with One Leg
Doolittle, J. Body Scissors
Eidson, B. Little Brother
Farrell, K. American Satan
Fenwick, E. P. Two Names for Death
Fitzsimmons, C. Crimson Ice
Forbes, S. Buried in So Sweet a Place
Fuller, T. Harvard Has a Homicide
    Reunion with Murder
    Three Thirds of a Ghost
Gill, Josephine. House That Died
Gillette, W. Astounding Crime on Torrington Road
Gillmore, I. H. June Jeopardy
Gillmore, R. Opal Pin
Gilmore, J. Blue Flame
Giroux, L., Jr. Rishi
Gladstone, E. Operation S.H.A.R.E.
Goldberg, M. Anatomy Lesson
Goldthwaite, E. K. Root of Evil
Green, T. J. Flowered Box
Greenan, R. H. 5 titles
Gresham, E. Lucifer Was Tall
Gutcheon, B. Still Missing
Hancock, H. I. Inspector Henderson
Haring, D. Left for Dead!
Hartman, D. Family Skeletons
Hatch, M. R. P. Berkeley Street Mystery
Healy, J. So Like Sheep
    Staked Goat
    Swan Dive
Heatter, B. Golden Stag
Heyman, E. L. Thomas Crown Affair
Higgins, G. V. 12 titles
Hirschhorn, R. Pride of Healers
Holt, W. Savage Snow
Hudson, J. Case of Need
Irwin, I. H. Body Rolled Downstairs
    Many Murders
    Murder Masquerade
    Poison Cross Mystery
Jones, C. R. Rum Row Murders
Juniper, A. Very Proper Death
Kelly, S. all 4 titles
Kimbrough, K. Kathrine, the Returned
    Susannah, the Righteous

Kinsley, L. Red-Light Victim
Klein, Z. Still Among the Living
Knight, K. L. Mortal Words
    Trace Elements
Knight, K. M. They're Going to Kill Me
Langton, J. Memorial Hall Murder
    Murder at the Gardner
Lathen, E. Something in the Air
Lawrence, Kelly. Gone Shots
Levon, F. Max Cat
Logan, M. Killing in Venture Capital
Lorimer, G. False Gods
McAleer, J. Coign of Vantage
McCloy, H. Burn This
    Question of Time
    Sleepwalker
McCurtin, P. Boston Bust-Out
McDonald, G. Confess Fletch
    Flynn
MacLeod, C. Family Vault
    Palace Guard
    Recycled Citizen
    Withdrawing Room
McNeil, J. Little Brother
Malcolm-Smith, G. Lady Finger
Martin, W. Back Bay
Martyn, W. Bathurst Complex
Masiello, J. Family Trouble
Matheson, D. Stray Cat
Merwin, Sam, Jr. Knife in My Back
Meyer, L. Paperback Thriller
Michaels, Grant. Body to Dye For
Minahan, J. Great Harvard Robbery
Montague, C. H. Written in Red
Morton, A. Branch for the Baron
Murphy, Gloria. Bloodties
    Play-Room
Murray, Lt. M. M. Dog Detective and His Young
    Master
Musello, D. Mystic Lakes
Neggers, C. Claim the Crown
Ness, T. T. Short of Murder
Nile, D. Terror at Deepcliff
Paisner, D. Obit
Palmer, M. both titles
Parker, R. B. 8 titles
Paul, Elliot. Waylaid in Boston
Pendleton, D. Boston Blitz
Philbrick, W. R. Ice for the Eskimo
    Paint It Black
    Shadow Kills
Quick, D. Fifth Dagger
Reeves, R. Doubting Thomas
    Peeping Thomas
Reid, J. Offering
Reynolds, J. L. And Leave Her Lay Dying
    Man Who Murdered God
Rivers, C. Indecent Behavior
Robinson, J. H. Boston Conspiracy
Rockwood, H. Clarice Dyke, the Female Detective
    Donald Dyke, the Yankee Detective
    Harry Pinkurten, the King of Detectives
    Nat Foster, the Boston Detective
Romano, D. Banacek
Rosen, R. Fadeaway
Rosen, S. Death and Blintzes
Ross, Clarissa. Gemini in Darkness
Ross, W. E. D. One Louisberg Square
St. John, N. Medici Ring
Saralegui, Jorge. Looker
Savage, E. H. Chronological History of the Boston Watch and Police
    Police Records and Recollections
Scarlett, R. all 5 titles
Schofield, W. G. Payoff in Black
Scott, Mansfield. Behind Red Curtains
Severy, M. Darrow Enigma
Shubin, S. Never Quite Dead
Silver, V. Death of a Radcliffe Roommate
Skehan, E. M. Bullet for Georgie
Smith, A. T. Death in the Cards
Smith, R. C. Secret Singing
    Wild Justice
Stackelberg, G. Double Agent

Stephenson, N. Zodiac
Storm, M. Cry, Tiger!
Story, W. Cemeteries Are for Dying
    Final Thesis
Tapply, W. 6 titles
Taylor, M. I. Man Who Awoke
Thomas, Dicey. Statutory Murder
Tilton, A. Beginning with a Bash
Waitt, I. Death a la King
Walker, W. Dime to Dance By
Wells, T. at least 9 titles
White, Ned. Very Bad Thing
Wolk, G. 400 Brattle Street
Young, A. Wicked Stepmother

BRAZIL (See also: Rio de Janeiro; South America)

Aarons, E. S. Assignment—Amazon Queen
Alexander, Jan. Bishop's Palace
Anthony, P. Amazon Slaughter
Benton, K. 24th Level
Brewer, G. Appointment in Hell
Caillou, A. Assault on Kolchak
Cameron, L. Girl with the Dynamite Bangs
Canning, V. Man from the Turkish Slave
Carter, Nick. Amazon
    Master Assassin
    Ten Times Dynamite
Charles, R. Three Days to Live
Deutsch, D. G. Bend in the River
Dourado, A. Bells of Agony
Fish, R. L. 5 titles
Fonseca, R. Bufo & Spalanzini
Footner, H. Scarred Jungle
Ghose, Z. Don Bueno
Gregor, P. Jump Into the Sun
Haring, D. Treasure Chest Girl
Hastings, Michael. Snake and the Arrow
Higgins, J. Last Place God Made
Kirk, L. Farm at Sante Fe
Leonard, C. L. Fourth Funeral
Leslie, P. Diving Dames Affair
Lindsay, D. T. Wings Over the Amazon
McCutchan, P. Screaming Dead Balloons
McDonald, G. Carioca Fletch
MacLean, A. River of Death
Middlemiss, R. Parrot Man
Mills, A. Gentleman of Rio
Murphy, W. B. Timber Line
Neilan, S. Braganza Pursuit
Norwood, V. Drums Along the Amazon
Pattinson, J. Petronov Plan
Pendleton, D. Blood Fever
    Blood of the Lion
Perry, Ritchie. Fall Guy
    One Good Death Deserves Another
    Presumed Dead
Ribeiro, J. U. Sergeant Getulio
Robeson, K. Death Green
    Ten Ton Snakes
Rosenberger, J. Mato Grosso Horror
Sarto, B. Tigress of Brazil
Sherman, D. King Jaguar
Spinelli, M. Assignment Without Glory
Stivers, D. Amazon Slaughter
Thackeray, K. Counterflood
Wilson, Gar. Amazon Strike

BRITISH GUIANA. See: Guyana.

BRITISH HONDURAS. See: Belize.

BRUSSELS (Brus. See also: Antwerp; Belgium)

Albrand, M. Meet Me Tonight
Babson, M. Fatal Fortune
Baker, W. H. Brussels Dossier
Bickers, R. Scent of Mayhem
Fennerton, W. Jensen Scenario
Gainham, S. Takeover Bid
Lambert, R. Monsieur Faux-Pas
May, P. Hidden Faces
Porter, Joyce. Kaleidoscope
Simenon, G. Lodger
Stonehouse, J. Ralph

Settings Index — CALIFORNIA / 1225

BUCHAREST (Buch. See also: Rumania; Balkans)
Household, G. Lives and Times of Bernardo Brown
Mason, V. W. Bucharest Ballerina Murders
Williams, V. Fox Prowls

BUDAPEST (Buda. See also: Hungary)
Aarons, E. S. Assignment—Budapest
Carter, Nick. Devil's Cockpit
    Ebony Cross
Fagyas, M. Fifth Woman
Frank, P. Affair of State
Gallico, P. Trial by Terror
Gielgud, V. Death in Budapest
Mason, V. W. Budapest Parade Murders
Melville, Alan. Danube Flows Red
Napier, M. Budapest Risk
Parker, Robert. Headquarters Budapest
Pickering, R. E. Himself Again
Rosenberger, J. Budapest Action
Sentjurc, I. Prayer for an Assassin
Sjowall, M. Man Who Went Up in Smoke
Tickell, J. Yolan of the Plains

BUENOS AIRES (Buen. A. See also: Argentina; South America)
Bruce, J. Live Wire
Cumberland, M. Which of Us Is Safe?
Denevi, M. Rosa at Ten O'Clock
Desmond, H. Doorway to Death
Heberden, M. V. Engaged to Murder
Kaplan, A. War of the Raven
Leonard, C. L. Sinister Shelter
McCurtin, P. Deadliest Game
Pollard, A. O. Deal in Death
Puig, M. Buenos Aires Affair
Romsey, P. Lidless Eye
Sage, D. 22 Brothers

BULGARIA (Bulg. See also: Balkans; Macedonia)
Braddon, G. Death Rings No Bell
Carter, Nick. Pursuit of the Eagle
Gilman, D. Elusive Mrs. Pollifax
Grey, A. Bulgarian Exchange
Gulyashki, A. Zakhov Mission
Haddad, C. A. Academic Factor
Hossent, H. Fear Business
Littell, R. October Circle
Orvis, K. Night Without Darkness
Pendleton, D. Battle Lines
Thompson, A. A. Message from Absalom

BURMA (See also: Far East)
Atlee, P. Star Ruby Contract
Becker, S. Blue-Eyed Shan
Blankenship, W. D. Tiger Ten
Carr, R. Love in Burma
    Red Tiger
Carter, Nick. List
Cleary, J. Forests of the Night
Cooper, Brian. Van Langeren Girl
Derby, M. Echo of a Bomb
Douie, M. Pointing Man
Eggar, A. Hatanee
Fielding, H. Palace Tales
Gilman, D. Incident at Badamya
Harvester, S. Dragon Road
Hild, J. Barrabas Fix
Johnston, G. H. Death Takes Small Bites
Kenmore, F. J. Southeast of Mandalay
Kilgore, A. Opium Eater
Lowis, C. C. District Bungalow
    Four Blind Mice
MacLeod, R. Cave of Bats
Macao, M. Rape of Sun Lee Fong
Marlowe, G. Burma Battle
Mason, V. W. Trouble in Burma
Mitton, G. E. Green Moth
Mundy, M. Pagan Pagoda
Nimse, G. Take What You Want
Pruitt, J. N. Burma Strike
Roberts, M. Mask for Crime
Rosenberger, J. Burma Probe
    Hell Wind in Burma

Savi, G. B. Last Lap
Wager, W. Blue Leader
Walker, Greg. Battle Zone
Ward, B. E. M. Viper's Vengeance
Wynd, O. Sumatra Seven Zero

CAIRO (See also: Egypt; Africa, North)
Brewer, G. Appointment in Cairo
Burke, L. J. Cairo Counterplot
Caillou, A. Alien Virus
Carter, Nick. Cairo Mafia
Corrigan, M. Baby Face
Dekker, C. Silence So Deadly
Evans, K. Oasis of Fear
Flagg, J. Woman of Cairo
Flett, A. Never Shake a Skeleton
Gough, L. Sandstorm
Heckstall-Smith, A. Man with Yellow Shoes
Hedges, S. G. Diamond Duel
Hocking, A. Nile Green
Hone, J. Private Sector
Jarvis, H. W. House of Silence
Kay, C. Thieves Fall Out
King, F. Raya
Kneale, B. Appointment in Cairo
MacGrath, H. Carpet from Baghdad
Manchester, W. Beard the Lion
Martyn, W. Cairo Crisis
Mason, V. W. Cairo Garter Murders
Mosley, L. O. Cat and the Mice
Pearce, M. all 3 titles
Rhodes, K. It Happened in Cairo
Robeson, K. Pharaoh's Ghost
Sheraton, N. Cairo Ring
Smith, Don. Secret Mission: Cairo
Stivers, D. Cairo Countdown
Tabori, G. Original Sin
Thorne, E. P. Chinese Poker
Tute, W. Cairo Sleeper
Wilson, Gar. Rim of Fire
York, A. Combination

CALCUTTA (See also: Bombay; New Delhi; India)
Abraham, C. S. Benjamin & Co.
Baker, W. H. Angry Night
Carter, Nick. Night of the Avenger
Collier, R. Pay-Off in Calcutta
Rushton, C. No Beast So Fierce
Sinclair, Fredric. Drop One, Carry Four
Tokson, E. Appointment in Calcutta

CALIFORNIA (Calif. See also: Los Angeles; Sacramento; San Diego; San Francisco; West)
Abercrombie, B. Run for Your Life
Adams, F. R. King's Crew
Adleman, R. H. Annie Deane
Adler, W. Madeline's Miracles
Ainsworth, E. Death Cues the Pageant
Alexander, Irene. Revenge Can Wait
Alexander, Jan. House at Rose Point
    House of Fools
Alexander, K. Private Investigation
Alexander, M. Birthmark of Fear
Allen, Anita. False Face of Death
Altman, T. Intruder
Alverson, C. Not Sleeping, Just Dead
Ames, L. House of Haddon
    Hungry Sea
Anderson, W. C. Penelope, the Damp Detective
Andrews, V. C. If There Be Thorns
Anonymous. Running Down a Double
Anthony, D. Organization
    Stud Game
Anzelon, R. Goblin Tree
Arden, W. Deal in Violence
Ardies, T. Palm Springs
Armstrong, C. 10 titles
Arthur, R. Somebody's Walking Over My Grave
Ashby, K. Climb a Dark Cliff
    Crown Valley
Ashe, G. Rabble of Rebels
Ashton, S. Santa Ana Wind

Babcock, D. V. Hannah Says Foul Play
Baker, M. Hilltop Murder
Ball, J. Cool Cottontail
Ballard, W. T. Murder Can't Stop
Barker, P. Carver
Barmby, C. James Cope
Barnes, L. J. Bitter Finish
Barns, G. M. Deadly Summer
Barry, J. E. Uranium Murders
Bass, M. Dirty Money
Bauman, C. Secret of Haverly House
Bechdolt, F. R. Mutiny
Beck, K. K. Murder in a Mummy Case
Benet, J. Private Killing
Bennett, R. A. Which One?
Bercovici, E. So Little Cause for Caroline
Berne, K. Bare Acquaintances
    Shock Value
Biggers, E. D. Chinese Parrot
    Keeper of the Keys
Birkley, D. both titles
Bishop, G. Apparition
Black, C. Wanting
Blankenship, W. D. Programmed Man
Bloomfield, R. 5 titles
Blunt, D. Dead Giveaway
Bocca, G. Fourth Horseman
Bonner, G. Taken at the Flood
Booth, C. G. Gold Bullets
    Murder at High Tide
    Sinister House
Borton, D. Kane
Boucher, A. Case of the Seven Sneezes
Bradbury, R. Death Is a Lonely Business
Bradfield, S. History of Luminous Motion
Bradley, Muriel. at least 4 titles
Braly, M. On the Yard
Braun, R. A. Murder, Four Miles High
Breen, J. L. Listen for the Click
    Loose Lips
    Touch of the Past
Brisco, P. Horror at Gull House
Brodeur, P. Stunt Man
Brown, Carter. at least 47 titles
Browne, W. D. Dew of Slumber
Bryant, D. Killing Wonder
Buchanan, J. D. Red Dog
Buckley, J. Beyond Murder
Burks, A. L. Tight Rope
Burnett, W. R. Cool Man
    Dark Hazard
    High Sierra
Busch, N. Titan Game
Byrne, R. Dam
Cadnum, M. Nightlight
Cain, J. M. Double Indemnity
    Mildred Pierce
    Past All Dishonor
    Postman Always Rings Twice
Caine, H. T. Carpenter, Detective
Cake, P. Pro-Am Murders
Cameron, E. E. Curse of the Casa Del Monte
    House on the Beach
Cameron, O. Catch a Tiger
    Fire Trap
    Silent One
Camp, William. Jacobs Park Killings
    Night Beat
Cardiff, S. Speaking Stones
Carey, Bernice. all 8 titles
Carrel, M. Case of the Innocent Witness
Carter, Nick. Red Rebellion
Caspary, V. Man Who Loved His Wife
Cassels, L. Bad Investment
Castle, F. Dead and Kicking
    Lovely and Lethal
Causey, J. O. Frenzy
    Killer Take All!
Chaber, M. E. Hangman's Harvest
Chalmers, S. Affair of the Gallows Tree
Chambers, P. probably all 18 titles
Chambers, W. Bring Me Another Murder
    Dead Men Leave No Fingerprints
    Once Too Often

C

1226 / CALIFORNIA

C

Chandler, R. 6 titles
Charteris, L. Saint to the Rescue
Chase, J. H. at least 20 titles
Chase, K. Where There's a Will
Chaytor, L. Course in Murder
Chesbro, G. Veil
Chester, P. Murder Forestalled
Cheyney, P. Dames Don't Care
Child, N. Murder Comes Home
Church, G. Race with the Sun
Chute, V. both titles
Clark, Dale. Death Wore Fins
    Narrow Cell
    Red Rods
    Run for the Money
Clarke, R. Murderers Are Silent
Clason, C. B. Murder Gone Minoan
    Poison Jasmine
Claudia, S. Madness at the Castle
Clement, H. Any Old Port in a Storm
    By Dawn's Early Light
Cleveland, J. Minus One Corpse
Clifton, B. Murder Specialist
Coffey, B. Voice of the Night
Colby, L. Touch of Evil
Collins, Mary. Dog Eat Dog
    Only the Good
Collins, Michael. Chasing Eights
Colter, E. Gull Cove Murders
Connor, K. P. Blood Moon
Conrad, B. Endangered
Conroy, Albert. Mr. Lucky
Cook, Bruce. Mexican Standoff
Cooper, P. J. Inheritance
    Restaurant
Correll, A. B. Murder Is an Art
Coulter, H. G. Death Comes to Casanova
Cousins, E. G. Weekend with Maxwell
Cox, I. E. Murder Among Friends
Craig, M. Flash Point
    Ten Thousand Several Doors
    To Play the Fox
    Were He a Stranger
Crane, F. Black Cypress
Crane, R. Tongue of Treason
Crawford, L. Ransom
Creasey, J. Blight
Crighton, R. E. Million Dollar Lift
Crowe, J. all 6 titles
Cullen, C. Don't Get Caught
Cunningham, C. Silent Murder
Currier, J. L. Cargo of Fear
Da Cruz, D. Double Kill
Daemer, W. Case of the Lonely Lovers
Daniel, J. Play Melancholy Baby
Daniels, D. Beaumont Tradition
    Castle Morvant
    Vineyard Chapel
Daniels, L. On the Run
Daniels, N. Rape of a Town
Davidson, J. Sex Cult Murders
Davies, Melissa. Face of Chalk
Davis, Gwen. Aristocrats
Davis, K. Words Can Kill
Davis, L. R. Threat of Dragons
Davis, N. Sally's in the Alley
Dawson, J. Kindred Crimes
Dean, Dudley. Lila My Lovely
Delacorta. Alba
Deming, R. Anything But Saintly
    Death of a Pusher
Dennis, R. C. both titles
De Puy, E. S. Hospital Homicides
    Long Knife
Derrick, L. Brotherhood of Blood
    Skyhigh Betrayers
De Sario, J. P. Sanctuary
Deutschman, D. Signals
Devon, G. Bad Desire
Dewey, T. B. Can a Mermaid Kill?
    Girl in a Punchbowl
    Girl with the Sweet Plump Knees
    Go, Honeylou
Dixon, H. V. 7 titles

Dodson, S. Sausalito
Dorrance, J. Fighting Hearts
Dowdell, D. K. Hawk Over Hollyhedge Manor
Drew, J. H. Edge of the Tightrope
Drummond, J. K. Thy Sting, Oh Death
    'Tis the Season to Be Dying
Dudgeon, R. My Price Is Murder
Dudley, O. all 3 titles
Duncan, D. Madrone Tree
    Shade of Time
Dundee, R. Inferno
Dunlap, S. Bohemian Connection
    Equal Opportunity Death
    Last Annual Slugfest
Dunne, D. Inconvenient Woman
Dunning, J. Looking for Ginger North
Durrant, T. Marble Forest
Du Soe, R. C. Devil Thumbs a Ride
Dyer, G. Three-Cornered Wound
Eberhart, M. G. Escape the Night
Eby, L. Velvet Fleece
Echard, M. Before I Wake
    Who Killed Frankie Leash?
Edgley, L. Fear No More
Egan, L. Case for Appeal
Eldredge, G. Murder in the Stratosphere
Elkins, C. Wicked Slice
Elliott, Richard. Master File
Ellis, J. B. Mysterious Dr. Oliver
Ellis, V. Death Comes Like a Thief
Engstrand, S. More Deaths Than One
    Sling and the Arrow
Ericson, L. Deadly Advice
Evans, John. If You Have Tears
Fair, A. A. 24 titles
Falk, L. Mystery of the Sea Horse
Farr, C. House of Secrets
    Sinister House
Farr, J. Lady and the Snake
Farrar, H. Murder Goes to School
Farrell, H. Such a Gorgeous Kid Like Me
Fay, D. Black Pearl of Passion
Femling, J. Backyard
    Hush, Money
Fickling, G. G. 5 titles
Field, P. Someone Is Watching
Fine, P. H. Troubled Waters
Finney, J. House of Numbers
    Night People
Fisher, S. Take All You Can Get
Fitzgerald, A. J. Pamela's Place
Fitzsimmons, C. One Man's Poison
    Tied for Murder
Fleischman, A. S. Venetian Blonde
Fletcher, D. Beyond Recall
Flynn, J. M. 7 titles
Fogelson, G. Jewel: Undercover Cop
Foley, R. This Woman Wanted
Forbes, J. D. Murder in Full View
Fox, J. M. Coven
    Wheel Is Fixed
Foxx, J. Wildfire
Francis, Robin. Button, Button
Franklin, K. Murder at Shirttail Flats
Fray, A. And Kill Once More
Freeman, K. W. Murder Sets the Pace
Frost, J. Warlord
Frost, J. V. Portrait in Black
Gamble, M. L. Diamond of Deceit
Gardiner, D. Transatlantic Ghost
Gardner, E. S. at least 15 titles
Garfield, B. Necessity
Garvin, R. M. FORTEC Conspiracy
Gates, H. L. Death Counts Five
Gault, W. C. 7 titles
George, P. Come Blond, Come Murder
    Cool Murder
Gilligan, R. Chinese Restaurants Never Serve
    Breakfast
    Live Oaks Also Die
Goddard, K. Alchemist
Goeney, W. M. Moment of Truth
Goldman, L. Fall Guy for Murder
    Tiger by the Tail

Goldman, R. L. Hartwell Case
Goldsmith, B. Blue Numbers
Goldstein, A. D. Nobody's Sorry He Got Killed
    You're Never Too Old to Die
Gordons. Big Frame
    Case of the Talking Bug
    Night After the Wedding
    Operation Terror
Gottesfeld, G. Blood Harvest
Goulart, R. 6 titles
Grafton, S. all 7 titles
Greenleaf, S. State's Evidence
Gregory, J. Emerald Murder Trap
    House of the Opal
    Maid of the Mountain
Gregory, Stephan. Frame Up
Gruber, F. Silver Tombstone
    Twilight Man
Hale, Jennifer. Secret of Devil's Cave
Hall, M. B. Emma Chizzit and the Queen Anne
    Killer
Hall, O. M. Murder City
    So Many Doors
Hall, R. L. Murder at San Simeon
Ham, B. Rolling Vengeance
Hammett, D. Dain Curse
    Red Harvest
Hammil, J. Limbo
Hammonds, M. OPEC Objective
Hankins, A. P. Cole of Spyglass Mountain
Hansen, J. 8 titles
Hansen, R. P. 6 titles
Harding, R. Bay City Burnout
Haring, D. Cool Ones
    Lady on a Short Fuse
    Little Big Shot!
Harrington, R. E. Seven of Swords
Harris, A. Baroni
Harriss, W. Bay Psalm Book Murder
Hart, Jeanne. Fetish
    Some Die Young
Hartman, D. Massacre at Russian River
Hastings, B. Demon Within
Hasty, J. E. Angel with Dirty Wings
Hawthorne, J. Golden Fleece
Hayes, R. Hungarian Game
Hayward, R. Trapped
Head, M. Smell of Money
Heard, H. F. Reply Paid
Heath, E. Murder of a Mystery Writer
Heath, M. 7 titles
Heller, M. So I'm a Heel
Henderson, M. R. If I Should Die
Hicks, H. B. Castle at Jade Cove
Himmel, R. Two Deaths Must Die
Hitchens, B. End of the Line
    Grudge
    Man Who Followed Women
Hitchens, D. 11 titles
Holden, A. Girl on the Beach
Holland, M. Fallen Angel
Homes, G. 8 titles
Hornsby, W. both titles
Houser, L. Lake of Fire
Houston, D. Shadows on the Moon
Houston, J. D. Continental Drift
Howard, Clark. Hunters
    Killings
    Mark the Sparrow
Howard, J. A. Death Audit
    Murder in Mind
Hubler, R. Chase
Hughston, D. You Stand Accused
Hurd, F. Nightmare at Mountain Aerie
Hutter, A. D. Death Mechanic
Hyman, J. Echoes
Ing, D. Blood of Eagles
Jackson, O. T. Dark Love, Dark Magic
Jason, S. Valley of Death
Jeter, K. W. In the Land of the Dead
Johnson, C. Clinic
Johnson, Diane. Shadow Knows
Johnson, G. Moon Country

Johnston, V. Flight to Yesterday
    Mourning Trees
Johnston, W. And Loving It
Judd, C. Jerusalem Camp
Kaminsky, S. M. Catch a Falling Clown
Kane. Model Killer
    Morgue the Merrier
    Murder in Striplicate
Kane, F. Esprit de Corpse
Katcher, L. Now Is the Time
Kaufman, P. Pandora
Keene, D. Dead in Bed
    Home Is the Sailor
    Live Again, Love Again
    Take a Step to Murder
Kelston, R. Murder's End
Kennealy, J. Polo in the Rough
Kent, F. House at Canterbury
Ketchum, J. Cover
Kinsburn, E. Wizard's Spyglass
Kirby, D. Death at My Heels
Kirsch, J. Bad Moon Rising
Kittredge, M. Murder in Mendocino
Knight, C. 15 titles
Koontz, D. R. Midnight
    Phantoms
    Vision
Kraft, G. Screwdriver
Krentz, J. A. Legacy
Lacy, E. Napalm Bugle
Lamb, J. J. Chinese Straight
Lambert, R. Piece of the Moon
Lambirth, F. E. Rivard House
Lamm, R. California Conspiracy
La Pierre, J. Children's Games
    Unquiet Grave
La Pointe, D. Flames Over the Castle
Larsen, G. D. Kilbourne Connection
    180 Degree Murder
Larson, C. Matthew's Hand
Lawson, W. B. Dalton Boys in California
Laymon, R. Funland
    Tread Softly
Lee, T. Monster of Lazy Hook
Leitfred, R. B. Corpse That Spoke
    Death Cancels the Evidence
Leslie, Jean. 6 titles
Levine, R. M. Bad Blood
Levinson, R. Playhouse
Lewellen, T. C. Billikin Courier
Lewis, E. Death and the Single Girl
    Here Today, Dead Tomorrow
Libby, A. F. Long Fast Ride
Lipke, K. Rain on the Roof
Lipsky, E. Devil's Daughter
Little, C. Blackout
Livingston, Jayson. Point Blank
Long, Jeff. Angels of Light
Lord, J. Sixty-Nine Diamonds
Lupoff, R. A. Comic Book Killer
Lynch, J. four titles
Lynds, D. Crossfire
Lyon, D. 7 titles
Lyons, A. At the Hands of Another
    Fast Fade
    Killing Floor
McAllister, A. L. House of Vengeance
McCall, J. J. Downbeat on a Debutante
McCall, L. L. On the Run
McConnell, F. Frog King
McCurtin, P. Vendetta
McDaniel, D. Dagger Affair
McDermid, F. See No Evil
McDonald, G. Confess Fletch
MacDonald, J. D. Green Ripper
Macdonald, J. R. Find a Victim
    Name Is Archer
MacDonald, P. Guest in the House
Macdonald, R. 11 titles
MacDonald, W. C. Gloved Saskia
McDowell, G. Reprieve of Roger Maine
McDonell, M. Althea
MacGowan, A. Who Is This Man?
MacKenzie, D. Kyle Contract

MacKenzie, J. A. Rahab Link
McKimmey, J. Run If You're Guilty
    Squeeze Play
    Winner Take All
MacLean, Alistair. Goodbye California
MacLeod, Ruth. Mendocino Menace
MacManus, Y. With Fate Conspire
McNamara, J. D. Blue Mirage
    Fatal Command
    First Directive
MacNeil, N. Death Ride
    Spy Catchers
McPartland, J. Big Red's Daughter
    Face of Evil
    Last Night
    Ripe Fruit
Mahannah, F. Broken Angel
    Golden Goose
    Stopover for Murder
    Yellow Hearse
Mainwaring, D. One Against the Earth
Makris, J. N. Nightshade
Mankiewicz, D. M. Trial
Mannon, M. M. all 3 titles
Manor, J. all 4 titles
Marble, D. Sail Into Silence
Marfield, D. Ghost on the Balcony
Marin, A. C. Storm of Spears
Mark, A. Ethical Man
Marks, H. K. Triad
Marlowe, D. J. Operation Drumfire
Marshall, R. Sucker Punch
Martell, C. Halsey and the Dead Ringer
    Halsey and the Fine Art of Murder
Mascott, T. Wife Who Ran Away
Mason, G. With Soul So Dead
Mason, R. Someone and Felicia Warwick
Masterton, W. 12 titles
Matera, L. Smart Money
Matheson, R. Stir of Echoes
Matthews, C. Dive Into Death
Mavity, N. B. 5 titles
Maxwell, A. E. Gatsby's Vineyard
    Just Another Day in Paradise
    Just Enough Light to Kill
Maybridge, S. J. Double for Danger
Mayfair, F. Over My Dead Body
Melchior, I. Marcus Device
Miles, Cassie. Handle with Care
Miles, J. Silver Bullet Gang
Millar, K. Three Roads
Millar, M. 10 titles
Miller, Marc. Death at the Easel
Miller, Wade. Girl from Midnight
    Kiss Her Goodbye
    Kitten with a Whip
Millhauser, B. Whatever Goes Up
Mills, Harry. Woman Stealer
Mitchell, Kirk. Black Dragon
Moeller, M. J. Scarlet Reckoning
Moffat, G. Rage
Moody, S. Penny Pinching
Morella, J. Ince Affair
Morgan, P. Death Car Surfside
Morrow, S. Rules of the Game
Morrow, W. C. Blood-Money
Muller, M. 5 titles
Murphy, M. Dangerous Legacy
Murray, W. Hard Knocker's Luck
    Tip on a Dead Crab
    When the Fat Man Sings
Nakagawa, K. S. Rendezvous of Mysteries
Nash, A. all 4 titles
Nash, J. R. Dark Fountain
Nava, M. How Town
Neely, R. 5 titles
Nelson, H. L. Island of Escape
Nichols, L. Twilight
Nickolae, B. Finders Keepers
Nielsen, H. 6 titles
Nielsen, V. both titles
Norris, K. Mystery House
    Secret of the Marshbanks
Nunn, K. Tapping the Source

O'Brien, S. Night of the Scorpion
    Shadow of the Caravan
Obstfeld, R. Brain Wave
    Dead-End Option
O'Connor, R. S. Murder Won't Wait
O'Farrell, W. Golden Key
    Gypsy, Go Home
Offord, L. G. Glass Mask
    Smiling Tiger
O'Hanlon, J. D. Murder at 300 to 1
Oksner, C. M. Burdens of Proof
Olsen, D. B. 12 titles
O'Malley, P. Affair of John Donne
    Affair of Jolie Madame
    Affair of the Blue Pig
    Affair of the Bumbling Briton
Oppenheimer, J. Rattlesnakes and Roses
O'Rourke, F. Private Anger, and Flight and Pursuit
    P's Progress
Oster, J. Rancho Maria
Ostrum, H. Three to Get Ready
Owen, D. Girl Possessed
    Juice Town
Packard, F. From Now On
Pagano, J. Condemned
Page, C. G. Mist Over Morrow Bay
    Secret of the East Wind
Page, M. Reclining Nude
Palmer, P. K. Turquoise/Yellow Case
Palmer, S. Omit Flowers
    Puzzle of the Pepper Tree
    Unhappy Hooligan
Pearce, G. Orphans
Pearson, R. Probable Cause
Pendleton, D. 5 titles
Perdue, V. Alarum and Excursion
    Singing Clock
Petievich, G. Quality of the Informant
Phillips, M. Death Spiral
Pilpel, R. H. High Anxiety
Platt, K. Princess Stakes Murder
    Pushbutton Butterfly
Pohlman, M. D. Problem of Virtue
Porter, R. N. Rest Hollow Mystery
Posard, C. Stranglehold
Potter, J. A. Talent for Dying
Prather, R. S. Ride a High Horse
    Slap Happy
Priestley, J. B. Doomsday Men
Pronzini, B. 9 titles
Queen, E. Madman Theory
    Room to Die In
Quentin, P. Puzzle for Fiends
Quinn, J. Silicon Valley Slaughter
Rabe, P. Kill the Boss Good-By
Race, P. Killer Take All
Radcliffe, J. Blackwood
Ranier, P. J. Scared Stiff
Rath, V. 7 titles
Ray, R. Hit Man Cometh
Rayter, J. Asking for Trouble
Reese, J. Looters
Reeves, Robert. Cellini Smith, Detective
Renn, C. Violent Air
Richardson, M. Portrait of Fear
Rico, D. Daisy Dilemma
    Nightmare of Eyes
Rigsby, H. As a Man Falls
    Calliope Reef
    Kill and Tell
    Lucinda
Ritchie, R. W. Deep Furrows
Roberts, W. D. at least 13 titles
Robertson, C. Red Chameleon
Robeson, K. 5 titles
Robinson, David. Confession of Andrew Clare
Rosellini, G. Deadly Intent
Rosenberger, J. Silicon Valley Connection
Rosenthal, N. C. Silenced Witnesses
Ross, Clarissa. Spectral Mist
Ross, Gene. Lady, Throw Me a Curve
    Two Smart Dames
Ross, J. A. Risky Pleasure
Ross, Morgan. Any Number Can Die!

C

1228 / CALIFORNIA

Ross, Paul. Dynamite Monster Boogie Concert
    Hitchhike Killer
    Valley of Death
Roszak, T. Dreamwatcher
Roudybush, A. Blood Ties
Ryan, Jenna. Suspended Animation
Ryder, S. Three on the Road
Ryerson, F. Seven Suspects
Sadler, M. Circle of Fire
St. John, G. Invisible Trap
Salas, F. What Now My Love
Sanders, G. Crime on My Hands
Sapir, R. Dr. Quake
Savage, M. Coach Draws Near
Sawyer, C. H. J. Alfred Prufrock Murders
    Murder in Gray and White
Saxby, C. Death Joins the Woman's Club
    Death Wore Roses
    Out of It All
Saxon, J. A. Half-Past Mortem
Scannell, D. Hood
Scarpetta, F. Torture Contract
Schenk, J. Caves of Darkness
Scott, Thurston. Cure It with Honey
Sears, R. M. Golden Sentinels
    Grangerfjord Monks
    Heir of Grangerfjord Castle
Shattuck, R. Half-Haunted Saloon
    Wedding Guest Sat on a Stone
Sheldon, W. J. Man Who Paid His Way
Sherman, P. J. Sleep off the Highway
Shippey, L. Girl Who Wanted Experience
    Where Nothing Ever Happens
Shriber, I. S. Last Straw
Silva, D. Come Thirteen
Simmons, M. K. Cameron Hill
    Diamonds of Alcazar
Simon, R. L. California Roll
Simonson, S. Larkspur
Simpson, C. H. Life in the Mines
Sims, L. V. Death Is a Family Affair
    Murder Is Only Skin Deep
    To Sleep, Perchance to Kill
Singer, S. Free Draw
    Spit in the Ocean
Siracco, S. Low Bite
Smith, L. R. Revolting Development
Smith, R. A. Keeper
Smoke, S. Trick of the Night
Snyder, Z. K. Heirs of Darkness
Spencer, J. both titles
Sprague, J. C. Dynasty of Fear
Stadley, P. Autumn of a Hunter
Stanton, K. Seek, Strike and Destroy
Steele, C. Yellow Scourge
Stein, A. M. We Saw Him Die
Stein, S. Resort
Stevenson, F. Dark Odyssey
    Ides of November
    Shadow on the House
Stivers, D. 7 titles
Stone, A. L. Julie
Strahan, K. C. Hobgoblin House
Streib, D. California Shakedown
Swanton, S. Sweetheart
Taylor, S. W. Man with My Face
Teilhet, D. L. Big Runaround
    Broken Face Murders
Telfer, D. Guilty Ones
Terhune, A. P. Black Gold
    Grudge Mountain
Thayer, L. 9 titles
Thomas, Ross. Chinaman's Chance
    Fourth Durango
Thompson, A. L. Love, the Sorcerer
Thompson, J. Nothing Man
Thornburg, N. Cutter and Bone
    To Die in California
Title, E. Face in the Mirror
Toombs, J. Fog Maiden
Trask, K. Dead Men Do Tell
Trimble, L. Cargo for the Styx
    Date for Murder
    Nothing to Lose But My Life
    Surfside Caper

Trott, S. Housewife and the Assassin
    Pursued by the Crooked Man
Tucker, W. Dove
Turney, C. Other One
Usher, J. both titles
Valentine, D. Unorthodox Methods
Vance, J. H. Fox Valley Murders
    Pleasant Grove Murders
Vernier, P. California Factor
Von Elsner, D. Pour a Swindle Through a Loophole
    Who Says a Corpse Has to Be Dull
Waddell, E. L. Murder at Drake's Anchorage
Wade, A. Isle of Peril
Wade, B. Pop Goes the Queen
Walker, Irma. Lucifer Wine
Wallace, D. R. Turquoise Dragon
Wallace, Patricia. Deadly Grounds
Wambaugh, J. Secrets of Harry Bright
Ward, E. C. Coast Highway 1
    Nice Little Beach Town
Warmbold, J. White Hand
Washburn, L. J. Wild Night
Waters, T. A. Lost Victim
    Psychedelic Spy
Way, I. S. House on Sky High Road
Wayland, P. Counterstroke
Webb, J. Damned Lovely
Welles, K. Gambler's Girl
Wells, S. Footsteps in the Air
    Murder Is Not Enough
    Witches' Pond
Werlin, M. Shadow Play
Werner, G. One Helluva Blow
Westheimer, D. Going Public
Weston, Garnett. Dead Men Are Dangerous
    Murder in Haste
White, L. Death Takes the Bus
Whitney, P. A. Emerald
    Flaming Tree
Whittington, H. Doomsday Affair
    One Deadly Dawn
Wilcox, C. Silent Witness
    Third Figure
    Watcher
Wilderness, D. O. Sinsation of a Sintury
Williams, B. Borderline Case
Williams, M. This House Is Burning
Wilmer, D. Dead Fall
Wings, M. She Came in a Flash
Winston, D. Death Watch
Winter, B. Night Was Made for Murder
Wissmann, R. Desert of Darkness
Wolf, J. Two Shadows for Death
Wolfe, S. Last Billable Hour
Wood, W. P. Gangland
    Rampage
Wormser, R. Invader
    Nice Girl Like You
Worth, C. Trail of the Serpent
Wuamett, V. Teardown
Wyka, F. Wishful Thinking
Zane, L. Brenda
Zannos, S. Trust the Liar

CAMBODIA (Camb. See also: Far East)
Ballinger, B. S. Spy at Angkor Wat
Carter, Nick. Cambodia
Casey, R. J. Cambodian Quest
    Four Faces of Siva
Hild, J. Rivers of Flesh
Lansing, J. Cambodia Kill-Zone
Pendleton, D. Cambodian Clash
St. John, David. Festival for Spies
Sandberg, B. Brass Diamonds
Wright, Wilbur. Carter's Castle

CANADA (Can. See also: Montreal; Ottawa;
    Toronto; Winnipeg; Vancouver)
Aeby, J. Pipes of Margaree
Allan, L. at least 18 titles
Anderson, A. Affair at Timber Lake
Anderson, I. all 7 titles
Apple, A. E. Mr. Chang of Scotland Yard
Arvonen, H. at least 6 titles

Bagley, D. Landslide
Bailey, Eric. Cradle's Revenge
Baird, T. Way to the Old Sailor's Home
Bennett, R. D. Sector 12
Bettany, G. Scarbrow
    Silent Mountain
    Villainy
Bindloss, H. Harden's Escape
Binns, O. Clancy of the Mountain Police
    Hazard of the Snows
    Lady of the North Star
    Trail of Adventure
Blankenship, W. D. Yukon Gold
Bonnamy, F. Man in the Mist
Boyd, A. No Man's Woman
Boyd, H. One Night of Murder
Brillant, J. M. Vision of Murder
Brown, Carter. Seven Sirens
Buchan, J. Sick Heart River
Burke, J. If It Weren't for Sex . . I'd Have to Get a
    Job
Cade, P. Death Slams the Door
Cahill, J. Flying with the Mounties
Campbell, Reginald. Policeman from Eton
Campbell, William. all 3 titles
Carleton, S. LaChance Mine Mystery
Carter, Alixe. No Tears for Peggy Perle
Carter, Nick. High Yield in Death
Case, R. O. Wings North
Cassells, J. Picaroon Goes West
Castle, J. Flight Into Danger
Chadwick, J. A. Enemy Outpost
Chalmers, J. W. Horseman in Scarlet
Clare, J. Passionate Invaders
Cocking, R. Die with Me, Lady
    Weep No More, Lady
Cody, H. A. Long Patrol
Connor, R. Corporal Cameron
    Patrol of the Sun Dance Trail
Craig, A. all 9 titles
Craig, John. If You Want to See Your Wife Again
    In Council Rooms Apart
Cresswell, M. Murder in a Road Gang
Cullum, R. at least 10 titles
Curwood, J. O. Philipp Steele of the Northwest
    Mountain Police
Cushing, E. L. Blood on My Rug
Dallas, J. Night of the Storm
Daniels, D. Jade Green
Dawson, C. Murder Point
Dean, A. Encounter with Evil
De Mar, P. Gnome Mine Mystery
Dennis, R. MacTaggart's War
Derrick, L. Deep Cover Blast-Off
    Mankill Sport
    Quebec Connection
Disney, D. C. 17th Letter
Dix, M. Flame of the Khan
Dixon, M. Special Delivery
Dobie, P. Pawn to Queen
Dorrance, E. Get Your Man
Dorrance, J. Long Arm of the Mounted
    Never Fire First
Douglas, L. W. Always Anonymous Beast
    Ninth Life
Douthwaite, L. C. at least 7 titles
Dutton, J. S., Jr. Underground
Dyker, B. Get Your Man
Eddenden, A. E. Good Year for Murder
Engel, H. 5 titles
Erskine, L. Y. 11 titles
Estey, D. Bonner Deception
Farr, C. at least 6 titles
Footner, H. 5 titles
Forrest, A. E. Silent Guests
Fossom, J. Cop in the CLoset
Foster, Marion. Monarchs Are Flying
Francis, D. Edge
Fraser, W. A. Blood Lilies
    Bulldog Carney
    Red Meekins
Fry, A. Revenge of Annie Charlie
Fry, P. Harsh Evidence
Garner, H. all 3 titles

Settings Index

Gatenby, R. Fugitive Affair
Gaunt, M. B. Leases of Death
Goodchild, G. 5 titles
Hagen, M. A. Dig Me Later
Hamilton, D. Interlopers
    Ravagers
    Terrorizers
Harcourt, P. Cover for a Traitor
Harris, J. N. Weird World of Wes Beattie
Hawkshaw. Benwell Mystery
Heald, T. Murder at Moose Jaw
Helwig, D. Old Wars
    Sound Lake Laughter
Henderson, J. Copperhead
Hendryx, J. B. most of the 58 titles
Higgins, D. W. Passing of a Race
Hill, H. Spectre Gold
Herron, S. Miro
Hyde, C. Icarus Seal
    Wave
Innes, H. Atlantic Fury
    Campbell's Kingdom
    High Stand
    Land God Gave to Cain
Janes, J. R. Watcher
Jardin, R. Devil's Mansion
Jason, S. Death Race
John, O. Disinformer
Johnson, L. Heads for Death
    Murder Began Yesterday
Johnston, Madeleine. Death Casts a Lure
Keirstad, B. S. Brownsville Murders
Kelland, C. B. Case of the Nameless Corpse
Kendall, R. S. both titles
Kennedy, M. Escape to Quebec
Kilgore, A. Canadian Killing Ground
Knox, A. Raider's Moon
Kyle, D. Raft of Swords
Lamb, J. J. Losers Take All
Lancaster, G. B. Law-Bringers
Lehner, A. P. When the Trail Calls
Lewis, R. Fenokee Project
Lincoln, V. Swan Island Murders
Lindblad, J. Zap Day
Little, P. Who Was He?
Longstreth, T. M. 8 titles
Lotz, J. all 3 titles
Lovelady, G. K. Beyond the Rim
Lovell, M. 5 titles
Lund, T. Murder of Dave Brandon
    Robbery at Portage Bend
    Weston of the Royal North-West Mounted Police
McClean, J. S. Aerie
McClintock, G. Wolves at Cooking Lake
McCoy, T. Treasure of the Yukon
McDonald, A. Black Deeds in Whitehorse
McFarlane, L. Agent of the Falcon
    Mystery of Spider Lake
    Snow Hawk
McKechnie, N. K. Saddleroom Murder
Mackie, J. Sinners Twain
McLeish, D. both titles
Macmillan, A. Mountie Patrol
Maling, A. From Thunder Bay
Marchant, B. Canadian Farm Mystery
    Mysterious Inheritance
Marlowe, G. Espionage!
Marshall, Robin. Campbell of the Mounties
Martin, I. K. Billions
Martyn, W. Death by the Lake
Marvin, S. Chateau in the Shadows
Merington, M. Searle of the Mounted
Millar, M. Air That Kills
    Fire Will Freeze
    Weak-Eyed Bat
Mitchell, Ken. Meadowlark Connection
Moffat, J. 8 titles
Moore, A. Royce of the Royal Mounted
Mott, L. White Darkness
Mounce, D. Shield Project
Mowery, W. B. 9 titles
Murray, W. L. Trail's End
Newton, D. Double Crossed

Nicole, Claudette. House at Hawk's End
North, J. River Rising
O'Donnell, L. Death Schuss
O'Grady, R. Bleak November
Olson, O. N. Mountie on Trial
O'Rourke, F. Concannon
Osborne, L. Keys of Hell
Packard, F. Hidden Door
    Sin That Was His
Parker, Gilbert. Northern Lights
    Pierre and His People
Paul, J. Oil by Murder
Peterson, G. Klondike Kalamity
Pollock, J. C. Centrifuge
Prichard, H. November Joe, the Detective of the Woods
Pronzini, B. Starvation Camp
Quogan, A. Fine Art of Murder
Reilly, H. Compartment K
Richard, S. Terror at Nelson Woods
Ridley, N., Jr. Stolen Nugget of Gold
Roberts, M. Prey of the Strongest
Robeson, K. 8 titles
Roper, G. G. Death on an Island
Ross, D. Out of the Night
Ross, Marilyn. at least 8 titles
Sandford, L. E. Wilson of the Mounted
Saxby, A. Comrades Three!
Scott, J. M. Unknown River
Shannon, D. Lodestar Legacy
Shaw, Stanely. Siren of the Snows
Shelley, S. Bowmanville Break
Shields, C. Swann
Shields, D. Just Before Dawn
Short, L. Barren Land Murders
Smiley, V. Cove of Fear
Smith, Christine. Murder Most Strange
Smith, F. A. Dragon's Breath
Smith, R. A. Kramer Project
Stark, R. Blackbird
Stead, R. J. C. both titles
Steele, H. all 7 titles
Stoddard, C. all 15 titles
Streib, D. Terror for Sale
Switzer, R. I Was Going Anyway
Templeton, G. both titles
Templeton, J. Dead or Alive
Terman, D. Free Flight
Thayer, L. Still No Answer
Thurley, N. Murder Strikes North
Tivey, T. B. Riddle of the Snows
    Trapline
Toombs, J. J. Restless Obsession
Treynor, A. M. all 4 titles
Vanardy, V. Up Against It
Van de Water, F. F. Havoc
Vermandel, J. G. Scratch a Lover
Vipond, D. Night of the Shooting Star
Walker, D. Black Dougal
    Mallabec
Walker, Rowland. Blue Ridge Patrol
Walters, L. Dead Reckoning
Wees, F. S. M'Lord, I Am Not Guilty
Weston, Garnett. Legacy of Fear
    Murder on Shadow Island
Weyman, R. C. Sherlock Holmes and the Mark of the Beast
Wheatley, D. Strange Story of Linda Lee
White, S. A. 9 titles
Whitney, J. L. H. Whisper of Shadows
Whitney, P. A. Feather on the Moon
Williams, V. Dead Man Manor
Winward, W. Judas Cloak
Wood, T. 6 titles
Wright, E. Body Surrounded by Water
Wright, L. R. Chill Rain in January
    Sleep While I Sing
    Suspect
Wynne-Jones, T. Odd's End
Yates, B. Dead in the Water
York, T. Trapper
Young, D. Agent Provocateur
Young, Scott. Murder in a Cold Climate
Zaremba, E. Beyond Hope

CARIBBEAN / 1229

CANARY ISLANDS (Can. Is. See also: Spain; Madrid; Barcelona; Majorca)
Atlee, P. Silken Baroness
Harding, R. Appointment in Tenerife
MacLeod, R. Legacy from Tenerife
Serafin, D. Port of Light
Walsh, J. M. Danger Zone

CAPE COD (See also: Boston; Massachusetts; New England)
Abbot, A. Creeps
Aldyne, N. Cobalt
Arnold, M. Cape Cod Caper
Barroll, C. Strange Place for Murder
Benson, B. Burning Fuse
Boyer, R. Billingsgate Shoal
Bramhall, M. Button, Button
    Murder Is an Evil Business
Buck, C. N. Portuguese Silver
Cameron, E. E. Place of Mischief
Carpenter, C. Sleight of Hand
Clark, M. H. Where Are the Children?
Damore, L. Cache
Diamond, F. Love Me to Death
Dickens, M. Room Upstairs
Farnsworth, M. Dark Wood
Farr, C. House of Treachery
Fitzsimmons, C. Death Rings a Bell
Forbes, S. Welcome, My Dear, to Belfry House
Foy, G. Asia Rip
Gresham, E. Puzzle in Paisley
Irwin, I. H. all 5 titles
Johnston, V. Phantom Cottage
Kiker, D. both titles
Kingsley, B. Black Angel
Knight, K. M. 14 titles
Lincoln, J. C. Out of the Fog
    Ownley Inn
Lockwood, M. Mystery at Lonesome End
McCaffrey, A. Mark of Merlin
MacIsaac, F. Wild Man of Cape Cod
McMullen, M. Dangerous Funeral
Mead, R. Moses Bottle
    Nightingale Trivet
Murphy, J. F. Quonsett
Ostrander, I. Island of Intrigue
    McCarty, Incog.
Parker, R. B. Promised Land
Phillips, Carey. Cape Cod Caper
Reilly, H. Double Man
Ross, Marilyn. Dark Stars Over Seacrest
Rossi, B. Muzzle Blast
Scott, J. D. Sea File
Shay, F. Murder on Cape Cod
Simmons, M. K. Captain's House
Stratton, R. Decorated Corpse
Taylor, P. A. 23 titles
Welles, E. Captain's Walk
Wiley, E. Death's Pale Face
Yates, M. Widow's Walk

CAPE TOWN (See also: South Africa; Johannesburg; Transvaal)
Creasey, J. Call the Toff
Drin, M. Signpost to Fear
Drummond, June. Black Unicorn
    Welcome, Proud Lady
Harris, P. Cry Hold!
    Letters of Discredit
Penrose, M. both titles
Richmond, M. Masked Terror
Scobie, A. Cape Town Affair
Stone, D. Too Deep Then

CARACAS (See also: Venezuela; South America)
Carter, Nick. Agent Counter Agent
Coxe, G. H. One Minute Past Eight
Guernsey, P. Angel Falls

CARIBBEAN (Carib. See also: West Indies; individual West Indies countries)
Arnett, J. Zaitech Sting
Arnold, S. J. Creole

CARIBBEAN

Atlee, P. Fer-de-Lance Contract
    Rockabye Contract
Atwood, M. Bodily Harm
Bagley, D. Wyatt's Hurricane
Ballem, J. Marigot Run
Barron, H. Big Score
Bell, Josephine. Wilberforce Legacy
Bingley, D. E. Caribbean Crisis
Black, I. S. Caribbean Strip
Blochman, L. G. Blow-Down
Boothby, G. Kidnapped President
Boylan, M. S. Passion of Gabrielle
Bretonne, A. M. Dark Talisman
Buchanan, J. D. Prince of Malta
Burnett, W. R. Widow Barony
Cade, S. Slade's Marauders
Caidin, M. Three Corners to Nowhere
Cairns, C. Great Gorme
Calmer, N. Avima Affair
Canning, V. Delivery of Furies
Carr, A. H. Z. Finding Maubee
Carter, Nick. Caribbean Coup
    Death Message: Oil 74-2
    Doctor Death
    War from the Clouds
Chaber, M. E. Gallows Garden
Chambers, W. Dry Tortugas
Charteris, L. Saint on the Spanish Main
Chesbro, G. Turn Loose the Dragon
Christie, A. Caribbean Mystery
Clifford, F. Hunting-Ground
Coffman, V. Curse of the Island Pool
    Enemy of Love
    Isle of the Undead
Conroy, Albert. Looters
Cotler, G. Mission in Black
Coulter, C. Impulse
Coxe, G. H. Barotique Mystery
    Woman with a Gun
Cronin, M. Caribbean Kidnap
    One Jump Ahead
Cutter, J. Big One
Daniels, D. Island of Evil
    Raxl, Voodoo Princess
    Strange Paradise
Daniels, V. Mendoza's Treasure
Darby, R. Death Boards the Lazy Lady
Dark, J. Black Napoleon
Davey, J. Murder in Paradise
Dickinson, P. Walking Dead
Dodson, D. B. Man Who Ran Away
Douglass, D. M. all 3 titles
Eberhart, M. G. House of Storm
Farr, C. Dark Citadel
    Heiress to Corsair Keep
    Mansion Malevolent
    Mansion of Menace
Fenisong, R. Ill Wind
Ferguson, N. Black Coral
Flagg, J. Paradise Gun
Fleming, I. Doctor No
Flynn, J. Viva McHugh
Forbes S. But I Wouldn't Want to Die There
    Don't Die on Me, Billie Jean
    Will and Last Testament of Constance Cobble
Fuller, W. Brad Dolan's Blonde Cargo
Garth, D. Thunderbird
Gilford, C. B. Dead Man Out
Granger, B. Hemingway's Notebook
Graves, R. L. Black Gold of Malverde
Grissom, K. Drop-Off
Halliday, B. Violence Is Golden
Hamilton, D. Intimidators
    Mona Intercept
Heatter, B. Devlin's Triangle
Herzog, A. Aries Rising
Hild, J. Barrabas Sting
Holding, E. S. Speak of the Devil
Holland, I. Kilgaren
Holt, Samuel. What I Tell You Three Times Is False
Hutton, A. Edge of the Deep
Jamieson, L. both titles
Johnston, R. Red Sky in the Morning
Kains, J. Curse of the Golden Skull
Kaiser, J. Black Pearl
Kauffman, R. W. Money to Burn
Key, S. A. Mark of Cain
Lauder, P. Noble Lord
Levin, J. Snow
Linscott, G. Whiff of Sulphur
Littlepage, L. Murder-by-the-Sea
Long, Duncan. Night Stalkers
Lyall, G. Shooting Script
McCloy, H. Goblin Market
McCray, M. Black Palm
    Blue Water Contract
MacDonnell, J. E. Caribbean Striker
McFather, N. Whispering Island
Mansfield, P. H. Final Exposure
Marlowe, D. J. Route of the Red Gold
Marlowe, H. Passage by Night
Marquand, J. P. Last Laugh, Mr. Moto
Mersereau, J. Corpse Came Ashore
Moore, Robin. Caribbean Caper
Mounce, D. R. Operation Cuttlefish
Mountford, A. M. Beneath the Night Sky
Moyes, P. Angel Death
    Black Girl, White Girl
    To Kill a Coconut
Muir, T. Death in Soundings
Mulholland, P. H. Calypso Murders
O'Donnell, L. Tachi Tree
Orenstein, F. Paradise of Death
Orgill, D. Ride a Tiger
Orr, M. Tejera Secrets
Page, C. G. Storm Clouds Over Paradise
Pendleton, D. Helldust Cruise
Perry, T. Island
Plantz, D. Marked for Death
Prather, R. S. Dead Man's Walk
Puissesseau, R. Someone Will Die Tonight in the Caribbean
Queen, E. Killer Touch
Reid, D. Caribbean Crisis
Rhys, J. Wide Sargasso Sea
Richards, P. President Has been Kidnapped
Robeson, K. Dagger in the Sky
    Mystery on Happy Bones
Robison, H. Rat Alley
Rohmer, S. Island of Fu Manchu
Rosenberger, J. Caribbean Caper
    Satan Strike
Ross, Philip. White Flower
Runyon, C. Color Him Dead
    To Kill a Dead Man
Sale, R. Not Too Narrow—Not Too Deep
Sandberg, P. L. King's Point
Sanders, J. Hat of Authority
Sapir, R. Voodoo Die
Saxby, C. Even Bishops Die
Schutz, B. M. Things We Do for Love
Sheckley, R. Calibre .50
Shelby, P. Tides
Sprechman, J. R. Caribe
Stanton, K. Cold Blue Death
    Evil Cargo
    Sargasso Secret
Stevenson, W. Booby Trap
Stivers, D. White Fire
Stone, N. at least 5 titles
Stribling, T. S. Clues of the Caribbees
Sugar, A. Enforcer
Tattersall, J. Damnation Reef
Tiger, J. Wipeout
Van Hearn, J. Don't Betray Me
Walker, M. Code Name Rapier
Weeks, J. Limbo Touch
Wells, T. Hark, Hark, the Watchdogs Bark
Westlake, D. E. I Gave at the Office
    Who Stole Sassi Manoon?
Wetherell, J. Maiden of Glory Island
Williams, A. Widow's War
Willis, T. Most Beautiful Girl in the World
Winthrop, W. Island of the Accursed
Woodhouse, M. Phil and Me
Zelman, A. Right Moves

CASABLANCA (Casa. See also: Morocco; Africa, North; Tangier)
Carter, Nick. Casbah Killers
    Safari for Spies
Corrigan, M. Madame Sly
Leopold, C. Casablack
Ross, Clarissa. Casablanca Intrigue

CENTRAL AMERICA (Cent. Am. See also: individual countries)
Ahern, J. Cocaine Run
Allende, I. Of Love and Shadows
Ash, W. Ride a Paper Tiger
Bostram, H. Pressure Point
Brand, N. Death in the Forest
Breckling, G. J. River of Fire
Carter, Nick. Death Squad
    Law of the Lion
    Mayan Connection
    Tropical Deathpact
Chantler, D. T. Capablanca Opening
Charles, C. A. Liar's Dice
Church, G. Bombs Burst Once
Coles, M. Dangerous by Nature
Crosby, J. Take No Prisoners
Fennell, G. Killer Patrol
Franklin, C. Trembling Thread
Gill, T. Jungle Harvest
Haring, D. Deal Me Out!
    Love Me and Die
Harris, Roger. L.S.D. Dossier
Hastings, Michael. Death Across the Tamagash
Hild, J. Barrabas Edge
Hilton, J. President's Agent
Holmes, D. C. Velvet Ape
Hough, S. B. Mission in Guemo
Keene, D. Flight by Night
Kilgore, A. Killer Genesis
    Slaughter Run
Koehler, R. P. Blue Parakeet Murders
    Salute to Murder
Levey, R. A. Dictators Die Hard
McCray, M. Death Machine Contract
MacKenzie, D. Night Boat from Puerto Vedra
Marin, A. C. Rise with the Wind
Morris, Jim. Silvernail
Owen, Richard. Nightmare
Pendleton, D. New War
    Rogue Force
Quinn, J. Mercenary Kill
Robeson, K. Golden Peril
    Headless Men
    Man of Bronze
    They Died Twice
Ronns, E. Passage to Terror
Stivers, D. Red Menace
Stone, R. Flag for Sunrise
Sydell, E. Diplomatic Immunity
Thomas, R. Missionary Stew
Thurston, R. For the Silverfish
Tippette, G. China Blue
Tolman, H. Hero by Proxy
Van Vors, B. L. End of the River
White, R. W. Sanibel Flats
Woolrich, C. Savage Bride

CEYLON (Cey.)
Aarons, E. S. Assignment—Ceylon
Beaty, D. Temple Tree
Christie, S. both titles
Creighton, J. A. Mask of Evil
Harvester, S. Moonstone Jungle
Hild, J. Butchers of Eden
Jones, H. L. Temporary A.S.P. Smith
Lambot, I. Come Back and Die
Leslie, J. Perahera
Sela, O. Portuguese Fragment
Stivers, D. Tech War
Wheatley, D. Dangerous Inheritance

CHANNEL ISLANDS (Chan. Is. See also: England)
Bonett, J. No Grave for a Lady
Bonfiglioli, K. Something Nasty in the Woodshed

Settings Index

Conway, J. D. Island of Fear
Ferguson, J. Death Comes to Perigord
Graham, J. Game of Heroes
Hardwick, Michael. Bergerac
La Garde, H. Tide Waits for No Man
Le Huray, C. P. Death for a Holiday
Patterson, J. M. Doubly Dead
Robinson, Derek. Kramer's War
Royce, K. Channel Assault
Saville, A. Bergerac and the Moving Finger
Seymour, Arabella. Dangerous Deceptions
Tickell, J. Appointment with Venus
Troy, S. Waiting for Oliver
Vane, P. Here Is the Evidence
Volk, G. Cliffs of Sark

CHARLESTON (See also: West Virginia; South Carolina; South)
Carr, J. D. Dark of the Moon
Clark, P. both titles
Edwards, Cassie. Love's Legacy
Fleming, T. F. Dreams of Glory
Ford, L. Road to Folly
Hayward, R. Soft Arms of Death
Long, L. B. House of the Deadly Nightshade
Macomber, D. Clearing in the Fog
Mitchell, I. Asylum
O'Farrell, W. Causeway to the Past
Robinson, Patricia. Something to Hide
Ross, A. B. Murder Cure
Sprinkle, P. H. Murder in the Charleston Manner

CHICAGO (Chi. See also: Illinois; Midwest)
Acre, S. Yellow Overcoat
Albert, M. H. Untouchables
Anderson, G. Sit-In
Anderson, G. C. . . . As They Do Unto Me
Anonymous. Mysteries of Chicago
Ashenhurst, J. World's Fair Murders
Ballinger, B. S. Body Beautiful
    Body in the Bed
    Portrait in Smoke
Balmer, E. Achievements of Luther Trant
    Breath of Scandal
    Dragons Drive You
    Keeban
Barry, Joe. Fall Guy
    Third Degree
    Triple Cross
Barry, M. Chicago Slaughter
Baynes, J. Meet Morocco Jones in the Case of the Syndicate Hoods
Belanger, C. Five Man War
Benson, C. Corpses Don't Kill
Benson, O. G. Cain's Woman
Blake, E. Jade Green Cats
Blank, M. Shadowchase
Bloch, R. American Gothic
Bonnamy, F. Death by Appointment
Booth, C. B. Mr. Clackworthy
Brod, D. C. Murder in Store
Brown, F. 8 titles
Browne, H. Pork City
Brunner, B. Face of Night
Bryson, L. Gloved Hand
Burnett, W. R. Goodbye, Chicago
    Little Caesar
    Silver Eagle
Burroughs, E. R. Efficiency Expert
    Girl from Farris's
Campbell, R. W. 7 titles
Capelli, A. Chicago Payoff
Carroll, C. Chicago
Carroll, J. Baby Killer
Carroll, Leslie. Blackmailer and the Blonde
Carroll, Loren. Wild Onion
Cashman, J. Gentleman from Chicago
Caspary, V. Evvie
Charteris, L. Call for the Saint
Christian, K. Death and Bitters
Churchill, J. Grime and Punishment
Clark, E. C. Fatal Element
Clason, C. B. Dragon's Cave
    Fifth Tumbler

    Man from Tibet
    Purple Parrot
Collins, M. A. 5 titles
Cook, B. Sex Life
Cormack, B. Racket
Cormany, M. Lost Daughter
    Red Winter
    Rich or Dead
Corne, M. E. Death at a Masquerade
    Magnet for Murder
Corrigan, M. Dumb As They Come
Craig, M. S. Gillian's Chain
    Third Blonde
Crump, P. Burn, Killer, Burn
Crunden, A. B. Chicago Winter's Tale
D'Amato, B. Hands of Healing Murder
    Hardball
Derrick, L. Computer Kill
    Inca Gold Hijack
Dewey, T. B. 10 titles
Di Pego, G. Keeper of the City
Dixon, M. Crime Wave
Donohue, H. E. F. Higher Animals
Eagle, J. Hoodlums
Eberhart, M. G. 6 titles
Eckert, A. W. Scarlet Mansion
Eden, R. Loot
Edwards, J. G. 6 titles
Elliott, W. J. Snatched Dame
Elrod, P. N. all 3 titles
Engleman, P. Catch a Falling Angel
Engling, R. Body Mortgage
Evans, John. Halo for Satan
    Halo in Blood
    Halo in Brass
Fairman, P. W. Glass Ladder
    Search for a Dead Nympho
Forbes, S. Sad, Sudden Death of My Fair Lady
Fox, G. R. Fangs of the Serpent
Fox, T. C. Cops
Fredericks. E. J. Shakedown Hotel
Freeman, M. J. Case of the Blind Mouse
    Scarf on the Scarecrow
Garfield, B. Death Sentence
Gash, Joe. both titles
Gettel, R. Twice Burned
Gillian, M. Warrant for a Wanton
Glasmon, K. Public Enemy
Gordon, W. Jim the Penman
Gordons. Case File: FBI
    FBI Story
Gorman, E. Murder in the Wings
Granger, B. El Murders
    Public Murders
Grant, M. Gangdom's Doom
Grecco, Johnny. Call Her Savage
Greeley, A. at least 7 titles
Greenburg, D. Philly
Greenlee, S. Spook Who Sat by the Door
Gregorich, B. Dirty Proof
Griffith, B. Time for Frankie Coolin
Gross, M. S. To the Dark Tower
Gruber, F. Gold Gap
    Leather Duke
    Navy Colt
    Scarlet Feather
Haas, J. L. Vendetta
Haring, D. Manhattan 5-6742
Harris, L. M. Pickled Poodles
Harrison, William. In a Wild Sanctuary
Hausfeld, R. Menace
Hawkins, O. Chicago Hustle
Hecht, B. Thousand and One Afternoons in Chicago
Heed, R. Ghosts Never Die
Herber, W. Death Paints a Portrait
    King-Sized Murder
Himmel, R. Beyond Desire
    I Have Gloria Kirby
    Rich and the Damned
    Twenty-Third Web
Hodges, C. G. Murder by the Pack
    Naked Villainy
Hoyne, T. T. Intrigue on the Upper Level

Izzi, E. 6 titles
James, F. Killer in the Kitchen
Janson, H. 34 titles
Jenkins, J. 12 titles
Jerome, O. F. Murder at Avalon Arms
    Red Kite Clue
Johnson, E. R. Cardinalli Contract
Johnson, M. C. Damned Trifles
Kahn, M. A. Canaan Legacy
Kaminsky, S. M. When the Dark Man Calls
    You Bet Your Life
Kantor, H. Big Stopper
Katz, M. J. Murder Off the Glass
Keeler, H. S. at least 16 titles
Keene, D. at least 6 titles
King, Ramona. Steal Away
King, S. Between Murders
Kisner, J. Slice of Life
Klasne, W. Street Cops
Klawans, H. L. Informed Consent
    Sins of Commission
Knebel, F. Convention
Lait, J. Put on the Spot
Latimer, Jonathan. Headed for a Hearse
    Lady in the Morgue
    Sinners and Shrouds
Laurence, R. Fast Buck
Le Jemlys. Lawyer Manton of Chicago
Levin, M. Compulsion
Linton, D. Enough Rope
    Kill and Desire
    Lips of Death
    Shrouds Are Cheap
Lloyd, W. Bergen Worth
Lore, P. Looking Glass Murders
    Murder Behind Closed Doors
Lorimer, G. Acquittal
Lynch, L. Against Odds
    Sealed Verdict
McConnell, F. D. Murder Among Friends
MacDonald, J. D. One Fearful Yellow Eye
McGivern, W. P. But Death Runs Faster
    Heaven Ran Last
    Matter of Honor
    Very Cold for May
McGraw, L. Hatchett
MacHarg, W. Blind Man's Eyes
    Indian Drum
Mackenzie, S. Assault!
    Sniper
McManus, J. Out of the Blue
Maling, A. Bent Man
    Dingdong
    Go-Between
    Lover and Thief
Markham, S. It's Not Easy to Die
Marshall, S. Some Like It Hot
Martins, R. Cinch
    Sandman
Masterton, G. Headlines
Mazzarro, E. Bootleg Angel
    Chicago Dateline
    One Death in the Red
Merwin, B. Girl and the Bill
Michaels, Barbara. Search the Shadows
Michaels, Jan. Into the Night
Miller, Rex. Slob
Morgan, Dean. Roston Outfit in Chicago
Nash, J. R. Crime Story
Nielsen, H. Gold Coast Nocturne
O'Donnell, S. Runaway Wife
Old Spicer. Three Finger Marks
Olesker, J. B. No Place Like Home
Ozaki, M. K. at least 6 titles
Paretsky, S. 6 titles
Parrish, R. Case and the Girl
Paulsen, G. Clutterkill
    Sweeper
Payne, W. Scarred Chin
Pendleton, D. Chicago Wipeout
    Killing Urge
    Save the Children
Peters, Bill. Blondes Die Young

CHICAGO

Pinkerton, A. F. Dyke Darrel, the Railroad Detective
    Jim Cummings
    Marked for Life
    Saved at the Scaffold
Plum, M. Killing of Judge MacFarlane
    Murder at the World's Fair
Postgate, J. W. Private Detective No. 39
Pruitt, A. both titles
Quill, M. 6 titles
Ramm, C. Chicago Assault
Raskin, E. Westing Game
Raymond, C. S. Men on the Dead Man's Chest
Razio, R. Blondie Beg Your Bullet
Rea, M. P. Compare These Dead!
    Curtain for Crime
    Death of an Angel
Rice, C. 10 titles
Richberg, D. Shadow Men
Robertson, Stephen. Blood Tells
    Decoys
    Handyman
Robeson, K. Sky Walker
Roeburt, J. Al Capone
    Mobster
Ronald, J. Murder for Cash
Rosemoor, P. Crimson Holiday
    Double Images
    Ticket to Nowhere
Rosenberger, J. Death Merchant
    Ninja Nightmare
Ross, Sam. He Ran All the Way
Russell, C. M. Case of the Topaz Flower
    Dreadful Reckoning
    Tiny Diamond
Saber, R. O. at least 8 titles
Saberhagen, F. Matter of Taste
Sapir, R. Union Bust
Sarto, B. Chicago Dames
Scarpetta, F. Mafia Wipe-Out
Scotland, J. Seventh Man
Shaw, Wade. Jewel of Desire
Sherer, M. W. Option on Death
Shura, M. F. Shop on Threnody Street
Simmons, J. Lamplighter
Slim, I. Trick Baby
Smalley, D. E. Stumbling
Smith, C. M. all 6 titles
Smith, Mark. Death of the Detective
Smith, T. L. Thief Who Came to Dinner
Spencer, R. H. Fifth Script
    Monastery Nightmares
    Missing Bishop
    Regis Arms Caper
Sprinkle, P. H. Murder at the Markham
Stark, Inspector. Western Ferret
Starrett, V. 5 titles
Storm, M. Chicago Terror
    Dame in My Bed
Straus, R. Pengard Awake
Strobel, M. Ice Before Killing
Sutton, R. Long Lines
Targ, W. Case of Mr. Cassidy
Thayer, J. S. Hess Cross
Theroux, P. Chicago Loop
Thomas, Ross. Porkchoppers
Thorne, P. Murder in the Fog
    Secret Toll
    Sheridan Road Mystery
    Spiderweb Clues
Tiger, J. Death Hits the Jackpot
Tine, R. Red Heat
Torrio, V. all 4 titles
Ullman, J. M. Good Night, Irene
    Lady on Fire
    Venus Trap
Van Sickle, V. A. Wrong Body
Vedder, J. K. Last Doorbell
Vinton, A. Mystery in Green
Von Hoffman, N. Organized Crimes
Wagoner, D. Man in the Middle
Walker, R. W. Burning Obsession
    Dying Breath
Wallace, E. On the Spot
Wallace, I. Golden Room

Waller, L. "K"
Warren, V. Runaround
Watkins, M. Chicago
Webster, H. K. Sealed Trunk
Weisman, J. Three Faces of Death
Welton, A. D. 27th Ride
Weverka, R. Sting
White, D. Southern Daughter
Whitney, P. A. Red Is for Murder
Wight, N. Death in the Inner Office
Williams, K. both titles
Wills, T. Mine to Avenge
Winski, N. Chicago Deathwinds
Wolfe, G. Pandora by Holly Hollander
Yastrow, S. Undue Influence
Zubro, M. R. Simple Suburban Murder
    Why Isn't Becky Twitchell Dead?

CHILE (See also: South America)
Boothby, G. In Strange Company
Breslin, P. Interventions
Carter, Nick. Inca Death Squad
Dekker, C. Femme Fatale
De Villiers, G. Death in Santiago
Dodge, D. Long Escape
    Plunder of the Sun
Fielding, J. Trance
Ganachilly, A. Whispering Death
Hudson, C. Final Act
Robeson, K. Man Who Shook the Earth
Schwartz, A. No Country for Old Men

CHINA (See also: Peking; Shanghai; Formosa; Hong Kong; Mongolia; Far East)
Aarons, E. S. Assignment—Manchurian Doll
Abdullah, A. Remittance-Woman
Aldridge, J. Statesman's Game
Ames, J. B. Emerald Buddha
Amor, P. F. People's Republic
Anne-Mariel. Rendezvous in Peking
Appel, B. Four Roads to Death
Ballinger, B. S. Chinese Mask
Barker, A. Dragon in Spring
Becker, S. Chinese Bandit
Black, G. Dragon for Christmas
Block, T. Skyfall
Bonavia, D. China Lovers
Boothby, G. Doctor Nikola
Brent, M. Moonraker's Bride
Caillou, A. Assault on Ming
Cannell, C. Guardian of the Cup
Carter, Nick. Defector
    14 Seconds to Hell
    Operation Starvation
    Red Guard
Cleary, J. High Road to China
Collins, G. Chinese Red
Comber, L. Strange Cases of Magistrate Pao
Cordell, A. Bright Cantonese
Creasey, J. Death in the Rising Sun
Crossen, K. F. Tortured Death
Dawe, C. Plotters of Peking
Derby, M. Echo of a Bomb
Ellinger, G. Ricksha Clue
Footman, R. China Spy
Garvin, R. M. Talbott Agreement
George, P. Commander-1
Gibbs, G. F. Vanishing Idol
Gilman, D. Mrs. Pollifax on the China Station
Gluck, S. Thieves' Honour
Hampshire, A. C. Dragon's Claws
Hardy, R. Wings of the Wind
Harknett, T. Crown: Bamboo Shoot-Out
Harvester, S. Shadows in a Hidden Land
Hebden, M. Killer for the Chairman
Hume, F. Mandarin's Fan
Hurd, F. China Silk
Hutton, M. Chinese Girl
Hyer, R. Riceburner
Johnson, S. Doomsday Deposit
Jones, Jack. Journey Into Death
Keck, M. Behind the Devil Screen
Kennedy, J. R. Chairman
Kilgore, A. China Bloodhunt

Lenton, D. Blue Mandarin
M—, Mr. Chest of Opium
Macao, M. Return of the Opium Wars
Mathews, F. A. Staircase of Surprise
Meagher, G. E. Tomorrow's Horizon
Mills, A. Escapade
Miln, L. J. Soul of China
Milton, N. D. China Option
Montalbano, W. D. Death in China
Mosher, J. S. Liar Dice
Nabarro, D. North from Singapore
Nathan, R. S. White Tiger
Neebel, R. Yunnan Terminus
Norman, James. all 3 titles
O'Grady, L. Lady Jane
Packard, F. Dragon's Jaw
Payn, J. By Proxy
Pendleton, D. Fastburn
    Hong Kong Hit List
Pentecost, H. Chinese Nightmare
Phillips, L. Split Bamboo
St. John, David. Mongol Mask
Sapir, R. Assassins Playoff
    Chinese Puzzle
Sheldon, W. J. Yellow Music Kill
Sherman, D. White Mandarin
Simon, R. L. Peking Duck
Sinclair, D. Temple Dogs Guard My Fate
Siris, P. Peking Mandate
Skoggard, B. China Hand
Starrett, V. Laughing Buddha
Sullivan, S. M. Super Man Chu
Taylor, Theodore. Body Trade
Teed, G. H. Murder in Manchuria
    Tiger of Canton
Teilhet, H. T. Assassins
Thomey, T. Flight to Takla-Ma
Thompson, S. L. Countdown to China
Thorne, E. P. Smith of Cheng Su
Trenhaile, J. Gates of Exquisite View
    Scroll of Benevolence
Van Gulik, R. 18 titles
Wallace, E. Tomb of T'sin
Wees, F. S. Last Concubine
West, K. House That Chak Built
Wheatley, D. Island Where Time Stands Still
Wilson, Gar. China Command
Yardley, H. O. Crows Are Black Everywhere

CHURCH
Anthony, M. D. Becket Factor
Birmingham, G. A. Hymn Tune Mystery
Byfield, B. N. Solemn High Murder
Gilbert, M. Close Quarters
Harpur, P. Serpent's Circle
Haymon, S. T. Ritual Murder
Heald, T. Unbecoming Habits
Holland, I. Death at St. Anselm's
Howie, E. No Face to Murder
Hughes, Babette. Murder in Church
L'Engle, M. Severed Wasp
Nash, S. Unhallowed Murder
Papazoglou, O. Sanctity
Prantera, A. Strange Loop
Rendell, R. Heartstones
Williams, David. Holy Treasure

CINCINNATI (Cin. See also: Ohio; Cleveland; Columbus; Midwest)
Clark, M. B. Model Corpse
DeBrosse, J. Serpentine Wall
Gilla, E. N. Cap and Gown for a Shroud
McCombs, R. L. F. Clue in Two Flats
Pyle, A. M. Murder Moves In
    Pure Murder
    Trouble Making Toys
Reston, J. Knock at Midnight
Valin, J. all 8 titles

CLEVELAND (Cleve. See also: Ohio; Cincinnati; Columbus; Midwest)
Ballenger, D. Blood for Breakfast
Bolton, R. L. Sleep with the Angels

Settings Index

Collins, M. A. Bullet Proof
    Butcher's Dozen
    Dark City
Dye, W. H. Devil's Cameo
Eastman, R. Pendulum
Foster, R. Laughing Buddha Murders
Haring, D. Murder Doll
Harrington, W. Trial
Livingston, M. J. Prodigy
MacDougall, J. K. Weasel Hunt
Martin, J. E. Flip Side of Life
    Mercy Trap
Martin, Robert. Key to the Morgue
    Sleep, My Love
Pendleton, D. Cleveland Pipeline
Rabe, P. Bring Me Another Corpse
Roberts, Les. Full Cleveland
    Pepper Pike
Shriber, I. S. Invitation to Murder
    Pattern for Murder
Tidyman, E. Line of Duty

COLOMBIA (Colom. See also: South America)
Browne, G. A. Green Ice
Carter, Nick. Plot for the Fourth Reich
Chacko, D. White Gamma
Cunningham, Chet. Colombia Crackdown
Daley, R. Faint Cold Fear
Graves, R. L. Platinum Bullet
Manrique, J. Columbian Gold
Pendleton, D. Line of Fire
Rosenberger, J. Mission Deadly Snow
Schmidt, Dan. Death Camp Colombia
Shervell, G. Killer Cola
Stein, A. M. Only the Guilty
Stivers, D. Fire and Maneuver
Wilson, Gar. Nightmare Merchants
Woods, Stuart. White Cargo

COLORADO (Colo. See also: Denver; West)
Adler, W. Natural Enemies
Allegreto, M. Night of Reunion
Barrett, W. Death of a Stranger
Beres, M. Sunstrike
Black, Campbell. Piper
Brandt, T. Run, Brother, Run!
Brett, Stephen. Some Die Hard
Burns, R. Avenging Angel
    Farnsworth Score
    Ground Money
Campbell, R. W. Plugged Nickel
Carter, Nick. Human Time Bomb
Chance, L. Cutting Edge
Chrysostom Society. Carnage at Christhaven
Clason, C. B. Blind Drifts
Cline, C. T. Quarry
Davidson, D. M. Catering to Nobody
Dean, E. Murder a Mile High
Derrick, L. Radiation Hit
Downing, W. Clear Case of Murder
Dramann, A. Last Victim
Dreher, S. Captive in Time
Dunning, J. Holland Suggestions
Dvorkin, D. Ursus
Earley, F. Moving Target
Edmunds, B. Beware the Crimson Cord!
Faust, R. Wolf in the Clouds
Forest, R. One Step Ahead
Franklin, K. High San Juan
    Silvercat
Gardiner, D. Lion in Wait
Guinn, W. Death Lies Deep
Halliday, B. Murder Wears a Mummer's Mask
Hamilton, D. Steel Mirror
Hawkins, E. H. Wellspring
Hill, A. H. Murder on the Mountain
Hinchman, J. Secrets in the Snow
Howard, J. A. I Like It Tough
Karr, Lee. Beware My Love
Karr, Leona. Falcon's Cry
    Treasure Hunt
Kimbrough, K. Unseen Torment
King, Stephen. Misery

Kruger, P. Bronze Claws
    Cold Ones
    If the Shroud Fits
    Weave a Wicked Web
Kunst, E. Mystery of Evangeline Fairfax
MacDonald, E. House at Gray Eagle
McGerr, P. Catch Me If You Can
Mayer, Suzanne. In for Life
Mechem, P. both titles
Mitchell, Sara. Walk in Deep Shadows
Moore, Barbara. Doberman Wore Black
Murphy, T. Aspen Incident
Nelson, H. L. 9 titles
Oliphant, B. J. Dead in the Scrub
    Unexpected Corpse
Overholser, S. Molly and the Gold Baron
Parker, M. Which Mrs. Torr
Parrish, R. Strange Case of Cavendish
Paulson, G. Murphy
Pearl, J. Time to Kill . . . A Time to Die
Pendleton, D. Colorado Kill-Zone
    Mountain Rampage
Perry, T. both titles
Rodell, V. Free-Lance Murder
Roderus, F. Rain Rustlers
    Video Vandal
Rowley, W. H. Concerto for Murder
Sandberg, P. L. Wolf Mountain
Saul, J. Creature
Saxby, C. Death in the Sun
Scherf, M. Always Murder a Friend
Schier, N. Death Goes Skiing
    Death on the Slopes
    Murder by the Book
Shovald, A. Kill the Competition
Stevens, Diane. Labyrinth
Stivers, D. Dead Zone
Taylor, J. R. Old Stonewall, the Colorado Detective
Thacker, C. G. Slalom to Terror
Thomas, C. Narrow Gauge to Murder
Tracy, L. Terms of Surrender
Vail, C. Porcelain Dolls Don't Bleed
Vaile, W. N. Mystery of the Golconda
Walker, Irma. Murder in 25 Words or Less
White, L. Operation—Murder
Whitney, P. Domino
Willoughby, L. D. Frontier Detective
Yaffe, J. Mom Meets Mer Maker
    Nice Murder for Mom

COLUMBUS (See also: Ohio; Cincinnati; Cleveland; Midwest)
McGrew, F. Taste of Death
Martin, Robert. Catch a Killer

CONGO. See: Belgian Congo.

CONNECTICUT (Conn. See also: New England)
Acheson, E. Red Herring
Aiken, R. Ghost Hunters
Armstrong, C. Unsuspected
Armstrong, M. Murder in Stained Glass
Avery, R. Fast Man with a Dollar
    Murder a Day!
Bachman, R. Thinner
Balmer, E. Five Fatal Words
Barber, W. A. Pencil Points to Murder
Barker, E. Cobra Candlestick
Blankenship, W. D. Brotherly Love
Blayne, S. Terror in the Night
Blizard, M. Conspiracy of Silence
    Late, Lamented Lady
Booton, K. Andrew's Wife
Boyers, B. White Mazurka
Brandel, M. Murder in the Family
Brennan, J. P. Adventures of Lucius Leffing
    Chronicles of Lucius Leffing
Bronson, F. W. Bulldog Has the Key
    Uncas Island Murders
Bronte, L. 6 titles
Brown, Carter. Murderer Among Us
    Sex Clinic
Burke, R. Here Lies the Body

CONNECTICUT / 1233

Caldwell, T. Late Clara Beame
Cambry, C. K. Personal
Carpenter, C. Peabody Experiment
Caspary, V. Bedelia
    Secret of Elizabeth
Cassidy, B. Corpse in the Picture Window
    Floater
Chambers, D. Some Day I'll Kill You
Coffin, C. Dogwatch
Collins, Michael. Nightrunners
Cores, L. Let's Kill George
Correy, L. Star Driver
Coxe, G. H. 7 titles
Crosby, L. Midsummer Night's Murder
    Too Many Doors
Curtiss, U. 8 titles
Dalton, P. Silent, Silken Shadows
Daly, E. Evidence of Things Seen
Daniels, D. House of Stolen Memories
    Lady of the Shadows
Dank, G. Friends Till the End
    Going Out in Style
Davis, J. R. Right to Die
Davis, L. R. Reference to Death
    Taste of Vengeance
Davis, T. Murder on Alternate Tuesdays
Dean, R. G. Murder by Marriage
    What Gentleman Strangles a Lady?
Dempsey, A. Red Falcons
Derrick, L. Animal Game
Disney, D. C. Death in the Back Seat
    30 Days Hath September
Disney, D. M. 31 titles
Dolson, H. all 4 titles
Drew, M. A. Diabolist
Du Bois, T. 5 titles
Du Bois, W. Case of the Haunted Brides
Duff, B. Ask No Questions
Dutton, C. J. Clutching Hand
Eberhart, M. G. Fighting Chance
    Murder in Waiting
Eichler, A. Moment for Murder
Eulo, K. House of Caine
Eyre, M. Presence
Fenisong, R. Jenny Kissed Me
Fenwick, E. Disturbance on Berry Hill
    Poor Harriet
Fischer, B. Bleeding Scissors
Foley, R. 11 titles
Footner, H. Murder Runs in the Family
    Whip-Poor-Will Mystery
Forbes, S. Bury Me in Gold Lame
Forrest, R. 9 titles
Gartland, H. Globe Hollow Mystery
Gatenby, R. Nightmare Chrysalis
Gerson, N. Special Agent
    State Trooper
Giles, G. E. Target for Murder
Glendinning, R. Ultimate Game
Goldthwaite, E. K. Scarecrow
Goulart, R. Even the Butler Was Poor
    Ghosting
    Graveyard of My Own
Grandower, E. Seaview Manor
Grant, C. L. Hour of the Oxrun Dead
Green, A. K. Chief Legatee
Green, Sharon. Haunted House
Greene, J. E. Bridge at Branfield
Guernsey, P. Unhallowed Ground
Haring, D. Killer for Kicks
    Kiss of Death
    Lovely But Cold
    Peel Me a Peach
Harnan, T. Signal for Danger
Harrington, W. Skin Deep
Hatch, M. R. P. Bank Tragedy
Hawk, J. House of Sudden Sleep
Hayes, J. Act of Rage
    Third Day
Hazeltine, H. Sable Lorcha
Heberden, M. V. Murder Cancels All Debts
    That's the Spirit
    Tragic Target
    Vicious Pattern

C

Highland, D. Death Is a Dark Man
Hill, K. both titles
Hintze, N. Listen, Please Listen
Holland, R. Danger on Cue
Homesley, L. Blondy's Boy Friend
Howarth, C. M. Eyes in the Night
Hunt, P. Murder Among the Nudists
    Murder for Breakfast
Iams, J. Corpse of the Old School
James, Rebecca. House Is Dark
Johns, V. P. Shady Doings
Johnston, V. Crystal Cat
Kahn, S. Mall
Kains, J. Witch's Tower Mystery
Kashner, R. Graceful Exit
Kelman, J. Prime Evil
Kendrick, B. Odor of Violets
King, C. D. Arrogant Alibi
Kirkpatrick, J. Woman at Dead Oaks
Kittredge, M. Dead and Gone
    Fatal Diagnosis
    Poison Pen
Klass, D. Night of the Tyger
Landon, H. Hands Unseen
Lanham, E. Death in the Wind
    Death of a Corinthian
    Double Jeopardy
    Six Black Camels
Lathen, E. Place for Murder
Lauferty, L. Hungry House
Leonard, C. L. Stolen Squadron
Letton, J. Incident at Hendon
Levin, I. Deathtrap
Lincoln, N. S. Secret of Mohawk Pond
Linzee, D. Death in Connecticut
    Housebreaker
Lippincott, D. Savage Ransom
Livingston, A. Trackless Death
Lockridge, F. Golden Man
Lockridge, R. Murder in False-Face
Lord, G. She Never Grew Old
Ludlum, R. Matlock Paper
Lynch, M. Creighton's Castle
McCloy, H. Changeling Conspiracy
    Long Body
    Two-Thirds of a Ghost
MacFadyen, V. Bittern Point
McGerr, P. For Richer, for Poorer
McHugh, F. Y. Bluethorne
    Shadow Acres
McMullen, M. Country Kind of Death
    Welcome to the Grave
McShea, S. Hometown Heroes
Mace, M. Headlong for Murder
Mack, C. K. Chameleon Variant
Mallet, A. House on Eagle Ledge
Marden, D. With Penalty and Interest
Mario, Q. Death Drops Delilah
Marlowe, S. Translation
Maxim, J. R. Bannerman Effect
Maxwell, H. K. Girl in a Mask
May, J. S. Devil of Dragon House
Mix, T. Question of Judgement
Murphy, W. B. Leonardo's Law
North, Gerry. Meet Gerry North
O'Neill, J. P. Mystic Policeman
Owen, P. Mystery of a Country Inn
Papazoglou, O. Once and Always Murder
Penfield, C. both titles
Pentecost, H. 9 titles
Philips, J. 9 titles
Pintoff, E. Zachary
Polan, M. L. Second Seed
Queen, E. Cop Out
    Inspector Queen's Own Case
Randolph, M. Breathe No More
Rathbone, R. A. Death in the Drawing Room
Reilly, H. 6 titles
Richard, S. Ashley Hall
Robeson, K. Red Moon
Rogers, J. T. Red Right Hand
Ronns, E. Catspaw Ordeal
    Gift of Death
Roos, K. Grave Danger

Ross, Clarissa. Glimpse Into Terror
Ross, Marilyn. Memory of Evil
Rowe, A. Up to the Hilt
St. John, G. Secret of Kensington Manor
Saunders, L. Devil's Den
Schneider, J. A. Darkness Falls
Seabrooke, J. P. Four Knocks on the Door
    Shadow Hall
Shane, S. Diamonds in the Dumpling
Siller, V. Complete Stranger
    Hell with Elaine
Simenon, G. Man on the Bench in the Barn
    Rules of the Game
Simpson, H. R. Rendezvous Off Newport
Skedgell, M. Farm Boy
Smith, Rosamund. Nemesis
Smithies, R. H. R. Shoplifter
Spear, E. G. Witch of Blackbird Pond
Steel, K. Imposter
    Judas, Incorporated
Stevens, F. She Left a Silver Slipper
Steward, D. Acupuncture Murders
Strange, J. S. Black Hawthorn
    Clue of the Second Murder
    Night of Reckoning
Sutton, H. Sacrifice
Taylor, H. B. Duplicate
    Triumverate
Tessier, T. Rapture
Thayer, L. 5 titles
Tibbles, G. Latest Mrs. Adams
Tracy, D. Death Calling—Collect
Travis, E. Under the Influence
Tryon, T. Night of the Moonbow
    Other
Tyler, E. Murder on the Bluff
Vance, L. J. No Man's Land
Walker, H. Case of the Missing Gardener
Wallis, J. H. Mystery of Vaucluse
Walton, G. L. Oscar Montague—Paranoic
Waugh, H. at least 17 titles
Waugh, M. Living Dead
Wells, Carolyn. 7 titles
Wells, T. How to Kill a Man
Weston, George. Wondering Moon
Wickham, H. Clue of the Primrose Petal
Wilde, P. 5 titles
Winslow, P. G. Cry in the City
Wolzien, V. Fortieth Birthday Party
    Murder at the PTA Luncheon
Wood, S. Murder of a Novelist
Woods, Stockton. Game Bet
    Laughing Man

COPENHAGEN (Copen. See also: Denmark;
    Greenland; Scandinavia)
Albrand, M. Nightmare in Copenhagen
Anker, J. Two Dead Men
Ardman, H. Endgame
Bodelsen, A. One Down
    Think of a Number
Heller, F. Emperor's Old Clothes
Kyle, E. Mirror Dance
MacLeod, Robert. Dragonship
Nielsen, H. Stranger in the Dark
Nielsen, T. Gallowsbird's Song
Oram, J. Copenhagen Affair
Peters, Elizabeth. Copenhagen Connection

CORSICA (Cors. See also: France; Marseilles; Nice;
    Paris; Mediterranean Island)
Anonymous. Columbia
Atkey, P. Juniper Rock
Buck, P. School for Slaughter
Deane, S. No Tears for the Dead
Grant, James. Island of Gold
Hammond, L. Life to Lose
Joseph, G. Needle in a Haystack
Newman, B. Death to the Spy
Philips, A. Girl Out in Corsica
Smith, Don. Corsican Takeover
    Secret Mission: Corsica
Swift, B. Mission Code: Granite Island
Welcome, J. Wanted for Killing

COSTA RICA (See also: Central America)
Goldman, J. A. Waldorf
Lantigua, J. Burn Season
Rathbone, J. Zdt
Roberts, Les. Costa Rica Chaos

CRETE (See also: Greece; Athens; Mediterranean
    Island)
Ayrton, E. Cretan
Hammond, M. Theseus Code
Hay, F. There Was No Moon
Highsmith, P. Two Faces of January
Palmer, J. Cretan Cipher
Stewart, M. Moon-Spinners
Swift, B. Mission Code: Minotaur
Yorke, M. Mortal Remains

CUBA (See also: Havana; West Indies; Caribbean)
Booth, C. G. Kings Die Hard
Boothby, G. Across the World for a Wife
Buchanan, J. D. Professional
Buckley, W. F, Jr. Mongoose, R.I.P.
    See You Later, Alligator
Catto, M. Banana Men
Dekker, C. Pin It on the Doll
Doliner, R. Orange Air
Dolph, J. Dead Angel
Duncan, Lee. Fidel Castro Assassinated
Fuller, W. Tight Squeeze
Hild, J. Eye of the Fire
Holden, L. Caribbean Conspiracy
Hunt, H. Whisper Her Name
Kent, A. Corpse to Cuba
Lewis, N. Cuban Passage
    Small War Made to Order
Mason, V. W. Yellow Arrow Murders
Mayer, E. E. Cobra Team
Null, G. Cuban Expedition
Richards, C. Gentle Assassin
Rosenberger, J. Castro File
Runyon, P. Night Jump—Cuba
Sanderson, D. No Charge for Framing
Taylor, C. D. Counterstrike
Terman, D. Shell Game
Thayer, J. S. Ringer
Underwood, J. Headlong
Walsh, P. E. Murder in Baracoa
Whittington, H. Rebel Woman
Willard, T. Bold Forager
Willets, G. Anita, the Cuban Spy
Yates, M. T. Death Sends a Cable

CYPRUS (See also: Mediterranean Island)
Appleby, John. Bad Summer
Bird, M. J. Aphrodite Inheritance
Blackstock, C. Mr. Christopoulos
Everitt, B. Cold Front
Gage, W. H. Appointment with Dishonor
Grant, Roderick. Private Vendetta
Haggard, W. Expatriots
    Protectors
Hocking, A. Night's Candles
    So Many Doors
Kaye, M. M. Death Walked In Cyprus
MacLeod, R. Property in Cyprus
Mather, B. With Extreme Prejudice
Nash, D. Not Yours the Island
Nicole, Claudette. Mistress of Orion Hall
Summerton, M. Ghost Flowers
Wills, C. M. Clue of the Golden Ear-Ring
Winch, A. Rape of Aphrodite

CZECHOSLOVAKIA (Czech. See also: Prague)
Blackstock, C. Encounter
Block, Lawrence. Cancelled Czech
Carter, Nick. Dubrovnik Massacre
Copp, D. Pursuit of Agent M
Davidson, L. Night of Wenceslas
Desmond, H. Hand of Vengeance
Littell, R. Amateur
MacInnes, H. Snare of the Hunter
MacLean, Alistair. Last Frontier
Paterson, N. Man on a Tight Rope

Pollock, J. C. Crossfire
Robeson, K. Shape of Terror
Ross, Philip. Talley's Truth
Ross, Regina. Face of Danger
Rushton, C. Bloody with Spurring
Sinclair, O. Bitter Sweet Summer
Skvorecky, J. Mournful Demeanour of Lieutenant Boruvka
Smith, Jonathan. Come Back
Stein, A. M. Finger

DALLAS (See also: Austin; Texas; Houston; San Antonio; Southwest)
Abshire, R. K. Dallas Drop
    Gants
    Turnaround Jack
Aubrey, E. Sherlock Holmes in Dallas
Banks, Joan. Death Claims
Carlton, M. Hot Oil
Clifton, G. Burn Sugar Burn
Coggins, P. Lady Is the Tiger
Crane, F. Flying Red Horse
Duncan, W. G. Cannon's Mouth
    Last Seen Alive
    Rafferty's Rules
Estes, C. C. Eavesdropping on Death
    Moon Gate
Gray, A. W. In Defense of Judges
Head, L. Terrarium
Jerina, C. Sweet Jeopardy
    Tall Dark Alibi
Lackey, M. Burning Water
Mathis, E. See No Evil
Miller, Rex. Stone Shadow
Mills, D. F. Dark Room
Moran, R. Dallas Down
Nisbet, J. Lethal Injection
Risenhoover, C. C. Wine, Murder, and Blueberry Sundaes
Rooth, A. R. Eye of the Beholder
Sanders, W. F. Whip Hand

DAMASCUS (See also: Syria; Middle East)
Arvay, H. Damascus Countdown
Dekker, C. Wink from a Witch
Kaplan, H. Damascus Cover
Leasor, J. Passport for a Pilgrim
Levy, Joseph. Operation Damascus
Vange, N. Spy in Damascus

DELAWARE (Dela. See also: South)
Brandt, C. Right to Remain Silent
Howard, H. Sleep for the Wicked
Poe, E. A., Jr. House Party Murders
White, L. Night of the Rape

DENMARK (Den. See also: Copenhagen; Greenland; Scandinavia)
Bodelsen, A. Consider the Verdict
    Straus
Eden, D. Shadow Wife
Elvestad, S. Case of Robert Robertson
Orum, P. Nothing But the Truth
    Whipping Boy
Rosenhayn, P. Joe Jenkins' Case Book
Rosenkrantz, P. Man in the Basement

DENVER (See also: Colorado; West)
Allegretto, M. Blood Stone
    Dead of Winter
    Death on the Rocks
Battin, B. W. Boogey Man
Burns, R. 7 titles
Cooke, William. Nemesis Conjecture
Cresswell, J. Charades
    Free Fall
Downing, W. 3 titles
Flynn, J. Bannerman
Janson, H. Lady, Mind That Corpse
Karr, L. Housesitter
Kimbrough, K. Twisted Cameo
McCaffrey, A. Stitch in Snow
McConnell, V. Double Daughter

Monson, B. Scorpion Sapphire
Montgomery, Y. Obstacle Course
    Scavengers
Orde, A. J. Death and the Dogwatcher
    Little Neighborhood Murder
Paulsen, G. Kill Fee
    Night Rituals
Ramm, C. Denver Strike
Spivey, A. J. Michael

DETROIT (Det. See also: Michigan; Midwest)
Allyn, D. Cheerio Killings
Barry, M. Detroit Massacre
Caval, P. Girls in Bondage
Clark, A. C. Crime Partners
    Death List
Effinger, G. A. Shadow Money
Estleman, L. D. 16 titles
Garnet, A. H. Santa Claus Killer
Goines, D. Dopefiend
Howes, R. Night of the Garter Murder
Jackson, J. A. all 3 titles
Janson, H. Kill This Man
Kantner, R. all 5 titles
Kienzle, W. X. all 12 titles
Lang, B. Crockett on the Loose
Lathen, E. Murder Makes the Wheels Go Round
Leonard, E. 6 titles
Litwak, L. Waiting for the News
Logan, T. all 4 titles
Marlett, M. Another Day Toward Death
    Death Has a Thousand Doors
Miller, D. T. Blood Link
Murphy, W. B. Blood Ties
Pendleton, D. Detroit Deathwatch
Q, J. Bunnies
Ramm, C. Detroit Combat
Rossi, B. Mafia Death Watch
St. George, M. Jigsaw
Santiago, V. J. Dead End Delivery
Smith, V. E. Jones Men
Weisman, J. Evidence
    Heroin Triple Cross
    Starlight Motel Incident

DISTRICT OF COLUMBIA. See: Washington D.C.

DJAKARTA (See also: Indonesia; Bali; Borneo; Java; New Guinea; Sumatra)
Carter, Nick. Judas Spy
    Time Clock of Death
Roberts, M. K. Jakarta Coup
Sloan, J. P. Last Cold-War Cowboy

DOMINICAN REPUBLIC (Dom. Rep. See also: West Indies; Caribbean)
Siller, V. Road

DUBLIN (Dub. See also: Ireland; Belfast)
Brady, John. Kaddish in Dublin
    Stone of the Heart
    Unholy Ground
Cleary, C. P. Death in the Life Department
Connolly, C. Voice
Dillon, E. Death in the Quadrangle
Easterman, D. Brotherhood of the Tomb
Fallon, A. C. Blood Is Thicker
Gill, B. Death of a Joyce Scholar
    McGarr at the Dublin Horse Show
Joyce, J. Off the Record
Lawton, C. Double Fix
Loraine, P. Dublin Nightmare
Lovell, M. Spy Who Got His Feet Wet
McGinley, P. Goosefoot
Perrin, R. Jewels
Queneau, R. We Always Treat Women Too Well
Redmond, L. Death Is So Kind
Stein, A. M. Shoot Me Dacent
White, W. J. One for the Road
Wilkinson, B. Run, Mongoose

DUTCH GUIANA. See: Surinam.

DUTCH WEST INDIES. See: Indonesia.

ECUADOR (Ecua. See also: South America)
Edwards, P. Valley of Vultures
Keitges, J. Dawn and Vengeance
Pruitt, J. N. Special Operations Command
Wallace, C. H. Tailwind to Danger

EDINBURGH (Edin. See also: Scotland; Glasgow; Hebrides)
Bramble, F. Strange Case of Deacon Brodie
Brett, Simon. So Much Blood
Claridge, Marten. Nobody's Fool
Crockett, S. R. Kid McGhie
Granger, B. November Man
Hely, E. Mark of Displeasure
Holt, V. Snare of Serpents
Hood, E. Wake for Donald
Kelly, M. Dead Man's Riddle
Kirk, R. Lord of the Hollow Dark
Knight, Alanna. Bloodline
    Deadly Beloved
    Enter Second Murderer
McCrumb, S. Paying the Tiger
M'Govan, J. all 7 titles
McGregor, I. Death Wore a Diadem
McKelway, S. C. Edinburgh Caper
M'Levy, J. Curiosities of Crime in Edinburgh
    Sliding Scale of Life
Mann, Jessica. Charitable End
Mitchell, G. My Bones Will Keep
Munro, H. Brain Robbers
Piper, P. Death in the Canongate
Rankin, I. Knots & Crosses
Ross, Angus. Edinburgh Exercise
Ross, Marilyn. Curse of Black Charlie
Stephens, R. Cruciform Mark
Swan, A. S. Mask of Gold

EGYPT (See also: Cairo; Africa, North)
Aarons, E. S. Assignment—The Cairo Dancers
Aldridge, J. I Wish He Would Not Die
Alter, R. E. Thieves Like Us
Barber, N. Women of Cairo
Beecher, W. Mayday Man
Boothby, G. Pharos, the Egyptian
Brown, W. F. Thursday at Noon
Caldecott, M. Son of the Sun
Christie, A. Death Comes As the End
    Death on the Nile
    Murder on the Nile
Cook, R. Sphinx
Cooper, C. Turkish Spy
Dekker, C. Cutie Cursed
    Lay Low, My Lovely
El Hakim, T. Maze of Justice
Elliott, Janice. Life on the Nile
Ellison, E. Tomb of Horror
Elsworthy, A. L. Death Glides In
Follett, K. Key to Rebecca
Garth, D. Eastward in Eden
Griffiths, A. Bid for Empire
Harrington, R. E. Aswan High
Harvester, S. Breastplate for Aaron
Hastings, M. Veiled Isis
Holden, J. R. Spider Flies Again
    Suez Patrol
    Suez Side Ace
Hymers, J. Utter Death
Jackman, S. Game of Soldiers
Jordan, D. Nile Green
Kabal, A. M. Adversary
Lange, J. Easy Go
    Last Tomb
Leader, C. Nightmare on the Nile
Leasor, J. Never Had a Spanner on Her
Leighton, T. Night of the Sphinx
McKinley, F. B. Death Sails the Nile
Mann, Jack. Egyptian Nights
Mann, Jessica. Death Beyond the Nile
Mastero Storyteller. Welcome to the Torture Chamber
Mundy, T. Mystery of Khubu's Tomb
Munslow, B. No Safe Road

Nelson, R. F. Dogheaded Death
Pape, G. Scorpion Sanction
Parsons, A. Death by the Nile
Peters, Elizabeth. 5 titles
Rathborne, S. Masked in Mystery
Rees, G. Secret of the Suez Canal
Rohmer, S. 6 titles
Sackville, O. Curse of Amen-Tah
Salisbury, C. Autumn in Araby
Sinclair, F. Drop One, Carry Four
Stevenson, F. House at Luxor
Sugar, A. Aswan Assignment
Taylor, P. W. Murder in the Suez Canal
Teed, G. H. Bottom of Suez
Van Ash, C. Fires of Fu Manchu
Walsh, J. M. King's Messenger
Weigall, A. King Who Preferred Midnight
Wheatley, D. Quest of Julian Day
    Sultan's Daughter
White, P. Cairo
Whittemore, E. Nile Shadows
Wilson, G. Aswan Hellbox
Wood, Barbara. Hounds and Jackals
Wynne, F. E. Mediterranean Mystery
Zorro. Gray Creatures

EL SALVADOR (See also: Central America)
De Villiers, G. Game of Eyes Only
Montalbano, W. Sinners of San Ramon
Roberts, M. K. Commando Squad
Rosenberger, J. Slaughter in El Salvador

ENGLAND (Eng. Here is a selection of books with
    English settings non-British authors. See
    also: next entry; Channel Islands; Isle of
    Man)
Alexander, Joan. One Summer Day
Allison, E. M. A. Through the Valley of Death
Allison, W. Alias Richard Power
    Turnstile of Night
Ambler, J. Hunters
Amey, L. Major Deception
Andrews, C. Affair of the Malacca Stick
Arnold, M. Toby's Folly
Asher, M. Black Wind
Astley, J. Fall of Midas
Atwater, J. D. Time Bomb
Austin, Alex. Salt and Pepper
Avallone, M. London, Bloody London
    One More Time
B. and R. Helen Ashwood, the Female Detective
Balmer, E. Waylaid by Wireless
Banner, M. Q37
Barry, N. Sherbourne's Folly
Batson, G. Gift of Murder
Baxt, G. Affair at Royalties
    Alfred Hitchcock Murder Case
Bell, Donna. Scandalous Miss
Bennett, E. D. Gower Court Manor
Bennett, J. M. Local Matter
Bennett, Janice. Haunted
Berckman, E. 11 titles
Bernard, R. Death Takes a Sabbatical
Bernard, T. Moonshadow Mansion
Biggers, E. D. Agony Column
Biggle, L., Jr. Quallsford Inheritance
Black, E. B. Ravenelle Riddle
Blair, A. Through the Eyes of Evil
Blaker, R. Jefferson Secret
Bleeck, O. Highbinders
Bloch, R. Jekyll Legacy
    Night of the Ripper
Bonner, G. Castlecourt Diamond Case
Borowitz, A. Jack the Ripper Walking Tour
    Murder
Boutell, A. Death Brings a Storke
    Tell Death to Wait
Bowker, R. Dover Beach
Boyer, B. H. Solstice Cipher
Boyer, R. L. Giant Rat of Sumatra
Bradley, M. H. Hanging Matter
Bradshaw, H. Pasha's Web
Brandner, G. London
Bristowe, A. Tunnel

Bronte, L. Lord Satan
Brookes, O. Gatherer
    Widow of Ratchets
Brooks, A. T. White Camellias
Brown, Carter. at least 6 titles
Brown, R. A. Sherlock Holmes and the Mysterious
    Friend of Oscar Wilde
Buchanan, P. Sounder of Swine
Buck, P. Death in the Castle
Buckley, W. F. High Jinx
    Saving the Queen!
Burt, M. Granville Crypt Murders
Burton, Anthony. Coventry Option
Byrd, M. Fly Away, Jill
Byrne, R. Tunnel
Cameron, S. Death in the House
    Late Gentleman
    Some Die Telling
Campbell, H. R. 5 titles
Campbell, Ramsey. Doll Who Ate His Mother
Carmichael, F. Night Is My Enemy
Carr, J. D. at least 29 titles
Carter, Nick. 6 titles
Cashman, J. Cook General
    Kid Glove Charlie
Caspary, V. Husband
Chapman, H. W. Limmerston Hall
Charles, I. Grenencourt
Chester, Sarah. Dancing on the Wind
Cheyney, J. Secret of Giltham Hall
Chimenti, F. Web of Allyngrood
Clark, Cecily. Ravensley Manor
Clark, G. Baroness of Bow Street
    Dulcie Blight
Clark, M. H. Anastasia Syndrome
Clark, Mark. Ripper
Claudia, S. Clock and Bell
Cleaver, A. Summerstorm
Clift, D. Spy in the House
Coffman, V. 8 titles
Coker, C. Balmoral Nude
Collins, R. Case of the Philosopher's Ring
Cooke, M. B. Clutch of Circumstance
Coppel, Alfred. Dragon
Crane, F. Applegreen Hat
Creighton, M. both titles
Crichton, M. Great Train Robbery
Crossen, K. F. Big Dive
Cummings, M. Royal Conspiracy
Cunningham, E. V. Assassin Who Gave Up His
    Gun
Curle, R. Who Goes Home?
Cutter, L. all 3 titles
Dall, J. Death of a Revolutionist
Damer, A. Too Lively to Live
Daniels, N. Magnetic Man
Darby, C. at least 14 titles
Davidson, T. L. Murder in the Laboratory
Davis, B. Trevena's Daughter
Davis, Mildred. Third Half
Davis, R. H. In the Fog
Dean, S. F. X. Ceremony of Innocence
    It Can't Be My Grave
DeAndrea, W. L. Snark
De La Torre, L. Detections of Dr. Sam: Johnson
    Dr. Sam: Johnson, Detector
    Elizabeth Is Missing
    Return of Dr. Sam: Johnson, Detector
Delving, M. 6 titles
Derleth, A. 11 titles
Devon, M. Miss Osborne Misbehaves
Dibdin, M. Last Sherlock Holmes Story
Dickson, Carr. Bowstring Murders
Dickson, Carter. 21 titles
Dirckx, J. H. Dr. Thorndyke's Dilemma
Disch, T. M. Prisoners
Dobyns, S. Man of Little Evils
Doherty, P. C. Death of a King
Domatilla, J. Last Crime
Donaldson, N. Goodbye, Dr. Thorndyke
Dorner, M. Freeze Frame
Drago, F. Devil's Church
Dunn, C. Gabrielle's Gamble
Eastvale, M. As the Sparks Fly

Eden, M. Conquest Before Autumn
Edwards, Anne. Survivors
Eliot, A. Return to Aylforth
Elkins, A. J. Murder in the Queen's Armes
Ellis, E. S. Eye of the Sun
Elmblad, M. Outrageous Fortune
Estleman, L. D. Dr. Jekyl and Mr. Holmes
    Sherlock Holmes vs. Dracula
Evans, C. L. Nemesis Wife
Exbrayat, C. Ravishing Idiot
Eyre, K. W. Monk's Court
Farmer, J. Sedona
Farmer, P. Legend of Piper's Hole
Fish, R. L. Gross Carriage of Justice
    Incredible Schlock Homes
    Memoirs of Schlock Homes
    Murder League
Fisher, Graham. Plot to Kill Wallis Simpson
Fiske, D. Bound to Murder
Fleming, H. P. Bloodline and Feathers
Fletcher, Jessica. Gin and Daggers
Flores, J. Hawkshead
Folliott, D. Signpost to Murder
Footner, H. Anybody's Pearls
Ford, J. M. Scholars of the Night
Fox, G. F. Terror Over London
Franklin, M. 5th of November
Fraser, F. L. Screaming Portrait
Friesner, E. M. Druid's Blood
Frome, D. 14 titles
Gallico, P. Too Many Ghosts
Galton, R. Spy with a Cold Nose
Garfield, B. Paladin
Garrett, Randall. Too Many Magicians
Garwood, J. Guardian Angel
Gay, V. Spy at the Gate
Gayle, N. Death Follows a Formula
    Sinister Crag
Gellis, R. Sing Witch, Sing Death
George, E. Great Deliverance
    Well-Schooled in Murder
Giroux, E. X. all 3 titles
Gluck, S. Great London Mystery
Gollomb, J. Girl in the Fog
Grant, M. Shadow Beware
Greene, M. Winter's Flame
Greenleaf, S. G. Three Knaves
Greenwood, L. B. all 3 titles
Grey, N. Foxglove Summer
Grimes, M. 10 titles
Grove, M. You'll Die Laughing
Guthrie, A. B., Jr. Murder in the Cotswolds
Hall, G. Silver Strand
Hall, R. L. Benjamin Franklin Takes the Case
    Exit Sherlock Holmes
    King Edward Plot
Halliday, F. Case of Indelicate Champagne
Hamilton, V. Traitorous Heart
Handler, D. Man Who Lived by Night
Hanshew, T. W. World's Finger
Hardy, L. Requiem for a Redhead
Hargrave, L. Clara Reeve
Haring, D. 5 titles
Harris, Marilyn. Bledding Sorrow
Hart, C. G. Settling of Accounts
Hartenfels, J. Doctor Death
Haughey, T. B. all 5 titles
Hawkes, E. Shadow of the Moth
Heard, H. F. Notched Hairpin
    Taste for Honey
Heberden, M. V. To What Dread End
Heller, F. London Adventures of Mr. Collin
Heller, K. all 3 titles
Henderson, B. Nikrova's Passion
Hershman, M. Target for Terror
Hesky, O. Life Sentence
Higgins, M. Changeling
    Unholy Sanctuary
    Witch Alone
Highsmith, P. Story-Teller
Hild, J. Barrabas Thrust
Hodel, M. P. Enter the Lion
Hodgson, A. Golden Ballast
Holland, I. De Maury Papers

ENGLAND

Holmes, N. Nobody's Fault
Holzer, H. Psychic Detective: The Unicorn
Howard, E. Murderer in the Garden
Howatch, S. at least 5 titles
Hubell, N. Adventures of Creighton Holmes
Huber, B. Death and the Dowager
Huff, T. E. Meet a Dark Stranger
    Nine Bucks Row
Hufford, S. Trial of Innocence
Hughes, Z. Fortress London
Hunt, Charlotte. Gemini Revenged
    Gilded Sarcophagus
    Lotus Vellum
Hurd, F. Curse of the Moors
    Rommany
    Secret of Awen Castle
Hynd, N. False Flags
Ind, A. Sino-Variant
Jackson, M. J. A. Punjat's Ruby
Janifer, L. M. Woman Without a Name
Jeffers, H. P. Murder Most Irregular
Johnston, V. Hour Before Midnight
Jorgensen, H. R. Red Lacquer Case
Kamm, D. Cliff's Head
Kary, E. Midnight Lace
Kauffman, R. W. Beg Pardon, Sir!
Kellerman, F. Quality of Mercy
Kelly, N. In the Shadow of King's
Kenney, S. Garden of Malice
Kent, E. Who?
Kilgore, A. Buckingham Blowout
Kilpatrick, S. Wake All the Dead
Kimbrough, K. Joanne, the Unpredictable
    Shadow Over Pleasant Heath
King, Alison. Dreamer, Lost in Terror
    Marcia, the Innocent
King, L. W. Rochemer Hag
Kingsbury, M. Beware the Fog
Klein, E. Blackmailer
Knott, F. Write Me a Murder
Kummer, F. A. Green God
    Web
Kurland, M. Death by Gaslight
    Infernal Device
Kyd, T. Cover His Face
La Barre, H. Blackwood's Daughter
Laker, R. Smuggler's Bride
Landon, H. 5 titles
Lange, J. Venom Business
Larsen, G. Dorothy and Agatha
Latham, L. Identity Crisis
La Tourrette, J. Previous Lady
Laumer, K. Afrit Affair
    Gold Bomb
Law, E. Sealed Knot
Layman, E. M. Airesboro Castle
Lee, Lydia. Magnificent Mirabelle
Lehmkuhl, D. Woman in the Moon
Lewis, Canella. Sensitive Encounter
Lientz, G. all 5 titles
Lindley, E. Brackenroyd Inheritance
    Devil in Crystal
Linzee, D. Belgravia
Litzinger, B. Watch It, Dr. Adrian
Livingston, W. Mystery of Burnleigh Manor
Lomas, G. R. Hostages
Lord, J. Bannerman Case
Luhrs, V. Longbow Murder
McCloy, H. Further Side of Fear
McDaniel, D. Rainbow Affair
McDowell, R. Wimbledon
McErlean, S. Mask of Silence
MacKay, A. M. Triad Conspiracy
McKnight, C. Gravetide
McMullen, M. Grave Without Flowers
    Pimlico Plot
    Something of the Night
Madden, A. W. Amberley Diamonds
Maling, A. Rheingold Route
Mann, P. Steal Big
Markham, V. 6 titles
Marlow, E. Falconridge
    Lady at Lyon House
    Master of Phoenix Hall
    Midnight at Mallyncourt

Martin, K. Vanessa
Mason, C. B. Deadly Impulse
Matthias, L. A. Pandora Plague
Merrell, B. Sign of Death
Meyer, N. West End Horror
Michaels, B. 5 titles
Miller, Lanora. Quickthorn
Mitchelson, A. Earthquake Machine
    Hellbirds
Moffett, C. Bishop's Purse
Mooney, J. Trail of the Barrow
Moore, Robin. London Switch
Morton, P. Province of Darkness
Muller, M. There Hangs the Knife
Mullin, A. Spy
Murray, P. Free Agent
Nelson, C. M. Barren Harvest
Nichols, S. House of Rancour
    Silsby
Noone, E. Daughter of Darkness
Norman, Elizabeth. Castle Cloud
    If the Reaper Ride
O'Grady, L. Artist's Daughter
O'Grady, R. Pippin's Journal
Olden, M. Golden Kill
O'Neill, A. High Bid for Murder
Oram, J. Stone-Cold Dead in the Market Affair
Orde, L. Eagles
    Heritage
Paar, A. Watcher in the Garden
Palmer, S. Adventure of the Marked Man
    Puzzle of the Silver Persian
Parker, Beatrice. Betrayal at Blackcrest
    Come to Castlemoor
Parnell, A. Lovespell
Patrick, Q. Cottage Sinister
    Death Goes to School
    Murder at Cambridge
Payes, R. C. Bride of Fury
    Devil's Court
Pearlman, G. Adventures of Sherlock Holmes'
    Smarter Brother
Pearson, E. L. Sherlock Holmes and the Drood
    Mystery
Peltz, R. S. Dustman to Ashes
Pendleton, D. Assault on Soho
Peters, Elizabeth. Camelot Caper
    Deeds of the Disturber
    Murders of Richard III
Peterson, Audrey. Deadly Rehearsal
    Death in Wessex
    Elegy in a Country Graveyard
    Nocturne Murder
Pinkerton, A. F. Whitechapel Murders
Piper, E. Stand-In
Plum, J. Secret of Benjamin Square
Polk, D. House on the Black Moor
Porter, M. E. Road to Ruin
Post, M. D. Bradmoor Mystery
    Sleuth of St. James's Square
Poyer, J. Tunnel War
Pritchett, A. Karamour
    Legacy of Evil
    Malpas Legacy
    Mill Reef Hall
Queen, E. Study in Terror
Quinn, A. Satyr Ring
Ragosta, M. King John's Treasure
Randell, C. Curse of Deepwater
    Mallory Grange
    Whisper of Fear
Ratcliffe, S. Castle Captive
Raymond, M. Long Journey Home
Revell, L. Party for the Shooting
Rice, Louise. By Whose Hand?
Richmond, D. Dunkirk Directive
Rider, A. Safe Place
Rigg, J. Slipperdown Chant
Robbins, A. On the Trail of Blood
Roberts, J. L. Castlereagh
    Jade Vendetta
    Ravenswood
Robeson, K. Sea Magician
Robinson, Peter. 5 titles
Roby, M. L. 6 titles

Roffey, J. Hostile Witness
Romaine, D. Shadow of Evil
Roosevelt, E. Murder at the Palace
Root, G. T. Bird in the Hand
Rosenheim, A. Tormenting of Lafayette Jackson
Rosenthal, E. Advanced Calculus of Murder
Ross, Dana. Demon of the Darkness
    This Shrouded Night
Ross, Marilyn. at least 7 titles
Roth, H. Shadow of a Lady
Rowan, D. Silver Wood
Ruben, W. S. Murder: Love Story
Rubens, B. Sunday Best
Ryan, Jenna. Carnival
Ryck, F. Loaded Gun
Saberhagen, F. Holmes-Dracula File
St. Clair, K. Room Beneath the Stairs
St. James, B. Witch
St. John, N. both titles
Sale, R. For the President's Eyes Only
Sebastian, M. both titles
Shannon, Dell. Manson Curse
Shepherd, E. both titles
Sherman, R. Jigsaw
Shoebridge, M. Ranleigh Court
Shulman, S. Bride of Devil's Leap
    Castlecliff
    Daughters of Astaroth
Siegel, B. Adventures of Richard O'Boy
Simenon, G. Maigret's Revolver
Sladek, J. Black Aura
    Invisible Green
Smith, Wynne. Rushmoreland Rubies
Souvestre, P. Slippery As Sin
Stafford, C. Honour of Ravensholme
    House by Exmoor
Stanford, A. Mission in Sparrow Brush Lane
Stang, J. A. Shadows on the Sceptered Isle
Stashower, D. Adventures of the Ectoplasmic Man
Stephenson, M. House on Wrath Moor
Stevens, S. B. Shrieking Shadow of Penporth Island
Stevenson, F. Kilmeny in the Dark Wood
Stivers, D. Firecross
    Royal Flush
Stokes, M. L. Case of the Judas Spoon
Straub, P. Julia
Swain, F. You'll Hang, My Love
Swiggett, H. Strongbox
Taylor, B. Kindness of Strangers
Taylor, G. E. Death of Jason Darby
Teilhet, D. L. Odd Man Pays
Theirry, J. F. Adventure of the Eleven Cuff-Buttons
Thomas, F. all 4 titles
Tidyman, E. Goodbye, Mr. Shaft
Tine, R. Uneasy Lies the Head
Tourney, L. all 5 titles
Trevelyan, J. Greythorne
Troy, J. Haunted Honeymoon
Vance, L. J. Bandbox
    Black Bag
    Red Masquerade
Vasilos, T. Past Tense
Vaughan, S. Royal Game
Vernon, K. R. Phantom of Fonthill Park
Villiers, M. Serpent of Lilith
Wagner, S. Cove in Darkness
Wakefield, M. E. Secret at Midwinter End
Wallace, C. H. Highflight to Hell
Wallace, C. M. Waking Dream
Waller, L. Embassy
Warren, B. C. Lost Bride of Hatfield Castle
Wasser, M. Priory
Watkins, R. H. Master of Revels
Waugh, H. Shadow Guest
Weenolsen, H. Trial of Jenny Sykes
Wees, F. S. Mystery of the Creeping Man
Wellman, M. W. Sherlock Holmes' War of the
    Worlds
Werner, P. Swirling Mists of Cornwall
West, E. Night Is a Time for Listening
West, Pamela. Yours Truly, Jack the Ripper
White, Alicen. Evil That Walks Invisible
Whitney, P. A. Hunter's Green
Williams, J. B. Baronet's Crime
Williamson, M. Death in the Picture

E

1238 / ENGLAND

Willock, R. Night of the Visitor
Wilson, Gar. Missile Menace
    Viper Factor
Wilson, M. Wind of Death
Withers, J. Echo in a Dark Room
Wood, Barbara. Curse This House
Woodbridge, H. H. Dig: Two Heads Wanted
Woodley, R. Deadly Encounter
Wright, E. Death in the Old Country
York, E. Medea Legend
York, H. Malverne Manor
    Tremorra Towers
Zochert, D. Murder in the Hellfire Club

ENGLAND (Eng. Here is a representative listing of British authors who principally use English settings. See also: previous entry; Channel Islands; Isle of Man)

Abbey, Ruth
A'Beckett, A. W.
Adams, D
Adams, Herbert
Adams, S.
Addiscombe, J.
Adye, J.
Aiken, Joan
Ainsworth, H.
Aird, C.
Alais, E. W.
Alan, M.
Alding, P.
Alexander, John
Alexander, Ruth
Alington, C. A.
Allan, S.
Allardyce, P.
Allbeury, T.
Allen, A.
Allen, G.
Allen, M.
Allerton, Mark
Allington, M.
Amberley, R.
Ames, D.
Anderson, J. R. L.
Andover, H.
Anson, L.
Appleton, G. W.
Applin, A.
Armour, R. C.
Armstrong, A.
Armstrong, R.
Arnold, J.
Arnold, R.
Ashe, G.
Ashford, J.
Ashton, C.
Askew, A.
Atkey, B.
Austen-Leigh, L.
Austwick, J.
Babson, M.
Bailey, Elliott
Bailey, H. C.
Baker, I.
Balfour, H.
Balham, J.
Ball, B.
Ballinger, W. A.
Bamburg, L.
Barclay, B.
Barling, C.
Barnard, R.
Barnett, G.
Barnett, J.
Baron, P.
Barrett, F.
Barrington, P.
Barry, C.
Bawden, N.
Baxter, G.
Bayfield, W. J.
Beckett, M.
Begbie, G.

Bell, Josephine
Bell, V.
Bellairs, G.
Belloc, H.
Bennett, A.
Bennetts, P.
Bentley, E. C.
Bentley, J.
Berkeley, A.
Bessell, J. P.
Bidson, L.
Bingham, J.
Black, Ladbroke
Black, Lionel
Blackburn, J.
Blackmore, J.
Blair, A.
Blake, N.
Bobin, J. W.
Bodkin, M. M.
Boland, J.
Bolt, B.
Bolton, J.
Bouchier, W.
Bowers, D.
Boyle, C. N.
Bracey, A.
Braddon, M. E.
Brady, N.
Bramah, E.
Branch, P.
Brand, C.
Brandon, C.
Brandon, G.
Brandon, J.
Branston, F.
Brebner, P.
Brent, N.
Brett, S.
Bridges, R.
Bridges, V.
Brinton, H.
Brisbane, C.
Brock, A.
Brock, L.
Brooks, C.
Brooks, E. S.
Brooks, L. H.
Brown, A. C.
Browne, D. G.
Bruce, L.
Bruton, E.
Bryce, C.
Bude, J.
Bullivant, C. H.
Bulwer-Lytton, E.
Burke, J.
Burke, T.
Burley, W. J.
Burnaby, N.
Burnett, G.
Burt, M.
Burton, Miles
Busby, R.
Bush, C.
Butler, Ragan
Cadell, E.
Campbell, R. T.
Cannan, J.
Capes, B.
Cargill, L.
Carmichael, H.
Carnac, C.
Carr, J.
Carter, Y.
Carvic, H.
Cassells, J.
Cecil, H.
Chance, J. N.
Chance, Stephen
Chancellor, J.
Channon, E. M.
Chapman, R.
Chester, G.

Chesterton, G. K.
Cheyney, P.
Chittenden, F. A.
Christie, A.
Clandon, H.
Clark, Douglas
Cleeves, A.
Clement, F. A.
Clevely, H.
Clinton-Baddeley, V. C.
Clouston, J. S.
Cobb, B.
Cobb, T.
Cockin, J.
Cody, L.
Coggin, J.
Cohen, A.
Cole, G. H. D.
Collins, G.
Collins, W.
Connington, J. J.
Conrad, C.
Cooke, M. E.
Cookson, C.
Coram, C.
Corbett, Mrs.
Corbett, J.
Courage, J.
Cowdroy, J.
Cowen, F.
Crauford, W. H. L.
Crawford, R.
Creasey, J.
Crispin, E.
Crombie, M.
Cromwell, A. G. E.
Cronin, M.
Cross, L.
Cross, Mark
Cullingford, G.
Culpan, M.
Curties, H.
Dacre, R.
Dalman, M.
Dalton, M.
Dane, C.
Daniel, R.
Dark, R.
Darlington, W. A.
Davies, L. P.
Davis, George
Davis, H. C.
Davis, R.
Davison, G.
Dawe, C.
Deane, D.
Deane, N.
De Crespigny, P. C.
Delannoy, B.
Desmond, H.
Despard, L.
Dickens, C.
Dickson, Grierson
Dignam, C. B.
Dilnot, G.
Dix, M. B.
Dolphin, R.
Donavan, J.
Donovan, D.
Douglas, George
Doyle, A. C.
Drax, P.
Drummond, C.
Drummond, J.
Dudley, E.
Duke, W.
Du Maurier, D.
Duncan, F.
Duncan, W. M.
Durbridge, F.
Durham, D.
Durham, M.
East, R.
Easton, N.

Settings Index   ENGLAND / 1239

Eden, D.
Edgar, A.
Edgar, J.
Edwards, W.
Egleton, C.
Emerson, D.
Ephesian
Erskine, M.
Esmond, H.
Evans, G.
Everton, F.
Eyles, L.
Fairlie, G.
Falkirk, R.
Farjeon, B. L.
Farjeon, J. J.
Farmer, B. J.
Farnol, J.
Farrar, S.
Ferrars, E.
Farrer, K.
Field, K.
Field, Mora
Fielding, A.
Fitt, M.
Fleming, Joan
Fletcher, David
Fletcher, J. S.
Fletcher, R. J.
Flynn, B.
Foster, R. Francis
Fowler, S.
Fox-Davies, A. C.
Foxall, R.
Francis, B.
Frankau, G.
Franklin, C.
Fraser, A.
Fraser, James
Frazer, M.
Fredman, M.
Freeman, R. A.
Fremlin, C.
Froest, F.
Fuller, R.
Furnivall, G.
Fyfield, F.
Gale, J.
Gallon, T.
Gammon, D. J.
Garrett, W.
Garve, A.
Gask, A.
Gerard, F.
Gerard, M.
Gibbons, H. H. C.
Gielgud, V.
Gilbert, A.
Gilbert, M.
Giles, K.
Gloag, John
Goodchild, G.
Goodman, J.
Goodwin, J.
Gore, W.
Gorell, L.
Goyne, R.
Graaf, P.
Graeme, B.
Graham, Carolyn
Graham, Neill
Graham, Winifred
Grant, Richard
Gray, B.
Gray, D.
Graydon, W. M.
Green, Glint
Greenwood, J.
Gregg, C. F.
Grex, L.
Gribble, L.
Grierson, E.
Grierson, F.
Griffith, G.

Gunn, V.
Haggard, W.
Hale, E.
Halliday, M.
Hamilton, B.
Hamilton, E.
Hamilton, F. S.
Hardinge, R.
Hardwick, Mollie
Hardy, A. S.
Hare, C.
Hare, R.
Harris, Rosemary
Harris-Burland, J. B.
Harrison, R.
Hart, I. R. G.
Hart, Roy
Hastings, Macdonald
Hastings, P.
Hawton, H.
Haymon, S. T.
Haynes, A.
Heald, T.
Herman, H.
Hervey, E.
Hext, H.
Heyer, G.
Hichens, R.
Hill, H.
Hill, H. E.
Hill, R.
Hilton, J. B.
Hobson, H.
Hobson, P.
Hocking, A.
Hodder-Williams, C.
Hollingsworth, L.
Holmes, G.
Holt, Gavin
Holt, H.
Holt, V.
Hope, C.
Hope, S.
Horler, S.
Hornung, E. W.
Hubbard, P. M.
Hull, R.
Hume, D.
Hume, F.
Hunt, K.
Hunter, A.
Hunter, J.
Hurt, F.
Hutchinson, H.
Hyland, S.
Hyne, C. J. C.
Hythe, G.
Innes, M.
Ironside, J.
Islay, N.
Ison, G.
Jackson, L.
Jackson, M.
Jacobs, T. C. H.
James, Bill
James, P. D.
Jardine, W.
Jeffries, R.
Jenkins, H.
Jepson, E.
Jepson, S.
Jobson, H.
Johnson, Z.
Jon, M.
Jones, B.
Jones, E.
Keate, E. M.
Kelly, M.
Kelly, Susan
Kemp, H.
Kennedy, M.
Kernahan, C.
Kernahan, Mrs. C.
Keverne, R.

Kiddy, M. G.
King, Frank
Kingston, C.
Knight, L. A.
Kyle, S.
Ladline, R.
Laing, K.
Lane, G.
Larbalestier, P.
Launay, D.
Laurence, J.
Leaderman, G.
Le Fanu, J. S.
Leighton, M. C.
Lemarchand, E.
Lenehan, J. C.
Le Queux, W.
Lester, F.
Lester, V.
Lewis, J.
Lewis, Michael
Lewis, Roy
Lewis, T.
Ley, A. C.
Leyton, P.
Limnelius, G.
Llewellyn, R.
Locke, G. E.
Loder, V.
Lorac, E. C. R.
Lovesey, P.
Lowndes, M. B.
Lucas, N.
Luck, P.
Lustgarten, E.
Lynn, M.
MacDonald, P.
McGirr, E.
McGuire, P.
Mackenzie, A.
MacKenzie, D.
MacKenzie, N.
Mackenzie, S.
McLean, A. C.
MacLean, Arthur
McLeave, H.
MacLeod, H. C.
McNeilly, W.
McShane, M.
Maddock, S.
Magee, M.
Magnay, W.
Maguire, M.
Makin, W. J.
Malcolm, J.
Malloch, P.
Mann, Jack
Manton, P.
March, J.
March, M.
Marlowe, F.
Marlowe, P.
Marric, J. J.
Marsden, A.
Marsh, Jean
Marsh, John
Marsh, Richard
Marshall, I.
Marshall, L.
Marston, E.
Martin, A. R.
Martin, Richard
Martyn, W.
Masterman, W. S.
Maybury, A.
Mayhew, M.
Meade, L. T.
Meadows, C.
Meek, M. R. D.
Melville, Alan
Melville, J.
Meriton, P.
Meynell, L.
Mills, O.

E

Millward, E. J.
Milne, A. A.
Milne, J.
Mitchell, G.
Moore, A.
Morice, A.
Morland, N.
Morris, T. B.
Morrison, A.
Morrissey, J. L.
Mortimer, J.
Morton, A.
Morton, G.
Moyes, P.
Muir, Dexter
Murray, A.
Murray, E. J.
Murray, Stephen
Neel, J.
Newman, B.
Newman, G. F.
Nichols, B.
Norman, F.
Norsworthy, G.
North, G.
O'Duffy, E.
O'Hara, Kenneth
O'Hara, Kevin
Oliver, A.
Oppenheim, E. P.
Orde-Powlett, N.
Osborne, M.
Parsons, A.
Payn, J.
Payne, L.
Penn, J.
Perowne, B.
Pertwee, R.
Peters, Ellis
Peterson, M.
Petrie, R.
Philips, G. N.
Phillips, C.
Phillips, H. L.
Phillips, Mike
Phillpotts, E.
Philmore, R.
Picton, B.
Plummer, T. A.
Pollard, A. O.
Poole, M.
Porter, J.
Postgate, R.
Powell, P. H.
Price, A.
Priestley, J. B.
Procter, M.
Proudfoot, W.
Punshon, E. R.
Quin, B. G.
Quiroule, P.
Radford, E.
Radley, S.
Randall, R.
Redmond-Howard, L. G.
Rees, A. J.
Reeve, Christopher
Reid, D.
Remenham, J.
Rendall, R.
Rhea, N.
Rhode, J.
Richardson, Robert
Robbins, C.
Robertson, C.
Rodd, R.
Roffman, J.
Rogers, B.
Rolls, A.
Ronald, J.
Ross, Jonathan
Rowland, J.
Royce, K.
Ruegg, J.

Rushton, C.
Ryan, R. R.
Ryland, C.
Saddler, K. A.
Sanders, B.
Sandys, J.
Sayers, D. L.
Scott, J. S.
Scott, Sutherland
Scott, Will
Seamark
Sennocke, T. J. R.
Sergeant, A.
Shand, W.
Sharp, D.
Sheahan, K. M.
Shearing, J.
Sheldon, R.
Shore, P. R.
Silverman, M. R.
Simon
Simmons, R.
Simpson, D.
Sims, G.
Sims, G. R.
Slate, J.
Smith, D. W.
Smith, H. M.
Smith, Joan
Smith, Shelley
Snaith, J. C.
Sonin, R.
Soutar, A.
Southworth, L.
Spain, N.
Spiller, A.
Sprigg, C. S.
Stand, M.
Stanners, H. H.
Staynes, J.
Steed, N.
Stone, Austin
Stone, S.
Story, J. T.
Straker, J. F.
Street, J.
Strong, B.
Strong, L. A. G.
Stuart, D.
Swinson, A.
Sykes, W. S.
Symonds, F. A.
Symons, B.
Symons, J.
Symons, M.
Tack, A.
Tattersall, J.
Taylor, A.
Temple-Ellis, N. A.
Terris, E. W.
Tey, J.
Thomas, A.
Thomson, B.
Thorndike, R.
Thorne, G.
Thynne, M.
Toye, S.
Trench, J.
Trent, P.
Trevor, R.
Trow, M. J.
Troy, K.
Troy, S.
Truss, S.
Turner, Bill
Turner, J.
Turner, J. V.
Tyrer, W.
Underwood, M.
Upward, A.
Urquhart, P.
Usher, F.
Usher, G.
Vahey, J. H.

Valentine, D.
Vane, D.
Vane, N.
Van Greenaway, P.
Verner, G.
Verron, R.
Vickers, R.
Vincent, K.
Vine, B.
Vivian, E. C.
Vivian, F.
Volk, G.
Vosper, G. V.
Vulliany, C. E.
Waddell, M.
Wade, H.
Wainwright, J.
Wakefield, H. R.
Walker, P. N.
Walker, R.
Wallace, C.
Wallace, E.
Walling, R. A. J.
Walsh, J. M.
Ward, J.
Warden, F.
Warden, G.
Warner, D.
Warner, M.
Warren, J.
Warren, J. R.
Warriner, T.
Waters
Watson, C.
Watson, H. B. M.
Waye, C.
Webb, A.
Webster, F. A. M.
Welford, M.
Wentworth, P.
Weymouth, A.
Whaley, F. J.
Wheeler, H. E.
White, E. L.
White, F. M.
White, R. J.
Whitechurch, V. L.
Whitelaw, D.
Willett, H.
Williamson, Audrey
Willis, T.
Willock, C.
Wills, C. M.
Wilson, Colin
Wilson, G. M.
Wilson, Gregory
Wilson, P. W.
Wise, Arthur
Witting, C.
Wodehouse, P. G.
Woden, G.
Wood, A.
Wood, E.
Wood, Mrs. H.
Woods, S.
Woodthorpe, R. C.
Worth, M.
Wright, J.
Wynne, A.
Wynnton, P.
Yates, D.
York, J.
Yorke, M.

ETHIOPIA (Ethio. See also: Africa, North)
Aarons, W. B. Assignment Sheba
Allbeury, T. Girl from Addis
Atlee, P. Judah Lion Contract
Carter, Nick. Z Document
Cody, L. Rift
Hild, J. Vultures of the Horn
McCurtin, P. Somali Smashout
Trench, J. Beyond the Atlas

Settings Index

FAR EAST (See also: individual countries)
Aarons, E. S. Assignment—Helene
    Assignment—Sulu Sea
Agniel, L. D. Pressure Point
Alexander, D. Coltray
Alexander, G. all 4 titles
Ambler, E. Night-Comers
    Passage of Arms
Arnold, W. China Gate
Balaban, J. B. Coming Down Again
Ballinger, B. S. Spy in the Java Sea
Beaufort, T. Whatever Happened to Rosie Dunn?
Binns, O. Red Token
Black, G. Bitter Tea
    Moon for Killers
    Night Run from Java
Bloodworth, D. Any Number Can Play
Bok. Dragons to Slay
    Vampires of the China Coast
Bond, L. Red Phoenix
Boothby, G. Beautiful White Devil
Boulle, P. Ears of the Jungle
Butler, R. Fingernail Beach
Carter, Nick. Dragonfire
    Vulcan Disaster
Crowder, K. Asian Eyes
Cushman, D. Opium Flower
    Port Orient
Dark, J. Bamboo Bomb
Davis, F. M. Kiss the Tiger
Derby, M. Out of Asia Alive
Downes, H. Opium Stratagem
Duncan, R. L. Temple Dogs
Edwards, P. Laughing Death
Egleton, C. Gone Missing
Footman, R. Once a Spy
Givens, J. Friend in the Police
Glemser, B. Grand Opening
Gluck, S. Dragon in Harness
Goodchild, G. Black Orchid
Gordons. Menace
Hall, Adam. Pekin Target
    Quiller's Run
Hamilton, A. Wyss Pursuit
Hardy, R. Face of Jalanath
Haring, D. Ends of the Earth
Harvester, S. Bamboo Screen
    Tiger in the North
Hayes, Ralph. Death Makers Conspiracy
Haythorne, J. None of Us Cared for Kate
Heffernan, W. Corsican
Hervey, H. Black Parrot
Horn, H. Murder at Linpara
Horton, G. Edge of Hazard
Hurd, D. Smile on the Face of the Tiger
Kaplan, A. Dragon Fire
Laing, A. Dr. Scarlett
Lustbader, E. V. Black Heart
McLaughlin, W. R. D. Syndicate of Evil
Mair, G. B. Girl from Peking
Marquand, J. P. No Hero
Mason, V. W. Sulu Sea Murders
Mather, B. Midnight Gun
Merritt, D. Hatch's Mission
Mills, A. Blue Spider
    Intrigue Island
Moffitt, I. Retreat of Radiance
Newton, J. E. Java Edge
Packard, F. 5 titles
Patterson, H. Sad Wind from the Sea
Phillips, J. A. Pagoda
Proud, F. M. Golden Triangle
Pruitt, J. N. Striker One Down
Roberts, M. K. Pathet Vengeance
Robeson, K. Flaming Falcons
    Thousand-Headed Man
Sandberg, B. Chinese Spur
Saul, J. Next Best Thing
Schoonover, J. Bangkok Collection
Silliphant, S. Silver Star
Snell, E. Yellow Seven
Stacpoole, H. D. House of Crimson Shadows
Stone, S. C. S. Dragon's Eye
    Spies

Straub, P. Koko
Thayer, J. S. Earhart Betrayal
Thorne, E. P. Black Sunset
    House of the Fragrant Lotus
Vivian, E. C. Forbidden Door
Walsh, J. M. Face Value
    Island Alert
Wingate, J. Seawayman
Woodman, M. Medusa Kiss

FIJI (See also: South Pacific)
Arthur, F. all 4 Spearpoint titles
Dekker, C. Hurricane Is a Blonde
Drinkwater, C. Abundance of Rain
Journet, T. Troupe of Star-Crossed Killers
Stuart, I. Dark Crusader
Vandercook, J. W. Murder in Fiji

FINLAND (Fin. See also: Helskini; Scandinavia)
Gardner, J. Icebreaker
Grayson, Rupert. Escape with Gun Cotton
Low, O. To His Just Deserts
Lyall, G. Most Dangerous Game
Risku, C. White Midnight
Smith, F. E. Devil Behind Me
Vicary, J. Ice Maiden
Wilson, Gar. Power Gambit
Wuorio, E. L. Midsummer Lokki

FLORENCE (See also: Italy; Milan; Naples; Rome;
    Sardinia; Sicily; Venice)
Barnao, J. HammerLocke
Coker, C. Other David
Dibdin, M. Rich Full Death
Fletcher, Dorothy. Music Master
Gault, M. Face of Death
Gilbert, M. Etruscan Net
Griffin, J. Florentine Madonna
Inchbald, P. Or the Bambino Dies
    Tondo for Short
Lippard, G. Ladye Annabel
Lorrimer, C. Voice in the Dark
Michaels, B. Grey Beginning
Nabb, M. 7 titles
Stein, A. M. One Dip Dead
Thomas, H. W. Long Shadow

FLORIDA (Fla. See also: Jacksonville; Miami;
    Tampa; South)
Adams, E. L. Gambler's Throw
Alter, R. E. Carny Kill
    Swamp Sister
Ard, W. All I Can Get
Beatty, E. Jupiter Missile Mystery
    River in the Sun
Becker, S. Juice
Beechcroft, W. Position of Ultimate Trust
Benedict, L. Fatal Flower
Bennett, R. D. Rendezvous 2.2
Biggers, E. D. Love Insurance
Blacir, A. Unwitting Witness
Bowen, N. Hear No Evil
Brace, T. Murder Goes in a Trailer
    Murder Goes to the Dogs
Brackeen, S. Delfina
Braly, M. Master
Breen, R. Adam's Child
Brent, R. L. Liquidator
Brewer, G. at least 14 titles
Brody, M. Teaser Set to Kill
Brown, Carter. Death of a Doll
Caidin, M. Maryjane Tonight at Angels Twelve
Caillou, A. Swamp War
Carmichael, F. Said the Spider to the Fly
Carrier, W. Bay of the Damned
Carter, Nick. 5 titles
Chambers, W. Bright Star of Danger
    In Savage Surrender
Chase, E. R. Dark Corners
Chase, J. Mark of the Red Diamond
Chase, J. H. 14 titles
Chelton, J. My Deadly Angel
Christian, A. G. Harani Trail

FLORIDA / 1241

Churchill, L. Grinning Ghoul
    Shadows and Shadows
Claymore, T. Reunion in Florida
Cline, C. T., Jr. Missing Persons
    Reaper
Colby, R. Make Mine Vengeance
    Quaking Widow
Collins, Stuart. Burn Down
Conroy, Al. Blood Run
    Strangle Hold!
Conty, J.-P. Big Secret, Suzuki
Conway, N. Omega Operation
Cooper, C. R. Action in Diamonds
Coram, R. America's Heroes
    Narcs
Corrigan, M. Love for Sale
Coxe, G. H. Never Bet Your Life
Crabb, N. Ralph
Crane, F. Murder on the Purple Water
Crews, L. Option to Die
Crockett, L. Sandman
Cullimore, A. Good Place to Hide
Daly, C. J. Hidden Hand
Davis, Gordon. Ring Around Rosy
Dean, R. G. Layoff
Dent, L. Lady Afraid
Derrick, L. Cryogenic Nightmare
    Demented Empire
De Witt, J. Murder on Shark Island
Dietrich, R. Be My Victim
    One for the Road
Donohue, M. Sutter's Sands
Drake, Alison. Black Moon
    Tango Key
Du Bois, T. Rogue's Coat
Duncan, L. Point of Violence
Eberhart, M. G. Another Man's Murder
    Unidentified Woman
    White Dress
Edwards, Jame. Terror by Design
Evans, E. Shadowland
Feegel, J. R. Autopsy
    Death Sails the Bay
Fickling, G. G. Bombshell
Flanders, R. Silver Threads
Floyd, M. Secret of Saraband
Flynn, J. M. Surfside 6
Foley, R. Wild Night
Foster, R. Bier for a Chaser
Freemantle, B. Charlie Muffin's Uncle Sam
Friedman, M. Hurricane Season
Fuller, W. Back Country
    Girl in the Frame
    Goat Island
    Pace That Kills
Glendinning, R. Terror in the Sun
    Who Evil Thinks
Goulart, R. Wisemann Originals
Granger, B. Schism
Green, A. What a Body!
Green, E. P. Sneaks
Greth, L. Nightmare!
Gunter, A. C. Don Belasco of Key West
Hagen, P. Dark Journey Home
Hale, C. He's Late This Morning
    Murder in Tow
Hale, Jennifer. Beyond the Dark
    House of Strangers
    House on Key Diablo
    Stormhaven
Hall, Jim. Tropical Squeeze
    Under Cover of Daylight
Halleran, T. both titles
Halliday, B. 6 titles
Haring, D. Countdown to Murder!
    Dames Come Deep-Freeze
Harrington, W. Scorpio 5
Harrison, W. Strip the Town Naked
Hayes, J. No Escape
Heatter, B. Scarred Man
Hiassen, C. Double Whammy
    Skin Tight
Higgins, Joan. Little Death Music
Hild, J. Firestorm U.S.A.

F

Hill, Kim. Death on Demand
Hillgarth, A. Change for Heaven
Hilton, J. B. Sunset Law
Himmel, R. I'll Find You
Hinchman, J. Dreamspinner
Hirschfeld, B. Key West
Holden, L. Hide-Out
Holley, H. Blood on the Beach
Houston, M. B. Yonder
Huber, F. Axx Goes South
Hunter, J. D. Florida Is Closed Today
Hunter, R. W. Net of Fear
Hurst, E. H. Mystery Island
Janeschutz, T. Hidden Lake
Janson, H. Bewitched
    Hell's Angel
    Milady Took the Rap
Johnson, J. L. Nine Lives of Alphonse
Johnston, V. White Pavilion
Jordan, L. Operation: Perfidia
Kallen, L. Piano Bird
Kane, H. My Darlin' Evangeline
Karr, Lee. Dark Cries of Gray Oaks
Kauffmann, L. Waldo
Keene, D. 6 titles
Kelley, L. That's No Way to Die
Kendrick, B. 5 titles
Kennedy, B. Uninvited Guest
Kerr, B. Damned If He Does
    Shakedown
King, R. Case of the Redoubled Cross
    Faces of Danger
    Malice in Wonderland
Kingsley, B. Blind Chance
Knight, K. M. Silent Partner
Knotts, R. And the Deep Blue Sea
Koenig, J. Floater
Koperwas, S. Easy Money
Lariar, L. Day I Died
Latimer, Jonathan. Dead Don't Care
Law, J. Shadow of the Palms
Leonard, E. Split Images
    Stick
Leslie, John. Blood on the Keys
    Killer in Paradise
Leventhal, S. Black Marble Pool
Lewis, Jack. Night for Evil
Lippincott, D. Home
Lockridge, F. Murder by the Book
Lockridge, R. Death by Association
    Troubled Journey
Lordahl, J. A. Those Subtle Weeds
Lutz, J. 5 titles
Lynch, M. Silken Web
McBain, E. 10 titles
McDonald, C. P. Gulf Stream
    Patch
MacDonald, J. D. 25 titles
McDowell, M. Cold Moon Over Babylon
McGregor, T. J. Kin Dread
    On Ice
Mackenzie-Lamb, E. Labyrinth
McKernan, V. Osprey Reef
McKnight, B. 10 titles
MacLean, Alistair. Fear Is the Key
McLendon, J. Deathwork
McMahon, T. P. Jink
Maling, A. Loophole
Manson, W. Deadly Game
Marchant, B. Secret of the Everglades
Marlowe, D. J. Name of the Game Is Death
    Never Live Twice
    Operation Whiplash
Martin, A. Kastle Krags
Matthiessen, P. Killing Mister Watson
Mayfield, S. Lonely Terror
Merkin, R. South Florida Book of the Dead
Merle, R. Day of the Dolphin
Messmann, J. Bullet for the Bride
Metcalfe, W. Two Weeks Before Murder
Michaels, Jan. Only Witness
Morgan, S. Too Rich to Live
Murphy, J. Long Reconnaissance
Murphy, W. B. Death Sentence

Murray, M. Sunshine Corpse
Muse, P. Eight Candles Glowing
Neely, E. J. Chateau Laurens
Nelson, Mildred. Island
Norman, G. Midnight Water
    Sweetwater Ranch
Norton, A. Opal-Eyed Fan
O'Rourke, W. Criminal Tendencies
Pace, T. all 3 titles
Packard, F. Four Stragglers
Pairo, P. Winner's Cut
Palmtag, D. Starling Street
Patti, P. Silhouettes
Patton, C. Fatal Analysis
Payne, A. This'll Slay You
Peck, R. N. Hallapoosa
Pendleton, D. Hammerhead Reef
    Paramilitary Plot
    Thermal Thursday
    White Line War
Philbrick, W. R. Crystal Blue Persuasion
    Neon Flamingo
    Tough Enough
Plumb, C. Murderous Move
Pope, E. Colcorton
Powell, R. And Hope to Die
    Shark River
    Shell Game
    Shot in the Dark
Pratt, T. Barefoot Mailman
Provost, G. Without Mercy
Ramm, C. Florida Firefight
Ransome, S. 11 titles
Rea, M. P. Blackout at Rehearsal
    Death Walks the Dry Tortugas
Reilly, H. Lament for the Bride
Reiss, B. Flamingo
Richards, W. Dead Man's Tide
Roche, A. S. In the Money
    Pleasure Buyers
Rohde, W. L. Uneasy Lies the Head
Rohmer, S. Moon Is Red
Rome, A. My Kind of Game
Ronns, E. Dark Destiny
    I Can't Stop Running
Russon, J. Living Things
Sanchez, T. Mile Zero
Sax, A. Salt Cat Bank
Serrian, M. Night Runners
Shedd, G. C. Lady of Mystery House
Siller, V. Lonely Breeze
    Mood for Murder
Singer, N. Diamond Stud
Smitten, R. Godmother
Somers, S. Romany Curse
Spillane, M. By-Pass Control
Springer, C. Smuggler's Moon
Sproul, K. Mystery of the Closed Car
Stanford, D. Bargain in Blood
Sterling, S. Dead Right
Stone, Elna. Dark Masquerade
Strange, J. S. Strangler Fig
Terhune, A. P. Secret of Sea-Dream House
Thacker, C. G. Fatal Amusement
Thames, C. H. Violence Is Golden
Thayer, L. Five Bullets
    Jaws of Death
Thomas, D. Gulf Coast Run
Thompson, W. C. Suitcase Full of Money
Toole, W. Death in Deep Shadows
Tracy, D. 5 titles
Tralins, R. Ring-a-Ding UFOs
Walker, Irma. Murdoch Legacy
Walker, R. W. Razor's Edge
Ware, J. Faxon Secret
Watson, S. Weep No More My Brother
Webb, J. F. Craigshaw Curse
Welles, E. Spaniard's Gift
Werry, R. R. Casket for a Lying Lady
Westcott, C. T. Half a Kick from Home
Westlake, D. E. Trust Me on This
White, L. 5 titles
Whiteley, L. S. Snakes in the Garden
Whitney, P. A. Dream of Orchids
    Poinciana

Whittington, H. at least 6 titles
Wilder, R. Walk with Evil
Williams, C. All the Way
    Go Home, Stranger
    Man on the Run
    Talk of the Town
Winston, D. Mayeroni Myth
    Trificante Treasure
Worts, G. F. Red Darkness
Yarnell, D. Mantrap
Zachary, H. One Day in Hell

FORMOSA (Includes Taiwan. See also: Far East; China)
Ang, L. Butcher's Wife
Marlowe, D. J. Operation Checkmate
Quigley, J. Secret Soldier
Wood, C. Taiwan

FRANCE (Fr. Monaco is included here. See also: Marseilles; Nice; Paris; Corsica)
Aarons, E. S. Girl on the Run
A'Beckett, A. W. Hard Luck
Abro, B. July 14 Assassination
Aiken, Joan. Foul Matter
    Smile of the Stranger
Albert, M. Gargoyle Conspiracy
    Operation Lila
    Pink Panther
Albrand, M. Day in Monte Carlo
    None Shall Know
Allain, M. at least 4 of 5 titles
Allbeury, T. Lantern Network
    Time Without Shadows
Allen, Warner. Death Fungus
Ambler, E. Epitaph for a Spy
    Kind of Anger
Ames, D. Corpse Diplomatique
Ames, J. Dark Carnival
Anderson, J. Storm Castle
Annesley, M. Agent Intervenes
Anonymous. Titled Counterfeiter
Anthony, Evelyn. Occupying Power
    Voices on the Wind
Arley, C. Dead Man's Bay
    Ready Revenge
Arnold, M. Death on the Dragon's Tongue
Ashe, G. Death from Below
    Elope to Death
    Rogue's Ransom
    Wait for Death
Audemars, P. most of the 30 titles
Aufricht-Ruda, H. Case for the Defendant
Aveline, C. all titles
Bair, P. Gypsum Flower
Baker, W. H. Destination Dieppe
Ballard, K. G. Gauge of Deception
Bark, C. V. See the Living Crocodiles
Barker, A. Big Fix
Barker, C. H. Devil's Brood
Barr, R. Triumphs of Eugene Valmont
Barrett, J. Monte Carlo Stories
Barron, E. Marcel Levignet
Barwick, J. Devil at the Crossroads
Base, R. Foreign Object
Baskerville, B. St. Cloud Affair
Batten, J. Riviera Blues
Beardmore, G. Thousand Witnesses
Beare, G. Snake on the Grave
Beeding, F. 6 titles
Bell, Josephine. House Above the River
Bellairs, G. 10 titles
Belletto, R. Eclipse
Belot, A. Flower of Crime
    Men Are What Women Make Them
Bennett, Kem. Dangerous Knowledge
Bentley, J. Mr. Marlow Chooses Wine
Berckman, E. Journey's End
    Lament for Four Brides
    Voice of Air
Beresford, J. D. Decoy
Beresford, L. What's at the End?
Bernanos, G. Crime
Bernede, A. both titles

Settings Index

FRANCE / 1243

Berry, J. Don't Betray Me
Beste, R. V. Faith Has No Country
Blackstock, C. Gallant
Bocca, G. Nadine
Boileau, P. most of the 10 titles
Boissiere, A. both titles
Bond, M. 7 titles
Boothby, G. Woman of Death
Bordeaux, H. House That Died
Boulle, P. Noble Profession
Bower, M. Skipper Anne
Boyle, K. Frenchman Must Die
Bradley, Michael. Corsican Cross
Brahms, C. Casino for Sale
Bramson, K. Case of Dr. Morel
Brason, J. Fourth Arm
Braun, M. G. Operation Jealousy
Brennan, R. Toledo Dagger
Brewer, G. Mediterranean Caper
Bridge, A. Emergency in the Pyrenees
Bright, A. Golden Earnest
Brooker, C. Dark Mosaic
Brown, H. J. Duffy
Browne, D. G. House of the Sword
Browne, E. Murder by Appointment
Buckingham, N. Storm in the Mountains
Burge, R. J. There Is a Destiny
Burke, R. Frightened Pigeon
Bush, C. Case of the Climbing Rat
Butler, Gerald. Choice of Two Women
Butterworth, M. Man Who Broke the Bank at Monte Carlo
  Soundless Scream
Calef, N. Frantic
Calvin, H. It's Different Abroad
Campbell, A. Juggernaut
  Keep Away from Water
Canfield, M. Tuscany Madonna
Canler, M. Autobiography of a French Detective
Canning, V. 5 titles
Carfax, C. Sleeping Salamander
Carr, G. Ice-Axe Murders
Carr, J. D. Captain Cut-Throat
  Emperor's Snuff Box
Carstairs, J. P. Gardenias Bruise Easily
Carter, Nick. Gallagher Plot
  Man Who Sold Death
Castle, A. Wolf-Lure
Catalan, H. all 3 titles
Chadwick, C. Moving House of Foscaldo
Charles, R. Flight of the Raven
Charteris, L. Saint and the Templar Treasure
Chase, J. H. Not Safe to Be Free
  You Have Yourself a Deal
Cheyney, P. Dark Interlude
Christie, A. Murder on the Links
  Mystery of the Blue Train
Christin, P. Ranks of the Black Order
Clare, A. Child of the Menhir
Claretie, J. Crime of the Boulevard
Coffman, V. at least 7 titles
Coles, M. 5 titles
Connell, V. Monte Carlo Mission
Conte, M. Cassie
Cooper, P. J. My Lady Evil
Coppee, F. Guilty Man
Coppel, Alec. Moment to Moment
Cort, N. French Entrapment
Courage, J. Affair Ravel
Cousin, M. Where Did the Girls Go?
Crane, C. Coast of Fear
Creasey, J. Toff and the Deep Blue Sea
Crofts, F. W. Cask
Crosby, J. Affair of Strangers
Cross, B. Nightwalkers
Cross, J. Grave of Heroes
Cumberland, M. at least 31 titles
Cutter, J. Talent for Revenge
Daley, R. Dangerous Edge
Daniels, D. Monte Cristo
Dard, F. Man of the Avenue
Davis, B. Fourth Day of Fear
Davis, D. S. God Speed the Night
Dawe, C. Black Spider

De Bremont, A. Black Opal
De Gramont, S. Lives to Give
Deighton, L. Yesterday's Spy
De Jean, G. Who Killed Lord Brixham?
Dekobra, M. Operation Magali
Delacorta. Lola
D'Erigny, S. Mysterious Madame S
Des Cars, G. Brute
Desmond, H. Turn Back from Death
De Teramond, G. Mystery of Lucien Delorme
Detzer, K. Broken Three
Dewhurst, E. After the Ball
Didelot, F. Seventh Juror
Diplomat. Scandal in the Chancery
Dodge, D. To Catch a Thief
Downes, D. Orders to Kill
Du Boisgobey, F. most of the 67 titles
Dumas, C. R. Second Bureau
Du Maurier, D. Scapegoat
E-7. Romance of a Spy
Eberhart, M. G. White Cockatoo
Edwards, Alexander. Last of Sheila
Edwards, G. Mystery of the Lyons Mail
Egerton, D. Design for an Accident
Eliot, A. Shadows Waiting
Elkins, A. J. Old Bones
Ellerbeck, R. Rose . . . Rose . . . Where Are You?
Everard, H. Sketches in France
Fairlie, G. Double the Bluff
  Scissors Cut Paper
  They Found Each Other
Farjeon, J. J. Sinister Inn
Farmlet, C. Fair in the Fearless Old Fashion
Farrere, C. House of the Secret
Faust, R. Tombs of Blue Ice
Fear, W. H. Killers
Ferm, B. Vengeance of Valdone
Ferrars, E. Hunt the Tortoise
Fickling, G. G. Honey on Her Tail
Flagg, J. Murder in Monaco
Fleming, I. Casino Royale
Forbes, C. Stone Leopard
Forrest, A. Captain Justice
Forsyte, C. Diving Death
France, V. Naked Five
Franklin, C. Fear Runs Softly
  Trembling Thread
Franklin, M. Destructors
Franklin, S. Malcontents
Freeling, N. 16 titles
Freemantle, B. Deaken's War
Freyer, F. Black, Black Hearse
Friedman, M. Temporary Ghost
Frith, W. Sack of Monte Carlo
Frost, F. Secret Agent Number One
Fry, P. Thick Blue Sweater
  Yellow Trousers
Gaboriau, E. most if not all 16 titles
Gaite, F. Brief Candles
  Come and Go
  Family Matter
Gallico, P. Zoo Gang
Gardner, J. Liquidator
Garrett, R. Murder and Magic
Garth, D. Tortured Angel
Gaston, B. Death Dealers
Gates, H. L. House of Murder
Gavin, C. None Dare Call It Treason
Geddes, P. Hangman
Gibbs, G. F. Splendid Outcast
Gilbert, A. Passenger to Nowhere
Gilbert, H. Hotels with Empty Rooms
Gill, E. Crime Coast
Gill, J. Kiki
Glazier, S. Lost Provinces
Glen, E. Secret of Villa Vanestra
Goldie, B. Green Tabloids
Goodchild, G. Monster of Grammont
Gordon, E. Chaperone
Gouze, R. Quiet Game of Bambu
Graeme, B. La Belle Laurine
Graeme, D. Inn of the Thirteen Swords
  Monsieur Blackshirt
  Sword of Monsieur Blackshirt

  Vengeance of Monsieur Blackshirt
Graham, Winston. Night Without Stars
Granger, B. Shattered Eye
Grant-Adamson, L. Guilty Knowledge
Gray, B. House of the Lost
Greene, G. Tenth Man
Greville, H. Un Mystere
Gribble, L. She Died Laughing
Grierson, F. Mysterious Mademoiselle
Griffiths, A. Rome Express
Guil, J. One Crime Too Many
Gunter, A. C. City of Mystery
  That Frenchman
Haines, W. W. Target
Halkett, R. Where Every Prospect Pleases
Hallatt, W. Suppression
Halliday, M. Go Ahead with Murder
  Murder Week-End
Hambledon, P. Murder's No Picnic
Hamilton, E. Casino Mystery
Hardy, A. S. both titles
Harris, J. Spring of Malice
Harris, Macdonald. Treasure of Sainte-Foy
Hastings, P. Field of the Forty Footsteps
Healey, B. Death in Three Masks
  Waiting for a Tiger
Heatter, B. Mutilator
Heaven, C. Place of Stones
Hebden, M. 14 titles
Hebert, A. In the Shadow of the Wind
Heckstall-Smith, A. Where There Are Vultures
Heilgers, L. Somewhere in France
Helterman, J. Blue Frogs
Hertz, G. Foreign Harry Complot
Higgins, J. Cold Harbour
Highsmith, P. Boy Who Followed Ripley
  Ripley Under Ground
  Ripley's Game
Hill, C. Jackdaw
Hill, Reginald. Collaborators
Hilton, J. B. Moondrop to Murder
Hiscott, L. Bishop's Move
Hitchcock, R. Sea Wrack
Holt, V. King of the Castle
Horler, S. Checkmate
  Evil Chateau
  Grim Game
  Princess After Dark
Hougron, J. Question of Character
Hughes, D. Pork Butcher
Hugill, R. Peril in Provence
Hume, D. Bring 'Em Back Dead!
Humes, H. L. Underground City
Hunter, A. Honfleur Decision
Hunter, J. D. Flying Cross
Hynd, N. Revenge
Imber, H. House of the Apricots
Irving-James, T. Dinner After Death
Jacobs, T. C. H. 8 titles
Jacquemard-Senecal. both titles
James, Maryl. Brandy on the Rocks
Janson, H. Invasion
Japrisot, S. Lady in the Car with Glasses and a Gun
  One Deadly Summer
  10:30 from Marseilles
  Trap for Cinderella
Jarvie, C. G. Vicious Circuit
Jason. High Litre Lolita
Jepson, S. Fear in the Wind
Jerrold, B. Two Lives
Jessup, R. Deadly Duo
  Night Boat to Paris
Johns, W. E. No Motive for Murder
Johnstone, I. Cannes
Jones, B. Layers of Deceit
  Testament of Evil
Jordan, L. Toy Cupboard
Kartun, D. Courier
Kassak, F. Come Kill with Me
Kelly, M. Twenty-Fifth Hour
Kent, S. Lions at the Kill
Kenyon, L. Challenge at Le Mans
  Countdown at Monaco
Kenyon, M. Free-Range Wife

F

Kimbro, J. Twilight Return
King, Robert. Red Spy at Night
Kingston, C. Infallible System
    Shadow of Monte Carlo and other stories
Kirst, H. H. Hero in the Tower
Koehler, R. P. Puppets of Chance
Koontz, D. Hanging On
Laborde, J. Dominici Affair
    Privileged Character
Lacy, E. Sex Castle
Lambert, R. Crime in Quarantine
    Mediterranean Murder
Lange, J. Scratch One
Le Bailly, P. Watch of Evil
Leblanc, M. most or all 23 titles
Lees, D. Zodiac
Lem, S. Chain of Chance
LeQueux, W. Court of Honour
Leroux, G. most of the 29 titles
Leslie, P. Bastard Brigade
    Hell for Tomorrow
Lestienne, V. Furioso
Level, M. Shadow
Levy, B. Missing Matisse
    Shining Mischief
Lewis, Canella. Music of Aquarius
Leyford, H. Murder Man
Linscott, G. Healthy Body
Lister, S. Delorme in Deep Water
Locke, W. J. Joyous Adventures of Aristide Pujol
Lodwick, J. First Steps Inside the Zoo
Loraine, P. Day of the Arrow
    Death Wishes
    Last Shot
Lovell, M. Spy Who Fell Off the Back of the Bus
Lowndes, M. B. Chink in the Armor
    Uttermost Farthing
Luard, N. Orion Line
Luddecke, W. J. Thursday at Noon
Lyall, G. Midnight Plus One
Macardle, D. Dark Enchantment
McCloy, H. Smoking Mirror
McConnor, V. Provence Puzzle
    Riviera Puzzle
McCutcheon, H. Black Attendant
McGann, M. Liar's Dice
McHale, T. Alinsky's Diamond
MacInnes, Helen. Agent in Place
    Assignment in Brittany
MacKenzie, D. Knife Edge
    Postscript to a Dead Letter
    Raven and the Paperhangers
MacLean, Alistair. Caravan to Vaccares
    Way to Dusty Death
MacLeod, Robert. Cargo Risk
Malet, L. 120 Rue de la Gare
Malm, D. To the Castle
Malot, H. Story Without a Moral
Manceron, G. Deadlier Sex
Markham, V. Song of Doom
Marlowe, A. Red Rocking Bird
Marlowe, S. Search for Bruno Heidler
Marsh, N. Spinsters in Jeopardy
Marsland, A. Cache-Cache
    Classic Death
Martin, Shane. Saracen Shadow
Marton, G. Obelisk Conspiracy
Marvin, S. Summer of Fear
Mary, J. Mendon Mystery
Maske, J. Cherbourg Mystery
    Saint-Malo Mystery
Mason, A. E. W. 5 titles
Mason, Howard. Proud Adversary
Massey, R. Crime in the Boulevard Raspail
Maybury, A. I Am Gabriella!
    Moonlit Door
Mayo, J. Hammerhead
Meadow, H. Uncertain Glory
Mercer, I. Man Gets Into His Tomb
Messer, M. Mouse Trap
Minton, P. Orphan of the Shadows
    Secret Melody
Mitchell, S. W. Adventures of Francois
Monsarrat, N. Castle Garac

Monteilhet, H. Andromache
    Return from the Ashes
    Road to Hell
Moore, I. Chateau Sinister
Moray, H. That Woman
Morrell, D. Blood Oath
Morton, A. Baron in France
Morton, P. Destiny's Child
Mountjoy, H. Minister of Police
Munro, J. Man Who Sold Death
Murray, M. Breakfast with a Corpse
    Good Luck to the Corpse
    King and the Corpse
Murray, W. H. Dark Rose the Phoenix
Mykel, A. W. Salamandra Glass
Newman, B. Maginot Line Murder
Nicolaysen, B. Perilous Passage
Nisot, E. Shortly After Midnight
Noel, S. Prelude to Murder
O'Brien, H. V. Four-and-Twenty Blackbirds
O'Brine, M. Pale Moon Rising
O'Farrell, W. Grow Young and Die
    Snakes of St. Cyr
Offutt, A. Operation: Super Ms.
Ohnet, G. Great Marl-Pit
    Woman of Mystery
Old Sleuth. Giant Detective in France
Oppenheim, E. P. 21 titles
Orczy, B. Castles in the Air
    Man in Gray
    Spy of Napoleon
Orgill, D. Days of Darkness
    Jasius Pursuit
Orvis, K. Into a Dark Mirror
Osborn, D. French Decision
Oughton, F. Two Lives of Robert Ledru
Palmer, B. Blind Man's Mark
    Flesh and Blood
Paris, A. Arrowheart
Parker, Robert. Ticket to Oblivion
Paul, B. Seventeenth Stair
Peart, R. Angels of Death
Peck, L. Tough Pitch
Pell, F. Hangman's Hill
Pendleton, D. 5 titles
Pendower, J. Widow from Spain
Penmare, W. Man Who Could Stop War
Perry, R. Fool's Mate
Pertwee, R. Such an Enmity
Peterson, Audrey. Murder in Burgundy
Pilgrim, D. Emperor's Secret
Pollitz, E. A. Forty-First Thief
Pons, S. Mademoiselle B.
Post, M. D. Monsieur Jonquelle, Prefect of Police
Praviel, A. Murder of Monsieur Fualdes
Preedy, G. Fourth Chamber
Price, A. '44 Vintage
    Other Paths to Glory
Radford, E. Death at the Chateau Noir
Radford, J. P. All of Our Aircraft Are Missing
Renard, M. all 4 titles
Renaud, J. J. Phantom Violin
Resnick, M. Eros at Zenith
Revelli, G. Commander Amanda Nightingale
Reynaud-Fourton, A. Reluctant Assassin
Reynolds, B. Whereabouts Unknown
Reynolds, Q. Man Who Wouldn't Talk
Richard, Ross. Murder on the Monte
Richardson, A. Rose of Kantara
Rippon, M. all 4 titles
Rives, A. Incident
Robeson, K. Black, Black Witch
Roche, R. M. Clermont
Rochester, G. E. Worst Squadron in France
Rohmer, E. S. Bianca in Black
Ross, Marilyn. Sinister Garden
Rostand, R. D'Artagnan Signature
Roudybush, A. Gastronomic Murder
Rowland, H. C. Sultana
Rushton, C. Devil's Power
Russell, C. E. Adventures of the D.C.I.
Rutherford, D. Black Leather Murders
Ryck, F. Sacrificial Pawn
    Undesirable Company
    Woman Hunt

St. John, David. Diabolus
    On Hazardous Duty
Saltmarsh, M. Clouded Moon
San Antonio. Crooks' Hill
    Hatchet Man
    Tough Justice
Sanders, B. To Catch a Spy
Sanders, John. Firework for Oliver
Sanders, Lawrence. Passion for Molly T
Sarasin, J. G. Fleur de Lys
    Mystery of Martin Guerre
Sarto, B. Death by the Seine
    Riviera Nights
Saul, J. R. Birds of Prey
Scarpetta, F. Body Count
    Die, Killer, Die
    Stone Killer
Schmidt, Dan. Ring of Fire
Scholefield, A. Point of Honour
Scott, Ralph. Unknown Quest
Scott, Jeremy. Angels in Your Beer
Scribner, F. K. Secret of Fontellac
Service, R. W. House of Fear
Seton, G. V Plan
    W Plan
Sharkey, J. Honestly, Now!
Shearing, J. Forget-Me-Not
    Lady and the Arsenic
Sheppard, S. Monte Carlo
Shulman, S. Lady of Arlac
Sieveking, L. Tomb with a View
Simenon, G. most titles set in Paris or elsewhere in France
Simmel, J. M. Wind and the Rain
Simpson, H. R. Junior Year Abroad
    Three Day Alliance
Skeggs, D. Estuary Pilgrim
Sloan, C. Wings of Death
Smith, Don. Man Who Played Thief
    Payoff
Souvestre, P. Fantomas
    Nest of Spies
Sparroy, M. Leper's Bell
Steeman, A. Night of the 12th-13th
Stein, A. M. Moonmilk and Murder
    Rolling Heads
    Snare Andalucian
Stephenson, R. Festival Death
Stevenson, A. French Inheritance
Stevenson, B. E. Destroyer
    Kingmakers
    Villa Aurelia
Steward, S. M. Murder Is Murder Is Murder
Stewart, Mary. Madam, Will You Talk?
    Nine Coaches Waiting
    Thunder on the Right
Stewart, Michael. Belle
Stringer, D. Yesterday Man
Strong, M. Danger Feeds My Fear
Stuart, John. Ashes to Ashes
Summerton, M. Nightingale at Noon
Tarrant, J. Rommel Plot
Tattersall, I. Society of Nobles
Taylor, Domini. Siege
Teed, G. H. Mystery of the Seine
Teilhet, H. T. Double Agent
    Private Undertaking
Terrall, R. Madam Is Dead
Thomas, Craig. Wolfsbane
Thomas, Leslie. Ormerod's Landing
Thompson, G. Nobody Cared for Kate
Thomson, J. Long Revenge
Thurston, T. Portrait of a Spy
Tickell, J. Villa Mimosa
Tomerlin, J. Comeback
Tom-Gallon, N. Monsieur Zero
Toussaint-Samat, J. both titles
Travers, H. Madame Aubrey Dines with Death
Travis, E. Finders, Keepers
Trevanian. Summer of Katya
Usher, F. Stairway to Murder
Vance, E. Reprisal
Vance, L. J. Alias the Lone Wolf
Vestal, S. Wine Room Murder

Vignant, J. F. Alpine Affair
Walker, Mark. Cassis . . . Resort to Vengeance
Wallis, R. S. Blood from a Stone
Warden, G. Nut-Browne Mayd
Warriner, T. Death's Dateless Night
Waters. Experiences of a French Detective
Watson, Clarissa. Last Plane from Nice
    Runaway
Way, P. Super-Celeste
Webb, A. both titles
Weil, B. Dossier IX
Weismiller, E. Serpent Sleeping
Welcome, J. Hell Is Where You Find It
    Run for Cover
Wellsley, J. Wine of Vengeance
West, E. Man Running
Weyman, S. J. Man in Black
Wharton, A. Two of Diamonds
Wheatley, D. 6 titles
White, A. Long Fuse
    Long Silence
    Long Watch
Whitelaw, D. League of St. Louis
Wilden, T. To Die Elsewhere
Wiles, J. Short Walk Abroad
Wilkinson, B. Proceed at Will
Williams, C. Wrong Venus
Williams, V. Mannequin
    Pigeon House
    Red Mass
Williamson, C. N. Berry Goes to Monte Carlo
Wills, C. M. Colonel's Foxhound
Wilson, G. M. Do Not Sleep
Wise, A. Naughty Girls
Woods, K. Murder in a Walled Town
Yates, D. 5 titles
York, A. Dark Passage
Young, M. Chateau in Brittany

FRANKFURT (Frank. See also: Germany; Berlin;
    Hamburg; Munich)
Kuby, E. Rosemarie
Malcolm, J. Discourse with Shadows
Monteilhet, H. Murder at the Frankfurt Book Fair

FRENCH ANTILLES (Fr. Ant. See also: West
    Indies; Caribbean)
Ambler, E. Doctor Frigo
Myers, B. Nightfall

FUTURE (Here listed are books explicitly set at a
    time later than that of writing. Year and
    place of setting are given where identified.
    See also: Past)
Abrahams, P. Tongues of Fire
Agnew, S. Canfield Decision (Wash. D.C., 1983)
Alexander, P. Show Me a Hero (Eng., ca.1990)
Allbeury, T. All Our Tomorrows
Allen, R. Captain Gardner of the International
    Police
Amis, K. Russian Hide-and-Seek
Anderson, I. F. Cypher 8
Arch, E. L. both titles
Arlen, M. Hell! Said the Duchess
Arrigi, M. Ordinary Man (NYC)
Asimov, I. Caves of Steel
    Naked Sun
    Robots and Empire
    Robots of Dawn
Bachman, R. Running Man
Ball, J. First Team
Barker, Nicholas. Red Ice (ship, 1990)
Barrow, D. Zilov Bombs
Basile, G. V. Eye of the Eagle (2000 A.D.)
    The Jackal Helix (2000 A.D.)
    The Sting of the Scorpion
Bass, R. Lime's Crisis (1997)
Bayley, B. J. Knights of the Limits
Baylus, R. F. People Exchange (NYC, 2086)
Bear, D. Keeping Time (NYC, 1999)
Bear, G. Queen of Angels (L.A., 2000s)
Belloc, H. But Soft—We Are Observed (Eng., 1979)
Betancourt, J. Rememory
Bickham, J. Day Seven (Houston, 1994)

Biggle, L. all 5 titles
Bishop, G. Shuttle People
Blair, J. M. Landscape of Darkness
Bolton, J. M. Mission: Tori
Borowitz, A. Jack the Ripper Talking Tour Murder
    (Eng., 1988)
Bova, B. Cyberbooks (NYC)
    Future Crime
Bowker, R. Dover Beach (Eng.)
    Replica
Boyd, J. Last Starship from Earth
Brain, J. Finger of Fire
Brin, D. Earth (2038)
    Sundiver (2200s)
Brown, D. Day of the Cheetah (1996)
    Silver Tower (1992)
Brown, Michael. Idiot Played Rachmaninov
Brown, R. G. Sibyl Sue Blue (1990s)
    Waters of Centaurus (1990s)
Burdick, E. Fail-Safe (1967)
Burke, John. Hotel Cosmos
Caidin, M. Prison Ship (2000s)
Caro, D. R. Man in the Dark Suit
Cassilis, R. Madness of the People
Chamberlain, W. Red January (U.S., 1969)
Christian, J. Five Gates to Armageddon (Jerus.,
    1985)
Clark, Curt. Anarchaos
Clark, E. Send in the Lions (1985)
Clark, W. Special Relationship (1977)
Clement, H. all 3 titles
Cohen, B. Blood on the Moon
    Taking of Satcon Station
Cole, W. V. Park Avenue (NYC)
Condon, R. Entwining (1984, Wash. D.C.)
    Prizzi's Glory (1992)
Cook, W. W. Round Trip to the Year 2000 (U.S.,
    2000)
Cooper, E. Prisoner of Fire (1990s)
Cordell, A. If You Believe the Soldiers (Eng.)
Corley, E. Jesus Factor (U.S.)
Coyle, H. Bright Star
Craig, D. Alias Man (Eng., 1970s)
    Contact Lost (Eng., 1970s)
    Message Ends (Eng., 1970s)
Cudlip, D. R. Comprader (U.S.)
Cussler, C. Deep Six (1989)
    Dragon (1993)
    Night Probe! (1989)
    Vixen 03 (U.S., 1988)
D'Agneau, M. Eeny Meeny Miny Mole
Dalmas, J. Varkaus Conspiracy (1995)
Daventry, L. Man of Double Deed (2090)
Dawson, L. Time Before Genesis
Deegan, J. J. Beyond the Fourth Door
Delahaye, M. Third Day (Mid. East, 1988)
Del Martia, A. Interstellar Espionage
    Space Pirates
Domatilla, J. Last Crime (Eng.)
Donne, M. Claret, Sandwiches and Sin (Afr., 1979)
Donnelly, D. Nearing Storm
Dozois, G. Nightmare Blue
Drake, David. Lacey and His Friends
Dunleavy, S. Very First Lady (Wash. D.C., 1985)
Dvorkin, D. Budspy
Dzagoyan, R. Aristotle System
Easton, T. A. Sparrowhawk
Edmondson, G. C. Takeover
Edwards, Nicky. Stealing Time
Effinger, G. A. Exile Kiss
    Fire in the Sun (2000s)
    When Gravity Fails
Egleton, C. Judas Mandate (Eng.)
    Last Post for a Partisan (Eng.)
    Piece of Resistance (Eng.)
Elgin, S. H. Star-Anchored, Star Angered
Elliott, Richard. Sword of Allah (1991)
Engling, R. Body Mortgage
Evans, E. E. Man of Many Minds
Evans, J. Midas Men (Russ., 1984)
Farren, M. Armageddon Crazy
Fast, J. Mortal Gods (2226)
Faust, J. C. Company Man
    Death of Honor (2000s)

Filbrun, J. S. Gemini Rising (1998)
Finlay, F. Cruel Trade (Ire.)
Finlay, I. Azanian Assignment (S. Afr., 1981)
Fisher, D. E. Hostage to One (1990)
Forbes, B. Endless Game (Eng, 1988)
    Song at Twilight
Forbes, C. Year of the Golden Ape (S.F., 1977)
Forsyth, F. Devil's Alternative (1982)
    Fourth Protocol (1988)
    Negotiator (U.S., 1990s)
Foster, A. D. Alien Nation (L.A.)
Fowler, S. Adventure of the Blue Room (Eng., 1990)
Fox, Peter. Doomsday Device (2000)
Franklin, J. Rat Race
Free, C. Soft Kill
Freed, D. China Card (1984)
Friewalds, J. Famine Plot (1980)
Gardner, J. Golgotha
Garn, Jake. Night Launch (1990s)
Gawron, J. M. Algorithm
Gibson, William. Count Zero
    Neuromancer
Gilden, M. Surfing Samurai Robots
Goddard, K. Balefire (L.A., 1984)
Goldin, S. Mindflight
Gottfried, C. Steel Eye
Goulart, R. 9 titles
Gray, C. Murder in Millenium VI
Green, T. M. Barking Dogs (Toronto, 1999)
Green, M. Delphi Calculus
Gridban, V. Lonely Astronomer (ca.1990)
    Master Must Die (1990)
Gunn, J. Star Bridge
Haiblum, I. Hand of Ganz
    Identity Plunderers
    Out of Sync
Haining, P. Hero
Haldemann, J. All My Sins Remembered
    Buying Time
    Hemingway Hoax (1996)
Hamilton, B. Brighton Murder Trial (1940s)
Harding, R. Bay City Burnout (Calif.)
    Blood Highway
    Fire and Ice
    Outrider
Harkon, F. Spawn of Space
Harness, C. L. Venetian Court
Harrington, R. E. Aswan High (Egypt, 1984)
Harris, L. Masada Plan (1979)
Harrison, H. Make Room! Make Room!
    Stainless Steel Rat for President (3000s)
    Stainless Steel Rat Gets Drafted
    Stainless Steel Rat Is Born (3000s)
Harrison, P. Storming Intrepid
Hashian. Shanidar (Iran, 1995)
Hastings, M. M. City of Endless Night (Ger., 2151)
Hawkey, R. Wild Card (U.S.)
Heard, H. F. Doppelgangers (1997)
Herbert, F. Dragon in the Sea (2000s)
Hill, Reginald. One Small Step
Hinz, C. Liege-Killer
Hoch, E. D. Fellowship of the Hand (2000s)
    Frankenstein Factory (2000s)
    Transvection Machine (2000s)
Hogan, J. P. Endgame Enigma
    Inherit the Stars
    Mirror Maze (2000)
Holly, J. H. Mind Traders
Hoyle, T. Vail (Eng.)
Hoyne, T. T. Intrigue on the Upper Level (Chi.)
Hudner, K. Heirs of the Kingdom
Hughes, G. Green Fire
Hunt, G. Planet X
Hurd, D. Send Him Victorious (Eng., 1975)
Hyman, T. Giant Killer (1984)
Ing, D. Soft Targets (1980-1)
James, D. Fall of the Russian Empire (Russ., 1986)
Janifer, L. Knave and the Game
Janson, H. Unseen Assassin
Javor, F. A. Rim-World Legacy
Jenkins, G. Fireprint
Johnson, S. God Bless America (U.S., 1976)
Johnson, W. O. Hammered Gold (L.A., 1984)
Jones, D. Barbarossa Red (1989)

Rubicon One (Mid. East, 1986)
Winter Palace (Russia, 1991)
Kadrey, R. Metrophage (L.A., 2000s)
Keeler, H. S. Box from Japan (Chi., 1942)
Kelly, T. J. Lost in Space and the Mortgage Due
Kerr, Katherine. Polar City Blues
Kilian, M. Northern Exposure (Ottawa)
Killough, L. Doppleganger Gambit
    Dragon's Teeth (Kan. City, 2000s)
    Spider Play (Kan. City)
Kilroy-Silk, R. Ceremony of Innocence (1984–2020)
Koman, V. Jehovah Contract
Koontz, D. R. Night Chills (Maine, 1977)
Kurland, M. Psi Hunt (U.S.)
Kurtz, K. Legacy of Lehr
Kytle, R. Star Griffin (2100s)
    Fire and Ice
Lamm, R. California Conspiracy (Calif., 1992)
    1988 (1988)
Land, J. Alpha Deception
Lang, K. Trans Mercurian
Laumer, K. Once There Was a Giant
    Other Side of Time
    Retief
    Reward for Retief
Lee, S. Dunn's Conundrum (Wash. D.C.)
Legge, R. Hawk
Leinster, M. Doctor to the Stars
Lippincott, D. E Pluribus Bang! (Wash. D.C.)
Long, F. B. John Carstairs, Space Detective
Lord, Graham. God and All His Angels (Eng.)
Lorrah, J. Vulcan Academy Murders
Lowe, S. Aurora (U.S., 1987)
Luna, K. Operation Orbit
McCarry, C. Better Angels (U.S., 1990s)
McCarthy, A. One Woman Lost (Wash. D.C., 1992)
McDonald, Raymond. Mad Scientist
McKinney, J. Kaduna Memories (NYC, 2000s)
McKinney, R. L. Kamchatka Incident (Russ., 1993)
McQuay, M. Deadliest Show in Town (2000s)
    Escape from New York (NYC, 1977)
    Hot Time in Old Town (2000s)
    Odds Are Murder (2000s)
    When Trouble Beckons (2000s)
Mackin, R. Fire Storm (Seattle, 1999)
    Gulf Attack (Texas, 1999)
Madden, T. A. Outbanker
Maddock, L. all 4 titles
Madsen, D. U.S.S.A.
Maine, C. E. Count-Down
Major, H. M. Alien Trace
Mann, Paul. Libyan Contract
Marriott, H. P. F. Iron Detective of Germany
Mather, A. Raid (Australia)
Matthews, Clyde. Ides of March Conspiracy
Merwin, S., Jr. Killer to Come
Michelmore, R. Adventure in Venus
Miller, Steve. Agent of Change
    Carpe Diem
Milton, N. D. China Option (China)
Mitchell, A. Bodyguard
Mitchell, V. E. Enemy Unseen (2200s)
Moore, C. L. Doomsday Morning
Moran, R. Dallas Down (1999)
Moreno, P. Digital Justice
Morris, Janet. Active Measures
    Forty-Minute War
    Threshold
Morris, Jim. Sheriff of Purgatory (Ark., 1996)
Mullin, C. Very British Coup (Eng., 1989)
Naha, E. Paradise Plot
    Suicide Plague
Nelson, W. Siege of Buckingham Palace (Eng., ca.1985)
Newman, K. Night Mayor
Niven, L. 5 titles
Noel, A. A. Murder on Usher's Planet
    Speaker to Heaven
Noel, S. I Killed Stalin (1959)
Nolan, W. F. Look Out for Space
    Space for Hire
Norwood, W. Stranded
    Trapped

Oppenheim, E. P. Wrath to Come (Fr., 1950)
O'Riordan, R. Cadre One
Panshin, A. all 3 titles
Pape, G. Scorpion Sanction (Egypt)
Pearson, P. Postscript for Malpas (Scot., 1985)
Peters, D. Mind-Force Warrior (2021)
Phillips, M. Brain Twisters
    Impossibles (NYC, 1972)
    Supermind (1973)
Pohl, F. Cool War
    Gladiator-at-Law
Pratt, F. Double Jeopardy
Quest, R. Countdown to Doomsday
    Fenton Affair
Quick, W. T. Systems
Raphael, R. President Must Die (Wash. D.C., 1990s)
Reaves, J. M. both titles
Reed, D. V. Murder in Space
Reeves-Stephens, G. Dark Matter (L.A., 1995)
Resnick, M. Second Contact (2065)
Reynolds, M. 6 titles
Ritner, P. Red Carpet for the Shah
Robens, H. Hambro's Itch
Robinett, S. Man Responsible (2000s)
    Stargate
Robinson, F. M. Great Divide (late 1980s)
Ross, D. D. Argus Gambit
Royce, K. 10,000 Days (Mid. East, 1984)
Ruff, I. Dark Red Star (Eng., 1990s)
Schlossstein, S. Kensei (Jap., 1985)
Schmidt, Dennis. Dark Paradise
Schmitz, J. H. all 5 titles
Scortia, T. N. Blowout!
Scott, H. No Exit (Moscow)
Seaver, T. Beanball (NYC)
Sebastian, T. Spy in Question (Moscow, 1990)
Shagan, S. Pillars of Fire (Mid. East, 1992)
Shatner, W. Tekwar (L.A., 2100s)
Shea, M. Tomorrow's Men (Eng.)
Sheckley, R. Hunter/Victim
    Victim Prime
Shirley, J. Black Hole of Carcosa
Simmons, G. Murdock (hosp., 2010)
Sloane, B. Blown Dead (NYC, 2026)
    Hot Zone (NYC)
Smith, G. H. Second War of Worlds
Smith, L. N. Probability Broach (1987)
Sohl, J. Altered Ego (2000s)
Spencer, J. both titles (Calif., 1997)
Spicer, M. Final Act (Eng., 2006)
Spruill, S. G. Imperator Plot
    Paradox Planet (2100)
    Psychopath Plague
Stapp, R. More Perfect Union (U.S., 1981)
Stein, B. Croesus Conspiracy (1982–4)
Stith, J. E. Deep Quarry
    Redshift Rendezvous
Stryker, H. NYPD 2025 (NYC, 2025)
Taylor, C. D. Counterstrike (Cuba)
Tennant, E. Last of the Country House Murders
Thompson, E. P. Sykaos Papers (Eng., 1990s)
Tine, R. Midnight City (NYC, 2000s)
    Uneasy Lies the Head (Eng.)
Topol, A. Fourth of July War (Iran, 1983)
Tower, Stella. Yesterday's Bones
Tregarron, Y. Murderer's Island
Trenhaile, J. Mahjong Spies (H. Kong)
Tucker, W. Time Bomb
    Wild Talent
Tyson, J. A. Scarlet Tanager (Wash. D.C., 1930)
Vance, J. 8 titles
Van Lhin, E. Police Your Planet
Verron, R. Day of the Dust (Eng.)
Vinge, J. D. Catspaw
Vinge, V. Marooned in Real Time
Wallace, Ian. 6 titles
Washburn, R. C. Jury of Death (Midwest, 1950)
Waters, T. A. Centerforce
Watt-Evans, L. Nightside City
Way, P. Super-Celeste
Webb, S. Adventures of Terra Tarkington
Weber, J. Defcon One
Weiner, A. Station Gehenna
Weisman, J. Watchdogs (Wash. D.C., 1988)

Wesley, M. Sixth Seal (Eng.)
West, Pamela. 20/20 Vision
Wheatley, D. Black August (Eng.)
Whitmore, E. D.E.A.D.
Wilhelm, K. Dark Door
Williamson, Jack. Mazeway
Wilson, F. P. Dydeetown World
Wilson, Gahan. Eddy Deco's Last Caper
Winslow, P. G. I, Martha Adams
Womack, J. Ambient (NYC)
Wood, Bari. Lightsource (late 1980s)
Woods, Brett. Britannia Obsession (Wash. D.C., 1987)
Wright, S. F. Prelude in Prague (1938)
Wulffson, D. Point-Blank (Mex., 1994)
Yaeger, C. H. Counterfeit Hostage (Russ., 1992)
    Hunger for Heroes (1992)
Yermakov, N. Journey from Flesh
Zahn, T. Coming of Age
Zessa, C. Paris 2005 (Paris, 2005)

GENEVA (See also: Switzerland; Zurich)
Ambler, E. Intercom Conspiracy
Beeding, F. Little White Hag
    Seven Sleepers
Carr, J. D. In Spite of Thunder
Carter, Nick. Nowhere Weapon
Carvic, H. Miss Seeton Sings
Diplomat. Slow Death at Geneva
Eskapa, S. Secret-Keeper
Freemantle, B. Runaround
Golan, M. Geneva Crisis
Macauley, R. Mystery at Geneva
Moyes, P. Death on the Agenda
Myers, P. Deadly Crescendo
Nisot, E. False Witness
    Hazardous Holiday
    Twelve to Dine
    Unnatural Deeds
Oldfeld, P. Death of a Diplomat
Title, E. All Through the Night
Torr, D. Treason Line
Upton, R. Golden Fleecing
Walker, M. Code Name: Judas
Whitman, J. T. Geneva Accord

GEORGIA (Ga. See also: Atlanta; South)
Alexander, Jan. Moon Garden
Ballard, M. F. Deadly Promise
Balmer, E. Golden Hoard
Bottoms, D. Easter Weekend
Brent, R. L. Cocaine Connection
Brewer, G. Backwoods Teaser
Brooks, H. Without a Warrant
Carr, J. B. Man with Bated Breath
Cline, C. T., Jr. Prey
Cranford, B. Rattlesnake Master
Daniels, D. Night Shadow
    Unearthly
Daniels, H. R. Girl in 304
Derrick, L. Divine Death
    Dixie Death Squad
Dexter, P. Paris Trout
Dickey, J. Deliverance
Diehl, W. Hooligans
Dougall, L. Earthly Purgatory
Dykes, L. Savannah Score
Feegel, J. R. Malpractice
Field, Medora. both titles
Fitz, J. D. Graven Image
Gordon, Arthur. Reprisal
Gray, Angela. Nightmare at Riverview
Haring, D. Spanish Harlem
Harris, A. L. Deliver Us from Evil
Harris, Charlaine. Real Murders
Hopkins, L. C. Black Buck
Jessup, R. Cry Passion
    Cunning and the Haunted
Kay, T. After Eli
    Dark Thirty
Keene, D. Farewell to Passion
Kennedy, S. Passage to Violence
Kimbrough, K. Barbara, the Valiant
    Millijoy, the Determined
McCrumb, S. Sick of Shadows

Settings Index

MacDonald, J. D. Crossroads
McShane, M. Just a Face in the Dark
Mann, Jessica. Funeral Sites
Matschat, C. H. Murder at Okefenokee
Mettler, G. Down Home
Moore, R. A. Death in the Past
Murphy, W. B. Final Crusade
Nicole, Claudette. Circle of Secrets
Packer, V. Dark Don't Catch Me
Parkhurst, J. Southern Moon
Pendleton, D. Savannah Swingsaw
Ross, Marilyn. Long Night of Fear
Savage, James. Girl in a Jam
Siegel, D. How Still My Love
Stivers, D. Deathbites
Strickland, B. Shadowshow
Upchurch, B. Scarborough Hall
Vance, S. Spook
Walsh, P. E. KKK
Webb, Sharon. Pestis 18
Wellard, J. Snake in the Grass
Whitney, P. A. Lost Island
Williams, B. A. Pirate's Purchase
Woods, Sherryl. Reckless
    Stolen Moments
Woods, Stuart. Chiefs
    Grass Roots
    Under the Lake

GERMANY (Ger. Both East and West Germany are included here. See also: Frankfurt; Hamburg; Munich; Berlin)
Abdullah, A. Man on Horseback
Albrand, M. Door Fell Shut
    Linden Affair
    Rhine Replica
Allain, M. Yellow Document
Allbeury, T. Only Good German
    Special Collection
Andreas, F. all 4 titles
Angellotti. M. P. Three Black Bags
Annesley, M. Spy Against the Reich
Anonymous. Shrewtzer Castle
Ashe, S. I Am Saxon Ashe
Bachmann, L. P. Lorelei
    Phoenix
Ballard, K. G. Gauge of Deception
Beech, W. Article 92: Murder-Rape
Beeding, F. Not a Bad Show
Behn, N. Shadowboxer
Berckman, E. Evil of Time
    Finger to Her Lips
    Strange Bedfellow
Bernard, J. Burning Fuse
Betteridge, D. Dictator's Destiny
    Escape of General Gerard
    Potsdam Murder Plot
Beymer, W. G. Middle of Midnight
Blackburn, J. Ring of Roses
Blagowidow, G. Last Train from Berlin
Bontly, T. Giant's Shadow
Brodeur, P. Sick Fox
Brunner, J. Wear the Butcher's Medal
Buchanan, J. Crossfire Kill
Buckley, W. F. Stained Glass
Burke, J. W. Three Day Pass—to Kill
Butler, Gwendoline. Brides of Friedberg
Butterworth, W. E. Court-Martial
Cargill, L. Lady Was Elusive
Carney, D. Square Circle
Carr, J. D. Castle Skull
Carter, N. Bright Blue Death
    Korean Tiger
    Reich Four
Chance, J. N. Killer Reaction
Chapman, John. Look, No Hans!
Charlesworth, M. Glass House
Charteris, L. Getaway
Chase, J. H. Whiff of Money
Cleri, M. Six Graves to Munich
Coles, M. Drink to Yesterday
    No Entry
    Now or Never
    Pray Silence

Conot, R. Nuremberg Gift
Cook, Nick. Angel, Archangel
Cook, T. H. Orchids
Cort, N. Alpine Gambit
Cory, D. Pilgrim on the Island
Craig, W. Strasbourg Legacy
Cross, J. Dark Road
D'Amore, G. V. ESPolska Ploy
Davidson, L. Making Good Again
Day, W. B. Man from M.O.D.
Deighton, L. Winter
Delamare, G. Midnight King
Dial, J. Echoes of War
Di Mona, J. To the Eagle's Nest
Duncan, A. Official Secret
Dunne, C. Retrieval
Elkins, A. J. Deceptive Clarity
    Fellowship of Fear
Esser, R. Paper Chase
Evans, W. P. Double Cross Squadron
Fallon, M. Testament of Caspar Schultz
Fanger, H. Life for a Life
Farr, C. Castle on the Rhine
Ferguson, J. Terror on the Island
Firth, A. Tall, Balding, Thirty-Five
Fischer, E. Berlin Indictment
Forbes, C. Leader and the Damned
Ford, Hilary. Bella on the Roof
Forsyth, F. Odessa File
Fox, J. M. Cheese from a Mousetrap
Frank, L. Cause of the Crime
Freeling, N. Dresden Green
    Gadget
Fuller, S. Dead Pigeon on Beethoven Street
Gaite, F. Far Traveler
Gardiner, W. J. Man on the Left
Gibbs, G. F. Golden Bough
    Silver Death
    Yellow Dove
Glendinning, R. Mission to Murder
Goodchild, G. Q33
Gordon, Alex. Cipher
Gray, B. Six Feet of Dynamite
Grayson, R. Thieves' Highway
Gregor, M. Town Without Pity
Gurr, D. Ring Master
Hall, Adam. Quiller KGB
    Striker Portfolio
Hall, Michael. Once Upon a Crime
Hallahan, W. H. Trade
Hardy, J. L. Recoil
Harrington, W. English Lady
    Search for Elizabeth Brandt
Hart-Davis, D. Level Five
Hastings, M. M. City of Endless Night
Hawthorne, J. Professor's Sister
Hebden, M. Mask of Violence
Hedges, J. Gold Plated Hearse
Helitzer, F. Hans, Who Goes There?
Herlin, H. Friends
    Solo Run
Heywood, J. Berkut
Higgins, J. Day of Judgement
    Eagle Has Landed
Hittleman, C. K. 36 Hours
Hogan, R. J. Aces of the White Death
    Bat Staffel
    Vultures of the White Death
Holt, Gavin. Dark Street
Hunter, J. D. Expendable Spy
    One of Us Works for Them
    Tin Cravat
Innes, H. Air Bridge
Jacques, N. Dr. Mabuse, Master of Mystery
Janson, H. Nyloned Avenger
Johnson, J. L. Handful of Dominoes
Jones, V. Monument of Terror
Jute, A. Zaharoff Commission
Kail, R. Swastika
Kastner, E. Missing Miniature
Kemeny, J. A. Strands of War
Kennedy, J. D. Rain of Death
Kennedy, W. P. Himmler Equation
Kenrick, T. 81st Site

GERMANY / 1247

Keystone, O. Major Crime
Kielland, A. Dangerous Honeymoon
King, Frank. Crooks' Cross
Knopp, J. M. Eternal Reich
Kozhevnikov, V. Shield and Sword
Latimer, J. Border of Darkness
Lee, Elsie. Dark Moon, Lost Lady
    Romance on the Rhine
    Sinister Abbey
LeQueux, W. Behind the German Lines
    More Secrets of Potsdam
Lucas, R. Who Dares to Live
McCormick, J. Last Seen Alive
McGarrity, M. Passing Advantage
McKenna, M. Nightfighter Spy
Mackenzie, A. M. Dusseldorf
MacKenzie, D. Double Exposure
MacLean, Alistair. Where Eagles Dare
Mans, A. On the Shores of Night
Marchmont, A. W. Dash for a Throne
Marlowe, S. Trouble Is My Name
Martin, H. Sleeping Girls Don't Lie
Mason, Howard. Red Bishop
Maxwell, K. Equinox
Melchior, I. Code Name: Grand Guignol
    Eva
    Haigerloch Project
    Order of Battle
    V-3
Miehe, U. Puma
Moore, Dorinne. Caverns of Falkenhorst
Morgulas, J. Torquemada Principle
Neuman, F. Maneuvers
Newman, B. Traveling Executioner
Nicholson, R. Passion for Treason
Nolan, F. Alert State Black
    Mittenwald Syndicate
    Ritter Double-Cross
    Wolf-Trap
O'Neill, F. Secret Country
Palmer, L. Night Music
Paris, A. Teeth of the Wolf
Parish, J. Hour of the Unicorn
Parsons, Mrs. Castle of Wolfenbach
    Mysterious Warning
Pendleton, D. Bloodsport
    Trojan Horse
Persico, J. E. Spiderweb
Peters, Elizabeth. Borrower of the Night
    Trojan Gold
Peters, R. Bravo Romeo
Pinkham, W. Second Oldest Profession
Preedy, G. R. Painted Angel
Price, Anthony. New Kind of War
Price, Ashland. Enemy in My Arms
Puccetti, R. Death of the Fuhrer
Rabe, P. Shroud for Jesso
Ramsey, E. Kummersdorf Connection
Raven, S. Sabre Squadron
Revere, J. D. Assassin
Robertson, Charles. Elijah Conspiracy
Robinson, B. F. Trail of the Dead
Rochester, G. E. Return of Grey Shadow
    Secret Squadron in Germany
Rohmer, R. Hour of the Fox
Rohmer, S. Day the World Ended
Rosenberger, J. Methuselah Factor
Rosenkrantz, P. Magistrate's Own Case
Rostov, M. Eroica
    Night Hunt
Rushton, C. Murder in Bavaria
    No Second Stroke
Saffron, R. Demon Device
St. George, G. Proteus Pact
Saltmarsh, M. Indigo Death
Scott, C. Hitler's Bomb
Sela, O. Exchange of Eagles
Semenov, J. Himmler Ploy
Seton, G. Red Colonel
    W Plan
Seymour, G. Contract
Shapiro, L. Sealed Verdict
Shaw, B. Nazi Hunter
Sherwood, J. Disappearance of Dr. Bruderstein

G

Short, C. Black Room
　　Dark Lantern
Simmel, J. M. Cain '67
　　Dear Fatherland
　　Love Is Just a Word
Sinclair, Michael. Sonntag
Sinstadt, G. Fidelio Score
Siodmak, C. Third Ear
Sleath, E. Orphan of the Rhine
Smith, R. A. Fox Trap
Spetz, S. Nuke Hill
Storm, J. Dark Emerald
Sussman, B. J. Crooked Cross
Tarrant, J. Clauberg Trigger
Taylor, Andrew. Toyshop
Teilhet, D. L. Talking Sparrow Murders
Tellet, R. Draught of Lethe
Thomas, Leslie. Orange Wednesday
Thomas, P. Code Name: Rubble
　　Spy
Thomas, Ross. Cold War Swap
　　Eighth Dwarf
Thompson, S. L. Recovery
Tiger, J. Code Name: Little Ivan
Tobias, K. Lady in the Lightning
Trevor, E. Damocles Sword
Vance, E. Escape
Von Tautphoeus, Baroness. Cyrilla
Wager, W. Time of Reckoning
Walser, M. No Man's Land
Watson, H. B. M. Alise of Astra
Watson, P. Nazi's Wife
Weill, G. Fuhrer Seed
Wheatley, D. Faked Passports
　　Scarlet Imposter
　　Second Seal
　　They Used Dark Forces
White, Alan. Long Night's Walk
Williams, V. Crouching Beast
Willis, T. Lions of Judah
Wilson, A. Wallace Intervenes
Wilson, Gar. Bonn Blitz
　　Main Offensive
　　Ultimate Terror
Winward, W. Ball Bearing Run
　　Canaris Fragments
Wormser, R. Torn Curtain

GHANA (See also: Africa)
Birmingham, M. Heat of the Sun

GIBRALTAR (Gib.)
Anderson, M. Tales of the Rock
Benady, S. Sherlock Holmes in Gibraltar
Berrow, N. Terror in the Fog
Betteridge, D. Gibraltar Conspiracy
Biggers, E. D. Inside the Lines
Horler, S. Bullet for the Countess
McCutchan, P. Gibraltar Road
Newman, B. Death Under Gibraltar
Perowne, B. Gibraltar Prisoner
　　Raffles' Crime in Gibraltar

GLASGOW (See also: Scotland; Edinburgh; Hebrides)
Anonymous. Alfred Leslie
Boyce, C. Blooding Mr. Naylor
Boyd, E. Dark Number
Carver, S. Died O'Wednesday
Dekker, C. Wax Model
Devine, D. M. My Brother's Killer
Fraser, S. Night in George Square
Knox, B. 13 titles
Lindsay, F. Jill Rips
McIlvanney, W. Laidlaw
　　Papers of Tony Veitch
MacNaught, T. P. Recollections of a Glasgow Detective Officer
Malloch, P. Break-Through
　　11.20 Glasgow Central
　　Lady of No Compassion
Miller, H. Mourning Brooch
Munro, H. Clutha Plays a Hunch
　　Who Told Clutha

Rae, H. C. Marksman
Ross, Marilyn. Phantom of the Snow
Swan, A. S. Maclure Mystery
Tremaine, J. Maggie
Turnbull, P. 6 titles
West, P. E. Madeleine

GREECE (See also: Athens; Balkans; Crete; Macedonia)
Aiken, Joan. Butterfly Picnic
　　Last Movement
Appleby, J. Aphrodite Means Death
Arundale, P. Bread and Olives
Ballinger, B. S. Beacon in the Night
Bell, Josephine. Catalyst
Bennett, Janice. House of Athena
Black, I. S. Man on the Bridge
Blake, P. Escape to Athena
Brett, S. Mrs. Pargeter's Package
Brunner, J. Good Men Do Nothing
Bryon, C. Foreign Matter
Carter, Nick. Assassin—Code Name Vulture
　　Liquidator
　　Seven Against Greece
　　Ultimate Code
Cole, G. D. H. Greek Tragedy
Colman, G. D. Reckless Passage
Davidson, A. Out from the Shadows
Davis, D. S. Enemy and Brother
Davis, H. C. Perhaps to Kill
Dickinson, P. Lizard in the Cup
Divomlikoff, L. Traitor
Edwards, Jane. Dangerous Odyssey
Emmett, R. Trojan Horses
Filgate, C. M. Runway to Death
Fisher, N. Rise at Dawn
Forbes, C. Heights of Zervos
Francis, E. Elena
Gage, N. Eleni
Goddard, R. Into the Blue
Goshgarian, G. Atlantis Fire
Gruber, F. Greek Affair
Haden, P. Angry Island
Harvey, J. Coup D'Etat
Hawkins, F. N. Ritter's Gold
Higgins, J. Night Judgment at Sinos
Hodge, J. A. Strangers in Company
Horton, G. Monk's Treasure
Innes, H. Levkas Man
Jason, S. Grecian Bloodbath
Jones, James. Touch of Danger
Katcher, L. Blind Cave
Kirton, J. Greek Fire
Lathen, E. When in Greece
Loraine, P. Dead Men of Sestos
MacInnes, H. Decision at Delphi
　　Double Image
McManus, L. Operation Backlash
Markham, R. Colonel Sun
Martin, Shane. Myth Is Murder
Mather, M. Damian
Maybury, A. Walk in the Paradise Garden
Michaels, B. Sea King's Daughter
Mitchell, G. Come Away, Death
Mitchell, J. Death and Bright Water
Moody, S. Penny Wise
Morley, E. Sinister Isle of Love
Muir, Jean. Smiling Medusa
Nielsen, H. Shot on Location
O'Donnell, P. Dead Man's Handle
Osborne, H. Arcadian Affair
Paris, A. Graven Image
Parker, Derek. Trade of Angels
Patterson, H. Dark Side of the Island
Pendower, J. Traitor's Island
Phillifent, J. T. Corfu Affair
Rosenblum, R. Cover Stories
Ross, Marilyn. Night of the Phantom
Scott, Douglas. Operation Artemis
Sheen, G. Assignment Greece
Smithson, R. L. Dowry of Danger
Stallworth, L. Pot Shot
Stewart, M. My Brother Michael
　　This Rough Magic

Streib, D. Deadly Crusader
Swift, B. Mission Code: Acropolis
Unsworth, B. Idol Hunter
Vasilos, T. Wolf's Prey
Wheatley, D. Dangerous Inheritance
　　Mayhem in Greece
White, J. M. Moscow Papers
Whitney, P. A. Seven Tears for Apollo
Wilk, M. Eliminate the Middle Man
Wilson, G. Harvest Hell
Wilson, I. Empty Tigers
Worboys, A. Lion of Delos
Yorke, M. Grave Matters

GREENLAND (Green. See also: Denmark; Copenhagen; Scandinavia)
Axton, D. Prison of Ice
Higgins, J. East of Desolation
Kyle, D. In Deep
MacLean, Alistair. Night Without End
Raven, J. Pinnacle of Ice
Rosenberger, J. Greenland Mystery
Scott, J. M. Snowstone

GRENADA (See also: West Indies)
Pendleton, D. Death Wind

GUATEMALA (Guat. See also: Central America)
Amos, A. Pray for a Miracle
Clifford, F. Amigo, Amigo
Daniels, D. Maya Temple
Earley, F. Ransom in Jade
Graves, R. L. Quicksilver
Hill, R. L. Evil That Men Do
Knight, K. M. Bells for the Dead
Leonard, P. G. Phantom of the Sacred Well
McLarty, N. Chain of Death
Murphy, W. B. Time Trial
O'Donnell, P. Last Day in Limbo
Stivers, D. Death Strike
　　Ironman
　　Warlord of Azatlan
Wilson, Gar. Barracuda Run

GUIANA (See also: Guyana; Surinam; South America)
Coxe, G. H. Assignment in Guiana

GUYANA (See also: Guiana; Surinam; South America)
Aarons, W. B. Assignment Tiger Devil
Adams, M. Mudland
Capon, P. Amongst Those Missing
Coxe, G. H. Man on a Rope
Davies, W. X. Operation Choke Point
Hesla, S. Hawthorn Conspiracy
Wallbridge, C. S. Through a Glass Darkly
Wilson, Gar. Terror in Guyana

HAITI (See also: West Indies; Caribbean)
Arnett, J. Death Force
Ballinger, W. A. Drums of the Dark Gods
Becker, S. Rendezvous in Haiti
Binns, O. Treasure of Christophe
Buck, P. Deadly Birdman
Carter, Nick. Black Death
　　Terrible Ones
Case, Jim. Hellfire in Haiti
Cullimore, A. Bad Day in the Bahamas
Daniels, D. Dark Island
Davison, J. Devil's Horsemen
Graeme, D. Drums Beat Red
Greene, G. Comedians
Hayes, R. Illegal Entry
Hogan, R. J. Flight from the Grave
McCurtin, P. Battle Pay
Marlowe, D. Nightshade
Pendleton, D. Haitian Hit
Phillips, J. A. Deadly Mermaid
Roscoe, T. Murder on the Way!
Ross, Marilyn. Haiti Circle
Smith, Don. Haitian Vendetta
Teed, G. H. Voodoo Island

Thorne, E. P. Assignment Haiti
    Caribbean Affair
Vandercook, J. Murder in Haiti
Wheatley, D. Strange Conflict

HAMBURG (Hamb. See also: Germany; Berlin; Frankfurt; Munich)
Baker, W. H. It Happened in Hamburg
McDougall, M. C. Chase the Snowman
Pendleton, D. Blowout
Ross, A. Hamburg Switch
Skinner, M. Somewhere in Hamburg

HANOI (See also: Viet Nam; Saigon; Far East)
Blacker, I. R. Search and Destroy
Carter, Nick. Asian Mantrap
    Hanoi

HAVANA (See also: Cuba; West Indies; Caribbean)
Barry, M. Havana Hit
Carpentier, A. Chase
Carter, Nick. Death Mission; Havana
Colton, M. Big Woman
Coxe, G. H. Murder in Havana
    Woman at Bay
Cutler, R. Gates of Sagittarius
Darby, R. Death Conducts a Tour
Davis, Gordon. I Came to Kill
Dudley, F. Havana Hotel Murders
Goldman, L. Black Fire
Green, E. P. Perfect Fools
Greene, G. Our Man in Havana
Gross, S. Havana X
Guenter, C. H. Dead Drop in Havana
Haring, D. Honey-Blonde Blues!
Harrigan, S. Cuban Heel
Sanger, J. Case of the Missing Corpse
Spewack, S. Murder in the Gilded Cage
Sylvester, R. Big Boodle
Wade, R. Knave of Eagles

HAWAII (Haw. Principally Honolulu settings)
Aresbys. Mark of the Dead
    Murder at Red Pass
Arnold, M. Menehune Murders
Avallone, M. Hawaii Five-O
    Terror in the Sun
Barroll, C. Shadow Man
Beck, K. K. Peril Under the Palsm
Bickerton, D. King of the Sea
Biggers, E. D. Black Camel
    House Without a Key
Bingham, C. It Happened in Hawaii
Blair, Alma. Dark Side of Paradise
Burke, W. Time of Innocence
Carter, Nick. Doomsday Formula
    Hawaii
Cassiday, B. Girl in the Trunk
Castle, F. Hawaiian Eye
Coffman, V. Chinese Door
    House of Sandalwood
    Orchid Tree
Corrigan, M. Honolulu Snatch
Crane, R. Paradise Trap
Davis, Mildred. Strange Corner
Deptula, W. both titles
Dewey, T. B. Too Hot for Hawaii
Dudley, D. What Dark Secret
Eyre, K. W. Sandalwood Fan
Fair, A. A. Some Women Won't Wait
Farr, C. Island of Evil
Fisher, Michael. Cries from the Darkness
Ford, L. Honolulu Story
Glendinning, R. Death Match
Hamilton, D. Betrayers
Hamilton, I. Never Die in Honolulu
Harris, H. Angry Battalion
Hintzi, N. Aloha Means Goodbye
Huntsberry, W. E. both titles
Jason. Honolulu Slay Ride
Joyce, D. Matter of Time
Katkov, N. Blood and Orchids
Kaufman, J. Jewel of the Seas

Knebel, F. Dave Sulkin Cares!
Knight, C. Affair of the Ginger Lei
    Affair of the Splintered Heart
Laflin, J. Silent Kind of War
Long, Max. all 3 titles
Lustbader, E. V. Zero
McCurtin, P. Bloodbath
Marquand, J. P. Think Fast, Mr. Moto
Mason, V. W. Branded Spy Murders
Morgan, P. Hagn Dead Hawaiian Style
    Scarlet Surf at Makaha
Morrison, R. Tree of Evil
Nash, N. R. East Wind, Rain
Pendleton, D. Hawaiian Hellground
Prather, R. S. Dance with the Dead
Raines, J. Big Island
Rogers, M. I. H. Horror in Hawaii
St. Clair, R. Mystery in Hawaii
Schuler, F. Pearl Harbor Cover-Up
Sharpe, A. Vanishing Bridegroom
Sheridan, J. Kahuna Killer
    Mamo Murders
    Waikiki Widow
Steven, E. E. Kat and Copy-Cat
Stivers, D. Iron God
Streib, D. Hawaiian Takeover
Stuart, H. L. Ginger Flower
Swigart, R. Toxin
    Vector
Teilhet, D. L. Feather Cloak Murders
Vandercook, J. W. Murder in Hawaii
Von Elsner, D. Countdown for a Spy
    How to Succeed at Murder Without Really Trying
    Those Who Prey Together Slay Together
Walker, Irma. Maunaloa Curse
Wallace, V. Eyes Upon a Wet Grave
Webb, J. F. Bride of Cairngorn
    Is This Coffin Taken?
    Somewhere Within This House
Whitney, P. A. Silversword
Whittington, H. Brass Monkey
Wilson, G. Dragon's Kill
Wylie, P. Spy Who Spoke Porpoise
Yates, M. T. Murder by the Yard
Zimmelman, L. Honolulu Red

HEBRIDES (See also: Scotland; Edinburgh; Glasgow)
Barr, R. Dark Island
Black, G. Big Wind for Summer
Bridge, A. Dangerous Islands
Campbell, Karen. Thunder on Sunday
Devine, A. D. U-Boat in the Hebrides
Dickinson, P. Seals
Ferrars, E. Wandering Widows
Grayson, R. Death Stalk
Grindal, R. Over the Sea to Die
Hebden, M. Dark Side of the Island
John, O. McGregor's Island
Kirk, R. Old House of Fear
Knox, B. Devilweed
McLarty, D. Deep Blue Seize
McLean, A. C. Death on All Hallows
MacVicar, A. Killings on Kersivay
Pugh, M. Last Place Left
Ross, Marilyn. Loch Sinister
Roy, A. All Evil Shed Away
Williams, V. Portcullis Room

HELSKINKI (See also: Finland; Scandinavia)
Fleming, Joan. You Won't Let Me Finish
Granger, B. British Cross
Joensuu, M. Harjunpaa and the Stone Murders
Kilhlman, C. Downfall of Gerdt Bladh
Sariola, M. both titles
Smith, K. N. Country of the Heart

HISTORICAL SETTINGS. See: Past.

HOLLAND (Holl. See also: Amsterdam)
Aarons, E. S. Assignment—Lowlands
Albrand, M. No Surrender

Arley, C. Matter of Opportunity
Ashe, S. Saxon Ashe . . . Secret Agent
Baddock, J. Radar Job
Brent, N. No Space for Murder
Brierley, D. Blood Group O
Canning, V. House of the Seven Flies
Clive, J. Last Liberator
Freeling, N. 5 titles
Janson, H. Silken Menace
Jones, T. Dutch Treat
Koning, H. De Witt's War
Lawman, A. Hounds of Spring
McCarthy, M. Cannibals and Missionaries
MacLean, A. Floodgate
Maartens, M. Sin of Joost Avelingh
Mandel, P. Black Ship
Marlowe, A. Thunder in the Kirk
Moyes, P. Death and the Dutch Uncle
Norton, A. At Sword's Point
Perry, Ritchie. Dutch Courage
Sanders, R. Dutch Justice
Scott, Annjeanette. Count of Van Rheeden Castle
Simenon, G. Crime in Holland
White, A. Long Night's Walk

HONDURAS (See also: Central America)
Stivers, D. Kill School

HONG KONG (H. Kong. See also: China; Shanghai; Peking; Formosa; Far East; Macao)
Ames, J. Perilous Quest
Atlee, P. Kowloon Contract
Bennett, J. Dragon
Black, G. Eyes Around Me
Bobker, L. R. Flight of a Dragon
Brown, Carter. Bird in a Guilt-Edged Cage
    Chinese Donavan
    Hong Kong Caper
Brown, Wenzell. Hong Kong Aftermath
Browne, W. City of Masks
Carter, Nick. 5 titles
Chaber, M. E. Jade for a Lady
    Man in the Middle
Clavell, J. Noble House
Cohan, T. Opium
Cooke, D. C. 14th Agent
Coqhoun, K. Filthy Rich
Corrigan, M. Sin of Hong Kong
Crane, F. Three Days in Hong Kong
Crowcraft, P. That Man Bolt
Daniels, D. Affair in Hong Kong
    House of the Seven Courts
Daniels, N. Baron of Hong Kong
Dark, J. Assignment Hong Kong
Davis, F. M. Secret: Hong Kong
Davis, J. G. Years of the Hungry Tiger
Dekker, C. Danger Doll
Dodge, D. Hooligan
Drake, F. Double Identity
Driscoll, P. Pangolin
Freemantle, B. Inscrutable Charlie Muffin
Gash, Jonathan. Jade Woman
Gerson, N. B. All That Glitters
Gilman, D. Mrs. Pollifax and the Hong Kong Buddha
Hall, Adam. Mandarin Cypher
Harcourt, P. Agents of Influence
Harding, R. S. L. Demon of Hong Kong
Hartland, M. Down Among the Dead Men
Hartmann, M. Tigers of Deceit
Hutton, A. Ivory Slave
Kenrick, T. Neon Tough
Key, S. A. Cain's Chinese Puzzle
Konkel, K. G. E. Glorious East Wind
Lambert, D. Triad
Leather, S. Hungry Ghost
Le Carre, J. Honourable Schoolboy
Lustbader, E. V. Jian
McCurtin, P. Operation Hong Kong
McLachlan, I. Seventh Hexagram
Manson, W. Chinese Conundrum
Marshall, W. 13 titles

Mason, V. W. Hong Kong Airbase Murders
Mason-Parker, S. Wind and the Water
Mather, B. Hour of the Dog
Matthews, Clayton. Hong Kong
Maybury, A. Jeweled Daughter
Mills, A. Stowaway
Milton, J. Death Makers
Morton, A. Baron and the Chinese Puzzle
Norman, E. Hang Me in Hong Kong
O'Callaghan, D. Scavengers
Pence, J. Armed and Dangerous
Pereira, M. Pigeon's Blood
Peters, Bryan. Hong Kong Kill
Rosenberger, J. Hong Kong Massacre
Ross, Clarissa. Jade Princess
Schorr, M. Seize the Dragon
Scott, Justin. Widow of Desire
Sela, O. Bengali Inheritance
Sheldon, W. J. House of Happy Mayhem
Stewart, I. Peking Payoff
Stewart, W. T. Gaff Lee, Detective
Trenhaile, J. Spies
Wheatley, D. Bill for the Use of a Body
Whittle, A. Hong Kong Club
Wilson, Gar. Weep, Moscow, Weep

HONOLULU. See: Hawaii.

HOSPITAL (Hosp.)
Bachmann, L. Bitter Lake
Bayne, I. Death and Benedict
Bayne-Powell, I. Death Enters the Ward
Bell, Josephine. Murder in Hospital
    No Escape
    Trouble in Hunter Ward
    Wolf! Wolf!
Berliner, R. Hiding Places
Binder, O. O. Hospital Horror
Bramhall, M. Tragedy in Blue
Brand, C. Green for Danger
Bryan, M. Intent to Kill
Calderwood, C. Bonesetter's Brawl
Candy, E. Which Doctor?
Carroll, J. Baby Killer
Clark, M. H. Cradle Will Fall
Cohen, Anthea. Angel of Death
    Angel of Vengeance
    Angel Without Mercy
    Guardian Angel
Collee, J. Kingsley's Touch
Cook. R. Coma
Craig, R. Trauma
Curtiss, E. M. Nine Doctors and a Madman
Curtiss, U. Danger: Hospital Zone
Davis, M. Hospital Murders
    Murder Without Weapons
De Puy, E. S. Hospital Homicides
    Long Knife
Di Fiore, F. Mask
Eberhart, M. G. From This Dark Stairway
    Glass Slipper
    Patient in Room 18
Edwards, J. G. all 8 titles
Eyles, A. W. Murder in Hospital
Fast, J. Bright Face of Danger
Fitz, J. D. Viper's Bite
Francis, B. Death on the Roof
Gill, B. M. Victims
Green, Gerald. Hostage Heart
Greene, J. E. Madmen Die Alone
Hastings, C. Bonaventure
Holding, E. S. Miasma
Horvitz, L. Compton Effect
Hubbard, M. A. Murder at St. Dennis
Joshua, B. Drop of Murder
Katz, W. Facemaker
Kerr, J. Emergency Room
Kittredge, M. Dead and Gone
    Fatal Diagnosis
Klavans, H. L. Informed Concent
    Sins of Commission
Klein, D. M. Beauty Sleep
Kramer, Y. Primal Scene
Lambirth, F. Behind the Door

Lees, H. Death in the Doll's House
    Prescription for Murder
Leonard, G. Beyond Control
Little, C. Black Corridors
    Black Smith
    Black Stocking
    Black Thumb
McClintock, A. Case of the Three Broken Necks
McCully, W. Doctors Beware!
McEvoy, H. Jones, A., Finds the Body
Marsh, N. Nursing-Home Murder
Mix, T. Question of Judgement
Munder, L. Therapy for Murder
Neuman, F. Seclusion Room
Olgin, H. A. Cover Up
Palmer, M. Sisterhood
Perry, F. Mystery of the Girl in Blue
Perry, J. D. Murder Walks the Corridors
Platt, R. Letting Blood
Pronin, B. Syndrome
Ravin, N. Seven North
Reiter, B. P. Saturday Night Knife and Gun Club
Robinson, L. R. Blood Run
Ross, A. B. Murder Cure
Royce, K. Woodcutter Operation
Sapir, R. Murder Ward
Scott, Sutherland. Murder in the Mobile Unit
Simmons, G. Murdock
Sinclair, Fiona. Dead of a Physician
Sobel, I. P. Dr. Monte Cristo
Spruill, S. Painkiller
Trevor, E. Theta Syndrome
Truax, R. Accident Ward Mystery
Wakefield, R. I. Death the Sure Physician
Ward, R. Sandman
Way, J. H. Dream Watch
Wilkinson, Sandra. Brain Death
Wilkinson, S. D. Death on Call
Williamson, B. G. Death Stalks the Ward
Wilson, R. C. Icefire

HOUSTON (See also: Texas; Austin; Dallas; San Antonio; Southwest)
Anderson, Rex. My Dead Brother
    Night Calls
Baker, Susan. My First Murder
Barthelme, P. Brainfade
    Tart, with a Silken Finish
Bickham, J. Day Seven
Brandon, J. Predator's Waltz
Cooley, M. You'll Hear from Us
Cooper, S. R. Houston in the Rearview Mirror
Cunningham, Chet. Houston Hellground
Dale, J. A. Long Distance
Donahue, J. Confessor
    Lady Loved Too Well
    Pray to the Hustlers' God
Furman, L. Shadow Line
Goldman, L. Judd for the Defense #2
Hilborn, A. Personal Justice
Holmes, A. Wake of a Lawyer
Irving, C. Trial
Lansdale, J. R. Act of Love
Lindsey, D. L. Cold Mind
    Heat from Another Sun
    Mercy
    Spiral
Moore, Robin. Search and Destroy
Mosiman, B. S. Wireman
Ramm, C. Houston Attack
Saunders, L. Smoke Screen
Stevens, Linda. Shadowplay
Wolfe, J. Drilling for Death

HUNGARY (Hung. See also: Budapest)
Baker, W. H. Inexpendable
Blackstock, C. Knock at Midnight
Bridge, A. Tightening String
De Villiers, G. Countess and the Spy
Fagyas, M. Widowmaker
Graeme, B. Trail of the White Knight
Klein, E. Parachutists
Luard, N. Warm and Golden War
Moore, Edward. Mysteries of Hungary

Newton, D. Red Judas
Parker, Robert. Passport to Peril
Roby, M. L. Hidden Book
Vance, L. J. Woman in the Shadow
Wheatley, D. Traitor's Gate
Williams, V. Three of Clubs

ICELAND (Ice.)
Bagley, D. Running Blind
Decker, J. Death Gambit
Dobner, M. P. Sea Wind
Dunne, C. Black Ice
Kilian, M. Valkyrie Project
MacLeod, Robert. Incident in Iceland
Marlowe, S. Danger Is My Line
Pendleton, D. Blood Heat Zero

IDAHO (Ida. See also: West)
Ahern, J. D.E.A.T.H. Hunters
Burroughs, R. Fugitive Feet
Dobbins, P. H. Murder Moon
Easton, L. Driven Flesh
Lane, G. Stolen Scar
La Pierre, J. Cruel Mother
Loban, E. H. Calloused Eye
McCall, W. Aim for the Heart
    Dead Aim
Maning, K. Swastika
Offord, L. G. Clues to Burn
Pendleton, D. Brothers in Blood
Robeson, K. Glass Mountain
Shaw, R. Running
Wren, M. K. Seasons of Death

ILLINOIS (Ill. See also: Chicago; Midwest)
Allen, Glen. Ace Squadron
Balmer, E. Shield of Silence
Barry, Joe. Pay-Off
Baylor, D. B. Fatal Obsession
Brod, D. C. Error in Judgment
Browne, H. Taste of Ashes
Brucker, M. Girl Named Marica
Burkey, D. Rain Lover
Cannell, D. Mum's the Word
Casey, R. J. Third Owl
Cohen, Charles. Silver Linings
    Those Lake View Wives
Cook, E. Forbidden Tower
Crane, F. Golden Box
Cromie, A. Lucky to Be Alive?
Curtis, W. A. Strange Adventures of Mr. Middleton
Davis, D. S. Shock Wave
Dewey, T. B. Deadline
    Handle with Fear
    Hue and Cry
    Sad Song Singing
Dundee, W. D. Burning Season
    Skintight Shroud
Eatock, M. Haunted Heirloom
    See No Evil
Eberhart, M. G. Danger in the Dark
    Fair Warning
Evans, Fallon. Pistols and Pedagogues
Everson, D. 5 titles
Fonseca, E. H. Affair at the Grotto
Foote-Smith, E. Never Say Die
Grandower, E. Secret Room of Morgate House
Guthrie, Al. both titles
Hanley, E. Guilty As Charged
Hinkemeyer, M. T. Order of the Arrow
Howard, J. A. Bullet-Proof Martyr
Jenkins, J. Courtney
    Hilary
    Karlyn
    Paige
Johnson, R. Lady in Dread
Jorgenson, N. Circle of Vengeance
Keeler, H. S. Chameleon
Kenyon, M. Whole Hog
Knotts, R. Meeting by Moonlight
Lobaugh, E. K. I Am Afraid
    She Never Reached the Top
Lore, P. Who Killed the Pie Man?
MacDonald, J. D. Death Trap

Settings Index

McInerny, R. 11 titles
Maxwell, W. So Long, See You Tomorrow
Neidig, W. J. Fire Flingers
Nevins, F. M. Ninety Million Dollar Mouse
O'Brien, Darcy. Murder in Little Egypt
Pendleton, D. Monday's Mob
Plum, M. Dead Man's Secret
Postgate, J. W. Woman's Devotion
Potts, J. Go, Lovely Rose
Pulver, M. M. Ashes to Ashes
    Unforgiving Minutes
Rice, C. Eight Faces at Three
Roberts, D. Beginning of a Crime
Rosenberger, J. Death Trap
Runyon, C. Black Moth
Russell, C. M. 5 titles
Scott, Denis. Beckoning Shadow
Skom, E. Mark Twain Murder
Spencer, R. H. Abu Wahab Caper
    Echoes of Zero
    Stranger City Caper
Stevens, S. B. Bloodstone Inheritance
Stokes, M. L. Wolf Howls Murder
Truscott, L. K. Rules of the Road
Tucker, W. 6 titles
Unekis, R. Chase
Vale, R. M. House on Rainbow Leap
Van Atta, W. Good Place to Work and Die
    Hatchet Man
    Shock Treatment
Walker, R. N. Brain Watch
Wallis, J. H. Woman He Chose
Warren, V. Brandon Returns
Webster, H. K. Who Is the Next?
Whitehead, J. House on the Hill
Wilder, T. Eighth Day
Wolfe, G. Castleview

INDIA (See also: Bombay; Calcutta; New Delhi; Indian Ocean)
Abdullah, A. Red Stain
Abraham, C. S. Five Plus Four
Aiken, Joan. Lightning Tree
Andrul. Wayside
Angus, J. Scorpion's Nest
Arnold, Edwin. Queen's Justice
Ashton, M. Nana's Talisman
Aylward, M. Harper's Luck
Ballinger, W. A. Carrion Eaters
Banerjea, S. B. Indian Detective Stories
    Tales of Bengal
Blochman, L. G. Bengal Fire
    Bombay Mail
    Red Snow at Darjeeling
    Wives to Burn
Breem, W. Leopard and the Cliff
Bruce, K. Fakir's Curse
    Sliding Death
Campbell, H. Secret Brotherhood
Carnac, N. Indigo
Carter, Nick. Arms of Vengeance
    Double Identity
Casberg, M. A. all 3 titles
Channing, M. King Cobra
    Nine Lives
Cleary, J. Faraway Drums
Cooke, D. C. c/o American Embassy
Cooper, Brian. Mission for Betty Smith
    Touch of Thunder
    Van Langeren Girl
Cox, E. C. all 3 titles
Creasey, J. Wings of Peace
Dellbridge, J. Moles of Death
Drummond, I. Necklace of Skulls
Easterman, D. Ninth Buddha
Easton, J. Ferrol Bond
Edwards, P. Holocaust Auction
Egleton, C. Death of a Sahib
Eliade, M. Two Tales of the Occult
Emery, J. I. Tiger of Baragunga
Ferguson, J. Secret Road
Fforde, B. Trotter
Fisher, Richard. Indian Police
Friedman, M. Fault Tree

Ganpat. Speakers in Silence
Gould, N. Rajah's Racer
Griffiths, A. Before the British Raj
Hales, A. G. Gore of the Guides
Handley, L. Luxury Tour
Hart-Davis, D. Man-Eaters of Jassapur
Hirtt, H. Heat of Winter
Holt, V. India Fan
Ironside, E. Very Private Enterprise
Jenkinson, E. J. Gates of Doom
Kaye, M. M. Death Walked in Kashmir
Keating, H. R. F. 12 titles
King, F. Act of Darkness
Levett-Yeats, S. Galahad of the Creeks
McCloskey, W. Mallore Affair
McMunn, G. Black Velvet
Marlow, E. Danger in Dahlkari
Marlowe, S. Killers Are My Meat
Marqusse, M. Slow Turn
Mason, A. E. W. Sapphire
Mather, B. 5 titles
Morton, A. Baron Goes East
Mukerji, D. G. Secret Listeners of the East
Mundy, T. at least 12 titles
Murari, T. N. Imperial Agent
Parsons, A. No Alibi for Murder
Penny, F. Romance of a Nautch Girl
Penny, F. E. 7 titles
Perrin, A. Tales That Are Told
Peters, Ellis. Death to the Landlords!
Richardson, M. Song of India
Roadarmel, P. Kaligarh Fault
Rosenberger, J. Hell in Hindu Land
    Hindu Trinity Affair
Ross, Clarissa. Kashmiri Passions
Sahgal, N. Plans for Departure
St. John, David. Towers of Silence
Sathianadhan, K. Detective Janaki
Selwyn, F. Sergeant Verity and the Imperial
    Diamond
Seton, G. K Code Plan
Shannon, A. Black Scorpion
Sidwa, B. N. Crow Eaters
Snyder, C. M. Flaw in the Sapphire
Soutar, A. Chosen of the Gods
Sparling, J. North of Delhi, East of Heaven
Taylor, Meadows. Confessions of a Thug
Taylor, P. W. Murder in the Taj Mahal
Thorne, E. P. Bengali Spider Plan
    Black Sadhu
    Death Rust
    Ganges Mud
Tracy, L. Sirdar's Sabre
Vance, L. J. Bronze Bell
Vandyopadhyaya, S. B. Adventures of Mrs. Russell
Wheatley, D. Rape of Venice
Wilson, A. Crimson Dacoit
    Devil's Cocktail
    Mystery of Tunnel 51
Wilson, G. Night of the Thuggee
Woodruff, P. Call the Next Witness
Wren, P. C. Dew and Mildew

INDIAN OCEAN (Ind. O. See also: India; Bombay; Calcutta; Ceylon; New Delhi)
Chase, J. Betrayal in Eden
Francis, B. Death on the Atoll
Hild, J. Barrabas Fire
Innes, H. Strode Venturer
Lisle, E. By Unseen Hands
O'Brine, M. Dodos Don't Duck
Poyer, J. Operation Malacca
Stanton, K. Whirlwind Beneath the Sea

INDIANA (Ind. See also: Indianapolis; Midwest)
Adler, T. On Murder's Skirts
Appleman, P. Shame the Devil
Bonnamy, F. Rope of Sand
Brown, F. Dead Ringer
Cameron, K. at least 6 titles
Carkeet, D. Double Negative
Cody, C. S. Witching Night
Cooper, J. L. Grasshopper Summer
Daniels, D. House on Circus Hill

Decker, J. Death Comes Home
De Weese, J. Hour of the Cat
Endore, G. Detour at Night
Frommer, S. H. Murder in C Major
Gatenby, R. Hanged for a Sheep
Hays, H. R. Stranger on the Highway
Hensley, J. L. all 15 titles
Kingsley, M. J. Shadow Over Elveron
Lewin, M. Z. Enemies Within
    Missing Woman
Lowe, K. Haze of Evil
McClintick, M. all 4 titles
McElfresh, A. Keep Back the Dark
McInerny, R. Body and Soil
    Cause and Effect
    Savings and Loam
Meredith, M. House of a Thousand Candles
Rickett, F. both titles
Russell, A. J. Devalino Caper
Russell, C. M. Between Us and Evil
    Careless Mrs. Christian
    June, Moon, and Murder
    Lament for William
Saber, R. O. Deadly Lover
Sapir, R. Power Play
Stratton, Thomas. Mind-Twisters Affair
Vachss, A. Blossom
Wolf, Sarah. Long Chain of Death

INDIANAPOLIS (See also: Indiana; Midwest)
Hayes, J. Desperate Hours
James, M. Night Glow
Kenyon, L. Revenge at Indy
Lewin, M. Z. 9 titles
Stark, R. Rare Coin Score
Tierney, R. Stone Veil

INDONESIA (Indon. See also: Djakarta; Bali; Borneo; Java; New Guinea; Sumatra)
Atlee, P. Ill Wind Contract
    Makassar Strait Contract
Carey, B. Dangerous Isles
Daniels, J. R. Firegold
Derby, M. Sunlit Ambush
Duncan, R. L. In the Enemy Camp
East, M. McCreary Moves In
Harvester, S. Golden Fear
Holmes, G. Surabaya
Koch, C. J. Year of Living Dangerously
Luceno, J. Rainchaser
McCurtin, P. Guns of Palembang
Rosenberger, J. Operation Skyhook
Stacpoole, H. D. Tales of Mynheer Amayat

IOWA (Ia. See also: Midwest)
Atwater, M. M. Crime in Corn-Weather
Boyd, C. B. Revenge in "The Convent"
Brown, Carter. Silken Nightmare
Campbell, R. W. Red Cent
Collins, Max. 9 titles
Deming, R. What's the Matter with Helen?
Gorman, E. Grave's Retreat
    Night of Shadows
    What the Dead Men Say
Greenleaf, S. Fatal Obsession
Gruber, F. Fourth Letter
    Laughing Fox
Howard, H. Room 37
Hultman, H. J. This Murderous Shaft
Janson, H. Devil's Highway
    Lilies for My Lovely
Jeffery, R. Mine
Lafore, L. Nine Seven Juliet
Millhiser, M. Nella Waits
Parrish, P. Escape the Past
Plum, M. Susanna, Don't You Cry!
Price, Nancy. Sleeping with the Enemy
Rice, C. Thursday Turkey Murders
Rich, V. Cooking School Murders
Schmitt, L. F. Shyster Lawyer
Strieber, W. Billy

IRAN (See also: Iraq; Teheran; Middle East)
Aarons, E. S. Assignment—Moon Girl

IRAN

Adams, R. Star of Persia
Brackett, L. Silent Partner
Bulliet, R. Tomb of the Twelfth Iman
Carter, Nick. Slaughter Day
Chubin, B. Feet of a Snake
Clavell, J. Whirlwind
Copeland, W. Five Hours from Isfahan
De Villiers, G. Versus the C.I.A.
Easterman, D. Last Assassin
Epstein, E. J. Cartel
Fink, S. Hailing Sign
Flagg, J. Persian Cat
Hamizrachi, Y. Golden Lion and the Sun
Harvester, S. Unsung Road
Hashian. Shanidar
Hayes, R. Scorpio Cipher
Hild, J. Plains of Fire
Janson, H. Auctioned
    Desert Fury
    Persian Pride
Jason, S. Appointment in Iran
Landon, C. Flag in the City
Pendleton, D. Teheran Wipeout
Rider, R. Dyed for Death
Schmidt, Dan. Flight 666
Sheckley, R. White Death
Somerville-Large, P. Couch of Earth
Strong, T. Fifth Hostage
Topol, A. Fourth of July War
Wiltse, D. Wedding Guest

IRAQ (See also: Iran; Terehan; Middle East)
Quinnell, A. J. Snap Shot
Scott, A. Unknown Path

IRELAND (Ire. Both Ireland and Northern Irland included here. See also: Belfast; Dublin)
Addison, H. R. Recollections of an Irish Police Magistrate
Albert, T. N. Tales of an Ulster Detective
Allan, O. Green Bushes
Anonymous. Last Drop of '68
Anthony, E. No Enemy But Time
Atlee, P. Shankill Road Contract
Baker, W. H. Treasure Hunters
Ballinger, W. A. Green Grassy Slopes
    Rebellion
Banville, J. Birchwood
    Book of Evidence
Birmingham, G. A. Fidgets
    Lost Lawyer
    Search Party
Blake, N. Private Wound
Bodkin, M. M. White Magic
Brandon, B. Cliffs of Night
Brennan, E. Whispering Walls
Brewster, D. Heart's Grown Brutal
Bringle, M. Man in the Moss-Colored Trousers
Brydon, S. Guns Over the Border
Buchanan, R. W. Father Anthony
Caswell, H. Never Wed an Old Man
Christopher, J. Little People
Clancy, A. Blind Plot
Cleeve, B. Death of a Painted Lady
    Death of a Wicked Servant
    Vote X for Treason
Clifford, F. Wild Justice
Coffman, V. Beckoning
    Cliffs of Dread
Connor, R. I Am Death
Cooper, Lynna. Hour of the Harp
Cowen, F. Curse of the Clodaghs
Crofts, F. W. Sir John Magill's Last Journey
Crowe, C. Abbeygate
    Tower of Kilraven
Curry, G. L. Portrush Mystery
Curtis, Robert. Irish Police Officer
Daniel, M. Bold Thing
Daniels, D. Cormac Legend
    Mirror of Shadows
Davis, D. S. Habit of Fear
Denning, M. Beyond the Prize
De St. Jorre, J. Patriot Game

Dillon, E. Death at Crane's Court
    Sent to His Account
Douglas, Aleck. Murder Hole Road
Douglas, C. N. Amberleigh
Dowling, R. Mystery of Killard
    Old Corcoran's Money
    Skeleton Key
    Sweet Inisfail
Driscoll, P. In Connection with Kilshaw
Du Bois, T. Cavalier's Corpse
    Shannon Terror
Dunn, N. J. Vultures of Erin
Dunne, L. Ringleader
Dunsany, L. Curse of the Wise Woman
Dwyer-Joyce, A. Moonlit Way
    Rainbow Glass
    Reach for the Shadows
    Storm of Wrath
Eden, D. Whistle for the Crows
Everett, P. Death in Ireland
Finlay, F. Cruel Trade
Fitzgerald, A. J. Blackthorn
Fletcher, J. S. Golden Spur
Flood, N. To Killashea
Foley, L. both titles
Forbes, S. Terror Touches Me
Ford, Hilary. Castle Malindine
Forrest, Wilma. Last Hope House
Fry, P. Bright Green Waistcoat
Gallie, M. You're Welcome to Ulster!
Garve, A. House of Spiders
Gaskin, C. Edge of Glass
Gilford, C. B. Crooked Shamrock
Gill, B. 5 titles
Gray, B. Conquest in Ireland
Greeley, A. M. Rite of Spring
Griffin, J. Ring of Kerry
Guinness, K. D. Fisherman's End
Harris, Andrea. Irish Affair
Heath, M. 6 titles
Hely, S. Sign of the Serpent
Henderson, L. Final Glass
Henry, Michael. Murder in the Old Jail
Herron, S. Hound and the Fox and the Harper
    Through the Dark and Hairy Wood
    Whore-Mother
Higgins, J. Confessional
    Savage Day
Hild, J. No Sanctuary
Hollyock, D. Innocent Madness
Hynes, J. Wild Colonial Boy
Innes, M. Journeying Boy
Jones, K. O. To the Dark Tower Came
Karr, L. Castle of Crushed Shamrocks
Keating, H. R. F. Dog It Was That Died
Kebbe, J. Armalite Maiden
Kent, N. Hint of Murder
Kenyon, M. May You Die in Ireland
    100,000 Welcomes
    Rapist
    Shooting of Dan McGrew
Kerr, A. W. Shadow of Drumcarnett
Kickham, C. Knocknagow
Knoll, A. Stolen Bride of Glengarra Castle
La Tourrette, J. Joseph Stone
Lowell, J. R. Irish Game
Macardle, D. Earth-Bound
McCaffrey, A. Kitternan Legacy
McCartan, D. Operation Emerald
McCullough, E. M. Five Devils of Kilmainham
McCurtin, P. Green Hell
MacDermott, W. R. Foughilotra
McGinley, P. Bogmail
    Devil's Diary
    Trick of the Ga Bolga
McMullen, M. My Cousin Death
McNamara, M. M. Sovereign Solution
Meade, L. T. Home of Silence
Michaels, S. Summary Justice
Molloy, P. Legacy of Demons
Morgan, C. Devil's Cavern
Murphy, D. J. Milesian Chief
Murphy, W. B. Hand of Lazarus
Newman, G. F. Testing Ground

Nichols, S. Serpent's Tooth
Nicole, Claudette. Cliffs of Death
    Dark Whispers
    Haunting of Drumroe
O'Brien, F. Third Policeman
O'Flaherty, L. Informer
O'Grady, R. O'Houlihan's Jest
O'Mahoney, T. P. Lynch Years
O'Neill, D. Life Has No Price
Ostrander, K. Ghosts of Ballyduff
    Sea Tower
O'Sullivan, J. B. Blacklash
    Cold Chisel
    There Is an S.O.S.
Patterson, H. Cry of the Hunter
    Pay the Devil
Paul, B. Curse of Halewood
Pendleton, D. Countdown to Chaos
    Defenders and Believers
Phillifent, J. T. Mad Scientist Affair
Pim, S. Common or Garden Crime
Piper, P. Woman Delia
Platt, K. Murder in Rosslare
Polk, D. Tower of the Crow
Polland, M. Little Spot of Bother
    Thicker Than Water
Powell, M. Waiting Game
Power, M. S. Darkness in the Eye
Poyer, J. Shooting of the Green
Randell, C. Black Candle
Reeves, F. Deadly Inheritance
Reid, D. Beat on an Orange Drum
Richardson, M. Candle in the Wind
Roby, M. L. House at Kilgallen
Rodney, B. Owl Flies Home
Rosenberger, J. Shamrock Smash
St. James, I. Killing Anniversary
Seaman, D. Bomb That Could Lip-Read
Seymour, G. Field of Blood
Shreve, L. G. Tides of Sligo
Sinclair, D. Third Force
Somerville-Large, P. Living Dog
Spain, P. Blood Scenario
Stevenson, F. Curse of the Concullens
Stoker, B. Snake's Pass
Strong, T. Whisper Who Dares
Tennant, E. Woman Beware Woman
Thum, M. Abbey Court
Thynne, R. Irish Holidays
Tierney, P. Power of Lismara
Turk, S. A. Secret of Carickfirneagh Castle
Walsh, M. Danger Under the Moon
Welcome, J. Reasons of Hate
Welles, E. Fahnworth Manor
Westbury, H. Frederick Hazzleden
White, S. Fighting Irish
White, T. D. My Name Is Norval
Woods, Stuart. Run Before the Wind
Wylie, N. both titles

ISLE OF MAN (See also: England; Channel Islands)
Bellairs, G. 6 titles
Duncan, F. Murder in Man
Estey, D. Lost Tale
Fraser, Anthea. Island in Waiting

ISRAEL (Isr. See also: Jerusalem; Tel Aviv; Middle East)
Aricha, A. Flying Camel
Arnold, M. Zadok's Treasure
Baker, I. Justice for Judas
Bannister, J. Shards
Bax, R. Death Beneath Jerusalem
Betcherman, B. Stiletto
Callard, M. City Called Holy
Carter, Nick. Assignment: Israel
Courter, G. Code Ezra
Falkirk, R. Twisted Wire
Gordon, N. Jerusalem Diamond
Haddad, C. A. Bloody September
    Moroccan
    Operation Apricot
Hadley, J. Night-Blooming Cereus
Haggard, W. Visa to Limbo

Harvester, S. Zion Road
Hesky, O. Different Night
Hoffenberg, J. 17 Ben Gurion
Hunter, J. H. Banners of Blood
Jason, S. Sealed with Blood
Johnson, J. L. Code Name Sebastian
Kaplan, H. Bullets of Palestine
Karlin, W. Extras
Kemelman, H. Monday the Rabbi Took Off
Kenan, A. Road to Ein Harod
Klinger, H. Lust for Murder
Kriss, G. First Loyalty
Lane, A. Revelations
Latham, A. Orchids for Mother
Leonard, E. Hunted
McFarlane, I. Jerusalem Conspiracy
Meisels, A. Six Other Days
O'Neill, A. Da Vinci Road
Operator 1384. Black Arab
Pendleton, D. Death Has a Name
    Hellbinder
Rogers, B. Doomsday Scroll
Sachar, H. M. Man on the Camel
Sapir, R. Last Temple
Shahar, D. His Majesty's Agent
Singer, S. M. For Dying You Always Have Time
Tucker, W. This Witch
Vicas, V. Impromptu Imposter
Walsh, J. E. Man Who Buried Jesus
Weisman, J. Blood Cries
Whittemore, E. Jericho Mosaic
Wilson, G. Return to Armageddon
Yariv, F. Safe Haven

ISTANBUL (Istan. See also: Turkey; Middle East;
    Balkans)
Ambler, E. Light of Day
Carter, Nick. Istanbul
Fleming, Joan. When I Grow Rich
Forsyte, C. Diplomatic Death
Hayes, Ralph. Turkish Mafia Conspiracy
Hughes, D. T. Istanbul Elopement
Morris, R. C. Memoirs of an Ottoman Secret Agent
Pollock, D. Lair of the Fox
Ross, Clarissa. Istanbul Nights
Smith, Don. Secret Mission: Istanbul
Stein, A. M. Deadly Delight
Tokson, E. Harem Games
Unsworth, B. Rage of the Vulture
Walsh, J. M. Death at His Elbow
Wheatley, D. Eunuch of Stanboul
Whitney, P. A. Black Amber
Wilson, G. Phoenix in Flames

ITALY (It. See also: Florence; Milan; Naples; Rome;
    Sardinia; Sicily; Venice)
Aarons, E. S. Assignment—Lili Lamaris
    Assignment—Palermo
    Assignment—Sorrento Siren
Albrand, M. After Midnight
    Without Orders
Ambler, E. Send No More Roses
Anonymous. Autobiography of an Italian Police
    Officer
Anthony, Evelyn. Malaspiga Exit
Arnold, Ralph. Fish and Company
Arpino, G. Crime of Honor
Arrighi, M. Turkish White
Ashe, G. Life for a Death
Bagley, D. Golden Keel
Baker, W. H. Dogs of War
Baskerville, B. By Whose Hand?
Beeding, F. Black Arrows
    Six Proud Walkers
Bennett, Dorothy. Curious Were Killed
Bentley, N. Events of That Week
Black, Clementina. Pursuit of Camilla
Black, Lionel. Two Ladies in Verona
Brande, D. Most Beautiful Lady
Brown, Carter. Seidlitz and the Super-Spy
Bryan, J. Contessa Came Too
Buchan, James. Davy Chadwick
Butler, R. Italian Assets
Butterworth, M. Villa on the Shore

Cameron, L. Amphorae Pirates
Canning, V. Castle Minerva
Carter, Nick. Mark of Cosa Nostra
Cassiday, B. Operation Goldkill
Chaber, M. E. Lonely Walk
Cleary, J. Peter's Pence
    Safe House
Cleeve, B. You Must Never Go Back
Clewes, H. Epitaph for Love
Coffman, V. Demon Tower
Coker, C. Vines of Ferrara
Coles, M. Man in the Green Hat
Cook, Bob. Questions of Identity
Cornelisen, A. Any Four Women Could Rob the
    Bank of Italy
Cory, D. Intrigue
Cowen, F. Hounds of Carvello
Crighton, R. E. Red for Terror
Crookenden, I. Horrible Revenge
Dacre, C. Zofloya
Dalton, M. Wife of Baal
Daniels, D. Magic Ring
Dark, J. Spy from the Grave
Davidson, A. Siren's Lure
Davis, S. His Father's Ghost
De Bilio, B. Vendetta Con Brio
Dekker, C. Step Into Fire
De Villiers, G. West of Jerusalem
Dibden, M. Ratking
    Vendetta
Dickens, F. Three Cheers for the Good Guys
Donovan, D. Scarlet Seal
Downes, D. Red Rose for Maria
Duane, A. Hadrian Ransom
Du Maurier, D. Flight of the Falcon
Farr, C. Villa of Shadows
Fenisong, R. Schemers
Ferrars, E. Alibi for a Witch
Fisher, N. Walk at a Steady Pace
Fitzgerald, N. Imagine a Man
Flagg, J. Dear, Deadly Beloved
    Lady and the Cheetah
Fletcher, Dorothy. Late Contessa
Follett, E. Villa of the Scorpions
Forbes, H. Detective in Italy
Forgione, L. Men of Silence
Fraser, J. In Place of Reason
Fraser, M. C. Satanist
Fruttero, C. Sunday Woman
Gilbert, M. Death in Captivity
Gill, B. McGarr and the Sienese Conspiracy
Glanville, B. Catacomb
Godey, J. Fatal Beauty
Gollin, J. Verona Passamezzo
Greene, H. Flags at Doney
Gruber, F. Etruscan Bull
Gunn, V. All Change for Murder
Haggard, W. Hard Sell
Halidom, M. Y. Poison Ring
Halliday, L. Devil's Door
Harris, Rosemary. Double Snare
Hathaway, M. Silence at Nightingales
Highsmith, P. Talented Mr. Ripley
Hitchcock, L. Ducetti Heir
Holland, I. Lost Madonna
Holme, T. At the Lake of Sudden Death
Holt, Gavin. Sole Survivor
Hosegood, L. Minotaur Garden
Hotchner, A. E. Dangerous American
Howlett, J. Christmas Spy
Hume, F. Creature of the Night
Hummel, G. F. Summer Lightning
Innes, H. Angry Mountain
    Dead and Alive
    Lonely Skier
Irwin, W. Julius Caesar Murder Case
Jay, W. Fear in Borzano
John, O. Thirty Days Hath September
Johns, D. Beatrice Mystery
Johnston, V. Etruscan Smile
Jones, H. W. Shot on Location
Kennedy, W. P. Toy Soldiers
Knight, K. M. Invitation to Vengeance
La Barre, H. Florentine Win

Lathom, F. Italian Mysteries
La Tourrette, J. Pompeii Scrolls
    Shadows in Umbria
Lee, Elsie. Clouds Over Vellanti
Lee, John. Lago
Lem, S. Chain of Chance
Leonard, C. L. Treachery in Trieste
Leslie, P. Splintered Sunglasses Affair
Lewis, R. H. Death in Verona
Linscott, G. Murder Makes Tracks
Livingston, W. Mystery of Villa Sinestre
Lombardi, C. Lighting Seven Candles
Loraine, P. Angel of Death
    Mafia Kiss
Lynch, F. Stranger at the Wedding
McEvoy, M. Calabrian Summer
McGinnis, E. L. Strasburg Collection
MacGrath, H. Cellini Plaque
MacInnes, H. North from Rome
MacLeod, R. Cut in Diamonds
MacPherson, M. Protege
Maddock, S. Conspirators in Capri
Marshall, R. Mission to Siena
    Wary Transgressor
Marvin, S. Secret of the Villa Como
Masterson, W. Hunter of the Blood
Mather, B. Geth Straker
Maxwell, V. Way of the Tamarisk
Mayo, J. Let Sleeping Girls Lie
Meade, E. Murder Squad
Melton, W. Nine Lives to Pompeii
Meredith, K. L. Golden Chalice
Meynell, L. Thirteen Trumpeters
Michaels, B. Wings of the Falcon
Mills, Hugh. In Pursuit of Evil
Moore, Dorinne. Masquerade at Monfalcone
Moore, Robin. Italian Connection
Morgan, R. Golden Hoard
Moyes, P. Dead Men Don't Ski
Nabb, M. Prosecutor
Newman, B. Mussolini Murder Plot
Nixon, Alan. Item 7
North, J. Legend of the Thirteenth Pilgrim
O'Brine, M. Mills
    No Earth for Foxes
Old Sleuth. Giant Detective Among the Italian
    Brigands
    Old Ironsides Among the Italian Brigands
Oppenheim, E. P. Daughter of the Marionis
Orgill, D. Astrid Factor
    Death Brings
Paradise, M. Face of an Angel
Pears, I. Raphael Affair
Pendower, J. Operation Carlo
Pendleton, D. Tuscany Terror
Pollack, C. Mystery of Rapallo
Price, A. October Men
Prokosch, F. Tale for Midnight
Quinn, Simon. Human Factor
Quinnell, A. J. Man on Fire
Radcliffe, A. Italian
    Mysteries of Udolpho
Ragosta, M. J. Taverna in Terrazzo
Raven, S. Brother Cain
Ridgway, J. Treasure of the Cosa Nostra
Rosenblum, R. Good Thief
Ross, Bradley. No Margin for Terror
Ross, Marilyn. Castle Malice
Ross, W. E. D. Dark Villa of Capri
Rossiter, E. Lemon Garden
Rutherford, D. 5 titles
Sawkins, R. H. Snow in Paradise
Sciascia, L. One Way or Another
Seeber, G. C. Abduction
Seymour, G. Red Fox
Shelley, M. Valperga
Siciliano, E. Diamante
Slater, N. Falcon
Smith, Don. Padrone
Snell, E. Blue Murder
Snelling, L. Heresy
Somers, J. Brethren of the Axe
Stanhope, L. S. Di Montranzo
Steegmuller, F. Silence at Salerno

Stein, A. M. Lend Me Your Ears
Stern, R. M. Bright Road to Fear
Stevenson, A. Coil of Serpents
Stone, D. Tired Spy
Strutton, B. Glut of Virgins
Summerton, M. Dark and Secret Place
Swift, B. Mission Code: Survival
Swindells, M. Corsican Woman
Tabbuchi, A. Vanishing Point
Taylor, M. A. Appointment in Verona
Thompson, V. Scarlet Iris
Toye, N. Twice Murdered Man
Tyler, A. Chase the Wind
Vance, J. Strange Notions and The Dark Ocean
Van Rjndt, P. Tetramachus Collection
Waller, L. Coast of Fear
Watson, G. Black Jack
Webster, E. all 8 titles
West, M. L. Big Story
    Daughter of Silence
    Salamander
White, S. Terror in Turin
Whitten, L. Killing Pace
Williams, T. all 3 titles
Williams, V. Courier to Marrakesh
Williamson, T. Connector
Withers, E. L. Heir Apparent
Yorke, R. M. P. Haunted Palace
Young, G. Code-Name Caruso

JACKSONVILLE (Jack. See also: Florida; Miami; Tampa; South)
Humes, L. R. Bridge to Nowhere
Levison, E. all 3 titles

JAKARTA. See: Djakarta.

JAMAICA (Jam. See also: West Indies; Caribbean)
Ashe, R. Hurricane Wake
Battle, L. Habit of the Blood
Carter, Nick. Jamaican Exchange
Cave, H. B. Disciples of Dread
Chadwick, J. Web of Evil
Dark, J. Operation Scuba
Eberhart, M. G. Enemy in the House
    Speak No Evil
Elman, R. Breadfruit Lotteries
Fleming, I. Man with the Golden Gun
Greig, M. Whispers in the Sun
Hadley, J. Deadly Ackee
Heath, M. Castlereagh
Keegan, M. Ice, Wind and Fire
Lange, J. Grave Descend
Morris, John. all 3 titles
Murray, M. Neat Little Corpse
Revere, J. D. Born to Kill
Rohmer, S. Virgin in Flames
Ryder, J. Cry of the Halidon
Scott, V. Kreutzman Formula
Shearing, J. Golden Violet
Terrall, R. Sand Dollars
Tidyman, E. Shaft's Carnival of Killers
White, S. King of Kingston
Wilson, Gar. Kingston Carnage

JAPAN (Jap. See also: Tokyo; Far East)
Barry, L. Sudden Silence
Bellah, J. W. Brass Gong Tree
Black, G. Dead Man Calling
Blood, A. Jade Rabbit
Broinowski, A. Take One Ambassador
Browne, Courtney. Ancient Pond
Cade, Robin. Fear Dealers
Carter, Nick. Christmas Kill
    Day of the Dingo
    Sign of the Prayer Shawl
Cleary, J. Phoenix Tree
Cogan, M. Black Rain
Daniels, Paul. Transister Girls
Duncan, R. L. Day the Sun Fell
    Fire Storm
Fernandes, J. R. Yokohama Hood
Finnegan, S. It Blows Up in Your Face
Fleming, I. You Only Live Twice

Forve, G. Ofanu
French, R. R. Spy Is Forever
Gilchrist, A. Death of an Admiral
Graves, R. L. Argon Furnace
Harvester, S. Copper Butterfly
Hayes, S. K. Tulku
King, Francis. Custom House
Knapp, G. C. Stranglehold
Leader, C. Wreath of Cherry Blossoms
Lustbader, E. V. White Ninja
McMahon, T. P. Mayday
M., A. Wooing of Webster
Matsumoto, S. Points and Lines
    Voice
Melville, J. all 7 titles
Murphy, W. B. Temple Dogs
Natsuki, S. Innocent Journey
    Murder at Mt. Fuji
Nichols, L. Key to Midnight
Nishimura, K. Mystery Train Disappears
Norman, E. Kill Me in Atami
    Kill Me in Roppongi
    Kill Me in Yokohama
Olden, M. Dai-Sho
    Oni
Pendleton, D. Invisible Assassins
Queen, E. Guess Who's Coming to Kill You?
Rampo, Edogawa. Japanese Tales of Mystery and Imagination
Rance, J. Bullet Train
Roberts, J. H. February Plan
Robeson, K. Jui San
Rosenberger, J. Nipponese Nightmare
Royce, K. Bustillo
Schlossstein, S. Kensei
Seward, J. Assignment: Find Cherry
    Cave of the Chinese Skeletons
    Eurasian Virgins
    Frogman Assassination
Takagi, A. both titles
Thayer, L. Two Ways to Die
Togawa, M. Kiss of Fire
Van de Wetering, J. Inspector Saito's Small Satori
Wheatley, D. Bill for the Use of a Body
Whitney, P. A. Moonflower
Wilson, Gar. Ninja Blood
Wynd, O. Walk Softly, Men Praying

JAVA (See also: Indonesia; Bali; Borneo; Djakarta; New Guinea; Sumatra)
Carter, Nick. Time Clock of Death
Crisp, F. Fazackerley's Millions

JERUSALEM (Jerus. See also: Israel; Tel Aviv; Middle East)
Bayer, W. Pattern Crimes
Blackburn, J. Flame and the Wind
Carter, Nick. Jerusalem File
Christian, J. Five Gates to Armageddon
Christie, Agatha. Appointment with Death
Dixon, R. Going to Jerusalem
Gross, J. This Year in Jerusalem
Kellerman, J. Butcher's Theatre
Kemelman, H. One Fine Day the Rabbi Bought a Cross
Klawans, H. L. Jerusalem Code
Littell, B. Dolorosa Deal
Mandino, O. Christ Commission
Sapir, R. Body
Simon, R. L. Raising the Dead

JOHANNESBURG (Johan. See also: South Africa; Cape Town; Transvaal)
Brechin, D. Nic Barber I.D.B.
Harman, N. Yours Truly, Angus MacIvor
Monig, C. Once Upon a Crime
Moodie, E. Great Shakes
O'Keefe, B. Diamonds Can Be Dangerous
Seuffert, M. Trespassers Will Die
Severn, R. Stalk a Long Shadow

JORDAN (See also: Middle East)
Lyall, G. Uncle Target
Roberts, T. A. Shy Moon

KANSAS (Kan. See also: Midwest)
Adleman, R. H. Bloody Benders
Blankenship, W. D. Leavenworth Irregulars
Booth, C. B. Amateur Detectives
Chase, J. H. No Orchids for Miss Blandish
Conway, J. W. Something or Nothing
Derrick, L. Dodge City Bombers
Dold, G. 6 titles
Epperson, S. K. Brother Lowdown
Flanders, R. Easy Access
Forbes, S. Grieve for the Past
    If Two of Them Are Dead
Jackson, B. Flameout
Keeling, D. J. Case of Innocence
Kingsley-Smith, T. Forsaken
Pendleton, D. Prairie Fire
Picard, N. Bum Steer
Reese, J. Weapon Heavy
Ruse, P. Alumni Murders
Sherburne, J. Death's Gray Angel

KANSAS CITY (Kan. City. See also: Missouri; St. Louis; Midwest)
Battin, B. W. Programmed for Terror
DeCoursey, V. Enter This Night
Eliot, G. F. Federal Bullets
Head, M. Accomplice
Johnson, E. R. Judas
Killough, L. Dragon's Teeth
    Spider Play
Maloney, J. J. I Speak for the Dead
Morelli, S. Deal Me Out
Roper, L. V. Hookers Don't Go to Heaven
Roscoe, M. Death Is a Round Black Ball
    One Tear for My Grave
    Riddle Me This
Russell, Randy. Hot Wire
Vincent, L. M. Final Dictation

KENTUCKY (Ky. See also: Louisville; South)
Anderson, James. Lovers and Other Killers
Anderson, U. S. King of the Roses
Anderson, Virginia. Blood Lies
    King of the Roses
Buchanan, P. Murder of Crows
Buck, C. N. Mountain Justice
Carr, Jess. Intruder in the Wind
Caudill, H. M. Slender Is the Thread
Clark, D. P. Poison Speaks Softly
    Roll, Jordan, Roll
Cobb, I. S. Judge Priest Turns Detective
Crane, F. Daffodil Blonde
    Death in Lilac Time
Cunningham, A. B. 19 titles
Daingerfield, F. That Gay Nineties Murder
Damien, C. Appleshaw
Daniels, D. Lanier Riddle
Echard, M. I Met Murder on the Way
Grafton, C. W. all 3 titles
Halliday, B. Taste for Violence
Hayes, J. Winner's Circle
Hill, D. C. Deadly Messiah
Hoff, B. J. Dark River Legacy
Kingsley, M. J. Black Man, White Man
Knight, Barbara. Woodsedge
Large, M. H. Twelfth Juror
Lauben, P. Nice Sound Alibi
    Surfeit of Alibis
Leonard, E. Moonshine War
Long, L. B. To the Dark Tower
Lyons, A. W. Murder at Prospect, Kentucky
McCafferty, T. Pet Peeves
McDowell, R. E. Hound's Tooth
Morgan, Kate. Slay at the Races
Morrell, D. First Blood
Nicole, Claudette. Bloodroots Manor
Nolan, J. C. Sudden Squall
Parmer, C. Murder at the Kentucky Derby
Thayer, G. Dark Rider
Thompson, F. Transgressor
Walker, Ira. Someone's Stolen Nellie Grey
Windham, S. Missing

Settings Index

KENYA (See also: Africa, East)
Bagley, D. Legacy
　Windfall
Barstow, P. Night Is for Hunting
Catanach, J. N. Brideprice
Duchi, D. Assassins on Safari
Farrington, J. Hand
Fearon, D. Nairobi Nightcap
Garrigues, E. Grass Rain
Gicheru, M. Double-Cross
　Two in One
Hayes, Ralph. Scavenger Kill
Hutton, A. Passport to Peril
Jacks, O. Autumn Heroes
Jones, R. W. Manipulator
Kaye, M. M. Later Than You Think
Leslie, N. Death Comes to Kenya
Leslie-Melville, B. That Nairobi Affair
McDonald, G. Fletch Too
McQuillan, K. Deadly Safari
Makoloo, O. Two Young to Die
Mwangi, M. Kill Me Quick
Ngugi Wa Thiong'o. Petals of Blood
Ng'weno, H. Man from Pretoria
Peverett, A. Death Stalks in Kenya
Proffitt, N. Edge of Eden
Rosen, G. H. Black Money
Stoneham, C. T. Kenya Mystery
Waugh, H. Murder on Safari
Wilson, Gar. Terror in the Dark

KOREA (Kor. Both North and South Korea included here. See also: Far East)
Atlee, P. Last Domino Contract
Browne, M. Dragon Strike
Carter, Nick. Korean Kill
　Korean Tiger
Crane, R. Sergeant and the Queen
　Sgt. Corbin's War
　Strikeback!
Davis, F. M. Naked and the Lost
Forrest, Williams. Stigma
Harvester, S. Troika
Howe, R. W. Flight of the Cormorants
Murphy, W. B. Eleventh Hour
Newton, M. Korea Kill
Roberts, Mark. Korean Carnage
Rosenberger, J. Operation Thunderbolt
Sheldon, W. J. Gold Bait
Smith, Don. Secret Mission: North Korea
Stokes, M. L. Under Cover of Night
Stroup, W. Mark of Pak San Ri
Wilson, G. Korean Killground

KUWAIT (Kuw. See also: Middle East)
Arvay, H. Operation Kuwait
De Villiers, G. Kill Kissinger
Wilson, Gar. Gulf of Fire

LAOS (See also: Far East)
Ballinger, B. S. Spy in the Jungle
Lewis, N. Single Pilgrim
Little, L. In the Village of the Man
Meiring, D. Brinkman

LAS VEGAS (Las Veg. See also: Nevada; Reno; West)
Ahern, J. Hard Way
Andersen, I. Big Night
Ard, W. Mr. Trouble
Ballard, W. T. Dealing Out Death
　Murder Last Vegas Style
　Pretty Miss Murder
　Seven Sisters
Barry, M. Desert Stalker
Beckner, M. Money Plays
Cameron, L. File on a Missing Redhead
Carter, Nick. Eight Card Stud
　Mind Poisoners
Clark, A. C. Kenyatta's Last Hit
Cox, W. R. Murder in Vegas
Demaris, O. Vegas Legacy
Derrick, L. Blood on the Strip

Douglas, C. N. Crystal Days
　Crystal Nights
Duff, J. P. Dangerous to Know
Duncan, R. L. Serpent's Mark
Einstein, C. Blackjack Hijack
Fair, A. A. Spill the Jackpot!
Fisher, S. No House Limit
Foley, R. Call It Accident
Foster, R. Blonde and Beautiful
Franklin, M. Vegas
Frazer, R. C. Mark Kilby and the Secret Syndicate
Garrett, F. Mob War
Goldman, W. Heat
Goldthwaite, E. K. Cut for Partners
Gray, A. W. Size
Gruber, F. Honest Dealer
Haring, D. Assassins Take All
　Honey-Warm and Hungry
　Lovely and Lethal
Herries, N. My Private Hangman
Howard, V. Murder with Love
Joey. Joey Collects
Kane. Sing, Baby, Sing Sing
Kijewski, K. Katwalk
Lamb, J. J. Nickel Straight
MacDonald, J. D. Only Girl in the Game
Moore, Arthur. Las Vegas
Morgan, D. M. Money Leads to Murder
Murphy, W. B. Trace and 47 Miles of Rope
　Two Steps from Three East
Nichols, L. Eyes of Darkness
Paul, Elliot. Black and the Red
Pendleton, D. Bone Yard
　Vegas Vendetta
Perriam, W. Sin City
Perry, T. Butcher's Boy
Petievich, G. Shakedown
Prather, R. S. Find This Woman
Ramm, C. Vegas Vengeance
Reese, J. Omar, Fats and Trixie
Renek, J. Las Vegas Strip
Rice, J. Night Stalker
Rome, D. Christina
Rossi, B. Las Vegas Vengeance
Scherf, M. If You Want a Murder Well Done
　To Cache a Millionaire
Schorr, M. Ace of Diamonds
Sederberg, A. 60 Hours of Darkness
Shaw, W. Out for Kicks
Stivers, D. Blood Mark
Thackrey, T. Aces and Eights
Thomas, C. Cactus Shroud
Tucker, W. Procession of the Damned
Waer, J. Murder in Las Vegas
Williams, B. Stranger to Herself

LEBANON (Leb. See also: Beirut; Middle East)
Arathorn, D. Kamal
Atiyah, E. Donkey from the Mountains
　Lebanon Paradise
Benedictus, D. Rabbi's Wife
Cleary, J. Season of Doubt
Griswold, G. Red Pawns
Hild, J. Skyjack
Jay, C. Arms for Adonis
Katcha, V. Don't Look Down
Keller, B. Baghdad Defections
McCurtin, P. Spoils of War
Osborne, H. Pay-Day
Pendleton, D. Assault
Seymour, G. At Close Quarters
Stewart, M. Gabriel Hounds
Tyndall, J. Death in Lebanon

LEIPZIG (Leip. See also: Germany)
Clifford, F. Naked Runner
White, J. D. Leipzig Affair

LIBYA (See also: Africa, North)
Carter, Nick. Bloodtrail to Mecca
Case, Jim. Assault Into Libya
Coppel, A. Show Me a Hero
Edwards, P. Fist of Fatima
Emmett, R. Devil's Finger

Evans, K. No Cause for Dying
Graham, J. Bloody Passage
Home, M. Place of Little Birds
James, Stuart. Spy Is Falling
Leib, F. A. Fire Arrow
Lewis, N. Suitable Case for Corruption
Maning, K. Bloodstorm
Pendleton, D. Libya Connection
Rosenberger, J. Laser War
Skimin, R. Libyan Warlord
Smith, Don. Libyan Contract
Stillman, R. Tracker

LIMA (See also: Peru; South America)
Houston, R. Cholo
Levey, R. A. Murder in Lima
Pendleton, D. Twisted Path
Stevens, G. Spider

LISBON (See also: Portugal; Madeira)
Benton, K. Sole Agent
Brennan, F. H. Memo to a Firing Squad
Caillou, A. Assault on Loveless
Delman, D. Murder in the Family
Fish, R. L. Hochmann Miniatures
Footner, H. Unneutral Murder
Gifford, T. Man from Lisbon
Lambert, D. Judas Code
MacKenzie, D. Spreewald Collection
Patterson, H. To Catch a King
Pires, J. C. Ballad of Dog's Beach
Prokosch, F. Conspirators
Rich, K. Lucifer Mask
Robeson, K. Hate Genius
Telfair, R. Target for Tonight
Weber, R. Troubleshooter

LITHUANIA (Lith.)
Annesley, M. Spies in the Web

LONG ISLAND (L.I. See also: New York; New York City; Rochester)
Adams, S. H. Flying Death
Adamson, L. Cat in the Manger
Albrand, M. Taste of Terror
Alexander, Irene. Ninth Life
Anthony, Max. Gun-Men's Wake
Aronson, H. Establishment of Innocence
Ashbrook. H. Most Immoral Murder
　Murder Makes Murder
　Murder of Steven Kester
Austin, H. Drink the Green Water
Barrett, Monte. Pelham Murder Case
Barry, Jerome. Strange Relations
Bentley, J. Call Off the Corpse
Bentley, J. L. Duane of the FBI
Bigelow, O. Peacock Season
Bogart, W. Murder Is Forgetful
Bonnell, J. F. Death Over Sunday
Bonney, J. L. Death by Dynamite
Booth, C. B. House of Rogues
　Seaside Mystery
　Telltale Plot
Box, E. Death Likes It Hot
Brewster, E. V. Surprise Party Murder
Bruce, G. Claim of the Fleshless Corpse
Burke, R. Murder on High Heels
Cameron, D. C. Grave Without Grass
Carrington, E. S. Crimson Goddess
Chamberlain, G. A. In Defense of Mrs. Maxon
Charteris, L. Lady on a Train
Chase, A. M. Peril at the Spy Nest
Chichester, J. J. House of the Moving Room
Clancy, E. A. Fast Money
Clarkson, L. Shadow of John Wallace
Cobb, I. S. Murder Day by Day
Coleman, C. Nightmare in July
Conners, B. F. Hampton Sisters
Crane, C. Someone at the Door
　Summer Girl
Crosby, L. Night Attack
Curle, R. Corruption
Dane, J. Y. Cabana Murders
Daniels, D. Dark Villa

Darby, R. Beauty Sleep
Davey, J. Touch of Stagefright
Davis, Mildred. Invisible Border
Debrett, H. Before I Wake
De Forrest, B. Snows of Yesterday
Delman, D. Nice Murderers
    One Man's Murder
De Mille, N. Gold Coast
De Pre, J. Die, Jessica, Die
Early, J. Razzamatazz
Eberhart, M. G. Nine O'Clock Tide
    Witness at Large
Ehrlich, J. Drowning
Farrington, F. Little Game
Fenisong, R. Wench Is Dead
Fielding, Joy. Deep End
Fischer, B. Silent Dust
Fitzsimmons, C. Manville Murders
    Mystery at Hidden Harbor
    No Witness!
Flusser, M. Squeal Man
Foster, I. Moorwood Legacy
Frost, L. Murder at Large
Gibson, W. B. Grove of Doom
Gillespie, R. B. Deathstorm
    Last of the Honeywells
Glidden, M. W. both titles
Goldthwaite, E. K. First You Have to Find Him
    Sixpenny Dame
Green, E. P. Rotten Apples
Griffin, A. J. Ocean of Fire
    Spirit of Brynmaster Oaks
Haring, D. Emergency Operator
    Mayhem, It's Marvelous
    Take Me!
Harris, L. Hamptons
Hawthorne, V. Diary of Evil
    Sweet Deadly Passion
Heyward, D. Pulitzer Prize Murders
Hildick, W. Vandals
Hinkemeyer, M. T. Dark Below
    Lilac Night
    Order of the Arrow
Hobhouse, A. Hangover Murders
Holding, E. S. 6 titles
Hopkins, S. both titles
Hubbard, Regina. Curse of Nightwind
Hubbard, Richard. Daughter of Despair
Isaacs, S. Compromising Positions
Johns, A. Traffic with Evil
Johnson, S. Walk a Winter Beach
Johnston, V. 5 titles
Johnston, W. Tragedy at the Beach Club
Jones, C. R. Van Norton Murders
Jones, E. Who Killed Gregory?
Jordan, E. Devil and the Deep Blue Sea
    Life of the Party
Kane, H. Frenzy of Evil
Kelland, C. B. Double Treasure
Kelsey, V. Bride Dined Alone
Kendall, J. Playing for Keeps
Kenrick, T. Kidnap Kid
King, S. If I Die Before I Wake
Klein, N. Terror by Night
Knight, K. M. Rendezvous with the Past
    Terror by Twilight
Kutak, R. I Am the Cat
Lacy, E. Devil for the Witch
Laflin, J. Spy Who Didn't
Lariar, L. Win, Place and Die!
Lathen, E. Stitch in Time
Lauferty, L. Crimson Thread
Leonard, G. Ice Cathedral
Liddon, E. S. Riddle of the Russian Princess
Lilly, J. Death in B-Minor
Linakis, S. Killing Ground
Livingston, A. Double Cross
    Night of Crime
Loring, A. 13th Doll
Lottman, E. Hemlock Tree
McCaffrey, A. Ring of Fear
McCloy, H. Change of Heart
    Deadly Truth
McGivern, W. P. Savage Streets

McGurk, S. Big Dig
McRoyd, A. Death in Costume
Malmar, M. Never Say Die
Mancini, A. Menage
Martyn, W. Return of Anthony Trent
Mason, V. W. Seeds of Murder
Matheson, D. Ninth Life
Maxxe, R. Arcade
Mayfield, S. Stranger in the House
Moxley, F. W. Glassy Pond
Nazel, J. Delta Crossing
Ostrander, I. Tattooed Arm
Palmer, S. Miss Withers Regrets
Parker, M. Death Do Us Part
    Intriguer
Pentecost, H. Die After Dark
    Homicidal Horse
    Sow Death, Reap Death
Philbin, T. Yearbook Killer
Philips, J. Death Delivers a Postcard
Popkin, Z. So Much Blood
Potts, J. Death of a Stray Cat
Puzo, M. Godfather
Queen, E. Egyptian Cross Mystery
Quick, D. Cry in the Night
    Something Evil
Raison, M. M. No Weeds for the Widow
Reach, J. Blind Gambit
Reeve, A. B. Adventuress
    Stars Scream Murder
Ridgway, J. Hardly a Man Is Now Alive
Roberts, W. A. Haunting Hand
Robeson, K. Cartoon Crimes
    Dr. Time
Ronns, E. Say It with Murder
Ross, Clarissa. Drifthaven
Roueche, B. Fago
    Feral
Rud, A. M. Rose Bath Riddle
    Stuffed Men
Ryerson, F. Borgia Blade
Schley, S. M. Dream Sinister
Scott, Denis. Murder Makes a Villain
Scott, L. Living Dead Man
Scott, M. D. Van Dyne Collection
Seabrooke, J. P. Green Bag
Serrian, M. Captured
Shane, S. Lady in Danger
Sloane, W. To Walk the Night
Smith, L. D. Corpse with the Listening Ear
    Death Is Thy Neighbor
    Follow This Fair Corpse
Smith, W. K. Sultan's Skull
Steel, K. Crooked Shadow
Stevenson, F. Bianca
Stokes, M. L. Dying Room
Stone, Hampton. Strangler Who Couldn't Let Go
Stout, D. Hell Gate
Strange, J. S. Picture of the Victim
Teta, J. Clock at Ravenswood
Thayer, L. Alias Dr. Ely
    Man's Enemies
    Persons Unknown
    That Affair at the Cedars
Todd, P. Blood All Over
Tyson, J. A. Rhodendron Man
Vanardy, V. Lady of the Night Wind
Watkins, R. H. Air Murders
    Half a Clew
Watson, Clarissa. Bishop in the Back Seat
    Runaway
    Somebody Killed the Messenger
Webb, L. J. Walking the Dusk
Weinman, I. Hampton Heat
Welles, K. See No Evil
Wells, Carolyn. 11 titles
Werner, P. Secret at Orient Point
Westermann, J. Exit Wounds
    High Crimes
Westlake. D. E. Bank Shot
Wheelock. D. Murder at Montauk
White, L. 5 titles
Whitney, P. A. Golden Unicorn
    Rainsong

Wiles, D. X Factor
Williams, V. Clock Ticks On
    Masks Off at Midnight
Willoughby, J. Crimsoned Millions
Winston, D. Trap
Worts, G. F. Blue Lacquered Box

LOS ANGELES (L.A. See also: California;
    Sacramento; San Diego; San Francisco;
    West)
Adams, C. F. Decoy
    What Price Murder
Alexander, M. Curtis Wives
Allen, E. C. Laguna Contracts
Allen, S. Murder in Hollywood
    Murder on the Glitter Box
Ames, C. Gorgonzola, Won't You Please Come
    Home?
Amo, G. Come Nightfall
Andersen, U. S. Hard and Fast
Andrews, C. Butterfly Murder
Aricha, A. Journey Toward Death
Armour, J. Killer's Category
Armstrong, C. 8 titles
Ashton, A. Phantom Reflection
Babcock, D. V. Gorgeous Ghoul
    Homicide for Hannah
Bacar, J. Avenue of the Stars
Baker, L. Cheaters
Ball, J. 7 titles
Ballard, W. T. Say Yes to Murder
    Walk in Fear
Ballinger, B. S. Heir Hunters
    Law
    Not I, Said the Vixen
Banks, R. E. both titles
Bannister, W. Portrait of Death
Barkley, D. Freeway
Barnes, D. all 5 titles
Barry, M. Los Angeles Holocaust
Base, R. Matinee Idol
Baxt, G. Neon Graveyard
    Talking Pictures Murder
Baynes, J. Peeping Tom Murders
Bear, G. Queen of Angels
Bellem, R. L. Dan Turner, Hollywood Detective
Berckman, E. She Asked for It
Berger, P. Deadly Kisses
Bergman, A. Hollywood and Le Vine
Bergquist, L. Your Shot, Darling!
Beynon, J. Cypress Man
Bishop, M. G. Scylla
Bishop, P. Citadel Run
    Sand Against the Tide
Black, J. D. Trouble Man
Bloch, R. Lori
    Night-World
    Psycho II
Blodgett, M. Captain Blood
Blumenthal, J. Tinseltown Murders
Bogar, J. Payoff for Paula
Booth, C. G. Cat and the Clock
Booth, E. With Sirens Screaming
Boston, C. K. Silver Jackass
Boucher, A. Case of the Baker Street Irregulars
    Case of the Crumpled Knave
    Case of the Solid Key
Boyer, C. Mosaic Earring
Boyers, B. Murder by Proxy
Boyles, W. Wild Ride
Brackett, L. No Good from a Corpse
Bradbury, R. Graveyard for Lunatics
Braham, H. Call Me Deadly
Braudy, S. Who Killed Sal Mineo?
Braun, W. Murder in Hollywood
Breen, J. L. Gathering Place
Brent, L. W. One Man's Crime
Brett, J. Who'd Hire John Brett?
Brown, Carter. at least 32 titles
Brown, F. His Name Was Death
    Murderers
    Wench Is Dead
Brown, Rudd. Killing in Real Estate
Buchanan, J. L.A. Gang War

Settings Index   LOS ANGELES

Bugliosi, V. T. Shadow of Cain
Bunker, E. Little Boy Blue
Burnett, W. R. Nobody Lives Forever
    Romelle
Byers, C. A. Inverness Murder
Cagle, G. Payola!
Cain, N. all 5 titles
Cain, P. Fast One
Caine, H. T. Hollywood Heroes
Cameron, L. Hot Car
    Outsider
Campbell, R. W. 5 titles
Carleson, D. V. Body Glow
Carmichael, F. Pen Is Deadlier
Carr, K. Don't Bet on Living, Alice
    You're Hired; You're Dead
Carrel, M. Emerald Heart
Carson, R. Golden Years Caper
    Quality of Mercy
Caspary, V. Weeping and the Laughter
Castle, F. Violent Hours
Chaber, M. E. Day It Rained Diamonds
    Flaming Man
    Softly in the Night
Chais, P. Final Cut
Chandler, R. High Window
    Killer in the Rain
    Little Sister
    Long Goodbye
Charbonneau, L. And Hope to Die
Chase, J. H. Eve
    What's Better Than Money?
Chastain, T. Case of the Burning Bequest
Child, N. Diamond Ransom Murders
Childs, T. Cold Turkey
Chittenden, M. Beyond the Rainbow
Clad, N. Taste for Brilliants
Clark, A. C. Cry Revenge
Clarke, R. Synonym for Murder
Clason, C. B. Green Shiver
    Whispering Ear
Cline, J. Forever Beat
Clothier, P. Dirty-Down
Cochran, A. Two Plus Two
Coffey, B. Surrounded
Cohen, O. R. at least 6 titles
Colby, R. 5 titles
Collins, Mary. Death Warmed Over
Collins, Michael. Slasher
Colter, E. Cheer for the Dead
Colton, M. Double Take
Conteris, H. Ten Percent of Life
Cook, Bruce. Rough Cut
Cope, H. Death Stalks the Fleet
Copper, B. most if not all 52 of the Mike Faraday books
Corres, P. "Beverly Hills" Browning
Corrington, J. W. White Zone
Cox, W. R. Tycoon and the Tigress
Craig, John. Superdude
Crain, W. W. Psycho Squad
Crais, R. Monkey's Raincoat
    Stalking the Angel
Crawford, O. Execution
Creighton, J. Half Interest in Murder
Crooker, H. Hollywood Murder Mystery
Crosby, V. Fast-Death Factor
Cunningham, E. V. 8 titles
Curtis, W. Red Dragon
Dana, R. Death Was the Echo
Daniels, D. Larrabee Heiress
Daniels, N. Arrest and Trial
    Missing Witness
    One Angry Man
Davidson, M. Thursday Woman
Dejeans, E. Double House
Dekker, C. Double or Nothing
Dekker, C. Woman in Marble
Dekobra, M. Hangman Never Waits
    Lady Is a Vamp
    Madonna in Hollywood
Delacorta. Vida
De Larrabeiti, M. Hollywood Takes
De Marco, G. Canvas Prison

Demaris, O. 5 titles
Deming, R. at least 7 titles
Denning, Mark. Ransom
Derrick, L. Assassination File
    Showbiz Wipeout
    Target Is H
De Sario, J. P. Limbo
Deverell, W. Platinum Blues
Dewey, T. B. 7 titles
Dexter, B. I'll Sing You the Death of Bill Brown
DiChiara, R. Dick and the Devil
    Hard-Boiled
Dickinson, W. Dead Man Talks Too Much
Dillinger, J. Adrenaline
Disney, D. C. Golden Swan Murder
Dodge, D. Shear the Black Sheep
Dooley, R. Flashback
Dratler, J. J. Judas Fire
    Pitfall
Duff, J. P. Run from Death
    Some Die Young
    Who Dies There?
Duke, W. Fair Prey
Dunne, J. G. True Confessions
Eachus, I. Raid on the Bremerton
Eby, L. Blood Runs Cold
    Death Begs the Question
    Hell Hath No Fury
Echard, M. Stand-In for Death
Eden, R. Short Skirts
Edgley, L. Angry Heart
    Dirty Business
    Judas Goat
Edingtons. Monk's Hood Murders
    Murder to Music
    Studio Murder Mystery
Egan, L. 25 titles
Eichler, A. Election by Murder
Eldredge, G. Death for the Surgeon
Eldridge, M. Lightning May Strike Anywhere
Elliott, David. Blue Movie
Elliott, Tom. Dwelling
Ellroy, J. 8 titles
Enders, R. Tight Squeeze
Endore, G. Methinks the Lady—
Ephron, A. Bruised Fruit
Evans, K. L. Feast for Spiders
Eversz, R. Bottom Line Is Murder
    False Profit
Fair, A. A. Beware the Curves
Farr, J. Deadly Combo
Farrell, H. What Ever Happened to Baby Jane?
Fast, J. Inner Circle
Fawcette, S. Murder at the 1984 Summer Games
Fenady, A. J. both titles
Ferrigno, R. Horse Latitudes
Fickling, G. G. Girl on the Prowl
    Naughty But Dead
Fielding, J. Transformation
Fisher, S. Big Dream
    Giveaway
    I Wake Up Screaming
    Image of Hell
Fitzsimmons, C. Evil Men Do
Fleming, Robert. Night Freight Murders
Fliegel, R. Next to Die
Flowers, C. It Never Rains in Los Angeles
Fluke, J. Final Appeal
    Video Kill
Flynn, C. H. Washed in the Blood
Ford, L. Devil's Stronghold
Forrest, K. V. Amateur City
    Beverly Malibu
    Murder at the Nightwood Bar
Forward, R. L. Owl
Foster, A. D. Alien Nation
Foster, R. Invisible Man Murders
Fox, J. M. 10 titles
Francis, W. Bury Me Not
    Rough on Rats
Frank, W. I. God for One More Ride
Franklin, M. at least 8 titles
Fray, A. Built for Trouble
    Dame's the Game
    Dice Spelled Murder

Frazer, R. C. Hollywood Hoax
Fritch, C. E. Negative of a Nude
Gale, C. Golden Eyes
Galloway, D. Lamaar Ransom—Private Eye
Gardner, E. S. about 83 titles
Gault, W. C. 17 titles
Gavin, T. Last Film of Emile Vico
Gibbons, C. Murder in Hollywood
Gifford, T. Hollywood Gothic
Gilden, M. Surfing Samurai Robots
Gless, E. G. Murder at Tall Tip
Goddard, K. Balefire
Goines, D. Inner City Hoodlum
Goldberg, G. J. Heart Payments
Goldman, R. L. Murder of Harvey Blake
Goodis, D. Of Missing Persons
Gordon, R. Dead Level
Gordons. 5 titles
Gottesfeld, G. Violet Closet
Graham, Anthony. Death Business
    No Sale for Haloes
Grant, J. Mace!
Gray, B. Conquest in California
Grayson, Rupert. Gun Cotton in Hollywood
Green, G. Heartless Light
Green, Kate. Shattered Moon
Greenleaf, S. Ditto List
Gregory, M. Triplets
Grote, W. Cain's Girl Friend
Grove, M. You'll Die, Darling
    You'll Die Today
    You'll Die When You Hear This
Gruber, F. 8 titles
Hallas, R. You Play the Black and the Red Comes Up
Hallinan, T. both titles
Hamilton, N. Killer's Rights
    Shape of Fear
Handler, D. Man Who Died Laughing
Hansen, J. 5 titles
Hansl, A. Call from L.A.
Haring, D. Any Guy Can Die in Bed!
    Cry Twice, Kitten!
    Death Wears a Lady's Smile
    Temptress Touch
Harrington, R. E. Quintain
Harris, N. In the Shadows
Harris, Timothy. Good Night and Goodbye
    Heat Wave
Harriss, W. Timor Mortis
Hausfeld, R. Bullets for Blondes
Haycox, E. Rough Air
Hayes, H. Where the Truth Lies
Hays, L. Harry-O #2
Haywood, G. A. both titles
Heath, C. Old Scores to Settle
    Small But Deadly Wars
    Ten Percent of Trouble
Heath, E. Death Takes a Dive
    Murder Pool
Hecht, B. I Hate Actors!
Heinecke, H. J. And the Winds Blew
Henderson, M. R. By Reas Of
    Killing Game
Heyes, D. Kill
    Kiss-Off
Heyman, E. L. Dead Heat on a Merry-Go-Round
Hitchens, B. F.O.B. Murder
    One-Way Ticket
Hitchens, D. Fools Gold
    Sleep with Slander
    Stairway to an Empty Room
Hoffenberg, J. Desperate Adversaries
Hoffman, L. Fear Among the Shadows
Holland, M. Glass Heart
Holmes, H. H. both titles
Holt, Samuel. One of Us Is Wrong
Holton, L. 9 titles
Horgan, M. Dames Is My Undoing
Horwitz, M. Bloody Silks
Howard, J. A. Die on Easy Street
Howe, M. J. Mother Shadow
Huggins, R. all 4 titles
Hughes, B. Murder in Church
Hughes, D. B. Bamboo Blonde

L

LOS ANGELES

Davidian Report
In a Lonely Place
Hunt, H. Lovers Are Losers
Hunt, M. V. Mystery of Daria Kane
Huston, F. Rich Get It All
Hutton, J. F. Too Good to Be True
Hyams, J. Murder at the Academy Awards
Hyman, J. Eyes of a Stranger
Ingersol, J. Rose Can Kill
Irvine, R. R. Freeze Frame
    Horizontal Hold
    Jump Cut
    Ratings Are Murder
Israel, P. Hush Money
Jahn, M. Switch
Janson, H. Gunsmoke In Her Eyes
    Sweetheart, Here's Your Grave
Jason, S. Coffin Corner U.S.A.
    Hollywood Assassin
Jerome, O. F. Five Assassins
Johnson, B. B. Death of a Blue-Eyed Soul Brother
    Mother of the Year
Johnson, E. R. God Keepers
Johnson, M. Clone People
Johnson, W. O. Hammered Gold
Johnston, V. House Above Hollywood
Johnston, W. Banyon
Jones, E. R. Alarm
Jones, G. E. Trap
Judd, H. Shadow of a Doubt
Kadrey, R. Metrophage
Kahn, J. Echo Vector
Kaminsky, S. M. 11 titles
Kane, A. Slaughter's Big Rip-Off
Kane, F. About Face
    Bare Trap
    Dead Rite
    Mourning After
Kane, H. Peter Gunn
Kastle, H. Sunset People
Katz, M. J. Last Dance in Redondo Beach
Keating, H. R. F. Go West, Inspector Ghote
Keene, D. at least 6 titles
Kelland, C. B. Murder Makes an Entrance
Kellerman, F. Milk and Honey
    Ritual Bath
    Sacred and Profane
Kellerman, J. 5 titles
Kerr, J. Emergency Room
Kincaid, D. Sunset Bomber
Knight, C. Affair of the Corpse Escort
    Affair of the Fainting Butler
Knight, D. both titles
Koehler, R. P. Murder Expert
    Murder in the Green Sedan
    Steps to Murder
Kolb, K. Couch Trip
Koman, V. Jehovah Contract
    Solomon's Knife
Koontz, D. R. Bad Place
    Whispers
Kraft, G. Bloody Mary
    Bullshoot
    Let's Rob Roy
Kramer, George. Remarkable Murder
Krich, R. M. Where's Mommy Now?
La Fountaine, G. Two Minute Warning
Land, M. Quicksand
Langham, J. R. both titles
Lariar, L. He Died Laughing
Larsen, G. Paramount Kill
Larson, C. Muir's Blood
    Someone's Death
Laumer, K. Deadfall
Lawrence, A. both titles
Lawson, S. Scorpio
Lee, Edward. both titles
Leonard, E. Get Shorty
Leslie, Jean. Hair of the Dog
Lewis, Lange. Birthday Murder
    Juliet Dies Twice
    Meat for Murder
    Murder Among Friends
Lewis, Margo. Concept for Murder
Lewis, S. Cowboy Blues

Linington, E. all 14 titles
Linklater, J. L. at least 6 titles
Lochte, D. Laughing Dog
    Sleeping Dog
Locke, R. D. Taste of Brass
Lockhart, M. Nobody Dies in Chinatown
Loraine, P. Ask the Rattlesnake
Lorne, D. Sight Unseen
Lovesey, P. Keystone
Ludlow, I. all 3 titles
Ludwig, J. Little Boy Lost
Luther, M. L. both titles
Lyons, A. 5 titles
Lysaght, B. both titles
McCall, L. L. Tapping at the Window
McCardell, R. C. Diamond from the Sky
MacCargo, J. T. Faces of Murder
McConnor, V. Limbo
    Man Who Knew Hammett
McCoy, H. I Should Have Stayed Home
    They Shoot Horses, Don't They?
McCray, M. D. C. Death March
McDermid, F. Ghost Wanted
McDonald, G. Fletch Won
    Fletch's Moxie
Macdonald, J. R. Meet Me at the Morgue
    Way Some People Die
Macdonald, R. Moving Target
Macdonald, R. Barbarous Coast
    Ferguson Affair
    Instant Enemy
McDonnell, G. Intruder from the Sea
    My Sister, Good Night
McElwain, B. Fatal Games
McGivern, W. P. Reprisal
MacKenzie, J. A. Omega Document
McManis, J. A. Hooded Asp
McMurdie, A. L. Nightmare Hall
MacNeil, N. Two Guns for Hire
McPartland, J. Wild Party
Magee, B. Columbo and the Samurai Sword
Mandell, M. Killer Instinct
Mann, E. A. Portals
Marble, M. S. both titles
Marlowe, D. J. Operation Deathmaker
Martin, A. L. Crimson Frame
    Death on a Ferris Wheel
    Fear Comes Calling
Martinez, A. Jigsaw John
Martinez, S. A. Target for Terror
Martyn, W. Chromium Cat
Masterton, G. Tengu
Matcha, J. Prowler in the Night
Matheson, R. Ride the Nightmare
    Someone Is Bleeding
Mayo, N. Benefit
Meggs, B. Saturday Games
Melchior, I. Watchdogs of Abaddon
Meyer, N. Target Practice
Miles, K. Double Eagle
Millar, M. Beast in View
    Stranger in My Grave
Millard, O. Missing Person
Miller, G. Black Glove
Miller, Tony. Night Calls
Miller, V. B. Angel's Blood
Miller, Wade. Big Guy
    Tiger's Wife
Millington, F. Crime Across the Way
Mitchell, Blake. Sacrifice
Mitchell, S. Double Bluff
    Lonely Shroud
Montecino, M. Crosskiller
Moore, P. Death Drives the Lead Car
Morgan, John. Death to Comrade X
Morgan, M. Decoy
    Nine More Lives
Morgan, P. Too Mini Murders
Morse, L. A. all 3 titles
Mosley, W. Devil in a Blue Dress
Murphy, W. B. Smoked Out
Murray, W. Getaway Blues
    Killing Touch
    King of the Nightcap
Myers, P. B. Hollywood Murder

Naha, E. On the Edge
    Razzle-Dazzle
Nash, N. R. Radiance
Nathanson, J. Puzzle for Experts
Nava, M. Goldenboy
Nazel, J. Devil Dolls
Neely, R. No Certain Life
Newland, N. M. Walk to Your Grave
Newman, B. Spy in the Brown Derby
Newton, M. Blood Sport
Nielsen, H. Borrow the Night
    Woman on the Roof
Nixon, Allan. Goodnight, Garrity
Noguchi, T. T. Physical Evidence
    Unnatural Causes
Nolan, W. F. Death Is for Losers
    White Cad Cross-Up
Norst, J. Colors
    Lethal Weapon
Nuetzel, C. both titles
Obstfeld, R. Goulden Fleece
O'Callaghan, M. Death Is Forever
    Hit and Run
Odlum, J. Mirabilis Diamond
O'Hanlon, J. D. As Good As Murdered
    Murder at Malibu
Olgin, H. A. Cover Up
Olsen, D. B. at least 7 titles
O'Toole, M. Red Mist
Paige, R. Door to December
Palmer, L. Cat-Eye
Palmer, S. Cold Poison
    Puzzle of the Happy Hooligan
    Rook Takes Knight
Panger, D. Mask of Abraham Morgenstern
Parker, R. B. Savage Place
Parker, T. J. Laguna Heat
    Little Saigon
Patrick, A. Beyond the Law
Paul, Elliot. Black Gardenia
Peeples, S. A. Man Who Died Twice
Pender, L. Hit and Run
Pendleton, D. 7 titles
Perdue, V. Case of the Foster Father
    Case of the Grieving Monkey
    He Fell Down Dead
Perry, T. Big Fish
    Metzger's Dog
Peters, B. Big H
Petievich, G. Earth Angels
    Money Men and One-Shot Deal
    To Die in Beverly Hills
    To Live and Die in L.A.
Phillips, R. B. Gun Play
Pierce, D. M. Down in the Valley
    Hear the Wind Blow, Dear
    Roses Love Sunshine
Platt, K. 5 titles
Plunkett, J. She'll Get Hers
Prather, R. S. 29 titles
Presnell, F. G. Too Hot to Handle
Preston, J. Heil! Hollywood
Pronin, B. Syndrome
Pryor, L. Viper
Queen, E. 5 titles
Quentin, P. Suspicious Circumstances
Quinn, J. Crystal Kill
Rabe, P. It's My Funeral
    Stop This Man!
    War of the Dons
Race, P. Self-Made Widow
Racina, T. Sweet Revenge
Raison, M. M. Murder in a Lighter Vein
    Nobody Loves a Dead Man
Ramm, C. L.A. Wars
Rawlings, P. Fade to Black
Rawson, T. I Want to Live!
Ray, R. Bloody Murdock
    Dial "M" for Murdock
    Merry Christmas, Murdock
    Murdock for Hire
Reach, J. Storm Over Hollywood
    Sunset Strip
Reed, Rex. Personal Effects
Reese, J. Pity Us All

Reeves, Robert. No Love Lost
Reeves-Stevens, G. Dark Matter
Rhodes, V. Groomed for Murder
Rice, C. April Robin Murders
Richardson, J. H. Spring Street
Richardson, Scott. King of the Shadows
Rico, D. Passion Flower Puzzle
Rider, S. Misplaced Corpse
Rifkin, S. McQuaid
Robb, T. N. Flip Side
Roberts, Les. Infinite Number of Monkeys
    Not Enough Horses
    Snake Oil
Robeson, K. Seven Agate Devils
Robinett, S. Final Option
    Unfinished Business
Rock, P. Hickey and Boggs
Rodgers, M. J. For Love or Money
Rolfe, E. Glass Room
Rosaire, F. White Night
Rosmanith, O. L. Signature to a Crime
Ross, Marilyn. Behind the Purple Veil
Ross, Paul. Freebie and the Bean
Ross, S. Hang-Up
    Ready for the Tiger
Rotsler, W. Vice Squad
Rovin, J. both titles
Rowson, M. Wasteland
Rubel, J. L. No Business for a Lady
Rubel, M. Flex
Rubin, R. Annulment
Rustan, J. Tangled Snarl
Ryerson, F. Shadows
Sadler, M. Deadly Innocents
    Here to Die
St. Pierre, D. Marshal
Sale, R. Benefit Performance
    Lazarus #7
    Passing Strange
Sanchez, T. Zoot-Suit Murders
Sanders, B. Starshine Connection
Sanders, G. Stranger at Home
Sangster, J. Snowball
Santiago, V. J. Detour to a Funeral
Sapir, R. Brain Drain
Sauer, R. Game of the Silence
Saul, O. Dark Side of Love
Saxby, C. Death Over Hollywood
    Murder at the Mike
Saxon, J. A. Liability Limited
Saxon, V. Hollywood Hitman
Scarpetta, F. Death to the Mafia
Schiffer, M. Colors
Schorr, M. Blindside
    Diamond Rock
    Eye for an Eye
Schwartz, R. B. Frozen Stare
Scott, R. Shakedown
Shagan, S. City of Angels
    Vendetta
Shah, D. K. As Crime Goes By
Shannon, D. all 36 titles
Shatner, W. Tekwar
Simon, R. L. both titles
Simpson, P. Partners in Time
Sinclair, M. Goodbye, L.A.
    Only in L.A.
    Tough Luck L.A.
Smith, P. C. Nothing But Blood
Smoke, S. Deliver Us from Evil
    Pacific Edge
Sohl, J. Odious Ones
Solomon, B. Gone Man
    Open Shadow
Spain, J. all 3 titles
Stadley, P. Black Leather Barbarians
Stanley, J. Bogart 48
Stanley, R. Hippy Cult Murders
Starr, Jimmy. all 3 titles
Steeber, M. One If by Night
Steiner, S. Murder on Her Mind
Stewart, L. Panic on Page One
Stewart, S. Big Rip-Off
Stilgebauer, E. Star of Hollywood

Stinson, J. Double Exposure
    Double Take
    Low Angles
    Truck Shot
Stivers, D. 5 titles
Stratford, M. Sniper
Stratton, C. Dead on Arrival
    Hostages
    Runaway
Sutton, Jefferson. Cassady
Sutton, Jessica. Kill or Cure
Szollosi, T. Proving
Taylor, A. F. How I Made a Million Dollars
Taylor, F. House of the Hunter
Taylor, S. S. all 3 titles
Tebbetts-Taylor, E. Now I Law Me Down to Die
Telushkin, J. Final Analysis of Dr. Stark
    Unorthodox Murder of Rabbi Wahl
Thayer, L. Guilty!
Thomey, T. And Dream of Evil
    Killer in White
Thompson, G. Cup of Death
    Murder Mystery
Thompson, J. Grifters
Thoreau, D. Book of Numbers
    Good Book
    Satanic Condition
Thornburg, N. Dreamland
Thorp, R. Nothing Lasts Forever
    Rainbow Drive
Tine, R. Beverly Hills Cop II
Tolkin, M. Player
Tralins, R. Dragnet '67
Trask, M. Murder in Brief
Trevor, E. Theta Syndrome
Trevor, L. all 3 titles
Treynor, B. all 3 titles
Trinian, J. House of Evil
Truesdell, J. Be Still, My Love
    Morgue the Merrier
Vasquez, R. Giant Killer
Verner, G. Con Man
Von Elsner, D. Don't Just Stand There, Do
    Someone
Vowell, D. both titles
Wager, W. Blue Moon
Walk, C. E. Green Seal
Walker, G. Suspect
Walker, T. P. Recall
Wallace, F. L. both titles
Wallace, Randall. Blood of the Lamb
Wallace, Robert. Death Under Contract
Wambaugh, J. Black Marble
    Delta Star
    Golden Orange
    New Centurions
Ward, Donald. Death Takes the Stage
Warga, W. Hardcover
Warren, B. Fandom Is a Way of Death
Warren, D. Case of Rape
    Scarlet Starlet
Washburn, L. J. Dead Stick
Webb, J. 9 titles
Weisman, J. Quadraphone Homicide
West, O. Pit
Westbrook, R. Left-Handed Policeman
    Nostalgia Kills
Westheimer, D. Avila Gold
Weston, C. Poor, Poor Ophelia
    Rouse the Demon
    Susannah Screaming
Weston, Garnett. Undertaker Dies
Weverka, R. Griff
Wheatley, D. Such Power Is Dangerous
White, L. T. Me, Detective
White, Teri. Bleeding Hearts
    Fault Lines
    Tightrope
Whitfield, R. Death in a Bowl
Whittington, H. Don't Speak to Strange Girls
Wick, C. Dark House, Dark Road
Wiles, D. Death Flight
Wilk, M. Moving Picture Boys
Williams, B. Make a Killing

    Stranger to Herself
    Well-Dressed Corpse
Williams, B. A. End to Mirth
Williamson, A. M. Black Sleeves
Wilmer, D. Memo for Murder
Wilson, Dana. Make with the Brains, Pierre
Winski, N. L.A. Massacre
Wolff, B. Hyde and Seek
Wolfson, V. Nothing Happens to Children in
    Beverly Hills
Wormser, R. Hanging Heiress
Wyka, F. Regression
Yariv, F. P. Last Exit
Young, C. Todd Dossier
Zindel, P. When Darkness Falls

LOUISIANA (La. See also: New Orleans; South)
Anderson, S. L. Shadows Across the Bayou
Arkham, C. Deadly Friendship
Austin, Marilyn. Blackwater Bayou
Barrett, Monte. Murder at Belle Camille
Barron, A. Serpent in the Shadows
Bellamann, H. Victoria Grandolet
Blake, J. Midnight Waltz
Brown, Sandra. Slow Heat in Heaven
Burke, J. L. Heaven's Prisoners
Camp, W. Sinister Island
Carter, A. S. Adopted Face
Cockrell, F. Dark Waters
Conaway, J. World's End
Crane, F. Buttercup Case
Crawford, R. A. Image of Evil
Crecy, J. Night Hunters
Crosby, J. Dear Judgment
Daingerfield, F. Ghost House
Daniels, D. at least 6 titles
Davenport, F. Secret of the Bayou
Eberhart, M. G. With This Ring
Effinger, G. A. Felicia
Eyre, M. Return to Gravesend
Fitzgerald, A. J. House of Tragedy
Fleming, Jane. Hawthorn Wood
Fletcher, M. M. Scorpion of Chateau Laverria
Footner, H. Trial by Water
Fuller, C. Soldier's Play
Glenning, R. Corpse Sat Up
Grimwood, K. Voice Outside
Hall, G. Blue Taper
Harris, C. Sweet and Deadly
Hayworth, E. Evil at Bayou Laforche
Heath, M. Calderwood
    Legend of Blackhurst
    Marshwood
Herber, W. Live Bait for Murder
Hitchens, D. In a House Unknown
Hubbard, M. A. Murder Takes the Veil
Hughes, M. E. Precious in His Sight
Hurd, F. House of Shadows
Kane, F. Poison Unknown
Karl, M. S. Death Notice
    Killer's Ink
Keene, D. Big Kiss-Off
    Bring Him Back Dead
    Notorious
Kimbrough, K. Shriek in the Midnight Tower
Knoblock, K. T. Murder in the Mind
    Take Up the Bodies
Kruger, P. Message from Marise
Landers, G. Deer Killers
Long, A. R. It's Death, My Darling!
    Murder Goes South
Louis, J. Madelaine
McCray, M. Louisiana Firestorm
MacIvers, S. Cry of the Wind
    Night Without End
Martin, Carl. Delta Deputies
Matschat, C. H. Murder at the Black Crook
Maxwell, P. Bewitching Grace
    Dark Masquerade
    Plantation Inn
    Stranger at Plantation Inn
Milburn, E. Wings of Darkness
Mitchelmore, G. Natural Weapon
Morris, Elizabeth. Teaspoon of Murder

L

Nicole, Claudette. When the Wind Cries
Nicole, Claudia. Moonwater
Nottingham, P. Hatred's Web
Percy, W. Thanatos Syndrome
Reddoch, J. Night of the Hellebore
Redman, J. Death by the Riverside
Robeson, K. Quest of the Spider
Ronns, E. Death Is My Shadow
Ross, Sam. Tight Corner
Rydell, F. Annalisa
St. John, G. Shadow on Spanish Swamp
Sellars, M. House on Black Bayou
Shuman, M. K. Frenchman's Blood
Stone, H. Heiress of Bayou Vache
Talmage, A. Dark Over Acadia
Tracy, D. Look Down on Her Dying
    Naked She Died
Weston, H. G. House of False Faces
Wilcox, James. Miss Undine's Living Room
Wood, C. Shadow from the Bogue
Woodrell, D. Muscle for the Wing
    Under the Bright Lights

LOUISVILLE (See also: Kentucky; South)
Amrin, E. First Angel
Birkett, J. Last Private Eye
    Queen's Mare
Colby, R. Captain Must Die
Haring, D. His Own Executioner
McDowell, E. Bloodline to Murder
    In at the Kill
    Stamped for Death
    Three for the Gallows
Revell, L. No Pockets in Shrouds
Sellers, M. Raise the Dark Gambler

MACAO (See also: China; Far East; Shanghai;
    Peking; Formosa; Hong Kong)
Black, G. Golden Cockatrice
Booth, Martin. Jade Pavilion
Carney, D. Macau
Carter, Nick. Macao
Fleischman, A. S. Look Behind You, Lady
Hardy, L. Nightshade Ring
Harknett, T. Crown: Macao Mayhem
Tokson, E. When Dragons Dance

MACEDONIA (Maced. See also: Balkans; Bulgaria;
    Greece; Yugoslavia)
Allen, T. Jade Elephants

MADAGASCAR
Haworth, J. Heart of Stone

MADEIRA (See also: Portugal; Lisbon)
Farnsworth, M. Castle That Whispered
Ferrars, E. Skeleton Staff
    Witness Before the Fact
Goddard, R. Past Caring
White, Alicen. Watching Eye

MADISON (See also: Wisconsin; Midwest)
Derleth, A. Death by Design
    Narracong Riddle

MADRID (See also: Spain; Barcelona; Canary
    Islands; Majorca)
Bagby, G. Body in the Basket
Carter, Nick. Code Name: Werewolf
Chaber, M. E. Man Inside
Cory, D. Hammerhead
Fletcher, Dorothy. Meeting in Madrid
Larreta, A. Last Portrait of the Duchess of Alba
Lee, John. Caught in the Act
Marlowe, S. Drum Beat—Madrid
Moore, G. Theodosius de Zulvin, the Monk of
    Madrid
Naughton, E. Case in Madrid
Rathbone, J. Lying in State
Roos, A. Few Days in Madrid
Serafin, D. Christmas Rising
    Madrid Underground
    Saturday of Glory

Strachan, T. S. Short Weekend
Wilson, Gar. Fair Game

MAINE (See also: New England)
Abbott, A. Third Tower
Abbott, S. Whispering Gables
Anderson, J. Hooray for Homicide
    Murder of Sherlock Holmes
Angus, S. Arson and Old Lace
Barber, W. A. Drawn Conclusion
Bishop, M. Widow's Walk
Blizard, M. Men in Her Death
Bonnamy, F. Blood and Thirsty
Boorstin, P. Glory Hand
Borthwick, J. S. Down East Murders
    Student Body
Bradley, M. H. Nice People Murder
Brean, H. Clock Strikes Thirteen
Burleigh, D. Q. Kristiana Killers
Bushall, A. Shadowdance
Calin, A. Multitude of Shadows
Clark, B. Deathstalk
Combes, S. M. Caly
Coolidge, E. L. Maine Girl
Cooper, Lynna. Stark Island
Daly, E. Deadly Nightshade
    Unexpected Night
Daniels, D. at least 12 titles
Dantz, W. R. Pulse
Dean, R. G. Affair at Lover's Leap
De Blasis, C. Night Child
Dibner, M. Ransom Run
Dickson, M. Octavia's Hill
Disney, D. M. Find the Woman
    Voice from the Grave
Eldridge, G. D. Millbank Case
Ellis, J. Walk a Tightrope
Esteven, J. While Murder Waits
Fahy, C. Lyssa Syndrome
Fairman, P. W. That Girl
Farr, C. at least 8 titles
Fennelly, P. Cuckoos on the Hearth
Findley, T. Telling of Lies
Fitzpatrick, J. Serena
Fuller, Anne. Death on the Outer Shoal
Gerry, M. S. Sound of Water
Gibson, W. Crime Over Casco
Gilman, D. Tightrope Walker
Gladstone, E. Enigma
Gordon, E. Freer's Cove
Gould, J. R. Long Silence
Hatch, M. R. P. Strange Disappearance of Eugene
    Comstocks
Hermes, M. Phoenix Nest
Holland, R. S. Minot's Folly
    Mystery of the "Opal"
Holt, H. J. Midnight at Mears House
Hood, M. P. all 6 titles
Hopkins, N. M. Racoon Lake Mystery
Hougan, C. Romeo Flag
Howe, F. Legacy of Lanshore
Hufford, S. Cove's End
Johnston, V. Other Karen
    Presence in an Empty Room
Kalish, R. Bloodtide
Kenney, S. Graves in Academe
    One Fell Swoop
Kimbrough, K. Augusta, the First
    Jane, the Courageous
    Margaret, the Faithful
    Rachel, the Possessed
King, Stephen. It
Koontz, D. R. Night Chills
Kyle, R. Nice Guys Finish Last
Laing, A. Cadaver of Gideon Wyck
Landon, H. Gray Magic
    Owl's Warning
Leffingwell, A. Mystery of Bar Harbor
Lemke, Karen. Down East Detective
Letton, J. Cragsmoor
Livingston, N. Magic for Murder
McCurtin, P. Cosa Nostra
MacLeod, C. Gladstone Bag
Martyn, W. Murder Island

Matheson, R. Hell House
Mayor, D. It's an Ill Wind
Meservey, R. Masquerade Into Madness
Michaels, B. Crying Child
Morison, B. J. all 4 titles
Nebel, F. Fifty Roads to Town
Nichols, S. Widow's Walk
Nicole, Claudette. Dark Mill
Nightingale, U. Bitters Wood
Noone, E. Seacliffe
Norwood, H. Death Down East
Ogilvie, E. Bellwood
    Dancer in Yellow
    Dreaming Summer
    When the Music Stopped
Orford, E. Maze
Orr, C. Wailing Rock Murders
Osborne, D. Fog Island
Packard, F. Miracle Man
Parker, R. B. Early Autumn
    Wilderness
Patterson, A. M. Heaviest Pipe
Pendleton, D. Island Deathtrap
Philbrick, W. R. Slow Dancer
Phillips, J. Hermit's End
Pollack, E. Rowan Tree Crop
Potts, J. Troublemaker
Potts, Ron. Black Moon
Pronzini, B. Games
Reilly, H. Thirty-First Bullfinch
Reiss, B. Casco Deception
Revell, L. Silver Spade
Rich, V. Baked-Bean Supper Murders
Rinehart, M. R. Yellow Room
Roberts, W. D. Girl Who Wasn't There
    Invitation to Evil
Robeson, K. Squeaking Goblin
Ronns, E. Million Dollar Murder
    Murder Money
Ross, Clarissa. Corridors of Fear
    Durrell Towers
    Out of the Fog
Ross, Dana. Figure in the Shadows
    Lodge Sinister
Ross, Marilyn. at least 33 titles
Ross, W. E. D. Twilight Web
    Yesteryear Phantom
Rowe, A. Curiosity Killed a Cat
    Fatal Purchase
    Little Dog Barked
Russell, R. Point of Reference
Sanborn, R. B. Murder on the Aphrodite
Saul, J. Second Child
Saum, K. Murder Is Relative
Scott, A. Falcon's Island
Shannon, Doris. Punishment
Sloane, W. Edge of Running Water
Stein, A. M. Coffin Country
    Nose for It
Stern, P. V. D. Love Is the One with Wings
Strange, J. S. Bell in the Fog
Stuart, E. Shaking Shadow
Swann, F. Brass Key
Tapply, W. G. Dead Meat
Thayer, L. Accident, Manslaughter or Murder?
Turnbull, M. Return of Jenny Weaver
Van de Water, F. F. Alibi
Van de Wetering, J. Maine Massacre
    Murder by Remote Control
Warren, P. Ghost at Ravenkill Manor
    Ravenkill
Webb, J. F. Carnavaron's Castle
Wells, Carolyn. Murder on Parade
    Vanishing of Betty Varian
Westbrook, P. D. Infra Blood
    Red Herring Murder
Williams, B. A. Dreadful Night
    Mischief
    Pascal's Mill
    Silver Forest
Worrell, J. Sting of the Bee

MAJORCA (Maj. See also: Spain; Barcelona;
    Madrid; Canary Islands)

Angus, W. Murder in Mallorca
Asher, Miriam. Nightmare in Eden
Ashford, J. Double Run
Bryan, M. Murder in Majorca
Canning, V. Manasco Road
Carr, G. Holiday with Murder
Crosby, J. Nightfall
Dodson, S. Majorca
Gale, A. Harvest of Terror
Gilruth, S. Drown Her Remembrance
Hild, J. Red Hammer Down
Hintze, N. Cry Witch
Jeffries, R. 14 titles
MacLeod, R. All Other Perils
Mercer, I. Mission to Majorca
O'Brine, M. Passport for Treason
Sims, G. R. Who Is Cato?
Tabori, P. Murder in Majorca

MALAYA. See: Malaysia.

MALAYSIA (Mal. Malaya included here. See also: Far East)
Aarons, E. S. Assignment—White Rajah
Black, G. Time for Pirates
Carter, Nick. Cobra Kill
Catanach, J. N. White Is the Color of Death
Clifford, H. Studies in Brown Humanity
Collis, M. Dark Door
Derby, M. Big Water
    Malayan Rose
    Tigress
Fleischman, A. S. Malay Woman
Harvester, S. Yesterday Walkers
Kauffman, F. Coconut Wireless
Keon, M. Durian Tree
Lilley, T. Projects Section
Maugham, W. S. Ah King
Meade, D. C. Death Over Her Shoulder
    Fatal Shadows
Packard, F. Gold Skull Murders
Scott, B. Prayer Mat
    Secret of the Elephants
Sheen, G. Malayan Story
Sherlock, J. Ordeal of Major Grigsby
Thorne, E. P. Jungle Hut
Trevor, E. Burning Shore
Varney, G. Bungalow of Dead Birds
Yorke, S. Agency House, Malaya

MALI (See also: Africa, West)
Capstan. Inkosi-Carver Investigates

MALLORCA. See: Majorca.

MALTA (See also: Mediterranean Island)
Bagley, D. Freedom Trap
Butler, Gwendoline. Coffin in Malta
Butterworth, M. Vanishing Act
Cass, Z. Island of the Seven Hills
Cutter, J. Maltese Vengeance
Galway, R. C. Assignment Malta
Hedges, S. G. Malta Mystery
Howard, H. Secret of Simon Cornell
Lindsay, K. Suspense
MacLeod, R. Killing in Malta
Maddock, S. Gentlemen of the Night
Mullally, F. Malta Conspiracy
Stuart, Mrs. A. T. Chronicles of a Service Life in Malta

MANILA (See also: Philippines; Far East)
Coxe, G. H. Dangerous Legacy
Kennedy, J. Paper Chase
Knight, C. Affair of the Circus Queen
Lamot, I. Let the Witness Die
Langdon, J. Vicious Circuit
McQuinn, D. E. Wake in Darkness
Marshall, William. Manila Bay
    Whisper
Orbison, K. Key to the Case
Robeson, K. Screaming Man
Teed, G. H. Five in Fear

MARSEILLES (Mars. See also: France; Nice; Paris; Corsica)
Caillou, A. Marseilles
Lefevre, C. Murder in Marseilles
Leonard, C. L. Search for a Scientist
Malo, V. G. Murder on the Mistral
Moore, Robin. French Connection II
Pereira, M. Singing Millionaire
Simpson, H. R. Gathering of Gunmen
    Jumpmaster
Smith, Don. Marseilles Enforcer
Thomas, Louis. Good Children Don't Kill

MARYLAND (Md. See also: Baltimore)
Beechcroft, W. Image of Evil
Bellah, J. W. Bones of Napoleon
Blizard, M. Dark Corner
Brode, R. Clue of the Curious Cat
Broun, D. Egypt's Choice
Cain, J. M. Galatea
    Magician's Wife
Chase, Samantha. Needlepoint
Coffin, C. Mare's Nest
Coffin, G. Forgotten Fleet Mystery
Creighton, J. A. Inn of Evil
Daiger, K. S. both titles
Daniels, D. Blackthorn
    Emerald Hill
    Lily Pond
Disney, D. C. Balcony
    Strawstack
Du Breuil, L. Legend of Molly Moor
Finch, P. In a Place Dark and Secret
Fletcher, L. Strange Blue Yawl
Footner, H. Dark Ships
    Island of Fear
    Ramshackle House
Ford, L. 6 titles
Frome, D. Strange Death of Martin Green
Gaines, A. While the Wind Howled
Garton, R. Trade Secrets
Hamilton, D. Date with Darkness
    Night Walker
Haring, D. Beatnik Babe
Hart, F. N. Hide in the Dark
Hayes, W. E. all 3 titles
Horn, P. Chesapeake Project
Johnson, M. W. Let's Go Play at the Adams'
Karlin, W. Lost Armies
Kelley, P. A. Sleightly Lethal
Kingsbury, M. Island of Fog
Kummer, F. A. Scarecrow Murders
    Twisted Face
Lincoln, N. S. Fifth Latchkey
    Thirteenth Letter
Lippincott, D. Nursery
Longstreet, S. Crime
McGerr, P. Murder Is Absurd
McMullen, M. Other Shoe
Michaels, B. Prince of Darkness
    Walker in Shadows
Norton, A. Snow Shadow
    White Jade Fox
Ostrander, K. Foxfire Cove
Padget, M. House of Strangers
Pendleton, D. Iranian Hit
Peters, Elizabeth. Love Talker
Putre, J. W. Small and Incidental Murder
Rainey, R. Cult .45
Revell, L. Bus Station Murders
Rice, C. Telefair
Roberts, N. Night Moves
Robins, R. Murder at Bayside
Ronns, E. Point of Peril
St. Clair, D. Lady's Not for Living
St. John, G. Night of Evil
Sapir, R. Murder Ward
Sterling, S. Big Ear
Sucher, D. Dead Men Don't Marry
Sutphen, V. T. In Jeopardy
Tracy, D. Big X
    How Sleeps the Beast
    Round Trip
Truscott, L. K. Dress Gray

Ware, J. Thorne House
Welles, E. Waterview Manor
White, L. Crimshaw Memorandum
    Marilyn K.
Winston, D. Adventuress
    Love of Lucifer

MASSACHUSETTS (Mass. See also: Boston; Cape Cod; New England)
Angus, D. Death on Jerusalem Road
August, J. Advance Agent
Baker, C. Gay Head Conspiracy
Batson, G. Strange Boarders
Benson, B. all titles
Biederman, M. Post No Bonds
Blackmur, L. L. Love Lies Slain
Blake, N. Morning After Death
Boyer, R. Gone to Earth
    Penny Ferry
    Whale's Footprints
Bramhall, M. Tragedy in Blue
Brean, H. Hardly a Man Is Now Alive
Bretonne, A. M. Gallows Stands in Salem
Buchanan, P. Parliament of Owls
Byfield, B. N. Harder Thing Than Triumph
Cameron, D. C. Murder's Coming
Cardiff, S. Fool's Apple
Carew, J. Samantha
Carey, C. Chekhov Proposal
Carleton, M. Swan Sang Once
Carr, J. B. Death Whispers
Cassidy, S. J. Altar Boy
Chamberlain, Elinor. Snare for Witches
Clugston, K. Murderer in the House
Coburn, A. Goldilocks
    Love Nest
    Trespassers
Collins, Jackson. Voltan Treasure
Cormier, R. After the First Death
Coxe, G. H. Eye Witness
Coyne, J. E. House of Exile
Craig, P. R. Beautiful Place to Die
Curtiss, P. E. Gay Conspirators
Curtiss, U. 5 titles
Dalmas, H. Fowler Formula
Dana, M. Lake Mystery
Daniels, D. Two Worlds of Peggy Scott
Daniels, H. R. Accused
    House on Greenapple Road
Dean, S. F. X. Nantucket Soap Opera
Decker, D. Devil's Punchbowl
Dessart, G. Man Died Here
Disney, D. M. Enduring Old Charms
Dodge, Langdon. Midsummer Madness
Dyer, G. Adriana
Eberhart, M. G. Wolf in Man's Clothing
Ehrlich, M. Big Boys
Farnsworth, M. Evil That Waited
Fast, J. Watchful at Night
Forbes, S. Terrors of the Earth
Foster, I. Sabath Quest
Fried, B. Concerto in the Key of Death
Fuller, T. Keep Cool, Mr. Jones
Futrelle, M. Secretary of Frivolous Affairs
Goode, G. W. King Dan, the Factory Detective
Graat, H. Devil and Ben Camden
Graham, J. A. Arthur
Green, A. K. Doctor Izard
    XYZ
Gunning, S. Hot Water
Hagerty, H. J. Jasmine Trail
Harris, L. Don't Be No Hero
Hart, S. Martha's Vineyard Affair
Hawkes, J. Julian's House
Healy, J. Yesterday's News
Healy, J. M. Blunt Darts
Highsmith, P. Deep Water
Hough, J. Guardian
Jordan, E. Trap
Kains, J. Devil Mask Mystery
Kalish, R. Bloodmoon
Kallen, L. Tanglewood Murder
Katzenbach, J. Day of Reckoning
Kelman, J. While Angels Sleep

Kemelman, H. 7 titles
Kimbrough, K. Rebecca, the Mysterious
Langton, J. 5 titles
Leonard, A. B. Judson Murder Case
Leslie, W. Love or Whatever It Is
Lifson, D. S. Headless Victory
Lincoln, J. C. Blair's Attic
Littlefield, A. Which Mrs. Bennett
Logan, M. C.A.T. Caper
Long, L. B. Legacy of Evil
Lovesmith, J. Legacy of Fear
Lowndes, M. B. Lizzie Borden
Lynch, M. Pale Hand of Danger
    Where Shadows Lie
McCarty, J. Deadly Resurrection
McCloy, H. Imposter
McDonald, G. Running Scared
McFarlane, L. Murder Tree
McHugh, F. Y. Shadow Over Mount Sharon
MacLeod, C. 9 titles
McMullen, M. Bad News Man
Mailer, N. Tough Guys Don't Dance
Malcolm-Smith, G. Come Out, Come Out
Marsten, R. Even the Wicked
Mason, V. W. Vesper Service Murders
Miller, G. W. Thunder Rise
Norris, K. Black Flamingo
O'Brien, L. Sweet William Is Dead
Osborn, D. Murder on Martha's Vineyard
Page, K. H. Body in the Belfry
Parker, R. B. Pale Kings and Princes
    Playmates
Patrick, W. Spirals
Paul, B. In-Laws and Outlaws
Pearson, R. Seizing of Yankee Green Mall
Pendleton, D. Savage Fire
    War Against the Mafia
Pickard, N. 5 titles
Pidgin, C. F. Chronicles of Quincy Adams Sawyer,
    Detective
    Hidden Man
Popkin, Z. Murder in the Mist
Quick, D. Doctor Looks at Murder
Randall, F. E. Haldane Station
Randall, W. Deadly the Daring
Rennert, M. 3 titles
Reybold, M. Inspector's Opinion
Rich, V. Nantucket Diet Murders
Rich, W. Brain-Waves and Death
Ritter, M. Caroline, Caroline
Robeson, K. Hex
    Nightwitch Devil
Ronns, E. Terror in the Town
Roof, K. M. Murder on the Salem Road
Roos, K. Murder on Martha's Vineyard
Ross, Clarissa. at least 6 titles
Ross, Dan. Cliffhaven
Ross, Marilyn. Don't Look Behind You
Russell, E. S. Nice Enough to Murder
    She Should Have Cried on Monday
Ryan, Jenna. Cast in Wax
Rydell, F. If She Should Die
    No Questions Asked
St. Clair, E. Sandcastle Murders
Saul, J. R. Comes the Blind Fury
Sax, A. Death in the Colony
Saxton, M. Danger Road
Scribner, H. My Mysterious Clients
Shattuck, R. Snark Was a Boojum
Sherman, D. Riddle
Silver, V. Death of a Harvard Freshman
Smith, Rosamund. Soul/Mate
Smith, R. N. Death Be Nimble
Smolens, J. Winter by Degrees
Stagge, J. Death's Old Sweet Song
    Three Fears
Stansberry, D. Spoiler
Stephan, L. Murder R.F.D.
    Reprise
Stevenson, F. Dark Encounter
    Witch's Crossing
Strange, J. S. Unquiet Grave
Stratton, R. One Among None
Sumner, C. R. Withdraw Thy Foot

Tapply, W. G. Dead Winter
    Vulgar Boatman
Tessier, T. Rapture
Tilton, A. 7 titles
Trevelyan, J. Landsend Terror
Vandergriff, A. Bell Tower of Wyndspelle
    Wyndspelle
    Wyndspelle's Child
Van Hazinga, C. House on Gannet's Point
Wagner, E. Case of Bottled Murder
Walker, W. Immediate Prospect of Being Hanged
    Rules of the Knife Fight
Wallis, R. S. No Bones About It
Waltch, L. M. Fearful Symmetry
    Third Victim
Waters, T. A. In the Halls of Evil
Wells, Carolyn. 7 titles
Wells, T. 5 titles
Wender, T. Knight Must Fall
Wernick, S. Blood Tide
Wheeler, G. Easy Come
Wickware, F. Dangerous Ground
Williams, S. Mystery in Red
Winsor, R. Always Lock Your Bedroom Door
    Corpse That Walked
Wright, L. R. Perfect Corpse
Young, E. A. Luke Darby
Zaroulis, N. L. Poe Papers

MAURITIUS
Shill, J. C. Murder in Paradise

MEDICAL SETTINGS. See: Hospital.

MEDITERRANEAN ISLAND (Med. Is. See also:
    Corsica; Crete; Cyprus; Majorca;
    Sardinia; Sicily)
Ames, D. Lucky Jane
Birmingham, G. A. Island Mystery
Brand, C. Tour de Force
Canning, V. Python Project
Fitt, M. Late Uncle Max
Howard, L. Invitation to Paradise
Innes, H. Medusa
Oliver, M.-A. Antipodes
Quayle, A. On Such a Night
Taffrail. Jade Lizard

MELANESIA (See also: New Caledonia)
Corris, P. Cargo Club

MELBOURNE (Melb. See also: Australia; Adelaide;
    Sydney; Solomon Islands; Tasmania)
Afford, M. Blood on His Hands!
Bridges, R. This House Is Haunted
Corris, P. Baltic Business
Duckworth, C. Steps to the High Garden
Galbally, F. Juryman
Gray, D. Murder in Melbourne
Greenwood, K. both titles
Hume, F. Mystery of a Hansom Cab
Jillett, N. Copycat
Koch, C. J. Boys in the Island
Law, M. J. Death in the Spring
Lewis, Catherine. Unable by Reason of Death
Mace, H. And Death Came Too
    Death of a Golden Goose
Michaelis, A. Ingram Intervenes
North, Eric. Chip on My Shoulder
    Name Is Smith
Oxlade, B. Death in Brunswick
Preston, James. Racing Axes
Quinn, P. E. Jewelled Belt
Stutley, S. J. Melbourne Mystery
Wallace, Robert. Payday
Westlaw, S. Mystery of Lombardy Chambers
Williamson, D. Removalists
Wright, June. Faculty of Murder

MEMPHIS (See also: Tennessee; Nashville; South)
Dana, R. Death of a Millionaire
Falkner, W. C. White Rose of Memphis
Foote, S. September September
Wells, Charlie. Last Kill

MESOPOTAMIA (Mesop. See also: Turkey; Middle
    East)
Christie, A. Murder in Mesopotamia

MEXICO (Mex. See also: Mexico City)
Aarons, E. S. Come Back My Love
Adams, H. When Rich Men Die
Adkins, B. all 3 titles
Ahern, J. Master of D.E.A.T.H.
Ames, R. Dangerous One
Angus, S. Dead to Rites
Ardies, T. Their Man in the White House
Atlee, P. Death Bird Contract
Bagley, D. Vivero Letter
Bannister, W. Counterfeit Death
Barnao, J. LockeStep
Bedford-Jones, H. Shadow
Bellah, J. Imperial Express
Biart, L. Clients of Doctor Bernagius
Blackburn, J. Young Man from Lima
Blanc, S. Green Stone
    Rose Window
    Yellow Villa
Brizzolara, J. Wirecutter
Buchan, Stuart. Fleeced
Buckingham, B. both titles
Burleson, C. W. Mexican Affair
Caillou, A. Death Charge
Cain, J. M. Serenade
Calder-Marshall, A. Way to Santiago
Carlton, B. In the Foxes' Lair
Carter, Nick. 6 titles
Cassidy, John. Assassination on Maya Bay
Chadwick, C. Cactus
Chambers, W. Action at World's End
    You Can't Get Away by Running
Chance, L. Baja Run
Charbonneau, L. Lair
Chase, K. Killer Be Killed
Chute, V. Wayward Angel
Coffey, B. Wall of Masks
Cohen, A. A. Acts of Theft
Content, N. Hideaway
Craig, Rianna. On Executive Orders
Crane, F. Ultraviolet Widow
Crawford, William. Chinese Connection
Cronin, M. Sweet Water
Crumley, J. Pigeon Shoot
Currier, J. L. Cargo of Fear
Curtiss, U. In Cold Pursuit
Cutter, J. Vengeance Mountain
Darby, R. If This Be Murder
Davis, N. Mouse in the Mountain
Denham, R. Recipe for a Crime
Denning, M. Die Fast, Die Happy
Deptula, W. Naked Mistress
Derrick, L. Baja Bandidos
    Mexican Brown
Dewey, T. B. Golden Hooligan
Downing, T. 8 titles
Duff, J. P. Run from Death
Edwards, P. Glyphs of Gold
Elias, A. J. Sonora Mutation
Elkins, A. J. Curses!
Ellson, H. Killer's Kiss
Falk, L. Slave Market of Mucar
Faust, R. Death Fires
Fickling, G. G. Dig a Dead Doll
Fleetwood, H. Young Fair God
Flynn, J. It's Murder, McHugh
Flynn, J. M. Danger Zone
    Screaming Cargo
Ford, R. Ultimate Good Luck
Fox, J. M. Save Them for Violence
Frost, J. V. Silver Shine
Fuentes, C. Hydra Head
Gerard, F. Prisoner of the Pyramid
Gilman, D. Unexpected Mrs. Pollifax
Graham, J. Wrath of God
Grayson, Rupert. Gun Cotton in Mexico
Grew, W. Murder Has Many Faces
Hamilton, D. Frighteners
    Menacers
    Retaliators

Settings Index MICHIGAN / 1263

Hanson, J. W. Brother Berserk
Haring, D. Take Off, Baby
Harper, Richard. Death Raid
Harris, D. Last Scam
Harrison, H. Montezuma's Revenge
Harshorne. Mexican Assassin
Hartman, D. Mexico Kill
Heath, C. A-Team
Heath, P. Assassins for Tomorrow
Hebden, M. Pel Among the Pueblos
Hedges, J. Mexican Mourning
Hines, J. Talons of the Hawk
    Third Wife
Homes, G. Street of the Crying Woman
Howard, H. Routine Investigation
Howard, V. Murder on Her Mind
Hume, F. Harlequin Opal
Hunt, H. Guadalajara
    Maelstrom
Ibarguengoitia, J. both titles
Janson, H. Death Wore a Petticoat
Karl, M. S. Mobius Man
Keener, J. Borderline
Kelly, B. Tuna Is Not for Eating
Kelly, J. Music from Another Room
Kennedy, G. Murder on Location
Kirk, L. Cuernavaca Question
Knight, C. Affair of the Black Sombrero
Knight, K. M. 7 titles
Knye, C. House That Fear Built
Koehler, R. P. Hooded Vulture Murders
Lacy, E. Moment of Untruth
Lange, O. Incident at La Junta
Leonard, P. G. Prey of the Eagle
Levine, Larry. Treasure
Lindop, A. E. Judas Figures
    Singer Not the Song
Lindsey, D. L. Black Gold, Red Death
MacDonald, J. D. Damned
    Dress Her in Indigo
    Empty Trap
MacLean, Arthur. Mission to Mexico
MacLean, J. Deadfall
MacNeil, N. Mexican Slay Ride
Madsen, A. Borderlines
Maling, A. Decoy
Markson, D. Going Down
Marlowe, D. J. Operation Hammerlock
Marlowe, S. Cawthorn Journals
Masterson, W. Dark Fantastic
    Last One Kills
Mathews, W. C. King Cobra
Millar, M. Ask for Me Tomorrow
Miller, W. 5 titles
Morgan, Dean. Rostron Outfit in Mexico
Muir, Jean. Stranger, Tread Light
Murphy, W. B. Survival Course
Murray, C. Day of the Dead
Murray, W. King of the Nightcap
Nash, C. Murder Is My Shadow
North, J. High Valley
Oliver, L. Mexican Adventure
O'Rourke, F. High Dive
Paradis, V. A. Cocaine Caper
Patterson, H. Dillinger
    Thunder at Noon
Paul, P. Night of the Jaguar
Pendleton, D. Acapulco Rampage
Peters, Elizabeth. Night of Four Hundred Rabbits
Phillips, J. House of Darkness
Phillips, J. A. Suitable for Framing
Prather, R. S. Darling, It's Death
Queen, E. Kiss and Kill
    Last Score
Quentin, P. Follower
    Run to Death
Rabe, P. Time Enough to Die
Rattray, R. Fan of Dirty Green
Rayter, J. Stab in the Dark
Rilla, W. Dispensable Man
Roberts, Les. Carrot for the Donkey
Robeson, K. Hell Below
Roper, R. Mexico Days
Rosenberger, J. Mexican Hit

Rowan, D. Shadow of the Volcano
Russell, C. M. Ill Met in Mexico
Salas, F. What Now My Love
Scarpetta, F. Icepick in the Spine
Sharp, M. Falseface
Shepherd, John. Lights, Camera, Murder
Snyder, G. Tomb Seven
Stark, R. Damsel
Stein, A. M. 8 titles
Stivers, D. Scorched Earth
Streib, D. House of Silence
Swain, J. Man Who Walked Through Walls
Travis, Gerry. Big Bite
Twist, P. Gilded Hideaway
Wagner, G. Passionate Land
Walker, Greg. Machete
Warren, G. Laughing Widow
Westheimer, D. Olmec Head
Weverka, R. One Minute to Eternity
Wheatley, D. Unholy Crusade
Whitaker, H. Mystery of the Barranca
White, L. Mexico Run
Whitlach, J. Gannon's Line
Williams, B. Tumulto
    Well-Dressed Skeleton
Wilson, Gar. Jungle Sweep
Winston, D. Castle of Closing Doors
Wright, R. B. Tourists
Wulffson, D. Point-Blank

MEXICO CITY (Mex. City. See also: Mexico)
Barry, M. Killing Run
Brown, Carter. Murder Wears a Mantilla
Cheyney, P. Don't Get Me Wrong
Eberhart, M. G. Wings of Fear
Gatenby, R. Whisper of Evil
Highsmith, P. Game for the Living
Horton, John. Black Legend
Lindsey, D. L. In the Lake of the Moon
Lucas, C. Unfinished Business
Millar, M. Listening Walls
Morales, P. Victim for Hire
Palmer, S. Puzzle of the Blue Banderilla
Prather, R. S. Pattern for Panic
Quentin, P. Puzzle for Pilgrims
Stivers, D. Into the Maze
Taibo, P. I. Easy Thing
Trimble, L. Dead and the Deadly
    Till Death Do Us Part
Van Meter, D. A. Body of Evidence
Waer, J. 17 and Black
Weintraub, S. Mexican Slay Ride
Wilson, David. Park Avenue Executioner

MIAMI (See also: Florida; Jacksonville; Tampa; South)
Ahern, J. Miamigrad
Banko, D. Very Dead with a Twist
Barry, M. Miami Marauder
Barth, R. Deadly Climate
Brace, T. Murder Goes Fishing
Brown, Carter. Graves, I Dig!
Buchanan, E. Nobody Lives Forever
Buchanan, J. Miami War Zone
Chaber, M. E. Bonded Dead
Chambers, D. Case of Caroline Animus
    Darling, This Is Death
Chandler, B. Behind the Badge
Charteris, L. Saint in Miami
Chase, E. R. Dangerous Places
Colby, R. Kim
    Murder Mistress
Conners, T. Combat Zone—Miami
Crawford, Max. Six Key Cut
Davis, Maggie. Miami Midnight
Deane, J. Moon Over Miami
De Borchgrave, A. Monimbo
Ellin, S. Bind
    Star Light, Star Bright
Ernst, P. Lady, Get Your Gun
Fisher, D. E. Last Flying Tiger
Foster, R. Too Late for Mourning
Frazer, R. C. Mark Kilby and the Miami Mob
Fuller, W. Brad Dolan's Miami Manhunt

Grave, S. all 6 titles
Hall, Adam. Quiller Barracuda
Halliday, B. at least 52 titles
Haring, D. A. O. Caper
    Big-Time Baby!
    Don't Die on Me, Diana
    Filthy Ones
Heyman, E. L. Miami Undercover
Hiassen, C. Tourist Season
Kastle, H. Miami Golden Boy
Keene, D. Miami 59
Kendrick, B. Eleven of Diamonds
King, R. Murder Masks Miami
King, T. J. Noose of Red Beads
La France, M. Miami Murder-Go-Round
Leonard, E. Cat Chaser
    La Brava
Levine, P. To Speak for the Dead
McGregor, T. J. Dark Fields
    Death Sweet
    Kill Flash
Macklin, M. Thin Edge of Mania
Malina, F. Some Like 'Em Shot
Montalbano, W. D. Powder Burn
Palmer, T. Transfer
Pendleton, D. Miami Massacre
    Wild Card
Reach, J. Murder Over Miami
Robeson, K. Red Snow
Rome, A. Lady in Cement
    Miami Mayhem
Russell, C. M. Murder Steps In
Sapir, R. Kill or Cure
Sarto, B. Miami for Murder
Scarpetta, F. Mafia Massacre
Schley, S. M. Dr. Toby Finds Murder
Smith, R. K. Sadie Shapiro in Miami
Stivers, D. Miami Crush
Taylor, Matt. Neon Flamingo
Terhune, A. P. Black Caesar's Clan
Williford, C. 5 titles
Winters, M. Miami, One Way

MICHIGAN (Mich. See also: Detroit; Midwest)
Armstrong, A. Case of the Weird Sisters
Beek, J. R. Bradford's Trials
Bramhall, M. Murder Is Contagious
Brennan, A. 5 titles
Brucker, M. Poison Party
Bunn, T. Worse Than Death
Byfield, B. N. Forever Wilt Thou Die
Cameron, D. C. White for a Shroud
Cloutier, H. Murder, Absolutely Murder
Coffin, P. Search for My Great Uncle's Head
Creeth, E. H. Deerlover
Davis, D. S. Town of Masks
Dodge, M. L. Sticks and Stones
Dreyer, M. M. Beckoning Hands
Garnet, A. H. Maze
Garth, D. Fire on the Wind
Goff, G. Black Dog
Green, C. Scarlet Venus
Greenbaum, L. Out of Shape
Hale, C. 10 titles
Hall, F. H. In the Lamb White Days
Harrington, J. No One Knows My Name
Henry, C. Welcome Home, Lily Glow
Howes, R. Case of the Copy-Hook Killing
    Death Dupes a Lady
    Death Rides a Hobby
    Murder at Maneuvers
Kakonis, T. Criss-Cross
    Michigan Roll
Kent, F. Opal Legacy
Lang, B. Brand of Fear
    Perdition Express
Leonard, E. Big Bounce
    Killshot
Lippincott, D. Unholy Mourning
Loban, E. H. Signed in Yellow
MacDonald, J. D. Price of Murder
MacVeigh, S. Corpse and the Three Ex-Husbands
Magoon, C. I Smell the Devil
Marlett, M. Escape While I Can

Martin, C. H. PK Factor
Martin, Robert. Echoing Shore
Mayhew, G. A. Murder at Daybreak
Mead, S. How to Succeed at Business Spying by Trying
Millar, K. Dark Tunnel
Millar, M. Vanish in an Instant
Nielsen, H. Crime Is Murder
Osborn, D. Open Season
Patch, D. E. L. all 5 titles
Plum, M. Murder at the Hunting Club
Pohlman, M. D. Problem of Evil
Porter, M. E. Mercy of the Court
Prentis, J. H. Case of Doctor Horace
Roberts, W. D. Murder at Grand Bay
Robeson, K. Devil's Playground
    Monsters
Shriber, I. S. Murder Well Done
Sibbald, G. Dodge Boys
Smith, Mark. Toyland
Spike, P. Night Letter
Thall, M. Let Sleeping Afghans Lie
Toombs, J. J. Heart of Winter
    Point of Lost Souls
Traver, R. Anatomy of a Murder
    Laughing Whitefish
    People vs. Kirk
    Small-Town D.A.
Valentine, J. Trouble in Thor
Welles, P. Angels in the Snow
    Members Only
Wolf, Sarah. Long Chain of Death

MICRONESIA
Kluge, P. F. Day That I Die

MIDDLE EAST (Mid. East. See also: individual countries)
Aarons, E. S. Assignment—Afghan Dragon
    Assignment—Karachi
    Assignment—Zoraya
Aarons, W. B. Assignment 13th Princess
Ahern, J. Surgical Strike
Aldridge, J. Mockery in Arms
Ambler, E. Levanter
Aricha, A. Phoenix
Arvay, H. Piraeus Plot
    Stranglehold
Atlee, P. Spice Route Contract
Awin, M. Silence Over Sinai
Bachmann, L. Bitter Lake
Bagley, D. Spoilers
Ballinger, B. S. Source of Fear
Barrett, Michael. Ten Against Nura
Beare, G. Bee Sting Deal
    Bloody Sun at Noon
    Very Breath of Hell
Bennett, K. Devil's Current
Benton, K. Craig and the Midas Touch
Black, Lionel. Arafat Is Next!
Blankfort, M. Behold the Fire
Boothby, G. Bid for Freedom
Bowser, J. No Sanctuary
Buck, P. Black Gold Briefing
Caillou, A. Assault on Fellawi
    Dead Sea Submarine
    Sword of God
    Who'll Buy My Evil?
Canning, V. His Bones Are Coral
Carter, Nick. Day of the Mahdi
    Green Wolf Connection
    Middle East Massacre
    Terms of Vengeance
Case, Jim. Sword of the Prophet
Charles, R. Clash of Hawks
Chase, P. Deadly Crusade
Childs, M. Taint of Innocence
Christian, J. Persian Death-Trap
Connell, C. Most Delicious Evil
Connelly, M. Souvenir from Qam
Coppel, Alfred. Thirty-Four East
Cox, R. Ground Zero
Coyle, H. Sword Point
Cronin, M. Marksman
Crowder, H. Ambush at Osirak
Da Cruz, D. Captive City
    Landfall Finesse
Davidson, L. Long Way from Shiloh
Delacorte, P. Levantine
Delahaye, M. Third Day
De Mille, N. By the Waters of Babylon
Derrick, L. Hell's Hostages
Dickinson, Peter. Poison Oracle
Edmonds, H. Red Desert
Edwards, Samuel. Exploiters
Emmett, R. King, Bishop, Knight
Evans, Jonathan. Misfire
Fairbairn, D. Street 8
Faqir, F. Nisanit
Farhi, M. Last of Days
Fitzgerald, G. Druze Document
Fulton, E. G. Vengeance, My Love
Garbo, N. Cabal
Garner, W. Andra Fiasco
Garrett, F. Counter Attack
Gibbs, G. F. Road to Bagdad
Gilbert, M. Ninety-Second Tiger
Graham, B. Spy or Die
Green, W. M. Man Who Called Himself Devlin
Groner, A. Mene Tekel
Gruber, F. Bridge of Sand
Guenter, C. H. Dead in Aqaba
Haddad, C. A. Bloody September
Haggard, W. Median Line
    Powder Barrell
Hamilton, Adam. Yashar Pursuit
Harvester, S. Assassins Road
Harwood, R. Genoa Ferry
Hastings, M. Devil's Spy
Heath, C. Operation Desert Sun
Heller, F. Thousand and Second Night
Holt, G. E. By Favour of Allah
Household, G. Arabesque
    Doom's Caravan
Jackont, A. Borrowed Time
John, O. Dead on Time
Johnston, R. Black Camels of Qashran
Jones, D. Rubicon One
Kalb, M. In the National Interest
Kane, H. Tripoli Documents
Kaplan, A. Scorpion
Kilgore, A. Slave of the Warmonger
Laflin, J. Temple at Ilumquh
Lane, K. Gambit
Lee, Elsie. Drifting Sands
Lyall, G. Judas Country
McAdam, P. Arabian Assault
MacAlister, I. Driscoll's Diamonds
MacKinnon, A. Red-Winged Angel
MacLean, R. Baited Blonde
MacLeod, R. Place of Mists
Marchment, A. W. By Snare of Love
Mason, C. Hostage
Mason, Robert. More News from Middle East
Maugham, R. Man with Two Shadows
Meiring, D. Talk with the Angels
    Wildcatter
Melville-Ross, A. Blindfold
    Shaw's War
Merek, J. Blackbird
Merritt, B. Patmos Conspiracy
Moore, Robin. Dubai
Moss, W. S. Bats with Baby Faces
Mundy, T. Jimgrim and Allah's Peace
    King in Check
O'Brine, M. Dagger Before Me
O'Connor, D. Slender Chance
Operator 1384. Jackals of the Secret Service
Osmond, M. Curtains of Solomon
Pace, E. Saberlegs
Paul, A. Present from Hugo
Pendleton, D. Hellfire Crusade
Pereira, M. Angel Came Down
Peters, Elizabeth. Dead Sea Cipher
Ponthier, F. Assignment Basra
Poyer, D. Gulf
Pugh, M. Murmur of Destiny
Quinnell, A. J. Mahdi

Rathbone, J. With My Knives I Know I'm Good
Roberts, D. Journey from Baghdad
Roberts, T. A. Heart of a Dog
Rohmer, S. Egyptian Nights
    Mask of Fu Manchu
Rosenberger, J. Miracle Mission
    Psychotron Plot
    Vengeance of the Golden Hawk
Rowe, J. Aswan Solution
Royce, K. 10,000 Days
St. Clair, L. Fortune in Death
Sandys, J. Stripe for a Stripe
Scanlon, N. Quinn
Schiff, B. Vatican Target
Seymour, G. Home Run
Shagan, S. Pillars of Fire
Shamis, G. Crack in the House of God
Sheckley, R. Time Limit
Sherwood, J. Undiplomatic Exit
Sigel, E. Kermanshah Transfer
Spouse, M. Hammerword Technique
Stacey, T. Deadline
    Worm in the Rose
Starnes, R. Flypaper War
Stivers, D. Rain of Doom
Thorne, E. p. They Never Come Back
Tiger, J. Doomdate
Tippin, G. L. Arab
Topol, A. Woman of Valor
Tripp, M. Kilo Forty
Tyndall, J. Death in the Jordan
Van Vors, B. L. Prince and the Sufi
Waugh, A. Mule on the Minaret
West, M. L. Tower of Babel
Williamson, T. Doomsday Contract
Winston, P. Assignment in Bahrein

MIDDLE WEST. See: Midwest.

MIDWAY ISLAND (Midway Is.)
Yates, M. T. Midway to Murder

MIDWEST (See also: the twelve individual states)
August, J. Troubled Star
Austin, Anne. Avenging Parrot
    Murder Backstairs
    Murdered But Not Dead
    One Drop of Blood
Bloch, R. Terror
Blochman, L. G. Clues for Dr. Coffee
    Diagnosis: Homicide
    Recipe for Homicide
Booth, C. B. Kidnapping Syndicate
Borgenicht, M. Don't Look Back
Boyd, M. Murder in the Stacks
Branson, H. C. Last Year's Blood
Braun, L. J. 11 titles
Brown, F. Night of the Jabberwock
Burnett, W. R. Asphalt Jungle
    Little Man, Big World
    Vanity Row
Chehak, S. T. Harmony
Corrigan, M. I Like Danger
Cox, T. R. Shadows of One Another
Coughlin, W. J. Stalking Man
Davis, D. S. Judas Cat
Dean, R. G. Murder in Mink
    Murder Through the Looking Glass
Deming, R. Tweak the Devil's Nose
De Weese, J. Nightmare in Pewter
Dewey, T. B. Mean Streets
Dorian, P. Streaker Murders
Dwight, O. Close His Eyes
Eberhart, M. G. Pattern
Echard, M. Dark Fantastic
Fackler, E. Arson
Flanders, R. Key
Foote-Smith, E. Gentle Albatross
Gatenby, R. Aim to Kill
Givens, C. G. Big Mike
    Rose Petal Murders
Goldman, R. L. Death Plays Solitaire
    Murder Behind the Mike
    Murder Without Motive
    Snatch

Settings Index MONTANA / 1265

Gorman, E. Blood Game
Gosling, P. Backlash
Hanson, V. Death Walks the Post
Heelan, K. Heartland
Heffernan, D. Murder at Sunset Gables
Helseth, H. E. Brothers Brannigan
Herrington, L. Carry My Coffin Slowly
Hickok, F. Eye for an Eye
Howie, E. Cry Murder
    Murder for Two
Hubbard, M. A. Sister Simon's Murder Case
    Step Softly on My Grave
Hultman, H. J. Death at Windward Hill
    Find the Woman
Janson, H. Tension
Johnson, E. R. Mongo's Back in Town
Kelly, J. Protection
Livingston, A. In Cold Blood
Lowe, K. Catalyst
    No Tears for Shirley Minton
MacDonald, J. D. You Live Once
McKimmey, J. Cornered!
    Perfect Victim
Marino, N. both titles
Marlowe, M. F.B.I. Girl
Mills, R. Leading Lady
Monahan, J. Big Stan
Montgomery, I. Golden Dress
Moseley, D. Dead of Summer
Murphy, M. Borrowed Alibi
Nowak, J. Death at the Crossings
Ordway, P. Face in the Shadows
Peck, M. S. Bed by the Window
Post, M. Candidate for Murder
Potter, D. Way of an Eagle
Potts, J. Lightning Strikes Twice
Rimel, D. W. Curse of Cain
Roberts, Lee. Case of the Missing Lovers
    Pale Door
Rogers, S. You Leave Me Cold!
    You'll Be Sorry!
Roueche, B. Black Weather
Russell, C. M. 5 titles
Rutledge, N. Beware the Hoot Owl
    Preying Mantis
    Wanted for Murder
Scott, M. S. Crime Hound
Seifert, A. Shadows Tonight
Smith, Mitchell. Stone City
Sohl, J. Prelude to Peril
Spence, M. Rebekka Moon
Spencer, R. Radish River Caper
Spillane, M. Long Wait
Stark, R. Butcher's Moon
    Slayground
Stein, A. M. Case of the Absent-Minded Professor
Taylor, D. Five in Judgment
Thomas, C. Prominent Among the Mourners
Tucker, W. Red Herring
Wallace, F. Front Man
Wallis, R. S. Cold Bed in the Clay
    Too Many Bones
Washburn, R. C. Jury of Death
Webster, H. K. Butterfly
Wilmot, R. P. Death Rides a Painted Horse
Wormser, R. Late Mrs. Five
Wylie, P. Danger Mansion

MILAN (See also: Italy, Florence; Naples; Rome; Sardinia; Sicily; Venice)
Ambler, E. Cause for Alarm
Carter, Nick. Massacre in Milan
Creasey, J. Prince for Inspector West
Eco, U. Foucault's Pendulum
Hunter, Robin. Quarry's Contract
Scerbanenco, G. Duca and the Milan Murders
Tute, W. Next Saturday in Milan

MILWAUKEE (Milw. See also: Wisconsin; Madison; Midwest)
Brown, F. Here Comes a Candle
Duhart, W. H. Deadly Pay-Off
Foth, K. Cure
Gault, W. C. Bloody Bokhara
Thornburg, N. Knockover

MINNEAPOLIS (Mpls. See also: Minnesota; Midwest)
Anonymous. Bob Younger's Fate
Barkin, J. Hot Streak
Brennan, D. Badge of Honor
Breslin, C. Unholy Child
Gifford, T. Cavanaugh Quest
Gorman, E. Night Kills
Hall, Steve. Rape of the Nicollet Mall Mannequin
Hart, E. Hallowed Murder
Helgerson, J. Slow Burn
Hunsburger, H. E. Death Signs
Lake, M. D. Amends for Murder
    Cold Comfort
Logue, M. Red Lake of the Heart
Loomis, N. Murder Goes to Press
Odlum, J. Nine Lives Are Not Enough
O'Donohoe, N. April Snow
    Wind Chill
Sanford, J. Rules of Prey
    Shadow Prey
Seeley, M. Whistling Shadow
Simonsen, S. J. Below Third Street
Taylor, L. A. 5 titles
Williams, Bob. Ozark Flats

MINNESOTA (Minn. See also: Minneapolis; Midwest)
Arctander, J. W. Guilty?
Adams, H. Murder
Becklund, J. Golden Fleece
Bestor, G. C. Prelude to Murder
Boardman, N. S. Wine of Violence
Brennan, D. Insurrection!
    Lay-Over Town
Claire, M. Drowning Wire
Clark, M. H. Cry in the Night
Dorner, M. Nightmare
Douglas, C. N. Counterprobe
    Probe
Enger, L. L. Comeback
Fluke, J. Winter Chill
Gores, J. Wolf Time
Greene, J. E. Laughing Loon
Guest, J. Killing Time in St. Cloud
Hinkemeyer, M. T. Fields of Eden
    Fourth Down
    Summer Solstice
    Time to Reap
Hong, E. Wild Blue Berries
Hopkins, A. T. Have a Lovely Funeral
Kelsey, V. Whisper Murder!
Kruger, P. Weep for Willow Green
McInerny, R. Frigor Mortis
Mead, R. D. You'll Never Take Me
O'Donohoe, N. Open Season
O'Malley, P. Affair of Swan Lake
O'Meara, W. Minnesota Gothic
Pender, L. Traitor's Dispatch
Pendleton, D. Violent Streets
Seeley, M. 5 titles
Siegel, B. Death in White Bear Lake
Stanley, S. Rogue's Castle
Taylor, L. A. Poetic Justice
    Shed Light on Death
Thayer, S. Saint Mudd
Walker, Gertrude. So Deadly Fair
Wallis, R. S. Forget My Fate
Watson, L. In a Dark Time
Wolffe, K. Death's Long Shadow

MISSISSIPPI (Miss. See also: South)
Bakker, K. Sea Treasure
Boles, P. D. Mississippi Run
Bristow, G. Two and Two Make Twenty-Two
Buchanan, P. Requiem of Sharks
Burnes, C. Deadly Breed
    Measure of Deceit
Chaze, E. Wettermark
Craddock, C. E. Story of Dulciehurst
Daniels, D. House of Many Doors
Eberhart, M. G. Cup, the Blade or the Gun
Eliot, A. Stranger at Pembroke
Faulkner, W. all 3 titles
Foote, S. Follow Me Down

Ford, L. Murder with Southern Hospitality
Grisham, J. Time to Kill
Hannah, B. Nightwatchman
Hawkins, D. In Memory of Murder
Hays, S. B. Go Down, Death
Holloway, E. H. Cobweb House
Judson, W. Kilman's Landing
Kimbrough, K. Thanesworth House
Mosiman, B. S. Deadly Affections
Murfi, L. Magnolia Curse
Pauley, B. A. Voices Long Hushed
Pearson, A. Murder by Degrees
Rosenberg, S. When the Bough Breaks
Scafidel, J. R. Wit's End
Sellars, M. Cry of the Cat
Stein, A. M. . . . And High Water
Thompson, Monroe. Blue Room
Vance, W. Homicide Lost
Weill, G. Bonnet Man
Whitten, L. H. Moon of the Wolf
Wilson, Charles. Nightwatcher
Zumwalt, E. Masquerade of Evil

MISSOURI (Mo. See also: Kansas City; St. Louis; Midwest)
Allen, E. V. Voices in the Wind
Bannon, P. Whisper Murder Softly
Behn, N. Seven Silent Men
Cassiday, B. Buried Motive
Cleary, J. Vortex
Cusick, R. T. Scarecrow
Dawson, C. B. Remind Me to Forget
Dent, L. Lady in Peril
Ginty, E. B. Missouri Legend
Gruber, F. Hungry Dog
Howie, E. No Face to Murder
Keene, D. My Flesh Is Sweet
Krasner, W. Death of a Minor Poet
    Resort to Murder
Lutz, J. Bonegrinder
    Truth of the Matter
Moor, E. Shadowed Porch
Neighbors, J. E. Hatchet Job
Randolph, V. Camp-Meeting Murders
Rhodes, R. Sons of Earth
Robeson, K. Evil Gnome
    Talking Devil
Rosenberger, J. Armageddon, USA!
Roueche, B. Last Enemy
Seifert, A. Deeds Ill Done
    3 Blind Mice
Smith, M. A. Legacy of the Lake
Thompson, P. Rainbow Ribbon
Thornburg, N. Black Angus
Woodrum, L. Stumble Upon the Dark Mountains

MONACO. See: France.

MONGOLIA (See also: China; Russia)
Dark, J. Sword of Genghis Khan
Edwards, P. Needles of Death
Harvest, S. Nameless Road
Oliver, L. Mongolian Interlude

MONTANA (Mont. See also: West)
Adams, C. F. Shady Lady
Ashley, J. Secrets of the Heart
Berthold, M. P. Local Call
Bonnamy, F. Death on a Dude Ranch
Bradley, Muriel. Murder in Montana
Burke, J. L. Black Cherry Blues
Cameron, O. Butcher's Wife
Cleary, J. Sound of Lightning
Crecy, J. Winter Keeper
Finch, P. Trespass
Grady, J. Shadow of the Condor
Guthrie, A. B. Genuine Article
    No Second Wind
    Playing Catch-Up
    Wild Pitch
Hufford, S. Delicate Deceit
Hugo, R. Death and the Good Life
Joscelyn, A. Golden Bowl
Lassiter, A. King of the Mountain
Millard, J. Thunderbolt and Lightfoot

Moffat, G. Grizzly Trail
Paul, Elliot. Fracas in the Foothills
Pronzini, B. Last Days of Horse-Shy Halloran
Reid, R. S. Big Sky Blues
Rinehart, M. R. State vs. Elinor Norton
Sapir, R. Last War Dance
Scherf, M. 9 titles
Siller, V. Somber Memory
    Under a Cloud
Simpson, C. H. Life in the Far West
Stevens, C. D. Printer's Devil
Stout, R. Death of a Dude
Van Gieson, J. Raptor
West, S. G. Amos
Zochert, D. Another Weeping Woman

MONTE CARLO. See: France.

MONTREAL (Montr. See also: Canada; Ottawa;
    Toronto; Vancouver; Winnipeg)
Apple, A. E. Mr. Chang's Crime Ray
Atlee, P. Canadian Bomber Contract
Black, Lawrence. Tanner's Tiger
Brett, Martin. Darker Traffic
    Dum-Dum for the President
    Hot Freeze
Bryan, M. Intent to Kill
Buell, J. Four Days
    Pyx
Curtis, Richard. Death in the Crease
Cushing, E. L. Murder Without Regret
Deverell, W. Mindfield
Gagnon, M. By Hate Possessed
Hardin, P. Frightened Dove
McFarlane, L. Streets of Shadow
Malloch, P. Hardiman's Landing
Marcott, J. Hard to Kill
Moore, B. Revolution Script
    Wreath for a Redhead
Newman, J. Dead Man's Tears
Orvis, K. Damned and Destroyed
Pape, G. Chain Reaction
Pendleton, D. Canadian Crisis
Phillips, E. Buried on Sunday
    Where There's a Will
Power, P. both titles
Smith, Joan. Brush with Death
Torgerson, E. D. Murderer Returns
Trevanian. Main
Vermandel, J. G. 5 titles
Wayland, P. Double Defector

MOROCCO (Mor. See also: Casablanca; Tangier;
    Africa, North)
Binns, O. Three Black Dots
Brothers, W. P. Morocco Episode
Byfield, B. N. Parcel of Their Fortunes
Carter, Nick. Blood of the Falcon
Coriola. Intrigue in Morocco
Daniels, D. Affair in Marakesh
Drummond, I. Tank of Sacred Eels
Eliot, A. Incident at Villa Rahmana
Garth, D. Three Roads to a Star
Gilman, D. Mrs. Pollifax and the Whirling Dirvish
Goodchild, G. Road to Marrakesh
Gordons. Tiger on My Back
Gray, D. For Richer for Richer
Grenier, R. Marrakesh One-Two
Hyne, C. J. C. Marriage of Kettle
Innes, H. Strange Land
Jason, S. Blood Debt
Leader, C. Murder in Marrakech
Leonard, C. L. Fanatic of Fez
MacAlister, I. Strike Force 7
McConnell, M. Clinton Is Assigned
MacLeod, R. Cargo Risk
Neebel, R. Wargamer
Sands, M. Maroc 7
Seton, G. Colonel Grant's Tomorrow
Sherry, J. Loring Affair
Smith, Don. Secret Mission: Morocco
Timperley, R. Devil's Paradise
Weston, Garnett. Hidden Portal

Williamson, S. Glory Trap
Winston, P. Doomsday Vendetta

MOSCOW (See also: Russia; Mongolia)
Arvay, H. Moscow Intercept
Bannerman, D. Gamov Factor
Barling, T. Olympic Sleeper
Binyon, T. J. Swan Song
Bruce, J. Flash Point
Burch, J. Lubyanka
Carter, Nick. Moscow
    13th Spy
Chambers, P. Moscow Manhunt
Chaber, M. E. So Dead the Rose
    Wild Midnight Falls
Charles, R. Steel Killer
Cullen, R. Soviet Sources
Datesh, J. N. Moscow Tape
Dickey, F. Burial in Moscow
Doherty, K. Long Day's Dying
Evans, P. Englishman's Daughter
Flannery, S. Gulag
    Kremlin Conspiracy
Francis, D. Trial Run
Frayn, M. Russian Interpreter
Freemantle, B. Kremlin Kiss
    Rules of Engagement
Garve, A. Murder in Moscow
Grant, D. Moscow 500
Grant, M. Romanoff Jewels
Green, G. Karpov's Brain
Hall, Adam. Scorpion Signal
Harvester, S. Moscow Road
Hunt, H. Kremlin Conspiracy
Hunter, Matthew. Kremlin Armoury
    Schiller
Jackson, J. O. Dzerzhinsky Square
Jones, D. Russian Spring
Kaminsky, S. M. 5 titles
Kaplan, H. Chopin Express
Lippincott, D. Salt Mine
Littell, R. Mother Russia
Low, I. His Master's Voice
Madsen, D. U.S.S.A.
Mair, G. B. Death's Foot Forward
Mefford, W. H. Games of 80
Moody, J. Moscow Magician
Moss, R. Moscow Rules
Murphy, W. B. Dangerous Games
    High Priest
Newman, B. Moscow Murder
Neznansky, F. Body in Sokolniki Park
    Deadly Games
    Fair at Sokolniki
Olcott, A. Murder at the Red October
Ovalov, L. S. Comrade Spy
Pape, G. Music Wars
Patterson, J. Jericho Commandment
Pearson, W. Chessplayer
Pendleton, D. Moscow Massacre
Pieczenik, S. R. Mind Palace
Quinnell, A. J. In the Name of the Father
Redgate, J. Last Decathlon
Redwood, A. Deadline Moscow
Robertson, C. Red Chameleon
Robeson, K. Red Spider
Ross, Clarissa. Moscow Mists
Salisbury, J. Moscow Gold
Scott, H. No Exit
Sebastian, T. Spy in Question
Sela, O. Kremlin Control
Semyonov, J. Himmler Ploy
    Petrovka 38
Shub, J. L. Moscow by Nightmare
Smith, Don. Secret Mission: The Kremlin Plot
Smith, M. C. Gorky Park
Tack, A. Spy Who Wasn't Exchanged
Thayer, C. W. Moscow Interlude
Tiger, J. Countertrap
Topol, E. Red Square
Vacha, R. Moscow 1980
Vallance, D. Man in the Lubianka
Wood, A. Red Square

MOZAMBIQUE (Mozam. See also: Africa, East)
Carter, Nick. N3 Conspiracy
Driscoll, P. Barboza Credentials
Hardy, R. Rivers of Darkness
Scobie, A. Murder a la Mozambique
Trew, A. Chalk Circle
Wilson, David. Murder in Mozambique

MUNICH (See also: Germany; Berlin; Frankfurt;
    Hamburg)
Daniels, N. Hunt Club
Dowdell, D. K. House in Munich
Horstman, T. Kessler Alliance
Huch, R. Deruga Trial
Kirst, H. H. Time for Payment
    Time for Scandal
    Time for Truth
MacLeod, R. Witchdance in Bavaria
Mullally, F. Munich Involvement
Orde, L. Munich 10
Smith, Don. Secret Mission: Munich
Ulrich, M. Bank Robbery

NAMIBIA. See: South West Africa.

NAPLES (See also: Italy; Florence; Milan; Rome;
    Sardinia; Sicily; Venice)
Anonymous. Cavern of Horrors
Baker, L. Preying Streets
Crookenden, I. Mysterious Murder
Curtiss, E. M. Dead Dogs Bite
Davies, J. See Naples and Die
Dekker, C. Kiss from a Killer
Dowling, G. Neopolitan Reel
Harris, John. Picture of Defeat
Holme, T. Neopolitan Streak
Maddock, S. Gentlemen of the Night
Marshall, R. You Find Him—I'll Fix Him
Nathenson, J. See Naples and Die
Rabe, P. House in Naples
Stagg, J. Nightmare in Naples
Veraldi, A. Payoff
Wheatley, D. Rising Storm

NASHVILLE (Nashv. See also: Tennessee; Memphis;
    South)
Holden, L. Compton Connection
Kaye, M. Grand Old Opry Murders
Patterson, J. Thomas Berryman Number
Pendleton, D. Tennessee Smash
Sadler, B. Nashville with a Bullet

NASSAU (See also: Bahamas; West Indies;
    Caribbean)
Dietrich, R. My Body
Lange, J. Drug of Choice
McCulley, W. Blood on Nassau's Moon

NEBRASKA (Neb. See also: Omaha; Midwest)
Barnes, R. C. Silent Thunder
Black, Robert. Death Angel
Chehak, S. T. Story of Annie D.
Eberhart, M. G. Mystery of Hunting's End
Fleet, C. Place Like Hessberg
Forest, R. Secrets of Tyrone
Ham, B. Nebraska Nightmare
Kempley, W. Probability Factor
Pettit, M. Need to Kill
Portnoy, H. N. Hot Rain
Saul, J. Nathaniel
Stark, R. Jugger
Travis, Gretchen. Too Old to Die
Wiltse, D. Home Again

NEPAL
Carr, G. Corpse at Camp Two
Carter, Nick. Katmandu Contract
    Operation Snake
Coulter, S. Stranger Called the Blues
Court, K. But Don't Go Alone
Davidson, P. Katmandu Affair
Hart-Davis, D. Heights of Rimring
Hauser, T. Hanneman's War
Leigh, S. Dark Labyrinth

Settings Index

Luceno, J. Rock Bottom
Martin, Nancy. Black Bridge to China
Mason, R. Fever Tree
Schmidt, Dan. Red Firestorm
Wilkins, K. Quantum Web

NETHERLANDS. See: Holland.

NEVADA (Nev. See also: Las Vegas; Reno; West)
Adams, C. F. Crooking Finger
  Sabotage
Armour, J. Saturday Night Massacre
Bergon, F. Shoshone Mike
Brent, L. Who Dares?
Butler, Michael. Gauntlet
Chaber, M. E. Born to Be Hanged
Chase, J. H. One Bright Summer Morning
Clark, A. C. Kenyatta's Escape
Corbett, D. Deadline Death
Cox, W. R. Death on Location
Daniels, N. Lady for Sale
Dewey, T. B. Nude in Nevada
Dodge, D. Bullets for the Bridegroom
Eberhart, M. G. El Rancho Rio
Fisher, Herb. Doctor Death
Fitzgerald, A. J. Devil's Gate
Fluke, J. Dead Giveaway
Hagen, L. Winter Roses
Ham, B. Highway Warriors
Haring, D. Dangerous Decor
  "V" for Vixen
Heath, M. Secrets Can Be Fatal
Hillerman, T. Skinwalkers
Holden, J. Dangerous Legacy
Homes, G. Build My Gallows High
Johnston, V. Howling in the Woods
Johnstone, W. Carnival
Kane, F. Due or Die
Lane, J. R. Static
Loghry, E. Shadow of Deceit
McCray, M. Red Man Contract
McKimmey, J. Man with the Gloved Hand
Marlowe, D. J. Four for the Money
Morgan, Dean. Four Guns to Carson City
  Nevada Alibi
Olden, M. They've Killed Anna
Owen, D. Girl Possessed
Queen, E. And on the Eighth Day
Ralston, G. Chain Reaction
  Murder's Money
Roberts, W. D. Dangerous Legacy
  Search for Willie
Ross, Z. H. One Corpse Missing
  Three Down Vulnerable
Ryan, Jenna. Southern Cross
Schopen, B. Big Silence
  Desert Look
Strahan, K. C. Desert Lake Mystery
  Desert Moon Mystery
Taylor, M. A. Red Is for Shrouds
  Return to Murder
Trevor, E. Night Stop
Van der Zee, J. Stateline
Winski, N. Nevada Nightmare
Wire, H. C. Marked Man
Worts, G. F. Laughing Girl

NEW CALEDONIA (See also: Melanesia)
Roberts, Mark. Poisoned Paradise

NEW DELHI (See also: India; Bombay; Calcutta)
Bahadur, K. P. Murder in the Delhi Mail
Carter, Nick. Holy War
  Sign of the Cobra
Peters, Ellis. Mourning Raga

NEW ENGLAND (New Eng. See also: the six
    individual states)
Adams, S. H. Secret of Lonesome Cove
Aldrich, T. B. Stillwater Tragedy
Allan, Dina. Melody of Murder
Allen, A. J. New England Gothic
Altman, T. Black Christmas
Babson, M. Trail of Ashes

Bagby, G. Corpse Candle
Benchley, N. Hunter's Moon
Benedict, L. Lucifer Cult
Bernard, R. Deadly Meeting
Blair, H. L. Three Saw the Murder
Blake, E. Death Down East
Borneman, E. Tremolo
Bradford, S. W. Tender Prey
Bramhall, M. Murder Solves a Problem
Bronson, F. W. Nice People Don't Kill
Brown, Carter. Terror Comes Creeping
Brown, D. F. Grimm Death
Carew, J. Run, Nurse, Run
Carleton, M. Bride Regrets
  Night of the Good Children
Carlson, D. Miss Mary's Husbands
Chambers, W. E. Death Toll
Chase, A. M. Danger in the Dark
Chipperfield, R. O. Trigger of Conscience
Clauson, C. Jaws of Circumstance
Coburn, A. Widow's Walk
Converse, F. Into the Void
Converse, F. H. Mystery of a Diamond
Cook, R. Fever
Corby, J. Farewell to the Castle
  Nightmare Legacy
Crabb, A. Ghosts
Crandall, E. White Violets
Cross, A. Sweet Death, Kind Death
Crowe, C. Northwater
Daly, C. J. Man in the Shadows
Daniels, D. Voices on the Wind
Dannett, S. Defy the Tempest
Dean, S. F. X. By Frequent Anguish
  Death and the Mad Heroine
De Vincent, E. Tower Park
De Weese, J. Reimann Curse
Disney, D. C. Crimson Friday
Disney, D. M. 8 titles
Du Bois, T. 6 titles
Dutton, C. J. 5 titles
Eberhart, M. G. Jury of One
Ellery, J. Family Affairs
Esteven, J. By Night at Dinsmore
  Door of Death
Eustis, H. Horizontal Man
Fenisong, R. Villainous Company
Fenwick, E. Goodbye, Aunt Elva
Findley, F. Counterfeit Corpse
Fischer, B. Girl Between
  House of Flesh
  Kill to Fit
Foley, R. Back Door to Death
  Bones of Contention
  Put out the Light
Forbes, S. All for One and One for Death
  Business of Bodies
  Encounter Darkness
  Relative to Death
Ford, F. Ninth Candle
Foster, M. Humdrum House
Foster, W. B. From Six to Six
Fredericks, J. Everybody's Ready to Die
Fuller, A. Blood on the Common
Gardiner, D. Beer for Psyche
Grant, C. L. Last Call of Mourning
Greenan, R. Secret Life of Algernon
  Pendleton
Gresham, E. Prisoner's Base
Hayes, J. Long Dark Night
Head, A. Everybody Adored Cara
Heath, E. A. Affair at Tideways
Hirschhorn, R. Target Mayflower
Holbrook, M. Wanted: A Murderess
Holding, E. S. Widow's Mite
Holland, I. Trelawny
Jackson, G. Witch's Moon
Jansen, L. M. Bride of the Shadows
Jordan, E. Page Mr. Pomeroy
Julian, R. Murder in Focus
Kamarck, L. Bellringer
King, R. Lethal Lady
Koehler, R. P. Doctor's Murder Case
Lathen, E. Pick Up Sticks

NEW ENGLAND / 1267

Lawrence, Hilda. Blood Upon the Snow
  Time to Die
Livingston, A. Monk of Hambledon
Lynch, M. at least 6 titles
MacDonald, P. J. Little Sister
  Unforgiven
McHenry, J. Spectre of the Forest
McNamara, J. J. Billion Dollar Catch
Mainwaring, M. Murder at Midyears
Malan, E. Cobwebs and Clues
Mayor, D. Last Call for Lissa
Michaels, Barbara. Into the Darkness
Monette, P. Taking Care of Mrs. Carroll
Murphy, W. B. Dead Letter
Noone, E. Dark Cypress
Oellrichs, I. Murder Makes Us Gay
Ogilvie, E. Face of Innocence
Owen, H. C. Ways of Death
Patrick, Q. Grindle Nightmare
Payne, W. Overlook House
Pentecost, H. 5 titles
Petersen, H. D.A.'s Daughter
Philips, J. Murder Arranged
Pilgrim, C. Silent Slain
Porcelain, S. E. Crimson Cat Murders
Potts, J. Little Lie
Queen, E. 6 titles
Randall, F. E. Place of Sapphires
Reagan, T. B. Caper
Reilly, H. Murder on Angler's Island
Reisner, M. Four Witnesses
  Hunted
Rinehart, M. R. Wall
Roberts, W. D. Ghosts of Harrel
  Key Witness
  King's Pawn
Rogers, K. Vantage Point
Ronns, E. Net
Roos, K. Requiem for a Blonde
Roscoe, T. Only in New England
Ross, F. Sleeping Dogs
Rowe, A. Curiosity Killed the Cat
Rowland, H. C. Peddler
Russell, E. S. Fortunate Island
Rutledge, N. Easy to Murder
Rydell, F. They're Not Home Yet
Salinger, S. S. Reckless Abandon
Saul, J. Hellfire
Selig, E. B. Mariner's End
Serrester, L. Frog Murders
Sherry, E. Call the Witness
Smith, F. S. House and the Tower
Snodgrass, G. M. Crestwood Traps
Spalding, J. Spider Island
Sproul, K. Death and the Professor
Stagge, J. Scarlet Circle
Steeves, H. R. Good Night, Sheriff
Stone, G. Z. Dear Deadly Cara
Storm, M. Edge of Danger
Stratton, G. Killing Cousins
Talbot, H. Rim of the Pit
Thielen, B. Open Season
Thomas, W. Stranger in the Land
Thompson, J. Kill-Off
Tryon, T. Lady
Tyler, C. W. both titles
Walton, E. Witch House
Warren, P. Apprentice to Terror
Wells, Carolyn. Anybody But Anne
  Mystery Girl
  Tannahill Tangle
  Where's Emily?
Whipple, K. Fires at Fitch's Folly
  Murders at Loon Lake
Whitney, P. A. Sea Jade
Wilkinson, R. H. Mad Murder
Wilkinson, S. D. Death on Call
Williams, V. Clue of the Rising Moon
Winston, D. Emerald Station
  Inheritance
Winter, A. Whispering Caverns
Withers, E. L. House on the Beach
Woodbury, D. O. both titles
Yglesias, H. Sweetsir

NEW GUINEA (See also: Indonesia; Djakarta; Bali; Borneo; Java; Sumatra)
Binns, O. By Papuan Waters
  Lady of the Miniature
Boothby, G. Crime of the Under-Seas
Grimshaw, B. Coral Palace
Halls, G. Voice of the Crab
Harvester, S. Paradise Men
Hastings, M. Satan's Bay
Herndon, E. Morning Morning True
Innes, H. Solomon's Seal
Jay, C. Beat Not the Bones
Jay, G. M. Feast of the Dead
Jones, Howard. Tropical Tales
Lambert, E. Veterans
Lindall, E. Time Too Soon
MacAlister, I. Skylark Mission
McCarthy, D. Fate of O'Loughlin
McCurtin, P. Body Count
MacDonnell, J. E. Colt & Co. in the Valley of Gold
Mather, A. Deep Gold
Muir, Denis. Death Defies the Doctor
Nolan, R. W. Treasure of Loatani Point
South, M. Curse of the Sightless Fish
Vandercook, J. M. Murder in New Guinea
Wallace, T. Mystery of DS 24
  Skyriders
Wood, C. Kago

NEW HAMPSHIRE (N.H. See also: New England)
Aldrich, T. B. Out of His Head
Avallone, M. Man from AVON
Badgley, A. V. Rembrandt Decisions
Banks, Russell. Affliction
Block, Lawrence. Case of the Pornographic Photos
Borgenicht, M. Extreme Remedies
Brett, H. Promises to Keep
Campbell, Bethany. Dead Opposite
Charles, Spencer. Mystery on the Mount
Douglas, L. W. Mystery of Crooknose
Drown, M. Plowing Up a Snake
Fischer, B. Fools Walk In
Frederics, M. Emergency Exit
Green, A. They Died Laughing
Gresham, E. Puzzle in Parchment
Hatch, M. R. P. Missing Man
Heatter, B. Act of Violence
Holden, R. Snow Fury
Hurd, F. Secret of Canfield House
Hyde, C. Jericho Falls
Landon, H. Forbidden Door
Lathen, E. Come to Dust
Lathrop, G. P. In the Distance
Leonard, C. Other Maritha
Letton, J. Haunting of Cliffside
  Jenny and I
McIntire, M. Old-Fashioned Murder
McNab, O. Horror Story
Orenstein, Frank. Candidate for Murder
Orr, C. Dartmouth Murders
Ottolengui, R. Conflict of Evidence
Palmer, R. Orion Was Rising
Parsons, C. M. Secret of the Sea
Ross, Marilyn. Shorecliff
Samson, J. Auctioneer
Sherman, Steve. Maple Sugar Murders
  White Mountain Murders
Slattery, J. Juliet Effect
Stewart, E. Rock Rude
Stewart, R. Sixth Sense
Thomas, M. Y. Crystal Shadows
Wallis, J. H. Niece of Abraham Pein
Weesner, T. True Detective
Whitney, P. A. Silverhill
Williams, T. Followed Man

NEW JERSEY (N.J. See also: Newark; Trenton)
Ames, R. Awake and Die
Anonymous. Orphan Seamstress
  Devil Drives
Ard, W. No Angels for Me
Arden, W. Dark Power
Bagby, G. Corpse with the Purple Thighs
Bahr, E. J. Help, Please
Ballard, F. Ladies of the Jury
Balmer, E. Torn Letter
Beck, H. C. Death by Clue
Block, Lawrence. Specialists
Bonner, G. Girl at Central
Booton, K. Runaway Home!
Bradley, J. If Hate Could Kill
Bruno, A. Bad Luck
Cafferty, J. Death on the Boardwalk
Caldwell, B. Vanderleigh Legacy
Callahan, J. Ace of Death
Cameron, L. Barca
  Tancredi
Chamberlain, G. A. Red House
Clark, M. H. Cradle Will Fall
Clinch, C. Perth Amboy Mystery
Collins, M. A. Midnight Haul
Crane, C. People Next Door
Cunningham, E. V. Alice
Davis, L. R. Barren Heritage
  Evidence Unseen
Demaris, O. Ricochet
Drayton, R. Hell's Belles
Engleman, P. Dead in Center Field
  Murder-in-Law
  Who Shot Longshot Sam?
Erdman, P. Palace
Fischer, J. High Stakes
Fox, G. Warlord's Hill
Gates, N. Hush Hush Johnson
Gilmore, C. C. Atlantic City Proof
  Bad Room
Goldsmith, N. Atlantic City Murder Mystery
Goodis, D. Burglar
  Somebody's Done For
Gottlieb, N. Stinger
Grant, C. L. In a Dark Dream
  Pet
Grant, M. Shadow Strikes
Gunther, M. Epidemic 9
Haaf, B. T. Crystal Pawns
Hall, Parnell. Favor
Halleran, E. E. Thirteen Toy Pistols
Hanson, V. Mystery for Mary
Haring, D. 13 titles
Heberden, M. V. Drinks on the Victim
  Murder Goes Astray
Hilary, R. Pieces of Cream
Hobart, D. B. Clue of the Leather Noose
Holt, A. Bier for a Hussy
Howie, E. Murder at Stone House
Hunvald, H. Masterpiece of Nice Mr. Breen
Hustad, D. Perfect Family
Iams, J. Girl Meets Body
Kane, H. Crumpled Cup
  Run for Doom
Keith, C. Hiding Place
  Missing, Presumed Dead
Kent, B. Under the Boardwalk
Kilgore, K. Something for Nothing
Klaich, D. Heavy Gilt
Knebel, F. Trespass
Kozloff, C. Ondine
Lathen, E. Murder to Go
Leavitt, A. J. Shame the Devil
Leonard, C. L. Secret of the Spa
Leonard, E. Glitz
Levinrew, W. Murder on the Palisades
Little, C. Black Gloves
  Black-Headed Pins
  Black Iris
  Black Piano
McGarrity, M. Neon Caesar
McMullen, M. Man with Fifty Complaints
Mallory, R. New Jersey Showdown
Martyn, W. Scarlett Murder
Mason, V. W. Spider House
Meredith, D. W. Christmas Card Murders
Moroso, J. A. Listening Man
Murphy, W. B. Atlantic City
  Bay City Blast
  Trace
Napier, M. Possession of Elizabeth Calder
Noel, S. Few Die Well
Noone, E. Second Secret
North, H. Expressway
O'Donnell, L. Babes in the Woods
Oellrichs, I. at least 5 titles
Packer, V. Something in the Shadows
Pendleton, D. Jersey Guns
Pentecost, H. Steel Palace
Pettit, M. Axmann Agenda
Pikser, J. Junk on the Hill
Pratt, F. Cunning Mulatto
Propper, M. Ticker-Tape Murder
Queen, E. Halfway House
Quinn, Seabury. Devil's Bride
Reagan, T. B. Inside-Out Heist
Rider, J. W. both titles
Riley, D. Rite of Expiation
Robeson, K. Giggling Ghosts
  Midas Man
Ronns, E. Corpse Hangs High
  Decoy
Rosten, L. King Silky!
Rothberg, A. Stalking Horse
Ryan, S. Death Never Sleeps
Sadler, M. Mirror Image
Saperstein, A. Camp
Sapir, R. Created: The Destroyer
  Mafia Fix
Sauter, E. Hunter
  Hunter and the Ikon
Scarpetta, F. Kill!
Scherf, M. Case of the Kippered Corpse
  Corpse Grows a Beard
Scoppettone, S. Some Unknown Person
Shane, S. Baby in the Ash Can
Simmons, M. K. Gypsy Grove
Smith, Edgar. Reasonable Doubt
Spain, T. Time to Kill
Stark, R. Deadly Edge
  Man with the Getaway Face
Stevens, S. Dead City
Stevenson, B. E. That Affair at Elizabeth
Stratton, Ted. Tourist Trap
Swem, C. L. Werewolf
Teague, R. You Can't Ignore Murder
Terhune, A. P. Blundell's Last Guest
  Letters of Marque
  Loot!
  Unseen!
Thayer, L. 8 titles
Turnbull, M. Coast Road Murder
Wahl, A. H. Handsome, But Dead
Walker, P. Altar
Wallmann, M. M. both titles
Waterhouse, J. Playing for Keeps
Wells, Carolyn. 5 titles
Westlake, D. E. Jimmy the Kid
Wheeler, E. L. Fritz to the Front
Whitney, P. A. Winter People
Wise, W. Amazon Factor
Wolff, W. A. Murder at Endor
Wylie, P. Murderer Invisible
Yates, G. W. Body That Wasn't Uncle
Zawadsky, P. Demon of Raven's Cliff

NEW MEXICO (N. Mex. See also: Albuquerque; Sante Fe; Southwest)
Aeby, J. Serena
Ames, D. Murder Beings at Home
Ames, N. Whisper in the Forest
Apodaca, R. S. Waxen Image
Armstrong, M. Blue Santo Murder Mystery
Benchley, P. Rummies
Berne, K. False Impressions
Boniface, M. Wings of Death
Bowen, J. Man Without a Head
Brown, F. Far Cry
Castle, F. Murder in Red
Crane, F. Amethyst Spectacles
  Horror on the Ruby X
  Polkadot Murder
  Turquoise Shop
Crawford, William. Stryker
Curtiss, U. Forbidden Garden
  Hours to Kill

Settings Index

Dean, S. F. X. Such Pretty Toys
Derrick, L. Terror in Taos
Eberhart, M. G. Chiffon Scarf
Farnsworth, M. Companion to Evil
    Cross for Tomorrow
Faust, R. Burning Sky
Griffiths, J. Snake Charmer
Hall, D. J. Perilous Sanctuary
Hamilton, D. Assignment: Murder
    Infiltrators
    Silencers
Head, L. Crystal Clear Case
Hillerman, T. 6 titles
Johnston, V. Shadow Behind the Curtain
Kazan, E. Assassins
Kelland, C. B. Death Keeps a Secret
King, Harold. Paradigm Red
Knight, C. Death of a Big Shot
Koehler, R. P. Here Come the Dead
    Road House Murders
    Sing a Song of Murder
    Some Try Murder
Kunetka, J. W. Shadow Man
Lange, O. Red Snow
Layne, M. M. Balloon Affair
Lipsky, E. Lincoln McKeever
Lummis, C. F. King of the Broncos
McMullen, M. Gift Horse
Magnuson, J. Ghost Dancing
Masterson, W. Undertaker Wind
Maxwell, A. E. Steal the Sun
Meredith, D. R. Sheriff and the Folsom Man Murders
Moore, Barbara. Wolf Whispered Death
Mosler, B. Y. Horror at the Hacienda
Murphy, W. B. Date with Death
Nichols, J. American Blood
Noyes, S. Shadowbox
O'Malley, P. Affair of the Red Mosaic
O'Rourke, F. Man Who Found His Way
Parker, F. M. Shadow Man
Pendleton, D. Blood and Thunder
    Wednesday's Wrath
Reilly, H. Day She Died
Rifkin, S. Snow Rattlers
Robeson, K. Glass Man
Roderus, F. Dead Heat
Ronns, E. Don't Cry, Beloved
Rosemoor, P. Ambushed
Ryan, F. C. Murder on the Ranch
Satterthwait, W. At Ease with the Dead
Scarpetta, F. Kiss of Death
Smith, M. C. Stallion Gate
Spicer, B. Act of Anger
    Kellogg Junction
Stern, R. M. 7 titles
Stivers, D. Shadow Warriors
Stowe, J. L. Winter Stalk
Swarthout, G. Skeletons
Thackrey, T. Preacher
Thomas, C. Hearse Horse Snickered
Thurlo, A. Black Mesa
Trimble, L. Tragedy in Turquoise
Van Ettan, T. Dead Kachina Man
Whittington, H. Ticket to Hell
Williamson, A. Secret Gold
Wilson, Brownlow. Devil's Staircase
Winston, D. Devil's Daughter
    Secrets of Cromwell Crossing
Wiseman, T. Savage Day
Withers, E. L. Salazar Grant
Woods, C. Night Chant

NEW ORLEANS (New Or. See also: Louisiana; South)
Ames, J. E. both titles
Anonymous. Mysteries of New Orleans
Arnold, M. Death of a Voodoo Doll
Atlee, P. Green Wound
Barnes, L. Cities of the Dead
Bedford-Jones, H. Mardi-Gras Mystery
Boyles, W. Killing Trade
Bristow, G. Gutenberg Murders
    Invisible Host
    Mardi-Gras Murders
Buntline, N. Mysteries and Miseries of New Orleans
Burke, J. L. Morning for Flamingos
    Neon Rain
Carr, J. D. Deadly Hall
    Ghosts' High Noon
    Papa La-Bas
Carson, B. Torment Was a Woman
Chaber, M. E. Hearse of Another Color
Claymore, T. Appointment in New Orleans
    Dead Men Don't Answer
Colbert, J. No Special Hurry
    Profit and Sheen
Conaway, J. Big Easy
Conroy, Al. Murder Mission!
Cooke, S. G. Treasure of Rodolfo Fierro
Corrington, J. W. Civil Death
    Project Named Desire
    So Small a Carnival
Coulson, J. Fear Stalks the Bayou
Coxe, G. H. One Way Back
Craddock, I. Yazoo Mystery
Crane, F. Indigo Necklace
Dailey, J. Masquerade
Dale, Alan. Ned Bachman, the New Orleans Detective
Daniels, D. Dark Stage
    Ghost Song
Davis, J. M. White Rook
Day, C. Hacker
Denoux, O. Big Kiss
    Grim Reaper
Derrick, L. Mardi Gras Massacre
Dillmann, J. Blood Warning
    French Quarter Killers
    Unholy Matrimony
Donaldson, D. J. Cajun Nights
Dorsett, D. Dueling Oaks
Drayton, R. Anyone's Grief
Du Breuil, L. Mirror Image
Eberhart, M. G. Bayou Road
Ellis, J. Wexford
Fair, A. A. Owls Don't Blink
Fawcette, S. Computer Criminals
Feibleman, P. S. Charlie Boy
Fennelly, T. Closet Hanging
    Glory Hole Murders
    Kiss Yourself Goodbye
Fleming, Rudd. Cradled in Murder
Gibson, W. B. Mask of Mephisto
Greene, F. N. Into the Night
Griffiths, Gertrude. Secret of the Shadow
Halliday, B. Michael Shayne's Long Chance
    Murder and the Married Virgin
Hancock, H. I. Detective Johnson of New Orleans
Harris, T. Black Sunday
Hines, J. Legend of Witchwynd
Holcombe, W. H. Mystery of New Orleans
Holden, G. Deadlier Than the Male
Irish, W. Waltz Into Darkness
Kains, J. Whispering Cat Mystery
Knoblock, K. T. There's Been Murder Done
Lee, T. House of Montague
Leonard, E. Bandits
Leslie, Lynn. Street of Dreams
Lobaugh, E. K. Shadows in Succession
Locke, D. House of Two Wives
Long, A. R. Murder by Scripture
Long, L. B. Crucible of Evil
    Lemoyne Heritage
Lutz, J. Right to Sing the Blues
McCurtin, P. New Orleans Holocaust
MacDonald, J. D. Murder for the Bride
Montecino, M. Big Time
Morrow, S. Insiders
Ogan, G. Murder in the Wind
    To Kill a Judge
Otis, G. H. Bourbon Street
Parker, F. M. Assassins
Parker, R. H. Final Four
Pendleton, D. New Orleans Knockout
Perkins, K. Voodoo'd
Pinkerton, M. Woman's Revenge
Potter, J. L. Kill, Sweet Charity, Kill
Pronzini, B. Masques
Richards, C. Marble Jungle
Robinson, Sue. Amendment
Roper, L. V. Emerald Chicks Caper
    Red Horse Caper
Scarpetta, F. Counterattack
Shankman, S. Now Let's Talk of Graves
Shuman, M. K. Caesar Clue
    Maya Stone Murders
Smith, Julie. New Orleans Mourning
Stivers, D. Cult War
Stone, E. M. both titles
Thayer, L. Guilt Edged
Thorne, E. Flight Hostess
Treat, L. D As in Dead
Vanderveer, S. Death for the Lady
Ward, W. Murderer of New Orleans
Wells, Charlie. Let the Night Cry
Wills, G. At Button's
Wiltz, C. Diamond Before You Die
    Killing Circle
Womack, S. Murphy's Fault
York, Thomas. Desireless

NEW YORK CITY (NYC. See also: New York; Long Island; Rochester)
Aaron, D. Agent of Influence
Aarons, E. S. 5 titles
Abbey, K. Beyond the Dark
    Run with the Hare
Abbot, A. 7 titles
Abbot, W. J. Philip Derby, Reporter
Abdullah, A. Bungalow on the Roof
Abrahams, R. D. Death in 1-2-3
Adams, F. U. both titles
Adams, G. Swindle
Adcock, T. L. Precinct 19
    Sea of Green
Aiken, A. W. all 5 titles
Albrand, M. Final Encore
    Manhattan North
Alden, W. Lost Million
Aldis, D. Murder in a Haystack
Alexander, David. 14 titles
Alexander, L. Big Stick
    Speak Softly
Allan, D. at least 4 titles
Allan, F. both titles
Allan, H. Tragic Case of John Renold
Allan, L. Five for One
    Jungle Crime
    Man on the Twenty-Fourth Floor
    Masked Stranger
Alleman, R. Therapist
Allen, S. Murder in Manhattan
Altman, A. Heaven and Hell
Altman, T. Dark Places
Anderson, M. Her Mother's Husband
Anderson, P. Pleasure Business
Andress, L. Caper
Andrews, Mark. Bomb Squad
    Return of Jack the Ripper
Andrews, P. Cop Story
Andrews, S. all 3 titles
Anonymous. Charley Hunter
    Dark Masquerade
    Man from the West
    Mysteries of New York
    Mysterious Marksman
    Orphan Seamstress
    Smiling Corpse
    Strange Stories of a Detective
    Wilfred Montressor
Anthony, Evelyn. Assassin
    Rendezvous
Appel, B. Brain Guy
    Dark Stain
    Life and Death of a Tough Guy
    Raw Edge
Archer, R. both titles
Ard, W. 9 titles
Arden, W. Deadly Legacy
Arleo, J. Grand Street Collector
Armstrong, C. Dream Walker
    Lay On, MacDuff!
    Mischief
Arnold, E. Quicksand

Arrighi, M. 6 titles
Arthur, B. Swiftly to Evil
Asbury, H. both titles
Ashbrook, H. Murder Comes Back
    Murder of Cecily Thane
    Purple Onion Mystery
Ashe, D. Shroud for Grandmama
Ashe, G. Man Who Stayed Alive
    No Need to Die
Ashwood-Collins, A. Deadly Resolutions
Asimov, I. Caves of Steel
    Murder at the ABA
    Puzzles of the Black Widowers
Asinof, E. Name of the Game Is Murder
Auster, P. City of Glass
    Ghosts
Austin, Anne. Black Pigeon
Austin, H. Drink the Green Water
Avallone, M. at least 21 titles
Avery, A. A. Anything for a Quiet Life
Avery, R. Murder on the Downbeat
Axelrod, G. Blackmailer
Babbin, J. Bloody Soaps
    Prime Time Corpse
Bacon, J. D. Medusa's Head
Bacon, P. Inward Eye
Bagby, G. 42 titles
Baker, C. Pool Ticket .025
Baker, R. Conspiracy
Baker, S. S. both titles
Baker, W. H. Take Death for a Lover
Ball, E. H. all 3 titles
Ballard, P. D. Brothers in Blood
    Death Brokers
Ballinger, B. S. 7 titles
Banks, E. Mystery of Frances Farrington
Barber, M. Britz of Headquarters
Barber, W. A. Deed Is Drawn
    Drawback to Murder
    Murder Draws a Line
    Noose Is Drawn
Barbour, A. M. That Mainwaring Affair
Bardin, J. F. all 4 titles
Barker, A. Apollo Legacy
Barker, W. Only the Good Die
Barlay, B. Satan Comes Across
Barnes, J. Outside the Law
Barrett, Monte. Murder Off Stage
    Wedding March Murder
Barron, H. High Cost of Murder
Barry, B. Murder Among Friends
Barry, Jerome. 6 titles
Barry, Joe. Homicide Hotel
Barry, M. Harlem Showdown
    Night Raider
Bart, S. Ruby Sweetwater and the Ringo Kid
Barth, R. 5 titles
Basinsky, E. Big Steal
Batson, G. Design for Murder
Baxt, G. 9 titles
Bayard, F. Death and Lilacs
Bayer, O. W. Eye for an Eye
Bayer, W. Blind Side
    Peregrine
    Switch
Baylus, R. F. People Exchange
Bayne, S. Turning Sword
Bear, D. Keeping Time
Bechdolt, J. Wages of Peril
Beeckman, R. Last Woman
Beinhart, L. No One Rides for Free
    You Get What You Pay For
Bell, A. Out of Circulation
Bell, M. S. Waiting for the End of the World
    Washington Square Ensemble
Bellak, G. Third Friday
Belmar, H. New York by Night
Belsky, D. Murder Is for Keeps
    One for the Money
    South Street Confidential
Benedict, G. Case of the Deadly Drops
Benjamin, Edla. Murder Without Makeup
Benjamin, P. Squeeze Play
Bennett, Jay. Catacombs

Bennett, Liza. Madison Avenue Murder
    Seventh Avenue Murder
Bensen, D. R. Sherlock Holmes in New York
Benson, T. Death Wears a Mask
    Strictly Private
Benton, J. Marji and the Kidnap Plot
Benton, J. L. Talent for Murder
Berg, B. Hide and Seek
Berger, T. Who Is Teddy Villanova?
Bergman, A. Big Kiss-Off of 1944
Bergman, L. Walk Softly, Walk Deadly
Bernhard, R. S. Girls in 5J
Berry, Carole. Good Night, Sweet Prince
    Letter of the Law
    Year of the Monkey
Betcherman, B. Suspicions
Bierstadt, E. H. Satan Was a Man
Biracree, T. Red Berets
    Torch
Bird, B. Death in Four Colors
    Downbeat for a Dirge
Black, C. Apology
Black, D. Murder at the Met
Black, J. Dead Run
Blackwelder, S. Price of Heaven
Blake, P. Double Griffin
Blake, W. D. My Time or Yours
Blaney, C. E. Child Slaves of New York
    Millionaire Detective
    Young Buffalo in New York
Blankfort, M. Widow-Makers
Blau, E. Keys to Billy Trillo
Blayne, S. Gay Ghastly Holiday
Blazer, J. S. Deal Me Out
Bleeck, O. Procane Chronicle
Bliss, A. Camden Ruby Murder
Bliss, T. Broadway Butterfly Murders
Blizard, M. Watch Sinister
Blochman, L. G. See You at the Morgue
Block, C. B. Art for Keeps
Block, Lawrence. 15 titles
Block, Libbie. Bedeviled
Blood, M. both titles
Bloom, M. T. 13th Man
Blumenthal, J. Case of the Hardboiled Dicks
Blunt, G. Cold Eye
Bly, N. Mystery of Central Park
Bogard, D. Pardon My Body
Bogart, W. Hell on Friday
    Murder Man
Bohjalian, C. A. Killing in the Real World
Bohle, E. Wife Who Died Twice
Bond, E. Evil in the House
Bonner, G. Black Eagle Mystery
Bonney, J. L. Murder Without Clues
Booth, C. B. Deceiver's Door
Booth, L. F. both titles
Borgenicht, M. 5 titles
Bosse, M. J. Incident at Naha
Botein, B. Prosecutor
Bourjaily, V. Game Men Play
Boutelle, C. Artificial Fate
    Beyond the End
Bova, B. Cyberbooks
Bowen, Michael. Badger Game
Bowen, R. S. both titles
Box, E. Death in the Fifth Position
Boyd, F. Flesh Peddlers
    Johnny Staccato
Boyle, T. Only the Dead Know Brooklyn
    Post-Mortem Effects
Brace, T. Murder Goes to the World's Fair
Bradley, M. H. Murder in Room 700
Brady, C. T. Corner in Coffee
Bram, C. Holt Tight
Brand, M. Six Golden Angels
Brandel, M. Rain Before Seven
Brean, H. Darker the Night
    Matter of Fact
    Traces of Brillhart
Brenn, G. J. Voices
Breslin, J. all 3 titles
Brett, Michael. all 10 titles
Brett, Michael. Diamond Kill

Brett, Mike. both titles
Brewer, J. Get Dumm!
Brez, E. M. Those Dark Eyes
Bringle, M. Murder Most Gentrified
Bromell, H. Follower
Bronson-Howard, G. Birds of Prey
    Black Book
    Enemy to Society
Brothers, J. Ox
Broun, D. Counterweight
    Subject of Harry Egypt
Brown, Carter. at least 9 titles
Brown, F. Murder Can Be Fun
Brown, H. Penthouse Killings
Brown, J. Night of Terror
Brown, J. E. Incident at 125th Street
Brown, Wenzell. at least 8 titles
Browner, J. Death of a Punk
Bruce, G. both titles
Brucker, M. There Goes the Bride
Bruno, A. Bad Blood
    Bad Guys
Brussel, J. A. Just Murder, Darling
Bryant, Matt. Cue for Murder
Bryce, L. Romance of an Alter Ego
Buck, C. N. Alias Red Ryan
    Marked Men
Bugliosi, V. T. Lullaby and Goodnight
Buntline, N. Mysteries and Miseries of New York
Buranelli, P. Big Nick
    News Reel Murder
Burdette, Charles. Gambler
Burgess, G. Find the Woman
    Ladies in Boxes
Burke, J. F. all 5 titles
Burke, R. 5 titles
Burkholz, H. Strange Bedfellows
Burne, G. Murder to Music
Burnham, H. Murder of Lalla Lee
Byfield, B. N. Solemn High Murder
Byrne, R. Skyscraper
Caldwell, A. B. No Tears Shed
    Turquoise Hazard
Calin, H. J. Rocks and Ruin
Cameron, D. C. And So He Had to Die
    Death at Her Elbow
    Dig Another Grave
Cameron, L. Block Busters
Campbell, R. W. Malloy's Subway
Campbell, S. Below the Dead-Line
Canavor, F. Rape One
Cannon, C. both titles
Cannon, P. H. Pulptime
Caputi, A. Storms and Son
Cardiff, S. Inner Steps
Carey, Charles. Van Suyden Sapphires
Carey, M. Vice Squad Cop
Carlson, P. M. Murder Unrenovated
    Rehearsal for Murder
Carmello, C. La Mattanza
Carpenter, C. Deadhead
    Games Murderers Play
    Only Her Hairdresser Knew
Carpenter, H. K. Whistling in the Dark
Carpenter, M. Experiment Perilous
Carroll, Joy. Glitter Girl
Carson, B. She Died Downtown
Carter, M. Call Me Killer!
Carter, Nicholas. Death Has Green Eyes
    Empire of Crime
    Park Avenue Murder!
Carter, Nick. 5 titles
Caspary, V. Laura
    Murder in the Stork Club
    Ruth
Cassiday, B. While Murder Waits
Cassina, L. Cop's Blood
Castoire, M. Gold Shield
Caunitz, W. Black Sand
    One Police Plaza
    Suspects
Cavanagh, A. Children Are Gone
Chalmers, S. House of Two Green Eyes
Chamberlain, G. A. Great Van Suttart Mystery

Settings Index

NEW YORK CITY

Chambers, D. Frightened Man
    Last Secret
    She'll Be Dead by Morning
    Too Like the Lightning
Chambers, R. all 3 titles
Chambers, R. W. Tracer of Lost Persons
Chambers, W. E. Redemption Factor
Champlin, V. Shadowed by a Detective
Chandler, D. Glass Totem
Chanslor, T. both titles
Charteris, L. Call for the Saint
    Saint in New York
    Saint on Guard
Charyn, J. 6 titles
Chase, A. M. Party at the Penthouse
    Twenty Minutes to Kill
Chase, J. Green Jade Necklace
Chase, J. H. Try This One for Size
    Twelve Chinks and a Woman
Chastain, T. 6 titles
Cheatham, L. Marriage Pact
Chesbro, G. 7 titles
Chester, Ann. Slightly Imperfect
Chevigny, P. Criminal Mischief
Chichester, J. J. Bigamist
    Sanderson: Master Rogue
    Silent Cracksman
Child, R. W. Vanishing Men
Chiu, T. Port Arthur Chicken
Christian, N. all 3 titles
Christmas, J. all 3 titles
Christopher, Constance. Dead Man's Flower
Cirni, J. both titles
Clancy, E.A . Watched Out
Clarins, D. Woman in the Window
    Woman Who Knew Too Much
Clark, M. H. Stranger Is Watching
    While My Pretty One Sleeps
Clarke, D. H. Murderer's Holiday
Clauson, C. Gloyne Murder
Cleary, J. Spearfield's Daughter
Cline, E. First Prize
Cochran, R. G. Victoria Pruitt Comes to Town
Coe, T. Don't Lie to Me
    Jade in Aries
    Kinds of Love, Kinds of Death
    Murder Among Children
Coffaro, K. Gently Into Night
Coffey, B. Face of Fear
Cohane, M. E. Murder One!
Cohen, James. Mindbender
Cohen, O. R. 5 titles
Cohen, S. Angel Face
    330 Park
Cohen, S. P. Heartless
    Island of Steel
Cohler, D. K. Freemartin
    Gamemaker
Colburn, L. Death in a Small World
Colby, R. Secret of the Second Door
Cole, Derek. Blonde on Ice
Cole, W. V. Park Avenue
Collins, H. Cut Me In
Collins, J. H. Great Taxi-Cab Mystery
Collins, Michael. 7 titles
Collison, W. 6 titles
Coltrane, J. Talon
Conant, P. Dr. Gatskill's Blue Shoes
Conde, N. In the Deep Woods
    Religion
Condon, F. Dancing Doll
Condon, R. Death of a Politician
    Prizzi's Family
    Prizzi's Honor
Connable, A. Twelve Trains to Babylon
Connell, E. I Had to Kill Her
Cook, R. Brain
Cook, S. Sharing
Cook, T. H. Blood Innocents
    Flesh and Blood
    Killing of the Fallow Deer
    Night Secrets
Cooke, J. C. Vera Gerard Case
Coombs, M. Moment of Need

Corcoran, W. Dark Waters
Corder, E. Bite
Cores, L. Corpse de Ballet
    Misty Curtain
    Painted for the Kill
Cornell, L. Poison Case Number 10
Coughlin, T. G. Hero of New York
Coulter, C. False Pretenses
Count, E. W. Hundred Percent Squad
Coverdale, H. both titles
Cowan, S. Bitter Justice
Cox, W. R. Death Comes Early
Coxe, G. H. Fashioned for Murder
    Fifth Key
Coyne, P. J. Manuscript for Murder
Craig, Jonathan. at least 10 titles
Crane, C. Wife Found Slain
Crane, F. Cinnamon Murder
    Pink Umbrella
Cranston, C. Murder on Fifth Avenue
Crawford, J. R. Philosopher's Murder Case
Creasey, J. Murder, London-New York
    Toff in New York
Creed, W. Death Wears a Green Hat
Crockett, J. Lullaby with Lugers
Cronin, G. P. both titles
Cronley, J. Cheap Shot
Crooker, H. Crime in Washington Mews
    Man About Broadway
Crosby, J. Party of the Year
Crosby, K. Strange Case of Eleanor Cuyler
Cross, A. 6 titles
Crossen, K. F. Case of the Curious Heel
    Case of the Phantom Fingerprints
Crozier, A. O. Magnet
Csida, J. Crime Is of the Essence
Cudahy, S. Trojan Gold
Cullen, C. Deadly Chase
Cunningham, E. V. 8 titles
Cunningham, P. Bear's Requiem
Currie, B. Officer 666
Curtis, N. M. all 3 titles
Curtiss, P. E. Wanted: A Fool
Cutter, J. Manhattan Revenge
    Vendetta
Da Cruz, D. Fire Kill
Dade, R. Execution Night
    Torturer
Daintrey, L. Gold
Daley, J. A. Spicy Lady
Daley, R. Hands of a Stranger
    Man with a Gun
    To Kill a Cop
    Year of the Dragon
Dallas, R. Master Mind
D'Alton, M. Fatal Finish
Dalton, P. 90 Gramercy Park
Daly, C. J. 8 titles
Daly, E. 9 titles
Dana, F. Murder at the New York World's Fair
Dana, M. Master Mind
    Mystery of the Third Parrot
    Within the Law
Dane, J. Y. Christmas Tree Murders
    Grasp at Straws
    Murder Cum Laude
Daniels, C. L. Bronze Buddha
Daniels, D. Summer House
    Veil of Treachery
Daniels, N. Captive
    Deadly Game
    Mausoleum Key
Daniels, Paul. Naked Streets
Darby, R. Murder with Orange Blossoms
Davies, F. Cross of Gold Affair
Davies, G. Portrait of Susan
Davis, D. S. 10 titles
Davis, E. There Was an Old Woman
Davis, F. C. 11 titles
Davis, J. G. Fear No Evil
Davis, Mildred. Room Upstairs
    Sound of Insects
Davis, P. Dancer's Death
Day, L. both titles

Dean, A. Snipe Hunt
Dean, E. Wax Basket Murder
Dean, G. Case of Marie Corwin
    Case of the Fifth Key
Dean, R. G. Murder of Convenience
    Murder on Margin
    On Ice
    Sutton Place Murders
Dean, S. all 9 titles
De Andrea, W. L. 5 titles
Deane, J. Great Pretender
Deaver, J. W. Always a Thief
    Death of a Blue Movie Star
    Manhattan Is My Beat
DeGrave, P. Keep the Baby, Faith
    Unholy Moses
Dejeans, E. Moreton Mystery
    Romance of a Million Dollars
Dekker, C. Sign of the Server
Dekker, J. Manhunt in Manhattan
De Laguna, F. Arrow Points to Nowhere
Delancey, R. Murder Below Wall Street
De Lillo, D. Running Dog
Dell, A. Johnny on the Spot
Delman, D. Dead Faces Laughing
    Liar's League
Demarest, A. Murder on Every Floor
Demarest, P. G. House on Washington Place
De Mexico, N. R. Madman on a Drum
De Mille, N. at least 6 titles
De Mirjian, A. Not a Clue
Denbow, W. Chandler
Dentinger, J. all 3 titles
Denver, P. Dead on Time
De Pre, J. Aquarius, My Evil
    Third Woman
Derrick, L. Countdown to Terror
    Hijacking Manhattan
De Steiguer, W. Jewels for a Shroud
Deutsch, A. V. Starett
De Villiers, G. Operation New York
Devon, D. G. Shattered Mask
    Temple Kent
Devoor, A. Oliver Iverson
Dexter, L. Case of the Brooklyn Mobsters
Diamond, F. Murder in Five Columns
    Murder Rides a Rocket
    Widow Maker
Diamond, G. Black Midnight
Dickenson, F. Kill 'Em with Kindness
Dietl, B. One Tough Cop
Dines, M. Abrams and Jones, Homicide
Dixon, S. Too Late
Docherty, J. L. He Won't Need It Now
Doctorow, E. L. Billy Bathgate
Dodson, D. B. Looking for Zoe
Doe, J. Eye-Witness
Doherty, E. J. Broadway Murders
Doliner, R. On the Edge
Dolph, J. all 5 titles
Dooley, H. H. Last Rights
Dougall, B. I Don't Scare Easy
Downey, T. Splendid Executioner
Drake, A. Steel Noose
Drake, D. all 3 titles
Drake, L. Medical Center Murders
Drennen, R. Murder Beat
Droge, E. F. Honor Legion
    In the Highest Tradition
Drummond, June. Trojan Mule
Du Bois, T. Death Tears a Comic Strip
    High Tension
    Late Bride
Du Bois, W. Case of the Deadly Diaries
Ducker, B. Bankroll
Dudgeon, R. at least 8 titles
Dudowicz, E. Thirty-Second Floor
Duff, B. Central Park Murder
Dunham, M. Stilled Life
Dunne, D. People Like Us
Duris, G. Real Endings
Early, J. Donato & Daughter
Eastman, E. Mouse with Red Eyes
Eastman, R. O. Mysteries of Blair House

N

Eberhard, F. G. Microbe Murders
    13th Murder
Eberhardt, W. F. both titles
Eberhart, M. G. 9 titles
Edgar, K. I Hate You to Death
Edwards, Stafford. Money Order Murder
Egerton, J. K. Soul Laid Bare
Ehrlich, M. Spin the Glass Web
Eichler, A. 5 titles
Einstein, C. Bloody Spur
    Last Laugh
    Naked City
Eisinger, J. Walls Came Tumbling Down
Elbert, J. Very Cagey Lady
Elias, A. J. Bowman Test
Elias, D. Gory Details
Eller, J. both titles
Ellin, S. 5 titles
Ellington, R. Exit for a Dame
    Just Killing Time
    Shoot the Works
Elliott, W. J. Dope Devils
Ellis, J. B. Something Else
Ellson, H. Duke
    I'll Fix You
    Tomboy
Ely, D. Seconds
Endicott, J. S. Crime Inc.
Endicott, S. Mayor Harding of New York
Enefer, D. Dark Kiss
    Deadly Quiet
    Long Chance
England, G. A. Greater Crime
English, A. Edge of Violence
English, R. Sugarplum Staircase
Enright, R. E. both titles
Erickson, N. W. Splinters of Fear
Ericson, W. Fallen Angel
Ernst, P. Bronze Mermaid
    Hangman's Hat
Erskine, F. Naked Murder
Ethan, J. B. all 3 titles
Eulo, K. Nocturnal
Fairlie, G. No Sleep for Macall
Fairman, P. W. To Catch a Crooked Girl
Falk, L. Golden Circle
Falkner, L. Murder Off Broadway
Falstein, L. both titles
Farrell, Maud. Skid
Farrington, F. Strangers in 7A
Fast, H. Confession of Joe Cullen
Fast, J. Model for Murder
    Street of Fear
    Walk in Shadow
Fauley, W. F. Queenie
Faur, M. P. Friendly Place to Die
Fearing, K. Big Clock
    Generous Heart
    Loneliest Girl in the World
Fenisong, R. 16 titles
Fenster, B. Last Page
Fenwick, E. P. Murder in Haste
Ferguson, N. Putting Out
Ferguson, W. B. M. Escape to Eternity
    Shayne Case
Ferm, B. Edge of Beauty
Ferris, W. Across 110th
Fetta, E. L. all 3 titles
Fiaschetti, M. You Gotta Be Rough
Fickling, G. G. Blood and Honey
Field, E. What Nigel Knew
Field, T. Killer's Carnival
Fielding, H. Equal Partners
    Straight Out
Fields, A. V-J Day
Findley, F. Man in the Middle
    Murder Makes Me Mad
    My Old Man's Badge
    Waterfront
Finley, G. Death Strikes Out
Finley, S. Case of the Black Sheep
Firth, N. W. Manhattan Bombshell
Fischer, B. 7 titles
Fish, R. L. Trials of O'Brien

Fisher, D. E. Crisis
    Katie's Terror
Fisher, Rudolph. Conjure Man Dies
Fisher, S. Winter Kill
Fitzpatrick, J. Dreamwalker
Fitzsimmons, C. Girl in the Cage
    Moving Finger
    Whispering Widow
Fleetwood, H. Order of Death
Fleming, E. Murder Takes a Honeymoon
Fletcher, Lucille. Blindfold
    Eighty Dollars to Stamford
    Mirror Image
Fliegel, R. Art of Death
    Organ Grinder's Monkey
    Time to Kill
Flora, F. Park Avenue Tramp
Flynn, D. Murder in A-Flat
    Murder Isn't Enough
    Murder on the Hudson
    Ordinary Murder
Flynn, W. J. Barrel Mystery
Foley, P. Yellow Circle
Foley, R. 17 titles
Footner, H. 23 titles
Ford, B. Show Business
Forester, B. M. In Strict Confidence
Forman, H. J. both titles
Forrest, D. Great Dinosaur Robbery
Forrester, I. L. Dangerous Inheritance
Foster, M. Crooked
    Whistling Man
Foster, R. Girl from Easy Street
Foster, Robert Frederick. Cab No. 44
Fowler, K. All the Skeletons in All the Closets
Fox, D. Ethel Opens the Door
    Handwriting on the Wall
    Man Who Convicted Himself
Foy, G. Asia Rip
Frances, S. D. Day the Island Almost Sank
    Fault in Our Stars
    Panic in the Streets
Frank, W. Chalk Face
Frankel, S. Aleph Solution
Franklin, Edgar. In and Out
Franklin, Eugene. all 3 titles
Franklin, S. Chickens in the Airshaft
Frazer, A. Fall of Marty Moon
Frazer, R. C. Mark Kilby Solves a Murder
    Mark Kilby Stands Alone
    Mark Kilby Takes a Risk
Fredericks, A. Film of Fear
    Little Fortune
Freeborn, P. Stark Truth
Freeman, L. Case on Cloud Nine
    Psychiatrist Says Murder
Friedman, H. Tunnel
Friedman, K. Case of Lone Star
    Frequent Flier
    Greenwich Killing Time
    When the Cat's Away
Friedman, P. Reasonable Doubt
Friedman, R. Insurrection of Hippolytus Brandenburg
Frimmer, S. Dead Matter
Frost, B. all 4 titles
Fuller, R. Eve of Judgment
    Ordeal
Fuller, S. Dark Page
Fulton, C. Vidocq of New York
Fulton, E. 5 titles
Furst, A. Shadow Trade
Futrelle, J. Diamond Master
    Simple Case of Susan
Futrelle, M. Lieutenant What's-His-Name
Gage, N. Bones of Contention
Gallagher, G. I Found Him Dead
Gallagher, M. Quicksilver
Gallagher, R. Doomsday Committee
    One-Armed Murderer
    Stewardess Strangler
Gallant, G. S. Living Image
Gallico, P. Hand of Mary Constable
Galwey, R. C. Assignment New York

Gant, M. Queen Street
Gard, O. Seventh Chasm
Gardiner, D. What Crime Is It?
Garfield, B. Death Wish
Garrity. Dragon Hunt
Gartland, H. House of Cards
Garys, W. Detonator
Gatenby, R. Evil Is As Evil Does
Gates, H. L. Scarlet Fan
Gattzden, M. O.D. at Sweet Claude's
Gayle, N. Death in the Glass
Geller, M. 6 titles
George, D. R. Death Meets the Deadline
George, T. both titles
Gerrity, D. J. Numbers Man
    Plastic Man
Gibbs, A. Murder Between Drinks
Gibson, W. Mother Goose
    Quarter of Eight
    Voodoo Death
Giles, R. Shamus
Gillespie, R. 5 titles
Gillmore, R. Alster Case
    Ebony Bed Murder
Giniger, H. Rasons of the Heart
Gipe, G. Coney Island Quickstep
Gladstone, E. Taste of Deception
Glazner, J. M. Big Apple Money Is Rotten to the Core
Glick, C. Laughing Buddha
Gluck, S. 8 titles
Godey, J. 7 titles
Gold, D. Park
Goldman, W. Marathon Man
Goldsborough, R. 5 titles
Goldsmith, G. Murder on His Mind
Goldstein, A. D. Person Shouldn't Die Like That
Goldthwaite, E. K. Marble Forest
Gollin, J. Eliza's Galiardo
Gollomb, J. Curtain of Storm
    Portrait Invisible
    Subtle Trail
Goodis, D. Nightfall
Goodman, G. Killing in the Market
Goodrich, D. L. Paint Me a Million
Gordon, H. Dead on Arrival
Gordon, I. Burden of Guilt
Gordon, K. Jumpin' Jupiter
Gorman, E. Murder on the Aisle
Gould, H. Double Bang
    Fort Apache, the Bronx
    One Dead Debutante
Gould, J. Never Too Rich
Grace, A. Wharf Sinister
Grafton, S. Most Dangerous Game
Graham, J. A. Aldeburg Cezanne
    Something in the Air
Graham, Whidden. Crimson Hairs
Grandower, E. Rivergate House
Granovetter, M. both titles
Grant, M. 24 titles
Grayson, Rupert. Gun Cotton—Adventure Nine
Grecco, J. Manhattan Massacre
Green, A. K. 9 titles
Green, W. M. See How They Run
Greenan, R. H. Nightmare
Greenberg, D. Exes
    Love Kills
    Nanny
Gregory, F. L. Cipher of Death
Gregory, M. House on Carroll Street
Gresham, E. Pawn in Jeopardy
Grew, W. Doubles in Death
Grey, H. Portrait of a Mobster
Greig, M. Fire in His Hand
Griff. Brooklyn Moll Shoots Bedmate
    Demon Barber of Broadway
    Vice Queens on Broadway
Griswold, G. Checkmate by the Colonel
Gropper, M. H. Is No One Innocent?
Gross, K. Fine Line
Grove, M. You'll Die Tonight
Grove, W. Man Who Said No
Gruber, F. 6 titles

Settings Index   NEW YORK CITY / 1273

Guare, J. Landscape of the Body
Gunter, A. C. Dr. Burton's Success
Haddam, J. Not a Creature Was Stirring
Haggard, P. all 4 titles
Haiblum, I. Bad Neighbors
    Murder in Yiddish
Hailey, J. P. all 4 titles
Hall, G. Witch's Suckling
Hall, G. H. End Is Known
Hall, Parnell. 5 titles
Hallahan, W. H. Catch Me, Kill Me
    Dead of Winter
    Search for Joseph Tully
Halliday, B. Armed . . . Dangerous . . .
    She Woke to Darkness
Halliday, F. Ambler
    Chocolate Mousse Murders
Halpern, J. Jade Unicorn
Hamill, D. Machine
    Stomping Ground
Hamill, E. T. Child Killer
    Sadist
    Slasher
Hamill, P. Deadly Piece
    Guns of Heaven
Hammett, D. Thin Man
Hammock, C. S. Why Murder the Judge?
Hammond, C. So Violent My Love
Handler, D. Man Who Would Be F. Scott
    Fitzgerald
Handley, A. Kiss Your Elbow
Hannon, E. Doors
Harben, W. N. Caruthers Affair
Hardwick, R. Hawk
Haring, D. at least 234 titles
Harper, O. It's Never Too Late to Mend
Harragan, S. Sin Is a Redhead
Harrington, Joseph. all 3 titles
Harrington, Joyce. Dreemz of the Night
Harrington, W. Mister Target
Harris, C. A. Con Man
Harris, Colver. Hide and Go Seek
Harris, L. M. Protector
Harris, R. Honor Bound
Harrison, Bruce. A-100
Harrison, C. both titles
Harvey, J. N. By Reason of Insanity
Harvey, M. Clue of the Clock
    Dragon of Lung Wang
    House of Seclusion
    Mystery of the Hidden Room
Hastings, B. Don't Cry Little Girl
Hastings, George. Philip Henson M.D.
Hastings, W. S. Man in the Brown Derby
Hatvary, G. E. Suiter
Hauser, T. Agatha's Friends
    Beethoven Conspiracy
    Dear Hannah
Hausfeld, R. Big Kill
    Eddie Gorgon Calls the Tune
    Eddie Gorgon Takes the Rap
    One Step to Death
Hawkes, R. Kill for It
    NARC
Hawthorne, J. 5 titles
Hayes, J. Deep End
Hays, L. Once Upon a Time in America
Hazard, F. Hex Murder
Hazel, Henry. Three Golden Balls
Healy, E. P. both titles
Heard, H. F. Murder by Reflection
Hearn, D. Bad August
Hebach, L. Murder of Bishop Conrad
Heberden, M. V. 10 titles
Hecht, B. Count Bruga
    Florentine Dagger
    1001 Afternoons in New York
Heffernan, W. Broderick
    Ritual
    Toltec
Heller, L. Murder in Makeup
Hendricks, M. Money to Burn
Henriquez, R. A. Four Way Proof
Hentoff, N. both titles

Herrick, M. J. When Last Seen . . .
Hershman, M. Guilty Witness
Hervey, M. Brooklyn Angel
Herzog, D. Undercover Woman
Higginson, H. W. Bad Murder by the Arch
Highsmith, P. Blunderer
    Dog's Ransom
    Found in the Street
Hild, J. No Safe Place
Hillstrom, T. Riddle
Himes, C. all 9 titles
Hinkle, V. Murder After a Fashion
Hirschberg, C. Florentine Finish
Hirschfeld, B. Dreamers and Dealers
Hitchcock, A. Rope
Hitchens, D. Baxter Letters
Hjortsberg, W. Falling Angel
Hoch, E. D. Shattered Raven
Hochstein, P. Fatal Fetish
Hodgkin, M. R. Dead Indeed
Hoffecker, D. M. Wall Street Murders
Hogan, E. J. Tight Case
Hogarth, E. Goose Is Cooked
Holbrook, M. Suitable for Framing
Holden, R. P. Penthouse Murders
Holland, I. 7 titles
Hollander, L. Exhibit
Honig, D. Severith Style
Horan, J. D. New Vigilantes
Horansky, R. Dead Ahead
Hornblow, A. Argyle Case
    Profligate
Horovitz, I. Indian Wants the Bronx
Horvitz, L. Causes Unknown
    Compton Effect
Howard, Hampton. Friends, Russians, and
    Countryman
Howard, Hartley. at least 19 titles
Howe, J. M. Accessory for Murder
Hoyt, R. Cool Runnings
Huber, F. V. Apple Crunch
Hudiberg, E. Killer's game
Hudson, W. C. J. P. Dunbar
    Jack Gordon, Knight Errant, Gotham 1883
    Man with a Thumb
Hughes, D. B. 5 titles
Hughes, R. Ladies' Man
Hull, H. Close Her Pale Blue Eyes
Hunter, E. Big Fix
    Horse's Head
    Matter of Conviction
Hurley, G. Have You Seen This Man?
Hurwood, B. J. Rip-Off!
Hutton, W. R. Broadway Racket
Hynd, N. Sandler Inquiry
Iams, J. Death Draws the Line
    Into Thin Air
Iannuzzi, J. N. Courthouse
    Part 35
Irish, W. Deadline at Dawn
    Phantom Lady
Irwin, T. D. Collusion
Irwin, W. House of Mystery
    Red Button
Israel, Peter. If I Should Die Before I Die
    I'll Cry When I Kill You
Israel, Philip. Me and Brenda
Jacks, J. Murder on the Wild Side
Jackson, B. Operation Burning Candle
Jackson, Felix. So Help Me God
Jackson, G. Court of Shadows
Jacobs, H. Juror
Jaediker, K. Tall, Dark and Dead
Jaffe, M. Death Goes to a Party
Jaffe, S. Other Anne Fletcher
Jahn, M. Death Games
    Killer on the Heights
    Night Rituals
    Quark Maneuver
James, Robert. Death Wears Pink Shoes
Janifer, L. M. Final Fear
    You Can't Escape
Janson, H. This Woman Is Death
    When Dames Get Tough

Jarvis, F. G. Murder at the Met
Jason, P. Entangled
Jason, S. 6 titles
Jeffers, H. P. 5 titles
Jenkins, W. Man Who Feared
Jenks, G. C. Stop Thief!
Jerome, O. F. Corpse Awaits
    Murder As Usual
Jessup, H. W. Van Beck Will
Jessup, R. Lowdown
    Threat
Joey. Hit #29
John, A. Judas Voice
Johns, F. Square Emerald
Johns, V. P. Murder by the Day
    Servant's Problem
Johnson, K. Blue Sunshine
Johnson, O. Max Fargus
    Sixty-First Second
Johnson, Sandy. CUPPI
Johnston, J. Paint Her Face Dead
    Pray for Ricky Foster
Johnston, V. Face in the Shadows
    People on the Hill
    Stone Maiden
Johnston, W. 5 titles
Johnston, W. Barney
    Get Smart!
    Marriage Cage
Jones, C. R. King Murder
    Torch Murder
Jones, Craig. Too Late to Be Good
Jones, I. Clue of the Hungry Corpse
Jordan, E. After the Verdict
    Girl in the Mirror
    Night Club Mystery
Joshua, B. Drop of Murder
Judson, W. Alice and Me
Kahn, S. New York, N.Y.
Kamarck, L. Dinosaur
    Zinsser Implant
Kaminsky, S. M. Smart Moves
Kane. at least 5 titles
Kane, F. 22 titles
Kane, H. 42 titles
Kantor, Hal. Blown Away
Kantor, M. Signal Thirty-Two
Kaplan, A. Killing for Charity
Karney, J. at least 7 titles
Karp, D. Hardman
Kastle, H. Death Squad
Kastle, H. D. Countdown to Murder
    Hot Prowl
Katz, W. Open House
    Surprise Party
Kauffman, R. W. Share and Share Alike
    Spider's Web
Kaufman, W. I Hate Blondes
Kaye, M. 5 titles
Keene, D. Bye, Baby Bunting
    Mrs. Homicide
    Too Hot to Hold
Keith, C. Diamond-Studded Typewriter
Kelland, C. B. 6 titles
Keller, H. A. Death Sits In
Kelly, B. all 4 titles
Kelly, M. A. Park Lane South
Kendrick, B. 10 titles
Kennedy, M. It Began in New York
Kenrick, T. Blast
    Chicago Girl
    Nighttime Guy
    Two Lucky People
Kent, E. House Opposite
Keyes, E. Double Dare
Keystone, O. Arsenic for the Teacher
Kidde, J. Prophetess
Kieran, J. Come Murder Me
King, F. Down and Dirty
    Night Vision
    Sleeping Dogs Die
    Take the D Train
King, I. She's a Cop, Ain't She?
King, O. B. Five Million in Cash

N

King, R. Crime of Violence
  Holiday Homicide
  Murder by the Clock
Kingsley, S. Detective Story
Kirkwood, J. P.S. Your Cat Is Dead
Kittredge, R. Skylight
Klainer, J. A. Judas Gene
Klein, N. No! No! the Woman!
Klein, T. E. D. Nighttown
Klinger, H. Essence of Murder
  Murder Off Broadway
  Wanton for Murder
Knight, Adam. I'll Kill You Next!
  Murder for Madame
  Stone Cold Blonde
  Triple Slay
Knight, K. M. Exit a Star
Knight, W. E. Tiger Tame
Knister, B. Dating Service
Knott, F. Wait Until Dark
Koenig, J. Little Odessa
Koenig, L. Neighbor
  Rockabye
Kootz. both titles
Kotzwinkle, W. Midnight Examiner
Kramer, K. Kiss Me Quick
Kramer, Y. Primal Scene
Krasney, S. A. Death Cries in the Street
  Design for Dying
  Homicide Call
  Homicide West
Krone, C. Blood Wrath
Krumgold, J. Thanks to Murder
Kurnitz, H. Invasion of Privacy
Kuttner, P. Man Who Lost Everything
Kwitney, J. Shakedown
Kyle, R. Blackmail, Inc.
  Model for Murder
  Some Like It Cool
Lachman, C. In the Name of the Law
Lacy, E. at least 11 titles
Laflin, J. Spy Who Loved America
Lait, J. Beast of the City
  Gangster Girl
Lake, P. A. Leffert's Disease
Lamb, A. Greenhouse
Land, M. Last Flight
Landon, H. 9 titles
Lanham, E. 5 titles
Lantry, M. Assignment New York
Lariar, L. 5 titles
Larkin, R. T. Godmother
Larosa, L. J. Random Factor
Larsen, E. Not a Through Street
Latham, B. all 5 titles
Lathen, E. 6 titles
Lawrence, J. D. all 4 titles
Lawrence, J. I. Tower of Terror
Lawrence, Michael. Naked and Alone
Lawrence, S. Daughters of Music
Lawson, W. B. Jesse James at Coney Island
  Jesse James in New York
Lazarus, M. Neighborhood Watch
Lebhar, B. Black Eye Snapshot
Le Breton, A. Rififi in New York
Lee, Babs. Measured for Murder
  Model Is Murdered
Lee, G. R. G-String Murders
Lee, Jennette. Dead Right
  Green Jacket
Lee, Linda. One by One
Lee, Norma. Beautiful Gunner
  Broadway Jungle
  Lover—Say It with Mink!
Lees, H. Dark Device
Leffingwell, A. Nine Against New York
Leinster, M. Murder Will Out
L'Engle, M. Severed Wasp
Leonard, F. Box 100
Leonard, G. Beyond Control
Leuci, B. all 3 titles
Leverage, H. Whispering Wires
Levine, E. Double Jeopardy
Levine, Lawrence. New York One

Levinrew, W. Murder from the Grave
Levon, F. Much Ado About Murder
Lewerth, M. Stuyvesant Square
Lewis, Arthur Henry. Apaches of New York
  Boss, and How He Came to Rule New York
  Confessions of a Detective
Lewis, I. both titles
Lewis, Stephen. Monkey Rope
Lewis, T. Rooftops
Lewis, William. Gala
Lieberman, H. City of the Dead
  Nightbloom
  Shadow Dancers
Link, W. Prescription: Murder
Linzer, G. Troupe
Lipsky, E. Kiss of Death
  Murder One
  People Against O'Hara
Lipsyte, M. Hot Type
Little, C. Black Coat
  Black Curl
  Black House
  Black Shrouds
Livingston, A. Light Fingered Ladies
Livingston, Jack. Die Again, Macready
  Nightmare File
  Piece of the Silence
Lloyd, N. Robberies Co., Ltd.
Lobell, N. D. Shadow and the Blot
Lockridge, F. 30 titles
Lockridge, R. 14 titles
Logan, C. One of These Seven
Long, Manning. Dull Thud
  False Alarm
  Here's Blood in Your Eye
  Savage Breast
Longbaugh, H. No Way to Treat a Lady
Longo, L. Family on Vendetta Street
Lord, G. Murder's Little Helper
Lorens, M. K. Deception Island
  Ropedancer's Falle
Loring, A. Mark of Satan
Lourie, R. First Loyalty
Love, W. F. Chartreuse Clue
Luehrmann, A. Curious Case of Marie Dupont
  Other Brown
Lundy, M. Baby Farm
Lupica, M. all 3 titles
Luska, S. As It Was Written
Lustbader, E. V. Ninja
Lutz, J. Jericho Man
  Shadowtown
  SWF Seeks Same
Lynch, L. Danger Line
  Lost Witness
Lynds, D. Charlie Chan Returns
Lynn, J. Professor
Lyon, W. Criminal Court
Lyons, D. Flower of Evil
Lyons, N. President Is Coming to Lunch
McAlary, M. Buddy Boys
McBain, E. Another Part of the City
  Downtown
  Guns
McCloy, H. 8 titles
McConnor, V. Amadora
McCormack, T. Strictly Amateur
McCretton, M. Beauty Can Kill
McCully, W. Death Rides Tandem
McCurtin, P. 6 titles
McDonald, G. Safekeeping
MacDonald, J. D. Nightmare in Pink
MacDonald, P. Dark Wheel
MacDougald, R. Blushing Monkey
  Deaths of Lora Karen
  Whistling Legs
McDowell, E. Lost World
McDowell, M. Gilded Needles
  Katie
McDowell, R. Mercy Man
McFarlane, A. E. Behind the Bolted Door?
McGerr, P. Death in a Million Living Rooms
  Follow, As the Night
  Seven Deadly Sisters

McGill, G. Rough Cut
McGirr, E. Murderous Journey
McGivern, W. P. 5 titles
MacGrath, H. Drums of Jeopardy
  Green Stone
  World Outside
McGurk, S. Grand Central Murders
MacHarg, W. Affairs of O'Malley
McInerny, R. Noonday Devil
MacInnes, H. Neither Five Nor Three
McIntyre, J. T. In the Dead of Night
  Museum Murder
MacIsaac, F. Don't Let Him Burn!
  Hole in the Wall
  Murder C.O.D.
  Vanishing Professor
McIver, N. J. Assassin Prepares
  Come Back, Alice Smythereene!
McKenzie, D. J. Wall Street Wonder
McKinney, J. Kaduna Memories
McLaughlin, R. Nothing to Report
  Pending Investigation
McMahan, J. Footwork
McMorrow, T. both titles
McMullen, M. 6 titles
McRoyd, A. Double Shadow Murders
  Golden Goose Murders
MacVeigh, S. Grand Central Murder
Maas, P. Made in America
Macao, M. New York Necromancy
Madderom, G. Jewels That Got Away
Malcolm-Smith, G. If a Body Meet a Body
  Square Peg
Malina, F. Murder Over Broadway
Maling, A. Koberg Link
Malley, L. all 3 titles
Mallory, D. Target Manhattan
Mallory, R. Harlem Hit
Manchester, J. Run, Thief, Run!
Mancini, A. Minnie Santangelo and the Evil Eye
  Minnie Santangelo's Mortal Sin
  Yellow Gardenia
Mandeville, C. Last Days of New York
Manly, A. S. Secrets of a Dark Plot in New York Society
Manly, M. Old Specie, the Treasury Detective
Mann, P. Dog Day Afternoon
Manners, D. X. Dead to the World
Manson, W. Duke
Maracotta, L. Hide-and-Seek
Marasco, R. Burnt Offerings
Marcus, A. A. Make Way for Murder
Mardon, D. In for a Penny
Marfield, D. Man with a Paper Skull
  Mystery of King Cobra
  Mystery of the East Wind
  Sword in the Pool
Mario, Q. Murder in the Opera House
  Murder Meets Mephisto
Markson, D. Epitaph for a Dead Beat
  Epitaph for a Tramp
Marlowe, D. J. 6 titles
Marlowe, D. Catch the Brass Ring
  Model for Murder
  Turn Left for Murder
Marmor, A. both titles
Maron, M. 6 titles
Marsh, P. Devil's Daughter
Marshall, William. New York Detective
Marsten, R. Big Man
  Runaway Black
Martin, I. K. Regan and the Manhattan File
Martyn, W. Anthony Trent, Master Criminal
  Recluse of Fifth Avenue
  Triumphant Prodigal
Mason, Clifford. all 3 titles
Massey, M. Through the Lens
Masters, J. D. 6 titles
Masur, H. Q. 13 titles
Matera, L. Hidden Agenda
Matheson, R. Fury on Sunday
Mathewson, Joseph. both titles
Matteson, S. Murder at the Spa
Matthews, B. Last Meeting

Settings Index

NEW YORK CITY / 1275

Matthews, Clyde. Ides of March Conspiracy
Matthews, J. B. Indictment
Maurice, A. B. Riddle of the Rovers
Maxim, J. Abel/Baker/Charley
Maxwell, M. Ernest Gray
Maxwell, T. Kiss Me Once
    Saberdene Variations
Mayo, D. Murder at the Big Store
Mearson, L. all 3 titles
Merrick, Mark. Great Travers Case
Merrick, Mollie. Upper Case
Merritt, A. Creep, Shadow!
    Seven Footprints to Satan
Merwin, S., Jr. Death in the Sunday Supplements
    Matter of Policy
    Message from a Corpse
    Murder in Miniatures
Messmann, J. Jogger's Moon
    Promise for Death
    Revenger
    Stiletto Signature
Meyers, Annette. Big Killing
    Tender Death
Meyers, Martin. Kiss and Kill
    Reunion for Death
Meyers, Manny. Last Mystery of Edgar Allan Poe
Michaels, A. Diamonds
Michaels, P. Come, Follow Me
Michel, M. S. Psychiatric Murders
    Sweet Murder
    X-Ray Murders
Miller, A. Colfax Book-Plate
Miller, B. E. Death Deal
    Set-Up
Miller, F. C. Savage Street
Miller, Judi. Catch Me If You Can
    I'll Be Wearing a White Carnation
    Phantom of the Soap Opera
    Save the Last Dance for Me
Miller, V. Fernanda
Miller, V. B. all 9 titles
Mills, James. One Just Man
    Panic in Needle Park
    Prosecutor
    Seventh Power
Milton, David. Hyte Maneuver
Minahan, J. 5 titles
Minick, M. Kung Fu Avengers
Minton, P. Dark of Memory
Mitchell, D. L. In Times Square
Mitchell, L. Parachute Murder
Mitchell, W. Goldfish Murders
Mochan, B. Brass Knuckles
Monsky, M. Looking Out for #1
Montague, J. Whose Millions?
Moore, H. F. S. Death at 7:10
Moore, Robin. Set-Up
Moran, C. Killer's Caress
Morette, E. Sturgis Wager
Morgan, Dean. Murder on Coney Island
Morgan, W. L. Ice Man
Morley, C. Haunted Bookshop
Moroso, J. A. People Against Nancy Preston
Morris, C. Pinkerton Ferret
Morris, Jim. Spurlock: Sheriff of Purgatory
Morrow, S. Dancing with a Tiger
Morton, G. Perrin Murder Case
Morton, W. Murderer
    Mystery of the Human Bookcase
Mulkeen, T. P. both titles
Mullen, C. Thereby Hangs a Corpse
Mumford, E. W. Out of the Ashes
Murari, T. N. Shooter
Murphy, Dallas. Lover Man
Murphy, Haughton. 5 titles
Murphy, W. B. 12 titles
Naha, E. Con Game
Napier, G. Dear Hungarian Friend
Neely, R. five titles
Neiderman, A. Devil's Advocate
Nemec, D. Mad Blood
Nevins, F. N. 120-Hour Clock
Newell, A. Who Killed Cavelotti?

Newman, C. Knock-Off
    Midtown South
    Sixth Precinct
Newman, G. F. Guvnor
    Men with the Guns
Newman, O. Unmasking a King
Niall, M. Run Like a Thief
Nichols, F. Angel Face
    Loner
Nickolay, M. Brother and Sister
Nicolai, C. Killer Is Loose
Nicole, M. Code Name: Love
Nicolet, C. C. Death of a Bridge Expert
Nile, D. Evil Men Do
Nisot, E. Sleepless Men
Noel, S. Empire of Evil
Nolan, F. Kill Petrosino!
Norden, E. Ultimate Solution
Novak, R. all 3 titles
Nusser, R. Walking After Midnight
Nyland, G. Mr. South Burned His Mouth
Oakroyd, S. Maybe He's Dead
OCork, S. Hell Bent for Heaven
    Murder of Muriel Lake
O'Dell, J. W. Loan Shark
Odlum, J. Morgue Is Always Open
O'Donnell, L. 19 titles
O'Farrell, W. 6 titles
O'Hanlon, J. D. Murder at Coney Island
O'Higgins, H. J. Adventures of Detective Barney
    Detective Duff Unravels It
Old Sleuth. at least 16 titles
Olden, M. Giri
    Gossip
    Informant
    Poe Must Die
Olesker, H. all 3 titles
Oppenheim, E. P. Other Romilly
Orde, L. Night They Stole Manhattan
    Tiger's Claw
Orenstein, F. both titles
Ormond, F. Three Keys
Osborn, J. J. Man Who Owned New York
Osborne, W. H. all 5 titles
Osbourne, L. Peril
Oster, J. 5 titles
Ostrander, I. 8 titles
Ostrander, K. Image Seller
Ottolengui, R. Artist in Crime
    Crime of the Century
    Final Proof
Ottum, R. both titles
Oursler, W. Departure Delayed
    Folio on Florence White
    Trial of Vincent Doon
Packard, F. 11 titles
Packer, V. Thrill Kids
    Young and Violent
Padgett, L. Day He Died
Page, M. Fast Company
    Shadowy Third
Page, S. Legend in Blue Steel
Page, S. H. Fool's Gold
    Sinister Cargo
    Tragic Curtain
Pahlow, G. Somebody Shot the Captain
Paley, F. Rumble on the Docks
Palmer, P. Murder from Heaven
Palmer, S. 8 titles
Panati, C. Pleasuring of Rory Malone
Panbourne, O. Varanoff Tradition
Papazoglou, O. Death's Savage Passion
    Sweet, Savage Death
    Wicked, Loving Murder
Paradise, V. Girl Died Laughing
Paris, M. Mystery
Parke, F. G. First Night Murder
Parker, M. Along Came a Spider
Pastor, T. Night Scenes in New York
Patrick, Q. Danger Next Door
    Death for Dear Clara
Patrick, Vincent. both titles
Patterson, I. Standish Gaunt Case

Patterson, J. Midnight Club
Patterson, R. N. Escape the Night
Paul, B. 9 titles
Paul, R. Bond Street Burlesque
    Thomas Street Horror
Pearl, J. Lepke
    Victims
Peckham, R. Murder in Strange Houses
Peebles, N. N. both titles
Pele. World Cup Murder
Pender, L. Deja Vu
Pendleton, D. 6 titles
Penn, Steele. Clerk Barton's Crime
Pentecost, H. 40 titles
Percy, C. Death Is Skin Deep
Perrin, F. V. Don
Perry, M. Final Cut
Perry, W. Home in the Dark
    Kremlin Watcher
    Murder at the U.N.
Peters, E. Die for Love
Peters, R. both titles
Peters, S. Park Is Mine
Peterson, Keith. Rain
    Rough Justice
    There Fell a Shadow
Philbin, T. 7 titles
Philips, J. 13 titles
Phillips, C. B. Someone Killed Her Husband
Phillips, D. G. Master Rogue
Phillips, J. A. Case of the Shivering Chorus Girls
Phillips, M. Impossibles
Phillips, Steven. Resisting Arrest
Picano, F. Lure
Pierce, N. Messenger from Munich
Piesman, M. Unorthodox Practices
Pike, R. L. Mute Witness
    Police Blotter
    Quarry
Pines, P. Tin Angel
Piper, E. 5 titles
Pitman, W. D. Quincunx Case
Pitts, D. This City Is Ours
Platt, K. Dead As They Come
Platt, R. Swaying Corpse
Poate, E. M. Behind Locked Doors
    Doctor Bentiron: Detective
Pollack, R. Episode
Pollitz, E. A. Empire State
Popkin, Z. Death of Innocence
    Death Wears a White Gardenia
    No Crime for a Lady
    Time Off for Murder
Porcelain, S. E. Purple Pony Murders
Posner, R. Mafia Man
    Seven-Ups
Post, M. D. Corrector of Destinies
Potts, J. 7 titles
Powers, E. both titles
Poynter, B. Murder on 47th Street
    Murillo Mystery
Probst, M. Winter Losses
Procter, A. Murder in Manhattan
Pronzini, B. Eye
    Fan
Prosper, J. Gold-Killer
Purtell, J. Tiffany Caper
Quarry, N. 6 titles
Quartermain, J. Rock of Diamond
Queen, E. 26 titles
Quentin, P. 7 titles
Quinn, J. all 3 titles
Quint, N. American Spy Story
Rae, C. M. Sarah Cobb
Rafferty, S. S. Die Laughing
Raines, J. Unbalanced Acts
Rainey, R. Porn Tapes
    Venus Underground
Raison, M. M. Phantom of Forty-Second Street
Ralston, G. A. Deadly, Deadly Art
Ramm, C. Deadly in New York
Ramsay, D. Descent Into the Dark
    Four Steps to Death
    Little Murder Music

N

Rand, Steve. All Her Vices
Randall, B. Fan
    Last Man on the List
Randall, J. Broadway Bounty
Randall, W. R. Crystal Eye
Randisi, R. J. 5 titles
Ransome, S. Death Checks In
Raskin, E. Tattooed Potato
Rathbone, C. K. both titles
Rathbone, S. Miss Pauline of New York
Rauch, C. Spy on Riverside Drive
Ravel, J. Lady Cop
Rawlings, F. Lisping Man
Rawls, P. Streets of Blood
Rawson, C. Death from a Top Hat
    Footprints on the Ceiling
    Great Merlini
Reach, J. Late Last Night
    Danger—Girls Working!
Reardon, J. Big Time Tommy Sloan
Reed, W. Motive for Murder
    Time to Kill
Reeve, A. B. 17 titles
Reeves, Robert. Dead and Done For
Reilly, H. 16 titles
Reiss, B. Summer Fires
Reno, M. R. Final Proof
Resnicow, H. 6 titles
Reuben, S. Julian Solo
Rice, C. Having Wonderful Crime
    Sunday Pigeon Murders
Richards, A. To Market, to Market
Richards, C. Death of an Angel
Rickett, F. Stalked
Riddell, G. Murder with Music
Riddell, J. John Riddell Murder Case
Ridgway, J. Adam's Fall
Riefe, A. Conspirators
    Lady Killers
Rieman, T. Vamp Till Ready
Riess, C. High Stakes
Rifkin, S. Ladyfingers
    McQuaid in August
Rigsby, H. Clash of Shadows
Ring, A. Killers Play Tough
Rivers, G. Killing House
Robbins, T. Master of Murder
Roberts, P. Tender Prey
Roberts, W. A. Mind Reader
    Top-Floor Killer
Robertson, Alexander. Irish Monte Cristo's Search
    Old Specie, the Treasury Detective
Robeson, K. 35 titles
Robins, E. Secret That Was Kept
Robinson, A. Dick and Jane
Robinson, E. H. Scarred Hand
Robinson, L. R. Blood Run
Roche, A. S. at least 13 titles
Rockwood, H. Harry Sharpe, the New York Detective
    Neil Nelson, the Veteran Detective
Roeburt, J. 9 titles
Rogers, J. T. Once in a Red Moon
Rohde, R. H. Hunted Down
Rohde, W. L. Heel
Rohmer, S. 5 titles
Ronald, J. She Got What She Asked For
Ronns, E. Art Studio Murders
    Death in a Lighthouse
    Glass Cage
    No Place to Live
Roos, K. 13 titles
Root, P. Devil on the Stairs
Roote, M. Badge 373
Rosen, R. Saturday Night Dead
Rosen, V. Gun in His Hand
Rosenbaum, R. Murder at Elaine's
Rosenberg, P. Contact on Cherry Street
    Point Blank
Rosenberg, S. N. Brenda Maneuver
Rosenberger, J. Blueprint Invisibility
    Manhattan Wipeout
    Operation Overkill
Rosenfeld, A. Trigger Man

Ross, Albert. If I Knew What I Was Doing
Ross, Barnaby. Drury Lane's Last Case
    Tragedy of X
    Tragedy of Y
Ross, Bradley. Soft Touch
Ross, C. Voice from the Grave
Ross, I. T. all 5 titles
Rossi, B. Head Crusher
    Triggerman
Rosten, L. Silky!
Roth, H. Button, Button
    Crimson in the Purple
    Mask of Glass
    Sleeper
Rowe, A. Deadly Intent
    Too Much Poison
Rowland, H. C. Return of Frank Clamart
Royal, M. House of Mystery
Ruhen, C. Violent Ones
Russell, R. Reunion
Rutledge, N. Cry Murder
    Emily Will Know
Rutman, L. Clash of Eagles
Sachs, E. N. Octangle
Sackett, S. Emerald Angel
Sadler, M. Touch of Death
Sadlier, A. T. Phileas Fox, Attorney
Sagola, M. J. both titles
Saint, H. F. Memoirs of an Invisible Man
St. Dennis, M. both titles
Saks, E. E. Innocents on Broadway
Salter, M. Cat's-Paw
Sanborn, B. X. Doom-Maker
Sanders, D. To Catch a Thief
Sanders, Lawrence. 11 titles
Sanders, Leonard. Act of War
Sandroff, R. Fighting Back
Sann, P. Dead Heat
Santiago, S. Undercover
Santiago, V. J. Eye for an Eye
Santini, R. Disenchanted Diva
    Swell Style of Murder
Saperstein, D. Fatal Reunion
Sapir, R. Bressio
    Mugger Blood
    Quest
Sargent, P. Black Valentine
Sarto, B. Bowery Birdie
    Manhattan Terrors
Saunders, C. C. Design for Treachery
Saunders, L. Columnist Murder
Sauter, E. Predators
Savage, R. H. Checked Through, Missing Trunk No. 17580
Scaduto, A. Terrible Time to Die
Scaparro, J. Worst Enemies
Scarborough, C. Stryker
Scarpetta, F. Times Square Connection
Scherf, M. 6 titles
Schisgall, O. Devil's Daughter
Schley, S. M. Who'd Shoot a Genius?
Schneider, J. A. Stryker's Children
Schoenfeld, H. Let Them Eat Bullets
Schor, A. Line by Line
Schulman, S. After Delores
    People in Trouble
Schwartz, A. Blowtop
Schwarz, B. Ransom for Miss LeGrun
Scott, J. Normandie Triangle
    Rampage
    Treasure for Treasure
Scott, L. 5 titles
Scott, Mansfield. Black Circle
Scott, R. T. M. 8 titles
Scott-Heron, G. Vulture
Seabrooke, J. P. Woman in 919
Seaver, T. Beanball
Seligson, T. Kidd
Sellars, E. K. Murder a la Mode
Selman, R. Once Upon a Crime
Seton, A. Dragonwyck
Shane, S. Lady in a Million
    Lady in Lilac
Shannon, Doris. Family Money

Shannon, J. Devil's Passkey
Shapiro, H. Murder in Soho
Shapiro, W. F. Eddie Black
Sharkey, J. both titles
Sharp, W. Murder of the Honest Broker
Shaw, J. T. Blood on the Curb
Shay, F. Charming Murder
Sheehan, P. P. House with a Bad Name
Sheldon, S. Naked Face
    Rage of Angels
Shenkin, E. Brownstone Gothic
Sher, J. Cold Companion
Sherburne, J. Death's Clenched Fist
Sheridan, J. Chinese Chop
Sherlock, J. State of Emergency
Sherrill, K. Midnight Lightning
Sherry, E. 6 titles
Shiffrin, A. B. Twilight Walk
Short, C. Big Cat
Siddall, R. B. Travers
Sideman, A. Murder on Both Sides
Siegel, J. Ruby
Silber, D. Confessions
Silberstang, E. Losers, Weepers
Siller, V. It Had to Be You
    Paul's Apartment
    Watchers
Simenon, G. Maigret in New York's Underworld
Simmons, M. K. Girl with the Key
Simon, L. Irving Solution
Simon, R. A. Weekend Mystery
Slattery, K. Broadway Lady
    Night Was a Lady Crying
    No Caution for Caroline
    You Can't Bring 'Em Back
Slavitt, D. R. Agent
Slesar, H. Enter Murderers
    Grey Flannel Shroud
    Thing at the Door
Sloane, Ben. both titles
Smiley, J. Duplicate Keys
Smith, Dennis. Glitter and Ash
Smith, E. E. Miss Melville Regrets
    Miss Melville's Revenge
Smith, F. Broadcast Murders
Smith, J. C. S. both titles
Smith, K. N. Catching Fire
    Elegy for a Soprano
    Watcher
Smith, L. D. Girl Hunt
Smith, Martin. Canto for a Gypsy
Smith, Mitchell. Daydreams
Smith, W. K. Bowery Murder
Smith, Y. Banana Murders
Smithies, R. H. R. Academic Question
Snell, D. Lights, Camera . . . Murder
Snow, K. Night Waking
Snow, W. Golden Nightmare
Solomita, S. Force of Nature
    Forced Entry
    Twist of the Knife
Somerville, C. Artist in Crime
Somerville, I. Scattered Death
Sommers, B. Hold Back the Night
Sorrele, R. Kiss/Kill
Spatz, H. D. Death on the Nose
Spewack, S. Skyscraper Murder
Spillane, M. 18 titles
Sprechman, J. R. Caribe
Springs, J. Kansas
Sproul, K. Birthday Murder
Squerent, W. Your Golden Jugular
Stade, G. Confessions of a Lady Killer
Stagg, C. H. Silver Sandals
    Thornley Colton, Blind Detective
Stanley, F. G. Murder Leaves a Ring
Stanley, O. Legal Fire
Stark, M. Run for Your Life!
Stark, R. Black Ice Score
    Hunter
Stark, S. Too Many Sinners
Stashower, D. Elephants in the Distance
Sted, R. They All Bleed Red
Steel, K. 5 titles

Settings Index

NEW YORK CITY

Steele, C. Invisible Empire
    March of the Flame Marauders
    Masked Invasion
Steele, J. House of Iron Men
Steeley, R. D. Hot Ice
Stein, A. M. Lock and Key
    Pistols for Two
Stephens, R. N. Mystery of Murray Davenport
Sterling, S. 17 titles
Sterling, T. House Without a Door
Stern, R. M. Tower
Stevens, S. Go Down Dead
    Rat Pack
Stevenson, B. E. 5 titles
Stewart, E. Heads
    Privileged Lives
Stewart, F. M. Mephisto Waltz
Stewart, F. S. Crippled Hand
Stewart, J. Boudoirs Are My Beat
Stewart, R. Apparition
    Possession of Joel Delaney
    Sixth Sense
Stinson, H. Fingerprints
Stivers, D. Hard Kill
    Tower of Terror
Stockbridge, G. 5 titles
Stockwell, G. Candy Killings
    Embarrassed Murderer
Stokes, M. L. Case of the President's Heads
    Lady Lost Her Head
Stone, Hampton. 17 titles
Stout, R. 44 titles
Stovall, W. Minus Pool
Stowell, W. A. Marston Murder Case
    Mystery of the Singing Walls
Strange, J. S. 10 titles
Stratton, R. Smack Goddess
Streiber, W. Wolfen
Stringer, A. at least 7 titles
Strong, Harrington. Brand of Silence
Stoud, C. Close Pursuit
    Sniper's Moon
Stryker, H. NYPD 2025
Stuart, Anthony. Force Play
Stuart, W. L. Dead Lie Still
    Night Cry
Sudak, E. Icepick in Ollie Birk
Sugar, A. Kill City
Suyker, B. Death Scene
Swaim, D. H. L. Mencken Murder Case
Tanenbaum, R. K. Depraved Indifference
    No Lesser Plea
Tarkenton, F. Murder at the Super Bowl
Taubes, F. Run . . . Run . . . Run
Taylor, Matt. Famous McGarry Stories
Teagle, M. both titles
Telfair, R. Corpse That Talked
Templeton, C. Act of God
    Kidnapping of the President
Terrall, R. They Deal in Death
Texier, C. Panic Blood
Thatcher, J. Nightgleams
Thayer, L. 11 titles
Thayer, T. Illustrious Corpse
Thomas, A. E. Double Cross
Thomas, E. Death Rides the Dragon
    Yellow Magic
Thomas, Jim. Cross Purposes
Thompson, J. Child of Rage
Thompson, V. Green Ray
Thurman, S. "Mad Dog" Coll
Tidyman, E. Shaft
    Shaft Among the Jews
Tine, R. Midnight City
Toepfer, R. G. Endplay
Topor, T. Bloodstar
    Coda
Torbett, D. Kick-In
    On Trial
Torgerson, E. D. Cold Finger Curse
Torres, E. Carlito's Way
    Q & A
Tosches, N. Cut Numbers
Towne, S. Death Out of Thin Air

Tracy, L. Bartlett Mystery
    House of Peril
Tracy, V. Moment After
    Personal Appearance of a Lioness
Train, A. at least 10 titles
Traubel, H. Metropolitan Opera Murders
Travis, Grethen. She Fell Among Thieves
Treat, L. 5 titles
Tree, G. Case Against Butterfly
    Case Against Myself
Trevor, E. Penthouse
Trigoboff, J. Bone Orchard
Trotta, G. Veronica Died Monday
Tuccille, J. Wall Street Blues
Tucker, J. B. He's Dead—She's Dead: Details at
    Eleven
    Man Who Looked Like Howard Cosell
Turnbull, M. Rogues' March
Tyger, T. Hellfire
Uccello, L. Death of a Renaissance Man
Uhnak, D. 7 titles
Ullman, A. Sorry, Wrong Number
Upton, P. Satan's Sabbath
Upton, R. Killing in Real Estate
Vachss, A. H. Blue Belle
    Flood
    Hard Candy
    Strega
Valdez, P. Satan's Sabbath
Vanardy, V. 5 titles
Van Atta, W. Adam Sleep
Vance, L. J. at least 11 titles
Van de Water, F. F. Hidden Ways
    Plunder
Van Dine, S. S. 11 titles
Van Urk, V. both titles
Veiller, B. Bait for a Tiger
    Trial of Mary Dugan
Veley, C. Night Whispers
Venning, M. Jethro Hammer
    Murder Through the Looking Glass
Violett, E. Double Take
Waddell, C. C. Juror No. 17
    Midnight to High Noon
Wager, W. 58 Minutes
    Otto's Boy
Walk, C. E. Time Lock
Walker, Gerald. Cruising
Wall, D. C. One Cried Murder
Wallace, A. Passion Pulls the Trigger
Wallace, F Little Hercules
Wallace, I. Almighty
Wallace, R. 11 titles
Wallis, J. H. 5 titles
Walsh, P.E. Murder Room
Walsh, T. 8 titles
Ward, E. Five for Bridge
Ward, Harold. "Vulture" Strikes
Ward, R. Sandman
Warren, P. Nurse at Brooding Mansion
Warren, V. Brandon in New York
    By Fair Means or Foul
Watson, Clarissa. Fourth Stage of Gainsborough
    Brown
Waugh, H. 6 titles
Webster, H. K. Ghost Girl
    Whispering Man
Weil, J. Real Cool Cat
Weill, G. Woman's Eyes
Wein, J. Roommate
Wein, L. Mayhem in Manhattan
Weiner, H. Crime on the Cuff
Weinman, I. Tailor's Dummy
    Virgil's Ghost
Weinstein, H. East Coast Crisis
Weir, H. C. Miss Madelyn Mack, Detective
Wellard, J. Moment in Time
Wells, A. M. Murderer's Choice
    Sin of Angels
    Talent for Murder
Wells, Carolyn. 23 titles
West, J. B. Bullets Are My Business
    Eye for an Eye
    Never Kill a Cop
    Taste for Blood

West, R. F. Crystal Clear
Westlake, D. E. 16 titles
Wheat, C. Dead Man's Thoughts
    Where Nobody Dies
Wheelock, D. Dead Giveaway
White, G. M. Fast Life in New York
    New York by Night
White, L. 10 titles
White, M. Out of the Night
White, S. E. Sign at Six
White, Teri. Max Trueblood and the Jersey
    Desperado
Whitney, P. A. Quicksilver Pool
    Window on the Square
Whitney, S. Singled Out
Wilcox, C. McCloud
    New Mexico Connection
Wilkinson, Sandra. Brain Death
Williams, Alan. Room Service
Williams, Alexander. Death Over Newark
    Murder in the WPA
Williams, Henry. How to Murder Your Wife
Williams, H. L. Steel Safe
Williams, H. S. Witness of the Sun
Williams, J. B. Leaves from the Notebook of a New
    York Detective
    Secret Compact
Williams, Peter. Appointment at Midnight
    So Long, My Lady
Williams, S. In the Tenth Moon
Williamson, C. N. Lord John in New York
Wills, T. You'll Get Yours
Wilmot, R. P. Blood in Your Eye
    Murder on Monday
Wilson, David. Corpse Maker
    Killing
Wilson, Gahan. Everybody's Favorite Duck
Wilson, M. A. Footsteps Behind Her
    Stalk the Hunter
Wiltse, D. Fifth Angel
    Serpent
Winchester, J. Solitary Man
Winder, R. No Admission
Winslow, P. G. Rockefeller Gift
Wise, A. Blood-Red Rose
Wiser, H. F. Deadly Stakes
Wishman, S. Nothing Personal
Wohl, J. P. Nirvana Contracts
Wolfe, C. Murder at La Marimba
Wolfe, L. Wasted
Wolff, W. A. Manhattan Night
    Trial of Mary Dugan
Wolfson, M. Silk and Sin
Wolfson, P. J. Bodies Are Dust
Wolk, G. Man Who Dealt in Blood
Wolk, M. Beast on Broadway
    Big Picture
Womack, J. Ambient
Wood, B. Killing Gift
Wood, W. Secret Paper
Woodrow, W. Burned Evidence
    Pawns of Murder
Woodward, H. both titles
Woolfolk, W. Naked Hunter
    Run While You Can
Woolrich, C. Black Angel
    Bride Wore Black
Wormser, R. Communist's Corpse
    Man with the Wax Face
Worth, C. Corpse That Knew Everybody
Worts, G. E. Dangerous Young Man
Wright, Jim. Last Frame
Wright, R. Disappearance of Kimball Webb
Wright, W. Blonde Target
Wylie, P. Savage Gentleman
Xantippe. Death Catches Up with Mr. Kluck
Yaffe, J. Nothing But the Night
Yates, G. W. There Was a Crooked Man
Yates, M. Death Casts a Vote
Yates, P. Death Comes to Dinner
    Death in the Hands of Talent
    Dress Circle Murders
Yglesias, R. Murderer Next Door
Yorck, R. L. So Cold the Night
Young, R. E. Murder at Mansions

N

Yudkoff, A. Circumstances Beyond Control
Zeiger, A. Serenade for a Shylock
Ziran, G. Counsellor
Zore, H. Alibi Off Broadway
Zuckerman, A. Tiger Kittens

NEW YORK STATE (N.Y. See also: Long Island; New York City; Rochester)
Alcott, C. Dungeons of Crowley Hall
Alexander, Jan. Second House
Allen, E. O. Hounds of the Moon
Alverson, C. Fighting Back
Ard, W. Like Ice She Was
Armstrong, C. Black-Eyed Stranger
    Innocent Flower
Austin, H. It Couldn't Be Murder
    Murder in Triplicate
    Murder of a Matriarch
Avallone, M. Fallen Angel
Bacheller, I. A. House of the Three Ganders
Bagby, G. My Dead Body
    Ring Around a Murder
Ballard, K. G. Bar Sinister
Bank, L. H. 17 Farrington Way
Barrington, M. Stop on the Green Light!
Barth, R. Furnished for Murder
Beam, M. Murder in a Shell
Benchley, N. Catch a Falling Spy
Bennett, Jay. Death Is a Silent Room
Biggers, E. D. Seven Keys to Baldpate
Blochman, L. G. Rather Cool for Mayhem
Block, L. Girl with the Long Green Heart
Blumberg, G. Hit Woman
Bond, E. Clouded Mirror
Booton, K. Troubled House
Borgenicht, M. Margin for Doubt
    Tomorrow Trap
    True or False
Brand, M. Granduca
Branson, H. C. Case of the Giant Killer
    Fearful Passage
Broun, D. From 9 O'Clock to Jamaica Bay
Brown, Carter. Had I But Groaned
Browne, H. Thin Air
Bunn, T. Closet Bones
Camp, Wadsworth. Gray Mask
Campbell, J. Homing
Carlson, P. M. Audition for Murder
    Murder Is Academic
    Murder Misread
Carr, J. D. Panic in Box C
Carter, Nick. Weapon of Night
Carter, N. V. Mooncalf Murders
Cartrell, P. Sin of Sister Betty
Chadwick, C. Cactus
Chambers, D. Death Against Venus
    Rope for an Ape
Chambers, R. W. Flaming Jewel
Cherkas, M. Secret Affairs
Chesbro, G. Language of Cannibals
Chichester, J. J. King of Diamonds
    Rogues of Fortune
Chimenti, F. Silent Room
Chipperfield, R. O. Above Suspicion
    Man in the Jury Box
    Unseen Hand
Coe, T. Wax Apple
Collins, Michael. Walk a Black Wind
Collins, Michelle. both titles
Collins, M. A. Nice Weekend for Murder
Collison, W. Red-Haired Alibi
Connors, B. F. Dancehall
Cooper, J. F. Ways of the Hour
Corby, J. As Deadly Does
    Riverwood
Corren, G. Place on Dark Island
Costello, M. J. Midsummer
    Sleep Tight
Coxe, G. H. Groom Lay Dead
Coyne, J. Hunting Season
Craig, Jonathan. So Young, So Wicked
Crane, C. 6 titles
Cross, A. James Joyce Murder
Crow, C. P. No More Monday Mornings

Cushman, C. F. I Wanted to Murder
Cutler, R. Medusa Syndrome
Cutter, J. Psycho Soldiers
Dalton, P. Darkening Willows
Daly, E. Death and Letters
    Night Walk
    Nothing Can Rescue Me
Daniels, D. at least 18 titles
Daniels, Paul. Motel Girl
Davis, Christopher. Dog Horse Rat
Davis, D. S. Black Sheep, White Lamb
Davis, F. C. High Heel Homicide
Davis, M. Voice on the Telephone
Davis, T. Terror on Compass Lake
Deal, B. H. Waiting to Hear from William
Dean, A. 14 titles
Dean, G. Murder on Stilts
DeAndrea, W. L. Azreal
    Hog Murders
    Killed on the Rocks
    Killed with a Passion
Debrett, H. Lonly Way to Die
Delman, D. Death of a Nymph
    Sudden Death
Deming, R. Hit and Run
Dickson, Carter. Graveyard to Let
Disney, D. M. Hospitality of the House
Dobner, M. Gingerbread House
    Heather
Dobyns, S. 6 titles
Dorf, F. Reasonable Madness
Dougall, B. Singing Corpse
Drachman, T. S. Reason for Madness
    Something for the Birds
DuBois, T. 5 titles
Dudgeon, R. Murder—So What!
Duncombe, F. Death of a Spinster
Dunn, J. A. Death Gamble
Dutton, C. J. Crooked Cross
    Out of the Darkness
Eberhard, F. G. Super-Gangster
Eberhart, M. G. Alpine Condo Crossfire
    Another Woman's House
    Danger Money
    Unknown Quantity
Ehlrich, J. Cry, Baby
    Slow Burn
Einstein, C. No Time at All
Eliot, A. Dark Beneath the Pines
Ellin, S. Stronghold
Ellis, K. M. Dolores Divine, Guilty or Innocent?
England, G. A. Alibi
Fagan, N. both titles
Farris, J. Captors
Fenisong, R. Snare for Sinners
Fenwick, E. Passenger
    Silent Cousin
Ferguson, W. B. M. Black Company
    Riddle of the Rose
Ferm, B. False Idols
Fischer, B. 8 titles
Fish, R. L. Handy Death
Fisher, D. Variations on a Theme
Fisher, S. Night Before Murder
Fitzsimmons, C. Bainbridge Murder
Fleming, I. Spy Who Loved Me
Fletcher, Dorothy. Brand Inheritance
Foley, R. Ape in Velvet
    Hundredth Door
    Man in Shadow
Footner, H. House with the Blue Door
Foster, M. Trap
Fox, D. Doom Dealer
Fox, G. F. One Wife's Ways
    Witness This Woman
Freytag, J. Amber Palace
Frost, W. A. Marworth Mystery
Fuller, T. This Is Murder, Mr. Jones
Fulton, E. Fatal Flashback
Gallagher, G. Chord in Crimson
Gatenby, R. Deadly Relations
    Season of Danger
Gearon, J. Velvet Well
Gibbs, G. F. Triangle Man

Gilbert, N. R. Affair at Pine Court
Giles, G. E. 3 Died Variously
Gill, J. Dead of Summer
Gillespie, R. Little Sally Does It Again
Gilman, D. Nun in the Closet
Gluck, S. Blind Fury
Godey, J. Gun and Mr. Smith
Goldfluss, H. E. Judgment
Goldsmith, M. M. Double Jeopardy
Goldthwaite, E. K. Don't Mention My Name
Gordon, K. Bride's Bouquet
Grace, Alicia. Head of Medusa
Grady, F. P. Sergeant Death
Green, A. K. 9 titles
Gresham, E. Puzzle in Parquet
Grey, D. Tracking of K.K.
Gruber, F. Talking Clock
Hall, Stephanie. Whisper in the Dark
Harding, W. H. Rainbow
Haring, D. at least 14 titles
Haring, F. Greek Revival
Harper, D. Hanged Men
Hart, F. N. Bellamy Trial
Hastings, B. Don't Walk Home Alone
Hayes, Ralph. Deadly Prey
Heald, A. Shadow Under White Face
Heberden, M. V. Lobster Pick Murder
    They Can't All Be Guilty
Helm, J. both titles
Highland, D. 153 Oakland Street
Highsmith, P. Glass Cell
    This Sweet Sickness
Hilliard, J. Morgan's Castle
Hirsch, L. Murder Steals the Show
Hirschfeld, B. Secrets
Hoch, E. D. City of Brass
Holden, J. Nurse at the Castle
Holding, E. S. Unfinished Crime
    Virgin Huntress
Holland, I. Counterpoint
    Flight of the Archangel
    Tower Abbey
Holland, R. Hunter
Horvitz, L. Blood Moon
Howie, E. Murder for Christmas
Hudson, W. C. Dugdale Millions
Hunt, P. Murders at Scandal House
Hunter, E. Every Little Crook and Nanny
Irving, A. Deadline
Jackson, B. Programmer
Jackson, C. R. Quintus Oakes
Jagoda, R. Friend in Deed
James, Rebecca. Storm's End
James, Susan. Foul Deeds
Jeffers, A. Screen for Murder
Johnson, A. P. Hush, Winifred Is Dead
Johnson, B. B. Bad Day for a Black Brother
Johnson, Paul . Killing the Blues
Johnson, Philip. Hung Until Dead
Johnston, V. Along a Dark Path
Johnston, W. Waddington Cipher
Jones, Jennifer. all 3 titles
Kallen, L. Introducing C. B. Greenfield
    Little Madness
Kane, H. Laughter Came Screaming
    Two Must Die
Kauffman, R. W. Miss Frances Baird, Detective
Kenne, D. Sleep with the Devil
Kelland, C. B. Lady and the Giant
Kelley, L. P. Deadlocked!
Kelley, W. Tyree Legend
Kelly, J. Appalachin
Kelman, J. Where Shadows Fall
Kenrick, T. Seven Day Soldiers
Kent, W. Woman in Purple Pajamas
Kessner, L. Spy Next Door
King, C. D. Careless Corpse
King, H. Hahnemann Sequela
King, R. 8 titles
Kinney, T. Devil Take the Foremost
Klein, N. Destroying Angel
Knevels, G. By Candle-Light
    Diamond Rose Mystery
Knight, Adam. Knife at My Back

Settings Index — NEW YORK STATE / 1279

Kunstler, J. H. Blood Solstice
Kyle, R. Kill Now, Pay Later
Lacy, E. Pity the Honest
Laffin, J. I'll Die Tonight
Laiken, D. Death Among Strangers
    Killing Time in Buffalo
Land, J. To Walk the Night
Lane, J. Kill Me Tonight
    Murder Menagerie
    Murder Spoils Everything
Langley, L. Osiris Died in Autumn
Lariar, L. Death Paints the Picture
Lathen, E. Banking on Death
    Going for the Gold
    Sweet and Low
Lathrop, G. P. Would You Kill Him?
Latimer, Jonathan. Murder in the Madhouse
Lawrence, Hilda. Death of a Doll
Liddy, G. G. Monkey Handlers
Liebeler, J. M. You, the Jury
Lilly, J. Death Thumbs a Ride
    Seven Sisters
Livingston, A. Guilty Accuser
    On the Right Wrists
Lockridge, F. Murder Out of Turn
    Pinch of Poison
    Tangled Cord
    Ticking Clock
Lockridge, R. 22 titles
Long, Manning. Bury the Hatchet
    Vicious Circle
Lorens, M. K. Sweet Narcissus
Low, G. Invitation to Kill
Ludlum, R. Osterman Weekend
Lupton, L. Murder Without Tears
Lynch, D. C. Ventry
Lynch, J. Face to Face
McCahery, J. Grave Undertaking
McCall, D. Triphammer
McCloy, H. Mr. Splitfoot
    Panic
    Through a Glass, Darkly
McCully, W. Doctors Beware!
McCutcheon, G. B. Daughter of Anderson Crow
MacDonald, H. C. Death Walks Softly
MacDonald, J. D. All These Condemned
    Judge Me Not
    On the Run
MacGrath, H. Blue Rajah Murder
McKnight, C. House in the Shadows
McMahon, T. P. Hubschmann Effect
McNamara, E. Once Over Deadly
MacNeil, N. Hot Dam
Macrae, T. all 3 titles
MacVeigh, S. Murder Under Construction
Mace, M. Motto for Murder
Madsen, D. Black Plume
Mallory, A. Apperson's Folly
    Black Valley Murders
    House of Carson
    Mysteries of Black Valley
Maloney, R. Nixon Recession Caper
Manners, D. X. Memory of a Scream
Manson, W. Man Called Black
    Talent for Violence
Marasco, R. Parlor Games
Marfield, D. Mandarin's Sapphire
Marlowe, D. J. Shake a Crooked Town
Martyn, W. Last Scourge
Maxon, J. G. Progeny
Melville, Annabelle. Rue the Reservoir
Miller, Merle. Secret Understanding
Miller, V. Hide the Children
Mills, H. Mossbank Murder
Moorhouse, H. Gauntlet of Alceste
    Golden Scarab
Morland, C. Legacy of Winterwyck
Moroso, J. A. Quarry
Morton, W. Little Lady Lost
    Masquerade
Mosley, L. O. So I Killed Her
Mullen, C. Good Place for Murder
Murphy, W. B. Getting Up with Fleas
    Sole Survivor

Myers, I. B. Give Me Death
Mygatt, G. Nightmare
Napier, M. Child of Satan
Naylor, H. R. Mystery of Monastery Farm
Neiderman, A. Brainchild
    Playmates
    Reflection
    Someone's Watching
Nichols, A. Third Child
Nichols, F. Be Silent, Love
Nicholson, M. Siege of the Seven Suitors
Nicolson, J. U. Fingers of Fear
Nile, D. Mistress of Farrondale
Noone, E. Heirloom of Tragedy
Oates, J. C. Because It is Bitter and Because It Is My Heart
    Mysteries of Winterthurn
O'Brien, Meg. Salmon in the Soup
OCork, S. End of the Line
    Sports Freak
O'Donnell, L. Sleeping Beauty Murders
Ogburn, D. Will and the Deed
Olmsted, H. J. Hot Diary
Orenstein, F. Killing in Real Estate
Orvis, K. Disinherited
Ostrander, I. 6 titles
Packer, V. Alone at Night
    Girl on the Best Seller List
    Hare in March
Padgett, L. Brass Ring
Page, S. H. Resurrection Murder Case
Partridge, B. Ainsley Case
Patrick, Q. Death and the Maiden
Patterson, I. Eppworth Case
Paul, R. Tragedy at Tiverton
Pember-Hiller, G. Run Corpse, Run
Pendleton, D. Meltdown
Pentecost, H. Deadly Trip
    Honeymoon with Death
    Kill and Kill Again
Peterson, Keith. Trapdoor
Philips, J. Murder Clear, Track Fast
Phillips, R. R. Death Smiles
Piper, E. Lady and Her Doctor
Plagemann, B. Boxwood Maze
Poate, E. M. Murder on the Brain
Powell, F. House on the Hudson
Pronzini, B. Running of Beasts
Queen, E. Copper Frame
    Finishing Stroke
    House of Brass
Quentin, P. Man in the Net
Quintano, D. Weekend at the Villa
Randall, F. E. Hedgerow
Randolph, M. Grim Grow the Lilacs
Ransome, S. Shroud for Shylock
Rauch, C. Deep Disturbance
    Landlady
Rawson, C. Headless Lady
    No Coffin for the Corpse
Reagan, T. B. Blood Money
Reed, D. V. I Thought I'd Die
Reed, W. Marked for Murder
    No Sign of Murder
Reeve, A. B. Film Mystery
    Mystery Mind
Reilly, H. 5 titles
Rice, Laverne. Well-Dressed for Murder
Ridgway, J. People in Glass House
Rigsby, H. Tulip Tree
Rinehart, M. R. Bat
    Swimming Pool
Roberts, Lee. Death of a Ladies' Man
    Suspicion
Robeson, K. 6 titles
Robinson, Anthony. Whole Truth
Ronns, E. They All Ran Away
Roos, A. Speaking of Murder
Roos, K. Cry in the Night
Roosevelt, E. Hyde Park Murder
Rosenblum, R. Sweetheart Deal
Ross, B. Tragedy of Z
Ross, Marilyn. Face in the Shadows
Rossi, B. Blood Oath

Roth, H. Content Assignment
Ryan, A. Dead White
Sadler, M. Falling Man
St. Clare, D. Saratoga Mantrap
St. John, G. Dark Watch
    Secret of Dresden Farm
    Sinister Voice
Salvato, S. A. Briarcliff Manor
Sanders, Lawrence. Sixth Commandment
Sanders, M. K. Bride Laughed Once
Sapir, R. Murder's Shield
Sarrantonio, A. Cold Night
Scherf, M. Green Plaid Pants
Schubert, J. D. Keep
Scott, Dana. Five Fatal Letters
Scott, Milton. Dear, Dead Harry
Seabrooke, J. P. Eyewitness
Seeley, C. Storm Fear
Sharkey, J. Par for the Corpse
Shaw, J. T. It Happened at the Lake
Sherburne, J. Death's Pale Horse
Sherry, E. Tears for Jessie Hewitt
Shreve, A. Eden Close
Shriber, I. S. Dark Arbor
    Family Affair
    Head Over Heels in Murder
Siller, V. Curtain Between
    Widower
Simmons, M. K. Willow Pond
Sinclair, R. B. It Couldn't Be Murder
Singer, L. That's the House, There
Smith, Garret. I Did It!
Smith, T. L. Devil and Webster Daniels
Smithies, R. H. R. Disposing Mind
Spillane, M. Twisted Thing
Spinell, R. Dies Irae
Stanford, D. Slaughtered Lovelies
Stanwood, B. Seventh Child
Stark, R. Green Eagle Score
    Seventh
Starr, Jonathan. Grapevine
Steel, K. Ambush House
    Murder in G-Sharp
Stein, A. M. Cradle and the Grave
Stephan, L. Murder Most Distressing
Stern, R. M. Cry Havoc
    These Unlucky Deeds
Stevenson, B. E. House Next Door
Stevenson, R. Ice Blues
    On the Other Hand
Stockbridge, G. Satan's Death Blast
Stout, R. Double for Death
    Hand in the Glove
    Some Buried Caesar
Strange, J. S. Murder on the Ten-Yard Line
Stream, A. C. Third Bullet
Strobel, M. Kiss and Kill
Sutton, E. Dead Fingers
Swiggett, H. Corpse in the Derby Hat
Taylor, E. A. Murder at Vassar
Taylor, Edith. Serpent Under It
Taylor, H. B. Trouble with Tycoons
Taylor, R. W. Scandal
Terhune, A. P. Amateur Inn
Thayer, L. 6 titles
Thompson, V. Mr. Guelpa
Tibbetts, G. F. Mystery of Kun-Ja-Muck Cave
Tomerlin, J. Return to Vikki
Train, A. Hermit of Turkey Hollow
Travis, Gretchen. Cottage
    Two Spruce Lane
Treat, L. 7 titles
Tremonte, J. Devil's House
Turnbull, A. S. Wedding Bargain
Van Arsdale, W. Professor Knits a Shroud
Vance, E. Secret Thread
Vance, L. J. Bandbox
Van Deusen, D. Garden Club Murders
Van de Water, F. F. Eye of Lucifer
    Still Waters
Van Dine, S. S. Winter Murder Case
Van Raalte, J. Walls Are High
Veder, B. Playing with Fire
Venning, M. Man Who Slept All Day

Vernon, J. Lindbergh's Son
Wade, H. So Lovely to Kill
Wallace, R. Murder Stalks a Billion
Walsh, T. Action of the Tiger
    Face of the Enemy
    Tenth Point
Warwick, C. My Pal, the Killer
Waters, T. A. Blackwood Cult
Waugh, H. Madam Will Not Dine Tonight
Waugh, M. Back from the Dead
Webb, J. F. No Match for Murder
Webster, H. K. Alleged Great-Aunt
Wells, Carolyn. 16 titles
Westlake, D. E. Drowned Hope
    Help I Am Being Held Prisoner
    Killing Time
    Killy
Westminster, A. Moon in Shadow
Weston, H. G. Mystic Manor
Wetherell, J. Her Stepfather's House
Wharton, A. White Ghost of Fenwick Hall
White, L. Hostage for a Hood
    House Next Door
White, Matthew. Affair at Islington
Whitney, P. A. Stone Bull
    Thunder Heights
Widdemer, M. Red Castle Women
Wilcox, S. F. Dry White Tear
    St. Lawrence Run
Wilhelm, K. Sweet, Sweet Poison
Wilkins, W. A. Cleverdale Mystery
Willard, J. Cat and the Canary
    Thorne Theatre Mystery
Williams, D. Second Sight
Winsor, R. Three Motives for Murder
Witten, T. M. Place
Wolman, D. Little Boy Lost
Wood, B. Tribe
Wood, C. Tabloid Murders
Wright, M. Murder on Polopel
Wylie, P. Corpses at Indian Stones

NEW ZEALAND (N.Z. See also: Auckland; Wellington)
Alien. Devil's Half Acre
Bagley, D. Snow Tiger
Ball, J. Kiwi Contract
Beam, F. Sealed and Dispatched
    Vicar Done It
    Vicar Investigates
    With Murder in Mind
Billing, G. Alpha Trip
Brown, Michael. Idiot Played Rachmaninov
Burfield, E. After Midnight
    Last Day of Summer
Calder, J. O'Rourke Affair
Cooper, Barbara. all 4 titles
Crawford, J. T. both titles
Denman, P. Man Who Guided Missiles
Eden, D. Bride by Candlelight
    Cat's Prey
    Lamb to the Slaughter
Francis, Charles. Ask a River
Gee, M. all 5 titles
Graeme-Holder, W. Decker
Hoare, H. A. Now and for Ever
Hunt, Eve. Girl on the Run
Jay, S. both titles
Joseph, G. Trial and Error
Journet, T. Deathwishers
    God Killers
Keinzley, F. Time to Prey
McClenaghan, J. Moving Target
McGregor, M. Drifting Mist
    Glowing Dark
    House at Lake Taupo
    Whispering Echo
MacKenzie, A. Splash of Red
Manning, A. Timber and Top Dressing
Mantell, L. all 5 titles
Marsh, N. Colour Scheme
    Died in the Wool
    Photo-Finish
    Vintage Murder

Messenger, E. 10 titles
Murray, F. Invitation to Danger
Owen, C. Philip Loveluck
Packer, V. Evil Friendship
Peter, C. Ask a River
Potter, J. Going West
Richmond, M. Troubled Heritage
Salter, E. Death in a Mist
Sandford, K. Dead Reckoning
Satchell, W. both titles
Scott, Gavin. Hot Pursuit
Scott, Mary. Such Nice People
Scott, Rosie. Glory Days
Sherwood, J. Botanist at Bay
Stellenbach, B. Not Even a Mouse
Stephenson, R. Body in My Arms
Subond, V. House Over Hell Valley
Taylor, William. Mask of the Clown
Wake, V. F. Mists of Ravensfall
Wilson, Gar. Cold Dead
Wilson, Guthrie. Feared and the Fearless

NEWARK (See also: New Jersey; Trenton)
Hilary, R. Behind the Fact
    Pillows of the Community
    Snake in the Grasses
Holden, L. Dead Wrong
Levinrew, W. For Sale—Murder
Paul, G. Little Killer
Sohland, A. Evidence Circumstantial
Toma, D. Airport Affair

NICARAGUA (Nic. See also: Central America)
Brinkley, J. Circus Master's Mission
Carter, Nick. Ice Trap Terror
Chacko, D. Black Chamber
Davis, Patti. Deadfall
Elman, R. Menu Cypher
Overgard, W. Few Good Men
Pendleton, D. Backlash

NICE (See also: France; Marseilles; Paris; Corsica)
Kenrick, T. Only Good Body's a Dead One
Leslie, P. Finger in the Sky Affair
Read, P. P. Villa Golitsyn

NIGERIA (Nig. See also: Africa, West)
Dickinson, P. Tefuga
Garba, M. T. both titles
Irungu, J. Boarder Runners
Klop, T. Harmattan
Mangut, J. Have Mercy
Nwokolo, C. Extortionist
Thorpe, V. Exterminators
    Instrument

NORTH CAROLINA (N.C. See also: South)
Ballard, M. F. Raven Rock
Brent, R. L. Invitation to a Strangling
Buchanan, C. Black Cloak Murders
Burt, K. N. Red Lady
Cantrell, L. W. Ridge
Cook, M. B. In Hot Blood
Cooney, C. B. both titles
Coyne, J. Child of Shadows
Daniels, D. Woman in Silk and Shadows
Ehle, J. Widow's Trial
Forbes, S. Go to Thy Death Bed
Haas, B. Daisy Canfield
Hardy, W. Little Sin
Hay, J. Hidden Woman
    Winning Clue
Hyde, C. Crestwood Heights
Johnston, V. Girl on the Beach
Kimbrough, K. Spectre of Dolphin Cove
Knowlton, R. A. Court of Crows
Kosner, A. My Sister Ophelia
Lockridge, R. Death in a Sunny Place
McBriarty, D. Snowshot
    Whitewater VI
McCullough, K. G. Programmed for Danger
MacGrath, H. Green Stone
MacKay, A. both titles

Malone, M. Time's Witnesses
    Uncivil Seasons
Maner, W. Image Killer
Maron, M. Bloody Kin
Moore, H. F. S. Murder Goes Rolling Along
Ogburn, D. Death on the Mountain
Poate, E. M. Trouble at Pinelands
Polsky, T. Cudgel
Poyer, D. C. Hatteras Blue
Ross, James. They Don't Dance Much
Saab, P. Sweetwater Point Motel
Schutz, B. M. Embrace the Wolf
Squire, E. D. Kill the Messenger
Talbot, H. Hangman's Handyman
Winston, D. Gallows Way
Zachary, H. Bloodrush
    Murder in White
    To Guard the Right

NORTH DAKOTA (N. Dak. See also: Midwest)
Beeching, J. Dakota Project
Murphy, W. B. Blue Smoke and Mirrors
O'Malley, P. Affair of Chief Strongheart
Scherf, M. Don't Wake Me Up While I'm Driving
Stark, R. Score

NORTHWEST (N.W. See also: Oregon; Washington)
Anderson, C. Reasonable Doubt
Bainbridge, C. Hard Corps
Cutter, J. Sullivan's Revenge
Davis, K. Dead to Rights
Fogle, J. Drugstore Cowboy
Hanson, Dirk. Incursion
Hinds, R. W. Tunnel to Doom
Keeble, J. Yellowfish
Lake, J. Silent Scream
Olsen, J. Missing Persons
Saul, J. R. Cry for the Strangers
Sellers, M. Night Shadows

NORWAY (Nor. See also: Oslo; Scandinavia)
Barnard, R. Death in a Cold Climate
    Death in Purple Prose
Bingham, J. Night's Black Agent
Carr, G. Lewker in Norway
Christiansen, S. Two Living and One Dead
Crecy, J. Evil Among Us
Elvestad, S. Man Who Plundered the City
Engstrand, S. Spring 1940
Francis, Clare. Wolf Winter
Francis, D. Slay-Ride
Fullerton, A. Special Dynamic
Griffiths, E. Water Widow
Hamilton, D. Terminators
Innes, H. Blue Ice
Kielland, A. Live Dangerously
Lewis, David. Andromeda Assignment
Lie, J. Devil's Birthday
Lyall, G. Blame the Dead
MacAlan, P. Valkyrie Directive
Maitland, J. A. Sartoroe
Perry, Ritchie. Your Money and Your Wife
Purser, P. Peregrination 22
Robeson, K. Haunted Ocean
Rovin, J. Destination: Norway
Viller, F. Black Tortoise
White, A. Long Midnight
Whitney, P. A. Listen for the Whisperer

OCEAN. See: Ship.

OHIO (See also: Cincinnati; Cleveland; Columbus; Midwest)
Anthony, D. Midnight Lady and Mourning Man
Arden, W. Goliath Scheme
Bandy, E. Blackstock Affair
Biggle, L., Jr. Interface for Murder
Brackett, L. Eye for an Eye
    Tiger Among Us
Brennan, L. A. Death at Flood Tide
Burtis, T. Flying Blood
Cain, J. M. Rainbow's End

Campbell, M. E. Scandal Has Two Faces
Carl, L. S. Ashes to Ashes
Carrel, M. Tears of Blood
Chaber, M. E. As Old As Cain
Chacko, D. Gage
    Price
Chamberlain, A. Tall Dark Man
Churchill, L. Death Rides a Black Steed
Clark, W. A. Girl on the Volkswagen Floor
Corne, M. E. Death at the Manor
Crowell, W. Murder in Mocking Valley
Cullinan, T. Eighth Sacrament
Dear, W. C. "Please . . . Don't Kill Me"
Dominic, R. B. Attending Physician
    Murder Out of Commission
Elliott, B. One Is a Lonely Number
Falkner, L. M
Gilbert, M. A. Office Party
Gosling, P. Hoodwink
    Monkey Puzzle
Hale, C. Going, Going, Gone
Hardin, P. Hidden Grave
Haring, D. Death Is My Mistress
Harrington, W. Power
    Which the Justice, Which the Thief
Hintze, N. You'll Like My Mother
Hoff, B. J. Domino Image
Hultman, H. J. Murder on Route 40
Janson, H. Gun Moll for Hire
Johnson, B. B. That's Where the Cat's At, Baby
Johnson, G. both titles
King, R. Diagnosis: Murder
Lacy, E. Room to Swing
Lanning, G. Pedestal
Leeke, J. Sudden Ice
McConnaughey, J. Three for the Money
MacDougall, J. K. Death and the Maiden
McGrew, F. Murder by Mail
Maddux, B. J. Veil Withdrawn
Marlett, M. Devil Builds a Chapel
Martin, J. E. 95 File
Martin, Robert. 8 titles
Miles, J. Blackmailer
Miller, Judi. Cry in the Night
Morse, F. V. Black Eagles Are Flying
Olson, D. If I Don't Tell
Presnell, F. G. No Mourners Present
    Send Another Coffin
Roberts, Lee. If the Shoe Fits
    Little Sister
    Once a Widow
Robeson, K. Nevlo
Shriber, I. S. As Long As I Live
    Body for Bill
Stevenson, L. L. Big Game
Stokes, M. L. Iron Tiger

OKINAWA
Hearndon, E. Island Quarry

OKLAHOMA (Okla. See also: Oklahoma City; Tulsa; Southwest)
Adams, Clifton. Whom Gods Destroy
Allen, T. B. Short Life
Anderson, E. Thieves Like Us
Berkey, B. F. Keys to Tulsa
Bickham, J. Miracleworker
Cole, D. Murder at the White Tulip
Cooper, S. R. Man in the Green Chevy
    Other People's Houses
Cornell, L. Murder Case Number 33
Cunningham, W. Pretty Boy
Derrick, L. Oklahoma Firefight
Elder, M. Wolf Hunt
Hager, J. both titles
Jackson, K. 3 titles
Knickmeyer, S. both titles
Lehrer, J. Sooner Spy
Mechem, K. Frame for Murder
Miles, J. Dally with a Deadly Doll
    Night Hunters
Moore, Robin. Big Paddle
Reagan, T. B. Bank Job
Robeson, K. Derrick Devil

Rossi, B. Scarfaced Killer
Sandstrom, E. K. Death Down Home
Thompson, Jim. King Blood
Williams, C. Big Bite
Wright, M. Army Post Murders

OKLAHOMA CITY (Okla. City. See also: Oklahoma; Tulsa; Southwest)
Hillerman, T. Fly on the Wall
Thiessen, V. My Brother, Cain
Thomas, Ross. Briarpatch

OMAHA (See also: Nebraska; Midwest)
Forsyth, B. Expo '98: Sherlock Holmes in Omaha
Moss, J. Arson Job
Reynolds, W. J. 5 titles

OPERA. See: Theatre.

OREGON (Oreg. See also: Portland; Northwest)
Anderson, C. Without a Trace
Barry, I. House of Deadly Night
Bennett, M. L. Murder Once Done
Biderman, B. Paper Cuts
Brautigan, R. Hawkline Monster
Brennan, A. Castle Mirage
Byron, J. TNT for Two
Cooper, P. J. Moonblood
    Shuddering Fair One
Cunningham, C. Demons of Highpoint House
Derrick, L. High Disaster
Eby, L. Case of the Malevolent Twin
Echard, M. If This Be Treason
Farr, C. House on the Cliffs
Goodwin, H. Home for the Heart
Haynes, C. Perpetual Check
Heath, M. Return to Clerycastle
Holliday, Dolores. Blue House
Hoyt, R. Manna Enzyme
    Siskiyou Two-Step
Janson, H. Angel, Shoot to Kill
Kennedy, N. Village Tale
Kohler, V. Rainy North Woods
Lee, Bernie. Murder at Musket Beach
Lee, T. Summer Shock
Meyers, A. Murder Ends the Song
Mitcheltree, T. Terror in Room 201
Munn, V. Touch a Wild Heart
Nicole, Claudette. Haunted Heart
Offord, L. G. Walking Shadow
Olsen, D. B. Cats Have Tall Shadows
Pendleton, D. Council of Kings
Pronzini, B. Lighthouse
Stack, A. Lust Killer
Strahan, K. C. Footprints
    Meriweather Mystery
    October House
Trimble, L. Give Up the Body
Walker, Greg. Springblade
Wilhelm, K. Hamlet Trap
    Smart House
Wren, M. K. 5 titles

ORIENT. See: Far East; individual countries.

OSLO (See also: Norway; Scandinavia)
Henege, T. Death of a Shipowner
Nielsen, H. False Witness
Roberts, R. Crayfish Club

OTTAWA (See also: Canada; Montreal; Toronto; Vancouver; Winnipeg)
Adams, I. S—Portrait of a Spy
Champagne, P. Fair Affair
Kilian, M. Northern Exposure
Rohmer, R. Ultimatum
Sale, Medora. Murder in Focus

PAKISTAN (Pak.)
Hartland, M. Frontier of Fear
Hubbard, P. M. Custom of the Country
Jay, C. Yellow Turban

Leasor, J. Frozen Assets
    Passport to Peril
Lewis, R. H. Where Agents Fear to Tread
McLeave, H. Borderline Case
Mundy, M. Death Is a Tiger
Rosenberger, J. Pakistan Kill Ground

PALESTINE. See: Israel.

PANAMA (Pan. See also: Central America)
Amos, A. Fatal Harvest
    Panic in Paradise
Arnett, J. Panama Dead
Chambers, W. Navy Murders
Conrad, B. Stars Give Warning
Coxe, G. H. Candid Imposter
    Death at the Isthmus
Derrick, L. Panama Power Play
Knight, K. M. Death Came Dancing
    Tainted Token
    Trademark of a Traitor
Roberts, Mark. Canal Zone Conquest
Robertson, C. Strike Zone
Rosenberger, J. Kronos Plot
    Nightmare in Panama
Thomas, E. Shadow of Chu-Seng
Wolfe, M. Panama Paradox
Yarborough, C. Condor Conspiracy

PARAGUAY (Parag. See also: South America)
Lieberman, H. Climate of Hell
Masters, D. Spiral of Death
Pendleton, D. Guerrilla Games
Pickering, P. Wild About Harry

PARIS (See also: France; Nice; Marseilles)
Abdullah, A. Trail of the Beast
Adams, I. End Game in Paris
Albert, M. H. 7 titles
Albrand, M. Mask of Alexander
    Remembered Anger
Allan, J. Who's Next?
Anders, K. T. Legacy of Fear
Andrews, C. Affair of the Syrian Dagger
Annesley, M. Spy-Counter Spy
Anthony, Evelyn. Return
Appleton, G. W. Frozen Hearts
Armstrong, A. Spies in Amber
Ash, W. Take-Off
Aveline, C. Passenger on the U
Bachmann, L. P. Ultimate Act
Barak, M. Enigma
Barker, W. Himitsu Attack
Baron, S. End of the Line
Bass, R. Emerald Illusion
Behr, E. Getting Even
Benoit, T. City of Light
Black, E. B. Crime of the Chromium Bowl
Blackmore, J. Angel's Tear
Boileau, P. Living and the Dead
Boland, J. Counterpol in Paris
Bonner, P. H. Hotel Tallyrand
Boulle, P. Photographer
Bourne, P. And Bay the Moon
    Fall of the Eagle
Bove, E. Murder of Suzy Pommier
Bowick, D. M. Tapestry of Death
Brady, J. Paris One
Brenning, L. H. 5 titles
Brickhill, P. Deadline
Briskin, J. Naked Heart
Bunker, J. Diamond Cut Diamond
Butterworth, M. Black Look
    Virgin on the Rocks
Campbell, A. Click of the Gate
    Desire to Kill
    No Light Came On
    Spiderweb
Campden, J. Hundredth Acre
Carco, F. Noose of Sin
    Perversity
Carr, J. D. Corpse in the Waxworks
    Four False Weapons
    It Walks by Night

Carter, Nick. Jewel of Doom
　　Nowhere Weapon
　　Operation Starvation
　　Parisian Affair
Catalan, H. Soeur Angele and the Embarrassed
　　Ladies
Catto, M. Sam Casanova
Cheyney, P. You'd Be Surprised
Christopher, J. Murder-Go-Round
Clement, H. Darling Lili
Coen, F. Plunderers
Coffman, V. Masque by Gaslight
　　Small Tawny Cat
　　Veronique
Cole, K. S. I'm Afraid I'll Live
Cory, D. This Traitor, Death
Crane, F. Murder in Blue Street
Creasey, J. Toff Goes Gay
Cumberland, M. at least 21 titles
Cutter, J. American Vengeance
Daniels, N. Spy Ghost
Dark, J. Reluctant Assassin
Deighton, L. Expensive Place to Die
Dekobra, M. Prince or Clown
Delacorta. Diva
　　Nana
Demouzon. Mouche
De Pont-Jest, R. Case of Dr. Plemon
Dickson, Carter. Unicorn Murders
Didelot, F. 5 titles
Dorland, M. Double-Cross Circuit
Du Boisgobey, F. many/most of the 67 titles
Eberstadt, I. Natural Victims
Echenoz, J. Cherokee
Edwards, Anne. Miklos Alexandrovitch Is Missing
Egleton, C. Seven Days to a Killing
Ellin, S. House of Cards
Ely, D. Trot
Endore, G. Werewolf of Paris
Fairlie, G. Stone Blunts Scissors
Fick, C. Disturbance in Paris
Fighton, G. Z. Ghost of Passy
Fisher, N. Last Assignment
Fishter, J. F. Ambassador of Death
Fleming, Joan. Good and the Bad
　　Hell's Belle
Flynn, J. M. Warlock
Foster, T. Murder in the Rue de Bac
Fowler, S. Who Murdered Reynard?
Fox, J. M. Dark Crusade
Frances, S. D. Sad and Tender Flesh
Fredericks, A. Blue Lights
　　One Million Francs
Freeling, N. Those in Peril
Friedman, M. Magic Mirror
Fry, P. Brown Suede Jacket
　　Long Overcoat
Fytton, F. Nation Within
Gascar, P. Lambs of Fire
Gavin, C. Light Woman
Goldberg, M. Karamanov Equations
Goron, M. F. both titles
Graeme, B. Cherchez la Femme
　　Lady in Black
　　Man from Michigan
Graeme, R. Blackshirt Finds Trouble
Grant, M. Zemba
Gray, B. Big Brain
Grayson, Richard. 5 titles
Green, Gerald. Faking It
Greenfield, I. A. High Terror
Greenwood, E. French Farce
Grierson, F. 6 titles
Groc, L. Bus That Vanished
Gurin, P. Adventures with Dangerous Women
Haedrich, M. Crack in the Mirror
Harcourt, P. At High Risk
Haring, D. Lady You're Loaded
Harrington, W. Oberst
Harrison, M. Exploits of Chevalier Dupin
Hart, C. G. Escape from Paris
Head, M. Accomplice
　　Murder at the Flea Club
Hebden, M. Eyewitness

Hely, E. Dominant Third
Hemyng, B. Women of Paris
Herber, W. Almost Dead
Hering, H. A. Hunt the Tiger
Herrick, M. J. When Last Seen . . .
Hodges, A. Body in the Car
　　Embassy Murder
Holt, V. Demon Lover
Hotchner, A. E. Man Who Lived at the Ritz
Howard, H. War Toys
Hughes, Z. Fires of Paris
Hunt, H. Violent Ones
Hutin, P. Shadow Jury
Israel, P. French Kiss
　　Stiff Upper Lip
Jacobs, T. C. H. Target for Terror
James, Martin. Night Train
Japrisot, S. Goodbye, Friend
Jepson, S. Noise in the Night
Johnston, Gunnar. Two Kings
Johnston, V. House on the Left Bank
　　House with Dark Mirrors
Joyce, T. R. S.P.Y.S.
Kane, F. Maid in Paris
Kartun, D. Beaver to Fox
Kaufelt, D. A. Souvenir
Kessel, J. Bernan Affair
Knight, Adam. Girl Running
Kotzwinkle, W. Fata Morgana
Lacroix, J. P. Innocent Gunman
Lacy, E. Go for the Body
Law, J. Gemini Trip
Legaret, J. Tightrope
Lenton, D. Crooks of Paris
Leroux, G. Kiss That Killed
Leslie, P. Cold Snap
Levene, P. Ambrose in Paris
Levi, P. Knit One, Drop Two
Lodwick, J. Love Bade Me Welcome
Lucas, N. Red Stranger
Lyons, N. Champagne Blues
McConnor, V. French Doll
　　I Am Vidocq
　　Paris Puzzle
McCutcheon, P. Executioners
McGerr, P. Fatal in My Fashion
MacGrath, H. Wolves of Chaos
MacKenzie, N. Fear Stalks the City
Maas, E. Lady at Bay
Machard, A. Wolf Man
Malet, L. Rats of Montsouris
Malm, D. On a Fated Night
Malo, V. G. And Why Not?
Mara, B. French for Murder
　　This Gun for Gloria
Marder, I. Paris Bit
Marlowe, S. Drum Beat—Dominque
Marshall, B. Accounting
Merrick, W. Packard Case
Millar, R. Half a Corpse
Mills, A. Apache Girl
　　Cafe in Montparnasse
　　Paris Agent
Miln, L. J. Purple Mask
Mitchell, E. Plotters of Paris
Moffett, C. Master Mind
　　Seine Mystery
　　Through the Wall
Monteilhet, H. Prisoner of Love
Mooney, J. Millionaire's Folly
Morgan, Dean. Contract for Homicide
Muir, A. Red Carnation
Mullin, A. Spy
Nason, L. H. Contact Mercury
Netzen, K. To Win and to Lose
Newman, B. Otan Plot
Noel, S. Storm Over Paris
Noro, F. Do No Evil
Ohnet, G. Poison Dealer
Old Sleuth. Terrible Youth
Oppenheim, E. P. Seeing Life
Owen, H. C. Adventures of Antoine
Pace, L. Deception by Design
Page, M. Set a Thief

Paul, Elliot. Hugger-Mugger in the Louvre
　　Mayhem in B-Flat
　　Murder on the Left Bank
　　Mysterious Mickey Finn
Perowne, B. Singular Conspiracy
Peters, L. Tarakian
Peterson, B. Peripheral Spy
Phillips, C. Walk in the Dark
Porter, J. Chinks in the Curtain
Powell, L. Black Casket
Poynter, B. Disappearance of Mary Amber
Randolph, E. Paris in September
Raphael, J. N. Mystery of the Rue de Babylone
Reynolds, G. Victor Maury, the French Detective
Rhoads, J. W. Contract
Richmond, M. Evening in Paris
Robinson, E. M. Secret of the Swinging Room
Rollins, W. Ring and the Lamp
Ronald, E. B. Sort of Madness
Rosenberger, J. Paris Kill-Ground
Ross, W. E. D. Forbidden Castle
Roudybush, A. Death of a Moral Person
　　Female of the Species
　　House of the Cat
　　Suddenly in Paris
Rowland, H. C. Closing Net
Rutherland, D. Comes the Blind Fury
　　Creeping Flesh
St. Clair, L. Emerald Trap
St. Germain, G. Shadows of Death
St. James, B. April Thirtieth
　　Seven Dreamers
Saint-Laurent, C. Cautious Maiden
San Antonio. From A to Z
　　Stone Dead
　　Strangler
　　Thugs and Bottles
Saxe, R. B. Ghost Does a Richard III
Service, R. W. Master of the Microbe
Seton, G. K Code Plan
Shepherd, Joan. both titles
Sherard, R. H. Ghost's Revenge
Simenon, G. about 62 Maigret volumes, plus many
　　non-series titles
Simon, N. Coffin & Co.
Sinclair, Michael. How to Steal a Million
Smith, C. S. Chain of Circumstances
Smith, J. P. Blue Hour
　　Body and Soul
Sneddon, R. W. Monsieur X
Souvestre, P. Exploits of Juve
　　Limb of Satan
　　Messengers of Evil
　　Royal Prisoner
Spong, R. See If He Wins
Steeman, A. Six Dead Men
Stevens, S. Anvil Chorus
Steward, B. Evermore
Steward, S. M. Caravaggio Shawl
Strange, J. S. Catch the Gold Ring
Stuart, A. Seen and Not Heard
Stubbs, J. Painted Face
Sue, E. Mysteries of Paris
Suskind, P. Perfume
Tabori, P. Perdita's End
Teilhet, D. L. Murder in the Air
Thompson, V. Pointed Finger
Thomson, B. Richardson Goes Abroad
Torr, D. Diplomatic Cover
Travers, H. Madame Aubry and the Police
Treat, L. Venus Unarmed
Tyler, A. Chase the Storm
Vail, L. Murder! Murder!
Vance, L. J. Lone Wolf
Vexin, N. Murder in Montmartre
Vidocq. Life in Paris
　　Memoirs of Vidocq
Volkoff, V. both titles
Wallace, C. M. Fly by Night
Wallace, Irving. Plot
Waller, L. Trocadero
Ward, D. House in Paris
Warmbold, J. Third Way
Westlake, D. E. Castle in the Air

Settings Index

Weston, George. Wings of Destiny
Wheatley, D. Desperate Measures
    Prisoner in the Mask
    "V" for Vengeance
Wheeler, P. And the Bullets Were Made of Lead
White, G. M. When Tragedy Grins
Wickham, H. Boncouer Affair
    Trail of the Squid
Wilkinson, B. Night of the Short Knives
Wood, H. F. Englishman of the Rue Cain
Young, G. Devil's Passport
Zessa, C. Paris 2005

PAST (Here listed are books explicitly set at a time distinctly earlier than the time of writing. Year and place of setting are given where identified. See also: Future)

Abbey, R. Girl from the Sea (Eng.)
    Prisoner of the Manor (Eng.)
Abbott, S. Castle of Evil (1953, Rum.)
    River and the Rose (1860s, South)
Adams, H. Barbed Wire (1930s, S. Dak.)
    Fourth Widow (1930s, S. Dak.)
    Man Who Missed the Train (1934, S. Dak.)
    Missing Moon (1930s, S. Dak.)
    Murder (1930s, Minn.)
    Naked Liar (1930s, S. Dak.)
    Paint the Town Red (1930s, S. Dak.)
Adicks, R. Court of Owls (1860s, U.S.)
Aiken, Joan. Castle Barebane (1800s, Scot.)
    Deception (1800s, Eng.)
    Lightning Tree (1700s, Eng.)
    Smile of the Stranger (1790s, Eng.)
    Young Lady from Paris (ca.1850)
Ainsworth, P. Devil's Hole (1877, Australia)
Albert, M. H. Operation Lila (1942, Fr.)
    Untouchables (1930, Chi.)
Aldanov, M. Key (1917, Russ.)
Alexander, Jan. Darkwater (1860s, south)
Alexander, K. Songs of War (WWII)
Alexander, L. Big Stick (1870s, NYC)
    Speak Softly (ca.1890, NYC)
Allbeury, T. Lantern Network (WWII, Fr.)
    Time Without Shadows (WWII, Fr.)
Allen, E. O. Hounds of the Moon (1940s, N.Y.)
Allison, E. M. A. Through the Valley of Death (1379, Eng.)
Amis, K. Riverside Villas Murder (1930s, Eng.)
Amor, P. F. People's Republic (1960, China)
Anderson, Ian. 7 titles (1800s, Can.)
Anderson, J. Affair of the Blood-Stained Egg Cosy (1930s, Eng.)
    Affair of the Mutilated Mink Coat (1930s, Eng.)
Andrews, Mark. Return of Jack the Ripper (1888, NYC)
Andrews, Val. Sherlock Holmes and the Brighton Pavilion Mystery (1906, Eng.)
    Sherlock Holmes and the Eminent Thespian
Anonymous. Mystery of Marlborough House (ca.1800)
    Orphan Seamstress (1840s, N.J., NYC)
Anthony, E. Voices on the Wind (WWII, Fr.)
Appel, A. Time After Time (1917, Russ.)
Archer, Margaret. Gull Yard (1840, Eng.)
Argo, R. Year of the Monkey (Viet Nam)
Arnold, W. China Gate (1960s-1970s, Far East)
Arvonen, H. Sorrow for Angels (1890, Can.)
Ashton, A. Phantom Reflection (1935, L.A.)
Astley, J. Fall of Midas (ca.1900, Eng.)
Atiyah, E. Black Vanguard (1930s, Eng.)
Atlee, Barbara. Sacred Trusts (1928–1940)
Baddock, J. Emerald (1945, Berlin)
    Faust Conspiracy (1944, Eng.)
    Radar Job (1943, Holl.)
Bainbridge, B. Watson's Apology (1871, London)
Bair, P. Gypsum Flower (1944, Fr.)
Baird, T. Way to the Old Sailor's Home (1939, Can.)
Baker, Lucinda. Place of Devils (1879, Ariz.)
    Walk the Night Unseen (ca.1900, S.F.)
Baker, W. Destination Dieppe (1942, Fr.)
    Dogs of War (1945, It.)
    Inexpendable (1956, Hung.)

Rape of Berlin (1945, Berlin)
Strike North (1941, ship)
Baldwin, A. Last Heroes (WWII)
    Secret Warriors (WWII)
    Soldier Spies
Balling, L. C. Fourth Shot (1963)
Ballinger, W. A. Carrion Eaters (1947, India)
    Rebellion (1916, Ire.)
Bamford, F. Return of Cottington (1768, Eng.)
Banville, J. Birchwood (1800s, Ire.)
Barak, M. Enigma (1944, Paris)
Barber, N. Women of Cairo (1940s, Egypt)
Barlay, S. Cuban Confetti (1962)
Barling, T. Dance with Death (1960s, London)
    Dance with the Devil (1960s, London)
Barnard, R. Skeleton in the Grass (1936, Eng.)
Barnett, R. J. Jade and Fire (1948, Peking)
Barrett, Max. House Across the Park (1800s, Eng.)
Barry, Jane. Conscience of the King (early 1900s, Balkans)
Bart, S. Ruby Sweetwater and the Ringo Kid (1901, NYC)
Barton, J. Forest of Death (WWII)
    Kill Hitler (WWII)
    Lightning Strikes (WWII)
Barwick, J. Devil at the Crossroads (1940, Fr.)
    Hangman's Crusade (1941, Europe)
Bass, R. Emerald Illusion (1944, Paris)
Baxt, G. Alfred Hitchcock Murder Case (1925–1936, Eng.)
    Dorothy Parker Murder Case (1920s, NYC)
    Talking Pictures Murder (1929, L.A.)
    Tallulah Bankhead Murder Case (1952, NYC)
Becher, U. Woodchuck Hunt (1938, Switz.)
Beck, K. K. Death in a Deck Chair (1927, ship)
    Murder in a Mummy Case (1928, Calif.)
    Peril Under the Palms (1928, Haw.)
    Young Mrs. Cavendish and the Kaiser's Men (1919, S.F.)
Becker, S. Rendezvous in Haiti (1919, Haiti)
Beech, W. Article 92: Murder, Rape (1946, Ger.)
Beede, J. You Can Only Die Once
Behn, N. Seven Silent Men (1971, Mo.)
    Shadowboxer (1944, Ger.)
Beinhart, L. You Get What You Pay For (1984, NYC)
Bell, Donna. Scandalous Miss (1800s, Eng.)
Bellah, J. Imperial Express (1937, Mex.)
Bellamy, P. Prisoner of Ingecliff (1700s, Eng.)
Bennett, H. Wait Until Evening (WWII, Va.)
Bennett, J. M. Local Matter (1914, Eng.)
Bennett, Janice. Tempting Miss (1810)
Bennetts, P. Footsteps in the Fog (1800s, Eng.)
    Ring the Bell Softly (1865, Eng.)
    Voice in the Darkness (1870, Eng.)
Benoit, T. City of Light (Paris)
Bensen, D. R. Sherlock Holmes in New York (1901, NYC)
Benson, B. K. Who Goes There? (ca.1860, U.S.)
Bentley, P. House of Moreys (1809, Eng.)
    More Tales of the West Riding (Eng.)
    Tales of the West Riding (Eng.)
Berckman, E. Crown Estate (1200s, Eng.)
    Finger to Her Lips (1700s, Ger.)
    Long Arm of the Prince (ca.1600, Eng.)
Bergman, A. Big Kiss-Off of 1944 (1944, NYC)
    Hollywood and LeVine (1947, L.A.)
Bergon, F. Shoshone Mike (1911, Nev.)
Bernau, G. Candle in the Wind (1962)
Beste, R. V. Faith Has No Country (WWII, Fr.)
Beverley, J. Stanforth Secrets (1800s, Eng.)
    Stolen Bride (1800s, Eng.)
Bhabra, H. Gestures (1923–1946, Venice, Amst.)
Biggle, L., Jr. Glendower Conspiracy (1904, Wales)
    Quallsford Inheritance (1900, Eng.)
Binyon, T. J. Swan Song (1970s, Moscow)
Birkhim, M. Trust and Treason (1500s, Eng.)
Bishop, M. Killraven (Scot.)
    Widow's Walk (1870s, Maine)
Black, C. Death's Head (1945, Berlin)
Black, Laura. Castle Raven (1800s, Scot.)
    Glendraco (1860, Scot.)
    Strathgallant (1863, Eng.)
    Wild Cat (1862, Scot.)

Blackburn, J. Flame and the Wind (ca.30 A.D., Jerus.)
Blackstock, C. Factor's Wife (1816, Scot.)
    Knock at Midnight (1938, Hung.)
    Shirt Front (1936, Eng.)
Blagowidow, G. Last Train from Berlin (WWII, Ger.)
Blaine, R. Silver Setup (1948, Pa.)
    Tainted Jade (1948, Tex.)
Blair, M. Clanmire Tor (1800s, Eng.)
Blake, J. Midnight Waltz (ca.1850, La.)
Blake, P. Double Griffin (1944, NYC)
    Escape to Athens (1945, Greece)
Blake, V. Dark Guardian (Eng.)
Blake, W. D. My Time or Yours (1846, NYC)
Blankfort, M. Behold the Fire (WWI, Mid. East)
Bloch, R. American Gothic (1893, Chi.)
    Jekyll Legacy (1800s, Eng.)
    Night of the Ripper (1888, Eng.)
Block, L. Code of Arms (1940)
Blyth, J. Beset by Spies (1904)
Bok, C. Star Wormwood (1931, U.S.)
Boles, P. D. Limner (1870, Va.)
    Mississippi Run (1800s, Miss.)
Bond, C. Sweeney Todd, the Demon Barber of Fleet Street (early 1800s, London)
Bond, E. Evil in the House (1860s, NYC)
Booth, Martin. Jade Pavilion (1937-1948, Macao)
Borrie, H. Golden Heron (1930s)
Boulle, P. Noble Profession (WWII, Fr.)
Bourne, P. And Bay the Moon (1800s, Paris)
    Fall of the Eagle (1800s, Paris)
Bowen, Marjorie. Gorgeous Lovers
    Old Patch's Medley (1690–1795, London)
Bowen, Michael. Badger Game
Bower, M. Skipper Anne (ca.1810, Fr.)
Boyarsky, A. Shreiber (1945–6, Pol.)
Boyer, B. H. Solstice Cipher (1944, Eng.)
Boyer, R. L. Giant Rat of Sumatra (1893, Eng.)
Bradbury, R. Death Is a Lonely Business (1950, Calif.)
    Graveyard for Lunatics (1950s, L.A.)
Brady, L. Love Tap (1972, Wash. D.C.)
Brahms, C. Rappel 1910 (1910, Eng.)
Bram, C. Holt Tight (1940s, NYC)
Bramble, F. Strange Case of Deacon Brodie (1788, Edin.)
Brason, P. Fourth Arm (WWII, Fr.)
Brautigan. R. Dreaming of Babylon (1942, S.F.)
    Hawkline Monster (1902, Oreg.)
Breem, W. Leopard and the Cliff (1919, India)
Brent, M. Capricorn Stone (ca.1900, Eng.)
    Golden Urchin (1800s, Australia)
    Heritage of Shadows (1890s, Eng.)
    Kirkby's Changeling (1900, Eng.)
    Long Masquerade (late 1800s, Carib.)
    Merlin's Keep (1800s, Eng.)
    Moonraker's Bride (ca.1900, China)
    Stormswift (1800s, Eng.)
    Tregaron's Daughter (ca.1900, Venice)
Bridges, R. Bubble Moon (1700s)
    Cloud (1800s, Australia)
    On His Majesty's Service (1800s, Tas.)
    This House Is Haunted (1844–1939, Melb.)
Brierley, D. Big Bear, Little Bear (1948, Berlin)
Briggs, D. Standing Into Danger (1960s)
Brink, C. Bellini Look (1929, Venice)
Briskin, J. Naked Heart (1940s, Paris)
Bristowe, A. Tunnel (1900, Eng.)
Britton, C. Paybacks (1971, San Diego)
Bronte, L. Casino Greystone (1896, Conn.)
    Freedom Trail to Greystone (1860, Conn.)
    Gathering at Greystone (1812, Conn.)
    Greystone Heritage (1948, Conn.)
    Greystone Tavern (1776, Conn.)
    Lord Satan (1815, Eng.)
    Moonlight at Greystone (1924, Conn.)
Brooks, C. Blood on the Tracks (ca.1900, Eng.)
    Memoirs of Professor Moriarty (Eng.)
    Sherlock Holmes Revisited (Eng.)
Brophy, J. Day They Robbed the Bank of England (1900, Eng.)
Brown, R. A. Sherlock Holmes and the Mysterious Friend of Oscar Wilde (1895, Eng.)

1284 / PAST — Settings Index

Brown, W. F. Thursday at Noon (1962, Egypt)
Browne, H. Pork City (1930, Chi.)
Bryant, Will. Blue Russell (1899, West)
    Time for Heroes (ca.1920)
Buckingham, N. House Called Edenhythe (Eng.)
    Jade Dragon (1800s, Port.)
    Vienna Summer (1897, Vienna)
Buckley, W. F. High Jinx (1954, Eng.)
    Marco Polo, If You Can (1959)
    Mongoose R.I.P. (1963, Cuba)
    Saving the Queen (1940s, Eng.)
    See You Later, Alligator (1962, Cuba)
    Stained Glass (1950, Ger.)
    Story of Henri Tod (1961, Berlin)
Bugliosi, V. T. Lullaby and Goodnight (1920s, NYC)
Burch, J. Lubyanka (1978, Moscow)
Burke, John. Black Charade (ca.1890, Eng.)
    Devil's Footsteps (1888, Eng.)
    Ladygrove (ca.1890, Eng.)
Burke, W. Time of Innocence (1941, Haw.)
Burnett, W. R. Goodbye, Chicago (1928, Chi.)
Burroughs, R. Fugitive Feet (1944, Ida.)
Burton, Anthony. Coventry Option
Burton, B. J. Murder of Maria Marten (1827, Eng.)
Bushell, A. Shadowdance (1980, Maine)
Butler, Gwendoline. Brides of Friedberg (1800s, Ger.)
    Coffin for Pandora (1800s, Eng.)
    Coffin in Fashion (1960s, Eng.)
    Coffin on the Water (1946, Eng.)
    Coffin Underground (1978, Eng.)
    Red Staircase (1917, Russ.)
    Vesey Inheritance (1800s, Eng.)
Butler, Ragan. Captain Nash and the Honour of England (ca.1770, Eng.)
    Captain Nash and the Wroth Inheritance (1771, Eng.)
Butterworth, M. Virgin on the Rocks (1933, Paris)
Cable, M. Avery's Knot (1832, R.I.)
Cain, J. M. Past All Dishonor (1860s, Calif.)
Caine, J. Heathcliff (1800s, Eng.)
Caldecott, M. Son of the Sun
Callard, M. City Called Holy (1947, Isr.)
Cameron, K. Curse of Whispering Hills (1860s, Ind.)
    Evil at Whispering Hills (Ind.)
    Shadows on the Moon (Ind.)
Campbell, G. In the Shadow of Death (1790)
Campbell, P. Cedarhaven (1859, Wash.)
    Lush Valley (1890s)
Campbell, R. W. Circus Couronne (1914, Switz.)
Campsie, A. Clarinda Conspiracy
Cannon, P. H. Pulptime (1925, NYC)
Carlson, P. M. Murder Misread (1977)
Carmichael, F. Any Number Can Die (1920s)
    Victoria's House (ca.1900)
Carnac, N. Indigo (1857, India)
Carnell, J. Murder, Mystery and Mayhem (1936, Eng.)
Carr, J. D. Bride of Newgate (1815, Eng.)
    Captain Cut-Throat (1805, Fr.)
    Deadly Hall (1927, New Or.)
    Demoniacs (1757, Eng.)
    Devil in Velvet (1675, Eng.)
    Fire, Burn! (1829, Eng.)
    Ghosts' High Noon (1912, New Or.)
    Hungry Goblin (1869, Eng.)
    Most Secret (1670, 1815, Eng.)
    Murder of Sir Edmund Godfrey (1815, Eng.)
    Papa La-Bas (1858, New Or.)
    Scandal at High Chimneys (1865, Eng.)
    Witch of the Low Tide (1907, Eng.)
Carr, P. Lion Triumphant (1500s, Eng.)
    Miracle at St. Bruno's (1500s, Eng.)
    Witch from the Sea (1500s, Eng.)
Carroll, J. Firebird (1949, Wash. D.C.)
Carroll, R. Disappearance (1957–67, Europe)
Cashman, J. Cook General (1870s, Eng.)
    Gentleman from Chicago (1800s, Chi.)
    Kid Glove Charlie (1870s, Eng.)
Cassady, M. Alternate Casts (1800s)
Catanach, J. N. Brideprice (1960s, Kenya)
Chacko, D. Brick Alley (1960, Pa.)

Chalmers, J. W. Horseman in Scarlet (Can.)
Chalmers, S. Crime in Car 13 (1913, U.S.)
Chamberlain, Elinor. Snare for Witches (1663, Mass.)
Chamberlain, L. Other Side of the Door (1865, S.F.)
Chambers, R. W. Secret Service Operator 13 (1862, U.S.)
Champlin, T. King of the Highbinders (1880s, S.F.)
Chapman, H. W. Limmerston Hall (1800s, Eng.)
Chaput, W. J. Man on the Train (1944, Vt.)
Charles, I. Grenencourt (Eng.)
Charlesworth, M. Glass House (1970s, Ger.)
Charteris, L. Catch the Saint (1930s, Phil., Eng.)
    Saint and the Hapsburg Necklace (ca.1940, Vienna)
Cheatham, L. Marriage Pact (1830, NYC)
    Portrait of Emma (1700s, Boston)
    Secret of Saramount (ca.1900, South)
Cherkas, M. Red Shadows (1952)
    Secret Affairs (1952, N.Y.)
Chester, Sarah. Dancing on the Wind (Eng.)
Chevalier, H. For Us the Living (1929–41, S.F.)
Chevalier, P. Grudge (WWII, Eng.)
Cheyney, J. Secret of Giltham Hall (1600s, Eng.)
Childress, M. V for Victim (1942, Ala.)
Chimenti, F. Silent Room (1910, N.Y.)
    Web of Allynroad (1800s, Eng.)
Chittenden, M. Face in the Mirror
Chorlton, W. Rites of Sacrifice (1970, Tibet)
Christie, A. Death Comes As the End (2000 B.C., Egypt)
Clare, A. Child of the Menir (1700s, Fr.)
Clark, Cecily. Ravensley Manor (1800s, Eng.)
Clark, Dick. Murder on Tour (1978)
Clark, G. Baroness of Bow Street (ca.1810, Eng.)
    Dulcie Bligh (ca.1810, Eng.)
Clark, L. Murder of the Prime Minister (1812, Eng.)
Clark, Mark. Ripper (1888, Eng.)
Clarke, A. Lady in Black (1882, Eng.)
    Last Voyage (1939, Eng.)
Clarke, T. E. B. Murder at Buckingham Palace (1935, Eng.)
Cleary, J. City of Fading Light (1939, Berlin)
    Faraway Drums (1911, India)
    Golden Sabre (early 1900s, Russ.)
    High Road to China (1920s, China)
    Phoenix Tree (1945, Jap.)
Clement, H. Darling Lili (WWI, Paris)
Clements, A. Mistress of the Moor (1909, Scot.)
Clive, J. Last Liberator (1963, Holl.)
    Lion's Cage (WWII)
Cody, L. Rift (1974, Ethio.)
Coen, F. Plunderers (WWII, Paris)
Coffman, V. Dark Desire (1800s, Eng., Fr.)
    Dark Gondola (1790s, Venice)
    Dark Palazzo (1797, Venice)
    Demon Tower (1808, It.)
    Gaynor Women (1880s, Va.)
    House on the Moat (1810, Eng.)
    Hyde Place (1919, S.F.)
    Marsanne (ca.1820, Eng.)
    Masque by Gaslight (1858, Paris)
    Master of Blue Mire (1814, Eng.)
    Mist at Darkness (1821, Eng.)
    Mistress Devon (ca.1850, Boston)
    Moura (1815, Fr.)
    Orchid Tree (1930s, Haw.)
    Vampyre of Moura (1821, Fr.)
    Veronique (1790, Paris)
Coles, M. Drink to Yesterday (1917, Ger.)
Collins, L. Fall from Grace (WWII)
Collins, M. A. Bullet Proof (1937, Cleve.)
    Butcher's Dozen (Cleve.)
    Dark City (1935–6, Cleve.)
    Million Dollar Wound (1939–43, Chi.)
    Neon Mirage (1946, Chi.)
    No Cure for Death (1974, Ia.)
    True Crime (1934, Chi.)
    True Detective (1920s, Chi.)
Comber, L. Strange Cases of Magistrate Pao (ca.1100, China)
Condon, R. Prizzi's Family (late 1960s, NYC)
Connell, C. Meet Me at Philippi (ca.50 B.C., Rome)

    Most Delicious Poison (ca.50 B.C., Mid. East)
Connor, K. New Departure (1800s)
Conot, R. E. Ministers of Vengeance (1920s, S.F.)
Conteris, H. Ten Percent of Life (1956, L.A.)
Conway, L. Abbot's House (Eng.)
Cook, Nick. Angel, Archangel (1945, Ger.)
Cook, T. H. Streets of Fire (1963, Birmingham)
Cooke, S. G. Treasure of Rodolfo Fierro (1920s, N. Mex.)
Cooper, Brian. Genesis 38 (1903, Eng.)
Cooper, L. U. Lighted Room (1600s, Eng.)
Cooper, Lynna. Hour of the Harp (1800s, Ire.)
Cooper, M. H. When Fish Begin to Smell (1951, London)
Cooper, P. J. My Lady Evil (ca.1815, Fr.)
Copeland, W. Five Hours from Isfahan (1943, Iran)
Copp, D. S. Matter of Concealment (WWII)
Coppee, F. Guilty Man (1866, Fr.)
Copper, B. Dossier of Solar Pons (1920s, Eng.)
    Further Adventures of Solar Pons (Eng.)
    Necropolis (1800s, Eng.)
    Secret Files of Solar Pons (Eng.)
    Uncollected Cases of Solar Pons (Eng.)
Cormany, M. Red Winter (1983, Chi.)
Cort, N. all 5 titles (WWII)
Coulter, C. Calypso Magic (1813, W.I.)
Creasey, J. Masters of Bow Street (1739–1829, Eng.)
Creighton, M. Dynamiters (1886, London)
    Royal Flush (ca.1890, London)
Crichton, M. Great Train Robbery (1855, Eng.)
Crichton, W. Donnelly Murders (1800s, U.S.)
Crider, B. Galveston Gunman (1800s, Tex.)
Crofts, F. W. Cask (1910–12, Fr.)
Crookenden, I. Horrible Revenge (1500s, It.)
Crowder, K. Iron Web (WWII, S. Afr.)
Crowley, D. Riddle Me a Murder (1365, Eng.)
Crunden, A. B. Chicago Winter's Tale (WWI, Chi.)
Cummings, M. Royal Conspiracy (1800s, Eng.)
Cunningham, C. Demons of Highpoint House (1910, Oreg.)
Curties, T. J. H. Saint Botolph's Priory (ca.1640, Eng.)
Curtis, N. M. Matricide's Daughter (mid 1830s, NYC)
    Star of the Fallen (mid 1830s, NYC)
    Victim's Revenge (mid 1830s, NYC)
Cutler, R. Gates of Sagittarius (1939, Havana)
Dacre, C. Zofloya (1400s, It.)
Daingerfield, F. That Gay Nineties Murder (1890, Ky.)
Daley, J. A. Spicy Lady (1968, NYC)
Daley, R. Dangerous Edge (1952, Fr.)
Dalton, P. Darkening Willows (ca.1910, N.Y.)
Daniels, D. Attic Rope (La.)
    Bell (1892, Maine)
    Blackthorn (1903, Md.)
    Child of Darkness (1911, N.Y.)
    Circle of Guilt (ca.1910, S.F.)
    Cliffside Castle (1890, N.Y.)
    Conover's Folly (1890, Maine)
    Dance in Darkness (1890, N.Y.)
    Dark Stage (1892, New Or.)
    Dark Villa (ca.1900, L.I.)
    Darkhaven (1890, N.Y.)
    Duncan Dynasty (1885, La.)
    Guardian of Willow House (1915, N.Y.)
    House of Many Doors (Miss.)
    House of Stolen Memories (1800s, Conn.)
    House on Crocus Hill (1895, Ind.)
    In the Shadows (N.Y.)
    Journey Into Terror (ca.1860, S.C.)
    Lady of the Shadow (Conn.)
    Lanier Riddle (1890, Ky.)
    Leland Legacy (1890, Ky.)
    Man from Yesterday (ca.1900, N.Y.)
    Marble Leaf (N.Y.)
    Marriott Hall (1880, Maine)
    Mistress of Falcon Hill (1867, La.)
    Monte Carlo (ca.1900, Fr.)
    Mostly by Moonlight (1871, Maine)
    Night Shadow (1895, Ga.)
    Poison Flower (1895, Vt.)
    Possessed (1890, Maine)
    Saratoga (1880s, N.Y.)

Settings Index

Shadow of a Man (1890, La.)
Shadows from the Past (1890, N.Y.)
Silent Halls of Ashenden (N.Y.)
Summer House (ca.1900, NYC)
Templeton Memoirs (1890, N.Y.)
Tidemill (1895, Va.)
Tormented (1883, La.)
Unearthly (1880, Ga.)
Vineyard Chapel (1918, Calif.)
Voices on the Wind (1895, New Eng.)
Web of Peril (N.Y.)
Whistle in the Wind (1885, La.)
Willow Weep (1889, N.Y.)
Darby, C. Falcon and the Moon (1886, Eng.)
  Falcon for a Witch (ca.1910, Eng.)
  Falcon Rising (1818, Eng.)
  Falcon Sunset (1916, Eng.)
  Falcon Tree (1841, Eng.)
  Falcon's Claw (1399, Eng.)
  Flaunting Moon (1644, Eng.)
  King's Falcon (1644, Eng.)
  Season of the Falcon (1774, Eng.)
Darty, P. Wailing Winds of Juneau Abbey (1890, Alaska)
  Widowed Bride of Raven Oaks (1860s, Ala.)
Davenport, F. Secret of the Bayou (La.)
Davenport, J. Murder at Bill's O'Jacks (1832, Eng.)
Davis, Christopher. Dog Horse Rat (1970s, N.Y.)
Davis, J. M. Murder of Frau Schultz (1944, Russ.)
Davis, Lindsay. Shadows in Bronze (70 A.D., Rome)
  Silver Pigs (70 A.D., Rome)
Davis, Robert. Kimura (1970, S.F.)
DeAndrea, W. L. Five O'Clock Lightning (1953, NYC)
  Lunatic Fringe (1896, NYC)
De Blasis, C. Night Child (1865, Maine)
De Gramont, S. Lives to Give (WWII, Fr.)
Deighton, L. SS-GB (1941, Eng.)
  Spy Sinker (1977–1987)
  Winter (1900–1945)
Dekobra, M. Diamond Queen (1900, Trans.)
De La Torre, L. Detections of Dr. Sam: Johnson (ca.1770, Eng.)
  Dr. Sam: Johnson, Detector (ca.1770, Eng.)
  Elizabeth Is Missing (1753, Eng.)
  Exploits of Dr. Sam: Johnson (ca.1770, Eng.)
  Heir of Douglas (1700s, Scot.)
  Return of Dr. Sam: Johnson, Detector (ca.1770, Eng.)
De Lillo, D. Libra (1960s)
De Marco, G. Canvas Prison (1949, L.A.)
  October Heat (1934, S.F.)
Demarest, P. G. House on Washington Place (1860s, NYC)
Deming, R. What's the Matter with Helen? (1933, Ia.)
Dennis, E. M. Mr. Coleman, Gent (1664, Eng.)
Dennis, R. MacTaggart's War (1940, Can.)
De Pre, J. Die, Jessica, Die (1910, L.I.)
  Sound of Dying Roses (1871, Va.)
  Third Woman (1912, NYC)
Derleth, A. Adventure of the Orient Express (1930s, Europe)
  Adventure of the Unique Dickensians (1930s, Eng.)
  Casebook of Solar Pons (1930s, Eng.)
  Chronicles of Solar Pons (1930s, Eng.)
  In re Sherlock Holmes (1930s, Eng.)
  Memoirs of Solar Pons (1930s, Eng.)
  Mr. Fairlie's Final Journey (1930s, Eng.)
  Praed Street Dossier (1930s, Eng.)
  Praed Street Papers (1930s, Eng.)
  Reminiscences of Solar Pons (1930s, Eng.)
  Return of Solar Pons (1930s, Eng.)
  Three Problems for Solar Pons (1930s, Eng.)
Devine, D. This Is Your Death (1962, Eng.)
Devlin, E. Hide and Seek (1961)
Devon, M. Miss Osborne Misbehaves (ca.1810, Eng.)
Devoore, A. Oliver Iverson (1890, NYC)
Dexter, P. Paris Trout (1940s, Ga.)
Dial, J. Echoes of War (WWII, Ger.)
Dibdin, M. Last Sherlock Holmes Story (1888, Eng.)

Rich Full Death (1855, Florence)
DiChiara, R. Dick and the Devil (1949, L.A.)
Dickinson, P. Perfect Gallows (1940s, Eng.)
Dicks, T. Mounties: Great March West (Can.)
  Mounties: Massacre in the Hills (Can.)
  Mounties: Wardrums of the Blackfoot (Can.)
Dickson, Carter. Fear Is the Same (1795, Eng.)
Diehl, W. 17 (1930s, U.S.)
Dillmann, J. Blood Warning (1980, New Or.)
  French Quarter Killers (1976, New Or.)
  Unholy Matrimony (1974, New Or.)
Disney, D. M. At Some Forgotten Door (1886, Conn.)
  Testimony by Silence (1880s, Conn.)
  That Which Is Crooked (1898–1946, Conn.)
Ditton, J. Copley's Hunch (WWII)
Dobyns, S. Dancer with One Leg (1970s, Boston)
Doctorow, E. L. Billy Bathgate (1930s, NYC)
Dodson, D. B. Last Command (1942)
Doherty, P. C. Angel of Death (1299, Eng.)
  Crown in Darkness (1286, Scot.)
  Death of a King (1344, Eng.)
  Fate of Princes (1483–5, Eng.)
  Satan in St. Mary's (1290s, Eng.)
  Serpent Among the Lilies (1429, Eng.)
  Spy in Chancery (1290s, Eng.)
  Whyte Hart (1404, Eng.)
Dold, G. 6 titles (1950s, Kan.)
Doliner, R. Thin Line (1963, Viet Nam)
  Twelfth of April (1920–58)
Donaldson, N. Goodbye, Dr. Thorndyke (1943, Eng.)
Donovan, D. Scarlet Seal (ca.1500, It.)
Doody, M. Aristotle Detective (332 B.C., Athens)
Doran, J. In the Depths of the First Degree (1862, Va.)
Dorsetts, D. Dueling Oaks (New Or.)
Douglas, Ben. Challenge at Castle Gap (1912, Tex.)
Douglas, C. N. Amberleigh (1890s, Ire.)
  Good Night, Mr. Holmes (1890s, London)
Douglas, John. Blind Spring Rambler (1923, W. Va.)
  Haunts (1985, W. Va.)
Dourado, A. Bells of Agony (1700s, Brazil)
Downes, D. Scarlet Thread (WWII)
Downing, D. Red Eagles (1944)
Dreher, S. Captive in Time (1871, Colo.)
Driscoll, P. Heritage (1945–62, Algeria)
Drown, M. Plowing Up a Snake (1956, N.H.)
Drummond, John. Behind Dark Shutters (1890s, Scot.)
Drummond, June. Slowly the Poison (1911, S. Afr.)
  Unsuitable Miss Pelham
Du Breuil, L. Legend of Molly Moor (Md.)
Dudley, E. Picaroon (1700s, Eng.)
Du Maurier, D. Jamaica Inn (ca.1815, Eng.)
  My Cousin Rachel (1800s, Eng.)
Dunn, C. Gabrielle's Gamble (1800s, Eng.)
Durand, L. Daddy (early 1940s)
  Jaguar (1920s)
E-7. Romance of a Spy (WWII, Fr.)
Easterman, D. Ninth Buddha (1921, India)
Eastvale, M. As the Sparks Fly (1800s, Eng.)
Eberhart, M. G. Bayou Road (1863, New Or.)
  Casa Madrone (1906, S.F.)
  Family Fortune (ca.1860, W. Va.)
Echard, M. Dark Fantastic (1870s, Midwest)
Eckert, A. W. Scarlet Mansion (1800s, Chi.)
Eco, U. Name of the Rose (1327, It.)
Eddenden, A. E. Good Year for Murder (1940, Can.)
Eden, D. Bella (1800s, Eng.)
  Samantha (1800s, Eng.)
  Sleep in the Woods (1800s, Eng.)
Eden, M. Murder of Lawrence of Arabia (1930s, Saud. Arab.)
Edgar, J. Dancer's Daughter (Eng.)
Edwards, Cassie. Love's Legacy (1865, Charleston)
Edwards, H. All Night at Mr. Stanyhursts (1783, Eng.)
Edwards, H. S. Missing Man (1700s, Eng.)
Edwards, R. Captain's Lady (Eng.)
Egleton, C. October Plot (WWII, Eng.)
  Russian Enigma (1962)

Winter Touch (1956, Eng.)
Eickhoff, R. L. Hand to Execute
Elder, M. Prometheus Operation (1945, U.S.)
Elliott, David. Blue Movie
Ellis, J. Wexford (1852, New Or.)
Ellroy, J. Big Nowhere (1950, L.A.)
  Black Dahlia (1940s, L.A.)
  Clandestine (1951, L.A.)
  L.A. Confidential (1950s, L.A.)
Elon, A. Timetable (1944)
Elrod, P. N. Bloodcircle (1930s, Chi.)
  Bloodlust (1930s, Chi.)
  Lifeblood (1930s, Chi.)
Elsna, H. Cast a Long Shadow (1905, Eng.)
  Cherished Ones (ca.1910, Eng.)
Emerick, L. Web of Evil (1887, Pa.)
Emerson, D. Gate of Honour (1820)
  Murder in the Family (1840, Eng.)
Endore, G. Werewolf of Paris (1871, Paris)
Engleman, P. Catch a Falling Angel (1969, Chi.)
  Dead in Center Field (1961, N.J.)
  Who Shot Longshot Sam? (1974, N.J.)
Epstein, E.J. Cartel (1953, Iran)
Esmond, H. Darsham's Folly (Eng.)
  Eye Stones (1800s, Eng.)
Estey, D. Lost Tale (WWII, Isle of Man)
Estleman, L. D. Dr. Jekyll and Mr. Holmes (1890s, Eng.)
  Sherlock Holmes vs. Dracula (1890, Eng.)
  Whiskey River (1928–31, Det.)
Evans, Alan. Audacity (1918, ship)
  Thunder at Dawn (WWII)
Evans, Audrey. So Pitifully Slain (1500s, Eng.)
Eyre, M. Girl in the Tiffany Dress (1810, Pitt.)
Fagyas, M. Devil's Lieutenant (1909, Vienna)
Fairbairn, R. Devil Kinsmere (1670, Eng.)
Fairlie, G. They Found Each Other (WWII, Fr.)
Falkirk, R. all titles in Blackstone series (1820s, Eng.)
Falkner, H. Arlett's Death (early 1980s, Syd.)
Fantoni, B. Mike Dime (1948, Phil.)
Farmer, J. Sedona (1838, Eng.)
Farmer, P. J. Adventure of the Peerless Peer (1916, Afr.)
Farnol, J. all Shrig titles (ca.1815–1820, Eng.)
Farnsworth, M. Evil That Waited (1904, Mass.)
Farrant, S. Lady of Rogan's Tower (Eng.)
  Reluctant Paragon (1800s, Eng.)
  Touch of Terror (1860s, Eng.)
Ferrand, G. House of Glass (Venice)
  Moonmist (1840, Eng.)
Feuer, L. Case of the Revolutionist's Daughter (1881, Eng.)
Fields, A. V-J Day (1945, NYC)
Findley, T. Famous Last Words (WWII)
Fisher, Alan. Yangtze (1937, Shanghai)
Fisher, Graham. Plot to Kill Wallis Simpson (1936, Eng.)
Flannery, S. Trinity Factor (WWII)
Fleming, H. K. Day They Kidnapped Queen Victoria (1867, Eng.)
Fleming, Jane. Hawthorn Wood (La.)
Fleming, Joan. Every Inch a Lady (1950s, Eng.)
  Screams from a Penny Dreadful (1800s, Eng.)
  Too Late! Too Late! the Maiden Cried (1800s, Eng.)
Fleming, T. F. Dreams of Glory (1780, Charleston)
Fletcher, Donna. San Francisco Surrender (1873, S.F.)
Fletcher, J. S. At the Blue Bell Inn (1600s, Eng.)
Flohr, W. Lotus Deception (1966–8)
Flores, J. Hawkshead (1800s, Eng.)
Flynn, C. H. Washed in the Blood (1938, L.A.)
Flynn, J. Bannerman (1916, Denver)
  Border Incident (1916)
Follett, J. Churchill's Gold (1941, ship)
  Mirage (1967)
  U-700 (1941)
Follett, K. Key to Rebecca (1942, Egypt)
  Man from St. Petersburg (1914, Eng.)
  Storm Island (WWII)
Foote, S. September September (1957, Memphis)
Forbes, C. Heights of Zervos (1941, Greece)
  Leader and the Damned (WWII, Ger.)

Forbes, S. Buried in So Sweet a Place (1918, Boston)
    Deadly Kind of Lonely (1939, Tex.)
    Go to Thy Death Bed (1891, N.C.)
    Grieve for the Past (1930s, Kan.)
    Sad, Sudden Death of My Fair Lady (1933, Chi.)
    She Was Only the Sheriff's Daughter (1940s, Tex.)
Ford, E. Such Bitter Business (1800s, Eng.)
Ford, Hilary. Bride for Bedivere (1800s, Eng.)
    Castle Malindine (1860s, Ire.)
Forrest, A. Balance of Dangers (ca.1804)
    Captain Justice (1804, Fr.)
    Pandora Secret (1804, Eng.)
Forrest, Wilma. Anne of Destiny House (Scot.)
    Last Hope House (1855, Ire.)
Forsyte, C. Decoding of Edwin Drood (1860s, Eng.)
Forsythe, B. Expo '98: Sherlock Holmes in Omaha (1898, Omaha)
Fowles, J. Maggot (1700s)
Fox, G. Warlord's Hill (1940s, N.J.)
Fox, G. F. Terror Over London (1888, London)
Fox, Joseph, Jr. Tancred (ca.1100)
Foxall, R. Amorous Rogue (ca.1750, Eng.)
    Dark Forest (1807, Eng.)
    Little Ferret (1807, Eng.)
    Noble Pirate (ca.1750, Eng.)
    Silver Goblet (1808, Eng.)
    Society of the Dispossessed (ca.1750, Eng.)
Foxx, J. Freebooty (1863, S.F.)
Francis, C. Night Sky (1935–45)
    Wolf Winter (1950s, Nor.)
Frank, W. I. Good for One More Ride (early 1900s, L.A.)
Frankland, E. P. Murders at Crossby (900s, Eng.)
Franzen, J. Twenty-Seventh City (1984, St. Louis)
Freeborn, R. Russian Crucifix (1860, Eng.)
Freeling, N. Sand Castles (Holl.)
Freytag, J. Amber Palace (N.Y.)
Friedman, M. Hurricane Season (1950s, Fla.)
    Paper Phoenix (1975, S.F.)
Friesner, E. M. Druid's Blood (1800s, Eng.)
Frizell, B. Timetable for the General (WWII)
Fuller, C. Soldier's Play (1944, La.)
Furst, A. Night Soldiers (1934–45, Europe)
Fytton, F. Nation Within (ca.1960, Paris)
Gadda, C. E. That Awful Mess on the Via Merulana (1927, Rome)
Gainham, S. Mythmaker (1946, Vienna)
    Place in the Country (1946, Austria)
    Stone Roses (1948, Prague)
Gaither, F. O. Double Muscadine (1850s, South)
Galloway, D. Lamaar Ransom—Private Eye (WWII, L.A.)
Galsworthy, J. On Forsyte 'Change
Garbo, N. Cabal (1967, Mid. East)
Gardner, J. Flamingo (1930s, Shanghai)
    Secret Families (1964)
    Secret Generations (1909–35, Eng.)
    Secret Houses (1940s)
Garfield, B. Paladin (WWII, Eng.)
    Romanov Succession (1941, Europe)
    Tripwire (1880s, West)
Garth, D. Fire on the Wind (Mich.)
Garwood, J. Bride (Scot.)
    Guardian Angel (1815, London)
Gaskin, C. Charmed Circle (WWII, Scot.)
Gast, K. P. Dil Dies Hard (1915, Wash.)
Gavin, C. Light Woman (1871, Paris)
    None Dare Call It Treason (1941, Fr.)
Gavin, T. Last Film of Emile Vico (1938, L.A.)
Gay, V. Spy at the Gate (1804, Eng.)
Gaynor, M. Chicago Joe and the Showgirl (1944, Eng.)
Gellis, R. Sing Witch, Sing Death (ca.1900, Eng.)
Geron, F. Blooding (WWII)
Gerson, J. Death Squad London (1936, London)
    Death's Head Berlin (1934, Berlin)
    Deathwatch (1939, London)
Giancol, A. Three Racketeers (1920s)
Gibbs, M. A. Amateur Governess (1897, Eng.)
Gilbert, Anna. Family Likeness (1800s, Eng.)
    Flowers for Lilian (1800s, Eng.)
    Images of Rose (1883, Eng.)
    Look of Innocence (ca.1890, Eng.)
    Miss Bede Is Staying (1800s, Eng.)
    Walk in the Wood (WWII, Eng.)
Gilbert, M. Death in Captivity (WWII, It.)
Gilman, D. Incident at Badamya (1950, Burma)
Gilmore, C. C. Atlantic City Proof (ca.1928, N.J.)
Gipe, G. Coney Island Quickstep (1891, NYC)
Glazier, S. Lost Provinces (1907–11, Fr.)
Goddard, R. Painting the Darkness (1882, Eng.)
Godfrey, E. Case of the Cold Murderer (1969, Toronto)
Goldberg, G. J. Heart Payments (1966, L.A.)
Goldsmith, B. Blue Numbers (1973, Calif.)
Goodchild, G. Saskatoon Patrol (ca.1900, Can.)
    Trooper O'Neill (1890s, Can.)
Goodman, G. S. Mysterious Abduction (1770s, Austria)
Gordon, R. Medical Witness (1936, Eng.)
    Private Life of Dr. Crippin (1909, Eng.)
    Private Life of Jack the Ripper (1888, Eng.)
Gores, J. Hammett (1928, S. F.)
Gorman, E. Blood Game (1892, Midwest)
    Death Ground (1890s)
    Grave's Retreat (1884, Ia.)
    Guild (1890s)
    Night of Shadows (1890, Ia.)
    What the Dead Men Say (1898, Ia.)
Goulart, R. Curse of the Obelisk (1897)
Gowing, N. Wire (1981, Pol.)
Grace, A. Wharf Sinister (ca.1860, NYC)
Graeme, B. Cherchez la Femme (1800s, Paris)
    Lady in Black (1800s, Paris)
    Trail of the White Knight (1919, Hung.)
Graeme, D. Inn of the Thirteen Swords (ca.1600, Fr.)
    Monsieur Blackshirt (ca.1600, Fr.)
    Sword of Monsieur Blackshirt (ca. 1600, Fr.)
    Vengeance of Monsieur Blackshirt (ca.1600, Fr.)
Grafton, C. W. Rope Began to Hang the Butcher (1941, Ky.)
Graham, J. Wrath of God (1922, Mex.)
Graham, W. Wreck of the Grey Cat (1898, Eng.)
Grandower, E. Blackbourne Hall (ca.1910)
    Rivergate House (1920s, NYC)
    Secret Room of Morgate House (1896, Ill.)
Grant, D. Emerald Decision (1940, Eng.)
Grant, William. Collison Course (1800s, Colo.)
    Colorado Special (1800s, Colo.)
    Gold Train (1800s, West)
    Iron Horse (1800s, West)
    Trackwalker (1800s, West)
Graves, R. L. Argon Furnace (1942, Jap.)
Graves, W. Mumberley Inheritance (1900, Eng.)
Gray, Angela. Lattimore Arch (1895, Wash. D.C.)
    Nightmare at Riverview (1885, Ga.)
Gray, Caroline. Third Life (1932)
Gray, D. S. Heydrich Deception (1939)
Grayson, Richard. 7 titles (ca.1900, Paris)
Green, F. L. Odd Man Out (1920s, Belfast)
Green, W. M. Romanov Connection (ca.1920, Russ.)
Greene, G. Tenth Man (1945, Fr.)
Greene, H. Flags at Doney (1956, It.)
Greene, M. Forever Love
    Winter's Flame (1895, Eng.)
Greenwald, K. Lost Adventures of Sherlock Holmes
Greenwood, K. Cocaine Blues (1920s, Melb.)
    Flying Too High (1920s, Melb.)
Greenwood, L. B. Sherlock Holmes and the Case of Sabina Hall (1890s, Eng.)
    Sherlock Holmes and the Case of the Raleigh Legacy (ca.1890, London)
    Sherlock Holmes and the Thistle of Scotland (1890, Eng.)
Gretton, M. S. Crumplin! (1491, Eng.)
Grey, H. Portrait of a Mobster (1920s, NYC)
Grierson, E. Massingham Affair (1890s, Eng.)
Grossbach, R. Cheap Detective (1940, S.F.)
Guild, N. Berlin Warning (1941)
    Chain Reaction (1944)
Gunn, N. M. Key of the Chest (ca.1900, Scot.)
Gurr, D. Ring Master (WWII, Ger.)
H., I. Phantoms of the Cloister (1420, Eng.)

Haines, W. W. Target (1944, Fr.)
Halkin, J. Hantu
Hall, B. Passion of Dracula (1911, Eng.)
Hall, D. J. Crowd Is Silent (WWII, Europe)
Hall, R. L. Benjamin Franklin Takes the Case (1757, Eng.)
    Exit Sherlock Holmes (1906, Eng.)
    King Edward Plot (1906, Eng.)
    Murder at San Simeon (1934, Calif.)
Hall, Rodney. Captivity Captive (1898, Australia)
Hambly, B. Quirinal Hill Affair (116, Rome)
    Those Who Hunt the Night (1907, London)
Hamilton, M. A. Special Providence (1917, Eng.)
Hamilton, P. Gas Light (1800s, Eng.)
Hamilton, V. Traitorous Heart (1800s, Eng.)
Hammer, D. L. 22nd Man
Hammond, M. Theseus Code (1943, 1978, Crete)
Hammond, M. A. Land of Gold (1800s, S.F.)
Hanley, E. Guilty As Charged (1930s, Ill.)
Harding, Bret. all 10 titles (West)
Harding, W. H. Rainbow (1925, N.Y.)
Hardwick, Michael. Nightbone (1800s, Eng.)
    Prisoner of the Devil (1895, Eng.)
    Private Life of Dr. Watson
    Regency Rake (ca.1820, Eng.)
    Regency Revenge (ca.1820, Eng.)
    Regency Royal (ca.1820, Eng.)
    Sherlock Holmes (1902, Eng.)
Hardy, R. Wings of the Wind (1964, China)
Hargrave, L. Clara Reeve (1800s, Eng.)
Harrington, W. English Lady (1931–WWII, Ger.)
    Oberst (1944, Paris)
    Search for Elizabeth Brandt (1938–45, Ger.)
Harris, Joanna. Worldly Innocent
Harris, John. Covenant with Death (WWI)
    Fox from His Lair (WWII)
    Picture of Defeat (1942, Naples)
    Sunset at Sheba (1914, S. Afr.)
Harrison, M. Exploits of Chevalier Dupin (1800s, Paris)
    I, Sherlock Holmes (1881–91, Eng.)
Harrison, R. all 9 titles (1890s, Eng.)
Hart, C. G. Escape from Paris (1940, Paris)
Hartland, M. Down Among the Dead Men (1970s, H. Kong)
Harwicke, G. Acting on Information Received (1960s)
Hastings, M. Devil's Spy (1917, Mid. East)
Hastings, P. Act of Darkness (1890s, Eng.)
    Conservatory (1871, Eng.)
    Field of the Forty Footsteps (1790s, Fr.)
Hatfield, M. Spy Fever
Hawkes, E. Shadow of the Moth (1917, London)
Hayes, J. M. Grey Pilgrim (1940, Ariz.)
Hayes, L. Challoners of Bristol (1811, R.I.)
    Harlequin House (1869, S.C.)
Hays, L. Once Upon a Time in America (1933–68, NYC)
Head, M. Accomplice (1934, Paris; 1935, Kan. City)
Heard, H. F. Black Fox (1870s)
Heath, M. House of the Strange Women (1800s, Calif.)
Heatter, B. Einstein Plot (1941)
    London Gun (WWII)
Heaven, C. Castle of Eagles (1847, Vienna)
    Craven Legacy (1840, Eng.)
    Fires of Glenloch (1700s, Scot.)
Hebert, A. In the Shadow of the Wind (1936, Fr.)
Heffernan, W. Broderick (1920s, NYC)
Heller, K. Man's Illegal Life (1722, London)
    Man's Loving Family (1727, Eng.)
    Man's Storm (1703, London)
Helterman, J. Blue Frogs (1800s, Fr.)
Hely, S. Sign of the Serpent (1700s, Ire.)
Hering, H. A. Hunt the Tiger (1781, Paris)
Herlin, H. Grishin (1918, Russ.)
    Solo Run (ca.1975, Ger.)
Hervey, E. Governess (1870, Eng.)
    Into the Valley of Death (1870s, Eng.)
    Man of Gold (1874, Eng.)
Heyer, G. Black Moth (1800s, Eng.)
    Quiet Gentleman (1800s, Eng.)
    Regency Buck (1800s, Eng.)

Settings Index — PAST

Heyes, D. Kill (1938, L.A.)
Heywood, J. Berkut (1945, Ger.)
Hicks, H. B. Castle at Jade Cove (1884, Calif.)
Higgins, G. V. Trust (1967, Boston)
Higgins, J. Cold Harbour (1944, Fr.)
    Day of Judgement (1963, Ger.)
    Eagle Has Landed (1943, Ger.)
    Last Place God Made (1938, Brazil)
    Luciano's Luck (1943, Sic.)
    Night of the Fox (WWII)
    Season in Hell (1983)
Hill, P. Devil of Aske (1700s, Eng.)
Hill, Reginald. Collaborators (WWII, Fr.)
Hilton, J. Knight Without Armour (ca.1915, Russ.)
Hilton, J. B. Dead-Nettle (1904, Eng.)
    Gamekeeper's Gallows (1877, Eng.)
    Mr. Fred (Eng.)
    Quiet Stranger (Eng.)
    Rescue from the Rose (1911, Eng.)
    Some Run Crooked (1958, Eng.)
Hirschfeld, B. Bonnie and Clyde (1932, U.S.)
Hirschhorn, R. Target Mayflower (1944, New Eng.)
Hirt, H. Heat of Winter (1952, India)
Hitchcock, R. Attack the Lusitania! (1915)
    Sea Wrack (1940, Fr.)
Hitt, J. A. Sherlock Holmes and the Curious
    Adventure of the Clockwork Prince
    (1899, London)
Hodel, M. P. Enter the Lion (1875, Eng.)
Hodge, J. A. Here Comes a Candle (1812, Mass.)
    Maulever Hall (Eng.)
    Winding Stair (1806, Port.)
Hogan, J. P. Proteus Operation (1939)
Hollyock, D. Innocent Madness (1838, Ire.)
Holmes, N. Nobody's Fault (1970s, Eng.)
Holt, V. Captive (1800s, Eng.)
    Demon Lover (1800s, Paris)
    Lord of the Far Island (ca. 1900, Eng.)
    Road to Paradise (1800s, Eng.)
    Secret Woman (1800s, Eng.)
    Silk Vendetta (1800s)
    Time of the Hunter's Moon (1800s, Eng.)
Hood, E. Wake for Donald (1820s, Edin.)
Horan, J. D. Peking Agent (1962)
Horler, S. Blanco Case (1876, Eng.)
    Man of Evil (1600s, Eng.)
Hotchner, A. E. Man Who Lived at the Ritz (1940, Paris)
Howard, E. Murderer in the Gaden (ca.1900, Eng.)
Howley, B. Stalking Horse (1972)
Hubell, N. Adventures of Creighton Holmes (1930s, Eng.)
Huff, T. E. Nine Bucks Row (ca.1890, Eng.)
Huffman, L. House Behind the Mint (1870s, S.F.)
Hughart, B. Bridge of Birds (ca.1000, Peking)
    Story of the Stone (ca.1000, Peking)
Hughes, M. E. Precious in His Sight (1960s, La.)
Hughes, T. J. Queen's Mate (1943, ship)
Humes, H. L. Underground City (WWII, Fr.)
Hunter, E. Lizzie (1890s, U.S.)
Hunter, J. D. Expendable Spy (1945, Ger.)
    Flying Cross (1918, Fr.)
    Tailspin (1945, Europe)
    Tin Cravat (1945, Ger.)
Hunter, S. Master Sniper (WWII)
    Spanish Gambit (1930s, Sp.)
Hurd, F. Curse of the Moors (Eng.)
    House on Russian Hill (1800s, S.F.)
    Secret of Awen Castle (Eng.)
Hutchinson, H. G. Crowsborough Beacon (late 1700s, Eng.)
Hylton, S. Caprice
    Carridice Chain (WWI, Eng.)
    Crimson Falcon (ca.1900, Vienna)
Hyman, T. Seven Days to Petrograd (1917, Russ., train)
Hynd, N. Flowers from Berlin (1939, U.S.)
    Khrushev Objective (1956)
    Truman's Spy (1950, U.S.)
Iddesleigh, W. S. N. Charms (1751, Eng.)
Ignatius, D, Agents of Influence (ca.1970, Beirut)
Ireland, W. H. Catholic (1200s)

Gondez the Monk (1200s)
Irish, W. Waltz Into Darkness (1880, New Or.)
Irving, C. Angel of Zin (1943, Pol.)
    Axis (1936–40)
Irwin, R. Mysteries of Algiers (1960, Algiers)
Irwin, W. Julius Caesar Murder Case (ca.50 B.C., It.)
Isaacs, S. Shining Through (WWII, Berlin)
Jackman, S. Game of Soldiers (1948, Egypt)
    Operation Catcher (1944, Yem.)
Jackson, Eileen. Autumn Lace (1800s, Wales)
Jackson, M. J. A. Arabian Pearl (ca.1900, train)
    Punjat's Ruby (1899, Eng.)
James, Donald. House of Janus (ca.1945)
    Shadow of the Wolf (1941, Eng.)
Jameson, F. Green Fire (1968, S. Am.)
Jameson, S. Before the Crossing (1939, Eng.)
Janeway, H. This Passionate Land (1850s, South)
Janson, H. Invasion (1944, Fr.)
Jarrett, P. Throwaway Man (1943)
Jeaffreson, J. C. Live It Down (1830s)
Jefferis, B. Beloved Lady (1400s, Eng.)
Jeffers, H. P. Adventure of the Stalwart Companions (1880, NYC)
    Murder on Mike (1939, NYC)
    Rag Doll Murder (1935, NYC)
    Rubout at the Onyx (1935, NYC)
Jenkins, Dan. Fast Copy (1930s, Tex.)
Jerrold, B. Two Lives (1830s, Fr.)
Johnston, V. Fateful Summer (1910, L.I.)
    House on Bostwick Square (1880s, Eng.)
    House on the Left Bank (1870, Paris)
    I Came to the Highlands (1800s, Scot.)
    Late Mrs. Fonsell (1800s, L.I.)
    Man at Windmere (1857, Eng.)
    Masquerade in Venice (1880, Venice)
    Silver Dolphin (1840s, L.I.)
Johnston, W. Banyon (1937, L.A.)
Jones, F. Master and Maid (1915, Toronto)
Jones, H. W. Death and the Trumpets of Tuscany (1950s, Venice)
    Shot on Location (ca.1968, It.)
Jones, J. S. Time of the Wolf (1942, Vienna)
Jones, K. O. To the Dark Tower Came (1840s, Ire.)
Jones, M. Season of the Strangler (1969, Ala.)
Jones, R. D. Fenris Option (WWII)
Jones, R. P. Country Code
    Man Who Killed Hitler (WWII, Berlin)
Jones, T. Dutch Treat (1940, Holl.)
Jordan, L. Hidden Fires (ca.1900, Tex.)
Judd, C. Jerusalem Camp
Jupp, R. F. Chancery Lane Tragedy (1815, London)
Jute, A. Zaharoff Commission (WWII, Ger.)
Kail, N. Swastika (WWII, Ger.)
Kaminsky, S. M. Bullet for a Star (1940, L.A.)
    Buried Caesars (1942, L.A.)
    Catch a Falling Clown (ca.1942, Calif.)
    Down for the Count (1942, L.A.)
    Fala Factor (ca.1942, L.A.)
    He Done Her Wrong (ca.1942, L.A.)
    High Midnight (1942, L.A.)
    Howard Hughes Affair (1942, L.A.)
    Man Who Shot Lewis Vance (1942, L.A.)
    Murder on the Yellow Brick Road (ca. 1940, L.A.)
    Never Cross a Vampire (1942, L.A.)
    Poor Butterfly (1942, S.F.)
    Smart Moves (1942, NYC)
    Think Fast, Mr. Peters (1942, L.A.)
    You Bet Your Life (ca.1940, Chi.)
Kane, C. J. Blood and Sable (WWI, Russ.)
Kantor, Hal. Big Stopper (1920s, Chi.)
    Blown Away (1915–1948, NYC)
Kaplan, A. War of the Raven (1939, Buen. A.)
Karr, Lee. Beware My Love (1800s, Colo.)
    Dark Cries of Gray Oaks (1880s, Fla.)
Kartun, D. Courier (1940, Fr.)
Kary, E. Midnight Lace (1844, London)
Katkov, N. Blood and Orchids (1930, Haw.)
Kaufelt, D. A. Souvenir (1942, Paris)
Kavaler, R. Doubting Castle (late 1800s)
Kavanaugh, C. Bride of Lenore (1891, Va.)
Kay, T. After Eli (1939, Ga.)
Keane, C. Crossing (1945, ship)

Keating, H. R. F. Murder of the Maharajah (1930, India)
    Remarkable Case of Burglary (1871, Eng.)
Kelland, C. B. Dangerous Angel (1870s, S.F.)
    Lady and the Giant (1869, N.Y.)
    Monitor Affair (1860s, NYC)
Kellerman, F. Quality of Mercy (1593, Eng.)
Kelly, J. Appalachin (1950s, N.Y.)
Kelly, M. That Girl in the Alley (1936, Eng.)
Kelly, T. J. Terror by Gaslight (1800s, Phil.)
Kelton, E. Stand Proud (ca.1905, Tex.)
Kemeny, J. A. Strands of War (WWII, Ger.)
Keneally, T. Victim of the Aurora (1910, Antarctic)
Kennedy, W. Legs (1920s, U.S.)
Kennedy, W. P. Himmler Equation (1944, Ger.)
Kenrick, T. Faraday's Flowers (1940, Shanghai)
Keppel, C. Madam, You Must Die (1798, Eng.)
    Villains (1744, Eng.)
    When I Say Goodbye (1700s, Eng.)
Ker, A. Adeline Saint Julian (1632)
    Edric the Forester (1066)
Kerr, Philip. March Violets (1936, Berlin)
    Pale Criminal (1938, Berlin)
Kerr, R. Stuart Legacy (1800s, Scot.)
Kerrigan, J. Phoenix Assault (1945, Berlin)
Kessel, J. Bernan Affair (1921, Paris)
Kidd, E. Sweet Secrets (ca.1900)
Kiefer, W. Lingala Code (1960s, Bel. Congo)
Kilian, M. Dance on a Sinking Ship (1935, ship)
Kimbrough, K. Augusta, the First (1742, Maine)
    Barbara, the Valiant (1859, Ga.)
    Dorothy, the Terrified (1863, South)
    Jane, the Courageous (1771, Maine)
    Joanne, the Unpredictable (1834, Eng.)
    Kathrine, the Returned (1900, Boston)
    Marcia, the Innocent (1845, Eng.)
    Margaret, the Faithful (1783, Maine)
    Millijoy, the Determined (1858, Ga.)
    Patricia, the Beautiful (1787, Va.)
    Rachel, the Possessed (1798, Maine)
    Rebecca, the Mysterious (1822, Mass.)
    Susannah, the Righteous (1807, Boston)
    Thanesworth House (1800s, Miss.)
Kinder, K. Raven and the Dove (1876, Eng.)
King, Benjamin. Bullet for Stonewall (ca.1860, U.S.)
King, F. Act of Darkness (1930s, India)
    Raya (1942, Cairo)
King, H. Four Days (1953, U.S.)
King, L. W. Rochemer Hag (1800s, Eng.)
King, Ramona. Steal Away (1930s, Chi.)
Kingsley, B. Black Angel (1933, Cape Cod)
Kingsley-Smith, T. Forsaken (1930s, Kan.)
    Murder of an Old-Time Movie Star (1930s, L.A.)
Kirsch, J. Bad Moon Rising (1960s, Calif.)
Kirst, H. H. Hero in the Tower (1940, Fr.)
    Night of the Generals (1942–56, Ger.)
    Nights of the Long Knives (1933–9, Ger.)
    Twilight of the Generals (1938, Berlin)
Kisner, J. Slice of Life (1945, Chi.)
Klein, E. Parachutists (1944, Hung.)
Kleypas, L. Give Me Tonight (1880)
Knight, Alanna. Bloodline (1800s, Edin.)
    Deadly Beloved (1800s, Edin.)
    Enter Second Murderer (1800s, Edin.)
    Killing Cousins (1871, Scot.)
Knight, S. Requiem at Rogano (1902, Eng.)
Knox, A. Raider's Moon (ca.1790, Can.)
Koning, H. De Witt's War (1941, Holl.)
    Petersburg-Cannes Express (1900, train)
Konsalik, H. G. Strike Force Ten (1945, Russ.)
Koontz, D. R. Hanging On (WWII, Fr.)
Kotzwinkle, W. Fata Morgana (1861, Paris)
Kozhevnikov, V. Shield and Sword (WWII, Ger.)
Krauth, N. Matilda, My Darling (1890s, Australia)
Kriz, J. Karsten's Flats (1938, Tex.)
Kruse, J. Red Omega (1951)
Kurland, M. Death by Gaslight (ca.1890, Eng.)
    Infernal Device (ca.1890)
Kyle, D. Black Camelot (1944)
    King's Commissar (1918, Russ.)
    Stalking Point (WWII)
La Fountaine, G. Scott-Dunlap Ring (1870s, U.S.)
Laidlaw, R. Linton Porcupine (1500s, Eng.)

Laiken, D. Killing Time in Buffalo (1967, N.Y.)
Laine, A. Melancholy Virgin (1800s, Eng.)
    Reluctant Heiress (ca.1802, Eng.)
Laker, R. Smuggler's Bride (1809, Eng.)
Lambe, G. Mysteries of Ferney Castle (1600s, Eng.)
Lambert, D. Golden Express (1940, train)
    Judas Code (1941, Lisbon)
    Vendetta (1942, Russ.)
Land, Jane. These Tiger's Hearts (1860s, Vienna)
Lane, Jane. Conies in the Hay (Eng.)
Lane, Willoughby. Sherlock Holmes and the Wood Green Empire Mystery (1918)
Langley, B. Churchill Diamonds (1898)
    Traverse of the Gods (1944, Switz.)
Lanigan, C. Bound by Love (1914)
Larreta, A. Last Poirtrait of the Duchess of Alba (1802, Madrid)
Larsen, G. Dorothy and Agatha (1937, Eng.)
    Paramount Kill (1945, L.A.)
Latham, B. all 5 titles (1930s, NYC)
Lathom, F. Astonishment!! (1700s)
    Mysterious Free-Booter (1500s)
    Unknown (ca.1530, Eng.)
Lathy, T. P. Invisible Enemy (1600s, Pol.)
La Tourrette, J. House on Octavia Street (1899, S.F.)
Laumer, K. Deadfall (1948, L.A.)
Law, E. Sealed Knot (1811, Eng.)
Lawman, A. Hounds of Hell (1940, Holl.)
Lawrence, Ken. Berlin Message (WWII)
Leasor, J. Unknown Warrior (WWII)
Lee, Elsie. Silence Is Golden (1860s, Eng.)
Lee, John. Lago (WWII, It.)
    Lake of the Diamond (WWII)
    Ninth Man (1942, Wash. D.C.)
    Stalag Texas (1946, Tex.)
    Thirteenth Hour (1944, Berlin)
Lee, Lydia. Magnificent Mirabelle (1800s, Eng.)
Lee, V. Penelope Brandling (1700s, Wales)
Lee, W. W. Rogue's Gold (West)
    Rustler's Venom (West)
Leighton, T. Night of the Sphinx (1936, Egypt)
    Phoenix Formula (WWII)
Leonard, P. G. Phantom of the Sacred Well (1879, Guat.)
Leopold, C. Casablack (1942, Casa.)
Lescroart, J. T. Rasputin's Revenge (1916, Russ.)
Leslie, P. Bastard Brigade (WWII, Fr.)
    Catapult Ultimatum (WWII)
    Cold Snap (1940, Paris)
    Death Mail (WWII, Prague)
Leslie, Susan. Unfinished Tapestry (1850, Eng.)
Lestienne, V. Furioso (WWII, Fr.)
Levey, M. Affair on the Appian Way (ancient Rome)
Levi, P. Head in the Soup (1972, Eng.)
Le Voleur. For Love of a Bedouin Maid (1797)
Lewerth, M. Stuyvesant Square (1878, NYC)
Lewis, N. Cuban Passage (1959, Cuba)
    March of the Long Shadows (1947, Sicily)
Ley, A. C. At Dark of Moon (1804, Eng.)
    Fatal Assignation (1816, Eng.)
    Letters for a Spy (ca.1800, Eng.)
    Masquerade of Vengeance (1816, Eng.)
    Reputation Dies (1816, London)
    Tenant of Chesdene Manor (ca.1820, Eng.)
Lientz, G. Crown vs. Dr. Watson (1894, Eng.)
    Death at Appledore Towers (1890s, Eng.)
    Honour of the Yorkshire Light Artillery (1890, Eng.)
    Lost Heir (1895, Eng.)
    Murder at the Diogenes Club (1890s, Eng.)
Limonov, E. Memoirs of a Russian Punk (Russ.)
Lincoln, N. S. Lost Despatch (1865, Wash. D.C.)
Lindley, E. Brackroyd Inheritance (1800s, Eng.)
Linscott, G. Murder, I Presume (1874, Eng.)
Linzee, D. Death in Connecticut (1971, Conn.)
Lipsky, E. Devil's Daughter (1880s, S.F.)
    Lincoln McKeever (1890s, N. Mex.)
Litewka, A. Warsaw (WWII, Warsaw)
Litvinoff, E. Blood on the Snow (ca. 1920, Russ.)
Litwak, L. Waiting for the News (1939–43, Det.)
Llosa, M. V. Who Killed Palomino Molero? (1950s, Peru)
Lockhart, M. Nobody Dies in Chinatown (1950s, L.A.)

Lofts, N. Jassy (1800s, Eng.)
Long, H. Golden Cat
Long, Martin. Dark Gateway (1880s, Syd.)
    Garden House (1880s, Syd.)
    Music Room (1880s, Syd.)
Lovesey, P. all Sgt. Cribb titles (ca. 1880, Eng.)
    Bertie and the Seven Bodies (1890, Eng.)
    Bertie and the Tinman (1886, Eng.)
    False Inspector Dew (1921, ship)
    Keystone (1915, L.A.)
    On the Edge (1946, Eng.)
    Rough Cider (1964, Eng.)
Lowell, J. R. Irish Game (1800s, Ire.)
Lowndes, M. B. Lizzie Borden (1890s, Mass.)
Lucas, R. Who Dare to Live (WWII, Ger.)
Ludlum, R. Rhineman Exchange (WWII)
    Scarlatti Inheritance (1918–1944)
Luhrs, V. Longbow Murder (1100s, Eng.)
Lupoff, R. Lovecraft's Book (1927)
Lynch, F. Dangerous Magic (ca.1910, Scot.)
Lynch, M. Blacktower (1800s, Eng.)
    Creighton's Castle (1920s, Conn.)
    Night of the Moonrose (1892, U.S.)
    Road to Midnight (1888, U.S.)
    Where Evil Waits (1782, New Eng.)
    Witches' Holiday (ca.1900, U.S.)
Lynx, J. J. Prince of Thieves (ca.1900, Eng.)
Lyons, D. Flower of Evil (NYC)
Lyons, N. Haunting of Abbotsgarth (1900, Eng.)
MacAlan, P. Doomsday Decree (ca.1945)
    Valkyrie Directive (1940, Nor.)
MacAlister, I. Skylark Mission (1941, New Guinea)
MacBeth, G. Kind of Treason (ca.1940, Eng.)
McCaffrey, A. Mark of Merlin (1945, Cape Cod)
McCammon, R. R. Wolf's Hour (1941, Europe)
McCarry, C. Bride of the Wilderness
    Secret Lovers (1960, Europe)
    Tears of August (1963)
McCarthy, M. Cannibals and Missionaries (1975, Holl.)
McCloy, H. Smoking Mirror (1940, Fr.)
McConnor, V. I Am Vidocq (1823, Paris)
MacDonald, E. House at Grey Eagle (1904, Colo.)
McDonald, G. Safekeeping (1940s, NYC)
McDowell, M. Gilded Needles (1882, NYC)
    Jack and Susan in 1953 (1953)
    Jack and Susan in 1913 (1913)
    Jack and Susan in 1933 (1933)
    Katie (1871, NYC)
McEvoy, M. Calabrian Summer (WWII, It.)
    Peril at Polvellyn (1800s, Eng.)
McEwan, I. Innocent (1955, Berlin)
McFadden, G. V. Preventive Man (1829, Eng.)
    Turning Sword (ca.1815, Eng.)
McGill, G. War Story (WWII, Berlin)
McGrath, P. Grotesque (1949, Eng.)
McGregor, I. Death Wore a Diadem (1860, Edin.)
McHugh, F. Y. Blackthorne (ca.1910, Conn.)
McIvers, S. Cry of the Wind (1800s, La.)
    Night Without End (ca.1870, La.)
MacKinnon, C. Finding Hoseyn (1977, Teheran)
McKnight, C. Gravetide (1800s, Eng.)
MacLean, Alistair. Breakheart Pass (1870s, West)
    Force 10 to Navarone (WWII, Yugos.)
    Guns of Navarone (WWII, Turk.)
    Partisans (1943, Yugos.)
    San Andreas (WWII, ship)
McQuay, M. Escape from New York (1977, NYC)
McQuinn, D. E. Targets (1969, Saigon)
Maass, E. Lady at Bay (1672, Paris)
Maass, J. Gouffé Case (1889, Paris)
Madden, A. W. Amberley Diamonds (1800s, Eng.)
Madsen, D. Black Plume (1835–52, N.Y.)
Magezis, J. Vanishing Act
Malcolm, J. Discourse with Shadows (1945, Frank.)
Malet, L. 120 Rue de la Gare (WWII, Fr.)
    Rats of Montsouris (Paris)
Malm, D. Claire (1847, Eng.)
Man, J. Lion's Share (1976)
Mancini, A. Yellow Gardenia (1929, NYC)
Mandel, P. Black Ship
Mandino, O. Christ Commission (36 A.D., Jerus.)
Manners, A. Singing Swans (1800s, Scot.)
    Stone Maiden (ca.1905, Scot.)

Margolin, P. Heartstone (1960, U.S.)
Mariner, D. Chatham Rats (WWII)
Markham, V. Scamp (ca.1720, Eng.)
Markstein, G. Cooler (1944, Eng.)
    Ultimate Issue (1961)
Marlow, E. Danger at Dahlkari (1800s, India)
    Falconridge (1800s, Eng.)
    Lady at Lyon House (1800s, Eng.)
    Master of Phoenix Hall (1888, Eng.)
    Midnight at Mallyncourt (1800s, Eng.)
Marlowe, S. 1956 (1956)
    Valkyrie Encounter (1944, Berlin)
Marshall, B. Accounting (1933, Paris)
Marshall, William. New York Detective (1883, NYC)
Marston, E. Merry Devils (ca.1590, Eng.)
    Queen's Head (1588, Eng.)
    Trip to Jerusalem (1590, Eng.)
Martin, A. E. Sinners Never Die (1895, Australia)
Martin, Caroline. Blue Ridge Mystery (1860, S.C.)
Martin, H. Sleeping Girls Don't Lie (1951, Ger.)
Martin, V. Mary Reilly (1800s, Eng.)
Massey, C. Bride of Inveroce (1800s, Scot.)
    Polmarram Tower (1830, Eng.)
Massie, A. Death of Men (1978, Rome)
Masterton, G. Condor (WWII)
    Headlines (1949, Chi.)
    Ikon (1962)
Mather, B. Hour of the Dog (1941, H. Kong)
Mathieson, T. Devil and Ben Franklin (1734, Phil.)
    Great "Detectives"
Matthias, L. A. Pandora Plague (1902, Eng.)
Matthiessen, P. Killing Mister Watson (1800s, Fla.)
Maxim, J. R. Time Out of Mind (1880s, NYC)
Maxwell, A. E. Steal the Sun (1945, N. Mex.)
Maxwell, P. Secret of Mirror House (ca.1870, South)
Maxwell, T. Kiss Me Once (1942, NYC)
    Kiss Me Twice (1945)
Maxwell, W. So Long, See You Tomorrow (1920s, Ill.)
May, J. S. Devil of Dragon House (1858, Conn.)
    Heritage of Shadows (South)
Mayhew, M. Master of Aysgarth (1832, Eng.)
    Owlers (1700s, Eng.)
Mazzaro, E. Bootleg Angel (1920s, Chi.)
    One Death in the Red (1920s, Chi.)
Meiring, D. Brinkman (1960, Laos)
    Wildcatter (1970s, Mid. East)
Melchior, I. Code Name: Grand Guignol (1944, Ger.)
    Eva (1944, Ger.)
    Haigerloch Project (1945, Ger.)
    Order of Battle (WWII, Ger.)
    Sleeper Agent (WWII, Europe)
Melville, J. Raven's Forge (1800s, Eng.)
Mendoza, E. City of Wonders (ca.1900, Sp.)
Merritt, D. My Sister's Keeper (1960s)
Messenger, E. Golden Dawns the Sun (1860s, N.Z.)
Meyer, N. Seven-Per-Cent Solution (ca.1890)
    West End Horror (ca.1890, Eng.)
Meyers, Manny. Last Mystery of Edgar Allan Poe (1846–7, NYC)
Michaels, B. Black Rainbow (1855, Eng.)
    Greygallows (1842, Eng.)
    Master of Blacktower (1853, Scot.)
    Patriot's Dream (1860s, U.S.)
    Wings of the Falcon (1860, It.)
    Wizard's Daughter (1857, Eng.)
Milburn, E. Wings of Darkness (ca.1860, La.)
Miles, G. Evil Mark (1820s, Eng.)
Miln, L. J. Purple Mask (1803, Paris)
Mitchell, Kirk. Black Dragon (1943, Calif.)
    With Siberia Comes a Chill (1945, S.F.)
Mitchell, S. W. Adventures of Francois (1790s, Fr.)
Mitchelson, A. Earthquake Machine (1906, Eng.)
    Hellbirds (ca.1905, Eng.)
Moen, J. John Moe, Double Agent (WWII)
Molloy, M. Black Dwarf (WWII)
Montague, J. Clock Tower (1900, Eng.)
Moon, G. Corpse! (1936, London)
Moore, Edward. Mysteries of Hungary (1400s, Hung.)
Moore, Robin. Big Paddle (1933, Okla.)

Settings Index

Moray, H. That Woman (ca.1790, Fr.)
Morella, J. Ince Affair (1924, Calif.)
Morgulas, J. Torquemada Principle (1938, Ger.)
    Twelfth Power of Evil
Morison, B. J. Beer and Skittles (1972, Maine)
    Champagne and a Gardener (ca.1969, Maine)
    Port and a Star Boarder (1972, Maine)
    Voyage of the Chianti (ca.1973, Maine)
Morland, C. Legacy of Winterwyck (1842, N.Y.)
Morley, Des. Children of Fear
Morley, G. T. Deeds of Darkness (1500s)
Morris, R. C. Memoirs of an Ottoman Secret Agent (1497, Istanbul)
Morris, W. F. Strange Case of Gunner Rawley (WWI)
Morrison, A. Hole in the Wall (1800s, Eng.)
Morton, P. Province of Darkness (1800s, Eng.)
Mosher, H. F. Stranger in the Kingdom (1952, Vt.)
Mosley, W. Devil in a Blue Dress (1948, L.A.)
Motta, L. Flames on the Bosphorus (1453, Turk.)
Mountjoy, H. Minister of Police (1700s, Fr.)
Muller, M. Beyond the Grave (1894, Calif.)
Mullin, A. Spy (1776, Paris, London)
Murari, T. N. Imperial Agent (ca.1900, India)
Murphy, D. J. Fatal Revenge (1670)
    Milesian Chief (1798, Ire.)
Murphy, Roberta. Acts of Darkness (1913, London)
Murray, F. Belchamber Scandal (1860s, Eng.)
Mustoo, T. Deerstalker (1900, Berlin)
Myers, A. Murder at Plums (1800s, Eng.)
    Murder in a Pug's Parlour (1800s, Eng.)
    Murder in the Limelight (1800s, Eng.)
Names, L. D. Cowboy Conspiracy (1912, Ariz.)
Nash, J. R. Dark Fountain (1927, Calif.)
Nash, N. R. East Wind, Rain (1941, Haw.)
Neely, R. Shadows from the Past (1942, NYC)
    Walter Syndrome (1938, NYC)
Neilan, S. Air of Glory
    Braganza Pursuit (1800s, Brazil)
Neill, R. Hangman's Cliff (1700s)
Neilson, M. Bride of Alderburn
    Dark Path
Nelson, R. F. Dogheaded Death (1st century, Egypt)
Netzen, K. To Win and to Lose (1940, Paris)
    all 5 series books (WWII)
Neuman, F. Maneuvers (1962, Ger.)
Nichols, S. House of Rancour (1800s, Eng.)
    Rachel (ca.1770, Pa.)
    Serpent's Tooth (1845, Ire.)
    Silsby (1600s, Eng.)
Nicholson, R. Passion for Treason (WWII, Ger.)
Nicolaysen, B. Perilous Passage (WWII, Fr.)
Niland, D. Dead Men Running (1916, Australia)
Nile, D. Evil Men Do (NYC)
    Mistress of Farrondale (ca.1880, N.Y.)
Nolan, F. Kill Petrosino! (ca.1900, NYC)
    Mittenwald Syndicate (1945, Ger.)
    Oshawa Project (ca.1946)
    White Nights, Red Dawn (1915, Russ.)
    Wolf Trap (WWII, Ger.)
Noonan, M. Magwitch (ca.1850, Australia)
Noone, E. Corridor of Whispers (1800s, Pa.)
    Dark Cypress (New Eng.)
    Daughter of Darkness (1890s, Eng.)
    Heirloom of Tragedy (N.Y.)
    Seacliffe (Maine)
    Second Secret (1860s, N.J.)
    Victorian Crown (ca.1870, W. Va.)
Norman, Elizabeth. Castle Cloud (1850, Eng.)
    If the Reaper Ride (ca.1850, Eng.)
North, John. Sherlock Holmes and the Arabian Princess (1902)
    Sherlock Holmes and the Germany Nanny (1902, Eng.)
Norton, A. Opal-Eyed Fan (ca.1850, Fla.)
Oates, J. C. Mysteries of Winterthurn (1800s, N.Y.)
O'Brien, S. Shadow of the Caravan (1862, Calif.)
O'Brine, M. Pale Moon Rising (1942, Fr.)
O'Grady, L. Artist's Daughter
O'Hagen, J. Roman Death (45 B.C., Rome)
Olden, M. Poe Must Die (1840, NYC)
Olshaker, M. Blood Race (1936, Berlin)
Orczy, B. Man in Gray (ca.1810, Fr.)
    Spy of Napoleon (ca.1810, Fr.)

O'Rourke, F. Man Who Found His Way (1927, N. Mex.)
Ostrander, K. Image Seller (1800s, NYC)
O'Toole, G. J. A. Cosgrove Report (1868, Wash. D.C.)
Oughton, F. Two Lives of Robert Ledru (Fr.)
Overgard, W. Few Good Men (1931, Nic.)
    Shanghai Tango (1931, Shanghai)
P., F. H. Castle of Caithness (1200s, Scot.)
Page, M. Set a Thief (1911, Paris)
Palliser, C. Quincunx (1800s, Eng.)
Palmer, J. Haunted Cavern (ca.1450, Scot.)
    Mystery of the Black Tower (1300s)
Palmer, S. Adventure of the Marked Man (1890s, Eng.)
Palmer, W. J. Detective and Mr. Dickens (1800s, Eng.)
Paretti, S. Maria Canossa (1943, Rome)
Paris, A. Teeth of the Wolf (1945, Ger.)
Parker, Beatrice. Come to Castlemoor (1800s, Eng.)
    Jamintha (1800s, Eng.)
Parker, F. M. Assassins (1847, New Or.)
    Shadow Man (1846, N. Mex.)
Parker, Gerrard. Prism (WWII)
Parkhurst, J. Southern Moon (1800s, Ga.)
Parnell, A. Lovespell (1870, Eng.)
    Whispers at Midnight (1700s, Va.)
Partridge, B. Ainsley Case (1885, N.Y.)
Patrick, W. Blood Winter (1917, Berlin)
Patterson, H. Dillinger (1934, Mex.)
    Pay the Devil (1865, Ire.)
    Thunder at Noon (1930, Mex.)
    To Catch a King (1940, Lisbon)
    Valhall Exchange (1944, Austria)
Pattinson, J. Dead Men Rise Up Never (1938, Eng.)
Paul, B. Chorus of Detectives (1920, NYC)
    Credenza for Caruso (1910, NYC)
    Prima Donna at Large (1915, NYC)
Paul, J. Secret of Sherlock Holmes
Paul, R. Bond Street Burlesque (1857, NYC)
    Thomas Street Horror (1836, NYC)
    Tragedy at Tiverton (1832, N.Y.)
Pauley, B. A. Blood Kin (1864, Tenn.)
    Voices Long Hushed (1880s, Miss.)
Paulsen, G. Murphy (1890s, Colo.)
Payes, R. C. Bride of Fury (ca.1890, Eng.)
    Devil's Court (1720, Eng.)
Pearce, M. Mamur Zapt and the Donkey-Vous (1908, Cairo)
    Mamur Zapt and the Night of the Dog (1908, Cairo)
    Mamur Zapt and the Return of the Carpet (1908, Cairo)
Pearlman, G. Adventures of Sherlock Holmes' Smarter Brother (1891, Eng.)
Pearson, D. Loom of Tancred (1800s, Eng.)
Pearson, E. L. Sherlock Holmes and the Drood Mystery (1914, Eng.)
Peart, R. Angels of Death (1942, Fr.)
Peck, R. N. Hallapoosa (1930s, Fla.)
Peeples, S. A. Man Who Died Twice (1922, L.A.)
Pember, R. Jack the Ripper (1888, Eng.)
Perowne, B. Raffles of the Albany (ca.1900, Eng.)
    Raffles of the M.C.C. (ca.1905, Eng.)
    Singular Conspiracy (1844, Paris)
Perrin, R. Jewels (1907, Dublin)
Perry, A. all 11 titles (1880s, London)
Perry, Robin. Welcome to a Hero (1962, Wash. D.C.)
Persico, J. E. Spiderweb (ca.1946, Ger.)
Perutz, L. Master of the Day of Judgment (1909, Vienna)
Peters, Elizabeth. Crocodile on the Sandbank (1880, Egypt)
    Curse of the Pharaohs (ca.1900, Egypt)
    Deeds of the Disturber (ca.1898, Eng.)
    Lion in the Valley (1896, Egypt)
    Mummy Case (late 1800s, Egypt)
Peters, Ellis. all 17 Cadfael titles (1100s, Eng.)
Peterson, G. Klondike Kalamity (1888, Can.)
Petrie, G. Branch Bearers (1860, Eng.)
    Dorking Gap Affair (1870s, Eng.)
    Monstrous Regiment (1800s, Eng.)
Pettit, M. Need to Kill (1983, Neb.)

Phillips, J. Greenwood (ca.1865, South)
Pickering, P. Blue Gate of Babylon (1960, Berlin)
Pierce, G. King's Ransom (Eng.)
Pilgrim, D. Emperor's Servant (ca.1808, Fr.)
Pilpel, R. H. To the Honor of the Fleet (1912, ship)
Pintoff, E. Zachary (1945, Conn.)
Piper, P. Margot Leck (1880s, Eng.)
Player, R. Month of the Mangled Models (1800s, Eng.)
Plum, J. Secret of Benjamin Square (1800s, Eng.)
Ponthier, F. Assignment Basra (1940s, Mid. East)
Pope, D. Convoy (1942)
    Decoy (WWII)
Porter, M. E. Road to Ruin (1800s, Eng.)
Post, M. D. Methods of Uncle Abner (ca.1850, Va.)
    Silent Witness (ca.1850, Va.)
    Uncle Abner, Master of Mysteries (ca.1850, Va.)
Potter, J. Death in the Forest
    Trail of Blood (1536, Eng.)
Poyer, J. Tunnel War (1911, Eng.)
Pratt, A. Franks: Duellist (ca.1810, Eng.)
Praviel, A. Murder of Monsieur Fualdes (1817, Fr.)
Preedy, G. R. Bagatelle
    Fourth Chamber (1600s, Fr.)
    Painted Angel (1809–11, Ger.)
Price, Anthony. '44 Vintage (1944, Fr.)
    New Kind of War (1945, Ger.)
    Soldier No More (1957, Fr.)
Price, Ashland. Enemy in My Arms (WWII, Ger.)
Price, J.-A. Doomsday Ship (WWII, ship)
    Operation Night Hawk (WWII)
Priestley, J. B. Bright Shadow (1946, Eng.)
Pritchett, A. Karamour (Eng.)
    Legacy (1800s, Eng.)
    Malpas Legacy (1800s, Eng.)
    Mill Reef Hall (Eng.)
Proffitt, N. Embassy House (1970, Viet Nam)
Prokosch, F. Tale for Midnight (1500s, It.)
Pronzini, B. Firewind (1800s)
    Hangings (1890s, Calif.)
    Last Days of Horseshy Halloran (1878, Mont.)
    Quincannon (1893, S.F.)
    Starvation Camp (1800s, Can.)
Puccetti, R. Death of the Fuhrer (WWII, Ger.)
Queen, E. And on the Eighth Day (1943, Nev.)
    Study in Terror (1888, Eng.)
Queneau, R. We Always Treat Women Too Well (1916, Dub.)
Radcliffe, A. Castles of Athlin and Dunbayne (Middle Ages, Scot.)
    Mysteries of Udolpho (1600s, It.)
    Sicilian Romance (1580, Sic.)
Rae, C. M. Sarah Cobb (1800s, NYC)
Rae, H. C. Rookery (ca.1850, Eng.)
Rafferty, S. S. Fatal Flourishes (ca.1750, U.S.)
Ragosta, M. J. Loren Veiled (ca.1905, Pa.)
    Witness to Treason (1200s, Eng.)
Randall, J. Broadway Bounty (1800s, NYC)
Randisi, R. J. Ham Reporter (1912, NYC)
Raoul. Fortune Spins Auburn (WWI)
Rathbone, J. Lying in State (1975, Madrid)
Rauch, C. Spy on Riverside Drive (1943, NYC)
Raygor, L. Catherine's Twins (post WWII, Berlin)
Raynes, J. Legacy of the Wolf (1857, Scot.)
Reardon, J. Big Time Tommy Sloane (1950s, NYC)
Reese, S. 9 titles (West)
    Weapon Heavy (1800s, Kan.)
Reiss, B. Casco Deception (WWII, Maine)
Reynolds, G. Victor Maury, the French Detective (1807, Paris)
Rhoads, J. W. Contract (1957, Paris)
Rhys, J. Wide Sargasso Sea (1830s, Carib.)
Richards, C. Death of an Angel (1890s, NYC)
    Marble Jungle (1890s, New Or.)
Richards, D. Double Game (1939, Berlin)
Richards, T. Virgel Directive (late 1930s)
Richmond, D. Dunkirk Directive (WWII, Eng.)
Riefe, B. Auldearn House (1930s, Scot.)
Rigg, P. Pencarnan (1920, Wales)
    Slipperdown Chant (ca.1910, Eng.)
Robb, T. N. Flip Side (1956, L.A.)
Robbins, A. On the Trail of Blood (1671, London)
Robert, L. Dipo Flight

1290 / PAST   Settings Index

Roberts, J. L. Castlereagh (1819, Eng.)
    Jade Vendetta (1894, Eng.)
    Ravenswood (1800s, Eng.)
    Wilderness Inn (1795, West)
Roberts, J. M. SPQR (70 B.C., Rome)
Roberts, P. Tender Prey (1930s, NYC)
Roberts, W. D. Devil's Double (1856, Calif.)
    Hellfire Heritage (late 1800s, Calif.)'
    Jaubert Ring (1895, S.F.)
    Radkin Revenge (1862, Calif.)
    Search for Willie (ca.1900, Nev.)
    Stuart Strain (1850, Calif.)
    White Jade (1885, Calif.)
Robertson, C. Directive 16 (1940)
    Omega Deception (1943)
    Strike Zone (1941, Panama)
Robinson, Derek. Eldorado Network (1941, Eng.)
Rockwood, H. Walt Wheeler, the Scout Detective (1862, Va.)
Roeburt, J. Al Capone (1919–29, Chi.)
    Mobster (1929, Chi.)
    Sing Out, Sweet Homicide (1925, NYC)
Rogers, G. Scandal in Eden (ca.1930, S.F.)
Rohmer, R. Hour of the Fox (1944, Ger.)
Romanes, J. Berlin Breakout (1948, WWII)
    Raid (WWII)
Roof, K. M. Murder on the Salem Road (ca.1850, Mass)
Roosevelt, E. Hyde Park Murder (1935, N.Y.)
    Murder and the First Lady (ca.1940, Wash. D.C.)
    Murder at Hobcaw Barony (ca.1940, S. Car.)
    Murder at the Palace (1942, Eng.)
    Murder in the Blue Room (1942, Wash. D.C.)
    Murder in the Oval Office (1934, Wash. D.C.)
    Murder in the Rose Garden (1936, Wash. D.C.)
    White House Pantry Murder (1941, Wash. D.C.)
Roosevelt, J. Family Matter (1943, U.S.)
Roscoe, T. Only in New England (1911)
    To Live and Die in Dixie (1902, Va.)
Rose, G. Bright Adventure (ca.1905, S. Am.)
    Clear Road to Archangel (1917, Russ.)
Rosen, G. H. Black Money (1970, Kenya)
Rosen, S. Death and Blintzes (1935, Boston)
Rosen, V. Gun in His Hand (1931, NYC)
Ross, Clarissa. Dancing Years (1933, ship)
    Face in the Pond (1870, Eng.)
    Istanbul Nights (1861, Istan.)
    Kashmiri Passions (1856, India)
    Moscow Mists (Moscow)
Ross, Dana. Demon of the Darkness (1889, Eng.)
    Figure in the Shadows (1894, Maine)
    Raven and the Phantom (1880s, Phil.)
Ross, F. Shining Day (WWII, Eng.)
Ross, Marilyn. Curse of Black Charlie (1775, Edin.)
    Dark Towers of Fog Island (1877, Can.)
    Death's Dark Music (1919, Scot.)
    Ghost and the Garret (1837, Eng.)
    Ghost Ship of Fog Island (1870, Can.)
    Phantom of the Snow (1854, Glasgow)
    Pleasure's Daughter (ca.1670, Eng.)
    Satan's Rock (1900, Can.)
    Shadows Over Briarcliff (1884, Eng.)
    Temple of the Darkness (1665, Eng.)
    Vampire Contessa (1880s, Eng.)
Ross, W. E. D. Twilight Web (1892, Maine)
    Whispering Gallery (1884, Va.)
Rossiter, J. Dark Flight (WWII)
Rostov, M. Careless Feast (WWII, Vienna)
    Night Hunt (1962, Ger.)
Rouviere, H. Lussington Abbey (1200s)
Royce, K. Channel Assault (1942, Chan. Is.)
Royde-Smith, N. Altar-Piece (ca.1910, Eng.)
Rubel, M. Flex (1958, L.A.)
Russell, A. Larksong at Dawn (Scot.)
Russell, W. C. Tragedy of Ida Noble (1838, ship)
Rutman, L. Clash of Eagles (1939, NYC)
Saberhagen, F. Holmes-Dracula File (1897, Eng.)
Sachar, H. M. Man on the Camel (ca.1972, Isr.)
Sackett, S. Emerald Angel (1800s, NYC)

Saffron, R. Demon Device (1917, Ger.)
Sage, R. Record Mystery (1860s, Australia)
St. Clair, L. Obsessions (1918–58, U.S.)
St. George, G. Proteus Pact (WWII, Ger.)
St. James, B. April Thirtieth (ca.1800, Paris)
    Seven Dreamers (1800s, Paris)
St. James, I. Killing Anniversary (1916, Ire.)
St. John, N. Guinevere's Gift (ca.1905, Eng.)
    Medici Ring (1874, Boston)
    Wychwood (1800s, Eng.)
Salisbury, C. Autumn in Araby (1869, Egypt)
    Dark Inheritance (1845, Eng.)
    Mallion's Pride (1862, Eng.)
    Winter Bride (1856, Eng.)
Salvato, S. A. Briarcliff Manor (ca.1850, N.Y.)
Sanchez, T. Zoot-Suit Murders (1943, L.A.)
Sanders, J. Cromwell's Cavalier (1650s, Eng.)
    Firework for Oliver (1654, Fr.)
    Hat of Authority (1656, Carib.)
    Roundhead Retreat (1600s)
    Without Trumpet or Drum (1600s)
Sanders, Leonard. Act of War (WWII, NYC)
Sanders, R. Dutch Justice (WWII, Holl.)
Sandys, R. A. Act of Betrayal (WWII)
Sarasin, J. G. Fleur de Lys (1600s, Fr.)
    Mystery of Martin Guerre (1500s, Fr.)
Satterthwait, W. Miss Lizzie (1921, Mass.)
Scherf, M. Don't Wake Me While I'm Driving (1920s, N. Dak.)
Schnurr, W. Johnny Death (1933–4, U.S.)
Schofield, H. A. Private Kind of War (1941)
    Red Light Red Light (WWII)
Scholefield, A. Alpha Raid (WWI)
    King of the Golden Valley (1939)
    Sea Cave (1920s, S. Afr.)
Schorr, M. Bully! (1903, U.S.)
Schubert, J. D. Keep (1880s, N.Y.)
Schuler, F. Pearl Harbor Cover-Up (1941, Haw.)
Scoppettone, S. Some Unknown Person (1906–1977, N.J.)
Scott, C. Hitler's Bomb (WWII, Ger.)
Scott, Douglas. Gift of Artemis (WWII)
    Shadows (WWII)
Scott, Honoria. Castle of Strathmay (1200s)
Scott, J. Normandie Triangle (WWII, NYC)
    Pride of Royals (WWI)
Seaman, D. Chase Royal (1867, Eng.)
Sebastian, M. Bow Street Brangle (ca.1820, Eng.)
    Bow Street Gentleman (ca.1820, Eng.)
Seilaz, A. Veil of Silence (ca.1900, Tex.)
Sela, O. Exchange of Eagles (1940, Ger.)
    Petrograd Consignment (1919, Russ.)
Sellars, M. House on Black Bayou (1700s, La.)
Selwyn, F. Cracksman on Velvet (1800s, Eng.)
    Sergeant Verity and the Blood Royal (1860, Pa.)
    Sergeant Verity and the Imperial Diamond (1800s, India)
    Sergeant Verity and the Swell Mob (ca.1860, Eng.)
    Sergeant Verity Presents His Compliments (1860, Eng.)
Semenov, J. Himmler Ploy (WWII, Ger.)
Sennocke, T. J. R. Inquests Bewraying (1930–1, Eng.)
    Inquests by Jury (1937, Eng.)
    Inquests on the Deceased (1933–4, Eng.)
Seton, A. Dragonwyck (1840s, NYC)
Seymour, Arabella. Dangerous Deception (1938, Chan. Is.)
Shaffer, E. A. Major Washington (1754, Va.)
Shah, D. K. As Crime Goes By (1947, L.A.)
Shannon, Doris. Family Money (1914, NYC)
Shapiro, S. Time to Remember (1963)
Sharp, Allan. Case of the Dancing Bees (1914, Eng.)
    Meyringen Papers (1894, Switz.)
    Unsolved Case of Sherlock Holmes
Shaw, B. Days of Power, Nights of Fear (1950s, Wash. D.C.)
Shaw, Stanley. Sherlock Holmes and the 1902 Fifth Test (1902, Eng.)
    Sherlock Holmes Meets Annie Oakley (1887, Eng.)
Shearing, J. Airing in a Closed Carriage (1889, Eng.)

    Aunt Beardie (1794, Eng.)
    Blanche Fury (1848–50, Eng.)
    Fetch (1870, Eng.)
    For Her to See (1800s, Eng.)
    Forget-Me-Not (1800s, Fr.)
    Golden Violet (1860, Jam.)
    Lady and the Arsenic (1869, Fr.)
    Laura Sarelle (1700s, Eng.)
    Mignonette
    Moss Rose (1800s, Eng.)
Sheffield, C. Erasmus Magister (1700s)
Sheldon, R. Harsh Evidence (1874, Eng.)
Shelley, M. Valperga (1200s, It.)
Shelley, S. Bowmanville Break (1943, Can.)
    Francine (1944, Sp.)
Shenkin, E. Brownstone Gothic (1871, NYC)
    Midsummer's Nightmare (1923, U.S.)
Sheppard, S. Four Hundred (1872, Eng.)
    Monte Carlo (WWII, Fr.)
Sherburne, J. Death's Bright Arrow (1894, Ky.)
    Death's Clenched Fist (1890, NYC)
    Death's Gray Angel (1890, Kan.)
    Death's Pale Horse (1880s, N.Y.)
Sheridan, A. M. Summoned to Darkness (1891, Venice)
Sherlock, J. Amindra Gamble (1940, ship)
Sherman, D. Man Who Loved Mata Hari (WWII)
    Traitor (1780)
Sherridane, D. Heart of a Gangster (1920s, S.F.)
Sherwood, J. Shot in the Arm (1937, Eng.)
Shimer, R. H. Cricket Cage (1886, Seattle)
Shoebridge, M. Ranleigh Court (1800s, Eng.)
Short, C. Black Room (1892, Ger.)
Short, L. Barren Land Murders (1940, Can.)
Shreve, L. G. Tides of Sligo (1979, Ire.)
Shreve, S. R. Children of Power (1954, Wash. D.C.)
Shulman, S. Bride of Devil's Leap (1800s, Eng.)
    Lady of Arlac (1892, Fr.)
Sidhwa, B. N. Crow Eaters (ca.1900, India)
Siegel, B. Adventures of Richard O'Boy (1850s, Eng.)
Silberrad, U. L. Green Pastures
Simmel, J. M. Sybil Cipher (1950s, Berlin)
Simmons, Steven. Body Blows (1970s, Calif.)
Simons, H. Landing (1942, Wash. D.C.)
Simonsen, S. J. Below Third Street (1920s, Mpls.)
Simpson, G. E. Fair Warning (WWII)
Sinclair, A. Facts in the Case of E. A. Poe (1811, U.S.)
Sinclair, C. Lallie
Singer, N. Shakedown Kid (1930s, U.S.)
Skoggard, B. China Hand (ca.1948, China)
Skvorecky, J. End of Lientenant Boruvka (1968, Prague)
    Return of Lieutenant Boruvka (1970s, Toronto)
Slater, I. Forbidden Zone
Slavitt, D. R. Ringer (1942, U.S.)
Sloan, C. Wings of Death (WWII, Fr.)
Slotkin, R. Return of Henry Starr (ca.1920)
Smith, B. D. Dreamspinner
Smith, Catherine. Barozzi (1500s, Venice)
Smith, Joan. 3 titles (1800s, Eng.)
Smith, M. C. Stallion Gate (1945, N. Mex.)
Smith, Shelley. Afternoon to Kill (ca.1910, Eng.)
Smith, Wynne. Rushmoreland Rubies (1800s, Eng.)
Spear, E. G. Witch of Blackbird Pond (1687, Conn.)
Spencer, R. H. Missing Bishop (1969, Chi.)
Spencer, Scott. Secret Anniversaries (1940, Wash. D.C)
Spike, P. Night Letter (1940, Mich.)
Spivey, A. J. Michael (1930s, Denver)
Spong, R. See If He Wins (1944, Paris)
Squire, R. Portrait of Barbara (1891, Fr.)
Stafford, C. Honour of Ravensholme (1800s, Eng.)
    Moira (Scot.)
Stanford, A. Mission in Sparrow Brush Lane (1943, Eng.)
Stanley, J. Bogart '48 (1948, L.A.)
Stanley, S. Rogue's Castle (Minn.)
Stanley, W. Cloud Nineteen (WWII)
Stanwood, D. Seventh Royale (1942–1978)
Stashower, D. Adventures of the Ectoplasmic Man

Settings Index — PAST

(1910, Eng.)
Steed, N. Black Eye (1937, Eng.)
  Black Mail (1930s, Eng.)
Steiber, R. High Castle (1926, Austria)
Stein, B. Manhattan Gambit (1943)
Stephenson, M. House on Wrath Moor (1800s, Eng.)
Stevens, R. T. Flight from Bucharest (1918, Europe)
Stevens, S. Anvil Chorus (1975, Paris)
Stevenson, F. Curse of the Concullens (1865, Ire.)
  Dark Odyssey (ca.1845, Calif.)
  Ides of November (1950s, Calif.)
  Kilmeny in the Dark Wood (1800s, Eng.)
  Shadow on the House (1905, Calif.)
  Witch's Crossing (1870, Mass.)
Stevenson, W. Eclipse (1941)
Steverner, C. J. Death of a Borgia (ca.1400, Rome)
Steward, B. Evermore (1889, Paris)
  Lincoln Diddle (1860s, U.S.)
Steward, S. M. Caravaggio Shawl (1937, Paris)
  Murder Is Murder Is Murder (1937, Fr.)
Stone, Elna. Visions of Esmaree (1930s, South)
Storey, R. Angel of Death (1916)
Stout, D. Caroline Skeletons (1944, S. Car.)
Stowers, C. Innocence Lost (1987, Tex.)
Stratham, F. P. From Love's Ashes (1935, Atlanta)
Straub, P. Mystery (1960s, Wis.)
Stringer, D. Yesterday Man (WWII, Fr.)
Strong, T. Fifth Hostage (1980, Iran)
  Whisper Who Dares (1976, Ire.)
Stuart, H. L. Ginger Flower (1900–44, Haw.)
Stubbs, J. Case of Kitty Ogilvie (1700s, Scot.)
  Dear Laura (1890s, Eng.)
  Golden Crucible (1906, S.F.)
  My Grand Enemy (1750s, Eng.)
  Painted Face (1902, Paris)
Sturrock, J. Captain Bolton's Corpse (ca.1800, Eng.)
  Conspiracy of Poisons (ca.1800, Eng.)
  Pangersbourne Murders (ca.1800, Eng.)
  Suicide Most Foul (1815, Belg.)
  Thistlewood Plot (1820, Eng.)
  Village of Rogues (ca.1800, Eng.)
  Wicked Way to Die (ca.1800, Eng.)
  Wilful Lady (1802, Eng.)
Suskind, P. Perfume (1700s, Paris)
Sussman, B. J. Crooked Cross (WWII, Ger.)
  Shanghai (1945, Shanghai)
Sutcliffe, K. Heart Possessed (Eng.)
  Love's Illusion (1890s, London)
Swaim, D. H. L. Mencken Murder Case (1948, NYC)
Swift, B. Mission Code: Snow Queen (1943, Arctic)
Swinson, A. Sergeant Cork's Casebook (ca.1890, Eng.)
  Sergeant Cork's Second Casebook (ca.1890, Eng.)
Sykes, Mrs. S. Margiana (1400s)
Symons, J. Blackheath Poisonings (1890s, Eng.)
  Bland Beginning (1924, Eng.)
  Death's Darkest Face (1936, 1966, Eng.)
  Detling Murders (1800s, Eng.)
  Sweet Adelaide (1880s, Eng.)
Tanenbaum, R. K. No Lesser Plea (1970s, NYC)
Tarrant, J. Clauberg Trigger (1945, Ger.)
  Rommel Plot (WWII, Fr.)
Taschdjian, C. Peking Man Is Missing (1940s, Peking)
Tattersall, J. Chanter's Chase (ca.1800, Eng.)
  Damnation Reef (ca.1890, Carib.)
  Dark at Noon (Wales)
  Lady Ingram's Retreat (1808, Eng.)
  Lyonesse Abbey (early 1800s, Eng.)
  Midsummer Masque (1803, Eng.)
  Wild Hunt (1809, Eng.)
  Witches of All Saints (1811, Eng.)
Taylor, Andrew. Second Midnight (1939–1963)
Taylor, Barry. Deadfall Trap (1971, Tib.)
  Shadow Tiger (1963, Saigon)
Taylor, Fred. Walking Shadows (WWII)
Taylor, Frederick. Kinder Garden (1948, Berlin)
Taylor, G. E. Death of Jason Darby (1778, Eng.)
Taylor, L. A. Poetic Justice (1982, Minn.)
Tempest, S. Winter of Fear (1872, Eng.)
Terman, D. Shell Game (1962, Cuba)

Thatcher, J. Nightgleams (ca.1900, NYC)
Thayer, J. S. Earhart Betrayal (1946, Far East)
  Hess Cross (1942, Chi.)
  Pursuit (1944, U.S.)
  Stettin Secret (1947, Pol.)
Thayer, S. Saint Mudd (1934, Minn.)
Thomas, Craig. Wolfsbane (1963, Fr.)
Thomas, D. Belladonna (1880, Eng.)
  Jekyll, Alias Hyde (1884, Eng.)
  Mad Hatter Summer (1800s, Eng.)
  Ripper's Apprentice (1892, London)
Thomas, D. Captain Wunder (1907)
Thomas, F. Sherlock Holmes and the Golden Bird (1890, Eng.)
  Sherlock Holmes and the Masquerade Murder (ca.1890, Eng.)
  Sherlock Holmes and the Sacred Sword (1890, Eng.)
  Sherlock Holmes and the Treasure Train (1890s, Eng.)
Thomas, Leslie. Ormerod's Landing (1940, Fr.)
Thomas, M. L. Lady True's Gate (1800s, Eng.)
Thomas, Ross. Eighth Dwarf (1946, Ger.)
Thompson, E. To Catch a Rainbow (1868, Australia)
Thompson, J. King Blood (ca.1900, Okla.)
  Pop. 1280 (late 1800s, South)
Thomsen, F. Second Lady Cameron (1800s, Scot.)
Thorndike, R. Amazing Quest of Doctor Syn (1780, Eng.)
  Courageous Exploits of Doctor Syn (ca.1780, Eng.)
  Doctor Syn (ca.1780, Eng.)
  Doctor Syn on the High Seas (ca.1780, ship)
  Doctor Syn Returns (ca.1780, Eng.)
  Further Adventures of Doctor Syn (ca.1780, Eng.)
  Shadow of Doctor Syn (ca.1780, Eng.)
Thornton, F. J. Snake Harvest (1898, Phil.)
Thum, M. Abbey Court (1800s, Ire.)
  Fernwood (1893, Va.)
Thurman, S. "Mad Dog" Coll (1932, NYC)
Thynne, R. Boffin's Find (1850s, Australia)
Tickell, J. Villa Mimosa (WWII, Fr.)
Tippette, G. Bank Robber (1800s, West)
  Wilson's Gold (1800s, West)
  Wilson's Luck (1800s, West)
Tokson, E. Cavender's Balkan Quest (ca.1914, Balkans)
  Harem Games (1908, Istan.)
  When Dragons Dance (1900, Macao)
Tomlinson, G. On a Field of Black (1875, Pa.)
Tone, T. Full Cry (1907, Va.)
  Lady on the Line (1899, U.S.)
Torrio, V. Bootlegger (1920s, Chi.)
  Executioner (1920s, Chi.)
Tourney, L. all 5 titles (ca.1602, Eng.)
Tozer, B. Riddle of the Forest (1890s, Eng.)
Tracy, D. Editor (1932, U.S.)
Traver, R. Laughing Whitefish (1800s, Mich.)
Travis, T., Jr. Lamia (1968, Chi.)
Tremaine, J. Maggie (ca.1900, Glasgow)
Trevelyan, J. Greythorne (1800s, Eng.)
Trevelyan, R. all 5 titles (mid 1800s, Eng.)
Trevor, E. Damocles Sword (ca.1941, Eng.)
Trow, M. J. all 9 titles (1891–1910, Eng.)
Truscott, L. K. Army Blue (1969, Saigon)
  Dress Gray (1960s, Md.)
Tryon, T. Night of the Moonbow (1938, Conn.)
  Other (1930s, Conn.)
Tucker, J. Blaze of Riot (1933, Berlin)
Tucker, J. B. Man Who Looked Like Howard Cosell (1983, NYC)
Tunstall, B. Shiny Night (1800s, Eng.)
Turnbull, A. S. Wedding Bargain (1935, N.Y.)
Turnbull, P. Claws of the Gryphon (1944)
Turpin, A. Little Medicine Bottle (1930s)
Tyler, W. T. Man Who Lost the War (1945–7, Europe)
  Rogue's March (ca.1970, Belg. Congo)
Tynan, K. Agatha (1926, Eng.)
Ulam, A. Kirov Affair (1934–82, Russ.)
Unsworth, B. Idol Hunter (1908, Greece)

Rage of the Vulture (1908, Istan.)
Unsworth, M. Wild Winds (1800s, Scot.)
Vale, R. M. House on Rainbow Leap (1865, Ill.)
Van Ash, C. Fires of Fu Manchu (1917, Egypt)
Vance, J. Strange Notions and The Dark Ocean (1950s, It., ship)
Vandergriff, A. Bell Tower of Wyndspelle (ca.1770, Mass.)
  Wyndspelle (ca.1770, Mass.)
  Wyndspelle's Child (1815, Mass.)
Van Gulik, R. all 18 titles (600s, China)
Van Rjndt, P. Last Message to Berlin (1940)
Vaughan, M. Discretion of Dominick Ayres (1896, Eng.)
Vaughan, R. Valkyrie Mandate (1963, Saigon)
Vaughan, S. Royal Game (Eng.)
Vaughn, Robert. Sherlock Holmes: The Adventures of the Ancient Gods (U.S.)
Vernon, K. R. Phantom of Fonthill Park (1847, Eng.)
Villiers, M. Serpent of Lilith (ca.1860, Eng.)
Vincent, C. Garden of Satan (1892, U.S.)
Vine, B. Fatal Inversion (1976, Eng.)
Von Hoffman, N. Organized Crimes (1929, Chi.)
Vosper, G. V. Squire of Landrewn (1838, Eng.)
Wacht, L. Mission to Warsaw (WWII, Warsaw)
Wagner, G. Season of Assassins (1940s)
Wagner, S. Cove in Darkness (ca.1700, Eng.)
Walk, C. E. Paternoster Ruby (1892, U.S.)
Walker, R. Women in Whitehall (1917, Eng.)
Walker, T. Mission Accomplished (1950)
Wallace, E. Devil Man (1875, Eng.)
Wallace, I. Golden Room (ca.1900, Chi.)
Walsh, J. E. Man Who Buried Jesus (30 A.D., Isr.)
Walsh, R. Mycroft Memoranda (1888, Eng.)
Warner, Richard. Netley Abbey (1300s)
Warren, B. C. Last Bride of Hatfield Castle (1852, Eng.)
Warren, P. Castle of Dreams (ca.1860, U.S.)
Washburn, L. J. Dead Stick (1920s, L.A.)
  Dog Heavies (1920s, Tex.)
  Wild Night (1920s, Calif.)
Watson, L. In a Dark Time (1973, Minn.)
Watson, P. Nazi's Wife (WWII, Ger.)
Weatherby, W. J. Coronation
Webb, A. both titles (WWII, Fr.)
Webb, J. F. Somewhere Within This House (1887, Haw.)
Weenolsen, H. Trial of Jenny Sykes (1685, Eng.)
Weismiller, E. Serpent Sleeping (WWII, Fr.)
Weissman, J. Zodiac Killer (1960s, S.F.)
Wellman, M. W. Sherlock Holmes's War of the Worlds (1902, Eng.)
Werner, P. Secret at Orient Point (late 1800s, L.I.)
  Swirling Mists of Cornwall (1887, Eng.)
West, F. W. Welsh Courtship (1745, Wales)
West, Pamela. Yours Truly, Jack the Ripper (1888, London)
West, P. E. Madeleine (1857, Glasgow)
Westlake, D. E. Gangway! (1874, S.F.)
  High Jinx (1938, Switz.)
  Transylvania Station (1890s, Rum.)
Weston, H. G. House of False Faces (1860s, La.)
  Mystic Manor (1890, N.Y.)
Wetherell, J. Dark Wing (1871, Wash.)
Weyman, R. C. Sherlock Holmes and the Mark of the Beast (1891, Can.)
Weyman, S. J. Man in Black (1637, Fr.)
Wheatley, D. Code Word—Golden Fleece (1939, Pol.)
  Come Into My Parlour (1941, Russ.)
  Dark Secret of Josephine (1793–4, W.I.)
  Desperate Measures (1814–5, Belg., Paris)
  Evil in a Mask (1806–9, Russ., Port.)
  Gateway to Hell (1953, Arg.)
  Irish Witch (1812–4, U.S., Ire.)
  Launching of Roger Brook (1783–7, Fr., Eng.)
  Man Who Killed the King (1793–4, Fr.)
  Prisoner in the Mask (1890s, Paris)
  Rape of Venice (1796–8, India, Venice)
  Ravishing of Lady Mary Ware (1909–12, Port., Russ.)
  Rising Storm (1789–92, Naples, Fr.)
  Second Seal (1914, Vienna, Ger.)

Shadow of Tyburn Tree (1787–9, Scand., Russ.)
Sultan's Daughter (1798–9, Egypt, Fr.)
They Used Dark Forces (1943, Ger.)
Traitor's Gate (1942, Hung.)
Vendetta in Spain (1906, Sp.)
Wanton Princess (1800–05)
White, Alan. Long Day's Dying (WWII)
    Long Drop (WWII, Belg.)
    Long Fuse (WWII, Fr.)
    Long Hand of Death (WWII)
    Long Midnight (WWII, Nor.)
    Long Night's Walk (WWII, Holl.)
    Long Silence (WWII, Fr.)
    Long Watch (WWII, Fr.)
White, R. J. Smartest Grave (1901, Eng.)
    Women of Peasenhall (1902, Eng.)
White, S. Operation Raven (1940, Eng.)
White, S. E. Gray Dawn (1850s, S.F.)
Whiteson, L. White Snake (1973, Rhod.)
Whitney, P. A. Quicksilver Pool (ca.1806, NYC)
    Sea Jade (1870s, New Eng.)
    Trembling Hills (1906, S.F.)
    Window on the Square (1870s, NYC)
Whittemore, E. Nile Shadows (1942, Egypt)
Wiat, P. Phantasmagoria (1800s)
Wilder, T. Eighth Day (ca.1900, Ill.)
Williams, Bob. Ozark Flats (1894, Mpls.)
Williams, Emlyn. Dr. Crippen's Diary (1883–1910, Eng.)
Williams, G. M. Pomeroy (1903, Eng.)
Williams, G. P. Deadly Illusion (ca.1972)
Williams, J. A. Jacob's Ladder (ca.1965, W. Afr.)
Willis, T. Lions of Judah (1939, Ger.)
Willoughby, L. D. Frontier Detective (1881, Colo.)
Wilson, F. P. Black Wind (WWII)
Wilson, P. W. Black Tarn (1909, Eng.)
    Bride's Castle (1893, Eng.)
    Old Mill (1912, Eng.)
Wimberly, C. Emerald Tears of Foxfire Manor (1864, S. Car.)
Winslow, P. G. Windsor Plot (WWII)
Winston, D. Adventuress (ca.1900, Md.)
    Gallows Way (1858, N.C.)
    Haversham Legacy (1860s, Wash. D.C.)
Winward, W. Ball Bearing Run (1943, Ger.)
    Canaris Fragments (1945, Ger.)
    Hammerstrike (1942, Eng.)
    Judas Cloak (1947, Can.)
    Seven Minutes Past Midnight (1945, Berlin)
Wise, D. Spectrum (1965)
Wiseman, T. Children of the Ruins (WWII)
    Day Before Sunrise (1945, Berlin)
    Game of Secrets (1947, Wash. D.C.)
    Savage Day (1945, N. Mex.)
Withers, E. L. Heir Apparent (1941, It.)
Wood, Barbara. Curse This House (1857, Eng.)
    Night Trains (WWII, Pol.)
Wood, H. H. Dig: Two Heads Wanted (1847, Eng.)
Woolrich, C. Doom Stone (1757–1941, U.S.)
York, E. Medea Legend (Eng.)
York, H. Malverne Manor (1800s, Eng.)
    Tremorra Towers (1870, Eng.)
    Venetian Charade (1881, Venice)
York, T. Trapper (1931, Can.)
Yurick, S. Richard A (1962)
Zaroulis, N. L. Poe Papers (1890s, Mass.)
Zochert, D. Murder in the Hellfire Club (1775, Eng.)
Zodrow, J. R. Sins of War (1942)

PEKING (See also: China; Shanghai; Formosa; Hong Kong; Far East; Mongolia; Macao)
Aarons, E. S. Assignment—Peking
Barnett, R. J. Jade and Fire
Becker, S. Last Mandarin
Bennett, James. Spinach Jade
Carter, Nick. Peking/The Tulip Affair
Clark, E. Chinese Burn
Daniels, N. Baron's Mission to Peking
Drake, F. Appointment in Peking
Epstein, C. Murder in China
Hughart, B. both titles
Jones, Margaret. Confucius Enigma
Larany, D. Big Red Sun
Marquand, J. P. Thank You, Mr. Moto
Smith, Don. Peking Connection
    Secret Mission: Peking
Taschdjian, C. Peking Man Is Missing

PENNSYLVANIA (Pa. See also: Philadelphia; Pittsburgh)
Aswad, B. Family Passions
    Winds of the Old Days
Black, R. J. Killing of the Golden Goose
Blaine, R. Silver Setup
Booton, K. Quite by Accident
    Time Running Out
    Toy
Brown, C. B. Wieland
Buranelli, P. Happy Nightmare
Caldwell, A. B. Death Rattle
Carr, J. D. Poison in Jest
Chacko, D. Brick Alley
Chamberlain, G. A. Night at Lost End
Chase, J. Behind the Purple Mask
    Gold Imp
Clark, W. C. Murder Goes to Bank Night
Colbron, G. I. Club Car Mystery
Constantine, K. C. all 9 titles
Davies, G. Terror at Dearcliff House
Davis, F. C. Deep Lay the Dead
    Graveyard Never Closes
    Let the Skeletons Rattle
Day, Deforest. August Ice
    Cold Killing
Delman, D. He Who Digs a Grave
Duncan, R. L. In the Blood
Dyer, G. Storm Is Rising
Emerick, L. Web of Evil
Eppley, L. Murder in the Cellar
Gibbs, G. F. Castle Rock Mystery
    Out of the Dark
Green, A. K. House in the Mist
Greth, R. . . . Now You Don't
Hall, G. Juliet Room
Haring, D. Lawless Lady
    Madam Blood
Hart, C. G. Flee from the Past
Highsmith, P. Cry of the Owl
    Edith's Diary
Holland, R. S. How Murder Speaks
Hultman, H. J. Ready for Death
Hunter, J. D. Spies, Inc.
Janson, H. Sugar and Vice
John, C. Witching
Keith, C. Crayfish Dinner
    Rich Uncle
Kelland, C. B. Mark of Treachery
Kelley, P. A. Sleightly Murder
Koontz, D. R. After the Last Race
Laing, P. If I Should Murder
Letton, J. Allegra's Child
Leverage, H. Phantom Alibi
Lippincott, N. Murder at Glen Athol
Long, A. R. Corpse at the Quill Club
    Once Acquitted
McCormick, C. Resume for Murder
MacNeil, N. Third on a Seesaw
Martin, H. R. House on the Marsh
Massey, M. Left Hand Left
Mayo, K. Mounted Justice
Michaels, B. House of Many Shadows
    Someone in the House
Millard, J. Mansion of Evil
Mullen, V. Toy Tree
Murphy, W. B. Lucifer's Weekend
Myers, I. B. Murder Yet to Come
Nichols, S. Rachel
    Sunless Day
    That Dark Inn
Noone, E. 5 titles
O'Donnell, L. Cop Without a Shield
Pendleton, D. Flesh Wounds
Plagemann, B. Wolfe's Cloister
Popkin, Z. Dead Man's Gift
Powell, R. Don't Catch Me
Propper, M. Station Wagon Murder
Pulver, M. M. Murder at the War
Ragosta, M. J. Lorena Veiled
Ransome, S. 7 titles
Reilly, H. Doll's Trunk Murder
Reisner, M. House of Cobwebs
Roper, G. Midnight Intruder
Rowe, J. N. Judas Squad
St. Clair, E. Provenance House
    Singing Harp
Seidman, R. J. Bucks County Idyll
Shallit, J. Yell Bloody Murder
Spatz, H. D. Murder with Long Hair
Stagge, J. 7 titles
Steele, C. Army of the Dead
Stein, A. M. Nowhere?
Stilson, C. B. Seven Blue Diamonds
Stivers, D. Strike Force
Stone, A. American Pep
Strange, J. S. Make My Bed Soon
Tomlinson, G. On a Field of Black
Treat, L. O As in Omen
Turnbull, M. Madame Judas
Weber, R. Grave-Maker's House
Whitney, P. A. Snowfire
Williams, Margery. Thing in the Woods
Williamson, Chet. McKain's Dilemma
    Reign
Winslow, J. Griffin Towers
Yates, P. Curtain Call for Murder

PERSIA. See: Iran.

PERU (See also: South America)
Andrews, P. Amazon Gold
Barry, M. Peruvian Nightmare
Benton, K. Craig and the Jaguar
Carter, Nick. Night of the Condor
    Red Rays
Hale, M. Empire on Arumac
Hebden, M. Portrait in a Dusty Frame
Helfgott, D. Buried
Leamer, L. Assignment
Leonard, C. L. Pursuit in Peru
Leroux, G. Bride of the Sun
Llosa, M. V. Who Killed Palomino Molero?
Murphy, W. B. Master's Challenge
Myers, M. R. Journey to Cuzco
Stein, A. M. Up to No Good
Webb, V. Little Lady Killing

PHILADELPHIA (Phil. See also: Pennsylvania; Pittsburgh)
Barry, M. Philadelphia Blow-Up
Berckman, E. Blind Villain
Biddle, A. J. D. Word for Word and Letter for Letter
Blum, R. Simultaneous Man
Booton, K. Who Knows Julie Gordon?
Bourgeau, A. Seduction
    Wolfman
Brown, C. B. Arthur Mervyn
    Ormond
Carr, J. D. Burning Court
Charteris, L. Catch the Saint
Chase, J. Blue Shadow Mystery
Conroy, Al. Death Grip
Delman, D. Last Gambit
Dexter, P. God's Pocket
Dugan, J. K. Badge of Honor
    Special Operations
Fantoni, B. Mike Dime
Fitzmaurice, E. Circumstantial Evidence
Ford, L. Philadelphia Murder Story
Ford, M. F. Shadow of Murder
Freind, S. F. God's Children
Fuller, C. Zooman and the Sign
Goodis, D. 5 titles
Hallahan, W. H. Keeper of the Children
Harrison, C. Break and Enter
Holland, R. S. House of Delusion
    Panelled Room
Kelly, T. J. Terror by Gaslight
Krasney, S. A. Mania for Blondes
    Morals Squad

Kyd, T. Blood Is a Beggar
    Blood of Vintage
    Blood on the Bosom Divine
Lewis, Arthur H. Copper Beeches
Liebman, R. Grand Jury
Lippard, G. Quaker City
Long, A. R. Death Looks Down
    Symphony in Murder
    Triple Cross Murders
McGivern, W. P. Big Heat
    Shield for Murder
McMullen, M. Death by Bequest
    Funny, Jonas, You Don't Look Dead
Malek, D. O. Fair Game
Mallowe, M. Meat Man
Marchant, W. Firebird
Masterton, G. Death Dream
Mathieson, T. Devil and Ben Franklin
Morris, A. P. Mark Magic, Detective
Morris, C. Cap Colt, the Quaker Detective
O'Neil, K. Death Strikes at Heron House
    Mooney Moves Around
    Ninth Floor: Middle City Tower
Pendleton, D. Panic in Philly
Platt, R. Letting Blood
Powell, R. False Colors
Propper, M. 12 titles
Roberts, Gillian. Caught Dead in Philadelphia
    Philly Stakes
Ronns, E. Black Orchid
    Gang Rumble
Ross, Dana. Raven and the Phantom
Sauter, E. Skeletons
Savidge, E. C. Wallingford
Scarberry, A. S. Dimpled Racketeer
Selwyn, F. Sergeant Verity and the Blood Royal
Shallit, J. Billion Dollar Body
    Kiss the Killer
    Lady, Don't Die on My Doorstep
Shubin, S. Holy Secrets
Solmssen, A. R. G. Rittenhouse Square
Spicer, B. 5 titles
Thornton, F. J. Snake Harvest
Wheeler, E. L. Fritz to the Front
Whitten, L. Killing Pace
Wideman, J. E. Philadelphia Fire
Williams, S. Aconite Murders
    Murder of Miss Betty Sloan
Witley, A. F. Dangerously Blonde
Zachary, F. N. Cradle and All

PHILIPPINES (Philip. See also: Manila; Far East)
Came, B. Rice Wine
Case, Jim. Philippine Hardpunch
Chamberlain, E. Appointment in Manila
Crisp, F. Manila Stranger
Culverwell, D. Days of Yellow
Del Mar, D. Blood Pearls of Sulu
Fox, G. Amok
Jones, R. F. Blood Tide
Kenyon, M. Sorry State
Lynch, D. Bad Fortune
    Deathly Pale
    Killing Frost
McCurtin, P. Moro
Mason, V. W. Fort Terror Murders
Olden, M. Sword of Vengeance
Pendleton, D. Whipsaw
Thomas, Ross. Out on the Rim

PHOENIX (See also: Arizona; Tucson; Southwest)
Altman, T. True Bride
Barry, M. Phoenix Inferno
Brown, F. Five-Day Nightmare
Dunlap, S. Pious Deception
Gage, E. Phoenix No More
Gallagher, S. Valley of Lights
Hawley, S. R. Deadly Secrets
Hughes, D. B. Expendable Man
Jance, J. Minor in Possession
Kelland, C. B. Counterfeit Gentleman
Maling, A. Shroeder's Game
Martin, C. C. Godchildren
Martori, J. Street Fights

Wohl, J. P. Blind Trust Kills

PITTSBURGH (Pitt. See also: Pennsylvania; Philadelphia)
Creed, W. Death Comes Grinning
Dwyer, D. Legacy of Terror
Eyre, M. Girl in the Tiffany Dress
Gat, N. Nevsky's Return
Guy, D. Man Who Loved Dirty Books
Paul, B. First Gravedigger
    Your Eyelids Are Growing Heavy
Rinehart, M. R. Case of Jennie Brice
Stone, E. C. Fear Rides the Fog
Whitfield, R. Green Ice

POLAND (Pol. See also: Warsaw)
Annesley, M. Vanished Vice-Counsel
Anonymous. Secret Mission
Conway, P. Escape to Danger
Gowing, N. Wire
Hagar, J. Shadow of the Eagle
Iams, J. Shot of Murder
Irving, C. Angel of Zin
Lathy, T. P. Invisible Enemy
MacInnes, H. While Still We Live
Marchmont, A. W. In the Case of Freedom
Nasielski, A. Ace of Spades
Royce, K. Fall Out
Ruff, I. Orphan Soldier
Sebastian, T. Spy Shadow
Simpson, J. Fine and Private Place
Thayer, J. S. Stettin Secret
Wheatley, D. Code-Word—Golden Fleece
Wilkinson, R. H. Zittaw the Cruel
Wood, Barbara. Night Trains

PORTLAND (See also: Oregon; Northwest)
Haynes, C. Bishop's Gambit
Larson, C. Portlnd Murders
Margolin, P. M. Last Innocent Man
Trimble, L. Blondes Are Skin Deep
Williams, W. Take the Money and Die

PORTUGAL (Port. See also: Lisbon; Madeira)
Bosak, S. Gammon
Boyle, T. Cold Stove League
Bridge, A. Malady in Madeira
    Portuguese Escape
Buckingham, N. Jade Dragon
Canning, V. Birdcage
Charteris, L. Saint in Pursuit
De Villiers, G. Portuguese Defection
Fleming, Joan. Death of a Sardine
Greenland, F. Misericordia Drop
Grey, N. Dark Sun, Pale Shadows
Hodge, J. A. Winding Stair
Holton, L. Deliver Us from Wolves
Knight, L. A. Pawn
Lee, Babs. Passport to Oblivion
Lee, Elsie. Satan's Coast
L'Engle, M. Arm of the Starfish
McCray, M. Contract: Terror Summit
MacKenzie, D. Raven's Longest Night
MacLeod, Robert. Burial in Portugal
    Salvage Job
Pemberton, M. Guilty Secret
Souza, E. Blue Rum
Spencer, E. Death of Captain Shand
Teixeira, B. Flowers for the Executioner
Walker, D. Diamonds for Moscow
Walker, Martin. Infiltrator
Wheatley, D. Evil in a Mask
    Ravishing of Lady Mary Ware
Yorke, R. M. P. Valley of Collares

PORTUGUESE EAST AFRICA. See: Mozambique.

PORTUGUESE WEST AFRICA. See: Angola.

PRAGUE (See also: Czechoslovakia)
Chase, J. H. Have This One on Me
Cleeve, B. Exit from Prague
Crecy, J. My Face Beneath the Stone

Drummond, I. Diamonds of Loreta
Gainham, S. Stone Roses
George, J. Kill Dog
Heym, S. Hostages
Hostovsky, E. Missing
Leslie, P. Death Mail
MacLeod, R. Problem in Prague
Skvorecky, J. End of Lieutenant Boruvka
    Miss Silver's Past
Smith, Don. Secret Mission: Prague
Wheatley, D. Curtain of Fear
Wilson, Gar. Doomsday Syndrome

PUERTO RICO (P. Rico. See also: San Juan; West Indies; Caribbean)
Adamson, M. J. February Face
Carter, Nick. Filthy Five
    San Juan Inferno
Dane, Mark. Felicia
Gayle, N. Murder at 28:10
    Sentry-Box Murder
Ingersol, J. Game Called Murder
Ives, J. Marchant Woman
Jason, S. Suicide in San Juan
Knight, Adam. Sunburned Corpse
Lathen, E. Longer the Thread
Nessen, R. First Lady
Pendleton, D. Caribbean Kill
Sheppard, M. Strangers in the Sun
Stark, R. Dame
Strother, E. W. Island of Terror
Telfair, R. Good Luck, Sucker

RAILWAY. See: Train.

RELIGIOUS SETTINGS. See: Church.

RENO (See also: Nevada; Las Vegas; West)
Adams, T. E. Sinful Cowboy
Anderson, Susan. Shadow Dance
Arre, H. Corpse by the River
Cain, J. M. Jelous Woman
    Sinful Woman
Denning, M. Din of Inequity
Evans, D. No Slightest Whisper
Ford, L. Reno Rendezvous
Hamilton, D. Removers
Haring, D. Hell's Little Angel!
Homes, G. No Hands on the Clock
Land, M. Dream Buyers
Quentin, P. Puzzle for Wantons
Roderus, F. Turn-Out Man
Ross, John. Devil's Gate Road
Torrey, R. 42 Days for Murder

RHODE ISLAND (R.I. See also: New England)
Bond, E. Waiting Eyes
Cable, M. Avery's Knot
Cohen, James. Disappearance
Disney, D. M. Did She Fall or Was She Pushed?
Dutton, C. J. Shadow on the Glass
Eliot, G. F. Navy Spy Murders
Footner, H. Easy to Kill
Ford, L. Invitation to Murder
Hayes, L. Challoners of Bristol
Hinch, D. Death at Newport
Lamb, A. Greystones
Lamb, M. Chains of Gold
Lambert, D. Murder in Newport
Rosen, R. D. Strike Three You're Dead
Sapir, R. Spies
Whitney, P. Spindrift
Wolff, G. Providence

RHODESIA (Rhod. Includes Zimbabwe. See also: Africa)
Adams, A. Quimby
Ballinger, W. A. Call It Rhodesia
Butler, K. R. Fall of Rock
Carter, Nick. Rhodesia
Creasey, J. Sleep
Early, R. Time of Madness
Gilman, D. Mrs. Pollifax on Safari

Hartmann, M. Game for Vultures
Hunter, R. W. Congo Diamonds
Langley, B. War of the Running Fox
McCurtin, P. Massacre at Umtali
MacKenzie, N. Strange Happening
MacKinnon, C. K. Flame Lily
    Lost Hyena
Rothwell, H. T. No Honour Amongst Spies
Whiteson, L. White Snake

RICHMOND (See also: Virginia; South)
Edwards, Anne. Child of Night

RIO DE JANEIRO (Rio de J. See also: Brazil; South America)
Bernstein, K. Senator's Ransom
Caillou, A. Terror in Rio
Carter, Nick. Assignment: Rio
    Carnival for Killing
    Checkmate in Rio
Chaber, M. E. Six Who Ran
Colby, E. Bossa Nova Bed
Derrick, L. Rampage in Rio
Fallon, G. Rendezvous in Rio
Fish, R. L. Always Kill a Stranger
    Diamond Bubble
    Fugitive
    Xavier Affair
Fonseca, R. High Art
Harvey, M. Vengeance of the Ivory Skull
Howard, V. Rendezvous in Rio
Kelsey, V. Owl Sang Three Times
    Satan Has Six Fingers
Mason, V. W. Rio Casino Intrigue
Morgan, Dean. Roston Outfit in Rio
Pierson, E. Good Neighbor Murder
Seymour, H. In the Still of the Night
Stirling, E. K. Unsuspected Conduct

ROCHESTER (Roch. See also: New York; Long Island; New York City)
Dean, A. Call Me Pandora
    Deadly Contact
    Foggy, Foggy Dew
Haring, D. Blondes Can Be Bitter!
O'Brien, Meg. Daphne Decisions

ROMANIA. See: Rumania.

ROME (See also: Italy; Florence; Milan; Naples; Sardinia; Sicily; Venice)
Airth, R. Snatch
Alexander, Mrs. Crumpled Leaf
Arrighi, M. Navona 1000
Bagot, R. Roman Mystery
Ballinger, W. A. Starlet for a Penny
Banks, O. Caravaggio Obsession
Bentley, J. Macedonian Mixup
Benton, K. Spy in Chancery
Bonner, P. H. S.P.Q.R.
Bracken, C. P. Roman Ring
Breton, T. Pentecost Project
Calvin, H. Italian Gadget
Carter, Nick. Massacre in Milan
    Our Agent in Rome Is Missing
Close, R. Boheme Connection
Collin, R. O. Imbroglio
Colombo, P. Throw Back the Little Ones
Connell, C. Meet Me at Philippi
Coppel, A. Land of Mirrors
Daniels, M. Passport to Terror
Davis, Lindsey. Shadows in Bronze
    Silver Pigs
Dekker, C. Don't Bother to Knock
Durston, P. E. H. Mortissimo
Fleetwood, H. Foreign Affairs
    Girl Who Passed for Normal
    Roman Magic
Gadda, C. E. That Awful Mess on Via Merulana
Gardner, A. Six-Day Week
Gash, Jonathan. Vatican Rip
Geddes, P. State of Corruption
Goodchild, G. Spanish Steps
Habe, H. Poisoned Stream
Hambly, B. Quirinal Hill Affair
Hanna, D. Vacant Throne
Heller, F. Mr. Collin Is Ruined
Howard, H. Secret of Simon Cornell
Jason, S. Instant Dead
Jaye, P. Body's Name Was Jones
Jones, P. Month of the Pearl
Kennedy, E. Fixes
Lester, T. Episode in Rome
Levey, M. Affair on the Appian Way
Linzee, D. Discretion
Llewellyn, C. Masks of Rome
Longstreet, S. Ambassador
Lorac, E. C. R. Murder on a Monument
McGivern, W. P. Margin of Terror
McGuire, P. Spanish Steps
McInerny, R. Romanesque
MacKintosh, M. Roman Adventure
Marcus, C. Mark Castle—Cable Address: Rome
Marlowe, S. Peril Is My Pay
Marsh, N. When in Rome
Massie, A. Death of Men
Maybury, A. Terracotta Palace
Mewshaw, M. Year of the Gun
Meyer, K. Bishop's Room
Morley, E. Intrigue in Rome
Murphy, W. F. Roman Enigma
Murray, W. Mouth of the Wolf
Nixon, W. Strategic Compromise
Norwood, F. Pope Must Die
O'Brine, M. Killers Must Eat
O'Hagen, J. Death and a Madonna
    Roman Death
O'Neal, V. Beecher
O'Neill, F. Roman Circus
Paretti, S. Maria Canossa
Pearson, J. Kindness of Dr. Avicenna
Pendleton, D. Assault on Rome
Peters, Elizabeth. Seventh Sinner
    Street of the Five Moons
Pierce, R. Run, Traitor, Run
Rejaunier, J. Affair in Rome
Revell, L. See Rome and Die
Revere, J. D. Vatican Kill
Roberts, J. M. SPQR
Rosenberger, J. Massacre in Rome
Rostand, R. Killing in Rome
Rothstein, R. Hand of Fatima
Rotsstein, A. N. Judgment in St. Peter's
Rutherford, D. Stop at Nothing
Scotti, R. A. both titles
Smith, Joan. Follow That Blonde
Stainton, A. Sweet Rome
Stein, A. M. Sitting Up Dead
Stevermer, C. J. Death of a Borgia
Stuart, Anthony. Vicious Circles
Timperley, R. Spell of the Hanged Man
Tine, Robert. State of Grace
West, Morris. Lazarus
Wilson, Gar. Hostaged Vatican
Wlaschin, K. To Kill the Pope
Wolk, G. Leopold Contract

RUMANIA (Rum. See also: Bucharest; Balkans)
Aarons, E. S. Assignment—Mara Tirana
Abbott, S. Castle of Evil
Francis, Maurice. First Light Fraser
Gheorghiu, C. V. Immortals of the Mountain
McDaniel, D. Vampire Affair
Nile, D. Vampire Cameo
Rosenberger, J. Roumanian Question
Ross, R. Falls the Shadow
Sandulescu, J. Carpathian Caper
Sharkey, J. Creature Creeps
Stoker, B. Dracula
Stuart, Anthony. That Man Gull
Westlake, D. E. Transylvania Station
Williams, Eric. Dragoman Pass

RUSSIA (Russ. See also: Moscow; Mongolia)
Aarons, E. S. Assignment—Suicide
Adler, W. Trans-Siberian Express
Ahern, J. Captain Blood
    Origin of a Vendetta
Aksyonov, V. Island of Crimea
Aldanov, M. Key
Aleshkovsky, Y. Hand
Allbeury, T. Consequence of Fear
    Man with the President's Mind
    Moscow Quadrille
Appel, A. Time After Time
Bannerman, D. Pipeline from Hell
Bax, R. Came the Dawn
    Red Escapade
Behn, N. Kremlin Letter
Bernstein, K. Intercept
Block, Lawrence. Tanner's Twelve Swingers
Buchanan, J. Invasion from U.S.S.R.
Buck, P. Operation Icicle
Burgess, A. Honey for the Bears
    Tremor of Intent
Butler, Gwendoline. Red Staircase
Campbell, G. Wild and Weird
Carter, Nick. Black Sea Bloodbath
    Crossfire Red
    Operation Petrograd
Charles, R. Arctic Assignment
Chernenok, M. Losing Bet
Clark, Eric. Black Gambit
Cleary, J. Golden Sabre
Coles, M. Alias Uncle Hugo
Conan, A. Psi Delegation
Corrigan, M. Girl from Moscow
Creasey, J. Prophet of Fire
Crossland, R. L. Red Ice
Daniels, N. Spy Hunt
Davis, J. M. Murder of Frau Schultz
De Halsalle, H. Woman Spy
De Mille, N. Charm School
Dostoevski, F. M. Brothers Karamazov
    Crime and Punishment
Drummond, A. Scented Death
Duranty, W. Gold Train
Edelman, M. Call on Kuprin
Edmonds, H. Trail of the Lonely River
Elliott, Scott. Borzoi Control
Evans, J. Midas Men
Ferguson, A. Random Track to Peking
Freemantle, B. Face Me When You Walk Away
Garfield, B. Kolchak's Gold
Garrett, F. Polar Assault
Garve, A. Ashes of Loda
Grayson, Rupert. Gun Cotton Goes to Russia
Halkin, J. Hantu
Hall, Adam. Northlight
    Sinkiang Executive
Harvester, S. Red Road
Herlin, H. Grishin
Hild, J. Barrabas Raid
    Gulag War
    Kremlin Devils
    Sakhalin Breakout
Hope, C. G. Second Plan
Hoyt, R. Head of State
Hyman, T. Seven Days to Petrograd
Ingram, E. M. Game and the Candle
James, D. Fall of the Russian Empire
John, H. Carnellian Circle
John, O. Beam of Black Light
    Shadow in the Sea
Jones, Dennis. Winter Palace
Kaledin, V. K. Flash D 13
Kaminsky, S. M. Cold Red Sunrise
Kane, C. J. Blood and Sable
Kenmore, F. J. Wire Window
Kiddy, M. G. Devil's Dagger
Kilgore, A. Siberian Alternative
Kilian, M. Blood of the Czars
King, K. D. Ursula
Konsalik, H. G. Strike Force Ten
Korotyukov, A. It's Hard to Be a Russian Spy
Kyle, D. Cage of Ice
    King's Commisar
Laflin, J. Reluctant Spy
Lambert, D. Man Who Was Saturday
    Vendetta
    Yermakov Transfer
Lawrence, Hadley. Intruder

Settings Index

Lear, J. Death in Leningrad
LeQueux, W. Strange Tales of a Nihilist
    In the Tsar's Dominions
Lescroart, J. T. Rasputin's Revenge
Lieberman, H. Green Train
Limonov, E. Memoirs of a Russian Punk
Lipatov, V. Village Detective
Litvinov, E. Blood on the Snow
McCutchan, P. Man from Moscow
    Moscow Coach
McEnery, J. Black Inheritance
MacKenzie, N. In Great Danger
McKinney, R. L. Kamchatka Incident
McLeave, H. Double Exposure
Marchant, B. Dangerous Mission
Marlowe, S. Death Is My Comrade
Morris, M. E. Alpha Bug
Morton, V. Yellow Ticket
Niesewand, P. Fallback
Nolan, F. White Nights, Red Dawn
Olcott, A. May Day in Magadan
Old Sleuth. American Detective in Russia
Osborne, G. Traitor's Gate
Pawle, L. Strange Coast
Pendleton, D. Ice Cold Kill
    Terminal Velocity
Porter, J. Neither a Candle Nor a Pitchfork
    Package Included Murder
    Sour Cream with Everything
Richmond, M. Red Claws
Robeson, K. Fortress of Solitude
Rose, G. Clear Road to Archangel
Rosenberger, J. Escape from Gulag Taria
    Fatal Formula
Rosenblum, R. Mushroom Cave
Rovin, J. Destination: Stalingrad
Royce, K. Fall Out
Ruse, G. A. Houndstooth
Ryck, F. Green Light, Red Catch
Sangster, J. Foreign Exchange
Saxon, P. This Spy Must Die
Scott, Justin. Cossack's Bride
Scott, R. T. M. Mad Monk
Sela, O. Petrograd Assignment
Seton, G. Eye for an Eye
Seymour, G. Archangel
Smith, Carmichael. Atomsk
Spang, M. G. Spy Who Longed for Home
Stivers, D. Duelling Missiles
Stohlman, R. Overflowing Rain
Streib, D. Counter Force
Thomas, Craig. Firefox Down
    Snow Falcon
Tine, R. Broken Eagle
Topol, E. Red Gas
Ulam, A. Kirov Affair
Vance, C. G. Grave for a Russian
Van Rjndt, P. Blueprint
Wallace, E. Book of All Power
Wees, F. S. Country of the Strangers
Wentworth, P. Red Stephan
Wheatley, D. 5 titles
White, E. L. Elephant Never Forgets
Williams, Alan. Beria Papers
    Gentleman Traitor
Williams, David. Treasure in Roubles
Wilson, Gar. Show of Force
Yaeger, C. H. Counterfeit Hostage
Zimmerman, R. D. Blood Russian
    Cross and the Sickle

SACRAMENTO (See also: California; Los Angeles;
    San Diego; San Francisco; West)
Kijewski, K. Catapult

SAIGON (See also: Viet Nam; Hanoi; Far East)
Cain, J. 5 titles
Carter, Nick. Saigon
Chase, J. H. Lotus for Miss Quon
Eickhoff, R. L. Hand to Execute
Kasper, R. C. Love Spy, Love
Klawitter, J. Crazyhead
Leader, C. Cargo to Saigon

McQuinn, D. E. Targets
Magnuson, T. Small Gust of Wind
Mason, V. W. Saigon Singer
Saxon, P. Woman of Saigon
Taylor, Barry. Shadow Tiger
Truscott, L. K. Army Blue
Vaughan, R. Valkyrie Mandate

ST. LOUIS (See also: Missouri; Kansas City;
    Midwest)
Beach, E. R. Joshua Humble
Bent, S. Buchanan of "The Press"
Dean, R. G. Murder Makes a Merry Widow
Dunn, D. Murder's Web
Franklin, M. Justice Has No Sword
Franzen, J. Twenty-Seventh City
Komo, D. Clio Browne: Private Investigator
Krell, E. D. Killer Cops
Lawson, W. B. Frank James in St. Louis
Lutz, J. 5 titles
Meskil, P. Sin Pit
Nevins, F. M. 120-Hour Clock
Pendleton, D. Missouri Deathwatch
    St. Louis Showdown
Sapir, R. Sweet Dreams
Scarpetta, F. Slaughterhouse
Smith, T. L. Money War
Tucker, W. Warlock

SALT LAKE CITY (See also: Utah; West)
Cook, T. H. Tabernacle
Irvine, R. Angel's Share
    Baptism for the Dead
    Gone to Glory
Levitt, J. R. Carnivores
Maling, A. Lucky Devil
Pett, S. Sirens
Stewart, G. Tenth Virgin
    Zarahemia Vision
Thurman, A. R. Whitewashed Tomb

SAN ANTONIO (See also: Texas; Austin; Dallas;
    Houston; Southwest)
Brandon, J. Fade the Heat
Davis, J. F. Chinese Label
Dekker, C. Dark Angel of Fire
Ford, K. Sky Fighters
Janson, H. Honey, Take My Gun
Marlowe, D. J. Operation Counterpunch
North, S. Jasmine for My Grave
Risenhoover, C. C. Blood Bath
    Dead Even

SAN DIEGO (See also: California; Los Angeles;
    Sacramento; San Francisco; West)
Adams, C. F. Black Door
    Contraband
Bass, M. Bandini Affair
    Moving Finger
Carney, W. Rose Exterminator
Cunningham, Chet. Avenger
Douglas, B. Bloody Precinct
Fleischman, A. S. Straw Donkey Case
Gilbert, D. L. Black Star Murders
    Murder Begins at Home
Hays, L. Harry-O
Higgs, E. C. Happy Man
Lange, J. Binary
Masterson, W. Slow Gallows
Mathews, W. C. King Cobra
Miller, Wade. 8 titles
Morgan, D. M. Lovely Night to Kill
Oppenheimer, J. Trouble at the Gabourys'
Pendleton, D. Resurrection Day
    San Diego Siege
Pronzini, B. Double
Purtill, R. Murdercon
Rogers, Charles. 1199
Stowell, W. A. Wake of the Setting Sun
Wallace, Patricia. Small Favors
Wells, S. Death Is My Name
Williams, P. C. Mission Bay Murder

SAN FRANCISCO (S.F. See also: California; Los
    Angeles; Sacramento; San Diego; West)
Adams, C. F. Up Jumped the Devil
Aiken, E. Love and I
Alexander, Jan. Jade Figurine
Alexander, K. Time After Time
Alverson, C. Goodey's Last Stand
Anderson, J. A. Society Ball Murders
Anderson, Poul. all 3 TY titles
Archer, F. Malabang Pearl
    Turquoise Spike
    Widow Watchers
Aresbys. Who Killed Coralie?
Atherton, G. Avalanche
Babula, W. According to St. John
    St. John's Baptism
Baker, Lucinda. Walk the Night Unseen
Barish, S. Reasonable Doubt
Barry, M. Bay Prowler
Bartholomew, C. Second Sight
Beal, M. F. Angel Dance
Beck, K. K. Unwanted Attentions
    Young Mrs. Cavendish and the Kaiser's Men
Bedford-Jones, H. Shadow
Bennett, Dorothy. Murder Unleashed
Bezzerides, A. I. Thieves Market
Biderman, B. Genesis Files
Biederman, M. Makover
Biggers, E. D. Behind That Curtain
    Fifty Candles
Blair, M. Final Ring
Blaney, C. E. King of the Opium Ring
Booth, C. G. Those Seven Alibis
Booth, E. Broken Window
Bosse, M. F. Man Who Loved Zoos
Boucher, A. Case of the Seven of Calvary
Bowman, R. J. House of Blue Lights
Boyle, J. Boston Blackie
Bradford, K. Footprints
Braly, M. Shake Him Till He Rattles
Brautigan, R. Dreaming of Babylon
    Willard and His Bowling Trophies
Bretnor, R. Killing in Swords
Brooks, A. One Enchanted Summer
Brykczynski, T. Caged
Bucci, M. Court of the Stone Children
Budd, C. Scarlet Sandals
Burnham, H. Telltale Telegram
Byrd, M. California Thriller
    Finders Weepers
Calhoun, C. W. Until Proven Guilty
Capelli, A. Frisco Hi-Jack
Carpenter, G. Night Tide
Carter, Nick. Mind Poisoners
Chamberlain, Esther. Coast of Chance
Chamberlain, L. Other Side of the Door
Chambers, W. Dog Eat Dog
    Thirteen Steps
Champlin, T. King of the Highbinders
Chang, L. Year of the Tiger
Charleston, W. Hero Rat
Chevalier, H. For Us the Living
Cheyney, P. Can Ladies Kill?
Clarke, R. Death of a Flower Child
Coffman, V. Fear of Heights
    High Terrace
    Hyde Place
Cohen, I. R. Passover Commando
Cohen, S. Diane Game
Collins, Mary. Dead Center
    Fog Comes
    Sister of Cain
Combs, D. Sleepwalker
Conot, R. E. Ministers of Vengeance
Cooke, G. M. Man Behind the Mask
Corrigan, M. Lady of China Street
Corris, P. Big Drop
    Heroin Annie
Crane, F. 6 titles
Curzon, D. From Violent Men
Daniels, D. Circle of Guilt
    Juniper Hill
Davis, K. 5 titles

Davis, Robert. Kimura
Dean, Sara. Traverse
De Bra, L. Ways That Are Wary
Dekker, C. Paper Doll
De Marco, G. Frisco Blues
    October Heat
Denning, M. Shades of Gray
Dixon, H. V. Killer in Silk
Dodge, A. M. Eye of the Peacock
Dodge, D. Death and Taxes
    It Ain't Hay
Dong, E. Heart Beat
Doyle, C. W. Shadow of Quong Lung
Drury, Rev. S. Startling and Thrilling Narrative
Duncan, D. Bramble Bush
Dunlap, S. 5 titles
Dyer, G. Catalyst Club
    Five Fragments
    Long Death
    People Ask Death
Eberhart, M. G. Casa Madrone
Edwards, Alexander. Black Bird
Emery, G. Front for Murder
Eshleman, J. M. both titles
Eyre, K. W. Chinese Box
    Sandalwood Fan
Fair, A. A. Some Slips Don't Show
    Top of the Heap
Falk, L. Hydra Monster
Fawcette, S. Time Runs Out at the Democratic Convention
Fessier, M. Fully Dressed and in His Right Mind
Fickling, G. G. Stiff As a Broad
Finnegan, R. Bandaged Nude
    Many a Monster
Fisher, S. Hell-Black Night
    Saxon's Ghost
Fitzsimmons, C. Sudden Silence
Fletcher, Donna. San Francisco Surrender
Flynn, J. Blood on Frisco Bay
    Body for McHugh
    Five Faces of Murder
    McHugh
Flynn, J. M. Ring Around a Rogue
Folder, L. Rocky Libido in San Francisco
Forbes, C. Year of the Golden Ape
Ford, L. Siren in the Night
Foxx, J. Freebooty
Fraser, E. Emerald Necklace
    Mystery of the Star Sapphire
Frey, J. N. Killing in Dreamland
    Long Way to Die
Freytag, J. Mercenary
Gann, E. K. Of Good and Evil
Gardner, E. S. Case of the Backward Mule
    Case of the Substitute Face
    Murder up My Sleeve
Garlington, P. Aces & Eights
Gates, H. L. Laughing Peril
    Murder in the Fog
Gillette, P. Chinese Godfather
Gilmer, J. L. Hell Has No Exit
    Hell Is Forever
Girard, B. Cool Jade
Gold, H. Slave Trade
Goldsmith, G. Layout for a Corpse
Goodis, D. Dark Passage
Gores, J. 7 titles
Gosling, P. Running Duck
Grant, Linda. both titles
Grant, M. Green Eyes
Green, Kate. Night Angel
Greenleaf, S. Beyond Blame
    Death Bed
    Grave Error
    Toll Call
Greenwald, N. Lady Cat
Gregory, J. Case for Mr. Paul Savoy
    Ladyfingers
Grossbach, R. Cheap Detective
Gunn, J. Deadlier Than the Male
Hamilton, C. Twilight Forest
Hammett, D. 8 titles
Hammond, M. A. Land of Gold

Hardin, R. Amateur Hour
Haring, D. San Francisco Shakedown
Harper, O. Opium Smugglers of Frisco
Hartman, D. City of Blood
    Death in the Air
    Death on the Docks
    Duel for Cannons
Held, P. Take My Face
Hellerstein, H. Wired
Helmore, T. Affair at Quala
Holzer, H. W. Red Chindvit Conspiracy
House, B. Curse of the Mandarin's Fan
Huffman, L. House Behind the Mint
Hurd, F. House on Russian Hill
Hurlbut, E. H. Lanagan, Amateur Detective
James, B. both titles
Jones, Cleo. Case of the Fragmented Woman
Kains, J. Green Lama Mystery
    Laughing Dragon Mystery
Kaminsky, S. M. Poor Butterfly
Kane, F. Guilt-Edged Frame
    Line-Up
Keating, H. Murder by Death
Kelland, C. B. Dangerous Angel
Kenneally, G. P. Nobody Wins
Kenneally, J. Polo Anyone?
    Polo Solo
    Polo's Ponies
    Polo's Wild Card
Kenrick, T. Tough One to Lose
Kinlay, A. Killers Cannot Live
Kinsburn, E. Tong Men and a Million
Kuttner, H. Murder of a Wife
    Murder of Ann Avery
    Murder of Eleanor Pope
Kuttner, P. Absolute Proof
Lang, H. Corpse on the Hearth
Lantigua, J. Heat Lightning
Laurence, G. One Bang-Up Job
Lee, Elsie. Sam Benedict
Leitfred, R. H. Man Who Was Murdered Twice
Lescroart, J. T. Dead Irish
Leslie, Jean. Shoes for My Love
Levin, D. California Street
Lipman, C. House of Evil
Loraine, P. Voices in an Empty Room
Loughead, F. H. Man Who Was Guilty
Lovell, B. E. both titles
Lynch, J. Bragg's Hunch
MacAvoy, R. A. Tea with the Black Dragon
McDonald, G. Who Took Toby Rinaldi?
MacGowan, A. Million Dollar Suitcase
    Mystery Woman
    Seventh Passenger
    Shaken Down
McKimmey, J. Blue Mascara Tears
MacLean, Alistair. Golden Gate
McRae, D. All the Muscle You Need
Maddren, G. Case of the Johannesberg Riesling
Mair, G. B. Jade Cat
Mallory, R. San Francisco Vendetta
Mandell, M. Butcher Block
Marko, Z. Scratch a Thief
Marlowe, D. Somebody's Sister
Martel, J. Partners
Martin, Kenneth. Billy's Brother
Martini, S. P. Simeon Chamber
Matera, L. Good Fight
    Radical Departure
    Where Lawyers Fear to Tread
Mavity, N. P. Man Who Didn't Mind Hanging
Maylon, B. J. Corpse with Knee Action
Merrick, Mollie. Mysterious Mr. Frame
Mersereau, J. Murder Loves Company
Michaels, M. C. Through the Eyes of the Dead
Michelson, M. Yellow Journalist
Miller, Marc. Plaid Shroud
    Room, Board and Death
Miner, V. Murder in the English Department
Minton, P. Fog Hides the Fury
    Thunder Over the Reefs
Mitchell, Kirk. With Siberia Comes a Chill
Montadon, P. Intruders
Morgan, Seth. Homeboy

Morgan, W. Enforcer
Morrow, J. T. Prophet
Morrow, S. Murder May Follow
Muller, M. 9 titles
Murphy, W. B. Pigs Get Fat
Murray, Lynne. Termination Interview
Nava, M. Little Death
Neely, R. Sexton Woman
Nelson, H. L. Copper Lady
    Dead Giveaway
    Fountain of Death
    Title Is Murder
Nelson, Mildred. Dark Stone
Nicolai, C. Murder in the Fine Arts
Nisbet, J. Gourmet
Offord, L. G. Murder on Russian Hill
    My True Love Lies
    9 Dark Hours
    Skeleton Key
Oleck, H. L. Singular Fury
Olsen, D. B. Clue in the Clay
O'Marie, C. A. Advent of Dying
    Missing Madonna
    Novena for Murder
Orpet, F. Murder's No Accident
Palmer, S. Hildegarde Withers Makes the Scene
Park, O. Chinatown Connection
Pendleton, D. California Hit
    Doomsday Disciples
Pike, R. L. Bank Job
    Deadline 2 A.M.
    Gremlin's Grampa
    Reardon
Potter, J. A. If I Should Die Before I Wake
Pronzini, B. 10 titles
Queen, E. Four Johns
Quentin, P. Puzzle for Puppets
Quinn, T. Great Bridge Conspiracy
Raison, M. M. Gay Mortician
Rath, V. 6 titles
Rayter, J. Victim Was Important
Reed, C. Big Scratch
Reed, I. Last Days of Louisiana Red
Rhodes, Daniel. Adversary
Rigsby, H. Murder for the Holidays
Ring, D. Peddler
Rivera, W. L. Panic Walks Alone
Roan, T. Dragon Strikes Back
Roberts, W. D. Jaubert Ring
Robeson, K. Death Machine
Rock, P. Dirty Harry
Rodgers, M. J. Taste of Death
Rogers, G. Scandal in Eden
Rogers, J. C. Foul Play
Rogers, L. Crime Has No Friends
Roscoe, M. Slice of Hell
Rosenthal, E. Calculus of Murder
Russell, Alan. No Sign of Murder
Ruyle, J. 22 titles
Ryan, J. both titles
Ryerson, F. Fear of Fear
St. Clair, M. Daddy's Gone a'Hunting
St. Martin, T. Jill
Santiago, V. J. Kill or Be Killed
Sapir, R. Holy Terror
Saralegui, J. Last Rites
    Shadow Stalker
Scortia, T. N. Nightmare Factor
Shankman, S. Impersonal Attractions
Sherridane, D. Heart of a Gangster
Siler, J. Triangles of Fire
Silver, H. Bogus Lover
Simpson, Robert. Welcome Danger
Sims, G. Hunters Point
Singer, S. Full House
    Samson's Deal
    Suicide King
Smith, Julie. 5 titles
Spade, D. San Francisco by Night
Stacpoole, H. D. Mystery of Uncle Ballard
Stanley, J. Dark Side
Stern, R. M. Will
Stewart, A. Devil's Toy
Strahan, K. C. Death Traps

Settings Index   SCOTLAND / 1297

Streib, D. Karate Killers
Stuart, A. Catspaw
    Catspaw II
Stubbs, J. Golden Crucible
Swaim, L. Killing
Taylor, E. A. Cable Car Murder
Taylor, S. W. Grinning Gismo
Teilhet, D. L. Crimson Hair Murders
    Ticking Terror Murders
Thayer, L. 5 titles
Thompson, G. Lupe
Thompson, J. Ironside
Thompson, L. S. both titles
Thoreau, D. City at Bay
    Dynasty of Power
Trimble, L. Design for Dying
Trinian, J. North Beach Girl
    Scratch a Thief
Upton, R. Farberge Egg
    Who'd Want to Kill Old George?
Valentine, D. Collector of Photographs
Valley, M. Magnum Force
Vance, J. House on Lily Street
    View from Chickweed's Window
Van der Zee, J. Blood Brotherhood
Van Dycke, T. Not with My Neck
Vardeman, R. E. Screaming Knife
Walcott, E. A. both titles
Walker, W. Two Dude Defense
Wallace, M. Case of Loyalties
    Primary Target
Wallace, R. Yellow Shadows of Death
Wambaugh, J. Choirboys
Ward, S. Odds Against Linda
Warmbold, J. June Mail
Warner, R. Murder on the Air
Webb, V. Little Lady Killing
Weiss, M. All Points Bulletin
    No Go on Jackson Street
Weissman, J. Zodiac Killer
Welch, P. Murder by the Book
Westlake, D. E. Gangway!
White, S. E. Gray Dawn
Whitney, P. A. Trembling Hills
Wick, C. Faceless Man
Wilcox, C. 17 titles
Wiley, H. Copper Mask
    Jade
    Manchu Blood
    Murder by the Dozen
Willeford, C. Pick-Up
Williams, B. Conflict of Interest
    Matter of Confidence
Williams, C. Nothing in Her Way
Wilson, G. Welcome to the Feast
Wilson, L. This Deadly Dark
Worley, W. My Dead Wife
Yarbro, C. Q. Beastnights
    Music When Sweet Voices Die
Zackel, F. both titles
Zimmerman, B. Blood Under the Bridge

SAN JUAN (See also: Puerto Rico; West Indies; Caribbean)
Adamson, M. J. April When They Woo
    May's New Fangled Mirth
    Not Till a Hot January
O'Donnell, L. Murder Under the Sun

SANTE FE (See also: New Mexico; Albuquerque; Southwest)
Farnsworth, M. Great Stone Heart
Hughes, D. B. Blackbirder
    Ride the Pink Horse
McKnight, B. Downwind
Maxwell, A. E. Art of Survival
Mayer, R. Search
Morgan, Dean. Assignment to Sante Fe
Reilly, H. Follow Me
Satterthwait, W. Wall of Glass
Schier, N. Demon of the Opera
Stevens, Phyllis. Stepwives
Whitney, P. A. Turquoise Mask

SARDINIA (Sard. See also: Italy; Florence; Milan; Naples; Rome; Sicily; Venice)
Miller, Wade. Mad Baxter
Townend, Peter. Zoom!

SAUDI ARABIA (Saud. Arab. See also: Middle East)
Carter, Nick. Arab Plague
    Lethal Prey
Dewar, E. Perfumes of Arabia
Durie, L. This Yellow Slave
Eden, M. Murder of Lawrence of Arabia
Evans, K. Rich Way to Die
Gerard, F. Prince of Paradise
Hastings, Michael. Sands of Khali
Innes, H. Doomed Oasis
Ludlum, R. Icarus Agenda
MacAlister, I. Valley of the Assassins
Marlowe, H. Seven Pillars to Hell
Marlowe, S. Manhunt Is My Mission
Peel, K. J. Twelfth Night of Ramadan
Pendleton, D. Desert Strike
San Antonio. Knights of Arabia
Turner, E. Your Secret Is in a Well

SCANDINAVIA (Scand. See also: individual countries)
Bagley, D. Tightrope Men
Creasey, J. Legion of the Lost
Forbes, C. Cover Story
Hamilton, Donald. Vanishers
Wheatley, D. Shadow of Tyburn Tree
Woods, Stuart. Deep Lie
York, A. Co-Ordinator

SCHOOL. See: Academia.

SCOTLAND (Scot. See also: Edinburgh; Glasgow; Hebrides)
Aiken, Joan. Castle Barebane
Anthony, Elizabeth. Dramatic Murder
Arnold, M. Lament for a Lady Laird
Bannister, J. Going Down of the Sun
Barrett, C. F. Douglas Castle
Beaton, M. C. all 5 titles
Bishop, M. Killraven
Black, G. Cold Jungle
Black, Laura. Castle Raven
    Glendraco
    Wild Cat
Blackstock, C. Factor's Wife
    Shadow of Murder
Bland, J. Death in Waiting
Blickle, K. North Sea Mistress
Boyd, M. S. Mystery of the Castle
Buchan, J. 5 titles
Buckingham, N. Call of Glengarron
Burgess, L. Halloween
Caird, J. all 5 titles
Campbell, C. Murder on the Moors
    Murder up the Glen
    Red Glen
Campbell, H. R. Murder Set to Music
Carr, J. D. Case of the Constant Suicides
Carter, Nick. Pressure Point
Chalmers, S. Blood on the Heather
    Greater Punishment
Cleaton, I. Outsider
Clements, A. Christabel's Room
    Highland Fire
    Mistress of the Moor
Clements, E. H. High Tension
    Perhaps a Little Danger
Collee, J. Kingsley's Touch
Cork, B. Unnatural Hazard
Corrigan, M. Riddle of Double Island
Courage, J. Nightingales Never Sing
Craig, B. Scobie in September
Creasey, J. Flood
Crofts, F. W. Groote Park Murder
Cross, C. Masque of Enchantment
Crowe, C. Talisman
Davies, E. Widow's Necklace
Davies, L. P. Assignment Abacus

Deane, N. Secret Errand
De La Torre, L. Heir of Douglas
Devine, D. Sunk Without Trace
Devine, D. M. Doctors Also Die
    Fifth Cord
    His Own Appointed Day
    Illegal Tender
Dick, A. MacAlister Looks On
Dipper, A. Golden Virgin
Doherty, P. C. Crown in Darkness
Donnelly, J. Bane
Dorer, N. You Will Like It Here
Dorien, R. House of Dread
Douglas, G. House with the Green Shutters
Drummond, John. Behind Dark Shutters
Duff, D. Loch Spy
Duncan, W. M. Murder of a Cop
Dunnett, A. End of Term
    No Thanks to the Duke
Dunstan, M. "Live On"
Durie, L. Traill Case
Elgin, M. Return to Glenshael
    Visibility Nil
Farr, C. Castle on the Loch
Ferguson, J. Dark Geraldine
    Night in Glengyle
Ferrars, E. In at the Kill
Fletcher, J. S. Copper Box
Forrest, Wilma. Anne of Destiny House
Foster, John. Searchers
Fraser, Antonia. Wild Island
Friedman, M. Paper Phoenix
Frost, K. Death Registers at the Eagle Arms
Galwey, G. V. Murder on leave
Gardiner, D. Seventh Mourner
Gardiner, G. At the House of Dree
Garrett, W. Secret of the Hills
Garwood, J. Bride
Gaskin, C. Charmed Circle
Gaston, B. Death Crag
    Deep Green Death
    Drifting Death
George, E. Payment in Blood
Goldie, B. Piper of Arristoun
Goodchild, G. Dear Old Gentleman
Gordon, E. Birdwatcher
Gordon, N. Factory on the Cliff
Graham, A. Follow the Little Pictures!
    Murder Disqualifies
Grant, Roderick. Stalking of Adrian Lawford
Gray, B. Conquest in Scotland
Grayson, R. Whisky Murders
Gunn, N. M. Blood Hunt
    Key of the Chest
    Silver Bough
Halliday, D. Dolly and the Singing Bird
Hamilton, D. Devastators
Hamilton, H. At Night to Die
Hammond, G. 16 titles
Hart-Davis, D. Fire Falcon
Hastings, MacDonald. Cork on the Water
Hayes, L. Dark Legend
Heaven, C. Fires of Glenlochy
Hild, J. Barrabas Kill
Hill, L. Daggers Drawn
Hill, P. Whitton's Folly
Honeycombe, G. Neither the Sea Nor the Sand
Howarth, D. Group Flashing Two
Howatch, S. Waiting Sands
Hubbard, P. M. Causeway
    Graveyard
    Whisper in the Glen
Huff, A. P. Key to Hawthorn Heath
Hull, R. Last First
Hunter, A. Gabrielle's Way
    Gently North-West
    Gently with Love
Hutchinson, H. Lost Golfer
Innes, H. North Star
    Sabotage Broadcast
Innes, M. Lament for a Maker
Jamison, A. Lairds of Turriff Hall
Johnston, V. Deveron Hall
    I Came to the Highlands

Jones, H. M. Scottish Chieftains
Kelly, M. Write on Both Sides of the Paper
Kerr, R. Stuart Legacy
Kerrigan, P. Survival Game
Kippax, J. Scar
Knight, Alanna. 5 titles
Knox, B. 22 titles
Knox, R. A. Double Cross Purposes
    Still Dead
Kyle, E. Mally Lee
Langley, B. Avenge the Belgrano
Law, J. Death Under Par
Lechmere, D. In Deadly Peril
Lee, Elsie. Mansion of the Golden Windows
Leslie, M. Cavanaugh Keep
Lewis, Deborah. Lady in the Tapestry
    Voices Out of Time
Lewis, R. Of Singular Purpose
Lillie, H. Listening Silence
Linklater, E. House of Gair
Llewellyn, S. Deadeye
Lovell, M. Spy Who Barked in the Night
Lyall, F. Croaking of the Raven
    Death and the Remembrancer
    Death in Time
Lyell, W. D. House in Queen Anne Square
Lynch, F. Dangerous Magic
MacArthur, D. W. Landfall
    Mystery of the "David M"
McCloy, H. One That Got Away
MacClure, V. House of Dearth
McCutchan, P. Coach North
McCutcheon, H. Killer's Moon
    Red Sky at Night
McEwen, H. Children of the Mists
McGown, J. Murder Movie
McKeand, G. Lady Glenroy
MacKinnon, A. Cormorant's Isle
    Dead on Departure
    House of Darkness
    Map of Mistrust
MacKintosh, M. Double Dealers
MacLeod, A. all 3 titles
MacLeod, R. Money Mountain
McNeilly, W. Case of the Stag at Bay
McShane, M. Night's Evil
MacVicar, A. at least 17 titles
Mac. John O'Howgate
Mair, A. Douglas Affair
Mair, G. B. Live, Love, and Cry
Malcolm, M. Headless Beings
Malloch, P. Fugitive's Road
    Walk In, Death
Manners, A. Singing Swans
    Stone Maiden
Manton, P. Murder in the Highlands
Marsh, John. Operation Snatch
Marshall, Edison. Death Bell
Massey, C. Bride of Invercoe
Maybury, A. Dark Star
Meek, M. R. D. Split Second
Meldrum, D. S. Conquest of Charlotte
Michaels, B. Master of Blacktower
Miles, K. Bullet Hole
Mitchell, G. My Bones Will Keep
    Winking at the Brim
Moffat, G. Miss Pink at the Edge of the World
    Over the Sea to Death
    Snare
Morris, E. Five Fowlers
Muir, A. Blue Bonnet
    Satyr Mask
    Shadow on the Left
    Third Warning
Muir, T. Death on the Loch
    Death Under Virgo
Munro, H. Clue for Clutha
Ogilvie, E. Devil in Tartan
    Silent Ones
Ostrander, K. Doom of Glendour
P., F. H. Castle of Caithness
Parker, Richard. Gingerbread Man
Paterson, A. J. B. Mist from Yarrow
Paul, W. Lion Rampant

Pearson, P. Postscript for Malpas
Peck, W. Warrielaw Jewel
Pendleton, D. Time to Kill
Peters, Elizabeth. Legend on Green Velvet
Rae, H. C. Few Small Bones
    Saturday Epic
    Shooting Gallery
    Skinner
Randall, R. Watchman's Stone
Randell, C. Weeping Tower
Raynes, J. Legacy of the Wolf
Reznek, L. Medicine Man
Richmond, M. Traitor's Harvest
Riefe, B. Auldearn House
Rochester, G. E. Dead Man's Gold
Roe, C. F. both titles
Ross, Angus. Aberdeen Conundrum
Ross, Clarissa. Face in the Pond
Ross, Dan. Castle on the Cliff
Ross, Marilyn. Cauldron of Evil
    Cellars of the Dead
    Death's Dark Music
    Waiting in the Shadows
Roy, A. Curtained Sleep
    Devil in the Darkness
Ruell, P. Castle of the Demon
Rushton, C. Terror Tower
Russell, A. Larksong at Dawn
Saxon, P. Satan's Child
Sayers, D. L. Five Red Herrings
Scott, Annjeanette. Castle for the Left Hand
Scott, B. C. Midnight Heather of Bridee Castle
Scott, G. Water Horse
Scott, Honoria. Castle at Strathway
Scott, M. D. J. Drumbuie House
Sheffield, C. Erasmus Magister
Shulman, S. Prisoner of Garve
Sinclair, Michael. Dollar Covenant
Sinclair, O. Hearts by the Tower
Smith, Clark. Speaking Eye
Stafford, C. Moira
Stand, M. Death Came with Darkness
Stern, R. M. I Hide, We Seek
    Manuscript for Murder
Stevenson, A. Mask of Treason
Stevenson, D. E. Crooked Adam
Stevenson, T. Murder at the Bar
Stewart, Lois. Dark Rendezvous at Dungariff
Stewart, Mary. Wildfire at Midnight
Stuart, V. Darnley's Bride
Stubbs, J. Case of Kitty Ogilvie
Taffrail. Shetland Plan
Tain, I. Cherrycake Death
Tavis, A. Duke's Day
Thomas, Martin. Laird of Evil
Trocchi, A. Young Adam
Urquhart, M. Grey Man
Venters, A. Kennedy's Killing
Vicary, J. Castle at Glencarris
Walker, D. Ash
    Storm and the Silence
    Winter of Madness
Walsh, M. Man in Brown
Warden, F. Love That Lasts
Warrick, M. Bandit Trust
    Yawning Lion
West, M. L. Summer of the Red Wolf
Wheatley, D. Malinsay Massacre
Whitelaw, D. Horror on the Loch
Wilkinson, R. Big Still
Williams, P. C. Tartan Murders
Willock, R. I, Victoria Strange
Wills, C. Defeat of a Detective
Wilson, Gar. Iron Claymore
Wurr, H. J. all 3 titles
Wynne, A. Loving Cup
    Murder in Thin Air
    Murder of a Lady

SEA. See: Ship.

SEATTLE (See also: Washington; Northwest)
Anderson, James. Lovers and Other Killers
Arre, H. Golden Shroud
Beck, K. K. Body in the Volvo
Brock, S. Just Around the Coroner
Castle, Jayne. Fatal Fortune
Curtis, W. Red Heroin
Derrick, L. Northwest Contract
Dietz, W. C. Matrix Man
Edwards, Alexander. McQ
Elmblad, M. Little Company
Emerson, E. W. 5 titles
Hoyt, R. Decoys
    Fish Story
    30 for a Harry
Huebner, F. D. Joshua Sequence
    Judgment by Fire
    Picture Postcard
Iles, B. Murder in Mink
Jance, J. A. 7 titles
Kelsey, V. Fear Came First
McQuinn, D. E. Shadow of Lies
Mackin, R. Fire Storm
Pearson, R. Undercurrents
Pendleton, D. Firebase Seattle
Reed, Harlan. Swing Music Murder
Rice, J. Night Strangler
Ross, Z. H. Overdue for Death
Shimer, R. H. Cricket Cage
Silliphant, S. Slender Thread
Thornberg, N. Lion at the Door
Warden, M. Dead Ringer
    Death Beat
    Topless Corpse
    Wasps in the Woodpile
Warren, V. Invitation to Kill
Wilson, B. Dog Collar Murders
    Murder in the Collective

SENEGAL (Sen. See also: Africa, West)
Chase, J. H. This Is for Real
O'Neil, K. Death at Dakar

SHANGHAI (See also: China; Peking; Formosa; Hong Kong; Far East; Mongolia; Macao)
Booth, C. G. General Died at Dawn
Corrigan, M. Shanghai Jezebel
Dekker, C. Run for Your Life
Dekobra, M. Honeymoon in Shanghai
Dodge, S. Shanghai Incident
Fisher, Alan. Yangtze
Fleischman, A. S. Murder's No Accident
    Shanghai Flame
Gardner, J. Flamingo
Ile, T. Shanghai Nights
Kenrick, T. Faraday's Flowers
Marshall, W. Shanghai
Mason, V. W. Shanghai Bund Murders
Morland, N. Concrete Maze
    Sing a Song of Cyanide
Overgard, W. Shanghai Tango
Smith, Don. China Coaster
Sussman, B. J. Shanghai
Thorne, P. That Evening in Shanghai

SHIP
Aarons, E. S. Sinners
Adams, C. F. And Sudden Death
Adams, E. L. Death Charter
    Murder in the Hurricane
Addis, H. Dark Voyage
Allen, Will. Contraband Cruises
Allison, W. Secret of the Sea
Ames, J. Frightened Heart
Anderson, J. R. L. Death in the North Sea
Anderson, James. Angel of Death
Andrews, P. Drug Runner
Anonymous. By the Fore Barbette
Antill, E. Murder in Mid-Atlantic
Ard, W. Babe in the Woods
    Girl for Danny
Arliss, J. Shark Bait Affair
Armstrong, R. Sinister Widow at Sea
Austin, H. Lilies for Madame

Settings Index

Avallone, M. Assassins Don't Die in Bed
Babson, M. Cruise of a Deathtime
    Murder Sails at Midnight
Baker, H. Cartwright Is Dead, Sir!
Baker, W. H. Strike North
Barker, Nicholas. Red Ice
Barry, C. Death of a First Mate
Bax, R. Red Escapade
Beach, E. L. Cold Is the Sea
Beck, K. K. Death in a Deck Chair
Bell, Josephine. Fennister Affair
Benchley, N. Sail a Crooked Ship
Bentley, J. Mr. Marlow Takes to Rye
Berckman, E. Hovering Darkness
Blake, C. Deadly Legacy
Blake, N. Widow's Cruise
Blanc, S. Sea Troll
Blochman, L. G. Midnight Sailing
Block, T. H. Forced Landing
Boothby, G. Bid for Fortune
    Ocean Secret
Borthwick, J. S. Bodies of Water
Bosworth, A. R. Full Crash Dive
Bradley, David. Lodestar Project
Brandon, A. Full Circle
Brandon, J. Mr. Pennington Comes Through
    Murder on the High Seas
Bream, F. Corpse on the Cruise
Brean, H. Traces of Merrilee
Brewer, M. Windward Passage
Bunce, F. So Young a Body
Burton, Miles. Murder in Absence
Cable, B. Double Scoop
Callison, B. Thunder of Crude
Cameron, O. Owl and the Pussycat
Cannon, J. Web of Terror
Carr, J. D. Blind Barber
Carter, Nick. Deep Sea Death
    Sea Trap
Carver, S. Died o'Wednesday
Cawley, R. Shockwave
Chambers, D. Blonde Died First
Charles, E. F. Death Crosses the Line
Charles, H. Miss Seeton at the Helm
Charles, R. Scream of the Dove
Charteris, L. Saint Overboard
Childers, E. Riddle of the Sands
Clancy, T. Hunt for Red October
Clark, M. H. Caribbean Blues
Clarke, A. Cabin 3033
Clements, C. Hell Ship to Kuma
    Satan Takes the Helm
Cobb, B. Corpse at Casablanca
Cole, G. D. H. Greek Tragedy
Collins, D. Ordeal
    Simple Simon Smith
    Vulnerable
Collins, G. Channel Million
Compton, G. High Tide for Hanging
Connell, R. Murder at Sea
Connolly, V. Five Ports to Danger
Coonts, S. Final Flight
Cornwell, B. Crackdown
    Wildtrack
Coxe, G. H. Inland Passage
Cranston, C. Murder Maritime
Creasey, J. Toff on Board
Crofts, F. W. Enemy Unseen
    Loss of the Jane Vosper
Croudace, G. Scarlet Bikini
Cussler, C. Pacific Vortex
Danton, R. Ship of Hate
DeAndrea, W. L. Killed in Paradise
Dearden, R. L. Care of the Commander
Derrick, L. Deepsea Shootout
Deverell, W. High Crimes
Dickson, Carter. Nine—and Death Makes Ten
Divine, A. D. Terror in the Thames
Dodge, D. Angel's Ransom
Douglas, Gavin. Rough Passage
Douglass, D. M. Many Brave Hearts
Drago, F. Cruise with Death
Drax, P. High Seas Murder
Du Bois, T. Face of Hate

Eberhart, M. G. Five Passengers from Lisbon
    Patient in Cabin C
Edgar, K. Honduras Double Cross
Edmonds, H. Death Ship
Ellis, W. Knife Edge
Emery, S. At Nine Bells
Evans, Alan. Audacity
Filer, T. Man on Watch
Finer, A. Deepwater
Finley, G. Secret of Love
Finney, J. Assault on a Queen
Fish, R. L. Rub-a-Dub-Dub
Fitzsimmons, C. This—Is Murder!
Flagg, J. Death and the Naked Lady
Fletcher, L. Girl in Cabin B54
Follett, J. Churchill's Gold
Footner, H. Dangerous Cargo
Forbes, S. Name's Death, Remember Me?
Forsythe, R. Pleasure Cruise Mystery
Gardner, J. Win, Lose or Die
Garrett, F. Blood Beach
Garve, A. Hero for Leanda
Gibbs, G. F. Foul Weather
Gibbs, T. Running Fix
Gibson, G. Captain Incognito
Gielgud, V. Necessary End
Gill, E. Crime de Luxe
Gilruth, S. Corpse for Charybdis
Gollin, J. Broken Consort
Gorman, E. Several Deaths Later
Gould, S. Murder of the Admiral
Graeme, B. Hate Ship
    Mystery on the Queen Mary
    Racing Yacht Mystery
Granger, B. Queen's Crossing
Grantham, G. Mystery of the S.S. "Timor"
Green, W. M. Avery's Fortune
Gregg, M. Dhow Patrol
Grimshaw, B. Kris-Girl
Groom, P. Temperamental Journey
Gruppe, H. Truxton Cipher
Hagen, M. A. Murder—But Natch
Hamilton, B. Too Much of Water
Hannay, J. F. W. Gin and Ginger
Harper, Olive. Caught in Mid-Ocean
Harper, R. J. Dragonhead Deal
Harris, Colver. Murder in Amber
Harris, J. Road to the Coast
Harrison, H. QEII Is Missing
Hawk, J. Mid-Ocean Tragedy
Hebden, M. Pride of Dolphins
Higgins, J. Storm Warning
Hild, J. Barrabas War
    Red Vengeance
Hilton, J. Ship of the Damned
Hocking, A. Mediterranean Murder
Holding, E. S. Lady Killer
Holton, L. Touch of Jonah
Howes, R. Callao Clue
    Death on the Bridge
    Nasty Name Murders
Hufford, S. Midnight Sailing
Hughes, T. J. Queen's Mate
Hull, J. H. Angela
Hunter, J. White Phantom
Innes, H. 5 titles
James, Robert. Board Stiff
Jenkins, G. Grue of Ice
Johnson, J. L. Trackless Seas
Johnston, R. Angry Ocean
    Stowaway
Joseph, A. Logan
Joseph, M. To Kill the Potemkin
Kane, F. Conspirators
    Crime of Their Life
Keane, C. Crossing
    Heir
Keene, D. Passage to Samoa
Keinzley, F. Cottage at Chapelyard
Kenmore, F. J. Jasmine Sloop
Keyes, M. Dead Parrot
Kilian, M. Dance on a Sinking Ship
King, C. D. Obelists at Sea
King, R. 5 titles

Knight, Adam. Sumburned Corpse
Knight, C. Affair of the Scarlet Crab
Knight, F. Captain of the "Calabar"
Knight, Maxwell. Crime Cargo
Kytle, R. Last Voyage
Lanham, E. One Murder Too Many
    Passage to Danger
Laumer, K. Drowned Queen
Leroux, G. Floating Prison
Little, C. Grey Mist Murders
Llewellyn, S. Blood Orange
Lockridge, F. Voyage Into Violence
Lockridge, R. Inspector's Holiday
Loder, V. Ship of Secrets
Lorenz, F. Rage at Sea
Lovesey, P. False Inspector Dew
Lowden, D. Bandersnatch
McCloy, H. She Walks Alone
McCutchan, P. Redcap
McGerr, P. Save the Witness
MacIsaac, F. Death Rides the Deep
MacKinnon, A. No Wreath from Manuela
McLaughlin, W. R. D. Sabotage at Sea!
MacLean, Alistair. 5 titles
Mainwaring, M. Murder in Pastiche
Marsh, N. Clutch of Constables
    Swinging in the Shrouds
Martin, Shane. Wake for Mourning
Martyn, W. Murder Walks the Deck
Maxwell, V. Way of the Tamarisk
Michelet, J. Orion's Belt
Miller, J. M. T. On a Dead Man's Chest
Miller, Wade. Nightmare Cruise
Montross, D. Fellow-Traveler
Morton, A. Baron on Board
Muir, D. Midnight Admirals
Murray, M. No Duty on a Corpse
Nash, S. Death Over Deep Water
Nelson, M. Crusoe Test
Neville, M. Hateful Voyage
Norman, D. N. Thunder Station
Norris, F. Shanghaied
North, Gerry. Gerry North Collects
O'Brine, M. Corpse to Cairo
Ockley, G. T. Devil on Board
O'Neill, E. A. Rotterdam Delivery
Oppenheim, E. P. Bird of Paradise
    Strange Case of Mr. Jocelyn Thew
Packard, F. Devil's Mantle
Page, C. G. Beyond the Windswept Sea
Palmer, J. Above and Below
Patrick, Q. S.S. Murder
Pattinson, J. Contact Mr. Delgado
    Mystery of the Gregory Kotovsky
    Precious Cargo
Patton, D. K. Murder on the Pacific
Pendleton, D. Crude Kill
Peterson, Audrey. Murder in Burgundy
Pilpel, R. H. To the Honor of the Fleet
Pleasants, W. S. Stingaree Murders
Price, J.-A. Doomsday Ship
Price, W. Death Is a Stowaway
Quentin, D. Perilous Voyage
Radcliffe, G. In the Grip of the Brute
Reed, Douglas. Rule of Three
Reed, Harlan. Case of the Crawling Cockroach
Rhodes, K. Crime on a Cruise
Richmond, M. Cabin Nineteen
Riesenberg, F. Left-Handed Passenger
Rinehart, M. R. After-House
Robeson, K. Mystery Under the Sea
    Red Terrors
    Sargasso Ogre
Rosenberger, J. Caribbean Blood Moon
    Iron Swastika Plot
    Zembya Expedition
Ross, C. Dancing Years
Ross, H. H. Mystery of the Lotus Queen
Ross, W. E. D. Fogbound
Rostand, R. Cross Currents
Roth, H. Too Many Doctors
Russell, W. C. Tale of Two Tunnels
    Tragedy of Ida Noble
Sale, R. Death at Sea

S

Salisbury, C. Dolphin Summer
Sapir, R. Ship of Death
Savage, E. Two If by Sea
Saxby, C. Death Cuts the Film
Schaill, W. S. Cabot Station
Scott, Justin. Shipkiller
Scott, Mansfield. Phantom Passenger
Sears, R. M. Port of No Return
Shaw, F. H. Atlantic Murder
Shaw, J. T. Derelict
Sherlock, J. Amindra Gamble
Shore, V. B. Murder on the Glass Floor
Simons, R. Murder First Class
Slater, I. Deep Chill
    Sea Gold
Smith, M. C. Polar Star
Smith, Wilbur. Eye of the Tiger
Snow, C. P. Death Under Sail
Spicer, B. Taming of Carney Wilde
Stahl, R. Death Stalks "The Wild Goose"
Stanley, B. Alscott Experiment
Stanton, K. Operation Sea Monster
Starrett, V. Murder on "B" Deck
Stein, A. M. Kill Is a Four-Letter Word
Stephens, E. Submariner
Stephenson, H. M. Yo-Ho, and a Bottle of Rum!
Stone, A. L. Decks Ran Red
Streib, D. Predators
Symons, B. Jane Carberry and the Laughing
    Fountain
Tack, A. Death Takes a Dive
Taylor, C. D. Boomer
Taylor, P. W. Murder in the Flagship
Teed, G. H. Killer Aboard
    Murder Ship
Thayer, L. Dead Reckoning
    Last Trump
    Lightning Strikes Twice
Thorndike, R. Doctor Syn on the High Seas
Thurman, S. Night After Night
Tonkin, P. Coffin Ship
Townend, W. Night's Black Agent
Trask, K. Murder Incidental
Trew, A. Antonov Project
    Running Wild
Trott, N. Monkey Boat
Vance, J. Strange Notions and The Dark Ocean
Vance, L. J. Lone Wolf's Last Prowl
    Lone Wolf's Son
    Sheep's Clothing
Villars, E. Normandie Affair
Webb, F. Caviar Cruise
Wells, Carolyn. Bronze Hand
Wells, S. Murder Is Not Enough
Wheatley, D. Murder Off Miami
    Uncharted Seas
White, L. Rich and Dangerous Game
Whitfield, R. Virgin Kills
Whitman, H. E. O. Pirate of Pittsburgh
Wilkinson, R. Murder on the High Seas
Willard, T. Strike Fighters
Williams, C. Aground
    Dead Calm
Williams, V. Fog
Wilson, G. Atlantic Scramble
    Sea of Savages
Wilson, J. R. Round Voyage
Wilson, M. A. Panic-Stricken
Wilson, S. Greatest Crime
Wood, J. Friday Run
    Lisa Bastian
Worts, G. F. Silver Fang
Wynd, O. Death the Red Flower
Yates, M. T. Hush-Hush Murders
York, A. Captivator
    Fascinator
York, J. Voyage with Murder

SIAM. See: Thailand.

SICILY (Sic. See also: Italy; Florence; Milan; Naples;
    Rome; Sardinia; Venice)
Anonymous. Avenger
Bishop, S. Onlooker
Brydon, S. Manhunt in Sicily
Charteris, L. Vendetta for the Saint
Clifford, F. Another Way of Dying
Crookenden, I. Fatal Secrets
Curtis, J. A. K. Sicilian Mysteries
Gielgud, V. To Bed at Noon
Higgins, J. In the Hour Before Midnight
    Luciano's Luck
Howlett, J. Tango November
Larkin, R. T. Honor Thy Godmother
Lewis, N. March of the Long Shadows
Llewellyn, C. Lady of the Labyrinth
McEvoy, M. Castle Doom
MacKintosh, M. Sicilian Affair
Marchmont, A. W. My Lost Self
Montague, E. Demon of Sicily
Moore, J. Zeluco
Peterson, Jim. Sicilian Slaughter
Radcliffe, A. Sicilian Romance
Rossmann, J. Mind-Masters
Sciascia, L. Equal Danger
    Mafia Vendetta
    Man's Blessing
Sinclair, Fiona. Meddle with the Mafia
Urquhart, M. Bitter Lemon Mob

SIERRA LEONE (See also: Africa, West)
Daniels, N. Operation S-L
Harris, J. Funny Place to Hold a War

SINGAPORE (Sing. See also: Far East)
Aarons, E. S. Assignment—Nuclear Nude
Ball, J. Singapore
Black, G. Suddenly, at Singapore . . .
Bogart, W. Singapore
Carter, Nick. Singapore Sling
Corrigan, M. Singapore Downbeat
Crisp, F. Chandu Men
Crisp, P. A. In the Shadow of the Dragon
Dekker, J. Singapore Set-Up
Derby, M. Five Nights in Singapore
    Ghost Blonde
    Sun in the Hunter's Eyes
Foxx, J. Jade Figurine
Kirk, L. Man on the Raffles Verandah
Leib, F. A. Sea Lion
MacBeth, G. Kind of Treason
Mason, V. W. Singapore Exile Murders
Murray, M. Doctor and the Corpse
Nicholas, J. Asbestos Mask
Nunn, F. Blue Haze
Pereira, M. Pigeon's Blood
Pitt, R. Month of the Evil Moon
Rideout, H. M. Dragon's Blood
Sherwood, J. Two Died in Singapore
Stewart, I. Seizing of Singapore
Thomas, Ross. Singapore Wink

SOLOMON ISLANDS (Sol. Is. See also: Australia;
    South Pacific)
Frazer, M. Four Jealous Men
Seton, Georgina. Bring Another Glass
Stevens, K. M. Panic in the Solomons

SOUTH (See also: the 14 individual states)
Abbot, S. River and the Rose
Alexander, David. Bloodstain
Alexander, Jan. Darkwater
Allerton, Mary. Shadow and the Web
Arnold, J. Prettybelle
Blackmon, A. both titles
Boggs, M. Scissors, Paper, Stone
Burton, C. D. Long Goodnight
Caine, P. Virus
Chetham, L. Secret of Saramount
Childers, V. Things Undone
Clemeau, C. Ariadne Clue
Cohen, O. R. May Day Mystery
Daingerfield, F. Linden Walk Tragedy
Day, Dianne. Obsidian
Deal, B. Long Way to Go
Deasy, M. Coriola Affair
Dixon, M. Heartlanders
Ellis, Julie. Daughter's Promise
Ellis, M. No Man for Murder
Fonseca, E. H. Thirteenth Bed in the Ballroom
Fox, J. M. Free Ride
Gaither, F. O. Double Muscadine
Gallo, D. Sin in the South
Garland, N. Crime of Innocence
Garrison, C. both titles
Gatenby, R. Third Identity
Givens, C. G. Jig-Time Murders
Gonzales, J. Follow That Hearse!
Greene, W. Death in the Deep South
Greer, B. Holloween
Grubb, D. Shadow of My Brother
Hardwick, R. Plotters
    Season to Be Deadly
Harrington, J. Family Reunion
Harris, C. Secret Rage
Hawkins, D. Headsman's Holiday
    Walls of Silence
Hay, J. Bellamy Case
Hilldrup, R. P. To Die for a Golden Leaf
Hines, J. Slashed Portrait
Holden, G. Killer Loose!
    Something's Happened to Kate
    Sound an Alarm
    Velvet Target
Janeway, H. This Passionate Land
Jensen, R. J. House That Samael Built
Johnson, E. R. Cage Five Is Going to Break
Johnston, W. W. Wheels of Death
Jones, M. Cry in Absence
    Last Things
Kane, F. Liz
Keene, D. Dangling Carrot
    Too Black for Heaven
Keene, F. Pattern in Black and Red
Kelly, T. J. Murder in the Magnolias
Kent, D. Knife Is Silent
Kimbrough, K. Dorothy, the Terrified
Lawrence, H. Pavilion
Lermina, J. Chase
Liddon, E. S. Riddle of the Florentine Folio
Logue, J. Replay: Murder
McCarthy, D. Killing at the Big Tree
McClelland, M. G. Manitou Island
McCorkle, J. July 7th
Macomber, D. Return to Octavia
Maxwell, P. Secret of Mirror House
May, J. S. Heritage of Shadows
Mills, William. Those Who Blink
Morrow, S. Moonlighters
Mosiman, B. S. Bloodland
Nordan, R. All Dressed Up to Die
Ogburn, D. Ra-Ta-Plan—!
Phillips, J. Greenwood
Poyer, D. C. Shiloh Project
Rifkin, S. Murderer Vine
Rigsby, H. Avenger
Rilla, W. Dispensable Man
Robertson, L. Back Country Crimes
Robison, G. Dark Lady
Rock, P. Tick . . . Tick . . . Tick
Sapir, R. Chained Reaction
Shaara, M. Herald
Shivers, L. Here to Get My Baby Out of Jail
Short, C. Blue-Eye Boy
Stacy, O. Murder at Cypress Hall
Stone, Elna. Secret of the Willows
    Visions of Esmaree
Taylor, J. R. Macon Moore, the Southern Detective
Terrall, R. Killer Is Loose Among Us
Thomas, Ross. Fools in Town Are on Our Side
Thompson, J. Pop. 1280
Trehearne, E. Storm at Midnight
Van Deusen, D. Murder Bicarb
Vandergriff, A. Sisters of Sorrow
Vincent, R. Blacklash
Walk, C. E. Silver Blade
Warden, L. Murder on Wheels
White, L. Death of a City
Williams, C. Big City Girl
Winston, D. Flight of a Fallen Angel

SOUTH AFRICA (S. Afr. See also: Cape Town; Johannesburg; Transvaal)
Anthony, N. Diamond Racket
Ashe, G. Promise of Diamonds
Avallone, M. Blazing Affair
Bagley, M. Mohembo Crossing
Brechin, D. Uncut Diamonds
Brownlee, F. Colonel Wanzi
Bryden, H. A. both titles
Burmeister, J. Running Scared
Chase, J. H. Vulture Is a Patient Bird
Christie, A. Man in the Brown Suit
Crosbie, J. Gun Runners
Croudace, G. Blackadder
    Motives for Murder
Crowder, K. Iron Web
Davis, B. Conspiracy of Eagles
Deane, N. Look at Murder
    Murder Ahead
Desmond, H. Jacaranda Murders
    Lady, Where Are You?
    Murder Strikes at Dawn
    Silent Witness
Dodge, D. Troubleshooter
Driscoll, P. Spearhead
    Wilby Conspiracy
Drummond, June. 6 titles
Du Camp, A. Twana
E., W. T. I.D.B.
Ebersohn, W. Closed Circle
    Divide the Night
    Lonely Place to Die
Eland, C. Desperate Search
Eskapa, S. Blood Fugue
Finlay, I. Azanian Assignment
Francis, D. Smokescreen
Frost, W. A. Man Between
Galgut, D. Sinless Season
Gardiner, G. Pattern of Chance
Gates, N. Decoy in Diamonds
Glanville, E. Fair Colonist
Godfrey, P. Death Under the Table
Goff, O. Eye of the Peacock
Graham, Mark. Harbinger
Gray, D. Baby Face
Grayson, Rupert. Gun Cotton, Secret Agent
Greene, L. P. at least 16 titles
Harris, P. Final Set
Hartmann, M. Shadow of the Leopard
Hayes, R. Satan Stone
Hickman, H. Bachelor Party
Hild, J. Some Chose Hell
Hornblow, A. Mask
Hume, F. Traitor in London
Jacobson, D. Dance of the Sun
Jason, S. African Contract
    Man from White Hat
Jenkins, G. In Harm's Way
    River of Diamonds
Justin, D. Shard's Rock
Langley, B. Blood River
Leroux, E. One for the Devil
    Third Eye
McClure, J. 8 titles
MacKenzie, N. Dark Night
    Death Holds His Court
Meynell, L. Danger Round the Corner
Milne, S. False Witness
    Hammer of Justice
    Stiff Silk
Mitford, B. at least 5 titles
Niesewand, P. Member of the Club
O'Keefe, B. Gold Without Glitter
Peter, J. Runaway
Radford, E. Murder Magnified
Rosenberger, J. Invasion of the Clones
Ruff, H. L. Duel with Diamonds
Sampson, V. Murder of Paul Rougier
Scholefield, A. Sea Cave
Seymour, G. Song in the Morning
Sheldon, L. V. I.D.B. in South Africa
Sibson, F. H. Breeze from the Backveld
Taube, L. S. Diamond Boomerang
Taylor, P. W. Murder in the Game Reserve

Vahey, J. H. Mr. Nemesis
Van Rensburg, H. Man with Two Ties
Van Wijk, J. L. Iselane
Van Zyl, P. R. Prosecutor
Von Linsingen, F. W. B. Pressure-Gauge Murder
Webster, E. C. Pot Holes
Webster, P. Kruger's Gold
Wells, A. W. All This Is Ended
Westrup, W. Old McBein
Wheatley, D. Fabulous Valley
Whishaw, F. Diamond of Evil
Whitney, P. A. Blue Fire
Wilson, Gar. Time Bomb
Wilson, Snoo. Soul of the White Ant
York, J. Safari with Fear

SOUTH AMERICA (S. Am. See also: individual countries)
Atlee, P. Black Venus Contract
Bagley, D. High Citadel
Bandolier, S. Murder Manana
Barrett, Michael. Last Flowers
Berrow, N. Claws of the Cougar
Boorstin, P. Savage
Caillou, A. Plotters
Carter, A, Infernal Desire Machines of Doctor Hoffman
Carter, Nick. Death Hand Play
Chambers, W. Coast of Intrigue
Clifford, F. Act of Mercy
Cory, D. Johnny Goes West
Dundas, L. all 3 titles
Ellin, S. Panama Portrait
Faust, R. Long Count
Fox, C. Sweet Bait of Money
Grae, C. Winged Dancer
Hall, Adam. Volcanoes of Sam Domingo
Hamilton, D. Annihilators
Haring, D. 36-24-Forty-Five
Harwood, R. Guilt Merchants
Hild, J. Death Deal
Holbrook, M. Crime Wind
Household, G. Three Sentinels
Jameson, F. Green Fire
Judd, A. Tango
Laflin, J. Spy in White Gloves
Kaplan, A. Hour of the Assassins
Le May, A. One of Us is a Murderer
Luceno, J. Head Hunters
Luigi, B. Lost Underworld
Marlowe, S. Murder Is My Dish
Marquand, J. P. It's Loaded, Mr. Bauer
Messmann, J. Ransom!
Mills, A. Pursued
Neebel, R. Immediate Action
Oppenheim, E. P. Man and His Kingdom
Ordway, P. Teak Forest
Packer, B. J. Caro
Pattinson, J. Last Stronghold
Pendleton, T. Hodak
Pollard, A. O. Death Game
Q., J. Survivor
Reed, E. Passport to Panic
Robeson, K. Blood Countess
    Dust of Death
    Freckled Shark
    Spook Hole
Rose, G. Bright Adventure
Rossiter, J. Deadly Green
Salkeld, M. Missing from the Shelf
Sangster, J. Your Friendly Neighborhood Death Dealer
Sickelmore, R. Osrick
Szulc, T. Diplomatic Immunity
Tiger, J. Mission Impossible
Tracy, L. Terms of Surrender
Trevor, J. Savage Game
Wahloo, P. Assignment
Wheatley, D. Star of Ill-Omen
Wickham, H. Jungle Terror
Williams, A. Snake Water
Woodhouse, M. Moon Hill
Woolrich, C. Black Alibi

SOUTH CAROLINA (S.C. See also: Charleston; South)
Ball, J. In the Heat of the Night
Ballard, M. F. Cry at Dusk
Blackwood, S. Lamontane
Breaznell, G. Star of Sutherland
Cohen, O. R. Gray Dusk
Daniels, D. Journey Into Terror
Disney, D. C. Hangman's Tree
Dunn, J. A. House on Doubloon Inlet
Govan, C. N. Plantation Murder
Guild, N. Old Acquaintance
Haring, D. Time for Tempting
Hart, C. G. 7 titles
Hayes, L. Harlequin House
Head, A. Always in August
Holland, I. Darcourt
Holman, H. all 5 titles
Hunt, Clarence. Small Town Corpse
Jefferson, B. W. Small Town Murder
Joseph, A. Killers at Sea
King, R. Duenna to a Murder
Lara, J. Soulcatcher
Long, L. B. Witch Tree
Marlowe, D. J. Vengeance Man
Martin, Caroline. Blue Ridge Mystery
Nightingale, U. Dawn Comes Soon
Piper, D. Plot
Roosevelt, E. Murder at Hobcaw Barony
Stout, D. Caroline Skeletons
Wimberly, C. Emerald Tears of Foxfire Manor

SOUTH DAKOTA (S. Dak. See also: Midwest)
Adams, H. 7 titles
Hubbard, M. A. Murder at St. Dennis
Jordan, C. Carol in the Dark
O'Brien, Dan. Spirit of the Hills

SOUTH PACIFIC (S. Pac. See also: individual islands or countries)
Adams, H. By Order of the Five
Alben, A. Our Man in Mongoa
Bannerman, D. Call of Honor
Becke, L. 6 titles
Binns, O. Secret Pearls
Boothby, G. Lady of the Island
Brown, Carter. No Blonde Is an Island
Bullivant, C. H. Unbarred Door
Carey, Basil. Dead Man's Shadow
Carter, Nick. Death Island
Cotler, G. Bottletop Affair
Dana, R. Murder in Paradise
Elston, A. V. Murder by Mandate
Forsythe, R. Murder on Paradise Island
Gluck, S. Deeper Scar
Grimshaw, B. at least 9 titles
Haring, D. Crime Cutie
Hastings, Michael. Green Silence
Hild, J. Pacific Payload
Innes, M. Appleby on Ararat
Jones, Howard. Tropical Tales
Kelly, Vince. Guarded Pearls
    Storm-Tossed
Kinney, J. Locket for Tawi
McGuire, P. Burial Service
McLaren, J. Stories of Fear
Murphy, W. B. Coin of the Realm
Nisbet, H. Children of Hermes
Parker, Gilbert. Cumner's Son
Peel, C. D. Nightdive
Pentecost, H. Brass Chills
Pugh, E. Rogues' Paradise
Rivere, A. Wantons of Betrayal
Robeson, K. Deadly Dwarf
    Fantastic Island
Rostand, R. Viper's Game
Sabre, D. Murder by Bamboo
Sackville, O. Island of Ghosts
    McLoon of the South Seas
Safroni-Middleton, A. No Extradition
Silliphant, S. Steel Tiger
Stock, R. Beach Combings
Streib, D. Cargo Gods
Thomson, B. South Sea Yarns

Trevor, E. Shoot
Walsh, J. M. Girl of the Islands
Wheatley, D. White Witch of the South Seas
Wickham, H. Scarlet X
Williams, V. Return of Clubfoot
Wilson, Gar. Search and Destroy
Young, G. Vengeance of Hurrican Williams

SOUTH WEST AFRICA (S. W. Africa)
Carter, J. Diamond Mercenaries
Cornell, F. C. Rip Van Winkle of the Kalahari
Harris, Rex. Hand in Diamonds
Jenkins, G. Twist of Sand
Stander, S. Flight from the Hunter

SOUTHWEST (S.W. See also: 4 individual states)
Abbey, E. Monkey Wrench Gang
Anderson, R. Cover Her with Roses
Ashe, G. Long Search
Braly, M. Felony Tank
Chase, J. H. Come Easy—Go Easy
Collins, Jackson. Himmler Plague
Cooper, W. Death Has a Thousand Doors
Creasey, J. Drought
Curtiss, U. Out of the Dark
Dessart, G. Cry for the Lost
Dobbins, P. H. Death Trap
Dodge, J. Not Fade Away
Dunning, L. Keller's Bomb
Earley, F. Hot Pursuit
Garfield, B. Hit
Goldsmith, M. M. Detour
Hamilton, D. Ambushers
    Death of a Citizen
    Intriguers
Jason, S. Slaughter in September
Jones, R. P. Heisters
Keene, D. If the Coffin Fits
    My Flesh Is Sweet
Kingsbury, C. L. Mystery of the Carroll Ranch
L'Amour, L. Haunted Mesa
Leland, C. T. Mean Time
Locke, D. Drawstring
MacDonald, J. D. Purple Place for Dying
MacNeil, N. Death Takes an Option
Matthews, C. Nylon Nightmare
Miller, J. M. T. Weatherby
Neider, C. Authentic Death of Hendry Jones
Niall, M. Bad Day at Black Rock
Nielsen, H. Detour
Pronzini, B. Panic!
Quammen, D. Zolta Configuration
Ripley, C. Murder Walks Alone
Roberts, J. H. Burning Sky
St. Clair, E. A. Murder Unplanned
Shaffer, J. Peterbilt to Laredo
Spicer, B. Adversary
Spike, P. Last Rites
Stephens, Reed. Man Who Risked His Life
Taylor, R. W. Doomsday Square
Thorpe, E. Night I Caught the Sante Fe Chief
Weiss, M. L. Death Hitches a Ride
West, D. Wish Me Dead
White, L. Hijack
Wormser, R. Drive East on 66
Zollinger, N. Lautrec

SOVIET UNION. See: Russia.

SPAIN (Sp. See also: Barcelona; Madrid; Canary
    Islands; Majorca)
Allen, S. No Marks for Trying
Ames, D. Landscape with Corpse
    Man in the Tricorn Hat
    Man with Three Chins
    No Mourning for the Matador
Arliss, J. Lady Killer Affair
Atkey, P. Blue Water Murder
Ballard, K. G. Bar Sinister
    Coast of Fear
Barclay, J. Unknown
Barker, A. If Anything Should Happen to Me

Beeding, F. Four Armourers
    Hell Let Loose
    Hidden Kingdom
    Mr. Bobadil
Benson, E. P. Bulls of Ronda
Berrow, N. It Howls at Night
Beste, R. V. Next Time I'll Pay My Own Way
Bird, K. Mozart Fiddle
Bonett, J. Better Dead
    No Time to Kill
    Private Face of Murder
    This Side Murder
Bradshaw, A. Crimson Stain
Bridge, A. Episode at Toledo
Brown, Alan. Princess
Brown, Antony. Slay Me Suddenly
Bruce, L. Death on the Black Sands
Burmeister, J. Someone Else's War
Carter, Nick. 6 titles
Charteris, L. Thieves' Picnic
Cleife, P. Pinchbeck Masterpiece
Clifford, F. Green Fields of Eden
    Spanish Duet
    Third Side of the Coin
Coles, M. Knife for the Juggler
Cordell, A. To Slay the Dreamer
Corrigan, M. Riddle of the Spanish Circus
Cory, D. 8 titles
Creasey, J. Mists of Fear
Davidson, H. C. Queen of the Black Hand
Davidson, Leif. Sardine Deception
Deane, N. Death in the Spanish Sun
De Mille, J. Castle in Spain
Denby, E. Mrs. W's Last Sandwich
Dines, M. Operation—Kill or Be Killed
Dixon, J. E. Killers in the Sun
Dodge, D. Carambola
Douglas, M. Prey by Night
    Pure Sweet Hell
Duras, M. Ten-Thirty on a Summer Night
Eden, D. Marriage Chest
Egerton, D. Hour of Truth
Ellery, J. Death on the Circuit
Erickson, L. Arena of Fear
Farjeon, J. J. Peril in the Pyrenees
Farr, C. Web of Horror
Fernandez, A. Castle of Lugas
Fitzgerald, K. Quiet Under the Sun
Frances, S. D. To Love and Yet to Die
Fry, P. Paint-Stained Flannels
Galway, R. C. Assignment Andalusia
Goldston, R. C. Catafalque
Gosling, P. Woman in Red
Gray, B. Calamity Conquest
Green, Sarah. Festival of St. Jago
Gruber, F. Spanish Prisoner
Haggard, W. Scorpion's Tail
Halidom, M. Y. Son of Desolation
Halliday, D. Dolly and the Cookie Bird
Harper, S. Necessary Evil
Harrison, E. Fatal Hour
Hebden, M. Errant Knights
Henaghan, J. Azor!
Hocking, A. Mediterranean Murder
Hopkins, R. Raid on the Villa Joyosa
Hossent, H. Memory of Treason
Household, G. Olura
Hunter, S. Spanish Gambit
Jacobs, T. C. H. Deadly Race
    Woman Who Waited
Janson, H. Contraband
    Deadly Mission
    Untamed
Johnston, V. I Came to a Castle
Kershaw, R. Blood-Red Earth
Keyes, F. P. Station Wagon in Spain
Lamb, M. Last Nazi
Lange, J. Odds On
    Zero Cool
Lansdale, N. White Island
Larsen, G. Atascadero Island
Lathom, F. Castle of Ollada
Leonard, C. Steps to Murder

Lodwick, J. Somewhere a Voice Is Calling
Lovell, M. Apple Spy in the Sky
Luard, Nicholas. Robespierre Serial
Lyon, B. White Crow
McCutcheon, H. Treasure of the Sun
McEvoy, M. Queen of Spades
McGerr, E. Funeral Was in Spain
McGivern, W. P. Caper of the Golden Bulls
    Choice of Assassins
McGuire, P. O. Fiesta for Murder
MacInnes, H. Message from Malaga
MacKenzie, D. Raven in Flight
MacKintosh, M. Appointment in Andalusia
MacLeod, R. Mayday from Malaga
Marlowe, D. J. Operation Stranglehold
Marlowe, S. Jeopardy Is My Job
Marshall, J. Follow a Shadow
Martyn, D. Sinister Legacy
Mason, A. E. W. Summons
Mendoza, E. City of Wonders
Messmann, J. Inheritors
Mitchell, G. Twenty-Third Man
Montalban, M. V. Murder in the Central
    Committee
Mundy, M. Death Cries Ole
Murphy, J. El Greco Puzzle
    Pay on the Way Out
Norman, B. Matter of Mandrake
Oldsey, B. Spanish Season
Oliver, M.-A. Study in Lilac
Ordway, P. Night of Reckoning
Palmer, J., Jr. Mystic Sepulchre
Pendower, J. Anxious Lady
Perowne, B. Tilted Moon
Polland, M. Package to Spain
Prichard, K. Chronicles of Don Q
    Don Q's Love Story
    New Chronicles of Don Q
Rathbone, J. Bloody Marvelous
    Carnival!
    Raving Monarchist
Reade, B. Ibeza Syndicate
Revelli, G. Amanda in Spain
Rhodes, Russell. Herod Conspiracy
Richmond, M. Passport to Danger
Rising, L. She Who Was Helena Cass
Roos, K. Scent of Mystery
    Suddenly One Night
Ross, Angus. Ampurias Exchange
    Burgos Contract
Rossiter, J. Golden Virgin
    Rope for General Dietz
St. John, David. Return from Vorkuta
Sanderson, D. Cry Wolfram
Saxon, A. Run in Diamonds
Serafin, D. Angel of Torremolinos
    Body in Cadiz Bay
Sheldon, S. Sands of Time
Shelley, S. Francine
Smith, Don. Death Stalk in Spain
Spicer, B. Burned Man
    Day of the Dead
Stark, J. Greek Virgin
Stein, A. M. Snare Andalucian
Symons, J. Plot Against Roger Rider
Tarmey, M. Outrage
Tilden, F. Spanish Prisoner
Townend, Peter. Out of Focus
Vizetelly, E. A. Scorpion
Wahloo, P. Lorry
Walker, George. Three Spaniards
Wallace, B. E. Man Who Could Not Swim
Walsh, J. M. Spies in Spain
Weil, J. Spy Who Came Home to Die
West, E. Man Running
Whalley, P. Villains
Wheatley, D. Golden Spaniard
    Vendetta in Spain
Worboys, A. Every Man a King
Yates, G. W. Body That Came by Post
Yeldham, P. But She Won't Lie Down

SRI LANKA. See: Ceylon.

Settings Index

STOCKHOLM (Stock. See also: Sweden; Scandinavia)
Donnel, C. P. Murder-Go-Round
Drew, P. Deep in the Dark Country
Eden, D. Waiting for Willa
Lang, M. Death Awaits Thee
Martenson, J. Death Calls on the Witches
Regis, J. Copper House
Siwertz, S. Goldman's
Sjowall, M. 6 titles

SUDAN (See also: Africa)
Farjeon, J. J. Dangerous Beauty
McCarry, C. Miernik Dossier

SUMATRA (Sum. See also: Indonesia; Djakarta; Bali; Borneo; Java; New Guinea)
Aarons, E. S. Assignment—Sumatra
Barnes, R. Water from the Moon
Cleary, J. Long Pursuit

SURINAM (Suri. See also: South America)
Coxe, G. H. Double Identity
Newell, R. Star House
Rosenberger, J. Surinam Affair

SWAZILAND
Van Rensburg, H. Death in a Dark Pool

SWEDEN (Swed. See also: Stockholm; Scandinavia)
Aarons, E. S. Assignment—Black Viking
Carter, Nick. Bright Blue Death
Coffman, V. Looking-Glass
Covington, J. Operative
Craig, P. Gate of Ivory, Gate of Horn
Hamilton, D. Wrecking Crew
Hogstrand, O. all 3 titles
Hubert, T. Trap
Katz, R. Ziggurat
Lang, M. No More Murders
    Wreath for the Bride
Lee, Elsie. Barrow Sinister
MacKenzie, A. M. Swedish Mysteries
Peters, E. Silhouette in Scarlet
Regis, J. No. 13 Toroni
Sjowall, M. Cop Killer
    Murder at the Savoy
    Roseanna
Starnes, R. Requiem in Utopia
Strong, T. Last Mountain
Sundman, P. O. Two Days, Two Nights
Walter, H. Bullet for Charles
White, E. L. Step in the Dark

SWITZERLAND (Switz. See also: Geneva; Zurich)
Albrand, M. Hunted Woman
Ames, D. Crime Out of Mind
Arnold, Elliott. Code of Conduct
Baker, P. Minnie Swan
Barstow, P. Glacier Run
Becher, U. Woodchuck Hunt
Bellairs, G. Death of a Shadow
Bennett, Dorothea. Under the Skin
Bordeaux, H. Murder Party
Brewer, G. Devil in Davos
Bridge, A. Numbered Account
Burkholz, H. Mulligan's Seed
Campbell, R. W. Circus Couronne
Canning, V. Panther's Moon
Carling, J. R. Weird Picture
Carr, G. Murder on the Matterhorn
Carter, Nick. Counterfeit Agent
    Eyes of the Tiger
Cartwright, J. Horse of Darius
Cleeve, B. Assignment to Vengeance
Dark, J. Sea Scrape
Denning, M. Swiss Abduction
Drummond, June. Cable-Car
Duerrenmatt, F. Dangerous Game
    Judge and His Hangman
    Pledge
    Quarry
Edwards, Anne. Haunted Summer
    Survivors

Erdman, P. Billion Dollar Sure Thing
    Last Days of America
Fairchild, W. Swiss Arrangement
Fleming, I. On Her Majesty's Secret Service
Fletcher, L. . . . And Presumed Dead
Flynn, J. Five Faces of Murder
Forbes, C. Terminal
Gair, M. Snow Job
Gaskin, C. File on Devlin
Gialanella, V. Frankenstein
Gilman, D. Palm for Mrs. Pollifax
Greene, H. Cancelled Accounts
Griswold, G. Pinned Man
Guild, N. Lost and Found Man
Haggard, W. Visa to Limbo
Henissart, P. Margin of Error
Hocking, A. Cat's Paw
Hossent, H. No End to Fear
Kavanaugh, C. Deception
Kelso, J. Ghost Skier
Knight, K. M. High Rendezvous
Lakin, R. Angel Take Care
Langley, B. Traverse of the Gods
Lunn, P. Evil in High Places
McCrae, E. House of the Whispering Winds
MacInnes, H. Pray for a Brave Heart
MacLeod, R. Path of Ghosts
    Pay-Off in Switzerland
Mair, G. B. Kisses from Satan
Marlowe, A. Winnowing Winds
Marlowe, S. Francesca
    Summit
Marvin, S. Chalet Bougy-Villars
Masterson, W. Man on a Nylon String
Maxfield, H. S. Legacy of a Spy
Messer, M. Castle for Sale
Meynell, L. Die by the Book
Minton, P. Engraved in Evil
Mitford, B. Fordham's Feud
Moyes, P. Season of Snows and Sins
Myers, P. Deadly Sonata
Pearson, D. A. G. Golden Stone
Penmare, W. Scorpion
Plain, J. Secret of the Snows
Quest, E. Silver Castle
Rey, P. Out
Reynolds, B. Accessory After the Fact
    Affair at the Chateau
Ross, P. Good Death
Ryp, E. Deadly Bonds
Scott, J. M. Other Half of the Orange
Sharp, Allen. Meyringen Papers
Shaw, L. Innocent Deception
Shaw, Patricia. Never Paint a Stranger
Sherwood, J. Limericks of Lachasse
Snell, E. Murder in Switzerland
Somerville-Large, P. Hang Glider
Stand, M. Death Came in Lucerne
Stanley, M. Swiss Conspiracy
Stein, A. M. Alp Murder
    Garbage Collector
Summerton, M. Ring of Mischief
Townend, Paul. Died O' Wednesday
    Man on the End of the Rope
Trevanian. Eiger Sanction
Walker, D. Devil's Plunge
Waller, L. Swiss Account
Westlake, D. E. High Jinx
White, Ared. Spy Night
Williams, Alan. Shah-Mak
Wood, S. Death in Lord Byron's Room

SYDNEY (Syd. See also: Australia; Adelaide; Melbourne; Solomon Islands; Tasmania)
Anderson, Jessica. Ordinary Lunacy
Bacia, J. Shadows of Power
Baker, S. J. Gig
Barrett, R. G. Boys from Binjiwunyawunya
    Real Thing
    You Wouldn't Be Dead for Quids
Beeby, O. all 4 titles
Beede, J. You Can Only Die Once
Berrow, N. Eleventh Plague
Blaque, F. Stand Over

Breck, Leon. Love Among Thieves
Brown, Carter. Coffin Bird
Bunce, S. No Sainted City
Carroll, W. J. all 3 titles
Claremont, R. To Sleep, to Die
Cleary, J. 8 titles
Cook, K. Bloodhouse
Corrigan, M. Sydney for Sin
Corris, P. 7 titles
Crane, R. Key of Corruption
Cutcheon, Edgar. Black Feather
Day, M. both titles
DeBrune, A. Dagger and Cord
Eipper, C. Shadowing Secrets
Elliott, P. Silent Bullet
Falkner, H. Arlett's Death
Fletcher, James. All the Dead Lay Down
Flower, P. Crisscross
Fraser, Ron. After-Dark
Galway, R. C. Assignment Sydney
Gardiner, H. Murder in Haste
Geason, S. Shaved Fish
Godwin, J. Requiem for a Rat
Hamilton, I. Persecutor
    Thrill Machine
Hann, D. Deserters
    Put In, Take Out
    Yellow Witch
Haring, D. 10 titles
Hoffman, K. Blackmarket Brains
Howard, Tom. All Possible Avenues
    Dead Lucky
Jefferis, B. Undercurrent
Kaufman, M. Container
Kelly, Vince. Greedy Ones
    Last Minute Clue
    Racket Buster
Kensch, O. Death Is a Habit
Lambert, Elizabeth. Sleeping House Party
Long, Martin. all 3 titles
McNab, C. all 3 titles
Mann, L. Murder in Sydney
Martin, A. E. Death in the Limelight
Moffitt, I. Colour Man
Moss, W. Down an Alley Filled with Cats
Neville, M. 6 titles
North, Eric. Who Killed Marie Westhoven?
Pratt, A. Great "Push" Experiment
Reid, D. Showdown in Sydney
Robertson, M. To Ripen or to Kill
Rowe, Jennifer. Murder by the Book
Ruhen, C. Rebels
Scot-Bernard, P. Sex Is a Deadly Exercise
Sherlock, A. B. Yellow Beetle
Singer, B. Don't Slip, Delaney
Spencer, Julian. Shooting Sequence
Stivens, D. Wide Arch
West, Charles. Destruction Man
    Stonefish
Whitman, C. all 3 titles
Wright, Steve. Drop in the Ocean
Yates, R. Social Death

SYRIA (Syr. See also: Damascus; Middle East)
Barton, D. R. Once in Aleppa
Bayne, S. Agent Extraordinary
Carter, Nick. Thunderstrike in Syria
Easterman, D. Seventh Sanctuary
Household, G. High Place
Imber, H. House of the Apricots
Pendleton, D. Cold Judgment
Poyer, D. Med
Shagan, S. Discovery

TAHITI (See also: South Pacific)
Atlee, P. Paper Pistol Contract
Bestor, G. C. Postage Stamp Murder
Gardner, A. Assignment in Tahiti
McCormick, C. Club Paradis Murders
Powell, S. W. 6 titles
Vance, J. H. Deadly Isles

TAIWAN. See: Formosa.

TAMPA (See also: Florida; Jacksonville; Miami; South)
Crews, L. Extreme Close-Up
    Kill Cue
Doyle, J. T. Epitaph for a Loser
Lederer, M. Adriatic Formula
Powell, T. 5 titles
Rosenberger, J. Project Andromeda
Whittington, H. Humming Box

TANGANYIKA (Tang. See also: Tanzania; Africa; Zanzibar)
Edqvist, D. Black Sister
Scholey, J. Dead Past

TANGIER (See also: Morocco; Casablanca; Africa, North)
Ames, D. They Journey by Night
Baker, W. H. Guardians
Bayer, W. Tangier
Carstairs, J. P. No Wooden Overcoat
    Smell of Peardrops
Carter, Nick. Omega Terror
    Terror Code
Corrigan, M. Golden Angel
Crane, F. Coral Princess Murders
Dickson, Carter. Behind the Crimson Blind
Fry, P. Grey Sombrero
Gilruth, S. Snake Is Living Yet
Jackson, M. Nightmare in Morocco
Luard, N. Dirty Area
McCutcheon, H. Yet She Must Die
Mason, V. W. Deadly Orbit Mission
    Two Tickets to Tangier
O'Brine, M. Deadly Interlude
Rougvie, C. Tangier Assignment
Royce, K. Soft-Footed Moor
Seymour, H. Intrigue in Tangier
Summers, K. Design for Death
Teilhet, H. T. Terror in Tangier
Verner, G. Faceless Ones
Wallace, E. Man from Morocco
Wilkinson, L. Appointment in Tangier

TANZANIA (Tanz. See also: Tanganyika; Zanzibar; Africa)
Blair, J. Danger at Olduvai
Rhodes, Richard. Last Safari

TASMANIA (Tas. See also: Australia; Adelaide; Melbourne; Sydney; Melbourne; Solomon Islands)
Bridges, H. Creaking Door
    House of Storms
Bridges, R. Negrohead
    On His Majesty's Service
    Owl Is Abroad
    Soul of the Sword
Butler, R. South of Hell's Gates
Hay, W. Escape of the Notorious Sir William Heans
Koch, C. J. Boys in the Island
Mace, H. House of Hate
    Murder Among Those Present
Parker, Richard. Boy on a Chain
Rowcroft, C. Bushranger of Van Diemen's Land
    Life and Adventures of William Thornby in Old Van Diemen's Land
    Tales of the Colonies
Vogel, H. B. Gentleman Garnet

TEHERAN (See also: Iran; Middle East)
MacKinnon, C. Finding Hoseyn
Mayo, J. Once in a Lifetime
Pace, E. Nightingale
Pendleton, D. Teheran Wipeout

TEL AVIV (See also: Israel; Jerusalem; Middle East)
Hesky, O. Sequin Syndicate
    Serpent's Smile
    Time for Treason
Litvinoff, E. Falls the Shadow

TENNESSEE (Tenn. See also: Memphis; Nashville; South)
Alexander, Jan. Devil's Dance
Bourgeau, A. Elvis Murders
    Lonely Way to Die
    Murder at the Cheatin' Heart Motel
Bradley, M. H. Murder in the Family
Cameron, K. 5 titles
Carey, Webster. Walking Tall
Carmack, J. Tell-Tale Clock Mystery
Carroll, L. S. Bullet Creek
Chapman, M. Glen Hazard
Christopher, E. E. Invisibles
Clark, D. P. Just for the Bride
Constiner, M. Hearse of a Different Color
Farris, J. Sharp Practice
Ford, L. Burn Forever
Hagan, C. Redemption
Ham, B. Tennessee Terror
Heath, W. L. Violent Saturday
Kendrick, B. Out of Control
McCrumb, S. If Ever I Return, Peggy-O
MacDonald, P. J. No Way Home
McGivern, W. P. Summit
Morris, W. R. Twelfth of August
Musick, J. R. His Brother's Crime
Pauley, B. A. Blood Kin
Seifert, S. Death Stops at the Old Stone Inn
Warren, R. P. Meet Me in the Green Glen
Whitney, P. A. Glass Flame
Wingate, W. Shotgun

TEXAS (Tex. See also: Dallas; Houston; San Antonio; Southwest)
Abshire, R. Shaman Tree
Allan, F. K. Death in Gentle Grove
Amos, A. Borderline Murder
Austin, Anne. Wicked Woman
Azolakov, A. Contractees Die Young
Baker, A. both titles
Bannerman, W. B. Santos, Border Detective
Barron, A. Bride of Menace
    Dark Vengeance
    Murder Is a Gentle Kiss
    Strange Legacy
Barry, J. E. Skeleton in Concrete
Barthelme, P. Push, Meet Shove
Battin, B. W. Demented
Bay, A. Coyote Cried Twice
Becker, S. Covenant with Death
Bell, J. One More Time
Bird, S. M. Do Evil Cheerfully
Blaine, R. Tainted Jade
Bloch, R. Psycho
    Psycho House
Boniface, M. Murder As an Ornament
    Venom in Eden
Borthwick, J. S. Case of the Hook-Billed Kites
Bramlett, J. Trouble—Texas Style
Brandon, J. Deadbolt
Brown, R. D. Hazzard
Brown, Sandra. Best Kept Secrets
Cameron, E. both titles
Carlton, B. Moonshell
Case, P. Death Blade
Charteris, L. Saint on Guard
Chase, A. M. Murder of a Missing Man
Clifford, C. L. While the Bells Rang
Cohen, B. Coliseum
Conley, R. J. Killing Time
Crawford, M. Waltz Across Texas
Crider, B. all 8 titles
Cunningham, A. B. Death of a Bullionaire
Dean, R. G. Murder Most Opportune
Derrick, L. Supergun Mission
Dewlin, A. Twilight of Honor
Douglas, B. Challenge at Castle Gap
Downing, T. Death Under the Moonflower
    Last Trumpet
    Murder on Tour
Duncan, W. G. Fatal Sisters
    Wrong Place, Wrong Time
Estes, C. C. Unhappy New Year

Fackler, E. Barbed Wire
Forbes, S. Deadly Kind of Lonely
    She Was Only the Sheriff's Daughter
    Some Poisoned by Their Wives
Fox, H. B. Murder in a Small Town—Perhaps
Freeman, M. J. Murder of a Midget
Galloway, J. Toothache Tree
Gardner, J. For Special Services
Gatenby, R. Season of Danger
Gray, A. W. Bino
Greene, A. C. Santa Claus Bank Robbery
Halliday, B. Murder Is My Business
Ham, B. Personal War
Hannay, J. F. W. Thirteenth Floor
Haring, D. Big Contract
    Halo for My Honey
Harrington, W. Partners
Holden, R. P. Death on the Border
Hopkins, K. Campus Corpse
Howard, C. Dirt Rich
Howard, J. A. Murder Takes a Wife
Hughes, D. B. Candy Kid
Irsfeld, J. H. Rat's Alley
Jenkins, Dan. Fast Copy
Jordan, L. Hidden Fires
Kellerman, D. both titles
Kelton, E. Stand Proud
Kingery, D. Paula
Kistler, M. Night of the Tiger
Kriz, J. Karsten's Flats
La Fountaine, G. Flashpoint
Lane, J. Like a Man
Lansdale, J. R. Cold in July
    Nightrunners
    Savage Season
Leach, C. Blood Games
Lee, G. R. Mother Finds a Body
Levinson, S. both titles
Lingo, A. E. Murder in Texas
McCollom, R. And Then They Die
McDonald, G. Buck Passes Flynn
McLendon, J. Eddie Macon's Run
Mackin, R. Gulf Attack
Mandelkau, J. Leo Wyoming Caper
Martin, L. 7 titles
Mathis, E. 7 titles
Maxwell, R. Minus Man
Meredith, D. R. Murder by Deception
    Murder by Impulse
    Sheriff and the Branding Iron Murders
    Sheriff and the Panhandle Murders
Morgan, Dean. Rostron Outfit to Texas
Newcomb, K. Pandora Man
Nighbert, D. F. Strikezone
O'Farrell, W. Wetback
O'Malley, F. Best Go First
Parker, M. Death Makes a Deal
Pendleton, D. Texas Storm
    Trial
Perkins, K. Moccasin Murders
Pirtle, C. Last Deadly Lie
Potter, J. A. Needle
Putnam, G. P. Hot Oil
Reasoner, J. M. Texas Wind
Reeves, Ruth. Lament for a Lonesome Corpse
Reid, J. Deer in Water
Reynolds, Clay. Agatite
Riley, B. Guilty Parties
Roberts, Lee. Judas Journey
Robertson, D. Ideal, Genuine Man
Romberg, N. Spirit Stalker
Roos, K. One False Move
St. Mox, E. A. Heart of Oak Detective
Sanders, Leonard. Texas Noon
Sapir, R. Final Death
Seilaz, A. Veil of Silence
Smith, J. V. Beastmaker
Smith, Z. Z. Very Private Island
Stark, R. Handle
Stein, A. M. Blood on the Stars
Stein, P. Grand Scam
Stivers, D. Night Heat
    Texas Showdown

Settings Index

Storm, E. Firing Line
Stowers, C. Innocence Lost
Tell, D. Murder at Red Rock Ranch
Thompson, J. Killer Inside Me
    Texas by the Tail
Thompson, T. Celebrity
Ullman, A. Naked Spur
Wallace, R. Uniformed Killers
Walsh, Robert. Violent Hours
Washburn, L. J. Dog Heavies
Webb, M. G. 3 titles
Werry, R. R. Hammer Me Home
White, J. M. Game of Troy
Wingate, A. Death by Deception
    Eye of Anna
Woody, W. Mistress of Horror House
Wozencraft, K. Rush

THAILAND (Thai. See also: Bangkok; Far East)
Aarons, E. S. Assignment—Cong Hai Kill
Ballinger, B. S. Spy in Bangkok
Black, G. Wind of Death
Decker, J. Deadly Snow
De Villiers, G. Death on the River Kwai
Duncan, W. R. Queen's Messenger
Emmett, R. Ride the Tiger
Gilman, D. Mrs. Pollifax and the Golden Triangle
Harvester, S. Battle Road
    Dragon Road
Mills, James. Truth About Peter Harley
Pendleton, D. Devil's Horn
    Tiger War
Sheldon, W. J. Red Flower Kill
Springer, J. Deeper Danger

THEATRE
Anthony, Elizabeth. Ballet of Death
    Ballet of Fear
Applin, A. Stage Door
Baker, R. M. Death Stops the Rehearsal
Bell, Jospehine. Death at Half-Term
Bird, P. Staged for Death
Brand, C. Death of Jezebel
Brandon, J. G. Murder on the Stage
Brett, Simon. 6 titles
Bromley, G. Midsummer Night's Crime
Bude, J. Death Steals the Show
Carlson, P. M. Rehearsal for Murder
Cassady, M. Alternate Casts
Colburn, L. Death of a Prima Donna
Collins, Michelle. Premiere at Willow Run
Crispin, E. Case of the Gilded Fly
    Swan Song
Crozier, J. Murder in Public
Daniels, D. Castle Morvant
Davis, K. Forza Trap
Dayle, D. Death in the Theatre
Dentinger, J. Death Mask
    First Hit of the Season
    Murder on Cue
Dewhurst, E. Playing Safe
Elder, M. Phantom in the Wings
Fletcher, David. Don't Whistle "MacBeth"
Francis, B. Death in Act IV
Fyfe, H. H. Player's Tragedy
Graeme, B. No Clues for Dexter
Graham, Caroline. Death of a Hollow Man
Gray, D. No Quarter for a Star
Hanna, D. Opera House Murders
Holland, R. Danger on Cue
Holt, Gavin. Death Takes the Stage
    No Curtains for Cora
Jarvis, F. G. Murder at the Met
Keating, H. R. F. Death of a Fat God
Kennedy, Adrienne. Deadly Triplets
Lang, M. Death Awaits Thee
Lee, G. R. G-String Murders
Lewis, William. Gala
Littlepage, L. Murder-by-the-Sea
Lockridge, R. Old Die Young
Long, A. M. Lady Saw Red
Loraine, P. Exit with Intent
McDuff, E. M. Murder in the Theatre
Mario, Q. Murder in the Opera House
Marsh, N. Light Thickens
    Opening Night
    Vintage Murder
Marston, E. Queen's Head
Martin, A. E. Death in the Limelight
Melville, J. Raven's Forge
Miller, J. Save the Last Dance for Me
Mitchell, G. Death at the Opera
Morice, A. Death in the Round
    Murder in Mimicry
    Murder in Outline
    Sleep of Death
Munro, H. Brain Robbers
Murphy, Haughton. Murder Takes a Partner
Myers, A. Murder in the Limelight
Paul, B. Cadenza for Caruso
    Chorus of Detectives
    Fourth Wall
    Prima Donna at Large
Peters, Ellis. Funeral of Figaro
Plummer, T. A. Muse Theatre Murder
Reeves, J. Murder with Muskets
Resnicow, H. Gold Curse
    Gold Deadline
    Gold Gamble
Roos, K. Made Up to Kill
Schier, N. Demon of the Opera
Smith, K. N. Catching Fire
Stewart, A. Devil's Toy
Suyker, B. Death Scene
Traubel, H. Metropolitan Opera Murders
Verner, G. Show Must Go On
Wall, D. C. One Cried Murder
Ward, Donald. Death Takes the Stage
Whitehead, B. Playing God
Williamson, Audrey. both titles
Wilmot, J. R. Death in the Stalls
Yarbro, C. Q. Music When Sweet Voices Die
Zilinsky, U. Happy English Child

TIBET (Tib.)
Carter, Nick. Red Guard
Channing, M. White Python
Chorlton, W. Rites of Sacrifice
Cleary, J. Pulse of Danger
Cory, D. Johnny Goes East
Davidson, L. Rose of Tibet
Easton, J. Dog-Face
    Red Sap
Edwards, P. Deadly Cyborgs
Evarts, H. G. Turncoat
Fallon, M. Year of the Tiger
Hamilton, N. Tomorrow in Katmandu
Harvester, S. Chinese Hammer
Hild, J. Barrabas Heist
Langley, B. East of Everest
MacKenzie, N. Seven Days to Death
McLeave, H. Under the Icefall
Mason, V. W. Himalayan Assignment
Mather, B. Break in the Line
Miller, T. K. Sherlock Holmes on the Roof of the World
Mondol, P. Operation Tibet
Mundy, T. Old Ugly Face
    Ramsden
    Thunder Dragon Gate
Murray, W. H. Five Frontiers
Patterson, H. Iron Tiger
Pelham, A. Fortress of Ashes
Robeson, K. Meteor Menace
Savarin, J. Gunship
Smith, Don. Secret Mission: Tibet
Taylor, Barry. Deadfall Trap
Wincor, R. Sherlock Holmes in Tibet

TOKYO (See also: Japan; Far East)
Aarons, E. S. Assignment—Tokyo
Barker, W. Shibo Discipline
Bender, W., Jr. Tokyo Intrigue
Bruce, J. Hot Line
Carter, Nick. Temple of Fear
Corrigan, M. Lady from Tokyo
Crane, R. Operation Vengeance
    Time Running Out
Dark, J. Assignment Tokyo
Derrick, L. Tokyo Purple
De Villiers, G. Hostage in Tokyo
Duncan, R. L. Dragons at the Gate
Ellis, Michael. Score at Tea-Time
Goble, N. Condition Green: Tokyo
Hann, D. Michiko
Kenrick, D. Death in a Tokyo Family
Lustbader, E. V. Miko
McPartland, J. Affair in Tokyo
    Danger for Breakfast
    Tokyo Doll
Marquand, J. P. Stopover: Tokyo
Matsumoto, S. Inspector Imanishi Investigates
Middleton, T. Operation Tokyo
Miller, L. Operation Godiva
Norman, E. 5 titles
Pendleton, D. Code of Dishonor
    Siege
Perrelli, N. Terror in Tokyo
Randall, D. Dragon Lover
Roberts, J. H. Q Document
St. John, David. One of Our Agents Is Missing
St. Moore, A. Angel Face Tatters the Kimono
Sheldon, W. J. Blue Kimono Kill
Stanley, G. Death in Tokyo
Stanley, J. Samurai Six
Title, E. Circle of Deception
Togawa, M. both titles
Walker, S. Tokyo Escapade
Warnock, W. Frozen Secrets

TORONTO (See also: Canada; Montreal; Ottawa; Vancouver; Winnipeg)
Batten, J. Straight No Chaser
Case, D. Wolf Tracks
Cushing, E. L. Unexpected Corpse
Dawson, D. L. Last Rights
Engel, H. Victim Must Be Found
Franklin, Edwina. No Pain, No Gaine
Godfrey, E. Case of the Cold Murderer
    Murder Behind Locked Doors
Gordon, Alison. Dead Pull Hitter
Green, T. M. Barking Dogs
Jones, F. Master and Maid
Keller, D. One Way Street
Kelley, T. P. Tapestry Triangle
Law, Alexander. To an Easy Grave
Lovell, A. Flying Time
Malloch, P. Cop-Lover
Millar, M. Devil Loves Me
    Invisible Worm
    Iron Gates
    Wall of Eyes
Phillips, E. O. Sunday's Child
Porter, Anna. Mortal Sins
Reeves, J. all 3 titles
Ritchie, S. Hollow Woman
    Work for a Dead Man
Ross, H. Fleur de Lys Affair
Sale, Medora. Murder in a Good Cause
    Murder on the Run
Shea, S. Victims
Skvorecky, J. Return of Lieutenant Boruvka
Smith, Joan. Capriccio
Watson, P. Alter Ego
Wees, F. S. Faceless Enemy
    Keys of My Prison
    Where Is Jenny Now?
Wood, T. Live Bait
Wright, E. 5 titles
Wright, R. B. Final Things
Zaremba, E. Reason to Kill
    Work for a Million

TRAIN
Adler, W. Trans-Siberian Express
Alexander, Ruth. Rome Express
Burton, Miles. Death in the Tunnel
Byrne, R. Mannequin
Carter, Nick. Butcher of Belgrade
Chalmers, S. Crime in Car 13
Christie, A. Murder on the Orient Express
Coolidge, E. L. Mountain Limited

Davis, T. Full Fare for a Corpse
Denbie, R. Death on the Limited
Dent, L. Lady to Kill
Downing, T. Lazy Lawrence Murders
    Vultures in the Sky
Fisher, Laine. Fare Prey
Forbes, C. Avalanche Express
Fox, J. M. Free Ride
Francis, D. Edge
Gordons. Campaign Train
Greene, G. Stamboul Train
Gribble, L. Murder First Class
Hagen, M. A. Plant Me Now
Highsmith, P. Strangers on a Train
Hughes, D. B. Dread Journey
Hyde, C. Maxwell's Train
Hyman, T. Seven Days to Petrograd
Jackson, M. J. A. Arabian Pearl
Japrisot, S. 10:30 from Marseilles
Karlin, W. Crossover
King, C. D. Obelists en Route
Koning, H. Petersburg-Cannes Express
Lambert, D. Golden Express
    Yermakov Transfer
Lieberman, H. Green Train
Little, C. Great Black Kanba
McCutchan, P. Overnight Express
MacLean, Alistair. Breakheart Pass
MacVeigh, S. Streamlined Murder
Nebel, F. Sleepers East
Stockbridge, G. Corpse Cargo
Tucker, W. Last Stop
Ware, J. Detour to Denmark
Yarborough, C. Murder on the Long Straight

TRANSVAAL (Trans. See also: South Africa; Cape Town; Johannesburg)
Dekobra, M. Diamond Queen

TRENTON (See also: New Jersey; Newark)
Gallison, K. Death Tape
    Unbalanced Accounts

TRINIDAD (Trin. See also: West Indies; Caribbean)
Brown, Wenzell. Rum and Coca-Cola Murders
Coxe, G. H. One Hour to Kill
Underwood, M. Arm of the Law
Vandercook, J. W. Murder in Trinidad

TUCSON (See also: Arizona; Phoenix; Southwest)
Brown, F. Lenient Beast
Creighton, J. Evil Is the Night
Hall, Matthew. Nightmare Logic
Homes, G. Hill of the Terrified Monk
Michaels, Lewis. No Exit for a Blonde!
Nielsen, H. Killer in the Street
Reid, D. Death Waits in Tucson

TULSA (See also: Oklahoma; Oklahoma City; Southwest)
Sasser, C. W. Homicide

TUNISIA (Tun. See also: Africa, North)
Benton, K. Craig and the Tunisian Tangle
Davis, Maggie. Rommel's Gold
Evans, K. Shadows of Violence
Henissart, P. Narrow Exit
Highsmith, P. Tremor of Forgery
Jacobs, T. C. H. Target for Terror
Jepson, S. Death Gong
McCutchan, P. Sladd's Evil
Operator 1384. Catacombs of Death
Pendower, J. Mission in Tunis
Rutherford, D. Kick Start
Stevens, E. S. Veil
Summerton, M. Sand Rose

TURKEY (Turk. See also: Istanbul; Middle East; Balkans)
Aarons, E. S. Assignment—Ankara
Angus, S. Death of a Hittite
Arnold, M. Exit Actors, Dying
Atlee, P. Underground Cities Contract
Bartram, G. Aelian Fragment
    Fair Game
Carter, Nick. Strike Force Terror
    Turkish Bloodbath
Daniel, D. Ark
Davison, Geoffrey. Chessboard Spies
Drummond, I. Stench of Poppies
Farrere, C. Man Who Killed
Fleming, Joan. Nothing Is the Number When You Die
Forsyte, C. Murder with Minarets
Garve, A. Ascent of D-13
Gilman, D. Amazing Mrs. Pollifax
Heggy, J. P. Grab
Katz, R. Spoils of Ararat
Kemal, Y. Sea-Crossed Fisherman
Luther, R. Intermind
MacLean, Alistair. Guns of Navarone
Mason, V. W. Dardanelles Derelict
Motta, L. Flames on the Bosphorus
Moyzisch, L. C. Operation Cicero
Munro, J. Innocent Bystanders
Pendleton, D. Double Crossfire
Rathbone, J. Diamonds Bid
    Hand Out
    Kill Cure
    Trip Trap
Rosenberger, J. Enigma Project
Roudybush, A. Sybaritic Death
Saltmarsh, M. Highly Inflammable
Settle, M. L. Blood Tie
Stevenson, A. Turkish Rondo
West, R. W. Destroyer
Westall, W. Sacred Crescents
Wood, C. Death in Ankara

UGANDA (See also: Africa)
Arnett, J. Genocide Express
Hayes, R. Track of the Beast
Watkins, L. Killing of Idi Amin
Westlake, D. E. Kahawa
Zake, S. J. L. Truckful of Gold

UNITED STATES (U.S. Here is a selection of titles by non-U.S. authors which use non-specific or varying U.S. settings. See also: each of the fifty states; Washington D.C.; Puerto Rico; Virgin Islands)
Alexander, Gordon. Silent Witness
Allbeury, T. Man with the President's Mind
    Pay Any Price
    Twentieth Day of January
Baker, W. H. Blood Trail
Ballinger, W. A. Naked from a Well
Bell, Josephine. Adventure with Crime
Bogar, J. Dinah for Danger
Brennan, R. Man Who Walked Like a Dancer
Bryant, P. Two Hours to Doom
Byrom, J. Thou Shouldst Be Living
Cheyney, P. Don't Get Me Wrong
    Poison Ivy
Como, L. both titles
Conty, J.-P. Canal Street
Cooper, Craig. at least 5 titles
Corrigan, M. All Brides Are Beautiful
    Naked Lady
    Shanghai Jezebel
Corris, P. "Box Office" Browning
    Browning Takes Off
Coughlin, W. J. Destruction Committee
Crane, A. One Night of Fear
Curtis, Robert. Smoky Cell
Drummond, I. Power of the Bug
Dudgeon, R. Suicide Sheet
Elias, D. Cause of the Screaming
Elliott, W. J. Bren Hardy, Tough Dame
    Tough Ghosts
Fleming, I. Diamonds Are Forever
    Live and Let Die
Forsyth, F. Negotiator
Francis, D. Blood Sport
"G-Man." all 4 titles
Gardner, J. Understrike
Gosling, P. Hoodwink
Grahame, M. both titles
Hansen, V. Murder with Menaces
Haring, D. Dames Are Dynamite
    Sooner Your Die
Hausfeld, R. Murder Madness
    Night of Terror
    Shadow of Death
James, Max. Death Is Where You Meet It
Jepson, E. Grinning Avenger
Johnson, Duff. Chiseller
Kane. Fatal Frame
Kane, M. Sucker Trap
Kennedy, E. all 5 titles
Kensch, O. Image of Death
Kirby, D. Carnival of Death
    Death Man
Laffin, J. Devil's Emissary
Lewis, T. Boldt
Lynford, R. Sweet, Blonde and Ghoulish
McCutchan, P. Dead Line
Marshall, R. Blondes' Requiem
    Hit and Run
    Lady, Here's Your Wreath
Martyn, W. Death Fear
    Men Without Faces
Mitchell, S. most if not all 15 titles
Morelli, S. Take It and Like It
Morton, A. Affair for the Baron
Moscovit, A. Judgment Day Archives
Muller, P. Danger—Dame at Work
    Hasty Heiress
    Lady Is Lethal
    Slay Time
Oppenheim, E. P. World's Great Snare
O'Sullivan, J. B. Don't Hang Me Too High
    I Die Possessed
Pulman, J. Fixation
Rattan, J. Crime Buster
Robertson, S. R. Murder Makes Me Mad
Rome, D. Cannibals
    Cleaver
    Sandra
Saint, E. all 3 titles
Slattery, K. Girl Without a Name
    Tenth Street Killer
    Two-Fisted Killer
Smith, T. D. Now Try the Morgue
Steeber, M. Same Song, Next Verse
Steward, P. Gaboreau the Terrible
Sutherland, W. Death Rides the Air Line
Tate, R. Emperor on Ice
Tracy, L. No Other Way
Valdez, P. Feline Frame-Up
    Flight Into Horror
Ward, Harold. Blood of a Buddha
    Vulture
Warren, V. Farewell by Death
Wheatley, D. Irish Witch
    Strange Story of Linda Lee
Whitelaw, D. Murder in Motley

UNIVERSITY. See: Academia.

URUGUAY (Urug. See also: South America)
Daniels, N. License to Kill
De Villiers, G. Angel of Vengeance

U.S.S.R. See: Russia.

UTAH (See also: Salt Lake City; West)
Bellamy, J. Mistress of Ghosthaven
Conroy, Al. Soldato!
Derrick, L. Aryan Onslaught
George, P. Final Steal
Hild, J. Barrabas Fallout
Jones, C. Prophet Motive
Keller, K. Final Landscapes
Mailer, N. Executioner's Song
Mayer, R. Execution
Moffat, G. Stone Hawk
Pollock, T. Rainbow Man
Robeson, K. Mad Mesa
Shattuck, R. Said the Spider to the Fly

Settings Index

Snyder, G. Ogden Enigma

VANCOUVER (Van. See also: Canada; Montreal; Ottawa; Toronto; Winnipeg)
Ardies, T. Kosygin Is Coming
Atlee, P. White Wolverine Contract
Bonner, M. Shapes That Creep
Bowers, E. Ladies' Night
Deverell, W. Needles
Gough, L. 5 titles
Kent, Winona. Skywatcher
Layhew, J. Rx for Murder
Moore, C. His Lordship's Arsenal
Moore, M. Field Work
Pendleton, D. Hell's Gate
Shannon, Doris. Little Girls Lost
Slade, M. Ghoul
    Headhunter

VENEZUELA (Venez. See also: Caracas; South America)
Braun, M. G. Apostles of Violence
De Villiers, G. Que Viva Guevara
East, R. Pearl Choker
Ekert-Rotholz, A. Checkpoint Orinoco
Halliday, B. Caught Dead
Mason, V. W. Maracaibo Mission
Owen, Richard. Eye of the Gods
Paulsen, G. Death Specialists
Quinnell, A. J. Siege of Silence
Roberts, Mark. Maracaibo Massacre
Williams, L. Tropical Murder

VENICE (See also: Italy; Florence; Milan; Naples; Rome; Sardinia; Sicily)
Aarons, E. S. Assignment—The Girl in the Gondola
Aiken, Joan. Blackground
Albrand, M. Mask of Alexander
Anne-Mariel. Murder in Venice
Bhabra, H. Gestures
Boothby, G. Farewell, Nikola
Brent, M. Tregaron's Daughter
Brink, C. Bellini Look
Canning, V. Venetian Bird
Carter, Nick. Mission to Vengeance
Caudwell, S. Thus Was Adonis Murdered
Coffman, V. Dark Gondola
    Dark Palazzo
Coker, C. Hand of the Lion
Ehrlich, M. Reincarnation in Venice
Ferrand, G. House of Glass
Flagg, J. Death's Lovely Mask
Friedman, M. Venetian Mask
Gash, Jonathan. Gondola Scam
Healey, B. Last Ferry from the Lido
    Stone Baby
    Vespucci Papers
Hedges, S. G. Venetian Summer Mystery
Highsmith, P. Those Who Walk Away
Hill, R. Another Death in Venice
Hodge, J. A. One Way to Venice
Holme, T. all 3 titles
Inchbald, P. Short Break in Venice
Jacobs, T. C. H. Secret Power
Jason, S. Venetian Vendetta
Johnston, V. Masquerade in Venice
Jones, H. W. Death and the Trumpets of Tuscany
Low, O. Murky Shadows
MacInnes, H. Venetian Affair
Maning, K. Killpoint
Marshall, R. Mission to Venice
Maybury, A. Ride a White Dolphin
Pendower, J. Trap for Fools
Poynter, B. Disappearance of Mary Amber
Robertson, C. Clash of Steel
Rowan, H. Overture in Venice
Rudorff, R. Venice Plot
S., T. I. Violin and Vendetta
Sager, G. Formula
Sheckley, R. Game of X
Sheridan, A. M. Summoned to Darkness
Sklepowich, E. Death in a Serene City
Smith, Caroline. Barozzi
Spark, M. Territorial Rights

Stein, A. M. Cheating Butler
Sterling, T. Evil of the Day
    Silent Siren
Symons, J. Criminal Comedy of the Contented Couple
Unsworth, B. Stone Virgin
Vesey, A. H. Clock and the Key
Vivian, H. Mysteries of Venice
Wallace, Irving. Pigeon Project
Wheatley, D. Rape of Venice
Wilkinson, Sarah. Ruffian Boy
York, H. Venetian Charade

VERMONT (Vt. See also: New England)
Abbey, K. And Let the Coffin Pass
Abrahams, P. Hard Rain
Ashbrook, H. Murder of Sigurd Sharon
Babe, T. Billy Irish
Barber, W. A. Murder Enters the Picture
Borgenicht, M. Booked for Death
Brandon, W. Dangerous Dead
Brean, H. Wilders Walk Away
Brookhouse, C. Wintermute
Campbell, B. Pros and Cons
Cardiff, S. Severing Line
Carmichael, F. Exit the Body
    Exit Who?
    Murder in the Rerun
Carpenter, C. Cat Got Your Tongue?
Chapin, C. Three Died Beside the Marble Pool
Chaput, W. J. Man on the Train
Colburn, L. Death Through the Mill
Comfort, B. Grave Consequences
    Green Mountain Murder
    Vermont Village Murder
Cornish, C. Dead of Winter
Crane, Caroline. Circus Day
Daniels, D. Poison Flower
    Yesterday's Evil
Disney, D. M. Money for the Taking
Dutton, C. J. House by the Road
Emery, S. House That Whispered
Farnsworth, M. Menace of Marble Hill
Foley, R. Girl on a High Wire
Fought, C. A. Rabble's Curse
Frail, E. J. Cult
Garland, I. Abandon Hope
Gordon, E. Freebody Heiress
Hansen, R. P. Back to the Wall
    Mark Three for Murder
Harris, Rosemary. Three Candles for the Dark
Hastings, D. G. Death at the Depot
Hayes, J. Ways of Darkness
Holder, W. Case of the Dead Divorcee
Hughes, R. Unholy Communion
Judd, M. Husband of the Corpse
    Murder Is a Best Seller
Koenig, J. Smuggler's Notch
Levin, I. Dr. Cook's Garden
Loomis, P. Pure As the Driven Snow
McAllister, A. Look Over Your Shoulder
McHale, T. Lady from Boston
Markham, V. Dead Are Prowling
Mayor, A. Borderlines
    Open Season
Merrill, P. J. Slender Thread
Morella, J. Dark Memories
Mosher, H. F. Stranger in the Kingdom
Packer, V. Come Destroy Me
Pelley, W. D. Blue Lamp
Pentecost, H. Where the Snow Was Red
Philips, J. Laughter Trap
    Murder in Marble
    Thursday's Folly
Pronzini, B. Night Screams
Resnicow, H. Crossword Hunt
    Seventh Crossword
Richard, S. Intruder at Maison Benedict
Rohde, W. L. High Red for Dead
Rossi, B. Killing Machine
Smith, Alison. Rising
    Someone Else's Grave
Stein, A. M. Chill Factor
Strange, J. S. Reasonable Doubt

Sucher, D. Dead Men Don't Give Seminars
Taschdjian, C. Classified Death
Thielen, B. Charm of Finches
Wayland, P. Waiting Game
Wells, Carolyn. Killer Room with the Tassels
    Spooky Hollow
Westbrook, P. D. It Boils Down to Murder
    Sting of Death
Wheeler, H. C. We Have Always Lived in the Castle
Whitaker, L. Return to Hawkeston Hall
Winston, D. Lotteries

VIENNA (See also: Austria)
Andersch, A. Redhead
Bettauer, H. Viennese Love
Buckingham, N. Return to Vienna
    Vienna Summer
Callas, T. City of Kites
Charteris, L. Saint and the Hapsburg Necklace
Colbron, G. I. Joe Muller, Detective
Crisp, N. J. Ninth Circle
Crisp, W. Spytrap
Daniels, N. Some Die Running
Duke, M. Bormann Receipt
Eden, M. Gilt-Edged Traitor
Ellis, Julie. Rendezvous in Vienna
Fagyas, M. Devil's Lieutenant
Farr, C. Room of Secrets
Fletcher, Dorothy. Farewell to Vienna
Gainham, S. Mythmaker
    Time Right Deadly
Greene, G. Third Man
Hall, G. H. Watcher at the Door
Heaven, C. Castle of Eagles
Hylton, S. Crimson Falcon
Jones, J. S. Time of the Wolf
La Barre, H. Stranger in Vienna
Land, Jane. These Tiger's Hearts
Leather, E. Vienna Elephant
Lewis, F. J. Climax
Lorac, E. C. R. Murder in Vienna
McCutcheon, H. Suddenly, in Vienna
Maddock, S. Doorway to Danger
Marlowe, S. Passport to Peril
Milton, J. Baron Sinister
Oppenheim, E. P. Last Train Out
Page, A. So Late, Monsieur Calone
Payne, L. Vienna Blood
Perutz, L. Master of the Day of Judgment
Pick, M.. League of Liars
Pickering, R. E. Himself Again
Posey, C. A. Red Danube
Rainey, R. Hit Parade
Rosmanith, O. L. Storm Clouds Over Vienna
Rostov, M. Careless Feast
Rothberg, A. Great Waltz
Simmel, J. M. Caesar Code
Slote, A. Lazarus in Vienna
Storm, J. Bitter Rubies
Streib, D. Seeds of Evil
Vance, L. J. Dead Ride Hard
Vreeland, F. Dishonored
Weissl, A. Mystery of the Green Car
Wheatley, D. Second Seal
Wuorio, E. L. Woman with the Portuguese Basket

VIET NAM (See also: Hanoi; Saigon; Far East)
Acres, M. Viet Rampage
Anne-Mariel. Tigress of the Evening
Argo, R. Year of the Donkey
Baker, W. H. Dead and the Damned
    Judas Diary
Buchanan, J. Saigon Slaughter
Cain, J. Dinky-Dau Death
Care, W. Vietnam Spook Show
Cassidy, J. Station in the Delta
Collingwood, C. Defector
Coonts, S. Flight of the Intruder
Cross, E. B. Ninth Dragon
Crowther, J. Firebase
Daniels, N. Operation VC
Derrick, L. Jungle Blitz
Diehl, W. Thai Horse

VIET NAM

Doliner, R. Thin Line
Elegant, R. S. Kind of Treason
Garfield, B. Last Bridge
Harvester, S. Battle Road
Heath, L. C. CW2
Helm, E. all 4 titles
Honig, L. For Your Eyes Only
Kempley, W. Invaders
Lansing, J. at least 5 titles
Lassiter, A. Triangle
McAllister, B. Dream Baby
McCray, M. Deadly Reunion
McCurtin, P. Golden Triangle
Maning, K. MIA
Maurer, D. A. Dying Place
Murphy, W. B. Walking Wounded
Pendleton, D. 5 titles
Proffitt, N. Embassy House
Rivers, G. Five Fingers
Rohan, D. Browning Touch
Ross, W. Bamboo Terror
Sadler, B. Cry Havoc
Taylor, C. D. War Ship
Whittington, H. Burden's Mission
Williams, Alan. Tale of the Lazy Dog
Wolfe, M. Chinese Fire Drill
    Man on a String
    Two-Star Pigeon
Zlotnik, D. Black Market

VIRGIN ISLANDS (Vir. Is.)
Barbour, R. H. Death in the Virgins
Charles, I. When Only the Bougainvillia Blooms
Davis, Mildred. Scorpion
Dietrich, R. Steve Bentley's Calypso Caper
Ellington, R. Stone Cold Dead
Farrer, H. G. How Evil the Word
Jevons, M. Murder at the Margin
Johns, V. P. Hush, Gabriel!
Morrow, S. Season of Evil
Riefe, A. Tyger at Bay
Scarpetta, F. Kill Them All
Stein, A. M. Home and Murder
Whitney, P. A. Columbella

VIRGINIA (Va. See also: Richmond; South)
Aarons, E. S. Assignment—Treason
Acheson, E. Murder to Hounds
Andrews, V. C. Flowers in the Attic
    Seeds of Yesterday
Anthony, D. Blood on a Harvest Moon
Atkins, T. Blue Man
Barton, G. Ambassador's Trunk
Bennett, H. Wait Until Evening
Berliner, R. Manhood Ceremony
Blain, W. E. Passion Play
Boles, P. D. Limner
Brown, R. M. Wish You Were Here
Carr, J. Murder on the Appalachian Trail
Carr, J. D. Dead Man's Knock
Claudia, S. Master of Foxhallow
Coffman, V. Gaynor Women
Cohen, O. R. Romance in Crimson
Colby, R. Lament for Julie
Cornwell, P. D. Postmortem
Crosby, John. Take No Prisoners
Daniels, D. Curse of Mallory Hall
    Illusion at Haven's Edge
    Nightfall
    Tidemill
Dean, R. G. Case of Joshua Locke
Demijohn, T. Black Alice
De Pre, J. Sound of Dying Roses
Devine, S. both titles
Disney, D. M. 5 titles
Doran, J. In the Depths of the First Degree
Eberhart, M. G. Hunt with the Hounds
Fitzgerald, J. Belle Haven
Flannagan, R. Country Court
Ford, L. False to Any Man
    Town Cried Murder
Foxe, J. Hampton Classic
Fredericks, A. Mark of the Rat

Gaines, A. Old Must Die
    Voodoo Goat
Grey, R. both titles
Hale, Jennifer. Ravensridge
Hay, J. "No Clue!"
Henle, T. Death Files for Congress
Hintze, N. Stone Carnation
Hoffman, W. Godfires
    Walk to the River
Holland, I. Grenelle
Hornig, D. 5 titles
James, L. Triple Mirror
Johns, V. P. Singing Widow
Kavanaugh, C. Bride of Lenore
Kevern, B. Dark Eden
Kimbrough, K. Patricia, the Beautiful
Koehler, R. P. Tread Gently, Death
Laing, P. Brief Case of Murder
Lee, Elsie. Winegarden
Leonard, C. L. Deadline for Destruction
Lincoln, N. S. Meredith Mystery
    Moving Finger
Long, Manning. Short Shrift
McCloy, H. Slayer and the Slain
McCrumb, S. Lovely in Her Bones
    Windsor Knot
McCullough, K. Night Prowlers
McDonald, G. Fletch's Fortune
McKinney, R. L. Death in a Small Southern Town
McNamara, L. B. Pilgrim's End
Mack, E. Death of a Portrait
Maner, W. Deadly Nightshed
    Die of a Rose
Marsten, R. Murder in the Navy
Martin, David. Lie to Me
Michaels, B. Be Buried in the Rain
    Patriot's Dream
    Witch
Ostrander, K. Specter of the Dunes
Packer, V. Whisper His Sin
Parnell, A. Whispers at Midnight
Peden, W. H. Twilight at Monticello
Pendleton, D. Day of Mourning
Peters, Elizabeth. Devil-May-Care
Post, M. D. Methods of Uncle Abner
    Silent Witness
    Uncle Abner, Master of Mysteries
Ramm, C. Operation Norfolk
Revell, L. Kindest Use of a Knife
Robeson, K. Devil on the Moon
Rockwood, H. Walt Wheeler, the Scout Detective
Ronns, E. State Department Murders
Roscoe, T. To Live and Die in Dixie
Ross, Clarissa. Ghosts of Grantmeer
Ross, Marilyn. Mask of Evil
Ross, W. E. D. Dark Is My Shadow
    Whispering Gallery
    Whispers in the Night
Rossi, B. No Quarter Given
Ruter, P. S. Reminiscences of a Virginia Physician
Sapir, R. Death Check
Scott, J. R. Woman in Question
Seward, W. W. Skirts of the Dead Night
Shaffer, E. A. Major Washington
Siller, V. Echo of a Bomb
    Old Friend
Stapleton, D. Corpse and Robbers
Thomas, E. Dancing Death
Thum, M. Fernwood
Tone, T. Full Cry
Walk, C. E. Yellow Circle
Webster, J. Four-Pools Mystery
Whipple, K. Killings in Carter Cave
Whitney, P. A. Rainbow in the Mist
    Singing Stones

WALES
Anonymous. Mystery of Woodcroft
Ashby, R. C. Death on Tiptoe
    Out Went the Taper
Ashe, M. A. Ring of Roses
Bailey, H. C. Mr. Fortune Finds a Pig
Biggle, L., Jr. Glendower Conspiracy

Blaisdell, A. Nightmare
Boore, W. H. both titles
Brand, C. Cat and Mouse
C., L. G. Bertram's Right
Carnac, C. Impact of Evidence
Carr, G. 6 titles
Chance, S. Septimus and the Stone of Offering
Christie, A. Unexpected Guest
Clements, E. H. Other Island
Cory, D. Circe Complex
Covertside, N. Secret of a Hollow Tree
Cowan, G. K. both titles
Craig, D. Double Take
Creasey, J. Toff at Butlin's
Daniel, G. Welcome Death
Delving, M. Die Like a Man
Devine, A. D. Admiral's Million
Downes, J. Mountain Decameron
Dudley, E. To Love and to Perish
Elson, J. Romance of the Castle
Eyerly, J. Leonardo Touch
Farjeon, J. J. Greenmask
Finley, G. Kiss a Stranger
Fletcher, H. L. V. Miss Agatha
Gallie, B. Strike for a Kingdom
Goyne, R. Missing Minx
Graham, Alan. Who Killed Gerald Cruden?
Graham, Winston. Woman in the Mirror
Gray, B. Leave It to Conquest
Gunn, V. Death on Shivering Sands
Hardie, D. W. F. Riddle of the Cambrian Venus
Harris-Burland, J. B. Disc
Healey, B. Blanket of the Dark
Hill, Peter. Enthusiast
Howard, Londen. Foxglove Country
Hubbard, P. M. Dancing Man
Hunter, A. Gently to the Summit
Hurst, H. S. Dark Is My Destiny
Jackson, Eileen. Autumn Lace
James, Hallam. Fair Isle Jumper Mystery
John, O. Sabotage
Jones, Mervyn. Two Women and Their Man
Jones, R. W. Cop Out
    Green Reapers
    Saving Grace
Kamm, D. Secret of Manly Stones
Keating, J. Son of Judith
Knight, L. A. Paying Guest
Lee, V. Penelope Brandling
Lewis, N. Every Man's Brother
Lewis, Roy. Distant Banner
    Witness My Death
Lovell, M. Ghost of Megan
McGirr, E. Entry of Death
MacLeod, C. Curse of the Giant Hogweed
Markham, V. Death in the Dusk
Mayse, S. Merlin's Web
Melville, J. Nun's Castle
Millward, E. J. Copper Bottle
Moffat, G. Die Like a Dog
    Persons Unknown
Murphy, Roberta. Enchanted
Niall, I. Village Policeman
Norton, O. Corpse-Bird Cries
O'Hara, K. Searchers of the Dead
Ormerod, R. Alibi Too Soon
    Seeing Red
Payne, L. Take the Money and Run
Peters, Ellis. City of Gold and Shadows
Priestley, J. B. Benighted
Rees, A. J. Brink
Remenham, J. Righteous Abel
Richardson, S. Green Cape
Rigg, J. Pencarnan
Rutland, H. Bleeding Hooks
Sanford, U. Poisoned Anemones
Secombe, H. Welsh Fargo
Sladen-Smith, F. At Last We Are Alone
Stafford, C. Teville Obsession
Sullivan, M. A. Owen Castle
Tattersall, J. Dark at Noon
Thomas, Murray. Buzzards Pick the Bones
Troy, S. Swift to Its Close
Ullman, A. Night Man

Settings Index

Vahey, J. H. Storm Lady
Verner, G. Dene of the Secret Service
Walters, L. Dragon's Eye
Walton, W. Sins of the Fathers
Warden, F. Farm in the Hills
Warner, M. Death in Time
Wellsley, J. Castle on the Mountain
West, F. W. Welsh Courtship
Williams, David. Divided Treasure
    Murder for Treasure
Williams, Raymond. Volunteers

WARSAW (See also: Poland)
Annesley, M. Room 14
Hall, Adam. Warsaw Document
Litewka, A. Warsaw
Simpson, Ronald. End of a Diplomat
Swift, B. Mission Code: Springboard
Tripp, M. Wife-Smuggler
Wacht, L. Mission to Warsaw

WASHINGTON D.C. (Wash. D.C.)
Adkins, J. Deadline for Final Art
Adler, W. American Quartet
    American Sextet
    Casanova Embrace
Aellen, R. Redeye
Agnew, S. Canfield Decision
Alner, J. Z. Capital Murder
Anderson, Patrick. Busy Bodies
    President's Mistress
    Sinister Forces
Anonymous. President Vanishes
Anthony, E. Avenue of the Dead
Archer, J. Shall We Tell the President?
Avallone, M. Missing!
Banks, C. Girls on the Row
Barton, G. Pembroke Mason Affair
    Strange Adventures of Bromley Barnes
Bartram, G. White Peril
Bass, M. R. Force Red
Baxter, T. Hailstone
Bayer, O. W. Brutal Question
Beechcroft, W. Pursuit of Fear
    Secret Kills
Benford, T. B. Hitler's Daughter
Black, Angus. Slipknot
Black, C. Asterisk Destiny
Blacker, I. R. Kilroy Gambit
Blake, R. Stripped for Murder
Blatty, W. P. Legion
Bonnamy, F. Dead Reckoning
    King Is Dead on Queen Street
    Portrait of the Artist as Dead Man
Borgenicht, M. Corpse in Diplomacy
Bowen, Michael. Washington Deceased
Box, E. Death Before Bedtime
Brady, L. Love Tap
Bunn, T. Closing Costs
Burnes, C. Fear Familiar
Cain, J. M. Institute
Calde, M. A. Shadowboxer
Calmer, N. Avima Affair
Carroll, J. Firebird
    Madonna Red
Carter, Nick. 5 titles
Charteris, L. Saint Steps In
Clark, M. H. Stillwatch
Cody, J. P. Search and Destroy
    Top Secret Kill
Coffin, G. Murder in the Senate
Cohen, W. S. Double Man
Condon, R. Entwining
Coonts, S. Under Siege
Da Cruz, D. Vulcan's Hammer
Davey, J. Undoubted Deed
Davis, D. S. Old Sinners Never Die
Davis, Gordon. Counterfeit Kill
    House Dick
Dean, R. G. Body Was Quite Cold
    Case of Joshua Locke
Deane, P. Time for Treason
Decker, J. Death's Little Sister
Denker, H. Place for the Mighty

    Warfield Syndrome
Derrick, L. Capitol Hell
Dietrich, R. 7 titles
Dillon, W. Deadly Intrusion
Diplomat. 5 titles
Disney, D. C. Explosion
Dominic, R. B. 6 titles
Donnel, C. P. Murder-Go-Round
Doyle, J. T. Deadly Resurrection
Drury, A. Decision
Dunleavy, S. Very First Lady
Eberhart, M. G. Man Next Door
Ehrlichman, J. both titles
Evans, J. P. Vanishing Vector
Feiffer, J. White House Murder Case
Footner, H. Nation's Missing Guest
Ford, L. 8 titles
Fox, V. J. Pentagon Case
Futrelle, J. Elusive Isabel
Gaines, A. Omit Flowers, Please
Gann, E. K. Bad Angel
Garbo, N. Confrontation
Garfield, B. Line of Succession
Garland, R. C. Zalea
Gerould, G. H. Midsummer Mystery
Gillis, J. Chain Saw
Godey, J. Talisman
Goode, B. Senator's Nude
Goodrum, C. A. all 3 titles
Gordons. Power Play
Grady, J. Hard Bargains
    Runner in the Street
    Six Days of the Condor
Gray, Angela. Lattimore Arch
Green, A. K. Filigree Ball
Gross, Martin. Red President
Guild, N. President's Men
Halliday, B. Violent World of Michael Shayne
Hamilton, D. Murderer's Row
Harrington, R. E. Death of a Patriot
Hart, F. N. Crooked Lane
Haughey, T. B. Case of the Unbolted Lightning
Hay, J. Melwood Mystery
    That Washington Affair
    Unlighted House
Heffernan, W. Caging of the Raven
Henkin, H. Crisscross
Henley, W. Roman Solution
Hermann, W. Operation Intrigue
Hillerman, T. Talking God
Hirschfeld, B. Kingpin
Horton, F. W., Jr. Technocrats
Houk, L. C. V. Girl in Question
Hudson, C. Insider Out
Huebner, F. D. Black Rose
Hunter, G. Death Warrant
Huston, H. C. both titles
Hyman, T. Russian Woman
James, L. Caliph Intrigue
    Capital Hill Affair
Jason, S. Corporate Caper
Jerina, C. Flirting with Disaster
Johnson, S. Panther Jones for President
Johnston, W. Get Smart Once Again!
Jute, A. Eight Days in Washington
Kamarck, L. Informed Source
Karp, D. Brotherhood of Velvet
Kelly, J. Diplomatic Incident
Kennedy, A. Debt of Honor
Knebel, F. Dark Horse
    Seven Days in May
    Vanished
Knowland, H. Madame Baltimore
Kummer, F. A. Death at Eight Bells
    Design for Murder
Kurland, M. Last President
Lambert, D. Red House
    Trance
Larkin, R. T. For Godmother and Country
Latham, A. Orchids for Mother
Law, J. Big Payoff
Lee, John. Ninth Man
Lee, S. Dunn's Conundrum
Leonard, C. L. Secrets for Sale

Levy, D. L. Potomac Conspiracy
Lincoln, N. S. 16 titles
Lippincott, D. E Pluribus Bang!
Lowell, E. Tell Me No Lies
Ludlum, R. Chancellor Manuscript
    Icarus Agenda
McCall, A. Holocaust
McCarthy, A. One Woman Lost
McCarthy, J. R. Special Agent
McGerr, P. Is There a Traitor in the House?
    Legacy of Danger
    Pick Your Victim
McGhee, E. Last Caesar
MacInnes, H. I and My True Love
McLeish, R. Man Who Wasn't There
Mace, M. Blondes Don't Cry
Manson, W. Very Black Deed
Marlowe, S. Homicide Is My Game
    Mecca for Murder
    Violence Is My Business
Martin, M. Ravens of Rockhurst
Mason, V. W. Washington Legation Murders
Matthews, Clyde. Ides of March Conspiracy
Merritt, D. Hatch's Conspiracy
Meyer, L. both titles
Michaels, Barbara. Ammie, Come Home
    Shattered Silk
    Smoke and Mirrors
Milton, David. As Peace Lay Dying
Moore, Robin. Chinese Ultimatum
Moore, William. Last Surprise
Morice, A. Murder in Mimicry
Morris, A. P. Head Hunter
Morris, C. Stolen Letter
Moyes, P. Black Widower
Munder, L. Therapy for Murder
Murphy, W. B. Line of Succession
    Rain of Terror
Nessen, R. First Lady
O'Brien, R. C. Report from Group 17
O'Connor, B. One-Shot War
Oran, D. Z Warning
Osborn, D. Love and Treason
O'Toole, G. Cosgrove Report
Patrick, K. Death Is a Tory
Pearson, W. Chessplayer
Pease, W. D. Playing the Dozens
Pendleton, D. Dead Man Running
    Washington IOU
Perrett, G. Executive Privilege
Perry, Robin. Welcome for a Hero
Peterson, J. Balance of Power
Philips, P. At Bay
Picard, S. Notebooks
Pierson, E. Defense Rests
Plum, M. Murder of a Redhaired Man
    State Department Cat
Powell, R. All Over But the Shooting
    Lay That Pistol Down
    Shoot If You Must
Prager, J. S. Newman Factor
Pronzini, B. Acts of Mercy
Ramm, C. Terror in D.C.
Raphael, R. President Must Die
Ravin, N. Evidence
    Seven North
Revell, L. Men with Three Eyes
Rinehart, M. R. Man in Lower Ten
Roberts, Carey. Touch a Cold Door
Roberts, Nora. Brazen Virtues
    Sacred Sins
Robeson, K. Blood Ring
    Merchants of Disaster
    Smiling Dogs
Robinson, L. W. Assassin
Rodgers, M. J. Bloodstone
Rogers, J. T. Stopped Clock
Rogers, R. M. Negotiator
Roosevelt, E. 5 titles
Ross, Frank. 65th Tape
Ross, L. Q. Adventure in Washington
Roudybush, A. Before the Ball Was Over
    Capital Crime
    Sybaritic Death

Russell, A. J. Pour the Hemlock
Salinger, P. On the Instructions of My Government
Sanders, Lawrence. Capitol Crimes
Santiago, V. J. This Gun for Justice
Sapir, R. Head Men
Scherf, M. Dead: Senate Office Building
Schutz, B. M. All the Old Bargains
    Tax in Blood
Scott, J. R. Cab of the Sleeping Horse
    Man in Evening Clothes
    Red Emeralds
Serling, R. J. Air Force One Is Haunted
    President's Plane Is Missing
Sheldon, W. J. Rites of Murder
Shobin, D. Seeding
Shreve, S. R. Children of Power
Siller, V. Good Night, Ladies
    One Alone
Simons, H. Landing
Smith, Martin. Analog Bullet
Sohmer, S. Favorite Son
Spencer, Scott. Secret Anniversaries
Spore, K. Death of a Scavenger
Spruill, S. Painkiller
Stark, R. Mourner
Starnes, R. And When She Was Bad She Was
    Murdered
    Another Mug for the Bier
    Other Body in Grant's Tomb
Steele, C. Blood Reign of the Dictator
    Legions of the Death Master
Stein, A. M. Death Takes a Paying Guest
Stewart, E. They've Shot the President's Daughter
Stringer, A. Story Without a Name
Swaybill, R. E. Final Witness
Swerdlow, J. Code Z
Taylor, John. Patterns of Abuse
Taylor, W. Admiral's a Spy
Teilhet, D. L. Fear Makers
Thacker, C. G. Dream Spinners
Thomas, Ross. 6 titles
Thompson, S. L. Airburst
Thornburg, E. We've Been Waiting for You
Toomay, P. On Any Given Sunday
Truman, M. all 10 titles
Tully, A. Brahmin Arrangement
Tyler, W. T. Shadow Cabinet
Tyson, J. A. Scarlet Tanager
Ullman, B. E. Voluptuaries
Valentine, P. W. Crime Scene at "O" Street
Vanhee, G. G. Night Strike
Van Orsdell, J. Ragland
Victoroff, J. I. Wild Type
Von Elsner, D. Ace of Spies
Wallace, Irving. R Document
Wallace, R. Green Glare Murders
Wallis, J. H. Capitol City Mystery
Wartofsky, V. Prescription for Justice
Wayland, P. Double Defector
Weber, R. Company Spook
Weisman, J. Watchdogs
Werner, P. If Truth Be Known
West, J. B. Cobra Venom
White, L. House on K Street
    Rafferty
Whitehurst, B. Death on Capitol Hill
Whitten, L. H. Progeny of the Adder
Wilhelm, K. City of Cain
Wilkinson, B. Last Clear Chance
Winston, D. Haversham Legacy
    Long and Living Shadow
    Mira
Wolfson, M. In the Long Run We Are All Dead
Woods, Brett. Britannia Obsession
Woolfolk, W. President's Doctor
Yardley, H. O. Blonde Countess
    Red Sun of Nippon

WASHINGTON state (Wash. See also: Seattle; Northwest)
Adams, L. Z. Mirror Murder
Adkins, J. Cookie
Ashe, G. Death in the Trees
Ball, J. Chief Tallon and the S.O.R.
    Police Chief
    Trouble for Tallon
Barns, G. M. Murder Walks the Stairs
    Only the Losers Win
Barry, I. Darkness at Mantia
Brandner, G. Aardvark Affair
Brock, S. all 4 titles
Campbell, P. Cedarhaven
    Lush Valley
Castle, Jayne. Chilling Deception
Chittenden, M. Findlay's Landing
Delmonico, A. Eyrie of an Eagle
Derrick, L. Quaking Terror
Elkins, A. J. Dark Place
Emerson, E. W. Black Hearts and Slow Dancing
    Help Wanted: Orphans Preferred
Farr, F. Elephant Valley
Freeman, S. Fair Weather Foul
Gaines, A. No Crime Like the Present
Gast, K. P. Dil Dies Hard
Gillis, J. Killers of Starfish
Hawkins, J. Violent City
Herbrand, J. Dangerous House
    Lost Heritage
Higman, D. Pranks
Huston, H. C. With Murder for Some
Hyde, C. Wave
Johnson, N. T. Too Hot to Handle
Jones, N. Case of the Hanging Lady
    Ride the Dark Storm
Kendall, K. Death Rides the Storm
Kevern, B. Darkness Falling
    Key
Lamson, D. Whirlpool
La Point, D. Picture of Death
Leffland, E. Mrs. Munck
Lehman, D. Getbacks of Mother Superior
Marion, E. Keys to the House
Montgomery, I. Death Won a Prize
Moore, E. Shallow Runs the River
Nisbet, J. Death Puppet
Olson, D. B. Devious Design
Paul, C. Child Is Missing
Pender, L. Sky Pirate
Rife, E. A. Broken Promise
Roberts, W. D. Act of Fear
    Sniper
Rule, A. Possession
St. John, Darby. Westgate Mystery
Sears, R. M. Spirit of Cove Island
Smith, Janet. Sea of Troubles
Stewart, J. Before It's Too Late
Trimble, L. 5 titles
Weeks, D. Cape Murders
    Friday Harbor Murders
Wetherell, J. Cottage at Avalanche
    Dark Wing

WELLINGTON (See also: New Zealand; Auckland)
Burfield, E. New Mrs. Rainier
Hunter, H. Case for Punishment
    Inclination to Murder

WEST (See also: individual states)
Allen, G. Jaws of Death
Ames, N. My Path Belated
Anthony, W. Men of Mystery
Barbour, A. M. At the Time Appointed
Blair, C. Crystal Destiny
Bowman, J. House of Hate
Bryant, W. Blue Russell
Byrne, R. Mannequin
Cooper, C. R. Mystery of the Four Abreast
Corkill, L. Fish Lane
Craig, M. Cranes of Ibycus
Crumley, J. Last Good Kiss
    Wrong Case
Cunningham, John. Wait Till Dark
Dewey, T. B. My Love Is Violent
Dickey, P. Lincoln Highwayman
Eberhart, M. G. Man Missing
Fine, P. H. Night Trains
Fox, J. M. Crunch
Frazee, S. Sky Block
Gardiner, D. Drink for Mr. Cherry
Garfield, B. Tripwire
Gibbs, G. F. Hunted
Grant, M. Shadow—Destination Moon
Grant, William. Gold Train
    Iron Horse
    Trackwalker
Green, A. K. Mayor's Wife
Guthrie, A. B. Murders at Moon Dance
Gutteridge, L. Killer Pine
Hale, C. Ghost River
Harding, Bret. all 10 titles
Hawkins, W. E. Cowled Menace
Henderson, H. H. Queen of Spades
Humphreys, R. Hunch
Isely, R. K. Strange Code of Justice
Jackson, D. Cut of the Ax
Jeter, K. W. Death Arms
Kay, N. Trouble in the Air
Kruger, P. Bullet for a Blonde
Lynch, L. Mountain Mystery
Lynde, F. Grafters
McKimmey, J. Long Ride
MacLean, Alistair. Breakheart Pass
Mande, E. E. Spirit of Melissa Norgate
Mantle, B. In the House of Another
Millhiser, M. Willing Hostage
Overholser, S. Molly and the Confidence Men
Packard, F. Wire Devils
Peel, C. D. Flameout
Powell, R. Say It with Bullets
Reed, J. D. Free Fall
Reese, J. Sharpshooter
    Texas Gold
    Weapon Heavy
    Wes Hardin's Gun
Reid, D. Babcock Boys
Roberson, J. Smoketree
Roberts, J. L. Wilderness Inn
Robeson, K. Tunnel Terror
Sanders, C. W. Murder Trail
Sangster, J. Blackball
Short, L. Last Hunt
Snow, C. H. Bonanza Murder Case
    Highgrade Murder
    Lakeside Murder
    Sign of the Death Circle
Spilken, A. Burning Moon
Stevens, Diane. Valley of the Shadows
Taylor, J. R. Gipsy Blair, the Western Detective
Teilhet, H. T. Rim of Terror
Troy, J. Web of Murder
Tuttle, W. C. most of the 82 titles

WEST INDIES (W.I. See also: individual countries; Caribbean)
Anderson, J. R. L. Death in the Caribbean
Bennett, D. Carrion Crows
Bickham, J. Dropshot
Coulter, C. Calypso Magic
Desmond, H. Edge of Horror
Dobson, M. Touchstone
East, R. Twenty-Five Sanitary Inspectors
Footner, H. Obeah Murders
Gaskin, C. Fiona
Grace, A. Hawksbill Manor
Grove, M. You'll Die Tomorrow
Gulliver, H. Kill with Style
Haggard, W. Telemann Touch
Hamilton, D. Detonators
Heberden, M. V. Murder Follows Desmond
    Shannon
Lecomber, B. Dead Weight
    Turn Killer
Mason, Howard. Body Below
Mathewson, W. Immediate Release
Owen, R. White Slave
Pattinson, J. Angry Island
    Paradise in the Sun
Potter, Jennifer. Taking of Agnes
Root, P. Evil Became Them

Settings Index

Sager, G. Run, Sheep, Run
Smith, Shelley. This Is the House
Waugh, A. Island in the Sun
Wheatley, D. Dark Secret of Josephine
Williams, David. Treasure Up in Smoke
York, A. Tallant for Disaster
    Tallant for Trouble
Zachary, H. Top Level Death

WEST VIRGINIA (W. Va. See also: Charleston; South)
Anthony, D. Blood on a Harvest Moon
Ashley, S. Stalking Blind
Bird, B. Hawk Watch
    Never Wake a Dead Man
Davis, D. S. Clay Hand
Douglas, John. Blind Spring Rambler
    Haunts
    Shawnee Alley Fire
Eberhart, M. G. Family Fortune
Evans, E. Wintershade
Fitz, J. D. Devon Maze
Grubb, D. Watchman
    You Never Believe Me
Hoff, B. J. Storm at Daybreak
    Tangled Web
Livingston, Jack. Hell-Bent for Election
McCaig, D. Man Who Made the Devil Glad
McCrumb, S. Highland Laddie Gone
Montague, M. P. In Calvert's Valley
Nicole, M. Thick As Thieves
Noone, D. Victorian Crown
Pedneau, D. 5 titles
Peters, Elizabeth. Naked Once More
Salem, R. New Blood
Stout, R. Too Many Cooks

WINNIPEG (See also: Canada; Montreal; Ottawa; Toronto; Vancouver)
Silver, A. Good Time Charlie's Back in Town Again

WISCONSIN (Wis. See also: Madison; Milwaukee; Midwest)
Allis, S. Nightwind
Bloomfield, R. Stranger in Town
Brock, R. Tarn House
Canyon, C. Junior League Murders
Carrier, W. Death of a Chancellor
Clason, C. B. Death Angel
Collins, Max. Slasher
Coulson, J. Stone of Blood
Delmonico, A. Chateau Chaumond
Derleth, A. 9 titles
Dormer, M. Family Closets
Eberhart, M. G. Hangman's Whip
Edgley, L. False Face

Fonseca, E. H. Affair at the Grotto
    Death Below the Dam
Hanson, V. Casual Slaughters
Kruger, P. Finish Line
Kutchin, V. Strange Case of John R. Graham
Landers, G. Hunting Shack
Loken, C. Boy Next Door
Lord, G. Murder, Plain and Fancy
McConnell, F. Blood Lake
Machin, M. L. Outrageous Fortune
Millstead, T. Behind You
Nonweiler, A. Murder on the Pike
O'Finn, T. Happy Holiday!
Ozaki, M. K. Inquest
    Wake Up and Scream
Pender, L. Taste of Treason
Reidinger, P. Intimate Evil
Rice, C. Trial by Fury
Riggs, J. R. 5 titles
Roberts, W. D. Face of Danger
Rogers, S. Don't Look Behind You!
Russell, C. M. I Heard the Death Bell
Stirling, E. K. Chain Letter
Stratton, Thomas. Invisibility Affair
Straub, P. Mystery
Tadrack, M. Mistress of Evil
Von Elsner, D. You Can't Do Business with Murder
Wells, Carolyn. Deep-Lake Mystery
Winslow, H. Into Thin Air
Zimmerman, R. D. Mindscream

WYOMING (Wyo. See also: West)
Avallone, M. Lust Is No Lady
Baird, T. Poor Millie
Conley, R. J. Wilder and Wilder
Davis, T. Full Fare for a Corpse
Ferguson, W. B. M. Wyoming Tragedy
Ford, L. Old Lover's Ghost
Friedman, P. Rage
Gallagher, R. Murder by Gemini
Gibbs, G. F. Anything Can Happen
Kelland, C. B. Sinister Strangers
Lynch, L. Woman's Tragedy
Morrell, D. Totem
Parker, M. Murder in Jackson Hole
Peterson, Geoff. Medicine Dog
Robeson, K. Green Eagle
Roderus, F. Oil Rig
Ryan, C. Black Gravity
Seeley, M. Eleven Came Back
Stout, R. Mountain Cat
Szanto, G. Not Working
Williamson, Chilton. Desert Light

YEMEN (Yem. See also: Middle East)
Harvester, S. Treacherous Road

Jackman, S. Operation Catcher
Rosenberger, J. Night of the Peacock

YUGOSLAVIA (Yugos. See also: Belgrade; Balkans; Macedonia)
Brett, Martin. Flee from Terror
Canning, V. Forest of Eyes
Carter, N. Hour of the Wolf
    Turncoat
Cook, W. Taxi to Dubrovnik
Durrell, L. White Eagles Over Serbia
Footman, R. Always a Spy
Gainham, S. Silent Hostage
Gray, B. Follow the Lady
Hossent, H. Run for Your Death
Ingram, E. M. Unafraid
Karlin, W. Crossover
Laric, P. Maribor Remembered
Leonard, C. Hostage in Illyria
Leonard, C. L. Treachery in Trieste
MacLean, Alistair. Force 10 from Navarone
    Partisans
Marlowe, S. Drum Beat—Marianne
Quinton, A. Ragusa Theme
Rothberg, A. Thousand Doors
Sayer, W. W. Outlaws of Yugo-Slavia
Smith, Don. Dalmatian Tapes
    Perilous Holiday
Stein, A. M. Never Need an Enemy
Stout, R. Black Mountain
Symons, J. Man Who Lost His Wife
Travis, Grethen. Holiday of Fear
Wilson, Gar. Belgrade Deception
Woodhouse, M. Rock Baby

ZAIRE. See: Belgian Congo.

ZAMBIA. (See also: Africa)
Gilman, D. Mrs. Pollifax on Safari

ZANZIBAR (Zanz. See also: Tanzania; Tanganyika; Africa)
Aarons, W. B. Assignment Tyrant's Bride
Kaye, M. M. House of Shade
Keast, F. Final Caliph
Mason, V. W. Zanzibar Intrigue

ZIMBABWE. See: Rhodesia.

ZURICH (See also: Switzerland; Geneva)
Albrand, M. Zurich/AZ900
Duerrenmatt, F. Execution of Justice
Rooth, A. R. Ninth Car
Willock, R. Street of the Small Steps

SERIES INDEX

Series Index

A-Team; C. Heath
    R. Renauld
Abbot, Sgt. Bill; J. Penn
Abbot, John; B. Whitaker
Abbott, Pat and Jean; F. Crane
Abbott, Samuel G.; J. R. Langham
Abel, Luke; N. Cain
Able Team; D. Stivers
Abner, Uncle; M. D. Post
"Ace," The; S. Horler
Ace, Harvey; M. Horwitz
Acton, Kit (Marsden); M. Bramhall
Adam, Eve; J. Skvorecky
Adam 12; M. Stratford
    C. Stratton
Adams, Insp.; L. Hollingsworth
Adams, Adelaide; A. Blackmon
Adams, Anthony; T. Brace
Adams, Bradley; M. Dekobra
Adams, Charlie; R. Boyer
Adams, Donald O'Keefe; D. Sage
Adams, Hilda; M. R. Rinehart
Adams, Samantha; S. Shankman
    A. Story
Adjusters, The; P. Winston
Adkins, Harry; R. Foxall
Adrano, Johnny; Michael Bradley
Adrian, Insp. Christopher; M. R. Silverman
Agutter, Charlie; S. Llewellyn
Ainsworth, Martin; M. Underwood
Alba; Delacorta
Albany, Jack; J. Godey
Alberg, Sgt. Karl; L. R. Wright
Aldington, Rev. Claire; I. Holland
Aletter, Finney; Y. Montgomery
Allain, Insp.; B. Graeme
Allan, Rocky; V. Rath
Allard, Nick; B. Barclay
    Roger Harris
Allen, Peter; L. Anson
Alleyn, Roderick; N. Marsh
Allison, John; R. Meade
Allport, Det. Insp.; F. Everton
Aloha, Johnny; D. Keene
Alvarez, Insp. Enrique; R. Jeffries
Amayat, Mynheer; H. D. Stacpoole
Amberdon, Telzey; J. Schmitz
Ambers, Marilyn; E. St. Clair
American Avenger; R. Emmett
Ames, Martin; A. Eichler
Ames, Sid; H. W. Roden
Ames, William; L. Freeman
Amiss, Robert; R. D. Edwards
Amsterdam, Johnny; Michael Lawrence
Anders, Insp./Supt.; H. Jobson
Anders, Jonathan; C. Nicole
Anders, Tad; T. Allbeury
Anderson, Judge; J. Wagner
Anderson, Ben; G. Compton
Anderson, Christine; M. Mace
Anderson, Everett; K. S. Daiger
Anderson, Lou (Shifty); W. Murray
Anderson, Sgt. Pepper; L. Trevor
Anderson, Insp. Tom; L. Southworth
Anderwelt, Hermann; E. Douglass
Angel Eyes; W. B. Longley
Angel, Fitzroy Maclean; M. Ripley
Angele, Soeur; H. Catalan
Anhalt, Mici; L. O'Donnell
Annesley, George; F. Everton
Annie, Polack; J. Lait
Anstruther, Bill; J. Nicholas
Anstruther, Colin; J. Plain
Anthony, Wade; Eric Heath
Anthropol Detective Agency; L. Trimble
Antigua Players; J. Gollin
Antoine; H. C. Owen
Antonio, San; San Antonio
Antony, Mark; C. Curzon
Appleby, John; M. Innes
Appleby, Pecos; R. P. Koehler
April, Johnny; M. Roscoe
Aragon, Tom; M. Millar
Arbuthnot, Montrose; N. A. Temple-Ellis

Archer, Lew; John Macdonald
    John Ross Macdonald
    Ross Macdonald
Archer, Matt; Clay Henry
Archer, Maxwell; H. Clevely
Archer, Oceola; Joseph Baker Carr
Archie; N. Morland
Argand, Jan; J. Rathbone
Argee, Trigger; J. Schmitz
Argyle, Albert; J. T. Story
Aristo Autos; J. Leasor
Ark, Simon; E. D. Hoch
Armiston, Oliver; F. I. Anderson
Armitage, Bryan; B. Cobb
Armitage, Stephen; H. McLeave
Armstrong, Inspector; A. White
Arnholt; G. Latta
Arnold, Insp.; Miles Burton
Arrest and Trial; N. Daniels
Arrow, Frank; W. Deptula
Arrow, Sgt. Steve; L. Mantell
Artifex, Simon; R. Keverne
Asbestos, Jim; L. F. Schmitt
Asch, Jacob; Arthur Lyons
Asenath, Lady; B. Thomson
Ash, Andrew; F. Grierson
Ashden, Geoff; R. Westall
Ashe, Saxon; Saxon Ashe
Ashe, Steve; J. A. Howard
Ashenden; W. S. Maugham
Asher, Tim; H. J. Hultman
Ashley, Robert Lee; Chester K. Steele
Ashton, Insp. Carol; C. McNab
Ashton, Simon; E. Antill
Assassin, The; P. McCurtin
Assassin, The; J. D. Revere
Aswell, Peter; Wenzell Brown
Attar; Robert Graham
Atwell, Sgt. Nick; M. Underwood
Aubrey, Madame; H. Travers
Audley, David; A. Price
Audran, Marid; G. A. Effinger
Austen, William; A. Hocking
Austin, Steve; M. Caiden
Autos, Aristo; J. Leasor
Avenger, The; K. Robeson
Avenger, American; R. Emmett
Avengers, The; N. Daniels
    D. Enefer
    J. Garforth
    K. Laumer
    P. MacNee
    J. Peel
Avengers, The New; J. Carter
    J. Cartwright
    P. Cave
    W. Harris
Aveyard, William; James Fraser
Axbrewder, Mick; R. Stephens
Aylwin, Jerome; A. Curry

Bablon, Severac; S. Rohmer
Bader, Rex; Mack Reynolds
Badge of Honor; J. K. Dugan
Baggs, Henry Napoleon; C. H. Bullivant
Baier, Kate; G. Slovo
Bailey, Supt. Geoffrey; F. Fyfield
Bailey, Hilary Dunsany III; H. Bailey
Bailey, Hilea; H. Bailey
Bailey, Jane; M. Dobson
Bailey, Stuart; R. Huggins
Bailhache, Insp.; H. Phillips
Bain, Joe; J. H. Vance
Bain, Joshua; J. A. MacKenzie
Baines, Scattergood; C. B. Kelland
Baird, Frances; R. W. Kauffman
Baker, Insp./Supt.; O. Mills
Baker, Charles A.; H. C. Huston
Baker, Larry; Carter Brown
Baker, Paul; B. Norman
Baldwin, Mark; Alixe Carter
Baldwin, T. T.; S. OCork
Baley, Elijah; I. Asimov
Ballard, David and Michelle; C. G. Page

Ballard, Greg; D. Sinclair
Balm, Gilead; B. Capes
Balzac, Mario; K. C. Constantine
Banacek; D. Romano
Banion, Dan; R. Finnegan
Banks, Insp. Alan; Peter Robinson
Banner, Rex; Robert Chapman
Bannerman; J. Flynn
Bannerman, Paul; J. R. Maxim
Banning, Bill; N. Easton
Bannion, Burns; E. Norman
Bannister, Guy; M. Crossley
Barcello, Lee; S. Ransome
Barclay, George; Ernest Paul
Baretta; A. Patrick,
    T. Racina
Barlach, Hans; F. Duerrenmatt
Barlow; R. A. J. Walling
Barlow, Supt. Charles; Elwyn Jones
Barlowe, Insp; C. I. D. Smith
Barnaby, Capt.; L. T. White
Barnaby, Insp.; C. Howard
    H. Shaw
Barnaby, Insp. Tom; Caroline Graham
Barnard, Insp.; T. C. H. Jacobs
Barne, Richard; E. G. Cousins
Barnes, Berkeley; Eugene Franklin
Barnes, Bromley; G. Barton
Barnes, Ezell; R. Hilary
Barnes, John; R. Ottolengui
Barnett, Cory; B. E. Miller
Barney, Al; J. H. Chase
Baron, The; A. Morton
Baron, Bruce; N. Daniels
Baron, Hugo; Michael Brett
Barrabas, Nile; J. Hild
Barradine, Lord; E. Jepson
Barrie, Dennis; A. Reynolds
Barrin, John; Gret Lane
Barron, Peter and Janet; R. Darby
Barrow, Charles; F. J. Price, Jr.
Barrow, Jake; N. Quarry
Barrows, Winston; M. L. Eades
Barry, Insp.; A. Rowe
Barry, Alun; Kenneth O'Hara
Barth, Kay; N. Schier
Bartlett, Nell; D. Elias
Bartley, John; C. J. Dutton
Barton, Dick; Anonymous
    Dick Barton
    M. Dorrell
    Elwyn Jones
    L. Pryce
    A. Radnor
    G. Webb
Baruk, Bimbashi; S. Rohmer
Bascombe, Carver; K. Davis
Basil, Insp.; P. Hobson
Basnet, Andrew; E. Ferrars
Bass, Insp.; S. Truss
Bass, Stanley; D. Anthony
Bassett, Insp. George; C. Ryland
Bassett, Supt. Henry; P. Burden
Bassett, Justin; R. Stratton
Bastian, Lt. Andy; R. Wormser
Bastide, Insp. Roger; H. R. Simpson
Bastion, Prof. Luther; Gavin Holt
Bastion, William; R. Harrison
Bates, Norman; R. Bloch
Bathurst, Anthony; B. Flynn
Bathurst, Neil; L. L. Lynch
Batman; N. Adams
    M. Barr
    C. S. Gardiner
    Bob Kane
    W. Lyon
    Frank Miller
    Alan Moore
    P. Moreno
    G. Morrison
    D. O'Neil
    L. Wein
    R. Wenk
Battle, Supt.; A. Christie

B

B

Batts, Singer; T. B. Dewey
Baum, Alfred; D. Kartun
Bawtry, Sam; D. Enefer
Baxter, Insp. Richard; Margaret Moore
Baxter, Tory; M. Blair
Baynes, Dr. Douglas; V. Bell
Beagle, Lutie and Amanda; T. Chanslor
Beagle, Otis; C. K. Boston
    F. Gruber
Beale, Edward; R. Penny
Bear, Win; L. N. Smith
Beaufoy; H. Drummond
Beaumont; P. Barthelme
Beaumont, Insp. Henry; M. E. Atkins
Beaumont, J. P.; J. A. Jance
Beaumont, Jack; M. McDowell
Beck, Insp.; C. Ryland
Beck, Luke; P. Conway
Beck, Martin; M. Sjowall
Beck, Paul; M. M. Bodkin
Beckett, Lee; J. Crowe
Becq, Raoul; W. LeQueux
Beddoes, Sgt.; R. W. Jones
Bede, Simon; B. N. Byfield
Beef, Sgt.; L. Bruce
Beeke, William; E. S. Brooks
Beetham-Saunders, Dr. Villiers; W. LeQueux
Behrens, Samuel; Michael Gilbert
Belcourt, Robert; C. Rougvie
Beldrum, Archibald; L. F. Hay
Bell; E. R. Punshon
Bell, Garnett; C. H. Bullivant
Bell, John; L. T. Meade
Bell, Samuel; B. Freemantle
Bellamy, Harker; S. Horler
Bellamy, John; T. C. H. Jacobs
Bellcroix, Stephen; D. Craig
Bellman; W. L. DeAndrea
Belot, Frederic; C. Aveline
Belsize, Christopher; V. Rendall
Ben the Tramp; J. J. Farjeon
Benasque, Mike; A. Caillou
Benbow, Angela; C. H. Sawyer
Bencolin, Henri; J. D. Carr
Bendilow, Supt. Edmund; Carleton Wallace
Benedict, Jerry; E. Ronns
Benedict, Sam; H. L. Oleck,
    Brad Williams
Benham, John; M. Home
Benjamin, Paul; B. Garfield
Bennett, Fred; Elliott Lewis
Bennett, Jim; Robert Martin
Bennett, Maggie; A. Stuart
Bennett, Reid; T. Wood
Bennion, Roger; H. Adams
Benskin, Police Constable; E. P. Oppenheim
Bent, John; H. C. Branson
Bentiron, Dr. Thaddeus; E. M. Poate
Bentley, Steve; R. Dietrich
Beresford, Michael; L. Le Grand
Beresford, Tommy & Tuppence; A. Christie
Berets, Black; M. McCray
Bergerac, Jim; Michael Hardwick
    A. Saville
Berkley, George Stanhope; L. Meynell
Bernal, Insp. Luis; D. Serafin
Bernard, Paul; S. Gluck
Bernhardt, Alan; Collin Wilcox
Berresford, May; C. H. Bullivant
Bertie; P. Lovesey
Beryl; W. LeQueux
Besserley, General; E. P. Oppenheim
Best, Petunia; B. Chetwynd
Beverley, Jim; A. Marsden
Bey, Nur; J. Rathbone
Biggers; G. Stanley
Biggles; W. E. Johns
Bignon, Orestes; F. Didelot
Billings, Joshua; Taffrail
Binton, Margaret; R. Barth
Bionic Woman; E. Lottman
Birch, Jefferson; W. W. Lee
Birdseye, Miriam; N. Spain
Birdwood, Verity "Birdy"; J. Rowe

Birge, Sam; W. Krasner
Birkett, Insp. Sam; L. Payne
Birney, Joe; J. Livingston
Birnkov, Anton; M. Chernenok
Birtley, Mr.; C. A. Alington
Bishop, Adrienne; J. Ellery
Bishop, Prof. Harry; C. Haynes
Bishop, Hugo; S. Rattray
Bishop, Robin; G. Homes
Bishop, Shauna; J. J. Montague
Bizzy-Quizzy; Professor Bowker
Black, Capt.; M. Pemberton
Black, Insp.; Anonymous
Black, Supt.; J. N. Chance
Black; W. Manson
Black; J. Nazel
Black Berets; M. McCray
Black Eagles; J. Lansing
Black, Johnny; N. Steed
Black, Jonathan; R. Garnett
Black Pearl; W. D. Roberts
Black, Peter; L. A. G. Strong
Black, Thomas; E. W. Emerson
Black Whip; J. Brearley
Black Widowers; I. Asimov
Blackburn, Jeffery; M. Afford
Blacker, Insp.; Anonymous
Blackgrove, Tim; I. MacKintosh
Blackshirt; B. Graeme
    R. Graeme
Blackshirt, Lord; B. Graeme
Blackshirt, Monsieur; D. Graeme
Blackstone, Edmund; R. Falkirk
Blackthorne; Lincoln; G. Marsh
Blackwood, Riley; V. Starrett
Blade, Jud; K. Jackson
Blain, Barney; Carter Brown
Blaine, Larry; L. R. Davis
Blair, Margot; K. M. Knight
Blair, Mike; H. Searls
Blair, Nigel; L. F. Hay
Blair, Major Peter; J. R. L. Anderson
Blaise, Modesty; P. O'Donnell
Blake; W. LeQueux
Blake, Arab & Andy; Richard Powell
Blake, Jana; J. C. Conaway
Blake, Jonathan; J. N. Chance
Blake, Red; Edward Lee
Blake, Sexton; D. Ames
    Anonymous
    R. C. Armour
    W. Arthur
    J. Ascott
    W. H. Baker
    W. A. Ballinger
    W. J. Bayer
    L. Bidston
    Ladbroke Black
    A. Blair
    S. Blake
    S. Blakesley
    J. W. Bobin
    G. Bowman
    J. G. Brandon
    J. Brearley
    T. C. Bridges
    C. Brisbane
    E. S. Brooks
    L. H. Brooks
    Jonathan Burke
    Lewis Carlton
    Philip Chambers
    Gilbert Chester
    S. Christie
    H. Clevely
    J. Creasey
    G. Dilnot
    M. B. Dix
    Rex Dolphin
    L. C. Douthwaite
    S. Drew
    J. Drummond
    A. Edgar
    W. Edwards

    R. C. Elliott
    L. Essex
    Gwyn Evans
    F. D. Fawcett
    R. Francis Foster
    M. Frazer
    C. Vernon Frost
    E. J. Gannon
    J. Garforth
    C. Gates
    H. H. C. Gibbons
    N. Goddard
    R. Goyne
    B. Gray
    R. M. Graydon
    W. M. Graydon
    V. J. Hanson
    R. Hardinge
    A. S. Hardy
    Edwin Harrison
    C. Hayter
    Harry Egbert Hill
    C. M. Hincks
    W. B. Home-Gall
    S. Hood
    S. Hope
    D. H. Hyde
    L. Jackson
    W. Jardine
    G. Johns
    J. G. Jones
    A. Kent
    Hilary King
    A. Kirby
    Jack Lewis
    Derek Long
    Arthur MacLean
    W. McNeilly
    A. Maxwell
    M. Mead
    P. Meriton
    O. Merland
    H. C. Miln
    Andrew Murray
    Edgar Joyce Murray
    M. Osborne
    A. Parsons
    W. J. Passingham
    J. N. Pentelow
    B. Perowne
    G. N. Philips
    M. Poole
    R. H. Poole
    J. Purley
    P. Quiroule
    G. Rees
    Desmond Reid
    W. Reynolds
    Ross Richards
    P. Saxon
    W. W. Sayer
    H. Scott
    E. Semphill
    S. G. Shaw
    W. Shute
    A. Skene
    J. Stagg
    J. Stamper
    Richard Standish
    W. E. Stanton-Hope
    J. T. Story
    D. Stuart
    G. Sydney
    J. Sylvester
    F. A. Symonds
    G. H. Teed
    Martin Thomas
    H. Townley
    W. Tyrer
    P. Urquhart
    G. Verner
    W. P. Vickery
    F. Warwick
    T. C. Wignall
    Richard Williams

Blakeney, Sir Percy; B. Orczy
Blanc, Insp.; B. St. James
Blancanales, Pol; D. Stivers
Bland, Insp.; J. Symons
Blatchington, Everard; G. D. H. Cole
Blayde, Supt.; J. Wainwright
Blayne, Sebastian; S. Blayne
Blaze, Joe; R. Novak
Blessingay, Insp.; G. J. Barrett
Blessington, Charles; J. Sherwood
Bligh, Dulcie; G. Clark
Blinkwell, Prof.; S. Fowler
Bliss, Insp.; J. Remenham
Bliss, Jim; Christopher Booth
Bliss, Vicky; Elizabeth Peters
Blissberg, Harvey; R. Rosen
Blixen, Nils-Frederik; C. Larson
Blood, Mark; A. Morgan
Blood, Capt. Peter; R. Sabatini
Bloodworth, Leo; D. Lochte
Bloom, John Isidore; E. Warman
Bloomer, Theo; J. Hadley
Blow, Dr. William; K. Hopkins
Blue, Sibyl Sue; R. G. Brown
Blunt, Mortimer; M. Cranston
Blunt, Sandy; P. Yates
Bly, Dorrit; F. Bunce
Bobbie; I. Farquhar
Boddy, John; T. Thurston
Bodine, Jack; T. Bunn
Body Smasher; J. Stacy
Bodyguard, The; R. Reinsmith
Boggs, Sam; M. Washburn
Bognor, Simon; T. Heald
Bolan, Mack; D. Pendleton
    Jim Peterson
Boles, Orson; E. Chaze
Bolland, Henry; H. Andover
Bolsover, John; U. L. Silberrad
Bolt, Dave; Richard Curtis
Bolt, John; R. Hawkes
Bolt, John; Gayle Stone
    D. Unkefer
Bomfortune, Raoul; H. C. Bailey
Bonaparte, Napoleon; A. W. Upfield
Bond, Christopher; W. Martyn
Bond, Israel; S. Weinstein
Bond, James; Ian Fleming
    J. Gardner
    R. Markham
    Christopher Wood
Bondurant, Victor; J. G. Edwards
Bone, Supt.; J. Staynes
Bonner; R. Harding
Bonner, Cas; Charles Ryan
Bonner, Dol; R. Stout
Boone, Jefferson; J. Messmann
Booth, Silas; J. L. Linklater
Bordelon, Johnny; G. Ogan
Borden, Steve; B. Dougall
Borg, Steven; C. A. Posey
Borges, Insp.; J. Bonett,
    J. & E. Bonett
Borgia, Cesare; R. Sabatini
Borgneff, Vasily; H. Burkholz
Borham, John; G. Brodie
Borker, Billy; F. Hardy
Boruvka, Lt.; J. Skvorecky
Bounty Hunter; W. Boyles
Bounty, Peter; T. Downing
Bourne, Insp.; R. C. Finney
Bourne, "Daddy"; G. V. Galwey
Bourne, Jason; R. Ludlum
Bowers, Peter; J. H. Hulland
Bowlong, Colonel; Anonymous
Bowman, Supt.; J. Burrows
Bowman, Glenn; Hartley Howard
Box, Virginia; J. Moffatt
Boxer Unit; N. Cort
Boyd, Danny; Carter Brown
Boyd, Felix; S. Campbell
Boyd, Nile; G. Jackson
Boyne, Jerry; A. MacGowan
Bracewell, Nicholas; E. Marston

Bracken, Donald; J. S. Blazer
Bradbury, Insp.; N. Longmate
Brade, Capt. Courtney; K. Wolffe
Brade, Simon; H. R. Campbell
Bradfield, Peter; C. Witting
Bradford, Hank; M. Warden
Bradley, Supt.; Colin Robertson
Bradley, Adela Beatrice Lestrange; G. Mitchell
Bradley, Ben; W. G. Forbes
Bradley, Bill; G. Tree
Bradley, Jason; G. Larsen
Bradley, Luke; H. Pentecost
Bradley, Rupert "Brad"; E. B. Ronald
Bradshaw, Charlie; S. Dobyns
Bradshaw, Noah; Madeleine Johnston
Bradshawe, Jane; M. A. Allen
Brady, Franklin; A. McRoyd
Brady, Pete; M. S. Karl
Bragg, John; Henry Wade
Bragg, Sgt. Joseph; R. Harrison
Bragg, Peter; J. Lynch
Brain, Big; G. Brandner
Brain, Colonel; H. Cecil
Bramley, Insp.; A. Broome
Brand, Hilary; H. Brand
Brand, Jake; R. L. Brent
Brand, Mark; J. J. Connington
Brandeis, Kyle; W. Ash
Brandon, Anthony; Bryan Peters
Brandon, Mark; V. Warren
Brandstetter, Dave; J. Hansen
Brandt, Miss; M. Lawrence
Brannigan, Supt.; Andrew MacKenzie
Branscombe, Geoffrey; H. Matheson
Branson, Al; R. P. Koehler
Branson, John Lloyd; D. R. Meredith
Brant, Mason; N. M. Hopkins
Braxton, Colonel; M. D. Post
Bray; W. LeQueux
Bray, Insp. Bernard; C. S. Sprigg
Breck, Adam; K. Orvis
Bredder, Joseph; L. Holton
Bredon, Miles; R. A. Knox
Breed, Barr; B. S. Ballinger
Breen, Jim; J. Karney
Breeze, Benedict; I. Bayne
Brendel, Ernst; J. C. Masterman
Brennan, Michael; F. Zackel
Brent, Carey; M. W. Glidden
Brent, Dudley; D. Marfield
Brent, Jimmy; H. Kemp
Brent, Jimmy; Ed Martin
Brent, Mike; G. Fennell
Brentford, Insp.; S. B. Hough
Brett, Alan; Robert Garrett
Brett, Brian; C. Monig
Brett, Chester; Gwyn Evans
Brett, Chico; Kevin O'Hara
Brett, Dixon; Chris Allen
    Anonymous
    P. W. Batten
    T. S. King
    T. Mayne
    G. Prout
    R. Saville
    S. R. Shepherd
    Anthony Thomas
    Richard Worth
    J. Wylde
Brett, Mike; Keith Campbell
Brett, Reginald; L. Tracy
Brewer, William; H. McElroy
Brews, Insp.; V. Loder
Brewster, Amy; S. Merwin, Jr.
Brice, Richard; C. Junor
Brichter, Sgt. Peter; M. M. Pulver
Briconi; B. Baskerville
Briercliffe, Ronald; F. Beeding
Brierly, Herman; W. Levinrew
Briganti, Robert; P. McCurtin
Briggs; R. L. Fish
Briggs, Tommy; D. MacDonald
Bright, Rosie; Judge Ruegg
Bright, Susan; M. McDowell

Brill, Janna; L. Killough
Brindle, Max; A. S. Fleischman
Brinklow, Sgt.; H. Footner
Brisco, Sam; P. Hamill
Britain, William; J. Courage
Britland, Jane; R. L. Gerard
Brock, Supt. "Badger"; J. Bingham
Brock, Insp. David; R. J. White
Brock, John; D. Skirrow
Brockie, William; W. Brockie
Brodsky, Dan; E. Rosenthal
Brogan, Cole; J. Poyer
Brogan, Jerry; J. L. Breen
Bromley, Barry; N. Gould
Bronson, Richard; P. Rawls
Brook, Roger; D. Wheatley
Brooke, Clay; H. Crooker
Brooke, Loveday; C. L. Pirkis
Brooks, Mike; H. T. Rothwell
Broom, Andrew; R. McInerny
Broom, Herbert; F. Hurt
Brosky, Lt. Kevin; E. Naha
Brown, Father; G. K. Chesterton
Brown, Angel; G. Montrose
Brown, Benvenuto; E. Gill
Brown, Forsythia; R. C. Payes
Brown, Deputy Sheriff Jake; D. Cameron
Brown, Jane & Dagobert; D. Ames
Brown, Nick; R. Coram
Brown, Rusty; C. Regan
Brown, Vee; C. J. Daly
Browne, Carl; B. Ham
Browne, Freddie; M. Poole
Browning, Richard; P. Corris
Bruce, James; R. Johnston
Brunel, Jacques; C. Gavin
Bruno, Brother Felipe; Marjorie Bowen
Brunt, Insp. Thomas; J. B. Hilton
Bryant, John; Richard Grayson
Bryce, Emily & Henry; M. Scherf
Bryce, Kevin; D. Valentine
Bryden, Avis; E. Phillpotts
Buchan, Insp.; S. Barlay
Buchanan, Johnny; J. Brenner
    K. T. McCall
Buck, Insp.; A. Marsden
Buckby, Lionel; John Gloag
Buckle, Ebenezer; N. Brady
Budd, Lanny; U. Sinclair
Budd, Robert; G. Verner
Buell, Martin; M. Scherf
Buffum, Mr.; H. de Selincourt
Bull, George; M. Kennedy
Bull, Homer; L. Lariar
Bullion, Simon; M. B. Dix
Bullock, Hlene; B. N. Byfield
Bulman, George; R. Holdstock
    J. Raymond
Bulstrode, Jimmy; M. Van Vorst
Bunce, Dr. Nathaniel; E. M. Curtiss
Bunker, Terry; Paul Ross
Bunn, Smiler; B. Atkey
Burford, Insp. Archie; V. MacClure
Burgess, Iron; Old Sleuth
Burgess, Insp. Jim; C. Franklin
Burke; A. Vachss
Burke, Insp./Supt. Curtis; R. Trevor
Burke, Eleanora; V. Perdue
Burke, Jerry; Asa Baker
Burke, Shamus; H. M. Webster
Burke's Law; R. Fuller
Burlane, James; R. Hoyt
Burmann, Cheviot; B. Cobb
Burnell, John; F. Vivian
Burnivel, Insp.; E. Candy
Burns, Carl; B. Crider
Burns, Jim; F. Penny
Burr, Jason; D. Kent
Burr, Thad; Anonymous
Burra, Parra; J. Hawke
Burrell, Jacob; G. Boothby
Burrill, William; Adam Gordon MacLeod
Burroughs, Julian; W. B. Murphy
Burton; E. P. Oppenheim

Burton, Dr.; A. C. Gunter
Burton, Insp.; G. E. Locke
Burton, Major Dick; M. Beckett
Bushyhead, Chief Mitchell; J. Hager
Butcher, The; S. Jason
Butler; P. Kirk
Butler, Morgan; D. Anthony
Butler, Patrick; J. D. Carr
Button, Harry; J. Barbette
Byrd, Ferris; A. Stuart
Byrne, Insp.; E. C. Vivian
Byrnes, Insp.; J. Hawthorne
    Unknown

CAT; S. Andrews
C.O.B.R.A.; J. Rosenberger
Cable, Bret; B. Callison
Cable, Sarah; M. Hartland
Cabot, Philip; R. McDougald
Cadee, Don; S. Dean
Cadfael, Brother; Ellis Peters
Cadman, Insp.; C. Rushton
Caesare, Rosie; R. Santini
Cage, Allen; E. R. Jones
Cage, B. F.; P. Israel
Cage, Huntington; A. Riefe
Cain; B. Freeborn
Cain; S. A. Key
Cain, Cabot; A. Caillou
Cain, Jenny; N. Picard
Caine, Nick; D. Zochert
Cainsforth, Duncan; J. Maske
Cairn, Donald; V. Loder
Calder, Daniel John; Michael Gilbert
Calder, Keith; G. Hammond
Calderwood, Harry; P. A. Kelley
Caldwell, Prof.; M. K. Ozaki
Cale, Martyn; P. Long
Caliban; P. Warren
Callaghan, Slim; P. Cheyney
Callaghan, "Steel"; M. Chesney
Callahan, Brock; W. C. Gault
Callahan, Dirty Harry; D. Hartman
    W. Morgan
    P. Rock
    J. C. Stinson
    M. Valley
Callan, David; J. Mitchell
Calloway, Sarah; J. Warmbold
Cam, Insp.; J. Cockin
Camberwell, Ronald; J. S. Fletcher
Camellion, Richard; J. Rosenberger
Camelot, Charles; P. Israel
Cameron, Sgt./Corp.; R. Connor
Cameron, Janice; J. Sheridan
Cameron, Paul; W. Wright
Campbell, Humphrey; G. Homes
Campbell, Pat; E. Colter
Campbell, Susan; P. Heneker
Campenhaye, Paul; J. S. Fletcher
Campion, Albert; Margery Allingham
    Youngman Carter
Cane, David; J. Courage
Cannon; P. Denver
    D. Enefer
    R. Gallagher
Cannon, Curt; Curt Cannon
Cannon, Dave; M. Delving
Cantini, Angel; R. Eversz
Canuck, Johnny; J. Moffatt
Capliostro, Count; R. Sabatini
Capricon, Supt. Merlin; P. G. Winslow
Carberry, Jane; B. Symons
Carberry, Letitia; M. R. Rinehart
Carbo; J. Quartermain
Cardby, Mick; David Hume
Cardiff, Insp./Supt.; D. Gray
Cardigan, Burgess (Buzz); D. Rico
Cardigan, Peter; Monte Barrett
Cardinal; S. Blakesley
Cardinal, Insp. James; M. Walton
Carding, Hugh; G. Collins
Cardolini, Frank; D. J. Gerrity
Carew; S. Blakesley

Cargunka, D. C. O.; W. H. Hodgson
Carlisle, Kenneth; Carolyn Wells
Carlito; E. Torres
Carlton, Insp. Giles; H. Phillips
Carlyle, Carlotta; Linda Barnes
Carmichael, Agnes; Anthea Cohen
Carmichael, Justine; K. Chase
Carmichael, Michael; P. Durst
Carnaby-King, Det. Sgt.; P. N. Walker
Carnacki; W. H. Hodgson
Carner, Mary; Z. Popkin
Carney; Stuart Martin
Carolan; F. A. M. Webster
Carolus, Lucian; E. Ascher
Carpenter, Mr.; H. L. Peacock
Carpenter, Ace; H. T. Caine
Carpenter, Chips; G. Eldredge
Carr, Charles; G. Petievich
Carr, Dan; Willard K. Smith
Carradine, Steven; M. K. Robertson
Carrados, Max; E. Bramah
Carrick, Webb; B. Knox
Carrington, Derek; B. Netton
Carrington, F. T.; J. S. Clouston
Carroll, David; O. R. Cohen
Carroll, Jimmy; H. McCutcheon
Carruthers; R. L. Fish
Carruthers, John; E. C. Cox
Carson, Don; A. Pruitt
Carson, Trader; John Barnett
Carstairs; N. Davis
Carstairs, "Apples"; S. Myles
Carstairs, Brett; S. Horler
Carstairs, John; F. B. Long
Carstairs, Dr. Richard; A. De O.
Carter; E. R. Punshon
Carter, Jack; T. Lewis
Carter, John; K. T. Jones
Carter, Insp. Neil; E. Dewhurst
Carter, Nick; Nicholas Carter
    Nick Carter
Carter, Ralph; T. Lilley
Carter, Steve; A. R. Long
Carter, Tony; David Hume
Carter, Trim; Nicholas Carter
Cartwright, Bill; P. Morgan
Caruso, Enrico; B. Paul
Carvalho, Pepe; M. V. Montalban
Carvel, Kelly; N. Daniels
Carver, Fred; J. Lutz
Carver, Rex; V. Canning
Caryll, Victor; G. Fairlie
Casanova, Jaques; R. Sabatini
Case, Charlie; J. Spencer
Casey, Flash; P. Ayres
    S. Bristol
    G. H. Coxe
Casey, Dr. Peter; R. Mead
Casey, Phil; H. Lugar
Cash, Sam; B. Crump
Caspian, Dr. Alexander; John Burke
Cass, Jeff; R. Severn
Cassella, Tony; L. Beinhart
Cassidy, Horatio; J. Crosby
Cassidy, Lew; T. Maxwell
Castain, Ricky; W. H. Baker
Castang, Henri; H. Freeling
Casteel Family; V. C. Andrews
Castle, Darby; Jan Michaels
Castle, Julian; J. Crown
Castle, Peter; G. Davison
Castleman, Marc; R. Kutak
Castleton, James; C. A. Alington
Cato, Dr. Paul; L. T. Meade
Cauldron, Insp.; S. Fowler
Caution, Lemmy; P. Cheyney
Cavannagh, John; Ian Anderson
Cavender, Alec; E. Tokson
Cawthorne, Supt.; R. Silverwood
Cayley, Lois; Grant Allen
Cellini, Dr. Emmanuel; M. Halliday
Cervantes, Antonio "Chico"; Bruce Cook
Chace, Insp.; V. Loder

Chad, Denis; Mary Archer
Chadwick, Geoffrey; E. O. Phillips
Chadwick, John; G. Cobden
Chalice, Harry; Donald MacKenzie
Challis, Bart; W. F. Nolan
Challis, Prof. Ronald; Shane Martin
Challoner, Humphrey; R. A. Freeman
Chambers, Peter; H. Kane
Chambrun, Pierre; H. Pentecost
Chameleon; J. La Plante
Champnell, Augustus; Richard Marsh
Chan, Charlie; M. Avallone
    E. D. Biggers
    D. Lynds
Chan, David; C. Leader
Chance, Det. Insp.; G. R. Sims
Chance, John Newton; J. N. Chance
Chandos; D. Yates
Chane, Alexander; Ralph Hayes
Chaney, Ace; C. Garrison
Chang, Mr.; A. E. Apple
Channay, Gilbert; E. P. Oppenheim
Chantecoq; A. Bernede
Chaos, Jacob; Shelley Smith
Chard, Peter; G. Verner
Chard, Simon; B. Malim
Charles, Mrs. Edwina; M. Warner
Charleston, Sheriff Chick; A. B. Guthrie, Jr.
Charlesworth, Insp.; C. Brand
Charlesworth, Sgt.; J. S. Fletcher
Charlesworth, James; J. Sandys
Charlie's Angels; M. Franklin
Charlton, Insp.; C. Witting
Chase; N. Daniels
Chase, Nick; N. Cort
Chatham, Erik; R. Neebel
Chavasse, Paul; M. Fallon
Chee, Jim; T. Hillerman
Cheri-Bibi; G. Leroux
Cherrington, Richard; G. Daniel
    D. Rees
Cherry, Insp.; P. Van Greenaway
Chesterfield, Henry; Clive Brooks
Chetwynd, Dr.; L. T. Meade
Chetwynd, Dennis; H. J. Fidler
Cheyney, Colonel Allen; P. Cosgrave
Chill; J. Sherman
Chillders, Dr. Russell V.; J. Sherman
Chipstead, "Bunny"; S. Horler
Chisholm, Paul; A. W. Eyles
Chitterwick, Ambrose; A. Berkeley
Chopper Cop; Paul Ross
Chopper Cops; R. Mackin
Chorley, Insp. Bill; F. C. Tickner
Christie, Bob; James Preston
Christy, Gordon; Barbara Moore
Christopher, Bob; R. R. Irvine
Christopher, James; Curtis Steele
Christopher, Paul; C. McCarry
Chucky, Insp.; C. Brand
Church, Johnny; V. Howard
Cigarini, Giuseppi; G. Frankau
Circle of Thirteen; W. M. Graydon
Circle, Secret; G. Null
Cirret, Antoine; E. Hely
Clackworthy, Amos; Christopher B. Booth
Clamart, Frank; H. C. Rowland
Clancy, Lt.; R. L. Pike
Clancy, Jack; K. K. Beck
Clancy, Peter; L. Thayer
Clane, Terry; E. S. Gardner
Clapp, Lt. Austin; Wade Miller
Claremont, Clarice; C. Cranston
Clark, Clark Clark; S. S. Baker
Clarke, Henry; Waters
Clarke, Horace; I. Lewis
Clarkson-Parry, James; B. G. Quin
Claw, Tut; V. A. Paradis
Clay, Colonel; Grant Allen
Clay, Cutty; H. MacGrath
Clay, Capt. Homer; P. Lauben
Clay, Lucien; R. Gore-Browne
Clay, Stephen; S. E. Porcelain
Claymore, Tod; T. Claymore

Clayton, Jack; S. Gluck
Clayton, Jeff; W. Ward
Cleary, Jack; David Elliott
    M. Lockhart
    T. N. Robb
Cleek, Hamilton; H. P. Hanshew
    M. E. Hanshew
    T. W. Hanshew
Clegg, Samson; R. H. Clark
Clemons, Frank; T. H. Cook
Clerihew, Mr.; Warner Allen
    E. C. Bentley
Cleveland, John; S. Fowler
Clifford, Bob; Leroy Scott
Clift, Cornelius; E. Heath
Clinton, Hortense; M. Hagen
Clouseau, Insp.; F. Waldman
Clown, Crimson; J. McCulley
Club, Catalyst; G. Dyer
Club, Union; I. Asimov
Clubfoot; D. Valentine
    V. Williams
Cluer, Dan; W. B. M. Ferguson
Cluff, Sgt. Caleb; G. North
Clume, Asaph; R. L. Goldman
Clunk, Joshua; H. C. Bailey
Cluthra; H. Munro
Clymping, Viscount; V. Gielgud
Cobb, Ira; R. Winsor
Cobb, Matt; W. L. DeAndrea
Cockrill, Insp.; C. Brand
Cody; D. Brierley
Cody, John; Jim Case
Coffee, Dr.; L. G. Blochman
Coffin, Sgt./Insp. John; Gwendoline Butler
Colby, Al; D. Dodge
Cole, Carter; F. C. Davis
Cole, Elvis; R. Crais
Cole, Harlan; J. Donahue
Cole, Schyler; Frederick C. Davis
Coll, Matthew; R. H. Lewis
Collier, Hugh; M. Dalton
Collin, Mr.; F. Heller
Collins; B. Hitchens
Collins, Barnabas; Marilyn Ross
Collins, Lizzie; E. L. Long
Colorado, Kat; K. Kijewski
Colson, Capt.; A. White
Colt, Thatcher; A. Abbot
Colton, Thornley; C. H. Stagg
Coltray, Stosh; D. Alexander
Columbo; H. Clement
    L. Hays
    A. Lawrence
    B. Magee
Colwyn, David; A. J. Rees
Cominsec, Agent of; Ralph Hayes
Commandos, Israeli; A. Sugar
Con, Val; Steve Miller
Conacher, Steve; Adam Knight
Condon; D. Jordan
Condor, The; J. Grady
Condor, Bart; W. Wright
Cone, Timothy; Lawrence Sanders
Conger, Jake; R. Goulart
Conley, Sgt. Chuck; J. M. Fox
Conlin, Capt./Insp.; Clement Wood
Connell, Dan; J. Foxx
Connell, David; J. Weatherhead
Connor, Doc; J. Dolph
Connors; S. M. Gardenhire
Connors, Liz; Susan Kelly
Conquest, Norman; B. Gray
Conquez, Joe; Clifford Mason
Conrad, Clive; Frank King
Conroy, Insp. Thomas; H. Asbury
Considine, Steve; R. P. Wilmot
Constantine, Dr.; M. Thynne
Continental Op; D. Hammett
Contrell, Roman; E. R. Chase
Conway, Brian Dinsmore; Simon Stone
Conway, George; L. T. Meade
Conway, Rupert; E. Leather
Cook, Barney; H. J. O'Higgins

Cool, Bertha; A. A. Fair
Cooley, Dade; G. Thompson
Cooper, Iris; K. K. Beck
Cooperman, Benny; H. Engel
Cop, Chopper; Paul Ross
Copp, Joe; D. Pendleton
Coppersmith; R. J. Griffin
Coquenil, Paul; C. Moffett
Corbett, Hugh; P. C. Doherty
Corbin, Ben; R. Crane
Corby, Insp.; Lettice Cooper
Cord, Talos; Robert MacLeod
Cordry, Jason; J. D. O'Hanlon
Corey, Lee; T. Williamson
Cork, Captain; S. S. Rafferty
Cork, Sgt.; A. Swinson
Cork, Montague; MacDonald Hastings
Corleone, Michael; M. Puzo
Cormack, Alan; J. Baddock
Cornelius, Jerry; M. Moorcock
Cornell, Dr. Alexander; M. Scott Michel
    Milton Scott
Cornford, Insp.; M. Kennedy
Cornish, Katherine (Kay); Virginia Hanson
Cornish, Nicholas; A. MacKenzie
Corridon, Martin "Brick Top"; R. Marshall
Corrigan, "Biff"; W. Morton
Corrigan, Mark; M. Corrigan
Corrigan, Tim; E. Queen
Corti, Insp. Franco; P. Inchbald
Cory, Dr. Patrick; C. Siodmak
Cosgrove; M. M. Innes
Costain, Ricky; W. H. Baker
Costaine, Tony; N. MacNeil
Costello; J. Nicholson
Costello, Patrick; Richard Hall
Cotten, Neal; Sam S. Taylor
Cotter, Wellington; Martin Long
Cotterell, Martin; J. Trench
Cotton, Gunston; Rupert Grayson
Coulson, Rex; J. Mann
Countdown WWIII; W. X. Davies
Counter Force; D. Streib
Courtenay, Det. Insp.; N. Berrow
Courtney, Maggie; A. Pearson
Coward, Tom; R. Base
Coyle; J. Philips
Coyne, Brady; W. G. Tapply
Crader, Carl; E. D. Hoch
Craft, Sebald; I. Patterson
Crag, Osborne; S. Elvestad
Cragg, Sam; F. Gruber
Craggs, Mrs.; H. R. F. Keating
Craggs, John; C. A. Alington
Cragin, Cliff; E. H. Price
Craig, Prof.; Babette Hughes
Craig, Sgt.; I. Jefferies
Craig, Alan; Malcolm Gray
Craig, John; J. Munro
Craig, Nat; E. Dudley
Craig, Peter; K. Benton
Craig, Steve; B. Winter
Craig, Tom; V. Van Urk
Craine, Paul; E. P. Healy
Cramer, Insp.; R. Stout
Crammond, Roger; T. Muir
Crandel, Ben; Murray Sinclair
Crane, Bill; Jonathan Latimer
Crane, Lionel; D. Stuart
Crane, Paul; Wade Curtis
Cranfurd, Liane; S. Gilruth
Cranley, Nick; M. Storm
Cranmer, Steve; S. Knickmeyer
Cranston, Lamont; W. B. Gibson
    M. Grant
Crawford; D. Cushman
Crawford, Jack; Thomas Harris
Crawford, Tango; E. Gunton
Crawford, Thea; Jessica Mann
Crawley, Ray; P. Corris
Cray, Joseph P.; E. P. Oppenheim
Craythorne, Major Jonathan; Arthur Douglas
Creevy, Winston; J. Lord
Creighton, Peter; A. Livingston

Crewe; V. Vanardy
Crewe; John R. Watson
Cribb, Sgt.; P. Lovesey
Crichton, Tessa; A. Morice
Criddle, Adrian; B. Strong
Crime Minister, The; I. Barclay
Crisis Aversion Team; S. Andrews
Crispin, John; R. Foxall
Crockett, Fred; B. Lang
Croft, Joshua; W. Satterthwait
Croker, Danby; R. A. Freeman
Crole, Simon; R. H. Leitfred
Crombie, Sam; G. H. Coxe
Cromwell, Burt; Inspector Stark
Crook, Arthur; Anthony Gilbert
Crosley, Lee; R. Tralins
Cross, Inspector; H. Slesar
Crow, Insp. John; R. Lewis
Crow, Anderson; G. B. McCutcheon
Crow, Martin; G. Norsworthy
Crow, Titus; B. Lumley
Crowder, George; H. Pentecost
Crowley, Vince; Bill Kelly
Crown, John; T. Harknett
Crown, Steve; D. Streib
Croyd; I. Wallace
Crupper, Jo; T. Le Breton
Cruz, Sgt. Carlos; Marilyn Wallace
Crymes, Charity; E. Phillpotts
Cuddy, John Francis; J. F. Healy
Cullinan, Timothy; O. Martin
Cummings, Insp.; Paul McGuire
Cunliffe, Dr. Richard John; H. Frankish
Cunningham, "Brains"; E. P. Thorne
Cunningham, John; G. Hammond
Curfew, Max; J. Brunner
Curtis, Hugh; P. Somers
Curtis, Lyle; E. L. Fetta
Curwen, Insp. Peter; R. Vickers
Curzon, Amanda; F. Usher
Cutting, Samuel; P. D. Westbrook
Cyber, Adam; P. Heath

Dack, Capt.; P. Meriton
Daguerre, Christian; C. Stevens
Dahlquist, Serendipity; D. Lochte
Dain, Stephen; R. Sheckley
Dakar, Ahmad; R. Werry
Dakkers, Sam; Mike Brett
Dakota; G. A. Ralston
Dale, Barlow; R. Siverns
Dale, Edward; W. Chesney
Dale, Insp. James; J. C. Cooper
Dale, Jimmie; F. Packard
Dale, Martin; H. Landon
Dale, Martin; Maxwell Scott
Dalgliesh, Adam; P. D. James
Dallas, Supt. Brett; M. G. Hugi
Dallenger; R. Harding
Dalmas; R. Chandler
Dalton Boys, The; W. B. Lawson
Dalziel, Supt. Andrew; Reginald Hill
Damiot, Insp.; V. McConnor
Dan, Lingo; P. Pollard
Danby, Don; Griff
Dance, Charlie; T. Barling
Dancer, April; M. Avallone
    S. Latter
    P. Leslie
Dane, Bartholomew; Rex Dark
Dane, Timothy; W. Ard
Danevitch, Michael; D. Donovan
Danforth, Abigail Patience; M. J. A. Jackson
Dangerfield, Maxine; C. Franklin
Daniel, Vic; D. M. Pierce
Daniels, Supt.; G. Baxter
Daniels, Charmian; Jennie Melville
Daniels, Webster; Terrence Lore Smith
Danning, David; D. Von Elsner
Dante, Joe; C. Newman
Darblay, Insp. Jean; Mollie Hardwick
Darby, Patrish; The Aresby's
Darcy, Lord; R. Garrett
    M. Kurland

D

Dare, Susan; M. G. Eberhart
Darington, Peter; D. V. Duff
Dark, Charlie; B. Garfield
Dark Shadows; Marilyn Ross
Darling, Kiss; J. Yardley
Darrell, Frank; S. Strand
Darren, Graham; A. Lenton
Darroch, Mike; A. MacKinnon
Darrow, Percy; S. E. White
Dartanian, Alex; R. Rainey
Dartley, Richard; I. Barclay
Darwin, Erasmus; C. Sheffield
Darzek, Jan; L. Biggle
Davenant, P. J.; F. S. Hamilton
Davenport, Lucas; J. Sandford
Davie, Dr.; V. C. Clinton-Baddeley
Davies, Bill; Sara Elizabeth Mason
Davies, Dangerous; L. Thomas
Davies, John; Margot Bennett
Davis, John George; J. Ripley
Davis, Lisa; L. M. Waltch
Davison, Gilbert; R. J. Fletcher
Dawe, Archer; J. S. Fletcher
Dawlish, Patrick; G. Ashe
Dawson, Chief Insp.; B. Copplestone
Dax, Saturnin; M. Cumberland
Day, Julian; D. Wheatley
Dazaar; Nicholas Carter
Deacon, William; H. Brean
Deadly Force; M. Dixon
Dean, Garry; P. Whelton
Dean, Jeffrey; W. Warga
Dean, Marc; P. Buck
Dean, Paul; B. Francis
Dean, Samson; Mike Phillips
Deane, Robert; J. W. Vandercook
Deane, Sarah; J. S. Borthwick
Death, Dr.; Zorro
Death Merchant, The; J. Rosenberger
Death Squad; F. Colter
Decker, Bill; L. Treat
Decker, Paul; A. I. Albert
Decker, Paul; G. Hackforth-Jones
Decker, Peter; F. Kellerman
Decker, Tyger (Tygrus Gerald); A. Riefe
Dee, Judge; R. Van Gulik
Dee, Mr.; D. Cory
Deene, Carolus; L. Bruce
Deering, Insp./Supt.; Simon
Defenders, The; J. Ahern
Defenders, The; R. Fuller
Defoe, Chase; Deforest Day
de Gier, Detective; J. Van de Wetering
de Goede, Demosthenes H.; J. Lermina
DeGraaf, Dr. Garritt; B. D'Amato
de Grandin, Jules; Seabury Quinn
DeHavilland, Mr.; J. N. Chance
Dekker, Carl; C. Dekker
Dekker, Johnny; J. Dekker
Dekker, Josh; A. Webb
de la Bath, Hubert Bonisseur; J. Bruce
Delafield, Kate; K. V. Forrest
de Lancey, Marka; B. Frost
Delaney; B. Singer
Delaney, Al; T. B. Black
Delaney, Edward X.; Lawrence Sanders
Delaney, Joe; F. Archer
Delaroy, "Steeley"; W. E. Johns
Delaware, Alex; J. Kellerman
Delmasso; W. LeQueux
Delphond, Stanley; F. Halliday
Demarrest, Jack; R. L. Gerard
de Mazareen, Lady Molly; B. Orczy
Dempsey; J. Raymond
    Jack Savage
Dene, Dorcas; George R. Sims
Dene, Michael; G. Verner
Dene, Trevor; V. Williams
Denning, Ned; M. Sebastian
Dennison; A. Lassiter
Denson, John; R. Hoyt
Denton, Micky; F. Kane
Denton, Wat; Nicholas Carter
Department of Dead Ends; R. Vickers

Department of Unexplained Deaths; Derek Raymond
Derben, Insp. Frank; P. A. Foxall
de Richleau, Duke; D. Wheatley
de Rohan, Raoul; J. Graeme
de Rosny, Baron; S. Weyman
Derrick, Richard; H. B. M. Watson
De Sales, Francis; T. Boyle
de Silva; Jose; R. L. Fish
Desouza, Frank; F. Olbrich
d'Espinal, Harcourt; B. Healey
Destroyer, The; R. Sapir
    W. B. Murphy
Detroit Police Department; T. Logan
Deutsch, Richard; J. Christian
Deventer, Piet; J. R. L. Anderson
Deveraux; B. Granger
Devereaux, Johnny; J. Roeburt
Deveril, Peter; H. Innes
Deville, Rufus; J. Noy
Devlin, Brock; Scott Mitchell
Devlin, Liam; J. Higgins
Devlin, Timothy; B. Heatter
Devon, Michael; R. Pennington
Devore, Dennis; Dorothy Bennett
DeWitt, Manny; P. Rabe
Dewpond, D'Arcy; W. Slater
Dexter, Charles; J. Fredman
Diamond, Red; M. Schorr
Diavolo, Don; S. Towne
Dice, Commander Allan; Peter Hill
Dick, Magic; Old Sleuth
Dickerson, Joseph; E. K. Goldthwaite
Dickins, Insp. John; E. P. Oppenheim
Didier, Insp. Auguste; A. Myers
Diego, Lt.; V. Kelsey
di Ganzarello, Alexxandro; I. Drummond
Digburn, Howard; B. Sanders
Digby, Insp.; I. Wray
Digby, Athelstan; W. F. Harvey
Digger, The; W. B. Murphy
Di Gris, Slippery Jim; H. Harrison
Dilke, Matthew; L. Gutteridge
DiMarco, Jeff; D. M. Disney
Dime, Mike; B. Fantoni
Dimmock, Alfred; F. Russell
Dingle, James; G. Osborne
di Palma; Laura; L. Matera
Disbro, Gil; J. E. Martin
Disher, Will Scott
Ditteridge, Supt.; E. Ferrars
Dix, Constantine; B. Pain
Dixon; E. Wallace
Dixon, George; G. Dixon
    R. Edwards
    T. Willis
Dixon, Sgt. Joe; R. Wormser
Doan; N. Davis
Dobbins, P. C.; P. Froud
Dobbs, John; R. B. Saxe
Dobbs, Insp. Ronald; Christina Blake
Dodds, Septimus; Sutherland Scott
Docker, Insp.; H. Pink
"Dog"; A. Del Martia
    F. Harkon
Doight, Henry; B. Symons
Dolan, Brand; W. Fuller
D'Oliveres, D'Arcy; David Foster
Dollanganger, Cathy; V. C. Andrews
Dollanganger, Chris; V. C. Andrews
Dolling, Ursula; J. S. Clouston
Donahue, Lorna; Katharine Hill
Donan, Gil; M. P. Hood
Donavan, Paul; Carter Brown
Donelli, Joe; Sherryl Woods
Doner, Dan (DeeDee); F. Shay
Donnegan, Lt. Peter; D. Quick
Donoghue, Insp. Fabian; P. Turnbull
Donovan; W. LeQueux
Donovan; L. Parker
Donovan; J. Philips
Donovan, Barry; Steve Wright
Donovan, Dick; Dick Donovan
Donovan, Jeanne; M. R. Henderson

Donovan, Max; R. W. Nolan
Doome, Sheridan; S. Fisher
    S. Gould
Doowinkle, John; H. Klingsberg
Dormouse, The; Frank King
Dorrington, Horace; Arthur Morrison
Dortmunder, John; D. E. Westlake
Dougal, William; Andrew Taylor
Douglas, Brian; John Lee
Douglas, Catherine; S. Sheldon
Douglas, Michael; J. D. Forbes
Douglas, Micky; A. Infante
Dove, Fidelity; D. Durham
Dowling, Father Roger; R. McInerny
Downey, Corporal; J. B. Hendryx
Downs, Insp.; V. Sampson
Doyle, Matt; D. L. Gilbert
Doyle, Patrick Michael; A. Newell
Doyne, Dennis; C. Baines
Draco, Pete; Richard Foster
Dragnet; R. Deming
    D. Knight
    R. Tralins
    D. Vowell
Dragoon, Ransom; F. Diamond
Drake, Desmond; Sea-Lion
Drake, Dexter; E. Barker
Drake, Earl; Dan J. Marlowe
Drake, John; W. H. Baker
    W. A. Ballinger
    P. Leslie
    W. McNeilly
Drake, Simon; M. Maguire
Drake, Simon; H. Nielsen
Drake, Stephen; C. Wilcox
Drake, Steve; R. Ellington
Drakov, Anton; J. Winters
Draper, Carl; G. C. Dukes
Dreamer, The; W. M. Duncan
Drew, Adam; Virginia Hanson
Drew, James; W. Garrett
Drew, Sgt. Ronnie; F. Vivian
Drewer, Timothy; Hilary Landon
Drewry, Chief Insp.; N. Burnaby
Drex, Quentin; Gwyn Evans
Drexel, Michael; G. Usher
Dreyer; F. P. Wilson
Driffield, Sir Clinton; J. J. Connington
Drink, William; S. Finnegan
Driscoll, Clifford; W. L. DeAndrea
Driscoll, Stuff; R. King
Drost, Theodore; W. LeQueux
Drum, Chester; S. Marlowe
Drummond, Bulldog; G. Fairlie
    H. C. McNeile
    H. Reymond
Drury, Insp. Dennis; W. S. Sykes
Drury, Dynamite; L. P. Greene
Drury, Frank; P. Marlowe
Dryden, Ben; M. Hartmann
Du Cas, Insp.; H. Imbert-Terry
Duane, Stephen; J. L. Benton
Ducane, Kenneth; J. Bingham
DuCrane, Johnny; J. DuCrane
Dudley, Phyllis; R. A. Freeman
Duff, John; H. J. O'Higgins
Duff, MacDougal; C. Armstrong
Duffy, Insp./Supt.; N. Fitzgerald
Duffy, Nick; D. Kavanagh
Duggan, Bud; M. Geller
Duker, Casson; W. Mole
Du Lane, Lois; E. Saint
Dulcet, Dove; Christopher Morley
Duluth, Peter; P. Quentin
Dumas, Max; Carter Brown
Dumphry, Ernest; B. Pain
Dunbar, Cliff; W. Harriss
Dundas, Michael; V. Rath
Dundee, James F. "Bonnie"; Anne Austin
Dunjer; I. Haiblum
Dunlap, Constance; A. B. Reeve
Dunn, Dave; M. Avallone
Dunn, Jim; H. L. Nelson
Dunn, Micah; M. K. Shuman

Series Index

Dupin, C. Auguste; M. Brelich
    M. Harrison
    E. A. Poe
Dupuy, M.; Anthony Gilbert
Durell, Sam; E. S. Aarons
    W. B. Aarons
Durkin, Dan; A. M. Chase
Durkin, James; A. Stringer
Durston, John; W. LeQueux
Dust, Joe; P. Graaf
DuVivien, Johnny; N. Spain
Dwyer, Jack; E. Gorman
Dyer, Henry; R. H. Ring
Dyke, Toby; E. (X.) Ferrars
Dynes, Lathom; H. Robertson

Eady, Quentin; E. P. Thorne
Eagle Force; Dan Schmidt
Eagle, John; P. Edwards
Eagle, Ken; M. Geller
Eagles, Black; J. Lansing
Eason, Dr. Scott; D. Weeks
East, Floyd; C. Rushton
East, Mark; Hilda Lawrence
Easter, Bill; J. Blackburn
Easy, John; R. Goulart
Eddie, Crying; Donald MacKenzie
Eddison, Bob; M. Delving
Edwards, Jane Amanda; Charlotte Murray Russell
Egerton, Scott; Anthony Gilbert
Egg, Montague; D. L. Sayers
Egypt, Harry; D. Broun
Ehrengraf, Martin; L. Block
Eichord, Jack; Rex Miller
87th Precinct; E. McBain
Eisenberg, Aaron; P. Chase
Eldon, Bill; E. S. Gardner
Eliot, Charlotte; E. M. Filgate
Elizabeth; F. Kilpatrick
Elizalde, Lt. Felix; W. Marshall
Elk, Insp.; E. Wallace
Elliott, Maggie; E. A. Taylor
Ellis, Capt. Guy; G. E. Rochester
Ellis, Tony; R. P. Koehler
Ellison (Pitt), Charlotte; A. Perry
Elton, Fox; Ared White
Elver, Horace Augustus; G. Dilnot
Emerson, Amelia Peabody; Elizabeth Peters
Emery, Val; G. Dilnot
Emory, Jason; Kootz
Emp, Insp. H.; S. Horler
Enforcer, The; A. Sugar
England, Anthony; W. J. Elliott
Entwhistle, Ebbie; F. A. M. Webster
Epton, Rosa; M. Underwood
Equalizer; D. G. Deutsch
Erridge, Matt; A. M. Stein
Esposito, January; G. Dowling
Essex, Steve; S. Waldron
Eszterhazy, Dr.; A. Davidson
Evans, Insp.; R. W. Jones
Evans, Insp.; W. J. Makin
Evans, Educated; E. Wallace
Evans, Homer; Elliot Paul
Evans, Louisa; Jane Johnston
Evans, Michael; B. Graham
Everhard, Donald; P. Steward
Eversleigh, Peter; R. Goyne
Ewart, Edgar; A. E. Walter
Ewart, George; W. LeQueux
Executioner, The; D. Pendleton
    Jim Peterson
Expediter, The; P. Edwards
Eyes, Angel; W. B. Longley

Fable, Horatio; A. Bonnard
Face, Twisted; G. Davison
Fahy, Frank; V. Kelly
Faide, Major; H. Wade
Fair, Prosper; B. Atkey
Fairbanks, Hank; E. Dean
Fairfield, Peggy; E. S. Liddon
Fairr, Melville; M. Venning
Fairweather, Doran; Mollie Hardwick

Falco, Marcus Didius; Lindsey Davis
Falcon; J. Crozier
Falcon, Supt.; D. Yates
Falcon, The; D. Drake
Falconer, Geoffrey; W. LeQueux
Falkenstein, Jesse; L. Egan
Fan Tan; D. Dell
Fane, Martin & Richard; M. Halliday
Fang, Wu; Roland Daniel
Fanks, Octavius; F. Hume
Fannin, Harry; D. Markson
Fanshaw, Jim; M. Poole
Fansler, Kate; A. Cross
Fantomas; M. Allain
    P. Souvestre
Faraday, Matt; William Grant
Faraday, Micah; L. T. Meade
Faraday, Mike; B. Copper
Farne, Max; R. Butler
Faro, Insp. Jeremy; Alanna Knight
Farrant, Harry; Lord Gorell
Farrant, Michael; P. G. Larbalestier
Farrel, John; B. Hitchens
Farrel, Mike; Carter Brown
Farrell, Bruno; E. Mazzaro
Farrell, Johnny; J. Farrell
    H. Lugar
Farrow, Marcus Aurelius; Angus Ross
Farthing family; John Gardner
Fathers, Insp. Harry; D. W. Smith
Fatso, Dr.; J. Ruyle
Faulkner, Reggie; E. Snell
Faunce, John; M. E. Braddon
Featherstone, Monte; M. Gardner
Fedora, Johnny; D. Cory
Feiffer, Insp. Harry; W. Marshall
Fell, Gideon; J. D. Carr
Fellows, Fred; H. Waugh
Felse Family; E. Pargeter
    Ellis Peters
Feltham, Peter; B. Mather
Felton, Ray; John Marsh
Fen, Gervase; E. Crispin
Fenby, Insp.; R. Hull
Fenchurch, John; D. Fiske
Fender, Ludovic; P. Geddes
Fender, Martin; J. Sublett
Fenian, "Nails"; H. D. Steward
Fenn, Christopher; M. L. Stokes
Fennell, Geoff; E. P. Thorne
Fenner, Dave; J. H. Chase
Fenner, Jack; G. H. Coxe
Fenner, Maxwell; L. F. Booth
Fenton, Horace Spurgeon; J. T. Story
Fenton, Lawrie; M. Annesley
Fenwick, Sgt.; R. Batchelor
Ferenc, Dr.; Richard Savage
Ferguson, Detective; N. S. Lincoln
Fernand, Monsieur; B. Orczy
Ferne; J. N. Chance
Ferron, Les; D. Keene
Feston, Bernard; K. Fitzgerald
Ffellowes, Brigadier; S. E. Lanier
Fiddler; A. E. Maxwell
Field, Fabian; D. Donovan
Fielding, Henry Arthur; D. Sharp
Fielding, Kit; Dick Francis
Fillinger, Insp.; Paul McGuire
Finch, Insp.; J. Thomson
Finch, Martyn; P. Cleife
Finch, Septimus; M. Erskine
Finley, Peter; M. Lupica
Finnegan, John; N. Forrest
Finney, Mary; M. Head
Fire-Bomb Jack; Old Sleuth
Firebrace, Capt.; Seafarer
Firth, Ian; Ludovic Peters
Fish, Horace; B. Pain
Fisher, Horne; G. K. Chesterton
Fisher, Phryne; Kerry Greenwood
Fitzgerald, Ed; D. Flynn
Fitzgerald, Fiona; W. Adler
Fitzgerald, Homer; Charlotte Murray Russell
Fitzgerald, Kevin; T. Topor

Flack, Jeremy; J. Maske
Flagg, Insp.; J. Cassells
    W. M. Duncan
Flagg, Conan; M. K. Wren
Flagg, Steven; W. B. Day
Flagg, Webster; V. P. Johns
Flamm, Greg; I. Wilson
Flannery, Jimmy; Robert Campbell
Flatchley, John; J. McCulley
Flecheux, Robert; Demouzon
Fleck, Peter; R. Clapperton
Flecker, James; Josephine Pullein-Thompson
Fleming, Insp.; J. Cameron
Fleming, Jack; P. N. Elrod
Fleming, Roger; S. Harvester
Fletch; G. McDonald
Fletcher, Irwin M.; G. McDonald
Fletcher, Jessica; J. Anderson
    Jessica Fletcher
Fletcher, Johnny; F. Gruber
Fletcher, Norman Stanley; Jonathan Marshall
    Paul Victor
Fletcher, Stephen; G. Davison
Fletcher, Virgil; G. P. Cronin
Flick, Robert; J. Ehrlich
Flicker, Gil; E. J. Millward
Flint, Artemus; B. Goldsweig
Flint, Phineas; C. Walk
Flique, Anatole; C. G. Booth
Flower, Insp.; Moira Field
Flush, Clifford; P. Branch
Flute, Adam; D. Launay
Flynn; E. Flower
Flynn, M. Newton
Flynn, Capt.; E. L. Long
Flynn, Francis Xavier; G. McDonald
Flynn, Terry; Joe Gash
    B. Granger
Flynn, Xavier; J. Braine
Folly, Supt.; J. York
Fontaine, Danny; W. Ard
Fontaine, Solange; F. T. Jesse
Fontana, Sheriff Mac; E. W. Emerson
Force; J. Decker
Force, Check; Ralph Hayes
Force, Counter; G. Wilson
Force, Eagle; Dan Schmidt
Force Five; J. Rovin
Ford, Alan; Carolyn Wells
Ford, Ashton; D. Pendleton
Ford, Brad; Hank Hobson
Fordingham, Brian; S. Horler
Fordney, Professor; A. Ripley
Forge, Barney; R. Starnes
Forrest, Dan; W. Beechcroft
Forrester, Michael; F. S. Wees
Forsythe, Robert; E. X. Giroux
Fortescue, John; C. Brandon
Fortune, Chester; T. H. Stone
Fortune, Dan; Michael Collins
Fortune, Hannibal; L. Maddock
Fortune, Reggie; H. C. Bailey
Fortune, Temple; T. C. H. Jacobs
Fortune's Friends; K. Reynolds
Fosse, Guy; E. Cannon
Foster, Insp.; Anonymous
Foster, Harry; A. Cullimore
Four Just Men; E. Wallace
Fowler, Barney; M. D. Pohlman
Fowler, Dan; G. F. Eliot
Fowler, Grant; P. Richards
Fowler, Timothy; C. Harris
Fowlkes, Freddie; G. M. Bowman
Fox, Paul; D. Mounce
Fox, Tecumseh; R. Stout
Fox, Supt. Tommy; G. Ison
Foy, Supt. Francis; Lionel Black
Fraleigh, Sgt. Finnbar; J. D. McNamara
Frame, Reynold; H. Brean
Frampton, Andrew; T. A. Plummer
Franck, Cesar Augustus; A. M. Pyle
Francois; S. W. Mitchell
Frankenstein; D. F. Glut
    M. W. Shelley

F

F

Franklin, Alton Benjamin "Rooster"; Randy Russell
Franklin, Ev; F. Orenstein
Franklin, Margo; J. Jenkins
Frant, Arabella; D. Fearon
Fraser, Alan; H. Desmond
Fraser, Geoffrey; Elliot Bailey
Fraser, James; J. Wood
Frass; J. Chancellor
Frayne, Ambrose and Dominque; J. T. McIntosh
Frazer, Tim; F. Durbridge
Frederickson, Robert; G. Chesbro
Freedman, Benny; M. Bass
Freeman, John; J. Ironside
Freeman, Jub; L. Treat
Freer, Virginia; E. Ferrars
French, Alan; J. Gollin
French, Bill; C. Hale
French, Joseph; F. W. Crofts
Frend, Max; B. Chetwynd
Frere, Royston; W. J. Elliott
Friedman, Kinky; K. Friedman
Friendly, Abe; R. Neely
Frost, Insp.; H. Maynard Smith
Frost, Gerald; S. Horler
Frost, Hank; A. Kilgore
Frost, Henry; Josephine Bell
Frost, Jack; R. Wingfield
Frost, Reuben; Haughton Murphy
Fry, Pete; P. Fry
Fu Manchu; S. Rohmer
    C. Van Ash
Furling, Richard; F. Grierson
Furneaux, Insp.; G. Holmes
    L. Tracy
Furnival, Insp.; A. Haynes
Furnival, Matthew; S. Phillips
Furnivall; G. Butler
Fury, Jackson; C. Jerina
Fusil, Insp.; P. Alding
Fyles, Sgt./Insp.; R. Cullum
Fyodorov, Yuri; Gayle Stone
    D. Unkefer

G-8; R. J. Hogan
Gabriel, Vic; Dan Schmidt
Gaden, Supt.; P. H. Powell
Gaffney, Supt. John; G. Ison
Gail and Mitch; Gordons
Gail, John; S. D. Frances
Gaines, Vicky; F. Diamond
Galbreath, D.A. Carey; W. McCully
Gale, Gabriel; G. K. Chesterton
Gale, Simon; G. Verner
Gall, Joe; P. Atlee
    J. A. Phillips
Gallagher, Gale; G. Gallagher
Gallagher, Gordon; J. J. Savarin
Gallyon, Gale; R. Buxton
    S. Gordon
Galt; J. Gollomb
Galt, Jason; M. Lovell
Galt, Oliver; V. France
Gamadge, Clara; E. Boylan
Gamadge, Henry; E. Daly
Gamble, Charlie; D. Matheson
Gane, Paul; M. Woodman
Gannon, Mike; D. Ballenger
Gant, Michael; C. Thomas
Gantian, Colonel; C. Dawe
Gants; R. Abshire
Gantt, Barney; J. S. Strange
Gard, Billy; W. A. Dupuy
Garde, Vance; J. La Plante
Garden, Ben; T. Pace
Garfield, Mr.; F. R. Buckley
Garfield, Grant; C. Franklin
Garfield, Lucas; Frank Ross
Garfin, Mike; Martin Brett
Garnett, Insp.; R. Philmore
Garnett, David; C. Egleton
Garnish, Harry; F. McConnell
Garratt, Frank; P. Wentworth
Garrett; Glen Cook

Garrett, Barney; D. Franklin
Garrett, Charles; Frederick Nolan
Garrett, Colin; G. Brandner
Garrett, Henry; G. D. Larsen
Garrett, Mike; R. Blaine
Garrison, Roger; J. Rovin
Garrison, Victor; D. Kirby
Garrity, Tony; Allan Nixon
Garroway, Pete; P. Garroway
    G. Usher
Garson; E. Raskin
Garstang; R. A. J. Walling
Garth; W. Camp
Garth, Insp.; H. Blayn
    M. Karta
Garton, Joe; G. Hackforth-Jones
Gates, Ben; R. Kyle
Gates, Carol; L. Colburn
Gault, Captain; W. H. Hodgson
Gaunt, Jonathan; Robert MacLeod
Gaunt, Michael; G. Braddon
Gautier, Insp. Jean-Paul; Richard Grayson
Gavin, Rod; John Quinn
Gaylord, Supt.; W. M. Duncan
Gently, Insp./Supt.; A. Hunter
Gently, Dirk; Douglas Adams
George, Edwin; C. A. Goodrum
Gerard; A. C. Doyle
Gerard, Phillip; J. Dentinger
Gerber, Mack; E. Helm
Gerson, Keith; J. Vance
Gethryn, Anthony; P. MacDonald
Ghent, Insp.; B. Francis
Ghost, The; R. B. Saxe
Ghote, Insp. Ganesh; H. R. F. Keating
Gibbon, Insp.; Barbara Cooper
Gibbons, Bert; A. Bruno
Gibson, Christopher; I. Montgomery
Gibson, Glen; J. Bentley
Gibson, Henry; D. MacKail
Gibson, Jeremiah X. "Gibby"; Hampton Stone
Gideon, Commander George; W. V. Butler
    J. Creasey
    J. J. Marric
Gidleigh, Insp.; S. Truss
Gifford, Adam; A. Lejeune
Gilchrist; L. T. Meade
Gilead, Justin; W. B. Murphy
Gilette, Jenny; E. Gresham
    R. Grey
Gill; N. Morland
Gill, Eve; S. Jepson
Gillard, Patrick; M. Duffy
Gilles, M.; J. Decrest
Gilliant, Supt.; J. Wainwright
Gilly, Mr.; W. M. Duncan
Gilmartin, Supt. Lawrence; C. Barry
Gimblet, Mr.; Mrs. C. Bryce
Girl from H.A.R.D.; J. Moffatt
Girl from U.N.C.L.E.; M. Avallone
    S. Latter
    P. Leslie
Girland, Mark; J. H. Chase
Glauberman, Alex; Dick Cluster
Glencannon, Mr.; G. Gilpatric
Glendower, Tobias; M. Arnold
Glenne, Al; M. G. Braun
Glenning, Paula; Anna Clarke
Glick, Murray; M. J. Katz
Gloom, Insp.; Frank King
Glover, Insp.; M. Evermay
Glover, Insp.; L. Lamb
Glover, Derek; S. C. Mason
Glowery, Prof. James; A. Lejeune
Godbold, Insp.; B. Bolt
Goddin, Haggai; O. John
Godfrey, Jim; B. E. Stevenson
Godwin, Cynthia; G. Beare
Gold, Alexander; H. Resnicow
Gold, Marty; M. Kaye
Gold, Lt. Max; O. R. Cohen
Gold, Lt. Ronnie; G. Paulsen
Golden, Sammy; Jack Webb

Goldstein, Sgt. Jay; Marilyn Wallace
Good, Carl; R. O. Saber
Good, Simon; George Davis
Goodey, Joe; C. Alverson
Goodwin, Archie; R. Goldsborough
    R. Stout
Gordon, Alison; W. Wager
Gordon, Ben; I. T. Ross
Gordon, Chet; K. Millar
Gordon, Ellie; K. Berne
Gordon, Insp. Hugh; S. Gilruth
Gordon, Lindsay; V. McDermid
Gordon, Yudel; W. Ebersohn
Gore, Colonel Wyckham; L. Brock
Gorgon, Eddie; R. Hausfeld
Gorham, Insp.; J. Cowdroy
Gorman, Butch; R. E. Howard
Gorodish, Serge; Delacorta
Gorse, Ernest Ralph; P. Hamilton
Goss, Nathaniel; C. Willock
Gossett, Malcolm; E. P. Oppenheim
Gotch, Shark; A. R. Wetjen
Goulburn, Richard; J. S. Fletcher
Gould, Bart; J. Hilton
    J. Milton
Gould, Harry; R. Obstfeld
Gould, Skipper; R. Kalish
Grady, Lt. Bill; I. S. Shriber
Grafton, Jake; S. Coonts
Graham, Angel; Richard Russell
Graham, Davina; E. Anthony
Graham, Kate; J. Arliss
Graham, Peter; B. Thompson
Graham, Richard; J. Welcome
Grainger, Supt. Paul; F. Sinclair
Gramport, Insp.; G. Barnett
Granby, Colonel; F. Beeding
Grandison, Capt; B. Bolt
Grant, Alan; G. Daviot
    J. Tey
Grant, Basil; G. K. Chesterton
Grant, Casey; D. Rico
Grant, Celia; J. Sherwood
Grant, David; G. B. Mair
Grant, Dean; R. W. Walker
Grant, Douglas; F. N. Millar
Grant, Duncan; G. Seton
Grant, Harry; B. Freeborn
Grant, Laurie; M. MacKintosh
Grant, Michael; Roland Daniel
    C. Thomas
Grant, Patrick; M. Yorke
Grant, Rupert; G. K. Chesterton
Grant, Sam; J. Pattinson
Grant, Victor; J. B. Ethan
Granville, Clive; M. McKenna
Graves, Insp.; W. J. Makin
Gray; D. Cory
Gray, Insp.; P. Piper
Gray, Colin; M. Channing
Gray, Cordelia; P. D. James
Gray, Linda; D. Cory
Gray, Michael; H. Kuttner
Gray, Lt. Vern; E. Lanham
Graydon, Kendal; H. E. Wheeler
Grayle, Barnaby; W. W. Sayer
Grayleigh, Peter; Colin Robertson
Grayling, Lester; L. J. Lynwood
Great Merlini, The; C. Rawson
Greaves, Emma; Lionel Black
Green, Gregory George Gordon; J. Mann
Green, Horatio; B. Nichols
Green, Jeff; C. Keith
Green, Kelly; L. Starr
Green, Noah; N. Hentoff
Greene, "Tubby"; R. Goyne
Greenfield, C. B.; L. Kallen
Greenleaf, Mr.; H. O. Yardley
Greensleeves; W. M. Duncan
Greenway, Lt. Claude; L. S. Thompson
Greer, James; N. Gayle
Gregg, Avery; R. P. Koehler
Gregory, Miss; P. Gibbon

Gregory, Dan; L. Jamieson
Gregory, Scott; R. Stratton
Gresham, Hubert; J. F. Fraser
Gretton, Beverley; H. Cadett
Grey, Colwin; A. J. Rees
Grey, Jennifer; J. Jenkins
Grey, Roman; Martin Smith
Grey, Scout; R. L. Bellamy
Grey Shadow; G. E. Robinson
Greybreek; A. MacVicar
Griddle, L. F. "Scoop"; T. Polsky
Grierson, Insp.; H. J. Wurr
Grierson, David; I. Stuart
Griffin, Hamo; W. Hawes
Grigson, Denzil; A. Broome
Grijpstra, Detective; J. Van de Wetering
Grisman, Saul; D. Morrell
Grist, Simon; T. Hallinan
Grofield, Alan; R. Stark
Grogan, Insp.; M. Neville
Groode, Mr.; G. Griswold
Gross, Sam; J. P. Wohl
Grundt, Adolph; D. Valentine
    V. Williams
Gryce, Ebenezer; A. K. Green
Guardians, The; P. Saxon
Guarnaccia, Marshal; M. Nabb
Gubb, Philo; E. P. Butler
Guelpa, Mr.; V. Thompson
Guild, Leo; E. Gorman
Guinness, Ray; N. Guild
Guiu, Lonia; M.-A. Oliver
Gull, Vladimer; Anthony Stuart
Gulliver, Insp.; G. Burnett
Gunner, Aaron; G. A. Haywood
Gunning, Ed; W. J. Elliott
Gunther, Bernhard; Philip Kerr
Gunther, Lt. Joe; A. Mayor
Guttman, Max; A. D. Goldstein
Guy, Brian; J. Ridgway
Guzman, Felix; Peg Case

Haden, Stephen; N. J. Crisp
Hagee, Jack; C. J. Henderson
Haggerty, Leo; B. M. Schutz
Haham, David; C. A. Haddad
Haig, Alec; A. Haig
Haig, "Digger"; S. H. Courtier
Haig, Leo; L. Block
    C. Harrison
Haig, Tubby; Anonymous
Hailey, Eustace; A. Wynne
Hale, Jim; R. Knotts
Hale, Max; G. H. Coxe
Hale, Max; K. Sandford
Haledjian, Dr.; D. J. Sobol
Hales, Ann; M. Ingate
Halifax, Dr.; L. T. Meade
Hall, Satan; C. J. Daly
Hall, "Tubby"; P. Hambledon
Hallam, Anthony; R. J. Buckley
Hallam, Lucas; L. J. Washburn
Hallan, Insp.; George Douglas
Haller, Mike; M. Byrd
Halleran, Charlie; G. Gottesfeld
Halley, Sid; D. Francis
Halliday, David; H. Baldwin Taylor
Halliday, Willie; M. Fredman
Halloran; D. Gethin
Halloran, Meg; J. La Pierre
Halsey, Mick; C. Martell
Halstead, Arthur; W. E. Hayes
Hambledon, Rupert; J. Dellbridge
Hambledon, Tommy; M. Coles
Hamel, Neil; J. Van Gieson
Hamill, Cub; D. McCaig
Hamilton, Anthony; F. Frost
Hamilton, Gil; L. Niven
Hamm, Steve; H. Bostrom
Hammer, Mike; M. Spillane
Hammond, Crane; F. Carmichael
Hanard, Richard; V. Beynon-Harris
Hanaud, Insp.; A. E. W. Mason

Hand, Christopher; S. H. Page
Handyman, The; J. Messmann
Hanks, Arly; Joan Hess
Hanlon, George; E. E. Evans
Hanlon, Red; Mollie Merrick
Hannasyde, Supt.; G. Heyer
Hannay, Richard; J. Buchan
    J. Smithers
Hannegan, Edge; B. E. Lovell
Hannibal, Joe; W. D. Dundee
Hanvey, Jim; O. R. Cohen
Harald, Lt. Sigrid; M. Maron
Harald, Simon; J. Welcome
Hard Corps; C. Bainbridge
Hardin, Bart; David Alexander
Hardin, Mark; L. Derrick
Harding, Prof.; H. H. Morrell
Harding, Derek; M. Worth
Hardman, Jim; Ralph Dennis
Hardy, Bren; W. J. Elliott
Hardy, Cliff; P. Corris
Hardy, Patrick; Martin Meyers
Harker; N. Hollander
Harker, Hawthorne Albert; M. Olden
Harkness, William; M. Warrick
Harland, John; R. Foley
Harland, Robert; B. F. Robinson
Harlequin, George; M. L. West
Harley, John; A. Tack
Harley, Paul; S. Rohmer
Harman, Mike; J. M. Walsh
Harmas, Steve; J. H. Chase
Harmon, Prof. Robert; R. Elman
Harpe, Angela; James D. Lawrence
Harper; M. Aylward
Harper, Bill; P. Ernst
Harper, Stephen; Walter C. Brown
Harpur, Insp. Colin; Bill James
Harragan, Steve; S. Harragan
Harrigan; P. O'Malley
Harrigan, Tex; A. Derleth
Harrington Convent; E. Shepherd
Harris, Abbie; A. Dean
Harris, Jim and Kate; T. MacRae
Harris, Leonard; R. Keverne
Harris, Paul; G. Black
Harris, Sam; M. Cronin
Harrison, Clay; Clifton Robins
Harrison, Rick; J. Stacy
Harrison, Steve; R. E. Howard
Harrow, Insp.; Shipley Adams
Harry, Dirty; D. Hartman
    W. Morgan
    P. Rock
    J. Stinson
    M. Valley
Harry-O; L. Hays
Hart, Jonathan and Jennifer; R. Bowdler
Hart, Stephen; J. Barton
Harter; John Douglas
Hartley, Hashknife; W. C. Tuttle
Hartley, James; N. Vane
Hartley, Roger; George Ellinger
Harty, Cass; J. Y. Dane
Harvard, Bingham; V. Vanardy
Harvard, Paul; C. H. Gibbs-Smith
Harvester, Steve; J. M. Fox
Harvey; D. Hurd
Haskell, Insp.; W. Sutherland
Haskell, Ellie Simons; D. Cannell
Haskell, Vejay; S. Dunlap
Hassett, Ben; H. De Hamel
Hastings, Bill and Coco; L. G. Offord
Hastings, Lt. Frank; B. Pronzini
    C. Wilcox
Hastings, Jefferson; J. Hay
Hastings, Jimmy; C. G. Givens
Hastings, Stanley; Parnell Hall
Haswell, Jimmie; H. Adams
Hatch, Cyrus; Frederick C. Davis
Hatch, Jake; Robert Campbell
Hatcher, Amos; O. Banks
Hatcher, Frank; D. Merritt

Hatfield, Prof. Paul; S. Rogers
Havilland, Antony; V. Gielgud
Havoc, Johnny; J. Jakes
Hawaii Five-O; M. Avallone
    H. Harris
Hawk, Michael; D. Streib
Hawk, Nathan; B. McKnight
Hawk, Street; J. Roberts
Hawke, Dixon; Anonymous
    J. Creasey
Hawke, Matt; C. Cunningham
Hawkehurst, Valentine; M. E. Braddon
Hawker, James; C. Ramm
Hawkes, A. B. C.; Ephesian
Hawkins, J. D.; W. R. Philbrick
Hawkins, Tony; H. Harrison
Hawks, Joaquin; B. S. Ballinger
Hawks, Star; R. Goulart
Hawthorne, Nimue; G. Linscott
Haydon, Stuart; D. L. Lindsey
Hayduke, George; E. Abbey
Hayes, Father; P. Leslie
Hayes, Judith; A. Porter
Hayes, Julia; D. S. Davis
Hayes, Lee; E. Lacy
Haygarth School; Jack North
Haynes, Sherwood; J. Symons
Hazard, Bill; P. Marlowe
Hazard, Eric; L. Crosby
Hazell, James; P. B. Yuill
Hazell, Thorpe; V. L. Whitechurch
Hazelrigg, Insp.; M. Gilbert
Hazzard; R. Keverne
Hazzard, Cheney; R. D. Brown
Head, Insp.; E. C. Vivian
Head, Norman; L. T. Meade
Headcorn, Insp.; A. Campbell
Headhunters, The; J. Weisman
Headley, Insp.; T. B. Morris
Heald, Max; H. Hossent
Hearne, Bunjy; T. Craig
Heath, Jennifer; A. Tyler
Heather, Arthur; W. LeQueux
Hedley, Marshall; F. A. Fawkes
Hedley, Paul; B. Healey
Heffernan (or Hefferman), Hooky; L. Meynell
Heimrich, Merton; F. & R. Lockridge
    R. Lockridge
    R. & F. Lockridge
Heine; E. Wallace
Heldar, Sally & Johnny; H. Hamilton
Heller, Carl; F. Roderus
Heller, Jesse; D. Kellerman
Heller, Nate; M. A. Collins
Hellier, James; M. Cronin
Helm, Ben; B. Fischer
Helm, Matt; D. Hamilton
Hemingway, Clarence E.; J. Maske
Hemlock, Jonathan; Trevanian
Hemmingway, Insp.; G. Heyer
Hemyock, Maurice; D. G. Browne
Henderson, Insp.; C. Barling
    P. Barrington
Henley, Jack; S. Kay
Hennings, Rachel; J. L. Breen
Henry, Ben; M. Weiss
Henry, George Herbert; J. Sharkey
Henry, Gil; C. W. Grafton
Henry, Kate; Alison Gordon
Henry, Rush; Joe Barry
Henshaw, Susan; V. Wolzien
Hepburn, Maurice; Lord Gorell
Hern, Rowland; N. Olde
Hero, Alexander; P. Gallico
Hero, Pepperoni; B. Kelly
Heron, Felix; G. Verner
Heron, Patrick; C. Brogan
Herring, Timothy; M. Torrie
Herrivell, Richard; J. Bentley
Herron, Julia; P. Cheyney
Hetherege, Millicent; R. Bernard
Hetzel, Miro; J. Vance
Hewes-Bradford, Barrington; A. Hamilton

H

Hewitt, Jefferson; J. Reese
Hewitt, Martin; Arthur Morrison
Heysen, Pete; I. Hamilton
Higgins, Cuthbert; C. F. Gregg
Higgins, Matthew; Means Davis
Highway; Garnett Weston
Hildreth, Lady Jane; M. Spicer
Hill, Asmun; H. Hawton
Hill, Dave; B. Adkins
Hill, Sgt. Judy; J. McGown
Hillary, Charles; F. McGrew
Hiller, Gregory; Jack Laflin
Hillsden, Alec; B. Forbes
Hiscock, Insp.; Jeremy Potter
Hite, Quinny; R. Burke
Hitman, The; K. Ross
Hitman, The; N. Winski
Hoag, Stewart; D. Handler
Hobbs, Sgt.; Michael Lewis
Hockney, Robert; A. De Borchgrave
Hodson, Mr.; Margaret Bidwell
Hoeffler; P. O'Malley
Hogg, Miss; A. Lee
Hoggerty, Gentle; Griff
    B. Sarto
Hogget, Ron; James Mitchell
Holden, David; J. Ahern
Holden, Nikki; E. R. Chase
Holderly Hall; K. Cameron
Holland, Mark; P. Myers
Holliday, Felix; Arthur E. Jones
Holliday, Hiram; P. Gallico
Holly, Insp.; R. Postgate
Holman, Rick; Carter Brown
Holmes, Bill; G. F. Hughes
Holmes, Creighton; N. Hubell
Holmes, J. Zinsheimar; H. Kellock
Holmes, Sherlock; Val Andrews
    A. Arnold
    S. Benady
    D. R. Bensen
    R. H. Bibolet
    L. Biggle, Jr.
    Joellen Bland
    R. L. Boyer
    Clive Brooks
    R. A. Brown
    T. Bullimore
    A. Burgess
    P. H. Cannon
    J. D. Carr
    D. Charlton
    S. K. Chettur
    J. S. Clouston
    M. Creighton
    M. D'Agneau
    M. Dibdin
    C. N. Douglas
    Adrian Conan Doyle
    Arthur Conan Doyle
    W. E. Dudley
    D. Dvorkin
    L. D. Estleman
    M. Fantina
    L. Feuer
    C. Fischer
    C. Fisher
    J. Forster
    B. Forsythe
    G. Frow
    L. Garland
    W. Gillette
    P. Giovanni
    G. Gooden
    G. Gravatt
    O. Gray
    K. Greenwald
    L. B. Greenwood
    R. L. Hall
    L. Halliwell
    D. L. Hammer
    Michael Hardwick
    M. Harrison
    P. Hartley
    J. Hershey
    J. A. Hitt
    M. P. Hodel
    G. R. Holms
    J. C. Iraldi
    M. Jaffee
    H. P. Jeffers
    K. Jones
    T. J. Kelly
    M. Kurland
    M. Lambe
    W. Lane
    J. T. Lescoart
    F. A. Leslie
    G. Lientz
    H. A. Litzinger
    B. MacNamara
    B. Majeski
    R. Mallett
    C. Marowitz
    L. A. Matthias
    R. Mauro
    N. Meyer
    T. K. Miller
    A. Mitchelson
    Roberts Morgan
    T. Mustoo
    C. Muusmann
    J. Nassivera
    J. North
    A. Nowlan
    G. Nown
    S. Palmer
    J. Paul
    G. Pearlman
    R. Pearsall
    E. L. Pearson
    G. Petrie
    R. Piercy
    M. Powell
    E. Queen
    C. Redmond
    F. Richardson
    E. C. Roberts
    S. C. Roberts
    D. Rosa
    P. Ryan
    F. Saberhagen
    J. Shakley
    A. Sharp
    L. Sharp
    Stanley Shaw
    F. Sherrod
    D. O. Smith
    G. H. Smith
    R. Smullyan
    V. Starrett
    D. Stashower
    A. M. Stokes
    F. Thomas
    M. J. Trow
    N. Utechin
    C. Van Ash
    R. Vaughn
    R. Walsh
    A. C. Ward
    J. Watson
    M. W. Wellman
    R. C. Weyman
    R. Wincor
Holmes, William; C. V. Bark
Holt, Essington; Robert Wallace
Holt, Samuel; S. Holt
Holton, Paul; Charlotte Hunt
Homberg, Julia; S. Gainham
Homes, Schlock; R. L. Fish
Homes, Shylock; J. K. Bangs
Homes, Stately; A. Porges
Honegger, George; J. S. Strange
Honeybath, Charles; M. Innes
Hood, Adam; N. Rich
Hood, Charles; J. Mayo
Hood, Mark; James Dark
Hook, The; B. Latham
Hook, Insp.; Gret Lane
Hook, Sam; H. T. Teilhet
    M. Tolman
Hope, Matthew; E. McBain
Hopkins, Sgt.; V. Sampson
Hopkins, John; Roland Daniel
Hopkins, Sgt. Lloyd; J. Ellroy
Hopton, Insp.; J. C. Woodiwiss
Horn, Max; B. Sloane
Horne, Charles; W. Tucker
Horne, Harry; J. Gonzales
Horne, Lewis; M. Molloy
Hornsley, Michael; E. Salter
Horoscope, Ptolemy; Anonymous
Horrocks, Mr.; C. J. C. Hyne
Horton; L. Butler
Horwitz, Lt. Jacob; D. Delman
Hoskins, Insp. Sam; R. Dacre
Houghton, Bill; M. Culpan
Houston, Sam; E. S. De Puy
Howard, Anthony; H. McCutcheon
Howard, Kent; Kent Howard
Howard, Roz; S. Kenney
Howard, Russell; A. E. Jobson
Howard, Tom; Tom Howard
Howden, John; W. Mills
Howe, Larry; Eugene Franklin
Hoyland, Mr.; P. C. Williams
Hoyland, Tamara; Jessica Mann
Hubbard, Mike; M. Seuffert
Hudson; T. A. Fraser
Huff, Percy Aloysius; C. Edwards
Huggins, Barney; M. Shelley
Hughes, Elwyn; D. W. F. Hardie
Hughes, Matt; Aylwin Lee Martin
Hughes, Nora; L. R. Davis
Hugo, John; A. Green
Huish, Martin; S. Horler
Hull, Sara; J. R. Piggin
Humble, Mr.; F. Bunce
Humbleby, Insp.; E. Crispin
Hume, Hampton; B. Bird
Hume, Laurie; W. M. Duncan
Hume, Morris; William Robertson
Hunt, Elsie Mae; A. M. Stein
Hunt, Frederick; Lillian Day
Hunt, Lucius; J. Wellard
Hunt, Seth; M. O. Rolfe
Hunter, The; Ralph Hayes
Hunter, Adam; N. Conway
Hunter, Bounty; W. Boyles
Hunter, Ed & Am; F. Brown
Hunter, Max; W. T. Ballard
Hunter, Nazi; M. Mandell
Hunter, Pete; A. A. Marcus
Hunter, Philip; M. Procter
Hunter, Robert Lee; E. Sauter
Hunter, Sam; L. A. Morse
Hunter, Tony; R. G. Dean
Hunters, The; P. Tabori
Huntington, Colin; G. Condon
Hussy, Joe; C. Dunne
Huuygens, Kek; R. L. Fish
Hyde, Anne; A. S. Swan
Hyde, Barney; N. Brent
Hyde, John Byron; B. Wolff
Hyde, John George Norman; J. Boland
Hyer, Hank; K. Steel

I Spy; J. Tiger
Iceman; J. Nazel
Iff, Simon; A. Crowley
Ike, Nimble; Old Sleuth
Illusionist, The; J. P. Radford
Inch, Insp. John; J. Templeton
Inch, Johnny; J. F. Straker
Indermill, Bonnie; C. Berry
Ingelram, Raymond; G. Household
Ingram; A. Michaelis
Ingram, John; C. Williams
Inman, Tommy; Martha Webb
Inquisitor, The; Simon Quinn
Invaders, The; Rafe Bernard
    K. Laumer

P. Leslie
Irish, Jeremiah; N. Child
Iron Burgess; Old Sleuth
Ironside; J. Thompson
Irving, Paul; L. Grex
Irving, Rip; O. Mills
Iskirlak, Nuri; Joan Fleming
Israeli Commandos; A. Sugar
It Takes a Thief; G. Brewer
Ivorsen, Eric; R. Spencer
Ixell, Baron; O. Schisgall

J, Anna; P. Swan
Jacara; V. Norwood
Jack, Captain; M. Pemberton
Jack the Juggler; Old Sleuth
Jacks, Wilton; J. H. Wallis
Jackson, Ed; Nora Roberts
Jackson, Insp. John Jay "Jailbird"; D. T. Lindsay
Jackson, Juliet; M. Turnbull
Jackson, Kane; W. Arden
Jackson, William; W. B. Murphy
Jacobs, Callista; K. L. Knight
Jacoby, Miles; R. J. Randisi
Jacoby, Quentin; J. C. S. Smith
Jacovich, Milan; Les Roberts
Jaeger, Curt; M. Mandell
Jagedinski, Anna; P. Swan
Jagger, Mick; W. Garner
Jaggers; J. Templer
James, Insp.; R. Bax
James, Harry; K. Giles
James, Jesse; W. B. Lawson
James, Jessica; M. O'Brien
James, Mike; Denis Scott
Jameson, Cass; C. Wheat
Jamison, J. J.; L. A. Taylor
Janaki; K. Sathianadhan
Janson, Hank; H. Janson
Jansson, Willa; L. Matera
Jantarro, John Kenneth Galbraith; S. Ritchie
Jardino, Robbie; N. Singer
Jarnegan; C. Moran
Jarrett, Rev. Jabal; F. Bream
Jasen, Commodore; E. P. Oppenheim
Jason; J. N. Chance
Jason; Jason
Jason, Alex; A. Sugar
Jason, Julius; A. Hope
Jat, Captain; W. H. Hodgson
Jaxon, Wood; M. S. Michel
Jaz, Doctor; M. Vivian
Jazine, Earl; E. D. Hoch
Jeffrey, Arthur; H. K. Webster
Jellipot, Mr.; S. Fowler
Jenkins, Joe; P. Rosenhayn
Jenkyn, Matthew; P. C. Doherty
Jenner, Jimmy; J. Milne
Jennerton; E. P. Oppenheim
Jensen, Lt. Christopher; L. Langley
Jensen, Peter; P. Wahloo
Jeremy, John; Jeffrey Montague
Jericho, John; H. Pentecost
Jerningham, Peter; I. B. Meyers
Joey; Joey
Johnson, Insp.; D. Batchelor
Johnson, Coffin Ed; C. Himes
Johnson, Helen; E. Dewhurst
Johnson, Johnson; D. Halliday
Johnson, Dr. Sam; L. de la Torre
Johnson, Steve; H. L. Nelson
Johnson, Wellaby; O. Booth
Jolivet, Insp.; J. Shepherd
Jolly, Sgt.; David Fletcher
Jolson, Ben; R. Goulart
Joly; A. S. Hardy
Jones, Barnabas; M. L. Stokes
Jones, Cleopatra; R. Goulart
Jones, Glyn; G. Osborne
Jones, Grave Digger; C. Himes
Jones, Guinevere; Jayne Castle
Jones, Jason; K. F. Crossen
Jones, Jupiter; T. Fuller
Jones, Liberty; M. McCracken
Jones, Morocco; J. Baynes
Jones, Pine-Top; J. T. Story
Jones, Russell; M. Mundy
Jones, Samuel; V. G. Mathison
Jones, Tom; A. Puckett
Jones, Zachary; H. Steirman
Jonquelle, Monsieur; M. D. Post
Jonson, Ben; P. Levi
Jordan; L. Butler
Jordan, Dan; Harlan Reed
Jordan, Jack; William Du Bois
Jordan, Marc; R. M. Laurenson
Jordan, Scott; H. Q. Masur
Jorkens, Joseph; Lord Dunsany
Journey, Jack; J. R. Nash
Jow, Jonathan; W. J. Makin
Joyce, Michael; L. Cornell
Judd, Clinton; L. Goldman
Judd for the Defense; L. Goldman
Judd, George; E. Bruton
Judd, Humphrey; V. L. Whitechurch
Jugg, Jack; D. Suddaby
Jurnet, Insp. Ben; S. T. Haymon
Jury, Insp. Richard; M. Grimes
Justice, Capt. John Valcourt; A. Forrest
Justice, Peter; F. Duncan
Justice, William; J. Arnett
Justus, Jake & Helen; C. Rice
Jutt, Lavie; Marguerite Barclay

Kaine, Daniel & Jennifer; B. J. Hoff
Kale, Stephen; M. Jon
Kamus of Kadizar; J. M. Reaves
Kane, Insp.; R. Scarlett
Kane, Adam; W. R. Burnett
Kane, Andy; Carter Brown
Kane, Ben; N. Stone
Kane, Elias; S. G. Spruill
Kane, Martin; Kane
Kane, Sugar; L. Marshall
Kane, Tom; D. Jordan
Kao, Li; B. Hughart
Karemos, Helen; E. Zaremba
Karlov, Vladimer; Ralph Hayes
Karns, Joe; G. De Weese
Karp, Roger "Butch"; R. K. Tanenbaum
Kate, Lady; Anonymous
Kauffman, Insp. Max; T. Chastain
Kavanagh, Knock-Out; B. Stuart
Kay, Bromley; J. M. Walsh
Kaye, Simon; H. Waugh
Kearney, Daniel, Associates; J. Gores
Kearny, Max; R. Goulart
Keate, Sarah; M. G. Eberhart
Keaton, Kyra; T. Tone
Keats, Colin; V. B. Shore
Keeble, Magnus; A. Wood
Keefe, Michael; Michael Wolfe
Keegan; B. Ball
Keel, Daniel; T. A. Schock
Keen, Franklyn; H. Long
Keen, Gregory; L. Hardy
Keene, Arnold; Eric Wood
Keene, Max; R. O. Saber
Keene, Oliver; J. M. Walsh
Keith, Harrison; Nicholas Carter
Keith, John; N. Daniels
Kellaway, Bill; Gwyn Evans
Keller; N. De Mille
Keller, Konstantin; H. H. Kirst
Kellerway, Detective; W. H. L. Crauford
Kelling, Sarah; C. MacLeod
Kellog, Casey; C. Weston
Kells, Michael; P. Cheyney
Kelly, Lt.; H. Roth
Kelly, Aloysius; B. Worsley-Gough
Kelly, Clovis; J. Babbin
Kelly, Homer; J. Langton
Kelly, Jack; G. Petievich
Kelly, Joe; R. Avery
Kelly, Joseph, L. Ford
Kelly, Ned; C. Hayter
Kelly, Prof. Neil; S. F. X. Dean
Kelly, Samuel Moses; J. F. Burke
Kelsey, Insp.; E. Page
Kelso, Sgt. George; M. McClintick
Kemp, Lennox; M. R. D. Meek
Kendall, Insp.; J. J. Farjeon
Kendall, William; P. Chase
Kendrick, Don; A. MacKinnon
Kendry, Veil; G. C. Chesbro
Kennedy, Bill; L. Charteris
Kennedy, Craig; A. B. Reeve
Kennedy, George; G. Kennedy
Kennedy, Jerry; G. V. Higgins
Kenny, Mike; E. Dillon
Kent, Addison; H. Moorhouse
Kent, Brice; G. E. Giles
Kent, Charlotte; M. Kittredge
Kent, Christopher; J. Boswell
Kent, Larry; D. Haring
Kent, Temple; D. G. Devon
Kenton, Malcolm; S. Harvester
Kenworthy, Supt. Simon; John Buxton Hilton
Kenyatta; Al C. Clark
Kenyon, Sidney; N. J. Crisp
Keogh, Father; A. E. Lindop
Kerr, Constable; P. Alding
Kerrigan, Lt.; J. Harrington
Kerrigan, Peter; N. Gordon
Kerry, Daniel "Red"; S. Rohmer
Kerry, Don; J. Ashford
Ker(r)wood, Charles Douglas; Allan Duncan
Kettle, Owen; C. J. C. Hyne
Kettle, Sebastian; J. D. White
Keyes; J. N. Chance
Keyne, Skelton; C. Wood
Kham, Chin Kwang; Richard Foster
Khan, Asaf; Afghan
Kharduni; A. Soutar
Kidd, Randy; Dagmar
Kidnadze, Gyp; K. Vincent
Kiet, Supt. Bamsan; Gary Alexander
Kilby, Insp.; J. C. Lenehan
Kilby, Mark; R. C. Frazer
Kilgerrin, Paul; Charles L. Leonard
Killain, Johnny; Dan J. Marlowe
Killers, The; K. Netzen
Killinger, Jedediah, III; P. K. Palmer
Killsquad; F. Garrett
Killy, Francis Xavier; Simon Quinn
Kilpi, Osmo; M. Sariola
Kincaid, Rogan; H. Talbot
Kincaid, Tom; W. R. Cox
Kinderman, Lt. Bill; W. P. Blatty
King, Frank; Frank King
King, Jason; R. Miall
King, Mike; Graham Fisher
King, Reefe; A. Barker
King, Sam; R. E. Banks
King, Wylie; L. Saunders
Kirby, Brent; R. E. Howard
Kirby, Grant; C. Richards
Kirby, Jacqueline; Elizabeth Peters
Kirby, William; S. Horler
Kirk, Ashton; J. T. MacIntyre
Kirk, General Charles; J. Blackburn
Kirk, Devlin; Rex Burns
Kirk, Steven; D. Hornig
Kirlin, Claude "Snake"; A. Bourgeau
Klaw, Moris; S. Rohmer
Klick, Chris; W. McCall
Kline, John; P. Martin
Knickman, Insp.; A. Eichler
Knight, Clarence; Frank King
Knight Rider; G. A. Larson
Knight, Sam; D. K. Cohler
Knightly, Charles; S. Horler
Knollis, Gordon; F. Vivian
Knowles, Colin; R. East
Knowles, Randy; H. Holzer
Knox, Algernon; E. P. Oppenheim
Knox, Jonathan; R. E. McDowell
Koa, Komako; Max Long
Koenig, Charles; R. Swigart
Koesler, Father Bob; W. X. Kienzle
Kohl, Andre; P. Salinger

Kojak; Abby Mann
  V. B. Miller
Kolarova, Viera; E. Powers
Kolchak, Carl; J. Rice
Kollin, Lars; O. Hogstrand
Koravitch, Captain Ivan; V. L. Whitechurch
Koregorvsky; A. Wood
Kovack, Shaun; S. Morelli
Kovacks, Riley; G. De Marco
Kovak, Sheriff Milton; S. R. Cooper
Koval, Stash; R. Peters
Kowalski, Spaceman; Teri White
Koyala; J. C. Beecham
Kozminski, Abraham; Q. Downes
Krag, Asbjorn; S. Elvestad
Krahmer, Lt. Ben; S. A. Krasney
Krales, Josh; H. Gould
Kramer, Lt.; J. McClure
Kramer, Phil; P. Kruger
Kreutzemark, Prof.; F. Beeding
Krim, Major; D. Marfield
Krim, Harvey; E. V. Cunningham
Krug, Al; C. Weston
Kurger, Dan; M. Cormany
Kruger, Herbie; J. Gardner
Kusak, Handsome; C. Rice
Kuvakin, Ivan; A. Olcott
Kyd, Thomas; Timothy Harris
Kyle, Insp.; R. Vickers
Kyle, Jack; R. Abshire
Kyle, Tim; Robin Moore
Kynnersley, Sir John; A. C. Fox-Davies

La Bas, Papa; I. Reed
Lacaita, Nigel; W. A. MacKenzie
Lacy, A. Lincoln; M. Strobel
Laidlaw, Insp. Jack; W. McIlvanney
Laidman, Insp. Martin; S. Seaton
Laing, Patric; P. Laing
Laird, Andrew; R. MacLeod
Lam, Donald; A. A. Fair
Lamb, Insp. Ernest; P. Wentworth
Lamb, Sgt. Johnny; J. Donavan
Lambert, Valerie; J. Allan
Lanagan, Jack; E. H. Hurlbut
Lanark, Ryne; S. Robertson
Lancey, Sgt.; L. P. Greene
Land, Hannah; A. MacKay
Land, Marty; David Alexander
Landon, Arnold; Roy Lewis
Landon, Geoffrey; G. Sinstadt
Landon, Harvey; J. Pattinson
Landshark; I. Zacharia
Lane, Drury; B. Ross
Lane, Jimmy; F. Ryerson
Lane, Lorimer; Carolyn Wells
Lane, Paul; F. & R. Lockridge
Lang, Sherwood; C. D. Warren
Langham, Insp. Neville; R. Daniel
Langley, Bill; P. Meriton
Langley, Ingrid; M. Duffy
Langley, Tom; J. Monmouth
Langtry, Jimmy; Francis Leslie
Lannihan, Wolf; Lawrence Sanders
Lanson, Mike; J. H. Bond
Lantz, Tony; C. Mullen
Lanyard, Michael; L. J. Vance
Larch, Marian; B. Paul
Largo, Lou; W. Ard
Larkin, Jim; M. Russell
Larose, Gilbert; A. Gask
Larren, Simon; R. Charles
Larrimore, Tracy; J. Paull
Larson, Abe; S. A. Krasney
Lash, Lynn; L. Dent
Lash, Simon; F. Gruber
Last Ranger; C. Sargent
La Stanza, Dino; O. Denoux
Latham, Grace; L. Ford
Latimer, Charles; E. Ambler
Latimer, Charles & James; F. Gaite
Latin, Max; N. Davis
Laurance, Annie; C. G. Hart
Lavendale, Ambrose; E. P. Oppenheim

Lavender, Jimmie; V. Starrett
Lawless, Frank H.; Rolf Bennett
Lawrence, Merrick; N. W. Firth
Lawson, Loretta; Joan Smith
Lawson, Peter; M. Bolton
Layton, Anne & David; Marion Roberts
Leaphorn, Joe; T. Hillerman
Leather, Danny; D. Lawrence
Leathermouth; C. Dawe
Le Breton, Miles; J. Esteven
Lecain, Insp.; F. Didelot
Lecoq, Monsieur; E. Gaboriau
Lector, Dr. Hannibal; Thomas Harris
Lee, P. C.; E. Wallace
Lee, Anna; L. Cody
Lee, Sgt./Insp. Brian "Bonny"; George Douglas
Lee, Gaff; W. L. Stewart
Lee, Gerry; K. Hopkins
Lee, Gypsy Rose; G. R. Lee
Lee, Judith; Richard North
Lee, Largely; Evelyn Harris
Lee, Marc; Bob Ham
Lee, Nelson; J. Andrews
  Anonymous
  E. S. Brooks
  A. Cartwright
  R. Hardinge
  Maxwell Scott
  G. H. Teed
Lee, Norma "Nicky"; Norma Lee
Lee, Quong; T. Burke
Leffing, Lucius; J. P. Brennan
Left, Richard; C. Forsyte
LeGrande, Richard; I. R. Blacker
Leidl, Constance; K. Wilhelm
Leigh, Simon; R. Temple
Leighton, Shirley; P. Ernst
Leith, Gwynn; V. B. Shore
Leith, Lester; E. S. Gardner
Leithen, Edward; J. Buchan
Leland, Joseph; R. Thorp
Leland, Quinn; Franklin M. Davis
Lemaire, Miriam; C. Stanton
Lennox, Insp./Supt.; J. Wainwright
Lennox, Bill; W. T. Ballard
Lennox, Bill; John Shepherd
Lenorme, Ursula; T. W. Speight
Leopold, Captain; E. D. Hoch
LeQueux, William; W. LeQueux
Leric, Det. Insp.; R. Busby
Le Roux, Frank; Hosanna Brown
Leroy, J. R. "Rick"; B. Perowne
Leslie, Supt.; W. M. Duncan
Lessinger; R. Essex
Lester, Edward; E. Levison
Lester, "Tiger"; D. Betteridge
Lestrade, Insp.; M. J. Trow
Levert, M.; J. Toussaint-Samat
Levin, Roger; A. Furst
Levine, Abe; D. E. Westlake
LeVine, Jack; A. Bergman
Levy, Lt.; E. S. Holding
Lewis, Butch; D. Klein
Lewis, Gregory; D. Frome
Lewis, Jenny & Hunter; E. Gresham
  R. Grey
Lewis, Louis; R. Pertwee
Lewker, Abercrombie; G. Carr
  S. Styles
Liberator, The; N. Deane
Li Kao; B. Hughart
Lime, Harry; O. Welles
Lincoln, John Abraham; D. Dodge
Lincoln, Matt; E. Garth
Lindon, Insp. Bob; C. Whitman
Lindsey, Ralph; Ben Benson
Linge, Malko; G. De Villiers
Lingemann, Jack; Susan Kelly
Linh, Thibong; T. Roscoe
Link, Barry; Vigilant
Linkum, Sam; H. Mitgang
Linley; Lord Dunsany
Linnear, Nicholas; E. V. Lustbader
Linnet, Birdie; G. Linscott

Lintott, Insp. John; J. Stubbs
Linz, Baroness Clara; E. P. Oppenheim
Lion, Talbot; S. Victor
Lipinski, Insp.; G. Griffith
Liquidator, The; R. L. Brent
Lisle, Darina; J. Laurence
Lissendale, Gerald; S. Horler
Little, Jim; Maude Parker
Littlejohn, Thomas; G. Bellairs
Llorca, Juan; D. Ames
Lloyd, Insp.; J. McGown
Lloyd, Sheriff Bill; W. Reed
Loams, Turlock; J. Ruyle
Locke, Ferrers; J. Andrews
  Anonymous
  E. S. Brooks
  P. A. Clarke
  S. Hope
  G. E. Rochester
  Steve Rogers
  Hedley Scott
  J. Sylvester
  Francis Warwick
  St. John Watson
  X
Locke, Jeremy; M. Challis
Locke, John; S. Silliphant
Locke, John; Ted Wood
Locke, Kim; K. F. Crossen
  C. Richards
Locken, Mike; R. Rostand
Lockington, Lacey; R. H. Spencer
Lockwood, Bill; B. Latham
Logan; A. Joseph
Logan, Mike; Henry Holt
Lohmann, Insp. Ernst; J. Gerson
Lomax, Jacob; M. Allegretto
Londe, Joseph; E. P. Oppenheim
Lone Wolf, The; M. Barry
Lone Wolf, The; L. J. Vance
Lonergan, Leatherface; P. Renwick
Long, Chester; C. Carpenter
Long, Sgt. Jerry; J. M. Fox
Long, Lydford; H. Carstairs
Long, Michael; G. A. Larson
Long, Pusher; D. Miall
Lonnie the Fed; H. Lugar
Lonto, Tony; E. R. Johnson
Loomis, Clay; Leonard Sanders
Lord, Ferrers; S. Drew
Lord, Michael; C. Daly King
Lorimer, Graham; I. Stuart
Loring, Carole; B. Carlton
Lott, Insp.: H. Wade
Lou; R. Buxton
  D. Rogan
Louis, Ben; E. S. Russell
Love, Jason; J. Leasor
Love, Pharoah; G. Baxt
Lovejoy; Jonathan Gash
Lovel, Jack; O. J. Currington
Lovelace, Clarisse; N. Aldyne
Lovick, Insp.; G. M. Wilson
Low, Ambrose; H. Cecil
Low, Flaxman; K. Prichard
Lowe, Trevor; G. Verner
Lowell, Dr.; A. Merritt
Lowenkopf, Sgt. Shelly; R. Fliegel
Luccan, Rory; N. Morland
Lucias, Ben; R. Howes
Luck, Simon; John Marsh
Luckraft, Insp.; A. J. Reese
Ludlow, Adam; S. Nash
Lugar, Hans; H. Lugar
Lujack, Jimmy; D. Thoreau
Lumb, Tommy; L. Cross
Lumsden, Archie; M. Saltmarsh
Lund, Eric; R. S. Wallis
Lundberg, Nels; L. Saunders
Lupa, Auguste; J. T. Lescroart
Lupin, Arsene; M. Leblanc
Lurin; A. Morris
Luther, Frank; E. Lanham
Lydney, George; S. Fox

Lyle, Insp.; J. Wainwright
Lyle, Samuel; A. Crabb
Lynch, Bertram; J. W. Vandercook
Lynch, Colin; P. Mann
Lynley, Insp. Thomas; Elizabeth George
Lynn, Millie; C. H. Bullivant
Lynx; Vigilant
Lynx, Jason; A. J. Orde
Lyon, Insp.; P. Winn
Lyons, Carl; D. Stivers
Lyons, Pauline; Elizabeth Anthony
Lyson, Charles; E. P. Oppenheim

McAdden, Ric; C. Leader
McAllister; A. Train
MacAllister, Frank; R. Perry
MacAllister, Ross; C. Coram
McAlpin, Insp. William; R. H. R. Smithies
McAlpine, Philip; A. Diment
MacArthur, Ian; S. Jepson
Macauley, Mr.; R. Thorndyke
Macauley, Mike; N. Marino
McBain, Vicky; Colin Robertson
Macbeth, Hamish; M. C. Beaton
McBride, Rex; C. F. Adams
McCaig, Insp./Supt.; H. C. Rae
McCale, Duke; Gerald Brown
McCall, Andrew; M. Carrel
McCall, Bert; N. MacNeil
McCall, Matt; C. C. Risenhoover
McCall, Mike; C. Leader
McCall, Mike; E. Queen
McCallum; A. McGregory
MacCallum, Duncan; A. MacKinnon
MacCallum, Ivor; Carter Brown
McCann; Operator 1384
MacCardle, Cam; T. Halleran
McCarthy, Patrick Aloysius; G. Brandon
 J. G. Brandon
McCarty, Timothy; I. Ostrander
McCauley, Quint; D. C. Brod
McCleary, Mike; T. J. MacGregor
McClintock, Shirley; B. J. Oliphant
McCloud; C. Wilcox
 Davis Wilson
McClue, Ferris; H. Wickham
McConaughy, Miles; A. D. H. Smith
McCone, Sharon; M. Muller
McCorkle, Mac; Ross Thomas
McCoy; G. Clifton
McCoy, Johnny; J. Wolfe
McCoy, Ross; S. Gluck
McCracken, Blaine; J. Land
MacCray, Philip; O. F. Jerome
McCunn, Duncan; J. Buchan
MacDonald, Lynn; K. C. Strahan
McDonald, Paul; Julie Smith
MacDonald, Insp. Robert; E. C. R. Lorac
McDumont, Insp. Walter; H. Garner
McFall, Nina; E. Fulton
McFarland, Mac; D. Kiker
MacFarlane, Rev. P. J.; A. MacVicar
McFee, Al; N. W. Firth
McFoy, Bernard; J. M. Shrog
McGarr, Insp.; B. Gill
McGarry, Dan; Matt Taylor
McGarvey, Kirk; D. J. Hagberg
McGee, Travis; John D. MacDonald
McGinty, Slade; J. Pendower
M'Govan, James; J. M'Govan
McGrath, Peter; Michael Brett
McGregor; H. Kane
MacGregor, Capt. James Donald; Robert Mason
McGregor, Rob; T. Dicks
McGuffin, Amos; R. Upton
M'Guire, Insp.; G. Coverack
 J. Russell Warren
McGuire, Lt. Joe; J. L. Reynolds
McGurk, Gail; D. Marfield
McHugh; Jay Flynn
MacInnes, Kevin; F. Bandy
Macintosh, Isabel; H. Resnicow
McIntyre, Mac; M. E. Corne
MacKay, Insp.; E. L. Cushing

McKay, Ellis; L. A. G. Strong
McKay, Robin; John Morris
McKechnie; B. Hitchens
McKee, Insp. Christopher; H. Reilly
McKeene, Deville; R. Walker
McKellar, Ross; N. N. Peebles
McKeller, Insp.; H. McCutcheon
McKelvie, Graydon; M. Harvey
McKenna, Patience Campbell; O. Papazoglou
McKenna, Scott Waydon; J. Rosenberger
McKenzie, Alex; J. S. Borthwick
McKenzie, Shane; R. Magowan
MacKenzie, Walter "Mac"; A. Guthrie
McKinnon, Todd; L. G. Offord
Maclain, Duncan; B. Kendrick
McLanahan, Patrick; Dale Brown
MacLane, Drew; D. Morrell
MacLaren, Supt. Steve; B. Scott
McLean, Insp.; G. Goodchild
McLean, Anne "Davvie" Davenport; Margaret Taylor
 Yates
Maclean, Gregor; R. Copeland
 H. McLeave
MacLean, Roy; B. Gaston
McLeish, Supt. John; J. Neel
MacLeod, Neil; Allan Campbell McLean
McLintock, Bruce; A. MacVicar
MacLurg, Marcus; R. Petrie
MacMorgan; R. Striker
McMurdo, Andy; N. Morland
McNab, Constable; H. Footner
MacNab, Francis; J. Ferguson
Macnaughton-Innes, Lionel; A. Griffiths
MacNeil, Harry; H. P. Jeffers
MacNeill, Supt.; W. M. Duncan
McNeill, Anne & Jeffrey; T. Du Bois
McNinch, Constable Robert; T. A. Albert
Macomber, Elisha; K. M. Knight
McPhee, Sheriff Peter; D. McBriarty
MacPherson, Elizabeth; S. McCrumb
McQuaid, Damian; S. Rifkin
Macrae, Hawk; A. Barker
Macready, Sheriff; H. Holman
Macsporran, Insp.; L. Hill
MacTavish, Alonzo; P. Cheyney
McTavish, Stoner; S. Dreher
McTurk, Commander; C. J. C. Hyne
MacVeigh, Andy & Sue; S. MacVeigh
McVeigh, Mike; R. Emmett
McWhinney, Trish; B. Comfort
MacWhorter, Angus; H. S. Keeler
MacWilliams, Eve; M. Blizard

MIA Hunter; Jack Buchanan
M-Squad; D. Saunders
Maasten, Nicholas; O. Sela
Macall, Johnny; G. Fairlie
Mace; J. Grant
Mace, Insp.; R. Keverne
Mack, Dr. Johnny; T. S. Drachman
Mack, Madelyn; H. C. Weir
Macklin, Brett; I. Ludlow
Macklin, Peter; L. D. Estleman
Madden, David; D. M. Disney
Madden, Joseph; V. J. Santiago
Maddox; Martin Walker
Maddox, Ivor; E. Linington
Madero, Jose Manuel; G. Homes
Madigan, Lt.; E. Lanham
Madigan, Cash; B. Cassiday
Mado, George; W. Tute
Magaracz, Nick; K. Gallison
Magellan, Philip; A. Fletcher
 P. McCurtin
 F. Scarpetta
Magic Dick; Old Sleuth
Magic, Mark; Anthony P. Morris
Magic Man, The; D. Bannerman
Magill, Moss; Dorothy Gardiner
Magnum, Cuddy; M. Malone
Maguire, Blue; Teri White
Maguire, Joe; J. P. Radford
Maguire, Johnny; R. Himmel
Mahon, Ambrose; S. H. Courtier

Mahoney, John; S. Flannery
Mahoney, Wallace; S. Flannery
Mahoun, Nicky; Clark Smith
Maidment, Richard; M. Cronin
Maitland, Antony; S. Woods
Maitland, George; M. Severy
Maitland, Jim; H. C. McNeile
Major, The; John Ross
Major, Aubrey St. John; L. P. Greene
Makepeace; J. Raymond
 Jack Savage
Malcolm, Mr.; G. Fairlie
Malcolm, James "Solo"; N. Graham
Malcolm, Richard; J. Grady
Malins, Tommy; M. B. Dix
Mallaby, James; Bruce Norman
Mallard, Insp./Supt. "Duck"; A. Spiller
Mallett, Insp.; C. Hare
Mallett, Supt.; M. Fitt
Mallett, Dan; F. Parrish
Mallett, William; D. Orgill
Mallin, David; R. Ormerod
Mallory; R. Chandler
Mallory; M. A. Collins
Mallory, Capt.; Alistair MacLean
Mallory, Sgt.; T. J. R. Sennock
Mallory, James Maxfield; R. C. Smith
Mallory, Vic; J. H. Chase
Malloy, Chance; L. Dent
Malloy, Jim; C. Stoddard
Malone, Jim; T. C. H. Jacobs
Malone, John J.; L. M. Harris
 C. Rice
Malone, Kenneth; M. Phillips
Malone, Lawrence; G. H. Teed
Malone, Ryder; J. W. Rider
Malone, Scobie; J. Cleary
Malone, Steven; N. Morland
Maltravers, Augustus; Robert Richardson
Man from U.N.C.L.E.; M. Avallone
 Joel Bernard
 J. Hunter Holly
 P. Leslie
 D. McDaniel
 J. Oram
 J. T. Phillifent
 Thomas Stratton
 H. Whittington
Man, George; K. Heller
Man, Magic, The; D. Bannerman
Manchenil, Bolivar; D. M. Douglass
Manciple, Prof. Gideon; K. Hopkins
Mancuso, Eddie; H. Burkholz
Mandarin, Dr. Rance; Zorro
Mandell-Essington, Francis; J. S. Clouston
Manderton, Insp.; V. Williams
Mandrake, Professor; J. & E. Bonett
Mandrake, Oliver; J. Haythorne
Mandrell, Augustus; F. McAuliffe
Manfred, Judge; A. R. Hilliard
Mann, Tiger; M. Spillane
Mannering, John; A. Morton
Mannering, Randolph; S. Paternoster
Manners, Dr.; J. P. McGinity
Manners, Harley; C. J. Dutton
Manners, Silas; J. Moffatt
Manning, Supt; B. Cobb
Manning, Johnny; M. Dines
Mannister; E. P. Oppenheim
Mannix; M. Avallone
 J. T. MacCargo
Mansel, Jonah; D. Yates
Manson, Doctor Harry; E. Radford
Manton, Simon; M. Underwood
Manwaering, Phillip; D. Newton
Mappin, Amos Lee; H. Footner
Marauders; M. McGann
Marburg; L. T. Meade
March, Colonel; J. D. Carr
 C. Dickson
March, Insp. Christopher; M. Durham
March, Erik; G. G. Fickling
March, Justin; S. Horler
March, Milo; M. E. Chaber

M

March, Septimus; L. Bamburg
Margetson, Sgt./Insp./Supt.; E. M. Keate
Margolis, Eddie; S. P. Cohen
Maria, Black; J. Slate
Marker, Frank; A. Marriott
    A. Southcott
Markey, Dawn; C. Burnes
Markham; Lawrence Block
Marklin, Peter; N. Steed
Marklove, Helen; W. LeQueux
Marks, Jonathan; G. M. Barnes
Marksman, The; P. McCurtin
    F. Scarpetta
Marle, Jeff; J. D. Carr
Marley, James; Philip Ross
Marley, Lawrence; J. Walker
Marlow, Supt. "Cissie"; G. Dickson
Marlow, Daisy; D. M. Morgan
Marlow, Dick; J. Bentley
Marlow, Peter; J. Hone
Marlow, Sam; A. J. Fenady
Marlowe, Greg; Greg Marlowe
Marlowe, Philip; R. Chandler
    H. Conteris
    R. B. Parker
Marne, John; W. Keenan
Maroc, Jake; E. V. Lustbader
Marple, Jane; A. Christie
Marquis, Sir Henry; M. D. Post
Marrell, Peter; Stanley Hopkins, Jr.
Marritt, Richard; T. Hauser
Marryat, Stephen; M. Leek
Marsden, Insp. Christopher; E. Backhouse
Marsden, Eric; Anthony Graham
Marsh, Dr. Clio; J. Bannister
Marsh, Emma; E. Dean
Marsh, Harry; J. Bannister
Marsh, Jack; D. Franklin
Marsh, John; J. N. Chance
Marsh, Kate; Gret Lane
Marshall, Sgt./Insp.; B. Newman
Marshall, Bill; E. Woodward
Marshall, George; C. Barling
    P. Barrington
Marshall, John; M. Denning
Marshall, John & Suzy; J. M. Fox
Marshall, Megan; Michelle Collins
Marshall, Nick; G. Mitcham
Marsham, Peter; L. Cross
Marston, Paul; R. Eversz
Marten, Balthazar; M. J. Adamson
Martin, Insp.; R. Amberley
Martin; W. LeQueux
Martin, Anthony; W. Francis
Martin, Ben; J. Messmann
Martin, Chris; A. Roome
Martin, Insp. Clancy; Wallace Jackson
Martin, Supt. Donald; M. Bardsley
Martin, Emil; M. A. Taylor
Martin, George; F. Beeding
Martin, Jim; F. Sleath
Martin, John; Colin Robertson
Martin, Ray; R. Reinsmith
Martin, Tavy; D. Winsor
Martin, William; K. Stanton
Martineau, Insp.; M. Procter
Martini, David; R. Raine
Martinson, Arthur; C. Fitzsimmons
Martinson, John; H. Clevely
Martiny, Paul; W. Haggard
Martyn, Valentine; N. Gould
Marvin, Dr. Joan; L. Eyles
Marvin, Pete; B. Edmunds
Marwood, Colonel; A. C. Fox-Davies
Mary Helen, Sister; Sister Carol O'Marie
Mason, Chief Insp.; R. Armstrong
Mason, Paul; C. Leader
Mason, Perry; T. Chastain
    E. S. Gardner
    W. McCleery
Mason, Randolph; M. D. Post
Mason, Tom; M. R. Zubro
Massey, Miss; M. Michelson
Massey, Richard; V. Siller

Master, Murder; J. Rosenberger
Master, Ninja, The; W. Barker
Masters, Carl; L. L. Lynch
Masters, Insp./Supt. George; Douglas Clark
Masters, J. C. K. "Jiggers"; A. Rud
Masuto, Sgt. Masao; E. V. Cunningham
Mata, Hoani; V. M. Grayland
Mather, Robert; B. Graeme
Matson, Gunnar; Breni James
Matson, Patrick; M. Baldwin
Matthews, Sheriff Charles Timothy; D. R. Meredith
Matthews, Freye; J. Palmer
Matthews, James; W. Oursler
Max, Gaston; S. Rohmer
Maxim, Major Harry; G. Lyall
Maxwell, Georgia Lee; M. Friedman
Maxwell, Mahlon; L. Killough
May, Dr. Tina; Sarah Kemp
Mayberry, Noel; G. Tree
Maybridge, Insp. Tom; B. M. Gill
Mayhew, Stephen; D. B. Olsen
Maynard, Garrett; H. Swiggett
Mayo, Asey; Phoebe Atwood Taylor
Mayo, Insp. Gil; M. Eccles
Mead, Selena; P. McGerr
Meatyard, Chief Constable George; S. Horler
Mechante, Lady; G. Burgess
Medford, Insp.; H. Roth
Medford, Joe; J. Starr
Medina, David; A. M. Kabal
Meiklejohn, Charlie; K. Wilhelm
Meldrum, "Tiny"; A. Glanville
Melrose, John; W. Mills
Melville, Susan; E. E. Smith
Mendoza, Julian; J. Ronald
Mendoza, Luis; Dell Shannon
Menendez, Insp.; S. Blanc
Mensing, Loren; F. M. Nevins, Jr.
Mercenaries; Jon Hart
Mercenary, The; P. Buck
Mercenary, The; A. Kilgore
Mercer, Penny & Vincent; H. Clandon
Merchant, Death, The; J. Rosenberger
Meredith, Insp.; J. Bude
Meredith, Lt.; D. Ramsay
Meredith, John; F. Gerard
Merlini, Great; C. Rawson
Merlotti, Nick; J. Deane
Merriman, Mike; Jonathan Burke
Merrion, Desmond; Miles Burton
Merritt, Vic; Jake Cafferty
    James Callahan
Merrivale, Henry; J. D. Carr
    C. Dickson
Mersey, Supt.; F. A. Clement
Meynell, David; I. Baker
Miami Vice; S. Grave
Micklem, Don; R. Marshall
Middleton, Edward; Wardon Curtis
Migglewade, Montague; E. Hale
Mikhalovitch, Vladimir; W. LeQueux
Milano, Johnny; S. Ellin
Mildmay, Geoffrey; B. Wilkinson
Miles, Don; L. Kenyon
Miles, Robert; D. Everard
Miller, Alan; P. Hunt
Miller, Doc; H. Peterson
Miller, James; M. B. Dix
Miller, Nick; Harry Patterson
Millhone, Kinsey; S. Grafton
Millington, Earl of; G. Hackforth-Jones
Mills; M. O'Brine
Millwall, Insp.; J. Sandys
Milodragovitch, Milo; J. Crumley
Milton, Arthur; L. Henderson
Mind-Masters; I. Ross
    J. F. Rossmann
Minder; A. Masters
Minister, Crime; I. Barclay
Minoque, Sgt. Matt; John Brady
Minter, Supt.; E. Wallace
Miro; S. Herron
Mission Impossible; J. Tiger
    M. Walker

Mitchell, Insp.; N. S. Lincoln
Mitchell, Sgt./Lt. Charley; W. A. Wolff
Mitchell, Peter; G. W. Cooke
Mitchell, Robert Leory; R. Ottolengui
Mitchell, Scott; J. Harvey
Mitchell, Insp. Steven; Josephine Bell
Mitchell, William; H. A. Wrenn
Mod Squad; R. Deming
    William Johnston
Mogabe, Juman; R. Mackin
Moh, Li; J. Cowdroy
Mohamed, Insp. Raj; I. Sousa
Mohune, Peter; P. Groom
Molloy, Claire; Joan Hess
Mom; J. Yaffe
Monaghan, Rosie; A. McDonald
Mondo; A. Destefano
Mongo; G. Chesbro
Monk, Cummings King; M. P. Shiel
Monk, Dittany; A. Craig
Monk, Osbert; A. Craig
Monk, Richard; M. Underwood
Montero, Insp.; S. Nash
Montgomery, Kirke; A. Mallory
Montgomery, Insp. Richard; S. Shepherd
Montigny, Pierre; E. D. Torgerson
Montrose, Dr. Jean; C. F. Roe
Moodrow, Stanley; S. Solomita
Moody, Hank; R. Chambers
Moody, Nathaniel; E. C. Lester
Moon Man; F. C. Davis
Moon, Manville; R. Deming
Moon, Martin; L. Malloy
Mooney, Supt.; D. Magarshack
Mooney, Lt. Frank; H. Lieberman
Mooney, Jerry; K. O'Neil
Moore, John; J. Logue
Moore, Toussaint M.; E. Lacy
Moran, Jigger; J. Roeburt
Moran, P.; P. Wilde
Morane, Bob; H. Vernes
Morck, Insp. Jonas; P. Orum
Moreau, Birge; V. Vanardy
Morell, Dr.; E. Dudley
Moreno, Pedro; P. Morales
Moreton, Commander; D. Boyle
Moretti, Paddy; J. Sherburne
Morgan, Inspector; O. Crawfurd
Morgan, Connie; J. B. Hendryx
Morgan, David; R. Owen
Morgan, Elwyn; S. Farrar
Morgan, Glyn; Rosa Lambert
Morgan, Gutsy; Duff Johnson
Morgan, Mordecai "Maudie"; P. Lacey
Morgan, Rain; L. Grant-Adamson
Morganthau, Molly; G. Bonner
Moriarty, Prof.; Clive Brooks
    J. Gardner
Morini, Johnny; Al Conroy
Morley, Pat; James Burke
Mornington, Anthony; M. B. Dix
Morrison, Dan; J. Shallitt
Morrison, Hugh; F. Orenstein
Morrison, Nigel; N. Fisher
Morro, Nick; P. Buranelli
Morse, Insp.; C. Dexter
Mortdecai, Charlie; K. Bonfiglioli
Morthoe, Julian; P. M. Wilson
Mortimer, Teddy; G. F. Turner
Morton, Constable James; R. Harrison
Moseley, Sgt. Hoke; C. Willeford
Mosley, Insp.; J. Greenwood
Moss, Max; S. L. Thompson
Moss, Phil; B. Knox
Mosson, Major; L. Cargill
Most Deadly Game, The; R. Gallagher
Mostyn, Colonel; M. Hebden
Moto, Mr.; J. P. Marquand
Mott, Miss; E. P. Oppenheim
Mott, Sgt. Angus; C. Curzon
Mott, Daisy Jane; Jennifer Jones
Moult, Winslow; B. L. Jacot
Mounsell, Captain; W. W. Dixon
Mudhed, Solon; Anonymous

Muffin, Charlie; B. Freemantle
Muir, George; F. Grierson
Mulcahaney, Norah; L. O'Donnell
Mulcahy, Eugene; J. Street
Muldoon, Hart; J. Flagg
Muldrew, Gordon; L. Allan
Mulheisen, Sgt.; J. A. Jackson
Muller, "Dusty"; A. Glanville
Muller, Joe; G. I. Colbron
    A. Groner
Muller, Paul; Paul Muller
Mulligan, Patrick; B. Orczy
Mulligan, Tim; A. M. Stein
Mulroy, J. D.; R. Werry
Mulvaney, Ed; J. Ahern
Mundy, Al; G. Brewer
Munro, Peter; I. S. Black
Murder Master; J. Rosenberger
Murder She Wrote; J. Anderson
Murdoch, Bruce; N. Deane
Murdock, Kent; G. H. Coxe
Murdock, Matt; R. Ray
Murdock, Rachel & Jennifer; D. B. Olsen
Murgatroyd, William; W. H. Osborne
Murmur, Heron; S. Harvester
Murphy, Patsy; Nicholas Carter
Murphy, Frank; D. Lynch
Murray, Bill; A. Colin
Mustard, Buddy; Roland Daniel
Mycroft, Mr.; H. F. Heard
Myrl, Dora; M. M. Bodkin
Mystic Rebel; R. Syvertsen

N, Mrs.; D. S. Davis
Naik, Kesho; E. C. Cox
Nairn, David; M. Hartland
Nameless; B. Pronzini
Narayan, Capt. Prem; M. A. Casberg
Nash, Aubrey; T. Davis
Nash, Capt. George; Regan Butler
Nash, Monty; R. Telfair
Nazi Hunter; M. Mandell
Nebraska; W. J. Reynolds
Necessary, Nathan; Ken Jackson
Necroscope; B. Lumley
Nelson, Ed; F. Norman
Nelson, Capt. Gridley; R. Fenisong
Ness, Eliot; M. A. Collins
Nettlefield, Harry; W. LeQueux
Neuman, Lt. Jacob; J. Oster
Nevers, Billy; J. M. Glazner
Nevsky, Yuri; D. Gat
New Avengers; J. Carter
    J. Cartwright
    P. Cave
    W. Harris
Newberry, Millicent; Jennette Lee
Newman, Victor; D. Sucher
Newsom, Insp.; F. Stewart
Newton, Anthony; E. Wallace
Nicholls, Insp. Trevor; G. Peters
Nichols, Capt.; L. Colcord
Nicholson, Hedley; M. Kelly
Nicholson, Nick; R. Barr
Nicolson, Lloyd; P. Wayland
Nicolson, Supt. Mark; R. Charles
Night Hawk; J. Brearley
Nighthawk; S. Horler
Nightingale, Amanda; G. Revelli
Nightingale, Insp. Brett; M. Kelly
Night Stalkers; Duncan Long
Nikola, Dr.; G. Boothby
Nilsen, Pam; Barbara Wilson
Nilsen, Sgt. Rudolf; E. Griffiths
Nimble Ike; Old Sleuth
Ninja Master, The; W. Barker
Nipper; Maxwell Scott
Noble, Branders; A. Richard Martin
Noble, Nick; A. Boucher
Noble, Stewart; M. MacKintosh
Nolan, Frank; Max Collins
Nolan, John; C. Nicolai
Noon, Ed; M. Avallone
Norgil; M. Grant

Norrington, Jennifer; I. Drummond
Norris, Mrs.; D. S. Davis
Norroy, Yorke; G. Bronson-Howard
Norse, Rae; J. Esteven
North, Mr. & Mrs.; F. & R. Lockridge
North, Edward; Colin Robertson
North, Gerry; Gerry North
North, Hugh; Van Wyck Mason
North, Nora; M. Duke
North, Pam & Jerry; F. & R. Lockridge
Northeast, Guy; J. Cannan
Norton, Dave; P. Malloch
Norton, Les; R. G. Barrett
Novak, Jack; Howard Hunt
Nudger, Al; J. Lutz

Oakes, Blackford; W. F. Buckley
Oakes, Boysie; J. Gardner
Oakes, Quintus; C. R. Jackson
Oath, Hamish; D. Durrant
O'Breen, Fergus; A. Boucher
O'Brien, Kenneth; E. Gellibrand
O'Brien, Patrick; I. H. Irwin
O'Brien, Sarah; M. Marlett
O'Connor, Father; D. G. Rowlands
O'Connor, Lefty; B. Shannon
O'Day, Chauncey; A. Gaines
O'Day, Double; Gwyn Evans
O'Dea, Rita Gardella; A. Coburn
O'Dell, Barry; R. O. Chipperfield
Odell, Philip; L. Powell
Odom, Hiram; M. Boniface
O'Hagan, Captain; S. Rohmer
O'Hannay, James; C. Rushton
Ohara, Isamu; N. Hamilton
O'Hara, Pixie; D. Sturrock
O'Hara, Terence; P. Costello
Ohms, Sheerluck; W. Ion
O'Kelly, Michael the; M. O'Brine
Okewood, Desmond; D. Valentine
    V. Williams
Okoro, Paul; V. Thorpe
Old Man in the Corner; B. Orczy
Old Sleuth; Anonymous
    Old Sleuth
O'Leary; B. Graeme
O'Leary, Lance; M. G. Eberhart
Oliver, Mrs. Ariadne; A. Christie
Oliver, Gideon; A. J. Elkins
Oliver, Ted; J. Horton
Oliverez, Elena; M. Muller
Olson, Sheriff John Charles; M. G. Chute
O'Malley, Supt.; M. Kenyon
O'Malley, W. B. MacHarg
O'Malley, Ben; B. Lysaght
O'Malley, Brian; Roland Daniel
O'Malley, Shaun; Gene Ross
O'Mara, Sgt.; M. Sandford
O'Mara, Shaun; P. Cheyney
O'Meara, Donald Briggs; D. Bannerman
O'Neil, Dallas; J. B. Jenkins
O'Neil, Tod; J. K. Stafford
O'Neill, Jim; D. M. Disney
O'Neill, Peggy; M. D. Lake
Op, Continental; D. Hammett
Opara, Christie; D. Uhnak
Operator 5; Curtis Steele
Ord, Insp.; Austen Allen
Orde, Bobby; S. E. White
Orient, Dr. Owen; F. Lauria
Orlando, Marcus; G. Frankau
Ormiston, Colonel; J. M. Walsh
Ormsberry, Van Dusen; J. S. Strange
O'Roarke, Jocelyn; J. Dentinger
O'Rourke, Terence; L. J. Vance
Orsen; D. Wheatley
Ortiz, Johnny; R. M. Stern
Osgood, John; J. Ahern
O'Shaunnessey; Jessica Ryan
Otani, Supt. Tetsuo; James Melville
Otis, Miss; B. Sarto
Otley, Gerald; M. Waddell
O'Toole, Bridget; F. McConnell
O'Toole, Bryon; R. Thurston

Outrider; R. Harding
Overload series; B. Ham
Owen, Bobby; E. R. Punshon
Owen, Capt. Garth; M. Pearce
Owen, Dr. Hillis; A. M. Welles
Owen, Richard; M. Sharp
Owens, Molly; S. Overholser
O'Wynn, Winnie; Bertram Atkey
Oxman, E. L.; J. Lutz
    B. Pronzini
Ozmar; E. Hulme-Beaman

P Division; P. Turnbull
Pace, Jake and Hildy; R. Goulart
Pace, Quentin; R. Denbie
Packard, James; R. C. Galway
Padillo, Michael; Ross Thomas
Padre, The; R. Goyne
Pagan, Billy; Randolph Bedford
Pagan, Frank; Campbell Armstrong
Page, Geoffrey; V. L. Whitechurch
Pagett, Private; W. P. Drury
Palfrey, Dr.; J. Creasey
Palmer, Harry; L. Deighton
Palmer-Jones, George; A. Cleeves
Pamplemousse, Monsieur Aristide; M. Bond
Pancho, Don; B. Buckingham
Panton, Colin; P. Purser
Pao, Magistrate; L. Comber
Paola and George; G. Sampson
Parable, Titus; Anonymous
Paradise, Mike; J. Canon
Pardoe, Chief Insp.; D. Bowers
Parent, Maurice; J. Lermina
Parew, Thibault; G. Eldredge
Pargeter, Melita; S. Brett
Paris, Charles; Simon Brett
Paris, Evan; J. Louis
Paris, Wade; Ben Benson
Parker, Insp.; J. Austwick
Parker; R. Stark
Parker, Claire; L. Gough
Parker, Ellis; F. Pratt
Parker, Dr. Eric; T. T. Noguchi
Parker, Jerry; J. Gunn
Parkins, Christopher; R. L. Dearden
Parks, Eddie; G. Ade
Parmalee, Bill; P. Wilde
Parnell, Tim; Don Smith
Parodi, Don Isidro; J. L. Borges
Parr, Depty; F. I. Anders
Parrish; M. F. Harris
Parrott, Liz; Manning Long
Parry, Franklin; R. Keverne
Parry, Insp. Lane; M. Sarsfield
Pascal, Lt.; H. Pentecost
Paschal, Mrs.; Anonymous
Paternoster, Colonel; R. Inchbald
Paterson, Ross; K. Field
Patras, Commissaire; F. Grierson
Patten, Insp. Richard; R. Ormerod
Patten, Roger; A. A. Randall
Patterson, Jock; P. N. Walker
Pavlov, Gregory (Grisha); Jessica Ryan
Payne, Detective; Old Sleuth
Payne, Madeline; L. L. Lynch
Payne, Sham; K. Secrist
Peace, Commander Geoffrey; G. Jenkins
Peacemaker, The; A. Hamilton
Peachy, St. George; F. Starnes
Peacock, Percy; C. Fitzsimmons
Peak, Hugo; D. Mackail
Pearson, Supt. Andrew; E. Shepherd
Pearson, Insp. Jack; Roland Daniel
Peck, Judge Ephraim; A. Derleth
Peckover, Insp. Harry; M. Kenyon
Pedersen, Carl; Jeanne Hart
Pedley, Ben; S. Sterling
Pel, Insp. Clovis; M. Hebden
Pelazoni, Lexey Jane; L. Head
Pelham, Pel; A. E. Martin
Pellew, Gregory; V. Gielgud
Pemberty, Dick; P. Conde
Pendlebury, Mr.; A. Webb

Pendragon, John Hawkdale; R. Trevelyan
Penetrator, The; L. Derrick
Penk, Insp.; W. Gore
Pennington, Arthur Stukeley; G. Brandon
    J. G. Brandon
Pennington, Peter; E. Snell
Pennoyer, Miles; Margery Lawrence
Penny, Mr.; M. Moiseiwitsch
Penny, Alice; A. Bliss
Penny, Archibald; Wallace Jackson
Pennyfeather, A.; D. B. Olsen
Pepper, Supt.; Frank A. Smith
Pepper, Mr.; B. Thomson
Pepper, Amanda; Gillian Roberts
Peregrine Connection; R. York
Perfect, Johnny; J. Noel
Perkins, Andrea; C. Coker
Perkins, Ben; R. Kantner
Perkins, Bruce; J. Lilly
Perkins, Douglas; M. Babson
Perkins, R. I.; R. Garnett
Perks, Matilda; R. C. Woodthorpe
Peroni, Insp. Achille; T. Holme
Perrin, Christopher; C. Waye
Perry, Justin; J. D. Revere
Persad, Kala; Headon Hill
Pete, Blue; L. Allan
Peters, Anna; J. Law
Peters, Casey; H. F. S. Moore
Peters, Eric; O. R. Cohen
Peters, J. D.; H. Clevely
Peters, Toby; S. Kaminsky
Petersen, Brian; J. P. Cody
Petrella, Patrick; M. Gilbert
Petrie, Amos; J. V. Turner
Petros, Mikael Josef; James Anderson
Petrosino, Joe; Frederick Nolan
Pettengill, Insp.; A. Rowe
Pettigrew, Francis; C. Hare
Pettiweather, Penelope; J. A. Salmonson
Phantom, The; L. Falk
Phantom, Gray; Herman Landon
Phelan, Lt.; M. K. Ozaki
Phelan, Johnny; J. P. Duff
Phelps, Chet; G. Childerness
Phenwick Women; K. Kimbrough
Phibes, Dr.; W. Goldstein
Philis; Ritchie Perry
Phillips, Bino; A. W. Gray
Phillips, Nathan; N. O'Donohoe
Philpotts, Freddy; A. B. Caldwell
Phin, Thackeray; J. Sladek
Phoenix Force; G. Wilson
Phoenix, Joe; A. W. Aiken
    Anonymous
Pibble, James; P. Dickinson
Picaroon, The; J. Cassells
Picaroon, The; Herman Landon
Pickett, Jonas; Michael Gilbert
Pierce, Insp.; R. A. J. Walling
Pig, Lord; N. Lombard
Pike, Abe; E. Glanville
Pilgrim, Mr.; D. Cory
Pilgrim, The; M. Cronin
Pilgrim, Black; G. Stanley
Pilkington; W. Caine
Pinaud, Monsieur; P. Audemars
Pinch, Dearborn V.; E. P. Green
Pincher; C. M. Hincks
Pincus, Silky; L. Rosten
Pine, Paul; H. Browne
    J. Evans
Pink, Melinda; G. Moffat
Pink, Norman; M. McShane
Pinkerton, Private; H. Ashton
Pinkerton Detective Agency; W. H. Baker
    D. Reid
    R. Story
Pinkerton, Evan; D. Frome
Pinner, Jocelyn; B. Norman
Piper, John; H. Carmichael
Piper, Katherine "Peter"; A. R. Long
Piper, Peter; N. B. Mavity
Piron, Jim; E. McGirr

Pitkin, Mr.; B. Boothroyd
Pitt, Insp.; J. F. Straker
Pitt, Dirk; C. Cussler
Pitt, Insp. Thomas; A. Perry
Placard, Nicholas; Demouzon
Place, Thackeray; K. Williams
Plante, Guy; J. Palmer
Pleydell, Bertram; J. Smithers
    D. Yates
Plotkin, Sylvia; G. Baxt
Plummer, Jeff; D. Lees
Plush, Paul; O. Keystone
Poe, Christopher; R. C. Brown
Poe, Edgar Allan; D. Madsen
    M. Olden
    A. Sinclair
    B. Steward
Poggioli, Henry; T. S. Stribling
Point Team; J. B. Hadley
Pointer, Insp.; A. Fielding
Poirot, Hercule; A. Christie
Pol, Charles; Alan Williams
Policewoman; L. Trevor
Pollard, Insp./Supt. Tom; E. Lemarchand
Pollifax, Emily; D. Gilman
Pollok, William; G. Grogan
Polo, Nick; J. Kennealy
Pond, Mr.; G. K. Chesterton
Pons, L. Rees; C. D. King
Pons, Solar; B. Copper
    A. Derleth
Ponsonby, Peter; Jean Leslie
Ponting, Bob; B. Bolt
Pontivy, Papa; B. Newman
Poole, Insp.; Henry Wade
Port, Daniel; P. Rabe
Porter, Appleton; M. Lovell
Porter, Ben and Carrie; E. Travis
Porter, Harry; E. Naha
Poskitt, Mr.; J. S. Fletcher
Posse, Insp.; A. Alington
Post, Dr. Anthony; A. Irving
Potter, Brock; A. Maling
Potter, Eugenia; V. Rich
Potter, Hiram; R. Foley
Pottle, Mr.; R. Connell
Povin, General Stepan; J. Trenhaile
Powder, Lt. Leroy; M. Z. Lewin
Powell, Ricvhard; A. Fowles
Power, Mike; P. Denver
Power, William; H. Clandon
Powers, Johnny; J. Rayter
Powers, Will; I. Zacharia
Powledge, Lt.; M. P. Rea
Poynings, Roger; Michael Burt
Preacher; T. Thackrey
Precinct, 87th; E. McBain
Precinct Siberia; T. Philbin
Preed, Mr.; Ladbroke Black
Prehznev, Anton; W. LeQueux
Prentice, John; Sea-Lion
Prentis, Insp.; E. Backhouse
Prentiss, Agatha Welch; V. P. Johns
Prescot, Julian; Julian Prescot
Preston, Johnny; P. Chester
Preston, Mark; Peter Chambers
Priam, Lady Margaret; J. Christmas
Price, Jimmy "Wiggly; J. J. Chichester
Price, Ronald; J. Cannan
Pride; E. P. Oppenheim
Pride, Duncan; A. Frazer
Pride, Jeff; J. Heneghan
    A. O'Neill
Pride, Nassim; R. Petrie
Priest, Judge; I. S. Cobb
Priestley, Dr. Lancelot; J. Rhode
Prike, Leonidas; L. G. Blochman
Primrose, John; L. Ford
Prince, Cliveden; A. Reubens
Prince, David; G. Webb
Prince, Henry; C. F. Gregg
Prince, Napoleon; M. Edginton
Pringle, G. D. H.; N. Livingston
Pringle, Romney; C. Ashdown

Prisoner, The; T. M. Disch
    D. Motter
    H. Stine
Private Eye; B. Pronzini
Probyn, Insp.; Morley Adams
Probyn, Julia; A. Bridge
Professionals, The; Ken Black
Pross, David; J. T. Savarin
Protection Ltd.; N. Harman
Protector, The; R. Rainey
Protector, The; I. Zacharia
Prouse, Dalton; J. McCulley
Pry, Paul; E. S. Gardner
Prye, Paul; M. Millar
Psycho Squad; R. Dade
Pujol, Aristide; W. J. Locke
Puma, Joe; W. C. Gault
    R. Scott
Purbright, Insp. Walter; C. Watson
Purdue, Chance; R. H. Spencer
Pursuivant, Judge Keith Hilary; M. W. Wellman
Pusser, Sheriff Buford; Webster Carey
    W. R. Morris
Putnam, Sgt. David; L. Stephan
Pym, Henry; W. J. Burley
Pym, John; D. C. Murray
Pym, Nicholas; J. Sanders
Pym, Mrs. Palmyra; N. Morland
Pynchon, Whit; D. Pedreau
Pyne, Parker; A. Christie

Q, Don; K. Prichard
Q33; G. Goodchild
Quade, Oliver; F. Gruber
Quaile, Insp.; J. M. Walsh
Quan, Samuel; G. Begbie
Quane, Crispin; E. Kilvington
Quantrill, Insp. Douglas; S. Radley
Quarles, Christopher; P. Brebner
Quarles, Francis; J. Symons
Quarry; M. A. Collins
Quarry, Simon; Robin Hunter
Quarshie, Dr.; J. Wyllie
Quartz, Dr.; Nicholas Carter
Quayle, Everard Peter; P. Cheyney
Quayle, Hilary; M. Kaye
Quayle, Ian; A. Caillou
Quayle, Kit; J. Aldridge
Quayle, Peter; P. Trent
Quayne, Maxwell; F. A. Symonds
Queen, Ellery; E. Queen
Queen, Richard; E. Queen
Queen's Investigator; M. Cooney
Quentin, Andrew; A. Peterson
Quentin, Peter; R. Quest
Quero, Mercedes; G. E. Locke
Quest, Philip; Peter Townend
Quest, Philip; N. Vane
Quill, Insp.; C. Brahms
Quill, Supt.; L. Lamb
Quiller; Adam Hall
Quin, Harley; A. Christie
Quin, Sebastian; S. Horler
Quincannon, John; M. Muller
    B. Pronzini
Quince, Dion; P. Cake
    T. L. Welch
Quincy; T. Racina
Quinn; H. Carmichael
Quinn; N. Scanlon
Quinn, Rupert; Alan Williams
Quinney, Joe; H. A. Vachell
Quint, Peter; H. Austin
Quintain, Richard; W. H. Baker
    W. A. Ballinger
Quinto, Gimiendo Hernandez; James Norman
Quirke, Adam; V. Gribdan
Quist, Gregory; W. C. MacDonald
Quist, Julian; H. Pentecost
Qwilleran, Jim; L. J. Braun

Race, Colonel; A. Christie
Race, Blue Jean Billy; C. W. Tyler
Race, Christopher; C. N. Williamson

Rachmaninoff, Lt. Nicky; R. Westbrook
Radcliff; R. Mallory
Radkin, Joseph; B. Biderman
Radnitz, Herman; J. H. Chase
Radoub, Jacques; H. D. Stacpoole
Raeburn, Mark; M. Gair
Rafferty; W. G. Duncan
Rafferty, Neil; C. Wiltz
Raffles, A. J.; David Fletcher
    G. Greene
    E. W. Hornung
    B. Perowne
    P. Tremayne
Raffles, Mrs. A. J. Van; J. K. Bangs
Ragnon, Tom; R. Harper
Railton family; John Gardner
Rainey, Jim; P. McCurtin
Raker; D. Scott
Ralston, Deb; Lee Martin
Ramsay, Andrea Reid; C. H. Matschat
Ramsay, David; C. H. Matschat
Ramsay, Steve; C. H. Wallace
Ramsdale, Lucy; H. Dolson
Ramsey, Hec; D. Owen
Ramsey, Rick; R. Santini
Rand; E. D. Hoch
Randall, D. C.; The Gordons
Randall, Mark; C. Eland
Randollph, Rev. C. P. "Con"; C. M. Smith
    T. L. Smith
Randolph, Snooky; G. Dank
Raneleigh, Arthur; M. L. Luther
Ranger, Last; C. Sargent
Rankin, James; J. Grady
Rankin, Tommy; M. Propper
Ransome, Rogue; Dean Morgan
Ransome, Steve; Dean Ransome
Rant, Stephen; H. E. Wheeler
Raphael, Dr. Louis; A. Muir
Rason, Insp. George; D. Durham
    R. Vickers
Rason, Det. Insp. J.; D. Durham
    S. Kyle
    R. Vickers
Rater, Oliver; E. Wallace
Ratichon, Hector; B. Orczy
Ratlin, Sgt.; J. Roffman
Ravel, Claude; B. Jones
Raven, Freddie; M. Lundy
Raven, John; D. MacKenzie
Raven, Richard; J. Griffin
Ravenhill, Anthony; R. Francis Foster
Rawlings, "Little John"; J. Minahan
Raye, Cristina; B. Grimshaw
Raymond, Sgt.; N. Longmate
Rayne, Brigadier; P. Coke
Razio, Rick; R. Razio
Razoni, Ed; W. B. Murphy
Read, Anthony; S. Toye
Read, Vernon; Maxwell Scott
Reamer, Donald; W. M. Duncan
Reardon, Lt. Jim; R. L. Pike
Recks; M. F. Harris
Rector, Pete; V. Siller
Reddman, Joe; W. Downing
Reddy, Irving Martin; I. Zacharia
Reece, Caitlin; L. W. Douglas
Reed, Sgt. Bob; C. Drummond
Reed, James; J. Sangster
Reed, Lal; C. Wood
Reeder, J. G.; E. Wallace
Reeder, Paul; Robert C. Dennis
Rees, Idewald; B. Mather
Regan, Jack; J. Balham
    I. K. Martin
Regan, Insp. Michael; E. Hale
Regan, Paddy; D. Rutherford
Regina; Dagmar
Register, Mark; Arthur Douglas
Rehm, Jimmy; W. Herber
Reid, Andrea; C. H. Matschat
Reilly, Harry; G. Corbin
Remington, Cliff; R. Obstfeld
Remington, J. A.; R. Ladline

Remover, The; Roland Daniel
Remsen; D. Montrose
Renard, Hercule; P. Audemars
Renfrew, Douglas; L. Y. Erskine
Renko, Arkady; M. C. Smith
Rennert, Hugh; T. Downing
Renwick, Roger; H. MacInnes
Renzler, Mark; P. Engleman
Repington; S. Horler
Resistance; G. St. Germain
Resnick, Charles; John Harvey
Resnick, Slots; M. Geller
Retief, Jame; K. Laumer
Revel, Michael; N. Berrow
Revenger, The; J. Messmann
Rex, Nigel; G. Goodchild
Reynolds, Insp.; Elaine Hamilton
Reynolds, Maxine; M. Grove
Rezaire, Jimmie; A. Armstrong
Rhineheart, Michael; J. Birkett
Rhoden, Steven; Ira Walker
    Irma Walker
Rhodenbarr, Bernie; L. Block
Rhodes, Sheriff Dan; B. Crider
Rhodes, James; D. Gober
Rhymer, Arnold; U. Key
Rhys, Insp. Madoc; A. Craig
Riam, George; D. O. Woodbury
Rice, Bill; M. Stand
Rice, Miles Standish; B. Kendrick
Richards, Paul; D. Dallas
Richardson, P. C.; B. Thomson
Richardson, Dr. Paul; H. L. Klawans
Richmond, Frank; Anthony Graham
Rickman, Colonel; J. M. White
Rickman, Roy; D. Craig
Rider, Knight; G. A. Larson
Ridgway, Martin; P. Helm
Ridley, Nat; N. Ridley, Jr.
Ridoser; Arthur Morris
Rig Warrior; W. W. Johnstone
Rigby, Dorothy Mayotte; T. Heald
Riggs, Bingo; C. Rice
Riley, Pete; P. Quinn
Rillington, Anthony; N. Orde-Powlett
Rim-Fire; C. Ballew
Ringer, The; E. Wallace
Ringrose, John; E. Phillpotts
Ringway, Stephen; S. M. Lott
Ringwood, Richard; K. Farrer
Rintoul, Linus; J. Edmonds
Riordan, Matthew; F. D. Huebner
Riordan, Patrick; R. Gilligan
Riordan, Preston John; S. Hanlon
Rios, Henry; M. Nava
Ripley; Lord Dunsany
Ripley, Charles; J. Wainwright
Ripley, John; The Gordons
Ripley, Tom; P. Highsmith
Rivers, Ed; T. Powell
Rivers, Julian; C. Carnac
Rivington, Paul; G. Verner
Rizzi, Capt.; T. Sterling
Roadblaster; P. Hofrichter
Roath, Sheila; D. Craig
Robak, Donald; J. L. Hensley
Roberts, Amanda; Sherryl Woods
Roberts, George; M. Symons
Roberts, Mitch; G. Dold
Roberts, Randy; Carter Brown
Robicheaux, Dave; J. L. Burke
Robins, Constable; M. Stand
Robins Family; T. Chastain
Robocop; E. Naha
Rock, Johnny; B. Rossi
Rockford Files; M. Jahn
Rockwell, Chris; D. Linzee
Rockwell, Rocky; J. Iams
Rodd, Aaron; E. P. Oppenheim
Roden, Jess; A. B. Cunningham
Rodway, Insp.; J. K. Ryland
Roersch, Sgt. Edmund; H. Kastle
Roff, Sergei; Charles Russell
Rogers, Bull; A. Brede

Rogers, Insp. George; Jonathan Ross
Rogers, Huntoon; C. Knight
Rogers, John; Jonathan Ross
Rogers, Pogy; Z. H. Ross
Roharik, Larry; J. M. Eshleman
Roi, Leo; P. Lore
Rolf, Sergei; Charles Russell
Rolfe, Helga; J. H. Chase
Rolfe, Simon; J. L. Bonney
Rolfe, Zach; J. J. Lamb
Rollison, Richard; W. V. Butler
    J. Creasey
Roman, Dan; E. Mathis
Rome, Tony; A. Rome
Romm, Sebastian; P. Freund
Rook, Howie; S. Palmer
Roosevelt, Eleanor; E. Roosevelt
Roosevelt, Theodore; Lawrence Alexander
Rope, Charlie; J. Eller
Roper, Insp./Supt. Douglas; Roy Hart
Roper, Max; K. Platt
Roper, Piers; K. Follett
Roque, Konrad; G. Morton
Rosher, Insp. Alf; J. S. Scott
Ross, Supt.; J. J. Connington
Ross, Charity; J. Bickham
Ross, Insp. Gordon; Lord Gorell
Ross, Jack; B. Schopen
Ross, Martin; A. Allyson
Ross, Mike; K. Carr
Ross, Paul; P. Heneker
Rossi, Lt. Dino; E. Fulton
Rostetter, Tommy; A. Campbell
Rostnikov, Insp. Porfiry; S. M. Kaminsky
Roston Outfit; Dean Morgan
Roth, Max; H. Arvay
Rouletabille, Joseph; G. Leroux
Rourke, Peter; D. C. Cooke
Rourke, Timothy; J. Wolf
Rowlands, Bill; Norman Lucas
Rowley, Sgt. Tony; R. Busby
Royce, Rupert; J. Aldridge
Rudd, Insp.; J. Thomson
Rudd, Hugh; H. C. Davis
Rudd, Matt; R. Deming
Ruff, Peter; E. P. Oppenheim
Rugger; R. Thurston
Rumford, John; G. H. Teed
Rumpole, Horace; J. Mortimer
Rune; J. W. Deaver
Rusby, Myles; V. Markham
Rushton, Grant; G. H. Teed
Russell, Alan; N. Fitzgerald
Russell, Col. Charles; W. Haggard
Russell, Franklin; R. M. Baker
Rutherford, Anthea and Justin; A. C. Ley
Rutherford, Jumbo; N. Leslie
Ryan, Lt.; M. Scherf
Ryan, Bill; M. Morgan
Ryan, Blackie; A. Greeley
Ryan, Charlie; J. C. Lenehan
Ryan, Frank; E. Leonard
Ryan, Jack; T. Clancy
Ryan, Jim; P. Ernst
Ryan, Monsignor John Blackwood; A. Greeley
Ryan, Maggie; P. M. Carlson
Ryan, Sean; B. Cleeve
Ryder, Dick; H. B. M. Watson
Ryder, Harry; R. Footman
Ryder, William (Tiny); W. Boyles
Rye, Bill; J. Spain
Ryker, Joe; N. De Mille
    E. T. Hamill
Ryland, Garth; J. R. Riggs
Rymal, Balmy; A. Stringer
Ryvet, Insp.; C. Carnac

S-Com; Steve White
SOB's; J. Hild
Saber, Insp. Joel; Gavin Holt
Saber, Sarah; D. Linzee
Sabin, Mr.; E. P. Oppenheim
Sabin, Rachel; W. Warga
Sader, Jim; D. Hitchens

S

Safford, Ben; R. B. Dominic
Sage, Malcolm; H. Jenkins
Saigon Commandos; J. Cain
Saint, The; L. Charteris
St. Amand, Jean Henri; D. L. Teilhet
St. Clair, Theophilus; A. Griffiths
St. Cyr, Claudine; Ian Wallace
St. Francis School; E. S. Brooks
St. George, Philip; M. Avallone
St. Ives, Philip; O. Bleeck
St. James, Kiel; E. Chaze
St. James, Quin; T. J. MacGregor
St. John, Jeremiah; W. Babula
St. Vincent, Britt; I. Ross
    J. F. Rossman
Saito, Insp.; J. Van de Wetering
Salis, Jo; W. O. Greener
Salisbury, Arthur; R. Crawford
Sallis, Oscar; F. Usher
Sallust, Gregory; D. Wheatley
Sally the Sleuth; Barreau
Salmond, Andrew; L. Dundas
Salter, Insp. Charlie; E. Wright
Saltfleet, Insp. Gregory; Colin Wilson
Samson, Capt.; Gavin Douglas
Samson, Albert; Michael Z. Lewin
Samson, Bernard; L. Deighton
Samson, Jake; S. Singer
Samson, John; M. Tripp
San Antonio; San Antonio
Sand, Robert; M. Olden
Sanders, Commissioner; F. Gerard
    E. Wallace
Sanders, Insp. John; Medora Sale
Sanderson, Insp.; David Hume
Sanderson, Maxwell; J. J. Chichester
Sanderson, Phil; L. Grex
Sands, Insp.; M. Millar
Sands, Jim; R. J. Casey
Sandyman, Mr.; N. Graham
Sanford, Joe; F. M. Proud
Sant; W. LeQueux
Santangelo, Minnie; A. Mancini
Santos; W. B. Bannerman
Sarel, Richard; J. Bryan
Sargeant, Peter; E. Box
Sark, Mortimer; J. Hawk
Sars, Dr. Lao; Eric North
Sasha; A. Wood
Satan, Dr.; P. Ernst
Saturday, Johnny; L. Goldman
Saumarez, John; C. Dane
Saunders, Insp.; Scober
Saunders, Insp.; V. M. Steele
Saunders, Jeff; M. Bar-Zohar
Savage, Doc; K. Robeson
Savage, John; J. Trevor
Savage, Marc; M. Eden
Savage, Mark; L. Payne
Savage, Matt; Craig Cooper
Savage, Myra; M. McShane
Savage, Rampion; James Turner
Savage, Spencer Monroe; P. Theroux
Savage, Steve; David Lewis
Savile, Justin; M. Malone
Saville, Bill; Roland Daniel
Savoy, Paul; J. Gregory
Sawyer, Pete; M. Albert
Sawyer, Quincy Adams; C. F. Pidgin
Saxe, Christopher; S. Shane
Saxon; Les Roberts
Saxon, Alan; K. Miles
Saxon, Ludovic; J. Cassells
Sayers, Michael; E. P. Oppenheim
Sayler, Catherine; Linda Grant
Scant, Jerry; L. A. Knight
Scaramouche; R. Sabatini
Scarf, Paul; Raymond Boyd
Scarfe, Det. Sgt.; J. Goodwin
Scarlet Pimpernel; B. Orczy
Scarlett, Doctor; A. Laing
Scarlett, John; B. Bolt
Scarlett, Peter; S. Horler
Schaefer, William; D. Estow

Schmidt, Insp.; G. Bagby
Schofield, Peter; T. B. Dewey
Schwartz, Gadgets; D. Stivers
Schwartz, Lenny; I. Weinman
Schwartz, Rebecca; Julie Smith
Scipio, Danny; T. Gates
Scorpion Squad; E. Helm
Scott, Aline; Alison Drake
Scott, John; S. Picard
Scott, Philip; Hartley Howard
Scott, Shell; D. Knight
    R. S. Prather
Scott, Spider; K. Royce
Scotter, Mr.; T. Warriner
Scudamore, Laura; R. Armstrong
Scudder, Matthew; L. Block
Scylla; W. Goldman
Seals; S. Mackenzie
Search; R. Weverka
Seary, Major Hutton; John Ross
Sebastian; J. L. Johnson
Second Bureau; C. R. Dumas
Secret Agent; W. H. Baker
    W. A. Ballinger
    P. Leslie
    W. McNeilly
Secret Agent X-9; D. Hammett
Secret Circle; G. Null
Secret City; D. Storm
Seddall, Harry; J. K. Mayo
Seeton, Emily; H. Carvic
    Hampton Charles
Segrove, James; D. Durham
    R. Vickers
Segundo, Martin; B. Langley
Seidlitz, Mavis; Carter Brown
Selbon, Paul & Peter; J. McCulley
Selby, Doug; E. S. Gardner
Selby, Pete; Jonathan Craig
Selden, Dick; W. S. Masterman
Semlake, Insp.; J. Varnam
Seng-Chu; E. Thomas
Sergeant, Jock; D. DaCruz
Sessions, Frank; H. Waugh
Seton, Mike; T. C. H. Jacobs
Severance, Grace; M. Scherf
Severn, Insp.; G. Bromley
Severson, Knute; T. Wells
Sevrel, Insp.; C. Worth
Shade, Rene; D. Woodrell
Shadow, The; W. B. Gibson
    M. Grant
Shadowers, The; D. Fox
Shadows, Dark; Marilyn Ross
Shaeffer, Beowulf; L. Niven
Shaft, John; E. Tidyman
Shand, Dale; D. Enefer
Shandy, Prof. Peter; C. MacLeod
Shane, Insp.; S. Truss
Shane, Peter; F. Bonnamy
Shaner, Hana; R. Greth
Shanley, Joseph; Jack Webb
Shannon, Supt.; C. Ryland
Shannon, Clinton; Lee Roberts
Shannon, Desmond; M. V. Heberden
Shannon, John J.; C. F. Adams
Shannon, Lucy; D. Belsky
Shannon, Michael; G. Bowman
Shannon, Patrick; J. Quinn
Shapiro, Nathan; F. & R. Lockridge
    R. Lockridge
Shard, Simon; P. McCutchan
Shark, Tiger; K. Stanton
Sharman, Nick; M. Timlin
Sharp, Terence Everard Christopher; J. M. Howard
Sharpe, Morrison; L. Cargill
Sharpshooter, The; B. Rossi
Sharretts, B. K.; P. H. Woodward
Shaw, Emma; H. W. Jones
Shaw, Commander Esmonde; P. McCutchan
Shaw, James; I. Haiblum
Shaw, Paul; M. Sadler
Shayne, Michael; B. Halliday
Shea, Tim; J. Delmont

Shearer, Frank; R. Crawford
Shelley, Insp.; John Rowland
Sheridan, David; C. Davy
Sheridan, Jim; V. Torrio
Sheridan, Timothy Seamus Wolfe; S. F. Wilcox
Sheringham, Roger; Anthony Berkeley
Sherman, Phil; Don Smith
Sherman, Winston Marlowe; M. K. Lorens
Sherriff, Michael; P. McAdam
Sherwood, Insp.; J. Bude
Shield, The; P. McAdam
Shields, Jefferson; P. Carlon
Shigata, Mark; A. Wingate
Shimoni, Tami; O. Hesky
Shirley, Patrick C.; O. Mills
Shock, Ben; P. Buchanan
Shoestring, Eddie; P. Ableman
Sholmes, Herlock; Charles Hamilton
    P. Todd
Sholto, Sam; D. Hart-Davis
Shomar, Shomri; H. Klinger
Shomes, Kerlock; T. Gross
Shone, Radford; Headon Hill
Shore, Jemima; Antonia Fraser
Short, Augustus; Richard Marsh
Shrig, Jasper; J. Farnol
Shulman, Con; Blair Johns
    Hank Spencer
Sidel, Isaac; J. Charyn
Sikiti; F. Brownlee
Silber; Gunnar Johnson
Silence, John; A. Blackwood
Silent Invasion; M. Cherkas
Silk, Dorian; S. Harvester
Silk, Lou; J. H. Chase
Silk, Steve; J. B. O'Sullivan
Silver, Insp. Jim; Henry Holt
Silver, Maud; P. Wentworth
Silvestri, Guy; M. Rennert
Simmons, Bernard; F. & R. Lockridge
    R. Lockridge
Simmons, Ralph; R. B. Gillespie
Simon, Benjamin; G. Dean
Simon, Grant; H. Pentecost
Simpson; R. L. Fish
Simpson, Arthur Abdel; E. Ambler
Simpson, Tim; J. Malcolm
Sims, Det. Insp.; F. Grierson
Sin, Dr. Yen; D. E. Keyhoe
Sinclair, Alex; D. W. MacArthur
Sinclair, Arthur; W. S. Masterman
Sinclair, John "Chant"; D. Cross
Sinclair, Matt; T. Fennelly
Sinclair, Steve; J. Decker
Singer, Jacob; G. Baxt
Sinkage, Matt; M. Cherkas
Skane, Insp.; D. Marfield
Skarratt, Insp.; J. S. Fletcher
Skrene, Vincent; F. Richardson
Slade; D. Bagley
Slade, Detective Insp.; V. Grey
Slade, Anthony; L. Gribble
Slade, Ben; H. Burkholz
Slade, Geoffrey; F. Lester
Slade, John; R. Essex
Slade, Mac; J. Blumenthal
Slade, Nicholas; R. C. Woodthorpe
Slane, Insp.; S. Maddock
Slane, Jasper; E. P. Oppenheim
Slappey, Forian; O. R. Cohen
Slate, Veronica; L. Crews
Slattery, Mike; D. R. Dunn
Slaughter; H. Clement
    A. Kane
Slavin, Vitaly; J. Semenov
Slayton, Ben; B. Sanders
Sleep, Sam; S. Finnegan
Sleuth, Satan; M. Avallone
Sloan, Insp. C. D.; C. Aird
Slocum, Capt.; H. D. Stacpoole
Slone, Maggie; Elizabet M. Stone
Smaile, Oliver; J. Adye
Small, Rabbi David; H. Kemelman
Smallpiece, Colin; F. J. Kenmore

Series Index   TANCRED, DR. BENJAMIN / 1333

Smarles, Insp. Joshua; M. Urquhart
Smart, Maxwell; William Johnston
Smiley, George; J. Le Carre
Smith, Captain; The Edingtons
Smith, Inspector; S. Troy
Smith, Don Alvaredo y Miraflores; Capstan
Smith, Aurelius; R. T. M. Scott
Smith, Beau; Z. H. Ross
Smith, Benbow; P. Wentworth
Smith, Black John; J. B. Hendryx
Smith, Brad; J. Bickham
Smith, Cellini; Robert Reeves
Smith, Daye; F. Usher
Smith, Jill; S. Dunlap
Smith, Joe; Horace Smith
Smith, John; W. Blassingame
Smith, John; H. Pentecost
Smith, John; M. Plum
Smith, John; J. Sangster
Smith, Kim; J. Boland
Smith, Lancelot Carolus; N. Berrow
Smith, Mackensie; M. Truman
Smith, Nayland; S. Rohmer
Smith, Necessary; K. F. Crossen
Smith, Oliver Thomas Trentham; F. Dare
Smith, Supt. Owen; J. Barnett
Smith, T. B.; E. Wallace
Smith, Temporary A. S. P.; H. L. Jones
Smith, Tusk; H. Zachary
Smith, William Wilfeborce; W. Haggard
Smith, Xenia; A. Meyers
Smolinsky, Joshua; C. Sinclair
Smyth, Millard; E. M. Boyd
Sneed, Insp. Terry; G. F. Newman
Sniper; M. Acres
    D. Kramer
Snow, John; R. H. Sawkins
Snubbins, Samuel; C. M. Hincks
Soldier for Hire; M. K. Roberts
    R. Skimin
Soldon, Sgt. Louis; B. Turner
Solo, Napoleon; M. Avallone
    Joel Bernard
    J. Hunter Holly
    P. Leslie
    D. McDaniel
    J. Oram
    J. T. Phillifent
    Thomas Stratton
    H. Whittington
Sommers, Harry; P. Whalley
Sommers, Jaime; E. Lottman
Space; W. F. Nolan
Spade, Danny; D. Ambler
Spade, Richard; B. B. Johnson
Spade, Sam; D. Hammett
Spalding, Eric; W. C. Harvey
Spanner, J. T.; T. Chastain
Spargo; J. D. Scott
Sparrow; C. Murphy
Sparrow, Charlie; T. Ardies
Speare, Luke; Frederick C. Davis
Spearman, Henry; H. Jevons
Spearpoint, Insp.; F. Arthur
Spears, Simon; V. Gielgud
Special Operation Executive; J. H. Crisp
Special Operations Command; J. N. Pruitt
Special Squad; D. Franklin
Specialist, The; J. Cutter
Specialist, The; E. Lecale
Speed, Bill; J. B. Donovan
Speed, Martin; G. Elliott
    M. G. Hugi
    John Norman
Speed, Maxwell; R. Starnes
Speer, Giff; D. Tracy
Spence, Supt. Ben; M. Allen
Spence, Margo Franklin; J. Jenkins
Spence, Philip; J. Jenkins
Spencer, Dick; N. Winski
Spencer, John; Lou Smith
Spencer, Tony; O. Beeby
Spenser; Robert B. Parker
Spicer, Robert; M. Danvers

Spider, The; J. McCulley
Spider, The; R. T. M. Scott
    G. Stockbridge
Spink, Captain; Morley Roberts
Spinnet, Phineas; A. Soutar
Spooner, Sara; J. Kelman
Spotted Moon, Charlie; C. Q. Yarbro
Spraggue, Michael; L. J. Barnes
Spratt, Sgt.; George Douglas
Spring, Penelope; M. Arnold
Spring, Terry; J. Kains
Springblade; Greg Walker
Springfield, Mr.; J. Sandys
Springfield, Judd; Alison Smith
Squad, Ms.; M. Endfield
Stafford family; B. Mather
Stafford, Max; D. Bagley
Stainton, Insp. Alec; Stephen Murray
Stallard, Vincent; G. Beare
Stand, Nathan; J. Kern
Standiford; D. Shoubridge
Standish, John; K. Netzen
Standish, Kaye and Mike; J. E. Gurdon
Standish, Ronald; H. C. McNeile
Standish, Tiger; S. Horler
Stanley, Hagar; F. Hume
Stannard, Rand; R. L. Hershatter
Stanton, Hugh; R. Vickers
Star, Black; J. McCulley
Star Hawks; R. Goulart
Stark, Joanna; M. Muller
Stark, John; T. Harknett
Stark, Robert; M. Schorr
Starr, Jason; P. Heath
Starsky & Hutch; M. Franklin
Starte, Roger & Kate; Eric Williams
Stash; R. Peters
Stash, T. D.; W. R. Philbrick
Staunton, Insp. Robert; Peter Hill
Staveley, George; Clifton Robbins
Stears, Giovanni; F. O'Neill
Steel, Alan; Colin Robertson
Steel, Raeburn; C. Brooks
Steele, Argus; Babs Lee
Steele, Lt. Donovan; J. D. Masters
Steele, Jim; D. Chambers
Steele, John; J. Odlum
Steele, Insp. Malcome; Mansfield Scott
Steele, Sir Nicolas; M. Pemberton
Steele, Rocky; John B. West
Steele, Skyrocket; R. Goulart
Steer, Corporal Laury; L. C. Douthwaite
Steevens, Stonewall; M. G. Kiddy
Stein, Gertrude; S. M. Steward
Stenton, Jack; T. Dexter
Stern, Sandy; S. Turow
Stevens, Insp.; B. Graeme
Stevens, Dave; K. A. Saddler
Stevens, Gavin; W. Faulkner
Stevens, Jim; D. Smith
Stewart, Allan; V. Siller
Steytler, Det. Sgt.; S. Milne
Stiffson, Mr.; H. Jenkins
Stock, Matthew; L. Tourney
Stockwell, "Spider"; J. R. Holden
Stoddart, Insp.; A. Haynes
Stokes, Harvey; Nicholas Carter
Stole, Sebastian; C. Wogan
Stone; D. Keene
Stone, Arnold; R. J. McLaughlin
Stone, Curt; J. Seward
Stone, Fleming; Carolyn Wells
Stone, J. Rockingham; R. Armstrong
Stone, Mark; Jack Buchanan
Stone, "Rolling"; K. Laing
Stone, Shep; J. Jacks
Stoner, Harry; J. Valin
Stoner, Mark; R. Hayes
Stonewall; M. K. Roberts
    R. Skimin
Storey, Rosika; H. Footner
Storm, Insp.; J. M. Walsh
Storm, Christopher; W. A. Barber
Strachey, Donald; R. Stevenson

Straight, Ricky; G. Morgan
Straker, Geth; B. Mather
Strang, Jim; G. Dilnot
Strang, John & Sally; H. Brinton
Strange, James; E. B. Quinn
Strange, Jeff; A. Gaines
Strange, Jimmy; E. Dudley
Strange, Violet; A. K. Green
Strange Report; John Burke
Strangely, Peter; E. B. Black
Strangeways, Nigel; N. Blake
Stranleigh, Lord; Robert Barr
Stratton, Mark; R. T. Bickers
Straun, Insp. Angus; B. Cork
Straussman; G. Davison
Street, Dee; H. Wakefield
Street Hawk, The; J. Roberts
Streeter, Joe; J. F. Burke
Strickland, Insp.; G. Dilnot
Strickland, Jack; H. Balfour
Strike Fighters; T. Willard
Striker, Jason; P. Anthony
Strong, Max; R. Dudgeon
Strong, Mike; P. Cagney
Strong, Philip; W. Oursler
Strong, Robert; Colin Robertson
Struthers, Dixie T.; L. V. Sims
Stryker, Colin; William Crawford
Stryker, Lt. Jack; P. Gosling
Stryker, John; D. Barnes
Stryker, Sgt. Mark; J. Cain
Stuart, David; J. K. MacDougall
Stuart, Scott; G. Coffin
Stubbs, John; R. T. Campbell
Stubbs, Prof. Marcus; E. Radford
Sturrock, Jeremy; Jeremy Sturrock
Styles, Peter; J. Philips
Sullivan, Bob; F. Mullally
Sullivan, Giles; H. Resnicow
Sullivan, Hank; A. R. Rooth
Sullivan, Jack; J. Cutter
Sultan, Wm. (Sultan's Harem); H. Austin
Summer, Jack; R. Goulart
Summers; S. Horler
Summers, "Doc"; F. Marlowe
Summers, Steve; J. Manor
Sumuru; S. Rohmer
Sun Hill Police Station; John Burke
Surgical Strike; J. Ahern
Sussman, Andy; M. J. Katz
Sutherland, Chief of Police; F. Eberhard
Sutherland, John; L. Galloway
Swain, Insp. Alfred; Donald Thomas
Swain, Ape; D. Da Cruz
Swain, Matthew; M. McQuay
Swan, C. J.; R. Philmore
Sweetwater, Caleb; A. K. Green
Swift, Leighton; C. R. Jones
Swift, Loren; D. Hornig
Swinton, Insp; P. Flower
Swinton, Insp.; I. Greig
Switch; M. Jahn
Sydenham; D. Seaman
Syfret, Lord; A. Kenealy
Symon, York; E. Wallace
Syn, Dr.; R. Thorndyke

T-Man; B. Sanders
TNT; D. Masters
Tabor, Chester C.; M. Cruz
Taffin; L. Mallet
Taggart; Ralph Hayes
Taine, Roger; G. Household
Takemura, Cobb; R. Swigart
Talbot, Clem; T. P. Mulkeen
Tallant, Col. Munro; A. York
Talley, Tom; Philip Ross
Tallis, Roger; J. Rossiter
Tallon, Jack; J. Ball
Tamar, Hilary; S. Caudwell
Tamara; E. Ambler
Tamiko, Tina; P. Bishop
Tan, Fan; D. Dell
Tancred, Dr. Benjamin; G. D. H. Cole

T

T

Tandy, Michael "Napper"; N. Shepherd
Tangent, Peter; Lawrence Sanders
Tanner; M. Newton
Tanner, Evan; L. Block
Tanner, John Marshall; S. Greenleaf
Tansey, Insp. Dick; J. Penn
Target, Kinsey; Griff
    Hank Spencer
Tarleton, Dr. Frank; A. Upward
Tarleton, John; F. F. Van de Water
Tarrant, Trevis; C. D. King
Tate, Ann; C. Burnes
Tatlock, Tyler; D. Donovan
Taverner, Dr.; D. Fortune
Taylor, Pete; R. D. Abrahams
Taylor, Richard; Anonymous
Teal, Insp. Claude Eustace; L. Charteris
Tealeaf, Timothy; W. W. Hill
Team, Able; D. Stivers
Team Three; C. Cunningham
Teed, Russell; D. Montrose
Tejeda, Lt. Roger; W. Hornsby
Telefair, Kitty; F. Stevenson
Tellford, Jeff; D. Fisher
Tempest, Ashley, A. C. Fox-Davies
Tempest, Bill; W. Shand
Templar, Simon; L. Charteris
Temple, Evelyn; Lord Gorell
Temple, Paul; F. Durbridge
    Paul Temple
Templeton, Paul; R. Goyne
Tepper, Sally; Frank King
Teresa, Sister Mary; M. Quill
Terhune, Theodore I.; B. Graeme
Terminator, The; John Quinn
Tern, Bill; B. E. Wallace
Terrel, Timothy; S. Maddock
Terrell, Frank; J. H. Chase
Terrence, Michael & "Terry"; G. Brandon
Terry, Matt; J. Luceno
Tewkesbury, Mr.; H. Cecil
Thackeray, Constable; P. Lovesey
Thane, Colin; B. Knox
Thanet, Insp. Luke; D. Simpson
Thatcher family; P. Yates
Thatcher, John Putnam; E. Lathen
Thatcher, Steve; F. C. Davis
Then Came Bronson; William Johnston
    C. Stratton
Theobald, Kate; Lionel Black
Theron, Thomas; R. Reeves
Thew, Insp.; D. G. Browne
Thirlstane, Jock; W. Russell
Thomas, Ethel; C. Fitzsimmons
Thomas, Lizzie; A. Oliver
Thomassy, George; S. Stein
Thompson, Chief Insp.; Peter Drax
Thompson, Dr. Alec; E. McGhee
Thompson, Jake; Evelyn Cameron
Thompson, Michael; P. C. Williams
Thompson, Mike; J. Paull
Thompson, Pat; R. G. Dean
Thorn; Jim Hall
Thorndyke, John; J. H. Dirckx
    N. Donaldson
    R. A. Freeman
    A. C. Ward
Thorne, Insp./Supt. George; J. Penn
Thorne, Tommy; Charles H. Snow
Thornton, Bo; Greg Walker
Three, Team; C. Cunningham
Thunderbolt, The; J. McCulley
Thunstone, John; M. W. Wellman
Thursby, Roger; H. Cecil
Thursday, Max; Wade Miller
Thyrde, Derek; B. Denham
Tibbett, Henry & Emmy; P. Moyes
Tibbett, John; L. Payne
Tibbs, Virgil; J. Ball
Tierney, James; J. A. Moroso
Tiger Shark; K. Stanton
Tinker; E. Jepson
Tintagel, Lord & Lady; F. Draco
Tish; M. R. Rinehart

Titterton, Adrian; Edward Brown
Tobin; E. Gorman
Tobin, Insp.; Dorothy B. Hughes
Tobin, Art; J. Lutz
    B. Pronzini
Tobin, Matthew; A. Caillou
Tobin, Mitchell; T. Coe
Toby, Quentin; S. M. Schley
Todd, Insp.; J. Halstead
Todd, Fraser; H. L. Jones
Todd, Irving; P. Conde
Todd, Jerry; M. J. Freeman
Toff, The; W. V. Butler
    J. Creasey
Toklas, Alice; S. M. Steward
Toland, Nick; W. L. Story
Tolefree, Philip; R. A. J. Walling
Tompkins, Tommy; F. Branston
Tonelli, Pietro; Alexander Williams
Tong, Harry; E. Burgess
Tope, Insp.; Ben Ames Williams
Tope, Edward; H. C. Davis
Topham, Mr.; C. R. Gull
Toplitt, Kingsley; G. Stockwell
Torrent, Andrew; L. Cores
Torreyton, Dick; E. F. Charles
Torry, Derek; J. Gardner
Touchfeather, Katy; J. Sangster
Tower, Hugo; V. France
Townsend, Schuyler; F. Gordon
Townshend, Mr.; J. M. Cobban
Tozzi, Mike; A. Bruno
Track, Dan; J. Ahern
    P. Andrews
Tracker, Nat; R. Stillman
Trackman, Martin; Anonymous
Tracy, Devlin; W. B. Murphy
Tracy, Dick; Anonymous
    M. A. Collins
    C. Gould
    William Johnston
Tracy, John; T. Wallace
Tracy, Noel; Alex Fraser
Tracy, Philip "Spike"; H. Ashbrook
Traherne, Sydney; M. St. Dennis
Train, Rick; B. Fischer
Trant, Luther; E. Balmer
Trant, Timothy; Q. Patrick
    P. Quentin
Trapp, Capt. Ralph "Rat"; J. W. Corrington
Traveler, Moroni; R. Irvine
Travers, Insp.; P. Barrington
Travers, Ludovic; C. Bush
Travis, Sheila; P. H. Sprinkle
Treadgold, Insp.; A. Weymouth
Treadgold, Horace B.; V. Williams
Treasure, Mark; D. Williams
Tredennick, Angeline; R. B. Sanborn
Tree, Ms.; M. A. Collins
Trees, Peter; John Q
Tregarde, Diana; M. Lackey
Trelawney; A. Melville-Ross
Trelawny, Edward; A. R. Long
Trelawny, John; G. Goodchild
Treloar, Septimus; Stephen Chance
Tremaine, Mordecai Euripides; F. Duncan
Tremayne, Charles; N. MacKenzie
Trent, Anthony; W. Martyn
Trent, Gregory; A. Seifert
Trent, Maria; H. Kane
Trent, Philip; E. C. Bentley
Trenton, Garaway; J. P. Carstairs
Trenton, Hilda; D. Lyon
Trenton, Richard; Anne Burton
Trethowan, Insp. Perry; R. Barnard
Trevellyan, Insp. Nick; Susan Kelly
Trevor, Carole; J. Philips
Treynor, Jimmy; A. Livingston
Trill, Vincent; D. Donovan
Triple Threat; Gayle Stone
    D. Unkefer
Trosper, Alan; W. Hood
Trothe, Edmund; R. Llewellyn
Trotter, Tuddleton; H. S. Keeler

Trotti, Comissario; T. Williams
Troy, David; Alan Gardner
Troy, Jeff & Haila; K. Roos
Truscott, Bill; Griff
Tuck, Richard; Lange Lewis
Tucker, Charity; P. Buchanan
Tucker, Coleridge, III; I. Drummond
Tucker, Mike; B. Coffey
Tucker, Roy; A. Kennedy
Tucker, Sam; J. A. Potter
Tudor, Mark; A. Nash
Tuke, Harvey; D. G. Browne
Tully, Jasper; D. S. Davis
Tumbler, Hector; S. Crabtree
Tupper, Amy; Josephine Bell
Turk, Capt. Rupert; A. S. Long
Turnbuckle, Henry; J. Ritchie
Turnbull, Roger; J. Tyndall
Turner, Dan; R. L. Bellem
Turner, Milo; F. M. Nevins, Jr.
Tutt, Ephraim; A. Train
Tuttlebury, Erasmus; W. C. Platts
Tweed; C. Forbes
Twelves, Jim; W. F. Shannon
Twin, Anthony Nicholas; D. Masters
Twins, Avenging; J. McCulley
Twombley, Jabez; Sidney Williams
Twotoes, Tommy; David Alexander
Tyler, Dennis; Diplomat
Tyler, Jeff; J. L. Potter
Tyler, Julia; L. Revell
Tyler, Nat; Warren Miller
Tyler, Ralph; M. Valentine
Tyson, Henry; F. A. Kummer
Tyson-Tyree, Annie; D. Pedneau

U.N.C.L.E., Girl from; M. Avallone
    S. Latter
    P. Leslie
U.N.C.L.E., Man from; M. Avallone
    Joel Bernard
    J. Hunter Holly
    P. Leslie
    D. McDaniel
    J. Oram
    J. T. Phillifent
    Thomas Stratton
    H. Whittington
Ukridge; P. G. Wodehouse
Union Club; I. Asimov
Unwin, Harriet; E. Hervey
Urban, Robert; C. H. Guenter
Urizar, Miguel; H. McCloy
Ursula, Sister; A. Boucher
    H. H. Holmes
Useless, Trooper; L. P. Greene
Usher, Ambrose; J. Davey
Utley, Gabe; G. Stewart

V., Monsieur; A. Upward
Vachell, Supt.; E. Huxley
Valcour, Lt.; Rufus King
Valentine, Claudia; Marele Day
Valentine, Dan; N. Aldyne
Valeshoff; E. Ambler
Vallance, BIll; W. Proudfoot
Vallon, Johnny; P. Cheyney
Valmont, Eugene; Robert Barr
Vampire Files; P. N. Elrod
Van der Valk, Insp.; N. Freeling
Van der Valk, Arlette; N. Freeling
Van Dusen, Prof. Augustus S. F. X.; J. Futrelle
Van Kill, Hendrik; S. Bayne
Van Larsen, Max; G. Baxt
Van Loan, Richard Curtis; Robert Wallace
Vanardy, Cuthbert; H. Landon
Vance, Philo; W. Butterfield
    J. Riddell
    S. S. Van Dine
Vane, Sydney; N. Islay
Vaness, Richard; M. Black
Vanessa, Sarah; J. Storm
Vanner, Rick; M. V. Heberden
Varallo, Vic; L. Egan

Varney, Chick; Jerome Barry
Vaughan, Barry and Dee; J. Jordan
Vaughan, Valentine; R. T. Hopkins
Velvet, Nick; E. D. Hoch
Venables, Tessie; H. Holley
Vendetta; I. Zacharia
Venn, Sgt.; L. Brock
Venneker, Paul; P. Geddes
Verdean, Gillian; T. Gibbs
Vereker, Anthony; R. Forsythe
Verity, Mr.; P. Antony
Verity, Sgt. William; F. Selwyn
Vernet, Van; L. L. Lynch
Vernon, Larry; D. Bateson
Verrell, Anthony; B. Graeme
Verrell, Richard; B. Graeme
Veseloffsky, Baron; S. Horler
Vesey, Horace; W. Gerrare
Vice, Miami; S. Grave
Vickary, Grant; R. Hobart
Vicop; M. Newton
Victor, Emma; M. Wings
Vidocq; P. Bourne
Vigilante, The; I. Ludlow
Vigilante, The; V. J. Santiago
Villiers, Anthony; A. Panshin
Villiers, Francis; B. Rodney
Vincent, Johnny; J. Calder
Vine, Gil; S. Sterling
Vivanti, Paul; S. Horler
Vokes, Major T. P.; H. R. Addison
Von Helsing, Alicia; J. Mathewson
von Kaz, Baron; D. L. Teilhet
von Kopf, Olga; H. De Halsalle
Vorobeitchik, Wenceslas; A. Steeman
Voss, Abelard; D. C. Cameron
Vulture, The; Harold Ward

Wace, Fadiman; Roger Simons
Wade; G. Bristow
Wade, Hilda; Grant Allen
Wade, Nyla; V. McConnell
Wager, Gabriel; Rex Burns
Wagstaffe, Michael; M. Arlen
Wainwright, James; B. Mather
Wake, Insp.; C. Kingston
Walk, Insp. John; R. Daniel
Walker; M. D. Post
Walker, Amos; L. D. Estleman
Walker, Calico Jack; P. Bishop
Wallace, Brendan; M. Brewer
Wallace, Brett; W. Barker
Wallace, Leonard; Alexander Wilson
Wallace, Michael; Roland Daniel
Wallingford, James Rufus; G. R. Chester
Wallion, Maurice; J. Regis
Walsh, Lt. Marty; O. R. Cohen
Waltz, John; C. McCormick
Wanawake, Penny; S. Moody
Wanzi, Corporal; F. Brownlee
Warbots; G. H. Stine
Ward, Albert; F. Greco
Ward, Clayton; R. Merwin
Ward, Eric; Roy Lewis
Ward, Peter; David St. John
Ward, Watson; B. Delannoy
Ware, Anthony; S. Wells
Ware, Drexel; C. Andrews
Warfield, Stephen; D. Chacko
Waring, Scarsdale; T. Stanleyan King
Warlock, Mike; P. Haggard
Warlord, The; J. Frost
Warner, William; M. Sylvester
Warren, James; James Warren
Warrender, Elizabeth; G. D. H. Cole
Warrington-Reeve, Claude; Josephine Bell
Warshawksi, V. I.; S. Paretsky
Warwick, John; J. McCulley
Watchman, Sam; B. Garfield
Waterlow, Roger; C. MacKenzie
Watson, Mr.; Dorothy Gardiner
Watson, Sheriff Jug; H. Zachary
Wayne, Morgan; M. Blood

Wayne, Pamela; M. O'Nair
Wayne, Rodney; A. G. E. Cromwell
Wayne, Steve; T. Harknett
Wayward, Carl; L. Treat
Weatherby, Artie; J. M. T. Miller
Weatherley, Kate; M. Birmingham
Weaver, Nicky; N. Weaver
Weaver, T. S.; D. Keith
Webb, Chief Insp. David; Anthea Fraser
Webb, John & Anne; F. G. Presnell
Webber, Insp. John; A. Oliver
Webley; L. Maddock
Webster, Dallas; D. Stanford
Webster, Danile; R. Sale
Wedgewood, Nat; J. Fairfax-Blakeborough
Weigand, Bill; F. & R. Lockridge
Welch, Agatha; V. P. Johns
Wells, Prof.; F. Grierson
Wells, Clifford; N. S. Bortner
Wells, John; K. Peterson
Welpton, Sam; J. A. Saxon
Welt, Nicky; H. Kemelman
Wentworth, Lyon; R. Forrest
Wentworth, Richard; R. T. M. Scott
  G. Stockbridge
Wesley, Sheridan; H. Waugh
West, Ambrose; P. Levene
West, Delilah; M. O'Callaghan
West, Helen; F. Fyfield
West, Henry Highland; J. Nazel
West, Honey; G. G. Fickling
West, Janine; E. Welles
West, Roger; J. Creasey
Westborough, Theocritus Lucius; C. B. Clason
Westlake, Hugh; J. Stagge
Weston, Mrs. Caywood; E. Thomas
Weston, Dick; T. Lund
Weston, Geoffrey; T. B. Haughey
Weston, James; James Warren
Weston, Tommy; W. Sheridan
Wetzon, Leslie; A. Meyers
Wexford, Insp.; R. Rendell
Weybridge, Lady; Rex Sandys
Wharton, Sam; D. Buckingham
Wheat, Whitney; J. Lane
Wheeler, Al; Carter Brown
Whelan, Dick; Laurence Dwight Smith
Whippletree, Sheriff Emil; M. T. Hinkemeyer
Whispering Hills; K. Cameron
Whistler; Robert Campbell
Whitby, Supt.; N. Morland
White, Al; G. Holden
White, George; M. M. Mannon
White, Lace; Jeannette Covert Nolan
White, Col. Peregrine; B. Spicer
Whitfield, Bob; R. A. Moore
Whitney, Whit; D. Dodge
Wick, Christer; Maria Lang
Widgeon, Insp.; Alan Thomas
Widowers, Black; I. Asimov
Widows; L. La Plante
Wield, Insp.; Glint Green
Wigan, James; B. J. Farmer
Wiggin, Gramps; E. S. Gardner
Wigglesworth, Augustus; H. S. Carter
Wilbur, Keightley; F. Danby
Wilcox, Carl; Harold Adams
Wilde, Carney; B. Spicer
Wilde, Jonas; A. York
Wilkins, Insp.; J. Anderson
Wilkins, Insp.; F. Beeding
Wilkins, Insp.; Murray Thomas
Will, Willowdene; H. Sutcliffe
Willard, Nell; M. Lynch
Williams, Chief Insp.; H. Clevely
Williams, George; J. Di Mona
Williams, Paul; H. C. McDonald
Williams, Race; C. J. Daly
Williams, Remo; W. B. Murphy
  R. Sapir
Willing, Basil; H. McCloy
Willis, George; W. Hughes
Willows, Jack; L. Gough

Willum, Persis; Clarissa Watson
Willoughby, Hugh James; Gayle Stone
  D. Unkefer
Wilshaw, David; A. O. Pollard
Wilson, Cyrus; A. H. Garnet
Wilson, Dick; K. Sproul
Wilson, Francesca; J. Neel
Wilson, Supt. Henry; G. D. H. Cole
Wilt, Henry; T. Sharpe
Wimble, "One Week"; H. Burnham
Wimsey, Lord Peter; D. L. Sayers
Wine, Moses; Roger L. Simon
Winfield, Carter; D. L. Gilbert
Winfield, Jane; A. Peterson
Wing; J. Reach
Wingate, Caledonia; C. H. Sawyer
Wingate, Mac; Brian Swift
Winkley, Mr.; H. Rutland
Winkman, Jake; D. Von Elsner
Winslow, Steve; J. P. Hailey
Winston, Peter; J. Laflin
  P. Winston
Winston, Stoney; J. Stinson
Winter, Charles; C. Egleton
Winter, Rabbi Daniel; J. Telushkin
Winter, Holly; S. Conant
Winter, Insp./Supt. William; Gwendoline Butler
Winterbottom, Lettie; L. Cutter
Winters, Matt; I. Oellrichs
Winterstone, Lord; N. Lombard
Wintino, Dave; E. Lacy
Wintringham, Dr. David; Josephine Bell
Wise, Insp.; Anonymous
Wise, Justus; A. W. Barrett
Wise, Pennington; Carolyn Wells
Witherall, Leonidas; A. Tilton
Withers, Hildegarde; S. Palmer
Woar, Hazlitt; G. W. Yates
Wolfe, Nero; R. Goldsborough
  R. Stout
Wolff, Rick; R. Mackin
Wolfram, Hugo; R. Graves
Wong; H. Wiley
Woodfield, Will; E. Foote-Smith
Woodhead, Alister; E. H. Clements
Woodruff, Bernard; G. Dank
Woods, Insp.; D. E. Muir
Woodward, James Rowland, VII; J. S. Blazer
Woodward, Tony; J. Baddock
Woolf, Dave; B. Bannerman
Woolfe, Miss; Winifred Graham
Woolrich, Tony; M. M. Raison
Wordsworth, Ken; S. Hey
Wortenheimer, Silas; D. Learmonth
Worthing, Martha; J. K. Drummond
Worthington, Elizabeth Lamb; B. J. Morison
Wragge, Arnold "Tiger"; P. Capon
Wraithlea, Commander; P. Walker Taylor
Wrayne, Daphne; Mark Cross
Wren, Insp.; N. A. Temple-Ellis
Wren, Russel; T. Berger
Wright, David; J. F. Straker
Wright, Eddie; C. Mullen
Wu, Lily; J. Sheridan
Wulff, Burt; M. Barry
Wyatt; D. Gethin
Wycherley, Dr. Xavier; M. Rittenberg
Wycliffe, Supt. Charles; W. J. Burley
Wyman, Michael; Bob Cook
Wyndham Saga; S. Nichols
Wynnton, Robert; S. Horler

X, Secret Agent; B. House

Yamamura, Trygve; P. Anderson
Yard, John; Ralph Hayes
Yardley, John; R. Garnett
Yates, Susan; E. L. Fetta
Yeadings, Supt. Mike; C. Curzon
Yedder, Ira; E. Bond
Yeoman, Giles; M. Woodhouse
Ygrec, Insp. Maurice; M. Rippon
Yeoman; R. Jackson
York, Insp.; M. Durham

York, Supt. Richard; A. Williamson
York, Sherrett; Gavin Holt
Yorke, Roland; Mrs. Henry Wood
Young, Bernard; Eric Wood
Young, Simon; J. Trenhaile
Young, Wilson; G. Tippette
Youngblood, Kyle; Herb Fisher

Z, Department; J. Creasey
Z-Comm; K. Maning
Zaleski, Prince; M. P. Shiel
Zalman, Jerry; G. Kraft
Zambra, Sebastian; Headon Hill
Zanca, Joe; J. N. Frey
Zane, Martin; L. Trimble

Zane, Thornton; M. Massey
Zen, Insp. Aurelio; M. Dibdin
Zevich, F. T.; A. Bourgeau
Zharkov, Alexander; W. B. Murphy
Zimmerman, Lt. Al; T. George
Zondi, Sgt.; J. McClure
Zordan, Anna; J. Eastwood

SERIES CHARACTER CHRONOLOGY

Series Character Chronology

YEAR	CHARACTER	TYPE	COUNTRY	BOOK TYPE	NUMBER OF BOOKS	AUTHOR
1878	Ebenezer Gryce	police	A	hb	13	A. K. Green
1878	James M'Govan	police	B	hb	7	J. M'Govan
1887	Insp. Byrnes	police	A	hb	5	J. Hawthorne
1887	Sherlock Holmes (1)	private	B	hb	9	A. C. Doyle
1888	Dick Donovan	police	B	hb	15	D. Donovan
1889	Nick Carter	private	A	pb	571	Nicholas Carter
1891	Old Sleuth	private	A	pb	(8)	Old Sleuth
1891	Robert Spicer	private	B	pb	(6)	M. Danvers
1892	John Barnes		A	hb	5	R R. Ottolengui
1892	Dr. Quartz	criminal	A	pb	12	Nicholas Carter
1894	Nimble Ike	amateur	A	pb	(6)	Old Sleuth
1895	Capt. Owen Kettle	adventurer	B	hb	(15)	C. J. C. Hyne
1895	Dr. Nikola	criminal	B	hb	5	G. Boothby
1897	Jesse James	criminal	A	pb	(10)	W. B. Lawson
1898	Paul Beck	private	B	hb	6	M. M. Bodkin
1898	Patsy Murphy	private	A	pb	10	Nicholas Carter
1899	Trim Carter	private	A	pb	5	Nicholas Carter
1899	Harrison Keith	private	A	pb	51	Nicholas Carter
1899	Francis Mandell-Essington	adventurer	B	hb	7	J. S. Clouston
1899	A. J. Raffles	criminal	B	hb	17	E. W. Hornung B. Perowne D. Fletcher G. Greene
1899	Caleb Sweetwater	police	A	hb	5	A. K. Green
1902	Mark Spicer		A	pb	14	Old Sleuth
1902	Nat Tyler		A	pb	(6)	Warren Miller
1903	Jim Godfrey	amateur	B	hb	6	B. Stevenson
1904	Tony Clark		A	pb	36	Dick Stewart
1904	Burt Cromwell		A	pb	36	Inspector Stark
1904	Tod O'Neil		A	pb	34	J. K. Stafford
1905	Scarlet Pimpernel	adventurer	B	hb	13	Baroness Orczy
1906	Felix Boyd	private	A	pb	6	Scott Campbell
1906	Nelson Lee	private	B	pb	21	various hands
1906	Augustus S. F. X. Van Dusen	private	A	hb	7	J. Futrelle
1907	Sexton Blake	private	B	pb	1591	various hands
1907	Arsene Lupin	criminal	F	hb	16	M. Leblanc
1907	Joseph Rouletabille	amateur	F	hb	5	G. Leroux
1907	Ashley Tempest	private	B	hb	(5)	A. C. Fox-Davies
1907	Dr. John Thorndyke	private	B	hb	30	R. A. Freeman N. Donaldson J. H. Dirckx
1908	Four Just Men	adventurer	B	hb	5	E. Wallace
1908	J. Rufus Wallingford	criminal	A	hb	5	G. R. Chester
1909	Insp. Furneaux	police	B	hb	(15)	G. Holmes L. Tracy
1909	Fleming Stone	private	A	hb	61	Carolyn Wells
1910	Jeff Clayton	private	A	pb	32	W. Ward
1910	Hamilton Cleek	police	B	hb	12	T. W. Hanshew M. E. Hanshew H. P. Hanshew
1910	Insp. Hanaud	police	B	hb	6	A. E. W. Mason
1911	Father Brown	amateur	B	hb	6	G. K. Chesterton
1911	Letitia Carberry	amateur	A	hb	6	M. R. Rinehart
1911	Commissioner Sanders	police	B	hb	15	E. Wallace F. Gerard
1912	Smiler Bunn	criminal	B	hb	9	B. Atkey
1912	Richard Duvall	private	A	hb	5	A. Fredericks
1912	Craig Kennedy	private	A	hb	26	A. B. Reeve
1912	Edward Leithen	private	B	hb	7	John Buchan
1912	Judge Priest	amateur	A	hb	7	I. S. Cobb
1913	Dr. Fu Manchu	criminal	B	hb	16	S. Rohmer C. Van Ash
1913	Ferrars Lord	private	B	pb	8	S. Drew
1913	Sgt. Jasper Shrig	police	B	hb	(11)	J. Farnol
1914	Max Carrados	amateur	B	hb	5	E. Bramah
1914	Michael Lanyard	criminal	A	hb	8	L. J. Vance
1915	P. J. Davenant	amateur	B	hb	6	F. S. Hamilton
1915	Fantomas	criminal	F	hb	12	P. Souvestre M. Allain
1915	Richard Hannay	amateur	B	hb	7	John Buchan J. Smithers
1915	Dr. Syn	criminal	B	hb	7	R. Thorndyke
1916	Martin Dale		B	pb	5	Maxwell Scott
(1916)	Insp. Mitchell	police	A	hb	(10)	N. S. Lincoln
1916	Connie Morgan	adventurer	A	hb	10	J. B. Hendryx
1917	Jimmie Dale	adventurer	A	hb	5	F. Packard
(1917)	Tubby Haig	private	B	pb	(60)	anonymous
1917	Timothy McCarty	amateur	A	hb	5	I. Ostrander
1918	Dr. Adolph Grundt	spy	B	hb	7	D. Valentine V. Williams
1918	Anthony Trent	criminal	B	hb	25	W. Martyn

YEAR	CHARACTER	TYPE	COUNTRY	BOOK TYPE	NUMBER OF BOOKS	AUTHOR
1919	Peter Clancy	amateur	A	hb	60	L. Thayer
1919	Pennington Wise	private	A	hb	8	Carolyn Wells
1920	Corporal Downey	police	A	hb	15	J. B. Hendryx
1920	Bulldog Drummond	adventurer	B	hb	19	H. C. McNeile
						G. Fairlie
						H. Reymond
						J. Smithers
1920	Reggie Fortune	police	B	hb	22	H. C. Bailey
1920	Bertram Pleydell	amateur	B	hb	9	D. Yates
1920	Hercule Poirot	private	B	hb	41	A. Christie
1920	Ephraim Tutt	private	A	hb	13	A. Train
1921	John Bartley	private	A	hb	8	C. J. Dutton
1921	Blue Pete	adventurer	B	hb	20	L. Allan
1921	Gunston Cotton	spy	B	hb	14	Rupert Grayson
1921	Paul Harvey	private	B	hb	5	S. Rohmer
1921	Francis McNab	private	B	hb	6	J. Ferguson
1921	Jonah Mansel	amateur	B	hb	12	D. Yates
1921	Cuthbert Vanardy	adventurer	A	hb	5	Herman Landon
1922	Tommy & Tuppence Beresford	amateur	B	hb	5	A. Christie
1922	Jerry Boyne	private	A	hb	5	A. MacGowan
1922	Dixon Brett	private	B	pb	53	various hands
1922	Cheri-Bibi	adventurer	F	hb	5	G. Leroux
1922	Blue Pete		B	hb	19	L. Allan
1922	Douglas Renfrew	police	A	hb	9	L. Y. Erskine
1923	Jim Hanvey	private	A	hb	6	O. R. Cohen
1923	Insp. Luckraft	police	B	hb	7	A. J. Rees
1923	Graydon McKelvie		A	hb	5	M. Harvey
1923	Aurelius Smith	spy	A	hb	7	R. T. M. Scott
1923	Supt. Henry Wilson	police	B	hb	25	G. D. H. Cole
1923	Lord Peter Wimsey	amateur	B	hb	16	D. L. Sayers
1924	Insp. Joseph French	police	B	hb	32	F. W. Crofts
1924	Col. Anthony Gethryn	amateur	B	hb	12	P. MacDonald
1924	Chullunder Ghose	adventurer	B	hb	5	T. Mundy
1924	Col. Wyckham Gore	amateur	B	hb	7	L. Brock
1924	Jimmie Haswell	private	B	hb	9	H. Adams
1924	Jimgrim	spy	B	hb	12	T. Mundy
1924	Ferrers Locke	private	B	pb	33	various hands
1924	Aubrey Major	adventurer	B	hb	(19)	L. P. Greene
1924	Insp. Pointer	police	B	hb	23	A. Fielding
1924	Insp. George Rason	police	B	hb	(9)	D. Durham
						R. Vickers
1924	Insp. J. Rason	police	B	hb	(8)	S. Kyle
1924	Anthony Ravenhill	amateur	B	hb	(7)	R. F. Foster
1924	J. G. Reeder	police	B	hb	5	E. Wallace
1924	Insp. Sims	police	B	hb	13	F. Grierson
1925	Charlie Chan	police	A	hb	8	E. D. Biggers
						D. Lynds
						M. Avallone
1925	Peter Creighton	private	A	hb	5	A. Livingston
1925	Sgt. Elk	police	B	hb	5	E. Wallace
1925	Supt. Laurence Gilmartin	police	B	hb	(15)	C. Barry
1925	Dr. Eustace Hailey	amateur	B	hb	28	A. Wynne
(1925)	Hashknife Hartley	private	A	hb	(26)	W. C. Tuttle
1925	Dr. Lancelot Priestley	amateur	B	hb	72	J. Rhode
1925	Roger Sheringham	amateur	B	hb	10	A. Berkeley
1925	Madame Rosika Storey	amateur	A	hb	8	H. Footner
1925	Richard Verrell	criminal	B	hb	30	B. Graeme
						R. Graeme
1925	Paul Vivanti	criminal	B	hb	6	S. Horler
1926	Supt. Battle	police	B	hb	5	A. Christie
1926	Ben	amateur	B	hb	8	J. J. Farjeon
1926	Gilbert Larose	police	B	hb	28	A. Gask
1926	Nat Ridley	private	A	pb	15	N. Ridley, Jr.
1926	Mortimer Sark	amateur	B	hb	5	J. Hawk
1926	Sir Arthur Sinclair	police	B	hb	(18)	W. S. Masterman
1926	Ludovic Travers	amateur	B	hb	63	C. Bush
1926	Philo Vance	amateur	A	hb	12	S. S. Van Dine
1927	Anthony Bathurst	amateur	B	hb	53	B. Flynn
1927	Miles Bredon	amateur	B	hb	5	R. Knox
1927	Chandos	adventurer	B	hb	10	D. Yates
1927	Martin Dale	criminal	B	hb	9	Herman Landon
1927	Sgt. Trevor Dene	police	B	hb	5	V. Williams
1927	Sir Clinton Driffield	police	B	hb	17	J. J. Connington
1927	Scott Egerton	amateur	B	hb	10	Anthony Gilbert
1927	Philip MacCray		A	hb	5	O. F. Jerome
1927	Jimmie Rezaire	private	B	hb	5	Anthony Armstrong
1927	Race Williams	private	A	hb	8	C. J. Daly
1928	Prof. Luther Bastian	amateur	B	hb	(17)	Gavin Holt
1928	Wu Fang	criminal	B	hb	(6)	Roland Daniel
1928	Col. Alistair Granby	spy	B	hb	17	F. Beeding
1928	Comm. Denzil Grigson	police	B	hb	(8)	A. Broome

Series Character Chronology

YEAR	CHARACTER	TYPE	COUNTRY	BOOK TYPE	NUMBER OF BOOKS	AUTHOR
1928	Insp. Cuthbert Higgins	police	B	hb	35	C. F. Gregg
1928	Sgt. Patrick Aloysius McCarthy	police	B	hb	(53)	J. G. Brandon / G. Brandon
1928	Lynn MacDonald	private	A	hb	7	K. C. Strahan
1928	Bill Saville	police	B	hb	(6)	Roland Daniel
1928	Insp. Shane	police	B	hb	6	S. Truss
1928	Maud Silver	private	B	hb	32	P. Wentworth
1928	Simon Templar	adventurer	B	hb	50+	L. Charteris
1928	Sir Leonard Wallace	spy	B	hb	(8)	Alexander Wilson
1929	Insp. Napoleon Bonaparte	police	B	hb	29	A. W. Upfield
1929	Dame Beatrice Bradley	amateur	B	hb	66	Gladys Mitchell
1929	Albert Campion	amateur	B	hb	27	M. Allingham / Y. Carter
1929	Insp. Carter & Sgt. Bell	police	B	hb	5	E. R. Punshon
1929	Insp. Hugh Collier	police	B	hb	(14)	M. Dalton
1929	Continental Op	private	A	hb	10	D. Hammett
1929	Insp. Frost	police	B	hb	7	H. M. Smith
1929	Insp. Alan Grant	police	B	hb	6	G. Daviot / J. Tey
1929	Col. Duncan Grant	spy	B	hb	7	G. Seton
1929	Sarah Keate	amateur	A	hb	7	M. Eberhart
1929	Insp. McLean	police	B	hb	66	G. Goodchild
1929	Harley Manners	amateur	A	hb	6	C. Dutton
1929	Peter Piper	amateur	A	hb	5	N. B. Mavity
1929	Insp. John Poole	police	B	hb	8	Henry Wade
1929	Ellery Queen	amateur	A	hb	45	E. Queen
1929	Tommy Rankin	police	A	hb	14	M. Propper
1929	Maxwell Sanderson	criminal	A	hb	5	J. J. Chichester
1929	Jim Sands	amateur	A	hb	5	R. J. Casey
1929	Insp. Jim Silver	police	B	hb	(15)	Henry Holt
1929	Supt. Anthony Slade	police	B	hb	(35)	L. Gribble
1929	Jimmy Traynor	private	A	hb	5	A. Livingston
1929	Lt. Valcour	police	A	hb	11	Rufus King
1929	Anthony Vereker	amateur	B	hb	6	R. Forsythe
1929	Insp. Williams	police	B	hb	(5)	H. Clevely
1930	Harker Bellamy	spy	B	hb	11	S. Horler
1930	Henri Bencolin	police	A	hb	6	J. D. Carr
(1930)	Insp. Archie Burford	police	B	hb	7	V. MacClure
1930	Hugh Carding	private	B	hb	7	G. Collins
1930	Joshua Clunk	private	B	hb	12	H. C. Bailey
1930	Thatcher Colt	police	A	hb	8	A. Abbot
1930	James F. Dundee	police	A	hb	5	Anne Austin
1930	Prof. Henry Fielding	amateur	B	hb	(9)	D. Sharp
1930	Insp. Kane	police	A	hb	5	R. Scarlett
1930	Insp. Christopher McKee	police	A	hb	31	H. Reilly
1930	Amos Lee Mappin	amateur	A	hb	10	H. Footner
1930	Jeff Marle	amateur	A	hb	6	J. D. Carr
1930	Jane Marple	amateur	B	hb	16	A. Christie
1930	Kate Marsh	amateur	B	hb	8	G. Lane
1930	Desmond Merrion	amateur	B	hb	61	M. Burton
1930	Gordon Muldrew	police	B	hb	(7)	Luke Allan
1930	Capt. Hugh North	spy	A	hb	25	V. W. Mason
1930	Evan Pinkerton	amateur	A	hb	12	D. Frome
1930	Sebastian Quin	amateur	B	hb	5	S. Horler
1930	Insp. Reynolds	police	B	hb	(8)	Elaine Hamilton
(1930)	Jerry Scant	amateur	B	hb	(5)	L. A. Knight
1930	Insp. Skane	police	A	hb	5	D. Marfield
1930	Ronald Standish	private	B	hb	5	H. C. McNeile
1930	Insp. John Swinton	police	B	hb	5	I. Greig
1930	Philip Tracy	amateur	A	hb	7	H. Ashbrook
1930	Dennis Tyler	police	A	hb	7	Diplomat
1930	Daphne Wrayne	private	B	hb	47	Valentine / Mark Cross
1931	Ronald Camberwell	private	B	hb	10	J. S. Fletcher
1931	Major Peter Castle	spy	B	hb	(6)	Gilderoy Davison
1931	Asaph Clume	private	A	hb	6	R. L. Goldman
1931	Lamont Cranston	adventurer	A	pb	54	Maxwell Grant / W. B. Gibson
1931	Insp. Cummings	police	B	hb	(5)	P. McGuire
1931	Col. Peter Gantian	spy	B	hb	(11)	C. Dawe
1931	Clay Harrison	private	B	hb	5	Clifton Robbins
1931	Paul Irving	private	B	hb	(7)	L. Grex
1931	Insp. Wilton Jacks	police	A	hb	6	J. H. Wallis
1931	Mr. Jellipot	private	B	hb	(10)	S. Fowler
1931	Insp. MacDonald	police	B	hb	46	E. C. R. Lorac
1931	Asey Mayo	amateur	A	hb	24	P. A. Taylor
1931	Li Moh	amateur	B	hb	6	J. Cowdroy
1931	Peter Shane	amateur	A	hb	8	F. Bonnamy
1931	Black John Smith		A	hb	18	J. B. Hendryx
1931	Insp. Stevens	police	B	hb	13	B. Graeme
1931	Twisted Face	criminal	B	hb	(8)	Gilderoy Davison

YEAR	CHARACTER	TYPE	COUNTRY	BOOK TYPE	NUMBER OF BOOKS	AUTHOR
1931	Insp. John Walk	police	B	hb	(7)	Roland Daniel
1931	Hildegarde Withers	amateur	A	hb	17	S. Palmer
1932	Insp. Barnard	police	B	hb	(14)	T. C. H. Jacobs
1932	Mick Cardby	private	B	hb	(27)	David Hume
1932	Gordon Craigie (Dept. Z)	spy	B	hb	29	J. Creasey
1932	Insp. Fillinger	police	B	hb	(6)	P. McGuire
(1932)	Insp. Andy Frampton	police	B	hb	(48)	T. A. Plummer
1932	Christopher Hand	private	A	hb	5	S. H. Page
1932	J. R. Leroy		B	hb	5	B. Perowne
1932	Lessinger	criminal	B	hb	8	R. Essex
1932	Insp. Michael Lord	police	A	hb	6	C. D. King
1932	Insp. Jules Maigret	police	F	hb	78+	G. Simenon
(1932)	Insp. Jack Pearson	police	B	hb	(5)	R. Daniel
1932	Amos Petrie	police	B	hb	7	J. V. Turner
1932	Dr. L. Rees Pons	amateur	A	hb	5	C. D. King
1932	Tiger Standish	spy	B	hb	12	S. Horler
1932	Philip Tolefree	private	B	hb	22	R. A. J. Walling
1933	Supt. Edmund Bendilow	police	B	hb	(5)	Carlton Wallace
1933	Christopher Bond	private	B	hb	9	W. Martyn
1933	Supt. Robert Budd	police	B	hb	(25)	G. Verner
1933	Major Dick Burton	amateur	B	hb	6	M. Beckett
1933	Rex Coulson	adventurer	B	hb	6	Jack Mann
1933	Duke de Richleau	spy	B	hb	11	D. Wheatley
1933	Dr. Gideon Fell	amateur	A	hb	25	J. D. Carr
1933	Trevor Lowe	amateur	B	hb	(14)	G. Verner
1933	Perry Mason	private	A	hb	87+	E. S. Gardner
						T. Chastain
(1933)	Colonel Ormiston	spy	B	hb	(11)	J. M. Walsh
1933	Constable Bobby Owen	police	B	hb	35	E. R. Punshon
1933	Arthur Stukely Pennington	amateur	B	hb	(30)	J. G. Brandon
						G. Brandon
1933	Hugh Rennert	police	A	hb	6	T. Downing
1933	P. C. Richardson	police	B	hb	8	B. Thomson
1933	Charlie Ryan		B	hb	5	J. C. Lenehan
1933	Phineas Spinnet	private	B	hb	(14)	A. Soutar
1933	"Doc" Summers		B	hb	(5)	F. Marlowe
1933	Timothy Terrel	spy	B	hb	(18)	S. Maddock
1934	Insp. Roderick Alleyn	police	B	hb	33	N. Marsh
1934	Major Jack Atherley	amateur	B	hb	(8)	C. Ashton
1934	Biggles	amateur	b	hb	(95)	W. E. Johns
1934	Sgt. Geoffrey Boscobell	police	B	hb	13	C. M. Wills
1934	Capt. Flynn	adventurer	B	hb	(11)	E. L. Long
1934	Insp. Head	police	B	hb	(12)	E. C. Vivian
1934	Richard Herrivell	amateur	B	hb	9	John Bentley
1934	Grace Latham and/or John Primrose	amateur	A	hb	16	L. Ford
1934	Sir Henry Merrivale	amateur	A	hb	24	Carter Dickson
						J. D. Carr
1934	Judge Ephraim Peck	amateur	A	hb	11	A. Derleth
1934	Gregory Sallust	spy	B	hb	11	D. Wheatley
1934	Mr. Swan	amateur	B	hb	5	R. Philmore
1934	Paul Templeton	private	B	hb	13	R. Goyne
1934	Insp. Treadgold	police	B	hb	7	A. Weymouth
1934	Nero Wolfe	private	A	hb	53+	R. Stout
						R. Goldsborough
1935	Sheriff Rocky Allan	police	A	hb	6	V. Rath
1935	Insp. Victor Bonderant	police	A	hb	7	J. G. Edwards
1935	Freddie Browne	amateur	B	hb	(8)	M. Poole
1935	Bill Crane	private	A	hb	5	J. Latimer
1935	Mr. De Havilland	amateur	B	hb	(12)	J. N. Chance
1935	Jane Amanda Edwards	amateur	A	hb	12	C. M. Russell
1935	Jack Fenner	amateur	A	hb	7	G. H. Coxe
1935	Laurie Fenton	spy	B	hb	(14)	M. Annesley
1935	Lt. Bill French	police	A	hb	13	C. Hale
1935	James Greer	amateur	A	hb	5	N. Gayle
(1935)	Dixon Hawke	private	B	pb	25	anonymous
1935	Sgt. Hemingway	police	B	hb	8	G. Heyer
1935	Percy Huff	amateur	B	hb	(6)	C. Edwards
1935	Henry Hyer	private	A	hb	9	K. Steel
1935	Elisha Macomber	amateur	A	hb	16	K. M. Knight
1935	Lawrence Malone		B	pb	5	G. H. Teed
1935	Insp. Meredith	police	B	hb	(26)	J. Bude
1935	Mr. Moto	spy	A	hb	6	J. P. Marquand
1935	Kent Murdock	amateur	A	hb	23	G. H. Coxe
1935	Patrick O'Brien	police	A	hb	5	I. H. Irwin
1935	Mrs. Palmyra Pym	police	B	hb	28	N. Morland
1935	Lt. Peter Quint	police	A	hb	5	H. Austin
1935	Grant Rushton		B	hb	(5)	G. H. Teed
1935	Doc Savage	adventurer	A	pb	182	K. Robeson
1935	Insp. Schmidt	police	A	hb	51	G. Bagby
1935	Insp. Shelley	police	B	hb	(17)	J. Rowland
1935	Nigel Strangeways	private	B	hb	16	N. Blake

Series Character Chronology / 1343

YEAR	CHARACTER	TYPE	COUNTRY	BOOK TYPE	NUMBER OF BOOKS	AUTHOR
1936	Sir John Appleby	police	B	hb	35	M. Innes
1936	Insp. Edward Beale	police	B	hb	8	R. Penny
1936	Sgt. William Beef	police	B	hb	8	L. Bruce
1936	Roger Bennion	amateur	B	hb	27	H. Adams
1936	Robin Bishop	amateur	A	hb	5	G. Homes
1936	Simon Brade	amateur	A	hb	7	Harriette Campbell
1936	Chester Brett	private	B	hb	(6)	G. Evans
1936	Insp. Cheviot Burmann	police	B	hb	(42)	B. Cobb
1936	David Cane	amateur	B	hb	(6)	J. Courage
1936	Lemmy Caution	police	B	hb	12	P. Cheyney
(1936)	Clive Conrad	private	B	hb	(21)	Frank King
1936	Arthur Crook	private	B	hb	51	Anthony Gilbert
1936	Bartholomew Dane	private	B	hb	(8)	Rex Dark
1936	Dr. Septimus Dodds	private	B	hb	(11)	Sutherland Scott
1936	Peter Duluth	amateur	A	hb	8	P. Quentin
1936	Barney Gantt	amateur	A	hb	8	J. S. Strange
1936	Insp. Gidleigh	police	B	hb	24	S. Truss
1936	Gregory George	private	B	hb	8	Jack Mann
						Gordon Green
1936	Jupiter Jones	amateur	A	hb	5	T. Fuller
1936	Anne & Jeffrey McNeill	amateur	A	hb	19	T. Du Bois
1936	Sir John Meredith	police	B	hb	17	F. Gerard
1936	Dick Pemberty	spy	B	hb	(10)	P. Conde
(1936)	"Rem" Remington		B	hb	6	R. Ladline
1936	Insp. Ryvet	police	B	hb	6	C. Carnac
1936	Irving Todd	police	B	hb	(7)	P. Conde
(1936)	Insp. Wake	police	B	hb	(7)	C. Kingston
1936	Theocritus Lucius Westborough	amateur	A	hb	10	C. B. Clason
1936	Dr. Hugh Westlake	amateur	A	hb	9	J. Stagge
1936	Tony Woolrich	amateur	A	hb	5	M. M. Raison
1937	Maxwell Archer	private	B	hb	(7)	H. Clevely
1937	Insp. Harry Charlton	police	B	hb	11	C. Witting
1937	Jason Cordry	amateur	A	hb	5	J. O'Hanlon
1937	Gerald Frost	adventurer	B	hb	7	S. Horler
1937	Insp. Headcorn	police	B	hb	5	Alice Campbell
1937	Peter Justice	adventurer	B	hb	(5)	F. Duncan
1937	Oliver "O.K." Keene	spy	B	hb	(12)	J. M. Walsh
1937	Sgt. Johnny Lamb	police	B	hb	5	J. Donavan
1937	Capt. Ben Lucias	police	A	hb	6	R. Howes
1937	Capt. Duncan Maclain	private	A	hb	13	B. Kendrick
1937	Insp. John Mallett	police	B	hb	6	C. Hare
1937	John Mannering	criminal	B	hb	47	Anthony Morton
1937	Insp. Steven Mitchell	police	B	hb	13	Josephine Bell
1937	Mr. Pendlebury	amateur	B	hb	(9)	A. Webb
1937	Huntoon Rogers	amateur	A	hb	18	C. Knight
1937	Doug Selby	police	A	hb	9	E. S. Gardner
1937	Lt. Timothy Trant	police	A	hb	8	Q. Patrick
						P. Quentin
1937	Dr. David Wintringham	amateur	B	hb	12	Josephine Bell
1937	Leonidas Witherall	amateur	A	hb	8	A. Tilton
1938	Sgt. Peter Bradfield	police	B	hb	9	C. Witting
1938	Slim Callaghan	private	B	hb	10	P. Cheyney
1938	Humphrey Campbell	private	A	hb	5	G. Homes
1938	Mary Carner	private	A	hb	5	Z. Popkin
1938	Norman Conquest	adventurer	B	hb	51	B. Gray
1938	Sgt. Paul Dean	police	B	hb	(5)	B. Francis
1938	Michael Dundas	amateur	A	hb	8	V. Rath
1938	Insp. Septimus Finch	police	B	hb	21	M. Erskine
1938	Cyrus Hatch	amateur	A	hb	8	F. C. Davis
1938	Tony Hunter	private	A	hb	10	R. G. Dean
1938	Supt. Mallett	police	B	hb	(19)	M. Fitt
1938	Lt. Stephen Mayhew	police	A	hb	7	D. B. Olsen
1938	The Great Merlini	amateur	A	hb	5	C. Rawson
1938	Peter Mohune	spy	B	hb	(5)	P. Groom
1938	Insp. George Muir	police	B	hb	15	F. Grierson
1938	Richard Rollison	adventurer	B	hb	61	J. Creasey
						W. V. Butler
1938	Insp. Joel Saber	police	B	hb	(6)	Gavin Holt
1938	Paul Temple	amateur	B	hb	14	F. Durbridge
						P. Temple
1938	Basil Willing	amateur	A	hb	13+	H. McCloy
(1939)	Insp. William Austen	police	B	hb	(29)	Anne Hocking
1939	Peter & Janet Barron	amateur	B	hb	5	R. Darby
1939	Luke Bradley	police	A	hb	5	H. Pentecost
(1939)	Insp. Cadman	police	B	hb	(5)	C. Rushton
1939	Tod Claymore	amateur	B	hb	8	T. Claymore
1939	Insp. Bill Cromwell	police	B	hb	43	V. Gunn
1939	Patrick Dawlish	spy	B	hb	50	G. Ashe
1939	Homer Evans	amateur	A	hb	9	Elliot Paul
1939	Peter Grayleigh	adventurer	B	hb	14	Colin Robertson
1939	Supt. Gordon Knollis	police	B	hb	(11)	F. Vivian

YEAR	CHARACTER	TYPE	COUNTRY	BOOK TYPE	NUMBER OF BOOKS	AUTHOR
1939	Donald Lam	private	A	hb	29	A. A. Fair
1939	John J. Malone	private	A	hb	14	C. Rice
1939	Dick Marlowe	private	B	hb	(6)	L. M. Harris John Bentley
1939	Philip Marlowe	private	A	hb	8	R. Chandler
1939	Bruce Murdoch	spy	B	hb	7	H. Conteris N. Deane
1939	Rachel & Jennifer Murdock	amateur	A	hb	13	D. B. Olsen
1939	Fergus O'Breen	private	A	hb	6	A. Boucher
1939	Papa Pontivy	spy	B	hb	(16)	B. Newman
1939	Sheriff Jess Roden	police	A	hb	21	A. B. Cunningham
1939	Desmond Shannon	private	A	hb	17	M. V. Heberden
1939	Mike Shayne	private	A	hb	69	B. Halliday
1939	Jim Steele	amateur	A	hb	7	D. Chambers
1939	Edward Trelawny	amateur	A	hb	(6)	A. R. Long
1939	Matt Winters	amateur	A	hb	(7)	I. Oellrichs
1939	Alister Woodhead	spy	B	hb	(13)	E. H. Clements
1940	Jane Carberry	amateur	B	hb	(5)	B. Symons
1940	Saturnin Dax	police	B	hb	(34)	M. Cumberland
1940	Toby Dyke	amateur	B	hb	5	E. X. Ferrars
1940	Earl of Millington		B	hb	(5)	G. Hackforth-Jones
1940	Supt. Roger Ellerdine	police	B	hb	11	C. M. Wills
1940	Johnny Fletcher & Sam Cragg	amateur	A	hb	14	F. Gruber
1940	Henry Gamadge	amateur	A	hb	16	E. Daly
1940	Capt. Bill Grady	police	A	hb	8	I. S. Shriber
1940	Tommy Hambledon	spy	B	hb	26	M. Coles
1940	Elsie May Hunt & Tim Mulligan	amateur	A	hb	18	A. M. Stein
1940	Rex McBride	private	A	hb	6	C. F. Adams
1940	Pam & Jerry North	amateur	A	hb	26	F. Lockridge
1940	"Peter" Piper	amateur	A	hb	(6)	A. R. Long
1940	Christopher Storm	amateur	A	hb	7	W. A. Barber
1940	Haila & Jeff Troy	amateur	A	hb	9	K. Roos
1940	Harvey Tuke	police	B	hb	7	D. G. Browne
1941	Pat & Jean Abbott	amateur	A	hb	(26)	F. Crane
1941	John Bent	private	A	hb	7	H. C. Branson
1941	Mike Brett	spy	B	hb	6	Keith Campbell
1941	Insp. Cockrill	police	B	hb	7	C. Brand
1941	Quinny Hite	private	A	hb	5	R. Burke
1941	Insp. Thomas Littlejohn	police	B	hb	57	G. Bellairs
1941	Sgt. Mallory	police	B	pb	5	T. J. R. Sennocke
(1941)	Jim Malloy	police	A	hb	(9)	C. Stoddard
1941	Buddy Mustard	private	B	hb	(16)	Roland Daniel
1941	Liz Parrott	amateur	A	hb	7	Manning Long
1941	Theodore I. Terhune	amateur	B	hb	8	B. Graeme
1942	Jack "Flash" Casey	amateur	A	hb	7	G. H. Coxe
1942	Roger Fleming		B	hb	(7)	P. Ayres S. Harvester
1942	Paul Kilgerrin	private	A	hb	11	C. L. Leonard
1942	"Tiger" Lester	spy	B	hb	12	D. Betteridge
1942	Insp. Gridley Nelson	police	A	hb	13	R. Fenisong
1942	Dr. Stanislaus Alexander Palfrey	spy	B	hb	33	J. Creasey
1942	Marshal Ben Pedley	police	A	hb	9	S. Sterling
1942	Francis Pettigrew	private	B	hb	5	C. Hare
1942	Lt. Richard Tuck	police	A	hb	5	Lange Lewis
1942	Insp. Roger West	police	B	hb	42	J. Creasey
1943	Martin Ames	amateur	A	hb	6	A. Eichler
1943	Supt. John Bellamy	police	B	hb	(7)	T. C. H. Jacobs
1943	Arab & Andy Blake	amateur	A	hb	5	R. Powell
1943	Steve Carter	private	A	hb	(7)	A. R. Long
1943	Rush Henry	private	A	hb	(5)	Joe Barry
1943	Insp. Carl Knickman	police	A	hb	6	A. Eichler
1943	Lydford Long	amateur	B	hb	13	H. Carstairs
1943	Alonzo MacTavish	criminal	B	pb	7	P. Cheyney
1943	John Marshall	private	B	hb	13	J. M. Fox
1943	Dr. Morelle	amateur	B	hb	15	E. Dudley
1943	Jim O'Neill	police	A	hb	5	D. M. Disney
1944	Kit Acton	amateur	A	hb	5	M. Bramhall
1944	Maria Black	amateur	B	hb	5	J. Slate
1944	Lanny Budd	spy	A	hb	7	U. Sinclair
1944	Garry Dean	amateur	A	hb	6	P. Whelton
1944	Gervase Fen	amateur	B	hb	11	E. Crispin
1944	Insp. Grogan	police	B	hb	(19)	M. Neville
1944	Albie Harris	amateur	A	hb	6	A. Dean
1944	Dr. Harry Manson	police	B	hb	(35)	E. Radford
1944	Martin Speed		B	hb	9	G. Elliott
1944	Mordecai Tremaine	amateur	B	hb	(6)	M. G. Hugi John Norman F. Duncan
1945	Sgt. Peter Bradfield	police	B	hb	9	C. Witting
1945	Peter Eversleigh	amateur	B	hb	6	R. Goyne
(1945)	Insp. Alan Frazer	police	B	hb	(33)	H. Desmond

Series Character Chronology

YEAR	CHARACTER	TYPE	COUNTRY	BOOK TYPE	NUMBER OF BOOKS	AUTHOR
1945	Jub Freeman	police	A	hb	10	L. Treat
1945	Ben Helm	private	A	hb	6	B. Fischer
1945	Asmun Hill		B	hb	(6)	H. Hawton
1945	Patrick Laing	amateur	A	hb	6	P. Laing
1945	Jenny Gilette (Lewis) & Hunter Lewis	amateur	A	hb	6	R. Grey
1945	Sir Abercrombie Lewker	amateur	B	hb	18	S. Styles
1945	Dr. Sam: Johnson	amateur	A	hb	5+	L. de la Torre
1945	Prof. A. Pennyfeather	amateur	A	hb	6	D. B. Olsen
1945	Solar Pons	private	A	hb	16	A. Derleth
						B. Copper
1945	Insp. Julian Rivers	police	B	hb	15	C. Carnac
1945	Steve Silk	private	B	hb	(15)	J. B. O'Sullivan
1945	Prof. John Stubbs	amateur	B	hb	7	R. T. Campbell
1945	Mitch Taylor	police	A	hb	7	L. Treat
1945	Insp. York	police	B	hb	(5)	M. Durham
1946	Supt. Andrew Ash	police	B	hb	13	F. Grierson
1946	Insp. William Bastian	police	B	hb	(5)	Richard Harrison
1946	Lt. Austin Clapp	police	A	hb	7	Wade Miller
1946	Major Brains Cunningham	spy	B	hb	(15)	E. P. Thorne
1946	Jeff DiMarco	amateur	A	hb	8	D. M. Disney
1946	Johnny DuVivien	amateur	B	hb	5	N. Spain
1946	Insp. Flagg	police	B	hb	(33)	J. Cassells
						W. M. Duncan
1946	Grant Garfield	private	B	hb	(20)	C. Franklin
1946	Insp. Merton Heimrich	police	A	hb	25	F. Lockridge
						R. Lockridge
1946	Charles Horne	private	A	hb	5	W. Tucker
1946	Hank Janson	private	B	pb	214	Hank Janson
(1946)	Insp. "Duck" Mallard	police	B	hb	(17)	A. Spiller
1946	Miss Otis	criminal	B	pb	(18)	B. Sarto
1946	Paul Pine	private	A	hb	5	John Evans
						H. Browne
1946	John Prentice	adventurer	B	hb	(5)	Sea-Lion
1946	Insp. Michael Regan	police	B	hb	5	E. Hale
1946	Dick Tracy	police	A	pb	11	C. Gould
						Anonymous
						M. A. Collins
						W. Johnston
1947	Silas Booth	private	A	hb	(6)	J. L. Linklater
1947	Roger Brook	spy	B	hb	12	D. Wheatley
1947	Peter Chambers	private	A	hb	35	H. Kane
1947	Insp. Garth	police	B	hb	6	H. Blayn
						N. Karta
1947	Mike Hammer	private	A	hb	12+	M. Spillane
1947	Insp. Hazelrigg	police	B	hb	8	M. Gilbert
1947	Ed & Am Hunter	amateur	A	hb	7	F. Brown
1947	Capt. Steve Johnson	police	A	hb	5	H. L. Nelson
1947	Scott Jordan	private	A	hb	12	H. Q. Masur
1947	Johnny Liddell	private	A	hb	31	Frank Kane
1947	Mac	private	A	hb	17	T. B. Dewey
1947	Supt. Arthur Manning	police	B	hb	(7)	B. Cobb
1947	Insp. Dick Mason	police	B	hb	9	R. Armstrong
1947	Insp. Lancelot Carolus Smith	police	B	hb	5	N. Berrow
1947	Max Thursday	private	A	hb	6	Wade Miller
1947	Julia Tyler	amateur	A	hb	7	L. Revell
1947	Gil Vine	private	A	hb	8	S. Sterling
1948	Jane & Dagobert Brown	amateur	B	hb	12	D. Ames
1948	Rev. Martin Buell	amateur	A	hb	7	M. Scherf
1948	Doc Connor	amateur	A	hb	5	J. Dolph
1948	Mark Corrigan	spy	B	hb	30	M. Corrigan
1948	Roger Crammond	amateur	B	hb	8	T. Muir
1948	Insp. Peter Curwen	police	B	hb	(7)	R. Vickers
(1948)	Johnny Dekker	private	B	pb	17	J. Dekker
1948	Steve Drake	private	A	hb	5	R. Ellington
1948	Jeremiah X. Gibson	police	A	hb	18	Hampton Stone
1948	Eve Gill	amateur	B	hb	6	S. Jepson
1948	Insp. Andy McMurdo	police	B	hb	(8)	N. Morland
1948	Philip Odell	private	B	hb	(5)	Lester Powell
1948	Supt. Sandyman	police	B	hb	(7)	Neill Graham
1949	Lew Archer	private	A	hb	19	J. Macdonald
						J. R. Macdonald
						R. Macdonald
1949	Dr. Douglas Baynes	amateur	B	hb	6	V. Bell
1949	Miriam Birdseye	amateur	B	hb	6	N. Spain
1949	Charles Blessington	spy	B	hb	(5)	J. Sherwood
1949	Nick Cranley	private	B	pb	(15)	M. Storme
1949	Judge Dee	police	B	hb	18	R. van Gulik
1949	Jim Dunn	private	A	hb	8	H. L. Nelson
1949	Temple Fortune	private	B	hb	(20)	T. C. H. Jacobs
1949	Carney Wilde	private	A	hb	7	B. Spicer
1950	Sam Birge	police	A	hb	6	W. Krasner

YEAR	CHARACTER	TYPE	COUNTRY	BOOK TYPE	NUMBER OF BOOKS	AUTHOR
1950	George Dixon	police	B	hb	(6)	T. Willis
						George Dixon
						Rex Edwards
1950	Johnny Maguire	private	A	pb	6	R. Himmel
1950	Insp. Ambrose Mahon	police	B	hb	(7)	S. H. Courtier
1950	Lefty O'Connor		B	pb	(7)	B. Shannon
1950	Insp. Ronald Price	police	B	hb	5	J. Cannan
1950	John Ripley	police	A	hb	5	Gordons
1950	Shell Scott	private	A	pb	39	R. S. Prather
						David Knight
1950	John Cornelius Franklin Scotter	private	B	hb	7	T. Warriner
1950	Danny Spade	private	B	pb	36	D. Ambler
						D. Spade
1950	Luke Speare & Schuyler Cole	private	A	hb	6	F. C. Davis
1950	Sumuru	criminal	A	pb	5	S. Rohmer
1951	Rex Banner	amateur	B	hb	(7)	Robert Chapman
1951	Jim Bennett	private	A	hb	(12)	Robert Martin
1951	Hugo Bishop	amateur	B	hb	6	S. Rattray
1951	Glenn Bowman	private	B	hb	(38)	H. Howard
1951	Chico Brett	private	B	hb	16	Kevin O'Hara
1951	Steve Conacher	private	A	hb	8	Adam Knight
1951	Montague Cork	amateur	B	hb	5	Macdonald Hastings
1951	Timothy Dane	private	A	hb	9	W. Ard
1951	Hubert Bonisseur de la Bath	spy	F	hb	16	J. Bruce
1951	Simon Drake	private	A	hb	6	H. Nielsen
1951	Insp. George Felse (and family)	police	B	hb	13	E. Pargeter
1951	Joe Gall	spy	A	pb	23	J. A. Phillips
						P. Atlee
1951	Carl Good	private	A	pb	(6)	R. O. Saber
1951	Insp. Hugh Gordon	police	B	hb	7	S. Gilruth
1951	Jacare		B	pb	(6)	V. Norwood
1951	Lonnie	police	B	pb	6	H. Lugar
1951	Vicky McBain	private	B	hb	8	Colin Robertson
1951	Insp. George Marshall	police	B	hb	(12)	P. Barrington
						C. Barling
1951	Michael the O'Kelly	adventurer	B	hb	7	M. O'Brine
1951	Capt. Wade Paris	police	A	hb	10	Ben Benson
1951	Lt. Romano	police	A	hb	9	David Alexander
1951	Laura Scudamore	criminal	B	hb	7	R. Armstrong
1951	Max Strong	private	Au	pb	(23)	R. Dudgeon
1952	Johnny April	private	A	hb	5	M. Roscoe
1952	Dick Barton			hb	7	various hands
1952	Red Benton			pb	5	M. Clinten
1952	Steve Harragan	private	A	hb	9	S. Harragan
1952	Hooky Heffern(m)an	private	B	hb	21	L. Meynell
1952	Kent Howard		B	pb	6	Kent Howard
1952	Milo March	private	A	hb	21	M. E. Chaber
1952	John Piper	private	B	hb	(37)	H. Carmichael
1952	Father Shanley	amateur	A	hb	9	J. Webb
1952	Insp. Smith	police	B	hb	(10)	S. Troy
1953	James Bond	spy	B	hb	25+	I. Fleming
						R. Markham
						John Gardner
						Christopher Wood
1953	Mark Brandon	private	B	hb	7	V. Warren
1953	Carl Dekker		Au	pb	(10)	C. Dekker
1953	Insp. Patrick Duffy	police	B	hb	9	N. Fitzgerald
1953	Johnny Fedora	spy	B	hb	(16)	D. Cory
1953	Gentle Hoggerty		B	pb	6	Griff
						B. Sarto
1953	Barney Hyde	private	B	hb	9	N. Brent
1953	Pine-Top Jones		B	pb	10	B. Harding
1953	Andy Kane		Au	pb	5	Carter Brown
(1953)	Larry Kent	private	Au	pb	(334)	D. Haring
1953	Ralph Lindsey	police	A	hb	7	Ben Benson
1953	Johnny Macall	private	B	hb	6	G. Fairlie
1953	Richard Maidment		B	hb	(6)	M. Cronin
1953	William Mitchell	private	B	hb	5	H. A. Wrenn
1953	Hart Muldoon	adventurer	A	pb	5	J. Flagg
1953	Ed Noon	private	A	hb	32+	M. Avallone
1953	Joe Puma	private	A	pb	8	R. Scott
						W. C. Gault
1953	Gregory Quist	private	A	hb	9	W. C. MacDonald
1954	Don Cadee	private	A	hb	9	S. Dean
1954	Steve Craig	private	B	hb	(9)	B. Winter
1954	Brad Dolan	adventurer	A	pb	6	W. Fuller
1954	Gil Donan	police	A	hb	5	M. P. Hood
1954	Horatio Green	amateur	B	hb	5	B. Nichols
1954	Bart Hardin	amateur	A	hb	8	David Alexander
1954	Insp. Simon Manton	police	B	hb	(13)	M. Underwood
1954	Insp. Harry Martineau	police	B	hb	(14)	M. Procter

Series Character Chronology

YEAR	CHARACTER	TYPE	COUNTRY	BOOK TYPE	NUMBER OF BOOKS	AUTHOR
1954	Lt. Pascal	police	A	hb	6	H. Pentecost
1954	Insp. Pitt	police	B	hb	(7)	J. F. Straker
1954	San Antonio	police	F	hb	11	San Antonio
1954	Rampion Savage	amateur	B	hb	12	James Turner
1954	Ludovic Saxon	adventurer	B	hb	(21)	J. Cassells
1954	John & Sally Strang	amateur	B	hb	(6)	H. Brinton
1954	Larry Vernon	private	B	hb	(6)	D. Bateson
1955	Insp. William Baker	police	B	hb	(8)	O. Mills
1955	Marc Brody	amateur	Au	pb	79	M. Brody
1955	Brock Callahan	private	A	hb	13	W. C. Gault
1955	Nicholas Carnish		B	hc	(6)	A. MacKenzie
1955	John Chadwick	private	B	hb	7	G. Cobden
1955	Carolus Deene	amateur	B	hb	23	L. Bruce
1955	Supt. Michael Drexel	police	B	hb	5	G. Usher
1955	Chester Drum	private	A	pb	20	S. Marlowe / R. S. Prather
1955	Sam Durell	spy	A	pb	48	E. S. Aarons / W. B. Aarons
1955	Insp. George Gently	police	B	hb	38+	A. Hunter
1955	Commander George Gideon	police	B	hb	26	J. J. Marric / W. V. Butler / J. Creasey
1955	Miss Hogg	private	B	hb	9	A. Lee
1955	Sugar Kane	private	B	hb	29	L. Marshall
(1955)	Malcolm Kenton	spy	B	hb	(5)	S. Harvester
1955	Solo Malcolm	private	B	hb	(37)	Neill Graham
1955	Hiram Potter	amateur	A	hb	11	Rae Foley
1955	Mavis Seidlitz	private	Au	pb	13	Carter Brown
1955	Pete Selby	police	A	pb	10	Jonathan Craig
1956	Steve Carella (87th Precinct)	police	A	pb	41+	E. McBain
1956	Quentin Eady	amateur	B	hb	(6)	E. P. Thorne
1956	Michael Grant	private	B	hb	(7)	Roland Daniel
1956	Daniel Port	private	A	pb	6	P. Rabe
1956	Julia Probyn	spy	B	hb	7	A. Bridge
1956	Richard Quintain	spy	B	pb	16	W. H. Baker / W. A. Ballinger
1956	Nathan Shapiro	police	A	hb	12	F. Lockridge / R. Lockridge
1956	Daye Smith	amateur	B	hb	(13)	F. Usher
1956	Ambrose Usher	amateur	B	hb	7+	J. Davey
1956	Al Wheeler	police	Au	pb	59	Carter Brown
1957	Bill Banning	private	B	hb	8	Nat Easton
1957	Steve Bentley	amateur	A	pb	9	R. Dietrich
1957	Danny Boyd	private	Au	pb	33	Carter Brown
1957	Insp. Bradbury	police	B	hb	5	N. Longmate
(1957)	Supt. Bradley	police	B	hb	(11)	Colin Robertson
1957	Johnny Buchanan	private	Au	pb	22	K. T. McCall
1957	Prof. Ronald Challis	amateur	B	hb	5	Shane Martin
1957	Insp. John Coffin	police	B	hb	18+	Gwendoline Butler
1957	Brad Ford	private	B	hb	5	H. Hobson
1957	Pete Fry	private	B	hb	15	P. Fry
1957	Insp. "Digger" Haig	police	B	hb	(6)	S. H. Courtier
1957	Nathan Hawk	private	A	pb	12	B. McKnight
1957	Insp. Michael Hornsley	police	B	hb	5	E. Salter
1957	Grave-Digger Jones & Coffin Ed Johnson	police	A	pb	8	C. Himes
1957	Morocco Jones	private	A	pb	5	Jack Baynes
1957	Insp. Lovick	police	B	hb	(15)	G. M. Wilson
1957	Mark Raeburn	private	B	hb	6	M. Gair
1957	Pete Schofield	private	A	pb	9	T. B. Dewey
1957	Colin Thane & Bill Moss	police	B	hb	20+	B. Knox
1957	Honey West	private	A	pb	11	G. G. Fickling
1958	Burns Bannion	private	A	pb	(8)	Earl Norman
1958	Jake Barrow	private	A	pb	6	N. Quarry
1958	Clutha	private	B	hb	7	H. Munro
1958	Tony Costaine & Bert McCall	private	A	pb	7	N. MacNeil
1958	Matt Erridge	amateur	A	hb	23	A. M. Stein
1958	Ben Gates	private	A	pb	5	R. Kyle
1958	Richard Graham	amateur	B	hb	5	J. Welcome
1958	Jeff Green	private	A	hb	5	C. Keith
1958	Max Heald	spy	B	hb	6	H. Hossent
1958	Martin Kane	private	Au	pb	14	Kane
1958	Gen. Charles Kirk	spy	B	hb	(8)	J. Blackburn
1958	Insp. Gregory Pellew	police	B	hb	11	V. Gielgud
1958	M. Pinaud	police	B	hb	27	P. Audemars
1958	Julian Prescot	private	B	hb	9	J. Prescot
1958	Insp. Purbright	police	B	hb	12	Colin Watson
1958	Col. Charles Russell	spy	B	hb	25+	W. Haggard
1958	Supt. Swinton	police	B	hb	(7)	P. Flower
1958	Garaway Trenton		B	hb	7	J. P. Carstairs

YEAR	CHARACTER	TYPE	COUNTRY	BOOK TYPE	NUMBER OF BOOKS	AUTHOR
1959	Col. Richard Barne	amateur	B	hb	(6)	E. G. Cousins
1959	Father Joseph Bredder	amateur	A	hb	11	L. Holton
1959	Chief Fred Fellows	police	A	hb	11	H. Waugh
1959	James Fraser		B	hb	(5)	James Wood
1959	Mark Kilby	private	A	pb	6	R. C. Frazer
1959	Johnny Killain	private	A	pb	5	D. J. Marlowe
1959	Lou Largo	private	A	pb	6	W. Ard
1959	McHugh	spy	A	pb	5	J. Flynn
1959	Monty Nash	spy	A	pb	5	R. Telfair
1959	Patrick Petrella	police	B	hb	5+	M. Gilbert
1959	Ed Rivers	private	A	pb	5	T. Powell
1959	Rocky Steele	private	A	pb	6	J. B. West
1959	Insp. Henry Tibbett	police	B	hb	18+	P. Moyes
1959	Insp. Fadiman Wace	police	B	hb	16	R. Simons
1960	Insp. Herbert Broom	police	B	hb	(6)	F. Hurt
1960	Sgt. Caleb Cluff	police	B	hb	11	G. North
1960	Simon Good	criminal	B	hb	6	George Davis
1960	Insp. Paul Grainger	police	B	hb	5	Fiona Sinclair
1960	Matt Helm	spy	A	pb	25+	D. Hamilton
1960	Lt. Luis Mendoza	police	A	hb	38	Dell Shannon
1960	Commander Esmonde Shaw	spy	B	hb	21+	P. McCutchan
1960	Dorian Silk	spy	B	hb	(12)	S. Harvester
1960	Giff Speer	police	A	pb	9	D. Tracy
1961	Supt. Bradley	police	B	hb	11	Colin Robertson
1961	George Crowder	amateur	A	hb	7	H. Pentecost
1961	Stephen Dain	police	A	pb	5	R. Sheckley
1961	David Danning	private	A	pb	8	D. von Elsner
1961	Jesse Falkenstein	private	A	hb	12	L. Egan
1961	Adam Flute	private	B	hb	6	D. Launay
1961	Paul Harris	amateur	B	hb	13+	G. Black
1961	Hoeffler & Harrigan	spy	A	hb	7	P. O'Malley
1961	Rick Holman	private	Au	pb	35	Carter Brown
1961	Mark Preston	private	B	hb	35+	Peter Chambers
1961	Dale Shand	private	B	hb	(13)	D. Enefer
1961	George Smiley	spy	B	hb	7+	J. LeCarre
1961	John Putnam Thatcher	amateur	A	hb	20+	Emma Lathen
1961	Vic Varallo	police	A	hb	13	L. Egan
1962	Pierre Chambrun	amateur	A	hb	23	H. Pentecost
1962	Paul Chavasse	spy	B	hb	6	M. Fallon
1962	Supt. Adam Dalgliesh	police	B	hb	9+	P. D. James
1962	Charmian Daniels	police	B	hb	12+	Jennie Melville
1962	Capt. Jose da Silva	police	A	hb	10	R. L. Fish
1962	Earl Drake	criminal	A	pb	12	D. J. Marlowe
1962	Ian Firth	private	B	hb	(6)	Ludovic Peters
1962	William Holmes	spy	B	hb	7	C. V. Bark
1962	Adam Ludlow	amateur	B	hb	5	S. Nash
(1962)	Slade McGinty	private	B	hb	(5)	J. Pendower
1962	Antony Maitland	private	B	hb	48	Sara Woods
1962	Nameless ("Harry Palmer" in films)	spy	B	hb	7+	L. Deighton
1962	Parker	criminal	A	pb	16	R. Stark
1962	Claude Ravel	spy	B	hb	(9)	Bradshaw Jones
1962	Bernard Simmons	police	A	hb	7	F. Lockridge R. Lockridge
1962	Insp. Joshua Smarles	police	B	hb	8	M. Urquhart
1962	Insp. Van der Valk	police	B	hb	11+	N. Freeling
1962	Steve Wayne	private	B	hb	(9)	T. Harknett
1963	Larry Baker	amateur	Au	pb	6	Carter Brown
1963	Lt. Lee Barcello	police	A	hb	6	S. Ransome
1963	Hilary Brand	adventurer	B	pb	10	Hilary Brand H. Janson
1963	Jan Darzek	private	A	hb	5+	L. Biggle
1963	Brock Devlin	private	B	hb	(12)	Scott Mitchell
(1963)	Supt. Frank Drury	police	B	hb	(5)	P. Marlowe
1963	Bart Gould	spy	A	pb	8	Joseph Hilton J. Milton
1963	David Grant	spy	B	hb	10	G. Mair
1963	Insp. George Judd	police	B	hb	5	E. Bruton
1963	Simon Larren	spy	B	hb	(10)	R. Charles
1963	Insp. Marcus MacLurg	police	B	hb	(5)	R. Petrie
1963	James Packard	spy	B	hb	12	R. C. Galway
1963	Supt. Donald Reamer	police	B	hb	13	W. M. Duncan
1964	Martin Ainsworth	spy	B	hb	5	M. Underwood
1964	Insp. Salvador Borges	police	B	hb	6	J. Bonett
1964	Webb Carrick	police	B	hb	14+	B. Knox
1964	Jimmy Carroll		B	hb	(5)	H. McCutcheon
1964	Nick Carter	spy	A	pb	261	Nick Carter
1964	Bart Condor	private	B	hb	(6)	W. Wright
1964	Ben Corbin		A	pb	6	Robert Crane
1964	Talos Cord	spy	B	hb	6	Robert MacLeod
1964	Insp. Wilfred Dover	police	B	hb	10	J. Porter
1964	Kate Fansler	amateur	A	hb	10+	A. Cross

Series Character Chronology

YEAR	CHARACTER	TYPE	COUNTRY	BOOK TYPE	NUMBER OF BOOKS	AUTHOR
1964	Insp. Ganesh Ghote	police	B	hb	18+	H. R. F. Keating
1964	Alan Grofield	criminal	A	pb	7	R. Stark
1964	Gregory Hiller	spy	A	pb	5	J. Laflin
1964	Charles Hood	spy	B	hb	(6)	J. Mayo
1964	John Keith	spy	A	pb	8	N. Daniels
1964	Homer Kelly	private	A	hb	7+	J. Langton
1964	Dr. Jason Love	spy	B	hb	9+	J. Leasor
1964	Travis McGee	adventurer	A	pb	21	J. D. MacDonald
1964	Sgt. Ivor Maddox	police	A	hb	13	E. Linington
1964	Insp. Trevor Nicholls	police	B	hb	7	G. Peters
1964	Boysie Oakes	spy	B	hb	9	J. Gardner
1964	Nicholas Pym		B	hb	5	John Sanders
1964	Bill Rice	private	B	hb	(8)	M. Stand
1964	Rabbi David Small	amateur	A	hb	9+	H. Kemelman
1964	Curt Stone	private	A	hb	5	J. Seward
1964	Peter Styles	amateur	A	hb	18	J. Philips
1964	Insp. Reg Wexford	police	B	hb	15+	R. Rendell
1965	Modesty Blaise	spy	B	hb	28+	P. O'Donnell
1965	Johnny Canuck	private	B	hb	8	J. Moffatt
1965	Dr. Emmanuel Cellini	amateur	B	hb	11	Michael Halliday
1965	John Gail	spy	B	pb	7	S. Frances
1965	Joaquin Hawks	spy	A	pb	5	B. S. Ballinger
1965	Paul Hedley	amateur	B	hb	7	B. Healey
(1965)	Mark Hood	spy	B	pb	(14)	James Dark
1965	Insp. Bill Houghton	police	B	hb	5	M. Culpan
1965	Insp. Harry James	police	B	hb	9	K. Giles
1965	John Jericho	amateur	A	hb	6	H. Pentecost
1965	Quiller	spy	B	hb	14+	Adam Hall
1965	Kelly Robinson & Alexander Scott	spy	A	pb	7	J. Tiger
1965	Maxwell Smart	spy	A	pb	9	W. Johnston
1965	Napoleon Solo	spy	A	pb	22	various hands
1965	Virgil Tibbs	police	A	hb	9	J. Ball
1965	Dick Van Loan	adventurer	A	pb	22	R. Wallace
1965	Peter Ward	spy	A	pb	10	D. St. John
(1966)	Jonathan Blake	private	B	hb	(34)	J. N. Chance
1966	Mike Brooks	spy	B	hb	5	H. T. Rothwell
1966	James Christopher	spy	A	pb	11	Curtis Steele
1966	Barnabas Collins	amateur	A	pb	32	Marilyn Ross
1966	Tim Corrigan	police	A	pb	6	E. Queen
1966	Jules de Grandin	private	A	hb	7	Seabury Quinn
1966	Mike Faraday	private	B	hb	52+	B. Copper
1966	Haggai Godin	spy	B	hb	6	O. John
1966	Insp. Hallan	police	B	hb	(11)	George Douglas
1966	Timothy Herring	amateur	B	hb	6	M. Torrie
1966	Phil Kramer	private	A	hb	5	P. Kruger
1966	Pete McGrath	private	A	hb	10	Michael Brett
1966	Scobie Malone	policq	Au	hb	7+	J. Cleary
1966	Jim Piron	private	B	hb	9	E. McGirr
1966	Emily Pollifax	amateur	A	hb	9+	D. Gilman
1966	Jim Qwilleran	amateur	A	hb	11+	L. J. Braun
(1966)	Supt. Charles Ripley	police	B	hb	(7)+	J. Wainwright
1966	Secret Agent X	spy	A	pb	8	B. House
1966	Knute Severson	police	A	hb	16+	Tobias Wells
1966	Insp. Christopher Dennis Sloan	police	B	hb	12+	C. Aird
1966	Evan Tanner	spy	A	pb	7	Lawrence Block
1966	Mitch Tobin	amateur	A	hb	5	T. Coe
1966	Jonas Wilde	spy	B	hb	9	A. York
1966	Giles Yoeman	spy	B	hb	5	M. Woodhouse
1967	George Barclay	private	B	hb	5	Ernest Paul
1967	Martin Beck	police	S	hb	10	M. Sjowall
1967	Dave Cannon	amateur	A	hb	5	M. Delving
1967	Sgt. Carnaby-King	police	B	hb	(11)+	P. N. Walker
1967	Lord Darcy	amateur	A	hb	5+	R. Garrett
1967	Dr. Davie	amateur	B	hb	5	V. C. Clinton-Baddeley
1967	Supt. Folly	police	B	hb	6	J. York
1967	Dan Fortune	private	A	hb	15+	Michael Collins
1967	Insp. Matthew Furnival	police	B	hb	(5)	Stella Phillips
1967	Insp. Robert Fusil	police	B	hb	14	P. Alding
1967	Dr. Paul Holton	amateur	A	pb	6	Charlotte Hunt
1967	Kek Huuygens	criminal	A	hb	5	R. L. Fish
1967	Sgt. Masao Masuto	police	A	hb	7+	E. V. Cunningham
1967	Paul Muller	private	B	hb	15	P. Muller
1967	Insp. Tom Pollard	police	B	hb	17+	E. Lemarchand
1967	Sgt. Bob Reed	police	B	hb	5	C. Drummond
1967	Sebastian	spy	A	hb	5+	J. L. Johnson
1968	Insp. Anders	police	B	hb	15	H. Jobson
1968	Insp. William Aveyard	police	B	hb	9	James Fraser
1968	Sam Bawtry		B	hb	(10)	D. Enefer
1968	Tommy Briggs	private	B	hb	6	D. MacDonald
1968	Angel Brown	adventurer	B	hb	13	G. Montrose
1968	James Dingle & Glyn Jones		B	hb	(5)	G. Osborne

YEAR	CHARACTER	TYPE	COUNTRY	BOOK TYPE	NUMBER OF BOOKS	AUTHOR
1968	Ludovic Fender	spy	B	hb	5+	P. Geddes
1968	James Hellier		B	hb	(6)	M. Cronin
1968	Kane Jackson	private	A	hb	5	W. Arden
1968	Johnson Johnson	amateur	B	hb	6+	D. Halliday
1968	Insp. Simon Kenworthy	police	B	hb	17	J. B. Hilton
1968	Tony Lonto	police	A	hb	5+	E. R. Johnson
1968	Supt. James Pibble	police	B	hb	6+	P. Dickinson
1968	Pete Riley	private	B	hb	(5)	P. Quinn
1968	Insp. George Rogers	police	B	hb	17+	Jonathan Ross
1968	Ben Safford	amateur	A	hb	7+	R. B. Dominic
1968	Marc Savage	spy	B	hb	5	M. Eden
1968	Matt Savage		B	hb	(6)	Craig Cooper
1968	Emily Seeton	amateur	B	hb	8+	H. Carvic H. Charles
1968	Phil Sherman	spy	A	pb	21	Don Smith
1968	Supt. Charles Wycliffe	police	B	hb	16+	W. J. Burley
1969	Steve Austin	spy	A	pb	5	M. Caidin
1969	Mack Bolan	adventurer	A	pb	164+	D. Pendleton Jim Peterson
1969	Cabot Cain	adventurer	A	pb	6	A. Caillou
1969	Bill Cartwright	spy	A	pb	10	P. Morgan
1969	Peter Craig	spy	B	hb	7	Kenneth Benton
1969	Insp. John Crow	police	B	hb	8	Roy Lewis
1969	Paul Decker		B	hb	6	G. Hackforth-Jones
1969	G-8	spy	A	pb	9	R. J. Hogan
1969	Lt. Frank Hastings	police	A	hb	16+	C. Wilcox B. Pronzini
1969	Insp. Leric	police	B	hb	5	R. Busby
1969	Malko Linge	spy	F	pb	16	G. de Villiers
1969	George Mado	spy	B	hb	6	W. Tute
1969	Insp. George Masters	police	B	hb	26+	Douglas Clark
1969	Jennifer Norrington, Allessandro Di Ganzarello, Coleridge Tucker	adventurer	B	hb	9	Ivor Drummond
1969	Philip St. Ives	private	A	hb	5+	O. Bleeck
1969	Kate Theobald	amateur	B	hb	(6)	Lionel Black
1969	Richard Wentworth	adventurer	A	pb	14	R. T. M. Scott G. Stockbridge
1970	Dr. David Audley	spy	B	hb	18+	A. Price
1970	Dave Brandstetter	private	A	hb	12+	J. Hansen
1970	Butcher	police	A	pb	35	S. Jason
1970	Sgt. Cribb	police	B	hb	8	P. Lovesey
1970	Tessa Crichton	amateur	B	hb	23	A. Morice
1970	Supt. Andrew Dalziel	police	B	hb	15+	Reginald Hill
1970	John Dortmunder	criminal	A	hb	7+	D. E. Westlake
1970	Marcus Aurelius Farrow	spy	B	hb	20+	Angus Ross
1970	Jonathan Gaunt	police	B	hb	10+	Robert MacLeod
1970	Patrick Grant	amateur	B	hb	5	M. Yorke
1970	Joe Leaphorn	police	A	hb	7+	T. Hillerman
1970	William Martin	spy	A	pb	11	K. Stanton
1970	Sgt. Robert Mather	police	B	hb	9	B. Graeme
1970	Constance Morrison-Burke	amateur	B	hb	5	J. Porter
1970	Max Roper	private	A	hb	7	K. Platt
1970	Spider Scott	criminal	B	hb	8+	K. Royce
1970	John Shaft	private	A	hb	7	E. Tidyman
1970	Paul Shaw	private	A	hb	6	M. Sadler
1971	Dirty Harry Callahan	police	A	pb	16	various hands
1971	Cannon	private	A	hb	8	various hands
1971	Capt. Colson		B	hb	(5)	Alan White
1971	Jim Di Griz	police	B	hb	7+	H. Harrison
1971	Insp. Finch	police	B	hb	16+	J. Thomson
1971	Lt. Kramer	police	B	hb	7+	J. McClure
1971	Turlock Loams	private	A	hb	22+	J. Ruyle
1971	"Nameless"	private	A	hb	22+	B. Pronzini
1971	Johnny Ortiz	police	A	hb	6+	R. M. Stern
1971	Julian Quist	amateur	A	hb	16	H. Pentecost
1971	Donald Robak	private	A	hb	11+	J. L. Hensley
1971	Albert Samson	private	A	hb	7+	M. Z. Lewin
1971	Kitty Telfair	amateur	A	pb	6	F. Stevenson
1971	Matthew Tobin	adventurer	A	pb	7	A. Caillou
1971	Remo Williams	police	A	pb	83+	R. Sapir W. B. Murphy
1972	Steve Austin		A	hb	(5)	M. Caidin
1972	Mario Balzac	police	A	hb	9+	K. C. Constantine
1972	Lee Beckett	private	A	hb	6+	J. Crowe
1972	Dick Benson	adventurer	A	pb	36	K. Robeson
1972	Edmund Blackstone	police	B	hb	6	R. Falkirk
1972	Richard Camellion	spy	A	pb	70+	J. Rosenberger
1972	Lt. Jacob Horowitz	police	A	hb	10+	D. Delman
1972	Jacqueline Kirby	amateur	A	hb	5+	Elizabeth Peters
1972	Johnny Morini	adventurer	A	pb	5	Al Conroy

Series Character Chronology

YEAR	CHARACTER	TYPE	COUNTRY	BOOK TYPE	NUMBER OF BOOKS	AUTHOR
1972	Norah Mulcahaney	police	A	hb	13+	L. O'Donnell
1972	Philis	spy	B	hb	13	Ritchie Perry
1972	Hilary Quayle	amateur	A	hb	5+	Marvin Kaye
1972	Randy Roberts	private	Au	pb	5	Carter Brown
1972	Jeremy Sturrock	police	B	hb	7	Jeremy Sturrock
1973	Supt. Charles Barlow	police	B	hb	6	Elwyn Jones
1973	Major Peter Blair	police	B	hb	8	J. R. L. Anderson
1973	Simon Bognor	police	B	hb	10+	T. Heald
1973	John Bolt	police	A	pb	9	R. Hawkes
1973	Jefferson Boone	adventurer	A	pb	6	J. Messmann
1975	Chick Charleston	police	A	hb	5	A. B. Guthrie
1973	Dakota	private	A	pb	5	G. Ralston
1973	John Eagle	spy	A	pb	14	Paul Edwards
1973	Conan Flagg	amateur	A	hb	6	M. K. Wren
1973	Mark Hardin	adventurer	A	pb	53	L. Derrick
1973	Jefferson Hewitt	private	A	hb	11	John Reese
1973	Alex Jason	adventurer	A	pb	6	A. Sugar
1973	Deputy Marshal Sam McCloud	police	A	pb	6	C. Wilcox / David Wilson
1973	Hawk Macrae	adventurer	A	pb	5	Albert Barker
1973	Mace	adventurer	A	pb	8	L. Chang / C. K. Fong
1973	Philip Magellan	adventurer	A	pb	22	F. Scarpetta / P. McCurtin / A. Fletcher
1973	Ben Martin	adventurer	A	pb	6	J. Messmann
1973	Frank Nolan	criminal	A	pb	7+	M. A. Collins
1973	Melinda Pink	amateur	B	hb	12+	G. Moffat
1973	Dirk Pitt	amateur	A	hb	10+	C. Cussler
1973	Jeff Pride	amateur	A	pb	5	A. O'Neill / J. Heneghan
1973	Ed Razoni & William Jackson	police	A	pb	7	W. B. Murphy
1973	Johnny Rock	adventurer	A	pb	16	B. Rossi
1973	John Samson	police	B	hb	(10)+	M. Tripp
1973	Specialist		B	pb	5	E. Lecale
1973	John Stark	adventurer	B	pb	12	J. Hedges
1973	Moses Wine	private	A	hb	6+	R. L. Simon
1973	Burt Wulff	adventurer	A	pb	14	M. Barry
1974	Insp. Enrique Alvarez	police	B	hb	14+	R. Jeffries
1974	Jacob Ashe	private	A	hb	10+	A. Lyons
1974	Black Widowers	amateur	A	hb	5+	I. Asimov
1974	Jake Brand	adventurer	A	pb	5	R. L. Brent
1974	Henri Castang	police	B	hb	12+	N. Freeling
1974	Rose Epton	private	B	hb	14+	M. Underwood
1974	Irwin M. Fletcher	amateur	A	hb	9+	G. Mcdonald
1974	Jim Hardman	private	A	pb	12	Ralph Dennis
1974	Max Kaufman	police	A	hb	5+	T. Chastain
1974	Francis Xavier Killy	spy	A	pb	6	Simon Quinn
1974	Lt. Kojak	police	A	pb	9	V. B. Miller
1974	Andrew Laird	private	B	hb	7+	R. MacLeod
(1974)	Insp. Lennox	police	B	hb	(10)+	J. Wainwright
1974	David Mallin	private	B	hb	(14)	R. Ormerod
1974	Rev. C. P. Randollph	amateur	A	hb	7	C. M. Smith / T. L. Smith
1974	John Raven	police	B	hb	13+	D. MacKenzie
1974	Mike Ross	private	A	pb	7	K. Carr
1974	Sgt. Joe Ryker	police	A	pb	8	N. DeMille / E. T. Hamill
1974	Britt St. Vincent		A	pb	5	J. F. Rossmann / I. Ross
1974	Supt. Simon Shard	police	B	hb	9+	P. McCutchan
1974	Spenser	private	A	hb	17+	Robert B. Parker
1974	Jason Striker	adventurer	A	pb	5	P. Anthony
1974	Taggart	spy	A	pb	6	R. Hayes
1974	Sgt. William Verity	police	B	hb	5+	F. Selwyn
1974	Henry Highland West		A	pb	7	J. Nazel
1975	Sgt. Nick Atwell	police	B	hb	5	M. Underwood
1975	Huntington Cage	private	A	pb	6	A. Riefe
1975	Supt. Merlin Capricorn	police	B	hb	6	P. G. Winslow
1975	Alexander Chane	adventurer	A	pb	5	R. Hayes
1975	Amelia Emerson	amateur	A	hb	5+	Elizabeth Peters
1975	Insp. Harry Feiffer	police	B	hb	13	W. Marshall
1975	Grijpstra & DeGier	police	B	hb	7+	J. Van de Wetering
1975	Patrick Hardy	private	A	pb	5	Martin Meyers
1975	Joseph Madden	adventurer	A	pb	6	V. J. Santiago
1975	Insp. Morse	police	B	hb	8+	C. Dexter
1975	Molly Owens		A	hb	6	S. Overholser
1975	Charles Paris	amateur	B	hb	15+	Simon Brett
1975	Dr. Quarshie	amateur	A	hb	8	J. Wyllie
1975	Jack Regan	police	B	hb	10+	I. K. Martin / J. Balham

YEAR	CHARACTER	TYPE	COUNTRY	BOOK TYPE	NUMBER OF BOOKS	AUTHOR
1975	Max Roth	spy	B	pb	(9)	H. Arvay
1975	Isaac Sidel	police	A	hb	5+	J. Charyn
1975	Robert Urban		A	pb	7	C. H. Gunther
1975	Gabriel Wager	police	A	hb	8+	Rex Burns
1975	Lyon Wentworth	amateur	A	hb	7+	R. Forrest
1975	John Yard	adventurer	A	pb	5	R. Hayes
1976	Carver Bascombe	private	A	pb	8+	K. Davis
1976	Charlie Bradshaw	private	A	hb	6+	S. Dobyns
1976	Insp. Thomas Brunt	police	B	hb	6	J. B. Hilton
1976	Mrs. Charles	amateur	B	hb	(7)	M. Warner
1976	David Grierson	private	B	hb	(5)	I. Stuart
1976	Al Nudger	private	A	hb	7+	J. Lutz
1976	Blackford Oakes	spy	A	hb	8+	W. F. Buckley
1976	Anna Peters	private	A	hb	5	J. Law
1976	Brock Potter	amateur	A	hb	5	A. Maling
1976	Quarry	criminal	A	pb	5+	M. A. Collins
1976	Jim Rainey	adventurer	A	pb	18	P. McCurtin
1976	Richard Raven		B	hb	11	J. Griffin
1976	Alf Rosher	police	B	hb	10	J. S. Scott
1976	Matthew Scudder	private	A	pb	10+	L. Block
1976	Starsky & Hutch	police	A	pb	8	M. Franklin
1976	Mark Treasure	amateur	B	hb	14+	David Williams
1976	Janine West	amateur	A	pb	5	E. Welles
1977	Cadfael	amateur	B	hb	18+	Ellis Peters
1977	Insp. Neil Carter	police	B	hb	5+	E. Dewhurst
1977	Charlie's Angels	private	A	pb	5	M. Franklin
1977	Father Roger Dowling	amateur	A	hb	12+	R. McInerny
1977	Robert Frederickson	private	A	hb	9+	G. Chesbro
1977	Vladimir Gull	spy	B	hb	6	Anthony Stuart
1977	Matthew Hope	private	A	hb	9+	E. McBain
1977	Lovejoy	amateur	B	hb	13+	Jonathan Gash
1977	Sharon McCone	private	A	hb	11+	M. Muller
1977	Insp. McGarr	police	A	hb	8+	B. Gill
1977	Amos McGuffin	private	A	hb	5+	R. Upton
1977	Dan Mallett	amateur	B	hb	7+	F. Parrish
1977	Charlie Muffin	spy	B	hb	9+	B. Freemantle
1977	Toby Peters	private	A	hb	15+	S. M. Kaminsky
1977	Bernie Rhodenbarr	criminal	A	hb	5+	L. Block
1977	Jemima Shore	amateur	B	hb	9+	Antonia Fraser
1977	Persis Willum	amateur	A	hb	5+	Clarissa Watson
1978	Sgt. Steve Arrow	police	B	hb	5	L. Mantell
1978	Tory Baxter	amateur	A	pb	8	M. Blair
1978	Dr. Russell V. Chillders	private	A	pb	7	J. Sherman
1978	Matt Cobb	amateur	A	hb	6+	W. L. DeAndrea
1978	Virginia Freer	amateur	B	hb	7+	E. Ferrars
1978	Insp. Jean-Paul Gautier	police	B	hb	7+	R. Grayson
1978	Chance Purdue	private	A	hb	5	R. H. Spencer
1978	Insp. Douglas Quantrill	police	B	hb	7+	S. Radley
1978	Maxine Reynolds	amateur	A	pb	7	M. Grove
1978	Horace Rumpole	private	B	pb	8+	J. Mortimer
1978	Pete Sawyer	private	A	hb	8+	M. H. Albert
1978	Peter Shandy	amateur	A	hb	8+	C. MacLeod
1978	Terry Spring	amateur	A	pb	6	J. Kains
1978	Geoffrey Weston	private	A	pb	6+	T. B. Haughey
1978	Yoeman		B	hb	13	Robert Jackson
1979	Lt. Luis Bernal	police	B	hb	6+	D. Serafin
1979	Butler		A	pb	12	P. Kirk
1979	Keith Calder	amateur	B	hb	16+	G. Hammond
1979	Devereaux	spy	A	hb	10+	B. Granger
1979	Margo Franklin & Philip Spence	private	A	pb	13	Jerry Jenkins
1979	C. B. Greenfield	amateur	A	hb	5+	L. Kallen
1979	Sarah Kelling	amateur	A	hb	10+	C. MacLeod
1979	Father Bob Koesler	amateur	A	hb	12+	W. X. Kienzle
1979	Wallace & John Mahoney	spy	A	pb	7+	S. Flannery
1979	Billy Nevers	private	A	pb	5	J. M. Glazner
1979	Supt. Tetsuo Otani	police	B	hb	12	James Melville
1979	Insp. Clovis Pel	police	B	hb	14+	M. Hebden
1979	Insp. Thomas Pitt	police	B	hb	10+	A. Perry
1979	Owen Smith	police	B	hb	5+	J. Barnett
1979	Penelope Spring and Toby Glendower	amateur	A	pb	8+	M. Arnold
1979	John Marshall Tanner	private	A	hb	6+	S. Greenleaf
1980	Fred Bennett	police	A	pb	7	Elliott Lewis
1980	Hank Bradford	amateur	A	pb	5	M. Warden
1980	Jim Chee	police	A	hb	8+	T. Hillerman
1980	Hank Frost	adventurer	A	pb	17	A. Kilgore
1980	Cliff Hardy	private	Au	pb	13+	P. Corris
1980	Michael Hawk	adventurer	A	pb	14	D. Streib
1980	Insp. Ben Jurnet	police	B	hb	5+	S. T. Haymon
1980	Simon Kaye	private	A	pb	6	H. Waugh
1980	Insp. Kelsey	police	B	hb	7+	E. Page
1980	Anna Lee	private	B	hb	6+	L. Cody

Series Character Chronology

YEAR	CHARACTER	TYPE	COUNTRY	BOOK TYPE	NUMBER OF BOOKS	AUTHOR
1980	Ray Martin	private	A	pb	10	R. Reinsmith
1980	Insp. Achille Peroni	police	B	hb	5	T. Holme
1980	Appleton Porter	spy	A	hb	14+	M. Lovell
1980	Matthew Stock	amateur	A	hb	5+	L. Tourney
1980	Harry Stoner	private	A	hb	8+	J. Valin
1980	Amos Walker	private	A	hb	11+	L. Estleman
1981	Jim Bergerac		B	pb	7	Michael Hardwick / A. Saville
1981	Nick Chase	spy	A	pb	5	N. Cort
1981	Martin Coll	amateur	B	hb	5+	R. H. Lewis
1981	Marc Dean	adventurer	A	pb	9	Peter Buck
1981	Insp. Fabian Donoghue	police	B	hb	6+	P. Turnbull
1981	Marshal Guarnaccia	police	B	hb	7+	M. Nabb
1981	Lt. Sigrid Harald	police	A	pb	6+	M. Maron
1981	Tamara Hoyland	spy	B	hb	5+	Jessica Mann
1981	Curt Jaeger		A	pb	5	M. Mandell
1981	Insp. Richard Jury	police	A	hb	10+	M. Grimes
1981	Bill Lockwood	private	A	pb	5	B. Latham
1981	MacMorgan	adventurer	A	pb	7	R. Striker
1981	Mike McVeigh		A	pb	5	R. Emmett
1981	Insp. Porfiry Rostnikov	police	A	hb	6+	S. M. Kaminsky
1981	Ben Slayton	police	A	pb	5	Buck Sanders
1981	Julie Smith	police	A	pb	6+	S. Dunlap
1981	Stonewall	adventurer	A	pb	5	R. Skimin
1981	Sister Mary Teresa	amateur	A	hb	6+	M. Quill
1981	Insp. Luke Thanet	police	B	hb	9+	Dorothy Simpson
1981	Perry Trethowan	police	B	hb	5+	R. Barnard
1981	Brett Wallace	adventurer	A	pb	15+	W. Barker
1981	Eric Ward	private	B	hb	8+	Roy Lewis
1981	Carl Wilcox	amateur	A	pb	8+	Harold Adams
1981	Mac Wingate		A	pb	11	Brian Swift
1982	Able Team	adventurer	A	pb	51	Dick Stivers
1982	Charlie Adams	amateur	A	hb	6+	R. Boyer
1982	Peter Bragg	private	A	pb	7	J. Lynch
1982	William Dougal	amateur	B	hb	6+	Andrew Taylor
1982	Rod Gavin		A	pb	6	John Quinn
1982	Neil Kelly	amateur	A	hb	6+	S. F. X. Dean
1982	Arnold Landon	amateur	B	hb	5+	Roy Lewis
1982	Kinsey Millhone	private	A	hb	7+	S. Grafton
1982	Gideon Oliver	amateur	A	hb	6+	A. Elkins
1982	Phoenix Force	adventurer	A	pb	49+	Gar Wilson
1982	John Rawlings	police	A	hb	6	J. Minahan
1982	Mark Savage	private	B	hb	5	L. Payne
1982	Tweed	spy	B	hb	7+	C. Forbes
1982	V. I. Warshawski	private	A	hb	6+	S. Paretsky
1983	Nile Barrabas		A	pb	37+	J. Hild
1983	Andrew Basnet	amateur	B	hb	6+	E. Ferrars
1983	Reed Bennett	police	A	hb	7+	Ted Wood
1983	Margaret Binton	amateur	A	hb	6+	R. Barth
1983	Sgt. Joseph Bragg & Constable James Morton	police	B	hb	9+	Ray Harrison
1983	Agnes Carmichael	criminal	B	hb	9+	Anthea Cohen
1983	Steve Crown		A	pb	9	D. Streib
1983	Alex Dartanian		A	pb	6	R. Rainey
1983	Ed Fitzgerald	amateur	A	hb	5+	D. Flynn
1983	Alexander Gold	amateur	A	hb	5+	H. Resnicow
1983	Serge Gorodish & Alba	criminal	F	hb	6+	Delacorta
1983	Jennifer Gray		A	pb	6	Jerry Jenkins
1983	Eric Ivorsen	adventurer	A	pb	5	Rick Spencer
1983	Michael Long		A	pb	5	G. A. Larson
1983	Mallory	amateur	A	hb	5+	M. A. Collins
1983	Insp. Mosley	police	B	hb	6	J. Greenwood
1983	Aristide Pamplemousse	amateur	B	hb	7+	M. Bond
1983	Insp. Richard Patten	police	B	hb	7+	R. Ormerod
1983	Justin Perry		A	pb	5	J. D. Revere
1983	Insp. Charlie Salter	police	A	hb	7+	Eric Wright
1983	Bernard Samson	spy	B	hb	6+	L. Deighton
1983	Jake Samson	amateur	A	hb	5+	S. M. Singer
1983	Ralph Simmons	amateur	A	hb	5+	R. Gillespie
1983	Mark Stryker		A	pb	12	Jonathan Cain
1983	Supt. George Thorne	police	B	hb	5+	J. Penn
1983	Devlin Trace	private	A	pb	8+	W. Murphy
1983	Supt. Mike Yeadings	police	B	hb	6+	Claire Curzon
1984	Lou "Shifty" Anderson	amateur	A	hb	5+	William Murray
1984	Black Berets	adventurer	A	pb	14	M. McCray
1984	Jenny Cain	amateur	A	pb	6+	N. Pickard
1984	Brady Coyne	private	A	hb	9+	W. G. Tapply
1984	John Francis Cuddy	private	A	hb	5+	J. M. Healy
1984	Dennison		A	pb	6	A. Lassiter
1984	Robert Forsythe	private	A	hb	8+	E. X. Giroux
1984	Celia Grant	amateur	B	hb	7+	J. Sherwood

YEAR	CHARACTER	TYPE	COUNTRY	BOOK TYPE	NUMBER OF BOOKS	AUTHOR
1984	James Hawker		A	pb	11	C. Ramm
1984	Carl Heller	private	A	pb	6	F. Roderus
1984	Patience McKenna	amateur	A	hb	5+	O. Papazoglou
1984	Elizabeth MacPherson	amateur	A	pb	5+	S. McCrumb
1984	Nebraska	private	A	hb	5+	W. J. Reynolds
1984	Deb Ralston	police	A	hb	7+	Lee Martin
1984	Eleanor Roosevelt	amateur	A	hb	8+	E. Roosevelt
1984	Garth Ryland	amateur	A	hb	5+	J. R. Riggs
1984	Tim Simpson	amateur	B	hb	7+	John Malcolm
1984	Jack Sullivan	adventurer	A	pb	11	J. Cutter
1984	Dan Track		A	pb	12	J. Ahern
1984	Penny Wanawake	amateur	B	hb	6+	Patrick Andrews S. Moody
1984	Insp. David Webb	police	B	hb	8+	Anthea Fraser
1985	J. P. Beaumont	police	A	pb	8	J. A. Jance
1985	Thomas Black	private	A	pb	5+	E. W. Emerson
1985	Burke	private	A	hb	5+	A. Vachss
1985	Harry Calderwood	amateur	A	pb	5+	P. A. Kelley
1985	Dr. Alex Delaware	amateur	A	hb	5+	J. Kellerman
1985	Jack Dwyer	private	A	hb	6+	E. Gorman
1985	Fiddler	private	A	hb	5+	A. E. Maxwell
1985	Paula Glenning	amateur	B	hb	6	A. Clarke
1985	Insp. Colin Harpur	police	B	hb	(5)+	Bill James
1985	Mark Holland	amateur	B	hb	6+	P. Myers
1985	Insp. Lestrade	police	B	hb	9+	M. J. Trow
1985	Hamish Macbeth	police	A	hb	5+	M. C. Beaton
1985	Rain Morgan	amateur	B	hb	5+	L. Grant-Adamson
1985	G. D. H. Pringle	amateur	B	hb	6+	N. Livingston
1985	John Blackwood Ryan	amateur	A	hb	8+	A. Greeley
1985	Maggie Ryan	amateur	A	pb	6+	P. M. Carlson
1985	Giles Sullivan and Isabel Macintosh	amateur	A	pb	5	H. Resnicow
1985	Anthony Nicholas Twin		A	pb	7	D. Masters
1986	John Cody	adventurer	A	pb	5	Jim Case
1986	Doran Fairweather	amateur	B	hb	5+	Mollie Hardwick
1986	Jimmy Flannery	amateur	A	pb	6+	Robert Campbell
1986	Ashton Ford	adventurer	A	pb	6+	D. Pendleton
1986	Reuben Frost	amateur	A	hb	5+	H. Murphy
1986	David & Jennifer Kaine	amateur	A	pb	5+	B. J. Hoff
1986	Keyes	private	B	hb	(5)	J. N. Chance
1986	Claire Malloy	amateur	A	hb	5+	J. Hess
1986	Peter Marklin	amateur	B	hb	5+	N. Steed
1986	Ben Perkins	private	A	pb	5+	R. Kantner
1986	Dan Rhodes	police	A	hb	5+	B. Crider
1986	Mark Stone	adventurer	A	pb	14+	Jack Buchanan
1987	Jack Eichord	private	A	pb	5+	Rex Miller
1987	Garrett	private	A	pb	5+	Glen Cook
1987	Stanley Hastings	private	A	hb	6+	Parnell Hall
1987	Ben Kane		A	pb	7	N. Stone
1987	Annie Laurance	amateur	A	pb	6+	C. G. Gart
1987	Mike McCleary and Quin St. James	police	A	pb	5+	T. J. MacGregor
1987	Charlie Meiklejohn & Constance Leidl	private	A	hb	5+	K. Wilhelm
1987	Robert Miles	private	A	pb	5+	D. Everson
1987	Nick Polo	private	A	hb	5+	J. Kennealy
1987	Andrew Quentin and Jane Winfield	amateur	A	hb	5+	A. Peterson
1987	Rafferty	private	A	pb	6+	W. G. Duncan
1987	Mitch Roberts	private	A	pb	6+	G. Dold
1987	Insp./Supt. Roper	police	B	hb	6+	R. Hart
1988	Matt Faraday		A	pb	8	W. Grant
1988	David Holden	adventurer	A	pb	12+	J. Ahern
1988	Nina McFall	amateur	A	pb	6+	E. Fulton
1989	Luke Abel		A	pb	6	Nicholas Cain
1989	Vic Gabriel		A	pb	6+	Dan Schmidt
1989	Marc Lee and Carl Browne		A	pb	8+	B. Ham
1989	Lt. Donovan Steele	police	A	pb	6+	J. D. Masters
1989	Bo Thornton		A	pb	6+	Greg Walker

(1) Many later authors used this character for novels, as well as for plays, usually adapted from Doyle's stories; these later volumes are not included in this count. See the Series Index.

FILM INDEX

A

FILM TITLE	STUDIO	YEAR	DIRECTOR	SCREENWRITER	SOURCE AUTHOR/WORK	SERIES
A Toi de Jouer Callaghan	?	1954	Willy Rozier	Xavier Vallier	Peter Cheyney (Sorry You've Been Troubled)	Slim Callaghan
Abbey Grange	*Stoll	1922	George Ridgwell	Patrick L. Mannock	A. C. Doyle (Return of Sherlock Holmes)	Sherlock Holmes (Ellie Norwood)
Abbott and Costello Meet Dr. Jekyll and Mr. Hyde	Universal	1953	Charles Lamont	Lee Loeb	R. L. Stevenson (Strange Case of Dr. Jekyll and Mr. Hyde)	
Abbott and Costello Meet Frankenstein	Universal	1948	Charles T. Barton	John Grant, Robert Lees, Frederic I. Rinaldo	M. W. Shelley (Frankenstein)	
Abbott and Costello Meet the Ghosts	Universal	1948	Charles T. Barton	John Grant, Robert Lees, Frederic I. Rinaldo	M. W. Shelley (Frankenstein)	
Abbott and Costello Meet Frankenstein				John Grant		
Abominable Dr. Phibes	AIP	1971	Robert Fuest	James Whiton, William Goldstein	novel: W. Goldstein (Dr. Phibes)	Dr. Anton Phibes (Vincent Price)
Above Suspicion	MGM	1943	Richard Thorpe	Keith Winter, Melville Baker, Patricia Coleman	H. MacInnes	
Absinthe	MGM	1929	Lionel Barrymore	Willard Mack	J. W. MacConaughy (Madame X)	
Madame X						
Accidental Death	Merton Park	1963	Geoffrey Nethercott	Arthur LaBern	E. Wallace (Jack o' Judgment)	
Accomplice	Pathe	1946	Walter Colmes	Irving Elman, Frank Gruber	F. Gruber (Simon Lash, Private Detective)	Simon Lash (Richard Arlen)
Account Rendered	Major	1957	Peter Graham Scott	Barbara S. Harper	P. Barrington	George Marshall (Ewen Solon)
Accused	Paramount	1948	William Dieterle	Ketti Frings	J. Truesdell (Be Still, My Love)	
Accused	Paramount	1988	Jonathan Kaplan	Tom Topor	novel: D. Chiel	
Accused of Murder	Republic	1956	Joe Kane	W. R. Burnett	W. R. Burnett (Vanity Row)	
Ace of Spades	Real Art	1935	George Pearson	Gerard Fairlie	J. C. Fraser	
Ace Up Your Sleeve	Ameri.-Int.	1975	Ivan Passer	Jesse Lasky, Jr., Pat Silver	J. H. Chase (Ace Up My Sleeve)	
Crime and Passion						
Across 110th Street	UA	1972	Barry Shear	Luther Davis	W. Ferris	
Across the Bridge	IPF	1957	Ken Annakin	Guy Elmes, Denis Freeman	G. Greene (Nineteen Stories)	
Across the Pacific	*World	1914	Edward Carewe	Edward Carewe	C. E. Blaney	
Across the Pacific	*Warner	1926	Roy del Ruth	D. F. Zanuck	C. E. Blaney	
Act of Aggression (?)	Gaumont	1975	Gerard Pires	Jean-P. Mauchette, Gerard Pires	J. Buell (Shrewsdale Exit)	
Act of Mercy	Cavalcade	1962	Anthony Asquith	John Mortimer	F. Clifford	
Guns of Darkness						
Act of Murder	UI	1949	Michael Gordon	Michael Blankfort, Robert Thoeren	E. Lothar (Mills of God)	
Live Today for Tomorrow						
Action Man	Comacico	1967	Jean Delannoy	Alphonse Boudard, Jean Delannoy	J. Flynn	
Hoodlum's Sun						
Leather and Nylon						
Action of the Tiger	Claridge	1957	Terence Young	Robert Carson, Peter Myers	J. Wellard	
Actors and Sin	UA	1952	Ben Hecht	Ben Hecht	B. Hecht (Actor's Blood)	
Address Unknown	Columbia	1944	William C. Menzies	Kressmann Taylor, Herbert Dalmas	K. Taylor	
Adulteress	Times Film	1959	Marcel Carne	Charles Spaak, Marcel Carne	E. Zola (Therese Raquin)	
Therese Raquin						
Adventure, Inc	*?	1928	Fred Sauer	?	A. Christie (Secret Adversary)	Tommy & Tuppence Beresford (Carlo Aldini, Eva Gray)
Adventures in Diplomacy	*Eclair	1914	?	Albert Simonin	J. Futrelle (Elusive Isabel)	
Adventures of Arsene Lupin	Chavane	1956	Jacques Becker	Jacques Becker	M. Leblanc (headnote)	Arsene Lupin
Adventures of Captain Kettle	*Kettle	1922	Meyrick Milton	C. J. C. Hyne	C. J. C. Hyne	Captain Kettle (Charles Kettle)

Film Index — AMATEUR GENTLEMAN / 1357

Title	Studio	Year	Director	Writer	Character (Actor)
Adventures of Scaramouche	Capitole	1964	Antonio Isasmendi	Arthur Rigel / Colin Mann / Antonio Isasmendi	R. Sabatini (Scaramouche) / Scaramouche (Gerald Barray)
Adventures of Sherlock Holmes	TCF	1939	Alfred Werker	Edwin Blum / William Drake	W. Gillette (Sherlock Holmes) / Sherlock Holmes (Basil Rathbone)
Adventures of Sherlock Holmes' Smarter Brother	TCF	1975	Gene Wilder	Gene Wilder	/ Sherlock Holmes (Douglas Wilmer)
Affair at the Novelty Theatre	*Stoll	1924	Hugh Croise	Hugh Croise	novel: G. Pearlman / Old Man (Rolf Leslie)
Affair Nina B	Cinedis	1961	Robert Siodmak	Roger Nimier / Robert Siodmak	B. Orczy (Old Man in the Corner)
Affair of Three Nations	*Gold Roost.	1915	Arnold Daly / Ashley Miller	?	J. M. Simmel (Affair of Nina B)
Afraid to Talk	Universal	1932	Edward L. Cahn	Tom Reed	J. McIntyre
After Dark	*Kalem	1913	Sidney Olcott	Gene Gaunthier	G. Sklar (Merry-Go-Round)
After Dark	*Buckland	1915	Warwick Buckland	?	D. Boucicault
After Dark	*World	1915	Frederick Thompson	?	D. Boucicault
After Dark, My Sweet	Avenue	1990	James Foley	Robert Redlin / James Foley	D. Boucicault / Jim Thompson
After Midnight / Captain Carey, U.S.A.	Paramount	1950	Mitchell Leisen	Robert Thoeren	M. Albrand
After the Verdict	*Tschechowa	1929	Henrik Galeen	Alma Reville	R. Hichens
Against All Odds	Columbia	1984	Taylor Hackford	Eric Hughes	G. Homes (Build My Gallows High)
Agatha	Warner	1979	Michael Apted	Kathleen Tynan / Arthur Hopcraft	K. Tynan
Agatha Christie's Endless Night / Endless Night	Brit. Lion	1981	Sidney Gilliat	Sidney Gilliat	A. Christie (Endless Night)
Age of Indiscretion	MGM	1935	Edward Ludwig	Lenore Coffee	T. D. Irwin (Collusion)
Agency	RSI	1980	George Kaczender	Noel Hynd	novel: P. Gottlieb
Agent 8 3/4 / Hot Enough for June	Rank	1963	Ralph Thomas	Lukas Heller	L. Davidson (Night of Wenceslas)
Agent Trouble	BAC	1987	Jean-Pierre Mocky	Jean-Pierre Mocky / John Pielmeier	M. J. Bosse (Man Who Loved Zoos)
Agnes of God	Columbia	1985	Norman Jewison	John Pielmeier	John Pielmeier
Agony Column	*Warner	1926	Roy del Ruth	Edward T. Lowe, Jr.	E. D. Biggers
Ah Bakudan	Toho-Japan	1964	Kihachi Okamoto	Kihachi Okamoto	W. Irish (Dead Man Blues)
Al Capone	Allied Art.	1959	Richard Wilson	Malvin Wald / Henry F. Greenberg	novel: J. Roeburt
Alias Ladyfingers	*Metro	1921	Bayard Veiller	Lenore J. Coffee	J. Gregory (Ladyfingers)
Alias the Lone Wolf	*Columbia	1927	Edward H. Griffith	Edward H. Griffith / Dorothy Howell	L. J. Vance
Alias the Night Wind	*Fox	1923	Joseph Franz	Robert N. Lee	V. Vanardy
Alibi	*Viagraph	1916	Paul Scardon	George H. Plympton	G. A. England
Alibi	Twickenham	1931	Leslie S. Hiscott	H. Fowler Mear	M. Morton
Alien Nation	TCF	1988	Graham Baker	Rockne S. O'Bannon	A. Christie (Murder of Roger Ackroyd) novel: A. D. Foster
All People Will Be Brothers	Roxy	1973	Alfred Vohrer	Manfred Purzer	J. M. Simmel (Cain '67)
All the Winners	*Samuelson	1920	Geoffrey H. Malins	?	A. Applin (Wicked)
All the World to Nothing	*Pathe	1916	Henry King	Stephen Fox	W. Martyn
All This, and Heaven Too	Warner	1940	Anatole Litwak	Casey Robinson	Rachel Field
Almost Married	TCF	1932	William C. Menzies / Marcel Varnel	Wallace Smith / Guy Bolton	A. A. Soutar (Devil's Triangle)
Alphabet Murders	MGM	1966	Frank Tashlin	David Pursall / Jack Seddon	A. Christie (ABC Murders) / Hercule Poirot (Tony Randall)
Alraune	Styria	1952	Arthur M. Rabenalt	Fritz Rotter	H. H. Ewers
Alster Case	*Essanay	1915	J. Charles Haydon	?	R. Gillmore
Amateur	TCF	1982	Charles Jarrott	Robert Littell / Diana Maddox	R. Littell
Amateur Gentleman	*Stoll	1920	Maurice Elvey	?	J. Farnol
Amateur Gentleman	*First Nat.	1926	Sidney Olcott	Lillie Hayward	J. Farnol

A

FILM TITLE	STUDIO	YEAR	DIRECTOR	SCREENWRITER	SOURCE AUTHOR/WORK	SERIES
Amateur Gentleman	Criterion	1936	Thornton Freeland	Clemence Dane Sergei Nolbandov Edward Knoblock	J. Farnol	
Amazing Adventure Amazing Quest of Mr. Ernest Bliss Riches and Romance Romance and Riches	Klement	1936	Alfred Zeisler	John L. Balderston	E. P. Oppenheim (Amazing Quest of Mr. Ernest Bliss)	
Amazing Dr. Clitterhouse	First Nat	1938	Anatole Litvak	John Wexley John Huston	B. Lyndon	
Amazing Partnership	*Stoll	1921	George Ridgwell	Charles Barnett	E. P. Oppenheim	
Amazing Quest of Mr. Ernest Bliss	*Hepworth	1920	Henry Edwards	?	E. P. Oppenheim	
Amazing Quest of Mr. Ernest Bliss Amazing Adventure Riches and Romance Romance and Riches	Klement	1936	Alfred Zeisler	John L. Balderston	E. P. Oppenheim	
Ambushers	Columbia	1967	Henry Levin	Herbert Baker	D. Hamilton	Matt Helm (Dean Martin)
American Dream See You in Hell, Darling	Warner	1966	Robert Gist	Mann Rubin	N. Mailer	
American Friend	Filmverlag	1977	Wim Wenders	Wim Wenders	P. Highsmith (Ripley's Game)	
American Prisoner	BIP	1929	Thomas Bentley	Eliot Stannard Garnett Weston	E. Phillpotts	
Amorous Adventures of Moll Flanders	Paramount	1965	Terence Young	Denis Cannan Roland Kibbee	D. Defoe (Fortunes and Misfortunes of the Famous Moll Flanders)	
Amsterdam Affair	Trio	1968	Gerry O'Hara	Edmund Ward	N. Freeling (Love in Amsterdam)	Insp. Van der Valk (Wolfgang Kieling)
Anatomy of a Murder	Columbia	1959	Otto Preminger	Wendell Mayes	R. Traver	
And Hope to Die	?	1972	Rene Clement	Sebastian Japrisot	D. Goodis (Black Friday)	
And Jimmy Went to the Rainbow's Foot	Roxy	1971	Alfred Vohrer	Manfred Purzer	J. M. Simmel (Caesar Code) novel: R. Grossbach	
And Justice for All	Columbia	1979	Norman Jewison	Valerie Curtin Barry Levinson		
And Now the Screaming Starts	Amicus	1974	Roy Ward Baker	Roger Marshall	D. Case (Fengriffin)	
And Then There Were None	TCF	1945	Rene Clair	Dudley Nichols	A. Christie (Ten Little Niggers)	
And Then There Were None Ten Little Indians	Corpo	1976	Peter Collinson	Enrique Llovet	A. Christie (Ten Little Niggers)	
Anderson Tapes	Columbia	1971	Sidney Lumet	Erich Krohnke	Lawrence Sanders	
Angel, Angel, Down We Go Cult of the Damned	Am. Inter	1958	Robert Thom	Frank Pierson Robert Thom	novel: W. Johnston	
Angel Esquire	*Gaumont	1919	W. P. Kellino	George Pearson	E. Wallace	
Angel Heart	Tri-Star	1987	Alan Parker	Alan Parker	W. Hjortsberg (Falling Angel)	
Angel Street Gas Light	Brit. Nat.	1940	Thorold Dickinson	A. R. Rawlinson Bridget Boland	P. Hamilton (Gas Light)	
Angry Hills	MGM	1959	Robert Aldrich	A. I. Bezzerides	L. Uris	
Angry Silence	Beaver	1960	Guy Green	Bryan Forbes	novel: John Burke	
Anna the Adventuress	*Hepworth	1920	Cecil M. Hepworth	Blanche McIntosh	E. P. Oppenheim	
Another Man's Poison	Angel	1951	Irving Rapper	Val Guest	L. Sands (Intent to Murder)	
Another Man's Shoes	*Universal	1922	Jack Conway	Victor Bridges Raymond L. Shrock	V. Bridges	
Any Number Can Play	MGM	1949	Mervyn LeRoy	Richard Brooks	E. H. Heth	
Any Number Can Win Basement Melody Big Grab	Cipra	1963	Henri Verneuil	Albert Simonin Michel Audiard Henri Berneuil	J. Trinian (Big Grab)	
Anyone for Venice? Honey Pot It Comes Up Murder Mr. Fox of Venice	UA	1966	J. L. Mankiewicz	J. L. Mankiewicz	T. Sterling (Evil of the Day)	

Film Index

Title	Studio	Year	Director	Writer	Character (Actor)
Anything Might Happen	Real Art	1934	George A. Cooper	H. Balfour	
Appointment with Death	Cannon	1988	Michael Winner	H. Fowler Mear / Anthony Shaffer / Peter Buchanan / Michael Winner / Nicholas Phipps; A. Christie	Hercule Poirot (Peter Ustinov)
Appointment with Venus Island Rescue	Brit. Film	1951	Ralph Thomas	J. Tickell	
April Fool's Day	Hometown	1986	Fred Walton	Danilo Bach	
April Is a Deadly Month	Sara	1987	Laurent Heynemann	Laurent Heynemann / Bertrand Tavernier / Philippe Boucher; novel: Jeff Rovin / Derek Raymond (Devil's Home on Leave)	
Arabesque	Donen	1966	Stanley Donen	Julian Mitchell / Stanley Price / Pierre Marton; Alex Gordon (Cipher)	
Ardent Room	UFA	1962	Julien Duvivier	Charles Spaak / Julien Duvivier; J. D. Carr (Burning Court)	
Argyle Case	*Warwick	1917	Ralph Ince	Frederic Chapin / Ralph Ince; H. Ford	
Argyle Case	Warner	1929	Howard Bretherton	Harvey Thew; H. Ford	
Arizona	*All Star	1913	Lawrence B. McGill	?; Augustus Thomas	
Arizona	*Arrcraft	1918	Douglas Fairbanks / Albert Parker	Douglas Fairbanks; Augustus Thomas	
Arm at the Left	CCFC	1965	Claude Sautet	Charles Williams / Fouli Elia / Claude Sautet; C. Williams (Aground)	
Armadale	*Gaumont	1916	Richard Garrick	?; W. Collins	
Armageddon	Lira	1977	Alain Jessua	Alain Jessua; D. Lippincott (Voice of Armageddon)	
Army of Shadows	Corono-Fono	1969	J.-P. Melville	J.-P. Melville; J. Kessel	
Arrest Bulldog Drummond	Paramount	1939	James Hogan	Stuart Palmer; H. C. McNeile (Final Count)	Bulldog Drummond (John Howard)
Arrivederci, Baby! Drop Dead, Darling	Paramount	1967	Ken Hughes	Ken Hughes / Ronald Harwood; R. Deming (Careful Man)	
Arsenal Stadium Mystery	GFD	1939	Thorold Dickinson	Thorold Dickinson / Donald Bull; L. Gribble	Insp. Slade (Leslie Banks)
Arsene Lupin	*London	1916	George L. Tucker	Kenelm Foss; E. Jepson	Arsene Lupin (Gerald Ames)
Arsene Lupin	*Vitagraph	1917	Paul Scardon	Garfield Thompson / Paul Potter; E. Jepson	Arsene Lupin (Earle Williams)
Arsene Lupin, Detective	Film d'Art	1937	H. Diamant-Berger	H. Diamant-Berger; M. Leblanc (Jim Barnett Intervenes)	Arsene Lupin (Jules Barry)
Arsene Lupin vs. Sherlock Holmes	*Vitascope	1910	Viggo Larsen	?	Arsene Lupin (Paul Otto)
Arsenic and Old Lace	Warner	1944	Frank Capra	Julius J. Epstein / Philip G. Epstein; J. Kesselring	
Arsenio Lupin	Pereda	1945	?	?; M. Leblanc (Arsene Lupin Versus Holmlock Shears)	Arsene Lupin (?)
Ashes and Diamonds	Film Polski	1961	Andrzej Wajda	Andrzej Wajda / Jerzy Andrejewski; J. Andrzeyevski	
Aspern	Oxala	1981	Eduardo de Grigorio	Michael Graham; H. James (Aspern Papers)	
Asphalt Jungle	MGM	1950	John Huston	Ben Maddow / John Huston; W. R. Burnett	
Assassin Venetian Bird	Brit. Film	1952	Ralph Thomas	Victor Canning; V. Canning (Venetian Bird)	
Assassin for Hire	Merton	1951	Michael McCarthy	Rex Rienits; R. Rienits	
Assassination Bureau	Heathfield	1969	Basil Dearden	Michael Relph / Wolf Mankowitz; J. London	
Assault	Rank	1971	Sidney Hayers	John Kruse; K. Young (Ravine)	
Assault Force ffoulkes North Sea Hijack	Universal	1980	Andrew V. McLaglen	Jack Davies; J. Davies (Esther, Ruth and Jennifer)	
Assault on a Queen	Paramount	1966	Jack Donahue	Rod Serling; J. Finney	

A

FILM TITLE	STUDIO	YEAR	DIRECTOR	SCREENWRITER	SOURCE AUTHOR/WORK	SERIES
Assault on Agathon	Nine Net.	1976	Laslo Benedek	Alan Caillou	A. Caillou	Cabot Cain (Nico Minardos)
Assignment	Nordisk	1977	Mats Arehn	Lars Magnas Janson / Ingemar Ejre / Mats Arehn	P. Wahloo	
Assignment in Brittany	MGM	1943	Jack Conway	Anthony Veiller / William H. Wright / Howard Emmett Rogers	H. MacInnes	
Assignment K	Mazurka	1967	Val Guest	Val Guest / Bill Strutton / Maurice Foster	H. Howard (Department K)	Philip Scott (Stephen Boyd)
Assignment—Paris	Columbia	1952	Robert Parrish	William Bowers	P. Gallico (Trial by Terror)	
Assignment Redhead	Anglo Amal.	1962	Maclean Rogers	Maclean Rogers	L. Hardy (Requiem for a Redhead)	
Million Dollar Manhunt						
Asylum	Amicus	1972	Roy Ward Baker	Robert Bloch	novel: W. Johnston	
At Bay	*Gold Roost.	1915	George Fitzmaurice	Ouida Bergere	P. Philips	
At the Mercy of Tiberius	*Samuelson	1920	Fred Leroy Granville	?	A. J. Wilson	
Price of Silence						
At the Villa Rose	*Stoll	1920	Maurice Elvey	Sinclair Hill	A. E. W. Mason	
At the Villa Rose	Twickenham	1930	Leslie Hiscott	Cyril Twyford	A. E. W. Mason	
Mystery at the Villa Rose						
At the Villa Rose	APBC	1939	Walter Summers	Doreen Montgomery	A. E. W. Mason	
House of Mystery						
Attempt to Kill	Merton Park	1961	Royston Morley	Richard Harris	E. Wallace (Lone House Mystery)	
Attention, the Kids Are Watching	Adel	1978	Serge Leroy	Christopher Frank / Serge Leroy	P. L. Dixon (Children Are Watching)	
Auction Mart	*Brit. Act.	1920	Duncan Macrae	Adrian Brunel	S. Tremayne	
Audrey Rose	UA	1977	Robert Wise	Frank De Felitta	F. De Felitta	
Avalanche	*Artcraft	1919	George Fitzmaurice	Ouida Bergere	G. Atherton	
Avalanche	PRC	1946	Irving Allen	Andrew Holt	K. Boyle	
Avalanche Express	Lorimar	1979	Mark Robson	Abraham Polonsky	C. Forbes	
Avec un Elastique	?	1964	J.-L. Tacchella	Jean Valere / J.-L. Tacchella	C. Williams (Big Bite)	
Avenger	Monogram	1933	Edwin L. Marin	Brown Holmes / Tristan Tupper	J. Goodwin	
Awakening	Solofilm	1980	Mike Newell	Allan Scott / Chris Bryant / Clive Exton	B. Stoker (Jewel of the Seven Stars)	
Baby, Take a Bow	Fox	1934	Harry Lachman	Philip Klein	J. P. Judge (Square Crooks)	
Baby, the Rain Must Fall	Columbia	1965	Robert Mulligan	Horton Foote	H. Foote (Traveling Lady)	
Bachelor's Folly	Gaumont	1931	T. Hayes Hunter	Angus MacPhail / Robert Stevenson	E. Wallace (Calendar)	
Calendar						
Back from the Dead	TCF	1957	Charles M. Warren	Catherine Turney	C. Turney (Other One)	
Back to God's Country	*First Nat.	1919	David M. Hartford	?	J. O. Curwood	
Back to God's Country	*Universal	1927	Irvin Willat	Charles Logue	J. O. Curwood	
Back to God's Country	Universal	1953	Joseph Pevney	Tom Reed	J. O. Curwood	
Back to Life	*Postman	1925	Whitman Bennett	Harry Chandlee	A. Soutar (Back from the Dead)	
Backfire!	Merton Park	1962	Paul Almond	Robert Stewart	E. Wallace (headnote)	
Background to Danger	Warner	1943	Raoul Walsh	W. R. Burnett	E. Ambler (Uncommon Danger)	
Bad Blonde	Hammer	1953	Reginald Leborg	Richard Landau / Guy Elmes	M. Catto (Flanagan Boy)	
Flanagan Boy						
Bad Company	RKO	1931	Tay Garnett	Thomas Buckingham	J. Lait (Put on the Spot)	
Bad Day at Black Rock	MGM	1955	John Sturges	Millard Kaufman	M. Niall	

Title	Studio	Year	Director	Writer	Source/Notes
Bad for Each Other	Columbia	1953	Irving Rapper	Irving Wallace, Horace McCoy	H. McCoy (Scalpel)
Bad Seed	Warner	1956	Mervyn LeRoy	John Lee Mahin	M. Anderson
Badge of Policeman O'Roon	*Eclair	1913	?	?	O. Henry (Trimmed Lamp)
Badge 373	Paramount	1973	Howard W. Koch	Pete Hamill	novel: M. Roote
Badlanders	MGM	1958	Delmer Daves	Richard Collins	W. R. Burnett (Asphalt Jungle)
Balaoo	*Eclair	1913	?	?	G. Leroux
Balcony	Reade-Ster.	1963	Joseph Strick	Ben Maddow	J. Genet
Banana Boat	Patina	1975	Sidney Hayers	David Pursall	
Banana Peel				Jack Seddon	M. Hebden (What Changed Charlie Farthing)
What Changed Charlie Farthing					
Banana Peel	Omnia	1963	Marcel Ophuls	Claude Sautet, Daniel Boulanger, Marcel Ophuls	C. Williams (Nothing in the Way)
Band of Outsiders	Anouchka	1964	Jean-Luc Godard	Jean-Luc Godard	D. Hitchens (Fools' Gold)
Bandbox	*Hodgkinson	1919	Roy William Neill	Roy Somerville	L. J. Vance
Bank Shot	UA	1974	Gower Champion	Wendell Mayes	D. E. Westlake
Banker's Double	*Edison	1915	Langdon West	?	S. Campbell (Below the Dead-Line)
Barbarous Street	Films/Tour	1984	Gilles Behat	Gilles Behat, Jean Vautrin	D. Goodis (Street of the Lost)
Barnes Murder Case	*Stoll	1924	Sinclair Hill	Sinclair Hill	E. P. Oppenheim (Conspirators)
Conspirators					
Barton Mystery	*Stoll	1920	Harry Roberts	R. Byron-Webber	W. Hackett
Barton Mystery	B&D	1932	Henry Edwards	?	W. Hackett
Barton Mystery	?	1948	Charles Spaak	Albert Siminon	W. Hackett
Basement Melody	Cipra	1963	Henri Verneuil	Michel Audiard, Henri Verneuil	J. Trinian (Big Grab)
Any Number Can Win					
Big Grab					
Bat	*UA	1926	Roland West	Roland West	M. R. Rinehart
				Julian Josephson	
Bat	AA	1959	Crane Wilbur	Crane Wilbur	M. R. Rinehart
Bat Whispers	UA	1930	Roland West	Roland West	M. R. Rinehart (Bat)
Batman	TCF	1966	Leslie Martinson	Lorenzo Semple, Jr.	novel: W. Lyon
					Batman (Adam West)
					Batman (Michael Keaton)
Batman	Warner	1989	Tim Burton	Sam Hamm, Warren Skaaren	novel: C. S. Gardiner
Battling Bellhop	Warner	1937	Michael Curtiz	Seton I. Miller	Francis Wallace (Kid Galahad)
Kid Galahad					
Bawlerout	*Reliance	1913	Oscar C. Apfel	?	F. Halsey
Bear Island	Columbia	1980	Don Sharp	Don Sharp, David Butler, Murray Smith	A. MacLean
Beast of Marseilles	Dial	1957	Hugo Fregonese	John Baines	R. Croft-Cooke (Seven Thunders)
Seven Thunders					
Beast of the City	MGM	1932	Charles Brabin	John Lee Mahin	novel: J. Lait
Beast with Five Fingers	Warner	1947	Robert Florey	Curt Siodmak	W. F. Harvey
Beat the Devil	Romulus	1953	John Huston	Truman Capote, John Huston	J. Helvick
Beautiful Jim, of the Blankshire Regiment	*B&C	1914	Maurice Elvey	Eliot Stannard	J. S. Winter
Because of the Cats	Cine-Vog	1973	Fons Rademakers	Hugo Claus	N. Freeling
					Insp. Van der Valk (Bryan Marshall)
					Martin Beck (Jan Decleir)
Beck	Filmcase	1992	Jacob Bijl	Jacob Bijl	M. Sjowall (Locked Room)
Bedelia	Corfield	1946	Lance Comfort	Jay Drater, Moie Charles, Herbert Victor, Vera Caspary, Roy Ridley	V. Caspary
Bedroom Window	DEG	1987	Curtis Hanson	Isadore Goldsmith, Curtis Hanson	A. Holden (Witnesses)

B

FILM TITLE	STUDIO	YEAR	DIRECTOR	SCREENWRITER	SOURCE AUTHOR/WORK	SERIES
Beetle	*Barker	1919	Alexander Butler	Helen Blizzard	R. Marsh	
Before Dawn	RKO	1933	Irving Pichel	Marian Dix / Garrett Fort / Ralph Block	E. Wallace (Sergeant Sir Peter)	
Before I Wake Shadow of Fear	Gibraltar	1955	Al Rogell	Robert Westerby	H. Debrett	
Beggar in Purple	*Pathe	1920	Edgar Lewis	?	A. Soutar	
Beggars of Life	Paramount	1928	William A. Wellman	Benjamin Glazer / Jim Tully	J. Tully	
Behind Masks Jeanne of the Marshes	*Fam. Play.	1921	Frank Reicher	Katherine Stuart	E. P. Oppenheim (Jeanne of the Marshes)	
Behind That Curtain	Fox	1929	Irving Cummings	Sonya Levien / Clarke Silvernail	E. D. Biggers	Charlie Chan (E. L. Park)
Behind the Headlines	Kenilworth	1956	Charles Saunders	Allan MacKinnon	R. Chapman	
Behind the Mask	Columbia	1932	John Francis Dillon	Jo Swerling	E. P. Oppenheim (Jeanne of the Marshes)	
Behold a Pale Horse	Columbia	1964	Fred Zinnemann	J. P. Miller	E. Pressburger (Killing a Mouse on Sunday)	
Behold This Woman	Vitagraph	1924	J. Stuart Blackton	Marian Constance	E. P. Oppenheim (Hillman)	
Believers	Orion	1987	John Schlesinger	Mark Frost	N. Conde (Religion)	
Bella Donna	*Fam. Play.	1915	Hugh Ford / Edwin S. Porter	Hugh Ford	R. Hichens	
Bella Donna	*Fam. Play	1923	George Fitzmaurice	Ouida Bergere	R. Hichens	
Bella Donna	Twickenham	1934	Robert Milton	Vera Allinson / H. Fowler Mear	R. Hichens	
Bellamy Trial	MGM	1928	Monta Bell	Monta Bell	F. N. Hart	
Bellman and True	Hand-Made	1987	Richard Loncraine	Desmond Lowden / Richard Loncraine / Michael Wearing	D. Lowden	
Belonging	*Stoll	1922	F. Martin Thornton	Leslie H. Gordon	O. Wadsley	
Ben	Cinerama	1972	Phil Karlson	Gilbert A. Ralston	novel: G. A. Ralston	
Benson Murder Case	Paramount	1930	Frank Tuttle	Bartlet Cormack	S. S. Van Dine	Philo Vance (William Powell)
Bentley's Conscience	*Ideal	1922	Denison Clift	Denison Clift	P. Trent	
Beryl Coronet	*Franco-Bri.	1912	Georges Treville		A. C. Doyle (Adventures of Sherlock Holmes)	Sherlock Holmes (Georges Treville)
Beryl Coronet	*Stoll	1921	Maurice Elvey	Charles Barnett	A. C. Doyle (Adventures of Sherlock Holmes)	Sherlock Holmes (Eille Norwood)
Betrayed	United Art.	1988	Costa-Gavras	Joe Eszterhas		
Betty	MK2	1992	Claude Chabrol	Claude Chabrol		
Between Life and Death	*Ambrosio	1912	?	?		
Beverly Hills Cop II	Paramount	1987	Tony Scott	Larry Ferguson / Warren Skaaren		
Beware, My Lovely	RKO	1952	Harry Horner	Mel Dinelli	M. Dinelli (Man)	
Beyond the Curtain	Rank	1960	Compton Bennett	Compton Bennett / John Cresswell	A. J. Wallis (Thunder Above)	
Beyond the Forest	Warner	1949	King Vidor	Lenore Coffee	S. Engstrand	
Beyond the Limit Honorary Consul	World Film	1983	John Mackenzie	Christopher Hampton	G. Greene (Honorary Consul)	
Beyond the River Bottom of the Bottle	TCF	1956	Henry Hathaway	Sidney Boehm	G. Simenon (Bottom of the Bottle)	
Beyond This Place Web of Evidence	Georgefield	1959	Jack Cardiff	Kenneth Taylor	A. J. Cronin	
Bid for Fortune	*Unity-Super	1917	Sidney Morgan	Sidney Morgan	G. Boothby	Dr. Nikola (A. Harding Steerman)
Big Boodle Night in Havana	UA	1957	Richard Wilson	Jo Eisinger	R. Sylvester	
Big Bounce	Warner	1969	Alex March	Robert Dozier	E. Leonard	
Big Caper	UA	1957	Robert Stevens	Martin Berkeley	L. White	

B

Title	Studio	Year	Director	Writer	Character (Actor)
Big Chance	Major	1957	Peter Graham Scott	P. Barrington (headnote)	
Big Chief	Continental	1960	Henri Verneuil	O. Henry (Whirligigs)	
Big Clock	Paramount	1948	John Farrow	K. Fearing	
Big Easy	Columbia	1987	Jim McBride	J. Conaway (?)	
Big Fix	Universal	1978	Jeremy Paul Kagan	R. L. Simon	Moses Wine (Richard Dreyfus)
Big Gamble	RKO	1931	Fred Niblo	O. R. Cohen (Iron Chalice)	
Big Game	RKO	1936	George Nicholl, Jr.	F. McGrew Willis	
Big Grab	Cipra	1963	Henri Verneuil	Irwin Shaw	
Any Number Can Win				Albert Siminon	
Basement Melody				Michel Audiard	
				Henri Verneuil	
Big Heat	Columbia	1953	Fritz Lang	Sydney Boehm	
Big House	MGM	1930	George Hill	Frances Marion	
Big Knife	UA	1955	Robert Aldrich	James Poe	
				C. Odets	
Big Night	UA	1951	Joseph Losey	Stanley Ellin	
				S. Ellin (Dreadful Summit)	
				Joseph Losey	
Big Operator	Gaumont	1976	Claude Pinoteau	Michel Audiard	
				Claude Pinoteau	
Big Sleep	Warner	1946	Howard Hawks	William Faulkner	Philip Marlowe (Humphrey Bogart)
				Leigh Brackett	
				Jules Furthman	
				R. Chandler	
Big Sleep	UA	1977	Michael Winner	Michael Winner	Philip Marlowe (Robert Mitchum)
				R. Chandler	
Big-Town Round-Up	*Fox	1921	Lynn Reynolds	W. M. Raine	
Billion Dollar Brain	Lowndes	1967	Ken Russell	L. Deighton	Harry Palmer (Michael Caine)
Billy Bathgate	Buena Vista	1991	Robert Benton	Tom Stoppard	
				E. L. Doctorow	
Birds	Universal	1963	Alfred Hitchcock	Evan Hunter	
				D. Du Maurier (Apple Tree)	
Birds of Prey	*Columbia	1927	William James Craft	Dorothy Howell	
				G. Bronson-Howard	
Birds of Prey	ATP	1931	Basil Dean	Basil Dean	
				A. A. Milne (Fourth Wall)	
Birthday Party	Continental	1968	William Friedkin	H. Pinter	
Bishop Misbehaves	MGM	1935	E. A. Dupont	Harold Pinter	
				Leon Gordon	
				F. Jackson	
Bishop's Misadventures					
Bishop Murder Case	MGM	1930	Nick Grinde	George Auerbach	Philo Vance (Basil Rathbone)
			David Burton	Lenore J. Coffee	
				S. S. Van Dine	
Bishop's Misadventures	MGM	1935	E. A. Dupont	Leon Gordon	
Bishop Misbehaves				George Auerbach	
				F. Jackson (Bishop Misbehaves)	
Bitch	Spritebowl	1979	Gerry O'Hara	Gerry O'Hara	
				Monja Danischewsky	
Bitter Springs	Ealing	1950	Ralph Smart	W. P. Lipscomb	
Bizarre, Bizarre	Lenauer	1937	Marcel Carne	Jacques Prevert	
Black Angel	Universal	1946	Roy William Neill	Roy Chanslor	
				Jackie Collins	
				novel: C. King	
Black Bag	*Universal	1922	Stuart Paton	George Hively	
Black Bird	*MGM	1926	Tod Browning	Waldemar Young	
				J. S. Clouston (His First Offense)	
Black Bird	Columbia	1975	David Giler	David Giler	C. Woolrich
				L. J. Vance	
Black Box	*Universal	1915	Otis Turner	Otis Turner	novel: T. Browning (Mocking Bird)
				novel: A. Edwards	
Black Camel	TCF	1931	Hamilton MacFadden	Barry Connors	novel: E. P. Oppenheim
				Philip Klein	Charlie Chan (Warner Oland)
				E. D. Biggers	
Black Christmas	Ambassador	1974	Bob Clark	Roy Moore	
Black Coffee	Twickenham	1931	Leslie Hiscott	Brock Williams	Hercule Poirot (Austin Trevor)
				novel: L. Hays	
				A. Christie	
Black Doll	Universal	1938	Otis Garrett	H. Fowler Mear	
Black Eagle	Columbia	1948	Robert Gordon	Harold Buckley	W. E. Hayes
				Edward Huebsch	O. Henry (Roads of Destiny)
				Hal Smith	
Black Eye	Warner	1974	Jack Arnold	Mark Haggard	J. Jacks (Murder on the Wild Side)
				Jim Martin	
Black Glove	Hammer	1954	Terence Fisher	Ernest Borneman	E. Borneman (?) (Tremelo)
Face the Music					

B

FILM TITLE	STUDIO	YEAR	DIRECTOR	SCREENWRITER	SOURCE AUTHOR/WORK	SERIES
Black Limelight	ABPC	1938	Paul L. Stein	Dudley Leslie Walter Summers	G. Sherry	
Black Marble	AVCO	1980	Harold Becker	Joseph Wambaugh	J. Wambaugh	
Black Mask	WB-FN	1935	Ralph Ince	Paul Gangelin Frank Launder Michael Barringer	B. Graeme (Blackshirt)	Richard Verrell (Ellis Irving)
Black Orchid	Paramount	1958	Martin Ritt	Joseph Stefano		
Black Pearl	*Rayart	1928	Scott Pembroke	Arthur Hoerl	novel: E. Ronns	
Black Peter	*Stoll	1922	George Ridgwell	Patrick L. Mannock Geoffrey H. Malins	W. Woodrow A. C. Doyle (Return of Sherlock Holmes)	Sherlock Holmes (Eille Norwood)
Black Rain	Paramount	1989	Ridley Scott	Craig Bolotin Warren Lewis	novel: Mike Cogan	
Black Secret	*Pathe	1920	George B. Seitz	Bertram Millhauser	R. W. Chambers (In Secret)	
Black Sheep	*AB	1915	J. Farrell MacDonald	?	E. Yates	
Black Spider	*B&C	1920	William J. Humphrey	William J. Humphrey	C. Dawe	
Black Sun	Stockholm	1978	Arne Mattson	Per Wahloo Arne Mattson	P. Wahloo (Lorry)	
Black Sunday	Paramount	1977	John Frankenheimer	Ernest Lehman Kenneth Ross Ivan Moffat	T. Harris	
Black Swan	TCF	1942	Henry King	Ben Hecht Seton I. Miller	R. Sabatini	
Black Watch	Fox	1929	John Ford	John Stone James K. McGuinness	T. Mundy (King of the Khyber Rifles)	
Black Widow	TCF	1954	Nunnally Johnson	Nunnally Johnson	P. Quentin	
Black Windmill	Universal	1974	Don Siegel	Leigh Vance	C. Egleton (Seven Days to a Killing)	
Blackboard Jungle	MGM	1955	Richard Brooks	Richard Brooks	E. Hunter	
Blackguard	*UFA	1925	Graham Cutts	Alfred Hitchcock	R. Paton (Autobiography of a Blackguard)	
Blackmail	BI	1929	Alfred Hitchcock	Alfred Hitchcock Benn W. Levy Charles Bennett Garnett Weston	C. Bennett	
Blackmailed	Gen. Film	1950	Marc Allegret	Hugh Mills Roger Vadim	E. Myers (Mrs. Christopher)	
Blackout Murder by Proxy	Hammer	1954	Terence Fisher	Richard Landau	H. Nielsen (Gold Coast Nocturne)	
Blackout Danger Within	Lesslie	1959	Don Chaffey	Bryan Forbes Frank Harvey	M. Gilbert (Death in Captivity)	
Blade Runner	Ladd	1982	Ridley Scott	Hampton Fancher David People	P. K. Dick (Do Androids Dream of Electric Sheep?)	
Blague Dans le Coin	?	1963	Maurice Labro	Charles Spaak Gerard Carlier Maurice Labro	Carter Brown (Curtains for a Chorine)	
Blanche Fury	Cineguild	1948	Marc Allegret	Audrey E. Lindop Cecil McGivern Hugh Mills	J. Shearing	
Bleak House	*Ideal	1920	Maurice Elvey	William J. Elliott	C. Dickens	
Bleak House	*Master	1922	H. B. Parkinson	Frank Miller	C. Dickens	
Blind Adventure	Viagraph	1918	Wesley Ruggles	George H. Plympton	E. D. Biggers (Agony Column)	
Blind Alley	Columbia	1939	Charles Vidor	Philip MacDonald Michael Blankfort Albert Duffy	J. Warwick	
Blind Date Chance Meeting	Ind. Art.	1959	Joseph Losey	Ben Barzman Millard Lampell Hope Loring	L. Howard	
Blind Goddess	*Fam. Play.	1926	Victor Fleming	Louis D. Lighton Gertrude Orr	A. Train	

Film Index   BLUE DIAMOND / 1365

Title	Studio	Year	Director	Writer	Source	Character
Blind Goddess	Gainsboro.	1948	Harold French	Muriel Box Sydney Box	P. Hastings	
Blind Justice	Real Art	1934	Bernard Vorhaus	Vera Allinson	A. Ridley (Recipe for Murder)	
Blind Man's Eyes	*Metro	1919	John Ince	June Mathis	W. MacHarg	
Blind Terror	Filmways	1971	Richard Fleischer	Brian Clemens	novel: W. Hughes	
So No Evil						
Blindfold	Universal	1966	Philip Dunne	Philip Dunne W. H. Menger	L. Fletcher	
Blonde from Peking	Comacico	1968	Nicolas Gessner	Nicolas Gessner Marc Behm	J. H. Chase (You Have Yourself a Deal)	
Peking Blonde						
Blonde Ice	Classics	1948	Jack Bernhard	Jacques Vilfrid Kenneth Gamet	W. Chambers (Once Too Often)	
Blonde Like That!	Cocinor	1963	Jean Jabely	Jacques Robert Felecien Marceau	J. H. Chase (Miss Shumway Waves a Wand)	
Blonde Sinner	Kenwood	1956	J. Lee Thompson	John Cresswell Joan Henry	J. Henry (Yield to the Night)	
Yield to the Night						
Blonde Vampire	*Physioc	1922	Wray Physioc	?	novel: D. Mooers	
Blondes for Danger	Wilcox	1938	Jack Raymond	Gerald Elliott	E. Price (Red for Danger)	
Blood and Roses	E.G.E.	1961	Roger Vadim	Roger Vadim Roger Vailland Claude Brule Claude Martin	J. S. Le Fanu (In a Glass Darkly)	
Blood Beast from Outer Space	New Art	1965	John Gilling	Jim O'Connolly	F. Crisp (Night Callers)	
Blood Brothers	Warner	1978	Robert Mulligan	Walter Newman	R. Price	
Blood Feast	Box Office	1963	Hershell G. Lewis	Allison Louise Down	novel: L. E. Murphy	
Blood from the Mummy's Tomb	Hammer	1971	Michael Carreras Seth Holt	Christopher Wicking	B. Stoker (Jewel of the Seven Stars)	
Blood Money	*Granger	1921	Fred Goodwins	?	C. H. Bullivant	
Blood on My Hands	UI	1949	Norman Foster	Leonardo Bercovici Walter Bernstein	G. Butler (Kiss the Blood Off My Hands)	
Kiss the Blood Off My Hands				Hugh Gray		
Blood Relatives	Filmel	1978	Claude Chabrol	Ben Maddow Claude Chabrol R. Sydeny	E. McBain	Steve Carella (Donald Sutherland)
Blood Simple	River Road	1984	Joel Coen	Ethan Coen Joel Coen	J. and E. Coen	
Blood Spattered Bride	Morgana	1972	Vicente Aranda	Vicente Aranda Michel Audiard	J. S. Le Fanu (In a Glass Darkly)	
Blood to the Head	Rivers	1956	Gilles Grangier	Gilles Grangier	G. Simenon (Young Cardinaud)	
Bloodhounds of Broadway	Columbia	1989	Howard Brookner	Howard Brookner Colman deKay	D. Runyon	
Bloodline	Paramount	1979	Terence Young	Laird Koenig	S. Sheldon	
Sidney Sheldon's Blood-line						
Bloodlust	Cinegraf	1961	Ralph Brooke	Ralph Brooke	R. Connell (Variety)	
Bloodsuckers	Grafton	1970	Michael Burrowes	Julian More	S. Raven (Doctors Wear Scarlet)	
Doctors Wear Scarlet						
Incense for the Damned						
Bloody Mama	AIP	1969	Roger Corman	Robert Thom	novel: R. Thom	
Bloody Morning	Peking	1992	Shaohong Li	Mao Xiao Shaohong Li	G. G. Marquez (Chronicle of a Death Foretold)	
Blow Out	Filmways	1981	Brian De Palma	Brian De Palma Geoffrey H. Malins	novel: N. Williams	
Blue Carbuncle	*Stoll	1923	George Ridgwell	Patrick L. Mannock	A. C. Doyle (Adventures of Sherlock Holmes)	Sherlock Holmes (Eille Norwood)
Blue City	Paramount	1986	Michelle Manning	Lukas Heller Walter Hill	K. Millar	
Blue Dahlia	Paramount	1946	George Marshall	Raymond Chandler	R. Chandler	
Blue Diamond	*Viascope	1910	?	?	M. Leblanc (Arsene Lupin Versus Holmlock Shears)	Arsene Lupin (?)

B

B

FILM TITLE	STUDIO	YEAR	DIRECTOR	SCREENWRITER	SOURCE AUTHOR/WORK	SERIES
Blue Envelope Mystery	*Vitagraph	1916	Wilfred North	Helen Duey and/or A. Van Buren Powell	S. Kerr (Blue Envelope)	
Blue Lamp	Ealing	1950	Basil Dearden	T. E. B. Clarke	T. Willis	George Dixon (Jack Warner)
Blue Mountains Mystery	*South.Cross	1921	Raymond Longford Lottie Lyell	Alexander Mackendrick Lottie Lyell	Harrison Owen (Mount Marunga Mystery)	
Blue Sunshine	Ellanby	1978	Jeff Lieberman	Jeff Lieberman		
Blue, White and Perfect	TCF	1941	Herbert I. Leeds	Samuel G. Engel	novel: K. Johnson Bordon Chase (Diamonds of Death)	Michael Shayne (Lloyd Nolan)
Boat from Shanghai Chin-Chin-Chinaman	Real Art	1931	Guy Newall	Brock Williams Guy Newall	P. Walsh (Chin-Chin-Chinaman)	
Body Parts	Paramount	1991	Eric Red	Eric Red Norman Snider Patricia Herskovic Joyce Taylor	P. Boileau (Choice Cuts)	
Body Snatcher	RKO	1945	Robert Wise	Philip MacDonald Carlos Keith	R. L. Stevenson	
Bombay Mail	Universal	1934	Edwin L. Marin	Tom Reed L. G. Blochman	L. G. Blochman	
Bombsight Stolen	Gainsbor.	1941	Anthony Asquith	Anatole de Grunwald J. O. C. Orton	G. Kerr (Cottages to Let)	
Bonaventure Thunder on the Hill	UI	1951	Douglas Sirk	Oscar Saul Andrew Solt	C. Hastings	
Bones Old Bones of the River	Gainsbor.	1938	Marcel Varnel	Marriott Edgar Val Guest J. O. C. Orton	E. Wallace	Commissioner Sanders (Wyndham Goldie)
Bonnie and Clyde	Warner	1967	Arthur Penn	David Newman Robert Benton	novel: B. Hirschfeld	
Book of Numbers	AVCO	1973	Raymond St. Jacques	Larry Spiegel	R. D. Pharr	
Boomerang	*KB	1913	Thomas H. Ince	C. Gardner Sullivan	W. H. Osborne	
Boomerang	*National	1919	Bertram Bracken	Franklyn Hall	W. H. Osborne	
Born Reckless	Fox	1930	John Ford	Dudley Nichols	D. H. Clarke (Louis Beretti)	
Born Reckless Louis Beretti	Warner	1959	Howard W. Koch	Richard Landau		
Born to Gamble	Liberty	1934	Phil Rosen	E. Morton Hough	novel: M. Rogers	
Born to Kill	RKO	1947	Robert Wise	Eve Greene Richard Macaulay	E. Wallace (Forty-Eight Short Stories) J. Gunn (Deadlier Than the Male)	
Born to Win	UA	1971	Ivan Passer	David Scott Milton		
Bosambo Sanders of the River	London	1935	Zoltan Korda	Lajos Biro Jeffrey Dell Arthur Wimperis	novel: M. Roote E. Wallace	Commissioner Sanders (Leslie Banks)
Boscombe Valley Mystery	*Stoll	1922	George Ridgwell	Patrick L. Mannock Geoffrey H. Malins	A. C. Doyle (Adventures of Sherlock Holmes)	Sherlock Holmes (Eille Norwood)
Bosun's Mate	*London	1914	Harold Shaw	?	W. W. Jacobs (Captains All)	
Bosun's Mate	Anvil	1953	Richard Warren	?	W. W. Jacobs (Captains All)	
Bottom of the Bottle Beyond the River	TCF	1956	Henry Hathaway	Sidney Boehm	G. Simenon	
Bottom of the Well	*Vitagraph	1917	John Robertson	?	F. U. Adams	
Boulevard Nights	Warner	1979	Michael Pressman	Desmond Nakano	novel: D. Gram	
Boy Cried Murder	UI	1966	George Breakston	Robin Estridge	W. Irish (Dead Man Blues)	
Boy on a Dolphin	TCF	1957	Jean Negulesco	Ivan Moffat Dwight Taylor	D. Divine	
Boys from Brazil	TCF	1978	Franklin Schaffner	Heywood Gould	I. Levin	
Boys in Brown	Gainsboro.	1949	Montgomery Tully	Montgomery Tully	R. Beckwith	

Film Index   BRONZE BELL / 1367

Title	Studio	Year	Director	Screenwriter	Source	Notes		B
Brain	Stross	1962	Freddie Francis	Robert Stewart	C. Siodmak			
Vengeance				Philip Mackie				
Bram Stoker's Dracula	Columbia	1992	Francis F. Coppola	John Kruse	B. Stoker (Dracula)			
Branded	*Gaumont-B.	1920	C. C. Calvert	James V. Hart	G. Biss			
Brandy for the Parson	Group Three	1952	John Eldridge	Paul Rooff	G. Household (Tales of Adventurers)			
				John Dighton				
				Walter Meade				
				Alfred O'Shaughnessy				
Brasher Doubloon	MGM	1947	John Brahm	Dorothy Hannah	R. Chandler (High Window)	Philip Marlowe (George Montgomery)		
High Window								
Brass Bowl	*Edison	1914	?	?	L. J. Vance			
Brass Bowl	*Fox	1924	Jerome Storm	Thomas Dixon, Jr.	L. J. Vance			
Brass Bullet	*Universal	1920	Ben Wilson	Walter Woods	F. R. Adams (Pleasure Island)			
Brass Target	MGM	1978	John Hough	Alvin Boretz	F. Nolan (Oshawa Project)			
Brat Farrar	Hammer	1950	?	?	J. Tey			
Break in the Circle	Hammer	1954	Val Guest	Robert Westerby	P. Loraine			
				Val Guest				
Breakheart Pass	UA	1975	Tom Gries	Alistair MacLean	A. MacLean			
Breaking Point	*Fam. Play.	1924	Herbert Brenon	Edfrid Bingham	M. R. Rinehart			
				Julie Herne				
Breaking Point	Warner	1950	Michael Curtiz	Ranald MacDougall	E. Hemingway (To Have and Have Not)			
Breaking Point	Butcher	1960	Lance Comfort	Peter Lambert	L. Meynell			
Great Armored Car Swindle								
Breakout	Lesslie	1959	Don Chaffey	Bryan Forbes	M. Gilbert (Death in Captivity)			
Danger Within				Frank Harvey				
Breakup	Films Boet.	1970	Claude Chabrol	Claude Chabrol	C. Armstrong (Balloon Man)			
Breath of Scandal	*Schulberg	1924	Louis Gasnier	Eve Unsell	E. Balmer			
Breathless Moment	*Universal	1924	Robert F. Hill	Raymond L. Shrock	M. Bryant (Redemption of Richard)			
				William E. Wing				
				Harvey Gates				
Bride	*Metropol.	1926	Edward Dillon	Finis Fox	S. Olivier			
Bride	Colgems	1985	Frank Roddam	Lloyd Fonvielle	M. W. Shelley (Frankenstein)			
Bride of Frankenstein	Universal	1935	James Whale	William Hurlbut	M. W. Shelley (Frankenstein)			
				John L. Balderston				
Bride of the Lake	Twickenham	1934	Maurice Elvey	H. Fowler Mear	D. Boucicault (Colleen Bawn)			
Lily of Kilarney								
Bride Wore Black	Carosse	1968	Francois Truffaut	Francois Truffaut	C. Woolrich			
				Jean-Louis Richard				
Brigadier Gerard	*Barker	1915	Bert Haldane	Roland Talbot	A. C. Doyle (Exploits of Brigadier Gerard)	Brigadier Gerard (Lewis Walter)		
Brighton Mystery	*Stoll	1924	Hugh Croise	Hugh Croise	B. Orczy (Old Man in the Corner)	Old Man (Rolf Leslie)		
Brighton Rock	APL	1947	John Boulting	Graham Greene	G. Greene			
Young Scarface				Terrence Rattigan				
Brink's Job	Universal	1978	William Friedkin	Walon Green	N. Behn (Big Stick-Up at Brink's!)			
British Agent	Warner	1934	Michael Curtiz	Laird Doyle	H. B. Lockhart (Memoirs of a British Agent)			
British Intelligence	Warner	1940	Terry Morse	Lee Katz	A. P. Kelly (Three Faces East)			
Enemy Agent				John Kangan				
Broad Daylight	CCFC	1960	Rene Clement	Paul Gegauff	P. Highsmith (Talented Mr. Ripley)	Tom Ripley (Alain Delon)		
Lust for Evil				Rene Clement				
Purple Noon								
Broadway	Universal	1929	Paul Fejos	Edward T. Lowe, Jr.	P. Dunning			
				Charles Furthman				
Broadway	Universal	1942	William A. Seiter	Felix Jackson	P. Dunning			
				John Bright				
Broken Blossoms	*Artcraft	1917	D. W. Griffith	D. W. Griffith	T. Burke (Limehouse Nights)			
Broken Blossoms	Universal	1936	Hans Brahm	Emlyn Williams	T. Burke (Limehouse Nights)			
Bronze Bell	*Ince	1921	James W. Horne	Del Andrews	L. J. Vance			
				Louis Stevens				

B

FILM TITLE	STUDIO	YEAR	DIRECTOR	SCREENWRITER	SOURCE AUTHOR/WORK	SERIES
Brooding Eyes	*Banner	1926	Edward J. Le Saint	Mary Alice Scully Pierre Gendron	J. Goodwin (Paid in Full)	
Brother Orchid	Warner	1940	Lloyd Bacon	Earl Baldwin	L. Brady	
Brotherhood	Paramount	1968	Martin Ritt	Lewis John Carlino	novel: L. J. Carlino	
Brotherhood of Satan	Four Star	1970	Bernard McEveety	William Welch	novel: L. Q. Jones	
Brotherhood of the Yakuza Yakuza	Warner	1975	Sydney Pollack	Paul Schrader Robert Towne	novel: L. Schrader	
Brothers in Law	Tudor	1957	Roy Boulting	Frank Harvey Jeffrey Dell Roy Boulting	H. Cecil	Roger Thursby (Ian Carmichael)
Brothers Karamazov Murderer Dimitri Karamazov	Terra	1931	Fyodor Ozep	Leonhard Frank Fyodor Ozep Victor Trivas Erich Engel	F. M. Dostoevskii	
Brothers Karamazov	Fincine	1948	Giacomo Gentilomo	Giacomo Gentilomo Gaspare Cataldo Alberto Vecchietti Giogio Pala	F. M. Dostoevskii	
Brothers Karamazov	MGM	1957	Richard Brooks	Richard Brooks	F. M. Dostoevskii	
Brothers Karamazov	Mosfilm	1968	Ivan Piriev	Ivan Piriev	F. M. Dostoevskii	
Brothers Rico	Columbia	1957	Phil Karlson	Lewis Meltzer Ben Perry	G. Simenon	
Brown Wallet	First Nat.	1936	Michael Powell	Ian Dalrymple	S. Aumonier (Miss Bracegirdle and Others)	
Bruce-Partington Plans	*Stoll	1922	George Ridgwell	Patrick L. Mannock Geoffrey H. Malins	A. C. Doyle (His Last Bow)	Sherlock Holmes (Eille Norwood)
Brute	*Fam. Play. Du Daumou	1914 1987	? Claude Guillemot	? Claude Guillemot	F. A. Kummer G. Des Cars	
Build My Gallows High Out of the Past	RKO	1947	Jacques Tourneur	Geoffrey Homes	G. Homes	
Bulldog Drummond	*Astra	1922	Oscar Apfel	B. E. Doxat-Pratt	H. C. McNeile	Bulldog Drummond (Carlyle Blackwell)
Bulldog Drummond	Goldwyn	1929	F. Richard Jones	Wallace Smith Sidney Howard	H. C. McNeile	Bulldog Drummond (Ronald Colman)
Bulldog Drummond at Bay	ABPC	1937	Norman Lee	James Parrish	H. C. McNeile	Bulldog Drummond (John Lodge)
Bulldog Drummond at Bay	Columbia	1947	Sidney Salkow	Frank Gruber	H. C. McNeile	Bulldog Drummond (Ron Randell)
Bulldog Drummond Comes Back	Paramount	1937	Louis King	Edward T. Lowe	H. C. McNeile (Female of the Species)	Bulldog Drummond (John Howard)
Bulldog Drummond in Africa	Paramount	1938	Louis King	Garnett Weston	H. C. McNeile (Challenge)	Bulldog Drummond (John Howard)
Bulldog Drummond Strikes Back	UA	1934	Roy Del Ruth	Nunnally Johnson	H. C. McNeile (Knock-Out)	Bulldog Drummond (Ronald Colman)
Bulldog Drummond Strikes Back	Columbia	1947	Frank McDonald	Edna Anhalt Edward Anhalt	H. C. McNeile (Knock-Out)	Bulldog Drummond (Ron Randell)
Bulldog Drummond's Bride	Paramount	1939	James Hogan	Stuart Palmer Garnett Weston	H. C. McNeile ("Sapper": The Best Short Stories)	Bulldog Drummond (John Howard)
Bulldog Drummond's Peril	Paramount	1938	James Hogan	Stuart Palmer	H. C. McNeile (Third Round)	Bulldog Drummond (John Howard)
Bulldog Drummond's Revenge	Paramount	1937	Louis King	Edward T. Lowe	H. C. McNeile (Return of Bulldog Drummond)	Bulldog Drummond (John Howard)
Bulldog Drummond's Secret Police	Paramount	1939	James Hogan	Garnett Weston	H. C. McNeile (Temple Tower)	Bulldog Drummond (John Howard)
Bulldog Drummond's Third Round	*Astra	1925	Sidney Morgan	Sidney Morgan	H. C. McNeile (Third Round)	Bulldog Drummond (Jack Buchanan)
Bulldog Sees It Through	ABPC	1940	Harold Huth	Doreen Montgomery	G. Fairlie (Scissors Cut Paper)	

Title	Studio	Year	Director	Writer	Notes
Bullet for Pretty Boy	AI	1970	Larry Buchanan	Henry Rosenbaum	novel: M. Avallone
Bullitt	Warner	1968	Peter Yates	Alan R. Trustman	R. Pike (Mute Witness)
Bullshot	HandMade	1983	Dick Clement	Harry Kleiner	R. House (Bullshot Crummond)
				Ron House	
				Diz White	
				Alan Shearman	
Bunny Lake Is Missing	Wheel	1965	Otto Preminger	John Mortimer	E. Piper
				Penelope Mortimer	
Burden of Proof	*Davies	1918	Julius Steger	Samuel M. Weller	V. Sardou (Diplomates)
Burglar	*World	1917	Harley Knoles	Virginia T. Hudson	A. Thomas (Editha's Burglar)
Burglar	Columbia	1957	Paul Wendkos	David Goodis	D. Goodis
Burglar	Nelvana	1987	Hugh Wilson	Joseph Loeb III	L. Block (headnote)
				Matthew Weisman	
				Hugh Wilson	
Burglar and the Girl	*DeForest	1928	Hugh Croise	?	M. Boulton
Burglar and the Lady	*Sun Photo.	1915	Herbert Blache	Langdon McCormick	O. Harper
Burglars	Verneuil	1971	Henri Verneuil	Vaha Katcha	D. Goodis (Burglar)
				Henri Verneuil	
Buried Treasure	*Cosmpolitan	1921	George D. Baker	George D. Baker	F. B. Austin (On the Borderland)
Burn	Grimaldi	1970	Gillo Pontecorvo	Franco Solinas	novel: N. Gant
				Giorgio Arlorio	
Burn Out	New World	1975	Daniel Mann	Trevor Wallace	E. Ambler (Journey Into Fear)
Journey Into Fear					
Burndown	M.C.E.G.	1990	James Allen	Anthony Barwick	S. Collins (Burn Down)
				Colin Stewart	
Burned Evidence	Continental	1929	?	?	W. Woodrow
Burnt Offerings	PEA Films	1976	Dan Curtis	William F. Nolan	R. Marasco
				Dan Curtis	
Busman's Honeymoon	MGM	1940	Arthur B. Woods	Monckton Hoffe	D. L. Sayers
Haunted Honeymoon				Angus MacPhail	
				Harold Goldman	
Busy Body	Paramount	1967	William Castle	Ben Starr	D. E. Westlake
Busybody	Laterna	1969	Bent Christensen	?	J. Popplewell
But Not for Me	Paramount	1959	Walter Lang	Michael Hayes	novel: E. Ronns
Butch Minds the Baby	Universal	1942	Albert S. Rogell	Leonard Spigelgass	D. Runyon (Guys and Dolls)
Butcher, Baker, Nightmare Maker	Internat.	1982	William Asches	Stephen Breimer	novel: R. Natale
Night Warning				Alan Jay Glueckman	
Nightmare Maker					
Butterfly	*World	1915	?	O. A. C. Lund	H. K. Webster
Butterfly	Par Par	1981	Matt Cimber	John Goff	J. M. Cain
				Matt Cimber	
Butterfly on the Shoulder	Action	1978	Jacques Deray	Jean-Cl. Carriere	J. Gearon (Velvet Well)
				Tonino Guerra	
				Roger Smith	
CC and Company	AVCO	1970	Seymour Robbie	?	novel: M. Roote
Caballero's Way	*Eclair	1914	?	Joanne Court	O. Henry (Heart of the West)
Cairo	MGM	1963	Wolf Rilla	Seton I. Miller	W. R. Burnett (Asphalt Jungle)
Calcutta	Paramount	1947	John Farrow	Angus MacPhail	novel: Alex Morrison
Calendar	Gaumont-B.	1931	T. Hayes Hunter	Robert Stevenson	E. Wallace
Bachelor's Folly					
Calendar	Gainsbor.	1948	Arthur Crabtree	Geoffrey Kerr	E. Wallace
Calico Cat	*Edison	1914	?	?	C. M. Thompson
Call Harry Crown	TCF	1974	John Frankenheimer	Robert Dillon	M. Franklin (99 44/100% Dead)
99 and 44/100% Dead					
Callaghan Remet Ca	?	1960	Willy Rozier	Xavier Vallier	P. Cheyney
Callan	EMI	1974	Don Sharp	James Mitchell	J. Mitchell (Magnum for Schneider) Slim Callaghan David Callan (Edward Woodward)
Called Back	*Thanhauser	1912	?	?	H. Conway
Called Back	*Gold Reel	1914	Otis Turner	James Dayton	H. Conway
Called Back	*London	1914	George L. Tucker	?	H. Conway
Called Back	*Amalgamated	1922	W. J. Lincoln	W. J. Lincoln	H. Conway

Peter Wimsey
(Robert Montgomery)

FILM TITLE	STUDIO	YEAR	DIRECTOR	SCREENWRITER	SOURCE AUTHOR/WORK	SERIES
Called Back	Real Art	1933	Jack Harris	Reginald Denham	H. Conway	
Calling Bulldog Drummond	MGM	1951	Victor Saville	Howard E. Rogers Gerald Ferlie Arthur Wimperis	G. Fairlie	Bulldog Drummond (Walter Pidgeon)
Calling Philo Vance	Warner	1940	William Clemens	Tom Reed	S. S. Van Dine (Kennel Murder Case)	Philo Vance (James Stephenson)
Calvert's Valley	*Fox	1922	Jack Dillon	Jules Furthman	M. P. Montagu (In Calvert's Valley)	
Cameron of the Mounted	*Hodkinson	1922	Henry MacRae	?	R. Connor (Corporal Cameron)	Allan Cameron (Gaston Glass)
Campbell's Kingdom	Rank	1957	Ralph Thomas	Robin Estridge Hammond Innes	H. Innes	
Canary Murder Case	Paramount	1929	Malcolm St. Clair	Florence Ryerson Albert Shelby LeVino Herman J. Mankiewicz S. S. Van Dine	S. S. Van Dine	Philo Vance (William Powell)
Cancel My Reservation	Warner	1972	Paul Bogart	Arthur Marx Robert Fisher	L. L'Amour (Broken Gun)	
Candidate for Murder	Merton Park	1962	David Villiers	Lukas Heller	E. Wallace (headnote)	
Candles at Nine	Brit Nat.	1944	John Harlow	Basil Mason	A. Gilbert (Mouse Who Wouldn't Play Ball)	
Candleshoe	Disney	1977	Norman Tokar	John Harlow David Swift Rosemary A. Sisson	M. Innes (Christmas at Candleshoe)	
Cape Fear	UI	1962	J. Lee Thompson	James R. Webb	J. D. MacDonald (Executioners)	
Cape Fear	Universal	1991	Martin Scorsese	Wesley Strick	J. D. MacDonald (Executioners)	
Caper of the Golden Bulls Carnival of Thieves	Embassy	1967	Russell Rouse	Ed Waters David Moessinger	W. P. McGivern	
Caprice	TCF	1967	Frank Tashlin	Jay Jayson Frank Tashlin	novel: J. Withers	
Captain Applejack	Warner	1931	Hobart Henley	Maude Fulton	W. Hackett	
Captain Blood	WB-FN	1935	Michael Curtiz	Casey Robinson	R. Sabatini (Captain Blood, His Odyssey)	Capt. Peter Blood (Errol Flynn)
Captain Blood, Fugitive Captain Pirate	Columbia	1952	Ralph Murphy	Robert Libott Frank Burt John Meredyth Lucas	R. Sabatini (Chronicles of Captain Blood)	Capt. Peter Blood (Louis Hayward)
Captain Carey, U.S.A. After Midnight	Paramount	1950	Mitchell Leisen	Robert Thoeren	M. Albrand (After Midnight)	
Captain Clegg Night Creatures	Universal	1962	Peter Graham Scott	Anthony Hinds Barbara S. Harper	R. Thorndyke (Dr. Syn)	
Captain Khorshid	Farabi	1988	Naser Taghvai	Naser Taghvai	E. Hemingway (To Have and Have Not) novel: C. Houghton	
Captain of the Guard	Universal	1930	Paul Fejos John S. Robertson	Arthur Ripley		
Captain Pirate Captain Blood, Fugitive	Columbia	1952	Ralph Murphy	Robert Libott Frank Burt John Meredyth Lucas	R. Sabatini (Chronicles of Captain Blood)	Capt. Peter Blood (Louis Hayward)
Captain Starlight	*Spencer's	1911	Alfred Rolfe	?	R. Boldrewood (Robbery Under Arms)	
Captive City	Paramount	1963	Joseph Anthony	Guy Elmes Eric Bercovici Marc Brandel	J. Appleby	
Conquered City						
Caravan to Vaccares	Rank	1974	Geoffrey Reeve	Paul Wheeler Joseph Forest	A. MacLean	
Cardboard Box	*Stoll	1923	George Ridgwell	Geoffrey H. Malins Patrick L. Mannock	A. C. Doyle (His Last Bow)	Sherlock Holmes (Eille Norwood)
Careful, He Might Hear You	Syme	1983	Carl Schultz	Michael Jenkins	S. L. Elliott	
Carey Treatment	MGM	1972	Blake Edwards	James P. Bonner Jack Andrews	J. Hudson (Case of Need)	
Caribbean Mystery	TCF	1945	Robert Webb	Leonard Praskins	J. W. Vandercook (Murder in Trinidad)	

CASTLE OF CRIMES / 1371

C

Title	Studio	Year	Director	Writer	Source / Character
Carnival of Thieves Caper of the Golden Bulls	Embassy	1967	Russell Rouse	Ed Waters David Moessinger	W. P. McGivern (Caper of the Golden Bulls)
Carpet from Bagdad	*Selig	1915	Colin Campbell	Colin Campbell	H. MacGrath
Carrington, V.C.	Remus	1954	Anthony Asquith	John Hunter	D. Christie
Court Martial					
Carry-Cot	Mallard	1973	Andrew Sinclair	Andrew Sinclair	A. Thynne
Carter Case	*Oliver	1919	Donald MacKenzie	John W. Gray Julius J. Epstein	A. B. Reeve (headnote)
Casablanca	Warner	1942	Michael Curtiz	Phillip G. Epstein Howard Koch	J. J. Epstein
Case Against Mrs. Ames	Paramount	1936	William A. Seiter	Gene Towne Graham Baker	A. S. Roche
Case of Elinor Norton State vs. Elinor Norton	TCF	1935	Hamilton MacFadden	Ross Franken Philip Klein	M. R. Rinehart (State vs. Elinor Norton)
Case of Identity	*Stoll	1921	Maurice Elvey	William J. Elliott	A. C. Doyle (Adventures of Sherlock Holmes) — Sherlock Holmes (Eille Norwood)
Case of Jonathan Drew Lodger	*Gainsbor.	1926	Alfred Hitchcock	Eliot Stannard Alfred Hitchcock	M. B. Lowndes (Lodger)
Case of Lady Camber	*Broadwest	1920	Walter West	Benedict James	H. A. Vachell
Case of Mrs. Pembroke Two Against the World	Warner	1936	William McGann	Michel Jacoby	L. Weitzenkorn (Five Star Final)
Case of the Black Cat	First Nat.	1936	William McGann	F. Hugh Herbert	E. S. Gardner (Case of the Caretaker's Cat) — Perry Mason (Ricardo Cortez)
Case of the Black Parrot	Warner	1941	Noel M. Smith	Robert E. Kent	B. E. Stevenson (Mystery of the Boule Cabinet)
Case of the Curious Bride	First Nat.	1935	Michael Curtiz	Tom Reed	E. S. Gardner — Perry Mason (Warren William)
Case of the Frightened Lady	Pennant	1940	George King	Edward Dryhurst	E. Wallace (Frightened Lady)
Case of the Howling Dog	Warner	1934	Alan Crosland	Ben Markson	E. S. Gardner — Perry Mason (Warren William)
Case of the Lucky Legs	First Nat.	1935	Archie L. Mayo	Brown Holmes Ben Markson	E. S. Gardner — Perry Mason (Warren William)
Case of the Missing Blonde Corpse in the Morgue Lady in the Morgue	Universal	1938	Otis Garrett	Jerry Chodorov Eric Taylor Robertson White	J. Latimer (Lady in the Morgue) — Bill Crane (Preston Foster)
Case of the Stuttering Bishop	First Nat.	1937	William Clemens	Don Ryan	E. S. Gardner — Perry Mason (Donald Woods)
Case of the Vanished Bonds	*Edison	1914	Langdon West	?	S. Campbell (Below the Dead-Line)
Case of the Velvet Claws	First Nat.	1936	William Clemens	Tom Reed	E. S. Gardner — Perry Mason (Warren William)
Casino Murder Case	MGM	1935	Edwin L. Marin	Florence Ryerson Edgar Allan Woolf	S. S. Van Dine — Philo Vance (Paul Lukas)
Casino Royale	Fam. Art.	1967	John Huston Ken Hughes Val Guest Robert Parrish Joe McGrath	Wolf Mankowitz John Law Michael Sayers	I. Fleming — James Bond (David Niven)
Cassandra Crossing	AVCO	1977	George Pan Cosmatos	Tom Mankiewicz Robert Katz	novel: R. Katz
Cast a Dark Shadow	Frobisher	1955	Lewis Gilbert	John Cresswell	J. Green (Murder Mistaken)
Castle of Crimes House of the Arrow	ABPC	1940	Harold French	Doreen Montgomery	A. E. W. Mason (House of the Arrow) — Insp. Hanaud (Kenneth Kent)

1372 / CASTLE OF DOOM — Film Index

FILM TITLE	STUDIO	YEAR	DIRECTOR	SCREENWRITER	SOURCE AUTHOR/WORK	SERIES
Castle of Doom	Dreyer	1931	Carl T. Dreyer	Carl T. Dreyer / Christian Jul	J. S. Le Fanu (In a Glass Darkly)	
Not Against the Flesh						
Strange Adventure of David Gray						
Vampire						
Cat	Valoria	1971	P. Granier-Deferre	P. Granier-Deferre / Pascal Jardin	G. Simenon	
Cat and Mouse	Anvil	1958	Paul Rotha	Paul Rotha	M. Halliday	
Desperate Men						
Cat and the Canary	*Universal	1927	Paul Leni	Alfred A. Cohn / Robert F. Hill / Walter A. Cohn	J. Willard	
Cat and the Canary	Paramount	1939	Elliott Nugent	Walter De Leon / Lynn Starling	J. Willard	
Cat and the Canary	Grenadier	1981	Radley Metzger	Radley Metzger	J. Willard	
Cat Chaser	Vestron	1989	Abel Ferrara	Elmore Leonard / Jim Borrelli / Alan Sharp	Elmore Leonard	
Cat Creeps	Universal	1930	Rupert Julian	Gladys Lehman / William Hurlbut	J. Willard (Cat and the Canary)	
Cat o' Nine Tails	Spettacolli	1971	Dario Argento	Dario Argento	novel: P. J. Gillette	
Catacombs	Parroch	1964	Gordon Hessler	Dan Mainwaring	Jay Bennett	
Woman Who Wouldn't Die						
Catamount Killing	Atlas	1974	Krzysztof Zanussi	Julian More / Sheila More	J. H. Chase (I Would Rather Stay Poor)	
Catch Me a Spy	Ludgate	1971	Dick Clement	Dick Clement / Ian La Frenais	G. Marton	
Cat's Paw	Lloyd	1934	Sam Taylor	Sam Taylor	C. B. Kelland	
Catspaw	*Edison	1916	George A. Wright		W. H. Osborne	
Cave on Thundercloud	*Essanay	1915	?	?	M. R. Rinehart (Book of Tish)	Letitia Carberry (?)
Caves of Night	Columbia	?	?	?	J. Christopher	
Cecile Est Mort	Continental	1943	Maurice Tourneur	J.-P. Le Chanois	G. Simenon (Maigret and the Spinster)	Jules Maigret (Albert Prejean)
Celestial City	*Brit. Inst.	1929	Joe Orton	Joe Orton	B. Orczy	
Chairman	Apjac	1969	J. Lee Thompson	Ben Maddow	J. R. Kennedy	
Most Dangerous Man in the World						
Chalk Garden	Quota	1963	Ronald Neame	John Michael Hayes	E. Bagnold	
Challenge	Reliance	1948	Jean Yarbrough	Frank Gruber / Irving Elman	H. C. McNeile	Bulldog Drummond (Tom Conway)
Chamber of Horrors	Rialto	1940	Norman Lee	Norman Lee / Gilbert Gunn	E. Wallace (Door with Seven Locks)	
Door with Seven Locks						
Chance Meeting	Indep. Art.	1959	Joseph Losey	John Argyle / Ben Barzman / Millard Lampell	L. Howard (Blind Date)	
Change of Mind	Sagittarus	1969	Kris Peterson	Seeleg Lester / Richard Wesson	novel: C. Stratton	
Channings	*Master Film House	1920	Edwin J. Collins	William J. Elliott	H. Wood	
Chant of Jimmie Blacksmith	Universal	1978	Fred Schepsi	Fred Schepsi	T. Keneally	
Charade		1964	Stanley Donen	Peter Stone	novel: P. H. Stone	
Charge Is Murder	MGM	1963	Boris Sagal	Henry Denker	A. Dewlen (Twilight of Honor)	
Twilight of Honor						
Charles Augustus Milverton	*Stoll	1922	George Ridgwell	Patrick L. Mannock / Geoffrey H. Malins	A. C. Doyle (Return of Sherlock Holmes)	Sherlock Holmes (Eille Norwood)
Charley Varrick	Universal	1973	Don Siegel	Howard Rodman / Dean Riesner	J. Reese (Looters)	
Charlie Chan and the Curse of the Dragon Queen	Am. Cinema	1980	Clive Donner	Stan Burns / David Axelrod	novel: M. Avallone	Charlie Chan (Peter Ustinov)

C

Title	Distributor	Year	Director	Writer	Source
Charlie Chan Carries On	TCF	1931	Hamilton MacFadden	Philip Klein Barry Connors	E. D. Biggers (Warner Oland) Charlie Chan
Charlie Chan in Rio	TCF	1941	Harry Lachman	Samuel G. Engel Lester Ziffren	E. D. Biggers (Black Camel) (Sidney Toler) Charlie Chan
Charlie Chan's Chance	Fox	1932	John Blystone	Barry Connors Philip Klein	E. D. Biggers (Behind That Curtain) (Warner Oland) Charlie Chan
Charlie Chan's Courage	TCF	1934	George Hadden	Seton I. Miller	E. D. Biggers (Chinese Parrot) (Warner Oland) Charlie Chan
Charlie Chan's Greatest Case	TCF	1933	Hamilton MacFadden	Lester Cole Marion Orth	E. D. Biggers (House Without a Key) (Warner Oland) Charlie Chan
Charlie Chan's Murder Cruise	TCF	1940	Eugene Forde	Robertson White Lester Ziffren	E. D. Biggers (Charlie Chan Carries On) (Sidney Toler) Charlie Chan
Charlie Muggin	Euston	1979	?	?	B. Freemantle (Charlie Muffin)
Chase	Columbia	1946	Arthur Ripley	Philip Yordan	C. Woolrich (Black Path of Fear)
Chase	Columbia	1966	Arthur Penn	Lillian Hellman	H. Foote
Chase a Crooked Shadow	ABP	1958	Michael Anderson	David D. Osborn Charles Sinclair	play: A. Shaughnessy (Double Cut)
Chautauqua Trouble with Girls	MGM	1969	Peter Tewkesbury	Arnold Peyser Lois Peyser	D. Keene
Cheap Detective	Columbia	1978	Robert Moore	Neil Simon	novel: R. Grossbach
Cheaters at Play	Fox	1932	Hamilton MacFadden	M. S. Boylan	L. J. Vance (Lone Wolf's Son)
Cheating Cheaters	*Young	1919	Allan Dwan	Kathryn Stuart	M. Marcin
Cheating Cheaters	*Universal	1927	Edward Laemmle	Charles A. Logue James T. O'Donoghue	M. Marcin
Cheating Cheaters	Universal	1934	Richard Thorpe	Gladys Unger James Mulhauser Allen Rivkin	M. Marcin
Cheerful Fraud	*Universal	1927	William A. Seiter	Leigh Jacobson Sam Mintz Rex Taylor William A. Seiter Harvey Thew	K. R. G. Browne (Following Ann)
Cheri-Bibi	Dist. Par.	1938	Leon Mathot	?	G. Leroux (Pierre Fresnay) Cheri-Bibi
Chicago	*DeMille	1927	Frank Urson	Lenore J. Coffee	M. Watkins
Chicago Deadline	Paramount	1949	Lewis Allen	Warren Duff	T. Thayer (One Woman)
Chicago Joe and the Showgirl	Polygram	1990	Bernard Rose	David Yallow	novel: M. Gaynor
Chick	*Brit. Lion	1928	A. V. Bramble	Eliot Stannard	E. Wallace
Chick	B&D	1936	Michael Hankinson	Irving Leroy Daniel Wheddon Gerard Fairlie Cyril Gardner D. B. Wyndham-Lewis	E. Wallace
Child's Play	Paramount	1972	Sidney Lumet	Leon Prochnik	R. Marasco
Chin-Chin-Chinaman Boat from Shanghai	Real Art	1931	Guy Newall	Brock Williams Guy Newall	P. Walsh
China Syndrome	Columbia	1979	James Bridges	Mike Gray T. S. Cook James Bridges	novel: B. Wohl
Chinatown	Paramount	1974	Roman Polanski	Robert Towne	screenplay: R. Towne
Chinese Bungalow	*Stoll	1926	Sinclair Hill	?	M. Osmond
Chinese Bungalow	Neo-Art	1930	J. B. Williams Arthur W. Barnes	J. B. Williams Marian Osmond James Corbett	M. Osmond
Chinese Bungalow Chinese Den	Pennant	1940	George King	A. R. Rawlinson George Wellesley	M. Osmond
Chinese Den Chinese Bungalow	Pennant	1940	George King	A. R. Rawlinson George Wellesley	M. Osmond (Chinese Bungalow)

C

FILM TITLE	STUDIO	YEAR	DIRECTOR	SCREENWRITER	SOURCE AUTHOR/WORK	SERIES
Chinese Parrot	*Jewel	1927	Paul Leni	J. Grubb Alexander	E. D. Biggers	Charlie Chan (K. Sojin)
Chinese Puzzle	*Ideal	1919	Fred Goodwins	Fred Goodwins	M. Bower	
Chinese Puzzle	Twickenham	1932	Guy Newall	H. Fowler Mear	M. Bower	
Choice of Assassins	Rome Paris	1967	Philippe Fourastie	Remo Forlani Philippe Fourastie	W. P. McGivern	
Choirboys	Lorimar	1978	Robert Aldrich	Christopher Knopf	J. Wambaugh	
Christmas Holiday	Universal	1944	Robert Siodmak	Herman J. Mankiewicz	W. S. Maugham	
Chronicle of a Death Foretold	Italmedia	1987	Francesco Rosi	Francesco Rosi Tonino Guerra	G. G. Marquez	
Cinema Murder	*Cosmopol.	1920	George D. Baker	Frances Marion	E. P. Oppenheim (Other Romilly)	
Circle	IA	1948	W. Lee Wilder	Heinz Herald Guy Endore	H. Herald (Burning Bush)	
Vicious Circle						
Woman in Brown						
Circular Staircase	*Selig	1915	Edward J. LeSaint	?	M. R. Rinehart	
Circus of Fear	Am. Inter.	1967	John Moxey	Peter Welbeck	E. Wallace (headnote)	
Psycho-Circus						
Circus Queen Murder	Columbia	1933	Roy William Neill	Jo Swerling	A. Abbot (About the Murder of the Circus Queen)	Thatcher Colt (Adolphe Menjou)
City Across the River	UI	1949	Maxwell Shane	Maxwell Shane Dennis Cooper Irving Shulman	I. Shulman (Amboy Dukes)	
City After Midnight	Monarch	1957	Compton Bennett	Compton Bennett	J. D. Carr (Emperor's Snuff Box)	
That Woman Opposite						
City of Purple Dreams	*Selig	1918	Colin Campbell	Gilson Willets	Anonymous	
City of Silent Men	*Lasky	1921	Tom Forman	Frank Condon	J. Moroso (Quarry)	
City of Sin	Lynn-Romero	1959	John Cromwell	Edgar Romero	novel: D. O'Callaghan (Scavengers)	
Scavengers						
Clairvoyant	?	?	?	?	H. Clement	
Clash by Night	Eternal	1963	Montgomery Tully	Maurice J. Wilson Montgomery Tully	R. Croft-Cooke	
Escape by Night						
Clayton Treasure Mystery	Fox Brit.	1938	Manning Haynes	Edward Dryhurst	N. Gordon (Shakespeare Murders)	
Clean Slate	Films/Tour	1981	Bertrand Tavernier	Jean Aurenche Bertrand Tavernier	J. Thompson (Pop. 1280)	
Population 1280						
Cleopatra Jones	Warner	1973	Jack Starrett	Max Julien Sheldon Keller	novel: R. Goulart	Cleopatra Jones (Tamara Dobson)
Cleopatra Jones and the Casino of Gold	Warner	1975	Chuck Ball	William Tennant	novel: R. Goulart	Cleopatra Jones (Tamara Dobson)
Climax	Universal	1944	George Waggner	Curt Siodmak Lynn Starling	novel: F. J. Lewis	
Cloak and Dagger	Carr	1984	Richard Franklin	Tom Holland	W. Irish (Dead Man Blues)	
Clockmaker	Lira	1974	Bertrand Tavernier	Jean Aurenche Pierre Bost	G. Simenon (Watchmaker of Everton)	
Watchmaker of Saint-Paul						
Clockwork Orange	Warner	1971	Stanley Kubrick	Stanley Kubrick	A. Burgess	
Closing Net	*Gold Roost.	1915	Edward Jose	George B. Seitz	H. C. Rowland	
Club Extinction	Prism	1989	Claude Chabrol	Sollace Mitchell	N. Jacques (Dr. Mabuse, Master of Mystery)	
Dr. M.						
Clue	Polygram	1985	Jonathan Lynn	Jonathan Lynn John Landis	novel: M. McDowell	
Clue of the New Pin	Brit. Lion	1929	Arthur Maude	Kathleen Hayden	E. Wallace	
Clue of the New Pin	Merton Park	1960	Allan Davis	Philip Mackie	E. Wallace	Supt. Meredith (Bernard Lee)
Clue of the Silver Key	Merton Park	1961	Gerard Glaister	Philip Mackie	E. Wallace	Supt. Meredith (Bernard Lee)
Clue of the Twisted Candle	Merton Park	1960	Allan Davis	Philip Mackie	E. Wallace	
Coast of Chance	*Selig	1913	Oscar Eagle	?	E. Chamberlain	

Coast of Skeletons	Towers	1964	Robert Lynn	Anthony S. Veitch	E. Wallace (Sanders of the River)	Commissioner Sanders (Richard Todd)
Cobra	Cannon	1986	George Pan Cosmatos	Peter Welbeck	P. Gosling (Running Duck)	
Code Name: Emerald	MGM	1985	Martin Starger	Sylvester Stallone	R. Bass (Emerald Illusion)	
Code of Scotland Yard	Brit. Lion	1946	George King	Ronald Bass	E. Percy (Play with Fire)	
Shop at Sly Corner				Katherine Strueby		
Coffy	Am. Int.	1973	Jack Hill	Jack Hill		
Cold River	Cold River	1982	Fred G. Sullivan	Fred G. Sullivan	novel: P. W. Fairman	
Cold Steel	*Meyberg	1921	Sherwood MacDonald	Monte Katterjohn	W. Judson	
Cold Sweat	Corona	1971	Terence Young	Shimon Wincelberg	G. C. Shedd (In the Shadow of the Hills)	
From the Boys				Albert Simonin	R. Matheson (Ride the Nightmare)	
Collector	Columbia	1965	William Wyler	Stanley Mann	J. Fowles	
				John Kohn		
Colleen Bawn	*Kalem	1911	Sidney Olcott	Gene Gauntier	D. Boucicault	
Colleen Bawn	*Aust. Life	1911	Gaston Mervale	?	D. Boucicault	
Colleen Bawn	*Yankee	1911	?	?	D. Boucicault	
Colleen Bawn	*Stoll	1924	W. P. Kellino	Eliot Stannard	D. Boucicault	
Loves of Colleen Bawn						
Color Me Blood Red	Box Office	1965	Hershell G. Lewis	Hershell G. Lewis	novel: H. G. Lewis	
Colorado Pluck	*Fox	1921	Jules Furthman	Jules Furthman	G. Goodchild (Colorado Jim)	
Colorado Territory	Warner	1949	Raoul Walsh	John Twist	W. R. Burnett (High Sierra)	
				Edmund H. North		
Colors	Orion	1988	Dennis Hopper	Michael Schiffer		
Coma	MGM	1978	Michael Crichton	Michael Crichton	novel: Joel Norst	
Come Back, Charleston Blue	Warner	1972	Mark Warren	Bontche Schweig	R. Cook	
					C. Himes (Heat's On)	
Come Dance with Me	Kingsley	1960	Michel Boisrond	Annette Wademant	K. Roos (Blonde Died Dancing)	
Come-On	Anglo-Am.	1956	Russell Birdwell	Warren Douglas	W. Chambers	
				Whitman Chambers		
Come to My House	*Fox	1928	Alfred E. Green	Marion Orth	A. S. Roche	
Comedians	MGM	1967	Peter Glenville	Graham Greene	G. Greene	
Comedy of Terrors	Alta Vista	1963	Jacques Tourneur	Richard Matheson	novel: Elsie Lee	
Committed	Vision Int.	1991	William A. Levey	Simon Last	S. Claudia (Clock and Bell)	
				Paul Mason		
Compromising Positions	Paramount	1985	Frank Perry	Susan Isaacs	S. Isaacs	
Compulsion	TCF	1959	Richard Fleischer	Richard Murphy	M. Levin	
Concorde—Airport 1979	Universal	1979	David Lowell Rich	Eric Roth	novel: K. Stewart	
				Jennings Lang		
Condemned to Death	Twickenham	1932	Walter Forde	Bernard Merivale	G. Goodchild (Jack O'Lantern)	
				H. Fowler Mear		
				Brock Williams		
Condemned to Life	Allied	1962	Basil Dearden	Janet Green	novel: W. Drummond (Life for Ruth)	
Life for Ruth				John McCormick		
Condorman	Disney	1981	Charles Jarrott	Marc Sturdivant	R. Sheckley (Game of X)	
				Glen Caron		
				Mickey Rose		
Conduct Unbecoming	Allied Art.	1975	Michael Anderson	Robert Enders	B. England	
Cone of Silence	Baring	1960	Charles Frend	Robert Westerby	D. Beaty	
Trouble in the Sky				Jeffrey Dell		
Confessions	*Stoll	1925	W. P. Kellino	Lydia Hayward	B. Reynolds (Confession Corner)	
Confidence Man	*Fam. Play.	1924	Victor Heerman	Paul Sloane	L. Y. Erskine	
Confidential Agent	Warner	1945	Herman Shumlin	Robert Buckner	G. Greene	
Confidential Agent	Warner	1955	Orson Welles	Orson Welles	O. Welles (Mr. Arkadin)	
Mr. Arkadin						
Confidentially Yours	du Carrosse	1983	Francois Truffaut	Francois Truffaut	C. Williams (Long Saturday Night)	
Finally, Sunday				Suzanne Schiffman		
Let It Be Sunday				Jean Aurel		
Conflict	*Universal	1921	Stuart Paton	George C. Hull	C. B. Kelland	

Gravedigger Jones (Godfrey Cambridge) Coffin Ed Johnson (Raymond St. Jacques)

C

C

FILM TITLE	STUDIO	YEAR	DIRECTOR	SCREENWRITER	SOURCE AUTHOR/WORK	SERIES
Conflict	WB-FN	1945	Curtis Bernhardt	Arthur T. Horman Dwight Taylor	novel: Alex Morrison	
Conformist	Mars	1971	Bernardo Bertolucci	Bernardo Bertolucci	A. Moravia	
Conjure Wife Night of the Eagle	Am. Inter.	1962	Sidney Hayers	Charles Beaumont Richard Matheson George Baxt	F. Leiber, Jr.	
Conquered City Captive City	Paramount	1963	Joseph Anthony	Guy Elmes Eric Bercovici Marc Brandel	J. Appleby (Captive City)	
Conqueror Worm Edgar Allan Poe's Conqueror Worm Witch-Finder General	Tigon Brit.	1968	Michael Reeves	Michael Reeves Tom Baker Louis M. Hayward	R. Bassett (Witch-Finder General)	
Conspiracy	*Fam. Play	1914	Allan Dwan	?	R. Baker	
Conspiracy	RKO	1930	Christy Cabanne	Beulah Marie Dix	R. Baker	
Conspirator	MGM	1949	Victor Saville	Sally Benson Gerard Fairlie	H. Slater	
Conspirators	*Stoll	1924	Sinclair Hill	Sinclair Hill	E. P. Oppenheim	
Conspirators	Warner	1944	Jean Negulesco	Vladimir Pozner Leo Rosten	F. Prokosch	
Contraband	*Fam. Play.	1925	Alan Crosland	Jack Cunningham	C. B. Kelland	
Convict 99	*Gaumont	1919	G. B. Samuelson	?	M. C. Leighton	
Convicted	Columbia	1938	Leon Barsha	Edgar Edwards William Bowers	W. Irish (Six Nights of Mystery)	
Convicted	Columbia	1950	Henry Levin	Fred Niblo, Jr. Seton I. Miller	M. Flavin (Criminal Code)	
Cool Breeze	MGM	1972	Barry Pollack	Barry Pollack	W. R. Burnett (Asphalt Jungle)	
Cool Hand Luke	Warner	1967	Stuart Rosenberg	Donn Pearce	Donn Pearce	
Cop	Atlantic	1987	James B. Harris	Frank R. Pierson James B. Harris	J. Ellroy (Blood on the Moon)	Sgt. Lloyd Hopkins (James Woods)
Cop Hater	Barbizon	1957	William Berke	Henry Kane	E. McBain	Steve Carella (Robert Loggia)
Cop-Out Stranger in the House	De Grunwald	1967	Pierre Rouve	Pierre Rouve	G. Simenon (Strangers in the House)	
Copper Beeches	*Fran.-Brit.	1912	Georges Treville	?	A. C. Doyle (Adventures of Sherlock Holmes)	Sherlock Holmes (Georges Treville)
Copper Beeches	*Stoll	1921	Maurice Elvey	William J. Elliott	A. C. Doyle (Adventures of Sherlock Holmes)	Sherlock Holmes (Eille Norwood)
Cops and Robbers	UA	1973	Aram Avakian	Donald E. Westlake	D. E. Westlake	
Cops' Sunday	Filmax	1983	Michel Vianey	Michel Vianey	A. Coburn (Off Duty)	
Cordelia the Magnificent	*Zierler	1923	George Archainbaud	Frank S. Beresford	L. Scott	
Corpse Came C.O.D.	Columbia	1947	Henry Levin	George Bricker Dwight Babcock	J. Starr	
Corpse in the Morgue Case of the Missing Blonde Lady in the Morgue	Universal	1938	Otis Garrett	Eric Taylor Robertson White	J. Latimer (Lady in the Morgue)	Joe Medford (George Brent)
Corridor of Mirrors	Apollo	1948	Terence Young	Rudolph Cartier Edana Romney	C. Massie	Bill Crane (Preston Foster)
Corrupt Order of Death	Vigo	1983	Robert Faenza	Robert Faenza Eunio de Concini Hugh Fleetwood	H. Fleetwood (Order of Death)	
Corsair	UA	1931	Roland West	Josephine Lovett	W. Green	
Cottage to Let Bombsight Stolen	Gainsbor.	1941	Anthony Asquith	Anatole de Grunwald J. O. C. Orton	G. Kerr (Cottages to Let)	

CRIME AND PUNISHMENT / 1377

C

Cotton Comes to Harlem	UA	1969	Ossie Davis	Arnold Perl Ossie Davis	C. Himes	Gravedigger Jones (Godfrey Cambridge) Coffin Ed Johnson (Raymond St. Jacques)
Couch	Warner	1962	Owen Crump	Robert Bloch	novel: R. Bloch	
Counsel for the Defense	*King	1925	Burton King	Arthur Hoerl	L. Scott	
Count Dracula	Fenix	1970	Jess Franco	Jess Franco Peter Welbeck Augusto Finochi Carlo Fadda Milo G. Cuccia Dietmar Behnke	B. Stoker (Dracula)	
Counterattack One Against Seven	Columbia	1945	Zoltan Korda	John Howard Lawson	J. Stevenson	
Counterfeit Traitor	Paramount	1962	George Seaton	George Seaton	A. Klein	
Country Beyond	*Fox	1926	Irving Cummings	Irving Cummings Ernest Maas	J. O. Curwood	
Country Beyond	TCF	1936	Eugene Forde	Lamar Trotti Adele Comandini	J. O. Curwood	
Courier	Euston	1988	Frank Deasy Joe Lee	Frank Deasy	novel: Gerald Cole	
Court Marshall Carrington, V.C.	Remus	1954	Anthony Asquith	John Hunter	D. Christie (Carrington, V.C.)	
Covenant with Death	Warner	1967	Lamont Johnson	Larry Marcus Saul Levitt	S. Becker	
Crack in the Mirror	TCF	1960	Richard Fleischer	Mark Canfield	M. Haedrich	
Crack-Up	RKO	1946	Irving Reis	John Paxton Ben Bengal Ray Spencer	Fredric Brown (Madman's Holiday)	
Crackerjack Man with 100 Faces	Gainsbor.	1938	Albert de Courville	A. R. Rawlinson Michael Pertwee Basil Mason	W. B. M. Ferguson	
Crash	*First Nat.	1928	Eddie Cline	Charles Kenyon	F. Packard (Night Operator)	Douglas Renfrew (James Newill)
Crashing Through	Monogram	1939	Elmer Clifton	Sherman Lowe	L. Y. Erskine (Renfrew Rides the Range)	
Craze	Harbour	1973	Freddie Francis	Aben Kandel Herman Cohen	H. Seymour (Infernal Idol)	
Crazy Joe	Bright-P. Rome-Paris	1973	Carlo Lizzani	Lewis John Carlino	novel: M. Barone	
Crazy Pete	Rialto	1965	Jean-Luc Godard	Jean-Luc Godard	L. White (Obsession)	
Creature with the Blue Hand	*?	1967	Alfred Vohrer	Alex Berg	E. Wallace (Blue Hand)	
Creeping Shadow Limping Man	BIP	1931	John Orton	John Orton	W. Scott (Man)	Disher (Franklin Dyall)
Crime	Solaris	1984	Salvatore Nocita	Vittorio Bonicelli	G. Bernanos	
Crime and Passion Ace Up Your Sleeve	Am.-Int.	1975	Ivan Passer	Jesse Lasky, Jr. Pat Silver	J. H. Chase (Ace Up My Sleeve)	
Crime and Punishment	*?	1913	I. Vronsky	?	F. M. Dostoevskii	
Crime and Punishment	*Arrow	1917	Lawrence McGill	?	F. M. Dostoevskii	
Crime and Punishment	*Moscow Art	1927	?	?	F. M. Dostoevskii	
Crime and Punishment	*?	1929	Robert Weine	?	F. M. Dostoevskii	
Crime and Punishment	Columbia	1935	Josef Von Sternberg	S. K. Lauren Joseph Anthony	F. M. Dostoevskii	
Crime and Punishment	Gen. Prod.	1935	Pierre Chenal	Marcel Ayme Pierre Chenal Christian Stengel Wladimir Strijenski	F. M. Dostoevskii	
Crime and Punishment	Terrafilm	1948	Hampe Faustman	Bertil Malmberg Sven Stople	F. M. Dostoevskii	
Crime and Punishment	Pathe	1957	Georges Lampin	Charles Spaak	F. M. Dostoevskii	
Crime and Punishment	Mosfilm	1970	Lev Kulijanov	Lev Kulijanov Nikolai Figurovski	F. M. Dostoevskii	

1378 / CRIME AND PUNISHMENT — Film Index

C

FILM TITLE	STUDIO	YEAR	DIRECTOR	SCREENWRITER	SOURCE AUTHOR/WORK	SERIES
Crime and Punishment	Villealfa	1984	Aki Kaurismaki	Aki Kaurismaki Pauli Pentti	F. M. Dostoevskii	
Crime and Punishment USA	AA	1958	Denis Sanders	Walter Newman	F. M. Dostoevskii (Crime and Punishment)	
Crime at Blossoms	B&D	1933	Maclean Rogers	Maclean Rogers	M. Shairp	
Crime by Night	Warner	1944	William Clemens	Richard Weil Joel Malone	G. Homes (Forty Whacks)	
Crime Doctor	RKO	1934	John Robertson	Jane Murfin	I. Zangwill (Big Bow Mystery)	
Crime Unlimited	WB-FN	1935	Ralph Ince	Brock Williams Ralph Smart	D. Hume	
Crime Without Passion	Paramount	1934	Ben Hecht Charles MacArthur	Ben Hecht Charles MacArthur	B. Hecht (Collected Stories of Ben Hecht)	
Crimes at the Dark House	Pennant	1940	George King	Edward Dryhurst Frederick Hayward H. F. Maltby	W. Collins (Woman in White)	
Criminal at Large Frightened Lady	Brit. Lion	1932	T. Hayes Hunter	Angus MacPhail Bryan Edgar Wallace	E. Wallace (Case of the Frightened Lady)	
Criminal Code	Columbia	1931	Howard Hawks	Fred Niblo, Jr. Seton I. Miller	M. Flavin	
Criminal Within Murder at Glen Athol	Invincible	1935	Frank R. Strayer	John W. Krafft	N. Lippincott (Murder at Glen Athol)	
Crimson Circle	*Kinema	1922	George Ridgwell	Patrick L. Mannock	E. Wallace	
Crimson Circle	New Era	1930	Friedrich Zelnik	Howard Gaye	E. Wallace	
Crimson Circle	Wainwright	1936	Reginald Denham	Howard Irving Young	E. Wallace	
Crimson City	Warner	1928	Archie Mayo	Anthony Coldeway	novel: A. Coldeway	
Crimson Gardenia	*Goldwyn	1919	Reginald Barker		R. Beach	
Criss Cross	Universal	1949	Robert Siodmak	Daniel Fuchs	D. Tracy	
Crooked Billet	*Gainsbor.	1929	Adrian Brunel	Angus MacPhail	D. Titheradge	
Crooked Man	*Stoll	1923	George Ridgwell	Geoffrey H. Malins Patrick L. Mannock	A. C. Doyle (Memoirs of Sherlock Holmes)	Sherlock Holmes (Eille Norwood)
Crooked Road	Argo	1964	Don Chaffey	J. Garrison Don Chaffey	M. West (Big Story)	
Crooks in Clover Penthouse	MGM	1933	W. S. Van Dyke	Frances Goodrich Albert Hackett	A. S. Roche (Penthouse)	
Cross-Country	Filmline	1983	Paul Lynch	John Hunter William Gray	H. D. Kastle	
Cross Currents	B&D	1935	Adrian Brunel	Adrian Brunel Pelham Leigh Amann	W. G. Elliott (Nine Days' Blunder)	
Cross Up Tiger by the Tail	Tempean	1955	John Gilling	John Gilling Willis Goldbeck	J. Mair (Never Come Back)	
Crossfire	RKO	1947	Edward Dmytryk	John Paxton	R. Brooks (Brick Foxhole)	
Crossing the Line	Palace	1991	David Leland	Don McPherson	W. McIlvanney (Big Man)	
Crosstrap	Unifilms	1962	R. Hartford-Davis	Philip Wrestler	J. N. Chance (headnote)	
Crouching Beast	Stafford	1935	W. Victor Hanbury	?	V. Williams	
Crown v. Stevens	WB-FN	1936	Michael Powell	Brock Williams	L. Meynell (Third Time Unlucky)	
Crucial Test	*Edison	1911	?		R. H. Davis (Ranson's Folly)	
Cruising	UA	1980	William Friedkin	William Friedkin	G. Walker	
Cry Baby Killer	Allied Art.	1958	Jus Addis	Leo Gordon Melvin Levy	novel: Joseph Hilton	
Cry in the Night	Warner	1956	Frank Tuttle	David Dortort	W. Masterson (All Through the Night)	
Cry of the City	TCF	1948	Robert Siodmak	Richard Murphy	H. E. Helseth (Chair for Martin Rome)	
Cry of the Owl	Italfrance	1987	Claude Chabrol	Claude Chabrol Odila Barskil	P. Highsmith	
Cry Terror	MGM	1958	Andrew L. Stone	Andrew L. Stone	novel: A. L. Stone	
Cry Tough	UA	1959	Paul Stanley	Harry Kleiner	I. Shulman	
Cry Uncle	Cambist	1971	John G. Avildsen	David Odell	M. Brett (Lie a Little, Die a Little)	
Cry Wolf	Warner	1947	Peter Godfrey	Catherine Turney	M. Carleton	

D

Title	Studio	Year	Director	Writer	Source/Character
Cult of the Damned	Am. Inter.	1958	Robert Thom	Robert Thom	novel: W. Johnston (Angel, Angel, Down We Go)
Angel, Angel, Down We Go					
Curlytop	*Fox	1924	Maurice Elvey	Frederick Hatton	T. Burke (Whispering Windows)
Curse of Drink	*Weber	1922	Harry O. Hoyt	Harry O. Hoyt	C. E. Blaney
Curse of Frankenstein	Hammer	1957	Terence Fisher	Jimmy Sangster	M. W. Shelley (Frankenstein)
Curse of the Werewolf	Hospur	1961	Terence Fisher	John Elder	G. Endore (Werewolf of Paris)
Curtain at Eight	Majestic	1933	E. Mason Hopper	Edward T. Lowe	O. R. Cohen (Backstage Mystery)
Cutter and Bone	Gurian	1981	Ivan Passer	Jeffrey Alan Fiskin	N. Thornburg
Cutter's Way					
Cutter's Way	Gurian	1981	Ivan Passer	Jeffrey Alan Fiskin	N. Thornburg (Cutter and Bone)
Cutter and Bone					
Cynara	Goldwyn	1933	King Vidor	Frances Marion	R. Gore-Brown (Imperfect Lover)
				Lynn Starling	
Cynthia-of-the-Minute	*Artco	1920	Perry Vekroff	Leah Baird	L. J. Vance
Daddy's Gone A-Hunting	Nat. Gen.	1969	Mark Robson	Larry Cohen	novel: Mike St. Clair
Dames Get Along	CICO-Pathe	1954	Bernard Borderie	Lorenzo Semple, Jr.	P. Cheyney (Dames Don't Care) Lemmy Caution (Eddie Constantine)
				Bernard Borderie	
				Jacques Vilfrid	
Damned	Brit. Lion	1961	Joseph Losey	Evan Jones	H. L. Lawrence (Children of the Light)
These Are the Damned					
Dancer and the King	*World	1914	E. Artaud	Edwin Carewe	C. E. Blaney
Dancing Men	*Stoll	1923	George Ridgwell	Geoffrey H. Malins	A. C. Doyle (Return of Sherlock Holmes) Sherlock Holmes (Eille Norwood)
				Patrick L. Mannock	
Dandy in Aspic	Columbia	1968	Laurence Harvey	Derek Marlowe	D. Marlowe
			Anthony Mann		
Danger Ahead	Criterion	1940	Ralph Staub	Edward Halperin	L. Y. Erskine (Renfrew's Long Trail) Douglas Renfrew (James Newill)
Danger Island	TCF	1939	Herbert I. Leeds	Peter Milne	J. W. Vandercook (Murder in Trinidad) Mr. Moto (Peter Lorre)
Mr. Moto in Danger Island					
Mr. Moto on Danger Island					
Danger on the Air	Universal	1938	Otis Garrett	Betty Laidlow	Xantippe (Death Catches Up with Mr. Kluck)
				Robert Lively	
Danger Route	Amicus	1967	Seth Holt	Meade Roberts	A. York (Eliminator) Jonas Wilde (Richard Johnson)
				Robert Stewart	
Danger Signal	Warner	1945	Robert Florey	Adele Commandini	P. Bottome (Murder in the Bud)
				C. Graham Baker	
Danger Within	Lesslie	1959	Don Chaffey	Bryan Forbes	M. Gilbert (Death in Captivity)
Breakout				Frank Harvey	
Dangerous Afternoon	Theatrecr.	1961	Charles Saunders	Brandon Fleming	G. Anstruther
Dangerous Blondes	Columbia	1943	Leigh Jason	Richard Flournoy	K. Roos (If the Shroud Fits)
				Jack Henley	
Dangerous Corner	RKO	1934	Phil Rosen	Anne M. Chapin	J. B. Priestley
				Madeleine Ruthven	
Dangerous Crossing	TCF	1953	Joseph M. Newman	Leo Townsend	J. D. Carr (Dead Sleep Lightly)
Dangerous Davies	ITC	1980	Val Guest	Val Guest	L. Thomas Dangerous Davies (Bernard Cribbens)
				Leslie Thomas	
Dangerous Days	Em. Authors	1920	Reginald Barker	Charles Kenyon	M. R. Rinehart
Dangerous Female	Warner	1931	Roy del Ruth	Maude Fulton	D. Hammett (Maltese Falcon) Sam Spade (Ricardo Cortez)
Maltese Falcon				Lucien Hubbard	
				Brown Holmes	
				Dashiell Hammett	
Dangerous Lies	*Fam. Play.	1921	Paul Powell	Mary O'Connor	E. P. Oppenheim (headnote)
Dangerous Partners	MGM	1945	Edward L. Cahn	Marion Parsonnet	O. W. Bayer (Paper Chase)
Dangerous to Know	Paramount	1938	Robert Florey	William R. Lipman	E. Wallace (On the Spot)
				Horace McCoy	
Dans la Gueule du Loup	Panda	1961	Jean-Chas. Dudremet	Michel Lebrun	J. H. Chase (Just Another Sucker)
				Jean-Chas. Dudremet	
Dark Corner	TCF	1946	Henry Hathaway	Jay Dratler	L. Q. Ross
				Bernard Schoenfeld	

D

FILM TITLE	STUDIO	YEAR	DIRECTOR	SCREENWRITER	SOURCE AUTHOR/WORK	SERIES
Dark Eyes of London Human Monster	Argyle	1939	Walter Summers	Patrick Kirwan Walter Summers	E. Wallace	
Dark Eyes of London Dead Eyes of London	Rialto	1961	Alfred Vohrer	John F. Argyle Trygve Larsen	E. Wallace	
Dark Hazard	First Nat.	1934	Alfred E. Green	Ralph Block Brown Holmes	W. R. Burnett	
Dark Hour	Chester.	1936	Charles Lamont	Ewart Adamson	S. Gluck (Last Trap)	Paul Bernard (Berton Churchill)
Dark Mirror	*Paramount	1920	Charles Giblyn	E. Magnus Ingleton	L. J. Vance	
Dark of the Sun Mercenaries	MGM	1968	Jack Cardiff	Quentin Werty Adrian Spies	Wilbur Smith (Train from Katanga)	
Dark Page	Columbia	1952	Phil Karlson	Ted Sherdeman Eugene Ling James Poe	S. Fuller	
Dark Passage	Warner	1947	Delmar Daves	Delmar Daves	D. Goodis	
Dark Past	Columbia	1948	Rudolph Mate	Malvin Wald Oscar Saul Philip MacDonald Michael Blankfort Albert Duffy	J. Warwick (Blind Alley)	
Dark Secret	Nettlefold	1949	Maclean Rogers	A. R. Rawlinson Moie Charles	M. Shairp (Crime at Blossoms)	
Dark Shadows House of Dark Shadows	MGM	1970	Dan Curtis	Sam Hall Gordon Russell	novel: Marilyn Ross (House of Dark Shadows)	Barnabas Collins (Jonathan Frid)
Dark Stairway	WB-FN	1938	Arthur Woods	Brock Williams Basil Dillon	M. Eberhart (From This Dark Stairway)	
Dark Tower	Warner	1943	John Harlow	Reginald Purdell Brock Williams	A. Woollcott	
Dark Waters	UA	1944	Andre de Toth	Joan Harrison Marian Cockrell Arthur Horman	F. Cockrell	
Dark Wind	Seven Arts	1991	Errol Morris	Eric Bergren Neal Jimenez Mark Horowitz	T. Hillerman	Jim Chee (Lou Diamond Phillips) Joe Leaphorn (Fred Ward) Travis McGee (Rod Taylor)
Darker Than Amber	Nat. Gen.	1970	Robert Clouse	Ed Waters	J. D. MacDonald	
Darkman	Universal	1990	Sam Raimi	Chuck Pfarrer Sam Raimi Ivan Raimi Daniel Goldline Joshua Goldin	novel: Randall Boyle	
Darling Lili	Paramount	1970	Blake Edwards	Blake Edwards William Peter Blatty		
Das Indische Tuch	Rialto	1963	Alfred Vohrer	Harald G. Peterson Georg Hurdalek	E. Wallace (Frightened Lady)	
Daughter of Darkness	Kenilworth	1947	Lance Comfort	Max Catto	M. Catto (They Walk Alone)	
Daughter of the Dragon	Paramount	1931	Lloyd Corrigan	Lloyd Corrigan Monte Katterjohn Sidney Buchman	S. Rohmer (Daughter of Fu Manchu)	Fu Manchu (Warner Oland)
Daughter of Two Worlds	*First Nat.	1920	James Young	James Young Edmund Golding	L. Scott	
Dawn	*Lucoque	1917	H. Lisle Lucoque	Pauline Lewis	H. R. Haggard	
Dawning	TVS-Vista	1988	Robert Knights	Moira Williams	Jennifer Johnston (Old Jess)	
Day of Days	*Fam. Play.	1914	Daniel Frohman	?	L. J. Vance	
Day of the Dolphin	AVCO Emb.	1973	Mike Nichols	Buck Henry	R. Merle	
Day of the Jackal	Universal	1973	Fred Zinnemann	Kenneth Ross	F. Forsyth	

D

Title	Studio	Year	Director	Writer	Source
Day of the Owl	Panda Cin		Daminao Damiani	Daminao Damiani / Ugo Pirro	L. Sciascia (Mafia Vendetta)
Day the Fish Came Out	TCF	1967	Michael Cacoyannis	Michael Cacoyannis	novel: K. Cicellis
Day They Robbed the Bank of England	Summit	1960	John Guillermin	Richard Maibaum / Howard Clewes	J. Brophy
Daybreak	Gen. Films	1948	Compton Bennett	Muriel Box / Sidney Box	A. Meredith
Dazzling Miss Davison	*Mutual	1917	Frank Powell	?	
Dead Bang	Lorimar	1989	John Frankenheimer	Robert Foster	F. Warden
Dead Calm	Roadshow	1989	Phillip Noyce	Terry Hayes	novel: E. Naha
Dead Certainty	*Broadwest	1920	George Dewhurst	P. L. Mannock	C. Williams
Dead End	UA	1937	William Wyler	Lillian Hellman	N. Gould / S. Kingsley
Dead Eyes of London	Rialto	1961	Alfred Vohrer	Trygve Larsen	E. Wallace (Dark Eyes of London)
Dark Eyes of London					
Dead Heat on a Merry-Go-Round	Columbia	1968	Bernard Girard	Bernard Girard	novel: E. L. Heyman
Dead Image	Warner	1964	Paul Heinreid	Oscar Millard	novel: Robert Thomas (Dead Ringer)
Dead Ringer				Albert Beich	
Dead Man's Float	Andromeda	1980	Pete Sharp	Roger Carr	Roger Carr
Dead Men Are Dangerous	Welwyn	1939	Harold French	Victor Kendall / Harry Hughes / Vernon Clancy	H. C. Armstrong (Hidden)
Dead Men Tell No Tales	*Vitagraph	1920	Tom Terriss	Lillian Chester	E. W. Hornung
Dead Men Tell No Tales	Brit. Nat.	1939	David Macdonald	George R. Chester / Walter Summers / Stafford Dickins / Doreen Montgomery / Emlyn Williams	F. Beeding (Norwich Victims)
Dead of Night	Ealing	1945	Basil Dearden	Angus MacPhail / John Baines / T. E. B. Clarke	E. F. Benson (Room in the Tower)
Dead on a Rainy Sunday	Incite	1986	Joel Santoni	Philippe Setbon	Joan Aiken
Dead on Course	Hammer	1952	Terence Fisher	John Gilling	M. Black
Wings of Danger					
Dead Pigeon on Beethoven Street	Bavaria	1972	Samuel Fuller	Samuel Fuller	novel: S. Fuller
Dead Reckoning	Columbia	1947	John Cromwell	Oliver H. P. Garrett / Steve Fisher / Allen Rivkin	novel: Alex Morrison
Dead Ringer	Warner	1964	Paul Heinreid	Oscar Millard	novel: Robert Thomas
Dead Image					
Dead Ringers	Astral	1988	David Cronenberg	David Cronenberg / Norman Snider	Bari Wood (Twins)
Dead Run	Universal	1967	Christian-Jaque	Christian-Jaque / Michel Levine / Pascal Jardin / Danny Tyber	R. Sheckley
Dead Secret	*Monopol	1913	Nicholas Webster	Stanner E. V. Taylor ?	W. Collins
Dead to the World	National	1961	David Cronenberg	John Roeburt	E. Ronns (State Department Murders)
Dead Zone	EMI	1984	David Cronenberg	Jeffrey Boam	Stephen King
Deadfall	Salamander	1967	Bryan Forbes	Bryan Forbes	D. Cory
Deadlier Than the Male	Santor	1966	Ralph Thomas	Jimmy Sangster / David Osborn / Liz Charles-Williams	novel: H. Reymond
					Bulldog Drummond (Richard Johnson)
Deadline	TCF	1952	Richard Brooks	Richard Brooks	novel: J. Eastwood
Deadline U.S.A.					
Deadline at Dawn	RKO	1946	Harold Clurman	Clifford Odets	W. Irish
Deadline U.S.A.	TCF	1952	Richard Brooks	Richard Brooks	novel: J. Eastwood (Deadline)
Deadline					
Deadly Affair	Lumet	1966	Sidney Lumet	Paul Dehn	J. Le Carre (Call for the Dead)
Deadly Bees	Amicus	1967	Freddie Francis	Robert Bloch / Anthony Marriott	H. F. Heard (Taste of Honey)

Film Index   DEADLY BEES / 1381

George Martin (Hugh Williams)

Richard Vaness (Zachary Scott)

D

FILM TITLE	STUDIO	YEAR	DIRECTOR	SCREENWRITER	SOURCE AUTHOR/WORK	SERIES
Deadly Circuit	Telema	1983	Claude Miller	Michel Audiard / Jacques Audiard	M. Behm (Eye of the Beholder)	
Deadly Duo	UA	1962	Reginald LeBorg	Owen Harris	R. Jessup	
Deadly Encounter	?	1979	?	R. John Hugh	novel: R. Woodley	
Deadly Friend	Warner	1987	Wes Craven	Bruce Joel Rubin	D. Henstell (Friend)	
Deadly Game / Third Party Risk	Hammer	1955	Daniel Birt	Daniel Birt	N. Bentley (Third Party Risk)	
Deadly Is the Female / Gun Crazy	UA	1949	Joseph H. Lewis	MacKinlay Kantor / Millard Kaufman	M. Kantor (Author's Choice)	
Deadly Record	Ind. Art.	1959	Lawrence Huntington	Vivian A. Cox / Lawrence Huntington	N. W. Hooke	
Deadly Trap	Corona	1971	Rene Clement	Sidney Buchman / Eleanor Perry	A. Cavanagh (Children Are Gone)	
Dear Fatherland, Be at Peace	Constantin	1976	Roland Kirk	Roland Kirk	J. M. Simmel (Dear Fatherland)	
Dear Murderer	Gainsbor.	1947	Arthur Crabtree	Muriel Box / Sydney Box / Peter Rogers	S. L. Clowes	
Death at a Broadcast / Death at Broadcasting House	Phoenix	1934	Reginald Denham	Basil Mason	V. Gielgud (Death at Broadcasting House)	
Death at a Broadcast	Phoenix	1934	Reginald Denham	Basil Mason	V. Gielgud	
Death Croons the Blues	St. Margar.	1937	David Macdonald	H. Fowler Mear / Harry Alan Towers	J. Ronald	
Death Drums Along the River	Big Ben	1963	Lawrence Huntington	Nicholas Roeg / Maisie Sharman	E. Wallace (Sanders of the River)	Commissioner Sanders (Richard Todd)
Death Goes to School	Independent	1953	Stephen Clarkson	Stephen Clarkson	S. Davis (Death in Seven Hours)	
Death in Brunswick	Roadshow	1990	John Ruane	John Ruane / Boyd Oxlade	B. Oxlade	
Death in High Heels	Marylebone	1947	Lionel Tomlinson	?	C. Brand	
Death Kiss	Worldwide	1933	Edward L. Marin	Barry Barringer / Gordon Kahn	M. St. Dennis	
Death of a Beauty / End of Belle / Passion of Slow Fire	Lux	1961	Edouard Molinaro	Jean Anoulin	G. Simenon (Belle)	
Death of a Champion	Paramount	1939	Robert Florey	Stuart Palmer / Cortland Fitzsimmons	F. Gruber (Brass Knuckles)	Oliver Quade (Lynne Overman)
Death on the Diamond	MGM	1934	Edward Sedgwick	Harvey Thew / Joseph Sherman / Ralph Spence	C. Fitzsimmons	
Death on the Nile	Paramount	1978	John Guillermin	Anthony Shaffer	A. Christie	Hercule Poirot (Peter Ustinov)
Death on the Set / Murder on the Set	Twickenham	1935	Leslie S. Hiscott	Michael Barringer	V. MacClure	Archie Burford (Garry Marsh)
Death Takes a Holiday	Paramount	1934	Mitchell Leisen	Maxwell Anderson / Gladys Lehman	Walter Ferris	
Death Trap	Merton Park	1962	John Moxey	John Roddick / Wendell Mayes	E. Wallace (headnote)	
Death Wish	Paramount	1974	Michael Winner	Henry Suso	B. Garfield	
Deathsport	New World	1978	Henry Suso / Allan Arkush	Donald Stewart	novel: W. Hughes	
Deathtrap	Warner	1982	Sidney Lumet	Jay Presson Allen / Barbara Turner	I. Levin	
Deathwatch	Beverly	1966	Vic Morrow	Vic Morrow	J. Genet (Maids and Deathwatch)	
Deception	Warner	1946	Irving Rapper	John Collier / Joseph Than	E. Walter (Jealousy)	
Decision Before Dawn	TCF	1951	Anatole Litvak	Peter Viertel	G. Howe (Call It Treason)	

Title	Studio	Year	Director	Writer	Notes
Decks Ran Red	MGM	1958	Andrew L. Stone	Andrew L. Stone	novel: A. L. Stone
Deep	Casablanca	1977	Peter Yates	Virginia Stone Peter Benchley Tracy Keenan Wynn	P. Benchley
Deep Water	Hamster	1981	Michel Deville	Michel Deville Florence Delay Christopher Frank	P. Highsmith
Defector	Seven Arts	1966	Raoul Levy	Robert Guenette Peter Francke Raoul Levy	P. Thomas (Spy)
Defenders of the Law	Standard	1931	Joseph Levering	Hampton Del Ruth Louis Heifetz	novel: H. Del Ruth
Definite Object	*Eros	1920	Edgar J. Camiller	Edgar J. Camiller	J. Farnol
Delavine Affair	Croydon	1954	Douglas Pierce	George Fisher	Robert Chapman (Winter Wears a Shroud) Rex Banner (Peter Reynolds)
Deliverance	Warner	1972	John Boorman	James Dickey	J. Dickey
Delta Factor	Spillane	1970	Tay Garnett	Tay Garnett	M. Spillane
Delta Force	Cannon	1986	Menahem Golan	James Bruner Menahem Bolan	novel: J. Norst
Demon	*Metro	1918	George D. Baker	George D. Baker	C. N. Williamson
Demon Barber of Fleet Street Sweeney Todd, the Demon Barber of Fleet Street	King	1936	George King	Frederick Hayward H. F. Maltby	G. D. Pitt (Sweeney Todd, the Demon Barber of Fleet Street)
Der Falscher von London	Rialto	1961	Harald Reinl	Johannes Kai	E. Wallace (Forger)
Der Grune Bogenschutze	Rialto	1960	Jurgen Roland	Wolfgang Menge	E. Wallace (Green Archer)
Der Morder	Aurora	1978	Ottokar Runze	Ottokar Runze	G. Simenon (Murderer)
Der Schwarze Abt	Rialto	1963	Franz J. Gotlieb	Franz J. Gotlieb	E. Wallace (Black Abbot)
Der Unheimliche Monch	Rialto	1965	Harald Reinl	Johannes Kai Joachim Bartsch	E. Wallace (Terror)
Der Zinker	Ondra	1931	Carl Lamac Max Fric	Fred Denger Rudolf Katcher Egon Eis Otto Eis	E. Wallace (Squeaker)
Der Zinker	Rialto	1963	Alfred Vohrer	H. G. Petersson	E. Wallace (Squeaker)
Descent Into Hell	Partner's	1986	Francis Girod	Francis Girod Jean-Loup Dabadie	D. Goodis (Wounded and the Slain)
Desert Attack Ice-Cold in Alex	ABPC	1958	J. Lee Thompson	J. Lee Thompson Christopher Landon T. J. Morrison	C. Landon (Ice-Cold in Alex)
Desert Fury	Paramount	1947	Lewis Allen	Robert Rossen A. I. Bezzerides	R. Stewart (Desert Town)
Desert Sands	UA	1955	Lesley Selander	Ramona Stewart George W. George George F. Slavin Danny Arnold	J. Robb (Punitive Action)
Design for Murder Trunk Crime	Charter	1939	Roy Boulting	Francis Miller	E. Percy (Trunk Crime)
Desire in the Dust	TCF	1960	William F. Claxton	Charles Lang	H. Whittington
Despair	Bavaria At.	1978	Werner Fassbinder	Tom Stoppard	V. Nabokoff-Sirin
Desperate Hours	Paramount	1955	William Wyler	Joseph Hayes	J. Hayes
Desperate Hours	MGM	1990	Michael Cimino	Lawrence Konner Mark Rosenthal Joseph Hayes	J. Hayes
Desperate Man	Merton Park	1959	Peter Maxwell	James Eastwood	P. Somers (Beginner's Luck)
Desperate Men Cat and Mouse	Anvil	1958	Paul Rotha	Paul Rotha	M. Halliday (Cat and Mouse)
Desperate Moment	BFM	1953	Compton Bennett	Patrick Kirwan George H. Brown	M. Albrand
Desperate Search	MGM	1952	Joseph Lewis	Walter Doniger	A. Mayse
Destroying Angel	*Edison	1915	Richard Ridgely	Richard Ridgely	L. J. Vance

Hugh Curtis (Conrad Phillips)

D

D

FILM TITLE	STUDIO	YEAR	DIRECTOR	SCREENWRITER	SOURCE AUTHOR/WORK	SERIES
Destroying Angel	*Beck	1923	W. S. Van Dyke	Leah Baird	L. J. Vance	
Destructors	Kettledrum	1974	Robert Parrish	Judd Bernard	novel: M. Franklin	
Marseilles Contract						
Detective	Facet	1954	Robert Hamer	Thelma Schnee	G. K. Chesterton (Innocence of Father Brown)	Father Brown
Father Brown				Robert Hamer		(Alec Guinness)
Detective	TCF	1968	Gordon Douglas	Abby Mann	R. Thorp	Joseph Leland
						(Frank Sinatra)
Detective Story	Paramount	1951	William Wyler	Philip Yordan	S. Kingsley	
				Robert Wyler		
Detour	Prod. Rel.	1946	Edgar G. Ulmer	Martin Goldsmith	M. M. Goldsmith	
Detour	Williams	1992	Wade Williams	Roger Hull	M. M. Goldsmith	
				Wade Williams		
Dette de Haine	*Film d'Art	1915	?	?	G. Ohnet (Debt of Hatred)	
Devil Commands	Columbia	1941	Edward Dmytryk	Robert D. Andrews	W. Sloane (Edge of Running Water)	
				Milton Gunzberg		
Devil-Doll	MGM	1936	Todd Browning	Todd Browning	A. Merritt (Burn, Witch, Burn)	
				Garrett Fort		
				Erich Von Stroheim		
				Guy Endore		
Devil Makes Three	MGM	1952	Andrew Marton	Jerry Davis	L. P. Bachmann (Kiss of Death)	
Devil Rides Out	Hammer	1968	Terence Fisher	Richard Matheson	D. Wheatley	Duke de Richleau
Devil's Bride						(Christopher Lee)
Devil Thumbs a Ride	RKO	1947	Felix Feist	Felix Feist	R. C. Du Soe	
Devil to Pay	*Pathe	1920	Ernest C. Warde	Jack Cunningham	F. N. Greene	
Devil's Agent	Dalton	1962	John P. Carstairs	Robert Westerby	H. Habe (Agent of the Devil)	
Devil's Bride	Hammer	1968	Terence Fisher	Richard Matheson	D. Wheatley (Devil Rides Out)	Duke de Richleau
Devil Rides Out						(Christopher Lee)
Devil's Chaplain	*Rayart	1919	Duke Worne	Arthur Hoerl	G. Bronson-Howard	
Devil's Chaplain	*Trem Carr	1929	Duke Worne	Arthur Hoerl	G. Bronson-Howard	
Devil's Circus	*MGM	1926	B. Christiansen	B. Christiansen	novel: B. Christiansen	
Devil's Daffodil	Omnia	1962	Akos Rathony	Basil Dawson	E. Wallace (Daffodil Mystery)	
				Donald Taylor		
Devil's Foot	*Stoll	1921	Maurice Elvey	William J. Elliott	A. C. Doyle (His Last Bow)	Sherlock Holmes
						(Eille Norwood)
Devil's Own	Hammer	1966	Cyril Frankel	Nigel Kneale	P. Curtis	
Witches						
Devil's Profession	*Arrow	1915	F. C. S. Tudor	F. C. S. Tudor	G. de St. W. James	
Devil's Rain	Bryanston	1975	Robert Fuest	Gabe Essoe	novel: M. Willis	
				James Ashton		
				Gerald Hopman		
Diabolique	Cinedis	1955	H. G. Clouzot	H. G. Clouzot	P. Boileau (Woman Who Was)	
Fiends				Jerome Geromini		
				Rene Masson		
				Frederic Grendel		
Dial "M" for Murder	Warner	1954	Alfred Hitchcock	Frederick Knott	F. Knott	
Dial 999	Merton Park	1955	Montgomery Tully	Montgomery Tully	B. Graeme (Way Out)	
Way Out						
Diamond	Gibraltar	1954	Montgomery Tully	John C. Higgins	M. Procter (Rich Is the Treasure)	
Diamond Wizard						
Diamond Man	*Davidson	1924	Arthur Rooke	Eliot Stannard	E. Wallace (headnote)	
Diamond Wizard	Gibraltar	1954	Montgomery Tully	John C. Higgins	M. Procter (Rich Is the Treasure)	
Diamond						
Diamonds Are Forever	UA	1971	Guy Hamilton	Richard Maibaum	I. Fleming	James Bond
				Tom Mankiewicz		(Sean Connery)
Diana and Destiny	*Windsor	1916	F. Martin Thornton	?	C. Garvice	

Dick Tracy	Touchstone	1990	Warren Beatty	Jim Cash Jack Epps, Jr. Victor Kendall	novel: M. A. Collins	Dick Tracy (Warren Beatty)
Dick Turpin	Stoll	1933	W. Victor Hanbury John Stafford		W. H. Ainsworth (Rookwood)	
Dick Turpin's Ride to York	*Stoll	1922	Maurice Elvey	Leslie H. Gordon	W. H. Ainsworth (Rookwood)	
Dickson's Diamonds	Edison	1914	Langdon West	Scott Campbell	S. Campbell (Below the Dead-Line)	
Die Bande des Schreckens	Rialto	1960	Harald Reinl	J. Joachim Bartsch Wolfgang Schnitzler	E. Wallace (Terrible People)	
Die! Die! My Darling Fanatic	Hammer	1965	Silvio Narizzano	Richard Matheson	A. Blaisdell (Nightmare)	
Die Gruft mit dem Ratselschloss	Rialto	1964	Franz J. Gotlieb	R. A. Stemmle	E. Wallace (Angel Esquire)	
Die Hard	TCF	1988	John McTiernan	Jeb Stuart Steven E. deSouza	R. Thorp (Nothing Lasts Forever)	John McClane (Bruce Willis)
Die Harder	TCF	1990	Renny Harlin	Steven E. deSouza Doug Richarson	W. Wager (58 Minutes)	John McClane (Bruce Willis)
Die Racker	Ulrich	1960	Karl Anton	Gustav Kampendonk Rudolph Cartier	E. Wallace (Avenger)	
Die Rot Kreis	Rialto	1959	Jurgen Roland	Wolfgang Menge Trygve Larsen	E. Wallace (Crimson Circle)	
Die Seltsame Grafin	Rialto	1961	Josef von Baky	R. A. Stemmle	E. Wallace (Strange Countess)	
Die Tur mit den Sieben Schlosser	Rialto	1962	Alfred Vohrer	Harald G. Petersson	E. Wallace (Door with Seven Locks)	
Die Verschwundene Miniatur	Carlton	1954	Carl-Heinz Schroth	Erich Kastner	E. Kastner (Missing Miniature)	
Died on a Rainy Sunday	Incite	1986	Joel Santoni	Joel Santoni Philippe Setbon	Joan Aiken	
Dillinger	Am. Int.	1973	John Milius	John Milius	novel: H. Clement	
Diplomacy	*Fam. Play.	1926	Marshall Neilan	Benjamin Glazer	V. Sardou (Diplomates)	
Diplomatic Courier	TCF	1952	Henry Hathaway	Casey Robinson Liam O'Brien	P. Cheyney (Sinister Errand)	
Diplomatic Immunity	Fries	1991	Peter Mario	Randall Frakes Jim Trombetta Richard Donn	Theodore Taylor (Stalker)	Michael Kells (Tyrone Power)
Dirty Hands Innocents with Dirty Hands	Films Boet.	1975	Claude Chabrol	Claude Chabrol	R. Neely (Damned Innocents)	
Dirty Harry	Warner	1971	Don Siegel	Harry Julian Fink Rita M. Fink Dean Riesner	novel: P. Rock	Harry Callahan (Clint Eastwood)
Dirty Mary, Crazy Larry	TCF	1974	John Hough	Leigh Chapman Antonio Santean	R. Unekis (Chase)	
Dirty Tricks	Filmplan	1980	Alvin Rakoff	William Norton, Sr. Eleanor E. Norton Thomas Gifford Camille Gifford	T. Gifford (Glendower Legacy)	
Disappearance	Hemmings	1977	Stuart Cooper	Paul Mayersberg	D. Marlowe (Echoes of Celandine)	
Disappearance of the Judge	*Barker	1919	Alexander Butler	?	C. R. Gull (Lost Judge)	
Dishonored	Paramount	1931	Josef Von Sternberg	Daniel N. Rubin Josef Von Sternberg	novel: F. Vreeland	
Dishonoured Lady	UA	1947	Robert Stevenson	Edmund H. North	M. B. Lowndes (Letty Lynton)	
Disreputable Mr. Raegan	*Edison	1910	?	?	R. H. Davis (Gallegher)	
Diva	Galaxie	1981	Jean-Jacq. Beineix	Jean-Jacq. Beineix Jean Van Hamme	Delacorta	Serge Gorodish (Richard Bohringer) Alba (Thuy An Luu)
Do You Know This Voice?	Brit. Lion	?	?	?	E. Berckman	
Doc Savage ... The Man of Bronze Man of Bronze	Warner	1975	Michael Anderson	George Pal	R. Robeson (Man of Bronze)	Doc Savage (Ron Ely)
Dock Brief Trial and Error	MGM	1962	James Hill	Pierre Rouve	J. Mortimer (Three Plays)	
Dr. Jekyll	Whodunit	1981	Walerian Borowczyk	Walerian Borowczyk	R. L. Stevenson (Strange Case of Dr. Jekyll and Mr. Hyde)	

D

D

FILM TITLE	STUDIO	YEAR	DIRECTOR	SCREENWRITER	SOURCE AUTHOR/WORK	SERIES
Dr. Jekyll and Mr. Hyde	*Selig	1908	?	?	R. L. Stevenson (Strange Case of Dr. Jekyll and Mr. Hyde)	
Dr. Jekyll and Mr. Hyde	*Nordisk	1910	?	?	R. L. Stevenson (Strange Case of Dr. Jekyll and Mr. Hyde)	
Dr. Jekyll and Mr. Hyde	*Thanhauser	1912	?	?	R. L. Stevenson (Strange Case of Dr. Jekyll and Mr. Hyde)	
Dr. Jekyll and Mr. Hyde	*Kinemacolor	1913	?	?	R. L. Stevenson (Strange Case of Dr. Jekyll and Mr Hyde)	
Dr. Jekyll and Mr. Hyde	*Imp	1913	Herbert Brenon	Herbert Brenon	R. L. Stevenson (Strange Case of Dr. Jekyll and Mr. Hyde)	
Dr. Jekyll and Mr. Hyde	*Fam. Play.	1920	John S. Robertson	Clara S. Beranger	R. L. Stevenson (Strange Case of Dr. Jekyll and Mr. Hyde)	
Dr. Jekyll and Mr. Hyde	Paramount	1931	Rouben Mamoulian	Samuel Hoffenstein Percy Heath	R. L. Stevenson (Strange Case of Dr. Jekyll and Mr. Hyde)	
Dr. Jekyll and Mr. Hyde	MGM	1941	Victor Fleming	John Lee Mahin	R. L. Stevenson (Strange Case of Dr. Jekyll and Mr. Hyde)	
Doctor Jekyll and Sister Hyde	Hammer	1971	Roy Ward Baker	Brian Clemens	R. L. Stevenson (Strange Case of Dr. Jekyll and Mr. Hyde)	
Dr. Jekyll's Dungeon of Death	New Amer.	1982	James Wood	James Mathers	R. L. Stevenson (Strange Case of Dr. Jekyll and Mr. Hyde)	
Dr. M	Prism	1989	Claude Chabrol	Sollace Mitchell	R. L. Stevenson (Strange Case of Dr. Jekyll and Mr. Hyde)	
Club Extinction						
Dr. Mabuse, Gambler	*Ufa	1922	Fritz Lang	Thea von Harbou	N. Jaques (Dr. Mabuse, Master of Mystery)	
Dr. Mabuse, Master of Mystery	*Bioscop	1927	?	?	N. Jaques (Dr. Mabuse, Master of Mystery)	
Dr. Nikola	*Nordisk	1909	?	?	G. Boothby	Dr. Nikola (?)
Doctor No	UA	1962	Terence Young	Richard Maibaum Johanna Harwood Berkely Mather	I. Fleming	James Bond (Sean Connery)
Doctor Phibes Rises Again	AIP	1972	Robert Fuest	Robert Fuest Robert Blees	novel: W. Goldstein	Dr. Anton Phibes (Vincent Price)
Doctor Rameau	*Fox	1915	Will S. Davis	Will S. Davis	G. Ohnet	
Dr. Strangelove	Columbia	1964	Stanley Kubrick	Stanley Kubrick Terry Southern Peter George	P. Bryant (Two Hours to Doom)	
Dr. Syn	Gaumont-Br.	1937	Roy William Neill	Roger Burford Michael Hogan	R. Thorndyke	Dr. Syn (George Arliss)
Dr. Syn Alias the Scarecrow	Disney	1962	James Neilson	Robert Westerby	R. Thorndyke (Doctor Syn)	Dr. Syn (Patrick McGoohan)
Doctors Wear Scarlet	Grafton	1970	Terence Fisher	Paul Tabori Terence Fisher	S. Raven	
Bloodsuckers						
Incense for the Damned						
Dog Day Afternoon	Warner	1975	Sidney Lumet	Frank Pierson	P. Mann	
Dog Eat Dog	Ajay	1963	Ray Nazarro Albert Zugsmith	Robert Hill Michael Elkins	R. Bloomfield (headnote)	
Dogs of War	UA	1980	John Irvin	Gary DeVore George Malko	F. Forsyth	
Domino Killings	Ass. Gen.	1977	Stanley Kramer	Adam Kennedy	A. Kennedy (Domino Principle)	Roy Tucker (Gene Hackman)
Domino Principle						
Domino Principle	Ass. Gen.	1977	Stanley Kramer	Adam Kennedy	A. Kennedy	Roy Tucker (Gene Hackman)
Domino Killings						
Don Chicago	Brit Nat.	1945	Maclean Rogers	Austin Melford	C. E. B. Roberts	
Don Is Dead	Universal	1973	Richard Fleischer	Marvin H. Albert	N. Quarry	
Don Q, Son of Zorro	*Elton	1925	Donald Crisp	Jack Cunningham	K. Prichard (Don Q's Love Story)	Don Q (Douglas Fairbanks)
Donovan Affair	Columbia	1929	Frank R. Capra	Howard J. Green Dorothy Howell	O. Davis	
Donovan's Brain	UA	1953	Felix Feist	Felix Feist	C. Siodmak	
Don't Bother to Knock	TCF	1952	Roy Baker	Daniel Taradash	C. Armstrong (Mischief)	
Don't Ever Leave Me	Rank	1949	Arthur Crabtree	Robert Westerby	Anthony Armstrong (headnote)	
Don't Just Stand There	Universal	1967	Ron Winston	Charles Williams	C. Williams (Wrong Venus)	
Don't Look Now	Casey	1973	Nicolas Roeg	Allan Scott Chris Bryant	D. Du Maurier (Not After Midnight)	
Doomed Cargo	Gaumont	1936	Albert de Courville	Frank Launder Sidney Gilliat	A. Ridley (Wrecker)	
Seven Sinners						

D

Film	Studio	Year	Director	Writer	Source
Door with Seven Locks	Rialto	1940	Norman Lee	L. DuGarde Peach / Austin Melford	E. Wallace
Chamber of Horrors					
Dossier 51	Elefilm	1978	Michel Deville	Norman Lee / Gilbert Gunn / John Argyle / Gilles Perrault / Michel Deville	G. Perrault
51 File					
Double	Merton Park	1963	Lionel Harris	Lindsay Galloway / John Roddick	E. Wallace
Double-Barrelled Detective Story	Saloon	1965	Adolfas Mekas	Adolfas Mekas	M. Twain
Double Con	Universal	1973	Larry Yust	T. Raewyn / A. Neuberg / Larry Yust	I. Slim (Trick Baby)
Trick Baby					
Double Confession	Reynolds	1950	Ken Annakin	William Templeton / Ralph Keene	J. Garden (All on a Summer's Day)
Double Cross Roads	Fox	1930	Alfred L. Werker / George Middleton	George Brooks / Howard Estabrook / Gladys Lehman / Jack Cunningham	W. Lipman (Yonder Grow the Daisies)
Double Door	Paramount	1934	Charles Vidor		E. McFadden
Double Identity	Warner	1940	Ray Enright	Barry Trivers / Bertram Millhauser	J. O. Curwood (River's End)
River's End					
Double Indemnity	Paramount	1944	Billy Wilder	Billy Wilder / Raymond Chandler	J. M. Cain
Double Life	Universal	1947	George Cukor	Ruth Gordon / Garson Kanin	novel: M. W. Wellman
Double Life of Mr. Alfred Burton	*Lucky Cat	1919	Arthur Rooke	Kenelm Foss / Frank Tarloff / Alfred Hayes	E. P. Oppenheim
Double Man	Albion	1967	Franklin Schaffner		H. S. Maxfield (Legacy of a Spy)
Double Negative	Quandrant	1980	George Bloomfield	Thomas Hedley, Jr. / Charles Dennis	K. Millar (Three Roads)
Double Tour	CCFC	1959	Claude Chabrol	Janis Allen / Paul Gegauff	S. Ellin (Key to Nicholas Street)
Web of Passion					
Down Our Street	Paramount	1932	Harry Lachman	Harry Lachman	Ernest George (Belle)
Down River	Gaumont	1931	Peter Godfrey	Ralph G. Bettinson	Seamark
Down Three Dark Streets	UA	1954	Arnold Laven	The Gordons / Bernard Schoenfeld	Gordons (Case File: FBI)
Down Under Donovan	*Stoll	1922	Harry Lambart	Forbes Dawson	E. Wallace
Downfall	Merton Park	1964	John Moxey	Robert Stewart	E. Wallace (headnote)
Dracula	Universal	1931	Tod Browning	Garrett Fort	B. Stoker
Horror of Dracula	Hammer	1957	Terence Fisher	Jimmy Sangster	B. Stoker
Dracula	Latglen	1974	Dan Curtis	Richard Matheson	B. Stoker
Dracula	Universal	1979	John Badham	W. D. Richter	H. Deane
Dracula, Prince of Darkness	Hammer	1965	Terence Fisher	John Sansom / Anthony Hinds	B. Stoker (Dracula)
Dracula Sucks	Kodiak	1979	Philip Marshak	Darryl A. Marshak / David J. Kern	B. Stoker (Dracula)
Dracula's Daughter	Universal	1936	Lambert Hillyer	Garrett Fort	B. Stoker (Dracula's Guest)
Dragon Murder Case	Warner	1934	H. B. Humberstone	F. Hugh Herbert / Robert Lee	S. S. Van Dine
Dragonwyck	TCF	1946	Joseph Mankiewicz	Joseph Mankiewicz	A. Seton
Dream Street	*Griffith	1921	D. W. Griffith	Roy Sinclair	T. Burke (Limehouse Nights)
Dream Woman	*Blache	1914	Alice Blache	?	Wilkie Collins (Woman in White)
Dressed to Kill	TCF	1941	Eugene Forde	Stanley Rauh / Manning O'Connor	R. Burke (Dead Take No Bows)
Dressed to Kill	Cinema 77	1980	Brian De Palma	Brian De Palma	novel: C. Black
Driver	TCF	1978	Walter Hill	Walter Hill	novel: C. B. Phillips

John Ripley (Broderick Crawford)

Philo Vance (Warren William)

Michael Shayne (Lloyd Nolan)

D

FILM TITLE	STUDIO	YEAR	DIRECTOR	SCREENWRITER	SOURCE AUTHOR/WORK	SERIES
Drop Dead, Darling	Paramount	1967	Ken Hughes	Ken Hughes	R. Deming (Careful Man)	
Arrivederci, Baby!						
Drowning Pool	Warner	1975	Stuart Rosenberg	Ronald Harwood Tracy Keenan Wynn Lorenzo Semple, Jr. Walter Hill	J. R. Macdonald	Harper (Paul Newman)
Drug Store Cowboy	Avenue	1989	Gus Van Sant, Jr.	Gus Van Sant, Jr. Daniel Yost	J. Fogle	
Drums of Fu Manchu	Republic	1940	William Witney John English	Franklyn Adreon Norman S. Hall Morgan B. Cox Ronald Davidson Barney A. Sarecky Sol Shor	S. Rohmer	Fu Manchu (Henry Brandon)
Drums of Jeopardy	*Hoffman	1923	Roland G. Edwards	Arthur Hoerl	H. MacGrath	
Drums of Jeopardy	Tiffany	1931	George B. Seitz	Florence Ryerson	H. MacGrath	
Dry White Season	MGM	1989	Euzhan Palcy	Euzhan Palcy Colin Welland	A. Brink	
Duality of Man	*Wrench	1910	?	?	R. L. Stevenson (Strange Case of Dr. Jekyll and Mr. Hyde)	
Dublin Nightmare	Penington	1958	John Pomeroy	John Tully	P. Loraine	
Duds	*Goldwyn	1920	Thomas R. Mills	Harvey F. Thew	H. C. Rowland	
Duffy	Columbia	1968	Robert Parrish	Donald Cammell Harry Joe Brown, Jr.	novel: H. J. Brown, Jr.	
Dulcimer Street London Belongs to Me	GFD	1948	Sidney Gilliat	Sidney Gilliat J. B. Williams	N. Collins (London Belongs to Me)	
Dumb Man of Manchester	*Haggar	1908	William Haggar	?	B. F. Rayner	
Dummy	*Fam. Play.	1917	Francis E. Grandon	Eve Unsell	H. J. O'Higgins	
Dummy	Paramount	1929	Robert Milton	Herman Mankiewicz	H. J. O'Higgins	
Dust in the Sun	South. Int.	1958	Lee Robinson	W. P. Lipscomb Lee Robinson Joy Cavill	J. Cleary (Justin Bayard)	
Dusty Ermine Hideout in the Alps	Twickenham	1936	Bernard Vorhaus	L. DuGarde Peach Michael Hankinson Arthur Macrae Paul Hervey Fox H. Fowler Mear	N. Grant	
Dying Detective	*Stoll	1921	Maurice Elvey	William J. Elliott	A. C. Doyle (His Last Bow)	Sherlock Holmes (Eille Norwood)
Dynamite Man from Glory Jail Fool's Parade	Columbia	1971	Andrew V. McLaglen	James Lee Barrett	D. Grubb (Fool's Parade)	
Each Dawn I Die	Warner	1939	William Keighley	Norman Reilly Raine Warren Duff Charles Perry	J. Odlum	
Eagle Has Landed	ITC	1976	John Sturges	Tom Mankiewicz	J. Higgins	Liam Devlin (Donald Sutherland)
Eagle's Eye	*Foursquar	1918	George A. Lessey Wellington Playter	Courtney R. Cooper	W. J. Flynn	
Earl of Chicago	MGM	1939	Richard Thorpe	Lesser Samuels	Brock Williams	
East Lynne	*Harrison	1902	Dicky Harrison	Dicky Harrison	H. Wood	
East Lynne	*Selig	1908	?	?	H. Wood	
East Lynne	*Viagraph	1908	?	?	H. Wood	
East Lynne	*Precision	1910	George Nicholls or Theodore Marston	Theodore Marston	H. Wood	
East Lynne	*Thanhauser	1912			H. Wood	
East Lynne	*Barker	1913	Bert Haldane	Harry Engholm	H. Wood	
East Lynne	*Brightonia	1913	Arthur Charrington	?	H. Wood	
East Lynne	*AB	1915	Travers Vale	?	H. Wood	

Title	Studio	Year	Director	Writer	Source/Notes
East Lynne	*Fox	1916	Bertram Bracken	Mary Murillo	H. Wood
East Lynne	*Master	1922	H. B. Parkinson	W. C. Rowden	H. Wood
East Lynne	*Hardy	1922	Charles Hardy	?	H. Wood
East Lynne	*Fox	1925	Emmett Flynn	Lenore J. Coffee / Bradley King	H. Wood
East Lynne	TCF	1931	Frank Lloyd	Tom Barry	H. Wood
East Lynne Fiasco	*(Australia)	1917	John Cosgrove	?	H. Wood (East Lynne)
East Lynne in Bugville	*Crystal	1914	Phillips Smalley	?	H. Wood (East Lynne)
Easy Come, Easy Go	*Paramount	1928	Frank Tuttle	Florence Ryerson	O. Davis
Easy Pickings	*First Nat.	1929	George Archainbaud	Louis Stevens / William A. Burton	P. Cruger
Echo Murders	Brit. Nat.	1945	John Harlow	John Harlow	J. Sylvester (Terror of Tregarwith) Sexton Blake (David Farrar)
Echo of Barbara	Ind. Art.	1961	Sidney Hayers	John Kruse	Jonathan Burke
Eclipse	Celandine	1977	Simon Perry	Simon Perry	N. Wollaston
Eddie and the Cruisers	Aurora	1983	Martin Davidson	Martin Davidson / Arlene Davidson	P. F. Kluge
Eddie Macon's Run	Universal	1983	Jeff Kanen	Jeff Kanen	J. McLendon
Edgar Allan Poe's Conqueror Worm / Conqueror Worm / Witch-Finder General	Trigon	1968	Michael Reeves	Michael Reeves / Tom Baker / Louis M. Hayward	R. Bassett (Witch-Finder General)
Edge of Doom / Stronger Than Fear	RKO	1950	Mark Robson	Philip Yordan	L. Brady
Edge of Fury	UA	1958	Peter Lerner	Robert Gurney / Ted Berkman	R. M. Coates (Wisteria Cottage)
Edge of Sanity	Allied Vis.	1989	Gerard Kekoine	J. P. Felix	R. L. Stevenson (Strange Case of Dr. Jekyll and Mr. Hyde)
Edge of the City / Man Is Ten Feet Tall	MGM	1957	Martin Ritt	Robert Alan Aurther	novel: F. Pohl
Edith's Diary	Geissen.	1983	Hans Geissendoerfer	Hans Geissendoerfer / Frank Launder / Robert Edmunds	P. Highsmith
Educated Evans	WB-FN	1936	William Beaudine		E. Wallace / Educated Evans (Max Miller)
Eiger Sanction	Universal	1975	Clint Eastwood	Hal Dresner / Warren B. Murphy / Rod Whitaker	Trevanian / Jonathan Hemlock (Clint Eastwood)
Eight Million Ways to Die	PSO	1985	Hal Ashby	Oliver Stone / David Lee Henry	L. Block / Matthew Scudde (Jeff Bridges)
813	*Robertson	1921	Scott Sidney	W. Scott Darling	M. Leblanc / Arsene Lupin (Wedgewood Nowell)
Ein Sarg aus Hong-Kong	Leitienne	1964	Manfred R. Kohler	Manfred R. Kohler	J. H. Chase (Coffin from Hong Kong)
El Pediente	Argentina	1951	Leon Klimovsky	Ulyses P. de Murat / Samuel Eichelbaum	W. Irish (Dead Man Blues)
Eldorado Lode	*Edison	1913	?	?	H. B. M. Watson (Ifs and Ans)
Eleanor Cuyler	*Edison	1912	?	?	R. H. Davis (Van Bibber and others)
Electric Monster / Electronic Monster / Escapement	Anglo-Am.	1960	Montgomery Tully	Charles Eric Maine / J. MacLaren Ross	C. E. Maine (Escapement)
Electronic Monster / Electric Monster / Escapement	Anglo-Am.	1960	Montgomery Tully	Charles Eric Maine	C. E. Maine (Escapement)
Eleni	Warner	1985	Peter Yates	Steve Tesich	N. Gage
Elevator to the Gallows / Frantic	Lux	1958	Louis Malle	Roger Nimier / Louis Malle	N. Calef (Frantic)
11 Harrowhouse	TCF	1974	Aram Avakian	Anthony Squire / Jeffrey Bloom / Charles Grodin	G. A. Browne
Eleventh Commandment	*Gaumont	1924	George A. Cooper	Brandom Fleming / Adele Buffington	B. Fleming (Pillory)
Eleventh Commandment	Allied	1933	George Melford	Kurt Kempler	B. Fleming (Pillory)
Elinor Norton / Case of Elinor Norton	TCF	1935	Hamilton MacFadden	Ross Franken / Philip Klein	M. R. Rinehart (State vs. Elinor Norton)

E

E

FILM TITLE	STUDIO	YEAR	DIRECTOR	SCREENWRITER	SOURCE AUTHOR/WORK	SERIES
Ellery Queen and the Murder Ring	Columbia	1941	James Hogan	Eric Taylor Gertrude Purcell	E. Queen (Dutch Shoe Mystery)	Ellery Queen (Ralph Bellamy)
Ellery Queen and the Perfect Crime	Columbia	1941	James Hogan	Eric Taylor	E. Queen (Perfect Crime)	Ellery Queen (Ralph Bellamy)
Ellery Queen, Master Detective	Columbia	1940	Kurt Neumann	Eric Taylor	E. Queen	Ellery Queen (Ralph Bellamy)
Ellery Queen's Penthouse Mystery	Columbia	1941	James Hogan	Eric Taylor	E. Queen (Penthouse Mystery)	Ellery Queen (Ralph Bellamy)
Elusive Isabel	*Bluebird	1916	Stuart Paton	Raymond L. Shrock	J. Futrelle	
Elusive Pimpernel	*Stoll	1919	Maurice Elvey	Frederick Blachford	B. Orczy	Percy Blakeney (Cecil Humphrey)
Elusive Pimpernel	Brit. Lion	1950	Michael Powell Emeric Pressburger	Michael Powell Emeric Pressburger	B. Orczy	Percy Blakeney (David Niven)
Fighting Pimpernel				William Fairchild		
Embassy	Hemdale	1972	Gordon Hessler	John Bird	S. Coulter	
Emperor's Candlesticks	MGM	1937	George Fitzmaurice	Monckton Hoffe Harold Goldman	B. Orczy	
Empty Beach	Jethro	1985	Chris Thomson	Keith Dewhurst	P. Corris	Cliff Hardy (Bryan Brown)
Empty Hands	*Fam. Play.	1924	Victor Fleming	Carey Wilson	A. Stringer	
Empty House	*Stoll	1921	Maurice Elvey	William J. Elliott	A. C. Doyle (Return of Sherlock Holmes)	Sherlock Holmes (Eille Norwood)
Enchanted Hill	*Fam. Play.	1926	Irvin Willat	James S. Hamilton	P. B. Kyne	
End of Belle Death of a Beauty Passion of Slow Fire	Lux	1961	Edouard Molinaro	Jean Anouilh	G. Simenon (Belle)	
End of the Affair	Coronado	1955	Edward Dmytryk	Lenore Coffee	G. Greene	
End of the Game Getting Away with Murder Murder on the Bridge	MFG-T.R.A.	1975	Maximillian Schell	Maximillian Schell Arlene Sellers Bo Goldmann	F. Duerrenmatt (Judge and His Hangman)	
End of the Road	*Gem	1913	William R. Daley	Jack Byrne	E. Bulwer-Lytton (Ernest Malravers)	
End Play	Hexagon	1975	Tim Burstall	Tim Burstall	R. Braddon	
Endless Night Agatha Christie's Endless Night	Brit. Lion	1971	Sidney Gilliat	Sidney Gilliat	A. Christie	
Enemies of the Public Public Enemy	Warner	1931	William Wellman	Harvey Thew Kubec Glasmon John Bright	K. Glasmon (Public Enemy)	
Enemy Agent British Intelligence	Warner	1940	Terry Morse	Lee Katz	A. P. Kelly (Three Faces East)	
Enemy General	Columbia	1960	George Sherman	John Kangan Dan Pepper Burt Picard	novel: D. Pepper	
Enemy to Society	*Metro	1915	Edgar Jones	?	G. Bronson-Howard	
Enforcer Murder Inc.	U.S.Pict.	1951	Bretaigne Windust Raoul Walsh	Martin Rackin	novel: J. Eastwood (Murder Inc.)	
Enforcer	Warner	1976	James Fargo	Stirling Silliphant Dean Riesner	novel: W. Morgan	Harry Callahan (Clint Eastwood)
Engineer's Thumb	*Stoll	1922	George Ridgwell	Patrick L. Mannock Geoffrey H. Malins	A. C. Doyle (Adventures of Sherlock Holmes)	Sherlock Holmes (Eille Norwood)
England Made Me	Hemdale	1972	Peter Duffell	Peter Duffell Desmond Cory	G. Greene	
Englishman's Home	*B&C	1914	Ernest G. Batley	?	Guy Du Maurier	
Englishman's Home Mad Men of Europe	Aldwych	1940	Albert de Courville	Ian Hay Edward Knoblock	Guy Du Maurier	
Enigma	Archerwest	1983	Jeannot Szwarc	John Briley	M. Barak	
Enough Rope	Cocinor	1963	Claude Autant-Lara	Jean Aurenche Pierre Bost	P. Highsmith (Blunderer)	

E

Title	Studio	Year	Director	Writer	Source	Character (Actor)
Enter the Dragon	Warner	1973	Robert Clouse	Michael Allin		
Entertaining Mr. Sloane	Canterbury	1970	Douglas Hickox	Clive Exton	J. Orton	
Equator	Corso	1983	Serge Gainsbourg	Serge Gainsbourg	G. Simenon (Tropic Moon)	
Ernest Maltravers	*AB	1914	?	Travers Vale	E. Bulwer-Lytton	
Ernest Maltravers	*Ideal	1920	Jack Denton	Eliot Stannard	E. Bulwer-Lytton	
Escape	ATP	1930	Basil Dean	Basil Dean	J. Galsworthy	
Escape	TCF	1948	Joseph Mankiewicz	John Galsworthy	J. Galsworthy	
Escape	MGM	1940	Mervyn LeRoy	Philip Dunne	E. Vance	
				Arch Oboler		
				Marguerite Roberts		
Escape When the Door Opened						
Escape by Night	Eternal	1963	Montgomery Tully	Maurice J. Wilson	R. Croft-Cooke (Clash by Night)	
Clash by Night				Montgomery Tully		
Escape from New York	AVCO	1981	John Carpenter	John Carpenter	M. McQuay	
				Nick Castle		
Escape from Zahrein	Paramount	1961	Ronald Neame	Robin Estridge	M. Barrett (Appointment in Zahrein)	
Escape in the Desert	Warner	1945	Edward A. Blatt	Thomas Job	R. Sherwood (Petrified Forest)	
Escape to Athena	ITC	1979	George Pan Cosmatos	Edward Anhalt	novel: P. Blake	
				Richard S. Lochte		
Escapement	Anglo-Am.	1960	Montgomery Tully	Charles Eric Maine	C. E. Maine	
Electric Monster				J. MacLaren Ross		
Electronic Monster						
Escort Girl	RKO	1986	Bob Swaim	Bob Swaim	P. Theroux (Doctor Slaughter)	
				Edward Behr		
Half Moon Street						
Eternal Struggle	*Metro	1923	Reginald Barker	J. G. Hawks	G. B. Lancaster (Law Bringers)	
				Monte Katterjohn		
Eugene Aram	*Cricks	1914	Edwin J. Collins	Edwin J. Collins	E. Bulwer-Lytton	
Eugene Aram	*Edison	1915	Richard Ridgely	Richard Ridgely	E. Bulwer-Lytton	
Eugene Aram	*Davidson	1924	Arthur Rooke	Kinchen Wood	E. Bulwer-Lytton	
Eva	Interopa	1962	Joseph Losey	Hugo Butler	J. H. Chase (Eve)	
				Evan Jones		
Eve, the Devil's Woman						
Eve, the Devil's Woman	Interopa	1962	Joseph Losey	Hugo Butler	J. H. Chase (Eve)	
Eva				Evan Jones		
Evelyn Prentice	MGM	1934	William K. Howard	Lenore Coffee	W. E. Woodward	
Every Little Crook and Nanny	MGM	1972	Cy Howard	Cy Howard	E. Hunter	
				Jonathan Axelrod		
				Robert Klane		
Everybody Does It	TCF	1949	Edmund Goulding	Nunnally Johnson	J. M. Cain (Career in C Major)	
Everything Is Thunder	Gaumont	1936	Milton Rosmer	Marion Dix	J. L. Hardy	
Evil That Men Do	ITC	1984	J. Lee Thompson	David Lee Henry	R. L. Hill	
				John Crowther		
Evil Under the Sun	EMI	1982	Guy Hamilton	Anthony Shaffer	A. Christie	Hercule Poirot (Peter Ustinov)
Evil Women Do	*Bluebird	1916	Rupert Julien	E. J. Clawson	E. Gaboriau (Clique of Gold)	
Ex-Flame	Liberty	1930	Victor Halperin	George Draney	H. Wood (East Lynne)	
				Herbert Farjeon		
Mixed Doubles						
Excess Baggage	Real Art	1933	Redd Davis	H. Fowler Mear	H. M. Raleigh	
Exiles	*Fox	1923	Edmund Mortimer	Fred Jackson	R. H. Davis (Exile)	
Exorcist	Warner	1973	William Friedkin	William P. Blatty	W. P. Blatty	
Exorcist III	TCF	1990	William P. Blatty	William P. Blatty	W. P. Blatty (Legion)	
Experiment in Terror	Columbia	1962	Blake Edwards	The Gordons	Gordons (Operation Terror)	Lt. Bill Kinderman (Lee J. Cobb)
						Lt. Bill Kinderman (George C. Scott)
						John Ripley (Glenn Ford)
Grip of Fear						
Experiment Perilous	RKO	1944	Jacques Tourneur	Warren Duff	M. Carpenter	
Expiation	*Stoll	1922	Sinclair Hill	Sinclair Hill	E. P. Oppenheim	
Exploits of Elaine	Eclectic	1915	Louis Gasnier	Charles W. Goddard	A. B. Reeve	Craig Kennedy (?)
			George B. Seitz	George B. Seitz		

E

FILM TITLE	STUDIO	YEAR	DIRECTOR	SCREENWRITER	SOURCE AUTHOR/WORK	SERIES
Extreme Prejudice	Tri-Star	1987	Walter Hill	Deric Washburn, Harry Kleiner	novel: R. Dobbins	
Extremities	Atlantic	1986	Robert M. Young	Wm. Mastrosimone, Edwin Cook, Wendy Cutler, Andy Goldberg, Roger Stefens	W. Mastrosimone	
Eye of the Devil	Filmways	1966	J. Lee Thompson	Robin Estridge, Dennis Murphy	P. Loraine (Day of the Arrow)	
Eye of the Needle	King's Road	1981	Richard Marquand	Stanley Mann	K. Follett (Storm Island)	
Eyes in the Night	MGM	1941	Fred Zinnemann	Guy Trosper, Howard E. Rogers	B. Kendrick (Odor of Violets)	Duncan Maclain (Edward Arnold)
Eyes of Laura Mars	Columbia	1978	Irvin Kershner	John Carpenter, David Zelag Goodman		
Eyewitness	Allen	1970	John Hough	Ronald Harwood	novel: H. B. Gilmour	
Eyewitness Sudden Terror	TCF	1981	Peter Yates	Steve Tesich	M. Hebden	
Eyewitness Janitor						
FM—Frequency Murder	La Gueville	1988	Elisabeth Rappeneau	Elisabeth Rappeneau, Jacques Audiard	S. M. Kaminsky (When the Dark Man Calls)	
Face in the Night Menace in the Night	Gibraltar	1956	Lance Comfort	Norman Hudis	B. Graeme (Suspense)	
Face of a Stranger	Merton Park	1964	John Moxey	John Sherman	E. Wallace (headnote)	
Face the Music Black Glove	Hammer	1954	Terence Fisher	Ernest Borneman	E. Borneman (Tremolo)	
Faces in the Dark	Pennington	1960	David Eady	Ephraim Kogan, John Tully	P. Boileau	
Fade to Black	Am. Cinema	1980	Vernon Zimmerman	Vernon Zimmerman		
Fail-Safe	Columbia	1964	Sidney Lumet	Walter Bernstein	novel: R. Renauld	
Falcon Takes Over	RKO	1942	Irving Reis	Lynn Root, Frank Fenton	E. Burdick	Falcon (George Sanders)
					R. Chandler (Farewell, My Lovely)	
Fall Guy	RKO	1930	A. Leslie Pearce	Tim Whelan	G. Abbott	
Trust Your Wife						
Fall of a Saint	*Gaumont-B.	1920	W. P. Kellino	?	E. C. Scott	
Fallen Angel	TCF	1945	Otto Preminger	Harry Kleiner	M. Holland	
Fallen Idol Lost Illusion	Brit. Lion	1948	Carol Reed	Graham Greene, Leslie Storm, William Templeton	G. Greene (Basement Room)	
Fallen Sparrow	RKO	1943	Richard Wallace	Warren Duff	D. B. Hughes	
False Evidence	Stoll	1922	Harold Shaw	Frank Miller	E. P. Oppenheim	
False Evidence	Crusade	1937	Donovan Pedelty	Donovan Pedelty	R. Vickers (I'll Never Tell)	
False Faces	*Artcraft	1919	Irvin W. Willatt	Irvin W. Willatt	L. J. Vance	Michael Lanyard (Henry B. Walthall)
Family Business	Tri-Star	1989	Sidney Lumet	Vincent Patrick	V. Patrick	
Family Doctor	Templar	1957	Derek Twist	Derek Twist	J. Fleming (Deeds of Dr. Deadcert)	
Family Plot	Universal	1976	Alfred Hitchcock	Ernest Lehman	V. Canning (Rainbird Pattern)	
Family Secret	*Universal	1924	William Seiter	Lois Zellner	A. Thomas (Editha's Burglar)	
Fan	Paramount	1981	Edward Bianchi	Priscilla Chapman, John Harwell	B. Randall	
Fanatic Die! Die! My Darling	Hammer	1965	Silvio Narizzano	Richard Matheson	A. Blaisdell (Nightmare)	
Fantasia Among the Squares						
Fantasist	Oceanic	1971	Gerard Pires	Gerard Pires	C. Williams (Diamond Bikini)	
	ITC	1986	Robin Hardy	Robin Hardy	P. McGinley (Goosefoot)	
Fantomas	*Gaumont	1914	?	?	P. Souvestre	Fantomas (?)

Film Index   FIFTY ROADS TO TOWN / 1393

Title		Studio	Year	Director	Screenwriter	Source/Cast
Fantomas		*Fox	1921	Edward Sedgwick	Edward Sedgwick	P. Souvestre	Fantomas (?)
Fantomas		Braunberger	1934	Paul Fejos	?	P. Souvestre	Fantomas (Jean Galland)
Fantomas		Latino Con.	1946	Jean Sacha	Jean Louis Bouquet	P. Souvestre	Fantomas (?)
Fantomas		Lopert	1966	Andrew Hunebelle	Jean Halain Pierre Foucaud	P. Souvestre	Fantomas (Jean Marais)
Farewell, My Lovely		RKO	1945	Edward Dmytryk	John Paxton	R. Chandler	Philip Marlowe (Dick Powell)
Murder, My Sweet Farewell, My Lovely		AVCO	1975	Dick Richards	David Zelag Goodman	R. Chandler	Philip Marlowe (Robert Mitchum)
Fast and Loose		MGM	1939	Edwin L. Marin	Harry Kurnitz	M. Page (Fast Company)	Joel Sloane (Robert Montgomery)
Fast Company		MGM	1938	Edward Buzzell	Marco Page Harold Tarshis	M. Page	Joel Sloane (Melvyn Douglas)
Fast Walking		Lorimar	1982	James B. Harris	James B. Harris	E. Brawley (Rap)	
Fat Chance		TCF	1975	Peter Hyams	W. D. Richter	K. Laumer (Deadfall)	
Peeper							
Fatal Hour		*Metro	1920	George Terwilliger	Julian Burnham Gerald Butler	E. K. Chatterton (Marriages of Mayfair)	
Fatal Night		Anglofilm	1948	Mario Zampi	Kathleen Connors	M. Arlen (May Fair)	
Father Brown		Facet	1954	Robert Hamer	Thelma Schnee Robert Hamet	G. K. Chesterton (Innocence of Father Brown)	Father Brown (Alec Guinness)
Detective Father Brown, Detective		Paramount	1935	Edward Sedgwick	Henry Myers C. Gardner Sullivan	G. K. Chesterton (Wisdom of Father Brown)	Father Brown (Walter Connolly)
Fathom		TCF	1967	Leslie H. Martinson	Lorenzo Semple, Jr.	L. Forrester (Girl Called Fathom)	
Fear		Monogram	1946	Alfred Zeisler	Alfred Zeisler	F. M. Dostoevskii (Crime and Punishment)	
Suspense							
Fear in the Night		Paramount	1947	Maxwell Shane	Dennis Cooper Maxwell Shane	W. Irish (I Wouldn't Be in Your Shoes)	
Fear Is the Key		EMI	1972	Michael Tuchner	Robert Carrington	A. MacLean	
Fear Makers		Pacemaker	1958	Jacques Tournier	Elliot West Chris Appley	D. L. Teilhet	
Fear No More		Scaramouche	1961	Bernard Wiesey	Robert Bloomfield Maclean Rogers	L. Edgley	
Feathered Serpent		GS Enter.	1934	Maclean Rogers	Kathleen Butler	E. Wallace	
Federal Bullets		Monogram	1937	Karl Brown	Karl Brown	G. F. Eliot	
Female Fiends		Merton Park	1958	Montgomery Tully	J. McLaren Ross	P. Quentin (Puzzle for Fiends)	
Strange Awakening							
Fever in the Blood		Warner	1960	Vincent Sherman	Roy Huggins Harry Kleiner	W. Pearson	
ffolkes		Universal	1980	Andrew V. McLaglen	Jack Davies	J. Davies (Esther, Ruth and Jennifer)	
Assault Force North Sea Hijack							
Fiend Who Walked the West		TCF	1958	Gordon Douglas	Harry Brown Philip Yordan	E. Lipsky (Kiss of Death)	
Fiends		Cinedis	1955	H. G. Clouzot	H. G. Clouzot Jerome Geronimi Rene Masson	P. Boileau (Woman Who Was)	
Diabolique							
5th of November		Marseilles	1975	Don Sharp	Frederic Grendel John Gay	novel: M. Franklin	
Hennessy							
Fifty Candles		*Willat	1921	Irvin V. Willat	?	E. D. Biggers	
51 File		Elefilm	1978	Michel Deville	Gilles Perrault Michel Deville	G. Perrault (Dossier 51)	
Fifty Roads to Town		TCF	1937	Norman Taurog	George Marion, Jr. William Counselman	F. Nebel	

F

F

FILM TITLE	STUDIO	YEAR	DIRECTOR	SCREENWRITER	SOURCE AUTHOR/WORK	SERIES
Fifty-Two Pickup	Cannon	1986	John Frankenheimer	Elmore Leonard	E. Leonard	
Fighting Edge	*Warner	1926	Henry Lehrman	John Steppling Edward T. Lowe, Jr. Jack Wagner	W. M. Raine	
Fighting Mad	Criterion	1939	Sam Newfield	George Rosener		Douglas Renfrew (James Newill)
Fighting Pimpernel Elusive Pimpernel	Brit. Lion	1950	Michael Powell Emeric Pressburger	John Rathmell Michael Powell Emeric Pressburger	L. Y. Erskine (Renfrew Rides Again) B. Orczy (Elusive Pimpernel)	Percy Blakeney (David Niven)
Fighting Snub Reilly	*Stoll	1924	Andrew P. Wilson	?	E. Wallace (Forty-Eight Short Stories)	
File No. 113	*AB	1915	?	?	E. Gaboriau	
File of the Golden Goose	UA	1969	Sam Wanamaker	John C. Higgins James B. Gordon	novel: J. Watson	
File 113	Allied	1932	Chester M. Franklin	Francis Natteford	E. Gaboriau (File No. 113)	
Final Exam	Mot. Pict.	1981	Jimmy Huston	Jimmy Huston	novel: G. Meyer	
Final Option Who Dares Wins	Rank	1982	Ian Sharp	Reginald Rose	J. Follett (Tiptoe Boys)	
Final Problem	*Stoll	1923	George Ridgwell		A. C. Doyle (Memoirs of Sherlock Holmes)	Sherlock Holmes (Eille Norwood)
Finally, Sunday Confidentially Yours Let It Be Sunday	du Carrosse	1983	Francois Truffaut	Geoffrey H. Malins Patrick L. Mannock Francois Truffaut Suzanne Schiffman	C. Williams (Long Saturday Night)	
Find the Woman	*Cosmopol.	1922	Tom Terriss	Jean Aurel Dory Hobart	A. S. Roche	
Finders Keepers	CBS Theat.	1984	Richard Lester	Charles Dennis Ronny Graham Terence Marsh	C. Dennis (Next-to-Last Train Ride)	
Fine Pair	Cin. Center	1969	Francesco Maselli	Francesco Maselli Luisi Montagnana Larry Gelbart Virgil C. Leone	novel: C. Stratton	
Fire Flingers	*Jewel	1919	Rupert Julian	Waldemar Young Alex Lasker	W. J. Neidig	
Firefox	Warner	1982	Clint Eastwood	Wendell Willman	C. Thomas	
Firestarter	Universal	1984	Mark L. Lester	Stanley Mann	Stephen King	
Firm of Girdlestone	*London	1915	Harold Shaw	Bannister Berwin	A. C. Doyle	
First and the Last 21 Days 21 Days Together	London	1937	Basil Dean	Graham Greene Basil Dean	J. Galsworthy (Five Tales)	
First Blood	Orion	1982	Ted Kotcheff	Michael Kozoll William Sackheim Sylvester Stallone	D. Morrell	Rambo (Sylvester Stallone)
First Chronicles of Don Q	*B&C	1912	H. O. Martinek	Harold Brett	K. Prichard (Chronicles of Don Q)	Don Q (Charles Raymond)
First Comes Courage	Columbia	1943	Dorothy Arzner	Lewis Meltzer Melvin Levy George Sklar	E. Arnold (Commandos)	
First Deadly Sin	Filmways	1980	Brian Hutton	Mann Rubin	Lawrence Sanders	Edward Delaney (Frank Sinatra)
First Great Train Robbery Great Train Robbery	UA	1979	Michael Crichton	Michael Crichton	M. Crichton (Great Train Robbery)	
First Law	*Astra	1918	Lawrence McGill	Roy Somerville	G. Willets	
Fitzwilly	UA	1967	Delbert Mann	Isobel Lennart	Poynz Tyler (Garden of Cucumbers)	
Fitzwilly Strikes Back Fitzwilly	UA	1967	Delbert Mann	Isobel Lennart	Poynz Tyler (Garden of Cucumbers)	
Five Against the House	Columbia	1955	Phil Karlson	Sterling Silliphant William Bowers John Barnwell	J. Finney	

F

FOG FOR A KILLER

Title	Studio	Year	Director	Author
Five Ashore for Singapore	Numbre One	1967	Bernard T. Michel	Bernard T. Michel
Singapore, Singapore				
Five Fingers	TCF	1952	Joseph Mankiewicz	Pierre Kalfon
Operation Cicero				L. C. Moyzisch (Operation Cicero)
Five Star Final	Warner	1931	Mervyn LeRoy	Michael Wilson
				L. Weitzenkorn
Five Steps to Danger	UA	1957	Henry S. Kessler	Robert Lord
Five to One	Merton Park	1963	Gordon Flemyng	Byron Morgan
Flaming Forest	*Cosmopolit.	1926	Reginald Barker	Henry S. Kessler
Flamingo Road	Warner	1949	Michael Curtiz	Roger Marshall
				Waldemar Young D. Hamilton (Assignment: Murder)
				Robert Wilder E. Wallace (Thief in the Night)
				Edmund H. North J. O. Curwood
				R. Wilder
Flanagan Boy	Hammer	1953	Reginald Leborg	Richard Landau
Bad Blonde				Guy Elmes M. Catto
Flash of Green	Spectrafilm	1984	Victor Nunez	Victor Nunez
Flashpoint	HBO Pict.	1984	William Tannen	Dennis Shryack J. D. MacDonald
				Michael Butler G. La Fountaine
Flat 2	Merton Park	1962	Alan Cooke	Lindsay Galloway E. Wallace
Flesh and Fantasy	Universal	1943	Julien Duvivier	Ernest Pascal O. Wilde (Lord Arthur Savile's Crime)
				Samuel Hoffenstein
				Ellis St. Joseph
Flesh and the Fiends	Triad	1959	John Gilling	John Gilling R. L. Stevenson (Body Snatcher)
				Leon Griffiths
Flesh of the Orchid	Fox/Lira	1975	Patrice Chereau	Patrice Chereau J. H. Chase
				Jean-Claude Carriere
Fleshburn	Amiritraj	1984	George Gage	Beth Gage J. Ives (Fear in a Handful of Dust)
				George Gage
Fletch	Universal	1984	Michael Ritchie	Andrew Bergman G. McDonald
Flight from Destiny	Warner	1941	Vincent Sherman	Barry Trivers A. Berkeley (Trial and Error)
Flight of the Intruder	Paramount	1991	John Milius	Robert Dillon S. Coonts
				David Shaber
Flight of the Phoenix	TCF	1965	Robert Aldrich	Lukas Heller E. Trevor
Flim Flam Man	TCF	1967	Irvin Kershner	William Rose G. Owen (Ballad of the Flim Flam Man)
One Born Every Minute				Yakima Canutt
Floating Dutchman	Merton Park	1953	Vernon Sewell	Vernon Sewell N. Bentley
Floods of Fear	Rank	1958	Charles Crichton	Charles Crichton J. Hawkins
				Vivienne Knight
Floor Above	*Mutual	1914	James Kirkwood	? E. P. Oppenheim (headnote)
Florentine Dagger	Warner	1935	Robert Florey	Tom Reed B. Hecht
				Brown Holmes
Flowers in the Attic	NW-Fries	1987	Jeffrey Bloom	Jeffrey Bloom V. C. Andrews
Flying Eye	British	1955	William C. Hammond	William C. Hammond J. N. Chance (headnote)
				Ken Hughes
				Darrell Cating
Flying Fifty-Five	*Stoll	1924	A. E. Coleby	A. E. Coleby E. Wallace
Flying Fifty-Five	Admiral	1939	Reginald Denham	Victor Greene E. Wallace
				Vernon Clancey
				Kenneth Horne
Flying Squad	*Brit. Lion	1929	Arthur Maude	Kathleen Hayden E. Wallace
Flying Squad	Brit. Lion	1932	F. W. Kraemer	Bryan Edgar Wallace E. Wallace
Flying Squad	ABPC	1940	Herbert Brenon	Doreen Montgomery E. Wallace
Fog	Columbia	1934	Albert Rogell	Ethel Hill V. Williams
Fog	Compton	1965	James Hill	Dore Schary
Study in Terror				Donald Ford novel: E. Queen (Study in Terror)
Fog for a Killer	Eternal	1962	Montgomery Tully	Derek Ford
Out of the Fog				Montgomery Tully B. Graeme

Fletch
(Chevy Chase)

F

FILM TITLE	STUDIO	YEAR	DIRECTOR	SCREENWRITER	SOURCE AUTHOR/WORK	SERIES
Fog Over Frisco	Warner	1934	William Dieterle	Robert N. Lee	G. Dyer (Five Fragments)	
Follow That Horse	Cavalcade	1960	Alan Bromly	Eugene Solow Alfred Shaughnessy William Douglas Home Howard Mason	H. Mason (Photo Finish)	
Folly of Desire	*Red Feather	1916	George Loane Tucker	George Loane Tucker	A. Askew (Shulamite)	
Fool Killer	AA	1965	Servando Gonzalez	Morton Fine David Friedkin	H. Eustis	
Foolish Monte Carlo	*Wild Gun.	1922	William Humphrey	William Humphrey	C. Dawe (Black Spider)	
Fool's Parade	Columbia	1971	Andrew V. McLaglen	James Lee Barrett	D. Grubb	
Dynamite Man from Glory Jail						
Footfalls	*Fox	1921	Charles J. Brabin	?	W. D. Steele (Tower of Sand)	
Footsteps in the Fog	Film Loca.	1955	Arthur Lubin	Lenore Coffee Dorothy Reed Arthur Pierson	W. W. Jacobs (Sea Whispers)	
Footsteps in the Night Honeymoon Adventure	ATP	1931	Maurice Elvey	Rupert Downing John Paddy Carstairs Basil Dean	C. Fraser-Simpson	
For Pete's Sake	Rastar	1974	Peter Yates	Stanley Shapiro Maurice Richlin	novel: B. Street	
For the Love of Mike	Brit. Int.	1933	Monty Banks	Clifford Grey Frank Launder	H. F. Maltby	
For the Term of His Natural Life	*MacMahon	1908	Charles MacMahon	?	M. Clarke (His Natural Life)	
For the Term of His Natural Life	*Australas.	1927	Norman Dawn	Norman Dawn	M. Clarke (His Natural Life)	
For Them That Trespass	ABPC	1949	Alberto Cavalcanti	J. Lee Thompson William D. Home	E. Raymond	
For Your Eyes Only	UA	1981	John Glen	Richard Maibaum Michael G. Wilson	I. Fleming	James Bond (Roger Moore)
Forbidden Fruit	Cocinor	1952	Henri Verneuil	Jacques Companez Jean Mause Henri Verneuil	G. Simenon (Act of Passion)	
Forbidden Territory	Progress	1934	Phil Rosen	Dorothy Farnum Alma Reville	D. Wheatley	
Force of Evil	MGM	1948	Abraham Polonsky	Abraham Polonsky Ira Wolfert	I. Wolfert (Tucker's People)	
Force 10 from Navarone	AIP	1978	Guy Hamilton	Robin Chapman Carl Foreman George M. Fraser	A. MacLean	Capt. Mallory (Robert Shaw)
Forger	*Brit. Lion	1928	G. B. Samuelson	Edgar Wallace	E. Wallace	
Forgotten Faces	*Paramount	1928	Victor Schertzinger	Howard Estabrook Oliver H. P. Garrett	R. W. Child (Velvet Black)	
Forgotten Faces	Paramount	1936	E. A. Dupont	Brian Marlow Marguerite Roberts Robert M. Yost	R. W. Child (Velvet Black)	
Formula	MGM	1980	John G. Avildsen	Steve Shagan	S. Shagan	
Fort Apache, the Bronx	TCF	1981	Daniel Petrie	Heywood Gould	novel: H. Gould	
Fortune Is a Woman She Played with Fire	Harvel	1957	Sidney Gilliat	Sidney Gilliat Frank Launder Val Valentine	Winston Graham	
Fortunes of Captain Blood	Columbia	1950	Gordon Douglas	Michael Hogan	R. Sabatini	Capt. Peter Blood (Louis Hayward)
Forty Naughty Girls	RKO	1937	Edward Cline	John Grey	S.Palmer (headnote)	Hildegarde Withers (ZaSu Pitts)
Foul Play	*Edison	1911	?	?	C. Reade	
Foul Play	*Master	1920	W. C. Rowden	?	C. Reade	
Foul Play	Paramount	1978	Colin Higgins	Colin Higgins	novel: J. C. Rogers	

Film Index

Title	Studio	Year	Director	Writer	Source/Notes	Character
Four Boys and a Gun	UA	1957	William Berke	Philip Yordan / Leo Townsend	W. Wiener	
Four Dark Hours (Green Cockatoo / Race Gang)	New World	1937	William C. Menzies	Edward O. Berkman / Arthur Wimperis	G. Greene (headnote)	
Four Days' Wonder	Universal	1937	Sidney Salkow	Harvey Thew / Michael H. Uris	A. A. Milne	
Four Hours to Kill	Paramount	1935	Mitchell Leisen	Norman Krasna	N. Krasna (Small Miracle)	
Four Just Men	*Stoll	1921	George Ridgwell	George Ridgwell	E. Wallace	Four Just Men
Four Just Men (Secret Four)	Ealing	1939	Walter Forde	Angus MacPhail / Sergei Nolbandov / Roland Pertwee	E. Wallace	Four Just Men
Four Men and a Prayer	TCF	1938	John Ford	Richard Sherman / Sonya Levien / Walter Ferris	D. Garth	
Four Wall	*MGM	1928	William Nigh	Alice D. G. Miller / Frederick Forsyth	D. Burnet	
Fourth Protocol	Rank	1987	John Mackenzie	Richard Burridge	F. Forsyth	
Fourth Square	Merton Park	1961	Allan Davis	James Eastwood	E. Wallace (Four Square Jane)	
Foxhole in Cairo	Brit. Lion	1960	John Moxey	Leonard Mosley / Donald Taylor	L. O. Mosley (Cat and the Mice)	
Fragment of Fear	Columbia	1970	Richard C. Sarafian	Paul Dehn	J. Bingham	
Franchise Affair	ABPC	1950	Lawrence Huntington	Robert Hall / Lawrence Huntington	J. Tey	
Frankenstein	*Edison	1910	J. Searle Dawley	J. Searle Dawley	M. W. Shelley	
Frankenstein	Universal	1931	James Whale	Francis E. Faragoh / John L. Balderston / Garrett Fort / Robert Florey	M. W. Shelley	
Frankenstein General	New Star	1988	Deborah Roberts	Michael Kelly / Robert Deel	M. W. Shelley (Frankenstein)	
Frankenstein Must Be Destroyed	Hammer	1969	Terence Fisher	Anthony Nelson Keys / Bert Batt	M. W. Shelley (Frankenstein)	
Frankenstein: The True Story	MCA	1973	Jack Smight	Christo. Isherwood / Don Bachardy	M. W. Shelley (Frankenstein)	
Fraulein	TCF	1958	Henry Koster	Leo Townsend	J. McGovern	
Freebie and the Bean	Warner	1974	Richard Rush	Robert Kaufman	novel: P. B. Ross	
Freeway	New World	1988	Francis Delia	Darrell Fetry / Francis Delia	D. Barkley	
French Connection II	TCF	1975	John Frankenheimer	Robert Dillon / Laurie Dillon / Alexander Jacobs	novel: R. Moore	Popeye Doyle (Gene Hackman)
French Key	Republic	1946	Walter Colmes	Frank Gruber	F. Gruber	
Frenzy	Universal	1972	Alfred Hitchcock	Anthony Shaffer	A. La Bern (Goodbye Picadilly, Farewell Leicester Square)	
Friday the 13th	Paramount	1980	Sean S. Cunningham	Victor Miller	novel: S. Hawke	Johnny Fletcher (Albert Dekker)
Friends in San Rosario	*Selig	1912	?	?	O. Henry (Roads of Destiny)	
Friends of Eddie Coyle	Paramount	1973	Peter Yates	Paul Monash	G. V. Higgins	
Fright (Get Well Soon Visiting Hours)	Filmplan	1982	Jean Claude Lord	Brian Taggart	novel: K. Rembo	
Frightened Bride (Tall Headlines)	Grafton	1952	Terence Young	Audrey E. Lindop / Dudley Leslie	A. E. Lindop (Tall Headlines)	
Frightened Lady (Criminal at Large)	Brit. Lion	1932	T. Hayes Hunter	Angus MacPhail / Bryan Edgar Wallace	E. Wallace (Case of the Frightened Lady)	
Frightened Lady	Pennant	1940	George King	Edward Dryhurst	E. Wallace	
Frog (Case of the Frightened Lady)	Wilcox	1937	Jack Raymond	Ian Hay / Gerald Elliott	E. Wallace (Fellowship of the Frog)	Sgt. Elk (Gordon Harker)

F

FILM TITLE	STUDIO	YEAR	DIRECTOR	SCREENWRITER	SOURCE AUTHOR/WORK	SERIES
From Now On	*Fox	1920	Raoul Walsh	Raoul Walsh	F. Packard	
From Russia with Love	UA	1963	Terence Young	Richard Maibaum, Johanna Harwood	I. Fleming	James Bond (Sean Connery)
From the Boys						
Cold Sweat	Corona	1971	Terence Young	Shimon Wincelberg	R. Matheson (Ride the Nightmare)	
From the Valley of the Missing	*Fox	1915	Frank Powell	Clara S. Beranger, Jay Lewis	G. M. White	
Front Page Story	Lewis	1953	Gordon Parry	Jack Howells, William Fairchild, Guy Morgan	R. Gaines (Final Night)	
Fugitive						
On the Night of the Fire	GFD	1939	Brian Desmond Hurst	Brian Desmond Hurst, Patrick Kirwan, Terence Young	F. L. Green (On the Night of the Fire)	
Fugitive	RKO	1947	John Ford	Dudley Nichols	G. Greene (Power and the Glory)	
Fugitive Lady	Republic	1951	Sidney Salkow	John O'Dea	D. M. Disney (headnote)	
Fugitives	Fox	1929	William Beaudine	John Stone	R. H. Davis (Exiles)	
Full Circle	Fetter	1976	Richard Loncraine	Dave Humphries, Harry Bromley	P. Staub (Julia)	
Haunting of Julia						
Full Fathom Five	Concorde	1990	Carl Franklin	Bart Davis	Bart Davis	
Full House	TCF	1952	Henry Hathaway, Henry Koster, Henry King, Howard Hawks, Jean Negulesco	Lamar Trotti, Richard Breen, Ben Roberts, Ivan Goff, Walter Bullock, Nunnally Johnson	O. Henry (headnote)	
O. Henry's Full House						
Full Treatment						
Stop Me Before I Kill	Falcon	1961	Val Guest	Val Guest, Ronald Scott Thorn	R. S. Thorn	
Funeral in Berlin	Lowndes	1966	Guy Hamilton	Evan Jones	L. Deighton	Harry Palmer (Michael Caine)
Fury	TCF	1978	Brian De Palma	John Farris	J. Farris	
Fury at Furnace Creek	TCF	1948	H. B. Humberstone	Charles G. Booth, Winston Miller	D. Garth (Four Men and a Prayer)	
Fuzz	UA	1972	Richard A. Colla	Evan Hunter	E. McBain	Steve Carella (Burt Reynolds)
"G" Men	Warner	1935	William Keighley	Seton I. Miller	novel: H. K. Long	
Gables Mystery	BIP	1931	Harry Hughes	Harry Hughes	J. Celestin (Man at Six)	
Man at Six						
Gables Mystery	Welwyn	1938	Harry Hughes	Harry Hughes	J. Celestin (Man at Six)	
Gallagher	*Edison	1910	Edwin S. Porter	Edwin S. Porter	R. H. Davis	
Gambit	Universal	1966	Ronald Neame	Jack Davies, Alvin Sargent	novel: K. Lane	
Gamble in Lives	*B&C	1920	George Ridgwell	George Ridgwell	F. Stayton (Joan Danvers)	
Gamble with Heart	*Master	1923	Edwin J. Collins	Lucita Squiers	A. Carlyle	
Gamblers	*Lubin	1914	Barry O'Neil	George Terwilliger	C. Klein	
Gamblers	*Vitagraph	1919	Paul Scardon	Sam Taylor, Lucien Hubbard	C. Klein	
Gamblers	Warner	1929	Michael Curtiz	J. Grubb Alexander	C. Klein	
Game for Three Losers	Merton Park	1965	Gerry O'Hara	Roger Marshall	E. Lustgarten	
Game for Vultures	Columbia	1979	James Fargo	Philip Baird	M. Hartmann	
Game of Death	RKO	1945	Robert Wise	Norman Houston	R. Connell (Variety)	
Game of Liberty	*London	1916	George Loane Tucker	?	E. P. Oppenheim	
Under Suspicion						
Games	Universal	1967	Curtis Harrington	Gene Kearney	novel: H. Ellson	
Games of the Countess Dolingen of Gratz	Films Naut.	1981	Catherine Binet	Catherine Binet	B. Stoker (Dracula)	
Gang That Couldn't Shoot Straight	MGM	1971	James Goldstone	Waldo Salt	J. Breslin	

G

Title	Studio	Year	Director	Writer	Based on/Notes
Gang War / Odd Man Out	Two Cities	1947	Carol Reed	F. L. Green R. C. Sherriff	F. L. Green (Odd Man Out)
Gang War	TCF	1958	Gene Fowler, Jr.	Louis Vittes	O. Demaris (Hoods Take Over)
Gangster	AA	1947	Gordon Wiles	Daniel Fuchs	D. Fuchs (Low Company)
Garden Murder Case	MGM	1936	Edwin L. Marin	Bertram Millhauser	S. S. Van Dine novel; Philo Vance (Edmund Lowe)
Gas	Am. Inter.	1970	Roger Corman	Graham Armiage	novel: B. Hirschfeld
Gas Light	Brit. Nat.	1940	Thorold Dickinson	A. R. Rawlinson Bridget Boland	P. Hamilton
Angel Street				Jon Van Druten	
Gas Light / Murder in Thornton Square	MGM	1944	George Cukor	Walter Reisch John L. Balderston	P. Hamilton
Gaunt Stranger / Phantom Strikes	Ealing	1938	Walter Forde	Sidney Gilliat	E. Wallace (Ringer)
Gauntlet	Warner	1977	Clint Eastwood	Michael Butler Dennis Shryack	novel: M. Butler
Gay Adventure	Grosvenor	1936	Sinclair Hill	D. B. Wyndham Lewis	W. Hackett
Gay Lord Waring	*Bluebird	1916	Otis Turner	F. McGrew Willis	H. Townley
Gazebo	MGM	1959	George Marshall	George Wells	A. Coppel
Gazebo	Trianon	1971	Jean Girault	Claude Magnier Jacques Vilfrid	A. Coppel
Jo	ITC	1978	?	?	
Gemini Contenders	Paramount	1936	Lewis Milestone	Clifford Odets	R. Ludlum
General Died at Dawn	Palomar	1972	Bill Bain	Roger Marshall	C. G. Booth
Gentle Tale of Sex, Violence, Corruption and Murder					L. Moody (Ruthless Ones)
Romeo and Juliet, 1971					
What Became of Jack and Jill					
Gentleman After Dark	UA	1942	Edwin L. Marin	Patterson McNutt George Bruce	R. W. Child (Velvet Black)
Gentleman Burglar	*Edison	1908	Edwin S. Porter	Edwin S. Porter	M. Leblanc (headnote); Arsene Lupin (?)
Gentleman Burglar	*Selig	1915	?	?	M. Leblanc (Exploits of Arsene Lupin)
Gentleman's Fate	MGM	1931	Mervyn Le Roy	Leonard Praskins	K. U. P.
George Barnwell, the London Apprentice	*Hepworth	1913	Hay Plumb	Ivan Patrick Gore	G. Lillo (London Merchant)
Get Carter	MGM	1970	Mike Hodges	Mike Hodges	T. Lewis (Jack's Return Home); Jack Carter (Michael Caine)
Get-Rich-Quick-Wallingford	*Williamson	1916	Fred Niblo	Fred Niblo	G. R. Chester; J. Rufius Wallingford (?)
Get-Rich-Quick-Wallingford	*Paramount	1921	Frank Borzage	W. J. Lincoln ?	G. R. Chester; J. Rufius Wallingford (?)
Get-Rich-Quick-Wallingford / New Adventures of Get-Rich-Quick-Wallingford	MGM	1931	Sam Wood	W. J. Lincoln Charles MacArthur	G. R. Chester; J. Rufius Wallingford (William Haines)
Get Well Soon	Filmplan	1982	Jean Claude Lord	Brian Taggart	novel: K. Rembo
Fright					
Visiting Hours					
Getaway	First Art.	1972	Sam Peckinpah	Walter Hill	J. Thompson
Getting Away with Murder / Murder on the Bridge / End of the Game	MFG-T.R.A.	1975	Maxmillian Schell	Maximillian Schell Arlene Sellers Bo Goldmann	F. Duerrenmatt (Judge and His Hangman)
Ghost Breaker	*Lasky	1914	Oscar Apfel	James Montgomery Cecil B. DeMille	C. W. Goddard
Ghost Breaker	*Fam. Play.	1922	Alfred E. Green	Jack Cunningham Walter DeLeon	C. W. Goddard
Ghost Breakers	Paramount	1940	George Marshall	Walter DeLeon	C. W. Goddard
Ghost of John Holling / Mystery Liner	Monogram	1934	William Nigh	Wellwyn Totman	E. Wallace (Steward)
Ghost That Walks Alone	Columbia	1944	Lew Landers	Doris Shattuck Clarence U. Young	R. Shattuck (Wedding Guest Sat on a Stone)
Ghost Train	*Gainsboro.	1927	Geza M. Bolvary	?	A. Ridley

G

FILM TITLE	STUDIO	YEAR	DIRECTOR	SCREENWRITER	SOURCE AUTHOR/WORK	SERIES
Ghost Train	Gainsboro.	1931	Walter Forde	Angus MacPhail Lajos Biro	A. Ridley	
Ghost Train	City Prod.	1933	Lajos Lazar	Sidney Gilliat Laszlo Bekeffy	A. Ridley	
Ghost Train	Gainsboro.	1941	Walter Forde	Marriott Edgar Val Guest J. O. C. Orton Sidney Gilliat	A. Ridley	
Ghost Train	Dansk-Sv.	1976	Bent Christensen	Leif Panduro Bent Christensen	A. Ridley	
Ghoul	Gaumont	1933	T. Hayes Hunter	Roland Pertwee John Hastings Turner Frank King Leonard Hines L. DuGarde Peach Rupert Downing	Frank King	
Gideon of Scotland Yard	Columbia	1958	John Ford	T. E. B. Clarke	J. J. Marric (Gideon's Day)	George Gideon (Jack Hawkins)
Gideon's Day						
Gideon of Scotland Yard	Columbia	1958	John Ford	T. E. B. Clarke	J. J. Marric	George Gideon (Jack Hawkins)
Gift Supreme	*Macaulay	1920	Ollie L. Sellers	?	G. A. England	
Girl by the Roadside	*Bluebird	1918	Theodore Marston	John C. Brownell	V. Vanardy	
Girl from Mandalay	Republic	1936	Howard Bretherton	Wellyn Totman Endre Boehm	R. Campbell (Death in Tiger Valley)	
Girl Hunters	Colorama	1963	Roy Rowland	Mickey Spillane Roy Rowland Robert Fellows	M. Spillane	Mike Hammer (Mickey Spillane)
Girl in His House	*Vitagraph	1918	Tom Mills	Katharine Reed	H. MacGrath	
Girl in Pawn	Paramount	1934	Alexander Hall	William R. Lipman Sam Hellman Gladys Lehman	D. Runyon (Blue Plate Special)	
Little Miss Marker						
Girl in Room 17	UA	1953	Arnold Laven	Lawrence Roman	L. T. White (Harness Bull)	
Vice Squad						
Girl in the Dark	*Bluebird	1918	Stuart Paton	A. G. Kenyon	C. E. Walk (Green Seal)	
Girl in the Headlines	Viewfinder	1963	Michael Truman	Vivienne Knight Patrick Campbell	L. Payne (Nose on My Face)	Insp. Sam Birkett (Ian Hendry)
Model Murder Case						
Girl in the News	TCF	1940	Carol Reed	Sidney Gilliat Frank Launder	R. Vickers	
Girl in the Web	*Hampton	1920	Robert Thornby	Waldemar Young	G. Bonner (Miss Maitland, Private Secretary)	
Girl in the Woods	Republic	1958	Tom Gries	Oliver Crawford Marcel Klauber	O. Crawford (Blood on the Branches)	
Girl of the Port	Radio Pict.	1930	Bert Glennon	Beulah Marie Dix Charles Bennett	J. Russell (Far Wandering Men)	
Girl Was Young	Gaumont	1937	Alfred Hitchcock	Edwin Greenwood Anthony Armstrong Alma Reville Gerald Savory	J. Tey (Shilling for Candles)	
Young and Innocent						
Girl Who Dared	Republic	1944	Howard Bretherton	John K. Butler	Medora Field (Blood on Her Shoe)	
Girl with the Red Feather	*Selig	1915	?	?	M. Nicholson (Best Laid Schemes)	
Girly	Brigitte	1969	Freddie Francis	Brian Comport	B. Comport	
Mumsy, Nanny, Sonny and Girly						
Glass Bottom Boat	MGM	1966	Frank Tashlin	Everett Freeman	novel: B. Street	
Glass Cage	Hammer	1955	Montgomery Tully	Richard Landau	A. E. Martin (Common People)	
Glass Tomb						
Glass Cell	Roxy	1978	Hans Geissendoerfer	Hans Geissendoerfer Klaus Baedekerl	P. Highsmith	

G

Film	Studio	Year	Director	Writer	Source/Notes
Glass Key	Paramount	1935	Frank Tuttle	Kathryn Scola, Kubec Glasmon, Harry Ruskin	D. Hammett
Glass Key	Paramount	1942	Stuart Heisler	Jonathan Latimer	D. Hammett
Glass Tomb	Hammer	1955	Montgomery Tully	Richard Landau	A. E. Martin (Common People)
Glass Cage					
Glass Web	Universal	1953	Jack Arnold	Robert Blees, Leonard Lee	M. Ehrlich (Spin the Glass Web)
Glitter Dome	Thorn	1984	Stuart Margolin	Stanley Kallis	J. Wambaugh
Gloria Scott	*Stoll	1923	George Ridgwell	Geoffrey H. Malins, Patrick L. Mannock	A. C. Doyle (Memoirs of Sherlock Holmes) — Sherlock Holmes (Eille Norwood)
Godfather	Paramount	1972	Francis F. Coppola	Mario Puzo, Francis F. Coppola	M. Puzo — Vito Corleone (Marlon Brando)
Godfather, Part II	Paramount	1974	Francis F. Coppola	Francis F. Coppola, Mario Puzo	M. Puzo (Godfather) — Vito Corleone (Robert De Niro)
God's Clay	*Rooke	1919	Arthur Rooke	Arthur Rooke	A. Askew
God's Clay	First Nat.	1928	Graham Cutts	P. Maclean Rogers	A. Askew
God's Law and Man's	*Columbia	1917	John H. Collins	John H. Collins	P. Trent (Wife by Purchase)
God's Prodigal	*Int. Art.	1923	Bert Wynne	Louis Stevens	A. J. Russell
			Edward Jose		
Godsend	Cannon	1980	Gabrielle Beaumont	Olaf Pooley	B. Taylor
Going Crooked	*Fox	1926	George Melford	Keene Thompson, Albert S. Le Vino	Winchell Smith
Going in Style	Warner	1979	Martin Brest	Martin Brest	novel: R. Grossbach
Golden Child	Paramount	1986	Michael Ritchie	Dennis Feldman	novel: G. C. Chesbro
Golden Earrings	Paramount	1947	Mitchell Leisen	Abraham Polonsky, Frank Butler, Helen Deutsch	Y. Foldes
Golden Gate	ITC	1978	?	Judd Bernard	A. MacLean
Golden Heist	Warner	1975	Peter Duffell	Stephen Schneck	novel: W. Hughes
Hitler's Gold					
Inside Out					
Golden Pince-Nez	*Stoll	1923	George Ridgwell	Geoffrey H. Malins, Patrick L. Mannock	A. C. Doyle (Return of Sherlock Holmes) — Sherlock Holmes (Eille Norwood)
Golden Rendezvous	Film Trust	1977	Ashley Lazarus	Stanley Price	A. MacLean
Golden Salamander	Pinewood	1950	Ronald Neame	Ronald Neame, Victor Canning, Lesley Storm	V. Canning
Golden Snare	*Hartford	1921	David M. Hartford	James O. Curwood, David M. Hartford	J. O. Curwood
Golden Web	*Garrick	1920	Geoffrey H. Malins	Milton Rosmer	E. P. Oppenheim (Plunderers)
Golden Web	*Gotham	1926	Walter Lang	James Bell Smith	E. P. Oppenheim (Plunderers)
Goldfinger	UA	1964	Guy Hamilton	Richard Maibaum, Paul Dehn	I. Fleming — James Bond (Sean Connery)
Good Girls Beware	Corona	1957	Yves Allegret	Rene Wheeler, Jean Meckert	J. H. Chase (Miss Callaghan Comes to Grief)
Look Out, Girls					
Young Girls Reward					
Good Guys Always Win	MGM	1973	John Flynn	John Flynn	R. Stark (Outfit)
Outfit					
Good Guys Wear Black	Am. Cinema	1978	Ted Post	Bruce Cohn, Mark Medoff	novel: M. Franklin
Good Time Girl	Triton	1948	David Macdonald	Muriel Box, Sydney Box, Ted Willis	A. La Bern (Night Darkens the Streets)
Goodbye Charlie	TCF	1964	Vincente Minnelli	Harry Kurnitz	novel: M. H. Albert
Goodbye Gemini	Shafel	1970	Alan Gibson	Edmund Ward	J. Hall (Ask Agamemnon)
Gooseflesh	Paris Film	1963	Julien Duvivier	Rene Barjaval, Julien Duvivier	J. H. Chase (Come Easy—Go Easy)
Highway Pickup					
Gorgeous Bird Like Me	Films Caro.	1972	Francois Truffaut	Francois Truffaut, Jean-Louis Dabadie	H. Farrell (Such a Gorgeous Kid Like Me)
Such a Gorgeous Kid Like Me					

G

FILM TITLE	STUDIO	YEAR	DIRECTOR	SCREENWRITER	SOURCE AUTHOR/WORK	SERIES
Gorilla	*First Nat.	1927	Alfred Santell	Al Cohn Henry McCarty	R. Spence	
Gorilla	First Nat.	1930	Bryan Foy	W. Harrison Orkow Herman Ruby Ralph Spence	R. Spence	
Gorilla	TCF	1939	Alan Dwan	Rian James Sid Silvers	R. Spence	
Gorky Park	Orion	1983	Michael Apted	Dennis Potter	M. C. Smith	Arkady Renko (William Hurt)
Gracie Allen Murder Case	Paramount	1939	Alfred E. Green	Nat Perrin	S. S. Van Dine	Philo Vance (Warren William)
Grand Babylon Hotel	*Hepworth	1916	Frank Wilson	?	A. Bennett	
Grand Central Murder	MGM	1942	S. Sylvan Simon	Peter Ruric	S. MacVeigh	
Grand National Night Wicked Wife	Talisman	1953	Bob McNaught	Bob McNaught Val Valentine	D. Christie	
Grandeur and Decadence of a Small-Time Filmmaker	Hamster	1986	Jean-Luc Godard	Jean-Luc Godard		
Grandfather Smallweed	Brit. Sound	1928	Hugh Croise	?	C. Dickens (Bleak House)	
Granny Get Your Gun	FN-WB	1940	George Amy	Kenneth Gamet	E. S. Gardner (Case of the Dangerous Dowager)	
Grasp of Greed	*Bluebird	1916	Joseph De Grasse	Ida May Park	H. R. Haggard (Mr. Meeson's Will)	
Grasshopper	Nat. Gen.	1969	Jerry Paris	Jerry Belson Garry Marshall	M. McShane (Passing of Evil)	
Gray Dawn	*Hampton	1922	Eliot Howe Marie Jenney	E. Richard Schayer Jean Hersholt	S. E. White	
Gray Ghost	*Universal	1917	Stuart Paton	Stuart Paton	A. S. Roche (Loot)	
Gray Ghost	*Universal	1919	William C. Dowlan	Violet Clark	A. S. Roche (Loot)	
Gray Mask	*World	1915	Frank Crane	?	W. Camp	
Great Armored Car Swindle Breaking Point	Butcher	1960	Lance Comfort	Peter Lambert	L. Meynell (Breaking Point)	
Great Deception	*Kane	1926	Howard Higgin	Paul Bern	G. F. Gibbs (Yellow Dove)	
Great Hospital Mystery	TCF	1937	James Tinling	Bess Meredyth William Conselman Jerry Cady	M. Eberhart (headnote)	"Nurse Keats" (Jane Darwell)
Great Hotel Murder	TCF	1935	Eugene Forde	Arthur Kober	V. Starrett	
Great Impersonation	*Fam. Play.	1921	George Melford	Monte Katterjohn	E. P. Oppenheim	
Great Impersonation	Universal	1935	Alan Crosland	Frank Wood Eve Greene	E. P. Oppenheim	
Great Impersonation	Universal	1942	John Rawlins	W. Scott Darling	E. P. Oppenheim	
Great K&A Train Robbery	*Fox	1926	Lewis Seiler	John Stone	P. L. Ford	
Great Prince Shan	*Stoll	1924	A. E. Coleby	A. E. Coleby	E. P. Oppenheim	
Great Train Robbery First Great Train Robbery	UA	1979	Michael Crichton	Michael Crichton	M. Crichton	
Greater Than a Crown	*Fox	1925	Roy William Neill	Wyndham Gittens	V. Bridges (Lady from Long Acre)	
Greek Interpreter	*Stoll	1922	George Ridgwell	Patrick L. Mannock Geoffrey H. Malins	A. C. Doyle (Memoirs of Sherlock Holmes)	Sherlock Holmes (Eille Norwood)
Green Cloak	*Kleine	1915	?	Henry K. Webster Owen Davis	Y. Davis	
Green Cockatoo Four Dark Hours Race Gang	New World	1937	William C. Menzies	Edward O. Berkman Arthur Wimperis	G. Greene (headnote)	
Green Eyes	Chester. Individual	1934	Richard Thorpe	Andrew Moses	H. Ashbrook (Murder of Steven Kester)	
Green for Danger		1947	Sidney Gilliat	Sidney Gilliat Claude Guerney	C. Brand	Insp. Cockrill (Alastair Sim)
Green God	*Vitagraph	1918	Paul Scardon	?	F. A. Kummer	

Title	Studio	Year	Director	Writer	Character (Actor)
Green Ice	ITC	1981	Ernest Day	Edward Anhalt / Ray Hassett / Anthony Simmons / Robert de Laurentis / Sidney Gilliat / Frank Launder	G. A. Browne
Green Man	Brit. Lion	1956	Robert Day	John Hunter	F. Launder (Meet a Body)
Green Pack	Brit. Lion	1934	T. Hayes Hunter	Gordon Wellesley	E. Wallace
Green Scarf	B&A	1954	George M. O'Ferrall	G. W. Gifford	G. Des Cars (Brute)
Green Terror	*Gaumont	1919	W. P. Kellino	Louise Long	E. Wallace (Green Rust)
Greene Murder Case	Paramount	1929	Frank Tuttle	Bartlett Cormack	S. S. Van Dine / Philo Vance (William Powell)
Grell Mystery	*Vitagraph	1917	Paul Scardon	?	F. Froest
Grey Lady	*Nordisk	1909	Viggo Larsen	?	A. C. Doyle (Hound of the Baskervilles) / Sherlock Holmes (Viggo Larsen)
Grifters	Cineplex	1990	Stephen Frears	Donald Westlake	Jim Thompson
Grilling Inquisitor	Ariane	1981	Claude Miller	Claude Miller / Jean Herman / Michel Audiard	J. Wainwright (Brainwash)
Grip	*B&C	1915	Maurice Elvey	Eliot Stannard	J. S. Winter
Grip of Fear Experiment in Terror	Columbia	1962	Blake Edwards	Gordons	Gordons (Operation Terror)
Grip of the Strangler Haunted Strangler	Prod. Ass.	1958	Robert Day	Jan Read	novel: J. C. Cooper
Grissom Gang	Cinerama	1971	Robert Aldrich	John C. Cooper	J. H. Chase (No Orchids for Miss Blandish)
Groundstar Conspiracy	Universal	1972	Lamont Johnson	Leon Griffiths	L. Davies (Alien)
Grumpy	*Fam. Play.	1923	William De Mille	Matthew Howard	H. Hodges
Grumpy	Paramount	1930	George Cukor / Cyril Gardner	Clara Beranger / Doris Anderson	H. Hodges
Guardian	Universal	1990	William Friedkin	Steven Volk / Dan Greenburg / Ivan Foxwell	D. Greenburg (Nanny)
Guilt Is My Shadow	ABPC	1950	Roy Kellino	Roy Kellino / John Gilling	Peter Curtis (You're Best Alone)
Guilty	Monogram	1947	John Reinhardt	R. R. Presnell, Sr. / Maurice J. Wilson	W. Irish (Dancing Detective)
Guilty?	Gibraltar	1956	Edmond T. Greville	Ernest Dudley	M. Gilbert (Death Has Deep Roots)
Guilty As Charged	Paramount	1932	Erle Kenton	Arthur Kober / Frank Partos	D. N. Rubin (Riddle Me This!)
Guilty As Hell	Paramount	1932	Erle Kenton	Arthur Kober / Frank Partos	D. N. Rubin (Riddle Me This!)
Guilty As Charged Guilty Bystander	Film Class.	1950	Joseph Lerner	Don Ettlinger	Wade Miller / Max Thursday (Zachary Scott)
Guilty Man	*Paramount	1918	Irwin Willat	?	F. Coppee
Gumshoe	Columbia	1971	Stephen Frears	Neville Smith	novel: N. Smith
Gun Crazy Deadly Is the Female	UA	1949	Joseph H. Lewis	MacKinlay Kantor / Millard Kaufman	M. Kantor (Author's Choice)
Gun Moll	Pathe Con.	1953	Bernard Borderie	Jacques Berland / Bernard Borderie	P. Cheyney (Poison Ivy) / Lemmy Caution (Eddie Constantine)
Gun-Runner	*Tiffany	1929	Edgar Lewis	J. F. Netteford	A. Stringer
Gun Runners	UA	1958	Don Siegel	Daniel Mainwaring / Paul Monash	E. Hemingway (To Have and Have Not)
Gunrunners	UA	1958	Don Siegel	Daniel Mainwaring / Paul Monash	E. Hemingway (To Have and Have Not)
Guns of Darkness Act of Mercy	Cavalcade	1962	Anthony Asquith	John Mortimer	F. Clifford (Act of Mercy)
Guns of Navarone	Open Road	1961	J. Lee Thompson	Carl Foreman	A. MacLean / Capt. Mallory (Gregory Peck)
Gymkata Terrible Game	MGM	1985	Robert Clouse	Charles R. Carnes	D. T. Moore (Terrible Game)
Gypsy and the Gentleman	Rank	1958	Joseph Losey	Janet Green	N. W. Hooke (Darkness I Leave You)

G

FILM TITLE	STUDIO	YEAR	DIRECTOR	SCREENWRITER	SOURCE AUTHOR/WORK	SERIES
Half a Chance	*Reliance	1913	Oscar Apfel	?	F. S. Isham	
Half a Chance	*Hampton	1920	Robert Thornby	Fred Myron	F. S. Isham	
Half a Truth	*Stoll	1922	Sinclair Hill	Leslie H. Gordon	Rita	
Half Million Bribe	*Columbia	1916	Edgar Jones	Harry O. Hoyt	W. H. Osborne (Red Mouse)	
Half Moon Street	RKO	1986	Bob Swaim	Bob Swaim	P. Theroux (Doctor Slaughter)	
Halloween	Falcon Int.	1978	John Carpenter	John Carpenter / Debra Hill	novel: C. Richards	
Halloween II	Universal	1981	Rick Rosenthal	John Carpenter / Debra Hill	novel: J. Martin	
Hammer the Toff	Butcher	1952	Maclean Rogers	?	J. Creasey	Richard Rollison (John Bentley)
Hammerhead	Allen	1968	David Miller	William Bast / Herbert Baker	J. Mayo	Charles Hood (Vince Edwards)
Hammett	Zeotrope	1982	Wim Wenders	John Briley / Ross Thomas / Dennis O'Flaherty / Thomas Pope	J. Gores	
Hammond Mystery Undying Monster	TCF	1942	John Brahm	Lillie Hayward / Michel Jacoby	J. D. Kerruish (Undying Monster)	
Hand	Orion	1981	Oliver Stone	Oliver Stone	M. Brandel (Lizard's Tail)	
Hand of Peril	*Paragon	1916	Maurice Tourneur	Maurice Tourneur	A. Stringer	
Hands of a Strangler / Hands of Orlac	Riviera	1960	Edmond T. Greville	Edmond T. Greville / John Baines	M. Renard (Hands of Orlac)	
Hands of Orlac	*Pan-Film	1924	Robert Weine	Donald Taylor / Ludwig Nerz	M. Renard	
Hands of Orlac Mad Love	MGM	1935	Karl Freund	Guy Endore / P. J. Wolfson / John I. Balderston	M. Renard	
Hands of Orlac Hands of a Strangler	Riviera	1960	Edmond T. Greville	Edmond T. Greville / John Baines / Donald Taylor	M. Renard	
Hands of the Ripper	Hammer	1971	Peter Sasdy	L. W. Davidson	novel: E. S. Shew	
Hanged Man	Rank	1964	?	?	D. B. Hughes (Expendable Man)	
Hangover Square	TCF	1945	John Brahm	Barre Lyndon	P. Hamilton	
Hangup Superdude	Warner	1974	Henry Hathaway	John B. Sherry / Lee Lazich	B. Brunner (Face of Night)	
Hanky Panky	Columbia	1982	Sidney Poitier	Henry Rosenbaum / David Taylor	novel: L. Jarreau	
Happening	Horizon	1967	Eliot Silverstein	Frank R. Pierson / James D. Buchanan / Ronald Austin	novel: E. Curry	
Happy Thieves Once a Thief	UA	1962	George Marshall	John Gay	R. Condon (Oldest Confession)	
Hard Cash	*Edison	1913	Charles M. Seay	?	C. Reade	
Hard Cash	*Master	1921	Edwin J. Collins	Walter C. Rowden	C. Reade	
Hard Man	Columbia	1957	George Sherman	Leo Katcher	L. Katcher	
Hard Traveling	New World	1986	Dan Bessie	Dan Bessie	A. Bessie (Bread and a Stone)	
Harper Moving Target	Warner	1967	Jack Smight	William Goldman	J. Macdonald (Moving Target)	Harper (Paul Newman)
Harrassed Hero	Corsair	1954	Maurice Elvey	Brock Williams	E. Dudley	
Hate	*Metro	1922	Maxwell Karger	June Mathis	W. Camp (Communicating Door)	
Hate Ship	Brit. Int.	1929	Norman Walker	Monckton Hoffe / Eliot Stannard / Benn W. Levy	B. Graeme	
Hatter's Ghost	Horizons	1982	Claude Chabrol	Claude Chabrol	G. Simenon	
Haunted Bedroom	Edison	1914	?	?	Rita (Millionaire)	

Title	Year	Studio	Director	Writer	Source/Notes	Character (Actor)
Haunted Bell	1916	*Imp	Henry Otto	J. Grubb Alexander	J. Futrelle (Diamond Master)	
Haunted Honeymoon Busman's Honeymoon	1940	MGM	Arthur B. Woods	Monckton Hoffe Angus MacPhail Harold Goldman	D. L. Sayers (Busman's Honeymoon)	Peter Wimsey (Robert Montgomery)
Haunted House	1928	First Nat.	B. Christiansen	Richard Bee Lajos Biro	O. Davis	
Haunted Pajamas	1917	*Metro	Fred J. Balshofer	Fred J. Balshofer	F. P. Elliott	
Haunted Strangler Grip of the Strangler	1958	Prod. Ass.	Robert Day	Jan Read John C. Cooper	novel: J. C. Cooper (Grip of the Strangler)	
Haunted Summer	1988	Cannon	Ivan Passer	Lewis John Carlino		
Haunting	1963	Argyle	Robert Wise	Nelson Gidding	Anne Edwards S. Jackson (Haunting of Hill House)	
Haunting of Julia Full Circle	1976	Fetter	Richard Loncraine	Dave Humphries Harry Bromley	P. Staub (Julia)	
Haunting Shadows	1920	?	Henry King	?		
Having Wonderful Crime	1945	RKO	Edward Sutherland	Howard J. Green Stewart Sterling Parke Levy	M. Nicholson (House of a Thousand Candles) C. Rice	Jake Justus (George Murphy)
Hawk's Nest	1928	*First Nat.	B. Christiansen	James T. O'Donohoe Arthur Sheekman	novel: W. Gunning	
Hazard	1948	Paramount	George Marshall	Roy Chanslor	R. Chanslor	
He Died with His Eyes Open	1985	Swaine	Jacques Deray	Jacques Deray Michel Audiard	D. Raymond	
He Ran All the Way	1951	UA	John Berry	Guy Endore Hugo Butler	S. Ross	
Headline	1943	Corfield	John Harlow	Maisie Sharman	K. Attiwell (Reporter)	
Heads or Tails	1980	GEF	Robert Enrico	Ralph G. Bettinson Robert Enrico Marcel Julian Michel Audiard	A. Harris (Baroni)	
Hearse	1980	Marimark	George Bowers	Bill Bleich		
Heart and Soul Nonconformist Parson	1919	*Brit. Lion	A. V. Bramble	Eliot Stannard	novel: H. Clement R. Horniman (Nonconformist Parson)	
Heart of the Hills	1916	*Ediwon	Richard Ridgely	?	D. Whitelaw (Girl from the East)	
Heart of the Matter	1953	London	George M. O'Ferrell	Ian Dalrymple Lesley Storm	G. Greene	
Heart of the North	1938	First Nat.	Lewis Seiler	Lee Katz	W. B. Mowery	
Heart Trump for OSS 117 in Tokyo	1966	Valoria	Michel Boisrond	Vincent Sherman Pierre Foucaud Terence Young Marcel Mithois	J. Bruce (Hot Line)	OSS 117 (Frederick Stafford)
Hearts and Crosses	1913	*Eclair	?	?	O. Henry (Heart of the West)	
Heat	1987	Escalante	R. M. Richards	William Goldman	W. Goldman	
Heatwave House Across the Lake	1954	Hammer	Ken Hughes	Ken Hughes	K. Hughes (High Wray)	
Heatwave	1981	Roadshow	Philip Noyce	Marc Rosenberg Philip Noyce	novel: Timothy Harris	
Heaven Fell That Night Night Heaven Fell	1958	Kingsley	Roger Vadim	Roger Vadim Jacques Remy	A. Vidalie (Midnight Jewelers)	
Heliotrope	1920	*Cosmopolit.	George D. Baker	George D. Baker Alec Coppel Max Trell	R. W. Child (Velvet Black)	
Hell Below Zero	1954	Warwick	Mark Robson	Richard Maibaum	H. Innes (White South)	
Hell Is a City	1959	Hammer	Val Guest	Val Guest	M. Procter	Insp. Martineau (Stanley Baker)
Hell Is Empty	1967	Dominion	John Ainsworth	John Ainsworth Bernard Knowles John Fowler	J. F. Straker	
Hell Is Sold Out	1951	Zelstro	Michael Anderson	Guy Morgan Moie Charles	M. Dekobra	

H

1406 / HELL ON FRISCO BAY — Film Index

FILM TITLE	STUDIO	YEAR	DIRECTOR	SCREENWRITER	SOURCE AUTHOR/WORK	SERIES
Hell on Frisco Bay	Warner	1955	Frank Tuttle	Sydney Boehm Martin Rackin	W. P. McGivern (Darkest Hour)	
Hennessy	Marseilles	1975	Don Sharp	John Gay	novel: M. Franklin (5th of November)	
5th of November						
Her Bitter Lesson	*Selig	1912	Hardee Kirkland			
Her Fatal Sin	*Strand	1915	?	?	M. E. Braddon (Aurora Floyd)	
Her Fighting Chance	*Jacobs	1917	Edwin Carewe	?	M. E. Holmes	
Her First Appearance	*Edison	1910	Edwin S. Porter	?	J. O. Curwood (Back to God's Country)	
Her Last Affaire	Prod. Dist.	1935	Michael Powell	Ian Dalrymple	R. H. Davis (Van Bibber and others)	
Her Second Chance	*First Nat.	1926	Lambert Hillyer	Eve Unsell	W. W. Ellis (S.O.S.)	
Her Uncle	*London	1915	George Loane Tucker		W. Woodrow (Second Chance)	
Hero and the Terror	Cannon	1988	William Tannen	?	W. W. Jacobs (Short Cruises)	
					M. Blodgett	
Hero at Large	MGM	1980	Martin Davidson	Dennis Shryack Michael Blodgett		
Heroin Gang	MGM	1968	Brian Hutton	A. J. Carothers	novel: A. J. Carothers	
Sol Madrid				David Karp	R. Wilder (Fruit of the Poppy)	
Hickey and Boggs	UA	1972	Robert Culp	Walter Hill	novel: P. Rock	
Hidden Hand	Warner	1942	Ben Stoloff	Anthony Coldeway Raymond Schrock	Rufus King (Invitation to a Murder)	
Hidden Homicide	Luckwell	1958	Tony Young	Tony Young Bill Luckwell	P. Capon (Death at Shinglestrand)	
Hidden Room	Independent	1949	Edward Dmytryk	Alec Coppel	A. Coppel (Man About a Dog)	
Obsession						
Hidden Spring	*Yorke-Metro	1917	E. Mason Hopper	Fred J. Balshofer	C. B. Kelland	
Hideout	Brit. Lion	1948	Fergus McDonnell	Derek Neame Julian Orde	R. Westerby (Small Voice)	
Small Voice						
Hideout in the Alps	Twickenham	1936	Bernard Vorhaus	George Barraud L. DuGarde Peach Michael Hankinson Arthur Macrae Paul Hervey Fox H. Fowler Mear	N. Grant (Dusty Ermine)	
Dusty Ermine						
High and Low	Toho	1962	Akira Kurosawa	Akira Kurosawa Ryuzo Kikushima Eijiro Hisaita Hideo Oguni	E. McBain (King's Ransom)	
High Anxiety	TCF	1977	Mel Brooks	Mel Brooks Ron Clark Rudy DeLuca Barry Levinson		
High Ballin'	Am. Int.	1978	Peter Carter	Paul Edwards	novel: R. H. Pilpel	
High Bright Sun	Rank	1964	Ralph Thomas	Ian Stuart Black Bryan Forbes	novel: Richard Robinson	
McGuire Go Home!					I. S. Black	
High Command	ABFD	1936	Thorold Dickinson	Katherine Strueby Walter Meade Val Valentine	L. Robinson (General Goes Too Far)	
High Commissioner	Selmur	1968	Ralph Thomas	Wilfred Greatorex	J. Cleary	Scobie Malone (Rod Taylor)
Nobody Runs Forever						
High Hand	*Fav. Play.	1915	William D. Taylor	?	J. Futrelle	
High Road to China	Golden Har.	1983	Brian G. Hutton	Sandra W. Roland S. Lee Pogostin	J. Cleary	
High School Confidential	MGM	1958	Jack Arnold	Lewis Meltzer Robert Blees	novel: Morton Cooper	
High Sierra	First Nat.	1941	Raoul Walsh	John Huston W. R. Burnett	W. R. Burnett	
High Speed	*Hallmark	1920	Charles Miller	John J. Glavey	C. H. Stagg	

Film Index

H

Title	Studio	Year	Director	Writer(s)	Source	Character (Actor)
High Wall	MGM	1947	Curtis Bernhardt	Sydney Boehm / Lester Cole / Dorothy Hannah	A. R. Clark	
High Window / Brasher Doubloon	MGM	1947	John Brahm		R. Chandler	Philip Marlowe (George Montgomery)
Highest Bidder	*Goldwyn	1921	Wallase Worsley	Lloyd Lonergan / Rene Barjaval	M. Foster (Trap)	
Highway Pickup / Gooseflesh	Paris Film	1963	Julien Duvivier	Julien Duvivier	J. H. Chase (Come Easy—Go Easy)	
Highways by Night	RKO	1942	Peter Godfrey	Lynn Root / Frank Fenton	C. B. Kelland (Silver Spoon)	
Hill Girl	UGC	1990	Robin Davis	Robin Davis / Patrick Laurent / Alain Le Henry	Charles Williams	
His Lordship	*London	1915	George Loane Tucker	?	W. W. Jacobs (Short Cruises)	
His Lordship / Man of Affairs	Gaumont Br.	1937	Herbert Mason	Maude T. Howell / L. DuGarde Peach / Edwin Greenwood	N. Grant (Nelson Touch)	
His Official Wife	Tobis-Rora	1936	Erich Waschneck	Rolf Meyer / T. Echtermeier / Thea von Harbou	R. H. Savage (My Official Wife)	
His Robe of Honor	*Paralta	1918	Rex Ingram	Julian L. Lamothe	E. Dorrance	
His Wife's Friend	*Paramount	1920	Joseph De Grasse	R. Cecil Smith	J. B. Harris-Burland (White Rook)	
His Wife's Husband	*Pyramid	1922	Kenneth Webb	Dorothy Farnum	A. K. Green (Mayor's Wife)	
Hit and Run	Groupe	1959	Bernard Borderie	Jean Aurel	R. Marshall	
Hit and Run / Revenge Squad	Comworld	1982	Charles Braverman	Don Enright	L. Fletcher (Eighty Dollars to Stamford)	
Hit Man	MGM	1972	George Armitage	George Armitage	T. Lewis (Jack's Return Home)	
Hitler's Gold / Golden Heist / Inside Out	Warner	1975	Peter Duffell	Judd Bernard / Stephen Schneck	novel: W. Hughes (Inside Out)	
Hocussing of Cigarette	*Stoll	1924	Hugh Croise	Hugh Croise	B. Orczy (Old Man in the Corner)	Old Man (Rolf Leslie)
Holcroft Covenant	Thorn EMI	1985	John Frankenheimer	George Axelrod / Edward Anhalt / John Hopkins	R. Ludlum	
Hold-Up	AMLF	1985	Alexandre Arcady	Francis Veber / Daniel Saint-Hamont / Alexandre Arcady / Daniel Fuchs	J. Cronley (Quick Change)	
Hollow Triumph / Scar	Eagle-Lion	1948	Steve Sekely		M. Forbes	
Home at Seven / Murder on Monday	Brit. Lion	1952	Ralph Richardson	Anatole De Grunwald	R. C. Sherriff	
Home Before Dark	Warner	1958	Mervyn LeRoy	Eileen Bassing / Robert Bassing	E. Bassing	
Home Sweet Homicide	TCF	1946	Lloyd Bacon	F. Hugh Herbert	C. Rice	
Homicide for Three	Republic	1948	George Blair	Bradbury Foote / Albert DeMond	P. Quentin (Puzzle for Puppets)	
Honey Pot / Anyone for Venice? / It Comes Up Murder / Mr. Fox of Venice	UA	1966	J. L. Mankiewicz	J. L. Mankiewicz	T. Sterling (Evil of the Day)	
Honeymoon Adventure / Footsteps in the Night	ATP	1931	Maurice Elvey	Rupert Downing / John Paddy Carstairs / Basil Dean	C. Fraser-Simpson (Footsteps in the Night)	
Honeymoon Killers / Lonely Hearts Killers	Roxane	1969	Leonard Kastle	Leonard Kastle	novel: Paul Buck	
Honor First	*Fox	1922	Jerome Storm	Joseph F. Poland	G. F. Gibbs (Splendid Outcast)	
Honorary Consul / Beyond the Limit	World Film	1983	John Mackenzie	Christopher Hampton	G. Greene	
Honours Easy	BIP	1935	Herbert Brenon	Norman Watson / Roland Pertwee	R. Pertwee	Peter Duluth (Warren Douglas)

FILM TITLE	STUDIO	YEAR	DIRECTOR	SCREENWRITER	SOURCE AUTHOR/WORK	SERIES
Hoodlum's Sun						
Action Man	Comacico	1967	Jean Delannoy	Alphonse Boudard Jean Delannoy	J. Flynn (Action Man)	
Leather and Nylon						
Hopscotch	AVCO	1980	Ronald Neame	Brian Garfield Bryan Forbes	B. Garfield	
Hoordern Mystery	*Southwell	1920	Harry Southwell	M. F. Garwood	E. Finn	
Horizontal Lieutenant	MGM	1962	Richard Thorpe	George Wells	G. Cotler (Bottletop Affair)	
Hornet's Nest	*Vitagraph	1919	James Young	James Dayton	W. Woodrow	
Horrible Hyde	*Lubin	1915	Howell Hansel?	E. W. Sargent	R. L. Stevenson (Strange Case of Dr. Jekyll and Mr. Hyde)	
Horror of Dracula	Hammer	1957	Terence Fisher	Jimmy Sangster	B. Stoker (Dracula)	
Dracula						
Horror of Frankenstein	Hammer	1970	Jimmy Sangster	Jimmy Sangster Jeremy Burnham	M. Shelley (Frankenstein)	
Hostage	Heartland	1966	R. S. Doughten, Jr.	Robert Laning	C. Henry	
Hostage	Pinnacle	1992	Robert Young	Arthur Hopcraft	T. Allbeury (No Place to Hide)	
Hostages	Paramount	1943	Frank Tuttle	Lester Cole Frank Butler	S. Heym	
Hostile Takeover	S.C.Enter.	1988	George Mihalka	Stephen Zoller Michael A. Gilbert	Michael A. Gilbert (Office Party)	
Office Party						
Hostile Witness	Caralan	1968	Ray Milland	Jack Roffey	J. Roffey	
Hot Enough for June	Rank	1963	Ralph Thomas	Lukas Heller	L. Davidson (Night of Wenceslas)	
Agent 8 3/4						
Hot Ice	Pres. Day	1952	Kenneth Hume	Kenneth Hume	A. Melville (Week-End at Thrackley)	
Hot Rock	TCF	1972	Peter Yates	William Goldman	D. E. Westlake	John Dortmunder (Robert Redford)
How to Steal a Diamond in Four Uneasy Lessons						
Hot Rod Rumble	Nacirema	1957	Leslie H. Martinson	Meyer Dolinsky	novel: M. Dolinsky (Hot Rod Gang Rumble)	
Hot Spot	TCF	1941	H. B. Humberstone	Dwight Taylor	S. Fisher (I Wake Up Screaming)	
I Wake Up Screaming						
Hot Spot	Orion	1990	Dennis Hopper	Nona Tyson Charles Williams	Charles Williams (Hell Hath No Fury)	
Hotel Berlin	Warner	1945	Peter Godfrey Jack Gage	Jo Pagano Alvah Bessie	V. Baum (Hotel Berlin '43)	
Hotel Reserve	RKO	1944	Victor Hanbury Lance Comfort Max Greene	John Davenport	E. Ambler (Epitaph for a Spy)	
Hound of Blackwood Castle	Rialto	1968	Alfred Vohrer	Alex Berg	E. Wallace (headnote)	
Hound of the Baskervilles	*Vitaskop	1914	Rudolf Meinert	Richard Oswald	A. C. Doyle	Sherlock Holmes (Alwin Neuss)
Hound of the Baskervilles	*Stoll	1921	Maurice Elvey	William J. Elliott Dorothy Westlake	A. C. Doyle	Sherlock Holmes (Eille Norwood)
Hound of the Baskervilles	*Erda-Film	1929	Richard Oswald	Herbert Juttke G. C. Klaren	A. C. Doyle	Sherlock Holmes (Carlyle Blackwell)
Hound of the Baskervilles	Gaumont	1931	V. Gareth Gundrey	Edgar Wallace V. Gareth Gundrey	A. C. Doyle	Sherlock Holmes (Robert Rendel)
Hound of the Baskervilles	Ondra-Lamac	1937	Karl Lamac	C. von Stackelberg	A. C. Doyle	Sherlock Holmes (Bruno Guttner)
Hound of the Baskervilles	TCF	1939	Sidney Lanfield	Ernest Pascal	A. C. Doyle	Sherlock Holmes (Basil Rathbone)
Hound of the Baskervilles	Hammer	1959	Terence Fisher	Peter Bryan	A. C. Doyle	Sherlock Holmes (Peter Cushing)
Hound of the Baskervilles	Hemdale	1978	Paul Morrissey	Peter Cook Dudley Moore Paul Morrissey	A. C. Doyle	Sherlock Holmes (Peter Cook)
Hound of the Baskervilles	Mapleton	1983	Douglas Hickox	Charles Pogue	A. C. Doyle	Sherlock Holmes (Ian Richardson)

Title	Studio	Year	Director	Writer	Source/Notes	Cast
Hounds of Zaroff / Most Dangerous Game	RKO	1932	E. B. Schroedsack Irving Pichel	James A. Creelman	R. Connell (Variety)	
Hour Before the Dawn	Paramount	1944	Frank Tuttle	Michael Hogan Lesser Samuels	W. S. Maugham	
Hour of Glory / Small Back Room	Lond. Films	1949	Emeric Pressburger Michael Powell	Emeric Pressburger Michael Powell	N. Balchin	
Hour of Thirteen	MGM	1952	Harold French	Leon Gordon Howard Emmett Rogers	M. Porlock (X v. Rex)	
Hour of Thirteen	Hammer	1954	Ken Hughes	Ken Hughes	K. Hughes (High Wray)	
House Across the Lake / Heatwave						
House by the River	Fidelity	1950	Fritz Lang	Mel Dinelli	A. P. Herbert	
House in Marsh Road	Eternal	1960	Montgomery Tully	Maurice J. Wilson	L. Meynell	
House of a Thousand Candles	*Selig	1915	T. N. Heffron	Gilson Willets	M. Nicholson	
House of a Thousand Candles	Republic	1936	Arthur Lubin	H. W. Hanemann Endre Boehm	M. Nicholson	
House of Cards	Universal	1969	John Guillermin	Irving Ravetch Harriet Frank, Jr.	S. Ellin	
House of Dark Shadows / Dark Shadows	MGM	1970	Dan Curtis	Sam Hall Gordon Russell	novel: Marilyn Ross	Barnabas Collins (Jonathan Frid)
House of Fate / Muss 'Em Up	RKO	1936	Charles Vidor	Erwin Gelsey	J. E. Grant (Green Shadow)	
House of Fear	Universal	1928	Paul Leni	Alfred A. Cohn Tom Reed	W. Camp	
House of Fear	Universal	1939	Joe May	Peter Milne	W. Camp	
House of Fear	Universal	1945	Roy William Neill	Roy Chanslor	A. C. Doyle (Adventures of Sherlock Holmes)	Sherlock Holmes (Basil Rathbone)
House of Fright / Jekyll's Inferno / Two Faces of Dr. Jekyll	Hammer	1960	Terence Fisher	Wolf Mankowitz	R. L. Stevenson (Strange Case of Dr. Jekyll and Mr. Hyde)	
House of Games	Orion	1987	David Mamet	David Mamet	screenplay: D. Mamet	
House of Glass	*Select	1918	Emile Chautard	Charles E. Wittaker	M. Marcin	
House of Intrigue	AA	1959	Duilio Coletti	Duilio Coletti Ennio De Concini Giuseppi Scoponi Massimo Mida	H. J. Giskes (London Calling North Pole)	
House of Long Shadows	Cannon	1982	Peter Walker	Michael Armstrong	E. D. Biggers (Seven Keys to Baldpate)	
House of Marney	*Nettlefold	1926	Cecil M. Hepworth	Harry Hughes	J. Goodwin	
House of Menace / Kind Lady	MGM	1935	George B. Seitz	Bernard Schubert	E. Chodorov (Kind Lady)	
House of Mystery / At the Villa Rose	ABPC	1939	Walter Summers	Doreen Montgomery	A. E. W. Mason (At the Villa Rose)	Insp. Hanaud (Kenneth Kent)
House of Numbers	MGM	1957	Russell Rouse	Russell Rouse Don M. Mankiewicz	J. Finney	
House of Peril	Astra	1922	Kenelm Foss	Kenelm Foss Adeline Leitzbach	M. B. Lowndes (Chink in the Armour)	
House of Secrets	Chester.	1929	Edmund Lawrence	Sidney Hall	S. Horler	
House of Secrets	Chester.	1937	Roland D. Reed	John W. Krafft Robert Buckner	S. Horler	
House of Secrets / Triple Deception	Rank	1956	Guy Green	Bryan Forbes	S. Noel	
House of Silence	*Paramount	1918	Donald Crisp	Margaret Turnbull	E. Barron (Marcel Levignet)	
House of Strangers	TCF	1949	Joseph L. Mankiewicz	Philip Yordan	J. Weidman (I'll Never Go There Any More)	
House of the Arrow	Twickenham	1930	Leslie Hiscott	Cyril Twyford	A. E. W. Mason	Insp. Hanaud (Dennis Neilson-Terry)
House of the Arrow / Castle of Crimes	ABPC	1940	Harold French	Doreen Montgomery	A. E. W. Mason	Insp. Hanaud (Kenneth Kent)
House of the Arrow	ABPC	1953	Michael Anderson	Edward Dryhurst	A. E. W. Mason	Insp. Hanaud (Oscar Homolka)
House of the Lost Court	*Edison	1915	Charles Brabin	?	M. D'Alpins	
House of the Seven Hawks	Coronada	1959	Richard Thorpe	Jo Eisinger	V. Canning (House of the Seven Flies)	

H

FILM TITLE	STUDIO	YEAR	DIRECTOR	SCREENWRITER	SOURCE AUTHOR/WORK	SERIES
House of the Spaniard	IPF	1936	Reginald Denham	Basil Mason	A. Behrend	
House of Whispers	*Hankinson	1920	Ernest C. Warde	Jack Cunningham	W. Johnston	
House on Carroll Street	Orion	1987	Peter Yates	Walter Bernstein	novel: Mollie Gregory	
House on 92nd Street	TCF	1945	Henry Hathaway	Barre Lyndon / Charles G. Booth / John Monks, Jr.	novel: Alex Morrison	
House on Telegraph Hill	TCF	1951	Robert Wise	Elick Moll / Frank Partos	D. Lyon (Frightened Child)	
House on the Marsh	*London	1920	Fred Paul	?	F. Warden	
House Opposite	BIP	1931	Walter Summers	Walter Summers	J. J. Farjeon	
House Without a Key	*Pathe	1926	Spencer G. Bennett	Frank Leon Smith	E. D. Biggers	Ben (Frank Stanmore) / Charlie Chan (George Kuwa)
Housekeeper / Judgement in Stone	Rawifilm	1986	Ousama Rawi	Elaine Waisglass	R. Rendell (Judgement in Stone)	
Housekeeper's Daughter	UA	1939	Hal Roach	Rian James / Gordon Douglas	D. H. Clarke	
How Sir Andrew Lost His Vote	*Edison	1911	?	?	R. H. Davis (In the Fog)	
How the Hungry Man Was Fed	*Edison	1911	?	?	R. H. Davis (Van Bibber and others)	
How to Murder Your Wife	UA	1964	Richard Quine	George Axelrod	novel: H. Williams	
How to Steal a Diamond in Four Uneasy Lessons / Hot Rock	TCF	1972	Peter Yates	William Goldman	D. E. Westlake (Hot Rock)	John Dortmunder (Robert Redford)
How to Steal a Million	TCF	1966	William Wyler	Harry Kurnitz	novel: M. Sinclair	
How Women Love	*B.B. Prod.	1922	Kenneth Webb	Dorothy Farnum / George Farnum	I. L. Forrester (Dangerous Inheritance)	
Howling	AVCO	1980	Joe Dante	John Sayles / Terence H. Winkless	G. Brandner	
Howling II	Thorn EMI	1985	Philippe Mora	Robert Sarns / Gary Brandner	G. Brandner	
Howling 5: The Rebirth	Allied Vis.	1989	Neal Sundstrom	Clive Turner / Freddie Rowe	G. Brandner	
Human Cargo	TCF	1936	Allan Dwan	Jefferson Parker / Doris Malloy	K. Shepard (I Will Be Faithful)	
Human Factor	Bryanston	1975	Edward Dmytryk	Tom Hunter / Peter Powell	novel: S. Quinn	
Human Factor	Rank	1979	Otto Preminger	Tom Stoppard	G. Greene	
Human Monster / Dark Eyes of London	Argyle	1939	Walter Summers	Patrick Kirwan / Walter Summers	E. Wallace (Dark Eyes of London)	
Hunt for Red October	Paramount	1990	John McTiernan	John F. Argyle / Larry Ferguson	T. Clancy	Jack Ryan (Alec Baldwin)
Hunted Woman	*Vitagraph	1916	S. Rankin Drew	?	J. O. Curwood	
Hunted Woman	*Fox	1925	Jack Conway	Robert N. Lee	J. O. Curwood	
Hunting Party	UA	1971	Don Medford	William Norton / Gilbert Alexander / Lou Morheim	novel: J. Millard	
Huntingtower	*Welsh	1927	George Pearson	C. E. Whittaker	J. Buchan	Duncan McCunn (Harry Lauder)
Huntress	Ass. First	1923	Lynn Reynolds	Percy Heath	H. Footner	
Hustle	Paramount	1975	Robert Aldrich	Steve Shagan	S. Shagan (City of Angels)	
Hutch Stirs 'Em Up	*Ideal	1923	Frank H. Crane	Eliot Stannard	H. Harding (Hawk of Rede)	
Hyenas	Thelma	1992	Djibril D. Mambety	Djibril D. Mambety	F. Duerrenmatt (Visit)	
I Became a Criminal / They Made Me a Criminal / They Made Me a Fugitive	Gloria	1947	Alberto Cavalcanti	Noel Langley	J. Budd (Convict Has Escaped)	

Film Index					IN THE GRIP OF THE SINISTER ONE / 1411
I Cover the Waterfront		UA	1933	James Cruze	Wells Root / Jack Jevne / Max Miller	Max Miller
I Died a Thousand Times		Warner	1955	Stuart Heisler	W. R. Burnett	W. R. Burnett (High Sierra)
I Hate Actors		Septembre	1986	Gerard Krawozyk	Gerard Krawozyk	B. Hecht
I Killed the Count		Grafon	1939	Fred Zelnik	Laurence Huntington / Alec Coppel	A. Coppel
Who Is Guilty?						
I Love Trouble		Columbia	1947	S. Sylvan Simon	Roy Huggins	R. Huggins (Double Take)	Stuart Bailey (Franchot Tone)
I Love You Again		MGM	1940	W. S. Van Dyke II	Charles Lederer / George Oppenheimer / Harry Kurnitz	O. R. Cohen
I Married a Dead Man		Sara	1983	Robin Davis	Davis Laurent / Patrick Laurent	W. Irish
I, Monster		Amicus	1970	Stephen Weeks	Milton Subotsky	R. L. Stevenson (Strange Case of Dr. Jekyll and Mr. Hyde)
I Promised to Pay		Lynx	1961	Sidney Hayers	George Baxt	D. Bickerton (Payroll)
Payroll						
I Ring Doorbells		PRC	1946	Frank Strayer	Dick Irving Hyland / Raymond L. Shrock	R. Birdwell
I Saw What You Did		Universal	1965	William Castle	William McGivern	U. Curtiss (Out of the Dark)
I Start Counting		Triumverate	1969	David Greene	Richard Harris	A. E. Lindop
I Thank a Fool		MGM	1962	Robert Stevens	Karl Tunberg	A. E. Lindop
I, the Jury		UA	1953	Harry Essex	Harry Essex	M. Spillane	Mike Hammer (Biff Elliott)
I, the Jury		Am. Cinema	1982	Richard T. Heffron	Larry Cohen	M. Spillane	Mike Hammer (Armand Assante)
I Wake Up Screaming		TCF	1941	H. B. Humberstone	Dwight Taylor	S. Fisher
Hot Spot						
I Walk the Line		Columbia	1970	John Frankenheimer	Alvin Sargent	Madison Jones (Exile)
I Want to Live!		UA	1958	Robert Wise	Nelson Gilling / Don Mankiewicz	novel: T. Rawson
I Was an American Spy		Monogram	1951	Lesley Selander	Sam Roeca	Claire Phillips (Manila Espionage)
I Wouldn't Be in Your Shoes		Monogram	1948	William Nigh	Steve Fisher	W. Irish
Ice-Cold in Alex		ABPC	1958	J. Lee Thompson	J. Lee Thompson / Christopher Landon / T. J. Morrison	C. Landon
Desert Attack						
Ice Station Zebra		MGM	1968	John Sturges	Douglas Heyes	A. MacLean
Icy Breasts		Fox-Lira	1974	Georges Lautner	Georges Lautner / George Callahan	R. Matheson (Someone Is Bleeding)
I'll Get You for This		Kaydor	1951	Joseph M. Newman	William Rose	J. H. Chase
Lucky Nick Cain						
Illustrious Corpses		PEA	1975	Francesco Rosi	Francesco Rosi / Tonino Guerra / Lino Jannuzzi	L. Sciascia (Equal Danger)
Illustrious Prince		*Hawarth	1919	William Worthington	?	E. P. Oppenheim
I'm King of the Castle		Odessa	1989	Regis Wargnier	Regis Wargnier / Alain Le Henry	S. Hill
In a Lonely Place		Columbia	1950	Nicholas Ray	Andrew Solt	D. B. Hughes
In Case of Emergency		Columbia	1958	Claude Autant-Lara	Jean Aurenche / Pierre Bost	G. Simenon
Love Is My Profession						
In Cold Blood		Columbia	1967	Richard Brooks	Richard Brooks	T. Capote
In Defance of the Law		*Selig	1914	Colin Campbell	Colin Campbell	J. O. Curwood (Isobel)
In Full Cry		*Broadwest	1921	Einer J. Bruun	Benedict James / Frank Fowell	R. Marsh
In His Grip		*Gaumont	1921	C. C. Calvert	Paul Rooff	D. C. Murray
In Like Flint		TCF	1967	Gordon Douglas	Hal Fimberg	novel: B. Street
In the Balance		*Vitagraph	1917	Paul Scardon	Garfield Thompson	E. P. Oppenheim (Hillman)
In the Bishop's Carriage		*Fam. Play.	1915	Edwin S. Porter / J. Searle Dawley	Ben Schulberg	M. Michelson
In the Blood		*West	1923	Walter West	J. Bertram Brown	A. Soutar
In the Grip of the Sinister One		Rialto	1968	Alfred Vohrer	Ladislas Fodor	E. Wallace (headnote)

I

I

FILM TITLE	STUDIO	YEAR	DIRECTOR	SCREENWRITER	SOURCE AUTHOR/WORK	SERIES
In the Hands of the Spoilers	*Barker	1916	Leon Bary	?	S. Paternoster (Hand of the Spoiler)	
In the Heat of the Night	UA	1967	Norman Jewison	Stirling Silliphant	J. Ball	Virgil Tibbs (Sidney Poitier)
In the Hollow of Her Hand	*Select	1919	Charles Maigne	Charles Maigne	G. B. McCutcheon (Hollow of Her Hand)	
In the Next Room	First Nat.	1930	Edward Cline	James A. Starr, Harvey Gates	E. R. Belmont, and B. E. Stevenson (Mystery of the Boule Cabinet)	
In the Night	*Granger	1920	F. A. Richardson	Frank Fowell	J. Sutherland	
In the Wake of a Stranger	Crest	1959	David Eady	John Tully	I. S. Black	
Incense for the Damned	Grafton	1970	Michael Burrowes	Julian More	S. Raven (Doctors Wear Scarlet)	
Bloodsuckers						
Doctors Wear Scarlet						
Incident	MGM	1968	Larry Pearce	Nicholas E. Baehr	novel: M. Avallone	
Incident at Midnight	Merton Park	1963	Norman Harrison	Arthur LaBern	E. Wallace (headnote)	
Incomparable Bellairs	*London	1914	Harold Shaw	Bannister Merwin	A. Castle	
Incomparable Mistress						
Incomparable Mistress	*London	1914	Harold Shaw	Bannister Merwin	A. Castle (Incomparable Bellairs)	
Incomparable Bellairs						
Incubus	Film Vent.	1982	John Hough	George Franklin	Ray Russell	
Indiana Jones and the Last Crusade	Lucasfilm	1989	Steven Spielberg	Jeffrey Boam	novel: Rob McGregor	
Informer	BIP	1929	Arthur Robison	Benn W. Levy, Rolfe E. Vanlo	L. O'Flaherty	
Informer	RKO	1935	John Ford	Dudley Nichols	L. O'Flaherty	
Informers	Rank	1963	Ken Annakin	Alun Falconer, Paul Durst	D. Warner (Death of a Snout)	
Snout						
Underworld Informers						
Inheritance	Two Cities	1947	Charles Frank	Ben Travers	J. S. Le Fanu (Uncle Silas)	
Uncle Silas						
Innocent Bystanders	Sagitarius	1972	Peter Collinson	James Mitchell	J. Munro	John Craig (Stanley Baker)
Innocent Victim	Greenpoint	1989	Giles Foster	Gordon Williams	R. Rendell (Tree of Hands)	
Tree of Hands						
Innocents	Achilles	1960	Jack Clayton	William Archibald, Truman Capote, John Mortimer	H. James (Turn of the Screw)	
Innocents with Dirty Hands	Films Boet.	1975	Claude Chabrol	Claude Chabrol	R. Neely (Damned Innocents)	
Dirty Hands						
Inquest	Majestic	1931	G. B. Samuelson	Michael Barringer	M. Barringer	
Inquest	Charter	1939	Roy Boulting	Francis Miller	M. Barringer	
Inquisitor	Ariane	1981	Claude Miller	Claude Miller, Jean Herman, Michel Audiard	J. Wainwright (Brainwash)	
Grilling						
Inside Out	Warner	1975	Peter Duffell	Judd Bernard, Stephen Schneck	novel: W. Hughes	
Golden Heist						
Hitler's Gold						
Inside the Lines	*World	1918	David M. Hartford	Monte M. Katterjohn, Eward Adamson	E. D. Biggers	
Inside the Lines	RKO	1930	Roy J. Pomeroy	John Farrow	E. D. Biggers	
Inspector	Red Lion	1961	Phillip Dunne	Nelson Gidding	J. De Hartog	
Lisa						
Inspector Calls	Watergate	1954	Guy Hamilton	Desmond Davis, Frank Launder	J. B. Priestley	
Inspector Hornleigh on Holiday	20th Cent.	1939	Walter Forde	Sidney Gilliat	L. Grex (Stolen Death)	Insp. Hornleigh (Gordon Harker)
Inspector Maigret	Intermondia	1957	Jean Delannoy	R. M. Arlaud, Michel Audiard, Jean Delannoy	G. Simenon (Maigret Sets a Trap)	Insp. Maigret (Jean Gabin)
Maigret Sets a Trap						
Intent to Kill	Zonic	1958	Jack Cardiff	Jimmy Sangster	M. Bryan	

I

Title	Studio	Year	Director	Writer	Source	Notes
Interference	Paramount	1928	Roy J. Pomeroy	Hope Loring / Ernest Pascal	R. Pertwee	
Interlude	Universal	1957	Lothar Mendes	Daniel Fuchs / Franklin Coen / Inez Cocke	J. M. Cain (Serenade)	
Interlude	Columbia	1968	Douglas Sirk	Lee Langley / Hugh Leonard	J. M. Cain (Serenade)	
International Police / Interpol / Pickup Alley	Warwick	1957	John Gilling	John Paxton	novel: E. Ronns (Pickup Alley)	
Interpol / International Police / Pickup Alley	Warwick	1957	John Gilling	John Paxton	novel: E. Ronns (Pickup Alley)	
Intruder	Foxwell	1953	Guy Hamilton	Robin Maugham / John Hunter / Anthony Squire	R. Maugham (Line on Ginger)	
Intruder in the Dust	MGM	1949	Clarence Brown	Ben Maddow	W. Faulkner	Gavin Stevens (David Brian)
Invasion U.S.A.	Cannon	1985	Joseph Zito	James Bruner / Chuck Norris	novel: J. Frost	
Investigation of Murder / Laughing Policeman	TCF	1973	Stuart Rosenberg	Thomas Rickman	M. Sjowall (Laughing Policeman)	
Invincible Six	Paramount	1968	Jean Negulesco	Francesco De Feo / Francesco Thellung / Cleto Fontini	M. Barrett (Heroes of Yuca)	
Invisible Man	Universal	1933	James Whale	R. C. Sherriff	H. G. Wells	
Invisible Man	Calderon	1958	Alfredo Crevenna	Alfredo Salazar / Julio Alejandro	H. G. Wells	
Invisible Man's Revenge	Universal	1944	Ford Beebe	Bertram Millhauser	H. G. Wells (Invisible Man)	
Ipcress File	Lowndes	1964	Sidney J. Furie	Bill Canaway / James Doran	L. Deighton	Harry Palmer (Michael Caine)
Irish Luck	*Fam. Play	1925	Victor Heerman	Tom J. Geraghty / Alfred Hayes	N. Venner (Imperfect Imposter)	
Island in the Sun	TCF	1957	Robert Rossen	June Mathis	A. Waugh	
Island of Intrigue	*Metro	1910	Henry Otto	A. S. Le Vino	I. Ostrander	
Island Rescue / Appointment with Venus	Brit. Film	1951	Ralph Thomas	Nicholas Phipps	J. Tickell (Appointment with Venus)	
Isobel	*Davis	1920	Edwin Carewe	Edwin Carewe / Angus MacPhail	J. O. Curwood	
It Always Rains on Sunday	Ealing	1947	Robert Hamer	Robert Hamer / Henry Cornelius	A. La Bern	
It Comes Up Murder / Anyone for Venice? / Honey Pot / Mr. Fox of Venice	UA	1966	J. L. Mankiewicz	J. L. Mankiewicz	T. Sterling (Evil of the Day)	
It Happened in Broad Daylight	Praesens	1958	Ladislav Vajda	F. Duerrenmatt / Hans Jacoby / Ladislav Vajda	F. Duerrenmatt (Pledge)	
It Is Never Too Late to Mend	*Tait	1911	W. J. Lincoln	W. J. Lincoln	C. Reade	
It Is Never Too Late to Mend	*Edison	1913	Charles M. Seay	Charles M. Seay	C. Reade	
It Is Never Too Late to Mend	*Martin's Imperia	1917	Dave Aylott	Dave Aylott	C. Reade	
It Only Happens to the Living		1959	Tony Saytor	Pierre Larey / Jean Cosmos	R. Marshall (Things Men Do)	
It Shouldn't Happen to a Dog	TCF	1946	Herbert I. Leeds	Eugene Ling / Frank Gabrielson	E. Lanham	
It Started in Tokyo / Twenty Plus Two	AA	1961	Joseph M. Newman	Frank Gruber	F. Gruber (Twenty Plus Two)	
Italian Job	Oakhurst	1969	Peter Collinson	Troy Kennedy Martin	novel: T. K. Martin	
It's Alive	Larco	1977	Larry Cohen	Larry Cohen	novel: R. Woodley	

I

FILM TITLE	STUDIO	YEAR	DIRECTOR	SCREENWRITER	SOURCE AUTHOR/WORK	SERIES
It's Freezing in Hell	Koala	1990	Jean-Pierre Mocky	Jean-Pierre Mocky Andre Ruellan	E. Chaze (Black Wings Has My Angel)	
It's in the Blood	WB-FN	1938	Gene Gerrard	Reginald Purdell John Dighton J. O. C. Orton Brock Williams Basil Dillon	D. Whitelaw (Big Picture)	
Ivory Snuff Box	*World	1915	Maurice Tourneur	E. M. Ingleton	A. Fredericks	
Ivy	Universal	1947	Sam Wood	Charles Bennett	M. B. Lowndes (Story of Ivy)	
Jack Chanty	*Alliance	1915	Max Figman	Elliott Clawson	H. Footner	
Jack Sheppard	*London Film	1912	Percy Nash	?	J. B. Buckstone	
Jack Sheppard	*Broadoak	1923	Henry C. Taylor	?	W. H. Ainsworth	
Jack the Ripper	Mid Century	1958	Robert S. Baker	Jimmy Sangster	novel: S. James	
Jamaica Inn	Mayflower	1939	Alfred Hitchcock	Sidney Gilliat Joan Harrison J. B. Priestley Alma Reville	D. Du Maurier	
Jamaica Run	Paramount	1953	Lewis R. Foster	Lewis R. Foster	M. Murray (Neat Little Corpse)	
Janitor	TCF	1981	Peter Yates	Steve Tesich	novel: J. Minahan (Eyewitness)	
Eyewitness						
Jassy	Gen. Film	1947	Bernard Knowles	Dorothy Christie Campbell Christie Geoffrey Kerr	N. Lofts	
Jealousy	Paramount	1929	Jean De Limur	Garrett Fort Eugene Walter	E. Walter	
Jeanne of the Marshes	*Fam. Play.	1921	Frank Reicher	John D. Williams	E. P. Oppenheim	
Behind Masks						
Jekyll and Hyde... Together Again	Paramount	1982	Jerry Belson	Monica Johnson Harvey Miller Jerry Belson Michael Leeson	R. L. Stevenson (Strange Case of Dr. Jekyll and Mr. Hyde)	
Jekyll's Inferno	Hammer	1960	Terence Fisher	Wolf Mankowitz	R. L. Stevenson (Strange Case of Dr. Jekyll and Mr. Hyde)	
House of Fright						
Two Faces of Dr. Jekyll						
Jennifer Hale	TCF	1937	Bernard Mainwaring	Ralph Stock Bernard Mainwaring	R. Eden	
Jewel	Venture	1933	Reginald Denham	Basil Mason	E. Wallace (headnote)	
Jewel of the Nile	TCF	1985	Lewis Teague	Mark Rosenthal	novel: C. Lanigan	
Jewel Robbery	Warner	1932	William Dieterle	Erwin Gelsey	L. Fodor	
Jigsaw	Figaro	1962	Val Guest	Val Guest	H. Waugh (Sleep Long, My Love)	
Jigsaw	Universal	1968	James Goldstone	Quentin Werty	W. Ericson (Fallen Angel)	
Jigsaw Man	Fisz	1984	Terence Young	Jo Eisinger	Dorothea Bennett	
Jim Hanvey, Detective	Republic	1937	Phil Rosen	Joseph Krumgold Olive Cooper	O. R. Cohen	Jim Hanvey (Guy Kibbee)
Jim the Penman	*Fam. Play.	1915	Hugh Ford	Hugh Ford	C. L. Young	
Jim the Penman	*First Nat.	1921	Kenneth Webb	Dorothy Farnum	C. L. Young	
Jimmy Dale, Alias "The Grey Seal"	*Monmouth	1917	Henry McRae Webster	Mildred Considine	F. Packard (Adventures of Jimmie Dale)	Jimmie Dale (?)
Jimmy the Kid	Zephyr	1982	Gary Nelson	Sam Bobrick	D. E. Westlake	
Jo, the Crossing Sweeper	*Walturdaw	1910	?	?	C. Dickens (Bleak House)	
Jo, the Crossing Sweeper	*Barker	1918	Alexander Butler	Irene Miller	C. Dickens (Bleak House)	
John Heriot's Wife	*Anglo-Holl.	1920	B. E. Doxat-Pratt	B. E. Doxat-Pratt	A. Askew	
John Needham's Double	*Bluebird	1916	Lois Weber Philipps Smalley	Olga Printzlau	J. Hatton	

Fred Fellows (Jack Warner)

K

Title	Studio	Year	Director	Writer	Source
Johnny Angel	RKO	1945	Edwin L. Marin	Steve Fisher	C. G. Booth (Mr. Angel Comes Abroad)
Johnny Cool	UA	1963	William Asher	Frank Gruber	J. McPartland (Kingdom of Johnny Cool)
Johnny Handsome	Tri-Star	1989	Walter Hill	Joseph Landon	J. Godey (Three Worlds of Johnny Handsome)
Johnny on the Spot	Fancey	1954	Maclean Rogers	Ken Friedman	M. Cronin (Paid in Full)
Jokers	Universal	1967	Michael Winner	Maclean Rogers	
				Dick Clement	
				Ian La Frenais	
Jolly Bad Fellow	Tower	1964	Don Chaffey	Robert Hamer	C. E. Vulliamy (Don Among the Dead Men)
They All Died Laughing				Donald Taylor	
Jonathan	Iduna	1973	H. W. Giessendorfer	H. W. Giessendorfer	B. Stoker (Dracula)
Journey Into Fear	RKO	1943	Norman Foster	Orson Welles	E. Ambler
				Joseph Cotten	
Journey Into Fear	New World	1975	Daniel Mann	Trevor Wallace	E. Ambler
Burn Out					
Joy House	MGM	1964	Rene Clement	Pascal Jardin	D. Keene
Love Cage				Charles Williams	
				Rene Clement	
Joyless Street	*Sofar	1925	G. L. Pabst	Willy Haas	H. Bettaur (Viennese Love)
Joyous Adventures of Aristide Pujol	*Foss	1920	Frank Miller	Frank Miller	W. J. Locke
Judge Priest	TCF	1934	John Ford	Dudley Nichols	I. S. Cobb (Down Yonder with Judge Priest)
				Lamar Trotti	
Judgement in Stone	Rawifilm	1986	Ousama Rawi	Elaine Waisglass	R. Rendell
Housekeeper					
Juggernaut	JH Prod.	1936	Henry Edwards	Cyril Campion	A. Campbell
				H. Fowler Mear	
				Henrich Fraenkel	
Juggernaut	UA	1974	Richard Lester	Richard DeKoker	novel: A. Hine
				Alan Plater	
Julie	MGM	1956	Andrew L. Stone	Andrew L. Stone	A. L. Stone
July Pork Bellies	Rastar	1974	Peter Yates	Stanley Shapiro	novel: B. Street
For Pete's Sake				Maurice Richlin	
Jump for Glory	Criterion	1937	Raoul Walsh	John Meehan, Jr.	G. McDonell
When Thief Meets Thief				Harold French	
Just Ask for Diamond	Coverstop	1988	Stephen Bayly	Anthony Horowitz	A. Horowitz (Falcon's Malteser)
Just Before Nightfall	Films/Boet.	1971	Claude Chabrol	Claude Chabrol	E. Atiyah (Thin Line)
Justice	*Ideal	1917	Maurice Elvey	Eliot Stannard	J. Galsworthy
Juve Contre Fantomas	*Gaumont	1914	?	?	P. Souvestre (Exploits of Juve)
Juvenile Jungle	Coronado	1958	William Witney	Arthur T. Horman	novel: F. Counsel
Kaleidoscope	Warner	1966	Jack Smight	Robert Carrington	novel: M. Avallone
Bank Breaker				J.-H. Carrington	
Kamikaze '89	Ziegler	1982	Wolf Gremm	Robert Katz	P. Wahloo (Murder on the Thirty-First Floor)
				Wolf Gremm	
Kate Plus Ten	Wainwright	1938	Reginald Denham	Jack Hulbert	E. Wallace
				Jeffrey Dell	
Kazan	*Selig	1921	Berttram Bracken	Berttram Bracken	J. O. Curwood
Kazan	Columbia	1949	Will Jason	Arthur A. Ross	J. O. Curwood
Keane of Kalgoorlie	*Crick	1911	John Gavin	Agnes Gavin	Arthur Wright
Keep	Paramount	1983	Michael Mann	Michael Mann	F. P. Wilson
Keep Talking, Baby	UFA-Coma.	1961	Guy Le Frane	Roger Boussinot	D. Keene (Strange Witness)
				Yvon Samuel	
				Guy Le Frane	
Kennel Murder Case	Warner	1933	Michael Curtiz	Robert N. Lee	S. S. Van Dine
				Peter Milne	
				Robert Presnell	
Kensington Mystery	*Stoll	1924	Hugh Croise	Hugh Croise	B. Orczy (Old Man in the Corner)
Key Largo	Warner	1948	John Huston	Richard Brooks	M. Anderson
				John Huston	

Judge Priest
(Will Rogers)

Fantomas
(?)

Peter Jensen
(R. Werner Fassbinder)

Philo Vance
(William Powell)

Old Man
(Rolf Leslie)

1416 / KEY TO YESTERDAY — Film Index

FILM TITLE	STUDIO	YEAR	DIRECTOR	SCREENWRITER	SOURCE AUTHOR/WORK	SERIES
Key to Yesterday	*Fam. Play.	1914	Robert A. Dillon	Alfred Brenner	C. N. Buck	
Key Witness	MGM	1960	Phil Karlson	Sidney Michaels	F. Kane	
Kick-In	*Astra	1917	George Fitzmaurice	Ouida Bergere	W. Mack	
Kick-In	*Fam. Play.	1923	George Fitzmaurice	Ouida Bergere	W. Mack	
Kick-In	Paramount	1931	Richard Wallace	Bartlett Cormack	W. Mack	
Kid from Roaring Camp	*Champion	1911	?	?	Bret Harte (Bret Harte's Choice Bits)	
Kid Galahad	Warner	1937	Michael Curtiz	Seton I. Miller	Francis Wallace	
Bartling Bellhop						
Kid Galahad	Mirisch	1962	Phil Karlson	William Fay	Francis Wallace	
Kidnapping of the President	Sefel	1980	George Mendeluk	Richard Murphy	C. Templeton	
Kill-Off	Filmworld	1990	Maggie Greenwald	Maggie Greenwald	Jim Thompson	
Kill the Referee	Lira Eleph.	1984	Jean-Pierre Mocky	Jean-Pierre Mocky	A. Draper (Death Penalty)	
Killer	CFDC	1969	Claude Chabrol	Jacques Dreux	Nicholas Blake (Beast Must Die)	
Let the Beast Die				Paul Gegauff		
				Claude Chabrol		
Killer Elite	UA	1975	Sam Peckinpah	Marc Norman	R. Rostand	
				Stirling Silliphant		
Killer Inside Me	Warner	1976	Burt Kennedy	Edward Mann	J. Thompson	
				Robert Chamblee		
Killer of Killers	UA	1972	Michael Winner	Lewis John Carlino	novel: L. J. Carlino (Mechanic)	
Mechanic						
Killer Walks	Leontine	1952	Ronald Drake	Ronald Drake	G. Glennon (Gathering Storm)	
Killers	Universal	1946	Robert Siodmak	Anthony Veiller	E. Hemingway	
				John Huston		
Killers	Universal	1964	Don Siegel	Gene L. Coon	E. Hemingway	
Killing	UA	1956	Stanley Kubrick	Stanley Kubrick	L. White (Clean Break)	
				Jim Thompson		
Killing Affair	Hemdale	1988	David Saperstein	David Saperstein	R. Houston (Monday, Tuesday, Wednesday)	
Killing Dad	Scot. TV	1969	Michael Austin	Michael Austin	A. Quin (Berg)	
Kind Hearts and Coronets	Ealing	1949	Robert Hamer	Robert Hamer	R. Horniman (Israel Rank)	
				John Dighton		
Kind Lady	MGM	1935	George B. Seitz	Bernard Schubert	E. Chodorov	
House of Menace						
Kind Lady	MGM	1951	John Sturgis	Jerry Davis	E. Chodorov	
				Edward Chodorov		
				Charles Bennett		
King Murder	Chester.	1932	Richard Thorpe	Charles Reed Jones	C. R. Jones	King (Tyrone Power)
King of the Khyber Rifles	TCF	1954	Henry King	Ivan Goff	T. Mundy	
				Ben Roberts		
Kiss Before Dying	UA	1956	Gerd Oswald	Lawrence Roman	I. Levin	
Kiss Before Dying	Universal	1991	James Dearden	James Dearden	I. Levin	
Kiss Me Deadly	UA	1954	Robert Aldrich	A. I. Bezzerides	M. Spillane	Mike Hammer (Ralph Meeker)
Kiss of Death	TCF	1947	Henry Hathaway	Ben Hecht	E. Lipsky	
				Charles Lederer		
Kiss the Blood Off My Hands	Univ. Int.	1949	Norman Foster	Leonardo Bercovici	G. Butler	
Blood on My Hands				Walter Bernstein		
				Hugh Gray		
				Ben Maddow		
Kiss Tomorrow Goodbye	Warner	1950	Gordon Douglas	Harry Brown	H. McCoy	
Kitten with a Whip	Universal	1964	Douglas Heyes	Douglas Heyes	Wade Miller	
Klute	Warner	1971	Alan J. Pakula	Andy Lewis	novel: W. Johnston	
				Dave Lewis		
Knight Without Armor	London	1937	Jacques Feyder	Frances Marion	J. Hilton	
				Lajos Biro		

Knock on Any Door	Columbia	1949	Nicholas Ray	Arthur Wimperis Daniel Taradash John Monks, Jr.	W. Motley
Knocknagow	*Film/Ire.	1918	Fred O'Donovan	N. F. Patton	C. Kickham
Koenigsmark	Capital	1935	Maurice Tourneur	?	P. Benoit (Count Philip)
Kremlin Letter	TCF	1969	John Huston	John Huston Gladys Hill	N. Behn
Kronstadt	*Gaumont	1919	?	Max Pemberton	M. Pemberton
La Bete a L'Affut	?	1959	?	Pierre Chenal Michel Audiard Georges Tabet R. M. Arlaud	D. Keene (Moran's Woman)
La Pupa del Gangster	CCC	1974	Giorgio Capitani	Ernesto Castaldi Anthony Kimmins	W. Irish (Somebody on the Phone)
Laburnam Grove	ATP	1936	Carol Reed	Gordon Wellesley	J. B. Priestley
Labyrinth Reflection of Fear	Columbia	1971	William A. Fraker	Edward Hume Lewis John Carlino	S. Forbes (Go to Thy Death Bed)
Lackey and the Lady	*Brit. Act.	1919	Thomas Bentley	Thomas Bentley	T. Gallon
Lacquered Box	Haik	1932	Jean Kemm	?	A. Christie (Black Coffee)
Lad	Twickenham	1935	Henry Edwards	Gerard Faitie	E. Wallace (headnote)
Ladies Club	Heron Intl.	1986	A. K. Allen	Paul Mason Fran Lewis Ebeling	B. Black (Sisterhood)
Ladies in Retirement	Columbia	1941	Charles Vidor	Garrett Fort Reginald Denham	E. Percy
Ladies' Man	Paramount	1931	Lothar Mendes	Herman Mankiewicz	R. Hughes
Ladies' Man	Cyclops	1960	Jacques Cornu	Maurice Clavel Alain Cavalier Jacques Cornu	P. Quentin (Shadow of Guilt)
Ladies of the Jury	RKO	1932	Lowell Sherman	Marion Dix Salisbury Field John F. Ballard Eddie Welch	F. Ballard
Lady and the Doctor Lady and the Monster Tiger Man	Republic	1944	George Sherman	Dane Lussier Frederick Kohner	C. Siodmak (Donovan's Brain)
Lady and the Monster Lady and the Doctor Tiger Man	Republic	1944	George Sherman	Dane Lussier Frederick Kohner	C. Siodmak (Donovan's Brain)
Lady Audley's Secret	*Walturdaw	1906	?	?	M. E. Braddon
Lady Audley's Secret	*Kalem	1908	?	?	M. E. Braddon
Lady Audley's Secret	*Imp	1912	Otis Turner	Mary Asquith	M. E. Braddon
Lady Audley's Secret	*Fox	1915	Marshall Farnum	Eliot Stannard	M. E. Braddon
Lady Audley's Secret	*Ideal	1920	Jack Denton	Geoffrey H. Malins	M. E. Braddon
Lady Frances Carfax	*Stoll	1923	George Ridgwell	Patrick L. Mannock	A. C. Doyle (His Last Bow)
Lady from Long Acre	*Fox	1921	George E. Marshall	Paul Schofield	V. Bridges
Lady from Shanghai	Columbia	1948	Orson Welles	Orson Welles Alan Trustman	Sherwood King (If I Die Before I Wake)
Lady Ice	Tomorrow	1973	Tom Gries	Harold Clemens	novel: M. Braly (Master)
Lady in a Cage	Paramount	1964	Walter Grauman	Luther Davis	novel: R. Durand
Lady in Cement	TCF	1968	Gordon Douglas	Marvin H. Albert Jack Guss	A. Rome Tony Rome (Frank Sinatra)
Lady in the Car with Glasses and a Gun	Lira	1970	Anatole Litvak	Richard Harris Eleanor Perry	S. Japrisot
Lady in the Lake	MGM	1946	Robert Montgomery	Steve Fisher	R. Chandler Philip Marlowe (Robert Montgomery)
Lady in the Morgue Case of the Missing Blonde Corpse in the Morgue	Universal	1938	Otis Garrett	Raymond Chandler Eric Taylor Robertson White	J. Latimer Bill Crane (Preston Foster)
Lady Letmere's Jewelry	*Gaumont	1908	George R. Sims	?	G. R. Sims (Life We Live)

L

L

FILM TITLE	STUDIO	YEAR	DIRECTOR	SCREENWRITER	SOURCE AUTHOR/WORK	SERIES
Lady Mislaid	Welwyn	1958	David Macdonald	Frederick Gotfurt	K. Horne	
Lady Noggs—Peeress	*Progress	1929	Sidney Morgan	Sidney Morgan	E. Jepson	
Lady of Burlesque	Universal	1943	William Wellman	James Gunn	G. R. Lee (G-String Murders)	
Striptease Lady						
Lady of Death	Cine. Int.	1946	Carlos Christensen	Edmund Beloin	R. L. Stevenson (Suicide Club)	
Lady on a Train	Universal	1945	Charles David	Robert O'Brien	novel: L. Charteris	
Lady, or the Tiger?	*Edison	1908	?	?	F. R. Stockton	
Lady Takes a Flier	Universal	1958	Jack Arnold	Danny Arnold	novel: E. Ronns	
Lady Vanishes	Gaumont	1938	Alfred Hitchcock	Sydney Gilliat Frank Launder Alma Reville	E. L. White (Wheel Spins)	
Lady Vanishes	Hammer	1979	Anthony Page	George Axelrod Frank Launder Sidney Gilliat	E. L. White (Wheel Spins)	
Ladyfingers Alias Ladyfingers	*Metro	1921	Bayard Veiller	Lenore J. Coffee	J. Gregory	
Lair of the White Worm	Vestron	1988	Ken Russell	Ken Russell	B. Stoker	
Lancer Spy	TCF	1937	Gregory Ratoff	Philip Dunne	M. McKenna	
Laramie Trail	Republic	1944	John English	J. Benton Cheney	J. Gregory (Mystery at Spanish Hacienda)	
Larceny	Universal	1948	George Sherman	Herbert F. Margolis Louis Morheim William Bowers	L. Eby (Velvet Fleece)	
Larceny, Inc.	Warner	1942	Lloyd Bacon	Everett Freeman Edwin Gilbert	L. Perelman (Night Before Christmas)	
Last Bow	*Stoll	1923	George Ridgwell	Geoffrey H. Malins Patrick L. Mannock	A. C. Doyle (His Last Bow)	Sherlock Holmes (Eille Norwood)
Last Command	Paramount	1928	Josef von Sternberg	John S. Goodrich	novel: C. Houghton	
Last Embrace	UA	1979	Jonathan Demme	David Shaber	M. T. Bloom (13th Man)	
Last Escape	Oakmont	1970	Walter Grauman	Herman Hoffman	novel: M. Walker	
Last Express	Universal	1938	Otis Garrett	Edmund L. Hartmann	B. Kendrick	Duncan Maclain (Kent Taylor)
Last Grenade	Cinerama	1970	Gordon Flemyng	Kenneth Ware James Mitchell John Sherlock	J. Sherlock (Ordeal of Major Grigsby)	
Last Hour	Nettlefold	1930	Walter Forde	H. Fowler Mear	C. Bennett	
Last Journey	Twickenham	1935	Bernard Vorhaus	H. Fowler Mear John Soutar	J. J. Farjeon (Holiday Express)	
Last Known Address	Valoria	1970	Jose Giovanni	Jose Giovanni	J. Harrington	
Last Man to Hang	ACT	1956	Terence Fisher	Ivor Montagu Max Trell Gerald Bullett Maurice Elvey	G. Bullett (Jury)	
Last Mile	World Wide	1932	Sam Bischoff	Seton I. Miller	J. Wexley	
Last Mile	UA	1959	Howard W. Koch	Milton Subotsky Seton I. Miller	J. Wexley	
Last of Mrs. Cheyney	MGM	1929	Sidney Franklin	Hans Kraly Claudine West	F. Lonsdale	
Last of Mrs. Cheyney	MGM	1937	Richard Boleslawski George Fitzmaurice	Leon Gordon Samson Raphaelson Monckton Hoffe	F. Lonsdale	
Last of Philip Banter	Tesauro	1986	Herve Hachuel	Alvaro De La Huerta Herve Hachuel	J. F. Bardin	
Last of Sheila	Warner	1973	Herbert Ross	Stephen Sondheim Anthony Perkins	novel: A. Edwards	

L

Title	Studio	Year	Director	Writer	Source	Character
Last of the Lone Wolf	Columbia	1930	Richard Boleslavsky	James Whittaker / Dorothy Howell / John T. Neville / Frederick Knott	L. J. Vance (Lone Wolf)	Michael Lanyard (Bert Lytell)
Last Page	Exclusive	1952	Terence Fisher		J. H. Chase	
Manbait						
Last Shot You Hear	Lippert	1970	Gordon Hessler	Tim Shields	W. Fairchild (Sound of Murder)	
Last Summer in Tangiers	Ariana	1987	Alexandre Arcady	Alexandre Arcady / Alain Le Henry / Tito Topin	W. O'Farrell (Devil His Due)	
Last Turning	Lux	1939	Pierre Chenal	Charles Spaak / Alfred A. Cohn	J. M. Cain (Postman Always Rings Twice)	
Last Warning	Universal	1928	Paul Leni	Tom Reed / Robert F. Hill	W. Camp (House of Fear)	
Last Warning	Universal	1938	Al Rogell	Edmund L. Hartmann	J. Latimer (Dead Don't Care)	
Late Edwina Black	Gen. Film	1951	Maurice Elvey	Charles Frank / David Evans	W. Dinner	
Obsessed						
Laughing Policeman	TCF	1973	Stuart Rosenberg	Thomas Rickman	M. Sjowall	
Investigation of Murder						
Laura	TCF	1944	Otto Preminger	Jay Dratler / Samuel Hoffenstein / Betty Reinhardt / Ring Lardner, Jr. / Jerome Cady	V. Caspary	
Law and Disorder	Brit. Nat.	1939	David Macdonald	A. R. Rawlinson / Bridget Boland	J. Dell (Official Secret)	
Spies in the Air						
Spies of the Air						
Law and Disorder	Brit. Lion	1958	Charles Crichton	T. E. B. Clarke / Patrick Campbell / Vivienne Knight	D. Roberts (Smuggler's Circuit)	
Law and the Lady	MGM	1951	Edwin H. Knopf	Leonard Spigelgass / Karl Tunberg	F. Lonsdale (Last of Mrs. Cheyney)	
Law and the Woman	*Fam. Play.	1922	Penrhyn Stanlaws	Albert S. LeVino	C. Fitch (Woman in the Case)	
Lawyer Man	Warner	1932	William Dieterle	Rian James / James Seymour	M. Trell	
Lawyer Quince	*London	1914	Harold Shaw	?	W. W. Jacobs (Odd Craft)	
Lawyer Quince	*London	1924	Manning Haynes	Lydia Hayward	W. W. Jacobs (Odd Craft)	
Lay Off Blondes	CFF	1960	Maurice Cloche	Maurice Cloche	Carter Brown (Body)	
Le Cri du Cormoran le Soir Au-Dessus des Jonques	Gaumont	1970	Michel Audiard	Michel Audiard	E. Hunter (Horse's Head)	
Le Dernier de Six	Continental	1941	George Lacombe	Henri G. Clouzot	A Steeman (Six Dead Men)	
Le Dernier Reincarnation de Larsan	*Eclair	1914	Maurice Tourneur	Maurice Tourneur	G. Leroux (Perfume of the Lady in Black)	
Le Grand Frere	Gaumont	1982	Francis Girod	Francis Girod / Michel Grisolia	S. Ross (Ready for the Tiger)	
Le Grande Marnier	*Film d'Art	1913	?	?	G. Ohnet (Great Marl-Pit)	
Le Judgement de Minuit	Pallas	1932	Alexandre Esway	Jean Alley	E. Wallace (Ringer)	Ringer (?)
Le Mort Qui Tue	*Gaumont	1914	Andrew Charlot	?	P. Souvestre (Messengers of Evil)	Fantomas (?)
Le Mystere de la Chambre Jaune	*Eclair	1914	Maurice Tourneur	Maurice Tourneur	G. Leroux (Mystery of the Yellow Room)	Joseph Rouletabille (?)
Le Mystere de la Chambre Jaune	Alcina	1948	Henri Aisner	Vladimir Pozner	G. Leroux (Mystery of the Yellow Room)	Joseph Rouletabille (?)
Le Parfum de la Dame en Noir	Alcina	1949	Louis Daquin	Vladimir Pozner	G. Leroux (Perfume of the Lady in Black)	Joseph Rouletabille (?)
Le Salaire de Peche	?	1956	D. de la Patelliere	Roland Laudenbach / D. de la Patelliere	N. Rutledge (Emily Will Know)	
Le Silencieux	Gaumont	1972	Claude Pinoteau	Jean-Louis Dabadie	F. Ryck (Loaded Gun)	

L

FILM TITLE	STUDIO	YEAR	DIRECTOR	SCREENWRITER	SOURCE AUTHOR/WORK	SERIES
Le Tete d'un Homme	Vendal	1932	Julien Duvivier	Claude Pinoteau Louis Delapree Julien Duvivier Pierre Calmann	G. Simenon (Battle of Nerves)	Jules Maigret (Harry Bauer)
Le Voyageur de la Toussaint	Francinex	1942	Louis Daquin	Marcel Ayme Eugene Solow	G. Simenon (Strange Inheritance)	
League of Frightened Men	Columbia	1937	Alfred E. Green	Guy Endore	R. Stout	Nero Wolfe (Walter Connolly)
League of Gentlemen	Allied Film	1959	Basil Dearden	Bryan Forbes	J. Boland	Hyde (Jack Hawkins)
Leah Kleschna	Fam. Play.	1913	J. Searle Dawley	?	C. M. S. McLellan	
Learn, Baby, Learn	Winger	1969	Gordon Parks	Gordon Parks	G. Parks (Learning Tree)	
Learning Tree						
Learn, Baby, Learn	Winger	1969	Gordon Parks	Gordon Parks	G. Parks	
Leather and Nylon	Comacico	1967	Jean Delannoy	Alphonse Boudard Jean Delannoy	Jay Flynn (Action Man)	
Action Man						
Hoodlum's Sun						
Leave Her to Heaven	TCF	1945	John M. Stahl	Jo Swerling	B. A. Williams	
Leavenworth Case	*Bennett	1923	Charles Giblyn	Eve Stuyvesant	A. K. Green	
Leavenworth Case	Republic	1936	Lewis D. Collins	Albert DeMond Sidney Sutherland	A. K. Green	
Led Astray	*Vitagraph	1909	Van Dyke Brooke	?	Mrs. H. Wood (East Lynne)	
Legend of Hell House	Pilgrim	1973	Jean Hough	Richard Matheson	R. Matheson (Hell House)	
Legend of the Lawman	Am. Intl.	1977	Earl Bellamy	Howard B. Kreitsek	novel: W. Carey	
Walking Tall						Buford Pusser (Joe Don Baker)
Lemon Drop Kid	Paramount	1951	Sidney Lanfield	Edmund Hartmann Frank Tashlin Robert O'Brien	D. Runyon (Bloodhounds of Broadway)	
Leopard Lady	*DeMille	1928	Rupert Julian	Beulah Marie Dix Ardel Wray	E. C. Carpenter	
Leopard Man	RKO	1943	Jacques Tourneur	Edward Dein	C. Woolrich (Black Alibi)	
Lepke	Warner	1975	Menachem Golan	Wesley Lau Tamar Hoffs	novel: J. Pearl	
Les Canailles	Rivers	1960	Maurice Labro	R. M. Arlaud Louis Martin Claude Desailly Maurice Labro	Raymond Marshall (You Find Him—I'll Fix Him)	
Let 'Er Go Galleghe	*DeMille	1928	Elmer Clifton	Elliott Clawson	R. H. Davis (Gallegher)	
Let It Be Sunday	Vive. Dim.	1983	Francois Truffaut	Francois Truffaut Suzanne Schiffman Jean Aurel	C. Williams (Long Saturday Night)	
Confidentially Yours						
Finally, Sunday						
Let No Man Write My Epitaph	Columbia	1960	Philip Leacock	Robt. Presnell, Jr.	W. Motley	
Let the Beast Die	CFDC	1969	Claude Chabrol	Paul Gegauff Claude Chabrol	Nicholas Blake (Beast Must Die)	
Killer						
This Man Must Die						
Lethal Weapon	Warner	1987	Richard Donner	Shane Black	novel: J. Norst	
Let's Kill Uncle	Universal	1966	William Castle	Mark Rodgers	R. O'Grady	
Letter	*Paramount	1929	Jean De Limur	Garret Fort	W. S. Maugham	
Letter	Para. Pub.	1930	Louis Mercanton	?	W. S. Maugham	
Letter	First Nat.	1940	William Wyler	Howard Koch	W. S. Maugham	
Letty Lynton	MGM	1932	Clarence Brown	John Meehan Wanda Turchock	M. B. Lowndes	
L'Homme de Londres	Tavano	1943	Henri Decoin	Henri Decoin	G. Simenon (Newhaven-Dieppe)	
Libel	MGM	1959	Anthony Asquith	Anatole De Grunwald Karl Tunberg	E. Wooll	

Film Index

Title	Studio	Year	Director	Writer	Source/Notes	Character (Actor)
Liberation of L. B. Jones	Columbia	1970	William Wyler	Stirling Silliphant / Jesse Hill Ford	J. H. Ford (Liberation of Lord Byron Jones)	
License to Kill	MGM	1989	John Glen	Richard Maibaum / Michael G. Wilson	novel: John Gardner	James Bond (Timothy Dalton)
Life for Ruth	Allied	1962	Basil Dearden	Janet Green		
Condemned to Life						
Life for Sale	Continental	1929	?	John McCormick	novel: W. Drummond	
Life Goes On	B&D Para.	1932	Jack Raymond	?	S. Horler (In the Dark)	
Sorry You've Been Troubled				?	W. Hackett (Sorry You've Been Troubled)	
Life in the Balance	TCF	1955	Harry Horner	Robt. Presnell, Jr. / Leo Townsend	G. Simenon (headnote)	
Life of Rufus Dawes	*Spencer's	1911	Alfred Rolfe	Alfred Rolfe	M. Clarke (His Natural Life)	
Life Without Soul	*Ocean Film	1915	Joseph W. Smiley	Jesse J. Goldburg	M. Shelley (Frankenstein)	
Lightning Strikes Twice	Warner	1951	King Vidor	Lenore Coffee	M. Echard (Dark Fantastic)	
Lights and Shadows	MGM	1930	Robert Ober	Albert S. LeVino	P. Dunning (Night Hostess)	
Woman Racket			A. Kelly			
Lily of Kilarney	*BIP	1929	George Ridgwell	George Ridgwell	D. Boucicault (Colleen Bawn)	
Limbo Line	Trio	1968	Samuel Gallu	Donald James	V. Canning	
Limping Man	BIP	1931	John Orton	John Orton	W. Scott (Man)	
Creeping Shadows						Disher (Franklin Dyall)
Limping Man	Welwyn	1936	Walter Summers	Walter Summers	W. Scott (Man)	Disher (Francis L. Sullivan)
Line Engaged	Brit. Lion	1935	Bernard Mainwaring		J. De Leon	
Lion and the Lamb	Columbia	1931	George B. Seitz	Jack De Leon / Jack Celestin	E. P. Oppenheim	
Lion and the Mouse	*Lubin	1914	Barry O'Neil	Matt Taylor	A. Hornblow	
Lion and the Mouse	*Viagraph	1919	Tom Terriss	E. W. Sargent / Tom Terriss	A. Hornblow	
Lion and the Mouse	Warner	1928	Lloyd Bacon	Robert Lord	A. Hornblow	
Lion Man	*Universal	1920	Jack Wells / Albert Russell	Karl L. Coolidge / Joe Brandt	R. Parrish (Strange Case of Cavendish)	
Lion's Mouse	*Granger	1922	Oscar Apfel	William Pigott	C. N. Williamson	
Liquidator	MGM	1965	Jack Cardiff	? / Peter Yeldham	J. Gardner	Boysie Oakes (Rod Taylor)
Lisa	Red Lion	1961	Phillip Dunne	Nelson Gidding	J. De Hartog (Inspector)	
Inspector						
List of Adrian Messenger	Univ. Int.	1963	John Huston	Anthony Veiller	P. MacDonald	Anthony Gethryn (George C. Scott)
Little Caesar	First Nat.	1931	Mervyn LeRoy	Francis E. Faragoh / Robert N. Lee / Darryl Zanuck / Robert Lord	W. R. Burnett	
Little Drummer Girl	Pan Arts	1984	George Roy Hill	Loring Mandel	J. Le Carre	
Little Girl in a Big City	*Lumas	1925	Burton King	Victoria Moore	J. K. McCurdy	
Little Girl Who Lives Down the Lane	Braun	1976	Nicolas Gessner	Laird Koenig	L. Koenig	
Little Hour of Peter Wells	*Granger	1920	B. E. Doxat-Pratt	Eliot Stannard	D. Whitelaw	
Little Miss Marker	Paramount	1934	Alexander Hall	William R. Lipman / Sam Hellman / Gladys Lehman	D. Runyon (Blue Plate Special)	
Girl in Pawn						
Little Murders	TCF	1971	Alan Arkin	Jules Feiffer	J. Feiffer	
Little Sweetheart	Nelson	1988	Anthony Simmons	Anthony Simmons	A. Wise (Naughty Girls)	
Little Virtuous	Gaum. Int.	1968	Serge Korber	Claude Sautet / Michel Audiard	R. Marshall (But a Short Time to Live)	
Live and Let Die	UA	1973	Guy Hamilton	Tom Mankiewicz	I. Fleming	James Bond (Roger Moore) / Albert Argyle (Ian Hendry)
Live Now, Pay Later	Regal	1962	Jay Lewis	Jack Trevor Story	J. T. Story	
Live Today for Tomorrow	Univ. Int.	1949	Michael Gordon	Michael Blankfort / Robert Thoeren	E. Lothar (Mills of God)	
Act of Murder						

L

L

FILM TITLE	STUDIO	YEAR	DIRECTOR	SCREENWRITER	SOURCE AUTHOR/WORK	SERIES
Living Dangerously	BIP	1936	Herbert Brenon	Dudley Leslie Marjorie Deans Geoffrey Kerr	Reginald Simpson	
Living Daylights	UA	1987	John Glen	Richard Maibaum Michael G. Wilson	I. Fleming (Octopussy and The Living Daylights)	James Bond (Timothy Dalton)
Living Lies	Mayflower	1922	Emile Chautard	?	A. S. Roche (Plunder)	
Lizzie	MGM	1957	Hugo Haas	Mel Dinelli	S. Jackson (Bird's Nest)	
Loaded Dice	*Pathe	1918	Herbert Blache	Gilson Willets	E. H. Clark	
Locked Door	Feature	1929	George Fitzmaurice	C. Gardner Sullivan George Scarborough Earle Brown	C. Pollock (Sign on the Door)	
Locker 69	Merton Park	1962	Norman Harrison	Richard Harris	E. Wallace (headnote)	
Lodger Case of Jonathan Drew	*Gainsboro.	1926	Alfred Hitchcock	Eliot Stannard Alfred Hitchcock	M. B. Lowndes	
Lodger Phantom Fiend	Twickenham	1932	Maurice Elvey	Miles Mander Paul Rotha Ivor Novello H. Fowler Mear	M. B. Lowndes	
Lodger	TCF	1944	John Brahm	Barre Lyndon	M. B. Lowndes	
London After Midnight Hypnotist	*MGM	1927	Tod Browning	Tod Browning Waldemar Young	novel: M. Coolridge-Rask	
London Belongs to Me	GFD	1948	Sidney Gilliat	Sidney Gilliat J. B. Williams	N. Collins	
Dulcimer Street						
London by Night	*Barker	1913	Alexander Butler	Harry Engholm Rowland Talbot	C. Selby	
Lone Wolf	*Selznick	1917	Herbert Brenon	George E. Hall	L. J. Vance	Michael Lanyard (Bert Lytell)
Lone Wolf	*McKeown	1924	S. E. V. Taylor	S. E. V. Taylor	L. J. Vance	Michael Lanyard (Jack Holt)
Lone Wolf Returns	*Columbia	1926	Ralph Ince	J. Grubb Alexander	L. J. Vance	Michael Lanyard (Bert Lytell)
Return of the Lone Wolf Lone Wolf Returns	Columbia	1936	Roy William Neill	Joseph Krumgold Bruce Manning Lionel Hauser	L. J. Vance	Michael Lanyard (Melvyn Douglas)
Lone Wolf Spy Hunt	Columbia	1939	Peter Godfrey	Robert O'Connell Jonathan Latimer	L. J. Vance (Red Masquerade)	Michael Lanyard (Warren William)
Lonely Hearts	Toho	1983	Kon Ichikawa	Masaya Hidaka Ikuko Oya Kon Ichikawa	E. Hunter (Lady, Lady, I Did It!)	
Lonely Hearts Killers Honeymoon Killer	Roxane	1969	Leonard Kastle	Leonard Kastle	novel: Paul Buck (Honeymoon Killers)	
Lonely Road Scotland Yard Commands	ATP	1936	James Flood	James Flood Gerard Fairlie Anthony Kimmins	N. Shue	
Long Arm of Mannister	*Nat. Film	1919	Bertram Bracken	?	E. P. Oppenheim (Long Arm)	
Long Dark Hall	Five Oceans	1951	Anthony Bushell Reginald Beck	Nunnally Johnson W. E. C. Fairchild	E. Lustgarten (Case to Answer)	
Long Day's Dying	Junction	1968	Peter Collinson	Charles Wood	A. White	
Long Goodbye	UA	1973	Robert Altman	Leigh Brackett	R. Chandler	Philip Marlowe (Elliott Gould)
Long Haul	Marksman	1957	Ken Hughes	Ken Hughes	M. Mills	
Long Knife	Merton Park	1958	Montgomery Tully	Ian Stuart Black	S. Truss (Long Night)	
Long Memory	Europa	1952	Robert Hamer	Robert Hamer Frank Harvey	H. Clewes	
Long Wait	UA	1954	Victor Saville	Alan Green Lesser Samuels	M. Spillane	

Title	Studio	Year	Director	Writer	Source	Character
Longest Night	MGM	1936	Errol Taggart	Robert Andrews	C. Fitzsimmons (Whispering Window)	
Look Out, Girls	Corona	1957	Yves Allegret	Rene Wheeler	J. H. Chase (Miss Callaghan Comes to Grief)	
Good Girls Beware				Jean Meckert		
Young Girls Reward						
Loophole	Frankovich	1969	Frank R. Pierson	Frank R. Pierson	J. Le Carre	
Loophole	Walker	1980	John Quested	Jonathan Hales	R. Pollock	
Loot	*Universal	1919	William C. Dowlan	Violet Clark	A. S. Roche	
Loot	Perf. Arts	1970	Silvio Narizzano	Ray Galton	J. Orton	
				Alan Simpson		
Lord Arthur Savile's Crime	2RF Kamera	1968	Witold Lesiewicz	Witold Lesiewicz	O. Wilde	
Lord Camber's Ladies	BIP	1932	Benn W. Levy	Benn W. Levy	H. A. Vachell (Case of Lady Camber)	
				Edwin Greenwood		
				Gilbert Wakefield		
Lord Edgware Dies	Real Art	1934	Henry Edwards	H. Fowler Mear	A. Christie	Hercule Poirot (Austin Trevor)
Lord John in New York	*Gold Seal	1915	Edward J. LeSaint	Harvey Gates	C. N. Williamson	
Los Angeles Precinct 45	Columbia	1972	Richard Fleischer	Stirling Silliphant	J. Wambaugh (New Centurions)	
New Centurions						
Los Papeles de Aspern	Virginia	1991	Jordi Cadena	Jordi Cadena	Henry James (Aspern Papers)	
				Manuel Valls		
Loser Takes All	IFP	1956	Ken Annakin	Graham Greene	G. Greene	
Lost Continent	Hammer	1968	Michael Carreras	Michael Nash	D. Wheatley (Uncharted Seas)	
Lost House	*Majestic	1915	?	?	R. H. Davis (Man Who Could Not Lose)	
Lost Illusion	Brit. Lion	1948	Carol Reed	Graham Greene	G. Greene (Basement Room)	
Fallen Idol				Leslie Storm		
				William Templeton		
Lost Leader	Stoll	1922	George Ridgwell	William J. Elliott	E. P. Oppenheim	
Lost Man	Universal	1969	Robert Alan Aurthur	Robert Alan Aurthur	F. L. Green (Odd Man Out)	
Lost Moment	Universal	1947	Martin Gabel	Leonardo Bercovici	H. James (Aspern Papers)	
Lotusblueten fur Miss Quon	Rapid	1967	Jurgen Roland	James Brewer	J. H. Chase (Lotus for Miss Quon)	
Loudwater Mystery	*Broadwest	1921	Norman Macdonald	Norman Macdonald	E. Jepson	
Louis Beretti	Fox	1930	John Ford	Dudley Nichols	D. H. Clarke	
Born Reckless						
Love and Bullets	ITC	1978	Stuart Rosenberg	Wendell Mayes	novel: J. Heddon	
				John Melson		
Love and the Whirlwind	*Alliance	1922	Duncan Macrae	?	H. P. Lewis	
			Harold Shaw			
Love Cage	MGM	1964	Rene Clement	Pascal Jardin	D. Keene (Joy House)	
Joy House				Charles Williams		
				Rene Clement		
Love from a Stranger	Trafalgar	1937	Rowland V. Lee	Frances Marion	F. Vosper	
Love from a Stranger	Renown	1947	Richard Whorf	Philip MacDonald	F. Vosper	
Stranger Walked In						
Love Insurance	*Paramount	1920	Donald Crisp	Marion Fairfax	E. D. Biggers	
Love Is a Racket	Warner	1932	William A. Wellman	Courtney Terrett	R. James	
Such Things Happen						
Love Is My Profession	Columbia	1958	Claude Autant-Lara	Jean Aurenche	G. Simenon (In Case of Emergency)	
In Case of Emergency				Pierre Bost		
Love Is Only a Word	Roxy	1971	Alfred Vohrer	Manfred Purzer	J. M. Simmel (Love Is Just a Word)	
Love Letters	Paramount	1945	William Dieterle	Ayn Rand	C. Massie (Pity My Simplicity)	
Love Letters of a Star	Universal	1936	Lewis R. Foster	Lewis R. Foster	Rufus King (Case of the Constant God)	Lt. Valcour (C. Henry Gordon)
				Milton Carruth		
				James Mulhauser		
Love on the Spot	ATP	1932	Graham Cutts	John P. Carstairs	H. C. McNeile (Three of a Kind)	
				Reginald Purdell		
				Mary O'Hara		
Love Racket	*Ass. First	1924	Harry O. Hoyt	John F. Goodrich	B. K. Burns (Jury Woman)	
Love Racket	Warner	1929	William A. Seiter	Adele Commandini	B. K. Burns (Jury Woman)	

L

FILM TITLE	STUDIO	YEAR	DIRECTOR	SCREENWRITER	SOURCE AUTHOR/WORK	SERIES
Love Under Fire	TCF	1937	George Marshall	Gene Fowler Allen Rivkin Ernest Pascal	W. Hackett (Fugitives)	
Love Without Question	*Jans	1920	B. A. Rolfe	Violet Clark	W. Camp (Abandoned Room)	
Love's Boomerang	*Fam. Play.	1922	John S. Robertson	Josephine Lovett	D. C. Calthrop (Perpetua)	
Perpetua			Tom Geraghy	Helen Blizard		
Loves of Colleen Bawn	*Stoll	1924	W. P. Kellino	Eliot Stannard	D. Boucicault (Colleen Bawn)	
Colleen Bawn						
Loyalties	ATP	1933	Basil Dean	W. P. Lipscomb	J. Galsworthy	
Luck of Roaring Camp	*Edison	1910	Edwin S. Porter	Edwin S. Porter	Bret Harte (Bret Harte's Choice Bits)	
Luck of Roaring Camp	*Johnson	1911	?	?	Bret Harte (Bret Harte's Choice Bits)	
Luck of the Irish	*Mayflower	1920	Allan Dwan	?	H. MacGrath	
Lucky Nick Cain	Kaydor	1951	Joseph M. Newman	George Callahan William Rose	J. H. Chase (I'll Get You for This)	
I'll Get You for This						
Lucky Stiff	UA	1948	Lewis R. Foster	Lewis R. Foster	C. Rice	John J. Malone (Brian Donlevy)
Lunatic at Large	*Hepworth	1921	Henry Edwards	George W. Dewhurst	J. S. Clouston	Francis Mandell-Essington (Henry Edwards)
Lunatic at Large	*First Nat.	1927	Fred Newmeyer	Ralph Spence	J. S. Clouston	Francis Mandell-Essington (Jack Raymond)
Lupin the Gentleman Burglar	*Pasquali	1914	?	?	M. Leblanc (Exploits of Arsene Lupin)	Arsene Lupin (?)
Lure	*Shubert	1914	Alice Blache	Alice Blache	G. Scarborough	
Lure	Maude	1933	Arthur Maude	?	C. Cavendish	
Lure of the Swamp	TCF	1957	Hubert Cornfield	William George	G. Brewer (Hell's Our Destination)	
Lust for Evil	CCFC	1960	Rene Clement	Paul Gegauff Rene Clement	P. Highsmith (Talented Mr. Ripley)	Tom Ripley (Alain Delon)
Broad Daylight						
Purple Noon						
Lyons Mail	*Samuelson	1915	?	?	E. Moreau (Courier of Lyons)	
Lyons Mail	*Ideal	1916	Fred Paul	Benedict James	E. Moreau (Courier of Lyons)	
Lyons Mail	Twickenham	1931	Arthur Maude	H. Fowler Mear	E. Moreau (Courier of Lyons)	
McCabe and Mrs. Miller	Warner	1971	Robert Altman	Robert Altman Brian McKay	E. Naughton (McCabe)	
McGuffin	BBC	1985	Colin Bucksey	Michael Thomas	J. Bowen	
McGuire Go Home!	Rank	1964	Ralph Thomas	Ian Stuart Black	I. S. Black (High Bright Sun)	
High Bright Sun				Bryan Forbes		
Mackenzie Break	Brighton	1970	Lamont Johnson	William Norton	S. Shelley (Bowmanville Break)	
Mackintosh Man	Columbia	1973	John Huston	Walter Hill	D. Bagley (Freedom Trap)	Slade (Ian Bannen)
McQ	Warner	1974	John Sturges	Lawrence Roman	novel: A. Edwards	
M. Hire	Cinea	1989	Patrice Leconte	Patrice Leconte Patrick Dewolf	G. Simenon (Mr. Hire's Engagement)	
Macabre	Allied Art.	1958	William Castle	Robb White	T. Durrant (Marble Forest)	
Machine Gun McCain	Columbia	1970	Giuliano Montaldo	Mino Roli Giuliano Montaldo	O. Demaris (Candyleg)	
"Mad Dog" Coll	Columbia	1961	Burt Balaban	Edward Schreiber	novel: S. Thurman	
Mad Love	MGM	1935	Karl Freund	Guy Endore P. J. Wolfson John I. Balderston	M. Renard (Hands of Orlac)	
Hands of Orlac						
Mad Men of Europe	Aldwych	1940	Albert de Courville	Ian Hay Edward Knoblock	G. Du Maurier	
Englishman's Home						

Title	Studio	Year	Director	Writer	Source / Cast
Mad Room	Columbia	1969	Bernard Girard	Bernard Girard	E. Percy (Ladies in Retirement)
Mad Whirl	*Universal	1925	William A. Seiter	A. Z. Martin	R. W. Child (Fresh Waters)
Madame X	*Gold Roost.	1916	George F. Marion	Frederic Hatton	J. W. MacConaughy
Madame X	*Goldwyn	1920	Frank Lloyd	William E. Burlock	J. W. MacConaughy
				J. E. Nash	
				Frank Lloyd	
Madame X	MGM	1929	Lionel Barrymore	Willard Mack	J. W. MacConaughy
Absinthe					
Madame X	MGM	1937	Sam Wood	John Meehan	J. W. MacConaughy
Madame X	Universal	1965	David Lowell Rich	Jean Holloway	J. W. MacConaughy
Made in U.S.A.	Pathe	1967	Jean-Luc Godard	Jean-Luc Godard	R. Stark (Jugger)
Madhouse	AIP	1974	Jim Clark	Greg Morrison	Angus Hall (Qualtrough)
				Ken Levison	
Madigan	Universal	1968	Don Siegel	Henri Simoun	R. Dougherty (Commissioner)
				Abraham Polonsky	
				Harry Kleiner	
Madness of the Heart	Rank	1949	Charles Bennett	Charles Bennett	F. Sandstrom
Madonna of Avenue A	Warner	1929	Michael Curtiz	Ray Doyle	novel: M. Canfield
Madonna of the Seven Moons	Gainsbor.	1944	Arthur Crabtree	Brock Williams	M. Lawrence
				Roland Perrwee	
Madonna of the Sleeping Cars	*Natan	1929	?	?	M. Dekobra
Mafia	Panda	1968	Damiano Damiani	Damiano Damiani	L. Sciascia (Mafia Vendetta)
Day of the Owl				Ugo Pirro	
Magic	LeVine	1978	R. Attenborough	William Goldman	W. Goldman
Magnet of Doom	Spec. Lumb.	1963	Jean-P. Melville	Jean-P. Melville	G. Simenon
Magnum Force	Warner	1973	Ted Post	John Milius	novel: M. Valley
				Michael Cimino	
Maid for Murder	Asher	1962	Robert Asher	John Waterhouse	I. S. Black (We Must Kill Toni)
She'll Have to Go					
Maid of the Silver Sea	*Clark	1922	Guy Newall	Guy Newall	J. Oxenham
Maids	Mantis	1976	Christopher Miles	Robert Enders	J. Genet
				Christopher Miles	
Maigret a Pigalle	Rigante	1966	Mario Landi	Sergio Amidei	G. Simenon (Maigret in Montmartre)
				Mario Landi	Jules Maigret
					(Gino Cervi)
Maigret and the St. Fiacre Case	Cinedis	1959	Jean Delannoy	R. M. Arlaud	G. Simenon (Saint Fiacre Affair)
				Michel Audiard	Jules Maigret
				Jean Delannoy	(Jean Gabin)
Maigret Lays a Trap	Intermondia	1957	Jean Delannoy	R. M. Arlaud	G. Simenon (Maigret Sets a Trap)
Inspector Maigret				Michel Audiard	Jules Maigret
Maigret Sets a Trap				Jean Delannoy	(Jean Gabin)
Maigret Sees Red	Comacico	1963	Gilles Grangier	Jacques Robert	G. Simenon (Maigret and the Gangsters)
				Gilles Grangier	Jules Maigret
					(Jean Gabin)
Maigret Sets a Trap	Intermondia	1957	Jean Delannoy	R. M. Arlaud	G. Simenon
Inspector Maigret				Michel Audiard	Jules Maigret
Maigret Lays a Trap				Jean Delannoy	(Jean Gabin)
Maigret und Sein Grosster Fall	Intercont.	1966	Alfred Weidermann	Herbert Reinecker	G. Simenon (At the Gai-Moulin)
					Jules Maigret
					(Heinz Ruhmann)
Main Attraction	Seven Arts	1963	Daniel Petrie	John Patrick	novel: S. Michaels
Main Chance	Merton Park	1964	John Knight	Marguerite Roberts	E. Wallace (headnote)
Maisie	MGM	1939	Edwin L. Marin	Richard Harris	W. Collison (Dark Dame)
Majestic Hotel Cellars	Domaines	1945	Richard Portier	Mary McCall, Jr.	G. Simenon (Maigret and the Hotel Majestic)
				Charles Spaak	Jules Maigret
					(Albert Prejean)
Majorettes	Major	1988	Bill Hinzman	John Russo	J. Russo
Make Haste to Live	Republic	1954	William A. Seiter	Warren Duff	Gordons
Make Mine Mink	Rank	1960	Robert Asher	Michael Perrwee	P. Coke (Breath of Spring)
				Peter Blackmore	
Malaga	Ass. Brit.	1960	Laslo Benedek	David Osborn	D. MacKenzie (Scent of Danger)
Moment of Danger				Donald Ogden Stewart	
Malone	Orion	1987	Harley Cokliss	Christopher Frank	W. Wingate (Shotgun)

M

M

FILM TITLE	STUDIO	YEAR	DIRECTOR	SCREENWRITER	SOURCE AUTHOR/WORK	SERIES
Malpas Mystery	Ind. Art.	1960	Sidney Hayers	Paul Tabori Gordon Wellesley	E. Wallace (Face in the Night)	

Maltese Falcon
  Dangerous Female
	Warner	1931	Roy del Ruth	Maude Fulton
				Lucien Hubbard
				Brown Holmes
					D. Hammett	Sam Spade
						  (Ricardo Cortez)

Maltese Falcon	Warner	1941	John Huston	Dashiell Hammett John Huston	D. Hammett	Sam Spade (Humphrey Bogart)
Man and His Money	*Goldwyn	1919	Harry Beaumont	?	F. S. Isham	
Man About the House	Brit. Lion	1947	Leslie Arliss	Leslie Arliss J. B. Williams	F. B. Young	
Man About Town	TCF	1932	John Francis Dillon	Leon Gordon	D. Clift	
Man and the Beast Strange Case of the Man and the Beast	Sono	1951	Mario Soffici	Mario Soffici Carlos Marin Ulises Petit de Murat	R. L. Stevenson (Strange Case of Dr. Jekyll and Mr. Hyde)	
Man at Six Gables Mystery	BIP	1931	Harry Hughes	Harry Hughes Victor Kendall	J. Celesin	
Man at the Carlton Tower	Merton Park	1961	Robert Tronson	Philip Mackie	E. Wallace (Man at the Carlton)	
Man Behind the Mask	Rock	1936	Michael Powell	Ian Hay Syd Courtenay Jack Byrd	J. Futrelle (Chase of the Golden Plate)	
Man Called Back	World Wide	1932	Robert Florey	Stanley Haynes Robert Presnell Andrew Soutar	A. Soutar (Silent Thunder)	
Man Could Get Killed Welcome, Mr. Beddoes	Universal	1966	Ronald Neame	Richard Breen T. E. B. Clarke	D. Walker (Diamonds for Moscow)	
Man Detained	Merton Park	1961	Robert Tronson	Richard Harris	E. Wallace (Debt Discharged)	
Man from Headquarters	*Trem Carr	1928	Duke Worne	Arthur Hoerl	G. Bronson-Howard (Black Book)	
Man from Marrakech That Was George	Prodis	1966	Jacques Deray	H. Lanoe Jose Giovanni Jacques Deray	R. P. Jones (Heisters)	
Man from Nowhere	*Red Feather	1916	Henry Otto	William M. Clifford	Victor Bridges (?)	
Man from the Diner's Club	Columbia	1963	Frank Tashlin	Bill Blatry	novel: S. Baol	
Man Hunt	TCF	1941	Fritz Lang	Dudley Nichols	G. Household (Rogue Male)	
Man in Half Moon Street	Paramount	1944	Ralph Murphy	Charles Kenyon Garrett Fort	B. Lyndon	
Man in Hiding Mantrap	Hammer	1953	Terence Fisher	Paul Tabori Terence Fisher	S. Rattray (Queen in Danger)	
Man in Motley	*London	1916	Ralph Dewsbury	?	T. Gallon	
Man in the Attic	TCF	1953	Hugo Fregonese	Robt. Presnell, Jr. Barre Lyndon	M. B. Lowndes (Lodger)	Hugo Bishop (Paul Henreid)
Man in the Back Seat	Indep. Art.	1961	Vernon Sewell	Malcolm Hulke Eric Paice	E. Wallace (headnote)	
Man in the Middle	Pennebaker	1963	Guy Hamilton	Keith Waterhouse Willis Hall	H. Fast (Winston Affair)	
Man in the Net	UA	1959	Michael Curtiz	Reginald Rose	P. Quentin	
Man in the Raincoat	Cocinor	1958	Jules Duvivier	Rene Barjavel Jules Duvivier	J. H. Chase (Tiger by the Tail)	
Man in the Road	Gibraltar	1956	Lance Comfort	Guy Morgan	A. Armstrong (He Was Found in the Road)	
Man in the Shadow Pay the Devil	Universal	1957	Jack Arnold	Gene L. Coon	novel: H. Whittington	
Man in the Shadow	Merton Park	1957	Montgomery Tully	Stratford Davis	S. Davis (One Man's Secret)	
Man in the Steel Mask Man Without a Face Prisoner of the Skull Who?	Brit. Lion	1974	Jack Gold	John Gould	A. Budrys (Who?)	

MAN WHO VANISHED / 1427

Title	Studio	Year	Director	Screenplay	Source	Character (Actor)
Man in the Vault	RKO	1957	Andrew V. McLaglen	Burt Kennedy	F. Gruber (Lock and the Key)	
Man in the Water	Key West	1963	Mark Stevens	T. L. P. Swicegood	R. Sheckley	
Man Inside	*Universal	1916	John G. Adolfi	Raymond L. Schrock	N. S. Lincoln	
Man Inside	Warwick	1958	John Gilling	John Gilling	M. E. Chaber	Milo March (Jack Palance)
				David Shaw		
				Richard Maibaum		
Man Is Ten Feet Tall				Robert Alan Aurther		
Edge of the City	MGM	1957	Martin Ritt		novel: F. Pohl (Edge of the City)	
Man of Affairs						
His Lordship	Gaum. Brit.	1937	Herbert Mason	Maude T. Howell	N. Grant (Nelson Touch)	
				L. DuGarde Peach		
				Edwin Greenwood		
Man of Bronze						
Doc Savage—The Man of Bronze	Warner	1975	Michael Anderson	George Pal	K. Robeson	Doc Savage (Ron Ely)
				Joe Morhaim		
Man on a Tightrope	TCF	1953	Elia Kazan	Robert E. Sherwood	N. Paterson	
Man on Fire	Tri-Star	1987	Eli Chouraqui	Eli Chouraqui	A. J. Quinnell	
				Sergio Donati		
Man on the Box	*Lasky	1914	Cecil B. DeMille	Clara Beranger	H. MacGrath	
			Oscar Apfel			
			Wilfred Buckland			
Man on the Box	*Warner	1925	Charles Reisner	Charles A. Logue	H. MacGrath	
Man on the Eiffel Tower	A & T	1948	Burgess Meredith	Harry Brown	G. Simenon (Battle of Nerves)	Jules Maigret (Charles Laughton)
						Martin Beck (Carl-Gustav Lindstedt)
Man on the Roof	AB Svensk	1976	Bo Widerberg	Bo Widerberg	M. Sjowall (Abominable Man)	
Man Outside	Real Art	1933	George A. Cooper	H. Fowler Mear	D. Stuart	
Man Outside	Trio	1966	Samuel Gallu	Samuel Gallu	G. Stackelberg (Double Agent)	
				Julian Bond		
				Roger Marshall		
Man They Could Not Arrest	Gainsbor.	1931	T. Hayes Hunter	Arthur Wimperis	E. Wallace (headnote)	
				Angus MacPhail		
				T. Hayes Hunter		
Man They Couldn't Arrest	Gaum. Brit.	1933	T. Hayes Hunter	T. Hayes Hunter	A. J. Small	
Man-Trap	Paramount	1961	Edmund O'Brien	Ed Waters	J. D. MacDonald (Soft Touch)	
Man Who Bought London	*Windsor	1916	F. Martin Thornton	?	E. Wallace	
Man Who Changed	Real Art	1934	Henry Edwards	H. Fowler Mear	E. Wallace (Man Who Changed His Name)	
				Edgar Wallace		
Man Who Changed His Name	*Brit. Lion	1928	A. V. Bramble	Kathleen Hayden	E. Wallace	
Man Who Changed His Name	Real Art	1934	Henry Edwards	H. Fowler Mear	E. Wallace	
				Edgar Wallace		
Man Who Could Cheat Death	Hammer	1959	Terence Fisher	Jimmy Sangster	B. Lyndon (Man in Half Moon Street)	
Man Who Could Not Lose	*Favorite	1914	?	Robert A. Dillon	R. H. Davis	
Man Who Disappeared	Telecine	1951	Richard M. Grey	?	A. C. Doyle (Adventures of Sherlock Holmes)	Sherlock Holmes (John Longden)
Man with the Twisted Lip						
Man Who Finally Died	Magna	1962	Quentin Lawrence	Lewis Greifer	novel: John Burke	
				Louis Marks		
Man Who Haunted Himself	Excalibur	1970	Basil Dearden	Basil Dearden	A. Armstrong (Strange Case of Mr. Pelham)	
				Michael Relph		
Man Who Knew Too Much	GFD	1934	Alfred Hitchcock	A. R. Rawlinson	novel: Ruth Alexander	
				Charles Bennett		
				D. B. Wyndham Lewis		
				Edward Greenwood		
				Emlyn Williams		
Man Who Knew Too Much	Paramount	1956	Alfred Hitchcock	John Michael Hayes	novel: Ruth Alexander	
				Angus MacPhail		
Man Who Murdered	Terra	1931	Kurt Bernhardt	Heinz Goldberg	C. Farrere (Man Who Killed)	
				Herman Kosterliz		
				Harry Kahn		
Man Who Stayed at Home	*Hepworth	1915	Cecil H. Hepworth	?	J. E. H. Terry	
Man Who Stayed at Home	*Selznick	1920	George D. Baker	George D. Baker	J. E. H. Terry	
Man Who Vanished	*Edison	1914	Langdon West	?	S. Campbell (Below the Dead-Line)	

FILM TITLE	STUDIO	YEAR	DIRECTOR	SCREENWRITER	SOURCE AUTHOR/WORK	SERIES
Man Who Was Nobody	Merton Park	1960	Montgomery Tully	James Eastwood	E. Wallace	
Man Who Watched the Trains Go By	Stoss	1953	Harold French	Harold French	G. Simenon	
Paris Express						
Man Who Went Up in Smoke	Libik	1981	Peter Bacso	Wolfgang Muelbauer	M. Sjowall	Martin Beck (Derek Jacoby)
Man Who Won	*Vitagraph	1919	Paul Scardon	?	C. T. Brady	
Man Who Would Not Die	Centaur	1975	Robert Arkless	George Chesbro / Stephen Taylor / Robert Arkless	C. Williams (Sailcloth Shroud)	
Man Who Wouldn't Die	TCF	1942	Herbert I. Leeds	Arnaud d'Usseau	C. Rawson (No Coffin for a Corpse)	Michael Shayne (Lloyd Nolan)
Man Who Wouldn't Talk	TCF	1940	David Burton	Robert Ellis / Helen Logan / Lester Ziffren	H. Hall (Valiant)	
Man with a Cloak	MGM	1951	Fletcher Markle	Edward Ertinger / Frank Fenton	J. D. Carr (Third Bullet)	
Man with Bogart's Face	TCF	1980	Robert Day	Andrew J. Fenady	A. J. Fenady	Sam Marlow (Robert Sacchi)
Sam Marlow, Private Eye						
Man with My Face	UA	1951	Edward J. Montagne	Samuel W. Taylor / T. J. McGowan / Edward J. Montagne	S. W. Taylor	
Man with 100 Faces	Gainsbor.	1938	Albert de Courville	A. R. Rawlinson / Michael Pertwee / Basil Mason	W. B. M. Ferguson (Crackerjack)	
Crackerjack						
Man with the Deadly Lens	Columbia	1982	Richard Brooks	Richard Brooks	C. McCarry (Better Angels)	
Wrong Is Right						
Man with the Golden Gun	UA	1974	Guy Hamilton	Richard Maibaum / Tom Mankiewicz	I. Fleming	James Bond (Roger Moore)
Man with the Magnetic Eyes	Br. Found.	1945	Ronald Haines	Ronald Haines	R. Daniel	
Man with the Silver Eyes	AAA/Revcon	1985	P. Granier-Deferre	P. Granier-Deferre / G.-P. Sainderichin / William J. Elliott	R. Rossner (End of Someone Else's Rainbow)	
Man with the Twisted Lip	*Stoll	1921	Maurice Elvey	?	A. C. Doyle (Adventures of Sherlock Holmes)	Sherlock Holmes (Eille Norwood)
Man with the Twisted Lip	Telecine	1951	Richard M. Gray	?	A. C. Doyle (Adventures of Sherlock Holmes)	Sherlock Holmes (John Longden)
Man Who Disappeared						
Man with the X-Ray Eyes	Am. Int.	1963	Roger Corman	Robert Dillon / Ray Russell	novel: E. Sudak (X)	
X—The Man with the X-Ray Eyes						
Man with Two Faces	First Nat.	1934	Archie Mayo	Tom Reed / Niven Busch	A. Woollcott (Dark Tower)	
Man Within	Prod. Film	1947	Bernard Knowles	Muriel Box / Sydney Box	G. Greene	
Smugglers						
Man Without a Face	Brit. Lion	1974	Jack Gold	John Gould	A. Budrys (Who?)	
Man in the Steel Mask						
Prisoner of the Skull						
Who?						
Manbait	Exclusive	1952	Terence Fisher	Frederick Knott	J. H. Chase (Last Page)	
Last Page						
Manchurian Candidate	UA	1962	John Frankenheimer	George Axelrod / John Frankenheimer	R. Condon	
Mandarin Mystery	Republic	1936	Ralph Staub	John F. Larkin / Rex Taylor / Gertrude Orr / Cortland Fitzsimmons	E. Queen (Chinese Orange Mystery)	Ellery Queen (Eddie Quinlan)
Maneater	Heritage	1969	Samuel Fuller	Samuel Fuller / John Knightsbridge	V. Canning (His Bones Are Coral)	
Shark						
Manhandled	*Paramount	1924	Allan Dwan	Frank Tuttle	novel: A. Stringer	

Film Index

MASTER MIND / 1429

Title	Studio	Year	Director	Writer	Source/Notes
Manhattan	*Fam. Play.	1924	R. H. Burnside	Paul Sloane	J. Farnol (Definite Object)
Manhattan Knight	*Fox	1920	George A. Beranger	Frank W. Tuttle	G. Burgess (Find the Woman)
Manhattan Love Song	Monogram	1934	Leonard Fields	Paul H. Sloane	C. Woolrich
				David Silverstein	
				Leonard Fields	
Manhunter	Laurentis	1986	Michael Mann	Michael Mann	Thomas Harris (Red Dragon)
Maniac	Columbia	1963	Michael Carreras	Jimmy Sangster	M. Brandel (Time of the Fire)
Manslaughter	*Fam. Play.	1922	Cecil B. DeMille	Jeanie MacPherson	A. D. Miller
Manslaughter	Paramount	1930	George Abbott	George Abbott	A. D. Miller
Mantrap	Hammer	1953	Terence Fisher	Paul Tabori	S. Rattray (Queen in Danger)
Man in Hiding				Terence Fisher	
Marathon Man	Paramount	1976	John Schlesinger	William Goldman	W. Goldman
Margin for Error	TCF	1943	Otto Preminger	Lillie Hayward	C. Booth
Maria Marten	*Harrison	1902	Dicky Winslow	Dicky Winslow	Anonymous
Maria Marten	*Motograph	1913	Maurice Elvey	Maurice Elvey	Anonymous
Maria Marten	QTS	1928	Walter West	?	Anonymous
Maria Marten	George King	1935	George King	Randall Faye	
Marie du Port	Gordine	1949	Marcel Carne	Louis Chavance	G. Simenon (Chit of a Girl)
				Marcel Carne	
Mark	Stross	1961	Guy Green	Sidney Buchman	C. E. Israel
				Stanley Mann	
Mark of Cain	*Astra	1917	George Fitzmaurice	Philip Bartholomae	C. Wells
Mark of Cain	Two Cities	1948	Brian Desmond Hurst	Francis Crowdy	J. Shearing (Airing in a Closed Carriage)
				Christianna Brand	
				W. P. Lipscomb	
Mark of the Vampire	MGM	1935	Tod Browning	Guy Endore	novel: M. Coolridge-Rask (London After Midnight)
				Bernard Schubert	
Mark of the Whistler	Columbia	1944	William Castle	George Bricker	W. Irish (Borrowed Crime)
Marked Man					
Mark of the Whistler	Columbia	1944	William Castle	George Bricker	W. Irish (Borrowed Crime)
Marked Woman	*World Film	1914	O. A. C. Lund	Owen Davis	G. M. White
Marlowe	MGM	1969	Paul Bogart	Stirling Silliphant	R. Chandler (Little Sister)
Marnie	Universal	1964	Alfred Hitchcock	Jay Presson Allen	Winston Graham
Maroc 7	Rank	1967	Gerry O'Hara	David Osborn	novel: M. Sands
Marriage Lines	*Master	1921	Wilfred Noy	Wilfred Noy	J. S. Fletcher
Marriage of Convenience	Merton Park	1960	Clive Donner	Robert Stewart	E. Wallace (Three Oak Mystery)
Marseilles Contract	Kertledrum	1974	Robert Parrish	Judd Bernard	novel: M. Franklin (Destructors)
Destructors					
Marsupials: The Howling III	Bacannia	1987	Philippa Mora	Philippa Mora	G. Brandner (Howling III)
Martha	WDR	1973	Werner Fassbinder	Werner Fassbinder	C. Woolrich (Angels of Darkness)
Mary Regan	*First Nat	1919	Lois Weber	Tom Geraghty	L. Scott
Mask	*Selig	1921	Bertram Bracken	Bertram Bracken	A. Hornblow
Mask of Dimitrios	Warner	1944	Jean Negulesco	Arthur Lavon	E. Ambler
Mask of Fu Manchu	MGM	1932	Charles Brabin	Frank Gruber	S. Rohmer
			King Vidor	Irene Kuhn	
				Edgar Allan Woolf	
				John Willard	
Masque of the Red Death	Alta Vista	1964	Roger Corman	Charles Beaumont	
				R. Wright Campbell	
Masquerade	Fox	1929	Lumsden Hare	Malcolm S. Boylan	novel: Elsie Lee
			Russell J. Birdwell	F. H. Brennan	L. J. Vance (Brass Bowl)
Masquerade	Novus	1964	Basil Dearden	Michael Relph	V. Canning (Castle Minerva)
Operation Masquerade				William Goldman	
Shabby Tiger					
Masquerader	UA	1933	Richard Wallace	Howard Estabrook	K. C. Thurston
				Moss Hart	
Master Mind	*Lasky	1914	Oscar Apfel	Clara Beranger	M. Dana

M

FILM TITLE	STUDIO	YEAR	DIRECTOR	SCREENWRITER	SOURCE AUTHOR/WORK	SERIES
Master Mind	*Bennett	1920	Kenneth Webb	Kenneth Webb	M. Dana	
Master Mummer	*Edison	1915	Walter Edwin	Walter Edwin	E. P. Oppenheim	
Master Mystery	*Octagon	1919	Burton King	Arthur B. Reeve	novel: A. B. Reeve	
			E. Douglas Bingham	Charles A. Logue		
Master of Men	*Harma	1917	Wilfred Noy	?	E. P. Oppenheim	
Master of Merripit	*Clarendon	1915	Wilfred Noy	?	E. Phillpotts	
Maurizius Affair	Fran.-Lond.	1954	Julien Duvivier	Julien Duvivier	J. Wasserman (Maurizius Case)	
				Claire Devers		
Max and Jeremy	AMLF	1992	Claire Devers	Bernard Stora	Teri White (Max Trueblood and the Jersey Desperado)	
Maxwell Archer, Detective	RKO	1939	John P. Carstairs	Hugh Clevely	H. Clevely (Archer Plus 20)	Maxwell Archer (John Loder)
Meet Maxwell Archer				Katherine Strueby		
Mazarin Stone	*Stoll	1923	George Ridgwell	Geoffrey H. Malins	A. C. Doyle (Casebook of Sherlock Holmes)	Sherlock Holmes (Eille Norwood)
				Patrick L. Mannock		
Me—Gangster	Fox	1928	Raoul Walsh	Charles Francis Coe	C. F. Coe	
Mean Season	Orion	1985	Philip Borsos	Leon Piedmont	J. Katzenbach (In the Heat of the Summer)	
Mechanic	UA	1972	Michael Winner	Lewis John Carlino	novel: L. J. Carlino	
Killer of Killers						
Medusa Touch	Elan	1978	Jack Gold	John Briley	P. Van Greenaway	
				Jack Gold		
Meet Maxwell Archer	RKO	1939	John P. Carstairs	Hugh Clevely	H. Clevely (Archer Plus 20)	Maxwell Archer (John Loder)
Maxwell Archer, Detective				Katherine Strueby		
Meet Miss Marple	MGM	1961	George Pollock	David Pursall	A. Christie (4.50 from Paddington)	Jane Marple (Margaret Rutherford)
Murder, She Said				Jack Seddon		
				David Osborn		
Meet Mr. Callaghan	Pinnacle	1954	Charles Saunders	Brock Williams	G. Verner	Slim Callaghan (Derrick de Marney)
Meet Nero Wolfe	Columbia	1936	Herbert Biberman	Howard J. Green	R. Stout (Fer-de-Lance)	Nero Wolfe (Edward Arnold)
				Bruce Manning		
				Joseph Anthony		
Meet Sexton Blake	Anglo-Amer.	1944	John Harlow	John Harlow	A. Parsons (Mystery of the Stolen Despatches)	Sexton Blake (David Farrar)
Meet Simon Cherry	Hammer	1949	Godfrey Grayson	Gale Pedrick	G. Pedrick (Meet the Rev)	
				Godfrey Grayson		
				A. R. Rawlinson		
Meg the Lady	*London-Dip.	1916	Maurice Elvey	?	T. Gallon	
Melody Man	Columbia	1930	R. William Neill	Howard J. Green	novel: H. J. Green	
Melody of Death	*Stoll	1922	F. Martin Thornton	Leslie H. Gordon	E. Wallace	
Memento Mori	BBC	1992	Jack Clayton	Alan Kelley	M. Spark	
				Jeanie Sims		
				Jack Clayton		
Memoirs of an Invisible Man	Warner	1992	John Carpenter	Robert Collector	H. F. Saint	
				Dana Olsen		
				William Goldman		
Men in Her Life	Columbia	1931	William Beaudine	Robert Riskin	W. Fabian	
Men of Zanzibar	*Fox	1922	Rowland V. Lee	Dorothy Howell	R. H. Davis (Lost Road)	
Menace	Columbia	1932	Roy William Neill	Edward LeSaint	E. Wallace (Feathered Serpent)	
				Charles Logue		
				Roy Chanslor		
				Dorothy Howell		
Menace	Paramount	1934	Ralph Murphy	Anthony Veiller	P. MacDonald (R.I.P)	
				Chandler Sprague		
Menace in the Night	Gibraltar	1956	Lance Comfort	Norman Hudis	B. Graeme (Suspense)	
Face in the Night				John Sherman		
Mephisto Waltz	TCF	1971	Paul Wendkos	Ben Maddow	F. M. Stewart	
Mercenaries	MGM	1968	Jack Cardiff	Quentin Werty	Wilbur Smith (Train from Katanga)	
Dark of the Sun				Adrian Spies		
Mercy Merrick	*Edison	1913	Charles Brabin	Walter Edwin	Wilkie Collins (New Magdalen)	

Messenger of Death	Cannon	1988	J. Lee Thompson	Paul Jarrico	Rex Burns (Avenging Angel)
Meurtre en 45 Tours	Cite	1959	Etienne Perier	Dominique Fabre Etienne Perier Albert Valentin	P. Boileau (Heart to Heart)
Mexican's Gratitude	*Edison	1914	R. Ridgely		
Miami Blues	Orion	1990	George Armitage	George Armitage	O. Henry (Whirligigs) C. Willeford Hoke Moseley (Fred Ward)
Michael Shayne, Private Detective	TCF	1940	Eugene Forde	Stanley Rauh Manning O'Connor	B. Halliday (Private Practice of Michael Shayne) Michael Shayne (Lloyd Nolan)
Midnight	Congreg.	1980	John A. Russo	John A. Russo	J. A. Russo
Midnight Alibi	First Nat.	1934	Alan Crosland	Warren Duff	D. Runyon (Blue Plate Special)
Midnight Episode	Triangle	1950	Gordon Parry	Rita Barisse Reeve Taylor Paul Vincent Carroll David Evans William Templeton	G. Simenon (Monsieur la Souris)
Midnight Guest	*Universal	1923	George Archainbaud	?	F. M. White
Midnight in Paris	Dist. Films	1947	Georges Lecombe	Walter Klee	G. Simenon (Monsieur la Souris)
Midnight Lace	Universal	1960	David Miller	Ivan Goff Ben Roberts	J. Green (Matilda Shouted Fire)
Murder, My Sweet					
Midnight Life	*Gotham	1928	Scott Dunlap	Adele Buffington	R. W. Kauffman (Spider's Web)
Midnight Man	Universal	1974	Roland Kibbee Burt Lancaster	Roland Kibbee Burt Lancaster	D. Anthony (The Midnight Lady and the Mourning Man)
Midnight Mystery	RKO	1930	George B. Seitz	Beulah Marie Dix	H. I. Young (Hawk Island)
Mighty Quinn	MGM	1989	Carl Schenkel	Hampton Fancher	A. H. Z. Carr (Finding Maubee)
Mildred Pierce	Warner	1945	Michael Curtiz	Ranald MacDougall	J. M. Cain
Millie	RKO	1931	John Francis Dillon	Charles Kenyon Ralph Murphy	D. H. Clarke
Million a Minute	*Quality	1916	John W. Noble	Howard Irving Young	
Million Dollar Manhunt Assignment Redhead	Anglo Amal.	1962	Maclean Rogers	Maclean Rogers	H. Douglas L. Hardy (Requiem for a Redhead)
Million Dollar Mystery	*Thanhauser	1914	Howell Hansel	Lloyd F. Lonegan	novel: H. MacGrath

Million Eyes of Sumuru
  Sumuru
	Sumuru	1967	Lindsay Shouteff	Kevon Kavanagh	S. Rohmer Sumuru
					      (Shirley Eaton)

Millionaire	Warner	1931	John Adolfi	Julien Josephson Booth Tarkington	E. D. Biggers (Earl Derr Biggers Tells Ten Stories)
Millionaire Baby	*Selig	1915	Lawrence Marston	Gilson Willets	A. K. Green
Millionaires	*Warner	1926	Herman Raymaker	Raymond L. Shrock	E. P. Oppenheim (Inevitable Millionaires)
Mind Benders	Novus	1962	Basil Dearden	James Kennaway	J. Kennaway

Mind of Mr. Reeder
  Mysterious Mr. Reeder
	Grand Nat.	1939	Jack Raymond	Bryan Edgar Wallace
				Marjorie Gaffney
				Michael Hogan
					E. Wallace J. G. Reeder
					      (Will Fyffe)

Mind Over Motor	*Essanay	1915	E. H. Calvert	?	M. R. Rinehart (Book of Tish) Letitia Carberry (?)
Mind Over Motor	*Lascelle	1923	Ward Lascelle	H. Landers Jackson	M. R. Rinehart (Book of Tish) Letitia Carberry (Trixie Friganza)
Mine Own Executioner	London-Har.	1947	Anthony Kimmins	Nigel Balchin	N. Balchin
Ministry of Fear	Paramount	1944	Fritz Lang	Seton I. Miller	G. Greene
Miracle Man	*Paramount	1919	George Loane Tucker	George Loane Tucker Waldemar Young	F. Packard
Miracle Man	Paramount	1932	Norman McLeod	Samuel Hoffenstein	F. Packard
Miracles for Sale	MGM	1939	Tod Browning	Harry Ruskin Marion Parsonnet James Edward Grant	C. Rawson (Death from a Top Hat)
Mirage	Universal	1965	Edward Dmytryk	Peter Stone	W. Ericson (Fallen Angel)
Miriam Rozella	*Astra	1924	Sidney Morgan	Sidney Morgan	B. L. Farjeon
Mirror Crack'd	EMI	1980	Guy Hamilton	Jonathan Hales Barry Sandler	A. Christie (Mirror Crack'd from Side to Side) Jane Marple (Angela Lansbury)
Misery	Columbia	1990	Rob Reiner	William Goldman	Stephen King
Miss Bracegirdle Does Her Duty	*Gaumont	1926	Edwin Greenwood	?	S. Aumonier (Miss Bracegirdle and others)

M

FILM TITLE	STUDIO	YEAR	DIRECTOR	SCREENWRITER	SOURCE AUTHOR/WORK	SERIES
Miss Bracegirdle Does Her Duty	London	1936	Lee Grimes	?	S. Aumonier (Miss Bracegirdle and others)	
Miss Pinkerton	Warner	1932	Lloyd Bacon	Niven Busch Lillie Hayward	M. R. Rinehart	Hilda Adams (Joan Blondell)
Missing Million	Signet	1942	Phil Brandon	James Seymour	E. Wallace	
Missing People	Grand Nat.	1939	Jack Raymond	Lydia Hayward	E. Wallace (Mind of Mr. J. G. Reeder)	J. G. Reeder (Will Fyffe)
Missing Rembrandt	Twickenham	1932	Leslie S. Hiscott	Leslie S. Hiscott Cyril Twyford	A. C. Doyle (Return of Sherlock Holmes)	Sherlock Holmes (Arthur Wontner)
Missing Ten Days Spy in the Pantry Ten Days in Paris	Asher	1939	Tim Whelan	John Meehan, Jr. James Curtis	B. Graeme (Disappearance of Roger Tremayne)	
Missing Three-Quarter	*Stoll	1923	George Ridgwell	Geoffrey H. Malins Patrick L. Mannock	A. C. Doyle (Return of Sherlock Holmes)	Sherlock Holmes (Eille Norwood)
Missioner	*Stoll	1922	George Ridgwell	Paul Rooff	E. P. Oppenheim	
Mississippi Burning	Orion	1989	Alan Parker	Chris Gerolmo	novel: J. Norst	
Mississippi Mermaid	UA	1969	Francois Truffaut	Francois Truffaut	W. Irish (Waltz Into Darkness)	
Mist in the Valley	*Hepworth	1923	Cecil M. Hepworth	George Dewhurst	Dorin Craig	
Mr. Ace	Bogeaus	1946	Edwin L. Marin	Fred Finklehoff	novel: H. Christy	
Mr. & Mrs. North	MGM	1941	Robert B. Sinclair	S. K. Lauren	O. Davis	Pamela North (Gracie Allen) Jerry North (William Post, Jr.)
Mr. Arkadin	Warner	1955	Orson Welles	Orson Welles	O. Welles	
Mr. Barnes of New York	*Viagraph	1914	Maurice Costello Robert Gaillord	Eugene Mullin	A. C. Gunter	
Mr. Barnes of New York	*Goldwyn	1922	Victor Schertzinger		A. C. Gunter	
Mr. Denning Drives North	Brit. Lion	1951	Anthony Kimmins	Alec Coppel	A. Coppel	
Mr. Drew	ABPC	1949	Alberto Cavalcanti	J. Lee Thompson William D. Home	E. Raymond (For Them That Trespass)	
For Them That Trespass						
Mister Flow	Univ. Cin.	1936	Robert Siodmak	Henri Jeanson	G. Leroux (Man of a Hundred Masks)	
Mr. Fox of Venice Anyone for Venice? Honey Pot	UA	1966	J. L. Mankiewicz	J. L. Mankiewicz	T. Sterling (Evil of the Day)	
It Comes Up Murder						
Mr. Grex of Monte Carlo	*Lasky	1915	Frank Reicher	Marion Fairfax	E. P. Oppenheim	
Mr. Justice Raffles	*Hepworth	1921	Gerald Ames Gaston Quiribet	Blanche McIntosh	E. W. Hornung	A. J. Raffles (Gerald Ames)
Mr. Lyndon at Liberty	*London	1915	Harold Shaw		V. Bridges	
Mr. Majestyk	UA	1974	Richard Fleischer	Elmore Leonard	novel: E. Leonard	
Mr. Moses	Ross-Talbot	1964	Ronald Neame	Charles Beaumont Monja Danischewsky	M. Catto (Mister Midas)	
Mr. Moto in Danger Island Mr. Moto on Danger Island	TCF	1939	Herbert I. Leeds	Peter Milne	J. W. Vandercook (Murder in Trinidad)	Mr. Moto (Peter Lorre)
Mr. Moto on Danger Island Mr. Moto in Danger Island	TCF	1939	Herbert I. Leeds	Peter Milne	J. W. Vandercook (Murder in Trinidad)	Mr. Moto (Peter Lorre)
Mr. Potter of Texas	*San Antonio	1922	Leopold Wharton	George Rader	A. C. Gunter	
Mr. Reeder in Room 13 Mystery of Room 13	Brit. Nat.	1938	Norman Lee	Doreen Montgomery Victor Kendall Elizabeth Meehan	E. Wallace (Room 13)	J. G. Reeder (Gibb McLaughlin)
Mr. Wu	*Stoll	1922	Maurice Elvey	Fred. Blatchford	L. J. Miln	
Mr. Wu	*MGM	1927	William Nigh	Lorna Moon	L. J. Miln	
Mrs. Balfame	*Powell	1917	Frank Powell	Frank Powell	G. Atherton	
Mrs. Erricker's Reputation	*Hepworth	1920	Cecil M. Hepworth	Blanche McIntosh	T. Cobb	
Mrs. O'Malley and Mr. Malone	MGM	1950	Norman Taurog	William Bowers	Stuart Palmer (People vs. Withers and Malone)	John J. Malone (James Whitmore)

Film Index

MORD EM'LY / 1433

Title		Studio	Year	Director	Screenwriter	Source	Character (Actor)
Mrs. Pollifax, Spy		UA	1970	Leslie Martinson	C. A. McKnight	D. Gilman (Unexpected Mrs. Pollifax)	Emily Pollifax (Rosalind Russell)
Mrs. Pym of Scotland Yard		Hurley	1939	Fred Elles	Fred Elles / Nigel Morland / Peggy Barnwell	N. Morland (headnote)	Mrs. Pym (Mary Clare)
Mix Me a Person		Wessex	1962	Leslie Norman	Ian Dalrymple	J. T. Story	
Mixed Doubles		Liberty	1930	Victor Halparin	Roy Kerridge / George Draney		
Ex-Flame					Herbert Farjeon	Mrs. H. Wood (East Lynne)	
Mob		Columbia	1951	Robert Parrish	William Bowers	F. Findley (Waterfront)	
Remember That Face!							
Model Murder Case		Viewfinder	1963	Michael Truman	Vivienne Knight / Patrick Campbell	L. Payne (Nose on My Face)	
Girl in the Headlines							
Modern Dr. Jekyll and Mr. Hyde		*Selig	1910	?	?	R. L. Stevenson (Strange Case of Dr. Jekyll and Mr. Hyde)	
Modern Dr. Jekyll and Mr. Hyde		*Kalem	1913	?	?	R. L. Stevenson (Strange Case of Dr. Jekyll and Mr. Hyde)	
Modern Marriage		*F.X.B.	1923	Lawrence C. Windom	Dorothy Farnum	D. Vane (Lady Varley)	
Modesty Blaise		TCF	1966	Joseph Losey	Evan Jones	P. O'Donnell	Modesty Blaise (Monica Vitti)
Molly Maguires		Tamm	1970	Martin Ritt	Walter Bernstein	novel: J. O'Neill	
Moment of Danger		Ass. Brit.	1960	Laslo Benedek	David Osborn / Donald O. Stewart	D. MacKenzie (Scent of Danger)	
Malaga							
Moment to Moment		Universal	1966	Mervyn LeRoy	John Lee Mahin / Alec Coppel	novel: A. Coppel	
Mona Lisa		Handmade	1986	Neil Jordan	Neil Jordan / David Leland	novel: J. L. Novak	
Money Moon		*Alliance	1920	Fred Paul	Adrian Johnstone	J. Farnol	
Money Movers		South Aust.	1978	Bruce Beresford	Bruce Beresford	D. Minchin	
Money to Burn		*Gotham	1926	Walter Lang	James R. Smith	R. W. Kauffman	
Money Trap		MGM	1965	Burt Kennedy	Walter Bernstein	L. White	
Monk with a Whip		Rialto	1967	Alfred Vohrer	Alex Berg	E. Wallace (headnote)	
Monkey's Paw		*Magnet	1915	Sidney Northcote	?	W. W. Jacobs (Lady of the Barge)	
Monkey's Paw		*Artistic	1923	Manning Haynes	Lydia Hayward	W. W. Jacobs (Lady of the Barge)	
Monkey's Paw		RKO	1933	Wesley Ruggles / Ernest B. Schroedsack	Graham John	W. W. Jacobs (Lady of the Barge)	
Monkey's Paw		Kay	1948	Norman Lee	Norman Lee / Barbara Toy	W. W. Jacobs (Lady of the Barge)	
Monsieur la Souris		Dist. Films	1947	Georges Lecombe	Walter Klee	G. Simenon	
Midnight in Paris							
Monsieur Lecoq		*Thanhauser	1914	?	?	E. Gaboriau	Monsieur Lecoq (?)
Monte Carlo Nights		Monogram	1934	William Nigh	Norman Houston	E. P. Oppenheim (Mr. Billingham, the Marquis and Madelon)	
Moon in the Gutter		Gaumont	1983	Jean-J. Beineix	Jean-J. Beineix / Olivier Mergault	D. Goodis	
Moon of the Wolf		Filmways	1972	Daniel Petrie	Alvin Sapinsky	L. H. Whitten	
Moon-Spinners		Disney	1964	James Neilson	Michael Dyne	Mary Stewart	
Moonraker		UA	1979	Lewis Gilbert	Christopher Wood	novel: C. Wood (James Bond and Moonraker)	James Bond (Roger Moore)
Moonrise		Republic	1949	Frank Borage	Charles Haas	T. Strauss	
Moonshine Mountain		Creat. Com.	1967	Herschell G. Lewis	Charles Glore	novel: C. Glore	
White Trash on Moonshine Mountain							
Moonshine War		MGM	1970	Richard Quine	Elmore Leonard	E. Leonard	
Moonstone		*Selig	1915	Frank Crane	E. Magnus Ingleton	W. Collins	
Moonstone		Monach	1934	Reginald Barker	Adele Buffington	W. Collins	
Moontide		TCF	1942	Archie Mayo / Fritz Lang	John O'Hara	Willard Robertson	
Moorland Tragedy		GEM	1933	M. A. Wetherell	Allen Francis	B. Orczy (Unravelled Knots)	
Moral Sinner		*Fam. Play.	1924	Ralph Ince	J. Clarkson Miller	C. M. S. McLellan (Leah Kleschna)	
Mord Em'ly		*Welsh-Pear.	1922	George Pearson	Eliot Stannard	W. P. Ridge	Old Man (Moore Marriott)

FILM TITLE	STUDIO	YEAR	DIRECTOR	SCREENWRITER	SOURCE AUTHOR/WORK	SERIES
More Deadly Than the Male	World Dist.	1959	Robert Bucknell	Paul Chevalier	P. Chevalier	
More to Be Pitied Than Scorned	*Waldorf	1922	Edward Le Saint	?	C. E. Blaney	
Moriarty	*Goldwyn	1922	Albert Parker	Marion Fairfax	W. Gillette (Sherlock Holmes)	Sherlock Holmes (John Barrymore)
Morituri	TCF	1965	Bernard Wicki	Daniel Taradash	W. J. Luddecke	
Mormon Peril	*Master	1922	H. B. Parkinson	Frank Miller		
Trapped by the Mormons					Winifred Graham (Love Story of a Mormon)	
Morning After	Amer. Film.	1986	Sidney Lumet	James Hicks	novel: Eileen Lottman	
Mortal Storm	MGM	1940	Frank Borzage	Claudine West / George Froeschel / Andersen Ellis	P. Bottome	
Mortmain	*Vitagraph	1915	Theodore Marsten	Marguerite Bertsch	A. Train	
Moss Rose	TCF	1947	Gregory Ratoff	Jules Furthman / Tom Read / Niven Busch	J. Shearing	
Most Dangerous Game	RKO	1932	Ernest Schroedsack	James A. Creelman	R. Connell (Variety)	
Hounds of Zaroff						
Most Dangerous Man in the World / Chairman	Apjac	1969	J. Lee Thompson	Irving Pichel / Ben Maddow	J. R. Kennedy (Chairman)	
Most Dangerous Sin	Kingsley	1958	?	?	F. M. Dostoevskii (Crime and Punishment)	
Mothers Cry	First Nat.	1930	Hobart Henley	Lenore J. Coffee	H. G. Carlisle	
Mountain Music	Paramount	1937	Robert Florey	Duke Atteberry / Russell Crouse / Charles Lederer / John C. Moffitt	M. Kantor (Author's Choice)	
Moving Target / Harper	Warner	1967	Jack Smight	William Goldman	J. Macdonald	Harper (Paul Newman)
Moving Targets / Reunion	S. Aust.	1984	Chris Langman	Graham Hartley	K. Leopold (When We Ran)	
Mugger	Barbizon	1958	William Berke	Henry Kane	E. McBain	
Mumsy, Nanny, Sonny and Girly / Girly	Brigitte	1969	Freddie Francis	Brian Comport	B. Comport	
Murder	Brit. Int.	1930	Alfred Hitchcock	Alfred Hitchcock / Walter C. Mycroft / Alma Reville	C. Dane (Enter Sir John)	Sir John (Herbert Marshall)
Murder at Covent Garden	Twickenham	1932	Michael Barringer / Leslie Hiscott	Michael Barringer	W. J. Makin	
Murder at Glen Athol / Criminal Within	Invincible	1935	Frank R. Strayer	H. Fowler Mear / John W. Krafft	N. Lippincott	
Murder at Site Three	Seatle	1959	Francis Searle	Manning O'Brine	W. H. Baker (Crime Is My Business)	
Murder at the Baskervilles / Silver Blaze	Twickenham	1936	Thomas Bentley	H. Fowler Mear / Arthur Macrae	A. C. Doyle (Memoirs of Sherlock Holmes)	Sexton Blake (Geoffrey Toone) / Sherlock Holmes (Arthur Wontner)
Murder at the Gallop	MGM	1963	George Pollock	David Pursall / Jack Seddon	A. Christie (After the Funeral)	Jane Marple (Margaret Rutherford)
Murder by an Aristocrat	First Nat.	1936	Frank McDonald	James P. Cavanagh / Luci Ward / Roy Chanslor / Mignon G. Eberhart	M. G. Eberhart	
Murder by Death	Columbia	1976	Robert Moore	Neil Simon	novel: H. Keating	"Sally Keating" (Marguerite Churchill)
Murder by Decree	Ambassador	1979	Bob Clark	John Hopkins	novel: R. Weverka	Sherlock Holmes (Christopher Plummer)
Murder by Proxy / Blackout	Hammer	1954	Terence Fisher	Richard Landau	H. Nielsen (Gold Coast Nocturne)	
Murder by the Clock	Paramount	1931	Edward Sloman	Henry Myers	Rufus King	Lt. Valcour (William Boyd)

MURDER REPORTED

Murder Goes to College	Paramount	1937	Charles Riesner	Brian Marlow Robert Wyler Eddie Welch	K. Steel	Hank Hyer (Lynne Overman)
Murder in Reverse	Brit. Nat.	1946	Montgomery Tully	Montgomery Tully	Seamark (Out of the Dark)	
Murder in the Central Committee	Morgana	1982	Vicente Aranda	Vicente Aranda	M. V. Montalban	
Murder in the Family	Fox. Brit.	1938	Albert Parker	David Evans	J. Ronald	
Murder in the Private Car	MGM	1934	Harry Beaumont	Ralph Spence Edgar Allan Woolf Al Boasberg Harvey Thew	E. E. Rose (Rear Car)	
Murder on the Runaway Train						
Murder in Thornton Square Gas Light	MGM	1944	George Cukor	Jon Van Druten Walter Reisch John L. Balderston	P. Hamilton (Gas Light)	
Murder in Trinidad	TCF	1934	Louis King	Seton I. Miller	J. W. Vandercook	Bertram Lynch (Nigel Bruce)
Murder, Inc. Enforcer	U.S. Pict.	1951	Bretaigne Windust Raoul Walsh	Martin Rackin	novel: J. Eastwood	
Murder Is My Business	PRC	1946	Sam Newfield	Fred Myton	B. Halliday	Michael Shayne (Hugh Beaumont)
Murder Most Foul	MGM	1964	George Pollock	David Pursall Jack Seddon	A. Christie (Mrs. McGinty's Dead)	Jane Marple (Margaret Rutherford)
Murder, My Sweet Farewell, My Lovely	RKO	1945	Edward Dmytryk	John Paxton	R. Chandler (Farewell, My Lovely)	Philip Marlowe (Dick Powell)
Murder, My Sweet Matilda Midnight Lace	Universal	1960	David Miller	Ivan Goff Ben Roberts	J. Green (Matilda Shouted Fire)	
Murder of Dr. Harrigan	First Nat.	1936	Frank McDonald	Peter Milne Sy Bartlett Charles Belden	M. Eberhart (From This Dark Stairway)	"Sally Keating" (Kay Linaker)
Murder on a Bridal Path	RKO	1936	Edward Killy William Hamilton	Dorothy Yost Thomas Lennon Edmund North James Gow	S. Palmer (Puzzle of the Red Stallion)	Hildegarde Withers (Helen Broderick)
Murder on a Honeymoon	RKO	1935	Lloyd Corrigan	Seton I. Miller Robert Benchley	S. Palmer (Puzzle of the Pepper Tree)	Hildegarde Withers (Edna May Oliver)
Murder on Diamond Row Squeaker	London	1937	William K. Howard	Bryan Edgar Wallace Edward O. Berkman	E. Wallace (Squeaker)	
Murder on Monday Home at Seven	Brit. Lion	1952	Ralph Richardson	Anatole De Grunwald	R. C. Sherriff (Home at Seven)	
Murder on the Blackboard	RKO	1934	George Archainbaud	WillisGoldbeck	S.Palmer	Hildegarde Withers (Edna May Oliver)
Murder on the Bridge End of the Game Getting Away with Murder	MFG-T.R.A.	1975	Maximillian Schell	Maximillian Schell Arlene Sellers Bo Goldman	F. Duerrenmatt (Judge and His Hangman)	
Murder on the Campus On the Stroke of Nine	Chester.	1934	Richard Thorpe	Andrew Moses	W. Chambers (Campanile Murders)	
Murder on the Orient Express	EMI	1973	Sidney Lumet	Paul Dehn	A. Christie	Hercule Poirot (Albert Finney)
Murder on the Roof	Columbia	1930	George B. Seitz	F. Hugh Herbert	E. J. Doherty (Broadway Murders)	
Murder on the Runaway Train Murder in the Private Car	MGM	1934	Harry Beaumont	Ralph Spence Edgar Allan Woolf Al Boasberg Harvey Thew	E. E. Rose (Rear Car)	
Murder on the Second Floor	WB-FN	1932	William McGann	Roland Pertwee Challis Sanderson	F. Vosper	
Murder on the Set Death on the Set	Twickenham	1935	Leslie S. Hiscott	Michael Barringer	V. MacClure (Death on the Set)	Archie Burford (Garry Marsh)
Murder on the Yukon	Criterion	1940	Louis Gasnier	Milton Raison	L. Y. Erskine (Renfrew Rides)	Douglas Renfrew (James Newill)
Murder Reported	Fortress	1957	Charles Saunders	Doreen Montgomery	Robert Chapman (Murder for the Million)	

M

FILM TITLE	STUDIO	YEAR	DIRECTOR	SCREENWRITER	SOURCE AUTHOR/WORK	SERIES
Murder, She Said	MGM	1961	George Pollock	David Pursall / Jack Seddon	A. Christie (4.50 from Paddington)	Jane Marple (Margaret Rutherford)
Meet Miss Marple				David Osborn		
Murder Will Out	First Nat.	1930	Clarence Badger	J. Grubb Alexander	M. Leinster	
Murder with Pictures	Paramount	1936	Charles Barton	John C. Moffitt / Sidney Salkow	G. H. Coxe	Kent Murdock (Lew Ayres)
Murder Without Crime	Ass. Brit.	1950	J. Lee Thompson	J. Lee Thompson	J. L. Thompson	
Murderer	Cocinor	1963	Claude Autant-Lara	Jean Aurenche / Pierre Bost	P. Highsmith (Blunderer)	
Enough Rope						
Murderer Dimitri Karamazov	Terra	1931	Fyodor Ozep	Leonhard Frank / Fyodor Ozep / Victor Trivas / Erich Engel	F. M. Dostoevskii (Brothers Karamazov)	
Brothers Karamazov						
Murderer's Row	Columbia	1966	Henry Levin	Herbert Baker	D. Hamilton	Matt Helm (Dean Martin)
Murders in the Rue Morgue	*Rosenberg	1914	?	Sol A. Rosenberg	E. A. Poe (Prose Romances of Edgar A. Poe)	Dupin (?)
Murders in the Rue Morgue	Universal	1932	Robert Florey	Tom Reed / Dale Van Every / John Huston	E. A. Poe (Prose Romances of Edgar A. Poe)	Dupin (Leon Waycoff)
Murders in the Rue Morgue	AIP	1971	Gordon Hessler	Christopher Wicking / Henry Slesar	E. A. Poe (Prose Romances of Edgar A. Poe)	
Muscle Beach Party	Am. Int.	1964	William Asher	Robert Dillon	novel: Elsie Lee	
Musgrave Ritual	*Franco-Brit.	1912	Georges Treville	?	A. C. Doyle (Memoirs of Sherlock Holmes)	Sherlock Holmes (Georges Treville)
Musgrave Ritual	*Stoll	1922	George Ridgwell	Patrick L. Mannock	A. C. Doyle (Memoirs of Sherlock Holmes)	Sherlock Holmes (Eille Norwood)
Muss 'Em Up	RKO	1936	Charles Vidor	Geoffrey H. Malins / Erwin Gelsey	J. E. Grant (Green Shadow)	
House of Fate						
Mutiny	*Clark	1925	F. Martin Thornton	?	B. Bolt (Diana of the Islands)	
My Cousin Rachel	TCF	1952	Henry Koster	Nunnally Johnson	D. Du Maurier	
My Death Is a Mockery	Park Lane	1952	Tony Young	Douglas Baber	D. G. Baber	
My Gun Is Quick	UA	1957	George A. White	Richard Powell / Richard Collins	M. Spillane	Mike Hammer (Robert Bray)
My Lady's Garter	*Tourneur	1920	Maurice Tourneur	Lloyd Lonergan	J. Futrelle	
My Lady's Latchkey	*MacDonald	1921	Edwin Carewe	Finis Fox	C. N. Williamson (Second Latchkey)	
My Lord Conceit	*Stoll	1921	F. Martin Thornton	F. Martin Thornton	Rita	
My Lover, My Son	MGM	1970	John Newland	William Marchant / Jenni Hall / Brian Degas / Tudor Gates	E. Grierson (Reputation for a Song)	
My Name Is Julia Ross	Columbia	1945	Joseph H. Lewis	Muriel Roy Bolton	A. Gilbert (Woman in Red)	
My Official Wife	*Vitagraph	1914	James Young	Marguerite Bertsch / Eugene Millin	R. H. Savage	
My Sister and I	Burnham	1948	Harold Huth	A. R. Rawlinson / John Rees / Michael Medwin / Robert Westerby	E. Bonett (High Pavement)	
Mystere a Shanghai	Rapid	1950	Roger Blanc	Maurice Griffe / Jacques de Casembroot / S. A. Steeman	A. Steeman (Night of the 12th–13th)	
Mysteries of Paris	*Eclair	1909	?	?	E. Sue	
Mysteries of Paris	*SCAGL	1913	?	?	E. Sue	
Mysteries of Paris	Franco-Am.	1937	Felix Ganders	Felix Ganders	E. Sue	
Mysteries of Paris	Unidex	1962	Andre Hunnebelle	Jean Halain / Pierre Foucault / Diego Fabbri	E. Sue	

MYSTERY OF THE YELLOW ROOM / 1437

Title	Studio	Year	Director	Writer	Source	Character (Actor)
Mysterious Dr. Fu Manchu	Paramount	1929	Rowland V. Lee	Florence Ryerson / Lloyd Corrigan	S. Rohmer (Mystery of Dr. Fu Manchu)	Fu Manchu (Warner Oland)
Mysterious Mr. Reeder / Mind of Mr. Reeder	Grand Nat.	1939	Jack Raymond	Bryan Edgar Wallace / Marjorie Gaffney / Michael Hogan	E. Wallace (Mind of Mr. J. G. Reeder)	J. G. Reeder (Will Fyffe)
Mysterious Mr. Wong	Monogram	1935	William Nigh	Nina Howatt / Lew Levinson	H. S. Keeler (Sing Sing Nights)	
Mystery at the Villa Rose / At the Villa Rose	Twickenham	1930	Leslie Hiscott	James Herbuveaux / Cyril Twyford	A. E. W. Mason (At the Villa Rose)	Insp. Hanaud (Austin Trevor)
Mystery Girl	*Paramount	1919	William D. DeMille	Marion Fairfax	G. B. McCutcheon (Green Fancy)	
Mystery House	Warner	1938	Noel Smith	Sherman L. Lowe / Robertson White	M. Eberhart (Mystery of Hunting's End)	Sarah Keate (Ann Sheridan) / Lance O'Leary (Dick Purcell)
Mystery Liner / Ghost of John Holling	Monogram	1934	William Nigh	Wellwyn Trotman	E. Wallace (Steward)	
Mystery Mind	*Supreme	1920	Fred W. Sittenham / William S. Davis	Arthur B. Reeve / John W. Grey	novel: A. B. Reeve	
Mystery of a Hansom Cab	*Amalgamated	1911	W. J. Lincoln	?	F. Hume	
Mystery of a Hansom Cab	*B&C	1915	Harold Weston	Eliot Stannard	F. Hume	
Mystery of a Hansom Cab	*Pyramid	1925	Arthur Shirley	Arthur Shirley	F. Hume	
Mystery of Boscombe Vale	*Franco-Brit.	1912	Georges Treville	?	A. C. Doyle (Adventures of Sherlock Holmes)	Sherlock Holmes (Georges Treville) / Old Man (Rolf Leslie)
Mystery of Brudenell Court	*Stoll	1924	Hugh Croise	Hugh Croise	B. Orczy (Old Man in the Corner)	Old Man (Rolf Leslie)
Mystery of Dogstooth Cliff	*Stoll	1924	Hugh Croise	Hugh Croise	B. Orczy (Old Man in the Corner)	
Mystery of Edwin Drood	*Gaumont	1909	Arthur Gilbert	?	C. Dickens	
Mystery of Edwin Drood	*Films d'Art	1912	?	?	C. Dickens	
Mystery of Edwin Drood	*Blache	1914	Tom Terriss	Tom Terriss	C. Dickens	
Mystery of Edwin Drood	Universal	1935	Stuart Walker	John L. Balderston / Bradley King / Leopold Atlas / Gladys Unger	C. Dickens	
Mystery of Marie Roget	Universal	1942	Phil Rosen	Michael Jacoby	E. A. Poe (Tales)	Dupin (Patric Knowles)
Mystery of Mr. Bernard Brown	*Stoll	1921	Sinclair Hill	Mrs. Sydney Groome	E. P. Oppenheim	
Mystery of Mr. X	MGM	1934	Edgar Selwyn	Philip MacDonald / Howard Emmett Rogers / Monckton Hoffe	M. Porlock (X v. Rex)	
Mystery of Orcival	*AB	1916	J. Farrell MacDonald	?	E. Gaboriau	
Mystery of Room 13 / Mr. Reeder in Room 13	Brit. Nat.	1938	Norman Lee	Doreen Montgomery / Victor Kendall / Elizabeth Meehan	E. Wallace (Room 13)	J. G. Reeder (Gibb McLaughlin)
Mystery of the Diamond Belt	*Davidson	1914	Charles Raymond	Charles Raymond	Lewis Carlton	Sexton Blake (Phillip Kay) / Old Man (Rolf Leslie)
Mystery of the Khaki Tunic	*Stoll	1924	Hugh Croise	Hugh Croise	B. Orczy (Old Man in the Corner)	
Mystery of the Pink Villa	Twickenham	1930	Leslie Hiscott	Louis Mercanton / Renee Hervil	A. E. W. Mason (At the Villa Rose)	
Mystery of the Thirteenth Guest	Monogram	1943	William Beaudine	Charles Marlon / Tim Ryan / Arthur Hoerl	A. Trail (Thirteenth Guest)	
Mystery of the Villa Rose	Haik	1930	Louis Mercanton / Renee Hervil	Louis d'Yvre	A. E. W. Mason (At the Villa Rose)	
Mystery of the White Room	Universal	1939	Otis Garrett	Alex Gottlieb	J. G. Edwards (Murder in the Surgery)	
Mystery of the Yellow Room	*Realart	1919	Emile Chautard	Emile Chautard	G. Leroux	Insp. Hanaud (Leon Mathot)

M

FILM TITLE	STUDIO	YEAR	DIRECTOR	SCREENWRITER	SOURCE AUTHOR/WORK	SERIES
Mystery of the Yellow Room	Osso	1931	Marcel l'Herbier	?	G. Leroux	
Mystery of West Sedgwick	*Edison	1913	?	Margaret Turnbull	C. Wells (Gold Bag)	
Mystery Road	*Fam. Play.	1921	Paul Powell	Mary O'Connor	E. P. Oppenheim	
Naked City	Universal	1948	Jules Dassin	Malvin Wald Albert Maltz	screenplay: M. Wald	
Naked Edge	Glass	1961	Michael Anderson	Joseph Stefano	M. Ehrlich (First Train to Babylon)	
Naked Face	Cannon	1984	Bryan Forbes	Bryan Forbes	S. Sheldon	
Naked Kiss	AA	1965	Samuel Fuller	Samuel Fuller	novel: S. Fuller	
Naked Runner	Artanis	1967	Sidney J. Furie	Stanley Mann	F. Clifford	
Naked Spur	MGM	1953	Anthony Mann	Sam Rolfe	novel: A. Ullman	
Name of the Rose	TCF	1986	Jean-Jacques Annaud	Harold Jack Bloom Andrew Birkin Gerard Brach Howard Franklin Alain Godard	U. Eco	
Nancy Steele Is Missing	TCF	1937	George Marshall	Hal Long Gene Fowler	C. F. Coe (Ransom)	
Nanny	Hammer	1965	Seth Holt	Jimmy Sangster	E. Piper	
Narrowing Circle	Fortress	1955	Charles Saunders	Doreen Montgomery	J. Symons	
Native Son	Classic	1951	Pierre Chenal	Pierre Chenal Richard Wright	Richard Wright	
Naval Treaty	*Stoll	1922	George Ridgwell	Patrick L. Mannock Geoffrey H. Malins	A. C. Doyle (Memoirs of Sherlock Holmes)	Sherlock Holmes (Eille Norwood)
Negatives	Kettledrum	1968	Peter Medak	Peter Everett	P. Everett	
Neither the Sea Nor the Sand	Tigon	1972	Fred Burnley	Gordon Honeycombe Rosemary Davies	G. Honeycombe	
Net	*UA	1922	Kenneth Webb	Dorothy Farnum	Rex Beach	
Net	Gen. Film	1952	Anthony Asquith	William Fairchild	J. Pudney	
Project M7						
Nets of Destiny	Davidson	1924	Arthur Rooke	Eliot Stannard	M. Drake (Salving of a Derelict)	
Never a Dull Moment	Buena Vista	1967	Jerry Paris	A. J. Carothers	J. Godey (Thrill a Minute with Jack Albany)	Jack Albany (Dick Van Dyke)
Never Back Losers	Merton Park	1961	Robert Tronson	Lukas Heller	E. Wallace (Green Ribbon)	
Never Let Me Go	MGM	1953	Delmer Daves	Ronald Millar George Froeschel	R. Bax (Came the Dawn)	
Never Love a Stranger	AA	1959	Robert Stevens	Harold Robbins Richard Day	H. Robbins	
Never Mention Murder	Merton Park	1964	John Nelson Burton	Robert B. Stewart	E. Wallace (headnote)	
Never Say Never Again	Woodcote	1983	Irvin Kershner	Lorenzo Semple, Jr.	I. Fleming (Thunderball)	James Bond (Sean Connery)
Never Take Candy from a Stranger	Hammer	1961	Cyril Frankel	John Hunter		
New Adventures of Dr. Fu Manchu	Paramount	1930	Rowland V. Lee	Lloyd Corrigan Florence Ryerson	novel: R. Garis S. Rohmer (Devil Doctor)	Fu Manchu (Warner Oland)
Return of Dr. Fu Manchu						
New Adventures of Get-Rich-Quick Wallingford	MGM	1931	Sam Wood	Charles MacArthur	G. R. Chester (Get-Rich-Quick Wallingford)	J. Rufus Wallingford (William Haines)
Get-Rich-Quick Wallingford						
New Adventures of J. Rufus Wallingford	*Pathe	1916	Theodore Wharton	?	G. R. Chester (Get-Rich-Quick Wallingford)	J. Rufus Wallingford (Max Figman)
New Centurions Los Angeles Precinct 45	Columbia	1972	Richard Fleischer	Stirling Silliphant	J. Wambaugh	
New Leaf	Paramount	1970	Elaine May	Elaine May	J. Ritchie	
New Magdalen	*Powers	1910	Pierce Kingsley	Joseph A. Golden	Wilkie Collins	
New Magdalen	*Imp	1912	Herbert Brenon	?	Wilkie Collins	
New Magdalen	*Biograph	1914	Travers Vale	?	Wilkie Collins	
New York	*Fam. Play.	1927	Luther Reed	Forrest Halse	novel: B. Chambers	

N

Title	Studio	Year	Director	Writers	Source/Character
Next Man	Art. Ent.	1976	Richard C. Sarafian	Mort Fine / Alan R. Trustman / David M. Wolf / Michael Chapman / Richard C. Sarafian	
Nickel Ride	TCF	1975	Robert Mulligan	Eric Roth	
Night and Morning	*Clarenden	1915	Wilfred Noy	?	novel: M. T. Kaufman / E. Bulwer-Lytton
Night and the City	TCF	1950	Jules Dassin	Jo Eisinger	G. Kersh
Night at the Crossroads	Renoir	1932	Jean Renoir	?	G. Simenon (Crossroads Murders) / Jules Maigret (Pierre Renoir)
Night Caller Blood Beast from Outer Space	New Art	1965	John Gilling	Jim O'Connolly	F. Crisp (Night Callers)
Night Club Lady	Columbia	1932	Irvin Cummings	Robert Riskin	A. Abbot (About the Murder of the Night Club Lady) / Thatcher Colt (Adolphe Menjou)
Night Club Scandal	Paramount	1937	Ralph Murphy	Lillie Howard	D. N. Rubin (Riddle Me This!)
Night-Comers	Rank	1959	?	?	E. Ambler
Night Creatures Captain Clegg	Universal	1962	Peter Graham Scott	Anthony Hinds	R. Thorndyke (Dr. Syn)
Night Fighters Terrible Beauty	UA	1960	Tay Garnett	Barbara S. Harper / Robert W. Campbell	A. J. Roth (Terrible Beauty)
Night Has a Thousand Eyes	Paramount	1948	John Farrow	Barre Lyndon / Jonathan Latimer	G. Hopley
Night Has Eyes Terror House	ABPC	1942	Leslie Arliss	John Argyle / Leslie Arliss / Alan Kennington	A. Kennington
Night Heaven Fell Heaven Fell That Night	Kingsley	1958	Roger Vadim	Roger Vadim / Jacques Remy	A. Vidalie (Midnight Jewelers)
Night in Casablanca	UA	1946	Archie Mayo	Joseph Fields / Roland Kibbee	novel: D. Ames
Night in Havana Big Boodle	UA	1957	Richard Wilson	Jo Eisinger	R. Sylvester (Big Boodle)
Night in New Orleans	Paramount	1942	William Clemens	Jonathan Latimer	J. R. Langham (Sing a Song of Homicide)
Night Invader	WB-FN	1943	Herbert Mason	Brock Williams / Edward Dryhurst / Roland Pertwee	J. Bentley (Rendezvous with Death)
Night Journey	Brit. Nat.	1938	Oswald Mitchell	Jim Phelan / Maisie Sherman	J. Phelan (Ten-a-Penny People)
Night Moves	Warner	1975	Arthur Penn	Alan Sharp	novel: A. Sharp
Night Must Fall	MGM	1937	Richard Thorpe	John Von Druten	Emlyn Williams
Night Must Fall	MGM	1964	Karel Reisz	Clive Exton	Emlyn Williams
Night Nurse	Warner	1931	William A. Wellman	O. H. P. Garrett / Charles Kenyon	D. Macy
Night of January 16	Paramount	1941	William Clemens	Delmar Daves / Robert Pirosh / Eve Greene	A. Rand
Night of June 13	Paramount	1932	Stephen Roberts	Agnes Brand Leahy / Brian Marlow / William S. McNutt	F. Vreeland (June 13)
Night of Mystery	Paramount	1937	E. A. DuPont	Frank Partos / Gladys Unger	S. S. Van Dine (Greene Murder Case) / Philo Vance (Grant Richards)
Night of the Askari Whispering Death	Lord	1976	Juergen Goslar	Juergen Goslar / Scott Finch	D. Carney (Whispering Death)
Night of the Eagle Conjure Wife	Am. Int.	1962	Sidney Hayers	Charles Beaumont / Richard Matheson / George Baxt	F. Leiber, Jr. (Conjure Wife)
Night of the Following Day	Universal	1969	Hubert Cornfield	Hubert Cornfield / Robert Phippeny	L. White (Snatchers)
Night of the Generals	Horizon	1966	Anatole Litvak	Joseph Kessel / Paul Dehn	H. H. Kirst

N

FILM TITLE	STUDIO	YEAR	DIRECTOR	SCREENWRITER	SOURCE AUTHOR/WORK	SERIES
Night of the Hunter	UA	1955	Charles Laughton	James Agee	D. Grubb	
Night of the Juggler	Columbia	1980	Robert Butler	Bill Norton, Sr. Rick Natkin	W. P. McGivern	
Night of the Living Dead	Continental	1974	George A. Romero	John A. Russo	novel: J. Russo	
Night to Remember	Columbia	1942	Richard Wallace	Richard Flournoy Jack Henley	K. Roos (Frightened Stiff)	Jeff Troy (Brian Aherne) (Haila) Troy (Loretta Young)
Night Walker	Universal	1964	William Castle	Robert Bloch	novel: S. Stuart	
Night Warning Butcher, Baker, Nightmare Maker Nightmare Maker	Internat.	1982	William Asher	Stephen Breimer Alan Jay Blueckman	novel: R. Natale (Butcher, Baker, Nightmare Maker)	
Night Was Our Friend	Act	1951	Michael Anderson	Michael Pertwee Tony Williamson	M. Pertwee	
Night Watch	Avco Emb.	1973	Brian G. Hutton	Evan Jones	L. Fletcher	
Night Without Sleep	TCF	1952	Roy Baker	Frank Partos Elick Moll	E. Moll	
Night Without Stars	Europa	1951	Anthony Pelissier	Winston Graham	Winston Graham	
Nightcomers	Scimitar	1972	Michael Winner	Michael Hastings	novel: Michael Hastings	
Nightfall	Columbia	1957	Jacques Tourneur	Stirling Silliphant	D. Goodis	
Nightflyers	Vista	1987	T. C. Blake	Robert Jaffe	G. R. R. Martin	
Nightmare	Universal	1942	Tim Whelan	Dwight Taylor	M. Portlock (Mystery in Kensington Gore)	
Nightmare	UA	1956	Maxwell Shane	Maxwell Shane	C. Woolrich	
Nightmare Alley	TCF	1947	Edmund Goulding	Jules Furthman	W. L. Gresham	
Nightmare Honeymoon	MGM	1972	Nicholas Roeg	S. Lee Pogostin	L. Block (headnote)	
Nightmare in Chicago	Universal	1967	Elliot Silverstein Robert Altman	Donald Moessinger	W. P. McGivern (Killer on the Turnpike)	
Nightmare Maker Butcher, Baker, Nightmare Maker Night Warning	Internat.	1982	William Asher	Stephen Breimer Alan Jay Glueckman	novel: R. Natale (Butcher, Baker, Nightmare Maker)	
Nightwing	Polyc	1979	Arthur Hiller	Steve Shagan Bud Shrake Martin Cruz Smith	M. C. Smith	
Nine Forty-Five	WB-FN	1934	George King	Brock Williams	O. Davis (At 9:45)	
Nine Girls	Columbia	1944	Leigh Jason	Karen DeWolf Connie Lee	W. H. Pettit	
Nine Lives Are Not Enough	Warner	1941	A. E. Sutherland	Fred Niblo, Jr.	J. Odlum	
19 Red Roses	?	1974	?	?	T. Nielsen	
99 and 44/100% Dead Call Harry Crown	TCF	1974	John Frankenheimer	Robert Dillon	novel: M. Franklin (99 44/100% Dead)	
Ninth Guest	Columbia	1934	Roy William Neill	Garnett Weston	O. Davis	
No Abras Nunca Esa Puerta	Argentina	1952	C. H. Christensen	Alejandro Casona	W. Irish (Somebody on the Phone)	
No Down Payment	TCF	1957	Martin Ritt	Philip Yordan	J. McPartland	
No Escape	Welwyn	1936	Norman Lee	George Goodchild Frank Witty	G. Goodchild (No Exit)	
No Escape/No Exit No Escape	Welwyn	1936	Norman Lee	George Goodchild Frank Witty	G. Goodchild (No Exit)	
No Greater Love	*Selig	1915	?	?	W. Le Queux	
No Hands on the Clock	Paramount	1941	Frank McDonald	Maxwell Shane	G. Homes	Humphrey Campbell (Chester Morris)
No Man of Her Own	Paramount	1950	Mitchell Leisen	Sally Benson Catherine Turney	W. Irish (I Married a Dead Man)	
No Man's Land	*Metro	1918	Will S. Davis	Albert S. LeVino	L. J. Vance	
No Orchids for Miss Blandish	Alliance	1948	St. John L. Clowes	St. John L. Clowes	J. H. Chase	
No Place Like Homicide What a Carve Up!	New World	1961	Pat Jackson	Ray Cooney	Frank King (Ghoul)	

N

Title	Studio	Year	Director	Writer/Source	Character
No Pockets in a Shroud	Balzac	1975	Jean-Pierre Mocky	Jean-Pierre Mocky / Alain Moury	H. McCoy
No Resting Place	Lesslie	1951	Paul Rotha	Paul Rotha / Colin Lesslie / Michael Orrom / Gerald Healy	I. Niall
No Road Back	Gibraltar	1957	Montgomery Tully	Charles A. Leeds / Montgomery Tully	F. L. Cary (Madam Tic-Tac)
No Way Back	Concanen	1949	Stefan Osiecki	Stefan Osiecki / Derrick de Marney	T. Burke (Limehouse Nights)
No Way Out	Orion	1987	Roger Donaldson	Robert Garland	K. Fearing (Big Clock)
No Way to Treat a Lady	Paramount	1968	Jack Smight	John Gay	H. Longbaugh
Noble Bachelor	Stoll	1921	Maurice Elvey	William J. Elliott	A. C. Doyle (Adventures of Sherlock Holmes) — Sherlock Holmes (Eille Norwood)
Nobody Lives Forever	Warner	1946	Jean Negulesco	W. R. Burnett / Wilfred Greatorex	W. R. Burnett
Nobody Runs Forever / High Commissioner	Selmur	1968	Ralph Thomas		J. Cleary (High Commissioner) — Scobie Malone (Rod Taylor)
Nobody's Perfekt	Columbia	1981	Peter Bonerz	Tony Kenrick / James O. Curwood / David M. Hartford	T. Kenrick (Two for the Price of One)
Nomads of the North	*First Nat.	1920	David M. Hartford		J. O. Curwood
Non-Conformist Parson / Heart and Soul	*Brit. Lion	1919	A. V. Bramble	Eliot Stannard	R. Horniman
Non-Stop New York	Gaumont	1937	Robert Stevenson	Roland Pertwee / J. O. C. Orton / Kurt Siodmak / Derek Twist / E. V. H. Emmett	K. Attiwill (Sky Steward)
Noose for a Lady / Nora Prentiss	Insignia	1953	Wolf Rilla	Rex Rienits	G. Verner (Whispering Woman)
	Warner	1947	Vincent Sherman	N. Richard Nash / Philip MacDonald	novel: Alex Morrison
Norman Conquest / Park Plaza 605	B&A	1953	Bernard Knowles	Bernard Knowles / Albert Fennell / Bertram Ostrer / Clifford Witting	B. Gray (Dare-Devil Conquest) — Norman Conquest (Tom Conway)
North Sea Hijack / Assault Force ffoulkes	Universal	1980	Andrew V. McLaglen	Jack Davies	J. Davies (Esther, Ruth and Jennifer)
North Star	Sara Films	1982	P. Granier-Deferre	P. Granier-Deferre / Jean Aurenche / Michel Grisolia	G. Simenon (Lodger)
Northern Mystery	*Stoll	1924	Hugh Croise	Hugh Croise	B. Orczy (Old Man in the Corner) — Old Man (Rolf Leslie)
Northern Pursuit	Warner	1943	Raoul Walsh	Frank Gruber / Alvah Bessie	L. T. White (5,000 Trojan Horses)
Norwood Builder	*Stoll	1922	George Ridgwell	Patrick L. Mannock / Geoffrey H. Malins	A. C. Doyle (Return of Sherlock Holmes) — Sherlock Holmes (Eille Norwood)
Nosferatu	*Prana	1929	Friedrich W. Murnau	Henrik Galeen	B. Stoker (Dracula)
Not Against the Flesh / Castle of Doom / Strange Adventure of David Gray / Vampire	Dreyer	1931	Carl T. Dreyer	Carl T. Dreyer / Christian Jul	J. S. Le Fanu (In a Glass Darkly)
Not Guilty	*Bennett	1921	Sidney A. Franklin	J. Grubb Alexander	H. MacGrath (Parrot & Co.)
Nothing But the Best	Domino	1963	Clive Donner	Frederic Raphael	S. Ellin (Mystery Stories)
Nothing But the Night / Resurrection Syndicate	Charlemagne	1973	Peter Sasdy	Brian Hughes	J. Blackburn
Nothing But the Truth	Crone	1975	Henning Oernback	?	P. Orum
Notorious Landlady	Columbia	1962	Richard Quine	Larry Gelbart / Richard Quine / Blake Edwards	novel: I. Shulman
Notorious Miss Lisle	*First Nat.	1920	James Young	James Young	B. Reynolds

N

FILM TITLE	STUDIO	YEAR	DIRECTOR	SCREENWRITER	SOURCE AUTHOR/WORK	SERIES
Notorious Mrs. Carrick	*Stoll	1924	George Ridgwell	?	C. Procter (Pools of the Past)	
Notorious Sophie Lang	Paramount	1934	Ralph Murphy	Anthony Veiller	F. I. Anderson	Sophie Lang (Gertrude Michael)
Now Barrabas	Paramount	1949	Gordon Parry	Gordon Parry	W. D. Home	
Nowhere to Go	Ealing	1958	Seth Holt	Seth Holt / Kenneth Tynan	D. MacKenzie	
Number Seventeen	*Fox	1920	George A. Beranger	George A. Beranger	L. Tracy	
Number 17	Felner	1928	Geza M. Bolvary	Geza M. Bolvary	J. J. Farjeon	
Number 17	BIP	1932	Alfred Hitchcock	Alfred Hitchcock / Alma Reville / Rodney Ackland	J. J. Farjeon	
Number Six	Merton Park	1962	Robert Tronson	Philip Mackie	E. Wallace	
Nursemaid Who Disappeared	WB-FN	1939	Arthur Woods	Paul Gangelin	P. MacDonald	
Nurse's Secret	Warner	1941	Noel M. Smith	Connery Chappell / Anthony Coldeway	M. R. Rinehart (Miss Pinkerton)	
O. Henry's Full House / Full House	TCF	1952	Henry Hathaway / Henry Koster / Henry King / Howard Hawks / Jean Negulesco	Lamar Trotti / Richard Breen / Ben Roberts / Ivan Goff / Walter Bullock / Nunnally Johnson	O. Henry (headnote)	
OSS 117—Mission for a Killer	PAC-DA-MA	1966	Andre Hunabelle	Jean Halain / Pierre Foucaud / Andre Hunabelle	J. Bruce (Live Wire)	OSS 117 (Frederick Stafford)
Oakdale Affair	*World	1919	Oscar Apfel	?	E. R. Burroughs	
Obsessed / Late Edwina Black	Gen. Film	1951	Maurice Elvey	Charles Frank / David Evans	W. Dinner (Late Edwina Black)	
Obsession / Hidden Room	Independent	1949	Edward Dmytryk	Alec Coppel	A. Coppel (Man About a Dog)	
Obsession	Pathe	1954	Jean Delannoy	Antoine Blondin / Roland Laudenbach / Jean Delannoy	W. Irish (Dead Man Blues)	
Obsession	Cocinor	1959	Luchino Visconti	Pietrangeli / Giuseppi De Santis / Mario Alicata / Gianni Fuccini / Luchino Visconti	J. M. Cain (Serenade)	
Ocean's 11	Warner	1960	Lewis Milestone	Harry Brown / Charles Lederer	novel: G. C. Johnson	
October Man	World Film	1947	Roy Baker	Eric Ambler	novel: E. Britton	
Octopussy	Eon	1983	John Glen	George M. Fraser / Richard Maibaum / Michael G. Wilson	I. Fleming	James Bond (Roger Moore)
Octoroon	*Gaumont	1903	Dicky Winslow	Dion Boucicault	D. Boucicault	
Octoroon	*Kalem	1909	?	?	D. Boucicault	
Octoroon	Kalem	1913	Sidney Olcott	Gene Gauthier	D. Boucicault	
Odd Man Out	Two Cities	1947	Carol Reed	F. L. Green / R. C. Sherriff	F. L. Green	
Odds Against Tomorrow	UA	1959	Robert Wise	John O. Killens / Nelson Gidding	W. P. McGivern	
Odessa File	Columbia	1974	Ronald Neame	Kenneth Ross	F. Forsyth	
Off the Highway	*Prod. Dist.	1925	Tom Forman	George Markstein / Dorothy Farnum	T. Gallon (Tatterley)	
Offense	Tantallon	1973	Sidney Lumet	John Hopkins	J. Hopkins (This Story of Yours)	
Something Like the Truth						

Title	Studio	Year	Director	Writer/Source	Notes
Office Party Hostile Takeover	S.C. Enter.	1988	George Mihalka	Michael A. Gilbert / Stephen Zoller	M. A. Gilbert
Officer 666	*Kleine	1914	?	?	B. Currie
Officer 666	*Williamson	1916	Fred Niblo	W. J. Lincoln	B. Currie
Officer 666	*Goldwyn	1920	Harry Beaumont	Gerald C. Duffy	B. Currie
Old Bones of the River Bones	Gainsbor.	1938	Marcel Varnel	Marriott Edgar / Val Guest	E. Wallace (Bones)
Old Dark House	Universal	1932	James Whale	J. O. C. Orton / Benn W. Levy / R. C. Sherriff	J. P. Priestley (Benighted)
Old Dark House	Hammer	1963	William Castle	Robert Dillon	J. P. Priestley (Benighted)
Old Man	Brit. Lion	1931	Manning Haynes	Edgar Wallace	E. Wallace (Coat of Arms)
Old Rascal	Blue Dahlia	1992	Gerard Jourd'hui	Dominique Roulet / Gerard Jourd'hui	Fredric Brown (His Name Was Death)
Old Tin Can	Progefi	1967	Jacques Poitrenaud	Jean-Loup Dabadie / Jacques Poitrenaud / Albert Valentine / Michel Levine	D. Keene (Flight by Night)
On a Nice Summer Day	Prodis	1965	Jacques Deray	Michel Audiard / Didier Goulard / Maurice Fabre / Georges Bardawill / Jacques Deray	J. H. Chase (One Bright Summer Morning)
On Dangerous Ground	*World	1917	Robert Thornby	Frances Marion / A. I. Bezzerides	B. E. Stevenson (Little Comrade)
On Dangerous Ground	RKO	1952	Nicholas Ray	Nicholas Ray	G. Butler (Mad with Much Heart)
On Friday at Eleven World in My Pocket	Brit. Lion	961	Alvin Rakoff	Frank Harvey	J. H. Chase (World in My Pocket)
On Her Majesty's Secret Service	Eon	1969	Peter Hunt	Richard Maubaum / Simon Raven	I. Fleming / James Bond (George Lazenby)
On the Double	Deni-Capri	1961	Melville Shavelson	Jack Rose / Melville Shavelson	novel: Roger Fuller
On the Night of the Fire Fugitive	GFD	1939	Brian Desmond Hurst	Brian Desmond Hurst / Patrick Kirwan / Terence Young	F. L. Green
On the Run	Merton Park Chester.	1963	Robert Tronson	Richard Harris	E. Wallace (headnote)
On the Stroke of Nine Murder on the Campus		1934	Richard Thorpe	Andrew Moses	W. Chambers (Campanile Murders)
On the Waterfront	Columbia	1954	Elia Kazan	Budd Schulberg	B. Schulberg (Waterfront)
On the Yard	Midwest	1978	Raphael D. Silver	Malcolm Braly	M. Braly
On Thin Ice	*Warner	1925	Mal St. Clair	Darryl F. Zanuck	A. R. Colver (Dear Pretender)
On Trial	*Essanay	1917	James Young	James Young	E. L. Reizenstein
On Trial	Warner	1928	Archie Mayo	Robert Lord / Max Pollock	E. L. Reizenstein
On Trial	Warner	1939	Terry Morse	Don Ryan	E. L. Reizenstein
Once a Crook	TCF	1941	Herbert Mason	Roger Burford	E. Price
Once a Thief Happy Thieves	UA	1962	George Marshall	John Gay	R. Condon (Oldest Confession)
Once a Thief	MGM	1965	Ralph Nelson	Zekial Marko	J. Trinian (Scratch a Thief)
Once Upon a Time in America	Ladd	1984	Sergio Leone	Leonardo Benvenuti / Piero De Bernardi / Enrico Medioli / Franco Arcalli / Franco Ferrini	H. Grey (Hoods)
Once You Kiss a Stranger	Warner	1969	Robert Sparr	Frank Tarloff / Norman Katkov	P. Highsmith (Strangers on a Train)
One Against Seven Counterattack	Columbia	1945	Zoltan Korda	John Howard Lawson	Janet Stevenson (Counterattack)
One Born Every Minute Flim Flam Man	TCF	1967	Irvin Kershner	William Rose / Yakima Canutt	G. Owen (Ballad of the Flim Flam Man)

O

FILM TITLE	STUDIO	YEAR	DIRECTOR	SCREENWRITER	SOURCE AUTHOR/WORK	SERIES
One Deadly Summer	SNC	1983	Jean Becker	Sebastien Japrisot	S. Japrisot	
One-Eyed Jacks	Paramount	1961	Marlon Brando	Guy Trosper, Calder Willingham	C. Neider (Authentic Death of Hendry Jones)	
One for All						
President's Mystery	Republic	1936	Phil Rosen	Lester Cole, Nathaniel West	F. D. Roosevelt (President's Mystery Story)	
One Hour Before Dawn	*Hampton	1920	Henry King	Fred Myron, Fred Leon Smith	M. Scott (Behind Red Curtains)	
One Is Always Too Good to Women	CIC	1971	Michel Boisrond	Marcel Julian, Michel Boisrond	R. Queneau (We Always Treat Women Too Well)	
One Jump Ahead	Kenilworth	1955	Charles Saunders	Doreen Montgomery	Robert Chapman	
One Million Dollars	Rolfe	1915	John W. Noble	Arnold Fredericks	A. Fredericks (One Million Francs)	
One More Time	UA	1969	Jerry Lewis	Michael Pertwee	novel: M. Avallone	
One Night in Lisbon	Paramount	1941	Edward H. Griffith	Virginia Van Upp	J. Van Druten (There's Always Juliet)	
One Night in the Tropics	Universal	1940	A. E. Sutherland	Gertrude Purcell, Charles Grayson, Kathryn Scola, Frances Marion	E. D. Biggers (Love Insurance)	
One of Our Dinosaurs Is Missing	Disney	1975	Robert Stevenson	Bill Walsh	D. Forrest (Great Dinosaur Robbery)	
One of the Best	*Gainsboro.	1927	T. Hayes Hunter	Patrick L. Mannock	S. Hicks	
One of Those Things	A/S Nordisk	1971	Erik Balling	Erik Balling, Anders Bodelsen	A. Bodelsen (One Down)	
Hit and Run, Run, Run						
One Step to Eternity	Sirius	1955	Henri Decoin	Henri Decoin	P. McGerr (Follow, As the Night)	
Rope for Killing						
One Way Out	Columbia	1950	Henry Levin	J. de Baroncelli, William Bowers, Fred Niblo, Jr., Seton I. Miller	M. Flavin (Criminal Code)	
Convicted						
One Way Ticket	Columbia	1935	Herbert Biberman	Vincent Lawrence, Joseph Anthony, Oliver H. P. Garrett, Grover Jones	Ethel Turner	
One Way Ticket	Valoria	1971	Jose Giovanni	Jose Giovanni	H. E. Helseth (Chair for Martin Rome)	
One Wonderful Night	*Essanay	1914	E. H. Calvert	?	L. Tracy	
One Wonderful Night	*Universal	1922	Stuart Paton	?	L. Tracy	
Onion Field	AVCO	1979	Harold Becker	Joseph Wambaugh	J. Wambaugh	
Only Saps Work	Paramount	1930	Edwin H. Knopf, Cyril Gardner	Percy Heath, Joseph L. Mankiewicz, Sam Mintz	O. Davis (Easy Come, Easy Go)	
Only the Wind Knows the Answer	Roxy	1975	Alfred Vohrer	Manfred Purzer	J. M. Simmel (Wind and the Rain)	
Only When I Larf	Beeord	1968	Basil Dearden	John Salmon	L. Deighton	
Operation Cicero	TCF	1952	Joseph Mankiewicz	Michael Wilson	L. C. Moyzisch (Operation Cicero)	
Five Fingers						
Operation Cobra	Norsk	1979	Ola Solum	Ola Solum	A. Bodelsen	
Operation Masquerade	Novus	1964	Basil Dearden	Michael Relph, William Goldman	V. Canning (Castle Minerva)	
Masquerade						
Shabby Tiger						
Operation Undercover	UA	1974	Milton Katselas	Abby Mann, Ernest Tidyman	J. Mills (Report to the Commissioner)	(Rex) Banner (Paul Carpenter)
Report to the Commissioner						Richard Duvall (William Faversham)
Operator 13	MGM	1934	Richard Boleslavsky	Harvey Thew, Zelda Sears, Eve Greene	R. W. Chambers (Secret Service Operator 13)	
Spy 13						
Ordeal by Innocence	Cannon	1984	Desmond Davis	Alexander Stuart, Robert Faenza, Ennio de Concini	A. Christie	
Order of Death	Vigo	1983	Robert Faenza	Hugh Fleetwood	H. Fleetwood	
Corrupt						

Orders to Kill	Lynx	1958	Anthony Asquith	Paul Dehn	D. Downes
Orient Express	TCF	1934	Paul Martin	George St. George Paul Martin Carl Hovey Oscar Levant William Conselman	G. Greene (Stamboul Train)
Orion's Belt	New World	1987	Ola Solum	Richard Harris	J. Michelet
Orphans	Lorimar	1987	Alan J. Pakula	Lyle Kessler	L. Kessler
Osterman Weekend	Davis-Panz.	1983	Sam Peckinpah	Alan Sharp Ian Masters	R. Ludlum
Other	Rex-Bench.	1972	Robert Mulligan	Thomas Tryon	T. Tryon
Other Man	Brit. Lion	1932	Manning Haynes	?	E. Wallace (Nine Bears)
Other Men's Shoes	*Lewis	1920	Edgar Lewis	George D. Procter	A. Soutar
Other People's Money	*Thanhauser	1916	William Parke	Benedict James	E. Gaboriau
Other Person	*Granger	1921	B. E. Doxat-Pratt	Herman Raucher	F. Hume
Other Side of Midnight	TCF	1977	Charles Jarrott	Daniel Taradash	S. Sheldon
Other Side of the Door	*American	1916	Thomas Ricketts	Clifford Howard	L. Chamberlain
Odey	Open Road	1968	Dick Clement	Ian La Frenais Dick Clement	M. Waddell
					Gerald Otley (Tom Courtenay)
Our Man Flint	TCF	1965	Daniel Mann	Hal Fimberg Ben Starr	novel: J. Pearl
Our Man in Havana	Kingsmead	1960	Carol Reed	Graham Greene	G. Greene
Our Mother's House	Heron	1967	Jack Clayton	Jeremy Brooks Haya Harareet	J. Gloag
Out of the Clouds	Ealing	1955	Basil Dearden Michael Relph	Michael Relph John Eldridge Rex Reinits	J. Fores (Springboard)
Out of the Fog	Warner	1941	Anatole Litvak	Robert Rossen Jerry Wald Richard Macaulay	I. Shaw (Gentle People)
Out of the Fog Fog for a Killer	Eternal	1962	Montgomery Tully	Montgomery Tully	B. Graeme (Fog for a Killer)
Out of the Night	*Edison	1910	?		R. Beach (Laughing Bill Hyde)
Out of the Past Build My Gallows High	RKO	1947	Jacques Tourneur	Geoffrey Homes	G. Homes (Build My Gallows High)
Out of the Shadow	*Paramount	1919	Emile Chautard	Eve Unsell	E. W. Hornung (Shadow of a Rope)
Outback	NLT	1970	Ted Kotcheff	Evan Jones	K. Cook (Wake in Fright)
Outer Gate	Monogram	1937	Raymond Cannon	A. Laurie Brazee	O. R. Cohen
Outfit Good Guys Always Win	MGM	1973	John Flynn	John Flynn	R. Stark
Outside the Law	Universal	1930	Tod Browning	Tod Browning Lucien Hubbard Garrett Fort	novel: T. Browning
Outsider	*Rolfe	1917	William C. Dowlan	Charles A. Taylor	L. J. Vance (Nobody)
Outsider in Amsterdam	Veten. Ned.	1983	Wim Verstappen	Wim Verstappen Kees Holierhoek	J. van de Wetering
					de Gier (Rutger Hauer) Gripstra (Rijk de Gooyer)
Oval Diamond	*Thanhauser	1916	?	W. Eugene Moore	David Foster
Over My Dead Body	TCF	1942	Malcolm St. Clair	Edward James	J. D. O'Hanlon (As Good As Murdered)
					Jason Cordry (Milton Berle)
Overheard	Era	1930	Sinclair Hill	Leslie H. Gordon Harcourt Templeman	S. Aumonier
PT Raiders Ship That Died of Shame	Ealing	1955	Basil Dearden	John Whiting Michael Relph Basil Dearden	N. Monsarrat (Ship That Died of Shame)
Pace That Thrills	*First Nat.	1925	Webster Campbell	Byron Morgan	novel: R. Weber
Pagan	MGM	1929	W. S. Van Dyke	Dorothy Farnum	J. Russell (In Dark Places)

P

P

FILM TITLE	STUDIO	YEAR	DIRECTOR	SCREENWRITER	SOURCE AUTHOR/WORK	SERIES
Pagan Love	*Hodkinson	1920	Hugo Balin	?	A. Abdullah (Honorable Gentleman)	
Paid	MGM	1930	Sam Wood	Charles MacArthur	B. Veiller (Within the Law)	
Within the Law				Lucien Hubbard		
Paliser Case	*Goldwyn	1920	William Parke	Edfrid Bingham	E. Saltus	
Pallard the Punter	*Gaumont	1919	J. L. V. Leigh	George Pearson	E. Wallace (Grey Timothy)	
Pallet on the Floor	Mirage	1984	Lynton Butler	Martyn Sanderson	R. H. Morrieson	
				Robert Rising		
				Lynton Butler		
Pals First	*First Nat.	1926	Edwin Carewe	F. P. Elliott	L. W. Dodd	
				Olga Printzlau		
Panic in Needle Park	TCF	1971	Jerry Schatzberg	Joan Didion	J. Mills	
				John Gregory Dunne		
Panique	Filmsonor	1946	Julien Duvivier	Charles Spaak	G. Simenon (Mr. Hire's Engagement)	
				Julien Duvivier		
Panther's Moon	Univ. Int.	1950	George Sherman	George Zuckerman	V. Canning	
Spy Hunt				Leonard Lee		
Paper Mask	Film Four	1990	Christopher Morahan	John Collee	J. Collee	
Paper Orchid	Ganesh	1949	Roy Baker	Val Guest	A. La Bern	
Papered Down	*Essanay	1915	Lawrence C. Windom	?	M. R. Rinehart (Romantics)	
Parachute Jumper	Warner	1933	Alfred E. Green	John Francis Larkin	R. James (Some Call It Love)	
Paradine Case	Brit. Lion	1947	Alfred Hitchcock	David O. Selznick	R. Hichens	
				Alma Reville		
				James Bridie		
Paradise Garden	*Metro	1917	Fred J. Balshofer	Fred J. Balshofer	G. F. Gibbs	
				Richard V. Spencer		
Parallax View	Paramount	1974	Alan J. Pakula	David Giler	L. Singer	
				Lorenzo Semple, Jr.		
Paris at Midnight	*Metropolit.	1926	E. Mason Hopper	Frances Marion	H. Balzac (Le Pere Goriot)	
Paris by Night	Bri. Screen	1989	David Hare	David Hare	novel: David Hare	
Paris Express	Stoss	1953	Harold French	Harold French	G. Simenon (Man Who Watched the Trains Go By)	
Man Who Watched the Trains Go By						
Paris Trout	Viacom	1991	Stephen Gyllenhall	Pete Dexter	Pete Dexter	
Parisian Nights	*Gothic	1925	Al Santell	Kennedy Myron	R. Goyne	
Park Plaza 605	B&A	1953	Bernard Knowles	Bernard Knowles	B. Gray (Dare-Devil Conquest)	Norman Conquest
Norman Conquest				Albert Fennell		(Tom Conway)
				Bertram Ostrer		
				Clifford Witting		
Partner	Merton Park	1963	Gerard Glaister	John Roddick	E. Wallace (Million Dollar Story)	
Partners in Crime	Paramount	1937	Ralph Murphy	Garnett Weston	K. Steel (Murder Goes to College)	Hank Hyer
						(Lynne Overman)
Partners in Crime	Merton Park	1960	Peter Duffell	Robert Stewart	E. Wallace (Man Who Knew)	
Partners of the Night	*Goldwyn	1920	Paul Scardon	Charles Whittaker	L. Scott	
				Leroy Scott		
Party Girl	Victory	1930	Victor Halperin	Monte Katterjohn	E. Balmer (Dangerous Business)	Bob Clifford
				George Draney		(William B. Davidson)
				Victor Halperin		
Party Girl	MGM	1958	Nicholas Ray	George Wells	novel: M. H. Albert	
Pas Folla la Guepe	Marceau	1972	Jean Delannoy	Jean Delannoy	J. H. Chase (Just a Matter of Time)	
				Daniel Boulanger		
Pascali's Island	Avenue	1988	James Dearden	James Dearden	B. Unsworth	
Passage	Hemdale	1979	J. Lee Thompson	Bruce Nicolaysen	B. Nicolaysen (Perilous Passage)	
Passage from Hong Kong	Warner	1941	D. Ross Lederman	Fred Niblo, Jr.	E. D. Biggers (Agony Column)	
Passager Clandestin	Corona	1958	Ralph Habib	Maurice Auberge	G. Simenon (Stowaway)	
				Paul Andreota		
				Ralph Habib		
Passengers	Viaduc	1977	Serge Leroy	Serge Leroy	K. R. Dwyer (Chase)	
				Christopher Rank		

PERFECT CRIME

Title	Studio	Year	Director	Writer	Source / Character (Actor)
Passing of Mr. Quin	*Strand	1928	Julius Hagen	Leslie Hiscott	A. Christie (Mysterious Mr. Quin)
Passion of Slow Fire	Lux	1961	Edouard Molinaro	Jean Anouilh	G. Simenon (Belle)
Death of a Beauty					
End of Belle					
Passionate Adventure	*Gainsbor.	1924	Graham Cutts	Alfred Hitchcock	F. Stayton
Passionate Quest	*Warner	1926	J. Stuart Blackton	Marian Constance J. Stuart Blackton	E. P. Oppenheim
Passport to Treason	Mid-Century	1956	Robert S. Baker	Kenneth Hayles Norman Hudis	M. O'Brine
Pat Clancy's Adventure	*Edison	1912	?	?	O. Henry (Cabbages and Kings)
Patient in Room 18	Warner	1938	Bobby Connolly Crane Wilbur	Eugene Solow Robertson White	M. Eberhart
Patient Vanishes	Rialto	1941	Lawrence Huntington	John Argyle Edward Dryhurst David Hume	D. Hume (They Called Him Death)
This Man Is Dangerous					
Patriot Games	Paramount	1992	Philip Noyce	W. Peter Iliff Donald Stuart	T. Clancy
Paul Temple Returns	Nettlefold	1952	Maclean Rogers	Francis Durbridge	F. Durbridge (Paul Temple Intervenes) Paul Temple (John Bentley)
Paul Temple's Triumph	Nettlefold	1950	Maclean Rogers	A. R. Rawlinson	F. Durbridge (News of Paul Temple) Paul Temple (John Bentley)
Pawned	*Select	1922	Irvin V. Willat	Frank L. Packard Gene L. Coon	F. Packard
Pay the Devil	Universal	1957	Jack Arnold		novel: H. Whittington
Man in the Shadow					
Payment Deferred	MGM	1932	Lothar Mendes	Ernest Vadja Claudine West	J. Dell
Payoff	Filmauro	1978	Sergio Corbucci	Dino Maiuri Massima De Rita Luciano De Crescenzo Elvio Porta	A. Veraldi
Payroll	Lynx	1961	Sidney Hayers	George Baxt	D. Bickerton
I Promised to Pay					
Pearl of Death	Universal	1944	Roy William Neill	Bertram Millhauser	A. C. Doyle (Return of Sherlock Holmes) Sherlock Holmes (Basil Rathbone)
Peeper	TCF	1975	Peter Hyams	W. D. Richter	K. Laumer (Deadfall)
Fat Chance					
Peking Blonde	Comacico	1968	Nicolas Gessner	Nicolas Gessner Marc Behm Jacques Vilfrid	J. H. Chase (You Have Yourself a Deal)
Blonde from Peking					
Penelope	MGM	1966	Arthur Hiller	George Wells Willis Goldbeck	E. V. Cunningham
Penguin Pool Murder	RKO	1932	George Archainbaud		S. Palmer Hildegarde Withers (Edna May Oliver)
Penguin Pool Mystery					
Penguin Pool Mystery	RKO	1932	George Archainbaud	Willis Goldbeck	S. Palmer (Penguin Pool Murder) Hildegarde Withers (Edna May Oliver)
Penguin Pool Murder					
Penitentiary	Columbia	1938	John Brahm	Fred Niblo, Jr. Seton I. Miller	M. Flavin (Criminal Code)
Penniless Millionaire	*Broadwest	1921	Einar J. Bruun	Frank Fowell	D. C. Murray
Penthouse	MGM	1933	W. S. Van Dyke	Frances Goodrich Albert Hackett	A. S. Roche
Crooks in Clover					
People Against O'Hara	MGM	1951	John Sturges	John Monks, Jr.	E. Lipsky
People vs. Nancy Preston	*Stromberg	1925	Tom Forman	Marion Orth	J. Moroso (People Against Nancy Preston)
Perfect Alibi	ATP	1931	Basil Dean	Basil Dean A. A. Milne	A. A. Milne (Fourth Wall)
Birds of Prey					
Perfect Crime	FBO	1928	Bert Glennon	William LeBaron Ewart Adamson Victor Currier Randolph Bartlett	I. Zangwill (Big Bow Mystery)

P

1448 / PERFECT MURDER — Film Index

P

FILM TITLE	STUDIO	YEAR	DIRECTOR	SCREENWRITER	SOURCE AUTHOR/WORK	SERIES
Perfect Murder	Merchant	1989	Zafar Hai	Zafar Hai / H. R. F. Keating	H. R. F. Keating	Inspector Ghote (Naseeruddin Shah)
Perfect Sap	*First Nat.	1927	Howard Higgin	?	H. I. Young (Not Herbert)	
Perfume of the Lady in Black	Osso	1931	Marcel L'Herbier		G. Leroux	
Permission to Kill	AVCO	1975	Cyril Frankel	Robin Estridge	P. Loraine (W.I.L. One to Curtis)	
Perpetua	*Fam. Play.	1922	John S. Robertson	Josephine Lovett	D. C. Calthrop	
Love's Boomerang				Tom Geraghty		
Personal Affair	Two Cities	1953	Anthony Pelissier	Anthony Pelissier	L. Storm (Day's Mischief)	
Petrified Forest	Warner	1936	Archie L. Mayo	Charles Kenyon / Delmar Daves	R. Sherwood	
Phantom Buccaneer	*Essanay	1916	J. Charles Haydon	H. Tipton Steck	V. Bridges (Another Man's Shoes)	
Phantom Fiend Lodger	Twickenham	1932	Maurice Elvey	Miles Mander / Paul Rotha / Ivor Novello / H. Fowler Mear	M. B. Lowndes (Lodger)	
Phantom in the House	Trem Carr	1929	Phil Rosen	Arthur Hoerl	A. Soutar	
Phantom Lady	Universal	1944	Robert Siodmak	Bernard Schoenfeld	W. Irish	
Phantom Light	Gaumont	1934	Michael Powell	Ralph Smart / Austin Melford / J. Jefferson Farjeon	E. Price (Haunted Light)	
Phantom of Forty-Second Street	Prod. Rel.	1945	Albert Herman	Milton Raison	M. M. Raison	
Phantom of Paris	MGM	1931	John S. Robertson	Bess Meredyth / John Meehan / Edwin Justus Mayer	G. Leroux (Cheri-Bibi and Cecily)	Tony Woolrich (Dave O'Brien) Cheri-Bibi (John Gilbert)
Phantom of the Opera	*Universal	1925	Rupert Julian	Raymond Shrock / Elliot Clawson	G. Leroux	
Phantom of the Opera	Universal	1929	Rupert Julian / Edward Sedgwick	E. J. Clawson / Raymond L. Shrock / Tom Reed / Frank M. McCormack	G. Leroux	
Phantom of the Opera	Universal	1943	Arthur Lubin	Eric Taylor / Samuel Hoffenstein	G. Leroux	
Phantom of the Opera	Hammer	1962	Terence Fisher	John Elder	G. Leroux	
Phantom of the Opera	TCF	1989	Dwight H. Little	Duke Sandefur / Gerry O'Hara	G. Leroux	
Phantom of the Rue Morgue	Warner	1953	Roy Del Ruth	Harold Medford / James R. Webb	E. A. Poe (Prose Romances of Edgar A. Poe)	Dupin (Steve Forrest)
Phantom President	Paramount	1932	Norman Taurog	Walter De Leon / Harlan Thompson	G. F. Worts	
Phantom Strikes Gaunt Stranger	Ealing	1938	Walter Forde	Sidney Gilliat	E. Wallace (Ringer)	
Philip Steele	*Reliance	1912	?	?	J. O. Curwood (Philip Steele of the Northwest Mounted Police)	
Piccadilly Jim	*Selznick	1920	Wesley Ruggles	?	P. G. Wodehouse	
Piccadilly Jim	MGM	1936	Robert Z. Leonard	Charles Brackett / Edwin Knopf	P. G. Wodehouse	
Pickpocket	Lux	1963	Robert Bresson	Robert Bresson		
Pickup Alley International Police Interpol	Warwick	1957	John Gilling	John Paxton	F. M. Dostoevskii (Crime and Punishment) novel: E. Ronns	
Picpus	Continental	1942	Richard Pottier	J.-P. Le Chanois	G. Simenon (To Any Lengths)	Jules Maigret (Albert Prejean)
Picture Mommy Dead	Berkeley	1966	Bert I. Gordon	Robert Sherman	novel: Robert Sherman	
Pidgin Island	*Metro	1916	Fred J. Balshofer	Richard V. Spencer / Fred J. Balshofer	H. MacGrath	
Pigeon That Took Rome	Paramount	1962	Melville Shavelson	Melville Shavelson	D. Downes (Easter Dinner)	
Pilgrims of the Night	*Frothingham	1921	Edward Sloman	Edward Sloman	A. Partridge (Passers-By)	

Title	Studio	Year	Director	Cast	Notes
Pillaged	Ariane	1967	Alain Cavalier	Claude Sautet / Alain Cavalier	R. Stark (Score)
Pink Jungle	Univ. Int.	1968	Delbert Mann	Oscar Dancigers / Charles Williams	A. Williams (Snake Water)
Pink Panther	UA	1964	Blake Edwards	Blake Edwards / Maurice Richlin	novel: M. H. Albert; Insp. Clouseau (Peter Sellers)
Pink Panther Strikes Again	UA	1976	Blake Edwards	Blake Edwards / Frank Waldman	novel: F. Waldman; Insp. Clouseau (Peter Sellers)
Pink String and Sealing Wax	Ealing	1945	Robert Hamer	Diana Morgan / Robert Hamer	R. Pertwee
Pit and the Pendulum	Am. Int.	1961	Roger Corman	Richard Matheson	novel: L. Sheridan
Pit of Darkness	Butcher	1961	Lance Comfort	Lance Comfort	H. McCutcheon (To Dusty Death); Richard Logan (William Franklyn)
Pitfall	UA	1948	Andre De Toth	Karl Lamb	J. J. Drader
Place to Go	Excalibur	1963	Basil Dearden	Michael Relph / Clive Exton	M. Fisher (Bethnel Green)
Platinum High School Rich, Young and Deadly Trouble at 16	MGM	1960	Charles Haas	Robert Smith	novel: I. Shulman
Play Misty for Me	Universal	1971	Clint Eastwood	Jo Heins / Dean Riesner	novel: P. J. Gillette, q.v.
Playback	Merton Park	1962	Quentin Lawrnece	Robert B. Stewart	E. Wallace (headnote)
Pleasure Buyers	*Warner	1925	Chester Withey	Hope Loring / Louis D. Lighton	A. S. Roche
Pleydell Mystery	*Brit. Emp.	1916	Albert Ward	Albert Ward	A. Askew (Poison)
Plot Thickens Swinging Pearl Mystery	RKO	1936	Ben Holmes	Clarence U. Young / Jack Townley	S. Palmer (headnote)
Plunder	Brit. Dom.	1930	Tom Walls	W. P. Lipscomb	B. Travers
Plunder of the Sun	Warner	1953	John Farrow	Jonathan Latimer	D. Dodge
Plus the Whisky pour Callaghan	?	1954	Willy Rozier	Xavier Vallier	P. Cheyney
Poe's Tales of Terror Tales of Terror	Am. Int.	1962	Roger Corman	Richard Matheson	novel: E. Sudak (Tales of Terror)
Point Blank	MGM	1967	John Boorman	Alexander Jacobs / David Newhouse / Rafe Newhouse	R. Stark (Hunter)
Pointing Finger	*Stoll	1922	George Ridgwell	Paul Rooff	Rita
Pointing Finger	Real Art	1933	George Pearson	H. Fowler Mear	Rita
Poison	*Brit. Emp.	1916	Albert Ward	Albert Ward	A. Askew
Poison Pen	APBC	1939	Paul L. Stein	William Freshman / Doreen Montgomery / N. C. Hunter / Esther McCracken	R. Llewellyn
Pool of Flame	*Red Feather	1916	Otis Turner	F. McGrew Willis	L. J. Vance
Pope of Greenwich Village	MGM	1984	Stuart Rosenberg	Vincent Patrick	V. Patrick
Population 1280 Clean Slate	Films Tour	1981	Bertrand Tavernier	Jean Aurenche / Bertrand Tavernier	J. Thompson (Pop. 1280)
Porridge	Black Lion	1979	Dick Clement	Dick Clement / Ian Le Frenais	novel: P. Ableman
Port Afrique	Coronado	1956	Rudolph Mate	Frank Partos / John Cresswell	B. V. Dryer
Port of Missing Men	*Fam. Play.	1914	?	?	M. Nicholson
Portrait in Black	Universal	1960	Michael Gordon	Ivan Goff / Ben Roberts	I. Goff
Portrait in Smoke Wicked As They Come	Film Loca.	1956	Ken Hughes	Ken Hughes / Robert Westerby / Sigmund Miller	B. Ballinger
Portrait of a Mobster	Warner	1961	Joseph Pevney	Howard Browne	H. Grey
Portrait of Alison	Insignia	1955	Guy Green	Guy Green / Ken Hughes	F. Durbridge
Postmark for Danger					

Slim Callaghan (?)

Hildegarde Withers (ZaSu Pitts)

P

P

FILM TITLE	STUDIO	YEAR	DIRECTOR	SCREENWRITER	SOURCE AUTHOR/WORK	SERIES
Possession of Joel Delaney	ITC	1971	Waris Hussein	Matt Robinson Grimes Grice	R. Stewart	
Postman Always Rings Twice	MGM	1946	Tay Garnett	Harry Raskin Niven Busch	J. M. Cain	
Postman Always Rings Twice	Paramount	1981	Bob Rafelson	David Mamet	J. M. Cain	
Postmark for Danger	Insignia	1955	Guy Green	Guy Green Ken Hughes	F. Durbridge (Portrait of Alison)	
Portrait of Alison						
Power	MGM	1967	Byron Haskin	John Gay	F. M. Robinson	
Power and the Glory	RKO	1947	John Ford	Dudley Nichols	G. Greene	
Prairie Wife	*Eastern	1925	Hugo Ballin	Hugo Ballin	A. Stringer	
Prayer for the Dying	Goldwyn	1987	Mike Hodges	Edmund Ward Martin Lynch	J. Higgins	
Praying Mantis	Portman	1982	Jack Gold	Philip Mackie	H. Montellhet (Preying Mantises)	
Premature Burial	Am. Int.	1961	Roger Corman	Charles Beaumont Ray Russell	novel: M. H. Danne	
Premature Compromise	*Edison	1914	Charles Brabin	?	R. Barr (Young Lord Stranleigh)	Lord Stranleigh (?)
Prescription for Murder Family Doctor Prescription Murder Rx Murder	Templar	1957	Derek Twist	Derek Twist	J. Fleming (Deeds of Dr. Deadcert)	
Prescription Murder Family Doctor Prescription for Murder Rx Murder	Templar	1957	Derek Twist	Derek Twist	J. Fleming (Deeds of Dr. Deadcert)	
President	UFA	1961	Henri Verneuil	Michel Audiard Carey Wilson Cedric Worth Lynn Starling	G. Simenon (Premier)	
President Vanishes Strange Conspiracy	Paramount	1934	William A. Wellman		Anonymous	
President's Mystery One for All	Republic	1936	Phil Rosen	Lester Cole Nathaniel West	F. D. Roosevelt (President's Mystery Story)	
Presidio	Paramount	1988	Peter Hyams	Larry Ferguson	novel: Mike Cogan	
Presumed Innocent	Warner	1990	Alan J. Pakula	Frank Pierson Alan J. Pakula	S. Turow	
Pretty Maids All in a Row	MGM	1971	Roger Vadim	Gene Roddenberry	F. Pollini	Sandy Stern (Raul Julia)
Pretty Poison	TCF	1968	Noel Black	Lorenzo Semple, Jr.	S. Geller (She Let Him Continue)	
Prey	Concorde	1985	Vivian Pieters	Ton Ruys	C. Aird (Henrietta Who)	
Price of Silence At the Mercy of Tiberius	*Samuelson	1920	Fred L. Granville	?	A. J. Wilson (At the Mercy of Tiberius)	
Price of Silence	Eternal	1960	Montgomery Tully	Maurice J. Wilson	L. Meynell (One Step from Murder)	
Price of Things	UA	1930	Elinor Glyn	Lady Rhys Williams	E. Glyn	
Prime Cut	Cin. Cent.	1972	Michael Ritchie	Robert Dillon		
Prince of Tempters	*First Nat.	1926	Lothar Mendes	Paul Bern	novel: M. Roote E. P. Oppenheim (Ex-Duke)	
Princess of New York	*Fam. Play.	1921	Donald Crisp	Margaret Turnbull	C. Hamilton	
Priory School	*Stoll	1921	Maurice Elvey	Charles Barnett	A. C. Doyle (Return of Sherlock Holmes)	Sherlock Holmes (Eille Norwood)
Prison Breaker	Smith	1936	Adrian Brunel	Frank Witty	E. Wallace (headnote)	
Prisoner of the Skull Man in the Steel Mask Man Without a Face Who?	Brit. Lion	1974	Jack Gold	John Gould	A. Budrys (Who?)	
Private Lessons Philly	Farley	1981	Alan Myerson	Dan Greenburg	D. Greenberg (Philly)	
Private Life of Sherlock Holmes	UA	1970	Billy Wilder	Billy Wilder I. A. L. Diamond	novel: Michael Hardwick	Sherlock Holmes (Robert Stephens)

R

Title	Studio	Year	Director	Writer	Notes
Privilege	Worldfilm	1967	Peter Watkins	Norman Bognor Peter Watkins	novel: John Burke
Prize	MGM	1963	Mark Robson	Ernest Lehman	I. Wallace
Prize of Gold	Warwick	1955	Mark Robson	Robert Buckner John Paxton	M. Catto
Prizzi's Honor	TCF	1985	John Huston	Richard Condon Janet Reach	R. Condon
Professional	Cerito	1981	Georges Lautner	Michel Audiard	P. Alexander (Death of a Thin-Skinned Animal)
Professional Guest	King	1931	George King	H. Fowler Mear	W. Garrett
Project M7	Gen. Film	1952	Anthony Asquith	William Fairchild	J. Pudney (Net)
Net					
Project X	Paramount	1968	William Castle	Edmund Morris	L. P. Davies (Artificial Man)
Psycho	Paramount	1960	Alfred Hitchcock	Joseph Stefano	R. Bloch
Psycho-Circus	Am. Int.	1967	John Moxey	Peter Welbeck	E. Wallace (headnote)
Circus of Fear					
Public Defender	RKO	1931	J. Walter Ruben	Bernard Schubert	G. Goodchild (Splendid Crime)
Public Enemy	Warner	1931	William Wellman	Harvey Thew Kubec Glasmon	novel: K. Glasmon
Enemies of the Public				John Bright	
Public Prosecutor's Speech	Paramount	1931	Dimitri Buchowetzki	?	A. D Miller (Manslaughter)
Puppet on a Chain	Big City	1970	Don Sharp Geoffrey Reeve	Alistair MacLean Don Sharp Paul Wheeler	A. MacLean
Purple Noon	CCFC	1960	Rene Clement	Paul Gegauff Rene Clement	P. Highsmith (Talented Mr. Ripley)	Tom Ripley (Alain Delon)
Broad Daylight					
Lust for Evil					
Pursuing Vengeance	*Unity	1916	Martin Sabine	?	B. E. Stevenson (Mystery of the Boule Cabinet)	Jim Godfrey (Henry Mortimer)
Pursuit	MGM	1935	Edwin L. Marin	Wells Root	L. G. Blochman
Pursuit of D. B. Cooper	Polygram	1981	Roger Spottiswoode	Jeffrey Alan Fiskin	J. D. Reed (Free Fall)
Pursuit to Algiers	Universal	1945	Roy William Neill	Leonard Lee	A. C. Doyle (Return of Sherlock Holmes)	Sherlock Holmes (Basil Rathbone)
Pusher	UA	1960	Gene Milford	Harold Robbins	E. McBain	Steve Carella (Robert Lansing)
Pushover	Columbia	1954	Richard Quine	Roy Huggins	B. Ballinger (Rafferty)
Pyx	Cinerama	1973	Harvey Hart	Robert Schlitt	J. Buell
Q&A	Tri-Star	1990	Sidney Lumet	Sidney Lumet	E. Torres
Qualified Adventurer	*Stoll	1925	Sinclair Hill	Sinclair Hill	S. Jepson
Quarry	*Selig	1915	Lawrence Marston	Gilson Willets	J. Moroso
Queenie	*Fox	1921	Howard M. Mitchell	Dorothy Yost	W. F. Fauley
Question of Suspense	Luckwell	1961	Max Varnel	Lawrence Huntington	R. Vickers (headnote)
Quick Change	Warner	1990	Howard Franklin Bill Murray	Howard Franklin	J. Cronley
Quiet American	UA	1957	Joseph Mankiewicz	Joseph Mankiewicz	G. Greene
Quiet Place in the Country	Pea Cine.	1969	Elio Petri	Elio Petri Luciano Vincenzoni	novel: H. Clement
Quiller Memorandum	Foxwell	1966	Michael Anderson	Harold Pinter	Adam Hall (Berlin Memorandum)	Quiller (George Segal)
Quinney's	*Samuelson	1919	Rex Wilson	Roland Pertwee	H. A. Vachell
Quinney's	*Gaumont	1927	Maurice Elvey	John Longden	H. A. Vachell
Race Gang	New World	1937	William C. Menzies	Edward O. Berkman Arthur Wimperis	G. Greene (headnote)
Four Dark Hours					
Green Cockatoo					
Racket	*Paramount	1928	Lewis Milestone	Bartlett Cormack Harry Behn Del Andrews	B. Cormack
Racket	RKO	1951	John Cromwell Nicholas Ray	William W. Haines W. R. Burnett	B. Cormack

R

FILM TITLE	STUDIO	YEAR	DIRECTOR	SCREENWRITER	SOURCE AUTHOR/WORK	SERIES
Rafferty and the Gold Dust Twins	Warner	1975	Dick Richards	John Kaye	novel: Lillian Roberts	
Rafferty and the Highway Hustlers	Warner	1975	Dick Richards	John Kaye	novel: Lillian Roberts (Rafferty and the Gold Dust Twins)	
Rafferty and the Highway Hustlers Rafferty and the Gold Dust Twins						
Raffles	*Weber	1917	George Irving	Anthony Kelly	E. W. Hornung (Amateur Cracksman)	A. J. Raffles (John Barrymore)
Raffles	UA	1930	Harry D'Arrast George Fitzmaurice	Sidney Howard	E. W. Hornung (Amateur Cracksman)	A. J. Raffles (Ronald Colman)
Raffles	UA	1939	Sam Wood William Wyler	John Van Druton Sidney Howard F. Scott Fitzgerald	E. W. Hornung (Amateur Cracksman)	A. J. Raffles (David Niven)
Raffles, the Amateur Cracksman	*Viagraph	1905	?	?	E. W. Hornung (Amateur Cracksman)	A. J. Raffles (J. Barney Sherry)
Raffles, the Amateur Cracksman	*Universal	1925	King Baggott		E. W. Hornung (Amateur Cracksman)	A. J. Raffles (House Peters)
Rage	Warner	1972	George C. Scott	Harvey Thew	novel: P. Friedman	
Rage in Harlem	Miramax	1991	Bill Duke	Philip Friedman Dan Kleinman John Toles-Bey Bobby Crawford	C. Himes	Digger Jones (?) Coffin Ed Johnson (?)
Rage in Heaven	MGM	1941	W. S. Van Dyke Robert Sinclair	C. Isherwood Robert Thoeren	J. Hilton	
Raging Tide	Universal	1951	George Sherman	Ernest K. Gann	E. K. Gann (Fiddler's Green)	
Ragtime	Paramount	1981	Miles Forman	Michael Weller	E. L. Doctorow	
Raise the Titanic!	Assoc. Film	1980	Jerry Jameson	Adam Kennedy Eric Hughes	C. Cussler	Dirk Pitt (Richard Jordan)
Rambo: First Blood II	Tri-Star	1985	George Pan Cosmatos	Sylvester Stallone James Cameron	novel: D. Morrell	Rambo (Sylvester Stallone)
Rampage	DeLaurentis	1987	William Friedkin	William Friedkin	W. P. Wood	
Ramshackle House	*Tilford	1924	Harmon Wright	Coolidge Streeter	H. Footner	
Rank Outsider	*Broadwest	1920	Richard Garrick	Patrick L. Mannock	N. Gould	
Ransom	Lion Int.	1975	Caspar Wrede	Paul Wheeler	novel: P. Wheeler	
Ransom of Red Chief	*Edison	1911	?		O. Henry (Whirligigs)	
Ranson's Folly	*Edison	1910	Edwin S. Porter	Edwin S. Porter Charles Reade	R. H. Davis	
Ranson's Folly	*Edison	1915	Richard Ridgely	Richard Ridgely	R. H. Davis	
Ranson's Folly	*Inspir.	1926	Sidney Olcott	Lillie Hayward	H. R. Davis	
Rape	Cine-Vog	1973	Fons Rademakers	Hugo Claus	N. Freeling (Because of the Cats)	Insp. Van der Valk (Bryan Marshall)
Because of the Cats						Anthony Gethryn (Claude Horton)
Rasp	Film Eng.	1931	Michael Powell	J. J. Farjeon	P. MacDonald	
Rat	*Gainsbor.	1925	Graham Cutts	Graham Cutts	P. Bottome	
Rat	Imperator	1937	Jack Raymond	Hans Gulder Rameau Marjorie Gaffney Miles Malleson Romney Brent	P. Bottome	
Rats	Northshore	1982	Robert Clouse	Charles Eglee	J. Herbert	
Rattlerat	Spiegel	1987	Wim Verstappen	Wim Verstappen Rogier Proper	J. van de Wetering	
Raven	Am. Int.	1962	Roger Corman	Richard Matheson	novel: E. Sudak	
Ravishing Idiot	Belles Riv.	1964	Edouard Molinaro	Edouard Molinaro Andre Tabet Georges Tabet	C. Exbrayat	
Raw Deal	Int. Film	1986	John Irvin	Gary M. DeVore Norman Wexler	novel: W. Wager	

R

Title	Studio	Year	Director	Writer	Source	Notes
Razorback	McElroy	1984	Russell Mulcahy	Everett De Roche	P. Brennan	
Razumov	L'All. Cin.	1936	Marc Allegret	H. Wilhelm	J. Conrad (Under Western Eyes)	
Under Western Eyes						
Rear Window	Paramount	1954	Alfred Hitchcock	John Michael Hayes	W. Irish (After-Dinner Story)	
Rebecca	UA	1940	Alfred Hitchcock	Robert E. Sherwood, Joan Harrison	D. Du Maurier	
Reckless Age	*Universal	1924	Harry Pollard	Rex Taylor	E. D. Biggers (Love Insurance)	
Reckless Moment	Columbia	1949	Max Opuls	Henry Garson, Robert W. Soderberg, Mel Dinelli	E. S. Holding (Blank Wall)	
Recoil	*Goldwyn	1924	T. Hayes Hunter	Robert E. Kent, Gerald C. Duffy	R. Beach (Big Brother)	
Red Aces	*Brit. Lion	1929	Edgar Wallace	Edgar Wallace	E. Wallace	
Red Barn Crime	*Haggar	1908	?	?	Anonymous (Maria Marten)	
Red Circle	*Stoll	1922	George Ridgwell	Patrick L. Mannock, Geoffrey H. Malins	A. C. Doyle (His Last Bow)	Sherlock Holmes (Eille Norwood)
Red Dance	Fox	1928	Raoul Walsh	James A. Creelman	H. L. Gates (Red Dancer of Moscow)	
Red Danube	MGM	1949	George Sidney	Gina Kaus, Arthur Wimperis	B. Marshall (Vespers in Vienna)	
Red Dice	*DeMille	1926	William K. Howard	Jeanie MacPherson, Douglas Zoty	O. R. Cohen (Iron Chalice)	
Red Glove	*Universal	1919	J. D. McGowan	Hope Loring	D. Grant (Fifth Ace)	
Red-Haired Alibi	Capital	1932	Christy Cabanne	Edward T. Lowe	W. Collison	
Red-Headed League	*Stoll	1921	Maurice Elvey	William J. Elliott	A. C. Doyle (Adventures of Sherlock Holmes)	Sherlock Holmes (Eille Norwood)
Red Heat	Vestron	1988	Robert Collector	Robert Collector, Gary Drucker	novel: R. Tine	
Red House	Lesser	1947	Delmar Daves	Delmar Daves	G. A. Chamberlain	
Red Ibis	M. Films	1985	Jean-Pierre Mocky	Jean-Pierre Mocky, Andre Ruellan	Fredric Brown (Knock Three-One-Two)	
Red Lights	*Goldwyn	1923	Clarence G. Badger	Carey Wilson	E. E. Rose (Rear Car)	
Red Mark	*Cruze	1928	James Cruze	Julian Josephson	J. Russell	
Redhead	Europa	1962	Helmut Kaeutner	Helmut Kaeutner	A. Andersch	
Reflection of Fear	Columbia	1971	William A. Fraker	Edward Hume, Lewis John Carlino	S. Forbes (Go to Thy Death Bed)	
Labyrinth						
Reformation of Calliope	*Eclair	1913	?	?	O. Henry (Heart of the West)	
Regent's Park Mystery	*Stoll	1924	Hugh Croise	Hugh Croise	B. Orczy (Old Man in the Corner)	Old Man (Rolf Leslie)
Reigate Squires	*Fr.-Brit.	1912	Georges Treville	?	A. C. Doyle (Memoirs of Sherlock Holmes)	Sherlock Holmes (Georges Treville)
Reigate Squires	*Stoll	1922	George Ridgwell	Patrick L. Mannock, Geoffrey H. Malins	A. C. Doyle (Memoirs of Sherlock Holmes)	Sherlock Holmes (Eille Norwood)
Reincarnation of Peter Proud	Crosby	1974	J. Lee Thompson	Max Ehrlich, Sidney Sheldon	M. Ehrlich	
Remains to Be Seen	MGM	1953	Don Weis	Doris Malloy	H. Lindsay	
Remember Last Night?	Universal	1935	James Whale	Harry Clork, Dan Totheroh, Louise Henry	A. Hobhouse (Hangover Murders)	
Remember That Face Mob	Columbia	1951	Robert Parrish	William Bowers	F. Findley (Waterfront)	
Remittance Woman	*R-C	1923	Wesley Ruggles	Carol Warren	A. Abdullah	
Remo: The First Adventure	Orion	1985	Guy Hamilton	Christopher Wood	novel: W. Murphy	Remo Williams (Fred Ward)
Remote Control	MGM	1930	Malcolm St. Clair, Nick Grinde	Frank Butler	C. North	
Removalists	Seven Keys	1975	Tom Jeffrey	David Williamson	D. Williamson	
Renfrew of the Royal Mounted	Grand Nat.	1937	Al Herman	Charles Logue	L. Y. Erskine	Douglas Renfrew (James Newill)
Repeat Performance	Pathe	1947	Alfred Werker	Walter Bullock	W. O'Farrell	

R

FILM TITLE	STUDIO	YEAR	DIRECTOR	SCREENWRITER	SOURCE AUTHOR/WORK	SERIES
Report to the Commissioner	UA	1974	Milton Katselas	Abby Mann / Ernest Tidyman	J. Mills	
Operation Undercover						
Reporter	Corfield	1943	John Harlow	Maisie Sharman / Ralph G. Bettinson	K. Attiwill	
Reprieved	Monogram	1935	Lew Collins	Marion North / Charles Logue	H. S. Keeler (Sing Sing Nights)	
Sing Sing Nights						
Reprisal	Columbia	1956	George Sherman	David P. Harmon / Raphael Hayes / David Dortort	Arthur Gordon	
Resident Patient	*Stoll	1921	Maurice Elvey	William J. Elliott	A. C. Doyle (Memoirs of Sherlock Holmes)	Sherlock Holmes (Eille Norwood)
Resurrection Syndicate	Charlemagne	1973	Peter Sasdy	Brian Hughes	J. Blackburn (Nothing But the Night)	
Nothing But the Night						
Retour de Manivelle	Rank	1957	D. de la Patelliere	D. de la Patelliere / Julius J. Epstein / Charles Bair	J. H. Chase (There's Always a Price Tag)	
Return from the Ashes	Mirisch	1965	J. Lee Thompson		H. Monteilhet	
Return of Dr. Fu Manchu	Paramount	1930	Rowland V. Lee	Lloyd Corrigan / Florence Ryerson	S. Rohmer (Devil Doctor)	Fu Manchu (Warner Oland)
New Adventures of Dr. Fu Manchu						
Return of Sherlock Holmes	Fam. Play.	1929	Basil Dean	Garrett Fort / Basil Dean	A. C. Doyle (His Last Bow)	Sherlock Holmes (Clive Brook)
Return of Sophie Lang	Paramount	1936	George Archainbaud	Brian Marlow / Patterson McNutt	F. I. Anderson (Notorious Sophie Lang)	Sophie Lang (Gertrude Michael)
Return of the Frog	Imperator	1938	Maurice Elvey	Ian Hay / Gerald Eliott	E. Wallace (India-Rubber Men)	Insp. Elk (Gordon Harker)
Return of the Living Dead	Hemdale	1985	Dan O'Bannon	Dan O'Bannon	J. Russo	
Return of the Lone Wolf	*Columbia	1926	Ralph Ince	J. Grubb Alexander	L. J. Vance (Lone Wolf Returns)	
Lone Wolf Returns						
Return of the Pink Panther	UA	1974	Blake Edwards	Frank Waldman / Blake Edwards	novel: F. Waldman	Michael Lanyard (Bert Lytell) / Insp. Clouseau (Peter Sellers)
Return of the Scarlet Pimpernel	London	1937	Hans Schwartz	Lajos Biro / Arthur Wimperis / Adrian Brunel	B. Orczy (headnote)	Percy Blakeney (Barry K. Barnes)
Return of the Terror	First Nat.	1934	Howard Bretherton	Eugene Solow / Peter Milne	E. Wallace (Terror)	
Return of the Whistler	Columbia	1948	D. Ross Lederman	Edward Bock / Maurice Tombragel	W. Irish (Eyes That Watch You)	
Return to Sender	Merton Park	1963	Gordon Hales	John Roddick	E. Wallace (headnote)	
Reunion	South Aust.	1984	Chris Langman	Graham Hartley	K. Leopold (When We Ran)	
Revenge	UA	1928	Edwin Carewe	Finis Fox	novel: J. Warren	
Revenge Squad	Comworld	1982	Charles Braverman	Don Enright	L. Fletcher (Eighty Dollars to Stamford)	
Hit and Run						
Reward	TCF	1965	Serge Bourguignon	Serge Bourguignon / Oscar Millard	M. Barrett	
Rich, Young and Deadly	MGM	1960	Charles Haas	Robert Smith	novel: I. Shulman (Platinum High School)	
Platinum High School						
Trouble at 16						
Riches and Romance	Klement	1936	Alfred Zeisler	John L. Balderston	E. P. Oppenheim (Amazing Quest of Mr. Ernest Bliss)	
Amazing Adventure						
Amazing Quest of Mr. Ernest Bliss						
Romance and Riches						
Ricochet	Merton Park	1963	John Moxey	Roger Marshall	E. Wallace (Angel of Terror)	
Riddle of the Sands	Rank	1979	Tony Maylam	Tony Maylam / John Bailey	E. Childers	
Ride a Wild Pony	Disney	1975	Don Chaffey	Rosemary Anne Sisson	J. Aldridge (Sporting Proposition)	
Ride the Pink Horse	Univ. Int.	1947	Robert Montgomery	Ben Hecht / Charles Lederer	D. B. Hughes	

R

Title	Studio	Year	Director	Cast	Source
Rigged	Cinestar	1985	C. M. Cutry	John Goff / Jill Gurr	Reymond Marshall (Hit and Run)
Right to Love	*Paramount	1920	George Fitzmaurice	Ouida Bergere / Mary Murillo	C. Farrere (Man Who Killed)
Ringer	*Brit. Lion	1928	Arthur Maude	Edgar Wallace	E. Wallace
Ringer	Gainsboro.	1931	Walter Forde	Angus MacPhail / Robert Stevenson / Edgar Wallace	E. Wallace
Gaunt Stranger					
Ringer	Lond. Films	1952	Guy Hamilton	Val Valentine / Lesley Storm	E. Wallace
Riot	Paramount	1969	Buzz Kulik	James Poe	F. Elli
Rise and Fall of Legs Diamond	Warner	1960	Budd Boetticher	Joseph Landon	novel: O. H. Gaylord
Rise Up, Spy	Cathala	1982	Yves Boisset	Claude Veillot / Yves Boisset / Michel Audiard	G. Markstein (Chance Awakening)
Risk	Charter	1960	Roy Boulting / John Boulting	Nigel Balchin / Roy Boulting / Jeffrey Dell	N. Balchin (Sort of Traitors)
Suspect					
Rivals	Merton Park	1963	Max Varnel	John Roddick	E. Wallace (Elegant Edward)
River of Death	Breton	1990	Steve Carver	Edward Simpson / Andrew Deutsch	Alistair MacLean
River of Diamonds	Karat	1990	Robert J. Smawley	Hans Kuhle / Ian Yule	G. Jenkins
River of Stars	*Stoll	1921	F. Martin Thornton	Leslie H. Gordon / John Reinhardt	E. Wallace
River Pirate	*Fox	1928	William K. Howard	Benjamin Markson	C. F. Coe
River's End	*First Nat	1920	Marshall Neilan	Marion Fairfax	J. O. Curwood
River's End	Warner	1930	Michael Curtiz	Charles Kenyon	J. O. Curwood
River's End	Warner	1940	Ray Enright	Barry Trivers / Bertram Millhauser	J. O. Curwood
Double Identity					W. P. Lipscomb
Riverside Murder	Fox Brit.	1935	Albert Parker	Selwyn Jepson	A. Steeman (Six Dead Men)
Road House	Gaumont	1934	Maurice Elvey	Leslie Landau / Austin Melford / Leslie Arliss	W. Hackett
Road to Ein Harod	Sunrise	1990	Doron Eran	Rami Na'Aman	A. Kenan
Road to Fortune	Starcraft	1930	Arthur Varney	Hugh Broadbridge	H. Broadbridge (Moorland Terror)
Roadhouse Murder	RKO	1932	J. Walter Ruben	J. Walter Ruben / Gene Fowler	M. Level (headnote)
Roadhouse Nights	Paramount	1930	Hobart Henley	Garrett Fort	D. Hammett (Red Harvest)
Robbery Under Arms	*MacMahon's	1907	Charles MacMahon	Charles MacMahon	R. Boldrewood
Robbery Under Arms	*Pacific	1920	Kenneth Brampton	Kenneth Brampton	R. Boldrewood
Robbery Under Arms	Rank	1957	Jack Lee	Alexander Baron	R. Boldrewood / W. P. Lipscomb
Robbery Under Arms	ITC	1985	Ken Hannam / Donald Crombie	Graeme Koesveld / Tony Morphett	R. Boldrewood
Robin and the Seven Hoods	Warner	1964	Gordon Douglas	David R. Schwartz	novel: J. Pearl
Robocop	Orion	1987	Paul Verhoeven	Edward Neumeier / Michael Miner	novel: E. Naha
Robocop 2	Orion	1990	Irwin Kershner / Walon Green	Frank Miller	novel: E. Naha
Rogue Cop	MGM	1954	Roy Rowland	Sydney Boehm	W. P. McGivern
Rogue in Love	*London	1916	Bannister Merwin	Bannister Merwin	T. Gallon
Rogue in Love	*Diamond	1922	Albert Brouett	Harry Hughes	T. Gallon
Romance and Riches	Klement	1936	Alfred Zeisler	John L. Balderston	E. P. Oppenheim (Amazing Quest of Mr. Ernest Bliss)
Amazing Adventure					
Amazing Quest of Mr. Ernest Bliss					
Riches and Romance					
Romance of a Million Dollars	*Bachmann	1926	Tom Terriss	Arthur Hoerl	E. Dejeans

R

FILM TITLE	STUDIO	YEAR	DIRECTOR	SCREENWRITER	SOURCE AUTHOR/WORK	SERIES
Romance of Elaine	*Pathe	1915	George B. Seitz	Bertram Millhauser Charles W. Goddard George B. Seitz	A. B. Reeve	
Romance of Hefty Burke	*Edison	1910	?	?		
Romance of Mayfair	*Stoll	1925	Thomas Bentley	?	R. H. Davis (Exiles)	
Rome Express	Gaumont	1932	Walter Forde	Clifford Grey Sidney Gilliat Frank Vosper Ralph Stock	J. C. Snaith (Crime of Constable Kelly) novel: R. Alexander	
Romeo and Juliet, 1971 Gentle Tale of Sex, Violence, Corruption and Murder What Became of Jack and Jill?	Palomar	1972	Bill Bain	Roger Marshall	L. Moody (Ruthless Ones)	
Roof	Real Art	1933	George A. Cooper	H. Fowler Mear	D. Whitelaw	
Rooftops	New Visions	1989	Robert Wise	Terence Brennan	novel: R. Tine	
Room 13	Rialto	1964	Harald Reinl	Quentin Philips	E. Wallace	
Rooney	Rank	1958	George Pollock	Patrick Kirwan	C. Cookson	
Root of All Evil	Gainsbor.	1947	Brock Williams	Brock Williams	J. S. Fletcher	
Rope	Warner	1948	Alfred Hitchcock	Arthur Laurents Hume Cronyn Ben Hecht	P. Hamilton	
Rope for Killing One Step to Eternity	Sirius	1955	Henri Decoin	Henri Decoin J. C. Eger	P. McGerr (Follow, As the Night)	
Rosary Murders	First Take	1987	Fred Walton	Elmore Leonard Fred Walton	W. X. Kienzle	Father Bob Koesler (Donald Sutherland)
Roseanna	Svensk	1967	Hans Abramson	Hans Abramson	M. Sjowall	Martin Beck (Keve Hjelm)
Rosebud	UA	1975	Otto Preminger	Erik Lee Preminger Marjorie Kellogg	J. Hemingway	
Rosemary's Baby	Paramount	1968	Roman Polanski	Roman Polanski	I. Levin	
Rough Company Violent Men	Columbia	1954	Rudolph Mate	Harry Kleiner	D. Hamilton (Night Walker)	
Rough Cut	Paramount	1980	Donald Siegel	Francis Burns	D. Lambert (Touch the Lion's Paw)	
Rough Shoot Shoot First	UA	1953	Robert Parrish	Eric Ambler	G. Household	
Rough Sketch	Horizon	1949	John Huston	John Huston Peter Viertel	R. Sylvester	
Roxie Hart	TCF	1942	William A. Wellman	Nunnally Johnson	M. Watkins (Chicago)	
Rumble on the Docks	Columbia	1956	Fred F. Sears	Lou Morheim Jack DeWitt	F. Paley	
Run for the Sun	UA	1956	Roy Boulting	Dudley Nichols Roy Boulting	R. Connell (Variety)	
Runner Stumbles	TCF	1979	Stanley Kramer	Milan Stitt	M. Stitt	
Running Fight	*Paramount	1915	?	W. H. Osborne	W. H. Osborne	
Running Man	Peet	1963	Carol Reed	John Mortimer	S. Smith (Ballad of the Running Man)	
Running Man	Tri-Star	1987	Paul Michael Glaser	Stephen E. de Souza	R. Bachman	
Running Scared	Paramount	1972	David Hemmings	Clive Exton David Hemmings	G. McDonald	
Running Target	UA	1956	Marvin R. Weinstein	Marvin R. Weinstein Jack C. Couffer Conrad Hall	S. Frazee	
Running Water	*Stoll	1922	Maurice Elvey	Kinchen Wood	A. E. W. Mason	
Running Wild	Univ. Int.	1955	Abner Biberman	Leo Townsend	B. Benson (Girl in the Cage)	
Rush	MGM	1992	Lili Fini Zanuck	Pete Dexter	K. Wozencraft	
Russia House	MGM	1990	Fred Schepsi	Tom Stoppard	J. Le Carre	

Film Index

S

Title	Studio	Year	Director	Writer	Character (Actor)
Russian Roulette	ITC	1975	Lou Lombardo	Tom Ardies / Stanley Mann / Arnold Margolin	T. Ardies (Kosygin Is Coming)
Russians Are Coming, The Russians Are Coming	UA	1966	Norman Jewison	William Rose	N. Benchley (Off-Islanders)
Ruth of the Rockies	*Pathe	1920	George Marshall	?	J. McCulley (Broadway Bab)
Rx Murder	Templar	1957	Derek Twist	Derek Twist	J. Fleming (Deeds of Dr. Deadcert)
Family Doctor					
Prescription for Murder					
Prescription Murder					
Rynox	Film. Eng.	1931	Michael Powell	J. J. Farjeon	P. MacDonald
S.A.S. San Salvator	UGC	1982	Raoul Coutard	Gerard de Villiers	G. de Villiers (Game of Eyes Only) — Malko Linge (Miles O'Keeffe)
S.O.S	*Strand	1928	Leslie Hiscott	?	W. W. Ellis
S*P*Y*S	TCF	1974	Irvin Kershner	Malcolm Marmorstein / Lawrence J. Cohen / Fred Freeman	novel: T. R. Joyce
Sable Lorcha	*Triangle	1915	Lloyd Ingraham	Chester B. Clapp	H. Hazeltine
Sabotage	Gaum. Brit.	1936	Alfred Hitchcock	Charles Bennett / Ian Hay / Alma Reville / Helen Simpson	J. Conrad (Secret Agent)
Woman Alone					
Saboteur	TCF	1965	Bernard Wicki	E. V. H. Emmett / Daniel Taradash	W. J. Luddecke (Morituri)
Morituri					
Sacrifice	*Biograph	1909	D. W. Griffith	D. W. Griffith	O. Henry (Four Million)
Sail a Crooked Ship	Columbia	1961	Irving Brecher	Ruth Brooks Flippen / Bruce Geller	N. Benchley
Saint in London	RKO	1939	John P. Carstairs	Lynn Root / Frank Fenton	L. Charteris (Holy Terror) — Simon Templar (George Sanders)
Saint in New York	RKO	1938	Ben Holmes	Charles Kaufman / Mortimer Offner	L. Charteris — Simon Templar (Louis Hayward)
Saint in Palm Springs	RKO	1941	Jack Hively	Jerry Cady	L. Charteris (headnote) — Simon Templar (George Sanders)
St. Ives	Warner	1973	J. Lee Thompson	Berry Beckerman	O. Bleeck (Procane Chronicle) — Raymond St. Ives (Charles Bronson)
Saint Jack	Playboy	1979	Peter Bogdanovich	Peter Bogdanovich / Howard Sackler / Paul Theroux	P. Theroux
Saint Meets the Tiger	RKO	1941	Paul L. Stein	Leslie Arliss / Wolfgang Wilhelm / James Seymour / John Twist	L. Charteris (Meet the Tiger) — Simon Templar (Hugh Sinclair)
Saint Strikes Back	RKO	1939	John Farrow	Howard Browne	L. Charteris (She Was a Lady) — Simon Templar (George Sanders)
St. Valentine's Day Massacre	Corman	1967	Roger Corman	Howard Browne	novel: B. O'Hara
Saint's Double Trouble	RKO	1940	Jack Hively	Ben Holmes	L. Charteris (headnote) — Simon Templar (George Sanders)
Saint's Vacation	RKO	1941	Leslie Fenton	Leslie Charteris / Jeffrey Dell	L. Charteris (Getaway) — Simon Templar (Hugh Sinclair)
Salamander	ITC	1983	Peter Zinner	Robert Katz	M. West
Salomy Jane	*California	1914	J. Searle Dawley / Alex E. Beyfuss	?	Bret Harte (Stories in Light and Shadow)
Salomy Jane	*Alco	1915	?	?	
Salomy Jane	*Paramount	1923	George Melford	Waldemar Young / Angus MacPhail	Bret Harte (Stories in Light and Shadow)
Saloon Bar	Ealing	1940	Walter Forde	John Dighton / Michael Pertwee	F. Harvey
Salt and Pepper	UA	1968	Richard Donner	?	novel: Alex Austin — Richard Rollison (John Bentley)
Salute the Toff	Butcher	1951	Maclean Rogers	J. Creasey	
Salzburg Connection	TCF	1972	Lee H. Katzin	Oscar Millard	H. MacInnes

S

FILM TITLE	STUDIO	YEAR	DIRECTOR	SCREENWRITER	SOURCE AUTHOR/WORK	SERIES
Sam Marlow, Private Eye	TCF	1980	Robert Day	Andrew J. Fenady	A. J. Fenady (Man with Bogart's Face)	Sam Marlow (Robert Sacchi)
Man with Bogart's Face						
Sanctuary	TCF	1961	Tony Richardson	James Poe	W. Faulkner	
Sanders	Big Ben	1963	Lawrence Huntington	Harry Alan Towers	E. Wallace (Sanders of the River)	Gavin Stevens (Bradford Dillman)
Death Drums Along the River				Nicolas Roeg		Commissioner Sanders (Richard Todd)
Sanders of the River	London	1935	Zoltan Korda	Lajos Biro	E. Wallace	Commissioner Sanders (Leslie Banks)
Bosambo				Jeffrey Dell		
				Arthur Wimperis		
Sapphire	Artna	1959	Basil Dearden	Janet Green	novel: E. G. Cousins	
				Lukas Heller		
Satan Bug	UA	1965	John Sturges	James Clavell	I. Stuart	
				Edward Anhalt		
Satan in High Heels	Vega	1962	Jerald Intrator	John T. Chapman	novel: N. Chandler	
Satan Met a Lady	Warner	1936	William Dieterle	Brown Holmes	D. Hammett (Maltese Falcon)	
Scallywag	*Master	1921	Challis Sanderson	Walter C. Rowden	G. Allen	
Scandal for Sale	Universal	1932	Russell Mack	Ralph Graves	E. Gauvreau (Hot News)	
Scandal in Bohemia	*Stoll	1921	Maurice Elvey	William J. Elliott	A. C. Doyle (Adventures of Sherlock Holmes)	Sherlock Holmes (Eille Norwood)
Scandal in Paris	UA	1946	Douglas Sirk	Ellis St. Joseph	Vidocq (Memoirs of Vidocq)	
Thieves Holiday						
Scandal Sheet	Columbia	1952	Phil Karlson	Ted Sherdeman	S. Fuller (Dark Page)	
Dark Page				Eugene Ling		
				James Poe		
Scapegoat	MGM	1959	Robert Hamer	Gore Vidal	D. Du Maurier	
				Robert Hamer		
Scar	*World	1919	Frank Crane	Hamilton Smith	E. Gaboriau (headnote)	
Scar	Eagle-Lion	1948	Steve Sekely	Daniel Fuchs	M. Forbes (Hollow Triumph)	
Hollow Triumph						
Scarab Murder Case	B&D	1936	Michael Hankinson	Selwyn Jepson	S. S. Van Dine	Philo Vance (Wilfrid Hyde-White)
Scaramouche	*Metro	1923	Rex Ingram	Willis Goldbeck	R. Sabatini	Scaramouche (Ramon Navarro)
Scaramouche	MGM	1952	George Sidney	Ronald Miller	R. Sabatini	Scaramouche (Stewart Granger)
				George Froeschel		
Scarecrow	Oasis	1981	Sam Pilsbury	Michael Heath	R. H. Morrieson	
				Sam Pilsbury		
Scared Stiff	Paramount	1953	George Marshall	Herbert Baker	C. W. Goddard (Ghost Breakers)	
				Walter DeLeon		
				Ed Simmons		
				Norman Lear		
Scarface	UA	1932	Howard Hawks	Fred Pasley	A. Trail	
				W. R. Burnett		
				John Lee Mahin		
				Seton I. Miller		
				Ben Hecht		
Scarface	Universal	1983	Brian De Palma	Oliver Stone	A. Trail	
Scarlet Car	*Bluebird	1917	Joseph DeGrasse	William Parker	R. H. Davis	
Scarlet Car	*Universal	1923	Stuart Paton	George R. Chester	R. H. Davis	
Scarlet Claw	Universal	1944	Roy William Neill	Edmund L. Hartmann	A. C. Doyle (Hound of the Baskervilles)	Sherlock Holmes (Basil Rathbone)
Sherlock Holmes and the Scarlet Claw				Roy William Neill		
Scarlet Daredevil	*Wide World	1928	T. Hayes Hunter	Angus MacPhail	B. Orczy (Triumph of the Scarlet Pimpernel)	Percy Blakeney (Matheson Lang)
Scarlet Pimpernel	UA	1935	Harold Young	S. N. Behrman	B. Orczy	Percy Blakeney (Leslie Howard)
				Robert Sherwood		
				Arthur Wimperis		
				Lajos Biro		

Scarlet Runner	*Vitagraph	1916	Wallie Van	George H. Plympton	C. N. Williamson
Scarlet Weekend	MGM	1932	William P. S. Earle	Oliver Blake	W. Kent (Woman in Purple Pajamas)
Scattergood Baines	RKO	1941	Christy Cabanne	William Nobles Michael L. Simmons Edward T. Lowe	C.B.Kelland Scattergood Baines (Guy Kibbee)
Scavengers	Lynn-Romero	1959	John Crowell	Edgar Romero	novel: D. O'Callaghan
City of Sin					
Scent of Mystery	Scent/Myst.	1959	Jack Cardiff	William Roos Gerald Kersh	K. Roos (Ghost of a Chance)
School for Secrets	Two Cities	1946	Peter Ustinov	Peter Ustinov	novel: Delano Ames
Secret Flight					
Scobie Malone	Kingscroft	1975	Terry Ohlsson	Casey Robinson Graham Woodlock	J. Cleary (Helga's Web) Scobie Malone (Jack Thompson)
Scorpio	UA	1973	Michael Winner	David W. Rintels Gerald Wilson	novel: M. Roote
Scorpio Letters	MGM	1968	Richard Thorpe	Adrian Spies	V. Canning
Scotland Yard Commands	ATP	1936	James Flood	Jo Eisinger Gerard Fairlie	N. Shute (Lonely Road)
Lonely Road					
Scream and Scream Again	AIP	1969	Gordon Hessler	Christopher Wicking	P. Saxon (Disoriented Man)
Scream in the Dark	Republic	1943	George Sherman	Gerald Schnitzer Anthony Coldeway	J. Odlum (Morgue Is Always Open)
Screaming Mimi	Columbia	1957	Gerd Oswald	Anthony Kimmins Robert Blees	Fredric Brown
Sea God	Paramount	1930	George Abbott	George Abbott	J. Russell (Red Mark)
Sea Shall Not Have Them	Apollo	1954	Lewis Gilbert	Lewis Gilbert Vernon Harris	J. Harris
Sea Wolves	Lorimar	1981	Andrew V. McLaglen	Reginald Rose	J. Leasor (Boarding Party)
Sealed Lips	*World	1915	John Ince	Frank Condon	Maxwell Gray (Silence of Dean Maitland)
Sealed Valley	*Metro	1915	Lawrence Gill	Hulbert Footner	H. Footner
Sealed Verdict	Paramount	1948	Lewis Allen	Jonathan Latimer	L. Shapiro
Seance on a Wet Afternoon	AFM	1964	Bryan Forbes	Bryan Forbes	M. McShane Myra Savage (Kim Stanley)
Second Bureau	Comp. Fran. Prem.Staff.	1935	Pierre Billon	Bernard Zimmer Akos Tolnay	C. R. Dumas
Second Bureau		1936	W. Victor Hanbury	Reginald Long	C. R. Dumas
Second Floor Mystery	Warner	1930	Roy del Ruth	Joseph Jackson	E. D. Biggers (Agony Column)
Second Stain	*Stoll	1922	George Ridgwell	Patrick L. Mannock Geoffrey H. Malins	A. C. Doyle (Return of Sherlock Holmes) Sherlock Holmes (Eille Norwood)
Seconds	Paramount	1966	John Frankenheimer	Lewis John Carlino	D. Ely
Secret	Cin. Nat.	1975	Robert Enrico	Pascal Jardin	F. Ryck
Secret Agent	Gaum. Brit.	1936	Alfred Hitchcock	Charles Bennett Ian Hay Jesse Lasky, Jr. Alma Reville	W. S. Maugham (Ashenden)
Secret Beyond the Door	Univ. Int.	1948	Fritz Lang	Silvia Richards	Rufus King (Museum Piece No. 13)
Secret Call	Paramount	1931	Stuart Walker	Arthur Kober Eve Unsell	A. P. Terhune (Woman)
Secret Ceremony	Universal	1968	Joseph Losey	George Tabori	M. Denevi
Secret Document-Vienna	Davis	1954	Andrew Haguet	Andre Legrand	M. Dekobra (Widow with the Pink Gloves)
Secret Flight	Two Cities	1946	Peter Ustinov	Peter Ustinov	novel: Delano Ames
School for Secrets					
Secret Four	Ealing	1939	Walter Forde	Angus MacPhail Sergei Nolbandov Roland Pertwee	E. Wallace (Four Just Men) Four Just Men
Four Just Men					
Secret Friends	Whistling	1991	Dennis Potter	Dennis Potter	D. Potter (Ticket to Ride)
Secret of Deep Harbor	UA	1961	Edward L. Cahn	Owen Harris Wells Root	Max Miller (I Cover the Waterfront)

S

S

FILM TITLE	STUDIO	YEAR	DIRECTOR	SCREENWRITER	SOURCE AUTHOR/WORK	SERIES
Secret of Stamboul	GFD	1936	Andrew Marton	Richard Wainwright / Howard Irving Young / Noel Langley	D. Wheatley (Eunich of Stamboul)	
Spy in White						
Secret of the Hills	*Vitagraph	1921	Chester Bennett	E. Magnus Ingleton	W. Garrett	
Secret of the Moor	*Brit. Lion	1919	Lewis Willoughby	?	M. Gerard	
Secret of the Purple Reef	TCF	1960	William Witney	Harold Yablonsky / Gene Corman	D. Cottrell (Silent Reefs)	
Secret Service	*Paramount	1919	Hugh Ford	Beulah Marie Dix / Bernard Schubert	W. Gillette	
Secret Service	RKO	1931	J. Walter Ruben	Gerri J. Lloyd	W. Gillette	
Secret Six	MGM	1931	George Hill	Frances Marion	novel: F. Marion	
Secret Tent	Forward	1956	Don Chaffey	Jan Reed	E. Addyman	
Secret Ways	Univ. Int.	1960	Phil Karlson	Jean Hazlewood	A. MacLean (Last Frontier)	
Secret Witness	Columbia	1931	Thornton Freeland	Samuel Spewack	S. Spewack (Murder in the Gilded Cage)	
Terror by Night						
Secretary of Frivolous Affairs	*American	1915	Thomas Ricketts	Thomas Ricketts	M. Futrelle	
Secrets of Paris	*Bennett	1922	Kenneth Webb	Dorothy Farnum	E. Sue (Mysteries of Paris)	
Secrets of the Night	*Universal	1925	Herbert Blache	Edward J. Montagne	M. Marcin (Nightcap)	
Section des Disparus	C.I.C.C.	1956	Pierre Chenal	?	D. Goodis (Of Missing Persons)	
See No Evil	Filmways	1971	Richard Fleischer	Brian Clemens	novel: W. Hughes (Blind Terror)	
Blind Terror						
See Venice and Die	Cocinor	1964	Andre Versini	Jacques Robert / Andre Versini	R. Marshall (Mission to Venice)	
See You in Hell, Darling	Warner	1966	Robert Gist	Mann Rubin	N. Mailer (American Dream)	
American Dream						
Sentinel	Universal	1976	Michael Winner	Michael Winner / Jeffrey Konvitz	J. Konvitz	
Serenade	Warner	1956	Anthony Mann	Ivan Goff / Ben Roberts	J. M. Cain	
Set-Up	Merton Park	1963	Gerard Glaister	John Twist	E. Wallace (headnote)	
Seven Days in May	Paramount	1964	John Frankenheimer	Roger Marshall / Rod Serling	F. Knebel	
Seven Footprints to Satan	First Nat.	1929	Ben. Christensen	Richard Bee	A. Merritt	
Seven Graves for Rogan	Carnation	1983	Matt Cimber	John Goff / Matt Cimber / William Russell	M. Cleri (Six Graves to Munich)	
Time to Die						
Seven Keys to Baldpate	*Williamson	1916	Monte Luke	Alex C. Butler	E. D. Biggers	
Seven Keys to Baldpate	*Artcraft	1917	Hugh Ford	George M. Cohen / Hugh Ford	E. D. Biggers	
Seven Keys to Baldpate	*Fam. Play.	1925	Fred Newmeyer	Frank Griffin / Wade Boteler	E. D. Biggers	
Seven Keys to Baldpate	RKO	1930	Reginald Barker	Jane Murfin	E. D. Biggers	
Seven Keys to Baldpate	RKO	1935	William Hamilton / Edward Killy	Wallace Smith / Anthony Veiller	E. D. Biggers	
Seven Keys to Baldpate	RKO	1947	Lew Landers	Lee Loeb	E. D. Biggers	
Seven-Per-Cent Solution	Universal	1976	Herbert Ross	Nicholas Meyer	N. Meyer	Sherlock Holmes (Nicol Williamson)
Seven Sinners	Gaumont	1936	Albert de Courville	Frank Launder / Sidney Gilliat / L. DuGarde Peach / Austin Melford	A. Ridley (Wrecker)	
Doomed Cargo						
Seven Thieves	TCF	1960	Henry Hathaway	Sidney Boehm	S. Kent (Lions at the Kill)	
Seven Thunders	Dial	1957	Hugo Fregonese	John Baines	R. Croft-Cooke	
Beast of Marseilles						
Seven-Ups	TCF	1973	Philip D'Antoni	Albert Ruben / Alexander Jacobs	novel: R. Posner	
Seventh Cross	MGM	1944	Fred Zinnemann	Helen Deutsch	A. Seghers	

Seventh Juror	Orex	1962	Georges Lautner	Jacques Robert Pierre Laroche	F. Didelot
77, Park Lane	Fam. Play.	1931	Albert de Courville	Michael Powell Reginald Berkeley	W. Hackett
77 Rue Chalgrin	UA	1931	Albert de Courville	A. Seabourne Garrett Fort	W. Hackett (77, Park Lane)
70,000 Witnesses	Paramount	1932	Ralph Murphy	Robert N. Lee P. J. Wolfson Allen Rivkin	C. Fitzsimmons
Sexton Blake	*Gaumont	1909	C. Douglas Carlile	William McGrath C. Douglas Carlile	Sexton Blake (C. Douglas Carlile)
Sexton Blake and the Bearded Doctor	TCF	1935	George A. Cooper	Rex Hardinge	Sexton Blake (George Curzon) R. Hardinge (Blazing Launch)
Sexton Blake and the Hooded Terror	MGM	1938	George King	A. R. Rawlinson	Sexton Blake (George Curzon) P. Quiroule (Mystery of No. 13 Caversham Square)
Sh! The Octopus	Warner	1937	William McGann	George Bricker	R. Spence (Gorilla)
Shabby Tiger Masquerade Operation Masquerade	Novus	1964	Basil Dearden	Michael Relph	V. Canning (Castle Minerva)
Shadow	Real Art	1933	George A. Cooper	H. Fowler Mear Terence Egan	D. Stuart
Shadow Between	*Seal	1920	George Dewhurst	George Dewhurst	S. Hocking
Shadow Man Street of Shadows	Anglo-Am.	1953		Richard Vernon	L. Meynell (Creaking Chair)
Shadow of a Woman	Warner	1946	Joseph Santley	Whitman Chambers C. Graham Baker	V. Perdue (He Fell Down Dead)
Shadow of Doubt	MGM	1935	George B. Seitz	Wells Root	A. S. Roche
Shadow of Evil	*Brit. Art	1921	James Readon	Harry Hughes	C. Dawe
Shadow of Fear Before I Die	Gibraltar	1955	Al Rogell	Robert Westerby	H. Debrett (Before I Die)
Shadow of the Law	Paramount	1930	Louis Gasnier	Max Marcin John Farrow	J. Moroso (Quarry)
Shadow on the Wall	*Gotham	1925	Max Marcin Reeves Eason	Henry McCarty	J. B. Ellis (Picture on the Wall)
Shadow on the Wall	MGM	1949	Patrick Jackson	William Ludwig	H. Lees (Death in the Doll's House)
Shadows on the Stairs	Warner	1941	D. Ross Lederman	Anthony Coldeway	F. Vosper (Murder on the Second Floor)
Shaft	MGM	1971	Gordon Parks	John D. F. Black Ernest Tidyman	E. Tidyman	John Shaft (Richard Roundtree)
Shaft's Big Score	MGM	1972	Gordon Parks	Ernest Tidyman	E. Tidyman	John Shaft (Richard Roundtree)
Shake Hands with the Devil	Pennebaker	1959	Michael Anderson	Ivan Goff Ben Roberts	R. Conner
Shamus	Columbia	1973	Buzz Kulik	Marian Thompson Barry Beckerman	novel: R. Giles
Shanghai Gesture	UA	1941	Josef von Sternberg	Josef von Sternberg Karl Vollmoeller Geza Herczeg Jules Furthman	John Colton
Shanghai Surprise	MGM	1986	Jim Goddard	John Kohn Robert Bentley	T. Kenrick (Faraday's Flowers)
Share Out	Merton Park	1962	Gerard Glaister	Philip Mackie	E. Wallace (Jack o' Judgment)
Shark Maneater	Heritage	1969	Samuel Fuller	Samuel Fuller John Kingsbridge	V. Canning (His Bones Are Coral)
Sharky's Machine	Orion	1981	Burt Reynolds	Gerald DiPego	W. Diehl
Shattered	MGM	1991	Wolfgang Petersen	Wolfgang Petersen	R. Neely (Plastic Nightmare)
She Made Her Bed	Paramount	1934	Ralph Murphy	Casey Robinson Frank R. Adams	J. M. Cain (Baby in the Icebox)
She Played with Fire Fortune Is a Woman	Harvel	1957	Sidney Gilliat	Sidney Gilliat Frank Launder Val Valentine	Winston Graham (Fortune Is a Woman)

S

S

FILM TITLE	STUDIO	YEAR	DIRECTOR	SCREENWRITER	SOURCE AUTHOR/WORK	SERIES
She Shall Have Murder	Concanen	1950	Daniel Birt	Allen MacKinnon	D. Ames	Dagobert Brown (Derrick de Marney)
She Wolves	Rivers	1957	Luis Saslavsky	Luis Saslavsky Pierre Boileau Thomas Narcejac	P. Boileau (Prisoner)	
Demoniaque						
Shed No Tears	Pathe	1948	Jean Yarbrough	Brown Holmes Virginia Cook	D. Martin	
Sheep's Clothing	*Edison	1914	Charles M. Seay	Charles M. Seay	L. J. Vance	
She'll Have to Go	Asher	1962	Robert Asher	John Waterhouse	I. S. Black (We Must Kill Toni)	
Maid for Murder						
Sherlock Holmes	*Essanay	1916	Arthur Berthelet	H. S. Sheldon	W. Gillette	Sherlock Holmes (William Gilette)
Sherlock Holmes	*Goldwyn	1922	Albert Parker	Marion Fairfax Earle Brown	W. Gillette	Sherlock Holmes (John Barrymore)
Moriarty						
Sherlock Holmes	Fox	1932	William K. Howard	Bertram Millhauser	W. Gillette	Sherlock Holmes (Clive Brook)
Sherlock Holmes	TCF	1939	Alfred Werker	Edwin Blum William Drake	W. Gillette	Sherlock Holmes (Basil Rathbone)
Adventures of Sherlock Holmes						
Sherlock Holmes and a Study in Scarlet	Pac. Arts	1984	Eddy Graham	?	A. C. Doyle (Study in Scarlet)	Sherlock Holmes (voice: Peter O'Toole)
Sherlock Holmes and the Baskerville Case	Pac. Arts	1984	Eddy Graham	?	A. C. Doyle (Hound of the Baskervilles)	Sherlock Holmes (voice: Peter O'Toole)
Sherlock Holmes and the Deadly Necklace	Constantin	1962	Terence Fisher Frank Winterstein	Curt Siodmak	A. C. Doyle (Valley of Fear)	Sherlock Holmes (Christopher Lee)
Sherlock Holmes and the Great Murder Mystery	*Crescent	1908	?	?	E. A. Poe (Prose Romances of Edgar A. Poe)	Sherlock Holmes (?)
Sherlock Holmes and the Scarlet Claw	Universal	1944	Roy William Neill	Edmund L. Hartmann Roy William Neill Edward T. Lowe W. Scott Darling	A. C. Doyle (Hound of the Baskervilles)	Sherlock Holmes (Basil Rathbone)
Scarlet Claw						
Sherlock Holmes and the Secret Weapon	Universal	1943	Roy William Neill	Edmund L. Hartmann	A. C. Doyle (Return of Sherlock Holmes)	Sherlock Holmes (Basil Rathbone)
Sherlock Holmes and the Sign of Four	Pac. Arts	1984	Eddy Graham	?	A. C. Doyle (Sign of the Four)	Sherlock Holmes (voice: Peter O'Toole)
Sherlock Holmes and the Spider Woman	Universal	1944	Roy William Neill	Bertram Millhauser	A. C. Doyle (Sign of the Four)	Sherlock Holmes (Basil Rathbone)
Spider Woman						
Sherlock Holmes and the Valley of Fear	Pac. Arts	1984	Eddy Graham	?	A. C Doyle (Valley of Fear)	Sherlock Holmes (voice: Peter O'Toole)
Sherlock Holmes and the Voice of Terror	Universal	1942	John Rawlins	Lynn Riggs John Bright Robert D. Andrews	A. C. Doyle (His Last Bow)	Sherlock Holmes (Basil Rathbone)
Sherlock Holmes Faces Death	Universal	1943	Roy William Neill	Bertram Millhauser	A. C. Doyle (Memoirs of Sherlock Holmes)	Sherlock Holmes (Basil Rathbone)
Sherlock Holmes' Fatal Hour	Twickenham	1930	Leslie S. Hiscott	Cyril Twyford H. Fowler Mear Leslie S. Hiscott Arthur Wontner	A. C. Doyle (Memoirs of of Sherlock Holmes)	Sherlock Holmes (Arthur Wontner)
Sleeping Cardinal						
Shield for Murder	UA	1954	Edmund O'Brien Howard W. Koch	Richard A. Simmons John C. Higgins	W. P. McGivern	
Shining Through	TCF	1992	David Seltzer	David Seltzer	Susan Isaacs	
Ship from Shanghai	MGM	1930	Charles Brabin	John Howard Lawson	D. Collins (Ordeal)	
Ship That Died of Shame	Ealing	1955	Basil Dearden	John Whiting Michael Relph Basil Dearden	N. Monsarrat	
PT Raiders						
Shock Corridor	AA	1963	Samuel Fuller	Samuel Fuller	novel: M. Avallone	
Shock to the System	Corsair	1990	Jan Egleson	Andrew Klavan	Simon Brett	

S

Title	Studio	Year	Director	Writer	Notes
Shock Treatment	TCF	1964	Denis Sanders	Sidney Boehm	W. Van Atta
Shocker	UA	1961	Gottfried Reinhardt	Silvia Reinhardt	M. Gregor (Town Without Pity)
Town Without Pity				Georg Hurdalek	
Shoot	AVCO	1976	Harvey Hart	Dick Berg	D. Fairbairn
Shoot First	UA	1953	Robert Parrish	Eric Ambler	G. Household (Rough Shoot)
Rough Shoot					
Shoot It: Black, Shoot It: Blue	Lev.-Pick.	1974	Dennis McGuire	Dennis McGuire	P. Tyner (Shoot It)
Shoot the Pianist	Cocinor	1960	Francois Truffaut	Marcel Moussy	D. Goodis (Down There)
Shoot the Piano Player				Francois Truffaut	
Shoot the Piano Player	Cocinor	1960	Francois Truffaut	Marcel Moussy	D. Goodis (Down There)
Shoot the Pianist				Francois Truffaut	
Shooting Stars	Brit. Int.	1928	A. V. Bramble	John Orton	novel: E. C. Vivian
			Anthony Asquith	Anthony Asquith	
Shop at Sly Corner	Brit. Lion	1946	George King	Katherine Strueby	E. Percy (Play with Fire)
Code of Scotland Yard					
Short Cut to Hell	Paramount	1957	James Cagney	Ted Berkman	G. Greene (Gun for Sale)
				Raphael Blau	
Short Eyes	Paramount	1977	Robert M. Young	Miguel Pinero	M. Pinero
Slammer					
Short Work	Unabhängige	1967	Michael Kehlmann	Michael Kehlmann	J. Ashford (headnote)
				Carl Merz	
Shot in the Dark	Real Art	1933	George Pearson	H. Fowler Mear	G. Fairlie
Shot in the Dark	Chester.	1935	Charles Lamont	Charles Beldon	C. Orr (Dartmouth Murders)
Shot in the Dark	UA	1964	Blake Edwards	Blake Edwards	H. Kurnitz
				William P. Blatry	Insp. Clouseau (Peter Sellers)
Shulamite	*London	1915	George Loane Tucker	Kenelm Foss	A. Askew
Shuttered Room	Seven Arts	1967	David Greene	D. B. Ledrov	novel: J. Withers
				Nathaniel Tanchuck	
Shuttlecock	KM Films	1991	Andrew Piddington	Tim Rose Price	G. Swift
Si Muero Antes de Despertar	Argentina	1952	C. H. Christensen	Alejandro Casona	W. Irish (If I Should Die Before I Wake)
Sicilian	TCF	1987	Michael Cimino	Steve Shagan	M. Puzo
Side Street	RKO	1929	Malcolm St. Clair	Malcolm St. Clair	novel: M. St. Clair
				John Russell	
				George O'Hara	
				Eugene Walter	
Sidney Sheldon's Bloodline	Paramount	1979	Terence Young	Laird Koenig	S. Sheldon (Bloodline)
Bloodline					
Sign of the Four	*Thanhauser	1913	?	?	A. C. Doyle
Sign of the Four	*Stoll	1923	Maurice Elvey	Maurice Elvey	A. C. Doyle
Sign of the Four	ATP	1932	Graham Cutts	W. P. Lipscomb	A. C. Doyle
			Rowland V. Lee		
Sign of the Four	Mapleton	1983	Desmond Davis	Charles Pogue	A. C. Doyle
					Sherlock Holmes (Harry Benham)
					Sherlock Holmes (Eille Norwood)
					Sherlock Holmes (Arthur Wontner)
					Sherlock Holmes (Ian Richardson)
Sign of the Ram	Columbia	1948	John Sturgis	Charles Bennett	M. Ferguson
Sign on the Door	*Talmadge	1921	Herbert Brenon	Mary Murillo	C. Pollock
				Herbert Brenon	
Signpost to Murder	MGM	1964	George England	Sally Benson	M. Doyle
Silence of Dean Maitland	*Fraser	1914	?	?	Maxwell Gray
Silence of the Lambs	Orion	1991	Jonathan Demme	Ted Tally	Thomas Harris
Silencers	Columbia	1966	Phil Karlson	Oscar Saul	D. Hamilton
					Matt Helm (Dean Martin)
Silent Barrier	*Gibraltar	1920	William Worthington	Charles T. Dazey	L. Tracy
Silent Battle	*Bluebird	1916	Jack Conway	F. McGrew Willis	G. F. Gibbs
Silent Dust	Independent	1949	Lance Comfort	Michael Perrwee	R. Perrwee (Paragon)
Silent House	*Nettlefold	1929	Walter Forde	Walter Forde	J. G. Brandon
Silent Master	*Selznick	1917	Leonce Perret	Leonce Perret	E. P. Oppenheim (Seeing Life)

S

FILM TITLE	STUDIO	YEAR	DIRECTOR	SCREENWRITER	SOURCE AUTHOR/WORK	SERIES
Silent Partner	Carolco	1978	Daryl Duke	Curtis Hanson	A. Bodelsen (Think of a Number)	
Silent Witness	TCF	1932	Marcel Varnel	Douglas Doty	J. De Leon	
Silver Bears	EMI	1977	R. L. Hough		P. E. Erdman	
Silver Blaze	*Fran.-Brit.	1912	Ivan Passer	Peter Stone	A. C. Doyle (Memoirs of Sherlock Holmes)	Sherlock Holmes (Georges Treville)
			Georges Treville	?		
Silver Blaze	*Stoll	1923	George Ridgwell	Geoffrey H. Malins	A. C. Doyle (Memoirs of Sherlock Holmes)	Sherlock Holmes (Eille Norwood)
				Patrick L. Mannock		
Silver Blaze	Twickenham	1936	Thomas Bentley	H. Fowler Mear	A. C. Doyle (Memoirs of Sherlock Holmes)	Sherlock Holmes (Arthur Wontner)
Murder at the Baskervilles			Arthur Macrae	Arthur Macrae		
Silver Bridge	*Cairns	1920	Dallas Cairns	Eliot Stannard	H. P. Lewis	
Silver Car	*Vitagraph	1921	David Smith	Wyndham Martyn	W. Martyn (Secret of the Silver Car)	Anthony Trent (Earle Williams)
Silver King	*Lubin	1908	?	?	H. A. Jones	
Silver King	*Paramount	1919	George Irving	Burns Mantle	H. A. Jones	
Silver King	*Welsh-Pear.	1929	T. Hayes Hunter	Fenn Sherie	H. A. Jones	
Silver Streak	TCF	1976	Arthur Hiller	Colin Higgins		
Sin That Was His	*Selznick	1920	Hobart Henley	Edmund Goulding	novel: J. C. Rogers	
Sing Sing Nights	Monogram	1935	Lew Collins	Marion North	F. Packard	
Reprieved				Charles Logue	H. S. Keeler	
Singapore	Univ. Int.	1947	John Brahm	Seton I. Miller	novel: W. Bogart	
				Robert Thoeren		
Singapore, Singapore	Numbre One	1967	Bernard T. Michel	Bernard T. Michel	J. Bruce (Cold Spell)	
Five Ashore for Singapore				Pierre Kalfon		
Singer Not the Song	Rank	1961	Roy Ward Baker	Nigel Balchin	A. E. Lindop	
Single White Female	Columbia	1992	Barbet Schroeder	Don Roos	J. Lutz (SWF Seeks Same)	
Sinister Man	Merton Park	1961	Clive Bonner	Robert Stewart	E. Wallace	
Sinner Take All	MGM	1936	Errol Taggart	Leonard Lee	W. Chambers (Murder for a Wanton)	
				Walter Wise		
Sins of the Fathers	Paramount	1929	Ludwig Berger	E. Lloyd Shelton	novel: C. Houghton	
Sisters of Eve	*Trem Car	1928	Scott Pembroke	Arthur Hoerl	E. P. Oppenheim (Temptation of Tavernake)	
Sitting Target	MGM-EMI	1972	Douglas Hickox	Alexander Jacobs	L. Henderson	
Six Bridges to Cross	Gen. Film	1954	Joseph Pevney	Sidney Boehm	J. F. Dinneen (Anatomy of a Crime)	
Six Men	Planet	1951	Michael Law	Reed de Rouen	E. Radford	
				Michael Law		
				Richard Eastham		
Six Napoleons	*Stoll	1922	George Ridgwell	Patrick L. Mannock	A. C. Doyle (Return of Sherlock Holmes)	Sherlock Holmes (Eille Norwood)
				Geoffrey H. Malins		
633 Squadron	Mirisch	1964	Walter E. Grauman	James Clavell	F. E. Smith	
				Howard Koch		
Skull	Amicus	1965	Freddie Francis	Milton Subotsky	R. Bloch (Skull of the Marquis de Sade)	
Skullduggery	Universal	1970	Gordon Douglas	Nelson Gidding	Vercors (You Shall Know Them)	
			Richard Wilson			
Sky Bandits	Criterion	1940	Ralph Staub	Edward Halperin	L. Y. Erskine (Renfrew Rides the Sky)	Douglas Renfrew (James Newill)
Sky Riders	TCF	1976	Douglas Hickox	Jack De Witt	novel: L. Cameron	
				Stanley Mann		
				Garry Michael White		
Sky Terror	MGM	1972	John Guillermin	Tanley Greenberg	D. Harper (Hijacked)	
Skyjacked						
Skyjacked	MGM	1972	John Guillermin	Stanley Greenberg	D. Harper (Hijacked)	
Sky Terror						
Slammer	Paramount	1977	Robert M. Young	Miguel Pinero	M. Pinero (Short Eyes)	
Short Eyes						
Slate, Wyn & Me	Hemdale	1987	Don McLennan	Don McLennan	Georgia Savage (Slate and Wyn and Blanche McBride)	

Title	Studio	Year	Director	Writer	Source	Character
Slaughter	AIP	1972	Jack Starrett	Mark Hanna		Slaughter (Jim Brown)
Slaughter's Big Rip-Off	Am. Int.	1973	Gordon Douglas	Don Williams		Slaughter (Jim Brown)
Slave Market	*Fam. Play.	1917	Hugh Ford	Charles Johnson		
Slaves of Sumuru	Sumuru	1967	Lindsay Shonteff	Clara S. Beranger	F. A. Kummer (Painted Woman)	Sumuru (?)
Slayground	Thorn EMI	1983	Terry Bedford	Peter Welbeck		
Sleep My Love	UA	1948	Douglas Sirk	Trevor Preston	R. Stark	
				St. Clair McKelway	L. Q. Ross	
				Leo Rosten		
				Cyril Endfield		
				Decla Dunning		
Sleepers East	TCF	1934	Kenneth MacKenna	Lester Cole	F. Nebel	
Sleepers West	TCF	1941	Eugene Forde	Lou Breslow	F. Nebel (Sleepers East)	
				Stanley Rauh		
Sleeping Car Murders	Seven Arts	1965	Costa Gavras	Sebastien Japrisot	S. Japrisot (10:30 from Marseilles)	
				Costa Gavras		
Sleeping Car to Trieste	Two Cities	1948	John P. Carstairs	Allan MacKinnon	R. Alexander (Rome Express)	
				William D. Home		
Sleeping Cardinal	Twickenham	1930	Leslie S. Hiscott	Cyril Twyford	A. C. Doyle (Memoirs of Sherlock Holmes)	Sherlock Holmes (Arthur Wontner)
Sherlock Holmes's Fatal Hour				H. Fowler Mear		
				Leslie Hiscott		
				Arthur Wontner		
Sleeping Memory	*Metro	1917	George D. Baker	Albert S. Le Vino	E. P. Oppenheim (Great Awakening)	
Sleeping Tiger	Insignia	1954	Joseph Losey	Carl Foreman	M. Moisewitsch	
				Harold Buchman		
Sleeping with the Enemy	TCF	1991	Joseph Ruben	Ronald Bass	N. Price	
Slender Thread	Paramount	1965	Sydney Pollack	Stirling Silliphant	novel: S. Silliphant	
Sleuth	TCF	1972	Joseph Mankiewicz	Anthony Shaffer	A. Shaffer	
Slight Case of Murder	Warner	1938	Lloyd Bacon	Earl Baldwin	D. Runyon	
				Joseph Shrank		
Slightly Honorable	UA	1940	Tay Garnett	Ken Englund	F. G. Presnell (Send Another Coffin)	
				John Hunter Lay		
				Robert Allman		
Slightly Scarlet	Paramount	1930	Louis Gasnier	Howard Estabrook	novel: P. Heath	
			Edwin H. Knopf	Joseph Mankiewicz		
				Percy Heath		
Slightly Scarlet	RKO	1956	Allan Dwan	Robert Blees	J. M. Cain (Love's Lovely Counterfeit)	
Slippy McGee	*Morosco	1923	Wesley Ruggles	Marie Conway Oemler	M. C. Oemler	
Slippy McGee	Republic	1948	Albert Kelley	Norman S. Hall	M. C. Oemler	
				Jerry Gruskin		
Small Back Room	Lond. Films	1949	Emeric Pressburger	Emeric Pressburger	N. Balchin	
Hour of Glory			Michael Powell	Michael Powell		
Small Voice	Brit. Lion	1948	Fergus McDonnell	Derek Neame	R. Westerby	
Hideout				Julian Orde		
				George Barraud		
Smugglers	Prod. Film	1947	Bernard Knowles	Muriel Box	G. Greene (Man Within)	
Man Within				Sydney Box		
Snout	Rank	1963	Ken Annakin	Alun Falconer	D. Warner (Death of a Snout)	
Informers				Paul Durst		
Underworld Informers						
Snow Was Black	Tellus	1954	Luis Saslavsky	Luis Saslavsky	G. Simenon (Stain on the Snow)	
				Andre Tabet		
Snowball	Ind. Art.	1958	Pat Jackson	Anne Francis	J. Lake	
Snowbound	Gainsbor.	1948	David Macdonald	David Evans	H. Innes (Lonely Skier)	
				Keith Campbell		
So Evil My Love	Paramount	1948	Lewis Allen	Leonard Spigelgass	J. Shearing (For Her to See)	
				Ronald Millar		
So Long at the Fair	Gainsbor.	1951	Terence Fisher	Hugh Mills	A. Thorne	
			Antony Darnborough	Anthony Thorne		

S

S

FILM TITLE	STUDIO	YEAR	DIRECTOR	SCREENWRITER	SOURCE AUTHOR/WORK	SERIES
Social Buccaneer	Bluebird	1916	Jack Conway	Fred Myron	F. S. Isham	
Social Highwayman	*Playgoers	1914	?	?	E. P. Train	
Society Lawyer	MGM	1939	Edwin L. Marin	Frances Goodrich / Albert Hackett / Leon Gordon / Hugo Butler	A. S. Roche (Penthouse)	
Soho Gorilla	Rialto	1968	Alfred Vohrer	Freddy Gregor	E. Wallace (Dark Eyes of London)	
Soho Incident	Film Loca.	1956	Vernon Sewell	Ian Stuart Black	R. Westerby (Wide Boys Never Work)	
Spin a Dark Web						
Sol Madrid	MGM	1968	Brian Hutton	David Karp	R. Wilder (Fruit of the Poppy)	
Heroin Gang						
Soldier's Story	Caldix	1984	Norman Jewison	Charles Fuller	C. Fuller (Soldier's Play)	
Solitaire Man	MGM	1933	Jack Conway	James K. McGuinness	B. C. Spewack	
Solitary Child	Beacons.	1958	Gerald Thomas	Robert Dunbar	N. Bawden	
Solitary Cyclist	*Stoll	1921	Maurice Elvey	William J. Elliott	A. C. Doyle (Return of Sherlock Holmes)	Sherlock Holmes (Eille Norwood)
Solo for Sparrow	Merton Park	1962	Gordon Flemyng	Roger Marshall	E. Wallace (Gunner)	
Some Kind of Hero	Paramount	1982	Michael Pressman	James Kirkwood	J. Kirkwood	
Somebody Killed Her Husband	Columbia	1978	Lamont Johnson	Reginald Rose	novel: C. B. Phillips	
Someone at the Door	BIP	1936	Herbert Brenon	Marjorie Deans / Jack Davies	D. Christie	
Someone at the Door	Hammer	1950	Francis Searle	A. R. Rawlinson	D. Christie	
Something Like the Truth	Tantallon	1973	Sidney Lumet	John Hopkins	J. Hopkins (This Story of Yours)	
Offense						
Something to Hide	Avron	1973	Alastair Reid	Alastair Reid	N. Monsarrat	
Somewhere in France	*Triangle	1916	Charles Giblyn	?	R. H. Davis	
Son of His Father	*Paramount	1917	Victor Schertzinger	?	R. Cullum	
Son of the Immortals	*Bluebird	1916	Otis Turner	Bertram Grassby	L. Tracy	
Song of Sixpence	*Art Dramas	1917	Ralph Dean	?	F. A. Kummer	
Sons of Satan	*London	1915	George Loane Tucker	?	W. LeQueux	
Sonya and the Madman	Mostafá	19??	Hossam Mostafa	Mahmoud Dyab	F. M. Dostoevskii (Crime and Punishment)	
Sophie Lang	Paramount	1934	Ralph Murphy	Anthony Veiller	F. I. Anderson (Notorious Sophie Lang)	Sophie Lang (Gerrtude Michael)
Notorious Sophie Lang						
Sophie Lang Goes West	Paramount	1937	Charles Riesner	Doris Anderson / Brian Marlow / Robert Wyler	F. I. Anderson (Notorious Sophie Lang)	Sophie Lang (Gerrtude Michael)
Sorcerer	Suedfilm	1932	Alfred Vohrer	Knut Borris / G. Water	E. Wallace (Ringer)	
Sorcerer	Paramount	1977	William Friedkin	Walon Green	G. Arnaud (Wages of Fear)	
Wages of Fear						
Sorcery	SNEG	1962	Henri Decoin	Claude Accursi / Albert Husson / Henri Decoin	P. Boileau (Spells of Evil)	
Where the Truth Lies						
Sorry Wrong Number	Paramount	1948	Anatole Litvak	Lucille Fletcher	L. Fletcher	
Sorry You've Been Troubled	B&D Param.	1932	Jack Raymond	?	W. Hackett	
Life Goes On						
Soul of Pierre	*Biograph	1915	Travers Vale	?	G. Ohnet (Weird Gift)	
Sound of the Fury	UA	1951	Cyril Endfield	Jo Pagano	J. Pagano (Condemned)	
Try and Get Me						
Soupe aux Poulets	Gaumont	1963	Philipp Agostini	Michel Subiela / Rene Wheeler	E. McBain (Killer's Wedge)	
South Sea Bubble	*Gainsbor.	1928	T. Hayes Hunter	Angus MacPhail / Alma Reville	R. Pertwee	
Soylent Green	MGM	1973	Richard Fleischer	Stanley Greenberg	H. Harrison (Make Room! Make Room!)	
Spangles	*Universal	1926	Frank O'Connor	Leah Baird	novel: N. Revell	

Title	Studio	Year	Director	Writer	Credits	Character (Actor)
Spaniard's Curse	Wentworth	1958	Ralph Kemplen	Kenneth Hyde	E. Pargeter (Assize of the Dying)	
Spanish Cape Mystery	Republic	1935	Lewis D. Collins	Albert DeMond	E. Queen	Ellery Queen (Donald Cook)
Spanish Jade	*Paramount	1915	Tom J. Geraghty	Josephine Lovett	M. Hewlett	
Speckled Band	*Fran.-Brit.	1912	Georges Treville	?	A. C. Doyle (Adventures of Sherlock Holmes)	Sherlock Holmes (Georges Treville)
Speckled Band	*Stoll	1923	George Ridgwell	Geoffrey H. Malins, Patrick L. Mannock	A. C. Doyle (Adventures of Sherlock Holmes)	Sherlock Holmes (Eille Norwood)
Speckled Band	B&D	1931	Jack Raymond	W. P. Lipscomb	A. C. Doyle (Adventures of Sherlock Holmes)	Sherlock Holmes (Raymond Massey)
Speedy	*Lloyd	1928	Ted Wilde	John Grey, Lex Neal, Howard Emmett Rogers, Jay Howe	novel: R. Holman	
Spellbound	UA	1945	Alfred Hitchcock	Ben Hecht, Angus MacPhail	F. Beeding (House of Dr. Edwardes)	
Sphinx	Orion	1981	Franklin Schaffner	John Byrum	R. Cook	
Spider	TCF	1931	W. C. Menzies, Kenneth MacKenna	Barry Connors, Philip Klein	F. Oursler	
Spider	Admiral	1939	Maurice Elvey	Victor M. Greene, Kenneth Horne, Reginald Long	H. Holt (Midnight Mail)	Insp. Silver (Derrick de Marney)
Spider	TCF	1945	Robert Webb	Jo Eisinger	F. Oursler	
Spider Woman Sherlock Holmes and the Spider Woman	Universal	1944	Roy William Neill	W. Scott Darling, Bertram Millhauser	A. C. Doyle (Sign of the Four)	Sherlock Holmes (Basil Rathbone)
Spider's Web	Danziger	1960	Godfrey Grayson	Albert G. Miller, Eldon Howard	A. Christie	
Spies	Cinedis	1958	H. G. Clouzot	H. G. Clouzot, Jerome Jeronimi	E. Hostovsky (Midnight Patient)	
Spies in the Air	Brit. Nat.	1939	David Macdonald	A. R. Rawlinson, Bridget Boland	J. Dell (Official Secret)	
Law and Disorder						
Spies of the Air						
Spies Like Us	Warner	1985	John Landis	Dan Ackroyd, Lowell Ganz, Babaloo Mandell, Dave Thomas	novel: G. McGill	
Spies of the Air Law and Disorder Spies in the Air	Brit. Nat.	1939	David Macdonald	A. R. Rawlinson, Bridget Boland	J. Dell (Official Secret)	
Spikes Gang	UA	1974	Richard Fleischer	Irving Ravetch, Harriet Frank, Jr.	G. Tippette (Bank Gang)	
Spin a Dark Web Soho Incident	Film Loca.	1956	Vernon Sewell	Ian Stuart Black	R. Westerby (Wide Boys Never Work)	
Spiral Staircase	RKO	1946	Robert Siodmak	Mel Dinelli	E. L. White (Some Must Watch)	
Spiral Staircase	Raven	1975	Peter Collinson	Allan Scott, Chris Bryant, Mel Dinelli	E. L. White (Some Must Watch)	
Spiritism	Cinemato.	1965	Benito Alazraki	Rafael G. Travesi	W. W. Jacobs (Lady of the Barge)	
Splendid Coward	*Harma	1918	F. Martin Thornton	?	H. Townley	
Splendid Hazard	*First Nat.	1920	Alan Dwan	?	H. MacGrath	
Splendid Scapegrace	*Edison	1913	?	?	O. Henry (Whirligigs)	
Split	MGM	1968	Gordon Flemyng	Robert Sabaroff, Sam Greenlee	R. Stark (Seventh)	
Spook Who Sat by the Door	UA	1973	Ivan Dixon	Melvin Clay	S. Greenlee	
Spy	*Universal	1914	Otis Turner	James Dayton, Otis Turner	J. F. Cooper	
Spy	*?	1928	Fritz Lang	Thea von Harbou	T. von Harbou	

S

S

FILM TITLE	STUDIO	YEAR	DIRECTOR	SCREENWRITER	SOURCE AUTHOR/WORK	SERIES
Spy for a Day	Two Cities	1939	Mario Zampi	Anatole de Grunwald Hans Wilhelm Emeric Pressburger Ralph Block	S. Aumonier (Love-a-Duck)	
Spy Hunt Panther's Moon	Univ. Int.	1950	George Sherman	Tommy Thompson George Zuckerman Leonard Lee	V. Canning (Panther's Moon)	
Spy in Black U-Boat 29	Harefield	1939	Michael Powell	Emeric Pressberger Roland Pertwee	J. S. Clouston	
Spy in the Sky	AA	1958	W. Lee Wilder	Myles Wilder	A. S. Fleischman (Counterspy Express)	
Spy in White Secret of Stamboul	GFD	1936	Andrew Marton	Richard Wainwright Howard Irving Young Noel Langley	D. Wheatley (Eunich of Stamboul)	
Spy of Napoleon	Wardour	1936	Maurice Elvey	L. de Garde Peach Frederick Merrick Harold Simpson	B. Orczy	
Spy Ship	Warner	1942	B. Reeves Eason	Robert E. Kent	G. Dyer (Five Fragments)	
Spy 13 Operator 13	MGM	1934	Richard Boleslavsky	Harvey Thew Zelda Sears Eve Greene	R. W. Chambers (Secret Service)	
Spy Who Came in from the Cold	Paramount	1966	Martin Ritt	Paul Dehn Guy Trosper	J. Le Carre	George Smiley (Rupert Davies)
Spy Who Loved Me	UA	1977	Lewis Gilbert	Christopher Wood Richard Maibaum	novel: C. Wood (James Bond, the Spy Who Loved Me)	James Bond (Roger Moore)
Spy with a Cold Nose	Embassy	1966	Daniel Petrie	Ray Galton Alan Simpson	novel: R. Galton	
Square Crooks	*Fox	1928	Lewis Seiler	Becker Gardiner	J. P. Judge	
Squeaker	Brit. Lion	1930	Edgar Wallace	Edgar Wallace	E. Wallace	
Squeaker Murder on Diamond Row	London	1937	William K. Howard	Bryan Edgar Wallace Edward O. Berkman	E. Wallace	
Squeaker	Rialto	1964	Alfred Vohrer	Herbert Reinecker	E. Wallace (Ringer)	
Squeeze	Warner	1977	Michael Apted	Leon Griffiths	David Craig (Whose Little Girl Are You?)	
Srok Istekset Na Rassvete	Gruziafilm	1966	Nelli Nenova	Nelli Nenova Gennady Pulaja	W. Irish (Deadline at Dawn)	
Stage Fright	WB-FN	1950	Alfred Hitchcock	Whitfield Cook Alma Reville James Bridie	S. Jepson (Man Running)	Eve Gill (Jane Wyman)
Stain	*Eclectic	1914	Frank Powell	?	F. Halsey	
Stalag 17	Paramount	1953	Billy Wilder	Billy Wilder Edwin Blum	D. Bevan	
Stanton's Last Fling	*Edison	1913	Charles M. Seay	Charles M. Seay	H. B. M. Watson (Ifs and Ans)	
Star of Midnight	RKO	1935	Stephen Roberts	Howard J. Green Anthony Veiller Edward Kaufman	A. S. Roche	
Star Reporter	*Berwilla	1921	Duke Worne	?	W. Martyn (Mysterious Mr. Garland)	
Steele of the Royal Mounted	*Vitagraph	1925	David Smith	Jay Pilcher	J. O. Curwood (Philip Steele of the Royal North-West Mounted Police)	
Steelyard Blues	Warner	1972	Alan Myerson	David S. Ward		
Stella	TCF	1950	Claude Binyon	Claude Binyon	novel: Timothy Harris	
Stepford Wives	Fadsin	1975	Bryan Forbes	William Goldman	D. M. Disney (Family Skeleton)	
Stew in the Caribbean	Valoria	1967	Jacques Besnard	Pierre Foucard Michel Lebrun	I. Levin	
Stick	Universal	1985	Burt Reynolds	Elmore Leonard Joseph C. Stinson	A. Conroy (Looters)	
Stiletto	AVCO	1969	Bernard Kowalski	A. J. Russell	E. Leonard	
Still Waters Run Deep	*Ideal	1916	Fred Paul	Dane Stanton	H. Robbins	
Sting	Universal	1973	George Roy Hill	David S. Ward	T. Taylor	
					novel: R. Weverka	

Title	Studio	Year	Director	Cast	Source
Stingaree	*Kalem	1916	James W. Horne	James W. Horne / Becky Gardiner / Lynn Riggs	E. W. Hornung
Stingaree	RKO	1934	William A. Wellman		E. W. Hornung
Stock-Broker's Clerk	*Stoll	1922	George Ridgwell	Leonard Spigelgass / Patrick L. Mannock	A. C. Doyle (Memoirs of Sherlock Holmes)
Stolen Papers	*Franco-Br.	1912	Georges Treville	Geoffrey H. Malins / ?	A. C. Doyle (Memoirs of Sherlock Holmes)
Stone Cold Dead	Dimension	1980	George Mendeluk	George Mendeluk	H. Garner (Sin Sniper)
Stone Killer	Columbia	1973	Michael Winner	Gerald Wilson	J. Gardner (Complete State of Death)
Stone Leopard	ITC	1978	?	?	C. Forbes
Stop Me Before I Kill Full Treatment	Falcon	1961	Val Guest	Val Guest / Ronald Scott Thorn	R. S. Thorn (Full Treatment)
Stop Thief!	*Kleine	1915	George Fitzmaurice	?	Carlyle Moore
Stop Thief!	*Goldwyn	1920	Harry Beaumont	Charles Kenyon	Carlyle Moore
Stop, You're Killing Me	Warner	1952	Roy Del Ruth	James O'Hanlon	D. Runyon (Slight Case of Murder)
Stopover: Tokyo	TCF	1957	Richard L. Breen	Richard L. Breen / Walter Reisch	J. P. Marquand
Storm Fear	UA	1955	Cornell Wilde	Horton Foote	C. Seeley
Story of Shirley Yorke	Nettlefold	1948	Maclean Rogers	A. R. Rawlinson / Maclean Rogers / Kathleen Butler	H. A. Vachell (Case of Lady Camber)
Story of Temple Drake	Paramount	1933	Stephen Roberts	Oliver Garrett	W. Faulkner (Sanctuary)
Story-Teller	Common	1989	Rainer Boldt	Rainer Boldt / Dorothea Neukirchen / Wolf C. Schroder / Hans Kwiet	P. Highsmith
Story Without a Name Without Warning	*Paramount	1924	Irvin Willat	Arthur Stringer	novel: A. Stringer
Stowaway	Discifilm	1958	Lee Robinson	Lee Robinson / Ralph Habib	G. Simenon
Straight Is the Way	MGM	1934	Paul Sloane	Joy Cavill / Bernard Schubert	D. Burnet (Four Walls)
Straight Time	Warner	1978	Ula Grosbard	Alvin Sargent / Edward Bunker / Dustin Hoffman / Jeffrey Boam	E. Bunker (No Beast So Fierce)
Stranded in Arcady	*Astra	1917	Frank Crane	Philip Bartholomae	
Strange Adventure of David Gray Castle of Doom Not Against the Flesh Vampire	Dreyer	1931	Carl T. Dreyer	Carl T. Dreyer / Christian Jul	F. Lynde / J. S. Le Fanu (In a Glass Darkly)
Strange Affair	Paramount	1968	David Greene	Stanley Mann / Stephen Lonstreet	B. Toms
Strange Affair of Uncle Harry Uncle Harry	Universal	1945	Robert Siodmak	Keith Winter	T. Job (Uncle Harry)
Strange Awakening Female Fiends	Merton Park	1958	Montgomery Tully	J. McLaren Ross	P. Quentin (Puzzle for Fiends)
Strange Boarders	Gainsboro.	1938	Herbert Mason	Sidney Gilliat / A. R. Rawlinson	E. P. Oppenheim (Strange Boarders at Palace Crescent)
Strange Cargo	MGM	1940	Frank Borzage	Lawrence Hazard / Lesser Samuels	R. Sale (Not Too Narrow—Not Too Deep)
Strange Case of Dr. Jekyll and Mr. Hyde	Mosfilm	1987	Alexander Orlov	Alexander Orlov / Georgy Kapralov	R. L. Stevenson
Strange Case of Mary Page	*Essanay	1916	J. Charles Haydon	Frederick Lewis	F. Lewis
Strange Case of the Man and the Beast Man and the Beast	Sono	1951	Mario Soffici	Mario Soffici / Ulises P. de Murat / Carlos Marin	R. L. Stevenson (Strange Case of Dr. Jekyll and Mr. Hyde)
Strange Conspiracy President Vanishes	Paramount	1934	William A. Wellman	Carey Wilson / Cedric Worth	Anonymous (President Vanishes)
Strange Disappearance	*Imp	1915	George A. Lessey	Lynn Starling	A. K. Green
Strange Door	Univ. Int.	1951	Joseph Pevney	Raymond L. Shrock / Jerry Sackheim	R. L. Stevenson (New Arabian Nights)

S

FILM TITLE	STUDIO	YEAR	DIRECTOR	SCREENWRITER	SOURCE AUTHOR/WORK	SERIES
Strange Intruder	Anglo-Amal.	1957	Irving Rapper	David Evans Warren Douglas	H. Fowler (Shades Will Not Vanish)	
Stranger	*Paramount	1924	Joseph Henabery	Eidfrid Bingham Anthony Veiller	J. Galsworthy (Five Tales)	
Stranger	Int. Pict.	1946	Orson Welles	John Huston Orson Welles	novel: A. Veiller	
Stranger Came Home Unholy Four	Hammer	1954	Terence Fisher	Michael Carreras	G. Sanders	
Stranger in the House	De Grunwald	1967	Pierre Rouve	Pierre Rouve	G. Simenon (Strangers in the House)	
Stranger in Town	Tempean	1957	George Pollock	Norman Hudis Edward Dryhurst	F. A. Chittenden (Uninvited)	
Stranger Is Watching	MGM	1981	Sean S. Cunningham	Earl MacRauch Victor Miller	M. H. Clark	
Stranger Walked In Love from a Stranger	Renown	1947	Richard Whorf	Philip MacDonald	F. Vosper (Love from a Stranger)	
Strangers in the House Cop-Out	Lopert	1941	Henri Decoin	H.-G. Clouzot	G. Simenon	
Strangers of the Evening	Tiffany	1932	H. B. Humberstone	Stuart Anthony Warren B. Duff	T. Thayer (Illustrious Corpse)	
Strangers of the Night	Tiffany	1932	H. B. Humberstone	Stuart Anthony	T. Thayer (Illustrious Corpse)	
Strangers of the Evening Strangers on a Honeymoon	Gaumont Br.	1936	Albert de Courville	Sidney Gilliat Bryan Edgar Wallace Ralph Spence Laird Doyle	E. Wallace (Northing Tramp)	
Strangers on a Train	Warner	1951	Alfred Hitchcock	Julian Houston Raymond Chandler Czenzi Ormonde Whitfield Cook	P. Highsmith	
Stranglers of Bombay	Hammer	1959	Terence Fisher	David Z. Goodman	novel: S. James	
Straw Dogs	Cinerama	1971	Sam Peckinpah	David Z. Goodman Sam Peckinpah	G. M. Williams (Siege of Trencher's Farm)	
Straw Man	Hedgerley	1953	Donald Taylor	Donald Taylor	D. M. Disney	
Street of Chance	Paramount	1942	Jack Hively	Garrett Fort	C. Woolrich (Black Curtain)	
Street of No Return	Thunder	1991	Samuel Fuller	Jacques Bral Francois Besson	D. Goodis	
Street of Shadows Shadow Man	Anglo-Amal.	1953	Richard Vernon	Richard Vernon	L. Meynell (Creaking Chair)	
Street Without Joy	Films Vog	1938	Andre Hugon	?	H. Bettauer (Viennese Love)	
Strike It Rich	Millimeter	1990	James Scott	James Scott	G. Greene (Loser Takes All)	
Striptease Lady Lady of Burlesque	Universal	1943	William Wellman	James Gunn	G. R. Lee (G-String Murders)	
Stronger Than Desire	MGM	1939	Leslie Fenton	David Hertz William Ludwig	W. E. Woodward (Evelyn Prentice)	
Stronger Than Fear Edge of Doom	RKO	1950	Mark Robson	Philip Yordan	L. Brady (Edge of Doom)	
Studio Murder Mystery	Paramount	1929	Frank Tuttle	Frank Tuttle Ethel Doherty	Edingrons	
Study in Scarlet	*Samuelson	1914	George Pearson	Harry Engholm	A. C. Doyle	Sherlock Holmes (James Bragington)
Study in Scarlet	*Gold Seal	1914	Francis Ford	Grace Cunard	A. C. Doyle	Sherlock Holmes (Francis Ford)
Study in Scarlet	World Wide	1933	Edward L. Marin	Robert Florey Reginald Owen	A. C. Doyle	Sherlock Holmes (Reginald Owen)
Scarlet Ring Study in Terror Fog	Compton	1965	James Hill	Donald Ford Derek Ford	novel: E. Queen	Sherlock Holmes (John Neville)
Stuff That Dreams Are Made Of	Roxy	1972	Alfred Vohrer	Manfred Purzer	J. M. Simmel (Traitor Blitz)	

Film Index

Title	Studio	Year	Director	Writer	Source/Notes
Stunt Man	Simon	1980	Richard Rush	Lawrence B. Marcus / Richard Rush	P. Brodeur
Subway in the Sky	Orbit	1958	Muriel Box	Jack Andrews	novel: B. Birch
Such a Gorgeous Kid Like Me	Films Caro.	1972	Francois Truffaut	Francois Truffaut / Jean-Louis Dabadie	H. Farrell
Such Things Happen (Gorgeous Bird Like Me)	Warner	1932	William A. Wellman	Courtney Terrett	R. James (Love Is a Racket)
Love Is a Racket					
Sudden Fear	RKO	1952	David Miller	Lenore Coffee / Robert Smith	E. Sherry
Sudden Impact	Warner	1983	Clint Eastwood	Joseph C. Stinson	novel: J. C. Stinson; Harry Callahan (Clint Eastwood)
Sudden Terror Eyewitness	Allen	1970	John Hough	Ronald Harwood	M. Hebden (Eyewitness)
Suicide Club	*AB	1909	D. W. Griffith	Frank Woods	R. L. Stevenson
Suicide Club	*B&C	1914	Maurice Elvey	?	R. L. Stevenson
Suicide Club Trouble for Two	MGM	1936	J. Walter Ruben	Manuel Seff / Edward Paramore, Jr.	R. L. Stevenson
Suicide Club	Suicide	1987	James Bruce	Matthew Gaddis / Suzan Kouguell / Carl Caportoto	R. L. Stevenson
Sultana	*Balboa	1916	?	?	H. C. Rowland
Summer Heat	Atlantic	1987	Michie Gleason	Michie Gleason	L. Shivers (Here to Get My Baby Out of Jail)
Summer Storm	UA	1944	Douglas Sirk	Rowland Leigh / Douglas Sirk / Robert Thoeren	A. Chekhov (Shooting Party)
Sumuru Million Eyes of Sumuru	Sumuru	1967	Lindsay Shonteff	Kevon Kavanagh	S. Rohmer; Sumuru (Shirley Eaton)
Sun Shines Bright	Republic	1953	John Ford	Laurence Stallings	I. S. Cobb (Old Judge Priest); Judge Priest (Charles Winninger)
Sun-Up	*Bacon	1919	Oliver D. Bailey	Basil Dickey / John Daly / Stephen Oliver / James Booth	M. Marcin (Substitute Prisoner)
Sunburn	Hemdale	1979	Richard C. Sarafian		S. Ellin (Bind)
Sunday Woman	TCF Europa	1976	?	Agi Scarpelli	C. Fruttero
Super Fly	Warner	1972	Gordon Parks, Jr.	Philip Fenty	novel: P. Fenty
Superdude Hangup	Warner	1974	Henry Hathaway	John B. Sherry / Lee Lazich	B. Brunner (Face of Night)
Surgeon's Knife	Gibraltar	1957	Gordon Parry	Robert Westerby	A. Hocking (Wicked Flee); Insp. Austen (John Welsh)
Surprises of an Empty Hotel	*Vitagraph	1916	Theodore Marston	Jasper E. Brady	A. C. Gunter
Survival Run	Film Vent.	1980	Larry Spiegel	Larry Spiegel	novel: R. Hoskins
Survivor	Tuesday	1981	David Hemmings	David Ambrose	J. Herbert
Suspect	Universal	1945	Robert Siodmak	Bertram Millhauser / Arthur T. Horman	J. Ronald (This Way Out)
Suspect	Charter	1960	Roy Boulting / John Boulting	Nigel Balchin / Roy Boulting / Jeffrey Dell	N. Balchin (Sort of Traitors)
Risk					
Suspect	Tri-Star	1987	Peter Yates	Eric Roth	novel: Martin Meyers
Suspense	*Reicher	1919	Frank Reicher	Eve Unsell	I. Ostrander
Suspense Fear	Monogram	1946	Alfred Zeisler	Alfred Zeisler / Dennis Cooper	F. M. Dostoevskii (Crime and Punishment)
Suspicion	RKO	1941	Alfred Hitchcock	Samson Raphaelson / Joan Harrison / Alma Reville	F. Iles (Before the Fact)
Sweeney Todd, the Demon Barber of Fleet Street	*QTS	1928	Walter West	?	G. D. Pitt
Sweeney Todd, the Demon Barber of Fleet Street	King	1936	George King	Frederick Hayward / H. F. Maltby	G. D. Pitt
Sweet Ride	TCF	1968	Harvey Hart	Tom Mankiewicz	W. Murray

S

FILM TITLE	STUDIO	YEAR	DIRECTOR	SCREENWRITER	SOURCE AUTHOR/WORK	SERIES
Sweetheart	AMLF	1992	Michel Deville	Rosalinde Deville	A. Coburn	
Sweethearts and Wives	First Nat.	1930	Clarence Badger	Forrest Halsey	W. Hackett (Other Men's Wives)	
Swinging Pearl Mystery	RKO	1936	Ben Holmes	Clarence U. Young	S. Palmer (headnote)	Hildegarde Withers (ZaSu Pitts)
Plot Thickens				Jack Townley		
Switch	RFD	1963	Peter Maxwell	Philip Ridgeway	novel: P. Ridgeway	
				Colin Fraser		
Sword of Fate	*Screen Pl.	1921	Frances E. Grant	Frances E. Grant	H. Herman	
				Kate Gurney		
Sylvia	Paramount	1965	Gordon Douglas	Sydney Boehm	E. V. Cunningham	
Syndicate	Ass. Brit.	1968	Frederic Goode	Geoffrey Hays	Denys Rhodes	
Taffin	Un. Brit.	1988	Francis Megahy	David Ambrose	L. Mallet	
Take	Columbia	1974	R. Hartford-Davis	Del Reisman	G. F. Newman (Sir, You Bastard)	
				Franklin Coen		
Take My Life	Cineguild	1947	Ronald Neame	Winston Graham	Winston Graham	
				Valerie Taylor		
				Margaret Kennedy		
Taking of Pelham One Two Three	UA	1974	Joseph Sargent	Peter Stone	J. Godey	
Tales of Terror	Am. Int.	1962	Roger Corman	Richard Matheson	novel: E. Sudak	
Poe's Tales of Terror						
Talk About a Stranger	MGM	1952	David Bradley	Margaret Fitts	C. Armstrong (Albatross)	
Tall Headlines	Grafton	1952	Terence Young	Audrey E. Lindop	A. E. Lindop	
Frightened Bride				Dudley Leslie		
Tamara	Modern Art	1968	Hansjurgen Pohland	Hansjurgen Pohland	Hansjorg Martin (Sleeping Girls Don't Lie)	
Tamarind Seed	Jewel	1974	Blake Edwards	Blake Edwards	E. Anthony	
Tangled Evidence	Real Art	1934	George A. Cooper	H. Fowler Mear	P. C. De Crespigny	
Tangled Hearts	*Alliance	1920	William J. Humphrey	Adrian Johnstone	C. H. Bullivant (Wife Whom God Forgot)	
Wife Whom God Forgot						
Tangled Lives	*Fox	1917	J. Gordon Edwards	Mary Murillo	W. Collins (Woman in White)	
Target	Warner	1985	Arthur Penn	Howard Berk	novel: S. Hunter	
				Don Peterson		
Taste of Excitement	Trio	1969	Don Sharp	Brian Carton	B. Healey (Waiting for a Tiger)	
				Don Sharp		
Tatterly	*Lucoque	1916	H. Lisle Lucoque	Nellie E. Lucoque	T. Gallon	
Teeth of the Tiger	*Paramount	1919	Chet Withey	Roy Somerville	M. Leblanc	Arsene Lupin (David Powell)
Telefon	MGM	1977	Don Siegel	Peter Hyams	W. Wager	
				Stirling Silliphant		
Tell Him I Love Him	AMLF	1977	Claude Miller	Claude Miller	P. Highsmith (This Sweet Sickness)	
				Luc Beraud		
Temple Tower	Fox	1930	Donald Gallagher	Llewellyn Hughes	H. C. McNeile	Bulldog Drummond (Kenneth MacKenna)
Temptation	Universal	1946	Irving Pichel	Robert Thoeren	R. Hichens (Bella Donna)	
Temptation Harbour	ABPC	1947	Lance Comfort	Rodney Ackland	G. Simenon (Newhaven-Dieppe)	
				Frederick Gotfurt		
				Victor Skutezky		
Temptation of Carlton Earle	*Brit. Act.	1923	Wilfred Noy	S. H. Herkomer	S. M. During	
Temptress	Bushey	1949	Oswald Mitchell	Kathleen Butler	A. Campbell (Juggernaut)	
Ten Days in Paris	Asher	1939	Tim Whelan	John Meehan, Jr.	B. Graeme (Disappearance of Roger Tremayne)	
Missing Ten Days				James Curtis		
Spy in the Pantry						
Ten Days' Wonder	Hemdale	1971	Claude Chabrol	Paul Gegauff	E. Queen	
				Paul Gardner		
				Eugene Archer		
Ten Little Indians	TCF	1945	Rene Clair	Dudley Nichols	A. Christie (Ten Little Niggers)	
And Then There Were None						

T

Title	Studio	Year	Director	Cast/Crew	Source
Ten Little Indians	Seven Arts	1965	George Pollock	Peter Yeldham / Dudley Nichols / Peter Welbeck	A. Christie (Ten Little Niggers)
Ten Little Indians And Then There Were None	Corpo	1975	Peter Collinson	Enrique Llovet / Erich Krohnke	A. Christie (Ten Little Niggers)
Ten Little Indians	Breton	1990	Alan Birkinshaw	Jackson Hunsicker / Gerry O'Hara	A. Christie (Ten Little Niggers)
Ten Minute Alibi	Brit. Lion	1935	Bernard Vorhaus	Michael Hankinson / Vera Allinson	A. Armstrong
Ten Seconds to Hell	UA	1958	Robert Aldrich	Robert Aldrich / Tedd Sherman	L. P. Bachmann (Phoenix)
Ten Thirty P.M. Summer	UA	1966	Jules Dassin	Jules Dassin / Marguerite Duras	M. Duras (Ten-Thirty on a Summer Night)
Tenant	Marianne	1976	Roman Polanski	Roman Polanski / Gerard Brach	R. Topor
Tenth Victim	Embassy	1965	Elio Petri	Elio Petri / Ennio Flaiano / Tonino Guerra / Giorgio Salvoni	novel: R. Sheckley
Terence O'Rourke, Gentleman Adventurer	*Universal	1914	?	?	L. J. Vance
Term of Trial	Remus	1962	Peter Glenville	Peter Glenville	J. Barlow
Terminal Man	Warner	1974	Mike Hodges	Mike Hodges	M. Crichton
Terminator	Hemdale	1984	James Cameron	James Cameron / Gale Anne Hurd / William Wisher, Jr.	Shaun Hutson
Terrible Beauty Night Fighters	UA	1960	Tay Garnett	Robert W. Campbell	A. J. Roth
Terrible Game Gymkata	MGM	1985	Robert Clouse	Charles R. Carnes	D. T. Moore
Terrifying Bed	ZRF Camera	1968	Witold Lesiewicz	Witold Lesiewicz	W. Collins (After Dark)
Terror	Warner	1928	Roy del Ruth	Harvey Gates / Joseph Jackson	E. Wallace
Terror	ABPC	1938	Richard Bird	William Freshman	E. Wallace
Terror by Night Secret Witness	Columbia	1931	Thornton Freeland	Samuel Spewack	S. Spewack (Murder in the Gilded Cage)
Terror by Night	Universal	1946	Roy William Neill	Frank Gruber	A. C. Doyle (headnote) Sherlock Holmes (Basil Rathbone)
Terror House Night Has Eyes	ABPC	1942	Leslie Arliss	John Argyle / Leslie Arliss / Alan Kennington	A. Kennington (Night Has Eyes)
Terror of the Tongs	Hammer	1960	Anthony Bushell	Jimmy Sangster	novel: J. Sangster
Terrorists Ransom	Lion Int.	1975	Caspar Wrede	Paul Wheeler	P. Wheeler (Ransom)
Test of Honor	*Paramount	1919	John S. Robertson	Eve Unsell / Austin Melford	E. P. Oppenheim (Mr. Wingrave, Millionaire)
Thank Evans	WB-FN	1938	Roy William Neill	John Dighton	E. Wallace (Good Evans!) Educated Evans (Max Miller)
Thank You, Mr. Moto	TCF	1937	Norman Foster	John Meehan, Jr. / Norman Foster / Willis Cooper	J. P. Marquand Mr. Moto (Peter Lorre)
That Cold Day in the Park	Common.	1969	Robert Altman	Gillian Freeman	R. Miles
That Darn Cat	Disney	1965	Robert Stevenson	Gordons / Bill Walsh	Gordons (Undercover Cat)
That Man Bolt Thunderbolt To Kill a Dragon	Universal	1973	Henry Levin / David Lowell Rich	Quentin Werty / Charles Johnson	novel: P. Crowcraft
That Man George Our Man in Marrakech	Prodis	1966	Jacques Deray	H. Lanoe / Jose Giovanni / Jacques Deray	R. P. Jones (Heisters)
That Royle Girl	*Paramount	1925	D. W. Griffith	Paul Schofield	E. Balmer

T

FILM TITLE	STUDIO	YEAR	DIRECTOR	SCREENWRITER	SOURCE AUTHOR/WORK	SERIES
That Way with Women	Warner	1947	F. de Cordova	Leo Townsend Francis Swann	E. D. Biggers (Earl Derr Biggers Tells Ten Stories)	
That Woman Opposite	Monarch	1957	Compton Bennett	Compton Bennett	J. D. Carr (Emperor's Snuff Box)	
City After Midnight						
Then Came Bronson	MGM	1970	William Graham	Denne B. Petticlerc	novel: W. Johnston	
There Ain't No Justice	Ealing	1939	Penrose Tennyson	Penrose Tennyson Sergei Nolbandov James Curtis	J. Curtis	
Theresa Raquin	Times Film	1959	Marcel Carne	Charles Spaak Marcel Carne	E. Zola	
Adulteress						
These Are the Damned	Brit. Lion	1961	Joseph Losey	Evan Jones	H. L. Lawrence (Children of Light)	
Damned						
They All Died Laughing	Tower	1964	Don Chaffey	Robert Hamer Donald Taylor	C. E. Vulliamy (Don Among the Dead Men)	
Jolly Bad Fellow						
They Came by Night	TCF	1940	Harry Lachman	Sidney Gilliat Roland Pertwee Frank Launder Michael Hogan	B. Lyndon	
They Drive by Night	WB-FN	1938	Arthur Woods	Derek Twist	J. Curtis	
They Drive by Night	Warner	1940	Raoul Walsh	Jerry Wald Richard Macaulay	A. I. Bezzerides (Long Haul)	
They Gave Him a Gun	MGM	1937	W. S. Van Dyke	Cyril Hume Richard Maibaum Maurice Rapf	W. J. Cowen	
They Live by Night	RKO	1949	Nicholas Ray	Charles Schee Nicholas Ray	E. Anderson (Thieves Like Us)	
Twisted Road						
Your Red Wagon						
They Made Me a Criminal	Gloria	1947	Alberto Cavalcanti	Noel Langley	J. Budd (Convict Has Escaped)	
I Became a Criminal						
They Made Me a Fugitive						
They Made Me a Criminal	Gloria	1947	Alberto Cavalcanti	Noel Langley	J. Budd (Convict Has Escaped)	
I Became a Criminal						
They Made Me a Fugitive						
They Met in the Dark	IP-Excel.	1943	Karel Lamac	Anatole de Grunwald Miles Malleson Basil Bartlett Victor MacClure James Seymour Robert E. Thompson	A. Gilbert (Vanishing Corpse)	
They Shoot Horses, Don't They	Cinerama	1969	Sydney Pollack	James Poe	H. McCoy	
They Won't Believe Me	RKO	1947	Irving Pichel	Jonathan Latimer		
They Won't Forget	Warner	1937	Mervyn LeRoy	Aben Kandel Robert Rossen	G. McDonell (Death in the Deep South)	
Thief Who Came to Dinner	Warner	1973	Bud Yorkin	Walter Hill	T. L. Smith	Webster Daniels (Ryan O'Neal)
Thieves' Highway	TCF	1949	Jules Dassin	A. I. Bezzerides Ellis St. Joseph	A. I. Bezzerides (Thieves Market)	
Thieves Holiday	UA	1946	Douglas Sirk		Vidocq (Memoirs of Vidocq)	
Scandal in Paris						
Thieves Like Us	UA	1974	Robert Altman	Calder Willingham John Tewkesbury Robert Altman	E. Anderson	
Thin Man	MGM	1934	W. S. Van Dyke	Albert Hackett Frances Goodrich	D. Hammett	
Think Fast, Mr. Moto	TCF	1937	Norman Foster	Norman Foster Howard Ellis Smith	J. P. Marquand	Mr. Moto (Peter Lorre)
Think of a Number	Nordisk	1969	Kjaerulff-Schmidt	Kjaerulff-Schmidt	A. Bodelsen	

T

Title	Year	Studio	Director	Writer	Source/Notes	Character (Actor)
Third Clue	1934	Fox Brit.	Albert Parker	Michael Barringer	N. Gordon (Shakespeare Murders)	Peter Kerrigan (Robert Cochran)
				Lance Sieveking		
				Frank Atkinson		
Third Day	1965	Warner	Jack Smight	Burton Wohl	J. Hayes	
				Robert Presnell		
Third Degree	1914	*Lubin	Barry O'Neil	Clay M. Greene	A. Hornblow	
Third Degree	1919	*Vitagraph	Tom Terriss	Phil Lang	A. Hornblow	
Third Degree	1926	*Warner	Michael Curtiz	C. Graham Baker	A. Hornblow	
Third Man	1949	Brit. Lion	Carol Reed	Graham Greene	G. Greene	
Third Pary Risk (Deadly Game)	1955	Hammer	Daniel Birt	Daniel Birt	N. Bentley	
Third String	1914	*London	George Loane Tucker	?	W. W. Jacobs (Odd Craft)	
Third String	1932	Wold-Peas.	George Pearson	George Pearson	W. W. Jacobs (Odd Craft)	
				James Reardon		
Third Time Lucky	1948	Kenilworth	Gordon Parry	Gerald Butler	G. Butler (They Cracked Her Glass Slipper)	
Third Visitor	1950	Elvey	Maurice Elvey	Gerald Anstruther	G. Anstruther	
				David Evans		
Third Voice	1959	TCF	Hubert Cornfield	Hubert Cornfield	C. Williams (All the Way)	
Thirteen Lead Soldiers	1948	TCF	Frank McDonald	Irving Elman	H. C. McNeile (Sapper: The Best Short Stories)	Bulldog Drummond (Tom Conway)
13 Washington Square	1928	*Universal	Melville W. Brown	Harry O. Hoyt	L. Scott (No. 13 Washington Square)	
13 West Street	1962	Columbia	Philip Leacock	Bernard Schoenfeld	L. Brackett (Tiger Among Us)	
				Robert Presnell, Jr.		
Thirteen Women	1932	RKO	George Archainbaud	Bartlett Cormack	T. Thayer	
				Samuel Ornitz		
Thirteenth Chair	1919	*Acme	Leonce Perret	Leonce Perret	B. Veiller	
Thirteenth Chair	1929	MGM	Tod Browning	Elliott Clawson	B. Veiller	
Thirteenth Chair	1937	MGM	George Seitz	Marion Parsonnet	B. Veiller	
Thirteenth Guest	1932	Monogram	Albert Ray	Francis Hyland	A. Trail	
				Arthur Hoerl		
				Armitage Trail		
Thirteenth Hour	1932	*MGM	C. M. Franklin	Maxmillian Fabian	novel: S. Horler	
Thirteenth Juror	1927	*Jewel	Edward Laemmle	?	F. T. Hill	
Thirty Days at Hard Labor	1912	*Edison	?	?	O. Henry (Roads of Destiny)	
Thirty-Nine Steps	1935	Gaum. Brit.	Alfred Hitchcock	Charles Bennett	J. Buchan	Richard Hannay (Robert Donat)
				Ian Hay		
				Alma Reville		
Thirty-Nine Steps	1959	Rank	Ralph Thomas	Frank Harvey	J. Buchan	Richard Hannay (Kenneth More)
				Charles Bennett		
				Ian Hay		
				Alma Reville		
Thirty-Nine Steps	1978	Rank	Don Sharp	Michael Robson	J. Buchan	Richard Hannay (Robert Powell)
36 Hours	1964	MGM	George Seaton	George Seaton	novel: C. K. Hirtleman	
This Gun for Hire	1942	Paramount	Frank Tuttle	Albert Maltz	G. Greene (Gun for Sale)	
				W. R. Burnett		
This Man Is Dangerous Patient Vanishes	1941	Rialto	Lawrence Huntington	John Argyle	D. Hume (They Called Him Death)	Mick Cardby (James Mason)
				Edward Dryhurst		
				David Hume		
This Man Is Dangerous	1954	Sonofilm	Jean Sacha	Jacques Berland	P. Cheyney	Lemmy Caution (Eddie Constantine)
This Man Must Die Let the Beast Die	1969	CFDC	Claude Chabrol	Paul Gegauff	Nicholas Blake (Beast Must Die)	
				Claude Chabrol		
This Was a Woman	1948	Excelsior	Tim Whelan	Val Valentine	Joan Morgan	
Thomas Crown Affair	1968	UA	Norman Jewison	Alan R. Trustman		
Thor Bridge	1923	*Stoll	George Ridgwell	Geoffrey H. Malins	A. C. Doyle (Casebook of Sherlock Holmes)	Sherlock Holmes (Eille Norwood)
				Patrick L. Mannock		
Thou Shalt Not Steal	1917	*Fox	William Nigh	Adrian Johnson	E. Gaboriau (File No. 113)	

FILM TITLE	STUDIO	YEAR	DIRECTOR	SCREENWRITER	SOURCE AUTHOR/WORK	SERIES
Thread o' Scarlet	Gaumont	1930	Peter Godfred	Ralph G. Bettinson	J. J. Bell	
Three Days of the Condor	Paramount	1975	Sydney Pollack	Lorenzo Semple, Jr. David Rayfield	J. Grady (Six Days of the Condor)	
Three Faces East	*Prod. Dist.	1926	Rupert Julian	C. Gardner Sullivan Monte Katterjohn	A. P. Kelly	
Three Faces East	Warner	1930	Roy del Ruth	Oliver Garrett Arthur Caesar	A. P. Kelly	
Three in a Cellar Up in the Cellar	New Realm	1970	Theodore J. Flicker	Theodore J. Flicker	Angus Hall (Late Boy Wonder)	
Three Keys	*Banner	1925	Edward J. LeSaint	Robert Dillon	F. Ormond	
Three Live Ghosts	Schenck	1929	Thornton Freeland	Helen Hallett	F. S. Isham	
Three Live Ghosts	MGM	1935	H. B. Humberstone	C. Gardner Sullivan	F. S. Isham	
Three Rooms in Manhattan	Cocinor	1965	Marcel Carne	Jacques Sigurd Marcel Carne	G. Simenon (Three Beds in Manhattan)	
Three Sevens	*Vitagraph	1921	Chester Bennett	Calder Johnstone Dudley Leslie	P. P. Sheehan	
Three Silent Men	Butcher	1940	Daniel Birt	John Byrd	E. P. Thorne	
Three Strangers	Warner	1946	Jean Negulesco	John Huston Howard Koch	novel: Alex Morrison	
Three Students	*Stoll	1923	George Ridgwell	Geoffrey H. Malins Patrick L. Mannock	A. C. Doyle (Return of Sherlock Holmes)	Sherlock Holmes (Eille Norwood)
Three Weird Sisters	Brit. Nat.	1948	Dan Birt	Louise Birt Dylan Thomas David Evans	C. Armstrong (Case of the Weird Sisters)	
Three Witnesses	Twickenham	1935	Leslie Hiscott	Michael Barringer	S. Fowler	
Three Years with Thunderbolt	*South. Cr.	1910	John Gavin	?	A. Pratt	
Three's a Crowd	Republic	1945	Lesley Selander	Dane Lussier	M. Eberhart (Hasty Wedding)	
Thriller Story	Gaumont	1979	Alain Corneau	Alain Corneau George Perec	J. Thompson (Hell of a Woman)	
Through Fire and Water	*Ideal	1923	Thomas Bentley	Eliot Stannard	V. Bridges (Greensea Island)	
Through the Wall	*Vitagraph	1916	Rollin S. Sturgeon	Marguerite Bertsch	C. Moffett	
Thunder on the Hill	Univ. Int.	1951	Douglas Sirk	Oscar Saul	C. Hastings (Bonaventure)	
Bonaventure						
Thunderball	UA	1964	Terence Young	Richard Maibaum John Hopkins	I. Fleming	James Bond (Sean Connery)
Thunderbolt That Man Bolt	Universal	1973	Henry Levin David Lowell Rich	Quentin Werry Charles Johnson	novel: P. Crowcraft (That Man Bolt)	
To Kill a Dragon	UA	1974	Michael Cimino	Michael Cimino	novel: J. Millard	
Thundercloud	Barker	1919	Alexander Butler	?	T. Taylor (Still Waters Run Deep)	
Thunderbolt and Lightfoot	MGM	1970	Ralph Nelson	James Lee Barrett	novel: P. Rock	
Tick...Tick...Tick	*Eclectic	1914	Louis Gasnier	Theodore Wharton	C. Reade (Foul Play)	
Ticket-of-Leave Man	*AB	1914	Donald Mackenzie			
Ticket of Leave Man	*Barker	1918	Travers Vale	?	T. Taylor	
Ticket of Leave Man	King	1937	Bert Haldane	?	T. Taylor	
Tiger by the Tail Cross Up	Tempean	1955	George King	H. F. Maltby A. R. Rawlinson	T. Taylor	
Tiger in the Smoke	Rank	1956	John Gilling	John Gilling Willis Goldbeck	J. Mair (Never Come Back)	
Tiger Man Lady and the Doctor Lady and the Monster	Republic	1944	Roy Baker George Sherman	Anthony Pelissier Dane Lussier Frederick Kohner	M. Allingham C. Siodmak (Donovan's Brain)	
Tiger of San Pedro	*Stoll	1921	Maurice Elvey	William J. Elliott	A. C. Doyle (His Last Bow)	Sherlock Holmes (Eille Norwood)
Tiger Rose	Warner	1923	Sidney Franklin	Edmund Goulding Millard Webb	W. Mack	

Tiger Rose	Warner	1930	George Fitzmaurice	Harvey Thew Gordon Rigby DeLeon Anthony	W. Mack
Tiger's Coat	*Dial	1920	Roy Clements	?	E. Dejeans
Tigers Don't Cry	Rank	1978	?	?	J. Burmeister (Running Scared)
Tight Spot	Columbia	1955	Phil Karlson	William Bowers	L. Kantor (Dead Pigeon)
Timberjack	Republic	1954	Joe Kane	Allen Rivkin	D. Cushman
Time After Time	Warner	1979	Nicholas Meyer	Nicholas Meyer	K. Alexander
Time for Action	MGM	1957	Richard Thorpe	Charles Lederer	Irwin Shaw (Tip on a Dead Jockey)
Tip on a Dead Jockey					
Time Limit	Heath	1957	Karl Malden	Henry Denker	Henry Denker
Time to Die	Carnation	1983	Matt Cimber	John Goff Matt Cimber William Russell	M. Cleri (Six Graves to Munich)
Seven Graves for Rogan					
Time to Kill	TCF	1942	Herbert I. Lees	Clarence U. Young	R. Chandler (High Window)
Time to Remember	Merton Park	1962	Charles Jarrott	Arthur LaBern	E. Wallace (Man Who Bought London)
Time Without Pity	Harlequin	1957	Joseph Losey	Ben Barzman	Emlyn Williams (Someone Waiting)
Times Have Changed	*Fox	1923	James Flood	Jack Strumwasser	E. Davis
Tip on a Dead Jockey	MGM	1957	Richard Thorpe	Charles Lederer	Irwin Shaw
Time for Action					
To Catch a King	Gaylord	1983	?	John Michael Hayes	H. Patterson
To Catch a Thief	Paramount	1955	Alfred Hitchcock	Jules Furthman	D. Dodge
To Have and Have Not	Warner	1945	Howard Hawks	William Faulkner	E. Hemingway
To Have and to Hold	Merton Park	1963	Herbert Wise	John Sansom	E. Wallace (Lieutenant Bones)
To Kill a Dragon	Universal	1973	Henry Levin	Quentin Werty	novel: P. Crowcraft (That Man Bolt)
That Man Bolt			David Lowell Rich	Charles Johnson	
Thunderbolt					
To Kill a Mockingbird	Universal	1962	Robert Mulligan	Horton Foote	H. Lee
To Live and Die in L.A.	MGM	1985	William Friedkin	William Friedkin Gerald Petievich	G. Petievich
To the Devil—a Daughter	Hammer	1975	Peter Sykes	Chris Wicking John Peacock	D. Wheatley
To the Public Danger	Gen. Film	1948	Terence Fisher	T. J. Morrison Arthur Reid	P. Hamilton (Money with Menaces)
To What Red Hell	Strand	1929	Edwin Greenwood	Leslie Hiscott	P. Robinson
Together Brothers	TCF	1974	William A. Graham	Jack De Witt Joe Greene	novel: Jim Robinson
Tom Sawyer, Detective	Paramount	1939	Louis King	Lewis Foster Robert Yost Stuart Anthony	M. Twain
Tomorrow	Filmgroup	1972	Joseph Anthony	Horton Foote	W. Faulkner (Knight's Gambit)
Tong Man	*Haworth	1919	William Worthington	?	C. C. Westover (Dragon's Daughter)
Tony Rome	TCF	1967	Gordon Douglas	Richard L. Breen	A. Rome (Miami Mayhem)	Tony Rome (Frank Sinatra)
Too Dangerous to Live	WB-FN	1939	Anthony Hankey Leslie Norman	Paul Gangelin Connery Chappell Leslie Arliss	D. Hume	Mick Cardby (Edward Lexy)
Too Late for Tears	UA	1949	Byron Haskin	Roy Huggins	R. Huggins
Too Many Chefs	Warner	1978	Ted Kotcheff	Peter Stone	N. Lyons (Someone Is Killing the Great Chefs of Europe)
Someone Is Killing the Great Chefs of Europe					
Who Is Killing the Great Chefs of Europe?					
Too Many Crooks	*Vitagraph	1919	Ralph Ince	Edward J. Montagne	E. J. Rath
Too Many Crooks	*Fam. Play.	1927	Fred Newmeyer	Rex Taylor	E. J. Rath
Too Small My Friend	Films Quad.	1970	Eddy Matalon	Saddy Rebbot Jean-Claude Grimberg Eddy Matalon	J. H. Chase (Way the Cookie Crumbles)
Top Dog	*Windsor	1918	Arrigo Bocchi	Kenelm Foss	F. Hume
Topaz	Univ. Int.	1969	Alfred Hitchcock	Samuel Taylor	L. Uris

Michael Shayne
(Lloyd Nolan)

T

FILM TITLE	STUDIO	YEAR	DIRECTOR	SCREENWRITER	SOURCE AUTHOR/WORK	SERIES
Topkapi	UA	1964	Jules Dassin	Monja Danischewsky	E. Ambler (Light of Day)	
Torn Curtain	Universal	1966	Alfred Hitchcock	Brian Moore	novel: R. Wormser	
Torpedo Skin	Comacio	1970	Jean Delannoy	Jean Cau Jean Delannoy	F. Ryck (Woman Hunt)	
Torso Murder Mystery Traitor Spy	Rialto	1939	Walter Summers	Walter Summers John Argyle Jan Van Lusil Ralph G. Bettinson	T. C. H. Jacobs (Traitor Spy)	Insp. Barnard (Edward Lexy)
Torture Garden	Amicus	1968	Freddie Francis	Robert Bloch	R. Bloch (headnote)	
Touch of Evil	Universal	1958	Orson Welles	Orson Welles	W. Masterson (Badge of Evil)	
Touch of Larceny	Foxwell	1959	Guy Hamilton	Harry Keller Roger MacDougall Guy Hamilton Paul Winterton Ivan Foxwell	A. Garve (Megstone Plot)	
Touch of the Child	*Hepworth	1918	Cecil M. Hepworth	Blanche McIntosh	T. Gallon	
Tough Guys	Silver Sc.	1986	Jeff Kanew	James Orr	novel: Ian Don	
Tough Guys Don't Dance	Cannon	1987	Norman Mailer	Jim Cruickshank Norman Mailer	N. Mailer	
Towering Inferno	TCF	1974	John Guillermin Irwin Allen	Stirling Silliphant	R. M. Stern (Tower)	
Town Without Pity Shocker	UA	1961	Gortfried Reinhardt	Silvia Reinhardt Georg Hurdalek	M. Gregor	
Toy Soldiers	Tri-Star	1991	Daniel Petrie, Jr.	Daniel Petrie, Jr. David Koepp	W. P. Kennedy	
Traffic in Souls	*Imp	1913	George Loane Tucker	Walter McNamara George Loane Tucker		
Tragedy of Barnsdale Manor	*Stoll	1924	Hugh Croise	Hugh Croise	B. Orczy (Old Man in the Corner)	Old Man (Rolf Leslie)
Trail Beyond	Monogram	1934	Robert N. Bradbury	Lindsley Parsons	J. O. Curwood (Wolf Hunters)	
Trail of the Yukon	Monogram	1949	William X. Crowley	Oliver Drake	J. O. Curwood (Gold Hunters)	
Train	Fox-Lira	1973	P. Granier-Deferre	Pascal Jardin	G. Simenon	
Traitor Spy Torso Murder Mystery	Rialto	1939	Walter Summers	Walter Summers John Argyle Jan Van Lusil Ralph G. Bettinson	T. C. H. Jacobs	Insp. Barnard (Edward Lexy)
Traitor's Gate	Summit	1964	Freddie Francis	John Sansom	E. Wallace	
Trans-Siberian Express	ITC	1978	?	?	W. Adler	
Transit	Paris	1991	Rene Allio	Rene Allio	A. Seghers	
Trap for Cinderella	Gaumont	1965	Andre Cayatte	Jean Jourdeuil Sebastien Japrisot J. B. Rossi Jean Anouilh Andre Cayatte	S. Japrisot	
Trapeze	UA	1956	Carol Reed	James R. Webb	M. Catto (Killing Frost)	
Trapped by the Mormons Mormon Peril	*Master	1922	H. B. Parkinson	Frank Miller	Winifred Graham (Love Story of a Mormon)	
Trapper's Five Dollar Bill	*Edison	1911	?	?	O. Henry (Whirligigs)	
Travels with My Aunt	MGM	1972	George Cukor	Jay Presson Allen Hugh Wheeler	G. Greene	
Tread Softly	Albany	1952	David Macdonald	Gerald Verner	G. Verner (Show Must Go On)	
Tread Softly Stranger	Alderdale	1958	Gordon Parry	George Minter Denis O'Dell	J. Popplewell (Blind Alley)	
Tree of Hands Innocent Victim	Greenpoint	1989	Giles Foster	Gordon Williams	R. Rendell	
Tremane Case	*Stoll	1924	Hugh Croise	Hugh Croise	B. Orczy (Old Man in the Corner)	Old Man (Rolf Leslie)

Title	Studio	Year	Director	Screenwriter	Source	Character (Actor)
Trent's Last Case	*Broadwest	1920	Richard Garrick	P. L. Mannock	E. C. Bentley	Philip Trent (Gregory Scott)
Trent's Last Case	Fox	1929	Howard Hawks	Scott Darling	E. C. Bentley	Philip Trent (Raymond Griffith)
Trent's Last Case	Brit. Lion	1952	Herbert Wilcox	Pamela Wilcox Bower	E. C. Bentley	Philip Trent (Michael Wilding)
Trial	MGM	1955	Mark Robson	Don M. Mankiewicz	D. M. Mankiewicz	
Trial and Error	MGM	1962	James Hill	Pierre Rouve	J. Mortimer (Three Plays)	
Dock Brief						
Trial of Billy Jack	Taylor	1972	Frank Laughlin	Frank Christina / Teresa Christina	novel: H. Liebling	
Trial of Madame X	Invicta	1948	Paul England	Paul England / Bayard Veiller	J. W. MacConaughy (Madame X)	
Trial of Mary Dugan	MGM	1929	Bayard Veiller	Becky Gardiner	B. Veiller	
Trial of Mary Dugan	Parufamet	1931	Arthur Robison	Becky Gardiner / Arthur Robison	B. Veiller	
Trial of Mary Dugan	MGM	1941	Norman Z. McLeod	Bayard Veiller / Philip Klein	B. Veiller	
Trial of Vivienne Ware	Fox	1932	William K. Howard	Barry Connors	K. Ellis	
Trick Baby	Universal	1973	Larry Yust	T. Raewyn / A. Neuberg / Larry Yust	I. Slim	
Double Con						
Triple Deception	Rank	1956	Guy Green	Robert Buckner / Bryan Forbes	S. Noel (House of Secrets)	
House of Secrets						
Trisha's Spy	*Essanay	1915	?	?	M. R. Rinehart (Book of Tish)	
Triumph of Sherlock Holmes	Real Art	1934	Leslie S. Hiscott	H. Fowler Mear / Cyril Twyford / Arthur Wontner	A. C. Doyle (Valley of Fear)	Sherlock Holmes (Arthur Wontner)
Trooper O'Neill	*Fox	1922	C. R. Wallace / Scott Dunlap	William K. Howard	G. Goodchild	
Trouble at 16	MGM	1960	Charles Haas	Robert Smith	novel: I. Shulman (Platinum High School)	
Platinum High School						
Rich, Young and Deadly						
Trouble for Two	MGM	1936	J. Walter Ruben	Manuel Seff / E. E. Paramore, Jr.	R. L. Stevenson (Suicide Club)	
Suicide Club						
Trouble in Mind	Alive	1986	Alan Rudolph	Alan Rudolph	novel: R. S. Coburn	
Trouble in the Sky	Baring	1960	Charles Frend	Robert Westerby / Jeffrey Dell	D. Beary (Cone of Silence)	
Cone of Silence						
Trouble Man	TCF	1972	Ivan Nixon	John D. F. Black	novel: J. D. F. Black	
Trouble with Girls	MGM	1969	Peter Tewkesbury	Arnold Peyser / Lois Peyser	D. Keene (Chautauqua)	
Chautauqua						
Trouble with Harry	Paramount	1955	Alfred Hitchcock	John Michael Hayes	J. T. Story	
Trouble with Spies	Brigade	1987	Burt Kennedy	Burt Kennedy	M. Lovell (Apple Pie in the Sky)	
True Confessions	UA	1981	Ula Grosbard	John Gregory Dunne / Joan Didion	J. G. Dunne	
True Story of the Lyons Mail	*Samuelson	1915	George Pearson	Harry Engholm	E. Moreau (Courier of Lyons)	
Trunk Crime	Charter	1939	Roy Boulting	Francis Miller	E. Percy	
Design for Murder						
Trust Your Wife	RKO	1930	A. Leslie Pearce	Tim Whelan	G. Abbott (Fall Guy)	
Fall Guy						
Truth About Bebe Donge	UGC	1952	Henry Decoin	Maurice Auberge	G. Simenon (Trial of Bebe Donge)	
Try and Get Me	UA	1951	Cyril Endfield	Jo Pagano	J. Pagano (Condemned)	
Sound of the Fury						
Try This On for Size	Candice	1989	Guy Hamilton	Alex Medieff	J. H. Chase	Appleton Porter (Donald Sutherland)
Turf Conspiracy	*Broadwest	1918	Frank Wilson	Bannister Merwin	N. Gould	
Turn of the Screw	Guarko	1985	Eloy de la Iglesia	Gonzalo Golkoetxea / Eloy de la Iglesia / Angel Sastre	H. James	

T

FILM TITLE	STUDIO	YEAR	DIRECTOR	SCREENWRITER	SOURCE AUTHOR/WORK	SERIES
Turn of the Screw	Electric	1992	Rusty Lemorande	Rusty Lemorande	H. James	
Turn the Key Softly	Chiltern	1953	Jack Lee	John Brophy Maurice Cowan Jack Lee	J. Brophy	
Turning Point	Paramount	1952	William Dieterle	Warren Duff	H. McCoy (Corruption City)	
Twelve Angry Men	UA	1957	Sidney Lumet	Reginald Rose	R. Rose	
Twelve Good Men	WB-FN	1936	Ralph Ince	Sidney Gilliat Frank Launder	J. Rhode (Murders in Praed Street)	
21 Days First and the Last 21 Days Together	London	1937	Basil Dean	Graham Greene Basil Dean	J. Galsworthy (Five Tales)	
21 Days Together First and the Last 21 Days	London	1937	Basil Dean	Graham Greene Basil Dean	J. Galsworthy (Five Tales)	
Twenty Plus Two It Started in Tokyo	Allied Art.	1961	Joseph M. Newman	Frank Gruber	F. Gruber	
20,000 Pound Kiss	Merton Park	1963	John Moxey	Philip Mackie	E. Wallace (headnote)	
23 Paces to Baker Street	TCF	1956	Henry Hathaway	Nigel Balchin	P. MacDonald (Nursemaid Who Disappeared)	
Twice Told Tales	Admiral	1963	Sidney Salkow	Robert E. Kent	N. Hawthorne	
Twilight of Honor Charge Is Murder	MGM	1963	Boris Sagal	Henry Denker	A. Dewlen	
Twilight Women Women of Twilight	Romulus	1953	Gordon Parry	Anatole de Grunwald	S. Rayman (Women of Twilight)	
Twilight's Last Gleaming	Lorimar	1977	Robert Aldrich	Ronald M. Cohen Edward Huebsch	W. Wager (Viper Three)	
Twin	Le Gueville	1984	Yves Robert	Yves Robert Elizabeth Rappeneau	D. E. Westlake (Two Much!)	
Twin Pawns	*Acme	1919	Leonce Perret	Leonce Perret	W. Collins (Woman in White)	Geoffrey Peace
Twist of Sand	Christina	1967	Don Chaffey	Marvin H. Albert	G. Jenkins	(Richard Johnson)
Twisted Road They Live by Night Your Red Wagon	RKO	1949	Nicholas Ray	Charles Schnee Nicholas Ray	E. Anderson (Thieves Like Us)	
Two	Colmar	1974	Charles Trieschman	Charles Trieschman	novel: C. Trieschman	
Two Against the World Case of Mrs. Pembroke	Warner	1936	William McGann	Michel Jacoby	L. Weitzenkorn (Five Star Final)	
Two Faces of Dr. Jekyll House of Fright	Hammer	1960	Terence Fisher	Wolf Mankowitz	R. L. Stevenson (Strange Case of Dr. Jekyll and Mr. Hyde)	
Two Faces of January	Monaco	1986	Wolfgang Storch	Karl H. Willschrei Wolfgang Storch	P. Highsmith	
Two in the Dark	RKO	1936	Ben Stoloff	Seton I. Miller	G. Burgess (Two O'Clock Courage)	
Two-Letter Alibi	Paramount	1962	Robert Lynn	Roger Marshall	A. Garve (Death and the Sky Above)	
Two Living and One Dead	Swan	1961	Anthony Asquith	Lindsey Galloway	S. Christiansen	
Two Minute Warning	Universal	1976	Larry Peerce	Edward Hume	G. La Fountaine	
Two Mrs. Carrolls	Warner	1947	Peter Godfrey	Thomas Job	M. Vale	
Two O'Clock Courage	RKO	1945	Anthony Mann	Robert E. Kent Gordon Kahn	G. Burgess	
Two-Soul Woman	*Bluebird	1918	Elmer Clifton	Elmer Clifton	G. Burgess (White Cat)	
Two Thousand Maniacs	Box Office	1964	Hershell G. Lewis	Hershell G. Lewis	novel: H. G. Lewis	
U-Boat 29 Spy in Black	Harefield	1939	Michael Powell	Emeric Pressberger Roland Pertwee	J. S. Clouston (Spy in Black)	
Ugly Duckling	Hammer	1959	Lance Comfort	Sid Colin Jack Davies	R. L. Stevenson (Strange Case of Dr. Jekyll and Mr. Hyde)	
Unafraid	*Lasky	1915	Cecil B. DeMille	Cecil B. DeMille Laszlo Vadnay	E. M. Ingram	
Uncertain Glory	Warner	1944	Raoul Walsh	Max Brand	novel: H. Meadow	

Title	Studio	Year	Director	Writer	Source	Character (Actor)
Uncle Harry						
Strange Affair of Uncle Harry	Universal	1945	Robert Siodmak	Stephen Longstreet	T. Job	
Uncle Silas				Keith Winter		
Inheritance	Two Cities	1947	Charles Frank	Ben Travers	J. S. Le Fanu	
Under Cover	*Fam. Play.	1916	Robert Vignola	Dory Hobart	R. C. Megrue	
Under Cover Man	Paramount	1932	James Flood	Garrett Fort	J. Wilstach	
				Francis Faragoh		
				Thomson Burtis		
Under Suspicion	*London	1916	George Loane Tucker	?	E. P. Oppenheim (Game of Liberty)	
Under the Lash	*Paramount	1921	Sam Wood	J. E. Nash	A. Askew (Shulamite)	
Under the Red Robe	*Clarendon	1915	Wilfred Noy	Edward Rose	S. J. Weyman	
Under the Red Robe	New Worl	1937	Victor Seastrom	Lajos Biro	S. J. Weyman	
				Philip Lindsay		
				J. L. Hodgson		
				Arthur Wimperis		
Under Western Eyes	L'All. Cin.	1936	Marc Allegret	H. Wilhelm	J. Conrad	
Underground	Levy-Gard.	1970	Arthur Nadel	H. G. Lustig	novel: C. Stratton	
				Ron Bishop		
				Andy Lewis		
Undertaker Parlor Computer	Imperia	1976	Gerard Pires	Jean-P. Manchette	W. Kempley (Probability Factor)	
				Gerard Pires		
Underworld Informers	Rank	1963	Ken Annakin	Alun Falconer	D. Warner (Death of a Snout)	
Informers				Paul Durst		
Snout						
Undying Monster	TCF	1942	John Brahm	Lillie Hayward	J. D. Kerruish	
Hammond Mystery				Michel Jacoby		
Uneasy Terms	Brit. Nat.	1948	Vernon Sewell	Peter Cheyney	P. Cheyney	Slim Callaghan (Michael Rennie)
Unfaithful	Warner	1947	Vincent Sherman	David Goodis	W. S. Maugham (Letter)	
				James Gunn		
Unforbidden Sin	Continental	1929	?	?	R. Vickers	
Unholy Four	Hammer	1954	Terence Fisher	Michael Carreras	G. Sanders (Stranger at Home)	
Stranger Came Home						
Unholy Three	*MGM	1925	Tod Bornwing	Waldemar Young	T. Robbins	
Unholy Three	MGM	1930	Jack Conway	Elliot Nugent	T. Robbins	
				J. C. Nugent		
Unholy Wife	Universal	1957	John Farrow	Jonathan Latimer	novel: J. Roeburt	
Uninvited	Paramount	1944	Lewis Allen	Dodie Smith	D. Macardle (Uneasy Freehold)	
				Frank Partos		
Union City	Kinesis	1980	Mark Reichert	Mark Reichert	C. Woolrich (Nightwebs)	
Union Station	Paramount	1950	Rudolph Mate	Sydney Boehm	T. Walsh (Nightmare in Manhattan)	
Unknown Blonde	Majestic	1934	Hobart Henley	Leonard Field	T. D. Irwin (Collusion)	
				David Silverstein		
Unknown Purple	*Truart	1924	Roland West	?	R. West	
Unpaid Ransom	*Edison	1915	Langdon Scott	?	Scott Campbell (Below the Dead-Line)	Felix Boyd (?)
Unseen	Paramount	1945	Lewis Allen	Hagar Wilde	E. L. White (Midnight House)	
				Raymond Chandler		
Unsewing Machine	M. Films	1986	Jean-Pierre Mocky	Jean-Pierre Mocky	G. Brewer (Killer Is Loose)	
Unstoppable Man	Argo	1960	Terry Bishop	Alun Falconer	M. Gilbert (Amateur in Violence)	Insp. Hazelrigg (Marius Goring)
				Manning O'Brine		
				Terry Bishop		
Unsuitable Job for a Woman	Boyd	1981	Christopher Petit	Elizabeth MacKay	P. D. James	Cordelia Gray (Pippa Guard)
				Brian Scobie		
				Christopher Petit		
Unsuspected	Warner	1947	Michael Curtiz	Ranald MacDougall	C. Armstrong	
				Bess Meredyth		
Untamable	*Universal	1923	Herbert Blache	Hugh Hoffman	G. Burgess (White Cat)	
Up in the Cellar	New Realm	1970	Theodore J. Flicker	Theodore J. Flicker	Angus Hall (Late Boy Wonder)	
Three in a Cellar						

U

FILM TITLE	STUDIO	YEAR	DIRECTOR	SCREENWRITER	SOURCE AUTHOR/WORK	SERIES
Upstairs and Downstairs	Rank	1959	Ralph Thomas	Frank Harvey	R. S. Thorn	
Uptight	Paramount	1968	Jules Dassin	Jules Dassin, Ruby Dee	L. O'Flaherty (Informer)	
V. I. Warshawski	Buena Vista	1991	Jeff Kanew	Julian Mayfield, Edward Taylor, David Aaron Cohen, Nick Thiel	S. Paretsky (headnote)	
Valdez Is Coming	UA	1971	Edwin Sherin	Roland Kibee, David Rayfiel	E. Leonard	
Valiant	Fox	1929	William K. Howard	John Hunter Booth, Tom Barry	H. Hall	
Valley of Fear	*Samuelson	1916	Alexander Butler	Harry Engholm	A. C. Doyle	Sherlock Holmes (H. A. Sainsbury)
Valley of Fear Sherlock Holmes and the Deadly Necklace	Constantin	1962	Terence Fisher, Frank Winterstein	Curt Siodmak	A. C. Doyle	Sherlock Holmes (Christopher Lee)
Valley of Ghosts	*Brit. Lion	1928	G. B. Samuelson	Edgar Wallace	E. Wallace	
Valley of Silent Men	*Paramount	1922	Frank Borzage	John Lynch	J. O. Curwood	
Vampire Castle of Doom Not Against the Flesh Strange Adventure of David Gray	Dreyer	1931	Carl T. Dreyer	Carl T. Dreyer, Christian Jul	J. S. Le Fanu (In a Glass Darkly)	
Vampire Lovers	Hammer	1970	Roy Ward Baker	Tudor Gates, Harry Fine, Michael Style	J. S. Le Fanu (In a Glass Darkly)	
Van Bibber's Experiment	*Edison	1911	J. Searle Dawley	?	R. H. Davis (Gallegher)	
Vendetta	*Goldwyn	1921	George Jacoby	George Jacoby, Leo Lasko	A. C. Gunter (Mr. Barnes of New York)	
Venetian Affair	MGM	1966	Jerry Thorpe	E. Jack Neuman	H. MacInnes	
Venetian Bird Assassin	Brit. Film	1952	Ralph Thomas	Victor Canning	V. Canning	
Vengeance	Stross	1962	Freddie Francis	Philip Mackie	C. Siodmak (Donovan's Brain)	
Venom	Aribage	1981	Piers Haggard	John Kruse	A. Scholefield	
Verdict	Warner	1946	Don Siegel	Robert Carrington	I. Zangwill (Big Bow Mystery)	
Verdict	Anglo-Amal.	1964	David Eady	Peter Milne	E. Wallace (Big Four)	
Verdict	TCF	1982	Sidney Lumet	Arthur LaBern	B. C. Reed	
Verdict of the Heart	*Clarenden	1915	Wilfred Noy	David Mamet	C. Garvice	
Vertigo	Paramount	1958	Alfred Hitchcock	?	P. Boileau (Living and the Dead)	
				Alec Coppel, Samuel Taylor		
Vice Squad Girl in Room 17	UA	1953	Arnold Laven	Lawrence Roman	L. T. White (Harness Bull)	
Vice Squad	Embassy	1982	Gary A. Sherman	Sandy Howard, Kenneth Peters, Robert V. O'Neil	novel: W. Rotsler	
Vicious Circle The Circle Woman in Brown	UA	1948	W. Lee Wilder	Heinz Herald, Guy Endore	H. Herald (Burning Bush)	
Vicki	TCF	1953	Harry Horner	Dwight Taylor, Harold Greene	S. Fisher (I Wake Up Screaming)	
Vicky Van Woman Next Door	*Paramount	1919	Robert G. Vignola	Leo Townsend, Marion Fairfax	C. Wells	
Victim	Allied	1961	Basil Dearden	Janet Green, John McCormick	novel: W. Drummond	
Victor Frankenstein Terror of Frankenstein	Aspekt	1977	Calvin Floyd	Yvonne Floyd, Calvin Floyd	M. Shelley (Frankenstein)	

Film Index

Title	Studio	Year	Director	Writer	Notes
Villain	EMI-MGM	1971	Michael Tuchner	Dick Clement, Ian La Frenais, Al Lettieri	J. Barlow (Burden of Proof)
Vintage	MGM	1957	Jeffrey Hayden	Michael Blankfort	U. Keir
Violent Enemy	Trio	1969	Don Sharp	Edmund Ward	H. Marlowe (Candle for the Dead)
Violent Men	Columbia	1954	Rudolph Maté	Harry Kleiner	D. Hamilton (Night Walker)
Rough Company					
Violent Saturday	TCF	1955	Richard Fleischer	Sydney Boehm	W. L. Heath
Visit	TCF	1964	Bernhard Wicki	Ben Barzman	F. Duerrenmatt
Visiting Hours	Filmplan	1982	Jean Claude Lord	Brian Taggart	novel: K. Rembo
Fright					
Get Well Soon					
Voice in the Dark	*Goldwyn	1921	Frank Lloyd	Arthur F. Statter	R. E. Dyar
Voice in the Fog	*Lasky	1915	Frank Reicher	Hector Turnbull	H. MacGrath
Voice on the Wire	*Universal	1917	Stuart Paton	J. Grubb Alexander	E. H. Ball
			Ben Wilson		
Vous Pigez?	Dismage	1955	Pierre Chevalier	Victor Trivas, J. Doniol-Valcroze	P. Cheyney (Don't Get Me Wrong) (Lemmy Caution — Eddie Constantine)
W Plan	BIP	1930	Victor Saville	Victor Saville, Miles Malleson, Frank Launder	G. Seton (Duncan Grant — Brian Aherne)
Wages of Fear	Filmsonor	1953	H. G. Clouzot	H. G. Clouzot, Jerome Geronimi	G. Arnaud
Wages of Fear	Paramount	1977	William Friedkin	Walon Green	G. Arnaud
Sorcerer					
Wagons Roll at Night	Warner	1941	Ray Enright	Fred Niblo, Jr., Barry Trivers	Francis Wallace (Kid Galahad)
Wait Until Dark	Warner	1967	Terence Young	Robert Carrington, Jane-H. Carrington	F. Knott
Waiting Room for the Other Side	Cocinor	1964	Eberhard Keindorff	Alfred Vohrer, Johanna Sibelius	R. Marshall (Mission to Siena)
Walking Stick	Winkast	1970	Eric Till	George Bluestone	Winston Graham
Walking Tall	Cinerama	1973	Phil Karlson	Mort Briskin	novel: D. Warren (Buford Pusser — Joe Don Baker)
Walking Tall: Part 2	Am. Int.	1977	Earl Bellamy	Howard B. Kreitsek	novel: W. Carey (Buford Pusser — Bo Svenson)
Legend of the Lawman					
Walls Came Tumbling Down	Columbia	1946	Lothar Mendes	Wilfrid H. Pettitt	J. Eisinger
Wanted at Headquarters	*Universal	1919	Stuart Paton	Wallace Clifton	E. Wallace (headnote)
Ware Case	*Broadwest	1917	Walter West	J. Bertram Brown	G. Pleydell
Ware Case	*Film Mfg.	1928	H. Manning Haynes	Lydia Haywood, Roland Pertwee	G. Pleydell
Ware Case	Ealing	1938	Robert Stevenson	Robert Stevenson, E. V. H. Emmett	G. Pleydell
Warn That Man	APBC	1943	Lawrence Huntington	Vernon Sylvaine, Lawrence Huntington	V. Sylvaine
Warning Shot	Paramount	1967	Buzz Kulik	Mann Rubin	W. Masterson (711—Officer Needs Help)
Warriors	Paramount	1979	Walter Hill	David Shaber, Walter Hill	S. Yurick
Waste-Land	Cinedis	1960	Marcel Carné	Henri-Francois Rey, Marcel Carné	H. Ellison (Tomboy)
Watchers	Concorde	1988	Jon Hess	Bill Freed, Danien Lee	D. R. Koontz
Watchers II	Concorde	1990	Thierry Notz	Henry Dominic	D. R. Koontz (Watchers)
Watchmaker of Saint-Paul	Lira	1974	Bertrand Travenier	Jean Aurenche, Pierre Bost	G. Simenon (Watchmaker of Everton)
Clockmaker					
Waterfront	Conqueror	1950	Michael Anderson	John Brophy, Paul Soskin	J. Brophy
Waterfront Woman					
Waterfront Woman	Conqueror	1950	Michael Anderson	John Brophy, Paul Soskin	J. Brophy (Waterfront)
Waterfront					

1484 / WAY OF THE STRONG — Film Index

FILM TITLE	STUDIO	YEAR	DIRECTOR	SCREENWRITER	SOURCE AUTHOR/WORK	SERIES
Way of the Strong	*Metro	1919	Edwin Carewe	June Mathis	R. Cullum	
Way Out				Finis Fox		
Dial 999	Merton Park	1955	Montgomery Tully	Montgomery Tully	B. Graeme	
Way to the Gold	TCF	1957	Robert D. Webb	Wendell Mayes	W. D. Steele (Way to Gold)	
We Are Not Alone	First Nat.	1939	Edmund Goulding	James Hilton	J. Hilton	
				Milton Krims		
We Shall See	Merton Park	1964	Quentin Lawrence	Donal Giltinan	E. Wallace	
We Still Kill the Old Way	Cemo	1967	Elio Petri	Elio Petri	L. Sciascia (Man's Blessing)	
				Ugo Pirro		
Web of Evidence	Georgefield	1959	Jack Cardiff	Kenneth Taylor	A. J. Cronin (Beyond This Place)	
Beyond This Place						
Web of Passion	CCFC	1959	Claude Chabrol	Paul Gegauff	S. Ellin (Key to Nicholas Street)	
Double Tour						
Weekend of Shadows	Samson	1978	Tom Jeffrey	Peter Yeldham	H. Atkinson (Reckoning)	
Weird Woman	Universal	1944	Reginald Le Borg	Brenda Weisberg	F. Leiber, Jr. (Conjure Wife)	
				W. Scott Darling		
Welcome Danger	Paramount	1929	Clyde Bruckman	Paul Gerard Smith		
Welcome, Mr. Beddoes	Universal	1966	Ronald Neame	Richard Breen	novel: Robert Simpson	
Man Could Get Killed				T. E. B. Clarke	D. Walker (Diamonds for Moscow)	
We're on the Jury	RKO	1937	Ben Holmes	Franklin Coen	F. Ballard (Ladies of the Jury)	
West 11	Dial	1963	Michael Winner	Keith Waterhouse	L. Del Rivo (Furnished Room)	
				Willis Hall		
Western Prince Charming	*Edison	1912	?	?	O. Henry (Heart of the West)	Bill Crane
Westland Case	Universal	1937	Christy Cabanne	Robertson White	J. Latimer (Headed for a Hearse)	(Preston Foster)
What a Carve Up!	New World	1961	Pat Jackson	Ray Cooney	Frank King (Ghoul)	
No Place Like Homicide				Tony Hilton		
What a Girl!	Prodis	1960	Bernard Borderie	Marc-Gilb. Sauvajon	P. Cheyney (I'll Say She Does)	Lemmy Caution
				Bernard Borderie		(Eddie Constantine)
What Became of Jack and Jill?	Palomar	1972	Bill Bain	Roger Marshall	L. Moody (Ruthless Ones)	
Gentle Tale of Sex, Violence, Corruption						
and Murder						
Romeo and Juliet, 1971						
What Changed Charley Farthing	Patina	1975	Sidney Hayers	David Pursall	M. Hebden	
Banana Boat				Jack Seddon		
What Happened Then?	BIP	1934	Walter Summers	Walter Summers	L. T. Bradley	
What Price Murder	Speva	1957	Henry Verneuil	Annette Wademant	Raymond Marshall (Sucker Punch)	
				Francois Boyer		
				Henri Verneuil		
Whatever Happened to Aunt Alice?	Palomar	1969	Lee H. Katzin	Theodore Apstein	U. Curtiss (Forbidden Garden)	
Whatever Happened to Baby Jane?	Seven Arts	1962	Robert Aldrich	Lukas Heller	H. Farrell	
What's Bred . . . Comes Out in the Flesh	*Master	1916	Sidney Morgan	Sidney Morgan	G. Allen (What's Bred in the Bone)	
What's the Matter with Helen?	Raymax	1971	Curtis Harrington	Henry Farrell	novel: R. Deming	
When Eight Bells Toll	Rank	1971	Etienne Perier	Alistair MacLean	A. MacLean	
				Paul Stader		
When Greek Meets Greek	*West	1922	Walter West	?	P. Trent	
When It Was Dark	*Windsor	1919	Arrigo Bocchi	?	G. Thorne	
When the Door Opened	MGM	1940	Mervyn LeRoy	Arch Oboler	E. Vance (Escape)	
Escape				Marguerite Roberts		
When Thief Meets Thief	Criterion	1937	Raoul Walsh	John Meehan, Jr.	G. McDonell (Jump for Glory)	
Jump for Glory				Harold French		
When Tomorrow Comes	Universal	1939	John M. Stahl	Dwight Taylor	J. M. Cain (Serenade)	
Where Are the Children?	Columbia	1986	Bruce Malmuth	Jack Sholder	M. H. Clark	
Where Eagles Dare	Winkast	1968	Brian G. Hutton	Alistair MacLean	A. MacLean	

Film	Studio	Year	Director	Writers	Source/Notes
Where East Is East	MGM	1929	Tod Browning	Waldemar Young	novel: T. Browning
Where the Pavement Ends	*Metro	1923	Rex Ingram	Rex Ingram	J. Russell (Red Mark)
Where the Sidewalk Ends	TCF	1950	Otto Preminger	Ben Hecht / Frank Rosenberg / Victor Trivas / Robert E. Kent	W. L. Stuart (Night Cry)
Where the Spies Are	MGM	1965	Val Guest	Wolf Mankowitz / Val Guest / James Leasor	J. Leasor (Passport to Oblivion) / Dr. Jason Love (David Niven)
Where the Truth Lies	SNEG	1962	Henri Decoin	Claude Accursi / Albert Husson / Henri Decoin	P. Boileau (Spells of Evil)
Sorcery					
While the City Sleeps	RKO	1956	Fritz Lang	Casey Robinson	C. Einstein (Bloody Spur)
While the Patient Slept	First Nat.	1935	Ray Enright	Robert N. Lee / Eugene Solow / Brown Holmes	M. Eberhart / Sarah Keate (Aline MacMahon) / Lance O'Leary (Guy Kibbee)
Whirlpool	*Select	1918	Alan Crosland	Eve Unsell	V. Morton
Whirlpool	TCF	1950	Otto Preminger	Ben Hecht / Andrew Solt	G. Endore (Methinks the Lady—)
Whirlpool	Rank	1959	Lewis Allen	L. P. Bachmann	L. P. Bachmann (Lorelei)
Whispering Chorus	*Artcraft	1918	Cecil B. DeMille	Jeanie MacPherson	P. P. Sheehan
Whispering City	Quebec Prd.	1947	Fedor Ozep	Rian James / Leonard Lee	novel: Horace Brown
Whispering Death	Lord	1976	Juergen Goslar	Juergen Goslar / Scott Finch	D. Carney (Whispering Death)
Night of the Askari					
Whispering Smith	*Metropoliti.	1926	George Melford	Elliott J. Clawson	F. H. Spearman
Whispering Smith	Paramount	1948	Leslie Fenton	Frank Butler / Karl Lamb	F. H. Spearman
Whispering Wires	*Fox	1926	Albert Ray	L. G. Rigby	H. Leverage
Whispers	ITC	1991	Douglas Jackson	Anita Doohan	D. R. Koontz
Whistle Blower	Portreeve	1986	Simon Langton	Julian Bond	John Hale
Whistle Stop	UA	1946	Leonide Moguy	Philip Yordan	M. M. Wolff
Whistling in the Dark	MGM	1933	Elliott Nugent	Elliott Nugent / Robert MacGunigle	L. Gross
Whistling in the Dark	MGM	1941	S. Sylvan Simon	Harry Clork / Albert Mannheimer	L. Gross
White Alley	*Essanay	1916	?	?	C. Wells
White Circle	*Paramount	1920	Maurice Tourneur	Jack Gilbert / Jules Furthman	R. L. Stevenson (New Arabian Nights)
White Cockatoo	Warner	1935	Alan Crosland	Ben Markson / Lillie Hayward	M. Eberhart
White Face	Gainsboro.	1932	T. Hayes Hunter	Angus MacPhail / Bryan Edgar Wallace	E. Wallace
White Lie	*Gaumont	1914	?	?	W. LeQueux
White Mice	*Pinellas	1926	Edward H. Griffith	Randolph Bartlett	R. H. Davis
White Moll	*Fox	1920	Harry Millarde	E. Lloyd Sheldon	F. Packard
White of the Eye	Cannon	1987	Donald Cammell	Donald Cammell / China Cammell	M. Tracy (Mrs. White)
White Trash on Moonshine Mountain	Creat. Com.	1967	Hershell G. Lewis	Charles Glore	novel: C. Glore (Moonshine Mountain)
Moonshine Mountain					
Who?	Brit. Lion	1974	Jack Gold	John Gould	A. Budrys
Man in the Steel Mask					
Man Without a Face					
Prisoner of the Skull					
Who Dares Wins	Rank	1982	Ian Sharp	Reginald Rose	J. Follett (Tiptoe Boys)
Final Option					
Who Framed Roger Rabbit?	Touchstone	1988	Robert Zemeckis	Jeffrey Price / Peter Seamna	G. K. Wolf (Who Censored Roger Rabbit?)

W

FILM TITLE	STUDIO	YEAR	DIRECTOR	SCREENWRITER	SOURCE AUTHOR/WORK	SERIES
Who Is Guilty?	Grafton	1939	Fred Zelnik	Laurence Huntington	A. Coppel (I Killed the Count)	
I Killed the Count				Alec Coppel		
Who Is Hope Schuyler?	TCF	1942	Thomas Z. Loring	Arnaud d'Usseau	S. Ransome (Hearses Don't Hurry)	
Who Is Killing the Great Chefs of Europe?	Warner	1978	Ted Kotcheff	Peter Stone	N. Lyons (Someone Is Killing the Great Chefs of Europe)	
Someone Is Killing the Great Chefs of Europe						
Too Many Chefs						
Who Killed Aunt Maggie?	Republic	1940	Arthur Lubin	Stuart Palmer	Medora Field	
				Frank Gill, Jr.		
				Hal Finberg		
Who Killed John Savage?	WB-FN	1937	Maurice Elvey	Basil Dillon	P. MacDonald (Rynox)	
Who Killed the Cat?	Eternal	1966	Montgomery Tully	Maurice J. Wilson	A. Ridley (Tabitha)	
				Montgomery Tully		
Who Was Maddox?	Merton Park	1964	Geoffrey Nethercott	Roger Marshall	E. Wallace (Undisclosed Client)	
Who Was That Lady?	Columbia	1960	George Sidney	Norman Krasna	N. Krasna (Who Was That Lady I Saw You With?)	
Whole Truth	Valiant	1958	John Guillermin	Jonathan Latimer	P. Mackie	
Who'll Stop the Rain?	UA	1978	Karel Reisz	Judith Roscoe	R. Stone (Dog Soldiers)	
				Robert Stone		
Whose Wife?	*American	1917	Rollin S. Sturgeon	?	C. H. Bullivant	
Whosoever Shall Offend...	*Windsor	1919	Arrigo Bocchi	Kenelm Foss	F. M. Crawford	
Why Me?	Epic	1990	Gene Quintano	Donald E. Westlake	D. E. Westlake	
				Leonard Mass, Jr.		
Wicked As They Come	Film Loca	1956	Ken Hughes	Ken Hughes	B. Ballinger (Portrait in Smoke)	
Portrait in Smoke				Robert Westerby		
				Sigmund Miller		
Wicked Wife	Talisman	1953	Bob McNaught	Bob McNaught	D. Christie (Grand National Night)	
Grand National Night				Val Valentine		
Wicked Woman	MGM	1934	Charles Brabin	Florence Ryerson	Anne Austin	
				Zelda Sears		
Wicker Man	Brit. Lion	1973	Robin Hardy	Anthony Shaffer	R. Hardy	
Wickham Mystery	Samuelson	1931	G. B. Samuelson	?	J. McNally (Paper Chase)	
Widow Couderc	CFDC	1971	P. Granier-Deferre	Pascal Jardin	G. Simenon (Ticket of Leave)	
				P. Granier-Deferre		
Widow's Walk	Paradis	1987	P. Granier-Deferre	P. Granier-Deferre	A. Coburn	
				Dominique Roulet		
Wife, Husband and Friend	TCF	1939	Gregory Ratoff	Nunnally Johnson	J. M. Cain (Career in C Major)	
Wife Whom God Forgot	*Alliance	1920	William J. Humphrey	Adrian Johnstone	C. H. Bullivant	
Tangled Hearts						
Wilby Conspiracy	Optimus	1975	Ralph Nelson	Rod Amateau	P. Driscoll	
				Harold Nebenzal		
Wild Geese	Rank	1978	Andrew V. McLaglen	Reginald Rose	D. Carney	
Wild Geese II	Thorn EMI	1985	Peter Hunt	Reginald Rose	D. Carney (Square Circle)	
Wild Party	UA	1956	Harry Horner	John McPartland	J. McPartland	
Willard	Crosby	1971	Daniel Mann	Gilbert A. Ralston	S. Gilbert (Ratman's Notebooks)	
Winding Stair	*Fox	1926	John Griffith Wrap	?	A. E. W. Mason	
Window	RKO	1949	Ted Tetzlaff	Mel Dinelli	W. Irish (Dead Man Blues)	
Windows	UA	1980	Gordon Willis	Barry Siegel	novel: H. B. Gilmour	
Wine, Women and Horses	Warner	1937	Louis King	Roy Chanslor	W. R. Burnett (Dark Hazard)	
Wings of Danger	Hammer	1952	Terence Fisher	John Gilling	M. Black (Dead on Course)	
Dead on Course						
Wings of the Morning	*Fox	1919	J. Gordon Edwards	Charles Kenyon	L. Tracy (Rainbow Island)	
Winifred, the Shop Girl	*Viagraph	1916	George D. Baker	George Plympton	C. N. Williamson (Shop Girl)	
Winning of Miss Langton	*Edison	1910	Edwin S. Porter	Edwin S. Porter	R. H. Davis (Once Upon a Time)	Richard Vaness (Zachary Scott)
Winter Kills	AVCO	1979	William Richert	William Richert	R. Condon	
Winterset	RKO	1936	Alfred Santell	Anthony Veiller	Maxwell Anderson	
Wiser Sex	Paramoun:	1932	Berthold Viertel	Caroline Francke	C. Fitch (Woman in the Case)	
				Harry Hervey		

Film Index

WOMAN IN WHITE / 1487

Title	Studio	Year	Director	Cast	Source/Notes
Witch-Finder General	Tigon-Bri.	1968	Michael Reeves	Michael Reeves / Tom Baker / Louis M. Hayward	R. Bassett
Conqueror Worm					
Edgar Allan Poe's Conqueror Worm					
Witches	Hammer	1966	Cyril Frankel	Nigel Kneale	P. Curtis (Devil's Own)
Devil's Own					
Witching Hour	*Frohman	1916	George Irving	Anthony Kelly	A. Thomas
Witching Hour	*Fam. Play.	1921	William D. Taylor	Julia Crawford Ives / Anthony Veiller	A. Thomas
Witching Hour	Paramount	1934	Henry Hathaway	Salisbury Field	A. Thomas
With All Hands	Films Serna.	1986	Benoit Jacquot	Benoit Jacquot	
With Bridges Burned	*Edison	1910	?	?	J. Gunn (Deadlier Than the Male)
With Interest to Date	*Ediwon	1911	?	?	R. Beach (Laughing Bill Hyde)
Within the Law	*Williamson	1916	Monte Luke	W. J. Lincoln	R. Beach (Laughing Bill Hyde)
Within the Law	*Vitagraph	1917	William P. S. Earle	Violet Mallory / Eugene Mullin	B. Veiller
Within the Law	*Schenck	1923	Frank Lloyd	Frances Marion	B. Veiller
Within the Law	MGM	1939	Gustav Machaty	Charles Lederer / Edith Fitzgerald	B. Veiller
Without a Trace	TCF	1983	Stanley R. Jaffe	Beth Gutcheon	B. Gutcheon (Still Missing)
Without Apparent Motive	Valoria	1971	Philippe Labro	Philippe Labro / Jacques Lenzmann	E. McBain (Ten Plus One)
Without Regret	Paramount	1935	Harold Young	Doris Anderson / Charles Brackett	R. Pertwee (Interference)
Without Warning	*Paramount	1924	Irvin Willat	Arthur Stringer	novel: A. Stringer (Story Without a Name)
Story Without a Name					
Witness	CIC	1978	Jean-Pierre Mocky	Rodolfo Sonego	H. Judd (Shadow of a Doubt)
Witness	Paramount	1985	Peter Weir	Earl W. Wallace / William Kelley	novel: W. Kelley
Witness for the Defense	*Artcraft	1919	George Fitzmaurice	Ouida Bergere	A. E. W. Mason
Witness for the Prosecution	UA	1957	Billy Wilder	Billy Wilder / Harry Kurnitz / Larry Marcus	A. Christie
Witness Vanishes	Universal	1939	Otis Garrett	Robertson White / Harry O. Hoyt	J. Ronald (They Can't Hang Me!)
Wizard	*Fox	1927	Richard Rosson	Andrew Bennison	G. Leroux (Balaoo)
Wolf Hunters	*Ben Wilson	1926	Stuart Paton	?	J. O. Curwood
Wolf Hunters	Monogram	1950	Oscar Boetticher	W. Scott Darling	J. O. Curwood
Wolfen	Orion	1981	Michael Wadleigh	David Eyre / Michael Wadleigh	W. Strieber
Woman Alone	Gaum. Brit.	1936	Alfred Hitchcock	Charles Bennett / Ian Hay / Alma Reville / Helen Simpson / E. V. H. Emmett	J. Conrad (Secret Agent)
Sabotage					
Woman in Brown	UA	1948	W. Lee Wilder	Heinz Herald / Guy Endore	H. Herald (Burning Bush)
Circle					
Vicious Circle					
Woman in Grey	*Serico	1920	James Vincent	Walter Richard Hall / Mary McCall, Jr.	A. M. Williamson
Woman in Red	WB-FN	1935	Robert Florey	Peter Milne	Wallace Irwin (North Shore)
Woman in the Case	*Fam. Play.	1916	Hugh Ford	Anthony P. Kelly	C. Fitch
Woman in the Case	*Willough.	1916	George Willoughby	?	C. Fitch
Woman in the Dark	RKO	1934	Phil Rosen	Sada Cowan / Marcy Klauber	D. Hammett
Woman in the Window	RKO	1944	Fritz Lang	Charles Williams / Nunnally Johnson	J. H. Wallis (Once Off Guard)
Woman in White	*Gem	1912	?	?	W. Collins
Woman in White	*Thanhauser	1917	Ernest C. Warde	Lloyd Lonergan	W. Collins
Woman in White	*B&D	1929	Herbert Wilcox	Herbert Wilcox / Robert J. Cullin	W. Collins

Steve Carella (Jean-Louis Trintignant)

FILM TITLE	STUDIO	YEAR	DIRECTOR	SCREENWRITER	SOURCE AUTHOR/WORK	SERIES
Woman in White	Warner	1948	Peter Godfrey	Stephen M. Avery	W. Collins	
Woman Is a Stranger	Interfilm	1968	Rene Gainville	Jean-Louis Curtiss	J. H. Chase (Not Safe to Be Free)	
Woman Next Door	*Paramount	1919	Robert G. Vignola	Marion Fairfax	C. Wells (Vicky Van)	
Vicky Van						
Woman of Mystery	*AB	1916	Travers Vale	?	G. Ohnet	
Woman of Straw	Novus	1964	Basil Dearden	Michael Relph	C. Arley	
				Robert Muller		
				Stanley Mann		
Woman of the Iron Bracelets	*Progress	1920	Sidney Morgan	Sidney Morgan	F. Barrett	
Woman on the Beach	RKO	1947	Jean Renoir	Frank Davis	M. A. Wilson (None So Blind)	
				Jean Renoir		
				Michael Hogan		
Woman Racket	MGM	1930	Robert Ober	Albert S. LeVino	P. Dunning (Night Hostess)	
Lights and Shadows			A. Kelly			
Woman Who Came Back	*Paramount	1918	Robert G. Vignola	Beulah Marie Dix	C. M. S. McLellan (Leah Kleschna)	
Woman Who Dare	*California	1916	George E. Middleton	Leslie T. Peacock	A. M. Williamson	
Woman Who Wouldn't Die	Parroch	1964	Gordon Hessler	Dan Mainwaring	Jay Bennett (Catacombs)	
Catacombs						
Woman Wins	*Broadwest	1918	Frank Wilson	R. Byron-Webber	C. H. Bullivant	
				Kenelm Foss		
Woman's Law	*Arrow	1916	Lawrence McGill	Harvey Thew	Maravene Thompson	
Woman's Vengeance	Univ. Int.	1947	Zoltan Korda	Albert S. LeVino	A. Huxley (Mortal Coils)	
Women of Twilight	Romulus	1953	Gordon Parry	Aldous Huxley	S. Rayman	
Twilight Women				Anatole de Grunwald		
World in My Pocket	Brit. Lion	1961	Alvin Rakoff	Frank Harvey	J. H. Chase	
On Friday at Eleven						
Worldly Goods	Continental	1929	Phil Rosen	John Grey	A. Soutar	
				Scott Littleton		
World's Great Snare	*Fam. Play.	1916	Joseph Kaufman	?	E. P. Oppenheim	
Wrath of God	MGM	1972	Ralph Nelson	Ralph Nelson	J. Graham	
Wreck of the Mary Deare	MGM	1959	Michael Anderson	Eric Ambler	H. Innes (Mary Deare)	
Wrecker	Gainsboro.	1928	Geza M. Bolvary	Angus MacPhail	A. Ridley	
Wrecker	Columbia	1933	Albert Roge II	Jo Swerling	A. Ridley	
				Albert Roge II		
Wrecking Crew	Columbia	1968	Phil Karlson	William P. McGivern	D. Hamilton	Matt Helm (Dean Martin)
Wrong Box	Salamander	1966	Bryan Forbes	Larry Gelbart	R. L. Stevenson	
				Burt Shrevelove		
Wrong Is Right	Columbia	1982	Richard Brooks	Richard Brooks	C. McCarry (Better Angels)	
Man with the Deadly Lens						
X-The Man with the X-Ray Eyes	Am. Int.	1963	Roger Corman	Robert Dillon	novel: E. Sudak	
				Ray Russell		
Yakuza	Warner	1975	Sydney Pollack	Paul Schrader	novel: L. Schrader	
Brotherhood of the Yakuza				Robert Towne		
Year of the Dragon	MGM	1985	Michael Cimino	Oliver Stone	R. Daley	
				Michael Cimino		
Year of the Gun	Triumph	1991	John Frankenheimer	David Ambrose	M. Mewshaw	
Yellow Canary	TCF	1963	Buzz Kulik	Rod Serling	W. Masterson (Evil Come, Evil Go)	
Yellow Claw	*Stoll	1920	Rene Plaissetty	Gerard Fort Buckle	S. Rohmer	
Yellow Dog	Ord Halk	1932	Jean Tarride	?	G. Simenon (Face for a Clue)	Jules Maigret (Abel Tarride)
Yellow Face	*Stoll	1921	Maurice Elvey	William J. Elliott	A. C. Doyle (Memoirs of Sherlock Holmes)	Sherlock Holmes (Eille Norwood)

Z

Title	Studio	Year	Director	Writer	Source	Notes
Yellow Mask	Brit. Int.	1930	Harry Lachman	Val Valentine Miles Malleson George Arthurs Walter C. Mycroft W. David	E. Wallace (Traitor's Gate)	
Yellow Men and Gold	*Goldwyn	1922	Irvin Willat	Irvin Willat L. V. Jefferson	Gouverneur Morris	
Yellow Passport	Fox	1931	Raoul Walsh	Jules Furthman Guy Bolton	V. Morton (Yellow Ticket)	
Yellow Ticket	*Astra	1918	William Parke	Tom Cushing	V. Morton	
Yellow Ticket	Fox	1931	Raoul Walsh	Jules Furthman Guy Bolton	V. Morton	
Yellow Typhoon	*First Nat.	1920	Edward Jose	Monty Katterhorn John Cresswell	H. MacGrath	
Yield to the Night Blonde Sinner	Kenwood	1956	J. Lee Thompson	Joan Henry	J. Henry	
York Mystery	*Stoll	1924	Hugh Croise	Hugh Croise	B. Orczy (Old Man in the Corner)	Old Man (Rolf Leslie)
Yoru No Wana	Daiei	1967	Sokichi Tomimoto	Kazuro Funabashi	C. Woolrich (Black Angel)	
Yosemite Trail	*Fox	1922	Bernard J. Durning	Jack Strumwasser	R. Cullum (One-Way Trail)	
You Can't Beat the Law	Trem Carr	1928	Charles Hunt	Arthur Hoerl	novel: H. H. Van Loan	
You Can't Escape	Forth	1956	Wilfred Eades	Robert Hall	A. Kennington (She Died Young)	
You Can't See Round Corners	Amalgamated	1969	David Cahill	Doreen Montgomery Richard Lane	J. Cleary	
You Do It, Cutie	Prodis	1963	Bernard Borderie	Marc-G. Sauvajon Bernard Borderie	P. Cheyney (Your Deal, My Lovely)	Lemmie Caution (Eddie Constantine)
Your Turn, Darling						
You Only Live Twice	Eon	1967	Lewis Gilbert	Roald Dahl	I. Fleming	James Bond (Sean Connery)
You Pay Your Money	Butcher	1957	Maclean Rogers	Harry Jack Bloom Maclean Rogers	M. Cronin	
You'll Like My Mother	Universal	1972	Lamont Johnson	Jo Heims	N. A. Hinze	
Young and Innocent Girl Was Young	Gaum. Brit.	1937	Alfred Hitchcock	Charles Bennett Edwin Greenwood Anthony Armstrong Alma Reville Gerald Savory	J. Tey (Shilling for Candles)	
Young and Wild	Esla	1958	William Witney	Arthur T. Horman	novel: Morton Cooper	
Young Dillinger	AA	1965	Terroy O. Morse	Arthur Hoerl Don Zimbalist	novel: S. Stuart	
Young Don't Cry	Columbia	1957	Alfred L. Werker	Richard Jessup	R. Jessup	
Young Eve and Old Adam	*Union	1920	?	?	T. Gallon	
Young Girls Reward Good Girls Beware Look Out, Girls	Corona	1957	Yves Allegret	Rene Wheeler Jean Meckert	J. H. Chase (Miss Callaghan Comes to Grief)	
Young Savages	UA	1961	John Frankenheimer	Edward Anhalt J. P. Miller	E. Hunter (Matter of Conviction)	
Young Scarface Brighton Rock	APL	1947	John Boulting	Graham Greene Terence Rattigan	G. Greene (Brighton Rock)	
Young Sherlock Holmes	Paramount	1985	Barry Levinson	Chris Columbus	novel: A. Arnold	Sherlock Holmes (Nicholas Rowe)
Your Red Wagon They Live by Night Twisted Road	RKO	1949	Nicholas Ray	Charles Schee Nicholas Ray	E. Anderson (Thieves Like Us)	
Your Turn, Darling You Do It, Cutie	Prodis	1963	Bernard Borderie	Marc-G. Sauvagion Bernard Borderie	P. Cheyney (Your Deal, My Lovely)	Lemmie Caution (Eddie Constantine)
Yukon Flight	Criterion	1952	Ralph Staub	Edward Halperin	L. Y. Erskine (Renfew Rides North)	Douglas Renfrew (James Newill)
Yukon Gold	Monogram	1952	Frank McDonald	William Raynor	J. O. Curwood (Gold Hunters)	
Z	Reggane	1969	Costa-Gravas	Costa-Gravas Jorge Semprun	V. Vassilikos	
Zero Hour!	Paramount	1957	Hall Bartlett	Arthur Hailey	J. Castle (Flight Into Danger)	
Zoot Suit	Universal	1981	Luis Valdez	Luis Valdez	Luis Valdez	

SCREENWRITERS INDEX

Screenwriters Index

ABBOTT, GEORGE
Manslaughter. A. D. Miller
Sea God. J. Russell; Red Mark

ABRAMSON, HANS
Roseanna. M. Sjowall

ACCURSI, CLAUDE
Sorcery. P. Boileau; Spells of Evil

ACHARD, MARCEL
Midnight in Paris; G. Simenon; Monsieur la Souris

ACKLAND, RODNEY
No. 17. J. J. Farjeon
Temptation Harbour. G. Simenon; Newhaven-Dieppe

ACKROYD, DAN
Spies Like Us. G. McGill

ADAMS, FRANK R.
She Made Her Bed. J. M. Cain; Baby in the Icebox

ADAMSON, EWART
Dark Hour. S. Gluck; Last Trap
Inside the Lines. E. D. Biggers
Perfect Crime. I. Zangwill; Big Bow Mystery

ADREON, FRANKLYN
Drums of Fu Manchu. S. Rohmer

AGEE, JAMES
Night of the Hunter. D. Grubb

AGI
Sunday Woman. C. Fruttero

AINSWORTH, JOHN
Hell Is Empty. J. F. Straker

ALBERT, MARVIN H.
Don Is Dead. N. Quarry
Lady in Cement. A. Rome
Twist of Sand. G. Jenkins

ALDRICH, ROBERT
Chinese Parrot. E. D. Biggers
Ten Seconds to Hell. L. P. Bachmann; Phoenix

ALEJANDRO, JULIO
Invisible Man. H. G. Wells

ALEXANDER, GILBERT
Hunting Party. J. Millard

ALEXANDER, J. GRUBB
Gamblers. C. Klein
Haunted Bell. J. Futrelle; Diamond Master
Lone Wolf Returns. L. J. Vance
Murder Will out. M. Leinster
Not Guilty. H. MacGrath; Parrot & Co.
Voice on the Wire. E. H. Ball

ALICATA, MARIO
Obsession. J. M. Cain; Postman Always Rings Twice

ALLEN, JANIS
Double Negative. K. Millar; Three Roads

ALLEN, JAY PRESSON
Deathtrap. I. Levin
Marnie. Winston Graham
Travels with My Aunt. G. Greene

ALLEY, JEAN
Le Judgement de Minuit. E. Wallace; Ringer

ALLIN, MICHAEL
Enter the Dragon. M. Roote

ALLINSON, VERA
Bella Donna. R. Hichens
Blind Justice. A. Ridley; Recipe for Murder
Ten Minute Alibi. A. Armstrong

ALLIO, RENE
Transit. A. Seghers

ALSTON, EMMETT
Hunter's Blood. J. Cunningham

ALTMAN, ROBERT
McCabe and Mrs. Miller. E. Naughton; McCabe
Thieves Like Us. E. Anderson

AMANN, PELHAM LEIGH
Cross Currents. W. G. Elliott; Nine Days' Blunder

AMATEAU, ROD
Wilby Conspiracy. P. Driscoll

AMBLER, ERIC
October Man. E. Britton
Rough Shoot. G. Household
Wreck of the Mary Deare. H. Innes; Mary Deare

AMBROSE, DAVID
Survivor. J. Herbert
Taffin. L. Mallet
Year of the Gun. M. Mewshaw

AMIDAE, SERGIO
Maigret a Pigalle. G. Simenon; Maigret in Montmartre

ANDERSON, DORIS
Grumpy. H. Hodges
Sophie Lang Goes West. F. I. Anderson; Notorious Sophie Lang
Without Regret. R. Pertwee; Interference

ANDERSON, MAXWELL
Death Takes a Holiday. Walter Ferris

ANDREJEWSKI, JERZY
Ashes and Diamonds. J. Andrejewski

ANDREOTA, PAUL
Passager Clandestin. G. Simenon; Stowaway

ANDREWS, DEL
Bronze Bell. L. J. Vance
Racket. B. Cormack

ANDREWS, JACK
Caribbean Mystery. J. W. Vandercook; Murder in Trinidad
Subway in the Sky. B. Birch

ANDREWS, ROBERT D.
Devil Commands. W. Sloan; Edge of Running Water
Longest Night. C. Fitzsimmons; Whispering Window
Sherlock Holmes and the Voice of Terror. A. C. Doyle; His Last Bow

ANHALT, EDNA
Bulldog Drummond Strikes Back. H. C. McNeile; Knock-Out

ANHALT, EDWARD
Bulldog Drummond Strikes Back. H. C. McNeile; Knock-Out
Escape to Athena. P. Blake
Green Ice. G. A. Browne
Holcroft Covenant. R. Ludlum
Satan Bug. I. Stuart
Young Savages. E. Hunter; Matter of Conviction

ANOUILH, JEAN
Death of a Beauty. G. Simenon; Belle
Trap for Cinderella. S. Japrisot

ANSTRUTHER, GERALD
Third Visitor. G. Anstruther

ANTHONY, DELEON
Tiger Rose. W. Mack

ANTHONY, JOSEPH
Crime and Punishment. F. M. Dostoevskii
Meet Nero Wolfe. R. Stout; Fer-de-Lance
One-Way Ticket. Ethel Turner

ANTHONY, STUART
Strangers of the Evening. T. Thayer; Illustrious Corpse
Tom Sawyer, Detective. M. Twain

ANTHONY, WALTER
Cat and the Canary. J. Willard

APPLY, CHRIS
Fear Makers. D. L. Teilhet

APSTEIN, THEODORE
Whatever Happened to Aunt Alice? U. Curtiss; Forbidden Garden

ARANDA, VICENTE
Blood Spattered Bride. J. S. Le Fanu; In a Glass Darkly
Murder in the Central Committee. M. V. Montalban

ARCADY, ALEXANDRE
Hold-Up. J. Cronley; Quick Change
Last Summer in Tangiers. W. O'Farrell; Devil His Due

ARCALLI, FRANCO
Once Upon a Time in America. H. Grey; Hoods

ARCHER, EUGENE
Ten Days' Wonder. E. Queen

ARCHIBALD, WILLIAM
Innocents. H. James; Turn of the Screw

ARDIES, TOM
Russian Roulette. T. Ardies; Kosygin Is Coming

AREHN, MATS
Assignment. P. Wahloo

ARGENTO, DARIO
Cat o' Nine Tails. P. J. Gillette

ARGYLE, JOHN
Dark Eyes of London. E. Wallace
Door with Seven Locks. E. Wallace
Night Has Eyes. A. Kennington
This Man Is Dangerous. D. Hume; They Called Him Death
Traitor Spy. T. C. H. Jacobs

ARKLESS, ROBERT
Man Who Would Not Die. C. Williams; Sailcloth Shroud

ARLAUD, R. M.
Le Bete a L'Affut. D. Keene; Moran's Woman
Les Canailles. R. Marshall; You Find Him . . . I'll Fix Him
Maigret and the St. Fiacre Case. G. Simenon; Saint Fiacre Affair

ARLISS, LESLIE
Man About the House. F. B. Young
Night Has Eyes. A. Kennington
Road House. W. Hackett
Saint Meets the Tiger. L. Charteris; Meet the Tiger
Too Dangerous to Live. D. Hume

ARLORIO, GIORGIO
Burn. N. Gant

ARMITAGE, GEORGE
Hit Man. T. Lewis; Jack's Return Home
Miami Blues. C. Willeford

ARMITAGE, GRAHAM
Gas. B. Hirschfeld

ARMSTRONG, ANTHONY
Young and Innocent. J. Tey; Shilling for Candles

ARMSTRONG, MICHAEL
House of Long Shadows. E. D. Biggers; Seven Keys to Baldpate

ARNOLD, DANNY
Desert Sands. J. Robb; Punitive Action
Lady Takes a Flier. E. Ronns

ARTHURS, GEORGE
Yellow Mask. E. Wallace; Traitor's Gate

ASHTON, JAMES
Devil's Rain. M. Willis

ASQUITH, ANTHONY
Shooting Stars. E. C. Vivian

ASQUITH, MARY
Lady Audley's Secret. M. E. Braddon

A

ATKINSON, FRANK
Third Clue. N. Gordon; Shakespeare Murders

ATLAS, LEOPOLD
Mystery of Edwin Drood. C. Dickens

ATTEBERRY, DUKE
Mountain Music. M. Kantor; Author's Choice

AUBERGE, MAURICE
Passager Clandestin. G. Simenon; Stowaway
Truth About Bebe Donge. G. Simenon; Trial of Bebe Donge

AUDIARD, JACQUES
Deadly Circuit. M. Behm; Eye of the Beholder
FM—Frequency Murder. S. M. Kaminsky; When Dark Man Calls

AUDIARD, MICHEL
Any Number Can Win. J. Trinian
Big Operation. R. Airth; Snatch
Blood to the Head. G. Simenon; Young Cardinaud
Deadly Circuit. M. Behm; Eye of the Beholder
He Died with His Eyes Open. D. Raymond
Heads or Tails. A. Harris; Baroni
Inquisitor. J. Wainwright; Brainwash
La Bete a L'Affut. D. Keene; Moran's Woman
Le Cri du Cormoran le Soir Au-Dessus des Jonques. E. Hunter; Horse's Head
Little Virtuous. R. Marshall; But a Short Time to Live
Maigret and the St. Fiacre Case. G. Simenon; Saint Fiacre Affair
Maigret Sets a Trap. G. Simenon
On a Nice Summer Day. J. H. Chase; One Bright Summer Morning
President. G. Simenon; Premier
Professional. P. Alexander; Death of a Thin-Skinned Animal
Rise Up, Spy. G. Markstein; Chance Awakening

AUERBACH, GEORGE
Bishop Misbehaves. F. Jackson

AUREL, JEAN
Hit and Run. R. Marshall
Let It Be Sunday. C. Williams; Long Saturday Night

AURENCHE, JEAN
Clockmaker. G. Simenon; Watchmaker of Everton
In Case of Emergency. G. Simenon
Murderer. P. Highsmith; Blunderer
North Star. G. Simenon; Lodger
Population 1280. J. Thompson; Pop. 1280

AURTHUR, ROBERT ALAN
Edge of the City. F. Pohl
Lost Man. F. L. Green; Odd Man Out

AUSTIN, MICHAEL
Killing Dad. A. Quin; Berg

AUSTIN, RONALD
Happening. E. Curry

AVERY, STEPHEN MOREHOUSE
Woman in White. W. Collins

AXELROD, DAVID
Charlie Chan and the Curse of the Dragon Queen. M. Avallone

AXELROD, GEORGE
Holcroft Covenant. R. Ludlum
How to Murder Your Wife. H. Williams
Lady Vanishes. E. L. White; Wheel Spins
Manchurian Candidate. R. Condon

AXELROD, JONATHAN
Every Little Crook and Nanny. E. Hunter

AYLOTT, DAVE
It Is Never Too Late to Mend. C. Reade

AYME, MARCEL
Crime and Punishment. F. M. Dostoevskii
Le Voyageur de la Toussaint. G. Simenon; Strange Inheritance

BABCOCK, DWIGHT
Corpse Came C.O.D. J. Starr

BABER, DOUGLAS
My Death Is a Mockery. D. Baber

BACH, DANILO
April Fool's Day. J. Rovin

BACHARDY, DON
Frankenstein: The True Story. M. Shelley; Frankenstein

BACHMANN, LAWRENCE P.
Lorelei. L. P. Bachmann

BACON, LLOYD
Lion and the Mouse. A. Hornblow

BAEDEKERL, KLAUS
Glass Cell. P. Highsmith

BAEHR, NICHOLAS E.
The Incident. M. Avallone

BAILEY, JOHN
Riddle of the Sands. E. Childers

BAINES, JOHN
Dead of Night. E. F. Benson; Room in the Tower
Hands of Orlac. M. Renard
Seven Thunders. R. Croft-Cooke

BAIRD, LEAH
Cynthia-of-the-Minute. L. J. Vance
Destroying Angel. L. J. Vance
Spangles. N. Revell

BAIRD, PHILIP
Game for Vultures. M. Hartmann

BAKER, C. GRAHAM/GRAHAM
Case Against Mrs. Ames. A. S. Roche
Danger Signal. P. Bottome; Murder in the Bud
Shadow of a Woman. V. Perdue; He Fell Down Dead
Third Degree. A. Hornblow

BAKER, GEORGE D.
Buried Treasure. F. B. Austin; On the Borderland
Demon. C. N. Williamson
Heliotrope. R. W. Child; Velvet Black
Man Who Stayed Home. J.. E.. H. Terry

BAKER, HERBERT
Ambushers. D. Hamilton
Hammerhead. J. Mayo
Murderer's Row. D. Hamilton
Scared Stiff. C. W. Goddard; Ghost Breakers

BAKER, MELVILLE
Above Suspicion. H. MacInnes

BAKER, TOM
Witch-Finder General. R. Bassett

BALCHIN, NIGEL
Mine Own Executioner. N. Balchin
Singer Not the Song. A. E. Lindop
Suspect. N. Balchin; Sort of Traitors
23 Paces to Baker Street. P. MacDonald; Nursemaid Who Disappeared

BALDERSTON, JOHN
Amazing Quest of Mr. Ernest Bliss. E. P. Oppenheim
Bride of Frankenstein. M. W. Shelley; Frankenstein
Frankenstein. M. Shelley
Gas Light. P. Hamilton
Hands of Orlac. M. Renard
Mystery of Edwin Drood. C. Dickens

BALDWIN, EARL
Brother Orchid. L. Brady
Slight Case of Murder. D. Runyon

BALLARD, JOHN FREDERICK
Ladies of the Jury. F. Ballard

BALLIN, HUGO
Prairie Wife. A. Stringer

BALLING, ERIK
One of Those Things. A. Bodelsen; One Down

BALSHOFER, FRED J.
Haunted Pajamas. F. P. Elliott
Hidden Spring. C. B. Kelland
Paradise Garden. G. F. Gibbs
Pidgin Island. H. MacGrath

BARDAWILL, GEORGES
On a Nice Summer day. J. H. Chase; One Bright Summer Morning

BARISSE, RITA
Midnight Episode. G. Simenon; Monsieur la Souris

BARJAVAL, RENE
Gooseflesh. J. H. Chase; Come Easy—Go Easy
Man in the Raincoat. J. H. Chase; Tiger by the Tail

BARNETT, CHARLES
Amazing Partnership. E. P. Oppenheim
Beryl Coronet. A. C. Doyle; Adventures of Sherlock Holmes
Priory School. A. C. Doyle; Return of Sherlock Holmes

BARNWELL, JOHN
Five Against the House. J. Finney

BARNWELL, PEGGY
Mrs. Pym of Scotland Yard. N. Morland (headnote)

BARON, ALEXANDER
Robbery Under Arms. R. Boldrewood

BARRAUD, GEORGE
Small Voice. R. Westerby

BARRETT, JAMES LEE
Fool's Parade. D. Grubb
Tick . . . Tick . . . Tick. P. Rock

BARRINGER, BARRY
Death Kiss. M. St. Dennis

BARRINGER, MICHAEL
Black Mask. B. Graeme; Blackshirt
Death on the Set. V. MacClure
Inquest. M. Barringer
Murder at Covent Gardens. W. J. Makin
Third Clue. N. Gordon; Shakespeare Murders
Three Witnesses. S. Fowler

BARRY, TOM
East Lynn. H. Wood
Valiant. H. Hall

BARSKI, ODILA
Cry of the Owl. P. Highsmith

BARTHOLOMAE, PHILIP
Mark of Cain. C. Wells
Stranded in Arcady. F. Lynde

BARTLETT, BASIL
They Met in the Dark. Anthony Gilbert; Vanishing Corpse

BARTLETT, HALL
Zero Hour! J. Castle; Flight Into Danger

BARTLETT, RANDOLPH
White Mice. R. H. Davis

BARTLETT, SY
Murder of Dr. Harrigan. M. G. Eberhart; From This Dark Stairway

BARTSCH, J. JOACHIM
Der Unheimliche Monch. E. Wallace; Terror
Die Bade des Schreckens. E. Wallace; Terrible People

BARWICK, ANTHONY
Burndown. S. Collins; Burn Down

BARZMAN, BEN
Blind Date. L. Howard
Time Without Pity. E. Williams; Someone Waiting

BASS, RONALD
    Code Name: Emerald. R. Bass; Emerald Illusion
    Sleeping with the Enemy. N. Price
BASSING, EILEEN
    Home Before Dark. E. Bassing
BASSING, ROBERT
    Home Before Dark. E. Bassing
BAST, WILLIAM
    Hammerhead. J. Mayo
BATT, BART
    Frankenstein Must Be Destroyed. M. Shelley; Frankenstein
BAXT, GEORGE
    Conjure Wife. F. Leiber, Jr.
    Payroll. D. Bickerton
BEAUMONT, CHARLES
    Conjure Wife. F. Leiber, Jr.
    Masque of the Red Death. Elsie Lee
    Mr. Moses. M. Catto; Mister Midas
    Premature Burial. M. H. Danne
BEACH, REX
    Crimson Gardenia. R. Beach
BECKER, JACQUES
    Adventures of Arsene Lupin. M. Leblanc (headnote)
BECKERMAN, BARRY
    St. Ives. O. Bleeck; Procane Chronicle
    Shamus. R. Giles
BEE, RICHARD
    Haunted House. O. Davis
    Seven Footprints to Satan. A. Merritt
BEHAT, GILLES
    Barbarous Street. D. Goodis; Street of the Lost
BEHM, MARC
    Blonde from Peking. J. H. Chase; You Have Yourself a Deal
BEHN, HARRY
    Racket. B. Cormack
BEHNKE, DIETMAR
    Count Dracula. B. Stoker; Dracula
BEHR, EDWARD
    Half Moon Street. P. Theroux; Doctor Slaughter
BEHRMAN, S. N.
    Scarlet Pimpernel. B. Orczy
BEICH, ALBERT
    Dead Ringer. B. Thomas
BEINEIX, JEAN-JACQUES
    Diva. Delacorta
    Moon in the Gutter. D. Goodis
BEKEFFY, LASZLO
    Ghost Train. A. Ridley
BELDEN, CHARLES
    Murder of Dr. Harrigan. M. Eberhart; From This Dark Stairway
    Shot in the Dark. C. Orr; Dartmouth Murders
BELL, MONTA
    After Midnight. E. Fletcher-Allen
    Bellamy Trial. F. N. Hart
BELOIN, EDMUND
    Lady on a Train. L. Charteris
BELSON, JERRY
    Grasshopper. M. McShane; Passing of Evil
    Jekyll and Hyde . . . Together Again. R. L. Stevenson; Strange Case of Dr. Jekyll and Mr. Hyde
BENCHLEY, PETER
    Deep. P. Benchley
BENCHLEY, ROBERT
    Murder on a Honeymoon. S. Palmer; Puzzle of the Pepper Tree

BENGAL, BEN
    Crack-Up. F. Brown; Madman's Holiday
BENNETT, CHARLES
    Blackmail. C. Bennett
    Ivy. M. B. Lowndes; Story of Ivy
    Kind Lady. E. Chodorov
    Madness of the Heart. F. Sandstrom
    Man Who Knew Too Much. R. Alexander
    Sabotage. J. Conrad; Secret Agent
    Secret Agent. W. S. Maugham; Ashenden
    Sign of the Ram. M. Ferguson
    Thirty-Nine Steps. J. Buchan
    Young and Innocent. J. Tey; Shilling for Candles
BENNETT, COMPTON
    Beyond the Curtain. A. J. Wallis; Thunder Above
    That Woman Opposite. J. D. Carr; Emperor's Snuff Box
BENNISON, ANDREW
    Wizard. G. Leroux; Balaoo
BENSON, SALLY
    Conspirator. H. Slater
    No Man of Her Own. W. Irish; I Married a Dead Man
    Signpost to Murder. M. Doyle
BENTLEY, ROBERT
    Shanghai Surprise. T. Kenrick; Faraday's Flowers
BENTLEY, THOMAS
    Lackey and the Lady. T. Gallon
BENTON, ROBERT
    Bonnie and Clyde. B. Hirschfeld
BENVENUTI, LEONARDO
    Once Upon a Time in America. H. Grey; Hoods
BERANGER, CLARA
    Dr. Jekyll and Mr. Hyde. R. L. Stevenson; Strange Case of Dr. Jekyll and Mr. Hyde
    From the Valley of the Missing. G. M. White
    Grumpy. H. Hodges
    Man on the Box. H. MacGrath
    Master Mind. M. Dana
    Number Seventeen. L. Tracy
    Painted Woman. F. A. Kummer
BERAUD, LUC
    Tell Him I Love Him. P. Highsmith; This Sweet Sickness
BERCOVICI, ERIC
    Captive City. J. Appleby
BERCOVICI, LEONARDO
    Kiss the Blood Off My Hands. G. Butler
    Lost Moment. H. James; Aspern Papers
BERESFORD, BRUCE
    Money Movers. D. Minchin
BERESFORD, FRANK S.
    Bishop's Emeralds. H. Townley
    Cordelia the Magnificent. L. Scott
BERG, ALEX
    Creature with the Blue Hand. E. Wallace; Blue Hand
    Hound of Blackwood Castle. E. Wallace (headnote)
BERG, DICK
    Shoot. D. Fairbairn
BERGERE, OUIDA
    At Bay. P. Philips
    Avalanche. G. Atherton
    Bella Donna. R. Hichens
    Kick-In. W. Mack
    Right to Love. C. Farrere; Man Who Killed
    Witness for the Defence. A. E. W. Mason
BERGMAN, ANDREW
    Fletch. G. McDonald
BERGMAN, BORIS
    Twin. D. E. Westlake; Two Much!

BERGREN, ERIC
    Dark Wind. T. Hillerman
BERK, HOWARD
    Target. S. Hunter
BERKELEY, MARTIN
    Big Caper. L. White
BERKELEY, REGINALD
    77 Park Lane. W. Hackett
BERKMAN, EDWARD O.
    Four Dark Hours. G. Greene (headnote)
    Squeaker. E. Wallace
BERKMAN, TED
    Edge of Fury. R. M. Coates; Wisteria Cottage
    Short Cut to Hell. G. Greene; Gun for Sale
BERLAND, JACQUES
    Gun Moll. P. Cheyney; Poison Ivy
    This Man Is Dangerous. P. Cheyney
BERN, PAUL
    Great Deception. G. F. Gibbs; Yellow Dove
    Prince of Tempters. E. P. Oppenheim; Ex-Duke
BERNARD, JUDD
    Destructors. M. Franklin
    Inside Out. W. Hughes
BERNSTEIN, WALTER
    Fail-Safe. E. Burdick
    House on Carroll Street. Mollie Gregory
    Kiss the Blood Off My Hands. G. Butler
    Molly Maguires. J. O'Neill
    Money Trap. L. White
BERTOLUCCI, BERNARDO
    Conformist. A. Moravia
BERTSCH, MARGUERITE
    Mortmain. A. Train
    My Official Wife. R. H. Savage
    Through the Wall. C. Moffett
BESSIE, ALVAH
    Hotel Berlin. V. Baum; Hotel Berlin '43
    Northern Pursuit. L. T. White; 5,000 Trojan Horses
BESSIE, DAN
    Hard Traveling. A. Bessie; Bread and a Stone
BESSON, FRANCOIS
    Street of No Return. D. Goodis
BETTINSON, RALPH GILBERT
    Down River. Seamark
    Headline. K. Attiwill; Reporter
    Thread o' Scarlet. J. J. Bell
    Traitor Spy. T. C. H. Jacobs
BEZZERIDES, A. I.
    Angry Hills. L. Uris
    Desert Fury. R. Stewart; Desert Town
    Kiss Me, Deadly. M. Spillane
    On Dangerous Ground. G. Butler; Mad with Much Heart
    Thieves' Highway. A. I. Bezzerides; Thieves Market
BIJL, JACOB
    Beck. M. Sjowall; Locked Room
BINET, CATHERINE
    Games of the Countess Dolingen of Gratz. B. Stoker; Dracula
BINGHAM, ELFRID A.
    Breaking point. M. R. Rinehart
    Paliser Case. E. Saltus
    Stranger. J. Galsworthy; Five Tales
BINYON, CLAUDE
    Stella. D. M. Disney; Family Skeleton
BIRD, JOHN
    Embassy. S. Coulter
BIRKIN, ANDREW
    Name of the Rose. U. Eco

B

BIRO, LAJOS
- Ghost Train. A. Ridley
- Haunted House. O. Davis
- Knight Without Armour. J. Hilton
- Return of the Scarlet Pimpernel. B. Orczy (headnote)
- Sanders of the River. E. Wallace
- Scarlet Pimpernel. B. Orczy
- Under the Red Robe. S. J. Weyman

BIRT, DANIEL
- Third Party Risk. N. Bentley

BIRT, LOUISE
- Three Weird Sisters. C. Armstrong; Case of the Weird Sisters

BISHOP, RON
- Underground. C. Stratton

BISHOP, TERRY
- Unstoppable Man. M. Gilbert; Amateur in Violence

BLACHE, ALICE
- Lure. G. Scarborough

BLACK, IAN STUART
- High Bright Sun. I. S. Black
- Long Knife. S. Truss; Long Night
- Soho Incident. R. Westerby; Wide Boys Never Work

BLACK, JOHN D. F.
- Carey Treatment. J. Hudson; Case of Need
- Shaft. E. Tidyman
- Trouble Man. J. D. F. Black

BLACK, SHANE
- Lethal Weapon. J. Norst

BLACKMORE, PETER
- Make Mine Mink. P. Coke; Breath of Spring

BLACKTON, J. STUART
- Passionate Quest. E. P. Oppenheim

BLAIR, CHARLES
- Return from the Ashes. H. Monteilhet

BLAKE, OLIVER
- Scarlet Weekend. W. Kent; Woman in Purple Pajamas

BLANKFORT, MICHAEL
- Act of Murder. E. Lothar; Mills of God
- Blind Alley. J. Warwick
- Dark Past. J. Warwick; Blind Alley
- Vintage. U. Keir

BLATCHFORD, FREDERICK
- Elusive Pimpernel. B. Orczy
- Mr. Wu. L. J. Miln

BLATTY, WILLIAM PETER
- Darling Lili. H. Clement
- Exorcist. W. P. Blatty
- Exorcist III. W. P. Blatty; Legion
- Man from the Diner's Club. S. Baol
- Shot in the Dark. H. Kurnitz

BLAU, RAPHAEL
- Short Cut to Hell. G. Greene; Gun for Sale

BLEES, ROBERT
- Dr. Phibes Rises Again. W. Goldstein
- Glass Web. M. Ehrlich; Spin the Glass Web
- High School Confidential. Morton Cooper
- Screaming Mimi. F. Brown
- Slightly Scarlet. J. M. Cain; Love's Lovely Counterfeit

BLEICH, BILL
- Hearse. H. Clement

BLIZZARD, HELEN
- Beetle. R. Marsh
- Perpetua. D. C. Calthrop

BLOCH, ROBERT
- Asylum. W. Johnston
- Couch. R. Bloch
- Deadly Bees. H. F. Heard; Taste of Honey
- Night Walker. S. Stuart
- Torture Garden. R. Bloch (headnote)

BLOCHMAN, LAWRENCE G.
- Bombay Mail. L. G. Blochman

BLOCK, RALPH
- Before Dawn. E. Wallace; Sergeant Sir Peter
- Dark Hazard. W. R. Burnett
- Spy for a Day. S. Aumonier; Love-a-Duck

BLODGETT, MICHAEL
- Hero and the Terror. M. Blodgett

BLONDIN, ANTOINE
- Obsession. W. Irish; Dead Man Blues

BLOOM, HARRY JACK
- Naked Spur. A. Ullman
- You Only Live Twice. I. Fleming

BLOOM, JEFFREY
- 11 Harrowhouse. G. A. Browne
- Flowers in the Attic. V. C. Andrews

BLOOMFIELD, ROBERT
- Fear No More. L. Edgley

BLUESTONE, GEORGE
- Walking Stick. Winston Graham

BLUM, EDWIN
- Sherlock Holmes. W. Gillette
- Stalag 17. D. Bevan

BOAM, JEFFREY
- Dead Zone. Stephen King
- Indiana Jones and the Last Crusade. Rob McGregor
- Straight Time. E. Bunker; No Beast So Fierce

BOASBERG, AL
- Murder in the Private Car. E. E. Rose; Rear Car

BOBRICK, SAM
- Jimmy the Kid. D. E. Westlake

BOCK, EDWARD
- Return of the Whistler. W. Irish; Eyes That Watch You

BODELSEN, ANDERS
- One of Those Things. A. Bodelsen; One Down

BOEHM, ENDRE
- Girl from Mandalay. R. Campbell; Death in Tiger Valley
- House of a Thousand Candles. M. Nicholson

BOEHM, SYDNEY
- Big Heat. W. P. McGivern
- Bottom of the Bottle. G. Simenon
- Hell on Frisco Bay. W. P. McGivern; Darkest Hour
- High Wall. A. R. Clark
- Rogue Cop. W. P. McGivern
- Seven Thieves. S. Kent; Lions at the Kill
- Shock Treatment. W. Van Atta
- Six Bridges to Cross. J. F. Dinneen; Anatomy of a Crime
- Sylvia. E. V. Cunningham
- Union Station. T. Walsh; Nightmare in Manhattan
- Violent Saturday. W. L. Heath

BOGDANOVICH, PETER
- Saint Jack. P. Theroux

BOGNOR, NORMAN
- Privilege. John Burke

BOILEAU, PIERRE
- She Wolves. P. Boileau; Prisoner

BOISROND, MICHEL
- One Is Always Too Good to Women. R. Queneau; We Always Treat Women Too Well

BOISSET, YVES
- Prize of Peril. R. Sheckley; Tenth Victim
- Rise Up, Spy. G. Markstein; Chance Awakening

BOLAND, BRIDGET
- Gas Light. P. Hamilton
- Spies of the Air. J. Dell

BOLDT, RAINER
- Story-Teller. P. Highsmith

BOLOTIN, CRAIG
- Black Rain. Mike Cogan

BOLTON, GUY
- Almost Married. A. Soutar; Devil's Triangle
- Yellow Ticket. V. Morton

BOLTON, MURIEL ROY
- My Name Is Julia Ross. Anthony Gilbert; Woman in Red

BOLVARY, GEZA M.
- Number 17. J. J. Farjeon

BOND, JULIAN
- Man Outside. G. Stackelberg; Double Agent
- Whistle Blower. John Hale

BONICELLI, VITTORIO
- Crime. G. Bernanos

BONNER, JAMES P.
- Carey Treatment. J. Hudson; Case of Need

BOOTH, CHARLES G.
- Fury at Furnace Creek. D. Garth; Four Men and a Prayer
- House on 92nd St. Alex Morrison

BOOTH, JAMES
- Sunburn. S. Ellin; Bind

BOOTH, JOHN HUNTER
- Valiant. H. Hall

BORDERIE, BERNARD
- Dames Get Along. P. Cheyney; Dames Don't Care
- Gun Moll. P. Cheyney; Poison Ivy
- What a Girl! P. Cheyney; I'll Say She Does
- You Do It, Cutie. P. Cheyney; Your Deal, My Lovely

BORETZ, ALVIN
- Brass Target. F. Nolan; Oshawa Project

BORIS, ROBERT
- Some Kind of Hero. J. Kirkwood

BORNEMAN, ERNEST
- Face the Music. E. Borneman; Tremolo

BOROWCZYK, WALERIAN
- Dr. Jekyll. R. L. Stevenson; Strange Case of Dr. Jekyll and Mr. Hyde

BORRELLI, JIM
- Cat Chaser. Elmore Leonard

BORRIS, KNUT
- Sorcerer. E. Wallace; Ringer

BOST, PIERRE
- Clockmaker. G. Simenon; Watchmaker of Everton
- In Case of Emergency. G. Simenon
- Murderer. P. Highsmith; Blunderer

BOTELER, WADE
- Seven Keys to Baldpate. E. D. Biggers

BOUCHER, PHILIPPE
- April Is a Deadly Month. Derek Raymond; Devil's Home on Leave

BOUCICAULT, DION
- Octoroon. D. Boucicault

BOUDARD, ALPHONSE
- Action Man. J. Flynn

BOULANGER, DANIEL
- Banana Peel. C. Williams; Nothing in the Way
- Pas Falle la Guepe. J. H. Chase; Just a Matter of Time

BOULTING, ROY
- Brothers in Law. H. Cecil
- Suspect. N. Balchin; Sort of Traitors
- Twisted Nerve. Peter Evans

BOUQUET, JEAN LOUIS
- Fantomas. P. Souvestre

BOURGUIGNON, SERGE
  Reward. M. Barrett
BOUSSINOT, ROGER
  Keep Talking, Baby. D. Keene; Strange Witness
BOWER, PAMELA WILCOX
  Trent's Last Case. E. C. Bentley
BOWERS, WILLIAM
  Assignment—Paris. P. Gallico; Trial by Terror
  Convicted. M. Flavin; Criminal Code
  Five Against the House. J. Finney
  Larceny. L. Eby; Velvet Fleece
  Mrs. O'Malley and Mr. Malone. Stuart Palmer; People vs. Withers and Malone
  Mob. F. Findley; Waterfront
  Tight Spot. L. Kantor; Dead Pigeon
BOX, MURIEL
  Blind Goddess. P. Hastings
  Daybreak. A. Meredith
  Dear Murderer. S. L. Clowes
  Good Time Girl. A. La Bern; Night Darkens the Streets
  Man Within. G. Greene
BOX, SYDNEY
  Blind Goddess. P. Hastings
  Daybreak. A. Meredith
  Dear Murderer. S. L. Clowes
  Good Time Girl. A. La Bern; Night Darkens the Streets
  Man Within. G. Greene
BOYER, FRANCOIS
  What Price Murder. R. Marshall; Sucker Punch
BOYLAN, MALCOLM STUART
  Cheaters at Play. L. J. Vance; Lone Wolf's Son
  Masquerade. L. J. Vance; Brass Bowl
BRABIN, CHARLES
  Mercy Merrick. Wilkie Collins; New Magdalen
BRACH, GERARD
  Name of the Rose. U. Eco
  Tenant. R. Topor
BRACKEN, BERTRAM
  Mask. A. Hornblow
BRACKETT, CHARLES
  Piccadilly Jim. P. G. Wodehouse
  Without Regret. R. Pertwee; Interference
BRACKETT, LEIGH
  Big Sleep. R. Chandler
  Long Goodbye. R. Chandler
BRADY, JASPER E.
  Surprises of an Empty Hotel. A. C. Gunter
BRAL, JACQUES
  Street of No Return. D. Goodis
BRALY, MALCOLM
  On the Yard. M. Braly
BRAMPTON, KENNETH
  Robbery Under Arms. R. Boldrewood
BRAND, CHRISTIANNA
  Mark of Cain. J. Shearing; Airing in a Closed Carriage
BRANDEL, MARC
  Captive City. J. Appleby
BRANDNER, GARY
  Howling II. G. Brandner
BRANDT, JOE
  Lion Man. R. Parrish; Strange Case of Cavendish
BRAZEE, A. LAURIE
  Outer Gate. O. R. Cohen
BREEN, RICHARD L.
  Man Could Get Killed. D. Walker; Diamonds for Moscow
  O. Henry's Full House. O. Henry (headnote)
  Stopover: Tokyo. J. P. Marquand
  Tony Rome. A. Rome; Miami Mayhem

BREIMER, STEPHEN
  Butcher, Baker, Nightmare Maker. R. Natale
BRENNAN, F. H.
  Masquerade. L. J. Vance; Brass Bowl
BRENNAN, TERENCE
  Rooftops. R. Tine
BRENNER, ALFRED
  Key Witness. F. Kane
BRENON, HERBERT
  Dr. Jekyll and Mr. Hyde. R. L. Stevenson; Strange Case of Dr. Jekyll and Mr. Hyde
  Sign on the Door. C. Pollock
BRENT, ROMNEY
  Rat. P. Bottome
BRESLOW, LOU
  Sleepers West. F. Nebel; Sleepers East
BRESSON, ROBERT
  Pickpocket. F. M. Dostevskii; Crime and Punishment
BREST, MARTIN
  Going in Style. R. Grossbach
BRETT, HAROLD
  First Chronicles of Don Q. K. Prichard; Chronicles of Don Q
BREWER, JAMES
  Lotusblueten fur Miss Quon. J. H. Chase; Lotus for Miss Quon
BRICKER, GEORGE
  Corpse Came C.O.D. J. Starr
  Mark of the Whistler. W. Irish; Borrowed Crime
  Sh! The Octopus. R. Spence; Gorilla
BRIDGES, JAMES
  China Syndrome. B. Wohl
BRIDIE, JAMES
  Paradine Case. R. Hichens
  Stage Fright. S. Jepson; Man Running
BRIGHT, JOHN
  Broadway. P. Dunning
  Public Enemy. K. Glasmon
  Sherlock Holmes and the Voice of Terror. A. C. Doyle; His Last Bow
BRILEY, JOHN
  Enigma. M. Barak
  Hammerhead. J. Mayo
  Medusa Touch. P. Van Greenaway
BRISKIN, MORT
  Walking Tall. D. Warren
BROADBRIDGE, HUGH
  Road to Fortune. H. Broadbridge; Moorland Terror
BROOKE, RALPH
  Bloodlust. R. Connell; Variety
BROOKNER, HOWARD
  Bloodhounds of Broadway. D. Runyon
BROOKS, GEORGE
  Double Cross Roads. W. Lipman; Yonder Grow the Daisies
BROOKS, JEREMY
  Our Mother's House. J. Gloag
BROOKS, MEL
  High Anxiety. R. H. Pilpel
BROOKS, RICHARD
  Any Number Can Play. E. H. Heth
  Blackboard Jungle. E. Hunter
  Brothers Karamazov. F. M. Dostoevskii
  Deadline. J. Eastwood
  In Cold Blood. T. Capote
  Key Largo. M. Anderson
  Wrong Is Right. C. McCarry; Better Angels
BROPHY, JOHN
  Turn the Key Softly. J. Brophy
  Waterfront. J. Brophy

BROWN, EARL
  Locked Door. C. Pollock; Sign on the Door
  Sherlock Holmes. W. Gillette
BROWN, GEORGE H.
  Desperate Moment. M. Albrand
BROWN, HARRY
  Fiend Who Walked the West. E. Lipsky; Kiss of Death
  Kiss Tomorrow Goodbye. H. McCoy
  Man on the Eifel Tower. G. Simenon; Battle of Nerves
  Ocean's 11. G. C. Johnson
BROWN, HARRY JOE, JR.
  Duffy. H. J. Brown, Jr.
BROWN, J. BERTRAM
  In the Blood. A. Soutar
  Ware Case. G. Pleydell
BROWN, KARL
  Federal Bullets. G. F. Eliot
BROWNE, HOWARD
  Portrait of a Mobster. H. Grey
  St. Valentine's Day Massacre. B. O'Hara
BROWNELL, JOHN C.
  Girl by the Roadside. V. Vanardy
BROWNING, TOD
  Devil-Doll. A. Merritt; Burn, Witch, Burn!
  London After Midnight. M. Coolridge-Rask
  Outside the Law. T. Browning
BRUCE, GEORGE
  Gentleman After Dark. R. W. Child; Velvet Mask
BRULE, CLAUDE
  Blood and Roses. J. S. Le Fanu; In a Glass Darkly
BRUNEL, ADRIAN
  Auction Mart. S. Tremayne
  Cross Currents. W. G. Elliott; Nine Days' Blunder
  Return of the Scarlet Pimpernel. B. Orczy (headnote)
BRUNER, JAMES
  Delta Force. J. Norst
  Invasion U.S.A. J. Frost
BRYAN, PETER
  Hound of the Baskervilles. A. C. Doyle
BRYANT, CHRIS
  Awakening. B. Stoker; Jewel of the Seven Stars
  Spiral Staircase. E. L. White; Some Must Watch
BUCHANAN, JAMES D.
  Happening. E. Curry
BUCHMAN, HAROLD
  Sleeping Tiger. M. Moisewitsch
BUCHMAN, SIDNEY
  Daughter of the Dragon. S. Rohmer; Daughter of Fu Manchu
  Deadly Trap. A. Cavanagh; Children Are Gone
  Mark. C. E. Israel
BUCKINGHAM, THOMAS
  Bad Company. J. Lait; Put on the Spot
BUCKLE, GERARD FORT
  Yellow Claw. S. Rohmer
BUCKLEY, HAROLD
  Black Doll. W. E. Hayes
BUCKMAN, PETER
  Appointment with Death. A. Christie
BUCKNER, ROBERT
  Confidential Agent. G. Greene
  House of Secrets. S. Noel
  Prize of Gold. M. Catto
BUFFINGTON, ADELE
  Eleventh Commandment. B. Fleming; Pillory
  Midnight Life. R. W. Kauffman; Spider's Web
  Moonstone. W. Collins

BULL, DONALD
Arsenal Stadium Mystery. L. Gribble

BULLETT, GERALD
Last Man to Hang. G. Bullett; Jury

BULLOCK, WALTER
O. Henry's Full House. O. Henry (headnote)
Repeat Performance. W. O'Farrell

BUNKER, EDWARD
Straight Time. E. Bunker; No Beast So Fierce

BURFORD, ROGER
Doctor Syn. R. Thorndyke
Once a Crook. E. Price

BURLOCK, WILLIAM ELLIOT
Madame X. J. W. MacConaughy

BURNETT, W. R.
Accused of Murder. W. R. Burnett; Vanity Row
Background to Danger. E. Ambler; Uncommon Danger
High Sierra. W. R. Burnett
I Died a Thousand Times. W. R. Burnett; High Sierra
Nobody Lives Forever. W. R. Burnett
Racket. B. Cormack
Scarface. A. Trail
This Gun for Hire. G. Greene; Gun for Sale

BURNHAM, JEREMY
Horror of Frankenstein. M. W. Shelly; Frankenstein

BURNHAM, JULIE
Fatal Hour. E. Chatterton; Marriages of Mayfair

BURNS, FRANCIS
Rough Cut. D. Lambert; Touch the Lion's Paw

BURNS, STAN
Charlie Chan and the Curse of the Dragon Queen. M. Avallone

BURRIDGE, RICHARD
Fourth Protocol. F. Forsyth

BURT, FRANK
Captain Blood, Fugitive. R. Sabatini; Chronicles of Captain Blood
Fortunes of Captain Blood. R. Sabatini

BURTIS, THOMSON
Under Cover Man. J. Wilstach

BURTON, WILLIAM A.
Easy Pickings. P. Cruger

BUSCH, NIVEN
Man with Two Faces. A. Woollcott; Dark Tower
Miss Pinkerton. M. R. Rinehart
Moss Rose. J. Shearing
Postman Always Rings Twice. J. M. Cain

BUTLER, ALEX C.
Seven Keys to Baldpate. E. D. Biggers

BUTLER, DAVID
Bear Island. A. MacLean

BUTLER, FRANK
Golden Earrings. Y. Foldes
Hostages. S. Heym
Remote Control. C. North
Whispering Smith. F. N. Spearman

BUTLER, GERALD
Fatal Night. M. Arlen; May Fair
Third Time Lucky. G. Butler; They Cracked Her Glass Slipper

BUTLER, HUGO
Eva. J. H. Chase; Eve
He Ran All the Way. S. Ross
Society Lawyer. A. S. Roche; Penthouse

BUTLER, JOHN K.
Girl Who Dared. Medora Field; Blood on Her Shoe

BUTLER, KATHLEEN
Feathered Serpent. E. Wallace

Story of Shirley Yorke. H. A. Vachell; Case of Lady Camber
Temptress. A. Campbell; Juggernaut

BUTLER, LYNTON
Pallet on the Floor. R. H. Morrieson

BUTLER, MICHAEL
Flashpoint. G. La Fountaine
Gauntlet. M. Butler

BYRD, JACK
Man Behind the Mask. J. Futrelle; Chase of the Golden Plate

BYRNE, JACK
End of the Road. E. Bulwer-Lytton; Ernest Maltravers

BYRON-WEBBER, R.
Barton Mystery. W. Hackett
Woman Wins. C. H. Bullivant

BYRUM, JOHN
Sphinx. R. Cook

CACOYANNIS, MICHAEL
Day the Fish Came Out. K. Cicellis

CADINA, JORDI
Los Papeles de Aspern. H. James; Aspern Papers

CADY, JERRY
Great Hospital Mystery. M. G. Eberhart (headnote)
Saint in Palm Springs. L. Charteris (headnote)

CAESAR, ARTHUR
Three Faces East. A. P. Kelly

CAILLOU, ALAN
Assault on Agathon. A. Caillou

CALLAHAN, GEORGE
I'll Get You for This. J. H. Chase

CALMANN, PIERRE
Le Tete d'un Homme. G. Simenon; Battle of Nerves

CAMERON, JAMES
Rambo: First Blood Part II. D. Morrell
Terminator. S. Hutson

CAMILLER, EDGAR J.
Definite Object. J. Farnol

CAMMELL, CHINA
White of the Eye. M. Tracy; Mrs. White

CAMMELL, DONALD
White of the Eye. M. Tracy; Mrs. White

CAMPBELL, COLIN
In Defiance of the Law. J. O. Curwood; Isobel

CAMPBELL, KEITH
Snowbound. H. Innes; Lonely Skier

CAMPBELL, PATRICK
Girl in the Headlines. L. Payne; Nose on My Face
Law and Disorder. D. Roberts; Smuggler's Circuit

CAMPBELL, R. WRIGHT
Masque of the Red Death. Elsie Lee
Terrible Beauty. A. J. Roth

CAMPBELL, SCOTT
Dickson's Diamonds. S. Campbell; Below the Dead-Line

CAMPION, CYRIL
Juggernaut. A. Campbell

CAMPION, JOHN
Zero Hour! J. Castle; Flight Into Danger

CANAWAY, BILL
Ipcress File. L. Deighton

CANFIELD, MARK
Crack in the Mirror. M. Haedrich

CANNAN, DENIS
Amorous Adventures of Moll Flanders. D. Defoe; Fortunes and Misfortunes of the Famous Moll Flanders

CANNING, VICTOR
Golden Salamander. V. Canning
Venetian Bird. V. Canning

CAPORTOTO, CARL
Suicide Club. R. L. Stevenson

CAPOTE, TRUMAN
Beat the Devil. J. Helvick
Innocents. H. James; Turn of the Screw

CAREWE, EDWIN
Across the Pacific. C. E. Blaney
Dancer and the King. C. E. Blaney
Isobel. J. O. Curwood

CARLIER, GERARD
Blague Dans le Coin. Carter Brown; Curtains for a Chorine

CARLINO, LEWIS JOHN
Brotherhood. L. J. Carlino
Crazy Joe. M. Barone
Haunted Summer. A. Edwards
Mechanic. L. J. Carlino
Reflection of Fear. S. Forbes; Go to Thy Death Bed
Seconds. D. Ely

CARLISLE, C. DOUGLAS
Sexton Blake. W. M. Graydon; Five Years After

CARNE, MARCEL
Marie du Port. G. Simenon; Chit of a Girl
Therese Raquin. E. Zola
Three Rooms in Manhattan. G. Simenon; Three Beds in Manhattan
Waste-Land. H. Ellison; Tomboy

CARNES, CHARLES ROBERT
Terrible Game. D. T. Moore

CARON, GLEN
Condorman. R. Sheckley; Game of X

CAROTHERS, A. J.
Hero at Large. A. J. Carothers
Never a Dull Moment. J. Godey; Thrill a Minute with Jack Albany

CARPENTER, JOHN
Escape from New York. M. MacQuay
Eyes of Laura Mars. H. B. Gilmour
Halloween. C. Richards
Halloween II. J. Martin

CARPENTER, STEPHEN
Servants of Twilight. L. Nichols; Twilight

CARR, ROGER
Dead Man's Float. Roger Carr

CARRERAS, MICHAEL
Stranger Came Home. G. Sanders; Stranger at Home

CARRIERE, JEAN-CLAUDE
Butterfly on the Shoulder. J. Gearon; Velvet Well
Flesh of the Orchid. J. H. Chase

CARRINGTON, JANE-HOWARD
Kaleidoscope. M. Avallone
Wait Until Dark. F. Knott

CARRINGTON, ROBERT
Fear Is the Key. A. MacLean
Kaleidoscope. M. Avallone
Venom. A. Scholefield
Wait Until Dark. F. Knott

CARROLL, PAUL VINCENT
Midnight Episode. G. Simenon; Monsieur la Souris

CARRUTH, MILTON
Love Letters of a Star. Rufus King; Case of the Constant God

CARSON, ROBERT
    Action of the Tiger. J. Wellard
CARSTAIRS, JOHN PADDY
    Footsteps in the Night. C. Fraser-Simpson
    Love on the Spot. H. C. McNeile; Three of a
        Kind
CARTIER, RUDOLPH
    Corridors of Mirrors. C. Massie
    Der Racher. E. Wallace; Avenger
CARTON, BRIAN
    Taste of Excitement. B. Healey; Waiting for a
        Tiger
CASH, JIM
    Dick Tracy. M. A. Collins
CASONA, ALEJANDRO
    No Abras Nunca Esa Puerta. W. Irish; Somebody
        on the Phone
    Si Muero Antes de Despertar. W. Irish; If I
        Should Die Before I Wake
CASPARY, VERA
    Bedelia. V. Caspary
CASTALDI, ERNESTO
    La Pupa del Gangster. W. Irish; Somebody on
        the Phone
CASTLE, NICK
    Escape from New York. M. MacQuay
CATALDO, GASPARE
    Brothers Karamazov. F. M. Dostoevskii
CATLING, DARRELL
    Flying Eye. J. N. Chance (headnote)
CATTO, MAX
    Daughter of Darkness. M. Catto; They Walk
        Alone
CAU, JEAN
    Torpedo Skin. F. Ryck; Woman Hunt
CAVALIER, ALAIN
    Ladies' Man. P. Quentin; Shadow of Guilt
    Pillaged. R. Stark; Score
CAVANAGH, JAMES P.
    Murder at the Gallop. A. Christie; After the
        Funeral
CAVILL, JOY
    Stowaway. G. Simenon
CAYATTE, ANDRE
    Trap for Cinderella. S. Japrisot
CELESTIN, JACK
    Line Engaged. J. De Leon
CHABROL, CLAUDE
    Betty. G. Simenon
    Blood Relatives. E. McBain
    Breakup. C. Armstrong; Balloon Man
    Cry of the Owl. P. Highsmith
    Hatter's Ghosts. G. Simenon
    Innocents with Dirty Hands. R. Neely; Damned
        Innocents
    Just Before Nightfall. E. Atiyah; Thin Line
    Let the Beast Die. Nicholas Blake; Beast Must
        Die
CHAFFEY, DON
    Crooked Road. M. West; Big Story
CHAMBERS, WHITMAN
    Come-On. W. Chambers
    Shadow of a Woman. V. Perdue; He Fell Down
        Dead
CHAMBLEE, ROBERT
    Killer Inside Me. J. Thompson
CHANDLER, HARRY
    Back to Life. A. Soutar; Back from the Dead
CHANDLER, RAYMOND
    Blue Dahlia. R. Chandler
    Double Indemnity. J. M. Cain
    Lady in the Lake. R. Chandler
    Strangers on a Train. P. Highsmith
    Unseen. E. L. White; Midnight House
CHANSLOR, ROY
    Black Angel. C. Woolrich
    Hazard. R. Chanslor
    House of Fear. A. C. Doyle; Adventures of
        Sherlock Holmes
    Menace. E. Wallace; Feathered Serpent
    Murder by an Aristocrat. M. G. Eberhart
    Wine, Women and Horses. W. R. Burnett; Dark
        Hazard
CHAPIN, ANNE MORRISON
    Dangerous Corner. J. B. Priestley
CHAPIN, FREDERIC
    Argyle Case. H. Ford
CHAPMAN, JOHN T.
    Satan in High Heels. N. Chandler
CHAPMAN, LEIGH
    Dirty Mary, Crazy Harry. R. Unekis; Chase
CHAPMAN, MICHAEL
    Next Man. M. Z. Lewin
CHAPMAN, PRISCILLA
    Fan. B. Randall
CHAPMAN, ROBIN
    Force 10 from Navarone. A. MacLean
CHAPPELL, CONNERY
    Nursemaid Who Disappeared. P. MacDonald
    Too Dangerous to Live. D. Hume
CHARLES, MOIE
    Bedelia. V. Caspary
    Dark Secret. M. Sharp; Crime at Blossoms
    Hell Is Sold Out. M. Dekobra
CHARLES-WILLIAMS, LIZ
    Deadlier Than the Male. H. Reymond
CHARTERIS, LESLIE
    Saint's Vacation. L. Charteris; Getaway
CHAUTARD, EMILE
    Mystery of the Yellow Room. G. Leroux
CHAVANCE, LOUIS
    Marie du Port. G. Simenon; Chit of a Girl
CHENAL, PIERRE
    Crime and Punishment. F. M. Dostoevskii
    La Bete a L'Affut. D. Keene; Moran's Woman
    Native Son. R. Wright
CHENEY, J. BENTON
    Laramie Trail. J. Gregory; Mystery at Spanish
        Hacienda
CHEREAU, PATRICE
    Flesh of the Orchid. J. H. Chase
CHESBRO, GEORGE
    Man Who Would Not Die. C. Williams;
        Sailcloth Shroud
CHESTER, GEORGE RANDOLPH
    Dead Men Tell No Tales. E. W. Hornung
    Scarlet Car. R. H. Davis
CHESTER, LILIAN
    Dead Men Tell No Tales. E. W. Hornung
CHEVALIER, PAUL
    More Deadly Than the Male. P. Chevalier
CHEYNEY, PETER
    Uneasy Terms. P. Cheyney
CHODOROV, EDWARD
    Kind Lady. E. Chodorov
CHODOROV, JERRY
    Case of the Lucky Legs. E. S. Gardner
CHOURAQUI, ELIE
    Man on Fire. A. J. Quinnell
CHRISTENSEN, BENT
    Ghost Train. A. Ridley
CHRISTIAN-JACQUE
    Dead Run. R. Sheckley
CHRISTIANSEN, BENJAMIN
    Devil's Circus. B. Christiansen
CHRISTIE, CAMPBELL
    Jassy. N. Lofts
CHRISTIE, DOROTHY
    Jassy. N. Lofts
CHRISTINA, FRANK
    Trial of Billy Jack. H. Liebling
CHRISTINA, TERESA
    Trial of Billy Jack. H. Liebling
CIMBER, MATT
    Butterfly. J. M. Cain
    Time to Die. M. Cleri; Six Graves to Munich
CIMINO, MICHAEL
    Magnum Force. M. Valley
    Thunderbolt and Lightfoot. J. Millard
    Year of the Dragon. R. Daley
CLANCEY, VERNON
    Dead Men Are Dangerous. H. C. Armstrong;
        Hidden
    Flying Fifty-Five. E. Wallace
CLAPP, CHESTER B.
    Sable Lorcha. H. Hazeltine
CLARK, RON
    High Anxiety. R. H. Pilpel
CLARK, VIOLET
    Loot. A. S. Roche
    Love Without Question. W. Camp; Abandoned
        Room
CLARKE, T. E. B.
    Blue Lamp. T. Willis
    Dead of Night. E. F. Benson; Room in the
        Tower
    Gideon's Day. J. J. Marric
    Law and Disorder. D. Roberts; Smuggler's
        Circuit
    Man Could Get Killed. D. Walker; Diamonds
        for Moscow
CLAUS, HUGO
    Because of the Cats. N. Freeling
CLAVEL, MAURICE
    Ladies' Man. P. Quentin; Shadow of Guilt
CLAVELL, JAMES
    Satan Bug. I. Stuart
    633 Squadron. F. E. Smith
CLAWSON, ELLIOTT
    Evil Women Do. E. Gaboriau; Clique of Gold
    Jack Chanty. H. Footner
    Let 'Er Go Gallegher. R. H. Davis; Gallegher
    Phantom of the Opera. G. Leroux
    Thirteenth Chair. B. Veiller
    Whispering Smith. F. H. Spearman
CLAY, MELVIN
    Spook Who Sat by the Door. S. Greenlee
CLAYTON, JACK
    Memento Mori. M. Spark
CLEAVER, THOMAS MCKELVEY
    Saigon Commandos. Jonathan Cain; Mad
        Minute
CLEMENS, BRIAN
    Blind Terror. W. Hughes
    Doctor Jekyll and Sister Hyde. R. L. Stevenson;
        Strange Case of Dr. Jekyll and Mr. Hyde
CLEMENS, HAROLD
    Lady Ice. M. Braly; Master
CLEMENT, DICK
    Catch Me a Spy. G. Marton
    Jokers. M. Sands
    Otley. M. Waddell
    Porridge. P. Ableman
    Villain. J. Barlow; Burden of Proof

C

CLEMENT, RENE
Broad Daylight. P. Highsmith; Talented Mr. Ripley
Joy House. D. Keene

CLEVELY, HUGH
Meet Maxwell Archer. H. Clevely; Archer Plus 20

CLEWES, HOWARD
Day They Robbed the Bank of England. J. Brophy

CLIFFORD, WILLIAM M.
Man from Nowhere. V. Bridges

CLIFT, DENISON
Bentley's Conscience. P. Trent
Out to Win. R. Pertwee

CLIFTON, ELMER
Two-Soul Woman. G. Burgess; White Cat

CLIFTON, WALLACE
Wanted at Headquarters. E. Wallace (headnote)

CLOCHE, MAURICE
Lay Off Blondes. Carter Brown; Body

CLORK, HARRY
Remember Last Night? A. Hobhouse; Hangover Murders
Whistling in the Dark. L. Gross

CLOUZOT, HENRI-GEORGES
Diabolique. P. Boileau; Woman Who Was
Le Dernier des Six. A. Steeman; Six Dead Men
Spies. E. Hostovsky; Midnight Patient
Strangers in the House. G. Simenon
Wages of Fear. G. Arnaud

CLOWES, ST. JOHN L.
No Orchids for Miss Blandish. J. H. Chase

COCKRELL, MARIAN
Dark Waters. F. Cockrell

COE, CHARLES FRANCIS
Me—Gangster. C. F. Coe

COEN, ETHAN
Blood Simple. J. Coen

COEN, FRANKLIN
Interlude. J. M. Cain; Serenade
Take. G. F. Newman; Sir, You Bastard
We're on the Jury. F. Ballard; Ladies of the Jury

COEN, JOEL
Blood Simple. J. Coen

COFFEE, LENORE J.
Age of Indiscretion. T. D. Irwin; Collusion
Beyond the Forest. S. Engstrand
Bishop Murder Case. S. S. Van Dine
Chicago. M. Watkins
East Lynne. H. Wood
End of the Affair. G. Greene
Evelyn Prentice. W. E. Woodward
Footsteps in the Fog. W. W. Jacobs; Sea Whispers
Ladyfingers. J. Gregory
Lightning Strikes Twice. M. Echard; Dark Fantastic
Mothers Cry. H. G. Carlisle
Sudden Fear. E. Sherry

COHAN, GEORGE M.
Seven Keys to Baldpate. E. D. Biggers

COHEN, DAVID AARON
V. I. Warshawski. S. Paretski (headnote)

COHEN, HERMAN
Craze. H. Seymour; Infernal Idol

COHEN, LARRY
Daddy's Gone A-Hunting. Mike St. Clair
I, the Jury. M. Spillane
It's Alive. R. Woodley

COHEN, LAWRENCE J.
S*P*Y*S. T. R. Joyce

COHEN, RONALD M.
Twilight's Last Gleaming. W. Wager; Viper Three

COHN, ALFRED A.
Cat and the Canary. J. Willard
Gorilla. R. Spence
Last Warning. W. Camp; House of Fear

COHN, BRUCE
Good Guys Wear Black. M. Franklin

COLDEWAY, ANTHONY
Crimson City. A. Coldeway
Hidden Hand. Rufus King; Invitation to a Murder
Nurse's Secret. M. R. Rinehart; Miss Pinkerton
Scream in the Night. J. Odlum; Morgue Is Always Open
Shadows on the Stairs. F. Vosper; Murder on the Second Floor

COLE, LESTER
Charlie Chan's Greatest Case. E. D. Biggers; House Without a Key
High Wall. A. R. Clark
Hostages. S. Heym
President's Mystery. F. D. Roosevelt; President's Mystery Story
Sleepers East. F. Nebel

COLEBY, A. E.
Flying Fifty-Five. E. Wallace
Great Prince Shan. E. P. Oppenheim

COLEMAN, PATRICIA
Above Suspicion. H. MacInnes

COLETTI, DUILIO
House of Intrigue. H. J. Giskes; London Calling North Pole

COLIN, SID
Ugly Duckling. R. L. Stevenson; Strange Case of Dr. Jekyll and Mr. Hyde

COLLECTOR, ROBERT
Memoirs of an Invisible Man. H. F. Saint
Red Heat. R. Tine

COLLEE, JOHN
Paper Mask. J. Collee

COLLIER, JOHN
Deception. E. Walter; Jealousy

COLLINS, EDWIN J.
Eugene Aram. E. Bulwer-Lytton

COLLINS, JOHN H.
Wife by Purchase. P. Trent

COLLINS, RICHARD
Badlanders. W. R. Burnett; Asphalt Jungle

COLUMBUS, CHRIS
Young Sherlock Holmes. A. Arnold

COMFORT, LANCE
Pit of Darkness. H. McCutcheon; To Dusty Death

COMMANDINI, ADELE
Country Beyond. J. O. Curwood
Danger Signal. P. Bottome; Murder in the Bud
Love Racket. B. K. Burns; Jury Woman

COMPANEEZ, JACQUES
Forbidden Fruit. G. Simenon; Act of Passion

COMPORT, BRIAN
Mumsy, Nanny, Sonny and Girly. B. Comport

CONDON, FRANK
City of Silent Men. J. A. Moroso; Quarry
Sealed Lips. Maxwell Gray; Silence of Dean Maitland

CONDON, RICHARD
Prizzi's Honor. R. Condon

CONNORS, BARRY
Black Camel. E. D. Biggers
Charlie Chan Carries On. E. D. Biggers
Charlie Chan's Chance. E. D. Biggers; Behind That Curtain
Spider. F. Oursler
Trial of Vivienne Ware. K. Ellis

CONNORS, KATHLEEN
Fatal Night. M. Arlen; May Fair

CONSELMAN, WILLIAM
Fifty Roads to Town. F. Nebel
Great Hospital Mystery. M. G. Eberhart (headnote)
Orient Express. G. Greene; Stamboul Train

CONSIDINE, MILDRED
Jimmy Dale, Alias "The Grey Seal". F. Packard; Adventures of Jimmie Dale

CONSTANCE, MARIAN
Behold the Woman. E. P. Oppenheim; Hillman
Passionate Quest. E. P. Oppenheim

COOK, EDWIN
Extremities. W. Mastrosimone

COOK, PETER
Hound of the Baskervilles. A. C. Doyle

COOK, T. S.
China Syndrome. B. Wohl

COOK, VIRGINIA
"Shed No Tears." D. Martin

COOK, WHITFIELD
Stage Fright. S. Jepson; Man Running
Strangers on a Train. P. Highsmith

COOLIDGE, KARL L.
Lion Man. R. Parrish; Strange Case of Cavendish

COON, GENE L.
Killers. E. Hemingway; Men Without Women
Man in the Shadow. H. Whittington

COONEY, RAY
What a Carve Up! F. King; Ghoul

COOPER, COURTNEY RILEY
Eagle's Eye. W. J. Flynn

COOPER, DENNIS
City Across the River. I. Shulman; Amboy Dukes
Fear. F. M. Dostoevskii; Crime and Punishment

COOPER, JOHN C.
Grip of the Strangler. J. C. Cooper

COOPER, OLIVE
Jim Hanvey, Detective. O. R. Cohen

COOPER, WILLIS
Thank You, Mr. Moto. J. P. Marquand

COPPEL, ALEC
Hell Below Zero. H. Innes; White South
I Killed the Count. A. Coppel
Mr. Denning Drives North. A. Coppel
Moment to Moment. A. Coppel
Obsession. A. Coppel; Man About a Dog
Vertigo. P. Boileau; Living and the Dead

COPPOLA, FRANCIS FORD
Godfather. M. Puzo
Godfather, Part II. M. Puzo; Godfather

CORMACK, BARTLETT
Benson Murder Case. S. S. Van Dine
Greene Murder Case. S. S. Van Dine
Kick-In. W. Mack
Racket. B. Cormack
Thirteen Women. T. Thayer

CORMAN, GENE
Secret of the Purple Reef. D. Cottrell; Silent Reefs

CORNEAU, ALAIN
Thriller Story. J. Thompson; Hell of a Woman

CORNELIUS, HENRY
It Always Rains on Sunday. A. La Bern

CORNFIELD, HUBERT
Night of the Following Day. L. White; Snatchers
Third Voice. C. Williams; All the Way

CORNU, JACQUES
  Ladies' Man. P. Quentin; Shadow of Guilt
CORRIGAN, LLOYD
  Daughter of the Dragon. S. Rohmer; Daughter of Fu Manchu
  Mysterious Dr. Fu Manchu. S. Rohmer; Mystery of Dr. Fu Manchu
  Return of Dr. Fu Manchu. S. Rohmer; Devil Doctor
CORY, DESMOND
  England Made Me. G. Greene
COSMATOS, GEORGE PAN
  Cassandra Crossing. R. Katz
COSMOS, JEAN
  It Only Happens to the Living. R. Marshall; Things Men Do
COSTA-GRAVAS
  Z. V. Vassilikos
COTTEN, JOSEPH
  Hotel Reserve. E. Ambler; Journey Into Fear
COUFFER, JACK C.
  Running Target. S. Frazee
COURT, JOANNE
  Cairo. W. R. Burnett; Asphalt Jungle
COURTNEY, SYD
  Man Behind the Mask. J. Futrelle; Chase of the Golden Plate
COWAN, SADA
  Woman in the Dark. D. Hammett
COX, MORGAN L.
  Drums of Fu Manchu. S. Rohmer
COX, VIVIAN A.
  Deadly Record. N. W. Hooke
CRAWFORD, BOBBY
  Rage in Harlem. C. Himes; For Love of Imabelle
CRAWFORD, OLIVER
  Girl in the Woods. O. Crawford; Blood on the Branches
CREELMAN, JAMES ASHMORE
  Most Dangerous Game. R. Connell; Variety
  Red Dance. H. L. Gates; Red Dancer of Moscow
CRESSWELL, JOHN
  Beyond the Curtain. A. J. Wallis; Thunder Above
  Cast a Dark Shadow. J. Green; Murder Mistaken
  Port Afrique. B. V. Dryer
  Yield to the Night. J. Henry
CRICHTON, CHARLES
  Floods of Fear. J. Hawkins
CRICHTON, MICHAEL
  Coma. R. Cook
  First Great Train Robbery. M. Crichton; Great Train Robbery
CROISE, HUGH
  Affair at the Novelty Theatre. B. Orczy; Old Man in the Corner
  Brighton Mystery. B. Orczy; Old Man in the Corner
  Hocussing of Cigarette. B. Orczy; Old Man in the Corner
  Kensington Mystery. B. Orczy; Old Man in the Corner
  Mystery of Brudenell Court. B. Orczy; Old Man in the Corner
  Mystery of Dogstooth Cliff. B. Orczy; Old Man in the Corner
  Mystery of the Khaki Tunic. B. Orczy; Old Man in the Corner
  Northern Mystery. B. Orczy; Old Man in the Corner
  Regent's Park Mystery. B. Orczy; Old Man in the Corner
  Tragedy of Barnsdale Manor. B. Orczy; Old Man in the Corner
  York Mystery. B. Orczy; Old Man in the Corner

CRONENBERG, DAVID
  Dead Ringers. Bari Wood; Twins
CRONYN, HUME
  Rope. P. Hamilton
CROUSE, RUSSELL
  Mountain Music. M. Kantor; Author's Choice
CROWDY, FRANCIS
  Mark of Cain. J. Shearing; Airing in a Closed Carriage
CROWTHER, JOHN
  Evil That Men Do. R. L. Hill
CRUICKSHANK, JIM
  Tough Guys. I. Don
CUCCI, MILO
  Count Dracula. B. Stoker; Dracula
CULLEN, ROBERT J.
  Woman in White. W. Collins
CUMMINGS, IRVING
  Country Beyond. J. O. Curwood
CUNARD, GRACE
  Study in Scarlet. A. C. Doyle
CUNNINGHAM, JACK
  Contraband. C. B. Kelland
  Devil to Pay. F. N. Greene
  Don Q, Son of Zorro. K. Prichard; Don Q's Love Story
  Double Door. E. McFadden
  Ghost Breakers. C. W. Goddard
  House of Whispers. W. Johnston
  Tiger's Coat. E. Dejeans
CURRIER, VICTOR
  Perfect Crime. I. Zangwill; Big Bow Mystery
CURTELIN, JEAN
  Prize of Peril. R. Sheckley; Tenth Victim
CURTIN, VALERIE
  And Justice for All. R. Grossbach
CURTIS, JAMES
  Ten Days in Paris. B. Graeme; Disappearance of Roger Tremayne
  There Ain't No Justice. J. Curtis
CURTISS, JEAN-LOUIS
  Woman Is a Stranger. J. H. Chase; Not Safe to Be Free
CURWOOD, JAMES OLIVER
  Golden Snare. J. O. Curwood
  Nomads of the North. J. O. Curwood
CUSHING, TOM
  Yellow Ticket. V. Morton
CUTLER, WENDY
  Extremities. W. Mastrosimone
CUTTS, GRAHAM
  Rat. P. Bottome
DABADIE, JEAN-LOUIS
  Descent Into Hell. D. Goodis; Wounded and the Slain
  Old Tin Can. D. Keene; Flight by Night
  Le Silencieux. F. Ryck; Loaded Gun
  Such a Lovely Kid Like Me. H. Farrell; Such a Gorgeous Kid Like Me
DAHL, ROALD
  You Only Live Twice. I. Fleming
DAINTON, CHARLES
  Dick Turpin. W. H. Ainsworth; Rookwood
DALMAS, HERBERT
  Address Unknown. K. Taylor
DALRYMPLE, IAN
  Brown Wallet. S. Aumonier; Miss Bracegirdle and Others
  Heart of the Matter. G. Greene
  Her Latest Affaire. W. W. Ellis; S.O.S.
  Mix Me a Person. J. T. Story

DALY, JOHN
  Sunburn. S. Ellin; Bind
DAMIANI, DAMIANO
  Day of the Owl. L. Sciascia; Mafia Vendetta
DANCIGERS, OSCAR
  Pillaged. R. Stark; Score
DANE, CLEMENCE
  Amateur Gentleman. J. Farnol
DANISCHEWSKY, MONJA
  Bitter Springs. C. King
  Mr. Moses. M. Catto; Mister Midas
  Topkapi. E. Ambler; Light of Day
DARLING, W. SCOTT
  813. M. Leblanc
  Great Impersonation. E. P. Oppenheim
  Sherlock Holmes and the Secret Weapon. A. C. Doyle; Return of Sherlock Holmes
  Spider. F. Oursler
  Trent's Last Case. E. C. Bentley
  Weird Woman. F. Leiber, Jr.; Conjure Wife
  Wolf Hunters. J. O. Curwood
DASSIN, JULES
  10:30 P.M. Summer. M. Duras; Ten-Thirty on a Summer Night
  Uptight. L. O'Flaherty; Informer
DAVENPORT, JOHN
  Hotel Reserve. E. Ambler; Epitaph for a Spy
DAVES, DELMAR
  Dark Passage. D. Goodis
  Night of February 16. A. Rand
  Petrified Forest. R. E. Sherwood
  Red House. G. A. Chamberlain
DAVID, W.
  Yellow Mask. E. Wallace; Traitor's Gate
DAVIDSON, ARLENE
  Eddie and the Cruisers. P. F. Kluge
DAVIDSON, L. W.
  Hands of the Ripper. E. S. Shew
DAVIDSON, MARTIN
  Eddie and the Cruisers. P. F. Kluge
DAVIDSON, RONALD
  Drums of Fu Manchu. S. Rohmer
DAVIES, JACK
  Gambit. K. Lane
  North Sea Hijack. J. Davies
  Someone at the Door. D. Christie
  Ugly Duckling. R. L. Stevenson; Strange Case of Dr. Jekyll and Mr. Hyde
DAVIES, ROSEMARY
  Neither the Sea Nor the Sand. G. Honeycombe
DAVIS, BART
  Full Fathom Five. Bart Davis
DAVIS, DESMOND
  Inspector Calls. J. B. Priestley
DAVIS, FRANK
  Woman on the Beach. M. A. Wilson; None So Blind
DAVIS, JERRY
  Devil Makes Three. L. P. Bachmann; Kiss of Death
  Kind Lady. E. Chodorov
DAVIS, LUTHER
  Across 110th. Wally Ferris
  Lady in a Cage. R. Durand
DAVIS, OSSIE
  Cotton Comes to Harlem. C. Himes
DAVIS, OWEN
  Green Cloak. Y. Davis
DAVIS, ROBIN
  Hill Girl. C. Williams

DAVIS, STRATFORD
  Man in the Shadow. S. Davis; One Man's Secret

DAVIS, WILL S.
  Doctor Rameau. G. Ohnet

DAWLEY, J. SEARLE
  Frankenstein. M. Shelley

DAWN
  For the Term of His Natural Life. M. Clarke; His Natural Life

DAWSON, BASIL
  Devil's Daffodil. E. Wallace; Daffodil Mystery

DAWSON, FORBES
  Down Under Donovan. E. Wallace

DAY, RICHARD
  Never Love a Stranger. H. Robbins

DAYTON, JAMES
  Called Back. H. Conway
  Hornet's Nest. W. Woodrow
  Spy. J. F. Cooper

DAZEY, CHARLES T.
  Silent Barrier. L. Tracy

DEAN, BASIL
  Birds of Prey. A. A. Milne; Fourth Wall
  Escape. J. Galsworthy
  Footsteps in the Night. C. Fraser-Simpson
  Return of Sherlock Holmes. A. C. Doyle; His Last Bow
  21 Days. J. Galsworth; Five Tales

DEANS, MARJORIE
  Living Dangerously. R. Simpson
  Someone at the Door. D. Christie

DEARDEN, BASIL
  Man Who Haunted Himself. A. Armstrong; Strange Case of Mr. Pelham
  Ship That Died of Shame. N. Monsarrat

DEARDEN, JAMES
  Pascali's Island. B. Unsworth; Idol Hunter

DEASY, FRANK
  Courier. Gerald Cole

DE BARONCELLI, JACQUES
  Rope for a Killing. P. McGerr; Follow, As the Night

DE BERNARDI, PIERO
  Once Upon a Time in America. H. Grey; Hoods

DE CASEMBROOT, JACQUES
  Mystere a Shanghai. A. Steeman; Night of the 12th–13th

DECOIN, HENRI
  L'Homme de Londres. G. Simenon; Newhaven-Dieppe
  Rope for a Killing. P. McGerr; Follow, As the Night
  Sorcery. P. Boileau; Spells of Evil

DE CONCINI, ENNIO
  House of Intrigue. H. J. Giskes; London Calling North Pole
  Order of Death. H. Fleetwood

DE CRESCENZO, LUCIANO
  Payoff. A. Veraldi

DEE, RUBY
  Uptight. L. O'Flaherty; Informer

DEEL, ROBERT
  Frankenstein General Hospital. M. W. Shelley; Frankenstein

DE FELITTA, FRANK
  Audrey Rose. F. De Felitta

DE FEO, FRANCESCO
  Invincible Six. M. Barrett; Heroes of Yuca

DEGAS, BRIAN
  My Lover, My Son. E. Grierson; Reputation for a Song

DE GRUNWALD, ANATOLE
  Cottage to Let. G. Kerr; Cottages to Let
  Home at Seven. R. C. Sherriff
  Libel. E. Wooll
  Spy for a Day. S. Aumonier; Love-a-Duck
  They Met in the Dark. Anthony Gilbert; Vanishing Corpse
  Women of Twilight. S. Rayman

DEHN, PAUL
  Deadly Affair. J. Le Carre; Call for the Dead
  Fragment of Fear. J. Bingham
  Goldfinger. I. Fleming
  Murder on the Orient Express. A. Christie
  Night of the Generals. H. H. Kirst
  Orders to Kill. D. Downes
  Spy Who Came in from the Cold. J. Le Carre

DEIN, EDWARD
  Leopard Man. C. Woolrich; Black Alibi

DE KAY, COLMAN
  Bloodhounds of Broadway. D. Runyon

DEKOKER, RICHARD
  Juggernaut. A. Hine

DE LA HUERTA, ALVARID
  Last of Philip Banter. J. F. Bardin

DE LA IGLESIA, ELOY
  Turn of the Screw. H. James

DELANNOY, JEAN
  Action Man. J. Flynn
  Maigret and the St. Fiacre Case. G. Simenon; Saint Fiacre Affair
  Maigret Sets a Trap. G. Simenon
  Obsession. W. Irish; Dead Man Blues
  Pas Folle la Guepe. J. H. Chase; Just a Matter of Time
  Torpedo Skin. F. Ryck; Woman Hunt

DE LA PATELLIERE, DENYS
  La Salaire du Peche. N. Rutledge; Emily Will Know
  Retour de Manivelle. J. H. Chase; There's Always a Price Tag

DELAPREE, LOUIS
  Le Tete d'un Homme. G. Simenon; Battle of Nerves

DE LAURENTIS, ROBERT
  Green Ice. G. A. Browne

DELAY, FLORENCE
  Deep Water. P. Highsmith

DE LEON, JACK
  Line Engaged. J. De Leon

DE LEON, WALTER
  Big Gamble. O. R. Cohen; Iron Chalice
  Cat and the Canary. J. Willard
  Ghost Breakers. C. W. Goddard
  Phantom President. G. F. Worts

DELIA, FRANCIS
  Freeway. D. Barkley

DELL, JEFFREY
  Brothers in Law. H. Cecil
  Cone of Silence. D. Beaty
  Kate Plus Ten. E. Wallace
  Saint's Vacation. L. Charteris; Getaway
  Sanders of the River. E. Wallace
  Suspect. N. Balchin; Sort of Traitors

DEL RUTH, HAMPTON
  Defenders of the Law. H. Del Ruth

DELUCA, RUDY
  High Anxiety. R. H. Pilpel

DE MARNEY, DERRICK
  No Way Back. T. Burke; Limehouse Nights

DE MILLE, CECIL B.
  Ghost Breakers. C. W. Goddard
  Unafraid. E. M. Ingram

DE MOND, ALBERT
  Homicde for Three. P. Quentin; Puzzle for Puppets
  Leavenworth Case. A. K. Green
  Spanish Cape Mystery. E. Queen
  Woman in the Dark. D. Hammett

DE MURAT, ULYSSES PETIT
  El Pediente. W. Irish; Dead Man Blues
  Man and the Beast. R. L. Stevenson; Strange Case of Dr. Jekyll and Mr. Hyde

DENGER, FRED
  Der Unheimliche Monch. E. Wallace; Terror

DENHAM, REGINALD
  Called Back. H. Conway
  Ladies in Retirement. E. Percy

DENKER, HENRY
  Time Limit. H. Denker
  Twilight of Honor. A. Dewlin

DENNIS, CHARLES
  Double Negative. K. Millar; Three Roads
  Finders Keepers. C. Dennis; Next-to-Last Train Ride

DE PALMA, BRIAN
  Blow Out. N. Williams
  Dressed to Kill. Campbell Black

DERAY, JACQUES
  He Died with His Eyes Open. D. Raymond
  On a Nice Summer Day. J. H. Chase; One Bright Summer Morning
  Our Man in Marrakech. R. P. Jones; Heisters

DE RITA, MASSIMA
  Payoff. A. Veraldi

DE ROCHE, EVERETT
  Razorback. P. Brennan

DE ROUEN, REED
  Six Men. E. Radford

DESAILLY, CLAUDE
  Les Canailles. R. Marshall; You Find Him . . . I'll Fix Him

DE SANTIS, GIUSEPPI
  Obsession. J. M. Cain; Postman Always Rings Twice

DE SOUZA, STEPHEN E.
  Die Hard. R. Thorp; Nothing Lasts Forever
  Die Harder. W. Wager; 58 Minutes
  Running Man. R. Bachman

DEUTSCH, ANDREW
  River of Death. Alistair MacLean

DEUTSCH, HELEN
  Golden Earrings. Y. Foldes
  Seventh Cross. A. Seghers

DEVERS, CLAIRE
  Max and Jeremy. Teri White; Max Trueblood and the Jersey Desperado

DEVILLE, MICHEL
  Deep Water. P. Highsmith
  Dossier 51. G. Perrault

DEVILLE, ROSALINDE
  Sweetheart. A. Coburn

DE VILLIERS, GERARD
  S.A.S. San Salvator. G. de Villiers; Game of Eyes Only

DE VORE, GARY
  Dogs of War. F. Forsyth
  Raw Deal. W. Wager

DEWHURST, GEORGE W.
  Lunatic at Large. J. S. Clouston
  Mist in the Valley. Dorin Craig
  Shadow Between. S. Hocking

DEWHURST, KEITH
  Empty Beach. P. Corris

DEWITT, JACK
   Rumble on the Docks. F. Paley
   Sky Riders. L. Cameron
   Together Brothers. Jim Robinson

DEWOLF, KAREN
   Nine Girls. W. H. Pettitt

DEWOLF, PATRICK
   M. Hire. G. Simenon; Mr. Hire's Engagement

DEXTER, PETE
   Paris Trout. P. Dexter
   Rush. K. Wozencraft

DIAMANT-BERGER, HENRI
   Arsene Lupin Detective. M. Leblanc; Jim Barnett Intervenes

DIAMOND, I. A. L.
   Private Life of Sherlock Holmes. Michael Hardwick

DICKEY, BASIL
   Sun-Up. M. Marcin; Substitute Prisoner

DICKEY, JAMES
   Deliverance. J. Dickey

DICKINS, STAFFORD
   Dead Men Tell No Tales. F. Beeding; Norwich Victims

DICKINSON, THOROLD
   Arsenal Stadium Mystery. L. Gribble

DIDION, JOAN
   Panic in Needle Park. J. Mills
   True Confessions. J. G. Dunne

DIGHTON, JOHN
   Brandy for the Parson. G. Household; Tales of Adventurers
   It's in the Blood. D. Whitelaw; Big Picture
   Kind Hearts and Coronets. R. Horniman; Israel Rank
   Saloon Bar. F. Harvey
   Thank Evans. E. Wallace; Good Evans!

DILLON, BASIL
   Dark Stairway. M. G. Eberhart; From This Dark Stairway
   It's in the Blood. D. Whitelaw; Big Picture
   Who Killed John Savage? P. MacDonald; Rynox

DILLON, LAURIE
   French Connection II. R. Moore

DILLON, ROBERT A.
   Flight of the Intruder. S. Coonts
   French Connection II. R. Moore
   Key to Yesterday. C. N. Buck
   Man Who Could Not Lose. R. H. Davis
   Muscle Beach Party. Elsie Lee
   99 and 44/100% Dead. M. Franklin
   Old Dark House. J. B. Priestley; Benighted
   Prime Cut. M. Roote
   Three Keys. F. Ormond
   X. E. Sudak

DINELLI, MEL
   Beware, My Lovely. M. Dinelli; Man
   House by the River. A. P. Herbert
   Lizzie. S. Jackson; Bird's Nest
   Reckless Moment. E. S. Holding; Blank Wall
   Spiral Staircase. E. L. White; Some Must Watch
   Window. W. Irish; Dead Man Blues

DI PEGO, GERALD
   Sharky's Machine. W. Diehl

DIX, BEULAH MARIE
   Conspiracy. R. Baker
   Girl of the Port. J. Russell; Far Wandering Men
   Leopard Lady. E. C. Carpenter
   Midnight Mystery. H. I. Young; Hawk Island
   Secret Service. W. Gillette
   Woman Who Came Back. C. M. S. McLellan; Leah Kleschna

DIX, MARION
   Before Dawn. E. Wallace; Sergeant Sir Peter
   Everything Is Thunder. J. L. Hardy
   Ladies of the Jury. F. Ballard

DIXON, THOMAS, JR.
   Brass Bowl. L. J. Vance

DOHERTY, ETHEL
   Studio Murder Mystery. Edingtons

DOLINSKY, MEYER
   Hot Rod Rumble. M. Dolinsky; Hot Rod Gang Rumble

DOMINIC, HENRY
   Watchers II. D. R. Koontz; Watchers

DONATI, SERGIO
   Man on Fire. A. J. Quinnell

DONIGER, WALTER
   Desperate Search. A. Mayse

DONIOL-VALCROZE, JACQUES
   Vous Pigez. P. Cheyney; Don't Get Me Wrong

DONN, RICHARD
   Diplomatic Immunity. Theodore Taylor; Stalker

DOOHAN, ANITA
   Whispers. D. R. Koontz

DORAN, JAMES
   Ipcress File. L. Deighton

DORTORT, DAVID
   Cry in the Night. W. Masterson; All Through the Night
   Reprisal. Arthur Gordon

DOTY, DOUGLAS
   Silent Witness. J. De Leon

DOUGLAS, GORDON
   Housekeeper's Daughter. D. H. Clarke

DOUGLAS, WARREN
   Come-On. W. Chambers
   Strange Intruder. H. Fowler; Shades Will Not Vanish

DOWN, ALLISON LOUISE
   Blood Feast. L. E. Murphy

DOWNING, RUPERT
   Footsteps in the Night. C. Fraser-Simpson
   Ghoul. F. King

DOXAT-PRATT, B. E.
   Bulldog Drummond. H. C. McNeile
   John Heriot's Wife. A. Askew

DOYLE, LAIRD
   British Agent. H. B. Lockhart
   Strangers on a Honeymoon. E. Wallace; Northing Tramp

DOYLE, RAY
   Madonna of Avenue A. M. Canfield

DOZIER, ROBERT
   Big Bounce. E. Leonard

DRAKE, OLIVER
   Trail of the Yukon. J. O. Curwood; Gold Hunters

DRAKE, RONALD
   Killer Walks. G. Glennon; Gathering Storm

DRAKE, WILLIAM
   Sherlock Holmes. W. Gillette

DRANEY, GEORGE
   East Lynne. H. Wood
   Party Girl. E. Balmer; Dangerous Business

DRATLER, JAY
   Laura. V. Caspary

DRESNER, HAL
   Eiger Sanction. Trevanian

DREUX, JACQUES
   Kill the Referee. A. Draper; Death Penalty

DREYER, CARL THEODORE
   Strange Adventure of Donald Gray. J. S. Le Fanu; In a Glass Darkly

DRUCKER, GARY
   Red Heat. R. Tine

DRYHURST, EDWARD
   Clayton Treasure Mystery. N. Gordon; Shakespeare Murders
   Crimes at the Dark House. W. Collins; Woman in White
   Frightened Lady. E. Wallace
   House of the Arrow. A. E. W. Mason
   Night Invader. J. Bentley; Rendezvous with Death
   Stranger in Town. F. A. Chittenden; Uninvited
   This Man Is Dangerous. D. Hume; They Called Him Death

DUDLEY, ERNEST
   Guilty? M. Gilbert; Death Has Deep Roots

DUDRUMET, JEAN-CHARLES
   Dans la Gueude du Loup. J. H. Chase; Just Another Sucker

DUERRENMATT, FRIEDRICH
   It Happens in Broad Daylight. F. Duerrenmatt; Pledge

DUEY, HELEN
   Blue Envelope Mystery. S. Kerr; Blue Envelope

DUFF, WARREN
   Chicago Deadline. T. Thayer; One Woman
   Each Dawn I Die. J. Odlum
   Experiment Perilous. M. Carpenter
   Fallen Sparrow. D. B. Hughes
   Make Haste to Live. Gordons
   Midnight Alibi. D. Runyon; Blue Plate Special
   Strangers of the Evening. T. Thayer; Illustrious Corpse
   Turning Point. H. McCoy; Corruption City

DUFFELL, PETER
   England Made Me. G. Greene

DUFFY, ALBERT
   Blind Alley. J. Warwick
   Dark Past. J. Warwick; Blind Alley

DUFFY, GERALD C.
   Mr. Barnes of New York. A. C. Gunter
   Officer 666. B. Currie
   Recoil. R. Beach; Big Brother

DUNBAR, ROBERT
   Solitary Child. N. Bawden

DUNNE, JOHN GREGORY
   Panic in Needle Park. J. Mills
   True Confessions. J. G. Dunne

DUNNE, PHILIP
   Blindfold. L. Fletcher
   Escape. J. Galsworthy
   Lancer Spy. M. McKenna

DUNNETT, NIMIAN
   Restless Natives. N. Dunnett

DUNNING, DECLA
   Sleep My Love. L. Q. Ross

DURAS, MARGUERITE
   10:30 P.M. Summer. M. Duras; Ten-Thirty on a Summer Night

DURBRIDGE, FRANCIS
   Paul Temple Returns. F. Durbridge; Paul Temple Intervenes

DURST, PAUL
   Informers. D. Warner; Death of a Snout

D'USSEAU, ARNAUD
   Man Who Wouldn't Die. C. Rawson; No Coffin for the Corpse
   Who Is Hope Schuyler? S. Ransome; Hearses Don't Hurry

DUVIVIER, JULIEN
   Ardent Room. J. D. Carr; Burning Court
   Gooseflesh. J. H. Chase; Come Easy—Go Easy
   Le Tete d'un Homme. G. Simenon; Battle of Nerves

Man in the Raincoat. J. H. Chase; Tiger by the Tail
Maurizius Affair. J. Wasserman; Maurizius Case
Panique. G. Simenon; Mr. Hire's Engagement

DYAB, MAHMOUD
Sonya and the Madman. F. M. Dostoevskii; Crime and Punishment

DYNE, MICHAEL
Moon-Spinners. Mary Stewart

D'YVRE, LOUIS
Mystery of the Villa Rose. A. E. W. Mason; At the Villa Rose

EASTHAM, RICHARD
Six Men. E. Radford

EASTWOOD, JAMES
Desperate Man. P. Somers; Beginner's Luck
Fourth Square. E. Wallace; Four Square Jane
Man Who Was Nobody. E. Wallace

EBELING, FRAN LEWIS
Ladies Club. Betty Black; Sisterhood

EBERHART, MIGNON G.
Murder by an Aristocrat. M. G. Eberhart

ECHTERMEIER, T.
His Official Wife. R. H. Savage; My Official Wife

EDGAR, MARRIOTT
Bones. E. Wallace
Ghost Train. A. Ridley

EDMUNDS, ROBERT
Educated Evans. E. Wallace

EDWARDS, BLAKE
Darling Lili. H. Clement
Notorious Landlady. I. Shulman
Pink Panther. M. H. Albert
Pink Panther Strikes Again. F. Waldman
Return of the Pink Panther. F. Waldman
Shot in the Dark. H. Kurnitz
Tamarind Seed. E. Anthony

EDWARDS, EDGAR
Convicted. W. Irish; Six Nights of Mystery

EDWARDS, PAUL
High Ballin'. Richard Robinson

EDWIN, WALTER
Master Mummer. E. P. Oppenheim

EGAN, TERENCE
Shadow. D. Stuart

EGER, J. C.
Rope for a Killing. P. McGerr; Follow, As the Night

EGLEE, CHARLES
Rats. J. Herbert

EHRLICH, MAX
Reincarnation of Peter Proud. M. Ehrlich

EICHELBAUM, SAMUEL
El Pediente. W. Irish; Dead Man Blues

EIS, EGON
Der Zinker. E. Wallace; Squeaker

EIS, OTTO
Der Zinker. E. Wallace; Squeaker

EISINGER, JO
Big Boodle. R. Sylvester
House of the Seven Hawks. V. Canning; House of the Seven Flies
Jigsaw Man. Dorothea Bennett
Night and the City. G. Kersh
Scorpio Letters. V. Canning
Spider. F. Oursler

EJRE, INGEMAR
Assignment. P. Wahloo

ELDER, JOHN
Curse of the Werewolf. G. Endore; Werewolf of Paris
Phantom of the Opera. G. Leroux

ELDRIDGE, JOHN
Out of the Clouds. J. Fores; Springboard

ELIA, FOULI
Arm at the Left. C. Williams; Aground

ELKINS, MICHAEL
Dog Eat Dog. R. Bloomfield (headnote)

ELLES, FRED
Mrs. Pym of Scotland Yard. N. Morland (headnote)

ELLIN, STANLEY
Big Night. S. Ellin; Dreadful Summit

ELLIOTT, F. P.
Pals First. L. W. Dodd

ELLIOTT, GERALD
Blondes for Danger. E. Price; Red for Danger
Frog. E. Wallace; Fellowship of the Frog
Return of the Frog. E. Wallace; India-Rubber Men

ELLIOTT, WILLIAM J.
Bleak House. C. Dickens
Case of Identity. A. C. Doyle; Adventures of Sherlock Holmes
Channings. H. Wood
Copper Beeches. A. C. Doyle; Adventures of Sherlock Holmes
Devil's Foot. A. C. Doyle; His Last Bow
Dying Detective. A. C. Doyle; His Last Bow
Empty House. A. C. Doyle; Return of Sherlock Holmes
Hound of the Baskervilles. A. C. Doyle
Lost Leader. E. P. Oppenheim
Man with the Twisted Lip. A. C. Doyle; Adventures of Sherlock Holmes
Noble Bachelor. A. C. Doyle; Adventures of Sherlock Holmes
Red-Headed League. A. C. Doyle; Adventures of Sherlock Holmes
Resident Patient. A. C. Doyle; Memoirs of Sherlock Holmes
Scandal in Bohemia. A. C. Doyle; Adventures of Sherlock Holmes
Solitary Cyclist. A. C. Doyle; Return of Sherlock Holmes
Tiger of San Pedro. A. C. Doyle; His Last Bow
Yellow Face. A. C. Doyle; Memoirs of Sherlock Holmes

ELLIS, ANDERSEN
Mortal Storm. P. Bottome

ELLIS, ROBERT
Man Who Wouldn't Talk. H. Hall; Valiant

ELMAN, IRVING
Accomplice. F. Gruber; Simon Lash, Private Detective
Challenge. H. C. McNeile
Thirteen Lead Soldiers. H. C. McNeile; Sapper: The Best Short Stories

ELMES, GUY
Across the Bridge. G. Greene; Nineteen Stories
Captive City. J. Appleby
Flanagan Boy. M. Catto

ELVEY, MAURICE
Last Man to Hang. G. Bullett; Jury
Maria Marten. Anonymous
Sign of the Four. A. C. Doyle

EMMETT, E. V. H.
Non-Stop New York. K. Attiwill; Sky Steward
Sabotage. J. Conrad; Secret Agent
Ware Case. G. Pleydell

ENDERS, ROBERT
Maids. J. Genet

ENDFIELD, CYRIL
Sleep My Love. L. Q. Ross

ENDORE, GUY
Devil-Doll. A. Merritt; Burn, Witch, Burn!
Hands of Orlac. M. Renard
He Ran All the Way. S. Ross
League of Frightened Men. R. Stout
Mark of the Vampire. M. Coolridge-Rask; London After Midnight
Vicious Circle. H. Herald; Burning Bush

ENGEL, ERICH
Brothers Karamazov. F. M. Dostoevskii

ENGEL, SAMUEL G.
Blue, White and Perfect. Borden Chase; Diamonds of Death
Charlie Chan in Rio. E. D. Biggers; Black Camel

ENGHOLM, HARRY
East Lynne. H. Wood
London by Night. C. Selby
Study in Scarlet. A. C. Doyle
True Story of the Lyons Mail. E. Moreau; Courier of Lyons
Valley of Fear. A. C. Doyle

ENGLAND, PAUL
Trial of Madame X. J. W. MacConaughy; Madame X

ENGLUND, KEN
Slightly Honorable. F. G. Presnell; Send Another Coffin

ENRICO, ROBERT
Heads or Tails. A. Harris; Baroni

ENRIGHT, DON
Hit and Run. L. Fletcher; Eighty Dollars to Stamford

EPPS, JACK, JR.
Dick Tracy. M. A. Collins

EPSTEIN, JULIUS J.
Arsenic and Old Lace. J. Kesselring
Casablanca. J. J. Epstein
Return from the Ashes. H. Monteilhet

EPSTEIN, PHILIP G.
Arsenic and Old Lace. J. Kesselring
Casablanca. J. J. Epstein

ESSEX, HARRY
I, the Jury. M. Spillane

ESSOE, GABE
Devil's Rain. M. Willis

ESTABROOK, HOWARD
Double Cross Roads. W. Lipman; Yonder Grow the Daisies
Forgotten Faces. R. W. Child; Velvet Black
Masquerader. K. C. Thurston
Slightly Scarlet. P. Heath

ESTRIDGE, ROBIN
Boy Cried Murder. W. Irish; Dead Man Blues
Campbell's Kingdom. H. Innes
Escape from Zahrein. M. Barrett; Appointment in Zahrein
Eye of the Devil. P. Loraine; Day of the Arrow
Permission to Kill. P. Loraine; W.I.L. One to Curtis

ESZTERHAS, JOE
Betrayed. L. Fleischer

ETTINGER, EDWARD
Man Who Wouldn't Talk. H. Hall; Valiant

ETTLINGER, DON
Guilty Bystander. Wade Miller

EVANS, DAVID
Late Edwina Black. W. Dinner
Midnight Episode. G. Simenon; Monsieur la Souris
Murder in the Family. J. Ronald
Snowbound. H. Innes; Lonely Skier
Strange Intruder. H. Fowler; Shades Will Not Vanish
Third Visitor. G. Anstruther
Three Weird Sisters. C. Armstrong; Case of the Weird Sisters

Screenwriters Index

EVERETT, PETER
  Negatives. P. Everett
EXTON, CLIVE
  Awakening. B. Stoker; Jewel of the Seven Stars
  Entertaining Mr. Sloane. J. Orton
  Night Must Fall. E. Williams
  Place to Go. M. Fisher; Bethnel Green
  Running Scared. G. McDonald
EYRE, DAVID
  Wolfen. W. Streiber
FABBRI, DIEGO
  Mysteries of Paris. E. Sue
FABIAN, MAXIMILIAN
  Thirteenth Hour. S. Horler
FABRE, DOMINIQUE
  Meurtre en 45 Tours. P. Boileau; Heart to Heart
FABRE, MAURICE
  On a Nice Summer Day. J. H. Chase; One Bright Summer Morning
FADDA, CARL
  Count Dracula. B. Stoker; Dracula
FAENZA, ROBERT
  Order of Death. H. Fleetwood
FAIRBANKS, DOUGLAS
  Arizona. A. Thomas
FAIRCHILD, WILLIAM
  Embassy. S. Coulter
  Front Page Story. R. Gaines; Final Night
  Long Dark Hall. E. Lustgarten; Case to Answer
  Net. J. Pudney
FAIRFAX, MARION
  Love Insurance. E. D. Biggers
  Mr. Grex of Monte Carlo. E. P. Oppenheim
  Mystery Girl. G. B. McCutcheon; Green Fancy
  River's End. J. O. Curwood
  Sherlock Holmes. W. Gillette
  Vicky Van. C. Wells
FAIRLIE, GERARD
  Ace of Spades. J. C. Fraser
  Calling Bulldog Drummond. G. Fairlie
  Chick. E. Wallace
  Conspirator. H. Slater
  Lad. E. Wallace (headnote)
  Lonely Road. N. Shute
FALCONER, ALUN
  Informers. D. Warner; Death of a Snout
  Unstoppable Man. M. Gilbert; Amateur in Violence
FANCHER, HAMPTON
  Blade Runner. P. K. Dick; Do Androids Dream of Electric Sheep?
  Mighty Quinn. A. H. Z. Carr; Finding Maubee
FARAGOH, FRANCIS EDWARD
  Frankenstein. M. Shelley
  Little Caesar. W. R. Burnett
  Under Cover Man. J. Wilstach
FARJEON, HERBERT
  Ex-Flame. H. Wood; East Lynne
FARJEON, J. JEFFERSON
  Phantom Light. E. Price; Haunted Light
  Rasp. P. MacDonald
  Rynox. P. MacDonald
FARNHAM, JOE
  Bella Donne. R. Hichens
FARNUM, DOROTHY
  Forbidden Territory. D. Wheatley
  His Wife's Husband. A. K. Green; Mayor's Wife
  How Women Love. I. L. Forrester; Dangerous Inheritance
  Jim the Penman. C. L. Young
  Modern Marriage. D. Vane; Lady Varley
  Off the Highway. T. Gallon; Tatterley
  Pagan. J. Russell; In Dark Places
  Secrets of Paris. E. Sue; Mysteries of Paris

FARNUM, GEORGE
  How Women Love. I. L. Forrester; Dangerous Inheritance
FARRELL, HENRY
  What's the Matter with Helen? R. Deming
FARRIS, JOHN
  Fury. J. Farris
FARROW, JOHN
  Shadow of the Law. J. Moroso; Quarry
FASSBINDER, RAINER WERNER
  Martha. C. Woolrich; Angels of Darkness
FAULKNER, WILLIAM
  Big Sleep. R. Chandler
  To Have and Have Not. E. Hemingway
FAY, WILLIAM
  Kid Galahad. Francis Wallace
FAYE, RANDALL
  Maria Marten. Anonymous
FEIFFER, JULES
  Little Murders. J. Feiffer
FEIST, FELIX
  Devil Thumbs a Ride. R. C. Du Soe
  Donovan's Brain. C. Siodmak
FELDMAN, DENNIS
  Golden Child. G. C. Chesbro
FELIX, J. P.
  Edge of Sanity. R. L. Stevenson; Strange Case of Dr. Jekyll and Mr. Hyde
FELLOWS, ROBERT
  Girl Hunters. M. Spillane
FENADY, ANDREW J.
  Man with Bogart's Face. A. J. Fenady
FENNELL, ALBERT
  Park Plaza 605. B. Gray; Dare-Devil Conquest
FENTON, FRANK
  Falcon Takes Over. R. Chandler; Farewell, My Lovely
  Highways by Night. C. B. Kelland; Silver Spoon
  Man with a Cloak. J. D. Carr; Third Bullet
  Saint in London. L. Charteris; Holy Terror
FENTY, PHILIP
  Super Fly. P. Fenty
FERGUSON, LARRY
  Beverly Hills Cop II. R. Tine
  Hunt for Red October. T. Clancy
  Presidio. Mike Cogan
FERRINI, FRANCO
  Once Upon a Time in America. H. Grey; Hoods
FERRIS, WALTER
  Four Men and a Prayer. D. Garth
FETTY, DARRELL
  Freeway. D. Barkley
FIELD, LEONARD
  Unknown Blonde. T. D. Irwin; Collusion
FIELD, SALISBURY
  Ladies of the Jury. F. Ballard
  Witching Hour. A. Thomas
FIELDS, JOSEPH
  Night in Casablanca. D. Ames
FIELDS, LEONARD
  Manhattan Love Song. C. Woolrich
FIGUROVSKI, NIKOLAI
  Crime and Punishment. F. M. Dostoevskii
FINBERG, HAL
  In Like Flint. B. Street
  Our Man Flint. J. Pearl
  Who Killed Aunt Maggie? Medora Field
FINCH, SCOTT
  Whispering Death. D. Carney

FINE, HARRY
  Vampire Lovers. J. S. LeFanu; In a Glass Darkly
FINE, MORTON
  Fool Killer. H. Eustis
  Next Man. M. Z. Lewin
FINK, HARRY JULIAN
  Dirty Harry. P. Rock
FINK, R. M.
  Dirty Harry. P. Rock
FINKLEHOFF, FRED
  Mr. Ace. H. Christy
FINOCHI, AUGUSTO
  Count Dracula. B. Stoker; Dracula
FISHER, GEORGE
  Delavine Affair. R. Chapman; Winter Wears a Shroud
FISHER, ROBERT
  Cancel My Reservation. L. L'Amour; Broken Gun
FISHER, STEVE
  Dead Reckoning. Alex Morrison
  I Wouldn't Be in Your Shoes. W. Irish
  Johnny Angel. C. G. Booth; Mr. Angel Comes Aboard
FISHER, TERENCE
  Mantrap. S. Rattray; Queen in Danger
FISKIN, JEFFREY ALAN
  Cutter and Bone. N. Thornburg
  Pursuit of D. B. Cooper. J. D. Reed; Free Fall
FITTS, MARGARET
  Talk About a Stranger. C. Armstrong; Albatross
FITZGERALD, EDITH
  Within the Law. B. Veiller
FITZGERALD, F. SCOTT
  Raffles. E. W. Hornung; Amateur Cracksman
FITZSIMMONS, CORTLAND
  Death of a Champion. F. Gruber; Brass Knuckles
  Mandarin Mystery. E. Queen; Chinese Orange Mystery
FLAIANO, ENNIO
  Tenth Victim. R. Sheckley
FLEETWOOD, HUGH
  Order of Death. H. Fleetwood
FLEMING, BRANDON
  Dangerous Afternoon. G. Anstruther
  Eleventh Commandment. B. Fleming; Pillory
FLETCHER, LUCILLE
  Sorry Wrong Number. L. Fletcher
FLICKER, THEODORE J.
  Three in a Cellar. Angus Hall; Late Boy Wonder
FLIPPEN, RUTH BROOKS
  Sail a Crooked Ship. N. Benchley
FLOOD, JAMES
  Lonely Road. N. Shute
FLOREY, ROBERT
  Frankenstein. M. W. Shelley
  Study in Scarlet. A. C. Doyle
FLOURNOY, RICHARD
  Dangerous Blondes. K. Roos; If the Shroud Fits
  Night to Remember. K. Roos; Frightened Stiff
FLOYD, CALVIN
  Victor Frankenstein. M. Shelley; Frankenstein
FLOYD, YVONNE
  Victor Frankenstein. M. Shelley; Frankenstein
FLYNN, JOHN
  Outfit. R. Stark
FODOR, LADISLAS
  In the Grip of the Sinister One. E. Wallace (headnote)

FOLEY, JAMES
After Dark, My Sweet. Jim Thompson

FONTINI, CLETO
Invincible Six. M. Barrett; Heroes of Yuca

FONVIELLE, LLOYD
Bride. M. Shelley; Frankenstein

FOOTE, BRADBURY
Homicide for Three. P. Quentin; Puzzle for Puppets

FOOTE, HORTON
Baby, the Rain Must Fall. H. Foote; Traveling Lady
Storm Fear. C. Seeley
To Kill a Mockingbird. H. Lee
Tomorrow. W. Faulkner; Knight's Gambit

FOOTNER, HULBERT
Sealed Valley. H. Footner

FORBES, BRYAN
Angry Silence. John Burke
Danger Within. M. Gilbert; Death in Captivity
Deadfall. D. Cory
High Bright Sun. I. S. Black
Hopscotch. B. Garfield
House of Secrets. S. Noel
League of Gentlemen. J. Boland
Naked Face. S. Sheldon
Seance on a Wet Afternoon. M. McShane

FORD, DEREK
Study in Terror. E. Queen

FORD, DONALD
Study in Terror. E. Queen

FORD, HUGH
Bella Donna. R. Hichens
Jim the Penman. C. L. Young
Seven Keys to Baldpate. E. D. Biggers

FORD, JESSE HILL
Liberation of L. B. Jones. J. H. Ford; Liberation of Lord Byron Jones

FOREMAN, CARL
Force 10 from Navarone. A. MacLean
Guns of Navarone. A. MacLean
Sleeping Tiger. M. Moisewitsch

FOREST, JOSEPH
Caravan to Vaccares. A. MacLean

FORLANI, REMO
Choice of Assassins. W. P. McGivern

FORSYTH, FREDERICK
Fourth Protocol. F. Forsyth

FORT, GARRETT
Before Dawn. E. Wallace; Sergeant Sir Peter
Devil-Doll. A. Merritt; Burn, Witch, Burn!
Dracula. B. Stoker
Dracula's Daughter. B. Stoker; Dracula's Guest
Frankenstein. M. Shelley
Jealousy. E. Walter
Ladies in Retirement. E. Percy
Letter. W. S. Maugham
Man in Half Moon Street. B. Lyndon
Outside the Law. T. Browning
Return of Sherlock Holmes. A. C. Doyle; His Last Bow
Roadhouse Nights. D. Hammett; Red Harvest
70,000 Witnesses. C. Fitzsimmons
Street of Chance. C. Woolrich; Black Curtain
Under Cover Man. J. Wilstach

FOSS, KENELM
Arsene Lupin. E. Jepson
Double Life of Mr. Alfred Burton. E. P. Oppenheim
House of Peril. M. B. Lowndes; Chink in the Armour
Shulamite. A. Askew
Top Dog. F. Hume
When It Was Dark. G. Thorne
Whosoever Shall Offend. F. M. Crawford

FOSTER, LEWIS R.
Jamaica Run. M. Murray; Neat Little Corpse
Love Letters of a Star. Rufus King; Case of the Constant God
Lucky Stiff. C. Rice
Tom Sawyer, Detective. M. Twain

FOSTER, NORMAN
Thank You, Mr. Moto. J. P. Marquand
Think Fast, Mr. Moto. J. P. Marquand

FOSTER, ROBERT
Dead Bang. E. Naha

FOUCARD, PIERRE
Stew in the Caribbean. A. Conroy; Looters

FOUCAUD, PIERRE
Fantomas. P. Souvestre
Heart Trump for OSS 117 in Tokyo. J. Bruce; Hot Line
OSS 117—Mission for a Killer. J. Bruce; Live Wire

FOUCAULT, PIERRE
Mysteries of Paris. E. Sue

FOURASTIE, PHILIPPE
Choice of Assassins. W. P. McGivern

FOWELL, FRANK
In Full Cry. R. Marsh
In the Night. J. Sutherland
Penniless Millionaire. D. C. Murray

FOWLER, GENE
Love Under Fire. W. Hackett; Fugitives
Nancy Steele Is Missing. C. F. Coe; Ransom
Roadhouse Murder. M. Level (headnote)

FOWLER, JOHN
Hell Is Empty. J. F. Straker

FOX, FINIS
Bride. S. Olivier
My Lady's Latchkey. C. N. Williamson; Second Latchkey
Revenge. J. Warren
Way of the Strong. R. Cullum

FOX, PAUL HERVEY
Dusty Ermine. N. Grant

FOX, STEPHEN
All the World to Nothing. W. Martyn

FOXWELL, IVAN
Guilt Is My Shadow. P. Curtis; You're Best Alone
Touch of Larceny. A. Garve; Megstone Plot

FRAENKEL, HEINRICH
Juggernaut. A. Campbell

FRAKES, RANDALL
Diplomatic Immunity. Theodore Taylor; Stalker

FRANCIS, ALLEN
Moorland Tragedy. B. Orczy; Unravelled Knots

FRANCIS, ANNE
Snowball. J. Lake

FRANCKE, CAROLINE
Wiser Sex. C. Fitch; Woman in the Case

FRANCKE, PETER
Defector. P. Thomas; Spy

FRANCO, JESUS
Count Dracula. B. Stoker; Dracula

FRANK, CHARLES
Late Edwina Black. W. Dinner

FRANK, CHRISTOPHER
Attention, the Kids Are Watching. P. L. Dixon; Children Are Watching
Deep Water. P. Highsmith
Malone. W. Wingate; Shotgun

FRANK, HARRIET, JR.
Carey Treatment. J. Hudson; Case of Need
House of Cards. S. Ellin
Spikes Gang. G. Tippette; Bank Robber

FRANK, LEONHARD
Brothers Karamazov. F. M. Dostoevskii

FRANKEN, ROSS
Elinor Norton. M. R. Rinehart; State vs. Elinor Norton

FRANKENHEIMER, JOHN
Manchurian Candidate. R. Condon

FRANKLIN, GEORGE
Incubus. Ray Russell

FRANKLIN, HOWARD
Name of the Rose. U. Eco
Quick Change. J. Cronley

FRASER, COLIN
Switch. P. Ridgeway

FRASER, GEORGE MACDONALD
Force 10 from Navarone. A. MacLean
Octopussy. I. Fleming

FREDERICKS, ARNOLD
One Million Dollars. A. Fredericks; One Million Francs

FREED, BILL
Watchers. D. R. Koontz

FREEDMAN, FRED
S*P*Y*S. T. R. Joyce

FREEMAN, DENIS
Across the Bridge. G. Greene; Nineteen Stories

FREEMAN, EVERETT
Glass Bottom Boat. B. Street
Larceny, Inc. L. Perelman; Night Before Christmas

FREEMAN, GILLIAN
That Cold Day in the Park. R. Miles

FRENCH, HAROLD
Jump for Glory. G. McDonell
Man Who Watched the Trains Go By. G. Simenon

FRESHMAN, WILLIAM
Poison Pen. R. Llewellyn
Terror. E. Wallace

FRIEDKIN, DAVID
Fool Killer. H. Eustis

FRIEDKIN, WILLIAM
Cruising. G. Walker
Rampage. W. P. Wood
To Live and Die in L.A. G. Petievich

FRIEDMAN, KEN
Johnny Handsome. J. Godey; Three Worlds of Johnny Handsome

FRIEDMAN, PHILIP
Rage. P. Friedman

FRINGS, KETTI
Accused. J. Truesdell; Be Still, My Love

FROESCHEL, GEORGE
Mortal Storm. P. Bottome
Never Let Me Go. R. Bax; Came the Dawn
Scaramouche. R. Sabatini

FROST, MARK
Believers. N. Conde; Religion

FUCHS, DANIEL
Criss-Cross. D. Tracy
Gangster. D. Fuchs; Low Company
Hollow Triumph. M. Forbes
Interlude. J. M. Cain; Serenade

FUEST, ROBERT
Dr. Phibes Rises Again. W. Goldstein

FULLER, CHARLES
Soldier's Story. C. Fuller; Soldier's Play

FULLER, SAMUEL
Dead Pigeon on Beethoven Street. S. Fuller
Naked Kiss. S. Fuller
Shark. V. Canning; His Bones Are Coral
Shock Corridor. M. Avallone

FULTON, MAUDE
　Captain Applejack. W. Hackett
　Maltese Falcon. D. Hammett
FUNABASHI, KAZURO
　Yoru No Wana. C. Woolrich; Black Angel
FURTHMAN, CHARLES
　Broadway. P. Dunning
FURTHMAN, JULES
　Big Sleep. R. Chandler
　Calvert's Valley. M. P. Montagu; In Calvert's Valley
　Colorado Jim. G. Goodchild
　Moss Rose. J. Shearing
　Nightmare Alley. W. L. Gresham
　Shanghai Gesture. John Colton
　To Have and Have Not. E. Hemingway
　Yellow Ticket. V. Morton
GABRIELSON, FRANK
　It Shouldn't Happen to a Dog. E. Lanham
GADDIS, MATTHEW
　Suicide Club. R. L. Stevenson
GAFFNEY, MARJORIE
　Mind of Mr. J. G. Reeder. E. Wallace
　Rat. P. Bottome
GAGE, BETH
　Fleshburn. J. Ives; Fear in a Handful of Dust
GAGE, GEORGE
　Fleshburn. J. Ives; Fear in a Handful of Dust
GAINSBOURG, SERGE
　Equator. G. Simenon; Tropic Moon
GALEEN, HENRIK
　Nosferatu. B. Stoker; Dracula
GALLOWAY, LINDSAY
　Double. E. Wallace
　Flat 2. E. Wallace
　Two Living and One Dead. S. Christiansen
GALLU, SAMUEL
　Man Outside. G. Stackelberg; Double Agent
GALSWORTHY, JOHN
　Escape. J. Galsworthy
GALTON, RAY
　Loot. J. Orton
　Spy with a Cold Nose. R. Galton
GAMET, KENNETH
　Blonde Ice. W. Chambers; Once Too Often
　Case of the Stuttering Bishop. E. S. Gardner
　Granny Get Your Gun. E. S. Gardner; Case of the Dangerous Dowager
GANDERS, FELIX
　Mysteries of Paris. E. Sue
GANGELIN, PAUL
　Black Mask. B. Graeme; Blackshirt
　Nursemaid Who Disappeared. P. MacDonald
　Too Dangerous to Live. D. Hume
GANN, ERNEST K.
　Raging Tide. E. K. Gann; Fiddler's Green
GANZ, LOWELL
　Spies Like Us. G. McGill
GARDINER, BECKY
　Square Crooks. J. P. Judge
　Stingaree. E. W. Hornung
　Trial of Mary Dugan. B. Veiller
GARDNER, APRIL
　Chick. E. Wallace
GARDNER, PAUL
　Ten Days' Wonder. E. Queen
GARFIELD, BRIAN
　Hopscotch. B. Garfield
GARLAND, ROBERT
　No Way Out. K. Fearing; Big Clock

GARNETT, TAY
　Bad Company. J. Lait; Put on the Spot
　Delta Factor. M. Spillane
GARRETT, OLIVER H. P.
　Dead Reckoning. Alex Morrison
　Forgotten Faces. R. W. Child; Velvet Black
　Night Nurse. D. Macy
　One-Way Ticket. Ethel Turner
　Story of Temple Drake. W. Faulkner; Sanctuary
　Three Faces East. A. P. Kelly
GARRISON, J.
　Crooked Road. M. West; Big Story
GARSON, HENRY
　Reckless Moment. E. S. Holding; Blank Wall
GARWOOD, M. F.
　Hordern Mystery. E. Finn
GATES, HARVEY
　Breathless Moment. M. Bryant; Redemption of Richard
　In the Next Room. B. E. Stevenson; Mystery of the Boule Cabinet
　Lord John in New York. C. N. Williamson
　Terror. E. Wallace
GATES, TUDOR
　My Lover, My Son. E. Grierson; Reputation for a Song
　Vampire Lovers. J. S. Le Fanu; In a Glass Darkly
GAUNTHIER, GENE
　After Dark. D. Boucicault
　Colleen Bawn. D. Boucicault
　Octoroon. D. Boucicault
GAVIN, AGNES
　Keane of Kalgoorlie. Arthur Wright
GAVRAS, COSTA
　Sleeping Car Murders. S. Japrisot; 10:30 from Marseilles
GAY, JOHN
　Fifth of November. M. Franklin
　Happy Thieves. R. Condon; Oldest Confession
　No Way to Treat a Lady. H. Longbaugh
　Power. F. M. Robinson
GAYE, HOWARD
　Crimson Circle. E. Wallace
GEGAUFF, PAUL
　Broad Daylight. P. Highsmith; Talented Mr. Ripley
　Let the Beast Die. Nicholas Blake; Beast Must Die
　Ten Days' Wonder. E. Queen
　Web of Passion. S. Ellin; Key to Nicholas Street
GEISSENDOERFER, HANS W.
　Edith's Diary. P. Highsmith
　Glass Cell. P. Highsmith
　Jonathan. B. Stoker; Dracula
GELBART, LARRY
　Fine Pair. C. Stratton
　Notorious Landlady. I. Shulman
　Wrong Box. R. L. Stevenson
GELLER, BRUCE
　Sail a Crooked Ship. N. Benchley
GELSEY, ERWIN S.
　Jewel Robbery. L. Fodor
　Muss 'Em Up. J. E. Grant; Green Shadow
GENDRON, PIERRE
　Brooding Eyes. J. Goodwin; Paid in Full
GENTILOMO, GIACOMO
　Brothers Karamazov. F. M. Dostoevskii
GEORGE, GEORGE W.
　Desert Sands. J. Robb; Punitive Action
GEORGE, PETER
　Dr. Strangelove. P. Bryant; Two Hours to Doom
GEORGE, WILLIAM
　Lure of the Swamp. G. Brewer; Hell's Our Destination

GERAGHTY, TOM
　Irish Luck. N. Venner; Imperfect Imposter
　Mary Regan. L. Scott
GEROMINI, JEROME
　Diabolique. P. Boileau; Woman Who Was
　Wages of Fear. G. Arnaud
GESSNER, NICOLAS
　Blonde from Peking. J. H. Chase; You Have Yourself a Deal
GIDDING, NELSON
　Haunting. S. Jackson; Haunting of Hill House
　Inspector. J. De Hartog
　Odds Against Tomorrow. W. P. McGivern
　Skullduggery. Vercors; You Shall Know Them
GIFFORD, CAMILLE
　Dirty Tricks. T. Gifford; Glendower Legacy
GIFFORD, G. W.
　Green Terror. E. Wallace; Green Rust
GIFFORD, THOMAS
　Dirty Tricks. T. Gifford; Glendower Legacy
GILBERT, EDWIN
　Larceny, Inc. L. Perelman; Night Before Christmas
GILBERT, JACK
　White Circle. R. L. Stevenson; New Arabian Nights
GILBERT, LEWIS
　Sea Shall Not Have Them. J. Harris
GILBERT, MICHAEL A.
　Office Party. M. A. Gilbert
GILER, DAVID
　Black Bird. A. Edwards
　Parallax View. L. Singer
GILL, FRANK, JR.
　Who Killed Aunt Maggie? Medora Field
GILLIAT, SIDNEY
　Endless Night. A. Christie
　Fortune Is a Woman. Winston Graham
　Gaunt Stranger. E. Wallace; Ringer
　Ghost Train. A. Ridley
　Girl in the News. R. Vickers
　Green for Danger. C. Brand
　Green Man. F. Launder; Meet a Body
　Inspector Hornleigh on Holiday. L. Grex; Stolen Death
　Jamaica Inn. D. Du Maurier
　Lady Vanishes. E. L. White; Wheel Spins
　London Belongs to Me. N. Collins
　Rome Express. R. Alexander
　Seven Sinners. A. Ridley; Wrecker
　Strange Boarders. E. P. Oppenheim; Strange Boarders of Palace Crescent
　Strangers on a Honeymoon. E. Wallace; Northing Tramp
　They Came by Night. B. Lyndon
　Twelve Good Men. J. Rhode; Murders in Praed Street
GILLING, JOHN
　Dead on Course. Mansell Black
　Flesh and the Fiends. R. L. Stevenson; Body Snatchers
　Guilt Is My Shadow. P. Curtis; You're Best Alone
　Man Inside. M. E. Chaber
　Tiger by the Tail. J. Mair; Never Come Back
GILLING, NELSON
　I Want to Live! T. Rawson
GILTINAN, DONAL
　We Shall See. E. Wallace
GIOVANNI, JOSE
　Last Known Address. J. Harrington
　One Way Ticket. H. E. Helseth; Chair for Martin Rome
　Our Man in Marrakech. R. P. Jones; Heisters

G

GIRARD, BERNARD
  Dead Heat on a Merry-Go-Round. E. L. Heyman
  Mad Room. E. Percy; Ladies in Retirement
GIROD, FRANCIS
  Descent into Hell. D. Goodis; Wounded and the Slain
GITTENS, WYNDHAM
  Greater Than a Crown. V. Bridges; Lady from Long Acre
GLASMON, KUBEC
  Glass Key. D. Hammett
  Public Enemy. K. Glasmon
GLAVEY, JOHN J.
  High Speed. C. H. Stagg
GLAZER, BENJAMIN
  Beggars of Life. J. Tully
  Diplomacy. V. Sardou; Diplomates
GLEASON, MICHIE
  Summer Heat. L. Shivers; Here to Get My Baby Out of Jail
GLENVILLE, PETER
  Term of Trial. J. Barlow
GLORE, CHARLES
  Moonshine Mountain. C. Glore
GLUECKMAN, ALAN JAY
  Butcher, Baker, Nightmare Maker. R. Natale
GODARD, ALAIN
  Name of the Rose. U. Eco
GODARD, JEAN-LUC
  Band of Outsiders. D. Hitchens; Fool's Gold
  Crazy Pete. L. White; Obsession
  Grandeur and Decadence of a Small-Time Filmmaker. J. H. Chase (headnote)
  Made in U.S.A. R. Stark; Jugger
GODDARD, CHARLES W.
  Exploits of Elaine. A. B. Reeve
  Romance of Elaine. A. B. Reeve
GOFF, IVAN
  King of the Khyber Rifles. T. Mundy
  Midnight Lace. J. Green; Matilda Shouted Fire
  O. Henry's Full House. O. Henry (headnote)
  Portrait in Black. I. Goff
  Serenade. J. M. Cain
  Shake Hands with the Devil. R. Conner
GOFF, JOHN
  Butterfly. J. M. Cain
  Rigged. Raymond Marshall; Hit and Run
  Time to Die. M. Cleri; Six Graves to Munich
GOLAN, MENAHEM
  Delta Force. J. Norst
GOLD, JACK
  Medusa Touch. P. Van Greenaway
GOLDBECK, WILLIS
  Murder on the Blackboard. S. Palmer
  Penguin Pool Murder. S. Palmer
  Scaramouche. R. Sabatini
GOLDBERG, ANDY
  Extremities. W. Mastrosimone
GOLDBERG, HEINZ
  Man Who Murdered. C. Farrere; Man Who Killed
GOLDBURG, JESSE J.
  Life Without Soul. M. Shelley; Frankenstein
GOLDIN, JOSHUA
  Darkman. Randall Boyle
GOLDLINE, DANIEL
  Darkman. Randall Boyle
GOLDMAN, BO
  End of the Game. F. Duerrenmatt; Judge and His Hangman

GOLDMAN, HAROLD
  Busman's Honeymoon. D. L. Sayers
  Emperor's Candlesticks. B. Orczy
GOLDMAN, WILLIAM
  Heat. W. Goldman
  Magic. W. Goldman
  Marathon Man. W. Goldman
  Masquerade. V. Canning; Castle Minerva
  Memoirs of an Invisible Man. H. F. Saint
  Misery. Stephen King
  Moving Target. J. Macdonald
  Stepford Wives. I. Levin
GOLDSMITH, ISADORE
  Bedelia. V. Caspary
GOLDSMITH, MARTIN
  Detour. M. M. Goldsmith
GOLDSTEIN, WILLIAM
  Abominable Dr. Phibes. W. Goldstein; Dr. Phibes
GOLKOETXEA, GONZALO
  Turn of the Screw. H. James
GOODCHILD, GEORGE
  No Escape. G. Goodchild; No Exit
GOODIS, DAVID
  Burglar. D. Goodis
  Unfaithful. W. S. Maugham; Letter
GOODMAN, DAVID ZELAG
  Eyes of Laura Mars. H. B. Gilmour
  Farewell, My Lovely. R. Chandler
  Stranglers of Bombay. S. James
  Straw Dogs. G. M. Williams; Siege of Trencher's Farm
GOODRICH, FRANCES
  Penthouse. A. S. Roche
  Society Lawyer. A. S. Roche; Penthouse
  Thin Man. D. Hammett
GOODRICH, JOHN F.
  Last Command. C. Houghton
  Love Racket. B. K. Burns; Jury Woman
GOODWINS, FRED
  Chinese Puzzle. M. Bower
GORDON, JAMES B.
  File of the Golden Goose. J. Watson
GORDON, LEO
  Cry-Baby Killer. J. Hitton
GORDON, LEON
  Bishop Misbehaves. F. Jackson
  Hour of Thirteen. M. Porlock; X v. Rex
  Last of Mrs. Cheyney. F. Lonsdale
  Man About Town. D. Clift
  Society Lawyer. A. S. Roche; Penthouse
GORDON, LESLIE HOWARD
  Belonging. O. Wadsley
  Dick Turpin's Ride to York. W. H. Ainsworth; Rookwood
  "Half a Truth." Rita
  Melody of Death. E. Wallace
  Overheard. S. Aumonier
  River of Stars. E. Wallace
GORDON, RUTH
  Double Life. M. W. Wellman
GORDONS
  Down Three Dark Streets. Gordons; Case File: FBI
  Experiment in Terror. Gordons; Operation Terror
  That Darn Cat. Gordons; Undercover Cat
GORE, IVAN PATRICK
  George Barnwell, the London Apprentice. G. Lillo; London Merchant
GOSLAR, JUERGEN
  Whispering Death. D. Carney

GOTFURT, FREDERICK
  Lady Mislaid. K. Horne
  Temptation Harbour. G. Simenon; Newhaven-Dieppe
GOTTLIEB, ALEX
  Mystery of the White Room. J. G. Edwards; Murder in the Surgery
GOULARD, DIDIER
  On a Nice Summer Day. J. H. Chase; One Bright Summer Morning
GOULD, HEYWOOD
  Boys from Brazil. I. Levin
  Fort Apache, the Bronx. H. Gould
GOULD, JOHN
  Who? A. Budrys
GOULDING, EDMUND
  Daughter of Two Worlds. L. Scott
  Sin That Was His. F. Packard
  Tiger Rose. W. Mack
GOW, JAMES
  Murder on a Bridle Path. S. Palmer; Puzzle of the Red Stallion
GRAHAM, MICHAEL
  Aspern. H. James; Aspern Papers
GRAHAM, RONNY
  Finders Keepers. C. Dennis; Next-to-Last Train Ride
GRAHAM, WINSTON
  Night Without Stars. Winston Graham
  Take My Life. Winston Graham
GRANGIER, GILLES
  Blood to the Head. G. Simenon; Young Cardinaud
  Maigret Sees Red. G. Simenon; Maigret and the Gangsters
GRANIER-DEFERRE, PIERRE
  Cat. G. Simenon
  Man with the Silver Eyes. R. Rossner; End of Someone Else's Rainbow
  North Star. G. Simenon; Lodger
  Widow Couderc. G. Simenon; Ticket of Leave
  Widow's Walk. A. Coburn
GRANT, FRANCES E.
  Sword of Fate. H. Herman
GRANT, JAMES EDWARD
  Miracles for Sale. C. Rawson; Death from a Top Hat
GRANT, JOHN
  Abbott and Costello Meet Dr. Jekyll and Mr. Hyde. R. L. Stevenson; Strange Case of Dr. Jekyll and Mr. Hyde
  Abbott and Costello Meet Frankenstein. M. W. Shelley; Frankenstein
GRASSBY, BERTRAM
  Son of the Immortals. L. Tracy
GRAVES, RALPH
  Scandal for Sale. E. Gauvreau; Hot News
GRAY, HUGH
  Kiss the Blood Off My Hands. G. Butler
GRAY, MIKE
  China Syndrome. B. Wohl
GRAY, WILLIAM
  Cross-Country. H. D. Kastle
GRAYSON, CHARLES
  One Night in the Tropics. E. D. Biggers; Love Insurance
GRAYSON, GODFREY
  Meet Simon Cherry. G. Pedrick; Meet the Rev
GREATOREX, WILFRED
  High Commissioner. J. Cleary
GREEN, ALAN
  Long Wait. M. Spillane

GREEN, F. L.
  Odd Man Out. F. L. Green
GREEN, GUY
  Portrait of Alison. F. Durbridge
GREEN, HOWARD J.
  Donovan Affair. O. Davis
  Having Wonderful Crime. C. Rice
  Meet Nero Wolfe. R. Stout; Fer-de-Lance
  Melody Man. H. J. Green
  Star of Midnight. A. S. Roche
GREEN, JANET
  Gypsy and the Gentleman. N. W. Hooke; Darkness I Leave You
  Life for Ruth. W. Drummond
  Sapphire. E. G. Cousins
  Victim. W. Drummond
GREEN, WALON
  Brink's Job. N. Behn; Big Stick-Up at Brink's!
  Robocop 2. E. Naha
  Wages of Fear. G. Arnaud
GREENBERG, DAN
  Private Lessons. D. Greenberg; Philly
GREENBERG, HENRY F.
  Al Capone. J. Roeburt
GREENBERG, STANLEY R.
  Skyjacked. D. Harper; Hijacked
  Soylent Green. H. Harrison; Make Room! Make Room!
GREENE, EVE
  Born to Kill. J. Gunn; Deadlier Than the Male
  Great Impersonation. E. P. Oppenheim
  Night of January 16. A. Rand
  Operator 13. R. W. Chambers; Secret Service Operator 13
GREENE, GRAHAM
  Brighton Rock. G. Greene
  Comedians. G. Greene
  Fallen Idol. G. Greene; Basement Room and other stories
  First and the Last. J. Galsworthy; Five Tales
  Loser Takes All. G. Greene
  Our Man in Havana. G. Greene
  Third Man. G. Greene
GREENE, HAROLD
  Vicki. S. Fisher; I Wake Up Screaming
GREENE, JOE
  Together Brothers. Jim Robinson
GREENE, VICTOR M.
  Flying Fifty-Five. E. Wallace
  Spider. H. Holt; Midnight Mail
GREENHILL, DOROTHY
  Elder Brother. Anthony Gibbs
GREENLEE, SAM
  Spook Who Sat by the Door. S. Greenlee
GREENWALD, MAGGIE
  Kill-Off. J. Thompson
GREENWOOD, EDWARD
  Man Who Knew Too Much. R. Alexander
  Young and Innocent. J. Tey; Shilling for Candles
GREENWOOD, EDWIN
  Lord Camber's Ladies. H. A. Vachell; Case of Lady Camber
  Man of Affairs. N. Grant; Nelson Touch
GREGOR, FREDDY
  Soho Gorilla. E. Wallace; Dark Eyes of London
GREIFER, LEWIS
  Man Who Finally Died. John Burke
GREMM, WOLF
  Kamikaze '89. P. Wahloo; Murder on the Thirty-First Floor
GRENDEL, FREDERIC
  Diabolique. P. Boileau; Woman Who Was

GREVILLE, EDMOND T.
  Hands of Orlac. M. Renard
GREY, CLIFFORD
  For the Love of Mike. H. F. Maltby
  Rome Express. R. Alexander
GREY, JOHN W.
  Carter Case. A. B. Reeve (headnote)
  Forty Naughty Girls. S. Palmer (headnote)
  Mystery Mind. A. B. Reeve
  Speedy. R. Holman
  Worldly Goods. A. Soutar
GRICE, GRIMES
  Possession of Joel Delaney. R. Stewart
GRIFFE, MAURICE
  Mystere a Shanghai. A. Steeman; Night of the 12th–13th
GRIFFIN, FRANK
  Seven Keys to Baldpate. E. D. Biggers
GRIFFITH, D. W.
  Broken Blossoms. T. Burke; Limehouse Nights
  Sacrifice. O. Henry; Four Million
GRIFFITH, EDWARD H.
  Alias the Lone Wolf. L. J. Vance
GRIFFITHS, LEON
  Flesh and the Fiends. R. L. Stevenson; Body Snatchers
  Grissom Gang. J. H. Chase; No Orchids for Miss Blandish
  Squeeze. David Craig; Whose Little Girl Are You?
GRIMBERG, JEAN-CLAUDE
  Too Small, My Friend. J. H. Chase; Way the Cookie Crumbles
GRISOLIA, MICHEL
  Le Grand Frere. S. Ross; Ready for the Tiger
  North Star. G. Simenon; Lodger
GRODIN, CHARLES
  11 Harrowhouse. G. A. Browne
GROOME, MRS. SYDNEY
  Mystery of Mr. Bernard Brown. E. P. Oppenheim
GRUBER, FRANK
  Accomplice. F. Gruber; Simon Lash, Private Detective
  Bulldog Drummond at Bay. H. C. McNeile
  Challenge. H. C. McNeile
  French Key. F. Gruber
  Johnny Angel. C. G. Booth; Mr. Angel Comes Aboard
  Mask of Dimitrios. E. Ambler
  Northern Pursuit. L. T. White; 5,000 Trojan Horses
  Terror by Night. A. C. Doyle (headnote)
  Twenty Plus Two. F. Gruber
GRUSKIN, JERRY
  Slippy McGee. M. C. Oemler
GUENETTE, ROBERT
  Defector. P. Thomas; Spy
GUERNEY, CLAUD
  Green for Danger. C. Brand
GUERRA, TONINO
  Butterfly on the Shoulder. J. Gearon; Velvet Well
  Chronicle of a Death Foretold. G. G. Marquez
  Illustrious Corpses. L. Sciascia; Equal Danger
  Tenth Victim. R. Sheckley
GUEST, VAL
  Another Man's Poison. L. Sands; Intent to Murder
  Assignment K. H. Howard; Department K
  Bones. E. Wallace
  Break in the Circle. P. Loraine
  Dangerous Davies. L. Thomas
  Full Treatment. R. S. Thorn
  Ghost Train. A. Ridley
  Hell Is a City. M. Procter

  Jigsaw. H. Waugh; Sleep Long, My Love
  Paper Orchid. A. La Bern
  Where the Spies Are. J. Leasor; Passport to Oblivion
GUILLEMOT, CLAUDE
  Brute. G. Des Cars
GUNDREY, V. GARETH
  Hound of the Baskervilles. A. C. Doyle
GUNN, GILBERT
  Door with Seven Locks. E. Wallace
GUNN, JAMES
  Lady of Burlesque. G. R. Lee; G-String Murders
  Unfaithful. W. S. Maugham; Letter
GUNZBERG, MILTON
  Devil Commands. W. Sloane; Edge of Running Water
GURNEY, ROBERT
  Edge of Fury. R. M. Coates; Wisteria Cottage
GURR, JILL
  Rigged. Raymond Marshall; Hit and Run
GUSS, JACK
  Lady in Cement. A. Rome
GUTCHEON, BETH
  Without a Trace. B. Gutcheon; Still Missing
HAAS, CHARLES
  Moonrise. T. Strauss
HAAS, WILLY
  Joyless Street. H. Bettauer; Viennese Love
HABIB, RALPH
  Passager Clandestin. G. Simenon; Stowaway
HACHUEL, HERVE
  Last of Philip Banter. J. F. Bardin
HACKETT, ALBERT
  Penthouse. A. S. Roche
  Society Lawyer. A. S. Roche; Penthouse
  Thin Man. D. Hammett
HAGGARD, MARK
  Black Eye. J. Jacks; Murder on the Wild Side
HAI, ZAFAR
  Perfect Murder. H. R. F. Keating
HAILEY, ARTHUR
  Zero Hour! J. Castle; Flight Into Danger
HAINES, RONALD
  Man with the Magnetic Eyes. R. Daniel
HAINES, WILLIAM WISTER
  Racket. B. Cormack
HALAIN, JEAN
  Fantomas. P. Souvestre
  Mysteries of Paris. E. Sue
  OSS 117—Mission for a Killer. J. Bruce; Live Wire
HALES, JONATHAN
  Loophole. R. Pollock
  Mirror Crack'd. A. Christie; Mirror Crack'd from Side to Side
HALL, CONRAD
  Running Target. S. Frazee
HALL, FRANKLYN
  Boomerang. W. H. Osborne
HALL, GEORGE EDWARDES
  Dr. Jekyll and Mr. Hyde. R. L. Stevenson; Strange Case of Dr. Jekyll
  Queen's Evidence. L. Parr; Adam and Eve and Mr. Hyde
  Lone Wolf. L. J. Vance
HALL, JENNI
  My Lover, My Son. E. Grierson; Reputation for a Song
HALL, NORMAN S.
  Drums of Fu Manchu. S. Rohmer
  Slippy McGee. M. C. Oemler

H

HALL, ROBERT
Franchise Affair. J. Tey
You Can't Escape. A. Kennington; She Died Young

HALL, SAM
House of Dark Shadows. Marilyn Ross

HALL, SIDNEY
House of Secrets. S. Horler

HALL, WALTER RICHARD
Woman in Grey. A. M. Williamson

HALL, WILLIS
Man in the Middle. H. Fast; Winston Affair
West 11. L. Del Rivo; Furnished Room

HALLETT, HELEN
Three Live Ghosts. F. S. Isham

HALPERIN, EDWARD
Danger Ahead. L. Y. Erskine; Renfrew's Long Trail
Sky Bandits. L. Y. Erksine; Renfrew Rides the Sky
Yukon Flight. L. Y. Erskine; Renfrew Rides North

HALPERIN, VICTOR
Party Girl. E. Balmer; Dangerous Business

HALSEY, FORREST
New York. B. Chambers
Sweethearts and Wives. W. Hackett; Other Men's Wives

HAMER, ROBERT
Father Brown. G. K. Chesterton; Innocence of Father Brown
It Always Rains on Sunday. A. La Bern
Jolly Bad Fellow. C. E. Vulliamy; Don Among the Dead Men
Kind Hearts and Coronets. R. Horniman; Israel Rank
Long Memory. H. Clewes
Pink String and Sealing Wax. R. Pertwee
Scapegoat. D. Du Maurier

HAMILL, PETE
Badge 373. M. Roote

HAMILTON, GUY
Touch of Larceny. A. Garve; Megstone Plot

HAMILTON, JAMES SHELLEY
Enchanted Hill. P. B. Kyne

HAMM, SAM
Batman. C. S. Gardner

HAMMETT, DASHIELL
Maltese Falcon. D. Hammett

HAMMOND, WILLIAM C.
Flying Eye. J. N. Chance (headnote)

HAMPTON, CHRISTOPHER
Honorary Consul. G. Greene

HANEMANN, H. W.
House of a Thousand Shadows. M. Nicholson

HANKINSON, MICHAEL
Dusty Ermine. N. Grant
Ten Minute Alibi. A. Armstrong

HANNA, MARK
Slaughter. H. Clement

HANNAH, DOROTHY
High Window. R. Chandler

HANSON, CURTIS
Bedroom Window. A. Holden; Witnesses
Silent Partner. A. Bodelsen; Think of a Number

HARAREET, HAYA
Our Mother's House. J. Gloag

HARDINGE, REX
Sexton Blake and the Bearded Doctor. R. Hardinge; Blazing Launch Murder

HARDY, ROBIN
Fantasist. P. McGinley; Goosefoot

HARE, DAVID
Paris by Night. David Hare

HARLOW, JOHN
Candles at Nine. Anthony Gilbert; Mouse Who Wouldn't Play Ball
Echo Murders. J. Sylvester; Terror of Tregarwith
Meet Sexton Blake. A. Parsons; Mystery of the Stolen Despatches

HARMON, DAVID P.
Reprisal. Arthur Gordon

HARPER, BARBARA S.
Account Rendered. P. Barrington
Captain Clegg. R. Thorndyke; Dr. Syn

HARRIS, JAMES B.
Fast-Walking. E. Brawley; Rap

HARRIS, OWEN
Deadly Duo. R. Jessup
Secret of Deep Harbor. Max Miller; I Cover the Waterfront

HARRIS, RICHARD
Attempt to Kill. E. Wallace; Lone House Mystery
I Start Counting. A. E. Lindop
Lady in the Car with Glasses and a Gun. S. Japrisot
Locker 69. E. Wallace (headnote)
Main Chance. E. Wallace (headnote)
Man Detained. E. Wallace; Debt Discharged
On the Run. E. Wallace (headnote)
Orion's Belt. J. Michelet

HARRIS, VERNON
Sea Shall Not Have Them. J. Harris

HARRISON, JOAN
Dark Waters. F. Cockrell
Jamaica Inn. D. Du Maurier
Rebecca. D. Du Maurier
Suspicion. F. Iles; Before the Fact

HART, JAMES V.
Bram Stoker's Dracula. B. Stoker; Dracula

HART, MOSS
Masquerader. K. C. Thurston

HARTFORD, DAVID M.
Golden Snare. J. O. Curwood
Nomads of the North. J. O. Curwood

HARTLEY, GRAHAM
Reunion. K. Leopold; When We Ran

HARTMANN, EDMUND L.
Dangerous Partners. O. W. Bayer; Paper Chase
Last Express. B. Kendrick
Last Warning. J. Latimer; Dead Don't Care
Lemon Drop Kid. D. Runyon; Bloodhounds of Broadway
Scarlet Claw. A. C. Doyle; Hound of the Baskervilles
Sherlock Holmes and the Secret Weapon. A. C. Doyle; Return of Sherlock Holmes

HARTWELL, JOHN
Fan. B. Randall

HARVEY, FRANK
Brothers in Law. H. Cecil
Danger Within. M. Gilbert; Death in Captivity
Long Memory. H. Clewes
On Friday at Eleven. J. H. Chase; World in My Pocket
Thirty-Nine Steps. J. Buchan
Upstairs and Downstairs. R. S. Thorn

HARWOOD, JOHANNA
Doctor No. I. Fleming
From Russia with Love. I. Fleming

HARWOOD, RONALD
Arrivederci, Baby! R. Deming; Careful Man
Eyewitness. M. Hebden

HASSETT, RAY
Green Ice. G. A. Browne

HASTINGS, MICHAEL
Nightcomers. M. Hastings

HATTON, FREDERICK
Curlytop. T. Burke; Whispering Windows
Mad Whirl. R. W. Child; Fresh Waters

HAWKS, J. G.
Eternal Struggle. G. B. Lancaster; Law Bringers

HAY, IAN
Englishman's Home. G. Du Maurier
Frog. E. Wallace; Fellowship of the Frog
Man Behind the Mask. J. Futrelle; Chase of the Golden Plate
Return of the Frog. E. Wallace; India-Rubber Men
Sabotage. J. Conrad; Secret Agent
Secret Agent. W. S. Maugham; Ashenden
Thirty-Nine Steps. J. Buchan

HAYDEN, KATHLEEN
Clue of the New Pin. E. Wallace
Flying Squad. E. Wallace
Man Who Changed His Name. E. Wallace

HAYES, ALFRED
Double Man. H. S. Maxfield; Legacy of a Spy
Island in the Sun. A. Waugh

HAYES, JOHN MICHAEL
But Not for Me. E. Ronns
Chalk Garden. E. Bagnold
Man Who Knew Too Much. R. Alexander
Rear Window. W. Irish; After-Dinner Story
To Catch a Thief. D. Dodge
Trouble with Harry. J. T. Story

HAYES, JOSEPH
Desperate Hours (two versions). J. Hayes

HAYES, RAPHAEL
Reprisal. Arthur Gordon

HAYES, TERRY
Dead Calm. C. Williams

HAYLES, KENNETH
Passport to Treason. M. O'Brine

HAYNES, STANLEY
Man Behind the Mask. J. Futrelle; Chase of the Golden Plate

HAYS, GEOFFREY
Syndicate. Denys Rhodes

HAYWARD, FREDERICK
Crimes at the Dark House. W. Collins; Woman in White
Sweeney Todd, the Demon Barber of Fleet Street. G. D. Pitt

HAYWARD, LILLIE
Amateur Gentleman. J. Farnol
Margin for Error. C. Booth
Miss Pinkerton. M. R. Rinehart
Undying Monster. J. D. Kerruish
White Cockatoo. M. G. Eberhart

HAYWARD, LOUIS M.
Witch-Finder General. R. Bassett

HAYWARD, LYDIA
Confessions. B. Reynolds; Confession Corner
Laywer Quince. W. W. Jacobs; Odd Craft
Missing People. E. Wallace; Mind of Mr. J. G. Reeder
Monkey's Paw. W. W. Jacobs; Lady of the Barge
Ware Case. G. Pleydell

HAZARD, LAWRENCE
Strange Cargo. R. Sale; Not Too Narrow—Not Too Deep

HAZLEWOOD, JEAN
Secret Ways. A. MacLean; Last Frontier

HEALY, GERARD
No Resting Place. I. Niall

HEATH, MICHAEL
Scarecrow. R. H. Morrieson

HEATH, PERCY
Dr. Jekyll and Mr. Hyde. R. L. Stevenson; Strange Case of Dr. Jekyll and Mr. Hyde

Huntress. H. Footner
Only Saps Work. O. Davis; Easy Come, Easy Go
Slightly Scarlet. P. Heath

HECHT, BEN
Actors and Sin. B. Hecht; Actor's Blood
Black Swan. R. Sabatini
Crime Without Passion. B. Hecht; Collected Stories of Ben Hecht
Kiss of Death. E. Lipsky
Ride the Pink Horse. D. B. Hughes
Rope. P. Hamilton
Scarface. A. Trail
Spellbound. F. Beeding; House of Dr. Edwardes
Where the Sidewalk Ends. W. L. Stuart; Night Cry
Whirlpool. G. Endore; Methinks the Lady—

HEDLEY, THOMAS, JR.
Double Negative. K. Millar; Three Roads

HEIFETZ, LOUIS
Defenders of the Law. H. Del Ruth

HEIMS, JO
Play Misty for Me. P. J. Gillette
You'll Like My Mother. N. A. Hintze

HELLER, LUKAS
Blue City. K. Millar
Candidate for Murder. E. Wallace (headnote)
Flight of the Phoenix. E. Trevor
Hot Enough for June. L. Davidson; Night of Wenceslas
Never Back Losers. E. Wallace; Green Ribbon
Sapphire. E. G. Cousins
What Ever Happened to Baby Jane? H. Farrell

HELLMAN, LILLIAN
Chase. H. Foote
Dead End. S. Kingsley

HELLMAN, SAM
Little Miss Marker. D. Runyon; Blue Plate Special

HEMMINGS, DAVID
Running Scared. G. McDonald

HENLEY, JACK
Dangerous Blondes. K. Roos; If the Shroud Fits
Night to Remember. K. Roos; Frightened Stiff

HENRY, BUCK
Day of the Dolphin. R. Merle

HENRY, DAVID LEE
Eight Million Ways to Die. L. Block
Evil That Men Do. R. L. Hill

HENRY, JOAN
Yield to the Night. J. Henry

HENRY, LOUISE
Remember Last Night? A. Hobhouse; Hangover Murders

HERALD, HEINZ
Vicious Circle. H. Herald; Burning Bush

HERBERT, F. HUGH
Case of the Black Cat. E. S. Gardner; Case of the Caretaker's Cat
Dragon Murder Case. S. S. Van Dine
Home Sweet Homicide. C. Rice
Murder on the Roof. E. J. Doherty; Broadway Murders

HERBUVEAUX, JAMES
Mysterious Mr. Wong. H. S. Keeler; Sing Sing Nights

HERCZEG, GEZA
Shanghai Gesture. John Colton

HERKOMER, S. H.
Temptation of Carlton Earle. S. M. During

HERMAN, JEAN
Inquisitor. J. Wainwright; Brainwash

HERNE, JULIE
Breaking Point. M. R. Rinehart

HERSKOVIC, PATRICIA
Body Parts. P. Boileau; Choice Cuts

HERTZ, DAVID
Stranger Than Desire. W. E. Woodward; Evelyn Prentice

HERVEY, HARRY
Wiser Sex. C. Fitch; Woman in the Case

HERVIL, RENEE
Mystery at the Pink Villa. A. E. W. Mason; At the Villa Rose

HEYES, DOUGLAS
Ice Station Zebra. A. MacLean
Kitten with a Whip. Wade Miller

HEYNEMANN, LAURENT
April Is a Deadly Month. Derek Raymond; Devil's Home on Leave

HICKS, JAMES
Morning After. E. Lottman

HIDAKA, MASAYA
Lonely Hearts. E. McBain; Lady, Lady, I Did It!

HIGGINS, COLIN
Foul Play. J. C. Rogers
Silver Streak. J. C. Rogers

HIGGINS, JOHN C.
Diamond. M. Procter; Rich Is the Treasure
File of the Golden Goose. J. Watson
Shield for Murder. W. P. McGivern

HILL, DEBRA
Halloween. C. Richards
Halloween II. J. Martin

HILL, ETHEL
Fog. V. Williams

HILL, GLADYS
Kremlin Letter. N. Behn

HILL, JACK
Coffy. P. W. Fairman

HILL, ROBERT
Dog Eat Dog. R. Bloomfield (headnote)

HILL, ROBERT F.
Cat and the Canary. J. Willard
Last Warning. W. Camp; House of Fear

HILL, SINCLAIR
At the Villa Rose. A. E. W. Mason
Conspirators. E. P. Oppenheim
Expiation. E. P. Oppenheim
Qualified Adventurer. S. Jepson

HILL, WALTER
Blue City. K. Millar
Driver. C. B. Phillips
Drowning Pool. J. R. Macdonald
Getaway. J. Thompson
Hickey and Boggs. P. Rock
Mackintosh Man. D. Bagley; Freedom Trap
Thief Who Came to Dinner. T. L. Smith
Warriors. S. Yurick

HILTON, JAMES
We Are Not Alone. J. Hilton

HILTON, TONY
What a Carve Up! F. King; Ghoul

HINDS, ANTHONY
Captain Clegg. R. Thornyke; Dr. Syn
Dracula, Prince of Darkness. B. Stoker; Dracula

HINES, LEONARD
Ghoul. F. King

HISAITA, EIJIRO
High and Low. E. McBain; King's Ransom

HISCOTT, LESLIE S.
Missing Rembrandt. A. C. Doyle; Return of Sherlock Holmes
Passing of Mr. Quin. A. Christie; Mysterious Mr. Quin
Sherlock Holmes's Fatal Hour. A. C. Doyle; Memoirs of Sherlock Holmes
To What Red Hell. P. Robinson

HITCHCOCK, ALFRED
Blackguard. R. Paton; Autobiography of a Blackguard
Blackmail. C. Bennett
Case of Jonathan Drew. M. B. Lowndes; Lodger
Murder. C. Dane; Enter Sir John
No. 17. J. J. Farjeon
Passionate Adventure. F. Stayton

HIVELY, GEORGE
Black Bag. L. J. Vance

HOBART, DOTY
Find the Woman. A. S. Roche
Under Cover. R. C. Megrue

HODGES, MIKE
Get Carter. T. Lewis; Jack's Return Home
Terminal Man. M. Crichton

HODGSON, J. L.
Under the Red Robe. S. J. Weman

HOERL, ARTHUR
Black Pearl. W. Woodrow
Counsel for the Defense. L. Scott
Devil's Chaplain. G. Bronson-Howard
Drums of Jeopardy. H. MacGrath
Man from Headquarters. G. Bronson-Howard; Black Book
Mystery of the Thirteenth Guest. A. Trail; Thirteenth Guest
Phantom in the House. A. Soutar
Romance of a Million Dollars. E. Dejeans
Sisters of Eve. E. P. Oppenheim; Tempting of Tavernake
Thirteenth Chair. A. Trail
You Can't Beat the Law. H. H. Van Loan
Young Dillinger. S. Stuart

HOFFE, MONKTON
Busman's Honeymoon. D. L. Sayers
Emperor's Candlestick. B. Orczy
Hate Ship. B. Graeme
Last of Mrs. Cheyney. F. Lonsdale
Mystery of Mr. X. M. Porlock; X v. Rex

HOFFENSTEIN, SAMUEL
Dr. Jekyll and Mr. Hyde. R. L. Stevenson; Strange Case of Dr. Jekyll and Mr. Hyde
Flesh and Fantasy. O. Wilde; Lord Arthur Savile's Crime
Laura. V. Caspary
Miracle Man. F. Packard
Phantom of the Opera. G. Leroux

HOFFMAN, HERMAN
Last Escape. M. Walker

HOFFMAN, HUGH
Untamable. G. Burgess; White Cat

HOFFS, TAMAR
Lepke. J. Pearl

HOGAN, MICHAEL
Doctor Syn. R. Thorndyke
Fortunes of Captain Blood. R. Sabatini
Hour Before the Dawn. W. S. Maugham
Mind of Mr. J. G. Reeder. E. Wallace
They Came by Night. B. Lyndon

HOLIERHOEK, KEES
Outsider in Amsterdam. J. van de Wetering

HOLLAND, TOM
Cloak and Dagger. W. Irish; Dead Man Blues

HOLLOWAY, JEAN
Madame X. J. C. MacConaughy

HOLMES, BEN
Saint's Double. L. Charteris (headnote)

HOLMES, BROWN
Avenger. J. Goodwin
Case of the Lucky Legs. E. S. Gardner
Dark Hazard. W. R. Burnett

Florentine Dagger. B. Hecht
Maltese Falcon. D. Hammett
Satan Met a Lady. D. Hammett; Maltese Falcon
"Shed No Tears." D. Martin
While the Patient Slept. M. G. Eberhart

HOLT, ANDREW
Avalanche. K. Boyle

HOLT, SETH
Nowhere to Go. D. MacKenzie

HOME, WILLIAM DOUGLAS
Follow That Horse. H. Mason; Photo Finish
For Them That Trespass. E. Raymond
Sleeping Car to Trieste. R. Alexander; Rome Express

HOMES, GEOFFREY
Build My Gallows High. G. Homes

HONEYCOMBE, GORDON
Neither the Sea Nor the Sand. G. Honeycombe

HOPCRAFT, ARTHUR
Agatha. K. Tynan
Hostage. T. Allbeury; No Place to Hide

HOPKINS, JOHN
Holcroft Covenant. R. Ludlum
Murder by Decree. R. Weverka
Offense. J. Hopkins; This Story of Yours
Thunderball. I. Fleming

HOPMAN, GERALD
Devil's Rain. M. Willis

HORKHEIMER, H. M.
Arsene Lupin. M. Leblanc (headnote)

HORMAN, ARTHUR T.
Conflict. Alex Morrison
Dark Waters. F. Cockrell
Juvenile Jungle. F. Counsel
Suspect. J. Ronald; This Way Out
Young and Wild. Morton Cooper

HORNE, JAMES W.
Stingaree. E. W. Hornung

HORNE, KENNETH
Flying Fifty-Five. E. Wallace
Spider. H. Holt; Midnight Mail

HOROWITZ, ANTHONY
Just Ask for Diamond. A. Horowitz; Falcon's Malteser

HOROWITZ, MARK
Dark Wind. T. Hillerman

HOUGH, E. MORTON
Born to Gamble. E. Wallace; Forty-Eight Short Stories

HOUSE, RON
Bullshot. R. House; Bullshot Crummond

HOUSER, LIONEL
Lone Wolf Returns. L. J. Vance

HOUSTON, JULIAN
Strangers on a Honeymoon. E. Wallace; Northing Tramp

HOUSTON, NORMAN
Game of Death. R. Connell; Variety
Monte Carlo Nights. E. P. Oppenheim; Mr. Billingham, the Marquis and Madelon

HOVEY, CARL
Orient Express. G. Greene; Stamboul Train

HOWARD, CLIFFORD
Other Side of the Door. L. Chamberlain

HOWARD, CY
Every Little Crook and Nanny. E. Hunter

HOWARD, ELDON
Spider's Web. A. Christie

HOWARD, LILLIE
Night Club Scandal. D. N. Rubin; Riddle Me This!

HOWARD, MATTHEW
Groundstar Conspiracy. L. Davies; Alien

HOWARD, SANDY
Vice Squad. W. Rotsler

HOWARD, SIDNEY
Bulldog Drummond. H. C. McNeile
Raffles. E. W. Hornung; Amateur Cracksman

HOWARD, WALTER K.
Trooper O'Neill. G. Goodchild

HOWATT, NINA
Mysterious Mr. Wong. H. S. Keeler; Sing Sing Nights

HOWE, JAY
Speedy. R. Holman

HOWELL, DOROTHY
Alias the Lone Wolf. L. . Vance
Birds of Prey. G. Bronson-Howard
Donovan Affair. O. Davis
Last of the Lone Wolf. L. J. Vance; Lone Wolf
Men in Her Life. W. Fabian
Menace. E. Wallace; Feathered Serpent

HOWELL, MAUDE T.
His Lordship. N. Grant; Nelson Touch

HOWELLS, JACK
Front Page Story. R. Gaines; Final Night

HOYT, HARRY O.
Curse of Drink. C. E. Blaney
Half Million Bribe. W. H. Osborne; Red Mouse
13 Washington Square. L. Scott; No. 13 Washington Square
Wizard. G. Leroux; Balaoo

HUBBARD, LUCIEN
Gamblers. C. Klein
Maltese Falcon. D. Hammett
Outside the Law. T. Browning
Within the Law. B. Veiller

HUDIS, NORMAN
Face in the Night. B. Graeme; Suspense
Passport to Treason. M. O'Brine
Stranger in Town. F. A. Chittenden; Uninvited

HUDSON, VIRGINIA TYLOR
Burglar. A. Thomas; Editha's Burglar

HUEBSCH, EDWARD
Black Eagle. O. Henry; Roads of Destiny

HUET, J. H.
Lay Off Blondes. Carter Brown; Body

HUGGINS, ROY
Fever in the Blood. W. Pearson
I Love Trouble. R. Huggins; Double Take
Pushover. B. Ballinger; Rafferty
Too Late for Tears. R. Huggins

HUGH, R. JOHN
Deadly Encounter. R. Woodley

HUGHES, BRIAN
Nothing But the Night. J. Blackburn

HUGHES, ERIC
Against All Odds. G. Homes; Build My Gallows High
Raise the Titanic! C. Cussler

HUGHES, HARRY
Dead Men Are Dangerous. H. C. Armstrong; Hidden
House of Marney. J. Goodwin
Man at Six. J. Celestin
Rogue in Love. T. Gallon
Shadow of Evil. C. Dawe

HUGHES, KEN
Arrivederci, Baby! R. Deming; Careful Man
Flying Eye. J. N. Chance (headnote)
House Across the Way. K. Hughes; High Wray
Long Haul. M. Mills
Portrait of Alison. F. Durbridge

Wicked As They Come. B. Ballinger; Portrait in Smoke

HUGHES, LLEWELLYN
Temple Tower. H. C. McNeile

HULBERT, JACK
Kate Plus Ten. E. Wallace

HULKE, MALCOLM
Man in the Back Seat. E. Wallace (headnote)

HULL, GEORGE C.
Conflict. C. B. Kelland

HULL, ROGER
Detour. M. Goldsmith

HUME, CYRIL
They Gave Him a Gun. W. J. Cowen

HUME, DAVID
This Man Is Dangerous. D. Hume; They Called Him Death

HUME, EDWARD
Reflection of Fear. S. Forbes; Go to Thy Death Bed
Two Minute Warning. G. La Fountaine

HUME, KENNETH
Hot Ice. A. Melville; Week-End at Thrackley

HUMPHREY, WILLIAM J.
Black Spider. C. Dawe

HUMPHRIES, DAVE
Julia. P. Straub

HUNABELLE, ANDRE
OSS 117—Mission for a Killer. J. Bruce; Live Wire

HUNSICKER, JACKSON
Ten Little Indians. A. Christie; Ten Little Niggers

HUNTER, EVAN
Birds. D. Du Maurier; Apple Tree
Fuzz. E. McBain

HUNTER, JOHN
Carrington, V.C. D. Christie
Cross-Country. H. D. Kastle
Green Pack. E. Wallace
Intruder. R. Maugham; Line on Ginger
Never Take Candy from a Stranger. R. Garis

HUNTER, N. C.
Poison Pen. R. Llewellyn

HUNTER, T. HAYES
Man They Could Not Arrest. E. Wallace (headnote)
Man They Couldn't Arrest. A. J. Small

HUNTER, TOM
Human Factor. S. Quinn

HUNTINGTON, LAURENCE
Deadly Record. N. W. Hooke
Franchise Affair. J. Tey
I Killed the Count. A. Coppel
Question of Suspense. R. Vickers (headnote)
Warn That Man. V. Sylvaine

HURD, GALE ANN
Terminator. S. Hutson

HURDALEK, GEORG
Die Indische Tuch. E. Wallace; Frightened Lady
Town Without Pity. M. Gregor

HURLBUT, WILLIAM
Bride of Frankenstein. M. W. Shelley; Frankenstein

HURST, BRIAN DESMOND
On the Night of the Fire. F. L. Green

HUSSON, ALBERT
Sorcery. P. Boileau; Spells of Evil

HUSTON, JIMMY
Final Exam. G. Meyer

HUSTON, JOHN
  Amazing Dr. Clitterhouse. B. Lyndon
  Asphalt Jungle. W. R. Burnett
  Beat the Devil. J. Helvick
  High Sierra. W. R. Burnett
  Key Largo. M. Anderson
  Killers. E. Hemingway
  Kremlin Letter. N. Behn
  Maltese Falcon. D. Hammett
  Murders in the Rue Morgue. E. A. Poe; Prose Romances of Edgar A. Poe
  Stranger. A. Veiller
  Three Strangers. Alex Morrison
  We Were Strangers. R. Sylvester; Rough Edge

HUXLEY, ALDOUS
  Woman's Vengeance. A. Huxley; Mortal Coils

HYAMS, PETER
  Telefon. W. Wager

HYDE, KENNETH
  Spaniard's Curse. E. Pargeter; Assize of the Dying

HYLAND, DICK IRVING
  I Ring Doorbells. R. Birdwell

HYLAND, FRANCIS
  Thirteenth Chair. A. Trail

HYND, NOEL
  Agency. P. Gottlieb

ICHIKAWA, KON
  Lonely Hearts. E. McBain; Lady, Lady, I Did It!

ILIFF, W. PETER
  Patriot Games. T. Clancy

INCE, RALPH
  Argyle Case. H. Ford

INGLETON, E. MAGNUS
  Dark Mirror. L. J. Vance
  Ivory Snuff Box. A. Fredericks
  Moonstone. W. Collins
  Secret of the Hills. W. Garrett

INGRAM, REX
  Where the Pavement Ends. J. Russell; Red Mark

INNES, HAMMOND
  Campbell's Kingdom. H. Innes

ISAACS, SUSAN
  Compromising Positions. S. Isaacs

ISAMENDI, ANTONIO ISASI
  Adventures of Scaramouche. R. Sabatini; Scaramouche

ISHERWOOD, CHRISTOPHER
  Frankenstein: The True Story. M. W. Shelley; Frankenstein
  Rage in Heaven. J. Hilton

IVERS, JULIA CRAWFORD
  Witching Hour. A. Thomas

JACKSON, FELIX
  Broadway. P. Dunning

JACKSON, FRED
  Exiles. R. H. Davis

JACKSON, H. LANDERS
  Mind Over Motor. M. R. Rinehart; Book of Tish

JACKSON, JOSEPH
  Second Floor Mystery. E. D. Biggers; Agony Column
  Terror. E. Wallace

JACOBS, ALEXANDER
  French Connection II. R. Moore
  Point Blank. R. Stark; Hunter
  Seven-Ups. R. Posner
  Sitting Target. L. Henderson

JACOBSON, LEIGH
  Cheerful Fraud. K. R. G. Browne; Following Ann

JACOBY, GEORGE
  Vendetta. A. C. Gunter; Mr. Barnes of New York

JACOBY, HANS
  It Happens in Broad Daylight. F. Duerrenmatt; Pledge

JACOBY, MICHEL
  Mystery of Marie Roget. E. A. Poe; Tales
  Two Against the World. L. Weitzenkorn; Five Star Final
  Undying Monster. J. D. Kerruish

JACQUOT, BENOIT
  With All Hands. J. Gunn; Deadlier Than the Male

JAFFE, ROBERT
  Nightflyers. G. R. R. Martin

JAMES, BENEDICT
  Case of Lady Camber. H. A. Vachell
  In Full Cry. R. Marsh
  Lyons Mail. E. Moreau; Courier of Lyons
  Other Person. F. Hume

JAMES, DONALD
  Limbo Line. V. Canning

JAMES, EDWARD
  Over My Dead Body. J. D. O'Hanlon; As Good As Murdered

JAMES, RIAN
  Dragon Murder Case. S. S. Van Dine
  Gorilla. R. Spence
  Housekeeper's Daughter. D. H. Clarke
  Lawyer Man. M. Trell
  Whispering City. Horace Brown

JANNUZZI, LINO
  Illustrious Corpses. L. Sciascia; Equal Danger

JANSSON, LARS MAGNAS
  Assignment. P. Wahloo

JAPRISOT, SEBASTIEN
  And Hope to Die. D. Goodis; Black Friday
  One Deadly Summer. S. Japrisot
  Sleeping Car Murders. S. Japrisot; 10:30 from Marseilles
  Trap for Cinderella. S. Japrisot

JARDIN, PASCAL
  Cat. G. Simenon
  Dead Run. R. Sheckley
  Joy House. D. Keene
  Secret. F. Ryck; Undesirable Company
  Train. G. Simenon
  Widow Couderc. G. Simenon; Ticket of Leave

JARRICO, PAUL
  Messenger of Death. Rex Burns; Avenging Angel

JAYSON, JAY
  Caprice. J. Withers

JEANSON, HENRI
  Mister Flow. G. Leroux; Man of a Hundred Masks

JEFFERSON, L. V.
  Yellow Men and Gold. Gouverneur Morris

JENKINS, MICHAEL
  Careful, He Might Hear You. S. L. Elliott

JENNY, MARIE
  Gray Dawn. S. E. White

JEPSON, SELWYN
  Riverside Murder. A. Steeman; Six Dead Men
  Scarab Murder Case. S. S. Van Dine

JERONIMI, JEROME
  Spies. E. Hostovsky; Midnight Patient

JESSUA, ALAIN
  Armageddon. D. Lippincott; Voice of Armageddon

JESSUP, RICHARD
  Young Don't Cry. R. Jessup

JEVNE, JACK
  I Cover the Waterfront. Max Miller

JIMENEZ, NEAL
  Dark Wind. T. Hillerman

JOB, THOMAS
  Escape in the Desert. R. E. Sherwood; Petrified Forest
  Two Mrs. Carrolls. M. Vale

JOHN, GRAHAM
  Monkey's Paw. W. W. Jacobs; Lady of the Barge

JOHNSON, ADRIAN
  Thou Shalt Not Steal. E. Gaboriau; File No. 113

JOHNSON, CHARLES
  Slaughter's Big Rip-Off. A. Kane
  That Man Bolt. P. Crowcraft

JOHNSON, MONICA
  Jekyll and Hyde . . . Together Again. R. L. Stevenson; Strange Case of Dr. Jekyll and Mr. Hyde

JOHNSON, NUNNALLY
  Black Widow. P. Quentin
  Bulldog Drummond Strikes Back. H. C. McNeile; Knock-Out
  Everybody Does It. J. M. Cain; Career in C Major
  Long Dark Hall. E. Lustgarten; Case to Answer
  My Cousin Rachel. D. Du Maurier
  O. Henry's Full House. O. Henry (headnote)
  Roxie Hart. M. Watkins; Chicago
  Woman in the Window. J. H. Wallis; Once Off Guard

JOHNSTONE, ADRIAN
  Money Moon. J. Farnol
  Wife Whom God Forgot. C. H. Bullivant

JOHNSTONE, CALDER
  Three Sevens. P. P. Sheehan

JONES, CHARLES REED
  King Murder. C. R. Jones

JONES, EVAN
  Damned. H. L. Lawrence; Children of Light
  Eva. J. H. Chase; Eve
  Funeral in Berlin. L. Deighton
  Modesty Blaise. P. O'Donnell
  Night Watch. L. Fletcher
  Outback. K. Cook; Wake in Fright

JONES, GROVER
  One-Way Ticket. Ethel Turner

JORDAN, NEIL
  Mona Lisa. J. L. Novak

JOSEPHSON, JULIAN
  Bat. M. R. Rinehart
  Millionaire. E. D. Biggers; Earl Derr Biggers Tells Ten Stories
  Red Mark. J. Russell

JOURDEUIL, JEAN
  Transit. A. Seghers

JOURD'HUI, GERARD
  Old Rascal. Fredric Brown; His Name Was Death

JULIAN, MARCEL
  Heads or Tails. A. Harris; Baroni
  One Is Always Too Good to Women. R. Queneau; We Always Treat Women Too Well

JULIEN, MAX
  Cleopatra Jones. R. Goulart

JUTTKE, HERBERT
  Hound of the Baskervilles. A. C. Doyle

KAEUTNER, HELMUT
  Redhead. A. Andersch

KAHN, GORDON
  Death Kiss. M. St. Dennis
  Two O'Clock Courage. G. Burgess

KAHN, HARRY
  Man Who Murdered. C. Farrere; Man Who Killed

K

KAI, JOHANNES
　Der Falscher von London. E. Wallace; Forger
　Der Schwarze Abt. E. Wallace; Black Abbot

KALFON, PIERRE
　Five Ashore for Singapore. J. Bruce; Cold Spell

KALLIS, STANLEY
　Glitterdome. J. Wambaugh

KAMPENDONK, GUSTAV
　Die Racher. E. Wallace; Avenger

KANDEL, ABEN
　Craze. H. Seymour; Infernal Idol
　They Won't Forget. W. Greene; Death in the Deep South

KANE, HENRY
　Cop Hater. E. McBain
　Mugger. E. McBain

KANEW, JEFF
　Eddie Macon's Run. J. McLendon

KANGAN, JOHN
　British Intelligence. A. P. Kelly; Three Faces East

KANIN, GARSON
　Double Life. M. W. Wellman

KANTOR, MACKINLAY
　Deadly Is the Female. M. Kantor; Author's Choice

KAPRALOV, GEORGY
　Strange Case of Dr. Jekyll and Mr. Hyde. R. L. Stevenson

KARP, DAVID
　Sol Madrid. R. Wilder; Fruit of the Poppy

KASTLE, LEONARD
　Honeymoon Killers. Paul Buck

KASTNER, ERICH
　Die Verschwundene Miniatur. E. Kastner; Missing Miniature

KATCHA, VAHE
　Burglars. D. Goodis; Burglar

KATCHER, LEO
　Hard Man. L. Katcher

KATCHER, RUDOLF
　Der Zinker. E. Wallace; Squeaker

KATKOV, NORMAN
　Once You Kiss a Stranger. P. Highsmith; Strangers on a Train

KATTERHORN, MONTY
　Yellow Typhoon. H. MacGrath

KATTERJOHN, MONTE
　Cold Steel. G. C. Shedd; In the Shadow of the Hills
　Daughter of the Dragon. S. Rohmer; Daughter of Fu Manchu
　Eternal Struggle. G. B. Lancaster; Law Bringers
　Great Impersonation. E. P. Oppenheim
　Inside the Lines. E. D. Biggers
　Party Girl. E. Balmer; Dangerous Business
　Three Faces East. A. P. Kelly

KATZ, LEE
　British Intelligence. A. P. Kelly; Three Faces East
　Heart of the North. W. B. Mowery

KATZ, ROBERT
　Cassandra Crossing. R. Katz
　Kamikaze '89. P. Wahloo; Murder on the Thirty-First Floor
　Salamander. M. West

KAUFMAN, CHARLES
　Saint in New York. L. Charteris

KAUFMAN, EDWARD
　Star of Midnight. A. S. Roche

KAUFMAN, MILLARD
　Bad Day at Black Rock. M. Niall
　Deadly Is the Female. M. Kantor; Author's Choice

KAUFMAN, ROBERT
　Freebie and the Bean. P. B. Ross

KAURISMAKI, AKI
　Crime and Punishment. F. M. Dostoevskii

KAUS, GINA
　Red Danube. B. Marshall; Vespers in Vienna

KAVANAGH, KEVON
　Sumuru. S. Rohmer; Slaves of Sumuru

KAYE, JOHN
　Rafferty and the Gold Dust Twins. L. Roberts

KEARNEY, GENE
　Games. H. Ellson

KEATING, H. R. F.
　Perfect Murder. H. R. F. Keating

KEEFE, BARRIE
　Long Good Friday. R. Claughton

KEENE, RALPH
　Double Confession. J. Garden; All on a Summer's Day

KEHLMANN, MICHAEL
　Short Work. J. Ashford (headnote)

KEINDORFF, EBERHARD
　Waiting Room for the Other Side. R. Marshall; Mission to Siena

KEITH, CARLOS
　Body Snatcher. R. L. Stevenson

KELLER, HARRY
　Touch of Evil. W. Masterson; Badge of Evil

KELLER, SHELDON
　Cleopatra Jones. R. Goulart

KELLEY, ALAN
　Memento Mori. M. Spark

KELLEY, WILLIAM
　Witness. W. Kelley

KELLINO, ROY
　Guilt is My Shadow. P. Curtis; You're Best Alone

KELLOGG, MARJORIE
　Rosebud. J. Hemingway

KELLY, ANTHONY P.
　Raffles. E. W. Hornung; Amateur Cracksman
　Witching Hour. A. Thomas
　Woman in the Case. C. Fitch

KELLY, MICHAEL
　Frankenstein General Hospital. M. W. Shelley; Frankenstein

KEMPLER, K.
　Eleventh Commandment. B. Fleming; Pillory

KENDALL, VICTOR
　Dead Men Are Dangerous. H. C. Armstrong; Hidden
　Dick Turpin. W. H. Ainsworth; Rookwood
　Man at Six. J. Celestin
　Mr. Reeder in Room 13. E. Wallace; Room 13

KENNAWAY, JAMES
　Mind Benders. J. Kennaway

KENNEDY, ADAM
　Domino Principle. A. Kennedy
　Raise the Titanic! C. Cussler

KENNEDY, BURT
　Man in the Vault. F. Gruber; Lock and the Key
　Trouble with Spies. M. Lovell; Apple Spy in the Sky

KENNEDY, MARGARET
　Take My Life. Winston Graham

KENNINGTON, ALAN
　Night Has Eyes. A. Kennington

KENRICK, TONY
　Nobody's Perfekt. T. Kenrick; Two for the Price of One

KENT, ROBERT E.
　Case of the Black Parrot. B. E. Stevenson; Mystery of the Boule Cabinet
　Reckless Moment. E. S. Holding; Blank Wall
　Spy Ship. G. Dyer; Five Fragments
　Twice Told Tales. N. Hawthorne
　Two O'Clock Courage. G. Burgess
　Where the Sidewalk Ends. W. L. Stuart; Night Cry

KENYON, A. G.
　Girl in the Dark. C. E. Walk; Green Seal

KENYON, CHARLES
　Crash. F. Packard; Night Operator
　Dangerous Days. M. R. Rinehart
　Dick Turpin. W. H. Ainsworth; Rookwood
　Man in Half Moon Street. B. Lyndon
　Millie. D. H. Clarke
　Night Nurse. D. Macy
　Petrified Forest. R. E. Sherwood
　River's End. J. O. Curwood
　Stop Thief! Carlyle Moore
　Wings of the Morning. L. Tracy; Rainbow Island

KERN, DAVID J.
　Dracula Sucks. B. Stoker; Dracula

KERR, GEOFFREY
　Calendar. E. Wallace
　Jassy. N. Lofts
　Living Dangerously. R. Simpson

KERRIDGE, ROY
　Mix Me a Person. J. T. Story

KERSH, GERALD
　Scent of Mystery. K. Roos; Ghost of a Chance

KESSEL, JOSEPH
　Night of the Generals. H. H. Kirst

KESSLER, HENRY S.
　Five Steps to Danger. D. Hamilton; Assignment: Murder

KESSLER, LYLE
　Orphans. Lyle Kessler

KEYS, ANTHONY NELSON
　Frankenstein Must Be Destroyed. M. Shelley; Frankenstein

KIBBEE, ROLAND
　Amorous Adventures of Moll Flanders. D. Defoe; Fortunes and Misfortunes of the Famous Moll Flanders
　Midnight Man. D. Anthony; Midnight Lady and the Mourning Man
　Night in Casablanca. D. Ames
　Valdez Is Coming. E. Leonard

KIKUSHIMA, RYUZO
　High and Low. E. McBain; King's Ransom

KILLENS, JOHN O.
　Odds Against Tomorrow. W. P. McGivern

KIMMINS, ANTHONY
　Laburnum Grove. J. B. Priestley
　Lonely Road. N. Shute

KING, BRADLEY
　East Lynne. H. Wood
　Mystery of Edwin Drood. C. Dickens

KING, FRANK
　Ghoul. F. King

KINGSBRIDGE, JOHN
　Shark. V. Canning; His Bones Are Coral

KINGSLEY, PIERCE
　New Magdalen. Wilkie Collins

KIRK, ROLAND
　Dear Fatherland, Be at Peace. J. M. Simmel; Dear Fatherland

KIRKWOOD, JAMES
　Some Kind of Hero. J. Kirkwood

KIRWAN, PATRICK
　Bulldog Drummond at Bay. H. C. McNeile
　Dark Eyes of London. E. Wallace

Screenwriters Index

Desperate Moment. M. Albrand
On the Night of the Fire. F. L. Green
Rooney. C. Cookson

KJAERULFF-SCHMIDT, PALLE
Think of a Number. A. Bodelsen

KLANE, ROBERT
Every Little Crook and Nanny. E. Hunter

KLAREN, G. C.
Hound of the Baskervilles. A. C. Doyle

KLAUBER, MARCEL
Girl in the Woods. O. Crawford; Blood on the Branches
Woman in the Dark. D. Hammett

KLAVAN, ANDREW
Shock to the System. S. Brett

KLEIN, PHILIP
Baby, Take a Bow. J. P. Judge; Square Crooks
Black Camel. E. D. Biggers
Charlie Chan Carries On. E. D. Biggers
Charlie Chan's Chance. E. D. Biggers; Behind That Curtain
Elinor Norton. M. R. Rinehart; State vs Elinor Norton
Spider. F. Oursler
Trial of Vivienne Ware. K. Ellis

KLEINER, HARRY
Bullitt. R. Pike; Mute Witness
Cry Tough. I. Shulman
Extreme Prejudice. R. Dobbins
Fallen Angel. M. Holland
Fever in the Blood. W. Pearson
Madigan. R. Dougherty; Commissioner

KLEINMAN, DAN
Rage. P. Friedman

KNEALE, NIGEL
Devil's Own. P. Curtis

KNIGHT, VIVIENNE
Floods of Fear. J. Hawkins
Girl in the Headlines. L. Payne; Nose on My Face
Law and Disorder. D. Roberts; Smuggler's Circuit

KNOBLOCK, EDWARD
Amateur Gentleman. J. Farjeon
Englishman's Home. G. Du Maurier

KNOPF, CHRISTOPHER
Choirboys. J. Wambaugh

KNOPF, EDWIN
Piccadilly Jim. P. G. Wodehouse

KNOTT, FREDERICK
Dial "M" for Murder. F. Knott
Last Page. J. H. Chase

KNOWLES, BERNARD
Hell Is Empty. J. F. Straker
Park Plaza 605. B. Gray; Dare-Devil Conquest

KOBER, ARTHUR
Great Hotel Murder. V. Starrett
Guilty As Hell. D. N. Rubin; Riddle Me This!
Secret Call. A. P. Terhune; Woman

KOCH, HOWARD
Casablanca. J. J. Epstein
Letter. W. S. Maugham
633 Squadron. F. E. Smith
Three Strangers. Alex Morrison

KOENIG, LAIRD
Bloodline. S. Sheldon
Little Girl Who Lives Down the Lane. L. Koenig

KOEPP, DAVID
Toy Soldiers. W. P. Kennedy

KOESTVELD, GRAEME
Robbery Under Arms. R. Boldrewood

KOGAN, EPHRAIM
Faces in the Dark. P. Boileau

KOHLER, MANFRED R.
Sarg aus Hong Kong. J. H. Chase; Coffin from Hong Kong

KOHN, JOHN
Collector. J. Fowles
Shanghai Surprise. T. Kenrick; Faraday's Flowers

KOHNER, FREDERICK
Lady and the Monster. C. Siodmak; Donovan's Brain

KONNER, LAWRENCE
Desperate Hours. J. Hayes
Jewel of the Nile. C. Lanigan

KONVITZ, JEFFREY
Sentinel. J. Konvitz

KORBER, SERGE
Little Virtuous. R. Marshall; But a Short Time to Live

KOSTERLITZ, HERMAN
Man Who Murdered. C. Farrere; Man Who Killed

KOUGUELL, SUZAN
Suicide Club. R. L. Stevenson

KOZOLL, MICHAEL
First Blood. D. Morrell

KRAFFT, JOHN W.
House of Secrets. S. Horler
Murder at Glen Athol. N. Lippincott

KRALY, HANS
Last of Mrs. Cheyney. F. Lonsdale

KRASNA, NORMAN
Four Hours to Kill. N. Krasna
Who Was That Lady? N. Krasna; Who Was That Lady I Saw You With?

KRAWCZYK, GERARD
I Hate Actors. B. Hecht

KREITSEK, HOWARD B.
Walking Tall: Part 2. W. Carey

KRIMS, MILTON
We Are Not Alone. J. Hilton

KROHNKE, ERICH
Ten Little Indians. A. Christie; Ten Little Niggers

KRUMGOLD, JOSEPH
Jim Hanvey, Detective. O. R. Cohen
Lone Wolf Returns. L. J. Vance

KRUSE, JOHN
Assault. K. Young; Ravine
Echo of Barbara. Jonathan Burke
Vengeance. C. Siodmak; Donovan's Brain

KUBRICK, STANLEY
Clockwork Orange. A. Burgess
Dr. Strangelove. P. Bryant; Two Hours to Doom
Killing. L. White; Clean Break

KUHL, HANS
River of Diamonds. G. Jenkins

KUHN, IRENE
Mask of Fu Manchu. S. Rohmer

KULIJANOV, LEV
Crime and Punishment. F. M. Dostoevskii

KURNITZ, HARRY
Fast and Loose. M. Page; Fast Company
Goodbye Charlie. M. H. Albert
How to Steal a Million. M. Sinclair
I Love You Again. O. R. Cohen
Witness for the Prosecution. A. Christie

KUROSAWA, AKIRA
High and Low. E. McBain; King's Ransom

KWIET, HANS
Story-Teller. P. Highsmith

LA BERN, ARTHUR
Accidental Death. E. Wallace; Jack o' Judgment
Incident at Midnight. E. Wallace (headnote)
Time to Remember. E. Wallace; Man Who Bought London
Verdict. E. Wallace; Big Four

LABRO, MAURICE
Blague dans le Coin. Carter Brown; Curtains for a Chorine
Les Canailles. R. Marshall; You Find Him . . . I'll Fix Him

LABRO, PHILIPPE
Without Apparent Motive. E. McBain; Ten Plus One

LACHMAN, HARRY
Down Our Street. Ernest George; Belle

LA FRENAIS, IAN
Catch Me a Spy. G. Marton
Jokers. M. Sands
Otley. M. Waddell
Porridge. P. Ableman
Villain. J. Barlow; Burden of Proof

LAIDLOW, BETTY
Danger on the Air. Xantippe; Death Catches Up with Mr. Kluck

LAMB, KARL
Pitfall. J. J. Dratler
Whispering Smith. F. H. Spearman

LAMBERT, PETER
Breaking Point. L. Meynell

LAMOTHE, JULIAN L.
His Robe of Honor. E. Dorrance

LAMPELL, MILLARD
Blind Date. L. Howard

LANDAU, LESLIE
Riverside Murder. A. Steeman; Six Dead Men

LANDAU, RICHARD
Born Reckless. M. Rogers
Flanagan Boy. M. Catto
Glass Cage. A. E. Martin; Common People
Murder by Proxy. H. Nielsen; Gold Coast Nocturne

LANDI, MARIO
Maigret a Pigalle. G. Simenon; Maigret in Montmartre

LANDIS, JOHN
Clue. M. McDowell

LANDON, CHRISTOPHER
Ice-Cold in Alex. C. Landon

LANDON, JOSEPH
Johnny Cool. J. McPartland; Kingdom of Johnny Cool
Rise and Fall of Legs Diamond. O. H. Gaylord

LANE, RICHARD
You Can't See Round Corners. J. Cleary

LANG, CHARLES
Desire in the Dust. H. Whittington

LANG, JENNINGS
Concorde—Airport 1979. K. Stewart

LANG, PHIL
Third Degree. A. Hornblow

LANGLEY, LEE
Interlude. J. M. Cain; Serenade

LANGLEY, NOEL
Secret of Stamboul. D. Wheatley; Eunich of Stamboul
They Made Me a Fugitive. J. Budd; Convict Has Escaped

LANING, ROBERT
Hostage. C. Henry

LANOE, H.
Our Man in Marrakech. R. P. Jones; Heisters

LARDNER, RING, JR.
Laura. V. Caspary

LAREY, PIERRE
    It Only Happens to the Living. R. Marshall; Things Men Do

LARKIN, JOHN FRANCIS
    Mandarin Mystery. E. Queen; Chinese Orange Mystery
    Some Call It Love. R. James

LAROCHE, PIERRE
    Seventh Juror. F. Didelot

LARSEN, TRYGVE
    Die Rot Kreis. E. Wallace; Crimson Circle

LASKER, ALEX
    Firefox. C. Thomas

LASKO, LEO
    Vendetta. A. C. Gunter; Mr. Barnes of New York

LASKY, JESSE, JR.
    Ace Up Your Sleeve. J. H. Chase; Ace Up My Sleeve
    Secret Agent. W. S. Maugham; Ashenden

LAST, SIMON
    Committed. S. Claudia; Clock and Bell

LATIMER, JONATHAN
    Big Clock. K. Fearing
    Glass Key. D. Hammett
    Lone Wolf Spy Hunt. L. J. Vance; Red Masquerade
    Night Has a Thousand Eyes. G. Hopley
    Night in New Orleans. J. R. Langham; Sing a Song of Homicide
    Plunder of the Sun. D. Dodge
    Sealed Verdict. L. Shapiro
    They Won't Believe Me. G. McDonell
    Unholy Wife. J. Roeburt
    Whole Truth. P. Mackie

LAU, WESLEY
    Lepke. J. Pearl

LAUDENBACH, ROLAND
    Le Salaire du Peche. N. Rutledge; Emily Will Know
    Obsession. W. Irish; Dead Man Blues

LAUNDER, FRANK
    Black Mask. B. Graeme; Blackshirt
    Educated Evans. E. Wallace
    For the Love of Mike. H. F. Maltby
    Fortune Is a Woman. Winston Graham
    Girl in the News. R. Vickers
    Green Man. F. Launder; Meet a Body
    Inspector Hornleigh on Holiday. L. Grex; Stolen Death
    Seven Sinners. A. Ridley; Wrecker
    They Came by Night. B. Lyndon
    Twelve Good Men. J. Rhode; Murders in Praed Street
    W Plan. G. Seton

LAURANT, PATRICK
    Hill Girl. C. Williams

LAUREN, S. K.
    Crime and Punishment. F. M. Dostoevskii
    Mr. & Mrs. North. O. Davis

LAURENT, DAVIS
    I Married a Dead Man. W. Irish

LAURENT, PATRICK
    I Married a Dead Man. W. Irish

LAURENTS, ARTHUR
    Rope. P. Hamilton

LAUTNER, GEORGES
    Icy Breasts. R. Matheson; Someone Is Bleeding

LAVON, ARTHUR
    Mask. A. Hornblow

LAW, JOHN
    Casino Royale. I. Fleming

LAW, MICHAEL
    Six Men. E. Radford

LAWRENCE, VINCENT
    One-Way Ticket. Ethel Turner

LAWSON, JOHN HOWARD
    One Against Seven. J. Stevenson; Counterattack
    Ship from Shanghai. D. Collins; Ordeal

LAY, JOHN HUNTER
    Slightly Honorable. F. G. Presnell; Send Another Coffin

LAZICH, LEE
    Hangup. B. Brunner; Face of Night

LEAHY, AGNES BRAND
    Night of June 13. F. Vreeland

LEAR, NORMAN
    Scared Stiff. C. W. Goddard; Ghost Breakers

LEASOR, JAMES
    Where the Spies Are. J. Leasor; Passport to Oblivion

LEBARON, WILLIAM
    Perfect Crime. I. Zangwill; Big Bow Mystery

LEBRUN, MICHEL
    Dans la Gueule du Loup. J. H. Chase; Just Another Sucker
    Stew in the Caribbean. A. Conroy; Looters

LE CHANOIS, JEAN-PAUL
    Cecile Est Mort. G. Simenon; Maigret and the Spinster
    Picpus. G. Simenon; To Any Lengths

LECONTE, PATRICE
    M. Hire. G. Simenon; Mr. Hire's Engagement

LEDERER, CHARLES
    I Love You Again. O. R. Cohen
    Kiss of Death. E. Lipsky
    Mountain Music. M. Kantor; Author's Choice
    Ocean's 11. G. C. Johnson
    Ride the Pink Horse. D. B. Hughes
    Within the Law. B. Veiller

LEDROV, D. B.
    Shuttered Room. J. Withers

LEE, CONNIE
    Nine Girls. W. H. Pettitt

LEE, DAMIAN
    Watchers. D. R. Koontz

LEE, JACK
    Turn the Key Softly. J. Brophy

LEE, LEONARD
    Glass Web. M. Ehrlich; Spin the Glass Web
    Panther's Moon. V. Canning
    Pursuit to Algiers. A. C. Doyle; Return of Sherlock Holmes
    Sinner Take All. W. Chambers; Murder for a Wanton
    Whispering City. Horace Brown

LEE, NORMAN
    Door with Seven Locks. E. Wallace
    Monkey's Paw. W. W. Jacobs; Lady of the Barge

LEE, ROBERT N.
    Alias the Night Wind. V. Vanardy
    Dragon Murder Case. S. S. Van Dine
    Fog Over Frisco. G. Dyer; Five Fragments
    Hunted Woman. J. O. Curwood
    Kennel Murder Case. S. S. Van Dine
    Little Caesar. W. R. Burnett
    70,000 Witnesses. C. Fitzsimmons
    While the Patient Slept. M. G. Eberhart

LEEDS, CHARLES A.
    No Road Back. F. L. Cary; Madam Tic-Tac

LEES, ROBERT
    Abbott and Costello Meet Frankenstein. M. W. Shelley; Frankenstein

LE FRANE, GUY
    Keep Talking, Baby. D. Keene; Strange Witness

LEGRAND, ANDRE
    Secret Document—Vienna. M. Dekobra; Widow with the Pink Gloves

LE HENRY, ALAIN
    Hill Girl. C. Williams
    I'm King of the Castle. S. Hill
    Last Summer in Tangiers. W. O'Farrell; Devil His Due

LEHMAN, ERNEST
    Black Sunday. T. Harris
    Family Plot. V. Canning; Rainbird Pattern
    Prize. I. Wallace

LEHMAN, GLADYS
    Cat Creeps. J. Willard; Cat and the Canary
    Death Takes a Holiday. Walter Ferris
    Double Door. E. McFadden
    Little Miss Marker. D. Runyon; Blue Plate Special

LEIGH, ROWLAND
    Summer Storm. A. Chekhov; Shooting Party

LEITZBACH, ADELINE
    House of Secrets. S. Horler

LELAND, DAVID
    Mona Lisa. J. L. Novak

LEMORANDE, RUSTY
    Turn of the Screw. Henry James

LENNART, ISOBEL
    Fitzwilly. Poyntz Tyler; Garden of Cucumbers

LENNON, THOMAS
    Murder on a Bridle Path. S. Palmer; Puzzle of the Red Stallion

LENZMANN, JACQUES
    Without Apparent Motive. E. McBain

LEONARD, ELMORE
    Cat Chaser. Elmore Leonard
    Fifty-Two Pickup. Elmore Leonard
    Mr. Majestyk. Elmore Leonard
    Moonshine War. Elmore Leonard
    Rosary Murders. W. X. Kienzle
    Stick. Elmore Leonard

LEONARD, HUGH
    Interlude. J. M. Cain; Serenade

LEONE, SERGIO
    Once Upon a Time in America. H. Grey; Hoods

LEONE, VIRGIL C.
    Fine Pair. C. Stratton

LEROY, IRVING
    Chick. E. Wallace

LEROY, SERGE
    Attention, the Kids Are Watching. P. L. Dixon; Children Are Watching
    Passengers. K. R. Dwyer; Chase

LE SAINT, EDWARD J.
    Men of Zanzibar. R. H. Davis; Man of Zanzibar

LESIEWICZ, WITOLD
    Lord Arthur Saville's Crime. O. Wilde
    Terrifying Bed. W. Collins; After Dark

LESLIE, DUDLEY
    Black Limelight. G. Sherry
    Living Dangerously. R. Simpson
    Three Silent Men. E. P. Thorne

LESSLIE, COLIN
    No Resting Place. I. Niall

LESSON, MICHAEL
    Jekyll and Hyde . . . Together Again. R. L. Stevenson; Strange Case of Dr. Jekyll and Mr. Hyde

LESTER, SEELEG
    Change of Mind. C. Stratton

LETTIERI, AL
    Villain. J. Barlow; Burden of Proof

LEVANT, OSCAR
  Orient Express. G. Greene; Stamboul Train
LEVIEN, SONYA
  Behind That Curtain. E. D. Biggers
  Four Men and a Prayer. D. Garth
LEVINE, MICHEL
  Dead Run. R. Sheckley
  Old Tin Can. D. Keene; Flight by Night
LEVINO, ALBERT SHELBY
  Canary Murder Case. S. S. Van Dine
  Going Crooked. Winchell Smith
  Island of Intrigue. I. Ostrander
  Law and the Woman. C. Fitch; Woman in the Case
  No Man's Land. L. J. Vance
  Sleeping Memory. E. P. Oppenheim; Great Awakening
  Woman Racket. P. Dunning; Night Hostess
  Woman's Law. Maravene Thompson
LEVINSON, BARRY
  And Justice for All. R. Grossbach
  High Anxiety. R. H. Pilpel
LEVISON, KEN
  Madhouse. Angus Hall; Qualtrough
LEVITT, SAUL
  Covenant with Death. S. Becker
LEVY, BENN W.
  Blackmail. C. Bennett
  Hate Ship. B. Graeme
  Informer. L. O'Flaherty
  Lord Camber's Ladies. H. A. Vachell; Case of Lady Camber
LEVY, MELVIN
  Cry-Baby Killer. J. Hilton
  First Comes Courage. E. Arnold; Commandos
LEVY, PARKE
  Having Wonderful Crime. C. Rice
LEVY, RAOUL
  Defector. P. Thomas; Spy
LEWIS, ANDY
  Klute. W. Johnston
  Underground. C. Stratton
LEWIS, D. B. WYNDHAM
  Gay Adventure. W. Hackett
  Man Who Knew Too Much. R. Alexander
LEWIS, DAVE
  Klute. W. Johnston
LEWIS, EUGENE B.
  Haunting Shadows. M. Nicholson; House of a Thousand Shadows
LEWIS, FREDERICK
  Strange Case of Mary Page. F. Lewis
LEWIS, HERSHELL G.
  Color Me Blood Red. H. G. Lewis
  Two Thousand Maniacs. H. G. Lewis
LEWIS, JAY
  Front Page Story. R. Gaines; Final Night
LEWIS, PAULINE
  Dawn. H. R. Haggard
LEWIS, WARREN
  Black Rain. Mike Cogan
LI, SHAOHONG
  Bloody Morning. G. G. Marquez; Chronicle of a Death Foretold
LIBOTT, ROBERT
  Captain Blood, Fugitive. R. Sabatini; Chronicles of Captain Blood
  Fortunes of Captain Blood. R. Sabatini
LIEBERMAN, JEFF
  Blue Sunshine. K. Johnson
LIGHTON, LOUIS D.
  Blind Goddess. A. Train
  Pleasure Buyers. A. S. Roche

LINCOLN, W. J.
  Called Back. H. Conway
  Get-Rich-Quick-Wallingford. G. R. Chester
  It Is Never Too late to Mend. C. Reade
  Officer 666. B. Currie
  Within the Law. B. Veiller
LINDOP, AUDREY ERSKINE
  Blanche Fury. J. Shearing
  Tall Headlines. A. E. Lindop
LINDSAY, PHILIP
  Under the Red Robe. S. J. Weyman
LING, EUGENE
  Dark Page. S. Fuller
  It Shouldn't Happen to a Dog. E. Lanham
LIPMAN, WILLIAM R.
  Dangerous to Know. E. Wallace; On the Spot
  Little Miss Marker. D. Runyon; Blue Plate Special
LIPSCOMB, W. P.
  Bitter Springs. C. King
  Loyalties. J. Galsworthy
  Mark of Cain. J. Shearing; Airing in a Closed Carriage
  Plunder. B. Travers
  Robbery Under Arms. R. Boldrewood
  Sign of the Four. A. C. Doyle
  Speckled Band. A. C. Doyle; Adventures of Sherlock Holmes
LITTELL, ROBERT
  Amateur. R. Littell
LITTLETON, SCOTT
  Worldly Goods. A. Soutar
LIVELY, ROBERT
  Danger on the Air. Xantippe; Death Catches Up with Mr. Kluck
LLOVET, ENRIQUE
  Ten Little Indians. A. Christie; Ten Little Niggers
LLOYD, FRANK
  Madame X. J. W. MacConaughy
LLOYD, GERRIT J.
  Secret Service. W. Gillette
LOCHTE, RICHARD S.
  Escape to Athena. P. Blake
LOEB, JOSEPH, III.
  Burglar. L. Block (headnote)
LOEB, LEE
  Abbott and Costello Meet Dr. Jekyll and Mr. Hyde. R. L. Stevenson; Strange Case of Dr. Jekyll and Mr. Hyde
  Seven Keys to Baldpate. E. D. Biggers
LOGAN, HELEN
  Man Who Wouldn't Talk. H. Hall; Valiant
LOGUE, CHARLES A.
  Back to God's Country. J. O. Curwood
  Cheating Cheaters. M. Marcin
  Man on the Box. H. MacGrath
  Master Mystery. A. B. Reeve
  Menace. E. Wallace; Feathered Serpent
  Renfrew of the Royal Mounted. L. Y. Erskine
  Sing Sing Nights. H. S. Keeler
LONCRAINE, RICHARD
  Bellman & True. D. Lowden
LONEGAN, LLOYD F.
  Million Dollar Mystery. H. MacGrath
LONERGAN, LLOYD
  Highest Bidder. M. Foster; Trap
  My Lady's Garter. J. Futrelle
  Woman in White. W. Collins
LONG, HAL
  Nancy Steele Is Missing. C. F. Coe; Ransom
LONG, LOUISE
  Greene Murder Case. S. S. Van Dine

LONG, REGINALD
  Second Bureau. C. R. Dumas
  Spider. H. Holt; Midnight Mail
LONGDEN, JOHN
  Quinney's. H. A. Vachell
LONGSTREET, STEPHEN
  Uncle Harry. T. Job
LOOS, ANITA
  Lost House. R. H. Davis; Man Who Could Not Lose
LORD, ROBERT
  Five Star Final. L. Weitzenkorn
  Little Caesar. W. R. Burnett
  On Trial. E. L. Reizenstein
LORING, HOPE
  Blind Goddess. A. Train
  Interference. R. Pertwee
  Pleasure Buyers. A. S. Roche
  Red Glove. D. Grant; Fifth Ace
LOSEY, JOSEPH
  Big Night. S. Ellin; Dreadful Summit
LOVETT, JOSEPHINE
  Corsair. W. Green
  Perpetua. D. C. Calthrop
  Spanish Jade. M. Hewlett
LOWDEN, DESMOND
  Bellman & True. D. Lowden
LOWE, EDWARD T.
  Agony Column. E. D. Biggers
  Broadway. P. Dunning
  Bulldog Drummond Comes Back. H. C. McNeile; Female of the Species
  Bulldog Drummond's Revenge. H. C. McNeile; Return of Bulldog Drummond
  Curtain at Eight. O. R. Cohen; Backstage Mystery
  Fighting Back. W. M. Raine
  Red-Haired Alibi. W. Collison
  Scattergood Baines. C. B. Kelland
  Sherlock Holmes and the Secret Weapon. A. C. Doyle; Return of Sherlock Holmes
LOWE, SHERMAN L.
  Crashing Thru. L. Y. Erskine; Renfrew Rides the Range
  Mystery House. M. G. Eberhart; Mystery of Hunting's End
LOWRY, ROGER
  Negatives. P. Everett
LUCAS, JOHN MEREDYTH
  Captain Blood, Fugitive. R. Sabatini; Chronicles of Captain Blood
LUCKWELL, BILL
  Hidden Homicide. P. Capon; Death at Shinglestrand
LUCOQUE, H. LISLE
  Tatterly. T. Gallon
LUDWIG, WILLIAM
  Shadow on the Wall. H. Lees; Death in the Doll's House
  Stronger Than Desire. W. E. Woodward; Evelyn Prentice
LUMET, SIDNEY
  Q&A. E. Torres
LUND, O. A. C.
  Butterfly. H. K. Webster
LUSSIER, DANE
  Lady and the Monster. C. Siodmak; Donovan's Brain
  Three's a Crowd. M. G. Eberhart; Hasty Wedding
LUSTIG, H. G.
  Under Western Eyes. J. Conrad
LYELL, LOTTIE
  Blue Mountains Mystery. H. Owens; Mount Marunga Mystery

LYNCH, JOHN
   Valley of Silent Men. J. O. Curwood

LYNCH, MARTIN
   Prayer for the Dying. J. Higgins

LYNDON, BARRE
   Hangover Square. P. Hamilton
   House on 92nd St. Alex Morrison
   Lodger. M. B. Lowndes
   Man in the Attic. M. B. Lowndes; Lodger
   Night Has a Thousand Eyes. G. Hopley

LYNN, JONATHAN
   Clue. M. McDowell

LYTELL, BERT
   No Man's Land. L. J. Vance

MacARTHUR, CHARLES
   Crime Without Passion. B. Hecht; Collected Stories of Ben Hecht
   New Adventures of Get-Rich-Quick Wallingford. G. R. Chester; Get-Rich-Quick Wallingford
   Within the Law. B. Veiller

MACAULAY, RICHARD
   Born to Kill. J. Gunn; Deadlier Than the Male
   Out of the Fog. I. Shaw; Gentle People
   They Drive by Night. A. I. Bezzerides; Long Haul

McCALL, MARY, JR.
   Maisie. W. Collison; Dark Dame
   Woman in Red. Wallace Irwin; North Shore

McCARTY, HENRY
   Gorilla. R. Spence
   Shadow on the Wall. J. B. Ellis; Picture on the Wall

MacCLURE, VICTOR
   They Met in the Dark. Anthony Gilbert; Vanishing Corpse

McCORMACK, FRANK M.
   Phantom of the Opera. G. Leroux

McCORMICK, JOHN
   Life for Ruth. W. Drummond
   Victim. W. Drummond

McCORMICK, LANGDON
   Burglar and the Lady. O. Harper

McCOY, HORACE
   Bad for Each Other. H. McCoy; Scalpel
   Dangerous to Know. E. Wallace; On the Spot

McCRACKEN, ESTHER
   Poison Pen. R. Llewellyn

MACDONALD, NORMAN
   Loudwater Mystery. E. Jepson

MacDONALD, PHILIP
   Blind Alley. J. Warwick
   Body Snatcher. R. L. Stevenson
   Dark Past. J. Warwick; Blind Alley
   Love from a Stranger. F. Vosper
   Mystery of Mr. X. M. Porlock; X v. Rex
   Nora Prentiss. Alex Morrison

MacDOUGALL, RANALD
   Breaking Point. E. Hemingway; To Have and Have Not
   Mildred Pierce. J. M. Cain
   Unsuspected. C. Armstrong

MacDOUGALL, ROGER
   Touch of Larceny. A. Garve; Megstone Plot

McGIVERN, CECIL
   Blanche Fury. J. Shearing

McGIVERN, WILLIAM P.
   I Saw What You Did. U. Curtiss; Out of the Dark
   Wrecking Crew. D. Hamilton

McGOWAN, T. J.
   Man with My Face. S. W. Taylor

MCGRATH, JOHN
   Billion Dollar Brain. L. Deighton

McGRATH, WILLIAM
   70,000 Witnesses. C. Fitzsimmons

McGUINNESS, JAMES KEVIN
   Black Watch. T. Mundy; King of the Khyber Rifles
   Solitaire Man. B. C. Spewack

McGUIRE, DENNIS
   Shoot It: Black, Shoot It: Blue. P. Tyner; Shoot It

MacGUNIGLE, ROBERT
   Whistling in the Dark. L. Gross

McINTOSH, BLANCHE
   Anna the Adventuress. E. P. Oppenheim
   Mr. Justice Raffles. E. W. Hornung
   Mrs. Erricker's Reputation. T. Cobb
   Touch of the Child. T. Gallon

MacKAY, ELIZABETH
   Unsuitable Job for a Woman. P. D. James

McKELWAY, ST. CLAIR
   Sleep My Love. L. Q. Ross

MACKENDRICK, ALEXANDER
   Blue Lamp. T. Willis

MACKIE, PHILIP
   Clue of the New Pin. E. Wallace
   Clue of the Silver Key. E. Wallace
   Clue of the Twisted Candle. E. Wallace
   Man at the Carlton Tower. E. Wallace; Man at the Carlton
   Number Six. E. Wallace
   Praying Mantis. H. Monteilhet; Preying Mantises
   Share Out. E. Wallace; Jack o' Judgment
   20,000 Pound Kiss. E. Wallace (headnote)
   Vengeance. C. Siodmak; Donovan's Brain

MACKINNON, ALLAN
   Behind the Headlines. R. Chapman
   She Shall Have Murder. D. Ames
   Sleeping Car to Trieste. R. Alexander; Rome Express

McKNIGHT, C. A. [ROSALIND RUSSELL]
   Mrs. Pollifax, Spy. D. Gilman; Unexpected Mrs. Pollifax

MacLAREN-ROSS, J.
   Escapement. C. E. Maine

MacLEAN, ALISTAIR
   Breakheart Pass. A. MacLean
   Puppet on a Chain. A. MacLean
   When Eight Bells Toll. A. MacLean
   Where Eagles Dare. A. MacLean

McLENNAN, DON
   Slate, Wyn & Me. Georgia Savage; Slate and Wyn and Blanche McBride

MacMAHON, CHARLES
   Robbery Under Arms. R. Boldrewood

McNAMARA, WALTER
   Traffic in Souls. E. H. Ball

McNAUGHT, BOB
   Grand National Night. D. Christie

McNUTT, PATTERSON
   Gentleman After Dark. R. W. Child; Velvet Black
   Return of Sophie Lang. F. I. Anderson; Notorious Sophie Lang

McNUTT, WILLIAM SLAVENS
   Night of June 13. F. Vreeland

McPARTLAND, JOHN
   Wild Party. J. McPartland

MacPHAIL, ANGUS
   Busman's Honeymoon. D. L. Sayers
   Calendar. E. Wallace
   Crooked Billet. D. Titherage
   Dead of Night. E. F. Benson; Room in the Tower
   Four Just Men. E. Wallace
   Frightened Lady. E. Wallace; Case of the Frightened Lady
   Ghost Train. A. Ridley
   It Always Rains on Sunday. A. La Bern
   Man They Could Not Arrest. E. Wallace (headnote)
   Man Who Knew Too Much. R. Alexander
   Ringer. E. Wallace
   Saloon Bar. F. Harvey
   Scarlet Daredevil. B. Orczy; Triumph of the Scarlet Pimpernel
   South Sea Bubble. R. Pertwee
   Spellbound. F. Beeding; House of Dr. Edwardes
   White Face. E. Wallace
   Wrecker. A. Ridley

McPHERSON, DON
   Crossing the Line. W. McIlvanney; Big Man

MacPHERSON, JEANIE
   Manslaughter. A. D. Miller
   Red Dice. O. R. Cohen; Iron Chalice
   Whispering Chorus. P. P. Sheehan

MACRAE, ARTHUR
   Dusty Ermine. N. Grant
   Silver Blaze. A. C. Doyle; Memoirs of Sherlock Holmes

MacRAUCH, EARL
   Stranger Is Watching. M. H. Clark

MAAS, ERNEST
   Country Beyond. J. O. Curwood

MACK, WILLARD
   Madame X. J. W. MacConaughy

MADDOW, BEN
   Asphalt Jungle. W. R. Burnett
   Balcony. J. Genet
   Chairman. J. R. Kennedy
   Intruder in the Dust. W. Faulkner
   Kiss the Blood Off My Hands. G. Butler
   Mephisto Waltz. F. M. Stewart

MADDOX, DIANA
   Amateur. R. Littell

MAGNIER, CLAUDE
   Gazebo. A. Coppel

MAHIN, JOHN LEE
   Bad Seed. M. Anderson
   Beast of the City. J. Lait
   Dr. Jekyll and Mr. Hyde. R. L. Stevenson; Strange Case of Dr. Jekyll and Mr. Hyde
   Moment to Moment. A. Coppel
   Scarface. A. Trail

MAIBAUM, RICHARD
   Day They Robbed the Bank of England. J. Brophy
   Diamonds Are Forever. I. Fleming
   Doctor No. I. Fleming
   For Your Eyes Only. I. Fleming
   From Russia with Love. I. Fleming
   Goldfinger. I. Fleming
   Hell Below Zero. H. Innes; White South
   License to Kill. John Gardner
   Living Daylights. I. Fleming; Octopussy and the Living Daylights
   Man Inside. M. E. Chaber
   Man with the Golden Gun. I. Fleming
   Octopussy. I. Fleming
   On Her Majesty's Secret Service. I. Fleming
   Spy Who Loved Me. C. Wood; James Bond, the Spy Who Loved Me
   They Gave Him a Gun. W. J. Cowen
   Thunderball. I. Fleming

MAIGNE, CHARLES
   In the Hollow of Her Hand. G. B. McCutcheon; Hollow of Her Hand

MAILER, NORMAN
   Tough Guys Don't Dance. N. Mailer

MAINE, CHARLES ERIC
   Escapement. C. E. Maine

MAINWARING, BERNARD
  Jennifer Hale. R. Eden
MAINWARING, DANIEL
  Catacombs. Jay Bennett
  Gun Runners. E. Hemingway; To Have and Have Not
MAIURI, DINO
  Payoff. A. Veraldi
MALINS, GEOFFREY H.
  Abbey Grange. A. C. Doyle; Return of Sherlock Holmes
  Black Peter. A. C. Doyle; Return of Sherlock Holmes
  Blue Carbuncle. A. C. Doyle; Adventures of Sherlock Holmes
  Boscombe Valley Mystery. A. C. Doyle; Adventures of Sherlock Holmes
  Bruce-Partington Plans. A. C. Doyle; His Last Bow
  Cardboard Box. A. C. Doyle; His Last Bow
  Charles Augustus Milverton. A. C. Doyle; Return of Sherlock Holmes
  Crooked Man. A. C. Doyle; Memoirs of Sherlock Holmes
  Dancing Men. A. C. Doyle; Return of Sherlock Holmes
  Engineer's Thumb. A. C. Doyle; Adventures of Sherlock Holmes
  Final Problem. A. C. Doyle; Memoirs of Sherlock Holmes
  Gloria Scott. A. C. Doyle; Memoirs of Sherlock Holmes
  Golden Pince-Nez. A. C. Doyle; Return of Sherlock Holmes
  Greek Interpreter. A. C. Doyle; Memoirs of Sherlock Holmes
  His Last Bow. A. C. Doyle
  Lady Frances Carfax. A. C. Doyle; His Last Bow
  Mazarin Stone. A. C. Doyle; Casebook of Sherlock Holmes
  Missing Three-Quarter. A. C. Doyle; Return of Sherlock Holmes
  Musgrave Ritual. A. C. Doyle; Memoirs of Sherlock Holmes
  Naval Treaty. A. C. Doyle; Memoirs of Sherlock Holmes
  Norwood Builder. A. C. Doyle; Return of Sherlock Holmes
  Red Circle. A. C. Doyle; His Last Bow
  Reigate Squires. A. C. Doyle; Memoirs of Sherlock Holmes
  Second Stain. A. C. Doyle; Return of Sherlock Holmes
  Silver Blaze. A. C. Doyle; Memoirs of Sherlock Holmes
  Six Napoleons. A. C. Doyle; Return of Sherlock Holmes
  Speckled Band. A. C. Doyle; Adventures of Sherlock Holmes
  Stock-Broker's Clerk. A. C. Doyle; Memoirs of Sherlock Holmes
  Thor Bridge. A. C. Doyle; Casebook of Sherlock Holmes
  Three Students. A. C. Doyle; Return of Sherlock Holmes
MALKO, GEORGE
  Dogs of War. F. Forsyth
MALLE, LOUIS
  Elevator to the Gallows. N. Calef; Frantic
MALLESON, MILES
  Rat. P. Bottome
  They Met in the Dark. Anthony Gilbert; Vanishing Corpse
  W Plan. G. Seton
  Yellow Mask. E. Wallace; Traitor's Gate
MALLORY, VIOLET
  Within the Law. B. Veiller
MALLOY, DORIS
  Human Cargo. K. Shepard; I Will Be Faithful
  Remember Last Night. A. Hobhouse; Hangover Murders

MALMBERG, BERTIL
  Crime and Punishment. F. M. Dostoevskii
MALONE, JOEL
  Crime by Night. G. Homes; Forty Whacks
MALTBY, H. F.
  Crimes at the Dark House. W. Collins; Woman in White
  Sweeney Todd, the Demon Barber of Fleet Street. G. D. Pitt
  Ticket-of-Leave Man. T. Taylor
MALTZ, ALBERT
  Naked City. M. Wald
  This Gun for Hire. G. Greene; Gun for Sale
MAMBETY, DJIBRIL DIOP
  Hyenas. F. Duerrenmatt; Visit
MAMET, DAVID
  House of Games. D. Mamet
  Postman Always Rings Twice. J. M. Cain
  Verdict. B. C. Reed
MANCHETTE, JEAN-PATRICK
  Undertaker Parlor Computer. W. Kempley; Probability Factor
MANDEL, LORING
  Little Drummer Girl. J. Le Carre
MANDELL, BABALOO
  Spies Like Us. G. McGill
MANDER, MILES
  Lodger. M. B. Lowndes
MANKIEWICZ, DON M.
  House of Numbers. J. Finney
  I Want to Live! T. Rawson
  Trial. D. M. Mankiewicz
MANKIEWICZ, HERMAN J.
  Canary Murder Case. S. S. Van Dine
  Christmas Holiday. W. S. Maugham
  Dummy. H. J. O'Higgins
  Ladies' Man. R. Hughes
MANKIEWICZ, JOSEPH L.
  Dragonwyck. A. Seton
  Honey Pot. T. Sterling; Evil of the Day
  Only Saps Work. O. Davis; Easy Come, Easy Go
  Quiet American. G. Greene
  Slightly Scarlet. P. Heath
MANKIEWICZ, TOM
  Cassandra Crossing. R. Katz
  Diamonds Are Forever. I. Fleming
  Eagle Has Landed. J. Higgins
  Live and Let Die. I. Fleming
  Man with the Golden Gun. I. Fleming
  Sweet Ride. W. Murray
MANKOWITZ, WOLF
  Assassination Bureau. J. London
  Casino Royale. I. Fleming
  House of Fright. R. L. Stevenson; Strange Case of Dr. Jekyll and Mr. Hyde
  Where the Spies Are. J. Leasor; Passport to Oblivion
MANN, ABBY
  Detective. R. Thorp
  Report to the Commissioner. J. Mills
MANN, COLIN
  Adventures of Scaramouche. R. Sabatini; Scaramouche
MANN, EDWARD
  Killer Inside Me. J. Thompson
MANN, MICHAEL
  Keep. F. P. Wilson
  Manhunter. T. Harris; Red Dragon
MANN, STANLEY
  Collector. J. Fowles
  Eye of the Needle. K. Follett; Storm Island
  Firestarter. Stephen King
  Mark. C. E. Israel
  Naked Runner. F. Clifford
  Russian Roulette. T. Ardies; Kosygin Is Coming

Sky Riders. L. Cameron
Strange Affair. B. Toms
Woman of Straw. C. Arley
MANNHEIMER, ALBERT
  Whistling in the Dark. L. Gross
MANNING, BRUCE
  Lone Wolf Returns. L. J. Vance
  Meet Nero Wolfe. R. Stout; Fer-de-Lance
MANNOCK, PATRICK L.
  Abbey Grange. A. C. Doyle; Return of Sherlock Holmes
  Black Peter. A. C. Doyle; Return of Sherlock Holmes
  Blue Carbuncle. A. C. Doyle; Adventures of Sherlock Holmes
  Boscombe Valley Mystery. A. C. Doyle; Adventures of Sherlock Holmes
  Bruce-Partington Plans. A. C. Doyle; His Last Bow
  Cardboard Box. A. C. Doyle; His Last Bow
  Charles Augustus Milverton. A. C. Doyle; Return of Sherlock Holmes
  Crimson Circle. E. Wallace
  Crooked Man. A. C. Doyle; Memoirs of Sherlock Holmes
  Dancing Men. A. C. Doyle; Return of Sherlock Holmes
  Dead Certainty. N. Gould
  Engineer's Thumb. A. C. Doyle; Adventures of Sherlock Holmes
  Final Problem. A. C. Doyle; Memoirs of Sherlock Holmes
  Gloria Scott. A. C. Doyle; Memoirs of Sherlock Holmes
  Golden Pince-Nez. A. C. Doyle; Return of Sherlock Holmes
  Greek Interpreter. A. C. Doyle; Memoirs of Sherlock Holmes
  His Last Bow. A. C. Doyle
  Lady Frances Carfax. A. C. Doyle; His Last Bow
  Mazarin Stone. A. C. Doyle; Casebook of Sherlock Holmes
  Missing Three-Quarter. A. C. Doyle; Return of Sherlock Holmes
  Musgrave Ritual. A. C. Doyle; Memoirs of Sherlock Holmes
  Naval Treaty. A. C. Doyle; Memoirs of Sherlock Holmes
  Norwood Builder. A. C. Doyle; Return of Sherlock Holmes
  One of the Best. S. Hicks
  Rank Outsider. N. Gould
  Red Circle. A. C. Doyle; His Last Bow
  Reigate Squires. A. C. Doyle; Memoirs of Sherlock Holmes
  Second Stain. A. C. Doyle; Return of Sherlock Holmes
  Silver Blaze. A. C. Doyle; Memoirs of Sherlock Holmes
  Six Napoleons. A. C. Doyle; Return of Sherlock Holmes
  Speckled Band. A. C. Doyle; Adventures of Sherlock Holmes
  Stock-Broker's Clerk. A. C. Doyle; Memoirs of Sherlock Holmes
  Thor Bridge. A. C. Doyle; Casebook of Sherlock Holmes
  Three Students. A. C. Doyle; Return of Sherlock Holmes
  Trent's Last Case. E. C. Bentley
MANSE, JEAN
  Big Chief. O. Henry; Whirligigs
  Forbidden Fruit. G. Simenon; Act of Passion
MANTLE, BURNS
  Silver King. H. A. Jones
MARCEAU, FELECIEN
  Blonde Like That. J. H. Chase; Miss Shumway Waves a Wand
MARCHANT, WILLIAM
  My Lover, My Son. E. Grierson; Reputation for a Song

MARCIN, MAX
　Shadow of the Law. J. A. Moroso; Quarry

MARCUS, LARRY/LAWRENCE B.
　Covenant with Death. S. Becker
　Stunt Man. P. Brodeur
　Witness for the Prosecution. A. Christie

MARGOLIN, ARNOLD
　Russian Roulette. T. Ardies; Kosygin Is Coming

MARGOLIS, HERBERT F.
　Larceny. L. Eby; Velvet Fleece

MARIN, CARLOS
　Man and the Beast. R. L. Stevenson; Strange Case of Dr. Jekyll and Mr. Hyde

MARION, FRANCES
　Big House. J. Lait
　Cinema Murder. E. P. Oppenheim; Other Romilly
　Cynara. R. Gore-Brown; Imperfect Lover
　Knight Without Armour. J. Hilton
　Le Pere Goriot. H. Balzac
　Love from a Stranger. F. Vosper
　On Dangerous Ground. B. E. Stevenson; Little Comrade
　One Night in the Tropics. E. D. Biggers; Love Insurance
　Secret Six. F. Marion
　Within the Law. B. Veiller

MARION, GEORGE, JR.
　Fifty Roads to Town. F. Nebel

MARKO, ZEKIAL
　Once a Thief. J. Trinian; Scratch a Thief

MARKS, LEO
　Twisted Nerve. Peter Evans

MARKSON, BEN
　Case of the Howling Dog. E. S. Gardner
　Case of the Lucky Legs. E. S. Gardner
　White Cockatoo. M. G. Eberhart

MARKSTEIN, GEORGE
　Odessa File. F. Forsyth

MARLON, CHARLES
　Mystery of the Thirteenth Guest. A. Trail; Thirteenth Guest

MARLOW, BRIAN
　Forgotten Faces. R. W. Child; Velvet Black
　Murder Goes to College. K. Steel
　Night of June 13. F. Vreeland
　Return of Sophie Lang. F. I. Anderson; Notorious Sophie Lang
　Sophie Lang Goes West. F. I. Anderson; Notorious Sophie Lang

MARLOWE, DEREK
　Dandy in Aspic. D. Marlowe

MARMORSTEIN, MALCOLM
　S*P*Y*S. T. R. Joyce

MARRIOTT, ANTHONY
　Deadly Bees. H. F. Heard; Taste of Honey

MARSH, TERENCE
　Finders Keepers. C. Dennis; Next-to-Last Train Ride

MARSHAK, DARRYL A.
　Dracula Sucks. B. Stoker; Dracula

MARSHALL, GARRY
　Grasshopper. M. McShane; Passing of Evil

MARSHALL, ROGER
　And Now the Screaming Starts. D. Case; Fengriffin
　Five to One. E. Wallace; Thief in the Night
　Game for Three Losers. E. Lustgarten
　Man Outside. G. Stackelberg; Double Agent
　Ricochet. E. Wallace; Angel of Terror
　Set-Up. E. Wallace (headnote)
　Solo for Sparrow. E. Wallace; Gunner
　Two-Letter Alibi. A. Garve; Death and the Sky Above

What Became of Jack and Jill? L. Moody; Ruthless Ones
Who Was Maddox? E. Wallace; Undisclosed Client

MARSTON, THEODORE
　Aurora Floyd. M. E. Braddon
　East Lynne. H. Wood

MARTIN, A. Z.
　Mad Room. E. Percy; Ladies in Retirement

MARTIN, CLAUDE
　Blood and Roses. J. S. Le Fanu; In a Glass Darkly

MARTIN, JIM
　Black Eye. J. Jacks; Murder on the Wild Side

MARTIN, LOUIS
　Les Canailles. R. Marshall; You Find Him . . . I'll Fix Him

MARTIN, PAUL
　Orient Express. G. Greene; Stamboul Train

MARTIN, TROY KENNEDY
　Italian Job. T. K. Martin

MARTON, PIERRE
　Arabesque. Alex Gordon; Cipher

MARTYN, WYNDHAM
　Silver Car. W. Martyn; Secret of the Silver Car

MARX, ARTHUR
　Cancel My Reservation. L. L'Amour; Broken Gun

MASELLI, FRANCESCO
　Fine Pair. C. Stratton

MASON, BASIL
　Candles at Nine. Anthony Gilbert; Mouse Who Wouldn't Play Ball
　Crackerjack. W. B. M. Ferguson
　Death at Broadcasting House. V. Gielgud
　House of the Spaniard. A. Behrend
　Jewel. E. Wallace (headnote)

MASON, HOWARD
　Follow That Horse. H. Mason; Photo Finish

MASON, PAUL
　Committed. S. Claudia; Clock and Bell
　Ladies Club. Betty Black; Sisterhood

MASS, LEONARD, JR.
　Why Me? D. E. Westlake

MASSON, RENE
　Diabolique. P. Boileau; Woman Who Was

MASTERS, IAN
　Osterman Weekend. R. Ludlum

MASTROSIMONE, WILLIAM
　Extremities. W. Mastrosimone

MATALON, EDDY
　Too Small, My Friend. J. H. Chase; Way the Cookie Crumbles

MATHER, BERKLEY
　Doctor No. I. Fleming

MATHERS, JAMES
　Dr. Jekyll's Dungeon of Death. R. L. Stevenson; Strange Case of Dr. Jekyll and Mr. Hyde

MATHESON, RICHARD
　Comedy of Terrors. Elsie Lee
　Conjure Wife. F. Leiber, Jr.
　Devil Rides out. D. Wheatley
　Die! Die! My Darling. A. Blaisdell; Nightmare
　Dracula. B. Stoker
　Legend of Hell House. R. Matheson; Hell House
　Pit and the Pendulum. L. Sheridan
　Raven. E. Sudak
　Tales of Terror. E. Sudak

MATHIS, JUNE
　Blind Man's Eyes. W. MacHarg
　Hate. W. Camp; Communicating Door
　Island of Intrigue. I. Ostrander
　Way of the Strong. R. Cullum

MATTSON, ARNE
　Black Sun. P. Wahloo; Lorry

MAUCHETTE, JEAN-PATRICK
　Act of Aggression. J. Buell; Shrewsdale Exit

MAUGHAM, ROBIN
　Intruder. R. Maugham; Line on Ginger

MAY, ELAINE
　New Leaf. J. Ritchie

MAYER, EDWIN JUSTUS
　Phantom of Paris. G. Leroux; Cheri-Bibi and Cecily

MAYERSBERG, PAUL
　Disappearance. D. Marlowe; Echoes of Celandine

MAYES, WENDELL
　Anatomy of a Murder. R. Traver
　Bank Shot. D. E. Westlake
　Death Wish. B. Garfield
　Love and Bullets. J. Heddon
　Way to the Gold. W. D. Steele; Way to Gold

MAYFIELD, JULIAN
　Uptight. L. O'Flaherty; Informer

MAYLAM, TONY
　Riddle of the Sands. E. Childers

MEADE, WALTER
　Brandy for the Parson. G. Household; Tales of Adventurers
　High Command. L. Robinson; General Goes Too Far

MEAR, H(ARRY) FOWLER
　Alibi. M. Morton
　Anything Might Happen. H. Balfour
　Bella Donna. R. Hichens
　Black Coffee. A. Christie
　Chinese Puzzle. M. Bower
　Condemned to Death. G. Goodchild; Jack O'Lantern
　Death Croons the Blues. J. Ronald
　Dusty Ermine. N. Grant
　Excess Baggage. H. M. Raleigh
　Juggernaut. A. Campbell
　Last Hour. C. Bennett
　Last Journey. J. J. Farjeon; Holiday Express
　Lily of Kilarney. D. Boucicault; Colleen Bawn
　Lodger. M. B. Lowndes
　Lord Edgware Dies. A. Christie
　Lyons Mail. E. Moreau; Courier of Lyons
　Man Outside. D. Stuart
　Man Who Changed His Name. E. Wallace
　Murder at Covent Garden. W. J. Makin
　Pointing Finger. Rita
　Professional Guest. W. Garrett
　Roof. D. Whitelaw
　Shadow. D. Stuart
　Sherlock Holmes's Fatal Hour. A. C. Doyle; Memoirs of Sherlock Holmes
　Shot in the Dark. G. Fairlie
　Silent House. J. G. Brandon
　Silver Blaze. A. C. Doyle
　Tangled Evidence. P. C. De Crespigny
　Valley of Fear. A. C. Doyle

MECKERT, JEAN
　Look Out, Girls. J. H. Chase; Miss Callaghan Comes to Grief

MEDFORD, HAROLD
　Phantom of the Rue Morgue. E. A. Poe; Prose Romances of Edgar A. Poe

MEDIEFF, ALEX
　Try This On for Size. J. H. Chase

MEDIOLI, ENRICO
　Once Upon a Time in America. H. Grey; Hoods

MEDOFF, MARK
　Good Guys Wear Black. M. Franklin

MEDWIN, MICHAEL
　My Sister and I. E. Bonett; High Pavement

MEEHAN, ELIZABETH
　Mr. Reeder in Room 13. E. Wallace; Room 13

MEEHAN, JOHN, JR.
    Jump for Glory. G. McDonell
    Letty Lynton. M. B. Lowndes
    Madame X. J. C. MacConaughy
    Phantom of Paris. G. Leroux; Cheri-Bibi and Cecily
    Ten Days in Paris. B. Graeme; Disappearance of Roger Tremayne
    Thank Evans. E. Wallace; Good Evans!
MEKAS, ADOLFAS
    Double-Barrelled Detective Story. M. Twain
MELFORD, AUSTIN
    Don Chicago. C. E. B. Roberts
    Phantom Light. E. Price; Haunted Light
    Road House. W. Hackett
    Seven Sinners. A. Ridley; Wrecker
    Thank Evans. E. Wallace; Good Evans!
MELSON, JOHN
    Love and Bullets. J. Heddon
MELTZER, LEWIS
    Brothers Rico. G. Simenon
    First Comes Courage. E. Arnold; Commandos
    High School Confidential. Morton Cooper
MELVILLE, JEAN-PIERRE
    Army of Shadows. J. Kessel
    Magnet of Doom. G. Simenon
MENDELUK, GEORGE
    Stone Cold Dead. H. Garner; Sin Sniper
MENGE, WOLFGANG
    Der Grune Bogenschutze. E. Wallace; Green Archer
    Die Rot Kreis. E. Wallace; Crimson Circle
MENGER, W. H.
    Blindfold. L. Fletcher
MERCANTON, LOUIS
    Mystery of the Pink Villa. A. E. W. Mason; At the Villa Rose
MEREDYTH, BESS
    Great Hospital Mystery. M. G. Eberhart (headnote)
    Phantom of Paris. G. Leroux; Cheri-Bibi and Cecily
    Strangers of the Night. W. Hackett; Captain Applejack
    Unsuspected. C. Armstrong
MERGAULT, OLIVIER
    Moon in the Gutter. D. Goodis
MERIVALE, BERNARD
    Condemned to Death. G. Goodchild; Jack O'Lantern
MERRICK, FREDERICK
    Spy of Napoleon. B. Orczy
MERWIN, BANNISTER
    Firm of Girdlestone. A. C. Doyle
    Incomparable Bellairs. A. Castle
    Rogue in Love. T. Gallon
    Turf Conspiracy. N. Gould
MERZ, CARL
    Short Work. J. Ashford (headnote)
MESNIER, PAUL
    Cheri-Bibi. G. Leroux
METZGER, RADLEY
    Cat and the Canary. J. Willard
MEYER, NICHOLAS
    Seven-Per-Cent Solution. N. Meyer
    Time After Time. K. Alexander
MEYER, ROLF
    His Official Wife. R. H. Savage; My Official Wife
MICHAELS, SIDNEY
    Key Witness. F. Kane
MICHEL, BERNARD T.
    Five Ashore for Singapore. J. Bruce; Cold Spell

MIDA, MASSIMO
    House of Intrigue. H. J. Giskes; London Calling North Pole
MILES, CHRISTOPHER
    Maids. J. Genet
MILIUS, JOHN
    Dillinger. H. Clement
    Magnum Force. M. Valley
MILLAR, RONALD
    Never Let Me Go. R. Bax; Came the Dawn
    Scaramouche. R. Sabatini
    So Evil My Love. J. Shearing; For Her to See
MILLARD, OSCAR
    Dead Ringer. B. Thomas
    Reward. M. Barrett
    Salzburg Connection. H. MacInnes
MILLER, ALBERT G.
    Spider's Web. A. Christie
MILLER, ALICE D. G.
    Four Walls. D. Burnet
MILLER, CLAUDE
    Inquisitor. J. Wainwright; Brainwash
    Tell Him I Love Him. P. Highsmith; This Sweet Sickness
MILLER, FRANCIS
    Inquest. M. Barringer
    Trunk Crime. E. Percy
MILLER, FRANK
    Bleak House. C. Dickens
    False Evidence. E. P. Oppenheim
    Joyous Adventures of Aristide Pujol. W. J. Locke
    Robocop 2. E. Naha
    Trapped by the Mormons. Winifred Graham; Love Story of a Mormon
MILLER, HARVEY
    Jekyll and Hyde . . . Together Again. R. L. Stevenson; Strange Case of Dr. Jekyll and Mr. Hyde
MILLER, IRENE
    Jo, the Crossing Sweeper. C. Dickens; Bleak House
MILLER, J. CLARKSON
    Moral Sinner. C. M. S. McLellan; Leah Kleschna
MILLER, J. P.
    Behold a Pale Horse. E. Pressburger; Killing a Mouse on Sunday
    Young Savages. E. Hunter; Matter of Conviction
MILLER, MAX
    I Cover the Waterfront. Max Miller
MILLER, SETON I.
    Black Swan. R. Sabatini
    Calcutta. Alex Morrison
    Charlie Chan's Courage. E. D. Biggers; Chinese Parrot
    Convicted. M. Flavin; Criminal Code
    Criminal Code. M. Flavin
    "G" Men. H. K. Long
    Kid Galahad. Francis Wallace
    Last Mile. J. Wexley
    Ministry of Fear. G. Greene
    Murder in Trinidad. J. W. Vandercook
    Murder on a Honeymoon. S. Palmer; Puzzle of the Pepper Tree
    Penitentiary. M. Flavin; Criminal Code
    Scarface. A. Trail
    Singapore. W. Bogart
    Two in the Dark. G. Burgess; Two O'Clock Courage
MILLER, SIGMUND
    Wicked As They Come. B. Ballinger; Portrait in Smoke
MILLER, VICTOR
    Friday the 13th. S. Hawke
    Stranger Is Watching. M. H. Clark

MILLHAUSER, BERTRAM
    Black Secret. R. W. Chambers; In Secret
    Garden Murder Case. S. S. Van Dine
    Invisible Man's Revenge. H. G. Wells; Invisible Man
    Pearl of Death. A. C. Doyle; Return of Sherlock Holmes
    River's End. J. O. Curwood
    Romance of Elaine. A. B. Reeve
    Sherlock Holmes. W. Gillette
    Sherlock Holmes and the Spider Woman. A. C. Doyle; Sign of the Four
    Sherlock Holmes Faces Death. A. C. Doyle; Memoirs of Sherlock Holmes
    Suspect. J. Ronald; This Way Out
MILLIN, EUGENE
    My Official Wife. R. H. Savage
MILLS, HUGH
    Blackmailed. E. Myers; Mrs. Christopher
    Blanche Fury. J. Shearing
    So Long at the Fair. A. Thorne
MILNE, A. A.
    Birds of Prey. A. A. Milne; Fourth Wall
MILNE, PETER
    House of Fear. W. Camp
    Kennel Murder Case. S. S. Van Dine
    Mr. Moto in Danger Island. J. W. Vandercook; Murder in Trinidad
    Murder of Dr. Harrigan. M. G. Eberhart; From This Dark Stairway
    Return of the Terror. E. Wallace; Terror
    Verdict. I. Zangwill; Big Bow Mystery
    Woman in Red. Wallace Irwin; North Shore
MILTON, DAVID SCOTT
    Born to Win. M. Roote
MINER, MICHAEL
    Robocop. E. Naha
MINTER, GEORGE
    Tread Softly, Stranger. J. Popplewell; Blind Alley
MINTZ, SAM
    Cheerful Fraud. K. R. G. Browne; Following Ann
    Only Saps Work. O. Davis; Easy Come, Easy Go
MITCHELL, JAMES
    Callan. J. Mitchell; Magnum for Schneider
    Innocent Bystander. J. Munro
    Last Grenade. J. Sherlock; Ordeal of Major Grigsby
MITCHELL, JULIAN
    Arabesque. Alex Gordon; Cipher
MITCHELL, SOLLACE
    Dr. M. N. Jaques; Dr. Mabuse, Master of Mystery
MITHOIS, MARCEL
    Heart Trump for OSS 117 in Tokyo. J. Bruce; Hot Line
MOCKY, JEAN-PIERRE
    Agent Trouble. M. Bosse; Man Who Liked Zoos
    It's Freezing in Hell. E. Chaze; Black Wings Has My Angel
    Kill the Referee. A. Draper; Death Penalty
    No Pockets in a Shroud. H. McCoy
    Red Ibis. F. Brown; Knock Three-One-Two
    Unsewing Machine. G. Brewer; Killer Is Loose
MOESSINGER, DONALD
    Caper of the Golden Bulls. W. P. McGivern
    Nightmare in Chicago. W. P. McGivern; Killer on the Turnpike
MOFFAT, IVAN
    Black Sunday. T. Harris
    Boy on a Dolphin. D. Divine
MOFFITT, JOHN C.
    Mountain Music. M. Kantor; Author's Choice
    Murder with Pictures. G. H. Coxe

MOLINARO, EDOUARD
　Ravishing Idiot. C. Exbrayat

MOLL, ELICK
　House on Telegraph Hill. D. Lyon; Frightened Child
　Night Without Sleep. E. Moll

MONASH, PAUL
　Friends of Eddie Coyle. G. V. Kennedy
　Gun Runners. E. Hemingway; To Have and Have Not

MONKS, JOHN, JR.
　House on 92nd St. Alex Morrison
　Knock on Any Door. W. Motley
　People Against O'Hara. E. Lipsky

MONTAGNANA, LUISI
　Fine Pair. C. Stratton

MONTAGNE, EDWARD J.
　Man with My Face. S. W. Taylor
　Secrets of the Night. M. Marcin; Nightcap
　Too Many Crooks. E. J. Rath

MONTAGU, IVOR
　Last Man to Hang. G. Bullett; Jury

MONTALDO, GIULIANO
　Machine Gun McCain. O. Desmaris; Candyleg

MONTGOMERY, DOREEN
　At the Villa Rose. A. E. W. Mason
　Bulldog Sees It Through. G. Fairlie; Scissors Cut Paper
　Dead Men Tell No Tales. F. Beeding; Norwich Victims
　Flying Squad. E. Wallace
　House of the Arrow. A. E. W. Mason
　Mr. Reeder in Room 13. E. Wallace; Room 13
　Murder Reported. R. Chapman; Murder for the Million
　Narrowing Circle. J. Symons
　One Jump Ahead. R. Chapman
　Poison Pen. R. Llewellyn
　You Can't Escape. A. Kennington; She Died Young

MONTGOMERY, JAMES
　Ghost Breakers. C. W. Goddard

MOON, LORNA
　Mr. Wu. L. J. Miln

MOORE, BRIAN
　Torn Curtain. R. Wormser

MOORE, DUDLEY
　Hound of the Baskervilles. A. C. Doyle

MOORE, RAY
　Black Christmas. L. Hays

MOORE, VICTORIA
　Little Girl in a Big City. J. K. McCurdy

MOORE, W. EUGENE
　Oval Diamond. David Foster

MORA, PHILIPPE
　Marsupials: The Howling III. G. Brandner; Howling III

MORE, JULIAN
　Catamount Killings. J. H. Chase; I Would Rather Stay Poor
　Doctors Wear Scarlet. S. Raven

MORE, SHEILA
　Catamount Killings. J. H. Chase; I Would Rather Stay Poor

MORGAN, BYRON
　Five Star Final. L. Weitzenkorn
　Pace That Thrills. R. Weber

MORGAN, DIANA
　Pink String and Sealing Wax. R. Pertwee

MORGAN, GUY
　Front Page Story. R. Gaines; Final Night
　Hell Is Sold Out. M. Dekobra
　Man in the Road. A. Armstrong; He Was Found in the Road

MORGAN, SIDNEY
　Bid for Fortune. G. Boothby
　Bulldog Drummond's Third Round. H. C. McNeile; Third Round
　Lady Noggs—Peeress. E. Jepson
　Miriam Rozella. B. L. Farjeon
　What's Bred . . . Comes Out in the Flesh. G. Allen; What's Bred in the Bone
　Woman of the Iron Bracelets. F. Barrett

MORHAIM, JOE
　Man of Bronze. K. Robeson

MORHEIM, LOUIS
　Hunting Party. J. Millard
　Larceny. L. Eby; Velvet Fleece
　Rumble on the Docks. F. Paley

MORLAND, NIGEL
　Mrs. Pym of Scotland Yard. N. Morland (headnote)

MORPHETT, TONY
　Robbery Under Arms. R. Boldrewood

MORRIS, EDMUND
　Project X. L. P. Davies; Artificial Man

MORRISON, GREG
　Madhouse. Angus Hall; Qualtrough

MORRISON, T. J.
　Ice-Cold in Alex. C. Landon
　To the Public Danger. P. Hamilton; Money with Menaces

MORRISSEY, PAUL
　Hound of the Baskervilles. A. C. Doyle

MORROW, VIC
　Deathwatch. J. Genet; Maids and Deathwatch

MORTIMER, JOHN
　Act of Mercy. F. Clifford
　Bunny Lake Is Missing. E. Piper
　Innocents. H. James; Turn of the Screw
　Running Man. S. Smith; Ballad of the Running Man

MORTIMER, PENELOPE
　Bunny Lake Is Missing. E. Piper

MOSES, ANDREW
　Green Eyes. H. Ashbrook; Murder of Steven Kester
　Murder on the Campus. W. Chambers; Campanile Murders

MOSLEY, LEONARD
　Foxhole in Cairo. L. Mosley; Cat and the Mice

MOURY, ALAIN
　No Pockets in a Shroud. H. McCoy

MOUSSY, MARCEL
　Shoot the Pianist. D. Goodis; Down There

MUELBAUER, WOLFGANG
　Man Who Went Up in Smoke. M. Sjowall

MULHAUSER, JAMES
　Cheating Cheaters. M. Marcin
　Love Letters of a Star. Rufus King; Case of the Constant God

MULLER, ROBERT
　Woman of Straw. C. Arley

MULLIN, EUGENE
　Bottom of the Well. F. U. Adams
　Mr. Barnes of New York. A. C. Gunter
　Within the Law. B. Veiller

MURFIN, JANE
　Crime Doctor. I. Zangwill; Big Bow Mystery
　Seven Keys to Baldpate. E. D. Biggers

MURILLO, MARY
　East Lynne. H. Wood
　Ringer. E. Wallace
　Sign on the Door. C. Pollock
　Tangled Lives. W. Collins; Woman in White

MURPHY, DENNIS
　Eye of the Devil. P. Loraine; Day of the Arrow

MURPHY, RALPH
　Millie. D. H. Clarke

MURPHY, RICHARD
　Compulsion. M. Levin
　Cry of the City. H. E. Helseth; Chair for Martin Rome
　Kidnapping of the President. C. Templeton

MURPHY, WARREN B.
　Eiger Sanction. Trevanian

MYCROFT, WALTER C.
　Murder. C. Dane; Enter Sir John
　Yellow Mask. E. Wallace; Traitor's Gate

MYERS, HENRY
　Father Brown, Detective. G. K. Chesterton; Wisdom of Father Brown
　Murder by the Clock. Rufus King

MYERS, PETER
　Action of the Tiger. J. Wellard

MYTON, FRED
　Half a Chance. F. S. Isham
　Murder Is My Business. B. Halliday
　One Hour Before Dawn. M. Scott; Behind Red Curtains
　Social Buccaneer. F. S. Isham

MYTON, KENNEDY
　Parisian Nights. R. Goyne

NA'AMAN, RAMI
　Road to Ein Harod. A. Kenan

NAKANO, DESMOND
　Boulevard Nights. D. Gram

NARCEJAC, THOMAS
　She Wolves. P. Boileau; Prisoner

NASH, J. E.
　Madame X. J. W. MacConaughy
　Under the Lash. A. Askew; Shulamite

NASH, MICHAEL
　Lost Continent. D. Wheatley; Uncharted Seas

NASH, N. RICHARD
　Nora Prentiss. Alex Morrison

NATKIN, RICK
　Night of the Juggler. W. P. McGivern

NATTEFORD, J. FRANCIS
　File 113. E. Gaboriau; File No. 113
　Gun-Runner. A. Stringer

NEAL, LEX
　Speedy. R. Holman

NEAME, DEREK
　Small Voice. R. Westerby

NEAME, RONALD
　Golden Salamander. V. Canning

NEBENZAL, HAROLD
　Wilby Conspiracy. P. Driscoll

NEILL, ROY WILLIAM
　Scarlet Claw. A. C. Doyle; Hound of the Baskervilles

NELSON, RALPH
　Wrath of God. J. Graham

NENOVA, NELLI
　Srok Istekaet Na Rassvete. W. Irish; Deadline at Dawn

NERZ, LUDWIG
　Hands of Orlac. M. Renard

NEUBERG, A.
　Trick Baby. I. Slim

NEUKIRCHEN, DOROTHEA
　Story-Teller. P. Highsmith

NEUMAN, E. JACK
　Venetian Affair. H. MacInnes

NEUMEIER, EDWARD
　Robocop. E. Naha

NEVILLE, JOHN T.
  Last of the Lone Wolf. L. J. Vance; Lone Wolf
NEWALL, GUY
  Chin-Chin-Chinaman. P. Walsh
  Maid of the Silver Sea. J. Oxenham
NEWHOUSE, DAVID
  Point Blank. R. Stark; Hunter
NEWHOUSE, RAFE
  Point Blank. R. Stark; Hunter
NEWMAN, DAVID
  Bonnie and Clyde. B. Hirschfeld
NEWMAN, WALTER
  Bloodbrothers. R. Price
  Crime and Punishment USA. F. M. Dostoevskii; Crime and Punishment
NIBLO, FRED, JR.
  Convicted. M. Flavin; Criminal Code
  Criminal Code. M. Flavin
  Get-Rich-Quick-Wallingford. G. R. Chester
  Nine Lives Are Not Enough. J. Odlum
  Passage from Hong Kong. E. D. Biggers; Agony Column
  Penitentiary. M. Flavin; Criminal Code
  Wagons Roll at Night. Francis Wallace; Kid Galahad
NICHOLS, DUDLEY
  Fugitive. G. Greene; Power and the Glory
  Informer. L. O'Flaherty
  Judge Priest. I. S. Cobb; Down Yonder with Judge Priest
  Louis Beretti. D. H. Clarke
  Man Hunt. G. Household; Rogue Male
  Run for the Sun. R. Connell; Variety
  Ten Little Indians. A. Christie; Ten Little Niggers
  Ten Little Niggers. A. Christie
NICOLAYSEN, BRUCE
  Passage. B. Nicolaysen; Perilous Passage
NIMIER, ROGER
  Affair of Nina B. J. M. Simmel
  Elevator to the Gallows. N. Calef; Frantic
NOBLES, WILLIAM
  Scarlet Weekend. W. Kent; Woman in Purple Pajamas
NOLAN, WILLIAM F.
  Burnt Offerings. R. Marasco
NOLBANDOV, SERGEI
  Amateur Gentleman. J. Farnol
  Four Just Men. E. Wallace
  There Ain't No Justice. J. Curtis
NORMAN, MARC
  Killer Elite. R. Rostand
NORRIS, CHUCK
  Invasion U.S.A. J. Frost
NORTH, EDMUND H.
  Colorado Territory. W. R. Burnett; High Sierra
  Dishonoured Lady. M. B. Lowndes; Letty Lynton
  Flamingo Road. R. Wilder
  Murder on a Bridle Path. S. Palmer; Puzzle of the Red Stallion
NORTH, MARION
  Sing Sing Nights. H. S. Keeler
NORTON, ELEANOR ELIAS
  Dirty Tricks. T. Gifford; Glendower Legacy
NORTON, WILLIAM
  Hunting Party. J. Millard
  Mackenzie Break. S. Shelly; Bowmanville Break
NORTON, WILLIAM, SR.
  Dirty Tricks. T. Gifford; Glendower Legacy
  Night of the Juggler. W. P. McGivern
NOVELLO, IVOR
  Lodger. M. B. Lowndes

NOY, WILFRED
  Marriage Lines. J. S. Fletcher
NOYCE, PHILLIP
  Heatwave. Timothy Harris
NUGENT, ELLIOTT
  Unholy Three. T. Robbins
  Whistling in the Dark. L. Gross
NUGENT, J. C.
  Unholy Three. T. Robbins
NUNEZ, VICTOR
  Flash of Green. J. D. MacDonald
OAKSEY, JOHN
  Dead Cert. D. Francis
O'BANNON, DAN
  Return of the Living Dead. J. Russo
O'BANNON, ROCKNE S.
  Alien Nation. A. D. Foster
OBOLER, ARCH
  Escape. E. Vance
O'BRIEN, LIAM
  Diplomatic Courier. P. Cheyney; Sinister Errand
O'BRIEN, ROBERT
  Lady on a Train. L. Charteris
  Lemon Drop Kid. D. Runyon; Bloodhounds of Broadway
O'BRINE, MANNING
  Murder at Site Three. W. H. Baker; Crime Is My Business
OBROW, JEFFREY
  Servants of Twilight. L. Nichols; Twilight
O'CONNELL, ROBERT
  Lone Wolf Returns. L. J. Vance
O'CONNOLLY, JIM
  Night Caller. F. Crisp; Night Callers
O'CONNOR, MANNING
  Dressed to Kill. R. Burke; Dead Take No Bows
  Michael Shayne, Private Detective. B. Halliday; Private Practice of Michael Shayne
O'CONNOR, MARY
  Dangerous Lies. E. P. Oppenheim (headnote)
  Mystery Road. E. P. Oppenheim
O'DEA, JOHN
  Fugitive Lady. D. M. Disney (headnote)
ODELL, DAVID
  Cry Uncle. M. Brett; Lie a Little, Die a Little
O'DELL, DENIS
  Tread Softly, Stranger. J. Popplewell; Blind Alley
ODETS, CLIFFORD
  Deadline at Dawn. W. Irish
  General Died at Dawn. C. G. Booth
O'DONOGHUE, JAMES T.
  Cheating Cheaters. M. Marcin
O'DONOHOE, JAMES T.
  Hawk's Nest. W. Gunning
OEMLER, MARIE CONWAY
  Slippy McGee. M. C. Oemler
OFFNER, MORTIMER
  Saint in New York. L. Charteris
O'FLAHERTY, DENNIS
  Hammett. J. Gores
OGUNI, HIDEO
  High and Low. E. McBain; King's Ransom
O'HANLON, JAMES
  Slight Case of Murder. D. Runyon
O'HARA, GEORGE
  Side Street. M. St. Clair
O'HARA, GERRY
  Bitch. Jackie Collins

Phantom of the Opera. G. Leroux
Ten Little Indians. A. Christie; Ten Little Niggers
O'HARA, JOHN
  Moontide. Willard Robertson
O'HARA, MARY
  Love Racket. B. K. Burns; Jury Woman
OLIVER, STEPHEN
  Sunburn. S. Ellin; Bind
OLSEN, DANA
  Memoirs of an Invisible Man. H. F. Saint
O'NEIL, ROBERT VINCENT
  Vice Squad. W. Rotsler
OPHULS, MARCEL
  Banana Peel. C. Williams; Nothing in the Way
OPPENHEIMER, GEORGE
  I Love You Again. O. R. Cohen
ORDE, JULIAN
  Small Voice. R. Westerby
ORKOW, W. HARRISON
  Gorilla. R. Spence
ORLOV, ALEXANDER
  Strange Case of Dr. Jekyll and Mr. Hyde. R. L. Stevenson
ORMONDE, CZENZI
  Strangers on a Train. P. Highsmith
ORNITZ, SAMUEL
  Thirteen Women. T. Thayer
ORR, GERTRUDE
  Blind Goddess. A. Train
  Mandarin Mystery. E. Queen; Chinese Orange Mystery
ORR, JAMES
  Tough Guys. I. Don
ORROM, MICHAEL
  No Resting Place. I. Niall
ORTH, MARION
  Charlie Chan's Greatest Case. E. D. Biggers; House Without a Key
  Come to My House. A. S. Roche
  People vs. Nancy Preston. J. A. Moroso; People Against Nancy Preston
ORTON, J. O. C.
  Bones. E. Wallace
  Cottage to Let. G. Kerr; Cottages to Let
  Ghost Train. A. Ridley
  It's in the Blood. D. Whitelaw; Big Picture
  Non-Stop New York. K. Attiwill; Sky Steward
ORTON, JOE
  Celestial City. B. Orczy
ORTON, JOHN
  Everything Is Thunder. J. L. Hardy
  Limping Man. W. Scott; Man
  Shooting Stars. E. C. Vivian
OSBORN, DAVID
  Deadlier Than the Male. H. Reymond
  Maroc 7. M. Sands
  Moment of Danger. D. MacKenzie; Scent of Danger
  Murder, She Said. A. Christie; 4.50 from Paddington
OSBORN, DAVID D.
  Chase a Crooked Shadow. A. Shaughnessy; Double Cut
OSBORNE, W. H.
  Running Fight. W. H. Osborne
O'SHAUGHNESSY, ALFRED
  Brandy for the Parson. G. Household; Tales of Adventurers
OSIECKI, STEFAN
  No Way Back. T. Burke; Limehouse Nights

OSTRER, BERTRAM
　　Park Plaza 605. B. Gray; Dare-Devil Conquest
OSWALD, RICHARD
　　Hound of the Baskervilles. A. C. Doyle
OXLADE, BOYD
　　Death in Brunswick. B. Oxlade
OYA, IKUKO
　　Lonely Hearts. E. McBain; Lady, Lady, I Did It!
OZEP, FYODOR
　　Brothers Karamazov. F. M. Dostoevskii
PACKARD, FRANK L.
　　Pawned. F. L. Packard
PAGANO, JO
　　Hotel Berlin. V. Baum; Hotel Berlin '43
　　Try and Get Me. J. Pagano; Condemned
PAGE, MARCO
　　Fast Company. Marco Page
PAICE, ERIC
　　Man in the Back Seat. E. Wallace (headnote)
PAKULA, ALAN J.
　　Presumed Innocent. S. Turow
PAL, GEORGE
　　Man of Bronze. K. Robeson
PALA, GIOGIO
　　Brothers Karamazov. F. M. Dostoevskii
PALCY, EUZHAN
　　Dry White Season. A. Brink
PALMER, STUART
　　Arrest Bulldog Drummond. H. C. McNeile; Final Count
　　Bulldog Drummond's Bride. H. C. McNeile; Sapper: The Best Short Stories
　　Bulldog Drummond's Peril. H. C. McNeile; Third Round
　　Death of a Champion. F. Gruber; Brass Knuckles
　　Who Killed Aunt Maggie? Medora Field
PANDURO, LEIF
　　Ghost Train. A. Ridley
PARAMORE, EDWARD E., JR.
　　Baby, Take a Bow. J. P. Judge; Square Crooks
　　Trouble for Two. R. L. Stevenson; Suicide Club
PARK, IDA MAY
　　Grasp of Greed. H. R. Haggard; Mr. Meeson's Will
PARKER, ALAN
　　Angel Heart. W. Hjortsberg; Falling Angel
　　Mississippi Burning. J. Norst
PARKER, JEFFERSON
　　Human Cargo. K. Shepard; I Will Be Faithful
PARKER, WILLIAM
　　Scarlet Car. R. H. Davis
PARKS, GORDON
　　Learned Tree. G. Parks
PARRISH, JAMES
　　Bulldog Drummond at Bay. H. C. McNeile
PARRY, GORDON
　　Now Barabbas. W. D. Home
PARSONNET, MARION
　　Dangerous Partners. O. W. Bayer; Paper Chase
　　Miracles for Sale. C. Rawson; Death from a Top Hat
　　Thirteenth Chair. B. Veiller
PARSONS, LINDSLEY
　　Trail Beyond. J. O. Curwood; Wolf Hunters
PARTOS, FRANK
　　Guilty As Hell. D. N. Rubin; Riddle Me This!
　　House on Telegraph Hill. D. Lyon; Frightened Child
　　Night of Mystery. S. S. Van Dine; Greene Murder Case

Night Without Sleep. E. Moll
Port Afrique. B. V. Dryer
PASCAL, ERNEST
　　Flesh and Fantasy. O. Wilde; Lord Arthur Savile's Crime
　　Hound of the Baskervilles. A. C. Doyle
　　Interference. R. Pertwee
　　Love Under Fire. W. Hackett; Fugitives
PASLEY, FRED
　　Scarface. A. Trail
PATON, STUART
　　Loot. A. S. Roche
PATRICK, JOHN
　　Main Attraction. S. Michaels
PATRICK, VINCENT
　　Family Business. V. Patrick
　　Pope of Greenwich Village. V. Patrick
PATTON, N. F.
　　Knocknagow. C. Kickham
PAXTON, JOHN
　　Crack-Up. F. Brown; Madman's Holiday
　　Crossfire. R. Brooks; Brick Foxhole
　　Farewell, My Lovely. R. Chandler
　　Pickup Alley. E. Ronns
　　Prize of Gold. M. Catto
PEACH, L. DU GARDE
　　Dusty Ermine. N. Grant
　　Ghoul. F. King
　　His Lordship. N. Grant; Nelson Touch
　　Seven Sinners. A. Ridley; Wrecker
　　Spy of Napoleon. B. Orczy
PEACOCK, JOHN
　　To the Devil—a Daughter. D. Wheatley
PEACOCK, LESLIE T.
　　Woman Who Dared. A. M. Williamson
PEARCE, DONN
　　Cool Hand Luke. Donn Pearce
PEARSON, GEORGE
　　Angel Esquire. E. Wallace
　　Pollard the Punter. E. Wallace; Grey Timothy
　　Third String. W. W. Jacobs; Odd Craft
PECKINPAH, SAM
　　Straw Dogs. G. M. Williams; Siege of Trencher's Farm
PEDELTY, DONOVAN
　　I'll Never Tell. R. Vickers
PEDRICK, GALE
　　Meet Simon Cherry. G. Pedrick; Meet the Rev
PELISSIER, ANTHONY
　　Personal Affair. L. Storm; Day's Mischief
　　Tiger in the Smoke. M. Allingham
PEMBERTON, MAX
　　Kronstadt. M. Pemberton
PENTTI, PAULI
　　Crime and Punishment. F. M. Dostoevskii
PEOPLE, DAVID
　　Blade Runner. P. K. Dick; Do Androids Dream of Electric Sheep?
PEPPER, DAN
　　Enemy General. D. Pepper
PEREC, GEORGES
　　Thriller Story. J. Thompson; Hell of a Woman
PERIER, ETIENNE
　　Meurtre en 45 Tours. P. Boileau; Heart to Heart
PERKINS, ANTHONY
　　Last of Sheila. A. Edwards
PERL, ARNOLD
　　Cotton Comes to Harlem. C. Himes
PERRAULT, GILES
　　Dossier 51. G. Perrault

PERRET, LEONCE
　　Silent Master. E. P. Oppenheim; Seeing Life
　　Thirteen Chairs. B. Veiller
　　Twin Pawns. W. Collins; Woman in White
PERRIN, NAT
　　Gracie Allen Murder Case. S. S. Van Dine
PERRY, BEN
　　Brothers Rico. G. Simenon
PERRY, CHARLES
　　Each Dawn I Die. J. Odlum
PERRY, ELEANOR
　　Lady in the Car with Glasses and a Gun. S. Japrisot
PERRY, SIMON
　　Eclipse. N. Wollaston
PERTWEE, MICHAEL
　　Crackerjack. W. B. M. Ferguson
　　Make Mine Mink. P. Coke; Breath of Spring
　　Night Was Our Friend. M. Pertwee
　　One More Time. M. Avallone
　　Salt and Pepper. Alex Austin
　　Silent Dust. R. Pertwee; Paragon
PERTWEE, ROLAND
　　Four Just Men. E. Wallace
　　Ghoul. F. King
　　Honours Easy. R. Pertwee
　　Madonna of the Seven Moons. M. Lawrence
　　Murder on the Second Floor. F. Vosper
　　Night Invader. J. Bentley; Rendezvous with Death
　　Non-Stop New York. K. Attiwill; Sky Steward
　　Quinney's. H. A. Vachell
　　Spy in Black. J. S. Clouston
　　They Came by Night. B. Lyndon
　　Ware Case. G. Pleydell
PETERS, KENNETH
　　Vice Squad. W. Rotsler
PETERSEN, DON
　　Target. S. Hunter
PETERSEN, WOLFGANG
　　Shattered. R. Neely; Plastic Nightmare
PETERSSON, HARALD G.
　　Das Indische Tuch. E. Wallace; Frightened Lady
　　Der Zinker. E. Wallace; Squeaker
　　Die Tur mit den Sieben Schlosser. E. Wallace; Door with the Seven Locks
PETIEVICH, GERALD
　　To Live and Die in L.A. G. Petievich
PETIT, CHRISTOPHER
　　Unsuitable Job for a Woman. P. D. James
PETRI, ELIO
　　Quiet Place in the Country. H. Clement
　　Tenth Victim. R. Sheckley
　　We Still Kill the Old Way. L. Sciascia; Man's Blessing
PETRIE, DAN, JR.
　　Big Easy. J. Conaway
　　Toy Soldiers. W. P. Kennedy
PETTICLERC, DENNE BART
　　Then Came Bronson. W. Johnston
PETTITT, WILFRID H.
　　Walls Came Tumbling Down. J. Eisinger
PEYSER, ARNOLD
　　Trouble with Girls. D. Keene; Chautauqua
PEYSER, LOIS
　　Trouble with Girls. D. Keene; Chautauqua
PFARRER, CHUCK
　　Darkman. Randall Boyle
PHELAN, JIM
　　Night Journey. J. Phelan; Ten-a-Penny People
PHILIPS, QUENTIN
　　Room 13. E. Wallace

Screenwriters Index

PHIPPENY, ROBERT
  Night of the Following Day. L. White; Snatchers
PHIPPS, NICHOLAS
  Appointment with Venus. J. Tickell
PICARD, BURT
  Enemy General. D. Pepper
PIEDMONT, LEON
  Mean Season. J. Katzenbach; In the Heat of Summer
PIELMEIER, JOHN
  Agnes of God. J. Pielmeier
PIERSON, ARTHUR
  Footsteps in the Fog. W. W. Jacobs; Sea Whispers
PIERSON, FRANK R.
  Anderson Tapes. Lawrence Sanders
  Cool Hand Luke. Donn Pearce
  Dog Day Afternoon. P. Mann
  Happening. E. Curry
  Looking Glass War. J. Le Carre
  Presumed Innocent. S. Turow
PIETERS, VIVIAN
  Prey. C. Aird; Henrietta Who
PIETRANGELI, ANTONIO
  Obsession. J. M. Cain; Postman Always Rings Twice
PIGOTT, WILLIAM
  Lion Man. R. Parrish; Strange Case of Cavendish
PILCHER, JAY
  Steele of the Royal Mounted. J. O. Curwood; Philip Steele of the Royal Northwest Mounted Police
PINERO, MIGUEL
  Short Eyes. M. Pinero
PINOTEAU, CLAUDE
  Big Operator. R. Airth; Snatch
  Le Silencieux. F. Ryck; Loaded Gun
PINTER, HAROLD
  Birthday Party. H. Pinter
  Quiller Memorandum. Adam Hall; Berlin Memorandum
PIRES, GERARD
  Act of Aggression. J. Buell; Shrewsdale Exit
  Fantasia Among the Squares. C. Williams; Diamond Bikini
  Undertaker Parlor Computer. W. Kempley; Probability Factor
PIRIEV, IVAN
  Brothers Karamazov. F. M. Dostoevskii
PIROSH, ROBERT
  Night of January 16. A. Rand
PIRRO, UGO
  Day of the Owl. L. Sciascia; Mafia Vendetta
  We Still Kill the Old Way. L. Sciascia; Man's Blessing
PLATER, ALAN
  Juggernaut. A. Hine
PLYMPTON, GEORGE H.
  Alibi. G. A. England
  Blind Adventure. E. D. Biggers; Agony Column
  Scarlet Runner. C. N. Williamson
  Winifred the Shop Girl. C. N. Williamson; Shop Girl
POE, JAMES
  Big Knife. C. Odets
  Dark Page. S. Fuller
  Riot. F. Elli
  Sanctuary. W. Faulkner
  They Shoot Horses, Don't They? H. McCoy
POGOSTIN, LEE
  High Road to China. J. Cleary
  Nightmare Honeymoon. L. Block (headnote)

POGUE, CHARLES
  Hound of the Baskervilles. A. C. Doyle
  Sign of the Four. A. C. Doyle
POHLAND, HANSJURGEN
  Tamara. Hansjorg Martin; Sleeping Girls Don't Lie
POITRENAUD, JACQUES
  Old Tin Can. D. Keene; Flight by Night
POLAND, JOSEPH FRANKLIN
  Honor First. G. F. Gibbs; Splendid Outcast
POLANSKI, ROMAN
  Rosemary's Baby. I. Levin
  Tenant. R. Topor
POLLOCK, BARRY
  Cool Breeze. W. R. Burnett; Asphalt Jungle
POLLOCK, MAX
  On Trial. E. L. Reizenstein
POLONSKY, ABRAHAM
  Avalanche Express. C. Forbes
  Force of Evil. I. Wolfert; Tucker's People
  Golden Earrings. Y. Foldes
  Madigan. R. Dougherty; Commissioner
  Nuts. T. Topor
POOLEY, OLAF
  Godsend. B. Taylor
POPE, THOMAS
  Hammett. J. Gores
PORTA, ELVIO
  Payoff. A. Veraldi
PORTER, EDWARD S.
  Gallegher. R. H. Davis
  Gentleman Burglar. M. Leblanc (headnote)
  Luck of Roaring Camp. Bret Harte; Bret Harte's Choice Bits
  Winngs of Miss Langton. R. H. Davis; Once Upon a Time
POTTER, DENNIS
  Gorky Park. M. C. Smith
  Secret Friends. D. Potter; Ticket to Ride
POTTER, PAUL
  Arsene Lupin. E. Jepson
POWELL, A. VAN BUREN
  Blue Envelope Mystery. S. Kerr; Blue Envelope
POWELL, FRANK
  Mrs. Balfame. G. Atherton
POWELL, MICHAEL
  Elusive Pimpernel. B. Orczy
  77, Park Lane. W. Hackett
  Small Back Room. N. Balchin
POWELL, PETER
  Human Factor. S. Quinn
POWELL, RICHARD
  My Gun Is Quick. M. Spillane
POZNER, VLADIMIR
  Conspirators. F. Prokosch
  Le Mystere de la Chambre Jaune. G. Leroux; Mystery of the Yellow Room
  Le Parfum de la Dame en Noire. G. Leroux; Perfume of the Lady in Black
PRASKINS, LEONARD
  Caribbean Mystery. J. W. Vandercook; Murder in Trinidad
  Gentleman's Fate. K. U. P.
PREMINGER, ERIK LEE
  Rosebud. J. Hemingway
PRESNELL, ROBERT, JR.
  Let No Man Write My Epitaph. W. Motley
  Life in the Balance. G. Simenon (headnote)
  Man in the Attic. M. B. Lowndes; Lodger
  Third Day. J. Hayes
  13 West Street. L. Brackett; Tiger Among Us

PRESNELL, ROBERT R., SR.
  Guilty. W. Irish; Dancing Detective
  Kennel Murder Case. S. S. Van Dine
  Man Called Back. A. Soutar; Silent Thunder
PRESSBURGER, EMERIC
  Elusive Pimpernel. B. Orczy
  Small Back Room. N. Balchin
  Spy for a Day. S. Aumonier; Love-a-Duck
  Spy in Black. J. S. Clouston
PRESTON, TREVOR
  Slayground. R. Stark
PREVERT, JACQUES
  Bizarre, Bizarre. J. S. Clouston; His First Offense
PRICE, JEFFREY
  Who Framed Roger Rabbit? G. K. Wolf; Who Censored Roger Rabbit?
PRICE, STANLEY
  Arabesque. Alex Gordon; Cipher
  Golden Rendezvous. A. MacLean
PRICE, TIM ROSE
  Shuttlecock. G. Swift
PRIESTLEY, J. B.
  Jamaica Inn. D. Du Maurier
PRINTZLAU, OLGA
  John Needham's Double. J. Hatton
  Pals First. L. W. Dodd
PROCHNIK, LEON
  Child's Play. R. Marasco
PROCTOR, GEORGE DUBOIS
  Other Men's Shoes. A. Soutar
PROPER, ROGIER
  Rattlerat. J. van de Wetering
PUCCINI, GIANNI
  Obsession. J. M. Cain; Postman Always Rings Twice
PULAJA, GENNADY
  Srok Istekaet Na Rassvete. W. Irish; Deadline at Dawn
PURCELL, GERTRUDE
  Ellery Queen and the Murder Ring. E. Queen; Dutch Shoe Mystery
  One Night in the Tropics. E. D. Biggers; Love Insurance
PURDELL, REGINALD
  Dark Tower. A. Woollcott
  It's in the Blood. D. Whitelaw; Big Picture
  Love on the Spot. H. C. McNeile; Three of a Kind
PURSALL, DAVID
  Alphabet Murders. A. Christie; ABC Murders
  Murder at the Gallop. A. Christie; After the Funeral
  Murder Most Foul. A. Christie; Mrs. McGinty's Dead
  Murder, She Said. A. Christie; 4.50 from Paddington
  What Changed Charley Farthing? M. Hebden
PURZER, MANFRED
  All People Will Be Brothers. J. M. Simmel; Cain '67
  And Jimmy Went to the Rainbow's Foot. J. M. Simmel; Caesar Code
  Love Is Only a Word. J. M. Simmel; Love Is Just a Word
  Only the Wind Knows the Answer. J. M. Simmel; Wind and the Rain
  Stuff That Dreams Are Made Of. J. M. Simmel; Traitor Blitz
PUZO, MARIO
  Godfather. M. Puzo
  Godfather, Part II. M. Puzo; Godfather
QUINE, RICHARD
  Notorious Landlady. I. Shulman

Q

RACKIN, MARTIN
    Hell on Frisco Bay. W. P. McGivern; Darkest Hour
    Murder, Inc. J. Eastwood
RADER, GEORGE
    Mr. Potter of Texas. A. C. Gunter
RAEWYN, T.
    Trick Baby. I. Slim
RAIMI, IVAN
    Darkman. Randall Boyle
RAIMI, SAM
    Darkman. Randall Boyle
RAINE, NORMAN REILLY
    Each Dawn I Die. J. Odlum
RAISON, MILTON
    Murder on the Yukon. L. Y. Erskine; Renfrew Rides North
    Phantom of Forty-Second Street. M. M. Raison
RALEY, RON
    Edge of Sanity. R. L. Stevenson; Strange Case of Dr. Jekyll and Mr. Hyde
RALSTON, GILBERT A.
    Ben. G. A. Ralston
    Willard. S. Gilbert; Ratman's Notebooks
RAMEAU, HANS GULDER
    Rat. P. Bottome
RAND, AYN
    Love Letters. C. Massie; Pity My Simplicity
RANK, CHRISTOPHER
    Passengers. K. R. Dwyer; Chase
RAPF, MAURICE
    They Gave Him a Gun. W. J. Cowen
RAPHAEL, FREDERIC
    Nothing But the Best. S. Ellin; Mystery Stories
RAPHAELSON, SAMSON
    Last of Mrs. Cheyney. F. Lonsdale
    Suspicion. F. Iles; Before the Fact
RAPPENEAU, ELIZABETH
    FM—Frequency Murder. S. M. Kaminsky; When Dark Man Calls
    Twin. D. E. Westlake; Two Much!
RASKIN, HARRY
    Postman Always Rings Twice. J. M. Cain
RATHMELL, JOHN
    Fighting Mad. L. Y. Erskine; Renfrew Rides Again
RATTIGAN, TERENCE
    Brighton Rock. G. Greene
RAUCHER, HERMAN
    Other Side of Midnight. S. Sheldon
RAUH, STANLEY
    Dressed to Kill. R. Burke; Dead Take No Bows
    Michael Shayne, Private Detective. B. Halliday; Private Practice of Michael Shayne
    Sleepers West. F. Nebel; Sleepers East
RAVEN, SIMON
    On Her Majesty's Secret Service. I. Fleming
RAVETCH, IRVING
    House of Cards. S. Ellin
    Spikes Gang. G. Tippette; Bank Robber
RAWLINSON, A. R.
    Chinese Bungalow. M. Osmond
    Crackerjack. W. B. M. Ferguson
    Dark Secret. M. Shairp; Crime at Blossoms
    Gas Light. P. Hamilton
    Man Who Knew Too Much. R. Alexander
    Meet Simon Cherry. G. Pedrick; Meet the Rev
    My Sister and I. E. Bonett; High Pavement
    News of Paul Temple. F. Durbridge
    Sexton Blake and the Hooded Terror. P. Quiroule; Mystery of No. 13 Caversham Square
    Someone at the Door. D. Christie
    Spies of the Air. J. Dell
    Story of Shirley Yorke. H. A. Vachell; Case of Lady Camber
    Strange Boarders. E. P. Oppenheim; Strange Boarders of Palace Crescent
    Ticket-of-Leave Man. T. Taylor
RAY, NICHOLAS
    On Dangerous Ground. G. Butler; Mad with Much Heart
    They Live by Night. E. Anderson; Thieves Like Us
RAYFIEL, DAVID
    Three Days of the Condor. J. Grady; Six Days of the Condor
    Valdez Is Coming. E. Leonard
RAYMOND, CHARLES
    Mystery of the Diamond Belt. Lewis Carlton
RAYNOR, WILLIAM
    Yukon Gold. J. O. Curwood; Gold Hunters
READ, JAN
    Grip of the Strangler. J. C. Cooper
    Secret Tent. E. Addyman
READ, TOM
    Moss Rose. J. Shearing
REARDON, JAMES
    Third String. W. W. Jacobs; Odd Craft
REBOT, SADDY
    Too Small, My Friend. J. H. Chase; Way the Cookie Crumbles
RED, ERIC
    Body Parts. P. Boileau; Choice Cuts
REDLIN, ROBERT
    After Dark, My Sweet. Jim Thompson
REED, KATHARINE
    Girl in His House. H. MacGrath
REED, TOM
    Back to God's Country. J. O. Curwood
    Bombay Mail. L. G. Blochman
    Calling Philo Vance. S. S. Van Dine; Kennel Murder Case
    Case of the Curious Bride. E. S. Gardner
    Case of the Velvet Claws. E. S. Gardner
    Florentine Dagger. B. Hecht
    Last Warning. W. Camp; House of Fear
    Murders in the Rue Morgue. E. A. Poe; Prose Romances of Edgar A. Poe
    Phantom of the Opera. G. Leroux
REES, JOAN
    My Sister and I. E. Bonett; High Pavement
REEVE, ARTHUR B.
    Master Mystery. A. B. Reeve
    Mystery Mind. A. B. Reeve
REEVES, MICHAEL
    Witch-Finder General. R. Bassett
REICHERT, MARK
    Union City. C. Woolrich; Nightwebs
REID, ALASTAIR
    Something to Hide. N. Monsarrat
REID, ARTHUR
    To the Public Danger. P. Hamilton; Money with Menaces
REID, DOROTHY
    Footsteps in the Fog. W. W. Jacobs; Sea Whispers
REINECKER, HERBERT
    Maigret und Sein Grosster Fall. G. Simenon; At the Gai-Moulin
    Squeaker. E. Wallace; Ringer
REINHARDT, BETTY
    Laura. V. Caspary
REINHARDT, JOHN
    River Pirate. C. F. Coe
REINHARDT, SILVIA
    Town Without Pity. M. Gregor
REINITS, REX
    Out of the Clouds. J. Fores; Springboard
REISCH, WALTER
    Gas Light. P. Hamilton
    Stopover: Tokyo. J. P. Marquand
REISMAN, DEL
    Take. G. F. Newman; Sir, You Bastard
RELPH, MICHAEL
    Assassination Bureau. J. London
    Man Who Haunted Himself. A. Armstrong; He Was Found in the Road
    Masquerade. V. Canning; Castle Minerva
    Out of the Clouds. J. Fores; Springboard
    Place to Go. M. Fisher; Bethnel Green
    Ship That Died of Shame. N. Monsarrat
    Woman of Straw. C. Arley
REMY, JACQUES
    Night Heaven Fell. A. Vidalie; Midnight Jewelers
RENOIR, JEAN
    Night at the Crossroads. G. Simenon; Crossroads Murders
    Woman on the Beach. M. A. Wilson; None So Blind
REVILLE, ALMA
    After the Verdict. R. Hichens
    Jamaica Inn. D. Du Maurier
    Murder. C. Dane; Enter Sir John
    No. 17. J. J. Farjeon
    Paradine Case. R. Hichens
    Sabotage. J. Conrad; Secret Agent
    Secret Agent. W. S. Maugham; Ashenden
    South Sea Bubble. R. Pertwee
    Stage Fright. S. Jepson; Man Running
    Suspicion. F. Iles; Before the Fact
    Thirty-Nine Steps. J. Buchan
    Young and Innocent. J. Tey; Shilling for Candles
REY, HENRI-FRANCOIS
    Waste-Land. H. Ellison; Tomboy
REYNOLDS, LYNN
    Big-Town Round-Up. W. M. Raine
RICHARD, JEAN-LOUIS
    Bride Wore Black. C. Woolrich
RICHARDS, SILVIA
    Secret Beyond the Door. Rufus King; Museum Piece No. 13
RICHARDSON, DOUG
    Die Harder. W. Wager; 58 Minutes
RICHARDSON, TONY
    Dead Cert. D. Francis
RICHERT, WILLIAM
    Winter Kills. R. Condon
RICHLIN, MAURICE
    For Pete's Sake. B. Street
    Pink Panther. M. H. Albert
RICHTER, W. D.
    Dracula. H. Deane
    Peeper. K. Laumer; Deadfall
RICKETTS, THOMAS
    Secretary of Frivolous Affairs. M. Futrelle
RICKMAN, THOMAS
    Laughing Policeman. M. Sjowall
RIDGELY, RICHARD
    Destroying Angel. L. J. Vance
    Eugene Aram. E. Bulwer-Lytton
    Ranson's Folly. R. H. Davis
RIDGEWAY, PHILIP
    Switch. P. Ridgeway
RIDGWELL, GEORGE
    Four Just Men. E. Wallace
    Joan Danvers. F. Stayton
    Lily of Kilarney. D. Boucicault; Colleen Bawn

RIDLEY, ROY
    Bedelia. V. Caspary
RIENITS, REX
    Assassin for Hire. R. Rienits
    Noose for a Lady. G. Verner; Whispering Woman
RIESNER, DEAN
    Charley Varrick. J. Reese; Looters
    Dirty Harry. P. Rock
    Enforcer. W. Morgan
    Play Misty for Me. P. J. Gillette
RIGBY, GORDON
    Tiger Rose. W. Mack
RIGBY, L. G.
    Whispering Wires. H. Leverage
RIGEL, ARTHUR
    Adventures of Scaramouche. R. Sabatini; Scaramouche
RIGGS, LYNN
    Sherlock Holmes and the Voice of Terror. A. C. Doyle; His Last Bow
    Stingaree. E. W. Hornung
RINALDO, FREDERIC I.
    Abbott and Costello Meet Frankenstein. M. W. Shelley; Frankenstein
RINTELS, DAVID W.
    Scorpio. M. Roote
RIPLEY, ARTHUR
    Captain of the Guard. C. Houghton
RISING, ROBERT
    Pallet on the Floor. R. H. Morrieson
RISKIN, ROBERT
    Men in Her Life. W. Fabian
    Night Club Lady. A. Abbot; About the Murder of the Night Club Lady
RITCHEY, WILL M.
    Arsene Lupin. M. Leblanc (headnote)
    Whispering Smith. F. H. Spearman
RITCHIE, MICHAEL
    Golden Child. G. C. Chesbro
RIVKIN, ALLEN
    Cheating Cheaters. M. Marcin
    Dead Reckoning. Alex Morrison
    Love Under Fire. W. Hackett; Fugitives
    70,000 Witnesses. C. Fitzsimmons
    Timberjack. D. Cushman
ROACH, JANET
    Prizzi's Honor. R. Condon
ROBBINS, HAROLD
    Never Love a Stranger. H. Robbins
    Pusher. E. McBain
ROBERT, JACQUES
    Blonde Like That. J. H. Chase; Miss Shumway Waves a Wand
    Maigret Sees Red. G. Simenon; Maigret and the Gangsters
    See Venice and Die. R. Marshall; Mission to Venice
    Seventh Juror. F. Didelot
ROBERT, YVES
    Twin. D. E. Westlake; Two Much!
ROBERTS, BEN
    King of the Khyber Rifles. T. Mundy
    Midnight Lace. J. Green; Matilda Shouted Fire
    O. Henry's Full House. O. Henry (headnote)
    Portrait in Black. I. Goff
    Serenade. J. M. Cain
    Shake Hands with the Devil. R. Conner
ROBERTS, MARGUERITE
    Escape. E. Vance
    Forgotten Faces. R. W. Child; Velvet Black
    Main Attraction. S. Michaels

ROBERTS, MEADE
    Danger Route. A. York; Eliminator
ROBINSON, CASEY
    All This, and Heaven Too. Rachel Field
    Captain Blood. R. Sabatini; Captain Blood—His Odyssey
    Diplomatic Courier. P. Cheyney; Sinister Errand
    Scobie Malone. J. Cleary; Helga's Web
    She Made Her Bed. J. M. Cain; Baby in the Icebox
    While the City Sleeps. C. Einstein; Bloody Spur
ROBINSON, MATT
    Possession of Joel Delaney. R. Stewart
ROBISON, ARTHUR
    Trial of Mary Dugan. B. Veiller
ROBINSON, LEE
    Stowaway. G. Simenon
ROBSON, MICHAEL
    Thirty-Nine Steps. J. Buchan
RODDENBERRY, GENE
    Pretty Maids All in a Row. F. Pollini
RODDICK, JOHN
    Death Trap. E. Wallace (headnote)
    Double. E. Wallace
    Partner. E. Wallace; Million Dollar Story
    Return to Sender. E. Wallace (headnote)
    Rivals. E. Wallace; Elegant Edward
RODGERS, MARK
    Let's Kill Uncle. R. O'Grady
RODMAN, HOWARD
    Charley Varrick. J. Reese; Looters
ROEBURT, JOHN
    Dead to the World. E. Ronns; State Department Murders
ROECA, SAM
    I Was an American Spy. Claire Phillips; Manila Espionage
ROEG, NICOLAS
    Death Drums Along the River. E. Wallace; Sanders of the River
ROFFEY, JACK
    Hostile Witness. J. Roffey
ROGE, ALBERT, II
    Wrecker. A. Ridley
ROGERS, HOWARD EMMETT
    Assignment in Brittany. H. MacInnes
    Calling Bulldog Drummond. G. Fairlie
    Eyes in the Night. B. Kendrick; Odor of Violets
    Hour of Thirteen. M. Porlock; X v. Rex
    Mystery of Mr. X. M. Porlock; X v. Rex
    Speedy. R. Holman
ROGERS, P. MACLEAN
    Crime at Blossoms. M. Shairp
    Feathered Serpent. E. Wallace
    God's Clay. A. Askew
    Johnny on the Spot. M. Cronin; Paid in Full
    Million Dollar Manhunt. L. Hardy; Requiem for a Redhead
    Story of Shirley Yorke. H. A. Vachell; Case of Lady Camber
    You Pay Your Money. M. Cronin
ROLAND, SANDRA WEINTRAUB
    High Road to China. J. Cleary
ROLFE, ALFRED
    Life of Rufus Dawes. Marcus Clarke; His Natural Life
ROLFE, SAM
    Naked Spur. A. Ullman
ROLI, MINO
    Machine Gun McCain. O. Demaris; Candyleg
ROMAN, LAWRENCE
    Kiss Before Dying. I. Levin
    McQ. A. Edwards
    Vice Squad. L. T. White; Harness Bull

ROMERO, EDGAR
    Scavengers. D. O'Callaghan
ROMNEY, EDANA
    Corridor of Mirrors. C. Massie
ROOFF, PAUL
    Branded. G. Biss
    In His Grip. D. C. Murray
    Missioner. E. P. Oppenheim
    Pointing Finger. Rita
ROOKE, ARTHUR
    God's Clay. A. Askew
ROOS, DON
    Single White Female. J. Lutz; SWF Seeks Same
ROOS, WILLIAM
    Scent of Mystery. K. Roos; Ghost of a Chance
ROOT, LYNN
    Falcon Takes Over. R. Chandler; Farewell, My Lovely
    Highways by Night. C. B. Kelland; Silver Spoon
    Saint in London. L. Charteris; Holy Terror
ROOT, WELLS
    I Cover the Waterfront. Max Miller
    Pursuit. L. G. Blochman
    Secret of Deep Harbor. Max Miller; I Cover the Waterfront
    Shadow of Doubt. A. S. Roche
ROSCOE, JUDITH
    Who'll Stop the Rain? R. Stone; Dog Soldiers
ROSE, EDWARD
    Under the Red Robe. S. J. Weyman (2 versions)
ROSE, JACK
    On the Double. Roger Fuller
ROSE, MICKEY
    Condorman. R. Sheckley; Game of X
ROSE, REGINALD
    Man in the Net. P. Quentin
    Sea Wolves. J. Leasor; Boarding Party
    Somebody Killed Her Husband. C. B. Phillips
    Twelve Angry Men. R. Rose
    Who Dares Wins. J. Follett; Tiptoe Boys
    Wild Geese. D. Carney
    Wild Geese II. D. Carney; Square Circle
ROSE, WILLIAM
    Flim Flam Man. G. Owen; Ballad of the Flim Flam Man
    I'll Get You for This. J. H. Chase
    Russians Are Coming, The Russians Are Coming. N. Benchley; Off-Islanders
ROSENBAUM, HENRY
    Bullet for Pretty Boy. M. Avallone
    Hanky Panky. L. Jarreau
ROSENBERG, FRANK
    Where the Sidewalk Ends. W. L. Stuart; Night Cry
ROSENBERG, MARC
    Heatwave. Timothy Harris
ROSENBERG, SOL A.
    Murders in the Rue Morgue. E. A. Poe; Prose Romances of Edgar A. Poe
ROSENER, GEORGE
    Fighting Mad. L. Y. Erskine; Renfrew Rides Again
ROSENTHAL, MARK
    Desperate Hours. J. Hayes
    Jewel of the Nile. C. Lanigan
ROSI, FRANCESCO
    Chronicles of a Death Foretold. G. G. Marquez
    Illustrious Corpses. L. Sciascia; Equal Danger
ROSS, ARTHUR A.
    Kazan. J. O. Curwood
ROSS, J. MCLAREN
    Strange Awakening. P. Quentin; Puzzle for Fiends

ROSS, KENNETH
  Black Sunday. T. Harris
  Day of the Jackal. F. Forsyth
  Odessa File. F. Forsyth

ROSSEN, ROBERT
  Desert Fury. R. Stewart; Desert Town
  Out of the Fog. I. Shaw; Gentle People

ROSSI, J. B.
  Trap for Cinderella. S. Japrisot

ROSTEN, LEO
  Conspirators. F. Prokosch
  Sleep My Love. L. Q. Ross

ROTH, ERIC
  Concorde—Airport 1979. K. Stewart
  Nickel Ride. M. T. Kaufman
  Suspect. Martin Meyers

ROTHA, PAUL
  Cat and Mouse. M. Halliday
  Lodger. M. B. Lowndes
  No Resting Place. I. Niall

ROTTER, FRITZ
  Alraune. H. H. Ewers

ROULET, DOMINIQUE
  Old Rascal. Fredric Brown; His Name Was Death
  Widow's Walk. A. Coburn

ROUSE, RUSSELL
  House of Numbers. J. Finney

ROUVE, PIERRE
  Dock Brief. J. Mortimer; Three Plays
  Stranger in the House. G. Simenon; Strangers in the House

ROWDEN, WALTER COURTENAY
  East Lynne. H. Wood
  Foul Play. C. Reade
  Hard Cash. C. Reade
  Scallywag. G. Allen

ROWE, FREDDIE
  Howling 5: The Rebirth. G. Brandner

ROWLAND, ROY
  Girl Hunters. M. Spillane

RUANE, JOHN
  Death in Brunswick. B. Oxlade

RUBEN, ALBERT
  Seven-Ups. R. Posner

RUBEN, J. WALTER
  Roadhouse Murder. M. Level (headnote)

RUBIN, BRUCE JOEL
  Deadly Friend. D. Henstell; Friend

RUBIN, DANIEL N.
  Dishonored. F. Vreeland

RUBIN, MANN
  American Dream. N. Mailer
  First Deadly Sin. Lawrence Sanders
  Warning Shot. W. Masterson; 711—Officer Needs Help

RUBY, HERMAN
  Gorilla. R. Spence

RUDOLPH, ALAN
  Trouble in Mind. R. S. Coburn

RUELLAN, ANDRE
  It's Freezing in Hell. E. Chaze; Black Wings Has My Angel
  Red Ibis. F. Brown; Knock Three-One-Two

RUNZE, OTTOKAR
  Der Morder. G. Simenon; Murderer

RURIC, PETER
  Grand Central Murder. S. MacVeigh

RUSH, RICHARD
  Stunt Man. P. Brodeur

RUSKIN, HARRY
  Glass Key. D. Hammett
  Miracles for Sale. C. Rawson; Death from a Top Hat

RUSSELL, A. J.
  Stiletto. H. Robbins

RUSSELL, GORDON
  House of Dark Shadows. Marilyn Ross

RUSSELL, JOHN
  Side Street. M. St. Clair

RUSSELL, KEN
  Lair of the White Worm. B. Stoker

RUSSELL, RAY
  Premature Burial. M. H. Danne
  X—The Man with the X-Ray Eyes. E. Sudak

RUSSELL, WILLIAM
  Time to Die. M. Cleri; Six Graves to Munich

RUSSO, JOHN A.
  Majorettes. J. Russo
  Midnight. J. Russo
  Night of the Living Dead. J. Russo

RUTHVEN, MADELEINE
  Dangerous Corner. J. B. Priestley

RUYS, TON
  Prey. C. Aird; Henrietta Who

RYAN, DON
  Case of the Stuttering Bishop. E. S. Gardner
  On Trial. E. L. Reizenstein

RYAN, TIM
  Mystery of the Thirteenth Guest. A. Trail; Thirteenth Guest

RYERSON, FLORENCE
  Canary Murder Case. S. S. Van Dine
  Casino Murder Case. S. S. Van Dine
  Drums of Jeopardy. H. MacGrath
  Easy Come, Easy Go. O. Davis
  Mysterious Dr. Fu Manchu. S. Rohmer; Mystery of Dr. Fu Manchu
  Return of Dr. Fu Manchu. S. Rohmer; Devil Doctor
  Wicked Woman. Anne Austin

SABAROFF, ROBERTS
  Split. R. Stark; Seventh

SACKHEIM, JERRY
  Strange Door. R. L. Stevenson; New Arabian Nights

SACKHEIM, WILLIAM
  First Blood. D. Morrell

SACKLER, HOWARD
  Saint Jack. P. Theroux

SAINDERICHIN, GUY-PATRICK
  Man with the Silver Eyes. R. Rossner; End of Someone Else's Rainbow

ST. CLAIR, MALCOLM
  Side Street. M. St. Clair

ST. GEORGE, GEORGE
  Orders to Kill. D. Downes

SAINT-HAMONT, DANIEL
  Hold Up. J. Cronley; Quick Change

ST. JOSEPH, ELLIS
  Flesh and Fantasy. O. Wilde; Lord Arthur Savile's Crime
  Scandal in Paris. Vidocq; Memoirs of Vidocq

SALAZAR, ALFREDO
  Invisible Man. H. G. Wells

SALKOW, SIDNEY
  Fugitive Lady. D. M. Disney (headnote)
  Murder with Pictures. G. H. Coxe

SALMON, JOHN
  Only When I Larf. L. Deighton

SALT, ANDREW
  Whirlpool. G. Endore; Methinks the Lady—

SALT, WALDO
  Gang That Couldn't Shoot Straight. J. Breslin

SALVONI, GIORGIO
  Tenth Victim. R. Sheckley

SAMUEL, YVON
  Keep Talking, Baby. D. Keene; Strange Witness

SAMUELS, LESSER
  Earl of Chicago. Brock Williams
  Hour Before the Dawn. W. S. Maugham
  Long Wait. M. Spillane
  Strange Cargo. R. Sale; Not Too Narrow—Not Too Deep

SANDEFUR, DUKE
  Phantom of the Opera. G. Leroux

SANDERSON, CHALLIS
  Murder on the Second Floor. F. Vosper

SANDERSON, MARTYN
  Pallet on the Floor. R. H. Morrieson

SANDLER, BARRY
  Mirror Crack'd. A. Christie; Mirror Crack'd from Side to Side

SANGSTER, JIMMY
  Curse of Frankenstein. M. Shelley; Frankenstein
  Deadlier Than the Male. H. Reymond
  Intent to Kill. M. Bryan
  Jack the Ripper. S. James
  Man Who Could Cheat Death. B. Lyndon; Amazing Dr. Clitterhouse
  Maniac. M. Brandel; Time of the Fire
  Nanny. E. Piper
  Terror of the Tongs. J. Sangster

SANSOM, JOHN
  Dracula, Prince of Darkness. B. Stoker; Dracula
  Face of a Stranger. E. Wallace (headnote)
  To Have and To Hold. E. Wallace; Lieutenant Bones
  Traitor's Gate. E. Wallace

SANTEAN, ANTONIO
  Dirty Mary, Crazy Larry. R. Unekis; Chase

SANTONI, JOEL
  Dead on a Rainy Sunday. Joan Aiken

SAPERSTEIN, DAVID
  Killing Affair. R. Houston; Monday, Tuesday, Wednesday

SAPINSLEY, ALVIN
  Moon of the Wolf. L. H. Whitten

SARAFIAN, RICHARD C.
  Next Man. M. Z. Lewin

SARECKY, BARNEY A.
  Drums of Fu Manchu. S. Rohmer

SARGENT, ALVIN
  Gambit. K. Lane
  I Walk the Line. Madison Jones; Exile
  Nuts. T. Topor
  Straight Time. E. Bunker; No Beast So Fierce

SARGENT, E. W.
  Horrible Hyde. R. L. Stevenson; Strange Case of Dr. Jekyll and Mr. Hyde
  Lion and the Mouse. A. Hornblow

SARNS, ROBERT
  Howling II. G. Brandner

SASLAVSKY, LUIS
  She Wolves. P. Boileau; Prisoner
  Snow Was Black. G. Simenon; Stain on the Snow

SASTRE, ANGEL
  Turn of the Screw. H. James

SAUL, OSCAR
  Bonaventure. C. Hastings
  Dark Past. J. Warwick; Blind Alley
  Silencers. D. Hamilton

SAUTET, CLAUDE
   Arm at the Left. C. Williams; Aground
   Banana Peel. C. Williams; Nothing in the Way
   Little Virtuous. R. Marshall; But a Short Time to Live
   Pillaged. R. Stark; Score
SAUVAJON, MARC-GILBERT
   What a Girl! P. Cheyney; I'll Say She Does
   You Do It, Cutie. P. Cheyney; Your Deal, My Lovely
SAVILLE, VICTOR
   W Plan. G. Seton
SAVORY, GERALD
   Young and Innocent. J. Tey; Shilling for Candles
SAYERS, MICHAEL
   Casino Royale. I. Fleming
SAYLES, JOHN
   Howling. G. Brandner
SCARBOROUGH, GEORGE
   Locked Door. C. Pollock; Sign on the Door
SCARPELLI
   Sunday Woman. C. Fruttero
SCHARY, DORE
   Fog. V. Williams
SCHAYER, E. RICHARD
   Gray Dawn. S. E. White
SCHELL, MAXIMILIAN
   Murder on the Bridge. F. Duerrenmatt; Judge and His Hangman
SCHEPSI, FRED
   Chant of Jimmie Blacksmith. T. Keneally
SCHIFFER, MICHAEL
   Colors. J. Norst
SCHIFFMAN, SUZANNE
   Let It Be Sunday. C. Williams; Long Saturday Night
SCHLITT, ROBERT
   Pyx. J. Buell
SCHNECK, STEPHEN
   Inside Out. W. Hughes
SCHNEE, CHARLES
   They Live by Night. E. Anderson; Thieves Like Us
SCHNEE, THELMA
   Father Brown. G. K. Chesterton; Innocence of Father Brown
SCHNITZER, GERALD
   Scream in the Dark. J. Odlum; Morgue Is Always Open
SCHNITZLER, WOLFGANG
   Der Grune Bogenschutze. E. Wallace; Green Archer
   Die Bande des Schreckens. E. Wallace; Terrible People
SCHOENFELD, BERNARD C.
   Dark Cover. L. Q. Ross
   Down Three Dark Streets. Gordons; Case File: FBI
   Phantom Lady. W. Irish
   Straight Is the Way. D. Burnet; Four Walls
SCHOFIELD, PAUL
   That Royle Girl. E. Balmer
SCHRADER, PAUL
   Yakuza. L. Schrader
SCHREIBER, EDWARD
   "Mad Dog" Coll. S. Thurman
SCHRODER, WOLF CHRISTIAN
   Story-Teller. P. Highsmith
SCHUBERT, BERNARD
   Kind Lady. E. Chodorov
   Mark of the Vampire. M. Coolridge-Rask; London After Midnight

Public Defender. G. Goodchild; Splendid Crime
Secret Service. W. Gillette
SCHULBERG, BEN
   In the Bishop's Carriage. M. Michelson
SCHULBERG, BUDD
   On the Waterfront. B. Schulberg; Waterfront
SCHWARTZ, DAVID R.
   Robin and the Seven Hoods. J. Pearl
SCHWEIG, BONTCHE
   Come Back, Charleston Blue. C. Himes; Heat's On
SCOBIE, BRIAN
   Unsuitable Job for a Woman. P. D. James
SCOLA, KATHRYN
   Glass Key. D. Hammett
   One Night in the Tropics. E. D. Biggers; Love Insurance
SCOPONI, GIUSEPPI
   House of Intrigue. H. J. Giskes; London Calling North Pole
SCOTT, ALLAN
   Awakening. B. Stoker; Jewel of the Seven Stars
   Don't Look Now. D. Du Maurier; Not After Midnight
   Spiral Staircase. E. L. White; Some Must Watch
SCOTT, JAMES
   Strike It Rich. G. Greene; Loser Takes All
SCOTT, LEROY
   Partners of the Night. L. Scott
SCOTT, PETER GRAHAM
   Big Chance. P. Barrington (headnote)
SCULLY, MARY ALICE
   Brooding Eyes. J. Goodwin; Paid in Full
SEABOURNE, A.
   77 Rue Chalgrin. W. Hackett; 77, Park Lane
SEAMNA, PETER
   Who Framed Roger Rabbit? G. K. Wolf; Who Censored Roger Rabbit?
SEARS, ZELDA
   Operator 13. R. W. Chambers; Secret Service Operator 13
   Wicked Woman. Anne Austin
SEATON, GEORGE
   Counterfeit Traitor. A. Klein
   36 Hours. C. K. Hittleman
SEAY, CHARLES M.
   It Is Never Too Late to Mend. C. Reade
   Sheep's Clothing. L. J. Vance
   Stanton's Last Fling. H. B. M. Watson; Ifs and Ans
SEDDON, JACK
   Alphabet Murders. A. Christie; ABC Murders
   Murder at the Gallop. A. Christie; After the Funeral
   Murder Most Foul. A. Christie; Mrs. McGinty's Dead
   Murder, She Said. A. Christie; 4.50 to Paddington
   What Changed Charley Farthing? M. Hebden
SEDGWICK, EDWARD
   Fantomas. P. Souvestre
SEFF, MANUEL
   Trouble for Two. R. L. Stevenson; Suicide Club
SEITER, WILLIAM A.
   Cheerful Fraud. K. R. G. Browne; Following Ann
SEITZ, GEORGE BRACKETT
   Closing Net. H. C. Rowland
   Exploits of Elaine. A. B. Reeve
   Romance of Elaine. A. B. Reeve
SELLERS, ARLENE
   Murder on the Bridge. F. Duerrenmatt; Judge and His Hangman

SELTZER, DAVID
   Shining Through. S. Isaacs
SELZNICK, DAVID O.
   Paradine Case. R. Hichens
SEMPLE, LORENZO, JR.
   Batman. W. Lyon
   Daddy's Gone A-Hunting. Mike St. Clair
   Drowning Pool. J. R. Macdonald
   Fathom. L. Forrester; Girl Called Fathom
   Never Say Never Again. I. Fleming; Thunderball
   Parallax View. L. Singer
   Pretty Poison. S. Geller; She Let Him Continue
   Three Days of the Condor. J. Grady; Six Days of the Condor
SEMPRUN, JORGE
   Z. V. Vassilikos
SERLING, ROD
   Assault on a Queen. J. Finney
   Seven Days in May. F. Knebel
   Yellow Canary. W. Masterson; Evil Come, Evil Go
SETBON, PHILIPPE
   Dead on a Rainy Sunday. Joan Aiken
SEWELL, VERNON
   Floating Dutchman. N. Bentley
SEYMOUR, JAMES
   Lawyer Man. M. Trell
   Missing Million. E. Wallace
   Saint Meets the Tiger. L. Charteris; Meet the Tiger
   They Met in the Dark. Anthony Gilbert; Vanishing Corpse
SHABER, DAVID
   Flight of the Intruder. S. Coonts
   Last Embrace. M. T. Bloom; 13th Man
   Warriors. S. Yurick
SHAFFER, ANTHONY
   Appointment with Death. A. Christie
   Death on the Nile. A. Christie
   Evil Under the Sun. A. Christie
   Frenzy. A. La Bern; Goodbye Piccadilly, Farewell Leicester Square
   Sleuth. A. Shaffer
   Wicker Man. R. Hardy
SHAGAN, STEVE
   Formula. S. Shagan
   Hustle. S. Shagan; City of Angels
   Nightwing. M. C. Smith
   Sicilian. M. Puzo
SHANE, MAXWELL
   City Across the River. I. Shulman; Amboy Dukes
   Fear in the Night. W. Irish; I Wouldn't Be in Your Shoes
   Fear in the Night. C. Woolrich; Nightmare
   Nightmare. C. Woolrich
   No Hands on the Clock. G. Homes
SHAPIRO, STANLEY
   For Pete's Sake. B. Street
SHARMAN, MAISIE
   Death Goes to School. S. Davis; Death in Seven Hours
   Headline. K. Attiwill; Reporter
   Night Journey. J. Phelan; Ten-a-Penny People
SHARP, ALAN
   Cat Chaser. Elmore Leonard
   Night Moves. A. Sharp
   Osterman Weekend. R. Ludlum
SHARP, DON
   Bear Island. A. MacLean
   Puppet on a Chain. A. MacLean
   Taste of Excitement. B. Healey; Waiting for a Tiger
SHATTUCK, DORIS
   Ghost That Walks Alone. R. Shattuck; Wedding Guest Sat on a Stone

SHAUGHNESSY, ALFRED
   Follow That Horse. H. Mason; Photo Finish

SHAVELSON, MELVILLE
   On the Double. R. Fuller
   Pigeon That Took Rome. D. Downes; Easter Dinner

SHAW, DAVID
   Man Inside. M. E. Chaber

SHAW, IRWIN
   Big Game. F. Wallace

SHEARMAN, ALAN
   Bullshot. R. House; Bullshot Crummond

SHEEKMAN, ARTHUR
   Hazard. R. Chanslor

SHELDON, E. LLOYD
   Sins of the Fathers. C. Houghton
   White Moll. F. Packard

SHELDON, H. S.
   Sherlock Holmes. W. Gillette

SHELDON, SIDNEY
   Remains to Be Seen. H. Lindsay

SHERDEMAN, TED
   Dark Page. S. Fuller

SHERIE, FENN
   Silver King. H. A. Jones

SHERLOCK, JOHN
   Last Grenade. J. Sherlock; Ordeal of Major Grigsby

SHERMAN, JOHN
   Face in the Night. B. Graeme; Suspense

SHERMAN, JOSEPH
   Death on the Diamond. C. Fitzsimmons

SHERMAN, RICHARD
   Four Men and a Prayer. D. Garth

SHERMAN, ROBERT
   Picture Mommy Dead. Robert Sherman

SHERMAN, TEDD
   Ten Seconds to Hell. L. P. Bachmann; Phoenix

SHERMAN, VINCENT
   Heart of the North. W. B. Mowery

SHERRIFF, R. C.
   Invisible Man. H. G. Wells
   Odd Man Out. F. L. Green
   Old Dark House. J. B. Priestley; Benighted

SHERRY, JOHN B.
   Hangup. B. Bernard; Face of Night

SHERWOOD, ROBERT E.
   Man on a Tightrope. N. Paterson
   Rebecca. D. Du Maurier
   Scarlet Pimpernel. B. Orczy

SHEVELOVE, BURT
   Wrong Box. R. L. Stevenson

SHIELDS, TIM
   Last Shot You Hear. W. Fairchild; Sound of Murder

SHIRLEY, ARTHUR
   Mystery of a Hansom Cab. F. Hume

SHOLDER, JACK
   Where Are the Children? M. H. Clark

SHOR, SOL
   Drums of Fu Manchu. S. Rohmer

SHRAKE, BUD
   Nightwing. M. C. Smith

SHRANK, JOSEPH
   Slight Case of Murder. D. Runyon

SHROCK, RAYMOND L.
   Another Man's Shoes. V. Bridges
   Breathless Moment. M. Bryant; Redemption of Richard
   Elusive Isabel. J. Futrelle
   Hidden Hand. Rufus King; Invitation to a Murder
   I Ring Doorbells. R. Birdwell
   Man Inside. N. S. Lincoln
   Millionaires. E. P. Oppenheim; Inevitable Millionaires
   Phantom of the Opera. G. Leroux
   Strange Disappearance. A. K. Green

SHRYACK, DENNIS
   Flashpoint. G. La Fountaine
   Gauntlet. M. Butler
   Hero and the Terror. M. Blodgett

SHULMAN, IRVING
   City Across the River. I. Shulman; Amboy Dukes

SIBELIUS, JOHANNA
   Waiting Room for the Other Side. R. Marshall; Mission to Siena

SIEGEL, BARRY
   Windows. G. Simenon

SIEVEKING, LANCE
   Third Clue. N. Gordon; Shakespeare Murders

SIGURD, JACQUES
   Three Rooms in Manhattan. G. Simenon; Three Beds in Manhattan

SILLIPHANT, STIRLING
   Enforcer. W. Morgan
   Five Against the House. J. Finney
   In the Heat of the Night. J. Ball
   Killer Elite. R. Rostand
   Liberation of L. B. Jones. J. H. Ford; Liberation of Lord Byron Jones
   Marlowe. R. Chandler; Little Sister
   New Centurians. J. Wambaugh
   Nightfall. D. Goodis
   Slender Thread. S. Silliphant
   Telefon. W. Wager
   Towering Inferno. R. M. Stern; Tower

SILVER, PAT
   Ace Up Your Sleeve. J. H. Chase; Ace Up My Sleeve

SILVERNAIL, CLARKE
   Behind That Curtain. E. D. Biggers

SILVERS, SID
   Gorilla. R. Spence

SILVERSTEIN, DAVID
   Manhattan Love Song. C. Woolrich
   Unknown Blonde. T. D. Irwin; Collusion

SIMENON, GEORGES
   Night at the Crossroads. G. Simenon; Crossroads Murders

SIMMONS, ANTHONY
   Green Ice. G. A. Browne
   Little Sweetheart. A. Wise; Naughty Girls

SIMMONS, ED
   Scared Stiff. C. W. Goddard; Ghost Breakers

SIMMONS, MICHAEL L.
   Scattergood Baines. C. B. Kelland

SIMMONS, RICHARD ALAN
   Shield for Murder. W. P. McGivern

SIMON, NEIL
   Cheap Detective. R. Grossbach
   Murder by Death. H. Keating

SIMON, ROGER L.
   Big Fix. R. L. Simon

SIMONIN, ALBERT
   Adventures of Arsene Lupin. M. Leblanc (headnote)
   Any Number Can Win. J. Trinian
   From the Boys. R. Matheson; Ride the Nightmare

SIMOUN, HENRI
   Madigan. R. Dougherty; Commissioner

SIMPSON, ALAN
   Loot. J. Orton
   Spy with a Cold Nose. R. Galton

SIMPSON, EDWARD
   River of Death. Alistair MacLean

SIMPSON, HAROLD
   Spy of Napoleon. B. Orczy

SIMPSON, HELEN
   Sabotage. J. Conrad; Secret Agent

SIMS, JEANIE
   Memento Mori. M. Spark

SINCLAIR, ANDREW
   Blue Blood. A. Thynne; Carry-Cot

SINCLAIR, CHARLES
   Chase a Crooked Shadow. A. Shaughnessy; Double Cut

SINCLAIR, ROY
   Dream Street. T. Burke; Limehouse Nights

SIODMAK, KURT/CURT
   Beast with Five Fingers. W. F. Harvey
   Climax. F. J. Lewis
   Non-Stop New York. K. Attiwill; Sky Steward
   Valley of Fear. A. C. Doyle

SIODMAK, ROBERT
   Affair of Nina B. J. M. Simmel

SIRK, DOUGLAS
   Summer Storm. A. Chekhov; Shooting Party

SISSON, ROSEMARY ANNE
   Candleshoe. M. Innes; Christmas at Candleshoe
   Ride a Wild Pony. J. Aldridge; Sporting Proposition

SKAAREN, WARREN
   Batman. C. S. Gardner
   Beverly Hills Cop II. R. Tine

SKLAR, GEORGE
   First Comes Courage. E. Arnold; Commandos

SKUTEZKY, VICTOR
   Temptation Harbour. G. Simenon; Newhaven-Dieppe

SLAVIN, GEORGE F.
   Desert Sands. J. Robb; Punitive Action

SLESAR, HENRY
   Murders in the Rue Morgue. E. A. Poe; Prose Romances of Edgar A. Poe

SLOANE, PAUL H.
   Confidence Man. L. Y. Erskine
   Manhattan. J. Farnol; Definite Object
   Manhattan Knight. G. Burgess; Find the Woman

SLOMAN, EDWARD
   Pilgrims of the Night. A. Partridge; Passers-By

SMART, RALPH
   Crime Unlimited. D. Hume
   Phantom Light. E. Price; Haunted Light

SMITH, FRANK LEON
   House Without a Key. E. D. Biggers
   One Hour Before Midnight. M. Scott; Behind Red Curtains

SMITH, HAL
   Black Eagle. O. Henry; Roads of Destiny

SMITH, HAMILTON
   Scar. E. Gaboriau; File No. 113

SMITH, HOWARD ELLIS
   Think Fast, Mr. Moto. J. P. Marquand

SMITH, JAMES BELL
   Golden Web. E. P. Oppenheim; Plunderers

SMITH, JAMES R.
   Money to Burn. R. W. Kauffman

SMITH, MARTIN CRUZ
   Nightwing. M. C. Smith

SMITH, MURRAY
   Bear Island. A. MacLean
SMITH, NEVILLE
   Gumshoe. N. Smith
SMITH, PAUL GERARD
   Welcome Danger. R. Simpson
SMITH, R. CECIL
   His Wife's Friend. J. B. Harris-Burland; White Rook
SMITH, ROBERT
   Platinum High School. I. Shulman
   Sudden Fear. E. Sherry
SMITH, ROGER
   CC and Company. M. Roote
SMITH, WALLACE
   Almost Married. A. Soutar; Devil's Triangle
   Bulldog Drummond. H. C. McNeile
   Seven Keys to Baldpate. E. D. Biggers
SNIDER, NORMAN
   Body Parts. P. Boileau; Choice Cuts
   Dead Ringers. Bari Wood; Twins
SODERBERG, ROBERT W.
   Reckless Moment. E. S. Holding; Blank Wall
SOFFICI, MARIO
   Beast and the Man. R. L. Stevenson; Strange Case of Dr. Jekyll and Mr. Hyde
SOLINAS, FRANCO
   Burn. N. Gant
SOLOW, EUGENE
   Fog Over Frisco. G. Dyer; Five Fragments
   League of Frightened Men. R. Stout
   Patient in Room 18. M. G. Eberhart
   Return of the Terror. E. Wallace; Terror
   While the Patient Slept. M. G. Eberhart
SOLT, ANDREW
   Bonaventure. C. Hastings
   In a Lonely Place. D. B. Hughes
   Whirlpool. G. Endore; Methinks the Lady—
SOMERVILLE, ROY
   Bandbox. L. J. Vance
   First Law. G. Willets
   Teeth of the Tiger. M. Leblanc
SONDHEIM, STEPHEN
   Last of Sheila. A. Edwards
SONEGO, RODOLFO
   Witness. H. Judd; Shadow of a Doubt
SOSKIN, PAUL
   Waterfront. J. Brophy
SOUTAR, ANDREW
   Man Called Back. A. Soutar
SOUTAR, JOHN
   Last Journey. J. J. Farjeon; Holiday Express
SOUTHERN, TERRY
   Dr. Strangelove. P. Bryant; Two Hours to Doom
SPAAK, CHARLES
   Ardent Room. J. D. Carr; Burning Court
   Blague dans le Coin. Carter Brown; Curtains for a Chorine
   Crime and Punishment. F. M. Dostoevskii
   Last Turning. J. M. Cain; Postman Always Rings Twice
   Majestic Hotel Cellars. G. Simenon; Maigret and the Hotel Majestic
   Panique. G. Simenon; Mr. Hire's Engagement
   Therese Raquin. E. Zola
SPENCE, RALPH
   Death on the Diamond. C. Fitzsimmons
   Gorilla. R. Spence
   Lunatic at Large. J. S. Clouston
   Murder in the Private Car. E. E. Rose; Rear Car
   Strangers on a Honeymoon. E. Wallace; Northing Tramp

SPENCER, RAY
   Crack-Up. F. Brown; Madman's Holiday
SPENCER, RICHARD V.
   Paradise Garden. G. F. Gibbs
   Pidgin Island. H. MacGrath
SPEWACK, SAMUEL
   Secret Witness. S. Spewack; Murder in the Gilded Cage
SPIEGEL, LARRY
   Book of Numbers. R. D. Pharr
   Survival Run. R. Hoskins
SPIES, ADRIAN
   Dark of the Sun. W. Smith; Train from Katanga
   Scorpio Letters. V. Canning
SPIGELGASS, LEONARD
   Butch Minds the Baby. D. Runyon; Guys and Dolls
   Law and the Lady. F. Lonsdale; Last of Mrs. Cheyney
   So Evil My Love. J. Shearing; For Her to See
   Stingaree. E. W. Hornung
SPILLANE, MICKEY
   Girl Hunters. M. Spillane
SPRAGUE, CHANDLER
   Menace. P. Macdonald; R.I.P
SQUIERS, LUCITA
   Gamble with Hearts. A. Carlyle
SQUIRE, ANTHONY
   Intruder. R. Maugham; Line on Ginger
STALLINGS, LAURENCE
   Sun Shines Bright. I. S. Cobb; Old Judge Priest
STALLONE, SYLVESTER
   Cobra. P. Gosling; Running Duck
   First Blood. D. Morrell
   Rambo: First Blood Part II. D. Morrell
STANNARD, ELIOT
   American Prisoner. E. Phillpotts
   Beautiful Jim, of the Blankshire Regiment. J. S. Winter
   Case of Jonathan Drew. M. B. Lowndes; Lodger
   Chick. E. Wallace
   Colleen Bawn. D. Boucicault
   Diamond Man. E. Wallace (headnote)
   Ernest Maltravers. E. Bulwer-Lytton
   Grip. J. S. Winter
   Hate Ship. B. Graeme
   Hutch Stirs 'Em Up. H. Hancock; Hawk of Rede
   Justice. J. Galsworthy
   Lady Audley's Secret. M. E. Braddon
   Little Hour of Peter Wells. D. Whitelaw
   Mord Em'ly. W. P. Ridge
   Mystery of a Hansom Cab. F. Hume
   Nets of Destiny. M. Drake; Salving of a Derelict
   Nonconformist Parson. R. Horniman
   Silver Bridge. H. P. Lewis
   Through Fire and Water. V. Bridges; Greensea Island
STANTON, DANE
   Still Waters Run Deep. T. Taylor
STARLING, LYNN
   Cat and the Canary. J. Willard
   Climax. F. J. Lewis
   Cynara. R. Gore-Brown; Imperfect Lover
   President Vanishes. Anonymous
STARR, BEN
   Busy Body. D. E. Westlake
   Our Man Flint. J. Pearl
STARR, JAMES A.
   In the Next Room. E. R. Belmont
   In the Next Room. B. E. Stevenson; Mystery of the Boule Cabinet
STATTER, ARTHUR F.
   Voice in the Dark. R. E. Dyar

STECK, H. TIPTON
   Phantom Buccaneer. V. Bridges; Another Man's Shoes
STEEMAN, STANISLAUS ANDRE
   Mystere a Shanghai. A. Steeman; Night of the 12th–3th
STEFANO, JOSEPH
   Black Orchid. E. Ronns
   Naked Edge. M. Ehrlich; First Train to Babylon
   Psycho. R. Bloch
STEFENS, ROGER
   Extremities. W. Mastrosimone
STENGEL, CHRISTIAN
   Crime and Punishment. F. M. Dostoevskii
STEMMLE, R. A.
   Die Gruft mit dem Ratselschloss. E. Wallace; Angel Esquire
   Die Seltsame Grafin. E. Wallace; Strange Countess
STEPPLING, JOHN
   Fifty-Two Pickup. E. Leonard
STERLING, STEWART
   Having Wonderful Crime. C. Rice
STEVENS, LOUIS
   Bronze Bell. L. J. Vance
   Easy Pickings. P. Cruger
   God's Prodigal. A. J. Russell
STEVENSON, ROBERT
   Calendar. E. Wallace
   Ringer. E. Wallace
   Ware Case. G. Pleydell
STEWART, COLIN
   Burndown. S. Collins; Burn Down
STEWART, DONALD
   Patriot Games. T. Clancy
STEWART, DONALD OGDEN
   Moment of Danger. D. MacKenzie; Scent of Danger
STEWART, RAMONA
   Desert Fury. R. Stewart; Desert Town
STEWART, ROBERT
   Backfire! E. Wallace (headnote)
   Danger Route. A. York; Eliminator
   Downfall. E. Wallace (headnote)
   Marriage of Convenience. E. Wallace; Three Oak Mystery
   Never Mention Murder. E. Wallace (headnote)
   Partners in Crime. E. Wallace; Man Who Knew
   Playback. E. Wallace (headnote)
   Sinister Man. E. Wallace
   Vengeance. C. Siodmak; Donovan's Brain
STINSON, JOSEPH C.
   Stick. E. Leonard
   Sudden Impact. J. C. Stinson
STITT, MILAN
   Runner Stumbles. M. Stitt
STOCK, RALPH
   Jennifer Hale. R. Eden
   Rome Express. R. Alexander
STOLPE, SVEN
   Crime and Punishment. F. M. Dostoevskii
STONE, ANDREW L.
   Cry Terror. A. L. Stone
   Decks Ran Red. A. L. Stone
   Julie. A. L. Stone
STONE, JOHN
   Black Watch. T. Mundy; King of the Khyber Rifles
   Fugitives. R. H. Davis; Exiles
   Great K&A Train Robbery. P. L. Ford
STONE, OLIVER
   Eight Million Ways to Die. L. Bloch
   Hand. M. Brandel; Lizard's Tail

Scarface. A. Trail
Year of the Dragon. R. Daley

STONE, PETER
Charade. P. H. Stone
Mirage. W. Ericson; Fallen Angel
Silver Bears. P. E. Erdman
Taking of Pelham One Two Three. J. Godey
Who Is Killing the Great Chefs of Europe? N. Lyons; Someone Is Killing the Great Chefs of Europe

STONE, ROBERT
Who'll Stop the Rain? R. Stone; Dog Soldiers

STONE, VIRGINIA
Decks Ran Red. A. L. Stone

STOPPARD, TOM
Billy Bathgate. E. L. Doctorow
Despair. V. Nabokoff-Sirin
Human Factor. G. Greene
Russia House. J. Le Carre

STORA, BERNARD
Max and Jeremy. Teri White; Max Trueblood and the Jersey Desperado

STORCH, WOLFGANG
Two Faces of January. P. Highsmith

STORM, LESLEY
Fallen Idol. G. Greene; Basement Room and other stories
Golden Salamander. V. Canning
Heart of the Matter. G. Greene
Ringer. E. Wallace

STORY, JACK TREVOR
Live Now, Pay Later. J. T. Story

STREETER, COOLIDGE
Ramshackle House. H. Footner

STRICK, WESLEY
Cape Fear. J. D. MacDonald; Executioners

STRIJEUSKI, WLADIMIR
Crime and Punishment. F. M. Dostoevskii

STRINGER, ARTHUR
Story Without a Name. A. Stringer

STRUEBY, KATHERINE
High Command. L. Robinson; General Goes Too Far
Meet Maxwell Archer. H. Clevely; Archer Plus 20
Shop at Sly Corner. E. Percy; Play with Fire

STRUMWASSER, JACK
Times Have Changed. E. Davis
Yosemite Trail. R. Cullum; One-Way Trail

STRUTTON, BILL
Assignment K. H. Howard; Department K

STUART, ALEXANDER
Ordeal by Innocence. A. Christie

STUART, JEB
Die Hard. R. Thorp; Nothing Lasts Forever

STUART, KATHERINE
Jeanne of the Marshes. E. P. Oppenheim

STUART, KATHRYN
Cheating Cheaters. M. Marcin

STURDIVANT, MARC
Condorman. R. Sheckley; Game of X

STUYVESANT, EVE
Leavenworth Case. A. K. Green

STYLE, MICHAEL
Vampire Lovers. J. S. Le Fanu; In a Glass Darkly

SUBIELA, MICHEL
Soupe aux Poulets. E. McBain; Killer's Wedge

SUBOTSKY, MILTON
Last Mile. J. Wexley
I, Monster. R. L. Stevenson; Strange Case of Dr. Jekyll and Mr. Hyde
Skull. R. Bloch; Skull of the Marquis de Sade

SULLIVAN, C. GARDNER
Boomerang. W. H. Osborne
Father Brown, Detective. G. K. Chesterton; Wisdom of Father Brown
Locked Door. C. Pollock; Sign on the Door
Three Faces East. A. P. Kelly
Three Live Ghosts. F. S. Isham

SULLIVAN, FRED G.
Cold River. W. Judson

SUMMERS, WALTER
Black Limelight. G. Sherry
Dark Eyes of London. E. Wallace
Dead Men Tell No Tales. F. Beeding; Norwich Victims
House Opposite. J. J. Farjeon
Limping Man. W. Scott; Man
Return of Bulldog Drummond. H. C. McNeile; Black Gang
Traitor Spy. T. C. H. Jacobs
What Happened Then? L. T. Bradley

SUTHERLAND, SIDNEY
Leavenworth Case. A. K. Green

SWAIM, BOB
Half Moon Street. P. Theroux; Doctor Slaughter

SWANN, FRANCIS
That Way with Women. E. D. Biggers; Earl Derr Biggers Tells Ten Stories

SWERLING, JO
Behind the Mask. E. P. Oppenheim; Jeanne of the Marshes
Circus Queen Murder. A. Abbot; About the Murder of the Circus Queen
Leave Her to Heaven. B. A. Williams
Wrecker. A. Ridley

SWICEGOOD, T. L. P.
Man in the Water. R. Sheckley

SWIFT, DAVID
Candleshoe. M. Innes; Christmas at Candleshoe

SYDENY, R.
Blood Relatives. E. McBain

SYLVAINE, VERNON
Warn That Man. V. Sylvaine

TABET, ANDRE
Ravishing Idiot. C. Exbrayat
Snow Was Black. G. Simenon; Stain on the Snow

TABET, GEORGES
La Bete a L'Affut. D. Keene; Moran's Woman
Ravishing Idiot. C. Exbrayat

TABORI, GEORGE
Secret Ceremony. M. Denevi

TABORI, PAUL
Malpas Mystery. E. Wallace; Face in the Night
Mantrap. S. Rattray; Queen in Danger

TACCHELLA, JEAN-LOUIS
Avec un Elastique. C. Williams; Big Bite

TAGGART, BRIAN
Visiting Hours. K. Rembo

TAGHVAI, NASER
Captain Khorshid. E. Hemingway; To Have and Have Not

TALBOT, ROWLAND
Brigadier Gerard. A. C. Doyle; Exploits of Brigadier Gerard
London by Night. C. Selby

TALLMAN, ROBERT
Slightly Honorable. F. G. Presnell; Send Another Coffin

TALLY, TED
Silence of the Lambs. Thomas Harris

TANCHUCK, NATHANIEL
Shuttered Room. J. Withers

TARADASH, DANIEL
Don't Bother to Knock. C. Armstrong; Mischief
Knock on Any Door. W. Motley
Morituri. W. J. Luddecke
Other Side of Midnight. S. Sheldon

TARKINGTON, BOOTH
Millionaire. E. D. Biggers; Earl Derr Biggers Tells Ten Stories

TARLOFF, FRANK
Double Man. H. S. Maxfield; Legacy of a Spy
Once You Kiss a Stranger. P. Highsmith; Strangers on a Train

TARSHIS, HAROLD
Fast Company. Marco Page

TASHLIN, FRANK
Caprice. J. Withers
Lemon Drop Kid. D. Runyon; Bloodhounds of Broadway

TAVERNIER, BERTRAND
April Is a Deadly Month. Derek Raymond; Devil's Home on Leave
Population 1280. J. Thompson; Pop. 1280

TAYLOR, CHARLES A.
Outsider. L. J. Vance; Nobody

TAYLOR, DAVID
Hanky Panky. L. Jarreau

TAYLOR, DONALD
Devil's Daffodil. E. Wallace; Daffodil Mystery
Foxhole in Cairo. L. O. Mosley; Cat and the Mice
Hands of Orlac. M. Renard
Jolly Bad Fellow. C. E. Vulliamy; Don Among the Dead Men
Straw Man. D. M. Disney

TAYLOR, DWIGHT
Boy on a Dolphin. D. Divine
Conflict. Alex Morrison
I Wake Up Screaming. S. Fisher
Nightmare. M. Porlock; Mystery in Kensington Gore
Vicki. S. Fisher; I Wake Up Screaming
When Tomorrow Comes. J. M. Cain; Serenade

TAYLOR, EDWARD
V. I. Warshawski. S. Paretsky (headnote)

TAYLOR, ERIC
Ellery Queen and the Murder Ring. E. Queen; Dutch Shoe Mystery
Ellery Queen and the Perfect Crime. E. Queen; Perfect Crime
Ellery Queen, Master Detective. E. Queen
Ellery Queen's Penthouse Mystery. E. Queen; Penthouse Mystery
Lady in the Morgue. J. Latimer
Phantom of the Opera. G. Leroux

TAYLOR, JOYCE
Body Parts. P. Boileau; Choice Cuts

TAYLOR, KENNETH
Beyond This Place. A. J. Cronin

TAYLOR, KRESSMANN
Address Unknown. K. Taylor

TAYLOR, MATT
Lion and the Lamb. E. P. Oppenheim

TAYLOR, REEVE
Midnight Episode. G. Simenon; Monsieur la Souris

TAYLOR, REX
Cheerful Fraud. K. R. G. Browne; Following Ann
Mandarin Mystery. E. Queen; Chinese Orange Mystery
Reckless Age. E. D. Biggers; Love Insurance
Too Many Crooks. E. J. Rath

TAYLOR, S. E. V.
Lone Wolf. L. J. Vance

TAYLOR, SAMUEL W.
  Cat's Paw. C. B. Kelland
  Gambler. C. Klein
  Man with My Face. S. W. Taylor
  Topaz. L. Uris
  Vertigo. P. Boileau; Living and the Dead
TAYLOR, STEPHEN
  Man Who Would Not Die. C. Williams; Sailcloth Shroud
TAYLOR, VALERIE
  Take My Life. Winston Graham
TEMPLEMAN, HARCOURT
  Overheard. S. Aumonier
TEMPLETON, WILLIAM
  Double Confession. J. Garden; All on a Summer's Day
  Fallen Idol. G. Greene; Basement Room and other stories
  Midnight Episode. G. Simenon; Monsieur la Souris
TENNANT, WILLIAM
  Cleopatra Jones and the Casino of Gold. R. Goulart
TENNYSON, PENROSE
  There Ain't No Justice. J. Curtis
TERRETT, COURTNEY
  Love Is a Racket. R. James
TERRISS, TOM
  Lion and the Mouse. A. Hornblow
  Mystery of Edwin Drood. C. Dickens
TERWILLIGER, GEORGE W.
  Gamblers. C. Klein
TESICH, STEVE
  Eleni. N. Gage
  Eyewitness. J. Minahan
TEWKESBURY, JOAN
  Thieves Like Us. E. Anderson
THAN, JOSEPH
  Deception. E. Walter; Jealousy
THELLING, FRANCESCO
  Invincible Six. M. Barrett; Heroes of Yuca
THEROUX, PAUL
  Saint Jack. P. Theroux
THEW, HARVEY
  Argyle Case. H. Ford
  Cheerful Fraud. K. R. G. Browne; Following Ann
  Death on the Diamond. C. Fitzsimmons
  Duds. H. C. Rowland
  Four Days' Wonder. A. A. Milne
  Murder in the Private Car. E. E. Rose; Rear Car
  Operator 13. R. W. Chambers; Secret Service Operator 13
  Public Enemy. K. Glasmon
  Raffles, the Amateur Cracksman. E. W. Hornung; Amateur Cracksman
  Tiger Rose. W. Mack
  Woman's Law. Maravene Thompson
THIEL, NICK
  V. I. Warshawski. S. Paretsky (headnote)
THOEREN, ROBERT
  Act of Murder. E. Lothar; Mills of God
  Captain Carey, U.S.A. M. Albrand; After Midnight
  Rage in Heaven. J. Hilton
  Singapore. W. Bogart
  Summer Storm. A. Chekhov; Shooting Party
  Temptation. R. Hichens; Bella Donna
THOM, ROBERT
  Angel, Angel, Down We Go. W. Johnston
  Bloody Mama. R. Thom
THOMAS, DAVE
  Spies Like Us. G. McGill

THOMAS, DYLAN
  Three Weird Sisters. C. Armstrong; Case of the Weird Sisters
THOMAS, JAMES E.
  Predator. P. Monette
THOMAS, JOHN C.
  Predator. P. Monette
THOMAS, LESLIE
  Dangerous Davies. L. Thomas
THOMAS, MICHAEL
  McGuffin. J. Bowen
THOMAS, ROSS
  Hammett. J. Gores
THOMPSON, GARFIELD
  Arsene Lupin. E. Jepson
  In the Balance. E. P. Oppenheim; Hillman
THOMPSON, HARLAN
  Phantom President. G. F. Worts
THOMPSON, J. LEE
  For Them That Trespass. E. Raymond
  Ice-Cold in Alex. C. Landon
  Murder Without Crime. J. L. Thompson
THOMPSON, JIM
  Killing. L. White; Clean Break
THOMPSON, KEENE
  Going Crooked. Winchell Smith
THOMPSON, MARIAN
  Shake Hands with the Devil. R. Conner
THOMPSON, ROBERT E.
  They Shoot Horses, Don't They? H. McCoy
THOMPSON, TOMMY
  Spy for a Day. S. Aumonier; Love-a-Duck
THORN, RONALD SCOTT
  Full Treatment. R. S. Thorn
THORNE, ANTHONY
  So Long at the Fair. A. Thorne
THORNTON, F. MARTIN
  My Lord Conceit. Rita
TIDYMAN, ERNEST
  Report to the Commissioner. J. Mills
  Shaft's Big Score. E. Tidyman
TOLES-BEY, JOHN
  Rage in Harlem. C. Himes; For love of Imabelle
TOLNAY, AKOS
  Second Bureau. C. R. Dumas
TOMBRAGEL, MAURICE
  Return of the Whistler. W. Irish; Eyes That Watch You
TOPLIN, TITO
  Last Summer in Tangiers. W. O'Farrell; Devil His Due
TOPOR, TOM
  Accused. D. Chiel
TOTHEROH, DAN
  Remember Last Night? A. Hobhouse; Hangover Murders
TOTMAN, WELLYN
  Girl from Mandalay. R. Campbell
  Steward. E. Wallace
TOURNEUR, MAURICE
  Hand of Peril. A. Stringer
  Le Derniere Reincarnation de Larsan. G. Leroux; Perfume of the Lady in Black
  Le Mystere de la Chambre Jaune. G. Leroux; Mystery of the Yellow Room
TOWERS, HARRY ALAN
  Death Drums Along the River. E. Wallace; Sanders of the River
TOWNE, GENE
  Case Against Mrs. Ames. A. S. Roche

TOWNE, ROBERT
  Chinatown. R. Towne
  Yakuza. L. Schrader
TOWNLEY, JACK
  Plot Thickens. S. Palmer (headnote)
TOWNSEND, LEO
  Dangerous Crossing. J. D. Carr; Dead Sleep Lightly
  Four Boys and a Gun. W. Wiener
  Fraulein. J. McGovern
  Life in the Balance. G. Simenon (headnote)
  Running Wild. B. Benson; Girl in the Cage
  That Way with Women. E. D. Biggers; Earl Derr Biggers Tells Ten Stories
  Vicki. S. Fisher; I Wake Up Screaming
TOY, BARBARA
  Monkey's Paw. W. W. Jacobs; Lady of the Barge
TRAIL, ARMITAGE
  Thirteenth Guest. A. Trail
TRAVERS, BEN
  Inheritance. J. S. Le Fanu; Uncle Silas
TRAVESI, RAFAEL GARCIA
  Spiritism. W. W. Jacobs; Lady of the Barge
TRELL, MAX
  Hell Below Zero. H. Innes; White South
  Last Man to Hang. G. Bullett; Jury
TRIESCHMAN, CHARLES
  Two. C. Trieschman
TRIVAS, VICTOR
  Brothers Karamazov. F. M. Dostoevskii
  Vous Pigez? P. Cheyney; Don't Get Me Wrong
  Where the Sidewalk Ends. W. L. Stuart; Night Cry
TRIVERS, BARRY
  Flight from Destiny. A. Berkeley; Trial and Error
  River's End. J. O. Curwood
  Wagons Roll at Night. Francis Wallace; Kid Galahad
TROMBETTA, JIM
  Diplomatic Immunity. Theodore Taylor; Stalker
TROSPER, GUY
  Eyes in the Night. B. Kendrick; Odor of Violets
  One-Eyed Jacks. C. Neider; Authentic Death of Hendry Jones
  Spy Who Came in from the Cold. J. Le Carre
TROTTI, LAMAR
  Country Beyond. J. O. Curwood
  Judge Priest. I. S. Cobb; Down Yonder with Judge Priest
  O. Henry's Full House. O. Henry (headnote)
TROYAT, HENRI
  Big Chief. O. Henry; Whirligigs
TRUFFAUT, FRANCOIS
  Bride Wore Black. C. Woolrich
  Let It Be Sunday. C. Williams; Long Saturday Night
  Mississippi Mermaid. W. Irish; Waltz Into Darkness
  Shoot the Pianist. D. Goodis; Down There
  Such a Lovely Kid Like Me. H. Farrell; Such a Gorgeous Kid Like Me
TRUSTMAN, ALAN R.
  Bullitt. R. Pike; Mute Witness
  Lady Ice. M. Braly; Master
  Next Man. M. Z. Lewin
  Thomas Crown Affair. E. L. Heyman
TRYON, THOMAS
  Other. T. Tryon
TUCHOCK, WANDA
  Letty Lynton. M. B. Lowndes
TUCKER, GEORGE LOANE
  Folly of Desire. A. Askew; Shulamite
  Miracle Man. F. Packard
  Traffic in Souls. E. H. Ball

TUDOR, F. C. S.
 Devil's Profession. G. de S. W. James
TULLY, JIM
 Beggars of Life. J. Tully
TULLY, JOHN
 Faces in the Dark. P. Boileau
 In the Wake of a Stranger. I. S. Black
TULLY, MONTGOMERY
 Boys in Brown. R. Beckwith
 Clash by Night. R. Croft-Cooke
 Dial 999. B. Graeme; Way Out
 Murder in Reverse. Seamark; Out of the Dark
 No Road Back. F. L. Cary; Madam Tic-Tac
 Out of the Fog. B. Graeme; Fog for a Killer
 Who Killed the Cat? A. Ridley; Tabitha
TUNBERG, KARL
 I Thank a Fool. A. E. Lindop
 Law and the Lady. F. Lonsdale; Last of Mrs. Cheyney
 Libel. E. Wooll
TUPPER, TRISTAN
 Avenger. J. Goodwin
TURNBULL, HECTOR
 Voice in the Fog. H. MacGrath
TURNBULL, MARGARET
 House of Silence. E. Barron; Marcel Levignet
 Princess of New York. C. Hamilton
TURNER, BARBARA
 Deathwatch. J. Genet; Maids and Deathwatch
TURNER, CLIVE
 Howling 5: The Rebirth. G. Brandner
TURNER, JOHN HASTINGS
 Ghoul. F. King
TURNER, OTIS
 Black Box. E. P. Oppenheim
 Spy. J. F. Cooper
TURNEY, CATHERINE
 Back from the Dead. C. Turney; Other One
 Cry Wolf. M. Carleton
 No Man of Her Own. W. Irish; I Married a Dead Man
TUTTLE, FRANK W.
 Manhandled. A. Stringer
 Manhattan. J. Farnol; Definite Object
 Studio Murder Mystery. Edingtons
TWIST, DEREK
 Family Doctor. J. Fleming
 Non-Stop New York. K. Attiwill; Sky Steward
 They Drive by Night. J. Curtis
TWIST, JOHN
 Colorado Territory. W. R. Burnett; High Sierra
 Saint Strikes Back. L. Charteris; She Was a Lady
 Serenade. J M. Cain
TWYFORD, CYRIL
 House of the Arrow. A. E. W. Mason
 Missing Rembrandt. A. C. Doyle; Return of Sherlock Holmes
 Mystery at the Villa Rose. A. E. W. Mason; At the Villa Rose
 Sleeping Cardinal. A. C. Doyle; Memoirs of Sherlock Holmes
 Valley of Fear. A. C. Doyle
TYBER, DANNY
 Dead Run. R. Sheckley
TYNAN, KATHLEEN
 Agatha. K. Tynan
TYNAN, KENNETH
 Nowhere to Go. D. MacKenzie
TYSON, NONA
 Hot Spot. C. Williams; Hell Hath No Fury
UNGER, GLADYS
 Cheating Cheaters. M. Marcin
 Mystery of Edwin Drood. C. Dickens
 Night of Mystery. S. S. Van Dine; Greene Murder Case
UNSELL, EVE
 Breath of Scandal. E. Balmer
 Dummy. H. J. O'Higgins
 Her Second Chance. W. Woodrow; Second Chance
 Secret Call. A. P. Terhune; Woman
 Shadow of the Rope. E. W. Hornung
 Suspense. I. Ostrander
 Test of Honor. E. P. Oppenheim; Mr. Wingrave, Millionaire
 Whirlpool. V. Morton
URIS, MICHAEL H.
 Four Days' Wonder. A. A. Milne
USTINOV, PETER
 School for Secrets. Delano Ames
VADIM, ROGER
 Blackmailed. E. Myers; Mrs. Christopher
 Blood and Roses. J. S. Le Fanu; In a Glass Darkly
 Night Heaven Fell. A. Vidalie; Midnight Jewelers
VADJA, ERNEST
 Payment Deferred. J. Dell
VADNAY, LASZLO
 Uncertain Glory. H. Meadows
VAILLAND, ROGER
 Blood and Roses. J. S. Le Fanu; In a Glass Darkly
VAJDA, LADISLAV
 It Happens in Broad Daylight. F. Duerrenmatt; Pledge
VALDEZ, LUIS
 Zoot Suit. L. Valdez
VALENTIN, ALBERT
 Meurtre en 45 Tours. P. Boileau; Heart to Heart
 Old Tin Can. D. Keene; Flight by Night
VALENTINE, VAL
 Fortune Is a Woman. Winston Graham
 Grand National Night. D. Christie
 High Command. L. Robinson; General Goes Too Far
 Ringer. E. Wallace
 This Was a Woman. J. Morgan
 Yellow Mask. E. Wallace; Traitor's Gate
VALERE, JEAN
 Avec un Elastique. C. Williams; Big Bite
VALLIER, XAVIER
 A Toi de Jouer Callaghan. P. Cheyney; Sorry You've Been Troubled
 Callaghan Remet Ca. P. Cheyney (headnote)
 Plus de Whisky pour Callaghan. P. Cheyney; It Couldn't Matter Less
VALLS, MANUEL
 Los Papeles de Aspern. H. James; Aspern Papers
VANCE, LEIGH
 Black Windmill. C. Egleton; Seven Days to a Killing
VAN DINE, S. S.
 Canary Murder Case. S. S. Van Dine
VAN DRUTEN, JOHN
 Gas Light. P. Hamilton
 Raffles. E. W. Hornung; Amateur Cracksman
VAN EVERY, DALE
 Murders in the Rue Morgue. E. A. Poe; Prose Romances of Edgar A. Poe
VAN HAMME, JEAN
 Diva. Delacorta
VANLO, ROLFE E.
 Informer. L. O'Flaherty
VAN LUSIL, JAN
 Traitor Spy. T. C. H. Jacobs
VAN SANT, GUS, JR.
 Drugstore Cowboy. J. Fogle
VAN UPP, VIRGINIA
 One Night in Lisbon. J. Van Druten; There's Always Juliet
VAUTRIN, JEAN
 Barbarous Street. D. Goodis; Street of the Lost
VEBER, FRANCIS
 Hold-Up. J. Cronley; Quick Change
VECCHIETTI, ALBERTO
 Brothers Karamazov. F. M. Dostoevskii
VEILLER, ANTHONY
 Assignment in Brittany. H. MacInnes
 Killers. E. Hemingway; Men Without Women
 List of Adrian Messenger. P. MacDonald
 Notorious Sophie Lang. F. I. Anderson
 R.I.P. P. MacDonald
 Seven Keys to Baldpate. E. D. Biggers
 Star of Midnight. A. S. Roche
 Stranger. A. Veiller
 Winterset. Maxwell Anderson
 Witching Hour. A. Thomas
VEILLER, BAYARD
 Arsene Lupin. E. Jepson
 Trial of Mary Dugan. B. Veiller
VEILLOT, CLAUDE
 Rise Up, Spy. G. Markstein; Chance Awakening
VEITCH, ANTHONY SCOTT
 Coast of Skeletons. E. Wallace; Sanders of the River
VERNER, GERALD
 Tread Softly. G. Verner; Show Must Go On
VERNEUIL, HENRI
 Any Number Can Win. J. Trinian
 Big Chief. O. Henry; Whirligigs
 Burglars. D. Goodis; Burglar
 Forbidden Fruit. G. Simenon; Act of Passion
 What Price Murder. R. Marshall; Sucker Punch
VERNON, RICHARD
 Street of Shadows. L. Meynell; Creaking Chair
VERSINI, ANDRE
 See Venice and Die. R. Marshall; Mission to Venice
VERSTAPPEN, WIM
 Outsider in Amsterdam. J. van de Wetering
 Rattlerat. J. van de Wetering
VIANEY, MICHEL
 Cops' Sunday. A. Coburn; Off Duty
VICTOR, HERBERT
 Bedelia. V. Caspary
VIDAL, GORE
 Scapegoat. D. Du Maurier
VIERTEL, PETER
 Decision Before Dawn. G. Howe; Call It Treason
 We Were Strangers. R. Sylvester; Rough Sketch
VILFRID, JACQUES
 Blonde from Peking. J. H. Chase; You Have Yourself a Deal
 Dames Get Along. P. Cheyney; Dames Don't Care
 Gazebo. A. Coppel
VINCENZONI, LUCIANO
 Quiet Place in the Country. H. Clement
VISCONTI, LUCHINO
 Obsession. J. M. Cain; Postman Always Rings Twice
VITTES, LOUIS
 Gang War. O. Demaris; Hoods Take Over
VOLK, STEVEN
 Guardian. D. Greenburg; Nanny
VOLLMOELLER, KARL
 Shanghai Gesture. John Colton
VON DRUTEN, JOHN
 Night Must Fall. E. Williams

Screenwriters Index

VON HARBOU, THEA
  Dr. Mabuse, Gambler. N. Jacques; Dr. Mabuse, Master of Mystery
  His Official Wife. R. H. Savage; My Official Wife
  Spy. T. von Harbou

VON STACKELBERG, CARLA
  Hound of the Baskervilles. A. C. Doyle

VON STERNBERG, JOSEF
  Dishonored. F. Vreeland
  Shanghai Gesture. John Colton

VON STROHEIM, ERICH
  Devil-Doll. A. Merritt; Burn, Witch, Burn!

VOSPER, FRANK
  Rome Express. R. Alexander

WADEMANT, ANNETTE
  Come Dance with Me. K. Roos; Blonde Died Dancing
  What Price Murder. R. Marshall; Sucker Punch

WADLEIGH, MICHAEL
  Wolfen. W. Streiber

WAGNER, JACK
  Fighting Edge. W. M. Raine

WAHLOO, PER
  Black Sun. P. Wahloo; Lorry

WAINWRIGHT, RICHARD
  Secret of Stamboul. D. Wheatley; Eunich of Stamboul

WAISGLASS, ELAINE
  Judgement in Stone. R. Rendell

WAJDA, ANDRZEJ
  Ashes and Diamonds. J. Andrzeyevski

WAKEFIELD, GILBERT
  Lord Camber's Ladies. H. A. Vachell; Case of Lady Camber

WALD, JERRY
  Out of the Fog. I. Shaw; Gentle People
  They Drive by Night. A. Bezzerides; Long Haul

WALD, MALVIN
  Al Capone. J. Roeburt
  Dark Past. J. Warwick; Blind Alley
  Naked City. M. Wald

WALDMAN, FRANK
  Pink Panther Strikes Again. F. Waldman
  Return of the Pink Panther. F. Waldman

WALLACE, BRYAN EDGAR
  Flying Squad. E. Wallace
  Frightened Lady. E. Wallace; Case of the Frightened Lady
  Mind of Mr. J. G. Reeder. E. Wallace
  Squealer. E. Wallace
  Strangers on a Honeymoon. E. Wallace; Northing Tramp
  White Face. E. Wallace

WALLACE, EARL W.
  Witness. W. Kelley

WALLACE, EDGAR
  Hound of the Baskervilles. A. C. Doyle
  Man Who Changed His Name. E. Wallace
  Old Man. E. Wallace; Coat of Arms
  Ringer. E. Wallace
  Squeaker. E. Wallace
  Valley of Ghosts. E. Wallace

WALLACE, IRVING
  Bad for Each Other. H. McCoy; Scalpel

WALLACE, TREVOR
  Journey Into Fear. E. Ambler

WALSH, BILL
  One of Our Dinosaurs Is Missing. D. Forrest; Great Dinosaur Robbery
  That Darn Cat. Gordons; Undercover Cat

WALSH, RAOUL
  From Now On. F. Packard

WALTER, EUGENE
  Jealousy. E. Walter
  Side Street. M. St. Clair

WALTON, FRED
  Rosary Murders. W. X. Kienzle

WAMBAUGH, JOSEPH
  Black Marble. J. Wambaugh
  Onion Field. J. Wambaugh

WARD, ALBERT
  Poison. A. Askew

WARD, DAVID S.
  Steelyard Blues. Timothy Harris
  Sting. R. Weverka

WARD, EDMUND
  Amsterdam Affair. N. Freeling; Love in Amsterdam
  Goodbye Gemini. J. Hall; Ask Agamemnon
  Prayer for the Dying. J. Higgins
  Violent Enemy. H. Marlowe; Candle for the Dead

WARD, LUCI
  Murder by an Aristocrat. M. G. Eberhart

WARE, KENNETH
  Last Grenade. J. Sherlock; Ordeal of Major Grigsby

WARGNIER, REGIS
  I'm King of the Castle. S. Hill

WARREN, CAROL
  Honorable Gentleman. A. Abdullah

WASHBURN, DERIC
  Extreme Prejudice. R. Dobbins

WATER, G.
  Sorcerer. E. Wallace; Ringer

WATERHOUSE, JOHN
  She'll Have to Go. I. S. Black; We Must Kill Toni

WATERHOUSE, KEITH
  Man in the Middle. H. Fast; Winston Affair
  West 11. L. Del Rivo; Furnished Room

WATERS, ED
  Caper of the Golden Bulls. W. P. McGivern
  Darker Than Amber. J. D. MacDonald
  Man-Trap. J. D. MacDonald; Soft Touch

WATKINS, PETER
  Privilege. John Burke

WATSON, NORMAN
  Honours Easy. R. Pertwee

WEARING, MICHAEL
  Bellman & True. D. Lowden

WEBB, JAMES R.
  Cape Fear. J. D. MacDonald; Executioners
  Phantom of the Rue Morgue. E. A. Poe; Prose Romances of Edgar A. Poe
  Trapeze. M. Catto; Killing Frost

WEBB, KENNETH
  Master Mind. M. Dana

WEBB, MILLARD
  Tiger Rose. W. Mack

WEBSTER, HENRY KITCHELL
  Green Cloak. Y. Davis

WEIL, RICHARD
  Crime by Night. G. Homes; Forty Whacks

WEINSTEIN, MARVIN R.
  Running Target. S. Frazee

WEISBERG, BRENDA
  Weird Woman. F. Leiber, Jr.; Conjure Wife

WEISMAN, MATTHEW
  Burglar. L. Block (headnote)

WELBECK, PETER
  Circus of Fear. E. Wallace (headnote)
  Coast of Skeletons. E. Wallace; Sanders of the River
  Count Dracula. B. Stoker; Dracula
  Ten Little Indians. A. Christie

WELCH, EDDIE
  Ladies of the Jury. F. Ballard
  Murder Goes to College. K. Steel

WELCH, WILLIAM
  Brotherhood of Satan. L. Q. Jones

WELLAND, COLIN
  Dry White Season. A. Brink

WELLER, MICHAEL
  Ragtime. E. L. Doctorow

WELLER, SAMUEL M.
  Burden of Proof. V. Sardou; Diplomates

WELLES, ORSON
  Journey into Fear. E. Ambler
  Lady from Shanghai. Sherwood King; If I Die Before I Wake
  Mr. Arkadin. O. Welles
  Stranger. A. Veiller
  Touch of Evil. W. Masterson; Badge of Evil

WELLESLEY, GEORGE
  Chinese Bungalow. M. Osmond

WELLESLEY, GORDON
  Green Scarf. G. Des Cars; Brute
  Laburnum Grove. J. B. Priestley
  Malpas Mystery. E. Wallace; Face in the Night
  Peterville Diamond. L. Fodor; Jewel Robbery

WELLS, GEORGE
  Gazebo. A. Coppel
  Horizontal Lieutenant. G. Cotler; Bottletop Affair
  Party Girl. M. H. Albert
  Penelope. E. V. Cunningham

WENDERS, WIM
  American Friend. P. Highsmith; Ripley's Game

WERTY, QUENTIN
  Dark of the Sun. W. Smith; Train from Katanga
  Jigsaw. W. Ericson; Fallen Angel
  That Man Bolt. P. Crowcraft

WESSON, RICHARD
  Change of Mind. C. Stratton

WEST, CLAUDINE
  Last of Mrs. Cheyney. F. Lonsdale
  Mortal Storm. P. Bottome

WEST, ELLIOT
  Fear Makers. D. L. Teilhet

WEST, NATHANIAL
  President's Mystery. F. D. Roosevelt; President's Mystery Story

WEST, ROLAND
  Bat. M. R. Rinehart
  Bat Whispers. M. E. Rinehart; Bat

WESTERBY, ROBERT
  Break in the Circle. P. Loraine
  Cone of Silence. D. Beaty
  Devil's Agent. H. Habe; Agent of the Devil
  Dr. Syn Alias the Scarecrow. R. Thorndyke; Dr. Syn
  Don't Ever Leave Me. Anthony Armstrong (headnote)
  My Sister and I. E. Bonett; High Pavement
  Surgeon's Knife. A. Hocking; Wicked Flee
  Wicked As They Come. B. Ballinger; Portrait in Smoke

WESTLAKE, DONALD E.
  Cops and Robbers. D. E. Westlake
  Grifters. Jim Thompson
  Why Me? D. E. Westlake

WESTLAKE, DOROTHY
  Hound of the Baskervilles. A. C. Doyle

WESTON, GARNETT
    American Prisoner. E. Phillpotts
    Blackmail. C. Bennett
    Bulldog Drummond in Africa. H. C. McNeile; Challenge
    Bulldog Drummond's Bride. H. C. McNeile; Sapper: The Best Short Stories
    Bulldog Drummond's Secret Police. H. C. McNeile; Temple Tower
    Ninth Guest. O. Davis
    Partners in Crime. K. Steel; Murder Goes to College
WETHERELL, M. A.
    Moorland Tragedy. B. Orczy; Unravelled Knots
WEXLER, NORMAN
    Raw Deal. W. Wager
WEXLEY, JOHN
    Amazing Dr. Clitterhouse. B. Lyndon
WHARTON, THEODORE
    Ticket-of-Leave Man. C. Reade; Foul Play
WHEDDON, DANIEL
    Chick. E. Wallace
WHEELER, HUGH
    Travels with My Aunt. G. Greene
WHEELER, PAUL
    Caravan to Vaccares. A. MacLean
    Puppet on a Chain. A. MacLean
    Ransom. P. Wheeler
WHEELER, RENE
    Look Out, Girls. J. H. Chase; Miss Callaghan Comes to Grief
    Soupe aux Poulets. E. McBain; Killer's Wedge
WHELAN, TIM
    Fall Guy. G. Abbott
WHITAKER, ROD
    Eiger Sanction. Trevanian
WHITE, DIZZ
    Bullshot. R. House; Bullshot Crummond
WHITE, GARY MICHAEL
    Sky Riders. L. Cameron
WHITE, ROBB
    Macabre. T. Durrant; Marble Forest
WHITE, ROBERTSON
    Charlie Chan's Murder Cruise. E. D. Biggers; Charlie Chan Carries On
    Lady in the Morgue. J. Latimer
    Mystery House. M. G. Eberhart; Mystery of Hunting's End
    Patient in Room 18. M. G. Eberhart
    Westland Case. J. Latimer; Headed for a Hearse
    Witness Vanishes. J. Ronald
WHITING, JOHN
    Ship That Died of Shame. N. Monsarrat
WHITON, JAMES
    Abominable Dr. Phibes. W. Goldstein; Dr. Phibes
WHITTAKER, CHARLES E.
    House of Glass. M. Marcin
    Huntingtower. J. Buchan
    Partners of the Night. L. Scott
WHITTAKER, JAMES
    Last of the Lone Wolf. L. J. Vance; Lone Wolf
WICKING, CHRISTOPHER
    Blood from the Mummy's Tomb. B. Stoker; Jewel of the Seven Stars
    Murders in the Rue Morgue. E. A. Poe; Prose Romances of Edgar A. Poe
    Scream and Scream Again. P. Saxon; Disoriented Man
    To the Devil—a Daughter. D. Wheatley
WIDERBERG, BO
    Man on the Roof. M. Sjowall

WIENE, ROBERT
    Raskolnikov. F. M. Dostoevskii; Crime and Punishment
WILBUR, CRANE
    Bat. M. R. Rinehart
WILCOX, HERBERT
    Woman in White. W. Collins
WILDE, HAGAR
    Unseen. E. L. White; Midnight House
WILDER, BILLY
    Double Indemnity. J. M. Cain
    Private Life of Sherlock Holmes. Michael Hardwick
    Stalag 17. D. Bevan
    Witness for the Prosecution. A. Christie
WILDER, GENE
    Adventures of Sherlock Holmes' Smarter Brother. G. Pearlman
WILDER, MYLES
    Spy in the Sky. A. S. Fleischman; Counterspy Express
WILDER, ROBERT
    Flamingo Road. R. Wilder
WILHELM, HANS
    Spy for a Day. S. Aumonier; Love-a-Duck
    Under Western Eyes. J. Conrad
WILHELM, WOLFGANG
    Saint Meets the Tiger. L. Charteris; Meet the Tiger
WILLARD, JOHN
    Mask of Fu Manchu. S. Rohmer
WILLAT, IRVIN W.
    False Faces. L. J. Vance
    Yelloe Men and Gold. Gouverneur Morris
WILLETS, GILSON
    City of Purple Dreams. Anonymous
    House of a Thousand Candles. M. Nicholson
    Loaded Dice. E. H. Clark
    Millionaire Baby. A. K. Green
    Quarry. J. A. Moroso
WILLIAMS, BOB
    Accused of Murder. W. R. Burnett; Vanity Row
WILLIAMS, BROCK
    Black Coffee. A. Christie
    Chin-Chin-Chinaman. P. Walsh
    Condemned to Death. G. Goodchild; Jack O'Lantern
    Crime Unlimited. D. Hume
    Crown v. Stevens. L. Meynell; Third Time Unlucky
    Dark Stairway. M. G. Eberhart; From This Dark Stairway
    Dark Tower. A. Woolcott
    Harassed Hero. E. Dudley
    It's in the Blood. D. Whitelaw; Big Picture
    Madonna of the Seven Moons. M. Lawrence
    Meet Mr. Callaghan. G. Verner
    Night Invader. J. Bentley; Rendezvous with Death
    Nine Forty-Five. O. Davis; At 9:45
    Peterville Diamond. L. Fodor; Jewel Robbery
    Root of All Evil. J. S. Fletcher
WILLIAMS, CHARLES
    Arm at the Left. C. Williams; Aground
    Don't Just Stand There. C. Williams; Wrong Venus
    Hot Spot. C. Williams; Hell Hath No Fury
    Joy House. D. Keene
    Pink Jungle. A. Williams; Snake Water
    Woman in the Dark. D. Hammett
WILLIAMS, DON
    Slaughter. H. Clement
WILLIAMS, EMLYN
    Broken Blossoms. T. Burke; Limehouse Nights
    Dead Men Tell No Tales. F. Beeding; Norwich Victims

Man Who Knew Too Much. R. Alexander
WILLIAMS, GORDON
    Tree of Hands. R. Rendell
WILLIAMS, J. B.
    Chinese Bungalow. M. Osmond
    London Belongs to Me. N. Collins
    Man About the House. F. B. Young
WILLIAMS, JOHN D.
    Jealousy. E. Walter
WILLIAMS, MOIRA
    Dawning. Jennifer Johnston; Old Jess
WILLIAMS, LADY RHYS
    Price of Things. E. Glyn
WILLIAMS, WADE
    Detour. M. Goldsmith
WILLIAMSON, DAVID
    Removalists. D. Williamson
WILLIAMSON, TONY
    Night Watch. L. Fletcher
WILLINGHAM, CALDER
    One-Eyed Jacks. C. Neider; Authentic Death of Hendry Jones
    Thieves Like Us. E. Anderson
WILLIS, F. McGREW
    Big Gamble. O. R. Cohen; Iron Chalice
    Gay Lord Waring. H. Townley
    Pool of Flame. L. J. Vance
    Silent Battle. G. F. Gibbs
WILLIS, TED
    Good Time Girl. A. La Bern; Night Darkens the Streets
WILLMAN, WENDELL
    Firefox. C. Thomas
WILLSHREI, KARL HEINZ
    Two Faces of January. P. Highsmith
WILSON, CAREY
    Empty Hands. A. Stringer
    President Vanishes. Anonymous
    Red Lights. E. E. Rose; Rear Car
WILSON, GERALD
    Scorpio. M. Roote
    Stone Killer. J. Gardner; Complete State of Death
WILSON, HUGH
    Burglar. L. Block (headnote)
WILSON, MAURICE J.
    Clash by Night. R. Croft-Cooke
    Guilty? M. Gilbert; Death Has Deep Roots
    Price of Silence. L. Meynell; One Step from Murder
    Who Killed the Cat? A. Ridley; Tabitha
WILSON, MICHAEL
    Five Fingers. L. C. Moyzisch; Operation Cicero
WILSON, MICHAEL G.
    For Your Eyes Only. I. Fleming
    License to Kill. John Gardner
    Living Daylights. I. Fleming; Octopussy and The Living Daylights
    Octopussy. I. Fleming
WIMPERIS, ARTHUR
    Calling Bulldog Drummond. G. Fairlie
    Four Dark Hours. G. Greene (headnote)
    Knight Without Armour. J. Hilton
    Man They Could Not Arrest. E. Wallace (headnote)
    Red Danube. B. Marshall; Vespers in Vienna
    Return of the Scarlet Pimpernel. B. Orczy (headnote)
    Sanders of the River. E. Wallace
    Scarlet Pimpernel. B. Orczy
    Under the Red Robe. S. J. Weyman
WINCELBERG, SHIMON
    From the Boys. R. Matheson; Ride the Nightmare

Screenwriters Index

WING, WILLIAM E.
   Breathless Moment. M. Bryant; Redemption of Richard

WINKLESS, TERENCE H.
   Howling. G. Brandner

WINNER, MICHAEL
   Appointment with Death. A. Christie
   Big Sleep. R. Chandler
   Sentinel. J. Konvitz

WINSLOW, DICKY
   East Lynne. H. Wood
   Maria Marten. Anonymous

WINTER, KEITH
   Above Suspicion. H. MacInnes
   Uncle Harry. T. Job

WINTERTON, PAUL
   Touch of Larceny. A. Garve; Megstone Plot

WISE, WALTER
   Sinner Take All. W. Chambers; Murder for a Wanton

WISHER, WILLIAM, JR.
   Terminator. S. Hutson

WITTING, CLIFFORD
   Park Plaza 605. B. Gray; Dare-Devil Conquest

WITTY, FRANK
   No Escape. G. Goodchild; No Exit
   Prison Breakers. E. Wallace (headnote)

WOHL, BURTON
   Third Day. J. Hayes

WOLF, DAVID M.
   Next Man. M. Z. Lewin

WOLFERT, IRA
   Force of Evil. I. Wolfert

WOLFSON, P. J.
   Hands of Orlac. M. Renard
   70,000 Witnesses. C. Fitzsimmons

WONTNER, ARTHUR
   Sherlock Holmes's Fatal Hour. A. C. Doyle; Memoirs of Sherlock Holmes
   Triumph of Sherlock Holmes. A. C. Doyle; Valley of Fear

WOOD, CHARLES
   Long Day's Dying. A. White

WOOD, CHRISTOPHER
   Moonraker. C. Wood; James Bond and Moonraker
   Remo. W. B. Murphy
   Spy Who Loved Me. C. Wood; James Bond, the Spy Who Loved Me

WOOD, FRANK
   Great Impersonation. E. P. Oppenheim

WOOD, KINCHEN
   Eugene Aram. E. Bulwer-Lytton
   Running Water. A. E. W. Mason

WOODLOCK, GRAHAM
   Scobie Malone. J. Cleary; Helga's Web

WOODS, FRANK
   Suicide Club. R. L. Stevenson

WOODS, WALTER
   Brass Bullet. F. R. Adams; Pleasure Island

WOOLF, EDGAR ALLAN
   Casino Murder Case. S. S. Van Dine
   Mask of Fu Manchu. S. Rohmer
   Murder in the Private Car. E. E. Rose; Rear Car

WORTH, CEDRIC
   President Vanishes. Anonymous

WRAY, ARDEL
   Leopard Man. C. Woolrich; Black Alibi

WRESTLER, PHILIP
   Crosstrap. J. N. Chase (headnote)

WRIGHT, RICHARD
   Native Son. Richard Wright

WRIGHT, WILLIAM H.
   Assignment in Brittany. H. MacInnes

WYLER, ROBERT
   Detective Story. S. Kingsley
   Murder Goes to College. K. Steel
   Sophie Lang Goes West. F. I. Anderson; Notorious Sophie Lang

WYNDHAM-LEWIS, D. B.
   Chick. E. Wallace

WYNN, TRACY KEENAN
   Deep. P. Benchley
   Drowning Pool. J. R. Macdonald

XIAO, MAO
   Bloody Morning. G. G. Marquez; Chronicle of a Death Foretold

YABLONSKY, HAROLD
   Secret of the Purple Reef. D. Cottrell; Silent Reefs

YALLOP, DAVID
   Chicago Joe and the Showgirl. M. Gaynor

YELDHAM, PETER
   Liquidator. J. Gardner
   Ten Little Indians. A. Christie; Ten Little Niggers
   Weekend of Shadows. H. Atkinson; Reckoning

YORDAN, PHILIP
   Chase. C. Woolrich; Black Path of Fear
   Detective Story. S. Kingsley
   Edge of Doom. L. Brady
   Fiend Who Walked the West. E. Lipsky; Kiss of Death
   Four Boys and a Gun. W. Wiener
   House of Strangers. J. Weidman; I'll Never Go There Any More
   No Down Payment. J. McPartland
   Whistle Stop. M. M. Wolff

YOST, DANIEL
   Drugstone Cowboy. J. Fogle

YOST, DOROTHY
   Murder on a Bridle Path. S. Palmer; Puzzle of the Red Stallion
   Queenie. W. F. Fauley

YOST, ROBERT M.
   Forgotten Faces. R. W. Child; Velvet Black
   Tom Sawyer, Detective. M. Twain

YOUNG, CLARENCE UPSON
   Ghost That Walks Alone. R. Shattuck; Wedding Guest Sat on a Stone
   Plot Thickens. S. Palmer (headnote)
   Time to Kill. R. Chandler; High Window

YOUNG, HOWARD IRVING
   Crimson Circle. E. Wallace
   Million a Minute. H. Douglas
   Secret of Stamboul. D. Wheatley; Eunich of Stamboul

YOUNG, JAMES
   Daughter of Two Worlds. L. Scott
   Notorious Miss Lisle. B. Reynolds
   On Trial. E. L. Reizenstein

YOUNG, TERENCE
   Heart Trump for OSS 117 in Tokyo. J. Bruce; Hot Line
   On the Night of the Fire. F. L. Green

YOUNG, TONY
   Hidden Homicide. P. Capon; Death at Shinglestrand

YOUNG, WALDEMAR
   Black Bird. T. Browning; Mocking Bird
   Fire Flingers. W. J. Neidig
   Flaming Forest. J. O. Curwood
   Girl in the Web. G. Bonner; Miss Maitland, Private Secretary
   London After Midnight. M. Coolridge-Rask
   Miracle Man. F. Packard
   Salomy Jane. Bret Harte; Stories in Light and Shadow
   Unholy Three. T. Robbins
   Where East Is East. T. Browning

YULE, IAN
   River of Diamonds. G. Jenkins

YUST, LARRY
   Trick Baby. I. Slim

ZANUCK, DARRYL FRANCIS
   Across the Pacific. C. E. Blaney
   Little Caesar. W. R. Burnett
   On Thin Ice. A. R. Colver; Dear Pretender

ZEISLER, ALFRED
   Fear. F. M. Dostoevskii; Crime and Punishment

ZELLNER, LOIS
   Family Secret. A. Thomas; Editha's Burglar

ZIFFREN, LESTER
   Charlie Chan in Rio. E. D. Biggers; Black Camel
   Charlie Chan's Murder Cruise. E. D. Biggers; Charlie Chan Carries On
   Man Who Wouldn't Talk. H. Hall; Valiant

ZIMBALIST, DON
   Young Dillinger. S. Stuart

ZIMMER, BERNARD
   Second Bureau. C. R. Dumas

ZIMMERMAN, VERNON
   Fade to Black. R. Renaud

ZOLLER, STEPHEN
   Office Party. M. A. Gilbert

ZOTY, DOUGLAS
   Red Dice. O. R. Cohen; Iron Chalice

ZUCKERMAN, GEORGE
   Panther's Moon. V. Canning

DIRECTORS INDEX

Directors Index

ABBOTT, GEORGE
  Manslaughter. A. D. Miller
  Sea God. J. Russell; Red Mark
ABRAMSON, HANS
  Roseanna. M. Sjowall
ADDIS, JUS
  Cry-Baby Killer. J. Hilton
ADOLFI, JOHN G.
  Man Inside. N. S. Lincoln
  Millionaire. E. D. Biggers; Earl Derr Biggers Tells Ten Stories
AGOSTINI, PHILIP
  Soupe aux Poulets. E. McBain; Killer's Wedge
AINSWORTH, JOHN
  Hell Is Empty. J. F. Straker
AIZNER, HENRI
  Le Mystere de la Chambre Jaune. G. Leroux; Mystery of the Yellow Room
ALAZRAKI, BENITO
  Spiritism. W. W. Jacobs; Lady of the Barge
ALDRICH, ROBERT
  Angry Hills. L. Uris
  Big Knife. C. Odets
  Choirboys. J. Wambaugh
  Flight of the Phoenix. E. Trevor
  Grissom Gang. J. H. Chase; No Orchids for Miss Blandish
  Hustle. S. Shagan; City of Angels
  Kiss Me, Deadly. M. Spillane
  Ten Seconds to Hell. L. P. Bachmann; Phoenix
  Twilight's Last Gleaming. W. Wager; Viper Three
  Whatever Happened to Baby Jane? H. Farrell
ALLEGRET, MARC
  Blackmailed. E. Myers; Mrs. Christopher
  Blanche Fury. J. Shearing
ALLEGRET, YVES
  Look Out Girls. J. H. Chase; Miss Callaghan Comes to Grief
ALLEN, A. K. [Real name: JANET GREEK]
  Ladies Club. B. Black; Sisterhood
ALLEN, IRVING
  Avalanche. K. Boyle
ALLEN, IRWIN
  Towering Inferno. R. M. Stern; Tower
ALLEN, JAMES
  Burndown. S. Collins; Burn Down
ALLEN, LEWIS
  Chicago Deadline. T. Thayer; One Woman
  Desert Fury. Ramona Stewart; Desert Town
  Sealed Verdict. L. Shapiro
  So Evil My Love. J. Shearing; For Her to See Uninvited. D. Macardle; Uneasy Freehold
  Unseen. E. L. White; Midnight House
  Whirlpool. L. P. Bachmann; Lorelei
ALLIO, RENE
  Transit. A. Seghers
ALMOND, PAUL
  Backfire! E. Wallace (headnote)
ALTMAN, ROBERT
  Long Goodbye. R. Chandler
  McCabe and Mrs. Miller. E. Naughton; McCabe
  Nightmare in Chicago. W. P. McGivern; Killer on the Turnpike
  That Cold Day in the Park. R. Miles
  Thieves Like Us. E. Anderson
AMY, GEORGE
  Granny Get Your Gun. E. S. Gardner; Case of the Dangerous Dowager
ANDERSON, MICHAEL
  Chase a Crooked Shadow. A. Shaughnessy; Double Cut
  Hell Is Sold Out. M. Dekobra

House of the Arrow. A. E. W. Mason
Man of Bronze. K. Robeson
Naked Edge. M. Ehrlich; First Train to Babylon
Night Was Our Friend. M. Pertwee
Quiller Memorandum. Adam Hall; Berlin Memorandum
Shake Hands with the Devil. R. Conner
Waterfront. J. Brophy
Wreck of the Mary Deare. H. Innes; Mary Deare
ANNAKIN, KEN
  Across the Bridge. G. Greene; Nineteen Stories
  Double Confession. J. Garden; All on a Summer's Day
  Informers. D. Warner; Death of a Snout
  Loser Takes All. G. Greene
ANNAUD, JEAN-JACQUES
  Name of the Rose. U. Eco
ANTHONY, JOSEPH
  Captive City. J. Appleby
  Tomorrow. W. Faulkner; Knight's Gambit
ANTON, KARL
  Die Racher. E. Wallace; Avenger
APFEL, OSCAR
  Bawlerout. F. Halsey
  Bulldog Drummond. H. C. McNeile
  Half a Chance. F. S. Isham
  Lion's Mouse. C. N. Williamson
  Man on the Box. H. MacGrath
  Master Mind. M. Dana
  Oakdale Affair. E. R. Burroughs
APTED, MICHAEL
  Agatha. K. Tynan
  Gorky Park. M. C. Smith
  Squeeze. David Craig; Whose Little Girl Are You?
ARANDA, VICENTE
  Blood Spattered Bride. J. S. Le Fanu; In a Glass Darkly
  Murder in the Central Committee. M. V. Montalban
ARCADY, ALEXANDRE
  Hold-Up. J. Cronley; Quick Change
  Last Summer in Tangiers; W. O'Farrell; Devil His Due
ARCHAINBAUD, GEORGE A.
  Cordelia the Magnificent. L. Scott
  Easy Pickings. P. Cruger
  Midnight Guest. F. M. White
  Murder on the Blackboard. S. Palmer
  Penguin Pool Murder. S. Palmer
  Return of Sophie Lang. E. Anderson; Notorious Sophie Lang
  Thirteen Women. T. Thayer
AREHN, MATS
  Assignment. P. Wahloo
ARGENTO, DARIO
  Cat o' Nine Tails. P. J. Gillette
ARKIN, ALAN
  Little Murders. J. Feiffer
ARKLESS, ROBERT
  Man Who Would Not Die. C. Williams; Sailcloth Shroud
ARKUSH, ALLAN
  Deathsport. W. Hughes
ARLISS, LESLIE
  Man About the House. F. B. Young
  Night Has Eyes. A. Kennington
ARMITAGE, GEORGE
  Hit Man. Ted Lewis; Jack's Return Home
  Miami Blues. C. Willeford
ARNETT, JAMES
  Mackintosh Man. D. Bagley; Freedom Trap
ARNOLD, JACK
  Black Eye. J. Jacks; Murder on the Wild Side
  Glass Web. M. Ehrlich; Spin the Glass Web

High School Confidential. Morton Cooper
Lady Takes a Flier. E. Ronns
Man in the Shadow. H. Whittington
ARTAUD, E.
  Dancer and the King. C. E. Blaney
ARZNER, DOROTHY
  First Comes Courage. E. Arnold; Commandos
ASHBY, HAL
  Eight Million Ways to Die. L. Block
ASHER, ROBERT
  Make Mine Mink. P. Coke; Breath of Spring
  She'll Have to Go. I. S. Black; We Must Kill Toni
ASHER, WILLIAM
  Butcher, Baker, Nightmare Maker. R. Natale
  Johnny Cool. J. McPartland; Kingdom of Johnny Cool
  Muscle Beach Party. Elsie Lee
ASQUITH, ANTHONY
  Act of Mercy. F. Clifford
  Carrington, V.C. D. Christie
  Cottage to Let. G. Kerr; Cottages to Let
  Libel. E. Wooll
  Net. J. Pudney
  Orders to Kill. D. Downes
  Shooting Stars. E. C. Vivian
  Two Living and One Dead. S. Christiansen
ATTENBOROUGH, RICHARD
  Magic. W. Goldman
AUDIARD, MICHEL
  Le Cri du Cormoran le Soir Au-Dessus des Jonques. E. Hunter; Horse's Head
AURTHUR, ROBERT ALAN
  Lost Man. F. L. Green; Odd Man Out
AUSTIN, MICHAEL
  Killing Dad. A. Quin; Berg
AUTANT-LARA, CLAUDE
  In Case of Emergency. G. Simenon
  Murderer. P. Highsmith; Blunderer
AVAKIAN, ARAM
  Cops and Robbers. D. E. Westlake
  11 Harrowhouse. G. A. Browne
AVILDSEN, JOHN G.
  Cry Uncle. Michael Brett; Lie a Little, Die a Little
  Formula. S. Shagan
AYLOTT, DAVE
  It Is Never Too Late to Mend. C. Reade
BACON, LLOYD
  Brother Orchid. L. Brady
  Home Sweet Homicide. C. Rice
  Larceny, Inc. L. Perelman; Night Before Christmas
  Miss Pinkerton. M. R. Rinehart
  Slight Case of Murder. D. Runyon
BACSO, PETER
  Man Who Went Up in Smoke. M. Sjowall
BADGER, CLARENCE
  Murder Will Out. M. Leinster
  Red Lights. E. E. Rose; Rear Car
  Sweethearts and Wives. W. Hackett; Other Men's Wives
BADHAM, JOHN
  Dracula. H. Deane
BAGGOTT, KING
  Raffles, the Amateur Cracksman. E. W. Hornung; Amateur Cracksman
BAILEY, OLIVER D.
  Sun-Up. M. Marcin; Substitute Prisoner
BAIN, BILL
  What Became of Jack and Jill? L. Moody; Ruthless Ones

B

BAKER, GEORGE D.
　Buried Treasure. F. B. Austin; On the Borderland
　Cinema Murder. E. P. Oppenheim; Other Romilly
　Demon. C. N. Williamson
　Heliotrope. R. W. Child; Velvet Black
　Man Who Stayed Home. J. E. H. Terry
　Sleeping Memory. E. P. Oppenheim; Great Awakening
　Winifred the Shop Girl. C. N. Williamson; Shop Girl

BAKER, GRAHAM
　Alien Nation. A. D. Foster

BAKER, ROBERT S.
　Jack the Ripper. S. James
　Passport to Treason. M. O'Brine

BAKER, ROY WARD
　And Now the Screaming Starts. D. Case; Fengriffin
　Asylum. W. Johnston
　Doctor Jekyll and Sister Hyde. R. L. Stevenson; Strange Case of Dr. Jekyll and Mr. Hyde
　Don't Bother to Knock. C. Armstrong; Mischief
　Night Without Sleep. E. Moll
　October Man. E. Britton
　Paper Orchid. A. La Bern
　Singer Not the Song. A. E. Lindop
　Tiger in the Smoke. M. Allingham
　Vampire Lovers. J. L. Le Fanu; In a Glass Darkly

BALABAN, BURT
　"Mad Dog" Coll. S. Thurman

BALL, CHUCK
　Cleopatra Jones and the Casino of Gold. R. Goulart

BALLIN, HUGO
　Pagan Love. A. Abdullah; Honorable Gentleman
　Prairie Wife. A. Stringer

BALLING, ANDERS
　One of Those Things. A. Bodelsen; One Down

BALSHOFER, FRED J.
　Haunted Pajamas. F. P. Elliott
　Paradise Garden. G. F. Gibbs
　Pidgin Island. H. MacGrath

BANKS, MONTY
　For the Love of Mike. H. F. Maltby

BARKER, REGINALD
　Crimson Gardenia. R. Beach
　Dangerous Day. M. R. Rinehart
　Eternal Struggle. G. B. Lancaster; Law Bringers
　Flaming Forest. J. O. Curwood
　Moonstone. W. Collins
　Seven Keys to Baldpate. E. D. Biggers

BARNES, ARTHUR W.
　China Bungalow. M. Osmond

BARRINGER, MICHAEL
　Murder at Covent Garden. W. J. Makin

BARRYMORE, LIONEL
　Madame X. J. W. MacConaughy

BARSHA, LEON
　Convicted. W. Irish; Six Nights of Mystery

BARTLETT, HALL
　Zero Hour! J. Castle; Flight Into Danger

BARTON, CHARLES T.
　Abbott and Costello Meet Frankenstein. M. W. Shelley; Frankenstein
　Murder with Pictures. G. H. Coxe

BARY, LEON
　In the Hands of the Spoilers. S. Paternoster; In the Hands of the Spoiler

BATLEY, ERNEST G.
　Englishman's Home. Guy Du Maurier

BAYLY, STEPHEN
　Just Ask for Diamond. A. Horowitz; Falcon's Malteser

BEATTY, WARREN
　Dick Tracy. M. A. Collins

BEAUDINE, WILLIAM
　Educated Evans. E. Wallace
　Fugitives. R. H. Davis; Exiles
　Men in Her Life. W. Fabian
　Mystery of the Thirteenth Guest. A. Trail

BEAUMONT, GABRIELLE
　Godsend. B. Taylor

BEAUMONT, HARRY
　Man and His Money. F. S. Isham
　Murder in the Private Car. E. E. Rose; Rear Car
　Officer 666. B. Currie
　Stop Thief! Carlyle Moore

BECK, REGINALD
　Long Dark Hall. E. Lustgarten; Case to Answer

BECKER, HAROLD
　Black Marble. J. Wambaugh
　Onion Field. J. Wambaugh

BECKER, JACQUES
　Adventures of Arsene Lupin. M. Leblanc (headnote)

BECKER, JEAN
　One Deadly Summer. S. Japrisot

BEDFORD, TERRY
　Slayground. R. Stark

BEEBE, FORDE
　Invisible Man's Revenge. H. G. Wells; Invisible Man

BEHAT, GILLES
　Barbarous Street. D. Goodis; Street of the Lost

BEINEIX, JEAN-JACQUES
　Diva. Delacorta
　Moon in the Gutter. D. Goodis

BELL, MONTA
　After Midnight. E. Fletcher-Allen
　Bellamy Trial. F. N. Hart

BELLAMY, EARL
　Walking Tall: Part 2. W. Carey

BELSON, JERRY
　Jekyll and Hyde . . . Together Again. R. L. Stevenson; Strange Case of Dr. Jekyll and Mr. Hyde

BENEDEK, LASLO
　Assault on Agathon. A. Caillou
　Moment of Danger. D. MacKenzie; Scent of Danger

BENNETT, CHARLES
　Madness of the Heart. F. Sandstrom

BENNETT, CHESTER
　Secret of the Hills. W. Garrett
　Three Sevens. P. P. Sheehan

BENNETT, COMPTON
　Beyond the Curtain. A. J. Wallis; Thunder Above
　Desperate Moment. M. Albrand
　That Woman Opposite. J. D. Carr; Emperor's Snuff Box

BENNETT, SPENCER GORDON
　House Without a Key. E. D. Biggers

BENNETT, WHITMAN
　Back to Life. A. Soutar; Back from the Dead

BENTLEY, THOMAS
　American Prisoner. E. Phillpotts
　Lackey and the Lady. T. Gallon
　Romance of Mayfair. J. C. Snaith; Crime of Constable Kelly
　Silver Blaze. A. C. Doyle; Memoirs of Sherlock Holmes
　Through Fire and Water. V. Bridges; Greensea Island

BENTON, ROBERT
　Billy Bathgate. E. L. Doctorow

BERANGER, GEORGE A(NDRE)
　Manhattan Knight. G. Burgess; Find the Woman
　Number Seventeen. L. Tracy

BERESFORD, BRUCE
　Money Movers. D. Minchin

BERGER, LUDWIG
　Sins of the Fathers. C. Houghton

BERKE, WILLIAM
　Cop Hater. E. McBain
　Four Boys and a Gun. W. Wiener
　Mugger. E. McBain

BERNHARD, JACK
　Blonde Ice. W. Chambers; Once Too Often

BERNHARDT, CURTIS/KURT
　Conflict. Alex Morrison
　High Wall. A. R. Clark
　Man Who Murdered. C. Farrere; Man Who Killed

BERRY, JOHN
　He Ran All the Way. S. Ross

BERTHELET, ARTHUR
　Sherlock Holmes. W. Gillette

BERTOLUCCI, BERNARDO
　Conformist. A. Moravia

BESNARD, JACQUES
　Stew in the Caribbean. A. Conroy; Looters

BESSIE, DAN
　Hard Traveling. A. Bessie; Bread and a Stone

BEYFUSS, ALEX E.
　Salomy Jane. B. Harte; Stories in Light and Shadow

BIANCHI, EDWARD
　Fan. B. Randall

BIBERMAN, ABNER
　Running Wild. B. Benson; Girl in the Cage

BIBERMAN, HERBERT J.
　Meet Nero Wolfe. R. Stout; Fer-de-Lance
　One-Way Ticket. Ethel Turner

BIJL, JACOB
　Beck. M. Sjowall; Locked Room

BILLINGTON, KEVIN
　Interlude. J. M. Cain; Serenade

BILLON, PIERRE
　Second Bureau. C. R. Dumas

BINET, CATHERINE
　Games of the Countess Dolingen of Gratz. B. Stoker; Dracula

BINGHAM, E. DOUGLAS
　Master Mystery. A. B. Reeve

BINYON, CLAUDE
　Stella. D. M. Disney; Family Skeleton

BIRD, RICHARD
　Terror. E. Wallace

BIRDWELL, RUSSELL J.
　Come-On. W. Chambers
　Masquerade. V. Canning; Castle Minerva

BIRKINSHAW, ALAN
　Ten Little Indians. A. Christie; Ten Little Niggers

BIRT, DANIEL
　She Shall Have Murder. D. Ames
　Third Party Risk. N. Bentley
　Three Silent Men. E. P. Thorne
　Three Weird Sisters. C. Armstrong; Case of the Weird Sisters

BISCHOFF, SAM
　Last Mile. J. Wexley

BISHOP, TERRY
　Unstoppable Man. M. Gilbert; Amateur in Violence

Directors Index

BLACHE, ALICE
  Dream Woman. Wilkie Collins; Woman in White
  Lure. G. Scarborough

BLACHE, HERBERT
  Burglar and the Lady. O. Harper
  Loaded Dice. E. H. Clark
  Secrets of the Night. M. Marcin; Nightcap
  Untamable. G. Burgess; White Cat

BLACK, NOEL
  Pretty Poison. S. Geller; She Let Him Continue

BLACKTON, J. STUART
  Behold This Woman. E. P. Oppenheim; Hillman
  Passionate Quest. E. P. Oppenheim

BLAIR, GEORGE
  Homicide for Three. P. Quenton; Puzzle for Puppets

BLAKE, T. C.
  Nightflyers. G. R. R. Martin

BLANC, ROGER
  Mystere a Shanghai. A. Steeman; Night of the 12th–13th

BLATT, EDWARD A.
  Escape in the Desert. R. Sherwood; Petrified Forest

BLATTY, WILLIAM PETER
  Exorcist III. W. P. Blatty; Legion

BLOOM, JEFFREY
  Flowers in the Attic. V. C. Andrews

BLOOMFIELD, GEORGE
  Double Negative. K. Millar; Three Roads

BLYSTONE, JOHN G.
  Charlie Chan's Chance. E. D. Biggers; Behind That Curtain
  Dick Turpin. W. H. Ainsworth; Rookwood

BOCCHI, ARRIGO
  Top Dog. F. Hume
  When It Was Dark. G. Thorne
  Whosoever Shall Offend . . . F. M. Crawford

BOETTICHER, BUDD/OSCAR
  Rise and Fall of Legs Diamond. O. H. Gaylord
  Wolf Hunters. J. O. Curwood

BOGART, PAUL
  Cancel My Reservation. L. L'Amour; Broken Gun
  Marlowe. R. Chandler; Little Sister

BOGDANOVICH, PETER
  Saint Jack. P. Theroux

BOISROND, MICHEL
  Come Dance with Me. K. Roos; Blonde Died Dancing
  Heart Trump for OSS 117 in Tokyo. J. Bruce; Hot Line
  One Is Always Too Good to Women. R. Queneau; We Always Treat Women Too Well

BOISSET, YVES
  Prize of Peril. R. Sheckley; Tenth Victim
  Rise Up, Spy. G. Markstein; Chance Awakening

BOLDT, RAINER
  Story-Teller. P. Highsmith

BOLESLAVKSY [BOLESLAWSKI], RICHARD
  Last of Mrs. Cheyney. F. Lonsdale
  Last of the Lone Wolf. L. J. Vance; Lone Wolf
  Operator 13. R. W. Chambers; Secret Service Operator 13

BOLVARY, GEZA M.
  Ghost Train. A. Ridley
  No. 17. J. J. Farjeon
  Wrecker. A. Ridley

BONERZ, PETER
  Nobody's Perfekt. T. Kenrick; Two for the Price of One

BONNER, CLIVE
  Sinister Man. E. Wallace

BOORMAN, JOHN
  Deliverance. J. Dickey
  Point Blank. R. Stark; Hunter

BORDERIE, BERNARD
  Dames Get Along. P. Cheyney; Dames Don't Care
  Gun Moll. P. Cheyney; Poison Ivy
  Hit and Run. R. Marshall
  What a Girl! P. Cheyney; I'll Say She Does
  You Do It, Cutie. P. Cheyney; Your Deal, My Lovely

BOROWCZYK, WALERIAN
  Dr. Jekyll. R. L. Stevenson; Strange Case of Dr. Jekyll and Mr. Hyde

BORSOS, PHILIP
  Mean Season. J. Katzenbach; In the Heat of Summer

BORZAGE, FRANK
  Get-Rich-Quick-Wallingford. G. R. Chester
  Moonrise. T. Strauss
  Mortal Storm. P. Bottome
  Strange Cargo. R. Sale; Not Too Narrow—Not Too Deep
  Valley of Silent Men. J. O. Curwood

BOULTING, JOHN
  Brighton Rock. G. Greene
  Risk. N. Balchin; Sort of Traitors

BOULTING, ROY
  Brothers in Law. H. Cecil
  Inquest. M. Barringer
  Run for the Sun. R. Connell; Variety
  Suspect. N. Balchin; Sort of Traitors
  Trunk Crime. E. Percy
  Twisted Nerve. Peter Evans

BOURGUIGNON, SERGE
  Reward. M. Barrett

BOWERS, GEORGE
  Hearse. H. Clement

BOX, MURIEL
  Subway in the Sky. B. Birch

BRABIN, CHARLES J.
  Beast of the City. J. Lait
  Footfalls. W. D. Steele; Tower of Sand
  House of the Lost Court. M D'Alpins
  Mask of Fu Manchu. S. Rohmer
  Premature Compromise. R. Barr; Young Lord Stranleigh
  Ship from Shanghai. D. Collins; Ordeal
  Splendid Scapegrace. O. Henry; Whirligigs
  Wicked Woman. A. Austin

BRACKEN, BERTRAM
  Boomerang. W. H. Osborne
  East Lynn. H. Wood
  Kazan. J. O. Curwood
  Long Arm of Mannister. E. P. Oppenheim; Long Arm
  Mask. A. Hornblow

BRADBURY, ROBERT N.
  Trail Beyond. J. O. Curwood; Wolf Hunters

BRADLEY, DAVID
  Talk About a Stranger. C. Armstrong; Albatross

BRAHM, JOHN/HANS
  Broken Blossoms. T. Burke; Limehouse Nights
  Hangover Square. P. Hamilton
  High Window. R. Chandler
  Lodger. M. B. Lowndes
  Penitentiary. M. Flavin; Criminal Code
  Singapore. W. Bogart
  Undying Monster. J. D. Kerruish

BRAMBLE, A. V.
  Chick. E. Wallace
  Man Who Changed His Name. E. Wallace
  Nonconformist Parson. R. Horniman
  Shooting Stars. E. C. Vivian

BRAMPTON, KENNETH
  Robbery Under Arms. R. Boldrewood

BRANDO, MARLON
  One-Eyed Jacks. C. Neider; Authentic Death of Hendry Jones

BRANDON, PHIL
  Missing Million. E. Wallace

BRAVERMAN, CHARLES
  Hit and Run. L. Fletcher; Eighty Dollars to Stamford

BREAKSTON, GEORGE
  Boy Cried Murder. W. Irish; Dead Man Blues

BRECHER, IRVING S.
  Sail a Crooked Ship. N. Benchley

BREEN, RICHARD L.
  Stopover: Tokyo. J. P. Marquand

BRENON, HERBERT
  Breaking Point. M. R. Rinehart
  Dr. Jekyll and Mr. Hyde. R. L. Stevenson; Strange Case of Dr. Jekyll and Mr. Hyde
  Flying Squad. E. Wallace
  Honours Easy. R. Pertwee
  Living Dangerously. R. Simpson
  Lone Wolf. L. J. Vance
  New Magdalen. Wilkie Collins
  Sign on the Door. C. Pollock
  Someone at the Door. D. Christie

BRESSON, ROBERT
  Pickpocket. F. M. Dostoevskii; Crime and Punishment

BREST, MARTIN
  Going in Style. R. Grossbach

BRETHERTON, HOWARD
  Argyle Case. H. Ford
  Girl from Mandalay. R. Campbell; Death in Tiger Valley
  Girl Who Dared. Medora Field; Blood on Her Shoe
  Return of the Terror. E. Wallace; Terror

BRIDGES, JAMES
  China Syndrome. B. Wohl

BROMLEY, HARRY
  Full Circle. P. Straub; Julia

BROMLY, ALAN
  Follow That Hearse. H. Mason; Photo Finish

BROOKE, RALPH
  Bloodlust. R. Connell; Variety

BROOKE, VAN DYKE
  Led Astray. Mrs. H. Woods; East Lynne

BROOKNER, HOWARD
  Bloodhounds of Broadway. D. Runyon

BROOKS, MEL
  High Anxiety. R. H. Pilpel

BROOKS, RICHARD
  Blackboard Jungle. E. Hunter
  Brothers Karamazov. F. M. Dostoevskii
  Deadline. J. Eastwood
  In Cold Blood. T. Capote
  Wrong Is Right. C. McCarry; Better Angels

BROUETT, ALBERT
  Rogue in Love. T. Gallon

BROWN, CLARENCE
  Intruder in the Dust. W. Faulkner
  Letty Lynton. M. B. Lowndes

BROWN, KARL
  Federal Bullets. G. F. Eliot

BROWN, MELVILLE W.
  13 Washington Square. L. Scott; No. 13 Washington Square

BROWNING, TOD
  Black Bird. T. Browning; Mocking Bird
  Devil-Doll. A. Merritt; Burn, Witch, Burn!

Dracula. B. Stoker
London After Midnight. M. Coolridge-Rask
Mark of the Vampire. M. Coolridge-Rask; London After Midnight
Miracles for Sale. C. Rawson; Death from a Top Hat
Outside the Law. T. Browning
Unholy Three. T. Robbins
Where East Is East. T. Browning

BRUCE, JAMES
Suicide Club. R. L. Stevenson

BRUCKMAN, CLYDE
Welcome Danger. R. Simpson

BRUNEL, ADRIAN
Crooked Billet. D. Titheradge
Cross Currents. W. G. Elliott; Nine Days' Blunder
Prison Breaker. E. Wallace (headnote)

BRUUN, EINAR J.
In Full Cry. R. Marsh
Penniless Millionaire. D. C. Murray

BUCHANAN, LARRY
Bullet for Pretty Boy. M. Avallone

BUCHOWETZKI, DIMITRI
Public Prosecutor's Speech. A. D. Miller; Manslaughter

BUCKLAND, WARWICK
After Dark. D. Boucicault

BUCKLAND, WILFRED
Man on the Box. H. MacGrath

BUCKNELL, ROBERT
More Deadly Than the Male. P. Chevalier

BUCKSEY, COLIN
McGuffin. J. Bowen

BURNLEY, FRED
Neither the Sea Nor the Sand. G. Honeycombe

BURNSIDE, R. H.
Manhattan. J. Farnol; Definite Object

BURROWES, MICHAEL
Doctors Wear Scarlet. S. Raven

BURSTALL, TIM
End Play. R. Braddon

BURTON, DAVID
Bishop Murder Case. S. S. Van Dine
Man Who Wouldn't Talk. H. Hall; Valiant

BURTON, JOHN NELSON
Never Mention Murder. E. Wallace (headnote)

BURTON, TIM
Batman. C. S. Gardner

BUSHELL, ANTHONY
Long Dark Hall. E. Lustgarten; Case to Answer
Terror of the Tongs. J. Sangster

BUTLER, ALEXANDER
Beetle. R. Marsh
Disappearance of the Judge. C. R. Gull; Lost Judge
Jo, the Crossing Sweeper. C. Dickens; Bleak House
London by Night. C. Selby
Thundercloud. T. Taylor; Still Waters Run Deep
Valley of Fear. A. C. Doyle

BUTLER, LYNTON
Pallet on the Floor. R. H. Morrieson

BUTLER, ROBERT
Night of the Juggler. W. P. McGivern

BUZZELL, EDWARD
Fast Company. M. Page

CABANNE, CHRISTY
Conspiracy. R. Baker
Lost House. R. H. Davis; Man Who Could Not Lose
Red-Haired Alibi. W. Collison
Scattergood Baines. C. B. Kelland
Westland Case. J. Latimer; Headed for a Hearse

CACOYANNIS, MICHAEL
Day the Fish Came Out. K. Cicellis

CADENA, JORDI
Los Papeles de Aspern. H. James; Aspern Papers

CAGNEY, JAMES
Short Cut to Hell. G. Greene; Gun for Sale

CAHILL, DAVID
You Can't See Round Corners. J. Cleary

CAHN, EDWARD L.
Dangerous Partners. O. W. Bayer; Paper Chase
Secret of Deep Harbor. Max Miller; I Cover the Waterfront

CAIRNS, DALLAS
Silver Bridge. H. P. Lewis

CALVERT, C(HARLES) C.
Branded. G. Biss
In His Grip. D. C. Murray

CALVERT, E(LISHA) H(ELM)
Mind Over Motor. M. R. Rinehart; Book of Trish
One Wonderful Night. L. Tracy

CAMERON, JAMES
Terminator. S. Hutson

CAMILLER, EDGAR J.
Definite Object. J. Farnol

CAMMELL, DONALD
White of the Eye. M. Tracy; Mrs. White

CAMPBELL, COLIN
Carpet from Bagdad. H. MacGrath
City of Purple Dreams. Anonymous
In Defiance of the Law. J. O. Curwood; Isobel

CAMPBELL, WEBSTER
Pace That Thrills. R. Weber

CANUTT, YAKIMA
Flim Flam Man. G. Owen; Ballad of the Flim Flam Man

CAPITANI, GIORGIO
La Pupa del Gangster. W. Irish; Somebody on the Phone

CAPRA, FRANK R.
Arsenic and Old Lace. J. Kesselring
Donovan Affair. O. Davis

CARDIFF, JACK
Beyond This Place. A. J. Cronin
Dark of the Sun. Wilbur Smith; Train from Katanga
Intent to Kill. M. Bryan
Liquidator. J. Gardner
Scent of Mystery. K. Roos; Ghost of a Chance

CAREWE, EDWIN
Across the Pacific. C. E. Blaney
Her Fighting Chance. J. O. Curwood; Back to God's Country
Isobel. J. O. Curwood
My Lady's Latchkey. C. N. Williamson; Second Latchkey
Pals First. L. W. Dodd
Revenge. J. Warren
Way of the Strong. R. Cullum

CARLILE, C. DOUGLAS
Sexton Blake. W. M. Graydon; Five Years After

CARNE, MARCEL
Bizarre, Bizarre. J. S. Clouston; His First Offense
Marie du Port. G. Simenon; Chit of a Girl
Therese Raquin. E. Zola
Three Rooms in Manhattan. G. Simenon; Three Beds in Manhattan
Waste-Land. H. Ellison; Tomboy

CARPENTER, JOHN
Escape from New York. M. McQuay
Halloween. C. Richards
Memoirs of an Invisible Man. H. F. Saint

CARRERAS, MICHAEL
Blood from the Mummy's Tomb. B. Stoker; Jewel of the Seven Stars
Lost Continent. D. Wheatley; Uncharted Seas
Maniac. M. Brandel; Time of the Fire

CARRUTH, MILTON
Love Letters of a Star. Rufus King; Case of the Constant God

CARSTAIRS, JOHN PADDY
Devil's Agent. H. Habe; Agent of the Devil
Meet Maxwell Archer. H. Clevely; Archer Plus 20
Saint in London. L. Charteris; Holy Terror
Sleeping Car to Trieste. R. Alexander; Rome Express

CARTER, PETER
High Ballin'. Richard Robinson

CARVER, STEVE
River of Death. Alistair MacLean

CASTLE, WILLIAM
Busy Body. D. E. Westlake
I Saw What You Did. U. Curtiss; Out of the Dark
Let's Kill Uncle. R. O'Grady
Macabre. T. Durrant; Marble Forest
Mark of the Whistler. W. Irish; Borrowed Crime
Night Walker. S. Stuart
Old Dark House. J. B. Priestley; Benighted
Project X. L. P. Davies; Artificial Man

CAVALCANTI, ALBERTO
For Them That Trespass. E. Raymond
They Made Me a Fugitive. J. Budd; Convict Has Escaped

CAVALIER, ALAIN
Pillaged. R. Stark; Score

CAYETTE, ANDRE
Trap for Cinderella. S. Japrisot

CHABROL, CLAUDE
Betty. G. Simenon
Blood Relatives. E. McBain
Breakup. C. Armstrong; Balloon Man
Cry of the Owl. P. Highsmith
Dirty Hands. R. Neely; Damned Innocents
Dr. M. N. Jacques; Dr. Mabuse, Master of Mystery
Hatter's Ghosts. G. Simenon
Just Before Nightfall. E. Atiyah; Thin Line
Let the Beast Die. N. Blake; Beast Must Die
Ten Days' Wonder. E. Queen
Web of Passion. S. Ellin; Key to Nicholas Street

CHAFFEY, DON
Crooked Road. M. West; Big Story
Danger Within. M. Gilbert; Death in Captivity
Jolly Bad Fellow. C. E. Vulliamy; Don Among the Dead Men
Ride a Wild Pony. J. Aldridge; Sporting Proposition
Secret Tent. E. Addyman
Twist of Sand. G. Jenkins

CHAMPION, GOWER
Bank Shot. D. E. Westlake

CHARLOT, ANDRE
Le Judgement de Minuit. E. Wallace; Ringer

CHARRINGTON, ARTHUR
East Lynne. H. Wood

CHAUTARD, EMILE
House of Glass. M. Marcin
Living Lies. A. S. Roche; Plunder
Mystery of the Yellow Room. G. Leroux
Out of the Shadow. E. W. Hornung; Shadow of the Rope

CHENAL, PIERRE
Crime and Punishment. F. M. Dostoevskii
Last Turning. J. M. Cain; Postman Always Rings Twice
Native Son. Richard Wright
Section des Disparus. D. Goodis; Of Missing Persons

CHEREAU, PATRICE
  Flesh of the Orchid. J. H. Chase
CHEVALIER, PIERRE
  Vous Pigez. P. Cheyney; Don't Get Me Wrong
CHOURAQUI, ELIE
  Man on Fire. A. J. Quinnell
CHRISTIAN-JACQUE
  Dead Run. R. Sheckley
CHRISTIANSEN, BENJAMIN
  Devil's Circus. B. Christiansen
  Haunted House. O. Davis
  Hawk's Nest. W. Gunning
  Seven Footprints to Satan. A. Merritt
CHRISTENSEN, BENT
  Busybody. J. Popplewell
  Ghost Train. A. Ridley
CHRISTENSEN, CARLOS HUGO
  Lady of Death. R. L. Stevenson; Suicide Club
  No Abras Nunca Esa Puerta. W. Irish; Somebody on the Phone
  Si Muero Antes de Despertar. W. Irish; If I Should Die Before I Wake
CIMBER, MATT
  Butterfly. J. M. Cain
  Time to Die. M. Cleri; Six Graves to Munich
CIMINO, MICHAEL
  Desperate Hours. J. Hayes
  Sicilian. M. Puzo
  Thunderbolt and Lightfoot. J. Millard
  Year of the Dragon. R. Daley
CLAIR, RENE
  Ten Little Niggers. A. Christie
CLARK, BOB
  Black Christmas. L. Hays
  Murder by Decree. R. Weverka
CLARK, JIM/JAMES B.
  Madhouse. Angus Hall; Qualtrough
CLARKSON, STEPHEN
  Death Goes to School. S. Davis; Death in Seven Hours
CLAXTON, WILLIAM F.
  Desire in the Dust. H. Whittington
CLAYTON, JACK
  Innocents. H. James; Turn of the Screw
  Memento Mori. M. Spark
  Our Mother's House. J. Gloag
CLEMENS, WILLIAM B.
  Calling Philo Vance. S. S. Van Dine; Kennel Murder Case
  Case of the Stuttering Bishop. E. S. Gardner
  Case of the Velvet Claws. E. S. Gardner
  Crime by Night. G. Homes; Forty Whacks
  Night in New Orleans. J. R. Langham; Sing a Song of Homicide
  Night of January 16. A. Rand
CLEMENT, DICK
  Bullshot Crummond. R. House
  Catch Me a Spy. G. Marton
  Otley. M. Waddell
  Porridge. P. Ableman
CLEMENT, RENE
  And Hope to Die. D. Goodis; Black Friday
  Broad Daylight. P. Highsmith; Talented Mr. Ripley
  Deadly Trap. A. Cavanagh
  Love Cage. D. Keene; Joy House
CLEMENTS, ROY S.
  Tiger's Coat. E. Dejeans
CLIFT, DENISON
  Bentley's Conscience. P. Trent
  Out to Win. R. Pertwee
CLIFTON, ELMER
  Crashing Thru. L. Y. Renfrew; Renfrew Rides the Range
  Let 'Er Go Gallegher. R. H. Davis; Gallegher
  Two-Soul Woman. G. Burgess; White Cat
CLINE, EDWARD F.
  Crash. F. Packard; Night Operator
  Forty Naughty Girls. S. Palmer (headnote)
  In the Next Room. E. R. Belmont
  In the Next Room. B. E. Stevenson; Mystery of the Boule Cabinet
CLOCHE, MAURICE
  Lay Off Blondes. Carter Brown; Body
CLOUSE, ROBERT
  Enter the Dragon. M. Roote
  Rats. J. Herbert
  Terrible Game. D. T. Moore
CLOUZOT, HENRI-GEORGES
  Diabolique. P. Boileau; Woman Who Was Spies. E. Hostovsky; Midnight Patient
  Wages of Fear. G. Arnaud
CLOWES, ST. JOHN L.
  No Orchids for Miss Blandish. J. H. Chase
CLURMAN, HAROLD
  Deadline at Dawn. W. Irish
COEN, JOEL
  Blood Simple. J. Coen
COHEN, LARRY
  It's Alive. R. Woodley
COKLISS, HARLEY
  Malone. W. Wingate; Shotgun
COLEBY, A. E.
  Flying Fifty-Five. E. Wallace
  Great Prince Shan. E. P. Oppenheim
COLETTI, DUILIO
  House of Intrigue. H. J. Giskes; London Calling North Pole
COLLA, RICHARD A.
  Fuzz. E. McBain
COLLECTOR, ROBERT
  Red Heat. R. Tine
COLLINS, EDWIN J.
  Channings. H. Wood
  Eugene Aram. E. Bulwer-Lytton
  Gamble with Hearts. A. Carlyle
  Hard Cash. C. Reade
COLLINS, JOHN H.
  God's Law and Man's. P. Trent; Wife by Purchase
COLLINS, LEWIS D.
  Leavenworth Case. A. K. Green
  Sing Sing Nights. H. S. Keeler
  Spanish Cape Mystery. E. Queen
COLLINSON, PETER
  Innocent Bystanders. J. Munro
  Italian Job. T. K. Martin
  Long Day's Dying. A. White
  Spiral Staircase. E. L. White; Some Must Watch
  Ten Little Indians. A. Christie; Ten Little Niggers
COLMES, WALTER
  Accomplice. F. Gruber; Simon Lash, Private Detective
  French Key. F. Gruber
COMFORT, LANCE
  Bedelia. V. Caspary
  Breaking Point. L. Meynell
  Daughter of Darkness. M. Catto; They Walk Alone
  Face in the Night. B. Graeme; Suspense
  Hotel Reserve. E. Ambler; Epitaph for a Spy
  Man in the Road. A. Armstrong; He Was Found in the Road
  Pit of Darkness. H. McCutcheon; To Dusty Death
  Silent Dust. R. Pertwee; Paragon
  Temptation Harbour. G. Simenon; Newhaven-Dieppe
  Ugly Duckling. R. L. Stevenson; Strange Case of Dr. Jekyll and Mr. Hyde
CONNOLLY, BOBBY
  Patient in Room 18. M. G. Eberhart
CONWAY, JACK
  Another Man's Shoes. V. Bridges
  Assignment in Brittany. H. MacInnes
  Haunted Woman. J. O. Curwood
  Silent Battle. G. F. Gibbs
  Solitaire Man. B. C. Spewack
  Unholy Three. T. Robbins
COOKE, ALAN
  Flat 2. E. Wallace
COOPER, GEORGE A.
  Anything Might Happen. H. Balfour
  Eleventh Commandment. B. Fleming; Pillory
  Man Outside. Donald Stuart
  Sexton Blake and the Bearded Doctor. R. Hardinge; Blazing Launch Murder
  Shadow. Donald Stuart
  Tangled Evidence. P. C. De Crespigny
COOPER, STUART
  Disappearance. D. Marlowe; Echoes of Celandine
COPPOLA, FRANCIS FORD
  Bram Stoker's Dracula. B. Stoker; Dracula
  Godfather. M. Puzo
  Godfather Part II. M. Puzo; Godfather
CORBUCCI, SERGIO
  Payoff. A. Veraldi
CORMAN, ROGER
  Bloody Mama. R. Thom
  Gas. B. Hirschfeld
  Masque of the Red Death. Elsie Lee
  Pit and the Pendulum. L. Sheridan
  Premature Burial. M. H. Danne
  Raven. E. Sudak
  St. Valentine's Day Massacre. B. O'Hara
  Tales of Terror. E. Sudak
  X. E. Sudak
CORNEAU, ALAIN
  Thriller Story. J. Thompson; Hell of a Woman
CORNFIELD, HUBERT
  Lure of the Swamp. G. Brewer; Hell's Our Destination
  Night of the Following Day. L. White; Snatchers
  Third Voice. C. Williams; All the Way
CORNU, JACQUES
  Ladies' Man. P. Quentin; Shadow of Guilt
CORRIGAN, LLOYD
  Daughter of the Dragon. S. Rohmer; Daughter of Fu Manchu
  Murder on a Honeymoon. S. Palmer; Puzzle of the Pepper Tree
COSGROVE, JOHN
  East Lynne Fiasco. H. Wood; East Lynne
COSMATOS, GEORGE PAN
  Cassandra Crossing. R. Katz
  Cobra. P. Gosling; Running Duck
  Escape to Athena. P. Blake
  Rambo: First Blood Part II. D. Morrell
COSTA-GRAVAS
  Betrayed. L. Fleischer
  Z. V. Vassilikos
COSTELLO, MAURICE
  Mr. Barnes of New York. A. C. Gunter
COUTARD, RAOUL
  S.A.S. San Salvator. G. de Villiers; Game of Eyes Only
CRABTREE, ARTHUR
  Calendar. E. Wallace
  Dear Murderer. S. J. Clowes
  Don't Ever Leave Me. Anthony Armstrong (headnote)
  Madonna of the Seven Moons. M. Lawrence

C

CRAFT, WILLIAM JAMES
  Birds of Prey. G. Bronson-Howard

CRANE, FRANK H.
  Gray Mask. W. Camp
  Hutch Stirs 'Em Up. H. Harding; Hawk of Rede
  Moonstone. W. Collins
  Scar. E. Gaboriau (headnote)
  Stranded in Arcady. F. Lynde

CRAVEN, WES
  Deadly Friend. D. Henstell; Friend

CREVENNA, ALFREDO
  Invisible Man. H. G. Wells

CRICHTON, CHARLES
  Floods of Fear. J. Hawkins
  Law and Disorder. D. Roberts; Smuggler's Circuit

CRICHTON, MICHAEL
  Coma. R. Cook
  Great Train Robbery. M. Crichton

CRISP, DONALD
  Don Q, Son of Zorro. K. Prichard; Don Q's Love Story
  House of Silence. E. Barron; Marcel Levignet
  Love Insurance. E. D. Biggers
  Princess of New York. C. Hamilton

CROISE, HUGH
  Affair at the Novelty Theatre. B. Orczy; Old Man in the Corner
  Brighton Mystery. B. Orczy; Old Man in the Corner
  Burglar and the Girl. M. Boulton
  Grandfather Smallweed. C. Dickens; Bleak House
  Hocussing of Cigarette. B. Orczy; Old Man in the Corner
  Kensington Mystery. B. Orczy; Old Man in the Corner
  Mystery of Brudenell Court. B. Orczy; Old Man in the Corner
  Mystery of Dogstooth Cliff. B. Orczy; Old Man in the Corner
  Mystery of the Khaki Tunic. B. Orczy; Old Man in the Corner
  Northern Mystery. B. Orczy; Old Man in the Corner
  Regent's Park Mystery. B. Orczy; Old Man in the Corner
  Tragedy of Barnsdale Manor. B. Orczy; Old Man in the Corner
  Tremarne Case. B. Orczy; Old Man in the Corner
  York Mystery. B. Orczy; Old Man in the Corner

CROMBIE, DONALD
  Robbery Under Arms. R. Boldrewood

CROMWELL, JOHN
  Dead Reckoning. Alex Morrison
  Racket. B. Cormack
  Scavengers. D. O'Callaghan

CRONENBERG, DAVID
  Dead Ringers. Bari Wood; Twins
  Dead Zone. Stephen King

CROSLAND, ALAN
  Case of the Howling Dog. E. S. Gardner
  Contraband. C. B. Kelland
  Great Impersonation. E. P. Oppenheim
  Midnight Alibi. D. Runyon; Blue Plate Special
  Whirlpool. V. Morton
  White Cockatoo. M. G. Eberhart

CROWLEY, WILLIAM X.
  Trail of the Yukon. J. O. Curwood; Gold Hunters

CRUMP, OWEN
  Couch. R. Bloch

CRUZE, JAMES
  I Cover the Waterfront. Max Miller
  Red Mark. J. Russell

CUKOR, GEORGE
  Double Life. M. W. Wellman
  Gas Light. P. Hamilton
  Grumpy. H. Hodges
  Travels with My Aunt. G. Greene

CULP, ROBERT
  Hickey and Boggs. P. Rock

CUMMINGS, IRVING
  Behind That Curtain. E. D. Biggers
  Country Beyond. J. O. Curwood
  Night Club Lady. A. Abbot; About the Murder of the Night Club Lady

CUNNINGHAM, SEAN S.
  Friday the 13th. S. Hawke
  Stranger Is Watching. M. H. Clark

CURTIS, DAN
  Burnt Offerings. R. Marasco
  Dracula. B. Stoker
  House of Dark Shadows. Marilyn Ross

CURTIZ, MICHAEL
  Breaking Point. E. Hemingway; To Have and Have Not
  British Agent. H. B. Lockhart
  Captain Blood. R. Sabatini; Captain Blood—His Odyssey
  Casablanca. J. J. Epstein
  Case of the Curious Bride. E. S. Gardner
  Flamingo Road. R. Wilder
  Gamblers. C. Klein
  Kennel Murder Case. S. S. Van Dine
  Kid Galahad. Francis Wallace
  Madonna of Avenue A. M. Canfield
  Man in the Net. P. Quentin
  Mildred Pierce. J. M. Cain
  River's End. J. O. Curwood
  Third Degree. A. Hornblow
  Unsuspected. C. Armstrong

CUTRY, C. M.
  Rigged. Raymond Marshall; Hit and Run

CUTTS, GRAHAM
  Blackguard. R. Paton; Autobiography of a Blackguard
  God's Clay. A. Askew
  Love on the Spot. H. C. McNeile; Three of a Kind
  Passionate Adventure. F. Stayton
  Rat. P. Bottome
  Sign of the Four. A. C. Doyle

DALEY, WILLIAM ROBERT
  End of the Road. E. Bulwer-Lytton; Ernest Maltravers

DALY, ARNOLD
  Affair of Three Nations. J. McIntyre (headnote)

DAMIAMI, DAMIANO
  Day of the Owl. L. Sciascia; Mafia Vendetta

DANTE, JOE
  Howling. G. Brandner

D'ANTONI, PHILIP
  Seven-Ups. R. Posner

DAQUIN, LOUIS
  Le Parfum de la Dame en Noire. G. Leroux; Perfume of the Lady in Black
  Le Voyageur la Toussaint. G. Simenon; Strange Inheritance

DARNBOROUGH, ANTONY
  So Long at the Fair. A. Thorne

DASSIN, JULES
  Naked City. M. Wald
  Night and the City. G. Kersh
  10:30 P.M. Summer. M. Duras; Ten-Thirty on a Summer Night
  Thieves' Highway. A. I. Bezzerides; Thieves Market
  Topkapi. E. Ambler; Light of Day
  Uptight. L. O'Flaherty; Informer

DAVES, DELMER
  Badlanders. W. R. Burnett; Asphalt Jungle
  Dark Passage. D. Goodis
  Never Let Me Go. R. Bax; Came the Dawn
  Red House. G. A. Chamberlain

DAVID, CHARLES
  Lady on a Train. L. Charteris

DAVIDSON, MARTIN
  Eddie and the Cruisers. P. F. Kluge
  Hero at Large. A. J. Carothers

DAVIS, ALLAN
  Clue of the New Pin. E. Wallace
  Clue of the Twisted Candle. E. Wallace
  Fourth Square. E. Wallace; Four Square Jane

DAVIS, DESMOND
  Ordeal by Innocence. A. Christie
  Sign of the Four. A. C. Doyle

DAVIS, OSSIE
  Cotton Comes to Harlem. C. Himes

DAVIS, REDD
  Excess Baggage. H. M. Raleigh

DAVIS, ROBIN
  Hill Girl. C. Williams
  I Married a Dead Man. W. Irish

DAVIS, WILL S.
  Doctor Rameau. G. Ohnet
  Mystery Mind. A. B. Reeve
  No Man's Land. L. J. Vance

DAWLEY, J. SEARLE
  Frankenstein. M. Shelley
  In the Bishop's Carriage. M. Michelson
  Leah Kleschna. C. M. S. McLellan
  Salomy Jane. B. Harte; Stories in Light and Shadow
  Van Bibber's Experiment. R. H. Davis; Gallegher

DAWN, NORMAN
  For the Term of His Natural Life. M. Clarke; His Natural Life

DAY, ERNEST
  Green Ice. G. A. Browne

DAY, ROBERT
  Green Man. F. Launder; Meet a Body
  Grip of the Strangler. J. C. Cooper
  Man with Bogart's Face. A. J. Fenady

DEAN, BASIL
  Birds of Prey. A. A. Milne; Fourth Wall
  Escape. J. Galsworthy
  First and the Last. J. Galsworthy; Five Tales
  Loyalties. J. Galsworthy
  Return of Sherlock Holmes. A. C. Doyle; His Last Bow

DEAN, RALPH
  Song of Sixpence. F. A. Kummer

DEARDEN, BASIL
  Assassination Bureau. J. London
  Blue Lamp. T. Willis
  Dead of Night. E. F. Benson; Room in the Tower
  League of Gentlemen. J. Boland
  Life for Ruth. W. Drummond
  Man Who Haunted Himself. A. Armstrong; Strange Case of Mr. Pelham
  Masquerade. V. Canning; Castle Minerva
  Mind Benders. J. Kennaway
  Only When I Larf. L. Deighton
  Out of the Clouds. J. Fores; Springboard
  Place to Go. M. Fisher; Bethnel Green
  Sapphire. E. G. Cousins
  Ship That Died of Shame. N. Monsarrat
  Victim. W. Drummond
  Woman of Straw. C. Arley

DEARDEN, JAMES
  Pascali's Island. B. Unsworth; Idol Hunter

DEASY, FRANK
  Courier. Gerald Cole

Directors Index

DECOIN, HENRI
L'Homme de Londres. G. Simenon; Newhaven—Dieppe
Rope for Killing. P. McGerr; Follow, As the Night
Sorcery. P. Boileau; Spells of Evil
Strangers in the House. G. Simenon
Truth About Bebe Donge. G. Simenon; Trial of Bebe Donge

DE CORDOVA, FREDERICK
That Way with Women. E. D. Biggers; Earl Derr Biggers Tells Ten Stories

DE COURVILLE, ALBERT
Crackerjack. W. B. M. Ferguson
Englishman's Home. G. Du Maurier
Seven Sinners. A. Ridley; Wrecker
77, Park Lane. W. Hackett
77 Rue Chalgrin. W. Hackett; 77, Park Lane
Strangers on a Honeymoon. E. Wallace; Northing Tramp

DE GRASSE, JOSEPH
Grasp of Greed. H. R. Haggard; Mr. Meeson's Will
His Wife's Friend. J. B. Harris-Burland; White Rook
Scarlet Car. R. H. Davis

DE GRIGORIO, EDUARDO
Aspern. H. James; Aspern Papers

DE LA IGLESIA, ELOY
Turn of the Screw. H. James

DELANNOY, JEAN
Action Man. J. Flynn
Maigret and the St. Fiacre Case. G. Simenon; Saint Fiacre Affair
Maigret Sets a Trap. G. Simenon
Obsession. W. Irish; Dead Man Blues
Pas Folle la Guepe. J. H. Chase; Just a Matter of Time
Torpedo Skin. F. Ryck; Woman Hunt

DE LA PATELLIERE, DENYS
La Salaire du Peche. N. Rutledge; Emily Will Know
Retour de Manivelle. J. H. Chase; There's Always a Price Tag

DELIA, FRANCIS
Freeway. D. Barkley

DE LIMUR, JEAN
Jealousy. E. Walter
Letter. W. S. Maugham

DEL RUTH, ROY
Across the Pacific. C. E. Blaney
Agony Column. E. D. Biggers
Bulldog Drummond Strikes Back. H. C. McNeile; Knock-Out
Maltese Falcon. D. Hammett
Phantom of the Rue Morgue. E. A. Poe; Prose Romances of Edgar A. Poe
Second Floor Mystery. E. D. Biggers; Agony Column
Stop, You're Killing Me. D. Runyon; Slight Case of Murder
Terror. E. Wallace
Three Faces East. A. P. Kelly

DE MILLE, CECIL B.
Man on the Box. H. MacGrath
Manslaughter. A. D. Miller
Unafraid. E. M. Ingram
Whispering Chorus. P. P. Sheehan

DE MILLE, WILLIAM C.
Grumpy. H. Hodges
Mystery Girl. G. B. McCutcheon; Green Fancy

DEMME, JONATHAN
Last Embrace. M. T. Bloom; 13th Man
Silence of the Lambs. Thomas Harris

DENHAM, REGINALD
Crimson Circle. E. Wallace
Death at Broadcasting House. V. Gielgud
Flying Fifty-Five. E. Wallace
House of the Spaniard. A. Behrend
Jewel. E. Wallace (headnote)
Kate Plus Ten. E. Wallace

DENTON, JACK
Ernest Maltravers. E. Bulwer-Lytton
Lady Audley's Secret. M. E. Braddon

DE PALMA, BRIAN
Blow Out. N. Williams
Dressed to Kill. Campbell Black
Fury. J. Farris
Scarface. A. Trail

DERAY, JACQUES
Butterfly on the Shoulder. J. Gearon; Velvet Well
He Died with His Eyes Open. D. Raymond
On a Nice Summer Day. J. H. Chase; One Bright Summer Morning
Our Man in Marrakech. R. P. Jones; Heisters

DE TOTH, ANDRE
Dark Waters. F. Cockrell
Pitfall. J. J. Dratler

DEVERS, CLAIRE
Max and Jeremy. Teri White; Max Trueblood and the Jersey Desperado

DEVILLE, MICHEL
Deep Water. P. Highsmith
Dossier 51. G. Perrault
Sweetheart. A. Coburn

DEWHURST, GEORGE
Dead Certainty. N. Gould
Shadow Between. S. Hocking

DEWSBURY, RALPH
Man in Motley. T. Gallon

DIAMANT-BERGER, HENRI
Arsene Lupin Detective. M. Leblanc; Jim Barnett Intervenes

DICKINSON, THOROLD
Arsenal Stadium Mystery. L. Gribble
Gas Light. P. Hamilton
High Command. L. Robinson; General Goes Too Far

DIETERLE, WILLIAM
Accused. J. Truesdell; Be Still, My Love
Fog Over Frisco. G. Dyer; Five Fragments
Jewel Robbery. L. Fodor
Lawyer Man. M. Trell
Love Letters. C. Massie; Pity My Simplicity
Satan Met a Lady. D. Hammett; Maltese Falcon
Turning Point. H. McCoy; Corruption City

DILLON, EDWARD
Bride. S. Olivier

DILLON, JACK/JOHN FRANCIS
Behind the Mask. E. P. Oppenheim; Jeanne of the Marshes
Calvert's Valley. M. P. Montagu; In Calvert's Valley
Man About Town. D. Clift
Millie. D. H. Clarke

DIXON, IVAN
Spook Who Sat by the Door. S. Greenlee

DMYTRYK, EDWARD
Crossfire. R. Brooks; Brick Foxhole
Devil Commands. W. Sloane; Edge of Running Water
End of the Matter. G. Greene
Farewell, My Lovely. R. Chandler
Human Factor. S. Quinn
Mirage. W. Ericson; Fallen Angel
Obsession. A. Coppel; Man About a Dog

DONAHUE, JACK
Assault on a Queen. J. Finney

DONALDSON, ROGER
No Way Out. K. Fearing; Big Clock

DONEN, STANLEY
Arabesque. Alex Gordon; Cipher
Charade. P. H. Stone

DONNER, CLIVE
Charlie Chan and the Curse of the Dragon Queen. M. Avallone
Marriage of Convenience. E. Wallace; Three Oak Mystery
Nothing But the Best. S. Ellin; Mystery Stories

DONNER, RICHARD
Lethal Weapon. J. Norst
Salt and Pepper. A. Austin

DOUGHTON, RUSSELL S., JR.
Hostage. C. Henry

DOUGLAS, GORDON
Detective. R. Thorp
Fiend Who Walked the West. E. Lipsky; Kiss of Death
Fortunes of Captain Blood. R. Sabatini
In Like Flint. B. Street
Kiss Tomorrow Goodbye. H. McCoy
Lady in Cement. A. Rome
Robin and the Seven Hoods. J. Pearl
Skullduggery. Vercors; You Shall Know Them
Slaughter's Big Rip-Off. A. Kane
Sylvia. E. V. Cunningham
Tony Rome. A. Rome; Miami Mayhem

DOWLAN, WILLIAM C.
Loot. A. S. Roche
Outsider. L. J. Vance; Nobody

DOXAT-PRATT, B. E.
John Heriot's Wife. A. Askew
Little Hour of Peter Wells. D. Whitelaw
Other Person. F. Hume

DRAKE, RONALD
Killer Walks. G. Glennon; Gathering Storm

DREW, S. RANKIN
Hunted Woman. J. O. Curwood

DREYER, CARL THEODORE
Strange Adventure of David Gray. J. S. Le Fanu; In a Glass Darkly

DUDREMET, JEAN-CHARLES
Dans la Gueule du Loup. J. H. Chase; Just Another Sucker

DUFFELL, PETER (JOHN)
England Made Me. G. Greene
Inside Out. W. Hughes
Partners in Crime. E. Wallace; Man Who Knew

DUKE, BILL
Rage in Harlem. C. Himes; For Love of Imabelle

DUKE, DARYL
Silent Partner. A. Bodelsen; Think of a Number

DUNLAP, SCOTT R.
Midnight Life. R. W. Kauffman; Spider's Web
Trooper O'Neill. G. Goodchild

DUNNE, PHILLIP
Blindfold. L. Fletcher
Inspector. J. De Hartog

DUPONT, E(WALD) A(NDRE)
Bishop Misbehaves. F. Jackson
Night of Mystery. S. S. Van Dine; Greene Murder Case

DURNING, BERNARD J.
Yosemite Trail. R. Cullum; One-Way Trail

DUVIVIER, JULIEN
Ardent Room. J. D. Carr; Burning Court
Flesh and Fantasy. O. Wilde; Lord Arthur Savile's Crime
Gooseflesh. J. H. Chase; Come Easy—Go Easy
Le Tete d'un Homme. G. Simenon; Battle of Nerves
Man in the Raincoat. J. H. Chase; Tiger by the Tail
Maurizius Affair. J. Wasserman; Maurizius Case
Panique. G. Simenon; Mr. Hire's Engagement

D

DWAN, ALLAN
Cheating Cheaters. M. Marcin
Conspiracy. R. Baker
Gorilla. R. Spence
Human Cargo. K. Shepard; I Will Be Faithful
Luck of the Irish. H. MacGrath
Manhandled. A. Stringer
Slightly Scarlet. J. M. Cain; Love's Lovely Counterfeit
Splendid Hazard. H. MacGrath

EADES, WILFRED
You Can't Escape. A. Kennington

EADY, DAVID
Faces in the Dark. P. Boileau
In the Wake of a Stranger. I. S. Black
Verdict. E. Wallace; Big Four

EAGLE, OSCAR
Coast of Chance. E. Chamberlain

EARLE, WILLIAM P. S.
Scarlet Runner. C. N. Williamson
Within the Law. B. Veiller

EASON, B. REEVES
Shadow on the Wall. J. B. Ellis; Picture on the Wall
Spy Ship. G. Dyer; Five Fragments

EASTWOOD, CLINT
Eiger Sanction. Trevanian
Firefox. C. Thomas
Gauntlet. M. Butler
Play Misty for Me. P. J. Gillette
Sudden Impact. J. C. Stinson

EDWARDS, BLAKE
Carey Treatment. J. Hudson; Case of Need
Darling Lili. H. Clement
Experiment in Terror. Gordons; Operation Terror
Pink Panther. M. H. Albert
Pink Panther Strikes Again. F. Waldman
Return of the Pink Panther. F. Waldman
Shot in the Dark. H. Kurnitz
Tamarind Seed. E. Anthony

EDWARDS, HENRY
Amazing Quest of Mr. Ernest Bliss. E. P. Oppenheim
Juggernaut. A. Campbell
Lad. E. Wallace (headnote)
Lord Edgware Dies. A. Christie
Lunatic at Large. J. S. Clouston
Man Who Changed His Name. E. Wallace

EDWARDS, J. GORDON
Tangled Lives. W. Collins; Woman in White
Wings of the Morning. L. Tracy; Rainbow Island

EDWARDS, ROLAND G.
Drums of Jeopardy. H. MacGrath

EDWIN, WALTER
Master Mummer. E. P. Oppenheim
Mercy Merrick. Wilkie Collins; New Magdalen

EGLESON, JAN
Shock to the System. S. Brett

ELDRIDGE, JOHN
Brandy for the Parson. G. Household; Tales of Adventurers

ELLES, FRED
Mrs. Pym of Scotland Yard. N. Morland (headnote)

ELVEY, MAURICE
Amateur Gentleman. J. Farnol
At the Villa Rose. A. E. W. Mason
Beautiful Jim, of the Blankshire Regiment. J. S. Winter
Beryl Coronet. A. C. Doyle; Adventures of Sherlock Holmes
Bleak House. C. Dickens
Case of Identity. A. C. Doyle; Adventures of Sherlock Holmes
Copper Beeches. A. C. Doyle; Adventures of Sherlock Holmes
Curly Top. T. Burke; Whispering Windows
Devil's Foot. A. C. Doyle; His Last Bow
Dick Turpin's Ride to York. W. H. Ainsworth; Rookwood
Dying Detective. A. C. Doyle; His Last Bow
Empty House. A. C. Doyle; Return of Sherlock Holmes
Footsteps in the Night. C. Fraser-Simpson
Grip. J. S. Winter
Harrassed Hero. E. Dudley
Hound of the Baskervilles. A. C. Doyle
Justice. J. Galsworthy
Late Edwina Black. W. Dinner
Lily of Killarney. D. Boucicault; Colleen Bawn
Lodger. M. B. Lowndes
Man with the Twisted Lip. A. C. Doyle; Adventures of Sherlock Holmes
Maria Marten. Anonymous
Meg the Lady. T. Gallon
Mr. Wu. L. J. Milne
Noble Bachelor. A. C. Doyle; Adventures of Sherlock Holmes
Priory School. A. C. Doyle; Return of Sherlock Holmes
Quinney's. H. A. Vachell
Red-Headed League. A. C. Doyle; Adventures of Sherlock Holmes
Resident Patient. A. C. Doyle; Memoirs of Sherlock Holmes
Return of the Frog. E. Wallace; India-Rubber Men
Road House. W. Hackett
Running Water. A. E. W. Mason
Scandal in Bohemia. A. C. Doyle; Adventures of Sherlock Holmes
Sign of the Four. A. C. Doyle
Solitary Cyclist. A. C. Doyle; Return of Sherlock Holmes
Spider. H. Holt; Midnight Mail
Spy of Napoleon. B. Orczy
Suicide Club. R. L. Stevenson
Third Visitor. G. Anstruther
Tiger of San Pedro. A. C. Doyle; His Last Bow
Who Killed John Savage? P. MacDonald; Rynox
Yellow Face. A. C. Doyle; Memoirs of Sherlock Holmes

ENDFIELD, CYRIL (RAKER)
Try and Get Me. J. Pagano; Condemned

ENGLAND, PAUL
Trial of Madame X. J. W. MacConaughy; Madame X

ENGLISH, JOHN
Drums of Fu Manchu. S. Rohmer
Laramie Trail. J. Gregory; Mystery at Spanish Hacienda

ENGLUND, GEORGE
Signpost to Murder. M. Doyle

ENRICO, ROBERT
Heads or Tails. A. Harris; Baroni
Secret. F. Ryck; Undesirable Company

ENRIGHT, RAY
River's End. J. O. Curwood
Wagons Roll at Night. Francis Wallace; Kid Galahad
While the Patient Slept. M. G. Eberhart

ERAN, DORON
Road to Ein Harod. A. Kenan

ESSEX, HARRY
I, the Jury. M. Spillane

ESWAY, ALEXANDRE
Le Judgement de Minuit. E. Wallace; Ringer

FAENZA, ROBERT
Order of Death. H. Fleetwood

FAIRBANKS, DOUGLAS
Arizona. A. Thomas

FARGO, JAMES
Enforcer. W. Morgan
Game for Vultures. M. Hartmann

FARNUM, MARSHALL
Lady Audley's Secret. M. E. Braddon

FARROW, JOHN
Big Clock. K. Fearing
Calcutta. Alex Morrison
Night Has a Thousand Eyes. G. Hopley
Plunder of the Sun. D. Dodge
Saint Strikes Back. L. Charteris; She Was a Lady
Unholy Wife. J. Roeburt

FASSBINDER, RAINER WERNER
Despair. V. Nabokoff-Sirin
Martha. C. Woolrich; Angels of Darkness

FAUSTMAN, LHAMPE
Crime and Punishment. F. M. Dostoevskii

FEARS, STEPHEN
Grifters. Jim Thompson

FEIST, FELIX E.
Devil Thumbs a Ride. R. C. Du Soe
Donovan's Brain. C. Siodmak

FEJOS, PAUL
Broadway. P. Dunning
Captain of the Guard. C. Houghton
Fantomas. P. Souvestre

FENTON, LESLIE
Saint's Vacation. L. Charteris; Getaway
Stronger Than Desire. W. E. Woodward; Evelyn Prentice
Whispering Smith. F. H. Spearman

FERRARA, ABEL
Cat Chaser. Elmore Leonard

FEYDER, JACQUES
Knight Without Armour. J. Hilton

FIELDS, LEONARD
Manhattan Love Song. C. Woolrich

FIGMAN, MAX
Jack Chanty. H. Footner

FISHER, TERENCE
Blackout. H. Nielsen; Gold Coast Nocturne
Curse of Frankenstein. M. Shelley; Frankenstein
Curse of the Werewolf. G. Endore; Werewolf of Paris
Dead on Course. M. Black
Devil Rides Out. D. Wheatley
Dracula. B. Stoker
Dracula, Prince of Darkness. B. Stoker; Dracula
Face the Music. E. Borneman; Tremolo
Frankenstein Must Be Destroyed. M. Shelley; Frankenstein
Hound of the Baskervilles. A. C. Doyle
House of Fright. R. L. Stevenson; Strange Case of Dr. Jekyll and Mr. Hyde
Last Man to Hang. G. Bullett; Jury
Last Page. J. H. Chase
Man Who Could Cheat Death. B. Lyndon; Amazing Dr. Clitterhouse
Mantrap. S. Rattray; Queen in Danger
Phantom of the Opera. G. Leroux
So Long at the Fair. A. Thorne
Stranger Came Home. G. Sanders; Stranger at Home
Stranglers of Bombay. S. James
To the Public Danger. P. Hamilton
Valley of Fear. A. C. Doyle

FITZMAURICE, GEORGE
At Bay. P. Phillips
Avalanche. G. Atherton
Bella Donna. R. Hichens
Emperor's Candlesticks. B. Orczy
Kick-In. W. Mack
Last of Mrs. Cheyney. F. Lonsdale
Locked Door. C. Pollock; Sign on the Door
Mark of Cain. C. Wells
Raffles. E. W. Hornung; Amateur Cracksman
Right to Love. C. Farrere; Man Who Killed
Stop Thief! Carlyle Moore
Tiger Rose. W. Mack
Witness for the Defense. A. E. W. Mason

Directors Index

FLEISCHER, RICHARD
Blind Terror. W. Hughes
Compulsion. M. Levin
Crack in the Mirror. M. Haedrich
Don Is Dead. N. Quarry
Mr. Majestyk. E. Leonard
New Centurions. J. Wambaugh
Soylent Green. H. Harrison; Make Room! Make Room!
Spikes Gang. G. Tippette; Bank Robber
Violent Saturday. W. L. Heath

FLEMING, VICTOR
Blind Goddess. A. Train
Dr. Jekyll and Mr. Hyde. R. L. Stevenson
Empty Hands. A. Stringer

FLEMYNG, GORDON
Five to One. E. Wallace; Thief in the Night
Last Grenade. J. Sherlock; Ordeal of Major Grigsby
Solo for Sparrow. E. Wallace; Gunner
Split. R. Stark; Seventh

FLICKER, THEODORE J.
Three in a Cellar. Angus Hall; Late Boy Wonder

FLOOD, JAMES
Lonely Road. N. Shute
Times Have Changed. E. Davis
Under Cover Man. J. Wilstach

FLOREY, ROBERT
Beast with Five Fingers. W. F. Harvey
Danger Signal. P. Bottome; Murder in the Bud
Dangerous to Know. E. Wallace; On the Spot
Death of a Champion. F. Gruber; Brass Knuckles
Florentine Dagger. B. Hecht
Man Called Back. A. Soutar; Silent Thunder
Mountain Music. M. Kantor; Author's Choice
Murders in the Rue Morgue. E. A. Poe; Prose Romances of Edgar A. Poe
Woman in Red. Wallace Irwin; North Shore

FLOYD, CALVIN
Victor Frankenstein. M. Shelley; Frankenstein

FLYNN, EMMETT J.
East Lynne. H. Wood

FLYNN, JOHN
Outfit. R. Stark

FOLEY, JAMES
After Dark, My Sweet. Jim Thompson

FORBES, BRYAN
Deadfall. D. Cory
Naked Face. S. Sheldon
Seance on a Wet Afternoon. M. McShane
Stepford Wives. I. Levin
Wrong Box. R. L. Stevenson

FORD, FRANCIS
Study in Scarlet. A. C. Doyle

FORD, HUGH
Jim the Penman. C. L. Young
Secret Service. W. Gillette
Seven Keys to Baldpate. E. D. Biggers
Slave Market. F. A. Kummer; Painted Woman
Woman in the Case. C. Fitch

FORD, JOHN
Black Watch. T. Mundy; King of the Khyber Rifles
Four Men and a Prayer. D. Garth
Fugitive. G. Greene; Power and the Glory
Gideon's Day. J. J. Marric
Informer. L. O'Flaherty
Judge Priest. I. S. Cobb; Down Yonder with Judge Priest
Louis Beretti. D. H. Clarke
Sun Shines Bright. I. S. Cobb; Old Judge Priest

FORDE, EUGENE
Charlie Chan's Murder Cruise. E. D. Biggers; Charlie Chan Carries On
Country Beyond. J. O. Curwood
Dressed to Kill. R. Burke; Dead Take No Bows
Great Hotel Murder. V. Starrett
Michael Shayne, Private Eye. B. Halliday; Private Practice of Michael Shayne
Sleepers West. F. Nebel; Sleepers East

FORDE, WALTER
Condemned to Death. G. Goodchild; Jack O'Lantern
Four Just Men. E. Wallace
Gaunt Stranger. E. Wallace; Ringer
Ghost Train. A. Ridley
Inspector Hornleigh on Holiday. L. Grex; Stolen Death
Last Hour. C. Bennett
Peterville Diamond. L. Fodor; Jewel Robbery
Ringer. E. Wallace
Rome Express. R. Alexander
Saloon Bar. F. Harvey
Silent House. J. G. Brandon

FORMAN, MILOS
Ragtime. E. L. Doctorow

FORMAN, TOM
City of Silent Men. J. A. Moroso; Quarry
Off the Highway. T. Gallon; Tatterley
People vs. Nancy Preston. J. A. Moroso; People Against Nancy Preston

FOSS, KENELM
House of Peril. M. B. Lowndes; Chink in the Armour

FOSTER, GILES
Tree of Hands. R. Rendell

FOSTER, LEWIS R.
Jamaica Run. M. Murray; Neat Little Corpse
Love Letters of a Star. Rufus King; Case of the Constant God
Lucky Stiff. C. Rice

FOSTER, NORMAN
Journey into Fear. E. Ambler
Kiss the Blood Off My Hands. G. Butler
Thank You, Mr. Moto. J. P. Marquand
Think Fast, Mr. Moto. J. P. Marquand

FOURASTIE, PHILIPPE
Choice of Assassins. W. P. McGivern

FOWLER, GENE, JR.
Gang War. O. Demaris; Hoods Take Over

FOY, BRYAN
Gorilla. R. Spence

FRAKER, WILLIAM A.
Reflection of Fear. S. Forbes; Go to Thy Death Bed

FRANCIS, ALLEN
Moorland Tragedy. B. Orczy; Unravelled Knots

FRANCIS, FREDDIE
Craze. H. Seymour; Infernal Idol
Deadly Bees. H. F. Heard; Taste of Honey
Mumsy, Nanny, Sonny and Girlie. B. Comport
Skull. R. Bloch; Skull of the Marquis de Sade
Torture Garden. R. Bloch (headnote)
Traitor's Gate. E. Wallace
Vengeance. C. Siodmak; Donovan's Brain

FRANCO, JESUS
Count Dracula. B. Stoker; Dracula

FRANK, CHARLES
Uncle Silas. J. S. Le Fanu

FRANKEL, CYRIL
Never Take Candy from a Stranger. R. Garis
Permission to Kill. P. Loraine; W.I.L. One to Curtis
Witches. P. Curtis; Devil's Own

FRANKENHEIMER, JOHN
Black Sunday. T. Harris
Dead Bang. E. Naha
Fifty-Two Pickup. E. Leonard
French Connection II. R. Moore
Holcroft Covenant. R. Ludlum
I Walk the Line. Madison Jones; Exile
Manchurian Candidate. R. Condon
99 and 44/100% Dead. M. Franklin; 99 44/100% Dead
Seconds. D. Ely
Seven Days in May. F. Knebel
Year of the Gun. M. Mewshaw
Young Savages. E. Hunter; Matter of Conviction

FRANKLIN, CARL
Full Fathom Five. Bart Davis

FRANKLIN, CHESTER M.
File 113. E. Gaboriau; File No. 113
Thirteenth Hour. S. Horler

FRANKLIN, HOWARD
Quick Change. J. Cronley

FRANKLIN, RICHARD
Cloak and Dagger. W. Irish; Dead Man Blues

FRANKLIN, SIDNEY A.
Last of Mrs. Cheyney. F. Lonsdale
Not Guilty. H. MacGrath; Parrot & Co.
Tiger Rose. W. Mack

FRANZ, JOSEPH
Alias the Night Wind. V. Vanardy

FREARS, STEPHEN
Gumshoe. N. Smith

FREELAND, THORNTON
Amateur Gentleman. J. Farnol
Secret Witness. S. Spewack; Murder in the Gilded Cage
Three Live Ghosts. F. S. Isham

FREGONESE, HUGO
Man in the Attic. M. B. Lowndes; Lodger
Seven Thunders. R. Croft-Cooke

FRENCH, HAROLD
Blind Goddess. P. Hastings
Dead Men Are Dangerous. H. C. Armstrong; Hidden
Hour of Thirteen. M. Porlock; X v. Rex
House of the Arrow. A. E. W. Mason
Man Who Watched the Trains Go By. G. Simenon

FREND, CHARLES
Cone of Silence. D. Beaty

FREUND, KARL
Hands of Orlac. M. Renard

FRIC, MAX
Der Zinker. E. Wallace; Squeaker

FRIEDKIN, WILLIAM
Birthday Party. H. Pinter
Brink's Job. N. Behn; Big Stick-Up at Brink's!
Cruising. G. Walker
Exorcist. W. P. Blatty
Guardian. D. Greenburg; Nanny
Rampage. W. P. Wood
To Live and Die in L.A. G. Petievich
Wages of Fear. G. Arnaud

FROHMAN, DANIEL
Day of Days. L. J. Vance

FUEST, ROBERT
Abominable Dr. Phibes. W. Goldstein; Dr. Phibes
Devil's Rain. M. Willis
Dr. Phibes Rises Again. W. Goldstein

FULLER, SAMUEL
Dead Pigeon on Beethoven Street. S. Fuller
Naked Kiss. S. Fuller
Shark. V. Canning; His Bones Are Coral
Shock Corridor. M. Avallone
Street of No Return. D. Goodis

FURIE, SIDNEY J.
Ipcress File. L. Deighton
Naked Runner. F. Clifford

FURTHMAN, JULES
Colorado Pluck. G. Goodchild; Colorado Jim

GABEL, MARTIN
  Lost Moment. H. James; Aspern Papers
GAGE, GEORGE
  Fleshburn. J. Ives; Fear in a Handful of Dust
GAGE, JACK
  Hotel Berlin. V. Baum; Hotel Berlin '43
GAILLORD, ROBERT
  Mr. Barnes of New York. A. C. Gunter
GAINSBOURG, SERGE
  Equateur. G. Simenon; Tropic Moon
GAINVILLE, RENE
  Woman Is a Stranger. J. H. Chase; Not Safe to Be Free
GALEEN, HENRIK
  After the Verdict. R. Hichens
GALLAGHER, DONALD
  Temple Tower. H. C. McNeile
GALLU, SAMUEL
  Double Agent. G. Stackelberg
  Limbo Line. V. Canning
GANDERS, FELIX
  Mysteries of Paris. E. Sue
GARDNER, CYRIL
  Grumpy. H. Hodges
  Only Saps Work. O. Davis; Easy Come, Easy Go
GARNETT, TAY
  Bad Company. J. Lait; Put on the Spot
  Delta Factor. M. Spillane
  Postman Always Rings Twice. J. M. Cain
  Slightly Honorable. F. G. Presnell; Send Another Coffin
  Terrible Beauty. A. J. Roth
GARRETT, OTIS
  Black Doll. W. E. Hayes
  Danger on the Air. Xantippe; Death Catches Up with Mr. Kluck
  Lady in the Morgue. J. Latimer
  Last Express. B. Kendrick
  Mystery of the White Room. J. G. Edwards; Murder in the Surgery
  Witness Vanishes. J. Ronald; They Can't Hang Me!
GARRICK, RICHARD
  Armadale. W. Collins
  Rank Outsider. N. Gould
  Trent's Last Case. E. C. Bentley
GASNIER, LOUIS
  Breath of Scandal. E. Balmer
  Exploits of Elaine. A. B. Reeve
  Murder on the Yukon. L. Y. Erskine; Renfrew Rides North
  Shadow of the Law. J. A. Moroso; Quarry
  Slightly Scarlet. P. Heath
  Ticket-of-Leave Man. C. Reade; Foul Play
GAVIN, JOHN
  Keane of Kalgoorlie. Arthur Wright
  Three Years with Thunderbolt. A. Pratt
GAVRAS, COSTA
  Sleeping Car Murders. S. Japrisot; 10:30 from Marseilles
GEISSENDOERFER, HANS C.
  Edith's Diary. P. Highsmith
  Glass Cell. P. Highsmith
  Jonathan. B. Stoker; Dracula
GENTILOMO, GIACOMO
  Brothers Karamazov. F. M. Dostoevskii
GERAGHTY, TOM J.
  Perpetua. D. C. Calthrop
  Spanish Jade. M. Hewlett
GEROLMO, CHRIS
  Mississippi Burning. J. Norst
GERRARD, GENE
  It's in the Blood. D. Whitelaw; Big Picture

GESSNER, NICOLAS
  Blonde from Peking. J. H. Chase; You Have Yourself a Deal
  Little Girl Who Lives Down the Lane. L. Koenig
GIBLYN, CHARLES
  Dark Mirror. L. J. Vance
  Leavenworth Case. A. K. Green
  Somewhere in France. R. H. Davis
GIBSON, ALAN
  Goodbye Gemini. J. Hall; Ask Agamemnon
GILBERT, ARTHUR
  Convict 99. M. C. Leighton
  Mystery of Edwin Drood. C. Dickens
GILBERT, LEWIS
  Cast a Dark Shadow. J. Green; Murder Mistaken
  Moonraker. C. Wood; James Bond and Moonraker
  Sea Shall Not Have Them. J. Harris
  Spy Who Loved Me. C. Wood; James Bond, the Spy Who Loved Me
  You Only Live Twice. I. Fleming
GILER, DAVID
  Black Bird. A. Edwards
GILL, LAWRENCE
  Sealed Valley. H. Footner
GILLIAT, SIDNEY
  Endless Night. A. Christie
  Fortune Is a Woman. Winston Graham
  Green for Danger. C. Brand
  London Belongs to Me. N. Collins
GILLING, JOHN
  Flesh and the Fiends. R. L. Stevenson; Body Snatcher
  Man Inside. M. E. Chaber
  Night Caller. F. Crisp; Night Callers
  Pickup Alley. E. Ronns
  Tiger by the Tail. J. Mair; Never Come Back
GIOVANNI, JOSE
  Last Known Address. J. Harrington
  One Way Ticket. H. E. Helseth; Chair for Martin Rome
GIRARD, BERNARD
  Dead Heat on a Merry-Go-Round. E. L. Heyman
  Mad Room. E. Percy; Ladies in Retirement
GIRAULT, JEAN
  Gazebo. A. Coppel
GIROD, FRANCIS
  Descent into Hell. D. Goodis; Wounded and the Slain
  Le Grand Frere. S. Ross; Ready for the Tiger
GIST, ROBERT
  American Dream. N. Mailer
GLAISTER, GERARD
  Clue of the Silver Key. E. Wallace
  Partner. E. Wallace; Million Dollar Story
  Set-Up. E. Wallace (headnote)
  Share Out. E. Wallace; Jack o' Judgment
GLASER, PAUL MICHAEL
  Running Man. R. Bachman
GLEASON, MICHIE
  Summer Heat. L. Shivers; Here to Get My Baby Out of Jail
GLEN, JOHN
  For Your Eyes Only. I. Fleming
  License to Kill. John Gardner
  Living Daylights. I. Fleming; Octopussy and The Living Daylights
  Octopussy. I. Fleming; Octopussy and The Living Daylights
GLENNON, BURT
  Girl of the Port. J. Russell; Far Wandering Men
  Perfect Crime. I. Zangwill; Big Bow Mystery

GLENVILLE, PETER
  Comedians. G. Greene
  Term of Trial. J. Barlow
GLYN, ELINOR
  Price of Things. E. Glyn
GODARD, JEAN-LUC
  Band of Outsiders. D. Hitchens; Fool's Gold
  Crazy Pete. L. White; Obsession
  Grandeur and Decadence of a Small-Time Filmmaker. J. H. Chase (headnote)
  Made in U.S.A. R. Stark; Jugger
GODDARD, JIM
  Shanghai Surprise. T. Kenrick; Faraday's Flowers
GODFREY, PETER
  Cry Wolf. M. Carleton
  Down River. Seamark
  Highways by Night. C. B. Kelland; Silver Spoon
  Hotel Berlin. V. Baum; Hotel Berlin '43
  Lone Wolf Spy Hunt. L. J. Vance; Red Masquerade
  Thread O'Scarlet. J. J. Bell
  Two Mrs. Carrolls. M. Vale
  Woman in White. W. Collins
GOLAN, MENACHEM
  Delta Force. J. Norst
  Lepke. J. Pearl
GOLD, JACK
  Medusa Touch. P. Van Greenaway
  Praying Mantis. H. Monteilhet; Preying Mantises
  Who? A. Budrys
GOLDEN, JOSEPH A.
  New Magdalen. Wilkie Collins
GOLDSTONE, JAMES
  Gang That Couldn't Shoot Straight. J. Breslin
  Jigsaw. W. Ericson; Fallen Angel
GONZALEZ, SERVANDO
  Fool Killer. H. Eustis
GOODE, FREDERIC
  Syndicate. Denys Rhodes
GOODWINS, FRED
  Blood Money. C. H. Bullivant
  Chinese Puzzle. M. Bower
GORDON, BERT I.
  Picture Mommy Dead. Robert Sherman
GORDON, MICHAEL
  Act of Murder. E. Lothar; Mills of God
  Portrait in Black. I. Goff
GORDON, ROBERT
  Black Eagle. O. Henry; Roads of Destiny
GOSLAR, JUERGEN
  Whispering Death. D. Carney
GOTTLIEB, FRANZ JOSEF
  Der Schwarze Abt. E. Wallace; Black Abbot
  Die Gruft mit dem Ratselschloss. E. Wallace; Angel Esquire
GOULDING, EDMUND
  Everybody Does It. J. M. Cain; Career in C Major
  Nightmare Alley. W. L. Gresham
  We Are Not Alone. J. Hilton
GRAHAM, EDDY
  Sherlock Holmes and a Study in Scarlet. A. C. Doyle; Study in Scarlet
  Sherlock Holmes and the Baskerville Case. A. C. Doyle; Hound of the Baskervilles
  Sherlock Holmes and the Sign of Four. A. C. Doyle; Sign of the Four
  Sherlock Holmes and the Valley of Fear. A. C. Doyle; Valley of Fear
GRAHAM, WILLIAM A.
  Then Came Bronson. W. Johnston
  Together Brothers. Jim Robinson

GRANDON, FRANCIS E.
Dummy. H. J. O'Higgins

GRANGIER, GILLES
Blood to the Head. G. Simenon; Young Cardinaud
Maigret Sees Red. G. Simenon; Maigret and the Gangsters

GRANIER-DEFERRE, PIERRE
Cat. G. Simenon
Man with the Silver Eyes. R. Rossner; End of Someone Else's Rainbow
North Star. G. Simenon; Lodger
Train. G. Simenon
Widow Couderc. G. Simenon; Ticket of Leave
Widow's Walk. A. Coburn

GRANT, FRANCES E.
Sword of Fate. H. Herman

GRANVILLE, FRED LEROY
At the Mercy of Tiberius. A. J. Wilson

GRAUMAN, WALTER E.
Lady in a Cage. R. Durand
Last Escape. M. Walker
633 Squadron. F. E. Smith

GRAYSON, GODFREY
Meet Simon Cherry. G. Pedrick; Meet the Rev
Spider's Web. A. Christie

GREEN, ALFRED E.
Come to My House. A. S. Roche
Dark Hazard. W. R. Burnett
Gracie Allen Murder Case. S. S. Van Dine
League of Frightened Men. R. Stout
Parachute Jumper. R. James; Some Call It Love

GREEN, GUY
Angry Silence. John Burke
House of Secrets. S. Noel
Mark. C. E. Israel
Portrait of Allison. F. Durbridge

GREENE, DAVID
I Start Counting. A. E. Lindop
Shuttered Room. J. Withers
Strange Affair. B. Toms

GREENE, MAX
Hotel Reserve. E. Ambler; Epitaph for a Spy

GREENWALD, MAGGIE
Kill-Off. Jim Thompson

GREENWOOD, EDWIN
Miss Bracegirdle Does Her Duty. S. Aumonier; Miss Bracegirdle and Others
To What Red Hell. P. Robinson

GREMM, WOLF
Kamikaze '89. P. Wahloo; Murder on the Thirty-First Floor

GREVILLE, EDMOND T.
Guilty? M. Gilbert; Death Has Deep Roots
Hands of Orlac. M. Renard

GREY, RICHARD M.
Man with the Twisted Lip. A. C. Doyle; Adventures of Sherlock Holmes

GRIES, TOM
Breakheart Pass. A. MacLean
Girl in the Woods. O. Crawford; Blood on the Branches
Lady Ice. M. Braly; Master

GRIFFITH, D. W.
Broken Blossoms. T. Burke; Limehouse Nights
Dream Street. T. Burke; Limehouse Nights
Sacrifice. O. Henry; Four Million
Suicide Club. R. L. Stevenson
That Royle Girl. E. Balmer

GRIFFITH, EDWARD H.
Alias the Lone Wolf. L. J. Vance
One Night in Lisbon. J. Van Druten; There's Always Juliet
White Mice. R. H. Davis

GRIMES, LEE
Miss Bracegirdle Does Her Duty. S. Aumonier; Miss Bracegirdle and Others

GRINDE, NICK
Bishop Murder Case. S. S. Van Dine
Remote Control. C. North

GROSBARD, ULA
Straight Time. E. Bunker; No Beast So Fierce
True Confessions. J. G. Dunne

GUEST, VAL
Assignment K. Hartley Howard; Department K
Break in the Circle. P. Loraine
Casino Royale. I. Fleming
Dangerous Davies. L. Thomas
Full Treatment. R. S. Thorn
Hell Is a City. M. Procter
Jigsaw. H. Waugh; Sleep Long, My Love
Where the Spies Are. J. Leasor; Passport to Oblivion

GUILLEMOT, CLAUDE
Brute. G. Des Cars

GUILLERMIN, JOHN
Day They Robbed the Bank of England. J. Brophy
Death on the Nile. A. Christie
House of Cards. S. Ellin
Skyjacked. D. Harper; Hijacked
Towering Inferno. R. M. Stern; Tower
Whole Truth. P. Mackie

GUNDRY, V. GARETH
Hound of the Baskervilles. A. C. Doyle

GYLLENHALL, STEPHEN
Paris Trout. P. Dexter

HAAS, CHARLES
Platinum High School. I. Shulman

HAAS, HUGO
Lizzie. S. Jackson; Bird's Nest

HABIB, RALPH
Passager Clandestin. G. Simenon; Stowaway
Stowaway. G. Simenon

HACHUEL, HERVE
Last of Philip Banter. J. F. Bardin

HACKFORD, TAYLOR
Against All Odds. G. Homes; Build My Gallows High

HADDEN, GEORGE
Charlie Chan's Courage. E. D. Biggers; Chinese Parrot

HAGEN, JULIUS
Passing of Mr. Quin. A. Christie; Mysterious Mr. Quin

HAGGAR, WILLIAM
Dumb Man of Manchester. B. F. Rayner

HAGGARD, PIERS
Venom. A. Scholefield

HAGUET, ANDREW
Secret Document—Vienna. M. Dekobra; Widow with the Pink Gloves

HAI, ZAFAR
Perfect Murder. H. R. F. Keating

HAINES, RONALD
Man with the Magnetic Eyes. R. Daniel

HALDANE, BERT
Brigadier Gerard. A. C. Doyle; Exploits of Brigadier Gerard
East Lynne. H. Wood
Ticket-of-Leave Man. T. Taylor

HALES, GORDON
Return to Sender. E. Wallace (headnote)

HALL, ALEXANDER
Little Miss Marker. D. Runyon; Blue Plate Special

HALL, GEORGE EDWARDES
Dr. Jekyll and Mr. Hyde. R. L. Stevenson; Strange Case of Dr. Jekyll and Mr. Hyde

HALPERIN, VICTOR
Ex-Flame. H. Wood; East Lynne
Party Girl. E. Balmer; Dangerous Business

HAMER, ROBERT
Father Brown. G. K. Chesterton; Innocence of Father Brown
It Always Rains on Sunday. A. La Bern
Kind Hearts and Coronets. R. Horniman; Israel Rank
Long Memory. H. Clewes
Pink String and Sealing Wax. R. Pertwee
Scapegoat. D. Du Maurier

HAMILTON, GUY
Diamonds Are Forever. I. Fleming
Evil Under the Sun. A. Christie
Force 10 from Navarone. A. MacLean
Funeral in Berlin. L. Deighton
Goldfinger. I. Fleming
Inspector Calls. J. B. Priestley
Intruder. R. Maugham; Line on Ginger
Live and Let Die. I. Fleming
Man in the Middle. H. Fast; Winston Affair
Man with the Golden Gun. I. Fleming
Mirror Crack'd. A. Christie; Mirror Crack'd from Side to Side
Remo: The First Adventure. W. B. Murphy
Ringer. E. Wallace
Touch of Larceny. A. Garve; Megstone Plot
Try This On for Size. J. H. Chase

HAMILTON, WILLIAM
Murder on the Bridle Path. S. Palmer; Puzzle of the Red Stallion
Seven Keys to Baldpate. E. D. Biggers

HAMMOND, WILLIAM C.
Flying Eye. J. N. Chance (headnote)

HANBURY, W. VICTOR
Crouching Beast. V. Williams
Dick Turpin. W. H. Ainsworth; Rookwood
Hotel Reserve. E. Ambler; Epitaph for a Spy
Second Bureau. C. R. Dumas

HANKEY, ANTHONY
Too Dangerous to Live. D. Hume

HANKINSON, MICHAEL
Chick. E. Wallace
Scarab Murder Case. S. S. Van Dine

HANNAM, KEN
Robbery Under Arms. R. Boldrewood

HANSEL, HOWELL
Horrible Hyde. R. L. Stevenson; Strange Case of Dr. Jekyll and Mr. Hyde
Million Dollar Mystery. H. MacGrath

HANSON, CURTIS
Bedroom Window. A. Holden; Witnesses

HARDY, CHARLES
East Lynne. H. Wood

HARDY, ROBIN
Wicker Man. R. Hardy

HARE, DAVID
Paris by Night. David Hare

HARE, LUMSDEN
Masquerade. L. J. Vance; Brass Bowl

HARLIN, RENNY
Die Harder. W. Wager; 58 Minutes

HARLOW, JOHN
Candles at Nine. Anthony Gilbert; Mouse Who Wouldn't Play Ball
Dark Tower. A. Woollcott
Echo Murders. J. Sylvester; Terror of Tregarwith
Headline. K. Attiwill; Reporter
Meet Sexton Blake. A. Parsons; Mystery of the Stolen Despatches

HARRINGTON, CURTIS
  Games. H. Ellson
  What's the Matter with Helen? R. Deming

HARRIS, JACK
  Called Back. H. Conway

HARRIS, JAMES B.
  Fast-Walking. E. Brawley; Rap

HARRIS, LIONEL
  Double. E. Wallace

HARRISON, NORMAN
  Incident at Midnight. E. Wallace (headnote)
  Locker 69. E. Wallace (headnote)

HART, HARVEY
  Pyx. J. Buell
  Shoot. D. Fairbairn
  Sweet Ride. W. Murray

HARTFORD, DAVID M.
  Back to God's Country. J. O. Curwood
  Golden Snare. J. O. Curwood
  Inside the Lines. E. D. Biggers
  Nomads of the North. J. O. Curwood

HARTFORD-DAVIS, ROBERT
  Crosstrap. J. H. Chase (headnote)
  Take. G. F. Newman; Sir, You Bastard

HARVEY, LAURENCE
  Dandy in Aspic. D. Marlowe

HASKIN, BYRON
  Power. F. M. Robinson
  Too Late for Tears. R. Huggins

HATHAWAY, HENRY
  Bottom of the Bottle. G. Simenon
  Dark Corner. L. Q. Ross
  Diplomatic Courier. P. Cheyney; Sinister Errand
  Hangup. B. Brunner; Face of Night
  House on 92nd Street. Alex Morrison
  Kiss of Death. E. Lipsky
  O. Henry's Full House. O. Henry (headnote)
  Seven Thieves. S. Kent; Lions at the Kill
  23 Paces to Baker Street. P. MacDonald; Nursemaid Who Disappeared
  Witching Hour. A. Thomas

HAWKS, HOWARD
  Big Sleep. R. Chandler
  Scarface. A. Trail
  To Have and Have Not. E. Hemingway
  Trent's Last Case. E. C. Bentley

HAYDEN, JEFFREY
  Vintage. U. Keir

HAYDON, J. CHARLES
  Alster Case. R. Gillmore
  Phantom Buccaneer. V. Bridges; Another Man's Shoes
  Strange Case of Mary Page. F. Lewis

HAYERS, SIDNEY
  Assault. K. Young; Ravine
  Conjure Wife. F. Leiber, Jr.
  Echo of Barbara. John Burke
  Malpas Mystery. E. Wallace; Face in the Night
  Payroll. D. Bickerton
  What Changed Charley Farthing. M. Hebden

HAYNES, H. MANNING
  Clayton Treasure Mystery. N. Gordon; Shakespeare Murders
  Lawyer Quince. W. W. Jacobs; Odd Craft
  Monkey's Paw. W. W. Jacobs; Lady of the Barge
  Old Man. E. Wallace; Coat of Arms
  Other Man. E. Wallace; Nine Bears
  Ware Case. G. Pleydell

HAYWARD, FREDERICK
  Elder Brother. Anthony Gibbs

HECHT, BEN
  Actors and Sin. B. Hecht; Actor's Blood
  Crime Without Passion. B. Hecht; Collected Stories of Ben Hecht

HEERMAN, VICTOR
  Confidence Man. L. Y. Erskine
  Imperfect Imposter. N. Venner

HEFFRON, RICHARD T.
  I, the Jury. M. Spillane

HEFFRON, T. N.
  House of a Thousand Candles. M. Nicholson

HEISLER, STUART
  Glass Key. D. Hammett
  I Died a Thousand Times. W. R. Burnett; High Sierra

HEMMINGS, DAVID
  Running Scared. G. McDonald
  Survivor. J. Herbert

HENABERY, JOSEPH
  Stranger. J. Galsworthy; Five Tales

HENDERSON, CLARK
  Saigon Commandos. Jonathan Cain; Mad Minute

HENLEY, HOBART
  Captain Applejack. W. Hackett
  Mothers Cry. H. G. Carlisle
  Roadhouse Nights. D. Hammett; Red Harvest
  Sin That Was His. F. Packard
  Unknown Blonde. T. D. Irwin; Collusion

HENREID, PAUL
  Dead Ringer. B. Thomas

HEPWORTH, CECIL M(ILTON)
  Anna the Adventuress. E. P. Oppenheim
  House of Marney. J. Goodwin
  Man Who Stayed at Home. J. E. H. Terry
  Mist in the Valley. Dorin Craig
  Mrs. Erricker's Reputation. T. Cobb
  Touch of the Child. T. Gallon

HERMAN, ALBERT
  Phantom of Forty-Second Street. M. M. Raison
  Renfrew of the Royal Mounted. L. Y. Erskine

HERSHOLT, JEAN
  Gray Dawn. S. E. White

HERVIL, RENEE
  Mystery of the Villa Rose. A. E. W. Mason; At the Villa Rose

HESS, JON
  Watchers. D. R. Koontz

HESSLER, GORDON
  Catacombs. Jay Bennett
  Embassy. S. Coulter
  Last Shot You Hear. W. Fairchild; Sound of Murder
  Murders in the Rue Morgue. E. A. Poe; Prose Romances of Edgar A. Poe
  Scream and Scream Again. P. Saxon; Disoriented Man

HEYES, DOUGLAS
  Kitten with a Whip. Wade Miller

HEYNEMANN, LAURENT
  April Is a Deadly Month. Derek Raymond; Devil's Home on Leave

HICKOX, DOUGLAS
  Entertaining Mr. Sloane. J. Orton
  Hound of the Baskervilles. A. C. Doyle
  Sitting Target. L. Henderson
  Sky Riders. L. Cameron

HIGGIN, HOWARD
  Great Deception. G. F. Gibbs; Yellow Dove
  Perfect Sap. H. I. Young; Not Herbert

HIGGINS, COLIN
  Foul Play. J. C. Rogers

HILL, GEORGE
  Big House. J. Lait
  Secret Six. F. Marion

HILL, GEORGE ROY
  Little Drummer Girl. J. Le Carre
  Sting. R. Weverka

HILL, JACK
  Coffy. P. W. Fairman

HILL, JAMES
  Study in Terror. E. Queen

HILL, ROBERT F.
  Breathless Moment. M. Bryant; Redemption of Richard

HILL, SINCLAIR
  China Bungalow. M. Osmond
  Conspirators. E. P. Oppenheim
  Expiation. E. P. Oppenheim
  Gay Adventure. W. Hackett
  Half a Truth. Rita
  Mystery of Mr. Bernard Brown. E. P. Oppenheim
  Overheard. S. Aumonier
  Qualified Adventurer. S. Jepson

HILL, WALTER
  Driver. C. B. Phillips
  Extreme Prejudice. R. Dobbins
  Johnny Handsome. J. Godey; Three Worlds of Johnny Handsome
  Warriors. S. Yurok

HILLER, ARTHUR
  Nightwing. M. C. Smith
  Penelope. E. V. Cunningham
  Silver Streak. J. C. Rogers

HILLYER, LAMBERT
  Dracula's Daughter. B. Stoker; Dracula's Guest
  Her Second Chance. W. Woodrow; Second Chance

HINZMAN, BILL
  Majorettes. J. Russo

HISCOTT, LESLIE
  Alibi. M. Morton
  Black Coffee. A. Christie
  Death on the Set. V. MacClure
  House of the Arrow. A. E. W. Mason
  Missing Rembrandt. A. C. Doyle; Return of Sherlock Holmes
  Murder at Covent Garden. W. J. Makin
  Mystery at the Villa Rose. A. E. W. Mason; At the Villa Rose
  Mystery of the Pink Villa. A. E. W. Mason; At the Villa Rose
  S.O.S. W. W. Ellis
  Sleeping Cardinal. A. C. Doyle; Memoirs of Sherlock Holmes
  Three Witnesses. S. Fowler
  Triumph of Sherlock Holmes. A. C. Doyle; Valley of Fear

HITCHCOCK, ALFRED
  Birds. D. Du Maurier; Apple Tree
  Blackmail. C. Bennett
  Dial "M" for Murder. F. Knott
  Family Plot. V. Canning; Rainbird Pattern
  Frenzy. A. La Bern; Goodbye Piccadilly, Farewell Leicester Square
  Jamaica Inn. D. Du Maurier
  Lady Vanishes. E. L. White; Wheel Spins
  Lodger. M. B. Lowndes
  Man Who Knew Too Much. R. Alexander (2 versions)
  Marnie. Winston Graham
  Murder. C. Dane; Enter Sir John
  Paradine Case. R. Hichens
  Psycho. R. Bloch
  Rear Window. W. Irish; After-Dinner Story
  Rebecca. D. Du Maurier
  Rope. P. Hamilton
  Sabotage. J. Conrad; Secret Agent
  Secret Agent. W. S. Maugham; Ashenden
  Spellbound. F. Beeding; House of Dr. Edwardes
  Stage Fright. S. Jepson; Man Running
  Strangers on a Train. P. Highsmith

Suspicion. F. Iles; Before the Fact
Thirty-Nine Steps. J. Buchan
To Catch a Thief. D. Dodge
Topaz. L. Uris
Torn Curtain. R. Wormser
Trouble with Harry. J. T. Story
Vertigo. P. Boileau; Living and the Dead
Young and Innocent. J. Tey; Shilling for Candles

HIVELY, JACK
Saint in Palm Springs. L. Charteris (headnote)
Saint's Double Trouble. L. Charteris (headnote)
Street of Chance. C. Woolrich; Black Curtain

HODGES, MIKE
Get Carter. Ted Lewis; Jack's Return Home
Prayer for the Dying. J. Higgins
Terminal Man. M. Crichton

HOFFMAN, DUSTIN
Straight Time. E. Bunker; No Beast So Fierce

HOFFMAN, MICHAEL
Restless Natives. N. Dunnett

HOGAN, JAMES
Arrest Bulldog Drummond. H. C. McNeile; Final Count
Bulldog Drummond's Bride. H. C. McNeile; The Best Short Stories
Bulldog Drummond's Peril. H. C. McNeile; Third Round
Bulldog Drummond's Secret Police. H. C. McNeile; Temple Tower
Ellery Queen and the Murder Ring. E. Queen; Dutch Shoe Mystery
Ellery Queen's Penthouse Mystery. E. Queen; Penthouse Mystery
Perfect Crime. E. Queen

HOLMES, BEN
Plot Thickens. S. Palmer (headnote)
Saint in New York. L. Charteris
We're on the Jury. F. Ballard; Ladies of the Jury

HOLT, SETH
Blood from the Mummy's Tomb. B. Stoker; Jewel of the Seven Stars
Danger Route. A. York; Eliminator
Nanny. E. Piper
Nowhere to Go. D. MacKenzie

HOPPER, DENNIS
Colors. J. Norst
Hot Spot. C. Williams; Hell Hath No Fury

HOPPER, E. MASON
Curtain at Eight. O. R. Cohen; Backstage Mystery
Hidden Spring. C. B. Kelland
Paris at Midnight. H. Balzac; Le Pere Goriot

HORNE, JAMES W.
Bronze Bell. L. J. Vance

HORNER, HARRY
Beware, My Lovely. M. Dinelli; Man
Life in the Balance. G. Simenon (headnote)
Vicki. S. Fisher; I Wake Up Screaming
Wild Party. J. McPartland

HOUGH, JOHN
Dirty Mary, Crazy Larry. R. Unekis; Chase
Brass Target. F. Nolan; Oshawa Project
Eyewitness. M. Hebden
Incubus. Ray Russell
Legend of Hell House. R. Matheson; Hell House

HOUGH, R. L.
Silent Witness. J. De Leon

HOWARD, CY
Every Little Crook and Nanny. E. Hunter

HOWARD, WILLIAM K.
Evelyn Prentice. W. E. Woodward
Red Dice. O. R. Cohen; Iron Chalice
River Pirate. C. F. Coe
Sherlock Holmes. W. Gillette
Squeaker. E. Wallace
Trial of Vivienne Ware. K. Ellis
Valiant. H. Hall

HOWE, ELIOT
Gray Dawn. S. E. White

HOYT, HARRY O.
Curse of Drink. C. E. Blaney
Love Racket. B. K. Burns; Jury Woman

HUGHES, HARRY
Gables Mystery. J. Celestin; Man at Six
Man at Six. J. Celestin

HUGHES, KEN
Arrivederci, Baby! R. Deming; Careful Man
Casino Royale. I. Fleming
House Across the Way. K. Hughes; High Wray
Long Haul. M. Mills
Wicked As They Come. B. Ballinger; Portrait in Smoke

HUGHES, ROBERT C.
Hunter's Blood. J. Cunningham

HUGON, ANDRE
Street Without Joy. H. Bettauer; Viennese Love

HUMBERSTONE, H. BRUCE
Dragon Murder Case. S. S. Van Dine
Fury at Furnace Creek. D. Garth; Four Men and a Prayer
I Wake Up Screaming. S. Fisher
Strangers of the Evening. T. Thayer; Illustrious Corpse
Three Live Ghosts. F. S. Isham

HUME, KENNETH
Hot Ice. A. Melville; Week-End at Thrackley

HUMPHREY, WILLIAM J.
Black Spider. C. Dawe
Foolish Monte Carlo. C. Dawe; Black Spider
Wife Whom God Forgot. C. H. Bullivant

HUNABELLE, ANDRE
Fantomas. P. Souvestre
Mysteries of Paris. E. Sue
OSS 117—Mission for a Killer. J. Bruce; Live Wire

HUNT, CHARLES
You Can't Beat the Law. H. H. Van Loan

HUNT, PETER
On Her Majesty's Secret Service. I. Fleming
Wild Geese II. D. Carney; Square Circle

HUNTER, T. HAYES
Calendar. E. Wallace
Frightened Lady. E. Wallace; Case of the Frightened Lady
Ghoul. F. King
Green Pack. E. Wallace
Man They Could Not Arrest. E. Wallace (headnote)
Man They Couldn't Arrest. A. J. Small
One of the Best. S. Hicks
Recoil. R. Beach; Big Brother
Scarlet Daredevil. B. Orczy; Triumph of the Scarlet Pimpernel
Silver King. H. A. Jones
South Sea Bubble. R. Pertwee
White Face. E. Wallace

HUNTINGTON, LAWRENCE
Deadly Record. N. W. Hooke
Death Drums Along the River. E. Wallace; Sanders of the River
Franchise Affair. J. Tey
This Man Is Dangerous. D. Hume; They Called Him Death
Warn That Man. V. Sylvaine

HURST, BRIAN DESMOND
Mark of Cain. J. Shearing; Airing in a Closed Carriage
On the Night of the Fire. F. L. Green

HUSSEIN, WARIS
Possession of Joel Delaney. Ramona Stewart

HUSTON, JOHN
Asphalt Jungle. W. R. Burnett
Beat the Devil. J. Helvick
Casino Royale. I. Fleming
Final Exam. G. Meyer
Key Largo. M. Anderson
Kremlin Letter. N. Behn
List of Adrian Messenger. P. MacDonald
Mackintosh Man. D. Bagley; Freedom Trap
Maltese Falcon. D. Hammett
Prizzi's Honor. R. Condon
We Were Strangers. R. Sylvester; Rough Sketch

HUTH, HAROLD
Bulldog Sees It Through. G. Fairlie; Scissors Cut Paper
My Sister and I. E. Bonett; High Pavement

HUTTON, BRIAN G.
First Deadly Sin. Lawrence Sanders
High Road to China. J. Cleary
Night Watch. L. Fletcher
Sol Madrid. R. Wilder; Fruit of the Poppy
Where Eagles Dare. A. MacLean

HYAMS, PETER
Peeper. K. Laumer; Deadfall
Presidio. Mike Cogan

ICHIKAWA, KON
Lonely Hearts. E. McBain; Lady, Lady, I Did It!

INCE, JOHN
Beloved Adventurer. E. C. Hall
Blind Man's Eyes. W. MacHarg
Sealed Lips. Maxwell Gray; Silence of Dean Maitland

INCE, RALPH
Argyle Case. H. Ford
Black Mask. B. Graeme; Blackshirt
Crime Unlimited. D. Hume
Lone Wolf Returns. L. J. Vance
Moral Sinner. C. M. S. McLellan; Leah Kleschna
Too Many Crooks. E. J. Rath
Twelve Good Men. J. Rhode; Murders in Praed Street

INCE, THOMAS H.
Boomerang. W. H. Osborne

INGRAHAM, LLOYD
Sable Lorcha. H. Hazeltine

INGRAM, REX
His Robe of Honor. E. Dorrance
Scaramouche. R. Sabatini
Where the Pavement Ends. J. Russell; Red God

INTRATOR, JERALD
Satan in High Heels. N. Chandler

IRVIN, JOHN
Dogs of War. F. Forsyth
Raw Deal. W. Wager

IRVING, GEORGE
Raffles. E. W. Hornung; Amateur Cracksman
Silver King. H. A. Jones

ISASMENDI, ANTONIO ISASI
Adventures of Scaramouche. R. Sabatini; Scaramouche

JABELY, JEAN
Blonde Like That! J. H. Chase; Miss Shumway Waves a Wand

JACKSON, DOUGLAS
Whispers. D. R. Koontz

JACKSON, PATRICK
Shadow on the Wall. H. Lees; Death in the Doll's House
Snowball. J. Lake
What a Carve Up! F. King; Ghoul

JACOBY, GEORGE
Vendetta. A. C. Gunter; Mr. Barnes of New York

JACQUOT, BENOIT
With All Hands. J. Gunn; Deadlier Than the Male

JAFFE, STANLEY R.
Without a Trace. B. Gutcheon; Still Missing

JAMESON, JERRY
    Raise the Titanic! C. Cussler

JARROTT, CHARLES
    Amateur. R. Littell
    Condorman. R. Sheckley; Game of X
    Other Side of Midnight. S. Sheldon
    Time to Remember. E. Wallace; Man Who Bought London

JASON, LEIGH
    Dangerous Blondes. K. Roos; If the Shroud Fits
    Nine Girls. W. H. Pettitt

JASON, WILL
    Kazan. J. O. Curwood

JEFFREY, TOM
    Removalists. D. Williamson
    Weekend of Shadows. H. Atkinson; Reckoning

JESSUA, ALAIN
    Armageddon. D. Lippincott; Voice of Armageddon

JEWISON, NORMAN
    Agnes of God. J. Pielmeier
    . . . And Justice for All. R. Grossbach
    In the Heat of the Night. J. Ball
    Russians Are Coming, The Russians Are Coming. N. Benchley; Off-Islanders
    Soldier's Story. C. Fuller; Soldier's Play
    Thomas Crown Affair. E. L. Heyman

JOHNSON, LAMONT
    Covenant with Death. S. Becker
    Groundstar Conspiracy. L. P. Davies; Alien
    Mackenzie Break. S. Shelley; Bowmanville Break
    Somebody Killed Her Husband. C. B. Phillips
    You'll Like My Mother. N. Hintze

JOHNSON, NUNNALLY
    Black Widow. P. Quentin

JONES, EDGAR
    Enemy to Society. G. Bronson-Howard
    Half Million Bribe. W. H. Osborne; Red Mouse

JONES, F. RICHARD
    Bulldog Drummond. H. C. McNeile

JORDAN, NEIL
    Mona Lisa. J. L. Novak

JOSE, EDWARD
    Closing Net. H. C. Rowland
    God's Prodigal. A. J. Russell
    Yellow Typhoon. H. MacGrath

JOURD'HUI, GERARD
    Old Rascal. Fredric Brown; His Name Was Death

JULIAN, RUPERT
    Cat Creeps. J. Willard; Cat and the Canary
    Evil Women Do. E. Gaboriau; Clique of Gold
    Fire Flingers. W. J. Neidig
    Leopard Lady. E. C. Carpenter
    Phantom of the Opera. G. Leroux
    Three Faces East. A. P. Kelly

KACZENDER, GEORGE
    Agency. P. Gottlieb

KAEUTNER, HELMUT
    Redhead. A. Andersch

KAGAN, JEREMY PAUL
    Big Fix. R. L. Simon

KANE, JOE
    Accused of Murder. W. R. Burnett; Vanity Row
    Timberjack. D. Cushman

KANEW, JEFF
    Eddie Macon's Run. J. McLendon
    Tough Guys. I. Don
    V. I. Warshawski. S. Paretsky (headnote)

KAPLAN, JONATHAN
    Accused. D. Chiel

KARGER, MAXWELL
    Hate. W. Camp; Communicating Door

KARLSON, PHIL
    Ben. G. A. Ralston
    Brothers Rico. G. Simenon
    Dark Page. S. Fuller
    Five Against the House. J. Finney
    Key Witness. F. Kane
    Kid Galahad. Francis Wallace
    Secret Wars. A. MacLean; Last Frontier
    Silencers. D. Hamilton
    Tight Spot. L. Kantor; Dead Pigeon
    Walking Tall. D. Warren
    Wrecking Crew. D. Hamilton

KASTLE, LEONARD
    Honeymoon Killers. Paul Buck

KATSELAS, MILTON
    Report to the Commissioner. J. Mills

KATZIN, LEE H.
    Salzburg Connection. H. MacInnes
    Whatever Happened to Aunt Alice? U. Curtiss; Forbidden Garden

KAUFMAN, JOSEPH
    World's Great Snare. E. P. Oppenheim

KAURISMAKI, AKI
    Crime and Punishment. F. M. Dostoevskii

KAZAN, ELIA
    Man on a Tightrope. N. Paterson
    On the Waterfront. B. Schulberg; Waterfront

KEHLMANN, MICHAEL
    Short Work. J. Ashford (headnote)

KEIGHLEY, WILLIAM
    Each Dawn I Die. J. Odlum
    "G" Men. H. K. Long

KELLINO, ROY
    Guilt Is My Shadow. P. Curtis; You're Best Alone

KELLINO, W. P.
    Angel Esquire. E. Wallace
    Colleen Bawn. D. Boucicault
    Confessions. B. Reynolds; Confession Corner
    Fall of a Saint. E. C. Scott
    Green Terror. E. Wallace; Green Rust

KELLY, A.
    Woman Racket. P. Dunning; Night Hostess

KELLY, ALBERT
    Slippy McGee. M. C. Oemler

KEMM, JEAN
    Lacquered Box. A. Christie; Black Coffee

KEMPLEN, RALPH
    Spaniard's Curse. E. Pargeter; Assize of the Dying

KENNEDY, BURT
    Killer Inside Me. J. Thompson
    Money Trap. L. White
    Trouble with Spies. M. Lovell; Apply Spy in the Sky

KENTON, ERLE
    Guilty As Hell. D. N. Rubin; Riddle Me This!

KERSHNER, IRVIN
    Eyes of Laura Mars. H. B. Gilmour
    Flim Flam Man. G. Owen; Ballad of the Flim Flam Man
    Never Say Never Again. I. Fleming; Thunderball
    Robocop 2. E. Naha
    S*P*Y*S. T. R. Joyce

KESSLER, HENRY S.
    Five Steps to Danger. D. Hamilton; Assignment: Murder

KIBBEE, ROLAND
    Midnight Man. D. Anthony; Midnight Lady and the Mourning Man

KIKOINE, GERARD
    Edge of Sanity. R. L. Stevenson; Strange Case of Dr. Jekyll and Mr. Hyde

KILLY, EDWARD
    Murder on a Bridle Path. S. Palmer; Puzzle of the Red Stallion
    Seven Keys to Baldpate. E. D. Biggers

KIMMINS, ANTHONY
    Mine Own Executioner. N. Balchin
    Mr. Denning Drives North. A. Coppel

KING, BURTON
    Counsel for the Defense. L. Scott
    Little Girl in a Big City. J. K. McCurdy
    Master Mystery. A. B. Reeve

KING, GEORGE
    China Bungalow. M. Osmond
    Crimes at the Dark House. W. Collins; Woman in White
    Frightened Lady. E. Wallace
    Maria Marten. Anonymous
    Nine Forty-Five. O. Davis
    Professional Guest. W. Garrett
    Sexton Blake and the Hooded Terror. P. Quiroule; Mystery of No. 13 Caversham Square
    Shop at Sly Corner. E. Percy; Play with Fire
    Sweeney Todd, the Demon Barber of Fleet Street. G. D. Pitt
    Ticket-of-Leave Man. T. Taylor

KING, HENRY
    All the World to Nothing. W. Martyn
    Black Swan. R. Sabatini
    Haunting Shadows. M. Nicholson; House of a Thousand Candles
    King of the Khyber Rifles. T. Mundy
    O. Henry's Full House. O. Henry (headnote)
    One Hour Before Dawn. M. Scott; Behind Red Curtains

KING, LOUIS
    Bulldog Drummond Comes Back. H. C. McNeile; Female of the Species
    Bulldog Drummond in Africa. H. C. McNeile; Challenge
    Bulldog Drummond's Revenge. H. C. McNeile; Return of Bulldog Drummond
    Murder in Trinidad. J. W. Vandercook
    Tom Sawyer, Detective. M. Twain
    Wine, Women and Horses. W. R. Burnett; Dark Hazard

KIRK, ROLAND
    Dear Fatherland, Be at Peace. J. M. Simmel; Dear Fatherland

KIRKLAND, HARDEE
    Aurora Floyd. M. E. Braddon

KIRKWOOD, JAMES
    Floor Above. E. P. Oppenheim (headnote)

KJAERULFF-SCHMIDT, PALLE
    Think of a Number. A. Bodelsen

KLIMOVSKY, LEON
    El Pediente. W. Irish; Dead Man Blues

KNIGHT, JOHN
    Main Chance. E. Wallace (headnote)

KNIGHTS, ROBERT
    Dawning. Jennifer Johnston; Old Jess

KNOLES, HARLEY
    Burglar. A. Thomas; Edith's Burglar

KNOPF, EDWIN H.
    Law and the Lady. F. Lonsdale; Last of Mrs. Cheyney
    Only Saps Work. O. Davis; Easy Come, Easy Go
    Slightly Scarlet. P. Heath

KNOWLES, BERNARD
    Hell Is Empty. J. F. Straker
    Jassy. N. Lofts
    Man Within. G. Greene
    Park Plaza 605. B. Gray; Dare-Devil Conquest

KOCH, HOWARD W.
    Badge 373. M. Roote
    Born Reckless. M. Rogers

Last Mile. J. Wexley
Shield for Murder. W. P. McGivern

KOHLER, MANFRED R.
Sarg aus Hong-Kong. J. H. Chase; Coffin from Hong Kong

KORBER, SERGE
Little Virtuous. R. Marshall; But a Short Time to Live

KORDA, ZOLTAN
Counterattack. J. Stevenson
Sanders of the River. E. Wallace
Woman's Vengeance. A. Huxley; Mortal Coils

KOSTER, HENRY
Fraulein. J. McGovern
My Cousin Rachel. D. Du Maurier
O. Henry's Full House. O. Henry (headnote)

KOTCHEFF, TED
First Blood. D. Morrell
Outback. K. Cook; Wake in Fright
Who Is Killing the Great Chefs of Europe. N. Lyons; Someone Is Killing the Great Chefs of Europe

KOWALSKI, BERNARD
Stiletto. H. Robbins

KRAEMER, F. W.
Flying Squad. E. Wallace

KRAMER, STANLEY
Domino Principle. A. Kennedy
Runner Stumbles. M. Stitt

KRAWOZYK, GERARD
I Hate Actors. B. Hecht

KUBRICK, STANLEY
Clockwork Orange. A. Burgess
Dr. Strangelove. P. Bryant; Two Hours to Doom
Killing. L. White; Clean Break

KULIJANOV, LEV
Crime and Punishment. F. M. Dostoevskii

KULIK, BUZZ
Riot. F. Elli
Shamus. R. Giles
Warning Shot. W. Masterson; 711—Officer Needs Help
Yellow Canary. W. Masterson; Evil Come, Evil Go

KUROSAWA, AKIRA
High and Low. E. McBain; King's Ransom

LABRO, MAURICE
Blague dans le Coin. Carter Brown; Curtains for a Chorine
Les Canailles. R. Marshall; You Find Him . . . I'll Fix Him

LABRO, PHILIPPE
Without Apparent Motive. E. McBain; Ten Plus One

LACHMAN, HARRY
Baby, Take a Bow. J. P. Judge; Square Crooks
Charlie Chan in Rio. E. D. Biggers; Black Camel
Down Our Street. Ernest George; Belle
They Came by Night. B. Lyndon
Yellow Mask. E. Wallace; Traitor's Gate

LACOMBE, GEORGES
Le Dernier des Six. A. Steeman; Six Dead Men
Midnight in Paris. G. Simenon; Monsieur la Souris

LAEMMLE, EDWARD
Cheating Cheaters. M. Marcin
Thirteenth Juror. F. T. Hill

LAMAC, KARL/KAREL
Der Zinker. E. Wallace; Squeaker
Hound of the Baskervilles. A. C. Doyle
Sorcerer. E. Wallace; Ringer
They Met in the Dark. Anthony Gilbert; Vanishing Corpse

LAMBERT, HARRY
Down Under Donovan. E. Wallace

LAMONT, CHARLES
Abbott and Costello Meet Dr. Jekyll and Mr. Hyde. R. L. Stevenson; Strange Case of Dr. Jekyll and Mr. Hyde
Dark Hour. S. Gluck; Last Trap
Shot in the Dark. C. Orr; Dartmouth Murders

LAMPIN, GEORGES
Crime and Punishment. F. M. Dostoevskii

LANCASTER, BURT
Midnight Man. D. Anthony; Midnight Lady and the Mourning Man

LANDERS, LEW
Ghost That Walks Alone. R. Shattuck; Wedding Guest Sat on a Stone
Seven Keys to Baldpate. E. D. Biggers

LANDI, MARIO
Maigret a Pigalle. G. Simenon; Maigret in Montmartre

LANDIS, JOHN
Spies Like Us. G. McGill

LANFIELD, SIDNEY
Hound of the Baskervilles. A. C. Doyle
Lemon Drop Kid. D. Runyon; Bloodhounds of Broadway

LANG, FRITZ
Big Heat. W. P. McGivern
Dr. Mabuse, Gambler. N. Jacques; Dr. Mabuse, Master of Mystery
House by the River. A. P. Herbert
Man Hunt. G. Household; Rogue Male
Ministry of Fear. G. Greene
Moontide. Willard Robertson
Secret Beyond the Door. Rufus King; Museum Piece No. 13
Spy. T. Von Harbau
While the City Sleeps. C. Einstein; Bloody Spur
Woman in the Window. J. H. Wallis; Once Off Guard

LANG, WALTER
But Not for Me. E. Ronns
Golden Web. E. P. Oppenheim
Money to Burn. R. W. Kauffman

LANGMAN, CHRIS
Reunion. K. Leopold; When We Ran

LANGTON, SIMON
Whistle Blower. J. Hale

LARSEN, VIGGO
Arsene Lupin vs. Sherlock Holmes. M. Leblanc; Arsene Lupin vs. Holmlock Shears
Grey Lady. A. C. Doyle; Hound of the Baskervilles

LASCELLE, WARD
Mind Over Motor. M. R. Rinehart; Book of Tish

LAUGHLIN, FRANK
Trial of Billy Jack. H. Liebling

LAUGHTON, CHARLES
Night of the Hunter. D. Grubb

LAUTNER, GEORGES
Icy Breasts. R. Matheson; Someone Is Bleeding
Professional. P. Alexander; Death of a Thin-Skinned Animal
Seventh Juror. F. Didelot

LAVEN, ARNOLD
Down Three Dark Streets. Gordons; Case File: FBI
Vice Squad. L. T. White; Harness Bull

LAW, MICHAEL
Six Men. E. Radford

LAWRENCE, EDMUND
House of Secrets. S. Horler

LAWRENCE, QUENTIN
Man Who Finally Died. John Burke
Playback. E. Wallace (headnote)
We Shall See. E. Wallace

LAZAR, LAJOS
Ghost Train. A. Ridley

LAZARUS, ASHLEY
Golden Rendezvous. A. MacLean

LEACOCK, PHILIP
Let No Man Write My Epitaph. W. Motley
13 West Street. L. Brackett; Tiger Among Us

LEBORG, REGINALD
Deadly Duo. R. Jessup
Flanagan. M. Catto
Weird Woman. F. Leiber, Jr.; Conjure Wife

LECONTE, PATRICE
M. Hire. G. Simenon; Mr. Hire's Engagement

LEDERMAN, D. ROSS
Passage from Hong Kong. E. D. Biggers; Agony Column
Return of the Whistler. W. Irish; Eyes That Watch You
Shadows on the Stairs. F. Vosper; Murder on the Second Floor

LEE, JACK
Robbery Under Arms. R. Boldrewood
Turn the Key Softly. J. Brophy

LEE, JOE
Courier. Gerald Cole

LEE, NORMAN
Bulldog Drummond at Bay. H. C. McNeile
Door with Seven Locks. E. Wallace
Mr. Reeder in Room 13. E. Wallace; Room 13
Monkey's Paw. W. W. Jacobs; Lady of the Barge
No Exit. G. Goodchild

LEE, ROWLAND V.
Love from a Stranger. F. Vosper
Man of Zanzibar. R. H. Davis; Lost Road
Mysterious Dr. Fu Manchu. S. Rohmer; Mystery of Dr. Fu-Manchu
Return of Dr. Fu Manchu. S. Rohmer; Devil Doctor
Sign of the Four. A. C. Doyle

LEEDS, HERBERT I.
Blue, White and Perfect. Borden Chase; Diamonds of Death
It Shouldn't Happen to a Dog. E. Lanham
Man Who Wouldn't Die. C. Rawson; No Coffin for the Corpse
Mr. Moto in Danger Island. J. W. Vandercook; Murder in Trinidad
Time to Kill. R. Chandler; High Window

LE FRANE, GUY
Keep Talking, Baby. D. Keene; Strange Witness

LEHRMAN, HENRY
Fighting Edge. W. M. Raine

LEIGH, J. L. V.
Pallard the Punter. E. Wallace; Grey Timothy

LEISEN, MITCHELL
Captain Carey, U.S.A. M. Albrand; After Midnight
Death Takes a Holiday. W. Ferris
Four Hours to Kill. N. Krasna; Small Miracle
Golden Earrings. Y. Foldes
No Man of Her Own. W. Irish; I Married a Dead Man

LELAND, DAVID
Crossing the Line. W. McIlvanney; Big Man

LEMORANDE, RUSTY
Turn of the Screw. Henry James

LENI, PAUL
Cat and the Canary. J. Willard
Chinese Parrot. E. D. Biggers
Last Warning. W. Camp; House of Fear

LEONARD, ROBERT Z.
  Piccadilly Jim. P. G. Wodehouse
LEONE, SERGIO
  Once Upon a Time in America. H. Grey; Hoods
LERNER, JOSEPH
  Guilty Bystander. Wade Miller
LERNER, PETER
  Edge of Fury. R. M. Coates; Wisteria Cottage
LEROY, MERVYN
  Any Number Can Play. E. H. Heth
  Bad Seed. M. Anderson
  Escape. E. Vance
  Five Star Final. L. Weitzenkorn
  Gentleman's Fate. K. U. P.
  Home Before Dark. E. Bassing
  Little Caesar. W. R. Burnett
  Moment to Moment. A. Coppel
  They Won't Forget. W. Greene; Death in the Deep South
LEROY, SERGE
  Attention, the Kids Are Watching. P. L. Dixon; Children Are Watching
  Passengers. K. R. Dwyer; Chase
LE SAINT, EDWARD J.
  Brooding Eyes. J. Goodwin; Paid in Full
  Circular Staircase. M. R. Rinehart
  Lord John in New York. C. N. Williamson
  More to Be Pitied Than Scorned. C. E. Blaney
  Three Keys. F. Ormond
LESIEWICZ, WITOLD
  Lord Arthur Saville's Crime. O. Wilde
  Terrifying Bed. W. Collins; After Dark
LESSEY, GEORGE A.
  Eagle's Eye. W. J. Flynn
  Strange Disappearance. A. K. Green
LESTER, MARK L.
  Firestarter. Stephen King
LESTER, RICHARD
  Finders Keepers. C. Dennis; Next-to-Last Train Ride
  Juggernaut. A. Hine
LEVERING, JOSEPH
  Defenders of the Law. H. Del Ruth
LEVEY, WILLIAM A.
  Committed. S. Claudia; Clock and Bell
LEVIN, HENRY
  Ambushers. D. Hamilton
  Convicted. M. Flavin; Criminal Code
  Corpse Came C.O.D. J. Starr
  Murderer's Row. D. Hamilton
  That Man Bolt. P. Crowcraft
LEVINSON, BARRY
  Young Sherlock Holmes. A. Arnold
LEVY, BENN W.
  Lord Camber's Ladies. H. A. Vachell; Case of Lady Camber
LEVY, RAOUL
  Defector. P. Thomas; Spy
LEWIS, EDGAR
  Beggar in Purple. A. Soutar
  Gun-Runner. A. Stringer
  Other Men's Shoes. A. Soutar
LEWIS, HERSHELL GORDON
  Blood Feast. L. E. Murphy
  Color Me Blood Red. H. G. Lewis
  Moonshine Mountain. C. Glore
LEWIS, JAY
  Live Now, Pay Later. J. T. Story
LEWIS, JERRY
  One More Time. M. Avallone
LEWIS, JOSEPH H.
  Deadly Is the Female. M. Kantor; Author's Choice
  Desperate Search. A. Mayse
  My Name Is Julia Ross. Anthony Gilbert; Woman in Red
L'HERBIER, MARCEL
  Mystery of the Yellow Room. G. Leroux
  Perfume of the Lady in Black. G. Leroux
LI, SHAOHONG
  Bloody Morning. G. G. Marquez; Chronicle of a Death Foretold
LIEBERMAN, JEFF
  Blue Sunshine. K. Johnson
LINCOLN, W. J.
  Called Back. H. Conway
  It Is Never Too Late to Mend. C. Reade
  Mystery of a Hansom Cab. F. Hume
LITTLE, DWIGHT H.
  Phantom of the Opera. G. Leroux
LITVAK, ANATOLE
  All This, and Heaven Too. Rachel Field
  Amazing Dr. Clitterhouse. B. Lyndon
  Decision Before Dawn. G. Howe; Call It Treason
  Lady in the Car with Glasses and a Gun. S. Japrisot
  Night of the Generals. H. H. Kirst
  Out of the Fog. I. Shaw; Gentle People
  Sorry Wrong Number. L. Fletcher
LIZZANI, CARLO
  Crazy Joe. M. Barone
LLOYD, FRANK
  East Lynn. H. Wood
  Madame X. J. W. MacConaughy
  Voice in the Dark. R. E. Dyar
  Within the Law. B. Veiller
LOMBARDO, LOU
  Russian Roulette. T. Ardies; Kosygin Is Coming
LONCRAINE, RICHARD
  Bellman & True. D. Lowden
  Julia. P. Straub
LONGFORD, RAYMOND
  Blue Mountains Mystery. H. Owen; Mount Marunga Mystery
LORD, JEAN CLAUDE
  Visiting Hours. K. Rembo
LORD, ROBERT
  Lion and the Mouse. A. Hornblow
LORING, THOMAS Z.
  Who Is Hope Schuyler? S. Ransome; Hearses Don't Hurry
LOSEY, JOSEPH
  Big Night. S. Ellin; Dreadful Summit
  Blind Date. Leigh Howard
  Damned. H. L. Lawrence; Children of Light
  Eva. J. H. Chase; Eve
  Gypsy and the Gentleman. N. W. Hooke; Darkness I Leave You
  Modesty Blaise. P. O'Donnell
  Secret Ceremony. M. Denevi
  Sleeping Tiger. M. Moisewitsch
  Time Without Pity. E. Williams; Someone Waiting
LUBIN, ARTHUR
  Footsteps in the Fog. W. W. Jacobs; Sea Whispers
  House of a Thousand Candles. M. Nicholson
  Phantom of the Opera. G. Leroux
  Who Killed Aunt Maggie? M. Field
LUCOQUE, H. LISLE
  Dawn. H. R. Haggard
  Tatterly. T. Gallon
LUKE, MONTE
  Seven Keys to Baldpate. E. D. Biggers
  Within the Law. B. Veiller
LUMET, SIDNEY
  Anderson Tapes. Lawrence Sanders
  Child's Play. R. Marasco
  Deadly Affair. J. Le Carre; Call for the Dead
  Deathtrap. I. Levin
  Dog Day Afternoon. P. Mann
  Fail-Safe. E. Burdick
  Family Business. V. Patrick
  Morning After. E. Lottman
  Murder on the Orient Express. A. Christie
  Offense. J. Hopkins; This Story of Yours
  Q&A. E. Torres
  Twelve Angry Men. R. Rose
  Verdict. B. C. Reed
LUND, O. A. C.
  Marked Woman. G. M. White
LYELL, LOTTIE
  Blue Mountains Murder. H. Owen; Mount Marunga Mystery
LYNCH, PAUL
  Cross-Country. H. D. Kastle
LYNN, JONATHAN
  Clue. M. McDowell
LYNN, ROBERT
  Coast of Skeletons. E. Wallace; Sanders of the River
  Two-Letter Alibi. A. Garve; Death and the Sky Above
MacARTHUR, CHARLES
  Crime Without Reason. B. Hecht; Collected Stories of Ben Hecht
McBRIDE, JIM
  Big Easy. J. Conaway
McCARTHY, MICHAEL
  Assassin for Hire. R. Rienits
MACDONALD, DAVID
  Dead Men Tell No Tales. F. Beeding; Norwich Victims
  Death Croons the Blues. J. Ronald
  Good Time Girl. A. La Bern; Night Darkens the Street
  Lady Mislaid. K. Horne
  Snowbound. H. Innes; Lonely Skier
  Spies of the Air. J. Dell; Official Secret
  Tread Softly. G. Verner; Show Must Go On
McDONALD, FRANK
  Bulldog Drummond Strikes Back. H. C. McNeile; Knock-Out
  Murder by an Aristocrat. M. G. Eberhart
  Murder of Dr. Harrington. M. G. Eberhart; From This Dark Stairway
  No Hands on the Clock. G. Homes
  Thirteen Lead Soldiers. H. C. McNeile; Sapper: The Best Short Stories
  Yukon Gold. J. O. Curwood; Gold Hunters
MacDONALD, J. FARRELL
  Black Sheep. E. Yates
  Mystery of Orcival. E. Gaboriau
MACDONALD, NORMAN
  Loudwater Mystery. E. Jepson
MacDONALD, SHERWOOD
  Cold Steel. G. C. Shedd; In the Shadow of the Hills
McDONNELL, FERGUS
  Small Voice. R. Westerby
McEVEETY, BERNARD
  Brotherhood of Satan. L. Q. Jones
MacFADDEN, HAMILTON
  Black Camel. E. D. Biggers
  Charlie Chan Carries On. E. D. Biggers
  Charlie Chan's Greatest Case. E. D. Biggers; House Without a Key
  Cheaters at Play. L. J. Vance; Lone Wolf's Son
  Elinor Norton. M. R. Rinehart; State vs. Elinor Norton
McGANN, WILLIAM
  Case of the Black Cat. E. S. Gardner; Case of the Caretaker's Cat

Murder on the Second Floor. F. Vosper
Sh! The Octopus. R. Spence; Gorilla
Two Against the World. L. Weitzenkorn; Five Star Final

McGILL, LAWRENCE
Arizona. A. Thomas
Crime and Punishment. F. M. Dostoevskii
First Law. G. Willets
Woman's Law. M. Thompson

McGOWAN, J. P.
Red Glove. D. Grant; Fifth Ace

McGRATH, JOE
Casino Royale. I. Fleming

McGUIRE, DENNIS
Shoot It: Black, Shoot It: Blue. P. Tyner; Shoot It

McKAY, JAMES
Queen's Evidence. L. Parr; Adam and Eve

MacKENNA, KENNETH
Sleepers East. F. Nebel
Spider. F. Oursler

MACKENZIE, DONALD
Carter Case. A. B. Reeve (headnote)
Ticket-of-Leave Man. C. Reade; Foul Play

MACKENZIE, JOHN
Fourth Protocol. F. Forsyth
Honorary Consul. G. Greene
Long Good Friday. R. Claughton

McLAGLEN, ANDREW V.
Fool's Parade. D. Grubb
Man in the Vault. F. Gruber; Lock and the Key
North Sea Hijack. J. Davies; Esther, Ruth and Jennifer
Sea Wolves. J. Leasor; Boarding Party
Wild Geese. D. Carney

McLENNAN, DON
Slate, Wyn & Me. Georgia Savage; Slate and Wyn and Blanche McBride

McLEOD, NORMAN Z.
Miracle Man. F. Packard
Trial of Mary Dugan. B. Veiller

MacMAHON, CHARLES
For the Term of His Natural Life. Marcus Clarke; His Natural Life
Robbery Under Arms. R. Boldrewood

McNAUGHT, BOB
Grand National Night. D. Christie

MACRAE, ARTHUR
Silver Blaze. A. C. Doyle; Memoirs of Sherlock Holmes

MACRAE, DUNCAN
Auction Mart. S. Tremayne
Love and the Whirlwind. H. P. Lewis

MacRAE, HENRY
Cameron of the Mounted. R. Connor; Corporal Cameron

McTIERNAN, JOHN
Die Hard. R. Thorp; Nothing Lasts Forever
Hunt for Red October. T. Clancy
Predator. P. Monette

MACHATY, GUSTAV
Within the Law. B. Veiller

MACK, RUSSELL
Scandal for Sale. E. Gauvreau; Hot News

MAIGNE, CHARLES
In the Hollow of Her Hand. G. B. McCutcheon; Hollow of Her Hand

MAILER, NORMAN
Tough Guys Don't Dance. N. Mailer

MAINWARING, BERNARD
Jennifer Hale, R. Eden
Line Engaged. J. De Leon

MALDEN, KARL
Time Limit. H. Denker

MALINS, GEOFFREY H.
All the Winners. A. Applin; Wicked
Golden Web. E. P. Oppenheim; Plunderers
Greek Interpreter. A. C. Doyle; Memoirs of Sherlock Holmes

MALLE, LOUIS
Elevator to the Gallows. N. Calef; Frantic

MALMUTH, BRUCE
Where Are the Children? M. H. Clark

MAMBETY, DJIBRIL DIOP
Hyenas. F. Duerrenmatt; Visit

MAMET, DAVID
House of Games. D. Mamet

MAMOULIAN, ROUBEN
Dr. Jekyll and Mr. Hyde. R. L. Stevenson; Strange Case of Dr. Jekyll and Mr. Hyde

MANKIEWICZ, JOSEPH L.
Dragonwyck. A. Seton
Escape. J. Galsworthy
Honey Pot. T. Sterling; Evil of the Day
House of Strangers. J. Weidman; I'll Never Go There Any More
Operation Cicero. L. C. Moyzisch
Quiet American. G. Greene
Sleuth. A. Shaffer

MANN, ANTHONY
Dandy in Aspic. D. Marlowe
Naked Spur. A. Ullman
Serenade. J. M. Cain
Two O'Clock Courage. G. Burgess

MANN, DANIEL
Journey Into Fear. E. Ambler
Our Man Flint. J. Pearl
Willard. S. Gilbert; Ratman's Notebooks

MANN, DELBERT
Fitzwilly. Poyntz Tyler; Garden of Cucumbers
Pink Jungle. A. Williams; Snake Water

MANN, MICHAEL
Keep. F. P. Wilson
Manhunter. T. Harris; Red Dragon

MANNING, MICHELLE
Blue City. K. Millar

MARCH, ALEX
Big Bounce. E. Leonard

MARCIN, MAX
Shadow of the Law. J. Moroso; Quarry

MARGOLIN, STUART
Glitter Dome. J. Wambaugh

MARIN, EDWIN L.
Avenger. J. Goodwin
Bombay Mail. L. G. Blochman
Casino Murder Case. S. S. Van Dine
Death Kiss. M. St. Dennis
Fast and Loose. M. Page; Fast Company
Garden Murder Case. S. S. Van Dine
Gentleman After Dark. R. W. Child; Velvet Black
Johnny Angel. C. G. Booth; Mr. Angel Comes Aboard
Maisie. W. Collison; Dark Dame
Mr. Ace. H. Christy
Pursuit. L. G. Blochman
Society Lawyer. A. S. Roche; Penthouse
Study in Scarlet. A. C. Doyle

MARIO, PETER
Diplomatic Immunity. Theodore Taylor; Stalker

MARION, GEORGE F.
Madame X. J. W. MacConaughy

MARKHAM, MANSFIELD
Return of Raffles. E. W. Hornung (headnote)

MARKLE, FLETCHER
Man with a Cloak. J. D. Carr; Third Bullet

MARQUAND, RICHARD
Eye of the Needle. K. Follett; Storm Island

MARSHAK, PHILIP
Dracula Sucks. B. Stoker; Dracula

MARSHALL, GEORGE E.
Blue Dahlia. R. Chandler
Gazebo. A. Coppel
Happy Thieves. R. Condon; Oldest Confession
Hazard. R. Chanslor
Lady from Long Acre. V. Bridges
Love Under Fire. W. Hackett; Fugitives
Nancy Steele Is Missing. C. F. Coe; Ransom
Ruth of the Rockies. J. McCulley; Broadway Bab

MARSTON, LAWRENCE
East Lynne. H. Wood
Girl by the Roadside. V. Vanardy
Millionaire Baby. A. K. Green
Mortmain. A. Train
Quarry. J. A. Moroso
Woman in Black. W. Spence

MARSTON, THEODORE
Aurora Floyd. M. E. Braddon
Surprises of an Empty Hotel. A. C. Gunter

MARTIN, PAUL
Orient Express. G. Greene; Stamboul Train

MARTINEK, H. O.
First Chronicle of Don Q. K. Prichard; Chronicles of Don Q

MARTINSON, LESLIE H.
Batman. W. Lyon
Fathom. L. Forrester; Girl Called Fathom
Hot Rod Rumble. M. Dolinsky; Hot Rod Gang Rumble
Mrs. Pollifax, Spy. D. Gilman; Unexpected Mrs. Pollifax

MARTON, ANDREW
Devil Makes Three. L. P. Bachmann; Kiss of Death
Secret of Stamboul. D. Wheatley; Eunich of Stamboul

MASELLI, FRANCESCO
Fine Pair. C. Stratton

MASON, HERBERT
His Lordship. N. Grant; Nelson Touch
Night Invader. J. Bentley; Rendezvous with Death
Once a Crook. E. Price
Strange Boarders. E. P. Oppenheim; Strange Boarders of Palace Crescent

MATALAN, EDDY
Too Small, My Friend. J. H. Chase; Way the Cookie Crumbles

MATE, RUDOLPH
Dark Past. J. Warwick; Blind Alley
Port Afrique. B. V. Dryer
Union Station. T. Walsh; Nightmare in Manhattan

MATHOT, LEON
Cheri-Bibi. G. Leroux

MATTSON, ARNE
Black Sun. P. Wahloo; Lorry

MAUDE, ARTHUR
Clue of the New Pin. E. Wallace
Flying Squad. E. Wallace
Lure. C. Cavendish
Lyons Mail. E. Moreau; Courier of Lyons
Ringer. E. Wallace

MAXWELL, PETER
Desperate Man. P. Somers; Beginner's Luck
Switch. P. Ridgeway

MAY, ELAINE
New Leaf. J. Ritchie

MAY, JOE
House of Fear. W. Camp

MAYLAM, TONY
   Riddle of the Sands. E. Childers

MAYO, ARCHIE L.
   Case of the Lucky Legs. E. S. Gardner
   Crimson City. A. Coldeway
   Man with Two Faces. A. Woollcott; Dark Tower
   Moontide. Willard Robertson
   Night In Casablanca. D. Ames
   On Trial. E. L. Reizenstein
   Petrified Forest. R. E. Sherwood

MEDAK, PETER
   Negatives. P. Everett

MEDFORD, DON
   Hunting Party. J. Millard

MEGAHY, FRANCIS
   Taffin. L. Mallet

MEINERT, RUDOLF
   Hound of the Baskervilles. A. C. Doyle

MEKAS, ADOLFAS
   Double-Barrelled Detective Story. M. Twain

MELFORD, GEORGE
   Eleventh Commandment. B. Fleming; Pillory
   Going Crooked. Winchell Smith
   Great Impersonation. E. P. Oppenheim
   Salomy Jane. Bret Harte; Stories in Light and Shadow
   Scarlet Weekend. W. Kent; Woman in Purple Pajamas
   Whispering Smith. F. H. Spearman

MELVILLE, JEAN-PIERRE
   Army of Shadows. J. Kessel
   Magnet of Doom. G. Simenon

MENDELUK, GEORGE
   Kidnapping of the President. C. Templeton
   Stone Cold Dead. H. Garner; Sin Sniper

MENDES, LOTHAR
   Interference. R. Pertwee
   Ladies' Man. Rupert Hughes
   Payment Deferred. J. Dell
   Prince of Tempters. E. P. Oppenheim; Ex-Duke
   Walls Came Tumbling Down. J. Eisinger

MENZIES, WILLIAM CAMERON
   Address Unknown. K. Taylor
   Almost Married. A. Soutar; Devil's Triangle
   Four Dark Hours. G. Greene (headnote)
   Spider. F. Oursler

MERCANTON, LOUIS
   Letter. W. S. Maugham

MEREDITH, BURGESS
   Man on the Eifel Tower. G. Simenon; Battle of Nerves

MERVALE, GASTON
   Colleen Bawn. D. Boucicault

MERWIN, BANNISTER
   Rogue in Love. T. Gallon

METZGER, RADLEY
   Cat and the Canary. J. Willard

MEYER, NICHOLAS
   Time After Time. K. Alexander

MICHEL, BERNARD T.
   Five Ashore for Singapore. J. Bruce; Cold Spell

MIDDLETON, GEORGE E.
   Double Cross Roads. W. Lipman; Yonder Grow the Daisies
   Woman Who Dared. A. M. Williamson

MIHALKA, GEORGE
   Office Party. M. A. Gilbert

MILES, CHRISTOPHER
   Maids. J. Genet

MILESTONE, LEWIS
   General Died at Dawn. C. G. Booth
   Ocean's 11. G. C. Johnson
   Racket. B. Cormack

MILFORD, GENE
   Pusher. E. McBain

MILIUS, JOHN
   Dillinger. H. Clement

MILLAND, RAY
   Flight of the Intruder. S. Coonts
   Hostile Witness. J. Roffey

MILLARDE, HARRY
   White Moll. F. Packard

MILLER, ASHLEY
   Affair of Three Nations. J. McIntyre (headnote)

MILLER, CHARLES
   High Speed. C. H. Stagg

MILLER, CLAUDE
   Deadly Circuit. M. Behm; Eye of the Beholder
   Inquisitor. J. Wainwright; Brainwash
   Tell Him I Love Him. P. Highsmith; This Sweet Sickness

MILLER, DAVID
   Hammerhead. J. Mayo
   Midnight Lace. J. Green; Matilda Shouted Fire
   Sudden Fear. E. Sherry

MILLER, FRANK
   Joyous Adventures of Aristide Pujol. W. J. Locke

MILLS, TOM/THOMAS R.
   Duds. H. C. Rowland
   Girl in His House. H. MacGrath

MILTON, MEYRICK
   Adventures of Captain Kettle. C. J. C. Hyne

MILTON, ROBERT
   Bella Donna. R. Hichens
   Dummy. H. J. O'Higgins

MINNELLI, VINCENTE
   Goodbye Charlie. M. H. Albert

MITCHELL, HOWARD M.
   Queenie. W. F. Fauley

MITCHELL, OSWALD
   Night Journey. J. Phelan; Ten-a-Penny People
   Temptress. A. Campbell; Juggernaut

MOCKY, JEAN-PIERRE
   Agent Trouble. M. Bosse; Man Who Liked Zoos
   It's Freezing in Hell. E. Chaze; Black Wings Has My Angel
   Kill the Referee. A. Draper; Death Penalty
   No Pockets in a Shroud. H. McCoy
   Red Ibis. Fredric Brown; Knock Three-One-Two
   Unsewing Machine. D. Keene; Killer Is Loose
   Witness. H. Judd; Shadow of a Doubt

MOGUY, LEONIDE
   Whistle Stop. M. M. Wolff

MOLINARO, EDOUARD
   Death of a Beauty. G. Simenon; Belle
   Ravishing Idiot. C. Exbrayat

MONTAGNE, EDWARD
   Man with My Face. S. W. Taylor

MONTALDO, GIULIANO
   Machine Gun McCain. O. Demaris; Candyleg

MONTGOMERY, ROBERT
   Lady in the Lake. R. Chandler
   Ride the Pink Horse. D. B. Hughes

MOORE, ROBERT
   Cheap Detective. R. Grossbach
   Murder by Death. H. Keating

MORA, PHILIPPE
   Howling II. G. Brandner
   Marsupials: The Howling III. G. Brandner; Howling III

MORAHAN, CHRISTOPHER
   Paper Mask. J. Collee

MORGAN, SIDNEY
   Bulldog Drummond's Third Round. H. C. McNeile; Third Round
   Lady Noggs—Peeress. E. Jepson
   Miriam Rozella. B. L. Farjeon
   What's Bred . . . Comes Out in the Flesh. G. Allen; What's Bred in the Bone
   Woman of the Iron Bracelets. F. Barrett

MORLEY, ROYSTON
   Attempt to Kill. E. Wallace; Lone House Mystery

MORRIS, ERROL
   Dark Wind. T. Hillerman

MORRISSEY, PAUL
   Hound of the Baskervilles. A. C. Doyle

MORROW, VIC
   Deathwatch. J. Genet; Maids and Deathwatch

MORSE, TERRY O.
   British Intelligence. A. P. Kelly; Three Faces East
   On Trial. E. L. Reizenstein
   Young Dillinger. S. Stuart

MORTIMER, EDMUND
   Exiles. R. H. Davis

MOSTAFA, HOSSAM EL DINE
   Sonya and the Madman. F. M. Dostoevskii; Crime and Punishment

MOXEY, JOHN
   Angel of Terror. E. Wallace
   Circus of Fear. E. Wallace (headnote)
   Death Trap. E. Wallace (headnote)
   Downfall. E. Wallace (headnote)
   Face of a Stranger. E. Wallace (headnote)
   Foxhole in Cairo. L. O. Mosley; Cat and the Mice
   20,000 Pound Kiss. E. Wallace (headnote)

MULCAHY, RUSSELL
   Razorback. P. Brennan

MULLIGAN, ROBERT
   Baby, the Rain Must Fall. H. Foote; Traveling Lady
   Bloodbrothers. R. Price
   Nickel Ride. M. T. Kaufman
   Other. T. Tryon
   To Kill a Mockingbird. H. Lee

MURNAU, FRIEDRICH WILHELM
   Nosferatu. B. Stoker; Dracula

MURPHY, RALPH
   Captain Blood, Fugitive. R. Sabatini; Chronicles of Captain Blood
   Man in Half Moon Street. B. Lyndon
   Menace. P. MacDonald; R.I.P.
   Night Club Scandal. D. N. Rubin; Riddle Me This!
   Notorious Sophie Lang. F. I. Anderson
   Partners in Crime. K. Steel; Murder Goes to College
   70,000 Witnesses. C. Fitzsimmons
   She Made Her Bed. J. M. Cain; Baby in the Icebox

MURRAY, BILL
   Quick Change. J. Cronley

MYERSON, ALAN
   Private Lessons. D. Greenberg; Philly
   Steelyard Blues. Timothy Harris

NADEL, ARTHUR
   Underground. C. Stratton

NARIZZANO, SILVIO
   Die! Die! My Darling. A. Blaisdell; Nightmare
   Loot. J. Orton

NASH, PERCY
   Jack Sheppard. J. B. Buckstone

NAZARRO, RAY
   Dog Eat Dog. R. Bloomfield (headnote)

NEAME, RONALD
   Chalk Garden. E. Bagnold
   Escape from Zahrein. M. Barrett; Appointment in Zahrein
   Gambit. K. Lane
   Golden Salamander. V. Canning
   Hopscotch. B. Garfield
   Mr. Moses. M. Catto; Mister Midas

Odessa File. F. Forsyth
Take My Life. Winston Graham

NEGULESCO, JEAN
Boy on a Dolphin. D. Divine
Conspirators. F. Prokosch
Invincible Six. M. Barrett; Heroes of Yuca
Mask of Dimitrios. E. Ambler
Nobody Lives Forever. W. R. Burnett
O. Henry's Full House. O. Henry (headnote)
Three Strangers. Alex Morrison

NEILAN, MARSHALL
Diplomacy. V. Sardou; Diplomates
River's End. J. O. Curwood

NEILL, ROY WILLIAM
Bandbox. L. J. Vance
Black Angel. C. Woolrich
Circus Queen Murder. A. Abbot; About the Murder of the Circus Queen
Doctor Syn. R. Thorndyke
Greater Than a Crown. V. Bridges; Lady from Long Acre
House of Fear. A. C. Doyle; Adventures of Sherlock Holmes
Lone Wolf Returns. L. J. Vance
Melody Man. H. J. Green
Menace. E. Wallace; Feathered Serpent
Ninth Guest. O. Davis
Pearl of Death. A. C. Doyle; Return of Sherlock Holmes
Pursuit to Algiers. A. C. Doyle; Return of Sherlock Holmes
Scarlet Claw. A. C. Doyle; Hound of the Baskervilles
Sherlock Holmes and the Secret Weapon. A. C. Doyle; Return of Sherlock Holmes
Sherlock Holmes and the Spider Woman. A. C. Doyle; Sign of the Four
Sherlock Holmes Faces Death. A. C. Doyle; Memoirs of Sherlock Holmes
Terror by Night. A. C. Doyle (headnote)
Thank Evans. E. Wallace; Good Evans!

NEILSON, JAMES
Dr. Syn Alias the Scarecrow. R. Thorndyke; Dr. Syn
Moon-Spinners. Mary Stewart

NELSON, GARY
Jimmy the Kid. D. E. Westlake

NELSON, RALPH
Once a Thief. J. Trinian; Scratch a Thief
Tick . . . Tick . . . Tick. P. Rock
Wilby Conspiracy. P. Driscoll
Wrath of God. J. Graham

NENOVA, NELLI
Srok Istekaet Na Rassvete. W. Irish; Deadline at Dawn

NETHERCOTT, GEOFFREY
Accidental Death. E. Wallace; Jack o' Judgment
Who Was Maddox? E. Wallace; Undisclosed Client

NEUMANN, KURT
Ellery Queen, Master Detective. E. Queen

NEWALL, GUY
Chinese Puzzle. M. Bower
Maid of the Silver Sea. J. Oxenham

NEWELL, MIKE
Awakening. B. Stoker; Jewel of the Seven Stars

NEWFIELD, SAM
Fighting Mad. L. Y. Erskine; Renfrew Rides Again
Murder Is My Business. B. Halliday

NEWLAND, JOHN
My Lover, My Son. E. Grierson; Reputation for a Song

NEWMAN, JOSEPH M.
Dangerous Crossing. J. D. Carr; Dead Sleep Lightly
Lucky Nick Cain. J. H. Chase; I'll Get You for This
Twenty Plus Two. F. Gruber

NEWMEYER, FRED
Lunatic at Large. J. S. Clouston
Seven Keys to Baldpate. E. D. Biggers
Too Many Crooks. E. J. Rath

NIBLO, FRED
Big Gamble. O. R. Cohen; Iron Chalice
Get-Rich-Quick-Wallingford. G. R. Chester
Officer 666. B. Currie
Strangers of the Night. W. Hackett; Captain Applejack

NICHOLL, GEORGE, JR.
Big Game. F. Wallace

NICHOLLS, GEORGE
East Lynne. H. Wood

NICHOLS, MIKE
Day of the Dolphin. R. Merle

NIGH, WILLIAM
Four Walls. D. Burnet
Ghost of John Holling. E. Wallace; Steward
Mr. Wu. L. J. Miln
Monte Carlo Nights. E. P. Oppenheim; Mr. Billingham, the Marquis and Madelon

NIXON, IVAN
Trouble Man. J. D. F. Black

NOBLE, JOHN W.
I Wouldn't Be in Your Shoes. W. Irish
Million a Minute. H. Douglas
Mysterious Mr. Wong. H. S. Keeler; Sing Sing Nights
One Million Dollars. A. Fredericks; One Million Francs
Thou Shalt Not Steal. E. Gaboriau; File No. 113

NOCITA, SALVATORE
Crime. G. Bernanos

NORMAN, LESLIE
Mix Me a Person. J. T. Story
Too Dangerous to Live. D. Hume

NORTH, WILFRED
Blue Envelope Mystery. S. Kerr; Blue Envelope

NORTHCOTE, SIDNEY
Monkey's Paw. W. W. Jacobs; Lady of the Barge

NOTZ, THIERRY
Watchers II. D. R. Koontz; Watchers

NOY, WILFRED
Marriage Lines. J. S. Fletcher
Master of Men. E. P. Oppenheim
Master of Merripit. E. Phillpotts
Night and Morning. E. Bulwer-Lytton
Temptation of Carlton Earle. S. M. During
Under the Red Robe. S. J. Weyman
Verdict of the Heart. C. Garvice

NOYCE, PHILLIP
Dead Calm. C. Williams
Heatwave. Timothy Harris
Patriot Games. T. Clancy

NUGENT, ELLIOTT
Cat and the Canary. J. Willard
Whistling in the Dark. L. Gross

NUNEZ, VICTOR
Flash of Green. J. D. MacDonald

O'BANNON, DAN
Return of the Living Dead. J. Russo

OBER, ROBERT
Woman Racket. P. Dunning; Night Hostess

O'BRIEN, EDMUND
Man-Trap. J. D. MacDonald; Soft Touch
Shield for Murder. W. P. McGivern

O'BRIEN, JOHN B.
Bishop's Emeralds. H. Townley

OBROW, JEFFREY
Servants of Twilight. L. Nichols; Twilight

O'CONNOR, FRANK
Spangles. N. Revell

O'DONOVAN, FRED
Knocknagow. C. Kickham

OERNBAK, HENNING
Nothing But the Truth. P. Orum

O'FERRALL, GEORGE MORE
Green Scarf. G. Des Cars; Brute
Heart of the Matter. G. Greene

O'HARA, GERRY
Amsterdam Affair. N. Freeling; Love in Amsterdam
Bitch. Jackie Collins
Game for Three Losers. E. Lustgarten
Maroc 7. M. Sands

OHLSSON, TERRY
Scobie Malone. J. Cleary; Helga's Web

OKAMOTO, KIHACHI
Ah Bakudan. W. Irish; Dead Man Blues

OLCOTT, SIDNEY
After Dark. D. Boucicault
Amateur Gentleman. J. Farnol
Colleen Bawn. D. Boucicault
Octoroon. D. Boucicault
Ranson's Folly. R. H. Davis

O'NEIL, BARRY
Gamblers. C. Klein
Lion and the Mouse. A. Hornblow
Third Degree. A. Hornblow

OPHULS, MARCEL
Banana Peel. C. Williams; Nothing in the Way

OPULS, MAX
Reckless Moment. E. S. Holding; Blank Wall

ORLOV, ALEXANDER
Strange Case of Dr. Jekyll and Mr. Hyde. R. L. Stevenson

ORTON, JOE
Celestial City. B. Orczy

ORTON, JOHN
Creeping Shadows. W. Scott; Man

OSIECKI, STEFAN
No Way Back. T. Burke; Limehouse Nights

OSWALD, GERD
Kiss Before Dying. I. Levin
Screaming Mimi. Fredric Brown

OSWALD, RICHARD
Hound of the Baskervilles. A. C. Doyle

OTTO, HENRY
Haunted Bell. J. Futrelle; Diamond Master
Island of Intrigue. I. Ostrander
Man from Nowhere. V. Bridges

OZEP, FYODOR
Brothers Karamazov. F. M. Dostoevskii
Whispering City. Horace Brown

PABST, G. L.
Joyless Street. H. Bettauer; Viennese Love

PAGE, ANTHONY
Lady Vanishes. E. L. White; Wheel Spins

PAGLIERO, MARCELLO
Cheri-Bibi. G. Leroux

PAKULA, ALAN J.
Klute. W. Johnston
Orphans. Lyle Kessler
Parallax View. L. Singer
Presumed Innocent. S. Turow

PALCY, EUZHAN
Dry White Season. A. Brink

PARIS, JERRY
Grasshopper. M. McShane; Passing of Evil
Never a Dull Moment. J. Godey; Thrill a Minute with Jack Albany

P

PARKE, WILLIAM
Other People's Money. E. Gaboriau
Paliser Case. E. Saltus
Yellow Ticket. V. Morton

PARKER, ALAN
Angel Heart. W. Hjortsberg; Falling Angel

PARKER, ALBERT
Arizona. A. Thomas
Murder in the Family. J. Ronald
Riverside Murder. A. Steeman; Six Dead Men
Sherlock Holmes. W. Gillette
Third Clue. N. Gordon; Shakespeare Murders

PARKINSON, H. B.
Bleak House. C. Dickens
East Lynne. H. Wood
Trapped by the Mormons. Winifred Graham; Love Story of a Mormon

PARKS, GORDON
Learning Tree. G. Parks

PARKS, GORDON, JR.
Shaft. E. Tidyman
Shaft's Big Score. E. Tidyman
Super Fly. P. Fenty

PARRISH, ROBERT
Assignment—Paris. P. Gallico; Trial by Terror
Casino Royale. I. Fleming
Destructors. M. Franklin
Duffy. H. J. Brown, Jr.
Mob. F. Findley; Waterfront
Rough Shoot. G. Household

PARRY, GORDON
Front Page Story. R. Gaines; Final Night
Midnight Episode. G. Simenon; Monsieur la Souris
Now Barabbas. W. D. Home
Surgeon's Knife. A. Hocking; Wicked Flee
Third Time Lucky. G. Butler; They Cracked Her Glass Slipper
Tread Softly Stranger. J. Popplewell; Blind Alley
Women of Twilight. S. Rayman

PASSER, IVAN
Ace Up Your Sleeve. J. H. Chase; Ace Up My Sleeve
Born to Win. M. Roote
Cutter and Bone. N. Thornburg
Haunted Summer. A. Edwards
Silver Bears. P. E. Erdman

PATON, STUART
Black Bag. L. J. Vance
Conflict. C. B. Kelland
Elusive Isabel. J. Futrelle
Girl in the Dark. C. E. Walk; Green Seal
One Wonderful Night. L. Tracy
Scarlet Car. R. H. Davis
Voice on the Wire. E. H. Ball
Wanted at Headquarters. E. Wallace (headnote)
Wolf Hunters. J. O. Curwood

PAUL, FRED
House on the Marsh. F. Warden
Lyons Mail. E. Moreau; Courier of Lyons
Money Moon. J. Farnol
Mord Em'ly. W. P. Ridge
Still Waters Run Deep. T. Taylor

PEARCE, A. LESLIE
Fall Guy. G. Abbott

PEARSON, GEORGE
Ace of Spades. J. C. Fraser
Huntingtower. J. Buchan
Pointing Finger. Rita
Shot in the Dark. G. Fairlie
Study in Scarlet. A. C. Doyle
Third String. W. W. Jacobs; Odd Craft
True Story of the Lyons Mail. E. Moreau; Courier of Lyons

PECKINPAH, SAM
Getaway. J. Thompson
Killer Elite. R. Rostand
Osterman Weekend. R. Ludlum
Straw Dogs. G. M. Williams; Siege of Trencher's Farm

PEDELTY, DONOVAN
False Evidence. R. Vickers; I'll Never Tell

PEERCE, LARRY
Incident. M. Avallone
Two Minute Warning. G. La Fountaine

PELISSIER, ANTHONY
Night Without Stars. Winston Graham
Personal Affair. L. Storm; Day's Mischief

PEMBROKE, SCOTT
Black Pearl. W. Woodrow
Sisters of Eve. E. P. Oppenheim; Temptation of Tavernake

PENN, ARTHUR
Bonnie and Clyde. B. Hirschfeld
Chase. H. Foote
Night Moves. A. Sharp
Target. S. Hunter

PERIER, ETIENNE
Meurtre en 45 Tours. P. Boileau; Heart to Heart
When Eight Bells Toll. A. MacLean

PERRET, LEONCE
Silent Master. E. P. Oppenheim; Seeing Life
Thirteenth Chair. B. Veiller
Twin Pawns. W. Collins; Woman in White

PERRY, FRANK
Compromising Positions. S. Isaacs

PERRY, SIMON
Eclipse. N. Wollaston

PETERSEN, WOLFGANG
Shattered. R. Neely; Plastic Nightmare

PETERSON, KRIS
Change of Mind. C. Stratton

PETIT, CHRISTOPHER
Unsuitable Job for a Woman. P. D. James

PETRI, ELIO
Quiet Place in the Country. H. Clement
Tenth Victim. R. Sheckley
We Still Kill the Old Way. L. Sciascia; Man's Blessing

PETRIE, DANIEL
Fort Apache, the Bronx. H. Gould
Main Attraction. S. Michaels
Moon of the Wolf. L. Whitten
Spy with a Cold Nose. R. Galton

PETRIE, DANIEL, JR.
Toy Soldiers. W. P. Kennedy

PEVNEY, JOSEPH
Back to God's Country. J. O. Curwood
Portrait of a Mobster. H. Grey
Six Bridges to Cross. J. F. Dinneen; Anatomy of a Crime
Strange Door. R. L. Stevenson; New Arabian Nights

PHYSIOC, WRAY
Blonde Vampire. D. Mooers

PICHEL, IRVING
Before Dawn. E. Wallace; Sergeant Sir Peter
Most Dangerous Game. R. Connell; Variety
Temptation. R. Hichens; Bella Donna
They Won't Believe Me. G. McDonell

PIDDINGTON, ANDREW
Shuttlecock. G. Swift

PIERCE, DOUGLAS
Delavine Affair. R. Chapman; Winter Wears a Shroud

PIERSON, FRANK R.
Looking Glass War. J. Le Carre

PIETERS, VIVIAN
Prey. C. Aird; Henrietta Who

PILSBURY, SAM
Scarecrow. R. H. Morrieson

PINOTEAU, CLAUDE
Big Operation. R. Airth; Snatch
Le Silencieux. F. Ryck; Loaded Gun

PIRES, GERARD
Act of Aggression. J. Buell; Shrewsdale Exit
Fantasia Among the Squares. C. Williams; Diamond Bikini
Undertaker Parlor Computer. W. Kempley; Probability Factor

PIRIEV, IVAN
Brothers Karamazov. F. M. Dostoevskii

PLAISSETTY, RENE
Yellow Claw. S. Rohmer

PLAYTER, WELLINGTON
Eagle's Eye. W. J. Flynn

PLUMB, HAY
George Barnwell, the London Apprentice. G. Lillo; London Merchant

POHLAND, HANSJURGEN
Tamara. Hansjorg Martin; Sleeping Girls Don't Lie

POITIER, SIDNEY
Hanky Panky. L. Jarreau

POITRENAUD, JACQUES
Old Tin Can. D. Keene; Flight by Night

POLANSKI, ROMAN
Chinatown. R. Towne
Rosemary's Baby. I. Levin
Tenant. R. Topor

POLLACK, BARRY
Cool Breeze. W. R. Burnett; Asphalt Jungle

POLLACK, SYDNEY
Slender Threat. S. Silliphant
They Shoot Horses, Don't They? H. McCoy
Three Days of the Condor. J. Grady; Six Days of the Condor
Yakuza. L. Schrader

POLLARD, HARRY
Reckless Age. E. D. Biggers; Love Insurance

POLLOCK, GEORGE
Murder at the Gallop. A. Christie; After the Funeral
Murder, She Said. A. Christie; 4.50 from Paddington
Rooney. C. Cookson
Stranger in Town. F. A. Chittenden; Uninvited
Ten Little Indians. A. Christie; Ten Little Niggers

POLONSKY, ABRAHAM
Force of Evil. I. Wolfert; Tucker's People

POMEROY, JOHN
Dublin Nightmare. P. Loraine

POMEROY, ROY J.
Inside the Lines. E. D. Biggers
Interference. R. Pertwee

PONTECORVO, GILLO
Burn. N. Gant

PORTER, EDWIN S.
Bella Donna. R. Hichens
Gallagher. R. H. Davis
Gentleman Burglar. M. Leblanc (headnote)
Her First Appearance. R. H. Davis; Van Bibber and Others
In the Bishop's Carriage. M. Michelson
Luck of Roaring Camp. Bret Harte; Bret Harte's Choice Bits
Ranson's Folly. R. H. Davis
Winning of Miss Langton. R. H. Davis; Once Upon a Time

POST, TED
Good Guys Wear Black. M. Franklin
Magnum Force. M. Valley

POTTER, DENNIS
  Secret Friends. D. Potter; Ticket to Ride
POTTIER, RICHARD
  Majestic Hotel Cellars. G. Simenon; Maigret and the Hotel Majestic
  Picpus. G. Simenon; To Any Lengths
POWELL, FRANK
  Dazzling Miss Davison. F. Warden
  From the Valley of the Missing. G. M. White
  Mrs. Balfame. G. Atherton
  Stain. F. Halsey
POWELL, MICHAEL
  Brown Wallet. S. Aumonier; Miss Bracegirdle and others
  Crown v. Stevens. L. Meynell; Third Time Unlucky
  Elusive Pimpernel. B. Orczy
  Her Last Affair. W. W. Ellis; S.O.S.
  Man Behind the Mask. J. Futrelle; Chase of the Golden Plate
  Phantom Light. E. Price; Haunted Light
  Rasp. P. MacDonald
  Rynox. P. MacDonald
  Small Back Room. N. Balchin
  Spy in Black. J. S. Clouston
POWELL, PAUL
  Dangerous Lies. E. P. Oppenheim (headnote)
  Mystery Road. E. P. Oppenheim
PREMINGER, OTTO
  Anatomy of a Murder. R. Traver
  Bunny Lake Is Missing. E. Piper
  Fallen Angel. M. Holland
  Human Factor. G. Greene
  Laura. V. Caspary
  Margin for Error. C. Booth
  Rosebud. J. Hemingway
  Where the Sidewalk Ends. W. L. Stuart; Night Cry
  Whirlpool. G. Endore; Methinks the Lady—
PRESSBURGER, EMERIC
  Elusive Pimpernel. B. Orczy
  Small Back Room. N. Balchin
PRESSMAN, MICHAEL
  Boulevard Nights. D. Gram
  Some Kind of Hero. J. Kirkwood
PULAJA, GENNADY
  Srok Istekaet Na Rassvete. W. Irish; Deadline at Dawn
QUESTED, JOHN
  Loophole. R. Pollock
QUINE, RICHARD
  Moonshine War. E. Leonard
  Notorious Landlady. I. Shulman
  Pushover. B. Ballinger; Rafferty
QUINTANO, GENE
  Why Me? D. E. Westlake
QUIRIBET, GASTON
  Mr. Justice Raffles. E. W. Hornung
RABENALT, ARTHUR MARIA
  Alraune. H. H. Ewers
RADEMAKERS, FONS
  Because of the Cats. N. Freeling
RAFELSON, BOB
  Postman Always Rings Twice. J. M. Cain
RAINER, BOB
  Misery. Stephen King
RAKOFF, ALVIN
  Dirty Tricks. T. Gifford; Glendower Legacy
  World in My Pocket. J. H. Chase
RAPPENEAU, ELIZABETH
  FM—Frequency Murder. S. M. Kaminsky; When Dark Man Calls
RAPPER, IRVING
  Another Man's Poison. L. Sands; Intent to Murder
  Bad for Each Other. H. McCoy; Scalpel
  Deception. E. Walter; Jealousy
  Strange Intruder. H. Fowler; Shades Will Not Vanish
RATHONY, AKOS
  Devil's Daffodil. E. Wallace; Daffodil Mystery
RATOFF, GREGORY
  Lancer Spy. M. McKenna
  Moss Rose. J. Shearing
  Wife, Husband and Friend. J. M. Cain; Career in C Major
RAWI, ONSAMA
  Judgement in Stone. R. Rendell
RAWLINS, JOHN
  Great Impersonation. E. P. Oppenheim
  Sherlock Holmes and the Voice of Terror. A. C. Doyle; His Last Bow
RAY, ALBERT
  Thirteenth Guest. A. Trail
  Whispering Wires. H. Leverage
RAY, NICHOLAS
  In a Lonely Place. D. B. Hughes
  Knock on Any Door. W. Motley
  On Dangerous Ground. G. Butler; Mad with Much Heart
  Party Girl. M. H. Albert
  Racket. B. Cormack
  They Live by Night. E. Anderson; Thieves Like Us
RAYMAKER, HERMAN
  Millionaires. E. P. Oppenheim; Inevitable Millionaires
RAYMOND, CHARLES
  Mystery of the Diamond Belt. Lewis Carlton
RAYMOND, JACK
  Blondes for Danger. E. Price; Red for Danger
  Frog. E. Wallace; Fellowship of the Frog
  Mind of Mr. J. G. Reeder. E. Wallace
  Missing People. E. Wallace; Mind of Mr. J. G. Reeder
  Rat. P. Bottome
  Sorry You've Been Troubled. W. Hackett
  Speckled Band. A. C. Doyle; Adventures of Sherlock Holmes
READE, CHARLES
  Ranson's Folly. R. H. Davis
READON, JAMES
  Shadow of Evil. C. Dawe
RED, ERIC
  Body Parts. P. Boileau; Choice Cuts
REED, CAROL
  Fallen Idol. G. Greene; Basement Room
  Girl in the News. R. Vickers
  Laburnum Grove. J. B. Priestley
  Odd Man Out. F. L. Green
  Our Man in Havana. G. Greene
  Running Man. S. Smith; Ballad of the Running Man
  Third Man. G. Greene
  Trapeze. M. Catto; Killing Frost
REED, LUTHER
  New York. B. Chambers
REED, ROLAND
  House of Secrets. S. Horler
REEVE, GEOFFREY
  Caravan to Vaccares. A. MacLean
  Puppet on a Chain. A. MacLean
REEVES, MICHAEL
  Witch-Finder General. R. Bassett
REICHER, FRANK
  Jeanne of the Marshes. E. P. Oppenheim
  Mr. Grex of Monte Carlo. E. P. Oppenheim
  Suspense. I. Ostrander
  Voice in the Fog. H. MacGrath
REICHERT, MARK
  Union City. C. Woolrich; Nightwebs
REID, ALASTAIR
  Something to Hide. N. Monsarrat
REINHARDT, GOTTFRIED
  Town Without Pity. M. Gregor
REINHARDT, JOHN
  Guilty. W. Irish; Dancing Detective
REINL, HARALD
  Der Falsher von London. E. Wallace; Forger
  Der Unheimliche Monch. E. Wallace; Terror
  Die Bande des Schreckens. E. Wallace; Terrible People
  Room 13. E. Wallace
REIS, IRVING
  Crack-Up. Fredric Brown; Madman's Holiday
  Falcon Takes Over. R. Chandler; Farewell, My Lovely
REISNER, CHARLES
  Man on the Box. H. MacGrath
REISZ, KAREL
  Night Must Fall. E. Williams
  Who'll Stop the Rain? R. Stone; Dog Soldiers
RELPH, MICHAEL
  Out of the Clouds. J. Fores; Springboard
RENOIR, JEAN
  Night at the Crossroads. G. Simenon; Crossroads Murder
  Woman on the Beach. M. A. Wilson; None So Blind
REYNOLDS, BURT
  Sharky's Machine. W. Diehl
  Stick. E. Leonard
REYNOLDS, LYNN
  Big Town Round-Up. W. M. Raine
  Huntress. H. Footner
RICH, DAVID LOWELL
  Concorde—Airport 1979. K. Stewart
  Madame X. J. W. MacConaughy
  That Man Bolt. P. Crowcraft
RICHARDS, DICK
  Farewell, My Lovely. R. Chandler
  Rafferty and the Gold Dust Twins. L. Roberts
RICHARDS, R. M.
  Heat. W. Goldman
RICHARDSON, FRANKLAND A.
  In the Night. J. Sutherland
RICHARDSON, RALPH
  Home at Seven. R. C. Sherriff
RICHARDSON, TONY
  Dead Cert. D. Francis
  Sanctuary. W. Faulkner
RICHERT, WILLIAM
  Winter Kills. R. Condon
RICKETTS, THOMAS
  Other Side of the Door. L. Chamberlain
  Secretary of Frivolous Affairs. M. Futrelle
RIDGELY, RICHARD
  Destroying Angel. L. J. Vance
  Eugene Aram. E. Bulwer-Lytton
  Heart of the Hills. D. Whitelaw; Girl from the East
  Mexican's Gratitude. O. Henry; Whirligigs
  Ranson's Folly. R. H. Davis
RIDGWELL, GEORGE
  Abbey Grange. A. C. Doyle; Return of Sherlock Holmes
  Amazing Partnership. E. P. Oppenheim
  Black Peter. A. C. Doyle; Return of Sherlock Holmes
  Blue Carbuncle. A. C. Doyle; Adventures of Sherlock Holmes
  Boscombe Valley Mystery. A. C. Doyle; Adventures of Sherlock Holmes

R

Bruce-Partington Plans. A. C. Doyle; His Last Bow
Cardboard Box. A. C. Doyle; His Last Bow
Charles Augustus Milverton. A. C. Doyle; Return of Sherlock Holmes
Crimson Circle. E. Wallace
Crooked Man. A. C. Doyle; Memoirs of Sherlock Holmes
Dancing Men. A. C. Doyle; Return of Sherlock Holmes
Engineer's Thumb. A. C. Doyle; Adventures of Sherlock Holmes
Final Problem. A. C. Doyle; Memoirs of Sherlock Holmes
Four Just Men. E. Wallace
Gamble in Lives. F. Stayton; Joan Danvers
Gloria Scott. A. C. Doyle; Memoirs of Sherlock Holmes
Golden Pince-Nez. A. C. Doyle; Return of Sherlock Holmes
Lady Frances Carfax. A. C. Doyle; His Last Bow
Last Bow. A. C. Doyle; His Last Bow
Lily of Killarney. D. Boucicault; Colleen Bawn
Lost Leader. E. P. Oppenheim
Mazarin Stone. A. C. Doyle; Casebook of Sherlock Holmes
Missing Three-Quarter. A. C. Doyle; Return of Sherlock Holmes
Missioner. E. P. Oppenheim
Musgrave Ritual. A. C. Doyle; Memoirs of Sherlock Holmes
Naval Treaty. A. C. Doyle; Memoirs of Sherlock Holmes
Norwood Builder. A. C. Doyle; Return of Sherlock Holmes
Notorious Mrs. Carrick. C. Procter; Pools of the Past
Pointing Finger. Rita
Red Circle. A. C. Doyle; His Last Bow
Reigate Squires. A. C. Doyle; Memoirs of Sherlock Holmes
Second Stain. A. C. Doyle; Return of Sherlock Holmes
Silver Blaze. A. C. Doyle; Memoirs of Sherlock Holmes
Six Napoleons. A. C. Doyle; Return of Sherlock Holmes
Speckled Band. A. C. Doyle; Adventures of Sherlock Holmes
Stock-Broker's Clerk. A. C. Doyle; Memoirs of Sherlock Holmes
Thor Bridge. A. C. Doyle; Casebook of Sherlock Holmes
Three Students. A. C. Doyle; Return of Sherlock Holmes

RIESNER, CHARLES
Murder Goes to College. K. Steel
Sophie Lang Goes West. E. Anderson; Notorious Sophie Lang

RILLA, WOLF
Cairo. W. R. Burnett; Asphalt Jungle
Noose for a Lady. G. Verner; Whispering Woman

RIPLEY, ARTHUR
Chase. C. Woolrich; Black Path of Fear

RITCHIE, MICHAEL
Fletch. G. McDonald
Prime Cut. M. Roote

RITT, MARTIN
Black Orchid. E. Ronns
Brotherhood. L. J. Carlino
Edge of the City. F. Pohl
Molly Maguires. J. O'Neill
No Down Payment. J. McPartland
Nuts. T. Topor
Spy Who Came in from the Cold. J. Le Carre

ROACH, HAL
Housekeeper's Daughter. D. H. Clarke

ROBBIE, SEYMOUR
CC and Company. M. Roote

ROBERTS, DEBORAH
Frankenstein General Hospital. M. W. Shelley; Frankenstein

ROBERTS, HARRY
Barton Mystery. W. Hackett

ROBERTS, STEPHEN
Night of June 13. F. Vreeland
Star of Midnight. A. S. Roche
Story of Temple Drake. W. Faulkner; Sanctuary

ROBERTS, YVES
Twin. D. E. Westlake; Two Much!

ROBERTSON, JOHN S.
Bottom of the Well. F. U. Adams
Captain of the Guard. C. Houghton
Crime Doctor. I. Zangwill; Big Bow Mystery
Dr. Jekyll and Mr. Hyde. R. L. Stevenson; Strange Case of Dr. Jekyll and Mr. Hyde
Perpetua. D. C. Calthrop
Phantom of Paris. G. Leroux; Cheri-Bibi and Cecily
Test of Honor. E. P. Oppenheim; Mr. Wingrave, Millionaire

ROBINSON, ARTHUR
Informer. L. O'Flaherty

ROBINSON, LEE
Stowaway. G. Simenon

ROBISON, ARTHUR
Trial of Mary Dugan. B. Veiller

ROBSON, MARK
Avalanche Express. C. Forbes
Daddy's Gone A-Hunting. Mike St. Clair
Edge of Doom. L. Brady
Hell Below Zero. H. Innes; White South
Prize. I. Wallace
Prize of Gold. M. Catto
Trial. D. M. Mankiewicz

RODDAM, FRANK
Bride. M. Shelley; Frankenstein

ROEG, NICHOLAS
Don't Look Now. D. Du Maurier; Not After Midnight
Nightmare Honeymoon. L. Block (headnote)

ROGE, ALBERT, II
Wrecker. A. Ridley

ROGELL, AL
Before I Die. H. Debrett
Butch Minds the Baby. D. Runyon; Guys and Dolls
Fog. V. Williams
Last Warning. J. Latimer; Dead Don't Care

ROGERS, MACLEAN
Crime at Blossoms. M. Shairp
Dark Secret. M. Shairp; Crime at Blossoms
Don Chicago. C. E. B. Roberts
Feathered Serpent. E. Wallace
Hammer the Toff. J. Creasey
Johnny on the Spot. M. Cronin; Paid in Full
Million Dollar Manhunt. L. Hardy; Requiem for a Redhead
Paul Temple Returns. F. Durbridge; Paul Temple Intervenes
Paul Temple's Triumph. F. Durbridge; News of Paul Temple
Salute the Toff. J. Creasey
Story of Shirley Yorke. H. A. Vachell; Case of Lady Camber
You Pay Your Money. M. Cronin

ROLAND, JURGEN
Der Grune Bogenschutze. E. Wallace; Green Archer
Die Rot Kreis. E. Wallace; Crimson Circle
Lotusblueten fur Miss Quon. J. H. Chase; Lotus for Miss Quon

ROLFE, ALFRED
Captain Starlight. R. Boldrewood; Robbery Under Arms

Life of Rufus Dawes. Marcus Clarke; His Natural Life

ROLFE, B. A.
Love Without Question. W. Camp; Abandoned Room

ROMERO, GEORGE A.
Night of the Living Dead. J. Russo

ROOKE, ARTHUR
Diamond Man. E. Wallace (headnote)
Double Life of Mr. Alfred Burton. E. P. Oppenheim
Eugene Aram. E. Bulwer-Lytton
God's Clay. A. Askew
Nets of Destiny. M. Drake; Salving of a Derelict

ROSE, BERNARD
Chicago Joe and the Showgirl. M. Gaynor

ROSEN, PHIL
Born to Gamble. E. Wallace; Forty-Eight Short Stories
Dangerous Corner. J. B. Priestley
Forbidden Territory. D. Wheatley
Jim Hanvey, Detective. O. R. Cohen
Mystery of Marie Roget. E. A. Poe; Tales
Phantom in the House. A. Soutar
President's Mystery. F. D. Roosevelt; President's Mystery Story
Woman in the Dark. D. Hammett
Worldly Goods. A. Soutar

ROSENBERG, STUART
Cool Hand Luke. Donn Pearce
Drowning Pool. J. R. Macdonald
Laughing Policeman. M. Sjowall
Love and Bullets. J. Heddon
Pope of Greenwich Village. V. Patrick

ROSENTHAL, RICK
Halloween II. J. Martin

ROSI, FRANCESCO
Chronicle of a Death Foretold. G. G. Marquez
Illustrious Corpse. L. Sciascia; Equal Danger

ROSMER, MILTON
Everything Is Thunder. J. L. Hardy

ROSS, HERBERT
Last of Sheila. A. Edwards
Seven-Per-Cent Solution. N. Meyer

ROSSEN, RICHARD
Island in the Sun. A. Waugh
Wizard. G. Leroux; Balaoo

ROTHA, PAUL
Cat and Mouse. M. Halliday
No Resting Place. I. Niall

ROUSE, RUSSELL
Caper of the Golden Bulls. W. P. McGivern
House of Numbers. J. Finney

ROUVE, PIERRE
Stranger in the House. G. Simenon; Strangers in the House

ROWLAND, ROY
Girl Hunters. M. Spillane
Rogue Cop. W. P. McGivern

ROZIER, WILLY
A Toi de Jouer Callaghan. P. Cheyney; Sorry You've Been Troubled
Callaghan Remet Ca. P. Cheyney (headnote)
Plus de Whisky pour Callaghan. P. Cheyney; It Couldn't Matter Less

RUANE, JOHN
Death in Brunswick. B. Oxlade

RUBEN, J. WALTER
Public Defender. G. Goodchild; Splendid Crime
Roadhouse Murder. M. Level (headnote)
Secret Service. W. Gillette
Suicide Club. R. L. Stevenson

RUBEN, JOSEPH
Sleeping with the Enemy. N. Price

RUDOLPH, ALAN
  Trouble in Mind. R. S. Coburn
RUGGLES, WESLEY H.
  Agony Column. E. D. Biggers
  Monkey's Paw. W. W. Jacobs; Lady of the Barge
  Piccadilly Jim. P. G. Wodehouse
  Remittance Woman. A. Abdullah
  Slippy McGee. M. C. Oemler
RUNZE, OTTOKAR
  Der Morder. G. Simenon; Murderer
RUSH, RICHARD
  Freebie and the Bean. P. B. Ross
  Stunt Man. P. Brodeur
RUSSELL, ALBERT
  Lion Man. R. Parrish; Strange Case of Cavendish
RUSSELL, KEN
  Billion Dollar Brain. L. Deighton
  Lair of the White Worm. B. Stoker
RUSSO, JOHN A.
  Midnight. J. Russo
SABINE, MARTIN
  Pursuing Vengeance. B. E. Stevenson; Mystery of the Boule Cabinet
SACHA, JEAN
  Fantomas. P. Souvestre
  This Man Is Dangerous. P. Cheyney
SAGAL, BORIS
  Twilight of Honor. A. Dewlin
ST. CLAIR, MALCOLM
  Canary Murder Case. S. S. Van Dine
  Over My Dead Body. J. D. O'Hanlon; As Good As Murdered
  Remote Control. C. North
  Side Street. Mal St. Clair
  Thin Ice. A. R. Colver; Dear Pretender
ST. JACQUES, RAYMOND
  Book of Numbers. R. D. Pharr
SALKOW, SIDNEY
  Bulldog Drummond at Bay. H. C. McNeile
  Four Days' Wonder. A. A. Milne
  Twice Told Tales. N. Hawthorne
SAMUELSON, G. B.
  Convict 99. M. C. Leighton
  Forger. E. Wallace
  Inquest. M. Barringer
  Valley of Ghosts. E. Wallace
  Wickham Mystery. J. McNally; Paper Chase
SANDERS, DENIS
  Crime and Punishment USA. F. M. Dostoevskii; Crime and Punishment
  Shock Treatment. W. Van Atta
SANDERSON, CHALLIS
  Scallywag. G. Allen
SANGSTER, JIMMY
  Horror of Frankenstein. M. Shelley; Frankenstein
SANTELL, AL(FRED)
  Gorilla. R. Spence
  Parisian Nights. R. Goyne
  Winterset. Maxwell Anderson
SANTLEY, JOSEPH
  Shadow of a Woman. V. Perdue; He Fell Down Dead
SANTONI, JOEL
  Died on a Rainy Sunday. Joan Aiken
SAPERSTEIN, DAVID
  Killing Affair. R. Houston; Monday, Tuesday, Wednesday
SARAFIAN, RICHARD C.
  Next Man. M. Z. Lewin
  Sunburn. S. Ellin; Bind
SARGENT, JOSEPH
  Taking of Pelham One Two Three. J. Godey

SARGER, MARTIN
  Code Name: Emerald. R. Bass; Emerald Illusion
SASDY, PETER
  Hands of the Ripper. E. S. Shew
  Nothing But the Night. J. Blackburn
SASLAVSKY, LUIS
  She Wolves. P. Boileau; Prisoner
  Snow Was Black. G. Simenon; Stain on the Snow
SAUER, FRED
  Adventure, Inc. A. Christie; Secret Adversary
SAUNDERS, CHARLES
  Behind the Headlines. R. Chapman
  Dangerous Afternoon. G. Anstruther
  Meet Mr. Callaghan. G. Verner
  Murder Reported. R. Chapman; Murder for the Million
  Narrowing Circle. J. Symons
  One Jump Ahead. R. Chapman
SAUTET, CLAUDE
  Arm at the Left. C. Williams; Aground
SAVILLE, VICTOR
  Calling Bulldog Drummond. G. Fairlie
  Conspirator. H. Slater
  Long Wait. M. Spillane
  W Plan. G. Seton
SAYTOR, TONY
  It Only Happens to the Living. R. Marshall; Things Men Do
SCARDON, PAUL
  Alibi. G. A. England
  Arsene Lupin. E. Jepson
  Gamblers. C. Klein
  Green God. F. A. Kummer
  Grell Mystery. F. Froest
  In the Balance. E. P. Oppenheim; Hillman
  Man Who Won. C. T. Brady
  Partners of the Night. L. Scott
SCHAFFNER, FRANKLIN J.
  Boys from Brazil. I. Levin
  Double Man. H. S. Maxfield; Legacy of a Spy
  Sphinx. R. Cook
SCHATZBERG, JERRY
  Panic in Needle Park. James Mills
SCHELL, MAXIMILIAN
  Murder on the Bridge. F. Duerrenmatt; Judge and His Hangman
SCHENKEL, CARL
  Mighty Quinn. A. H. Z. Carr; Finding Maubee
SCHEPSI, FRED
  Chant of Jimmie Blacksmith. T. Keneally
  Russia House. J. Le Carre
SCHERTZINGER, VICTOR
  Forgotten Faces. R. W. Child; Velvet Black
  Mr. Barnes of New York. A. C. Gunter
  Son of His Father. R. Cullum
SCHLESINGER, JOHN
  Believers. N. Conde; Religion
  Marathon Man. W. Goldman
SCHROEDER, BARBET
  Single White Female. J. Lutz; SWF Seeks Same
SCHROEDSACK, ERNEST B.
  Monkey's Paw. W. W. Jacobs; Lady of the Barge
  Most Dangerous Game. R. Connell; Variety
SCHROTH, CARL-HEINTZ
  Die Verschwundene Miniatur. E. Kastner; Missing Miniature
SCHULTZ, CARL
  Careful, He Might Hear You. S. L. Elliott
SCHWARTZ, HANS
  Return of the Scarlet Pimpernel. B. Orczy (headnote)

SCORSESE, MARTIN
  Cape Fear. J. D. MacDonald; Executioner
SCOTT, GEORGE C.
  Rage. P. Friedman
SCOTT, JAMES
  Strike It Rich. G. Greene; Loser Takes All
SCOTT, PETER GRAHAM
  Account Rendered. P. Barrington
  Big Chance. P. Barrington (headnote)
  Captain Clegg. R. Thorndyke; Dr. Syn
SCOTT, RIDLEY
  Black Rain. M. Cogan
  Blade Runner. P. K. Dick; Do Androids Dream of Electric Sheep?
SCOTT, TONY
  Beverly Hills Cop II. R. Tine
SEARLE, FRANCIS
  Murder at Site Three. W. H. Baker; Crime Is My Business
  Someone at the Door. D. Christie
SEARS, FRED F.
  Rumble on the Docks. F. Paley
SEASTROM, VICTOR
  Under the Red Robe. S. J. Weyman
SEATON, GEORGE
  Counterfeit Traitor. A. Klein
  36 Hours. C. K. Hittleman
SEAY, CHARLES M.
  Hard Cash. C. Reade
  It Is Never Too Late to Mend. C. Reade
  Sheep's Clothing. L. J. Vance
  Stanton's Last Fling. H. B. M. Watson; Ifs and Ans
SEDGWICK, EDWARD
  Death on the Diamond. C. Fitzsimmons
  Fantomas. P. Souvestre
  Father Brown, Detective. G. K. Chesterton; Wisdom of Father Brown
  Phantom of the Opera. G. Leroux
SEILER, LEWIS
  Great K&A Train Robbery. P. L. Ford
  Heart of the North. W. B. Mowery
  Square Crooks. J. P. Judge
SEITER, WILLIAM A.
  Broadway. P. Dunning
  Case Against Mrs. Ames. A. S. Roche
  Cheerful Fraud. K. R. G. Browne; Following Ann
  Love Racket. B. K. Burns; Jury Woman
  Mad Whirl. R. W. Child; Fresh Waters
  Make Haste to Live. Gordons
  Witching Hour. A. Thomas
SEITZ, GEORGE B.
  Drums of Jeopardy. H. MacGrath
  Exploits of Elaine. A. B. Reeve
  In Secret. R. W. Chambers
  Kind Lady. E. Chodorov
  Lion and the Lamb. E. P. Oppenheim
  Midnight Mystery. H. I. Young; Hawk Island
  Murder on the Roof. E. J. Doherty; Broadway Murders
  Romance of Elaine. A. B. Reeve
  Shadow of Doubt. A. S. Roche
  Thirteenth Chair. B. Veiller
SEKELY, STEVE
  Hollow Triumph. M. Forbes
SELANDER, LESLEY
  Desert Sands. J. Robb; Punitive Action
  I Was an American Spy. Claire Phillips; Manila Espionage
  Three's a Crowd. M. G. Eberhart; Hasty Wedding
SELLERS, OLLIE L.
  Gift Supreme. G. A. England

SELTZER, DAVID
  Shining Through. S. Isaacs
SELWYN, EDGAR
  Mystery of Mr. X. M. Porlock; X v. Rex
SEWELL, VERNON
  Floating Dutchman. N. Bentley
  Man in the Back Seat. E. Wallace (headnote)
  Soho Incident. R. Westerby; Wide Boys Never Work
  Uneasy Terms. P. Cheyney
SHANE, MAXWELL
  City Across the River. I. Shulman; Amboy Dukes
  Fear in the Night. W. Irish; I Wouldn't Be in Your Shoes
  Fear in the Night. C. Woolrich; Nightmare
  Nightmare. C. Woolrich
SHARP, DON
  Bear Island. A. MacLean
  Callan. J. Mitchell
  Fifth of November. M. Franklin
  Puppet on a Chain. A. MacLean
  Taste of Excitement. B. Healey; Waiting for a Tiger
  Thirty-Nine Steps. J. Buchan
  Violent Enemy. H. Marlowe; Candle for the Dead
SHARP, IAN
  Who Dares Wins. J. Follett; Tiptoe Boys
SHARP, PETE
  Dead Man's Float. Roger Carr
SHAVELSON, MELVILLE
  On the Double. Roger Fuller
  Pigeon That Took Rome. D. Downes; Easter Dinner
SHAW, HAROLD
  Bosun's Mate. W. W. Jacobs; Captains All
  False Evidence. E. P. Oppenheim
  Firm of Girdlestone. A. C. Doyle
  Incomparable Bellairs. A. Castle
  Lawyer Quince. W. W. Jacobs; Odd Craft
  Love and the Whirlwind. H. P. Lewis
  Mr. Lyndon at Liberty. V. Bridges
SHEAR, BARRY
  Across 110th. W. Ferris
SHERIN, EDWIN
  Valdez Is Coming. E. Leonard
SHERMAN, GARY A.
  Vice Squad. W. Rotsler
SHERMAN, GEORGE
  Enemy General. D. Pepper
  Hard Man. L. Katcher
  Lady and the Monster. C. Siodmak; Donovan's Brain
  Larceny. L. Eby; Velvet Fleece
  Panther's Moon. V. Canning
  Raging Tide. E. K. Gann; Fiddler's Green
  Reprisal. Arthur Gordon
  Scream in the Dark. J. Odlum; Morgue Is Always Open
SHERMAN, LOWELL
  Ladies of the Jury. F. Ballard
SHERMAN, VINCENT
  Fever in the Blood. W. Pearson
  Flight from Destiny. A. Berkeley; Trial and Error
  Nora Prentiss. Alex Morrison
  Unfaithful. W. S. Maugham; Letter
SHIRLEY, ARTHUR
  Mystery of a Hansom Cab. F. Hume
SHONTEFF, LINDSAY
  Spy Story. L. Deighton
  Sumuru. S. Rohmer; Slaves of Sumuru
SHUMLIN, HERMAN
  Confidential Agent. G. Greene
SIDNEY, GEORGE
  Red Danube. B. Marshall; Vespers in Vienna
  Scaramouche. R. Sabatini
  Who Was That Lady? N. Krasna; Who Was That Lady I Saw You With?
SIDNEY, SCOTT
  813. M. Leblanc
SIEGEL, DON
  Black Windmill. C. Egleton; Seven Days to a Killing
  Charley Varrick. J. Reese; Looters
  Dirty Harry. P. Rock
  Gun Runners. E. Hemingway; To Have and Have Not
  Killers. E. Hemingway; Men Without Women
  Madigan. R. Dougherty; Commissioner
  Rough Cut. D. Lambert; Touch the Lion's Paw
  Telefon. W. Wager
  Verdict. I. Zangwill; Big Bow Mystery
SILVER, RAPHAEL D.
  On the Yard. M. Braly
SILVERSTEIN, ELLIOT
  Happening. E. Curry
  Nightmare Honeymoon. L. Block (headnote)
SIMMONS, ANTHONY
  Little Sweetheart. A. Wise; Naughty Girls
SIMON, S. SYLVAN
  Grand Central Murder. S. MacVeigh
  I Love Trouble. R. Huggins; Double Take
  Whistling in the Dark. L. Gross
SIMS, GEORGE R.
  Lady Letmere's Jewelry. G. R. Sims; Life We Live
SINCLAIR, ANDREW
  Blue Blood. A. Thynne; Carry-Cot
SINCLAIR, ROBERT B.
  Mr. & Mrs. North. O. Davis
  Rage in Heaven. J. Hilton
SIODMAK, ROBERT
  Affair Nina B. J. M. Simmel; Affair of Nina B
  Christmas Holiday. W. S. Maugham
  Criss-Cross. D. Tracy
  Cry of the City. H. E. Helseth; Chair for Martin Rome
  Killers. E. Hemingway; Men Without Women
  Mister Flow. G. Leroux; Man of a Hundred Masks
  Phantom Lady. W. Irish
  Spiral Staircase. E. L. White; Some Must Watch
  Strange Affair of Uncle Harry. T. Job; Uncle Harry
  Suspect. J. Ronald; This Way Out
SIRK, DOUGLAS
  Bonaventure. C. Hastings
  Interlude. J. M. Cain; Serenade
  Scandal in Paris. Vidocq; Memoirs of Vidocq
  Sleep My Love. L. Q. Ross
  Summer Storm. A. Chekhov; Shooting Party
SITTENHAM, FRED W.
  Mystery Mind. A. B. Reeve
SLOAN, PAUL
  Straight Is the Way. D. Burnet; Four Walls
SLOMAN, EDWARD
  Murder by the Clock. Rufus King
  Pilgrims of the Night. A. Partridge; Passers-By
SMALLEY, PHILLIPS
  East Lynne in Bugville. Mrs. H. Wood; East Lynne
  John Needham's Double. J. Hatton
SMART, RALPH
  Bitter Springs. C. King
SMAWLEY, ROBERT J.
  River of Diamonds. G. Jenkins
SMIGHT, JACK
  Frankenstein: The True Story. M. Shelley; Frankenstein
  Kaleidoscope. M. Avallone
  Moving Target. J. Macdonald
  No Way to Treat a Lady. H. Longbaugh
  Third Day. J. Hayes
SMILEY, JOSEPH W.
  Beloved Adventurer. E. C. Hall
  Life Without Soul. M. Shelley; Frankenstein
SMITH, DAVID
  Silver Car. W. Martyn; Secret of the Silver Car
  Steele of the Royal Mounted. J. O. Curwood; Philipp Steele of the Royal Northwest Mounted Police
SMITH, NOEL M.
  Case of the Black Parrot. B. E. Stevenson; Mystery of the Boule Cabinet
  Mystery House. M. G. Eberhart; Mystery of Hunting's End
  Nurse's Secret. M. R. Rinehart; Miss Pinkerton
SOFFICI, MARIO
  The Man and the Beast. R. L. Stevenson; Strange Case of Dr. Jekyll and Mr. Hyde
SOLEM, OLA
  Operation Cobra. A. Bodelsen
  Orion's Belt. J. Michelet
SOUTHWELL, HARRY
  Hordern Mystery. E. Finn
SPAAK, CHARLES
  Barton Mystery. W. Hackett
SPARR, ROBERT
  Once You Kiss a Stranger. P. Highsmith; Strangers on a Train
SPIEGEL, LARRY
  Survival Run. R. Hoskins
SPIELBERG, STEVEN
  Indiana Jones and the Last Crusade. Rob McGregor
SPOTTISWOODE, ROGER
  Pursuit of D. B. Cooper. J. D. Reed; Free Fall
SQUIRE, ANTHONY
  11 Harrowhouse. G. A. Browne
STADER, PAUL
  When Eight Bells Toll. A. MacLean
STAFFORD, JOHN
  Dick Turpin. W. H. Ainsworth; Rookwood
STAHL, JOHN M.
  Leave Her to Heaven. B. A. Williams
  When Tomorrow Comes. J. M. Cain; Serenade
STANLAWS, PENRHYN
  Woman in the Case. C. Fitch
STANLEY, PAUL
  Cry Tough. I. Shulman
STARRETT, JACK
  Cleopatra Jones. R. Goulart
  Slaughter. H. Clement
STAUB, RALPH
  Danger Ahead. L. Y. Erskine; Renfrew's Long Trail
  Mandarin Mystery. E. Queen; Chinese Orange Mystery
  Sky Bandits. L. Y. Erskine; Renfrew Rides the Sky
  Yukon Flight. L. Y. Erskine; Renfrew Rides North
STEGER, JULIUS
  Burden of Proof. V. Sardou; Diplomates
STEIN, PAUL L.
  Black Limelight. G. Sherry
  Poison Pen. R. Llewellyn
  Saint Meets the Tiger. L. Charteris; Meet the Tiger
STEVENS, MARK
  Man in the Water. R. Sheckley
STEVENS, ROBERT
  Big Caper. L. White

Directors Index

I Thank a Fool. A. E. Lindop
Never Love a Stranger. H. Robbins

STEVENSON, ROBERT
Dishonoured Lady. M. B. Lowndes; Letty Lynton
Non-Stop New York. K. Attiwill; Sky Steward
One of Our Dinosaurs Is Missing. D. Forrest; Great Dinosaur Robbery
That Darn Cat. Gordons; Undercover Cat
Ware Case. G. Pleydell

STOLOFF, BEN
Hidden Hand. Rufus King; Invitation to a Murder
Two in the Dark. G. Burgess; Two O'Clock Courage

STONE, ANDREW L.
Cry Terror. A. L. Stone
Decks Ran Red. A. L. Stone
Julia. A. L. Stone

STONE, OLIVER
Hand. M. Brandel; Lizard's Tail

STORCH, WOLFGANG
Two Faces in January. P. Highsmith

STORM, JEROME
Brass Bowl. L. J. Vance
Honor First. G. F. Gibbs; Splendid Outcast

STRAYER, FRANK R.
I Ring Doorbells. R. Birdwell
Murder at Glen Athol. N. Lippincott

STRICK, JOSEPH
Balcony. J. Genet

STURGEON, ROLLIN S.
Through the Wall. C. Moffett
Whose Wife? C. H. Bullivant

STURGIS, JOHN
Bad Day at Black Rock. M. Niall
Eagle Has Landed. J. Higgins
Kind Lady. E. Chodorov
McQ. A. Edwards
People Against O'Hara. E. Lipsky
Satan Bug. I. Stuart
Sign of the Ram. M. Ferguson

SULLIVAN, FRED G.
Cold River. W. Judson

SULLIVAN, FREDERICK
Mr. Meeson's Will. H. R. Haggard

SUMMERS, WALTER
At the Villa Rose. A. E. W. Mason
Dark Eyes of London. E. Wallace
House Opposite. J. L. Farjeon
Limping Man. W. Scott; Man
Return of Bulldog Drummond. H. C. McNeile; Black Gang
Traitor Spy. T. C. H. Jacobs
What Happened Then? L. T. Bradley

SUNDSTROM, NEAL
Howling 5: The Rebirth. G. Brandner

SUSO, HENRY
Deathsport. W. Hughes

SUTHERLAND, A. EDWARD
Having Wonderful Crime. C. Rice
Nine Lives Are Not Enough. J. Odlum
One Night in the Tropics. E. D. Biggers; Love Insurance

SWAIM, BOB
Half Moon Street. P. Theroux; Doctor Slaughter

SYKES, PETER
To the Devil—a Daughter. D. Wheatley

SZWARC, JEANNOT
Enigma. M. Barak

TACCHELLE, JEAN-LOUIS
Avec un Elastique. C. Williams; Big Bite

TAGGERT, ERROL
Longest Night. C. Fitzsimmons; Whispering Window
Sinner Take All. W. Chambers; Murder for a Wanton

TAGHVAI, NASER
Captain Khorshid. E. Hemingway; To Have and Have Not

TANNEN, WILLIAM
Flashpoint. G. La Fountaine
Hero and the Terror. M. Blodgett

TARRIDE, JEAN
Yellow Dog. G. Simenon; Face for a Clue

TASHLIN, FRANK
Alphabet Murders. A. Christie; ABC Murders
Caprice. J. Withers
Glass Bottom Boat. B. Street
Man from the Diner's Club. S. Baol

TAUROG, NORMAN
Fifty Roads to Town. F. Nebel
Mrs. O'Malley and Mr. Malone. Stuart Palmer; People vs. Withers and Malone
Phantom President. G. F. Worts

TAVERNIER, BERTRAND
Clockmaker. G. Simenon; Watchmaker of Everton
Population 1280. J. Thompson; Pop. 1280

TAYLOR, DONALD
Straw Man. D. M. Disney

TAYLOR, HENRY COCKRAFT
Jack Sheppard. W. H. Ainsworth

TAYLOR, SAM
Cat's Paw. C. B. Kelland

TAYLOR, STANNER E. V.
Dead Secret. W. Collins
Lone Wolf. L. J. Vance

TAYLOR, WILLIAM DESMOND
High Hand. J. Futrelle
Witching Hour. A. Thomas

TEAGUE, LEWIS
Jewel of the Nile. C. Lanigan

TENNYSON, PENROSE
There Ain't No Justice. J. Curtis

TERRISS, TOM
Dead Men Tell No Tales. E. W. Hornung
Find the Woman. A. S. Roche
Lion and the Mouse. A. Hornblow
Mystery of Edwin Drood. C. Dickens
Romance of a Million Dollars. E. Dejeans
Third Degree. A. Hornblow

TERWILLIGER, GEORGE W.
Fatal Hour. E. K. Chatterton; Marriages of Mayfair

TETZLAFF, TED
Window. W. Irish; Dead Man Blues

TEWKESBURY, PETER
Trouble with Girls. D. Keene; Chautauqua

THOM, ROBERT
Angel, Angel, Down We Go. W. Johnston

THOMAS, GERALD
Solitary Child. N. Bawden

THOMAS, RALPH
Appointment with Venus. J. Tickell
Campbell's Kingdom. H. Innes
Deadlier Than the Male. H. Reymond
High Bright Sun. I. S. Black
High Commissioner. J. Cleary
Hot Enough for June. L. Davidson; Night of Wenceslas
Thirty-Nine Steps. J. Buchan
Upstairs and Downstairs. R. S. Thorn
Venetian Bird. V. Canning

THOMPSON, FREDERICK
After Dark. D. Boucicault

THOMPSON, J. LEE
Cape Fear. J. D. MacDonald; Executioners
Chairman. J. R. Kennedy
Evil That Men Do. R. L. Hill
Eye of the Devil. P. Loraine; Day of the Arrow
Guns of Navarone. A. MacLean
Ice-Cold in Alex. C. Landon
Messenger of Death. Rex Burns; Avenging Angel
Murder Without Crime. J. L. Thompson
Passage. B. Nicolaysen; Perilous Passage
Reincarnation of Peter Proud. M. Ehrlich
Return from the Ashes. H. Monteilhet
St. Ives. O. Bleeck; Procane Chronicle
Yield to the Night. J. Henry

THOMSON, CHRIS
Empty Beach. P. Corris

THORNBY, ROBERT
Girl in the Web. G. Bonner; Miss Maitland, Private Secretary
Half a Chance. F. S. Isham
On Dangerous Ground. B. E. Stevenson; Little Comrade

THORNTON, F. MARTIN
Belonging. O. Wadsley
Diana and Destiny. C. Garvice
Diana of the Islands. B. Bolt
Man Who Bought London. E. Wallace
Melody of Death. E. Wallace
My Lord Conceit. Rita
River of Stars. E. Wallace
Splendid Coward. H. Townley

THORPE, JERRY
Venetian Affair. H. MacInnes

THORPE, RICHARD
Above Suspicion. H. MacInnes
Cheating Cheaters. M. Marcin
Earl of Chicago. B. Williams
Green Eyes. H. Ashbrook; Murder of Steven Kester
Horizontal Lieutenant. G. Cotler; Bottletop Affair
House of the Seven Hawks. V. Canning; House of the Seven Flies
King Murder. C. R. Jones
Murder on the Campus. W. Chambers; Campanile Murders
Night Must Fall. E. Williams
Scorpio Letters. V. Canning

TILL, ERIC
Walking Stick. Winston Graham

TINLING, JAMES
Great Hospital Mystery. M. G. Eberhart (headnote)

TOKAR, NORMAN
Candleshoe. M. Innes; Christmas at Candleshoe

TOMIMOTO, SOKICHI
Yoru No Wana. C. Woolrich; Black Angel

TOMLINSON, LIONEL
Death in High Heels. C. Brand

TOURNEUR, JACQUES
Comedy of Terrors. Elsie Lee
Ivory Snuff Box. A. Fredericks
My Lady's Garter. J. Futrelle

TOURNEUR, MAURICE
Cecile Est Morte. G. Simenon; Maigret and the Spinster
Hand of Peril. A. Stringer
Koenigsmark. P. Benoit; Count Philip
Le Derniere Reincarnation de Larsan. G. Leroux; Perfume of the Lady in Black
Le Mystere de la Chambre Jaune. G. Leroux; Mystery of the Yellow Room
White Circle. R. L. Stevenson; New Arabian Nights

TOURNIER, JACQUES
  Experiment Perilous. M. Carpenter
  Fear Makers. D. L. Teilhet
  Leopard Man. C. Woolrich; Black Alibi

TREVILLE, GEORGES
  Beryl Coronet. A. C. Doyle; Adventures of Sherlock Holmes
  Copper Beeches. A. C. Doyle; Adventures of Sherlock Holmes
  Musgrave Ritual. A. C. Doyle; Memoirs of Sherlock Holmes
  Mystery of Boscombe Vale. A. C. Doyle; Adventures of Sherlock Holmes
  Reigate Squires. A. C. Doyle; Memoirs of Sherlock Holmes
  Silver Blaze. A. C. Doyle; Memoirs of Sherlock Holmes
  Speckled Band. A. C. Doyle; Adventures of Sherlock Holmes
  Stolen Papers. A. C. Doyle; Memoirs of Sherlock Holmes

TRIESCHMAN, CHARLES
  Two. C. Trieschman

TRONSON, ROBERT
  Man at the Carlton Tower. E. Wallace; Man at the Carlton
  Man Detained. E. Wallace; Debt Discharged
  Never Back Losers. E. Wallace; Green Ribbon
  Number Six. E. Wallace
  On the Run. E. Wallace (headnote)

TRUFFAUT, FRANCOIS
  Bride Wore Black. C. Woolrich
  Let It Be Sunday. C. Williams; Long Saturday Night
  Mississippi Mermaid. W. Irish; Waltz Into Darkness
  Shoot the Piano Player. D. Goodis; Down There
  Such a Lovely Kid Like Me. H. Farrell; Such a Gorgeous Kid Like Me

TRUMAN, MICHAEL
  Girl in the Headlines. L. Payne; Nose on My Face

TUCHNER, MICHAEL
  Fear Is the Key. A. MacLean
  Villain. J. Barlow; Burden of Proof

TUCKER, GEORGE LOANE
  Arsene Lupin. E. Jepson
  Called Back. H. Conway
  Folly of Desire. A. Askew; Shulamite
  Game of Liberty. E. P. Oppenheim
  Miracle Man. F. Packard
  Shulamite. A. Askew
  Sons of Satan. W. Lequeux
  Third String. W. W. Jacobs; Odd Craft
  Traffic in Souls. E. H. Ball

TUDOR, F. C. S.
  Devil's Profession. G. de S. W. James

TULLY, MONTGOMERY
  Boys in Brown. R. Beckwith
  Clash by Night. R. Croft-Cooke
  Diamond. M. Procter; Rich Is the Treasure
  Escapement. C. E. Maine
  Glass Cage. A. E. Martin; Common People
  House in Marsh Road. L. Meynell
  Long Knife. S. Truss; Long Night
  Man in the Shadow. S. Davis; One Man's Secret
  Man Who Was Nobody. E. Wallace
  Murder in Reverse. Seamark; Out of the Dark
  No Road Back. F. L. Cary; Madam Tic-Tac
  Out of the Fog. B. Graeme; Fog of a Killer
  Price of Silence. L. Meynell; One Step from Murder
  Strange Awakening. P. Quentin; Puzzle for Fiends
  Way Out. B. Graeme
  Who Killed the Cat? A. Ridley; Tabitha

TURNER, OTIS
  Black Box. E. P. Oppenheim
  Called Back. H. Conway

  Gay Lord Waring. H. Townley
  Lady Audley's Secret. M. E. Braddon
  Pool of Flame. L. J. Vance
  Son of the Immortals. L. Tracy
  Spy. J. F. Cooper

TUTTLE, FRANK
  Benson Murder Case. S. S. Van Dine
  Cry in the Night. W. Masterson; All Through the Night
  Easy Come, Easy Go. O. Davis
  Glass Key. D. Hammett
  Greene Murder Case. S. S. Van Dine
  Hell on Frisco Bay. W. P. McGivern; Darkest Hour
  Hostages. S. Heym
  Hour Before the Dawn. W. S. Maugham
  Studio Murder Mystery. Edingtons
  This Gun for Hire. G. Greene; Gun for Sale

TWIST, DEREK
  Family Doctor. J. Fleming; Deeds of Dr. Deadcert

ULMER, EDGAR G.
  Detour. M. M. Goldsmith

URSON, FRANK
  Chicago. M. Watkins

USTINOV, PETER
  School for Secrets. Delano Ames

VADIM, ROGER
  Blood and Roses. J. S. Le Fanu; In a Glass Darkly
  Night Heaven Fell. A. Vidalie; Midnight Jewelers
  Pretty Maids All in a Row. F. Pollini

VAJDA, LADISLAV
  It Happens in Broad Daylight. F. Duerrenmatt; Pledge

VALDEZ, LUIS
  Zoot Suit. L. Valdez

VALE, TRAVERS
  Aurora Floyd. M. E. Braddon
  East Lynne. H. Wood
  Ernest Maltravers. E. Bulwer-Lytton
  New Magdalen. Wilkie Collins
  Soul of Pierre. G. Ohnet; Weird Gift
  Ticket-of-Leave Man. T. Taylor
  Woman of Mystery. G. Ohnet

VAN, WALLIE
  Scarlet Runner. C. N. Williamson

VAN DYKE, W. S., II
  Destroying Angel. L. J. Vance
  I Love You Again. O. R. Cohen
  Pagan. J. Russell; In Dark Places
  Penthouse. A. S. Roche
  Rage in Heaven. J. Hilton
  They Gave Him a Gun. W. J. Cowen
  Thin Man. D. Hammett

VAN SANT, GUS, JR.
  Drugstore Cowboy. J. Fogle

VARNEL, MARCEL
  Almost Married. A. Soutar
  Bones. E. Wallace
  Silent Witness. J. De Leon

VARNEL, MAX
  Question of Sixpence. R. Vickers (headnote)
  Rivals. E. Wallace; Elegant Edward

VARNEY, ARTHUR
  Road to Fortune. H. Broadbridge; Moorland Terror

VEILLER, BAYARD
  Ladyfingers. J. Gregory
  Trial of Mary Dugan. B. Veiller

VEKROFF, PERRY
  Cynthia-of-the-Minute. L. J. Vance

VERHOOVEN, PAUL
  Robocop. E. Naha

VERNEUIL, HENRI
  Big Chief. O. Henry; Whirligigs
  Big Grab. J. Trinian
  Burglars. D. Goodis; Burglar
  Forbidden Fruit. G. Simenon; Act of Passion
  President. G. Simenon; Premier
  What Price Murder. R. Marshall; Sucker Punch

VERNON, RICHARD
  Street of Shadows. L. Meynell; Creaking Chair

VERSINI, ANDRE
  See Venice and Die. R. Marshall; Mission to Venice

VERSTAPPEN, WIM
  Outsider in Amsterdam. J. van de Wetering
  Rattlerat. J. van de Wetering

VIANEY, MICHEL
  Cops' Sunday. A. Coburn; Off Duty

VIDOR, CHARLES
  Blind Alley. J. Warwick
  Double Door. E. McFadden
  Ladies in Retirement. E. Percy
  Muss 'Em Up. J. E. Grant; Green Shadow

VIDOR, KING
  Beyond the Forest. S. Engstrand
  Cynara. R. Gore-Brown; Imperfect Lover
  Lightning Strikes Twice. M. Echard; Dark Fantastic
  Mask of Fu Manchu. S. Rohmer

VIERTEL, BERTHOLD
  Wiser Sex. C. Fitch; Woman in the Case

VIGNOLA, ROBERT G.
  Under Cover. R. C. Megrue
  Vicky Van. C. Wells
  Woman Who Came Back. C. M. S. McLellan; Leah Kleschna

VILLIERS, DAVID
  Candidate for Murder. E. Wallace (headnote)

VINCENT, JAMES
  Woman in Grey. A. M. Williamson

VISCONTI, LUCHINO
  Obsession. J. M. Cain; Postman Always Rings Twice

VOHRER, ALFRED
  All People Will Be Brothers. J. M. Simmel; Cain '67
  And Jimmy Went to the Rainbow's Foot. J. M. Simmel; Caesar Code
  Creature with the Blue Hand; E. Wallace; Blue Hand
  Dark Eyes of London. E. Wallace
  Das Indische Tuch. E. Wallace; Frightened Lady
  Der Zinker. E. Wallace; Squeaker
  Die Tur mit dem Sieben Schlosser. E. Wallace; Door with the Seven Locks
  Hound of Blackwood Castle. E. Wallace (headnote)
  In the Grip of the Sinister One. E. Wallace (headnote)
  Love Is Only a Word. J. M. Simmel; Love Is Just a Word
  Monk with a Whip. E. Wallace (headnote)
  Only the Wind Knows the Answer. J. M. Simmel; Wind and the Rain
  Soho Gorilla. E. Wallace; Dark Eyes of London
  Squeaker. E. Wallace; Ringer
  Stuff That Dreams Are Made Of. J. M. Simmel; Traitor Blitz
  Waiting Room for the Other Side. R. Marshall; Mission to Siena

VON BAKY, JOSEF
  Die Seltsame Grafin. E. Wallace; Strange Countess

VON STERNBERG, JOSEF
  Crime and Punishment. F. M. Dostoevskii
  Dishonored. F. Vreeland
  Last Command. C. Houghton
  Shanghai Gesture. John Colton

Directors Index

VORHAUS, BERNARD
   Blind Justice. A. Ridley; Recipe for Murder
   Dusty Ermine. N. Grant
   Last Journey. J. J. Farjeon; Holiday Express
   Ten Minute Alibi. A. Armstrong

VRONSKY, I.
   Crime and Punishment. F. M. Dostoevskii

WADLEIGH, MICHAEL
   Wolfen. W. Strieber

WAGGNER, GEORGE
   Climax. F. J. Lewis

WAJDA, ANDRZEJ
   Ashes and Diamonds. J. Andrzeyevski

WALKER, NORMAN
   Hate Ship. B. Graeme

WALKER, PETER
   House of Long Shadows. E. D. Biggers; Seven Keys to Baldpate

WALKER, STUART
   Mystery of Edwin Drood. C. Dickens
   Secret Call. A. P. Terhune; Woman

WALLACE, C. R.
   Trooper O'Neill. G. Goodchild

WALLACE, EDGAR
   Red Aces. E. Wallace
   Squeaker. E. Wallace

WALLACE, RICHARD
   Fallen Sparrow. D. B. Hughes
   Kick-In. W. Mack
   Masquerader. K. C. Thurston
   Night to Remember. K. Roos; Frightened Stiff

WALLS, TOM
   Plunder. B. Travers

WALSH, RAOUL
   Background to Danger. E. Ambler; Uncommon Danger
   Colorado Territory. W. R. Burnett; High Sierra
   From Now On. F. Packard
   High Sierra. W. R. Burnett
   Jump for Glory. A. McDonell
   Me—Gangster. C. F. Coe
   Murder Inc. J. Eastwood
   Northern Pursuit. L. T. White; 5,000 Trojan Horses
   Red Dance. H. L. Gates; Red Dancer of Moscow
   They Drive by Night. A. I. Bezzerides; Long Haul
   Uncertain Glory. H. Meadows
   Yellow Ticket. V. Morton

WALTON, FRED
   April Fool's Day. J. Rovin
   Rosary Murders. W. X. Kienzle

WANAMAKER, SAM
   File of the Golden Goose. J. Watson

WARD, ALBERT
   Poison. A. Askew

WARDE, ERNEST C.
   Devil to Pay. F. N. Greene
   House of Whispers. W. Johnston
   Woman in White. W. Collins

WARGNIER, REGIS
   I'm King of the Castle. S. Hill

WARREN, CHARLES MARQUIS
   Back from the Dead. C. Turney; Other One

WARREN, MARK
   Come Back, Charleston Blue. C. Himes; Heat's On

WARREN, RICHARD
   Bosun's Mate. W. W. Jacobs; Captains All

WASCHNECK, ERICH
   His Official Wife. R. H. Savage; My Official Wife

WATKINS, PETER
   Privilege. John Burke

WEBB, KENNETH
   His Wife's Husband. A. K. Green; Mayor's Wife
   How Women Love. I. L. Forrester; Dangerous Inheritance
   Jim the Penman. C. L. Young
   Master Mind. M. Dana
   Net. R. Beach
   Secrets of Paris. E. Sue; Mysteries of Paris

WEBB, ROBERT D.
   Caribbean Mystery. J. W. Vandercook; Murder in Trinidad
   Spider. F. Oursler
   Way to the Gold. W. D. Steele; Way to Gold

WEBER, LOIS
   John Needham's Double. J. Hatton
   Mary Regan. L. Scott

WEBSTER, HARRY MCRAE
   Jimmy Dale, Alias "The Grey Seal". F. Packard; Adventures of Jimmie Dale

WEBSTER, NICHOLAS
   Dead to the World. E. Ronns; State Department Murders

WEEKS, STEPHEN
   I, Monster. R. L. Stevenson; Strange Case of Dr. Jekyll and Mr. Hyde

WEIDERMANN, ALFRED
   Maigret und Sein Grosster Fall. G. Simenon; At the Gai-Moulin

WEIGHT, HARMON
   Ramshackle House. H. Footner

WEINE, ROBERT
   Crime and Punishment. F. M. Dostoevskii
   Hands of Orlac. M. Renard

WEINSTEIN, MARVIN R.
   Running Target. S. Frazee

WEIR, PETER
   Witness. W. Kelley

WEIS, DON
   Remains to Be Seen. H. Lindsay

WELLES, ORSON
   Lady from Shanghai. Sherwood King; If I Die Before I Wake
   Mr. Arkadin. O. Welles
   Stranger. A. Veiller
   Touch of Evil. W. Masterson; Badge of Evil

WELLMAN, WILLIAM A.
   Beggars of Life. J. Tully
   Lady of Striptease. G. R. Lee; G-String Murders
   Love Is a Racket. R. James
   Night Nurse. D. Macy
   President Vanishes. Anonymous
   Public Enemy. K. Glasmon
   Roxie Hart. M. Watkins; Chicago
   Stingaree. E. W. Hornung

WELLS, JACK
   Lion Man. R. Parrish; Strange Case of Cavendish

WENDERS, WIM
   American Friend. P. Highsmith; Ripley's Friend
   Hammett. J. Gores

WENDKOS, PAUL
   Burglar. D. Goodis
   Mephisto Waltz. F. M. Stewart

WERKER, ALFRED L.
   Double Cross Roads. W. Lipman; Yonder Grow the Daisies
   Repeat Performance. W. O'Farrell
   Sherlock Holmes. W. Gillette
   Young Don't Cry. R. Jessup

WEST, LANGDON
   Banker's Double. S. Campbell; Below the Dead-Line
   Case of the Vanished Bonds. S. Campbell; Below the Dead-Line
   Dickson's Diamonds. S. Campbell; Below the Dead-Line
   Man Who Vanished. S. Campbell; Below the Dead-Line

WEST, ROLAND
   Bat. M. R. Rinehart
   Bat Whispers. M. R. Rinehart; Bat
   Corsair. W. Green
   Unknown Purple. Roland West

WEST, WALTER
   Brotherhood. E. Wallace; Double
   Case of Lady Camber. H. A. Vachell
   In the Blood. A. Soutar
   Maria Marten. Anonymous
   Sweeney Todd, the Demon Barber of Fleet Street. G. D. Pitt
   Ware Case. G. Pleydell
   When Greek Meets Greek. P. Trent

WESTON, HAROLD
   Mystery of a Hansom Cab. F. Hume

WETHERELL, M. A.
   Moorland Tragedy. B. Orczy; Unravelled Knots

WHALE, JAMES
   Bride of Frankenstein. M. W. Shelley; Frankenstein
   Frankenstein. M. W. Shelley
   Invisible Man. H. G. Wells
   Old Dark House. J. B. Priestley; Benighted
   Remember Last Night? A. Hobhouse; Hangover Murders

WHARTON, LEOPOLD
   Mr. Potter of Texas. A. C. Gunter

WHARTON, THEODORE
   New Adventures of J. Rufus Wallingford. G. R. Chester; Get-Rich-Quick Wallingford

WHELAN, TIM
   Nightmare. M. Porlock; Mystery in Kensington Gore
   Ten Days in Paris. B. Graeme; Disappearance of Roger Tremayne
   This Was a Woman. Joan Morgan

WHITE, GEORGE A.
   My Gun Is Quick. M. Spillane

WHORF, RICHARD
   Love from a Stranger. F. Vosper

WICKI, BERNHARD
   Morituri. W. J. Luddecke
   Visit. F. Duerrenmatt

WIDERBERG, BO
   Man on the Roof. M. Sjowall; Abominable Man

WIENE, ROBERT
   Raskolnikov. F. M. Doestoevskii; Crime and Punishment

WIESEN, BERNARD
   Fear No More. L. Edgley

WILBUR, CRANE
   Bat. M. R. Rinehart
   Patient in Room 18. M. G. Eberhart

WILCOX, HERBERT
   Trent's Last Case. E. C. Bentley
   Woman in White. W. Collins

WILDE, CORNELL
   Storm Fear. C. Seeley

WILDE, TED
   Speedy. R. Holman

WILDER, BILLY
   Double Indemnity. J. M. Cain
   Private Life of Sherlock Holmes. Michael Hardwick
   Stalag 17. D. Bevan
   Witness for the Prosecution. A. Christie

WILDER, GENE
   Adventure of Sherlock Holmes' Smarter Brother. G. Pearlman

WILDER, W. LEE
   Spy in the Sky. A. S. Fleischman; Counterspy Express
   Vicious Circle. H. Herald; Burning Bush

WILES, GORDON
   Gangster. D. Fuchs; Low Company

WILLAT, IRVIN V.
   Back to God's Country. J. O. Curwood
   Enchanted Hill. P. B. Kyne
   False Faces. L. J. Vance
   Fifty Candles. E. D. Biggers
   Guilty Man. F. Coppee
   Pawned. F. Packard
   Story Without a Name. A. Stringer
   Yellow Men and Gold. Gouverneur Morris

WILLIAMS, BROCK
   Root of All Evil. J. S. Fletcher

WILLIAMSON, WADE
   Detour. M. Goldsmith

WILLIS, GORDON
   Windows. H. B. Gilmour

WILLOUGHBY, GEORGE
   Woman in the Case. C. Fitch

WILLOUGHBY, LEWIS
   Secret of the Moor. M. Gerard

WILSON, ANDREW P.
   Fighting Snub Reilly. E. Wallace; Forty-Eight Short Stories

WILSON, BEN
   Brass Bullet. F. R. Adams; Pleasure Island
   Voice on the Wire. E. H. Ball

WILSON, FRANK
   Grand Babylon Hotel. A. Bennett
   Turf Conspiracy. N. Gould
   Woman Wins. C. H. Bullivant

WILSON, HUGH
   Burglar. L. Block (headnote)

WILSON, REX
   Quinney's. H. A. Vachell

WILSON, RICHARD
   Al Capone. J. Roeburt
   Big Boodle. R. Sylvester
   Skullduggery. Vercors; You Shall Know Them

WINDOM, LAWRENCE C.
   Modern Marriage. D. Vane; Lady Varley
   Papered Door. M. R. Rinehart; Romantics

WINDUST, BRETAIGNE
   Murder, Inc. J. Eastwood

WINNER, MICHAEL
   Appointment with Death. A. Christie
   Big Sleep. R. Chandler
   Death Wish. B. Garfield
   Jokers. M. Sands
   Mechanic. L. J. Carlino
   Nightcomers. Michael Hastings
   Scorpio. M. Roote
   Sentinel. J. Konvitz
   Stone Killer. J. Gardner; Complete State of Death

WINSLOW, DICKY
   East Lynne. H. Wood
   Maria Marten. Anonymous
   Octoroon. D. Boucicault

WINSTON, RON
   Don't Just Stand There. C. Williams; Wrong Venus

WINTERSTEIN, FRANK
   Valley of Fear. A. C. Doyle

WISE, HERBERT
   To Have and to Hold. E. Wallace; Lieutenant Bones

WISE, ROBERT
   Audrey Rose. F. De Felitta
   Body Snatcher. R. L. Stevenson
   Born to Kill. J. Gunn; Deadlier Than the Male
   Game of Death. R. Connell; Variety
   Haunting. S. Jackson; Haunting of Hill House
   House on Telegraph Hill. D. Lyon; Frightened Child
   I Want to Live! T. Rawson
   Odds Against Tomorrow. W. P. McGivern
   Rooftops. R. Tine

WITHEY, CHET/CHESTER
   Pleasure Buyers. A. S. Roche
   Teeth of the Tiger. M. Leblanc

WITNEY, WILLIAM
   Drums of Fu Manchu. S. Rohmer
   Juvenile Jungle. Firth Counsel
   Secret of the Purple Reef. D. Cottrell; Silent Reefs
   Young and Wild. Morton Cooper

WOOD, JAMES
   Dr. Jekyll's Dungeon of Death. R. L. Stevenson; Strange Case of Dr. Jekyll and Mr. Hyde

WOOD, SAM
   Ivy. M. B. Lowndes; Story of Ivy
   Madame X. J. W. MacConaughy
   New Adventures of Get-Rich-Quick Wallingford. G. R. Chester; Get-Rich-Quick Wallingford
   Raffles. E. W. Hornung; Amateur Cracksman
   Under the Lash. A. Askew; Shulamite
   Within the Law. B. Veiller

WOODS, ARTHUR
   Busman's Honeymoon. D. L. Sayers
   Dark Stairway. M. G. Eberhart; From This Dark Stairway
   Nursemaid Who Disappeared. P. MacDonald
   They Drive by Night. J. Curtis

WORNE, DUKE
   Devil's Chaplain. G. Bronson-Howard
   Man from Headquarters. G. Bronson-Howard; Black Book
   Mysterious Mr. Garland. W. Martyn

WORSLEY, WALLACE
   Highest Bidder. M. Foster; Trap

WORTHINGTON, WILLIAM
   Illustrious Prince. E. P. Oppenheim
   Silent Barrier. L. Tracy
   Tong Man. C. C. Westover; Dragon's Daughter

WRAY, JOHN GRIFFITH
   Winding Stair. A. E. W. Mason

WREDE, CASPAR
   Ransom. P. Wheeler

WRIGHT, GEORGE A.
   Catspaw. W. H. Osborne

WYLER, WILLIAM
   Collector. J. Fowles
   Dead End. S. Kingsley
   Desperate Hours. J. Hayes
   Detective Story. S. Kingsley
   How to Steal a Million. M. Sinclair
   Letter. W. S. Maugham
   Liberation of L. B. Jones. J. H. Ford; Liberation of Lord Byron Jones
   Raffles. E. W. Hornung; Amateur Cracksman

YARBROUGH, JEAN
   Challenge. H. C. McNeile
   Shed No Tears. D. Martin

YATES, PETER
   Bullitt. R. Pike; Mute Witness
   Deep. P. Benchley
   Eleni. N. Gage

   Eyewitness. J. Minahan
   For Pete's Sake. B. Street
   Friends of Eddie Coyle. G. V. Higgins
   Hot Rock. D. E. Westlake
   House on Carroll Street. Mollie Gregory
   Suspect. Martin Meyers

YORKIN, BUD
   Thief Who Came to Dinner. T. L. Smith

YOUNG, HAROLD
   Extremities. W. Mastrosimone
   Hostage. T. Allbeury; No Place to Hide
   Short Eyes. M. Pinero

YOUNG, JAMES
   Daughter of Two Worlds. L. Scott
   Hornet's Nest. W. Woodrow
   My Official Wife. R. H. Savage
   Notorious Miss Lisle. B. Reynolds
   On Trial. E. L. Reizenstein

YOUNG, TERENCE
   Action of the Tiger. J. Wellard
   Amorous Adventures of Moll Flanders. D. Defoe; Fortunes and Misfortunes of the Famous Moll Flanders
   Bloodline. S. Sheldon
   Corridor of Mirrors. C. Massie
   Doctor No. I. Fleming
   From Russia with Love. I. Fleming
   From the Boys. R. Matheson; Ride the Nightmare
   Jigsaw Man. Dorothea Bennett
   Tall Headlines. A. E. Lindop
   Thunderball. I. Fleming
   Wait Until Dark. F. Knott

YOUNG, TONY
   Hidden Homicide. P. Capon; Death at Shinglestrand
   My Death Is a Mockery. D. G. Baber

YUST, LARRY
   Trick Baby. I. Slim

ZAMPI, MARIO
   Fatal Night. M. Arlen; May Fair
   Spy for a Day. S. Aumonier; Love-a-Duck

ZANUCH, LILI FINI
   Rush. K. Wozencraft

ZANUSSI, KRZYSZTOF
   Catamount Killings. J. H. Chase; I Would Rather Stay Poor

ZEISLER, ALFRED
   Amazing Quest of Mr. Ernest Bliss. E. P. Oppenheim
   Fear. F. M. Dostoevskii; Crime and Punishment

ZELNIK, FRED
   I Killed the Count. A. Coppel

ZELNIK, FRIEDRICH
   Crimson Circle. E. Wallace

ZEMECKIS, ROBERT
   Who Framed Roger Rabbit. G. K. Wolf; Who Censored Roger Rabbit?

ZIMMERMAN, VERNON
   Fade to Black. R. Renaud

ZINNEMANN, FRED
   Behold a Pale Horse. E. Pressburger; Killing a Mouse on Sunday
   Day of the Jackal. F. Forsyth
   Eyes in the Night. B. Kendrick; Odor of Violets
   Seventh Cross. A. Seghers

ZINNER, PETER
   Salamander. M. West

ZITO, JOSEPH
   Invasion U.S.A. J. Frost

ZUGSMITH, ALBERT
   Dog Eat Dog. R. Bloomfield (headnote)